Standard & Poor's®
500 Guide

Standard & Poor's® 500 Guide

2011 Edition

Standard & Poor's

New York   Chicago   San Francisco
Lisbon   London   Madrid   Mexico City
Milan   New Delhi   San Juan   Seoul
Singapore   Sydney   Toronto

FOR STANDARD & POOR'S

Managing Director, Equity Research Services: Robert Barriera
Publisher: Frank LoVaglio

The *McGraw·Hill* Companies

ISBN   978-0-07-175490-3
MHID   0-07-175490-3

This publication is designed to provide accurate and authoritative information in regard to the subject matter covered. It is sold with the understanding that the publisher is not engaged in rendering legal, accounting, or other professional service. If legal advice or other expert assistance is required, the services of a competent professional person should be sought.

—From a declaration of principles jointly adopted by a committee of the American Bar Association and a committee of publishers

The companies contained in this handbook represented the components of the S&P 500 Index as of October 15, 2010.
Additions to or deletions from the Index will cause its composition to change over time.
Company additions and company deletions from the Standard & Poor's equity indexes do not in any way reflect an opinion on the investment merits of the company.

This book is printed on acid-free paper.

ABOUT THE AUTHOR

Standard & Poor's Financial Services LLC, a subsidiary of The McGraw-Hill Companies, Inc., is the nation's leading securities information company. It provides a broad range of financial services, including the respected Standard & Poor's ratings and stock rankings, advisory services, data guides, and the most closely watched and widely reported gauges of stock market activity—the S&P 500, S&P MidCap 400, S&P SmallCap 600, and the S&P Composite 1500 stock price indexes. Standard & Poor's products are marketed around the world and used extensively by financial professionals and individual investors.

Introduction

by **David M. Blitzer, Ph.D.**
Managing Director & Chairman of the Index Committee
Standard & Poor's

The S&P 500

Any Web site, television news program, newspaper, or radio report covering the stock market gives the latest results of a handful of stock indices, including the Dow Industrials, the NASDAQ, and the S&P 500. The Dow is the oldest, extending back over 100 years, and has covered only 30 stocks since shortly before the crash of 1929. The NASDAQ came to fame in the tech boom but ignores all the companies listed on the New York Stock Exchange. The S&P 500 is the index used by market professionals and institutional investors when they need to know what the stock market is doing. While there are several thousand stocks traded in the U.S. market, the S&P 500 covers the most significant ones, representing some three-quarters of the total value of all U.S. equities. Over $1.5 trillion invested through mutual funds, pensions, and exchange-traded funds track the S&P 500. These funds mimic what the index does—if the index rises, so do the funds. Further, when a stock is added to or dropped from the index, these trillions of dollars of funds buy, or sell, the stock. The S&P 500 is also the way the market and its condition is measured— for Wall Street, corporate earnings are the earnings per share calculated for the S&P 500, and the market's valuation is gauged by the price-earnings ratio on the S&P 500.

The S&P 500 and You, the Investor

If you picked up this book, you are probably interested in the stock market or stocks you might invest in; you may be wondering why institutional investors and market professionals focus so much attention on the 500 or what you can learn from the index. So, what can the index do? It can:

- Give you a benchmark for investment performance
- Tell you what kinds of stocks performed well or poorly in the past
- Let you see if today's valuations are higher or lower than in the past
- Help you compare one company or industry to another

We will look at these in turn before describing what's inside the S&P 500 and how S&P maintains the index.

Benchmarks: Monitoring investment performance—keeping score—is what separates occasional stock pickers from serious investors. People who chat about stocks with fellow workers or around the backyard barbeque rarely maintain records beyond the minimum level required to file their taxes. For these investors, stocks that go up are good and stocks that go down are disappointing; there is no serious analysis of what makes stocks move. Serious investors, whether institutional investors or individuals committed to managing their investments, know that understanding whether your stock selections work out requires knowing what the market did and how your portfolio compares to the market. This is where an index benchmark is essential.

The first question most investors have about their success is whether they are beating the market. A rough and ready answer can be found by comparing your portfolio's results to the S&P 500. More in-depth answers would either include dividends as well as price changes or would adjust for investment risks, or both. All the necessary data are widely available for the S&P 500 as well as being included in some brokerage statements and most mutual fund reports.

What went up and what went down: Simply looking at whether the market—the index—gained or lost can tell you a lot about what happened to your portfolio. For most portfolios and most stocks, the largest factor in their movements is how the overall market did. The second largest factor is often how similar stocks—in the same economic sector or industry—behaved. Because the S&P 500 covers 75 percent of the total value of the U.S. equity market, it is a very good indication of what the market did. The stocks in the index are all classified into sectors and industries, so you can use these segments of the index to see if your stocks did better or worse than others in the same sector.

There are 10 economic sectors that classify all the stocks in the S&P 500; the table following lists these sectors, the number of stocks in each, and the weight (based on market values) of each sector in the index. The performance of different sectors can be very different. Looking at the period from the recent low on March 9, 2009, to the end of November 2009, the financial sector gained 135%, materials and industrials each rose about 81% while telecommunication services gained "only" 24%. Before someone decides financial stocks are the all-time best remember that from the record high on October 9, 2007, to March 9th financials fell 59%, far more than any other sector. One comment heard from time to time is that no sector holds the leadership in the S&P 500 forever. Indeed, technology and financials have been trading the leadership back and forth for some 20 years. So be wary of anything that seems to overstay its welcome at the top of the list.

There are other classifications of stocks in the S&P 500. Not only are stocks assigned to an economic sector. They are also assigned to an industry group, an industry, and a sub-industry, using a classification standard called GICS® or the Global Industry Classification Standard.[1] There are 10 sectors, 24 industry groups, 68 industries, and 154 sub-industries. Separately from GICS, stocks are classified as growth or value stocks. Traditionally, growth stocks are those with fast-growing earnings, which offer investors the promise of higher earnings in the future. Value stocks are stocks believed to offer unrecognized values that are not reflected in the stock price. The classification is based on a number of financial ratios and measures, including earnings growth, price/earnings ratios, dividend yields, and similar measures. Although most investors hunt for growth stocks, value stocks tend to perform better over the long run. During periods of a few years or less, either one can easily outperform the other. Investors aren't the only people seeking growth; few if any companies want to be known as value stocks, and all want to be called growth stocks.

Market Valuations: The last few years certainly proved that there are times when markets go both up and down, sometimes by large amounts. The last 10 years of market moves are likely to be remembered for a long, long time. Through it all, what we really want to know is if stocks are really cheap and the market is likely to rise, or if stocks are overpriced and the market will tumble.

Economics tells us that a stock's value lies in the future earnings and dividends. Two convenient measures of how stock prices compare to earnings and dividends are the ratio of the price to earnings (P/E) and the dividend yield or percentage that the dividend is of the stock's price. Just as these are used for individual stocks, they are also used for the overall market by calculating these measures for the S&P 500. As of October 2010, the figures for the index were a P/E of 15.2 and a dividend yield of 2.0 percent. These numbers change as the market rises or falls and as company earnings and dividends change. Up-to-date numbers are published by Standard & Poor's on the Web at www.indices.standardandpoors.com and by various newspapers, magazines, and financial and investing Web sites.

---

[1]GICS(®) is maintained jointly by Standard & Poor's and MSCIBarra. Standard & Poor's Financial Services LLC is a subsidiary of the McGraw-Hill Companies, Inc.

A P/E of 15.2 for the index is significantly lower than the average since 1988 of 19.5. Many investors see a P/E below average as a sign that stocks are undervalued and that there are buying opportunities while a P/E far above the average is a caution sign. Earnings move up and down just as stock prices do, so both can affect the P/E ratio. Corporate earnings tend to fall in recessions and rise in good times, and these movements could distort P/E ratios.

Dividends have dropped out of fashion in the last two decades, and fewer investors seem to watch dividend yields. However, about 368 of the 500 stocks in the S&P 500 pay dividends, so the current dividend yield of 2.0 percent may tell us something about the market. Since the 1950s, the dividend yield on the S&P 500 has almost always been lower than the yield on U.S. treasury or high-grade corporate bonds. The bonds may be attractive for their safety, but they don't offer any opportunity for growth, although companies often raise their dividends as their earnings grow. In late 2008, this pattern reversed for awhile; the dividend yield of 2.3 percent topped the yield on 10-year U.S. treasuries.

Following the gyrations of 2008 another version of the P/E ratio has become popular with some analysts. Instead of looking at one year, the idea is to look at a longer period so that sharp short-term swings don't warp the figures. This approach, originally due to two academic economists[2] is to divide the current price by a 10-year average of earnings after the earnings' figures are adjusted for inflation. This figure gives a sense of the market's long-term relative value and long-run prospects that are less affected by recent economic and market gyrations. In March 2009, when the market made a deep low, this 10-year P/E was about 13 compared to a long-run average around 19 and it suggested stocks were cheap. As of October 2010, it was up to 15.2.

Both these measures may give some sense of whether the market is over- or under-priced. However, neither of these is even close to being a fail-safe guide to the stock market in any time period. Moreover, the wide price swings seen in 2007 through 2010 should remind all investors that the market constantly changes and evolves and must be approached with both care and respect.

Comparing One Company to Another: Suppose your neighbor or a coworker tells you about a stock you "have to own" because the P/E is only 10, much less than the overall market. Is it a buy? Maybe, or maybe not. The index and its components can tell you a lot about the stocks in the index as well as about the market. Stocks in the same industry or industry group often rise and fall together because the economic events and factors that affect one stock in an industry will affect others as well. When oil prices rise, most oil company stocks tend to do well. Rumors of changes in Medicare and other health care programs may affect all pharmaceutical stocks at once. One can compare data about a stock to the same information for similar stocks, to the industry or economic sector, and to the whole market. The S&P 500 and information about the stocks in it make this possible.

How does this help decide if a stock is cheap? Suppose the market's P/E as measured by the S&P 500 is 15 and the stock's P/E is 20, so it looks to be overpriced. Before forgetting about it, compare the data on the stock—P/E ratios, dividend yields, or other statistics—to similar stocks. The easiest way to find similar stocks is to use the sector and industry classifications from the S&P 500, as shown on the stock reports. As you do this with various stocks, you will begin to see that some sectors or industries seem to always have P/Es higher than the market while other sectors have low P/Es. Some sectors focus on growth stocks, which have high P/Es, while others focus on value stocks. You will notice similar patterns if you compare dividend yields. In fact, even looking for stocks that pay dividends will reveal some patterns.

---

[2]John Y. Campbell and Robert J. Shiller, "Valuation Ratios and the Long-Run Stock Market Outlook", *Journal of Portfolio Management*, winter 1998. Figures used in the text from www.dshort.com.

The stock market is shifting all the time, with some sectors becoming relatively more expensive and others fading from popularity. Within a sector there are similar movements among stocks as some move up faster while others may fade. It is useful to know how a stock compares to its peers in the same industry or sector as well as to understand how it compares to the entire market. Using the S&P 500 and the data shown on the stock reports, one can see these shifts and comparisons.

What's in the S&P 500

The S&P 500 Index consists of 500 stocks selected by Standard & Poor's to represent the U.S. stock market and, through the market, the U.S. economy. It is not the 500 "largest" stocks in the market. Rather, it is sometimes described as containing the leading stocks in leading industries. The stocks are selected based on published guidelines; all members of the S&P 500 must be U.S. companies. When they join the index, they must have market values of at least $3 billion, trade with reasonable liquidity, be profitable, and have at least half their shares available to investors. The selection of companies also considers the balance of economic sectors in the market and the index so that the index is a fair representation of the market as a whole.

The S&P 500 index is reported on television, Web sites and newspapers very widely. Data are also published on S&P's Web site at www.indices.standardandpoors.com. Many investors and investment analysts use the S&P 500 to help choose stocks, as described above. However it has many other investment uses: index mutual funds, exchange-traded funds (ETFs), futures, and options. Index mutual funds are mutual funds that track an index. The first funds, and the largest index funds today, track the S&P 500. Exchange-traded funds have grown in popularity in recent years. These are similar to index mutual funds except that they trade on an exchange and can by bought and sold at any time of day whereas mutual funds are only sold at prices based on the market close. The first U.S. ETF was based on the S&P 500; there are two large ETFs based on the S&P 500. In addition, numerous pension funds, endowments, and other institutional investments track the S&P 500. As of the end of 2007, over $1.5 trillion was invested in various investments that track the S&P 500 as closely as possible. This means that the fund tries to mimic the index, adding stocks when they are added to the index and matching any other adjustments in the index.

There are relatively few changes in the index; most of these changes are caused by mergers, acquisitions, and other corporate actions that remove companies from the index. Over the last several years, the index has seen about 30 changes each year where a "change" is one company added and one dropped. If one thinks of the index as a portfolio, it is amazingly stable compared to most mutual funds—the turnover in the S&P 500 is about 5 to 10 percent of its value each year, whereas mutual funds can see a turnover of over 100 percent in a single year. A typical change in the index occurs when a company is acquired and is dropped from the index and replaced with another company. At times, especially recently with the turmoil in the markets, companies in the index are removed because of bankruptcy.

While changes to the index don't occur every day, they can be important to some traders. Because so much money tracks the index, about 10 percent of the outstanding stock of any company in the index is bought by index funds, ETFs, and other index investors when a stock is added to the index. Further, this buying occurs over a relatively short period of time—a few weeks or less. The result is that stocks added to the S&P 500 often see their prices rise when they go into the index.

The S&P 500 index was created and is maintained by S&P. There is an Index Committee of S&P professional staff who oversee the index and are responsible for making necessary changes to assure that the index will be an accurate reflection of the U.S. equity markets. Because changes in the index can move the market, all the work done by the Index Committee is confidential until any changes to the index are announced. Moreover, because the changes can move the market, the announcements are made available to the public, and no one gets any advance notice before the public announcements on S&P's Web site.

Beyond various kinds of index funds and ETFs, there are other investment uses of the index—futures and options. These are derivatives based on the value of the index that offer investors—mostly institutional investors, but some individuals as well—opportunities to either hedge their positions or to easily establish a leveraged position in the index. Futures and options are usually seen as more complex and often riskier than buying stocks. Just as successful stock investing requires research and understanding, successful use of futures and options demands a solid understanding of how the instruments work and what the risks are. At times these can magnify the impact of shifts in the index. Furthermore, unlike stocks, futures and options have firm expiration dates that must be considered in any investment plan.

History

The S&P 500 celebrated its fiftieth anniversary in March 2007. However, its forebears go farther back. The S&P 500 is not the oldest index, an honor which goes to the Dow Jones Industrials. The 500 traces its lineage back to an index of 233 companies published weekly by The Standard Statistics Company beginning in 1923. That index was one of the first to have industry classifications to support investment analysis. In 1926, Standard Statistics began a daily index of 90 stocks. A decade and a half later, in 1941, Standard Statistics merged with Poor's Publishing to form S&P. In 1957 the indices were combined and gave us the S&P 500. A small number of companies in the current S&P 500 can trace their membership back to the 1920s, over 50 were members in 1957.

The index has seen various changes over the years as it kept up with the times and with developments in the market. Different industries have come and gone. Some of today's leading sectors were barely present or nonexistent in 1957. Technology is now a much bigger part of the index. Investment banks and brokerage houses were all private partnerships in 1957 and didn't begin to enter the index until the 1970s. In many ways the index's history is the history of the U.S. stock market.

Many investors, especially those who consider mutual funds, have seen data on the history of the U.S. stock market since 1926. That history is the S&P 500 and the 90 stock index that preceded the 500. Mutual funds and other investment products often compare their performance to the market; the market is the S&P 500. You might think that 500 stocks chosen simply to represent the market without any attempt to select "good" stocks that will beat the market might be an easy target to outperform. Actually, it is not; in fact, it is *very* difficult to consistently outperform the S&P 500 or most other broad-based indices. Research by Standard & Poor's and by various others shows that in a typical period of three or more years, fewer than one-third of mutual funds outperform the index. Further, a fund that managed to be in the lucky third that beat the index in the last three years has only a one-in-three chance of beating the index in the next three years. Why? First, index funds and ETFs are cheap, with very low expenses. Second, since it is very hard to know which stocks will go up first, it helps to own a lot of stocks.[3]

Today Standard & Poor's publishes literally hundreds of thousands of indices, covering over 80 stock markets in almost every country where there is a stock market. The largest indices have several times more stocks than the 500, including a global equity index with over 11,000 securities. At the other extreme there are narrow indices focused on a small sub-industry in one country. All these indices are used by investors, often in the same way the 500 can be used, as described here.

---

[3]On index results vs. mutual funds, see S&P's SPIVA reports on S&P's Web site or books by John Bogle or Burton Malkiel.

In conclusion

When you want to know how the market did, what went up or down, or whether your stock picks beat the market, the best place to look is the S&P 500.

S&P 500 Global Industry Classification Standard (GICS) Sectors
As of October 18, 2010

	Number of Companies	Percent of Market Capitalization
Consumer Discretionary	81	10.40
Consumer Staples	41	11.13
Energy	39	11.20
Financials	81	15.49
Health Care	51	11.55
Industrials	57	10.70
Information Technology	76	19.20
Materials	31	3.61
Telecommunication Services	9	3.13
Utilities	34	3.60

What You'll Find in This Book

In the pages that follow you will find an array of text and statistical data on 500 different companies spanning over 130 sub-industries. This information, dealing with everything from the nature of these companies' basic businesses, recent corporate developments, current outlooks, and select financial information relating to revenues, earnings, dividends, margins, capitalization, and so forth, might initially seem overwhelming. However, it's not that difficult. Just take a few moments to familiarize yourself with what you'll find on these pages.

Following is a glossary of terms and definitions used throughout this book. Please refer to this section as you encounter terms which need further clarification.

Glossary

S&P STARS – Since January 1, 1987, Standard & Poor's Equity Research Services has ranked a universe of common stocks based on a given stock's potential for future performance. Under proprietary STARS (STock Appreciation Ranking System), S&P equity analysts rank stocks according to their individual forecast of a stock's future total return potential versus the expected total return of a relevant benchmark (e.g., a regional index (S&P Asia 50 Index, S&P Europe 350 Index or S&P 500 Index), based on a 12-month time horizon. STARS was designed to meet the needs of investors looking to put their investment decisions in perspective.

S&P 12-Month Target Price – The S&P equity analyst's projection of the market price a given security will command 12 months hence, based on a combination of intrinsic, relative, and private market valuation metrics.

Investment Style Classification – Characterizes the stock as either a growth-or value-oriented investment, and, indicates the market value (size) of the company as large-cap, mid-cap or small-cap. Growth stocks typically have a higher price-to-earnings and price-to-cash flow ratio, that represents the premium that is being paid for the expected higher growth. Value stocks typically have higher dividends and more moderate P/E ratios consistent with their current return policies.

Qualitative Risk Assessment – The S&P equity analyst's view of a given company's operational risk, or the risk of a firm's ability to continue as an ongoing concern. The Qualitative Risk Assessment is a relative ranking to the S&P U.S. STARS universe, and should be reflective of risk factors related to a company's operations, as opposed to risk and volatility measures associated with share prices.

Quantitative Evaluations – In contrast to our qualitative STARS recommendations, which are assigned by S&P analysts, the quantitative evaluations described below are derived from proprietary arithmetic models. These computer-driven evaluations may at times contradict an analyst's qualitative assessment of a stock. One primary reason for this is that different measures are used to determine each. For instance, when designating STARS, S&P analysts assess many factors that cannot be reflected in a model, such as risks and opportunities, management changes, recent competitive shifts, patent expiration, litigation risk, etc.

S&P Quality Rankings (also known as **S&P Earnings & Dividend Rank-ings**) – Growth and stability of earnings and dividends are deemed key elements in establishing S&P's Quality Rankings for common stocks, which are designed to capsulize the nature of this record in a single symbol. It should be noted, however, that the process also takes into consideration certain adjustments and modifications deemed desirable in establishing such rankings. The final score for each stock is measured against a scoring matrix determined by analysis of the scores of a large and representative sample of stocks. The range of scores in the array of this sample has been aligned with the following ladder of rankings:

A+	Highest	B−	Lower
A	High	C	Lowest
A−	Above Average	D	In Reorganization
B+	Average	NR	Not Ranked
B	Below Average		

S&P Fair Value Rank – Using S&P's exclusive proprietary quantitative model, stocks are ranked in one of five groups, ranging from Group 5, listing the most undervalued stocks, to Group 1, the most overvalued issues. Group 5 stocks are expected to generally outperform all others. A positive (+) or negative (−) Timing Index is placed next to the Fair Value ranking to further aid the selection process. A stock with a (+) added to the Fair Value Rank simply means that this stock has a somewhat better chance to outperform other stocks with the same Fair Value Rank. A stock with a (−) has a somewhat lesser chance to outperform other stocks with the same Fair Value Rank. The Fair Value rankings imply the following: 5-Stock is significantly undervalued; 4-Stock is moderately undervalued; 3-Stock is fairly valued; 2-Stock is modestly overvalued; 1-Stock is significantly overvalued.

S&P Fair Value Calculation – The price at which a stock should trade at, according to S&P's proprietary quantitative model that incorporates both actual and estimated variables (as opposed to only actual variables in the case of S&P Quality Ranking). Relying heavily on a company's actual return on equity, the S&P Fair Value model places a value on a security based on placing a formula-derived price-to-book multiple on a company's consensus earnings per share estimate.

Insider Activity – Gives an insight as to insider sentiment by showing whether directors, officers and key employees who have proprietary information not available to the general public, are buying or selling the company's stock during the most recent six months.

Investability Quotient (IQ) – The IQ is a measure of investment desirability. It serves as an indicator of potential medium- to long-term return and as a caution against downside risk. The measure takes into account variables such as technical indicators, earnings estimates, liquidity, financial ratios and selected S&P proprietary measures.

Volatility – Rates the volatility of the stock's price over the past year.

Technical Evaluation – In researching the past market history of prices and trading volume for each company, S&P's computer models apply special technical methods and formulas to identify and project price trends for the stock.

Relative Strength Rank – Shows, on a scale of 1 to 99, how the stock has performed versus all other companies in S&P's universe on a rolling 13-week basis.

Global Industry Classification Standard (GICS) – An industry classification standard, developed by Standard & Poor's in collaboration with Morgan Stanley Capital International (MSCI). GICS is currently comprised of 10 sectors, 24 industry groups, 68 industries, and 154 sub-industries.

S&P Core Earnings – Standard & Poor's Core Earnings is a uniform methodology for adjusting operating earnings by focusing on a company's after-tax earnings generated from its principal businesses. Included in the Standard & Poor's definition are employee stock option grant expenses, pension costs, restructuring charges from ongoing operations, write-downs of depreciable or amortizable operating assets, purchased research and development, M&A related expenses and unrealized gains/losses from hedging activities. Excluded from the definition are pension gains, impairment of goodwill charges, gains or losses from asset sales, reversal of prior-year charges and provision from litigation or insurance settlements.

S&P Issuer Credit Rating – A Standard & Poor's Issuer Credit Rating is a current opinion of an obligor's overall financial capacity (its creditworthiness) to pay its financial obligations. This opinion focuses on the obligor's capacity and willingness to meet its financial commitments as they come due. It does not apply to any specific financial obligation, as it does not take into account the nature of and provisions of the obligation, its standing in bankruptcy or liquidation, statutory preferences, or the legality and enforceability of the obligation. In addition, it does not take into account the creditworthiness of the guarantors, insurers, or other forms of credit enhancement on the obligation. The Issuer Credit Rating is not a recommendation to purchase, sell, or hold a financial obligation issued by an obligor, as it does not comment on market price or suitability for a particular investor. Issuer Credit Ratings are based on current information furnished by obligors or obtained by Standard & Poor's from other sources it considers reliable. Standard & Poor's does not perform an audit in connection with any Issuer Credit Rating and may, on occasion, rely on unaudited financial information. Issuer Credit Ratings may be changed, suspended, or withdrawn as a result of changes in, or unavailability of, such information, or based on other circumstances.

Standard & Poor's Equity Research Services – Standard & Poor's Equity Research Services U.S. includes Standard & Poor's Investment Advisory Services LLC; Standard & Poor's

Equity Research Services Europe includes Standard & Poor's LLC- London; Standard & Poor's Equity Research Ser-vices Asia includes Standard & Poor's LLC's offices in Hong Kong and Singapore, Standard & Poor's Malaysia Sdn Bhd, and Standard & Poor's Information Services (Australia) Pty Ltd.

<u>**Abbreviations Used in S&P Equity Research Reports**</u>
CAGR – Compound Annual Growth Rate
CAPEX – Capital Expenditures
CY – Calendar Year
DCF – Discounted Cash Flow
EBIT – Earnings Before Interest and Taxes
EBITDA – Earnings Before Interest, Taxes, Depreciation and Amortization
EPS – Earnings Per Share
EV – Enterprise Value
FCF – Free Cash Flow
FFO – Funds From Operations
FY – Fiscal Year
P/E – Price/Earnings
PEG Ratio – P/E-to-Growth Ratio
PV – Present Value
R&D – Research & Development
ROA – Return on Assets
ROE – Return on Equity
ROI – Return on Investment
ROIC – Return on Invested Capital
SG&A – Selling, General & Administrative Expenses
WACC – Weighted Average Cost of Capital
Dividends on American Depository Receipts (ADRs) and American Depository Shares (ADSs) are net of taxes (paid in the country of origin).

REQUIRED DISCLOSURES

S&P Global STARS Distribution

In North America
As of September 30, 2010, research analysts at Standard & Poor's Equity Research Services North America recommended 39.2% of issuers with buy recommendations, 52.5% with hold recommendations and 8.3% with sell recommendations.

In Europe
As of September 30, 2010, research analysts at Standard & Poor's Equity Research Services Europe recommended 36.6% of issuers with buy recommendations, 43.2% with hold recommendations and 20.2% with sell recommendations.

In Asia
As of September 30, 2010, research analysts at Standard & Poor's Equity Research Services Asia recommended 46.8% of issuers with buy recommendations, 44.4% with hold recommendations and 8.8% with sell recommendations.

Globally
As of September 30, 2010, research analysts at Standard & Poor's Equity Research Services globally recommended 39.5% of issuers with buy recommendations, 50.2% with hold recommendations and 10.3% with sell recommendations.

5-STARS (Strong Buy): Total return is expected to outperform the total return of a relevant benchmark, by a wide margin over the coming 12 months, with shares rising in price on an absolute basis.

4-STARS (Buy): Total return is expected to outperform the total return of a relevant benchmark over the coming 12 months, with shares rising in price on an absolute basis.

3-STARS (Hold): Total return is expected to closely approximate the total return of a relevant benchmark over the coming 12 months, with shares generally rising in price on an absolute basis.

2-STARS (Sell): Total return is expected to underperform the total return of a relevant benchmark over the coming 12 months, and the share price not anticipated to show a gain.

1-STAR (Strong Sell): Total return is expected to underperform the total return of a relevant benchmark by a wide margin over the coming 12 months, with shares falling in price on an absolute basis.
Relevant benchmarks: In North America, the relevant benchmark is the S&P 500 Index, in Europe and in Asia, the relevant benchmarks are generally the S&P Europe 350 Index and the S&P Asia 50 Index.

For All Regions:
All of the views expressed in this research report accurately reflect the research analyst's personal views regarding any and all of the subject securities or issuers. No part of analyst compensation was, is, or will be directly or indirectly, related to the specific recommendations or views expressed in this research report.

Additional information is available upon request.
Other Disclosures

This report has been prepared and issued by Standard & Poor's and/or one of its affiliates. In the United States, research reports are prepared by Standard & Poor's Investment Advisory Services LLC ("SPIAS"). In the United States, research reports are issued by Standard & Poor's ("S&P"); in the United Kingdom by Standard & Poor's LLC ("S&P LLC"), which is authorized and regulated by the Financial Services Authority; in Hong Kong by Standard & Poor's LLC, which is regulated by the Hong Kong Securities Futures Commission; in Singapore by Standard & Poor's LLC, which is regulated by the Monetary Authority of Singapore; in Malaysia by Standard & Poor's Malaysia Sdn Bhd ("S&PM"), which is regulated by the Securities Commission; in Australia by Standard & Poor's Information Services (Australia) Pty Ltd ("SPIS"), which is regulated by the Australian Securities & Investments Commission; and in Korea by SPIAS, which is also registered in Korea as a cross-border investment advisory company.

The research and analytical services performed by SPIAS, S&P LLC, S&PM, and SPIS are each conducted separately from any other analytical activity of Standard & Poor's.

Standard & Poor's or an affiliate may license certain intellectual property or provide pricing or other services to, or otherwise have a financial interest in, certain issuers of securities, including exchange-traded investments whose investment objective is to substantially replicate the returns of a proprietary Standard & Poor's index, such as the S&P 500. In cases where Standard & Poor's or an affiliate is paid fees that are tied to the amount of assets that are invested in the fund or the volume of trading activity in the fund, investment in the fund will generally result in Standard & Poor's or an affiliate earning compensation in addition to the subscription fees or other compensation for services rendered by

Standard & Poor's. A reference to a particular investment or security by Standard & Poor's and/or one of its affiliates is not a recommendation to buy, sell, or hold such investment or security, nor is it considered to be investment advice.

Indexes are unmanaged, statistical composites and their returns do not include payment of any sales charges or fees an investor would pay to purchase the securities they represent. Such costs would lower performance. It is not possible to invest directly in an index. Standard & Poor's and its affiliates provide a wide range of services to, or relating to, many organizations, including issuers of securities, investment advisers, broker-dealers, investment banks, other financial institutions and financial intermediaries, and accordingly may receive fees or other economic benefits from those organizations, including organizations whose securities or services they may recommend, rate, include in model portfolios, evaluate or otherwise address.

For a list of companies mentioned in this report with whom Standard & Poor's and/or one of its affiliates has had business relationships within the past year, please go to: http://www.standardandpoors.com/products-services/articles/en/us/?assetID=1245187 982940

Disclaimers

This material is based upon information that we consider to be reliable, but neither S&P nor its affiliates warrant its completeness, accuracy or adequacy and it should not be relied upon as such. With respect to reports issued to clients in Japan and in the case of inconsistencies between the English and Japanese version of a report, the English version prevails. With respect to reports issued to clients in German and in the case of inconsistencies between the English and German version of a report, the English version prevails. Neither S&P nor its affiliates guarantee the accuracy of the translation. Assumptions, opinions and estimates constitute our judgment as of the date of this material and are subject to change without notice. Neither S&P nor its affiliates are responsible for any errors or omissions or for results obtained from the use of this information. Past performance is not necessarily indicative of future results.

This material is not intended as an offer or solicitation for the purchase or sale of any security or other financial instrument. Securities, financial instruments or strategies mentioned herein may not be suitable for all investors. Any opinions expressed herein are given in good faith, are subject to change without notice, and are only correct as of the stated date of their issue. Prices, values, or income from any securities or investments mentioned in this report may fall against the interests of the investor and the investor may get back less than the amount invested. Where an investment is described as being likely to yield income, please note that the amount of income that the investor will receive from such an investment may fluctuate. Where an investment or security is denominated in a different currency to the investor's currency of reference, changes in rates of exchange may have an adverse effect on the value, price or income of or from that investment to the investor. The information contained in this report does not constitute advice on the tax consequences of making any particular investment decision. This material is not intended for any specific investor and does not take into account your particular investment objectives, financial situations or needs and is not intended as a recommendation of particular securities, financial instruments or strategies to you. Before acting on any recommendation in this material, you should consider whether it is suitable for your particular circumstances and, if necessary, seek professional advice.

For residents of the U.K. – This report is only directed at and should only be relied on by persons outside of the United Kingdom or persons who are inside the United Kingdom and who have professional experience in matters relating to investments or who are high net worth persons, as defined in Article 19(5) or Article 49(2) (a) to (d) of the Financial Services and Markets Act 2000 (Financial Promotion) Order 2005, respectively.

For residents of Singapore – Anything herein that may be construed as a recommendation is intended for general circulation and does not take into account the specific investment objectives, financial situation or particular needs of any particular person. Advice should be sought from a financial adviser regarding the suitability of an investment, taking into account the specific investment objectives, financial situation or particular needs of any person in receipt of the recommendation, before the person makes a commitment to purchase the investment product.

For residents of Malaysia – All queries in relation to this report should be referred to Alexander Chia, Desmond Ch'ng, or Ching Wah Tam.

This investment analysis was prepared from the following sources: S&P MarketScope, S&P Compustat, S&P Industry Reports, I/B/E/S International, Inc.; Standard & Poor's, 55 Water St., New York, NY 10041.

Key Stock Statistics

Market Cap.—The stock price multiplied by the number of shares outstanding, based on market value calculated at the issue level.

Institutional Holdings—Shows the percent of total common shares held by financial institutions. This information covers some 2,500 institutions and is compiled by Vickers Stock Research Corporation, 226 New York Avenue, Huntington, N.Y. 11743

Value of $10,000 Invested 5 years ago—The value today of a $10,000 investment in the stock made 5 years ago, assuming year-end reinvestment of dividends.

Beta—The beta coefficient is a measure of the volatility of a stock's price relative to the S&P 500 Index (a proxy for the overall market). An issue with a beta of 1.5 for example, tends to move 50% more than the overall market, in the same direction. An issue with a beta of 0.5 tends to move 50% less. If a stock moved exactly as the market moved, it would have a beta of 1.0. A stock with a negative beta tends to move in a direction opposite to that of the overall market.

Per Share Data ($) Tables

Cash Flow—Net income plus depreciation, depletion, and amortization, divided by shares used to calculate earnings per common share. (See also: "Cash Flow" under Industrial Companies.)

Dividends—Generally total cash payments per share based on the ex-dividend dates over a 12-month period. May also be reported on a declared basis where this has been established to be a company's payout policy.

Earnings—The amount a company reports as having been earned for the year on its common stock based on generally accepted accounting standards. Earnings per share are presented on a "diluted" basis pursuant to FASB 128, which became effective December 15, 1997, and are generally reported from continuing operations, before extraordinary items. This reflects a change from previously reported *primary earnings per share*. Insurance companies report *operating earnings* before gains/losses on security transactions and *earnings* after such transactions.

Net Asset Value—Appears on investment company reports and reflects the market value of stocks, bonds, and net cash divided by outstanding shares. The % difference indicates the percentage premium or discount of the market price over the net asset value.

Payout Ratio—Indicates the percentage of earnings paid out in dividends. It is calculated by dividing the annual dividend by the earnings. For insurance companies, *earnings* after gains/losses on security transactions are used.

P/E Ratio High/Low—The ratio of market price to earnings—essentially indicates the valuation investors place on a company's earnings. Obtained by dividing the annual earnings into the high and low market price for the year. For insurance companies, *operating earnings* before gains/losses on security transactions are used.

Portfolio Turnover—Appears on investment company reports and indicates percentage of total security purchases and sales for the year to overall investment assets. Primarily mirrors trading aggressiveness.

Prices High/Low—Shows the calendar year high and low of a stock's market price.

Tangible Book Value; Book Value (See also: "Common Equity" under Industrial Companies)—Indicates the theoretical dollar amount per common share one might expect to receive from a company's tangible "book" assets should liquidation take place. Generally, book value is determined by adding the stated value of the common stock, paid-in capital and retained earnings and then subtracting intangible assets (excess cost over equity of acquired companies, goodwill, and patents), preferred stock at liquidating value and unamortized debt discount. Divide that amount by the outstanding shares to get book value per common share.

Income/Balance Sheet Data Tables

Banks

Cash—Mainly vault cash, interest-bearing deposits placed with banks, reserves required by the Federal Reserve, and items in the process of collection—generally referred to as float.

Commercial Loans—Commercial, industrial, financial, agricultural loans and leases, gross.

Common Equity—Includes common/capital surplus, undivided profits, reserve for contingencies and other capital reserves.

Deposits—Primarily classified as either *demand* (payable at any time upon demand of depositor) or *time* (not payable within 30 days).

Deposits/Capital Funds—Average deposits divided by average capital funds. Capital funds include capital notes/debentures, other long-term debt, capital stock, surplus, and undivided profits. May be used as a "leverage" measure.

Earning Assets—Assets on which interest is earned.

Effective Tax Rate—Actual income tax expense divided by net before taxes.

Gains/Losses on Securities Transactions—Realized losses on sales of securities, usually bonds.

Government Securities—Includes United States Treasury securities and securities of other U.S. government agencies at book or carrying value. A bank's major "liquid asset."

Investment Securities—Federal, state, and local government bonds and other securities.

Loan Loss Provision—Amount charged to operating expenses to provide an adequate reserve to cover anticipated losses in the loan portfolio.

Loans—All domestic and foreign loans (excluding leases), less unearned discount and reserve for possible losses. Generally considered a bank's principal asset.

Long-Term Debt—Total borrowings for terms beyond one year including notes payable, mortgages, debentures, term loans, and capitalized lease obligations.

Money Market Assets—Interest-bearing interbank deposits, federal funds sold, trading account securities.

Net Before Taxes—Amount remaining after operating expenses are deducted from income, including gains or losses on security transactions.

Net Income—The final profit before dividends (common/preferred) from all sources after deduction of expenses, taxes, and fixed charges, but before any discontinued operations or extraordinary items.

Net Interest Income—Interest and dividend income, minus interest expense.

Net Interest Margin—A percentage computed by dividing net interest income, on a taxable equivalent basis, by average earning assets. Used as an analytical tool to measure profit margins from providing credit services.

Noninterest Income—Service fees, trading, and other income, excluding gains/ losses on securities transactions.

Other Loans—Gross consumer, real estate and foreign loans.

% Equity to Assets—Average common equity divided by average total assets. Used as a measure of capital adequacy.

% Equity to Loans—Average common equity divided by average loans. Reflects the degree of equity coverage to loans outstanding.

% Expenses/Op. Revenues—Noninterest expense as a percentage of taxable equivalent net interest income plus noninterest income (before securities gains/losses). A measure of cost control.

% Loan Loss Reserve—Contra-account to loan assets, built through provisions for loan losses, which serves as a cushion for possible future loan charge-offs.

% Loans/Deposits—Proportion of loans funded by deposits. A measure of liquidity and an indication of bank's ability to write more loans.

% Return on Assets—Net income divided by average total assets. An analytical measure of asset-use efficiency and industry comparison.

% Return on Equity—Net income (minus preferred dividend requirements) divided by average common equity. Generally used to measure performance.

% Return on Revenues—Net income divided by gross revenues.

State and Municipal Securities—State and municipal securities owned at book value.

Taxable Equivalent Adjustment—Increase to render income from tax-exempt loans and securities comparable to fully taxed income.

Total Assets—Includes interest-earning financial instruments—principally commercial, real estate, consumer loans and leases; investment securities/ trading accounts; cash/money market investments; other owned assets.

Industrial Companies

Following data is based on Form 10K Annual Report data as filed with SEC.

Capital Expenditures—The sum of additions at cost to property, plant and equipment, and leaseholds, generally excluding amounts arising from acquisitions.

Cash—Includes all cash and government and other marketable securities.

Cash Flow—Net income (before extraordinary items and discontinued operations, and after preferred dividends) plus depreciation, depletion, and amortization.

Common Equity [See also "Tangible Book Value" under Per Share Data($) Tables]—Common stock plus capital surplus and retained earnings, less any difference between the carrying value and liquidating value of preferred stock.

Current Assets—Those assets expected to be realized in cash or used up in the production of revenue within one year.

Current Liabilities—Generally includes all debts/obligations falling due within one year.

Current Ratio—Current assets divided by current liabilities. A measure of liquidity.

Depreciation—Includes noncash charges for obsolescence, wear on property, current portion of capitalized expenses (intangibles), and depletion charges.

Effective Tax Rate—Actual income tax charges divided by net before taxes.

Interest Expense—Includes all interest expense on short/long-term debt, amortization of debt discount/premium, and deferred expenses (e.g., financing costs).

Long-Term Debt—Debts/obligations due after one year. Includes bonds, notes payable, mortgages, lease obligations, and industrial revenue bonds. Other long-term debt, when reported as a separate account, is excluded. This account generally includes pension and retirement benefits.

Net Before Taxes—Includes operating and nonoperating revenues (including extraordinary items not net of taxes), less all operating and nonoperating expenses, except income taxes and minority interest, but including equity in nonconsolidated subsidiaries.

Net Income—Profits derived from all sources after deduction of expenses, taxes, and fixed charges, but before any discontinued operations, extraordinary items, and dividends (preferred/common).

Operating Income—Net sales and operating revenues less cost of goods sold and operating expenses (including research and development, profit sharing, exploration and bad debt, but excluding depreciation and amortization).

% Long-Term Debt of Invested Capital—Long-term debt divided by total invested capital. Indicates how highly "leveraged" a business might be.

% Operating Income of Revenues—Net sales and operating revenues divided into operating income. Used as a measure of operating profitability.

% Net Income of Revenues—Net income divided by sales/operating revenues.

% Return on Assets—Net income divided by average total assets on a per common share basis. Used in industry analysis and as a measure of asset-use efficiency.

% Return on Equity—Net income less preferred dividend requirements divided by average common shareholders' equity on a per common share basis. Generally used to measure performance and industry comparisons.

Revenues—Net sales and other operating revenues. Includes franchise/ leased department income for retailers, and royalties for publishers and oil and mining companies. Excludes excise taxes for tobacco, liquor, and oil companies.

Total Assets—Current assets plus net plant and other noncurrent assets (intangibles and deferred items).

Total Invested Capital—The sum of stockholders' equity plus long-term debt, capital lease obligations, deferred income taxes, investment credits, and minority interest.

Insurance Companies

Life Insurance In Force—The total value of all life insurance policies including ordinary, group, industrial and credit. Generally the figure is reported before any amounts ceded, or the portions placed with other insurance companies.

Premium Income—The amount of premiums earned during the year is generally equal to the net premiums written plus any increase or decrease in earned premiums. The categories are divided into Life, Accident & Health, Annuity and Property & Casualty.

Net Investment Income—Income received from investment assets (before taxes) including bonds, stocks, loans and other investments (less related expenses).

Total Revenues—Includes premium income, net investment income and other income.

Property & Casualty Underwriting Ratios— Includes: Loss Ratio—losses and loss adjustment expenses divided by premiums earned; Expense Ratio—underwriting expenses divided by net premiums written; Combined Loss-Expense Ratio—Measures claims, losses and operating expenses against premiums. The total of losses and loss expenses, before policyholders' dividends, to premiums earned, e.g., at 106.0%, equivalent to a loss of six cents of every premium dollar before investment income and taxes.

Net Before Taxes—Total operating income before income taxes and security gains or losses. Generally will include any equity in income of subsidiaries.

Net Operating Income—Includes income from operations, before security gains or losses, and before results of discontinued operations and special items.

Net Income—Includes income from operations, after security gains or losses, and before results of discontinued operations and special items.

% Return On Revenues—Is the net operating income divided by the total revenues.

% Return On Assets—Is the net operating income divided by the mean/ average assets.

% Return On Equity—Is obtained by dividing the average common equity for the year into the net operating income, less any preferred stock dividend requirements.

Cash & Equivalent—Includes cash, accrued investment income and short- term investments (except when classified as investments by the company).

Premiums Due—Generally includes premiums owed but uncollected, agent's balances receivable and earned and unbilled premiums receivable.

Investment Assets—Includes all investments shown under the company's investment account. Bonds, values at cost, includes bonds and notes, debt obligations and any short-term investments. Stocks, values at market, includes common and preferred stocks in the investment portfolio. Loans, includes mortgage, policy and other loans.

% Investment Yield—Is the return received on the company's investment assets, and is obtained by dividing the average investment assets into the net investment income, before applicable income taxes.

Deferred Policy Costs—Reflect certain costs of acquiring insurance business which have been deferred. These costs are primarily related to the production of business such as commissions, expenses in issuing policies and certain agency expenses.

Total Assets—Includes total investments, cash and cash items, accrued investment income, premiums due, deferred policy acquisition costs, property and equipment, separate accounts and other assets.

Debt—Includes bonds, debentures, notes, loans and mortgages payable.

Common Equity—Consists of common stock, additional paid in capital, net unrealized capital gains or losses on investments, retained earnings—less treasury stock at cost.

Investment Companies

Total Investment Income—The sum of income received from dividends and interest on portfolio holdings.

Net Investment Income—The amount of income remaining after operating expenses are deducted from total investment income. The per share figure is generally reported by the company, or may be obtained by dividing the net investment income by the shares outstanding. This amount is available for the payment of distributions.

Realized Capital Gains—Represents the net gain realized on the sale of investments, as reported by the company in the statement of changes in net assets. Divide amount by shares outstanding to obtain per share figure.

% Net Investment Income/Net Assets—Measures return on net assets. Percentage is obtained by dividing net investment income by average net assets.

% Expenses/Net Assets—Generally measures cost control. Percentage is obtained by dividing operating expenses by average net assets.

% Expenses/Investment Income—Indicates the amount of income absorbed by expenses. Percentage is obtained by dividing operating expenses by total investment income.

Net Assets—Represents the total market value of portfolio securities, including net cash, short-term investments, and stocks and bonds at market.

% Change S&P "500"—Measures the percentage change in Standard & Poor's 500 stock price index, before reinvestment of dividends, and is a general indicator of overall stock market performance.

% Change AAA Bonds—Measures the percentage change in the Standard & Poor's high grade bond index, before reinvestment of interest, and is a measure of AAA bond price movements.

% Net Asset Distribution—Indicates the percentage breakdown of net assets in the following categories: a) net cash (cash receivables and other assets, less liabilities); b) short-term obligations (U.S. Government securities, commercial paper and certificates of deposit); c) bonds and preferred stocks; d) common stocks. To calculate the % net asset distribution, divide net assets into each of the above categories.

Real Estate Investment Trusts and Savings & Loans

Rental Income—Primarily income received from rental property.

Mortgage Income—Primarily income derived from mortgages.

Total Income—Includes rental and mortgage income, gains on sale of real estate and other.

General Expenses—Includes property operating expenses, real estate taxes, depreciation & amortization, administrative expenses and provision for losses.

Interest Expense—Includes interest paid on mortgage debt, convertible debentures, other debt obligations and short-term debt.

% Expenses/Revenues—Total expenses divided by revenues. The result represents the percentage of revenues (or the number of cents per dollar of income) absorbed by expenses.

Provision for Losses—Reserve charged to income for possible real estate losses.

Net Income—Profits for the year. This would include any gains/losses on the sale of real estate but exclude extraordinary items.

% Earnings & Depreciation/Assets—Obtained by dividing average assets into the sum of net income and depreciation expense (a measure of "cash flow" for REITs).

Total Assets—The sum of net investments in real estate and other assets.

Real Estate Investments—The sum of gross investments in real estate, construction in process and mortgage loans and notes before allowances for losses and accumulated depreciation.

Loss Reserve—Reserves set aside for possible losses on real estate investments.

Net Investment—Real estate investments less accumulated depreciation and loss reserves.

Cash—Cash on hand, cash in escrow and short-term investments.

S T Debt—Short-term obligations due and payable within one year of balance sheet date. This would include the current portion of long-term debt, mortgages and notes, bank loans and commercial paper.

Debt—Includes debentures, mortgages and other long-term debt due after one year of balance sheet date.

Equity—Represents the sum of shares of beneficial interest or common stock, convertible preferred stock when included as equity, capital surplus and undistributed net income.

Total Capitalization—Is the sum of the stated values of a company's total shareholders' equity including preferred, common stock and debt obligations.

Price Times Book Value Hi Lo—Indicates the relationship of a stock's market price to book value. Obtained by dividing year-end book values into yearly high/low range.

Utilities

Capital Expenditures—Represents the amounts spent on capital improvements to plant and funds for construction programs.

Capitalization Ratios—Reflect the percentage of each type of debt/equity issues outstanding to total capitalization. % DEBT is obtained by dividing total debt by the sum of debt, preferred, common, paid-in capital and retained earnings. % PREFERRED is obtained by dividing the preferred stocks outstanding by total capitalization. % COMMON, divide the sum of common stocks, paid-in capital and retained earnings by total capitalization.

Construction Credits—Credits for interest charged to the cost of constructing new plant. A combination of allowance for equity funds used during construction and allowance for borrowed funds used during construction—credit.

Depreciation—Amounts charged to income to compensate for the decline in useful value of plant and equipment.

Effective Tax Rate—Actual income tax expense divided by the total of net income and actual income tax expense.

Fixed Charges Coverage—The number of times income before interest charges (operating income plus other income) after taxes covers total interest charges and preferred dividend requirements.

Gross Property—Includes utility plant at cost, plant work in progress, and nuclear fuel.

Long-Term Debt—Debt obligations due beyond one year from balance sheet date.

Maintenance—Amounts spent to keep plants in good operating condition.

Net Income—Amount of earnings for the year which is available for preferred and common dividend payments.

Net Property—Includes items in gross property less provision for depreciation.

Operating Revenues—Represents the amount billed to customers by the utility.

Operating Ratio—Ratio of operating costs to operating revenues or the proportion of revenues absorbed by expenses. Obtained by dividing operating expenses including depreciation, maintenance, and taxes by revenues.

% Earned on Net Property—Percentage obtained by dividing operating income by average net property for the year. A measure of plant efficiency.

% Return on Common Equity—Percentage obtained by dividing income available for common stock (net income less preferred dividend requirements) by average common equity.

% Return on Invested Capital—Percentage obtained by dividing income available for fixed charges by average total invested capital.

% Return on Revenues—Obtained by dividing net income for the year by revenues.

Total Capitalization—Combined sum of total common equity, preferred stock and long-term debt.

Total Invested Capital—Sum of total capitalization (common-preferred-debt), accumulated deferred income taxes, accumulated investment tax credits, minority interest, contingency reserves, and contributions in aid of construction.

Finally, at the very bottom of the right-hand page, you'll find general information about the company: its address and telephone number, the names of its senior executive officers and directors (usually including the name of the investor contact), and the state in which the company is incorporated.

How to Use This Book to Select Investments

And so, at last, we come to the $64,000 question: Given this vast array of data, how might a businesswoman seeking to find out about her competition, a marketing manager looking for clients, a job seeker, and an investor use it to best serve their respective purposes?

If you are like one of the first three of these individuals—a businesswoman, a marketing manager, or a job seeker—your task will be arduous, to be sure, but this book will provide you with an excellent starting point and your payoff can make it all worthwhile. You will have to go through this book page by page, looking for those companies that are in the industries in which you are interested, that are of the size and financial strength that appeal to you, that are located geographically in your territory or where you're willing to relocate, that have been profitable and growing, and so forth. And then you will have to read about just what's going on at those companies by referring to the appropriate "Highlights" and "Business Summary" comments in these reports.

Of course, this book won't do it *all* for you. It is, after all, just a starting point, not a conclusive summary of everything you might need to know. It is designed to educate, not to render advice or provide recommendations. But it will get you pointed in the right direction.

Finally, what about an investor who wants to use this book to find good individual investments from among the 500 stocks in the S&P 500 Index? If you fall into that category, what should you do?

Well, you can approach your quest the same way that the businesswoman looking for information about her competitors, the marketing manager, and the job seeker approached theirs—by thumbing through this book page by page, looking for companies with high historical growth rates, generous dividend payout policies, wide profit margins, A+ Standard & Poor's Quality Rankings, or whatever other characteristics you consider desirable in stocks in which you might invest. In this case, however, we have made your job just a little bit easier.

We have already prescreened the 500 companies in this book for several of the stock characteristics in which investors generally are most interested, including Standard & Poor's Quality Rankings, growth records, and dividend payment histories, and we're pleased to present on the next several pages lists of those companies which score highest on the bases of these criteria. So if you, like most investors, find these characteristics important in potential investments, you might want to turn first to the companies on these lists in your search for attractive investments.

Good luck and happy investment returns!

Companies With Five Consecutive Years of Earnings Increases

This table, compiled from a computer screen of the stocks in this handbook, shows companies that have recorded rising per-share earnings for five consecutive years, have estimated 2010 EPS above those reported for 2009, pay dividends, and have Standard & Poor's Quality Rankings of A– or better.

Company	Business	S&P Quality Ranking	Fiscal Year End	EPS 2009 Actual $	EPS 2010 Estimate $	5 Yr. EPS % Growth Rate	Price	P/E on 2010 Est.	Yield
Baxter Intl	Mfr,dstr hospital/lab prod	A	Dec	3.59	3.98	13	49.16	12.4	2.4%
Becton, Dickinson	Health care pr:ind'l safety	A	Sep	4.99	5.08	15	74.75	14.7	2.0%
Brown-Forman'B'	Mkt whisky,wine prd/Lenox chin	A	Apr#	2.87	3.02	6	61.11	20.2	2.0%
C.H. Robinson Worldwide	Motor freight transportat'n	A+	Dec	2.13	2.30	12	71.21	31.0	1.4%
Colgate-Palmolive	Household & personal care	A+	Dec	4.37	4.77	13	74.90	15.7	2.8%
CVS Caremark Corp	Oper drug/health stores	A+	Dec	2.55	2.70	13	31.25	11.6	1.1%
Entergy Corp	Owns five operating utilities	A	Dec	6.29	6.80	8	76.12	11.2	4.4%
Hasbro Inc	Mfrs toys & games	A–	Dec	2.48	2.63	21	45.64	17.4	2.2%
Hudson City Bancorp	Savings bank,New Jersey	A	Dec	1.07	1.19	21	12.00	10.1	5.0%
Intl Bus. Machines	Lgst mfr business machines	A	Dec	10.01	11.50	17	138.85	12.1	1.9%
Kellogg Co	Convenience food products	A+	Dec	3.16	3.40	7	49.97	14.7	3.2%
Oracle Corp	Mkts database mgmt softwr	A–	May#	1.09	1.21	13	28.00	23.1	0.7%
Polo Ralph Lauren'A'	Retail apparel/home prd	A–	Mar+	4.73	5.11	11	92.91	18.2	0.4%
Praxair Inc	Ind'l gases/spcl coatings	A+	Dec	4.01	4.65	12	90.62	19.5	2.0%
Ross Stores	Apparel,shoes,linen retailer	A+	Jan+	3.54	4.25	26	55.74	13.1	1.1%
Sigma-Aldrich	Specialty chem prod	A+	Dec	2.80	3.15	10	60.65	19.3	1.1%
Smucker (J.M.)	Preserves: jellies & fillings	A+	Apr#	3.12	4.15	11	61.90	14.9	2.6%
TJX Companies	Off-price specialty stores	A+	Jan+	2.84	3.35	19	44.67	13.3	1.3%
Wal-Mart Stores	Operates discount stores	A+	Jan+	3.70	4.03	8	54.41	13.5	2.2%
Wisconsin Energy Corp	Hdlg:El & gas utility	A–	Dec	3.24	3.78	5	58.22	15.4	2.7%
Yum Brands	Oper family style restaurants	A	Dec	2.22	2.49	12	47.65	19.1	2.1%

#Actual 2010 EPS; P/E based on actual 2010 EPS.

+Actual 2010 EPS and Estimated 2011 EPS; P/E based on estimated 2011.

Chart data is as of the close October 8, 2010.

NOTE: All earnings estimates are Standard & Poor's projections.

S&P 500 STOCK SCREENS

Stocks With A+ Rankings

Based on the issues in this handbook, this screen shows stocks of all companies with Standard & Poor's Quality Rankings of A+.

Company	Business
Caterpillar Inc	Earthmoving mchy: diesel eng
C.H. Robinson Worldwide	Motor freight transportat'n
Coca-Cola Co	Major soft drink/juice co
Colgate-Palmolive	Household & personal care
CVS Caremark Corp	Oper drug/health stores
Danaher Corp	Mfr hand tools, auto parts
Ecolab Inc	Comm'l cleaning&sanitizing
Expeditors Intl, Wash	Int'l air freight forward'g
Exxon Mobil	World's leading oil co
Family Dollar Stores	Self-service retail stores
Genl Dynamics	Armored/space launch vehicles
Grainger (W.W.)	Natl dstr indus/comm'l prod
Hormel Foods	Meat & food processing
Johnson & Johnson	Health care products
Kellogg Co	Convenience food products
McCormick & Co	Spices, flavoring, tea, mixes

Company	Business
NIKE, Inc'B'	Athletic footwear
Omnicom Group	Major int'l advertising co
PepsiCo Inc	Soft drink:snack foods
Praxair Inc	Ind'l gases/spcl coatings
Procter & Gamble	Hshld, personal care, food prod
Ross Stores	Apparel, shoes, linen retailer
Sigma-Aldrich	Specialty chem prod
Smucker (J.M.)	Preserves: jellies & fillings
Stryker Corp	Specialty medical devices
Sysco Corp	Food distr & service systems
Target Corp	Depart/disc/spec stores
3M Co	Scotch tapes: coated abrasives
TJX Companies	Off-price specialty stores
United Technologies	Aerospace, climate ctrl sys
UnitedHealth Group	Manages health maint svcs
Wal-Mart Stores	Operates discount stores

Table based on data at the close of October 8, 2010.

S&P 500 STOCK SCREENS

Rapid Growth Stocks

The stocks below have shown strong and consistent earnings growth. Issues of rapidly growing companies tend to carry high price-earnings ratios and offer potential for substantial appreciation. At the same time, though, the stocks are subject to strong selling pressures should growth in earnings slow. Five-year earnings growth rates have been calculated for fiscal years 2005 through 2009 and the most current 12-month earnings.

Company	Business	Fiscal Year End	5 Yr. EPS Growth Rate %	EPS 2009 Actual $	EPS 2010 Estimate $	S&P Quality Rank	Price	P/E on 2010 Est.	Yield
Apple Inc	Personal computer systems	Sep	54	9.08	14.48	B	294.07	20.3	0.0%
Biogen Idec	Dvlp stge:immune sys pharma'ls	Dec	57	3.35	4.70	B	57.59	12.3	0.0%
Cerner Corp	Dvp hlthcare ind software pd	Dec	19	2.31	2.75	B+	86.24	31.4	0.0%
Cognizant Tech Solutions'A'	Computer software & svcs	Dec	29	1.78	2.27	B+	64.20	28.3	0.0%
Express Scripts	Health care management svcs	Dec	22	1.55	2.50	B+	48.30	19.3	0.0%
IntercontinentalExchange Inc	Energy commodity trad exch	Dec	52	4.27	5.89	NR	112.36	19.1	0.0%
Intl Bus. Machines	Lgst mfr business machines	Dec	17	10.01	11.50	A	138.85	12.1	1.9%
Oracle Corp	Mkts database mgmt softwr	May#	13	1.09	1.21	A-	28.00	23.1	0.7%
Ross Stores	Apparel,shoes,linen retailer	Jan+	26	3.54	4.25	A+	55.74	13.1	1.1%
Sigma-Aldrich	Specialty chem prod	Dec	10	2.80	3.15	A+	60.65	19.3	1.1%
Smucker (J.M.)	Preserves: jellies & fillings	Apr#	11	3.12	4.15	A+	61.90	14.9	2.6%
Stericycle Inc	Environmental mgmt svcs	Dec	23	2.03	2.45	B+	71.65	29.2	0.0%
TJX Companies	Off-price specialty stores	Jan+	19	2.84	3.35	A+	44.67	13.3	1.3%
Waters Corp	Mfr liquid chromatography inst	Dec	15	3.34	3.96	B+	70.79	17.9	0.0%
Yum Brands	Oper family style restaurants	Dec	12	2.22	2.49	A	47.65	19.1	2.1%

#Actual 2010 EPS; P/E based on actual 2010 EPS
+Actual 2010 EPS and Estimated 2011 EPS; P/E based on estimated 2011 EPS
Chart based on data at the close of October 8, 2010
NOTE: All earnings estimates are Standard & Poor's projections

S&P 500 STOCK SCREENS

Fast-Rising Dividends

Based on the issues in this handbook, the companies below were chosen on the basis of their five-year annual growth rate in dividends to the current 12-month indicated rate. All have increased their dividend payments each calendar year from 2005 to their current 12-month indicated rate.

Company	Divd. Paid 2005	Divd. Paid 2009	*Ind. Divd. Rate	**Divd. Growth Rate	Price	Yield
CenturyLink Inc	0.24	2.80	2.90	87.94	39.76	7.3%
AmerisourceBergen Corp	0.03	0.24	0.32	58.15	31.67	1.0%
Stryker Corp	0.09	0.50	0.60	51.04	49.68	1.2%
Texas Instruments	0.11	0.45	0.52	41.05	28.73	1.8%
Natl Semiconductor	0.08	0.32	0.40	38.48	13.03	3.1%
Yum Brands	0.22	0.78	1.00	37.65	47.65	2.1%
CSX Corp	0.22	0.88	1.04	37.63	57.49	1.8%
Darden Restaurants	0.24	0.90	1.28	36.30	44.12	2.9%
Ameriprise Financial	0.11	0.68	0.72	36.28	49.93	1.4%
Airgas Inc	0.23	0.70	1.00	35.92	67.85	1.5%
Lowe's Cos	0.10	0.35	0.44	33.05	22.70	1.9%
Cardinal Health	0.18	0.63	0.78	32.20	32.61	2.4%
Safeway Inc	0.10	0.37	0.48	31.63	21.19	2.3%
Monsanto Co	0.34	1.04	1.12	30.15	50.87	2.2%
Harris Corp	0.28	0.84	1.05	29.48	43.73	2.3%
Cummins Inc	0.30	0.70	1.05	28.78	92.91	1.1%
McDonald's Corp	0.67	2.05	2.44	28.20	76.10	3.2%
Ross Stores	0.19	0.54	0.64	28.02	55.74	1.1%
Tiffany & Co	0.28	0.68	1.00	27.79	48.51	2.1%
Intl Bus. Machines	0.78	2.15	2.60	26.64	138.85	1.9%
L-3 Communications Hldgs	0.50	1.40	1.60	25.22	70.78	2.3%
Norfolk Southern	0.48	1.36	1.44	25.01	60.53	2.4%
Hasbro Inc	0.33	0.80	1.00	23.92	45.64	2.2%
ITT Corp	0.36	0.81	1.00	23.49	47.91	2.1%
Lockheed Martin	1.05	2.34	3.00	23.36	70.10	4.3%
AFLAC Inc	0.44	1.12	1.20	23.31	54.35	2.2%
Walgreen Co	0.24	0.50	0.70	23.29	33.98	2.1%
Microchip Technology	0.45	1.36	1.37	22.08	30.97	4.4%
Medtronic, Inc	0.36	0.79	0.90	21.43	33.45	2.7%
TJX Companies	0.23	0.47	0.60	21.37	44.67	1.3%
Republic Services	0.33	0.76	0.80	21.31	31.22	2.6%
Murphy Oil	0.45	1.00	1.10	20.97	64.40	1.7%
Target Corp	0.36	0.66	1.00	20.30	54.20	1.8%
Hudson City Bancorp	0.27	0.59	0.60	19.97	12.00	5.0%
Xilinx Inc	0.26	0.58	0.64	19.68	26.08	2.5%
Praxair Inc	0.72	1.60	1.80	19.43	90.62	2.0%

Company	Divd. Paid 2005	Divd. Paid 2009	*Ind. Divd. Rate	**Divd. Growth Rate%	Price	Yield
Illinois Tool Works	0.59	1.24	1.36	19.20	48.43	2.8%
Grainger (W.W.)	0.92	1.78	2.16	18.12	123.00	1.8%
Automatic Data Proc	0.62	1.32	1.36	17.73	42.10	3.2%
Genl Dynamics	0.78	1.49	1.68	17.28	63.37	2.7%
NIKE, Inc'B'	0.50	1.00	1.08	17.02	82.04	1.3%
Linear Technology Corp	0.40	0.88	0.92	16.91	30.96	3.0%
Occidental Petroleum	0.76	1.30	1.52	16.41	83.18	1.8%
Gap Inc	0.16	0.34	0.40	16.17	18.21	2.2%
Best Buy	0.30	0.56	0.60	15.92	41.09	1.5%
Analog Devices	0.38	0.80	0.88	15.82	32.34	2.7%
Assurant Inc	0.31	0.59	0.64	15.70	40.89	1.6%
Clorox Co	1.12	1.92	2.20	15.62	68.15	3.2%
Becton, Dickinson	0.72	1.32	1.48	15.49	74.75	2.0%
PepsiCo Inc	0.98	1.75	1.92	14.93	65.75	2.9%
Caterpillar Inc	0.91	1.68	1.76	14.49	80.37	2.2%
United Technologies	0.88	1.54	1.70	14.31	72.91	2.3%
Deere & Co	0.61	1.12	1.20	14.25	75.35	1.6%
Parker-Hannifin	0.57	1.00	1.08	14.13	71.18	1.5%
Microsoft Corp	0.32	0.52	0.64	14.05	24.57	2.6%
Intel Corp	0.32	0.56	0.63	14.02	19.52	3.2%
VF Corp	1.10	2.37	2.40	13.87	84.33	2.8%
Leggett & Platt	0.62	1.01	1.08	13.42	23.75	4.5%
Robert Half Intl	0.28	0.48	0.52	13.42	26.53	2.0%
Colgate-Palmolive	1.11	1.72	2.12	13.08	74.90	2.8%
Northrop Grumman	1.01	1.69	1.88	13.05	62.29	3.0%
Williams Cos	0.25	0.44	0.50	13.05	19.72	2.5%
PG&E Corp	0.90	1.65	1.82	12.98	46.78	3.9%
Wisconsin Energy Corp	0.88	1.35	1.60	12.80	58.22	2.7%
Costco Wholesale	0.45	0.70	0.82	12.55	64.29	1.3%
CenterPoint Energy	0.40	0.76	0.78	12.49	16.09	4.8%
ConocoPhillips	1.18	1.91	2.20	12.42	59.61	3.7%
Procter & Gamble	1.09	1.72	1.93	12.22	61.86	3.1%
Ecolab Inc	0.35	0.56	0.62	12.08	51.64	1.2%
Sherwin-Williams	0.82	1.42	1.44	12.02	73.48	2.0%
Archer-Daniels-Midland	0.34	0.56	0.60	12.02	32.86	1.8%

*12-month indicated rate.   **Five-year annual compounded annual growth rate.   Chart based on data at the close of October 8, 2010.

S&P 500 STOCK SCREENS

Stock Reports

In using the Stock Reports in this handbook, please pay particular attention to the dates attached to each evaluation, recommendation, or analysis section. Opinions rendered are as of that date and may change often. It is strongly suggested that before investing in any security you should obtain the current analysis on that issue.

To order the latest Standard & Poor's Stock Report on a company, for as little as $3.00 per report, please call:

S&P Reports On-Demand at 1–800–292–0808.

Abbott Laboratories

STANDARD &POOR'S

S&P Recommendation BUY ★★★★☆

Price	12-Mo. Target Price	Investment Style
$52.56 (as of Oct 22, 2010)	$62.00	Large-Cap Growth

GICS Sector Health Care
Sub-Industry Pharmaceuticals

Summary This diversified life science company is a leading maker of drugs, nutritional products, diabetes monitoring devices, and diagnostics.

Key Stock Statistics (Source S&P, Vickers, company reports)

52-Wk Range	$56.79– 44.59	S&P Oper. EPS 2010E	4.18	Market Capitalization(B)	$81.154	Beta	0.27
Trailing 12-Month EPS	$3.41	S&P Oper. EPS 2011E	4.65	Yield (%)	3.35	S&P 3-Yr. Proj. EPS CAGR(%)	10
Trailing 12-Month P/E	15.4	P/E on S&P Oper. EPS 2010E	12.6	Dividend Rate/Share	$1.76	S&P Credit Rating	AA
$10K Invested 5 Yrs Ago	$14,170	Common Shares Outstg. (M)	1,544.0	Institutional Ownership (%)	67		

Price Performance

30-Week Mov. Avg. · · · 10-Week Mov. Avg. – – GAAP Earnings vs. Previous Year Volume Above Avg. STARS
12-Mo. Target Price — Relative Strength — ▲ Up ▼ Down ▶ No Change Below Avg. ★

Options: ASE, CBOE, P, Ph

Analysis prepared by **Herman B. Saftlas** on July 26, 2010, when the stock traded at **$ 48.93**.

Highlights

▶ We project that revenues will exceed $35 billion in 2010, up from 2009's $30.8 billion, lifted by an estimated contribution of about $2.9 billion from Solvay Group (acquired in mid-February 2010). We also forecast growth in established Abbott franchises such as Humira, which continues to grow faster than the overall self-injectable anti-TNF market. The Xience drug-eluting coronary stent should also continue to bolster vascular sales, while new products should support growth in nutritional and diagnostic products.

▶ We expect gross margins to expand modestly from 2009's 57.1%, helped by manufacturing efficiencies. But the SG&A and R&D ratios will probably increase somewhat, reflecting new product-related costs. The new U.S. health care reform law is expected to reduce EPS by $0.11 in 2010, which we think should be largely offset by EPS accretion of about $0.10 from the Solvay acquisition.

▶ After a projected adjusted effective tax rate of about 16.3% versus 2009's 16.8%, we forecast operating EPS of $4.18 for 2010. Lifted by new products, we see EPS rising to $4.65 in 2011.

Investment Rationale/Risk

▶ We believe Abbott's success with its targeted acquisition strategy will be a key driver for the above-average growth we forecast for ABT over the coming years. In mid-February 2010, ABT completed the $6.2 billion acquisition of the pharmaceuticals division unit of Belgium-based Solvay SA. We view this deal positively, as it gives ABT full rights to cholesterol drugs Tricor and Trilipix, and allows it to expand in vaccines and emerging foreign markets. The deal should also diversify ABT away from its reliance on Humira. We expect this acquisition to boost EPS by $0.10 in 2010 and $0.20 in 2011.

▶ Risks to our recommendation and target price include failure to integrate the Solvay acquisition, greater than expected competitive pressures in key markets, and possible pipeline setbacks.

▶ Our 12-month target price of $62 applies a premium-to-peers 14.8X multiple to our 2010 EPS estimate. We think this valuation is warranted in light of ABT's rapidly growing franchises in diversified health care markets. Our DCF model, which assumes a WACC of about 8.3% and terminal growth of 2%, also implies intrinsic value of $62.

Qualitative Risk Assessment

LOW	MEDIUM	HIGH

Our risk assessment reflects Abbott's operations in competitive markets and its exposure to the potential for generic competition. However, we believe the company has a relatively strong new product pipeline, with possible significant launches in both the medical device and pharmaceutical areas. We see the company as financially sound and having a strong balance sheet.

Quantitative Evaluations

S&P Quality Ranking A

D	C	B-	B	B+	A-	A	A+

Relative Strength Rank MODERATE
47
LOWEST = 1 HIGHEST = 99

Revenue/Earnings Data

Revenue (Million $)

	1Q	2Q	3Q	4Q	Year
2010	7,698	8,826	--	--	--
2009	6,718	7,495	7,761	8,790	30,765
2008	6,766	7,314	7,498	7,950	29,528
2007	5,290	6,371	6,377	7,221	25,914
2006	5,183	5,501	5,574	6,218	22,476
2005	5,383	5,524	5,384	6,047	22,338

Earnings Per Share ($)

	1Q	2Q	3Q	4Q	Year
2010	0.64	0.83	E1.05	E1.31	E4.18
2009	0.92	0.83	0.95	0.98	3.69
2008	0.60	0.85	0.69	0.89	3.03
2007	0.41	0.63	0.46	0.77	2.31
2006	0.56	0.40	0.46	-0.31	1.12
2005	0.53	0.56	0.44	0.63	2.16

Fiscal year ended Dec. 31. Next earnings report expected: NA. EPS Estimates based on S&P Operating Earnings; historical GAAP earnings are as reported.

Dividend Data (Dates: mm/dd Payment Date: mm/dd/yy)

Amount ($)	Date Decl.	Ex-Div. Date	Stk. of Record	Payment Date
0.400	12/11	01/13	01/15	02/15/10
0.440	02/19	04/13	04/15	05/15/10
0.440	06/11	07/13	07/15	08/15/10
0.440	09/16	10/13	10/15	11/15/10

Dividends have been paid since 1926. Source: Company reports.

Please read the Required Disclosures and Analyst Certification on the last page of this report.

The McGraw-Hill Companies

Abbott Laboratories

Business Summary July 26, 2010

CORPORATE OVERVIEW. Abbott Laboratories is a leading player in several growing health care markets. Through acquisitions, product diversification and R&D programs, ABT offers a wide range of prescription pharmaceuticals, infant and adult nutritionals, diagnostics, and medical devices.

During 2009, pharmaceuticals accounted for 53% of operating revenues, while nutritionals represented 17%, diagnostics contributed 12%, and vascular represented 9%. Sales of other products represented 9% of 2009 sales. Foreign sales accounted for 54% of total sales in 2009.

ABT's Pharmaceutical Products Group markets a wide array of human therapeutics. Major products include: Humira to treat rheumatoid arthritis and psoriatic arthritis ($5.5 billion in 2009 sales); Kaletra, an anti-HIV medication ($1.4 billion); TriCor/Trilipix, cholesterol treatments ($1.3 billion); Niaspan, a niacin-based cholesterol treatment ($855 million); and Lupron, a treatment for prostate cancer ($800 million). This division was augmented by the $6.2 billion purchase of the Solvay drug business in February 2010.

Nutritionals fall under U.S.-based Ross Products and Abbott Nutrition International. Products include leading infant formulas sold under the Similac and

Isomil names, as well as adult nutritionals, such as Ensure and ProSure for patients with special dietary needs, including cancer and diabetes patients. ABT also markets enteral feeding items.

Abbott Diabetes Care markets the Precision and FreeStyle lines of hand-held glucose monitors for diabetes patients. This division also markets data management and point-of-care systems, insulin pumps and syringes, and Glucerna shakes and nutrition bars tailored for diabetics.

Abbott Vascular markets coronary and carotid stents, catheters and guide wires, and products used for surgical closure. The principal product is the new Xience drug-eluting stent (DES), which was launched in July 2008 and is presently the leading product in the domestic DES market. Boston Scientific markets the Xience stent manufactured by Abbott under the Promus name, pursuant to an agreement with ABT.

Company Financials Fiscal Year Ended Dec. 31

Per Share Data ($)	2009	2008	2007	2006	2005	2004	2003	2002	2001	2000
Tangible Book Value	2.17	1.51	1.24	NM	2.89	2.22	2.90	1.93	1.14	4.54
Cash Flow	5.04	4.21	3.50	2.13	3.02	2.84	2.56	2.52	1.74	2.31
Earnings	3.69	3.03	2.31	1.12	2.16	2.02	1.75	1.78	0.99	1.78
S&P Core Earnings	3.61	2.86	2.31	1.16	2.01	1.90	1.95	1.62	0.77	NA
Dividends	1.56	1.41	1.27	1.16	1.09	1.03	0.97	0.92	0.82	0.74
Payout Ratio	42%	46%	55%	104%	50%	51%	55%	51%	83%	42%
Prices:High	57.39	61.09	59.50	49.87	50.00	47.63	47.15	58.00	57.17	56.25
Prices:Low	41.27	45.75	48.75	39.18	37.50	38.26	33.75	29.80	42.00	29.38
P/E Ratio:High	16	20	26	45	23	24	27	33	58	32
P/E Ratio:Low	11	15	21	35	17	19	19	17	42	16

Income Statement Analysis (Million $)										
Revenue	30,765	29,528	25,914	22,476	22,338	19,680	19,681	17,685	16,285	13,746
Operating Income	8,698	8,316	7,378	6,419	5,738	5,187	4,597	4,815	3,062	4,228
Depreciation	2,090	1,839	1,855	1,559	1,359	1,289	1,274	1,177	1,168	827
Interest Expense	520	528	593	416	241	200	146	239	307	114
Pretax Income	7,194	5,856	4,479	2,276	4,620	4,126	3,734	3,673	1,883	3,816
Effective Tax Rate	20.1%	19.2%	19.3%	24.6%	27.0%	23.0%	26.3%	23.9%	17.7%	27.0%
Net Income	5,746	4,734	3,606	1,717	3,372	3,176	2,753	2,794	1,550	2,786
S&P Core Earnings	5,599	4,473	3,609	1,787	3,158	2,972	2,971	2,561	1,233	NA

Balance Sheet & Other Financial Data (Million $)										
Cash	9,932	5,080	2,821	521	2,894	1,226	995	704	657	914
Current Assets	23,314	17,043	14,043	11,282	11,386	10,734	10,290	9,122	8,419	7,376
Total Assets	52,417	42,419	39,714	36,178	29,141	28,767	26,715	24,259	23,296	15,283
Current Liabilities	13,049	11,592	9,103	11,951	7,416	6,826	7,640	7,002	7,927	4,298
Long Term Debt	11,484	8,713	9,488	7,010	4,572	4,788	3,452	4,274	4,335	1,076
Common Equity	22,856	17,480	17,779	14,054	14,415	14,326	13,072	10,665	9,059	8,571
Total Capital	34,594	26,193	27,266	21,064	19,570	19,334	16,525	14,939	13,395	9,647
Capital Expenditures	1,089	1,288	1,656	1,338	1,207	1,292	1,247	1,296	1,164	1,036
Cash Flow	7,835	6,573	5,461	3,276	4,731	4,465	4,027	3,971	2,718	3,613
Current Ratio	1.8	1.5	1.5	0.9	1.5	1.6	1.3	1.3	1.1	1.7
% Long Term Debt of Capitalization	Nil	33.3	34.8	33.3	23.4	24.8	20.9	28.6	32.4	11.2
% Net Income of Revenue	18.7	16.0	13.9	7.6	15.1	16.1	14.0	15.8	9.5	20.3
% Return on Assets	NA	11.5	9.5	5.3	11.6	11.6	10.8	11.7	8.0	18.7
% Return on Equity	NA	26.9	22.7	12.1	23.5	23.2	23.2	28.3	17.6	34.8

Data as orig reptd.; bef. results of disc opers/spec. items. Per share data adj. for stk. divs.; EPS diluted. E-Estimated. NA-Not Available. NM-Not Meaningful. NR-Not Ranked. UR-Under Review.

Office: 100 Abbott Park Road, Abbott Park, IL 60064-6400.
Telephone: 847-937-6100.
Website: http://www.abbott.com
Chrmn & CEO: M.D. White

EVP & CFO: T.C. Freyman
EVP, Secy & General Counsel: L.J. Schumacher
Chief Acctg Officer & Cntlr: G.W. Linder
Treas: V. Yien

Investor Contact: L. Peepo (847-935-6722)
Board Members: R. Alpern, R. S. Austin, W. M. Daley, W. J. Farrell, H. L. Fuller, E. M. Liddy, P. N. Novakovic, W. A. Osborn, D. A. Owen, R. S. Roberts, S. C. Scott, III, W. D. Smithburg, G. F. Tilton, M. D. White

Founded: 1888
Domicile: Illinois
Employees: 73,000

Abercrombie & Fitch Co.

STANDARD &POOR'S

S&P Recommendation BUY ★★★★☆

Price	12-Mo. Target Price	Investment Style
$42.40 (as of Oct 22, 2010)	$52.00	Large-Cap Growth

GICS Sector Consumer Discretionary
Sub-Industry Apparel Retail

Summary This apparel retailer, which specializes in lifestyle branding, operates about 1,100 retail apparel stores across four brands.

Key Stock Statistics (Source S&P, Vickers, company reports)

52-Wk Range	$51.12–29.88	S&P Oper. EPS 2011E	1.85	Market Capitalization(B)	$3.743	Beta	1.64
Trailing 12-Month EPS	$1.05	S&P Oper. EPS 2012E	2.88	Yield (%)	1.65	S&P 3-Yr. Proj. EPS CAGR(%)	25
Trailing 12-Month P/E	40.4	P/E on S&P Oper. EPS 2011E	22.9	Dividend Rate/Share	$0.70	S&P Credit Rating	NA
$10K Invested 5 Yrs Ago	$9,179	Common Shares Outstg. (M)	88.3	Institutional Ownership (%)	94		

Price Performance

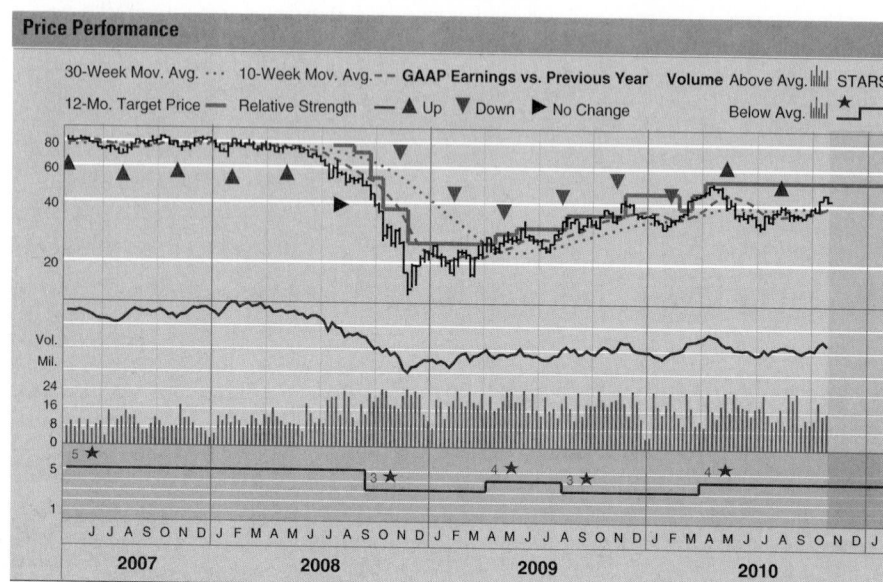

30-Week Mov. Avg. · · · 10-Week Mov. Avg. - - GAAP Earnings vs. Previous Year Volume Above Avg. STARS
12-Mo. Target Price — Relative Strength ▲ Up ▼ Down ► No Change Below Avg.

Options: ASE, CBOE, P, Ph

Analysis prepared by **Marie Driscoll, CFA** on August 20, 2010, when the stock traded at **$ 36.00**.

Highlights

► We see international expansion as the dominant growth theme for the next few years as ANF penetrates global markets with flagship stores for its A&F adult and kid business and in mall locations for Hollister. The fall opening of a Gilly Hicks in London will test whether this young woman's intimate brand has global demand as well. Same-store sales comparisons turned positive in FY 11 (Jan.) posting a +3% comp for the first half. A 20% increase in transactions per store in the July quarter suggests that lower prices (down about 15%), along with an improved assortment, are driving store traffic. We see more upside on back-to-school shopping.

► We estimate 11% sales growth for FY 11 and see 360 basis points (bps) of operating margin expansion to 7.6% of sales, on improved merchandise and gross margins, and leverage of store and distribution and marketing expenses.

► We see similar sales and productivity gains in FY 12. ANF has a 15% operating margin objective for FY 13 (versus 21% in FY 08), which we see as doable with the closure of underperforming domestic stores and the growing proportion of ecommerce and international.

Investment Rationale/Risk

► We see ANF continuing to invest in social media and a mobile commerce platform in FY 11, along with the pursuit of brand building and a ramp up of international expansion and new flagship locations. Some 12% of FY 10 sales were outside the U.S., where sales productivity and margins are substantially higher. U.K. Hollister stores, for example, average 6X the sales volume of a domestic Hollister. We expect the bulk of growth over the next five years to be from abroad.

► Risks to our recommendation and target price include weaker global economic growth than we project, negative same-store sales trends, and fashion and inventory risk.

► Our 12-month target price of $52 is 18X our FY 12 EPS estimate, which represents a modest premium to peers of 15% and is a 5% premium to ANF's five-year average forward P/E multiple. We believe operating performance was at a cyclical low in FY 10, but that the strong and rising global appeal of ANF brands will drive improved operating metrics and margin recovery in FY 11 and beyond.

Qualitative Risk Assessment

LOW	MEDIUM	HIGH

Our risk assessment reflects our view of ANF's strong balance sheet and cash flows, offset by a consumer base whose tastes change constantly.

Quantitative Evaluations

S&P Quality Ranking B+

D	C	B-	B	B+	A-	A	A+

Relative Strength Rank STRONG

78

LOWEST = 1   HIGHEST = 99

Revenue/Earnings Data

Revenue (Million $)

	1Q	2Q	3Q	4Q	Year
2011	687.8	745.8	--	--	--
2010	601.7	637.2	753.7	936.0	2,929
2009	800.2	845.8	896.3	998.0	3,540
2008	742.4	804.5	973.9	1,229	3,750
2007	657.3	658.7	863.5	1,139	3,318
2006	546.8	571.6	704.9	961.4	2,785

Earnings Per Share ($)

2011	-0.13	0.22	E0.57	E1.20	E1.85
2010	-0.26	-0.09	0.55	0.68	0.89
2009	0.69	0.87	0.72	0.78	3.05
2008	0.65	0.87	1.29	2.40	5.20
2007	0.62	0.72	1.11	2.14	4.59
2006	0.45	0.63	1.11	1.80	3.66

Fiscal year ended Jan. 31. Next earnings report expected: Mid November. EPS Estimates based on S&P Operating Earnings; historical GAAP earnings are as reported.

Dividend Data (Dates: mm/dd Payment Date: mm/dd/yy)

Amount ($)	Date Decl.	Ex-Div. Date	Stk. of Record	Payment Date
0.175	11/13	11/24	11/27	12/15/09
0.175	02/16	02/24	02/26	03/16/10
0.175	05/18	05/26	05/28	06/15/10
0.175	08/17	08/25	08/27	09/14/10

Dividends have been paid since 2004. Source: Company reports.

Please read the Required Disclosures and Analyst Certification on the last page of this report.

The McGraw-Hill Companies

Abercrombie & Fitch Co.

STANDARD &POOR'S

Business Summary August 20, 2010

CORPORATE OVERVIEW. Abercrombie & Fitch, established in 1892, operates four branded retail concepts: Abercrombie & Fitch (340 domestic, six international stores as of January 2010), abercrombie kids (205, four), Hollister Co. (507, 18), and Gilly Hicks (16), and e-commerce sites for each concept. Each targets a different age demographic, minimizing cannibalization, and all employ casual luxury positioning.

MARKET PROFILE. The company participates in the specialty apparel retail market targeted at youth, spanning the tween to young adult demographic. While the U.S. apparel market is considered mature, with demand mirroring population growth and a modicum related to fashion, the youth marketplace is generally considered attractive based on its spending clout. According to NPD consumer data, collectively, this group accounts for approximately 35% of total apparel spending, with the "sweet spot" being teenagers, who represent about 20%.

COMPETITIVE LANDSCAPE. The retail landscape is consolidating, with share accruing to the mass merchants and specialty chains while the traditional department store is losing ground. Specialty chains compete on customer knowledge garnered from daily interactions, focus groups and marketing in-

telligence, and this knowledge is often combined with high customer service levels to result in an attractive price/value equation for the consumer. ANF's target demographic is attracted to strong brands, as well as fashion and value, when determining apparel selections. The specialty channel holds the largest share of the apparel market at about 31% according to NPD Group and the sub-segment serving the youth demographic represents about 3% of total retail sales. With barriers to entry minimal (capital investment in merchandise, rent and labor expense) and potential returns on investment high and quick (four wall return on investment exceed 30% in 12 months for many specialty retailers), there was a steady flow of new industry participants through most of this decade, but more recently we've seen more store closures and slowed expansion plans. In addition to competing with other apparel retailers, regardless of channel, for youth discretionary spending, ANF competes with merchandise and services, especially consumer electronics and entertainment services.

Company Financials Fiscal Year Ended Jan. 31

Per Share Data ($)	2010	2009	2008	2007	2006	2005	2004	2003	2002	2001
Tangible Book Value	20.78	21.06	23.45	19.17	11.34	7.78	9.21	7.71	6.02	4.28
Cash Flow	3.59	5.57	7.21	6.18	5.02	3.39	2.73	2.50	2.05	1.85
Earnings	0.89	3.05	5.20	4.59	3.66	2.28	2.06	1.94	1.65	1.55
S&P Core Earnings	0.96	3.15	5.20	4.59	3.38	2.32	1.81	1.70	1.45	1.35
Dividends	0.70	0.70	0.70	0.60	0.50	0.50	Nil	Nil	Nil	Nil
Payout Ratio	79%	79%	13%	13%	14%	22%	Nil	Nil	Nil	Nil
Calendar Year	2009	2008	2007	2006	2005	2004	2003	2002	2001	2000
Prices:High	42.31	82.06	85.77	79.42	74.10	47.45	33.65	33.85	47.50	31.31
Prices:Low	16.95	13.66	67.72	49.98	44.17	23.07	20.65	14.97	16.21	8.00
P/E Ratio:High	48	27	16	17	20	21	16	17	29	20
P/E Ratio:Low	19	4	13	11	12	10	10	8	10	5

Income Statement Analysis (Million $)										
Revenue	2,929	3,540	3,750	3,318	2,785	2,021	1,708	1,596	1,365	1,238
Operating Income	398	686	912	794	661	453	398	370	313	284
Depreciation	239	225	184	146	124	106	66.6	56.9	41.2	30.7
Interest Expense	6.60	3.40	Nil	Nil	Nil	Nil	Nil	Nil	Nil	Nil
Pretax Income	120	451	759	672	549	353	335	316	277	261
Effective Tax Rate	33.9%	39.6%	37.4%	37.2%	39.2%	38.7%	38.8%	38.4%	39.0%	39.5%
Net Income	79.0	272	476	422	334	216	205	195	169	158
S&P Core Earnings	84.9	281	476	422	312	220	180	170	148	138

Balance Sheet & Other Financial Data (Million $)										
Cash	712	522	649	530	462	350	521	401	239	138
Current Assets	1,260	1,085	1,140	1,092	947	652	753	601	405	304
Total Assets	2,833	2,848	2,568	2,248	1,790	1,348	1,199	995	771	588
Current Liabilities	449	450	543	511	492	414	280	211	164	155
Long Term Debt	71.2	100	Nil	Nil	Nil	Nil	Nil	Nil	Nil	Nil
Common Equity	1,828	1,846	1,618	1,405	995	669	871	750	595	423
Total Capital	1,899	1,980	1,641	1,436	1,034	725	891	770	597	423
Capital Expenditures	175	368	403	403	256	185	99.1	93.0	127	153
Cash Flow	318	498	659	568	458	322	272	252	210	189
Current Ratio	2.7	2.4	2.1	2.1	1.9	1.6	2.7	2.8	2.5	2.0
% Long Term Debt of Capitalization	3.8	5.1	Nil	Nil	Nil	Nil	Nil	Nil	Nil	Nil
% Net Income of Revenue	2.7	7.7	12.7	12.7	12.0	10.7	12.0	12.2	12.4	12.8
% Return on Assets	2.8	10.1	19.8	20.9	21.0	15.8	18.5	22.1	24.8	30.2
% Return on Equity	4.3	15.7	31.5	35.2	40.1	28.3	25.3	29.0	33.1	43.1

Data as orig reptd.; bef. results of disc opers/spec. items. Per share data adj. for stk. divs.; EPS diluted. E-Estimated. NA-Not Available. NM-Not Meaningful. NR-Not Ranked. UR-Under Review.

Office: 6301 Fitch Path, New Albany, OH 43054.
Telephone: 614-283-6500.
Email: investor_relations@abercrombie.com
Website: http://www.abercrombie.com

Chrmn & CEO: M.S. Jeffries
EVP, CFO & Chief Acctg Officer: J.E. Ramsden
SVP, Secy & General Counsel: R.A. Robins, Jr.
Investor Contact: T.D. Lennox (614-283-6751)

Cntlr: B.P. Logan
Board Members: J. B. Bachmann, L. J. Brisky, A. M. Griffin, M. S. Jeffries, J. W. Kessler, E. M. Lee, C. R. Stapleton

Founded: 1892
Domicile: Delaware
Employees: 80,000

ACE Ltd

STANDARD &POOR'S

S&P Recommendation BUY ★★★★☆

Price	12-Mo. Target Price	Investment Style
$60.38 (as of Oct 22, 2010)	$68.00	Large-Cap Value

GICS Sector Financials
Sub-Industry Property & Casualty Insurance

Summary This specialty insurer provides commercial insurance and reinsurance for a diverse group of international clients. In July 2008, ACE redomesticated its holding company to Switzerland from the Cayman Islands.

Key Stock Statistics (Source S&P, Vickers, company reports)

52-Wk Range	$61.00– 47.09	S&P Oper. EPS 2010**E**	6.75	Market Capitalization(B)	$20.461	Beta	0.68
Trailing 12-Month EPS	$8.48	S&P Oper. EPS 2011**E**	7.30	Yield (%)	2.12	S&P 3-Yr. Proj. EPS CAGR(%)	NM
Trailing 12-Month P/E	7.1	P/E on S&P Oper. EPS 2010**E**	8.9	Dividend Rate/Share	$1.28	S&P Credit Rating	BBB+
$10K Invested 5 Yrs Ago	$13,370	Common Shares Outstg. (M)	338.9	Institutional Ownership (%)	91		

Price Performance

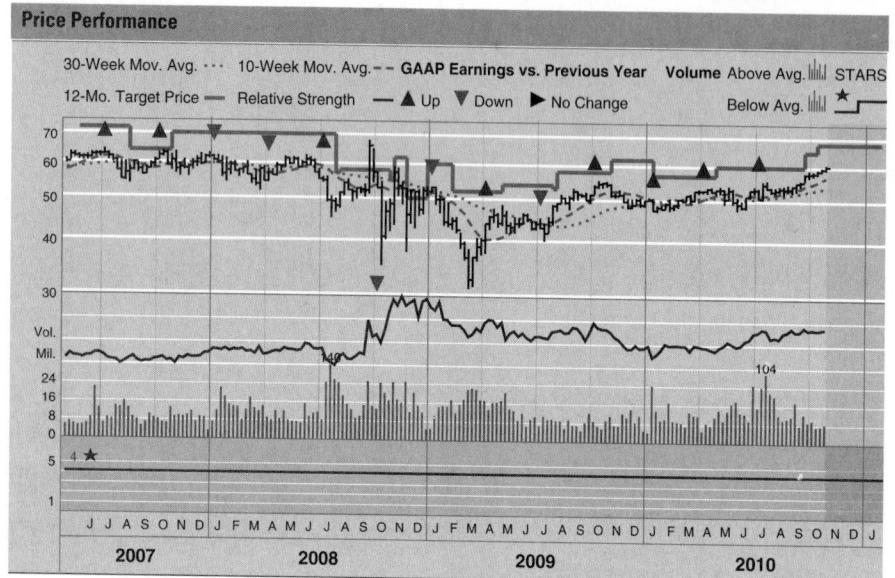

30-Week Mov. Avg. · · · 10-Week Mov. Avg. - - GAAP Earnings vs. Previous Year Volume Above Avg. ▏▍▏▎ STARS
12-Mo. Target Price — Relative Strength — ▲ Up ▼ Down ► No Change   Below Avg. ▏▍▏▎ ★

Options: ASE, CBOE, P, Ph

Qualitative Risk Assessment

LOW	MEDIUM	HIGH

Our risk assessment reflects our view of ACE as an opportunistic underwriter, offset by concerns we have about reserve levels in certain lines of business and the potential that credit quality in ACE's fixed income investment portfolio could deteriorate.

Quantitative Evaluations

S&P Quality Ranking   NR

D	C	B-	B	B+	A-	A	A+

Relative Strength Rank   MODERATE

69

LOWEST = 1   HIGHEST = 99

Revenue/Earnings Data

Revenue (Million $)

	1Q	2Q	3Q	4Q	Year
2010	3,949	3,760	--	--	--
2009	3,575	3,547	3,681	-4,272	15,075
2008	3,076	3,834	3,619	3,103	13,632
2007	3,549	3,468	3,642	3,495	14,154
2006	3,181	3,289	3,389	3,469	13,328
2005	3,148	3,258	3,494	3,188	13,088

Earnings Per Share ($)

	1Q	2Q	3Q	4Q	Year
2010	2.22	1.98	E1.63	E1.41	E6.75
2009	1.99	1.58	1.46	2.81	7.55
2008	1.11	2.20	0.16	0.06	3.53
2007	2.10	1.93	1.95	1.69	7.66
2006	1.45	1.72	1.73	1.99	6.90
2005	1.48	1.58	-0.43	0.69	3.31

Fiscal year ended Dec. 31. Next earnings report expected: Late October. EPS Estimates based on S&P Operating Earnings; historical GAAP earnings are as reported.

Highlights

► The 12-month target price for ACE has recently been changed to $68.00 from $68.00. The Highlights section of this Stock Report will be updated accordingly.

Investment Rationale/Risk

► The Investment Rationale/Risk section of this Stock Report will be updated shortly. For the latest News story on ACE from MarketScope, see below.

► 10/07/10 08:56 am ET ... S&P MAINTAINS BUY RECOMMENDATION ON SHARES OF ACE LIMITED (ACE 59.1****): ACE announced plans to acquire Malaysian insurer Jerneh Insurance Berhad for about $200M in a deal set to close in Q4. We believe this proposed purchase will enhance ACE's existing capabilities in that region. We also view positively ACE's plan of allocating some of its excess capital to an acquisition strategy that has included other accretive deals. We see ACE as a well run, opportunistic entity. We raise our target price by $3 to $68, assuming that the shares trade at 9.3X our $7.30 2011 EPS forecast, discounted to peers on our view of an asset mix riskier than some peers. / C.Seifert

Dividend Data (Dates: mm/dd Payment Date: mm/dd/yy)

Amount ($)	Date Decl.	Ex-Div. Date	Stk. of Record	Payment Date
0.310	11/19	12/15	12/17	01/11/10
0.310	02/25	03/29	03/31	04/12/10
0.330	05/19	07/23	07/27	08/17/10
0.330	08/12	09/29	10/01	10/22/10

Dividends have been paid since 1993. Source: Company reports.

ACE Ltd

Business Summary September 20, 2010

CORPORATE OVERVIEW. ACE Ltd. underwrites an array of insurance and rein-surance, and also provides funds to support underwriting capacity for Lloyd's syndicates managed by Lloyd's managing agencies. Net earned premiums to-taled $13.24 billion in 2009 (up 0.3% from $13.2 billion in 2008), with North American Insurance operations accounting for 43%, Overseas General Insur-ance for 39%, Global Reinsurance for 7%, and Life Insurance and Reinsurance for 11%. Underwriting results remained profitable in 2009, amid generally sta-ble claim trends, and the combined loss and expense ratio ended the year at 88.3%, versus 89.6% in 2008. Included in these results was the loss ratio, which totaled 58.8% in 2009, versus 60.6% in 2008. The expense ratio deterio-rated a bit, to 29.5% in 2009, from 29.0% in 2008.

Insurance - North America provides property and casualty insurance and reinsurance coverage, including excess liability, professional lines, satellite, excess property and political risk, to a diverse group of industrial, commercial and other enterprises.

Insurance - Overseas General includes the operations of ACE International, which provides property and casualty insurance, accident and health insur-ance and consumer-oriented products to individuals, mid-sized firms and large commercial clients. It also provides customized and comprehensive in-surance policies and services to multinational companies and their cross-

border subsidiaries. In addition, the segment includes the insurance opera-tions of ACE Global Markets, which mainly encompasses operations in the Lloyd's market.

Global Reinsurance includes the operations of ACE Tempest Re and several other subsidiaries that mainly provide property catastrophe reinsurance worldwide to insurers of commercial and personal property.

Life Insurance and Reinsurance includes the operations of ACE Tempest Re and ACE International Life and businesses of Combined Insurance. ACE Tem-pest Re offers traditional life reinsurance products, and an array of other rein-surance products aimed at helping life insurance companies manage their mortality, morbidity, lapse and/or capital market risks. ACE International Life offers individual life and group insurance and savings products in Indonesia, Thailand, Vietnam, Taiwan, UAE, China, Egypt, Europe and Latin America. On April 28, 2004, ACE sold approximately 65% of Assured Guaranty Ltd. (NYSE: AGO) in an initial public offering that netted ACE about $835 million.

Company Financials Fiscal Year Ended Dec. 31

Per Share Data ($)	2009	2008	2007	2006	2005	2004	2003	2002	2001	2000
Tangible Book Value	51.04	29.24	42.29	35.37	28.17	25.11	21.52	13.20	12.13	10.35
Operating Earnings	NA	NA	NA	NA	NA	NA	NA	NA	NA	NA
Earnings	7.55	3.53	7.66	6.90	3.31	3.88	5.25	0.27	-0.88	2.19
Dividends	1.45	1.09	1.06	0.98	0.90	0.82	0.74	0.66	0.58	0.48
Payout Ratio	19%	31%	14%	14%	27%	21%	14%	NM	NM	22%
Prices:High	55.64	68.00	64.32	61.90	56.85	45.98	42.80	44.98	43.19	43.94
Prices:Low	30.92	34.90	52.79	47.81	38.36	31.80	23.59	22.01	18.10	14.06
P/E Ratio:High	7	19	8	9	17	NM	NM	NM	NM	NM
P/E Ratio:Low	4	10	7	7	12	NM	NM	NM	NM	NM

Income Statement Analysis (Million $)										
Premium Income	NA	13,203	12,297	11,825	11,748	11,110	9,727	6,905	6,039	4,539
Net Investment Income	NA	2,062	1,918	1,601	1,264	1,013	901	812	803	781
Other Revenue	NA	-1,633	-61.0	-98.0	76.0	198	265	-489	-58.0	-39.0
Total Revenue	15,075	13,632	14,154	13,328	13,088	12,320	10,892	7,227	6,784	5,281
Pretax Income	3,077	1,567	3,160	2,831	1,317	1,439	1,794	-11.7	-247	598
Net Operating Income	NA	NA	NA	NA	NA	NA	NA	NA	NA	NA
Net Income	2,549	1,197	2,578	2,301	1,028	1,153	1,482	100	-158	517

Balance Sheet & Other Financial Data (Million $)										
Cash & Equivalent	669	867	926	917	850	807	817	NA	NA	NA
Premiums Due	NA	14,176	14,362	14,580	3,343	3,255	2,823	2,654	NA	NA
Investment Assets:Bonds	NA	34,015	36,171	31,587	27,361	22,891	19,312	NA	NA	NA
Investment Assets:Stocks	NA	2,609	1,837	1,713	1,507	1,266	562	NA	NA	NA
Investment Assets:Loans	NA	52.0	Nil	Nil	Nil	Nil	Nil	NA	NA	NA
Investment Assets:Total	46,515	40,547	41,779	36,601	31,922	26,925	22,555	17,555	15,197	13,064
Deferred Policy Costs	NA	1,214	1,121	1,077	930	944	1,005	832	679	573
Total Assets	77,980	72,057	72,090	67,135	62,440	56,183	49,317	43,874	37,186	31,837
Debt	NA	2,806	1,811	2,447	2,120	2,261	1,824	2,224	2,224	2,299
Common Equity	19,667	14,446	16,675	14,276	11,810	9,843	8,821	6,269	6,010	5,358
Property & Casualty:Loss Ratio	NA	60.6	61.6	52.3	74.5	70.6	64.6	73.7	83.9	65.6
Property & Casualty:Expense Ratio	NA	29.0	26.3	33.9	25.1	25.8	26.4	27.5	28.5	30.8
Property & Casualty Combined Ratio	88.3	89.6	87.9	86.2	99.6	96.4	91.0	101.2	112.4	96.4
% Return on Revenue	16.9	8.8	18.2	17.3	7.9	9.4	13.6	1.4	NM	9.8
% Return on Equity	14.9	7.7	16.4	17.6	9.5	11.9	19.2	1.2	NM	NA

Data as orig reptd.; bef. results of disc opers/spec. items. Per share data adj. for stk. divs.; EPS diluted. 2004-2000 data restated based on 2004 SEC Form 10-K/A. E-Estimated. NA-Not Available. NM-Not Meaningful. NR-Not Ranked. UR-Under Review.

Office: Barengasse 32, Zurich, Switzerland 8001.
Telephone: 41 43 456 76 00.
Email: investorrelations@ace.bm
Website: www.acelimited.com

Chrmn, Pres & CEO: E.G. Greenberg
Vice Chrmn: J. Keogh
COO: R.J. Rintala
CFO: P.V. Bancroft

Chief Acctg Officer: P.B. Medini
Investor Contact: H.M. Wilson (441-299-9283)
Board Members: M. G. Atieh, M. A. Cirillo-Goldberg, B. L. Crockett, E. G. Greenberg, R. M. Hernandez, J. Keogh, J. Krol, P. Menikoff, L. F. Mullin, T. J. Neff, R. Ripp, T. E. Shasta, O. Steimer

Founded: 1985
Domicile: Switzerland
Employees: 15,000

Adobe Systems Inc

STANDARD &POOR'S

S&P Recommendation HOLD ★★★☆☆

Price	12-Mo. Target Price	Investment Style
$28.21 (as of Oct 22, 2010)	$35.00	Large-Cap Growth

GICS Sector Information Technology
Sub-Industry Application Software

Summary This company provides software for multimedia content creation, distribution, and management.

Key Stock Statistics (Source S&P, Vickers, company reports)

52-Wk Range	$38.20–25.45	S&P Oper. EPS 2010E	1.60	Market Capitalization(B)	$14.351	Beta	1.69
Trailing 12-Month EPS	$0.90	S&P Oper. EPS 2011E	1.74	Yield (%)	Nil	S&P 3-Yr. Proj. EPS CAGR(%)	10
Trailing 12-Month P/E	31.3	P/E on S&P Oper. EPS 2010E	17.6	Dividend Rate/Share	Nil	S&P Credit Rating	BBB+
$10K Invested 5 Yrs Ago	$9,039	Common Shares Outstg. (M)	508.7	Institutional Ownership (%)	90		

Price Performance

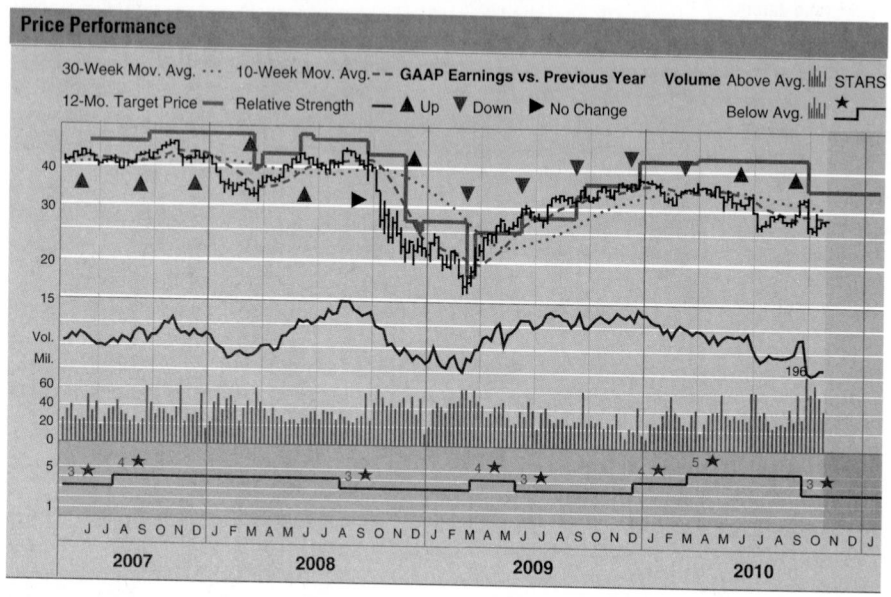

30-Week Mov. Avg. ··· 10-Week Mov. Avg. ‑ ‑ GAAP Earnings vs. Previous Year   Volume Above Avg. STARS
12-Mo. Target Price — Relative Strength ▲ Up ▼ Down ▶ No Change   Below Avg.

Options: ASE, CBOE, P, Ph

Analysis prepared by **Zaineb Bokhari** on October 06, 2010, when the stock traded at **$ 25.92**.

Highlights

➤ We estimate that sales will rise approximately 28% in FY 10 (Nov.) to about $3.8 billion, on our outlook for sales growth from Creative Suite 5 (CS5), and contribution from the acquisition of Omniture (October 2009). We see a very gradual improvement in the global economic environment and expect this to influence the ultimate sales trajectory of CS5, whose sales to date have tracked above those for CS4, but below the pace set by CS3. We see 7% sales growth in FY 11, propelled mainly by new products.

➤ Despite projected strong sales growth, we think FY 10 non-GAAP operating margins will widen modestly to 36.5%, from 35.1% in FY 09, reflecting the integration of Omniture. We expect the company to benefit from a recent restructuring, but expect expenses like R&D and sales and marketing to trend higher, as new products are launched and sales levels rise. We look for operating margins to remain flat in FY 11, as ADBE continues to invest in support of newer products.

➤ We estimate non-GAAP EPS of $1.60 in FY 10, then a rise to $1.74 for FY 11, excluding items such as restructuring and amortization charges.

Investment Rationale/Risk

➤ While still early, the upgrade cycle for Creative Suite 5 looks to be trailing the highly successful cycle for Creative Suite 3. Sales are being impacted by weakness in Japan, ADBE's second largest geographic region, and in education, the company's largest vertical market. We see the economic environment improving gradually through FY 11 and expect the trajectory of new product sales to be impacted by prevailing conditions. We look for ADBE to make acquisitions as it targets $5 billion in sales by FY 12.

➤ Risks to our recommendation and target price include weak demand for new products, loss of share to competing products or standards, and lack of support from makers of popular hardware platforms. Prolonged weakness in key markets is also a concern.

➤ We blend relative and intrinsic valuation measures to derive our 12-month target price of $35. In our DCF model, we incorporate assumptions for a 9.9% WACC and 3% terminal growth, resulting in a $42 value. In our P/E analysis, we apply a 16.3X multiple to our FY 11 estimate, the five-year average low we calculate for the shares, resulting in a value of about $28.

Qualitative Risk Assessment

LOW	**MEDIUM**	HIGH

Our risk assessment reflects the regularly changing nature of the software industry and our view that the success of new products will be impacted by the global economic environment. These factors are offset by our view of the company's size and market leadership, strong operating history, and solid balance sheet.

Quantitative Evaluations

S&P Quality Ranking   B+

D	C	B-	B	**B+**	A-	A	A+

Relative Strength Rank   WEAK

26

LOWEST = 1   HIGHEST = 99

Revenue/Earnings Data

Revenue (Million $)

	1Q	2Q	3Q	4Q	Year
2010	858.7	943.0	990.3	--	--
2009	786.4	704.7	697.5	757.3	2,946
2008	890.5	886.9	887.3	915.3	3,580
2007	649.4	745.6	851.7	911.2	3,158
2006	655.5	635.5	602.2	682.2	2,575
2005	472.9	496.0	487.0	510.4	1,966

Earnings Per Share ($)

	1Q	2Q	3Q	4Q	Year
2010	0.24	0.28	0.44	E0.46	E1.60
2009	0.30	0.24	0.26	-0.06	0.73
2008	0.38	0.41	0.35	0.46	1.59
2007	0.24	0.25	0.35	0.38	1.21
2006	0.17	0.20	0.16	0.30	0.83
2005	0.30	0.29	0.29	0.31	1.19

Fiscal year ended Nov. 30. Next earnings report expected: Mid December. EPS Estimates based on S&P Operating Earnings; historical GAAP earnings are as reported.

Dividend Data

No cash dividends have been paid since 2005.

Please read the Required Disclosures and Analyst Certification on the last page of this report.

The McGraw·Hill Companies

Adobe Systems Inc

Business Summary October 06, 2010

CORPORATE OVERVIEW. Adobe Systems (founded in 1982) is one of the world's largest software companies. It offers creative, business and mobile software and services used by consumers, artistic professionals, designers, knowledge workers, original equipment manufacturers, developers and enterprises for producing, managing, delivering and experiencing content across multiple operating systems, devices and media.

Some of the company's core products include: Acrobat (for document creation, distribution and management); Illustrator (to make graphic artwork); and Photoshop (for photo design, enhancement and editing). In December 2005, ADBE acquired Macromedia, a leading developer of software that enables the creation and consumption of digital content, for $3.5 billion in stock and related costs. Through this transaction, the company gained Macromedia's significant products, including Dreamweaver (Web development) and Flash (which provides an environment to produce dynamic digital content).

While acquisition activity had been minor in the two subsequent fiscal years, ADBE acquired Web analytics company Omniture for $1.8 billion in late FY 09 (Nov.). The company reasoned that its products offered the tools to create online content and, with Omniture, it could now help customers measure the efficacy of such content and thus allow them to better monetize it. The company recently announced, but has not completed, the purchase of Swiss enterprise content management software provider Day Software, for about $240 million.

The company's software runs on Microsoft Windows, Apple Mac OS, Linux, UNIX and other non-PC platforms. ADBE is making a push to provide solutions that can develop content for connected devices such as smartphones. ADBE participates in the Open Screen Project, with the aim of allowing developers of content to deliver their creations across connected devices that use the company's Flash and Adobe Air technologies. Begun in May 2008, the Open Screen Project had about 50 participants at the end of FY 09, including many top smartphone manufacturers.

CORPORATE STRATEGY. ADBE's indicated strategy is to address the needs of a variety of customers with offerings that support industry standards and can be deployed in a variety of contexts. We believe ADBE is focused on leveraging its market-leading software franchises with bundles and enhancements. Selling multiple products together has enabled ADBE to gain market share, increase penetration with existing customers, and expand its overall customer base. The Creative Suite is the company's flagship bundled offering. Macromedia was acquired to further this strategy.

Company Financials Fiscal Year Ended Nov. 30

Per Share Data ($)	2009	2008	2007	2006	2005	2004	2003	2002	2001	2000
Tangible Book Value	1.50	3.74	3.67	4.25	3.54	2.68	2.08	1.24	1.23	1.45
Cash Flow	1.26	2.09	1.74	1.33	1.31	1.03	0.65	0.52	0.53	0.65
Earnings	0.73	1.59	1.21	0.83	1.19	0.91	0.55	0.40	0.42	0.57
S&P Core Earnings	0.74	1.57	1.21	0.76	1.01	0.69	0.18	0.05	0.11	NA
Dividends	Nil	Nil	Nil	Nil	0.01	0.03	0.03	0.03	0.03	0.03
Payout Ratio	Nil	Nil	Nil	Nil	1%	3%	5%	6%	6%	6%
Prices:High	38.20	46.44	48.47	43.22	39.48	32.24	23.19	21.66	30.81	43.66
Prices:Low	15.70	19.49	37.20	25.98	25.80	17.15	12.29	8.25	11.10	13.36
P/E Ratio:High	52	29	40	52	33	35	42	55	74	77
P/E Ratio:Low	22	12	31	31	22	19	22	21	27	24

Income Statement Analysis (Million $)	2009	2008	2007	2006	2005	2004	2003	2002	2001	2000
Revenue	2,946	3,580	3,158	2,575	1,966	1,667	1,295	1,165	1,230	1,266
Operating Income	1,014	1,328	1,173	870	793	653	428	368	447	457
Depreciation	282	268	315	308	64.3	60.8	49.0	63.5	56.6	43.3
Interest Expense	3.41	10.0	Nil	Nil	Nil	Nil	Nil	Nil	Nil	Nil
Pretax Income	702	1,079	947	680	766	609	380	285	307	444
Effective Tax Rate	44.9%	19.2%	23.5%	25.6%	21.3%	26.0%	30.0%	32.8%	33.0%	35.1%
Net Income	387	872	724	506	603	450	266	191	206	288
S&P Core Earnings	392	860	721	466	515	343	86.7	20.6	51.7	NA

Balance Sheet & Other Financial Data (Million $)	2009	2008	2007	2006	2005	2004	2003	2002	2001	2000
Cash	1,904	2,019	946	772	421	376	190	184	219	237
Current Assets	2,474	2,735	2,573	2,884	2,009	1,551	1,329	814	767	878
Total Assets	7,256	5,822	5,714	5,963	2,440	1,959	1,555	1,052	931	1,069
Current Liabilities	845	763	852	677	480	451	437	377	314	315
Long Term Debt	1,000	350	Nil	Nil	Nil	Nil	Nil	Nil	Nil	Nil
Common Equity	4,864	4,410	4,650	5,152	1,864	1,423	1,101	674	617	753
Total Capital	5,864	4,878	4,799	5,223	1,943	1,502	1,119	674	617	755
Capital Expenditures	120	112	132	83.3	48.9	63.2	39.5	31.6	46.6	29.8
Cash Flow	669	1,140	1,039	814	667	511	315	255	262	331
Current Ratio	2.9	3.6	3.0	4.3	4.2	3.4	3.0	2.2	2.4	2.8
% Long Term Debt of Capitalization	17.1	7.2	Nil	Nil	Nil	Nil	Nil	Nil	Nil	Nil
% Net Income of Revenue	13.1	24.4	22.9	19.6	30.7	27.0	20.6	16.4	16.7	22.7
% Return on Assets	5.9	15.1	12.3	12.0	27.4	25.6	20.4	19.3	20.6	30.7
% Return on Equity	8.3	19.2	14.7	14.4	36.7	35.7	30.0	29.6	30.0	45.5

Data as orig reptd.; bef. results of disc opers/spec. items. Per share data adj. for stk. divs.; EPS diluted. E-Estimated. NA-Not Available. NM-Not Meaningful. NR-Not Ranked. UR-Under Review.

Office: 345 Park Avenue, San Jose, CA, USA 95110-2704.
Telephone: 408-536-6000.
Email: ir@adobe.com
Website: http://www.adobe.com

Co-Chrmn: J. Warnock
Co-Chrmn: C. Geschke
Pres & CEO: S. Narayen
EVP & CFO: M. Garrett

SVP & CTO: K. Lynch
Board Members: C. Baldwin, E. Barnholt, R. K. Burgess, M. R. Cannon, J. E. Daley, C. Geschke, S. Narayen, D. Rosensweig, R. Sedgewick, J. Warnock

Founded: 1983
Domicile: Delaware
Employees: 8,660

Advanced Micro Devices Inc

S&P Recommendation HOLD ★★★☆☆

Price	12-Mo. Target Price	Investment Style
$6.89 (as of Oct 22, 2010)	$8.00	Large-Cap Value

GICS Sector Information Technology
Sub-Industry Semiconductors

Summary This company is a leading producer of semiconductors that are used principally in computers and related products.

Key Stock Statistics (Source S&P, Vickers, company reports)

52-Wk Range	$10.24– 4.33	S&P Oper. EPS 2010**E**	0.38	Market Capitalization(B)	$4.648	Beta	2.17
Trailing 12-Month EPS	$1.74	S&P Oper. EPS 2011**E**	0.47	Yield (%)	Nil	S&P 3-Yr. Proj. EPS CAGR(%)	NM
Trailing 12-Month P/E	4.0	P/E on S&P Oper. EPS 2010**E**	18.1	Dividend Rate/Share	Nil	S&P Credit Rating	B+
$10K Invested 5 Yrs Ago	$3,153	Common Shares Outstg. (M)	674.6	Institutional Ownership (%)	56		

Price Performance

30-Week Mov. Avg. · · · 10-Week Mov. Avg. – – GAAP Earnings vs. Previous Year   Volume Above Avg. STARS
12-Mo. Target Price — Relative Strength   ▲ Up ▼ Down ► No Change   Below Avg. ★

Options: ASE, CBOE, P, Ph

Analysis prepared by **Clyde Montevirgen** on October 15, 2010, when the stock traded at **$ 7.04.**

Qualitative Risk Assessment

LOW	MEDIUM	HIGH

AMD is subject to the cyclical swings of the semiconductor industry, demand fluctuations for computer end-products, vacillation in average selling prices for chips, and strong competition from Intel, which is a much larger rival in microprocessors.

Quantitative Evaluations

S&P Quality Ranking   C

D	C	B-	B	B+	A-	A	A+

Relative Strength Rank   MODERATE

32

LOWEST = 1   HIGHEST = 99

Revenue/Earnings Data

Revenue (Million $)

	1Q	2Q	3Q	4Q	Year
2010	1,574	1,653	1,618	--	--
2009	1,177	1,184	1,396	1,646	5,403
2008	1,487	1,362	1,797	1,162	5,808
2007	1,233	1,378	1,632	1,770	6,013
2006	1,332	1,216	1,328	1,773	5,649
2005	1,227	1,260	1,523	1,838	5,848

Earnings Per Share ($)

2010	0.35	-0.06	-0.16	E0.11	E0.38
2009	-0.65	-0.49	-0.18	1.52	0.45
2008	-0.54	-1.14	-0.04	-2.32	-3.98
2007	-1.11	-1.09	-0.71	-3.06	-6.06
2006	0.38	0.18	0.27	-1.08	-0.34
2005	-0.04	0.03	0.18	0.21	0.40

Fiscal year ended Dec. 31. Next earnings report expected: Late January. EPS Estimates based on S&P Operating Earnings; historical GAAP earnings are as reported.

Dividend Data

No cash dividends have been paid.

Highlights

➤ We expect revenues to rise around 3% in 2011, following a projected 20% increase in 2010. Although we expect a period of inventory digestion over the near term and pricing pressure as competitors launch new products, we see PC demand improving next year, and believe new CPU and GPU product cycles will support average selling prices. We also think AMD can further penetrate the desktop PC market and gain traction in the server and mobile markets.

➤ We look for AMD's non-GAAP gross margins to widen to 46% from an anticipated 45% in 2010. Considering AMD's equity method of accounting for its stake in Globalfoundries, we generally see a less volatile gross margin structure, with fluctuations coming largely from sales mix. As new products are developed and released, we think R&D will rise at a faster rate, and see compensation-related expenses rising variably with sales. Overall, we expect the non-GAAP operating margin to be around 8% for 2010 and 2011.

➤ We think AMD's debt and interest payments will continue to weigh on its bottom line. Our non-GAAP estimates exclude equity income/losses from Globalfoundries.

Investment Rationale/Risk

➤ Our hold recommendation reflects our view of improving fundamentals, balanced by fair valuations. We are modeling below-peer revenue growth in 2011 due to a modest inventory correction and pricing pressure. Although we expect gross margins to contract from current levels, we believe AMD's revamped product portfolio and more flexible business model can lead to better profitability as sales rise, resulting in notable earnings growth. We also see adjusted profits and free cash flows leading to debt reduction, alleviating some financial risks. Based on these anticipated improvements, we think multiples should be above recent historical averages.

➤ Risks to our recommendation and target price include less-than-anticipated demand for computers, greater market share losses, and notable financial risk.

➤ Our 12-month target price of $8 is based on a blend of relative valuations. We apply a price-to-sales ratio of 1.1X to our forward 12-month sales per share estimate to derive a value of $10. We use a P/E multiple of 12X our 2011 EPS estimate, yielding a value of $6. Both multiples are above recent historical averages.

Please read the Required Disclosures and Analyst Certification on the last page of this report.

The McGraw·Hill Companies

Advanced Micro Devices Inc

STANDARD &POOR'S

Business Summary October 15, 2010

CORPORATE OVERVIEW. Advanced Micro Devices designs and sells digital integrated circuits (IC), including x86 microprocessors and chipsets for computers, embedded microprocessors for commercial and consumer applications, and, as a result of the company's acquisition of ATI Technologies in October 2006, graphics processors.

A microprocessor is an IC that serves as the central processing unit, or brain, of a computer. The performance of a processor is a critical factor for the performance of the computer. The main measures for microprocessor performance include: work-per-cycle, or how many instructions per cycle, clock speed, how fast the CPU's internal logic operates as measured by units of hertz, and power consumption. Other factors impacting performance include the number of cores on a microprocessor, bit rating of the microprocessor, memory size, and data access speed. AMD also sells chipsets, which send data between the microprocessor and the computer's input, display, and storage devices.

Embedded microprocessors are used in applications, such as industrial controls, point of sale/self-service kiosks, and casino gaming machines, among others. These chips require moderate-to-high performance and are relatively lower in cost, size, and power. The embedded market has grown at a healthy pace as customers, who generally used to design the embedded chips, are increasingly opting to use industry-standard x86 instruction architecture as a way to reduce costs and speed up time to market.

Graphics processors are used in computers to increase the speed of rendering images and to improve image resolution and color definition. In this business, AMD's discrete graphics processing unit (GPU) includes the relatively popular ATI Radeon products, which are widely utilized to improve graphics for video games and other multimedia functions.

The company has two reportable segments: Computing Solutions and Graphics. The Computing Solutions segment includes sales of microprocessors, chipsets, and embedded processors. The Graphics segment includes graphics, video and multimedia products, as well as revenues from the sale of video game consoles that include its technology.

Company Financials Fiscal Year Ended Dec. 31

Per Share Data ($)	2009	2008	2007	2006	2005	2004	2003	2002	2001	2000
Tangible Book Value	NM	NM	0.82	2.49	7.70	7.68	6.96	7.16	10.64	10.09
Cash Flow	2.22	-1.96	-3.72	1.36	3.14	3.54	2.08	-1.60	1.69	4.53
Earnings	0.45	-3.98	-6.06	-0.34	0.40	0.25	-0.79	-3.81	-0.18	2.95
S&P Core Earnings	-1.46	-2.32	-6.08	-0.35	0.38	-0.19	-1.08	-4.24	-0.49	NA
Dividends	Nil	Nil	Nil	Nil	Nil	Nil	Nil	Nil	Nil	Nil
Payout Ratio	Nil	Nil	Nil	Nil	Nil	Nil	Nil	Nil	Nil	Nil
Prices:High	10.04	8.08	20.63	42.70	31.84	24.95	18.50	20.60	34.65	48.50
Prices:Low	1.86	1.62	7.26	16.90	14.08	10.76	4.78	3.10	7.69	13.56
P/E Ratio:High	22	NM	NM	NM	80	NM	NM	NM	NM	16
P/E Ratio:Low	4	NM	NM	NM	35	NM	NM	NM	NM	5

Income Statement Analysis (Million $)	2009	2008	2007	2006	2005	2004	2003	2002	2001	2000
Revenue	5,403	5,808	6,013	5,649	5,848	5,001	3,519	2,697	3,892	4,644
Operating Income	615	255	94.0	1,238	1,451	1,452	748	-139	654	1,468
Depreciation	1,128	1,223	1,305	837	1,219	1,224	996	756	623	579
Interest Expense	438	375	390	126	105	112	110	71.3	61.4	60.0
Pretax Income	408	-2,313	-3,321	-115	33.7	116	-316	-1,258	-75.0	1,263
Effective Tax Rate	27.5%	NM	NM	NM	NM	5.05%	NM	NM	NM	20.3%
Net Income	213	-2,414	-3,379	-166	165	91.2	-274	-1,303	-60.6	1,006
S&P Core Earnings	-978	-1,401	-3,391	-170	155	-68.2	-373	-1,450	-161	NA

Balance Sheet & Other Financial Data (Million $)	2009	2008	2007	2006	2005	2004	2003	2002	2001	2000
Cash	2,676	1,096	1,889	1,380	633	918	968	429	427	591
Current Assets	4,275	2,379	3,816	3,963	3,559	3,228	2,900	2,020	2,353	2,658
Total Assets	9,078	7,675	11,550	13,147	7,288	7,844	7,094	5,619	5,647	5,768
Current Liabilities	2,210	2,226	2,625	2,852	1,822	1,846	1,452	1,372	1,314	1,224
Long Term Debt	4,252	4,702	5,031	3,672	1,327	1,628	1,900	1,780	673	1,168
Common Equity	648	-82.0	2,990	5,785	3,352	3,010	2,438	2,467	3,555	3,172
Total Capital	6,284	4,880	8,292	9,778	5,006	5,583	5,213	4,247	4,333	4,544
Capital Expenditures	466	624	1,685	1,857	1,513	1,440	570	705	679	805
Cash Flow	1,507	-1,191	-2,074	671	1,385	1,315	721	-547	562	1,585
Current Ratio	1.9	1.1	1.5	1.4	2.0	1.7	2.0	1.5	1.8	2.2
% Long Term Debt of Capitalization	67.7	96.4	60.7	37.6	26.5	29.2	36.4	41.9	15.5	25.7
% Net Income of Revenue	3.9	NM	NM	NM	2.8	1.8	NM	NM	NM	21.7
% Return on Assets	2.5	NM	NM	NM	2.2	1.2	NM	NM	NM	19.8
% Return on Equity	NM	NM	NM	NM	5.2	3.3	NM	NM	NM	39.1

Data as orig reptd.; bef. results of disc opers/spec. items. Per share data adj. for stk. divs.; EPS diluted. E-Estimated. NA-Not Available. NM-Not Meaningful. NR-Not Ranked. UR-Under Review.

Office: One AMD Place, Sunnyvale, CA 94088-3453.
Telephone: 408-749-4000.
Email: investor.relations@amd.com
Website: http://www.amd.com

Chrmn: B.L. Claflin
Pres & CEO: D.R. Meyer
COO, EVP & Chief Admin Officer: R.J. Rivet
SVP, CFO & Chief Acctg Officer: T. Seifert

SVP & CIO: A. Mahmoud
Investor Contact: R. Cotter (408-749-3887)
Board Members: W. A. Al Muhairi, W. M. Barnes, J. E. Caldwell, B. L. Claflin, C. Conway, N. M. Donofrio, H. P. Eberhart, D. R. Meyer, R. B. Palmer

Founded: 1969
Domicile: Delaware
Employees: 13,400

The McGraw-Hill Companies

AES Corporation (The)

STANDARD &POOR'S

S&P Recommendation BUY ★★★★☆

Price	12-Mo. Target Price	Investment Style
$12.31 (as of Oct 22, 2010)	$13.00	Large-Cap Growth

GICS Sector Utilities
Sub-Industry Independent Power Producers & Energy Traders

Summary The world's largest independent power producer, AES produces and distributes electricity in international and domestic markets.

Key Stock Statistics (Source S&P, Vickers, company reports)

52-Wk Range	$14.64–8.82	S&P Oper. EPS 2010E	0.79	Market Capitalization(B)	$9.774	Beta		1.39
Trailing 12-Month EPS	$0.66	S&P Oper. EPS 2011E	1.15	Yield (%)	Nil	S&P 3-Yr. Proj. EPS CAGR(%)		4
Trailing 12-Month P/E	18.7	P/E on S&P Oper. EPS 2010E	15.6	Dividend Rate/Share	Nil	S&P Credit Rating		BB-
$10K Invested 5 Yrs Ago	$7,962	Common Shares Outstg. (M)	794.0	Institutional Ownership (%)	72			

Price Performance

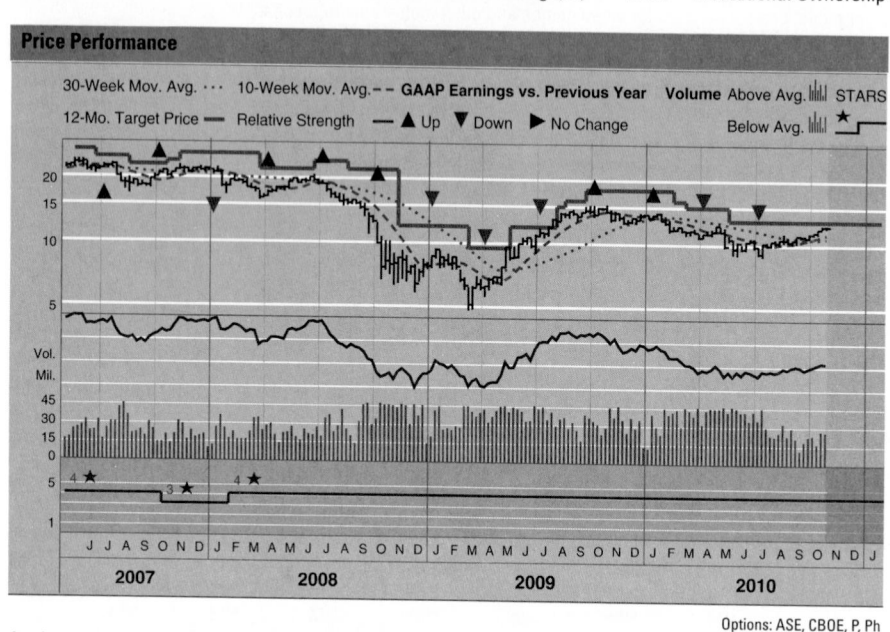

30-Week Mov. Avg. · · · 10-Week Mov. Avg. — — GAAP Earnings vs. Previous Year Volume Above Avg. STARS
12-Mo. Target Price — Relative Strength — ▲ Up ▼ Down ▶ No Change Below Avg. ★

Options: ASE, CBOE, P, Ph

Analysis prepared by **Christopher B. Muir** on September 01, 2010, when the stock traded at **$ 10.54**.

Highlights

➤ We see 2010's revenues rising 13% and 2011's 6.5%. We see unregulated 2010 revenues being helped by stabilizing commodity prices and new projects and acquisitions. We expect regulated revenues to rise, also helped by stabilizing commodity prices, partly offset by reduced demand in Chile related to the earthquake. We believe 2011 will be helped by slightly rising commodity prices and a weaker U.S. dollar.

➤ Our operating margin estimates are 22.2% for 2010 and 22.9% for 2011, versus 22.2% in 2009. For 2010, we expect higher per-revenue cost of sales for the regulated businesses, offset by lower per-revenue general & administrative expenses and unregulated cost of sales. Our pre-tax margin estimates are 15.3% for 2010 and 17.7% in 2011, versus 17.4% in 2009. We see lower non-operating income partly offset by lower net interest expense in 2010.

➤ We estimate 2010 operating EPS, excluding net nonrecurring gains of $0.05, of $0.79, a 34% decrease from 2009's $1.19, which excluded nonrecurring charges of $0.06, due to dilution related to the sale of stock. Our 2011 EPS forecast is $1.15, up 46%.

Investment Rationale/Risk

➤ We believe AES is a superior independent power producer. We think it should see above-average earnings growth and an improving balance sheet over the next couple of years, partly due to expansion projects. Results should also be helped by cost controls and strategic growth initiatives, which include a joint venture with China Investment Corp. and a pipeline of projects in advanced development, including plants not yet under construction, that total 8.0 gigawatts (GW) of traditional, 1.4 GW of wind, and 0.5 GW of solar generation capacity additions. We expect AES to add 1.5 GW of new capacity in 2010 and 0.7 GW in 2011.

➤ Risks to our recommendation and target price include financial statement revisions, currency fluctuations, political and regulatory uncertainty regarding utility rates and U.S. power margins, and counterparty default risk.

➤ The stock recently traded at 9.1X our 2011 EPS estimate, a 24% discount to independent power producer peers. Our 12-month target price of $13 is 11.3X our 2011 EPS estimate, a 21% discount to our peer target, as we see risk related to volatile exchange rates and an uncertain outlook for the global economy.

Qualitative Risk Assessment

LOW	MEDIUM	HIGH

Our risk assessment reflects the company's relatively large capitalization and mix of lower-risk regulated utility businesses in North America, offset by higher-risk merchant power operations and utility operations in emerging markets in South America, Eastern Europe, Central America and Asia.

Quantitative Evaluations

S&P Quality Ranking B

D	C	B-	B	B+	A-	A	A+

Relative Strength Rank STRONG

78

LOWEST = 1   HIGHEST = 99

Revenue/Earnings Data

Revenue (Million $)

	1Q	2Q	3Q	4Q	Year
2010	4,112	4,021	--	--	--
2009	3,269	3,335	3,695	3,820	14,119
2008	4,081	4,126	4,319	3,544	16,070
2007	3,121	3,344	3,471	3,673	13,588
2006	2,973	3,044	3,135	3,147	12,299
2005	2,663	2,668	2,782	2,973	11,086

Earnings Per Share ($)

	1Q	2Q	3Q	4Q	Year
2010	0.26	0.17	E0.26	E0.16	E0.79
2009	0.31	0.44	0.27	0.08	1.09
2008	0.35	1.31	0.22	-0.10	1.80
2007	0.18	0.41	0.14	0.01	0.73
2006	0.53	0.33	-0.51	0.07	0.43
2005	0.19	0.13	0.37	0.27	0.95

Fiscal year ended Dec. 31. Next earnings report expected: Early November. EPS Estimates based on S&P Operating Earnings; historical GAAP earnings are as reported.

Dividend Data

No cash dividends have been paid.

Please read the Required Disclosures and Analyst Certification on the last page of this report.

The McGraw-Hill Companies

AES Corporation (The)

STANDARD &POOR'S

Business Summary September 01, 2010

CORPORATE OVERVIEW. AES Corporation (AES) owns and operates a portfolio of electricity generation and distribution business in 29 countries through its subsidiaries and affiliates. The company has two principal businesses: generation and regulated utilities.

The generation business provides power for sale to utilities and other wholesale customers while the regulated utilities business distributes power to retail, commercial, industrial and governmental customers. In 2009, the generation unit contributed 51% of total revenues. It primarily sells electricity to utilities or other wholesale customers under power purchase agreements that are generally for five years or longer. The generation business also sells electricity to wholesale customers through competitive markets.

The remaining 49% of total revenues in 2009 came from the regulated utilities business. It markets electricity to residential, business, and government customers through integrated transmission and distribution systems.

The company also reports results geographically by segment. Latin American operations accounted for 67% of revenues, North American operations for 21%, European and African operations for 5%, Middle Eastern and Asian operations for 7%, and corporate activities for less than 0.1%. The company's largest exposures geographically are to Brazil (38%), the U.S. (18%), Chile (9%), Argentina (5%) and El Salvador (4%).

CORPORATE STRATEGY. AES pursues both a global and a local growth strategy to increase its business. The company's global strategy focuses on large-scale projects and pursues strategic initiatives. It concentrates on mergers and acquisitions, exploring opportunities in the climate change business such as the production of greenhouse gas reduction activities and related industries that involve environmental issues. The company also aims to mitigate exposure to price swings. In 2009, 65% of the revenues from its generation business was from plants that operate under PPAs of five years or longer for at least 75% of their output capacity. Additionally, 96% of its construction program capacity is subject to long-term contracts.

Company Financials Fiscal Year Ended Dec. 31

Per Share Data ($)	2009	2008	2007	2006	2005	2004	2003	2002	2001	2000
Tangible Book Value	4.29	2.64	1.91	1.97	NM	NM	NM	NM	2.87	5.21
Earnings	1.09	1.80	0.73	0.43	0.95	0.57	0.56	-4.81	0.87	1.42
S&P Core Earnings	1.10	0.53	0.65	0.78	1.04	0.51	0.94	-3.66	0.74	NA
Dividends	Nil	Nil	Nil	Nil	Nil	Nil	Nil	Nil	Nil	Nil
Payout Ratio	Nil	Nil	Nil	Nil	Nil	Nil	Nil	Nil	Nil	Nil
Prices:High	15.44	22.48	24.24	23.85	18.13	13.71	9.50	17.92	60.15	72.81
Prices:Low	4.80	5.80	16.69	15.63	12.53	7.56	2.63	0.92	11.60	34.25
P/E Ratio:High	14	12	33	55	19	24	17	NM	69	51
P/E Ratio:Low	4	3	23	36	13	13	5	NM	13	24

Income Statement Analysis (Million $)	2009	2008	2007	2006	2005	2004	2003	2002	2001	2000
Revenue	14,119	16,070	13,588	12,299	11,086	9,486	8,415	8,632	9,327	6,691
Depreciation	1,049	960	942	933	889	841	781	837	859	582
Maintenance	NA	NA	NA	NA	NA	NA	NA	NA	NA	NA
Fixed Charges Coverage	2.56	2.12	1.90	1.94	1.73	1.30	1.38	0.34	1.42	1.80
Construction Credits	NA	NA	NA	NA	NA	NA	NA	NA	NA	NA
Effective Tax Rate	24.6%	27.8%	42.4%	31.0%	31.9%	28.2%	30.3%	NM	28.7%	24.7%
Net Income	729	1,216	495	286	632	366	336	-2,590	467	648
S&P Core Earnings	732	344	447	526	693	332	564	-1,970	394	NA

Balance Sheet & Other Financial Data (Million $)	2009	2008	2007	2006	2005	2004	2003	2002	2001	2000
Gross Property	33,217	28,908	27,522	26,053	24,741	24,141	23,098	23,050	26,748	19,150
Capital Expenditures	2,520	2,840	2,425	1,460	1,143	892	1,228	2,116	3,173	2,150
Net Property	24,297	21,393	20,020	19,074	18,654	18,788	18,505	18,846	23,434	17,846
Capitalization:Long Term Debt	18,003	16,863	16,629	14,892	36,674	16,823	16,792	17,684	20,564	16,927
Capitalization:% Long Term Debt	79.4	82.1	84.0	83.1	95.7	91.1	96.3	102.0	78.8	77.9
Capitalization:Preferred	Nil	Nil	Nil	Nil	Nil	Nil	Nil	Nil	Nil	NA
Capitalization:% Preferred	Nil	Nil	Nil	Nil	Nil	Nil	Nil	Nil	Nil	NA
Capitalization:Common	4,675	3,669	3,164	3,036	1,649	1,645	645	-341	5,539	4,811
Capitalization:% Common	20.6	17.9	16.0	16.9	4.30	8.91	3.70	-1.97	21.2	22.1
Total Capital	28,856	25,082	24,282	21,818	40,655	20,758	19,293	19,142	29,537	24,752
% Operating Ratio	81.9	84.1	83.7	83.8	85.5	84.2	84.5	88.5	89.7	88.3
% Earned on Net Property	13.9	16.1	15.5	23.0	20.9	18.5	17.0	14.3	13.6	14.0
% Return on Revenue	5.2	7.6	3.6	2.3	5.7	3.9	4.0	NM	5.0	9.7
% Return on Invested Capital	12.2	12.7	16.7	16.3	7.0	13.6	13.6	21.6	7.3	9.8
% Return on Common Equity	17.5	35.6	15.9	12.3	48.5	33.4	221.1	NM	8.4	17.4

Data as orig reptd.; bef. results of disc opers/spec. items. Per share data adj. for stk. divs.; EPS diluted. E-Estimated. NA-Not Available. NM-Not Meaningful. NR-Not Ranked. UR-Under Review.

Office: 4300 Wilson Blvd Ste 1100, Arlington, VA 22203-4167.
Telephone: 703-522-1315.
Email: invest@aes.com
Website: http://www.aes.com

Chrmn: P.A. Odeen
Pres & CEO: P. Hanrahan
COO & EVP: A.R. Weilert
EVP & CFO: V.D. Harker

EVP, Secy & General Counsel: B.A. Miller
Investor Contact: A. Pasha (703-682-6552)
Board Members: S. W. Bodman, III, P. Hanrahan, T. Khanna, J. A. Koskinen, P. Lader, S. O. Moose, J. B. Morse, Jr., P. A. Odeen, C. O. Rossotti, S. Sandstrom

Founded: 1981
Domicile: Delaware
Employees: 27,000

The **McGraw-Hill** Companies

Aetna Inc.

STANDARD &POOR'S

S&P Recommendation BUY ★★★★☆

Price	12-Mo. Target Price	Investment Style
$31.20 (as of Oct 22, 2010)	$33.00	Large-Cap Blend

GICS Sector Health Care
Sub-Industry Managed Health Care

Summary This company is a leading U.S. provider of health care, dental, pharmacy, group life, disability, and long-term care benefits.

Key Stock Statistics (Source S&P, Vickers, company reports)

52-Wk Range	$35.96–25.00	S&P Oper. EPS 2010**E**	3.15	Market Capitalization(B)	$13.023	Beta	1.24
Trailing 12-Month EPS	$3.52	S&P Oper. EPS 2011**E**	3.10	Yield (%)	0.13	S&P 3-Yr. Proj. EPS CAGR(%)	7
Trailing 12-Month P/E	8.9	P/E on S&P Oper. EPS 2010**E**	9.9	Dividend Rate/Share	$0.04	S&P Credit Rating	A-
$10K Invested 5 Yrs Ago	$7,187	Common Shares Outstg. (M)	417.4	Institutional Ownership (%)	89		

Price Performance

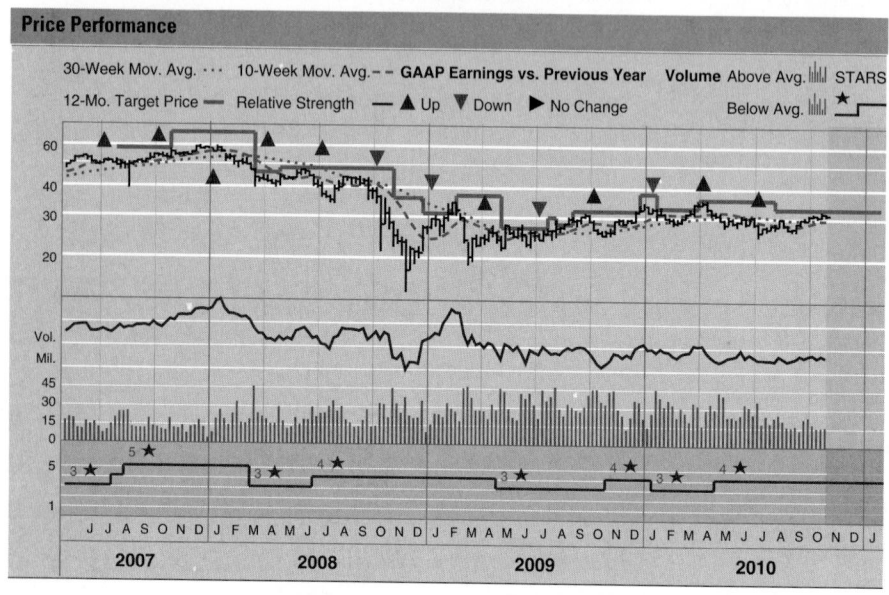

- 30-Week Mov. Avg. · · · ·   10-Week Mov. Avg. – – GAAP Earnings vs. Previous Year   Volume Above Avg. STARS
- 12-Mo. Target Price — Relative Strength — ▲ Up ▼ Down ► No Change   Below Avg.

Options: ASE, CBOE, P, Ph

Analysis prepared by **Phillip M. Seligman** on August 06, 2010, when the stock traded at **$ 30.11.**

Highlights

► We expect health care operating revenue to decline by 3.2% to $30.6 billion in 2010, following a 10% rise in 2009, when AET gained 1.2 million net new members via large commercial account wins and large gains in its Medicare Advantage (MA; Medicare managed care) and Medicaid units. We expect 575,000 fewer commercial risk and 120,000 fewerl commercial self-funded members, partly offset by slightly higher MA and Medicaid membership by year-end 2010.

► We estimate that medical costs in the commercial book will decline by 190 basis points as a percentage of premiums (medical loss ratio, MLR), on higher prices and the first half's reduction in reserves for medical costs related to prior-year and first-quarter 2010 claims. However, we expect the firm-wide medical loss ratio to decline by 150 bps on a lower MA premium rate and a higher mix of MA and Medicaid enrollment.

► We estimate 2010 operating EPS of $3.15 before one-time gains, versus 2009's $2.75 before one-time items and net realized capital gains. We project $3.10 for 2011, assuming higher MLRs under health care reform.

Investment Rationale/Risk

► We think AET has the size, scale, diversity, and financial flexibility to manage better than most insurers amid health care reform. But we expect the stock to be volatile, while AET waits for the rules on what constitutes medical costs starting 2011, given health care reform's required MLR floors. We are positive on AET's recently announced 12-year pact with CVS Caremark (CVS 30, Strong Buy), under which AET retains its pharmacy benefit management (PBM) unit with CVS administering the PBM services. Although the deal is expected to be accretive to AET's EPS starting in 2012, we think it will help offset some of the pressure on AET's MLRs caused by reform-based mandates. In addition, AET is working with Medicare to lift its marketing and enrollment sanctions by the next enrollment season.

► Risks to our recommendation and target price include intensified competition, a weaker economy, and adverse medical cost trends.

► We apply a multiple of 10.5X to our 2010 EPS estimate to derive our 12-month target price of $33. This multiple reflects a modest premium to peers given AET's turnaround efforts.

Qualitative Risk Assessment

LOW	MEDIUM	HIGH

Our risk assessment reflects AET's leadership in the highly fragmented managed care market. We see competition intensifying as consolidation has led the largest companies, including AET, to bump up against one another in more markets and geographies. Still, we believe AET's expanding product, market, and geographic diversity will permit stable operating performance over the long term.

Quantitative Evaluations

S&P Quality Ranking   B+

D	C	B-	B	B+	A-	A	A+

Relative Strength Rank   MODERATE

57

LOWEST = 1   HIGHEST = 99

Revenue/Earnings Data

Revenue (Million $)

	1Q	2Q	3Q	4Q	Year
2010	8,622	8,546	--	--	--
2009	8,615	8,671	8,722	8,756	34,764
2008	7,739	7,828	7,625	7,759	30,951
2007	6,700	6,794	6,961	7,144	27,600
2006	6,235	6,252	6,300	6,360	25,146
2005	5,427	5,497	5,701	5,867	22,492

Earnings Per Share ($)

2010	1.28	1.14	E0.65	E0.46	E3.15
2009	0.95	0.77	0.73	0.38	2.84
2008	0.85	0.97	0.58	0.42	2.83
2007	0.81	0.85	0.95	0.87	3.47
2006	0.65	0.67	0.85	0.80	2.96
2005	0.70	0.68	0.63	0.71	2.70

Fiscal year ended Dec. 31. Next earnings report expected: Late October. EPS Estimates based on S&P Operating Earnings; historical GAAP earnings are as reported.

Dividend Data (Dates: mm/dd Payment Date: mm/dd/yy)

Amount ($)	Date Decl.	Ex-Div. Date	Stk. of Record	Payment Date
0.040	09/25	11/10	11/13	11/30/09
0.040	09/24	11/10	11/15	11/30/10

Dividends have been paid since 2001. Source: Company reports.

Aetna Inc.

STANDARD &POOR'S

Business Summary August 06, 2010

CORPORATE OVERVIEW. In December 2000, Aetna sold its financial services and international operations for $5 billion ($35.33 a share, not adjusted) and the assumption of $2.7 billion of debt. AET shareholders received $35.33 a share in cash, plus one share of a new health care company named Aetna. Revenue contributions (excluding net investment and other income) from the company's business operations in 2009 were: Health Care 92.3%; Group Insurance 6.1%; and Large Case Pensions 1.6%.

The Health Care segment offers health maintenance organization (HMO), point-of-service (POS), preferred provider organization (PPO), and indemnity benefit products. The company had total health plan enrollment of 18,602,000 lives at June 30, 2010, up from 18,914,000 at December 31, 2009. Commercial risk enrollment was 5,133,000 lives, versus 5,614,000, while commercial administrative services (ASC; fee-based, self-funded accounts) was 11,887,000 lives, versus 11,821,000. Medicare enrollment was 451,000 lives, versus 433,000, while Medicaid enrollment was 1,131,000 lives, versus 1,046,000. The company also provided dental benefits to 13,912,000 members, versus 14,061,000, and

pharmacy benefits to 10,333,000 members, versus 11,013,000.

Group Insurance provides group life, disability and long-term care products. Group life contracts and group conversion policies totaled 41,050,000 at December 31, 2009, versus 41,673,000 at December 31, 2008.

Large Case Pensions manages various retirement products, including pension and annuity products, for defined benefit and defined contribution plans. Aetna has not marketed its Large Case Pensions products since 1993, but continues to manage the run-off of existing business. At December 31, 2009, assets under management totaled $11.2 billion, up from $10.7 billion at December 31, 2008.

Company Financials Fiscal Year Ended Dec. 31

Per Share Data ($)	2009	2008	2007	2006	2005	2004	2003	2002	2001	2000
Tangible Book Value	8.74	5.33	8.46	7.46	8.57	8.42	6.15	4.69	4.51	4.25
Cash Flow	NA	3.61	4.08	2.96	3.04	2.22	1.79	1.14	0.54	0.82
Earnings	2.84	2.83	3.47	2.96	2.70	1.94	1.48	0.64	-0.51	-0.23
S&P Core Earnings	2.92	3.17	3.39	2.96	2.55	1.71	1.51	0.19	-1.12	NA
Dividends	0.04	0.04	0.04	0.04	0.02	0.01	0.01	0.01	0.01	Nil
Payout Ratio	1%	1%	1%	1%	NM	NM	1%	2%	NM	Nil
Prices:High	34.91	59.80	60.00	52.48	49.68	31.89	17.56	12.98	10.67	10.59
Prices:Low	18.66	14.21	39.02	30.94	29.93	16.41	9.98	7.48	5.75	8.23
P/E Ratio:High	12	21	17	18	18	16	12	20	NM	NM
P/E Ratio:Low	7	5	11	10	11	8	7	12	NM	NM

Income Statement Analysis (Million $)	2009	2008	2007	2006	2005	2004	2003	2002	2001	2000
Revenue	34,764	30,951	27,600	25,146	22,492	19,904	17,976	19,879	25,191	26,819
Operating Income	NA	2,765	3,234	2,983	2,807	2,184	1,596	1,119	460	1,104
Depreciation	NA	378	322	270	204	182	200	302	598	588
Interest Expense	243	236	181	148	123	105	103	120	143	248
Pretax Income	1,901	2,174	2,796	2,587	2,547	1,899	1,442	545	-379	-39.0
Effective Tax Rate	32.9%	36.3%	34.5%	34.8%	35.8%	36.0%	35.2%	27.8%	NM	NM
Net Income	1,277	1,384	1,831	1,686	1,635	1,215	934	393	-292	-127
S&P Core Earnings	1,315	1,551	1,792	1,682	1,542	1,072	957	140	-639	NA

Balance Sheet & Other Financial Data (Million $)	2009	2008	2007	2006	2005	2004	2003	2002	2001	2000
Cash	1,204	1,180	2,078	880	1,378	1,595	1,655	2,017	1,631	2,204
Current Assets	NA	4,918	5,288	18,304	18,235	19,516	19,557	19,349	18,751	19,768
Total Assets	38,550	35,853	50,725	47,626	44,365	42,134	40,950	40,048	43,255	47,446
Current Liabilities	NA	7,555	7,675	7,103	7,617	7,011	7,368	7,719	8,139	10,003
Long Term Debt	3,640	3,638	3,269	2,442	1,156	1,610	1,614	1,633	1,591	Nil
Common Equity	9,504	8,186	10,038	11,009	12,167	9,081	7,924	6,980	9,890	10,127
Total Capital	NA	11,825	13,323	11,587	13,338	10,691	9,538	8,613	11,481	10,127
Capital Expenditures	NA	447	400	291	272	190	211	156	143	36.9
Cash Flow	NA	1,762	2,153	1,686	1,839	1,397	1,133	695	306	461
Current Ratio	0.8	0.7	0.7	2.6	2.4	2.8	2.7	2.5	2.3	2.0
% Long Term Debt of Capitalization	Nil	30.8	23.8	18.2	8.7	15.1	16.9	19.0	13.9	Nil
% Net Income of Revenue	3.7	4.5	6.6	6.7	7.6	6.4	5.2	2.0	NM	NM
% Return on Assets	3.4	3.2	3.7	3.7	3.8	2.9	2.3	0.9	NM	NM
% Return on Equity	NA	15.2	19.1	14.5	14.0	14.3	12.5	4.7	NM	NM

Data as orig reptd.; bef. results of disc opers/spec. items. Per share data adj. for stk. divs.; EPS diluted. E-Estimated. NA-Not Available. NM-Not Meaningful. NR-Not Ranked. UR-Under Review.

Office: 151 Farmington Avenue, Hartford, CT 06156.
Telephone: 860-273-0123.
Email: investorrelations@aetna.com
Website: http://www.aetna.com

Chrmn & CEO: R.A. Williams
Pres & COO: M.T. Bertolini
EVP & CFO: J. Zubretsky
SVP & General Counsel: W.J. Casazza

SVP & CIO: M. McCarthy
Investor Contact: J. Chaffkin (860-273-7830)
Board Members: F. M. Clark, Jr., B. Z. Cohen, M. J. Coye, R. N. Farah, B. H. Franklin, J. E. Garten, E. G. Graves, G. Greenwald, E. M. Hancock, R. J. Harrington, E. J. Ludwig, J. Newhouse, R. A. Williams

Founded: 1982
Domicile: Pennsylvania
Employees: 35,000

The McGraw·Hill Companies

AFLAC Inc

STANDARD &POOR'S

S&P Recommendation HOLD ★★★☆☆	**Price** $55.46 (as of Oct 22, 2010)	**12-Mo. Target Price** $51.00	**Investment Style** Large-Cap Growth

GICS Sector Financials
Sub-Industry Life & Health Insurance

Summary AFL provides supplemental health and life insurance in the U.S. and Japan. Products are marketed at worksites and help fill gaps in primary insurance coverage. Approximately 75% of revenues comes from Japan and 25% from the U.S.

Key Stock Statistics (Source S&P, Vickers, company reports)

52-Wk Range	$56.56– 39.91	S&P Oper. EPS 2010E	5.48	Market Capitalization(B)	$26.112	Beta	1.77
Trailing 12-Month EPS	$3.89	S&P Oper. EPS 2011E	5.94	Yield (%)	2.16	S&P 3-Yr. Proj. EPS CAGR(%)	7
Trailing 12-Month P/E	14.3	P/E on S&P Oper. EPS 2010E	10.1	Dividend Rate/Share	$1.20	S&P Credit Rating	A-
$10K Invested 5 Yrs Ago	$13,361	Common Shares Outstg. (M)	470.8	Institutional Ownership (%)	67		

Price Performance

30-Week Mov. Avg. · · · 10-Week Mov. Avg. – – GAAP Earnings vs. Previous Year   Volume Above Avg. STARS
12-Mo. Target Price — Relative Strength   ▲ Up ▼ Down ► No Change   Below Avg. ★

Options: ASE, CBOE, Ph

Analysis prepared by **Bret Howlett** on July 29, 2010, when the stock traded at **$ 50.01**.

Highlights

► We expect revenues to rise 10% to 12% in 2010, on contributions from new distribution outlets, the success of a new marketing campaign and introduction of products in Japan. We forecast sales growth of 12% to 13% at AFL Japan as the bank and Japan Post channels ramp up and on recent strong sales results of the revised medical product EVER, and the new child endowment product. We forecast that AFL Japan's pretax margins will expand to roughly 22% on an improved business mix and a decrease in the benefit ratio. Longer term, we believe AFL Japan's margins could contract slightly since the new child endowment product is less profitable than existing products.

► Due to challenging economic conditions in the U.S., we forecast a 5% to 6% sales decline there as consumers remain reluctant to purchase medical supplemental products. We expect revenue growth to be sluggish due to agent recruitment difficulties and lower new money yields.

► We estimate operating EPS of $5.48 for 2010 and $5.94 for 2011, excluding any realized investment gains or losses.

Investment Rationale/Risk

► We believe AFL is appropriately valued, trading at a significant premium to book value. We think AFL's investment portfolio presents investors with above average risk relative to the group, given its holdings of European bank hybrid bonds and European sovereign debt. While we think significant losses stemming from these investments are unlikely, we believe lower credit ratings could pressure AFL's capital position. However, we believe AFL maintains a strong capital position and generates consistent earnings, which should allow the company to increase its dividend and repurchase its shares in 2010. We believe AFL Japan will continue to be the growth engine and expect the unit's strong sales and margins to fuel EPS growth.

► Risks to our recommendation and target price include investment losses, unfavorable movements in the yen/dollar exchange rate, less organic premium growth than we forecast, and agent recruiting difficulties.

► Our 12-month target price is $51, or roughly 2.2X our 2010 book value per share estimate, below historical multiples.

Qualitative Risk Assessment

LOW	MEDIUM	HIGH

Our risk assessment reflects the potential for meaningful investment losses given AFL's large exposure to hybrid bonds of financial services companies, particularly European banks, and its exposure to European sovereign debt. This is offset by its strong market share position and solid risk-based capital ratio, and the company's consistent track record of share repurchases and dividend increases.

Quantitative Evaluations

S&P Quality Ranking   A

D	C	B-	B	B+	A-	A	A+

Relative Strength Rank   **STRONG**

76

LOWEST = 1   HIGHEST = 99

Revenue/Earnings Data

Revenue (Million $)

	1Q	2Q	3Q	4Q	Year
2010	5,065	4,980	--	--	--
2009	4,818	4,313	4,526	4,597	18,254
2008	4,267	4,336	3,691	4,260	16,554
2007	3,751	3,764	3,861	4,018	15,393
2006	3,559	3,697	3,672	3,687	14,616
2005	3,559	3,567	3,669	3,567	14,363

Earnings Per Share ($)

2010	1.35	1.23	E1.37	E1.35	E5.48
2009	1.22	0.67	0.77	0.53	3.19
2008	0.98	1.00	0.21	0.42	2.62
2007	0.84	0.84	0.85	0.78	3.31
2006	0.74	0.81	0.73	0.67	2.95
2005	0.64	0.66	0.90	0.72	2.92

Fiscal year ended Dec. 31. Next earnings report expected: Late October. EPS Estimates based on S&P Operating Earnings; historical GAAP earnings are as reported.

Dividend Data (Dates: mm/dd Payment Date: mm/dd/yy)

Amount ($)	Date Decl.	Ex-Div. Date	Stk. of Record	Payment Date
0.280	02/02	02/11	02/16	03/01/10
0.280	04/27	05/17	05/19	06/01/10
0.280	07/27	08/16	08/18	09/01/10
0.300	08/10	11/15	11/17	12/01/10

Dividends have been paid since 1973. Source: Company reports.

Please read the Required Disclosures and Analyst Certification on the last page of this report.

The **McGraw·Hill** Companies

AFLAC Inc

STANDARD &POOR'S

Business Summary July 29, 2010

CORPORATE OVERVIEW. Aflac provides supplemental health and life insurance in the U.S. and Japan. Most of Aflac's policies are individually underwritten and marketed at worksites through independent agents, with premiums paid by the employee. As of the end of 2009, Aflac believed it was the world's leading underwriter of individually issued policies marketed at work sites.

In 2009, Aflac Japan accounted for 75% of total revenues, compared to 72% in 2008. At December 31, 2009, Aflac Japan accounted for 85% of total company assets, down from 87% at year-end 2008. As of year-end 2009, Aflac Japan ranked first in terms of individual insurance policies in force, surpassing Nippon Life in March 2003.

Aflac Japan's insurance products are designed to help pay for costs that are not reimbursed under Japan's national health insurance system. Products include cancer life plans (28% of total Japanese sales in 2008; 34% in 2008); Rider MAX (3%; 5%), a rider for cancer life policies that provides accident and medical/sickness benefits; and EVER (36%; 34%), a stand-alone whole life medical plan. Aflac Japan also offers ordinary life products (29%; 23%) and other products (4%; 4%) such as living benefit life plans and care products.

During 2009, the number of licensed sales associates at AFL Japan rose to approximately 110,500 compared with 107,458 at December 31, 2008. The growth in licensed sales associates resulted primarily from individual agency recruitment.

Aflac U.S. sells cancer plans (18% of total U.S. sales in 2009; 19% in 2008) and various types of health insurance, including accident and disability (48%; 49%), fixed-benefit dental (5%; 5%), and hospital indemnity (18%; 16%). Other products include long-term care, short-term disability, and ordinary life policies (11%; 11%).

During 2009, the number of licensed sales associates at AFL U.S. rose 1.2% to approximately 75,300 agents. AFL recruited approximately 28,400 new sales associates in 2009.

Company Financials Fiscal Year Ended Dec. 31

Per Share Data ($)	2009	2008	2007	2006	2005	2004	2003	2002	2001	2000
Tangible Book Value	36.20	13.78	27.97	25.32	15.89	15.03	13.03	12.41	10.39	8.87
Operating Earnings	NA	NA	NA	NA	NA	NA	NA	1.56	1.34	1.21
Earnings	3.19	2.62	3.31	2.95	2.92	2.52	1.52	1.55	1.28	1.26
S&P Core Earnings	4.88	3.98	3.27	2.86	2.60	2.47	1.85	1.49	1.25	NA
Dividends	1.12	0.96	0.80	0.55	0.44	0.38	0.30	0.23	0.19	0.17
Payout Ratio	35%	366%	24%	19%	15%	15%	20%	15%	15%	13%
Prices:High	47.75	68.81	63.91	49.40	49.65	42.60	36.91	33.45	36.09	37.47
Prices:Low	10.83	29.68	45.18	41.63	35.50	33.85	28.00	23.10	23.00	16.78
P/E Ratio:High	15	26	19	17	17	17	24	22	28	30
P/E Ratio:Low	3	11	14	14	12	13	18	15	18	13

Income Statement Analysis (Million $)	2009	2008	2007	2006	2005	2004	2003	2002	2001	2000
Life Insurance in Force	128,652	123,200	98,027	87,855	80,610	80,496	69,582	56,680	46,610	51,496
Premium Income:Life	1,860	1,586	1,323	1,214	1,139	1,031	876	761	697	716
Premium Income:A & H	14,761	13,361	11,650	11,100	10,851	10,271	9,052	7,839	7,366	7,523
Net Investment Income	2,765	2,578	2,333	2,171	2,071	1,957	1,787	1,614	1,550	1,550
Total Revenue	18,254	16,554	15,393	14,616	14,363	13,281	11,447	10,257	9,598	9,720
Pretax Income	2,235	1,914	2,499	2,264	2,226	1,807	1,225	1,259	1,081	1,012
Net Operating Income	NA	NA	NA	NA	NA	NA	NA	825	720	657
Net Income	1,497	1,254	1,634	1,483	1,483	1,299	795	821	687	687
S&P Core Earnings	2,290	1,903	1,616	1,438	1,321	1,274	962	791	670	NA

Balance Sheet & Other Financial Data (Million $)	2009	2008	2007	2006	2005	2004	2003	2002	2001	2000
Cash & Equivalent	2,972	1,591	2,523	2,036	1,781	4,308	1,508	1,793	1,233	989
Premiums Due	764	920	732	535	479	417	547	435	347	301
Investment Assets:Bonds	70,731	67,495	55,410	50,686	47,551	48,024	42,893	37,483	31,677	31,305
Investment Assets:Stocks	24.0	27.0	22.0	25.0	84.0	77.0	73.0	258	245	236
Investment Assets:Loans	Nil	Nil	Nil	Nil	Nil	Nil	Nil	Nil	Nil	Nil
Investment Assets:Total	70,869	67,609	57,056	50,769	47,692	48,142	42,999	37,768	31,941	31,558
Deferred Policy Costs	8,533	8,237	6,654	6,025	5,590	5,595	5,044	4,277	3,645	3,685
Total Assets	84,106	79,331	65,805	59,805	56,361	59,326	50,964	45,058	37,860	37,232
Debt	2,599	1,721	1,465	1,420	1,050	1,141	1,409	1,312	1,000	956
Common Equity	8,417	6,639	8,795	8,341	7,927	7,573	6,646	6,394	5,425	4,694
% Return on Revenue	8.2	7.6	10.6	10.1	10.4	9.8	6.9	8.0	7.2	7.1
% Return on Assets	1.8	1.7	2.6	2.6	2.6	2.4	1.7	2.0	1.8	1.8
% Return on Equity	19.9	16.3	19.1	18.2	19.1	18.3	12.2	13.9	13.6	16.0
% Investment Yield	4.0	4.2	4.3	4.4	4.3	4.3	4.4	4.6	4.9	4.9

Data as orig reptd.; bef. results of disc opers/spec. items. Per share data adj. for stk. divs.; EPS diluted. E-Estimated. NA-Not Available. NM-Not Meaningful. NR-Not Ranked. UR-Under Review.

Office: 1932 Wynnton Road, Columbus, GA 31999.
Telephone: 706-323-3431.
Email: ir@aflac.com
Website: http://www.aflac.com

Chrmn & CEO: D.P. Amos
Pres, EVP, CFO & Treas: K. Cloninger, III
EVP & Chief Admin Officer: R.C. Davis
EVP, Secy & General Counsel: J.M. Loudermilk

SVP & Chief Acctg Officer: R.A. Rogers, Jr.
Investor Contact: K.S. Janke, Jr. (706-596-3264)
Board Members: D. P. Amos, J. S. Amos, II, P. S. Amos, II, M. H. Armacost, K. Cloninger, III, J. F. Harris, E. J. Hudson, D. W. Johnson, R. B. Johnson, C. B. Knapp, E. S. Purdom, B. K. Rimer, M. R. Schuster, D. G. Thompson, R. L. Wright, T. Yoshida

Founded: 1973
Domicile: Georgia
Employees: 8,057

Agilent Technologies Inc

STANDARD & POOR'S

S&P Recommendation BUY ★★★★☆

Price
$34.75 (as of Oct 22, 2010)

12-Mo. Target Price
$40.00

Investment Style
Large-Cap Blend

GICS Sector Information Technology
Sub-Industry Electronic Equipment Manufacturers

Summary This Hewlett-Packard (HPQ) spin-off is a diversified global manufacturer of test and measurement instruments, and life sciences and chemical analysis instruments.

Key Stock Statistics (Source S&P, Vickers, company reports)

52-Wk Range	$37.43–24.61	S&P Oper. EPS 2010**E**	1.94	Market Capitalization(B)	$12.036	Beta	1.36
Trailing 12-Month EPS	$1.18	S&P Oper. EPS 2011**E**	2.26	Yield (%)	Nil	S&P 3-Yr. Proj. EPS CAGR(%)	19
Trailing 12-Month P/E	29.5	P/E on S&P Oper. EPS 2010**E**	17.9	Dividend Rate/Share	Nil	S&P Credit Rating	BBB-
$10K Invested 5 Yrs Ago	NA	Common Shares Outstg. (M)	346.4	Institutional Ownership (%)	80		

Price Performance

30-Week Mov. Avg. · · · 10-Week Mov. Avg. – – GAAP Earnings vs. Previous Year   Volume Above Avg. STARS
12-Mo. Target Price — Relative Strength — ▲ Up ▼ Down ► No Change   Below Avg. ★

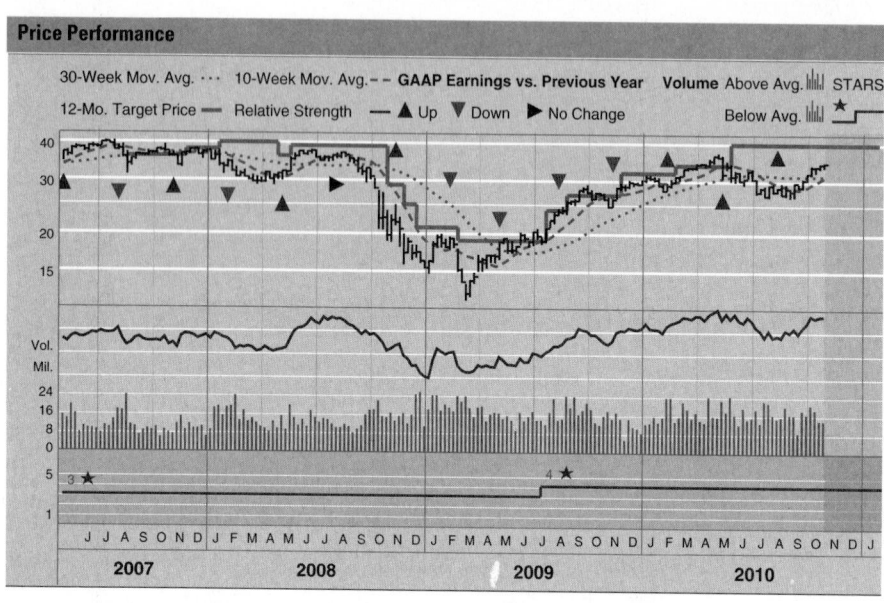

Options: ASE, CBOE, P, Ph

Analysis prepared by **Angelo Zino** on August 18, 2010, when the stock traded at **$29.28.**

Highlights

➤ We expect sales to rise 13% in FY 11 (Oct.) following our projection for a 20% increase in FY 10. We see revenues paced by growth in A's more cyclical electronic measurement end markets and aided by the acquisition of Varian. We see the chemical analysis business benefiting from growth in the food safety, petrochemical, and environment and forensic markets. In life sciences, we see sales driven by opportunities in pharmaceutical and biotech as well as academic and government.

➤ We project an annual gross margin of 55% in FY 11 versus our 54% margin outlook in FY 11, benefiting from higher volume and cost-cutting efforts. We expect A to recognize cost synergies of at least $75 million from its Varian deal over the next few quarters. We view positively previously completed cost-reduction moves, including the restructuring of A's electronic measurement group.

➤ We estimate operating EPS of $1.94 for FY 10, which excludes $0.25 in non-recurring charges, and $2.26 for FY 11. We model a 19% tax rate going forward. We think the Varian deal will aid expansion into high-growth adjacent markets, such as environmental analysis.

Investment Rationale/Risk

➤ We have a favorable view of the company's diversified end-market mix, with exposure to the non-cyclical life sciences and chemical analysis markets as well as cyclical electronic measurement markets. Over the longer term, we expect Agilent to focus on expanding aggressively through new product offerings in high-growth industries, complemented by opportunistic acquisitions in core markets. We forecast more stable demand and higher market share in both the chemical analysis and life science end-markets. We view the shares as attractively valued at current levels.

➤ Risks to our recommendation and target price include a weaker-than-expected global economy, narrower margins than we project, and weaker-than-anticipated traction for new product introductions.

➤ Our 12-month target price of $40 is based on our discounted cash flow analysis, which assumes a weighted average cost of capital of 10%, beta of 1.3X, and a terminal growth rate of 3%. Our target price is supported by a price-to-sales (P/S) ratio of 2.3X our FY 11 sales per share estimate of $17.69, near A's five-year historical average.

Qualitative Risk Assessment

LOW	MEDIUM	HIGH

Our risk assessment reflects the volatility of Agilent's results in the past, offset by recent efforts to streamline its businesses and divest parts of its portfolio that contributed to this variability.

Quantitative Evaluations

S&P Quality Ranking B-

D	C	B-	B	B+	A-	A	A+

Relative Strength Rank STRONG

83

LOWEST = 1   HIGHEST = 99

Revenue/Earnings Data

Revenue (Million $)

	1Q	2Q	3Q	4Q	Year
2010	1,213	1,271	1,384	--	--
2009	1,166	1,091	1,057	1,167	4,481
2008	1,393	1,456	1,444	1,481	5,774
2007	1,280	1,320	1,374	1,446	5,420
2006	1,167	1,239	1,239	1,328	4,973
2005	1,212	1,688	1,242	1,407	5,139

Earnings Per Share ($)

2010	0.22	0.31	0.58	E0.58	E1.94
2009	0.18	-0.29	-0.06	0.07	-0.09
2008	0.31	0.47	0.45	0.64	1.87
2007	0.36	0.30	0.45	0.46	1.57
2006	2.03	0.28	0.51	0.31	3.26
2005	0.10	0.11	0.10	-0.03	0.28

Fiscal year ended Oct. 31. Next earnings report expected: Mid November. EPS Estimates based on S&P Operating Earnings; historical GAAP earnings are as reported.

Dividend Data

No cash dividends have been paid.

Agilent Technologies Inc

Business Summary August 18, 2010

CORPORATE OVERVIEW. Agilent Technologies, which was spun off from Hewlett-Packard (HPQ) in 1999, provides investors with exposure to the communications, electronics, life sciences and chemical analysis industries. Agilent's revenues during FY 09 (Oct.) came from three business segments: electronic measurement 51% (60% in FY 08), bio-analytical measurement 45% (40%) and the semiconductor and board test business 4% (included with electronic measurement in FY 08). Starting in FY 10, Agilent will form three new operating segments from its existing businesses. The bio-analytical measurement segment will be separated into two operating segments, life sciences and chemical analysis. The electronic measurement segment will recombine electronic measurement and semiconductor and board test, which were reported separately in FY 09. Following this reorganization, Agilent will have three businesses -- life sciences, chemical analysis and electronic measurement.

The company's electronic measurement products compete in the communications test market and the general test market, which represented 39% and 61% of FY 09 segment revenues, respectively. The communications test market includes handset manufacturers, network equipment manufacturers and communications service providers. Agilent has a suite of fiber optic, broadband and data and wireless communications and microwave network products. General purpose test products and services are sold to the electronics

industry and other industries with significant electronic content, such as the aerospace and defense, computer and semiconductor industries. It sells electronic measurement products that are used for electronics manufacturing testing, parametric testing, and flat panel display (FPD) markets.

The bio-analytical measurement business focuses on the life sciences arena (47% of FY 09 segment sales) and the chemical analysis market (53% of FY 09 segment sales). Within life sciences, Agilent focuses on the pharmaceutical value chain in the areas of therapeutic research, discovery & development, clinical trials, and manufacturing and quality assurance and quality control. In the pharmaceutical and biopharmaceutical markets, Agilent's instruments help lower the cost of discovering and developing new drugs. It also has exposure to the academic and government market, which includes academic institutions, large government institutes and privately funded organizations. Chemical analysis focuses primarily on the following areas: petrochemical, environmental, homeland security and forensics, bioagriculture and food safety, and material science.

Company Financials Fiscal Year Ended Oct. 31

Per Share Data ($)	2009	2008	2007	2006	2005	2004	2003	2002	2001	2000
Tangible Book Value	4.86	4.81	6.75	7.79	7.39	6.42	5.09	8.44	9.95	10.37
Cash Flow	0.38	2.35	2.04	3.64	0.65	1.31	-3.02	-0.62	0.72	2.75
Earnings	-0.09	1.87	1.57	3.26	0.28	0.71	-3.78	-2.20	-0.89	1.66
S&P Core Earnings	-0.09	1.53	1.52	1.59	-0.11	0.27	-5.70	-3.10	-2.63	NA
Dividends	Nil	Nil	Nil	Nil	Nil	Nil	Nil	Nil	Nil	Nil
Payout Ratio	Nil	Nil	Nil	Nil	Nil	Nil	Nil	Nil	Nil	Nil
Prices:High	31.77	38.00	40.42	39.54	36.10	38.80	29.42	38.00	68.00	162.00
Prices:Low	12.02	14.76	30.26	26.96	20.11	19.51	18.35	10.50	18.00	38.06
P/E Ratio:High	NM	20	26	12	NM	55	NM	NM	NM	98
P/E Ratio:Low	NM	8	19	8	NM	27	NM	NM	NM	23

Income Statement Analysis (Million $)	2009	2008	2007	2006	2005	2004	2003	2002	2001	2000
Revenue	4,481	5,774	5,420	4,973	5,139	7,181	6,056	6,010	8,396	10,773
Operating Income	399	974	775	680	367	678	-363	-872	-44.0	1,548
Depreciation	162	179	191	170	186	292	362	735	734	495
Interest Expense	88.0	123	91.0	69.0	27.0	36.0	Nil	Nil	Nil	Nil
Pretax Income	7.00	815	670	1,528	306	440	-690	-1,547	-477	1,164
Effective Tax Rate	542.9%	15.0%	4.70%	5.96%	50.7%	20.7%	NM	NM	NM	35.0%
Net Income	-31.0	693	638	1,437	141	349	-1,790	-1,022	-406	757
S&P Core Earnings	-27.9	568	615	701	-55.1	137	-2,695	-1,438	-1,202	NA

Balance Sheet & Other Financial Data (Million $)	2009	2008	2007	2006	2005	2004	2003	2002	2001	2000
Cash	2,493	1,429	1,826	2,262	2,251	2,315	1,607	1,844	1,170	996
Current Assets	3,961	3,208	3,671	3,958	4,447	4,577	3,889	4,880	4,799	5,655
Total Assets	7,612	7,437	7,554	7,369	6,751	7,056	6,297	8,203	7,986	8,425
Current Liabilities	1,123	1,325	1,663	1,538	1,936	1,871	1,906	2,181	2,002	2,758
Long Term Debt	2,904	2,125	2,087	1,500	Nil	1,150	1,150	1,150	Nil	Nil
Common Equity	2,506	2,559	3,234	3,648	4,081	3,569	2,824	4,627	5,659	5,265
Total Capital	5,410	4,684	5,321	5,341	4,081	4,719	3,974	5,777	5,659	5,265
Capital Expenditures	128	154	154	185	139	118	205	301	881	824
Cash Flow	131	872	829	1,607	327	641	-1,428	-287	328	1,252
Current Ratio	3.5	2.4	2.2	2.6	2.3	2.4	2.0	2.2	2.4	2.1
% Long Term Debt of Capitalization	53.7	45.4	39.2	29.1	Nil	24.4	28.9	19.9	Nil	Nil
% Net Income of Revenue	NM	12.0	11.7	28.9	2.7	4.9	NM	NM	NM	7.0
% Return on Assets	NM	9.3	8.5	20.4	2.0	5.2	NM	NM	NM	10.9
% Return on Equity	NM	23.9	18.5	37.2	3.7	10.9	NM	NM	NM	17.5

Data as orig reptd.; bef. results of disc opers/spec. items. Per share data adj. for stk. divs.; EPS diluted. E-Estimated. NA-Not Available. NM-Not Meaningful. NR-Not Ranked. UR-Under Review.

Office: 5301 Stevens Creek Blvd, Santa Clara, CA 95051-7201.
Telephone: 408-553-2424.
Email: investor_relations@agilent.com
Website: http://www.agilent.com

Chrmn: J.G. Cullen
Pres & CEO: W.P. Sullivan
SVP, Secy & General Counsel: M.O. Huber
CFO: D. Hirsch

CTO: D.J. Solomon
Investor Contact: R. Gonsalves (408-345-8948)
Board Members: P. N. Clark, J. G. Cullen, H. Fields, R. J. Herbold, B. Koh, D. M. Lawrence, A. B. Rand, W. P. Sullivan

Founded: 1999
Domicile: Delaware
Employees: 16,800

Airgas Inc.

STANDARD &POOR'S

S&P Recommendation HOLD ★ ★ ★ ★ ☆

Price
$70.13 (as of Oct 22, 2010)

12-Mo. Target Price
$70.00

Investment Style
Large-Cap Growth

GICS Sector Materials
Sub-Industry Industrial Gases

Summary This leading distributor of industrial, medical and specialty gases and related equipment also distributes safety and other disposable supplies through its network of stores.

Key Stock Statistics (Source S&P, Vickers, company reports)

52-Wk Range	$70.23–41.82	S&P Oper. EPS 2011**E**	3.16	Market Capitalization(B)	$5.853	Beta		1.28
Trailing 12-Month EPS	$2.45	S&P Oper. EPS 2012**E**	3.63	Yield (%)	1.43	S&P 3-Yr. Proj. EPS CAGR(%)		13
Trailing 12-Month P/E	28.6	P/E on S&P Oper. EPS 2011**E**	22.2	Dividend Rate/Share	$1.00	S&P Credit Rating		BBB
$10K Invested 5 Yrs Ago	$26,787	Common Shares Outstg. (M)	83.5	Institutional Ownership (%)	75			

Price Performance

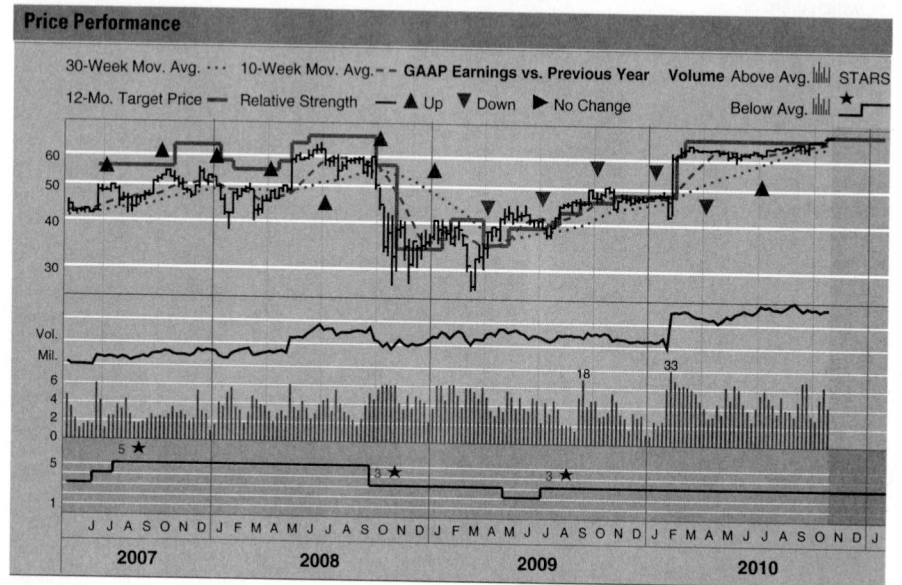

30-Week Mov. Avg. ···· 10-Week Mov. Avg. - - **GAAP Earnings vs. Previous Year** Volume Above Avg. STARS
12-Mo. Target Price — Relative Strength — ▲ Up ▼ Down ▶ No Change Below Avg.

Options: CBOE, Ph

Analysis prepared by **Mathew Christy, CFA** on October 14, 2010, when the stock traded at **$ 69.72.**

Highlights

▶ Following a sales decline of greater than 11% in FY 10 (Mar.), we see FY 11 sales gaining slightly more than 8%. Our forecast is based primarily on somewhat better pricing and volumes that should lead to higher overall same-store sales in FY 11. In addition, our forecast is based on the positive effects from our expectation of continued acquisitions. For FY 12, we forecast that revenue will rise by nearly 7%, on higher overall demand that we see leading to somewhat higher pricing and volumes.

▶ We believe operating margins will widen by about 1 percentage point in FY 11. Our forecast is based on higher operating margins from somewhat higher volumes, better asset utilization rates, increased pricing, and the positive effects of cost-cutting efforts, all partially offset by increased costs associated with the rollout of a new enterprise management software system. In FY 12, we forecast somewhat better operating margins on improved volume and pricing.

▶ On our projection for effective tax rates of 39% in FY 11 and 38% in FY 12, we expect operating EPS of $3.16 and $3.63 in the respective years.

Investment Rationale/Risk

▶ In February 2010, ARG rejected Air Products' (APD 82, Hold) $60 a share offer for the company, asserting that the proposed price significantly undervalued ARG. Following a series of increased offers (with the most recent at $65.50) and a partial victory by APD at ARG's latest annual meeting, the battle has moved to the courts due to disagreement over the outcome of the results for proposed changes to ARG's by-laws. In our opinion, a friendly deal could eventually be reached.

▶ Risks to our recommendation and target price include a negative resolution to the recent hostile acquisition offer from Air Products, and a renewed downturn in the economy.

▶ Our 12-month target price of $70 reflects our belief that ARG is an attractive acquisition target, considering its scale in packaged industrial gas. It is based on a weighted blend of historical chemical industry acquisition multiples applied to our forward 12-month estimates, including multiples of 1.14X our sales per share estimate, 8X our EBITDA estimate, and 22X our EPS estimate.

Qualitative Risk Assessment

LOW	MEDIUM	HIGH

Our risk assessment for Airgas reflects the company's acquisition strategy, its significant proportion of sales to the cyclical industrial manufacturing industry, and what we consider to be a relatively high level of debt.

Quantitative Evaluations

S&P Quality Ranking A-

D	C	B-	B	B+	A-	A	A+

Relative Strength Rank MODERATE

59

LOWEST = 1 HIGHEST = 99

Revenue/Earnings Data

Revenue (Million $)

	1Q	2Q	3Q	4Q	Year
2011	1,053	--	--	--	--
2010	979.3	962.3	942.1	980.4	3,864
2009	1,117	1,162	1,079	992.1	4,349
2008	915.1	1,007	1,008	1,087	4,017
2007	773.0	790.8	787.4	853.9	3,205
2006	690.7	714.4	702.4	746.9	2,830

Earnings Per Share ($)

	1Q	2Q	3Q	4Q	Year
2011	0.76	E0.78	E0.78	E0.81	E3.16
2010	0.66	0.65	0.56	0.47	2.34
2009	0.81	0.86	0.76	0.68	3.12
2008	0.63	0.60	0.67	0.76	2.66
2007	0.48	0.49	0.40	0.54	1.92
2006	0.38	0.38	0.41	0.45	1.62

Fiscal year ended Mar. 31. Next earnings report expected: Late October. EPS Estimates based on S&P Operating Earnings; historical GAAP earnings are as reported.

Dividend Data (Dates: mm/dd Payment Date: mm/dd/yy)

Amount ($)	Date Decl.	Ex-Div. Date	Stk. of Record	Payment Date
0.180	11/05	12/11	12/15	12/31/09
0.220	01/28	03/11	03/15	03/31/10
0.220	05/25	06/11	06/15	06/30/10
0.250	07/21	09/13	09/15	09/30/10

Dividends have been paid since 2003. Source: Company reports.

Please read the Required Disclosures and Analyst Certification on the last page of this report.

The McGraw·Hill Companies

Airgas Inc.

Business Summary October 14, 2010

CORPORATE OVERVIEW. Airgas has completed over 400 acquisitions over the past 25 years and has become the largest U.S. distributor of packaged gases and welding, safety, and related products, with an average market share of 25%, based on company data. ARG operated an integrated network of over 875 branch locations, 325 gas cylinder fill planters, 75 national/regional specialty gas laboratories, and other gas plants and facilities while marketing its products and services through sales representatives, retail stores, and has electronic, catalog, and telesales channels. The company had over 14,000 employees as of March 2010. Competitors in the packaged gas market include independent distributors (50% of the market), through a fragmented distribution network, as well as large distributors (25%), including Praxair, Linde AG, Air Liquide, Matheson Trigas and Valley National.

The distribution segment (89% of FY 10 (Mar.) total sales, 87.8% of earnings before interest and taxes (EBIT), and nearly 11% EBIT margins) purchases and distributes industrial, medical and specialty gases, process chemicals, and hardgoods. Products include industrial, specialty and medical gases, and welding, safety, and related products. Gas and rent revenues accounted for 60.7% of segment sales in FY 10, with hardgoods providing the remaining 39.3%. Industry segments served include manufacturing, service, construction, retail consumer establishments, transportation and utilities, and agriculture and mining.

The other operations segment (11%, 12.2%, 12.3%) produces and distributes certain gas products, principally dry ice, carbon dioxide, specialty gases, and nitrous oxide. The segment also includes the results of the company's National Welders, a producer and distributor of industrial gases. Customers include food processors, food services, pharmaceutical and biotech industries, and wholesale trade and grocery outlets.

The company has a fairly broad exposure to the overall U.S. economy, as it serves over 800,000 customers in multiple industries. As a percentage of total net sales, ARG estimates sales to the repair and maintenance segment accounted for 30%; industrial manufacturing 23%; energy and infrastructure construction 10%; medical 9%; petrochemical 7%; food products 6%; retail and wholesale trade 4%; analytical 3%; utilities 3%; transportation 2%; and other 3%.

Company Financials Fiscal Year Ended Mar. 31

Per Share Data ($)	2010	2009	2008	2007	2006	2005	2004	2003	2002	2001
Tangible Book Value	5.69	3.59	3.59	2.93	4.59	3.76	2.22	1.84	0.95	0.87
Cash Flow	5.15	5.75	4.90	3.66	3.14	2.64	2.25	2.05	1.74	1.71
Earnings	2.34	3.12	2.66	1.92	1.62	1.20	1.07	0.94	0.69	0.42
S&P Core Earnings	2.38	3.20	2.66	1.92	1.52	1.11	0.99	0.86	0.64	0.34
Dividends	0.76	0.56	0.28	0.24	0.18	0.16	Nil	Nil	Nil	Nil
Payout Ratio	32%	18%	11%	12%	11%	13%	Nil	Nil	Nil	Nil
Calendar Year	2009	2008	2007	2006	2005	2004	2003	2002	2001	2000
Prices:High	51.00	65.45	55.89	43.43	33.79	27.19	21.75	20.74	15.85	10.19
Prices:Low	26.29	27.09	39.00	31.65	21.15	19.82	15.27	11.75	6.38	4.63
P/E Ratio:High	22	21	21	22	21	23	20	22	23	24
P/E Ratio:Low	11	9	15	16	13	17	14	13	9	11

Income Statement Analysis (Million $)										
Revenue	3,864	4,349	4,017	3,205	2,830	2,411	1,895	1,787	1,636	1,629
Operating Income	658	746	676	489	396	315	255	238	198	198
Depreciation	235	221	190	147	128	112	88.0	79.8	72.9	86.8
Interest Expense	63.3	87.1	61.4	62.1	55.7	52.8	43.0	47.3	48.0	61.4
Pretax Income	314	429	371	257	208	148	128	109	78.4	48.9
Effective Tax Rate	37.5%	39.2%	38.9%	38.8%	37.4%	36.8%	37.1%	37.7%	38.0%	42.3%
Net Income	196	261	223	154	128	92.0	80.2	68.1	48.6	28.2
S&P Core Earnings	200	268	223	154	119	84.9	74.2	61.8	44.5	23.3

Balance Sheet & Other Financial Data (Million $)										
Cash	47.0	47.2	43.1	25.9	35.0	32.6	Nil	Nil	Nil	Nil
Current Assets	711	718	639	550	459	466	327	271	304	334
Total Assets	4,496	4,400	3,979	3,333	2,474	2,292	1,931	1,700	1,717	1,583
Current Liabilities	476	432	506	428	476	333	242	209	221	282
Long Term Debt	1,499	1,750	1,540	1,310	636	802	683	658	764	621
Common Equity	1,796	1,572	1,413	1,125	947	814	692	597	503	497
Total Capital	3,305	3,888	2,993	2,866	1,968	1,934	1,668	1,464	1,465	1,279
Capital Expenditures	253	352	267	244	214	168	93.7	68.0	58.3	65.9
Cash Flow	431	482	413	302	255	204	168	148	122	115
Current Ratio	1.5	1.7	1.3	1.3	1.0	1.4	1.3	1.3	1.4	1.2
% Long Term Debt of Capitalization	45.4	45.0	51.4	52.6	32.3	41.4	40.9	44.9	52.1	48.5
% Net Income of Revenue	5.1	6.0	5.6	4.8	4.5	3.8	4.2	3.8	3.0	1.7
% Return on Assets	4.4	6.2	6.1	5.3	5.4	4.3	4.4	4.0	2.9	1.7
% Return on Equity	11.7	17.5	17.6	14.9	14.5	12.2	12.4	12.4	9.7	5.8

Data as orig reptd.; bef. results of disc opers/spec. items. Per share data adj. for stk. divs.; EPS diluted. E-Estimated. NA-Not Available. NM-Not Meaningful. NR-Not Ranked. UR-Under Review.

Office: 259 North Radnor-Chester Road, Radnor, PA 19087-5283.
Telephone: 610-687-5253.
Email: investor@airgas.com
Website: http://www.airgas.com

Chrmn: J.C. van Roden, Jr.
Pres & CEO: P. McCausland
COO & EVP: M.L. Molinini
SVP & CFO: R.M. McLaughlin

SVP, Secy & General Counsel: R.H. Young, Jr.
Investor Contact: J. Worley (610-902-6206)
Board Members: W. T. Brown, J. P. Clancey, J. W. Hovey, R. C. III, R. L. Lumpkins, P. McCausland, T. B. Miller, Jr., P. A. Sneed, D. Stout, L. M. Thomas, E. Wolf, J. C. van Roden, Jr.

Founded: 1986
Domicile: Delaware
Employees: 14,000

Air Products and Chemicals Inc.

STANDARD &POOR'S

S&P Recommendation	HOLD ★★★☆☆	Price	12-Mo. Target Price	Investment Style
		$84.74 (as of Oct 22, 2010)	$88.00	Large-Cap Blend

GICS Sector Materials
Sub-Industry Industrial Gases

Summary This major producer of industrial gases and electronics and specialty chemicals also has interests in environmental and energy-related businesses.

Key Stock Statistics (Source S&P, Vickers, company reports)

52-Wk Range	$85.44– 64.13	S&P Oper. EPS 2010E	4.97	Market Capitalization(B)	$18.010	Beta	1.15
Trailing 12-Month EPS	$4.62	S&P Oper. EPS 2011E	5.55	Yield (%)	2.31	S&P 3-Yr. Proj. EPS CAGR(%)	10
Trailing 12-Month P/E	18.3	P/E on S&P Oper. EPS 2010E	17.1	Dividend Rate/Share	$1.96	S&P Credit Rating	A
$10K Invested 5 Yrs Ago	$17,500	Common Shares Outstg. (M)	212.5	Institutional Ownership (%)	84		

Price Performance

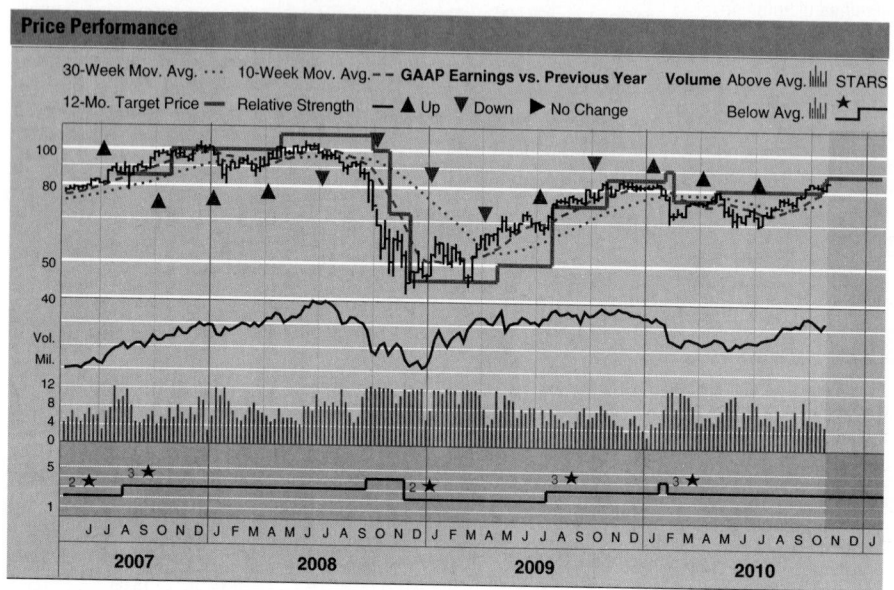

30-Week Mov. Avg. · · · 10-Week Mov. Avg. - - GAAP Earnings vs. Previous Year Volume Above Avg. STARS
12-Mo. Target Price — Relative Strength ▲ Up ▼ Down ▶ No Change Below Avg. ★

Options: CBOE, P, Ph

Qualitative Risk Assessment

LOW	MEDIUM	HIGH

Our risk assessment reflects the stable growth of the industrial gases industry versus commodity chemicals, and what we see as the company's relatively strong balance sheet, offset by volatile raw material cost exposure in the chemical segment.

Quantitative Evaluations

S&P Quality Ranking A

D	C	B-	B	B+	A-	A	A+

Relative Strength Rank STRONG

72

LOWEST = 1   HIGHEST = 99

Revenue/Earnings Data

Revenue (Million $)

	1Q	2Q	3Q	4Q	Year
2010	2,174	2,249	2,252	--	--
2009	2,195	1,955	1,976	2,129	8,256
2008	2,474	2,605	2,808	2,715	10,415
2007	2,410	2,451	2,574	2,603	10,038
2006	2,016	2,230	2,246	2,359	8,850
2005	1,991	2,003	2,078	2,071	8,144

Earnings Per Share ($)

2010	1.16	1.16	1.17	E1.30	E4.97
2009	0.42	0.89	0.54	1.14	3.00
2008	1.16	1.16	0.23	1.26	4.98
2007	1.03	1.02	1.28	1.35	4.67
2006	0.80	0.89	--	0.73	3.29
2005	0.72	0.75	0.82	0.79	3.08

Fiscal year ended Sep. 30. Next earnings report expected: NA. EPS Estimates based on S&P Operating Earnings; historical GAAP earnings are as reported.

Highlights

➤ The 12-month target price for APD has recently been changed to $88.00 from $85.00. The Highlights section of this Stock Report will be updated accordingly.

Investment Rationale/Risk

➤ The Investment Rationale/Risk section of this Stock Report will be updated shortly. For the latest News story on APD from MarketScope, see below.

➤ 10/21/10 12:54 pm ET ... S&P MAINTAINS HOLD OPINION ON SHARES OF AIR PRODUCTS & CHEMICALS (APD 84.6***): Sep-Q operating EPS of $1.35, vs. $1.14, exceeds our $1.30 estimate. Sales rose 10%, with volumes up 9% including a strong gain in electronics materials. Full FY 10 (Sep) operating EPS was $5.02 vs. $4.06. We boost our FY 11 EPS estimate by $0.15 to $5.55, helped by continued volume growth and strong equipment results. On the better EPS outlook, we boost our target price by $3 to $88. We note that a unfriendly merger with Airgas (ARG 70, Hold), if completed at the current $5.7B bid, would likely be operating EPS neutral to slightly accretive in first year before related costs. /R.O'Reilly-CFA

Dividend Data (Dates: mm/dd Payment Date: mm/dd/yy)

Amount ($)	Date Decl.	Ex-Div. Date	Stk. of Record	Payment Date
0.450	11/19	12/30	01/04	02/08/10
0.490	03/18	03/30	04/01	05/10/10
0.490	05/20	06/29	07/01	08/09/10
0.490	09/16	09/29	10/01	11/08/10

Dividends have been paid since 1954. Source: Company reports.

Please read the Required Disclosures and Analyst Certification on the last page of this report.

The McGraw-Hill Companies

Air Products and Chemicals Inc.

STANDARD &POOR'S

Business Summary October 12, 2010

CORPORATE OVERVIEW. Air Products & Chemicals is one of the largest global producers of industrial gases, and has a large specialty chemicals business. APD focuses on several areas for growth in industrial gases, including electronics, hydrogen for petroleum refining, health care, and Asia. International operations accounted for 54% of FY 09 (Sep.) sales.

The industrial gases businesses consists of nitrogen, oxygen, argon, hydrogen, helium, carbon monoxide, synthesis gas, and fluorine compounds for both merchant (44% of sales and 55% of profits in FY 09) and on-site tonnage (31%, 33%) customers. Sales of atmospheric gases (oxygen, nitrogen and argon) accounted for 21% of the total in FY 09. APD is the world's leading supplier of hydrogen (15% of total sales) and carbon monoxide products (HYCO) and helium. Beginning with the fourth quarter of FY 08, the European health care business (sales of $360 million in FY 07) has been reported as part of the merchant gases segment. APD has leading market positions in Spain, Portugal, and the U.K. Beginning in FY 08, the tonnage gases segment has also included the polyurethane intermediates business. The business had sales of $340 million in FY 07.

The electronics and performance materials segment (19%, 8%) supplies specialty gases (nitrogen trifluoride, silane, phosphine), tonnage gases, specialty and bulk chemicals, services and equipment to makers of silicone and semiconductors, displays and photovoltaic devices. Performance materials include epoxy and polyurethane additives, specialty amines, and surfactants for coatings, adhesives, personal care and cleaning products, and polyurethanes.

Equipment and energy (6%, 4%) includes cryogenic and gas processing equipment for air separation, gas processing, natural gas liquefaction (LNG), and hydrogen purification. The segment also includes 50%-owned ventures in power cogeneration and flue gas desulfurization facilities.

Company Financials Fiscal Year Ended Sep. 30

Per Share Data ($)	2009	2008	2007	2006	2005	2004	2003	2002	2001	2000
Tangible Book Value	17.10	18.21	22.01	17.59	16.03	15.45	12.99	13.33	10.79	10.78
Cash Flow	6.93	8.94	8.44	6.64	6.22	5.76	4.65	4.97	4.95	3.24
Earnings	3.00	4.98	4.67	3.29	3.08	2.64	1.79	2.36	2.12	0.57
S&P Core Earnings	2.74	4.56	4.65	2.94	3.01	2.63	1.66	1.67	1.70	NA
Dividends	1.79	1.70	1.48	1.34	1.25	1.04	0.88	0.82	0.78	0.74
Payout Ratio	60%	34%	32%	41%	41%	39%	49%	35%	37%	130%
Prices:High	85.44	106.06	105.02	72.45	65.81	59.18	53.07	53.52	49.00	42.25
Prices:Low	43.44	41.46	68.58	58.01	53.00	46.71	36.97	40.00	32.25	23.00
P/E Ratio:High	28	21	22	22	21	22	30	23	23	74
P/E Ratio:Low	14	8	15	18	17	18	21	17	15	40

Income Statement Analysis (Million $)	2009	2008	2007	2006	2005	2004	2003	2002	2001	2000
Revenue	8,256	10,415	10,038	8,850	8,144	7,411	6,297	5,401	5,717	5,496
Operating Income	1,995	2,360	2,179	1,777	1,700	1,567	1,218	1,319	1,313	1,407
Depreciation	840	869	840	763	728	715	640	581	573	576
Interest Expense	144	184	176	119	110	121	124	122	191	197
Pretax Income	837	1,479	1,376	1,049	998	851	565	784	737	118
Effective Tax Rate	22.2%	24.7%	21.9%	25.8%	26.4%	26.6%	26.0%	30.7%	29.7%	NM
Net Income	640	1,091	1,043	748	712	604	400	525	513	124
S&P Core Earnings	584	1,001	1,038	670	695	601	369	369	370	NA

Balance Sheet & Other Financial Data (Million $)	2009	2008	2007	2006	2005	2004	2003	2002	2001	2000
Cash	488	104	42.3	35.2	55.8	146	76.2	254	66.2	94.1
Current Assets	2,998	2,848	2,858	2,613	2,415	2,417	2,068	1,909	1,685	1,805
Total Assets	13,080	12,490	12,660	11,181	10,409	10,040	9,432	8,495	8,084	8,271
Current Liabilities	2,504	2,212	2,423	2,323	1,943	1,706	1,581	1,256	1,352	1,375
Long Term Debt	3,716	3,515	2,977	2,280	2,053	Nil	2,169	2,041	2,028	2,616
Common Equity	4,792	5,031	5,496	4,924	4,576	4,444	3,783	3,460	3,106	2,821
Total Capital	9,098	9,309	9,362	8,215	7,644	5,401	6,845	6,411	6,030	6,334
Capital Expenditures	1,179	1,085	1,055	1,261	930	706	613	628	708	768
Cash Flow	1,480	1,960	1,883	1,511	1,440	1,319	1,040	1,106	1,086	700
Current Ratio	1.2	1.3	1.2	1.1	1.2	1.4	1.3	1.5	1.2	1.3
% Long Term Debt of Capitalization	40.8	37.8	31.8	27.8	26.9	Nil	31.7	31.8	33.6	41.3
% Net Income of Revenue	7.8	10.5	10.4	8.5	8.7	8.2	6.4	9.7	9.0	2.3
% Return on Assets	5.0	8.7	8.7	6.9	7.0	6.2	4.5	6.3	6.3	1.5
% Return on Equity	13.0	20.7	20.0	15.8	15.8	14.7	11.1	16.0	17.3	4.3

Data as orig reptd.; bef. results of disc opers/spec. items. Per share data adj. for stk. divs.; EPS diluted. E-Estimated. NA-Not Available. NM-Not Meaningful. NR-Not Ranked. UR-Under Review.

Office: 7201 Hamilton Boulevard, Allentown, PA 18195-1501.
Telephone: 610-481-4911.
Website: http://www.airproducts.com
Chrmn, Pres & CEO: J. McGlade

SVP & CFO: P.E. Huck
SVP & General Counsel: J.D. Stanley
CTO: M. Alger
Treas: G.G. Bitto

Investor Contact: N. Squires (610-481-7461)
Board Members: M. L. Baeza, W. L. Davis, III, C. C. Deaton, M. J. Donahue, U. O. Fairbairn, W. D. Ford, E. E. Hagenlocker, E. Henkes, J. McGlade, M. G. McGlynn, L. S. Smith

Founded: 1940
Domicile: Delaware
Employees: 18,900

Akamai Technologies Inc

STANDARD &POOR'S

S&P Recommendation HOLD ★★★☆☆

Price $47.61 (as of Oct 22, 2010)	**12-Mo. Target Price** $45.00	**Investment Style** Large-Cap Growth

GICS Sector Information Technology
Sub-Industry Internet Software & Services

Summary This company develops and deploys solutions designed to accelerate and improve the delivery of Internet content and applications.

Key Stock Statistics (Source S&P, Vickers, company reports)

52-Wk Range	$53.06– 20.06	S&P Oper. EPS 2010**E**	0.86	Market Capitalization(B)	$8.646	Beta	0.80
Trailing 12-Month EPS	$0.80	S&P Oper. EPS 2011**E**	1.07	Yield (%)	Nil	S&P 3-Yr. Proj. EPS CAGR(%)	16
Trailing 12-Month P/E	59.5	P/E on S&P Oper. EPS 2010**E**	55.4	Dividend Rate/Share	Nil	S&P Credit Rating	NR
$10K Invested 5 Yrs Ago	$27,600	Common Shares Outstg. (M)	181.6	Institutional Ownership (%)	85		

Price Performance

30-Week Mov. Avg. ··· 10-Week Mov. Avg. -- **GAAP Earnings vs. Previous Year** **Volume** Above Avg. ⅲⅲ STARS
12-Mo. Target Price — Relative Strength — ▲ Up ▼ Down ► No Change Below Avg. ⅲⅲ ★

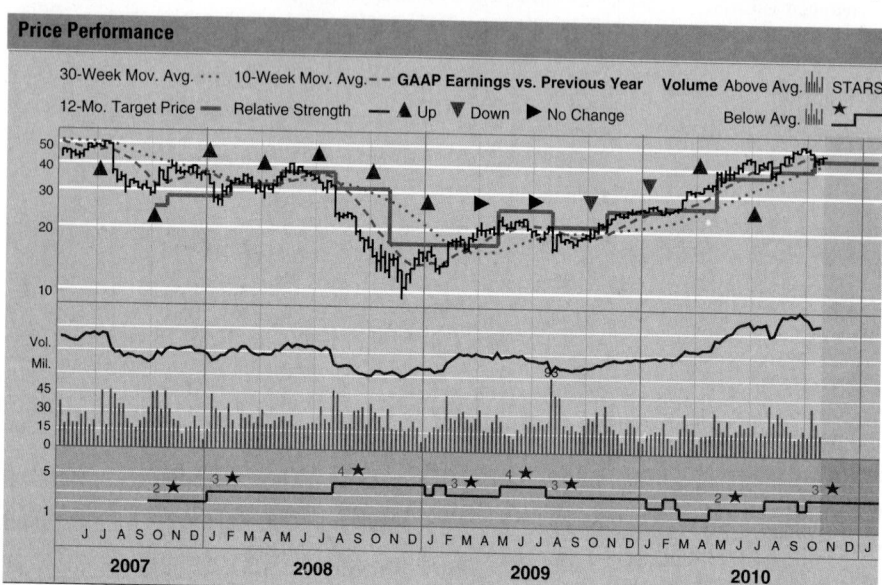

Options: ASE, CBOE, P, Ph

Analysis prepared by **Scott H. Kessler** on October 07, 2010, when the stock traded at **$ 44.27**.

Highlights

► We project that revenues will increase 17% in 2010 and 14% in 2011, reflecting what we consider solid secular growth, driven by the increasing use and importance of the Internet to distribute content and applications, and improving volumes, offset somewhat by the challenging global economy and pricing pressures.

► We think that annual gross, operating and net margins will be roughly steady from 2009 through 2011, reflecting scale and efficiency benefits, offset somewhat by pricing pressures and significant investment.

► AKAM has made some $450 million in acquisitions since late 2006, enhancing its capabilities regarding content and application transmission speeds, rich-media distribution, and peer-to-peer networks. In November 2008, it bought acerno for up to $100 million to build a more focused advertising business. A $100 million buy-back was announced in April 2009 and extended in April 2010. As of June 2010, AKAM had roughly $1.0 billion of net cash and marketable securities.

Investment Rationale/Risk

► AKAM has been a pioneer in content and application distribution. We believe this area will continue to grow notably, reflecting increasing demand for online video and software as a service (SaaS) offerings, but we think AKAM faces challenges related to weakened pricing in core products and services, online and mobile HD video perhaps gaining traction more gradually than some expect, and possibly some new competition in the value-added services area. We view the stock as fairly valued at recent levels.

► Risks to our opinion and target price include the potential for weakening of pricing, less robust demand for AKAM's solutions than we expect, and more significant competition.

► Our DCF analysis, with assumptions including a WACC of 10.7%, free cash flow growth averaging 15% from 2010 to 2014, and a terminal growth rate of 3%, leads to an intrinsic value of $45, which is our 12-month target price. We think DCF considerations constitute the best way to value AKAM, because certain non-cash items are very material to its results.

Qualitative Risk Assessment

LOW	MEDIUM	**HIGH**

Our risk assessment reflects what we view as rapidly evolving technologies, and notable and increasing competition.

Quantitative Evaluations

S&P Quality Ranking   B-

D	C	**B-**	B	B+	A-	A	A+

Relative Strength Rank   MODERATE
49
LOWEST = 1   HIGHEST = 99

Revenue/Earnings Data

Revenue (Million $)

	1Q	2Q	3Q	4Q	Year
2010	240.0	245.3	--	--	--
2009	210.4	204.6	206.5	238.3	859.8
2008	187.0	194.0	197.4	212.6	790.9
2007	139.3	152.7	161.2	183.2	636.4
2006	90.83	100.7	111.5	125.7	428.7
2005	60.10	64.65	75.71	82.66	283.1

Earnings Per Share ($)

	1Q	2Q	3Q	4Q	Year
2010	0.22	0.20	E0.20	E0.24	E0.86
2009	0.20	0.19	0.17	0.21	0.77
2008	0.20	0.19	0.18	0.22	0.79
2007	0.11	0.12	0.13	0.20	0.56
2006	0.07	0.07	0.08	0.12	0.34
2005	0.10	0.11	1.71	0.16	2.11

Fiscal year ended Dec. 31. Next earnings report expected: Late October. EPS Estimates based on S&P Operating Earnings; historical GAAP earnings are as reported.

Dividend Data

No cash dividends have been paid.

Please read the Required Disclosures and Analyst Certification on the last page of this report.

The McGraw·Hill Companies

Akamai Technologies Inc

STANDARD &POOR'S

Business Summary October 07, 2010

CORPORATE OVERVIEW. The Internet plays a crucial role in the way entities conduct business; however, it was not originally intended to accommodate the volume or complexity of today's demands. As a result, online information is often delayed or lost.

Akamai Technologies has developed solutions to accelerate and improve the delivery of Internet content and applications. Its solutions are designed to help customers enhance their revenues and reduce costs by maximizing the performance of their online businesses. Advancing website performance and reliability enable AKAM's customers to improve end-user experiences and promote more effective operations. Specifically, AKAM seeks to address issues related to performance, scalability and security. The company offers solutions focused on digital media distribution and storage, content and application delivery, application performance, on-demand managed services, and website intelligence. Importantly, we believe the company's offerings help clients monetize traffic and save/conserve capital.

CORPORATE STRATEGY. AKAM believes it has deployed the world's largest globally distributed computing platform, which includes more than 73,000 servers around the world. The company employs its proprietary solutions and specialized technologies such as advanced routing, load balancing, and data collection and monitoring to deliver customer content and applications. We perceive this platform and the related intellectual property as a notable competitive advantage the company will continue to leverage.

Although competition in this area has increased over the past few years, AKAM's focus on both dynamic (i.e., back and forth) distribution and segments beyond media and entertainment help insulate the company from substantial pricing pressures, in our view. Nonetheless, we believe lower-end business is more at risk given additional players entering the market.

We believe recent acquisitions have bolstered the company's base and breadth of technologies related to streaming rich media, enhancing distribution speeds, peer-to-peer networks, and online advertising. We see these areas contributing to significant growth, and expect AKAM to continue pursuing transactions that are not transformational in nature. We note that value-added services have been growing as a percentage of the company's revenues.

Company Financials Fiscal Year Ended Dec. 31

Per Share Data ($)	2009	2008	2007	2006	2005	2004	2003	2002	2001	2000
Tangible Book Value	6.81	6.04	5.47	4.10	3.19	NM	NM	NM	NM	2.02
Cash Flow	1.32	1.30	0.93	0.58	2.25	0.37	0.17	-1.01	-20.40	-1.98
Earnings	0.77	0.79	0.56	0.34	2.11	0.25	-0.25	-1.81	-23.59	-10.07
S&P Core Earnings	0.77	0.79	0.56	0.34	1.93	-0.16	-0.64	-2.05	-12.47	NA
Dividends	Nil	Nil	Nil	Nil	Nil	Nil	Nil	Nil	Nil	Nil
Payout Ratio	Nil	Nil	Nil	Nil	Nil	Nil	Nil	Nil	Nil	Nil
Prices:High	26.27	40.90	59.69	56.80	22.25	18.47	14.20	6.34	37.44	345.50
Prices:Low	12.29	9.25	27.75	19.57	10.64	10.74	1.18	0.56	2.52	18.06
P/E Ratio:High	34	52	NM	NM	11	74	NM	NM	NM	NM
P/E Ratio:Low	16	12	NM	NM	5	43	NM	NM	NM	NM

Income Statement Analysis (Million $)										
Revenue	860	791	636	429	283	210	161	145	163	89.8
Operating Income	348	313	217	124	98.5	69.2	30.1	-46.3	-131	-187
Depreciation	116	98.1	71.9	45.6	25.2	20.2	49.7	90.4	330	712
Interest Expense	2.84	2.83	3.09	3.17	5.33	10.2	18.3	18.4	18.9	8.93
Pretax Income	237	235	168	98.5	70.4	35.1	-28.7	-204	-2,434	-886
Effective Tax Rate	38.5%	38.1%	40.0%	41.7%	NM	2.20%	NM	NM	NM	NM
Net Income	146	145	101	57.4	328	34.4	-29.3	-204	-2,436	-886
S&P Core Earnings	144	145	101	57.2	300	-19.9	-75.6	-231	-1,286	NA

Balance Sheet & Other Financial Data (Million $)										
Cash	566	327	546	270	292	70.6	165	115	211	310
Current Assets	761	502	695	375	355	109	202	142	228	355
Total Assets	2,107	1,881	1,656	1,248	891	183	279	230	421	2,791
Current Liabilities	327	100	88.4	89.3	61.9	46.8	62.7	81.1	91.3	84.9
Long Term Debt	200	200	200	200	200	257	386	301	300	300
Common Equity	1,758	1,569	1,359	955	624	-126	-175	-168	17.2	2,404
Total Capital	1,958	1,769	1,559	1,155	824	131	211	133	317	2,705
Capital Expenditures	108	115	100	56.8	26.9	12.3	1.42	7.25	64.5	132
Cash Flow	248	243	173	103	353	54.6	20.5	-114	-2,106	-174
Current Ratio	6.0	5.0	7.9	4.2	5.7	2.3	3.2	1.7	2.5	4.2
% Long Term Debt of Capitalization	10.2	11.3	12.8	17.3	24.3	196.4	183.2	226.5	94.6	11.1
% Net Income of Revenue	17.0	18.4	15.9	13.4	115.9	16.4	NM	NM	NM	NM
% Return on Assets	7.3	8.2	7.0	5.4	61.1	14.9	NM	NM	NM	NM
% Return on Equity	8.8	9.9	8.7	7.3	131.7	NM	NM	NM	NM	NM

Data as orig reptd.; bef. results of disc opers/spec. items. Per share data adj. for stk. divs.; EPS diluted. E-Estimated. NA-Not Available. NM-Not Meaningful. NR-Not Ranked. UR-Under Review.

Office: 8 Cambridge Center, Cambridge, MA 02142-1413.
Telephone: 617-444-3000.
Email: ir@akamai.com
Website: http://www.akamai.com

Chrmn: G.H. Conrades
Pres: D. Kenny
CEO: P.L. Sagan
COO: R. Blumofe

SVP, CFO & Chief Acctg Officer: J.D. Sherman
Investor Contact: S. Smith (617-444-2804)
Board Members: G. H. Conrades, M. M. Coyne, II, C. K. Goodwin, J. A. Greenthal, D. Kenny, P. J. Kight, F. T. Leighton, G. A. Moore, P. L. Sagan, F. V. Salerno, N. Seligman

Founded: 1998
Domicile: Delaware
Employees: 1,750

The McGraw·Hill Companies

AK Steel Holding Corp

STANDARD &POOR'S

S&P Recommendation BUY ★★★★☆

Price	$13.35 (as of Oct 22, 2010)
12-Mo. Target Price	$19.00
Investment Style	Large-Cap Blend

GICS Sector Materials
Sub-Industry Steel

Summary This company produces flat-rolled carbon, stainless and electrical steels for the automotive, appliance, construction, electrical power generation and distribution markets.

Key Stock Statistics (Source S&P, Vickers, company reports)

52-Wk Range	$26.75– 11.34	S&P Oper. EPS 2010E	0.50	Market Capitalization(B)	$1.468	Beta	2.90
Trailing 12-Month EPS	$0.69	S&P Oper. EPS 2011E	1.84	Yield (%)	1.50	S&P 3-Yr. Proj. EPS CAGR(%)	NM
Trailing 12-Month P/E	19.4	P/E on S&P Oper. EPS 2010E	26.7	Dividend Rate/Share	$0.20	S&P Credit Rating	BB
$10K Invested 5 Yrs Ago	$19,926	Common Shares Outstg. (M)	110.0	Institutional Ownership (%)	61		

Price Performance

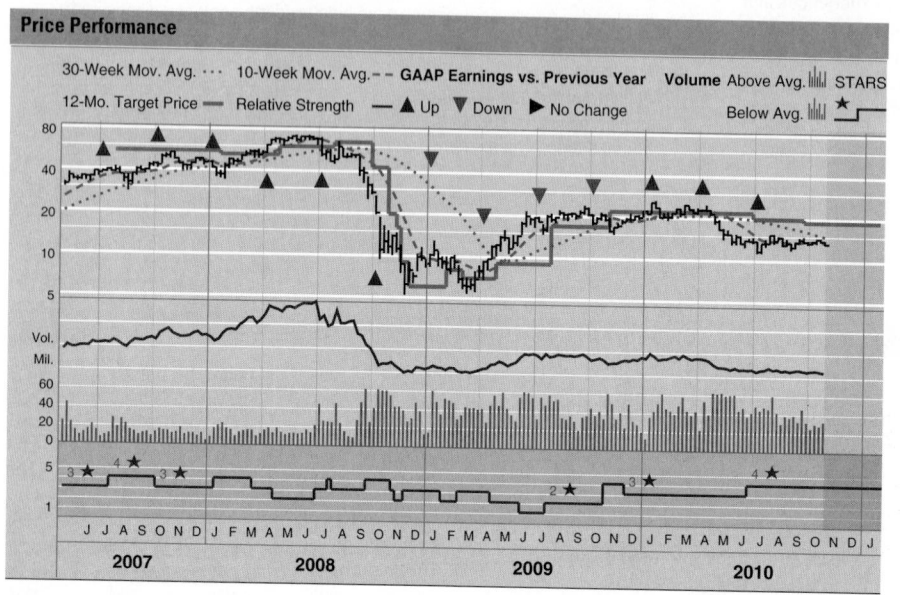

30-Week Mov. Avg. · · · · 10-Week Mov. Avg. – – GAAP Earnings vs. Previous Year Volume Above Avg. STARS
12-Mo. Target Price — Relative Strength — ▲ Up ▼ Down ▶ No Change Below Avg.

Analysis prepared by **Stuart J. Benway, CFA** on September 17, 2010, when the stock traded at **$ 13.79**.

Options: ASE, CBOE, P, Ph

Highlights

➤ Following a drop of 47% in 2009, we look for a nearly 50% sales increase in 2010, reflecting our expectation for a recovery in shipment volume and higher revenue per ton. Our forecast rests on several assumptions. First, S&P forecasts GDP growth of 2.8% in 2010, versus a decline in GDP of 2.6% in 2009. We see this resulting in rising demand for durable goods. Second, S&P Economics projects auto sales of 11.4 million units in 2010, up from 10.4 million in 2009. Third, we think that distributors will add to inventories in 2010. Fourth, we expect that sales will be aided by a more lucrative product mix.

➤ We look for a sizable improvement in margins and a return to operating profit in 2010, aided by higher volume and increased revenue per ton. After interest expense and taxes, we project operating EPS of $0.50 in 2010, versus an operating loss per share of $0.63 in 2009, which excludes unusual expense of $0.05.

➤ Longer term, we think earnings will rise on a gradual decline in pension and health care costs, greater internal sourcing of raw materials, and a more lucrative product mix.

Investment Rationale/Risk

➤ For the long term, we view AKS as poised for a turnaround. The company has cut costs and reduced funded debt and underfunded pension and health care liabilities. It also has obtained concessions on health care and retiree costs on its labor contracts, eliminating a sizable cost disadvantage versus other domestic steel companies. Thus, we think AKS now has a lower, more competitive cost structure, which should help boost earnings as steel demand recovers. Moreover, we believe that long-term results will also benefit from rising demand for the company's stainless/electrical steel products. We think the stock is attractively valued at a recent 7.5X our 2011 EPS estimate and with a dividend yield of nearly 1.5%.

➤ Risks to our recommendation and target price include declines in the volume of shipments and the average realized price per ton in 2011 instead of the increases we expect.

➤ Applying a multiple of 10.3X to our 2011 EPS estimate, at the low end of the historical range, we arrive at our 12-month target price of $19.

Qualitative Risk Assessment

LOW	MEDIUM	HIGH

Our risk assessment reflects AKS's exposure to the auto industry and other cyclical markets, along with its high ratio of total liabilities to assets versus peers. Partially offsetting these factors are AKS's debt reduction and cost-cutting in recent years.

Quantitative Evaluations

S&P Quality Ranking B-

D	C	B-	B	B+	A-	A	A+

Relative Strength Rank WEAK

17

LOWEST = 1   HIGHEST = 99

Revenue/Earnings Data

Revenue (Million $)

	1Q	2Q	3Q	4Q	Year
2010	1,406	1,596	--	--	--
2009	922.2	793.6	1,041	1,320	4,077
2008	1,791	2,237	2,158	1,459	7,644
2007	1,720	1,870	1,722	1,692	7,003
2006	1,436	1,497	1,554	1,582	6,069
2005	1,423	1,455	1,393	1,377	5,647

Earnings Per Share ($)

	1Q	2Q	3Q	4Q	Year
2010	0.02	0.24	E-0.10	E0.11	E0.50
2009	-0.67	-0.43	-0.06	0.36	-0.68
2008	0.90	1.29	1.67	-3.88	0.04
2007	0.56	0.98	0.97	0.95	3.46
2006	0.06	0.26	0.23	-0.45	0.11
2005	0.54	0.08	-0.26	0.37	0.01

Fiscal year ended Dec. 31. Next earnings report expected: Late October. EPS Estimates based on S&P Operating Earnings; historical GAAP earnings are as reported.

Dividend Data (Dates: mm/dd Payment Date: mm/dd/yy)

Amount ($)	Date Decl.	Ex-Div. Date	Stk. of Record	Payment Date
0.050	10/27	11/10	11/13	12/10/09
0.050	01/25	02/10	02/12	03/10/10
0.050	04/20	05/12	05/14	06/10/10
0.050	07/27	08/11	08/13	09/10/10

Dividends have been paid since 2008. Source: Company reports.

The McGraw·Hill Companies

AK Steel Holding Corp

STANDARD &POOR'S

Business Summary September 17, 2010

CORPORATE OVERVIEW. AK Steel Holding, the third largest integrated U.S. steelmaker in terms of production, sells premium quality coated, cold rolled and hot rolled carbon steel to the automotive, appliance and manufacturing markets, as well as to the construction industry and independent steel distributors and service centers.

Sales by market in 2009 were: automotive 36% (32% in 2008), appliance, industrial machinery, construction and manufacturing 31% (29%), and distribution and service centers 33% (34%).

Shipments in 2009 totaled 3,935,500 tons, versus 5,866,000 tons in 2008. In 2009, AKS incurred an $18 per ton operating loss, versus operating profit per ton of $124 in 2008.

CORPORATE STRATEGY. The company seeks to achieve sustained profitability by controlling costs and directing its marketing efforts toward those customers that require the highest quality flat-rolled steel with precise just-in-time delivery and technical support. AKS believes that its enhanced product quality and delivery capabilities, and its emphasis on customer technical support and product planning, are areas in which it excels in serving this market segment.

MARKET PROFILE. The primary factors affecting demand for steel products are economic growth in general and growth in demand for durable goods in particular. The two largest end markets for steel products in the U.S. are autos and construction. In 2009, these two markets accounted for 28.3% of shipments in the U.S. market. Other end markets include appliances, containers, machinery, and oil and gas. Distributors, also known as service centers, accounted for 20.6% of industry shipments in the U.S. market in 2009. Distributors are the largest single market for the steel industry in the U.S. Because distributors sell to a wide variety of OEMs, it is impossible to track the final destination of much of the industry's shipments. Consequently, demand for steel from the auto, construction and other industries may be higher than the shipment data would suggest. In terms of shipments, the size of the U.S. market was 62.2 million tons in 2009, and AKS's market share was 6.4%. In the U.S. market, consumption decreased at a compound annual growth rate (CAGR) of 7.9% from 2000 through 2009. Global steel production was 1.22 billion metric tons in 2009, versus 1.33 billion metric tons in 2008.

Company Financials Fiscal Year Ended Dec. 31

Per Share Data ($)	2009	2008	2007	2006	2005	2004	2003	2002	2001	2000
Tangible Book Value	7.71	8.43	7.51	3.44	1.30	0.92	NM	3.02	7.40	11.03
Cash Flow	1.30	1.84	5.22	1.95	1.86	2.29	-3.44	-2.32	1.41	3.45
Earnings	-0.68	0.04	3.46	0.11	0.01	0.28	-5.48	-4.42	-0.87	1.20
S&P Core Earnings	-0.88	2.41	3.43	1.00	0.84	2.70	-2.71	-1.06	-1.89	NA
Dividends	0.20	0.20	Nil	Nil	Nil	Nil	Nil	Nil	0.13	0.50
Payout Ratio	NM	500%	Nil	Nil	Nil	Nil	Nil	Nil	NM	42%
Prices:High	24.27	73.07	53.97	17.31	18.23	16.00	8.90	14.85	15.00	20.13
Prices:Low	5.39	5.20	16.13	7.58	6.23	3.65	1.74	6.45	7.50	7.50
P/E Ratio:High	NM	NM	16	NM	NM	57	NM	NM	NM	17
P/E Ratio:Low	NM	NM	5	NM	NM	13	NM	NM	NM	6

Income Statement Analysis (Million $)										
Revenue	4,077	7,644	7,003	6,069	5,647	5,217	4,042	4,289	3,994	4,612
Operating Income	147	930	860	409	397	139	155	331	370	586
Depreciation	217	202	196	204	205	219	222	225	245	248
Interest Expense	37.0	50.9	68.3	89.1	86.8	110	118	128	133	136
Pretax Income	-98.0	-6.90	591	-3.10	38.0	-193	-241	-803	-147	210
Effective Tax Rate	20.4%	NM	34.4%	NM	NM	NM	NM	NM	NM	37.0%
Net Income	-74.6	4.00	388	12.0	-0.80	30.5	-594	-476	-92.4	132
S&P Core Earnings	-97.0	269	385	110	92.4	295	-326	-125	-204	NA

Balance Sheet & Other Financial Data (Million $)										
Cash	462	563	714	519	520	377	54.7	283	101	86.8
Current Assets	1,630	2,003	2,427	2,548	2,246	2,107	1,358	1,700	1,548	1,522
Total Assets	4,275	4,677	5,197	5,518	5,488	5,453	5,026	5,400	5,226	5,240
Current Liabilities	741	734	973	932	903	747	779	860	954	890
Long Term Debt	606	633	653	1,115	1,115	1,110	1,198	1,260	1,325	1,388
Common Equity	881	963	875	417	220	197	-52.8	529	1,021	1,307
Total Capital	1,487	1,596	1,527	1,532	1,335	1,307	1,145	1,789	2,358	2,707
Capital Expenditures	134	167	104	76.2	174	98.8	79.6	93.8	109	138
Cash Flow	142	206	584	216	204	250	-373	-250	152	379
Current Ratio	2.2	2.7	2.5	2.7	2.5	2.8	1.7	2.0	1.6	1.7
% Long Term Debt of Capitalization	40.8	39.6	42.7	72.8	83.5	84.9	104.6	70.4	56.2	51.3
% Net Income of Revenue	NM	0.1	5.5	NM	NM	NM	NM	NM	NM	2.9
% Return on Assets	NM	0.1	7.2	NM	NM	NM	NM	NM	NM	2.5
% Return on Equity	NM	0.4	60.0	NM	NM	NM	NM	NM	NM	10.2

Data as orig reptd.; bef. results of disc opers/spec. items. Per share data adj. for stk. divs.; EPS diluted. E-Estimated. NA-Not Available. NM-Not Meaningful. NR-Not Ranked. UR-Under Review.

Office: 9227 Centre Pointe Drive, West Chester, OH 45069.
Telephone: 513-425-5000.
Website: http://www.aksteel.com
Chrmn, Pres & CEO: J.L. Wainscott

COO & EVP: J.F. Kaloski
EVP, Secy & General Counsel: D.C. Horn
Investor Contact: A.E. Ferrara, Jr. (513-425-2888)
SVP & CFO: A.E. Ferrara, Jr.

Board Members: R. A. Abdoo, J. S. Brinzo, D. C. Cuneo, W. K. Gerber, B. G. Hill, R. H. Jenkins, R. S. Michael, III, S. D. Peterson, J. A. Thomson, J. L. Wainscott

Founded: 1900
Domicile: Delaware
Employees: 6,500

The McGraw·Hill Companies

Alcoa Inc

STANDARD &POOR'S

S&P Recommendation BUY ★★★★☆

Price	12-Mo. Target Price	Investment Style
$12.72 (as of Oct 22, 2010)	$16.00	Large-Cap Value

GICS Sector Materials
Sub-Industry Aluminum

Summary Alcoa is one of the world's largest producers of aluminum and alumina.

Key Stock Statistics (Source S&P, Vickers, company reports)

52-Wk Range	$17.60– 9.81	S&P Oper. EPS 2010E	0.43	Market Capitalization(B)	$12.990
Trailing 12-Month EPS	$-0.28	S&P Oper. EPS 2011E	0.97	Yield (%)	0.94
Trailing 12-Month P/E	NM	P/E on S&P Oper. EPS 2010E	29.6	Dividend Rate/Share	$0.12
$10K Invested 5 Yrs Ago	$6,083	Common Shares Outstg. (M)	1,021.2	Institutional Ownership (%)	62

Beta	2.08
S&P 3-Yr. Proj. EPS CAGR(%)	NM
S&P Credit Rating	BBB-

Price Performance

30-Week Mov. Avg. · · · ·   10-Week Mov. Avg. – –   **GAAP Earnings vs. Previous Year**   Volume Above Avg. ▌▌▌ STARS
12-Mo. Target Price —   Relative Strength —   ▲ Up ▼ Down ▶ No Change   Below Avg. ▌▌▌ ★

Options: ASE, CBOE, P, Ph

Analysis prepared by **Leo J. Larkin** on October 14, 2010, when the stock traded at **$ 13.15**.

Highlights

➤ We expect a sales increase of 9.2% in 2011, following our forecast for an 11% rise in 2010. Our expectation for a further sales gain assumes U.S. real GDP growth of 2.4% in 2011, versus an estimated gain in GDP of 2.6% in 2010, and another year of growth in the global economy. We see higher volume in the downstream businesses on further increases in construction spending and auto sales. S&P forecasts a 2.2% rise in construction spending in 2011, versus a projected advance of 1.5% in 2010, and motor vehicle sales of 12.8 million units in 2011, versus 2010's expected level of 11.4 million units. We look for a higher aluminum price in 2011 on greater world demand and a continued decline in metal exchange inventories.

➤ We look for improved operating profits on higher realized prices for aluminum, increased volume, and production from new lower cost plants. After interest expense and taxes, we estimate EPS of $0.97 in 2011, versus projected operating EPS of $0.43 in 2010, which excludes unusual items totaling $0.32.

➤ Long term, we think EPS will rise on improving aluminum industry fundamentals and a shift to lower-cost aluminum plants.

Investment Rationale/Risk

➤ We think AA is attractively valued, recently trading at 13.5X our 2011 EPS estimate. We view AA as a special situation turnaround and a vehicle to benefit from an improvement in aluminum market fundamentals. In our opinion, AA's cost cutting, together with increased production from new lower-cost facilities, will result in a lower breakeven point, which in turn should lead to greater profitability and positive free cash flow over the business cycle. We are cautiously optimistic that the production discipline demonstrated by China in 2009 will continue and help boost the aluminum price. Market surpluses caused by the emergence of China as a net exporter in 2002 have been a drag on the aluminum price in recent years.

➤ Risks to our recommendation and target price include a decline in the price of aluminum in 2011 instead of the increase we project.

➤ Our 12-month target price of $16 is based on our view that the stock will trade at 16.5X our 2011 EPS estimate. Based on our target P/E, AA would trade just below the mid-point of its historical range of the past 10 years and at 2.0X its tangible book value at the end of 2010's third quarter.

Qualitative Risk Assessment

LOW	**MEDIUM**	HIGH

Our risk assessment reflects AA's exposure to cyclical markets such as autos and construction, offset by its large shares of the markets it serves.

Quantitative Evaluations

S&P Quality Ranking   B-

D	C	**B-**	B	B+	A-	A	A+

Relative Strength Rank   STRONG

73

LOWEST = 1   HIGHEST = 99

Revenue/Earnings Data

Revenue (Million $)

	1Q	2Q	3Q	4Q	Year
2010	4,887	5,187	5,287	--	--
2009	4,147	4,244	4,615	5,433	18,439
2008	6,998	7,245	6,970	5,688	26,901
2007	7,908	8,066	7,387	7,387	30,748
2006	7,244	7,959	7,631	7,840	30,379
2005	6,226	6,698	6,566	6,669	26,159

Earnings Per Share ($)

2010	-0.19	0.13	0.06	E0.11	E0.43
2009	-0.59	-0.32	-0.07	-0.27	-1.06
2008	0.36	0.67	0.37	-1.16	0.28
2007	0.77	0.81	0.64	0.74	2.95
2006	0.70	0.86	0.62	0.29	2.47
2005	0.30	0.53	0.33	0.24	1.40

Fiscal year ended Dec. 31. Next earnings report expected: Mid January. EPS Estimates based on S&P Operating Earnings; historical GAAP earnings are as reported.

Dividend Data (Dates: mm/dd Payment Date: mm/dd/yy)

Amount ($)	Date Decl.	Ex-Div. Date	Stk. of Record	Payment Date
0.030	01/25	02/03	02/05	02/25/10
0.030	04/22	05/05	05/07	05/25/10
0.030	07/23	08/04	08/06	08/25/10
0.030	10/01	11/03	11/05	11/25/10

Dividends have been paid since 1939. Source: Company reports.

Please read the Required Disclosures and Analyst Certification on the last page of this report.

The **McGraw·Hill** Companies

Alcoa Inc

STANDARD &POOR'S

Business Summary October 14, 2010

CORPORATE OVERVIEW. Alcoa is one of the world's largest producers of primary aluminum as well as one of the world's largest suppliers of alumina, an intermediate raw material used to make aluminum. In 2009, primary aluminum production totaled 3.6 million metric tons, versus 4.0 million metric tons in 2008; and alumina production totaled 14.3 million metric tons, versus 15.3 million metric tons in 2008.

MARKET PROFILE. The primary factor affecting demand for aluminum products is economic growth, in general, and growth in demand for durable goods, in particular. The three largest end markets for aluminum in North America are transportation, containers/packaging, and construction. In 2008 (latest available), these markets accounted for 62% of shipments in North America. In terms of primary production, the size of the world market was 23.4 million metric tons in 2009. Alcoa's market share was 15.4%. From 2000 through 2009, global consumption rose at a compound annual growth rate (CAGR) of 4.6%.

COMPETITIVE LANDSCAPE. Alcoa's direct competitors in the aluminum market are Aleris International, Inc., Aluminum Corp. of China, Century Aluminum,

Kaiser Aluminum, Norsk Hydro, United Company RUSAL and Quanex. Indirect competitors include mining companies that have aluminum and alumina operations, such as Vale, BHP Billiton and Rio Tinto. Led mostly by Alcoa and Alcan (now a subsidiary of Rio Tinto), consolidation of the industry accelerated in the late 1990s and thereafter.

However, the price of aluminum in the last economic expansion that ended in 2008's second half lagged the gains in other base metals such as carbon steel, copper and nickel by a wide margin. In our view, the reason for the less buoyant aluminum price is that exports from China have kept the aluminum market in overall surplus. Beginning in 2002, China became a net exporter of aluminum, and we believe that its production has become a drag on the aluminum price.

Company Financials Fiscal Year Ended Dec. 31

Per Share Data ($)	2009	2008	2007	2006	2005	2004	2003	2002	2001	2000
Tangible Book Value	6.90	7.61	12.75	8.53	6.96	6.72	5.36	3.27	4.96	6.19
Cash Flow	0.35	1.79	4.42	3.96	2.85	2.98	2.61	3.20	2.49	3.29
Earnings	-1.06	0.28	2.95	2.47	1.40	1.60	1.20	0.58	1.05	1.81
S&P Core Earnings	-1.09	-0.26	1.74	2.46	1.05	1.52	0.92	-0.17	0.17	NA
Dividends	0.26	0.68	0.68	0.60	0.60	0.60	0.60	0.60	0.60	0.50
Payout Ratio	NM	243%	23%	24%	43%	38%	50%	103%	57%	28%
Prices:High	16.51	44.77	48.77	36.96	32.29	39.44	38.92	39.75	45.71	43.63
Prices:Low	4.97	6.80	28.09	26.39	22.28	28.51	18.45	17.62	27.36	23.13
P/E Ratio:High	NM	NM	17	15	23	25	32	69	44	24
P/E Ratio:Low	NM	NM	10	11	16	18	15	30	26	13

Income Statement Analysis (Million $)										
Revenue	18,439	26,901	30,748	30,379	26,159	23,478	21,504	20,263	22,859	22,936
Operating Income	359	3,505	4,779	5,410	3,398	3,397	2,885	2,663	3,523	4,304
Depreciation	1,311	1,234	1,268	1,280	1,267	1,212	1,202	2,224	1,253	1,219
Interest Expense	470	574	401	384	339	270	314	350	393	427
Pretax Income	-1,498	792	4,491	3,432	1,933	2,204	1,669	925	1,641	2,812
Effective Tax Rate	NM	43.2%	34.6%	24.3%	22.8%	25.3%	24.2%	31.6%	32.0%	33.5%
Net Income	-985	229	2,571	2,161	1,233	1,402	1,034	498	908	1,489
S&P Core Earnings	-1,021	-210	1,511	2,154	924	1,334	777	-143	146	NA

Balance Sheet & Other Financial Data (Million $)										
Cash	1,481	762	483	506	762	457	576	344	512	315
Current Assets	7,022	8,150	8,086	9,157	8,790	7,493	6,740	6,313	6,792	7,578
Total Assets	38,455	37,822	38,803	37,183	33,696	32,609	31,711	29,810	28,355	31,691
Current Liabilities	5,414	7,279	7,166	7,281	7,368	6,298	5,084	4,461	5,003	7,954
Long Term Debt	8,974	8,509	6,371	5,910	5,279	5,346	6,692	8,365	6,388	4,987
Common Equity	12,397	11,680	15,961	14,576	13,318	13,245	12,020	9,872	10,614	11,366
Total Capital	25,195	23,162	24,847	23,103	20,892	20,852	20,911	20,087	18,927	18,892
Capital Expenditures	1,617	3,438	3,636	3,201	2,124	1,142	863	1,263	1,177	1,121
Cash Flow	324	1,461	3,839	3,441	2,498	2,612	2,234	2,720	2,159	2,706
Current Ratio	1.3	1.1	1.1	1.3	1.2	1.2	1.3	1.4	1.4	1.0
% Long Term Debt of Capitalization	35.6	36.7	25.6	25.6	25.3	25.6	32.0	41.6	33.8	26.4
% Net Income of Revenue	NM	0.9	8.3	7.1	4.7	6.0	4.8	2.5	4.0	6.5
% Return on Assets	NM	0.6	6.7	6.1	3.7	4.4	3.4	1.7	3.0	6.1
% Return on Equity	NM	1.7	10.2	15.5	9.3	11.1	9.4	4.9	8.2	16.9

Data as orig reptd.; bef. results of disc opers/spec. items. Per share data adj. for stk. divs.; EPS diluted. E-Estimated. NA-Not Available. NM-Not Meaningful. NR-Not Ranked. UR-Under Review.

Office: 390 Park Ave, New York, NY 10022-4608.
Telephone: 212-836-2674.
Email: investor.relations@alcoa.com
Website: http://www.alcoa.com

Chrmn, Pres & CEO: K. Kleinfeld
Pres: G.G. Morrison
EVP & CFO: C.D. McLane, Jr.
EVP & CTO: M.A. Zaidi

EVP & General Counsel: N.J. DeRoma
Board Members: A. D. Collins, Jr., K. S. Fuller, C. Ghosn, J. T. Gorman, J. M. Gueron, K. Kleinfeld, M. G. Morris, E. S. O'Neal, J. W. Owens, P. F. Russo, R. N. Tata, E. Zedillo

Founded: 1888
Domicile: Pennsylvania
Employees: 59,000

The McGraw-Hill Companies

Allegheny Energy Inc.

STANDARD &POOR'S

S&P Recommendation **BUY** ★★★★☆	Price $23.74 (as of Oct 22, 2010)	12-Mo. Target Price $30.00	Investment Style Large-Cap Blend

GICS Sector Utilities
Sub-Industry Electric Utilities

Summary This diversified energy company engages in electric generation, transmission, and delivery, and invests in and develops telecommunications and energy-related projects.

Key Stock Statistics (Source S&P, Vickers, company reports)

52-Wk Range	$26.79– 18.97	S&P Oper. EPS 2010E	2.58	Market Capitalization(B)	$4.027	Beta	0.90
Trailing 12-Month EPS	$2.32	S&P Oper. EPS 2011E	2.78	Yield (%)	2.53	S&P 3-Yr. Proj. EPS CAGR(%)	7
Trailing 12-Month P/E	10.2	P/E on S&P Oper. EPS 2010E	9.2	Dividend Rate/Share	$0.60	S&P Credit Rating	BBB-
$10K Invested 5 Yrs Ago	$9,325	Common Shares Outstg. (M)	169.6	Institutional Ownership (%)	80		

Price Performance

30-Week Mov. Avg. · · · · 10-Week Mov. Avg. – – GAAP Earnings vs. Previous Year Volume Above Avg. STARS
12-Mo. Target Price — Relative Strength — ▲ Up ▼ Down ► No Change Below Avg. ★

Options: ASE, CBOE, P

Analysis prepared by **Christopher B. Muir** on September 03, 2010, when the stock traded at **$ 23.53**.

Highlights

➤ We see 2010 revenues rising 12%, helped by both regulated and unregulated operations. We expect regulated utility revenues to increase 4.6%, benefiting from customer growth, transmission expansion, and a higher rate base. We look for unregulated revenues to rise 105% due to increased generation capacity factors, higher Pennsylvania rates, and greater capacity revenues. In 2011, we see revenues up 3.5%.

➤ We expect operating margins to rise to 26.5% in 2010, from 26.3% in 2009, as a result of lower per-revenue non-fuel operating expenses, partly offset by higher per-revenue fuel costs. We forecast operating margins of 27.3% in 2011. We expect pretax profit margins of 18.4% in 2010 and 19.1% in 2011, versus 18.9% in 2009. In 2010, we see higher interest expense, partly offset by higher nonoperating income.

➤ We forecast 2010 recurring EPS of $2.58, excluding $0.01 in nonrecurring charges, up 6.2% from $2.43 in 2009, excluding $0.12 of nonrecurring charges. Our 2011 EPS estimate is $2.78, a projected 7.8% increase.

Investment Rationale/Risk

➤ On February 11, FirstEnergy (FE 37, Buy) announced it intended to purchase AYE, pending approvals, for 0.667 FE shares per AYE share. We view the proposed deal positively, as we think it would lead to $530 million in annual cost savings by the end of five years. We also like the 2010 rate hike for POLR service in Pennsylvania followed by the elimination of rate caps, the absence of residential generation caps in Maryland, and purchased power cost recovery allowances in Virginia. We view positively AYE's debt to total capitalization ratio of 58.3% as of June 30, 2010, versus 59.3%, 59.6%, 61.5%, and 63.3% for the years ending 2009, 2008, 2007, and 2006, respectively.

➤ Risks to our recommendation and target price include lower-than-expected cash flows, a weaker-than-projected economy, and a failure to complete the proposed deal.

➤ Our 12-month target price of $30 reflects the proposed exchange ratio of 0.667 and FE's 12-month target price of $45. Using FE's recent $37 price, AYE shares traded at a 7.1% discount to the proposed transaction price, indicating, we believe, the market is starting to believe the deal may be completed.

Qualitative Risk Assessment

LOW	MEDIUM	HIGH

Our risk assessment reflects the company's mid-level capitalization and balanced sources of earnings, which include both low-risk regulated electric utility and higher-risk unregulated power generation operations.

Quantitative Evaluations

S&P Quality Ranking B

D	C	B-	B	B+	A-	A	A+

Relative Strength Rank MODERATE

38

LOWEST = 1   HIGHEST = 99

Revenue/Earnings Data

Revenue (Million $)

	1Q	2Q	3Q	4Q	Year
2010	1,049	945.7	--	--	--
2009	957.2	814.7	793.7	861.1	3,427
2008	875.0	953.5	849.6	707.8	3,386
2007	847.6	826.5	846.6	786.3	3,307
2006	845.6	722.2	816.6	737.0	3,121
2005	754.0	714.7	845.1	724.1	3,038

Earnings Per Share ($)

	1Q	2Q	3Q	4Q	Year
2010	0.52	0.71	E0.64	E0.66	E2.58
2009	0.79	0.43	0.45	0.64	2.31
2008	0.80	0.91	0.52	0.10	2.33
2007	0.65	0.45	0.67	0.65	2.43
2006	0.68	0.19	0.65	0.37	1.89
2005	0.24	-0.04	0.26	0.02	0.47

Fiscal year ended Dec. 31. Next earnings report expected: Late October. EPS Estimates based on S&P Operating Earnings; historical GAAP earnings are as reported.

Dividend Data (Dates: mm/dd Payment Date: mm/dd/yy)

Amount ($)	Date Decl.	Ex-Div. Date	Stk. of Record	Payment Date
0.150	02/25	03/04	03/08	03/22/10
0.150	05/20	06/03	06/07	06/21/10
0.150	07/08	09/09	09/13	09/27/10
0.150	10/07	12/09	12/13	12/27/10

Dividends have been paid since 2007. Source: Company reports.

Please read the Required Disclosures and Analyst Certification on the last page of this report.

The McGraw-Hill Companies

Allegheny Energy Inc.

STANDARD &POOR'S

Business Summary September 03, 2010

CORPORATE OVERVIEW. Allegheny Energy (AYE) is an integrated electric distribution and generation company operating in the Mid-Atlantic region. The company has two operating segments: Delivery and Services, which includes AYE's electric transmission and distribution (T&D) operations, and Generation and Marketing, which includes the company's generation and unregulated businesses.

AYE's three distribution businesses operate under the trade name Allegheny Power. West Penn operates a T&D system in southwestern, northern and south central Pennsylvania, serving approximately 714,900 customers as of December 31, 2009. Potomac Edison operates a T&D system in portions of West Virginia, Maryland and Virginia. AYE has agreed to sell the Virginia business and the sale should be completed imminently. Potomac Edison serves approximately 483,400 electric customers. Monongahela conducts a T&D business that serves roughly 383,600 electric customers in northern West Virginia. The Delivery Services segment also includes investments in transmission line projects (TrAIL and PATH) and Allegheny Ventures (includes unregulated energy-related businesses). The TrAIL project is expected to be completed in 2011.

Allegheny Energy Supply (AE Supply), AYE's primary unregulated generating division, ended 2009 with 7,015 megawatts (MW) of capacity. The division's capacity grew from 1999 to 2001 through the transfer of regulated power plants in Pennsylvania, Maryland, Virginia and Ohio from AYE's regulated utilities, acquisition of existing plants, and construction activities. Currently, AE Supply is contractually obligated to provide Potomac Edison and West Penn with the power that they need to meet a majority of their obligations, which represents a majority of AE Supply's operating capacity.

Monongahela owns or controls about 2,741 MW of generating capacity, most of which is delivered to AYE's electric utilities. Additionally, AYE owns a 40% interest (or 1,109 MW) in the Bath County pumped-storage hydroelectric power station.

As of December 31, 2009, about 78% of AYE's 9,756 MW of owned and controlled capacity was coal-fired, 9% was gas-fired, 12% was hydroelectric, and 1% was oil-fired.

Company Financials Fiscal Year Ended Dec. 31

Per Share Data ($)	2009	2008	2007	2006	2005	2004	2003	2002	2001	2000
Tangible Book Value	16.19	14.66	12.97	10.36	7.98	6.94	9.05	12.05	16.48	13.80
Earnings	2.31	2.33	2.43	1.89	0.47	0.99	-2.64	-4.00	3.73	2.84
S&P Core Earnings	2.42	2.08	2.28	1.90	0.45	0.56	-2.60	-4.22	3.24	NA
Dividends	0.60	0.60	0.15	Nil	Nil	Nil	Nil	1.29	1.72	1.72
Payout Ratio	26%	26%	6%	Nil	Nil	Nil	Nil	NM	46%	61%
Prices:High	35.97	64.75	65.48	46.25	32.32	20.20	13.09	43.86	55.09	48.75
Prices:Low	20.32	23.86	44.28	31.33	18.25	11.75	4.70	2.95	32.99	23.63
P/E Ratio:High	16	28	27	24	69	20	NM	NM	15	17
P/E Ratio:Low	9	10	18	16	39	12	NM	NM	9	8

Income Statement Analysis (Million $)	2009	2008	2007	2006	2005	2004	2003	2002	2001	2000
Revenue	3,427	3,386	3,307	3,121	3,038	2,756	2,472	2,988	10,379	4,012
Depreciation	282	274	277	273	308	299	327	309	302	248
Maintenance	NA	NA	NA	NA	NA	NA	NA	NA	288	230
Fixed Charges Coverage	3.18	3.59	4.54	2.80	1.39	1.28	-0.35	-1.21	3.38	3.11
Construction Credits	NA	NA	NA	NA	NA	NA	NA	13.0	11.5	7.28
Effective Tax Rate	38.0%	34.0%	37.6%	35.0%	46.1%	NM	NM	NM	35.2%	37.1%
Net Income	393	395	412	320	75.1	130	-334	-502	449	314
S&P Core Earnings	413	352	386	321	72.0	61.8	-329	-530	391	NA

Balance Sheet & Other Financial Data (Million $)	2009	2008	2007	2006	2005	2004	2003	2002	2001	2000
Gross Property	14,062	12,996	11,993	11,150	10,786	10,644	11,831	11,357	11,087	9,507
Capital Expenditures	1,166	994	848	447	306	266	254	403	463	402
Net Property	8,957	8,002	7,197	6,513	6,277	6,303	7,453	6,883	6,853	5,539
Capitalization:Long Term Debt	4,417	4,116	3,983	3,434	3,665	4,639	5,234	229	3,274	2,634
Capitalization:% Long Term Debt	58.7	59.1	61.1	62.3	58.8	77.4	77.5	10.6	54.7	60.2
Capitalization:Preferred	Nil	Nil	Nil	Nil	Nil	Nil	Nil	Nil	Nil	Nil
Capitalization:% Preferred	Nil	Nil	Nil	Nil	Nil	Nil	Nil	Nil	Nil	Nil
Capitalization:Common	3,113	2,851	2,535	2,080	1,695	1,354	1,516	1,932	2,710	1,741
Capitalization:% Common	41.3	40.9	38.9	37.7	98.6	22.6	22.5	89.4	45.3	39.8
Total Capital	7,686	8,314	7,877	6,462	6,228	6,733	7,713	3,358	7,090	5,372
% Operating Ratio	80.2	82.1	82.9	82.3	83.5	82.1	99.3	101.9	93.1	86.6
% Earned on Net Property	10.8	10.7	11.9	11.5	8.5	11.5	NM	NM	11.5	10.0
% Return on Revenue	11.5	11.7	12.5	10.2	2.5	4.7	NM	NM	4.3	7.8
% Return on Invested Capital	9.3	7.7	11.0	9.3	23.3	7.4	2.6	4.2	11.9	10.5
% Return on Common Equity	13.2	14.7	17.9	16.9	4.9	9.0	NM	NM	20.2	18.3

Data as orig reptd.; bef. results of disc opers/spec. items. Per share data adj. for stk. divs.; EPS diluted. E-Estimated. NA-Not Available. NM-Not Meaningful. NR-Not Ranked. UR-Under Review.

Office: 800 Cabin Hill Dr, Greensburg, PA 15601-1689.
Telephone: 724-837-3000.
Email: investorinfo@alleghenypower.com
Website: http://www.alleghenyenergy.com

Chrmn, Pres & CEO: P.J. Evanson
SVP & CFO: K.R. Oliver
Chief Acctg Officer & Cntlr: W.F. Wahl, III
Treas: B.E. Pakenham

Secy & General Counsel: D.M. Feinberg
Investor Contact: M. Kuniansky (724-838-6895)
Board Members: H. F. Baldwin, E. Baum, P. J. Evanson, C. F. Freidheim, Jr., J. L. Johnson, T. J. Kleisner, C. D. Pappas, S. H. Rice, G. E. Sarsten, M. H. Sutton

Founded: 1925
Domicile: Maryland
Employees: 4,383

The McGraw-Hill Companies

Allegheny Technologies Inc

STANDARD &POOR'S

S&P Recommendation HOLD ★★★★☆

Price	12-Mo. Target Price	Investment Style
$46.83 (as of Oct 22, 2010)	$49.00	Large-Cap Blend

GICS Sector Materials
Sub-Industry Steel

Summary This company is a leading producer of specialty metals for a wide variety of end markets.

Key Stock Statistics (Source S&P, Vickers, company reports)

52-Wk Range	$58.25–29.62	S&P Oper. EPS 2010E	1.21	Market Capitalization(B)	$4.616	Beta	1.87
Trailing 12-Month EPS	$0.95	S&P Oper. EPS 2011E	2.58	Yield (%)	1.54	S&P 3-Yr. Proj. EPS CAGR(%)	-18
Trailing 12-Month P/E	49.3	P/E on S&P Oper. EPS 2010E	38.7	Dividend Rate/Share	$0.72	S&P Credit Rating	BBB-
$10K Invested 5 Yrs Ago	$18,252	Common Shares Outstg. (M)	98.6	Institutional Ownership (%)	77		

Price Performance

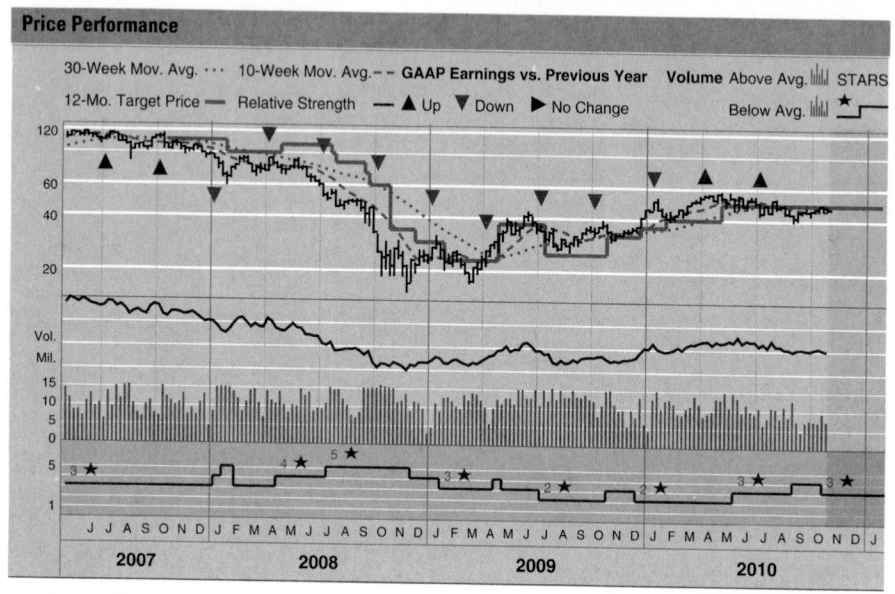

30-Week Mov. Avg. ···· 10-Week Mov. Avg. – – GAAP Earnings vs. Previous Year Volume Above Avg. STARS
12-Mo. Target Price — Relative Strength — ▲ Up ▼ Down ▶ No Change Below Avg. ★

Options: ASE, CBOE, P, Ph

Analysis prepared by **Leo J. Larkin** on October 15, 2010, when the stock traded at **$ 47.75**.

Highlights

➤ We project a 31% increase in sales in 2010, following the 42% decline in 2009. Our estimate reflects several assumptions. First, S&P estimates U.S. GDP growth of 2.6% in 2010, versus a decline of 2.6% in 2009. In our view, this will lead to a rebound in demand for durable goods and help boost shipments and prices for stainless steel. Second, after keeping their stainless inventories low in 2009, we think distributors will restock in 2010. Third, we think that sales of high-performance metals will recover as a result of the rebuilding of inventories in the aerospace supply chain following destocking in 2009.

➤ We look for a rebound in operating profit in 2010 on improved volume and firmer pricing, along with lower pension and other postretirement expenses. After interest expense and taxes, we project operating EPS of $1.21 in 2010, versus operating EPS of $0.17 in 2009, which excludes unusual expense of $0.17 in the second quarter.

➤ We think that consolidation in the stainless steel industry, along with a recovery in aerospace and other capital goods markets, will boost ATI's long-term earnings.

Investment Rationale/Risk

➤ We see ATI's long-term earnings rising on consolidation in the stainless steel industry. We believe the concentration of stainless steel production in fewer hands will lead to better industry pricing discipline and result in less volatile sales and profits over the business cycle. In our view, a decline in volatility should ultimately lead to higher valuations for ATI and other stainless steel producers. Also, we see long-term earnings rising on secular growth in the aerospace industry and other capital goods markets such as oil and gas, mining, and electrical power generation. With the shares recently trading with just modest upside to our target price, we would not add to positions.

➤ Risks to our recommendation and target price include a decline in prices for stainless steel and high performance metals in 2011 instead of the increase we project.

➤ Applying a multiple of 19X to our 2011 EPS estimate, toward the high end of ATI's range of the past 10 years, our 12-month target price for these volatile shares is $49. On this projected multiple, ATI would trade about in line with the P/E we apply to its specialty metals peers.

Qualitative Risk Assessment

LOW	MEDIUM	HIGH

Our risk assessment reflects ATI's exposure to cyclical markets such as aerospace and chemical processing, along with volatile raw material costs. Offsetting these factors are what we consider the company's solid shares of the markets it serves and its moderate balance sheet leverage.

Quantitative Evaluations

S&P Quality Ranking   B

D	C	B-	B	B+	A-	A	A+

Relative Strength Rank   MODERATE

36

LOWEST = 1   HIGHEST = 99

Revenue/Earnings Data

Revenue (Million $)

	1Q	2Q	3Q	4Q	Year
2010	899.4	1,052	--	--	--
2009	831.6	710.0	697.6	815.7	3,055
2008	1,343	1,461	1,392	1,113	5,310
2007	1,373	1,471	1,335	1,274	5,453
2006	1,041	1,211	1,288	1,397	4,937
2005	879.6	904.2	861.7	894.4	3,540

Earnings Per Share ($)

2010	0.18	0.36	E0.26	E0.35	E1.21
2009	0.06	-0.14	0.01	0.36	0.32
2008	1.40	1.66	1.45	1.15	5.67
2007	1.92	2.00	1.88	1.45	7.26
2006	1.00	1.37	1.58	1.63	5.59
2005	0.61	0.91	0.87	1.19	3.59

Fiscal year ended Dec. 31. Next earnings report expected: NA. EPS Estimates based on S&P Operating Earnings; historical GAAP earnings are as reported.

Dividend Data (Dates: mm/dd Payment Date: mm/dd/yy)

Amount ($)	Date Decl.	Ex-Div. Date	Stk. of Record	Payment Date
0.180	12/10	12/17	12/21	12/30/09
0.180	02/25	03/09	03/11	03/26/10
0.180	05/07	05/25	05/27	06/17/10
0.180	09/02	09/14	09/16	09/27/10

Dividends have been paid since 1996. Source: Company reports.

Please read the Required Disclosures and Analyst Certification on the last page of this report.

The McGraw-Hill Companies

Allegheny Technologies Inc

Business Summary October 15, 2010

In November 1999, Allegheny Technologies spun off all of the common stock of Teledyne Technologies Inc. (NYSE: TDY) and Water Pik Technologies, Inc. to ATI stockholders, and changed its name from Allegheny Teledyne Inc.

Following the spin-offs, ATI operates in three segments: Flat-Rolled Products, High Performance Metals, and Engineered Products. Markets for the three units include aerospace, oil and gas, transportation, food, chemical processing, consumer products, medical, and power generation.

The Flat-Rolled Products segment (49.6% of 2009 sales; $71.3 million of operating profits) consists of Allegheny Ludlum Corp., Rodney Metals, the Allegheny Rodney Strip division of Allegheny Ludlum, and the company's interest in a Chinese joint venture, Shanghai STAL Precision Stainless Steel Ltd. The companies in this segment produce, convert and distribute stainless steel sheet, strip and plate, precision rolled strip products, flat-rolled nickel-based alloys and titanium, silicon electrical steels and tool steels.

Shipments totaled 421,073 tons in 2009, versus 542,382 tons in 2008. The average realized price per ton was $3,600, versus $5,364 in 2008. Operating profits totaled $71.3 million in 2009, versus $377.4 million in 2008.

Competitors in flat-rolled stainless include AK Steel Holding and North American Stainless.

The High Performance Metals segment (42.6%; $235.7 million of operating profit) consists of Allvac, Allvac Ltd., Oremet-Wah Chang, Titanium Industries, and Rome Metals. These companies produce, convert and distribute nickel- and cobalt-based alloys and superalloys, titanium and titanium-based alloys, zirconium and zirconium chemicals, hafnium and niobium, tantalum and other special metals, primarily in long-product form. The unit's titanium products are sold mostly to aircraft and jet engine manufacturers.

Shipments of titanium mill products totaled 23,588 lbs. in 2009, versus 32,530 lbs. in 2008; shipments of nickel-based alloys were 32,562 lbs. in 2009, versus 42,525 lbs. in 2008; shipments of exotic alloys totaled 5,067 lbs. in 2009, versus 5,473 lbs. in 2008. Operating profits totaled $235.7 million in 2009, versus operating profit of $539 million in 2008.

Competitors in high performance and exotic metals include Titanium Metals Corp., RTI International Metals, Verkhnaya Salda Metallurgical Production Organization and UNITI and certain Japanese producers in the industrial and emerging markets.

Company Financials Fiscal Year Ended Dec. 31

Per Share Data ($)	2009	2008	2007	2006	2005	2004	2003	2002	2001	2000
Tangible Book Value	18.40	18.19	19.82	12.71	6.11	2.30	NM	3.15	9.42	10.51
Cash Flow	1.53	6.71	8.26	6.48	4.47	1.00	-2.96	0.30	0.91	2.80
Earnings	0.32	5.67	7.26	5.59	3.59	0.22	-3.87	-0.82	-0.31	1.60
S&P Core Earnings	0.73	4.42	7.12	5.92	3.76	0.26	-3.19	-2.17	-2.09	NA
Dividends	0.72	0.72	0.57	0.43	0.28	0.24	0.24	0.66	0.80	0.80
Payout Ratio	NM	13%	8%	8%	8%	109%	NM	NM	NM	50%
Prices:High	46.31	87.32	119.70	98.72	36.66	23.48	14.00	19.10	21.07	26.81
Prices:Low	16.92	15.00	80.00	35.47	17.30	8.64	2.10	5.21	12.50	12.50
P/E Ratio:High	NM	15	16	18	10	NM	NM	NM	NM	17
P/E Ratio:Low	NM	3	11	6	5	NM	NM	NM	NM	8

Income Statement Analysis (Million $)										
Revenue	3,055	5,310	5,453	4,937	3,540	2,733	1,937	1,908	2,128	2,460
Operating Income	211	973	1,256	970	452	87.7	-110	65.0	166	358
Depreciation	133	104	103	84.2	77.3	76.1	74.6	90.0	98.6	99.7
Interest Expense	21.4	38.3	4.80	23.3	38.6	35.5	27.7	34.3	29.3	34.4
Pretax Income	64.9	860	1,147	869	307	19.8	-280	-104	-36.4	209
Effective Tax Rate	41.5%	34.2%	34.9%	34.2%	NM	NM	NM	NM	NM	36.5%
Net Income	31.7	566	747	572	362	19.8	-313	-65.8	-25.2	133
S&P Core Earnings	71.5	441	733	605	378	23.3	-258	-176	-168	NA

Balance Sheet & Other Financial Data (Million $)										
Cash	709	470	623	502	363	251	79.6	59.4	33.7	26.2
Current Assets	1,998	1,929	2,249	1,988	1,484	1,160	743	812	926	1,023
Total Assets	4,346	4,170	4,096	3,282	2,732	2,316	1,885	2,093	2,643	2,776
Current Liabilities	625	694	704	646	561	493	395	342	333	414
Long Term Debt	1,038	495	507	530	547	553	504	509	573	491
Common Equity	2,012	1,961	2,224	1,493	800	426	175	449	945	1,039
Total Capital	3,161	2,524	2,731	2,023	1,347	979	679	958	1,671	1,689
Capital Expenditures	415	516	447	235	90.1	49.9	74.4	48.7	104	60.2
Cash Flow	150	670	850	656	439	95.9	-239	24.2	73.4	232
Current Ratio	3.2	2.8	3.2	3.1	2.6	2.4	1.9	2.4	2.8	2.5
% Long Term Debt of Capitalization	32.8	19.6	18.6	26.2	40.6	56.5	74.3	53.2	34.3	29.1
% Net Income of Revenue	1.0	10.7	13.7	11.6	10.2	0.7	NM	NM	NM	5.4
% Return on Assets	0.7	13.7	20.3	19.0	14.3	0.9	NM	NM	NM	4.8
% Return on Equity	1.6	27.1	40.2	49.9	59.0	6.6	NM	NM	NM	11.8

Data as orig reptd.; bef. results of disc opers/spec. items. Per share data adj. for stk. divs.; EPS diluted. E-Estimated. NA-Not Available. NM-Not Meaningful. NR-Not Ranked. UR-Under Review.

Office: 1000 Six PPG Pl, Pittsburgh, PA 15222-5479.
Telephone: 412-394-2800.
Website: http://www.alleghenytechnologies.com
Chrmn & CEO: L.P. Hassey

Pres & COO: R.J. Harshman
EVP, Secy & General Counsel: J.D. Walton
SVP & CFO: D.G. Reid
Chief Acctg Officer & Cntlr: K.D. Schwartz

Investor Contact: D.L. Greenfield (412-394-3004)
Board Members: D. C. Creel, J. C. Diggs, J. B. Harvey, L. P. Hassey, B. S. Jeremiah, M. J. Joyce, J. E. Rohr, L. J. Thomas, J. D. Turner
Founded: 1960
Domicile: Delaware
Employees: 8,500

Allergan Inc.

STANDARD &POOR'S

S&P Recommendation BUY ★★★★☆	**Price** $71.83 (as of Oct 22, 2010)	**12-Mo. Target Price** $83.00	**Investment Style** Large-Cap Growth

GICS Sector Health Care
Sub-Industry Pharmaceuticals

Summary This technology-driven global health care company develops and commercializes products in the eye care, neuromodulator, skin care and other specialty markets.

Key Stock Statistics (Source S&P, Vickers, company reports)

52-Wk Range	$72.98– 53.32	S&P Oper. EPS 2010E	3.17	Market Capitalization(B)	$21.795	Beta		0.94
Trailing 12-Month EPS	$2.64	S&P Oper. EPS 2011E	3.75	Yield (%)	0.28	S&P 3-Yr. Proj. EPS CAGR(%)		11
Trailing 12-Month P/E	27.2	P/E on S&P Oper. EPS 2010E	22.7	Dividend Rate/Share	$0.20	S&P Credit Rating		A+
$10K Invested 5 Yrs Ago	$16,951	Common Shares Outstg. (M)	303.4	Institutional Ownership (%)	89			

Price Performance

Options: ASE, CBOE, Ph

Analysis prepared by **Herman B. Saftlas** on October 19, 2010, when the stock traded at **$ 72.61**.

Highlights

➤ We see revenues rising about 10% in 2011, from the $4.75 billion that we estimate for 2010. Botox sales will likely show mid-teens growth, supported by firmer trends in consumer spending, and recently approved new indications for spasticity and migraines. Helped by DTC spending, we see robust gains in sales of Juvederm facial filler and Latisse eyelashes thickener. Sales of eye care pharmaceuticals should also rise, with gains in Lumigan and recently launched Ozurdex for macular edema more than offsetting generic erosion in the Alphagan line.

➤ We expect modest expansion in 2011 gross margins, benefiting from higher volume and manufacturing efficiencies. We look for the SG&A cost ratio to decrease, but for the R&D cost ratio to rise slightly on increased spending on new products. Non-operating expenses are likely to be slightly higher.

➤ After an estimated effective tax rate similar to the 28% that we forecast for 2010, we project operating EPS of $3.75 for 2011, up from a projected $3.17 for 2010. Results exclude goodwill amortization and other special items.

Investment Rationale/Risk

➤ We view Allergan as well positioned in ophthalmic drugs and aesthetics products. Although the soft economy has hurt certain lines, we see growth accelerating in 2011, helped by projected firming economic trends and new products. Despite competition from Dysport, we project Botox sales will exceed $1.6 billion in 2011, lifted by improved trends in consumer spending, greater penetration of foreign markets, and recently approved treatment indications for spasticity, and the prevention of chronic migraine headaches. Other new products that we expect to drive growth include Ozurdex for macular edema and Latisse for eyelash thickening.

➤ Risks to our recommendation and target price include a prolonged economic slump, greater-than-expected competitive pressures, and pipeline setbacks.

➤ Our 12-month target price of $83 applies an above-peers P/E of 22X to our EPS estimate for 2011. We believe this multiple is reasonable, given the superior EPS growth that we see for AGN. Our DCF model, which assumes a WACC of 9.9%, and terminal growth of 1%, also indicates an intrinsic value of about $83.

Qualitative Risk Assessment

LOW	MEDIUM	HIGH

Our risk assessment reflects the increased diversity of AGN's aesthetic products and markets via the acquisition of Inamed, our view of its strong focus on R&D, its leading market position in several ophthalmic drugs, and continued strong demand for Botox. However, we view the eye care and aesthetics markets as competitive, with the latter affected by the economic environment. We also note that certain pipeline products may not be successful.

Quantitative Evaluations

S&P Quality Ranking   B

D	C	B-	B	B+	A-	A	A+

Relative Strength Rank   STRONG

79

LOWEST = 1   HIGHEST = 99

Revenue/Earnings Data

Revenue (Million $)

	1Q	2Q	3Q	4Q	Year
2010	1,155	1,247	--	--	--
2009	1,007	1,131	1,141	1,224	4,504
2008	1,077	1,172	1,098	1,057	4,403
2007	886.5	988.1	993.7	1,091	3,939
2006	625.7	801.7	806.8	829.1	3,063
2005	527.2	591.0	606.1	594.9	2,319

Earnings Per Share ($)

2010	0.55	0.78	E0.78	E0.89	E3.17
2009	0.15	0.58	0.59	0.72	2.03
2008	0.36	0.48	0.55	0.50	2.57
2007	0.14	0.45	0.50	0.52	1.62
2006	-1.65	0.25	0.35	0.45	-0.44
2005	0.30	0.13	0.56	0.52	1.51

Fiscal year ended Dec. 31. Next earnings report expected: Late October. EPS Estimates based on S&P Operating Earnings; historical GAAP earnings are as reported.

Dividend Data (Dates: mm/dd Payment Date: mm/dd/yy)

Amount ($)	Date Decl.	Ex-Div. Date	Stk. of Record	Payment Date
0.050	10/22	11/05	11/09	11/30/09
0.050	02/04	02/17	02/19	03/12/10
0.050	04/30	05/14	05/18	06/08/10
0.050	08/02	08/13	08/17	09/07/10

Dividends have been paid since 1989. Source: Company reports.

Please read the Required Disclosures and Analyst Certification on the last page of this report.

The McGraw·Hill Companies

Allergan Inc.

Business Summary October 19, 2010

CORPORATE OVERVIEW. Allergan is a leading producer of ophthalmic, neuro-muscular and skin care pharmaceuticals, and, with its March 2006 acquisition of Inamed Corp., aesthetic products. Eye care drugs accounted for 47% of 2009 sales, Botox/neuromodulators 29%, skin care treatments 5%, urologics 2%, breast implants 6%, devices for obesity treatment 6%, and dermal fillers 5%. About 35% of 2009 sales were derived from foreign markets.

Eye care drugs include prescription and nonprescription products to treat eye diseases and disorders, including glaucoma, inflammation, infection, allergy, and dry eye. Important products are Alphagan, Alphagan P, and Combigan (sales of $415 million in 2009, versus $398 million in 2008), Lumigan ($457 million, versus $426 million) treatments, which are used to lower eye pressure in patients with open-angle glaucoma or ocular hypertension, and Restasis ($523 million, versus $444 million), for dry eye disease. Other eye care products include Acular, Alocril and Elestat, for seasonal allergic conjunctivitis; and Zymar and Ocuflox, for bacterial conjunctivitis.

Originally used for ophthalmic movement disorders, Botox (botulinum toxin type A) is also a widely accepted treatment for neuromuscular disorders and related pain. Botox has also garnered a rapidly growing market as a facial cosmetic agent. In 2002, the FDA approved the injectable drug for removing brow furrows and other facial wrinkles. We estimate that Botox sales are roughly equally divided between therapeutic indications and cosmetic uses. Botox accounts for over 80% of the total global neuromodulator drug market. Botox is also being studied for treating excessive sweating, post-stroke spasticity, back spasms, and migraines.

Skin care products include Zorac/Tazorac receptor-selective retinoids for acne and psoriasis; Aczone treatment for acne; Prevage and Avage facial aesthetic products; and Latisse, a drug used to produce longer, darker and thicker eyelashes. Aesthetic products include breast implants for aesthetic augmentation and reconstructive surgery following mastectomy, a range of dermal products to correct facial wrinkles, and the Lap-Band and Intragastric Balloon (BIB) systems for obesity treatment.

COMPETITIVE LANDSCAPE. Eye care competitors include Alcon Laboratories, Bausch & Lomb, Pfizer, Novartis, and Merck, while its skin care business competes against Dermik, a division of Sanofi-Aventis, Galderma, a joint venture between Nestle and L'Oreal, Medicis, Connetics, Novartis, Schering-Plough, and Johnson & Johnson.

Company Financials Fiscal Year Ended Dec. 31

Per Share Data ($)	2009	2008	2007	2006	2005	2004	2003	2002	2001	2000
Tangible Book Value	4.53	1.48	0.72	0.88	5.34	3.99	2.47	3.02	3.24	2.82
Cash Flow	2.89	2.75	2.32	0.08	1.82	1.69	0.03	0.42	1.19	1.09
Earnings	2.03	2.57	1.62	-0.44	1.51	1.41	-0.20	0.25	0.85	0.81
S&P Core Earnings	2.00	1.85	1.64	-0.42	1.36	1.26	-0.33	0.45	0.70	NA
Dividends	0.20	0.20	0.20	0.20	0.20	0.18	0.18	0.18	0.18	0.16
Payout Ratio	10%	8%	12%	NM	13%	13%	NM	73%	21%	20%
Prices:High	64.08	70.40	69.15	61.51	55.25	46.31	40.90	37.55	49.69	50.56
Prices:Low	35.41	28.95	52.50	46.29	34.51	33.39	35.83	24.53	29.50	22.25
P/E Ratio:High	32	27	43	NM	37	33	NM	NM	59	63
P/E Ratio:Low	17	11	32	NM	23	24	NM	NM	35	28

Income Statement Analysis (Million $)	2009	2008	2007	2006	2005	2004	2003	2002	2001	2000
Revenue	4,504	4,403	3,939	3,063	2,319	2,046	1,771	1,425	1,746	1,626
Operating Income	1,338	1,170	1,060	854	694	603	39.1	349	404	372
Depreciation	262	264	215	152	78.9	68.3	59.6	45.0	85.5	77.7
Interest Expense	76.9	62.0	72.7	60.2	12.4	18.1	15.6	17.4	21.4	19.8
Pretax Income	848	1,080	688	-19.5	599	532	-29.5	89.8	336	304
Effective Tax Rate	26.5%	27.0%	27.1%	NM	32.1%	28.9%	NM	28.0%	32.4%	29.0%
Net Income	621	786	501	-127	404	377	-52.5	64.0	227	215
S&P Core Earnings	610	567	507	-123	363	339	-87.3	118	187	NA

Balance Sheet & Other Financial Data (Million $)	2009	2008	2007	2006	2005	2004	2003	2002	2001	2000
Cash	1,947	1,110	1,158	1,369	1,296	895	508	774	782	774
Current Assets	3,106	2,271	2,124	2,130	1,826	1,376	928	1,200	1,325	1,326
Total Assets	7,537	6,791	6,579	5,767	2,851	2,257	1,755	1,807	2,046	1,971
Current Liabilities	812	697	716	658	1,044	460	383	404	490	433
Long Term Debt	1,491	1,635	1,630	1,606	57.5	570	573	526	521	585
Common Equity	4,823	4,010	3,739	3,143	1,567	1,116	719	808	977	874
Total Capital	6,353	5,652	5,551	4,836	1,626	1,689	1,294	1,337	1,499	1,459
Capital Expenditures	95.8	190	142	131	78.5	96.4	110	78.8	89.9	66.9
Cash Flow	883	843	716	25.0	483	445	7.10	109	312	293
Current Ratio	3.8	3.3	3.0	3.2	1.7	3.0	2.4	3.0	2.7	3.1
% Long Term Debt of Capitalization	23.5	28.9	29.8	33.2	3.5	33.8	44.3	39.4	34.7	40.1
% Net Income of Revenue	13.8	17.9	12.7	NM	17.4	18.4	NM	4.5	13.0	13.2
% Return on Assets	8.7	11.8	8.1	NM	15.8	18.8	NM	3.3	11.3	13.0
% Return on Equity	14.1	20.3	14.6	NM	30.1	41.1	NM	7.2	24.5	28.5

Data as orig reptd.; bef. results of disc opers/spec. items. Per share data adj. for stk. divs.; EPS diluted. E-Estimated. NA-Not Available. NM-Not Meaningful. NR-Not Ranked. UR-Under Review.

Office: 2525 Dupont Drive, Irvine, CA 92612.
Telephone: 714-246-4500.
Email: corpinfo@allergan.com
Website: http://www.alergan.com

Chrmn, CEO & Chief Admin Officer: D.E. Pyott
Pres: M. Ball
Vice Chrmn: H.W. Boyer
EVP & CSO: S.M. Whitcup

EVP & General Counsel: S.J. Gesten
Investor Contact: J. Hindman (714-246-4636)
Board Members: H. W. Boyer, D. Dunsire, M. R. Gallagher, G. S. Herbert, D. E. Hudson, R. A. Ingram, T. M. Jones, L. J. Lavigne, Jr., D. E. Pyott, R. T. Ray, S. J. Ryan, L. D. Schaeffer

Founded: 1948
Domicile: Delaware
Employees: 8,300

Allstate Corp (The)

STANDARD &POOR'S

S&P Recommendation HOLD ★★★☆☆	**Price** $32.79 (as of Oct 22, 2010)	**12-Mo. Target Price** $32.00	**Investment Style** Large-Cap Blend

GICS Sector Financials
Sub-Industry Property & Casualty Insurance

Summary Allstate, the second largest U.S. personal lines property-casualty insurer, also offers an array of life insurance and retirement savings products.

Key Stock Statistics (Source S&P, Vickers, company reports)

52-Wk Range	$35.51–26.86	S&P Oper. EPS 2010E	3.28	Market Capitalization(B)	$17.643	Beta	1.51
Trailing 12-Month EPS	$1.85	S&P Oper. EPS 2011E	4.15	Yield (%)	2.44	S&P 3-Yr. Proj. EPS CAGR(%)	2
Trailing 12-Month P/E	17.7	P/E on S&P Oper. EPS 2010E	10.0	Dividend Rate/Share	$0.80	S&P Credit Rating	A-
$10K Invested 5 Yrs Ago	$7,190	Common Shares Outstg. (M)	538.1	Institutional Ownership (%)	73		

Price Performance

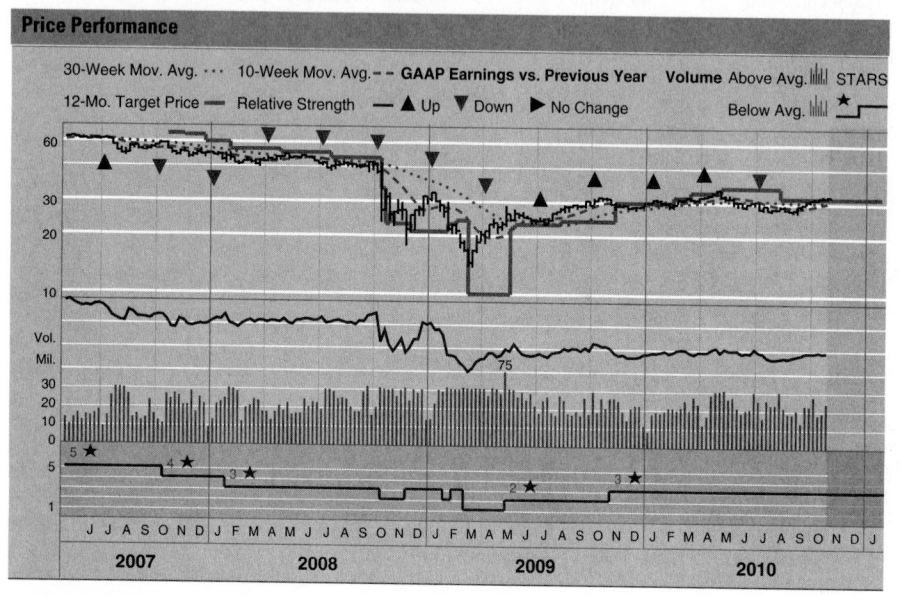

30-Week Mov. Avg. · · ·   10-Week Mov. Avg. – – –   GAAP Earnings vs. Previous Year   Volume Above Avg. | STARS
12-Mo. Target Price —   Relative Strength —   ▲ Up   ▼ Down   ▶ No Change   Below Avg. | ★

Options: ASE, CBOE, P, Ph

Analysis prepared by **Cathy A. Seifert** on August 06, 2010, when the stock traded at **$ 28.95.**

Highlights

➤ We expect operating revenues to be flat to down slightly in 2010, reflecting our forecast of flat to lower property-casualty earned premiums, and continued weakness in net investment income. Operating revenues in the first half of 2010 declined 1.2%, year to year, reflecting 1.0% lower property-casualty premiums, 11% higher life and annuity premiums, and an 8.1% decline in net investment income.

➤ We expect underwriting results to be modestly profitable in 2010, although we see margins contracting amid an ongoing deterioration in claim trends in several core lines. Underwriting margins should also contract if catastrophe losses return to "normal" levels. Catastrophe losses of $636 million in the first months of 2010, versus $818 million in the 2009 interim, led to a combined ratio of 96.8%, versus 100.0%. The combined ratio excluding catastrophes and prior year reserve re-estimates was 88.1% in the 2010 interim, versus 87.2% in the 2009 period.

➤ We estimate operating EPS of $3.28 in 2010 and $4.15 in 2011, versus $3.48 in 2009. Our operating EPS estimates assume a "normal" level of catastrophe losses and no significant reserve increases or asset writedowns.

Investment Rationale/Risk

➤ Our hold recommendation reflects our view that the shares are fairly valued versus peers, based on a ratio of price-to-tangible capital, which excludes goodwill and deferred acquisition costs. Under this framework, the shares trade at approximately 1.3X June 30, 2010, tangible capital, against an average of 1.2X for most property-casualty peers. We also believe ALL's invested asset mix is less liquid than many of its peers. At December 31, 2009, 11% (or $10.5 billion) of ALL's $97.2 billion of invested assets were classified as "level 3" under FAS fair value accounting rule 157. Level 3 assets are deemed the be the least liquid of a company's assets.

➤ Risks to our opinion and target price include a greater than anticipated erosion in underwriting and investment results and a greater than expected deterioration in the credit quality and liquidity of ALL's investment portfolio.

➤ Our 12-month target price of $32 assumes the shares will trade at about 7.7X our estimate of 2011 operating earnings per share, a discount to ALL's closest peers that we believe is warranted.

Qualitative Risk Assessment

LOW	MEDIUM	**HIGH**

Our risk assessment reflects our view of ALL's potential exposure to an outsized level of claims from catastrophes, partly offset by ALL's geographically diversified base of business. We also remain concerned about the level of illiquid assets in its investment portfolio.

Quantitative Evaluations

S&P Quality Ranking B+

D	C	B-	B	**B+**	A-	A	A+

Relative Strength Rank MODERATE

70

LOWEST = 1   HIGHEST = 99

Revenue/Earnings Data

Revenue (Million $)

	1Q	2Q	3Q	4Q	Year
2010	7,749	7,656	--	--	--
2009	7,883	8,490	7,582	8,058	32,013
2008	8,087	7,418	7,320	6,569	29,394
2007	9,331	9,455	8,992	8,991	36,769
2006	9,081	8,875	8,738	9,102	35,796
2005	8,705	8,791	8,942	8,945	35,383

Earnings Per Share ($)

	1Q	2Q	3Q	4Q	Year
2010	0.22	0.27	E0.83	E0.95	E3.28
2009	-0.51	0.72	0.41	0.96	1.58
2008	0.62	0.05	-1.71	-2.11	-3.07
2007	2.41	2.30	1.70	1.36	7.77
2006	2.19	1.89	1.83	1.93	7.84
2005	1.64	1.71	-2.36	1.59	2.64

Fiscal year ended Dec. 31. Next earnings report expected: Early November. EPS Estimates based on S&P Operating Earnings; historical GAAP earnings are as reported.

Dividend Data (Dates: mm/dd Payment Date: mm/dd/yy)

Amount ($)	Date Decl.	Ex-Div. Date	Stk. of Record	Payment Date
0.200	11/10	11/25	11/30	01/05/10
0.200	02/23	03/10	03/12	04/01/10
0.200	05/18	05/26	05/28	07/01/10
0.200	07/13	08/27	08/31	10/01/10

Dividends have been paid since 1993. Source: Company reports.

Please read the Required Disclosures and Analyst Certification on the last page of this report.

The McGraw·Hill Companies

Allstate Corp (The)

STANDARD &POOR'S

Business Summary August 06, 2010

CORPORATE OVERVIEW. Established in 1931 by Sears, Roebuck & Co., Allstate is the second largest U.S. personal lines property-casualty insurer (based on earned premiums), and the 16th largest life insurer (based on life insurance in force). It writes business mainly through a network of more than 14,000 exclusive agencies. ALL has also implemented a multi-access distribution model designed to allow customers to purchase company products through agents, over the Internet, via telephone, and through The Good Hands Network. ALL became an independent company in June 1995, when Sears, Roebuck & Co. spun off its 80% interest in the company.

The company's primary business is the sale of private passenger automobile and homeowners insurance, and it maintains national market shares of about 11% in each of these lines. ALL is licensed to write policies in all 50 states, the District of Columbia, Puerto Rico, and Canada. In 2009, property-liability net written premiums equaled $26.0 billion, down from $26.6 billion in 2008. Earned premiums totaled $26.2 billion in 2009, down from $27.0 billion in 2008. Of the 2009 total, standard automobile policies accounted for 63%, non-standard automobile policies 4%, homeowners' coverage 23%, and other (which includes commercial lines and other personal lines) for the remaining 10%. Underwrit-

ing results in 2009 improved amid a 38% drop in catastrophe claims, partly offset by an erosion in underlying claim trends. As a result, pretax underwriting profits surged to $995 million in 2009, from $164 million in 2008. The combined loss and expense ratio improved to 96.1% in 2009 versus 99.35 in 2008.

Allstate Financial (formerly Allstate Life) offers an array of life insurance, annuity, savings and investment and pension products through Allstate agents, financial institutions, independent agents and brokers, and direct marketing. Premiums and deposits totaled $5.1 billion in 2009 (down from nearly $11 billion in 2008 amid the absence of a $4.2 billion funding agreement). Of the 2009 total, interest-sensitive life insurance products accounted for 28%, traditional and other life insurance for 8%, accident and health products 9%, fixed deferred annuities 25%, indexed annuities 10%, fixed immediate annuities 6%, and bank deposits 14%.

Company Financials Fiscal Year Ended Dec. 31

Per Share Data ($)	2009	2008	2007	2006	2005	2004	2003	2002	2001	2000
Tangible Book Value	39.57	21.66	37.35	33.80	29.97	30.74	27.89	23.52	22.35	22.26
Operating Earnings	NA	NA	NA	NA	NA	NA	3.77	2.94	2.06	2.68
Earnings	1.58	-3.07	7.77	7.84	2.64	4.79	3.85	1.13	1.61	2.95
S&P Core Earnings	2.06	2.52	6.56	7.91	2.21	4.33	3.82	2.64	1.66	NA
Dividends	0.80	1.64	1.52	1.40	1.28	1.12	0.92	0.84	0.76	0.68
Relative Payout	51%	NM	20%	18%	48%	23%	24%	74%	47%	23%
Prices:High	33.50	52.90	65.85	66.14	63.22	51.99	43.27	41.95	45.90	44.75
Prices:Low	13.77	17.72	48.90	50.22	49.66	42.55	30.05	31.03	30.00	17.19
P/E Ratio:High	21	NM	8	8	24	11	11	37	29	15
P/E Ratio:Low	9	NM	6	6	19	9	8	27	19	6

Income Statement Analysis (Million $)	2009	2008	2007	2006	2005	2004	2003	2002	2001	2000
Life Insurance in Force	NA	NA	NA	NA	NA	NA	409,068	396,943	387,039	367,914
Premium Income:Life A & H	26,194	26,967	27,233	27,369	27,039	25,989	24,677	23,361	2,230	2,205
Premium Income:Casualty/Property.	1,958	1,895	1,866	1,964	2,049	2,072	2,304	2,293	22,197	21,871
Net Investment Income	4,444	5,622	6,435	6,177	5,746	5,284	4,972	4,854	4,796	4,633
Total Revenue	32,013	29,394	36,769	35,796	35,383	33,936	32,149	29,579	28,865	29,134
Pretax Income	1,248	-3,025	6,653	7,178	2,088	4,586	3,566	868	1,240	3,006
Net Operating Income	NA	NA	NA	NA	NA	NA	2,662	2,075	1,492	2,004
Net Income	854	-1,679	4,636	4,993	1,765	3,356	2,720	803	1,167	2,211
S&P Core Earnings	1,115	1,372	3,915	5,040	1,487	3,028	2,692	1,879	1,201	NA

Balance Sheet & Other Financial Data (Million $)	2009	2008	2007	2006	2005	2004	2003	2002	2001	2000
Cash & Equivalent	1,476	1,299	6,113	4,935	1,387	1,428	1,434	1,408	1,146	1,164
Premiums Due	4,839	4,842	4,879	4,789	4,739	4,721	4,386	6,958	6,674	3,802
Investment Assets:Bonds	78,766	68,608	94,451	98,320	98,065	95,715	87,741	77,152	65,720	60,758
Investment Assets:Stocks	7,768	5,596	7,758	7,777	6,164	5,895	5,288	3,683	5,245	6,086
Investment Assets:Loans	7,935	10,229	10,830	9,467	8,748	7,856	6,539	6,092	5,710	4,599
Investment Assets:Total	99,833	95,998	118,980	119,757	118,297	115,530	103,081	90,650	79,876	74,483
Deferred Policy Costs	5,470	8,542	5,768	5,332	5,802	4,968	4,842	4,385	4,421	4,309
Total Assets	132,652	134,798	156,408	157,554	156,072	149,725	134,142	117,426	109,175	104,808
Debt	5,910	5,659	5,640	4,620	4,887	5,291	5,073	4,161	3,894	3,862
Common Equity	16,692	12,641	21,851	21,846	20,186	21,823	20,565	34,128	17,196	17,451
Combined Loss-Expense Ratio	96.2	99.4	89.6	83.6	102.4	93.0	94.6	98.9	102.9	99.2
% Return on Revenue	2.7	NM	12.6	13.9	5.0	9.9	8.5	2.7	4.0	7.6
% Return on Equity	5.8	NM	21.2	23.8	8.4	15.8	14.3	2.4	6.7	13.0
% Investment Yield	4.6	5.2	5.3	5.2	4.9	4.8	5.1	5.7	6.2	6.4

Data as orig reptd.; bef. results of disc opers/spec. items. Per share data adj. for stk. divs.; EPS diluted. E-Estimated. NA-Not Available. NM-Not Meaningful. NR-Not Ranked. UR-Under Review.

Office: 2775 Sanders Road, Northbrook, IL 60062.
Telephone: 847-402-5000.
Website: http://www.allstate.com
Chrmn, Pres & CEO: T.J. Wilson, II

SVP & CFO: D. Civgin
SVP & General Counsel: M.C. Mayes
Secy: M.J. McGinn
Cntlr: S.H. Pilch

Board Members: F. D. Ackerman, R. D. Beyer, W. J. Farrell, J. M. Greenberg, R. T. LeMay, A. Redmond, H. J. Riley, Jr., J. I. Smith, J. Sprieser, M. A. Taylor, T. J. Wilson, II

Founded: 1953
Domicile: Delaware
Employees: 36,800

The McGraw-Hill Companies

Altera Corp

STANDARD &POOR'S

S&P Recommendation HOLD ★★★☆☆

Price $29.46 (as of Oct 22, 2010)	**12-Mo. Target Price** $32.00	**Investment Style** Large-Cap Growth

GICS Sector Information Technology
Sub-Industry Semiconductors

Summary This company is one of the largest makers of high-performance, high-density programmable logic devices (PLDs), and associated computer-aided engineering logic development tools.

Key Stock Statistics (Source S&P, Vickers, company reports)

52-Wk Range	$30.97– 19.23	S&P Oper. EPS 2010**E**	2.48	Market Capitalization(B)	$9.051	Beta	1.01
Trailing 12-Month EPS	$1.63	S&P Oper. EPS 2011**E**	2.64	Yield (%)	0.81	S&P 3-Yr. Proj. EPS CAGR(%)	50
Trailing 12-Month P/E	18.1	P/E on S&P Oper. EPS 2010**E**	11.9	Dividend Rate/Share	$0.24	S&P Credit Rating	NA
$10K Invested 5 Yrs Ago	$17,543	Common Shares Outstg. (M)	307.2	Institutional Ownership (%)	96		

Price Performance

30-Week Mov. Avg. · · · 10-Week Mov. Avg. - - **GAAP Earnings vs. Previous Year** Volume Above Avg. ▍▌▏ STARS
12-Mo. Target Price — Relative Strength — ▲ Up ▼ Down ▶ No Change Below Avg. ▍▌▏ ★

Options: ASE, CBOE, P, Ph

Analysis prepared by **Clyde Montevirgen** on October 20, 2010, when the stock traded at **$ 28.86.**

Highlights

➤ We see sales advancing 58% this year and 10% in 2011. Although we expect near-term order disruptions as customers digest excessive inventory, we believe healthy chip orders from the communications, computer, and industrial markets will support healthy longer-term growth, especially considering the proliferation of semiconductors in electronic devices and the replacement of ASICs with FPGAs. Also, we view favorably ALTR's 40 nanometer (nm) offerings, and think its relatively quick move onto this technology will help it gain market share.

➤ We believe the gross margin will be around 70% in 2011, modestly lower than projected 2010 levels. ALTR outsources its manufacturing, which contributes to relatively stable gross margins, but we see sales mix and modest pricing pressure causing a slight contraction from recent results. However, we think the adjusted operating margin will widen to around 46% in 2011 from a projected 44% in 2010, as sales grow faster than expenses.

➤ Our 2011 EPS estimate assumes a 14% effective tax rate and a 2% increase in the diluted share count.

Investment Rationale/Risk

➤ Our hold recommendation reflects our view of healthy fundamentals and valuations. Although we anticipate end-market demand softening due to economic uncertainty, and we remain wary about rising inventory in the supply chain, we believe ASIC displacement and market share gains with its 40nm offerings will support healthy long-term growth. With our view of relatively high profitability and with some financial leverage from ALTR's capital structure, we think return on equity will also continue to top the industry's. However, also considering the aforementioned risks, we think that fundamentals are largely reflected in the share price.

➤ Risks to our recommendation and target price include deteriorating economic conditions, market share losses, limited supply from foundry partners, and excessive inventory buildup.

➤ Our 12-month target price of $32 is based on a price-to-earnings multiple of 12X, near the industry average, applied to our 2011 EPS estimate. We believe this multiple is justified by ALTR's earnings growth, return on equity, and risk compared to other players in the industry.

Qualitative Risk Assessment

LOW	MEDIUM	HIGH

Our risk assessment reflects our view that Altera is subject to the sales swings of the semiconductor industry and competition from a larger rival. This is offset by the company's participation in a high-growth niche market.

Quantitative Evaluations

S&P Quality Ranking B

D	C	B-	**B**	B+	A-	A	A+

Relative Strength Rank MODERATE

63

LOWEST = 1 HIGHEST = 99

Revenue/Earnings Data

Revenue (Million $)

	1Q	2Q	3Q	4Q	Year
2010	402.3	469.3	--	--	--
2009	264.6	279.2	286.6	365.0	1,195
2008	336.1	359.9	356.8	314.5	1,367
2007	304.9	319.7	315.8	323.2	1,264
2006	292.8	334.1	341.2	317.4	1,286
2005	264.8	285.5	291.5	281.9	1,124

Earnings Per Share ($)

	1Q	2Q	3Q	4Q	Year
2010	0.50	0.58	E0.69	E0.71	E2.48
2009	0.15	0.16	0.19	E0.29	E0.86
2008	0.27	0.32	0.31	0.28	1.18
2007	0.21	0.22	0.20	0.20	0.82
2006	0.16	0.21	0.24	0.27	0.88
2005	0.17	0.18	0.21	0.19	0.74

Fiscal year ended Dec. 31. Next earnings report expected: NA. EPS Estimates based on S&P Operating Earnings; historical GAAP earnings are as reported.

Dividend Data (Dates: mm/dd Payment Date: mm/dd/yy)

Amount ($)	Date Decl.	Ex-Div. Date	Stk. of Record	Payment Date
0.050	01/26	02/08	02/10	03/01/10
0.050	04/20	05/06	05/10	06/01/10
0.060	07/20	08/06	08/10	09/01/10
0.060	10/19	11/08	11/10	12/01/10

Dividends have been paid since 2007. Source: Company reports.

Please read the Required Disclosures and Analyst Certification on the last page of this report.

The **McGraw·Hill** Companies

Altera Corp

STANDARD &POOR'S

Business Summary October 20, 2010

CORPORATE OVERVIEW. Altera Corp. is a worldwide supplier of programmable logic devices (PLDs), HardCopy brand structured application specific integrated circuits (ASICs), pre-defined design building blocks known as intellectual property cores, and associated software for logic development.

Most electronic devices use three types of digital integrated circuits: processors, memory, and logic. The logic semiconductors are used to manage the interchange and manipulation of digital signals within the system. There are three main types of logic chips: ASICs, application specific standard products (ASSPs), and PLDs.

PLDs are standard products, shipped blank for user programming. They are programmed at the customer's PC or workstation, using ALTR's proprietary software. Since the company's chips are programmed at a desktop and not at

a foundry, the customer has the ability to customize designs, an option that is limited in ASICs and ASSPs. Some of the other benefits of using PLDs include: enhanced design flexibility, shorter design cycles, lower up-front development costs, and the ability to get end-products to market faster. Although the design flexibility has resulted in a higher unit cost for some PLDs versus its logic counterparts, manufacturing technology is helping to eliminate the cost deferential and competitors in this segment are looking to displace ASICs and ASSPs with PLDs.

Company Financials Fiscal Year Ended Dec. 31

Per Share Data ($)	2009	2008	2007	2006	2005	2004	2003	2002	2001	2000
Tangible Book Value	3.66	2.73	2.74	4.46	3.52	3.42	2.93	2.95	2.89	3.21
Cash Flow	0.94	1.28	0.91	0.96	0.82	0.80	0.51	0.36	0.04	1.29
Earnings	0.84	1.18	0.82	0.88	0.74	0.72	0.40	0.23	-0.10	1.19
S&P Core Earnings	0.84	1.18	0.82	0.88	0.54	0.48	0.19	-0.02	-0.28	NA
Dividends	0.20	NA	0.12	Nil	Nil	Nil	Nil	Nil	Nil	Nil
Payout Ratio	24%	16%	15%	Nil	Nil	Nil	Nil	Nil	Nil	Nil
Prices:High	23.18	24.19	26.24	22.29	22.99	26.82	25.64	26.18	34.69	67.13
Prices:Low	13.92	12.99	18.00	15.54	15.96	17.50	10.30	8.32	14.66	19.63
P/E Ratio:High	28	21	32	25	31	37	64	NM	NM	56
P/E Ratio:Low	17	11	22	18	22	24	26	NM	NM	16

Income Statement Analysis (Million $)	2009	2008	2007	2006	2005	2004	2003	2002	2001	2000
Revenue	1,195	1,367	1,264	1,286	1,124	1,016	827	712	839	1,377
Operating Income	344	452	306	331	352	345	243	146	48.8	598
Depreciation	29.0	30.0	31.1	29.7	29.4	30.5	45.3	48.5	54.3	40.1
Interest Expense	5.09	15.5	Nil	Nil	Nil	Nil	Nil	Nil	Nil	Nil
Pretax Income	306	419	338	360	357	331	213	123	-13.0	744
Effective Tax Rate	17.8%	14.2%	14.1%	10.1%	21.9%	16.8%	27.0%	26.0%	NM	33.2%
Net Income	251	360	290	323	279	275	155	91.3	-39.8	497
S&P Core Earnings	251	360	290	323	204	182	70.7	-8.66	-106	NA

Balance Sheet & Other Financial Data (Million $)	2009	2008	2007	2006	2005	2004	2003	2002	2001	2000
Cash	1,547	1,217	1,021	738	788	580	259	255	145	496
Current Assets	2,042	1,627	1,534	1,735	1,495	1,537	1,270	1,176	1,129	1,769
Total Assets	2,293	1,880	1,770	2,215	1,823	1,747	1,488	1,372	1,361	2,004
Current Liabilities	490	386	490	598	555	468	385	241	247	756
Long Term Debt	500	503	250	1.30	3.87	Nil	Nil	Nil	Nil	Nil
Common Equity	1,085	800	861	1,608	1,326	1,279	1,102	1,131	1,115	1,248
Total Capital	1,585	1,302	1,111	1,609	1,330	1,279	1,102	1,131	1,115	1,248
Capital Expenditures	11.1	40.3	31.2	36.5	25.9	24.7	13.9	9.87	65.8	87.5
Cash Flow	280	390	321	353	308	306	200	140	14.5	537
Current Ratio	4.2	4.2	3.1	2.9	2.7	3.3	3.3	4.9	4.6	2.3
% Long Term Debt of Capitalization	31.5	38.6	22.5	0.1	0.3	Nil	Nil	Nil	NM	36.1
% Net Income of Revenue	21.0	26.3	23.0	25.1	24.8	27.1	18.8	12.8	NM	28.9
% Return on Assets	12.0	19.7	14.6	16.0	15.5	17.1	10.9	6.7	NM	28.9
% Return on Equity	26.6	43.3	23.5	22.5	21.0	23.1	13.9	8.1	NM	42.0

Data as orig reptd.; bef. results of disc opers/spec. items. Per share data adj. for stk. divs.; EPS diluted. E-Estimated. NA-Not Available. NM-Not Meaningful. NR-Not Ranked. UR-Under Review.

Office: 101 Innovation Drive, San Jose, CA 95134.
Telephone: 408-544-7000.
Email: inv_rel@altera.com
Website: http://www.altera.com

Chrmn, Pres & CEO: J.P. Daane
COO: W.Y. Hata
SVP, CFO & Chief Acctg Officer: R.J. Pasek
Secy & General Counsel: K.E. Schuelke

Investor Contact: S. Wylie (408-544-6996)
Board Members: J. P. Daane, R. J. Finocchio, Jr., K. McGarity, T. Nevens, K. A. Prabhu, J. C. Shoemaker, S. Wang

Founded: 1983
Domicile: Delaware
Employees: 2,551

The McGraw-Hill Companies

Altria Group Inc

STANDARD &POOR'S

S&P Recommendation **STRONG BUY** ★★★★★

Price $24.92 (as of Oct 22, 2010)	**12-Mo. Target Price** $28.00	**Investment Style** Large-Cap Blend

GICS Sector Consumer Staples
Sub-Industry Tobacco

Summary Altria Group (formerly Philip Morris Companies) is the largest U.S. cigarette producer. It spun off Kraft Foods in 2007 and its international cigarette operations in 2008.

Key Stock Statistics (Source S&P, Vickers, company reports)

52-Wk Range	$25.00– 17.81	S&P Oper. EPS 2010E	1.91	Market Capitalization(B)	$51.932	Beta	0.39
Trailing 12-Month EPS	$1.66	S&P Oper. EPS 2011E	2.01	Yield (%)	6.10	S&P 3-Yr. Proj. EPS CAGR(%)	6
Trailing 12-Month P/E	15.0	P/E on S&P Oper. EPS 2010E	13.0	Dividend Rate/Share	$1.52	S&P Credit Rating	BBB
$10K Invested 5 Yrs Ago	NA	Common Shares Outstg. (M)	2,084.0	Institutional Ownership (%)	60		

Price Performance

30-Week Mov. Avg. · · · ·   10-Week Mov. Avg. - - -   **GAAP Earnings vs. Previous Year**   **Volume** Above Avg. │.ıl.ıl STARS
12-Mo. Target Price —   Relative Strength —   ▲ Up ▼ Down ▶ No Change   Below Avg. │.ıl.ıl ★

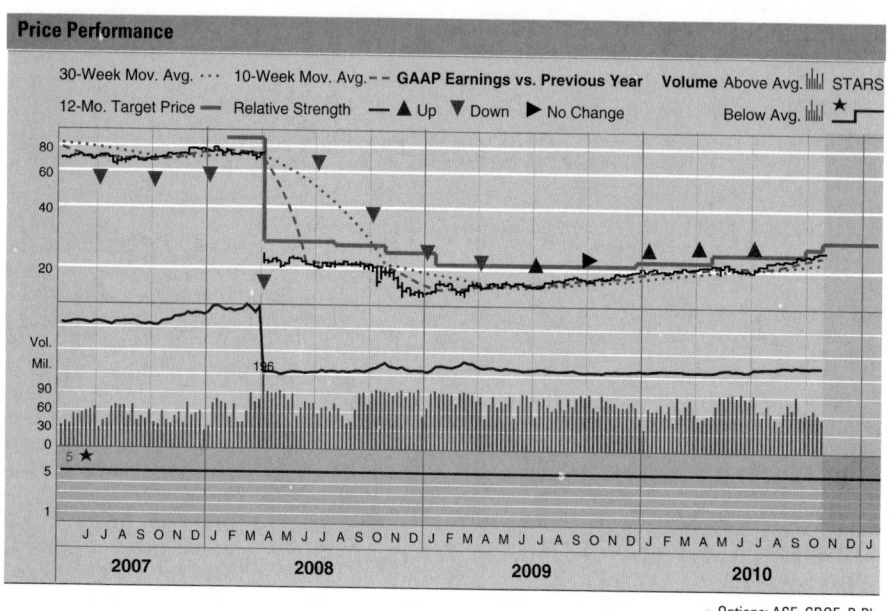

Options: ASE, CBOE, P, Ph

Analysis prepared by **Esther Y. Kwon, CFA** on October 20, 2010, when the stock traded at **$ 24.91**.

Highlights

▶ In March 2008, Altria completed the spinoff of Philip Morris International to shareholders with a share distribution ratio of one for one. The board of directors set Altria's initial dividend at a payout ratio of 75% and announced a $7.5 billion share repurchase program.

▶ We forecast that sales volumes will fall at a mid-single digit rate in 2010, moderating from a low double digit rate in 2009 on a significant hike in the federal excise tax on cigarettes, with brand investments, acquisitions, line extensions and new product introductions somewhat offsetting declining consumption. We see revenues rising about 1% and 3% on higher pricing in 2010 and 2011, respectively. Over the next several years, we expect MO's margins to widen on restructuring actions, including the closure of its Cabarrus facility, consolidation of all manufacturing in Richmond, VA, and $500 million of new SG&A expense reductions, up from $300 million estimated originally.

▶ On an effective tax rate of about 34%, we estimate 2010 EPS of $1.91, up from 2009 operating EPS of $1.75. For 2011, we forecast EPS of $2.01.

Investment Rationale/Risk

▶ In June 2009, President Obama signed the Family Smoking Prevention and Tobacco Control Act, granting the U.S. FDA the authority to regulate tobacco products. While we view this as a negative for the industry, it was well anticipated, and we see the restrictions solidifying market share leader Altria's dominant position and handicapping its smaller competitors. Operationally, we think Altria is likely to benefit from several factors over the next several years, including the integration of its recent acquisition of smokeless tobacco company UST and recent restructuring actions.

▶ Risks to our recommendation and target price include possible pressures on trading multiples as investors remain cautious about court trials, and potential increases in excise taxes and smoking bans at the state and local level.

▶ Our 12-month target price of $28 is based on historical and peer forward P/E multiples. We apply a multiple of 14X, above the average historical forward P/E and a slight premium to the domestic peer-average forward P/E, to our 2011 EPS estimate to calculate our target price. The shares recently provided a dividend yield of over 6%.

Qualitative Risk Assessment

LOW	MEDIUM	HIGH

MO is a large-cap company in an industry that is operationally very stable. However, the tobacco industry is beset by litigation. The company is subject to several ongoing legal actions, which could have a material impact on future cash flows.

Quantitative Evaluations

S&P Quality Ranking A

D	C	B-	B	B+	A-	A	A+

Relative Strength Rank MODERATE

69

LOWEST = 1   HIGHEST = 99

Revenue/Earnings Data

Revenue (Million $)

	1Q	2Q	3Q	4Q	Year
2010	3,951	4,341	--	--	--
2009	3,812	4,594	4,318	4,100	16,824
2008	3,604	4,179	4,341	3,833	15,957
2007	17,556	18,809	19,207	18,229	38,051
2006	24,355	25,769	25,885	25,398	101,407
2005	23,618	24,784	24,962	24,490	97,854

Earnings Per Share ($)

2010	0.39	0.50	E0.51	E0.45	E1.91
2009	0.28	0.49	0.42	0.35	1.54
2008	0.29	0.43	0.42	0.33	1.48
2007	1.01	1.05	1.24	1.03	4.33
2006	1.65	1.29	1.36	1.40	5.71
2005	1.24	1.40	1.38	1.09	5.10

Fiscal year ended Dec. 31. Next earnings report expected: NA. EPS Estimates based on S&P Operating Earnings; historical GAAP earnings are as reported.

Dividend Data (Dates: mm/dd Payment Date: mm/dd/yy)

Amount ($)	Date Decl.	Ex-Div. Date	Stk. of Record	Payment Date
0.340	12/16	12/28	12/30	01/11/10
0.350	02/24	03/11	03/15	04/09/10
0.350	05/20	06/11	06/15	07/09/10
0.380	08/27	09/13	09/15	10/12/10

Dividends have been paid since 1928. Source: Company reports.

Please read the Required Disclosures and Analyst Certification on the last page of this report.

The McGraw-Hill Companies

STANDARD &POOR'S

Altria Group Inc

Business Summary October 20, 2010

CORPORATE OVERVIEW. Altria Group (formerly Philip Morris Cos., Inc.) is a holding company for wholly owned and majority owned subsidiaries that make and market various consumer products, now primarily including cigarettes. Prior to the March 30, 2007, spinoff of Kraft Foods, Altria Group's reportable segments were domestic tobacco, international tobacco, North American food, international food and financial services. The spinoff of Philip Morris International was completed on March 28, 2008, at a one-for-one exchange rate.

Philip Morris U.S.A. (PM USA) is the largest U.S. tobacco company, with total U.S. cigarette shipments amounting to 148.7 billion units in 2009 (down 12.2% from 2008), accounting for 49.9% of total U.S. cigarette market shipments (down from 50.9% in 2008). Focus brands include Marlboro (the largest selling brand in the U.S.), Virginia Slims and Parliament in the premium category, and Basic in the discount category.

In January 2009, Altria completed the acquisition of UST Inc., the largest U.S. manufacturer and marketer of smokeless tobacco products, for $11.7 billion, which included the assumption of about $1.3 billion of debt.

Kraft Foods, the largest packaged food company in North America and sec-

ond largest in the world, was spun off on March 30, 2007, to MO shareholders as a tax-free stock dividend. MO shareholders received approximately 0.68 of a KFT share per MO share owned as a stock dividend at the end of March 2007, and cash in lieu of fractional shares.

In July 2002, MO sold its Miller Brewing Co. subsidiary to South African Brewers, plc., receiving $3.38 billion worth of shares in the newly formed company, SABMiller. As of December 31, 2009, this stake represented a 27.3% economic and voting interest.

CORPORATE STRATEGY. After considering a number of restructuring alternatives, including the possibility of separating Altria Group, Inc. into two, or potentially three, independent entities, the company in June 2007 announced that cigarette production for international markets would be shifted from U.S. facilities to European plants. It subsequently decided to spin off its international tobacco operations, with an effective date of March 28, 2008.

Company Financials Fiscal Year Ended Dec. 31

Per Share Data ($)	2009	2008	2007	2006	2005	2004	2003	2002	2001	2000
Tangible Book Value	NM	NM	3.97	NM	NM	NM	NM	NM	NM	NM
Cash Flow	1.69	1.58	4.79	6.57	5.92	5.35	5.22	6.10	4.93	4.50
Earnings	1.54	1.48	4.33	5.71	5.10	4.57	4.52	5.21	3.88	3.75
S&P Core Earnings	1.58	1.29	4.33	5.62	5.14	4.54	4.49	4.03	3.62	NA
Dividends	1.32	1.68	3.05	3.32	3.06	2.82	2.64	2.44	2.22	2.02
Payout Ratio	86%	1%	70%	58%	60%	62%	58%	47%	57%	54%
Prices:High	20.47	79.59	90.50	86.56	78.68	61.88	55.03	57.79	53.88	45.94
Prices:Low	14.50	14.34	63.13	68.36	60.40	44.50	27.70	35.40	38.75	18.69
P/E Ratio:High	13	54	21	15	15	14	12	11	14	12
P/E Ratio:Low	9	10	15	12	12	10	6	7	10	5

Income Statement Analysis (Million $)										
Revenue	16,824	15,957	38,051	70,324	68,920	63,963	60,704	62,182	72,944	63,276
Operating Income	6,627	5,229	14,892	19,705	19,004	17,929	17,663	18,476	18,039	16,396
Depreciation	291	215	980	1,804	1,675	1,607	1,440	1,331	2,337	1,717
Interest Expense	1,189	237	653	877	1,556	1,417	1,367	1,327	1,659	1,078
Pretax Income	4,877	4,789	13,257	16,536	15,435	14,004	14,760	18,098	14,284	13,960
Effective Tax Rate	34.2%	35.5%	30.9%	26.3%	29.9%	32.4%	34.9%	35.5%	37.9%	39.0%
Net Income	3,206	3,090	9,161	12,022	10,668	9,420	9,204	11,102	8,566	8,510
S&P Core Earnings	3,280	2,687	9,163	11,818	10,766	9,348	9,145	8,593	7,959	NA

Balance Sheet & Other Financial Data (Million $)										
Cash	1,871	7,916	6,498	5,020	6,258	5,744	3,777	565	453	937
Current Assets	10,576	16,527	28,919	26,152	25,781	25,901	21,382	17,441	17,275	17,238
Total Assets	36,677	27,215	57,211	104,270	107,949	101,648	96,175	87,540	84,968	79,067
Current Liabilities	7,992	7,642	18,782	25,427	26,158	23,574	21,393	19,082	20,141	25,949
Long Term Debt	11,185	6,839	11,046	14,498	17,868	18,683	21,163	21,355	18,651	19,154
Common Equity	4,072	2,828	18,554	39,619	35,707	30,714	25,077	19,478	19,620	15,005
Total Capital	16,064	14,662	33,610	68,496	71,945	67,714	64,110	56,832	52,768	40,824
Capital Expenditures	273	241	1,458	2,454	2,206	1,913	1,974	2,009	1,922	1,682
Cash Flow	3,497	3,305	10,141	13,826	12,343	11,027	10,644	12,433	10,903	10,227
Current Ratio	1.3	2.2	1.5	1.0	1.0	1.1	1.0	0.9	0.9	0.7
% Long Term Debt of Capitalization	69.6	46.6	30.0	21.2	24.8	27.6	33.0	37.6	35.3	46.9
% Net Income of Revenue	19.1	19.4	24.1	17.1	15.5	14.7	15.2	17.9	11.7	13.4
% Return on Assets	10.0	7.3	11.4	11.3	10.2	9.5	10.0	12.9	10.4	12.1
% Return on Equity	92.9	28.9	31.5	31.9	32.1	33.8	41.3	56.8	49.5	56.2

Data as orig reptd.; bef. results of disc opers/spec. items. Per share data adj. for stk. divs.; EPS diluted. E-Estimated. NA-Not Available. NM-Not Meaningful. NR-Not Ranked. UR-Under Review.

Office: 6601 W Broad St, Richmond, VA 23230-1723.
Telephone: 804-274-2200.
Website: http://www.altria.com
Chrmn & CEO: M.E. Szymanczyk

EVP & CFO: D.R. Beran
EVP & Chief Admin Officer: M.J. Barrington
EVP & CTO: J.R. Nelson
EVP & General Counsel: D.F. Keane

Investor Contact: C.B. Fleet (804-484-8222)
Board Members: E. E. Bailey, G. L. Baliles, J. T. Casteen, III, D. S. Devitre, T. F. Farrell, II, R. E. Huntley, T. W. Jones, G. Munoz, N. Sakkab, M. E. Szymanczyk

Founded: 1919
Domicile: Virginia
Employees: 10,000

The McGraw-Hill Companies

Amazon.com Inc

STANDARD &POOR'S

S&P Recommendation HOLD ★★★☆☆

Price	12-Mo. Target Price	Investment Style
$169.13 (as of Oct 22, 2010)	$165.00	Large-Cap Growth

GICS Sector Consumer Discretionary
Sub-Industry Internet Retail

Summary This leading online retailer sells a broad range of items from books to consumer electronics to home and garden products.

Key Stock Statistics (Source S&P, Vickers, company reports)

52-Wk Range	$170.17– 105.80	S&P Oper. EPS 2010E	2.61	Market Capitalization(B)	$75.741	Beta	1.18
Trailing 12-Month EPS	$2.42	S&P Oper. EPS 2011E	3.70	Yield (%)	Nil	S&P 3-Yr. Proj. EPS CAGR(%)	30
Trailing 12-Month P/E	69.9	P/E on S&P Oper. EPS 2010E	64.8	Dividend Rate/Share	Nil	S&P Credit Rating	A-
$10K Invested 5 Yrs Ago	$36,807	Common Shares Outstg. (M)	447.8	Institutional Ownership (%)	66		

Price Performance

30-Week Mov. Avg. · · · 10-Week Mov. Avg. – – GAAP Earnings vs. Previous Year   Volume Above Avg. STARS
12-Mo. Target Price — Relative Strength — ▲ Up ▼ Down ▶ No Change   Below Avg. ★

Options: ASE, CBOE, P, Ph

Qualitative Risk Assessment

LOW	MEDIUM	HIGH

Our risk assessment reflects AMZN's large market capitalization and leading position in the e-commerce industry, offset by increasing competition.

Quantitative Evaluations

S&P Quality Ranking   B-

D	C	B-	B	B+	A-	A	A+

Relative Strength Rank   STRONG
91
LOWEST = 1   HIGHEST = 99

Revenue/Earnings Data

Revenue (Million $)

	1Q	2Q	3Q	4Q	Year
2010	7,131	6,566	--	--	--
2009	4,889	4,651	5,449	9,519	24,509
2008	4,135	4,063	4,264	6,704	19,166
2007	3,015	2,886	3,262	5,673	14,835
2006	2,279	2,139	2,307	3,986	10,711
2005	1,902	1,753	1,858	2,977	8,490

Earnings Per Share ($)

	1Q	2Q	3Q	4Q	Year
2010	0.66	0.46	E0.51	E0.99	E2.61
2009	0.41	0.32	0.45	0.85	2.04
2008	0.34	0.37	0.27	0.52	1.49
2007	0.26	0.19	0.19	0.49	1.12
2006	0.12	0.05	0.05	0.23	0.45
2005	0.12	0.12	0.07	0.47	0.78

Fiscal year ended Dec. 31. Next earnings report expected: Late October. EPS Estimates based on S&P Operating Earnings; historical GAAP earnings are as reported.

Highlights

➤ The 12-month target price for AMZN has recently been changed to $165.00 from $155.00. The Highlights section of this Stock Report will be updated accordingly.

Investment Rationale/Risk

➤ The Investment Rationale/Risk section of this Stock Report will be updated shortly. For the latest News story on AMZN from MarketScope, see below.

➤ 10/22/10 09:22 am ET ... S&P REITERATES HOLD RECOMMENDATION ON SHARES OF AMAZON.COM (AMZN 164.97***): Q3 EPS of $0.51, vs. $0.45, is $0.03 shy of our est., as investments to spur growth adversely impacted margins. However, net sales rose 39%, as AMZN continues to capture significant share globally. We expect further margin compression over near the term as AMZN rolls out additional fulfillment centers. We are lowering our '10 and '11 EPS estimates to $2.61 and $3.70 from $2.70 and $3.80. But with sanguine long-term growth prospects, we are raising our DCF-based target price by $10 to $165. We think shares are fully valued, with AMZN trading at about 45X our '11 EPS view. /M. Souers

Dividend Data

No cash dividends have been paid.

Amazon.com Inc

STANDARD &POOR'S

Business Summary September 22, 2010

CORPORATE OVERVIEW. Since opening for business as "Earth's Biggest Bookstore" in July 1995, Amazon.com has expanded into a number of other product categories, including: apparel, shoes and jewelry; electronics and computers; movies, music and games; toys, kids and baby; sports and outdoors; home and garden; tools, auto and industrial; grocery; health and beauty; and digital downloads.

AMZN has virtually unlimited online shelf space, and can offer customers a vast selection of products through an efficient search and retrieval interface. The company personalizes shopping by recommending items which, based on previous purchases, are likely to interest a particular customer. Key Web site features also include editorial and customer reviews, manufacturer product information, secure payment systems, wedding and baby registries, customer wish lists, and the ability to view selected interior pages and search the entire contents of many books.

The company operates the following retail Web sites: www.amazon.com (U.S.), www.amazon.co.uk (U.K.), www.amazon.de (Germany), www.amazon.fr (France), www.amazon.co.jp (Japan), www.amazon.ca (Canada), www.amazon.cn (China), www.joyo.cn, www.shopbop.com, www.endless.com, and www.zappos.com. Amazon also designs, manufac-

tures and sells a wireless e-reading device, the Amazon Kindle. It focuses first and foremost on the customer experience by offering a wide selection of merchandise, low prices and convenience.

In addition to being the seller of record for a broad range of new products, AMZN allows other businesses and individuals to sell new, used and collectible products on its Web sites through its Merchant and Amazon Marketplace programs. The company earns fixed fees, sales commissions, and/or per-unit activity fees under these programs. AMZN also serves developers through Amazon Web Services, which provides access to technology infrastructure that developers can use to enable virtually any type of business.

Starting in 2003, the company began reporting results for two core segments: North America (52% of 2009 net sales) and International (48%). In 2009, media products accounted for 52% of net sales, electronics and other general merchandise 45%, and other 3%.

Company Financials Fiscal Year Ended Dec. 31

Per Share Data ($)	2009	2008	2007	2006	2005	2004	2003	2002	2001	2000
Tangible Book Value	7.35	4.44	2.30	0.58	0.15	NM	NM	NM	NM	NM
Cash Flow	2.51	2.28	1.76	0.93	1.07	1.56	0.27	-0.16	-0.80	-2.86
Earnings	2.04	1.49	1.12	0.45	0.78	1.39	0.08	-0.40	-1.53	-4.02
S&P Core Earnings	NA	1.41	1.12	0.48	0.83	1.27	0.02	-0.64	-2.49	NA
Dividends	Nil	Nil	Nil	Nil	Nil	Nil	Nil	Nil	Nil	Nil
Payout Ratio	Nil	Nil	Nil	Nil	Nil	Nil	Nil	Nil	Nil	Nil
Prices:High	145.91	97.43	101.09	48.58	50.00	57.82	61.15	25.00	22.38	91.50
Prices:Low	47.63	34.68	36.30	25.76	30.60	33.00	18.55	9.03	5.51	14.88
P/E Ratio:High	72	65	90	NM	64	42	NM	NM	NM	NM
P/E Ratio:Low	23	23	32	NM	39	24	NM	NM	NM	NM

Income Statement Analysis (Million $)	2009	2008	2007	2006	2005	2004	2003	2002	2001	2000
Revenue	24,509	19,166	14,835	10,711	8,490	6,921	5,264	3,933	3,122	2,762
Operating Income	1,386	1,129	926	629	553	508	349	193	35.1	-257
Depreciation	206	340	271	205	121	75.7	78.3	87.8	266	406
Interest Expense	34.0	71.0	77.0	78.0	92.0	107	130	143	139	131
Pretax Income	1,155	892	660	377	428	356	35.3	-150	-557	-1,411
Effective Tax Rate	21.9%	27.7%	27.9%	49.6%	22.2%	NM	NM	NM	NM	NM
Net Income	902	645	476	190	333	588	35.3	-150	-557	-1,411
S&P Core Earnings	NA	609	476	203	354	539	10.3	-242	-910	NA

Balance Sheet & Other Financial Data (Million $)	2009	2008	2007	2006	2005	2004	2003	2002	2001	2000
Cash	6,366	3,727	3,112	2,019	2,000	1,779	1,395	1,301	997	1,101
Current Assets	9,797	6,157	5,164	3,373	2,929	2,539	1,821	1,616	1,208	1,361
Total Assets	13,813	8,314	6,485	4,363	3,696	3,249	2,162	1,990	1,638	2,135
Current Liabilities	7,364	4,746	3,714	2,532	1,929	1,620	1,253	1,066	921	975
Long Term Debt	109	533	1,282	1,247	1,521	1,855	1,945	2,277	2,156	2,127
Common Equity	5,257	2,672	1,197	431	246	-227	-1,036	-1,353	-1,440	-967
Total Capital	5,388	3,205	2,479	1,678	1,767	1,628	909	924	716	1,160
Capital Expenditures	373	333	224	216	204	89.1	46.0	39.2	50.3	135
Cash Flow	1,108	985	747	395	454	664	114	-62.2	-291	-1,005
Current Ratio	1.3	1.3	1.4	1.3	1.5	1.6	1.5	1.5	1.3	1.4
% Long Term Debt of Capitalization	2.0	16.6	51.7	74.3	86.1	113.9	213.9	246.3	301.1	183.4
% Net Income of Revenue	3.7	3.4	3.2	1.8	3.9	8.5	0.7	NM	NM	NM
% Return on Assets	8.2	8.7	8.8	4.7	9.6	21.8	1.7	NM	NM	NM
% Return on Equity	22.8	33.3	58.5	56.1	NM	NM	NM	NM	NM	NM

Data as orig reptd.; bef. results of disc opers/spec. items. Per share data adj. for stk. divs.; EPS diluted. E-Estimated. NA-Not Available. NM-Not Meaningful. NR-Not Ranked. UR-Under Review.

Office: 1200 12th Avenue South, Seattle, WA 98144-2734.
Telephone: 206-266-1000.
Email: ir@amazon.com
Website: http://www.amazon.com

Chrmn, Pres & CEO: J.P. Bezos
COO: M.A. Onetto
SVP & CFO: T.J. Szkutak
SVP, Secy & General Counsel: L.M. Wilson

Chief Acctg Officer & Cntlr: S.L. Reynolds
Investor Contact: R. Eldridge (206-266-2171)
Board Members: T. A. Alberg, J. P. Bezos, J. S. Brown, W. B. Gordon, A. Monie, T. O. Ryder, P. Stonesifer

Founded: 1994
Domicile: Delaware
Employees: 24,300

The **McGraw-Hill** Companies

Ameren Corp

STANDARD &POOR'S

S&P Recommendation HOLD ★★★☆☆	**Price** $28.83 (as of Oct 22, 2010)	**12-Mo. Target Price** $29.00	**Investment Style** Large-Cap Value

GICS Sector Utilities
Sub-Industry Multi-Utilities

Summary Ameren is the holding company for the largest electric utility in the state of Missouri and several utilities in Illinois.

Key Stock Statistics (Source S&P, Vickers, company reports)

52-Wk Range	$29.45– 23.09	S&P Oper. EPS 2010**E**	2.67	Market Capitalization(B)	$6.893	Beta	0.71
Trailing 12-Month EPS	$2.41	S&P Oper. EPS 2011**E**	2.48	Yield (%)	5.34	S&P 3-Yr. Proj. EPS CAGR(%)	-3
Trailing 12-Month P/E	12.0	P/E on S&P Oper. EPS 2010**E**	10.8	Dividend Rate/Share	$1.54	S&P Credit Rating	BBB-
$10K Invested 5 Yrs Ago	$7,616	Common Shares Outstg. (M)	239.1	Institutional Ownership (%)	56		

Price Performance

30-Week Mov. Avg. · · · · 10-Week Mov. Avg. – – – GAAP Earnings vs. Previous Year Volume Above Avg. STARS
12-Mo. Target Price — Relative Strength — ▲ Up ▼ Down ► No Change Below Avg. ★

Options: P, Ph

Analysis prepared by **Justin McCann** on August 31, 2010, when the stock traded at **$ 27.61**.

Highlights

➤ Excluding $0.06 in net one-time gains, we expect operating EPS in 2010 to decline about 4% from 2009's $2.79, which excluded $0.01 of net one-time charges. Operating EPS in the first half of 2010 was aided by a strong second quarter, due to warmer weather and a return to full capacity of a major industrial customer. This was, however, more than offset by lower generation margins and nearly 12% more shares.

➤ For full-year 2010, we look for the Missouri and Illinois utilities to earn about $2.28 a share, and the generating segment about $0.39. For 2011, we expect the decline in EPS to reflect more common shares outstanding, reduced merchant generation margins, higher fuel costs, and a return to normal weather. We believe this will be partially offset by lower operating expenses due to AEE's cost-cutting measures.

➤ In July 2009, Illinois enacted a law that allowed electric and natural gas utilities to make rate adjustments that would recover the difference between their actual uncollectible accounts and the amount included in their previously approved base rates. In February 2010, the Illinois Commerce Commission (ICC) approved the adjustments that AEE's Illinois utilities had made.

Investment Rationale/Risk

➤ Although the stock is down about 1% year to date, it has rebounded about 17% from it 2010 low. In addition to market volatility, we believe the rebound has reflected the improved earnings outlook for 2010. This follows a 16% decline in 2009, which despite a 43% rebound from the year's low, partly reflected AEE's February announcement of a 39% cut in its dividend and a sharply reduced earnings outlook for the year. Confronted with rising environmental and financing costs, AEE considered the dividend cut essential for its financial strength.

➤ Risks to our recommendation and target price include a steep decline in power supply margins and a sharp drop in the average P/E ratio of AEE's peer group as a whole.

➤ AEE's 39% dividend cut in 2009 reduced its payout ratio from 91% of its operating EPS for 2009 to 55%. However, we expect the payout ratio to increase to about 62% of our EPS estimate for 2011. Following the recent rebound in the shares, the yield from the current dividend is about 5.6%, which is still well above the recent peer average of about 4.8%. Our 12-month target price is $29, a discount-to-peers multiple of 11.7X our EPS estimate for 2011.

Qualitative Risk Assessment

LOW	MEDIUM	HIGH

Our risk assessment reflects our expectation of steady cash flow from the company's regulated utilities, which have the benefit of fuel costs that are below the industry average. We believe that this, as well as the electric rate settlement agreement in Illinois, will be only partly offset by the impact of the current credit market environment and the economic slowdown.

Quantitative Evaluations

S&P Quality Ranking B

D	C	B-	**B**	B+	A-	A	A+

Relative Strength Rank MODERATE

54

LOWEST = 1 HIGHEST = 99

Revenue/Earnings Data

Revenue (Million $)

	1Q	2Q	3Q	4Q	Year
2010	1,916	1,704	--	--	--
2009	1,916	1,684	1,815	1,675	7,090
2008	2,081	1,790	2,060	1,908	7,839
2007	2,019	1,723	1,997	1,807	7,546
2006	1,800	1,550	1,910	1,620	6,880
2005	1,626	1,585	1,868	1,701	6,780

Earnings Per Share ($)

2010	0.43	0.64	E1.63	E-0.09	E2.67
2009	0.66	0.77	1.04	0.33	2.78
2008	0.66	0.98	0.97	0.27	2.88
2007	0.59	0.69	1.18	0.52	2.98
2006	0.34	0.60	1.42	0.30	2.66
2005	0.62	0.93	1.37	0.21	3.13

Fiscal year ended Dec. 31. Next earnings report expected: Early November. EPS Estimates based on S&P Operating Earnings; historical GAAP earnings are as reported.

Dividend Data (Dates: mm/dd Payment Date: mm/dd/yy)

Amount ($)	Date Decl.	Ex-Div. Date	Stk. of Record	Payment Date
0.385	02/12	03/08	03/10	03/31/10
0.385	04/27	06/07	06/09	06/30/10
0.385	08/13	09/07	09/09	09/30/10
0.385	10/08	12/06	12/08	12/31/10

Dividends have been paid since 1906. Source: Company reports.

Please read the Required Disclosures and Analyst Certification on the last page of this report.

The McGraw·Hill Companies

Ameren Corp

Business Summary August 31, 2010

CORPORATE OVERVIEW. Ameren Corporation (AEE) is a holding company that operates regulated electric and natural gas utilities and non-regulated businesses, including energy marketing, trading and consulting services, in Missouri and Illinois. AEE's Utility Operations segment is comprised of its electric generation and electric and gas transmission and distribution operations. The company's subsidiaries include Union Electric Company (UE), Central Illinois Light Company (CILCO), Central Illinois Public Service Company (CIPS), Ameren Energy Generating Company (Genco), CILCORP Inc., and Illinois Power Company (IP). In 2009, the company's electric services contributed 83.3% of its consolidated operating revenues (81.2% in 2008), while its gas services contributed 16.7% (18.8%).

CORPORATE STRATEGY. Although AEE has attempted to keep its rates low through disciplined cost control and efficient operations, the costs of nearly every aspect of its business have been rising at a rapid pace. Since new customer rates are usually based on historical costs after an approximate one-year regulatory review, by the time they have been implemented they are already inadequate to fully recover the current costs and to earn a fair return on the company's investment. AEE has determined that in order to deal with this problem more effectively (and to avoid customer shock at a sudden sharp increase in rates), it intends to seek smaller and more frequent rate increases. It also plans to seek automatic cost recovery mechanisms for its most expensive items, such as its fuel costs and environmental investments.

Company Financials Fiscal Year Ended Dec. 31

Per Share Data ($)	2009	2008	2007	2006	2005	2004	2003	2002	2001	2000
Tangible Book Value	29.04	28.10	27.48	26.80	25.08	24.92	23.19	24.95	24.26	23.34
Earnings	2.78	2.88	2.98	2.66	3.13	2.84	3.14	2.60	3.45	3.33
S&P Core Earnings	2.63	2.09	3.04	2.90	3.32	3.12	3.28	2.36	2.81	NA
Dividends	1.54	2.54	2.54	2.54	2.54	2.54	2.54	2.54	2.54	2.54
Payout Ratio	55%	88%	85%	95%	81%	89%	81%	98%	74%	76%
Prices:High	35.35	54.29	55.00	55.24	56.77	50.36	46.50	45.25	46.00	46.94
Prices:Low	19.51	25.51	47.10	47.96	47.51	40.55	42.55	34.72	36.53	27.56
P/E Ratio:High	13	19	18	21	18	18	15	17	13	14
P/E Ratio:Low	7	9	16	18	15	14	14	13	11	8

Income Statement Analysis (Million $)

	2009	2008	2007	2006	2005	2004	2003	2002	2001	2000
Revenue	7,090	7,839	7,546	6,880	6,780	5,160	4,593	3,841	4,506	3,856
Depreciation	801	742	681	661	632	557	519	431	406	382
Maintenance	NA	NA	NA	NA	NA	NA	NA	NA	382	368
Fixed Charges Coverage	2.88	3.21	3.33	3.48	4.32	3.81	3.61	4.04	4.65	4.86
Construction Credits	NA	NA	NA	NA	NA	NA	4.00	11.0	20.8	14.0
Effective Tax Rate	34.7%	33.7%	33.5%	32.7%	35.6%	34.7%	37.3%	38.3%	38.7%	39.7%
Net Income	612	605	618	547	628	530	506	382	475	457
S&P Core Earnings	578	440	632	597	666	582	530	347	387	NA

Balance Sheet & Other Financial Data (Million $)

	2009	2008	2007	2006	2005	2004	2003	2002	2001	2000
Gross Property	26,397	25,066	23,484	22,013	20,800	20,291	17,511	15,745	14,962	13,910
Capital Expenditures	1,704	1,896	1,381	992	947	806	682	787	1,103	929
Net Property	17,610	16,567	15,069	14,286	13,572	13,297	10,917	8,914	8,427	7,706
Capitalization:Long Term Debt	7,943	6,749	5,902	5,498	5,568	5,236	4,273	3,626	3,071	2,980
Capitalization:% Long Term Debt	50.3	49.2	46.7	45.5	46.7	47.4	49.5	48.6	47.8	48.3
Capitalization:Preferred	Nil	Nil	Nil	Nil	Nil	Nil	Nil	Nil	Nil	Nil
Capitalization:% Preferred	Nil	Nil	Nil	Nil	Nil	Nil	Nil	Nil	Nil	Nil
Capitalization:Common	7,853	6,963	6,752	6,583	6,364	5,800	4,354	3,842	3,349	3,196
Capitalization:% Common	49.7	50.8	53.3	54.5	53.3	52.6	50.5	51.4	52.2	51.7
Total Capital	16,207	15,964	14,722	14,241	14,047	13,075	10,653	9,339	8,144	7,884
% Operating Ratio	84.7	86.8	86.6	87.1	86.3	84.6	83.9	81.0	85.2	83.4
% Earned on Net Property	8.3	8.6	9.1	8.4	9.6	8.9	10.7	7.2	8.2	8.6
% Return on Revenue	8.6	7.7	8.4	8.0	9.3	10.3	11.0	9.9	10.6	11.9
% Return on Invested Capital	7.5	7.0	7.5	6.6	7.0	6.9	7.4	8.1	8.6	8.5
% Return on Common Equity	8.3	8.8	9.3	8.4	10.3	10.4	12.3	10.6	14.5	14.5

Data as orig reptd.; bef. results of disc opers/spec. items. Per share data adj. for stk. divs.; EPS diluted. E-Estimated. NA-Not Available. NM-Not Meaningful. NR-Not Ranked. UR-Under Review.

Office: 1901 Chouteau Avenue, St. Louis, MO 63103.
Telephone: 314-621-3222.
Email: invest@ameren.com
Website: http://www.ameren.com

Chrmn, Pres & CEO: T.R. Voss
SVP, CFO, Chief Acctg Officer & Cntlr: M.J. Lyons, Jr.
SVP, Secy & General Counsel: S.R. Sullivan
Treas: J.E. Birdsong

Investor Contact: D. Fischer (314-554-4859)
Board Members: S. F. Brauer, E. M. Fitzsimmons, W. J. Galvin, G. P. Jackson, J. C. Johnson, S. H. Lipstein, C. W. Mueller, H. Saligman, P. T. Stokes, T. R. Voss, S. R. Wilson, J. D. Woodard

Founded: 1881
Domicile: Missouri
Employees: 9,780

American Electric Power Co Inc

STANDARD &POOR'S

S&P Recommendation BUY ★★★★☆

Price $36.46 (as of Oct 25, 2010)	**12-Mo. Target Price** $41.00	**Investment Style** Large-Cap Value

GICS Sector Utilities
Sub-Industry Electric Utilities

Summary This electric utility holding company has subsidiaries operating in 11 states in the U.S.

Key Stock Statistics (Source S&P, Vickers, company reports)

52-Wk Range	$37.16–28.17	S&P Oper. EPS 2010**E**	3.12	Market Capitalization(B)	$17.480	Beta	0.61
Trailing 12-Month EPS	$2.42	S&P Oper. EPS 2011**E**	3.19	Yield (%)	4.61	S&P 3-Yr. Proj. EPS CAGR(%)	3
Trailing 12-Month P/E	15.1	P/E on S&P Oper. EPS 2010**E**	11.7	Dividend Rate/Share	$1.68	S&P Credit Rating	BBB
$10K Invested 5 Yrs Ago	$12,592	Common Shares Outstg. (M)	479.4	Institutional Ownership (%)	68		

Price Performance

30-Week Mov. Avg. · · · 10-Week Mov. Avg. - - GAAP Earnings vs. Previous Year Volume Above Avg. STARS
12-Mo. Target Price — Relative Strength — ▲ Up ▼ Down ▶ No Change Below Avg. ★

Options: ASE, CBOE, P, Ph

Analysis prepared by **Justin McCann** on October 25, 2010, when the stock traded at **$ 36.70**.

Highlights

► Excluding $0.49 in one-time charges, we expect 2010 operating EPS to increase about 5% from 2009's $2.97, which excluded a net one-time charge of $0.01. EPS in the first nine months of 2010 benefited from rate increases, very favorable weather, increased industrial sales, and lower operation and maintenance expenses, partially offset by increased depreciation and interest charges, a higher effective tax rate, and nearly 6% more shares outstanding.

► While full-year results in 2010 will benefit from the approval of more than $320 million in rate increases, results will remain restricted by the weakness in the economy and power markets. AEP's cost reduction program is expected to realize savings of approximately $150 million in 2010 and $200 million in 2011. Earnings in 2011 are also expected to benefit from a full-year of the rate increases implemented in 2010.

► We expect AEP's annual EPS growth rate to range between 2% and 4% in 2011 and 2012, but then increase to between 4% and 6% over the next few years, reflecting AEP's investments in its generation and transmission operations and a gradual recovery in the economy.

Investment Rationale/Risk

► While the sharp rise in the shares from their 52-week low and the reduced EPS growth rate projection for 2011 and 2012, has resulted in a lower level of expected appreciation, the recent recommendation by AEP management for a 9.5% increase in the dividend has enhanced the potential yield.

► Risks to our recommendation and target price include the potential for weaker than anticipated results from the company's retail and wholesale operations and a sharp decline in the average P/E multiple of the group as a whole.

► Following the recent recommendation for a 9.5% increase in the dividend by AEP's management, the projected yield (based on recent prices) would rise from about 4.6% to about 5.0%, well above the recent average for AEP's peers of 4.7%. Our 12-month target price is $41, which reflects a premium-to-peers P/E of 12.9X our EPS estimate for 2011.

Qualitative Risk Assessment

LOW	MEDIUM	HIGH

Our risk assessment reflects our view of the steady cash flow expected from the regulated utilities, with their low-cost fuel sources and generally supportive regulatory environments. The proceeds from the divestiture of most of AEP's high-risk unregulated energy businesses were used to enhance its balance sheet and financial strength.

Quantitative Evaluations

S&P Quality Ranking B

D	C	B-	B	B+	A-	A	A+

Relative Strength Rank MODERATE

43

LOWEST = 1   HIGHEST = 99

Revenue/Earnings Data

Revenue (Million $)

	1Q	2Q	3Q	4Q	Year
2010	3,569	3,360	--	--	--
2009	3,458	3,202	3,547	3,282	13,489
2008	3,467	3,546	4,191	3,236	14,440
2007	3,169	3,146	3,789	3,276	13,380
2006	3,108	2,936	3,594	2,984	12,622
2005	3,065	2,819	3,328	2,899	12,111

Earnings Per Share ($)

	1Q	2Q	3Q	4Q	Year
2010	0.72	0.28	E0.98	E0.47	E3.12
2009	0.81	0.68	0.93	0.50	2.97
2008	1.43	0.70	0.93	0.34	3.39
2007	0.68	0.64	1.02	0.52	2.86
2006	0.95	0.43	0.67	0.44	2.50
2005	0.90	0.57	0.94	0.23	2.63

Fiscal year ended Dec. 31. Next earnings report expected: Late October. EPS Estimates based on S&P Operating Earnings; historical GAAP earnings are as reported.

Dividend Data (Dates: mm/dd Payment Date: mm/dd/yy)

Amount ($)	Date Decl.	Ex-Div. Date	Stk. of Record	Payment Date
0.410	10/27	11/06	11/10	12/10/09
0.410	01/27	02/08	02/10	03/10/10
0.420	04/27	05/06	05/10	06/10/10
0.420	07/28	08/06	08/10	09/10/10

Dividends have been paid since 1909. Source: Company reports.

Please read the Required Disclosures and Analyst Certification on the last page of this report.

The McGraw-Hill Companies

American Electric Power Co Inc

STANDARD &POOR'S

Business Summary October 25, 2010

CORPORATE OVERVIEW. American Electric Power Co. (AEP) is a holding company that primarily operates electric utility services through its regulated subsidiaries. The utility services include the generation, transmission and distribution of electricity for sale to retail and wholesale customers in the U.S. AEP's non-regulated operations include the AEP River Operations subsidiary (formerly AEP MEMCO), which is engaged in the transportation of coal and dry bulk commodities, mainly on the Ohio, Illinois and lower Mississippi rivers. In 2009, the utility segment accounted for 94.4% of total revenues.

CORPORATE STRATEGY. AEP focuses on its core utility operations and seeks to deliver low-cost electric power to the communities it serves. The company plans to improve its efficiency and to maximize the power delivered from its generation facilities. In order to provide safe and reliable power, AEP will continue to make investments to upgrade its transmission and distribution infrastructure, as well as to be in compliance with the appropriate environmental standards. However, due to the conditions in the capital markets, the company's capital investments in 2009 were nearly $1.49 billion (37%) below its expenditures in 2008, and its projected expenditures for 2010 are $315 million

(12.6%) below its expenditures in 2009.

MARKET PROFILE. AEP provides electric utility services to over 5 million retail customers in 11 states over a total area of 197,500 square miles. AEP derived about 33% of its total utility operating revenues in 2009 from Ohio, 12% each from Texas and Virginia, 10% each from Indiana, Oklahoma and West Virginia, 5% from Kentucky, 3% from Louisiana, 2% each from Arkansas and Michigan, and about 1% from Tennessee. In 2009, the residential segment contributed 34.6% of utility retail revenues (32.0% in 2008), followed by commercial and industrial, which contributed 24.9% (23.4%) and 20.7% (22.2%), respectively. Wholesale sales accounted for 14.5% of total utility sales in 2009, down from 20.6% in 2007, while other sales accounted for the remainder. At the end of 2009, AEP had 100% ownership of 224,416 overhead circuit miles of transmission and distribution lines.

Company Financials Fiscal Year Ended Dec. 31

Per Share Data ($)	2009	2008	2007	2006	2005	2004	2003	2002	2001	2000
Tangible Book Value	27.31	26.09	25.17	24.88	22.87	21.31	19.74	19.67	20.92	20.72
Earnings	2.97	3.39	2.86	2.50	2.63	2.85	1.35	0.06	3.11	0.94
S&P Core Earnings	3.00	2.29	2.77	2.35	2.26	2.58	1.47	0.07	2.17	NA
Dividends	1.64	1.64	1.58	1.50	1.42	1.40	1.65	2.40	2.40	2.40
Payout Ratio	55%	48%	58%	60%	54%	49%	NM	NM	77%	255%
Prices:High	36.51	49.11	51.24	43.13	40.80	35.53	31.51	48.80	51.20	48.94
Prices:Low	24.00	25.54	41.67	32.27	32.25	28.50	19.01	15.10	39.25	25.94
P/E Ratio:High	12	14	19	17	16	12	23	NM	16	52
P/E Ratio:Low	8	8	15	13	12	10	14	NM	13	28

Income Statement Analysis (Million $)										
Revenue	13,489	14,440	13,380	12,622	12,111	14,057	14,545	14,555	61,257	13,694
Depreciation	1,660	1,571	1,513	1,467	1,318	1,300	1,299	1,377	1,383	1,062
Maintenance	1,205	NA	NA	NA	NA	NA	NA	NA	NA	NA
Fixed Charges Coverage	2.98	2.81	2.96	2.96	2.80	2.60	2.97	2.84	2.64	1.95
Construction Credits	82.0	45.0	33.0	30.0	21.0	NA	NA	NA	NA	NA
Effective Tax Rate	29.6%	31.9%	31.0%	32.7%	29.4%	33.7%	39.8%	79.3%	35.9%	66.4%
Net Income	1,362	1,368	1,144	992	1,029	1,127	522	21.0	1,003	302
S&P Core Earnings	1,373	924	1,107	934	883	1,021	573	21.1	698	NA

Balance Sheet & Other Financial Data (Million $)										
Gross Property	51,684	49,710	46,145	42,021	39,121	37,286	36,033	37,857	40,709	38,088
Capital Expenditures	2,896	3,960	3,556	3,528	2,404	1,693	1,358	1,722	1,832	1,773
Net Property	34,344	32,987	29,870	26,781	24,284	22,801	22,029	21,684	24,543	22,393
Capitalization:Long Term Debt	15,818	15,597	14,263	12,490	11,073	11,069	12,459	9,329	10,230	10,097
Capitalization:% Long Term Debt	54.6	59.3	58.6	57.0	54.9	56.5	61.3	56.9	55.4	55.6
Capitalization:Preferred	Nil	Nil	Nil	Nil	Nil	Nil	Nil	Nil	Nil	Nil
Capitalization:% Preferred	Nil	Nil	Nil	Nil	Nil	Nil	Nil	Nil	Nil	Nil
Capitalization:Common	13,140	10,693	10,079	9,412	9,088	8,515	7,874	7,064	8,229	8,054
Capitalization:% Common	45.4	40.7	41.4	43.0	45.1	43.5	38.7	43.1	44.6	44.4
Total Capital	30,699	31,418	29,072	26,802	25,032	24,403	24,290	21,523	24,523	23,554
% Operating Ratio	83.7	87.0	86.5	87.2	84.1	85.8	88.8	91.3	96.1	85.2
% Earned on Net Property	8.2	8.9	8.2	7.7	8.2	8.9	7.7	5.8	10.2	9.2
% Return on Revenue	10.1	9.5	8.6	7.9	8.5	8.0	3.6	0.1	1.6	2.2
% Return on Invested Capital	8.1	6.8	7.1	7.5	6.2	6.1	9.4	8.8	8.4	6.8
% Return on Common Equity	11.4	13.2	11.7	10.7	11.7	13.8	7.0	0.3	12.3	3.6

Data as orig reptd.; bef. results of disc opers/spec. items. Per share data adj. for stk. divs.; EPS diluted. E-Estimated. NA-Not Available. NM-Not Meaningful. NR-Not Ranked. UR-Under Review.

Office: 1 Riverside Plz, Columbus , OH 43215-2373.
Telephone: 614-716-1000.
Email: corpcomm@aep.com
Website: http://www.aep.com

Chrmn, Pres & CEO: M.G. Morris
COO: C.L. English
EVP & CFO: B.X. Tierney
SVP, Chief Acctg Officer & Cntlr: J.M. Buonaiuto

SVP & Treas: C.E. Zebula
Investor Contact: B. Rozsa (614-716-2840)
Board Members: E. R. Brooks, D. M. Carlton, J. F. Cordes, R. D. Crosby, Jr., L. A. Goodspeed, T. E. Hoaglin, L. A. Hudson, Jr., M. G. Morris, L. L. Nowell, III, R. L. Sandor, K. D. Sullivan, S. M. Tucker, J. F. Turner

Founded: 1906
Domicile: New York
Employees: 21,673

The McGraw-Hill Companies

American Express Co

STANDARD &POOR'S

S&P Recommendation **BUY** ★★★★☆	Price $39.03 (as of Oct 22, 2010)	12-Mo. Target Price $52.00	Investment Style Large-Cap Growth

GICS Sector Financials
Sub-Industry Consumer Finance

Summary American Express is a leading global payments and travel services company.

Key Stock Statistics (Source S&P, Vickers, company reports)

52-Wk Range	$49.19– 34.42	S&P Oper. EPS 2010**E**	3.40	Market Capitalization(B)	$46.961	Beta	2.01
Trailing 12-Month EPS	$2.71	S&P Oper. EPS 2011**E**	3.75	Yield (%)	1.84	S&P 3-Yr. Proj. EPS CAGR(%)	36
Trailing 12-Month P/E	14.4	P/E on S&P Oper. EPS 2010**E**	11.5	Dividend Rate/Share	$0.72	S&P Credit Rating	BBB+
$10K Invested 5 Yrs Ago	$9,053	Common Shares Outstg. (M)	1,203.2	Institutional Ownership (%)	81		

Price Performance

30-Week Mov. Avg. · · · 10-Week Mov. Avg. - - GAAP Earnings vs. Previous Year Volume Above Avg. STARS
12-Mo. Target Price — Relative Strength — ▲ Up ▼ Down ▶ No Change Below Avg. ★

Options: ASE, CBOE, P, Ph

Analysis prepared by **Rafay Khalid, CFA** on October 22, 2010, when the stock traded at **$ 39.56.**

Highlights

➤ We expect revenue growth of 12% in 2010 and 9% in 2011, reflecting our outlook for a gradual economic recovery to accelerate consumer and business spending. We expect AXP to remain cautious on customers' outstanding credit lines. We see sales increasing in all of AXP's divisions, with its U.S. card division posting the most robust gains.

➤ We project a pickup in expenses in 2010 and 2011, as we anticipate that marketing and promotional expenses will increase as AXP attempts to reinforce its brand presence. In addition, we foresee higher incentive compensation expense and technology spending, as we see the company investing in growth initiatives. However, we forecast a decline in loss provisions, reflecting our view of delinquency rates and unemployment stabilizing in 2010.

➤ Our EPS forecasts are $3.40 for 2010 and $3.75 for 2011. This compares to EPS of $1.55 in 2009, which included one-time items such as repayment of TARP funds and the repurchase of warrants.

Investment Rationale/Risk

➤ We believe that consumers and businesses will increase their spending in an improving economic environment. We think loss provisions in the global commercial, U.S. card and international card businesses will decline in 2010 and 2011, reflecting our outlook for lower delinquencies. We think AXP will take some of the savings from lower loss provisions and reinvest them to gain market share. In October, the U.S. Department of Justice sued AXP in a civil antitrust action over the company's rules that prevent merchants from providing discounts to consumers. While we believe this litigation will take time to resolve based on prior antitrust cases, we think it will create an overhang on the stock.

➤ Risks to our recommendation and target price include a significant slowdown in consumer and business spending, an increase in loss provisions, a weakening macroeconomic environment, and a decline in credit quality.

➤ Our 12-month target price of $52 is based on a historical discount P/E ratio of 13.9X our 2011 EPS estimate. We believe this discount is warranted, given the U.S. government's civil antitrust lawsuit against AXP.

Qualitative Risk Assessment

LOW	MEDIUM	HIGH

Our risk assessment reflects what we see as solid business fundamentals and a strong customer base. We view AXP as able to withstand a major global or U.S. economic downturn. Although we look for AXP to remain profitable, the extent of writedowns is uncertain due to national home price declines and high unemployment.

Quantitative Evaluations

S&P Quality Ranking A-

D	C	B-	B	B+	A-	A	A+

Relative Strength Rank WEAK

18

LOWEST = 1 HIGHEST = 99

Revenue/Earnings Data

Revenue (Million $)

	1Q	2Q	3Q	4Q	Year
2010	6,606	6,858	--	--	--
2009	5,926	6,092	6,016	6,489	26,730
2008	8,105	8,340	8,007	7,468	31,920
2007	7,631	8,199	7,953	7,364	31,557
2006	6,319	6,850	6,759	7,208	27,136
2005	5,672	6,090	6,068	6,437	24,267

Earnings Per Share ($)

	1Q	2Q	3Q	4Q	Year
2010	0.73	0.84	E0.90	E0.93	E3.40
2009	0.32	0.09	0.54	0.59	1.55
2008	0.90	0.57	0.74	0.27	2.48
2007	0.88	0.88	0.90	0.71	3.39
2006	0.70	0.78	0.78	0.76	3.01
2005	0.59	0.69	0.69	0.60	2.56

Fiscal year ended Dec. 31. Next earnings report expected: Late October. EPS Estimates based on S&P Operating Earnings; historical GAAP earnings are as reported.

Dividend Data (Dates: mm/dd Payment Date: mm/dd/yy)

Amount ($)	Date Decl.	Ex-Div. Date	Stk. of Record	Payment Date
0.180	11/23	01/07	01/11	02/10/10
0.180	03/22	03/30	04/01	05/10/10
0.180	05/24	06/30	07/02	08/10/10
0.180	09/27	10/06	10/08	11/10/10

Dividends have been paid since 1870. Source: Company reports.

Please read the Required Disclosures and Analyst Certification on the last page of this report.

The McGraw·Hill Companies

American Express Co

STANDARD &POOR'S

Business Summary October 22, 2010

CORPORATE OVERVIEW. American Express is a leading global payments and travel company. Its businesses are organized into two customer-focused groups -- global consumer and global business-to-business. Accordingly, U.S. card services and international card services are aligned within the global consumer group and global commercial services and global network & merchant services are alligned within the global business-to-business group.

U.S. Card Services includes the U.S. proprietary consumer card business, OPEN from American Express, the global Travelers Cheques and Prepaid Services business, and the American Express U.S. Consumer Travel Network.

International Card Services issues proprietary consumer and small business cards outside the U.S.

Global Commercial Services offers global corporate payment and travel-related products and services to large and midsized companies. It offers five primary products and services: Corporate Card, issued to individuals through a corporate account established by their employer and designed primarily for travel and entertainment spending; Corporate Purchasing Solutions, an account established by corporations to pay for everyday business expenses such as office and computer supplies; Buyer Initiated Payment, an electronic

solution for companies looking to streamline their payment processes; vPayment technology, which provides fast and efficient payment for large ticket purchases and permits the processing of large transactions with effective fraud; and American Express Business Travel, which helps businesses manage and optimize their travel expenses through a variety of travel-related products, services and solutions.

Global Network & Merchant Services consists of the merchant services businesses and global network services. Global Network Services develops and manages relationships with third parties that issue American Express branded cards. The Global Merchant Services businesses develop and manage relationships with merchants that accept American Express branded cards; authorize and record transactions; pay merchants; and provide a variety of value-added point of sale and back office services. In addition, in particular emerging markets, issuance of certain proprietary cards is managed within the Global Network Services business.

Company Financials Fiscal Year Ended Dec. 31

Per Share Data ($)	2009	2008	2007	2006	2005	2004	2003	2002	2001	2000
Tangible Book Value	9.53	7.61	8.22	7.52	8.50	12.83	11.93	10.62	9.04	8.81
Earnings	1.55	2.48	3.39	3.01	2.56	2.74	2.31	2.01	0.98	2.07
S&P Core Earnings	0.93	2.08	2.87	2.85	2.49	2.53	2.09	1.68	0.73	NA
Dividends	0.72	0.72	0.60	0.54	0.48	0.32	0.38	0.32	0.32	0.32
Payout Ratio	46%	29%	18%	18%	19%	12%	16%	16%	33%	15%
Prices:High	42.25	52.63	65.89	62.50	59.50	57.05	49.11	44.91	57.06	63.00
Prices:Low	9.71	16.55	50.37	49.73	46.59	47.32	30.90	26.55	24.20	39.83
P/E Ratio:High	27	21	19	21	23	21	21	22	58	30
P/E Ratio:Low	6	7	15	17	18	17	13	13	25	19

Income Statement Analysis (Million $)										
Cards in Force	87.9	92.4	86.4	78.0	71.0	65.4	60.5	57.3	55.2	51.7
Card Charge Volume	NA	NA	NA	NA	484,400	416,100	352,200	311,400	298,000	296,700
Premium Income	Nil	Nil	Nil	Nil	Nil	1,525	1,366	802	674	575
Commissions	3,372	4,317	4,343	4,333	4,236	4,079	3,484	3,521	3,969	4,165
Interest & Dividends	5,331	7,201	6,145	4,535	3,635	3,118	3,063	2,991	3,049	4,277
Total Revenue	26,730	31,920	31,557	27,136	24,267	29,115	25,866	23,807	22,582	23,675
Net Before Taxes	2,841	3,473	5,566	5,328	4,248	4,951	4,247	3,727	1,596	3,908
Net Income	2,137	2,871	4,048	3,729	3,221	3,516	3,000	2,671	1,311	2,810
S&P Core Earnings	1,101	2,412	3,426	3,531	3,144	3,244	2,723	2,245	986	NA

Balance Sheet & Other Financial Data (Million $)										
Total Assets	124,000	126,000	149,830	127,853	113,960	192,638	175,001	157,253	151,100	154,423
Cash Items	16,000	21,000	14,036	11,270	7,126	9,907	5,726	10,288	7,222	8,487
Investment Assets:Bonds	Nil	Nil	Nil	Nil	Nil	Nil	Nil	Nil	Nil	Nil
Investment Assets:Stocks	Nil	Nil	Nil	Nil	Nil	Nil	Nil	Nil	Nil	Nil
Investment Assets:Loans	30,010	40,659	53,436	50,248	40,801	35,942	33,421	29,003	27,401	26,884
Investment Assets:Total	54,347	53,185	67,472	61,518	62,135	60,809	57,067	53,638	46,488	43,747
Accounts Receivable	38,204	36,571	95,441	89,099	35,497	34,650	31,269	29,087	29,498	30,543
Customer Deposits	26,289	15,486	15,397	24,656	24,579	21,091	21,250	18,317	14,557	13,870
Travel Cheques Outstanding	5,975	6,433	7,197	7,215	7,175	7,287	6,819	6,623	6,190	6,127
Debt	52,338	69,034	73,047	57,909	30,781	33,061	30,809	16,819	8,288	5,211
Common Equity	14,000	12,000	11,029	10,511	10,549	16,020	15,323	13,861	12,037	11,684
% Return on Assets	1.7	2.0	2.9	3.1	2.1	1.9	1.8	1.7	0.9	1.9
% Return on Equity	16.5	24.3	37.6	35.4	24.2	22.4	20.6	20.6	11.1	25.8

Data as orig reptd.; bef. results of disc opers/spec. items. Per share data adj. for stk. divs.; EPS diluted. E-Estimated. NA-Not Available. NM-Not Meaningful. NR-Not Ranked. UR-Under Review.

Office: World Financial Ctr, 200 Vesey Street, New York, NY 10285-4814.
Telephone: 212-640-2000.
Website: http://www.americanexpress.com
Chrmn & CEO: K.I. Chenault

EVP & CFO: D.T. Henry
EVP & General Counsel: L.M. Parent
EVP & Cntlr: J. Amble
Treas: D.L. Yowan

Investor Contact: R. Stovall (212-640-5574)
Board Members: D. F. Akerson, C. Barshefsky, U. M. Burns, K. I. Chenault, P. Chernin, T. J. Leonis, T. J. Leonsis, J. Leschly, R. C. Levin, R. A. McGinn, E. D. Miller, Jr., S. S. Reinemund, R. D. Walter, R. A. Williams

Founded: 1868
Domicile: New York
Employees: 58,300

American International Group Inc

STANDARD &POOR'S

S&P Recommendation HOLD ★★★☆☆

Price
$41.56 (as of Oct 22, 2010)

12-Mo. Target Price
$43.00

GICS Sector Financials
Sub-Industry Multi-line Insurance

Summary AIG provides property, casualty, and life insurance, as well as other financial services, in 130 countries.

Key Stock Statistics (Source S&P, Vickers, company reports)

52-Wk Range	$45.90– 21.54	S&P Oper. EPS 2010**E**	5.17	Market Capitalization(B)	$5.616	Beta	3.76
Trailing 12-Month EPS	$-13.78	S&P Oper. EPS 2011**E**	5.20	Yield (%)	Nil	S&P 3-Yr. Proj. EPS CAGR(%)	NM
Trailing 12-Month P/E	NM	P/E on S&P Oper. EPS 2010**E**	8.0	Dividend Rate/Share	Nil	S&P Credit Rating	A-
$10K Invested 5 Yrs Ago	$345	Common Shares Outstg. (M)	135.1	Institutional Ownership (%)	54		

Price Performance

30-Week Mov. Avg. · · · 10-Week Mov. Avg. – – GAAP Earnings vs. Previous Year Volume Above Avg. STARS
12-Mo. Target Price — Relative Strength — ▲ Up ▼ Down ► No Change Below Avg. ★

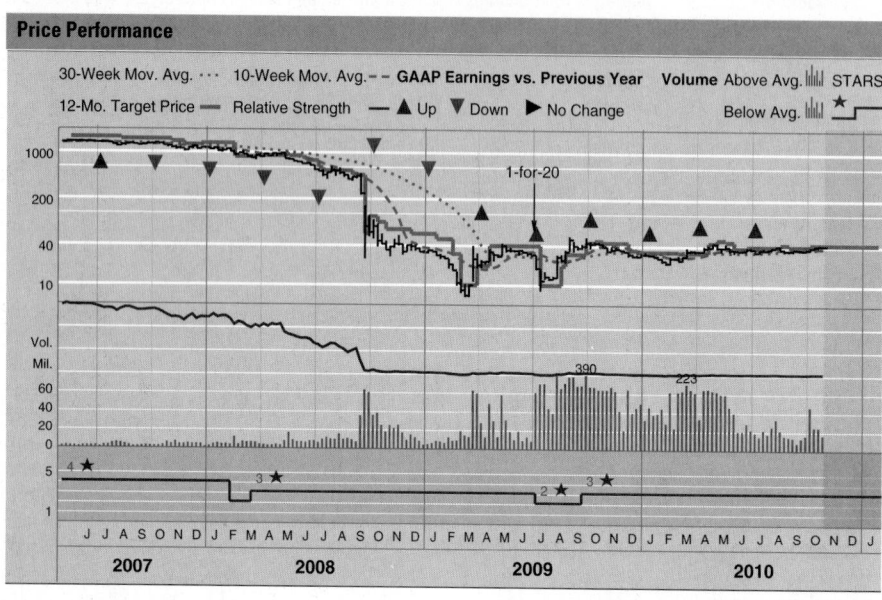

Options: ASE, CBOE, P, Ph

Qualitative Risk Assessment

LOW	MEDIUM	**HIGH**

AIG's outsized exposure (versus peers in the insurance industry) to the mortgage industry and the credit default swap market led to an emergency bailout by the Federal Reserve in 2008 and additional capital infusions in early 2009. Going forward, we believe there remains a high degree of execution risk as AIG seeks to restructure. We cannot rule out the need for additional capital infusions or further government intervention.

Quantitative Evaluations

S&P Quality Ranking C

D	**C**	B-	B	B+	A-	A	A+

Relative Strength Rank STRONG

77

LOWEST = 1   HIGHEST = 99

Highlights

➤ The 12-month target price for AIG has recently been changed to $43.00 from $45.00. The Highlights section of this Stock Report will be updated accordingly.

Investment Rationale/Risk

➤ The Investment Rationale/Risk section of this Stock Report will be updated shortly. For the latest News story on AIG from MarketScope, see below.

➤ 10/22/10 11:19 am ET ... S&P MAINTAINS HOLD RECOMMENDATION ON SHARES OF AMERICAN INTERNATIONAL GROUP (AIG 41.93***): AIG raised $17.8B from the initial public offering of AIA Group Ltd. The transaction resulted in AIG selling its 58% stake in AIA, or 7B shares, for HK$19.68, at the high end of the company's estimated range. We believe the transaction will increase AIG's book value given the capital gain from the sale. However, we continue to be concerned about the large amount of intangible assets on AIG's balance sheet, which we believe are vulnerable to impairment. We maintain our target price of $43, which assumes the shares trade at a discount to stated book value. /C. Seifert

Revenue/Earnings Data

Revenue (Million $)

	1Q	2Q	3Q	4Q	Year
2010	16,330	19,982	--	--	--
2009	20,458	29,525	26,049	--	96,004
2008	14,031	19,933	898.0	-23,758	11,104
2007	30,645	31,150	29,836	18,433	110,064
2006	27,259	26,743	29,199	29,993	113,194
2005	27,202	27,903	26,408	27,392	108,905

Earnings Per Share ($)

2010	-6.48	21.21	E0.85	E0.94	E5.17
2009	-39.60	2.30	0.68	-58.04	-86.30
2008	-61.80	-41.20	-181.00	-459.00	-756.80
2007	31.60	32.80	23.80	-41.40	47.80
2006	24.20	24.20	32.20	26.20	107.00
2005	29.00	34.20	13.20	3.40	79.80

Fiscal year ended Dec. 31. Next earnings report expected: Early November. EPS Estimates based on S&P Operating Earnings; historical GAAP earnings are as reported.

Dividend Data

No cash dividends have been paid on the common shares since September 2008.

Please read the Required Disclosures and Analyst Certification on the last page of this report.

The **McGraw·Hill** Companies

American International Group Inc

Business Summary August 29, 2010

American International Group provides an array of insurance and financial services in 130 countries and territories. Investigations several years ago by the New York Attorney General and the SEC into AIG's use of non-traditional insurance products and certain assumed reinsurance transactions culminated in a number of events, including the resignation of AIG's long-time CEO Maurice Greenberg; a writedown against earnings from 2000-2004 of nearly $4 billion; and a writedown of shareholders' equity of $2.26 billion. During 2005, AIG also incurred after-tax charges totaling $1.15 billion to settle numerous regulatory issues and $1.19 billion to boost loss reserves. During 2007 and 2008, AIG was confronted with the downward spiral of the U.S. residential mortgage market and subsequent deterioration in broader credit market conditions. To help replenish its capital, AIG in May 2008 raised $20 billion of new capital that included the sale of 196,710,525 common shares for $7.47 billion.

These moves proved insufficient, and in late September 2008, AIG was forced to accept an emergency line of credit from the Federal Reserve. To repay the Federal Reserve loan, AIG is undergoing a planned sale of its assets, including the December 2008 sale of Hartford Steam Boiler (HSB) to Munich Re for $742 million in cash and the assumption of $76 million of debt (less than the $1.2 billion AIG paid for HSB in 2000), the January 2009 sale of AIG Life Insurance Co. of Canada to BMO Financial Group for about $308 million in cash, and the June 2009 sale of 29.9 million shares of Transatlantic Holdings, Inc. (TRH) for

gross proceeds of $1.1 billion. As of March 2010, AIG had agreements to sell AIA Group to Prudential PLC for $35.5 billion, and American Life Insurance Co (ALICO) to MetLife, Inc. for $15.5 billion. The AIA sale to Prudential plc subsequently collapsed and AIG is reported to be preparing that unit for an initial public offering in Hong Kong. Subsequent revisions and additions to original terms have resulted in AIG receiving federal aid valued at approximately $173 billion and in trusts established for the benefit of the U.S. Treasury controlling approximately 77.9% of the voting power of AIG common stock. At December 31, 2009, total authorized and outstanding U.S. government support and assistance equaled $129.3 billion.

Revenues totaled $96.0 billion in 2009, versus $6.9 billion in 2008, as an 18% drop in premiums was offset by a surge in net investment income; much lower realized capital losses (of $6.9 billion versus $52.7 billion); a turnaround in the value of the credit default swap portfolio; and $11.5 billion of other income (versus other losses of $1.8 billion). Following a 3.3% decline in benefits and expenses, AIG reported net losses from continuing operations of $11.8 billion ($86.30 a share) in 2009, versus $97.6 billion ($737.12 a share) in 2008.

Company Financials Fiscal Year Ended Dec. 31

Per Share Data ($)	2009	2008	2007	2006	2005	2004	2003	2002	2001	2000
Tangible Book Value	256.03	347.20	683.00	759.20	602.60	554.60	487.80	406.40	398.80	339.60
Operating Earnings	NA	NA	NA	NA	NA	NA	NA	NA	NA	49.00
Earnings	-86.30	-756.80	47.80	107.00	79.80	75.00	70.60	42.00	41.40	48.20
S&P Core Earnings	-6.12	-388.40	66.20	107.20	87.00	75.40	77.80	52.60	41.20	NA
Dividends	Nil	12.40	14.60	12.60	11.00	5.60	4.40	3.56	3.16	2.81
Relative Payout	Nil	NM	31%	12%	14%	7%	6%	8%	8%	6%
Prices:High	55.90	1188	1459	1459	1469	1547	1327	1600	1966	2075
Prices:Low	8.22	25.00	1017	1150	998.20	1086	858.40	952.20	1320	1048
P/E Ratio:High	NM	NM	31	14	18	21	19	38	47	43
P/E Ratio:Low	NM	NM	21	11	13	14	12	23	32	22

Income Statement Analysis (Million $)	2009	2008	2007	2006	2005	2004	2003	2002	2001	2000
Life Insurance in Force	2,341,042	2,378,314	2,312,045	2,070,600	1,852,833	1,858,094	1,596,626	1,324,451	1,228,501	583,059
Premium Income:Life A & H	27,318	37,295	33,627	30,636	29,400	28,082	22,879	20,320	19,243	13,610
Premium Income:Casualty/Property.	30,664	46,222	45,682	43,451	41,872	40,607	31,734	24,269	19,365	17,407
Net Investment Income	25,239	12,222	28,619	25,292	22,165	18,434	16,662	15,034	14,628	9,824
Total Revenue	96,004	11,104	110,064	113,194	108,905	97,987	81,303	67,482	52,852	40,717
Pretax Income	-13,648	-108,761	8,943	21,687	15,213	14,950	13,908	8,142	8,139	8,349
Net Operating Income	NA	NA	NA	NA	105	NA	NA	NA	NA	5,737
Net Income	-10,383	-99,289	6,200	14,014	10,477	9,875	9,265	5,519	5,499	5,636
S&P Core Earnings	-5,877	-51,166	8,585	14,018	11,396	9,928	10,208	6,931	5,476	NA

Balance Sheet & Other Financial Data (Million $)	2009	2008	2007	2006	2005	2004	2003	2002	2001	2000
Cash & Equivalent	9,552	14,641	8,871	7,681	7,624	7,597	5,881	1,165	698	256
Premiums Due	16,549	17,330	18,395	17,789	15,333	15,137	14,166	13,088	11,647	11,832
Investment Assets:Bonds	396,982	404,134	428,935	417,865	385,680	365,677	309,254	243,366	200,616	102,010
Investment Assets:Stocks	17,840	21,143	41,646	30,222	23,588	17,851	9,584	7,066	7,937	7,181
Investment Assets:Loans	27,461	34,687	33,727	28,418	24,909	22,463	21,249	19,928	18,092	12,243
Investment Assets:Total	601,165	554,446	755,596	719,685	614,759	494,592	449,657	339,320	357,602	140,910
Deferred Policy Costs	40,814	45,782	43,150	37,235	33,248	29,736	26,398	22,256	17,443	10,189
Total Assets	847,585	860,418	1,060,505	979,414	853,370	798,660	678,346	561,229	492,982	306,577
Debt	113,298	137,054	162,935	186,866	78,625	66,850	57,877	50,076	34,503	5,801
Common Equity	40.0	52,690	95,801	101,677	86,317	80,607	71,253	59,103	52,150	39,619
Combined Loss-Expense Ratio	108.0	109.1	90.3	89.1	104.7	100.1	92.4	106.0	100.7	96.7
% Return on Revenue	NM	NM	5.6	12.4	9.6	10.1	11.4	8.2	10.5	13.8
% Return on Equity	NM	NM	6.3	14.9	12.6	13.1	14.2	9.9	11.0	15.5
% Investment Yield	4.1	2.0	3.9	3.8	3.7	3.9	4.1	4.8	4.5	7.4

Data as orig reptd.; bef. results of disc opers/spec. items. Per share data adj. for stk. divs.; EPS diluted. E-Estimated. NA-Not Available. NM-Not Meaningful. NR-Not Ranked. UR-Under Review.

Office: 70 Pine Street, New York, NY 10270-0094.
Telephone: 212-770-7000.
Website: http://www.aigcorporate.com
Chrmn: R.S. Miller, Jr.

Pres & CEO: B. Benmosche
EVP & CFO: D.L. Herzog
EVP & General Counsel: T.A. Russo
SVP & Chief Admin Officer: M.R. Cowan

Investor Contact: S.J. Bensinger
Board Members: B. Benmosche, S. N. Johnson, L. T. Koellner, D. H. Layton, C. S. Lynch, A. C. Martinez, G. L. Miles, Jr., H. S. Miller, R. S. Miller, Jr., M. W. Offit, R. A. Rittenmeyer, D. M. Steenland

Founded: 1967
Domicile: Delaware
Employees: 96,000

American Tower Corp

STANDARD &POOR'S

S&P Recommendation STRONG BUY ★★★★★	**Price** $50.22 (as of Oct 22, 2010)	**12-Mo. Target Price** $58.00	**Investment Style** Large-Cap Blend

GICS Sector Telecommunication Services
Sub-Industry Wireless Telecommunication Services

Summary This company operates the largest independent portfolio of wireless communications and broadcast towers in North America.

Key Stock Statistics (Source S&P, Vickers, company reports)

52-Wk Range	$52.34– 36.15	S&P Oper. EPS 2010E	0.99	Market Capitalization(B)	$20.145
Trailing 12-Month EPS	$0.81	S&P Oper. EPS 2011E	1.25	Yield (%)	Nil
Trailing 12-Month P/E	62.0	P/E on S&P Oper. EPS 2010E	50.7	Dividend Rate/Share	Nil
$10K Invested 5 Yrs Ago	$21,480	Common Shares Outstg. (M)	401.1	Institutional Ownership (%)	95

Beta	0.75
S&P 3-Yr. Proj. EPS CAGR(%)	10
S&P Credit Rating	BB+

Price Performance

30-Week Mov. Avg. ··· 10-Week Mov. Avg. – – **GAAP Earnings vs. Previous Year** **Volume** Above Avg. STARS
12-Mo. Target Price — Relative Strength — ▲ Up ▼ Down ▶ No Change Below Avg. ★

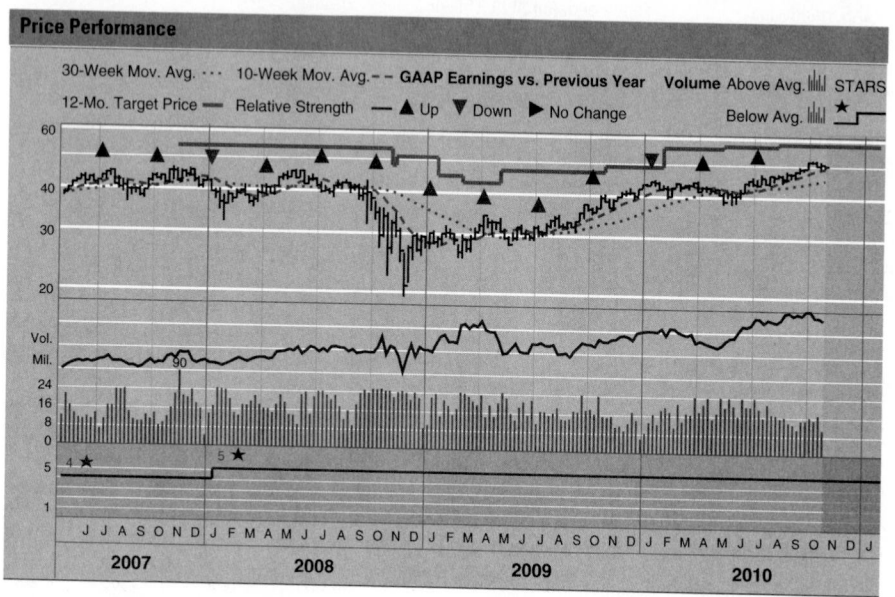

Options: ASE, CBOE, P, Ph

Analysis prepared by **James Moorman, CFA** on August 12, 2010, when the stock traded at **$ 45.92.**

Highlights

➤ Following an 8.2% revenue increase in 2009, we expect revenues to rise 11.9% in 2010 and 10.8% in 2011, reflecting higher lease activity per active tower and more new towers. We believe AMT will benefit from favorable tower industry trends, such as wireless carriers' demands to improve their network quality and coverage both in the U.S. and internationally.

➤ We are positive on AMT's operating discipline and look for operating expenses as a percentage of sales to decline in 2010 and 2011. We believe EBITDA margins, driven by higher tower utilization, will widen to 67.0% in 2010 and to 67.8% in 2011, up from 66.9% in 2009, which are levels well above the peer average. We believe this efficiency will enable free cash flow to increase to $789 million in 2010 and to $975 million in 2011, up from $641 million in 2009.

➤ We estimate EPS of $0.99 for 2010 and $1.25 for 2011, versus $0.61 posted in 2009. Our 2010 estimate includes projected stock option expense of $0.13.

Investment Rationale/Risk

➤ AMT is the market leader in the wireless tower industry, and we think further tower purchases will enable it to continue to achieve greater economies of scale. We believe the network upgrades to 4G, notably LTE and WiMAX, will provide an additional revenue boost over the next several years. AMT has an estimated 2010 net debt/EBITDA ratio of 3.1X, well below peers. We also expect AMT to continue to expand internationally in Mexico, Brazil, India, and Chile. AMT recently announced the planned purchase of an additional 4,450 towers in India. We consider the shares highly attractive for purchase and have a strong buy opinion on the shares.

➤ Risks to our recommendation and target price include slower demand in the tower lease business if carriers begin to cut back on spending. Another risk we see is the company's $4.2 billion of debt obligations.

➤ Our 12-month target price of $58 is largely based on 24X our free cash flow estimate for 2011, above the peer mean. Our target price also represents an enterprise value of 18.8X our 2011 EBITDA estimate, slightly above the industry average.

Qualitative Risk Assessment

LOW	MEDIUM	HIGH

Our risk assessment reflects the company's high total debt to total capitalization ratio, partly offset by our view of its steady cash flow and sufficient cash and investments to meet its working capital, capital expenditure and debt requirements.

Quantitative Evaluations

S&P Quality Ranking B

D	C	B-	B	B+	A-	A	A+

Relative Strength Rank MODERATE

50

LOWEST = 1   HIGHEST = 99

Revenue/Earnings Data

Revenue (Million $)

	1Q	2Q	3Q	4Q	Year
2010	454.4	469.9	--	--	--
2009	408.7	423.4	444.1	448.0	1,724
2008	382.2	393.7	409.3	408.3	1,594
2007	352.5	358.4	367.6	378.1	1,457
2006	320.4	325.9	333.5	337.7	1,317
2005	184.4	188.1	264.8	307.6	944.8

Earnings Per Share ($)

	1Q	2Q	3Q	4Q	Year
2010	0.24	0.25	E0.25	E0.26	E0.99
2009	0.14	0.13	0.17	0.16	0.59
2008	0.10	0.12	0.15	0.21	0.58
2007	0.05	0.03	0.14	-0.01	0.22
2006	-0.01	0.02	0.01	0.04	0.06
2005	-0.14	-0.14	-0.06	0.13	-0.44

Fiscal year ended Dec. 31. Next earnings report expected: Early November. EPS Estimates based on S&P Operating Earnings; historical GAAP earnings are as reported.

Dividend Data

No cash dividends have been paid.

Please read the Required Disclosures and Analyst Certification on the last page of this report.

The McGraw·Hill Companies

American Tower Corp

Business Summary August 12, 2010

CORPORATE OVERVIEW. American Tower Corp. operates the largest independent portfolio of wireless communications and broadcast towers in North America, based on the number of towers and revenue. The company's primary business is leasing antenna space on multi-tenant communications towers to wireless service providers and radio and television broadcast companies. The tower portfolio provides AMT with a recurring base of leased revenues from its customers and growth potential to add more tenants and equipment to these towers from its unused capacity. AMT also continues to expand its operations in Mexico, Brazil, and India, and plans to close on the acquisition of 4,450 towers in India in the third quarter.

PRIMARY BUSINESS DYNAMICS. Rental and management of the antenna sites is AMT's principal business, and accounted for 97% of revenue in the second quarter of 2010. AMT operated a tower portfolio of about 28,035 multi-user sites in the U.S., Mexico, Brazil, and India, as of June 30, 2010. The company signs service providers to long-term leases of usually five to 10 years that contain annual lease rate escalations of 3%-5%. Sprint Nextel, AT&T Wireless, and Verizon Wireless accounted for roughly 52% of AMT's 2009 tower revenue, putting AMT in a prime position for further market expansion projects, in our view. AMT could also benefit from increased data usage that

will require service providers to add capacity to cell sites, as well as from carriers that expand their networks. Carriers such as Leap Wireless, MetroPCS, and Clearwire are currently expanding their networks, and we believe this will boost growth. In addition, U.S. carriers spent close to $20 billion on 700MHz spectrum, and we believe they will use the spectrum to deploy 4G service starting in 2010 and continuing for several years.

International growth should benefit AMT in 2010, by our analysis. AMT has about 2,616 wireless towers and approximately 199 broadcast towers in Mexico, about 1,640 wireless towers in Brazil, approximately 2,871 sites in India, and 113 sites in Chile. Mexico, Brazil, and India accounted for roughly 15% of revenue in 2009. We expect Mexico and Brazil to conduct 3G spectrum auctions in 2010 and then to deploy 3G networks. We think these markets will continue to provide significant growth, as we believe they are also seeing significant data growth, which could lead to additional capacity requirements.

Company Financials Fiscal Year Ended Dec. 31

Per Share Data ($)	2009	2008	2007	2006	2005	2004	2003	2002	2001	2000
Tangible Book Value	NM	NM	2.41	0.88	0.74	NM	0.28	NM	1.94	2.06
Cash Flow	1.60	1.83	1.41	1.28	0.92	0.40	0.34	0.01	-0.05	0.55
Earnings	0.59	0.58	0.22	0.06	-0.44	-1.07	-1.17	-1.61	-2.35	-1.13
S&P Core Earnings	0.59	0.58	0.20	0.05	-0.50	-1.17	-1.35	-1.60	-2.50	NA
Dividends	Nil	Nil	Nil	Nil	Nil	Nil	Nil	Nil	Nil	Nil
Payout Ratio	Nil	Nil	Nil	Nil	Nil	Nil	Nil	Nil	Nil	Nil
Prices:High	43.84	46.10	46.53	38.74	28.33	18.75	12.00	10.40	41.50	55.50
Prices:Low	25.45	19.35	36.34	26.66	16.28	9.89	3.55	0.60	5.25	27.63
P/E Ratio:High	74	79	NM	NM	NM	NM	NM	NM	NM	NM
P/E Ratio:Low	43	33	NM	NM	NM	NM	NM	NM	NM	NM

Income Statement Analysis (Million $)	2009	2008	2007	2006	2005	2004	2003	2002	2001	2000
Revenue	1,724	1,594	1,457	1,317	945	707	715	788	1,134	735
Operating Income	NA	1,020	898	803	589	423	377	312	251	196
Depreciation	415	527	510	528	411	329	313	317	440	283
Interest Expense	250	254	240	217	224	264	280	257	309	186
Pretax Income	422	372	153	70.9	-130	-317	-305	-248	-567	-250
Effective Tax Rate	43.3%	36.4%	39.1%	58.9%	NM	NM	NM	NM	NM	NM
Net Income	238	236	92.7	28.3	-134	-239	-242	-315	-450	-190
S&P Core Earnings	238	236	85.6	24.6	-154	-261	-281	-313	-480	NA

Balance Sheet & Other Financial Data (Million $)	2009	2008	2007	2006	2005	2004	2003	2002	2001	2000
Cash	257	145	94.0	281	113	216	105	127	130	128
Current Assets	651	474	246	486	226	309	412	536	522	471
Total Assets	8,513	8,212	8,130	8,613	8,768	5,086	5,332	5,662	6,830	5,661
Current Liabilities	391	303	317	570	453	332	295	670	343	298
Long Term Debt	4,141	4,331	4,240	3,289	3,451	3,155	3,284	3,195	3,549	2,457
Common Equity	3,315	2,991	3,022	4,382	4,527	1,464	1,706	1,740	2,869	2,877
Total Capital	7,530	7,326	7,309	7,678	7,988	4,626	5,008	4,950	6,433	5,350
Capital Expenditures	250	243	154	127	88.6	42.2	61.6	180	568	549
Cash Flow	653	763	603	556	277	90.2	71.0	2.11	-9.72	93.1
Current Ratio	1.7	1.6	0.8	0.9	0.5	0.9	1.4	0.8	1.5	1.6
% Long Term Debt of Capitalization	55.0	59.1	58.6	42.9	43.2	68.2	65.6	64.5	55.2	45.9
% Net Income of Revenue	13.8	14.8	6.4	2.2	NM	NM	NM	NM	NM	NM
% Return on Assets	2.9	2.9	1.1	0.3	NM	NM	NM	NM	NM	NM
% Return on Equity	7.6	7.9	2.5	0.6	NM	NM	NM	NM	NM	NM

Data as orig reptd.; bef. results of disc opers/spec. items. Per share data adj. for stk. divs.; EPS diluted. E-Estimated. NA-Not Available. NM-Not Meaningful. NR-Not Ranked. UR-Under Review.

Office: 116 Huntington Avenue, Boston, MA 02116.
Telephone: 617-375-7500.
Email: ir@americantower.com
Website: http://www.americantower.com

Chrmn, Pres & CEO: J.D. Taiclet, Jr.
COO: W.H. Hess
EVP & CFO: T.A. Bartlett
EVP, Chief Admin Officer, Secy & General Counsel: E. DiSanto

SVP, Chief Acctg Officer & Cntlr: R.J. Meyer, Jr.
Investor Contact: M. Powell (617-375-7500)
Board Members: G. L. Cantu, R. P. Dolan, R. Dykes, C. F. Katz, J. A. Reed, P. D. Reeve, D. E. Sharbutt, J. D. Taiclet, Jr., S. L. Thompson

Founded: 1995
Domicile: Delaware
Employees: 1,420

Ameriprise Financial Inc

STANDARD &POOR'S

S&P Recommendation HOLD ★★★☆☆	Price $51.02 (as of Oct 22, 2010)	12-Mo. Target Price $45.00	Investment Style Large-Cap Growth

GICS Sector Financials
Sub-Industry Asset Management & Custody Banks

Summary This diversified financial services company, spun off from American Express in September 2005, provides insurance, investment and asset management services.

Key Stock Statistics (Source S&P, Vickers, company reports)

52-Wk Range	$52.10–34.14	S&P Oper. EPS 2010**E**	4.06	Market Capitalization(B)	$12.809	Beta	2.03
Trailing 12-Month EPS	$3.68	S&P Oper. EPS 2011**E**	4.93	Yield (%)	1.41	S&P 3-Yr. Proj. EPS CAGR(%)	21
Trailing 12-Month P/E	13.9	P/E on S&P Oper. EPS 2010**E**	12.6	Dividend Rate/Share	$0.72	S&P Credit Rating	A
$10K Invested 5 Yrs Ago	$16,214	Common Shares Outstg. (M)	251.0	Institutional Ownership (%)	91		

Price Performance

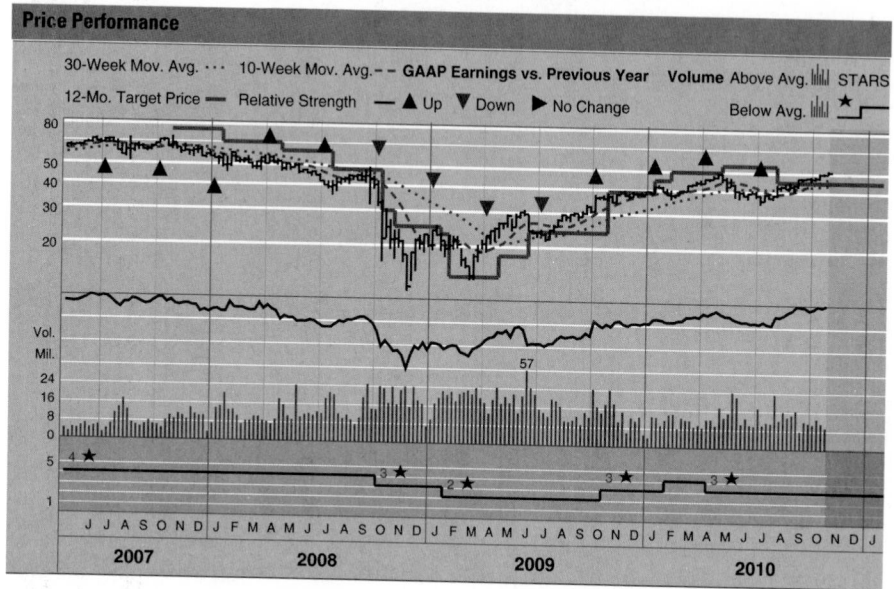

30-Week Mov. Avg. ··· 10-Week Mov. Avg. - - GAAP Earnings vs. Previous Year   Volume Above Avg. STARS
12-Mo. Target Price — Relative Strength   ▲ Up ▼ Down ▶ No Change   Below Avg. ★

Options: ASE, CBOE, P, Ph

Analysis prepared by **Matthew Albrecht** on July 30, 2010, when the stock traded at **$ 42.98.**

Highlights

▶ The recent Columbia Management acquisition is already helping the top line, and we think asset management and advice fees will grow nearly 40% this year. While we think relative fund performance has improved somewhat, sales trends remain uneven, particularly for domestic mutual funds. Variable annuity sales are helping to offset outflows from the fixed annuity business, which have been hurt by low interest rates, and sales of life, auto and home insurance products continue to improve. We expect revenues to rise more than 25% in 2010, helped by the acquisition, before more modest growth in 2011.

▶ We think the pretax margin will expand in 2010 despite rising distribution costs, as revenue growth outpaces the growth of core operating costs. We see further margin expansion in 2011 on efficiencies from the Columbia deal and revenue growth. We look for higher amortization of deferred acquisition costs too, though well below peak levels seen in 2008.

▶ We estimate EPS of $4.06 for 2010 and $4.93 for 2011.

Investment Rationale/Risk

▶ We believe AMP's focus on insurance products merits a lower valuation than some other asset managers. In our view, a rebound in client assets and improving relative fund performance should help average asset balances grow. We remain cautious on its investment portfolio, which includes residential and commercial mortgage securities and corporate debt and other asset-backed security holdings, but its outlook has improved. Asset balances are recovering, clients are re-engaging, and the Columbia acquisition should prove favorable to revenues and margins, but its valuation is appropriate.

▶ Risks to our recommendation and target price include potential market depreciation and greater regulatory concerns.

▶ AMP recently traded at 10.4X our 2010 EPS estimate, a discount to asset management peers. We expect the shares to trade at a peer discount due to AMP's revenue mix, with more reliance on insurance and annuity products. Our 12-month target price of $45 is equal to 9.5X our forward 12-month earnings estimate of $4.73.

Qualitative Risk Assessment

LOW	MEDIUM	HIGH

Our risk assessment reflects our view of the company's significant franchise value, offset by our concerns that the loss of the widely recognized American Express name could negatively affect AMP's ability to raise and retain client assets.

Quantitative Evaluations

S&P Quality Ranking   NR

D	C	B-	B	B+	A-	A	A+

Relative Strength Rank   STRONG

80

LOWEST = 1   HIGHEST = 99

Revenue/Earnings Data

Revenue (Million $)

	1Q	2Q	3Q	4Q	Year
2010	2,292	2,597	--	--	--
2009	1,716	1,874	1,946	2,269	7,946
2008	2,000	1,979	1,641	1,350	7,149
2007	2,096	2,204	2,227	2,319	8,909
2006	1,949	2,053	1,977	2,161	8,140
2005	1,847	1,895	1,873	1,869	7,484

Earnings Per Share ($)

	1Q	2Q	3Q	4Q	Year
2010	0.81	0.98	E1.05	E1.22	E4.06
2009	0.58	0.41	1.00	0.90	2.95
2008	0.82	0.93	-0.32	-1.69	-0.17
2007	0.68	0.81	0.83	1.08	3.39
2006	0.57	0.57	0.71	0.69	2.54
2005	0.71	0.61	0.50	0.44	2.26

Fiscal year ended Dec. 31. Next earnings report expected: NA. EPS Estimates based on S&P Operating Earnings; historical GAAP earnings are as reported.

Dividend Data (Dates: mm/dd Payment Date: mm/dd/yy)

Amount ($)	Date Decl.	Ex-Div. Date	Stk. of Record	Payment Date
0.170	10/21	10/29	11/02	11/16/09
0.170	02/03	02/10	02/12	02/26/10
0.180	04/26	05/05	05/07	05/21/10
0.180	07/28	08/04	08/06	08/20/10

Dividends have been paid since 2005. Source: Company reports.

Please read the Required Disclosures and Analyst Certification on the last page of this report.

The McGraw-Hill Companies

Ameriprise Financial Inc

Business Summary July 30, 2010

CORPORATE OVERVIEW. Ameriprise Financial completed its spinoff from American Express on September 30, 2005, and began trading on the New York Stock Exchange on October 3 under the symbol AMP. As of December 31, 2009, Ameriprise owned, managed and administered $458 billion of client assets and operated a network of more than 12,000 financial advisers. Ameriprise offers a broad assortment of products, including mutual funds, annuities and life insurance products. Ameriprise was originally named Investors Diversified Services before it was acquired by American Express in 1984. We think AMP will need to prove that it can grow and prosper without the benefits of its previous owner, American Express, which spun off the company in 2005. We believe the spinoff and marketing campaign have raised AMP's visibility among prospective clients and may also help attract and retain financial advisers. In terms of corporate governance, we view favorably the high proportion of independent directors on the board, but we would prefer that the company split the roles of chairman and CEO.

Ameriprise has five operating segments. Advice and Wealth Management (41% of net revenues in 2009, pretax loss) provides financial advice and full-service brokerage and banking services, primarily to retail clients, through its financial advisers. The Asset Management segment (18%, $60 million of pretax earnings) provides investment advice and investment products to retail and institutional clients. Threadneedle Investments predominantly provides international investment products and services, and RiverSource Investments predominantly provides products and services in the U.S. for domestic customers. Its domestic products are primarily distributed through the Advice and Wealth Management segment and third parties, while international products are mostly distributed through third parties. The Annuities segment (29%, $648 million of pretax earnings) provides RiverSource Life variable and fixed annuity products to retail clients, primarily through the Advice and Wealth Management segment. The Protection segment (25%, $496 million of pretax earnings) offers a variety of protection products to address the identified protection and risk management needs of retail clients including life, disability income and property-casualty insurance. The Corporate and Other segment consists of net investment income on corporate level assets, including unallocated equity and other revenues from various investments as well as unallocated corporate expenses. This segment, including intersegment eliminations, reduced net revenues by over $1 billion and incurred a pretax loss in 2009.

Company Financials Fiscal Year Ended Dec. 31

Per Share Data ($)	2009	2008	2007	2006	2005	2004	2003	2002	2001	2000
Tangible Book Value	30.75	22.41	34.81	31.10	30.75	6.45	NA	NA	NA	NA
Cash Flow	3.45	-0.74	4.11	3.21	2.26	NA	4.01	NA	NA	NA
Earnings	2.95	-0.17	3.39	2.54	2.26	2.80	3.00	NA	NA	NA
S&P Core Earnings	2.92	1.98	3.26	2.41	2.37	3.02	2.46	NA	NA	NA
Dividends	0.68	0.64	0.56	0.44	0.11	NA	NA	NA	NA	NA
Payout Ratio	23%	NM	17%	17%	5%	NA	NA	NA	NA	NA
Prices:High	40.00	57.55	69.25	55.79	44.78	NA	NA	NA	NA	NA
Prices:Low	13.50	11.74	51.31	40.30	32.00	NA	NA	NA	NA	NA
P/E Ratio:High	14	NM	20	22	20	NA	NA	NA	NA	NA
P/E Ratio:Low	5	NM	15	16	14	NA	NA	NA	NA	NA

Income Statement Analysis (Million $)	2009	2008	2007	2006	2005	2004	2003	2002	2001	2000
Income Interest	2,704	2,899	3,238	2,204	2,241	2,125	NA	NA	NA	NA
Income Other	5,242	4,250	5,671	5,936	5,243	4,645	NA	NA	NA	NA
Total Income	7,946	7,149	8,909	8,140	7,484	6,770	6,361	5,793	NA	NA
General Expenses	6,758	7,028	7,353	7,343	6,739	5,756	NA	NA	NA	NA
Interest Expense	268	288	367	116	73.0	78.0	NA	NA	NA	NA
Depreciation	120	204	173	166	164	NA	NA	NA	NA	NA
Net Income	722	-38.0	814	631	556	708	738	674	NA	NA
S&P Core Earnings	715	440	784	599	588	762	622	NA	NA	NA

Balance Sheet & Other Financial Data (Million $)	2009	2008	2007	2006	2005	2004	2003	2002	2001	2000
Cash	3,097	6,729	7,037	4,775	2,474	3,319	1,869	NA	NA	NA
Receivables	4,435	3,887	7,244	6,668	2,172	2,526	NA	NA	NA	NA
Cost of Investments	36,974	27,522	30,625	35,553	39,100	40,157	NA	NA	NA	NA
Total Assets	113,774	95,689	109,230	104,172	93,121	90,934	85,384	NA	NA	NA
Loss Reserve	Nil	Nil	Nil	Nil	Nil	Nil	NA	NA	NA	NA
Short Term Debt	Nil	Nil	Nil	Nil	Nil	Nil	NA	NA	NA	NA
Capitalization:Debt	2,249	2,027	2,018	2,225	1,833	1,878	NA	NA	NA	NA
Capitalization:Equity	9,273	6,191	7,810	7,925	7,687	8,058	7,288	NA	NA	NA
Capitalization:Total	12,125	8,218	9,828	10,150	9,520	9,936	NA	NA	NA	NA
Price Times Book Value:High	1.3	2.6	2.0	1.7	1.5	NA	NA	NA	NA	NA
Price Times Book Value:Low	0.4	0.5	1.5	1.2	1.0	NA	NA	NA	NA	NA
Cash Flow	842	166	987	759	556	NA	987	855	NA	NA
% Expense/Operating Revenue	88.4	105.2	88.6	90.2	90.0	86.2	NA	NA	NA	NA
% Earnings & Depreciation/Assets	0.8	0.2	0.9	0.1	0.1	NA	NA	NA	NA	NA

Data as orig reptd.; bef. results of disc opers/spec. items. Per share data adj. for stk. divs.; EPS diluted. E-Estimated. NA-Not Available. NM-Not Meaningful. NR-Not Ranked. UR-Under Review.

Office: 55 Ameriprise Financial Center, Minneapolis, MN 55474.
Telephone: 612-671-3131.
Website: http://www.ameriprise.com
Chrmn & CEO: J. Cracchiolo

EVP & CFO: W. Berman
EVP & General Counsel: J.C. Junek
SVP, Chief Acctg Officer & Cntlr: D.K. Stewart
SVP & Treas: J. Hamalainen

Investor Contact: L. Gagnon (612-671-2080)
Board Members: J. Cracchiolo, W. D. Knowlton, W. W. Lewis, S. S. Marshall, J. Noddle, H. Sarles, R. F. Sharpe, Jr., W. H. Turner
Founded: 1983
Domicile: Delaware
Employees: 9,793

AmerisourceBergen Corp

S&P Recommendation BUY ★★★★☆	

Price	**12-Mo. Target Price**	**Investment Style**
$32.06 (as of Oct 22, 2010)	$36.00	Large-Cap Blend

GICS Sector Health Care
Sub-Industry Health Care Distributors

Summary This distributor of pharmaceutical products and related health care services was formed via the August 2001 merger of Amerisource Health Corp. and Bergen Brunswig Corp.

Key Stock Statistics (Source S&P, Vickers, company reports)

52-Wk Range	$33.27– 22.07	S&P Oper. EPS 2010**E**	2.12	Market Capitalization(B)	$8.940	Beta	0.64
Trailing 12-Month EPS	$2.16	S&P Oper. EPS 2011**E**	2.35	Yield (%)	1.00	S&P 3-Yr. Proj. EPS CAGR(%)	14
Trailing 12-Month P/E	14.8	P/E on S&P Oper. EPS 2010**E**	15.1	Dividend Rate/Share	$0.32	S&P Credit Rating	BBB+
$10K Invested 5 Yrs Ago	NA	Common Shares Outstg. (M)	278.8	Institutional Ownership (%)	93		

Price Performance

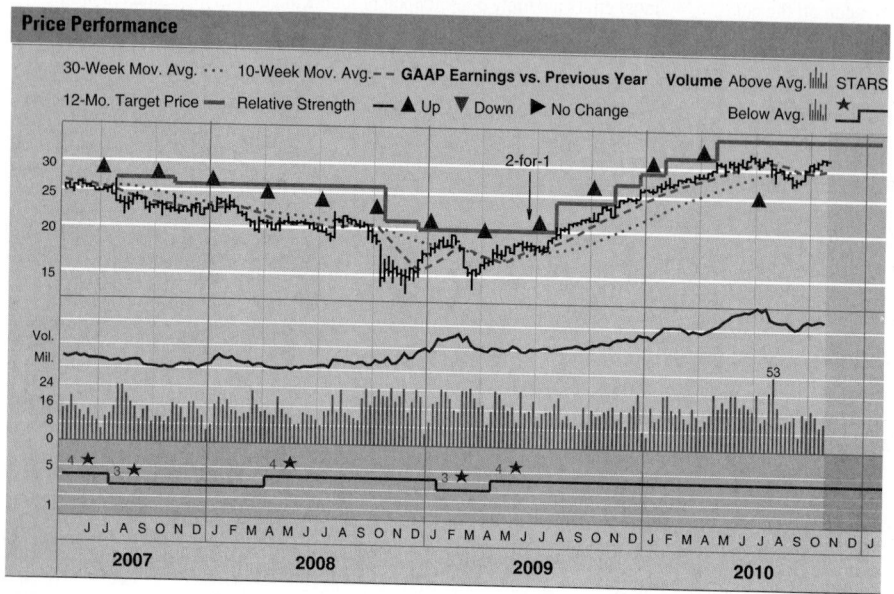

30-Week Mov. Avg. · · ·   10-Week Mov. Avg. – –   **GAAP Earnings vs. Previous Year**   Volume Above Avg. | STARS
12-Mo. Target Price —   Relative Strength —   ▲ Up   ▼ Down   ► No Change   Below Avg. | ★

Options: ASE, CBOE, P

Analysis prepared by **Herman B. Saftlas** on July 30, 2010, when the stock traded at **$ 29.91**.

Highlights

➤ We project revenue growth in FY 11 (Sep.) will slow to about 5%, from the 8% advance we forecast for FY 10, largely reflecting expected lower sales of generic Eloxatin (adversely affected by a recent litigation settlement), partly offset by sales of new generic versions of Lovenox and Gemzar. We see ABC's sales growth continuing to outpace the overall market, helped by new business, strong demand from ABC's largest customers, and generic drug launch timing.

➤ We see operating margins widening slightly on the positive impacts from generic drug and specialty drug penetration, increased fees from brand-name drug makers, and operating expense control. In our opinion, these positive factors should more than outweigh ABC's incremental spending on its enterprise resource planning software implementation.

➤ We estimate FY 11 operating EPS of $2.35, up from $2.12 indicated for FY 10 (excluding a $0.05 gain from the settlement of antitrust litigation). EPS comparisons should also benefit from share buybacks.

Investment Rationale/Risk

➤ We believe ABC has shown the resiliency to manage through this period of economic weakness and we expect it, like its peers, to benefit from health care reform. We also believe it has the wherewithal to hold its own and likely gain share in the competitive drug distribution market over the long haul. The company controls costs tightly, in our opinion, and we remain positive about its focus on generic and oncology drugs, which we view as among the fastest-growing and most profitable revenue drivers in the pharmaceutical market. In addition, ABC views acquisitions as a key part of its growth strategy, and we believe it has the cash flow and balance sheet needed for such transactions.

➤ Risks to our opinion and target price include intensified competition and loss of one or more major clients. Possible changes in Medicare Part D could also affect the business.

➤ Our 12-month target price of $36 applies a modest premium-to-peers multiple of 15.3X to our $2.35 EPS estimate for FY 11. Using a PEG ratio of 1.1, assuming a three-year EPS CAGR of 14%, we derive a P/E of 15.4X, also yielding a value of $36.

Qualitative Risk Assessment

LOW	MEDIUM	HIGH

Our risk assessment reflects what we view as ABC's improving financial performance, its ability to attract new accounts to more than compensate for account losses, and its healthy operating cash flow. However, we think the drug distribution arena is highly competitive, and that ABC is less diversified than many of its large health care distribution peers.

Quantitative Evaluations

S&P Quality Ranking   A-

D	C	B-	B	B+	A-	A	A+

Relative Strength Rank   MODERATE

60

LOWEST = 1   HIGHEST = 99

Revenue/Earnings Data

Revenue (Million $)

	1Q	2Q	3Q	4Q	Year
2010	19,336	19,301	19,602	--	--
2009	17,338	17,312	18,394	18,716	71,760
2008	17,279	17,756	17,997	17,158	70,190
2007	16,725	16,513	16,446	16,390	66,074
2006	14,653	15,221	15,686	15,643	61,203
2005	13,639	13,192	13,832	13,918	54,577

Earnings Per Share ($)

	1Q	2Q	3Q	4Q	Year
2010	0.52	0.63	0.57	E0.45	E2.12
2009	0.37	0.48	0.42	0.44	1.69
2008	0.33	0.41	0.35	0.37	1.45
2007	0.32	0.34	0.35	0.32	1.32
2006	0.24	0.31	0.29	0.31	1.13
2005	0.17	0.23	0.24	0.05	0.69

Fiscal year ended Sep. 30. Next earnings report expected: Early November. EPS Estimates based on S&P Operating Earnings; historical GAAP earnings are as reported.

Dividend Data (Dates: mm/dd Payment Date: mm/dd/yy)

Amount ($)	Date Decl.	Ex-Div. Date	Stk. of Record	Payment Date
0.080	11/12	11/19	11/23	12/07/09
0.080	01/27	02/10	02/12	03/01/10
0.080	05/13	05/20	05/24	06/07/10
0.080	08/12	08/20	08/24	09/07/10

Dividends have been paid since 2001. Source: Company reports.

STANDARD
&POOR'S

AmerisourceBergen Corp

Business Summary July 30, 2010

CORPORATE OVERVIEW. AmerisourceBergen Corp., one of the largest U.S. pharmaceutical distributors, began operation in August 2001, following the merger of Amerisource Health Corp. and Bergen Brunswig Corp. ABC accounted for the merger as an acquisition by Amerisource of Bergen.

The pharmaceutical distribution segment includes the AmerisourceBergen Drug Corporation (ABDC), AmerisourceBergen Specialty Group (ABSG) and the AmerisourceBergen Packaging Group (ABPG). ABDC distributes branded and generic pharmaceuticals, over-the-counter health care products, and home health care supplies and equipment to hospitals, pharmacies, mail order facilities, clinics, and alternate site facilities. ABSG ($15.6 billion of operating revenue in FY 09 (Sep.), versus $14.6 billion in FY 08) supplies goods and services to physicians and alternate care providers that specialize in disease states, such as oncology. ABPG repackages drugs from bulk to unit dose, unit of use, blister pack and standard bottle sizes.

National and retail drugstore chains, independent community drugstores, and pharmacy departments of supermarkets and mass merchandisers account for its retail market segment (32% of FY 09 total revenue), while the hospital/acute care, mail order and specialty pharmaceuticals markets together comprise its institutional market segment (68%). Revenues generated from sales to pharmacy benefit manager Medco Health Solutions (MHS) accounted for 17% of its total revenue in FY 09.

The "Other" segment is PharMerica's workers' compensation-related business, which provides pharmacy services to chronically and catastrophically ill patients under workers' comp programs, and provides pharmaceutical claims administration services for payors. On July 31, 2007, ABC spun off the PharMerica segment's long-term care business, a national dispenser of pharmaceutical products and services to patients in long-term care facilities. In October 2008, it sold the workers' comp business, which had total revenues and a loss before income taxes of about $404 million and $216 million, respectively in FY 08.

Company Financials Fiscal Year Ended Sep. 30

Per Share Data ($)	2009	2008	2007	2006	2005	2004	2003	2002	2001	2000
Tangible Book Value	NM	NM	0.03	3.96	3.69	4.31	3.61	2.61	0.90	1.20
Cash Flow	1.99	1.70	1.59	1.36	0.87	1.18	1.10	0.90	0.58	0.55
Earnings	1.69	1.45	1.32	1.13	0.69	1.02	0.97	0.79	0.52	0.48
S&P Core Earnings	1.70	1.41	1.23	1.04	0.62	0.78	0.93	0.76	0.42	NA
Dividends	0.21	0.15	0.10	0.05	0.03	0.03	0.03	0.03	Nil	Nil
Payout Ratio	12%	10%	8%	4%	4%	2%	3%	3%	Nil	Nil
Prices:High	26.58	24.30	28.28	24.48	21.09	16.00	18.36	20.71	18.00	13.42
Prices:Low	13.75	13.33	21.11	20.08	13.24	12.44	11.41	12.55	10.03	3.00
P/E Ratio:High	16	17	22	22	31	16	19	26	34	28
P/E Ratio:Low	8	9	16	18	19	12	12	16	19	6

Income Statement Analysis (Million $)	2009	2008	2007	2006	2005	2004	2003	2002	2001	2000
Revenue	71,760	70,190	66,074	61,203	54,577	53,179	49,657	45,235	16,191	11,645
Operating Income	992	919	912	814	723	978	963	804	302	217
Depreciation	90.0	82.1	104	96.9	81.2	87.1	71.0	61.2	21.6	16.1
Interest Expense	63.5	75.1	32.0	12.5	57.2	113	145	141	45.7	41.9
Pretax Income	824	761	7.85	741	469	760	726	572	202	160
Effective Tax Rate	37.9%	38.4%	37.1%	36.8%	37.7%	38.4%	39.2%	39.7%	38.6%	38.0%
Net Income	512	469	494	468	292	468	441	345	124	99.0
S&P Core Earnings	513	456	462	429	264	356	421	333	99.8	NA

Balance Sheet & Other Financial Data (Million $)	2009	2008	2007	2006	2005	2004	2003	2002	2001	2000
Cash	1,009	878	640	1,261	1,316	871	800	663	298	121
Current Assets	9,954	8,670	8,714	9,210	7,988	8,295	8,859	8,350	7,513	2,321
Total Assets	13,573	12,153	12,310	12,784	11,381	11,654	12,040	11,213	10,291	2,459
Current Liabilities	9,480	8,168	7,857	7,459	6,052	6,104	6,256	6,100	5,532	1,751
Long Term Debt	1,177	1,187	1,227	1,094	951	1,157	1,723	1,756	1,872	413
Common Equity	2,716	2,710	3,100	4,141	4,280	4,339	4,005	3,316	5,677	565
Total Capital	3,894	3,899	4,327	5,235	5,232	5,496	5,728	5,073	7,549	978
Capital Expenditures	146	137	118	113	203	189	90.6	64.2	23.4	16.6
Cash Flow	602	551	598	565	373	555	512	406	145	115
Current Ratio	1.1	1.1	1.1	1.2	1.3	1.4	1.4	1.4	1.4	1.3
% Long Term Debt of Capitalization	30.2	30.5	28.3	20.9	18.2	21.1	30.1	34.6	24.8	42.3
% Net Income of Revenue	0.7	0.7	0.7	0.8	0.5	0.9	0.9	0.8	0.8	0.9
% Return on Assets	4.0	3.8	3.9	3.9	2.5	4.0	3.8	3.2	1.9	4.4
% Return on Equity	18.9	16.2	13.6	11.1	6.8	11.2	12.1	11.2	4.0	22.1

Data as orig reptd.; bef. results of disc opers/spec. items. Per share data adj. for stk. divs.; EPS diluted. E-Estimated. NA-Not Available. NM-Not Meaningful. NR-Not Ranked. UR-Under Review.

Office: 1300 Morris Drive, Chesterbrook, PA 19087-5594.
Telephone: 610-727-7000.
Email: investorrelations@amerisourcebergen.com
Website: http://www.amerisourcebergen.com

Chrmn: R.C. Gozon
Pres & CEO: R.D. Yost
COO: D. Shane
EVP, CFO & Chief Acctg Officer: M.D. Dicandilo

SVP, Secy & General Counsel: J.G. Chou
Board Members: C. H. Cotros, R. W. Gochnauer, R. C. Gozon, E. E. Hagenlocker, J. E. Henney, K. W. Hyle, M. J. Long, H. W. McGee, R. D. Yost

Founded: 1985
Domicile: Delaware
Employees: 10,300

Amgen Inc

STANDARD &POOR'S

S&P Recommendation BUY ★★★★☆

Price	12-Mo. Target Price	Investment Style
$57.55 (as of Oct 22, 2010)	$66.00	Large-Cap Growth

GICS Sector Health Care
Sub-Industry Biotechnology

Summary Amgen, among the world's leading biotech companies, has major treatments for anemia, neutropenia, rheumatoid arthritis, psoriatic arthritis, psoriasis, cancer and osteoporosis.

Key Stock Statistics (Source S&P, Vickers, company reports)

52-Wk Range	$61.26– 50.26	S&P Oper. EPS 2010E	5.01	Market Capitalization(B)	$55.160	Beta	0.43
Trailing 12-Month EPS	$4.71	S&P Oper. EPS 2011E	5.27	Yield (%)	Nil	S&P 3-Yr. Proj. EPS CAGR(%)	10
Trailing 12-Month P/E	12.2	P/E on S&P Oper. EPS 2010E	11.5	Dividend Rate/Share	Nil	S&P Credit Rating	A+
$10K Invested 5 Yrs Ago	$7,844	Common Shares Outstg. (M)	958.5	Institutional Ownership (%)	79		

Price Performance

30-Week Mov. Avg. · · · · 10-Week Mov. Avg. - - **GAAP Earnings vs. Previous Year** **Volume** Above Avg. | STARS
12-Mo. Target Price — Relative Strength — ▲ Up ▼ Down ► No Change Below Avg. | ★

Options: ASE, CBOE, P, Ph

Analysis prepared by **Steven Silver** on October 14, 2010, when the stock traded at **$ 54.89**.

Highlights

➤ We forecast 2010 revenues of $14.9 billion, 2% above 2009's $14.6 billion, and 2011 revenues of $15.4 billion, which would represent 3% growth. We see growth driven by the launch of Prolia in the U.S. and in Europe, more than offsetting higher Medicaid rebates resulting from U.S. health care reform. We see AMGN managing the impacts of declining Aranesp sales over regulatory safety restrictions, and slowing Enbrel growth due to increased competition. Over the long term, we expect expanded indications for cancer drug Vectibix to renew sales growth in that franchise.

➤ We expect 2010 and 2011 adjusted operating margins of approximately 40%, in line with recent results. We see AMGN as having long-term expense leverage to support EPS amid revenue instability, although we anticipate higher costs in the near term, particularly in SG&A, due to the launch of Prolia.

➤ We estimate adjusted EPS of $5.01 in 2010 and $5.27 in 2011, excluding acquisition and restructuring expenses. We anticipate AMGN aggressively repurchasing shares, deploying its robust cash flows.

Investment Rationale/Risk

➤ Despite near-term headwinds due to U.S. health care reform and volatile foreign exchange rates, we have a favorable outlook for Prolia, as we see its recent approval for post-menopausal osteoporosis in Europe and the U.S. shifting investor focus to AMGN's long-term pipeline. We do, however, see AMGN being reliant on Prolia adoption, given our view of modest growth prospects to AMGN's mature core product roster. Ultimately, we expect Prolia to be approved for several cancer-induced bone loss conditions, and we forecast more than $2 billion in peak sales. With $14.5 billion in cash, we see AMGN as well funded to support earnings growth through share repurchases and acquiring new growth assets.

➤ Risks to our recommendation and target price include failure to gain market acceptance for Prolia and regulatory approval in expanded cancer uses, further regulatory restrictions on anemia drug sales, and increased competition.

➤ Our 12-month target price of $66 applies a 12.5X multiple to our 2011 adjusted EPS estimate, a discount to the large-cap sector peer average, on our view of a slowing growth profile.

Qualitative Risk Assessment

LOW	MEDIUM	HIGH

Our risk assessment reflects that the company's products are sold in highly competitive markets and are subject to government regulation. Changes to government reimbursement policies could significantly affect AMGN's revenues and profitability. Although adoption has been mild thus far, we believe that generic versions of several of AMGN's drugs pose a long-term threat in Europe.

Quantitative Evaluations

S&P Quality Ranking B+

D	C	B-	B	B+	A-	A	A+

Relative Strength Rank MODERATE

59

LOWEST = 1   HIGHEST = 99

Revenue/Earnings Data

Revenue (Million $)

	1Q	2Q	3Q	4Q	Year
2010	3,592	3,804	--	--	--
2009	3,308	3,713	3,812	3,809	14,642
2008	3,613	3,764	3,875	3,751	15,003
2007	3,687	3,728	3,611	3,745	14,771
2006	3,217	3,491	3,503	3,737	14,268
2005	2,833	3,172	3,154	3,271	12,430

Earnings Per Share ($)

2010	1.18	1.25	E1.24	E1.15	E5.01
2009	0.98	1.25	1.36	0.92	4.51
2008	1.04	0.87	1.09	0.91	3.90
2007	0.94	0.90	0.18	0.77	2.82
2006	0.82	0.01	0.94	0.71	2.48
2005	0.67	0.82	0.77	0.66	2.93

Fiscal year ended Dec. 31. Next earnings report expected: NA. EPS Estimates based on S&P Operating Earnings; historical GAAP earnings are as reported.

Dividend Data

No cash dividends have been paid.

Please read the Required Disclosures and Analyst Certification on the last page of this report.

The McGraw·Hill Companies

STANDARD &POOR'S

Amgen Inc

Business Summary October 14, 2010

CORPORATE OVERVIEW. Amgen, among the world's largest biotech companies, marketing five of the world's best-selling biotech drugs.

Epogen is a genetically engineered version of human erythropoietin (EPO), a hormone that stimulates red blood cell production in bone marrow. Its primary market is dialysis patients suffering from chronic anemia. Epogen sales were $2.57 billion in 2009 ($2.46 billion in 2008). Aranesp, a recombinant protein that stimulates the production of red blood cells in pre-dialysis and dialysis patients, is approved to treat anemia associated with chronic renal failure and cancer patients with chemotherapy-induced anemia (CIA).

Aranesp sales were $2.65 billion in 2009 ($3.14 billion in 2008). In 2007, Phase III trial data showed a higher rate of death when using Aranesp in treating anemia-of cancer (AoC) not associated with chemotherapy, an off-label prescribed use. Medicare removed AoC as a reimbursable use for Aranesp. During 2007, several studies emerged suggesting that Aranesp may foster tumor growth in several cancers when dosed at or above the approved 12 g/dl dose,

which has led to Medicare and FDA restrictions over its use.

Neupogen stimulates neutrophils (white blood cells that defend against bacterial infection) production in cancer patients whose natural neutrophils were destroyed by chemotherapy. In 2002, the FDA approved Neulasta, a long-acting white blood cell stimulant protecting chemo patients from infection. Total Neupogen and Neulasta 2009 sales were $4.64 billion ($4.66 billion in 2008).

Enbrel, acquired through the purchase of Immunex, (co-marketed with Wyeth) had 2009 sales of $3.49 billion ($3.60 billion in 2008) and is approved to treat rheumatoid arthritis (RA), psoriatic arthritis, and adults with moderate to severe chronic plaque psoriasis.

Company Financials Fiscal Year Ended Dec. 31

Per Share Data ($)	2009	2008	2007	2006	2005	2004	2003	2002	2001	2000
Tangible Book Value	8.81	5.79	3.03	3.36	5.08	4.08	4.06	2.80	4.99	4.16
Cash Flow	5.54	4.90	3.89	3.29	3.59	2.35	2.19	-0.82	1.28	1.24
Earnings	4.51	3.90	2.82	2.48	2.93	1.81	1.69	-1.21	1.03	1.05
S&P Core Earnings	4.50	4.08	2.74	2.48	2.77	1.58	1.50	-1.46	0.87	NA
Dividends	Nil	Nil	Nil	Nil	Nil	Nil	Nil	Nil	Nil	Nil
Payout Ratio	Nil	Nil	Nil	Nil	Nil	Nil	Nil	Nil	Nil	Nil
Prices:High	64.76	66.51	76.95	81.24	86.92	66.88	72.37	62.94	75.06	80.44
Prices:Low	44.96	39.16	46.21	63.52	56.19	52.00	48.09	30.57	45.44	50.00
P/E Ratio:High	14	17	27	33	30	37	43	NM	73	77
P/E Ratio:Low	10	10	16	26	19	29	28	NM	44	48

Income Statement Analysis (Million $)										
Revenue	14,642	15,003	14,771	14,268	12,430	10,550	8,356	5,523	4,016	3,629
Operating Income	6,658	6,726	6,631	6,022	5,689	4,636	3,758	2,501	2,003	1,761
Depreciation	1,049	1,073	1,202	963	841	734	686	447	266	212
Interest Expense	578	338	305	129	99.0	38.0	31.5	44.2	13.6	15.9
Pretax Income	5,204	5,250	3,961	4,020	4,868	3,395	3,173	-684	1,686	1,674
Effective Tax Rate	11.5%	20.1%	20.1%	26.6%	24.5%	30.4%	28.8%	NM	33.6%	32.0%
Net Income	4,605	4,196	3,166	2,950	3,674	2,363	2,260	-1,392	1,120	1,139
S&P Core Earnings	4,596	4,390	3,072	2,951	3,470	2,074	2,006	-1,683	936	NA

Balance Sheet & Other Financial Data (Million $)										
Cash	13,442	9,552	7,151	6,277	5,255	5,808	5,123	4,664	2,662	2,028
Current Assets	18,932	15,221	13,041	11,712	9,235	9,170	7,402	6,404	3,859	2,937
Total Assets	39,629	36,443	34,639	33,788	29,297	29,221	26,177	24,456	6,443	5,400
Current Liabilities	3,873	4,886	6,179	7,022	3,595	4,157	2,246	1,529	1,003	862
Long Term Debt	10,601	9,176	11,177	7,134	3,957	3,937	3,080	3,048	223	223
Common Equity	22,667	20,386	17,869	18,964	20,451	19,705	19,389	18,286	5,217	4,315
Total Capital	33,268	29,792	27,526	26,465	25,571	24,936	23,930	22,927	5,440	4,538
Capital Expenditures	530	672	1,267	1,218	867	1,336	1,357	658	442	438
Cash Flow	5,654	5,269	4,368	3,913	4,515	3,097	2,946	-945	1,386	1,350
Current Ratio	4.9	3.1	2.1	1.7	2.6	2.2	3.3	4.2	3.8	3.4
% Long Term Debt of Capitalization	31.9	30.8	33.9	27.0	15.5	15.8	12.9	13.3	4.1	4.9
% Net Income of Revenue	31.5	28.0	21.4	20.7	29.6	22.4	27.0	NM	27.9	31.4
% Return on Assets	12.1	11.8	9.3	9.4	12.6	8.5	8.9	NM	18.9	24.0
% Return on Equity	21.4	21.9	17.2	15.0	18.3	12.1	12.0	NM	23.5	31.0

Data as orig reptd.; bef. results of disc opers/spec. items. Per share data adj. for stk. divs.; EPS diluted. E-Estimated. NA-Not Available. NM-Not Meaningful. NR-Not Ranked. UR-Under Review.

Office: One Amgen Center Drive, Thousand Oaks, CA 91320-1799.
Telephone: 805-447-1000.
Email: investor.relations@amgen.com
Website: http://www.amgen.com

Chrmn & CEO: K.W. Sharer
Pres & COO: R.A. Bradway
SVP, Secy & General Counsel: D.J. Scott
SVP & CIO: T.J. Flanagan

CFO: J.M. Peacock
Investor Contact: A. Sood (805-447-1060)
Board Members: D. Baltimore, F. J. Biondi, Jr., J. D. Choate, V. D. Coffman, F. W. Gluck, R. M. Henderson, F. C. Herringer, G. S. Omenn, J. C. Pelham, J. P. Reason, L. D. Schaeffer, K. W. Sharer, R. D. Sugar, F. de Carbonnel

Founded: 1980
Domicile: Delaware
Employees: 17,200

The McGraw-Hill Companies

Amphenol Corp

STANDARD &POOR'S

S&P Recommendation BUY ★★★★★

Price $50.04 (as of Oct 25, 2010)

12-Mo. Target Price $63.00

Investment Style Large-Cap Growth

GICS Sector Information Technology
Sub-Industry Electronic Components

Summary This company makes connectors, cable, and interconnect systems for electronics, cable TV, telecommunications, aerospace, transportation, and industrial applications.

Key Stock Statistics (Source S&P, Vickers, company reports)

52-Wk Range	$50.44– 37.78	S&P Oper. EPS 2010**E**	2.70	Market Capitalization(B)	$8.693	Beta	1.40
Trailing 12-Month EPS	$2.58	S&P Oper. EPS 2011**E**	3.15	Yield (%)	0.12	S&P 3-Yr. Proj. EPS CAGR(%)	25
Trailing 12-Month P/E	19.4	P/E on S&P Oper. EPS 2010**E**	18.5	Dividend Rate/Share	$0.06	S&P Credit Rating	BBB-
$10K Invested 5 Yrs Ago	$24,772	Common Shares Outstg. (M)	173.7	Institutional Ownership (%)	93		

Price Performance

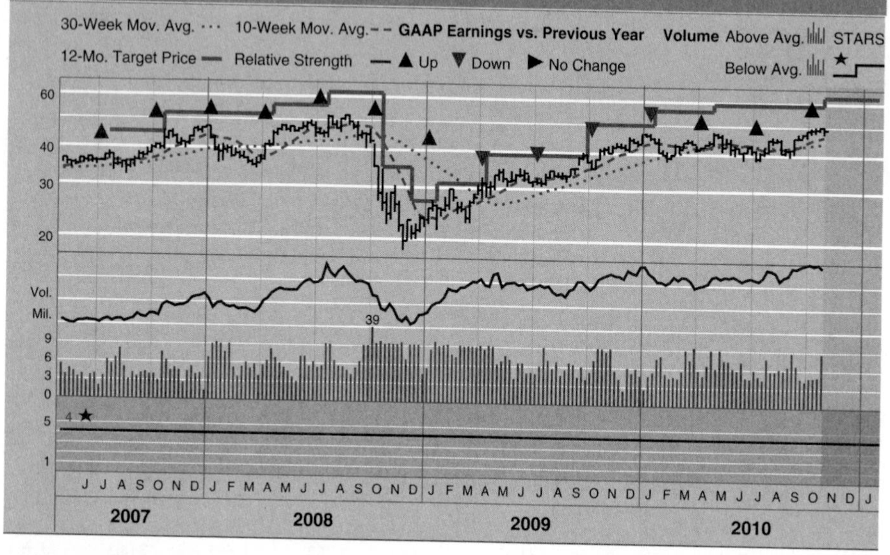
30-Week Mov. Avg. ···
10-Week Mov. Avg. – –
GAAP Earnings vs. Previous Year
Volume Above Avg.
STARS
12-Mo. Target Price
Relative Strength
▲ Up
▼ Down
▶ No Change
Below Avg.
60
40
30
20
Vol.
Mil.
39
9
6
3
0
5
4 ★
1
J J A S O N D J F M A M J J A S O N D J F M A M J J A S O N D J F M A M J J A S O N D J
2007
2008
2009
2010

Options: ASE, P, Ph

Analysis prepared by **Michael W. Jaffe** on October 25, 2010, when the stock traded at **$ 49.12**.

Highlights

- We forecast a 14% sales increase for 2011. Difficult economic conditions in the U.S., Western Europe, and elsewhere limited demand for APH's products for several quarters. However, on what now appear to be recovering U.S. and global economies, sales have revived over the past few quarters, and we see that trend continuing through 2011.
- We see the better sales trends that we forecast aiding margins in 2011. We also see profitability being assisted by APH's ongoing focus on proactive and aggressive cost controls. We expect these factors to outweigh the impact of higher commodity costs now being seen by Amphenol.
- APH's 32% year-to-year sales gain in 2010's third quarter reflected an ongoing upturn in demand in most of Amphenol's markets. Our forecast of continuing growth in 2011 sees APH's strongest gains continuing to come from military and aerospace, mobile devices and industrials markets. Our 2011 EPS forecast also compares with a 2010 period that excludes $0.11 of credits in the first nine months, with the one-time items related to tax benefits.

Investment Rationale/Risk

- We think the global economy has started to recover, and that Amphenol's business is in the midst of a revival. Moreover, we have a favorable outlook for APH's long-term prospects, on what we expect to be an ongoing expansion of the global communications infrastructure, increasing sophistication of military and space systems, and the use of more electronic devices in automobiles and other industrial products. Based on these factors and our relative P/E analysis, we view APH as undervalued.
- Risks to our recommendation and target price include a reversal of the recent improvement in global economic trends and a resultant lack of demand for APH's products.
- The shares recently traded at about 16X our 2011 EPS estimate, in the bottom half of APH's range of the past decade. Based on our belief that APH is in the midst of a business upturn, we think a higher valuation is merited. Our 12-month target price of $63 is based on a 20X multiple on our 2011 estimate, in the middle of its valuation range of the past decade, but at the top of APH's historical valuation at the current stage of earnings recovery.

Qualitative Risk Assessment

LOW | **MEDIUM** | HIGH

Our risk assessment reflects our view of the company's typically solid levels of cash flow and a strong business model, offset by the inherent cyclicality of APH's business.

Quantitative Evaluations

S&P Quality Ranking B+

D | C | B- | B | **B+** | A- | A | A+

Relative Strength Rank STRONG

72

LOWEST = 1 HIGHEST = 99

Revenue/Earnings Data

Revenue (Million $)

	1Q	2Q	3Q	4Q	Year
2010	771.0	884.8	948.5	--	--
2009	660.0	685.2	716.6	758.3	2,820
2008	770.7	846.8	863.7	755.3	3,236
2007	651.1	688.8	733.9	777.3	2,851
2006	569.0	606.6	636.4	659.4	2,471
2005	409.4	443.6	447.0	508.1	1,808

Earnings Per Share ($)

2010	0.56	0.74	0.78	**E**0.73	**E**2.70
2009	0.43	0.43	0.47	0.50	1.83
2008	0.54	0.61	0.63	0.56	2.34
2007	0.43	0.46	0.50	0.55	1.94
2006	0.32	0.29	0.37	0.43	1.40
2005	0.26	0.29	0.29	0.31	1.14

Fiscal year ended Dec. 31. Next earnings report expected: Late January. EPS Estimates based on S&P Operating Earnings; historical GAAP earnings are as reported.

Dividend Data (Dates: mm/dd Payment Date: mm/dd/yy)

Amount ($)	Date Decl.	Ex-Div. Date	Stk. of Record	Payment Date
0.015	10/26	12/14	12/16	01/06/10
0.015	01/28	03/15	03/17	04/07/10
0.015	04/29	06/14	06/16	07/07/10
0.015	07/29	09/13	09/15	10/06/10

Dividends have been paid since 2005. Source: Company reports.

Please read the Required Disclosures and Analyst Certification on the last page of this report.
Redistribution or reproduction is prohibited without written permission. Copyright ©2010 The McGraw-Hill Companies, Inc.

The McGraw·Hill Companies

STANDARD &POOR'S

Amphenol Corp

Business Summary October 25, 2010

CORPORATE OVERVIEW. Amphenol makes electrical, electronic and fiber optic connectors, interconnect systems, and coaxial and high-speed specialty cable. In 2009, APH derived 61% of its revenues from information technology and communications markets, 16% from industrial/automotive, and 23% from commercial aerospace and military. It derived 39% of its sales in North America, 19% in Europe, and 42% in Asia and elsewhere.

APH makes a broad range of interconnect products and assemblies (91% of 2009 revenues) for voice, video and data communications systems, commercial aerospace and military systems, automotive and mass transportation applications, and industrial and factory automation equipment. Its connectors and interconnect systems are mostly used to conduct electrical and optical signals for sophisticated electronic applications.

In communications, the company supplies connector and cable assembly products used in base stations for wireless communication systems and Internet networking equipment; smart card acceptor devices used in mobile telephones, set top boxes and other applications to facilitate reading data from smart cards; fiber optic connectors used in fiber optic transmissions; backplane and input/output connectors for servers and data storage devices, and

for linking PCs and peripheral equipment; and sculptured flexible circuits for integrating circuit boards.

APH also makes radio frequency connector products and antennas used in telecommunications, computer and office equipment, instrumentation equipment, local area networks and automotive electronics. Radio frequency connectors are also used in base stations, mobile communications devices and other components of cellular and personal communication networks.

The company believes it is the largest supplier of high-performance, military-specification, circular environmental connectors, generally used in sophisticated aerospace, military, commercial and industrial equipment. APH also makes industrial interconnect products, used in applications such as factory automation equipment, mass transportation applications and automotive safety products.

Company Financials Fiscal Year Ended Dec. 31

Per Share Data ($)	2009	2008	2007	2006	2005	2004	2003	2002	2001	2000
Tangible Book Value	1.73	0.35	1.00	NM	NM	NM	NM	NM	NM	NM
Cash Flow	2.39	2.86	2.38	1.79	1.42	1.13	0.80	0.66	0.76	0.88
Earnings	1.83	2.34	1.94	1.40	1.14	0.91	0.59	0.46	0.49	0.63
S&P Core Earnings	1.87	2.27	1.97	1.43	1.14	0.90	0.57	0.35	0.36	NA
Dividends	0.06	0.06	0.08	0.06	0.06	Nil	Nil	Nil	Nil	Nil
Payout Ratio	3%	3%	4%	4%	5%	Nil	Nil	Nil	Nil	Nil
Prices:High	47.14	52.28	47.24	35.25	23.10	18.76	16.03	12.94	14.50	17.59
Prices:Low	21.55	18.38	30.61	21.94	16.62	13.95	9.25	6.87	7.08	7.58
P/E Ratio:High	26	22	24	25	20	21	27	28	30	28
P/E Ratio:Low	12	8	16	16	15	15	16	15	15	12

Income Statement Analysis (Million $)	2009	2008	2007	2006	2005	2004	2003	2002	2001	2000
Revenue	2,820	3,236	2,851	2,471	1,808	1,530	1,240	1,062	1,104	1,360
Operating Income	587	724	635	518	394	315	241	209	229	287
Depreciation	98.5	91.3	82.3	72.6	50.7	38.8	37.0	34.8	46.7	42.8
Interest Expense	36.6	39.6	36.9	38.8	24.1	22.5	29.5	45.9	56.1	61.7
Pretax Income	447	582	501	373	308	247	158	123	135	173
Effective Tax Rate	26.7%	28.0%	29.5%	31.5%	33.0%	34.0%	34.0%	34.5%	38.2%	37.7%
Net Income	318	419	353	256	206	163	104	80.3	83.7	108
S&P Core Earnings	325	408	359	261	206	161	99.8	60.0	62.0	NA

Balance Sheet & Other Financial Data (Million $)	2009	2008	2007	2006	2005	2004	2003	2002	2001	2000
Cash	385	215	184	74.1	38.7	30.2	23.5	20.7	28.0	24.6
Current Assets	1,420	1,336	1,224	935	710	529	451	389	370	413
Total Assets	3,219	2,994	2,676	2,195	1,933	1,307	1,181	1,079	1,027	1,004
Current Liabilities	503	635	520	448	336	278	218	236	203	243
Long Term Debt	753	786	722	677	766	432	532	566	661	700
Common Equity	1,746	1,349	1,265	903	689	482	323	167	104	29.2
Total Capital	2,516	2,153	1,986	1,580	1,455	914	856	733	765	729
Capital Expenditures	59.8	107	104	82.4	57.1	44.3	30.2	18.8	38.6	53.1
Cash Flow	416	510	435	328	257	202	141	115	130	151
Current Ratio	2.8	2.1	2.4	2.1	2.1	1.9	2.1	1.6	1.8	1.7
% Long Term Debt of Capitalization	29.9	36.8	36.4	42.9	52.6	47.3	62.2	77.2	86.4	96.0
% Net Income of Revenue	11.3	13.0	12.4	10.3	11.4	10.7	8.4	7.6	7.6	7.9
% Return on Assets	10.2	14.8	14.5	12.4	12.7	13.1	9.2	7.6	8.2	11.7
% Return on Equity	20.5	32.1	32.6	32.1	35.2	40.6	42.4	59.3	125.7	NM

Data as orig reptd.; bef. results of disc opers/spec. items. Per share data adj. for stk. divs.; EPS diluted. E-Estimated. NA-Not Available. NM-Not Meaningful. NR-Not Ranked. UR-Under Review.

Office: 358 Hall Avenue, Wallingford, CT 06492.
Telephone: 203-265-8900.
Email: aphinfo@amphenol.com
Website: http://www.amphenol.com

Chrmn: M.H. Loeffler
Pres & CEO: R.A. Norwitt
SVP, CFO & Chief Acctg Officer: D.G. Reardon
Secy & General Counsel: E.C. Wetmore

Investor Contact: D. Reardon (203-265-8630)
Board Members: R. P. Badie, S. L. Clark, E. G. Jepsen, A. E. Lietz, M. H. Loeffler, J. R. Lord, R. A. Norwitt, D. H. Secord

Founded: 1932
Domicile: Delaware
Employees: 32,200

The **McGraw·Hill** Companies

Anadarko Petroleum Corp

STANDARD &POOR'S

| S&P Recommendation | HOLD ★★★☆☆ | Price $62.78 (as of Oct 25, 2010) | 12-Mo. Target Price $60.00 | Investment Style Large-Cap Blend |

GICS Sector Energy
Sub-Industry Oil & Gas Exploration & Production

Summary One of the largest independent exploration and production companies in the world, this U.S. concern has associated businesses in marketing, trading and minerals.

Key Stock Statistics (Source S&P, Vickers, company reports)

52-Wk Range	$75.07–34.54	S&P Oper. EPS 2010**E**	2.30	Market Capitalization(B)	$31.072	Beta	1.34
Trailing 12-Month EPS	$2.23	S&P Oper. EPS 2011**E**	2.22	Yield (%)	0.57	S&P 3-Yr. Proj. EPS CAGR(%)	-22
Trailing 12-Month P/E	28.2	P/E on S&P Oper. EPS 2010**E**	27.3	Dividend Rate/Share	$0.36	S&P Credit Rating	BBB-
$10K Invested 5 Yrs Ago	$15,031	Common Shares Outstg. (M)	494.9	Institutional Ownership (%)	82		

Price Performance

30-Week Mov. Avg. · · · 10-Week Mov. Avg. – – GAAP Earnings vs. Previous Year Volume Above Avg. STARS
12-Mo. Target Price — Relative Strength — ▲ Up ▼ Down ▶ No Change Below Avg. ★

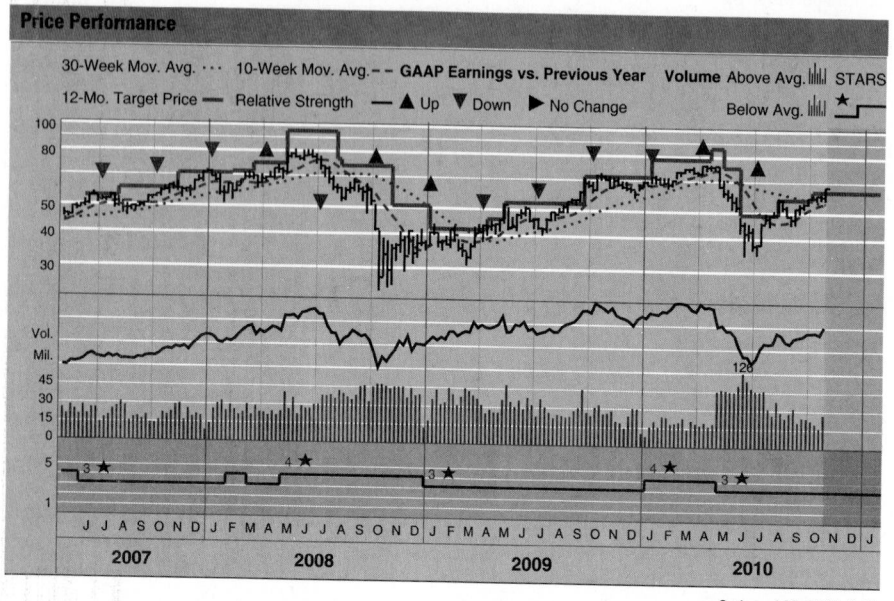

Options: ASE, CBOE, P, Ph

Analysis prepared by **Michael Kay** on October 25, 2010, when the stock traded at **$ 62.51**.

Highlights

▶ APC has raised 2010 production targets and shifted capital from the Gulf of Mexico (GOM) to onshore projects due to the deepwater drilling ban. APC is seeing success at Haynesville, Marcellus and Eagle Ford shales, providing exposure to low-cost resources, and sees 5%-7% production growth in 2010 and 7%-9% through 2014. We see a significant portion of this growth coming from onshore assets and see upside from APC's Niobrara acreage. APC is working on 13 "mega-projects", with first production expected in 2011. Given the extent of its success in the GOM, APC should be one of the major beneficiaries of the recent lifting of the deepwater drilling ban, but expect several months before drilling in the GOM ramps.

▶ APC plans capex of $5.3-$5.6 billion (vs. $4.7 billion) for 2010, with 36% for near-term projects, 22% for mega-projects, 20% for exploration, 11% for midstream, and 11% for shales. APC's cost structure and finding and development costs are improving, in our view.

▶ APC posted a 2009 per share loss of $2.13 ($0.97 non-cash loss). On production and price hikes, we see EPS of $2.30 (with a $0.31 non-cash gain) in 2010 and $2.22 in 2011.

Investment Rationale/Risk

▶ So far in 2010, focus has shifted to APC's 25% interest in the plugged Macondo well, where the Deepwater Horizon rig blew up and sank in April, and cleanup costs and compensation. Our hold recommendation is based on concerns and uncertainty over APC's liabilities. We expect APC to pursue all legal measures, as it has made clear its position that BP acted negligently. After a change in strategic focus fueled by acquisitions originally weakened its balance sheet and cost structure, APC has begun taken steps to lower debt levels and improve its cash position to over $3.3 billion. APC's growing domestic onshore oil and gas assets should help fund an active exploration program.

▶ Risks to our recommendation and target price include unfavorable changes in economic, industry or operating conditions, such as rising costs or difficulty in replacing reserves.

▶ We blend our NAV estimate of $63 with our DCF ($67; WACC 11%; terminal growth 3%) and peer-average relative metrics to arrive at our 12-month target price of $60. The shares have been under pressure in 2010, down over 20% since April 20, on concerns over financial liabilities related to the Gulf of Mexico oil spill.

Qualitative Risk Assessment

| LOW | MEDIUM | HIGH |

Our risk assessment reflects our view of APC's aggressive financial profile, and a business profile limited by participation in the cyclical, competitive and capital-intensive exploration and production sector, and by U.S. and international oil and gas operations that carry heightened political and operational risk.

Quantitative Evaluations

S&P Quality Ranking   B+

| D | C | B- | B | B+ | A- | A | A+ |

Relative Strength Rank   STRONG

89

LOWEST = 1   HIGHEST = 99

Revenue/Earnings Data

Revenue (Million $)

	1Q	2Q	3Q	4Q	Year
2010	3,139	2,604	--	--	--
2009	1,796	1,913	2,874	2,417	9,000
2008	2,978	2,786	6,149	3,810	15,723
2007	2,683	3,313	3,030	3,062	11,232
2006	1,701	1,809	3,498	3,179	10,187
2005	1,526	1,592	1,737	2,245	7,100

Earnings Per Share ($)

	1Q	2Q	3Q	4Q	Year
2010	1.43	-0.08	E0.34	E0.33	E2.30
2009	-0.73	-0.48	-0.40	0.46	-0.28
2008	0.50	0.03	4.62	1.70	6.84
2007	0.17	1.38	1.10	0.35	8.05
2006	1.22	1.43	2.98	0.40	6.02
2005	1.03	1.06	1.26	1.87	5.20

Fiscal year ended Dec. 31. Next earnings report expected: Early November. EPS Estimates based on S&P Operating Earnings; historical GAAP earnings are as reported.

Dividend Data (Dates: mm/dd Payment Date: mm/dd/yy)

Amount ($)	Date Decl.	Ex-Div. Date	Stk. of Record	Payment Date
0.090	11/11	12/07	12/09	12/23/09
0.090	02/16	03/08	03/10	03/24/10
0.090	05/18	06/07	06/09	06/23/10
0.090	08/03	09/03	09/08	09/22/10

Dividends have been paid since 1986. Source: Company reports.

Please read the Required Disclosures and Analyst Certification on the last page of this report.

Anadarko Petroleum Corp

Business Summary October 25, 2010

CORPORATE OVERVIEW. One of the largest independent E&P companies in the world, APC is engaged in the exploration, development, production, gathering, processing and marketing of natural gas, crude oil, condensate and NGLs. Major areas of operation are onshore in the U.S., in the deepwater Gulf of Mexico (GOM), and Algeria. APC also has production in China and exploration programs in Ghana and Brazil.

Proved oil and gas reserves rose 1% to 2,304 billion barrels of oil equivalent (boe) in 2009 (70% developed; 56% natural gas, 44% liquids). Production of 220 MMBOE, or 604,000 BOE/day, was up 7% from 2008.

CORPORATE STRATEGY. APC announced nine deepwater discoveries in three of the most attractive deepwater plays in the world in 2009. These results include five subsalt discoveries in the GOM, three offshore West Africa, and one in the pre-salt play offshore Brazil. Already in 2010, APC has announced a successful appraisal of the Tweneboa discovery offshore Ghana, a successful appraisal of the Lucius discovery in the GOM, a discovery offshore Mozambique at the Windjammer well in the Rovuma Basin, and a successful ap-

praisal of the Vito prospect in the GOM. We expect about 20%, or $1.06-$1.12 billion, of 2010 capex to be spent on exploration, most of it focused on APC's worldwide deepwater exploration program, which plans to drill about 30 exploration/appraisal wells. Up to 13 wells will be drilled offshore West Africa, 7-10 wells in the Gulf of Mexico, 4-6 wells in Brazil, 4-6 wells in Mozambique, and 3-5 wells in southeast Asia.

APC continues to advance current mega-projects in Ghana (Jubilee) and Algeria (El Merk), and expects each project to remain on schedule and within budget. The Jubilee field in Ghana is expected to start producing late this year, and in total, the three projects are expected to add more than 60,000 boe/d to APC production by 2012. APC plans to invest $1.17-$1.23 billion, or 22% of expected capex, on mega-projects in 2010.

Company Financials Fiscal Year Ended Dec. 31

Per Share Data ($)	2009	2008	2007	2006	2005	2004	2003	2002	2001	2000
Tangible Book Value	29.65	29.40	23.89	21.95	21.06	16.45	13.97	11.01	9.59	10.50
Cash Flow	7.08	14.13	14.23	10.28	8.04	6.05	5.01	3.74	2.09	3.64
Earnings	-0.28	6.84	8.05	6.02	5.20	3.18	2.46	1.61	-0.37	2.13
S&P Core Earnings	-0.25	5.13	1.65	6.09	5.22	3.27	2.47	1.53	-0.49	NA
Dividends	0.36	0.36	0.36	0.36	0.36	0.28	0.22	0.16	0.11	0.10
Payout Ratio	NM	5%	4%	6%	7%	9%	9%	10%	NM	5%
Prices:High	69.37	81.36	68.00	56.98	50.71	35.78	25.86	29.28	36.99	37.97
Prices:Low	30.88	24.57	38.40	39.51	30.01	24.00	20.14	18.39	21.50	13.78
P/E Ratio:High	NM	12	8	9	10	11	11	18	NM	18
P/E Ratio:Low	NM	4	5	7	6	8	8	11	NM	6

Income Statement Analysis (Million $)										
Revenue	8,210	14,640	15,892	10,187	7,100	6,067	5,122	3,860	8,369	5,686
Operating Income	NA	8,578	10,328	6,945	5,436	4,400	3,648	2,585	3,702	2,190
Depreciation, Depletion and Amortization	3,532	3,417	2,891	1,976	1,343	1,447	1,297	1,121	1,227	593
Interest Expense	702	742	1,214	655	201	352	253	203	92.0	Nil
Pretax Income	-108	5,429	6,329	4,238	3,895	2,477	1,974	1,207	-390	1,426
Effective Tax Rate	4.63%	40.0%	40.4%	34.0%	36.6%	35.2%	36.9%	31.2%	NM	42.2%
Net Income	-135	3,236	3,770	2,796	2,471	1,606	1,245	831	-176	824
S&P Core Earnings	-121	2,400	773	2,826	2,478	1,646	1,248	785	-243	NA

Balance Sheet & Other Financial Data (Million $)										
Cash	3,531	2,360	1,268	491	739	874	62.0	34.0	37.0	199
Current Assets	6,083	5,375	4,516	4,614	2,916	2,502	1,324	1,280	1,201	1,894
Total Assets	50,123	48,953	48,481	58,844	22,588	20,192	20,546	18,248	16,771	16,590
Current Liabilities	3,824	5,536	5,257	16,758	2,403	1,993	1,715	1,861	1,801	1,676
Long Term Debt	12,748	10,867	14,747	11,520	3,555	3,671	5,058	5,171	4,638	3,984
Common Equity	19,928	18,856	16,319	15,201	10,967	9,219	8,510	6,673	6,262	6,586
Total Capital	33,163	39,997	39,929	39,673	19,330	17,393	17,909	15,578	14,454	10,770
Capital Expenditures	4,352	4,801	4,246	1,086	3,408	3,064	2,772	2,388	3,316	1,708
Cash Flow	3,397	6,614	6,658	4,769	3,809	3,048	2,537	1,946	1,044	1,406
Current Ratio	1.6	1.0	0.9	0.3	1.2	1.3	0.8	0.7	0.7	1.1
% Long Term Debt of Capitalization	39.0	27.2	44.9	28.8	18.4	21.1	28.2	33.2	32.1	37.0
% Return on Assets	NM	6.6	7.0	6.9	11.5	7.9	6.4	4.7	NM	8.0
% Return on Equity	NM	18.4	24.2	21.3	24.4	17.9	16.1	12.8	NM	20.5

Data as orig reptd.; bef. results of disc opers/spec. items. Per share data adj. for stk. divs.; EPS diluted. E-Estimated. NA-Not Available. NM-Not Meaningful. NR-Not Ranked. UR-Under Review.

Office: 1201 Lake Robbins Drive, The Woodlands, TX 77380-1124.
Telephone: 832-636-1000.
Website: http://www.anadarko.com
Chrmn & CEO: J.T. Hackett

Pres & COO: R.A. Walker
SVP & CFO: R.G. Gwin
SVP, Chief Admin Officer & General Counsel: R.K. Reeves
Chief Acctg Officer: M. Douglas

Investor Contact: J. Colglazier (832-636-2306)
Board Members: R. J. Allison, Jr., J. R. Butler, Jr., L. R. Corbett, H. P. Eberhart, P. J. Fluor, P. M. Geren, III, J. R. Gordon, J. T. Hackett, P. R. Reynolds

Founded: 1985
Domicile: Delaware
Employees: 4,300

Analog Devices Inc.

STANDARD &POOR'S

S&P Recommendation	HOLD ★★★☆☆	Price $32.01 (as of Oct 22, 2010)	12-Mo. Target Price $32.00	Investment Style Large-Cap Growth

GICS Sector Information Technology
Sub-Industry Semiconductors

Summary This company manufactures high-performance integrated circuits (ICs) used in analog and digital signal processing applications.

Key Stock Statistics (Source S&P, Vickers, company reports)

52-Wk Range	$32.83– 25.26	S&P Oper. EPS 2010E	2.31	Market Capitalization(B)	$9.542	Beta	1.05
Trailing 12-Month EPS	$1.96	S&P Oper. EPS 2011E	2.46	Yield (%)	2.75	S&P 3-Yr. Proj. EPS CAGR(%)	20
Trailing 12-Month P/E	16.3	P/E on S&P Oper. EPS 2010E	13.9	Dividend Rate/Share	$0.88	S&P Credit Rating	A-
$10K Invested 5 Yrs Ago	$10,312	Common Shares Outstg. (M)	298.1	Institutional Ownership (%)	83		

Price Performance

30-Week Mov. Avg. · · · 10-Week Mov. Avg. - - **GAAP Earnings vs. Previous Year** Volume Above Avg. STARS
12-Mo. Target Price — Relative Strength — ▲ Up ▼ Down ► No Change Below Avg. ★

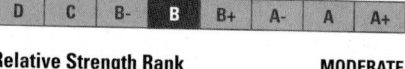

Options: ASE, CBOE, P, Ph

Analysis prepared by **Clyde Montevirgen** on August 23, 2010, when the stock traded at **$ 29.91**.

Highlights

➤ We expect revenues to rise about 8% in FY 11 (Oct.), compared to a projected 36% increase in FY 10. Although we are cautious of increasing inventory throughout the supply chain, we believe that growth will be supported by improving economic conditions and the greater usage of analog semiconductors as digital technology expands. We think recent design wins and increasing exposure to fast-growing segments within the automotive, industrial, and certain communications markets will aid top-line results.

➤ We are modeling a gross margin of 65% for FY 11, similar to the average result we expect for FY 10. We believe that benefits from higher plant utilization will balance changes in sales mix and products manufactured by foundries. We think that variable expenses, such as sales-related compensation, will increase with improving business conditions, and we see the non-GAAP operating margin staying around 32% for both fiscal years.

➤ Our EPS estimates assumes an effective tax rate of around 21% and a modest increase in the diluted share count.

Investment Rationale/Risk

➤ Our hold recommendation reflects our view of fair profitability and valuations. We believe that the company has done a good job improving its fixed cost structure and seeking growth in fast-growing segments, which should lead to above-average growth in FY 10. Margins are and should remain above ADI's stated long-term model; and based on our projections, we think return on equity will hover around the industry average. However, we see growth slowing in FY 11 as annual comparisons become more difficult. The share price implies relative multiples that are already around the industry average, which we think is appropriate.

➤ Risks to our recommendation and target price include slower traction for new products, worse-than-anticipated economic conditions, and a less favorable sales mix.

➤ Our 12-month target price of $32 is based on a price-to-earnings multiple of around 13X, near the industry average to account for our view of ADI's relative growth, return on equity, and risk, applied to our calendar 2011 EPS estimate.

Qualitative Risk Assessment

LOW	MEDIUM	HIGH

Our risk assessment reflects that ADI is subject to the sales cycles of the semiconductor industry, offset by our view of relatively stable chip pricing owing to high proprietary design content, broad end-markets, a leading market share in key converter and amplifier product categories and what we consider a lack of debt.

Quantitative Evaluations

S&P Quality Ranking **B**

D	C	B-	B	B+	A-	A	A+

Relative Strength Rank **MODERATE**

64

LOWEST = 1   HIGHEST = 99

Revenue/Earnings Data

Revenue (Million $)

	1Q	2Q	3Q	4Q	Year
2010	603.0	668.2	720.3	--	--
2009	476.6	474.8	492.0	571.6	2,015
2008	613.9	649.3	659.0	660.7	2,583
2007	645.9	614.7	637.0	648.5	2,511
2006	621.3	643.9	663.7	644.3	2,573
2005	580.5	603.7	582.4	622.1	2,389

Earnings Per Share ($)

2010	0.39	0.55	0.65	E0.69	E2.31
2009	0.08	0.18	0.22	0.36	0.85
2008	0.40	0.44	0.44	0.49	1.77
2007	0.45	0.37	0.44	0.31	1.51
2006	0.32	0.39	0.39	0.39	1.48
2005	0.28	0.31	0.32	0.18	1.08

Fiscal year ended Oct. 31. Next earnings report expected: Late November. EPS Estimates based on S&P Operating Earnings; historical GAAP earnings are as reported.

Dividend Data (Dates: mm/dd Payment Date: mm/dd/yy)

Amount ($)	Date Decl.	Ex-Div. Date	Stk. of Record	Payment Date
0.200	11/19	12/02	12/04	12/23/09
0.200	02/17	03/03	03/05	03/24/10
0.220	05/18	05/26	05/28	06/16/10
0.220	08/16	08/25	08/27	09/15/10

Dividends have been paid since 2003. Source: Company reports.

Please read the Required Disclosures and Analyst Certification on the last page of this report.

The McGraw-Hill Companies

Analog Devices Inc.

Business Summary August 23, 2010

CORPORATE OVERVIEW. Analog Devices designs, manufactures, and markets a broad line of high-performance analog, mixed-signal and digital signal processing (DSP) integrated circuits (ICs) that address a wide range of real-world signal processing applications. Real-world phenomena that these applications are designed for include light, sound, temperature, .motion and pressure. These phenomena are specifically analog in nature, and are manipulated for use in digital applications.

The expansion of broadband and wireless communications applications helps drive demand for analog and DSP chips. ADI's products are built into wireless telephones, base station equipment, and remote access servers, among others. The company's analog products are typically general purpose in nature and are used in a wide variety of equipment and systems. The company's chips are increasingly sold to PC and digital entertainment markets, as consumer equipment to handle voice, video and images becomes increasingly complex and sells to a wider audience.

Key markets are industrial, which accounted for approximately 52% of sales in FY 09 (Oct.), communications 25%, consumer 20%, and computer 3%. The cus-

tomer base is fairly broad: the 20 largest customers, excluding distributors, accounted for about 37% of sales in FY 09, and the largest customer, excluding distributors, accounted for approximately 5%. About 54% of FY 09 sales were derived from sales made through distributors.

CORPORATE STRATEGY. Analog Devices is a leading provider of high-performance analog and mixed-signal, and DSP integrated circuits, two of the faster growing segments within the broader semiconductor industry. We believe that the higher-end analog space will continue to attract new entrants given its anticipated growth rate, relatively dispersed market share, stable pricing, higher-margin sales, and low capital expenditures. Lending to less risk, we think chipmakers in this segment generally post less variable operating results and more stable free cash flows than most semiconductor makers, which tend to experience volatile swings during various stages of the industry's business cycle.

Company Financials Fiscal Year Ended Oct. 31

Per Share Data ($)	2009	2008	2007	2006	2005	2004	2003	2002	2001	2000
Tangible Book Value	7.78	7.46	6.71	9.17	9.61	9.66	8.42	7.50	7.20	5.90
Cash Flow	1.32	2.28	1.97	1.95	1.49	1.84	1.22	0.90	1.48	2.00
Earnings	0.85	1.77	1.51	1.48	1.08	1.45	0.78	0.28	0.93	1.59
S&P Core Earnings	0.84	1.74	1.45	1.46	0.29	0.91	0.20	-0.32	0.44	NA
Dividends	0.80	0.76	0.70	0.56	0.32	0.20	Nil	Nil	Nil	Nil
Payout Ratio	94%	43%	46%	38%	30%	14%	Nil	Nil	Nil	Nil
Prices:High	31.91	36.35	41.10	41.48	41.40	52.37	50.35	48.84	64.00	103.00
Prices:Low	17.82	15.29	30.19	26.07	31.71	31.36	22.58	17.88	29.00	41.31
P/E Ratio:High	38	21	27	28	38	36	65	NM	69	65
P/E Ratio:Low	21	9	20	18	29	22	29	NM	31	26

Income Statement Analysis (Million $)										
Revenue	2,015	2,583	2,546	2,573	2,389	2,634	2,047	1,708	2,277	2,578
Operating Income	478	782	916	771	703	852	552	405	675	924
Depreciation	140	153	155	172	156	153	168	238	210	157
Interest Expense	4.09	Nil	Nil	0.05	0.03	0.22	32.2	44.5	62.5	5.84
Pretax Income	297	666	659	664	588	733	382	140	507	866
Effective Tax Rate	16.8%	21.2%	24.0%	17.1%	29.4%	22.1%	21.9%	25.0%	29.7%	29.9%
Net Income	247	525	501	549	415	571	298	105	356	607
S&P Core Earnings	246	517	481	542	113	364	74.2	-118	170	NA

Balance Sheet & Other Financial Data (Million $)										
Cash	1,816	1,310	425	344	628	519	518	1,614	1,365	1,736
Current Assets	2,491	2,090	1,979	3,011	3,732	3,529	2,886	3,624	3,435	3,168
Total Assets	3,404	3,091	2,972	3,987	4,583	4,720	4,093	4,980	4,885	4,411
Current Liabilities	387	569	548	491	819	567	463	484	528	650
Long Term Debt	489	Nil	Nil	Nil	Nil	Nil	Nil	1,274	1,206	1,213
Common Equity	2,529	2,420	2,338	3,436	3,692	3,800	3,288	2,900	2,843	2,304
Total Capital	3,018	2,435	2,348	3,439	3,692	3,810	3,305	4,197	4,100	3,568
Capital Expenditures	56.1	157	142	129	85.5	146	67.7	57.4	297	275
Cash Flow	387	679	656	722	570	723	467	343	567	764
Current Ratio	6.4	3.7	3.6	6.1	4.6	6.2	6.2	7.5	6.5	4.9
% Long Term Debt of Capitalization	12.9	Nil	Nil	Nil	Nil	Nil	Nil	30.4	29.4	34.0
% Net Income of Revenue	12.3	20.3	19.6	21.4	17.4	21.7	14.6	6.2	15.7	23.6
% Return on Assets	7.6	17.3	14.3	12.8	8.9	13.0	6.6	2.1	7.7	18.3
% Return on Equity	10.0	22.1	17.3	15.4	11.1	16.1	9.6	3.7	13.8	31.0

Data as orig reptd.; bef. results of disc opers/spec. items. Per share data adj. for stk. divs.; EPS diluted. E-Estimated. NA-Not Available. NM-Not Meaningful. NR-Not Ranked. UR-Under Review.

Office: One Technology Way, Norwood, MA 02062-9106.
Telephone: 800-262-5643.
Email: investor.relations@analog.com
Website: http://www.analog.com

Chrmn: R. Stata
Pres & CEO: J.G. Fishman
CFO: D.A. Zinsner
CTO: S.H. Fuller

Chief Acctg Officer & Cntlr: S. Brennan
Investor Contact: M. Kohl (781-461-3759)
Board Members: J. Champy, J. L. Doyle, J. G. Fishman, J. C. Hodgson, Y. Istel, N. S. Novich, F. G. Saviers, P. J. Severino, K. J. Sicchitano, R. Stata

Founded: 1965
Domicile: Massachusetts
Employees: 8,300

Aon Corp.

STANDARD & POOR'S

S&P Recommendation	HOLD ★★★☆☆	Price $40.02 (as of Oct 22, 2010)	12-Mo. Target Price $39.00	Investment Style Large-Cap Blend

GICS Sector Financials
Sub-Industry Insurance Brokers

Summary This global provider of insurance brokerage services also offers consulting services and risk and insurance advice.

Key Stock Statistics (Source S&P, Vickers, company reports)

52-Wk Range	$44.34–35.10	S&P Oper. EPS 2010E	3.20	Market Capitalization(B)	$13.903	Beta	0.50
Trailing 12-Month EPS	$2.27	S&P Oper. EPS 2011E	3.45	Yield (%)	1.50	S&P 3-Yr. Proj. EPS CAGR(%)	7
Trailing 12-Month P/E	17.6	P/E on S&P Oper. EPS 2010E	12.5	Dividend Rate/Share	$0.60	S&P Credit Rating	BBB+
$10K Invested 5 Yrs Ago	$13,182	Common Shares Outstg. (M)	347.4	Institutional Ownership (%)	64		

Price Performance

30-Week Mov. Avg. · · · 10-Week Mov. Avg. - - GAAP Earnings vs. Previous Year Volume Above Avg. STARS
12-Mo. Target Price — Relative Strength ▲ Up ▼ Down ▶ No Change Below Avg. ★

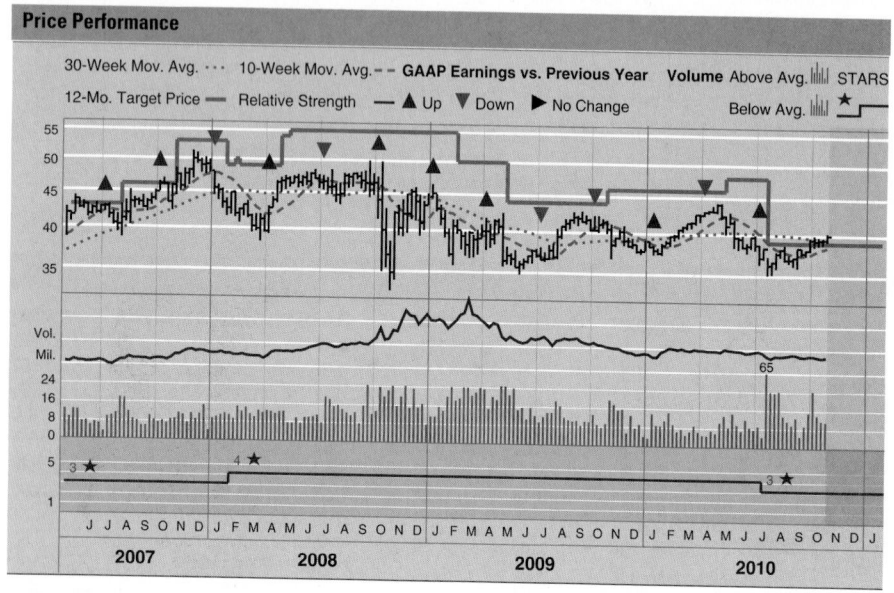

Options: ASE, CBOE, P, Ph

Analysis prepared by **Bret Howlett** on August 25, 2010, when the stock traded at **$36.48**.

Highlights

▶ We expect an organic brokerage revenue decline of 1%-2% in 2010, due to the difficult pricing environment and a decline in exposure units, partially offset by new business production. We forecast revenues increasing slightly, although we expect declining investment income to slow growth. We anticipate that the Asia-Pacific region will experience solid new business growth, and we expect 3% to 5% organic revenue growth. We see the adjusted margin for brokerage increasing to roughly 22%, helped by cost cuts and commission enhancements.

▶ We forecast organic revenue growth of up to 2% in consulting, despite challenging economic conditions. We believe AON is gaining market share in the business, fueled by recent key personnel additions, and we expect the improving economy to increase demand for its consulting services. We see the adjusted operating margin increasing to 16% on a lower cost structure and a more profitable business mix.

▶ We forecast adjusted EPS of $3.30 for 2010 and $3.60 for 2011. Our estimates exclude restructuring charges, integration expenses, and other items.

Investment Rationale/Risk

▶ Our hold recommendation reflects our opinion that AON will be adversely affected by the poor insurance pricing environment over the near term. We believe AON also faces considerable execution risk related to its proposed $4.9 billion acquisition of Hewitt Associates (HEW 49, Hold). While we think AON's business platform can drive organic growth in an unfavorable environment, we expect the company to face headwinds in brokerage in the U.S. and Europe as weak economies there pressure margins and volumes. We believe its aggressive cost-cutting initiatives, a share buyback program, exposure to reinsurance, and earnings contributions from the Asia-Pacific region will more than offset the impact from the difficult operating environment.

▶ Risks to our recommendation and target price include weaker organic revenue growth and margin pressure from a soft property and casualty market; currency risks; and potential additional contingent commission probes by international authorities.

▶ Our 12-month target price of $39 is about 10.8X our 2011 adjusted operating EPS estimate, below historical multiples.

Qualitative Risk Assessment

LOW	MEDIUM	HIGH

Our risk assessment reflects what we see as the company's well diversified operations and solid balance sheet, with low debt, offset by the loss of contingent commissions, business restructuring, a soft insurance pricing environment, lower exposures, potential for elevated amortization of intangible assets, and execution risk related to the proposed acquisition of Hewitt Associates.

Quantitative Evaluations

S&P Quality Ranking B+

D	C	B-	B	B+	A-	A	A+

Relative Strength Rank MODERATE

54

LOWEST = 1   HIGHEST = 99

Revenue/Earnings Data

Revenue (Million $)

	1Q	2Q	3Q	4Q	Year
2010	1,904	1,898	--	--	--
2009	1,846	1,882	1,794	2,073	7,595
2008	1,932	1,980	1,847	1,924	7,631
2007	1,798	1,866	1,775	2,032	7,471
2006	2,165	2,208	2,168	2,413	8,954
2005	2,464	2,456	2,387	2,530	9,837

Earnings Per Share ($)

2010	0.63	0.63	E0.72	E0.85	E3.20
2009	0.80	0.51	0.40	0.49	2.19
2008	0.56	0.55	0.53	0.43	2.06
2007	0.51	0.57	0.42	0.11	2.10
2006	0.57	0.53	0.27	0.57	1.86
2005	0.58	0.54	0.35	0.42	1.89

Fiscal year ended Dec. 31. Next earnings report expected: Early November. EPS Estimates based on S&P Operating Earnings; historical GAAP earnings are as reported.

Dividend Data (Dates: mm/dd Payment Date: mm/dd/yy)

Amount ($)	Date Decl.	Ex-Div. Date	Stk. of Record	Payment Date
0.150	01/12	01/28	02/01	02/15/10
0.150	04/21	04/29	05/03	05/17/10
0.150	07/19	07/29	08/02	08/16/10
0.150	10/07	10/28	11/01	11/15/10

Dividends have been paid since 1950. Source: Company reports.

Please read the Required Disclosures and Analyst Certification on the last page of this report.

The McGraw·Hill Companies

Aon Corp.

Business Summary August 25, 2010

CORPORATE OVERVIEW. Aon Corp. is a global provider of insurance broker-age services, insurance products, and risk and insurance advice, as well as other consulting services, conducting business in more than 120 countries and sovereignties. In 2009, AON was recognized by Business Insurance as the world's largest retail insurance broker as well as the largest worldwide rein-surance broker.

AON classifies its businesses into two operating segments: risk and insurance brokerage, and consulting. The risk and insurance brokerage segment ac-counted for 83% of total revenue from continuing operations in 2009, and the consulting segment 17%.

CORPORATE STRATEGY. AON employs a growth-through-acquisition strategy, which it believes has been vital in building its network of resources and capa-bilities. Over the past 21 years, AON has completed more than 443 acquisi-tions. In 2008, AON purchased a total of 31 companies, mostly related to its risk and insurance brokerage operations. However, in 2009, due to the chal-lenging economic conditions and turmoil in the financial markets, AON com-pleted only three major acquisitions.

IMPACT OF MAJOR DEVELOPMENTS. In July 2010, AON announced that its directors had approved an agreement to acquire Hewitt Associates (HEW 49,

Hold) for $4.9 billion. AON plans to finance the transaction using 50% cash and 50% stock, and the deal is expected to close in November 2010, subject to shareholder and regulatory approvals and customary closing conditions. The company believes the acquisition will be accretive to adjusted EPS in 2011 and GAAP EPS in 2012. We estimate cost synergies from the deal to exceed $360 million annually until 2013, and to result in AON's revenue mix changing to 60% insurance brokerage and 40% consulting.

In August 2008, AON announced plans to acquire Benfield, a leading reinsur-ance intermediary, for $1.75 billion. The transaction closed in November 2008 for $1.43 billion, due to a strengthening of the U.S. dollar versus the British pound. In connection with the transaction, AON announced a global restruc-turing program. AON expects the restructuring program to result in $155 mil-lion in charges, of which $55 million was already recorded in 2009. The com-pany expects $45 million in charges to be recorded in future earnings. The program is expected to save $84-$94 million, and $122 million of cumulative annualized savings by 2010.

Company Financials Fiscal Year Ended Dec. 31

Per Share Data ($)	2009	2008	2007	2006	2005	2004	2003	2002	2001	2000
Tangible Book Value	NM	NM	4.37	2.14	2.48	0.76	NM	NM	NM	NM
Cash Flow	3.02	2.74	2.67	2.54	2.69	2.62	3.06	2.57	1.98	3.08
Earnings	2.19	2.06	2.10	1.86	1.89	1.72	2.08	1.64	0.73	1.82
S&P Core Earnings	2.19	1.22	1.66	2.03	2.10	2.29	2.05	1.00	-0.06	NA
Dividends	0.60	0.60	0.60	0.75	0.60	0.60	0.60	0.83	0.90	0.87
Payout Ratio	27%	29%	29%	40%	32%	35%	29%	50%	123%	48%
Prices:High	46.19	50.00	51.32	42.76	37.14	29.44	26.79	39.63	44.80	42.75
Prices:Low	34.81	32.83	34.30	31.01	20.64	18.15	17.41	13.30	29.75	20.69
P/E Ratio:High	21	24	24	23	20	17	13	24	61	23
P/E Ratio:Low	16	16	16	17	11	11	8	8	41	11

Income Statement Analysis (Million $)										
Revenue	7,595	7,631	7,471	8,954	9,837	10,172	9,810	8,822	7,676	7,375
Operating Income	1,263	1,536	1,437	1,426	1,530	1,545	1,511	1,195	933	1,327
Depreciation	242	204	189	244	277	309	314	263	339	333
Interest Expense	122	126	138	129	125	136	137	158	167	-180
Pretax Income	949	863	1,024	920	965	880	1,110	793	399	854
Effective Tax Rate	28.2%	28.0%	34.4%	32.0%	33.5%	34.4%	38.3%	38.6%	43.5%	40.9%
Net Income	636	621	672	626	642	577	663	466	203	481
S&P Core Earnings	637	368	531	683	709	765	652	281	-19.4	NA

Balance Sheet & Other Financial Data (Million $)										
Cash	639	1,236	4,915	4,726	476	570	540	506	439	1,118
Current Assets	13,989	14,526	17,973	13,852	14,612	15,460	14,550	14,109	11,412	11,693
Total Assets	22,958	23,172	24,948	24,318	27,818	28,329	27,027	25,334	22,386	22,251
Current Liabilities	12,640	12,803	14,553	12,350	14,084	15,299	15,096	14,952	12,605	12,087
Long Term Debt	1,998	1,872	2,145	1,588	2,105	1,523	1,787	2,064	2,363	2,586
Common Equity	5,379	5,314	6,221	5,218	5,303	5,103	4,498	3,895	3,521	3,388
Total Capital	7,439	7,287	8,223	6,806	7,408	7,268	6,643	6,318	6,065	6,036
Capital Expenditures	140	103	170	152	126	80.0	185	278	281	179
Cash Flow	878	825	861	863	917	883	974	726	539	811
Current Ratio	1.1	1.1	1.2	1.1	1.0	1.0	1.0	0.9	0.9	1.0
% Long Term Debt of Capitalization	26.9	25.6	23.3	23.3	28.4	21.0	26.9	32.7	39.0	42.8
% Net Income of Revenue	8.4	8.1	9.0	7.0	6.5	5.7	6.8	5.3	2.6	6.5
% Return on Assets	2.8	2.6	2.7	2.4	2.3	2.1	2.5	2.0	0.9	2.2
% Return on Equity	11.9	10.8	11.8	11.9	12.3	12.0	15.8	12.6	5.9	14.9

Data as orig reptd.; bef. results of disc opers/spec. items. Per share data adj. for stk. divs.; EPS diluted. E-Estimated. NA-Not Available. NM-Not Meaningful. NR-Not Ranked. UR-Under Review.

Office: 200 East Randolph Street, Chicago, IL 60601.
Telephone: 312-381-1000.
Website: http://www.aon.com
Chrmn: L.B. Knight, III

Pres & CEO: G. Case
COO: A.M. Appel
EVP & CFO: C. Davies
EVP, Chief Admin Officer & CIO: G.J. Besio

Investor Contact: S. Malchow (312-381-3983)
Board Members: G. Case, F. Conti, C. A. Francis, J. C. Green, E. D. Jannotta, P. J. Kalff, L. B. Knight, III, J. M. Losh, R. E. Martin, A. J. McKenna, R. S. Morrison, R. B. Myers, R. C. Notebaert, J. W. Rogers, Jr., G. Santana, C. Y. Woo

Founded: 1919
Domicile: Delaware
Employees: 36,200

Apache Corp

STANDARD &POOR'S

S&P Recommendation STRONG BUY ★ ★ ★ ★ ★	**Price** $101.30 (as of Oct 22, 2010)	**12-Mo. Target Price** $133.00	**Investment Style** Large-Cap Blend

GICS Sector Energy
Sub-Industry Oil & Gas Exploration & Production

Summary One of the largest independent exploration and production companies in the U.S., Apache explores for, develops and produces natural gas, crude oil and natural gas liquids.

Key Stock Statistics (Source S&P, Vickers, company reports)

52-Wk Range	$111.00– 81.94	S&P Oper. EPS 2010E	9.52	Market Capitalization(B)	$36.901	Beta	1.19
Trailing 12-Month EPS	$7.66	S&P Oper. EPS 2011E	11.62	Yield (%)	0.59	S&P 3-Yr. Proj. EPS CAGR(%)	1
Trailing 12-Month P/E	13.2	P/E on S&P Oper. EPS 2010E	10.6	Dividend Rate/Share	$0.60	S&P Credit Rating	A-
$10K Invested 5 Yrs Ago	$17,467	Common Shares Outstg. (M)	364.3	Institutional Ownership (%)	79		

Price Performance

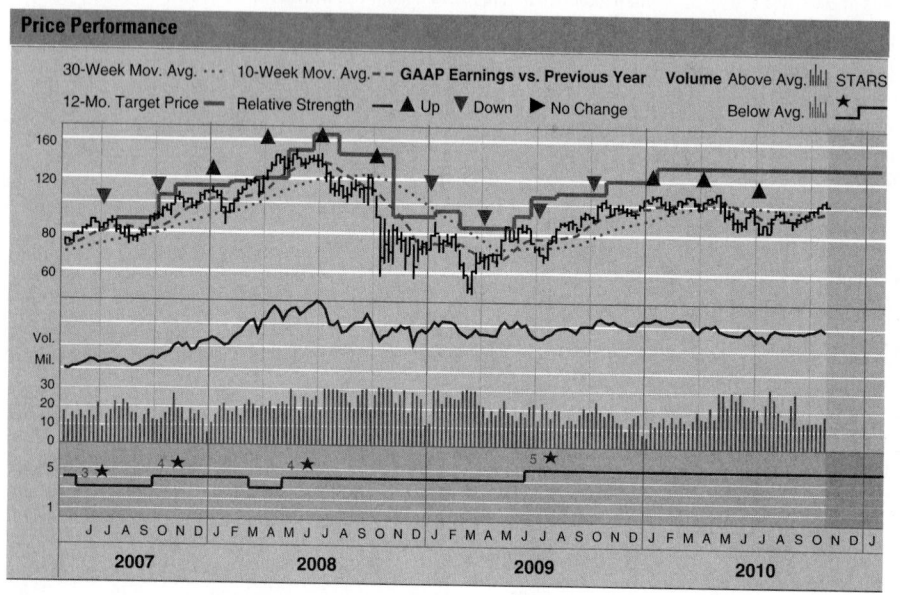

30-Week Mov. Avg. · · · 10-Week Mov. Avg. – – GAAP Earnings vs. Previous Year Volume Above Avg. STARS
12-Mo. Target Price — Relative Strength — ▲ Up ▼ Down ► No Change Below Avg.

Options: ASE, CBOE, P, Ph

Analysis prepared by **Michael Kay** on August 11, 2010, when the stock traded at **$ 92.80.**

Qualitative Risk Assessment

LOW	MEDIUM	HIGH

Our risk assessment for APA reflects its participation in a highly capital-intensive industry that derives value based on commodity prices that can be highly volatile. APA is a super-large exploration and production company diversified across major producing regions, focused on exploiting North American reserves and growing capital internationally.

Quantitative Evaluations

S&P Quality Ranking   A-

D	C	B-	B	B+	A-	A	A+

Relative Strength Rank   MODERATE

60

LOWEST = 1   HIGHEST = 99

Revenue/Earnings Data

Revenue (Million $)

	1Q	2Q	3Q	4Q	Year
2010	2,673	2,972	--	--	--
2009	1,634	2,093	2,332	2,570	8,615
2008	3,188	3,900	3,365	1,937	12,390
2007	1,997	2,468	2,499	3,014	9,978
2006	1,999	2,062	2,261	1,967	8,289
2005	1,662	1,759	2,061	2,102	7,584

Earnings Per Share ($)

2010	2.08	2.53	E2.37	E2.61	E9.52
2009	-5.25	1.31	1.30	1.72	-0.87
2008	3.03	4.28	3.52	-8.80	2.10
2007	1.47	1.89	1.83	3.19	8.39
2006	1.97	2.17	1.94	1.56	7.64
2005	1.67	1.76	2.05	2.35	7.84

Fiscal year ended Dec. 31. Next earnings report expected: Early November. EPS Estimates based on S&P Operating Earnings; historical GAAP earnings are as reported.

Highlights

▶ Production was up 9% in 2009, meeting APA's 6%-14% target, as international growth outweighed domestic declines on curtailed drilling activity as a result of lower prices. APA has a pipeline of about 10 projects set to begin production between 2009 and 2012, which should contribute about 150,000 boe/d of net new production. We see production from Van Gogh and Pyrenees in Australia, increased activity in the Granite Wash play and Horn River Basin, new processing capacity in Egypt, and Gulf of Mexico asset purchases from Devon Energy (DVN 64, Buy) boosting production 13% in 2010 and 20% in 2011.

▶ Production at Van Gogh and Pyrenees began in the first half of 2010. APA's 2009 capex was $4.1 billion, down close to 40%, on lower activity, and plans call for capex of $6 billion in 2010. Spending is expected to increase in every region and remain within cash flows.

▶ After operating EPS of $5.60 in 2009, down from 2008's $11.28, on lower prices, we see an advance to $9.52 in 2010 and $11.62 in 2011 on production and oil price gains. The debt-to-capital ratio is 22%, and the balance sheet remains one of the strongest among peers, in our view.

Investment Rationale/Risk

▶ APA is exploiting mature North American reserves and focusing capital on international development projects (offshore Australia, and the Salam gas plant in Egypt). We expect APA to protect its top-tier balance sheet, and we see cash flow funding projects. APA's pending acquisition of BP's assets in the Permian Basin, Canada and Egypt for $7 billion ($18/bbl of proved reserves, in line with recent deals) adds immense opportunity in three core operating regions. Investor concerns over a raised stake in the Gulf, from the pending $3.7 billion purchase of Mariner Energy (ME 23.50, Hold) have begun to subside, in our view, as we see little shelf impact, although we do see deepwater deferrals and higher costs.

▶ Risks to our opinion and target price include unfavorable changes to economic, industry and operating conditions, including increased costs, and difficulty replacing reserves.

▶ Our strong buy opinion reflects large crude oil projects, especially internationally, providing solid growth visibility. We blend our NAV estimate ($139) with DCF ($141; WACC of 11%, terminal growth of 3%) and relative metrics to derive our 12-month target price of $133.

Dividend Data (Dates: mm/dd Payment Date: mm/dd/yy)

Amount ($)	Date Decl.	Ex-Div. Date	Stk. of Record	Payment Date
0.150	12/11	01/20	01/22	02/22/10
0.150	03/11	04/20	04/22	05/21/10
0.150	05/12	07/20	07/22	08/23/10
0.150	09/24	10/20	10/22	11/22/10

Dividends have been paid since 1965. Source: Company reports.

Please read the Required Disclosures and Analyst Certification on the last page of this report.

Apache Corp

Business Summary August 11, 2010

CORPORATE OVERVIEW. One of the largest independent exploration and production (E&P) companies in the U.S., Apache Corp. (APA) explores for, develops and produces natural gas, crude oil and natural gas liquids (NGLs).

In North America, APA's interests are focused on the Gulf of Mexico, the Gulf Coast, East Texas, the Permian Basin, the Anadarko Basin, and the Western Sedimentary Basin of Canada. Outside of North America, APA has interests in Egypt, offshore Western Australia, offshore the U.K. in the North Sea, and onshore Argentina. APA's North American asset base comprises the U.S. Central region, U.S. Gulf Coast region and Canada region. Oil and liquids production, mainly from the U.S. Permian Basin and the Gulf of Mexico, made up nearly 40% of North American production and 46% of North American year-end estimated proved reserves.

At year-end 2009, Canada held approximately 22% of the company's estimated proved reserves. APA and EnCana Corporation (ECA) are 50% partners and control more than 400,000 acres in the Horn River Basin shale-gas play in northeast British Columbia.

Egypt holds APA's largest acreage position, with more than 11 million gross acres that provide considerable exploration and development opportunities. In addition to being the largest acreage holder in Egypt's Western Desert, APA believes it is also the largest producer of liquid hydrocarbons and natural gas in the Western Desert and the third largest in all of Egypt. In 2009, Egypt contributed 26% of total production and 13% of total estimated proved reserves.

In Australia, exploration activity is focused in the offshore Carnarvon, Gippsland and Browse Basins, where APA holds 4.3 million net acres. In 2009, the region increased production 40% and accounted for approximately 7% of total production and 13% of year-end estimated proved reserves.

Company Financials Fiscal Year Ended Dec. 31

Per Share Data ($)	2009	2008	2007	2006	2005	2004	2003	2002	2001	2000
Tangible Book Value	46.34	48.63	46.49	39.30	31.06	24.18	19.25	15.33	14.69	12.07
Cash Flow	6.57	25.68	15.41	13.19	12.22	8.81	6.67	4.55	5.30	4.46
Earnings	-0.87	2.10	8.39	7.64	7.84	5.04	3.35	1.80	2.37	2.48
S&P Core Earnings	-0.87	2.08	8.38	7.30	7.60	5.19	3.29	1.73	2.28	NA
Dividends	0.60	0.70	0.60	0.60	0.34	0.32	0.21	0.19	0.12	0.09
Payout Ratio	NM	33%	7%	8%	4%	6%	6%	11%	5%	4%
Prices:High	106.46	149.23	109.32	76.25	78.15	55.16	41.68	28.88	31.55	32.12
Prices:Low	51.03	57.11	63.01	56.50	47.45	36.79	26.26	21.12	16.56	13.91
P/E Ratio:High	NM	71	13	10	10	11	12	16	13	13
P/E Ratio:Low	NM	27	8	7	6	7	8	12	7	6

Income Statement Analysis (Million $)	2009	2008	2007	2006	2005	2004	2003	2002	2001	2000
Revenue	8,615	12,390	9,978	8,289	7,584	5,333	4,190	2,560	2,777	2,284
Operating Income	NA	8,988	7,224	5,753	5,792	4,119	3,241	1,048	2,146	1,310
Depreciation, Depletion and Amortization	2,500	7,952	2,348	1,816	1,416	1,222	1,073	844	821	584
Interest Expense	242	166	312	158	122	120	127	133	132	109
Pretax Income	326	932	4,673	4,010	4,206	2,663	1,922	899	1,199	1,204
Effective Tax Rate	187.1%	23.6%	39.8%	36.3%	37.6%	37.3%	43.0%	38.3%	39.7%	40.1%
Net Income	-284	712	2,812	2,552	2,624	1,670	1,095	554	723	721
S&P Core Earnings	-292	701	2,805	2,434	2,539	1,713	1,069	524	681	NA

Balance Sheet & Other Financial Data (Million $)	2009	2008	2007	2006	2005	2004	2003	2002	2001	2000
Cash	2,048	1,973	126	141	229	111	33.5	51.9	35.6	37.2
Current Assets	4,586	4,451	2,752	2,490	2,162	1,349	899	767	698	630
Total Assets	28,186	29,186	28,635	24,308	19,272	15,502	12,416	9,460	8,934	7,482
Current Liabilities	2,393	2,615	2,665	3,812	2,187	1,283	820	532	522	553
Long Term Debt	4,950	4,809	4,227	2,020	2,192	2,588	2,327	2,159	2,244	2,193
Common Equity	15,779	16,509	15,280	13,093	10,443	8,106	6,434	4,826	4,112	3,448
Total Capital	20,839	24,484	23,315	18,830	12,733	10,793	8,860	7,083	7,655	5,948
Capital Expenditures	3,631	5,973	5,807	3,892	3,716	2,456	1,595	1,037	1,525	1,011
Cash Flow	2,208	8,658	5,154	4,363	4,034	2,887	2,163	1,387	1,525	1,284
Current Ratio	1.9	1.7	1.0	0.7	1.0	1.1	1.1	1.4	1.3	1.1
% Long Term Debt of Capitalization	23.9	19.6	20.7	13.3	17.2	24.0	26.3	30.5	29.3	36.9
% Return on Assets	NM	2.5	10.6	11.7	15.1	12.0	10.0	6.0	8.8	11.1
% Return on Equity	NM	4.5	19.8	21.6	28.2	22.9	19.4	12.2	18.6	24.1

Data as orig reptd.; bef. results of disc opers/spec. items. Per share data adj. for stk. divs.; EPS diluted. E-Estimated. NA-Not Available. NM-Not Meaningful. NR-Not Ranked. UR-Under Review.

Office: 2000 Post Oak Blvd Ste 100, Houston, TX 77056-4400.
Telephone: 713-296-6000.
Website: http://www.apachecorp.com
Chrmn & CEO: G.S. Farris

Pres & CFO: R.B. Plank
COO: J.A. Crum
COO: R.J. Eichler
EVP & General Counsel: P.A. Lannie

Investor Contact: T. Chambers (713-296-6685)
Board Members: F. M. Bohen, G. S. Farris, R. M. Ferlic, E. C. Fiedorek, A. Frazier, Jr., P. A. Graham, J. A. Kocur, G. D. Lawrence, Jr., F. H. Merelli, R. D. Patton, C. Pitman

Founded: 1954
Domicile: Delaware
Employees: 3,452

Apartment Investment and Management Co

STANDARD &POOR'S

S&P Recommendation BUY ★★★★☆

Price	12-Mo. Target Price	Investment Style
$23.57 (as of Oct 22, 2010)	$25.00	Large-Cap Value

GICS Sector Financials
Sub-Industry Residential REITS

Summary This real estate investment trust is one of the largest U.S. owners and managers of multi-family apartment properties.

Key Stock Statistics (Source S&P, Vickers, company reports)

52-Wk Range	$24.21– 11.80	S&P FFO/Sh. 2010E	1.40	Market Capitalization(B)	$2.759	Beta	2.31
Trailing 12-Month FFO/Share	NA	S&P FFO/Sh. 2011E	1.50	Yield (%)	1.70	S&P 3-Yr. FFO/Sh. Proj. CAGR(%)	-2
Trailing 12-Month P/FFO	NA	P/FFO on S&P FFO/Sh. 2010E	16.8	Dividend Rate/Share	$0.40	S&P Credit Rating	BB+
$10K Invested 5 Yrs Ago	$12,355	Common Shares Outstg. (M)	117.0	Institutional Ownership (%)	94		

Price Performance

30-Week Mov. Avg. ···· 10-Week Mov. Avg. – – GAAP Earnings vs. Previous Year   Volume Above Avg. STARS
12-Mo. Target Price — Relative Strength — ▲ Up ▼ Down ▶ No Change   Below Avg. ★

Options: CBOE, P, Ph

Analysis prepared by **Royal F. Shepard, CFA** on August 11, 2010, when the stock traded at **$ 21.06.**

Highlights

► We think demand for apartments in many U.S. markets has turned positive, due to a declining home ownership rate and a limited amount of new supply. During the second quarter, AIV renewed existing leases at rates that were 1.9% above rents previously in place. Owing to an occupancy rate of 95.6%, as of June 30, we think the trust's pricing power will grow in coming periods. We estimate total revenues will decline about 10% in 2010, reflecting $1.3 billion in 2009 asset sales.

► We expect AIV to slow its disposition program in 2010, and begin considering new acquisitions in its core markets. We estimate the trust now derives more than 80% of operating income from its top 20 targeted markets. We anticipate new investments in coastal markets with limited competition from new construction activity.

► Our 2010 FFO per-share estimate of $1.40 reflects dilution from 2009 property sales and about a 1% decline in operating income on a same-property basis. We expect the trust to maintain the current annual dividend payout of $0.40 through 2010 in an effort to conserve cash.

Investment Rationale/Risk

► AIV holds what we view as a large and diversified portfolio of conventional and affordable residential properties. We think challenging economic conditions are beginning to ease for many apartment owners and may allow renewed rent growth in the second half of 2010. In our view, AIV has successfully repositioned its portfolio in attractive coastal markets. AIV also has recurring management fees that provide a degree of stability. We consider the shares undervalued, recently trading at 15.0X our 2010 FFO estimate of $1.40, a 20% discount to apartment REIT peers.

► Risks to our opinion and target price include slower-than-expected employment growth in AIV's markets, higher borrowing rates on floating rate debt, and a significant increase in new construction that creates competitive supply.

► Our 12-month target price of $25 is based partly on a multiple of 17.9X our 2010 FFO estimate of $1.40, a discount to peers and incorporating our view of AIV's below-average financial position. We blend in our net asset value model, based on recent transactions and a one-year cash return of 6.00%, leading to intrinsic value of $26.

Qualitative Risk Assessment

LOW	MEDIUM	HIGH

Our risk assessment for AIV reflects its a high level of financial leverage, offset by what we consider a manageable level of near-term debt maturities and improving operating performance.

Quantitative Evaluations

S&P Quality Ranking B-

D	C	B-	B	B+	A-	A	A+

Relative Strength Rank STRONG

77

LOWEST = 1   HIGHEST = 99

Revenue/FFO Data

Revenue (Million $)

	1Q	2Q	3Q	4Q	Year
2010	293.0	295.0	--	--	--
2009	297.5	299.1	296.4	302.8	1,196
2008	349.2	374.0	375.1	359.6	1,458
2007	413.1	426.4	426.7	455.0	1,721
2006	408.5	420.0	423.9	438.6	1,691
2005	361.6	372.3	386.8	400.9	1,522

FFO Per Share ($)

	1Q	2Q	3Q	4Q	Year
2010	0.37	0.49	E0.33	E0.34	E1.40
2009	0.42	0.44	0.31	0.25	1.55
2008	0.79	0.83	0.82	-0.34	1.45
2007	0.74	0.88	0.83	0.83	3.17
2006	0.68	0.73	0.74	0.91	3.07
2005	0.63	0.67	0.58	0.60	2.48

Fiscal year ended Dec. 31. Next earnings report expected: Early November. FFO Estimates based on S&P Funds From Operations Est..

Dividend Data (Dates: mm/dd Payment Date: mm/dd/yy)

Amount ($)	Date Decl.	Ex-Div. Date	Stk. of Record	Payment Date
0.100	10/29	11/18	11/20	11/30/09
0.100	12/18	12/29	12/31	01/29/10
0.100	04/29	05/19	05/21	06/01/10
0.100	07/29	08/18	08/20	08/31/10

Dividends have been paid since 1994. Source: Company reports.

Please read the Required Disclosures and Analyst Certification on the last page of this report.

The McGraw-Hill Companies

Apartment Investment and Management Co

STANDARD &POOR'S

Business Summary August 11, 2010

CORPORATE OVERVIEW. Apartment Investment and Management Co. is one of the largest U.S. multi-family residential REITs in terms of units. At December 31, 2009, it owned, held an equity interest in, or managed a geographically diversified portfolio of 870 properties, including about 135,654 apartment units, located in 44 states, the District of Columbia and Puerto Rico.

The trust conducts substantially all its business, and owns all its assets, through AIMCO Properties, L.P., of which AIV owns approximately a 91% interest. AIV operates in two segments: the ownership, operation and management of apartment properties; and the management of apartment properties for third parties and affiliates.

MARKET PROFILE. The U.S. housing market is highly fragmented, and is characterized broadly by two types of housing units -- multi-family and single-family. At the end of 2009, the U.S. Census Bureau estimated that there were 130.59 million housing units in the country, an increase of 0.9% from 2008. Partially due to the high fragmentation since residents have the option of either being owners or tenants (renters), the housing market can be highly competitive. Main demand drivers for apartments are household formation and em-

ployment growth. We estimate that 0.5 million new households were formed in 2009. Supply is created by new housing unit construction, which could consist of single-family homes, or multi-family apartment buildings or condominiums. The U.S. Department of Housing estimates that 0.55 million total housing units were started in 2009, down about 39% from 2008. Multi-family starts, for structures with more than five units, fell an estimated 63%.

With apartment tenants on relatively short leases compared to those of commercial and industrial properties, apartment REITs are generally more sensitive to changes in market conditions than REITs in other property categories. Results could be hurt by new construction that adds new space in excess of actual demand. Trends in home price affordability also affect both rent levels and the level of new construction, since the relative price attractiveness of owning versus renting is an important factor in consumer decision making.

Company Financials Fiscal Year Ended Dec. 31

Per Share Data ($)	2009	2008	2007	2006	2005	2004	2003	2002	2001	2000
Tangible Book Value	4.10	5.51	9.82	NA	NA	NA	NA	NA	18.90	23.33
Earnings	-2.34	-1.51	-1.14	-1.29	-1.25	-0.39	-0.25	0.94	0.23	0.52
S&P Core Earnings	-1.75	-1.51	-1.12	-1.29	-1.25	-0.39	-0.32	0.89	0.19	NA
Dividends	0.40	1.20	2.40	NA	NA	NA	NA	NA	3.12	2.80
Payout Ratio	NM	NM	NM	NM	NM	NM	NM	NM	NM	NM
Prices:High	17.09	43.67	65.79	59.17	44.14	39.25	42.05	51.46	50.13	50.06
Prices:Low	4.57	7.01	33.97	37.76	34.17	26.45	33.00	33.90	39.25	36.31
P/E Ratio:High	NM	1458	NM	NM	NM	NM	NM	55	NM	96
P/E Ratio:Low	NM	NM	NM	NM	NM	NM	NM	36	NM	70

Income Statement Analysis (Million $)										
Rental Income	1,141	1,351	1,641	1,630	1,460	1,402	1,446	1,292	1,298	1,051
Mortgage Income	Nil	Nil	Nil	Nil	Nil	Nil	Nil	Nil	Nil	Nil
Total Income	1,196	1,458	1,721	1,691	1,522	1,469	1,516	1,506	1,464	1,101
General Expenses	627	795	886	874	816	768	729	664	652	485
Interest Expense	324	369	422	408	368	367	373	340	316	270
Provision for Losses	21.5	4.18	3.95	2.78	1.37	Nil	Nil	Nil	Nil	Nil
Depreciation	444	459	473	471	412	369	328	289	364	330
Net Income	-217	-129	-48.1	-42.7	-27.9	55.7	70.7	175	107	99.2
S&P Core Earnings	-200	-183	-112	-124	-117	-35.5	-29.2	77.1	13.8	NA

Balance Sheet & Other Financial Data (Million $)										
Cash	81.3	300	210	230	330	293	98.0	97.0	820	1,068
Total Assets	7,906	9,403	10,607	10,290	10,017	10,072	10,113	10,317	8,323	7,700
Real Estate Investment	9,663	10,885	12,384	11,982	10,990	10,800	10,601	10,227	8,416	7,012
Loss Reserve	Nil	Nil	Nil	Nil	Nil	Nil	Nil	Nil	Nil	Nil
Net Investment	6,962	8,102	9,349	9,081	8,752	8,785	8,753	8,616	6,796	6,099
Short Term Debt	Nil	Nil	Nil	Nil	Nil	Nil	Nil	Nil	214	329
Capitalization:Debt	5,690	6,777	7,532	6,873	6,284	5,734	6,198	5,529	4,670	4,031
Capitalization:Equity	579	722	1,026	1,516	1,706	1,967	2,005	2,218	1,592	1,664
Capitalization:Total	7,342	8,632	9,838	9,165	9,436	9,246	9,580	9,180	7,904	7,037
% Earnings & Depreciation/Assets	2.6	3.3	4.2	4.2	3.8	4.2	3.9	5.0	5.9	1.5
Price Times Book Value:High	4.2	7.9	6.7	4.0	2.5	1.9	2.0	2.3	2.7	2.1
Price Times Book Value:Low	1.1	1.3	3.5	2.5	1.9	1.3	1.6	1.5	2.1	1.6

Data as orig reptd.; bef. results of disc opers/spec. items. Per share data adj. for stk. divs.; EPS diluted. E-Estimated. NA-Not Available. NM-Not Meaningful. NR-Not Ranked. UR-Under Review.

Office: 4582 S Ulster St Pkwy Ste 1100, Denver, CO 80237-2662.
Telephone: 303-757-8101.
Email: investor@aimco.com
Website: http://www.aimco.com

Chrmn & CEO: T. Considine
COO & Co-Pres: T.J. Beaudin
EVP & CFO: E.M. Freedman
EVP & Chief Admin Officer: M. Cortez

EVP & Treas: P.K. Fielding
Investor Contact: J. Martin (303-691-4440)
Board Members: J. N. Bailey, T. Considine, R. S. Ellwood, T. L. Keltner, J. Martin, R. A. Miller, K. M. Nelson, M. A. Stein

Founded: 1994
Domicile: Maryland
Employees: 3,500

The McGraw-Hill Companies

Apollo Group Inc

STANDARD &POOR'S

S&P Recommendation HOLD ★ ★ ★ ★ ★

Price	12-Mo. Target Price	Investment Style
$36.00 (as of Oct 22, 2010)	$40.00	Large-Cap Growth

GICS Sector Consumer Discretionary
Sub-Industry Education Services

Summary This provider of higher education programs for working adults offers educational programs and services throughout the U.S. and in a small number of foreign markets.

Key Stock Statistics (Source S&P, Vickers, company reports)

52-Wk Range	$75.10– 35.54	S&P Oper. EPS 2011E	4.20	Market Capitalization(B)	$5.294	Beta	0.07
Trailing 12-Month EPS	$3.62	S&P Oper. EPS 2012E	4.40	Yield (%)	Nil	S&P 3-Yr. Proj. EPS CAGR(%)	14
Trailing 12-Month P/E	9.9	P/E on S&P Oper. EPS 2011E	8.6	Dividend Rate/Share	Nil	S&P Credit Rating	NA
$10K Invested 5 Yrs Ago	$6,027	Common Shares Outstg. (M)	147.5	Institutional Ownership (%)	87		

Price Performance

30-Week Mov. Avg. · · ·   10-Week Mov. Avg. - -   **GAAP Earnings vs. Previous Year**   Volume Above Avg. STARS
12-Mo. Target Price —   Relative Strength —   ▲ Up   ▼ Down   ▶ No Change   Below Avg. ★

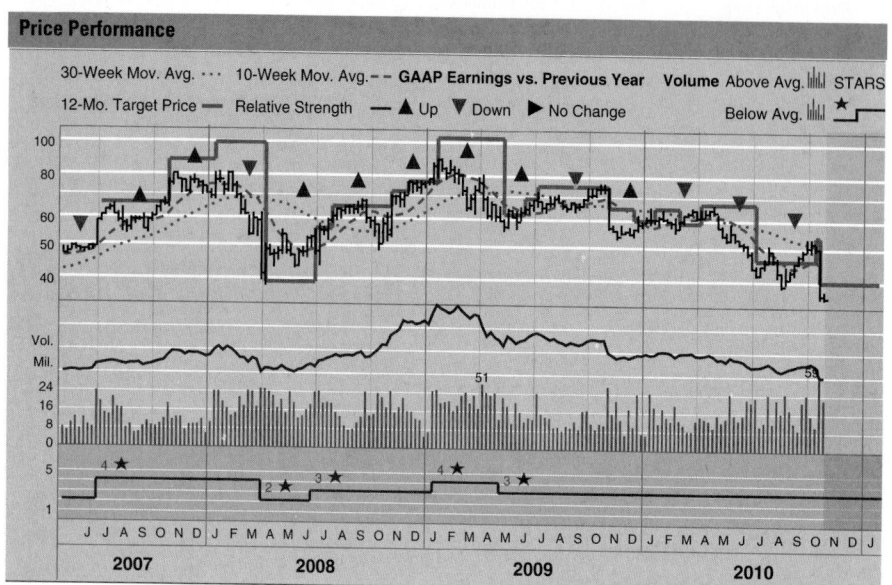

Options: ASE, CBOE, P, Ph

Qualitative Risk Assessment

LOW	MEDIUM	HIGH

Our risk assessment reflects a lack of consistent conditions in the for-profit education market, and APOL's frequent transformations of its business model. In the corporate governance area, we have a negative view of the near 100% voting control held by insiders through separate voting shares. We believe these factors are offset by what we view as APOL's consistently solid levels of cash flow and a healthy balance sheet.

Quantitative Evaluations

S&P Quality Ranking B+

D	C	B-	B	B+	A-	A	A+

Relative Strength Rank WEAK

5

LOWEST = 1   HIGHEST = 99

Highlights

▶ The 12-month target price for APOL has recently been changed to $40.00 from $54.00. The Highlights section of this Stock Report will be updated accordingly.

Investment Rationale/Risk

▶ The Investment Rationale/Risk section of this Stock Report will be updated shortly. For the latest News story on APOL from MarketScope, see below.

▶ 10/14/10 11:21 am ET ... S&P REITERATES HOLD OPINION ON SHARES OF APOLLO GROUP (APOL 37.2***): Aug-Q adjusted EPS of $1.31 vs. $1.10 meets our view. But APOL shares and peers are down sharply, as APOL sees a major decline in new students in the near-term, on proposed new government student lending rules. On top of new proposed regulations, APOL is near the 90% cut off point for revenues allowed from federal student loan usage, with an overall impact likely to be greater than we expected. We cut our FY 11 (Aug) EPS by $1.45 to $4.20, and start FY 12 at $4.40. We lower our target price by $14 to $40, 9.4X our calendar '11 estimate and low-end of APOL's historical range. /M.Jaffe

Revenue/Earnings Data

Revenue (Million $)

	1Q	2Q	3Q	4Q	Year
2010	1,270	1,070	1,337	1,259	4,926
2009	971.0	876.1	1,051	1,076	3,974
2008	780.7	693.6	835.2	831.4	3,141
2007	667.8	608.7	733.4	713.9	2,724
2006	628.9	569.6	653.6	624.2	2,478
2005	534.9	505.7	619.0	591.8	2,251

Earnings Per Share ($)

2010	1.54	0.67	1.16	0.32	3.72
2009	1.12	0.77	1.26	0.59	3.75
2008	0.83	-0.19	0.85	1.43	2.87
2007	0.65	0.35	0.75	0.60	2.35
2006	0.73	0.46	0.77	0.54	2.35
2005	0.58	0.47	0.77	0.58	2.39

Fiscal year ended Aug. 31. Next earnings report expected: Early January. EPS Estimates based on S&P Operating Earnings; historical GAAP earnings are as reported.

Dividend Data

No cash dividends have been paid.

Apollo Group Inc

Business Summary October 06, 2010

CORPORATE OVERVIEW. Historically, Apollo Group derived most of its revenues by providing higher education programs for working adults. It has several school units, but the large majority of its students have taken education programs at its University of Phoenix (UOP) unit. UOP offers its education programs at campuses, as well as through online programs. They consist mostly of associates, bachelors and masters degree programs in business, education, information technology, criminal justice and nursing. At May 31, 2010, APOL offered programs and services in 40 states, the District of Columbia, Puerto Rico, Canada, Latin America and Europe. Enrollment at UOP totaled 476,500 at May 31, 2010, up from 443,000 at August 31, 2009, 362,100 at August 31, 2008, and 313,700 at August 31, 2007.

CORPORATE STRATEGY. After falling to 3.3% in FY 06's (Aug.) third quarter (from 27.7% in FY 04's fourth quarter), Apollo's enrollment growth has revived, and stood at 13.3% in FY 10's third quarter (but down from 22.3% in FY 09's fourth quarter, which was the peak in this period of reviving enrollments). We attribute the initial downturn to changing demographic trends, greater competition and more regulatory scrutiny. Until a few years ago, APOL focused almost entirely on students who were older than the traditional 18-to-22 year-old college student, chiefly baby boomers. Yet, with the youngest baby boomers now over the age of 40, APOL began to seek students in other demographic categories. As a result, it began to place much more concentration on associate degrees, targeting younger students (with 45% of APOL's student count enrolled in associates programs at May 31, 2010). Yet, with persistence rates and loan repayment less favorable among its associates population, APOL has again moved back towards a focus on bachelors programs. Also, in an effort to boost student retention and student loan repayments, Apollo announced in June 2010, that it would soon require all prospective students with less than 24 credit hours to attend a free three week orientation program.

In October 2007, Apollo formed a $1 billion joint venture (Apollo Global) with the Carlyle Group, a private equity firm, to invest in the foreign education services sector. APOL committed up to $801 million (funding $440.5 million of $511.8 million in cash contributions made to Apollo Global through FY 09 year-end), and owned 86.1% of the venture as of mid-October 2009. We view this as an important step for APOL to expand its global footprint. In July 2009, Apollo Global purchased U.K.-based BPP Holdings plc (revenues of $263 million and pretax profit of $31.2 million in calendar 2008), which provides education and training to legal and financial professionals, for $602 million, net of and including certain items. This followed two much smaller foreign acquisitions in 2008.

Company Financials Fiscal Year Ended Aug. 31

Per Share Data ($)	2010	2009	2008	2007	2006	2005	2004	2003	2002	2001
Tangible Book Value	NA	44.33	4.56	3.62	3.40	3.73	4.89	5.23	3.60	2.47
Cash Flow	4.68	4.38	3.35	2.77	2.74	2.68	1.79	1.62	1.12	0.81
Earnings	3.72	3.75	2.87	2.35	2.35	2.39	0.77	1.30	0.87	0.60
S&P Core Earnings	5.42	4.08	2.87	2.35	2.42	2.30	0.72	1.22	0.79	0.52
Dividends	NA	Nil	Nil	Nil	Nil	Nil	Nil	Nil	Nil	Nil
Payout Ratio	Nil	Nil	Nil	Nil	Nil	Nil	Nil	Nil	Nil	Nil
Prices:High	66.69	90.00	81.68	80.75	63.26	84.20	98.01	73.09	46.15	33.31
Prices:Low	35.54	52.79	37.92	39.02	33.33	57.40	62.55	40.72	28.13	19.33
P/E Ratio:High	18	24	28	34	25	35	NM	56	53	56
P/E Ratio:Low	10	14	13	17	13	24	NM	31	32	32

Income Statement Analysis (Million $)	2010	2009	2008	2007	2006	2005	2004	2003	2002	2001
Revenue	4,926	3,974	3,141	2,724	2,478	2,251	1,798	1,340	1,009	769
Operating Income	1,520	1,229	829	697	738	767	481	428	293	194
Depreciation	147	117	79.7	71.1	67.3	54.5	43.2	40.3	35.2	32.7
Interest Expense	11.9	4.46	Nil	Nil	Nil	Nil	Nil	Nil	Nil	Nil
Pretax Income	1,001	1,040	783	657	668	730	456	402	266	175
Effective Tax Rate	NA	42.9%	39.2%	37.8%	37.9%	39.1%	39.1%	38.5%	39.4%	38.4%
Net Income	568	129	477	409	415	445	278	247	161	108
S&P Core Earnings	829	651	477	409	428	427	131	218	140	90.1

Balance Sheet & Other Financial Data (Million $)	2010	2009	2008	2007	2006	2005	2004	2003	2002	2001
Cash	1,285	968	486	370	355	595	677	800	610	375
Current Assets	2,253	1,880	1,170	925	803	835	855	950	730	487
Total Assets	3,601	3,263	1,860	1,450	1,283	1,303	1,452	1,378	980	680
Current Liabilities	1,794	1,755	866	744	596	518	465	335	264	182
Long Term Debt	168	128	Nil	Nil	Nil	Nil	Nil	Nil	15.5	14.8
Common Equity	1,356	1,158	834	634	604	707	957	1,027	699	482
Total Capital	1,557	7,966	849	634	604	707	957	1,027	715	497
Capital Expenditures	168	127	105	61.2	44.6	104	80.3	55.8	36.7	44.4
Cash Flow	715	698	556	480	482	499	321	287	196	141
Current Ratio	1.3	1.1	1.4	1.2	1.3	1.6	1.8	2.8	2.8	2.7
% Long Term Debt of Capitalization	10.8	9.4	Nil	Nil	Nil	Nil	Nil	Nil	2.2	3.0
% Net Income of Revenue	11.5	15.1	15.2	15.0	16.7	19.8	15.4	18.4	16.0	14.0
% Return on Assets	16.6	23.4	28.8	29.9	32.4	31.8	19.6	20.9	19.4	19.9
% Return on Equity	45.2	60.1	64.9	66.0	67.0	53.5	28.0	28.6	29.3	29.0

Data as orig reptd.; bef. results of disc opers/spec. items. Per share data adj. for stk. divs.; EPS diluted. E-Estimated. NA-Not Available. NM-Not Meaningful. NR-Not Ranked. UR-Under Review.

Office: 4025 S. Riverpoint Pkwy, Phoenix, AZ 85040.
Telephone: 480-966-5394.
Website: http://www.apollogrp.edu
Chrmn: J. Sperling

Pres & COO: J.L. D'Amico
Vice Chrmn: P. Sperling
Co-CEO: G.W. Cappelli
Co-CEO: C.B. Edelstein

Investor Contact: J. Pasinski (800-990-2765)
Board Members: T. C. Bishop, G. W. Cappelli, D. J. Deconcini, S. A. DiPiazza, Jr., C. B. Edelstein, S. J. Giusto, R. A. Herberger, Jr., A. Kirschner, K. S. Redman, J. R. Reis, M. F. Rivelo, J. Sperling, P. Sperling, G. Zimmer

Founded: 1981
Domicile: Arizona
Employees: 57,414

Apple Inc

STANDARD &POOR'S

S&P Recommendation | STRONG BUY ★★★★★

Price	**12-Mo. Target Price**	**Investment Style**
$307.47 (as of Oct 22, 2010)	$375.00	Large-Cap Growth

GICS Sector Information Technology
Sub-Industry Computer Hardware

Summary This company is a prominent provider of hardware and software, including the Macintosh (Mac) computer, the iPod digital media player, and the iPhone.

Key Stock Statistics (Source S&P, Vickers, company reports)

52-Wk Range	$319.00– 185.57	S&P Oper. EPS 2011**E**	18.46	Market Capitalization(B)	$280.893
Trailing 12-Month EPS	$15.15	S&P Oper. EPS 2012**E**	NA	Yield (%)	Nil
Trailing 12-Month P/E	20.3	P/E on S&P Oper. EPS 2011**E**	16.7	Dividend Rate/Share	Nil
$10K Invested 5 Yrs Ago	$55,241	Common Shares Outstg. (M)	913.6	Institutional Ownership (%)	69

Beta	1.43
S&P 3-Yr. Proj. EPS CAGR(%)	35
S&P Credit Rating	NR

Price Performance

30-Week Mov. Avg. · · · 10-Week Mov. Avg. - - **GAAP Earnings vs. Previous Year** Volume Above Avg. STARS
12-Mo. Target Price — Relative Strength — ▲ Up ▼ Down ► No Change Below Avg. ★

Options: ASE, CBOE, P, Ph

Analysis prepared by **Clyde Montevirgen** on October 19, 2010, when the stock traded at **$ 311.53**.

Highlights

► We estimate sales growth of 27% for FY 11 (Sep.), following a 52% advance in FY 10. We expect strong unit sales growth for iPhones, iPads, and MacBooks, and, consequently, we anticipate iTunes revenues advancing as AAPL's hardware sales promote downloads for Apps, music, and movies. We see iMac shipments rising modestly on product refreshes, but iPod units declining largely due to AAPL's large market share in this space and market saturation.

► We expect the gross margin to remain around 39% in FY 11, similar to FY 10 results. We believe the margins for the latest iPhone and iPad will improve slowly due to scale and cost-cutting efforts, balancing anticipated declining average selling prices for Macs and iPods. We look for expenses as a percentage of sales to remain around current levels as AAPL invests in new products, and we believe the operating margin will remain about 28%.

► Our FY EPS projections assume an effective tax rate around 26% and a modest increase in the share count.

Investment Rationale/Risk

► Our strong buy opinion reflects our favorable view of AAPL's growth. We are cautious about demand for consumer electronics products during a fragile economic recovery, and we are also concerned about pricing pressure on computers and MP3 players, but we think AAPL's iPhone, iPad, and MacBook products will provide secular and above-peers growth. With earnings growth expected to lead most mega- and large-cap technology companies, and considering AAPL's cash position, strong free cash flow generation, and relatively high return on equity (ROE), we believe multiples should be notably above those of the IT sector.

► Risks to our recommendation and target price include weak end-market demand, pricing pressure, competitive handset offerings, and poor execution of the iPad.

► Our 12-month target price of $375 is based on a P/E multiple of about 19X our calendar 2011 EPS estimate of $19.81, above the IT sector's to account for our view of relative growth, risk, and ROE. Our valuation is backed by our DCF model, which assumes a terminal growth rate of 4% and a weighted average cost of capital of around 12%, and yields a value of $400.

Qualitative Risk Assessment

LOW	MEDIUM	HIGH

Our risk assessment reflects our view of a seemingly ever-evolving market for consumer-oriented technology products, potential challenges associated with the company's growing size and offerings, and the critical importance to the company of founder and CEO Steve Jobs.

Quantitative Evaluations

S&P Quality Ranking B

D	C	B-	B	B+	A-	A	A+

Relative Strength Rank STRONG

83

LOWEST = 1　　　HIGHEST = 99

Revenue/Earnings Data

Revenue (Million $)

	1Q	2Q	3Q	4Q	Year
2010	15,683	13,499	15,700	20,343	65,225
2009	11,880	9,084	9,734	12,207	42,905
2008	9,608	7,512	7,464	7,895	32,479
2007	7,115	5,264	5,410	6,217	24,006
2006	5,749	4,359	4,370	4,837	19,315
2005	3,490	3,243	3,520	3,678	13,931

Earnings Per Share ($)

2010	3.67	3.33	3.51	4.64	15.15
2009	2.50	1.79	2.01	2.77	9.08
2008	1.76	1.16	1.19	1.26	5.36
2007	1.14	0.87	0.92	1.01	3.93
2006	0.65	0.47	0.54	0.62	2.27
2005	0.35	0.34	0.37	0.50	1.56

Fiscal year ended Sep. 30. Next earnings report expected: Late December. EPS Estimates based on S&P Operating Earnings; historical GAAP earnings are as reported.

Dividend Data

No cash dividends have been paid since 1996.

Please read the Required Disclosures and Analyst Certification on the last page of this report.

The McGraw-Hill Companies

Apple Inc

Business Summary October 19, 2010

CORPORATE OVERVIEW. Apple Inc. makes personal computers, mobile phones and portable digital music and video players and sells a variety of related software, services, peripherals and networking solutions.

Sales of Apple's computer, commonly known as Mac, made up approximately 35% of total revenues in calendar 2009. The company shipped over 11 million units of desktop and laptop computers, with laptop units selling roughly two times desktops. On a unit shipment basis, Macs grew around 13%, much faster than the mid-single digit growth that market researchers report for the PC industry. Mac revenues advanced as greater unit shipments offset deteriorating blended average selling prices, trends we believe will continue over the next couple of years.

AAPL's cellular phones, iPhones, made up over 26% of total 2009 revenues, with over 25 million iPhones sold. Compared to the 30% advance that market researchers reported for smartphone shipments in 2009, iPhone's 84% growth rate led to continued market share gains. This has been the fastest growing business over the past couple of years, and we see this trend continuing and becoming a larger proportion of total revenues. The company used to record

iPhone revenues on a subscription basis, but has since changed its revenue recognition practice and is now recording most of the iPhone's value up front, which should inflate iPhone revenues versus prior periods.

The company's personal media players, iPods, made up around 20% of total 2009 sales. Apple sold over 52 million of these in calendar 2009, and it believes that it currently has over 70% of the MP3 player market. Considering that the company has a large majority of the MP3 market share, and that this is largely a mature market, we believe Apple will likely face declining unit shipments and price deterioration in this business in coming years.

Music-related products, such as iTunes, made up roughly 10% of 2009 sales, while other peripherals/hardware and software/services comprised the remainder of 2009 total revenues.

Company Financials Fiscal Year Ended Sep. 30

Per Share Data ($)	2010	2009	2008	2007	2006	2005	2004	2003	2002	2001
Tangible Book Value	NA	34.66	23.04	16.27	11.47	8.83	6.36	5.61	5.54	5.59
Cash Flow	16.26	9.89	5.88	4.29	2.52	1.77	0.55	0.50	0.25	0.09
Earnings	15.15	9.08	5.36	3.93	2.27	1.56	0.36	0.10	0.09	-0.06
S&P Core Earnings	NA	9.08	5.36	3.93	2.27	1.47	0.22	-0.17	-0.19	-0.72
Dividends	NA	Nil	Nil	Nil	Nil	Nil	Nil	Nil	Nil	Nil
Payout Ratio	Nil	Nil	Nil	Nil	Nil	Nil	Nil	Nil	Nil	Nil
Prices:High	319.00	213.95	200.26	202.96	93.16	75.46	34.79	12.51	13.09	13.56
Prices:Low	190.25	78.20	79.14	81.90	50.16	31.30	10.59	6.36	6.68	7.22
P/E Ratio:High	21	24	37	52	41	48	98	NM	NM	NM
P/E Ratio:Low	13	9	15	21	22	20	30	NM	NM	NM

Income Statement Analysis (Million $)										
Revenue	65,225	42,905	32,479	24,006	19,315	13,931	8,279	6,207	5,742	5,363
Operating Income	19,412	12,474	6,748	4,726	2,645	1,829	499	138	164	-231
Depreciation	1,027	734	473	317	225	179	150	113	118	102
Interest Expense	NA	Nil	Nil	Nil	Nil	Nil	3.00	8.00	11.0	16.0
Pretax Income	18,540	12,066	6,895	5,008	2,818	1,815	383	92.0	87.0	-52.0
Effective Tax Rate	NA	31.8%	29.9%	30.2%	29.4%	26.4%	27.9%	26.1%	25.3%	NM
Net Income	14,013	8,235	4,834	3,496	1,989	1,335	276	68.0	65.0	-37.0
S&P Core Earnings	NA	8,235	4,834	3,496	1,989	1,259	164	-119	-137	-465

Balance Sheet & Other Financial Data (Million $)										
Cash	25,620	23,464	24,490	9,352	6,392	3,491	2,969	3,396	2,252	2,310
Current Assets	41,678	31,555	34,690	21,956	14,509	10,300	7,055	5,887	5,388	5,143
Total Assets	75,183	47,501	39,572	25,347	17,205	11,551	8,050	6,815	6,298	6,021
Current Liabilities	20,722	11,506	14,092	9,299	6,471	3,484	2,680	2,357	1,658	1,518
Long Term Debt	NA	Nil	Nil	Nil	Nil	Nil	Nil	Nil	316	317
Common Equity	47,791	31,640	21,030	14,532	9,984	7,466	5,076	4,223	4,095	3,920
Total Capital	47,791	31,640	21,705	15,151	10,365	7,466	5,076	4,223	4,640	4,503
Capital Expenditures	2,005	1,144	1,091	735	657	260	176	164	174	735
Cash Flow	15,040	8,969	5,307	3,813	2,214	1,514	426	181	183	65.0
Current Ratio	2.0	2.7	2.5	2.4	2.2	3.0	2.6	2.5	3.2	3.4
% Long Term Debt of Capitalization	Nil	Nil	Nil	Nil	Nil	Nil	Nil	Nil	6.8	7.0
% Net Income of Revenue	21.5	19.2	14.9	14.6	10.3	9.6	3.3	1.1	1.1	NM
% Return on Assets	21.7	19.7	14.9	16.4	13.9	13.6	3.7	1.0	1.1	NM
% Return on Equity	37.1	30.5	27.2	28.5	22.8	21.3	5.9	1.6	1.6	NM

Data as orig reptd.; bef. results of disc opers/spec. items. Per share data adj. for stk. divs.; EPS diluted. 2009 data as amended from SEC Form 10-K/A to reflect application of new accounting principles. E-Estimated. NA-Not Available. NM-Not Meaningful. NR-Not Ranked. UR-Under Review.

Office: 1 Infinite Loop, Cupertino, CA 95014.
Telephone: 408-996-1010.
Email: investor_relations@apple.com
Website: http://www.apple.com

CEO: S.P. Jobs
COO: T.D. Cook
Investor Contact: P. Oppenheimer (408-974-3123)
SVP & CFO: P. Oppenheimer

SVP, Secy & General Counsel: B. Sewell
Board Members: W. V. Campbell, M. S. Drexler, A. A. Gore, Jr., S. P. Jobs, A. Jung, A. Levinson

Founded: 1977
Domicile: California
Employees: 36,800

Applied Materials Inc

STANDARD &POOR'S

S&P Recommendation **BUY** ★★★★★	Price $12.13 (as of Oct 22, 2010)	12-Mo. Target Price $14.00	Investment Style Large-Cap Blend

GICS Sector Information Technology
Sub-Industry Semiconductor Equipment

Summary This company is the world's largest manufacturer of wafer fabrication equipment for the semiconductor industry.

Key Stock Statistics (Source S&P, Vickers, company reports)

52-Wk Range	$14.94– 10.27	S&P Oper. EPS 2010**E**	0.82	Market Capitalization(B)	$16.200	Beta	0.98
Trailing 12-Month EPS	$0.45	S&P Oper. EPS 2011**E**	1.32	Yield (%)	2.31	S&P 3-Yr. Proj. EPS CAGR(%)	NM
Trailing 12-Month P/E	26.9	P/E on S&P Oper. EPS 2010**E**	14.8	Dividend Rate/Share	$0.28	S&P Credit Rating	A-
$10K Invested 5 Yrs Ago	$7,728	Common Shares Outstg. (M)	1,336.1	Institutional Ownership (%)	79		

Price Performance

30-Week Mov. Avg. · · · 10-Week Mov. Avg. - - GAAP Earnings vs. Previous Year   Volume Above Avg. STARS
12-Mo. Target Price — Relative Strength — ▲ Up ▼ Down ▶ No Change   Below Avg. ★

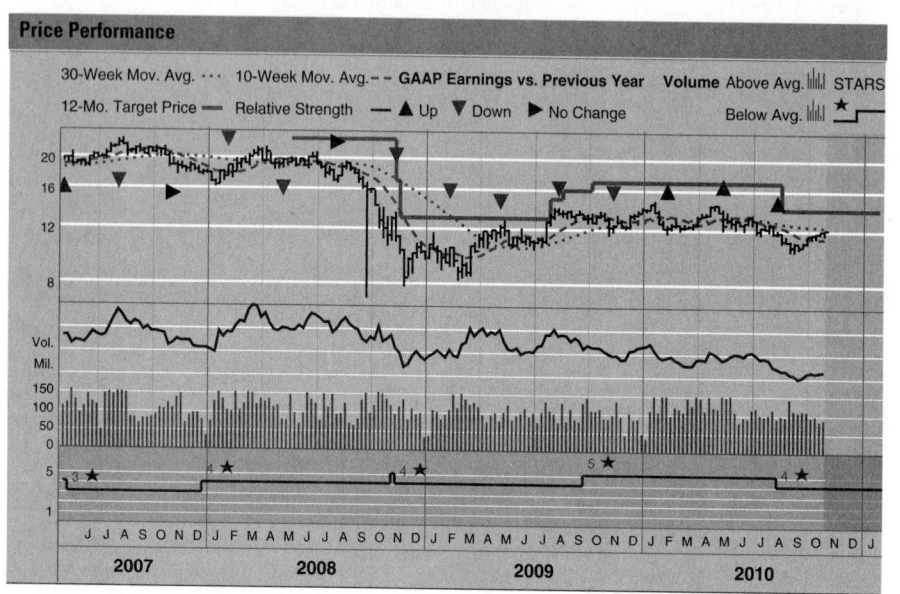

Options: ASE, CBOE, P, Ph

Analysis prepared by **Angelo Zino** on August 19, 2010, when the stock traded at **$ 11.42**.

Qualitative Risk Assessment

LOW	MEDIUM	HIGH

Our risk assessment reflects the historical cyclicality of the semiconductor equipment industry, a lack of visibility in the intermediate term, the dynamic nature of the change in semiconductor technology, and intense competition. This is offset by AMAT's market leadership, size, and what we see as its solid balance sheet.

Quantitative Evaluations

S&P Quality Ranking   B-

D	C	B-	B	B+	A-	A	A+

Relative Strength Rank   MODERATE

57

LOWEST = 1   HIGHEST = 99

Highlights

➤ We project sales to increase 16% in FY 11 (Oct.) following our outlook for an 84% rise in FY 10, as we see semiconductor customers investing in technology purchases and adding capacity. We expect semiconductor equipment sales to improve but at a slower pace going forward. We think flat panel display spending is being driven by improving consumer sentiment. We view solar as a large long-term growth driver and see segment sales being driven by China manufacturers expanding capacity. We believe some chipmakers are beginning to consider new fabs, which should lead to increased equipment spending in FY 11.

➤ We see gross margins of 45% in FY 11 versus our 39% margin projection in FY 10. We expect margins to benefit from higher volume and an ongoing manufacturing shift to Singapore. We anticipate margins being aided by a restructuring of AMAT's solar-related business, which we see resulting in annualized cost savings of at least $100 million upon completion in FY 11.

➤ We forecast operating EPS of $0.82 in FY 10, which excludes $0.17 of non-recurring charges, and $1.32 in FY 11. We model a tax rate of 31% for both FY 10 and FY 11.

Investment Rationale/Risk

➤ We have a favorable view of AMAT's valuation as well as its diversified end markets relative to peers. We think both semiconductor and flat panel equipment spending are poised to experience modest growth near term, as customers appear to be running at elevated capacity utilization levels. We believe AMAT's silicon systems group will see orders begin to flatten, as rising bookings in flash memory is likely to be offset by softer DRAM orders. We project greater solar-related orders, and more importantly, see the segment as profitable in FY 11. We see increasing share gains in both etch and reticle inspection. We view AMAT's financial and market share positions as superior to its peers.

➤ Risks to our recommendation and target price include a greater-than-expected slowdown in the global economy, which could weaken demand for chips and increase pricing pressures.

➤ We derive our 12-month target price of $14 by applying a peer-average price/sales (P/S) multiple of 1.70X to our calendar year 2011 sales per share forecast of $8.13. This ratio is below the company's three- and five-year historical averages of 2.6X and 2.8X, respectively.

Revenue/Earnings Data

Revenue (Million $)

	1Q	2Q	3Q	4Q	Year
2010	1,849	2,296	2,518	--	--
2009	1,333	1,020	1,134	1,526	5,014
2008	2,087	2,150	1,848	2,044	8,129
2007	2,277	2,530	2,561	2,367	9,735
2006	1,858	2,248	2,543	2,518	9,167
2005	1,781	1,861	1,632	1,718	6,992

Earnings Per Share ($)

	1Q	2Q	3Q	4Q	Year
2010	0.06	0.20	0.09	E0.30	E0.82
2009	-0.10	-0.19	-0.04	0.10	-0.23
2008	0.19	0.22	0.12	0.17	0.70
2007	0.29	0.29	0.12	0.30	1.20
2006	0.09	0.26	0.33	0.30	0.97
2005	0.17	0.18	0.23	0.15	0.73

Fiscal year ended Oct. 31. Next earnings report expected: Mid November. EPS Estimates based on S&P Operating Earnings; historical GAAP earnings are as reported.

Dividend Data (Dates: mm/dd Payment Date: mm/dd/yy)

Amount ($)	Date Decl.	Ex-Div. Date	Stk. of Record	Payment Date
0.060	12/08	02/22	02/24	03/17/10
0.070	03/08	05/24	05/26	06/16/10
0.070	06/09	08/23	08/25	09/15/10
0.070	09/14	11/22	11/24	12/15/10

Dividends have been paid since 2005. Source: Company reports.

Please read the Required Disclosures and Analyst Certification on the last page of this report.

The McGraw-Hill Companies

Applied Materials Inc

Business Summary August 19, 2010

CORPORATE OVERVIEW. At the end of FY 09 (Oct.), Applied Materials (AMAT) was the worldwide leader in the manufacturing of semiconductor capital equipment. AMAT divides its business into four segments: Silicon Systems Group, Applied Global Services, Display, and Energy and Environmental Solutions. The Silicon Systems Group, which accounted for 39% of FY 09 sales (49% in FY 08), is focused on developing and selling equipment for use in the front end of the semiconductor fabrication process. The silicon segment includes semiconductor capital equipment for etch, rapid thermal processing, deposition, chemical mechanical planarization, and metrology and inspection. AMAT's equipment in the silicon segment addresses most of the primary steps in chip fabrication.

The Applied Global Services segment, which represented 28% (29%) of FY 09 sales, provides solutions to optimize and increase productivity at customers fabs (semiconductor fabrication facilities). The segment includes products and services to improve the efficiency and reduce operating costs at semiconductor, display and solar customer factories. Applied Global Services products consist of spares, services, certain earlier generation products, and remanufactured equipment.

The Display segment, which comprised for 10% (12%) of FY 09 sales, develops equipment for the fabrication of flat panel displays. The segment develops equipment for manufacturing Liquid Crystal Displays (LCD's) for TVs, personal computers and other video-enabled devices. The Display segment also includes the design and manufacture of differentiated stand-alone equipment for the Applied SunFab Thin Film Line.

The Energy and Environmental Solutions segment accounted for 23% (10%) of sales in FY 09, and involves products targeting the solar photovoltaic (PV) cell market and energy efficient glass. AMAT offers manufacturing solutions for both wafer-based crystalline silicon (c-Si) and glass-based thin film applications to enable customers to increase the conversion efficiency and yields of PV devices.

Company Financials Fiscal Year Ended Oct. 31

Per Share Data ($)	2009	2008	2007	2006	2005	2004	2003	2002	2001	2000
Tangible Book Value	4.19	4.50	4.65	5.80	5.30	5.33	4.62	4.67	4.51	4.20
Cash Flow	-0.01	0.93	1.39	1.14	0.91	0.99	0.14	0.39	0.69	1.41
Earnings	-0.23	0.70	1.20	0.97	0.73	0.78	-0.09	0.16	0.46	1.20
S&P Core Earnings	-0.19	0.69	1.20	0.97	0.54	0.59	-0.33	-0.04	0.33	NA
Dividends	0.24	0.24	0.22	0.16	0.06	Nil	Nil	Nil	Nil	Nil
Payout Ratio	NM	34%	18%	16%	8%	Nil	Nil	Nil	Nil	Nil
Prices:High	14.22	21.75	23.00	21.06	19.47	24.75	25.94	27.95	29.55	57.50
Prices:Low	8.19	7.17	17.35	14.39	14.33	15.36	11.25	10.26	13.30	17.06
P/E Ratio:High	NM	31	19	22	27	32	NM	NM	65	48
P/E Ratio:Low	NM	10	14	15	20	20	NM	NM	29	14

Income Statement Analysis (Million $)	2009	2008	2007	2006	2005	2004	2003	2002	2001	2000
Revenue	5,014	8,129	9,735	9,167	6,992	8,013	4,477	5,062	7,343	9,564
Operating Income	53.4	1,695	2,665	2,517	1,748	2,313	440	683	1,538	3,149
Depreciation	291	320	268	270	300	356	382	388	387	362
Interest Expense	21.3	20.5	38.6	36.1	37.8	52.9	46.9	49.4	47.6	51.4
Pretax Income	-486	1,409	2,440	2,167	1,582	1,829	-212	341	1,104	2,948
Effective Tax Rate	NM	31.8%	29.9%	30.0%	23.5%	26.1%	NM	21.0%	29.8%	30.0%
Net Income	-305	961	1,710	1,517	1,210	1,351	-149	269	775	2,064
S&P Core Earnings	-257	936	1,710	1,511	905	1,017	-562	-65.2	558	NA

Balance Sheet & Other Financial Data (Million $)	2009	2008	2007	2006	2005	2004	2003	2002	2001	2000
Cash	2,215	2,101	1,203	861	990	2,282	1,365	1,285	1,356	1,648
Current Assets	5,689	6,664	6,606	6,081	9,449	10,282	8,371	8,073	7,782	8,839
Total Assets	9,574	10,906	10,654	9,481	11,269	12,093	10,312	10,225	9,829	10,546
Current Liabilities	1,939	2,946	2,373	2,436	1,765	2,288	1,641	1,501	1,533	2,760
Long Term Debt	201	202	202	205	407	410	456	574	565	573
Common Equity	7,095	7,449	7,821	6,651	8,929	9,262	8,068	8,020	7,607	7,104
Total Capital	7,297	7,808	8,023	6,856	9,336	9,672	8,524	8,594	8,172	7,677
Capital Expenditures	248	288	265	179	200	191	265	417	711	383
Cash Flow	-14.1	1,281	1,978	1,787	1,510	1,707	233	657	1,162	2,426
Current Ratio	2.9	2.3	2.8	2.5	5.4	4.5	5.1	5.4	5.1	3.2
% Long Term Debt of Capitalization	2.8	2.6	2.5	3.0	4.4	4.2	5.4	6.7	6.9	7.5
% Net Income of Revenue	NM	11.8	17.5	16.5	17.3	16.9	NM	5.3	10.5	21.6
% Return on Assets	NM	8.9	16.9	14.6	10.4	12.1	NM	2.7	7.6	23.5
% Return on Equity	NM	12.6	23.6	19.5	13.3	15.6	NM	3.4	10.5	35.3

Data as orig reptd.; bef. results of disc opers/spec. items. Per share data adj. for stk. divs.; EPS diluted. E-Estimated. NA-Not Available. NM-Not Meaningful. NR-Not Ranked. UR-Under Review.

Office: 3050 Bowers Avenue, Santa Clara, CA, United States 95054-3298.
Telephone: 408-727-5555.
Email: investor_relations@appliedmaterials.com
Website: http://www.appliedmaterials.com

Chrmn, Pres & CEO: M.R. Splinter
EVP & CFO: G.S. Davis
EVP & CTO: M. Pinto
SVP, Secy & General Counsel: J.J. Sweeney

Chief Acctg Officer & Cntlr: T. Timko
Board Members: S. R. Forrest, T. Iannotti, S. M. James, A. A. Karsner, G. H. Parker, D. D. Powell, W. P. Roelandts, J. E. Rogers, Jr., M. R. Splinter, R. H. Swan, A. J. de Geus

Founded: 1967
Domicile: Delaware
Employees: 12,619

Archer-Daniels-Midland Co

STANDARD &POOR'S

S&P Recommendation HOLD ★★★★★

Price	**12-Mo. Target Price**	**Investment Style**
$33.54 (as of Oct 22, 2010)	$33.00	Large-Cap Blend

GICS Sector Consumer Staples
Sub-Industry Agricultural Products

Summary This company is one of the world's leading agribusiness companies, with major market positions in agricultural processing and merchandising.

Key Stock Statistics (Source S&P, Vickers, company reports)

52-Wk Range	$33.72–24.22	S&P Oper. EPS 2011**E**	2.94	Market Capitalization(B)	$21.443	Beta	0.22
Trailing 12-Month EPS	$3.00	S&P Oper. EPS 2012**E**	3.10	Yield (%)	1.79	S&P 3-Yr. Proj. EPS CAGR(%)	5
Trailing 12-Month P/E	11.2	P/E on S&P Oper. EPS 2011**E**	11.4	Dividend Rate/Share	$0.60	S&P Credit Rating	A
$10K Invested 5 Yrs Ago	$15,265	Common Shares Outstg. (M)	639.3	Institutional Ownership (%)	69		

Price Performance

30-Week Mov. Avg. · · · 10-Week Mov. Avg. – – **GAAP Earnings vs. Previous Year** Volume Above Avg. STARS

12-Mo. Target Price — Relative Strength — ▲ Up ▼ Down ▶ No Change Below Avg.

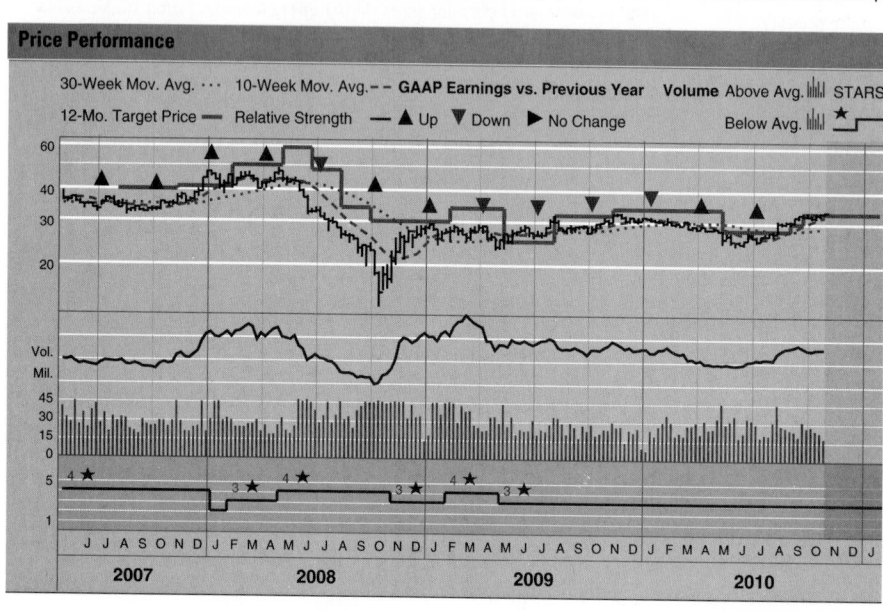

Options: ASE, CBOE, P, Ph

Analysis prepared by **Tom Graves, CFA** on September 10, 2010, when the stock traded at **$ 32.53**.

Qualitative Risk Assessment

LOW	**MEDIUM**	HIGH

Our risk assessment reflects the company's exposure to volatile commodity industry conditions, and moderately aggressive financial policies and leverage levels given the inherent cyclicality of the company's agricultural operations.

Quantitative Evaluations

S&P Quality Ranking A

D	C	B-	B	B+	A-	**A**	A+

Relative Strength Rank STRONG

71

LOWEST = 1 HIGHEST = 99

Revenue/Earnings Data

Revenue (Million $)

	1Q	2Q	3Q	4Q	Year
2010	14,921	15,913	15,145	15,703	61,682
2009	21,160	16,673	14,842	16,532	69,207
2008	12,828	16,496	18,708	21,784	69,816
2007	9,447	10,976	11,381	12,214	44,018
2006	8,627	9,299	9,123	9,547	36,596
2005	8,972	9,064	8,484	9,424	35,944

Earnings Per Share ($)

2010	0.77	0.88	0.65	0.69	3.00
2009	1.63	0.91	0.01	0.10	2.65
2008	0.68	0.73	0.80	0.58	2.79
2007	0.61	0.67	0.56	1.47	3.30
2006	0.29	0.56	0.53	0.62	2.00
2005	0.41	0.48	0.41	0.30	1.59

Fiscal year ended Jun. 30. Next earnings report expected: Early November. EPS Estimates based on S&P Operating Earnings; historical GAAP earnings are as reported.

Highlights

➤ In FY 11 (Jun.), we look for net sales to increase about 5% from the $61.7 billion reported for FY 10. We expect global economies to improve in FY 11, contributing to increased demand for products and services offered by ADM. Also, we expect ADM to benefit from some shifting in world agricultural trade that should increase demand for services provided by ADM. Over time, we believe ADM's market position will benefit from investment in new plants and cargo capacity. In FY 10, ADM's total expenditures for property, plant and equipment amounted to $1.61 billion.

➤ Near term, we look for ADM to benefit from a relatively large U.S. harvest of some major crops. In FY 10, ADM's reported EPS of $3.00 included a net negative impact of $0.14 from special items, including $0.11 of start-up costs related to new plants, $0.07 of debt buyback costs, and a $0.04 benefit related to changing LIFO valuations.

➤ Excluding any future LIFO adjustments, we project FY 11 EPS of $2.94, which includes increased caution regarding ADM's bioproducts business. For FY 12, we estimate EPS of $3.10

Investment Rationale/Risk

➤ As an internationally diversified agribusiness company, we think ADM is well positioned to outperform its peers based on scale and integration opportunities for the long term. While we think that global economic softness has slowed demand for ADM products, we think the company is well positioned to benefit from long-term global population growth and economic expansion.

➤ Risks to our recommendation and target price include adverse changes in plantings, government farm programs and policies, and from economic, operational, and industry conditions, such as commodity prices.

➤ Our 12-month target price of $33 is based on our view that the stock should trade at about 11.2X our estimate of year-ahead EPS, which would be a discount to a median and an average forward P/E for the stock over much of the past decade. We think the discount is warranted by a relatively lackluster economic environment and some concern about prospective increases in ethanol industry production capacity and higher commodity prices. The stock recently had an indicated dividend yield of about 1.9%.

Dividend Data (Dates: mm/dd Payment Date: mm/dd/yy)

Amount ($)	Date Decl.	Ex-Div. Date	Stk. of Record	Payment Date
0.140	11/05	11/17	11/19	12/10/09
0.150	02/04	02/16	02/18	03/11/10
0.150	05/06	05/18	05/20	06/10/10
0.150	08/05	08/17	08/19	09/09/10

Dividends have been paid since 1927. Source: Company reports.

The McGraw·Hill Companies

Archer-Daniels-Midland Co

STANDARD &POOR'S

Business Summary September 10, 2010

CORPORATE OVERVIEW. The successor to Daniels Linseed Co., founded in 1902, Archer Daniels Midland (ADM) is one of the world's largest agricultural processors, with a global network of processing plants. The company operates in four business segments: Oilseeds Processing (in FY 10 (Jun.), 37% of what ADM calls net sales and other operating income; 43% of FY 10 segment operating profit), Corn Processing (13%; 22%), Agricultural Services (41%; 21%), and Other (8%; 14%).

The Oilseeds Processing segment includes activities related to the processing of oilseeds, such as soybeans, cottonseed, sunflower seeds, canola, rapeseed, peanuts, and flaxseed, into vegetable oils and protein meals, principally for the food and feed industries. Partially refined oil is used to produce biodiesel or is sold to other manufacturers for use in chemicals, paints, and other industrial products, and refined oil can be further processed for use in the production of biodiesel. Cottonseed flour is sold primarily to the pharmaceutical industry, and cotton cellulose pulp is sold to the chemical, paper, and filter markets. Golden Peanut Co. LLC, a joint venture between ADM (50%) and Alimenta (U.S.A.) Inc., is a major supplier of peanuts to domestic and international markets. ADM's other ownership interests include a 16% ownership interest in Wilmar International Ltd., a leading agribusiness group in Asia.

The Corn Processing segment includes activities related to the production of syrup, starch, glucose, dextrose, and sweeteners used in the food and beverage industry, as well as activities related to the production, by fermentation, of alcohol, amino acids, and other specialty food and feed ingredients. Also, corn gluten feed and meal, plus distillers grains, are produced for use as animal feed ingredients. Ethyl alcohol may be produced for use as ethanol. ADM owns a 50% interest in Almidones Mexicanos S.A., which operates a wet corn milling plant in Mexico, and a 50% interest in Eaststarch C.V. (Netherlands), which owns interests in companies that operate wet corn milling plants in Bulgaria, Hungary, Slovakia, and Turkey.

The Agricultural Services segment utilizes the company's extensive grain elevator and transportation network to buy, store, clean and transport agricultural commodities, such as oilseeds, corn, wheat, milo, oats, rice, and barley, and resells these commodities primarily as feed ingredients and as raw materials to the agricultural processing industry. Agricultural Services includes activities of A.C. Toepfer International (ADM has an 80% interest), a global merchandiser of agricultural commodities and processed products.

Other operations include milling, processing, and financial activities.

Company Financials Fiscal Year Ended Jun. 30

Per Share Data ($)	2010	2009	2008	2007	2006	2005	2004	2003	2002	2001
Tangible Book Value	22.04	20.20	20.16	17.01	14.47	12.47	11.31	10.43	10.39	9.56
Cash Flow	4.41	3.80	3.91	4.36	3.00	2.60	1.82	1.69	1.64	1.44
Earnings	3.00	2.65	2.79	3.30	2.00	1.59	0.76	0.70	0.78	0.58
S&P Core Earnings	3.03	2.50	2.64	2.31	2.02	1.53	1.14	0.61	0.55	0.58
Dividends	0.58	0.54	0.49	0.43	0.37	0.32	0.27	0.24	0.20	0.19
Payout Ratio	19%	20%	18%	13%	19%	20%	36%	34%	25%	32%
Prices:High	33.72	33.00	48.95	47.33	46.71	25.55	22.55	15.24	14.85	15.80
Prices:Low	24.22	23.13	13.53	30.20	24.05	17.50	14.90	10.50	10.00	10.24
P/E Ratio:High	11	12	18	14	23	16	30	22	19	27
P/E Ratio:Low	8	9	5	9	12	11	20	15	13	18

Income Statement Analysis (Million $)	2010	2009	2008	2007	2006	2005	2004	2003	2002	2001
Revenue	61,682	69,207	69,816	44,018	36,596	35,944	36,151	30,708	23,454	20,051
Operating Income	3,357	3,420	3,188	2,743	2,450	2,015	1,432	1,423	1,424	1,272
Depreciation	912	743	721	701	657	665	686	644	567	572
Interest Expense	422	430	529	Nil	365	Nil	Nil	Nil	356	397
Pretax Income	2,585	2,534	2,624	3,154	1,855	1,516	718	631	719	522
Effective Tax Rate	NA	32.6%	31.3%	31.5%	29.3%	31.1%	31.1%	28.5%	28.9%	26.6%
Net Income	1,930	1,707	1,802	2,162	1,312	1,044	495	451	511	383
S&P Core Earnings	1,952	1,615	1,706	1,508	1,322	1,001	739	397	363	382

Balance Sheet & Other Financial Data (Million $)	2010	2009	2008	2007	2006	2005	2004	2003	2002	2001
Cash	1,046	1,055	1,265	2,087	2,334	1,430	1,412	765	844	676
Current Assets	10,279	19,408	25,455	15,122	11,826	9,711	10,339	8,422	7,363	6,150
Total Assets	23,693	23,104	25,790	25,118	21,269	18,598	19,369	17,183	15,416	14,340
Current Liabilities	374	8,885	14,621	7,868	6,165	5,367	6,750	5,147	4,719	3,867
Long Term Debt	7,174	7,848	7,690	4,752	4,050	3,530	3,740	3,872	3,111	3,351
Common Equity	14,631	13,499	13,490	11,253	9,807	8,433	7,698	7,069	6,755	6,332
Total Capital	21,805	21,577	21,653	16,537	14,614	12,743	12,092	11,485	10,498	10,327
Capital Expenditures	1,607	1,898	1,779	1,198	762	624	509	420	350	273
Cash Flow	2,842	2,450	2,523	2,863	1,969	1,709	1,180	1,095	1,078	955
Current Ratio	27.5	30.7	1.7	1.9	1.9	1.8	1.5	1.6	1.6	1.6
% Long Term Debt of Capitalization	32.9	36.4	35.5	28.7	27.7	27.7	30.9	33.7	29.6	32.4
% Net Income of Revenue	3.1	2.5	2.6	4.9	3.6	2.9	1.4	1.5	2.2	1.9
% Return on Assets	7.0	5.7	7.1	9.3	6.6	5.5	2.7	2.8	3.4	2.7
% Return on Equity	13.7	12.7	14.6	20.5	14.4	12.9	6.7	6.5	7.8	6.2

Data as orig reptd.; bef. results of disc opers/spec. items. Per share data adj. for stk. divs.; EPS diluted. E-Estimated. NA-Not Available. NM-Not Meaningful. NR-Not Ranked. UR-Under Review.

Office: 4666 Faries Parkway, Decatur, IL 62525.
Telephone: 217-424-5200.
Website: http://www.admworld.com
Chrmn, Pres & CEO: P. Woertz

EVP & CFO: S.R. Mills
EVP, Secy & General Counsel: D.J. Smith
Treas: V. Luthar
Investor Contact: D. Grimestad (217-424-4586)

Board Members: G. W. Buckley, M. H. Carter, P. Dufour, D. E. Felsinger, V. F. Haynes, P. J. Moore, A. M. Neto, T. F. O'Neill, K. R. Westbrook, P. Woertz

Founded: 1898
Domicile: Delaware
Employees: 29,300

The McGraw·Hill Companies

Assurant Inc.

STANDARD & POOR'S

S&P Recommendation HOLD ★★★☆☆

Price $41.37 (as of Oct 22, 2010)	**12-Mo. Target Price** $43.00	**Investment Style** Large-Cap Value

GICS Sector Financials
Sub-Industry Multi-line Insurance

Summary This company pursues a differentiated strategy of building leading positions in niche insurance markets.

Key Stock Statistics (Source S&P, Vickers, company reports)

52-Wk Range	$41.87 – 28.94	S&P Oper. EPS 2010**E**	4.85	Market Capitalization(B)	$4.408	Beta	1.51
Trailing 12-Month EPS	$4.10	S&P Oper. EPS 2011**E**	4.95	Yield (%)	1.55	S&P 3-Yr. Proj. EPS CAGR(%)	7
Trailing 12-Month P/E	10.1	P/E on S&P Oper. EPS 2010**E**	8.5	Dividend Rate/Share	$0.64	S&P Credit Rating	BBB
$10K Invested 5 Yrs Ago	$11,940	Common Shares Outstg. (M)	106.5	Institutional Ownership (%)	94		

Price Performance

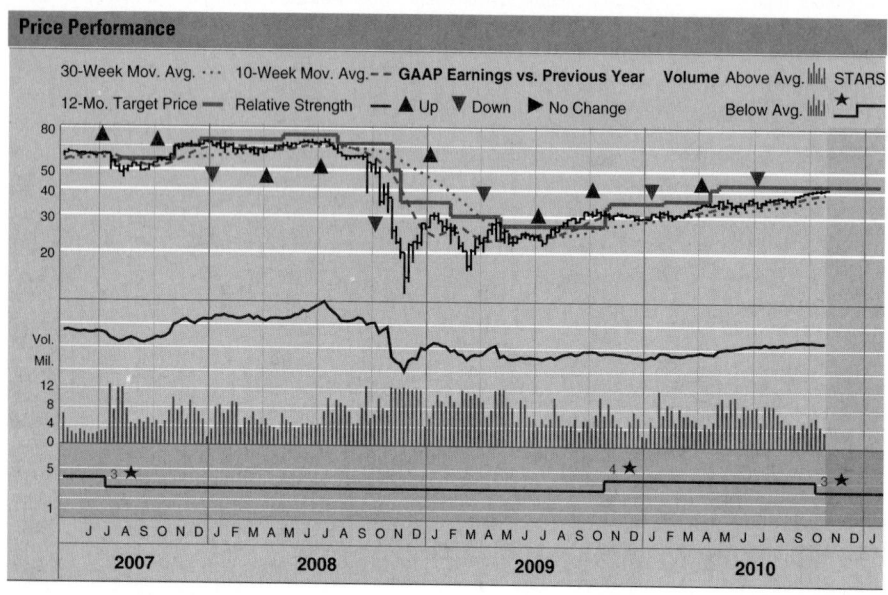

30-Week Mov. Avg. · · · 10-Week Mov. Avg. - - **GAAP Earnings vs. Previous Year** Volume Above Avg. STARS
12-Mo. Target Price — Relative Strength — ▲ Up ▼ Down ► No Change Below Avg. ★

Options: ASE, CBOE, P, Ph

Analysis prepared by **Bret Howlett** on October 20, 2010, when the stock traded at **$ 41.30**.

Highlights

➤ We expect premiums in the Solutions segment to fall 1%-3% in 2010, as weak consumer spending in the U.S. is only partially offset by international growth. We see earnings rising 4%-6% on an improved combined ratio, lower losses in the U.K., and expense reduction initiatives. We view favorably that Health has returned to profitability, and we believe that segment is on track to achieve a 4% after-tax margin by the end of the year. The Health segment has incurred sizable losses over the past year due to the recession, but pricing and plan design changes have improved results. We project earnings in Benefits to be up over 20% on higher margins from cost cuts and favorable underwriting results. Still, lower sales and enrollment should restrict revenue growth.

➤ We forecast modestly higher premiums in the Specialty Property segment on new business production and higher mortgage originations and average insured values. However, we are cautious longer term, due to the challenging housing market.

➤ We estimate operating EPS of $4.85 in 2010 and $4.95 in 2011, excluding realized investment gains or losses.

Investment Rationale/Risk

➤ Our hold recommendation reflects our belief that AIZ shares are fairly valued at current levels. We also believe there is a lack of catalysts that could drive upside to our earnings expectations in 2011 and beyond. We forecast strong operating earnings growth for AIZ in 2010, due to expense reductions and our view that the economic recovery will provide a boost to its economically sensitive businesses. Although AIZ is likely to face some top-line headwinds, we believe the company is on track to achieve better returns in all of its businesses. We think AIZ's underwriting expertise is strong, and that it has a high level of expertise in the specialized lines it markets. In our view, AIZ maintains a solid financial position, and we expect the company to use excess capital toward repurchasing its shares.

➤ Risks to our recommendation and target price include a slower-than-expected economic recovery, losses in Health, catastrophe risks, a sharp drop in demand for homeowners' coverage, and elevated investment losses.

➤ Our 12-month target price of $43 is 8.7X our 2011 operating EPS estimate, below AIZ's average historical multiple.

Qualitative Risk Assessment

LOW	MEDIUM	HIGH

Our risk assessment reflects the difficult operating environment for Assurant's Health and Specialty Property segments. Also, AIZ's Solutions business remains vulnerable to weak consumer spending. However, AIZ has a solid track record of disciplined capital management, and we believe the company's balance sheet is more conservatively positioned versus peers due to less debt and more conservative investment holdings.

Quantitative Evaluations

S&P Quality Ranking NR

D	C	B-	B	B+	A-	A	A+

Relative Strength Rank MODERATE

66

LOWEST = 1 HIGHEST = 99

Revenue/Earnings Data

Revenue (Million $)

	1Q	2Q	3Q	4Q	Year
2010	2,168	2,140	--	--	--
2009	2,088	2,274	2,157	2,182	8,701
2008	2,177	2,249	1,955	2,221	8,601
2007	2,057	2,065	2,148	2,183	8,454
2006	1,930	1,949	1,984	2,208	8,071
2005	1,862	1,874	1,879	1,882	7,498

Earnings Per Share ($)

	1Q	2Q	3Q	4Q	Year
2010	1.34	1.46	E1.03	E1.10	E4.85
2009	0.68	1.63	1.22	0.10	3.63
2008	1.57	1.59	-0.95	1.55	3.77
2007	1.45	1.36	1.56	1.01	5.38
2006	1.22	1.16	1.18	2.01	5.56
2005	0.82	0.92	0.74	1.03	3.50

Fiscal year ended Dec. 31. Next earnings report expected: Late October. EPS Estimates based on S&P Operating Earnings; historical GAAP earnings are as reported.

Dividend Data (Dates: mm/dd Payment Date: mm/dd/yy)

Amount ($)	Date Decl.	Ex-Div. Date	Stk. of Record	Payment Date
0.150	11/13	11/25	11/30	12/14/09
0.150	01/25	02/18	02/22	03/08/10
0.160	05/14	05/20	05/24	06/08/10
0.160	08/11	08/26	08/30	09/14/10

Dividends have been paid since 2004. Source: Company reports.

Assurant Inc.

STANDARD &POOR'S

Business Summary October 20, 2010

CORPORATE OVERVIEW. Assurant Inc. provides specialized insurance products in North America and other selected markets. The company was indirectly wholly owned by Fortis N.V. until February 2004, when Fortis sold about 65% of its stake via an IPO. In January 2005, Fortis sold 27.2 million shares of AIZ in a secondary public offering at $30.60 per share. In conjunction with the offering, Fortis issued $774 million of 7.75% bonds that were mandatorily exchangeable for up to 23.0 million shares of AIZ, or the cash value thereof, by January 2008. Fortis distributed most of its remaining AIZ shares to the holders of these bonds in January 2008, leaving it with about a 3% interest in AIZ. In August 2008, AIZ purchased one million shares of its common shares from Fortis.

As of March 2010, AIZ believed it was a leader or was aligned with clients who were leaders in creditor-placed homeowners insurance (based on servicing volume), manufactured housing homeowners insurance (based on the number of homes built), debt protection administration (based on credit card balances outstanding), group dental plans sponsored by employers (based on

the number of subscribers and master contracts in force), and pre-funded funeral insurance (based on the face amount of new policies sold).

On April 1, 2006, the company separated its Assurant Solutions unit into two business segments: Assurant Solutions and Assurant Specialty Property. In addition, with the creation of the new Assurant Solutions and Assurant Specialty Property segments, the company realigned the PreNeed segment under the new Assurant Solutions segment. In total, AIZ operates through four decentralized business segments: Assurant Solutions (35% of net earned premiums and other consideration in 2009); Assurant Specialty Property (26%); Assurant Health (25%); and, Assurant Employee Benefits (14%). AIZ also reports a fifth segment, Corporate and Other.

Company Financials Fiscal Year Ended Dec. 31

Per Share Data ($)	2009	2008	2007	2006	2005	2004	2003	2002	2001	2000
Tangible Book Value	31.11	19.06	NM	28.46	21.01	18.90	14.76	NA	NA	NA
Operating Earnings	NA	NA	NA	NA	NA	NA	NA	NA	NA	NA
Earnings	3.63	3.77	5.38	5.56	3.50	2.53	1.70	31.29	11.81	10.93
S&P Core Earnings	4.18	5.79	5.60	4.77	3.49	2.50	1.72	38.61	15.43	NA
Dividends	0.74	0.54	0.46	0.38	0.31	0.21	NA	NA	NA	NA
Relative Payout	20%	14%	9%	7%	9%	8%	NA	NA	NA	NA
Prices:High	33.37	71.31	69.77	56.78	44.68	31.29	NA	NA	NA	NA
Prices:Low	16.34	12.52	45.27	42.72	29.70	22.00	NA	NA	NA	NA
P/E Ratio:High	9	19	13	10	13	12	NA	NA	NA	NA
P/E Ratio:Low	5	3	8	8	8	9	NA	NA	NA	NA

Income Statement Analysis (Million $)										
Life Insurance in Force	123,383	123,383	136,530	137,507	157,203	166,452	169,787	192,984	203,660	NA
Premium Income:Life A & H	3,460	3,828	4,061	4,203	4,595	4,789	4,565	4,385	4,215	NA
Premium Income:Casualty/Property.	4,091	4,097	3,347	2,641	1,926	1,694	1,591	1,297	1,027	NA
Net Investment Income	699	774	799	737	687	635	607	632	712	691
Total Revenue	8,701	8,601	8,454	8,071	7,498	7,403	7,066	6,532	6,187	6,212
Pretax Income	710	563	1,011	1,096	656	536	259	370	206	194
Net Operating Income	NA	NA	NA	NA	NA	NA	NA	NA	NA	NA
Net Income	431	448	654	716	479	351	186	260	98.1	89.7
S&P Core Earnings	496	689	680	613	477	345	187	320	128	NA

Balance Sheet & Other Financial Data (Million $)										
Cash & Equivalent	1,474	1,185	954	1,125	NA	NA	NA	550	559	NA
Premiums Due	508	513	580	612	455	435	368	NA	NA	NA
Investment Assets:Bonds	9,967	8,591	10,126	9,118	8,962	9,178	8,729	NA	NA	NA
Investment Assets:Stocks	513	475	636	742	693	527	456	NA	NA	NA
Investment Assets:Loans	1,484	1,565	1,491	1,325	1,273	1,119	1,001	NA	NA	NA
Investment Assets:Total	13,158	12,067	13,747	12,429	12,516	13,472	10,924	10,029	9,601	NA
Deferred Policy Costs	2,505	2,651	2,895	2,398	2,022	1,648	1,394	NA	NA	NA
Total Assets	25,842	24,515	26,750	25,165	25,365	24,504	23,728	22,924	24,450	NA
Debt	972	972	972	972	972	972	1,946	975	NA	NA
Common Equity	4,853	3,710	4,089	3,833	3,778	3,768	2,832	3,346	3,452	NA
Combined Loss-Expense Ratio	74.7	76.4	92.0	91.4	90.8	92.4	93.3	NA	NA	NA
% Return on Revenue	5.0	5.2	7.7	8.9	6.4	4.9	2.6	4.0	1.6	1.4
% Return on Equity	10.1	11.5	16.5	18.7	12.8	10.6	6.7	NA	NA	NA
% Investment Yield	5.5	1.2	6.1	5.7	5.2	5.2	5.8	6.4	14.8	NA

Data as orig reptd.; bef. results of disc opers/spec. items. Per share data adj. for stk. divs.; EPS diluted. E-Estimated. NA-Not Available. NM-Not Meaningful. NR-Not Ranked. UR-Under Review.

Office: One Chase Manhattan Plaza, 41st Floor, New York, NY 10005.
Telephone: 212-859-7000.
Website: http://www.assurant.com
Chrmn: J.M. Palms

Pres & CEO: R.B. Pollock
Vice Chrmn: E.D. Rosen
EVP & CFO: M.J. Peninger
EVP & Treas: C.J. Pagano

Investor Contact: M. Kivett (212-859-7029)
Board Members: B. L. Bronner, H. L. Carver, J. N. Cento, A. R. Freedman, L. V. Jackson, D. B. Kelso, C. J. Koch, H. C. Mackin, J. M. Palms, R. B. Pollock, E. D. Rosen, J. A. Swainson

Founded: 1969
Domicile: Delaware
Employees: 15,000

The McGraw-Hill Companies

AT&T Inc

STANDARD &POOR'S

S&P Recommendation	**STRONG BUY** ★★★★★	Price $28.29 (as of Oct 22, 2010)	12-Mo. Target Price $33.00	Investment Style Large-Cap Value

GICS Sector Telecommunication Services
Sub-Industry Integrated Telecommunication Services

Summary AT&T Inc. (formerly SBC Communications) provides telephone and broadband service and holds full ownership of AT&T Mobility (formerly Cingular Wireless). AT&T Corp. was acquired in late 2005 and BellSouth in late 2006.

Key Stock Statistics (Source S&P, Vickers, company reports)

52-Wk Range	$29.43–23.78	S&P Oper. EPS 2010**E**	2.34	Market Capitalization(B)	$167.166	Beta	0.68
Trailing 12-Month EPS	$2.15	S&P Oper. EPS 2011**E**	2.47	Yield (%)	5.94	S&P 3-Yr. Proj. EPS CAGR(%)	5
Trailing 12-Month P/E	13.2	P/E on S&P Oper. EPS 2010**E**	12.1	Dividend Rate/Share	$1.68	S&P Credit Rating	A
$10K Invested 5 Yrs Ago	$15,949	Common Shares Outstg. (M)	5,909.0	Institutional Ownership (%)	57		

Price Performance

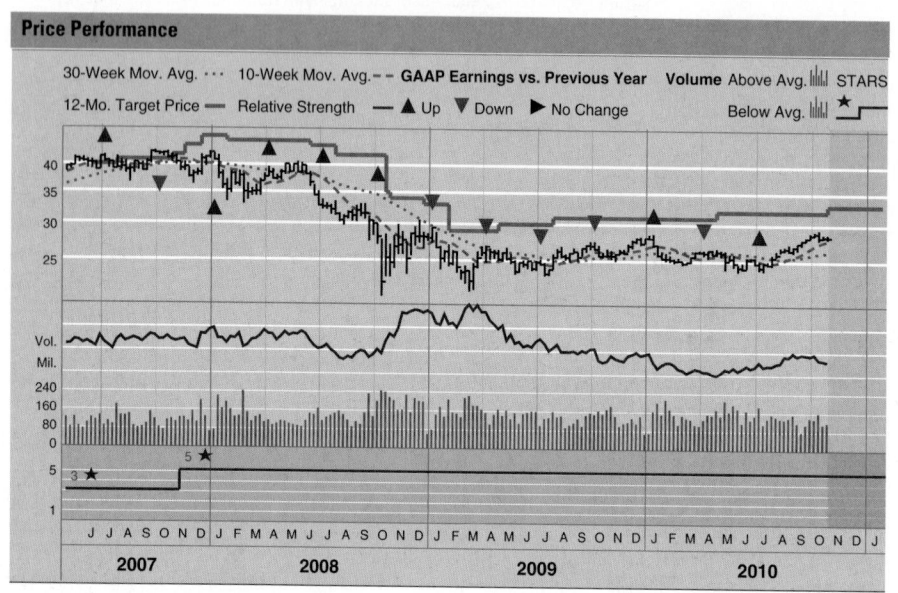

30-Week Mov. Avg. ···· 10-Week Mov. Avg. - - GAAP Earnings vs. Previous Year Volume Above Avg. STARS
12-Mo. Target Price — Relative Strength — ▲ Up ▼ Down ▶ No Change Below Avg. ★

Options: ASE, CBOE, P, Ph

Analysis prepared by **Todd Rosenbluth** on October 22, 2010, when the stock traded at **$ 28.34**.

Highlights

➤ We forecast that revenue will rise 2.0% in 2011, following a projected gain of 1.5% in 2010. We look for wireless revenue to advance 8% in 2011 on customer additions and growth in wireless data services. Meanwhile, we look for smaller revenue gains in the broadband business, helping to outweigh competitive and economic pressures in consumer and business voice operations.

➤ We see operating margins widening slightly to 19% in 2011 from our forecast for 2010. Despite high wireless handset subsidies used to gain and retain smartphone customers and pending integration of a wireless asset purchase, we believe wireless data and U-verse are generating improved profitability, and we see further benefits from workforce reductions undertaken in the past year. During the third quarter of 2010, operating margin expansion was below our projection due to high wireless customer acquisition costs.

➤ We estimate EPS of $2.34 for 2010 and $2.47 for 2011, up from $2.12 posted in 2009. We expect cash to begin to be used for share repurchases in 2011.

Investment Rationale/Risk

➤ We expect gains in consumer wireless and broadband to offset some wireline voice pressure, and we think the company's fundamentals will remain strong. The delayed recovery in enterprise is more dependent upon an improved labor market than T fixing its problems, in our opinion. Despite increased competition and risks that T could lose exclusivity of a key handset, we believe strong brand loyalty and an improved balance sheet are positives. We view T's above-average dividend as secure.

➤ Risks to our recommendation and target price include balance sheet weakness, increased competition that leads to unexpected customer losses, and worse-than-projected wireless services execution.

➤ We view T as undervalued, recently trading at a P/E of about 11.5X our 2011 estimate, a discount to the 13X for the broader market and the 14X of its telecom peers. Our 12-month target price of $33 is based on our relative analysis, which assumes a P/E of approximately 13X our 2011 EPS estimate to reflect T's strong industry leadership and above-average dividend yield. The dividend yield was recently about 6%.

Qualitative Risk Assessment

LOW	**MEDIUM**	HIGH

Our risk assessment reflects our view of the company's strong balance sheet and its power over suppliers, offset by the competitive nature of the telecom business and the integration challenges of numerous acquisitions.

Quantitative Evaluations

S&P Quality Ranking   B+

D	C	B-	B	**B+**	A-	A	A+

Relative Strength Rank   MODERATE

47

LOWEST = 1   HIGHEST = 99

Revenue/Earnings Data

Revenue (Million $)

	1Q	2Q	3Q	4Q	Year
2010	30,649	30,808	--	--	--
2009	30,571	30,734	30,855	30,858	123,018
2008	30,744	30,866	31,342	31,076	124,028
2007	28,969	29,478	30,132	30,349	118,928
2006	15,756	15,770	15,638	15,891	63,055
2005	10,248	10,328	10,320	12,966	43,862

Earnings Per Share ($)

2010	0.42	0.68	E0.63	E0.64	E2.34
2009	0.53	0.54	0.54	0.51	2.12
2008	0.57	0.63	0.55	0.41	2.16
2007	0.45	0.47	0.50	0.52	1.94
2006	0.37	0.46	0.56	0.50	1.89
2005	0.27	0.30	0.38	0.46	1.42

Fiscal year ended Dec. 31. Next earnings report expected: Late October. EPS Estimates based on S&P Operating Earnings; historical GAAP earnings are as reported.

Dividend Data (Dates: mm/dd Payment Date: mm/dd/yy)

Amount ($)	Date Decl.	Ex-Div. Date	Stk. of Record	Payment Date
0.420	12/18	01/06	01/08	02/01/10
0.420	03/26	04/07	04/09	05/03/10
0.420	06/25	07/07	07/09	08/02/10
0.420	09/24	10/06	10/08	11/01/10

Dividends have been paid since 1984. Source: Company reports.

AT&T Inc

STANDARD &POOR'S

Business Summary October 22, 2010

CORPORATE OVERVIEW. AT&T Inc. (T) combined SBC Communications with the acquired assets of AT&T Corp. following a November 2005 acquisition. At the end of 2006, T closed on its acquisition of BellSouth (BLS) for $86 billion in stock. As of September 2010, the company had 24.9 million consumer voice connections (down 11% from a year earlier), and 14 million consumer broadband customers (up 4%) along with business voice connections. With the acquisition of BLS, T took full control of Cingular Wireless, now the second largest U.S. carrier with 93 million subscribers (up 14% from a year earlier), including 3.4 million via acquisition, and expanded its wireline presence into the southeastern U.S. In early 2007, Cingular was renamed AT&T.

IMPACT OF MAJOR DEVELOPMENTS. In June 2006, T launched its new fiber-based network, which offers video and faster-speed broadband services. As of September 2010, the service, called U-verse, had been rolled out in part of T's operating territory with 2.7 million customers, up 51% from a year earlier. T has deployed the service to more than 26 million households and aims to deploy it to 30 million households by 2011. In April 2010, T said that it had signed up more than 22% of homes as customers with U-verse available for 30 months.

In mid-2007, T became the exclusive U.S. provider of the iPhone. Since then, it has launched multiple, faster versions of the product. T has been subsidizing the smartphone to drive customer demand and revenue per user. During 2009, more than 10 million iPhones were activated onto T's network; more than 11 million more were activated in the first nine months of 2010. Even with faster revenue growth and supporting customer loyalty in a competitive market, we think the iPhone has been earnings dilutive following new releases given T's subsidy of the product. However, we think margins have and will benefit in future periods as these customers mature. We believe T has a broad lineup of appealing smartphones and integrated devices used currently by approximately 39 million of its post-paid customers. In the first nine months of 2010, T added 3.1 million emerging devices, such as e-readers and the iPad, to its wireless data network.

COMPETITIVE LANDSCAPE. T faces competition in its consumer wireline and regional business operations from wireless, and has cable telephony overlapping with 75% of its overall wireline operations. We think this adds operating risk. Also, the weak U.S. economy has caused customers to reduce costs by dropping wireline and broadband connections.

Company Financials Fiscal Year Ended Dec. 31

Per Share Data ($)

	2009	2008	2007	2006	2005	2004	2003	2002	2001	2000
Tangible Book Value	NM	NM	NM	NM	8.29	11.77	11.09	9.51	8.62	7.38
Cash Flow	5.44	5.50	5.43	2.77	3.68	3.80	4.16	4.79	2.25	5.16
Earnings	2.12	2.16	1.94	1.89	1.42	1.50	1.80	2.23	2.14	2.32
S&P Core Earnings	2.11	1.39	1.66	1.82	1.24	1.22	1.50	1.21	1.39	NA
Dividends	1.64	1.60	1.42	1.33	1.29	1.25	1.37	1.07	1.02	1.01
Payout Ratio	77%	74%	73%	70%	91%	83%	76%	48%	48%	43%
Prices:High	29.46	41.94	42.97	36.21	25.98	27.73	31.65	40.99	53.06	59.00
Prices:Low	21.44	20.90	31.94	24.24	21.75	22.98	18.85	19.57	36.50	34.81
P/E Ratio:High	14	19	22	19	18	18	18	18	25	25
P/E Ratio:Low	10	10	16	13	15	15	10	9	17	15

Income Statement Analysis (Million $)

	2009	2008	2007	2006	2005	2004	2003	2002	2001	2000
Revenue	123,018	124,028	118,928	63,055	43,862	40,787	40,843	43,138	45,908	51,476
Depreciation	19,714	19,883	21,577	9,907	7,643	7,564	7,870	8,578	9,077	9,748
Maintenance	NA	NA	NA	NA	NA	NA	NA	NA	NA	NA
Construction Credits	NA	NA	NA	NA	36.0	31.0	37.0	58.0	119	81.0
Effective Tax Rate	32.4%	35.4%	34.0%	32.4%	16.3%	30.5%	32.9%	28.5%	36.1%	38.2%
Net Income	12,535	12,867	11,951	7,356	4,786	4,979	5,971	7,473	7,260	7,967
S&P Core Earnings	12,483	8,235	10,225	7,080	4,189	4,031	5,000	4,048	4,717	NA

Balance Sheet & Other Financial Data (Million $)

	2009	2008	2007	2006	2005	2004	2003	2002	2001	2000
Gross Property	230,552	218,579	210,518	202,149	149,238	136,177	133,923	131,755	127,524	119,753
Net Property	100,093	99,088	95,890	94,596	58,727	50,046	52,128	48,490	49,827	47,195
Capital Expenditures	17,335	20,335	17,717	8,320	5,576	5,099	5,219	6,808	11,189	13,124
Total Capital	174,406	176,415	197,561	193,009	96,727	77,544	69,607	62,705	58,476	54,079
Fixed Charges Coverage	6.4	6.6	6.0	5.8	4.4	6.9	7.0	6.9	6.6	8.0
Capitalization:Long Term Debt	64,720	60,872	57,255	50,063	26,115	21,231	16,060	18,536	17,133	16,492
Capitalization:Preferred	Nil	Nil	Nil	Nil	Nil	Nil	Nil	Nil	Nil	Nil
Capitalization:Common	101,900	96,347	115,367	115,540	54,690	40,504	38,248	33,199	32,491	30,463
% Return on Revenue	10.2	10.4	10.0	11.7	10.9	12.2	14.6	17.3	15.8	15.5
% Return on Invested Capital	8.9	8.3	7.6	4.9	6.5	7.0	9.0	11.4	12.9	16.6
% Return on Common Equity	12.7	12.2	10.4	8.6	10.1	12.6	16.7	22.6	23.1	27.9
% Earned on Net Property	21.6	23.7	21.4	13.4	11.3	11.6	12.9	17.5	22.4	22.9
% Long Term Debt of Capitalization	38.8	38.7	33.2	30.3	32.3	34.4	29.6	35.8	34.5	35.1
Capital % Preferred	Nil	Nil	Nil	Nil	Nil	Nil	Nil	Nil	Nil	Nil
Capitalization:% Common	61.2	61.3	66.8	67.8	67.7	65.6	70.4	64.2	65.5	64.9

Data as orig reptd.; bef. results of disc opers/spec. items. Per share data adj. for stk. divs.; EPS diluted. E-Estimated. NA-Not Available. NM-Not Meaningful. NR-Not Ranked. UR-Under Review.

Office: 2088 S Akard St, Dallas, TX 75202.
Telephone: 210-821-4105.
Website: http://www.att.com
Chrmn, Pres & CEO: R.L. Stephenson

EVP, CFO & Chief Acctg Officer: R. Lindner
EVP & General Counsel: D.W. Watts
SVP & Secy: A.E. Meuleman
SVP & Cntlr: J.J. Stephens

Investor Contact: D. Cessac (210-351-2058)
Board Members: G. F. Amelio, R. V. Anderson, J. H. Blanchard, J. Chico Pardo, J. P. Kelly, J. C. Madonna, L. M. Martin, J. B. McCoy, J. M. Roche, M. K. Rose, R. L. Stephenson, L. D. Tyson, P. P. Upton

Founded: 1983
Domicile: Delaware
Employees: 282,720

Autodesk Inc

STANDARD &POOR'S

S&P Recommendation	HOLD ★★★☆☆	Price $34.84 (as of Oct 22, 2010)	12-Mo. Target Price $29.00	Investment Style Large-Cap Growth

GICS Sector Information Technology
Sub-Industry Application Software

Summary This company develops, markets, and supports computer-aided design and drafting (CAD) software for use on desktop computers and workstations.

Key Stock Statistics (Source S&P, Vickers, company reports)

52-Wk Range	$35.18– 22.50	S&P Oper. EPS 2011E	0.87	Market Capitalization(B)	$7.919	Beta	2.11
Trailing 12-Month EPS	$0.75	S&P Oper. EPS 2012E	1.03	Yield (%)	Nil	S&P 3-Yr. Proj. EPS CAGR(%)	15
Trailing 12-Month P/E	46.5	P/E on S&P Oper. EPS 2011E	40.0	Dividend Rate/Share	Nil	S&P Credit Rating	NA
$10K Invested 5 Yrs Ago	$7,642	Common Shares Outstg. (M)	227.3	Institutional Ownership (%)	94		

Price Performance

30-Week Mov. Avg. ···   10-Week Mov. Avg. - - -   **GAAP Earnings vs. Previous Year**   Volume Above Avg. ▌▌▌▐   STARS
12-Mo. Target Price —   Relative Strength —   ▲ Up ▼ Down ▶ No Change   Below Avg. ▌▌▌▐ ★

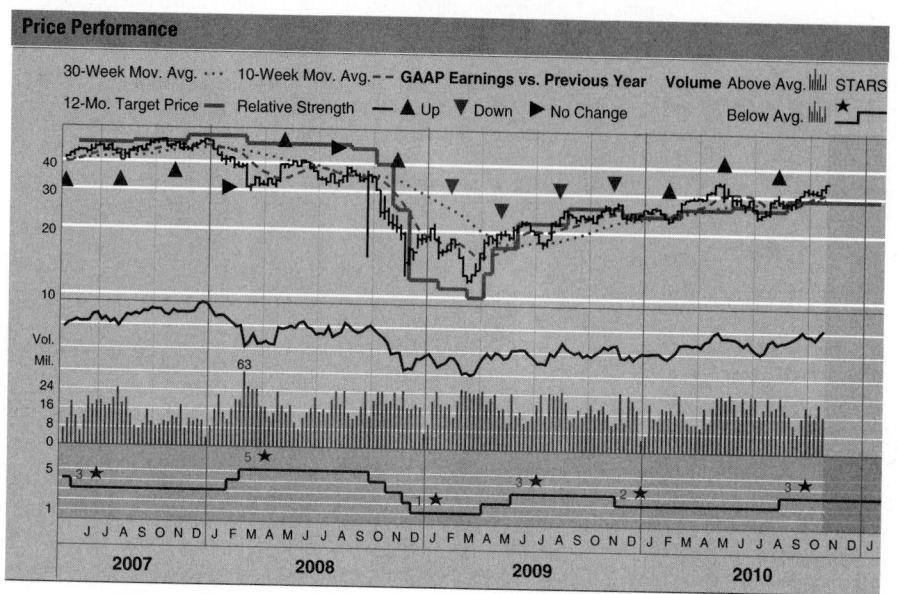

Options: ASE, CBOE, P, Ph

Analysis prepared by **Jim Yin, CFA** on August 17, 2010, when the stock traded at **$ 27.66**.

Highlights

▶ We estimate total revenues in FY 11 (Jan.) will rise 11%, following a 26% decline in FY 10. Our outlook is based on our view of a modest improvement in IT spending, even though we are concerned about a slowing global economy. We forecast a 16% rise in license revenues in FY 11 due to pent-up demand, as customers resume spending on new projects. We project 4.3% growth in maintenance revenues, reflecting stronger license revenues and a stronger renewal rate as some customers upgrade software. We note that the growth in maintenance revenues tends to lag that of license revenues.

▶ We see gross margins of 89% in FY 11, the same as in FY 10. We look for total operating expenses to decrease as a percentage of revenue due to further cost savings. We estimate that operating margins will widen to 14% in FY 11 from 3.8% in FY 10.

▶ Our EPS estimate is $0.87 for FY 11, up from $0.25 in FY 10. We project low-teen revenue growth in FY 11, and believe earnings will increase on further cost reductions and lower restructuring costs.

Investment Rationale/Risk

▶ We recently upgraded our recommendation to hold, from sell, based on our projection for stronger license revenues. Despite economic uncertainty, ADSK continues to signs new customers. We believe ADSK has not experienced the impact of economic uncertainty in Europe due to its long sales cycles. Additionally, the company has been controlling its expenses. Although we expect foreign currency exchange to be less favorable in FY 11, ADSK has a hedging program that should mitigate the impact.

▶ Risks to our opinion and target price include a weaker-than-expected economic recovery, weaker IT spending, significant loss in market share, and lower-than-expected cost savings from restructuring.

▶ Our 12-month target price of $29 is based on a blend of our discounted cash flow (DCF) and enterprise value (EV)-to-sales valuations. Our DCF model assumes a 13% weighted average cost of capital and 3% terminal growth, yielding intrinsic value of $30. From our EV-to-sales analysis, we derive a value of $28, based on an EV-to-sales ratio of 2.8X, almost in line with the industry's average of 2.7X.

Qualitative Risk Assessment

LOW	MEDIUM	HIGH

Our risk assessment reflects our concern about the financial crisis in Europe, the cyclical nature of ADSK's business, and intense competition in the computer-aided design market.

Quantitative Evaluations

S&P Quality Ranking   B

D	C	B-	B	B+	A-	A	A+

Relative Strength Rank   STRONG

87

LOWEST = 1   HIGHEST = 99

Revenue/Earnings Data

Revenue (Million $)

	1Q	2Q	3Q	4Q	Year
2011	474.6	472.8	--		--
2010	425.8	414.9	416.9	456.1	1,714
2009	598.8	619.5	607.1	489.8	2,315
2008	508.5	525.9	538.4	599.1	2,172
2007	436.0	449.6	456.8	497.4	1,840
2006	355.1	373.0	378.3	416.8	1,523

Earnings Per Share ($)

2011	0.16	0.25	E0.22	E0.24	E0.87
2010	-0.14	0.05	0.13	0.22	0.25
2009	0.41	0.39	0.45	-0.47	0.80
2008	0.34	0.39	0.35	0.40	1.47
2007	0.20	0.36	0.24	0.40	1.19
2006	0.31	0.30	0.38	0.33	1.33

Fiscal year ended Jan. 31. Next earnings report expected: Mid November. EPS Estimates based on S&P Operating Earnings; historical GAAP earnings are as reported.

Dividend Data

Quarterly cash dividends were discontinued after April 2005.

Please read the Required Disclosures and Analyst Certification on the last page of this report.

The McGraw-Hill Companies

Autodesk Inc

Business Summary August 17, 2010

CORPORATE OVERVIEW. Autodesk (ADSK) develops software solutions that enable customers in the architectural, engineering, construction, manufacturing, infrastructure, media and entertainment markets to create, manage and share their data and designs digitally. ADSK's software helps its customers to improve their designs before they actually begin the building process, thus saving time and money. The company is organized into four reportable operating segments: Platform Solutions and Emerging Business, which accounted for 36% of net revenue in FY 10 (Jan.), Architecture, Engineering and Construction (30%), Manufacturing (23%), and the Media and Entertainment segment (11%).

The targeted customers for its Platform Solutions and Emerging Business; Architecture, Engineering and Construction; and Manufacturing segments are those who design, build, manage or own building, manufacturing and infrastructure projects. Key products for these segments include AutoCAD, a general-purpose computer aided design (CAD) tool for design, modeling, drafting, mapping, rendering and facility management tasks; AutoCAD LT, a low-cost CAD package with 2D and basic 3D drafting capabilities; and Au-

todesk Inventor, a software that allows engineers to perform simulation and analysis on 3D models. Other products include Autodesk Mechanical Desktop, Autodesk Civil 3D, and Autodesk Revit products.

The Media and Entertainment segment develops digital systems and software for creating 3D animation, color grading, visual effects compositing, editing and finishing. Its products are used for PC and console game development, animation, film, television, and design visualization. Products include Autodesk 3ds Max, a 3D modeling and animation software package; Autodesk Flame, a digital system used by professionals to create and edit special visual effects in real-time; and Autodesk Inferno, which provides all the features of flame with film tools, and increased image resolution and color control for digital film work.

Company Financials Fiscal Year Ended Jan. 31

Per Share Data ($)	2010	2009	2008	2007	2006	2005	2004	2003	2002	2001
Tangible Book Value	3.68	2.89	3.14	3.07	2.06	2.07	2.07	1.84	2.20	1.85
Cash Flow	0.73	1.24	1.68	1.37	1.51	1.11	0.74	0.35	0.68	0.69
Earnings	0.25	0.80	1.47	1.19	1.33	0.90	0.52	0.14	0.40	0.40
S&P Core Earnings	0.31	1.18	1.49	1.19	1.05	0.67	0.33	-0.07	0.09	0.17
Dividends	NA	Nil	Nil	0.02	0.06	0.06	0.06	0.06	0.06	0.06
Payout Ratio	Nil	Nil	Nil	2%	5%	7%	12%	43%	15%	15%
Calendar Year	2009	2008	2007	2006	2005	2004	2003	2002	2001	2000
Prices:High	27.97	49.71	51.32	44.75	48.27	38.98	12.45	11.84	10.55	14.02
Prices:Low	11.70	12.45	36.74	29.56	26.20	12.10	6.41	5.09	6.05	4.86
P/E Ratio:High	NM	62	35	38	36	43	24	85	26	35
P/E Ratio:Low	NM	16	25	25	20	13	12	36	15	12

Income Statement Analysis (Million $)										
Revenue	1,714	2,315	2,172	1,840	1,523	1,234	952	825	947	936
Operating Income	246	543	539	440	414	314	0.16	99.7	195	208
Depreciation	112	102	49.8	43.9	43.7	51.9	50.3	48.8	62.9	68.8
Interest Expense	NA	Nil	Nil	2.10	Nil	Nil	Nil	Nil	Nil	Nil
Pretax Income	84.7	253	470	367	383	246	117	38.5	55.1	41.7
Effective Tax Rate	31.5%	27.3%	24.2%	21.0%	14.1%	10.1%	NM	17.1%	NM	NM
Net Income	58.0	184	356	290	329	222	120	31.9	90.3	93.2
S&P Core Earnings	71.7	271	362	292	258	161	74.4	-16.2	19.5	38.5

Balance Sheet & Other Financial Data (Million $)										
Cash	1,001	981	949	778	369	533	364	247	505	423
Current Assets	1,380	1,388	1,482	1,190	739	782	597	450	564	491
Total Assets	2,447	2,421	2,209	1,798	1,361	1,142	1,017	884	902	808
Current Liabilities	704	800	746	574	507	477	385	310	371	334
Long Term Debt	NA	Nil	Nil	Nil	Nil	Nil	Nil	Nil	Nil	Nil
Common Equity	1,474	1,311	1,231	1,115	791	648	622	569	529	460
Total Capital	1,474	1,333	1,231	1,115	791	648	629	571	529	473
Capital Expenditures	39.0	78.4	43.3	35.3	20.5	40.8	25.9	36.1	45.1	32.4
Cash Flow	170	286	406	334	373	273	171	80.7	153	162
Current Ratio	2.0	1.7	2.0	2.1	1.5	1.6	1.6	1.5	1.5	1.5
% Long Term Debt of Capitalization	Nil	Nil	Nil	Nil	Nil	Nil	Nil	Nil	Nil	Nil
% Net Income of Revenue	3.4	7.9	16.4	15.8	21.6	18.0	12.6	3.9	9.5	10.0
% Return on Assets	2.4	7.9	17.8	18.4	26.3	20.5	12.7	3.6	10.6	10.9
% Return on Equity	4.2	14.5	30.4	30.4	45.7	34.9	20.2	5.8	18.3	17.6

Data as orig reptd.; bef. results of disc opers/spec. items. Per share data adj. for stk. divs.; EPS diluted. E-Estimated. NA-Not Available. NM-Not Meaningful. NR-Not Ranked. UR-Under Review.

Office: 111 McInnis Parkway, San Rafael, CA 94903-2700.
Telephone: 415-507-5000.
Email: investor.relations@autodesk.com
Website: http://www.autodesk.com

Chrmn: C.W. Beveridge
Pres & CEO: C. Bass
COO & SVP: M. Chin
EVP, CFO & Chief Acctg Officer: M.J. Hawkins

SVP, Secy & General Counsel: P.W. Di Fronzo
Investor Contact: S. Pirri (415-507-6467)
Board Members: C. Bass, C. W. Beveridge, J. H. Dawson, P. Halvorsen, S. Maloney, M. T. McDowell, C. Robel, S. M. West

Founded: 1982
Domicile: Delaware
Employees: 6,800

Automatic Data Processing Inc.

STANDARD &POOR'S

| S&P Recommendation **BUY** ★★★★☆ | Price $43.80 (as of Oct 22, 2010) | 12-Mo. Target Price $47.00 | Investment Style Large-Cap Growth |

GICS Sector Information Technology
Sub-Industry Data Processing & Outsourced Services

Summary ADP, one of the world's largest independent computing services companies, provides a broad range of data processing services.

Key Stock Statistics (Source S&P, Vickers, company reports)

52-Wk Range	$45.74–26.46	S&P Oper. EPS 2011E	2.44	Market Capitalization(B)	$21.551	Beta	0.59
Trailing 12-Month EPS	$2.41	S&P Oper. EPS 2012E	2.59	Yield (%)	3.11	S&P 3-Yr. Proj. EPS CAGR(%)	5
Trailing 12-Month P/E	18.2	P/E on S&P Oper. EPS 2011E	18.0	Dividend Rate/Share	$1.36	S&P Credit Rating	AAA
$10K Invested 5 Yrs Ago	NA	Common Shares Outstg. (M)	492.0	Institutional Ownership (%)	75		

Price Performance

30-Week Mov. Avg. · · ·   10-Week Mov. Avg. - -   **GAAP Earnings vs. Previous Year**   Volume Above Avg. ▊▊▊ STARS

12-Mo. Target Price —   Relative Strength —   ▲ Up ▼ Down ▶ No Change   Below Avg. ▊▊▊ ★

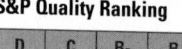

Options: ASE, CBOE, P, Ph

Analysis prepared by **Dylan Cathers** on October 13, 2010, when the stock traded at **$ 42.47**.

Highlights

▶ After revenue increased just 0.8% in FY 10 (Jun.), we look for a modest 3% rise in FY 11. We believe that the continued weak environment for employment will weigh on the company's core payroll and tax-filing business for the next few quarters at least. Levels of employment at clients remain muted, although there appear to be some improvements in retention rates. Revenue growth from Beyond Payroll should remain in the mid-single digits. The Dealer Services unit had some positive signs, as auto sales rebound. We see low prevailing interest rates reducing income from funds held for clients, but this should be partially offset by a slight increase in balances and lower borrowing costs.

▶ Operating margins narrowed in FY 10, and we do not expect any improvement in FY 11. We think modestly improving operational metrics and cost controls will be offset by investments in the sales force, new technologies, and recent acquisitions.

▶ Operating EPS was $2.37 in FY 10, excluding a tax benefit. We assume a modest level of share buybacks, and expect EPS of $2.44 in FY 11 and $2.59 in FY 12.

Investment Rationale/Risk

▶ Our buy opinion on the shares is based on valuation. We are seeing headwinds that will likely affect the company in the near term, namely low employment levels, continued weak U.S. vehicle sales, and low interest rates. However, we think conditions are improving. Further, over the longer term, we think the market for payroll outsourcing is relatively untapped, especially in the small and medium-sized business market and overseas, providing opportunities for future growth.

▶ Risks to our recommendation and target price include increased competition in the business process outsourcing market, an area into which ADP is venturing, which could lead to downward pressure on pricing and profit margins; a decrease in payrolls due to a weak economy; and failure of ADP to expand further into small and mid-sized businesses and international markets.

▶ Our 12-month target price of $47 is based on our relative valuation analysis, applying a roughly peer-average P/E of 18.8X to our calendar 2011 EPS estimate of $2.50.

Qualitative Risk Assessment

| LOW | MEDIUM | HIGH |

Our risk assessment reflects what we see as the company's strong balance sheet, steady cash inflow, and recurring revenue stream, offset by intense competition in payroll processing and the threat of new entrants into the marketplace.

Quantitative Evaluations

S&P Quality Ranking   **A**

| D | C | B- | B | B+ | A- | A | A+ |

Relative Strength Rank   **MODERATE**

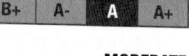

64

LOWEST = 1   HIGHEST = 99

Revenue/Earnings Data

Revenue (Million $)

	1Q	2Q	3Q	4Q	Year
2010	2,096	2,198	2,443	2,190	8,928
2009	2,182	2,203	2,375	2,108	8,867
2008	1,992	2,150	2,427	2,207	8,777
2007	1,755	1,874	2,171	2,000	7,800
2006	1,922	2,047	2,439	2,474	8,882
2005	1,855	1,994	2,349	2,302	8,499

Earnings Per Share ($)

2010	0.56	0.62	0.79	0.42	2.40
2009	0.54	0.59	0.80	0.69	2.63
2008	0.45	0.53	0.77	0.44	2.20
2007	0.39	0.45	0.65	0.35	1.83
2006	0.36	0.44	0.61	0.44	1.85
2005	0.35	0.42	0.57	0.44	1.79

Fiscal year ended Jun. 30. Next earnings report expected: Early November. EPS Estimates based on S&P Operating Earnings; historical GAAP earnings are as reported.

Dividend Data (Dates: mm/dd Payment Date: mm/dd/yy)

Amount ($)	Date Decl.	Ex-Div. Date	Stk. of Record	Payment Date
0.340	11/10	12/09	12/11	01/01/10
0.340	02/09	03/10	03/12	04/01/10
0.340	04/29	06/09	06/11	07/01/10
0.340	08/09	09/08	09/10	10/01/10

Dividends have been paid since 1974. Source: Company reports.

Please read the Required Disclosures and Analyst Certification on the last page of this report.

The McGraw·Hill Companies

STANDARD & POOR'S

Automatic Data Processing Inc.

Business Summary October 13, 2010

CORPORATE OVERVIEW. Automatic Data Processing (ADP) is the largest global provider of payroll outsourcing services based on revenue. The company also offers human resources outsourcing, tax filing, and benefits administration, with a broad range of data processing services in two business segments: employer and dealer.

Employer Services provides payroll, human resource, benefits administration, time and attendance, and tax filing and reporting services to more than 570,000 clients in North America, Europe, Australia, Asia and Brazil. Dealer Services provides transaction systems, data products and professional services to automobile and truck dealers and manufacturers worldwide.

MARKET PROFILE. The market for HR management services, which is the largest segment of ADP's Employer Services division, totaled $102.3 billion worldwide in calendar 2009, according to market researcher IDC. Between 2009 and 2014, IDC expects this area to expand at a compound annual growth rate (CAGR) of 4.6%, with the market in the U.S. increasing 4.3%, from $50.2 billion in 2009. For the more narrow processing services market, where ADP is the dominant company, IDC sees a CAGR of 3.7% in the U.S. between 2009 and 2014. In contrast, in the market for business process outsourcing (BPO) services, an area in which we see ADP expanding further, IDC expects a CAGR of

4.9% over the same time frame.

IMPACT OF MAJOR DEVELOPMENTS. In April 2006, ADP completed the sale of its Claims Services business for $975 million in cash, netting $480 million after taxes. In August 2006, ADP announced its intention to spin off its Brokerage Services business. The new public company, Broadridge Financial Services, which began trading on April 2, 2007, had sales of about $2 billion in FY 07 (Jun.), a high level of recurring revenues, and a revenue growth rate in the mid-single digits. This growth rate is below what we think the remaining Employer Services and Dealer Services units are capable of, especially given what we believe are strong overseas prospects. Further, the disposition of the Brokerage business (as well as the Claims sale) allows management to better concentrate on its two remaining businesses, in our opinion. With the Brokerage business spin-off complete, the new company distributed $690 million to ADP, which it used primarily for share buybacks, acquiring 40 million shares at a cost of about $2 billion in FY 07.

Company Financials Fiscal Year Ended Jun. 30

Per Share Data ($)	2010	2009	2008	2007	2006	2005	2004	2003	2002	2001
Tangible Book Value	5.19	4.72	3.97	3.93	5.21	4.55	4.23	4.57	5.25	4.97
Cash Flow	3.01	3.24	2.40	2.35	5.35	2.30	2.07	2.13	2.19	1.93
Earnings	2.40	2.63	2.20	1.83	1.85	1.79	1.56	1.68	1.75	1.44
S&P Core Earnings	2.37	2.58	2.11	1.78	1.85	1.60	1.38	1.42	1.49	1.31
Dividends	1.35	1.28	1.10	1.06	0.71	0.61	0.54	0.48	0.45	0.40
Payout Ratio	56%	49%	50%	58%	38%	34%	35%	28%	26%	27%
Prices:High	45.74	44.50	45.97	51.50	49.94	48.11	47.31	40.81	59.53	63.56
Prices:Low	26.46	32.03	30.83	43.89	42.50	40.37	38.60	27.24	31.15	41.00
P/E Ratio:High	19	17	21	28	27	27	30	24	34	44
P/E Ratio:Low	11	12	14	24	23	23	25	16	18	28

Income Statement Analysis (Million $)										
Revenue	8,928	8,867	8,777	7,800	8,882	8,499	7,755	7,147	7,004	7,018
Operating Income	2,081	2,138	1,832	1,795	1,967	1,948	1,745	1,793	1,952	1,938
Depreciation	309	308	106	289	289	304	307	275	279	321
Interest Expense	8.60	33.3	80.5	94.9	72.8	32.3	Nil	Nil	21.2	14.3
Pretax Income	1,863	1,905	1,812	1,624	3,486	1,678	1,495	1,645	1,787	1,525
Effective Tax Rate	NA	30.3%	35.9%	37.1%	19.2%	37.1%	37.4%	38.1%	38.4%	39.4%
Net Income	1,207	1,328	1,162	1,021	2,815	1,055	936	1,018	1,101	925
S&P Core Earnings	1,193	1,302	1,115	992	1,077	940	824	857	940	842

Balance Sheet & Other Financial Data (Million $)										
Cash	1,671	2,296	1,584	1,817	2,269	1,671	1,129	2,344	2,750	1,791
Current Assets	22,317	20,704	18,809	3,364	4,760	4,441	2,762	3,676	2,817	3,083
Total Assets	26,862	25,352	23,734	26,649	27,490	27,615	21,121	19,834	18,277	17,889
Current Liabilities	20,052	18,756	17,342	1,791	2,593	2,801	1,768	1,999	1,411	1,336
Long Term Debt	39.8	42.7	52.1	43.5	74.3	75.8	76.2	84.7	90.6	110
Common Equity	5,479	5,323	5,087	5,148	6,012	5,784	5,418	5,371	5,114	4,701
Total Capital	5,519	5,620	5,309	5,319	6,210	6,150	5,778	5,777	5,442	5,019
Capital Expenditures	103	158	181	173	292	196	196	134	146	185
Cash Flow	1,517	1,636	1,268	1,310	3,104	1,360	1,242	1,293	1,380	1,246
Current Ratio	1.1	1.1	1.1	1.9	1.8	1.6	1.6	1.8	2.0	2.3
% Long Term Debt of Capitalization	0.7	0.8	1.0	0.8	1.2	1.2	1.3	1.5	1.7	2.2
% Net Income of Revenue	13.5	15.0	13.2	13.1	31.7	12.4	12.1	14.2	15.7	13.2
% Return on Assets	4.6	5.4	4.6	3.8	10.2	4.3	4.6	5.3	6.1	5.3
% Return on Equity	22.4	25.5	22.7	18.3	47.7	18.8	17.3	19.4	22.4	19.9

Data as orig reptd.; bef. results of disc opers/spec. items. Per share data adj. for stk. divs.; EPS diluted. E-Estimated. NA-Not Available. NM-Not Meaningful. NR-Not Ranked. UR-Under Review.

Office: 1 Adp Blvd, Roseland, NJ 07068-1728.
Telephone: 973-974-5000.
Website: http://www.adp.com
Chrmn: L.A. Brun

Pres & CEO: G.C. Butler
CFO: F. Anderson, Jr.
CFO: C.R. Reidy
Chief Acctg Officer & Cntlr: A. Sheiness

Board Members: G. D. Brenneman, L. A. Brun, G. C. Butler, L. G. Cooperman, E. C. Fast, L. Gooden, R. G. Hubbard, J. P. Jones, III, S. T. Rowlands, E. T. Salem, G. L. Summe, H. Taub

Founded: 1949
Domicile: Delaware
Employees: 47,000

The McGraw-Hill Companies

AutoNation Inc

S&P Recommendation HOLD ★★★☆☆	**Price** $23.82 (as of Oct 22, 2010)	**12-Mo. Target Price** $24.00	**Investment Style** Large-Cap Blend

GICS Sector Consumer Discretionary
Sub-Industry Automotive Retail

Summary AutoNation, the largest U.S. retail auto dealer, owns and operates about 250 new vehicle franchises in 15 states.

Key Stock Statistics (Source S&P, Vickers, company reports)

52-Wk Range	$25.05– 16.99	S&P Oper. EPS 2010**E**	1.55	Market Capitalization(B)	$3.487	Beta		1.31
Trailing 12-Month EPS	$1.33	S&P Oper. EPS 2011**E**	1.79	Yield (%)	Nil	S&P 3-Yr. Proj. EPS CAGR(%)		21
Trailing 12-Month P/E	17.9	P/E on S&P Oper. EPS 2010**E**	15.4	Dividend Rate/Share	Nil	S&P Credit Rating		BB+
$10K Invested 5 Yrs Ago	$12,855	Common Shares Outstg. (M)	146.4	Institutional Ownership (%)	89			

Price Performance

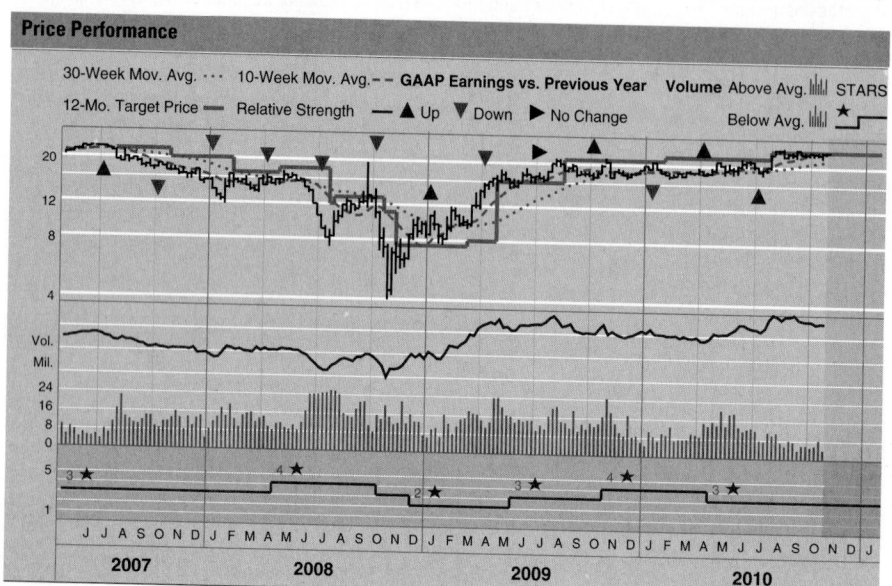

- 30-Week Mov. Avg. · · ·   10-Week Mov. Avg. - -   **GAAP Earnings vs. Previous Year**   Volume Above Avg. ▮▮▮ STARS
- 12-Mo. Target Price —   Relative Strength —   ▲ Up   ▼ Down   ▶ No Change   Below Avg. ▮▮▮ ★

Options: ASE, CBOE, P, Ph

Analysis prepared by **Efraim Levy, CFA** on October 20, 2010, when the stock traded at **$ 23.88**.

Highlights

► New vehicle sales in 2009 were hurt by the U.S. recession, weaker housing markets, and the credit crunch. In addition, several domestic branded AN dealerships were closed or received notices from automakers that they will be closed. We expect revenues to rise about 13% in 2010 and 11% in 2011, as the economy and consumer confidence should improve.

► For 2010, we project that higher industry volume and macroeconomic factors will bolster new and used vehicle sales. We expect new light vehicle sales volume to advance 10% in 2010, to 11.4 million units and rise further to 12.9 million units in 2011. Used vehicle sales prices have been rising in recent months. We believe SG&A expenses will increase as demand rebounds, but we also see cost-cutting positioning the company for improved profitability.

► We see AutoNation's 2010 and 2011 operating EPS rising on increased operating efficiencies. Although we expect a resurgence of capital spending in 2010 and 2011, we think cash flow will support share repurchases and expansion of the business internally and via acquisitions. Recent share repurchases contributed to our rising EPS forecast.

Investment Rationale/Risk

► The stock recently traded at P/E, price-to-free cash flow, and enterprise value-to-EBITDA multiples above peer averages, based on our 2011 estimates. We believe AN warrants a premium valuation given its above-peer-average net margins. Based on S&P's Core Earnings methodology, we believe AN's earnings quality for 2010 and 2011 will be high, as AutoNation does not offer its employees a pension plan. We view 2010 as the start of a multi-year uptrend in U.S. light vehicle sales.

► Risks to our recommendation and target price include lower multiples for automotive retailers, less-than-expected vehicle demand, and weaker pricing for new and used vehicles.

► Applying a P/E of about 15.8X, reflecting peer and historical P/E comparisons, to our 2011 EPS estimate of $1.79 leads to a value of about $28. Our DCF model, which assumes a weighted average cost of capital of 11.2%, a compound annual growth rate of 1.4% over the next 15 years, and terminal growth of 3%, calculates intrinsic value of approximately $19. Based on a weighted blend of these metrics, our 12-month target price is $24. We see cash flow remaining positive and sufficient to meet current needs.

Qualitative Risk Assessment

LOW	**MEDIUM**	HIGH

Our risk assessment reflects the cyclical nature of the automotive retailing industry, which is affected by interest rates, consumer confidence, and personal discretionary spending, offset by the company's highly variable cost structure.

Quantitative Evaluations

S&P Quality Ranking B-

D	C	**B-**	B	B+	A-	A	A+

Relative Strength Rank MODERATE

54

LOWEST = 1   HIGHEST = 99

Revenue/Earnings Data

Revenue (Million $)

	1Q	2Q	3Q	4Q	Year
2010	2,847	3,109	--	--	--
2009	2,412	2,615	2,916	2,815	10,758
2008	3,970	3,885	3,540	2,737	14,132
2007	4,395	4,559	4,602	4,214	17,692
2006	4,612	4,959	4,945	4,473	18,989
2005	4,561	5,019	5,188	4,485	19,253

Earnings Per Share ($)

	1Q	2Q	3Q	4Q	Year
2010	0.34	0.31	E0.43	E0.41	E1.55
2009	0.30	0.30	0.36	0.36	1.32
2008	0.31	0.30	-7.95	0.40	-6.89
2007	0.39	0.38	0.39	0.27	1.44
2006	0.37	0.33	0.40	0.35	1.45
2005	0.33	0.40	0.45	0.30	1.48

Fiscal year ended Dec. 31. Next earnings report expected: Late October. EPS Estimates based on S&P Operating Earnings; historical GAAP earnings are as reported.

Dividend Data

No cash dividends have been paid.

Please read the Required Disclosures and Analyst Certification on the last page of this report.

STANDARD &POOR'S

AutoNation Inc

Business Summary October 20, 2010

CORPORATE OVERVIEW. AutoNation's vehicle retailing unit segment operates in saturated markets, in our view. Although the company is the largest U.S. auto retailer, it controls only about 2% of the $1 trillion U.S. new and used car market. About 75% of total U.S. vehicle sales are to replace existing autos. AN's new auto retailing operations (53% of 2009 revenues) consist of about 245 dealerships.

The sale of used vehicles accounted for nearly 23% of revenues in 2009. Fixed operations provided 20% of sales, while finance and insurance and other accounted for the balance.

As of July 2010, investor Edward Lampert's ESL Investments Inc. owned about 55% of AutoNation's common shares. In January 2009, the company's directors approved agreements with certain automakers to permit ESL and certain affiliates to acquire 50% or more of the company. ESL has agreed to vote all shares above 50% in proportion to all non-ESL shares voted. Bill Gates controls about 12% of AutoNation's common shares through the Bill & Melinda Gates Foundation Trust and through Cascade Investment LLC.

CORPORATE STRATEGY. The company plans to maximize the return on its investment by using cash flow to purchase dealerships and buy back common shares, although given the current economic environment we expect this activity to be below the level of recent years. It also plans to divest non-core stores. In addition, AN intends to increase its mix of higher volume import and premium luxury stores. In 2009, 71% of new vehicle sales revenues were generated by import and luxury franchises; domestic franchises accounted for 29%.

Company Financials Fiscal Year Ended Dec. 31

Per Share Data ($)	2009	2008	2007	2006	2005	2004	2003	2002	2001	2000
Tangible Book Value	5.84	4.93	2.37	2.66	6.53	4.53	3.91	3.14	2.99	2.64
Cash Flow	1.76	-6.38	1.90	1.81	1.78	1.78	2.01	1.40	1.18	1.28
Earnings	1.32	-6.89	1.44	1.45	1.48	1.45	1.76	1.19	0.73	0.91
S&P Core Earnings	1.27	1.32	1.44	1.45	1.44	1.41	1.69	1.12	0.57	NA
Dividends	Nil	Nil	Nil	Nil	Nil	Nil	Nil	Nil	Nil	Nil
Payout Ratio	Nil	Nil	Nil	Nil	Nil	Nil	Nil	Nil	Nil	Nil
Prices:High	21.60	19.59	23.19	22.94	22.84	19.33	19.19	18.73	13.07	10.75
Prices:Low	7.62	3.97	14.65	18.95	17.91	15.01	11.61	9.05	4.94	4.63
P/E Ratio:High	16	NM	16	16	15	13	11	16	18	12
P/E Ratio:Low	6	NM	10	13	12	10	7	8	7	5

Income Statement Analysis (Million $)	2009	2008	2007	2006	2005	2004	2003	2002	2001	2000
Revenue	10,758	14,132	17,692	18,989	19,253	19,425	19,381	19,479	19,989	20,610
Operating Income	464	566	798	879	888	861	805	786	667	855
Depreciation	77.5	90.8	91.7	82.9	80.7	89.7	71.0	69.7	152	134
Interest Expense	78.7	177	247	267	191	159	143	125	43.7	248
Pretax Income	351	-1,423	459	542	623	607	591	618	401	525
Effective Tax Rate	33.3%	NM	37.3%	38.9%	36.5%	34.7%	14.4%	38.3%	38.9%	37.5%
Net Income	234	-1,225	288	331	396	396	506	382	245	328
S&P Core Earnings	225	234	288	331	385	385	486	359	192	NA

Balance Sheet & Other Financial Data (Million $)	2009	2008	2007	2006	2005	2004	2003	2002	2001	2000
Cash	174	111	32.8	52.2	244	107	171	176	128	82.2
Current Assets	2,251	2,554	3,238	3,386	3,880	3,678	3,990	3,629	3,153	4,176
Total Assets	5,407	6,014	8,480	8,607	8,825	8,699	8,823	8,585	8,065	8,830
Current Liabilities	1,863	2,456	2,902	3,031	3,412	3,411	3,810	2,981	2,578	3,141
Long Term Debt	1,105	1,226	3,917	1,558	484	798	808	643	647	850
Common Equity	2,303	2,198	3,474	3,713	4,670	4,263	3,950	3,910	3,828	3,843
Total Capital	3,416	3,424	5,446	5,496	5,340	5,218	4,935	5,500	5,329	5,570
Capital Expenditures	75.5	117	160	170	132	133	133	183	164	148
Cash Flow	312	-1,135	380	414	476	486	577	451	397	462
Current Ratio	1.2	1.0	1.1	1.1	1.1	1.1	1.0	1.2	1.2	1.3
% Long Term Debt of Capitalization	Nil	35.8	33.5	28.3	9.1	15.3	16.4	11.7	12.1	15.3
% Net Income of Revenue	2.2	NM	1.6	1.7	2.1	2.0	2.6	2.0	1.2	1.6
% Return on Assets	NA	NM	3.4	3.8	4.5	4.5	5.8	4.6	2.9	3.6
% Return on Equity	NA	NM	8.0	7.9	8.9	9.7	12.9	9.9	6.4	7.8

Data as orig reptd.; bef. results of disc opers/spec. items. Per share data adj. for stk. divs.; EPS diluted. E-Estimated. NA-Not Available. NM-Not Meaningful. NR-Not Ranked. UR-Under Review.

Office: 200 SW 1st Ave, Ft. Lauderdale, FL 33301.
Telephone: 954-769-6000.
Website: http://www.autonation.com
Chrmn & CEO: M.J. Jackson

Pres & COO: M.E. Maroone
EVP & CFO: M. Short
EVP, Secy & General Counsel: J.P. Ferrando
Chief Acctg Officer & Cntlr: M.J. Stephan

Board Members: R. J. Brown, R. L. Burdick, W. C. Crowley, D. B. Edelson, R. R. Grusky, M. J. Jackson, M. Larson, M. E. Maroone, C. A. Migoya

Founded: 1991
Domicile: Delaware
Employees: 18,000

The McGraw-Hill Companies

AutoZone Inc

STANDARD &POOR'S

S&P Recommendation HOLD ★★★☆☆

Price $234.72 (as of Oct 22, 2010)	**12-Mo. Target Price** $230.00

Investment Style Large-Cap Growth

GICS Sector Consumer Discretionary
Sub-Industry Automotive Retail

Summary This retailer of automotive parts and accessories operates over 4,000 AutoZone stores throughout most of the U.S. and in Mexico.

Key Stock Statistics (Source S&P, Vickers, company reports)

52-Wk Range	$234.98– 135.13	S&P Oper. EPS 2011**E**	16.87	Market Capitalization(B)	$11.034	Beta	0.47
Trailing 12-Month EPS	$14.98	S&P Oper. EPS 2012**E**	18.69	Yield (%)	Nil	S&P 3-Yr. Proj. EPS CAGR(%)	10
Trailing 12-Month P/E	15.7	P/E on S&P Oper. EPS 2011**E**	13.9	Dividend Rate/Share	Nil	S&P Credit Rating	BBB
$10K Invested 5 Yrs Ago	$29,939	Common Shares Outstg. (M)	47.0	Institutional Ownership (%)	85		

Price Performance

30-Week Mov. Avg. · · · 10-Week Mov. Avg. – – GAAP Earnings vs. Previous Year Volume Above Avg. STARS
12-Mo. Target Price — Relative Strength ▲ Up ▼ Down ► No Change Below Avg. ★

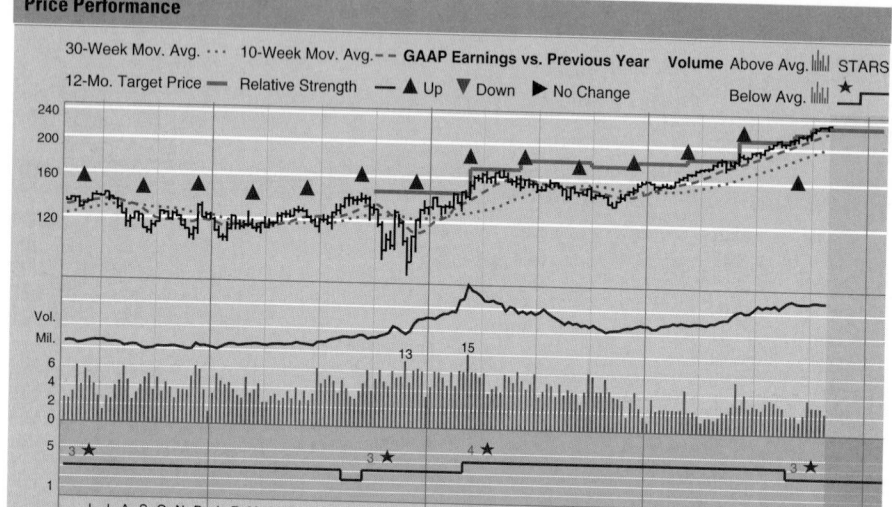

Options: ASE, CBOE, P, Ph

Analysis prepared by **Michael Souers** on September 24, 2010, when the stock traded at **$ 222.64**.

Highlights

► We see sales growth of 4.2% in FY 11 (Aug.), following an 8.0% advance in FY 10. This reflects our forecast of approximately 200 new stores in the U.S. and Mexico, along with same-store sales growth of 2% to 3%. While macroeconomic pressures are putting a financial strain on consumers, likely inducing them to delay preventive maintenance on their vehicles, we continue to view industry-specific drivers favorably, including the stabilization in miles driven and the increased number of vehicles that are seven years or older on the road.

► We look for a 20 basis point widening of operating margins, as supply chain efficiencies and increased sales of private-label products are partially offset by an increasing percentage of lower-margin commercial sales in the mix. We expect a slight leveraging of SG&A expenses on a modest comp-store sales increase.

► After modestly higher interest expense, taxes at an effective rate of 36.5%, and about 7% fewer shares due to AZO's active share repurchase program, we forecast that FY 11 operating EPS will increase 13%, to $16.88 from the $14.97 the company earned in FY 10.

Investment Rationale/Risk

► AutoZone maintains an industry-leading sales-to-square foot ratio, and sports higher gross, operating, and net margins than any of its peers in our coverage. In addition, we think long-term trends for the automotive aftermarket retail industry are extremely favorable, with an aging vehicle population and pent-up demand from recent maintenance deferrals. Near term, the recent stabilization in gasoline prices should help fuel spending on vehicle maintenance somewhat, and we believe AZO's recent comp performance has been quite impressive, given the macro challenges. However, following a significant recent increase in share price, we now find AZO appropriately valued.

► Risks to our recommendation and target price include a significant decline in consumer spending; a sharp rise in oil prices; a decrease in auto usage and miles driven; and declines in same-store-sales, which would cause expense deleverage.

► Our 12-month target price of $230, based on our DCF analysis, is equal to about 14X our FY 11 EPS estimate. Our DCF model assumes a weighted average cost of capital of 9.3% and a terminal growth rate of 3.0%.

Qualitative Risk Assessment

LOW	MEDIUM	HIGH

Our risk assessment reflects the cyclical and seasonal nature of the auto parts retailing industry, which is sensitive to various economic data points, offset by our view of the company's strong financial metrics and margins.

Quantitative Evaluations

S&P Quality Ranking B+

D	C	B-	B	B+	A-	A	A+

Relative Strength Rank STRONG

71

LOWEST = 1 HIGHEST = 99

Revenue/Earnings Data

Revenue (Million $)

	1Q	2Q	3Q	4Q	Year
2010	1,589	1,506	1,822	2,445	7,363
2009	1,478	1,448	1,658	2,232	6,817
2008	1,456	1,339	1,517	2,211	6,523
2007	1,393	1,300	1,474	2,003	6,170
2006	1,338	1,254	1,417	1,939	5,948
2005	1,286	1,204	1,338	1,882	5,711

Earnings Per Share ($)

2010	2.82	2.46	4.12	5.66	14.98
2009	2.23	2.03	3.13	4.43	11.73
2008	2.02	1.67	2.49	3.88	10.04
2007	1.73	1.45	2.17	3.23	8.53
2006	1.48	1.25	1.89	2.92	7.50
2005	1.52	1.16	1.86	2.66	7.18

Fiscal year ended Aug. 31. Next earnings report expected: Early December. EPS Estimates based on S&P Operating Earnings; historical GAAP earnings are as reported.

Dividend Data

No cash dividends have been paid.

AutoZone Inc

Business Summary September 24, 2010

CORPORATE OVERVIEW. AutoZone is the nation's leading specialty retailer and a leading distributor of automotive replacement parts and accessories, focusing primarily on do-it-yourself (DIY) consumers. As of August 29, 2009, the company operated 4,229 U.S. AutoZone stores, in 48 states, the District of Columbia and Puerto Rico, and 188 stores in Mexico. AZO also sells automotive diagnostic equipment and repair software through ALLDATA, and diagnostic and repair information, along with and parts and accessories, online at www.autozone.com.

The company's 4,417 stores represented 28.6 million sq. ft., up from 4,240 stores and 27.3 million sq. ft. a year earlier. Each store's product line includes new and remanufactured automotive hard parts, such as alternators, starters, water pumps, brake shoes and pads, carburetors, clutches and engines; maintenance items, such as oil, antifreeze, transmission, brake and power steering fluids, engine additives, protectants and waxes; and accessories, such as car stereos and floor mats. Parts are carried for domestic and foreign cars, sport utility vehicles, vans, and light trucks.

Stores, generally in high-visibility locations, range in size from about 4,000 sq. ft. to 8,100 sq. ft., with new stores increasingly using a larger format. As of August 29, 2009, AutoZone stores were principally in the following locations: 525 stores in Texas, 447 in California, 219 in Ohio, 208 in Illinois, 196 in Florida, 175 in Georgia, 164 in North Carolina, 150 in Tennessee, 145 in Michigan, 137 in Indiana, 119 in Arizona, 114 in New York, 109 in Pennsylvania, 108 in Louisiana and 100 in Missouri, with the rest in other states.

CORPORATE STRATEGY. AZO offers everyday low prices, and attempts to be the price leader in hard parts. Stores generally carry about 21,000 stock-keeping units. In addition to targeting the DIY customer, the company has a commercial sales program in the U.S. (AZ Commercial), which provides commercial credit and delivery of parts and other products to local, regional and national repair garages, dealers and service stations. As of August 29, 2009, 2,303 stores had commercial sales programs. The hub stores provide fast replenishment of key merchandise to support the DIY and commercial sales businesses. AZO does not perform repairs or installations.

Company Financials Fiscal Year Ended Aug. 31

	2010	2009	2008	2007	2006	2005	2004	2003	2002	2001
Per Share Data ($)										
Tangible Book Value	NA	NM	NM	1.52	2.35	1.15	NM	0.90	3.87	5.13
Cash Flow	NA	14.96	12.70	10.82	9.34	8.92	7.79	6.47	5.10	2.70
Earnings	14.98	11.73	10.04	8.53	7.50	7.18	6.56	5.34	4.00	1.54
S&P Core Earnings	NA	11.58	9.91	8.53	7.50	7.03	6.40	5.09	3.87	1.45
Dividends	NA	Nil	Nil	Nil	Nil	Nil	Nil	Nil	Nil	Nil
Payout Ratio	Nil	Nil	Nil	Nil	Nil	Nil	Nil	Nil	Nil	Nil
Prices:High	234.98	169.99	143.80	140.29	120.37	103.94	92.35	103.53	89.34	80.00
Prices:Low	152.32	125.80	84.66	103.40	83.81	77.76	70.35	58.21	59.20	24.37
P/E Ratio:High	16	14	14	16	16	14	14	19	22	52
P/E Ratio:Low	10	11	8	12	11	11	11	11	15	16
Income Statement Analysis (Million $)										
Revenue	7,363	6,817	6,523	6,170	5,948	5,711	5,637	5,457	5,326	4,818
Operating Income	1,493	1,357	1,294	1,215	1,239	1,114	1,106	1,028	889	646
Depreciation	NA	180	170	159	139	138	107	110	118	131
Interest Expense	159	148	121	119	110	104	93.0	84.8	79.9	101
Pretax Income	1,161	1,034	1,007	936	902	873	906	833	691	287
Effective Tax Rate	NA	36.4%	36.3%	36.4%	36.9%	34.6%	37.5%	37.9%	38.1%	38.8%
Net Income	738	657	642	596	569	571	566	518	428	176
S&P Core Earnings	NA	649	633	596	569	560	553	492	415	165
Balance Sheet & Other Financial Data (Million $)										
Cash	98.3	92.7	242	86.7	91.6	74.8	76.9	6.74	6.50	7.29
Current Assets	2,612	2,562	2,586	2,270	2,119	1,929	1,756	1,585	1,450	1,329
Total Assets	5,572	5,318	5,257	4,805	4,526	4,245	3,913	3,680	3,478	3,433
Current Liabilities	3,064	2,707	2,519	2,286	2,055	1,811	1,818	1,676	1,534	1,267
Long Term Debt	2,882	2,727	2,250	1,936	1,857	1,862	1,869	1,547	1,195	1,225
Common Equity	-739	-433	230	403	470	391	171	374	1,378	866
Total Capital	2,144	2,294	2,480	2,339	2,327	2,253	2,046	1,921	2,573	2,092
Capital Expenditures	NA	272	244	224	264	283	185	182	117	169
Cash Flow	NA	837	811	755	709	709	673	627	546	307
Current Ratio	0.9	1.0	1.0	1.0	1.0	1.1	1.0	0.9	0.9	1.0
% Long Term Debt of Capitalization	134.5	118.9	90.7	82.8	79.8	82.6	91.3	80.5	46.4	58.6
% Net Income of Revenue	10.0	9.6	9.8	9.7	9.6	10.0	10.0	9.5	8.0	3.6
% Return on Assets	13.6	12.4	12.8	12.8	13.0	14.0	14.7	14.5	12.4	5.2
% Return on Equity	NM	NM	202.8	136.5	132.3	203.1	207.7	97.4	27.5	18.9

Data as orig reptd.; bef. results of disc opers/spec. items. Per share data adj. for stk. divs.; EPS diluted. E-Estimated. NA-Not Available. NM-Not Meaningful. NR-Not Ranked. UR-Under Review.

Office: 123 South Front Street, Memphis, TN 38103-3607.
Telephone: 901-495-6500.
Email: investor.relations@autozone.com
Website: http://www.autozone.com

Chrmn, Pres & CEO: W.C. Rhodes, III
EVP, CFO & Treas: W.T. Giles
EVP, Secy & General Counsel: H.L. Goldsmith
SVP, Chief Acctg Officer & Cntlr: C. Pleas, III

SVP & CIO: J.A. Bascom
Investor Contact: B. Campbell (901-495-7005)
Board Members: W. C. Crowley, S. E. Gove, E. B. Graves, Jr., R. R. Grusky, J. R. Hyde, III, W. A. McKenna, G. R. Mrkonic, Jr., L. P. Nieto, Jr., W. C. Rhodes, III, T. W. Ullyot

Founded: 1979
Domicile: Nevada
Employees: 60,000

AvalonBay Communities Inc.

STANDARD & POOR'S

S&P Recommendation HOLD ★★★★☆

Price $110.08 (as of Oct 22, 2010)	**12-Mo. Target Price** $104.00	**Investment Style** Large-Cap Blend

GICS Sector Financials
Sub-Industry Residential REITS

Summary This real estate investment trust, formed via the 1998 merger of Bay Apartment Communities and Avalon Properties, specializes in upscale apartment communities.

Key Stock Statistics (Source S&P, Vickers, company reports)

52-Wk Range	$114.11– 66.90	S&P FFO/Sh. 2010E		Market Capitalization(B)	$9.375	Beta 1.36
Trailing 12-Month FFO/Share	NA	S&P FFO/Sh. 2011E	3.92	Yield (%)	3.24	S&P 3-Yr. FFO/Sh. Proj. CAGR(%) -4
Trailing 12-Month P/FFO	NA	P/FFO on S&P FFO/Sh. 2010E	4.19	Dividend Rate/Share	$3.57	S&P Credit Rating BBB+
$10K Invested 5 Yrs Ago	$16,756	Common Shares Outstg. (M)	28.1	Institutional Ownership (%)	NM	
			85.2			

Price Performance

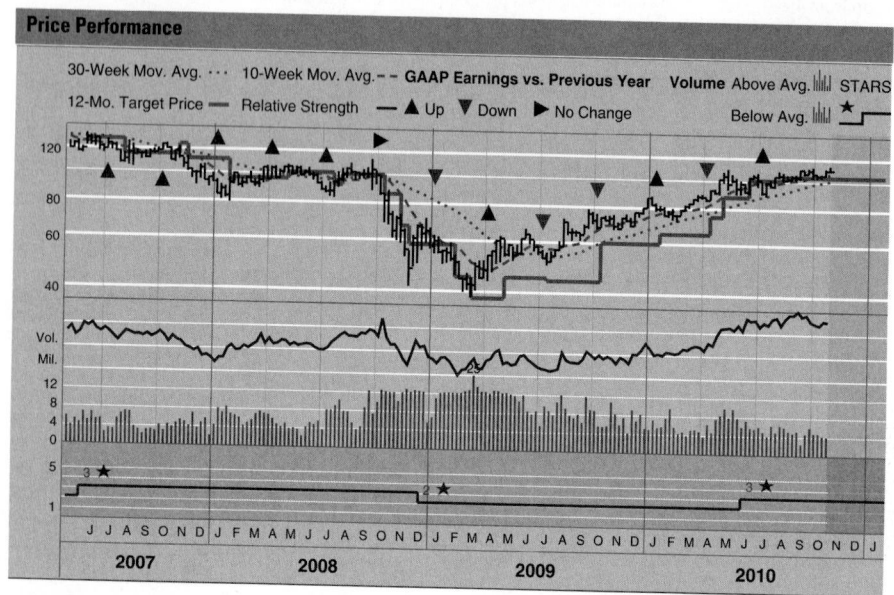

- 30-Week Mov. Avg. ···
- 10-Week Mov. Avg. - -
- GAAP Earnings vs. Previous Year
- Volume Above Avg.
- STARS
- 12-Mo. Target Price —
- Relative Strength
- ▲ Up ▼ Down ► No Change
- Below Avg.
- ★

Options: ASE, CBOE, P

Analysis prepared by **Royal F. Shepard, CFA** on August 11, 2010, when the stock traded at **$ 102.67**.

Highlights

➤ We expect improved pricing power for AVB's established properties in the second half of 2010. The trust's properties were full during the second quarter, at 96.5% occupancy. In our opinion, the strong demand reflects a trend away from home ownership, which hit a 10-year low in the second quarter according to the U.S. Census Bureau. Also, the competitive supply of new homes is modest, thanks to sharp drop in 2010 multi-family construction starts.

➤ We think AVB will move quickly to satisfy growing demand by reviving new development activities. As of June 30, 2010, it had seven communities under development at a total capital cost of $843.1 million. Moreover, in July, the trust started construction of three additional communities with 395 units at a total capital cost of $106.3 million. In our estimation, however, these properties will not contribute meaningfully to reported earnings until 2011.

➤ Our 2010 FFO per share forecast of $3.92, down from recurring FFO of $4.46 for 2009, reflects higher financing costs, inflationary increases in operating expenses, and about 4% more shares outstanding.

Investment Rationale/Risk

➤ We expect a better balance between supply and demand will lead to renewed rental growth during the second half of 2010. AVB's focus on upscale projects, in our view, may still make it vulnerable to excess inventories of single-family homes for rent. However, we think the trust's large pipeline of development projects holds value and will begin to add to earnings when new properties reach stable occupancy levels. We view the shares, recently trading at 24.5X our 2011 FFO per share estimate of $4.19, a 20% premium to peers, as appropriately reflecting our view of its above-average growth profile.

➤ Risks to our recommendation and target price include the potential for slower-than-expected employment growth; increased competition from unsold inventories of single-family homes; and less liquid credit markets that decrease investor demand for real estate assets.

➤ Our 12-month target price of $104 is based on applying a multiple of 24.8X to our 2010 FFO per share estimate of $4.19, a premium to apartment REIT peers on average. Our valuation reflects our view of AVB's relatively strong financial position, high quality properties, and large development pipeline.

Qualitative Risk Assessment

LOW	MEDIUM	HIGH

Our risk assessment reflects AVB's geographically diverse asset base and strong dividend coverage ratio.

Quantitative Evaluations

S&P Quality Ranking A-

D	C	B-	B	B+	A-	A	A+

Relative Strength Rank MODERATE

56

LOWEST = 1   HIGHEST = 99

Revenue/FFO Data

Revenue (Million $)

	1Q	2Q	3Q	4Q	Year
2010	215.8	220.9	--	--	--
2009	222.9	222.1	222.2	211.7	853.0
2008	204.2	211.2	218.5	220.4	854.2
2007	192.7	199.5	208.2	212.4	812.7
2006	175.2	180.7	187.7	193.8	737.3
2005	161.3	165.6	170.8	173.1	670.7

FFO Per Share ($)

	1Q	2Q	3Q	4Q	Year
2010	0.96	1.04	E0.95	E1.00	E3.92
2009	1.27	0.90	1.09	0.64	3.89
2008	1.24	1.26	1.28	0.30	4.07
2007	1.11	1.17	1.19	1.14	4.61
2006	1.15	1.03	1.11	1.09	4.38
2005	0.96	0.97	0.91	0.93	3.77

Fiscal year ended Dec. 31. Next earnings report expected: Late October. FFO Estimates based on S&P Funds From Operations Est..

Dividend Data (Dates: mm/dd Payment Date: mm/dd/yy)

Amount ($)	Date Decl.	Ex-Div. Date	Stk. of Record	Payment Date
0.893	12/10	12/29	12/31	01/15/10
0.893	02/10	03/29	03/31	04/15/10
0.893	05/19	06/28	06/30	07/15/10
0.893	09/07	09/29	10/01	10/15/10

Dividends have been paid since 1994. Source: Company reports.

Please read the Required Disclosures and Analyst Certification on the last page of this report.

The McGraw-Hill Companies

AvalonBay Communities Inc.

STANDARD &POOR'S

Business Summary August 11, 2010

CORPORATE OVERVIEW. AvalonBay Communities (AVB) is a real estate investment trust (REIT) specializing in the ownership of multi-family apartment communities. At December 31, 2009, AVB owned or held an interest in 172 apartment communities containing 50,364 apartment homes in 10 states and the District of Columbia, of which seven communities were under construction and seven communities were under reconstruction. AVB also owned a direct or indirect ownership interest in rights to develop an additional 28 communities; if developed in the manner expected, these would contain an estimated 7,180 apartment homes.

MARKET PROFILE. The housing market is highly fragmented and is broadly characterized by two types of housing units, multi-family and single-family. At the end of 2009, the U.S. Census Bureau estimated that there were 130.59 million housing units in the country, an increase of 0.9% from 2008. Partially on high fragmentation and the fact that residents have the option of either being owners or tenants (renters), the housing market can be highly competitive. Main demand drivers for apartments are household formation and employment growth. We estimate that 0.5 million new households were formed in 2009. Supply is created by new housing unit construction, which could consist of single-family homes, or multi-family apartment buildings or condominiums. The U.S. Department of Housing estimates that 554,000 housing units were started in 2009, down about 39% from 2007. Multi-family starts, for structures with more than five units, dropped significantly more, falling approximately 63%.

With apartment tenants on relatively short leases compared to those of commercial and industrial properties, we believe apartment REITs are generally more sensitive to changes in market conditions than REITs in other property categories. Results could be hurt by new construction that adds new space in excess of actual demand. Trends in home price affordability also affect both rent levels and the level of new construction, since the relative price attractiveness of owning versus renting is an important factor in consumer decision making.

Company Financials Fiscal Year Ended Dec. 31

Per Share Data ($)	2009	2008	2007	2006	2005	2004	2003	2002	2001	2000
Tangible Book Value	37.41	37.82	37.85	NA	NA	NA	NA	31.88	NA	29.31
Earnings	0.97	1.34	3.00	2.27	1.34	1.09	1.30	1.48	3.12	2.53
S&P Core Earnings	0.95	1.34	3.00	2.12	1.34	1.09	1.27	1.22	3.07	2.24
Dividends	3.57	5.38	3.33	NA	NA	NA	NA	NA	2.56	NA
Payout Ratio	NM	401%	111%	137%	NM	NM	NM	188%	82%	89%
Prices:High	87.82	113.07	149.94	134.60	92.99	75.93	49.71	52.65	51.90	50.63
Prices:Low	38.34	41.43	88.94	88.95	64.98	46.72	35.24	36.38	42.45	32.63
P/E Ratio:High	91	84	50	59	69	65	38	35	17	20
P/E Ratio:Low	40	31	30	39	48	40	27	24	14	13

Income Statement Analysis (Million $)	2009	2008	2007	2006	2005	2004	2003	2002	2001	2000
Rental Income	844	848	807	731	666	648	Nil	Nil	637	572
Mortgage Income	Nil	Nil	Nil	Nil	Nil	Nil	Nil	Nil	Nil	Nil
Total Income	852	854	813	737	671	648	610	639	642	573
General Expenses	374	436	346	236	376	368	192	247	229	203
Interest Expense	150	115	97.5	111	127	131	135	121	103	83.6
Provision for Losses	Nil	Nil	Nil	Nil	Nil	Nil	Nil	Nil	Nil	Nil
Depreciation	210	194	180	163	159	152	151	144	130	123
Net Income	77.8	114	248	180	108	86.3	100	121	249	211
S&P Core Earnings	76.1	104	239	159	98.9	76.7	87.6	85.7	213	NA

Balance Sheet & Other Financial Data (Million $)	2009	2008	2007	2006	2005	2004	2003	2002	2001	2000
Cash	106	259	210	146	48.0	4,921	4,744	4,813	4,479	4,286
Total Assets	7,458	7,173	6,736	5,813	5,165	5,068	4,910	4,952	4,664	4,397
Real Estate Investment	8,311	5,297	5,038	5,662	5,874	NA	5,431	5,369	4,838	4,875
Loss Reserve	Nil	Nil	Nil	Nil	Nil	NA	Nil	Nil	Nil	Nil
Net Investment	6,833	6,650	6,297	4,562	4,946	4,919	4,736	4,800	4,391	4,212
Short Term Debt	125	310	514	Nil	Nil	Nil	Nil	165	101	14.1
Capitalization:Debt	3,850	3,365	2,694	2,705	2,177	2,335	2,337	2,307	1,983	1,716
Capitalization:Equity	3,050	2,916	3,027	2,631	2,542	2,385	2,311	2,194	2,314	2,442
Capitalization:Total	6,906	6,290	5,534	5,194	4,738	4,741	2,336	4,579	4,353	4,208
% Earnings & Depreciation/Assets	3.9	8.7	6.8	6.2	5.2	NA	5.1	5.5	8.4	7.8
Price Times Book Value:High	2.3	3.0	4.0	4.0	2.8	NA	1.5	1.7	1.6	1.7
Price Times Book Value:Low	1.0	1.1	2.3	2.7	2.0	NA	1.1	1.1	1.3	1.1

Data as orig reptd.; bef. results of disc opers/spec. items. Per share data adj. for stk. divs.; EPS diluted. E-Estimated. NA-Not Available. NM-Not Meaningful. NR-Not Ranked. UR-Under Review.

Office: Ballston Tower, 671 North Glebe Road, Suite 800, Arlington, VA 22203.
Telephone: 703-329-6300.
Email: investments@avalonbay.com
Website: http://www.avalonbay.com

Chrmn & CEO: B. Blair
Pres: T.J. Naughton
COO: L.S. Horey
EVP & CFO: T.J. Sargeant

SVP, Secy & General Counsel: E.M. Schulman
Investor Contact: J. Christie (703-317-4747)
Board Members: B. Blair, B. A. Choate, J. J. Healy, Jr., T. J. Naughton, L. R. Primis, P. S. Rummell, H. Sarles, W. E. Walter

Founded: 1978
Domicile: Maryland
Employees: 1,877

Avery Dennison Corp

STANDARD &POOR'S

S&P Recommendation **BUY** ★★★★☆	Price $38.90 (as of Oct 22, 2010)	12-Mo. Target Price $50.00	Investment Style Large-Cap Blend

GICS Sector Industrials
Sub-Industry Office Services & Supplies

Summary This company is a leading worldwide manufacturer of pressure-sensitive adhesives and materials, office products, labels, retail systems and specialty chemicals.

Key Stock Statistics (Source S&P, Vickers, company reports)

52-Wk Range	$43.33–30.22	S&P Oper. EPS 2010E	2.70	Market Capitalization(B)	$4.113
Trailing 12-Month EPS	$2.50	S&P Oper. EPS 2011E	3.00	Yield (%)	2.06
Trailing 12-Month P/E	15.6	P/E on S&P Oper. EPS 2010E	14.4	Dividend Rate/Share	$0.80
$10K Invested 5 Yrs Ago	$8,874	Common Shares Outstg. (M)	105.7	Institutional Ownership (%)	88

Beta	1.45
S&P 3-Yr. Proj. EPS CAGR(%)	10
S&P Credit Rating	BBB

Price Performance

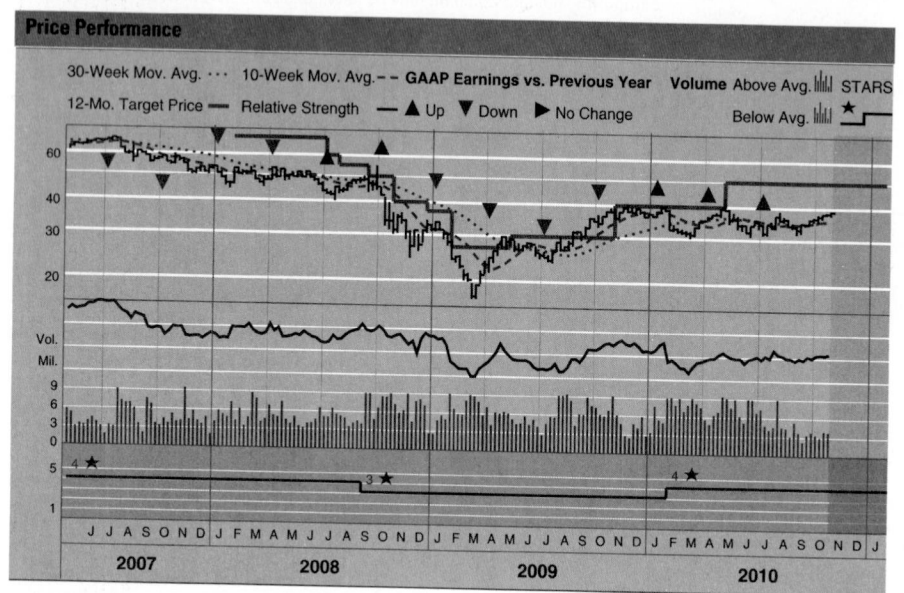

30-Week Mov. Avg. ··· 10-Week Mov. Avg. - - GAAP Earnings vs. Previous Year Volume Above Avg. STARS
12-Mo. Target Price — Relative Strength — ▲ Up ▼ Down ▶ No Change Below Avg. ★

Options: CBOE, P, Ph

Analysis prepared by **Richard O'Reilly, CFA** on July 30, 2010, when the stock traded at **$ 36.04.**

Qualitative Risk Assessment

LOW	MEDIUM	HIGH

Our risk assessment reflects the company's leading market shares in pressure-sensitive adhesives and office products, and our view of above-average growth rates in key end markets and relatively strong cash flow, offset by current sluggish markets.

Quantitative Evaluations

S&P Quality Ranking   B

D	C	B-	B	B+	A-	A	A+

Relative Strength Rank   STRONG

     72
LOWEST = 1   HIGHEST = 99

Revenue/Earnings Data

Revenue (Million $)

	1Q	2Q	3Q	4Q	Year
2010	1,555	1,680	--	--	--
2009	1,426	1,455	1,549	1,522	5,953
2008	1,645	1,829	1,725	1,512	6,710
2007	1,390	1,524	1,680	1,714	6,308
2006	1,337	1,410	1,418	1,411	5,576
2005	1,346	1,419	1,363	1,364	5,474

Earnings Per Share ($)

	1Q	2Q	3Q	4Q	Year
2010	0.51	0.79	E0.60	E0.55	E2.70
2009	-8.99	0.38	0.59	0.47	-7.21
2008	0.69	0.93	0.63	0.43	2.70
2007	0.80	0.87	0.59	0.81	3.07
2006	0.69	0.96	0.85	1.01	3.51
2005	0.58	0.89	0.86	0.57	2.90

Fiscal year ended Dec. 31. Next earnings report expected: Late October. EPS Estimates based on S&P Operating Earnings; historical GAAP earnings are as reported.

Dividend Data (Dates: mm/dd Payment Date: mm/dd/yy)

Amount ($)	Date Decl.	Ex-Div. Date	Stk. of Record	Payment Date
0.200	10/22	11/30	12/02	12/16/09
0.200	01/28	03/01	03/03	03/17/10
0.200	04/22	05/28	06/02	06/16/10
0.200	07/22	08/30	09/01	09/15/10

Dividends have been paid since 1964. Source: Company reports.

Highlights

▶ We project sales to increase about 7.5% in 2010, reflecting recovering consumer staples and retail apparel markets for the pressure-sensitive materials and retail information segments, higher selling prices, and unfavorable currency rates. The economically sensitive graphics and specialty tapes and films product lines should continue to recover on a healthier durable goods sector, but we expect the office products segment to stay soft in the second half of 2010, including for the back-to-school season.

▶ Margins in 2010 should be helped by better volumes and additional cost reductions, especially in retail information, although raw material costs will likely be higher in the second half. We project $70 million of additional restructuring savings this year on top of $115 million in 2009. We expect higher marketing spending in 2010, especially in office products, given new competitive pressures in labels.

▶ For 2010, we expect modestly lower interest expense but higher pension costs and a higher adjusted tax rate of about 22.5%, versus 12% in 2009. Our EPS estimate for 2010 excludes $0.25 of special charges in the first half.

Investment Rationale/Risk

▶ Our buy opinion is based on valuation. Organic sales declined through 2009, but rose 14% in the second quarter of 2010, as demand in end markets appears to be returning to pre-recession levels. We believe long-term fundamentals remain sound, with growth driven by the increasing use of non-impact printing systems for computers and for product tracking and information needs. We see a proliferation of high-quality graphics spurring sales of pressure-sensitive labels.

▶ Risks to our recommendation and target price include the potentially adverse impact of remaining antitrust investigations and related civil suits involving AVY, and an inability to introduce new products or raise selling prices in response to higher raw material costs.

▶ Our 12-month target price is $50. We value AVY shares using a P/E of about 18.5X our 2010 EPS projection, in line with the stock's historical premium to the S&P 500, reflecting what we view as a cyclical recovery in earnings. We believe AVY may raise its dividend and/or implement a stock buyback program.

STANDARD &POOR'S

Avery Dennison Corp

Business Summary July 30, 2010

CORPORATE OVERVIEW. Avery Dennison is the leading global manufacturer of pressure-sensitive technology and self-adhesive solutions for consumer products and label systems, including office products, product identification and control systems, and specialty tapes and chemicals.

Foreign operations accounted for 66% of sales in 2009.

The pressure-sensitive materials group (56% of sales and 72% of operating profits in 2009) includes Fasson- and JAC-brand pressure sensitive, self-adhesive coated papers, plastic films, metal foils, and fabrics in roll and sheet form; graphic and reflective decoration films and labels; and adhesives, protective coatings and electroconductive resins for industrial, automotive, aerospace, appliance, electronic, medical and consumer markets.

The office and consumer products group (14% and 37%) consists of consumer and office products such as pressure-sensitive labels; copier, laser and ink-jet printer labels and template software; presentation and organizing products (binders, sheet protectors, dividers); writing instruments and marking devices; security badge systems; and other products sold under the Avery, Marks-A-Lot, and Hi-Liter brands for office, home, and school uses.

Retail information services (22% and -5%) sell a variety of price marking and brand identification products for retailers, apparel manufacturers, distributors and industrial customers. Products include woven and printed labels; heat transfers; graphic and barcode tags; patches; integrated tags; price tickets; customer hard and soft good packaging; barcode printers; software; plastics fastening; and applications devices for use in identification, tracking and control applications. The segment reported a 15% decline in sales in 2009.

Other businesses (8% and -4%) consists of specialty fastening, bonding and sealing tapes sold in roll form; industrial and automotive labels, decoration films and graphics sold primarily to original equipment manufacturers; self-adhesive postal stamps and on-battery testing labels; and the radio frequency identification (RFID) business (inlays and labels). The RFID business had a net loss of about $30 million in each of 2005 and 2006, but the loss declined in both 2007 and 2008.

Company Financials Fiscal Year Ended Dec. 31

Per Share Data ($)	2009	2008	2007	2006	2005	2004	2003	2002	2001	2000
Tangible Book Value	NA	NM	NM	8.84	6.74	5.85	4.08	2.53	4.70	3.94
Cash Flow	-4.63	5.10	5.13	5.50	4.95	4.66	4.22	4.12	4.05	4.41
Earnings	-7.21	2.70	3.07	3.51	2.90	2.78	2.43	2.59	2.47	2.84
S&P Core Earnings	-1.71	2.20	2.98	3.48	2.66	2.51	2.05	2.02	1.81	NA
Dividends	1.22	1.65	1.61	1.57	1.53	1.49	1.45	1.35	1.23	1.11
Payout Ratio	NM	61%	52%	45%	53%	54%	60%	52%	50%	39%
Prices:High	40.14	55.00	71.35	69.31	63.58	66.60	63.75	69.70	60.50	78.50
Prices:Low	17.02	24.30	49.69	54.95	49.60	53.50	46.25	52.06	43.25	41.13
P/E Ratio:High	NM	20	23	20	22	24	26	27	24	28
P/E Ratio:Low	NM	9	16	16	17	19	19	20	18	14

Income Statement Analysis (Million $)										
Revenue	5,953	6,710	6,308	5,576	5,474	5,341	4,763	4,207	3,803	3,894
Operating Income	585	684	787	683	690	655	602	593	566	638
Depreciation	267	237	204	199	202	188	179	153	156	157
Interest Expense	85.3	122	111	55.5	57.9	58.5	57.7	43.7	50.2	54.6
Pretax Income	-791	271	375	426	367	373	335	365	360	426
Effective Tax Rate	5.59%	1.66%	19.1%	17.2%	20.4%	25.1%	27.5%	29.5%	32.4%	33.5%
Net Income	-747	266	304	353	292	280	243	257	243	284
S&P Core Earnings	-178	217	294	348	269	251	205	201	179	NA

Balance Sheet & Other Financial Data (Million $)										
Cash	138	106	71.5	58.5	98.5	84.8	29.5	22.8	19.1	11.4
Current Assets	1,733	1,930	2,058	1,655	1,558	1,542	1,441	1,216	982	982
Total Assets	5,003	6,036	6,245	4,294	4,204	4,399	4,105	3,652	2,819	2,699
Current Liabilities	1,868	2,058	2,478	1,699	1,526	1,387	1,496	1,296	951	801
Long Term Debt	1,089	1,545	1,145	502	723	1,007	888	837	627	773
Common Equity	1,363	1,750	1,989	1,681	1,512	1,549	1,319	1,056	929	828
Total Capital	2,451	3,295	3,376	2,261	2,235	2,647	2,274	1,968	1,647	1,695
Capital Expenditures	72.2	129	191	162	163	179	201	152	135	198
Cash Flow	-479	504	508	552	493	468	422	410	399	440
Current Ratio	0.9	0.9	0.8	1.0	1.0	1.1	1.0	0.9	1.0	1.2
% Long Term Debt of Capitalization	44.4	46.9	33.9	22.2	32.4	38.1	39.0	42.5	38.0	45.6
% Net Income of Revenue	NM	4.0	4.8	6.3	5.3	5.2	5.1	6.1	6.4	7.3
% Return on Assets	NM	4.3	5.8	8.3	6.8	6.6	6.3	7.8	8.8	10.7
% Return on Equity	NM	14.2	16.5	22.1	19.1	19.5	20.4	25.9	27.7	34.6

Data as orig reptd.; bef. results of disc opers/spec. items. Per share data adj. for stk. divs.; EPS diluted. E-Estimated. NA-Not Available. NM-Not Meaningful. NR-Not Ranked. UR-Under Review.

Office: 150 North Orange Grove Boulevard, Pasadena, CA 91103.
Telephone: 626-304-2000.
Email: investorcom@averydennison.com
Website: http://www.averydennison.com

Chrmn, Pres & CEO: D.A. Scarborough
SVP & CFO: M.R. Butier
SVP, Secy & General Counsel: S.C. Miller
SVP & CIO: R.W. Hoffman

CTO: D.N. Edwards
Investor Contact: E.M. Leeds (626-304-2029)
Board Members: B. A. Alford, P. K. Barker, R. Borjesson, J. T. Cardis, K. C. Hicks, P. W. Mullin, D. E. Pyott, D. L. Reed, D. A. Scarborough, P. T. Siewert, J. A. Stewart

Founded: 1935
Domicile: Delaware
Employees: 31,300

The McGraw-Hill Companies

Avon Products Inc.

STANDARD &POOR'S

S&P Recommendation HOLD ★★★☆☆

Price $34.43 (as of Oct 22, 2010)	**12-Mo. Target Price** $35.00

Investment Style Large-Cap Growth

GICS Sector Consumer Staples
Sub-Industry Personal Products

Summary This company is the world's leading direct marketer of cosmetics, toiletries, fashion jewelry, and fragrances and has more than 5 million sales representatives worldwide.

Key Stock Statistics (Source S&P, Vickers, company reports)

52-Wk Range	$36.39– 25.00	S&P Oper. EPS 2010**E**	2.02	Market Capitalization(B)	$14.769	Beta	1.56
Trailing 12-Month EPS	$1.47	S&P Oper. EPS 2011**E**	2.30	Yield (%)	2.56	S&P 3-Yr. Proj. EPS CAGR(%)	7
Trailing 12-Month P/E	23.4	P/E on S&P Oper. EPS 2010**E**	17.0	Dividend Rate/Share	$0.88	S&P Credit Rating	A-
$10K Invested 5 Yrs Ago	$14,682	Common Shares Outstg. (M)	429.0	Institutional Ownership (%)	85		

Price Performance

30-Week Mov. Avg. · · · 10-Week Mov. Avg. - - **GAAP Earnings vs. Previous Year** Volume Above Avg. STARS
12-Mo. Target Price — Relative Strength — ▲ Up ▼ Down ▶ No Change Below Avg. ★

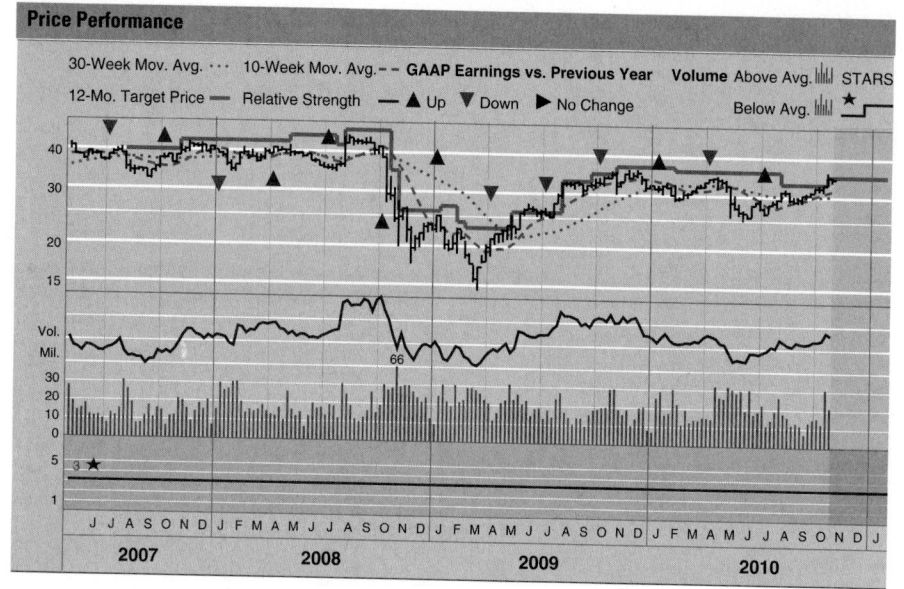

Options: ASE, CBOE, P, Ph

Analysis prepared by **Esther Y. Kwon, CFA** on October 13, 2010, when the stock traded at **$ 34.54**.

Highlights

► Our 2010 sales growth forecast is 8%, with modestly positive foreign currency. We expect growth to be led by Central & Eastern Europe, Western Europe/Middle East/Africa, and Latin America, with North America and China lagging. China appears to be having difficulty transitioning from beauty boutiques to the now-permitted direct sales channel. AVP had an improving local currency quarterly sales trend overall in 2009.

► We expect more cost savings benefits in 2010 from AVP's 2005 and 2009 multi-year restructuring plans and other cost reduction programs, following significant savings in 2008 and 2009. Also, the operating margin in 2010 should benefit from better sales leverage and a swing to positive foreign currency transaction effects (excluding Venezuela). Transaction effects involve not just the U.S. dollar but also the sale of euro-cost product into Central and Eastern Europe and the U.K.

► Our 2010 EPS estimate is $2.02, up from 2009's operating EPS of $1.72, excluding restructuring charges and one-time charges from recent changes involving the Venezuela currency.

Investment Rationale/Risk

► AVP's various restructuring and rationalization plans, including one announced in February 2009, entail reorganizing and downsizing the organization, implementing global manufacturing, and increasing supply chain efficiencies. AVP plans to reinvest the savings from these plans in marketing and R&D, and incentivizing its sales force. However, the benefits in 2009 were masked by foreign exchange issues and difficult economic conditions in many markets.

► Risks to our recommendation and target price include renewed weakness in the U.S. market, political and economic instability in international markets, competition from various sales channels, significant changes in foreign exchange rates, and unfavorable consumer reception of new products.

► Our 12-month target price of $35 is a blend of our historical and relative analyses. Our historical analysis applies a multiple of 18.3X, a discount to the 10-year historical average, to our 2010 EPS estimate, implying a value of $37. Our peer analysis applies a P/E multiple of 16.8X, in line with the peer average, for a value of $34.

Qualitative Risk Assessment

LOW	MEDIUM	HIGH

Our risk assessment reflects that demand for personal care products is usually static and not generally affected by changes in the economy or geopolitical factors. However, certain product categories, such as fragrances, may be more susceptible to adverse factors.

Quantitative Evaluations

S&P Quality Ranking A

D	C	B-	B	B+	A-	A	A+

Relative Strength Rank STRONG

79

LOWEST = 1   HIGHEST = 99

Revenue/Earnings Data

Revenue (Million $)

	1Q	2Q	3Q	4Q	Year
2010	2,490	2,679	--	--	--
2009	2,180	2,470	2,551	3,181	10,383
2008	2,502	2,736	2,645	2,808	10,690
2007	2,185	2,329	2,349	3,076	9,939
2006	2,003	2,080	2,059	2,623	8,764
2005	1,881	1,984	1,886	2,398	8,150

Earnings Per Share ($)

2010	0.10	0.39	E0.49	E0.72	E2.02
2009	0.27	0.19	0.36	0.62	1.45
2008	0.43	0.55	0.52	0.54	2.04
2007	0.34	0.26	0.32	0.30	1.22
2006	0.12	0.34	0.19	0.41	1.06
2005	0.36	0.69	0.35	0.40	1.81

Fiscal year ended Dec. 31. Next earnings report expected: Late October. EPS Estimates based on S&P Operating Earnings; historical GAAP earnings are as reported.

Dividend Data (Dates: mm/dd Payment Date: mm/dd/yy)

Amount ($)	Date Decl.	Ex-Div. Date	Stk. of Record	Payment Date
0.210	11/04	11/18	11/20	12/01/09
0.220	02/09	02/19	02/23	03/01/10
0.220	05/06	05/18	05/20	06/01/10
0.220	08/03	08/13	08/17	09/01/10

Dividends have been paid since 1919. Source: Company reports.

Please read the Required Disclosures and Analyst Certification on the last page of this report.

The **McGraw·Hill** Companies

Avon Products Inc.

Business Summary October 13, 2010

CORPORATE OVERVIEW. Avon Products, which began operations in 1886, is a global manufacturer and marketer of beauty and related products. Beginning in the fourth quarter of 2008, AVP changed its product categories from Beauty, Beauty Plus and Beyond Beauty to Beauty, Fashion and Home & Other. Beauty consists of cosmetics, fragrances, skin care and toiletries and accounted for 71% of sales in 2009. Fashion (17%) consists of fashion jewelry, watches, apparel, footwear, and accessories. Home & Other (12%) consists of gift and decorative products, housewares, entertainment & leisure, kids and nutrition. The company has operations in 65 countries and territories, including the U.S., and its products are distributed in 40 more. Geographically, 22% of 2009 sales were derived from North America, while Latin America accounted for 40%, Western Europe, the Middle East & Africa 12%, Central & Eastern Europe 14%, Asia-Pacific 9%, and China 3%. Operations outside North America accounted for 91% of segment operating profits in 2009. Sales are made to the ultimate customer mainly through a combination of direct selling and marketing by about 6.2 million independent Avon representatives.

In 2009, the number of active representatives rose 3% in North America, 10% in Latin America, 10% in Western Europe, the Middle East & Africa, 10% in Central & Eastern Europe, 6% in Asia-Pacific, 32% in China (from a low base), and 9% overall.

CORPORATE STRATEGY. AVP embarked on a multi-year restructuring plan in November 2005 in an effort to drive revenue and profit growth. The plan entails reorganizing and downsizing the organization, implementing global manufacturing, and increasing supply chain efficiencies. AVP expects restructuring benefits to help fund an increase in consumer research, marketing, and product development, which, in turn, is expected to enhance sales and ultimately profits. In fact, we saw an improvement in the year-to-year sales growth rate starting in mid-2006, but savings from the plan were not large enough to offset increases in the expenses mentioned above until 2008. Also in 2005, Avon started to implement a global supply chain strategy, which includes the development of a new common systems platform, known as enterprise resource planning (ERP).

In February 2009, AVP announced a new restructuring program, with implementation expected to start in the second half of 2009 and full implementation by 2012 to 2013.

Company Financials Fiscal Year Ended Dec. 31

Per Share Data ($)

	2009	2008	2007	2006	2005	2004	2003	2002	2001	2000
Tangible Book Value	2.16	0.76	1.66	1.79	1.68	2.02	0.79	NM	NM	NM
Cash Flow	1.88	2.41	1.55	1.42	2.10	2.05	1.63	1.34	1.10	1.20
Earnings	1.45	2.04	1.22	1.06	1.81	1.77	1.39	1.11	0.90	1.01
S&P Core Earnings	1.53	1.94	1.25	1.16	1.80	1.80	1.37	0.95	0.77	NA
Dividends	0.84	0.80	0.74	0.70	0.66	0.70	0.42	0.40	0.38	0.37
Payout Ratio	58%	39%	61%	66%	36%	40%	30%	36%	42%	37%
Prices:High	36.39	45.34	42.51	34.25	45.66	46.65	34.88	28.55	25.06	24.88
Prices:Low	14.40	17.45	31.95	26.16	24.33	30.81	24.47	21.75	17.78	12.63
P/E Ratio:High	25	22	35	32	25	26	25	26	28	25
P/E Ratio:Low	10	9	26	25	13	17	18	20	20	12

Income Statement Analysis (Million $)

	2009	2008	2007	2006	2005	2004	2003	2002	2001	2000
Revenue	10,383	10,690	9,939	8,764	8,150	7,748	6,876	6,228	5,995	5,715
Operating Income	1,370	1,558	1,176	1,146	1,289	1,361	1,162	1,029	951	886
Depreciation	181	158	145	160	140	135	124	125	109	97.1
Interest Expense	105	105	125	99.6	54.1	33.8	33.3	52.0	71.1	84.7
Pretax Income	926	1,238	796	704	1,124	1,188	994	836	666	691
Effective Tax Rate	32.2%	29.3%	33.0%	31.8%	24.0%	27.8%	32.1%	35.0%	34.7%	29.2%
Net Income	626	875	531	478	848	846	665	535	430	485
S&P Core Earnings	654	833	549	518	845	859	652	455	367	NA

Balance Sheet & Other Financial Data (Million $)

	2009	2008	2007	2006	2005	2004	2003	2002	2001	2000
Cash	1,312	1,105	963	1,199	1,059	770	694	607	509	123
Current Assets	4,189	3,557	3,515	3,334	2,921	2,506	2,226	2,048	1,889	1,546
Total Assets	6,833	6,074	5,716	5,238	4,763	4,148	3,562	3,328	3,193	2,826
Current Liabilities	2,275	2,912	3,053	2,550	2,502	1,526	1,588	1,976	1,461	1,359
Long Term Debt	2,308	1,456	1,168	1,171	766	866	878	767	1,236	1,108
Common Equity	1,273	675	712	790	794	950	371	-128	-74.6	-216
Total Capital	3,620	2,205	2,089	2,028	1,595	1,829	1,300	712	1,192	954
Capital Expenditures	297	381	279	175	207	250	163	127	155	194
Cash Flow	806	1,034	676	637	987	981	788	659	539	582
Current Ratio	1.8	1.2	1.2	1.3	1.2	1.6	1.4	1.0	1.3	1.1
% Long Term Debt of Capitalization	63.7	66.1	62.1	58.8	48.1	47.4	67.5	107.8	103.7	116.1
% Net Income of Revenue	6.0	8.2	5.3	5.4	10.4	10.9	9.7	8.6	7.2	8.5
% Return on Assets	9.7	14.9	9.7	9.6	19.0	21.9	19.3	16.4	14.3	18.1
% Return on Equity	64.3	126.3	70.7	60.3	97.2	128.0	545.8	NM	NM	NM

Data as orig reptd.; bef. results of disc opers/spec. items. Per share data adj. for stk. divs.; EPS diluted. E-Estimated. NA-Not Available. NM-Not Meaningful. NR-Not Ranked. UR-Under Review.

Office: 1345 Avenue Of The Americas, New York, NY 10105-0196.
Telephone: 212-282-5000.
Email: individual.investor@avon.com
Website: http://www.avoninvestor.com

Chrmn & CEO: A. Jung
SVP, Secy & General Counsel: K.K. Rucker
SVP & CIO: D. Herlihy
CFO: C.W. Cramb

Chief Acctg Officer & Cntlr: S. Ibbotson
Investor Contact: A.L. Chasen (212-282-5320)
Board Members: W. D. Cornwell, V. A. Hailey, F. Hassan, A. Jung, M. E. Lagomasino, A. S. Moore, P. S. Pressler, G. M. Rodkin, P. Stern, L. A. Weinbach

Founded: 1886
Domicile: New York
Employees: 41,000

Baker Hughes Inc

STANDARD &POOR'S

S&P Recommendation HOLD ★★★★★

Price	**12-Mo. Target Price**	**Investment Style**
$46.57 (as of Oct 22, 2010)	$52.00	Large-Cap Growth

GICS Sector Energy
Sub-Industry Oil & Gas Equipment & Services

Summary This company is one of the world's largest oilfield services companies, providing products and services to the energy industry.

Key Stock Statistics (Source S&P, Vickers, company reports)

52-Wk Range	$54.80– 35.62	S&P Oper. EPS 2010E	1.92	Market Capitalization(B)	$20.076	Beta	1.52
Trailing 12-Month EPS	$1.08	S&P Oper. EPS 2011E	2.84	Yield (%)	1.29	S&P 3-Yr. Proj. EPS CAGR(%)	33
Trailing 12-Month P/E	43.1	P/E on S&P Oper. EPS 2010E	24.3	Dividend Rate/Share	$0.60	S&P Credit Rating	A
$10K Invested 5 Yrs Ago	$9,441	Common Shares Outstg. (M)	431.1	Institutional Ownership (%)	87		

Price Performance

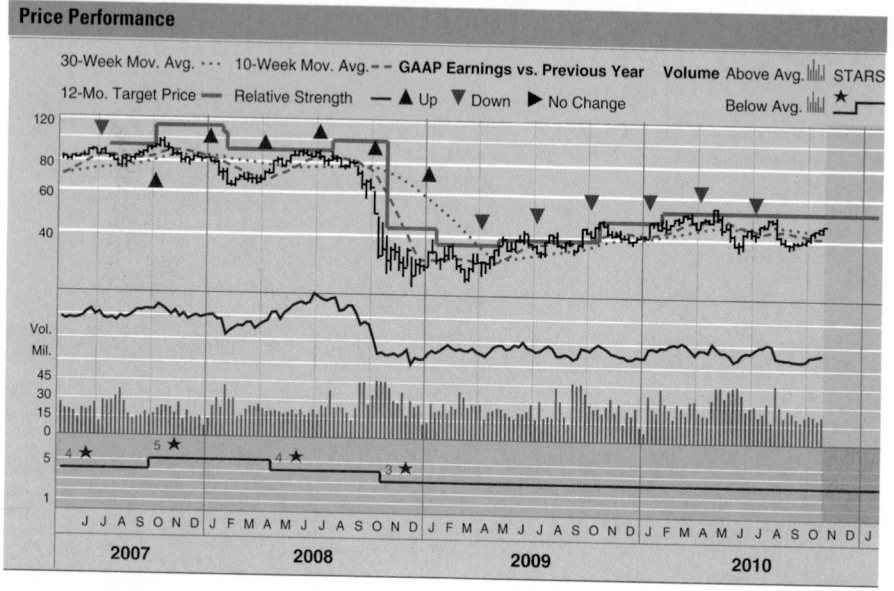

- 30-Week Mov. Avg. · · · · 10-Week Mov. Avg. – – GAAP Earnings vs. Previous Year Volume Above Avg. STARS
- 12-Mo. Target Price — Relative Strength — ▲ Up ▼ Down ► No Change Below Avg. ★

Options: ASE, CBOE, P, Ph

Analysis prepared by **Stewart Glickman, CFA** on August 27, 2010, when the stock traded at **$ 37.59**.

Highlights

- In late April, BHI completed its acquisition of the former BJ Services, adding a significant presence in the pressure pumping market and complementing its other existing oilfield services portfolio. We think the deal will enable BHI to better compete for international oilfield services contracts, given a broader set of offerings. However, we also see near-term challenges from the acquisition, including integration risk as well as a domestic pressure pumping market that may see pricing and utilization difficulties given chronically weak natural gas prices - although the uptick in interest in liquids-rich shale plays appears to be a positive.

- Long term, we see strong growth opportunities outside of North America and view this as a primary potential catalyst for BHI. With oil prices remaining fairly resilient so far this year for upstream operators, we expect capital spending growth in 2010, in contrast to the pullback in 2009, which should augur well for BHI's expansion plans.

- For 2010, we estimate EPS of $1.92, rising to $2.84 in 2011 on improved margin expectations.

Investment Rationale/Risk

- In 2011, we think BHI's growth prospects will improve. Recent stability in oil prices in the $70 per barrel range should help build overseas enthusiasm by upstream customers, and we also note a modestly improving U.S. rig count (albeit mainly on the strength of oil-directed activity). We expect BHI to undertake a more aggressive push into international markets, and now view BHI as better positioned to win integrated project management tenders.

- Risks to our recommendation and target price include lower energy prices; reduced drilling activity in international markets; slower-than-planned infrastructure build; higher-than-expected cost inflation; and integration risks associated with the recently completed BJ Services acquisition.

- Our discounted cash flow model, which assumes free cash flow growth of 11% per year for 10 years, and 3% thereafter, shows intrinsic value of about $48. Using multiples of 10X projected 2010 EBITDA and 11.5X estimated 2010 cash flows (below peers, which we see as merited on below-average projected 2010 ROIC), and blending these results with our DCF model, our 12-month target price is $52.

Qualitative Risk Assessment

LOW	MEDIUM	HIGH

Our risk assessment reflects BHI's exposure to volatile crude oil and natural gas prices, capital spending decisions by its exploration and production customers, and political risk associated with operating in frontier regions. Offsetting these risks is BHI's strong position in drilling and completion products.

Quantitative Evaluations

S&P Quality Ranking B

D	C	B-	B	B+	A-	A	A+

Relative Strength Rank STRONG

79

LOWEST = 1   HIGHEST = 99

Revenue/Earnings Data

Revenue (Million $)

	1Q	2Q	3Q	4Q	Year
2010	2,539	3,374	--	--	--
2009	2,668	2,336	2,232	2,428	9,664
2008	2,670	2,998	3,010	3,186	11,864
2007	2,473	2,538	2,678	2,740	10,428
2006	2,062	2,203	2,309	2,453	9,027
2005	1,643	1,768	1,785	1,989	7,186

Earnings Per Share ($)

	1Q	2Q	3Q	4Q	Year
2010	0.41	0.23	E0.50	E0.61	E1.92
2009	0.63	0.28	0.18	0.27	1.36
2008	1.27	1.23	1.39	1.41	5.30
2007	1.17	1.09	1.22	1.26	4.73
2006	0.93	4.14	1.09	1.02	7.21
2005	0.53	0.64	0.64	0.76	2.56

Fiscal year ended Dec. 31. Next earnings report expected: NA. EPS Estimates based on S&P Operating Earnings; historical GAAP earnings are as reported.

Dividend Data (Dates: mm/dd Payment Date: mm/dd/yy)

Amount ($)	Date Decl.	Ex-Div. Date	Stk. of Record	Payment Date
0.150	01/20	01/28	02/01	02/12/10
0.150	04/22	05/06	05/10	05/21/10
0.150	07/22	07/29	08/02	08/13/10
0.150	10/22	10/28	11/01	11/12/10

Dividends have been paid since 1987. Source: Company reports.

Baker Hughes Inc

STANDARD &POOR'S

Business Summary August 27, 2010

CORPORATE OVERVIEW. Baker Hughes was formed through the 1987 merger of Baker International Corp. and Hughes Tool Co. In 1998, it acquired seismic and wireline logging company Western Atlas, creating the third largest oilfield services company. BHI has operations in over 90 countries. North America accounted for 37% of total revenues in 2009, followed by the Europe, CIS and Africa region (30%) and the Middle East and Asia-Pacific region (21%). In 2005, the company reorganized its seven product-line focused divisions into three operating segments: Drilling & Evaluation; Completion & Production; and Western Geco (which provides reservoir imaging, monitoring and development services). In April 2006, however, BHI sold its 30% minority stake in seismic company Western Geco to the majority joint venture partner, Schlumberger. We like the deal for BHI, as we think it should enable BHI to focus on its core oilfield operations of drilling, completion and production.

The Drilling & Evaluation segment (48% of 2009 total oilfield revenues and 31% of 2009 total oilfield segment income) consists of four operating divisions: Baker Hughes Drilling Fluids, Hughes Christensen, INTEQ, and Baker Atlas. The products and services in this segment are typically used in the drilling of crude oil and natural gas wells.

Baker Hughes Drilling Fluids provides drilling and completion fluids, and fluid

environmental services. Fluids are used in order to control downhole pressure, clean the bottom of the well, and to cool and lubricate the drill bit and drill string. Hughes Christensen manufactures drill bit products, primarily Tri-cone roller cone drill bits and polycrystalline diamond compact (PDC) fixed cutter bits. INTEQ supplies directional and horizontal drilling services, coring services, subsurface surveying, logging-while-drilling, and measurement-while-drilling services.

Baker Atlas provides formation evaluation and perforating services for oil and natural gas wells. Formation evaluation involves measuring and analyzing specific physical properties of the rock in the vicinity of the wellbore to determine a reservoir's boundaries, hydrocarbon volume, and ability to produce fluids to the surface. Perforating services involve puncturing a well's steel casing and cement sheath with explosive charges; this creates a fracture in the formation, and provides a path for the hydrocarbons in the formation to enter the wellbore.

Company Financials Fiscal Year Ended Dec. 31

Per Share Data ($)	2009	2008	2007	2006	2005	2004	2003	2002	2001	2000
Tangible Book Value	18.18	16.89	15.14	11.58	9.42	7.35	5.87	6.05	5.69	4.64
Cash Flow	NA	7.35	6.36	8.85	3.68	2.69	1.59	1.56	2.32	2.14
Earnings	1.36	5.30	4.73	7.21	2.56	1.57	0.40	0.66	1.31	0.31
S&P Core Earnings	1.38	5.33	4.70	4.24	2.47	1.50	0.62	0.55	1.17	NA
Dividends	0.60	0.56	0.52	0.52	0.48	0.46	0.46	0.46	0.46	0.46
Payout Ratio	44%	11%	11%	7%	19%	29%	115%	70%	35%	148%
Prices:High	48.19	90.81	100.29	89.30	63.13	45.30	36.15	39.95	45.29	43.38
Prices:Low	25.69	24.40	62.26	60.60	40.73	31.56	26.90	22.60	25.76	19.63
P/E Ratio:High	35	17	21	12	25	29	90	61	35	NM
P/E Ratio:Low	19	5	13	8	16	20	67	34	20	NM

Income Statement Analysis (Million $)										
Revenue	9,664	11,864	10,428	9,027	7,186	6,104	5,293	5,020	5,382	5,234
Operating Income	NA	3,075	2,799	2,417	1,616	1,195	957	856	1,077	1,076
Depreciation, Depletion and Amortization	NA	637	521	434	382	374	349	302	345	612
Interest Expense	131	89.0	66.1	68.9	72.3	83.6	103	111	126	173
Pretax Income	611	2,319	2,257	3,737	1,279	780	328	380	662	236
Effective Tax Rate	31.1%	29.5%	32.9%	35.8%	31.6%	32.3%	45.1%	41.2%	33.7%	56.7%
Net Income	421	1,635	1,514	2,399	874	528	180	224	439	102
S&P Core Earnings	427	1,645	1,504	1,393	842	506	209	186	393	NA

Balance Sheet & Other Financial Data (Million $)										
Cash	1,595	1,955	1,054	750	697	319	98.4	144	45.4	34.6
Current Assets	6,225	7,145	5,456	4,968	3,840	2,967	2,524	2,556	2,697	2,487
Total Assets	11,439	11,861	9,857	8,706	7,807	6,821	6,302	6,401	6,676	6,453
Current Liabilities	1,613	2,511	1,618	1,622	1,361	1,236	1,302	1,080	1,212	988
Long Term Debt	1,785	1,775	1,069	1,074	1,078	1,086	1,133	1,424	1,682	2,050
Common Equity	7,284	6,807	6,306	5,243	4,698	3,895	3,350	3,397	3,328	3,047
Total Capital	9,084	8,966	7,791	6,617	6,004	5,214	4,611	4,988	5,221	5,255
Capital Expenditures	NA	1,303	1,127	922	478	348	405	317	319	599
Cash Flow	NA	2,272	2,035	2,832	1,257	902	529	525	783	714
Current Ratio	3.9	2.9	3.4	3.1	2.8	2.4	1.9	2.4	2.2	2.5
% Long Term Debt of Capitalization	19.7	19.8	13.7	16.2	18.0	20.8	24.6	28.6	32.2	39.0
% Return on Assets	3.6	15.1	16.3	29.1	12.0	8.0	2.8	3.4	6.7	1.5
% Return on Equity	6.0	24.9	26.2	48.3	20.4	14.6	5.3	6.7	13.8	3.3

Data as orig reptd.; bef. results of disc opers/spec. items. Per share data adj. for stk. divs.; EPS diluted. E-Estimated. NA-Not Available. NM-Not Meaningful. NR-Not Ranked. UR-Under Review.

Office: 2929 Allen Pkwy Ste 2100, Houston, TX 77019-2118.
Telephone: 713-439-8600.
Website: http://www.bakerhughes.com
Chrmn & CEO: C.C. Deaton

Pres & COO: M. Craighead
SVP & CFO: P.A. Ragauss
SVP & General Counsel: A.R. Crain, Jr.
CTO: D. Mathieson

Board Members: L. D. Brady, II, C. P. Cazalot, Jr., C. C. Deaton, E. P. Djerejian, A. G. Fernandes, C. W. Gargalli, P. Jungels, I, J. A. Lash, J. L. Nichols, J. L. Payne, H. J. Riley, Jr., J. W. Stewart, C. L. Watson

Founded: 1972
Domicile: Delaware
Employees: 34,400

The McGraw-Hill Companies

Ball Corp

STANDARD &POOR'S

S&P Recommendation BUY ★★★★☆

Price	12-Mo. Target Price	Investment Style
$61.38 (as of Oct 22, 2010)	$65.00	Large-Cap Blend

GICS Sector Materials
Sub-Industry Metal & Glass Containers

Summary Ball, one of the largest producers of metal beverage cans in the world, derives nearly 10% of its revenues from sales of hi-tech equipment to the aerospace industry.

Key Stock Statistics (Source S&P, Vickers, company reports)

52-Wk Range	$62.68–46.70	S&P Oper. EPS 2010E	4.55	Market Capitalization(B)	$5.621	Beta	0.61
Trailing 12-Month EPS	$3.53	S&P Oper. EPS 2011E	5.05	Yield (%)	0.65	S&P 3-Yr. Proj. EPS CAGR(%)	12
Trailing 12-Month P/E	17.4	P/E on S&P Oper. EPS 2010E	13.5	Dividend Rate/Share	$0.40	S&P Credit Rating	BB+
$10K Invested 5 Yrs Ago	$17,947	Common Shares Outstg. (M)	91.6	Institutional Ownership (%)	77		

Price Performance

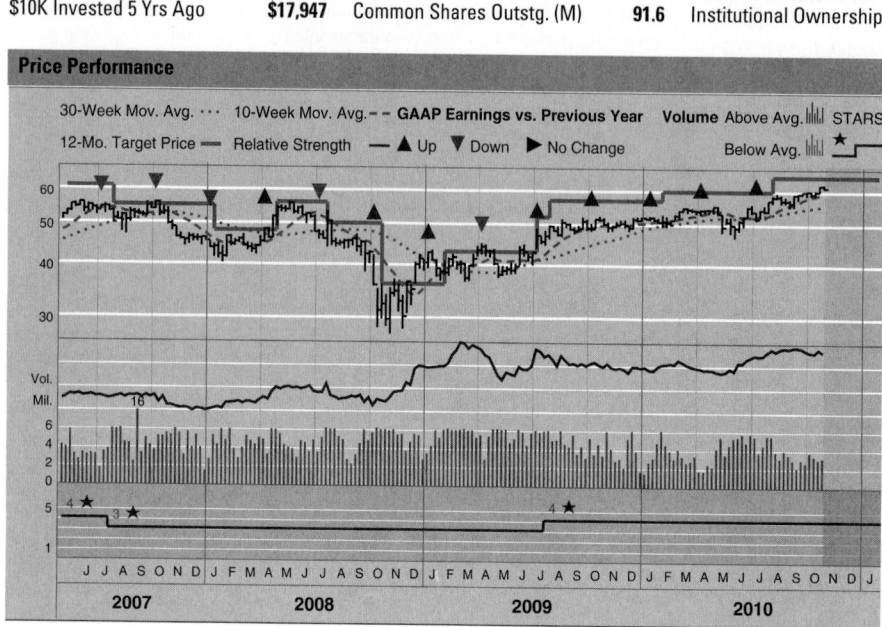

30-Week Mov. Avg. · · · 10-Week Mov. Avg. - - GAAP Earnings vs. Previous Year   Volume Above Avg. STARS
12-Mo. Target Price — Relative Strength — ▲ Up ▼ Down ▶ No Change   Below Avg. ★

Options: ASE, CBOE, P, Ph

Analysis prepared by **Stewart Scharf** on August 09, 2010, when the stock traded at **$ 58.82.**

Highlights

▶ We project mid single-digit sales growth for 2010, with modestly higher growth for 2011, driven primarily by increased demand for metal beverage containers in China, Brazil, and Western Europe. We also see steady growth for food cans, while aerosol can volume advances in the high-single digits. In our view, demand for energy and soft drink specialty cans should pick up, while aerospace segment bookings rebound.

▶ In our view, gross margins (before D&A) will widen somewhat in 2010, from 17.3% in 2009, reflecting supply chain initiatives, a better mix, and the elimination of higher-priced metal inventories. We look for EBITDA margins to widen further in 2010, from near 13% in 2009, based on improved productivity and synergies from plant acquisitions, which should offset a negative effect from a weak euro. Interest expense should rise due to additional debt resulting from acquiring AB InBev's plants.

▶ We project a higher effective tax rate of 32% for 2010, and estimate operating EPS of $4.55 (before a net $0.17 gain), and then an advance to $5.05 for 2011 (and assuming fewer shares).

Investment Rationale/Risk

▶ Our buy opinion is based on our valuation metrics, as well as our view of improving trends for beverage cans in emerging markets, a better cost structure, and strong free cash generation. We expect BLL to focus on its metal can operations following the pending sale of its plastics business.

▶ Risks to our recommendation and target price include negative foreign currency exchange; a decline in sales of imported beer and, to some extent, domestic soft drinks; cost pressures in Europe and China; supply disruptions due to strikes at facilities; integration problems; and, sharply higher raw material costs.

▶ At 13X our 2010 EPS estimate, the stock was recently trading modestly above BLL's closest peers and slightly below our projected P/E for the S&P 500 Index. Based on our relative metrics, including below-peer PEG (P/E-to-growth) and enterprise value-to-EBITDA ratios, we value the stock at $62. Our DCF model, which assumes a 3% perpetuity growth rate and a weighted average cost of capital of 7%, derives an intrinsic value of $68. Blending these valuations, our 12-month target price is $65.

Qualitative Risk Assessment

LOW	MEDIUM	HIGH

Our risk assessment reflects the seasonality and cyclicality inherent in the beverage can business, volatile raw material prices, and our view of BLL's high debt levels. These factors are offset by BLL's improving balance sheet, with solid credit quality and liquidity, and our expectations for solid cash flow.

Quantitative Evaluations

S&P Quality Ranking A-

D	C	B-	B	B+	A-	A	A+

Relative Strength Rank MODERATE

58

LOWEST = 1   HIGHEST = 99

Revenue/Earnings Data

Revenue (Million $)

	1Q	2Q	3Q	4Q	Year
2010	1,706	2,008	--	--	--
2009	1,586	1,926	1,969	1,864	7,345
2008	1,740	2,080	2,008	1,733	7,562
2007	1,694	2,033	1,992	1,756	7,475
2006	1,365	1,843	1,822	1,592	6,622
2005	1,324	1,552	1,584	1,291	5,751

Earnings Per Share ($)

	1Q	2Q	3Q	4Q	Year
2010	0.84	1.55	E1.45	E0.85	E4.55
2009	0.73	1.40	1.09	0.85	4.08
2008	0.85	1.02	1.05	0.36	3.29
2007	0.78	1.03	0.59	0.33	2.74
2006	0.43	1.23	1.02	0.46	3.14
2005	0.51	0.71	0.73	0.42	2.38

Fiscal year ended Dec. 31. Next earnings report expected: Late October. EPS Estimates based on S&P Operating Earnings; historical GAAP earnings are as reported.

Dividend Data (Dates: mm/dd Payment Date: mm/dd/yy)

Amount ($)	Date Decl.	Ex-Div. Date	Stk. of Record	Payment Date
0.100	10/28	11/27	12/01	12/15/09
0.100	01/27	02/25	03/01	03/15/10
0.100	04/28	05/27	06/01	06/15/10
0.100	07/28	08/30	09/01	09/15/10

Dividends have been paid since 1958. Source: Company reports.

Ball Corp

Business Summary August 09, 2010

CORPORATE OVERVIEW. Ball Corp. primarily manufactures rigid packaging products for beverages and foods. Two beverage companies account for a substantial part of its packaging sales: SABMiller plc and PepsiCo. BLL is comprised of five segments: Metal Beverage Packaging (Americas/Asia); Metal Beverage Packaging (Europe); Metal Food & Household Packaging (Americas); Plastic Packaging (Americas); and Aerospace and Technologies. The Aerospace and Technologies segment provides products and services to the defense and commercial markets, with U.S. government agencies accounting for 94% of the segment's sales in 2009. In June 2010, the company completed the purchase of the remaining 65% stake in JFP's Sanshui, China metal beverage can facility for $90 million in cash and assumed debt. The company recorded a $22 million ($0.24 a share) gain on the transaction. BLL produced more than 31 billion recyclable beverage cans in the U.S. and Canada in 2009, about 31% of the total market. Aluminum and steel beverage cans accounted for 63% of the company's net sales and 77% of EBIT in 2009.

The company's packaging products include aluminum and steel two-piece beverage cans, and two- and three-piece steel food cans. Metal Beverage Packaging (Americas and Asia) segment net sales represented 39% of the to-

tal in 2009 ($289 million of pretax earnings); Metal Beverage Packaging (Europe) 24% ($215 million); Metal Food and Household Packaging (Americas) 19% ($128 million); Plastic Packaging (Americas) 8.6% ($3.2 million loss); and Aerospace and Technologies 9.4% ($61 million). BLL entered the plastics business in 1995, when it began to make polyethylene terephthalate (PET) bottles. Sales volumes of metal food containers in North America tend to be highest from June through October due to seasonal vegetable and salmon packs. BLL believes this accounts for more than 30% of all North American metal beverage can shipments. In 2009, no customer accounted for more than 10% of sales. Sales outside of the U.S. account for about 30% of the total.

In 2009, BLL recorded a $0.32 gain on the sale of its stake in DigitGlobe in the second quarter, and a $0.12 charge mainly for closing two plastic packaging plants and costs related to its acquisition of AB InBev's plants.

Company Financials Fiscal Year Ended Dec. 31

Per Share Data ($)	2009	2008	2007	2006	2005	2004	2003	2002	2001	2000
Tangible Book Value	NM	NM	NM	NM	NM	NM	NM	NM	1.27	1.81
Cash Flow	7.09	6.36	5.47	5.55	4.30	4.49	3.81	2.68	0.44	1.81
Earnings	4.08	3.29	2.74	3.14	2.38	2.60	2.01	1.38	-0.93	0.54
S&P Core Earnings	3.92	2.78	3.31	2.30	2.54	2.67	2.12	1.10	-0.88	NA
Dividends	0.40	0.40	0.40	0.40	0.40	0.35	0.24	0.18	0.15	0.15
Payout Ratio	10%	12%	15%	13%	17%	13%	12%	13%	NM	28%
Prices:High	52.46	56.20	56.05	45.00	46.45	45.20	29.88	27.25	18.03	11.98
Prices:Low	36.50	27.37	43.51	34.16	35.06	28.26	21.15	16.30	9.52	6.50
P/E Ratio:High	13	17	20	14	20	17	15	20	NM	22
P/E Ratio:Low	9	8	16	11	15	11	11	12	NM	12

Income Statement Analysis (Million $)										
Revenue	7,345	7,562	7,475	6,622	5,751	5,440	4,977	3,859	3,686	3,665
Operating Income	945	926	914	729	697	739	663	458	127	445
Depreciation	285	297	281	253	214	215	206	149	153	159
Interest Expense	117	145	145	156	134	116	104	126	75.6	88.3	95.2
Pretax Income	551	467	377	462	362	436	331	245	-110	110
Effective Tax Rate	29.5%	31.5%	25.4%	28.5%	27.5%	31.9%	30.2%	34.3%	NM	38.9%
Net Income	388	320	281	330	262	296	230	159	-99.2	68.2
S&P Core Earnings	371	270	340	242	280	304	242	127	-96.0	NA

Balance Sheet & Other Financial Data (Million $)										
Cash	211	127	152	152	61.0	199	36.5	259	83.1	25.6
Current Assets	1,923	2,165	1,843	1,761	1,226	1,246	924	1,225	794	969
Total Assets	6,488	6,369	6,021	5,841	4,343	4,478	4,070	4,132	2,314	2,650
Current Liabilities	1,429	1,862	1,513	1,454	1,176	996	861	1,069	575	659
Long Term Debt	2,284	2,107	2,182	2,270	1,473	1,538	1,579	1,854	949	1,012
Common Equity	1,583	1,086	1,343	1,165	835	1,087	808	493	504	640
Total Capital	3,867	3,342	3,525	3,437	2,314	2,631	2,393	2,353	1,463	1,709
Capital Expenditures	187	307	309	280	292	196	137	158	68.5	98.7
Cash Flow	673	617	562	582	475	511	435	309	51.3	225
Current Ratio	1.4	1.2	1.2	1.2	1.0	1.3	1.1	1.1	1.4	1.5
% Long Term Debt of Capitalization	59.1	63.0	61.9	66.1	63.7	58.5	66.0	78.8	64.9	59.2
% Net Income of Revenue	5.3	4.2	3.8	5.0	4.5	5.4	4.6	4.1	NM	1.9
% Return on Assets	6.0	5.2	4.7	6.5	5.9	6.9	5.6	4.9	NM	2.5
% Return on Equity	29.1	26.3	22.4	32.7	27.2	31.2	35.4	32.0	NM	10.1

Data as orig reptd.; bef. results of disc opers/spec. items. Per share data adj. for stk. divs.; EPS diluted. E-Estimated. NA-Not Available. NM-Not Meaningful. NR-Not Ranked. UR-Under Review.

Office: 10 Longs Peak Dr, Broomfield, CO 80021-2510.
Telephone: 303-469-3131.
Website: http://www.ball.com
Chrmn & CEO: R.D. Hoover

Pres & COO: J.A. Hayes
SVP & CFO: S.C. Morrison
Chief Admin Officer & Secy: D.A. Westerlund
Treas: J.A. Knobel

Investor Contact: A.T. Scott (303-460-3537)
Board Members: R. W. Alspaugh, H. C. Fiedler, J. A. Hayes, R. D. Hoover, J. F. Lehman, G. R. Nelson, J. Nicholson, G. M. Smart, T. M. Solso, S. A. Taylor, II, E. H. Van Der Kaay

Founded: 1880
Domicile: Indiana
Employees: 14,500

Bank of America Corp

STANDARD &POOR'S

S&P Recommendation HOLD ★★★☆☆

Price	12-Mo. Target Price	Investment Style
$11.16 (as of Oct 25, 2010)	$14.00	Large-Cap Blend

GICS Sector Financials
Sub-Industry Other Diversified Financial Services

Summary This banking company, with operations in all 50 states and the District of Columbia, also provides international corporate financial services.

Key Stock Statistics (Source S&P, Vickers, company reports)

52-Wk Range	$19.86– 11.07	S&P Oper. EPS 2010E	0.05	Market Capitalization(B)	$111.978	Beta	2.29
Trailing 12-Month EPS	$-0.77	S&P Oper. EPS 2011E	1.62	Yield (%)	0.36	S&P 3-Yr. Proj. EPS CAGR(%)	NM
Trailing 12-Month P/E	NM	P/E on S&P Oper. EPS 2010E	NM	Dividend Rate/Share	$0.04	S&P Credit Rating	A
$10K Invested 5 Yrs Ago	$3,259	Common Shares Outstg. (M)	10,033.8	Institutional Ownership (%)	63		

Price Performance

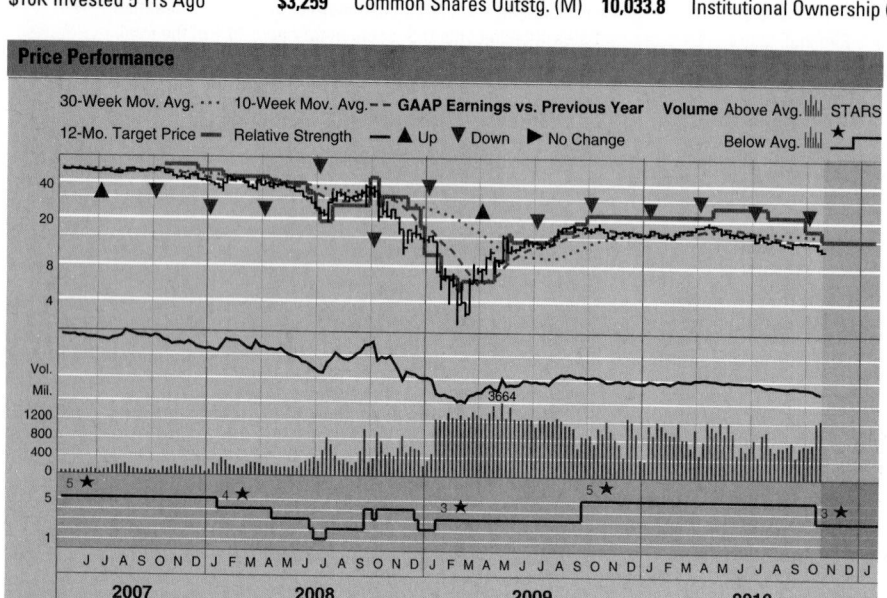

30-Week Mov. Avg. · · · 10-Week Mov. Avg. - - GAAP Earnings vs. Previous Year   Volume Above Avg. STARS
12-Mo. Target Price — Relative Strength — ▲ Up ▼ Down ▶ No Change   Below Avg.

Options: ASE, CBOE, P, Ph

Analysis prepared by **Erik Oja** on October 21, 2010, when the stock traded at **$ 11.75.**

Highlights

▶ Checking and debit card fees have declined sharply in the last year, due to a decision by BAC to make its products and fee structures more customer-friendly, in response to Regulation E and to the recent passing of US financial reform. However, we expect mortgage banking fees to remain strong in the final quarter of 2010, and likely into 2011, based on the volume of refinancing activity reported nationwide. This should help BAC's total noninterest income remain in the $15 billion per year range. Average earning assets will likely continue to decline due to poor loan demand from qualified borrowers. We look for trading results to remain volatile, and for investment banking and brokerage revenues to improve, albeit slowly. Overall, we expect revenues to decline 6.5% in 2010, but see modest growth in 2011.

▶ We forecast loan loss provisions of $31.0 billion in 2010, down from $48.6 billion in 2009. For 2011, we expect provisions to fall to $23.4 billion, and to remain the key driver of earnings growth at BAC in the 2010 to 2011 period.

▶ We expect EPS of $0.05 in 2010 and forecast $1.62 in 2011.

Investment Rationale/Risk

▶ BAC faces significant challenges related to its 2008 acquisition of Countrywide Financial, which are manifesting themselves in large repurchase requests from holders of mortgages that were securitized years ago by both companies. We think BAC will be able to work its way through this issue in an orderly way, but we are not sure of how this will affect capital and earnings in the next few years; thus our caution on the shares. In addition, the foreclosure crisis has cast a bright light on the banking industry's foreclosure practices, which may have been rushed, and which may lead to extensive delays in sales of nonperforming assets. However, we think BAC will remain well capitalized by new regulatory standards.

▶ Risks to our recommendation and target price include worse-than-expected credit conditions, greater-than-expected securities writedowns, and more onerous regulation.

▶ Our 12-month target price of $14 equates to about 1.15X our year-end projection for BAC's tangible book value, a discount to its historical levels.

Qualitative Risk Assessment

LOW	MEDIUM	HIGH

Our risk assessment reflects weak U.S. consumer trends, exposure to residential lending and credit cards, and a lower-than-historical tangible capital ratio, offset by what we see as a strong U.S. presence with a robust customer base.

Quantitative Evaluations

S&P Quality Ranking B

D	C	B-	B	B+	A-	A	A+

Relative Strength Rank WEAK

7

LOWEST = 1   HIGHEST = 99

Revenue/Earnings Data

Revenue (Million $)

	1Q	2Q	3Q	4Q	Year
2010	38,099	35,384	14,265	--	--
2009	45,417	40,736	33,135	31,162	150,450
2008	28,871	29,721	30,175	24,176	113,106
2007	30,447	32,409	29,347	26,987	119,190
2006	27,026	28,895	30,739	30,357	117,017
2005	19,168	21,222	21,621	22,280	83,980

Earnings Per Share ($)

2010	0.28	0.27	-0.77	E0.27	E0.05
2009	0.44	0.33	-0.26	-0.60	-0.29
2008	0.23	0.72	0.15	-0.48	0.55
2007	1.16	1.28	0.82	0.05	3.30
2006	1.07	1.19	1.18	1.16	4.59
2005	1.07	1.17	0.95	0.88	4.04

Fiscal year ended Dec. 31. Next earnings report expected: Late January. EPS Estimates based on S&P Operating Earnings; historical GAAP earnings are as reported.

Dividend Data (Dates: mm/dd Payment Date: mm/dd/yy)

Amount ($)	Date Decl.	Ex-Div. Date	Stk. of Record	Payment Date
0.010	01/27	03/03	03/05	03/26/10
0.010	04/28	06/02	06/04	06/25/10
0.010	07/28	09/01	09/03	09/24/10
0.010	10/25	12/01	12/03	12/24/10

Dividends have been paid since 1903. Source: Company reports.

Bank of America Corp

STANDARD &POOR'S

Business Summary October 21, 2010

CORPORATE OVERVIEW. Bank of America has operations in all 50 states, the District of Columbia and more than 40 foreign countries. In the U.S., it has about 6,000 retail banking centers and more than 18,000 ATMs. BAC reports the results of its operations through six business segments: Deposits, Global Card Services, Home Loans & Insurance, Global Banking, Global Markets, and Global Wealth & Investment Management.

Deposits includes the results from a comprehensive suite of products offered to consumers and small businesses, and generated 12% of revenues in 2009. Global Card Services mainly provides credit cards and related products to consumers and small businesses, and generated 24% of revenues in 2009. The Home Loans & Insurance segment provides consumer real estate products and services and a range of insurance products, and generated 14% of revenues in 2009. Global Banking provides a range of lending- and banking-related services to institutional clients around the globe, generating 19% of revenues in 2009. The Global Markets segment offers services to support institutional clients' investment and trading activities, and generated 17% of revenues in 2009. The Global Wealth & Investment Management group offers a range of banking, investment and brokerage services through its brokerage

force. The segment also includes BAC's 34% ownership in asset manager BlackRock (BLK 148, Hold), and generated 15% of revenues in 2009.

IMPACT OF MAJOR DEVELOPMENTS. On September 15, 2008, BAC agreed to acquire Merrill Lynch & Co., Inc. in a $50 billion all-stock transaction. The deal ultimately closed at a $29 billion purchase price due to the decline in BAC's stock. We think the deal is a good fit for BAC, particularly as it added 20,000 financial advisers and created cross-selling opportunities, but integration will likely be difficult.

On July 1, 2008, BAC acquired Countrywide Financial in a stock deal valued at $2.5 billion. Although the acquisition makes BAC a top U.S. mortgage originator, we believe it increased BAC's risk profile due to Countrywide's loan portfolio, which had a high proportion of option arm loans.

Company Financials Fiscal Year Ended Dec. 31

Per Share Data ($)	2009	2008	2007	2006	2005	2004	2003	2002	2001	2000
Tangible Book Value	11.09	7.14	11.54	12.18	13.18	12.41	12.34	12.59	11.65	10.66
Earnings	-0.29	0.55	3.30	4.59	4.04	3.69	3.57	2.96	2.09	2.26
S&P Core Earnings	-0.29	0.35	3.26	4.47	4.06	3.75	3.54	2.70	1.96	NA
Dividends	0.04	2.24	2.40	2.12	1.90	1.70	1.44	1.22	1.14	1.03
Payout Ratio	NM	407%	73%	46%	47%	46%	40%	41%	55%	46%
Prices:High	19.10	45.08	54.21	55.08	47.44	47.47	42.45	38.54	32.77	30.50
Prices:Low	2.53	10.01	40.61	40.93	41.13	38.51	32.13	26.98	22.50	18.16
P/E Ratio:High	NM	82	16	12	12	13	12	13	16	13
P/E Ratio:Low	NM	18	12	9	10	10	9	9	11	8

Income Statement Analysis (Million $)										
Net Interest Income	47,109	45,360	34,433	34,591	30,737	28,797	21,464	20,923	20,290	18,442
Tax Equivalent Adjustment	1,291	1,194	1,749	1,224	832	716	643	588	343	322
Non Interest Income	72,534	27,422	31,706	38,432	26,438	20,097	16,422	13,571	14,348	14,489
Loan Loss Provision	48,570	26,825	8,385	5,010	4,014	2,769	2,839	3,697	4,287	2,535
% Expense/Operating Revenue	55.8%	57.1%	56.0%	47.9%	50.4%	54.5%	52.2%	63.1%	59.8%	63.7%
Pretax Income	4,360	4,428	20,924	31,973	24,480	21,221	15,861	12,991	10,117	11,788
Effective Tax Rate	NM	9.48%	28.4%	33.9%	32.7%	33.4%	31.8%	28.8%	32.9%	36.2%
Net Income	6,276	4,008	14,982	21,133	16,465	14,143	10,810	9,249	6,792	7,517
% Net Interest Margin	2.65	2.98	2.60	2.82	2.84	3.26	3.36	3.75	3.68	3.22
S&P Core Earnings	-2,239	1,656	14,615	20,568	16,499	14,308	10,708	8,452	6,384	NA

Balance Sheet & Other Financial Data (Million $)										
Money Market Assets	396,341	251,570	303,389	302,482	294,292	197,308	153,090	115,687	81,384	76,544
Investment Securities	311,411	277,589	214,056	192,846	221,603	195,073	68,240	69,148	85,499	65,838
Commercial Loans	322,564	342,767	325,143	240,785	218,334	193,930	131,304	145,170	163,898	203,542
Other Loans	577,564	588,679	551,201	465,705	355,457	327,907	240,159	197,585	165,255	188,651
Total Assets	2,223,299	1,817,943	1,715,746	1,459,737	1,291,803	1,110,457	736,445	660,458	621,764	642,191
Demand Deposits	275,104	217,998	192,227	184,808	186,736	169,899	121,530	124,359	113,934	100,645
Time Deposits	716,507	664,999	612,950	508,689	447,934	448,671	292,583	262,099	259,561	263,599
Long Term Debt	438,521	268,292	197,508	146,000	100,848	98,078	75,343	67,176	68,026	72,502
Common Equity	194,236	139,351	142,394	132,421	101,262	99,374	47,926	50,261	48,455	47,556
% Return on Assets	0.3	0.2	0.9	1.5	1.4	1.5	1.5	1.4	1.1	1.2
% Return on Equity	3.8	2.9	10.8	18.1	16.3	19.2	22.0	18.7	14.1	16.3
% Loan Loss Reserve	3.8	2.5	1.3	0.4	1.4	1.7	1.7	2.0	2.1	1.7
% Loans/Deposits	99.0	105.5	105.5	304.3	87.4	84.4	89.7	88.4	97.8	107.7
% Equity to Assets	8.3	8.0	8.7	8.5	8.4	8.0	7.0	7.7	7.6	7.2

Data as orig reptd.; bef. results of disc opers/spec. items. Per share data adj. for stk. divs.; EPS diluted. E-Estimated. NA-Not Available. NM-Not Meaningful. NR-Not Ranked. UR-Under Review.

Office: 100 N Tryon St, Charlotte, NC 28255.
Telephone: 704-386-8486.
Website: http://www.bankofamerica.com
Chrmn: C.O. Holliday, Jr.

Pres & CEO: B.T. Moynihan
EVP & CFO: C.H. Noski
CTO: M. Gordon
Treas: M.D. Linsz

Investor Contact: K. Stitt (704-386-5667)
Board Members: S. S. Bies, W. P. Boardman, F. P. Bramble, V. W. Colbert, C. K. Gifford, C. O. Holliday, Jr., D. P. Jones, Jr., M. Lozano, W. E. Massey, T. J. May, B. T. Moynihan, D. E. Powell, C. O. Rossotti, T. M. Ryan, R. W. Scully

Founded: 1874
Domicile: Delaware
Employees: 302,000

The McGraw-Hill Companies

Bank of New York Mellon Corp (The)

STANDARD &POOR'S

S&P Recommendation BUY ★★★★☆	**Price** $25.27 (as of Oct 22, 2010)	**12-Mo. Target Price** $33.00	**Investment Style** Large-Cap Blend

GICS Sector Financials
Sub-Industry Asset Management & Custody Banks

Summary This company is a leader in securities processing, and also provides a complete range of banking, asset management and other financial services.

Key Stock Statistics (Source S&P, Vickers, company reports)

52-Wk Range	$32.65–23.78	S&P Oper. EPS 2010E	2.18	Market Capitalization(B)	$30.679	Beta	0.70
Trailing 12-Month EPS	$-0.54	S&P Oper. EPS 2011E	2.84	Yield (%)	1.42	S&P 3-Yr. Proj. EPS CAGR(%)	NM
Trailing 12-Month P/E	NM	P/E on S&P Oper. EPS 2010E	11.6	Dividend Rate/Share	$0.36	S&P Credit Rating	AA-
$10K Invested 5 Yrs Ago	$8,860	Common Shares Outstg. (M)	1,214.0	Institutional Ownership (%)	80		

Price Performance

30-Week Mov. Avg. · · · 10-Week Mov. Avg. - - GAAP Earnings vs. Previous Year   Volume Above Avg. STARS
12-Mo. Target Price — Relative Strength — ▲ Up ▼ Down ▶ No Change   Below Avg.

Options: ASE, CBOE, P, Ph

Qualitative Risk Assessment

LOW	MEDIUM	HIGH

Our risk assessment reflects what we view as solid fundamentals and diverse business lines. BK recently settled a $22.5 billion lawsuit by the Russian government alleging money laundering; it also significantly reduced the riskiest exposure of its securities portfolio. BK has provided stable earnings over the long term, and we believe it would be able to weather a prolonged economic downturn.

Quantitative Evaluations

S&P Quality Ranking B

D	C	B-	B	B+	A-	A	A+

Relative Strength Rank WEAK

22

LOWEST = 1   HIGHEST = 99

Highlights

▸ The 12-month target price for BK has recently been changed to $33.00 from $30.00. The Highlights section of this Stock Report will be updated accordingly.

Investment Rationale/Risk

▸ The Investment Rationale/Risk section of this Stock Report will be updated shortly. For the latest News story on BK from MarketScope, see below.

▸ 10/19/10 11:47 am ET ... S&P MAINTAINS BUY RECOMMENDATION ON SHARES OF BANK OF NEW YORK MELLON (BK 26.42****): Q3 EPS of $0.51, vs. a loss per share of $2.04, misses our $0.59 estimate, on higher than expected noninterest expenses. However revenues were better than we expected, driven by strong results in securities servicing and higher assets under management. On Q3 results, we reduce our '10 EPS estimate to $2.18 from $2.26. However, we keep our target price of $33, based on a premium to peers 3.7X estimate on our year-end tangible book value per share estimate of $8.90. This equals a peer-equivalent 11.6X multiple on our unchanged '11 EPS estimate of $2.84. /E. Oja

Revenue/Earnings Data

Revenue (Million $)

	1Q	2Q	3Q	4Q	Year
2010	--	--	--	--	--
2009	3,136	--	--	--	--
2008	3,745	4,078	4,262	3,367	16,339
2007	2,496	2,893	3,600	3,044	9,031
2006	2,074	2,276	2,219	2,493	9,062
2005	1,917	2,077	2,126	2,230	8,312

Earnings Per Share ($)

2010	0.50	0.55	E0.51	E0.62	E2.18
2009	0.28	0.23	-2.04	0.59	-0.93
2008	0.65	0.26	0.27	0.05	1.22
2007	0.60	0.59	0.56	0.61	2.38
2006	0.50	0.55	0.41	0.59	2.05
2005	0.52	0.55	0.54	0.56	2.15

Fiscal year ended Dec. 31. Next earnings report expected: NA. EPS Estimates based on S&P Operating Earnings; historical GAAP earnings are as reported.

Dividend Data (Dates: mm/dd Payment Date: mm/dd/yy)

Amount ($)	Date Decl.	Ex-Div. Date	Stk. of Record	Payment Date
0.090	01/20	01/28	02/01	02/09/10
0.090	04/20	04/28	04/30	05/11/10
0.090	07/20	07/28	07/30	08/10/10
0.090	10/19	10/27	10/29	11/09/10

Dividends have been paid since 1785. Source: Company reports.

Please read the Required Disclosures and Analyst Certification on the last page of this report.

The McGraw-Hill Companies

Bank of New York Mellon Corp (The)

STANDARD &POOR'S

Business Summary July 20, 2010

CORPORATE OVERVIEW. Bank of New York Mellon provides a comprehensive array of services that enable institutions and individuals to move and manage their financial assets in more than 100 markets worldwide. The company has several core competencies: institutional services, private banking, and asset management. Its global client base includes a broad range of leading financial institutions, corporations, government entities, endowments, and foundations.

Key products include advisory and asset management services to support the investment decision, trade execution, clearance and settlement capabilities, custody, securities lending, accounting, and administrative services for investment portfolios, sophisticated risk and performance measurement tools for analyzing portfolios, and services for issuers of both equity and debt securities.

CORPORATE STRATEGY. BK's strategy over the past decade has been to focus on scalable, fee-based securities servicing and fiduciary businesses, and it has achieved a top-three market share in most of its major product lines. The company attempts to distinguish itself competitively by offering products and services around the investment lifecycle.

By providing integrated solutions for clients' needs, BK strives to be the preferred partner in helping its clients succeed in the world's rapidly evolving financial markets. The company's key objectives include achieving positive operating leverage on an annual basis, successful integration of acquisitions and increasing the percentage of revenue and income derived from outside the U.S.

To achieve its top objectives, BK has grown both through internal reinvestments as well as the execution of strategic acquisitions to expand product offerings and increase market share in its scale businesses. Internal reinvestment occurs mainly through increased technology spending, staffing levels, marketing/branding initiatives, quality programs, and product development. The company invests in technology to improve the breadth and quality of its product offerings, and to increase economies of scale. BK has acquired over 90 businesses over the past 10 years, almost exclusively in its securities servicing and asset management areas.

Company Financials Fiscal Year Ended Dec. 31

Per Share Data ($)	2009	2008	2007	2006	2005	2004	2003	2002	2001	2000
Tangible Book Value	5.42	3.06	5.83	11.50	7.48	6.84	5.93	6.00	6.14	8.80
Earnings	-0.93	1.22	2.38	2.05	2.15	1.96	1.61	1.31	1.92	2.04
S&P Core Earnings	-0.99	1.05	2.33	2.01	2.11	1.83	1.55	1.07	1.65	NA
Dividends	0.51	0.96	0.95	0.91	0.87	0.84	0.81	0.81	0.76	0.70
Payout Ratio	NM	79%	40%	45%	40%	43%	50%	61%	40%	34%
Prices:High	33.62	49.90	50.26	42.98	35.71	36.94	35.50	49.29	61.61	62.94
Prices:Low	15.44	20.49	38.30	32.66	28.55	28.88	20.40	22.10	31.53	31.53
P/E Ratio:High	NM	40	21	21	17	19	22	37	32	31
P/E Ratio:Low	NM	17	16	16	13	15	13	17	16	15

Income Statement Analysis (Million $)	2009	2008	2007	2006	2005	2004	2003	2002	2001	2000
Net Interest Income	2,915	2,951	2,300	1,499	1,909	1,645	1,609	1,665	1,681	1,870
Tax Equivalent Adjustment	18.0	22.0	12.0	NA	29.0	30.0	35.0	49.0	60.0	54.0
Non Interest Income	10,141	12,329	9,232	5,337	4,888	4,613	3,971	3,261	3,386	2,959
Loan Loss Provision	332	131	-10.0	20.0	15.0	15.0	155	685	375	105
% Expense/Operating Revenue	73.2%	75.8%	70.4%	68.6%	65.7%	65.6%	65.9%	55.3%	54.4%	51.4%
Pretax Income	-2,208	1,939	3,225	2,170	2,367	2,199	1,762	1,372	2,058	2,251
Effective Tax Rate	NM	25.6%	31.0%	32.0%	33.6%	34.5%	34.3%	34.3%	34.7%	36.5%
Net Income	-814	1,442	2,227	1,476	1,571	1,440	1,157	902	1,343	1,429
% Net Interest Margin	1.82	1.92	2.08	2.01	2.36	2.07	2.22	2.62	2.57	2.96
S&P Core Earnings	-1,179	1,217	2,179	1,452	1,536	1,350	1,097	728	1,159	NA

Balance Sheet & Other Financial Data (Million $)	2009	2008	2007	2006	2005	2004	2003	2002	2001	2000
Money Market Assets	65,838	52,228	49,840	23,830	16,999	18,527	18,521	13,798	19,684	23,178
Investment Securities	56,049	39,435	48,698	21,106	27,326	23,802	22,903	18,300	12,862	7,401
Commercial Loans	3,797	7,205	4,766	5,925	13,252	12,624	13,646	20,335	19,034	21,327
Other Loans	32,892	35,774	43,465	31,868	27,474	23,157	21,637	11,004	16,713	14,934
Total Assets	212,224	237,009	197,656	103,370	102,074	94,529	92,397	77,564	81,025	77,114
Demand Deposits	33,477	55,816	32,372	19,554	18,236	17,442	14,789	13,301	12,635	13,255
Time Deposits	101,573	103,857	85,753	45,992	46,188	41,279	41,617	42,086	43,076	43,121
Long Term Debt	17,234	13,991	16,873	8,773	Nil	Nil	Nil	Nil	Nil	4,536
Common Equity	28,977	25,264	29,403	11,593	9,876	9,290	8,428	6,684	6,317	6,151
% Return on Assets	NM	0.7	1.5	1.4	1.6	1.5	1.4	1.1	1.7	1.9
% Return on Equity	NM	5.3	10.9	13.7	16.4	16.3	15.3	13.9	21.5	25.3
% Loan Loss Reserve	1.4	0.9	0.6	0.8	1.0	1.7	1.9	2.7	1.7	1.7
% Loans/Deposits	27.2	29.0	49.3	60.8	63.2	60.9	62.6	56.6	64.2	64.3
% Equity to Assets	8.8	12.6	13.6	10.5	9.7	9.5	8.9	8.2	7.9	7.4

Data as orig reptd.; bef. results of disc opers/spec. items. Per share data adj. for stk. divs.; EPS diluted. E-Estimated. NA-Not Available. NM-Not Meaningful. NR-Not Ranked. UR-Under Review.

Office: One Wall Street, New York, NY 10286.
Telephone: 212-495-1784.
Email: shareowner-svcs@bankofny.com
Website: http://www.bankofny.com

Chrmn & CEO: R.P. Kelly
Pres: G.L. Hassell
Vice Chrmn: C. Arledge
COO, EVP & CTO: K.D. Woetzel

EVP & CFO: T. Gibbons
Board Members: C. Arledge, R. E. Bruch, N. M. Donofrio, G. L. Hassell, E. F. Kelly, R. P. Kelly, R. J. Kogan, M. J. Kowalski, J. A. Luke, Jr., R. Mehrabian, M. A. Nordenberg, C. A. Rein, W. C. Richardson, S. C. Scott, III, J. P. Surma, Jr., W. W. von Schack

Founded: 1784
Domicile: Delaware
Employees: 42,200

The McGraw·Hill Companies

Bard (C.R.) Inc

STANDARD &POOR'S

S&P Recommendation HOLD ★★★☆☆

Price	12-Mo. Target Price	Investment Style
$83.01 (as of Oct 22, 2010)	$88.00	Large-Cap Growth

GICS Sector Health Care
Sub-Industry Health Care Equipment

Summary This diversified maker of therapeutic and diagnostic medical devices has exposure to the vascular, urology, oncology and specialty surgical markets.

Key Stock Statistics (Source S&P, Vickers, company reports)

52-Wk Range	$90.00– 74.87	S&P Oper. EPS 2010**E**	5.54	Market Capitalization(B)	$7.774	Beta	0.30
Trailing 12-Month EPS	$4.91	S&P Oper. EPS 2011**E**	6.15	Yield (%)	0.87	S&P 3-Yr. Proj. EPS CAGR(%)	11
Trailing 12-Month P/E	16.9	P/E on S&P Oper. EPS 2010**E**	15.0	Dividend Rate/Share	$0.72	S&P Credit Rating	A
$10K Invested 5 Yrs Ago	$13,557	Common Shares Outstg. (M)	93.6	Institutional Ownership (%)	87		

Price Performance

30-Week Mov. Avg. ··· 10-Week Mov. Avg. -- GAAP Earnings vs. Previous Year Volume Above Avg. STARS
12-Mo. Target Price — Relative Strength — ▲ Up ▼ Down ► No Change Below Avg.

Options: ASE, CBOE, P, Ph

Analysis prepared by **Phillip M. Seligman** on July 29, 2010, when the stock traded at **$ 77.80**.

Highlights

► We expect net sales in 2010 to climb about 8%, to $2.74 billion. Drivers we see include growth of about 13% in the vascular category, on gains in electrophysiology systems, angioplasty catheters and biopsy products; under 4% in urology, on easy comps, given distributor de-stocking in 2009 and increased sales of catheter stabilization devices offset by weak sales of Foley catheters; more than 6% in on-cology, on improved sales of ports and the vas-cular access ultrasound product line tempered by slower PICC (peripherally inserted central catheters) sales; and about 11% in surgical specialties on demand for soft tissue repair products. We see sales growth also aided by acquisitions.

► We forecast that gross margins in 2010 will be flat with 2009's 62%, as the benefits of cost im-provements are offset by lower production to reduce inventory in the first quarter. We also expect higher SG&A and R&D costs as a per-centage of sales.

► Excluding restructuring charges, our 2010 EPS estimate is $5.52, partly reflecting the dilutive impact of a recent acquisition, versus 2009's $5.09. We look for $6.15 in 2011.

Investment Rationale/Risk

► We maintain our hold recommendation on BCR shares, given the slower EPS growth (8%-9%) we see in 2010, versus 14% annual growth achieved in recent years. We think BCR must pick up the pace of new product offerings and, in this regard, we are encouraged by its prod-uct pipeline and planned growth in R&D invest-ment. We also view operating cash flow as healthy, which should enable BCR to make ad-ditional acquisitions. Nonetheless, we see a sustained decline in elective surgical proce-dure rates and hospital spending and increased regulatory requirements that appear to us to be extending the time before a product can launch.

► Risks to our recommendation and target price include intensified competition, reduced reim-bursement, and failure to commercialize new products in a timely fashion.

► Despite the slower three-year EPS growth rate we project, it is still modestly above peers and, hence, we believe a small premium valuation is appropriate. Applying a forward P/E to earnings growth ratio of 1.45X to our three-year project-ed growth rate of 11% and our 2010 EPS esti-mate, our 12-month target price is $88.

Qualitative Risk Assessment

LOW	MEDIUM	HIGH

Our risk assessment reflects the highly competitive environment in which BCR operates. In addition, hospital customers generate a large portion of revenues from Medicare, and are therefore subject to reimbursement risks that could reduce prices paid to suppliers. However, we believe BCR's product line is largely focused on areas that have not been subject to intense pricing pressure, and we think management has a solid track record in terms of identifying and integrating acquisitions.

Quantitative Evaluations

S&P Quality Ranking A

D	C	B-	B	B+	A-	A	A+

Relative Strength Rank MODERATE

48

LOWEST = 1 HIGHEST = 99

Revenue/Earnings Data

Revenue (Million $)

	1Q	2Q	3Q	4Q	Year
2010	650.8	673.9	--	--	--
2009	596.4	624.6	637.0	676.9	2,535
2008	584.0	617.1	616.8	634.2	2,452
2007	528.2	545.7	544.8	583.3	2,202
2006	467.5	498.2	498.9	520.9	1,986
2005	428.6	447.4	443.3	452.0	1,771

Earnings Per Share ($)

2010	1.24	1.29	E1.40	E1.48	E5.54
2009	1.10	1.11	1.31	1.08	4.60
2008	0.76	0.76	1.09	1.47	4.06
2007	0.95	0.91	0.96	1.01	3.84
2006	0.76	0.76	0.82	0.21	2.55
2005	0.75	0.79	0.83	0.75	3.12

Fiscal year ended Dec. 31. Next earnings report expected: Late October. EPS Estimates based on S&P Operating Earnings; historical GAAP earnings are as reported.

Dividend Data (Dates: mm/dd Payment Date: mm/dd/yy)

Amount ($)	Date Decl.	Ex-Div. Date	Stk. of Record	Payment Date
0.170	12/09	01/21	01/25	02/05/10
0.170	04/21	04/29	05/03	05/14/10
0.180	06/09	07/22	07/26	08/06/10
0.180	10/13	10/21	10/25	11/05/10

Dividends have been paid since 1960. Source: Company reports.

Please read the Required Disclosures and Analyst Certification on the last page of this report.

The McGraw-Hill Companies

Bard (C.R.) Inc

STANDARD
&POOR'S

Business Summary July 29, 2010

CORPORATE OVERVIEW. C.R. Bard offers a range of medical, surgical, diagnostic and patient care devices. Sales in 2009 came from urology (28%), vascular (27%), oncology (27%), surgical specialties (15%) and other (3%) products.

Bard's vascular products include percutaneous transluminal angioplasty catheters, guide wires, introducers and accessories, peripheral stents, vena cava filters and biopsy devices; electrophysiology products such as lab systems, and diagnostic therapeutic and temporary pacing electrode catheters; and fabrics, meshes and implantable vascular grafts.

Urological diagnosis and intervention products include Foley catheters, procedure kits and trays, and related urine monitoring and collection systems; urethral stents; and specialty devices for incontinence, endoscopic procedures, and stone removal. Newer products include the Infection Control Foley catheter that reduces the rate of urinary tract infections; a collagen implant and sling materials used to treat urinary incontinence; and brachytherapy services, devices, and radioactive seeds to treat prostate cancer.

Oncology products include specialty access catheters and ports; gastroenterological products (endoscopic accessories, percutaneous feeding devices and stents); biopsy devices; and a suturing system for gastroesophageal reflux disease.

Surgical specialties products include meshes for hernia and other soft tissue repairs; irrigation devices for orthopedic, laparoscopic and gynecological procedures; and topical hemostatic devices. In January 2003, Bard introduced the VentralexT hernia patch, a simplified intra-abdominal hernia repair technology characterized by minimal suturing, small incisions, and potentially shorter recovery times. In December 2007, Bard entered into a license agreement with Genzyme Corp. to manufacture and market the Sepramesh IP hernia repair product line and incorporate the related Sepra coating technology into the development of future hernia repair applications.

Company Financials Fiscal Year Ended Dec. 31

Per Share Data ($)	2009	2008	2007	2006	2005	2004	2003	2002	2001	2000
Tangible Book Value	13.34	11.62	10.73	9.46	10.39	7.26	5.35	4.84	3.97	2.53
Cash Flow	5.59	4.95	4.59	3.25	3.71	3.33	2.03	1.87	1.89	1.53
Earnings	4.60	4.06	3.84	2.55	3.12	2.82	1.60	1.47	1.38	1.04
S&P Core Earnings	4.80	3.96	3.86	2.96	2.86	2.29	1.73	1.27	1.21	NA
Dividends	0.66	0.62	0.58	0.54	0.50	0.47	0.45	0.43	0.42	0.41
Payout Ratio	14%	15%	15%	21%	16%	17%	28%	29%	31%	39%
Prices:High	88.43	101.61	95.33	85.72	72.79	65.13	40.80	31.97	32.47	27.47
Prices:Low	68.94	70.00	76.61	59.89	60.82	40.09	27.02	22.05	20.43	17.50
P/E Ratio:High	19	25	25	34	23	23	25	22	24	26
P/E Ratio:Low	15	17	20	23	19	14	17	15	15	17

Income Statement Analysis (Million $)										
Revenue	2,535	2,452	2,202	1,986	1,771	1,656	1,433	1,274	1,181	1,099
Operating Income	825	735	638	550	503	418	333	295	266	244
Depreciation	93.5	90.9	79.8	74.9	63.8	54.7	44.7	42.3	53.2	49.6
Interest Expense	11.8	12.1	11.9	16.9	12.2	12.7	12.5	12.6	14.2	19.3
Pretax Income	672	550	577	348	450	414	223	211	205	154
Effective Tax Rate	31.3%	24.3%	29.6%	21.7%	25.0%	26.9%	24.5%	26.5%	30.1%	30.6%
Net Income	460	417	406	272	337	303	169	155	143	107
S&P Core Earnings	475	407	409	317	309	244	182	134	126	NA

Balance Sheet & Other Financial Data (Million $)										
Cash	674	592	571	416	754	541	417	23.1	30.8	21.3
Current Assets	1,492	1,354	1,242	1,134	1,264	1,054	875	758	647	527
Total Assets	2,907	2,666	2,476	2,277	2,266	2,009	1,692	1,417	1,231	1,089
Current Liabilities	282	273	282	296	641	390	422	317	235	225
Long Term Debt	150	150	150	151	0.80	151	152	152	156	204
Common Equity	2,194	1,977	1,848	1,698	1,536	1,360	1,046	880	789	614
Total Capital	2,356	2,151	2,018	1,871	1,544	1,534	1,197	1,033	945	818
Capital Expenditures	48.1	50.6	50.7	70.4	97.2	74.0	72.1	41.0	27.4	19.4
Cash Flow	554	507	486	347	401	358	213	197	196	157
Current Ratio	5.3	5.0	4.4	3.8	2.0	2.7	2.1	2.4	2.8	2.3
% Long Term Debt of Capitalization	Nil	7.0	7.4	8.1	0.1	9.9	12.7	14.7	16.5	25.0
% Net Income of Revenue	18.2	17.0	18.5	13.7	19.0	18.3	11.8	12.2	12.1	9.7
% Return on Assets	NA	16.2	17.1	12.0	15.8	16.4	10.8	11.5	12.3	9.6
% Return on Equity	NA	21.8	22.9	16.8	23.3	25.2	17.5	18.6	20.4	18.0

Data as orig reptd.; bef. results of disc opers/spec. items. Per share data adj. for stk. divs.; EPS diluted. E-Estimated. NA-Not Available. NM-Not Meaningful. NR-Not Ranked. UR-Under Review.

Office: 730 Central Avenue, Murray Hill, NJ 07974.
Telephone: 908-277-8000.
Website: http://www.crbard.com
Chrmn & CEO: T.M. Ring

Pres & COO: J.H. Weiland
SVP & CFO: T.C. Schermerhorn
Chief Acctg Officer & Cntlr: F. Lupisella, Jr.
Treas: S.T. Lowry

Investor Contact: E.J. Shick (908-277-8413)
Board Members: D. M. Barrett, M. C. Breslawsky, T. K. Dunnigan, H. L. Henkel, J. C. Kelly, T. E. Martin, G. K. Naughton, T. M. Ring, T. G. Thompson, J. H. Weiland, A. Welters, T. L. White

Founded: 1907
Domicile: New Jersey
Employees: 11,000

Baxter International Inc

STANDARD &POOR'S

S&P Recommendation	**BUY** ★★★★☆	Price	12-Mo. Target Price	Investment Style
		$51.12 (as of Oct 22, 2010)	$58.00	Large-Cap Growth

GICS Sector Health Care
Sub-Industry Health Care Equipment

Summary This global medical products and services company provides critical therapies for people with life-threatening conditions.

Key Stock Statistics (Source S&P, Vickers, company reports)

52-Wk Range	$61.88– 40.25	S&P Oper. EPS 2010**E**	3.98	Market Capitalization(B)	$29.873	Beta	0.50
Trailing 12-Month EPS	$2.59	S&P Oper. EPS 2011**E**	4.30	Yield (%)	2.27	S&P 3-Yr. Proj. EPS CAGR(%)	7
Trailing 12-Month P/E	19.7	P/E on S&P Oper. EPS 2010**E**	12.8	Dividend Rate/Share	$1.16	S&P Credit Rating	A+
$10K Invested 5 Yrs Ago	$14,758	Common Shares Outstg. (M)	584.4	Institutional Ownership (%)	81		

Price Performance

30-Week Mov. Avg. · · · · 10-Week Mov. Avg. – – **GAAP Earnings vs. Previous Year** Volume Above Avg. ⅢⅢ STARS
12-Mo. Target Price — Relative Strength — ▲ Up ▼ Down ► No Change Below Avg. ⅢⅢ ★

Options: ASE, CBOE, P, Ph

Qualitative Risk Assessment

LOW	**MEDIUM**	HIGH

Our risk assessment reflects BAX's operations in a highly competitive business characterized by rapid technological change and new market entrants. In addition, the business entails regulatory and reimbursement risks, as well as liability risk from malfunctioning products. This is offset by our belief that health care products are largely immune to economic cycles, and that long-term demand should benefit from demographic growth of the elderly and a greater penetration of developing global markets.

Quantitative Evaluations

S&P Quality Ranking A

D	C	B-	B	B+	A-	**A**	A+

Relative Strength Rank STRONG

80

LOWEST = 1 HIGHEST = 99

Highlights

► The 12-month target price for BAX has recently been changed to $58.00 from $50.00. The Highlights section of this Stock Report will be updated accordingly.

Investment Rationale/Risk

► The Investment Rationale/Risk section of this Stock Report will be updated shortly. For the latest News story on BAX from MarketScope, see below.

► 10/21/10 12:50 pm ET ... S&P REITERATES BUY OPINION ON SHARES OF BAXTER INTERNATIONAL (BAX 50.94****): Q3 adjusted EPS rose 16% to $1.01, $0.04 ahead of our estimate. Excluding FX, sales increased 4%, lifted by gains in BioScience, Medication Delivery, and Renal Care. Margins benefited from improved SG&A and R&D cost ratios. We believe BAX is executing well on strategies aimed at improving market share in key franchises. We also see synergies from the planned combination of the Medication Delivery and Renal units. We are raising our target price by $8 to $58, applying a peer level P/E of 13.5X to our '11 EPS estimate of $4.30 (raised by $0.04). The dividend yields 2.3%. /H.Saftlas

Revenue/Earnings Data

Revenue (Million $)

	1Q	2Q	3Q	4Q	Year
2010	3,140	3,194	--	--	--
2009	2,824	3,123	3,145	3,470	12,562
2008	2,877	3,189	3,151	3,131	12,348
2007	2,675	2,829	2,750	3,009	11,263
2006	2,409	2,649	2,557	2,763	10,378
2005	2,383	2,577	2,398	2,491	9,849

Earnings Per Share ($)

2010	0.86	0.90	E0.97	E1.11	E3.98
2009	0.83	0.96	0.87	0.94	3.59
2008	0.67	0.85	0.74	0.91	3.16
2007	0.61	0.65	0.61	0.74	2.61
2006	0.43	0.47	0.57	0.66	2.13
2005	0.36	0.51	0.18	0.46	1.52

Fiscal year ended Dec. 31. Next earnings report expected: NA. EPS Estimates based on S&P Operating Earnings; historical GAAP earnings are as reported.

Dividend Data (Dates: mm/dd Payment Date: mm/dd/yy)

Amount ($)	Date Decl.	Ex-Div. Date	Stk. of Record	Payment Date
0.290	11/10	12/08	12/10	01/05/10
0.290	02/16	03/08	03/10	04/01/10
0.290	05/04	06/08	06/10	07/01/10
0.290	07/27	09/08	09/10	10/01/10

Dividends have been paid since 1934. Source: Company reports.

Please read the Required Disclosures and Analyst Certification on the last page of this report.

The **McGraw·Hill** Companies

Baxter International Inc

Business Summary July 27, 2010

CORPORATE OVERVIEW. Founded in 1931 as the first producer of commercially prepared intravenous (IV) solutions, Baxter International makes and distributes medical products and equipment, with a focus on the blood and circulatory system. In 2007, international sales accounted for 57% of the total. In March 2007, the company divested its Transfusion Therapies business.

The BioSciences unit (44% of 2009 sales) produces plasma-based and recombinant clotting factors for hemophilia, as well as biopharmaceuticals for immune deficiencies, cancer, and other disorders. It also offers biosurgery products for hemostasis, tissue sealing and tissue regeneration, vaccines, and blood processing and storage systems used by hospitals, blood banks and others. In addition, BAX sells a meningitis C vaccine, and is developing cell culture-derived vaccines for influenza, smallpox, Severe Acute Respiratory Syndrome and other diseases. Its most important Biosciences product is Advate, a recombinant blood-clotting agent produced without adding human or animal proteins in the cell culture, purification or final formulation process.

The Medication Delivery unit (38%) makes IV solutions and various specialty products such as critical-care generic injectable drugs, anesthetic agents, and nutrition and oncology products. The products work with devices such as drug-reconstitution systems, IV infusion pumps, nutritional compounding equipment, and medication management systems to provide fluid replenishment, general anesthesia, parenteral nutrition, pain management, antibiotic therapy, and chemotherapy.

Renal Care products (18%) comprise dialysis equipment and other products and services provided for kidney failure patients. BAX sells products for peritoneal dialysis (PD), including solutions, container systems and automated machines that cleanse patients' blood overnight while they sleep. The company also makes dialyzers and instrumentation for hemodialysis (HD). Another renal care product is Extraneal (icodextrin) solution, which facilitates increased fluid removal from the bloodstream during dialysis.

Company Financials Fiscal Year Ended Dec. 31

Per Share Data ($)	2009	2008	2007	2006	2005	2004	2003	2002	2001	2000
Tangible Book Value	8.08	6.79	7.53	6.42	3.61	2.45	1.74	1.53	3.44	2.43
Cash Flow	4.63	4.11	3.46	3.01	2.45	1.59	2.42	2.38	1.81	1.91
Earnings	3.59	3.16	2.61	2.13	1.52	0.62	1.52	1.67	1.09	1.24
S&P Core Earnings	3.66	2.99	2.68	2.24	1.38	0.52	1.25	1.30	0.53	NA
Dividends	1.07	0.91	0.72	0.58	0.58	0.58	0.58	0.58	0.58	0.15
Payout Ratio	30%	29%	28%	27%	38%	94%	38%	35%	53%	12%
Prices:High	60.99	71.53	61.09	48.54	41.07	34.84	31.32	59.90	55.90	45.13
Prices:Low	45.46	47.41	46.07	35.12	33.08	27.10	18.18	24.07	40.06	25.88
P/E Ratio:High	17	23	23	23	27	56	21	36	51	37
P/E Ratio:Low	13	15	18	16	22	44	12	14	37	21

Income Statement Analysis (Million $)										
Revenue	12,562	12,348	11,263	10,378	9,849	9,509	8,916	8,110	7,663	6,896
Operating Income	3,594	3,333	2,913	2,479	2,110	2,039	2,161	2,168	1,934	1,673
Depreciation	638	606	558	575	580	601	545	439	441	405
Interest Expense	117	165	136	101	166	99.0	118	71.0	108	124
Pretax Income	2,734	2,451	2,114	1,746	1,444	430	1,150	1,397	964	946
Effective Tax Rate	19.0%	17.8%	19.3%	19.9%	33.7%	10.9%	19.8%	26.1%	31.1%	22.0%
Net Income	2,205	2,014	1,707	1,398	958	383	922	1,033	664	738
S&P Core Earnings	2,248	1,906	1,757	1,467	864	323	756	794	313	NA

Balance Sheet & Other Financial Data (Million $)										
Cash	2,811	2,131	2,539	2,485	841	1,109	927	1,169	582	579
Current Assets	8,271	7,148	7,555	6,970	5,116	6,019	5,437	5,160	3,977	3,651
Total Assets	17,354	15,405	15,294	14,686	12,727	14,147	13,779	12,478	10,343	8,733
Current Liabilities	4,464	3,635	3,812	3,610	4,165	4,286	3,819	3,851	3,294	3,372
Long Term Debt	3,440	3,362	2,664	2,567	2,414	3,933	4,421	4,398	2,486	1,726
Common Equity	7,191	6,229	6,916	6,272	4,299	3,705	3,323	2,939	3,757	2,659
Total Capital	11,542	9,597	9,580	8,839	6,713	7,638	7,744	7,366	6,461	4,545
Capital Expenditures	1,014	954	692	526	444	558	789	734	669	101
Cash Flow	2,843	2,620	2,265	1,973	1,538	984	1,467	1,472	1,105	1,143
Current Ratio	1.9	2.0	2.0	1.9	1.2	1.4	1.4	1.3	1.2	1.1
% Long Term Debt of Capitalization	Nil	35.1	27.8	29.0	36.0	51.5	57.1	59.7	38.5	38.0
% Net Income of Revenue	17.6	16.3	15.2	13.5	9.7	4.0	10.3	12.7	8.7	10.7
% Return on Assets	NA	13.1	11.4	10.2	7.1	2.8	7.0	9.1	7.0	8.0
% Return on Equity	NA	30.6	25.9	26.4	23.9	10.8	29.4	30.9	20.7	24.6

Data as orig reptd.; bef. results of disc opers/spec. items. Per share data adj. for stk. divs.; EPS diluted. E-Estimated. NA-Not Available. NM-Not Meaningful. NR-Not Ranked. UR-Under Review.

Office: One Baxter Parkway, Deerfield, IL 60015.
Telephone: 847-948-2000.
Website: http://www.baxter.com
Chrmn, Pres & CEO: R.L. Parkinson, Jr.

CFO & Treas: R.J. Hombach
CSO: N.G. Riedel
Chief Acctg Officer & Cntlr: M.J. Baughman
Secy: S.A. Shinn

Investor Contact: M. Ladone (847-948-3371)
Board Members: W. E. Boomer, B. E. Devitt, J. D. Forsyth, G. D. Fosler, J. Gavin, III, P. S. Hellman, W. T. Hockmeyer, J. Martin, R. L. Parkinson, Jr., C. J. Shapazian, T. T. Stallkamp, K. J. Storm, A. P. Stroucken

Founded: 1931
Domicile: Delaware
Employees: 49,700

BB&T Corp

STANDARD &POOR'S

S&P Recommendation	BUY ★★★★☆	Price $22.62 (as of Oct 22, 2010)	12-Mo. Target Price $26.00	Investment Style Large-Cap Blend

GICS Sector Financials
Sub-Industry Regional Banks

Summary This financial holding company operates more than 1,800 financial centers in the Carolinas and several other states, mostly in the Southeast.

Key Stock Statistics (Source S&P, Vickers, company reports)

52-Wk Range	$35.72–21.72	S&P Oper. EPS 2010**E**	1.18	Market Capitalization(B)	$15.675	Beta	0.96
Trailing 12-Month EPS	$1.06	S&P Oper. EPS 2011**E**	2.82	Yield (%)	2.65	S&P 3-Yr. Proj. EPS CAGR(%)	33
Trailing 12-Month P/E	21.3	P/E on S&P Oper. EPS 2010**E**	19.2	Dividend Rate/Share	$0.60	S&P Credit Rating	A
$10K Invested 5 Yrs Ago	$6,975	Common Shares Outstg. (M)	693.0	Institutional Ownership (%)	51		

Price Performance

- 30-Week Mov. Avg. · · ·
- 10-Week Mov. Avg. – –
- GAAP Earnings vs. Previous Year
- Volume Above Avg. STARS
- 12-Mo. Target Price —
- Relative Strength —
- ▲ Up ▼ Down ▶ No Change
- Below Avg.

Options: ASE, CBOE, P, Ph

Qualitative Risk Assessment

LOW	MEDIUM	HIGH

Our risk assessment reflects the company's large-cap valuation, our view of the strong credit quality of its loan portfolio, and its history of profitability, offset by its exposure to the banking industry's current issues regarding funding and credit quality.

Quantitative Evaluations

S&P Quality Ranking B+

D	C	B-	B	B+	A-	A	A+

Relative Strength Rank WEAK

14

LOWEST = 1   HIGHEST = 99

Revenue/Earnings Data

Revenue (Million $)

	1Q	2Q	3Q	4Q	Year
2010	2,623	2,858	--	--	--
2009	2,740	2,633	2,685	2,790	10,818
2008	2,655	2,617	2,585	2,536	10,404
2007	2,543	2,690	2,719	2,747	10,668
2006	2,165	2,319	2,463	2,468	9,414
2005	1,760	1,918	2,036	2,118	7,831

Earnings Per Share ($)

	1Q	2Q	3Q	4Q	Year
2010	0.27	0.30	E0.30	E0.31	E1.18
2009	0.48	0.20	0.23	0.27	1.15
2008	0.78	0.78	0.65	0.51	2.71
2007	0.77	0.83	0.80	0.75	3.14
2006	0.79	0.79	0.77	0.46	2.81
2005	0.71	0.70	0.80	0.78	3.00

Fiscal year ended Dec. 31. Next earnings report expected: NA. EPS Estimates based on S&P Operating Earnings; historical GAAP earnings are as reported.

Highlights

- The 12-month target price for BBT has recently been changed to $26.00 from $38.00. The Highlights section of this Stock Report will be updated accordingly.

Investment Rationale/Risk

- The Investment Rationale/Risk section of this Stock Report will be updated shortly. For the latest News story on BBT from MarketScope, see below.

- 10/21/10 10:11 am ET ... S&P MAINTAINS BUY RECOMMENDATION ON SHARES OF BB&T (BBT 23.0****): Q3 EPS of $0.30, vs. $0.23, misses our $0.53 estimate, on a higher than expected loan loss provision, partly offset by better than expected noninterest income, driven by securities gains. On results, we are reducing our '10 EPS estimate to $1.18 from $1.42. However, we see strong signs of improving credit quality, in low formation of new nonperforming loans. To reflect peer multiples, we cut our target price by $12 to $26 based on a slight premium to peers 1.7X our year-end tangible book value per share estimate of $15.20. /E. Oja

Dividend Data (Dates: mm/dd Payment Date: mm/dd/yy)

Amount ($)	Date Decl.	Ex-Div. Date	Stk. of Record	Payment Date
0.150	02/23	04/07	04/09	05/03/10
0.150	06/22	07/07	07/09	08/02/10
0.150	06/22	09/02	09/07	08/02/10
0.150	08/24	10/13	10/15	11/01/10

Dividends have been paid since 1903. Source: Company reports.

The McGraw·Hill Companies

BB&T Corp

STANDARD &POOR'S

Business Summary July 26, 2010

CORPORATE OVERVIEW. BBT has bank operations providing loan, deposit and financial products primarily in the Southeast. BBT has seven reportable business segments: Banking Network, Mortgage Banking, Trust Services, Insurance Services, Investment Banking and Brokerage, Specialized Lending, and Treasury.

MARKET PROFILE. As of June 30, 2009, which is the latest available FDIC branch-level data, BBT had 1,820 branches and $114.4 billion in deposits, including, on a pro forma basis, the acquisition of Colonial Bancorp in August 2009.

BBT's footprint is relatively concentrated, as 61% of deposits are in North Carolina, Virginia and Florida. In North Carolina, BBT had 356 branches, $33.7 billion of deposits, and a deposit market share of 11.1%, ranking third. In Virginia, BBT had 390 branches, $20.0 billion of deposits, and a deposit market share of about 9.4%, ranking fourth. In Florida, BBT had 307 branches, $16.4 billion of deposits, and a deposit market share of about 4.1%, ranking fifth. These figures include $12.0 billion and 200 branches from the Colonial acquisition.

In Georgia, BBT had 172 branches, $11.1 billion of deposits, and a deposit market share of about 6.0%, ranking fifth. In Maryland, BBT had 128 branches, $6.6 billion of deposits, and a deposit market share of about 6.1%, ranking seventh. In South Carolina, BBT had 115 branches, $6.3 billion of deposits, and a deposit market share of about 9.1%, ranking third. In Alabama, including the Colonial acquisition, BBT had 88 branches, $5.8 billion of deposits, and a deposit market share of about 7.0%, ranking fourth. Almost all of BBT's current Alabama presence resulted from the Colonial transaction. In addition, BBT had a number one market ranking in West Virginia, was third in Kentucky, seventh in DC, and sixth in Tennessee. Finally, BBT had a small presence in Texas, Nevada and Indiana.

Company Financials Fiscal Year Ended Dec. 31

Per Share Data ($)	2009	2008	2007	2006	2005	2004	2003	2002	2001	2000
Tangible Book Value	13.77	11.86	12.73	11.04	11.76	12.26	11.66	12.04	13.50	11.91
Earnings	1.15	2.71	3.14	2.81	3.00	2.80	2.07	2.70	2.12	1.55
S&P Core Earnings	1.15	2.54	3.09	2.79	2.90	2.75	1.97	2.59	2.02	NA
Dividends	1.24	1.86	1.76	1.60	1.46	1.34	1.22	1.10	0.98	0.86
Payout Ratio	108%	67%	56%	57%	49%	48%	59%	41%	46%	55%
Prices:High	29.81	45.31	44.30	44.74	43.92	43.25	39.69	39.47	38.84	38.25
Prices:Low	12.90	18.71	30.36	38.24	37.04	33.02	30.66	31.03	30.24	21.69
P/E Ratio:High	26	17	14	16	15	15	19	15	18	25
P/E Ratio:Low	11	7	10	14	12	12	15	11	14	14

Income Statement Analysis (Million $)										
Net Interest Income	4,844	4,238	3,880	3,708	3,525	3,348	3,082	2,747	2,434	2,018
Tax Equivalent Adjustment	119	83.0	68.0	NA	82.7	NA	21.2	151	19.1	130
Non Interest Income	3,934	3,197	2,777	2,594	2,326	2,113	1,782	1,522	1,256	996
Loan Loss Provision	2,811	1,445	448	240	217	249	248	264	224	127
% Expense/Operating Revenue	56.2%	54.4%	54.6%	55.8%	53.4%	57.6%	63.6%	54.0%	60.1%	56.0%
Pretax Income	1,036	2,069	2,570	2,473	2,467	2,322	1,617	1,791	1,360	906
Effective Tax Rate	15.4%	26.6%	32.5%	38.2%	33.0%	32.9%	34.1%	27.8%	28.4%	30.8%
Net Income	853	1,519	1,734	1,528	1,654	1,558	1,065	1,293	974	626
% Net Interest Margin	3.66	3.63	3.52	3.74	3.89	4.04	4.06	4.25	4.17	3.56
S&P Core Earnings	728	1,406	1,707	1,514	1,608	1,529	1,012	1,241	927	NA

Balance Sheet & Other Financial Data (Million $)										
Money Market Assets	1,065	1,101	1,067	688	697	1,244	604	591	458	379
Investment Securities	34,545	33,219	23,428	22,868	20,489	19,173	16,317	17,655	16,662	13,851
Commercial Loans	49,820	50,480	44,870	41,300	37,655	34,321	12,429	7,061	6,551	5,894
Other Loans	56,387	48,189	46,037	41,611	36,739	33,228	49,151	44,079	38,985	33,561
Total Assets	165,764	152,015	132,618	121,351	109,170	100,509	90,467	80,217	70,870	59,340
Demand Deposits	22,365	16,225	14,260	14,726	13,477	12,246	11,098	7,864	6,940	5,064
Time Deposits	92,600	82,388	72,506	66,245	60,805	55,453	48,252	43,416	37,794	32,951
Long Term Debt	21,376	18,032	18,693	12,604	13,119	11,420	10,808	13,588	11,721	8,355
Common Equity	16,191	16,037	448	11,745	11,129	10,874	9,935	7,388	6,150	4,786
% Return on Assets	0.5	1.1	1.3	1.3	1.6	1.6	1.2	1.7	1.4	1.1
% Return on Equity	5.9	10.6	14.0	13.4	15.0	15.0	12.3	19.1	16.8	14.2
% Loan Loss Reserve	2.5	1.6	1.1	1.1	1.1	1.2	1.3	1.4	1.4	1.3
% Loans/Deposits	90.2	98.6	103.6	103.2	99.0	100.7	105.0	104.4	106.1	106.0
% Equity to Assets	10.1	9.0	9.6	9.9	10.5	10.9	10.1	9.0	8.4	7.9

Data as orig reptd.; bef. results of disc opers/spec. items. Per share data adj. for stk. divs.; EPS diluted. E-Estimated. NA-Not Available. NM-Not Meaningful. NR-Not Ranked. UR-Under Review.

Office: 200 West Second Street, Winston-Salem, NC 27101.
Telephone: 336-733-2000.
Website: http://www.bbandt.com
Chrmn, Pres & CEO: K.S. King

COO & EVP: C.L. Henson
EVP & CFO: D.N. Bible
EVP, Chief Acctg Officer & Cntlr: C.B. Powell
Treas: J. Nichols

Investor Contact: T. Gjesdal (336-733-3058)
Board Members: J. A. Allison, IV, J. S. Banner, K. D. Boyer, Jr., A. R. Cablik, R. E. Deal, B. J. Fitzpatrick, J. L. Glover, Jr., L. V. Hackley, J. P. Helm, J. P. Howe, III, K. S. King, J. H. Maynard, A. O. McCauley, J. H. Morrison, N. R. Qubein, T. E. Skains, T. N. Thompson, S. T. Williams

Founded: 1968
Domicile: North Carolina
Employees: 32,400

The McGraw-Hill Companies

Becton, Dickinson and Co

STANDARD &POOR'S

S&P Recommendation BUY ★★★★☆

Price	12-Mo. Target Price	Investment Style
$76.40 (as of Oct 22, 2010)	$87.00	Large-Cap Growth

GICS Sector Health Care
Sub-Industry Health Care Equipment

Summary This company provides a wide range of medical devices and diagnostic products used in hospitals, doctors' offices, research labs and other settings.

Key Stock Statistics (Source S&P, Vickers, company reports)

52-Wk Range	$80.56–66.20	S&P Oper. EPS 2010E	5.08	Market Capitalization(B)	$17.736	Beta	0.58
Trailing 12-Month EPS	$5.11	S&P Oper. EPS 2011E	5.45	Yield (%)	1.94	S&P 3-Yr. Proj. EPS CAGR(%)	8
Trailing 12-Month P/E	15.0	P/E on S&P Oper. EPS 2010E	15.0	Dividend Rate/Share	$1.48	S&P Credit Rating	AA-
$10K Invested 5 Yrs Ago	$16,291	Common Shares Outstg. (M)	232.1	Institutional Ownership (%)	81		

Price Performance

- 30-Week Mov. Avg. · · · ·   10-Week Mov. Avg. – – –   **GAAP Earnings vs. Previous Year**   **Volume** Above Avg. ▌▌▌ STARS
- 12-Mo. Target Price —   Relative Strength —   ▲ Up ▼ Down ► No Change   Below Avg. ▌▌▌ ★

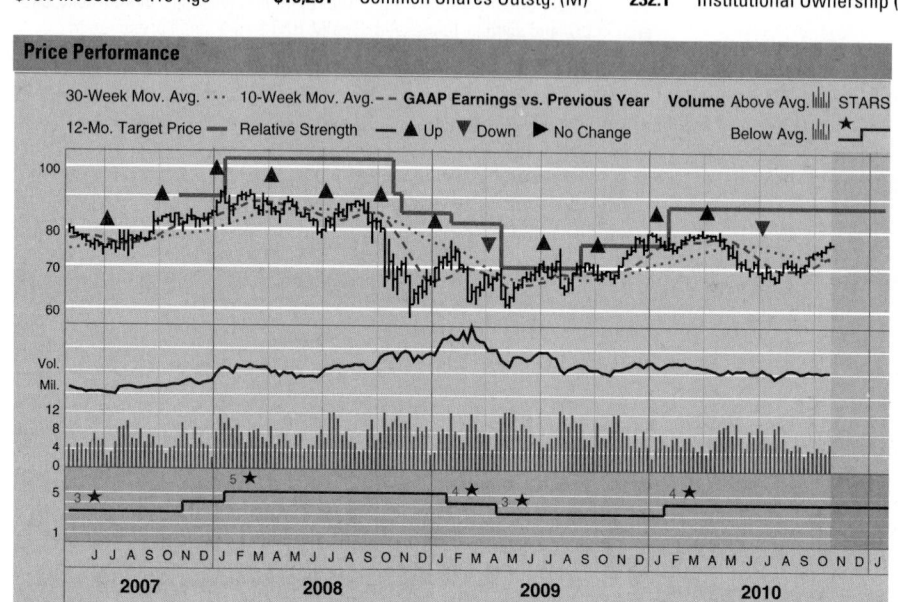

Options: CBOE, P, Ph

Analysis prepared by **Jeffrey Loo, CFA** on August 13, 2010, when the stock traded at **$ 71.06**.

Highlights

➤ We expect revenues to rise 5% in FY 10 (Sep.) and 6% in FY 11, inclusive of a neutral foreign exchange impact. We see the medical segment growing 6.6% and 5.4%, respectively, on global demand for diabetes care products, partially offset by slower H1N1 supply sales as the swine flu pandemic concerns has lessened. We believe diagnostics revenues will rise 4% and 5% on infectious disease testing products, but adversely affected by lower physician office visits, and see the biosciences revenues growing 5% in both years on solid cell analysis sales and aided partially by U.S. stimulus funding, which has been slow to roll out. We see gross margins declining 110 and 50 basis points (bps), mainly on higher resin costs, and but see operating margins declining 90 bps and 40 bps, aided by leverage.

➤ In August, BDX sold its ophthalmic systems unit and its surgical blades product platform. The assets generated approximately $200 million in annual revenue.

➤ Our FY 10 and FY 11 EPS estimates are $5.08 and $5.45, respectively.

Investment Rationale/Risk

➤ We believe the shares, recently trading at 12.8X our FY 11 EPS estimate, well below historical levels, are undervalued. We see steady growth from BDX's diversified product offering, and we are encouraged by strong global demand for BDX's safety, diabetes-care and disease-testing products, which we view as sustainable for the long term. In this regard, we note that the EU is working on safety legislation that could be adopted by member states in three years' time. Meanwhile, we view positively recent growth in the biosciences segment, driven by supplemental government funding for stem-cell research in Japan and increased demand for cell analysis products in the U.S.

➤ Risks to our opinion and target price include a slower-than-expected recovery in key life science markets, continued cutbacks in spending by the company's hospital customers, adverse patent litigation, and unfavorable foreign currency fluctuations.

➤ Our 12-month target price of $87 is derived by applying a multiple of 16X to our FY 2011 EPS estimate, slightly below historical levels.

Qualitative Risk Assessment

LOW	MEDIUM	HIGH

BDX's markets are competitive, and new product introductions by current and future competitors have the potential to significantly affect market dynamics. In addition, changes in domestic and foreign health care industry practices and regulations may result in increased pricing pressures and lower reimbursements for some of its products. However, we believe BDX's product line has more favorable demand and pricing characteristics than those in the medical equipment industry in general.

Quantitative Evaluations

S&P Quality Ranking   **A**

D	C	B-	B	B+	A-	A	A+

Relative Strength Rank   **MODERATE**

59

LOWEST = 1   HIGHEST = 99

Revenue/Earnings Data

Revenue (Million $)

	1Q	2Q	3Q	4Q	Year
2010	1,917	1,845	1,878	--	--
2009	1,734	1,741	1,820	1,898	7,161
2008	1,706	1,747	1,868	1,836	7,156
2007	1,502	1,576	1,631	1,651	6,360
2006	1,414	1,449	1,484	1,488	5,835
2005	1,288	1,366	1,381	1,379	5,415

Earnings Per Share ($)

	1Q	2Q	3Q	4Q	Year
2010	1.30	1.24	1.29	E1.23	E5.08
2009	1.26	1.06	1.38	1.25	4.92
2008	1.07	1.09	1.18	1.13	4.46
2007	0.51	0.92	0.95	0.98	3.36
2006	0.85	0.61	0.81	0.69	2.95
2005	0.74	0.71	0.73	0.47	2.66

Fiscal year ended Sep. 30. Next earnings report expected: Early November. EPS Estimates based on S&P Operating Earnings; historical GAAP earnings are as reported.

Dividend Data (Dates: mm/dd Payment Date: mm/dd/yy)

Amount ($)	Date Decl.	Ex-Div. Date	Stk. of Record	Payment Date
0.370	11/24	12/10	12/14	01/04/10
0.370	02/02	03/08	03/10	03/31/10
0.370	05/25	06/07	06/09	06/30/10
0.370	07/27	09/07	09/09	09/30/10

Dividends have been paid since 1926. Source: Company reports.

Please read the Required Disclosures and Analyst Certification on the last page of this report.

The McGraw-Hill Companies

Becton, Dickinson and Co

STANDARD &POOR'S

Business Summary August 13, 2010

Becton, Dickinson traces its roots to a concern started by Maxwell Becton and Fairleigh Dickinson in 1897. One of the first companies to sell U.S.-made glass syringes, BDX was also a pioneer in the production of hypodermic needles. The company now manufactures and sells medical supplies, devices, lab equipment and diagnostic products used by health care institutions, life science researchers, clinical laboratories, industry and the general public. In FY 09 (Sep.), 60% of the company's sales were generated from non-U.S. markets.

Major products in the core medical systems division (52% of FY 09 revenues) include hypodermic syringes and needles for injection, insulin syringes and pen needles for diabetes care, infusion therapy devices, prefillable drug delivery systems, and surgical blades and scalpels. The segment also markets specialty blades and cannulas for ophthalmic surgery procedures, anesthesia needles, critical care systems, elastic support products, and thermometers. The blood glucose monitoring and test strip business was sold in December 2006.

The diagnostics segment (31%) provides a range of products designed for the safe collection and transport of diagnostic specimens and instrumentation for analysis across a wide range of infectious disease testing, including health care-associated infections (HAIs). Its principal products and services include integrated systems for specimen collection; an extensive line of safety-engineered blood collection products and systems; plated media; automated blood culturing systems; molecular testing systems for sexually transmitted diseases and HAIs; microorganism identification and drug susceptibility systems; liquid-based cytology systems for cervical cancer screening; and rapid diagnostic assays. The segment also includes consulting services and customized, automated bar-code systems for patient identification and point-of-care data capture.

The biosciences unit (17%) provides research tools and reagents to clinicians and medical researchers studying genes, proteins and cells in order to better understand disease, improve diagnosis and disease management, and facilitate the discovery and development of novel therapeutics. Products include instrument systems for cell sorting and analysis, monoclonal antibody reagents and kits for diagnostic and research use, tools to aid in drug discovery and vaccine development, molecular biology products, fluid handling, cell growth and screening products.

Company Financials Fiscal Year Ended Sep. 30

Per Share Data ($)	2009	2008	2007	2006	2005	2004	2003	2002	2001	2000
Tangible Book Value	16.52	15.38	13.41	11.96	10.28	9.28	8.82	6.06	5.35	3.80
Cash Flow	6.39	5.89	5.09	4.52	4.36	3.57	3.54	2.92	2.76	2.58
Earnings	4.92	4.46	3.36	2.95	2.66	2.21	2.07	1.79	1.63	1.49
S&P Core Earnings	4.93	4.22	3.38	2.99	2.75	2.39	2.01	1.57	1.38	NA
Dividends	1.32	1.14	0.98	0.86	0.72	0.60	0.40	0.39	0.38	0.37
Payout Ratio	27%	26%	29%	29%	27%	27%	19%	22%	23%	25%
Prices:High	79.97	93.24	85.89	74.25	61.17	58.18	41.82	38.60	39.25	35.31
Prices:Low	60.40	58.14	69.30	58.08	49.71	40.90	28.82	24.70	29.96	23.75
P/E Ratio:High	16	21	26	25	23	26	20	22	24	24
P/E Ratio:Low	12	13	21	20	19	19	14	14	18	16

Income Statement Analysis (Million $)	2009	2008	2007	2006	2005	2004	2003	2002	2001	2000
Revenue	7,161	7,156	6,360	5,835	5,415	4,935	4,528	4,033	3,754	3,618
Operating Income	2,060	1,912	1,644	1,456	1,419	1,244	1,094	1,002	952	861
Depreciation	365	360	441	405	387	357	344	305	306	288
Interest Expense	69.8	66.2	46.0	66.0	55.7	29.6	73.1	33.3	47.1	78.3
Pretax Income	1,639	1,554	1,204	1,035	1,005	753	710	629	577	520
Effective Tax Rate	26.0%	27.4%	28.8%	27.0%	31.1%	22.6%	22.9%	23.6%	24.0%	24.4%
Net Income	1,213	1,128	856	756	692	583	547	480	438	393
S&P Core Earnings	1,216	1,068	863	766	714	628	523	417	364	NA

Balance Sheet & Other Financial Data (Million $)	2009	2008	2007	2006	2005	2004	2003	2002	2001	2000
Cash	1,946	1,030	511	1,000	1,043	719	520	243	82.1	49.2
Current Assets	4,647	3,615	3,131	3,185	2,975	2,641	2,339	1,929	1,763	1,661
Total Assets	9,305	7,913	7,329	6,825	6,072	5,753	5,572	5,040	4,802	4,505
Current Liabilities	1,777	1,417	1,479	1,576	1,299	1,050	1,043	1,252	1,265	1,354
Long Term Debt	1,488	953	956	957	1,061	1,172	1,184	803	1,902	780
Common Equity	5,143	4,936	4,362	3,836	3,284	3,037	2,863	2,450	2,288	1,912
Total Capital	6,831	5,924	5,318	4,793	4,345	4,328	4,200	3,396	4,321	2,823
Capital Expenditures	591	602	556	459	318	266	261	260	371	376
Cash Flow	1,578	1,488	1,297	1,161	1,080	940	889	783	742	679
Current Ratio	2.6	2.6	2.1	2.0	2.3	2.5	2.2	1.5	1.4	1.2
% Long Term Debt of Capitalization	21.8	16.1	17.9	20.0	24.4	27.1	28.2	23.6	44.0	27.6
% Net Income of Revenue	16.9	15.8	13.4	12.9	12.8	11.8	12.1	11.9	11.7	10.9
% Return on Assets	14.1	14.1	12.0	11.7	11.7	10.3	10.3	9.8	9.4	8.8
% Return on Equity	24.1	24.3	20.8	21.2	21.9	19.7	20.5	20.2	20.8	21.5

Data as orig reptd.; bef. results of disc opers/spec. items. Per share data adj. for stk. divs.; EPS diluted. E-Estimated. NA-Not Available. NM-Not Meaningful. NR-Not Ranked. UR-Under Review.

Office: One Becton Drive, Franklin Lakes, NJ 07417-1880.
Telephone: 201-847-6800.
Email: investor_relations@bdhq.bd.com
Website: http://www.bd.com

Chrmn & CEO: E.J. Ludwig
Pres & COO: V.A. Forlenza
EVP & CFO: D.V. Elkins
SVP & CTO: S.P. Bruder

SVP, Chief Acctg Officer & Cntlr: W.A. Tozzi
Investor Contact: P.A. Spinella (201-847-5453)
Board Members: B. L. Anderson, H. P. Becton, Jr., E. F. DeGraan, C. M. Fraser-Liggett, C. I. Jones, M. O. Larsen, E. J. Ludwig, A. Mahmoud, G. A. Mecklenburg, C. Minehan, J. F. Orr, W. J. Overlock, Jr., B. L. Scott, A. Sommer

Founded: 1897
Domicile: New Jersey
Employees: 29,116

The McGraw·Hill Companies

Bed Bath & Beyond Inc

STANDARD &POOR'S

S&P Recommendation BUY ★★★★☆

Price	12-Mo. Target Price	Investment Style
$44.02 (as of Oct 22, 2010)	$52.00	Large-Cap Growth

GICS Sector Consumer Discretionary
Sub-Industry Homefurnishing Retail

Summary This company operates a nationwide chain of more than 900 Bed Bath & Beyond superstores selling better-quality domestics merchandise and home furnishings. It also has retail stores under the names Christmas Tree Shops, Harmon and buybuy BABY.

Key Stock Statistics (Source S&P, Vickers, company reports)

52-Wk Range	**$48.52– 26.50**	S&P Oper. EPS 2011**E**	**2.76**	Market Capitalization(B)	**$11.406**	Beta	**1.15**
Trailing 12-Month EPS	**$2.66**	S&P Oper. EPS 2012**E**	**3.08**	Yield (%)	**Nil**	S&P 3-Yr. Proj. EPS CAGR(%)	**10**
Trailing 12-Month P/E	**16.6**	P/E on S&P Oper. EPS 2011**E**	**15.9**	Dividend Rate/Share	**Nil**	S&P Credit Rating	**BBB**
$10K Invested 5 Yrs Ago	**$11,296**	Common Shares Outstg. (M)	**259.1**	Institutional Ownership (%)	**94**		

Price Performance

30-Week Mov. Avg. · · · · 10-Week Mov. Avg.- - **GAAP Earnings vs. Previous Year** Volume Above Avg. ▐▌▐ STARS
12-Mo. Target Price — Relative Strength — ▲ Up ▼ Down ► No Change Below Avg. ▐▌▐ ★

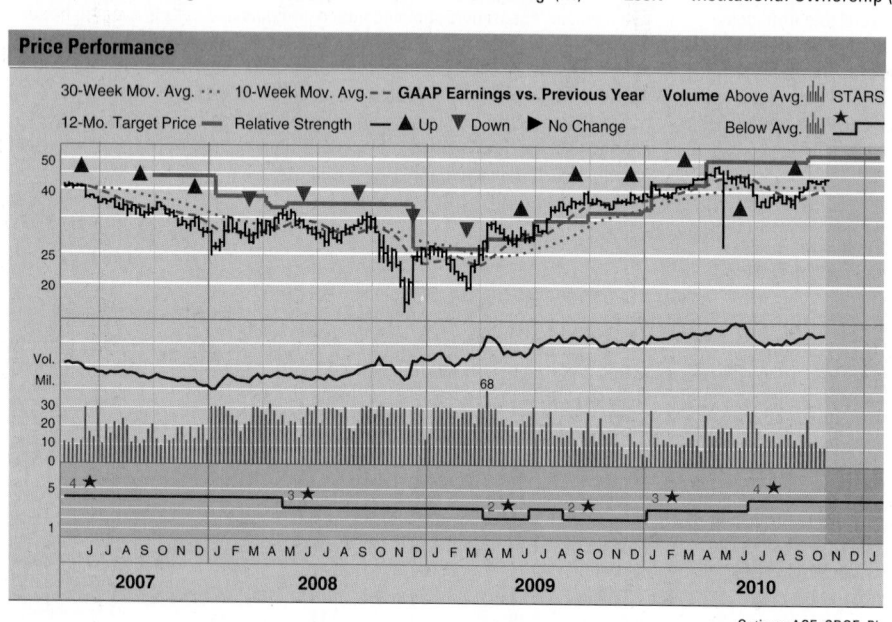

Options: ASE, CBOE, Ph

Analysis prepared by **Michael Souers** on September 24, 2010, when the stock traded at **$ 43.40**.

Highlights

▸ We expect sales to rise 8.7% in FY 11 (Feb.), following an 8.6% advance in FY 10. This reflects the projected addition of about 25 new Bed Bath & Beyond stores and a 5% same-store sales increase. We also anticipate the opening of approximately 10 new Christmas Tree Shops and 15 buybuy BABY stores. We see same-store sales reflecting slight increases in both foot traffic and average ticket.

▸ We expect gross margins to widen slightly, driven by a decrease in coupon redemptions and improved inventory management, partially offset by a negative product mix shift. We forecast a 120 basis point increase in operating margins, driven by gross margin improvement and continued cost-cutting efforts in payroll and advertising. In addition, we think BBBY will leverage fixed expenses on a solid expected comp-store sales increase.

▸ After slightly lower projected interest income, an anticipated effective tax rate of 38.7%, and a slightly lower diluted share count, we estimate FY 11 EPS of $2.76, a 20% increase from the $2.30 the company earned in FY 10. We see EPS of $3.08 in FY 12.

Investment Rationale/Risk

▸ We think BBBY shares are attractively priced, trading at about 14X our FY 12 EPS estimate, a discount to peers. In addition, we note the company's balance sheet includes over $6 of net cash per share. We expect continued market share gains for BBBY, with better merchandising and execution than peers. On the flip side, while we think the home furnishings industry is in the midst of reaching a cyclical bottom, plagued by cash-strapped consumers and a weak housing market, we expect it will take years for a solid recovery to build. BBBY is about 75% of the way to reaching its long-term goal of 1,300 stores, so we expect square footage growth to gradually slow.

▸ Risks to our recommendation and target price include an unexpected decline in consumer spending, an unanticipated shift in spending away from home-centric products, and miscues in BBBY's store expansion strategy.

▸ Our 12-month target price of $52, or about 17X our FY 12 EPS estimate, is based on our discounted cash flow analysis, which assumes a weighted average cost of capital of 10.3% and a terminal growth rate of 3.5%.

Qualitative Risk Assessment

LOW	MEDIUM	HIGH

Our risk assessment reflects the cyclical nature of the home furnishings retail industry, which relies heavily on consumer spending, and, to a lesser extent, housing turnover, offset by significant growth we see in major domestic metro markets and Canada.

Quantitative Evaluations

S&P Quality Ranking B+

D	C	B-	B	B+	A-	A	A+

Relative Strength Rank MODERATE

	68	

LOWEST = 1   HIGHEST = 99

Revenue/Earnings Data

Revenue (Million $)

	1Q	2Q	3Q	4Q	Year
2011	1,923	2,137	--	--	--
2010	1,694	1,915	1,975	2,244	7,829
2009	1,648	1,854	1,783	1,923	7,208
2008	1,553	1,768	1,795	1,933	7,049
2007	1,396	1,607	1,619	1,995	6,617
2006	1,244	1,431	1,449	1,685	5,810

Earnings Per Share ($)

2011	0.52	0.70	E0.64	E0.91	E2.76
2010	0.34	0.52	0.58	0.86	2.30
2009	0.30	0.46	0.34	0.55	1.64
2008	0.38	0.55	0.52	0.66	2.10
2007	0.35	0.51	0.50	0.72	2.09
2006	0.33	0.47	0.45	0.67	1.92

Fiscal year ended Feb. 28. Next earnings report expected: Early January. EPS Estimates based on S&P Operating Earnings; historical GAAP earnings are as reported.

Dividend Data

No cash dividends have been paid.

The McGraw-Hill Companies

Bed Bath & Beyond Inc

Business Summary September 24, 2010

CORPORATE OVERVIEW. Bed Bath & Beyond operates one of the largest U.S. chains of superstores selling domestics merchandise and home furnishings. BBBY stores predominantly range in size from 20,000 sq. ft. to 50,000 sq. ft., with some encompassing 100,000 sq. ft. The company has grown rapidly, from 34 stores at the end of FY 93 (Feb.) to 965 Bed Bath & Beyond stores in 49 states, the District of Columbia, Puerto Rico and Canada at year-end FY 10. BBBY opened 35 net new Bed Bath & Beyond Stores stores in FY 10, after opening 49 stores in FY 09; it expects to open 30 new stores in FY 11. During FY 10, total square footage of Bed Bath & Beyond stores grew 5.0%, to 33.7 million sq. ft., from 32.1 million sq. ft. Company stores are principally located in suburban areas of medium- and large-sized cities. These stores are situated in strip and power strip shopping centers, as well as in major off-price and conventional malls, and freestanding buildings.

In March 2002, the company acquired Harmon Stores, Inc., a health and beauty care retailer. The Harmon chain had 45 stores in three states at February 27, 2010, ranging in size from approximately 5,000 to 9,000 sq. ft.

In June 2003, BBBY acquired Christmas Tree Shops, a retailer of home decor, giftware, housewares, food, paper goods and seasonal products, for approximately $194.4 million, net of cash acquired. The company operated 61 Christmas Tree Shops in 15 states at year-end FY 10, ranging in size from 30,000 to 50,000 sq. ft.

In March 2007, BBBY acquired buybuy BABY, a retailer of infant and toddler merchandise, for approximately $67 million, net of cash acquired. The company operated 29 buybuy BABY stores in 14 states at year-end FY 10, ranging in size from 28,000 to 60,000 square feet.

Bed Bath & Beyond is also a partner in a joint venture that operates two stores in the Mexico City market under the name "Home & More".

Company Financials Fiscal Year Ended Feb. 28

Per Share Data ($)	2010	2009	2008	2007	2006	2005	2004	2003	2002	2001
Tangible Book Value	13.02	10.67	11.34	9.56	8.05	6.99	6.14	4.93	3.75	2.84
Cash Flow	3.01	2.32	2.69	2.56	2.29	1.96	1.59	1.25	0.94	0.75
Earnings	2.30	1.64	2.10	2.09	1.92	1.65	1.31	1.00	0.74	0.59
S&P Core Earnings	2.30	1.64	2.10	2.09	1.87	1.55	1.23	0.92	0.67	0.53
Dividends	Nil	Nil	Nil	Nil	Nil	Nil	Nil	Nil	Nil	Nil
Payout Ratio	Nil	Nil	Nil	Nil	Nil	Nil	Nil	Nil	Nil	Nil
Calendar Year	2009	2008	2007	2006	2005	2004	2003	2002	2001	2000
Prices:High	40.23	34.73	43.32	41.72	46.99	44.43	45.00	37.90	35.70	27.31
Prices:Low	19.11	16.23	27.96	30.92	35.50	33.88	30.18	26.70	18.70	11.00
P/E Ratio:High	17	21	21	20	24	27	34	38	48	46
P/E Ratio:Low	8	10	13	15	18	21	23	27	25	19

Income Statement Analysis (Million $)										
Revenue	7,829	7,208	7,049	6,617	5,810	5,148	4,478	3,665	2,928	2,397
Operating Income	1,165	850	996	1,026	990	890	724	555	409	319
Depreciation	184	176	158	136	111	97.5	84.6	74.8	62.5	46.7
Interest Expense	NA	Nil	Nil	Nil	Nil	Nil	Nil	Nil	Nil	Nil
Pretax Income	985	683	865	933	915	811	650	491	357	282
Effective Tax Rate	39.1%	37.8%	35.0%	36.3%	37.4%	37.8%	38.5%	38.5%	38.5%	39.0%
Net Income	600	425	563	594	573	505	399	302	220	172
S&P Core Earnings	600	425	563	594	557	470	370	277	200	155

Balance Sheet & Other Financial Data (Million $)										
Cash	1,528	670	224	988	652	851	867	617	429	239
Current Assets	3,563	2,563	2,080	2,699	2,072	2,097	1,969	1,594	1,227	886
Total Assets	5,152	4,269	3,844	3,959	3,382	3,200	2,865	2,189	1,648	1,196
Current Liabilities	1,150	953	1,014	1,145	990	874	770	680	511	353
Long Term Debt	NA	Nil	Nil	Nil	Nil	Nil	Nil	Nil	Nil	Nil
Common Equity	3,653	3,000	2,562	2,649	2,262	2,204	1,991	1,452	1,094	817
Total Capital	3,653	3,000	2,562	2,649	2,262	2,204	1,991	1,452	1,094	817
Capital Expenditures	154	216	358	318	220	191	113	135	121	140
Cash Flow	784	601	721	731	684	602	484	377	282	219
Current Ratio	3.1	2.7	2.1	2.4	2.1	2.4	2.6	2.3	2.4	2.5
% Long Term Debt of Capitalization	Nil	Nil	Nil	Nil	Nil	Nil	Nil	Nil	Nil	Nil
% Net Income of Revenue	7.7	5.9	8.0	9.0	9.9	9.8	8.9	8.2	7.5	7.2
% Return on Assets	12.7	10.5	14.4	16.2	17.4	16.7	15.8	15.8	15.4	16.7
% Return on Equity	18.0	15.3	21.6	24.2	25.7	24.1	23.2	23.7	23.0	25.0

Data as orig reptd.; bef. results of disc opers/spec. items. Per share data adj. for stk. divs.; EPS diluted. E-Estimated. NA-Not Available. NM-Not Meaningful. NR-Not Ranked. UR-Under Review.

Office: 650 Liberty Avenue, Union, NJ 07083.
Telephone: 908-688-0888.
Website: http://www.bedbathandbeyond.com
Co-Chrmn: L. Feinstein

Co-Chrmn & Secy: W. Eisenberg
Pres: A. Stark
CEO: S.H. Temares
COO & CTO: K. Wanner

Investor Contact: R. Curwin (908-688-0888)
Board Members: D. S. Adler, S. F. Barshay, W. Eisenberg, K. Eppler, L. Feinstein, P. R. Gaston, J. Heller, V. A. Morrison, S. H. Temares

Founded: 1971
Domicile: New York
Employees: 41,000

Bemis Co Inc

STANDARD &POOR'S

S&P Recommendation BUY ★★★★☆	Price $33.52 (as of Oct 22, 2010)	12-Mo. Target Price $36.00	Investment Style Large-Cap Blend

GICS Sector Materials
Sub-Industry Paper Packaging

Summary This company is a leading maker of a broad range of flexible packaging and pressure-sensitive materials.

Key Stock Statistics (Source S&P, Vickers, company reports)

52-Wk Range	$34.25– 25.42	S&P Oper. EPS 2010**E**	2.20	Market Capitalization(B)	$3.658	Beta	0.80
Trailing 12-Month EPS	$1.38	S&P Oper. EPS 2011**E**	2.50	Yield (%)	2.74	S&P 3-Yr. Proj. EPS CAGR(%)	15
Trailing 12-Month P/E	24.3	P/E on S&P Oper. EPS 2010**E**	15.2	Dividend Rate/Share	$0.92	S&P Credit Rating	BBB
$10K Invested 5 Yrs Ago	$16,531	Common Shares Outstg. (M)	109.1	Institutional Ownership (%)	72		

Price Performance

30-Week Mov. Avg. · · ·   10-Week Mov. Avg. – –   **GAAP Earnings vs. Previous Year**   Volume Above Avg. STARS
12-Mo. Target Price —   Relative Strength —   ▲ Up ▼ Down ▶ No Change   Below Avg.

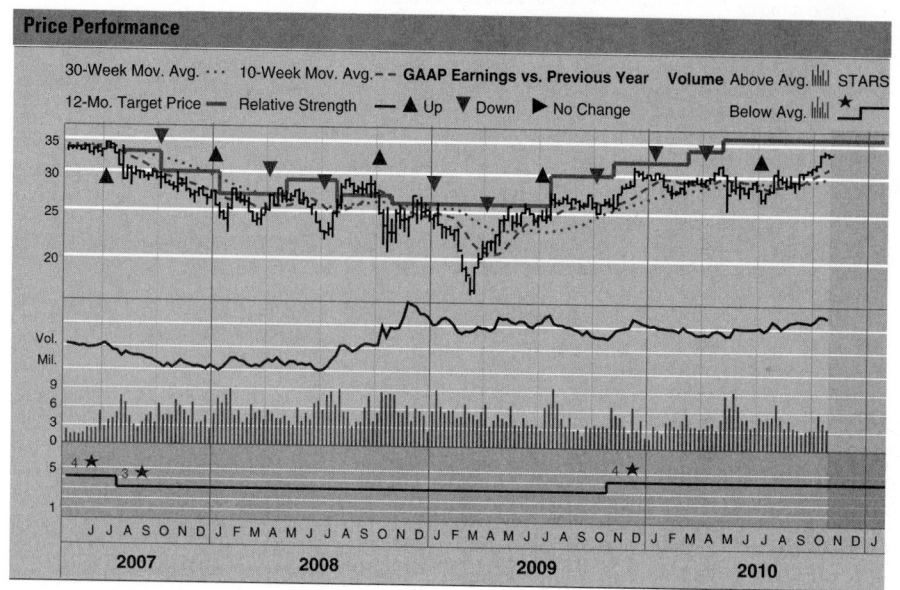

Options: ASE, CBOE, P

Analysis prepared by **Stewart Scharf** on October 19, 2010, when the stock traded at **$ 33.44.**

Highlights

➤ We expect organic sales (before Alcan's Food Americas unit and positive foreign currency) to advance in the mid-single digits in 2010, driven by increased demand for flexible packaging products in the Americas, and improving pressure-sensitive materials sales. We see innovative new products and recent acquisitions adding to total growth, with contributions from meat and cheese, and health and hygiene.

➤ In our view, gross margins will expand during 2010 and into 2011, from 20% in 2009, based on an improved sales mix from new higher-margin products, and better margins for graphics and technical pressure-sensitive products. Following a lag, pricing pass-throughs should offset higher, albeit stabilizing, resin costs. We look for operating margins (EBITDA) to widen modestly from 13.2% in 2009, as a decline in overhead costs due to accelerated synergies outweighs lower margins from Food Americas.

➤ We project an effective tax rate for 2010 of 36%, and operating EPS of $2.20 (before at least $0.27 of acquisition-related and other charges), advancing 14% to $2.50 in 2011.

Investment Rationale/Risk

➤ Our buy recommendation is based on our valuation metrics, along with what we see as the company's favorable cash flow and capital structure. Although BMS's debt ratio has risen due to financing related to its Alcan unit acquisition, we believe the deal will be a good strategic fit and cash generation will be sufficient to pay down debt.

➤ Risks to our recommendation and target price include another surge in commodity prices, softer global demand, and negative foreign exchange rates. We have some corporate governance concerns based on the CEO being a party to one or more related-party transactions.

➤ With the stock's recent dividend yield of 2.8%, versus 2% for the S&P 500 Index, and BMS's solid earnings track record, we apply an above five-year historical forward P/E of 18X to our 2010 EPS estimate to derive a value of $40. Based on our DCF analysis, the stock has an intrinsic value of $32, assuming a 3% terminal growth rate and an 8.3% weighted average cost of capital. Blending these valuations, we arrive at our 12-month target price of $36.

Qualitative Risk Assessment

LOW	MEDIUM	HIGH

Our risk assessment partly reflects challenging global economic conditions, volatile raw material prices and possible difficulty in integrating acquisitions. BMS has an S&P Quality Ranking of B+, which indicates average long-term earnings and dividend growth.

Quantitative Evaluations

S&P Quality Ranking   B+

D	C	B-	B	B+	A-	A	A+

Relative Strength Rank   STRONG

72

LOWEST = 1   HIGHEST = 99

Revenue/Earnings Data

Revenue (Million $)

	1Q	2Q	3Q	4Q	Year
2010	1,022	1,270	--	--	--
2009	843.4	866.4	898.9	905.9	3,515
2008	947.3	980.0	984.3	867.9	3,779
2007	909.1	921.8	905.7	912.7	3,649
2006	901.7	933.8	903.3	900.6	3,639
2005	831.9	879.9	870.1	892.1	3,474

Earnings Per Share ($)

	1Q	2Q	3Q	4Q	Year
2010	0.27	0.52	E0.58	E0.56	E2.20
2009	0.36	0.47	0.33	0.26	1.40
2008	0.42	0.46	0.44	0.33	1.65
2007	0.45	0.47	0.40	0.42	1.74
2006	0.35	0.46	0.45	0.39	1.65
2005	0.30	0.38	0.41	0.42	1.51

Fiscal year ended Dec. 31. Next earnings report expected: Late October. EPS Estimates based on S&P Operating Earnings; historical GAAP earnings are as reported.

Dividend Data (Dates: mm/dd Payment Date: mm/dd/yy)

Amount ($)	Date Decl.	Ex-Div. Date	Stk. of Record	Payment Date
0.225	10/29	11/12	11/16	12/01/09
0.230	02/04	02/11	02/16	03/01/10
0.230	05/06	05/13	05/17	06/01/10
0.230	07/29	08/11	08/13	09/01/10

Dividends have been paid since 1922. Source: Company reports.

Please read the Required Disclosures and Analyst Certification on the last page of this report.

The McGraw-Hill Companies

Bemis Co Inc

Business Summary October 19, 2010

CORPORATE OVERVIEW. Bemis Co., a leading North American producer of flexible packaging products, as well as pressure-sensitive materials, focuses primarily on the food industry (about 60% of sales). BMS expects combined food packaging sales going forward following the acquisition of Food Americas to range from 65% to 70% of total sales. Markets also include the chemicals, agribusiness, pharmaceutical, personal care products, electronics, automotive and graphic industries. BMS has 50 manufacturing plants (five leased) in 13 U.S. states and 10 countries.

Although BMS focuses on marketing its products in the U.S. (65% of 2009 net sales) and Europe (16%), it has broadened its reach to South America (17%), as well as Southeast Asia and Mexico, due to strong demand for barrier films to extend the shelf life of perishable foods. Canada accounted for 0.3% of sales, while 2.7% came from other regions.

The Flexible Packaging Products segment (85% of net sales in 2009; $385 million of operating profits) produces a wide range of consumer and industrial packaging products, including high barrier, polyethylene and paper products. High barrier products, which comprise more than 50% of net sales, include flexible polymer film structures and barrier laminates for food, medical and personal care products.

The Pressure Sensitive Materials segment (15%; $14 million in operating profits) produces printing products, decorative and sheet products, and technical products.

Flexible packaging competitors include Sealed Air, Sonoco Products, Amcor and Hood Packaging. Pressure-sensitive materials competitors include Avery Dennison, Acucote, Minnesota Mining and Manufacturing (3M), Ricoh, FLEXcon and Spinnaker Industries.

In January 2005, the company acquired majority ownership of Brazil-based Dixie Toga, a leading South American packaging company, for $250 million in cash (less than 6X Dixie's 2004 EBITDA). Dixie had annual sales of over $450 million in 2005. BMS controls 85% of Dixie's preferred shares.

BMS contributed $30 million to its U.S. pension plans in the second quarter of 2009, reflecting a lower funded status due to lower assets and increased liabilities. It contributed $15 million to the plan in early 2010, with no additional contributions likely during the year.

Company Financials Fiscal Year Ended Dec. 31

Per Share Data ($)	2009	2008	2007	2006	2005	2004	2003	2002	2001	2000
Tangible Book Value	9.90	6.72	9.70	7.31	6.29	7.48	5.81	4.11	4.39	4.76
Cash Flow	2.96	3.26	3.28	3.08	2.98	2.88	2.56	2.65	2.49	2.24
Earnings	1.40	1.65	1.74	1.65	1.51	1.67	1.37	1.54	1.32	1.22
S&P Core Earnings	1.39	1.40	1.67	1.64	1.48	1.65	1.32	1.28	1.02	NA
Dividends	0.90	0.66	0.84	0.76	0.72	0.64	0.56	0.52	0.50	0.48
Payout Ratio	64%	40%	48%	46%	48%	38%	41%	34%	38%	39%
Prices:High	31.41	29.70	36.53	34.99	32.50	29.49	25.58	29.12	26.24	19.66
Prices:Low	16.85	20.62	25.53	27.86	23.20	23.24	19.67	19.70	14.34	11.47
P/E Ratio:High	22	18	21	21	22	18	19	19	20	16
P/E Ratio:Low	12	12	15	17	15	14	14	13	11	9

Income Statement Analysis (Million $)	2009	2008	2007	2006	2005	2004	2003	2002	2001	2000
Revenue	3,515	3,779	3,649	3,639	3,474	2,834	2,635	2,369	2,293	2,165
Operating Income	464	443	468	492	472	420	384	401	384	363
Depreciation	159	163	159	152	151	131	128	119	124	108
Interest Expense	42.1	42.0	54.5	49.3	38.7	15.5	12.6	15.4	30.3	31.6
Pretax Income	245	269	290	289	282	294	240	268	228	212
Effective Tax Rate	36.5%	35.9%	36.0%	37.8%	40.3%	38.7%	38.4%	37.9%	38.2%	38.2%
Net Income	150	166	182	176	163	180	147	166	140	131
S&P Core Earnings	144	142	174	176	160	179	142	137	108	NA

Balance Sheet & Other Financial Data (Million $)	2009	2008	2007	2006	2005	2004	2003	2002	2001	2000
Cash	1,066	48.3	147	112	91.1	93.9	76.5	56.4	35.1	28.9
Current Assets	2,005	983	1,137	1,094	988	874	752	722	587	640
Total Assets	3,929	2,827	3,191	3,039	2,965	2,487	2,293	2,257	1,923	1,889
Current Liabilities	525	422	535	555	474	375	316	326	238	495
Long Term Debt	1,228	660	843	722	790	534	583	718	595	438
Common Equity	1,807	1,342	1,562	1,472	1,349	1,308	1,139	959	886	799
Total Capital	3,105	2,147	2,533	2,358	2,336	2,019	1,878	1,788	1,606	1,342
Capital Expenditures	89.2	121	179	159	187	135	106	91.0	117	100
Cash Flow	306	329	341	329	313	311	275	285	264	239
Current Ratio	3.9	2.3	2.1	2.0	2.1	2.3	2.4	2.2	2.5	1.3
% Long Term Debt of Capitalization	39.5	30.7	32.6	30.6	33.8	26.4	31.1	40.2	37.1	32.6
% Net Income of Revenue	4.3	4.4	5.0	4.8	4.7	6.3	5.6	7.0	6.1	6.0
% Return on Assets	4.5	5.5	5.8	5.9	6.0	7.5	6.5	7.9	7.4	7.6
% Return on Equity	9.5	11.5	12.0	12.5	12.2	14.7	14.0	17.9	16.7	17.1

Data as orig reptd.; bef. results of disc opers/spec. items. Per share data adj. for stk. divs.; EPS diluted. E-Estimated. NA-Not Available. NM-Not Meaningful. NR-Not Ranked. UR-Under Review.

Office: One Neenah Center, 4th Floor PO Box 669, Neenah, WI 54957-0669.
Telephone: 920-727-4100.
Website: http://www.bemis.com
Chrmn: J.H. Curler

Pres & CEO: H.J. Theisen
CFO: S.B. Ullem
CTO: R. Germonprez
Chief Acctg Officer & Cntlr: S.A. Jaffy

Investor Contact: M.E. Miller (920-527-5045)
Board Members: W. J. Bolton, J. H. Curler, D. S. Haffner, B. L. Johnson, T. Manganello, R. D. O'Shaughnessy, P. S. Peercy, E. N. Perry, W. J. Scholle, H. J. Theisen, H. A. Van Deursen, P. G. Weaver, G. C. Wulf

Founded: 1858
Domicile: Missouri
Employees: 20,400

Berkshire Hathaway Inc.

STANDARD &POOR'S

S&P Recommendation HOLD ★★★☆☆

Price $83.34 (as of Oct 22, 2010)	**12-Mo. Target Price** $88.00	**Investment Style** Large-Cap Blend

GICS Sector Financials
Sub-Industry Property & Casualty Insurance

Summary This holding company has interests in insurance, energy, financial services, publishing, retailing and manufacturing. Its investment portfolio included more than $59 billion of marketable equitable securities as of December 31, 2009.

Key Stock Statistics (Source S&P, Vickers, company reports)

52-Wk Range	$85.86– 64.72	S&P Oper. EPS 2010E	4.63	Market Capitalization(B)	$211.354	Beta	0.52
Trailing 12-Month EPS	$5.00	S&P Oper. EPS 2011E	5.00	Yield (%)	Nil	S&P 3-Yr. Proj. EPS CAGR(%)	NM
Trailing 12-Month P/E	16.7	P/E on S&P Oper. EPS 2010E	18.0	Dividend Rate/Share	Nil	S&P Credit Rating	AA+
$10K Invested 5 Yrs Ago	$14,941	Common Shares Outstg. (M)	1,007.6	Institutional Ownership (%)	22		

Price Performance

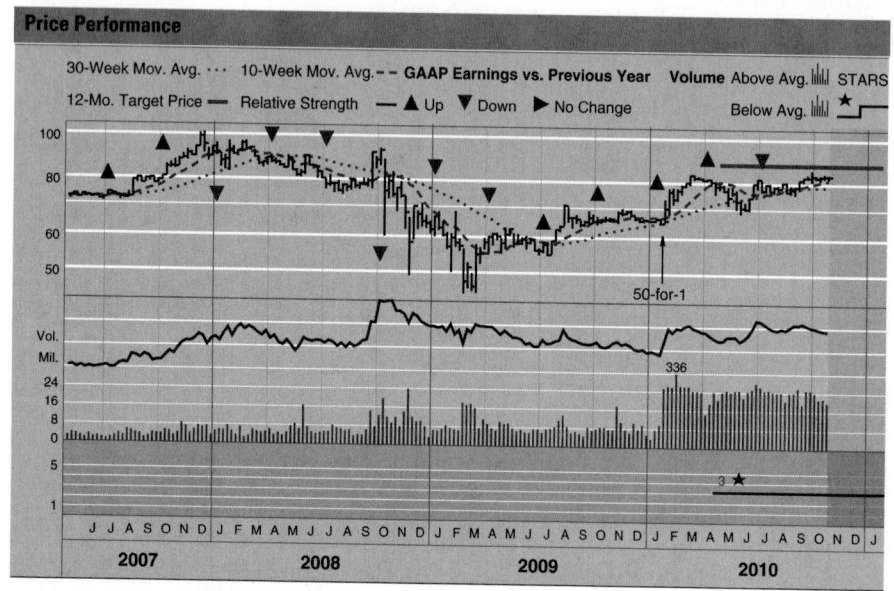

30-Week Mov. Avg. · · · 10-Week Mov. Avg. - - **GAAP Earnings vs. Previous Year** Volume Above Avg. STARS
12-Mo. Target Price — Relative Strength — ▲ Up ▼ Down ▶ No Change Below Avg. ★

50-for-1

336

3 ★

J J A S O N D J F M A M J J A S O N D J F M A M J J A S O N D J F M A M J J A S O N D J
2007   2008   2009   2010

Analysis prepared by **Cathy A. Seifert** on August 04, 2010, when the stock traded at **$ 80.76**.

Highlights

➤ We expect operating revenues in 2010 to advance by approximately 6%, as contributions from recent acquisitions are offset by economic-driven weakness in other areas (particularly in the first half of the year). We look for revenue growth in the insurance area (Berkshire's largest unit) to be above industry averages, primarily reflecting market share gains at GEICO and increased writings at certain reinsurance units.

➤ We project underwriting margins at GEICO to remain under pressure in 2010, reflecting a higher level of policy acquisition costs and some mixed claim trends. Underwriting margins in catastrophe-exposed lines of business may also come under some pressure in 2010 amid a forecasted resumption of "normal" levels of catastrophe losses. Margin improvements at other units (largely due to cost cuts) will likely enhance operating profits.

➤ We forecast operating earnings of $4.50 per share in 2010 and $5.00 per share in 2011, versus the $3.25 a share of operating earnings we calculate the company reported in 2009.

Investment Rationale/Risk

➤ Our Hold opinion reflects our view that the shares are appropriately valued on both a price/earnings and price/tangible book value basis. At current levels, the shares are trading at a premium to many of the company's closest peers (though peer comparisons are difficult given Berkshire's conglomerate-like business mix) and at the upper end of historical ranges.

➤ Risks to our opinion and target price include significant erosion in claim and premium pricing trends, and a more prolonged economic downturn, which would likely continue to dampen demand for many of Berkshire's products.

➤ Our 12-month target price of $88 assumes that the shares will trade at 19.6X our 2010 operating EPS forecast. This represents the upper end of Berkshire's historical average multiple, and is a premium to most of the company's insurance and reinsurance peers. We believe this premium is warranted in light of what we see as Berkshire's superior financial strength. Our target price also assumes the shares will trade at more than 2X estimated 2010 tangible book value per share.

Qualitative Risk Assessment

LOW	MEDIUM	HIGH

Our risk assessment reflects our positive view of the company's diversified revenue and earnings base and strong management team, offset by its exposure to catastrophe and investment losses. We also view chairman and CEO Warren Buffett's advanced age as a risk factor for the shares.

Quantitative Evaluations

S&P Quality Ranking   B+

D	C	B-	B	B+	A-	A	A+

Relative Strength Rank   MODERATE

48

LOWEST = 1   HIGHEST = 99

Revenue/Earnings Data

Revenue (Million $)

	1Q	2Q	3Q	4Q	Year
2010	32,037	31,709	--	--	--
2009	22,784	29,607	29,904	30,198	112,493
2008	25,175	30,093	27,926	24,592	107,786
2007	32,918	27,347	25,387	28,043	118,245
2006	22,763	24,185	2,536	26,231	98,539
2005	17,634	18,128	20,533	25,368	81,663

Earnings Per Share ($)

	1Q	2Q	3Q	4Q	Year
2010	1.51	0.80	E1.21	E1.25	E4.63
2009	-0.66	1.42	1.39	1.31	3.46
2008	0.40	1.24	0.45	0.05	2.15
2007	1.12	1.35	1.96	1.27	5.70
2006	1.00	1.01	1.20	1.55	4.76
2005	0.59	0.63	0.25	2.22	3.69

Fiscal year ended Dec. 31. Next earnings report expected: Early November. EPS Estimates based on S&P Operating Earnings; historical GAAP earnings are as reported.

Dividend Data (Dates: mm/dd Payment Date: mm/dd/yy)

Amount ($)	Date Decl.	Ex-Div. Date	Stk. of Record	Payment Date
50-for-l	11/03	--	--	01/21/10

Source: Company reports.

The McGraw-Hill Companies

Berkshire Hathaway Inc.

STANDARD &POOR'S

Business Summary August 04, 2010

CORPORATE OVERVIEW. Berkshire Hathaway is an insurance-based conglomerate. During 2009, segment operating revenues totaled $110.8 billion (down from $115.3 billion in 2008) and were derived as follows: GEICO Corp. 12%, General Re 5%, Berkshire Hathaway Reinsurance Group 6%, Berkshire Hathaway Primary Group 2%, investment income 5%, financial products 4%, Marmon 5%, McLane Company 28%, MidAmerican 10%, Shaw Industries 4%, and other businesses 19%.

The company has grown through acquisitions. On February 12, 2010, it acquired the 77.5% of Burlington Northern Santa Fe Corporation (BNSF) it did not already own for $100 a share (60% in cash and 40% in stock) for total consideration of $26.5 billion. One of its more significant transactions was the December 1998 acquisition of General Re Corp., the largest U.S.-based reinsurance group, in a stock transaction valued at about $22 billion. Among the more significant transactions in 2006 were the March purchase of PacifiCorp (a regulated electric utility) for $5.1 billion in cash and the July acquisition of 80% of Iscar Metalworking Companies for approximately $5 billion in cash. Berkshire acquired 60% of Marmon Holdings, Inc. (a private conglomerate) for $4.5 billion in March 2008. Berkshire acquired another 4.4% interest in Marmon in April 2008 for $329 million, and plans to acquire the remaining 35.6% of Marmon between 2011 and 2014. In late 2008, Berkshire invested $6.5 billion in

subordinated notes and preferred stock of Wm. Wrigley, Jr. Co. in connection with Mars, Inc's. acquisition of Wrigley.

Berkshire's common equity holdings had a market value of more than $59 billion at year-end 2009. The largest holdings were Coca-Cola (with a market value of $11.4 billion), Wells Fargo ($9.0 billion), American Express Co. ($6.1 billion) and Procter and Gamble ($5 billion). In October 2008, the company paid $8 billion to acquire newly issued 10% perpetual preferred stock of Goldman Sachs Group (GS) and General Electric (GE); and warrants (expiring in October 2013) to acquire up to 43.5 million GS common shares at $115 per share and up to 134.8 million GE common shares at $22.25 a share. In March 2009, Berkshire acquired a 12% convertible perpetual capital instrument without maturity and redemption date, issued by Swiss Re for $2.7 billion that is convertible into 120 million Swiss Re common shares. In April 2009, Berkshire acquired 3 million series A cumulative convertible perpetual preferred shares of Dow Chemical Co. (DOW) for $3 billion. Each share is convertible into 24.201 DOW common shares, subject to certain conditions.

Company Financials Fiscal Year Ended Dec. 31

Per Share Data ($)	2009	2008	2007	2006	2005	2004	2003	2002	2001	2000
Tangible Book Value	41.72	32.49	37.84	32.91	29.35	27.24	23.70	18.13	15.94	18.72
Operating Earnings	NA	NA	NA	NA	NA	NA	NA	NA	NA	NA
Earnings	3.46	2.15	5.70	4.76	3.69	3.17	3.54	1.86	0.35	1.46
S&P Core Earnings	4.28	2.21	4.20	4.30	2.06	2.67	2.72	1.70	-0.02	NA
Dividends	Nil	Nil	Nil	Nil	Nil	Nil	Nil	Nil	Nil	Nil
Payout Ratio	Nil	Nil	Nil	Nil	Nil	Nil	Nil	Nil	Nil	Nil
Prices:High	71.38	97.16	101.18	76.50	61.34	63.90	56.48	52.40	50.50	47.50
Prices:Low	44.82	49.02	69.20	56.78	52.24	53.70	40.30	38.50	39.54	27.02
P/E Ratio:High	21	45	18	16	17	20	16	28	NM	33
P/E Ratio:Low	13	23	12	12	14	17	11	21	NM	19

Income Statement Analysis (Million $)	2009	2008	2007	2006	2005	2004	2003	2002	2001	2000
Premium Income	27,884	25,525	31,783	23,964	21,997	21,085	NA	19,182	17,905	19,343
Net Investment Income	7,131	6,756	6,696	NA	NA	NA	4,191	NA	2,765	2,686
Other Revenue	77,478	75,505	79,766	74,575	59,666	53,297	59,668	17,984	16,998	11,947
Total Revenue	112,493	107,786	118,245	98,539	81,663	74,382	63,859	42,353	37,668	33,976
Pretax Income	11,979	7,574	20,161	16,778	12,791	10,936	12,020	6,435	1,469	5,587
Net Operating Income	NA	NA	NA	NA	NA	NA	NA	NA	-47.0	936
Net Income	8,055	4,994	13,213	11,015	8,528	7,308	8,151	4,286	795	3,328
S&P Core Earnings	9,947	5,127	9,739	9,954	4,767	6,148	6,275	3,919	-43.1	NA

Balance Sheet & Other Financial Data (Million $)	2009	2008	2007	2006	2005	2004	2003	2002	2001	2000
Cash & Equivalent	30,558	25,539	44,329	43,743	44,660	43,427	35,957	12,748	5,313	5,263
Premiums Due	5,295	4,961	4,215	NA	NA	NA	NA	NA	NA	NA
Investment Assets:Bonds	37,131	31,632	31,571	28,312	30,855	31,305	26,116	NA	36,509	32,567
Investment Assets:Stocks	56,562	49,073	74,999	61,533	46,721	37,717	35,287	NA	28,675	37,619
Investment Assets:Loans	13,989	13,942	12,359	NA	NA	NA	NA	NA	Nil	NA
Investment Assets:Total	140,282	116,182	118,929	87,738	79,269	66,876	78,029	87,356	67,158	71,823
Deferred Policy Costs	NA	NA	NA	NA	NA	NA	NA	NA	NA	NA
Total Assets	297,119	267,399	273,160	248,437	198,325	188,874	180,559	169,544	162,752	135,792
Debt	37,909	36,882	33,826	27,450	12,523	7,192	9,119	18,270	1,230	1,392
Common Equity	131,102	109,267	120,733	108,419	91,484	85,900	77,596	64,037	57,950	61,724
Property & Casualty:Loss Ratio	77.0	74.8	72.2	NA	NA	NA	NA	NA	79.9	85.7
Property & Casualty:Expense Ratio	18.2	17.9	18.4	NA	NA	NA	NA	NA	16.5	18.3
Property & Casualty Combined Ratio	95.2	92.7	90.6	88.1	87.9	89.1	94.2	93.8	96.4	104.0
% Return on Revenue	7.2	4.6	11.2	11.2	10.4	9.8	12.8	10.1	2.1	9.8
% Return on Equity	6.7	4.3	11.5	11.0	9.6	8.9	11.5	7.0	1.3	5.6

Data as orig reptd.; bef. results of disc opers/spec. items. Per share data adj. for stk. divs.; EPS diluted. Tangible book value per share based on combined A & B shares. E-Estimated. NA-Not Available. NM-Not Meaningful. NR-Not Ranked. UR-Under Review.

Office: 3555 Farnam St, Omaha, NE 68131.
Telephone: 402-346-1400.
Website: http://www.berkshirehathaway.com
Chrmn & CEO: W.E. Buffett

Vice Chrmn: C. Munger
SVP & CFO: M.D. Hamburg
Chief Acctg Officer & Cntlr: D.J. Jaksich
Secy: F.N. Krutter

Investor Contact: M. Hamburg (402-346-1400)
Board Members: H. G. Buffett, W. E. Buffett, S. B. Burke, S. Decker, W. H. Gates, III, D. S. Gottesman, C. Guyman, D. R. Keough, C. Munger, T. S. Murphy, R. L. Olson, W. Scott, Jr.

Founded: 1889
Domicile: Delaware
Employees: 222,000

Best Buy Co. Inc.

STANDARD &POOR'S

S&P Recommendation	BUY ★★★★☆		Price $42.74 (as of Oct 22, 2010)	12-Mo. Target Price $50.00	Investment Style Large-Cap Growth

GICS Sector Consumer Discretionary
Sub-Industry Computer & Electronics Retail

Summary This leading retailer of consumer electronics and entertainment software operates approximately 4,000 stores in the U.S., Canada, China and Europe.

Key Stock Statistics (Source S&P, Vickers, company reports)

52-Wk Range	$48.83– 30.90	S&P Oper. EPS 2011E	3.60	Market Capitalization(B)	$17.004	Beta		1.46
Trailing 12-Month EPS	$3.32	S&P Oper. EPS 2012E	3.91	Yield (%)	1.40	S&P 3-Yr. Proj. EPS CAGR(%)		8
Trailing 12-Month P/E	12.9	P/E on S&P Oper. EPS 2011E	11.9	Dividend Rate/Share	$0.60	S&P Credit Rating		BBB-
$10K Invested 5 Yrs Ago	$10,310	Common Shares Outstg. (M)	397.8	Institutional Ownership (%)	72			

Price Performance

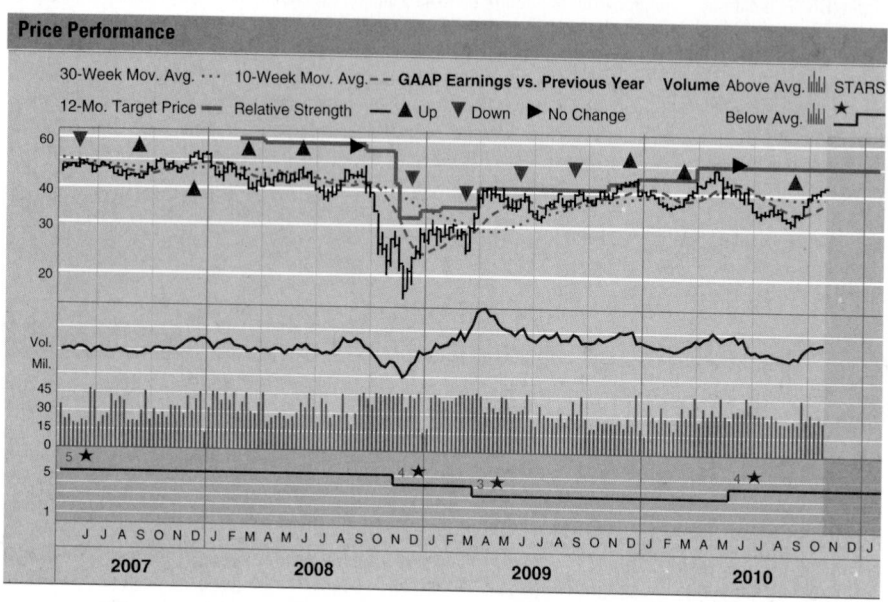

30-Week Mov. Avg. ··· 10-Week Mov. Avg. -- **GAAP Earnings vs. Previous Year** Volume Above Avg. STARS
12-Mo. Target Price — Relative Strength — ▲ Up ▼ Down ▶ No Change Below Avg.

2007 2008 2009 2010

Options: ASE, CBOE, P, Ph

Analysis prepared by **Michael Souers** on September 17, 2010, when the stock traded at **$ 36.94**.

Highlights

➤ We view BBY as the best-of-class U.S. consumer electronics retailer, based on its digital product focus, knowledgeable sales staff, and effective marketing campaigns. We think BBY's focus on advanced TVs, notebook computers, video gaming devices and mobile phones will support solid revenue growth near term.

➤ We project a 4.5% increase in revenues for FY 11 (Feb.), following a 10% advance in FY 10. We expect this growth to be driven by the opening of approximately 50-55 net new Best Buy stores worldwide, 75-100 Best Buy Mobile standalone stores and 10-15 Five Star stores in China. We also project an approximately 1% increase in comparable-store sales, given our forecast that consumer spending will remain pressured by macro factors. We expect a modest increase in operating margins, driven by a product mix shift and solid expense management.

➤ After taxes at an effective rate of 38.0% and flat interest expense, we project FY 11 EPS of $3.60, a 14% increase from the $3.15 the company earned in FY 10, excluding a restructuring charge. We see FY 12 EPS of $3.91.

Investment Rationale/Risk

➤ We favor BBY's recent decision to curb capital spending and strictly manage SG&A expenses in the current challenging macroeconomic environment. We also expect continued market share gains as BBY's customer-centric model should enable the company to continue to differentiate itself in a competitive marketplace. However, we are concerned that the industry faces a potential saturation of flat-panel TVs in the near term, and we think mass adoption of revolutionary products such as 3-D TVs may be several years away. Following a recent decline in the stock price, we think the shares are attractively valued at under 10X our FY 12 EPS estimate, a modest discount to historical averages and to the S&P 500.

➤ Risks to our recommendation and target price include sharp deterioration in the economic climate and consumer confidence, and failure to successfully execute strategic objectives.

➤ Our 12-month target price of $50, about 13X our FY 12 EPS projection, is based on our DCF analysis, which assumes a weighted average cost of capital of 10.9% and a terminal growth rate of 3.5%.

Qualitative Risk Assessment

LOW	**MEDIUM**	HIGH

Our risk assessment reflects what we view as BBY's strong balance sheet, sizable market share, numerous suppliers and buyers, and a history of profitability, offset by a highly competitive environment for consumer electronics retailing, with numerous rivals and strong price competition.

Quantitative Evaluations

S&P Quality Ranking B+

D	C	B-	B	**B+**	A-	A	A+

Relative Strength Rank STRONG

85

LOWEST = 1 HIGHEST = 99

Revenue/Earnings Data

Revenue (Million $)

	1Q	2Q	3Q	4Q	Year
2011	10,787	11,339	--	--	--
2010	10,095	11,022	12,024	16,553	49,694
2009	8,990	9,801	11,500	14,724	45,015
2008	7,927	8,750	9,928	13,418	40,023
2007	6,959	7,603	8,473	12,899	35,934
2006	6,118	6,702	7,335	10,693	30,848

Earnings Per Share ($)

2011	0.36	0.60	E0.67	E1.98	E3.60
2010	0.36	0.37	0.53	1.82	3.10
2009	0.43	0.48	0.13	1.35	2.39
2008	0.39	0.48	0.53	1.71	3.12
2007	0.47	0.47	0.31	1.55	2.79
2006	0.34	0.37	0.28	1.29	2.27

Fiscal year ended Feb. 28. Next earnings report expected: Mid December. EPS Estimates based on S&P Operating Earnings; historical GAAP earnings are as reported.

Dividend Data (Dates: mm/dd Payment Date: mm/dd/yy)

Amount ($)	Date Decl.	Ex-Div. Date	Stk. of Record	Payment Date
0.140	03/26	04/13	04/15	05/06/10
0.140	06/16	07/01	07/06	07/27/10
0.150	06/24	10/01	10/05	10/26/10

Dividends have been paid since 2003. Source: Company reports.

Please read the Required Disclosures and Analyst Certification on the last page of this report.

The McGraw-Hill Companies

STANDARD & POOR'S

Best Buy Co. Inc.

Business Summary September 17, 2010

CORPORATE OVERVIEW. This leading consumer electronics retailer operated, as of February 27, 2010, 1,069 Best Buy stores, 74 Best Buy Mobile stand-alone stores, 35 Pacific Sales showrooms, eight Magnolia Audio Video stores and six Geek Squad stand-alone stores in the U.S. BBY also operated 887 Car-phone Warehouse and 1,566 The Phone House Stores in Europe, 64 Canada Best Buy stores, 144 Future Shop stores in Canada, 158 Five Star stores in China, six Best Buy China stores, five Best Buy Mexico stores and one Best Buy Turkey store as of February 27, 2010.

U.S. Best Buy stores average approximately 39,000 retail square feet, and offer products in six revenue categories: consumer electronics (39% of FY 10 (Feb.) revenues), home office (34%), entertainment software (16%), appliances (4%), services (6%), and other (1%). Best Buy's largest category, consumer electronics, includes products such as televisions, digital cameras and accessories, digital camcorders and accessories, e-readers, DVD players, MP3 players and accessories, musical instruments, navigation products, home the-

ater audio systems and components, and mobile electronics including car stereo and satellite radio products.

CORPORATE STRATEGY. BBY's business strategy centers on meeting individual consumer electronics needs with end-to-end solutions, which involves greater employee involvement and increased services. BBY is committed to scaling BBY customer-centricity across the organization, and completed the transition of all remaining stores to the customer-centric operating model in FY 08. In FY 11, BBY plans to open 50-55 new Best Buy stores, the majority of which will be in the U.S., 75-100 small-format stores, primarily Best Buy Mobile stand-alone stores, and 10-15 Five Star stores in China.

Company Financials Fiscal Year Ended Feb. 28

Per Share Data ($)	2010	2009	2008	2007	2006	2005	2004	2003	2002	2001
Tangible Book Value	8.19	4.70	7.99	10.82	9.60	7.91	5.97	4.70	3.65	3.07
Cash Flow	5.25	4.25	4.40	3.80	3.16	2.76	2.41	1.91	1.91	1.18
Earnings	3.10	2.39	3.12	2.79	2.27	1.86	1.63	1.27	1.18	0.83
S&P Core Earnings	3.10	2.77	3.12	2.76	2.27	1.77	1.45	1.11	1.08	0.76
Dividends	0.56	0.54	0.46	0.36	0.31	0.50	0.27	Nil	Nil	Nil
Payout Ratio	18%	23%	15%	13%	14%	38%	17%	Nil	Nil	Nil
Calendar Year	2009	2008	2007	2006	2005	2004	2003	2002	2001	2000
Prices:High	45.55	52.98	53.90	59.50	18.03	41.47	41.80	35.83	33.42	39.50
Prices:Low	23.97	16.42	41.85	43.32	14.84	29.25	15.77	11.33	12.36	9.33
P/E Ratio:High	15	22	17	21	14	22	26	28	28	48
P/E Ratio:Low	8	7	13	16	11	16	10	9	10	11

Income Statement Analysis (Million $)										
Revenue	49,694	45,015	40,023	35,934	30,848	27,433	24,547	20,946	19,597	15,327
Operating Income	3,213	2,807	2,746	2,508	2,100	1,901	1,699	1,320	1,246	772
Depreciation	926	793	585	509	456	459	385	310	309	167
Interest Expense	94.0	94.0	62.0	Nil	30.0	44.0	31.0	25.0	2.00	6.90
Pretax Income	2,196	1,707	2,225	2,130	1,721	1,443	1,296	1,014	936	642
Effective Tax Rate	36.5%	39.5%	36.6%	35.3%	33.8%	35.3%	38.3%	38.7%	39.1%	38.3%
Net Income	1,317	1,003	1,407	1,377	1,140	934	800	622	570	396
S&P Core Earnings	1,317	1,163	1,407	1,364	1,140	873	704	538	512	361

Balance Sheet & Other Financial Data (Million $)										
Cash	1,916	498	1,438	1,205	681	470	2,600	1,914	1,855	747
Current Assets	10,566	8,192	7,342	9,081	7,985	6,903	5,724	4,867	4,611	2,929
Total Assets	18,302	15,826	12,758	13,570	11,864	10,294	8,652	7,663	7,375	4,840
Current Liabilities	8,978	8,435	6,769	6,301	6,056	4,959	4,501	3,793	3,730	2,715
Long Term Debt	1,104	1,126	627	590	178	528	482	828	813	181
Common Equity	6,964	4,643	4,484	6,201	5,257	4,449	3,422	2,730	2,521	1,822
Total Capital	8,103	6,071	5,151	6,826	5,435	4,977	3,904	3,558	3,334	2,003
Capital Expenditures	615	1,303	797	733	648	502	545	725	627	658
Cash Flow	2,243	1,796	1,992	1,886	1,596	1,393	1,185	932	925	563
Current Ratio	1.2	1.0	1.1	1.4	1.3	1.4	1.3	1.3	1.2	1.1
% Long Term Debt of Capitalization	13.6	18.6	12.2	8.6	3.3	10.6	12.3	23.3	24.4	9.0
% Net Income of Revenue	2.7	2.2	3.5	3.8	3.7	3.4	3.3	3.0	2.9	2.6
% Return on Assets	7.7	7.0	10.7	10.8	10.3	9.9	9.8	8.3	9.3	10.1
% Return on Equity	22.7	22.0	26.3	24.0	23.5	23.7	26.0	23.8	26.2	27.1

Data as orig reptd.; bef. results of disc opers/spec. items. Per share data adj. for stk. divs.; EPS diluted. E-Estimated. NA-Not Available. NM-Not Meaningful. NR-Not Ranked. UR-Under Review.

Office: 7601 Penn Avenue South, Richfield, MN 55423-3683.
Telephone: 612-291-1000.
Email: moneytalk@bestbuy.com
Website: http://www.bestbuy.com

Chrmn: R.M. Schulze
CEO: B.J. Dunn
EVP & CFO: J.L. Muehlbauer
EVP & Chief Admin Officer: T.R. Sheehan

SVP & Treas: R. Robinson
Investor Contact: J. Driscoll (612-291-6110)
Board Members: L. M. Caputo, B. J. Dunn, K. J. Higgins, R. James, E. S. Kaplan, S. Khosla, G. L. Mikan, III, M. H. Paull, R. M. Rebolledo, R. M. Schulze, H. Tyabji, G. R. Vittecoq

Founded: 1966
Domicile: Minnesota
Employees: 180,000

The McGraw-Hill Companies

Big Lots Inc

STANDARD &POOR'S

S&P Recommendation   BUY ★★★★☆

Price	12-Mo. Target Price	Investment Style
$33.50 (as of Oct 22, 2010)	$38.00	Large-Cap Blend

GICS Sector Consumer Discretionary
Sub-Industry General Merchandise Stores

Summary This leading broadline closeout retailer has over 1,370 Big Lots stores in 47 states.

Key Stock Statistics (Source S&P, Vickers, company reports)

52-Wk Range	$41.42–23.04	S&P Oper. EPS 2011**E**	2.85	Market Capitalization(B)	$2.531	Beta		1.14
Trailing 12-Month EPS	$2.81	S&P Oper. EPS 2012**E**	3.20	Yield (%)	Nil	S&P 3-Yr. Proj. EPS CAGR(%)		15
Trailing 12-Month P/E	11.9	P/E on S&P Oper. EPS 2011**E**	11.8	Dividend Rate/Share	Nil	S&P Credit Rating		BBB
$10K Invested 5 Yrs Ago	$28,979	Common Shares Outstg. (M)	75.6	Institutional Ownership (%)	NM			

Price Performance

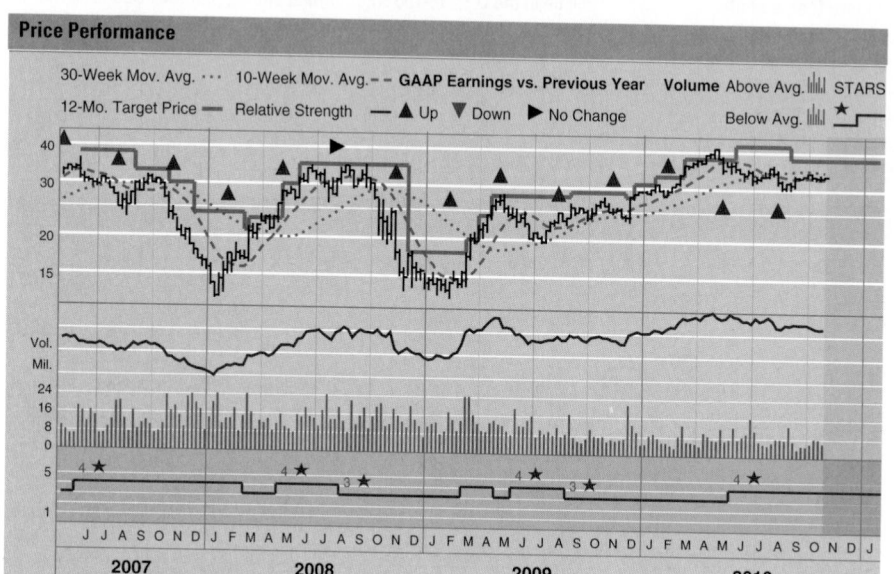

30-Week Mov. Avg. · · · ·   10-Week Mov. Avg. – –   **GAAP Earnings vs. Previous Year**   Volume Above Avg. ⅢⅢⅢ STARS
12-Mo. Target Price —   Relative Strength —   ▲ Up ▼ Down ▶ No Change   Below Avg. ⅢⅢⅢ ★

Options: P, Ph

Analysis prepared by **Jason N. Asaeda** on August 25, 2010, when the stock traded at **$ 30.34**.

Highlights

▶ In FY 11 (Jan.), we anticipate an increased focus on traffic-driving brand-name closeouts and "treasure hunt" items, and improved product quality and in-stock levels, particularly on consumables. We also look for a recovery in consumer demand for more discretionary-purchase categories to support a 4% same-store sales increase. In addition, we expect modest growth in selling square footage based on BIG's plan to open 80 new stores (40 net of closings), up from 52 new stores (22 net of closings) opened in FY 10. We believe the company will focus new store openings in its most successful trade areas in an effort to achieve high sales productivity. All told, we project net sales of $5.04 billion in FY 11.

▶ While BIG anticipates rising domestic and import freight costs and higher debit card fees in FY 11, operating margins are likely to widen on disciplined inventory management; planned advertising, utility and health care cost-saving initiatives; and expense leverage off projected same-store sales growth.

▶ Factoring in planned share repurchases, we see FY 11 EPS of $2.85, a 20% increase over FY 10's $2.37, before one-time items.

Investment Rationale/Risk

▶ Our buy recommendation is based on valuation. We look for BIG to weather a tough retail environment and to maintain strong cash flow in FY 11, supported by its efforts to raise sales productivity and lower its cost structure by better aligning products with customer preferences, by increasing the number of new stores in locations with better co-tenant mixes and/or demographics, and by building customer loyalty with the new Buzz Club Rewards program, which already has over 5 million members. Given what we see as its strong price-value proposition on brand-name merchandise, we also see potential for the company to gain incremental business as an increasing number of cost-conscious consumers seek out better deals on more discretionary-purchase goods.

▶ Risks to our recommendation and target price include sales shortfalls due to problems with merchandise availability and increased promotional activity by competitors.

▶ Our 12-month target price of $38 is based on a peer-discounted forward P/E multiple of 13.4X, which we believe is justified due to BIG's higher proportion of discretionary goods in its sales mix, applied to our FY 11 EPS estimate.

Qualitative Risk Assessment

LOW	MEDIUM	HIGH

Our risk assessment reflects our expectation of improving company fundamentals, supported by BIG's new merchandising and cost reduction initiatives, offset by what we see as a challenging retail environment that could hinder a turnaround.

Quantitative Evaluations

S&P Quality Ranking   B-

D	C	B-	B	B+	A-	A	A+

Relative Strength Rank   MODERATE

38

LOWEST = 1   HIGHEST = 99

Revenue/Earnings Data

Revenue (Million $)

	1Q	2Q	3Q	4Q	Year
2011	1,235	1,142	--		--
2010	1,142	1,087	1,035	1,463	4,727
2009	1,152	1,105	1,022	1,367	4,645
2008	1,128	1,085	1,031	1,412	4,656
2007	1,092	1,057	1,050	1,545	4,743
2006	1,099	1,051	1,041	1,395	4,430

Earnings Per Share ($)

	1Q	2Q	3Q	4Q	Year
2011	0.68	0.48	E0.26	E1.43	E2.85
2010	0.44	0.35	0.37	1.28	2.44
2009	0.42	0.32	0.15	1.00	1.89
2008	0.26	0.32	0.14	0.97	1.47
2007	0.13	0.04	0.02	0.83	1.01
2006	0.07	-0.12	-0.17	0.33	0.14

Fiscal year ended Jan. 31. Next earnings report expected: Early December. EPS Estimates based on S&P Operating Earnings; historical GAAP earnings are as reported.

Dividend Data

Proceeds from the sale of rights amounting to $0.01 a share were distributed in 2001.

Please read the Required Disclosures and Analyst Certification on the last page of this report.

The McGraw-Hill Companies

Big Lots Inc

STANDARD
&POOR'S

Business Summary August 25, 2010

CORPORATE OVERVIEW. Big Lot's strategy is to position itself as a preferred shopping destination for middle-income consumers seeking savings on brand-name closeouts and other value-priced merchandise. The company's product offerings range from everyday essentials such as food and other consumables, to more discretionary-purchase items, including furniture, holiday assortments, electronics, apparel, and small appliances. In our view, FY 07 (Jan.) was a transitional year for BIG, as the company slowed chain expansion in order to better focus on implementing operational changes to reverse a two-year trend of declining operating profits. Since then, we have seen BIG apply successful new merchandising and marketing strategies to further strengthen its financial performance. The company has over 1,370 Big Lots stores in 47 states.

CORPORATE STRATEGY. BIG's primary growth driver is expansion. The company seeks to build on its leadership position in broadline closeout retailing by expanding its market presence in both existing and new markets. From FY 00 through FY 05, the company increased its selling square footage at a compound annual growth rate (CAGR) of about 6% as it expanded its store count

from 1,230 to 1,502. In FY 06, BIG continued to expand its store base, adding 73 new stores. However, the company also accelerated the closure of underperforming locations as part of its What's Important Now (WIN) turnaround strategy, which was announced in November 2005. BIG closed 174 stores in FY 06, ending the fiscal year with 1,401 stores in 47 states.

WIN is aimed at improving BIG's financial performance via changes in the company's merchandising, cost structure, and real estate. As its first steps, BIG is attempting to raise the productivity of its chain by closing low-volume stores located mainly in small, rural, or weaker performing markets, and by moving from an opportunistic real estate strategy to one focused on its most successful trade areas. These areas include California, Arizona, Washington, New York and New Jersey. Between FY 07 and FY 09, the company closed 101 underperforming stores and opened only 39 new stores.

Company Financials Fiscal Year Ended Jan. 31

Per Share Data ($)	2010	2009	2008	2007	2006	2005	2004	2003	2002	2001
Tangible Book Value	12.35	9.61	13.34	11.10	9.47	9.54	9.51	8.83	8.11	8.28
Cash Flow	3.30	2.84	2.34	1.91	1.15	1.17	1.56	1.38	0.37	1.44
Earnings	2.44	1.89	1.47	1.01	0.14	0.27	0.77	0.65	-0.25	0.87
S&P Core Earnings	2.40	1.86	1.38	1.06	0.05	0.25	0.78	0.60	-0.32	0.83
Dividends	NA	Nil	Nil	Nil	Nil	Nil	Nil	Nil	Nil	Nil
Payout Ratio	Nil	Nil	Nil	Nil	Nil	Nil	Nil	Nil	Nil	Nil
Calendar Year	2009	2008	2007	2006	2005	2004	2003	2002	2001	2000
Prices:High	29.75	35.33	36.15	26.36	14.29	15.62	18.39	19.90	15.75	16.38
Prices:Low	12.62	12.40	15.35	11.83	10.06	11.05	9.92	9.75	7.15	8.25
P/E Ratio:High	12	19	25	26	NM	58	24	31	NM	19
P/E Ratio:Low	5	7	10	12	NM	41	13	15	NM	9

Income Statement Analysis (Million $)										
Revenue	4,727	4,645	4,656	4,743	4,430	4,375	4,174	3,869	3,433	3,277
Operating Income	388	334	315	276	141	172	222	231	43.4	249
Depreciation	74.9	78.6	88.5	101	115	104	93.7	85.7	72.0	64.5
Interest Expense	1.84	5.28	2.51	0.68	6.27	24.8	16.4	21.0	20.5	23.6
Pretax Income	323	250	239	170	20.9	43.3	113	125	-48.7	161
Effective Tax Rate	37.7%	38.0%	36.8%	34.0%	24.8%	29.8%	20.6%	39.5%	NM	39.5%
Net Income	201	155	151	113	15.7	30.4	89.9	75.7	-29.5	97.6
S&P Core Earnings	198	153	142	118	4.93	27.8	91.6	70.7	-36.7	92.6

Balance Sheet & Other Financial Data (Million $)										
Cash	284	34.8	37.1	282	1.71	2.52	174	160	NA	NA
Current Assets	1,123	871	891	1,149	994	1,035	1,134	NA	NA	NA
Total Assets	1,669	1,432	1,444	1,721	1,625	1,734	1,801	1,656	1,470	1,528
Current Liabilities	543	515	500	474	437	413	416	NA	NA	NA
Long Term Debt	NA	3.64	165	Nil	5.50	159	204	204	204	268
Common Equity	1,001	775	638	1,130	1,167	1,075	1,109	1,020	923	924
Total Capital	1,001	837	804	1,130	1,173	1,235	1,313	1,224	1,127	1,192
Capital Expenditures	78.7	88.7	60.4	35.9	68.5	135	170	110	NA	NA
Cash Flow	273	233	240	214	130	135	184	161	42.5	162
Current Ratio	2.1	1.7	1.8	2.4	2.3	2.5	2.7	NA	NA	NA
% Long Term Debt of Capitalization	Nil	0.4	20.6	Nil	0.5	12.9	15.5	16.7	18.1	22.5
% Net Income of Revenue	4.3	3.3	3.3	2.4	0.4	0.7	2.2	2.0	NM	3.0
% Return on Assets	13.0	10.8	9.6	6.7	0.9	1.7	5.2	4.8	NM	5.3
% Return on Equity	22.7	21.9	17.1	10.2	1.4	2.8	8.4	7.8	NM	8.8

Data as orig reptd.; bef. results of disc opers/spec. items. Per share data adj. for stk. divs.; EPS diluted. E-Estimated. NA-Not Available. NM-Not Meaningful. NR-Not Ranked. UR-Under Review.

Office: 300 Phillipi Road, Columbus, OH 43228-5311.
Telephone: 614-278-6800.
Website: http://www.biglots.com
Chrmn, Pres & CEO: S.S. Fishman

EVP, CFO & Chief Acctg Officer: J.R. Cooper
EVP, Secy & General Counsel: C.W. Haubiel, II
SVP & CIO: L.M. Bachmann
Investor Contact: T.A. Johnson (614-278-6622)

Board Members: J. Berger, S. S. Fishman, P. J. Hayes, D. T. Kollat, B. J. Lauderback, P. E. Mallott, R. Solt, J. R. Tener, D. B. Tishkoff

Founded: 1983
Domicile: Ohio
Employees: 35,600

Biogen Idec Inc

STANDARD &POOR'S

S&P Recommendation **SELL** ★★☆☆☆	Price $58.75 (as of Oct 22, 2010)	12-Mo. Target Price $53.00	Investment Style Large-Cap Growth

GICS Sector Health Care
Sub-Industry Biotechnology

Summary This major biopharmaceutical concern develops and markets targeted therapies for the treatment of multiple sclerosis, non-Hodgkin's lymphoma, and rheumatoid arthritis.

Key Stock Statistics (Source S&P, Vickers, company reports)

52-Wk Range	$60.28– 41.75	S&P Oper. EPS 2010E	4.72	Market Capitalization(B)	$14.213	Beta		0.69
Trailing 12-Month EPS	$3.93	S&P Oper. EPS 2011E	4.95	Yield (%)	Nil	S&P 3-Yr. Proj. EPS CAGR(%)		10
Trailing 12-Month P/E	15.0	P/E on S&P Oper. EPS 2010E	12.4	Dividend Rate/Share	Nil	S&P Credit Rating		BBB+
$10K Invested 5 Yrs Ago	$15,029	Common Shares Outstg. (M)	241.9	Institutional Ownership (%)	94			

Price Performance

30-Week Mov. Avg. · · · 10-Week Mov. Avg. – – **GAAP Earnings vs. Previous Year** Volume Above Avg. STARS
12-Mo. Target Price — Relative Strength ▲ Up ▼ Down ▶ No Change Below Avg. ★

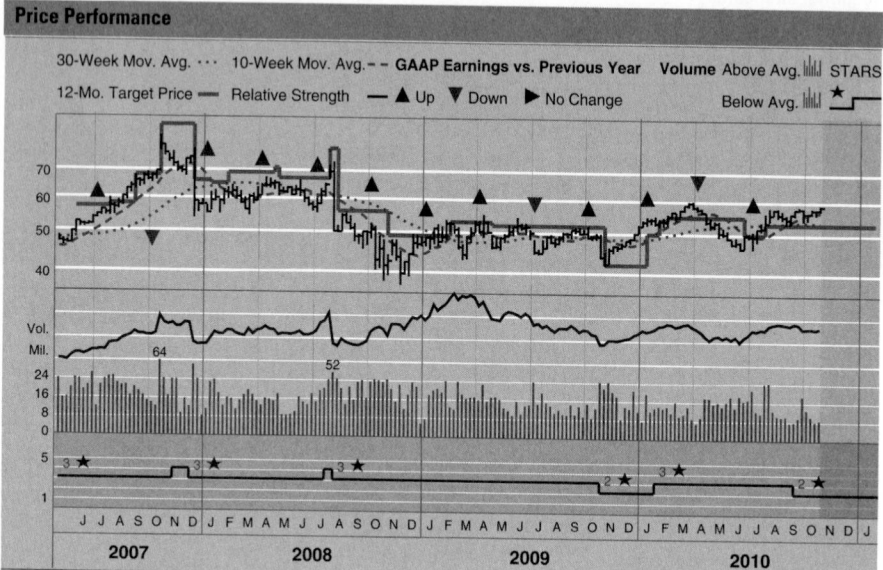

Options: ASE, CBOE, P, Ph

Analysis prepared by **Steven Silver** on October 15, 2010, when the stock traded at **$ 56.98.**

Highlights

▶ We estimate revenues to increase by about 6% in 2010 to $4.6 billion, with 2011 revenue growth of a modest 2% to $4.7 billion, due to new multiple sclerosis (MS) competition. We expect Tysabri to remain BIIB's key growth driver over the near-term as Avonex sales have moderated, relying on price hikes to offset slowing unit and share growth. However, we see a recently issued new Avonex patent extending to 2026, supporting core franchise cash flows. We forecast moderating Rituxan revenue growth, as ex-U.S. royalty agreements expire and competition increases.

▶ We expect operating expenses of 48% to 49% of total revenues in 2010 and 2011, compared to 50% in 2009. We see BIIB ramping expenses to support a more aggressive push to re-ignite Avonex usage. We are encouraged by its aggressive share repurchases of more than $2 billion since October 2009, with nearly 21 million shares repurchased during the second quarter of 2010. BIIB had $1.5 billion in cash and securities as of June 30, 2010.

▶ Our adjusted 2010 and 2011 EPS estimates of $4.72 and $4.95, respectively, exclude amortization of intangible assets.

Investment Rationale/Risk

▶ We view the share price as overvalued amid a rise in confirmed cases of brain infection PML to 68 in Tysabri patients, as of September 2010, and the recent FDA approval of Gilenya, an orally dosed therapy for multiple sclerosis. We remain wary of Tysabri's higher risk for PML as therapy duration increases, and expect Tysabri and Avonex's market share to be pressured by Gilenya's oral formulation. Although BIIB cited a favorable new patient trend for Tysabri in the second quarter of 2010, we see potential for more patients to take therapy breaks until an assay under development to stratify PML risk can ease safety concerns. We also see limited near-term pipeline catalysts, despite our view of several promising programs.

▶ Risks to our recommendation and target price include accelerating use of Tysabri due to easing safety concerns, slowing MS market competition, and BIIB successfully advancing its clinical pipeline.

▶ Our 12-month target price of $53 applies a 10.7X multiple to our 2011 EPS estimate, a discount to the large cap sector peer average, given our view of competitive and drug safety overhangs.

Qualitative Risk Assessment

LOW	MEDIUM	HIGH

Our risk assessment reflects that Biogen Idec sells products in competitive markets, and its biggest near-term growth driver faces safety concerns, requiring a comprehensive risk minimization program. The company also is engaged in the development of new drugs in new markets, outside of its core multiple sclerosis area of expertise.

Quantitative Evaluations

S&P Quality Ranking B

D	C	B-	B	B+	A-	A	A+

Relative Strength Rank MODERATE

61

LOWEST = 1   HIGHEST = 99

Revenue/Earnings Data

Revenue (Million $)

	1Q	2Q	3Q	4Q	Year
2010	1,109	1,213	--	--	--
2009	1,037	1,093	1,121	1,127	4,377
2008	942.2	993.4	1,093	1,069	4,098
2007	715.9	773.2	789.2	893.3	3,172
2006	611.2	660.0	703.5	708.3	2,683
2005	587.8	605.6	596.2	632.9	2,423

Earnings Per Share ($)

2010	0.80	1.12	E1.17	E1.21	E4.72
2009	0.84	0.49	0.95	1.06	3.35
2008	0.54	0.70	0.70	0.70	2.65
2007	0.38	0.54	0.41	0.67	1.99
2006	0.35	-0.50	0.45	0.32	0.62
2005	0.12	0.10	0.08	0.16	0.47

Fiscal year ended Dec. 31. Next earnings report expected: NA. EPS Estimates based on S&P Operating Earnings; historical GAAP earnings are as reported.

Dividend Data

No cash dividends have been paid.

Biogen Idec Inc

Business Summary October 15, 2010

CORPORATE OVERVIEW. Formed through the 2003 merger of IDEC Pharma-ceuticals and Biogen, Biogen Idec researches, develops and markets thera-peutics to treat cancer and autoimmune diseases.

BIIB's core franchise has been in autoimmune disorder multiple sclerosis, led by Avonex, approved by the FDA in 1996 to treat relapsing multiple sclerosis (MS), and in Europe in 1997. Avonex sales were $2.32 billion in 2009, up 8% from $2.2 billion in 2008. However, recent growth has been driven by price in-creases, as competition has slowed prescription growth. A new Avonex method of use patent issued in 2009 expires in 2026, extending the prior 2013 deadline. In May 2010, BIIB filed a lawsuit against rivals marketing similar be-ta interferons like Avonex, seeking sales royalties due to patent infringement.

Rituxan is a monoclonal antibody that binds to and eliminates CD-20 protein positive B-cells. The drug is approved for refractory non-Hodgkin's lym-phomas (NHL) and rheumatoid arthritis, and is co-marketed in the U.S. with Roche; BIIB receives joint business revenues on a percentage of sales basis, and royalties on ex-U.S. sales. Rituxan produced revenues to BIIB of about $1.09 billion in 2009, about 3% below 2008's $1.13 billion as ex-U.S. royalties began to expire. Rituxan is being explored for several new uses, but failed in progressive MS and lupus during 2008. A next-generation anti-CD20 candidate

under co-development, ocrelizumab, showed positive Phase III results for rheumatoid arthritis, but was discontinued in May 2010 due to safety con-cerns. BIIB would have received a lower royalty rate on ocrelizumab com-pared to Rituxan.

Tysabri, developed with Elan Corp., was approved for treating relapsing MS in late 2004. However, three cases of progressive multifocal leukoencephalopa-thy (PML) -- a rare, fatal nervous system disorder -- in 2005 prompted its re-moval from the market. Following safety evaluations and further data analy-ses, Tysabri was re-launched in the U.S. and Europe in 2006, with a stringent distribution program. As of June 30, 2010, BIIB cited more than 52,000 patients on Tysabri worldwide. As of September 2010, there have been 68 confirmed cases of PML in Tysabri patients, and the drug's label in the U.S. and Europe reflects higher PML risk as therapy duration passes two years. BIIB and Elan are developing an assay to identify patients with JC virus, which causes PML, for which data are expected in 2012. BIIB recognized $776 million of Tysabri revenues in 2009, 32% higher than the $588 million in 2008.

Company Financials Fiscal Year Ended Dec. 31

Per Share Data ($)	2009	2008	2007	2006	2005	2004	2003	2002	2001	2000
Tangible Book Value	11.69	8.70	6.44	9.60	8.38	7.08	6.85	7.25	6.22	4.63
Cash Flow	4.82	4.22	3.18	1.71	1.63	1.35	-4.57	0.88	0.62	0.39
Earnings	3.35	2.65	1.99	0.62	0.47	0.07	-4.92	0.85	0.59	0.36
S&P Core Earnings	3.32	2.76	2.01	0.69	0.16	-0.06	-5.13	0.54	0.34	NA
Dividends	Nil	Nil	Nil	Nil	Nil	Nil	Nil	Nil	Nil	Nil
Payout Ratio	Nil	Nil	Nil	Nil	Nil	Nil	Nil	Nil	Nil	Nil
Prices:High	55.34	73.59	84.75	52.72	70.00	68.13	42.15	71.40	75.00	77.65
Prices:Low	41.75	37.21	42.86	40.24	33.18	36.60	27.80	20.76	32.63	18.54
P/E Ratio:High	17	28	43	85	NM	NM	NM	84	NM	NM
P/E Ratio:Low	12	14	22	65	NM	NM	NM	24	NM	NM

Income Statement Analysis (Million $)	2009	2008	2007	2006	2005	2004	2003	2002	2001	2000
Revenue	4,377	4,098	3,172	2,683	2,423	2,212	679	404	273	155
Operating Income	1,723	1,832	1,260	1,117	756	483	14.6	285	137	60.6
Depreciation	428	462	380	376	402	439	61.3	10.2	6.31	4.74
Interest Expense	35.8	75.2	50.6	Nil	Nil	18.9	15.2	16.1	7.30	7.05
Pretax Income	1,333	1,149	852	492	256	64.1	-881	232	162	69.3
Effective Tax Rate	26.7%	31.8%	32.0%	56.6%	37.3%	60.9%	NM	36.0%	37.1%	17.2%
Net Income	970	783	638	214	161	25.1	-875	148	102	57.4
S&P Core Earnings	961	816	642	237	56.6	-21.6	-914	93.4	61.4	NA

Balance Sheet & Other Financial Data (Million $)	2009	2008	2007	2006	2005	2004	2003	2002	2001	2000
Cash	1,264	1,342	1,187	2,315	851	1,058	836	373	426	401
Current Assets	2,481	2,458	2,368	1,713	1,618	1,931	1,839	978	700	631
Total Assets	8,552	8,479	8,629	8,553	8,367	9,166	9,504	2,060	1,141	856
Current Liabilities	715	923	2,189	583	583	1,261	405	56.2	35.3	23.0
Long Term Debt	1,080	1,085	1,563	96.7	43.4	102	887	866	136	129
Common Equity	6,222	5,806	5,534	7,150	6,906	6,826	7,053	1,110	956	695
Total Capital	7,362	7,248	6,108	7,890	7,712	7,850	9,049	1,976	1,092	824
Capital Expenditures	166	276	284	198	318	361	301	166	0.07	31.4
Cash Flow	1,396	1,244	1,017	590	563	465	-814	158	108	62.1
Current Ratio	3.5	2.7	1.1	2.9	2.8	1.5	4.5	17.4	19.8	27.4
% Long Term Debt of Capitalization	14.7	15.0	0.9	1.2	0.6	1.3	9.8	43.8	12.4	15.7
% Net Income of Revenue	22.2	19.1	20.1	8.0	6.6	1.1	NM	36.6	37.3	37.1
% Return on Assets	11.4	9.2	7.4	2.5	1.8	0.3	NM	9.3	10.2	9.9
% Return on Equity	16.1	13.8	10.1	3.0	2.3	0.4	NM	14.3	12.3	13.4

Data as orig reptd.; bef. results of disc opers/spec. items. Per share data adj. for stk. divs.; EPS diluted. E-Estimated. NA-Not Available. NM-Not Meaningful. NR-Not Ranked. UR-Under Review.

Office: 14 Cambridge Center, Cambridge, MA 02142.
Telephone: 617-679-2000.
Website: http://www.biogenidec.com
Chrmn: W.D. Young

CEO: G.A. Scangos
COO: R. Hamm
EVP & CFO: P.J. Clancy
EVP & Secy: S.H. Alexander

Investor Contact: R. Jacobson (617-679-3710)
Board Members: A. J. Denner, C. D. Dorsa, C. C. Icahn, N. L. Leaming, R. C. Mulligan, R. W. Pangia, S. Papadopoulos, B. S. Posner, E. K. Rowinsky, G. A. Scangos, L. Schenk, S. A. Sherwin, W. D. Young

Founded: 1985
Domicile: Delaware
Employees: 4,750

BMC Software Inc

STANDARD &POOR'S

S&P Recommendation `HOLD` ★ ★ ★ ★ ★

Price $44.22 (as of Oct 22, 2010)	**12-Mo. Target Price** $41.00	**Investment Style** Large-Cap Blend

GICS Sector Information Technology
Sub-Industry Systems Software

Summary This company provides systems management software that improves the availability, performance and recovery of applications and data.

Key Stock Statistics (Source S&P, Vickers, company reports)

52-Wk Range	$44.68– 34.24	S&P Oper. EPS 2011**E**	2.26	Market Capitalization(B)	$7.899	Beta	0.68
Trailing 12-Month EPS	$2.24	S&P Oper. EPS 2012**E**	2.44	Yield (%)	Nil	S&P 3-Yr. Proj. EPS CAGR(%)	9
Trailing 12-Month P/E	19.7	P/E on S&P Oper. EPS 2011**E**	19.6	Dividend Rate/Share	Nil	S&P Credit Rating	BBB+
$10K Invested 5 Yrs Ago	$22,573	Common Shares Outstg. (M)	178.6	Institutional Ownership (%)	95		

Price Performance

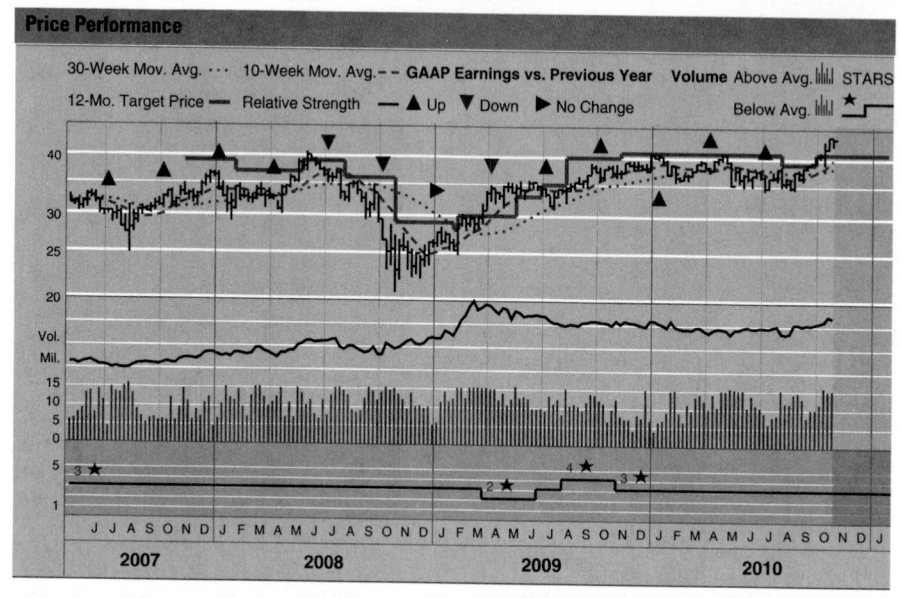

30-Week Mov. Avg. · · · 10-Week Mov. Avg. – – **GAAP Earnings vs. Previous Year** Volume Above Avg. ⃫⃫⃫ STARS
12-Mo. Target Price — Relative Strength — ▲ Up ▼ Down ▶ No Change Below Avg. ⃫⃫ ★

Options: ASE, CBOE, P, Ph

Analysis prepared by **Jim Yin, CFA** on September 27, 2010, when the stock traded at **$ 40.30.**

Highlights

➤ We expect revenues to increase 3.2% in FY 11 (Mar.), following a 2.1% advance in FY 10. Although we expect IT spending to rise about 5% in 2010, we think BMC and other software companies will grow slower than the IT industry. We believe most of the increased spending will be on hardware due to the severity of its decline during the downturn. We project flat revenues in the Mainframe Service Management segment and mid-single digit growth in the Enterprise Service Management business segment in FY 11. We think BMC will benefit from the growing interest in virtualization software, but this area currently accounts for a small portion of total revenues.

➤ We forecast gross margins of 78% in FY 11, down from 79% in FY 10. We expect operating expenses as a percentage of revenue to decline to 51%, from 52%, due to cost-saving initiatives and lower acquisition-related expenses. We believe operating margins in FY 11 will widen to 27%, from 26% in FY 10.

➤ Our EPS estimate for FY 11 is $2.26, up from $2.17 in FY 10, as a result of higher revenues and improved operating margins.

Investment Rationale/Risk

➤ Our hold recommendation reflects our concern about BMC's slow revenue growth. Although we expect IT spending to rise in 2010, sales cycles on large contracts remained elongated, as customers negotiate for more favorable terms. We also think revenues will be hurt by foreign currency exchange headwinds in FY 11. On the positive side, we think BMC can gain market share. Additionally, we project expanding operating margins, as the company has been effectively controlling its operating expenses.

➤ Risks to our recommendation and target price include a weaker-than-expected recovery in the global economy, heightened competition from large platform vendors, a decline in corporate spending on information technology, and greater pricing pressures.

➤ Our 12-month target price of $41 is based on a blend of our discounted cash flow (DCF) and P/E analyses. Our DCF model assumes an 11% weighted average cost of capital and 3% terminal growth, and yields an intrinsic value of $45. From our P/E analysis, we derive a value of $37 based on an industry P/E-to-growth ratio of 1.8X, or 16X our FY 11 EPS estimate of $2.26.

Qualitative Risk Assessment

LOW	MEDIUM	HIGH

Our risk assessment for BMC Software reflects our concern about the economic uncertainty in Europe and increased competition in its mainframe business from hardware vendors, offset by the company's cost-cutting measures.

Quantitative Evaluations

S&P Quality Ranking C

D	C	B-	B	B+	A-	A	A+

Relative Strength Rank STRONG

83

LOWEST = 1   HIGHEST = 99

Revenue/Earnings Data

Revenue (Million $)

	1Q	2Q	3Q	4Q	Year
2011	460.9	--	--	--	--
2010	450.0	461.8	508.1	491.3	1,911
2009	437.5	466.7	488.4	479.3	1,872
2008	385.0	420.7	459.0	466.9	1,732
2007	361.4	386.7	412.9	419.4	1,580
2006	348.3	361.8	380.3	407.9	1,498

Earnings Per Share ($)

	1Q	2Q	3Q	4Q	Year
2011	0.50	E0.53	E0.62	E0.61	E2.26
2010	0.44	0.50	0.59	0.64	2.17
2009	0.01	0.36	0.45	0.45	1.25
2008	0.27	0.38	0.45	0.46	1.57
2007	0.15	0.28	0.30	0.30	1.03
2006	-0.19	0.19	0.22	0.31	0.47

Fiscal year ended Mar. 31. Next earnings report expected: Late October. EPS Estimates based on S&P Operating Earnings; historical GAAP earnings are as reported.

Dividend Data

No cash dividends have been paid.

BMC Software Inc

Business Summary September 27, 2010

CORPORATE OVERVIEW. BMC Software is a leading provider of systems management, service management and automation solutions primarily for large enterprises. The company's software, called Business Service Management (BSM), helps customers increase productivity and reduce costs by automating IT processes and improving IT responses to business decisions and challenges. The company's products and services are used by over 16,000 companies, including 90% of the Fortune 100.

BMC's software business is organized in two segments. The Enterprise Service Management (ESM) business segment targets non-mainframe computing and addresses broad categories of IT management issues including Service Support, Service Assurance and Service Automation. ESM license revenue accounted for 57%, 61% and 54% of total software revenue in FY 10 (Mar.), FY 09 and FY 08, respectively.

The Mainframe Service Management (MSM) segment includes automated tools that enhance the performance and availability of database management systems on mainframe platforms. This segment includes BMC's mainframe performance monitoring and management product line, MAINVIEW. It also includes the management and recovery of IBM's DB2 and IMS databases.

MSM license revenue accounted for 43%, 39% and 46% of total software revenue in FY 10, FY 09 and FY 08, respectively.

BMC competes in a highly competitive industry. Its main competitors include International Business Machines Corporation, CA, Inc. and Hewlett-Packard.

BMC sells its software directly through its sales force and indirectly through resellers, distributors and systems integrators. The company also provides maintenance and support, which give customers the right to receive product upgrades. Product license and maintenance revenues accounted for 93% and 92% of total revenues in FY 10 and FY 09, respectively. BMC also provides professional services, which include implementation, integration and education services and contributed 7% and 8% of total revenues in FY 10 and FY 09, respectively.

Company Financials Fiscal Year Ended Mar. 31

Per Share Data ($)	2010	2009	2008	2007	2006	2005	2004	2003	2002	2001
Tangible Book Value	NM	NM	0.41	1.66	2.31	2.60	3.11	3.70	5.49	5.67
Cash Flow	2.78	1.89	2.01	1.79	1.40	1.33	1.03	1.25	0.78	1.42
Earnings	2.17	1.25	1.57	1.03	0.47	0.34	-0.12	0.20	-0.75	0.17
S&P Core Earnings	2.15	1.28	1.54	1.00	0.29	-0.03	-0.56	-0.01	-0.94	-0.19
Dividends	Nil	Nil	Nil	Nil	Nil	Nil	Nil	Nil	Nil	Nil
Payout Ratio	Nil	Nil	Nil	Nil	Nil	Nil	Nil	Nil	Nil	Nil
Calendar Year	2009	2008	2007	2006	2005	2004	2003	2002	2001	2000
Prices:High	40.73	40.87	37.05	33.67	21.68	21.87	19.84	23.00	33.00	86.63
Prices:Low	24.76	20.58	24.77	19.90	14.44	13.70	13.18	10.85	11.50	13.00
P/E Ratio:High	19	33	24	33	41	64	NM	NM	NM	NM
P/E Ratio:Low	11	16	16	19	27	40	NM	NM	NM	NM

Income Statement Analysis (Million $)	2010	2009	2008	2007	2006	2005	2004	2003	2002	2001
Revenue	1,911	1,872	1,732	1,580	1,498	1,463	1,419	1,327	1,289	1,504
Operating Income	622	573	464	413	334	264	162	349	400	336
Depreciation	176	121	88.2	161	205	222	259	248	376	315
Interest Expense	21.3	18.7	16.9	1.50	1.70	2.00	1.10	Nil	0.40	11.3
Pretax Income	504	364	434	301	204	98.2	-29.4	69.3	-231	60.4
Effective Tax Rate	19.5%	34.6%	27.8%	28.2%	50.0%	23.3%	NM	30.7%	NM	29.8%
Net Income	406	238	314	216	102	75.3	-26.8	48.0	-184	42.4
S&P Core Earnings	401	243	308	211	63.9	-5.94	-128	-3.42	-232	-46.6

Balance Sheet & Other Financial Data (Million $)	2010	2009	2008	2007	2006	2005	2004	2003	2002	2001
Cash	1,434	1,097	1,351	1,296	1,063	929	909	1,015	546	146
Current Assets	1,905	1,561	1,803	1,790	1,506	1,440	1,425	1,098	997	903
Total Assets	4,138	3,698	3,346	3,260	3,211	3,298	3,045	2,846	2,676	3,034
Current Liabilities	1,361	1,333	1,289	1,233	1,202	1,085	987	839	681	829
Long Term Debt	341	314	6.30	Nil	Nil	Nil	Nil	Nil	Nil	Nil
Common Equity	1,388	1,049	994	1,049	1,099	1,262	1,215	1,383	1,507	1,815
Total Capital	1,729	1,362	994	1,049	1,099	1,262	1,215	1,383	1,507	1,815
Capital Expenditures	22.1	28.0	38.4	33.7	24.1	57.7	50.4	23.6	64.3	183
Cash Flow	519	359	402	377	307	297	233	296	192	357
Current Ratio	1.4	1.2	1.4	1.5	1.3	1.3	1.4	1.3	1.5	1.1
% Long Term Debt of Capitalization	19.7	23.0	Nil	Nil	Nil	Nil	Nil	Nil	Nil	Nil
% Net Income of Revenue	21.3	12.7	18.1	13.7	6.8	5.1	NM	3.6	NM	2.8
% Return on Assets	10.4	6.8	9.5	6.7	3.1	2.4	NM	1.7	NM	1.4
% Return on Equity	33.3	23.3	30.7	20.1	8.6	6.1	NM	3.3	NM	2.4

Data as orig reptd.; bef. results of disc opers/spec. items. Per share data adj. for stk. divs.; EPS diluted. E-Estimated. NA-Not Available. NM-Not Meaningful. NR-Not Ranked. UR-Under Review.

Office: 2101 Citywest Boulevard, Houston, TX 77042-2827.
Telephone: 713-918-8800.
Email: investor@bmc.com
Website: http://www.bmc.com

Chrmn, Pres & CEO: R.E. Beauchamp
Investor Contact: S.B. Solcher
SVP & CFO: S.B. Solcher
SVP, Secy & General Counsel: D.M. Clolery

Chief Admin Officer: H.S. Castro
Board Members: J. E. Barfield, R. E. Beauchamp, G. L. Bloom, M. K. Gafner, M. J. Hawkins, S. A. James, P. T. Jenkins, L. J. Lavigne, Jr., K. O'Neil, T. C. Tinsley

Founded: 1980
Domicile: Delaware
Employees: 6,100

Boeing Co (The)

STANDARD &POOR'S

S&P Recommendation	BUY ★★★★☆		Price $71.26 (as of Oct 22, 2010)	12-Mo. Target Price $82.00	Investment Style Large-Cap Growth

GICS Sector Industrials
Sub-Industry Aerospace & Defense

Summary This company is the world's second largest manufacturer of both commercial jets (behind Airbus) and military weapons (behind Lockheed Martin).

Key Stock Statistics (Source S&P, Vickers, company reports)

52-Wk Range	$76.00– 47.18	S&P Oper. EPS 2010**E**	3.95	Market Capitalization(B)	$52.275	Beta	1.29
Trailing 12-Month EPS	$4.67	S&P Oper. EPS 2011**E**	4.45	Yield (%)	2.36	S&P 3-Yr. Proj. EPS CAGR(%)	-3
Trailing 12-Month P/E	15.3	P/E on S&P Oper. EPS 2010**E**	18.0	Dividend Rate/Share	$1.68	S&P Credit Rating	A
$10K Invested 5 Yrs Ago	$12,092	Common Shares Outstg. (M)	733.6	Institutional Ownership (%)	73		

Price Performance

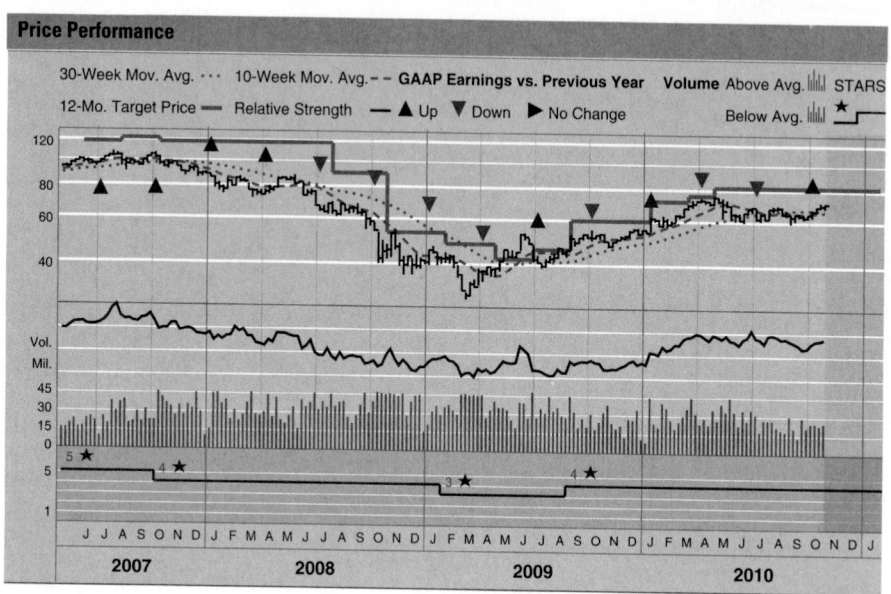

| 30-Week Mov. Avg. ···· | 10-Week Mov. Avg. – – | **GAAP Earnings vs. Previous Year** | Volume Above Avg. | STARS |
| 12-Mo. Target Price — | Relative Strength — | ▲ Up ▼ Down ▶ No Change | Below Avg. | ★ |

Options: ASE, CBOE, P, Ph

Analysis prepared by **Richard Tortoriello** on October 22, 2010, when the stock traded at **$ 71.50.**

Highlights

➤ We estimate a sales drop of 5.9% in 2010 on declines of 4% in aircraft shipments and 5% in defense sales, on cuts in programs including Brigade Combat Team Modernization, missile defense, and the C-17. For 2011, we project a 6% sales increase, driven entirely by Commercial Airplanes, on production increases for the 737 and 777 and the expected service entry of the 787. We project defense sales to remain flat in 2011. We note that third quarter 2010 Commercial Airplanes backlog rose 0.5%, the first rise in seven quarters, and Defense, Space, & Security backlog grew 2.9%, aided by a large FA-18/EA-18G order from the Navy.

➤ We estimate operating margins of 7.9% in 2010, down from 8.4% in 2009, on lower defense margins. For 2011 we expect a slight margin increase, to 8.1%, but see continued pressure on commercial margins due to initial production of the 787 and potential first delivery of the 747-8 Freighter.

➤ We estimate EPS of $3.95 for 2010 and $4.45 in 2011. We expect free cash flow of near zero in 2010, as Boeing increases inventory due to work on the 787 and 747-8, but project about $3 billion in 2011.

Investment Rationale/Risk

➤ We see several factors benefiting the shares. We expect emerging economies in Asia and the Middle East to continue to improve, which should sustain demand for narrow-body aircraft, supporting Boeing's total backlog of about 3,400 aircraft as of September 2010. In addition, U.S. airlines continue to take deliveries to improve fuel efficiency of aging fleets. Further, we expect the first quarter 2011 delivery of the 787 (first flight was in December 2009) to act as a catalyst for the stock, with about 850 aircraft recently on order. Finally, we view valuations, which are at or below historical averages, as attractive given our view that current income levels are depressed.

➤ Risks to our opinion and target price include a worsening financing or economic environment, further delays on major programs, and manufacturing issues.

➤ Our 12-month target price of $82 is based on an enterprise value-to-EBITDA multiple of 8.5X our 2011 EBITDA estimate. This compares favorably with BA's 20-year historical average EV-to-EBITDA multiple of 11.5X, and is slightly above a recent peer average multiple of 8.0X.

Qualitative Risk Assessment

LOW	MEDIUM	HIGH

Our risk assessment reflects BA's participation in highly cyclical, very competitive and capital-intensive businesses, offset by what we see as its long-term government contracts, its solid cash position and typically strong free cash flow generation, and a healthy backlog of business.

Quantitative Evaluations

S&P Quality Ranking B

D	C	B-	B	B+	A-	A	A+

Relative Strength Rank STRONG

72

LOWEST = 1   HIGHEST = 99

Revenue/Earnings Data

Revenue (Million $)

	1Q	2Q	3Q	4Q	Year
2010	15,216	15,573	16,967	--	--
2009	16,502	14,296	16,688	17,937	68,281
2008	15,990	16,962	15,293	12,664	60,909
2007	15,365	17,028	16,517	17,477	66,387
2006	14,264	14,986	14,739	17,541	61,530
2005	12,987	15,025	12,629	14,204	54,845

Earnings Per Share ($)

2010	0.70	1.06	1.12	E1.06	E3.95
2009	0.87	1.41	-2.22	1.77	1.87
2008	1.61	1.16	0.94	-0.12	3.65
2007	1.12	1.35	1.43	1.35	5.26
2006	0.88	-0.21	0.89	1.28	2.84
2005	0.64	0.70	1.26	0.59	3.19

Fiscal year ended Dec. 31. Next earnings report expected: Late January. EPS Estimates based on S&P Operating Earnings; historical GAAP earnings are as reported.

Dividend Data (Dates: mm/dd Payment Date: mm/dd/yy)

Amount ($)	Date Decl.	Ex-Div. Date	Stk. of Record	Payment Date
0.420	12/14	02/03	02/05	03/05/10
0.420	12/14	02/03	02/05	03/02/10
0.420	04/26	05/05	05/07	06/04/10
0.420	06/21	08/04	08/06	09/03/10

Dividends have been paid since 1942. Source: Company reports.

Boeing Co (The)

Business Summary October 22, 2010

CORPORATE OVERVIEW. Boeing is a global aerospace and defense giant that conducts business through three operating segments. Boeing Commercial Airplanes (BCA; 50% of revenues and 47% of operating profits in 2009) and EADS's Airbus division are the world's only makers of 150-plus seat passenger jets. Boeing Defense, Space & Security (49%, 51%) is the world's third largest military contractor behind Lockheed Martin Corp and England's BAE Systems. Boeing Capital Corp. (1%, 2%) primarily finances Boeing aircraft for airlines.

BCA's commercial jet aircraft family includes the 737 Next-Generation narrow body model and the 747, 767, 777 and 787 wide body models. The 787 (Dreamliner) is Boeing's newest model, and is scheduled for first delivery, following a more than two-year delay, in the final quarter of 2010. Boeing's upgraded 747-8 Freighter is also slated for delivery in the fourth quarter of 2010, with the passenger version scheduled for a year later. BCA also offers aviation support, aircraft modifications, spare parts, training, maintenance documents, and technical advice. Boeing had a commercial aircraft backlog at year-end 2009 of $251 billion.

Defense, Space & Security (BDS -- formerly Integrated Defense Systems) designs, develops and supports military aircraft, including fighters, transports, tankers, intelligence surveillance and reconnaissance aircraft, and heli-

copters; unmanned systems; missiles; space systems; missile defense systems; satellites and satellite launch vehicles; and communication, information and battle management systems. BDS's primary customer is the U.S. Department of Defense (80% of 2009 sales), but it also sells to NASA, international defense customers, civilian markets, and commercial satellite markets. Major programs include the AH-64 Apache and CH-47 Chinook helicopters, the C-17 Globemaster military transport, the V-22 Osprey tiltrotor aircraft, F/A-18E/F Super Hornet and F-15 Eagle fighter jets, as well as commercial and military satellites.

MARKET PROFILE. Based on total unit orders of 150-plus seat jetliners in the three years through 2009, Boeing and Airbus each control about half of the large commercial aircraft market. Demand for jetliners is driven primarily by growth in international air travel. Since 2002, passenger air traffic has grown by an average of over 6% annually. Although passenger air traffic declined 3.5% in 2009, the International Air Transport Agency predicts a 5.6% rise in 2010.

Company Financials Fiscal Year Ended Dec. 31

Per Share Data ($)	2009	2008	2007	2006	2005	2004	2003	2002	2001	2000
Tangible Book Value	NM	NM	3.78	NM	10.33	10.08	6.17	4.53	5.23	6.63
Cash Flow	4.21	5.26	7.18	4.76	5.08	4.00	2.68	2.46	5.52	4.14
Earnings	1.87	3.65	5.26	2.84	3.19	2.24	0.89	2.87	3.41	2.44
S&P Core Earnings	2.02	0.87	5.41	3.90	3.05	1.99	1.33	0.26	-0.06	NA
Dividends	1.68	1.60	1.40	1.20	1.00	0.77	0.68	0.68	0.68	0.56
Payout Ratio	90%	44%	27%	42%	31%	34%	76%	24%	20%	23%
Prices:High	56.56	88.29	107.83	92.05	72.40	55.48	43.37	51.07	69.85	70.94
Prices:Low	29.05	36.17	84.60	65.90	49.52	38.04	24.73	28.53	27.60	32.00
P/E Ratio:High	30	24	20	32	23	25	49	18	20	29
P/E Ratio:Low	16	10	16	23	16	17	28	10	8	13

Income Statement Analysis (Million $)										
Revenue	68,281	60,909	66,387	61,530	54,845	52,457	50,485	54,069	58,198	51,321
Operating Income	3,537	5,107	7,090	5,176	3,707	3,405	3,198	5,447	6,467	4,996
Depreciation	1,666	1,179	1,486	1,545	1,503	1,509	1,450	1,497	1,750	1,479
Interest Expense	339	524	196	593	653	685	800	730	650	445
Pretax Income	1,731	4,033	6,118	1,218	2,819	1,960	550	1,353	3,565	2,999
Effective Tax Rate	22.9%	33.5%	33.6%	NM	9.12%	7.14%	NM	63.6%	20.7%	29.0%
Net Income	1,335	2,684	4,058	2,206	2,562	1,820	718	492	2,827	2,128
S&P Core Earnings	1,442	619	4,177	3,042	2,450	1,616	1,074	203	284	NA

Balance Sheet & Other Financial Data (Million $)										
Cash	11,223	3,279	7,042	6,118	5,412	3,204	4,633	2,333	633	1,010
Current Assets	35,275	25,964	27,280	22,983	21,968	15,100	17,258	16,855	16,206	15,864
Total Assets	62,053	53,801	58,986	51,794	60,058	53,963	53,035	52,342	48,343	42,028
Current Liabilities	32,883	30,925	31,538	29,701	28,188	20,835	18,448	19,810	20,486	18,289
Long Term Debt	12,217	6,952	7,455	8,157	9,538	10,879	13,299	12,589	10,866	7,567
Common Equity	2,128	-1,264	9,004	4,739	11,059	11,286	8,139	7,696	10,825	11,020
Total Capital	15,149	5,658	17,649	12,896	22,664	23,255	21,438	20,285	21,868	18,587
Capital Expenditures	1,186	1,674	1,731	1,681	1,547	978	741	1,001	1,068	932
Cash Flow	3,001	3,833	5,544	3,751	4,065	3,329	2,168	1,989	4,577	3,607
Current Ratio	1.1	0.8	0.9	0.8	0.8	0.7	0.9	0.9	0.8	0.9
% Long Term Debt of Capitalization	80.7	122.9	42.2	63.3	42.1	46.8	62.0	62.1	49.7	40.7
% Net Income of Revenue	2.0	4.4	6.1	3.6	4.7	3.5	1.4	0.9	4.9	4.1
% Return on Assets	2.3	4.8	7.3	3.9	4.4	3.4	1.4	1.0	6.2	5.4
% Return on Equity	NM	NM	59.0	27.9	22.9	18.7	9.1	5.3	25.9	18.9

Data as orig reptd.; bef. results of disc opers/spec. items. Per share data adj. for stk. divs.; EPS diluted. E-Estimated. NA-Not Available. NM-Not Meaningful. NR-Not Ranked. UR-Under Review.

Office: 100 North Riverside Plaza, Chicago, IL 60606-1596.
Telephone: 312-544-2000.
Website: http://www.boeing.com
Chrmn, Pres & CEO: W.J. McNerney, Jr.

COO & CTO: J.J. Tracy
EVP & CFO: J.A. Bell
EVP & General Counsel: J.M. Luttig
Chief Admin Officer: R.D. Stephens

Investor Contact: R. Young (312-544-2140)
Board Members: J. H. Biggs, J. E. Bryson, D. L. Calhoun, A. D. Collins, Jr., L. Z. Cook, W. M. Daley, K. M. Duberstein, E. P. Giambastiani, Jr., E. M. Liddy, J. F. McDonnell, W. J. McNerney, Jr., S. C. Schwab, M. Zafirovski

Founded: 1916
Domicile: Delaware
Employees: 157,100

Boston Properties Inc

STANDARD &POOR'S

S&P Recommendation BUY ★★★★☆	**Price** $90.50 (as of Oct 22, 2010)	**12-Mo. Target Price** $92.00	**Investment Style** Large-Cap Blend

GICS Sector Financials
Sub-Industry Office REITS

Summary This real estate investment trust primarily owns office buildings in the Boston, Washington, DC, New York City, San Francisco and Princeton markets.

Key Stock Statistics (Source S&P, Vickers, company reports)

52-Wk Range	$91.23– 57.19	S&P FFO/Sh. 2010E	4.28	Market Capitalization(B)	$12.611	Beta	1.53
Trailing 12-Month FFO/Share	NA	S&P FFO/Sh. 2011E	4.20	Yield (%)	2.21	S&P 3-Yr. FFO/Sh. Proj. CAGR(%)	-1
Trailing 12-Month P/FFO	NA	P/FFO on S&P FFO/Sh. 2010E	21.1	Dividend Rate/Share	$2.00	S&P Credit Rating	A-
$10K Invested 5 Yrs Ago	$17,735	Common Shares Outstg. (M)	139.3	Institutional Ownership (%)	99		

Price Performance

30-Week Mov. Avg. · · · · 10-Week Mov. Avg. – – GAAP Earnings vs. Previous Year   Volume Above Avg. ▮▮▮▮ STARS
12-Mo. Target Price — Relative Strength — ▲ Up ▼ Down ▶ No Change   Below Avg. ▮▮▮▮ ★

[Price chart showing 2007, 2008, 2009, 2010 with volume and STARS ratings]

Options: ASE, CBOE, P

Analysis prepared by **Royal F. Shepard, CFA** on October 04, 2010, when the stock traded at **$ 83.25**.

Highlights

➤ We believe BXP is experiencing higher interest from tenants looking to lock in attractive rents at its high-quality properties, particularly in New York City and Washington, DC. We estimate occupancy will remain at close to 92.5% in 2010, above most rivals. Just under 14% of BXP's total space is subject to lease expiration by the end of 2011, a level we consider manageable. We estimate that total revenues will rise about 1%, absent any acquisitions, due to higher management fees and revenues from newly developed properties.

➤ BXP has built a large cash cushion, which it has begun to deploy toward acquisitions. In September 2010, it acquired 510 Madison Avenue in New York for $275 million. The trust has also agreed to acquire two properties in the Boston market, including the landmark John Hancock Tower for $930 million.

➤ Our 2010 FFO per share estimate of $4.28 reflects steady occupancy and higher third-party management fees, offset by dilution from recent debt and equity financing. BXP has initiated an "at the market" stock offering program for the sale of up to $400 million of common shares.

Investment Rationale/Risk

➤ In view of low tenant turnover, we think BXP's high-quality portfolio will hold up reasonably well in challenging market conditions. The trust faces minimal tenant turnover through 2011, which should limit any pressure on rents as leases renew. The potential of future fees from new development projects appears more limited until credit market conditions improve. On the other hand, we expect BXP to become more aggressive in closing acquisition opportunities as leasing metrics stabilize. We believe BXP's recent valuation of 19.5X our 2010 FFO per share estimate, a premium to peers, is warranted by its long-term growth potential.

➤ Risks to our recommendation and target price include national employment growth lagging our expectations, and lower-than-anticipated regional economic strength in BXP's markets.

➤ Our 12-month target price of $92 is based primarily on applying a multiple of 21.5X to our 2010 FFO per share estimate, a premium to office REITs serving less attractive suburban markets. We arrive at a $95 estimate of net asset value (NAV), based on recent market transactions and a one-year cash yield of 5.0%.

Qualitative Risk Assessment

LOW	MEDIUM	HIGH

Our risk assessment reflects what we see as BXP's large and diverse asset portfolio, its relatively unleveraged balance sheet, and consistent cash distribution.

Quantitative Evaluations

S&P Quality Ranking   B+

D	C	B-	B	B+	A-	A	A+

Relative Strength Rank   STRONG

74

LOWEST = 1   HIGHEST = 99

Revenue/FFO Data

Revenue (Million $)

	1Q	2Q	3Q	4Q	Year
2010	386.0	396.0	--	--	--
2009	377.5	389.5	377.3	377.9	1,522
2008	370.6	366.3	357.1	201.9	1,287
2007	360.7	372.2	368.6	380.8	1,482
2006	356.1	370.4	372.5	378.7	1,502
2005	356.2	360.6	361.8	366.3	1,438

FFO Per Share ($)

	1Q	2Q	3Q	4Q	Year
2010	1.23	1.12	E1.01	E1.08	E4.28
2009	1.11	1.32	1.31	1.05	4.61
2008	1.18	1.19	1.13	0.05	3.49
2007	0.42	0.32	0.32	1.22	4.64
2006	0.27	0.39	0.32	0.32	4.17
2005	0.23	0.16	0.16	0.24	4.31

Fiscal year ended Dec. 31. Next earnings report expected: Late October. FFO Estimates based on S&P Funds From Operations Est..

Dividend Data (Dates: mm/dd Payment Date: mm/dd/yy)

Amount ($)	Date Decl.	Ex-Div. Date	Stk. of Record	Payment Date
0.500	12/17	12/29	12/31	01/29/10
0.500	03/18	03/29	03/31	04/30/10
0.500	06/17	06/28	06/30	07/30/10
0.500	09/16	09/28	09/30	10/29/10

Dividends have been paid since 1997. Source: Company reports.

Please read the Required Disclosures and Analyst Certification on the last page of this report.

The McGraw·Hill Companies

Boston Properties Inc

Business Summary October 04, 2010

CORPORATE OVERVIEW. Boston Properties, founded in 1970, is a real estate investment trust (REIT) that develops, acquires, manages, operates, and is one of the largest U.S. owners of, Class A office properties. BXP conducts substantially all of its business through its limited partnership, of which it is the sole general partner, and holds an 84% economic interest.

At December 31, 2009, the property portfolio consisted of 146 properties, totaling 50.5 million net rentable sq. ft. and structured parking facilities for vehicles containing approximately 12.8 million sq. ft. The properties included 140 in-service office buildings and one hotel in Cambridge, Massachusetts. In addition, BXP had six buildings under development totaling 3.0 million sq. ft.

MARKET PROFILE The market for office leases is inherently cyclical. Local economic conditions, particularly the employment level, play an important role in determining competitive dynamics. Non-farm monthly payrolls declined through 2009, with an increase in the unemployment rate above 10%, from 7.2% as of December 2008.

The U.S. office market tends to track the overall economy on a lagged basis. At the end of December 2009, we believe the national vacancy rate was about 17.0%, an increase from a cyclical low of about 12.5% at the end of 2007. Go-

ing forward, we believe vacancy levels will continue to rise in 2010 due to a recessionary economic environment. In our opinion, BXP's principal markets, including Washington, DC, Manhattan, Boston, and San Francisco, are among the nation's strongest due to limited new construction activity in recent years. However, layoffs in the financial services sector, particularly in New York City, have pressured rents in recent months. In total, as of December 31, 2009, BXP had an office occupancy rate at established properties of 92.4%, much better than the national averages. Leases will expire on only about 9.1% of existing office space in 2010, limiting the trust's exposure to declining market rents.

Competition for leasing real estate is high. In addition, we believe that competition for the acquisition of new properties is intensifying from other REITs, private real estate funds, financial institutions, insurance companies and others. As a result, we think BXP could have difficulty finding new assets at attractive prices.

Company Financials Fiscal Year Ended Dec. 31

Per Share Data ($)	2009	2008	2007	2006	2005	2004	2003	2002	2001	2000
Tangible Book Value	32.01	29.14	30.72	27.45	25.92	26.61	22.51	20.79	19.34	19.02
Earnings	1.76	1.03	9.06	7.46	3.46	2.35	2.94	4.40	2.26	2.01
S&P Core Earnings	1.76	1.03	9.06	7.46	3.46	2.34	2.88	4.37	2.20	NA
Dividends	2.18	1.52	2.72	2.72	5.19	2.58	2.50	2.41	2.27	1.96
Payout Ratio	124%	NM	30%	36%	150%	110%	85%	55%	100%	96%
Prices:High	72.23	50.63	133.02	118.22	76.67	64.90	48.47	41.55	43.88	44.88
Prices:Low	29.30	19.69	87.78	72.98	56.66	42.99	34.80	32.95	34.00	29.00
P/E Ratio:High	41	60	15	16	22	28	16	9	19	22
P/E Ratio:Low	17	23	10	10	16	18	12	7	15	14

Income Statement Analysis (Million $)										
Rental Income	1,453	1,402	1,334	1,344	1,339	1,293	1,219	1,174	1,008	859
Mortgage Income	Nil	Nil	Nil	Nil	Nil	Nil	Nil	Nil	Nil	Nil
Total Income	1,522	1,488	1,482	1,502	1,438	1,400	1,310	1,235	1,033	879
General Expenses	601	588	554	557	545	528	498	464	351	300
Interest Expense	323	272	286	298	308	306	299	272	223	217
Provision for Losses	Nil	Nil	Nil	Nil	Nil	Nil	Nil	Nil	Nil	Nil
Depreciation	322	304	286	277	267	252	210	186	150	133
Net Income	231	125	1,098	874	393	255	290	420	215	153
S&P Core Earnings	231	125	1,094	874	393	254	284	413	203	NA

Balance Sheet & Other Financial Data (Million $)										
Cash	1,449	242	1,716	752	377	345	133	199	201	378
Total Assets	12,349	10,912	11,193	9,695	8,902	9,063	8,551	8,427	7,254	6,226
Real Estate Investment	11,100	10,618	10,250	9,552	9,151	9,291	8,983	8,671	7,458	6,113
Loss Reserve	Nil	Nil	Nil	Nil	Nil	Nil	Nil	Nil	Nil	Nil
Net Investment	9,066	8,850	8,718	8,160	7,886	8,148	7,981	7,848	6,738	5,526
Short Term Debt	310	100	Nil	Nil	Nil	Nil	Nil	Nil	282	194
Capitalization:Debt	6,608	6,172	5,492	4,559	4,679	4,733	5,005	3,336	4,033	3,415
Capitalization:Equity	4,446	3,531	3,669	3,223	2,917	2,936	2,400	2,160	1,754	1,648
Capitalization:Total	11,732	10,302	9,216	8,406	8,335	8,455	8,235	6,340	6,732	6,040
% Earnings & Depreciation/Assets	4.8	3.9	13.3	12.3	7.3	5.8	5.9	7.7	5.4	4.9
Price Times Book Value:High	2.3	4.5	4.3	4.3	3.0	2.4	2.1	2.0	2.3	2.4
Price Times Book Value:Low	0.9	1.3	2.9	2.7	2.2	1.6	1.5	1.6	1.8	1.5

Data as orig reptd.; bef. results of disc opers/spec. items. Per share data adj. for stk. divs.; EPS diluted. E-Estimated. NA-Not Available. NM-Not Meaningful. NR-Not Ranked. UR-Under Review.

Office: 800 Boylston St Ste 1900, Boston, MA 02199-8103.
Telephone: 617-236-3300.
Email: investor_relations@bostonproperties.com
Website: http://www.bostonproperties.com

Chrmn & CEO: M.B. Zuckerman
Pres: D.T. Linde
COO & EVP: E.M. Norville
SVP, CFO & Treas: M.E. LaBelle

SVP, Secy & General Counsel: F.D. Burt
Investor Contact: M. Walsh (617-236-3300)
Board Members: L. S. Bacow, Z. Baird, C. B. Einiger, J. A. Frenkel, D. T. Linde, A. J. Patricof, M. Turchin, D. A. Twardock, M. B. Zuckerman

Founded: 1970
Domicile: Delaware
Employees: 700

Boston Scientific Corp

STANDARD &POOR'S

S&P Recommendation | HOLD ★★★☆☆

Price	12-Mo. Target Price	Investment Style
$6.30 (as of Oct 22, 2010)	$7.00	Large-Cap Growth

GICS Sector Health Care
Sub-Industry Health Care Equipment

Summary This manufacturer of minimally invasive medical devices acquired its device rival Guidant Corp. in April 2006 for $27 billion in cash and stock.

Key Stock Statistics (Source S&P, Vickers, company reports)

52-Wk Range	$9.79– 5.04	S&P Oper. EPS 2010E	0.38	Market Capitalization(B)	$9.556	Beta	1.01
Trailing 12-Month EPS	$-1.76	S&P Oper. EPS 2011E	0.44	Yield (%)	Nil	S&P 3-Yr. Proj. EPS CAGR(%)	0
Trailing 12-Month P/E	NM	P/E on S&P Oper. EPS 2010E	16.6	Dividend Rate/Share	Nil	S&P Credit Rating	BBB-
$10K Invested 5 Yrs Ago	$2,637	Common Shares Outstg. (M)	1,516.9	Institutional Ownership (%)	86		

Price Performance

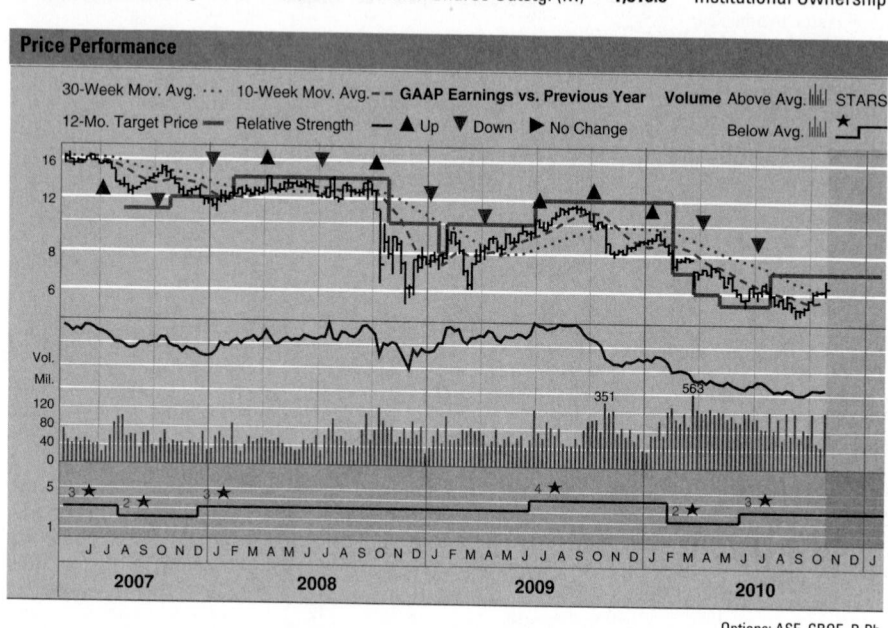

30-Week Mov. Avg. ···· 10-Week Mov. Avg. – – GAAP Earnings vs. Previous Year   Volume Above Avg. STARS
12-Mo. Target Price — Relative Strength — ▲ Up ▼ Down ▶ No Change   Below Avg.

Options: ASE, CBOE, P, Ph

Analysis prepared by **Phillip M. Seligman** on July 27, 2010, when the stock traded at **$ 5.93.**

Qualitative Risk Assessment

LOW	MEDIUM	**HIGH**

Our risk assessment reflects the company's operations within intensely competitive areas of the health care industry, and its dependence for growth on the development and commercialization of new products. In addition, a large percentage of customers are reimbursed by the federal Medicare program, and we believe the government is likely to reduce the pace of expenditure growth by lowering reimbursement rates for expensive medical devices such as defibrillators and cardiac stents.

Quantitative Evaluations

S&P Quality Ranking   C

D	**C**	B-	B	B+	A-	A	A+

Relative Strength Rank   **MODERATE**

70

LOWEST = 1   HIGHEST = 99

Highlights

▶ We see revenues declining less than 5% in 2010. We believe BSX lost some share from the recent, temporary implantable cardioverter defibrillator (ICD) recall, and we see the potential for permanent share loss in this market. We expect the ICD and stent markets to be challenging this year, and we think BSX will experience further margin erosion on a mix shift from its Taxus stent to the lower-margin PROMUS stent (due to the license and royalty agreement under which PROMUS is produced).

▶ We expect gross margins to contract, as the benefits of restructuring are outweighed by pricing pressures and product mix shift. We think R&D spending will be stable as a percentage of sales, but the SG&A cost ratio will rise as expenses are spread over a smaller base, BSX compensates personnel for commissions lost during its ICD recall, and the company increases investments in growth initiatives.

▶ We see adjusted EPS of $0.33 in 2010 and $0.43 in 2011, including amortization expense, given the ongoing recurring nature of such charges recorded by BSX in recent years.

Investment Rationale/Risk

▶ While BSX realized faster-than-expected growth of ICD sales in the second quarter, following the lifting of the recall, it was not a full recovery. Moreover, we think the recall and the company's recent advisory on three ICD models no longer sold (as reported in the Wall Street Journal) may have hurt its reputation and, hence, its ability to regain market share. We see this being offset by BSX's licensing agreement to market its PROMUS version of the successful XIENCE drug-eluting stent, its product pipeline -- which we view as promising despite recent launch delays -- and its planned emerging markets expansion. But we also see headwinds, including continued pricing pressures and deferral of procedures.

▶ Risks to our recommendation and target price include unfavorable litigation outcomes, a worse-than-expected product mix, intensified competition, and slow commercialization of new, key products.

▶ Our 12-month target price of $7.00 reflects a discount-to-peers 12X our 2010 cash EPS estimate of $0.59, before amortization expense of $0.26. We view this valuation as appropriate given the impact of BSX's ICD problems.

Revenue/Earnings Data

Revenue (Million $)

	1Q	2Q	3Q	4Q	Year
2010	1,960	1,928	--	--	--
2009	2,010	2,074	2,025	2,079	8,188
2008	2,046	2,024	1,978	2,002	8,050
2007	2,086	2,071	2,048	2,152	8,357
2006	1,620	2,110	2,206	2,065	7,821
2005	1,615	1,617	1,511	1,540	6,283

Earnings Per Share ($)

2010	-1.05	0.06	E0.07	E0.10	E0.38
2009	-0.01	0.10	0.13	-0.71	-0.68
2008	0.22	0.07	-0.04	-1.62	-1.38
2007	0.08	0.08	-0.18	-0.31	-0.33
2006	0.40	-3.21	0.05	0.19	-2.81
2005	0.42	0.24	-0.33	0.40	0.75

Fiscal year ended Dec. 31. Next earnings report expected: NA. EPS Estimates based on S&P Operating Earnings; historical GAAP earnings are as reported.

Dividend Data

No cash dividends have been paid.

The McGraw-Hill Companies

Boston Scientific Corp

STANDARD &POOR'S

Business Summary July 27, 2010

CORPORATE OVERVIEW. Boston Scientific develops and markets minimally invasive medical devices that are used in a broad range of interventional medical specialties, including interventional cardiology, cardiac rhythm management, peripheral intervention, electrophysiology, gynecology, oncology, urology and neuromodulation.

Within the cardiovascular market, the company sells products used to treat coronary vessel disease known as arteriosclerosis. The majority of BSX's cardiovascular products are used in percutaneous transluminal coronary angioplasty (PTCA) and percutaneous transluminal coronary rotational atherectomy. These products include PTCA balloon catheters, rotational atherectomy systems, guide wires, guide catheters, diagnostic catheters, and, more recently, a cutting balloon catheter. Other products include thrombectomy catheters, peripheral vascular stents, embolic protection filters, blood clot fil-

ter systems, and electrophysiology products.

BSX also sells balloon-expandable and self-expanding coronary stent systems. In early 2004, BSX launched Taxus, an Express stent coated with a polymer embedded with the anticancer compound paclitaxel. In January 2005, BSX launched its next-generation Taxus Liberte paclitaxel-eluting coronary stent in 18 Inter-Continental countries and in Europe. Taxus Liberte was launched in the U.S. in 2008. Through an agreement with Abbott Labs, BSX also sells the PROMUS everolimus-eluting stent system in the U.S. During 2009, drug-coated coronary stents accounted for 23% of total revenues.

Company Financials Fiscal Year Ended Dec. 31

Per Share Data ($)	2009	2008	2007	2006	2005	2004	2003	2002	2001	2000
Tangible Book Value	NM	NM	NM	NM	0.67	0.82	0.49	0.12	NM	0.33
Cash Flow	-0.13	-0.78	0.30	-1.90	1.12	1.60	0.79	0.64	0.22	0.68
Earnings	-0.68	-1.38	-0.33	-2.81	0.75	1.24	0.56	0.45	-0.07	0.46
S&P Core Earnings	0.49	-0.16	0.16	-2.75	1.39	1.27	0.50	0.33	-0.10	NA
Dividends	Nil	Nil	Nil	Nil	Nil	Nil	Nil	Nil	Nil	Nil
Payout Ratio	Nil	Nil	Nil	Nil	Nil	Nil	Nil	Nil	Nil	Nil
Prices:High	11.77	14.22	18.69	26.56	35.50	46.10	36.85	22.15	13.95	14.59
Prices:Low	6.08	5.41	11.27	14.43	22.80	31.25	19.10	10.24	6.63	6.09
P/E Ratio:High	NM	NM	NM	NM	47	37	66	49	NM	32
P/E Ratio:Low	NM	NM	NM	NM	30	25	34	23	NM	13

Income Statement Analysis (Million $)

	2009	2008	2007	2006	2005	2004	2003	2002	2001	2000
Revenue	8,188	8,050	8,357	7,821	6,283	5,624	3,476	2,919	2,673	2,664
Operating Income	2,141	2,159	2,158	-2,383	2,338	1,989	945	757	614	819
Depreciation	834	864	939	781	314	275	196	161	232	181
Interest Expense	407	468	570	435	90.0	64.0	46.0	43.0	59.0	70.0
Pretax Income	-1,308	-2,062	-569	-3,535	891	1,494	643	549	44.0	527
Effective Tax Rate	21.6%	NM	NM	NM	29.5%	28.9%	26.6%	32.1%	NM	29.2%
Net Income	-1,025	-2,072	-495	-3,577	628	1,062	472	373	-54.0	373
S&P Core Earnings	744	-231	240	-3,498	1,162	1,082	423	269	-77.0	NA

Balance Sheet & Other Financial Data (Million $)

	2009	2008	2007	2006	2005	2004	2003	2002	2001	2000
Cash	864	1,641	1,452	1,688	848	1,640	671	277	180	54.0
Current Assets	4,061	5,452	5,921	4,901	2,631	3,289	1,880	1,208	1,106	992
Total Assets	25,177	27,080	31,197	31,096	8,196	8,170	5,699	4,450	3,974	3,427
Current Liabilities	3,022	3,233	3,250	2,630	1,479	2,605	1,393	923	831	819
Long Term Debt	5,915	6,743	8,161	8,895	1,864	1,139	1,172	847	973	562
Common Equity	12,301	13,138	15,097	15,298	4,282	4,025	2,862	2,467	2,015	1,935
Total Capital	18,216	22,143	25,314	26,977	6,408	5,423	4,185	3,414	2,988	2,497
Capital Expenditures	312	362	363	341	341	274	188	112	121	76.0
Cash Flow	-191	-1,172	444	-2,796	942	1,337	668	534	178	554
Current Ratio	1.3	1.7	1.8	1.9	1.8	1.3	1.3	1.3	1.3	1.2
% Long Term Debt of Capitalization	32.5	30.5	34.5	33.0	29.1	21.0	28.0	24.8	32.6	22.5
% Net Income of Revenue	NM	NM	NM	NM	10.0	18.9	13.6	12.8	NM	14.0
% Return on Assets	NM	NM	NM	NM	7.7	15.3	9.3	8.9	NM	10.7
% Return on Equity	NM	NM	NM	NM	15.1	30.8	17.7	16.6	NM	20.4

Data as orig reptd.; bef. results of disc opers/spec. items. Per share data adj. for stk. divs.; EPS diluted. E-Estimated. NA-Not Available. NM-Not Meaningful. NR-Not Ranked. UR-Under Review.

Office: One Boston Scientific Pl, Natick, MA 01760-1537.
Telephone: 508-650-8000.
Email: investor_relations@bsci.com
Website: http://www.bostonscientific.com

Chrmn: P.M. Nicholas, Jr.
Pres & CEO: J.R. Elliott
COO & EVP: S.R. Leno
EVP & CFO: J.D. Capello

EVP, Chief Admin Officer, Secy & General Counsel: T.A. Pratt
Board Members: J. E. Abele, K. T. Bartlett, B. L. Byrnes, N. J. Connors, J. R. Elliott, M. A. Fox, R. Groves, E. Mario, N. J. Nicholas, Jr., P. M. Nicholas, Jr., U. E. Reinhardt, J. E. Sununu

Founded: 1979
Domicile: Delaware
Employees: 26,000

The McGraw-Hill Companies

Bristol-Myers Squibb Co

STANDARD &POOR'S

S&P Recommendation BUY ★★★★☆

Price	12-Mo. Target Price	Investment Style
$26.96 (as of Oct 22, 2010)	$30.00	Large-Cap Value

GICS Sector Health Care
Sub-Industry Pharmaceuticals

Summary Bristol-Myers Squibb is a leading global drugmaker, with strengths in cardiovascular, anti-infective and anticancer therapeutics.

Key Stock Statistics (Source S&P, Vickers, company reports)

52-Wk Range	$28.00– 21.67	S&P Oper. EPS 2010**E**	2.18	Market Capitalization(B)	$46.232	Beta	0.65
Trailing 12-Month EPS	$5.72	S&P Oper. EPS 2011**E**	2.35	Yield (%)	4.75	S&P 3-Yr. Proj. EPS CAGR(%)	6
Trailing 12-Month P/E	4.7	P/E on S&P Oper. EPS 2010**E**	12.4	Dividend Rate/Share	$1.28	S&P Credit Rating	A+
$10K Invested 5 Yrs Ago	$15,879	Common Shares Outstg. (M)	1,714.8	Institutional Ownership (%)	69		

Price Performance

30-Week Mov. Avg. · · · 10-Week Mov. Avg. - - GAAP Earnings vs. Previous Year Volume Above Avg. STARS
12-Mo. Target Price — Relative Strength ▲ Up ▼ Down ▶ No Change Below Avg. ★

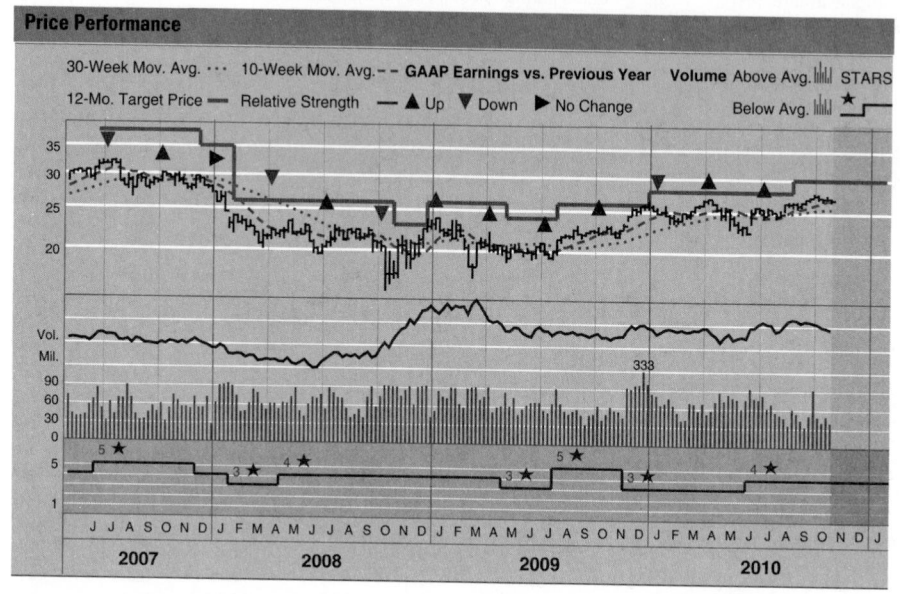

Options: ASE, CBOE, P, Ph

Analysis prepared by **Herman B. Saftlas** on August 19, 2010, when the stock traded at **$ 26.01**.

Qualitative Risk Assessment

LOW	**MEDIUM**	HIGH

In common with other large capitalization drugmakers, BMY is subject to generic challenges to its branded drugs, as well as risks associated with new drug development and regulatory approval. While we see promise in BMY's recent efforts to expand its pharmaceutical portfolio, we remain unsure if new products will be sufficient to offset the loss of patent protection on several key drugs over the 2011-2012 period. However, cost restructurings should help the bottom line.

Quantitative Evaluations

S&P Quality Ranking B+

D	C	B-	B	**B+**	A-	A	A+

Relative Strength Rank MODERATE

39

LOWEST = 1 HIGHEST = 99

Highlights

▸ We expect total sales from continuing operations in 2010 to rise about 5% from 2009's $18.8 billion, excluding sales of the Mead Johnson business, which was split off to shareholders in late 2009. Looking at the pharmaceutical portfolio, we see modestly higher sales of Plavix, with projected gains in the U.S. more than offsetting the impact of generic erosion abroad. Volume should also be augmented by gains in Abilify, Reyataz, oncology drugs, and new products such as Orencia for arthritis and Onglyza for type 2 diabetes.

▸ We see gross margins in 2010 similar to 2009's 73.3%. While we expect a ramp-up in R&D expenses on stepped-up new drug development, we see tight discipline on the SG&A line. We expect cost efficiencies to temper an anticipated negative impact of $0.12 a share from new health care reform legislation. We also expect EPS accretion of $0.05 from the Mead Johnson split-off.

▸ After an estimated tax rate of 23.5%, versus 22.2% in 2009, and a projected 14% decline in average shares, we forecast operating EPS of $2.18 for 2010. We see further EPS progress to $2.35 in 2011.

Investment Rationale/Risk

▸ In mid-August, the FDA granted priority review status for ipilimumab treatment for advanced melanoma, with an action scheduled for Dec. 25, 2010. The novel drug, which BMY obtained the 2009 purchase of Medarex, is also under review by European regulatory authorities. We believe the drug will likely obtain marketing clearance by the end of 2010, and achieve peak sales of close to $1 billion within five years. Earlier, BMY released favorable data on Sprycel, which showed that drug more effective than rivals in treating chronic myeloid leukemia. We see these drugs enhancing BMY's oncology franchise, which should help offset the effects of patent expirations on Plavix and other products.

▸ Risks to our recommendation and target price include increased competitive pressures in key product lines, and possible pipeline setbacks.

▸ Our 12-month target price of $30 is derived by applying a modest premium-to-peers P/E of 12.8X to our 2011 EPS estimate. Our DCF model, which assumes a WACC of 9.1% and terminal growth of 1%, also indicates intrinsic value near $30. The dividend recently yielded 4.8%.

Revenue/Earnings Data

Revenue (Million $)

	1Q	2Q	3Q	4Q	Year
2010	4,807	4,768	--	--	--
2009	4,322	4,665	4,788	5,033	18,808
2008	4,891	5,203	5,254	5,249	20,597
2007	4,317	4,757	4,893	5,381	19,348
2006	4,676	4,871	4,154	4,213	17,914
2005	4,532	4,889	4,767	5,019	19,207

Earnings Per Share ($)

2010	0.43	0.53	E0.53	E0.55	E2.18
2009	0.33	0.44	0.45	0.41	1.63
2008	0.32	0.36	0.30	0.61	1.59
2007	0.33	0.33	0.41	-0.07	0.99
2006	0.36	0.34	0.17	-0.07	0.81
2005	0.27	0.50	0.49	0.26	1.52

Fiscal year ended Dec. 31. Next earnings report expected: Late October. EPS Estimates based on S&P Operating Earnings; historical GAAP earnings are as reported.

Dividend Data (Dates: mm/dd Payment Date: mm/dd/yy)

Amount ($)	Date Decl.	Ex-Div. Date	Stk. of Record	Payment Date
0.320	12/21	12/30	01/04	02/01/10
0.320	03/02	03/30	04/04	05/03/10
0.320	06/09	06/30	07/02	08/02/10
0.320	09/07	09/29	10/01	11/01/10

Dividends have been paid since 1900. Source: Company reports.

Please read the Required Disclosures and Analyst Certification on the last page of this report.

The McGraw·Hill Companies

Bristol-Myers Squibb Co

Business Summary August 19, 2010

CORPORATE OVERVIEW. Bristol-Myers Squibb is a major global drugmaker, offering a wide range of prescription drugs. With the late 2009 split-off of the Mead Johnson nutritional products business, BMY is now solely a biopharmaceuticals company. In recent years, BMY also divested other non-core operations, including beauty care, orthopedic devices and imaging products. Foreign operations accounted for 36% of sales from continuing operations in 2009, down from 40% in 2008.

The company's largest selling drug is Plavix (sales of $6.1 billion in 2009), a platelet aggregation inhibitor for the prevention of stroke, heart attack and vascular disease. Plavix is produced through a joint venture with French drugmaker Sanofi-Aventis SA. Another important heart drug is Avapro/Avalide ($1.3 billion), an angiotensin II receptor blocker for hypertension.

The company's second biggest drug is Abilify ($2.6 billion), a psychotic agent used to treat schizophrenia and bipolar disorder. It is also used to treat major depression in combination with antidepressants. Principal oncology drugs are Erbitux ($683 million), a treatment for colorectal and head & neck cancers; Sprycel for leukemia ($421 million); and Ixempra ($109 million), a drug for advanced breast cancer.

Key anti-infective drugs are HIV/AIDS treatments such as Reyataz ($1.4 billion), Sustiva ($1.3 billion), and Baraclude ($734 million). BMY also offers Cefzil, Tequin, Maxipime, and other antibiotics. Other important drugs are Orencia, a treatment for rheumatoid arthritis ($602 million); Onglyza, a drug for type 2 diabetes; and Sinemet for Parkinson's disease.

In late December 2009, BMY completed the split-off of its Mead Johnson subsidiary (MJN 49, Hold) to BMY shareholders. Under terms of the deal, BMY's remaining 170 million MJN shares (an 83% interest) were exchanged for some 269 million BMY shares. BMY sold an initial 17% interest in Mead Johnson through an IPO, raising close to $1 billion.

During 2008, BMY sold its ConvaTec ostomy and wound care and its medical imaging businesses for a combined total of $4.5 billion in cash.

Company Financials Fiscal Year Ended Dec. 31

Per Share Data ($)	2009	2008	2007	2006	2005	2004	2003	2002	2001	2000
Tangible Book Value	4.80	3.17	2.14	1.68	2.28	1.76	1.62	0.88	1.70	3.96
Cash Flow	1.93	1.94	1.39	1.28	1.98	1.66	1.99	1.43	1.68	2.42
Earnings	1.63	1.59	0.99	0.81	1.52	1.21	1.59	1.05	1.29	2.36
S&P Core Earnings	1.59	1.24	1.02	0.88	1.43	1.24	1.57	1.07	0.67	NA
Dividends	1.25	1.24	1.12	1.12	1.12	1.12	1.12	1.12	1.10	0.98
Payout Ratio	77%	27%	113%	138%	74%	93%	70%	107%	85%	42%
Prices:High	26.62	27.37	32.35	26.41	26.60	31.30	29.21	51.95	73.50	74.88
Prices:Low	17.23	16.00	25.73	20.08	20.70	22.22	21.00	19.49	48.50	42.44
P/E Ratio:High	16	17	33	33	17	26	18	49	57	32
P/E Ratio:Low	11	10	26	25	14	18	13	19	38	18

Income Statement Analysis (Million $)										
Revenue	18,808	20,597	19,348	17,914	19,207	19,380	20,894	18,119	19,423	18,216
Operating Income	5,819	5,152	4,309	3,483	4,880	5,373	5,726	4,851	7,034	6,732
Depreciation	647	728	776	927	929	909	779	735	781	746
Interest Expense	184	333	457	498	349	310	277	410	182	108
Pretax Income	5,602	5,471	3,534	2,635	4,516	4,418	4,694	2,647	2,986	5,478
Effective Tax Rate	21.1%	24.1%	22.7%	23.1%	20.6%	34.4%	25.9%	16.4%	15.4%	25.2%
Net Income	3,239	3,155	1,968	1,585	2,992	2,378	3,106	2,034	2,527	4,096
S&P Core Earnings	3,149	2,465	2,024	1,727	2,808	2,448	3,043	2,076	1,321	NA

Balance Sheet & Other Financial Data (Million $)										
Cash	8,514	8,265	2,225	4,013	5,799	7,474	5,457	3,989	5,654	3,385
Current Assets	13,958	14,763	10,348	10,302	12,283	14,801	11,918	9,975	12,349	9,824
Total Assets	31,008	29,552	26,172	25,575	28,138	30,435	27,471	24,874	27,057	17,578
Current Liabilities	6,313	6,710	8,644	6,496	6,890	9,843	7,530	8,220	8,826	5,632
Long Term Debt	6,130	6,585	4,381	7,248	8,364	8,463	8,522	6,261	6,237	1,336
Common Equity	14,843	12,241	10,562	9,991	11,208	10,202	19,572	8,967	10,736	9,180
Total Capital	20,915	18,885	14,943	17,307	19,572	18,665	28,094	15,228	16,973	10,516
Capital Expenditures	730	941	843	762	738	676	937	997	1,023	589
Cash Flow	3,817	3,883	2,744	2,512	3,921	3,287	3,885	2,769	3,308	4,842
Current Ratio	2.2	2.2	1.2	1.6	1.8	1.5	1.6	1.2	1.4	1.7
% Long Term Debt of Capitalization	Nil	34.9	29.3	42.0	42.7	45.3	30.3	41.1	36.7	12.7
% Net Income of Revenue	17.2	15.3	10.2	8.8	15.6	12.3	14.9	11.2	13.0	22.5
% Return on Assets	NA	11.4	7.6	5.9	10.2	8.2	11.8	7.7	11.3	23.6
% Return on Equity	NA	27.7	19.2	15.0	27.9	23.8	16.8	22.5	25.4	46.0

Data as orig reptd.; bef. results of disc opers/spec. items. Per share data adj. for stk. divs.; EPS diluted. E-Estimated. NA-Not Available. NM-Not Meaningful. NR-Not Ranked. UR-Under Review.

Office: 345 Park Ave , New York, NY 10154-0037.
Telephone: 212-546-4000.
Website: http://www.bms.com
Chrmn: J.M. Cornelius

Pres, CEO & COO: L. Andreotti
EVP & CSO: E. Sigal
SVP, Secy & General Counsel: S. Leung
CFO: C. Bancroft

Investor Contact: J. Elicker (212-546-3775)
Board Members: L. Andreotti, L. B. Campbell, J. M. Cornelius, L. J. Freeh, L. H. Glimcher, M. Grobstein, L. Johansson, A. J. Lacy, V. L. Sato, T. D. West, Jr., R. S. Williams

Founded: 1887
Domicile: Delaware
Employees: 28,000

Broadcom Corp

STANDARD &POOR'S

S&P Recommendation	HOLD ★★★☆☆	**Price** $37.55 (as of Oct 22, 2010)	**12-Mo. Target Price** $38.00	**Investment Style** Large-Cap Blend

GICS Sector Information Technology
Sub-Industry Semiconductors

Summary This company provides semiconductors for broadband communications markets, including cable set-top boxes, cable modems, office networks, and home networking.

Key Stock Statistics (Source S&P, Vickers, company reports)

52-Wk Range	$38.47– 25.76	S&P Oper. EPS 2010**E**	2.02	Market Capitalization(B)	$16.834	Beta	1.41
Trailing 12-Month EPS	$1.19	S&P Oper. EPS 2011**E**	2.11	Yield (%)	0.85	S&P 3-Yr. Proj. EPS CAGR(%)	34
Trailing 12-Month P/E	31.6	P/E on S&P Oper. EPS 2010**E**	18.6	Dividend Rate/Share	$0.32	S&P Credit Rating	NA
$10K Invested 5 Yrs Ago	$13,365	Common Shares Outstg. (M)	503.5	Institutional Ownership (%)	90		

Price Performance

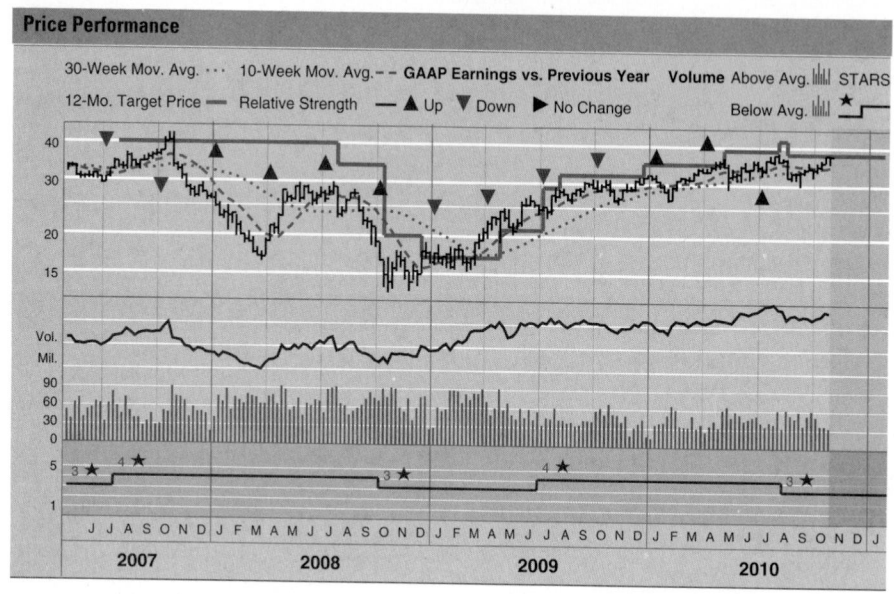

30-Week Mov. Avg. ···· 10-Week Mov. Avg. – – GAAP Earnings vs. Previous Year Volume Above Avg. STARS
12-Mo. Target Price — Relative Strength ▲ Up ▼ Down ▶ No Change Below Avg. ★

Options: ASE, CBOE, P, Ph

Analysis prepared by **Clyde Montevirgen** on August 17, 2010, when the stock traded at **$ 31.86**.

Highlights

▸ We anticipate sales will rise 46% in 2010 and 10% in 2011. Although we are concerned about rising inventory in the supply chain, we see expansion of broadband services and IT spending providing long-term growth opportunities for BRCM's broadband communication and enterprise networking businesses. We think that recent design wins for various combination wireless and mobile handset products will help boost mobile and wireless networking sales as its customers ramp production of new products. Generally, we believe BRCM has a well-diversified and innovative product portfolio, which has expanded its served available market and should lead to higher market share.

▸ We see the gross margin remaining in the 52% to 53% range over the next two years. Although varying sales mix could impact results, we believe that BRCM's fabless structure will help to keep gross margins relatively stable. Similarly, we expect the operating margin to be around 17% in 2010 and 2011, as sales growth balances higher expenses to support new products.

▸ Our 2011 earnings projections assume a 10% effective tax rate and a modest increase in the share count.

Investment Rationale/Risk

▸ Our hold recommendation reflects our view of improving fundamentals balanced by fair valuations. Through its focus on making integrated and multifunctional chips, we believe that BRCM is taking market share in relatively fast growing markets, which should lead to above-industry growth. The top-line advances should provide operating leverage and lead to improving profitability, in our opinion. Considering anticipated return on equity that should reach multi-year highs, we think relative multiples deserve to be above the industry average, which is already the case.

▸ Risks to our recommendation and target price include lower than anticipated enterprise spending, slower than anticipated orders for handset chips, and rising operating expenses.

▸ Our 12-month target price of $38 is based on a P/E multiple of 18X, above the peer average to account for our view of BRCM's relative earnings growth, return metrics, and risk, applied to our 2011 EPS estimate. Our DCF model, which assumes a WACC of around 11% and a terminal growth rate of 4%, implies an intrinsic value of $44.

Qualitative Risk Assessment

LOW	MEDIUM	HIGH

Our risk assessment reflects Broadcom's exposure to the sales cycles of the semiconductor industry, dependence on foundry partners for production, and greater reliance than most companies on stock-based compensation. This is partially offset by our view of a lack of debt and a broadening base of end users.

Quantitative Evaluations

S&P Quality Ranking B-

D	C	B-	B	B+	A-	A	A+

Relative Strength Rank STRONG

73

LOWEST = 1 HIGHEST = 99

Revenue/Earnings Data

Revenue (Million $)

	1Q	2Q	3Q	4Q	Year
2010	1,462	1,604	--	--	--
2009	853.4	1,040	1,254	1,343	4,490
2008	1,032	1,201	1,298	1,127	4,658
2007	901.5	897.9	950.0	1,027	3,776
2006	900.7	941.1	902.6	923.5	3,668
2005	550.3	604.9	695.0	820.6	2,671

Earnings Per Share ($)

	1Q	2Q	3Q	4Q	Year
2010	0.40	0.52	E0.57	E0.54	E2.02
2009	-0.19	0.03	0.16	0.11	0.13
2008	0.14	0.25	0.31	-0.32	0.41
2007	0.10	0.06	0.05	0.16	0.37
2006	0.20	0.18	0.19	0.08	0.64
2005	0.13	0.03	0.23	0.33	0.73

Fiscal year ended Dec. 31. Next earnings report expected: Late October. EPS Estimates based on S&P Operating Earnings; historical GAAP earnings are as reported.

Dividend Data (Dates: mm/dd Payment Date: mm/dd/yy)

Amount ($)	Date Decl.	Ex-Div. Date	Stk. of Record	Payment Date
0.080	01/27	02/17	02/19	03/08/10
0.080	05/20	06/02	06/04	06/21/10
0.080	08/12	08/25	08/27	09/13/10

Dividends have been paid since 2010. Source: Company reports.

Please read the Required Disclosures and Analyst Certification on the last page of this report.

The McGraw-Hill Companies

Broadcom Corp

Business Summary August 17, 2010

CORPORATE OVERVIEW. Founded in 1991, Broadcom is a global provider of semiconductors for wired and wireless communications. The company's products enable the delivery of voice, video, data and multimedia to and throughout the home, the office and the mobile environment. Broadcom's diverse product portfolio includes solutions for digital cable, satellite and Internet Protocol (IP) set-top boxes and media servers; high definition television (HDTV); high definition DVD players and personal video recording (PVR) devices; cable and DSL modems and residential gateways; high-speed transmission and switching for local, metropolitan, wide area and storage networking; System I/O server solutions; broadband network and security processors; wireless and personal area networking; cellular communications; global positioning system (GPS) applications; mobile multimedia and applications processors; mobile power management; and Voice over Internet Protocol (VoIP) gateway and telephony systems.

Revenues can be separated into three main target markets: Broadband Communications, Enterprise Networking, and Mobile and Wireless Networking. Broadband Communication products offer manufacturers a range of broad-

band communications and consumer electronics systems-on-a-chip (SoCs) that enable voice, video and data services over residential wired and wireless networks. Enterprise Networking enables a robust, scalable, secure and easy-to-manage network infrastructure for the carrier/service provider, data center, enterprise and small-to-medium-sized business, or SMB, markets. Its solutions aim to enable these networks to offer higher capacities and faster, more cost-efficient transport and management of voice, data and video traffic across wired and wireless networks. Mobile and Wireless Networking allows manufacturers to develop leading-edge mobile devices, enabling end-to-end wireless opportunities for the home, business and mobile markets. In 2009, net revenue by major target market was 34% broadband communications; 24% enterprise networking; and 38% mobile and wireless, with All Other making up the remainder.

Company Financials Fiscal Year Ended Dec. 31

Per Share Data ($)	2009	2008	2007	2006	2005	2004	2003	2002	2001	2000
Tangible Book Value	4.97	4.63	4.86	5.43	3.79	2.59	1.43	0.94	2.19	3.31
Cash Flow	0.33	0.60	0.48	0.73	0.85	0.59	-1.98	-5.20	-4.87	-1.59
Earnings	0.13	0.41	0.37	0.64	0.73	0.42	-2.19	-5.57	-7.19	-2.09
S&P Core Earnings	0.19	0.62	0.37	0.64	-0.04	-0.70	-2.31	-5.07	-6.87	NA
Dividends	Nil	Nil	Nil	Nil	Nil	Nil	Nil	Nil	Nil	Nil
Payout Ratio	Nil	Nil	Nil	Nil	Nil	Nil	Nil	Nil	Nil	Nil
Prices:High	32.29	29.91	43.07	50.00	33.28	31.37	25.10	35.57	93.00	183.17
Prices:Low	15.31	12.98	25.70	21.98	18.25	16.83	7.91	6.35	12.27	49.83
P/E Ratio:High	NM	73	NM	78	46	75	NM	NM	NM	NM
P/E Ratio:Low	NM	32	NM	34	25	40	NM	NM	NM	NM

Income Statement Analysis (Million $)										
Revenue	4,490	4,658	3,776	3,668	2,671	2,401	1,610	1,083	962	1,096
Operating Income	265	490	148	309	557	450	-30.4	-442	-573	-169
Depreciation	105	97.5	62.0	47.6	68.5	91.7	90.9	147	889	165
Interest Expense	NA	Nil	Nil	Nil	Nil	Nil	Nil	3.60	5.00	0.33
Pretax Income	72.2	222	219	367	392	294	-935	-1,939	-2,799	-692
Effective Tax Rate	9.60%	3.38%	2.70%	NM	NM	25.7%	NM	NM	NM	NM
Net Income	65.3	215	213	379	412	219	-960	-2,237	-2,742	-688
S&P Core Earnings	97.5	319	215	379	-25.7	-330	-1,011	-2,039	-2,617	NA

Balance Sheet & Other Financial Data (Million $)										
Cash	1,929	1,898	2,329	2,680	1,733	1,183	606	503	540	524
Current Assets	2,914	2,751	3,054	3,352	2,336	1,584	996	722	674	876
Total Assets	5,127	4,393	4,838	4,877	3,752	2,886	2,018	2,216	3,623	4,678
Current Liabilities	1,148	717	758	679	595	497	504	534	412	203
Long Term Debt	NA	Nil	Nil	Nil	Nil	Nil	Nil	1.21	4.01	Nil
Common Equity	3,892	3,607	4,036	4,192	3,145	2,366	1,490	1,645	3,207	4,475
Total Capital	3,892	3,607	4,036	4,192	3,145	2,366	1,490	1,646	3,211	4,475
Capital Expenditures	66.6	82.8	160	92.5	41.8	49.9	47.9	75.2	71.4	80.7
Cash Flow	170	312	275	427	480	310	-869	-2,090	-1,853	-523
Current Ratio	2.5	3.8	4.0	4.9	3.9	3.2	2.0	1.4	1.6	4.3
% Long Term Debt of Capitalization	Nil	Nil	Nil	Nil	Nil	Nil	Nil	0.1	0.1	Nil
% Net Income of Revenue	1.5	4.6	5.6	10.3	15.4	9.1	NM	NM	NM	NM
% Return on Assets	1.4	4.7	4.3	8.8	12.4	8.9	NM	NM	NM	NM
% Return on Equity	1.7	5.6	5.1	10.3	14.9	11.3	NM	NM	NM	NM

Data as orig reptd.; bef. results of disc opers/spec. items. Per share data adj. for stk. divs.; EPS diluted. E-Estimated. NA-Not Available. NM-Not Meaningful. NR-Not Ranked. UR-Under Review.

Office: 5300 California Avenue, Buildings 1-8, Irvine, CA 92617.
Telephone: 949-926-5000.
Email: investorinfo@broadcom.com
Website: http://www.broadcom.com

Chrmn: J.E. Major
Pres & CEO: S.A. McGregor
COO: N.Y. Kim
EVP & CFO: E.K. Brandt

EVP, Secy & General Counsel: A. Chong
Investor Contact: T.P. Andrew (949-926-5663)
Board Members: J. Amble, N. H. Handel, E. Hartenstein, J. E. Major, S. A. McGregor, W. T. Morrow, J. A. Swainson, R. E. Switz

Founded: 1991
Domicile: California

Brown-Forman Corp

S&P Recommendation HOLD ★★★★★

Price $61.93 (as of Oct 22, 2010)	
12-Mo. Target Price $64.00	
Investment Style Large-Cap Growth	

GICS Sector Consumer Staples
Sub-Industry Distillers & Vintners

Summary This leading distiller and importer of alcoholic beverages markets Jack Daniel's, Southern Comfort, Finlandia, Korbel and Bolla brands.

Key Stock Statistics (Source S&P, Vickers, company reports)

52-Wk Range	$65.05– 47.40	S&P Oper. EPS 2011**E**	3.06	Market Capitalization(B)	$5.548	Beta	0.73
Trailing 12-Month EPS	$2.96	S&P Oper. EPS 2012**E**	3.39	Yield (%)	1.94	S&P 3-Yr. Proj. EPS CAGR(%)	7
Trailing 12-Month P/E	20.9	P/E on S&P Oper. EPS 2011**E**	20.2	Dividend Rate/Share	$1.20	S&P Credit Rating	A
$10K Invested 5 Yrs Ago	$14,687	Common Shares Outstg. (M)	146.2	Institutional Ownership (%)	51		

Price Performance

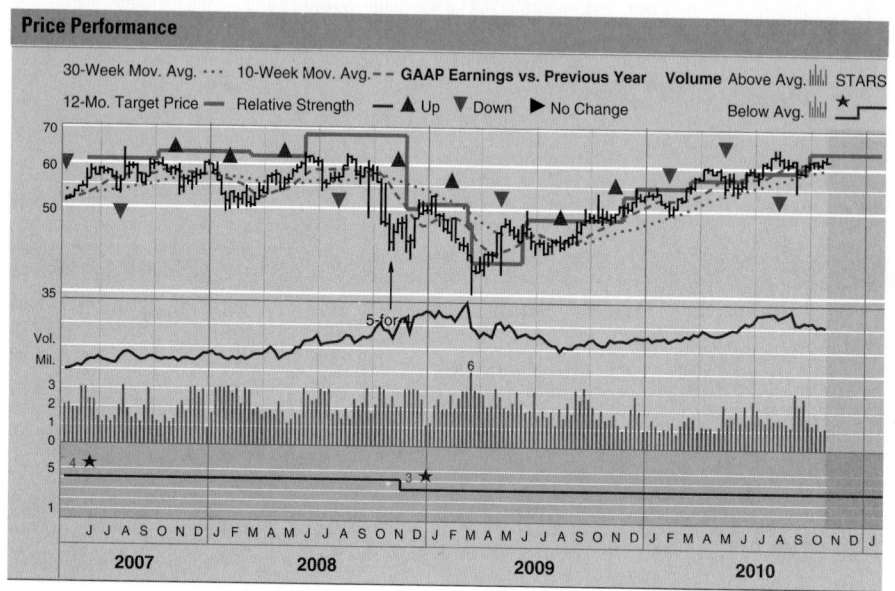

30-Week Mov. Avg. ··· 10-Week Mov. Avg. - - — GAAP Earnings vs. Previous Year Volume Above Avg. ▦ STARS
12-Mo. Target Price — Relative Strength — ▲ Up ▼ Down ▶ No Change Below Avg. ▦ ★

Analysis prepared by **Esther Y. Kwon, CFA** on September 23, 2010, when the stock traded at **$ 60.99**.

Highlights

▶ We forecast net sales growth (excluding excise taxes) of 1% in FY 11 (Apr.), on easier comparisons in the first half due to inventory drawdowns at distributors, more than reversing FY 10's 0.5% decline to approximately $2.5 billion. In constant currency, we see Jack Daniel's branded product sales rising, but we expect a decline in Southern Comfort, while Finlandia should continue to rise despite a negative foreign exchange impact. Long term, with 53% of FY 10 net sales from outside the U.S., we see Finlandia and, secondarily, Jack Daniel's driving more than 50% of net sales growth.

▶ We look for stable gross margins on cost efficiencies, offset by a lower-margin product and geographic mix and a continued high level of value added pack promotions. We forecast an uptick in operating expenses as BF elects to build out its own distribution in certain international markets, offset somewhat by lower media and advertising costs due to a greater emphasis on off-premise promotions.

▶ We estimate FY 11 EPS of $3.06. In June, directors authorized the repurchase of up to $250 million of shares through December 1, 2010.

Investment Rationale/Risk

▶ Long term, we look for continued strength in the global market, and we think spirits will continue to make successful inroads in the 21- to 27-year-old demographic. BF should continue to capitalize on what we see as positive industry trends with its strong portfolio of spirits and international reach, particularly with its Jack Daniel's brand. In the near term, however, we see an uneven recovery in the spirits category as we believe consumers will continue to selectively trade down and consumption shifts more rapidly to the lower-margin off-premise channel from on-premise.

▶ Risks to our recommendation and target price include an unexpected slowdown in the growth of top-performing brands. Also, we view BF's dual-class structure and the majority representation of insiders on its board of directors as corporate governance concerns.

▶ Our 12-month target price of $64 is supported by our P/E analysis, which applies a multiple of 21.0X, a premium to the stock's historical average of 19.6X and a premium to peers and the S&P 500, to our FY 11 EPS estimate of $3.06. We think a premium is fair given the company's higher international exposure.

Qualitative Risk Assessment

LOW	MEDIUM	HIGH

Brown-Forman is a large-cap competitor in an industry that has historically demonstrated relative stability. However, we believe the company's dual-class structure and the majority representation of insiders on its board of directors pose corporate governance concerns.

Quantitative Evaluations

S&P Quality Ranking A

D	C	B-	B	B+	A-	A	A+

Relative Strength Rank MODERATE
41
LOWEST = 1   HIGHEST = 99

Revenue/Earnings Data

Revenue (Million $)

	1Q	2Q	3Q	4Q	Year
2011	569.4	--	--	--	--
2010	570.8	698.8	637.4	561.9	2,469
2009	790.0	935.0	784.0	683.0	3,192
2008	739.0	893.0	877.0	772.0	3,282
2007	633.0	727.0	754.8	690.8	2,218
2006	547.0	666.0	637.0	594.0	2,444

Earnings Per Share ($)

	1Q	2Q	3Q	4Q	Year
2011	0.76	E0.95	E0.84	E0.51	E3.06
2010	0.81	0.99	0.73	0.49	3.02
2009	0.58	0.94	0.81	0.53	2.87
2008	0.58	0.83	0.74	0.65	2.85
2007	0.61	0.80	0.72	0.45	2.58
2006	0.57	0.73	0.78	0.49	2.56

Fiscal year ended Apr. 30. Next earnings report expected: Early December. EPS Estimates based on S&P Operating Earnings; historical GAAP earnings are as reported.

Dividend Data (Dates: mm/dd Payment Date: mm/dd/yy)

Amount ($)	Date Decl.	Ex-Div. Date	Stk. of Record	Payment Date
0.300	11/16	12/03	12/07	01/04/10
0.300	01/28	03/04	03/08	04/01/10
0.300	05/27	06/03	06/07	07/01/10
0.300	07/22	09/02	09/07	10/01/10

Dividends have been paid since 1960. Source: Company reports.

Brown-Forman Corp

STANDARD &POOR'S

Business Summary September 23, 2010

CORPORATE OVERVIEW. Brown-Forman Corp.'s origins date back to 1870. It is the world's fourth largest producer of distilled spirits. With a portfolio of well known brands, the company is best known for its popular Jack Daniel's Tennessee Whiskey, which continues to be its largest sales and profit producer.

Although many alcoholic beverage companies have moved in recent years to reduce their dependence on the highly mature brown spirits market, BF has remained whiskey-oriented. Its product line is stocked with well known whiskies, bourbons, vodkas, tequilas, rums, and liqueurs. Brands include Jack Daniel's, Southern Comfort, Tequila Herradura, el Jimador Tequila, and Canadian Mist. Global depletions of Jack Daniel's in FY 10 (Apr.) increased 2%, compared to 1% in FY 09. Statistics based on case sales rank Jack Daniel's as the largest selling American whiskey in the world, Canadian Mist as the second largest selling Canadian whiskey in the U.S. and the third largest in the world, and Southern Comfort as the largest selling domestic proprietary liqueur in the U.S. Other major alcoholic beverage lines include Fetzer and Bolla wines, Finlandia vodka, Chambord liqueur, and Korbel Champagnes.

International sales, consisting principally of exports of wines and spirits, in-

creased to 53% of total net revenues in FY 10 from 52% in FY 09. Beverage growth in recent years has come primarily from international markets for the company's spirits brands. The key export markets for brands include the U.K., Australia, Mexico, Poland, Germany, France, Spain, Italy, South Africa, China, Japan, Canada and Russia.

Until year-end FY 05, the consumer durables segment consisted of the Lenox Inc. subsidiary, which produced and marketed china, crystal and giftware under the Lenox and Gorham trademarks. The segment also included Dansk, a producer of tableware and giftware, Gorham, Kirk Steiff, and Hartmann Luggage. In July 2005, following a strategic review, the company agreed to sell Lenox. On September 1, 2005, BF consummated the sale of substantially all of Lenox to Department 56 for $196 million. Consumer durables was eliminated as a segment, and in May 2007, the sale of substantially all of the assets of Hartmann to Clarion Capital Partners was completed.

Company Financials Fiscal Year Ended Apr. 30

Per Share Data ($)	2010	2009	2008	2007	2006	2005	2004	2003	2002	2001
Tangible Book Value	3.81	3.03	2.24	1.42	6.79	4.55	3.43	1.93	6.17	5.40
Cash Flow	3.06	3.23	3.18	2.89	2.88	2.38	1.83	1.76	1.64	1.72
Earnings	3.02	2.87	2.85	2.58	2.56	2.02	1.69	1.45	1.33	1.36
S&P Core Earnings	3.03	2.62	2.82	2.54	2.52	1.90	1.66	1.24	1.11	1.22
Dividends	NA	0.81	2.25	0.62	0.73	0.64	0.58	0.58	0.54	0.51
Payout Ratio	NA	28%	79%	24%	29%	32%	34%	40%	41%	38%
Calendar Year	2009	2008	2007	2006	2005	2004	2003	2002	2001	2000
Prices:High	55.47	63.02	63.90	66.04	57.92	40.07	38.05	32.22	28.80	27.70
Prices:Low	34.97	40.46	50.54	52.22	37.30	34.24	24.10	23.48	23.06	16.75
P/E Ratio:High	18	22	22	26	23	20	23	22	22	20
P/E Ratio:Low	12	14	18	20	15	17	14	16	17	12

Income Statement Analysis (Million $)

	2010	2009	2008	2007	2006	2005	2004	2003	2002	2001
Revenue	2,469	2,481	3,282	2,806	2,444	2,729	2,577	2,378	1,958	1,924
Operating Income	715	730	735	627	560	513	473	429	408	438
Depreciation	5.00	55.0	52.0	44.0	44.0	58.0	56.0	55.0	55.0	64.0
Interest Expense	28.0	37.0	49.0	34.0	18.0	21.0	21.0	8.00	8.00	16.0
Pretax Income	682	630	644	586	559	476	388	373	348	366
Effective Tax Rate	NA	31.1%	31.7%	31.7%	29.3%	35.3%	33.5%	34.3%	34.5%	36.3%
Net Income	449	434	440	400	395	308	258	245	228	233
S&P Core Earnings	450	397	438	393	389	289	252	209	190	208

Balance Sheet & Other Financial Data (Million $)

	2010	2009	2008	2007	2006	2005	2004	2003	2002	2001
Cash	232	340	119	283	475	295	68.0	72.0	116	86.0
Current Assets	1,527	1,574	1,456	1,635	1,610	1,317	1,083	1,068	1,029	994
Total Assets	3,383	3,475	3,405	3,551	2,728	2,624	2,376	2,264	2,016	1,939
Current Liabilities	546	836	984	1,347	569	638	369	548	495	538
Long Term Debt	508	509	417	422	351	352	630	629	40.0	40.0
Common Equity	1,895	1,816	1,725	1,672	1,563	1,310	1,085	840	1,311	1,187
Total Capital	2,406	2,405	2,231	2,150	2,047	1,794	1,837	1,547	1,409	1,289
Capital Expenditures	34.0	49.0	41.0	58.0	52.0	49.0	56.0	119	71.0	96.0
Cash Flow	454	490	492	444	439	366	314	300	283	297
Current Ratio	2.8	1.9	1.5	1.2	2.8	2.1	2.9	1.9	2.1	1.8
% Long Term Debt of Capitalization	21.1	21.2	18.7	19.6	17.1	19.6	34.3	40.7	2.8	3.1
% Net Income of Revenue	18.2	17.5	13.4	14.3	16.2	11.3	10.0	10.3	11.6	12.1
% Return on Assets	13.1	12.6	12.7	12.7	14.7	12.3	11.1	11.4	11.5	12.5
% Return on Equity	24.2	24.5	26.7	24.7	27.5	25.6	26.8	22.8	18.3	20.9

Data as orig reptd.; bef. results of disc opers/spec. items. Per share data adj. for stk. divs.; EPS diluted. E-Estimated. NA-Not Available. NM-Not Meaningful. NR-Not Ranked. UR-Under Review.

Office: 850 Dixie Highway, Louisville, KY 40210-1038.
Telephone: 502-585-1100.
Website: http://www.brown-forman.com
Co-Chrmn: G.G. Brown, IV

Co-Chrmn & CEO: P.C. Varga
Vice Chrmn: J.S. Welch, Jr.
COO & EVP: M.I. McCallum
EVP & CFO: D.C. Berg

Investor Contact: T. Graven (502-774-7442)
Board Members: P. Bousquet-Chavanne, G. G. Brown, IV, M. S. Brown, Jr., B. L. Byrnes, J. D. Cook, S. A. Frazier, R. P. Mayer, W. E. Mitchell, W. M. Street, D. B. Stubbs, P. C. Varga, J. S. Welch, Jr.

Founded: 1870
Domicile: Delaware
Employees: 3,900

The McGraw·Hill Companies

Cabot Oil & Gas Corp

STANDARD
&POOR'S

S&P Recommendation	HOLD ★★★★★	Price	12-Mo. Target Price	Investment Style
		$30.88 (as of Oct 22, 2010)	$35.00	Large-Cap Growth

GICS Sector Energy
Sub-Industry Oil & Gas Exploration & Production

Summary Cabot is an independent oil and gas company engaged in development, exploration and production in North America.

Key Stock Statistics (Source S&P, Vickers, company reports)

52-Wk Range	$46.46– 26.62	S&P Oper. EPS 2010E	1.01	Market Capitalization(B)	$3.216	Beta	1.15
Trailing 12-Month EPS	$1.20	S&P Oper. EPS 2011E	0.25	Yield (%)	0.39	S&P 3-Yr. Proj. EPS CAGR(%)	-52
Trailing 12-Month P/E	25.7	P/E on S&P Oper. EPS 2010E	30.6	Dividend Rate/Share	$0.12	S&P Credit Rating	NA
$10K Invested 5 Yrs Ago	$14,465	Common Shares Outstg. (M)	104.1	Institutional Ownership (%)	NM		

Price Performance

30-Week Mov. Avg. · · · 10-Week Mov. Avg. - - GAAP Earnings vs. Previous Year Volume Above Avg. STARS
12-Mo. Target Price — Relative Strength — ▲ Up ▼ Down ► No Change Below Avg. ★

Options: ASE, CBOE, P, Ph

Analysis prepared by **Michael Kay** on October 15, 2010, when the stock traded at **$ 30.71**.

Highlights

▶ Production was up 8% to 103 Bcfe in 2009, on success at the Marcellus Shale, where gross production is over 200 Mmcf/d. COG is currently operating 7 horizontal rigs at Marcellus, where it has drilled 106 wells, completed 76 and plans to drill 75 wells in 2010. COG recently drilled its second Haynesville well, de-risking some of its acreage in the play. COG has been leasing acreage in the Eagle Ford Shale oil window to increase exposure to crude. We see a ramp in second-half volume as 30 Marcellus wells await completion. COG expects gross Marcellus production to surpass 250 Mmcf/d by year end and production growth of 21%-25%.

▶ In our view, a transformed asset base has lowered portfolio risk and improved drilling success. We expect focus in 2010 on Marcellus, but COG will also target the Haynesville and Eagle Ford shales, Cotton Valley Taylor Sands, James Lime, Hossten and Pettet formations.

▶ Operating EPS was $1.66 in 2009, down 28% on plunging gas prices. We see EPS of $1.01 in 2010 and $0.25 in 2011, reflecting higher production offset by lower realized prices due to less attractive hedges. COG sees 2010 capex at $725 million, versus $640 million in 2009.

Investment Rationale/Risk

▶ COG's core operating areas are performing well, with horizontal drilling programs in the Marcellus Shale and Texas moving ahead nicely, in our view. We see strong potential for its large undeveloped acreage at Marcellus, Haynesville and now Eagle Ford. In April, the Pennsylvania Department of Environmental Protection (DEP) issued a modified agreement to the consent order entered in November 2009 concerning environmental issues and alleged contamination of 14 water wells in Susquehanna County. We expect minimal effect on current drilling, as COG has no rigs in the area.

▶ Risks to our recommendation and target price include declining oil and gas prices, difficulty replacing reserves, and production declines.

▶ We believe the shares discount the potential from the Marcellus, Haynesville and Eagle Ford shales, but we are cautious on natural gas prices and see reduced upside potential for the shares. We blend our proved reserve NAV estimate ($42) with a target 7X enterprise value to 2011 EBITDA ($33) multiple, a premium to peers on expected double-digit production growth, and our DCF model ($32; 11% WACC, 3% terminal growth), for a 12-month target price of $35.

Qualitative Risk Assessment

LOW	MEDIUM	HIGH

Our risk assessment reflects that COG operates in a very capital-intensive industry that is cyclical and derives value from producing a commodity whose price is extremely volatile.

Quantitative Evaluations

S&P Quality Ranking B+

D	C	B-	B	B+	A-	A	A+

Relative Strength Rank MODERATE

41

LOWEST = 1   HIGHEST = 99

Revenue/Earnings Data

Revenue (Million $)

	1Q	2Q	3Q	4Q	Year
2010	212.6	195.5	--	--	--
2009	233.9	204.8	207.0	233.5	879.3
2008	219.7	248.9	244.8	232.5	945.8
2007	191.6	175.8	170.9	193.9	732.2
2006	214.8	190.8	184.7	171.7	762.0
2005	144.1	151.9	161.8	225.1	682.8

Earnings Per Share ($)

2010	0.28	0.21	E0.22	E0.28	E1.01
2009	0.46	0.24	0.37	0.34	1.42
2008	0.46	0.55	0.64	0.42	2.10
2007	0.50	0.42	0.36	0.43	1.71
2006	0.55	0.47	1.92	0.33	3.32
2005	0.21	0.36	0.34	0.59	1.50

Fiscal year ended Dec. 31. Next earnings report expected: Late October. EPS Estimates based on S&P Operating Earnings; historical GAAP earnings are as reported.

Dividend Data (Dates: mm/dd Payment Date: mm/dd/yy)

Amount ($)	Date Decl.	Ex-Div. Date	Stk. of Record	Payment Date
0.030	10/26	11/06	11/11	11/25/09
0.030	01/14	02/01	02/03	02/17/10
0.030	04/28	05/07	05/11	05/25/10
0.030	07/22	08/03	08/05	08/19/10

Dividends have been paid since 1990. Source: Company reports.

Please read the Required Disclosures and Analyst Certification on the last page of this report.

The McGraw·Hill Companies

Cabot Oil & Gas Corp

Business Summary October 15, 2010

CORPORATE OVERVIEW. Cabot Oil & Gas Corp. is an independent oil and gas company engaged in the development, exploitation and exploration of oil and gas properties in North America. In 2009, COG restructured operations, combining Rocky Mountain and Appalachia areas to form the North Region and combining the Anadarko Basin with the Texas and Louisiana areas to form the South Region. In 2009, COG sold substantially all of its Canadian properties.

In the North Region, activity is concentrated in northeast Pennsylvania and West Virginia in Appalachia, and in the Green River and Washakie Basins in Wyoming and the Paradox Basin in Colorado. COG spent $380 million, or 60% of 2009 capex, on the North Region, and has budgeted $447 million for 2010. Average daily production from the region in 2009 was 136.6 MMcfe/day, or 48% of total COG production.

The South Region is concentrated in east and south Texas, Oklahoma and Louisiana, with principal producing intervals in the Cotton Valley, Haynesville Shale, Pettet and James Lime formations. COG spent $238 million, or 37% of 2009 capex, on the South Region, and has budgeted $201 million for 2010. Average daily production from the region in 2009 was 145.5 MMcfe/day, or 52% of total COG production.

CORPORATE STRATEGY. In 2009, COG drilled 143 gross wells, with a success rate of 95%, compared to 432 gross wells with a success rate of 97% in 2008.

COG's proved reserves totaled 2,060 Bcfe at December 31, 2009, of which 98% was natural gas, up 6% from year-end 2008. In 2009, capital and exploration spending was $640 million, compared to $1.5 billion (including acquisitions) of total capex in 2008. At the end of 2009, 64% of total proved reserves were developed, and we estimate COG's reserve life to be 20 years.

Production increased 8% in 2009, to 103 Bcfe, compared to 95 Bcfe in 2008, due to increased production from the Marcellus Shale and from East Texas properties acquired in 2008, partly offset by sold Canadian assets and reduced activity in Oklahoma and Wyoming.

COG's interests are mainly held under customary mineral leases. These leases generally allow for the development of oil and gas on the properties, with terms ranging from 3-10 years. COG owns leasehold rights on about 2.9 million gross acres. COG's two largest fields are Branchfield Southeast in East Texas and Dimock in Susquehanna County, Pennsylvania. Additionally, COG is focusing on the acquired Angie field in East Texas. These three fields account for 43% of total proved reserves.

Company Financials Fiscal Year Ended Dec. 31

Per Share Data ($)	2009	2008	2007	2006	2005	2004	2003	2002	2001	2000
Tangible Book Value	17.49	NA	11.60	9.83	6.18	4.69	3.78	3.67	3.66	2.77
Cash Flow	3.99	4.31	3.36	4.57	2.58	1.94	1.27	1.18	1.41	0.93
Earnings	1.42	2.10	1.71	3.32	1.50	0.90	0.29	0.17	0.51	0.36
S&P Core Earnings	1.47	1.76	1.63	1.74	1.49	0.88	0.20	0.15	0.49	NA
Dividends	0.12	0.12	0.11	0.08	0.07	0.05	0.05	0.05	0.05	0.05
Payout Ratio	8%	6%	6%	2%	5%	6%	18%	32%	10%	15%
Prices:High	46.26	72.92	42.50	33.26	26.75	16.30	10.17	8.85	11.45	10.67
Prices:Low	17.84	19.18	27.87	19.13	13.72	9.57	7.50	5.92	5.42	4.69
P/E Ratio:High	33	35	25	10	18	18	35	53	22	30
P/E Ratio:Low	13	9	16	6	9	11	26	36	11	13

Income Statement Analysis (Million $)										
Revenue	879	946	732	762	683	530	509	354	447	369
Operating Income	NA	550	423	436	380	278	252	182	191	132
Depreciation, Depletion and Amortization	269	227	162	129	108	103	94.9	96.5	80.6	53.4
Interest Expense	59.0	36.4	17.2	18.4	22.5	22.0	23.5	25.3	20.8	22.9
Pretax Income	223	336	258	511	236	139	43.0	23.8	74.5	41.9
Effective Tax Rate	33.6%	37.1%	35.0%	37.1%	37.2%	36.2%	35.0%	32.3%	36.8%	39.3%
Net Income	148	211	167	321	148	88.4	28.0	16.1	47.1	25.5
S&P Core Earnings	153	178	159	172	148	87.2	19.1	14.4	45.1	NA

Balance Sheet & Other Financial Data (Million $)										
Cash	40.2	28.1	30.1	41.9	10.6	10.0	0.72	2.56	5.71	7.57
Current Assets	282	461	221	316	230	195	121	93.1	85.0	110
Total Assets	3,683	3,702	2,209	1,834	1,495	1,211	1,024	1,055	1,069	736
Current Liabilities	309	379	252	251	219	197	155	123	110	118
Long Term Debt	805	831	350	220	320	250	270	365	393	253
Common Equity	1,813	1,791	1,070	945	600	456	365	351	347	243
Total Capital	2,618	3,221	1,882	1,513	1,210	953	815	916	940	604
Capital Expenditures	611	1,454	557	467	351	207	122	103	127	99.4
Cash Flow	417	438	329	450	257	192	123	113	128	76.7
Current Ratio	0.9	1.2	0.9	1.3	1.1	1.0	0.8	0.8	0.8	0.9
% Long Term Debt of Capitalization	30.8	25.8	23.6	14.5	26.5	26.2	33.1	39.9	41.8	41.9
% Return on Assets	4.0	7.2	8.3	19.3	11.0	7.8	2.7	1.5	5.2	3.7
% Return on Equity	8.2	14.8	16.6	41.6	28.1	21.5	7.8	4.6	16.0	10.9

Data as orig reptd.; bef. results of disc opers/spec. items. Per share data adj. for stk. divs.; EPS diluted. E-Estimated. NA-Not Available. NM-Not Meaningful. NR-Not Ranked. UR-Under Review.

Office: 840 Gessner Rd Ste 1400, Houston, TX 77024.
Telephone: 281-589-4600.
Website: http://www.cabotog.com
Chrmn, Pres & CEO: D.O. Dinges

Investor Contact: S.C. Schroeder (281-589-4993)
Chief Acctg Officer & Cntlr: T. Roemer
Secy: L.A. Machesney
General Counsel: K. Cunningham

Board Members: R. J. Best, D. M. Carmichael, D. O. Dinges, J. R. Gibbs, R. L. Keiser, R. Kelley, P. D. Peacock, W. P. Vititoe

Founded: 1989
Domicile: Delaware
Employees: 567

Cameron International Corp

STANDARD & POOR'S

S&P Recommendation HOLD ★★★☆☆

Price	12-Mo. Target Price	Investment Style
$42.92 (as of Oct 22, 2010)	$44.00	Large-Cap Growth

GICS Sector Energy
Sub-Industry Oil & Gas Equipment & Services

Summary This company is a leading international manufacturer of oil and gas blowout preventers, flow control valves, surface and subsea production systems, and related oilfield services products.

Key Stock Statistics (Source S&P, Vickers, company reports)

52-Wk Range	$47.44–31.42	S&P Oper. EPS 2010E	2.26	Market Capitalization(B)	$10.396	Beta	1.58
Trailing 12-Month EPS	$1.98	S&P Oper. EPS 2011E	2.83	Yield (%)	Nil	S&P 3-Yr. Proj. EPS CAGR(%)	16
Trailing 12-Month P/E	21.7	P/E on S&P Oper. EPS 2010E	19.0	Dividend Rate/Share	Nil	S&P Credit Rating	BBB+
$10K Invested 5 Yrs Ago	$25,708	Common Shares Outstg. (M)	242.2	Institutional Ownership (%)	91		

Price Performance

- 30-Week Mov. Avg. · · · · 10-Week Mov. Avg. – – GAAP Earnings vs. Previous Year Volume Above Avg. ▥ STARS
- 12-Mo. Target Price — Relative Strength — ▲ Up ▼ Down ▶ No Change Below Avg. ▥ ★

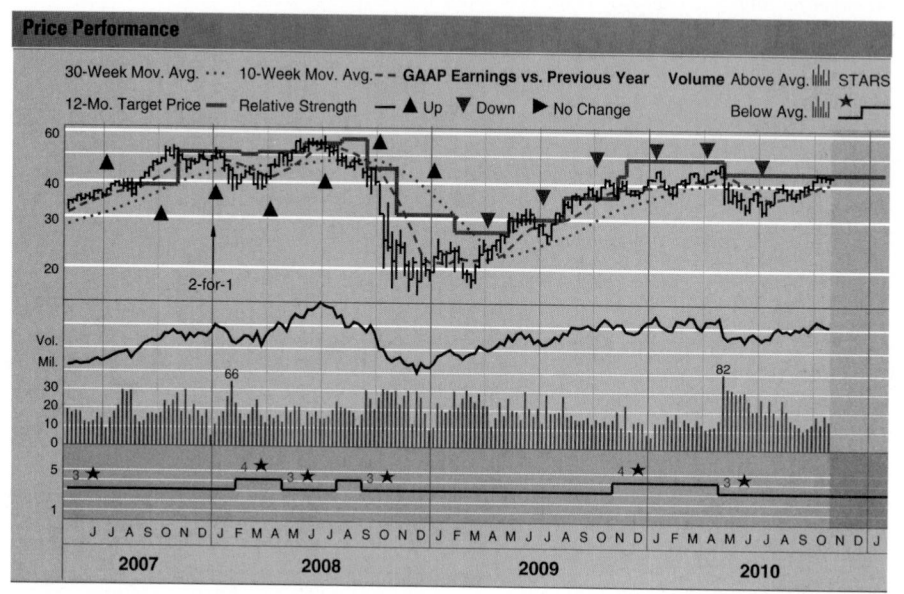

Analysis prepared by **Stewart Glickman, CFA** on August 05, 2010, when the stock traded at **$39.49**.

Options: ASE, CBOE, P, Ph

Qualitative Risk Assessment

LOW	MEDIUM	HIGH
		HIGH

Our risk assessment reflects CAM's exposure to volatile crude oil and natural gas prices, capital spending decisions made by its oil and gas producing customers, political risk associated with operating in frontier regions, an unclear regulatory environment, and legal risk associated with the U.S. Gulf of Mexico oil spill.

Quantitative Evaluations

S&P Quality Ranking   **B+**

D	C	B-	B	B+	A-	A	A+
				B+			

Relative Strength Rank   **MODERATE**

67

LOWEST = 1   HIGHEST = 99

Revenue/Earnings Data

Revenue (Million $)

	1Q	2Q	3Q	4Q	Year
2010	1,347	1,453	--	--	--
2009	1,257	1,270	1,232	1,464	5,223
2008	1,339	1,481	1,505	1,524	5,849
2007	997.0	1,139	1,186	1,344	4,666
2006	829.7	857.8	978.8	1,077	3,743
2005	547.9	594.8	636.6	738.6	2,518

Earnings Per Share ($)

	1Q	2Q	3Q	4Q	Year
2010	0.48	0.52	E0.58	E0.67	E2.26
2009	0.52	0.63	0.56	0.41	2.11
2008	0.55	0.65	0.73	0.67	2.60
2007	0.44	0.54	0.66	0.54	2.17
2006	0.24	0.32	0.39	0.42	1.36
2005	0.13	0.18	0.22	0.24	0.76

Fiscal year ended Dec. 31. Next earnings report expected: Early November. EPS Estimates based on S&P Operating Earnings; historical GAAP earnings are as reported.

Dividend Data

No cash dividends have been paid.

Highlights

- In early July, the Obama administration revised its drilling moratorium following successful industry-led legal challenges to the initial drilling ban announced May 28; the revised ban is scheduled to terminate November 30. We expect that, post-ban, new regulatory requirements will be enacted for blowout preventers (BOPs), which may include both equipment specifications as well as frequency of inspections. Depending on the extent to which BOP requirements are raised, CAM may benefit from increased BOP upgrade demand, and/or refurbishments. Either way, we also expect greater interest by rig contractors in arranging for CAM after-market support on installed BOPs. Based on data from RigLogix, we estimate that CAM has about a 50% market share of BOPs in the U.S. Gulf of Mexico.

- Second-quarter orders were $1.39 billion, despite no major project awards during the quarter. While Brazil looms as a potential catalyst for CAM, the timing of project awards remains uncertain.

- We project EPS of $2.26 in 2010, rising to $2.83 in 2011 on higher margins.

Investment Rationale/Risk

- We see several factors being potential tailwinds for CAM. First, potential regulatory changes could create near-term demand for BOPs, as well as increased annuity-like demand for aftermarket services. Second, the pickup in U.S. land activity, such as shale plays, is spurring higher demand for shorter-cycle businesses. Third, Brazil and other subsea demand remains a potential catalyst, although that may be more of a longer-term development. Nonetheless, in the near term, concerns remain over legal exposure to the Deepwater Horizon accident, given that it was a CAM blowout preventer that was installed on that rig.

- Risks to our recommendation and target price include lower oil and natural gas prices; new regulatory requirements that may affect CAM's manufacturing processes; and legal risk associated with the Deepwater Horizon accident.

- Our DCF model, assuming terminal growth of 3% and a WACC of 12.9%, indicates intrinsic value of about $58. Using below-peer multiples (due to legal risk) of 10.5X 2010 EBITDA, 12.0X 2010 operating cash flow, and blending with our DCF model, our 12-month target price is $44.

The **McGraw·Hill** Companies

Cameron International Corp

STANDARD &POOR'S

Business Summary August 05, 2010

CORPORATE OVERVIEW. Cameron International, an international provider of oil and gas pressure control equipment, is organized into three business segments: Drilling & Production Systems (DPS), Valves & Measurement (V&M), and Compression. Primary customers of DPS, V&M and Compression are major and independent oil and gas exploration companies, foreign national oil and gas companies, drilling contractors, pipeline companies, refiners, and other industrial and petrochemical processing companies. The company serves customers in North America (39% of 2009 revenues), Asia/Middle East (20%), Europe (15%), Africa (13%), South America (9.7%) and Other (3.3%).

Drilling & Production Systems (DPS; 65% of 2009 revenues and 67% of 2009 segment pretax income) manufactures pressure control equipment used at the wellhead in drilling, production and transmission of oil and gas, both onshore and offshore. Primary products include wellheads, drilling valves, blowout preventers, and control systems, marketed under the brand names Cameron, W-K-M, McEvoy, Willis, and Ingram Cactus. The segment also makes subsea production systems, which tend to be highly sophisticated technically. The company believes subsea capacity additions at manufactur-

ing plants in England, Brazil and Germany provide support for increased completions of subsea trees and associated manifolds, production controls and other equipment in the future.

Valves & Measurement (VMS; 23%, 23%), split out from the DPS division as a separately managed business in 1995, provides a full range of ball valves, gate valves, butterfly valves, and accessories used primarily to control pressures and direct oil and gas as they are moved from individual wellheads through transmission systems to refineries, petrochemical plants, and other processing centers. In September 2005, CAM announced an agreement to acquire substantially all of the flow control businesses of Dresser Inc.; the acquisition was completed in January 2006. The acquisition, which expanded the company's valve product line, totaled $217.5 million in cash and assumed debt. The acquired businesses were added to the company's V&M segment.

Company Financials Fiscal Year Ended Dec. 31

Per Share Data ($)	2009	2008	2007	2006	2005	2004	2003	2002	2001	2000
Tangible Book Value	9.04	6.88	6.67	5.11	4.40	3.83	3.81	3.39	2.92	2.69
Cash Flow	2.81	3.03	2.52	1.79	1.11	0.83	0.59	0.58	0.78	0.47
Earnings	2.11	2.60	2.17	1.36	0.76	0.44	0.26	0.28	0.44	0.13
S&P Core Earnings	2.12	2.63	2.27	1.43	0.73	0.34	0.17	0.12	0.21	NA
Dividends	Nil	Nil	Nil	Nil	Nil	Nil	Nil	Nil	Nil	Nil
Payout Ratio	Nil	Nil	Nil	Nil	Nil	Nil	Nil	Nil	Nil	Nil
Prices:High	42.49	58.53	53.83	28.91	21.55	14.19	13.90	14.90	18.25	20.97
Prices:Low	17.19	16.15	24.30	19.04	12.76	10.01	10.25	8.98	7.21	10.59
P/E Ratio:High	20	23	25	21	28	32	53	54	42	NM
P/E Ratio:Low	8	6	11	14	17	23	39	33	16	NM

Income Statement Analysis (Million $)										
Revenue	5,223	5,849	4,666	3,743	2,518	2,093	1,634	1,538	1,564	1,387
Operating Income	NA	1,023	814	605	340	232	164	196	251	215
Depreciation, Depletion and Amortization	157	98.7	81.5	101	78.4	82.8	83.6	77.9	83.1	75.3
Interest Expense	92.4	49.7	23.3	20.7	12.0	17.8	8.16	7.98	5.62	18.0
Pretax Income	643	872	708	489	263	133	77.6	85.1	143	43.8
Effective Tax Rate	26.0%	31.9%	29.3%	35.0%	34.9%	29.0%	26.2%	29.0%	31.0%	36.8%
Net Income	476	594	501	318	171	94.4	57.2	60.5	98.3	27.7
S&P Core Earnings	478	601	527	333	167	73.1	37.5	23.3	44.0	NA

Balance Sheet & Other Financial Data (Million $)										
Cash	1,861	1,621	740	1,034	362	227	292	274	112	16.6
Current Assets	4,714	4,056	3,072	2,908	1,728	1,205	1,148	1,018	965	688
Total Assets	7,725	5,902	4,731	4,351	3,099	2,356	2,141	1,998	1,875	1,494
Current Liabilities	2,296	2,112	1,693	1,628	922	528	680	375	378	346
Long Term Debt	1,232	1,256	742	745	444	458	204	463	459	188
Common Equity	3,920	2,320	2,095	1,741	1,595	1,228	1,137	1,041	976	842
Total Capital	5,174	3,662	2,909	2,577	2,078	1,727	1,387	1,550	1,477	1,069
Capital Expenditures	241	272	246	185	77.5	53.5	64.7	82.1	125	66.6
Cash Flow	632	692	582	419	250	177	141	138	181	103
Current Ratio	2.1	1.9	1.8	1.8	1.9	2.3	1.7	2.7	2.6	2.0
% Long Term Debt of Capitalization	23.8	34.3	26.2	28.9	21.4	26.5	14.7	29.9	31.1	17.6
% Return on Assets	7.0	11.2	11.0	8.5	6.3	4.2	2.8	3.1	5.8	1.9
% Return on Equity	15.2	26.9	26.1	19.1	12.1	8.0	5.3	6.2	10.6	3.6

Data as orig reptd.; bef. results of disc opers/spec. items. Per share data adj. for stk. divs.; EPS diluted. E-Estimated. NA-Not Available. NM-Not Meaningful. NR-Not Ranked. UR-Under Review.

Office: 1333 W Loop S Ste 1700, Houston, TX 77027-9118.
Telephone: 713-513-3300.
Website: http://www.c-a-m.com
Chrmn: S.R. Erikson

Pres & CEO: J.B. Moore
COO & EVP: J.D. Carne
SVP & CFO: C.M. Sledge
SVP & General Counsel: W.C. Lemmer

Investor Contact: R.S. Amann (713-513-3344)
Board Members: C. B. Cunningham, S. R. Erikson, P. J. Fluor, D. L. Foshee, J. B. Moore, M. E. Patrick, J. E. Reinhardsen, D. W. Ross, III, B. W. Wilkinson

Founded: 1994
Domicile: Delaware
Employees: 18,100

The McGraw-Hill Companies

Campbell Soup Co

STANDARD &POOR'S

S&P Recommendation SELL ★ ★ ☆ ☆ ☆

Price	12-Mo. Target Price	Investment Style
$36.37 (as of Oct 22, 2010)	$34.00	Large-Cap Growth

GICS Sector Consumer Staples
Sub-Industry Packaged Foods & Meats

Summary This company is a major producer of branded soups and other grocery food products.

Key Stock Statistics (Source S&P, Vickers, company reports)

52-Wk Range	$37.59–30.96	S&P Oper. EPS 2011E	2.62	Market Capitalization(B)	$12.220	Beta	0.27
Trailing 12-Month EPS	$2.42	S&P Oper. EPS 2012E	NA	Yield (%)	3.02	S&P 3-Yr. Proj. EPS CAGR(%)	7
Trailing 12-Month P/E	15.0	P/E on S&P Oper. EPS 2011E	13.9	Dividend Rate/Share	$1.10	S&P Credit Rating	A
$10K Invested 5 Yrs Ago	$14,455	Common Shares Outstg. (M)	336.0	Institutional Ownership (%)	36		

Price Performance

- 30-Week Mov. Avg. · · · ·
- 10-Week Mov. Avg. – –
- GAAP Earnings vs. Previous Year
- Volume Above Avg.
- STARS
- 12-Mo. Target Price —
- Relative Strength —
- ▲ Up ▼ Down ► No Change
- Below Avg.

Options: ASE, CBOE, P, Ph

Analysis prepared by **Tom Graves, CFA** on October 08, 2010, when the stock traded at **$35.48**.

Highlights

➤ In FY 11 (Jul.), we look for net sales to increase about 2% from the $7.68 billion reported for FY 10. Before special items, we estimate FY 11 EPS from continuing operations of $2.62, up from $2.47 in FY 10, which excludes about $0.05 of costs related to special items. In February 2010, CPB announced a plan to boost the performance of its U.S. condensed soup business. We expect efforts to include product improvements, further sodium reduction, changed packaging, improved shelving systems, and new marketing.

➤ In September 2010, CPB said that Douglas R. Conant plans to step down as the company's CEO at the end of FY 11, and his successor is expected to be Denise M. Morrison, who was elected COO, effective Oct. 1, 2010.

➤ Over the longer term, we look for Russia and China to become more significant contributors to CPB's overall growth. In May 2009, CPB said it had entered into a long-term agreement with Hellenic Bottling Company S.A. for the distribution of concentrated broth and other soup products in Russia.

Investment Rationale/Risk

➤ In our view, demand for soup has been surprisingly lackluster in the U.S. during the recent period of economic softness. We had expected that increased at-home meals would lead to stronger soup sales. Over the longer term, we expect CPB's overall revenue and profit growth prospects to be bolstered by new or enhanced products, increasingly portable packaging, and some expanded distribution, including overseas markets.

➤ Risks to our recommendation and target price include the possibility that consumer response to product improvement efforts, new CPB products and CPB marketing efforts will be better than anticipated, and that currency fluctuation will be more favorable than expected.

➤ Our 12-month target price of $34 reflects our view that the stock should trade at a discount to the average P/E we expect from a group of packaged food stocks. This reflects our concerns about the strength of the soup category and the promotional environment. The stock recently had an indicated dividend yield of 3.1%.

Qualitative Risk Assessment

LOW	MEDIUM	HIGH

Our risk assessment reflects the relatively stable nature of the company's end markets, our view of its strong cash flow, and corporate governance practices that we see as favorable relative to peers.

Quantitative Evaluations

S&P Quality Ranking A-

D	C	B-	B	B+	A-	A	A+

Relative Strength Rank MODERATE

36

LOWEST = 1   HIGHEST = 99

Revenue/Earnings Data

Revenue (Million $)

	1Q	2Q	3Q	4Q	Year
2010	2,203	2,153	1,802	1,518	7,676
2009	2,250	2,122	1,686	1,528	7,586
2008	2,185	2,218	1,880	1,715	7,998
2007	2,153	2,252	1,868	1,594	7,867
2006	2,002	2,159	1,728	1,454	7,343
2005	2,091	2,223	1,736	1,498	7,548

Earnings Per Share ($)

2010	0.87	0.74	0.49	0.33	2.42
2009	0.71	0.63	0.49	0.20	2.04
2008	0.69	0.67	0.14	0.24	1.76
2007	0.66	0.72	0.55	0.24	2.08
2006	0.69	0.58	0.35	0.20	1.82
2005	0.56	0.57	0.35	0.23	1.71

Fiscal year ended Jul. 31. Next earnings report expected: Late November. EPS Estimates based on S&P Operating Earnings; historical GAAP earnings are as reported.

Dividend Data (Dates: mm/dd Payment Date: mm/dd/yy)

Amount ($)	Date Decl.	Ex-Div. Date	Stk. of Record	Payment Date
0.275	11/18	12/28	12/30	02/01/10
0.275	03/25	03/31	04/05	05/03/10
0.275	06/24	07/01	07/06	08/02/10
0.275	09/23	10/07	10/12	11/01/10

Dividends have been paid since 1902. Source: Company reports.

Please read the Required Disclosures and Analyst Certification on the last page of this report.

The McGraw-Hill Companies

Campbell Soup Co

STANDARD &POOR'S

Business Summary October 08, 2010

CORPORATE OVERVIEW. Campbell Soup Co. is a major force in the U.S. packaged foods industry. The company, which traces its origins in the food business back to 1869, manufactures and markets a wide array of branded, prepared convenience food products worldwide.

In FY 10 (Jul.), operations outside the U.S. accounted for 29% of net sales and 21% of segment operating profits (before corporate expense). CPB's largest customer, Wal-Mart Stores, Inc., and its affiliates accounted for about 18% of CPB's net sales in FY 10.

The company reports results based on the following segments: U.S. Soup, Sauces and Beverages (48% of FY 10 sales, 64% of segment profits); Baking and Snacking (26%, 22%), International Soup, Sauces and Beverages (19%, 11%); and North America Foodservice (8%, 3%).

Campbell's U.S. Soup, Sauces and Beverages segment includes Campbell's condensed and ready-to-serve soups; Swanson broth, stocks and canned poultry; Prego pasta sauce; Pace Mexican sauce; Campbell's canned pasta,

gravies and beans; V8 juice and juice drinks; and Campbell's tomato juice.

The company's Baking and Snacking division includes Pepperidge Farm cookies, crackers, bakery and frozen products in the U.S.; and Arnotts biscuits in Australia and Asia Pacific. The International Soup, Sauces and Beverages segment includes soup, sauce and beverage businesses outside of the United States, including Europe, Latin America, the Asia Pacific region, the emerging markets of Russia and China, and the retail business in Canada.

The North America Food Service segment includes CPB's Away From Home operations, which represent the distribution of products such as soup, specialty entrees, beverage products, other prepared foods and Pepperidge Farm products through various foodservice channels in the U.S. and Canada.

Company Financials Fiscal Year Ended Jul. 31

Per Share Data ($)	2010	2009	2008	2007	2006	2005	2004	2003	2002	2001
Tangible Book Value	NM	NM	NM	NM	NM	NM	NM	NM	NM	NM
Cash Flow	3.19	2.78	2.47	2.79	2.52	2.39	2.20	2.11	2.05	2.19
Earnings	2.46	2.04	1.76	2.08	1.82	1.71	1.57	1.52	1.28	1.55
S&P Core Earnings	2.44	1.78	1.52	1.95	1.81	1.63	1.47	1.46	1.00	1.28
Dividends	1.08	1.00	0.88	0.80	0.72	0.68	0.63	0.63	0.63	0.90
Payout Ratio	44%	49%	50%	38%	40%	40%	40%	41%	49%	58%
Prices:High	37.59	35.80	40.85	42.65	39.98	31.60	30.52	27.90	30.00	35.44
Prices:Low	32.18	24.63	27.35	34.17	28.88	27.35	25.03	19.95	19.65	25.52
P/E Ratio:High	15	18	23	21	22	18	19	18	23	23
P/E Ratio:Low	13	12	16	16	16	16	16	13	15	16

Income Statement Analysis (Million $)	2010	2009	2008	2007	2006	2005	2004	2003	2002	2001
Revenue	7,676	7,586	7,998	7,867	7,343	7,548	7,109	6,678	6,133	6,664
Operating Income	1,611	1,532	1,564	1,541	1,445	1,483	1,394	1,376	1,442	1,470
Depreciation	251	264	271	23.0	289	279	260	243	319	266
Interest Expense	106	114	171	163	165	184	174	186	190	216
Pretax Income	1,242	1,079	939	1,149	1,001	1,030	947	924	798	987
Effective Tax Rate	NA	32.2%	28.5%	28.4%	24.6%	31.4%	31.7%	32.3%	34.2%	34.2%
Net Income	844	732	671	823	755	707	647	626	525	649
S&P Core Earnings	838	640	579	772	751	675	603	604	413	536

Balance Sheet & Other Financial Data (Million $)	2010	2009	2008	2007	2006	2005	2004	2003	2002	2001
Cash	254	51.0	81.0	71.0	657	40.0	32.0	32.0	21.0	24.0
Current Assets	1,687	1,551	1,693	1,578	2,112	1,512	1,481	1,290	1,199	1,221
Total Assets	6,276	6,056	6,474	6,445	7,870	6,776	6,675	6,205	5,721	5,927
Current Liabilities	2,065	1,628	2,403	2,030	2,962	2,002	2,339	2,783	2,678	3,120
Long Term Debt	1,945	2,246	1,633	2,074	2,116	2,542	2,543	2,249	2,449	2,243
Common Equity	929	728	1,318	1,295	1,768	1,270	874	387	-114	-247
Total Capital	2,874	2,974	3,251	3,369	3,884	3,812	3,417	2,636	2,335	1,996
Capital Expenditures	315	345	298	334	309	332	288	283	269	200
Cash Flow	1,095	996	942	1,106	1,044	986	907	869	844	915
Current Ratio	0.8	1.0	0.7	0.8	0.7	0.8	0.6	0.5	0.4	0.4
% Long Term Debt of Capitalization	67.7	75.5	49.4	61.6	54.5	66.7	74.4	85.3	104.9	112.4
% Net Income of Revenue	11.0	9.7	8.4	10.5	10.3	9.4	9.1	9.4	8.6	9.7
% Return on Assets	13.7	11.7	10.4	11.5	10.3	10.5	10.0	10.5	9.0	11.7
% Return on Equity	101.9	71.6	51.4	53.7	49.7	66.0	102.6	458.6	NM	NM

Data as orig reptd.; bef. results of disc opers/spec. items. Per share data adj. for stk. divs.; EPS diluted. E-Estimated. NA-Not Available. NM-Not Meaningful. NR-Not Ranked. UR-Under Review.

Office: 1 Campbell Pl, Camden, NJ 08103-1799.
Telephone: 856-342-4800.
Website: http://www.campbellsoupcompany.com
Chrmn: P.R. Charron

Pres & CEO: D.R. Conant
COO & EVP: D. Morrison
SVP, CFO & Chief Admin Officer: B.C. Owens
SVP & Chief Acctg Officer: A.P. DiSilvestro

Investor Contact: L.F. Griehs (856-342-6427)
Board Members: E. M. Carpenter, P. R. Charron, D. R. Conant, B. Dorrance, H. Golub, L. C. Karlson, R. W. Larrimore, M. A. Malone, S. Mathew, D. Morrison, W. D. Perez, C. R. Perrin, A. B. Rand, N. Shreiber, L. C. Vinney, C. C. Weber, A. D. van Beuren

Founded: 1869
Domicile: New Jersey
Employees: 18,400

CA Inc

STANDARD &POOR'S

S&P Recommendation HOLD ★★★★★	**Price** $22.87 (as of Oct 22, 2010)	**12-Mo. Target Price** $26.00	**Investment Style** Large-Cap Blend

GICS Sector Information Technology
Sub-Industry Systems Software

Summary This company (formerly Computer Associates International) develops systems software, database management systems, and applications software.

Key Stock Statistics (Source S&P, Vickers, company reports)

52-Wk Range	$23.91– 17.70	S&P Oper. EPS 2011**E**	1.74	Market Capitalization(B)	$11.801	Beta	0.88
Trailing 12-Month EPS	$1.52	S&P Oper. EPS 2012**E**	1.87	Yield (%)	0.70	S&P 3-Yr. Proj. EPS CAGR(%)	7
Trailing 12-Month P/E	15.1	P/E on S&P Oper. EPS 2011**E**	13.1	Dividend Rate/Share	$0.16	S&P Credit Rating	BBB
$10K Invested 5 Yrs Ago	$8,836	Common Shares Outstg. (M)	516.0	Institutional Ownership (%)	66		

Price Performance

30-Week Mov. Avg. ···   10-Week Mov. Avg. - -   **GAAP Earnings vs. Previous Year**   **Volume** Above Avg.||||| STARS
12-Mo. Target Price —   Relative Strength —   ▲ Up ▼ Down ▶ No Change   Below Avg.||||| ★

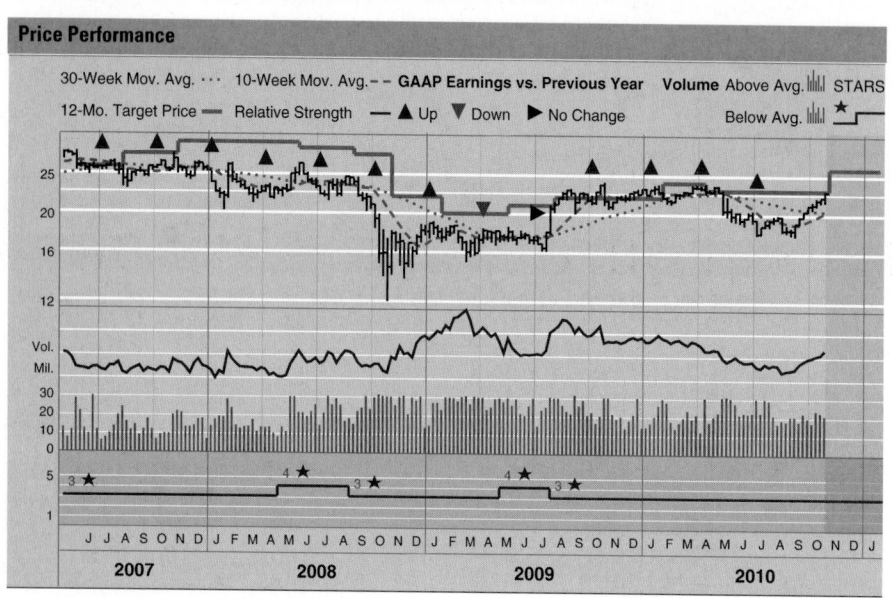

Options: ASE, CBOE, P, Ph

Qualitative Risk Assessment

LOW	MEDIUM	**HIGH**

Our risk assessment for the company reflects our concern about the financial crisis in Europe, weak spending in enterprise software, and modest underlying growth.

Quantitative Evaluations

S&P Quality Ranking   B-

D	C	**B-**	B	B+	A-	A	A+

Relative Strength Rank   **STRONG**

85

LOWEST = 1   HIGHEST = 99

Revenue/Earnings Data

Revenue (Million $)

	1Q	2Q	3Q	4Q	Year
2011	1,091	--	--	--	--
2010	1,050	1,072	1,128	1,103	4,353
2009	1,087	110.7	1,042	1,035	4,271
2008	1,025	1,067	1,100	1,085	4,277
2007	949.0	987.0	1,002	1,005	3,943
2006	927.0	950.0	971.0	948.0	3,796

Earnings Per Share ($)

2011	0.43	E0.44	E0.44	E0.45	E1.74
2010	0.37	0.41	0.49	0.19	1.47
2009	0.37	0.39	0.40	0.13	1.29
2008	0.24	0.26	0.31	0.14	0.93
2007	0.06	0.09	0.10	-0.04	0.22
2006	0.16	0.08	0.09	-0.07	0.26

Fiscal year ended Mar. 31. Next earnings report expected: Late October. EPS Estimates based on S&P Operating Earnings; historical GAAP earnings are as reported.

Highlights

▶ The 12-month target price for CA has recently been changed to $26.00 from $23.00. The Highlights section of this Stock Report will be updated accordingly.

Investment Rationale/Risk

▶ The Investment Rationale/Risk section of this Stock Report will be updated shortly. For the latest News story on CA from MarketScope, see below.

▶ 10/22/10 12:40 pm ET ... S&P MAINTAINS HOLD OPINION ON SHARES OF CA INC (CA 22.69***): Sep-Q EPS of $0.44, vs. $0.40, beats our estimate of $0.39. Revenues increased 3.5% to $1.11B, $15M above our forecast. The modest revenue growth reflects weakness in its mainframe business. However, we see that business stabilizing and stronger growth in its virtualization products, which were obtained through acquisitions. We raise our FY 11 (Mar.) EPS estimate by $0.11 to $1.74 and FY 12's by $0.13 to $1.87 on our higher revenue projection, reflecting the recent weakness in the U.S. dollar. We lift our target price by $3 to $26 on higher peer multiples. /J.Yin-CFA

Dividend Data (Dates: mm/dd Payment Date: mm/dd/yy)

Amount ($)	Date Decl.	Ex-Div. Date	Stk. of Record	Payment Date
0.040	11/05	11/13	11/17	11/30/09
0.040	02/04	02/11	02/16	03/16/10
0.040	05/12	05/26	05/31	06/16/10
0.040	07/28	08/05	08/09	08/19/10

Dividends have been paid since 1990. Source: Company reports.

STANDARD &POOR'S

CA Inc

Business Summary July 28, 2010

CORPORATE OVERVIEW. CA Inc. provides information technology (IT) management software, which helps customers better manage their IT infrastructure. The company has a broad portfolio of software products and services that span the areas of infrastructure management, IT security management, storage management, application performance management and business service optimization. The company's products and services include both mainframe and distributed solutions, each of which we estimate contribute about half of CA's revenues.

CORPORATE STRATEGY. In April 2007, CA announced a new strategy, Enterprise IT Management (EITM), for transforming the way companies manage their IT. The goal of EITM is to unify disparate elements of IT, including hardware, processes and people, so customers can have better control and manage these resources rather than replace existing IT investments. For example, CA's Unicenter Advanced Systems Management provides centralized management for virtualized and clustered server environments, enabling customers to assess and optimize network resources.

Key parts of CA's EITM strategy include:

Internal Product Development - CA plans to ship new versions of every major product, including those products obtained through acquisitions. The company has added headcount in India and Czech Republic research centers.

Strengthening Partner Relationships - CA intends to strengthen its global distribution by recruiting and educating channel partners on CA products and services. The company formed a Mid-Market and Storage organization that targets enterprises with 500-5,000 employees.

International Expansion - CA plans to invest in regions outside the U.S., especially in emerging markets such as China and India to increase the volume of enterprise sales. The company has also pursued small- and medium-sized customers in the Europe, Middle East and Africa (EMEA) region. International revenue comprised nearly 46% of total sales in FY 09 (Mar.), down from 48% in FY 08.

Company Financials Fiscal Year Ended Mar. 31

Per Share Data ($)	2010	2009	2008	2007	2006	2005	2004	2003	2002	2001
Tangible Book Value	NM	NM	NM	NM	NM	0.50	8.09	NM	NM	0.66
Cash Flow	2.01	1.56	1.21	0.47	1.22	0.24	0.17	0.60	-0.01	0.89
Earnings	1.47	1.29	0.93	0.22	0.26	0.02	-0.06	-0.46	-1.91	-1.02
S&P Core Earnings	1.48	1.31	0.97	0.23	0.26	0.22	0.02	-0.53	-2.05	-1.18
Dividends	0.16	0.16	0.16	0.16	0.08	0.08	0.08	0.08	0.08	0.08
Payout Ratio	11%	12%	17%	73%	31%	NM	NM	NM	NM	NM
Calendar Year	2009	2008	2007	2006	2005	2004	2003	2002	2001	2000
Prices:High	24.15	26.68	28.46	29.50	31.35	31.71	29.29	38.74	39.03	79.44
Prices:Low	15.13	12.00	22.86	18.97	26.04	22.37	12.39	7.47	18.31	18.13
P/E Ratio:High	16	21	31	NM	NM	NM	NM	NM	NM	NM
P/E Ratio:Low	10	9	25	NM	NM	NM	NM	NM	NM	NM

Income Statement Analysis (Million $)

	2010	2009	2008	2007	2006	2005	2004	2003	2002	2001
Revenue	4,353	4,271	4,277	3,943	3,796	3,530	3,276	3,116	2,964	4,198
Operating Income	1,631	1,377	1,137	560	836	504	417	421	-62.0	604
Depreciation	301	149	156	148	583	130	134	612	1,096	1,110
Interest Expense	76.0	95.0	370	126	41.0	106	Nil	172	227	344
Pretax Income	1,171	1,102	808	154	121	11.0	-54.0	-363	-1,385	-666
Effective Tax Rate	34.2%	37.0%	38.1%	21.4%	NM	NM	NM	NM	NM	NM
Net Income	771	694	500	121	156	13.0	-36.0	-267	-1,102	-591
S&P Core Earnings	768	704	522	122	155	136	7.10	-301	-1,185	-688

Balance Sheet & Other Financial Data (Million $)

	2010	2009	2008	2007	2006	2005	2004	2003	2002	2001
Cash	2,583	2,713	2,796	2,280	1,865	3,125	1,902	1,512	1,180	850
Current Assets	3,990	4,180	4,468	3,101	2,648	3,954	3,358	3,565	3,061	2,643
Total Assets	11,838	11,252	11,756	10,585	10,438	11,082	10,679	11,054	12,226	14,143
Current Liabilities	3,588	4,078	4,278	3,714	3,377	3,664	2,455	2,974	2,321	2,286
Long Term Debt	1,530	1,287	2,221	2,572	1,810	1,810	2,298	2,298	3,334	3,639
Common Equity	4,983	4,344	3,709	3,690	4,680	4,840	4,718	4,363	4,617	5,780
Total Capital	6,528	5,767	6,291	6,282	6,536	6,822	7,634	7,525	9,218	11,319
Capital Expenditures	79.0	83.0	117	150	143	69.0	30.0	30.0	25.0	89.0
Cash Flow	1,072	843	656	269	739	143	98.0	345	-6.00	519
Current Ratio	1.1	1.0	1.0	0.8	0.8	1.1	1.4	1.2	1.3	1.2
% Long Term Debt of Capitalization	23.4	22.3	36.2	41.1	27.7	26.5	30.1	30.5	36.2	32.1
% Net Income of Revenue	17.7	16.3	11.7	3.1	4.1	0.4	NM	NM	NM	NM
% Return on Assets	6.7	6.0	4.5	1.2	1.4	0.1	NM	NM	NM	NM
% Return on Equity	16.5	17.2	13.5	2.9	3.2	0.3	NM	NM	NM	NM

Data as orig reptd.; bef. results of disc opers/spec. items. Per share data adj. for stk. divs.; EPS diluted. E-Estimated. NA-Not Available. NM-Not Meaningful. NR-Not Ranked. UR-Under Review.

Office: One CA Plaza, Islandia, NY 11749.
Telephone: 800-225-5224.
Email: cainvestor@ca.com
Website: http://www.ca.com

Chrmn: A.F. Weinbach
CEO: W.E. McCracken
EVP & CFO: N. Cooper
EVP & Chief Admin Officer: P.J. Harrington, Jr.

EVP & CTO: D.F. Ferguson
Investor Contact: K. Doherty (212-415-6844)
Board Members: R. J. Bromark, G. J. Fernandes, K. Koplovitz, C. B. Lofgren, W. E. McCracken, R. Sulpizio, L. S. Unger, A. F. Weinbach, R. Zambonini

Founded: 1974
Domicile: Delaware
Employees: 13,800

The McGraw·Hill Companies

Capital One Financial Corp.

STANDARD &POOR'S

S&P Recommendation HOLD ★★★☆☆

Price	12-Mo. Target Price	Investment Style
$39.12 (as of Oct 22, 2010)	**$49.00**	Large-Cap Blend

GICS Sector Financials
Sub-Industry Consumer Finance

Summary This diversified consumer finance company is one of the largest issuers of Visa and MasterCard credit cards in the world.

Key Stock Statistics (Source S&P, Vickers, company reports)

52-Wk Range	$47.73–34.03	S&P Oper. EPS 2010E	6.83	Market Capitalization(B)	$17.869	Beta		1.79
Trailing 12-Month EPS	$5.46	S&P Oper. EPS 2011E	6.93	Yield (%)	0.51	S&P 3-Yr. Proj. EPS CAGR(%)		105
Trailing 12-Month P/E	7.2	P/E on S&P Oper. EPS 2010E	5.7	Dividend Rate/Share	$0.20	S&P Credit Rating		BBB
$10K Invested 5 Yrs Ago	$5,643	Common Shares Outstg. (M)	456.8	Institutional Ownership (%)	89			

Price Performance

30-Week Mov. Avg. ···   10-Week Mov. Avg. --   GAAP Earnings vs. Previous Year   Volume Above Avg. ▮▮▮ STARS
12-Mo. Target Price —   Relative Strength —   ▲ Up ▼ Down ▶ No Change   Below Avg. ▮▮▮ ★

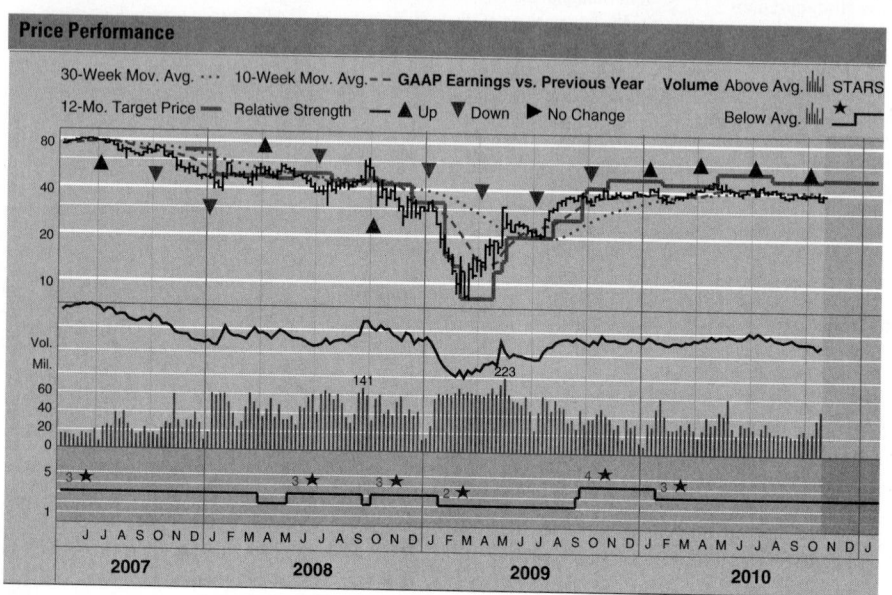

Options: ASE, CBOE, P, Ph

Analysis prepared by **Rafay Khalid, CFA** on October 19, 2010, when the stock traded at **$ 38.41**.

Highlights

► Following flat revenue in 2009, we expect revenues to increase in 2010 and 2011, on our outlook for an improving economy. However, we forecast a continued slowdown in loan growth, reflecting the company's tighter lending standards. Although regulation in its U.S. card business will likely hurt revenue due to a mandated change in minimum payment policies, we think COF will come up with alternative means to make up for some of the lost revenue.

► We expect loan loss provisions to decline in 2010 and 2011, on our outlook for lower delinquency levels. We look for charge-offs to continue declining for the rest of 2010 and in 2011, reflecting our view of credit improvement this year and unemployment levels peaking in mid-2010. We see an increase in expenses related to the integration of Chevy Chase Bank (acquired in early 2009) and a ramp-up of marketing expenses in the domestic credit card business to normal levels.

► We estimate operating EPS of $6.83 in 2010 and $6.93 in 2011. This compares with operating EPS of $0.84 in 2009, excluding one-time items.

Investment Rationale/Risk

► We see lower loss provisions in 2010, particularly as they relate to COF's commercial, auto, home, and credit card loans, reflecting our outlook for a decline in delinquency rates. We remain concerned about higher unemployment rates in the U.S. and the U.K., but we think peak levels will be lower than we previously expected. Uncertainty remains regarding the impact of recent credit card regulation, as fee income will likely come under pressure. But COF will likely attempt to recoup lost fee revenue from other facets of its business.

► Risks to our recommendation and target price include a decrease in consumer confidence; faster-than-expected deterioration in COF's mortgage portfolio; and higher-than-expected unemployment rates that would hurt credit quality.

► Our 12-month target price of $49 is based on a historical average tangible book value ratio of 1.42X our 2011 tangible book value per share estimate of $34.52. We believe this historical average is warranted, reflecting what we see as an improving economic environment.

Qualitative Risk Assessment

LOW	MEDIUM	HIGH

Our risk assessment reflects what we perceive as the risk of higher chargeoff and unemployment levels, offset by strong capital levels and favorable early delinquency trends.

Quantitative Evaluations

S&P Quality Ranking A-

D	C	B-	B	B+	A-	A	A+

Relative Strength Rank WEAK

28

LOWEST = 1   HIGHEST = 99

Revenue/Earnings Data

Revenue (Million $)

	1Q	2Q	3Q	4Q	Year
2010	5,091	4,642	4,722	--	--
2009	3,740	3,949	4,255	4,007	15,951
2008	4,936	4,269	4,469	4,137	17,856
2007	4,598	4,719	4,917	5,119	19,132
2006	3,737	3,607	2,826	4,021	15,191
2005	2,852	2,934	2,999	3,300	12,085

Earnings Per Share ($)

2010	1.58	1.78	1.79	E1.68	E6.83
2009	-0.38	-0.64	0.96	0.89	0.98
2008	1.70	1.24	1.03	-3.67	0.14
2007	1.62	1.89	-2.09	0.85	6.55
2006	2.86	1.78	1.89	1.14	7.62
2005	1.99	2.03	1.81	0.97	6.73

Fiscal year ended Dec. 31. Next earnings report expected: Late January. EPS Estimates based on S&P Operating Earnings; historical GAAP earnings are as reported.

Dividend Data (Dates: mm/dd Payment Date: mm/dd/yy)

Amount ($)	Date Decl.	Ex-Div. Date	Stk. of Record	Payment Date
0.050	10/29	11/06	11/11	11/20/09
0.050	01/28	02/10	02/12	02/22/10
0.050	04/29	05/07	05/11	05/20/10
0.050	07/29	08/09	08/11	08/20/10

Dividends have been paid since 1995. Source: Company reports.

Please read the Required Disclosures and Analyst Certification on the last page of this report.

The McGraw-Hill Companies

Capital One Financial Corp.

STANDARD &POOR'S

Business Summary October 19, 2010

CORPORATE OVERVIEW. Capital One Financial (COF) is one of the largest banks in the United States. It is a diversified banking corporation focused primarily on consumer and commercial lending and deposit origination. The company's principal business segments are national lending and local banking. The national lending segment consists of two sub-segments: U.S. Card, and Other National Lending. The Other National Lending sub-segment includes the Auto Finance sub-segment and International sub-segment.

The U.S. Card segment consists of domestic consumer credit card lending, national small business lending, installment loans and other unsecured consumer financial service activities. COF offers a wide variety of credit card and small business products, in addition to unsecured closed-end loans throughout the U.S., which it customizes to appeal to different consumer preferences and needs. Its product offerings are supported by extensive brand advertising. It routinely tests new products to develop products that appeal to different and changing consumer preferences. Its customized products include products offered to a wide range of consumer credit risk profiles, as well as products aimed at special consumer interests.

The Auto Finance segment consists of automobile and other motor vehicle financing activities. COF purchases retail installment contracts, secured by new and used automobiles or other motor vehicles, through dealer networks throughout the U.S. Additionally, it utilizes direct marketing, including the Internet, to offer automobile financing directly to consumers for the purchase of new and used vehicles, as well as refinancing of existing motor vehicle loans. As of December 31, 2009, COF was the fourth largest non-captive provider of auto financing in the U.S. In January 2005, it acquired Onyx Acceptance Corporation, an auto finance company that provides financing to franchised and select independent dealerships throughout the U.S. The company also completed the acquisition of Key Bank's non-prime auto loan portfolio in 2005. Similar to its credit card strategy, COF customizes product features, such as interest rate, loan amount and loan terms, enabling it to lend to customers with a wide range of credit profiles.

Company Financials Fiscal Year Ended Dec. 31

Per Share Data ($)	2009	2008	2007	2006	2005	2004	2003	2002	2001	2000
Tangible Book Value	26.90	27.28	27.89	28.30	33.99	33.98	25.75	20.44	15.33	9.94
Earnings	0.98	0.14	6.55	7.62	6.73	6.21	4.92	3.93	2.91	2.24
S&P Core Earnings	0.87	1.83	6.55	7.61	6.61	5.72	4.41	3.37	2.55	NA
Dividends	0.52	1.50	0.11	0.11	0.11	0.11	0.11	0.11	0.11	0.11
Payout Ratio	54%	NM	2%	1%	2%	2%	2%	3%	4%	5%
Prices:High	42.90	63.50	83.84	90.04	88.56	84.45	64.25	66.50	72.58	73.25
Prices:Low	7.80	23.28	44.40	69.30	69.09	60.04	24.91	24.05	36.40	32.06
P/E Ratio:High	44	NM	13	12	13	14	13	17	25	33
P/E Ratio:Low	8	NM	7	9	10	10	5	6	13	14

Income Statement Analysis (Million $)	2009	2008	2007	2006	2005	2004	2003	2002	2001	2000
Net Interest Income	7,697	7,149	6,530	5,100	3,680	3,003	2,785	2,719	1,663	1,589
Non Interest Income	5,286	6,692	8,054	6,997	6,358	5,900	5,416	5,467	4,420	3,034
Loan Loss Provision	4,230	5,101	2,637	1,476	1,491	1,221	1,517	2,149	990	718
Non Interest Expenses	7,417	8,210	8,078	6,967	5,718	5,322	4,857	4,586	4,058	3,148
% Expense/Operating Revenue	57.1%	59.3%	55.4%	57.6%	57.0%	59.8%	59.2%	56.0%	66.7%	68.1%
Pretax Income	1,336	582	3,870	3,653	2,829	2,360	1,827	1,451	1,035	757
Effective Tax Rate	26.2%	85.5%	33.0%	33.9%	36.1%	34.6%	37.0%	38.0%	38.0%	38.0%
Net Income	987	84.5	2,592	2,414	1,809	1,543	1,151	900	642	470
% Net Interest Margin	5.30	5.38	6.46	6.03	6.63	6.44	7.45	8.73	8.03	12.0
S&P Core Earnings	374	691	2,591	2,412	1,792	1,431	1,012	742	545	NA

Balance Sheet & Other Financial Data (Million $)	2009	2008	2007	2006	2005	2004	2003	2002	2001	2000
Money Market Assets	5,585	5,444	2,444	1,843	2,049	1,084	1,598	641	352	162
Investment Securities	38,910	31,003	19,782	15,452	14,350	9,300	5,867	4,424	3,116	1,697
Earning Assets:Total Loans	90,619	101,342	98,842	106,947	59,848	38,216	32,850	27,854	20,921	14,059
Total Assets	169,400	165,981	150,590	149,739	88,701	53,747	46,284	37,382	28,184	18,889
Demand Deposits	13,439	11,294	11,047	11,648	4,841	NA	Nil	Nil	Nil	Nil
Time Deposits	102,370	97,327	71,944	74,123	43,092	NA	22,416	17,326	12,839	8,379
Long Term Debt	15,438	16,735	20,237	20,217	14,863	Nil	14,813	8,124	Nil	4,051
Common Equity	26,589	23,516	24,294	25,235	14,129	8,388	6,052	4,623	3,324	1,963
% Return on Assets	0.6	0.1	1.7	2.0	2.5	3.1	2.8	2.7	2.7	2.9
% Return on Equity	3.9	0.4	10.5	12.3	16.1	21.4	21.6	22.6	24.3	27.0
% Loan Loss Reserve	4.6	4.5	2.9	2.0	3.0	3.9	4.9	6.2	4.0	3.7
% Loans/Deposits	78.3	93.0	114.5	124.7	124.8	149.1	146.5	160.8	162.9	167.8
% Loans/Assets	57.2	63.2	64.2	70.0	68.8	71.0	71.9	74.4	74.3	72.3
% Equity to Assets	14.9	15.1	16.5	16.5	15.8	14.4	12.8	12.1	11.2	10.8

Data as orig reptd.; bef. results of disc opers/spec. items. Per share data adj. for stk. divs.; EPS diluted. E-Estimated. NA-Not Available. NM-Not Meaningful. NR-Not Ranked. UR-Under Review.

Office: 1680 Capital One Drive, McLean, VA 22102-3407.
Telephone: 703-720-1000.
Email: investor.relations@capitalone.com
Website: http://www.capitalone.com

Chrmn, Pres & CEO: R.D. Fairbank
EVP, CFO & Chief Acctg Officer: G.L. Perlin
EVP & Cntlr: S.R. McFarland
SVP & Treas: S. Linehan

Secy & General Counsel: J.G. Finneran, Jr.
Investor Contact: M. Rowen (703-720-2455)
Board Members: E. R. Campbell, W. R. Dietz, R. D. Fairbank, P. W. Gross, A. F. Hackett, L. Hay, III, P. Leroy, M. A. Shattuck, III, B. H. Warner

Founded: 1993
Domicile: Delaware
Employees: 30,900

The McGraw-Hill Companies

Cardinal Health Inc

STANDARD &POOR'S

S&P Recommendation HOLD ★★★☆☆

Price $31.99 (as of Oct 22, 2010)	**12-Mo. Target Price** $38.00	**Investment Style** Large-Cap Blend

GICS Sector Health Care
Sub-Industry Health Care Distributors

Summary This company is one of the leading wholesale distributors of pharmaceuticals, medical/surgical supplies and related products to a broad range of health care customers.

Key Stock Statistics (Source S&P, Vickers, company reports)

52-Wk Range	$36.66– 28.22	S&P Oper. EPS 2011**E** 2.43	Market Capitalization(B) $11.234	Beta	0.73
Trailing 12-Month EPS	$1.78	S&P Oper. EPS 2012**E** 2.65	Yield (%) 2.44	S&P 3-Yr. Proj. EPS CAGR(%)	5
Trailing 12-Month P/E	18.0	P/E on S&P Oper. EPS 2011**E** 13.2	Dividend Rate/Share $0.78	S&P Credit Rating	BBB+
$10K Invested 5 Yrs Ago	NA	Common Shares Outstg. (M) 351.2	Institutional Ownership (%) 87		

Price Performance

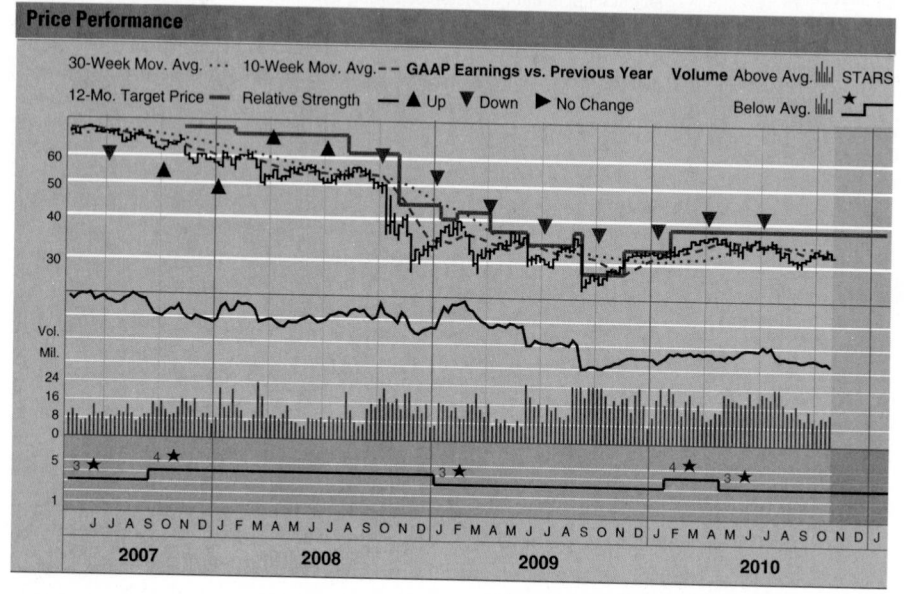

30-Week Mov. Avg. · · · 10-Week Mov. Avg. - - GAAP Earnings vs. Previous Year Volume Above Avg. STARS
12-Mo. Target Price — Relative Strength — ▲ Up ▼ Down ▶ No Change Below Avg.

Options: ASE, CBOE, P, Ph

Analysis prepared by **Herman B. Saftlas** on August 10, 2010, when the stock traded at **$ 32.72**.

Highlights

➤ We expect revenues to rise about 2.5% in FY 11 (Jun.), to about $101 billion. Sales in the Pharmaceutical segment should reflect low-single digit market growth, renewals of customer contracts, and a branded drug inflation rate similar to FY 10. Sales of nuclear medicines should benefit from the resolution of recent supply shortages. We also expect low single-digit market growth in the Medical segment, due to an anticipated normal flu season, and benefits from new marketing strategies and services.

➤ We project gross and operating margins to improve slightly in FY 11, with organic expenses expected to be flat with FY 10. However, expenses related to the new Healthcare Solutions business should result in a moderate increase in SG&A costs. We also expect a decline in interest expense.

➤ After a projected tax rate of 37%, versus FY 10's 37.5%, we estimate non-GAAP adjusted EPS of $2.43 for FY 11, up from the $2.22 reported for FY 10. Adjusted EPS exclude restructuring and acquisition-related costs, and various other non-recurring items.

Investment Rationale/Risk

➤ Representing one of the nation's three major pharmaceutical distribution companies, we see Cardinal well situated in its industry, with relationships with two major retail pharmacy chains generating over 40% of its revenues. We see CAH gaining good traction in its performance initiatives, including reducing the number of its generic drug suppliers and bolstering its generic drug sales, transforming its medical supply business, and expense control. Longer term, we believe health care reform will help lead to increased drug volumes for CAH and its peers. Meanwhile, we view CAH's cash flow as healthy, providing financial flexibility for business expansion, dividends and common share buybacks.

➤ Risks to our recommendation and target price include intensified competition, the loss of major accounts, consolidation trends in the U.S. retail pharmacy industry reducing the customer base, and unfavorable changes in contracts with drugmakers or retailers.

➤ Our 12-month target price of $38 is based on a peer-level multiple of 15.6X applied to our EPS estimate of $2.43 for FY 11.

Qualitative Risk Assessment

LOW	MEDIUM	HIGH

Our risk assessment reflects CAH's diversified products and services and what we believe are good growth prospects for its contract drugmaking and drug dispensing systems. However, we also see intense competition in the drug distribution market, and we believe that future drugmaker-distributor contract negotiations could be less favorable to distributors.

Quantitative Evaluations

S&P Quality Ranking B+

D	C	B-	B	B+	A-	A	A+

Relative Strength Rank WEAK

24

LOWEST = 1 HIGHEST = 99

Revenue/Earnings Data

Revenue (Million $)

	1Q	2Q	3Q	4Q	Year
2010	24,781	24,920	24,343	24,460	98,503
2009	24,321	25,075	24,918	25,199	99,512
2008	21,973	23,283	22,910	22,926	91,091
2007	20,938	21,785	21,867	22,263	86,852
2006	19,237	19,781	20,638	21,708	81,364
2005	17,796	18,555	19,103	19,457	74,911

Earnings Per Share ($)

2010	-0.17	0.64	0.62	0.54	1.62
2009	0.68	0.88	0.87	0.74	3.16
2008	0.82	0.89	1.02	0.89	3.62
2007	0.71	0.77	-0.01	0.61	2.08
2006	0.55	0.72	0.83	0.80	2.90
2005	0.50	0.47	0.84	0.59	2.40

Fiscal year ended Jun. 30. Next earnings report expected: Early November. EPS Estimates based on S&P Operating Earnings; historical GAAP earnings are as reported.

Dividend Data (Dates: mm/dd Payment Date: mm/dd/yy)

Amount ($)	Date Decl.	Ex-Div. Date	Stk. of Record	Payment Date
0.175	11/04	12/29	01/01	01/15/10
0.175	02/03	03/30	04/01	04/15/10
0.195	05/05	06/29	07/01	07/15/10
0.195	08/04	09/29	10/01	10/15/10

Dividends have been paid since 1983. Source: Company reports.

Please read the Required Disclosures and Analyst Certification on the last page of this report.

The McGraw-Hill Companies

Cardinal Health Inc

Business Summary August 10, 2010

CORPORATE OVERVIEW. Cardinal Health ranks as one of the nation's largest wholesalers of pharmaceuticals and medical products. On August 31, 2009, the company spun off to its shareholders stock in CareFusion Corp., a company formed from Cardinal's previous device businesses designed to prevent hospital medication errors and infections. CareFusion's stock trades on the NYSE under the symbol CFN.

The Pharmaceutical segment (91% of revenues in FY 10 (Jun.)) distributes pharmaceutical and related health care products to independent and chain drug stores, hospitals, alternate care centers, and supermarket and mass merchandiser pharmacies. The company also provides pharmaceutical repackaging and distribution for retail and mail order customers. Cardinal also offers third-party logistics support services, distributes therapeutic plasma to hospitals, clinics and other providers located in the U.S.

The company manufactures and markets generic pharmaceutical products for sale to hospitals, clinics and pharmacies in the United Kingdom. CAH also has a specialty pharmacy that provides prescription fulfillment and clinical care services directly to individual patients requiring highly intensive therapies. In July 2010, the company acquired Healthcare Solutions, a provider of data and services for oncology and specialty customers, for $517 million in cash, plus an additional $150 in future contingent payments.

Cardinal operates the world's largest network of nuclear pharmacies and is expanding its positron emission tomography (PET) agent manufacturing capabilities to support new drug development and the future of personalized medicine. This unit prepares and delivers radiopharmaceuticals for use in nuclear imaging and other procedures in hospitals and clinics. In addition, about 200 hospitals across the U.S. outsource the management of their inpatient pharmacy to Cardinal.

The Medical segment (9% of revenues) distributes medical-surgical products to ambulatory care centers, physician offices, clinical laboratories and hospitals across the U.S. and Canada. This unit also produces gloves, gowns, surgical drapes, scrubs and fluid management products. In addition, this segment conducts surgical and procedural kitting operations that assemble all necessary single-use surgical products and apparel for specific procedures into one kit, allowing clinicians to focus on the patient.

Company Financials Fiscal Year Ended Jun. 30

Per Share Data ($)	2010	2009	2008	2007	2006	2005	2004	2003	2002	2001
Tangible Book Value	8.48	7.30	4.26	4.12	8.52	8.20	7.05	12.10	11.50	9.50
Cash Flow	2.33	4.27	4.65	2.87	3.82	3.34	4.15	3.70	2.98	2.50
Earnings	1.62	3.16	3.62	2.07	2.90	2.40	3.47	3.12	2.45	1.88
S&P Core Earnings	1.39	3.16	3.64	3.08	2.88	2.16	3.14	2.78	2.26	1.69
Dividends	0.72	0.60	0.50	0.39	0.27	0.15	0.12	0.11	0.10	0.09
Payout Ratio	44%	19%	14%	19%	9%	6%	3%	4%	4%	5%
Prices:High	36.66	39.87	62.25	76.15	75.74	69.64	76.54	67.96	73.70	77.32
Prices:Low	29.69	24.87	27.79	56.41	61.15	52.85	36.08	50.00	46.60	56.67
P/E Ratio:High	23	13	17	37	26	29	22	22	30	41
P/E Ratio:Low	18	8	8	27	21	22	10	16	19	30

Income Statement Analysis (Million $)										
Revenue	98,503	99,512	91,091	86,852	81,364	74,911	65,054	50,467	44,394	47,948
Operating Income	1,627	2,488	2,594	2,485	2,474	2,555	2,694	3,723	2,216	1,893
Depreciation	254	399	375	322	393	410	299	266	244	281
Interest Expense	114	219	171	121	132	134	98.9	115	133	155
Pretax Income	1,212	1,667	1,957	1,252	1,835	1,629	2,238	2,127	1,701	1,332
Effective Tax Rate	NA	31.5%	32.3%	32.9%	32.2%	35.8%	31.9%	33.6%	33.8%	35.6%
Net Income	587	1,143	1,325	840	1,245	1,047	1,525	1,412	1,126	857
S&P Core Earnings	503	1,142	1,326	1,247	1,236	936	1,369	1,266	1,045	771

Balance Sheet & Other Financial Data (Million $)										
Cash	2,755	1,848	1,291	1,309	1,321	1,412	1,096	1,724	1,382	934
Current Assets	14,919	15,799	14,184	14,545	14,777	13,443	13,058	13,250	11,907	10,716
Total Assets	19,990	25,119	23,448	23,154	23,374	22,059	21,369	18,521	16,438	14,642
Current Liabilities	11,538	11,400	10,376	11,460	11,373	10,105	9,369	7,314	6,810	6,575
Long Term Debt	1,896	3,280	3,687	3,457	2,600	2,320	2,835	2,472	2,207	1,871
Common Equity	5,276	8,725	7,756	7,377	8,491	8,593	7,976	7,758	6,393	5,437
Total Capital	7,405	12,005	11,444	10,834	11,090	10,913	12,000	11,207	8,600	7,308
Capital Expenditures	256	533	376	1,630	443	572	410	423	285	341
Cash Flow	841	1,542	1,691	1,162	1,637	1,456	1,824	1,678	1,370	1,138
Current Ratio	1.3	1.4	1.4	1.3	1.3	1.3	1.4	1.8	1.7	1.6
% Long Term Debt of Capitalization	25.6	27.3	32.2	31.9	23.4	21.3	23.6	22.1	25.7	25.6
% Net Income of Revenue	0.6	1.2	1.5	1.0	1.5	1.4	2.3	2.8	2.5	1.8
% Return on Assets	2.6	4.7	5.7	3.6	5.5	4.8	7.7	8.1	7.2	6.4
% Return on Equity	8.4	13.9	17.5	10.6	14.6	12.6	19.5	20.0	19.0	17.4

Data as orig reptd.; bef. results of disc opers/spec. items. Per share data adj. for stk. divs.; EPS diluted. E-Estimated. NA-Not Available. NM-Not Meaningful. NR-Not Ranked. UR-Under Review.

Office: 7000 Cardinal Place, Dublin, OH 43017.
Telephone: 614-757-5000.
Website: http://www.cardinal.com
Chrmn & CEO: G.S. Barrett

EVP & Secy: S.T. Falk
EVP & CIO: P.B. Morrison
SVP & Chief Acctg Officer: S.G. Laws
SVP & Treas: J.M. Gomez

Board Members: C. F. Arnold, G. S. Barrett, G. A. Britt, C. S. Cox, C. Darden, B. L. Downey, J. F. Finn, G. B. Kenny, J. J. Mongan, R. C. Notebaert, D. W. Raisbeck, J. G. Spaulding

Founded: 1979
Domicile: Ohio
Employees: 31,200

The **McGraw·Hill** Companies

CareFusion Corp

STANDARD &POOR'S

S&P Recommendation HOLD ★★★☆☆

Price	12-Mo. Target Price	Investment Style
$24.70 (as of Oct 22, 2010)	$27.00	Large-Cap Growth

GICS Sector Health Care
Sub-Industry Health Care Equipment

Summary This leading maker of infusion pumps, dispensing systems, and respiratory and infection prevention products was spun off from Cardinal Health on August 31, 2009.

Key Stock Statistics (Source S&P, Vickers, company reports)

52-Wk Range	$30.08– 20.63	S&P Oper. EPS 2011E	1.63	Market Capitalization(B)	$5.492	Beta	NA
Trailing 12-Month EPS	$0.87	S&P Oper. EPS 2012E	1.87	Yield (%)	Nil	S&P 3-Yr. Proj. EPS CAGR(%)	14
Trailing 12-Month P/E	28.4	P/E on S&P Oper. EPS 2011E	15.2	Dividend Rate/Share	Nil	S&P Credit Rating	BBB-
$10K Invested 5 Yrs Ago	NA	Common Shares Outstg. (M)	222.4	Institutional Ownership (%)	77		

Price Performance

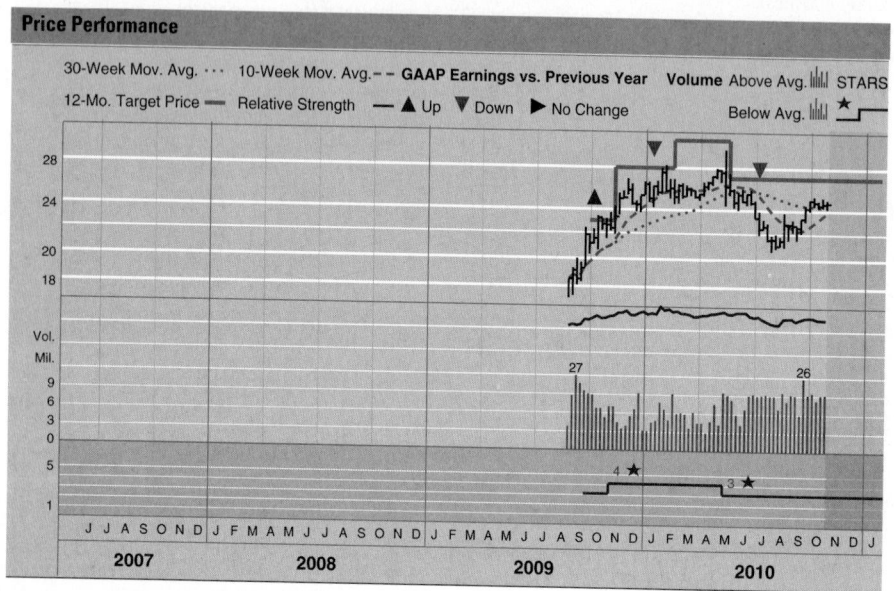

30-Week Mov. Avg. · · · · 10-Week Mov. Avg. – – GAAP Earnings vs. Previous Year Volume Above Avg. STARS
12-Mo. Target Price — Relative Strength — ▲ Up ▼ Down ► No Change Below Avg. ★

Analysis prepared by **Phillip M. Seligman** on August 16, 2010, when the stock traded at **$ 22.59**.

Highlights

➤ We expect CFN's revenue in FY 11 (Jun.) to rise 5%, to $4.13 billion, led by new products, the recent acquisition of IV (intravenous) device maker Medegen, and the fulfillment of a dispensing equipment contract deferred from FY 10. However, we see growth being limited by FY 10's H1N1-related revenue, resumption of Alaris infusion pump shipments in July 2009, and FY 10's favorable currency exchange rates. The company does not expect these top-line benefits to recur in FY 11.

➤ We forecast wider gross margins on an improved product mix. We also expect operating expenses to contract as a percentage of revenue, despite higher R&D spending, mainly on savings from a planned restructuring.

➤ We estimate EPS of $1.63 in FY 11, versus $1.42 in FY 10, but note that growth is masked by the $0.25 - $0.30 earned in FY 10 related to nonrecurring factors. We look for $1.87 in FY 12. We view CFN's $1 billion in cash as of June 30, 2010, and its expectations of operating cash flow of $425 million to $475 million in FY 11 as adequate for potential acquisitions.

Investment Rationale/Risk

➤ We expect CFN to benefit over the long term from hospitals seeking to reduce medication errors and hospital-acquired infection. We view CFN's expanding product portfolio as promising, and are positive on its plans to divest underperforming businesses and make more synergistic investments. But while we consider its view of a gradual thawing of hospital capital spending as encouraging, we expect hospitals to remain selective in their purchases, as their top priority for their limited budgets is IT projects, and we see increasing competition. We also believe it is too soon to determine how much CFN will benefit from rival Baxter's (BAX 46, Buy) infusion pump recall, and we see that being determined partly by BAX's success in replacing the pumps.

➤ Risks to our recommendation and target price include further declines in hospital capital spending, intensified competition, product recalls, and increased health care regulation.

➤ Our 12-month target price of $27 reflects a multiple of 20X our calendar 2010 EPS estimate of $1.35. This multiple is above peers' on our view of CFN's superior growth prospects.

Qualitative Risk Assessment

LOW	MEDIUM	HIGH

Our risk assessment reflects our belief that U.S. hospital capital spending will remain under pressure over the long term, limiting the sales growth of CFN's capital equipment, which represents about 40% of its business. Still, we expect these and CFN's disposables products to benefit from hospitals seeking to improve patient safety.

Quantitative Evaluations

S&P Quality Ranking NR

D	C	B-	B	B+	A-	A	A+

Relative Strength Rank MODERATE
52
LOWEST = 1　　　　HIGHEST = 99

Revenue/Earnings Data

Revenue (Million $)

	1Q	2Q	3Q	4Q	Year
2010	923.0	1,019	952.0	1,035	3,929
2009	1,167	1,167	1,076	1,091	4,501
2008	1,060	1,060	1,150	1,248	4,518
2007	--	--	--	--	3,478
2006	--	--	--	--	3,052
2005	--	--	--	--	--

Earnings Per Share ($)

2010	0.25	0.33	-0.04	0.23	0.77
2009	0.14	0.49	--	0.44	2.57
2008	--	--	--	--	--
2007	--	--	--	--	--
2006	--	--	--	--	--
2005	--	--	--	--	--

Fiscal year ended Jun. 30. Next earnings report expected: Early November. EPS Estimates based on S&P Operating Earnings; historical GAAP earnings are as reported.

Dividend Data

No cash dividends have been paid.

Please read the Required Disclosures and Analyst Certification on the last page of this report.

The McGraw-Hill Companies

STANDARD
&POOR'S

CareFusion Corp

Business Summary August 16, 2010

CORPORATE OVERVIEW. CareFusion Corp. is a global medical technology company with leading products and services designed to improve the safety and quality of health care. In 2008, Cardinal Health reorganized and consolidated the businesses comprising the majority of CareFusion into Cardinal Health's Clinical and Medical Products segment. CareFusion was incorporated in Delaware on January 14, 2009, for the purpose of holding the segment in connection with its planned spinoff, and transferred the equity interests of the entities that hold the assets and liabilities of the clinical and medical products businesses to CareFusion. Approximately 81% of the equity of CareFusion was spun off to Cardinal Health shareholders after the close of trading on August 31, 2009, and Cardinal plans to divest the remaining amount over time.

CFN consists of two segments: Critical Care Technologies and Medical Technologies and Services. Critical Care Technologies includes intravenous, or IV, infusion, medication and supply dispensing and respiratory care businesses that develop, manufacture and sell capital equipment and related dedicated and non-dedicated disposables. Medical Technologies and Services includes infection prevention and medical specialties products and services businesses that develop, manufacture and sell primarily single-use, disposable prod-

ucts and reusable surgical instruments. Its primary customers include hospitals, ambulatory surgical centers, clinics, long-term care facilities and physician offices in the U.S., and hospitals in 120 countries worldwide.

Primary product brands include: (1) Alaris IV infusion systems that feature proprietary software, Guardrails, an application that alerts the clinician when a parameter is outside the institution's pre-established limitations for that medication, thereby helping to reduce IV medication errors; (2) Pyxis automated medication dispensing systems that provide medication management and Pyxis automated medical supply dispensing systems; (3) AVEA and Pulmonetic Systems ventilation and respiratory products, and Jaeger and SensorMedics pulmonary products; (4) ChloraPrep products that help prevent vascular and surgical-site infections and MedMined software and services that help target and reduce hospital-acquired infections (HAIs); and (5) V. Mueller surgical instruments and related products and services.

Company Financials Fiscal Year Ended Jun. 30

Per Share Data ($)	2010	2009	2008	2007	2006	2005	2004	2003	2002	2001
Tangible Book Value	3.63	4.73	NA	NA	NA	NA	NA	NA	NA	NA
Cash Flow	1.54	3.45	NA	NA	NA	NA	NA	NA	NA	NA
Earnings	0.77	2.57	NA	NA	NA	NA	NA	NA	NA	NA
S&P Core Earnings	0.77	2.51	2.93	2.23	NA	NA	NA	NA	NA	NA
Dividends	NA	Nil	NA	NA	NA	NA	NA	NA	NA	NA
Payout Ratio	Nil	Nil	NA	NA	NA	NA	NA	NA	NA	NA
Prices:High	30.08	26.99	NA	NA	NA	NA	NA	NA	NA	NA
Prices:Low	20.63	17.25	NA	NA	NA	NA	NA	NA	NA	NA
P/E Ratio:High	39	11	NA	NA	NA	NA	NA	NA	NA	NA
P/E Ratio:Low	27	7	NA	NA	NA	NA	NA	NA	NA	NA

Income Statement Analysis (Million $)	2010	2009	2008	2007	2006	2005	2004	2003	2002	2001
Revenue	3,929	4,501	4,518	3,478	3,052	NA	NA	NA	NA	NA
Operating Income	714	856	945	691	573	NA	NA	NA	NA	NA
Depreciation	173	194	165	117	109	NA	NA	NA	NA	NA
Interest Expense	93.0	92.0	22.3	37.0	57.5	NA	NA	NA	NA	NA
Pretax Income	357	719	847	619	567	NA	NA	NA	NA	NA
Effective Tax Rate	NA	21.0%	21.8%	18.8%	18.8%	NA	NA	NA	NA	NA
Net Income	171	568	663	502	460	NA	NA	NA	NA	NA
S&P Core Earnings	172	568	663	502	NA	NA	NA	NA	NA	NA

Balance Sheet & Other Financial Data (Million $)	2010	2009	2008	2007	2006	2005	2004	2003	2002	2001
Cash	1,019	783	607	677	NA	NA	NA	NA	NA	NA
Current Assets	2,508	2,390	2,322	NA	NA	NA	NA	NA	NA	NA
Total Assets	7,943	8,349	8,329	7,876	NA	NA	NA	NA	NA	NA
Current Liabilities	753	762	762	NA	NA	NA	NA	NA	NA	NA
Long Term Debt	1,386	1,159	1,539	1,268	NA	NA	NA	NA	NA	NA
Common Equity	4,704	5,451	5,048	4,887	NA	NA	NA	NA	NA	NA
Total Capital	6,094	6,740	6,657	6,167	NA	NA	NA	NA	NA	NA
Capital Expenditures	127	129	188	115	105	NA	NA	NA	NA	NA
Cash Flow	344	762	828	620	569	NA	NA	NA	NA	NA
Current Ratio	3.3	3.1	2.9	3.2	NA	NA	NA	NA	NA	NA
% Long Term Debt of Capitalization	22.7	17.2	23.1	20.6	Nil	NA	NA	NA	NA	NA
% Net Income of Revenue	4.4	12.6	14.7	14.5	15.1	NA	NA	NA	NA	NA
% Return on Assets	NA	6.8	8.2	NA	NA	NA	NA	NA	NA	NA
% Return on Equity	NA	10.8	13.3	NA	NA	NA	NA	NA	NA	NA

Data as orig reptd.; bef. results of disc opers/spec. items. Per share data adj. for stk. divs.; EPS diluted. E-Estimated. NA-Not Available. NM-Not Meaningful. NR-Not Ranked. UR-Under Review.

Office: 3750 Torrey View Court, San Diego, CA 92130.
Telephone: 858-617-2000.
Website: http://www.carefusion.com
Chrmn & CEO: D. Schlotterbeck

COO: D. Winstead
EVP, Secy & General Counsel: J. Stafslien
SVP, Chief Acctg Officer & Cntlr: J. Maschal
CFO: E. Borkowski

Investor Contact: C. Cox (858-617-2020)
Board Members: P. Francis, R. Friel, J. Kosecoff, J. M. Losh, G. T. Lucier, E. Miller, M. D. O'Halleran, D. Schlotterbeck, R. Wayman

Employees: 15,000

The McGraw-Hill Companies

CarMax Inc

STANDARD &POOR'S

S&P Recommendation HOLD ★★★☆☆	**Price** $29.54 (as of Oct 22, 2010)	**12-Mo. Target Price** $26.00	**Investment Style** Large-Cap Growth

GICS Sector Consumer Discretionary
Sub-Industry Automotive Retail

Summary CarMax, the largest U.S. retailer of used vehicles, owns and operates more than 100 used car superstores in 49 markets.

Key Stock Statistics (Source S&P, Vickers, company reports)

52-Wk Range	$30.10– 18.62	S&P Oper. EPS 2011E	1.57	Market Capitalization(B)	$6.642	Beta	1.21
Trailing 12-Month EPS	$1.58	S&P Oper. EPS 2012E	1.63	Yield (%)	Nil	S&P 3-Yr. Proj. EPS CAGR(%)	12
Trailing 12-Month P/E	18.7	P/E on S&P Oper. EPS 2011E	18.8	Dividend Rate/Share	Nil	S&P Credit Rating	NA
$10K Invested 5 Yrs Ago	$21,421	Common Shares Outstg. (M)	224.9	Institutional Ownership (%)	98		

Price Performance

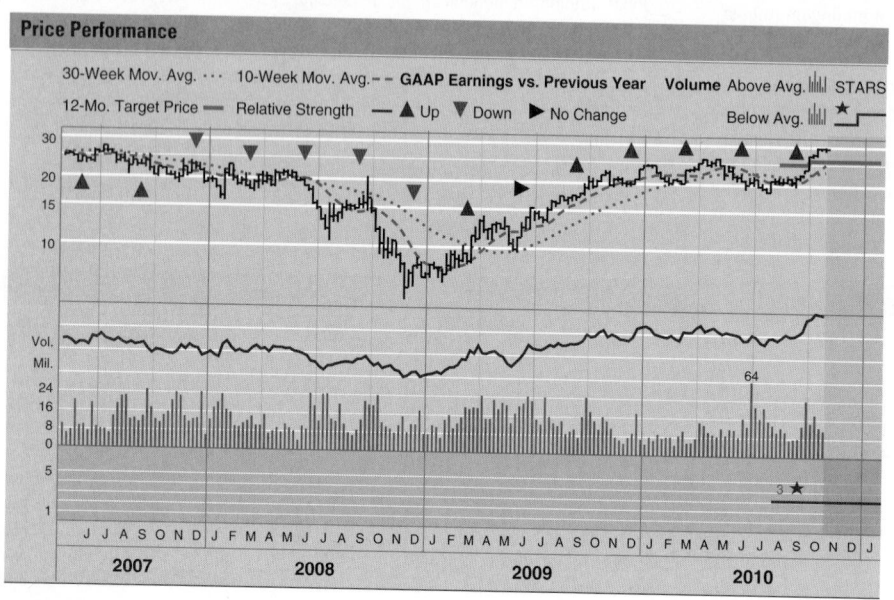

30-Week Mov. Avg. · · · 10-Week Mov. Avg. – – **GAAP Earnings vs. Previous Year** Volume Above Avg. STARS
12-Mo. Target Price — Relative Strength — ▲ Up ▼ Down ► No Change Below Avg. ★

Options: ASE, CBOE, P, Ph

Analysis prepared by **Efraim Levy, CFA** on September 22, 2010, when the stock traded at **$ 25.92**.

Highlights

▶ We expect revenues in FY 11 (Feb.) to rise 17.5%, through a combination of comparable-store sales growth and new store additions. Sales volume has been improving and average transaction price has been rising. The company opened three new stores in early FY 11. While SG&A expenses should rise as demand expands, we expect operating margins to improve during the fiscal year. In addition to its core used car superstores, CarMax also owns several new vehicle dealerships for selling a variety of automaker brands.

▶ For 2010 and 2011, we project that higher industry volume and macroeconomic factors will bolster new and used vehicle sales. The company plans to open between three and five used vehicle stores in FY 12 and between five and 10 in FY 13. As a result, we expect to see rising capital spending and depreciation and amortization charges during those years.

▶ We expect EPS to rise to $1.57 in FY 11 and then to $1.63 in FY 12, from $1.26 in FY 10. The balance sheet, with limited long-term debt, should support an increase in debt as the company resumes the addition of new stores to its portfolio.

Investment Rationale/Risk

▶ Based on our calendar 2010 P/E and price to free cash flow and total enterprise value to EBITDA estimates, KMX recently traded at a premium to the average of publicly traded automobile retailers in our analytical coverage. We believe the premium is warranted given KMX's better than peer net margin. We estimate adjusted free cash flow per share of $1.45 for FY 11 and $1.13 for FY 12, compared to $1.42 posted in FY 10. Rising investment in new facilities will limit capital available for other purposes.

▶ Risks to our recommendation and target price include a decrease in multiples for automotive retailers. In addition, demand for and pricing of used vehicles could be less than we expect, and credit for dealers and consumers could be more costly or difficult to obtain.

▶ We expect CarMax Auto Finance (CAF) to help deliver sales by providing financing for consumers, and we think CAF will make a solid profit contribution on its own. Based on historical and peer P/E comparisons, our 12-month target price is $26, or 16.7X our FY 11 EPS estimate of $1.57, toward the low end of KMX's historical range, but still above publicly traded automotive retailing peers.

Qualitative Risk Assessment

LOW	MEDIUM	HIGH

Our risk assessment reflects the cyclical nature of the automotive retailing industry, which is affected by interest rates, consumer confidence, and personal discretionary spending, offset by the company's variable cost structure.

Quantitative Evaluations

S&P Quality Ranking B+

D	C	B-	B	B+	A-	A	A+

Relative Strength Rank STRONG

92

LOWEST = 1   HIGHEST = 99

Revenue/Earnings Data

Revenue (Million $)

	1Q	2Q	3Q	4Q	Year
2011	2,319	2,342	--	--	--
2010	1,834	2,077	1,726	1,833	7,470
2009	2,209	1,839	1,456	1,471	6,974
2008	2,147	2,123	1,885	2,045	8,285
2007	1,885	1,930	1,768	1,883	7,466
2006	1,578	1,634	1,424	1,624	6,260

Earnings Per Share ($)

2011	0.45	0.48	E0.31	E0.34	E1.57
2010	0.13	0.46	0.33	0.33	1.26
2009	0.13	0.06	-0.10	0.17	0.27
2008	0.30	0.29	0.14	0.10	0.83
2007	0.27	0.25	0.21	0.19	0.92
2006	0.19	0.20	0.21	0.19	0.70

Fiscal year ended Feb. 28. Next earnings report expected: Late December. EPS Estimates based on S&P Operating Earnings; historical GAAP earnings are as reported.

Dividend Data

No cash dividends have been paid.

Please read the Required Disclosures and Analyst Certification on the last page of this report.

The McGraw·Hill Companies

CarMax Inc

Business Summary September 22, 2010

CORPORATE OVERVIEW. CarMax, Inc., is the largest U.S. retailer of used cars, based on data for FY 10 (Feb.). As of September 22, 2010, CarMax owned and operated 103 used car superstores. It also sells new vehicles at five locations under franchise agreements with four new car manufacturers. The company also provides financial services to customers through CarMax Auto Finance (CAF).

MARKET PROFILE. The automotive retailing industry is the largest retail trade sector in the U.S. It generates approximately $1.0 trillion in annual sales, comprising roughly 7% of GDP. The industry is highly fragmented, and we estimate that the 100 largest automotive retailers produce approximately 15% of industry revenues.

In its FY 10 10-K filing with the SEC, citing industry data from the CNW Group, CarMax said there were about 35 million used cars sold in the U.S. during calendar 2009, of which 15 million were estimated to be later-model, 1- to 6-year-old vehicles. While CarMax is the largest used auto retailer, it still represented only about 2% of the total late model used units sold.

During the past few years, Internet marketing has taken on great significance for the used vehicle and vehicle financing markets.

Our fundamental outlook for automotive retailers is positive, reflecting our view of improving sales prospects. We believe the industry has seen the bottom of the sales cycle. We still see a weak residential housing market, a difficult credit environment and relatively low consumer confidence limiting demand for big ticket items such as cars. However, bright spots include the sharp decline in gasoline prices from a peak above $4 a gallon and signs of economic improvement. We believe we could see increased year-over-year new vehicle sales volume for most months of 2010.

After U.S. light vehicle sales volume fell 21% in 2009, to 10.4 million units, we expect an 8.4% rebound, to 11.3 million units, in 2010. Publicly traded dealerships' general overweighting toward import and luxury brands should help them when demand likely rebounds with the economy. With expected higher sales, we look for dealer profits to improve in 2010.

Company Financials Fiscal Year Ended Feb. 28

Per Share Data ($)	2010	2009	2008	2007	2006	2005	2004	2003	2002	2001
Tangible Book Value	8.62	7.18	6.76	5.77	4.57	3.84	3.28	2.69	6.56	7.64
Cash Flow	1.53	0.52	1.04	1.08	0.82	0.63	0.63	0.52	0.65	0.55
Earnings	1.26	0.27	0.83	0.92	0.70	0.54	0.55	0.46	0.41	0.22
S&P Core Earnings	1.24	0.23	0.83	0.93	0.64	0.49	0.52	0.43	0.41	0.31
Dividends	Nil	Nil	Nil	Nil	Nil	Nil	Nil	Nil	Nil	Nil
Payout Ratio	Nil	Nil	Nil	Nil	Nil	Nil	Nil	Nil	Nil	Nil
Calendar Year	2009	2008	2007	2006	2005	2004	2003	2002	2001	2000
Prices:High	24.75	23.00	29.45	27.60	17.40	18.55	19.65	17.00	12.00	2.69
Prices:Low	6.92	5.76	18.57	13.87	12.32	9.02	6.23	6.45	1.94	0.66
P/E Ratio:High	20	85	35	30	25	35	36	37	29	12
P/E Ratio:Low	5	21	22	15	18	17	11	14	5	3

Income Statement Analysis (Million $)										
Revenue	7,645	6,989	8,200	7,598	6,260	5,260	4,598	3,970	3,518	2,501
Operating Income	514	156	347	362	165	124	119	90.7	168	104
Depreciation	58.3	54.7	46.6	34.6	26.7	20.1	16.2	14.9	16.3	18.1
Interest Expense	3.46	7.99	9.96	5.37	4.09	2.81	1.14	2.26	4.96	12.1
Pretax Income	453	96.8	297	323	240	185	189	157	146	73.5
Effective Tax Rate	37.8%	38.8%	38.7%	38.6%	38.3%	38.8%	38.5%	39.5%	38.0%	38.0%
Net Income	282	59.2	182	199	148	113	116	94.8	90.8	45.6
S&P Core Earnings	275	50.2	181	200	135	102	109	90.2	27.4	16.6

Balance Sheet & Other Financial Data (Million $)										
Cash	18.3	141	13.0	19.5	21.8	29.1	61.6	34.6	3.29	8.80
Current Assets	1,556	1,288	1,357	1,151	942	865	773	709	578	493
Total Assets	2,556	2,379	2,333	1,886	1,489	1,293	1,037	918	720	711
Current Liabilities	477	491	490	512	363	329	242	248	223	226
Long Term Debt	27.4	178	227	33.7	135	128	100	100	14.1	83.1
Common Equity	1,934	1,593	1,489	1,247	960	801	681	555	485	392
Total Capital	2,083	1,901	1,716	1,281	1,095	934	781	659	502	478
Capital Expenditures	22.4	186	253	192	194	230	181	122	41.4	10.8
Cash Flow	340	114	229	233	175	133	133	110	44.3	29.7
Current Ratio	3.3	2.6	2.8	2.2	2.6	2.6	3.2	2.9	2.6	2.2
% Long Term Debt of Capitalization	1.3	9.2	13.2	2.6	12.3	13.7	12.8	15.2	2.8	17.4
% Net Income of Revenue	3.7	0.9	2.2	2.6	2.4	2.1	2.5	2.4	2.6	1.8
% Return on Assets	11.4	2.5	8.6	11.7	10.6	9.6	11.9	11.6	12.7	6.6
% Return on Equity	16.0	3.8	13.3	17.8	16.8	15.2	18.9	18.2	20.7	12.4

Data as orig reptd.; bef. results of disc opers/spec. items. Per share data adj. for stk. divs.; EPS diluted. E-Estimated. NA-Not Available. NM-Not Meaningful. NR-Not Ranked. UR-Under Review.

Office: 12800 Tuckahoe Creek Pkwy, Richmond, VA 23238-1124.
Telephone: 804-747-0422.
Website: http://www.carmax.com
Chrmn: W.R. Tiefel

Pres & CEO: T.J. Folliard
EVP, CFO & Chief Acctg Officer: K. Browning
EVP & Chief Admin Officer: M.K. Dolan
SVP, Secy & General Counsel: E.M. Margolin

Investor Contact: K.D. Browning (804-747-0422)
Board Members: R. E. Blaylock, K. Browning, T. J. Folliard, J. E. Garten, S. D. Goodman, W. R. Grafton, E. H. Grubb, T. G. Stemberg, V. M. Stephenson, B. A. Stewart, W. R. Tiefel

Founded: 1996
Domicile: Virginia
Employees: 13,439

Carnival Corp

STANDARD &POOR'S

S&P Recommendation	HOLD ★★★☆☆	Price	12-Mo. Target Price	Investment Style
		$40.14 (as of Oct 22, 2010)	$42.00	Large-Cap Blend

GICS Sector Consumer Discretionary
Sub-Industry Hotels, Resorts & Cruise Lines

Summary Carnival Corp. and Carnival plc own businesses that operate more than 90 cruise ships, as well as tour companies in Alaska and Canada.

Key Stock Statistics (Source S&P, Vickers, company reports)

52-Wk Range	$44.21–28.71	S&P Oper. EPS 2010**E**	2.52	Market Capitalization(B)	$31.670	Beta	1.48
Trailing 12-Month EPS	$2.40	S&P Oper. EPS 2011**E**	2.72	Yield (%)	1.00	S&P 3-Yr. Proj. EPS CAGR(%)	UR
Trailing 12-Month P/E	16.7	P/E on S&P Oper. EPS 2010**E**	15.9	Dividend Rate/Share	$0.40	S&P Credit Rating	BBB+
$10K Invested 5 Yrs Ago	$9,490	Common Shares Outstg. (M)	789.0	Institutional Ownership (%)	55		

Price Performance

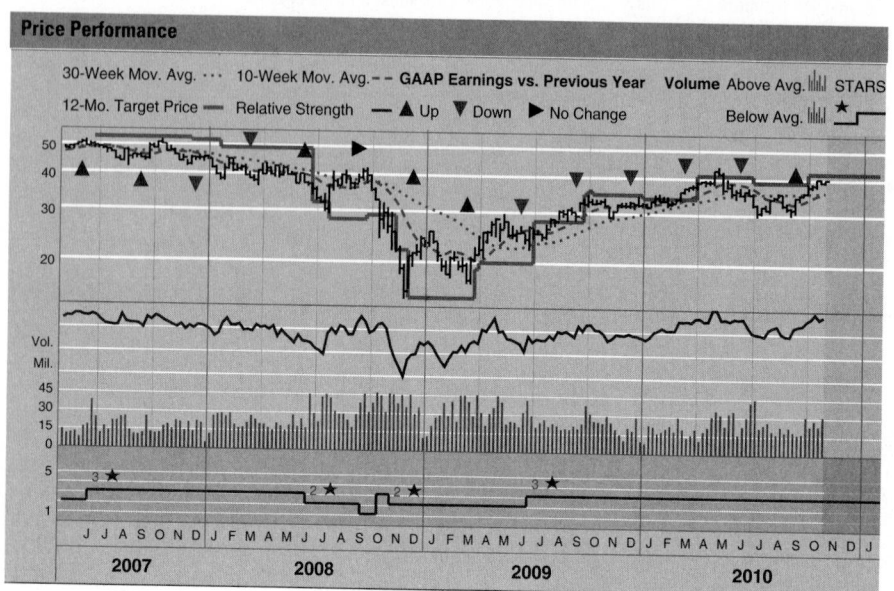

30-Week Mov. Avg. · · · 10-Week Mov. Avg. - - GAAP Earnings vs. Previous Year   Volume Above Avg. ▮▮▮ STARS
12-Mo. Target Price — Relative Strength — ▲ Up ▼ Down ► No Change   Below Avg. ▮▮▮ ★

Options: ASE, CBOE, P, Ph

Analysis prepared by **Preeti Rambhiya** on September 30, 2010, when the stock traded at **$38.30**.

Highlights

► In FY 11 (Nov.), we look for revenue to increase 8%, to $15.2 billion, from the $14.1 billion that we project for FY 10.

► In FY 11, we expect Carnival's net yield to increase by 3.5%, but we think that continued sector capacity growth amid challenging economic conditions could limit pricing gains as well as margin improvement. We caution that market volatility could pour cold water on both consumer optimism and discretionary spending. In FY 10, booking levels have been strong and pricing has picked up significantly.

► We believe the company's superb cost management has enabled Carnival to deliver strong operating performance versus expectations. In FY 11, we think a cost containment focus is likely to continue, but we expect the scope of further margin expansion to be limited. We look for Carnival's EBIT margin in FY 11 to be relatively flat with the 16.9% that we project for FY 10. For FY 11, we estimate EPS of $2.72, up from the $2.52 we project for FY 10, which excludes a net adverse impact of $0.03 from special items in FY 10's third quarter.

Investment Rationale/Risk

► We think that a key factor to monitor is whether yield growth momentum is maintained in the face of toughening comparisons and sticky unemployment. More importantly, we believe, the vast majority of the cost containment has been squeezed from commissions and selling expenses, which may prove unsustainable as the demand scenario improves.

► Downside risks to our target price and recommendation include material disappointments on pricing and advance bookings, significant deterioration in consumer confidence, and terrorism concerns. Rising oil prices are a risk, in our opinion, particularly as CCL does not hedge its fuel exposure.

► Our 12-month target price of $42 is derived from an equal blend of EV/EBITDA and P/E analyses and DCF valuation. Based on our FY 10 EBITDA estimate of $3.794 billion, we apply a multiple of 10.9X, a 10% premium to Carnival's five-year average, given the improved visibility we see, yielding a value of about $41. Our DCF analysis (WACC 8.6%, terminal growth rate of 2.5%) indicates an intrinsic value of about $44. Our P/E approach implies a value of about $41 a share.

Qualitative Risk Assessment

LOW	MEDIUM	HIGH

Our risk assessment reflects the capital intensity of the cruise sector and its sensitivity to economic cycles. This is offset by our view of Carnival's premier position in a consolidated industry with high barriers to entry, economies of scale, and Carnival's strong operating profile.

Quantitative Evaluations

S&P Quality Ranking   NR

D	C	B-	B	B+	A-	A	A+

Relative Strength Rank   STRONG

79

LOWEST = 1   HIGHEST = 99

Revenue/Earnings Data

Revenue (Million $)

	1Q	2Q	3Q	4Q	Year
2010	3,095	3,195	4,426	--	--
2009	2,864	2,948	4,139	3,206	13,157
2008	3,152	3,378	4,814	3,302	14,646
2007	2,688	2,900	4,321	3,124	13,033
2006	2,463	2,662	3,905	2,809	11,839
2005	2,396	2,519	3,605	2,567	11,087

Earnings Per Share ($)

2010	0.22	0.31	1.62	E0.34	E2.52
2009	0.32	0.33	1.33	0.24	2.23
2008	0.30	0.49	1.64	0.46	2.86
2007	0.35	0.48	1.64	0.44	2.95
2006	0.31	0.46	1.49	0.51	2.77
2005	0.42	0.49	1.36	0.43	2.70

Fiscal year ended Nov. 30. Next earnings report expected: Late December. EPS Estimates based on S&P Operating Earnings; historical GAAP earnings are as reported.

Dividend Data (Dates: mm/dd Payment Date: mm/dd/yy)

Amount ($)	Date Decl.	Ex-Div. Date	Stk. of Record	Payment Date
0.100	01/21	02/05	02/09	03/12/10
0.100	04/14	11/17	11/19	12/10/10

Dividends have been paid since 2010. Source: Company reports.

STANDARD &POOR'S

Carnival Corp

Business Summary September 30, 2010

CORPORATE OVERVIEW. Carnival Corp. is part of the world's largest cruise ship business, and has grown significantly through acquisitions and the addition of new ships. In 2003, Carnival merged with P&O Princess Cruises plc, which was renamed Carnival plc (CUK 40, Hold). As of September 2010, the combined Carnival operated 97 ships with capacity for more than 185,000 passengers. Also, Carnival has tour operations in Alaska and the Canadian Yukon.

With Carnival's dual listing company (DLC) format, there are separate stocks trading under the Carnival Corp. and Carnival plc names. Each company has retained its separate legal identity, but the two share a single senior executive management team, have identical boards of directors, and are run as if they were a single economic enterprise. In valuing the shares, we look at the combined financial results and equity base of the Carnival entities.

MARKET PROFILE. Looking ahead, we expect demand for cruise ship vacations to grow. In the U.S., we believe that most people have never taken a multi-night cruise ship vacation, and we expect that an aging U.S. population will lead to more interest in cruises. Also, we believe that a continued industry emphasis on providing ships with more features and the addition of more local ports will bolster passenger demand.

COMPETITIVE LANDSCAPE. We see Carnival enhancing its competitive position through the addition of new ships, which should encourage both returning and new customers. As of September 2010, Carnival had 11 new ships scheduled to be delivered between September 2010 and May 2014. However, one or more other ships could leave Carnival's fleet during this period.

In terms of capacity, Carnival was recently more than twice the size of its biggest competitor -- Royal Caribbean Cruises Ltd. (RCL 32, Buy).

Company Financials Fiscal Year Ended Nov. 30

Per Share Data ($)	2009	2008	2007	2006	2005	2004	2003	2002	2001	2000
Tangible Book Value	21.90	18.52	19.01	17.10	15.47	13.96	11.83	11.48	10.13	8.84
Cash Flow	3.85	4.39	4.24	3.89	3.91	3.13	2.46	2.38	2.21	2.08
Earnings	2.23	2.86	2.95	2.77	2.70	2.24	1.66	1.73	1.58	1.60
Dividends	Nil	1.60	1.38	1.03	0.80	0.52	0.44	0.42	0.42	0.42
Payout Ratio	Nil	56%	47%	37%	30%	23%	27%	24%	27%	26%
Prices:High	34.95	45.22	52.73	56.14	58.98	58.75	39.84	34.64	34.94	51.25
Prices:Low	16.80	14.85	41.70	36.40	45.78	39.75	20.34	22.07	16.95	18.31
P/E Ratio:High	16	6	18	20	22	26	24	20	22	32
P/E Ratio:Low	8	2	14	13	17	18	12	13	11	11

Income Statement Analysis (Million $)										
Revenue	13,157	14,646	13,033	11,839	11,087	9,727	6,718	4,368	4,536	3,779
Operating Income	3,463	3,921	3,826	3,601	3,541	2,985	1,968	1,444	1,448	1,233
Depreciation	1,309	1,249	1,101	988	902	812	585	382	372	288
Interest Expense	NA	466	367	312	330	284	195	111	121	41.4
Pretax Income	1,806	2,377	2,424	2,240	2,184	1,901	1,223	959	948	967
Effective Tax Rate	0.89%	1.98%	0.10%	NM	NM	2.47%	2.37%	NM	2.34%	0.11%
Net Income	1,790	2,330	2,408	2,279	2,257	1,854	1,194	1,016	926	965

Balance Sheet & Other Financial Data (Million $)										
Cash	538	650	943	1,163	1,178	643	1,070	667	1,421	189
Current Assets	NA	1,650	1,976	1,995	2,215	1,728	2,132	1,132	1,959	549
Total Assets	36,835	33,400	34,181	30,552	28,432	27,636	24,491	12,335	11,564	9,831
Current Liabilities	NA	5,781	7,260	5,415	5,192	5,034	3,315	1,620	1,480	1,715
Long Term Debt	9,097	7,735	6,313	6,355	5,727	6,291	6,918	3,012	2,955	2,099
Common Equity	22,035	19,098	19,963	18,210	16,972	15,760	13,793	7,418	6,591	5,871
Total Capital	31,947	27,914	26,276	24,565	22,699	22,051	20,711	10,430	9,546	7,970
Capital Expenditures	3,380	3,353	3,312	2,480	1,977	3,586	2,516	1,986	827	1,003
Cash Flow	3,099	3,579	3,509	3,267	3,159	2,666	1,779	1,398	1,298	1,253
Current Ratio	0.3	0.3	0.3	0.4	0.4	0.3	0.6	0.7	1.3	0.3
% Long Term Debt of Capitalization	28.5	27.7	24.0	25.9	25.2	28.5	33.4	28.9	31.0	26.3
% Net Income of Revenue	13.6	15.9	18.4	19.2	20.4	19.1	17.8	23.3	20.4	25.6
% Return on Assets	5.1	6.9	7.4	7.7	8.1	7.1	6.5	8.5	8.7	10.7
% Return on Equity	8.7	11.9	12.6	13.0	13.8	12.5	11.3	14.5	14.9	16.4

Data as orig reptd.; bef. results of disc opers/spec. items. Per share data adj. for stk. divs.; EPS diluted. E-Estimated. NA-Not Available. NM-Not Meaningful. NR-Not Ranked. UR-Under Review.

Office: Carnival Place MSCD925N, 3655 NW 87 Avenue, Miami, FL 33178-2428.
Telephone: 305-599-2600.
Website: http://www.carnivalcorp.com
Chrmn & CEO: M.M. Arison

Vice Chrmn & COO: H.S. Frank
SVP & CFO: D. Bernstein
SVP, Secy & General Counsel: A. Perez
Chief Acctg Officer & Cntlr: L. Freedman

Investor Contact: B. Roberts (305-406-4832)
Board Members: M. M. Arison, J. Band, R. H. Dickinson, A. W. Donald, P. L. Foschi, H. S. Frank, R. J. Glasier, M. A. Maidique, J. Parker, P. G. Ratcliffe, S. Subotnick, L. A. Weil, R. J. Weisenburger, U. Zucker

Founded: 1974
Domicile: Panama
Employees: 84,800

The McGraw·Hill Companies

Caterpillar Inc

STANDARD &POOR'S

S&P Recommendation BUY ★★★★☆

Price	12-Mo. Target Price	Investment Style
$78.33 (as of Oct 22, 2010)	$95.00	Large-Cap Blend

GICS Sector Industrials
Sub-Industry Construction & Farm Machinery & Heavy Trucks

Summary CAT, the world's largest producer of earthmoving equipment, is also a big maker of electric power generators and engines used in petroleum markets.

Key Stock Statistics (Source S&P, Vickers, company reports)

52-Wk Range	$81.20–50.50	S&P Oper. EPS 2010E	4.00	Market Capitalization(B)	$49.385	Beta	1.78
Trailing 12-Month EPS	$2.47	S&P Oper. EPS 2011E	5.25	Yield (%)	2.25	S&P 3-Yr. Proj. EPS CAGR(%)	41
Trailing 12-Month P/E	31.7	P/E on S&P Oper. EPS 2010E	19.6	Dividend Rate/Share	$1.76	S&P Credit Rating	A
$10K Invested 5 Yrs Ago	$18,204	Common Shares Outstg. (M)	630.5	Institutional Ownership (%)	66		

Price Performance

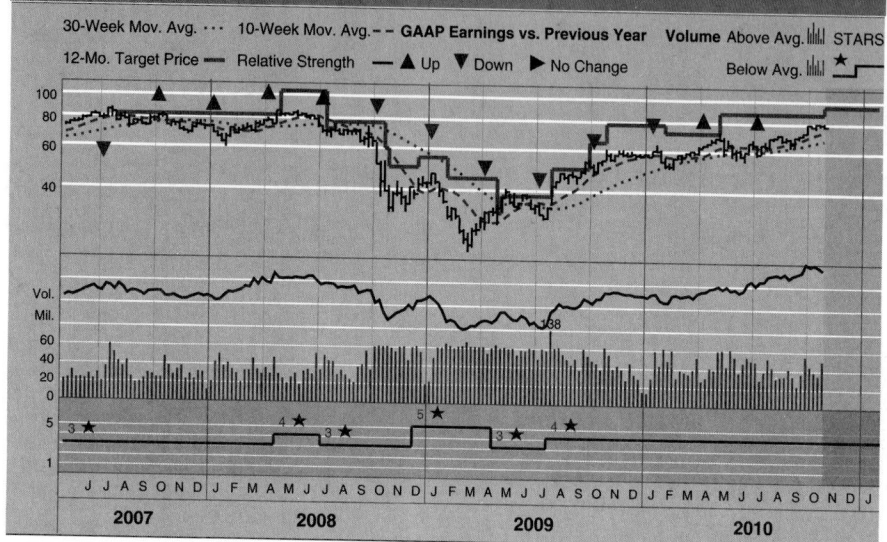

30-Week Mov. Avg. · · · 10-Week Mov. Avg. – – GAAP Earnings vs. Previous Year Volume Above Avg. STARS
12-Mo. Target Price — Relative Strength — ▲ Up ▼ Down ▶ No Change Below Avg. ★

Options: ASE, CBOE, P, Ph

Analysis prepared by **Michael W. Jaffe** on October 22, 2010, when the stock traded at **$ 78.89**.

Qualitative Risk Assessment

LOW	MEDIUM	HIGH

Our risk assessment reflects its leading position in many of the end markets it serves, offset by the highly cyclical nature of the construction equipment, agricultural equipment, and engine businesses.

Quantitative Evaluations

S&P Quality Ranking A+

D	C	B-	B	B+	A-	A	A+

Relative Strength Rank MODERATE 68

LOWEST = 1   HIGHEST = 99

Revenue/Earnings Data

Revenue (Million $)

	1Q	2Q	3Q	4Q	Year
2010	8,238	10,409	--	--	--
2009	9,225	7,975	7,298	7,898	32,396
2008	11,796	13,624	12,981	12,923	51,324
2007	10,016	11,356	11,442	12,144	44,958
2006	9,392	10,605	10,517	11,003	41,517
2005	8,339	9,360	8,977	9,663	36,339

Earnings Per Share ($)

	1Q	2Q	3Q	4Q	Year
2010	0.36	1.09	E1.08	E1.18	E4.00
2009	-0.19	0.60	0.64	0.36	1.43
2008	1.45	1.74	1.39	1.08	5.66
2007	1.23	1.24	1.40	1.50	5.37
2006	1.20	1.52	1.14	1.32	5.17
2005	0.81	1.08	0.94	1.20	4.04

Fiscal year ended Dec. 31. Next earnings report expected: NA. EPS Estimates based on S&P Operating Earnings; historical GAAP earnings are as reported.

Highlights

➤ We expect revenues to advance 15% in 2011. Weak global economies, tight credit markets and the resultant slowdowns in residential and commercial construction brought large sales declines in 2009 and in the early part of 2010. However, we think CAT's machinery business (its largest segment) is now in the midst of a recovery, on the seeming start of a global economic recovery and what appears to be the end of inventory destocking at CAT's dealers. We expect the forecasted gains to be driven in the near term by robust growth in CAT's operations in Asia/Pacific and Latin America, and increased demand in North America related to the need to replace aging and worn out equipment.

➤ We look for margins to widen in 2011, on the leverage that we see resulting from improved sales trends. We also expect margins to be aided by CAT's focus on improving operating efficiency, and incremental benefits from aggressive cost cuts implemented by CAT during its business downturn.

➤ Our 2011 forecast compares with a 2010 estimate that excludes $0.14 of charges related to the recently enacted U.S. health care bill.

Investment Rationale/Risk

➤ Depressed economic conditions greatly affected CAT's client markets in recent quarters. However, in light of aggressive stimulus packages put in place by governments throughout the world, we believe its business is in the process of recovery, and that it has also done a solid job of controlling costs. Based on these factors and our valuation model, we believe CAT's shares are undervalued.

➤ Risks to our opinion and target price include less robust than expected results from global stimulus packages, and worse than expected conditions in global credit markets.

➤ The shares recently traded at 15X our 2011 EPS forecast of $5.25, which is in the middle of CAT's typical valuation range as it moved further into business recoveries. We see the stock as undervalued based on our belief that government stimulus packages and improving credit conditions will allow its business to post a strong revival over the next few years, with CAT's recent streamlining actions likely to lead to robust earnings growth. We set our 12-month target price at $95, which is 18.1X our 2011 EPS forecast, and slightly above CAT's peak at a similar stage of its last business revival.

Dividend Data (Dates: mm/dd Payment Date: mm/dd/yy)

Amount ($)	Date Decl.	Ex-Div. Date	Stk. of Record	Payment Date
0.420	04/14	04/22	04/26	05/20/10
0.440	06/09	07/16	07/20	08/20/10
0.440	06/09	07/16	07/20	08/20/10
0.440	10/13	10/21	10/25	11/20/10

Dividends have been paid since 1914. Source: Company reports.

Please read the Required Disclosures and Analyst Certification on the last page of this report.

The McGraw-Hill Companies

Caterpillar Inc

STANDARD &POOR'S

Business Summary October 22, 2010

CORPORATE OVERVIEW. Caterpillar's distinctive yellow machines are in service in nearly every country in the world, with 69% of the company's revenues derived from outside of the U.S. in 2009 (67% in 2008). As of year-end 2009, 71% of CAT's independent dealers were located outside of the U.S. CAT operates in three principal lines of business: Machinery, Engines and Financial Products.

CAT's largest operating segment, the Machinery unit (56% of revenues and $1.0 billion of operating losses in 2009), makes earthmoving equipment. Operations include the design, manufacture, marketing and sale of construction, mining and forestry machinery including track and wheel tractors, track and wheel loaders, pipelayers, motor graders, wheel tractor-scrapers, track and wheel excavators, backhoe loaders, log skidders, log loaders, off-highway trucks, articulated trucks, paving products, skid steer loaders and related parts. This segment also includes logistics services for other companies and the design, manufacture, remanufacture, maintenance and servicing of rail-related products. The division's products are used predominantly in heavy construction (including infrastructure), general construction, mining, and

quarry/aggregates markets. These end markets are very cyclical and competitive.

The Engine segment (35% and operating profits of $1.5 billion) makes diesel, heavy fuel and natural gas reciprocating engines for both CAT's own earth-moving equipment and third-party customers. This segment designs, manufactures, markets and sells engines for Caterpillar machinery; electric power generation systems; locomotives; marine, petroleum, construction, industrial, agricultural and other applications; and related parts. This area also includes remanufacturing of Caterpillar engines and a variety of Caterpillar machine and engine components and remanufacturing services for other companies. The division's major end markets are petroleum, electric power generation, industrial and marine.

Company Financials Fiscal Year Ended Dec. 31

Per Share Data ($)	2009	2008	2007	2006	2005	2004	2003	2002	2001	2000
Tangible Book Value	9.61	5.51	14.88	7.07	9.77	8.34	6.48	5.51	5.75	5.97
Cash Flow	4.02	8.80	8.09	7.52	6.14	4.85	3.48	2.91	2.85	2.97
Earnings	1.43	5.66	5.37	5.17	4.04	2.88	1.57	1.15	1.16	1.51
S&P Core Earnings	2.03	4.56	5.46	5.48	4.05	2.76	1.50	0.20	0.16	NA
Dividends	1.68	1.68	1.32	1.10	0.91	0.78	0.71	0.70	0.69	0.67
Payout Ratio	117%	30%	25%	21%	23%	27%	45%	61%	59%	44%
Prices:High	61.28	85.96	87.00	82.03	59.88	49.36	42.48	30.00	28.42	27.56
Prices:Low	21.71	31.95	57.98	57.05	41.31	34.25	20.62	16.88	19.88	14.78
P/E Ratio:High	43	15	16	16	15	17	27	26	24	18
P/E Ratio:Low	15	6	11	11	10	12	13	15	17	10

Income Statement Analysis (Million $)										
Revenue	32,396	51,324	44,958	41,517	36,339	30,251	22,763	20,152	20,450	20,175
Operating Income	2,928	7,569	7,850	7,634	6,029	4,650	3,505	3,060	3,137	3,447
Depreciation	2,336	1,968	1,797	1,602	1,477	1,397	1,347	1,220	1,169	1,022
Interest Expense	389	1,427	1,420	1,297	1,028	750	716	800	942	980
Pretax Income	557	4,510	5,026	4,942	3,974	2,766	1,497	1,110	1,172	1,500
Effective Tax Rate	NM	21.1%	29.6%	28.4%	28.2%	26.4%	26.6%	28.1%	31.3%	29.8%
Net Income	895	3,557	3,541	3,537	2,854	2,035	1,099	798	805	1,053
S&P Core Earnings	1,277	2,867	3,604	3,748	2,860	1,951	1,052	133	98.7	NA

Balance Sheet & Other Financial Data (Million $)										
Cash	2,239	1,517	1,122	530	1,108	445	342	309	400	334
Current Assets	26,789	31,633	25,477	23,093	22,790	20,856	16,791	14,628	13,400	12,521
Total Assets	60,038	67,782	56,132	50,879	47,069	43,091	36,465	32,851	30,657	28,464
Current Liabilities	19,292	26,069	22,245	19,252	19,092	16,210	12,621	11,344	10,276	8,568
Long Term Debt	5,652	22,834	17,829	17,680	15,677	15,837	14,078	11,596	11,291	11,334
Common Equity	8,740	6,087	8,883	6,859	8,432	7,467	6,078	5,472	5,611	5,600
Total Capital	15,254	29,575	26,712	24,539	24,109	23,304	20,156	17,068	16,902	16,934
Capital Expenditures	2,316	4,011	3,040	2,675	2,415	2,114	1,765	1,773	1,968	1,388
Cash Flow	2,518	5,525	5,338	5,139	4,331	3,432	2,446	2,018	1,974	2,075
Current Ratio	1.4	1.2	1.2	1.2	1.2	1.3	1.3	1.3	1.3	1.5
% Long Term Debt of Capitalization	37.1	77.2	66.7	72.0	65.0	68.0	69.8	67.9	66.8	66.9
% Net Income of Revenue	2.8	6.9	7.9	8.5	7.9	6.7	4.8	4.0	3.9	5.2
% Return on Assets	1.4	5.7	6.6	7.2	6.3	5.1	3.2	2.5	2.7	3.8
% Return on Equity	12.1	47.5	45.0	46.3	35.9	30.0	19.0	14.4	14.4	19.0

Data as orig reptd.; bef. results of disc opers/spec. items. Per share data adj. for stk. divs.; EPS diluted. E-Estimated. NA-Not Available. NM-Not Meaningful. NR-Not Ranked. UR-Under Review.

Office: 100 N.E. Adams Street, Peoria, IL 61629.
Telephone: 309-675-1000.
Email: catir@cat.com
Website: http://www.cat.com

Chrmn: J.W. Owens
Pres: L.C. Calil
Vice Chrmn & CEO: D.R. Oberhelman
CFO: E.J. Rapp

CTO: T.L. Utley
Investor Contact: M. DeWalt (309-675-4549)
Board Members: W. Blount, D. M. Dickinson, J. T. Dillon, E. V. Fife, J. Gallardo, D. Goode, P. A. Magowan, D. R. Oberhelman, W. A. Osborn, J. W. Owens, C. D. Powell, E. B. Rust, Jr., S. C. Schwab, J. I. Smith

Founded: 1925
Domicile: Delaware
Employees: 95,290

CB Richard Ellis Group Inc

STANDARD &POOR'S

S&P Recommendation HOLD ★★★★★

Price	12-Mo. Target Price	Investment Style
$18.88 (as of Oct 22, 2010)	$19.00	Large-Cap Growth

GICS Sector Financials
Sub-Industry Real Estate Services

Summary CB Richard Ellis Group is a global commercial real estate services company.

Key Stock Statistics (Source S&P, Vickers, company reports)

52-Wk Range	$20.38– 9.98	S&P Oper. EPS 2010**E**	0.64	Market Capitalization(B)	$6.075	Beta	2.64
Trailing 12-Month EPS	$0.43	S&P Oper. EPS 2011**E**	1.06	Yield (%)	Nil	S&P 3-Yr. Proj. EPS CAGR(%)	67
Trailing 12-Month P/E	43.9	P/E on S&P Oper. EPS 2010**E**	29.5	Dividend Rate/Share	Nil	S&P Credit Rating	NA
$10K Invested 5 Yrs Ago	$12,348	Common Shares Outstg. (M)	321.8	Institutional Ownership (%)	97		

Price Performance

30-Week Mov. Avg. · · · · 10-Week Mov. Avg. - - **GAAP Earnings vs. Previous Year** **Volume** Above Avg. STARS
12-Mo. Target Price — Relative Strength — ▲ Up ▼ Down ▶ No Change Below Avg. ★

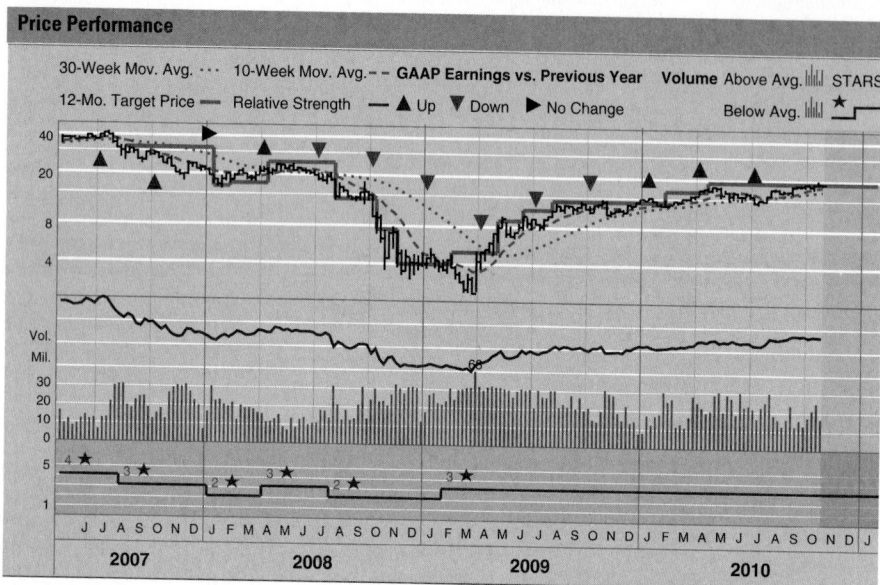

Options: ASE, CBOE, P, Ph

Analysis prepared by **Robert McMillan** on July 30, 2010, when the stock traded at **$ 16.94**.

Highlights

➤ After a 19% revenue decline in 2009 that stemmed from the global economic crisis, which caused sales and leasing activity to plummet, we see a rise of 25% in 2010 on an expected rebound in commercial real estate transactions. We look for CBG's property management and investment management businesses to recover before its sales and leasing business. We think the continuing, but gradual thawing of the credit markets and more prudent underwriting will contribute to an eventual and sustained pickup in the property sales and leasing business.

➤ During the 2010 second quarter, CBG's revenues rose 23%, while operating income surged on well-controlled expenses in CBG's low-fixed cost business. We were encouraged by growth in the Americas, Europe and the Asia-Pacific region. Revenues from sales and leasing activities jumped 61% and 29%, respectively, while commercial mortgage brokerage and investment management advanced 33% and 23%. Despite recent turbulence stemming from the European debt crisis, we expect CBG's business to sustain its momentum.

➤ We see EPS of $0.64 in 2010 and $1.06 in 2011.

Investment Rationale/Risk

➤ Longer term, however, we expect the company to benefit from its large size and broad array of products and services relative to peers. We think the global reach of CBG's operations helps generate economies of scale that few other real estate firms can match, helping create sustainable barriers to entry. Nevertheless, we see the shares remaining volatile until the turmoil in the financial markets abates.

➤ Risks to our recommendation and target price include lower-than-expected demand for office and industrial space, greater competition, and a further decline in financing activity for commercial real estate transactions.

➤ The stock recently traded at 25.7X our 2010 EPS estimate. Our 12-month target price of $19 reflects a multiple of about 29.6X our 2010 EPS forecast, on our assumption that the multiple will expand, as we see CBG's operating prospects improving. Although we believe the valuation multiple is rich relative to recent historical levels, we think the shares are appropriately valued at recent levels.

Qualitative Risk Assessment

LOW	MEDIUM	HIGH

Our risk assessment reflects CBG's position as one of the world's largest commercial real estate services firms, which should benefit from a worldwide rebound in demand for commercial real estate space and services.

Quantitative Evaluations

S&P Quality Ranking NR

D	C	B-	B	B+	A-	A	A+

Relative Strength Rank STRONG

71

LOWEST = 1   HIGHEST = 99

Revenue/Earnings Data

Revenue (Million $)

	1Q	2Q	3Q	4Q	Year
2010	1,026	1,172	--	--	--
2009	890.5	955.7	1,023	1,297	4,166
2008	1,231	1,315	1,300	1,283	5,129
2007	1,214	1,490	1,493	1,837	6,034
2006	903.5	751.3	967.9	1,409	4,032
2005	538.3	672.2	744.2	956.0	2,911

Earnings Per Share ($)

2010	-0.02	0.15	E0.23	E0.29	E0.64
2009	-0.14	-0.02	0.04	0.21	0.12
2008	0.10	0.08	0.15	0.03	0.34
2007	0.05	0.59	0.48	0.53	1.65
2006	0.16	0.27	0.39	0.53	1.35
2005	0.06	0.22	0.25	0.41	0.95

Fiscal year ended Dec. 31. Next earnings report expected: Late October. EPS Estimates based on S&P Operating Earnings; historical GAAP earnings are as reported.

Dividend Data

No cash dividends have been paid.

Please read the Required Disclosures and Analyst Certification on the last page of this report.

The McGraw-Hill Companies

CB Richard Ellis Group Inc

Business Summary July 30, 2010

CB Richard Ellis Group, Inc. is one of the largest global commercial real estate services companies in the world. The company's business is focused on several service competencies, including strategic advice and execution assistance for property leasing and sales, forecasting, valuations, origination and servicing of commercial mortgage loans, facilities and project management, and real estate investment management. CBG's primary business objective is to leverage its integrated global platform to garner an increasing share of industry revenues relative to competitors. CBG believes this will enable the company to maximize and sustain its long-term cash flow and increase long-term stockholder value. Management's strategy to achieve these business objectives consists of several elements: increasing revenues from large clients; capitalizing on cross-selling opportunities; continuing to grow the investment management business; expanding through fill-in acquisitions; and focusing on improving operating efficiency.

CBG's advisory services (30.8% of 2009 total consolidated revenues) include occupier/tenant and investor/owner services that meet a broad range of client needs, including real estate services, capital markets and valuation. The real estate services business offers a broad spectrum of services to occupiers/tenants and investors/owners. Real estate services include strategic advice and execution for owners, investors and occupiers of real estate in connection with the leasing, disposition and acquisition of property. Although we expect further economic improvement, we still believe that more stringent lending and credit conditions will continue to restrict commercial real estate buying activity over the next 12-18 months. However, we expect activity to improve over the dismal levels of the recent past, particularly in the Asia-Pacific region. Through its capital markets business, CBG offers comprehensive capital markets solutions, rather than separate sales and financing transactions. During 2009, this unit concluded more than $16.3 billion of capital markets transactions in the Americas, including $10.0 billion of investment sales transactions and $6.3 billion of mortgage loan originations. The valuation business provides valuation services that include market value appraisals, litigation support, discounted cash flow analyses, and feasibility and fairness opinions. During 2009, CBG completed over 30,000 valuation, appraisal and advisory assignments.

Company Financials Fiscal Year Ended Dec. 31

Per Share Data ($)	2009	2008	2007	2006	2005	2004	2003	2002	2001	2000
Tangible Book Value	NM	NM	NM	NM	NM	NM	NM	NA	NA	NA
Cash Flow	0.47	0.84	2.09	1.64	1.14	0.56	0.38	0.34	0.54	NA
Earnings	0.12	0.34	1.65	1.35	0.95	0.30	-0.11	0.15	0.32	NA
S&P Core Earnings	0.21	-1.30	1.71	1.33	0.94	0.30	NA	NA	NA	NA
Dividends	Nil	Nil	Nil	Nil	Nil	Nil	Nil	NA	NA	NA
Payout Ratio	Nil	Nil	Nil	Nil	Nil	Nil	Nil	NA	NA	NA
Prices:High	14.14	24.50	42.74	34.26	19.92	11.36	NA	NA	NA	NA
Prices:Low	2.34	3.00	17.49	19.46	10.40	6.03	NA	NA	NA	NA
P/E Ratio:High	NM	72	26	25	21	37	NA	NA	NA	NA
P/E Ratio:Low	NM	9	11	14	11	20	NA	NA	NA	NA

Income Statement Analysis (Million $)	2009	2008	2007	2006	2005	2004	2003	2002	2001	2000
Commissions	Nil	Nil	Nil	Nil	Nil	Nil	Nil	NA	NA	NA
Interest Income	6.13	18.0	29.0	9.80	9.30	4.30	6.00	NA	NA	NA
Total Revenue	4,166	5,129	6,034	4,032	2,911	2,365	1,949	1,170	675	NA
Interest Expense	189	167	163	45.0	54.3	65.4	71.3	NA	NA	NA
Pretax Income	-0.64	134	592	523	358	108	-41.0	48.8	42.5	NA
Effective Tax Rate	NM	85.4%	32.5%	37.9%	38.8%	40.2%	NM	61.7%	50.8%	NA
Net Income	33.3	73.7	388	319	217	64.7	-34.7	18.7	20.9	NA
S&P Core Earnings	58.5	-272	403	314	216	64.0	NA	NA	NA	NA

Balance Sheet & Other Financial Data (Million $)	2009	2008	2007	2006	2005	2004	2003	2002	2001	2000
Total Assets	5,039	5,818	6,243	5,945	2,816	2,272	2,213	1,325	1,359	NA
Cash Items	742	159	392	244	449	257	164	79.7	57.5	NA
Receivables	1,091	962	1,337	985	739	532	553	NA	NA	NA
Securities Owned	Nil	Nil	Nil	Nil	Nil	Nil	Nil	NA	NA	NA
Securities Borrowed	Nil	Nil	Nil	Nil	Nil	Nil	Nil	NA	NA	NA
Due Brokers & Customers	Nil	Nil	Nil	Nil	Nil	Nil	Nil	NA	NA	NA
Other Liabilities	1,883	1,937	2,428	1,906	1,138	809	833	NA	NA	NA
Capitalization:Debt	2,372	2,254	1,992	2,193	821	761	1,061	NA	NA	NA
Capitalization:Equity	629	1,211	989	1,182	794	560	333	251	257	NA
Capitalization:Total	3,157	3,465	3,244	3,573	1,622	1,321	1,394	779	794	NA
% Return on Revenue	0.8	1.4	6.4	7.8	7.4	2.7	NM	1.6	3.1	NA
% Return on Assets	0.7	1.2	6.4	7.2	8.5	2.8	NM	1.4	NA	NA
% Return on Equity	9.0	6.7	35.8	32.2	32.0	14.4	NM	7.4	NA	NA

Data as orig reptd.; bef. results of disc opers/spec. items. Per share data adj. for stk. divs.; EPS diluted. E-Estimated. NA-Not Available. NM-Not Meaningful. NR-Not Ranked. UR-Under Review.

Office: 11150 Santa Monica Blvd Ste 1600, Los Angeles, CA 90025-3385.
Telephone: 310-405-8900.
Website: http://www.cbre.com
Chrmn: R.C. Blum

Pres & CEO: W.B. White
Vice Chrmn: R. Wirta
COO & EVP: C.W. Frese, Jr.
EVP & Chief Acctg Officer: G. Borok

Investor Contact: N. Kormeluk (949-809-4308)
Board Members: R. C. Blum, P. M. Daniels, C. F. Feeny, B. M. Freeman, M. Kantor, F. V. Malek, J. J. Su, B. White, G. L. Wilson, R. Wirta

Founded: 2001
Domicile: Delaware
Employees: 29,000

CBS Corp

STANDARD &POOR'S

S&P Recommendation BUY ★★★★☆

Price	12-Mo. Target Price	Investment Style
$17.18 (as of Oct 22, 2010)	$18.00	Large-Cap Value

GICS Sector Consumer Discretionary
Sub-Industry Broadcasting & Cable TV

Summary This major operator of TV, radio, and outdoor advertising properties is one of the two companies created after the 2006 separation of the "old" Viacom into two public entities.

Key Stock Statistics (Source S&P, Vickers, company reports)

52-Wk Range	$18.20–11.40	S&P Oper. EPS 2010E	1.11	Market Capitalization(B)	$10.821	Beta	2.09
Trailing 12-Month EPS	$0.56	S&P Oper. EPS 2011E	1.24	Yield (%)	1.16	S&P 3-Yr. Proj. EPS CAGR(%)	10
Trailing 12-Month P/E	30.7	P/E on S&P Oper. EPS 2010E	15.5	Dividend Rate/Share	$0.20	S&P Credit Rating	BBB-
$10K Invested 5 Yrs Ago	NA	Common Shares Outstg. (M)	680.7	Institutional Ownership (%)	90		

Price Performance

30-Week Mov. Avg. · · · · 10-Week Mov. Avg. – – GAAP Earnings vs. Previous Year Volume Above Avg. STARS
12-Mo. Target Price — Relative Strength — ▲ Up ▼ Down ► No Change Below Avg.

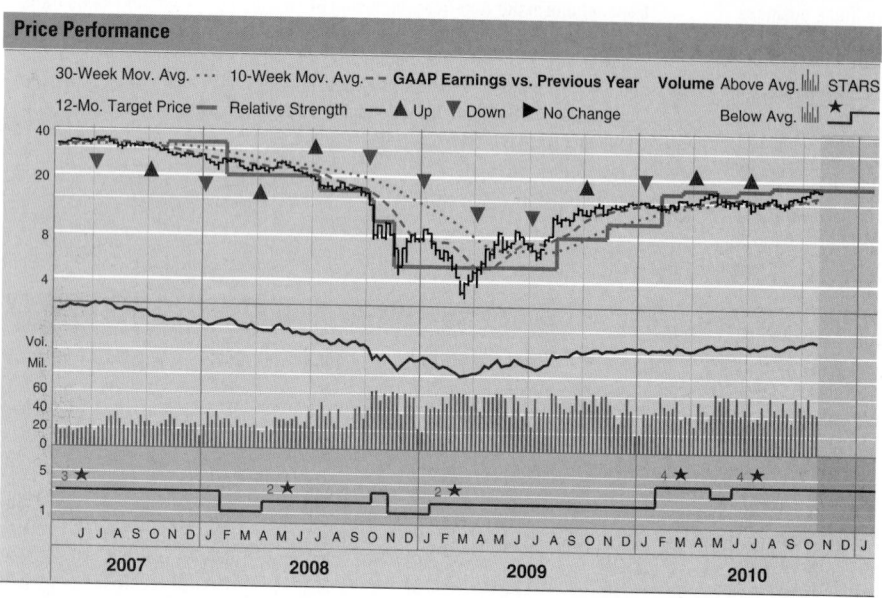

Options: ASE, CBOE, P

Analysis prepared by **Tuna N. Amobi, CFA, CPA** on August 05, 2010, when the stock traded at **$15.58**.

Highlights

➤ We project consolidated revenue growth of about 10% for 2010 to about $14.3 billion, mainly on strong affiliate and advertising revenue growth for the Entertainment, Cable Networks, and Local Broadcasting segments -- with the additional benefit of this year's upcoming political advertising cycle for the TV stations. We also anticipate a relatively modest recovery in the global Outdoor unit, on a gradual improvement in pricing power and occupancy levels (with further improvement in 2011). With some difficult comparisons, we expect 2011 consolidated revenues to advance about 5% to $15.0 billion, also assuming some relatively modest growth for the Publishing division.

➤ Over the next two years, we see sizable margin expansion, with the benefit of cost savings on recent restructuring measures driving a significant improvement in operating leverage. We see 42% adjusted EBIT growth in 2010, to $2.14 billion, and a relatively modest 7% in 2011, to nearly $2.29 billion.

➤ After D&A, reduced interest expense, and taxes, we see 2010 and 2011 operating EPS of $1.11 and $1.24, respectively -- assuming no major acquisitions, divestitures, or share buybacks.

Investment Rationale/Risk

➤ We think CBS's stronger-than-expected 2010 second quarter results showed signs of a cyclical upturn across virtually all of the company's core businesses -- with management's update indicating continued momentum into the third quarter. In particular, we note relatively strong gains for the CBS network during the recently concluded upfront season, even as the scatter ad market has stayed buoyant. We see other potential catalysts from a continued ramp-up of retransmission deals with pay TV providers, and longer-term publishing upside on growing e-books sales. We also note CBS's strong balance sheet with ample financial flexibility.

➤ Risks to our opinion and target price include a relatively high macroeconomic exposure to cyclical advertising businesses (nearly two-thirds of total revenues); corporate governance concerns related to voting control and board independence; and, foreign currency exposure.

➤ Based on what we see as an ample 1.6X 2010 P/E-to-growth (PEG) multiple, our 12-month target price is $18. We also note CBS's net operating loss carryforwards of about $1 billion. The stock recently provided a 1.3% dividend yield.

Qualitative Risk Assessment

LOW	MEDIUM	HIGH

Our risk assessment reflects what we view as CBS's steady free cash flow-generating businesses and ownership of some relatively well established traditional media brands, offset by exposure to cyclical ad-dependent businesses as well as potential structural challenges.

Quantitative Evaluations

S&P Quality Ranking B-

D	C	B-	B	B+	A-	A	A+

Relative Strength Rank STRONG

78

LOWEST = 1   HIGHEST = 99

Revenue/Earnings Data

Revenue (Million $)

	1Q	2Q	3Q	4Q	Year
2010	3,531	3,331	--	--	--
2009	3,160	3,006	3,350	3,498	13,015
2008	3,654	3,394	3,376	3,527	13,950
2007	3,658	3,375	3,281	3,759	14,073
2006	3,575	3,483	3,379	3,883	14,320
2005	5,577	5,876	5,943	3,828	14,536

Earnings Per Share ($)

	1Q	2Q	3Q	4Q	Year
2010	-0.04	0.22	E0.38	E0.44	E1.11
2009	-0.08	0.02	0.30	0.09	0.33
2008	0.36	0.61	-18.53	0.20	-17.43
2007	0.28	0.55	0.48	0.40	1.70
2006	0.31	0.64	0.42	0.43	1.79
2005	0.72	0.94	0.94	-6.07	-5.27

Fiscal year ended Dec. 31. Next earnings report expected: Early November. EPS Estimates based on S&P Operating Earnings; historical GAAP earnings are as reported.

Dividend Data (Dates: mm/dd Payment Date: mm/dd/yy)

Amount ($)	Date Decl.	Ex-Div. Date	Stk. of Record	Payment Date
0.050	11/16	12/09	12/11	01/01/10
0.050	02/23	03/09	03/11	04/01/10
0.050	05/26	06/08	06/10	07/01/10
0.050	08/20	09/08	09/10	10/01/10

Dividends have been paid since 2003. Source: Company reports.

Please read the Required Disclosures and Analyst Certification on the last page of this report.

The McGraw·Hill Companies

CBS Corp

STANDARD &POOR'S

Business Summary August 05, 2010

CORPORATE OVERVIEW. In its current form, the company is one of the two in-dependent public entities created after the early 2006 separation of the "old" Viacom (which was renamed CBS Corp., while the other entity adopted the "Vi-acom" name). Pursuant to the separation, each Class A and B shareholder of the "old" Viacom received 0.5 of a share of corresponding A or B stock of each of the new entities. We believe that CBS Corp. was the lower-growth entity resulting from the separation, and that it was targeted to value-oriented in-vestors.

The company is organized into five business reporting segments. The Enter-tainment segment (54% of 2009 revenue and 46% of adjusted EBIT) includes the CBS networks, CBS TV production and syndication, CBS Films and CBS In-teractive. Cable Networks (10% and 29%) comprises the Showtime Networks and CBS College Sports Network. Publishing (5% and 3%) comprises Simon & Schuster book publishers. The Local Broadcasting segment (18% and 28%) in-cludes 30 owned and operated (O&O) TV stations, as well as 130 radio sta-tions in 29 U.S. markets. The Outdoor unit (13% and -6%) operates billboards and out-of-home displays in the U.S. and abroad. In 2006, CBS sold its Para-mount Parks unit for $1.24 billion in cash.

CORPORATE STRATEGY. In June 2008, CBS acquired CNET Networks for about $1.8 billion in cash. CNET became the cornerstone of a new CBS Inter-active unit -- an online audience network with such verticals as Technology, Entertainment, Sports, News and Business. CBS's online video syndication network has several distribution partners such as AOL, Microsoft, Comcast, Joost, Bebo, Brightcove, Netvibes, Sling Media, and Veoh. In recent years, the company has divested several dozen radio stations (and some TV stations) in smaller markets. In May 2007, CBS acquired Last.fm, a music-based social network with nearly 20 million users in more than 200 countries, for $280 mil-lion in cash. In January 2006, CBS acquired College Sports Network cable channel for about $325 million in stock.

Company Financials Fiscal Year Ended Dec. 31

Per Share Data ($)	2009	2008	2007	2006	2005	2004	2003	2002	2001	2000
Tangible Book Value	NM	NM	NM	NM	NM	NM	NM	NM	NM	NM
Cash Flow	1.18	-16.64	2.34	2.36	-9.91	-16.62	2.77	3.55	3.31	3.04
Earnings	0.33	-17.43	1.70	1.79	-5.27	-17.56	1.62	2.48	-0.26	-0.60
S&P Core Earnings	0.49	-7.03	1.72	1.90	1.10	2.92	2.40	2.08	-0.76	NA
Dividends	0.20	1.06	0.94	0.68	0.56	0.50	0.24	Nil	Nil	Nil
Payout Ratio	61%	NM	55%	NM	NM	NM	15%	Nil	Nil	Nil
Prices:High	14.56	27.18	35.75	32.04	77.98	90.10	99.50	103.78	119.00	151.75
Prices:Low	3.06	4.36	25.57	23.85	59.86	60.18	66.22	59.50	56.50	88.63
P/E Ratio:High	44	NM	21	18	NM	NM	61	42	NM	NM
P/E Ratio:Low	9	NM	15	13	NM	NM	41	24	NM	NM

Income Statement Analysis (Million $)										
Revenue	13,015	13,950	14,073	14,320	14,536	22,526	26,585	24,606	23,223	20,044
Operating Income	NA	2,691	3,078	3,135	3,165	5,838	5,957	5,542	4,667	4,243
Depreciation	582	532	456	440	499	810	1,000	946	3,087	2,224
Interest Expense	542	547	571	566	720	719	776	848	963	822
Pretax Income	409	-12,593	2,052	2,036	-7,513	-13,676	2,861	3,695	656	436
Effective Tax Rate	44.7%	NM	40.0%	32.0%	NM	NM	55.9%	39.2%	NM	NM
Net Income	227	-11,673	1,231	1,383	-8,322	-15,060	1,435	2,207	-220	-364
S&P Core Earnings	329	-4,713	1,247	1,468	871	2,497	2,087	1,845	-656	NA

Balance Sheet & Other Financial Data (Million $)										
Cash	717	420	1,347	3,075	1,655	928	851	631	727	934
Current Assets	5,637	5,193	6,031	8,144	6,796	7,494	7,736	7,167	7,206	7,832
Total Assets	26,962	26,889	40,430	43,509	43,030	68,002	89,849	89,754	90,810	82,646
Current Liabilities	4,747	4,801	4,405	4,400	5,379	6,880	7,585	7,341	7,562	7,758
Long Term Debt	6,553	6,975	6,979	7,027	7,153	9,649	9,683	10,205	10,824	12,474
Common Equity	9,019	8,597	21,472	24,153	21,737	59,862	63,205	62,488	62,717	47,967
Total Capital	16,016	15,593	30,490	32,862	31,007	70,879	73,812	74,337	75,884	67,481
Capital Expenditures	262	474	469	394	376	415	534	537	515	659
Cash Flow	809	-11,142	1,687	1,822	-7,823	-14,250	2,435	3,152	2,867	1,860
Current Ratio	1.2	1.1	1.4	1.9	1.3	1.1	1.0	1.0	1.0	1.0
% Long Term Debt of Capitalization	40.9	44.7	24.8	21.0	23.1	13.6	13.1	13.7	14.3	18.5
% Net Income of Revenue	1.7	NM	8.8	9.7	NM	NM	5.4	9.0	NM	NM
% Return on Assets	0.8	NM	2.9	3.2	NM	NM	1.6	2.4	NM	NM
% Return on Equity	2.6	NM	5.5	5.9	NM	NM	2.3	3.5	NM	NM

Data as orig reptd.; bef. results of disc opers/spec. items. Per share data adj. for stk. divs.; EPS diluted. Data as orig. reptd., for "old" Viacom through third qtr. 2005. E-Estimated. NA-Not Available. NM-Not Meaningful. NR-Not Ranked. UR-Under Review.

Office: 51 West 52nd Street, New York, NY 10019-6188.
Telephone: 212-975-4321.
Website: http://www.cbscorporation.com
Chrmn: S.M. Redstone

Pres & CEO: L. Moonves
Vice Chrmn: S.E. Redstone
EVP & CFO: J.R. Ianniello
EVP & General Counsel: L.J. Briskman

Board Members: D. R. Andelman, J. A. Califano, Jr., W. S. Cohen, G. L. Countryman, C. K. Gifford, L. Goldberg, B. S. Gordon, L. M. Griego, A. Kopelson, L. Moonves, D. Morris, S. E. Redstone, S. M. Redstone, F. V. Salerno

Founded: 1986
Domicile: Delaware
Employees: 25,580

The McGraw-Hill Companies

Celgene Corp

S&P Recommendation STRONG BUY ★★★★★	**Price** $58.74 (as of Oct 22, 2010)	**12-Mo. Target Price** $74.00	**Investment Style** Large-Cap Growth

GICS Sector Health Care
Sub-Industry Biotechnology

Summary This company primarily develops and commercializes small molecule drugs for the treatment of bloodborne and solid tumor cancers and inflammatory disease.

Key Stock Statistics (Source S&P, Vickers, company reports)

52-Wk Range	$65.79– 48.02	S&P Oper. EPS 2010**E**	2.38	Market Capitalization(B)	$27.648	Beta	0.64
Trailing 12-Month EPS	$1.84	S&P Oper. EPS 2011**E**	2.96	Yield (%)	Nil	S&P 3-Yr. Proj. EPS CAGR(%)	25
Trailing 12-Month P/E	31.9	P/E on S&P Oper. EPS 2010**E**	24.7	Dividend Rate/Share	Nil	S&P Credit Rating	BBB+
$10K Invested 5 Yrs Ago	$22,750	Common Shares Outstg. (M)	470.7	Institutional Ownership (%)	84		

Price Performance

- 30-Week Mov. Avg. · · · 10-Week Mov. Avg. - - GAAP Earnings vs. Previous Year   Volume Above Avg. STARS
- 12-Mo. Target Price — Relative Strength — ▲ Up ▼ Down ▶ No Change   Below Avg. ★

Options: ASE, CBOE, P, Ph

Analysis prepared by **Steven Silver** on October 18, 2010, when the stock traded at **$ 58.21**.

Highlights

- ➤ We see 2010 revenues of $3.48 billion, 30% higher than in 2009, with 37% growth in Revlimid sales to $2.34 billion, and 2011 revenues of $4.37 billion, up 26%, with 21% higher Revlimid sales to $2.82 billion. We continue to see significant long-term growth for Revlimid, with new uses being explored in multiple blood cancers, and with its global expansion still in early stages. Further, we expect Vidaza and the recently acquired Abraxane to provide near-term revenue diversification.

- ➤ We forecast 2010 and 2011 gross margins above 92%, as CELG improves manufacturing efficiencies and discontinues sales of lower-margin drugs. We expect 2010 operating margin expansion to 39%, from 2009's 36%, and a further rise to 42% in 2011, driven by leverage from a global infrastructure after the 2008 purchase of Pharmion. We also view robust R&D investments favorably, as CELG expects to have 20 late-stage trials ongoing during 2010.

- ➤ We project adjusted EPS of $2.38 in 2010 and $2.96 in 2011, excluding amortization of intangible assets. We expect CELG to maintain a below-industry average tax rate of 20%-21%, on higher sales in lower tax jurisdictions.

Investment Rationale/Risk

- ➤ In our view, CELG holds the brightest growth prospects among large-cap biotech companies. We expect Revlimid to drive near-term revenue growth, bolstered by positive efficacy seen in first-line multiple myeloma studies, and its oral formulation and superior safety profile. We also have a favorable view of CELG's inflammation/immunology and cellular therapeutics pipelines complementing the core hematology/oncology franchise. We estimate CELG having around $2 billion in cash following the recently closed acquisition of Abraxis Bioscience for its cancer drug Abraxane, which is currently approved for metastatic breast cancer and in Phase III study for non-small cell lung cancer, and a $1.25 billion debt offering.

- ➤ Risks to our opinion and target price include slower-than-expected Revlimid sales growth, reimbursement issues for the drug, unfavorable defense of its patents, and clinical failure of CELG's earlier pipeline candidates.

- ➤ Our 12-month target price of $74 applies a 25X multiple to our 2011 adjusted EPS estimate of $2.96, a premium to large-cap peers on what we view as a superior earnings growth and pipeline outlook.

Qualitative Risk Assessment

LOW	MEDIUM	HIGH

Our risk assessment reflects the strong competition we see in the blood cancer treatment markets, particularly from Velcade in multiple myeloma. Further, in Thalomid and Revlimid, the company currently depends on two products in the same markets for the majority of its revenues. We also see inherent risk in CELG's drugs maintaining a competitive safety profile versus peers.

Quantitative Evaluations

S&P Quality Ranking   C

D	C	B-	B	B+	A-	A	A+

Relative Strength Rank   MODERATE

59

LOWEST = 1   HIGHEST = 99

Revenue/Earnings Data

Revenue (Million $)

	1Q	2Q	3Q	4Q	Year
2010	791.3	852.7	--	--	--
2009	605.1	628.7	695.1	761.0	2,690
2008	462.6	571.5	592.5	628.3	2,255
2007	293.4	347.9	349.9	414.6	1,406
2006	181.8	197.2	244.8	275.0	898.9
2005	112.4	145.7	129.5	149.3	536.9

Earnings Per Share ($)

2010	0.50	0.33	E0.63	E0.57	E2.38
2009	0.35	0.31	0.46	0.54	1.66
2008	-3.98	0.26	0.29	-0.33	-3.46
2007	0.14	0.13	0.09	0.18	0.54
2006	0.04	0.03	0.05	0.06	0.18
2005	0.13	0.03	Nil	0.01	0.18

Fiscal year ended Dec. 31. Next earnings report expected: Late October. EPS Estimates based on S&P Operating Earnings; historical GAAP earnings are as reported.

Dividend Data

No cash dividends have been paid.

STANDARD &POOR'S

Celgene Corp

Business Summary October 18, 2010

CORPORATE OVERVIEW. Celgene is a biopharmaceutical company focusing on the discovery, development and commercialization of products for the treatment of cancer and other severe, immune, inflammatory conditions. Its primary areas of expertise have been on hematological and solid tumor cancers, including multiple myeloma, myelodysplastic syndromes, chronic lymphocyte leukemia (CLL), non-Hodgkin's lymphoma (NHL), glioblastoma, and ovarian, pancreatic and prostate cancers.

CELG uses its small molecule technology to develop Immunomodulatory Drugs (IMiDs) and Selective Cytokine Inhibitory Drugs (SelCIDs), potent, orally available agents to fight acute and chronic diseases. Its primary focus to date has been treating multiple myeloma (MM), the second most commonly diagnosed blood cancer. According to the International Myeloma Foundation, there are an estimated 100,000 people in the U.S. with multiple myeloma and nearly 20,000 new cases diagnosed each year. The IMF estimates that multiple myeloma represents 1% of all cancers and accounts for 2% of cancer deaths.

To date, Celgene's primary marketed products have been Thalomid ($437 million sales in 2009) and Revlimid ($1.7 billion). Thalomid is CELG's version of thalidomide, an antiangiogenic agent capable of inhibiting blood vessel growth and down-regulating TNFa. In 1998, Thalomid was approved by the FDA to treat leprosy-related conditions. In 2006, FDA approved Thalomid to treat relapsed/refractory multiple myeloma. European rights to Thalomid were re-acquired in the March 2008 acquisition of Pharmion, and the drug was approved in Europe for front-line multiple myeloma in April 2008.

In December 28, 2005, FDA approved Revlimid, a successor analogue version of Thalomid, to treat patients with blood disorder myelodysplastic syndrome (MDS). Revlimid has subsequently been approved in the U.S., Europe and Japan, among other countries, for relapsed/refractory multiple myeloma, which has become its most lucrative indication. The drug is also being studied for amyloidosis, non-Hodgkin's lymphoma, and solid tumors including prostate, renal cell carcinoma, pancreatic and colorectal cancers. In 2009, a pivotal Phase III study, MM-015, showed a 50% reduction in progression-free survival in patients receiving Revlimid with melphalan and prednisone (MP) versus patients receiving MP alone as a multiple myeloma maintenance regimen after autologous stem cell transplant, and patients saw 75% progression-free survival improvement beyond nine cycles of therapy. We expect CELG to file the drug for earlier-stage MM use in major markets by early 2011. In August 2010, CELG received notice of a U.S. regulatory filing for a generic version of Revlimid and has responded with a challenge to the filing.

Company Financials Fiscal Year Ended Dec. 31

Per Share Data ($)	2009	2008	2007	2006	2005	2004	2003	2002	2001	2000
Tangible Book Value	7.55	5.37	6.80	4.83	1.48	1.06	0.93	0.85	1.03	1.00
Cash Flow	1.93	-3.13	0.60	0.23	0.23	0.18	0.06	-0.31	0.01	-0.05
Earnings	1.66	-3.46	0.54	0.18	0.18	0.16	0.04	-0.33	-0.01	-0.06
S&P Core Earnings	1.66	-3.45	0.55	0.19	0.05	0.08	-0.04	-0.33	-0.09	NA
Dividends	Nil	Nil	Nil	Nil	Nil	Nil	Nil	Nil	Nil	Nil
Payout Ratio	Nil	Nil	Nil	Nil	Nil	Nil	Nil	Nil	Nil	Nil
Prices:High	58.31	77.39	75.44	60.12	32.68	16.29	12.22	8.05	9.72	19.00
Prices:Low	36.90	45.44	41.26	31.51	12.35	9.37	5.04	2.83	3.60	4.58
P/E Ratio:High	35	NM	NM	NM	NM	NM	NM	NM	NM	NM
P/E Ratio:Low	22	NM	NM	NM	NM	NM	NM	NM	NM	NM

Income Statement Analysis (Million $)	2009	2008	2007	2006	2005	2004	2003	2002	2001	2000
Revenue	2,690	2,255	1,406	899	537	378	271	136	114	84.2
Operating Income	968	742	457	200	97.9	52.4	5.38	-31.0	-19.9	-23.9
Depreciation	126	149	31.5	25.7	14.3	9.69	8.03	5.18	5.09	3.72
Interest Expense	1.97	4.44	11.1	9.42	9.50	9.55	5.67	0.03	0.08	2.08
Pretax Income	976	-1,369	517	203	84.2	63.2	12.0	-101	-4.14	-18.8
Effective Tax Rate	20.4%	NM	56.2%	66.0%	24.4%	16.5%	NM	NM	NM	NM
Net Income	777	-1,534	226	69.0	63.7	52.8	12.8	-101	-2.90	-17.0
S&P Core Earnings	777	-1,528	230	71.5	10.8	25.0	-13.0	-88.6	-26.5	NA

Balance Sheet & Other Financial Data (Million $)	2009	2008	2007	2006	2005	2004	2003	2002	2001	2000
Cash	2,997	2,222	2,739	1,982	724	749	667	261	310	161
Current Assets	3,845	2,841	3,084	2,311	973	850	730	296	336	332
Total Assets	5,389	4,445	3,611	2,736	1,247	1,107	791	327	354	347
Current Liabilities	495	527	433	240	136	141	71.8	44.3	30.0	33.8
Long Term Debt	21.1	22.2	22.6	400	400	400	400	0.04	11.8	12.3
Common Equity	4,395	3,491	2,844	1,976	636	477	310	277	310	296
Total Capital	4,420	3,514	2,877	2,376	1,036	877	710	277	322	308
Capital Expenditures	93.4	77.4	64.4	46.1	35.9	36.0	11.2	11.1	7.87	9.64
Cash Flow	903	-1,385	258	94.7	77.9	62.4	20.8	-95.8	2.18	-13.3
Current Ratio	7.8	5.4	7.1	9.6	7.2	6.0	10.2	6.7	11.2	9.8
% Long Term Debt of Capitalization	Nil	0.6	0.8	16.8	38.6	45.6	56.3	0.0	3.7	4.0
% Net Income of Revenue	28.9	NM	16.1	7.7	11.9	14.0	4.7	NM	NM	NM
% Return on Assets	NA	NM	7.1	3.5	5.4	5.5	2.3	NM	NM	NM
% Return on Equity	NA	NM	9.4	5.3	11.4	13.0	4.3	NM	NM	NM

Data as orig reptd.; bef. results of disc opers/spec. items. Per share data adj. for stk. divs.; EPS diluted. E-Estimated. NA-Not Available. NM-Not Meaningful. NR-Not Ranked. UR-Under Review.

Office: 86 Morris Avenue, Summit, NJ 07901.
Telephone: 908-673-9000.
Email: info@celgene.com
Website: http://www.celgene.com
Chrmn: S.J. Barer
Pres, CEO & Secy: R.J. Hugin
SVP & CFO: J.A. Fouse
Chief Acctg Officer & Cntlr: A. Van Hoek
Treas: C.B. Elflein
Investor Contact: B.P. Gill (908-673-9530)
Board Members: S. J. Barer, M. D. Casey, C. S. Cox, R. L. Drake, R. J. Hugin, G. Kaplan, J. J. Loughlin, E. Mario, W. L. Robb
Founded: 1986
Domicile: Delaware
Employees: 2,813

The McGraw·Hill Companies

CenterPoint Energy Inc.

STANDARD &POOR'S

S&P Recommendation HOLD ★★★☆☆

Price	12-Mo. Target Price	Investment Style
$16.42 (as of Oct 22, 2010)	**$17.00**	Large-Cap Value

GICS Sector Utilities
Sub-Industry Multi-Utilities

Summary This Houston-based energy company (formerly Reliant Energy) is one of the largest electric and natural gas delivery companies in the U.S.

Key Stock Statistics (Source S&P, Vickers, company reports)

52-Wk Range	$16.56– 5.67	S&P Oper. EPS 2010E	1.07	Market Capitalization(B)	$6.925	Beta	0.73
Trailing 12-Month EPS	$1.05	S&P Oper. EPS 2011E	1.20	Yield (%)	4.75	S&P 3-Yr. Proj. EPS CAGR(%)	-3
Trailing 12-Month P/E	15.6	P/E on S&P Oper. EPS 2010E	15.3	Dividend Rate/Share	$0.78	S&P Credit Rating	BBB
$10K Invested 5 Yrs Ago	$16,528	Common Shares Outstg. (M)	421.8	Institutional Ownership (%)	70		

Price Performance

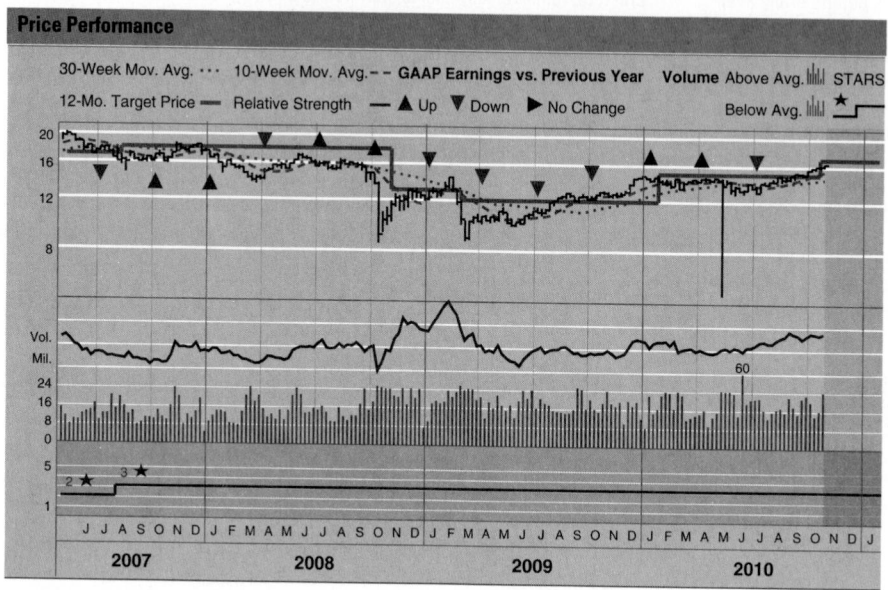

30-Week Mov. Avg. ···· 10-Week Mov. Avg. ‑ ‑ GAAP Earnings vs. Previous Year   Volume Above Avg. STARS
12-Mo. Target Price — Relative Strength — ▲ Up ▼ Down ▶ No Change   Below Avg. ★

Options: ASE, CBOE, P, Ph

Analysis prepared by **Justin McCann** on October 11, 2010, when the stock traded at **$ 16.17**.

Highlights

▸ We expect EPS in 2010 to increase about 5% from 2009's $1.01, which fell 22% from 2008's $1.30. Earnings in the first half of 2010 benefited from the more favorable weather and lower un-collected accounts at CNP's electric and gas utility operations, and from higher operating income at the interstate pipelines and field services operations. However, EPS was diluted by approximately 14% more shares. EPS in the first quarter was reduced by $0.05 due to federal legislation eliminating the tax deductibility of certain retiree health care costs.

▸ For full-year 2010, we expect EPS to benefit from higher operating margins in all of CNP's segments and a decline in its interest expense. This should, however, be partially offset by a higher effective tax rate and more shares outstanding. For 2011, we look for EPS to increase about 8% from anticipated results in 2010, reflecting an expected gradual recovery in both the economy and the energy markets.

▸ On June 30, 2010, CNP's Houston Electric subsidiary filed with the Texas Public Utility Commission a request for a $76 million increase in its distribution rates and an $18 million increase in its wholesale transmission rates.

Investment Rationale/Risk

▸ The stock is up about 11% year to date. This follows a 15% increase in 2009, and has reflected, in our view, CNP's improved financial strength, a well above peers yield from the dividend and the rebound in the utilities sector and the broader market. The stock had been badly hurt in early 2009 after CNP had announced a sharp reduction in its 2009 earnings outlook due to an increase in its projected pension expense. It was then further hurt by the impact of the economic downturn and the crisis in the credit markets.

▸ Risks to our recommendation and target price include a potential weakening of the company's financial strength, including a decreased ability to access capital markets on reasonable terms, and/or a large decline in the average P/E of the company's electric and gas utility peers.

▸ The dividend yield, recently at 4.8%, was above the recent electric and gas utility peer average of about 4.6%. Given the estimated 73% payout ratio on our EPS estimate for 2010, we believe the dividend is secure. Our 12-month target price is $17, reflecting a premium-to-peers P/E of approximately 14.2X our 2011 estimate.

Qualitative Risk Assessment

LOW	MEDIUM	HIGH

Our risk assessment reflects the strong and steady cash flow we expect from the Houston electric operations, which have a growing service territory; a low commodity risk profile; a generally supportive regulatory environment; and the gas purchase adjustment clauses that reduce the commodity risks related to the company's more diversified gas distribution operations.

Quantitative Evaluations

S&P Quality Ranking B

D	C	B-	B	B+	A-	A	A+

Relative Strength Rank STRONG

73

LOWEST = 1   HIGHEST = 99

Revenue/Earnings Data

Revenue (Million $)

	1Q	2Q	3Q	4Q	Year
2010	3,023	1,756	--	--	--
2009	2,766	1,640	1,576	2,299	8,281
2008	3,363	2,670	2,515	2,774	11,322
2007	3,106	2,033	1,882	2,602	9,623
2006	3,077	1,843	1,935	2,464	9,319
2005	2,762	1,932	2,073	3,212	9,722

Earnings Per Share ($)

	1Q	2Q	3Q	4Q	Year
2010	0.29	0.20	E0.29	E0.29	E1.07
2009	0.19	0.24	0.31	0.27	1.01
2008	0.36	0.30	0.39	0.25	1.30
2007	0.38	0.20	0.27	0.32	1.17
2006	0.28	0.61	0.26	0.20	1.33
2005	0.20	0.09	0.15	0.25	0.67

Fiscal year ended Dec. 31. Next earnings report expected: Late October. EPS Estimates based on S&P Operating Earnings; historical GAAP earnings are as reported.

Dividend Data (Dates: mm/dd Payment Date: mm/dd/yy)

Amount ($)	Date Decl.	Ex-Div. Date	Stk. of Record	Payment Date
0.195	01/21	02/11	02/16	03/10/10
0.195	04/22	05/12	05/14	06/10/10
0.195	07/22	08/12	08/16	09/10/10
0.195	10/21	11/12	11/16	12/10/10

Dividends have been paid since 1922. Source: Company reports.

Please read the Required Disclosures and Analyst Certification on the last page of this report.

The **McGraw·Hill** Companies

CenterPoint Energy Inc.

Business Summary October 11, 2010

CORPORATE OVERVIEW. CenterPoint Energy (formerly Reliant Energy) is a Houston-based energy delivery company with operations that include electric transmission and distribution (48.5% of operating income in 2009), interstate pipelines (22.8%), natural gas distribution (18.1%), field services (8.4%), competitive natural gas sales and services (1.9%), and other (0.3%).

MARKET PROFILE. The CenterPoint Energy Houston Electric (CEHE) utility serves more than 2 million customers in a 5,000 square mile territory that includes the cities of Houston and Galveston, TX, and (with the exception of Texas City), nearly all of the Houston/Galveston metropolitan area. Following the deregulation of the industry in Texas, wholesale and retail suppliers pay the company to deliver the electricity over its transmission lines. The natural gas subsidiary, CenterPoint Energy Resources Corp. (CERC), serves about 3.2 million residential, commercial and industrial customers in Arkansas, Louisiana, Minnesota, Mississippi, Oklahoma and Texas. In 2009, approximately 43% of total demand was accounted for by residential customers, and about 57% was from commercial and industrial customers.

CERC's interstate pipeline business owns and operates approximately 8,000 miles of gas transmission lines primarily located in Arkansas, Illinois, Louisiana, Missouri, Oklahoma and Texas. It also owns and operates six natural gas storage fields with a combined daily volume of about 1.2 billion cubic feet per day. CERC's field services business owns and operates around 3,700 miles of gathering pipelines and processing plants, and around 140 natural gas gathering systems in Arkansas, Oklahoma, Louisiana and Texas. In January 2007, CNP agreed to discontinue the development of its proposed pipeline with Spectra Energy (the spun-off gas transmission unit of Duke Energy) due to market conditions. The proposed pipeline (announced in June 2006) would have stretched from Texas to Pennsylvania.

Company Financials Fiscal Year Ended Dec. 31

Per Share Data ($)	2009	2008	2007	2006	2005	2004	2003	2002	2001	2000
Tangible Book Value	2.41	0.99	NM	NM	NM	NM	NM	NM	13.05	8.11
Earnings	1.01	1.30	1.17	1.33	0.67	0.61	1.37	1.29	3.14	2.68
S&P Core Earnings	1.05	1.31	1.31	1.18	0.75	0.65	1.28	2.17	3.00	NA
Dividends	0.76	0.73	0.68	0.60	0.40	0.40	0.40	1.07	1.50	1.50
Payout Ratio	75%	56%	58%	45%	60%	66%	29%	83%	48%	56%
Prices:High	14.87	17.35	20.20	16.87	15.14	12.32	10.49	27.10	50.45	49.00
Prices:Low	8.66	8.48	14.70	11.62	10.55	9.66	4.35	4.24	23.27	19.75
P/E Ratio:High	15	13	17	13	23	20	8	21	16	18
P/E Ratio:Low	9	7	13	9	16	16	3	3	7	7

Income Statement Analysis (Million $)	2009	2008	2007	2006	2005	2004	2003	2002	2001	2000
Revenue	8,281	11,322	9,623	9,319	9,722	8,510	9,760	7,923	46,226	29,339
Depreciation	743	708	631	599	541	490	625	616	911	906
Maintenance	NA	NA	NA	NA	NA	NA	NA	NA	NA	NA
Fixed Charges Coverage	1.80	2.14	1.95	1.80	1.35	1.15	1.37	1.80	3.33	2.60
Construction Credits	NA	NA	NA	NA	NA	NA	NA	NA	NA	NA
Effective Tax Rate	32.1%	38.3%	32.8%	12.6%	40.5%	NM	35.6%	35.0%	33.3%	32.9%
Net Income	372	447	399	432	225	206	420	386	919	771
S&P Core Earnings	386	451	444	384	254	224	390	642	868	NA

Balance Sheet & Other Financial Data (Million $)	2009	2008	2007	2006	2005	2004	2003	2002	2001	2000
Gross Property	14,770	14,006	13,250	12,567	11,558	10,963	11,812	11,409	24,214	15,260
Capital Expenditures	1,160	1,020	1,114	1,007	693	530	648	854	2,053	1,842
Net Property	10,788	10,296	9,740	9,204	8,492	8,186	11,812	11,409	15,857	15,260
Capitalization:Long Term Debt	9,119	10,181	8,364	7,802	8,568	7,193	10,783	9,194	6,448	5,701
Capitalization:% Long Term Debt	77.6	83.3	82.2	83.4	86.9	86.7	86.0	71.0	48.4	51.0
Capitalization:Preferred	Nil	Nil	Nil	Nil	Nil	Nil	Nil	Nil	Nil	10.0
Capitalization:% Preferred	Nil	Nil	Nil	Nil	Nil	Nil	Nil	Nil	Nil	0.09
Capitalization:Common	2,639	2,037	1,810	1,556	1,296	1,106	1,761	3,756	6,881	5,472
Capitalization:% Common	22.4	16.7	17.8	16.6	13.1	13.3	14.0	29.0	51.6	48.9
Total Capital	12,661	14,851	12,440	12,036	12,769	10,767	12,934	13,180	16,970	13,998
% Operating Ratio	88.6	91.2	89.7	89.5	91.9	91.5	85.8	85.8	96.6	94.9
% Earned on Net Property	10.7	12.7	12.5	11.8	11.3	10.6	21.8	17.2	12.8	13.2
% Return on Revenue	4.5	4.0	4.1	2.8	1.4	2.4	4.3	4.9	2.0	2.6
% Return on Invested Capital	7.8	7.3	8.5	8.3	7.9	7.6	11.1	14.7	11.2	10.3
% Return on Common Equity	15.9	23.2	23.7	30.3	18.7	14.4	26.4	10.3	14.8	14.3

Data as orig reptd.; bef. results of disc opers/spec. items. Per share data adj. for stk. divs.; EPS diluted. E-Estimated. NA-Not Available. NM-Not Meaningful. NR-Not Ranked. UR-Under Review.

Office: 1111 Louisiana Street, Houston, TX 77002-5230.
Telephone: 713-207-1111.
Email: info@reliantenergy.nl
Website: http://www.centerpointenergy.com

Chrmn: M. Carroll
Pres & CEO: D.M. McClanahan
EVP & CFO: G.L. Whitlock
EVP, Secy & General Counsel: S.E. Rozzell

SVP & Chief Acctg Officer: W.L. Fitzgerald
Investor Contact: M. Paulsen (713-207-6500)
Board Members: D. R. Campbell, M. Carroll, D. Cody, O. H. Crosswell, M. P. Johnson, J. M. Longoria, T. F. Madison, D. M. McClanahan, R. T. O'Connell, S. O. Rheney, R. A. Walker, P. S. Wareing, S. M. Wolff

Founded: 1882
Domicile: Texas
Employees: 8,810

CenturyLink Inc

STANDARD &POOR'S

S&P Recommendation HOLD ★★★★☆	Price $40.59 (as of Oct 22, 2010)	12-Mo. Target Price $36.00	Investment Style Large-Cap Blend

GICS Sector Telecommunication Services
Sub-Industry Integrated Telecommunication Services

Summary CTL acquired larger telecom peer Embarq in a stock deal in July 2009. Combined, the company provides voice service to 7 million customers and Internet service to 2 million customers in both rural towns and larger cities, like Las Vegas.

Key Stock Statistics (Source S&P, Vickers, company reports)

52-Wk Range	$40.78– 10.16	S&P Oper. EPS 2010E	3.41	Market Capitalization(B)	$12.236	Beta	0.74
Trailing 12-Month EPS	$3.33	S&P Oper. EPS 2011E	3.31	Yield (%)	7.14	S&P 3-Yr. Proj. EPS CAGR(%)	5
Trailing 12-Month P/E	12.2	P/E on S&P Oper. EPS 2010E	11.9	Dividend Rate/Share	$2.90	S&P Credit Rating	BBB-
$10K Invested 5 Yrs Ago	$15,958	Common Shares Outstg. (M)	301.4	Institutional Ownership (%)	76		

Price Performance

- 30-Week Mov. Avg. · · ·
- 10-Week Mov. Avg. – –
- 12-Mo. Target Price —
- Relative Strength —
- GAAP Earnings vs. Previous Year
- ▲ Up ▼ Down ► No Change
- Volume Above Avg. STARS
- Below Avg.

Analysis prepared by **Todd Rosenbluth** on August 09, 2010, when the stock traded at **$ 36.41**.

Highlights

➤ We forecast revenues of $7 billion in 2010 and $6.75 billion in 2011, down from $7.5 billion in 2009 on a pro forma basis including Embarq. Much of CTL's second-half 2009 reported revenues stemmed from the acquisition. We see pressure on voice services from ongoing access line losses, exacerbated by lower revenues from universal service funding, and the migration of wireless traffic from a customer, outweighing gains we expect from data services such as DSL.

➤ We look for EBITDA margins of 51% in 2010 and 52% in 2011, as we see cost synergies from billing and network integration. However, we expect to see increased selling and marketing costs in the second half of 2010. We look for depreciation charges to decline on a pro forma basis in 2010.

➤ Historically, CTL has repurchased shares on the open market, but with the company's current focus on merger integration and a new yet-to-be-approved deal, we do not expect additional repurchases in 2010. We estimate EPS of $3.41 in 2010 and $3.31 in 2011.

Investment Rationale/Risk

➤ While we believe the company is making progress integrating Embarq, we expect 2010 earnings pressure amid a decline in revenues even as cost synergies and room for greater broadband penetration exist. We also believe the planned stock-based acquisition of Qwest Communications (Q 6, Hold), subject to necessary approvals expected in mid-2011, adds new opportunities for expense synergies and dividend payout support, but also risks. We think Q faces tough competition in its consumer and enterprise segments and has greater debt leverage.

➤ Risks to our recommendation and target price include regulatory changes; an inability to smoothly integrate acquired assets; and an increase in customer migration or line losses.

➤ We think the shares, supported by a recent dividend yield of around 8%, are fairly valued. Our 12-month target price of $36 is based on an 11X P/E applied to our 2011 EPS estimate, a slight discount to multiples we expect for peers. At our target price, CTL would also trade at a discount on an enterprise value/EBITDA basis.

Qualitative Risk Assessment

LOW	MEDIUM	HIGH

Our risk assessment reflects what we see as CTL's relatively strong balance sheet and cash flow generation offset by the competitive nature of its markets and integration of a large acquisition.

Quantitative Evaluations

S&P Quality Ranking B+

D	C	B-	B	B+	A-	A	A+

Relative Strength Rank STRONG

71

LOWEST = 1   HIGHEST = 99

Revenue/Earnings Data

Revenue (Million $)

	1Q	2Q	3Q	4Q	Year
2010	1,800	1,772	--	--	--
2009	636.4	634.5	1,874	1,829	4,974
2008	648.6	658.1	650.1	643.0	2,600
2007	600.9	690.0	708.8	656.6	2,656
2006	611.3	608.9	619.8	607.7	2,448
2005	595.3	606.4	657.1	620.5	2,479

Earnings Per Share ($)

	1Q	2Q	3Q	4Q	Year
2010	0.84	0.88	E0.81	E0.79	E3.41
2009	0.67	0.69	0.50	0.76	2.55
2008	0.83	0.88	0.84	1.01	3.56
2007	0.68	1.00	1.01	1.05	3.72
2006	0.55	1.26	0.64	0.62	3.07
2005	0.59	0.64	0.64	0.59	2.49

Fiscal year ended Dec. 31. Next earnings report expected: Early November. EPS Estimates based on S&P Operating Earnings; historical GAAP earnings are as reported.

Dividend Data (Dates: mm/dd Payment Date: mm/dd/yy)

Amount ($)	Date Decl.	Ex-Div. Date	Stk. of Record	Payment Date
0.700	11/18	11/30	12/02	12/15/09
0.725	02/25	03/05	03/09	03/22/10
0.725	05/21	06/04	06/08	06/21/10
0.725	08/24	09/02	09/07	09/20/10

Dividends have been paid since 1974. Source: Company reports.

Please read the Required Disclosures and Analyst Certification on the last page of this report.

The McGraw·Hill Companies

CenturyLink Inc

Business Summary August 09, 2010

CORPORATE OVERVIEW. As of June 2010, CenturyLink Inc (formerly Century-Tel) operated 6.8 million telephone access lines, following the acquisition of Embarq in July 2009. The company also provided DSL broadband to 2.3 million customers (36% penetration of total addressable lines) and has partnered to offer wholesale satellite services to more than 594,000 customers through CTL's product bundles. In the first half of 2010, 44% of revenues were from voice services, 16% from network access services and the remainder from data and fiber transport services.

In early July 2009, CTL completed its planned acquisition of its larger, fellow telco Embarq Corp (EQ). The deal involved a swap of 1.37 CTL shares per EQ share and the assumption of $6 billion in debt. On a pro forma basis, the new company had 7.3 million access lines and 2.15 million DSL customers at the end of June 2009. Revenues would have been $1.96 billion during the second quarter of 2009 and EBITDA of $968 as a combined company, before any synergies. CTL believes it achieved $75 million of expense synergies from the merger during the second quarter of 2010 and expects to finish 2010 with a $330 million annualized synergy run rate.

In April 2010, CTL announced plans to acquire Qwest Communications (Q 6, Hold)), a wireline carrier currently with 9.4 million access lines, 3 million DSL customers and a stable enterprise segment. The deal, subject to necessary

approvals expected in mid-2011, is equal to $22 billion including the assumption of debt. We view the price to be fair and see opportunities for expense synergies (CTL expects $625 million on an annual basis) that can help CTL support its dividend. As of early August 2010, six of the 21 required state approvals had been received.

COMPETITIVE LANDSCAPE. We believe CTL faces challenges from technology substitution to cable telephony and to wireless. The penetration of the necessary broadband connection is smaller in the Tier II and Tier III markets in which CTL previously operated; as of late 2009, more than 65% of its access line customers had the option of cable broadband from companies such as Comcast. However, Embarq's operations included larger cities in Florida and Nevada that faced greater competition and were hurt by weakness in the housing market. At the end of the second quarter of 2010, CTL highlighted that its access lines declined 8% from a year earlier on a pro forma basis. This line loss rate remains higher than that of some peers, although it is lower than the 9% loss of a year earlier and the 11.5% access line loss Q had in the 12 months ended June 2010.

Company Financials Fiscal Year Ended Dec. 31

Per Share Data ($)	2009	2008	2007	2006	2005	2004	2003	2002	2001	2000
Tangible Book Value	NM	NM	NM	NM	1.41	NM	0.37	NM	NM	NM
Cash Flow	7.46	8.64	8.44	7.31	6.37	5.90	5.63	4.21	5.73	4.36
Earnings	2.55	3.56	3.72	3.07	2.49	2.41	2.38	1.33	2.41	1.63
S&P Core Earnings	2.77	3.33	3.37	2.52	2.30	2.36	2.35	1.08	1.21	NA
Dividends	2.80	1.61	0.26	0.25	0.24	0.23	0.22	0.21	0.20	0.19
Payout Ratio	110%	45%	7%	8%	10%	10%	9%	16%	8%	12%
Prices:High	37.16	42.00	49.94	44.11	36.50	35.54	36.76	35.50	39.88	47.31
Prices:Low	23.41	20.45	39.91	32.54	29.55	26.20	25.25	21.13	25.45	24.44
P/E Ratio:High	15	12	13	14	15	15	15	27	17	29
P/E Ratio:Low	9	6	11	11	12	11	11	16	11	15

Income Statement Analysis (Million $)	2009	2008	2007	2006	2005	2004	2003	2002	2001	2000
Revenue	4,974	2,600	2,656	2,448	2,479	2,407	2,381	1,972	2,117	1,846
Depreciation	975	524	536	524	532	501	471	412	473	388
Maintenance	NA	NA	NA	NA	NA	NA	NA	NA	NA	NA
Construction Credits	NA	NA	NA	NA	NA	NA	NA	NA	NA	NA
Effective Tax Rate	37.1%	34.7%	32.4%	37.4%	37.8%	38.4%	35.2%	35.3%	37.2%	39.0%
Net Income	511	3,294	418	370	334	337	345	190	343	231
S&P Core Earnings	551	342	377	302	307	330	339	153	171	NA

Balance Sheet & Other Financial Data (Million $)	2009	2008	2007	2006	2005	2004	2003	2002	2001	2000
Gross Property	15,557	8,869	8,666	7,894	7,801	7,431	3,455	6,668	5,839	5,915
Net Property	9,097	2,896	3,108	3,109	3,304	3,341	3,455	3,532	3,000	2,959
Capital Expenditures	755	287	326	314	415	385	378	386	507	450
Total Capital	17,221	7,311	6,962	5,604	5,993	6,172	6,588	6,666	4,425	5,082
Fixed Charges Coverage	3.2	3.8	3.9	4.4	3.6	3.6	3.4	2.3	3.4	3.2
Capitalization:Long Term Debt	7,254	3,294	2,734	2,413	2,376	2,762	3,109	3,578	2,088	3,050
Capitalization:Preferred	0.24	0.24	6.97	7.45	7.85	7.98	7.98	7.98	7.98	7.98
Capitalization:Common	9,461	3,163	3,402	3,184	3,609	3,402	3,471	3,080	2,329	2,024
% Return on Revenue	10.3	14.1	15.8	15.1	13.5	14.0	14.5	9.6	16.2	12.5
% Return on Invested Capital	7.5	7.5	9.5	9.8	8.8	8.6	8.6	7.4	12.2	9.4
% Return on Common Equity	8.1	11.1	12.7	10.9	9.5	9.8	10.5	7.0	15.7	12.0
% Earned on Net Property	20.6	24.2	25.5	20.8	38.2	36.9	35.0	31.5	34.6	35.0
% Long Term Debt of Capitalization	43.4	51.0	44.5	43.1	39.6	44.8	47.2	53.7	47.2	60.0
Capital % Preferred	Nil	Nil	0.1	0.1	0.1	0.1	0.1	0.1	0.2	0.2
Capitalization:% Common	56.6	49.0	55.4	56.8	60.2	55.1	52.7	46.2	52.6	39.8

Data as orig reptd.; bef. results of disc opers/spec. items. Per share data adj. for stk. divs.; EPS diluted. E-Estimated. NA-Not Available. NM-Not Meaningful. NR-Not Ranked. UR-Under Review.

Office: 100 CenturyLink Drive, Monroe, LA 71203.
Telephone: 318-388-9000.
Website: http://www.centurylink.com
Chrmn: W.A. Owens

Pres & CEO: G.F. Post, III
Vice Chrmn: H.P. Perry
Vice Chrmn: T.A. Gerke
COO & EVP: K.A. Puckett

Investor Contact: T. Davis (800-833-1188)
Board Members: V. Boulet, P. C. Brown, R. A. Gephardt, T. A. Gerke, W. B. Hanks, G. J. McCray, III, C. G. Melville, Jr., F. R. Nichols, W. A. Owens, H. P. Perry, G. F. Post, III, L. A. Siegel, J. R. Zimmel

Founded: 1968
Domicile: Louisiana
Employees: 20,200

Cephalon Inc

S&P Recommendation	HOLD ★★★☆☆	Price $64.10 (as of Oct 22, 2010)	12-Mo. Target Price $72.00	Investment Style Large-Cap Growth

GICS Sector Health Care
Sub-Industry Biotechnology

Summary This biopharmaceutical company markets and develops human therapeutics for the treatment of neurological disorders, pain indications and, most recently, oncology.

Key Stock Statistics (Source S&P, Vickers, company reports)

52-Wk Range	$72.87– 53.44	S&P Oper. EPS 2010**E**	7.11	Market Capitalization(B)	$4.820	Beta	0.46
Trailing 12-Month EPS	$4.99	S&P Oper. EPS 2011**E**	7.20	Yield (%)	Nil	S&P 3-Yr. Proj. EPS CAGR(%)	10
Trailing 12-Month P/E	12.9	P/E on S&P Oper. EPS 2010**E**	9.0	Dividend Rate/Share	Nil	S&P Credit Rating	NA
$10K Invested 5 Yrs Ago	$14,103	Common Shares Outstg. (M)	75.2	Institutional Ownership (%)	NM		

Price Performance

30-Week Mov. Avg. · · · · 10-Week Mov. Avg. – – GAAP Earnings vs. Previous Year Volume Above Avg. STARS
12-Mo. Target Price — Relative Strength ▲ Up ▼ Down ▶ No Change Below Avg.

Options: ASE, CBOE, P, Ph

Analysis prepared by **Steven Silver** on August 02, 2010, when the stock traded at **$ 58.24**.

Highlights

► We estimate 2010 sales of $2.71 billion, which would represent 24% growth over 2009, driven by contributions from products acquired from Mepha AG in April 2010. We forecast 9% sales growth in 2011, to about $2.97 billion. We expect the early 2012 patent expiration of Provigil to slow CEPH's revenue growth outlook, but we expect the impact to be mitigated by new approved uses for Nuvigil, wider adoption of Treanda in non-Hodgkin's lymphoma, and exposure to new markets through the Mepha deal.

► We expect gross margins to narrow from 87% in 2009 to around 84% in 2010 and 83% in 2011, as patients migrate from Provigil to the cheaper Nuvigil. We project operating margins of around 33% in 2010 and 31% in 2011, with operating margins further challenged by a ramp in investment in CEPH's biologics-focused pipeline and global infrastructure expansion. However, we see such efforts being supported by solid operational cash flows and a cash balance of $927 million as of June 30, 2010.

► Our 2010 and 2011 adjusted EPS estimates of $7.11 and $7.20 per share, respectively, exclude amortized intangible assets, restructuring and acquisition-related charges.

Investment Rationale/Risk

► Our recent downgrade to hold, from buy, reflects a more cautious view of CEPH's reliance on expanding Nuvigil's approved uses. While we are encouraged by CEPH's aggressive acquisition of biologic pipeline assets, we see few near-term catalysts and a less clear path to drive meaningful revenue growth to offset looming wakefulness franchise sales erosion. We still expect the FDA to approve Nuvigil for jet lag disorder at its new December 2010 action date given initial priority review status, but we are wary of its questioning of the drug's efficacy. We are encouraged by prospects for the Mepha AG acquisition to broaden CEPH's global sales reach and business mix.

► Risks to our recommendation and target price include failure to expand Nuvigil's product label, clinical failure of late-stage pipeline candidates, failure to expand the market for Fentora to offset erosion from generic Actiq, and further regulatory issues over product marketing.

► Our 12-month target price of $72 applies a 10.1X multiple to our 2010 adjusted EPS estimate, in line with our long-term growth outlook, but a discount to peers given CEPH's high exposure to generic drugs.

Qualitative Risk Assessment

LOW	MEDIUM	HIGH

Cephalon faces generic pressures in its pain franchise and in its wakefulness franchise in the coming years, and has been subject to regulatory oversight of its marketing practices and drug safety. Also, the company is developing new drugs for competitive markets, which we view as a highly risky endeavor.

Quantitative Evaluations

S&P Quality Ranking B-

D	C	B-	B	B+	A-	A	A+

Relative Strength Rank MODERATE
57
LOWEST = 1 HIGHEST = 99

Revenue/Earnings Data

Revenue (Million $)

	1Q	2Q	3Q	4Q	Year
2010	596.6	726.9	--	--	--
2009	514.4	539.0	535.2	562.9	2,192
2008	433.9	485.0	489.7	534.9	1,975
2007	437.0	447.2	438.4	450.0	1,773
2006	356.9	440.1	482.3	484.7	1,764
2005	280.0	286.0	309.5	336.4	1,212

Earnings Per Share ($)

2010	1.35	1.11	E1.70	E1.61	E7.11
2009	0.75	1.11	1.31	1.23	4.41
2008	0.52	0.80	1.42	0.15	2.92
2007	0.99	-0.06	-4.58	0.56	-2.88
2006	0.05	0.76	1.43	-0.08	2.08
2005	0.44	-4.29	0.50	0.30	-3.01

Fiscal year ended Dec. 31. Next earnings report expected: Late October. EPS Estimates based on S&P Operating Earnings; historical GAAP earnings are as reported.

Dividend Data

No cash dividends have been paid.

Cephalon Inc

STANDARD &POOR'S

Business Summary August 02, 2010

CORPORATE OVERVIEW. Cephalon develops, manufactures and markets therapeutics for the treatment of sleep disorders, neurodegenerative conditions and cancer.

CEPH's Provigil is approved for excessive daytime sleepiness (EDS) due to narcolepsy (a chronic, lifelong sleep disorder), obstructive sleep apnea/hypopnea syndrome and shift work sleep disorder. Provigil has patent protection until 2012. CEPH has developed Nuvigil, a single-isomer version of Provigil, with a longer duration of action and an improved side effect profile, which it launched in June 2009, and is transitioning Provigil users to Nuvigil. In October 2009, Teva Pharmaceuticals filed to produce a generic version of Nuvigil, which CEPH has challenged. Provigil/Nuvigil sales rose 11%, to $1.1 billion, in 2009, representing 51% CEPH's 2009 product sales.

CEPH's pain franchise sales fell by 3% in 2009, as Actiq sales for breakthrough cancer pain declined 15% to $230 million, due to generic competition. CEPH's Fentora, for the same indication, saw sales decline 9% in 2009, to $141 million. Following several deaths that occurred due to inappropriate prescribing and dosing, the FDA has delayed approving Fentora's use in non-cancer pain indications due to concerns over patient mis-use, pending an approved risk mini-

mization program. In June 2008, Watson Labs announced plans to seek a generic version of Fentora. CEPH filed to defend its patents.

In 2008, CEPH received FDA approval for Treanda for treatment of prevalent blood cancers chronic lymphocytic leukemia (CLL) and for relapsed indolent non-Hodgkin's lymphoma (NHL). To date, the majority of Treanda sales have come from CLL, but CEPH expects NHL sales to expand following the late 2009 publication of study data that showed Treanda outperformed the current standard of care. Treanda's patents expire in 2014. Treanda sales were $222 million in 2009, up from $75 million in 2008. In mid-2007, CEPH acquired North American rights to once-daily, extended-release muscle relaxant Amrix from ER Pharmaceuticals. In April 2008, CEPH received a patent extension extending market exclusivity to 2025, from the previously expected 2010 date. In October 2008, Mylan Pharmaceuticals filed to launch a generic version of Amrix. CEPH filed to defend its patents. Amrix sales were $114 million in 2009, up 55% over 2008.

Company Financials Fiscal Year Ended Dec. 31

Per Share Data ($)	2009	2008	2007	2006	2005	2004	2003	2002	2001	2000
Tangible Book Value	9.21	6.55	0.11	5.93	NM	NM	1.98	NM	NM	NM
Cash Flow	6.58	4.96	-1.02	3.75	-1.56	-0.37	2.01	3.12	-1.03	-2.42
Earnings	4.41	2.92	-2.88	2.08	-3.01	-1.31	1.44	2.84	-1.33	-2.51
S&P Core Earnings	4.44	3.13	3.44	2.14	-3.30	-1.43	0.90	2.08	-1.86	NA
Dividends	Nil	Nil	Nil	Nil	Nil	Nil	Nil	Nil	Nil	Nil
Payout Ratio	Nil	Nil	Nil	Nil	Nil	Nil	Nil	Nil	Nil	Nil
Prices:High	81.35	80.39	84.83	82.92	66.92	60.98	54.95	78.88	78.40	83.63
Prices:Low	52.55	56.20	64.65	51.58	37.35	41.58	36.92	35.82	36.38	29.88
P/E Ratio:High	18	28	NM	40	NM	NM	38	28	NM	NM
P/E Ratio:Low	12	19	NM	25	NM	NM	26	13	NM	NM

Income Statement Analysis (Million $)										
Revenue	2,192	1,975	1,773	1,764	1,212	1,015	715	507	267	112
Operating Income	763	533	450	428	249	282	201	132	37.8	-57.8
Depreciation	168	155	124	117	84.3	52.8	45.1	35.5	14.4	3.95
Interest Expense	90.3	28.5	19.8	67.0	25.2	50.4	28.9	38.2	73.1	Nil
Pretax Income	289	181	-68.4	238	-245	-28.2	130	62.4	-58.5	-93.7
Effective Tax Rate	27.2%	NM	NM	39.2%	NM	NM	35.6%	NM	NM	NM
Net Income	343	223	-192	145	-175	-73.8	83.9	175	-58.5	-93.7
S&P Core Earnings	345	239	230	149	-191	-80.6	51.1	140	-89.9	NA

Balance Sheet & Other Financial Data (Million $)										
Cash	1,648	524	826	497	205	574	1,116	486	549	36.6
Current Assets	2,566	1,330	1,422	1,198	1,049	1,180	1,370	786	734	141
Total Assets	4,658	3,169	3,506	3,045	2,819	2,440	2,382	1,689	1,389	308
Current Liabilities	1,338	1,422	2,006	1,377	1,279	216	138	120	107	80.8
Long Term Debt	362	3.69	3.79	225	763	1,284	1,409	861	867	55.1
Common Equity	2,262	1,503	1,302	1,309	612	830	770	643	399	165
Total Capital	3,658	1,585	1,362	1,607	1,486	2,209	2,225	1,556	1,265	220
Capital Expenditures	60.9	75.9	96.9	160	118	50.2	40.5	27.3	12.5	7.46
Cash Flow	511	378	-67.9	261	-90.6	-21.0	129	211	-49.7	-98.9
Current Ratio	1.9	0.9	0.7	0.9	0.8	5.5	9.9	6.6	6.9	1.7
% Long Term Debt of Capitalization	9.9	0.2	0.3	14.0	51.4	58.2	63.3	55.3	68.5	25.0
% Net Income of Revenue	15.6	11.3	NM	8.2	NM	NM	11.7	34.5	NM	NM
% Return on Assets	8.8	6.7	NM	4.9	NM	NM	4.1	11.2	NM	NM
% Return on Equity	18.2	15.9	NM	15.1	NM	NM	11.9	33.6	NM	NM

Data as orig reptd.; bef. results of disc opers/spec. items. Per share data adj. for stk. divs.; EPS diluted. E-Estimated. NA-Not Available. NM-Not Meaningful. NR-Not Ranked. UR-Under Review.

Office: 41 Moores Rd, Frazer, PA 19355-1113.
Telephone: 610-344-0200.
Email: investorrelations@cephalon.com
Website: http://www.cephalon.com

Chrmn, Pres & CEO: F. Baldino, Jr.
COO: K. Buchi
EVP, CFO & Chief Acctg Officer: W. Groenhuysen
EVP & Chief Admin Officer: C.A. Savini

EVP & CSO: J. Vaught
Investor Contact: C. Merritt (610-738-6376)
Board Members: F. Baldino, Jr., W. P. Egan, M. D. Greenacre, V. M. Kailian, K. E. Moley, C. A. Sanders, G. Wilensky, D. L. Winger

Founded: 1987
Domicile: Delaware
Employees: 3,026

Cerner Corp

S&P Recommendation	HOLD ★★★★★	Price $88.11 (as of Oct 22, 2010)	12-Mo. Target Price $87.00	Investment Style Large-Cap Growth

GICS Sector Health Care
Sub-Industry Health Care Technology

Summary This company is a leading supplier of health care information technology (HCIT) solutions, health care devices and related services.

Key Stock Statistics (Source S&P, Vickers, company reports)

52-Wk Range	$92.95–72.05	S&P Oper. EPS 2010E	2.75	Market Capitalization(B)	$7.267	Beta	0.99
Trailing 12-Month EPS	$2.53	S&P Oper. EPS 2011E	3.42	Yield (%)	Nil	S&P 3-Yr. Proj. EPS CAGR(%)	18
Trailing 12-Month P/E	34.8	P/E on S&P Oper. EPS 2010E	32.0	Dividend Rate/Share	Nil	S&P Credit Rating	NA
$10K Invested 5 Yrs Ago	$20,550	Common Shares Outstg. (M)	82.5	Institutional Ownership (%)	86		

Price Performance

30-Week Mov. Avg. · · · 10-Week Mov. Avg. – – GAAP Earnings vs. Previous Year Volume Above Avg. STARS
12-Mo. Target Price — Relative Strength — ▲ Up ▼ Down ▶ No Change Below Avg. ★

Options: ASE, CBOE, P, Ph

Analysis prepared by **Jeffrey Loo, CFA** on August 24, 2010, when the stock traded at **$ 73.34**.

Highlights

► We expect revenues to increase 11% in 2010 to $1.85 billion and 12% in 2011 to $2.08 billion, as Cerner sees the benefit of accelerating industry growth due to the American Recovery and Reinvestment Act of 2009 (ARRA), which incentivizes hospitals and clinicians to adopt health care information technology. We believe the recent release of the final "meaningful use" rules provides flexibility and will lead to broader adoption of health care IT, positively impacting the industry and CERN. We look for ARRA to drive solid bookings throughout 2010 aided by new clients. Approximately 25% of first-half sales in 2010 were from new clients. We expect this growth to be tempered somewhat by continued cautious levels of capital expenditures by Cerner's hospital customer base.

► We project gross margins to widen only 40 basis points (bps) in 2010 due to lower-margin system sales but aided by support and maintenance sales margins. But we see operating margins improving 200 bps on lower R&D cost and leverage, in spite of higher SG&A costs.

► Inclusive of stock compensation costs of $0.18 in 2010 and 2011, our EPS forecasts are $2.75 for 2010 and $3.42 for 2011.

Investment Rationale/Risk

► We believe the shares are fairly valued, recently trading at 27.0X and 21.9X our 2010 and 2011 EPS estimates, in line with peers. While we look for strong growth in health care information technology spending, driven by ARRA incentives as well as health care companies seeking to achieve additional cost efficiencies in the face of health care reform, we are concerned that implementation may be more complex and time-consuming than anticipated. Although we see hospital capex stabilizing, we expect it to remain below peak levels relative to sales.

► Risks to our recommendation and target price include increased competition for CERN's core HCIT products; and further slowdowns in hospital capex.

► Our 12-month target price of $87 is based on an in-line-with-peers PEG ratio of 1.75X, based on our 2010 EPS estimate of $2.75 and projected three-year EPS growth rate of 18%. We believe this high industry PEG ratio is appropriate due to the potential we see for robust growth from broad adoption of health care IT.

Qualitative Risk Assessment

LOW	MEDIUM	HIGH

Our risk assessment reflects CERN's established market position in the HCIT market and its broad customer base, weighed against a highly competitive environment for its products and services as well as the risk of technological obsolescence.

Quantitative Evaluations

S&P Quality Ranking B+

D	C	B-	B	B+	A-	A	A+

Relative Strength Rank STRONG

76

LOWEST = 1 HIGHEST = 99

Revenue/Earnings Data

Revenue (Million $)

	1Q	2Q	3Q	4Q	Year
2010	431.3	456.0	--	--	--
2009	392.3	403.8	409.4	466.3	1,672
2008	384.8	402.8	422.7	465.7	1,676
2007	365.9	386.6	372.9	394.5	1,520
2006	321.2	330.6	345.5	380.8	1,378
2005	262.5	277.8	294.6	325.8	1,161

Earnings Per Share ($)

2010	0.59	0.65	E0.71	E0.78	E2.75
2009	0.49	0.52	0.58	0.71	2.31
2008	0.44	0.42	0.54	0.86	2.26
2007	0.34	0.32	0.37	0.49	1.53
2006	0.25	0.29	0.33	0.48	1.34
2005	0.17	0.26	0.34	0.34	1.10

Fiscal year ended Dec. 31. Next earnings report expected: Late October. EPS Estimates based on S&P Operating Earnings; historical GAAP earnings are as reported.

Dividend Data

No cash dividends have been paid.

Cerner Corp

Business Summary August 24, 2010

CORPORATE OVERVIEW. Cerner Corp. is the largest standalone health care information technology (HCIT) company providing health care information technology solutions and devices and related services to health care organizations and consumers. Domestic (U.S.) revenues accounted for 84% of the total in 2009 (78% in 2008).

Revenues are derived from system sales, support and maintenance, and services. System sales (30% of revenues in 2009; 31% in 2008) includes sales of software, deployment period upgrade rights, installation fees, content subscriptions, transaction processing and hardware and sublicensed software. Support and maintenance (29%; 28%) includes ongoing support and services provided to clients. Services (39%; 38%) includes professional services excluding installation, and managed services. Reimbursed travel, which includes reimbursable out-of-pocket expenses related to client service activities, accounted for the remaining 2% (2%).

CORPORATE STRATEGY. Cerner intends to increase its market share by providing innovative solutions and services to existing and new clients as well as by capturing some potential clients who wish to upgrade their systems to

avail themselves of the incentives offered by the Health Information Technology for Economic and Clinical Health Act (HITECH) provisions of the American Recovery and Reinvestment Act (ARRA). We believe HCIT is in its nascent stages in the U.S., based on a recent article in FT Health magazine that estimated only about 20% of doctors' offices and 10% of hospitals currently utilize "some form" of HCIT.

Cerner, currently operating in over 25 countries, plans to increase its sales outside the U.S. as other countries realize the importance of HCIT. It also expects to increase its market share by making its offerings affordable to smaller community hospitals, critical access hospitals and physician practices, as well as by selling software as a service. It also plans to offer solutions beyond the HCIT market, similar to its current offerings, in the form of clinic, pharmacy and wellness services provided directly to employers.

Company Financials Fiscal Year Ended Dec. 31

Per Share Data ($)	2009	2008	2007	2006	2005	2004	2003	2002	2001	2000
Tangible Book Value	14.21	11.13	9.25	9.37	7.44	7.06	5.90	5.24	4.99	4.63
Cash Flow	3.81	3.42	2.72	2.88	2.57	2.07	1.54	1.43	0.07	2.01
Earnings	2.31	2.26	1.53	1.34	1.10	0.86	0.59	0.66	-0.61	1.48
S&P Core Earnings	2.31	2.32	1.53	1.34	0.96	0.73	0.41	0.48	0.37	NA
Dividends	Nil	Nil	Nil	Nil	Nil	Nil	Nil	Nil	Nil	Nil
Payout Ratio	Nil	Nil	Nil	Nil	Nil	Nil	Nil	Nil	Nil	Nil
Prices:High	85.97	59.81	66.17	50.58	49.26	26.95	23.25	28.53	30.75	32.44
Prices:Low	33.38	30.37	44.11	32.50	23.60	17.93	8.19	13.66	14.00	8.94
P/E Ratio:High	37	26	43	38	45	31	39	43	NM	22
P/E Ratio:Low	14	13	29	24	21	21	14	21	NM	6

Income Statement Analysis (Million $)										
Revenue	1,672	1,676	1,520	1,378	1,161	926	840	752	543	405
Operating Income	418	412	303	291	261	202	147	148	109	75.2
Depreciation	126	96.7	153	125	114	90.8	69.3	57.3	47.3	38.0
Interest Expense	8.49	10.6	11.9	0.70	5.86	6.15	7.02	5.56	4.43	7.32
Pretax Income	293	281	204	52.2	135	108	71.2	80.6	-63.3	172
Effective Tax Rate	33.9%	33.0%	37.7%	NM	36.2%	40.1%	39.9%	39.5%	NM	38.8%
Net Income	193	189	127	110	86.3	64.6	42.8	48.8	-42.4	105
S&P Core Earnings	193	194	127	110	75.3	54.9	29.4	35.2	24.9	NA

Balance Sheet & Other Financial Data (Million $)										
Cash	559	309	345	163	113	190	122	143	108	90.9
Current Assets	1,146	859	819	746	652	509	429	448	348	288
Total Assets	2,149	1,881	1,690	1,491	1,304	982	859	779	712	616
Current Liabilities	358	341	288	301	260	199	177	166	158	102
Long Term Debt	95.5	111	178	187	194	109	125	137	92.1	102
Common Equity	1,581	1,311	1,132	918	761	597	495	441	395	344
Total Capital	1,701	1,454	1,326	1,176	1,029	777	680	578	549	503
Capital Expenditures	131	108	181	131	64.8	44.2	26.8	33.2	25.7	16.2
Cash Flow	319	285	226	235	200	155	112	106	4.94	143
Current Ratio	3.2	2.5	2.8	2.5	2.5	2.6	2.4	2.7	2.2	2.8
% Long Term Debt of Capitalization	5.6	7.7	13.4	15.9	18.9	14.0	18.3	23.7	16.8	20.3
% Net Income of Revenue	11.6	11.3	8.4	8.0	7.4	7.0	5.1	6.5	NM	26.0
% Return on Assets	9.6	10.6	8.0	7.9	7.5	7.0	5.2	6.5	NM	16.5
% Return on Equity	13.4	15.4	12.4	13.1	12.7	11.8	9.1	11.7	NM	29.1

Data as orig reptd.; bef. results of disc opers/spec. items. Per share data adj. for stk. divs.; EPS diluted. E-Estimated. NA-Not Available. NM-Not Meaningful. NR-Not Ranked. UR-Under Review.

Office: 2800 Rockcreek Parkway, North Kansas City, MO 64117.
Telephone: 816-221-1024.
Email: invrelations@cerner.com
Website: http://www.cerner.com

Chrmn, Pres & CEO: N.L. Patterson
Vice Chrmn: C.W. Illig
COO & EVP: M.G. Valentine
EVP, CFO & Treas: M.G. Naughton

Chief Acctg Officer: M.R. Battaglioli
Investor Contact: A. Kells (816-201-2445)
Board Members: G. E. Bisbee, Jr., J. C. Danforth, L. M. Dillman, C. W. Illig, W. B. Neaves, N. L. Patterson, W. D. Zollars

Founded: 1980
Domicile: Delaware
Employees: 7,600

CF Industries Holdings Inc

STANDARD & POOR'S

S&P Recommendation HOLD ★★★★☆

Price	12-Mo. Target Price	Investment Style
$117.65 (as of Oct 22, 2010)	$112.00	Large-Cap Value

GICS Sector Materials
Sub-Industry Fertilizers & Agricultural Chemicals

Summary This company is a major manufacturer and distributor of nitrogen and phosphate fertilizer products in North America.

Key Stock Statistics (Source S&P, Vickers, company reports)

52-Wk Range	$120.35–57.56	S&P Oper. EPS 2010E	8.20	Market Capitalization(B)	$8.363
Trailing 12-Month EPS	$3.53	S&P Oper. EPS 2011E	8.55	Yield (%)	0.34
Trailing 12-Month P/E	33.3	P/E on S&P Oper. EPS 2010E	14.3	Dividend Rate/Share	$0.40
$10K Invested 5 Yrs Ago	$92,708	Common Shares Outstg. (M)	71.1	Institutional Ownership (%)	88

Beta	0.97
S&P 3-Yr. Proj. EPS CAGR(%)	9
S&P Credit Rating	NA

Price Performance

30-Week Mov. Avg. · · ·   10-Week Mov. Avg. – –   GAAP Earnings vs. Previous Year   Volume Above Avg. STARS
12-Mo. Target Price —   Relative Strength —   ▲ Up ▼ Down ► No Change   Below Avg.

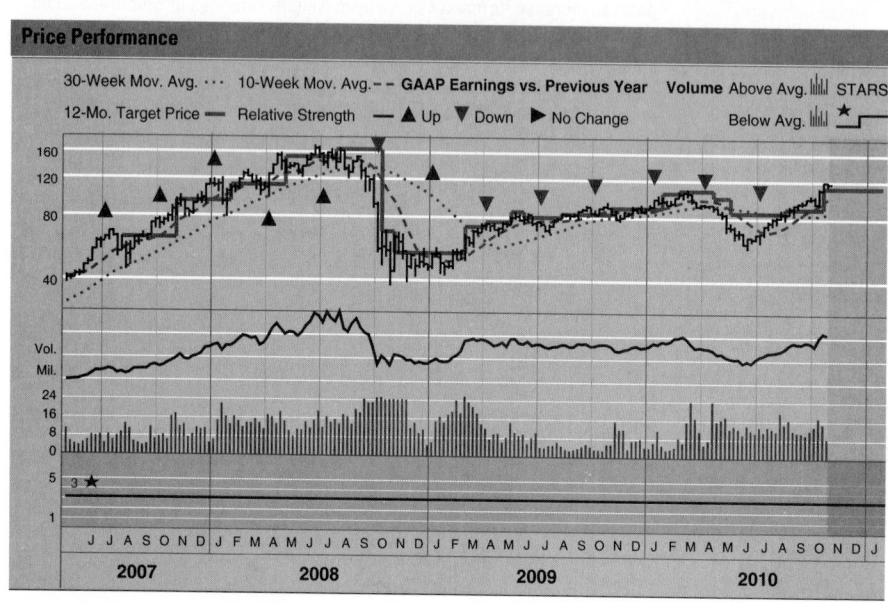

Options: ASE, CBOE, Ph

Analysis prepared by **Kevin Kirkeby** on October 08, 2010, when the stock traded at **$ 109.55**.

Highlights

➤ In April 2010, CF completed the acquisition of Terra Industries. We forecast GAAP revenues of $4.2 billion in 2010, including nearly nine months of contributions from Terra Industries, which was acquired in April. On a pro forma basis, we expect revenues to increase about 9% to $4.6 billion due to higher volumes and a higher average selling prices. We expect volume sales for the combined companies to rise 6%, due to inventory rebuilding and improved application rates. We think selling prices, which began to rise in mid-2010, will be higher on average in 2011, and contribute favorably to the $4.7 billion in revenues we forecast for next year.

➤ We expect margins to widen during 2010 due to the combination of higher selling prices and lower average input costs. However, integration-related expenses will be a partial offset, in our view. CF believes it can lower its cost structure by $135 million in the 18 months following the Terra transaction. We think input cost trends will be less favorable next year relative to selling prices, and will lead to a modest narrowing of margins for 2011.

➤ Our EPS estimate of $8.22 for 2010 excludes $2.73 of net special items (Terra breakup fee, mark-to-market fluctuations).

Investment Rationale/Risk

➤ CF increased its revenue base by about 60% through the April 2010 acquisition of Terra Industries, and is now among the largest global producers of phosphate and nitrogen. On account of the U.S. being a net importer of nitrogen fertilizer, we believe CF, as a domestic producer, benefits from a generally lower cost base, especially during periods of rising demand and selling prices. On this, and our view that post-acquisition debt levels are manageable, and we think valuations above the historic average are warranted.

➤ Risks to our recommendation and target price include difficulties integrating the Terra acquisition, increases in natural gas and sulfur costs, and more competitively priced imports due to a strengthening U.S. dollar.

➤ Our discounted cash flow model assumes relatively unchanged free cash flow for the next five years, a 10.8% cost of equity and 2.5% terminal growth, and calculates intrinsic value of $98. We apply a P/E of 15.5X to our four-quarter forward EPS estimate, which is above the historic average of 10X for CF, to yield a $126 value. Blending the two, we arrive at our 12-month target price of $112.

Qualitative Risk Assessment

LOW	MEDIUM	HIGH

Our risk assessment reflects the cyclical and seasonal nature of the agriculture industry and the company's reliance on the volatile natural gas industry for much of its raw materials, partly offset by the competitive advantage of having many overseas suppliers.

Quantitative Evaluations

S&P Quality Ranking NR

D	C	B-	B	B+	A-	A	A+

Relative Strength Rank STRONG 94

LOWEST = 1   HIGHEST = 99

Revenue/Earnings Data

Revenue (Million $)

	1Q	2Q	3Q	4Q	Year
2010	502.4	1,308	--		--
2009	680.6	991.0	430.1	506.7	2,608
2008	667.3	1,161	1,021	1,072	3,921
2007	447.7	848.9	582.9	852.5	2,757
2006	400.5	664.8	378.0	506.2	1,950
2005	459.3	626.7	359.4	463.0	1,908

Earnings Per Share ($)

	1Q	2Q	3Q	4Q	Year
2010	-0.09	1.54	E1.61	E2.00	E8.20
2009	1.28	4.33	0.78	1.04	7.42
2008	2.77	5.02	0.82	3.59	12.14
2007	1.02	1.65	1.52	2.38	6.57
2006	-0.45	0.77	0.13	0.14	0.60
2005	0.41	0.78	-1.81	-0.18	-0.66

Fiscal year ended Dec. 31. Next earnings report expected: Late October. EPS Estimates based on S&P Operating Earnings; historical GAAP earnings are as reported.

Dividend Data (Dates: mm/dd Payment Date: mm/dd/yy)

Amount ($)	Date Decl.	Ex-Div. Date	Stk. of Record	Payment Date
0.100	01/29	02/18	02/16	03/01/10
0.100	05/03	05/12	05/14	06/01/10
0.100	07/22	08/11	08/13	08/31/10
0.100	10/21	11/10	11/15	11/29/10

Dividends have been paid since 2005. Source: Company reports.

Please read the Required Disclosures and Analyst Certification on the last page of this report.

The McGraw-Hill Companies

CF Industries Holdings Inc

STANDARD &POOR'S

Business Summary October 08, 2010

CORPORATE OVERVIEW. CF Industries is a major manufacturer and distributor of nitrogen and phosphate fertilizer products in North America. In April 2010, CF completed the $4.7 billion acquisition of Terra Industries, boosting its revenue base by about 60%, based on 2009 figures. Principal products of the combined entity are ammonia, urea, urea ammonium nitrate solution (UAN), diammonium phosphate (DAP) and monoammonium phosphate (MAP). On a pro forma basis, the combined companies would have generated $4.2 billion in revenue during 2009, on sales of 11.8 million tons of nitrogen-related fertilizers and 2.1 million tons of phosphate fertilizers. Core markets and distribution facilities for the company are concentrated in the midwestern U.S. grain-producing states.

PRIMARY BUSINESS DYNAMICS. Nitrogen, phosphates and potash are the three primary plant nutrients that are essential for proper crop nutrition and maximum yields. There are no substitutes for them, and they are generally not substitutable for each other. Each of these fertilizers is actively traded in the global marketplace, with price being the primary means of differentiation. The U.S. is a net exporter of phosphate fertilizers, while it tends to import a significant amount of nitrogen-based product. Producers typically build their inventories ahead of the spring planting season when demand is the highest, and over the summer in advance of post-harvest fertilizer applications.

In 2009, natural gas purchases accounted for about 47% of the combined company's pro forma total cost of sales of nitrogen fertilizers and a substantially higher percentage of cash costs. CF uses, and plans to continue using, a combination of spot and term purchases of varied duration from a number of suppliers to maintain a reliable, competitively priced natural gas supply, and also uses certain financial instruments to hedge natural gas prices. It has developed a forward pricing program under which it traditionally sells about half of its nitrogen fertilizer, and this system provides some margin certainty.

CORPORATE STRATEGY. CF's manufacturing facilities are competitive, due, in our view, to their large scale and a modular configuration that allows it to adjust production to changing market conditions. Its distribution system is flexible and strategically located to serve its midwestern customers. The company's Donaldsonville, LA, nitrogen fertilizer facility is the largest in North America, and its Medicine Hat, Alberta, plant is the second largest, which gives it significant economies-of-scale advantages over its competitors. Through the purchase of Terra Industries, CF acquired interests in six nitrogen facilities in the U.S., as well as joint ventures in Trinidad and the United Kingdom.

Company Financials Fiscal Year Ended Dec. 31

Per Share Data ($)	2009	2008	2007	2006	2005	2004	2003	2002	2001	2000
Tangible Book Value	35.58	27.72	21.09	13.88	13.73	12.96	NA	NA	NA	NA
Cash Flow	9.48	13.93	8.06	2.32	1.11	3.21	1.57	2.14	0.77	1.57
Earnings	7.42	12.14	6.57	0.60	-0.66	1.23	-0.33	-0.51	-1.35	-0.47
S&P Core Earnings	7.30	11.91	6.56	0.63	-0.68	1.22	-0.35	NA	NA	NA
Dividends	0.40	0.40	0.08	0.08	0.02	NA	NA	NA	NA	NA
Payout Ratio	5%	3%	1%	13%	NM	NA	NA	NA	NA	NA
Prices:High	95.13	172.99	118.88	26.60	18.00	NA	NA	NA	NA	NA
Prices:Low	42.30	37.71	25.70	12.91	11.19	NA	NA	NA	NA	NA
P/E Ratio:High	13	14	18	44	NM	NA	NA	NA	NA	NA
P/E Ratio:Low	6	3	4	22	NM	NA	NA	NA	NA	NA

Income Statement Analysis (Million $)	2009	2008	2007	2006	2005	2004	2003	2002	2001	2000
Revenue	2,608	3,921	2,757	1,950	1,908	1,651	1,370	1,014	1,160	1,160
Operating Income	838	1,313	686	166	236	258	99.4	89.6	-32.1	97.6
Depreciation	101	101	84.5	94.6	97.5	109	105	108	102	112
Interest Expense	1.50	1.60	1.70	2.90	14.0	22.7	23.9	23.6	31.8	21.1
Pretax Income	694	1,180	627	81.8	110	132	-25.0	-38.3	-151	-40.1
Effective Tax Rate	35.4%	32.1%	31.8%	24.1%	NM	31.3%	NM	NM	NM	NM
Net Income	366	685	373	33.3	-36.2	67.7	-18.4	-28.1	-59.7	-25.8
S&P Core Earnings	360	671	372	34.9	-37.1	67.5	-19.7	NA	NA	NA

Balance Sheet & Other Financial Data (Million $)	2009	2008	2007	2006	2005	2004	2003	2002	2001	2000
Cash	882	625	861	25.4	37.4	72.8	169	NA	NA	NA
Current Assets	1,283	1,433	1,279	633	576	NA	526	NA	NA	NA
Total Assets	2,495	2,388	2,013	1,290	1,228	1,149	1,405	NA	NA	NA
Current Liabilities	480	818	629	353	341	NA	350	NA	NA	NA
Long Term Debt	4.70	Nil	4.90	4.20	4.20	4.01	255	NA	NA	NA
Common Equity	1,729	1,338	1,187	767	756	720	-0.79	NA	NA	NA
Total Capital	1,750	1,357	1,241	785	782	724	1,038	NA	NA	NA
Capital Expenditures	236	142	105	59.3	69.4	33.7	28.7	26.3	41.7	52.3
Cash Flow	467	785	457	128	61.3	176	86.6	118	42.3	86.2
Current Ratio	2.7	1.8	2.0	1.8	1.7	NA	1.5	NA	NA	NA
% Long Term Debt of Capitalization	0.3	Nil	0.4	0.5	0.5	0.6	24.6	Nil	NA	NA
% Net Income of Revenue	14.0	17.5	13.5	1.7	NM	4.1	NM	NM	NM	NM
% Return on Assets	15.0	31.1	22.6	2.6	NM	NA	NA	NA	NA	NA
% Return on Equity	23.8	54.2	38.2	4.4	NM	NA	NA	NA	NA	NA

Data as orig reptd.; bef. results of disc opers/spec. items. Per share data adj. for stk. divs.; EPS diluted. 2004 pro forma as adjusted; bal. sheet and book val. as of Jun. 30, 2005. Prior to 2005, per sh. data based on pro forma shs. E-Estimated. NA-Not Available. NM-Not Meaningful. NR-Not Ranked. UR-Under Review.

Office: 4 Parkway North, Suite 400, Deerfield, IL 60015-2590.
Telephone: 847-405-2400.
Website: http://www.cfindustries.com
Chrmn, Pres & CEO: S.R. Wilson

Chief Acctg Officer & Cntlr: R.A. Hoker
Treas: R.W. Selgrad
Secy & General Counsel: D.C. Barnard
Investor Contact: T. Huch (847-405-2515)

Board Members: R. C. Arzbaecher, W. W. Creek, W. Davisson, S. A. Furbacher, S. J. Hagge, D. R. Harvey, J. D. Johnson, E. A. Schmitt, S. R. Wilson

Founded: 1946
Domicile: Delaware
Employees: 1,600

The McGraw-Hill Companies

Chesapeake Energy Corp

S&P Recommendation BUY ★★★★☆

Price	**12-Mo. Target Price**	**Investment Style**
$21.16 (as of Oct 25, 2010)	$29.00	Large-Cap Blend

GICS Sector Energy
Sub-Industry Oil & Gas Exploration & Production

Summary As one of the largest independent exploration and production companies in the U.S., CHK focuses on U.S. onshore natural gas production east of the Rocky Mountains.

Key Stock Statistics (Source S&P, Vickers, company reports)

52-Wk Range	$29.22–19.62	S&P Oper. EPS 2010E	2.93	Market Capitalization(B)	$13.846	Beta	1.15
Trailing 12-Month EPS	$1.01	S&P Oper. EPS 2011E	2.69	Yield (%)	1.42	S&P 3-Yr. Proj. EPS CAGR(%)	-9
Trailing 12-Month P/E	21.0	P/E on S&P Oper. EPS 2010E	7.2	Dividend Rate/Share	$0.30	S&P Credit Rating	BB
$10K Invested 5 Yrs Ago	$7,543	Common Shares Outstg. (M)	654.3	Institutional Ownership (%)	72		

Price Performance

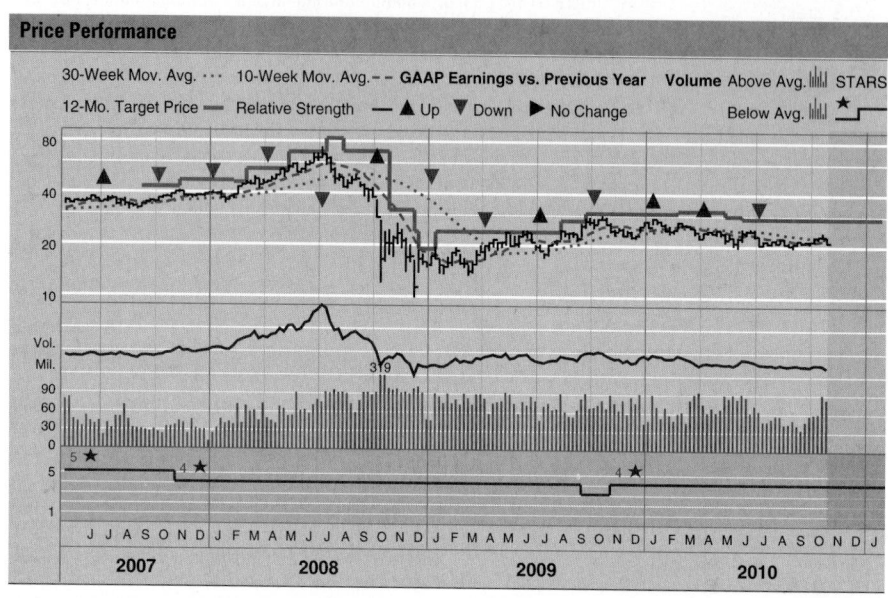

30-Week Mov. Avg. · · · 10-Week Mov. Avg. - - GAAP Earnings vs. Previous Year   Volume Above Avg. STARS
12-Mo. Target Price — Relative Strength — ▲ Up ▼ Down ► No Change   Below Avg.

Options: ASE, CBOE, P, Ph

Analysis prepared by **Michael Kay** on October 25, 2010, when the stock traded at **$ 21.20**.

Highlights

➤ In May, CHK stated plans to increase its focus on crude oil and lower debt, as it plans to raise $5 billion through asset sales (20% of Marcellus operations), JV's, and convertibles to repay $3.5 billion in debt and boost oil capex $1.5 billion over the next 24 months. CHK has since announced several liquids-rich opportunities (Granite Wash, Eagle Ford, Niobrara) as it attempts to add oil to its portfolio. We see production up 13% and 17% in 2010 and 2011. As of September, CHK ran 133 rigs, with 100 at natural gas shale plays and 21 rigs at unconventional liquid plays, with 12 at Granite Wash. CHK is aiming for a 50-rig program at liquids-rich plays in the next 12 months and plans to raise its liquid production mix from 10% currently to 15%-20% by year-end 2012.

➤ CHK has closed on five JV asset monetizations (most recently a $2.16 billion JV at Eagle Ford with CNOOC Ltd.), which we expect to increase shareholder value at five major shales, and intends to enter a JV at Niobrara. We believe JV funding has provided greater flexibility.

➤ On volume growth and hedges, we see EPS of $2.93 (with $0.01 non-cash gain) for 2010 and $2.69 for 2011, up from $1.91 ($0.46 loss) in 2009.

Investment Rationale/Risk

➤ CHK's aggressive acquisition strategy has seen it spend over $14 billion over the past 10 years, focused on unconventional natural gas plays. With turmoil in credit markets, and a highly leveraged balance sheet, CHK has monetized assets through JVs and is planning to sell certain non-Haynesville Shale producing assets in Louisiana for $225-$250 million and 20% of its Marcellus Shale operations. CHK believes it has built a solid position at 12 liquids-rich plays with 2.9 million net acres. CHK anticipates excess cash of $2 billion in 2010 for debt reduction. It sees drilling capex of $4.5-$4.6 billion per annum through 2012, up from $3.4 billion in 2009, and within its cash flow assumptions.

➤ Risks to our recommendation and target price include weaker economic and operating conditions, a sustained decline in natural gas prices, and difficulty replacing reserves.

➤ CHK has developed a dominant natural gas shale position, and we expect its expertise in unconventional drilling to carry over to liquids development. Our 12-month target price of $29 blends our proved NAV ($39) with our DCF ($26, assuming an 8.8% WACC; 3% terminal growth) and relative metrics ($27).

Qualitative Risk Assessment

LOW	MEDIUM	HIGH

Our risk assessment reflects CHK's business profile in a volatile, cyclical and capital-intensive segment of the energy industry. We believe CHK's financial strategy is aggressive, as it has been one of the most active acquirers in exploration and production, and one of the most active users of commodity hedges. This is partly offset by what we see as strong volume growth and good drilling prospects.

Quantitative Evaluations

S&P Quality Ranking   B-

D	C	B-	B	B+	A-	A	A+

Relative Strength Rank   **WEAK**

19

LOWEST = 1   HIGHEST = 99

Revenue/Earnings Data

Revenue (Million $)

	1Q	2Q	3Q	4Q	Year
2010	2,798	2,012	--	--	--
2009	1,995	1,673	1,811	2,222	7,702
2008	1,611	3,372	7,491	2,981	11,629
2007	1,580	2,105	2,027	2,089	7,800
2006	1,945	1,584	1,929	1,868	7,326
2005	783.5	1,048	1,083	1,751	4,665

Earnings Per Share ($)

2010	1.14	0.37	E0.64	E0.71	E2.93
2009	-9.63	0.39	0.30	-0.84	-9.57
2008	-0.29	-3.16	5.61	-1.51	1.14
2007	0.50	1.01	0.72	0.27	2.62
2006	1.44	0.82	1.13	0.96	4.35
2005	0.36	0.52	0.43	1.11	2.51

Fiscal year ended Dec. 31. Next earnings report expected: Late October. EPS Estimates based on S&P Operating Earnings; historical GAAP earnings are as reported.

Dividend Data (Dates: mm/dd Payment Date: mm/dd/yy)

Amount ($)	Date Decl.	Ex-Div. Date	Stk. of Record	Payment Date
0.075	12/18	12/30	01/04	01/15/10
0.075	03/08	03/30	04/01	04/15/10
0.075	06/21	06/29	07/01	07/15/10
0.075	09/01	09/29	10/01	10/15/10

Dividends have been paid since 2002. Source: Company reports.

Chesapeake Energy Corp

STANDARD &POOR'S

Business Summary October 25, 2010

CORPORATE OVERVIEW. As the largest producer of natural gas in the U.S. as of year-end 2008, Chesapeake Energy Corp. (CHK) is focused on discovering, acquiring and developing conventional and unconventional natural gas reserves onshore in the U.S., east of the Rocky Mountains, primarily in natural gas shale plays -- the Barnett Shale in the Fort Worth Basin, the Haynesville Shale in Louisiana, the Fayetteville Shale in the Arkoma Basin, and the Marcellus Shale in the Appalachian Basin. In 2009, CHK added the Eagle Ford Shale and Bossier play to its core properties of "Big 6" natural gas shale plays.

CHK operations are concentrated in six U.S. operating areas: Mid-Continent, Barnett Shale, Appalachian Basin, Permian and Delaware Basin, Ark-La-Tex, and South Texas and Texas Gulf Coast. Proved oil and gas reserves rose 18%, to 14.3 trillion cubic feet equivalent (Tcfe; 94% natural gas, 58% developed) in 2009. Oil and gas production rose 8%, to 906 billion cubic feet equivalent (92% natural gas), in 2009. We estimate CHK's 2009 organic reserve replacement at 343%. During 2009, CHK drilled 1,148 gross (831 net) operated wells and participated in 1,127 gross (99 net) wells operated by other companies. CHK's drilling success rate was 99% for company-operated wells. During 2009, CHK invested $2.941 billion in operated wells (using an average of 104 operated

rigs) and $439 million in non-operated wells (using an average of 60 non-operated rigs) for total drilling, completing and equipping costs of $3.38 billion.

MARKET PROFILE. From 1998 to the present, CHK has integrated an aggressive and technologically advanced drilling program with an active property consolidation program focused on small to medium-sized corporate and property acquisitions. Beginning in 2006, CHK shifted its strategy from drilling inventory capture to drilling inventory conversion. In doing so, CHK has de-emphasized its acquisitions of proved properties while further emphasizing its drilling program and converting its substantial backlog of drilling opportunities into proved developed producing reserves. CHK believes one of its most distinctive characteristics is its ability to increase its reserves and production organically. CHK conducts the most active drilling program in the U.S. and is active in most unconventional plays in the U.S. east of the Rockies, where it drills more horizontal wells than any other company in the industry.

Company Financials Fiscal Year Ended Dec. 31

Per Share Data ($)	2009	2008	2007	2006	2005	2004	2003	2002	2001	2000
Tangible Book Value	17.47	26.00	21.87	20.32	12.42	8.57	5.45	3.99	3.75	2.05
Cash Flow	11.26	5.21	6.87	7.36	5.05	3.56	2.61	1.54	2.52	3.67
Earnings	-9.57	1.14	2.62	4.35	2.51	1.53	1.20	0.17	1.51	3.01
S&P Core Earnings	-9.36	1.35	2.51	4.19	2.48	1.50	1.19	0.17	1.36	NA
Dividends	0.30	0.29	0.26	0.23	0.20	0.17	0.14	0.06	Nil	Nil
Payout Ratio	NM	26%	10%	5%	8%	11%	11%	35%	Nil	Nil
Prices:High	30.00	74.00	41.19	35.57	40.20	18.31	14.00	8.55	11.06	10.50
Prices:Low	13.27	9.84	27.27	26.81	15.06	11.70	7.27	4.50	4.50	1.94
P/E Ratio:High	NM	65	16	8	16	12	12	50	7	3
P/E Ratio:Low	NM	9	10	6	6	8	6	26	3	1

Income Statement Analysis (Million $)										
Revenue	7,702	11,629	7,800	7,326	4,665	2,709	1,717	738	969	628
Operating Income	NA	3,631	4,638	3,413	1,773	992	675	191	597	384
Depreciation, Depletion and Amortization	12,745	2,147	1,989	1,463	945	611	386	235	178	105
Interest Expense	113	314	675	301	220	167	154	111	98.3	86.3
Pretax Income	-9,288	1,186	2,341	3,255	1,493	805	501	67.1	438	196
Effective Tax Rate	37.5%	39.0%	38.0%	38.5%	36.5%	36.0%	38.0%	40.0%	39.9%	NM
Net Income	-5,830	723	1,451	2,003	948	515	311	40.3	263	456
S&P Core Earnings	-5,723	737	1,178	1,831	871	431	283	29.9	235	NA

Balance Sheet & Other Financial Data (Million $)										
Cash	307	1,749	1.00	2.52	60.0	6.90	40.6	248	125	3.50
Current Assets	2,446	4,292	1,396	1,154	1,183	568	342	435	361	167
Total Assets	29,914	38,444	30,734	24,417	16,118	8,245	4,572	2,876	2,287	1,440
Current Liabilities	2,688	3,621	2,761	1,890	1,964	964	513	266	173	163
Long Term Debt	12,295	14,184	10,950	7,376	5,490	3,075	2,058	1,651	1,329	945
Common Equity	11,444	16,297	11,170	9,293	4,598	2,672	1,180	758	617	282
Total Capital	24,636	34,244	27,046	21,944	13,469	7,172	3,982	2,559	2,097	1,270
Capital Expenditures	5,226	9,177	9,705	986	484	127	71.5	33.6	24.9	78.9
Cash Flow	6,892	2,837	3,346	3,377	1,851	1,087	674	265	439	556
Current Ratio	0.9	1.2	0.5	0.6	0.6	0.6	0.7	1.6	2.1	1.0
% Long Term Debt of Capitalization	51.8	41.4	47.4	33.6	40.8	42.9	51.7	64.5	63.4	74.4
% Return on Assets	NM	4.5	4.9	9.9	7.8	8.0	8.3	1.6	14.1	39.8
% Return on Equity	NM	5.3	13.3	27.6	24.9	24.7	29.7	4.4	58.1	NM

Data as orig reptd.; bef. results of disc opers/spec. items. Per share data adj. for stk. divs.; EPS diluted. E-Estimated. NA-Not Available. NM-Not Meaningful. NR-Not Ranked. UR-Under Review.

Office: 6100 North Western Avenue, Oklahoma City, OK 73118.
Telephone: 405-848-8000.
Website: http://www.chk.com
Chrmn & CEO: A.K. McClendon

COO & EVP: S.C. Dixon
EVP & CFO: M.C. Rowland
SVP, Chief Acctg Officer & Cntlr: M.A. Johnson
SVP, Treas & Secy: J. Grigsby

Investor Contact: J.L. Mobley (405-767-4763)
Board Members: R. K. Davidson, K. Eisbrenner, V. B. Hargis, F. Keating, C. T. Maxwell, A. K. McClendon, M. A. Miller, Jr., D. L. Nickles, F. B. Whittemore

Founded: 1989
Domicile: Oklahoma
Employees: 8,200

The McGraw-Hill Companies

Chevron Corp

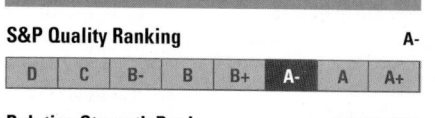
STANDARD &POOR'S

| S&P Recommendation **STRONG BUY** ★★★★★ | Price $84.55 (as of Oct 22, 2010) | 12-Mo. Target Price $98.00 | Investment Style Large-Cap Blend |

GICS Sector Energy
Sub-Industry Integrated Oil & Gas

Summary This global integrated oil company (formerly ChevronTexaco) has interests in exploration, production, refining and marketing, and petrochemicals.

Key Stock Statistics (Source S&P, Vickers, company reports)

52-Wk Range	$85.00– 66.83	S&P Oper. EPS 2010E	9.24	Market Capitalization(B)	$169.996	Beta	0.72
Trailing 12-Month EPS	$8.42	S&P Oper. EPS 2011E	9.68	Yield (%)	3.41	S&P 3-Yr. Proj. EPS CAGR(%)	33
Trailing 12-Month P/E	10.0	P/E on S&P Oper. EPS 2010E	9.2	Dividend Rate/Share	$2.88	S&P Credit Rating	AA
$10K Invested 5 Yrs Ago	$17,698	Common Shares Outstg. (M)	2,010.6	Institutional Ownership (%)	62		

Price Performance

- 30-Week Mov. Avg. ···
- 10-Week Mov. Avg. – –
- 12-Mo. Target Price —
- Relative Strength —
- GAAP Earnings vs. Previous Year
- ▲ Up ▼ Down ▶ No Change
- Volume Above Avg. STARS
- Below Avg. ★

Analysis prepared by **Tina J. Vital** on October 14, 2010, when the stock traded at **$ 83.20**.

Options: ASE, CBOE, P, Ph

Highlights

➤ We see minimal impact to CVX's oil and gas production but expect higher third quarter expenses from the U.S. Gulf of Mexico drilling moratorium (about 6% of CVX's output is from the Gulf of Mexico); in July, CVX estimated the impact at less than 10,000 b/d. We project third quarter oil & gas production will rise 1.1%, to 2.73 million boe per day, and we expect 1.6% growth, to 2.75 million boe per day, in 2010, on optimization efforts and increased gas sales in Thailand. Despite a base decline of 4%-5%, longer term, we expect field developments to permit annual production growth of about 2.6% between 2008 and 2013.

➤ On the downstream, as of September 2010, we project that U.S. Gulf Coast 3-2-1 refining crack spreads will narrow by about 5% in 2010 before widening about 16% in 2011. In January 2010, CVX began a restructuring study of its refining segment to make it smaller and less complex. Completion was slated for September 2010.

➤ We expect cost initiatives and an improved economic outlook to boost after-tax operating earnings by 84% in 2010 and 5% in 2011.

Investment Rationale/Risk

➤ CVX is reducing its refining footprint and focusing on large, long-lived upstream projects with higher margin and growth potential. We have a positive outlook for these prospects, given the company's 2005 purchase of Unocal and its on-going international "Big Five" developments. We consider CVX's reserve replacement rate to be solid, and we see improvement in its upstream costs.

➤ Risks to our recommendation and target price include declines in economic, industry and operating conditions. A pending 2003 lawsuit in Ecuador alleges environmental damage related to Texaco's prior operations, but we see little near-term financial impact since CVX has no operations there. (Texaco spent $40 million on a clean-up in Ecuador before leaving in 1997, at which time Ecuador released it from responsibility for its operations.)

➤ Blending our discounted cash flow ($99 per share, assuming a WACC of 7.7% and terminal growth of 3%) and relative market valuations, our 12-month target price is $98. This represents an enterprise value of about 5.1X our 2011 EBITDA estimate, a discount to U.S. supermajor peers.

Qualitative Risk Assessment

| **LOW** | MEDIUM | HIGH |

Our risk assessment reflects Chevron's diversified and strong business profile in volatile, cyclical and capital-intensive segments of the energy industry. We view its corporate governance practices as generally sound and its earnings as stable.

Quantitative Evaluations

S&P Quality Ranking A-

| D | C | B- | B | B+ | **A-** | A | A+ |

Relative Strength Rank MODERATE

| | 69 | |
LOWEST = 1   HIGHEST = 99

Revenue/Earnings Data

Revenue (Million $)

	1Q	2Q	3Q	4Q	Year
2010	46,741	51,051	--	--	--
2009	34,987	39,647	45,180	47,588	167,402
2008	65,903	78,310	73,615	43,145	264,958
2007	46,302	54,344	53,545	59,900	203,970
2006	54,624	53,536	54,212	47,746	210,118
2005	41,607	48,343	54,456	53,794	198,200

Earnings Per Share ($)

	1Q	2Q	3Q	4Q	Year
2010	2.27	2.70	E2.18	E2.20	E9.24
2009	0.92	0.87	1.92	1.53	5.24
2008	2.48	2.89	3.86	2.43	11.67
2007	2.18	2.52	1.75	2.32	8.77
2006	1.80	1.97	2.29	1.74	7.80
2005	1.28	1.76	1.64	1.86	6.54

Fiscal year ended Dec. 31. Next earnings report expected: Early November. EPS Estimates based on S&P Operating Earnings; historical GAAP earnings are as reported.

Dividend Data (Dates: mm/dd Payment Date: mm/dd/yy)

Amount ($)	Date Decl.	Ex-Div. Date	Stk. of Record	Payment Date
0.680	10/28	11/16	11/18	12/10/09
0.680	01/27	02/12	02/17	03/10/10
0.720	04/28	05/17	05/19	06/10/10
0.720	07/28	08/17	08/19	09/10/10

Dividends have been paid since 1912. Source: Company reports.

Please read the Required Disclosures and Analyst Certification on the last page of this report.

The **McGraw·Hill** Companies

Chevron Corp

Business Summary October 14, 2010

CORPORATE OVERVIEW. In October 2001, Chevron Corp. (CHV) and Texaco Inc. (TX) merged, creating the second largest U.S.-based oil company at the time, ChevronTexaco Corp. (CVX). In May 2005, the company changed its name to Chevron Corp.

CVX separately manages its upstream (or exploration and production; 26% of 2009 revenues and 91% of 2009 segment income), downstream (or refining, marketing and transportation; 72% and 5%), chemicals (1% and 4%) and other businesses, which includes its mining operations for coal and molybdenum, power generation, Chevron Energy Solutions (CES), and energy technology such as Chevron Technology Ventures (CTV) companies.

Net production of crude oil, natural gas liquids (NGLs) and natural gas rose 7%, to 2.678 million barrels of oil equivalent (boe) per day (69% liquids), in 2009, reflecting the start-up of the Blind Faith and Tahiti fields in the U.S. Gulf of Mexico in 2008 and the Agbami field in Nigeria in 2009, and the expansion of Tengiz in Kazakhstan. Net proved oil and gas reserves, including equity share in affiliates, rose 1.1%, to 11.31 billion boe (62% liquids, 73% developed) in 2009. Using data from John S. Herold, we estimate CVX's three-year (2006-2008) reserve replacement rate at 94%, below the peer average; three-

year finding and development costs at $23.48 per boe, above the peer average; three-year proved acquisition costs at $2.18 per boe, above the peer average; and reserve replacement costs at $18.43 per boe, above the peer average. We estimate CVX's 2009 organic reserve replacement rate at 115%.

As of December 31, 2009, CVX owned eight refineries and one asphalt plant (which was idled in early 2008, and is being operated as a terminal), and had interests in eight international refineries, for a total operable capacity of 2.158 million b/d (50% North America). CVX processes imported (85% of 2009 refinery inputs) and domestic (15%) crude oil in its U.S. refining operations. As of year-end 2009, it had a network of about 22,000 (44% U.S.) branded retail sites worldwide.

CVX's chemical segment includes the company's Oronite subsidiary and the 50%-owned Chevron Phillips Chemical Co. LLC (CPChem).

Company Financials Fiscal Year Ended Dec. 31

Per Share Data ($)	2009	2008	2007	2006	2005	2004	2003	2002	2001	2000
Tangible Book Value	43.48	40.93	34.66	29.71	25.99	21.47	16.98	14.80	15.92	15.54
Cash Flow	11.29	16.32	12.67	11.38	8.96	8.53	5.99	2.98	5.17	6.17
Earnings	5.24	11.67	8.77	7.80	6.54	6.14	3.57	0.54	1.85	3.99
S&P Core Earnings	5.04	10.90	8.34	7.88	6.62	5.88	3.50	1.22	1.66	NA
Dividends	2.66	2.53	2.26	2.01	1.75	1.53	1.43	1.40	1.33	1.30
Payout Ratio	51%	22%	26%	26%	27%	25%	40%	NM	72%	33%
Prices:High	79.82	104.63	95.50	76.20	65.98	56.07	43.50	45.80	49.25	47.44
Prices:Low	56.12	55.50	64.99	53.76	49.81	42.00	30.66	32.71	39.22	34.97
P/E Ratio:High	15	9	11	10	10	9	12	86	27	12
P/E Ratio:Low	11	5	7	7	8	7	9	61	21	9

Income Statement Analysis (Million $)										
Revenue	167,402	264,958	214,091	204,892	193,641	150,865	120,032	98,691	104,409	50,592
Operating Income	NA	45,238	33,936	35,748	27,129	21,542	49,336	28,848	16,031	15,834
Depreciation, Depletion and Amortization	12,110	9,528	8,309	7,506	5,913	4,935	5,384	5,231	7,059	2,848
Interest Expense	28.0	2.00	468	451	482	406	474	565	833	460
Pretax Income	18,528	43,057	32,274	32,046	25,293	20,636	12,850	4,213	8,412	9,270
Effective Tax Rate	43.0%	44.2%	41.8%	46.3%	43.9%	36.4%	41.6%	71.8%	51.8%	44.1%
Net Income	10,483	23,931	18,688	17,138	14,099	13,034	7,426	1,132	3,931	5,185
S&P Core Earnings	10,080	22,346	17,772	17,310	14,277	12,471	7,454	2,590	3,518	NA

Balance Sheet & Other Financial Data (Million $)										
Cash	8,822	9,560	8,094	11,446	11,144	10,742	5,267	3,781	3,150	2,630
Current Assets	37,216	36,470	39,377	36,304	34,336	28,503	19,426	17,776	18,327	8,213
Total Assets	164,621	161,165	148,786	132,628	125,833	93,208	81,470	77,359	77,572	41,264
Current Liabilities	26,211	32,023	33,798	28,409	25,011	18,795	16,111	19,876	20,654	7,674
Long Term Debt	9,829	6,083	6,753	7,679	12,131	10,456	10,894	10,911	8,989	5,153
Common Equity	91,914	86,648	77,088	73,684	66,722	48,575	40,022	36,176	37,120	21,761
Total Capital	102,456	104,739	95,532	93,219	90,315	66,471	57,601	53,009	52,524	31,822
Capital Expenditures	19,843	19,666	16,678	13,813	8,701	6,310	5,625	7,597	9,713	3,657
Cash Flow	22,593	33,459	26,997	24,644	20,012	17,969	12,810	6,363	10,990	8,033
Current Ratio	1.4	1.1	1.2	1.3	1.4	1.5	1.2	0.9	0.9	1.1
% Long Term Debt of Capitalization	Nil	5.8	7.3	8.2	13.4	15.7	18.9	20.6	17.1	16.2
% Return on Assets	6.4	15.4	13.3	13.3	12.9	14.9	9.4	1.5	5.1	12.7
% Return on Equity	NA	29.2	25.6	24.4	24.5	29.4	19.5	3.1	10.7	25.1

Data as orig reptd.; bef. results of disc opers/spec. items. Per share data adj. for stk. divs.; EPS diluted. Quarterly revs. incl. other inc. E-Estimated. NA-Not Available. NM-Not Meaningful. NR-Not Ranked. UR-Under Review.

Office: 6001 Bollinger Canyon Road, San Ramon, CA 94583-2324.
Telephone: 925-842-1000.
Email: invest@chevrontexaco.com
Website: http://www.chevrontexaco.com

Chrmn & CEO: J.S. Watson
Vice Chrmn & EVP: G. Kirkland
CFO: P.E. Yarrington
CTO: J.W. McDonald

Treas: P. Breber
Board Members: S. H. Armacost, L. F. Deily, R. E. Denham, R. J. Eaton, C. T. Hagel, E. Hernandez, Jr., F. G. Jenifer, G. Kirkland, S. A. Nunn, D. B. Rice, K. W. Sharer, C. R. Shoemate, J. G. Stumpf, R. D. Sugar, C. Ware, J. S. Watson

Founded: 1901
Domicile: Delaware
Employees: 64,000

The McGraw-Hill Companies

C.H. Robinson Worldwide Inc

STANDARD &POOR'S

S&P Recommendation BUY ★★★★☆

Price	12-Mo. Target Price	Investment Style
$72.52 (as of Oct 22, 2010)	$80.00	Large-Cap Growth

GICS Sector Industrials
Sub-Industry Air Freight & Logistics

Summary This global provider of multimodal transportation and logistics solutions has a network of over 230 offices in North America, South America, Europe, and Asia.

Key Stock Statistics (Source S&P, Vickers, company reports)

52-Wk Range	$72.99– 51.16	S&P Oper. EPS 2010**E**	2.30	Market Capitalization(B)	$12.028	Beta	0.81
Trailing 12-Month EPS	$2.18	S&P Oper. EPS 2011**E**	2.75	Yield (%)	1.38	S&P 3-Yr. Proj. EPS CAGR(%)	15
Trailing 12-Month P/E	33.3	P/E on S&P Oper. EPS 2010**E**	31.5	Dividend Rate/Share	$1.00	S&P Credit Rating	NA
$10K Invested 5 Yrs Ago	$25,620	Common Shares Outstg. (M)	165.9	Institutional Ownership (%)	78		

Price Performance

30-Week Mov. Avg. ··· 10-Week Mov. Avg. - - **GAAP Earnings vs. Previous Year** Volume Above Avg. STARS

12-Mo. Target Price — Relative Strength — ▲ Up ▼ Down ► No Change Below Avg. ★

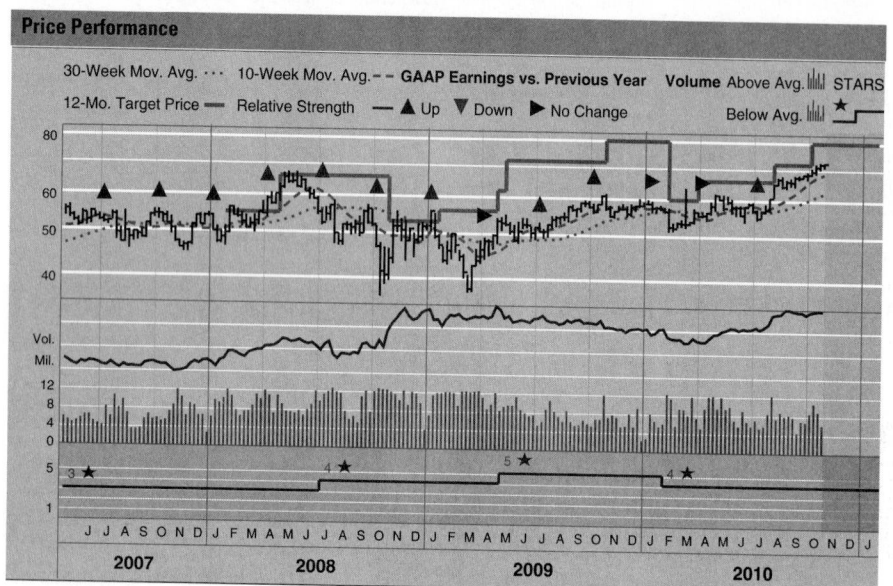

Options: ASE, CBOE, P, Ph

Analysis prepared by **Jim Corridore** on September 30, 2010, when the stock traded at **$ 70.43**.

Highlights

► For 2010, we see gross revenues rising about 15% on improving demand related to a strengthening U.S. economy, which has already led to increased shipping activity, although the overall economy is not robust. We believe CHRW will continue to gain market share as it increases penetration into existing accounts and adds new accounts. Gross revenues declined 12% in 2009, reflecting decreased volume and pricing for truck, intermodal, ocean, and air shipping services related to the weak U.S. economy.

► We expect operating margins to be impacted by rising purchased transportation costs, driven by higher capacity utilization rates among the trucking companies CHRW hires to transport goods. This should be partly offset by lower SG&A costs and a reduction in personnel costs as a percentage of revenues. We see operating margins of 7.3% for 2010, versus 7.7% in 2009.

► Our 2010 EPS estimate is $2.30, which is 8% growth over 2009's EPS of $2.13. We believe the quality of CHRW's earnings is high relative to most other transportation companies that we cover. For 2011, we see EPS growth of about 20%, to $2.75.

Investment Rationale/Risk

► We are positive on CHRW's history of strong returns on assets and equity relative to most other transportation companies. Also, CHRW has no long-term debt and has been a generator of cash over the past few years. We think the quality of its reported earnings is high relative to peers, as the company does not have a defined benefit pension plan. CHRW has shown an ability to leverage its non-asset model to generate profits during periods of declining demand, in our view, which has allowed it to financially outperform most peers during the current difficult economic climate.

► Risks to our recommendation and target price include the possibility of investor rotation out of transportation stocks, a potential further weakening of transport volumes, and sharply lower pricing related to excess industry transportation capacity.

► Our 12-month target price of $80 values the stock at 29X our 2011 EPS estimate of $2.75. Our valuation is above peer levels, but within CHRW's historical P/E range for the past five years of 17.5X to 36.1X earnings.

Qualitative Risk Assessment

LOW	MEDIUM	HIGH

Our risk assessment reflects CHRW's lack of long-term debt and our favorable view of its high quality of earnings and non-asset-based structure. This is only partially offset, in our view, by exposure to cyclical economic slowdowns and volatile transportation costs.

Quantitative Evaluations

S&P Quality Ranking A+

D	C	B-	B	B+	A-	A	A+

Relative Strength Rank STRONG

73

LOWEST = 1   HIGHEST = 99

Revenue/Earnings Data

Revenue (Million $)

	1Q	2Q	3Q	4Q	Year
2010	2,075	2,454	--	--	--
2009	1,688	1,926	1,955	2,008	7,577
2008	1,985	2,322	2,317	1,955	8,579
2007	1,619	1,880	1,865	1,952	7,316
2006	1,499	1,701	1,713	1,643	6,556
2005	1,215	1,405	1,485	1,584	5,689

Earnings Per Share ($)

2010	0.50	0.59	E0.59	E0.62	E2.30
2009	0.50	0.54	0.57	0.52	2.13
2008	0.50	0.52	0.54	0.52	2.08
2007	0.42	0.47	0.48	0.49	1.86
2006	0.33	0.38	0.40	0.42	1.53
2005	0.24	0.29	0.31	0.33	1.16

Fiscal year ended Dec. 31. Next earnings report expected: NA. EPS Estimates based on S&P Operating Earnings; historical GAAP earnings are as reported.

Dividend Data (Dates: mm/dd Payment Date: mm/dd/yy)

Amount ($)	Date Decl.	Ex-Div. Date	Stk. of Record	Payment Date
0.250	02/12	09/01	09/03	10/01/10

Dividends have been paid since 1997. Source: Company reports.

Please read the Required Disclosures and Analyst Certification on the last page of this report.

The McGraw·Hill Companies

C.H. Robinson Worldwide Inc

STANDARD &POOR'S

Business Summary September 30, 2010

CORPORATE OVERVIEW. With 2009 gross revenues of about $7.6 billion, C.H. Robinson Worldwide is one of the largest third-party logistics companies in North America. At February 2, 2010, the company provided multimodal transportation services and logistics solutions through a network of 235 offices in North America, South America, Europe and Asia. In 2009, gross profits were divided as follows: 88% from transportation, 9% from sourcing, and 3% from information services. Within the transportation segment, CHRW offers several modes of service, including trucks (86% of gross profits in the transportation segment in 2009), intermodal (3%), ocean (4%), air (3%), and miscellaneous (4%).

Through contracts with about 50,000 transportation companies, including motor carriers, railroads, and air freight and ocean carriers, the company maintains the largest network of motor carrier capacity in North America. One of the largest third-party providers of intermodal services in the U.S., it also provides air, ocean and customs services. In addition, CHRW operates value-added logistics services, including fresh produce sourcing, freight consolidation and cross-docking. In 2009, the company handled about 7.5 million shipments for more than 35,000 customers.

CORPORATE STRATEGY. CHRW has historically grown through internal growth, by expanding current offices, opening new branch offices and hiring additional sales people. Growth has also been augmented through selective acquisitions. In February 2005, the company acquired three produce sourcing and marketing companies: FoodSource Inc., FoodSource Procurement, LLC, and Epic Roots, Inc. The three companies had about $270 million in gross revenues in 2004. In the third quarter of 2005, CHRW purchased two freight forwarding businesses: Hirdes Group Worldwide and Bussini Transport S.r.l., with combined gross revenues of about $52 million in 2004. In May 2006, CHRW acquired certain assets of Paine Lynch and Associates, a third-party logistics company, for $30 million. In July 2007, CHRW purchased LXSI Services, a third-party domestic air and expedited services provider with gross revenues of about $25 million.

Company Financials Fiscal Year Ended Dec. 31

Per Share Data ($)	2009	2008	2007	2006	2005	2004	2003	2002	2001	2000
Tangible Book Value	4.14	4.46	4.47	3.86	3.11	2.60	2.09	1.59	1.23	0.85
Cash Flow	2.31	2.24	2.00	1.66	1.27	0.86	0.73	0.64	0.60	0.52
Earnings	2.13	2.08	1.86	1.53	1.16	0.80	0.67	0.56	0.49	0.42
S&P Core Earnings	2.13	2.08	1.86	1.53	1.16	0.79	0.63	0.56	0.47	NA
Dividends	0.25	0.90	0.75	0.57	0.36	0.26	0.18	0.13	0.11	0.08
Payout Ratio	12%	43%	0%	37%	31%	32%	27%	23%	21%	19%
Prices:High	61.69	67.36	58.19	55.18	41.70	28.20	21.50	17.70	16.13	16.44
Prices:Low	37.36	36.50	42.11	35.55	23.60	18.30	13.50	12.92	11.41	8.58
P/E Ratio:High	29	32	31	36	36	35	32	32	33	40
P/E Ratio:Low	18	18	23	23	20	23	20	23	23	21

Income Statement Analysis (Million $)	2009	2008	2007	2006	2005	2004	2003	2002	2001	2000
Revenue	7,577	8,579	7,316	6,556	5,689	4,342	3,614	3,294	3,090	2,882
Operating Income	615	598	534	439	345	235	195	171	153	134
Depreciation	30.5	26.9	24.1	23.9	18.5	11.8	11.0	14.0	19.1	17.3
Interest Expense	NA	Nil	Nil	Nil	Nil	Nil	Nil	Nil	Nil	Nil
Pretax Income	587	578	524	430	333	226	186	158	138	118
Effective Tax Rate	38.5%	37.9%	38.1%	37.9%	38.9%	39.3%	38.7%	39.0%	39.3%	39.5%
Net Income	361	359	324	267	203	137	114	96.3	84.0	71.2
S&P Core Earnings	361	359	324	267	203	136	107	94.9	79.8	NA

Balance Sheet & Other Financial Data (Million $)	2009	2008	2007	2006	2005	2004	2003	2002	2001	2000
Cash	386	497	455	349	231	166	199	133	116	79.9
Current Assets	1,307	1,348	1,389	1,256	1,085	846	717	589	503	460
Total Assets	1,834	1,816	1,811	1,632	1,395	1,081	908	778	683	644
Current Liabilities	732	698	758	687	612	453	381	343	324	346
Long Term Debt	NA	Nil	Nil	Nil	Nil	Nil	Nil	Nil	Nil	Nil
Common Equity	1,080	1,107	1,042	944	780	621	517	426	356	297
Total Capital	1,080	1,107	1,042	944	782	621	524	432	359	298
Capital Expenditures	34.5	23.8	43.7	43.2	21.8	34.7	8.57	17.3	17.1	15.5
Cash Flow	391	386	348	291	222	149	125	110	103	88.6
Current Ratio	1.8	1.9	1.8	1.8	1.8	1.9	1.9	1.7	1.6	1.3
% Long Term Debt of Capitalization	Nil	Nil	Nil	Nil	Nil	Nil	Nil	Nil	Nil	Nil
% Net Income of Revenue	4.8	4.2	4.4	4.1	3.6	3.2	3.2	2.9	2.7	2.5
% Return on Assets	19.8	19.8	18.8	17.6	16.4	13.8	13.5	13.2	12.7	12.2
% Return on Equity	33.0	33.4	32.7	31.0	29.0	24.1	24.2	24.6	25.7	26.2

Data as orig reptd.; bef. results of disc opers/spec. items. Per share data adj. for stk. divs.; EPS diluted. E-Estimated. NA-Not Available. NM-Not Meaningful. NR-Not Ranked. UR-Under Review.

Office: 14701 Charlson Rd, Eden Prairie, MN 55347-5076.
Telephone: 952-937-8500.
Website: http://www.chrobinson.com
Chrmn, Pres & CEO: J.P. Wiehoff

SVP, CFO & Chief Acctg Officer: C.M. Lindbloom
Treas: T.A. Renner
Secy & General Counsel: B.G. Campbell
Investor Contact: A. Freeman (952-937-7847)

Board Members: R. Ezrilov, W. M. Fortun, D. W. MacLennan, S. L. Polacek, R. K. Roloff, B. Short, J. B. Stake, M. W. Wickham, J. P. Wiehoff

Founded: 1905
Domicile: Delaware
Employees: 7,347

The McGraw-Hill Companies

Chubb Corp (The)

**STANDARD
&POOR'S**

S&P Recommendation **BUY** ★★★★☆	Price $57.92 (as of Oct 22, 2010)	12-Mo. Target Price $67.00	Investment Style Large-Cap Blend

GICS Sector Financials
Sub-Industry Property & Casualty Insurance

Summary One of the largest U.S. property-casualty insurers, Chubb has carved out a number of niches, including high-end personal lines and specialty liability lines coverage.

Key Stock Statistics (Source S&P, Vickers, company reports)

52-Wk Range	$59.18– 47.10	S&P Oper. EPS 2010**E**	5.82	Market Capitalization(B)	$18.219	Beta	0.47
Trailing 12-Month EPS	$6.70	S&P Oper. EPS 2011**E**	6.15	Yield (%)	2.56	S&P 3-Yr. Proj. EPS CAGR(%)	2
Trailing 12-Month P/E	8.6	P/E on S&P Oper. EPS 2010**E**	10.0	Dividend Rate/Share	$1.48	S&P Credit Rating	A+
$10K Invested 5 Yrs Ago	$15,316	Common Shares Outstg. (M)	314.5	Institutional Ownership (%)	84		

Price Performance

30-Week Mov. Avg. ··· 10-Week Mov. Avg. – – **GAAP Earnings vs. Previous Year** Volume Above Avg. |ılıl STARS
12-Mo. Target Price — Relative Strength ▲ Up ▼ Down ▶ No Change Below Avg. |ılıl ★

2007 2008 2009 2010

Options: ASE, CBOE, P, Ph

Highlights

▶ The 12-month target price for CB has recently been changed to $67.00 from $60.00. The Highlights section of this Stock Report will be updated accordingly.

Investment Rationale/Risk

▶ The Investment Rationale/Risk section of this Stock Report will be updated shortly. For the latest News story on CB from MarketScope, see below.

▶ 10/21/10 05:15 pm ET ... S&P MAINTAINS BUY RECOMMENDATION ON SHARES OF CHUBB CORPORATION (CB 58.36****): CB reports Q3 operating EPS of $1.69, vs. $1.56, above consensus, and our $1.19 view, amid better than expected underwriting results and impact of share buybacks. While our outlook is tempered by erosion in top line results, we note CB is growing its overseas business. We are raising our 2010 operating EPS estimate by $0.67 to $5.82 per CB guidance. We also raise 2011's estimate by $0.65 to $6.15. Our $67 target price (raised $7) assumes the shares trade at 11X our 2011 estimate, in line with the closest peers and the midpoint of CB's historical range. /C.Seifert

Qualitative Risk Assessment

LOW	MEDIUM	HIGH

Our risk assessment reflects our view that CB is a superior underwriter with sound capital and risk management practices and an attractive mix of business. This is offset by our concerns about the impact a prolonged economic slowdown could have on CB's business, and by its exposure to catastrophe and professional liability claims.

Quantitative Evaluations

S&P Quality Ranking   A

D	C	B-	B	B+	A-	A	A+

Relative Strength Rank   MODERATE

57

LOWEST = 1   HIGHEST = 99

Revenue/Earnings Data

Revenue (Million $)

	1Q	2Q	3Q	4Q	Year
2010	3,323	3,318	--	--	--
2009	2,965	3,266	3,320	-3,465	13,016
2008	3,489	3,354	3,303	3,075	13,221
2007	3,519	3,521	3,549	3,518	14,107
2006	3,506	3,445	3,451	3,601	14,003
2005	3,449	3,451	3,479	3,703	14,082

Earnings Per Share ($)

2010	1.39	1.59	E1.69	E1.58	E5.82
2009	0.95	1.54	1.69	2.03	6.18
2008	1.77	1.27	0.73	1.13	4.92
2007	1.71	1.75	1.87	1.68	7.01
2006	1.58	1.41	1.43	1.56	5.98
2005	1.18	1.23	0.60	1.46	4.47

Fiscal year ended Dec. 31. Next earnings report expected: Late October. EPS Estimates based on S&P Operating Earnings; historical GAAP earnings are as reported.

Dividend Data (Dates: mm/dd Payment Date: mm/dd/yy)

Amount ($)	Date Decl.	Ex-Div. Date	Stk. of Record	Payment Date
0.350	12/03	12/16	12/18	01/12/10
0.370	02/24	03/17	03/19	04/06/10
0.370	06/10	06/23	06/25	07/13/10
0.370	09/02	09/15	09/17	10/05/10

Dividends have been paid since 1902. Source: Company reports.

Please read the Required Disclosures and Analyst Certification on the last page of this report.

The McGraw·Hill Companies

Chubb Corp (The)

Business Summary July 26, 2010

CORPORATE OVERVIEW. Chubb Corp.'s property-casualty operations are divided into three strategic business units: Personal Lines (33% of net written insurance premiums in 2009); Commercial Insurance (42%); and Specialty Insurance (25%). Net written premiums totaled $11.08 billion in 2009, down 6% from net written premiums of $11.78 billion recorded in 2008. During 2009, 76% of CB's written premiums originated in the United States, while 24% was derived from overseas.

The Personal Lines division offers primarily automobile and homeowners insurance coverage. The company's products are typically targeted to individuals with upscale homes and automobiles, requiring more coverage choices and higher policy limits than are offered under standard insurance policies. Net written premiums totaled $3.7 billion in 2009 (down 2.6% from $3.8 billion in 2008), and were divided as follows: homeowners 64%, automobile 16%, and other (mainly personal article coverage) 20%.

Chubb Commercial Insurance underwrites an array of commercial insurance

policies, including those for multiple peril, casualty, workers' compensation, and property and marine coverage. Net written premiums totaled $4.66 billion in 2009 (down 6.6% from $4.99 billion in 2008) and were divided as follows: commercial casualty 32%, commercial multi-peril 24%, property and marine 27%, and workers' compensation 17%.

Chubb Specialty Insurance offers a variety of specialized executive protection and professional liability products for privately and publicly owned companies, financial institutions, professional firms, and health care organizations. Net written premiums totaled $2.74 billion in 2009 (down 5.5% from $2.90 billion in 2008), and were divided as follows: professional liability 88%, and surety 12%. Reinsurance assumed totaled $21 million in 2009, down from $64 million in 2008.

Company Financials Fiscal Year Ended Dec. 31

Per Share Data ($)	2009	2008	2007	2006	2005	2004	2003	2002	2001	2000
Tangible Book Value	50.03	36.63	37.31	32.57	28.56	25.06	21.50	18.67	17.81	18.58
Operating Earnings	NA	NA	NA	NA	NA	NA	NA	0.58	0.31	1.91
Earnings	6.18	4.92	7.01	5.98	4.47	4.01	2.23	0.65	0.32	2.01
S&P Core Earnings	6.14	5.58	6.41	5.63	3.87	3.63	2.08	0.42	0.19	NA
Dividends	1.40	1.32	1.45	1.00	1.08	0.78	0.72	0.70	0.68	0.66
Payout Ratio	23%	27%	21%	17%	24%	19%	32%	109%	NM	33%
Prices:High	53.79	69.39	55.99	54.73	49.73	38.73	34.65	39.32	43.31	45.13
Prices:Low	34.44	33.47	45.65	46.61	36.51	31.50	20.89	25.96	27.77	21.63
P/E Ratio:High	9	14	8	9	11	10	16	61	NM	23
P/E Ratio:Low	6	7	7	8	8	8	9	40	NM	11

Income Statement Analysis (Million $)										
Premium Income	11,331	11,828	11,946	11,958	12,176	11,636	10,183	8,035	6,656	6,146
Net Investment Income	1,649	1,732	1,738	1,580	1,408	1,256	1,118	997	983	957
Other Revenue	36.0	-339	423	465	12,675	286	93.2	57.7	115	6,294
Total Revenue	13,016	13,221	14,107	14,003	14,082	13,177	11,394	9,140	7,754	7,252
Pretax Income	2,954	2,537	3,937	3,525	2,447	2,068	934	168	-66.0	851
Net Operating Income	NA	NA	NA	NA	NA	NA	NA	201	111	681
Net Income	2,183	1,804	2,807	2,528	1,826	1,548	809	223	112	715
S&P Core Earnings	2,168	2,045	2,564	2,378	1,578	1,402	754	146	65.2	NA

Balance Sheet & Other Financial Data (Million $)										
Cash & Equivalent	511	491	489	449	427	392	1,044	1,644	691	720
Premiums Due	2,101	2,201	2,227	2,314	2,319	2,336	2,188	6,112	6,198	3,263
Investment Assets:Bonds	36,578	32,755	33,871	31,966	30,523	28,009	22,412	18,263	16,117	15,564
Investment Assets:Stocks	1,433	1,479	2,320	1,957	2,212	1,841	1,514	795	710	831
Investment Assets:Loans	Nil	Nil	Nil	Nil	Nil	Nil	Nil	Nil	Nil	Nil
Investment Assets:Total	42,004	38,738	40,081	37,693	34,893	31,504	26,934	21,279	17,784	17,001
Deferred Policy Costs	1,533	1,532	1,556	1,480	1,445	1,435	1,343	1,150	929	842
Total Assets	50,449	48,429	50,574	50,277	48,061	44,260	38,361	34,114	29,449	25,027
Debt	3,975	3,975	3,460	1,791	2,467	2,814	2,814	1,959	2,901	754
Common Equity	15,634	13,432	14,445	13,863	12,407	10,126	8,522	6,859	6,525	6,982
Property & Casualty:Loss Ratio	55.4	58.5	52.8	55.2	64.3	63.1	67.6	75.4	80.8	67.5
Property & Casualty:Expense Ratio	30.6	30.2	30.1	29.0	28.0	29.2	30.4	31.3	32.6	32.9
Property & Casualty Combined Ratio	86.0	88.7	82.9	84.2	92.3	92.3	98.0	106.7	113.4	100.4
% Return on Revenue	16.8	13.6	19.8	18.1	13.0	11.8	7.1	2.4	1.4	9.9
% Return on Equity	NA	12.9	19.8	19.2	16.2	16.6	10.5	3.3	1.7	10.8

Data as orig reptd.; bef. results of disc opers/spec. items. Per share data adj. for stk. divs.; EPS diluted. E-Estimated. NA-Not Available. NM-Not Meaningful. NR-Not Ranked. UR-Under Review.

Office: 15 Mountain View Road, Warren, NJ 07061-1615.
Telephone: 908-903-2000.
Email: info@chubb.com
Website: http://www.chubb.com

Chrmn, Pres & CEO: J.D. Finnegan
COO: J.J. Degnan
EVP & CFO: R.G. Spiro
EVP & General Counsel: M.A. Brundage

SVP & Chief Acctg Officer: J.J. Kennedy
Investor Contact: G.A. Montgomery (908-903-2365)
Board Members: Z. Baird, S. P. Burke, J. I. Cash, Jr., J. D. Finnegan, M. G. McGuinn, S. R. Pozzi, L. M. Small, J. Soderberg, D. Somers, K. H. Williams, J. M. Zimmerman, A. W. Zollar

Founded: 1967
Domicile: New Jersey
Employees: 10,200

CIGNA Corp.

STANDARD &POOR'S

S&P Recommendation [BUY] ★★★★☆

Price	12-Mo. Target Price	Investment Style
$36.17 (as of Oct 22, 2010)	$39.00	Large-Cap Growth

GICS Sector Health Care
Sub-Industry Managed Health Care

Summary CIGNA is one of the largest investor-owned employee benefits organizations in the U.S. Its subsidiaries are major providers of employee benefits offered through the workplace.

Key Stock Statistics (Source S&P, Vickers, company reports)

52-Wk Range	$39.26–27.20	S&P Oper. EPS 2010**E**	4.35	Market Capitalization(B)	$9.845	Beta		1.58
Trailing 12-Month EPS	$4.47	S&P Oper. EPS 2011**E**	4.60	Yield (%)	0.11	S&P 3-Yr. Proj. EPS CAGR(%)		7
Trailing 12-Month P/E	8.1	P/E on S&P Oper. EPS 2010**E**	8.3	Dividend Rate/Share	$0.04	S&P Credit Rating		BBB
$10K Invested 5 Yrs Ago	$9,555	Common Shares Outstg. (M)	272.2	Institutional Ownership (%)	83			

Price Performance

30-Week Mov. Avg. ··· 10-Week Mov. Avg. --- GAAP Earnings vs. Previous Year   Volume Above Avg. STARS
12-Mo. Target Price — Relative Strength   ▲ Up ▼ Down ▶ No Change   Below Avg. ★

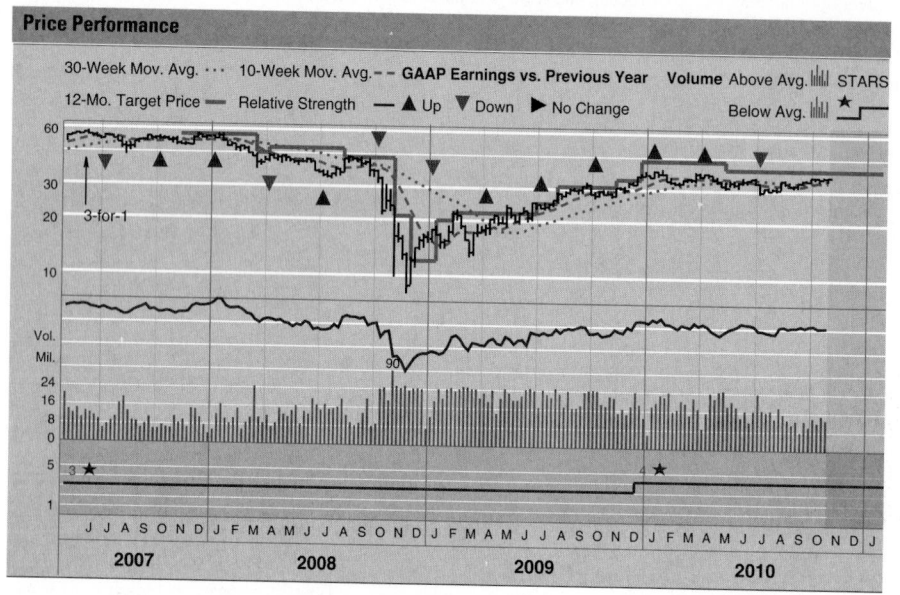

Options: ASE, CBOE, P, Ph

Analysis prepared by **Phillip M. Seligman** on August 12, 2010, when the stock traded at **$ 33.42**.

Highlights

➤ We look for health care segment revenue to rise about 14% in 2010, on higher premiums and 3% more members. We see medical enrollment growth driven by 98,000 additional Medicare Advantage (MA; Medicare health plan) Private Fee-for-Service members, mid single-digit growth in commercial middle-market (250 - 5,000 members) and select (50 - 250) accounts, and 40%-plus growth in individual/small business (2-50) market enrollment outweighing a mid single-digit decline in national account (5,000-plus) enrollment.

➤ We expect commercial medical costs to decline as a percentage of premiums (MCR: medical cost ratio), on the favorable impact of prior-year claims reserve development and lower utilization levels in the first half. However, we see a higher firmwide MCR partly on the higher percentage of MA enrollment. Elsewhere, we look for the more profitable group disability and life and international segments to continue to expand.

➤ We estimate operating EPS of $4.35 in 2010, versus $3.98 in 2009 before $0.75 of net one-time gains. We look for $4.60 in 2011.

Investment Rationale/Risk

➤ We believe CI lost a greater percentage of commercial members than peers in 2009 amid the soft economy. Hence, we are encouraged that its new products thus far appear to be enjoying strong retention rates and membership gains in the individual, small-group, and middle markets, outweighing national account losses. In addition, we think CI has made gains in improving its health care segment's operating cost structure, but has much more work to do. Elsewhere, we are also encouraged by CI's intention to focus more on its international business, given rising demand overseas for life, accident, and health products and private health insurance to supplement government-run programs. We also view CI as well capitalized and think its investment portfolio and cash flow is healthy.

➤ Risks to our recommendation and target price include intensified competition and higher-than-expected medical costs.

➤ Our 12-month target price of $39 assumes a slightly below-peer forward multiple of 9X our 2010 EPS estimate.

Qualitative Risk Assessment

LOW	MEDIUM	HIGH

Our risk assessment reflects our view of CI's improving cost structure, strong cash flow, diversity, and wide range of products. However, competition is intensifying in the managed care market, and CI's focus on maintaining pricing discipline in a weak economy has contributed to declines in enrollment.

Quantitative Evaluations

S&P Quality Ranking   B

D	C	B-	B	B+	A-	A	A+

Relative Strength Rank   MODERATE

62

LOWEST = 1   HIGHEST = 99

Revenue/Earnings Data

Revenue (Million $)

	1Q	2Q	3Q	4Q	Year
2010	5,205	5,353	--	--	--
2009	4,773	4,488	4,517	4,636	18,414
2008	4,569	4,863	4,852	4,817	19,101
2007	4,374	4,381	4,413	4,455	17,623
2006	4,107	4,098	4,137	4,205	16,547
2005	4,345	4,107	4,022	4,210	16,684

Earnings Per Share ($)

	1Q	2Q	3Q	4Q	Year
2010	1.02	1.06	E0.99	E0.92	E4.35
2009	0.76	1.58	1.19	1.19	4.73
2008	0.20	0.98	0.62	-0.78	1.04
2007	0.93	0.75	1.28	0.93	3.88
2006	0.96	0.78	0.93	0.76	3.44
2005	1.09	0.94	0.67	0.59	3.28

Fiscal year ended Dec. 31. Next earnings report expected: Early November. EPS Estimates based on S&P Operating Earnings; historical GAAP earnings are as reported.

Dividend Data (Dates: mm/dd Payment Date: mm/dd/yy)

Amount ($)	Date Decl.	Ex-Div. Date	Stk. of Record	Payment Date
0.040	02/24	03/09	03/11	04/12/10

Dividends have been paid since 1867. Source: Company reports.

Please read the Required Disclosures and Analyst Certification on the last page of this report.

The McGraw-Hill Companies

STANDARD &POOR'S

CIGNA Corp.

Business Summary August 12, 2010

CORPORATE OVERVIEW. CIGNA Corp., one of the largest U.S. employee benefits organizations, provides health care products and services and group life, accident and disability insurance.

Health Care offers group medical, dental, behavioral health and pharmacy services products. Medical products include consumer directed health plans (CDHPs), HMOs, network only, point-of-service (POS) plans, preferred provider organizations (PPOs), and traditional indemnity coverage. The health care products and services are offered through guaranteed cost, retrospectively experience-rated, administrative services only (ASO) and minimum premium funding arrangements. Under ASO, the employer or other plan sponsor self-funds all of its claims and assumes the risk for claim costs incurred. CI's CDHPs offer a modular product portfolio that provides a choice of benefits network and various funding, medical management, consumerism and health advocacy options for employers and consumers.

Medical covered lives as of June 30, 2010, totaled 11,365,000 (versus

11,040,000 as of December 31, 2009): 1,113,000 (1,001,000) guaranteed cost (commercial HMO and voluntary/limited benefits); 826,000 (761,000) experience-related indemnity; 147,000 (52,000) Medicare) and 9,279,000 (9,226,000) ASO.

Disability and Life, which provides employer-paid and voluntary life, accident and disability products, held group life insurance policies covering 4.7 million lives at year-end 2009, down from 6.2 million at year-end 2008. International operates in selected markets outside the U.S., providing individual and group life, accident and health, health care and pension products. CI's invested assets under management at year-end 2008 totaled $19.8 billion, versus $18.0 billion at year-end 2008.

Company Financials Fiscal Year Ended Dec. 31

Per Share Data ($)	2009	2008	2007	2006	2005	2004	2003	2002	2001	2000
Tangible Book Value	10.35	0.21	13.93	8.73	10.30	9.05	6.85	2.74	7.62	7.75
Operating Earnings	NA	NA	NA	NA	NA	NA	NA	NA	2.45	2.02
Earnings	4.73	1.04	3.88	3.44	3.28	3.81	1.47	-0.94	2.20	2.03
S&P Core Earnings	4.76	1.21	4.10	3.34	2.80	2.62	1.21	-0.24	1.77	NA
Dividends	0.04	NA	0.04	0.03	0.03	0.14	0.44	0.44	0.43	0.41
Relative Payout	1%	NA	1%	1%	1%	4%	30%	NM	19%	20%
Prices:High	38.12	NA	57.61	44.59	39.94	27.76	19.53	37.00	44.98	45.58
Prices:Low	12.68	NA	42.33	29.35	26.04	17.63	13.03	11.38	23.29	20.25
P/E Ratio:High	8	NA	15	13	12	7	13	NM	20	22
P/E Ratio:Low	3	NA	11	9	8	5	9	NM	11	10

Income Statement Analysis (Million $)	2009	2008	2007	2006	2005	2004	2003	2002	2001	2000
Life Insurance in Force	615,794	NA	475,346	NA	NA	NA	459,995	516,661	609,970	647,464
Premium Income:Life A & H	16,041	NA	15,008	13,641	13,695	14,236	15,441	15,737	15,367	16,328
Premium Income:Casualty/Property.	Nil	NA	Nil	Nil	Nil	Nil	Nil	Nil	Nil	Nil
Net Investment Income	1,014	NA	1,114	1,195	1,359	1,643	2,594	2,716	2,843	2,942
Total Revenue	18,414	19,101	17,623	16,547	16,684	18,176	18,808	19,348	19,115	19,994
Pretax Income	1,301	288	1,631	1,731	1,793	2,375	903	-569	1,497	1,497
Net Operating Income	NA	NA	NA	NA	NA	NA	NA	NA	1,101	983
Net Income	1,301	288	1,120	1,159	1,276	1,577	620	-397	989	987
S&P Core Earnings	1,309	335	1,180	1,127	1,090	1,082	509	-99.2	794	NA

Balance Sheet & Other Financial Data (Million $)	2009	2008	2007	2006	2005	2004	2003	2002	2001	2000
Cash & Equivalent	1,162	1,439	2,203	1,647	1,991	2,804	1,860	2,079	2,455	2,739
Premiums Due	7,958	NA	8,736	9,501	8,616	16,223	9,421	9,981	2,832	2,814
Investment Assets:Bonds	13,443	NA	12,081	12,155	14,947	16,136	17,121	27,803	23,401	24,776
Investment Assets:Stocks	113	NA	132	131	135	33.0	11,300	295	404	569
Investment Assets:Loans	5,071	NA	4,727	5,393	5,271	5,123	10,227	11,134	12,694	12,755
Investment Assets:Total	19,839	17,921	17,530	18,303	21,376	21,919	39,658	40,362	38,261	41,516
Deferred Policy Costs	943	NA	816	707	618	544	580	494	448	1,052
Total Assets	43,013	41,406	40,065	42,399	44,863	81,059	90,953	88,950	91,589	95,088
Debt	2,436	NA	1,790	1,294	1,338	1,438	1,500	1,500	1,627	1,163
Common Equity	5,417	3,592	4,748	4,330	5,360	5,203	4,465	3,665	5,055	5,634
Combined Loss-Expense Ratio	NA	NA	NA	NA	NA	NA	NA	NA	NA	NA
% Return on Revenue	7.1	1.5	6.4	7.0	7.6	8.7	3.3	NM	5.2	4.9
% Return on Equity	28.9	NA	24.7	23.9	24.2	32.2	15.3	NM	18.9	16.5
% Investment Yield	5.4	6.0	6.3	6.0	6.3	5.3	6.5	6.9	7.3	7.1

Data as orig reptd.; bef. results of disc opers/spec. items. Per share data adj. for stk. divs.; EPS diluted. E-Estimated. NA-Not Available. NM-Not Meaningful. NR-Not Ranked. UR-Under Review.

Office: Two Liberty Place, 1601 Chestnut Street, Philadelphia, PA 19192.
Telephone: 215-761-1000.
Website: http://www.cigna.com
Chrmn: I. Harris, Jr.

Pres & CEO: D.M. Cordani
EVP & General Counsel: C.A. Petren
EVP & CIO: P. Emond
CFO: T.A. McCarthy

Investor Contact: T. Detrick (215-761-1414)
Board Members: D. M. Cordani, I. Harris, Jr., J. E. Henney, P. Larson, R. Martinez, IV, J. Partridge, J. E. Rogers, Jr., J. P. Sullivan, C. C. Wait, E. C. Wiseman, D. F. Zarcone, W. D. Zollars

Founded: 1792
Domicile: Delaware
Employees: 29,300

The McGraw-Hill Companies

Cincinnati Financial Corp

STANDARD &POOR'S

S&P Recommendation HOLD ★★★☆☆

Price	12-Mo. Target Price	Investment Style
$30.49 (as of Oct 22, 2010)	$30.00	Large-Cap Blend

GICS Sector Financials
Sub-Industry Property & Casualty Insurance

Summary This insurance holding company markets primarily property and casualty coverage. It also conducts life insurance and asset management operations.

Key Stock Statistics (Source S&P, Vickers, company reports)

52-Wk Range	$30.70– 25.05	S&P Oper. EPS 2010E	1.43	Market Capitalization(B)	$4.960	Beta	0.72
Trailing 12-Month EPS	$3.13	S&P Oper. EPS 2011E	1.85	Yield (%)	5.25	S&P 3-Yr. Proj. EPS CAGR(%)	1
Trailing 12-Month P/E	9.7	P/E on S&P Oper. EPS 2010E	21.3	Dividend Rate/Share	$1.60	S&P Credit Rating	BBB
$10K Invested 5 Yrs Ago	$9,347	Common Shares Outstg. (M)	162.7	Institutional Ownership (%)	62		

Price Performance

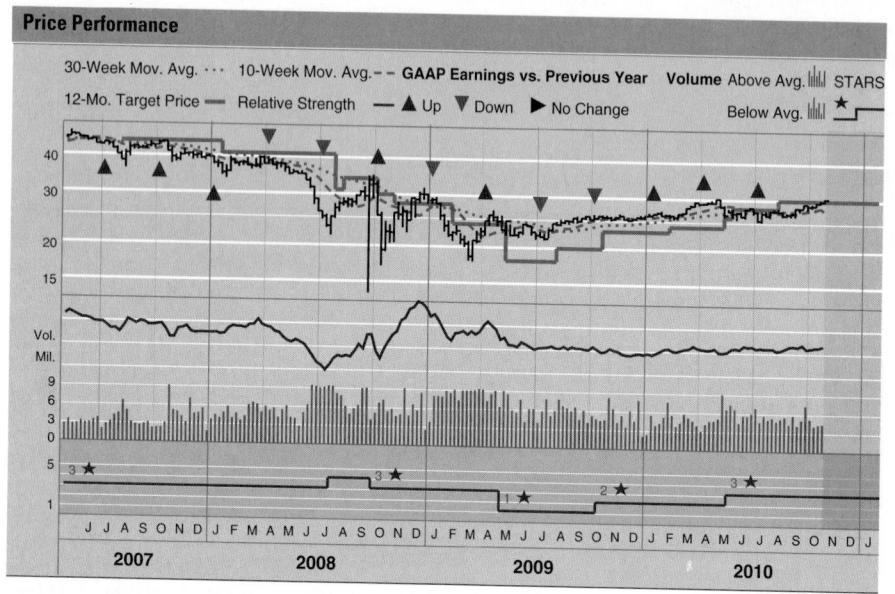

30-Week Mov. Avg. · · · 10-Week Mov. Avg. - - GAAP Earnings vs. Previous Year Volume Above Avg. STARS
12-Mo. Target Price — Relative Strength — ▲ Up ▼ Down ▶ No Change Below Avg.

Options: CBOE, P

Analysis prepared by **Cathy A. Seifert** on August 06, 2010, when the stock traded at **$ 27.47**.

Qualitative Risk Assessment

LOW	**MEDIUM**	HIGH

Our risk assessment reflects our view of the company as a fairly conservative underwriter with sound risk and capital management policies. However, CINF's investment allocation is more heavily weighted than peers toward equity holdings, although the company has taken steps to re-balance its investments.

Quantitative Evaluations

S&P Quality Ranking A

D	C	B-	B	B+	A-	**A**	A+

Relative Strength Rank MODERATE

70

LOWEST = 1   HIGHEST = 99

Revenue/Earnings Data

Revenue (Million $)

	1Q	2Q	3Q	4Q	Year
2010	887.0	878.0	--	--	--
2009	890.0	874.0	1,007	1,133	3,903
2008	704.0	917.0	1,186	1,018	3,824
2007	1,031	1,270	982.0	983.0	4,259
2006	1,607	981.0	967.0	995.0	4,550
2005	916.0	940.0	944.0	967.0	3,767

Earnings Per Share ($)

	1Q	2Q	3Q	4Q	Year
2010	0.42	0.17	E0.33	E0.48	E1.43
2009	0.22	-0.12	1.05	1.50	2.65
2008	-0.25	0.38	1.50	0.99	2.63
2007	1.11	2.02	0.72	1.11	4.97
2006	3.13	0.76	0.66	0.75	5.30
2005	0.81	0.89	0.66	1.03	3.40

Fiscal year ended Dec. 31. Next earnings report expected: Early November. EPS Estimates based on S&P Operating Earnings; historical GAAP earnings are as reported.

Dividend Data (Dates: mm/dd Payment Date: mm/dd/yy)

Amount ($)	Date Decl.	Ex-Div. Date	Stk. of Record	Payment Date
0.395	02/01	03/22	03/24	04/15/10
0.395	05/24	06/21	06/23	07/15/10
0.400	08/16	09/20	09/22	10/15/10
0.400	08/13	09/20	09/22	10/15/10

Dividends have been paid since 1954. Source: Company reports.

Highlights

▶ We expect property-casualty earned premiums to decline 1% to 2% in 2010, following a 2.6% drop in 2009. We see the effects of CINF's expansion being offset (albeit to a lesser degree) by price competition. Competition in many non-coastal regions (such as those where CINF operates) is expected to remain intense. Underwriting margins may narrow in 2010, particularly if catastrophe losses return to more "normal" levels. This impact may be offset by cost-cutting initiatives that CINF has undertaken.

▶ We estimate that net investment income will advance modestly in 2010, after declining 6.8% in 2009. The drop in investment income CINF experienced was worse than the results experienced by many of the company's peers, partly reflecting a different asset mix. CINF has taken steps in recent periods to shift its invested asset mix. As of December 31, 2009, 25% of CINF's invested assets were in equity securities (versus 33% at December 31, 2008). This compares to an industry average that we estimate at less than 15%.

▶ We estimate operating EPS of $1.43 in 2010 and $1.85 in 2011, versus $1.32 in 2009 and $2.10 in 2008.

Investment Rationale/Risk

▶ At current levels, we view the shares as adequately valued, and at a premium versus most peers, particularly on a price to operating earnings basis. Our outlook still reflects what we see as the dual challenges of continued price competition in many of CINF's core lines of business and a challenging investment environment. We believe CINF's results on both of those fronts lag many peers. We also see a high degree of execution risk in a number of the company's expansion strategies. We also note that the $1.58 indicated annual dividend exceeds our 2010 operating earnings per share estimate.

▶ Risks to our opinion and target price include a significant downturn in underwriting results (including an erosion in earned premiums and a significant narrowing of underwriting margins), and a greater than anticipated deterioration in investment results.

▶ Our 12-month target price of $30 assumes the shares will trade at approximately 16.2X our 2011 operating EPS estimate, a premium of at least 40% to most of the company's peers, and at the upper end of CINF's historical range.

Please read the Required Disclosures and Analyst Certification on the last page of this report.

The McGraw·Hill Companies

Cincinnati Financial Corp

Business Summary August 06, 2010

CORPORATE OVERVIEW. Cincinnati Financial Corp. (CINF) underwrites and sells property-casualty insurance primarily in the Midwest and Southeast, through a network of independent agents. Operations as of year-end 2009 were conducted in 37 states, through a network of approximately 1,680 independent insurance agencies, many of which own stock in the company. The company is licensed in all 50 states, the District of Columbia, and Puerto Rico. An ongoing geographical expansion plan is being implemented. Ten states accounted for about 68% of earned premium volume in 2009 (latest available): Ohio (21%), Illinois (9%), Indiana (7%), Pennsylvania (6%), North Carolina (5%), Georgia (5%), Michigan (4%), Virginia (4%), Wisconsin (4%), and Kentucky (3%).

Property-casualty net earned premiums totaled $2.9 billion in 2009, with commercial lines accounting for 76% and personal lines for 23% and excess and surplus lines for 1%. During 2009, commercial casualty lines of coverage accounted for 32% of commercial lines earned premiums, while commercial property lines coverage accounted for 22%, commercial auto for 18%, workers' compensation for 15%, special package coverages for 7%, surety and executive risk for 5%, and other for 1%. Personal auto accounted for 47% of personal lines earned premiums in 2009, homeowners' coverage for 40%, and other personal lines for 13%.

Underwriting results deteriorated in 2009 and 2008, largely due to an elevated level of catastrophe losses. The loss ratio in 2009 equaled 71.7% (including 5.7 points of catastrophe losses), versus 68.3% in 2008 (including 6.8 points of catastrophe losses). The expense ratio inched upward, to 32.8%, from 32.3%. Taken together, the combined ratio (before policyholder dividends) equaled 104.5% in 2009, a deterioration from 2008's combined ratio of 100.6%. (A combined ratio of under 100% indicates an underwriting profit, while one in excess of 100% signals an underwriting loss.)

Life, accident and health insurance is marketed through property-casualty agents and independent life insurance agents. This unit has been expanding its work site marketing activities, introducing a new product line and exploring expansion opportunities. Term life insurance represents this unit's largest product line. Life insurance earned premiums totaled $143 million in 2009, up from earned premiums of $126 million in 2008.

Company Financials Fiscal Year Ended Dec. 31

Per Share Data ($)	2009	2008	2007	2006	2005	2004	2003	2002	2001	2000
Tangible Book Value	29.38	22.67	32.94	39.38	34.88	35.60	35.10	31.42	33.62	33.80
Operating Earnings	NA	NA	NA	2.82	3.02	2.93	NA	1.67	1.17	0.82
Earnings	2.65	2.63	4.97	5.30	3.40	3.28	2.10	1.32	1.08	0.66
S&P Core Earnings	1.28	2.16	3.49	2.78	3.10	2.87	2.09	1.55	1.06	NA
Dividends	1.57	1.56	1.42	1.34	1.21	1.04	0.91	0.81	0.76	0.69
Relative Payout	59%	59%	29%	25%	35%	32%	43%	61%	71%	104%
Prices:High	29.66	40.24	48.45	49.19	45.95	43.52	38.01	42.90	38.94	39.29
Prices:Low	17.84	13.68	36.00	41.21	38.38	36.57	30.00	29.42	30.84	23.75
P/E Ratio:High	11	15	10	9	14	13	18	32	36	59
P/E Ratio:Low	7	5	7	8	11	11	14	22	29	36

Income Statement Analysis (Million $)	2009	2008	2007	2006	2005	2004	2003	2002	2001	2000
Life Insurance in Force	69,814	65,887	61,873	56,971	51,493	44,921	48,492	32,486	27,534	23,525
Premium Income:Life A & H	143	126	125	115	106	101	95.0	87.0	81.0	79.3
Premium Income:Casualty/Property.	2,911	3,010	3,125	3,163	3,058	2,919	2,653	2,391	2,071	1,828
Net Investment Income	501	537	608	570	526	492	465	445	421	415
Total Revenue	3,903	3,824	4,259	4,550	3,767	3,614	3,181	2,843	2,561	2,331
Pretax Income	582	540	1,192	1,329	823	800	480	279	221	109
Net Operating Income	NA	NA	NA	496	562	524	286	300	210	120
Net Income	432	429	855	930	602	584	374	238	193	118
S&P Core Earnings	208	354	602	487	549	512	372	279	189	NA

Balance Sheet & Other Financial Data (Million $)	2009	2008	2007	2006	2005	2004	2003	2002	2001	2000
Cash & Equivalent	557	1,009	226	202	119	306	91.0	112	93.0	60.3
Premiums Due	1,670	1,818	1,861	1,811	1,797	1,799	1,677	1,483	732	652
Investment Assets:Bonds	7,855	5,827	5,848	5,805	5,476	5,141	3,925	3,305	3,010	2,721
Investment Assets:Stocks	2,701	2,896	6,249	7,799	7,106	7,498	8,524	7,884	8,495	8,526
Investment Assets:Loans	Nil	Nil	Nil	Nil	Nil	Nil	Nil	Nil	Nil	Nil
Investment Assets:Total	10,643	8,890	12,261	13,759	12,702	12,677	12,527	11,257	11,571	11,316
Deferred Policy Costs	481	509	461	453	429	400	372	343	286	259
Total Assets	14,440	13,369	16,637	17,222	16,003	16,107	15,509	14,059	13,959	13,287
Debt	838	840	860	840	791	791	603	420	609	449
Common Equity	4,760	4,182	5,929	6,808	4,145	6,249	6,204	5,998	5,998	5,995
Combined Loss-Expense Ratio	104.5	100.6	90.3	94.3	89.2	89.8	94.7	98.4	104.9	112.5
% Return on Revenue	11.1	11.2	20.1	23.4	16.0	16.2	11.8	8.4	7.5	5.1
% Return on Equity	9.7	8.5	13.4	14.4	15.4	8.0	5.4	3.6	3.2	1.0
% Investment Yield	5.1	5.3	4.7	4.3	4.1	3.9	3.9	3.9	3.7	3.9

Data as orig reptd.; bef. results of disc opers/spec. items. Per share data adj. for stk. divs.; EPS diluted. E-Estimated. NA-Not Available. NM-Not Meaningful. NR-Not Ranked. UR-Under Review.

Office: 6200 South Gilmore Road, Fairfield, OH 45014-5141.
Telephone: 513-870-2000.
Email: investor_inquiries@cinfin.com
Website: http://www.cinfin.com

Chrmn: J.J. Schiff, Jr.
Pres & CEO: K.W. Stecher
SVP, CFO, Treas & Secy: S.J. Johnston
SVP & Chief Acctg Officer: E.N. Mathews

Investor Contact: H.J. Wietzel (513-870-2768)
Board Members: W. F. Bahl, G. T. Bier, L. Clement-Holmes, K. C. Lichtendahl, W. R. McMullen, G. W. Price, T. R. Schiff, J. J. Schiff, Jr., D. S. Skidmore, K. W. Stecher, J. F. Steele, Jr., L. R. Webb, E. A. Woods

Founded: 1950
Domicile: Ohio
Employees: 4,170

Cintas Corp

STANDARD &POOR'S

| S&P Recommendation **HOLD** ★★★★★ | Price **$28.08** (as of Oct 22, 2010) | 12-Mo. Target Price **$30.00** | Investment Style Large-Cap Growth |

GICS Sector Industrials
Sub-Industry Diversified Support Services

Summary A leader in the corporate identity uniform business, Cintas also provides entrance mats, cleaning services and supplies, first aid products, along with document management and shredding services.

Key Stock Statistics (Source S&P, Vickers, company reports)

52-Wk Range	$30.00– 23.10	S&P Oper. EPS 2011E	1.60	Market Capitalization(B)	$4.080	Beta	0.96
Trailing 12-Month EPS	$1.46	S&P Oper. EPS 2012E	1.70	Yield (%)	1.71	S&P 3-Yr. Proj. EPS CAGR(%)	7
Trailing 12-Month P/E	19.2	P/E on S&P Oper. EPS 2011E	17.6	Dividend Rate/Share	$0.48	S&P Credit Rating	A-
$10K Invested 5 Yrs Ago	$7,654	Common Shares Outstg. (M)	145.3	Institutional Ownership (%)	78		

Price Performance

30-Week Mov. Avg. · · · 10-Week Mov. Avg. - - GAAP Earnings vs. Previous Year Volume Above Avg. STARS
12-Mo. Target Price — Relative Strength — ▲ Up ▼ Down ▶ No Change Below Avg.

Analysis prepared by **Kevin Kirkeby** on September 30, 2010, when the stock traded at **$ 27.60.**

Options: ASE, CBOE, P, Ph

Highlights

➤ We forecast revenue growth of 3% in FY 11 (May), supported by a modest recovery in CTAS's rental unit, and acquisitions in its document management segment. Price competition was aggressive during much of FY 10, but we think it will lessen in coming quarters as the number of workers in industries served by CTAS rises. S&P is forecasting real GDP growth of 2.6% in calendar 2010 and 2.4% in 2011.

➤ We see margins largely unchanged during FY 11 as an improved sales performance and cost savings from facility closures and route consolidations offset rising wages and benefits. CTAS added to its sales force, even as the economy and rental volumes slowed last year. However, we think the sales team has reached the point where new business and additional work for existing customers are offsetting contract reductions. We are also assuming relatively flat diesel and natural gas prices, which are both sizable operating expenses, over the next year.

➤ Our EPS forecast of $1.60 in FY 11 reflects the 7.6 million shares CTAS has repurchased this fiscal year, mostly in August and September.

Investment Rationale/Risk

➤ Valuations have compressed during the past five years and are only modestly ahead of the S&P 500. We think this is partly due to slowing revenue growth, as CTAS's traditional customer base in manufacturing has generally been reducing headcount. At the same time, CTAS has been investing heavily in its non-uniform service offerings. Until these businesses mature and the economy improves to the point where employment moves steadily higher, we see muted net income growth.

➤ Risks to our recommendation and target price include renewed economic weakness, a rapid rise in fuel prices, declines in the prices CTAS receives for recycled paper, and regulatory changes that raise labor costs.

➤ Applying an 18.2X multiple, near the five-year average but ahead of the S&P 500, to our forward four-quarter EPS estimate, we calculate a value close to $30. Our DCF model yields an intrinsic value of $31, assuming a 9.0% weighted average cost of capital, 7% annual growth over the next five years, and 3% growth in perpetuity. Blending these valuation models results in our 12-month target price of $30.

Qualitative Risk Assessment

| LOW | MEDIUM | HIGH |

Our risk assessment reflects the company's leading position in its core business, other related services that we believe are showing growth, and what we view as a strong balance sheet and cash flow.

Quantitative Evaluations

S&P Quality Ranking A-

| D | C | B- | B | B+ | A- | A | A+ |

Relative Strength Rank MODERATE
56
LOWEST = 1   HIGHEST = 99

Revenue/Earnings Data

Revenue (Million $)

	1Q	2Q	3Q	4Q	Year
2011	923.9	--	--	--	--
2010	891.6	884.5	861.8	909.5	3,547
2009	1,002	985.2	908.6	878.7	3,775
2008	969.1	983.9	976.0	1,009	3,938
2007	914.2	923.3	905.4	964.1	3,707
2006	823.5	835.8	836.4	907.9	3,404

Earnings Per Share ($)

2011	0.40	E0.38	E0.39	E0.46	E1.60
2010	0.35	0.37	0.32	0.36	1.40
2009	0.51	0.47	0.47	0.03	1.48
2008	0.51	0.53	0.53	0.58	2.15
2007	0.53	0.51	0.48	0.57	2.09
2006	0.47	0.46	0.46	0.55	1.94

Fiscal year ended May 31. Next earnings report expected: Late December. EPS Estimates based on S&P Operating Earnings; historical GAAP earnings are as reported.

Dividend Data (Dates: mm/dd Payment Date: mm/dd/yy)

Amount ($)	Date Decl.	Ex-Div. Date	Stk. of Record	Payment Date
0.480	01/26	02/08	02/10	03/10/10

Dividends have been paid since 1984. Source: Company reports.

Please read the Required Disclosures and Analyst Certification on the last page of this report.

The McGraw·Hill Companies

STANDARD &POOR'S

Cintas Corp

Business Summary September 30, 2010

CORPORATE OVERVIEW. Cintas Corp. is North America's leading supplier of corporate uniforms, as well as a significant provider of related services. FY 09 (May) was the first time in 40 years that the company was unable to deliver an increase in revenues and net profits, reflecting the economic downturn. FY 10 marked the second time. The company reports financial results using four segments: Rental Uniforms and Ancillary Services, Uniform Direct Sales, Document Management, and First Aid, Safety & Fire Protection.

The Rental operating segment (72% of total revenues in FY 10 and 75% of gross profits, with a 43.6% margin) designs and manufactures corporate uniforms that it rents to its customers. Services provided to the rental markets by the company also include the cleaning of uniforms, as well as the provision of ongoing replacements as required by each customer. The company also offers ancillary products, including the rental or sale of entrance and special purpose mats, towels, mops, and linen products, as well as sanitation supplies and services and cleanroom supplies. It operates through about 7,700 local delivery routes (down from about 8,400 at the end FY 08 following route restructuring initiatives).

The Uniform Direct Sales segment (11%, 8%, and 30.6% margin) includes the

design, manufacture and direct sale of uniforms to CTAS's national account customers. In recent years, there has been an effort to offer more branded items in its catalogs alongside the traditional propriety uniform and apparel lines. This segment generally has less recurring business than the rental operations.

The First Aid, Safety and Fire Protection segment (10%, 9%, and 38.9% margin) provides first aid equipment, inspection, repair and recharging of portable fire extinguishers, fire suppression systems, and emergency and exit lights. In a short period of time, CTAS believes it has become the second-largest fire protection services company in the U.S., with capabilities in at least 42 of the top 50 cities. Although the company estimated the market for first aid and fire protection services to be about $4.5 billion a year, the recession and declines in non-residential construction prompted the company to re-evaluate its goals for this segment and cease providing fire protection services in certain smaller markets.

Company Financials Fiscal Year Ended May 31

Per Share Data ($)	2010	2009	2008	2007	2006	2005	2004	2003	2002	2001
Tangible Book Value	6.93	5.83	4.92	4.73	4.73	6.15	6.32	5.42	4.39	6.42
Cash Flow	2.41	2.50	3.10	2.96	2.78	2.43	2.26	2.12	1.95	1.82
Earnings	1.40	1.48	2.15	2.09	1.94	1.74	1.58	1.45	1.36	1.30
S&P Core Earnings	1.49	1.48	2.15	2.09	1.92	1.69	1.54	1.43	1.33	1.27
Dividends	0.48	0.46	0.39	0.35	0.32	0.32	0.29	0.27	0.25	0.22
Payout Ratio	34%	31%	18%	17%	16%	18%	18%	19%	18%	17%
Calendar Year	2009	2008	2007	2006	2005	2004	2003	2002	2001	2000
Prices:High	30.85	33.89	42.89	44.30	45.50	50.35	50.68	56.62	53.25	54.00
Prices:Low	18.09	19.51	31.14	34.57	37.51	39.51	30.60	39.15	33.75	23.17
P/E Ratio:High	22	23	20	21	23	29	32	42	39	42
P/E Ratio:Low	13	13	14	17	19	23	19	29	25	18

Income Statement Analysis (Million $)										
Revenue	3,547	3,775	3,938	3,707	3,404	3,067	2,814	2,687	2,271	2,161
Operating Income	564	653	726	713	674	614	602	539	478	459
Depreciation	152	158	149	135	127	120	117	115	101	90.2
Interest Expense	48.6	52.5	16.6	50.3	31.8	24.4	25.1	30.9	11.0	15.1
Pretax Income	344	362	531	534	522	477	432	396	372	356
Effective Tax Rate	NA	37.4%	36.8%	37.3%	37.3%	37.0%	37.0%	37.0%	37.0%	37.6%
Net Income	216	226	335	335	327	301	272	249	234	222
S&P Core Earnings	228	226	335	335	324	293	265	245	229	219

Balance Sheet & Other Financial Data (Million $)										
Cash	566	250	192	155	241	309	254	57.7	85.1	110
Current Assets	1,525	1,270	1,282	1,157	1,178	1,167	1,034	878	853	820
Total Assets	3,970	3,695	3,809	3,570	3,425	3,060	2,810	2,583	2,519	1,752
Current Liabilities	384	317	367	403	412	356	326	305	313	251
Long Term Debt	785	786	943	877	794	465	474	535	703	221
Common Equity	2,534	2,367	2,254	2,168	2,088	2,104	1,888	1,646	1,424	1,231
Total Capital	3,320	3,154	3,198	3,167	3,013	2,703	2,485	2,278	2,207	1,501
Capital Expenditures	111	160	190	181	157	141	113	115	170	147
Cash Flow	368	384	484	470	454	420	389	365	335	313
Current Ratio	4.0	4.0	3.5	2.9	2.9	3.3	3.2	2.9	2.7	3.3
% Long Term Debt of Capitalization	23.7	24.9	28.4	27.7	26.4	17.2	19.1	23.5	31.9	14.7
% Net Income of Revenue	6.1	6.0	8.5	9.0	9.6	9.8	44.4	9.3	10.3	10.3
% Return on Assets	5.6	6.0	9.1	9.6	10.1	10.2	10.1	9.8	11.0	13.3
% Return on Equity	8.8	9.8	15.2	15.7	15.6	15.1	15.4	16.2	17.6	19.6

Data as orig reptd.; bef. results of disc opers/spec. items. Per share data adj. for stk. divs.; EPS diluted. E-Estimated. NA-Not Available. NM-Not Meaningful. NR-Not Ranked. UR-Under Review.

Office: 6800 Cintas Boulevard, Cincinnati, OH 45262-5737.
Telephone: 513-459-1200.
Website: http://www.cintas.com
Chrmn: R.J. Kohlhepp

Pres & COO: J.P. Holloman
CEO: S.D. Farmer
Investor Contact: W.C. Gale (513-459-1200)
SVP, CFO & Chief Acctg Officer: W.C. Gale

Board Members: G. S. Adolph, G. V. Dirvin, R. T. Farmer, S. D. Farmer, J. Hergenhan, J. J. Johnson, R. J. Kohlhepp, D. C. Phillips, J. M. Scaminace, R. W. Tysoe
Founded: 1968
Domicile: Washington
Employees: 30,000

The McGraw-Hill Companies

Cisco Systems Inc

STANDARD &POOR'S

S&P Recommendation	STRONG BUY ★★★★★	Price $23.48 (as of Oct 22, 2010)	12-Mo. Target Price $29.00	Investment Style Large-Cap Growth

GICS Sector Information Technology
Sub-Industry Communications Equipment

Summary This company offers a complete line of routers and switching products that connect and manage communications among local and wide area computer networks employing a variety of protocols.

Key Stock Statistics (Source S&P, Vickers, company reports)

52-Wk Range	$27.74– 19.82	S&P Oper. EPS 2011**E**	1.54	Market Capitalization(B)	$131.142	Beta		1.27
Trailing 12-Month EPS	$1.33	S&P Oper. EPS 2012**E**	1.80	Yield (%)	Nil	S&P 3-Yr. Proj. EPS CAGR(%)		14
Trailing 12-Month P/E	17.7	P/E on S&P Oper. EPS 2011**E**	15.2	Dividend Rate/Share	Nil	S&P Credit Rating		A+
$10K Invested 5 Yrs Ago	$13,787	Common Shares Outstg. (M)	5,585.3	Institutional Ownership (%)	73			

Price Performance

Analysis prepared by **Ari Bensinger** on September 15, 2010, when the stock traded at **$ 21.63**.

Options: ASE, CBOE, P, Ph

Highlights

➤ Following an 11% sales increase in FY 10 (July), we see an additional 11% advance in FY 11, on higher networking product demand, aided by a product refresh cycle in core switching and routing. We believe the company has taken a more aggressive approach in targeting new market adjacencies, with new product announcements like unified computing (servers) and the Cius (tablets), as well as recent acquisitions, such as Tandberg (video conferencing), and Starent (wireless packet data).

➤ We look for FY 11 gross margins to narrow modestly, to 65%, as the benefits from higher sales volume are offset by a less favorable sales mix toward new products and higher component procurement and shipping costs. We believe CSCO will manage FY 11 costs prudently, and we see operating expenses rising at a slower rate than sales.

➤ After taxes at a 22% effective rate, we project FY 11 operating EPS of $1.54, including $0.18 of projected stock option expense, up from the $1.43 EPS posted for FY 10, which was before $0.10 of non-recurring items, mostly related to intangible asset amortization.

Investment Rationale/Risk

➤ We believe IT spending could weaken over the near term amid an uncertain macroeconomic outlook. Still, we see CSCO taking advantage of its broad-balanced portfolio, large established customer base, and strong cash position to gain market share from smaller networking rivals. We foresee a continued rapid increase in network bandwidth usage acting as a strong underlying growth driver for CSCO. We believe the shares, trading below peers on a P/E basis, do not adequately reflect CSCO's leading market position and strong profitability metrics.

➤ Risks to our recommendation and target price include a slower-than-expected recovery in enterprise and telecom spending, increased competition, and intensifying pricing pressures.

➤ Our 12-month target price of $29 equals a peer-average 19X our FY 11 EPS estimate of $1.54. We view the company's 7% free cash flow yield as one of the highest in the industry. Our discounted cash flow model, assuming a weighted average cost of capital of 11% and terminal growth of 3%, indicates an intrinsic value of just under $31.

Qualitative Risk Assessment

LOW	MEDIUM	HIGH

Our risk assessment for CSCO reflects the highly competitive nature of the industry in which it operates, balanced by our view of its strong financials, including $40 billion of cash and investments, and a dominant market position.

Quantitative Evaluations

S&P Quality Ranking — B+

D	C	B-	B	B+	A-	A	A+

Relative Strength Rank — MODERATE

62

LOWEST = 1   HIGHEST = 99

Revenue/Earnings Data

Revenue (Million $)

	1Q	2Q	3Q	4Q	Year
2010	9,021	9,815	10,368	10,836	40,040
2009	10,331	9,089	8,162	8,535	36,117
2008	9,554	9,831	9,791	10,364	39,540
2007	8,184	8,439	8,866	9,433	34,922
2006	6,550	6,628	7,322	7,984	28,484
2005	5,971	6,062	6,187	6,581	24,801

Earnings Per Share ($)

2010	0.30	0.32	0.37	0.33	1.33
2009	0.37	0.26	0.23	0.19	1.05
2008	0.35	0.33	0.29	0.33	1.31
2007	0.26	0.31	0.30	0.33	1.17
2006	0.20	0.22	0.22	0.25	0.89
2005	0.21	0.21	0.21	0.24	0.87

Fiscal year ended Jul. 31. Next earnings report expected: Early November. EPS Estimates based on S&P Operating Earnings; historical GAAP earnings are as reported.

Dividend Data

No cash dividends have been paid.

Please read the Required Disclosures and Analyst Certification on the last page of this report.

The **McGraw-Hill** Companies

Cisco Systems Inc

STANDARD &POOR'S

Business Summary September 15, 2010

CORPORATE OVERVIEW. Cisco Systems is the world's largest supplier of high-performance computer internetworking systems. The company's sales strategy is primarily based on distribution channel partners, with over 40,000 reseller partner sales representatives around the world. Geographically, FY 09 (Jul.) sales were distributed to the following regions: United States and Canada (54%), Europe (21%), the Emerging Markets (11%), Asia Pacific (10%), and Japan (4%).

Product families are categorized into four segments: switches (41% of total FY 09 product sales), routers (22%), advanced technologies (32%), and other. There are currently seven primary advanced technology segments: home networking, unified communications, security, storage area networking, wireless technology, application networking services, and video systems. The company also has a broad range of service offerings, including technical support services and advanced services.

In our view, the primary driver of company sales growth will be the advanced technologies segment. CSCO distinguishes its advanced technology sub-

segments as industry segments with the potential to become billion dollar businesses. We see the company continuing to identify additional advanced technology sub-segments in markets that build upon its networking expertise. The company is also actively developing a new wave of technologies, referred to as emerging technologies, including telepresence systems, physical security and digital media.

MARKET PROFILE. With a dominant market share of approximately 70% of the overall Ethernet switching market, we believe CSCO has become the de facto choice for Ethernet switches. We view the company's large installed base as a significant competitive advantage over peers. In the beginning of 2008, the company introduced its new Nexus series of switches that aims to unify storage and computing in data centers.

Company Financials Fiscal Year Ended Jul. 31

Per Share Data ($)	2010	2009	2008	2007	2006	2005	2004	2003	2002	2001
Tangible Book Value	NA	4.15	3.37	2.76	2.07	2.74	3.16	3.35	3.33	3.07
Cash Flow	1.68	1.35	1.59	1.40	1.10	1.02	0.91	0.72	0.52	0.17
Earnings	1.33	1.05	1.31	1.17	0.89	0.87	0.70	0.50	0.25	-0.14
S&P Core Earnings	1.31	1.06	1.30	1.15	0.88	0.70	0.52	0.28	0.12	-0.37
Dividends	NA	Nil	Nil	Nil	Nil	Nil	Nil	Nil	Nil	Nil
Payout Ratio	Nil	Nil	Nil	Nil	Nil	Nil	Nil	Nil	Nil	Nil
Prices:High	27.74	24.83	27.72	34.24	27.96	20.25	29.39	24.60	21.84	44.50
Prices:Low	19.82	13.61	14.20	24.82	17.10	16.83	17.53	12.33	12.24	11.04
P/E Ratio:High	21	24	21	29	31	23	42	49	87	NM
P/E Ratio:Low	15	13	11	21	19	19	25	25	49	NM

Income Statement Analysis (Million $)										
Revenue	40,040	36,117	39,540	34,922	28,484	24,801	22,045	18,878	18,915	22,293
Operating Income	11,194	9,153	11,189	10,034	8,380	8,451	7,738	6,477	4,941	2,257
Depreciation	2,030	1,768	1,744	1,413	1,293	1,009	1,443	1,591	1,957	2,236
Interest Expense	623	346	319	Nil	Nil	Nil	Nil	Nil	Nil	Nil
Pretax Income	9,415	7,693	10,255	9,461	7,633	8,036	6,992	5,013	2,710	-874
Effective Tax Rate	NA	20.3%	21.5%	22.5%	26.9%	28.6%	28.9%	28.6%	30.1%	NM
Net Income	7,767	6,134	8,052	7,333	5,580	5,741	4,968	3,578	1,893	-1,014
S&P Core Earnings	7,622	6,186	7,985	7,197	5,499	4,645	3,652	2,051	931	-2,641

Balance Sheet & Other Financial Data (Million $)										
Cash	39,861	35,001	26,235	3,728	3,297	4,742	3,722	3,925	9,484	4,873
Current Assets	51,421	44,177	35,699	31,574	25,676	13,031	14,343	13,415	17,433	12,835
Total Assets	81,130	68,128	58,734	53,340	43,315	33,883	35,594	37,107	37,795	35,238
Current Liabilities	19,233	13,655	13,858	13,358	11,313	9,511	8,703	8,294	8,375	8,096
Long Term Debt	12,188	10,295	6,393	6,408	6,332	Nil	Nil	Nil	Nil	Nil
Common Equity	44,285	38,647	34,353	31,480	23,912	23,174	25,826	28,029	28,656	27,120
Total Capital	59,569	48,972	40,875	37,898	30,250	23,184	25,916	28,039	28,671	27,142
Capital Expenditures	1,008	1,005	1,268	1,251	772	692	613	717	2,641	2,271
Cash Flow	9,797	7,902	9,796	8,746	6,873	6,750	6,411	5,169	3,850	1,222
Current Ratio	2.7	3.2	2.6	2.4	2.3	1.4	1.6	1.6	2.1	1.6
% Long Term Debt of Capitalization	20.5	21.0	15.6	16.9	20.9	Nil	Nil	Nil	Nil	Nil
% Net Income of Revenue	19.4	17.0	20.4	21.0	19.6	23.1	22.5	19.0	10.0	NM
% Return on Assets	10.4	9.7	14.4	15.2	14.5	16.5	13.7	9.6	5.2	NM
% Return on Equity	18.7	16.8	24.5	26.5	23.7	23.4	18.4	12.6	6.8	NM

Data as orig reptd.; bef. results of disc opers/spec. items. Per share data adj. for stk. divs.; EPS diluted. E-Estimated. NA-Not Available. NM-Not Meaningful. NR-Not Ranked. UR-Under Review.

Office: 170 West Tasman Drive, San Jose, CA 95134-1706.
Telephone: 408-526-4000.
Email: investor-relations@cisco.com
Website: http://www.cisco.com

Chrmn & CEO: J.T. Chambers
COO: R. Lloyd
EVP & CFO: F.A. Calderoni
SVP & Treas: D.K. Holland

SVP, Secy & General Counsel: M. Chandler
Investor Contact: L. Graves (408-526-6521)
Board Members: C. A. Bartz, M. M. Burns, M. D. Capellas, L. R. Carter, J. T. Chambers, B. L. Halla, J. L. Hennessy, R. M. Kovacevich, R. McGeary, M. K. Powell, A. Sarin, S. M. West, J. Yang

Founded: 1984
Domicile: California
Employees: 70,700

Citigroup Inc

STANDARD
&POOR'S

S&P Recommendation	**BUY** ★★★★☆	Price $4.11 (as of Oct 22, 2010)	12-Mo. Target Price $5.00	Investment Style Large-Cap Blend

GICS Sector Financials
Sub-Industry Other Diversified Financial Services

Summary This diversified financial services company provides a wide range of financial services to consumers and corporate customers in more than 100 countries and territories.

Key Stock Statistics (Source S&P, Vickers, company reports)

52-Wk Range	$5.07–3.11	S&P Oper. EPS 2010E	0.39	Market Capitalization(B)	$119.081	Beta	2.64
Trailing 12-Month EPS	$-0.12	S&P Oper. EPS 2011E	0.45	Yield (%)	Nil	S&P 3-Yr. Proj. EPS CAGR(%)	NM
Trailing 12-Month P/E	NM	P/E on S&P Oper. EPS 2010E	10.5	Dividend Rate/Share	Nil	S&P Credit Rating	BBB+
$10K Invested 5 Yrs Ago	$1,078	Common Shares Outstg. (M)	28,973.5	Institutional Ownership (%)	38		

Price Performance

30-Week Mov. Avg. · · · 10-Week Mov. Avg. – – GAAP Earnings vs. Previous Year Volume Above Avg. STARS
12-Mo. Target Price — Relative Strength — ▲ Up ▼ Down ▶ No Change Below Avg. ★

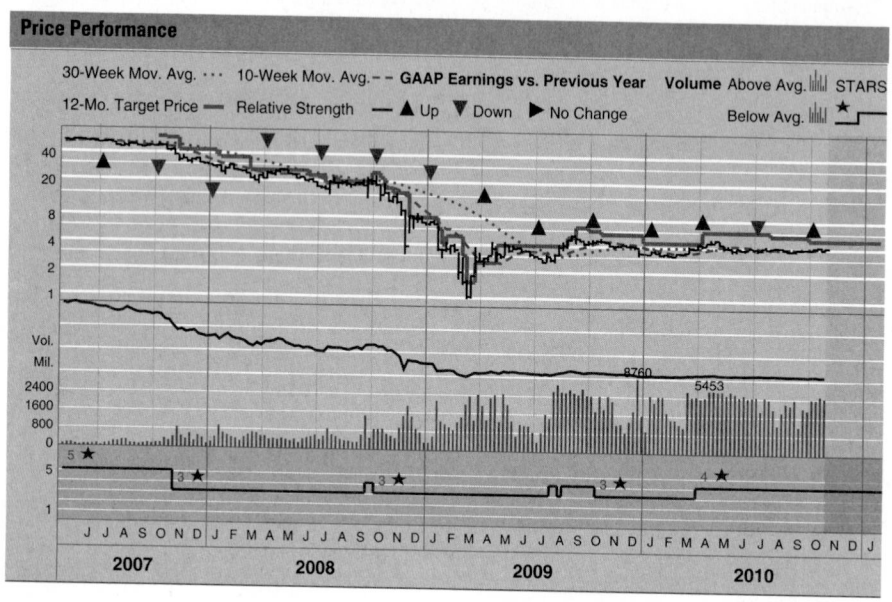

Options: ASE, CBOE, P, Ph

Highlights

► The 12-month target price for C has recently been changed to $5.00 from $5.50. The Highlights section of this Stock Report will be updated accordingly.

Investment Rationale/Risk

► The Investment Rationale/Risk section of this Stock Report will be updated shortly. For the latest News story on C from MarketScope, see below.

► 10/18/10 10:16 am ET ... RETRANSMIT - S&P MAINTAINS BUY RECOMMENDATION ON SHARES OF CITIGROUP INC. (C 4.06****): Q3 EPS of $0.07, vs. a loss per share of $0.23, misses our $0.11 estimate, on higher than expected loan loss provisions. However, our provisioning forecast was likely more aggressive than consensus, and Q3 provisions were significantly lower than Q2, a positive. On Q3 results, we are lowering our '10 EPS estimate to $0.39, from $0.43. We see improvements on track, and we keep our $5 target price, based on slightly below peers multiples of 10.9X on our unchanged forward four quarters EPS estimate of $0.46, and 1.15X our year end tangible book value per share estimate of $4.36. /E. Oja

Qualitative Risk Assessment

LOW	MEDIUM	**HIGH**

Our risk assessment reflects our view of C's exposure to risky assets on its balance sheet and to uncertain credit in domestic and international markets. It also reflects the possibility of attrition of C's customers and trading partners.

Quantitative Evaluations

S&P Quality Ranking   B

D	C	B-	**B**	B+	A-	A	A+

Relative Strength Rank   MODERATE

50

LOWEST = 1   HIGHEST = 99

Revenue/Earnings Data

Revenue (Million $)

	1Q	2Q	3Q	4Q	Year
2010	31,460	8,032	26,863	--	--
2009	32,178	36,811	27,070	11,947	108,006
2008	29,696	32,392	29,456	16,253	105,782
2007	43,021	45,802	43,197	27,209	159,229
2006	34,290	35,899	36,323	40,046	146,558
2005	28,620	28,837	31,147	31,714	120,318

Earnings Per Share ($)

2010	0.14	0.09	0.09	E0.12	E0.39
2009	-0.16	0.51	-0.23	-0.34	-0.76
2008	-1.04	-0.51	-0.71	-4.12	-4.72
2007	1.01	1.24	0.44	-1.99	0.72
2006	1.11	1.05	1.06	1.03	4.25
2005	0.98	0.91	0.97	0.98	3.82

Fiscal year ended Dec. 31. Next earnings report expected: Mid January. EPS Estimates based on S&P Operating Earnings; historical GAAP earnings are as reported.

Dividend Data

The most recent payment was in February 2009.

Citigroup Inc

STANDARD & POOR'S

Business Summary July 20, 2010

CORPORATE OVERVIEW. Following the market downturn and credit crisis, Citigroup decided to refocus on its core operations. It reorganized into three segments for reporting purposes. Citicorp consists of core banking operations for consumers and businesses, and includes its Regional Consumer Banking and Institutional Clients Group. Citi Holdings contains businesses and assets that the company no longer considers part of its core business, including its Brokerage and Asset Management, Local Consumer Lending, and Special Asset Pool units. Its Corporate and Other segment includes global staff functions and other corporate expenses.

The Regional Consumer Banking unit consists of C's four regional consumer banks that offer traditional banking services to retail customers, as well as its branded cards business and a small commercial banking business. It has roughly 4,000 branches in 39 countries, and in 2009, 68% of the unit's revenues were from outside North America, with a focus on emerging economies. The Institutional Clients Group includes securities and banking and transaction services units that provide corporate, institutional and high-net-worth clients with a wide range of banking and investment services and products. It has trading floors in about 75 countries and a proprietary network to handle client transactions that stretches to nearly 100 countries.

Citi Holdings contains a number of businesses and assets that the company intends to exit as quickly as practicable through divestitures, portfolio run-off and asset sales. At the end of 2009, the firm had already reduced the asset base of Holdings by about 40%, to $547 billion. C holds a 49% stake in the Morgan Stanley Smith Barney brokerage joint venture within the Brokerage and Asset Management unit. Morgan Stanley has options to purchase C's remaining stake in the JV over three years staring in 2012. This unit was also downsized in 2009 through the sale of Nikko Cordial Securities. The Local Consumer Lending unit held the majority of Holding's assets at year-end 2009, and includes a portion of the firm's North American mortgage business, retail partner cards, Western European cards and retail banking, CitiFinancial North America, Student Loan Corporation, and other global businesses. It divested a range of global card operations in 2009, and spun-off the majority of its Primerica stake in early 2010. About one half of assets in Local Consumer Lending consisted of U.S. mortgages at the end of 2009, which will likely see additional chargeoffs throughout 2010.

Company Financials Fiscal Year Ended Dec. 31

Per Share Data ($)	2009	2008	2007	2006	2005	2004	2003	2002	2001	2000
Tangible Book Value	4.15	4.41	9.95	14.14	12.76	11.72	10.75	9.70	15.49	12.84
Earnings	-0.76	-4.72	0.72	4.25	3.82	3.26	3.42	2.59	2.75	2.62
S&P Core Earnings	-1.53	-4.97	0.43	4.09	3.69	4.02	3.35	2.33	2.51	NA
Dividends	0.01	1.12	2.16	1.96	1.76	1.60	1.10	0.70	0.60	0.52
Payout Ratio	NM	NM	NM	46%	46%	49%	32%	27%	22%	20%
Prices:High	7.59	29.89	56.28	57.00	49.99	52.88	49.15	52.20	57.38	59.13
Prices:Low	3.26	3.05	28.80	44.81	42.91	42.10	30.25	24.48	34.51	35.34
P/E Ratio:High	NM	NM	78	13	13	16	14	20	21	23
P/E Ratio:Low	NM	NM	40	11	11	13	9	9	13	13

Income Statement Analysis (Million $)	2009	2008	2007	2006	2005	2004	2003	2002	2001	2000
Premium Income	3,020	3,221	3,132	3,202	3,132	3,993	3,749	3,410	13,460	12,429
Investment Income	29,178	44,319	58,273	41,409	28,833	22,728	18,937	21,036	26,949	27,562
Other Revenue	75,808	58,242	126,392	109,179	88,353	81,555	72,027	68,110	71,613	71,835
Total Revenue	108,006	105,782	159,229	146,558	120,318	108,276	94,713	92,556	112,022	111,826
Interest Expense	27,721	52,963	77,531	56,943	36,676	22,086	17,271	21,248	31,965	36,638
% Expense/Operating Revenue	71.1%	117.3%	87.3%	74.3%	75.5%	77.6%	72.2%	77.8%	80.5%	81.1%
Pretax Income	-7,799	-43,113	1,701	29,639	29,433	24,182	26,333	20,537	21,897	21,143
Effective Tax Rate	NM	45.6%	NM	27.3%	30.8%	28.6%	31.1%	34.1%	34.4%	35.6%
Net Income	-1,161	-23,125	3,617	21,249	19,806	17,046	17,853	13,448	14,284	13,519
S&P Core Earnings	-17,737	-26,217	2,154	20,311	19,114	20,934	17,424	12,000	12,943	NA

Balance Sheet & Other Financial Data (Million $)	2009	2008	2007	2006	2005	2004	2003	2002	2001	2000
Receivables	33,634	44,278	57,359	44,445	42,823	44,056	31,053	29,714	47,528	36,237
Cash & Investment	757,681	763,760	242,663	300,105	208,970	236,799	204,041	186,839	179,352	134,743
Loans	591,504	694,216	777,993	679,192	583,503	548,829	478,006	447,805	391,933	367,022
Total Assets	1,856,164	1,945,263	2,187,631	1,884,318	1,494,037	1,484,101	1,264,032	1,097,190	1,051,450	902,210
Capitalization:Debt	364,019	359,593	427,112	288,494	217,499	207,910	168,759	133,079	128,756	116,698
Capitalization:Equity	152,388	80,110	113,598	118,783	111,412	108,166	96,889	85,318	79,722	64,461
Capitalization:Total	518,992	501,223	540,710	408,277	330,036	317,201	284,251	219,797	210,003	182,904
Price Times Book Value:High	1.8	6.8	5.7	4.0	3.9	4.5	4.6	5.4	3.7	4.6
Price Times Book Value:Low	0.8	0.7	2.9	3.2	3.4	3.5	2.8	2.5	2.2	2.7
% Return on Revenue	NM	NM	2.3	22.0	16.5	15.7	18.8	14.5	12.8	12.9
% Return on Assets	NM	NM	0.2	1.3	1.3	1.2	1.5	1.3	1.5	1.6
% Return on Equity	NM	NM	3.1	18.5	18.0	16.6	19.5	11.6	19.7	22.2
Loans/Equity	5.8	8.0	6.3	5.5	5.2	5.1	5.1	3.6	5.3	5.6

Data as orig reptd.; bef. results of disc opers/spec. items. Per share data adj. for stk. divs.; EPS diluted. E-Estimated. NA-Not Available. NM-Not Meaningful. NR-Not Ranked. UR-Under Review.

Office: 399 Park Avenue, New York, NY, USA 10043.
Telephone: 212-559-1000.
Website: http://www.citigroup.com
Chrmn: R.D. Parsons

Pres: W. McNamee
CEO: V.S. Pandit
COO, Chief Admin Officer & CTO: D. Callahan
CFO: J.C. Gerspach

Board Members: A. J. Belda, T. C. Collins, B. Cowley, G. Franck, J. A. Grundhofer, R. L. Joss, A. N. Liveris, M. E. O'Neill, V. S. Pandit, R. D. Parsons, L. R. Ricciardi, J. Rodin, R. L. Ryan, A. M. Santomero, C. Scheurkogel, D. Taylor, W. S. Thompson, Jr., E. Zedillo

Founded: 1901
Domicile: Delaware
Employees: 269,000

Citrix Systems Inc

STANDARD &POOR'S

S&P Recommendation HOLD ★★★☆☆	**Price** $60.80 (as of Oct 22, 2010)	**12-Mo. Target Price** $60.00	**Investment Style** Large-Cap Growth

GICS Sector Information Technology
Sub-Industry Application Software

Summary This company is a leading developer and supplier of access infrastructure software and services.

Key Stock Statistics (Source S&P, Vickers, company reports)

52-Wk Range	$71.93– 36.75	S&P Oper. EPS 2010**E**	1.36	Market Capitalization(B)	$11.366	Beta	1.04
Trailing 12-Month EPS	$1.26	S&P Oper. EPS 2011**E**	1.58	Yield (%)	Nil	S&P 3-Yr. Proj. EPS CAGR(%)	20
Trailing 12-Month P/E	48.3	P/E on S&P Oper. EPS 2010**E**	44.7	Dividend Rate/Share	Nil	S&P Credit Rating	NR
$10K Invested 5 Yrs Ago	$23,048	Common Shares Outstg. (M)	186.9	Institutional Ownership (%)	93		

Price Performance

30-Week Mov. Avg. ··· 10-Week Mov. Avg. - - **GAAP Earnings vs. Previous Year** Volume Above Avg. ▮▮▮ STARS
12-Mo. Target Price — Relative Strength — ▲ Up ▼ Down ► No Change Below Avg. ▮▮▮ ★

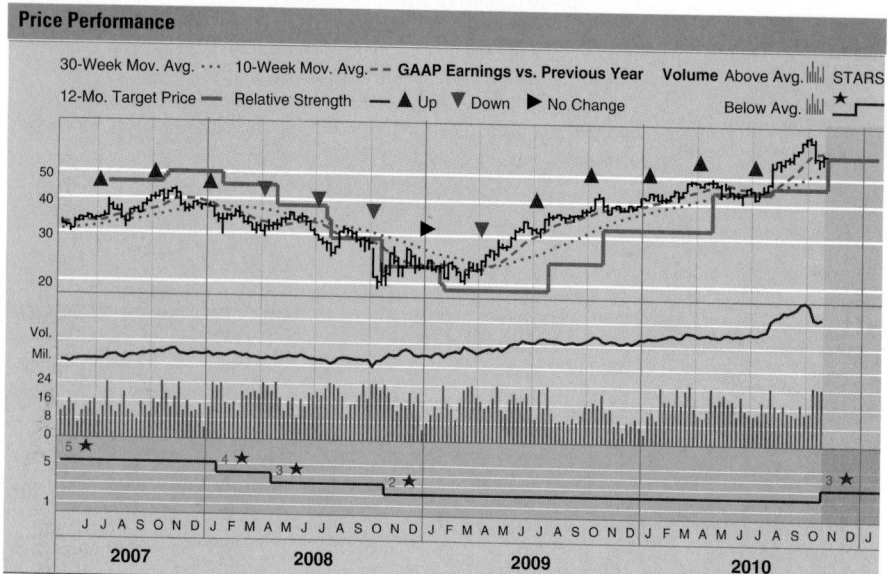

Options: ASE, CBOE, P, Ph

Qualitative Risk Assessment

LOW	MEDIUM	**HIGH**

Our risk assessment reflects rapidly changing technology and the competitive nature of the enterprise software market.

Quantitative Evaluations

S&P Quality Ranking   B+

D	C	B-	B	**B+**	A-	A	A+

Relative Strength Rank   MODERATE

45

LOWEST = 1   HIGHEST = 99

Revenue/Earnings Data

Revenue (Million $)

	1Q	2Q	3Q	4Q	Year
2010	414.3	458.4	--	--	--
2009	369.1	392.8	401.0	451.2	1,614
2008	377.0	391.7	398.9	415.7	1,583
2007	308.1	334.4	349.9	399.6	1,392
2006	260.0	275.5	277.9	321.0	1,134
2005	201.9	211.2	227.0	268.7	908.7

Earnings Per Share ($)

2010	0.25	0.25	E0.46	E0.40	E1.36
2009	0.04	0.23	0.29	0.47	1.03
2008	0.18	0.18	0.26	0.33	0.96
2007	0.20	0.29	0.33	0.33	1.14
2006	0.22	0.23	0.23	0.29	0.97
2005	0.22	0.16	0.23	0.32	0.93

Fiscal year ended Dec. 31. Next earnings report expected: Late October. EPS Estimates based on S&P Operating Earnings; historical GAAP earnings are as reported.

Dividend Data

No cash dividends have been paid.

Highlights

► The STARS recommendation for CTXS has recently been changed to 3 (hold) from 2 (sell) and the 12-month target price has recently been changed to $60.00 from $46.00. The Highlights section of this Stock Report will be updated accordingly.

Investment Rationale/Risk

► The Investment Rationale/Risk section of this Stock Report will be updated shortly. For the latest News story on CTXS from MarketScope, see below.

► 10/22/10 10:17 am ET ... S&P RAISES RECOMMENDATION ON SHARES OF CITRIX SYSTEMS TO HOLD FROM SELL (CTXS 58.83***): Q3 EPS of $0.46, vs. $0.29, beats our estimate of $0.36, aided by lower-than-expected taxes and higher interest income. Revenues rose 18% to $472M, $11M above our forecast, driven by strong demand for its data center infrastructure products. While bookings for desktop virtualization products declined sequentially from Q2 following the end of its upgrade program, we see accelerating growth in that segment. We increase our '10 EPS estimate $0.12 to $1.36 and '11's by $0.08 to $1.58. We raise our target price by $14 to $60, reflecting our higher revenue and EPS growth outlook. /J.Yin-CFA

The **McGraw·Hill** Companies

Citrix Systems Inc

STANDARD &POOR'S

Business Summary August 03, 2010

CORPORATE OVERVIEW. Citrix Systems (CTXS) designs, develops and markets server and desktop virtualization software solutions that enable users to access and share applications and files on-demand with a higher performance and level of security. CTXS's solutions help people conduct business in remote and mobile locations as they move from location to location, use multiple devices, and connect with a wide range of heterogeneous applications over wired, wireless and Internet networks.

CTXS organizes its products into three groups: Citrix Delivery Center, Online Services and Technical Services.

Citrix Delivery Center is focused on application virtualization, application networking and desktop virtualization. It includes Server Virtualization products, which allow servers to run multiple operating systems, thus enabling them to process multiple business applications. As a result, enterprises can reduce infrastructure costs by aggregating servers and data storage into pools of shared resources. The key product is Citrix XenServer, which was obtained through the acquisition of XenSource. CTXS and Microsoft entered into patent cross license and source code licensing agreements related to Microsoft's operating systems.

Another key application in Citrix Delivery Center is Citrix XenApp, previously

called Citrix Presentation Server, which runs the business logic of applications on a central server and displays the video on the users' computers. By keeping applications under a centralized control, it improves data security and reduces the costs of managing many different applications on every user's desktop. Other products include Citrix NetScaler and Citrix Repeater, which optimize the performance of a network by balancing the load and providing firewall protection.

Online Services are Web-based access and collaboration software and services. GoToMyPC allows users to remotely access PCs via the Internet. GoToMeeting enables online meetings, training sessions and collaborative gatherings. GoToAssist is an online solution that enables businesses to provide customer support over the Internet. GoToWebinar helps organizations conduct online events, such as large marketing events.

Technical Services include consulting, support, and training to help ensure that customers are achieving the maximum value of CTXS's products and services.

Company Financials Fiscal Year Ended Dec. 31

Per Share Data ($)	2009	2008	2007	2006	2005	2004	2003	2002	2001	2000
Tangible Book Value	5.89	4.13	3.59	3.92	2.68	2.80	3.24	2.57	2.48	2.94
Cash Flow	1.78	1.62	1.60	1.32	1.06	0.95	0.94	0.75	0.95	0.72
Earnings	1.03	0.96	1.14	0.97	0.93	0.75	0.74	0.52	0.54	0.47
S&P Core Earnings	1.02	0.99	1.14	0.97	0.74	0.48	0.23	-0.34	-0.19	NA
Dividends	Nil	Nil	Nil	Nil	Nil	Nil	Nil	Nil	Nil	Nil
Payout Ratio	Nil	Nil	Nil	Nil	Nil	Nil	Nil	Nil	Nil	Nil
Prices:High	43.78	38.95	43.90	45.50	29.46	26.00	27.86	24.70	37.19	122.31
Prices:Low	20.00	19.00	26.10	26.62	20.70	15.02	10.48	4.70	16.88	14.25
P/E Ratio:High	43	41	39	47	32	35	38	47	69	NM
P/E Ratio:Low	19	20	23	27	22	20	14	9	31	NM

Income Statement Analysis (Million $)	2009	2008	2007	2006	2005	2004	2003	2002	2001	2000
Revenue	1,614	1,583	1,392	1,134	909	741	589	527	592	471
Operating Income	344	295	297	267	233	212	189	145	216	172
Depreciation	139	124	85.2	63.6	22.0	33.6	34.3	41.4	79.6	50.2
Interest Expense	0.43	0.44	0.74	0.93	2.23	4.37	18.3	18.2	20.6	17.0
Pretax Income	194	197	251	243	226	164	161	113	153	135
Effective Tax Rate	1.48%	9.47%	14.5%	24.7%	26.2%	20.0%	21.0%	17.0%	31.0%	30.0%
Net Income	191	178	214	183	166	132	127	93.9	105	94.5
S&P Core Earnings	190	184	214	183	131	83.5	39.3	-60.5	-36.2	NA

Balance Sheet & Other Financial Data (Million $)	2009	2008	2007	2006	2005	2004	2003	2002	2001	2000
Cash	600	575	580	349	484	73.5	359	143	140	375
Current Assets	1,039	940	934	812	726	427	809	375	346	587
Total Assets	3,091	2,694	2,535	2,024	1,682	1,286	1,345	1,162	1,208	1,113
Current Liabilities	834	731	654	536	426	342	626	189	193	159
Long Term Debt	NA	Nil	Nil	Nil	31.0	Nil	Nil	334	346	330
Common Equity	2,189	1,918	1,838	1,464	1,203	925	707	622	647	593
Total Capital	2,189	1,918	1,838	1,464	1,234	925	707	955	994	923
Capital Expenditures	76.3	181	85.9	52.1	26.4	24.4	11.1	19.1	60.6	43.5
Cash Flow	330	302	300	247	188	165	161	135	185	145
Current Ratio	1.3	1.3	1.4	1.5	1.7	1.2	1.3	2.0	1.8	3.7
% Long Term Debt of Capitalization	Nil	Nil	Nil	Nil	2.5	Nil	Nil	34.9	34.8	35.8
% Net Income of Revenue	11.8	11.3	15.4	16.1	18.3	17.7	21.6	17.8	17.8	10.0
% Return on Assets	6.6	6.8	9.4	9.8	11.2	10.0	10.1	7.9	9.1	8.8
% Return on Equity	9.3	9.5	13.0	13.7	15.6	16.1	19.1	14.6	17.0	16.8

Data as orig reptd.; bef. results of disc opers/spec. items. Per share data adj. for stk. divs.; EPS diluted. E-Estimated. NA-Not Available. NM-Not Meaningful. NR-Not Ranked. UR-Under Review.

Office: 851 West Cypress Creek Road, Fort Lauderdale, FL 33309.
Telephone: 954-267-3000.
Email: investor@citrix.com
Website: http://www.citrix.com

Chrmn: T.F. Bogan
Pres & CEO: M.B. Templeton
SVP, CFO & Chief Acctg Officer: D.J. Henshall
Treas: K. Leopardi

Secy: A.G. Gomes
Investor Contact: E. Fleites (954-267-3000)
Board Members: T. F. Bogan, N. Caldwell, M. J. Demo, S. M. Dow, A. Hirji, G. E. Morin, G. Sullivan, M. B. Templeton

Founded: 1989
Domicile: Delaware
Employees: 4,816

Cliffs Natural Resources Inc

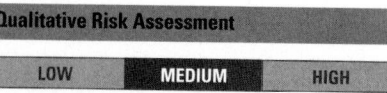

STANDARD &POOR'S

S&P Recommendation BUY ★★★★☆	**Price** $64.60 (as of Oct 22, 2010)	**12-Mo. Target Price** $78.00	**Investment Style** Large-Cap Growth

GICS Sector Materials
Sub-Industry Steel

Summary CLF is the largest supplier of iron ore pellets to the North American steel industry.

Key Stock Statistics (Source S&P, Vickers, company reports)

52-Wk Range	$76.17–32.87	S&P Oper. EPS 2010E	5.88	Market Capitalization(B)	$8.749	Beta	2.61
Trailing 12-Month EPS	$3.89	S&P Oper. EPS 2011E	6.84	Yield (%)	0.87	S&P 3-Yr. Proj. EPS CAGR(%)	76
Trailing 12-Month P/E	16.6	P/E on S&P Oper. EPS 2010E	11.0	Dividend Rate/Share	$0.56	S&P Credit Rating	BBB-
$10K Invested 5 Yrs Ago	$34,022	Common Shares Outstg. (M)	135.4	Institutional Ownership (%)	79		

Price Performance

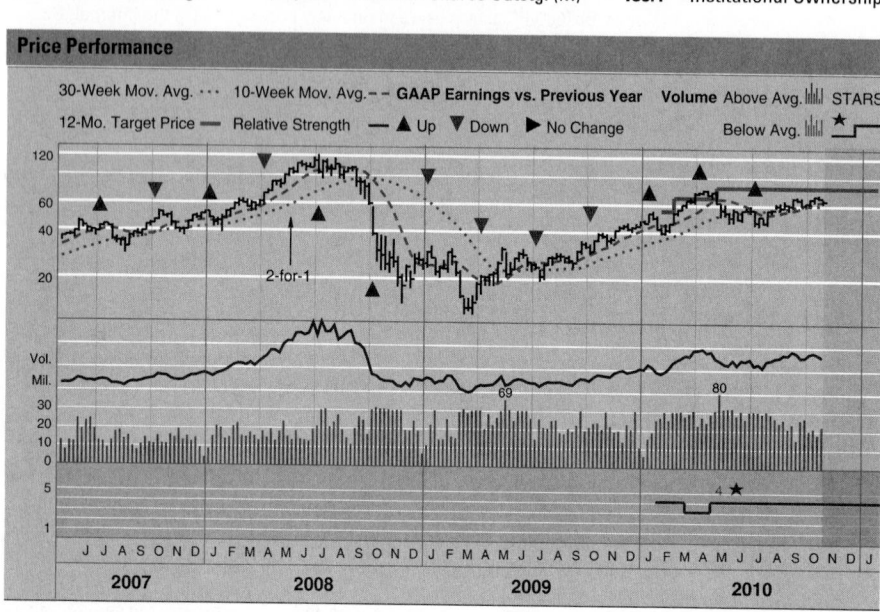

- 30-Week Mov. Avg. ···· 10-Week Mov. Avg. --- GAAP Earnings vs. Previous Year   Volume Above Avg. STARS
- 12-Mo. Target Price — Relative Strength — ▲ Up ▼ Down ► No Change   Below Avg. ★

Options: ASE, CBOE, P, Ph

Analysis prepared by **Leo J. Larkin** on August 10, 2010, when the stock traded at **$ 60.14**.

Highlights

➤ Excluding the August acquisition of coal operations from INR Energy, we look for an 88% sales increase in 2010 on higher volume and a rise in prices. Our forecast for a large sales increase rests on several assumptions. First, we look for U.S. GDP growth of 3.1% in 2010, after a 2.4% decline in 2009, and see global GDP growth of 3.8%, versus a drop of 1.8%. Second, we see a return to economic growth resulting in a rebound in steel production in both North America and Asia. Third, we believe steel mill inventories of iron and metallurgical coal finished 2009 at very low levels, and we expect mills to restock raw material inventories in 2010.

➤ On expected higher volume and prices for iron ore and metallurgical coal, we anticipate sharply higher operating income. After interest expense, taxes, and equity income, we project operating EPS of $5.88 for 2010, versus operating EPS of $1.03 posted in 2009 (excluding net unusual gains of $0.63). We estimate EPS of $6.84 in 2011.

➤ Long term, we see earnings rising on acquisitions, market share gains, further consolidation of the iron ore mining industry, and a secular rise in steel consumption in Asia.

Investment Rationale/Risk

➤ In our view, consolidation of the iron ore mining industry will result in generally firmer pricing and less volatile sales and profits over the course of the business cycle. Also, we think the company's strong market position in North America's iron ore market provides it with a solid platform for expansion in Asia and the ability to enter new markets such as ferrochrome. For the long term, we believe CLF's sales and earnings will rise on a combination of acquisitions, continued consolidation of the global iron ore mining industry, and a secular increase in steel consumption in most of Asia. We think the shares are attractively valued on a relative and absolute basis, recently trading at about 9.2X our 2011 EPS estimate.

➤ Risks to our recommendation and target price include a decline in the price of iron ore and metallurgical coal in 2011 instead of the increases we project.

➤ Our 12-month target price of $78 is 11.4X our 2011 EPS estimate of $6.84. On this projected multiple, the shares would trade just above the mid-point of their range over the past 10 years and at a discount to the P/E we apply to CLF's main iron ore mining peer.

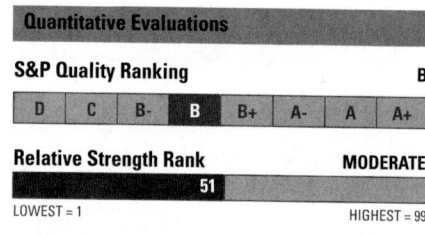

Qualitative Risk Assessment

LOW	MEDIUM	HIGH

Our risk assessment reflects the company's exposure to the highly cyclical demand for iron ore and metallurgical coal, offset by its large market share in iron ore.

Quantitative Evaluations

S&P Quality Ranking   B

D	C	B-	B	B+	A-	A	A+

Relative Strength Rank   MODERATE
51
LOWEST = 1   HIGHEST = 99

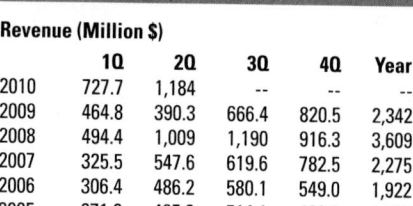

Revenue/Earnings Data

Revenue (Million $)

	1Q	2Q	3Q	4Q	Year
2010	727.7	1,184	--	--	--
2009	464.8	390.3	666.4	820.5	2,342
2008	494.4	1,009	1,190	916.3	3,609
2007	325.5	547.6	619.6	782.5	2,275
2006	306.4	486.2	580.1	549.0	1,922
2005	271.2	485.3	514.1	468.9	1,753

Earnings Per Share ($)

2010	0.69	1.92	E1.66	E1.75	E5.88
2009	-0.07	0.36	0.45	0.82	1.63
2008	0.16	2.57	1.61	0.47	4.76
2007	0.31	0.83	0.54	0.88	2.57
2006	0.34	0.77	0.84	0.67	2.60
2005	0.19	0.90	0.77	0.59	2.46

Fiscal year ended Dec. 31. Next earnings report expected: Late October. EPS Estimates based on S&P Operating Earnings; historical GAAP earnings are as reported.

Dividend Data (Dates: mm/dd Payment Date: mm/dd/yy)

Amount ($)	Date Decl.	Ex-Div. Date	Stk. of Record	Payment Date
0.088	01/12	02/11	02/16	03/01/10
0.140	03/11	05/12	05/14	06/01/10
.001 Spl.	03/11	05/12	05/14	06/01/10
0.140	07/13	08/11	08/13	09/01/10

Dividends have been paid since 2004. Source: Company reports.

Please read the Required Disclosures and Analyst Certification on the last page of this report.

The **McGraw·Hill** Companies

Cliffs Natural Resources Inc

STANDARD &POOR'S

Business Summary August 10, 2010

CORPORATE OVERVIEW. Cliffs Natural Resources, the largest producer of iron ore pellets in North America, primarily sells to integrated steel companies in the United States and Canada. The company manages and operates six North American iron ore mines located in Michigan, Minnesota and Eastern Canada that currently have a rated capacity of 38.1 million tons of iron ore pellet production annually, representing approximately 45.1% of total North American pellet production capacity. CLF is also a major supplier of direct-shipping lump and fines iron ore out of Australia and a significant producer of metallurgical coal.

Based on its percentage ownership of the North American mines CLF currently operates, its share of the rated pellet production capacity is currently 25.6 million tons annually, representing some 30.3% of total North American annual pellet capacity. In 2009, production totaled 19.6 million tons of iron ore pellets, including 17.1 million tons for the company's account and 2.5 million tons on behalf of steel company owners of the mines.

In 2009, the North American Iron Ore segment accounted for 62% of sales and had $275.5 million of operating profit; North American Coal accounted for 9%

of sales and incurred an operating loss of $71.9 million; Asia Pacific Iron Ore accounted for 23% of sales and had an operating profit of $87.2 million; and other operations accounted for 6% of sales and had $18.1 million of operating profit.

In 2009, the United States accounted for 45% of revenues, China 30%, Canada 10%, Japan 7%, and other countries 8%.

CORPORATE STRATEGY. The company seeks to achieve scale in the mining industry and focuses on serving the world's largest and fastest-growing steel markets. CLF plans to increase its business and presence as an international mining company by expanding both geographically and through the minerals it mines and markets. The company also intends to make acquisitions in minerals other than iron ore, such as metallurgical coal.

Company Financials Fiscal Year Ended Dec. 31

Per Share Data ($)	2009	2008	2007	2006	2005	2004	2003	2002	2001	2000
Tangible Book Value	17.97	14.20	13.35	9.12	7.28	4.76	2.72	0.98	4.63	4.97
Cash Flow	3.51	6.61	3.54	3.24	0.00	3.14	-0.10	-0.51	-0.21	0.37
Earnings	1.63	4.76	2.57	2.60	2.45	2.92	-0.43	-0.82	-0.40	0.22
S&P Core Earnings	1.85	4.48	2.38	2.67	2.40	2.16	-0.18	-1.07	-0.60	NA
Dividends	0.25	0.35	0.25	0.24	0.15	0.03	Nil	Nil	0.05	0.19
Payout Ratio	16%	7%	10%	9%	6%	1%	Nil	Nil	NM	87%
Prices:High	48.41	121.95	53.15	27.59	24.81	13.51	6.80	4.03	2.81	3.92
Prices:Low	11.80	13.73	23.00	15.70	11.70	4.85	1.84	1.96	1.71	2.46
P/E Ratio:High	30	26	21	10	10	5	NM	NM	NM	18
P/E Ratio:Low	7	3	9	6	5	2	NM	NM	NM	11

Income Statement Analysis (Million $)										
Revenue	2,342	3,609	2,275	1,933	1,753	1,207	825	599	374	430
Operating Income	589	1,201	473	445	403	146	-17.7	17.6	-33.8	20.4
Depreciation	237	201	107	73.9	48.6	29.3	26.7	25.5	15.4	12.9
Interest Expense	39.0	39.8	21.8	3.60	4.50	0.80	4.60	6.60	9.30	4.90
Pretax Income	225	681	370	388	368	286	-35.2	-57.3	-53.6	16.6
Effective Tax Rate	9.24%	21.2%	22.8%	23.4%	23.0%	NM	NM	NM	NM	NM
Net Income	205	516	270	280	273	321	-34.9	-66.4	-32.2	18.1
S&P Core Earnings	233	485	245	282	262	231	-14.8	-86.2	-48.4	NA

Balance Sheet & Other Financial Data (Million $)										
Cash	503	179	157	352	213	400	265	61.8	184	29.9
Current Assets	1,161	862	755	782	636	734	313	301	363	248
Total Assets	4,639	4,111	3,076	1,940	1,747	1,161	895	730	825	728
Current Liabilities	570	845	400	375	363	257	226	205	190	102
Long Term Debt	525	525	440	Nil	Nil	Nil	Nil	35.0	70.0	70.0
Common Equity	2,543	1,751	1,164	746	652	424	228	79.3	374	402
Total Capital	3,062	2,346	2,045	1,122	1,012	626	283	134	470	496
Capital Expenditures	116	183	200	120	97.8	60.7	20.1	8.60	9.20	17.8
Cash Flow	442	716	372	348	316	345	-8.20	-40.9	-16.8	31.0
Current Ratio	2.0	1.0	1.9	2.1	1.8	2.9	1.4	1.5	1.9	2.4
% Long Term Debt of Capitalization	17.2	22.4	21.5	Nil	Nil	Nil	Nil	26.1	14.9	14.1
% Net Income of Revenue	8.8	14.3	11.9	14.5	15.6	26.6	NM	NM	NM	4.2
% Return on Assets	4.7	14.4	10.6	15.2	18.3	31.4	NM	NM	NM	2.6
% Return on Equity	9.6	35.4	27.7	39.2	49.8	96.7	NM	NM	NM	4.5

Data as orig reptd.; bef. results of disc opers/spec. items. Per share data adj. for stk. divs.; EPS diluted. E-Estimated. NA-Not Available. NM-Not Meaningful. NR-Not Ranked. UR-Under Review.

Office: 200 Public Square, Suite 3300, Cleveland, OH 44114-2315.
Telephone: 216-694-5700.
Website: http://www.cliffsnaturalresources.com
Chrmn, Pres & CEO: J.A. Carrabba

EVP, CFO & Chief Admin Officer: L. Brlas
EVP & CTO: W. Brake, Jr.
Chief Acctg Officer & Cntlr: T.M. Paradie
Treas: S.M. Raguz

Board Members: R. C. Cambre, J. A. Carrabba, S. M. Cunningham, B. Eldridge, S. M. Green, J. K. Henry, J. F. Kirsch, F. R. McAllister, R. Phillips, R. K. Riederer, A. G. Schwartz

Founded: 1920
Domicile: Ohio
Employees: 5,404

The McGraw-Hill Companies

Clorox Co (The)

STANDARD &POOR'S

S&P Recommendation HOLD ★★★☆☆

Price	12-Mo. Target Price	Investment Style
$68.19 (as of Oct 22, 2010)	$69.00	Large-Cap Growth

GICS Sector Consumer Staples
Sub-Industry Household Products

Summary This diversified producer of household cleaning, grocery and specialty food products is also a leading producer of natural personal care products.

Key Stock Statistics (Source S&P, Vickers, company reports)

52-Wk Range	$69.00– 57.72	S&P Oper. EPS 2011**E**	4.57	Market Capitalization(B)	$9.474	Beta	0.42
Trailing 12-Month EPS	$4.24	S&P Oper. EPS 2012**E**	NA	Yield (%)	3.23	S&P 3-Yr. Proj. EPS CAGR(%)	8
Trailing 12-Month P/E	16.1	P/E on S&P Oper. EPS 2011**E**	14.9	Dividend Rate/Share	$2.20	S&P Credit Rating	BBB+
$10K Invested 5 Yrs Ago	$14,557	Common Shares Outstg. (M)	138.9	Institutional Ownership (%)	70		

Price Performance

- 30-Week Mov. Avg.
- 10-Week Mov. Avg.
- GAAP Earnings vs. Previous Year
- Volume Above Avg. STARS
- 12-Mo. Target Price
- Relative Strength
- ▲ Up ▼ Down ► No Change
- Below Avg.

Options: ASE, CBOE, P, Ph

Analysis prepared by **Michael Souers** on August 12, 2010, when the stock traded at **$ 64.43**.

Highlights

➤ We see sales growth of 3.0% in FY 11 (Jun.), following a 1.5% advance in FY 10. We expect a modestly negative impact from foreign currency translation due to a negative impact from the Venezuelan bolivar, and recategorization of Venezuela as hyperinflationary. While the recession has also dampened demand for some items in the natural home/personal care products categories, we view these areas as additive to CLX's growth for the long term, and expect CLX to continue to capture market share.

➤ We look for operating margins to widen about 10 basis points in FY 11 on continued benefits from cost reduction programs and slightly lower advertising expense, partially offset by narrowing gross margins as a result of commodity cost reinflation. CLX widened its operating margin (excluding restructuring costs) by 110 bps in FY 10, helped by pricing and cost savings.

➤ After slightly lower interest expense, and taxes at 34.0%, we project FY 11 EPS of $4.57, a 7.8% improvement from the $4.24 the company posted in FY 10.

Investment Rationale/Risk

➤ In recent years, CLX's performance has been positive but erratic, in our view, due to the seasonal nature of some businesses, the diverse categories in which it operates, and the timing of new product introductions. However, we think its level of product innovation is respectable and bolsters the company's pricing power and competitive stance. We view positively CLX's increased presence in the natural home/personal care products arena through Burt's Bees and Green Works.

➤ Risks to our recommendation and target price include increased competition and promotional activity that would affect profitability, poor consumer acceptance of new products, unfavorable foreign exchange, and potential challenges in the implementation of new enterprise resource planning system software.

➤ Our 12-month target price of $69 blends our historical and peer analyses. We apply a P/E below the 10-year historical average to our calendar 2011 EPS estimate for a $74 value. Our peer analysis uses a slight discount to the average peer multiple, for a $64 value.

Qualitative Risk Assessment

LOW	MEDIUM	HIGH

Our risk assessment reflects our view of stable demand for household and personal care products, which is generally not affected by changes in the economy or by geopolitical factors.

Quantitative Evaluations

S&P Quality Ranking A

D	C	B-	B	B+	A-	A	A+

Relative Strength Rank MODERATE

50

LOWEST = 1   HIGHEST = 99

Revenue/Earnings Data

Revenue (Million $)

	1Q	2Q	3Q	4Q	Year
2010	1,372	1,279	1,366	1,517	5,534
2009	1,384	1,216	1,350	1,500	5,450
2008	1,239	1,186	1,353	1,495	5,273
2007	1,161	1,101	1,241	1,344	4,847
2006	1,104	1,064	1,157	1,319	4,644
2005	1,048	1,000	1,086	1,254	4,388

Earnings Per Share ($)

2010	1.11	0.77	1.17	1.20	4.24
2009	0.91	1.08	1.09	1.20	3.81
2008	0.76	0.65	0.71	1.13	3.25
2007	0.73	0.59	0.84	1.07	3.22
2006	0.70	0.55	0.72	0.92	2.89
2005	0.50	0.72	0.75	1.00	2.88

Fiscal year ended Jun. 30. Next earnings report expected: Early November. EPS Estimates based on S&P Operating Earnings; historical GAAP earnings are as reported.

Dividend Data (Dates: mm/dd Payment Date: mm/dd/yy)

Amount ($)	Date Decl.	Ex-Div. Date	Stk. of Record	Payment Date
0.500	11/19	01/26	01/28	02/12/10
0.500	02/09	04/26	04/28	05/14/10
0.550	05/19	07/26	07/28	08/13/10
0.550	09/14	10/25	10/27	11/12/10

Dividends have been paid since 1968. Source: Company reports.

The **McGraw·Hill** Companies

Clorox Co (The)

Business Summary August 12, 2010

CORPORATE OVERVIEW. From its divestiture from The Procter & Gamble Company in 1969 through its January 1999 acquisition of First Brands and beyond, Clorox has expanded into a company with approximately $5.5 billion in annual sales, by focusing on building big-share brands in mid-sized categories. In November 2004, CLX completed the exchange of its ownership interest in a subsidiary for approximately 61.4 million of its shares held by Henkel KGaA, which represented about 29% of CLX's outstanding common stock prior to the exchange. The subsidiary transferred to Henkel contained CLX's existing insecticides and Soft Scrub cleaner businesses, its 20% interest in the Henkel Iberica, S.A. joint venture, and approximately $2.1 billion in cash.

As of FY 10 (Jun.), Clorox has four segments for reporting purposes: North America-Cleaning (34% of FY 09 sales and 37% of segmental profits); North America-Household (31% and 26%); North America-Lifestyle (15% and 24%); and International, which now includes Canada (20% and 13%). In FY 09, Wal-Mart Stores and its affiliated companies accounted for 27% of consolidated net sales.

Clorox's products include: laundry additives, including bleaches, under the Clorox, Clorox 2 and Javex brands; cleaning products, primarily under the Clorox, Formula 409, Liquid-Plumr, Pine-Sol, S.O.S., and Tilex brands; natural cleaning products under the Green Works brand (introduced in January 2008); water-filtration systems and filters under the Brita brand; professional cleaning products for institutional, janitorial, health care and food service markets; auto care products, primarily under the Armor All and STP brands; plastic bags, wraps and containers, under the Glad brand; cat litter products, primarily under the Fresh Step and Scoop Away brands; food products, primarily under the Hidden Valley and KC Masterpiece brands; charcoal products under the Kingsford and Match Light brands; and natural personal care products under the Burt's Bees brand. In FY 09, liquid bleach represented 13% of sales, trash bags 13%, and charcoal 10%.

CLX owns or leases and operates 23 manufacturing facilities in North America. The company also owns and operates 17 manufacturing facilities outside North America. CLX leases seven distribution centers located in North America and several other warehouse facilities.

Company Financials Fiscal Year Ended Jun. 30

Per Share Data ($)	2010	2009	2008	2007	2006	2005	2004	2003	2002	2001
Tangible Book Value	NM	NM	NM	NM	NM	NM	0.77	NM	0.24	1.38
Cash Flow	5.57	5.16	4.61	4.47	4.12	3.95	3.47	3.19	2.18	2.30
Earnings	4.26	3.81	3.25	3.22	2.89	2.88	2.55	2.33	1.37	1.36
S&P Core Earnings	4.26	3.70	3.15	3.26	2.94	2.73	2.43	2.26	1.63	1.11
Dividends	2.00	1.84	1.60	1.20	1.14	1.10	1.08	0.88	0.84	0.84
Payout Ratio	47%	48%	49%	37%	39%	38%	42%	38%	61%	62%
Prices:High	69.00	63.10	65.25	69.36	66.00	66.04	59.45	49.16	47.95	40.85
Prices:Low	58.96	45.67	47.48	56.22	56.17	52.50	46.50	37.40	31.92	29.95
P/E Ratio:High	16	17	20	22	23	23	23	21	35	30
P/E Ratio:Low	14	12	15	17	19	18	18	16	23	22

Income Statement Analysis (Million $)										
Revenue	5,534	5,450	5,273	4,847	4,644	4,388	4,324	4,144	4,061	3,903
Operating Income	1,291	1,208	1,116	1,059	967	1,011	1,069	1,046	942	895
Depreciation	185	190	193	192	188	190	197	191	190	225
Interest Expense	139	161	168	113	127	79.0	30.0	28.0	39.0	88.0
Pretax Income	925	811	693	743	653	731	840	802	498	487
Effective Tax Rate	NA	33.8%	33.5%	33.2%	32.2%	29.3%	35.0%	35.9%	35.3%	33.3%
Net Income	603	537	461	496	443	517	546	514	322	325
S&P Core Earnings	602	521	448	501	450	489	521	496	383	266

Balance Sheet & Other Financial Data (Million $)										
Cash	87.0	206	214	182	192	293	232	172	177	251
Current Assets	1,124	1,180	1,249	1,032	1,007	1,090	1,043	951	1,002	1,103
Total Assets	4,555	4,576	4,708	3,666	3,616	3,617	3,834	3,652	3,630	3,995
Current Liabilities	1,647	1,937	1,661	1,427	1,130	1,348	1,268	1,451	1,225	1,069
Long Term Debt	2,124	2,151	2,720	1,462	1,966	2,122	475	495	678	685
Common Equity	83.0	-175	-370	171	-156	-553	1,540	1,215	1,354	1,900
Total Capital	2,507	1,999	2,447	1,723	1,939	1,651	2,189	1,825	2,174	2,732
Capital Expenditures	203	197	170	147	180	151	172	205	177	192
Cash Flow	788	727	654	688	631	707	743	705	512	550
Current Ratio	0.7	0.6	0.8	0.7	0.9	0.8	0.8	0.7	0.8	1.0
% Long Term Debt of Capitalization	84.7	107.6	111.2	84.9	101.4	128.5	21.7	27.1	31.2	25.1
% Net Income of Revenue	10.9	9.9	8.7	10.2	9.5	11.8	12.6	12.4	7.9	8.3
% Return on Assets	13.2	11.6	11.0	13.6	12.2	13.9	14.6	14.3	8.4	7.8
% Return on Equity	NM	NM	NM	6613.3	NM	104.8	39.6	39.8	19.8	17.6

Data as orig reptd.; bef. results of disc opers/spec. items. Per share data adj. for stk. divs.; EPS diluted. E-Estimated. NA-Not Available. NM-Not Meaningful. NR-Not Ranked. UR-Under Review.

Office: 1221 Broadway, Oakland, CA, USA 94612-1888.
Telephone: 510-271-7000.
Email: investor_relations@clorox.com
Website: http://www.thecloroxcompany.com

Chrmn & CEO: D.R. Knauss
EVP & CFO: D.J. Heinrich
SVP & General Counsel: L. Stein
Chief Acctg Officer: T.D. Johnson

Secy: A.C. Hilt
Investor Contact: S. Austenfeld
Board Members: D. Boggan, Jr., R. H. Carmona, T. M. Friedman, G. J. Harad, D. R. Knauss, R. W. Matschullat, G. G. Michael, E. A. Mueller, J. L. Murley, P. Thomas-Graham, C. M. Ticknor

Founded: 1913
Domicile: Delaware
Employees: 8,300

CME Group Inc

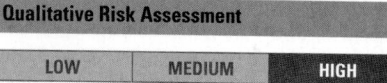
STANDARD &POOR'S

S&P Recommendation HOLD ★★★☆☆

Price	12-Mo. Target Price	Investment Style
$283.69 (as of Oct 22, 2010)	$332.00	Large-Cap Growth

GICS Sector Financials
Sub-Industry Specialized Finance

Summary The CME Group, a combination of the Chicago Mercantile Exchange and CBOT Holdings, is the world's largest futures exchange.

Key Stock Statistics (Source S&P, Vickers, company reports)

52-Wk Range	$353.03–234.50	S&P Oper. EPS 2010**E**	14.94	Market Capitalization(B)	$19.068	Beta	1.11
Trailing 12-Month EPS	$13.80	S&P Oper. EPS 2011**E**	16.59	Yield (%)	1.62	S&P 3-Yr. Proj. EPS CAGR(%)	11
Trailing 12-Month P/E	20.6	P/E on S&P Oper. EPS 2010**E**	19.0	Dividend Rate/Share	$4.60	S&P Credit Rating	AA
$10K Invested 5 Yrs Ago	$8,650	Common Shares Outstg. (M)	67.2	Institutional Ownership (%)	66		

Price Performance

30-Week Mov. Avg. · · · 10-Week Mov. Avg. - - ◼ GAAP Earnings vs. Previous Year Volume Above Avg. STARS
12-Mo. Target Price — Relative Strength — ▲ Up ▼ Down ► No Change Below Avg.

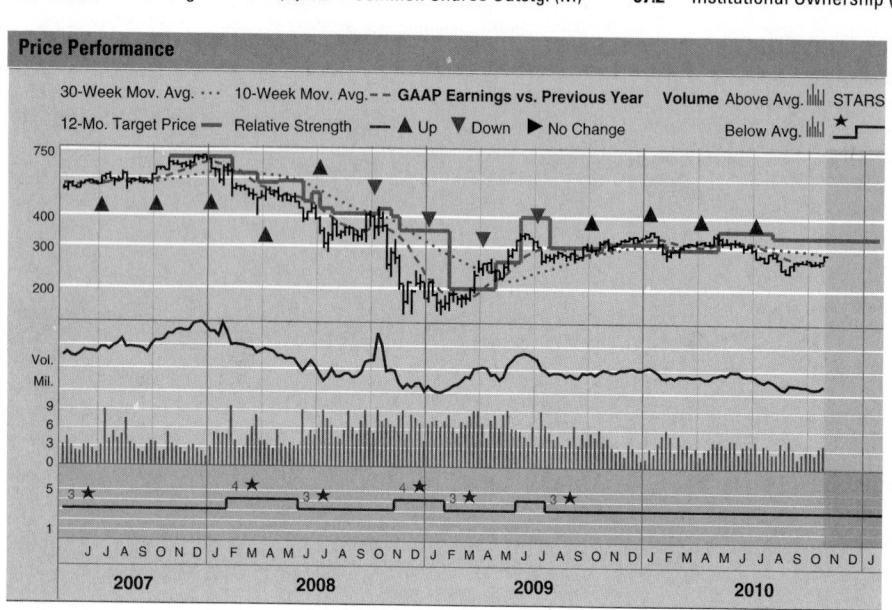

Options: ASE, CBOE, P, Ph

Analysis prepared by **Rafay Khalid, CFA** on July 30, 2010, when the stock traded at **$ 276.81**.

Highlights

➤ We forecast revenue growth of 14% in 2010 and 8% in 2011. We think trading volumes in 2010 and 2011 will improve over 2009, but they will remain below historical levels. In 2010, we foresee strength in domestic products and expansion into new international markets. Uncertainty about the direction of interest rates and the price of oil and gas continues in 2010, which should lead to a pick-up in hedging and speculative activity. But we forecast the average rate per contract will only increase 1% this year, compared to an 18% increase in 2009.

➤ We believe expenses on an absolute dollar basis will increase to $1.17 billion in 2010 and $1.20 billion in 2011, from $1.02 billion in 2009. Our expense forecast reflects our expectation for higher employee compensation costs, additional technology spending, and accelerating marketing expenses. But we forecast total expenses as a percentage of sales will decline to 39.1% in 2010 and 37.4% in 2011, compared to 39.2% in 2009. As a result, we see the operating margin rising to 60.9% in 2010 and 62.6% in 2011, from 60.8% in 2009.

➤ We forecast EPS of $14.94 in 2010 and $16.59 in 2011.

Investment Rationale/Risk

➤ Since the U.S. government passed the new financial reform legislation, we see derivatives products being cleared through a central exchange. While we believe CME has a first mover advantage in the clearing business, we think competition will be increasing, as we see new companies entering the business. We expect that the legislation will cause minimal impact on trading volume, reflecting our outlook for a long implementation period for the Volcker rule, which requires banks to have an ownership stake of 3% or less in a private equity or hedge fund.

➤ Risks to our recommendation and target price include intensified price competition, increased regulation that curbs speculative trading, a significant decline in trading volume, and a deterioration in the macroeconomic environment.

➤ Our 12-month target price of $332 is based on a historical average multiple of about 20X our 2011 EPS forecast. We believe a historical average is warranted, as we see increasing competition in the clearing business, offset by our view of an improving economy.

Qualitative Risk Assessment

LOW	MEDIUM	**HIGH**

Our risk assessment reflects potential volatility in results due to changes in futures trading volumes, recent acquisition activity in the sector, and a changing regulatory environment.

Quantitative Evaluations

S&P Quality Ranking NR

D	C	B-	B	B+	A-	A	A+

Relative Strength Rank MODERATE

64

LOWEST = 1 HIGHEST = 99

Revenue/Earnings Data

Revenue (Million $)

	1Q	2Q	3Q	4Q	Year
2010	693.2	813.9	--	--	--
2009	647.1	647.8	650.4	667.5	2,613
2008	625.1	563.2	681.0	691.8	2,561
2007	332.3	329.0	565.2	529.5	1,756
2006	251.7	282.2	274.7	281.3	1,090
2005	223.9	252.2	249.6	251.6	977.3

Earnings Per Share ($)

2010	3.62	4.12	E3.56	E3.66	E14.94
2009	3.00	3.33	3.04	3.04	12.41
2008	5.25	3.67	2.81	0.93	12.13
2007	3.69	3.57	3.87	3.75	14.93
2006	2.61	3.12	2.95	2.91	11.60
2005	2.04	2.36	2.22	2.18	8.81

Fiscal year ended Dec. 31. Next earnings report expected: Late October. EPS Estimates based on S&P Operating Earnings; historical GAAP earnings are as reported.

Dividend Data (Dates: mm/dd Payment Date: mm/dd/yy)

Amount ($)	Date Decl.	Ex-Div. Date	Stk. of Record	Payment Date
1.150	11/10	12/08	12/10	12/28/09
1.150	02/04	03/08	03/10	03/25/10
1.150	05/06	06/08	06/10	06/25/10
1.150	08/13	09/08	09/10	09/27/10

Dividends have been paid since 2003. Source: Company reports.

Please read the Required Disclosures and Analyst Certification on the last page of this report.

The McGraw-Hill Companies

CME Group Inc

Business Summary July 30, 2010

CORPORATE OVERVIEW. The largest futures exchange in the world, CME Group was formed in July 2007 from the merger of the Chicago Mercantile Exchange and CBOT Holdings. CME serves the risk management needs of clients worldwide through a diverse range of futures and options-on-futures products on its CME Globex electronic trading platform and on its trading floors. CME offers futures and options on futures primarily in four product areas: interest rates, stock indexes, foreign exchange, and commodities. CME is the leading exchange for trading Eurodollar futures, the world's most actively traded futures contract and a benchmark for measuring the relative value of U.S. dollar-denominated short-term fixed income securities.

CME operates its own clearing house, which clears, settles and guarantees every contract traded through its exchange. We view CME's internal clearing capabilities as a key competitive advantage as CME is able to capture the revenue associated with both the trading and clearing of its products. We expect CME to expand its clearing business by partnering with other exchanges, both domestically and abroad, and clearing over-the-counter (OTC) transactions.

In 2009, CME derived 83% of its revenue from fees associated with trading and clearing its products. These fees include per contract charges for trade execution, clearing and CME Globex fees. Within trading and clearing, the different products include commodities, equities, energy, foreign exchange, interest rates, and metals. CME Globex is the company's electronic platform through which it conducts more than 75% of CME's trading volume. Fees are charged at various rates based on the product traded, the method of trade, and the exchange trading privileges of the customer making the trade. Generally, members are charged lower fees than non-members. Certain customers benefit from volume discounts and limits on fees to encourage increased liquidity.

Company Financials Fiscal Year Ended Dec. 31

Per Share Data ($)	2009	2008	2007	2006	2005	2004	2003	2002	2001	2000
Tangible Book Value	NM	NM	NM	42.91	32.38	23.83	17.10	13.71	12.39	NA
Cash Flow	16.19	16.08	18.00	13.67	10.71	7.93	5.16	4.76	3.61	0.98
Earnings	12.41	12.13	14.93	11.60	8.81	6.38	3.60	3.13	2.33	-0.21
S&P Core Earnings	12.92	15.26	14.96	11.59	8.80	6.37	3.61	3.23	NA	NA
Dividends	4.60	9.60	3.44	2.52	1.84	1.04	0.63	Nil	NA	NA
Payout Ratio	37%	79%	23%	22%	21%	16%	18%	Nil	NA	NA
Prices:High	346.24	686.43	714.48	557.97	396.90	229.80	79.30	45.50	NA	NA
Prices:Low	155.06	155.49	497.00	354.50	163.80	72.50	41.35	35.00	NA	NA
P/E Ratio:High	28	57	48	48	45	36	22	15	NA	NA
P/E Ratio:Low	12	13	33	31	19	11	11	11	NA	NA

Income Statement Analysis (Million $)	2009	2008	2007	2006	2005	2004	2003	2002	2001	2000
Revenue	2,613	2,561	1,756	1,090	977	753	545	469	397	227
Operating Income	1,846	1,946	1,258	694	631	464	290	NA	NA	32.1
Depreciation	251	233	136	72.8	66.0	53.0	53.0	48.5	37.6	33.5
Interest Expense	134	56.5	115	92.1	57.0	19.0	8.74	15.9	9.48	NA
Pretax Income	1,438	1,248	1,096	672	508	368	206	154	114	-8.08
Effective Tax Rate	42.6%	42.7%	39.9%	39.4%	39.6%	40.2%	40.7%	39.0%	40.3%	41.3%
Net Income	826	715	659	407	307	220	122	94.1	68.3	-5.91
S&P Core Earnings	859	900	660	407	307	219	123	97.2	NA	NA

Balance Sheet & Other Financial Data (Million $)	2009	2008	2007	2006	2005	2004	2003	2002	2001	2000
Cash	303	608	4,744	3,872	904	660	442	339	292	75.0
Current Assets	6,699	19,112	4,987	4,030	3,783	2,695	4,723	3,215	2,818	267
Total Assets	35,651	48,133	20,306	4,307	3,969	2,857	4,873	3,355	2,958	381
Current Liabilities	6,524	18,643	4,076	2,755	2,830	2,026	4,288	2,889	2,544	197
Long Term Debt	2,015	2,966	Nil	Nil	Nil	Nil	Nil	2.33	8.22	NA
Common Equity	19,301	18,689	12,306	1,519	1,119	813	563	446	394	164
Total Capital	21,316	29,383	16,154	1,519	1,119	813	563	448	402	164
Capital Expenditures	158	200	164	87.8	85.6	67.0	63.0	56.3	16.3	11.2
Cash Flow	1,077	948	794	480	373	273	175	143	106	27.6
Current Ratio	1.0	1.0	1.2	1.5	1.3	1.3	1.1	1.1	1.1	1.4
% Long Term Debt of Capitalization	9.5	10.1	Nil	Nil	Nil	Nil	Nil	0.5	2.0	Nil
% Net Income of Revenue	31.6	27.9	37.5	37.4	31.4	29.2	22.5	20.1	17.2	NM
% Return on Assets	2.0	2.1	5.4	9.8	8.9	5.6	3.0	3.5	5.6	NM
% Return on Equity	4.4	4.6	9.5	30.9	31.7	31.9	24.2	27.1	33.0	NM

Data as orig reptd.; bef. results of disc opers/spec. items. Per share data adj. for stk. divs.; EPS diluted. E-Estimated. NA-Not Available. NM-Not Meaningful. NR-Not Ranked. UR-Under Review.

Office: 20 S Wacker Dr, Chicago, IL 60606-7408.
Telephone: 312-930-1000.
Email: info@cme.com
Website: http://www.cme.com

Chrmn: T.A. Duffy
Pres: P.S. Gill
Vice Chrmn: C.P. Carey
CEO: C.S. Donohue

COO: B.T. Durkin
Investor Contact: J. Peschier (312-930-8491)
Board Members: J. M. Bernacchi, T. S. Bitsberger, C. P. Carey, M. Cermak, D. H. Chookaszian, J. Clegg, R. F. Corvino, J. A. Donaldson, C. S. Donohue, T. A. Duffy, M. J. Gepsman, L. G. Gerdes, J. S. Ginsburg, D. R. Glickman, J. D. Hastert, G. J. Heraty, B. F. Johnson, G. M. Katler, P. B. Lynch, L. Melamed, W. Miller, II, J. Newsome, J. Niciforo, C. C. Odom, II, J. Oliff, J. L. Pietrzak, A. J. Pollock, J. F. Sandner, T. L. Savage, W. R. Shepard, H. J. Siegel, C. Stewart, D. A. Suskind, D. J. Wescott

Founded: 1898
Domicile: Delaware
Employees: 2,260

CMS Energy Corp

STANDARD & POOR'S

S&P Recommendation	HOLD ★★★☆☆	Price $18.69 (as of Oct 22, 2010)	12-Mo. Target Price $17.00	Investment Style Large-Cap Value

GICS Sector Utilities
Sub-Industry Multi-Utilities

Summary This energy holding company's principal subsidiary is Consumers Energy, the largest utility in Michigan and the sixth largest gas and 13th largest electric utility in the U.S.

Key Stock Statistics (Source S&P, Vickers, company reports)

52-Wk Range	$19.07– 13.00	S&P Oper. EPS 2010**E** 1.34	Market Capitalization(B) $4.302	Beta	0.59
Trailing 12-Month EPS	$0.97	S&P Oper. EPS 2011**E** 1.42	Yield (%) 4.49	S&P 3-Yr. Proj. EPS CAGR(%)	4
Trailing 12-Month P/E	19.3	P/E on S&P Oper. EPS 2010**E** 13.9	Dividend Rate/Share $0.84	S&P Credit Rating	BBB-
$10K Invested 5 Yrs Ago	$14,369	Common Shares Outstg. (M) 230.2	Institutional Ownership (%) NM		

Price Performance

30-Week Mov. Avg. · · · 10-Week Mov. Avg. - - GAAP Earnings vs. Previous Year   Volume Above Avg. STARS
12-Mo. Target Price — Relative Strength — ▲ Up ▼ Down ► No Change   Below Avg.

Options: ASE, CBOE, P, Ph

Analysis prepared by **Justin McCann** on September 13, 2010, when the stock traded at **$ 17.91**.

Highlights

▶ Excluding net one-time gains of $0.03, we expect operating EPS in 2010 to grow about 6% from 2009's $1.26. This would reflect a full year of annual surcharges of $91 million and $79 million (implemented in June and September 2009) for Energy Optimization and Renewable plans, and a $139.4 million electric rate increase. Since CMS had self-implemented a $179 million increase in May 2009, it had to refund the difference. It also had to refund the difference between the $65.9 million gas rate increase authorized in May 2010 and the $89 million increase it had self-implemented in November 2009.

▶ While operating EPS in the first half of 2010 was aided by rate increases and surcharges, this was partially offset by reduced gas sales due to the milder than normal winter weather. For 2011, we expect operating EPS to increase about 6% from anticipated results in 2010, reflecting CMS's investments in its rate base and a modest improvement in the local economy.

▶ On May 27, 2010, CMS announced that due to projected surplus generating capacity in its market, it was indefinitely deferring the development of an 830-megawatt clean coal power plant it planned to have operational in 2017.

Investment Rationale/Risk

▶ The shares were recently up about 13% year to date, reflecting, in our view, the recent 40% increase in the dividend and the rebound in the utility sector. This follows a nearly 57% gain in 2009 that primarily reflected an improved outlook for CMS's long-term earnings growth. It plans to invest about $6.4 billion in its Consumer Energy utility over the next five years, which should significantly add to its rate base and enable it to grow earnings at an average annual rate of 5% to 7%. We do not expect CMS to issue any new equity through 2012.

▶ Risks to our recommendation and target price include a slower-than-expected recovery in both the financial markets and the Michigan economy, as well as a decrease in the average P/E multiple of the group as a whole.

▶ Following the 40% increase in the dividend (effective with the November 2010 payment), the recent yield was around 4.7%, in line with the approximate average peer yield. The increase was made possible after the company reduced its five-year capital investment plan by about $1 billion. Our 12-month target price is $17, a modest discount-to-peers P/E of 12X our operating EPS estimate for 2011.

Qualitative Risk Assessment

LOW	MEDIUM	HIGH

Our risk assessment reflects the steady cash flow from the regulated electric and gas utility businesses, which operate within a generally supportive regulatory environment, and our view of a substantially improved financial risk profile.

Quantitative Evaluations

S&P Quality Ranking   B

D	C	B-	B	B+	A-	A	A+

Relative Strength Rank   MODERATE   **65**

LOWEST = 1   HIGHEST = 99

Revenue/Earnings Data

Revenue (Million $)

	1Q	2Q	3Q	4Q	Year
2010	1,967	1,340	--	--	--
2009	2,104	1,225	1,263	1,613	6,205
2008	2,184	1,365	1,428	1,844	6,821
2007	2,237	1,319	1,282	1,674	6,464
2006	2,032	1,396	1,462	1,920	6,810
2005	1,845	1,230	1,307	1,906	6,288

Earnings Per Share ($)

2010	0.35	0.39	E0.40	E0.30	E1.34
2009	0.31	0.21	0.29	0.03	0.83
2008	0.44	0.20	0.33	0.27	1.23
2007	-0.16	-0.26	0.34	-0.56	-0.62
2006	-0.13	0.30	-0.47	-0.16	-0.44
2005	0.74	0.12	-1.21	-0.09	-0.51

Fiscal year ended Dec. 31. Next earnings report expected: Early November. EPS Estimates based on S&P Operating Earnings; historical GAAP earnings are as reported.

Dividend Data (Dates: mm/dd Payment Date: mm/dd/yy)

Amount ($)	Date Decl.	Ex-Div. Date	Stk. of Record	Payment Date
0.150	01/29	02/04	02/08	02/26/10
0.150	04/19	05/05	05/07	05/28/10
0.150	07/19	08/04	08/06	08/31/10
0.210	10/22	11/03	11/05	11/30/10

Dividends have been paid since 2007. Source: Company reports.

CMS Energy Corp

STANDARD &POOR'S

Business Summary September 13, 2010

CORPORATE OVERVIEW. CMS Energy (CMS) is the energy holding company for Consumers Energy (formerly Consumers Power Co.), a regulated electric and gas utility serving Michigan's Lower Peninsula, and CMS Enterprises, which is engaged in U.S. and international energy-related businesses. CMS operates in three business segments: electric utility, gas utility, and enterprises. CMS's electric utility operations include generation, purchase, distribution and sale of electricity. CMS's gas utility purchases, transports, stores, distributes and sells natural gas. The Enterprises segment, through its various subsidiaries and equity investments, is engaged in diversified energy businesses, including independent power production, electric distribution, and natural gas transmission, storage and processing.

MARKET PROFILE. CMS's electric utility provides electricity to approximately 1.8 million customers in 61 of the 68 counties in the lower peninsula of Michigan. In 2009, the electric utility had total electric deliveries of 36 billion kWh. Consumers' electric utility customer base includes a mix of residential, com-

mercial and diversified industrial customers, the largest segment of which is the automotive industry, which accounted for about 5% of total electric revenues in 2009. In April 2007, CMS completed the sale of the Palisades 798-megawatt nuclear power plant to Entergy (ETR) for $363 million. The transaction included a 15-year power purchase agreement with ETR. The company's gas utility serves some 1.7 million customers in 46 of the 68 counties in Michigan's lower peninsula. The gas utility also owned 1,652 miles of transmission lines at the end of 2009, and 15 gas storage fields in Michigan, with a storage capacity of 307 bcf. The electric utility segment accounted for 54.9% of consolidated revenues in 2009 (52.8% in 2008); the gas utility segment 41.2% (41.5%); Enterprises 3.5% (5.4%), and, other 0.4% (0.3%).

Company Financials Fiscal Year Ended Dec. 31

Per Share Data ($)	2009	2008	2007	2006	2005	2004	2003	2002	2001	2000
Tangible Book Value	11.42	10.88	9.46	9.90	10.53	10.51	9.69	7.47	8.11	12.15
Earnings	0.83	1.23	-0.62	-0.44	-0.51	0.67	-0.30	-2.99	-2.53	0.36
S&P Core Earnings	1.08	1.01	-0.65	-0.16	-0.44	0.36	0.25	-3.75	-3.29	NA
Dividends	0.50	0.36	0.20	Nil	Nil	Nil	Nil	1.09	1.46	1.46
Payout Ratio	60%	29%	NM	Nil	Nil	Nil	Nil	NM	NM	NM
Prices:High	16.13	17.47	19.55	17.00	16.80	10.65	10.74	24.80	31.80	32.25
Prices:Low	9.98	8.33	14.98	12.09	9.70	7.81	3.41	5.45	19.49	16.06
P/E Ratio:High	19	14	NM	NM	NM	16	NM	NM	NM	NM
P/E Ratio:Low	12	7	NM	NM	NM	12	NM	NM	NM	NM

Income Statement Analysis (Million $)										
Revenue	6,205	6,821	6,464	6,810	6,288	5,472	5,513	8,687	9,597	8,998
Depreciation	590	629	540	576	525	431	428	403	530	637
Maintenance	220	193	201	326	249	256	226	211	263	298
Fixed Charges Coverage	1.70	2.05	3.38	1.18	-0.56	1.01	1.23	0.12	1.26	1.63
Construction Credits	NA	NA	NA	NA	NA	NA	NA	NA	NA	NA
Effective Tax Rate	34.3%	31.6%	63.3%	NM	NM	NM	NM	NM	NM	57.7%
Net Income	209	300	-126	-85.0	-98.0	127	-43.0	-416	-331	41.0
S&P Core Earnings	260	238	-145	-31.0	-93.1	63.4	40.6	-522	-431	NA

Balance Sheet & Other Financial Data (Million $)										
Gross Property	14,222	13,618	12,894	13,293	12,448	14,751	11,790	11,344	15,195	14,087
Capital Expenditures	818	792	1,263	670	593	525	535	747	1,262	1,032
Net Property	9,682	9,190	8,728	7,976	7,325	8,636	6,944	5,234	8,362	7,835
Capitalization:Long Term Debt	6,092	6,287	5,832	6,466	7,286	7,307	8,652	6,399	6,983	7,913
Capitalization:% Long Term Debt	68.2	69.9	71.0	72.2	73.8	75.8	84.5	85.0	78.7	77.0
Capitalization:Preferred	239	243	250	261	261	261	Nil	Nil	Nil	Nil
Capitalization:% Preferred	2.70	2.70	3.00	2.91	2.64	2.71	Nil	Nil	Nil	Nil
Capitalization:Common	2,602	2,463	2,130	2,234	2,322	2,072	1,585	1,133	1,890	2,361
Capitalization:% Common	29.1	27.4	25.9	24.9	23.5	21.5	15.5	15.0	21.3	23.0
Total Capital	9,724	9,145	8,323	9,234	10,566	11,123	11,010	8,058	9,834	11,221
% Operating Ratio	90.8	90.6	100.4	92.8	84.8	88.2	91.5	92.1	89.6	88.9
% Earned on Net Property	7.3	8.9	8.8	NM	NM	7.6	8.1	1.8	3.7	9.1
% Return on Revenue	3.4	4.4	NM	NM	NM	2.3	NM	NM	NM	0.5
% Return on Invested Capital	6.7	7.9	4.4	8.1	11.0	9.5	6.7	7.9	9.4	9.5
% Return on Common Equity	8.3	13.1	NM	NM	NM	6.3	NM	NM	NM	1.7

Data as orig reptd.; bef. results of disc opers/spec. items. Per share data adj. for stk. divs.; EPS diluted. E-Estimated. NA-Not Available. NM-Not Meaningful. NR-Not Ranked. UR-Under Review.

Office: One Energy Plaza, Jackson, MI 49201-2357.
Telephone: 517-788-0550.
Email: invest@cmsenergy.com
Website: http://www.cmsenergy.com

Chrmn: D.W. Joos
Pres & CEO: J.G. Russell
EVP & CFO: T.J. Webb
SVP & General Counsel: J.E. Brunner

Chief Acctg Officer & Cntlr: G.P. Barba
Investor Contact: L.L. Mountcastle (517-788-2590)
Board Members: M. S. Ayres, J. E. Barfield, S. E. Ewing, R. M. Gabrys, D. W. Joos, P. R. Lochner, Jr., M. T. Monahan, J. G. Russell, K. L. Way, J. B. Yasinsky

Founded: 1987
Domicile: Michigan
Employees: 8,039

Coach Inc.

STANDARD &POOR'S

| S&P Recommendation **STRONG BUY** ★★★★★ | Price $44.55 (as of Oct 22, 2010) | 12-Mo. Target Price $51.00 | Investment Style Large-Cap Growth |

GICS Sector Consumer Discretionary
Sub-Industry Apparel, Accessories & Luxury Goods

Summary COH designs, makes, and markets fine accessories for women and men, including handbags, weekend and travel accessories, outerwear, footwear, and business cases.

Key Stock Statistics (Source S&P, Vickers, company reports)

52-Wk Range	$44.97– 31.69	S&P Oper. EPS 2011**E**	2.65	Market Capitalization(B)	$13.249	Beta	1.63
Trailing 12-Month EPS	$2.33	S&P Oper. EPS 2012**E**	3.00	Yield (%)	1.35	S&P 3-Yr. Proj. EPS CAGR(%)	15
Trailing 12-Month P/E	19.1	P/E on S&P Oper. EPS 2011**E**	16.8	Dividend Rate/Share	$0.60	S&P Credit Rating	NA
$10K Invested 5 Yrs Ago	$14,049	Common Shares Outstg. (M)	297.4	Institutional Ownership (%)	87		

Price Performance

30-Week Mov. Avg. · · · 10-Week Mov. Avg. - - ■ GAAP Earnings vs. Previous Year Volume Above Avg. STARS
12-Mo. Target Price — Relative Strength — ▲ Up ▼ Down ► No Change Below Avg. ★

Options: ASE, CBOE, P, Ph

Analysis prepared by **Marie Driscoll, CFA** on September 10, 2010, when the stock traded at **$ 39.08**.

Highlights

▶ COH is developing its global business with a region-driven strategy -- a strong factory offering in regions where value is a high consumer priority (Japan and the U.S.) and heightened luxury positioning in Europe and China. COH is entering the $4 billion global men's bag and small leather goods market with the same regional focus. We see international expansion supporting global market share gains through 2015.

▶ COH intends to expand its retail distribution 10% in FY 11 (Jun.), emphasizing China, where sales doubled to $100 million in FY 10 and COH plans 30 new stores (+60% square footage) in FY 11. In the U.S., 30 new stores will include 10 each of men's only factory, factory and full price, and eight locations will open in Japan. We see mid single-digit wholesale growth driven by Europe and a +3% to +5% comp. We see 10.4% revenue growth (12.6% excluding the $70 million sales impact of a 53rd week in FY 10).

▶ We see 30 basis points of EBIT margin contraction to 31.6%, in FY 11 as COH invests in Reed Krakoff, Europe, and global infrastructure.

Investment Rationale/Risk

▶ We see favorable long-term sales and earnings prospects for COH, based as much on management's acumen as global brand potential. COH adeptly navigated the consumer pullback by lowering price points, increasing the value equation, and developing new marketing strategies to appeal to a younger audience. COH ended FY 10 on a strong note, with a June-quarter +6.3% North American comp along with a 10% rise in handbag penetration to 55%, and international momentum. COH's productivity and profitability metrics are double those of its specialty apparel peers, at an estimated $2,088 trailing 12-months sales per square foot and a 31.9% EBIT margin.

▶ Risks to our recommendation and target price include a sharp decline in consumer spending, risks associated with sourcing, fashion and inventory, and execution risk as COH expands internationally.

▶ Our $51 target price is 19.2X our FY 11 EPS estimate, a modest discount to COH's average five-year forward P/E of 21X and a 25% premium to a broad peer group of specialty apparel retailers.

Qualitative Risk Assessment

| LOW | MEDIUM | HIGH |

Our risk assessment reflects our view of COH's strong brand equity and rising cash flow, offset by a highly competitive market amid retail consolidation.

Quantitative Evaluations

S&P Quality Ranking B+

| D | C | B- | B | B+ | A- | A | A+ |

Relative Strength Rank STRONG

76

LOWEST = 1   HIGHEST = 99

Revenue/Earnings Data

Revenue (Million $)

	1Q	2Q	3Q	4Q	Year
2010	761.4	1,065	830.7	950.5	3,608
2009	752.5	960.3	739.9	777.7	3,230
2008	676.7	978.0	744.5	781.5	3,181
2007	529.4	805.6	625.3	652.1	2,612
2006	449.0	650.3	497.9	514.4	2,112
2005	344.1	531.8	415.9	418.7	1,710

Earnings Per Share ($)

2010	0.44	0.75	0.50	0.64	2.33
2009	0.44	0.67	0.36	0.46	1.91
2008	0.41	0.69	0.46	0.62	2.17
2007	0.31	0.57	0.39	0.42	1.69
2006	0.24	0.45	0.28	0.31	1.27
2005	0.17	0.34	0.23	0.25	1.00

Fiscal year ended Jun. 30. Next earnings report expected: NA. EPS Estimates based on S&P Operating Earnings; historical GAAP earnings are as reported.

Dividend Data (Dates: mm/dd Payment Date: mm/dd/yy)

Amount ($)	Date Decl.	Ex-Div. Date	Stk. of Record	Payment Date
0.075	11/19	12/03	12/07	12/28/09
0.075	02/04	03/04	03/08	03/29/10
0.150	05/17	06/04	06/08	07/06/10
0.150	08/18	09/02	09/07	10/04/10

Dividends have been paid since 2009. Source: Company reports.

Please read the Required Disclosures and Analyst Certification on the last page of this report.

The McGraw-Hill Companies

Coach Inc.

STANDARD &POOR'S

Business Summary September 10, 2010

CORPORATE OVERVIEW. Coach is a leading U.S. designer and marketer of high-quality accessories. Founded in 1941, COH has over the past several years transformed the Coach brand, building on its popular core categories by introducing new products in a broader array of materials, styles and categories. The company has also implemented a flexible sourcing and manufacturing model, which it believes enables it to bring a broader range of products to market more rapidly and efficiently.

MARKET PROFILE. Coach is the number one luxury accessories brand in the U.S., with an estimated 20% share of this estimated $8.3 billion market ($100+ handbags). In the 12 months ended June 2010, the category grew an estimated 3% to 5%, which COH easily outpaced. This sub-segment of the handbag/accessories market grew at an estimated 20% pace in 2007 and 2006, 17% in 2005, 30% in 2004, and 23% in 2003, before a flat 2008 and estimated 5%-10% decline in 2009. It remains one of the best-performing categories at retail. COH has been able to outpace industry growth as it executed its multi-channel growth strategy, and we believe COH has an estimated 20%+ U.S. handbag market share entering FY 11. The Japanese consumer makes up about 40% of the global luxury handbag market; COH estimates it holds 16% of the domestic

Japanese market, and aims to leverage its brand there by entering the men's small leather goods market. Developing markets represent the next leg of growth, supporting a global market projected at $25 billion in 2010. With a total of 41 locations in Greater China, COH currently holds an estimated 4% share of the market.

PRIMARY BUSINESS DYNAMICS. COH sells its products through direct-to-consumer and indirect channels, with the former accounting for 87% of total sales in FY 10 (Jun.), up from 84% in FY 09 and 55% in FY 05 via store expansion and comp store sales gains. As of July 3, 2010, direct-to-consumer channels included the Internet, direct mail catalogs, 342 North American retail stores, 121 North American factory stores, and 167 department store shop-in-shops, retail stores and factory stores in Japan. Indirect channels include an estimated 900 U.S. department store locations and 140 international department store, retail store and duty-free shop locations in 18 countries.

Company Financials Fiscal Year Ended Jun. 30

Per Share Data ($)	2010	2009	2008	2007	2006	2005	2004	2003	2002	2001
Tangible Book Value	4.01	4.41	3.73	4.52	2.57	2.07	2.00	1.11	0.67	0.43
Cash Flow	2.73	2.29	2.45	1.90	1.44	1.14	0.79	0.48	0.31	0.24
Earnings	2.33	1.91	2.17	1.69	1.27	1.00	0.68	0.40	0.24	0.19
S&P Core Earnings	2.33	1.91	2.17	1.69	1.26	0.91	0.61	0.35	0.21	0.17
Dividends	0.38	0.08	Nil	Nil	Nil	Nil	Nil	Nil	Nil	Nil
Payout Ratio	16%	4%	Nil	Nil	Nil	Nil	Nil	Nil	Nil	Nil
Prices:High	44.97	37.36	37.64	54.00	44.99	36.84	28.85	20.42	8.93	5.34
Prices:Low	32.96	11.41	13.19	29.22	25.18	24.51	16.88	7.26	4.30	2.50
P/E Ratio:High	19	20	17	32	35	37	42	52	38	28
P/E Ratio:Low	14	6	6	17	20	25	25	18	18	13

Income Statement Analysis (Million $)										
Revenue	3,608	3,230	3,181	2,612	2,112	1,710	1,321	953	719	616
Operating Income	1,276	1,095	1,280	1,074	830	679	487	274	163	130
Depreciation	127	123	101	80.9	65.1	57.0	42.9	30.2	25.5	24.1
Interest Expense	NA	NA	NA	Nil	Nil	1.22	0.81	0.70	1.12	2.26
Pretax Income	1,152	977	1,195	1,035	797	638	448	245	133	99.4
Effective Tax Rate	NA	36.2%	34.5%	38.5%	38.0%	36.9%	37.5%	37.0%	35.5%	35.6%
Net Income	735	623	783	637	494	389	262	147	85.8	64.0
S&P Core Earnings	735	625	783	637	492	356	236	129	74.9	58.3

Balance Sheet & Other Financial Data (Million $)										
Cash	696	800	699	557	143	155	263	229	94.0	3.69
Current Assets	1,303	1,396	1,386	1,740	974	709	706	449	288	152
Total Assets	2,467	2,564	2,274	2,450	1,627	1,347	1,029	618	441	259
Current Liabilities	529	460	451	408	342	266	182	161	159	104
Long Term Debt	24.2	25.1	2.58	2.87	3.10	3.27	3.42	3.54	3.62	3.69
Common Equity	1,505	1,696	1,516	1,910	1,189	1,033	782	427	260	148
Total Capital	1,530	1,721	1,545	1,950	1,223	1,041	842	453	279	152
Capital Expenditures	81.1	240	175	141	134	94.6	67.7	57.1	42.8	31.9
Cash Flow	862	746	884	717	559	446	305	177	111	88.2
Current Ratio	2.5	3.0	3.1	4.3	2.9	2.7	3.9	2.8	1.8	1.5
% Long Term Debt of Capitalization	1.6	1.5	0.2	0.1	0.3	0.3	0.4	0.8	1.3	2.4
% Net Income of Revenue	20.4	19.3	24.6	24.4	23.4	22.7	19.8	15.4	11.9	10.4
% Return on Assets	29.2	25.8	33.2	31.2	33.0	32.5	31.8	27.7	24.5	23.1
% Return on Equity	45.9	38.8	45.7	41.1	44.0	42.8	43.3	42.7	42.0	35.5

Data as orig reptd.; bef. results of disc opers/spec. items. Per share data adj. for stk. divs.; EPS diluted. E-Estimated. NA-Not Available. NM-Not Meaningful. NR-Not Ranked. UR-Under Review.

Office: 516 W 34th St, New York, NY 10001-1394.
Telephone: 212-594-1850.
Email: info@coach.com
Website: http://www.coach.com

Chrmn & CEO: L. Frankfort
COO & Co-Pres: J. Stritzke
EVP, CFO & Chief Acctg Officer: M.F. Devine, III
SVP, Secy & General Counsel: T. Kahn

Treas: N. Walsh
Investor Contact: M. Devine (212-594-1850)
Board Members: L. Frankfort, S. J. Kropf, G. W. Loveman, I. M. Menezes, I. R. Miller, M. E. Murphy, J. J. Zeitlin

Founded: 1941
Domicile: Maryland
Employees: 13,000

The McGraw·Hill Companies

Coca-Cola Co (The)

STANDARD &POOR'S

S&P Recommendation	**STRONG BUY** ★★★★★	**Price** $61.61 (as of Oct 22, 2010)	**12-Mo. Target Price** $68.00	**Investment Style** Large-Cap Growth

GICS Sector Consumer Staples
Sub-Industry Soft Drinks

Summary The world's largest soft drink company, KO also has a sizable fruit juice business.

Key Stock Statistics (Source S&P, Vickers, company reports)

52-Wk Range	$61.75– 49.47	S&P Oper. EPS 2010**E**	3.49	Market Capitalization(B)	$142.286	Beta		0.59
Trailing 12-Month EPS	$3.25	S&P Oper. EPS 2011**E**	3.82	Yield (%)	2.86	S&P 3-Yr. Proj. EPS CAGR(%)		8
Trailing 12-Month P/E	19.0	P/E on S&P Oper. EPS 2010**E**	17.7	Dividend Rate/Share	$1.76	S&P Credit Rating		A+
$10K Invested 5 Yrs Ago	$17,005	Common Shares Outstg. (M)	2,309.5	Institutional Ownership (%)	62			

Price Performance

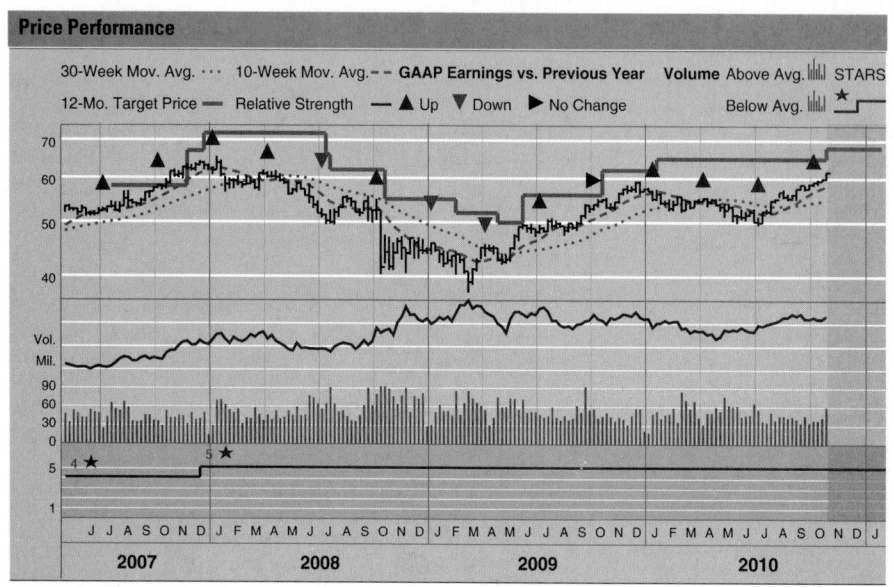

30-Week Mov. Avg. · · · 10-Week Mov. Avg. - - GAAP Earnings vs. Previous Year Volume Above Avg. STARS
12-Mo. Target Price — Relative Strength — ▲ Up ▼ Down ▶ No Change Below Avg. ★

Options: ASE, CBOE, P, Ph

Analysis prepared by **Esther Y. Kwon, CFA** on October 19, 2010, when the stock traded at **$ 60.45**.

Highlights

➤ For 2010, we project that sales will rise about 15% from 2009's $31 billion, on the purchase of the North American operations of Coca-Cola Enterprises and, to a lesser extent, higher prices, international volume growth, and positive foreign exchange. We look for mid-single digit growth in volumes, with carbonated volumes increasing at a low single digit rate and non-carbonated volumes rising at a high single digit rate. For 2011, we forecast sales growth of over 30%, driven by the inclusion of a full year of results from the acquisition.

➤ In 2010, we expect operating profit growth to accelerate as cost-cutting initiatives, positive operating leverage and more favorable commodity costs outweigh an unfavorable mix, with lower-margin emerging markets recovering faster than developed ones.

➤ Assuming an effective tax rate similar to 2009's 23%, we estimate EPS of $3.49 for 2010, up from operating EPS of $3.06 in 2009, which excludes asset impairment and restructuring charges, and $3.82 in 2011. KO's long-term financial objectives include 3% to 4% annual volume growth, 6% to 8% operating income growth, and EPS growth in the high single digits.

Investment Rationale/Risk

➤ In October 2010, KO completed the purchase of Coca-Cola Enterprises' (CCE 29, Hold) North American bottling operations for a total value of approximately $12.3 billion and sold to CCE its bottling operations in Norway and Sweden for $822 million. While we have an unfavorable view of the reduction in international exposure, we still see KO having an attractive relative international footprint, particularly in faster growing emerging markets, and capability to generate strong free cash flow, which we believe will be returned to shareholders through dividends and stock repurchases. We also see an opportunity to improve execution and reduce costs in North America.

➤ Risks to our recommendation and target price include adverse foreign currency movements, and unfavorable weather conditions in the company's markets.

➤ Our 12-month target price of $68 is based on an analysis of historical and comparative peer P/E multiples. KO's forward P/E has ranged between 16X and over 40X over the past few years. Given a more challenging economic environment, we think a multiple in the lower half of that range is appropriate.

Qualitative Risk Assessment

LOW	MEDIUM	HIGH

Our risk assessment for Coca-Cola Company reflects the relatively stable nature of the company's end markets, its dominant market share positions around the world, and our view of its strong balance sheet and cash flow.

Quantitative Evaluations

S&P Quality Ranking A+

D	C	B-	B	B+	A-	A	A+

Relative Strength Rank STRONG

71

LOWEST = 1   HIGHEST = 99

Revenue/Earnings Data

Revenue (Million $)

	1Q	2Q	3Q	4Q	Year
2010	7,525	8,674	8,426	--	--
2009	7,169	8,267	8,044	7,510	30,990
2008	7,379	9,046	8,393	7,126	31,944
2007	6,103	7,733	7,690	7,331	28,857
2006	5,226	6,476	6,454	5,932	24,088
2005	5,206	6,310	6,037	5,551	23,104

Earnings Per Share ($)

2010	0.69	1.02	0.88	E0.72	E3.49
2009	0.58	0.88	0.81	0.66	2.93
2008	0.64	0.61	0.81	0.43	2.49
2007	0.54	0.80	0.71	0.52	2.57
2006	0.47	0.78	0.62	0.29	2.16
2005	0.42	0.72	0.54	0.36	2.04

Fiscal year ended Dec. 31. Next earnings report expected: Early February. EPS Estimates based on S&P Operating Earnings; historical GAAP earnings are as reported.

Dividend Data (Dates: mm/dd Payment Date: mm/dd/yy)

Amount ($)	Date Decl.	Ex-Div. Date	Stk. of Record	Payment Date
0.440	02/18	03/11	03/15	04/01/10
0.440	04/22	06/11	06/15	07/01/10
0.440	07/22	09/13	09/15	10/01/10
0.440	10/21	11/29	12/01	12/15/10

Dividends have been paid since 1893. Source: Company reports.

Please read the Required Disclosures and Analyst Certification on the last page of this report.

The McGraw-Hill Companies

Coca-Cola Co (The)

STANDARD &POOR'S

Business Summary October 19, 2010

CORPORATE OVERVIEW. The Coca-Cola Company is the world's largest producer of soft drink concentrates and syrups, as well as the world's biggest producer of juice and juice-related products. Finished soft drink products bearing the company's trademarks have been sold in the U.S. since 1886, and are now sold in more than 200 countries. It owns or licenses more than 500 brands. Sales by operating segment in 2009 were derived as follows: North America (26.4% of revenues); Bottling Investments (26.4%); Europe (13.9%); Pacific (14.6%); Latin America (12.0%); Eurasia and Africa (6.4%); and Corporate (0.3%)

The company's business encompasses the production and sale of soft drink and non-carbonated beverage concentrates and syrups. These products are sold to the company's authorized independent and company-owned bottling/canning operations, and fountain wholesalers. These customers then either combine the syrup with carbonated water, or combine the concentrate with sweetener, water and carbonated water to produce finished soft drinks. The finished soft drinks are packaged in containers bearing the company's well-known trademarks, which include Coca-Cola, caffeine free Coca-Cola, Diet Coke (sold as Coke Light in many markets outside the U.S.), Cherry Coke, Coca-Cola Zero (sold as Coke Zero in some markets), Fanta, Full Throttle, Sprite, Diet Sprite/Sprite Zero, Barq's, Pibb Xtra, Mello Yello, Tab, Fresca, Powerade, Aquarius, and other products developed for specific markets. Other beverage products included enhanced water brands such as glaceau vitaminwater and smartwater. The company also markets Schweppes, Canada Dry, Crush and Dr. Pepper brands outside of the U.S. In 2009, concentrates and syrups for beverages bearing the trademark Coca-Cola or including the trademark Coke accounted for approximately 51% of the company's total concentrate sales.

In 2009, concentrate sales in the U.S. represented approximately 22% of KO's worldwide sales. About 51% of U.S. concentrate sales were beverage concentrates and syrups to 74 authorized bottlers in 393 licensed territories, 34% were fountain syrups sold to fountain retailers and 451 fountain wholesalers, and the remaining 15% were sales by the company of finished products.

KO has equity positions in approximately 38 unconsolidated bottling, canning and distribution operations for its products worldwide, including bottlers that accounted for approximately 56% of the company's worldwide unit case volume in 2009. Coca-Cola Enterprises (CCE) accounted for 47% of the company's U.S. concentrate sales.

Company Financials Fiscal Year Ended Dec. 31

Per Share Data ($)	2009	2008	2007	2006	2005	2004	2003	2002	2001	2000
Tangible Book Value	5.20	3.45	8.53	5.08	5.29	5.02	4.14	3.34	3.53	2.98
Cash Flow	3.46	2.94	3.00	2.56	2.43	2.36	2.11	1.93	1.92	1.19
Earnings	2.93	2.49	2.57	2.16	2.04	2.00	1.77	1.60	1.60	0.88
S&P Core Earnings	2.94	2.40	2.51	2.04	2.03	2.08	1.77	1.62	1.46	NA
Dividends	1.64	1.52	1.36	1.24	1.12	1.00	0.88	0.80	0.72	0.68
Payout Ratio	56%	61%	53%	57%	55%	50%	50%	50%	45%	77%
Prices:High	59.45	65.59	64.32	49.35	45.26	53.50	50.90	57.91	62.19	66.88
Prices:Low	37.44	40.29	45.56	39.36	40.31	38.30	37.01	42.90	42.37	42.88
P/E Ratio:High	20	26	25	23	22	27	29	36	39	76
P/E Ratio:Low	13	16	18	18	20	19	21	27	26	49

Income Statement Analysis (Million $)	2009	2008	2007	2006	2005	2004	2003	2002	2001	2000
Revenue	30,990	31,944	28,857	24,088	23,104	21,962	21,044	19,564	20,092	20,458
Operating Income	9,780	9,862	8,532	7,246	7,017	6,591	6,071	6,264	6,155	4,464
Depreciation	1,236	1,066	1,012	938	932	893	850	806	803	773
Interest Expense	355	438	456	220	240	196	178	199	289	447
Pretax Income	8,946	7,439	7,873	6,578	6,690	6,222	5,495	5,499	5,670	3,399
Effective Tax Rate	22.8%	21.9%	24.0%	22.8%	27.2%	22.1%	20.9%	27.7%	29.8%	36.0%
Net Income	6,824	5,807	5,981	5,080	4,872	4,847	4,347	3,976	3,979	2,177
S&P Core Earnings	6,842	5,595	5,827	4,797	4,854	5,063	4,350	4,021	3,654	NA

Balance Sheet & Other Financial Data (Million $)	2009	2008	2007	2006	2005	2004	2003	2002	2001	2000
Cash	9,213	4,979	4,308	2,590	4,767	6,768	3,482	2,345	1,934	1,892
Current Assets	17,551	12,176	12,105	8,441	10,250	12,094	8,396	7,352	7,171	6,620
Total Assets	48,671	40,519	43,269	29,963	29,427	31,327	27,342	24,501	22,417	20,834
Current Liabilities	13,721	12,988	13,225	8,890	9,836	10,971	7,886	7,341	8,429	9,321
Long Term Debt	5,059	2,781	9,329	1,314	1,154	1,157	2,517	2,701	1,219	835
Common Equity	24,799	20,472	21,744	16,920	16,355	15,935	14,090	11,800	11,366	9,316
Total Capital	30,456	24,130	27,269	18,842	17,861	17,542	16,944	14,900	13,027	10,509
Capital Expenditures	1,993	1,968	1,648	1,407	899	755	812	851	769	733
Cash Flow	8,060	6,873	6,993	6,018	5,804	5,740	5,197	4,782	4,782	2,950
Current Ratio	1.3	0.9	0.9	0.9	1.0	1.1	1.1	1.0	0.9	0.7
% Long Term Debt of Capitalization	16.6	11.5	12.9	7.0	6.5	6.6	14.9	18.1	9.4	7.9
% Net Income of Revenue	22.0	18.2	20.7	21.1	21.1	22.1	20.7	20.3	19.8	10.6
% Return on Assets	15.3	13.9	16.3	17.1	16.0	16.5	16.8	16.9	18.4	10.3
% Return on Equity	30.2	27.5	30.9	30.5	30.2	32.3	33.6	34.3	38.5	23.1

Data as orig reptd.; bef. results of disc opers/spec. items. Per share data adj. for stk. divs.; EPS diluted. E-Estimated. NA-Not Available. NM-Not Meaningful. NR-Not Ranked. UR-Under Review.

Office: 1 Coca Cola Plz NW, Atlanta, GA 30313-2499.
Telephone: 404-676-2121.
Website: http://www.coca-cola.com
Chrmn & CEO: M. Kent

Investor Contact: G. Fayard
EVP & CFO: G. Fayard
EVP & Chief Admin Officer: A.B. Cummings, Jr.
SVP & CTO: D.L. Strickland

Board Members: H. Allen, R. W. Allen, C. P. Black, B. Diller, A. Herman, M. Kent, D. R. Keough, M. E. Lagomasino, D. McHenry, S. A. Nunn, J. D. Robinson, III, P. V. Ueberroth, J. Wallenberg, J. B. Williams

Founded: 1886
Domicile: Delaware
Employees: 92,800

The McGraw-Hill Companies

Coca-Cola Enterprises Inc.

STANDARD &POOR'S

S&P Recommendation HOLD ★★★★☆	**Price** $24.63 (as of Oct 22, 2010)	**12-Mo. Target Price** $31.00	**Investment Style** Large-Cap Blend

GICS Sector Consumer Staples
Sub-Industry Soft Drinks

Summary This company is the world's largest bottler of Coca-Cola beverage products. Coca-Cola Co., which holds about 34% of CCE's common stock, has agreed to buy CCE's North American operations in exchange for a new CCE share and $10 for each old share.

Key Stock Statistics (Source S&P, Vickers, company reports)

52-Wk Range	$31.80– 18.75	S&P Oper. EPS 2010**E**	1.82	Market Capitalization(B)	$12.379	Beta	1.30
Trailing 12-Month EPS	$1.86	S&P Oper. EPS 2011**E**	2.02	Yield (%)	1.46	S&P 3-Yr. Proj. EPS CAGR(%)	9
Trailing 12-Month P/E	13.2	P/E on S&P Oper. EPS 2010**E**	13.5	Dividend Rate/Share	$0.36	S&P Credit Rating	A
$10K Invested 5 Yrs Ago	$13,563	Common Shares Outstg. (M)	502.6	Institutional Ownership (%)	53		

Price Performance

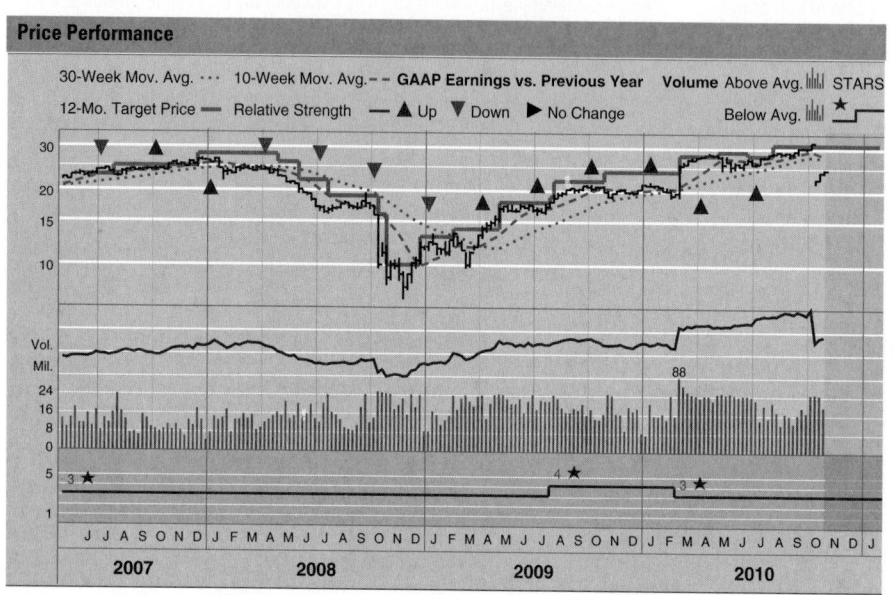

30-Week Mov. Avg. ···· 10-Week Mov. Avg. - - GAAP Earnings vs. Previous Year Volume Above Avg. STARS
12-Mo. Target Price — Relative Strength — ▲ Up ▼ Down ▶ No Change Below Avg. ★

Options: ASE, CBOE, P, Ph

Analysis prepared by **Esther Y. Kwon, CFA** on August 04, 2010, when the stock traded at **$ 29.41.**

Highlights

► In 2010, we see net revenues down about 1% from 2009's $21.6 billion. We project higher pricing in both North America and Europe, with lower volumes in North America and a low single-digit rise in Europe. We expect that North American volumes will remain sluggish on higher pricing and relative weakness in non-carbonated beverages, but we see some improvement in the economically sensitive take-home single-serve category.

► We see gross margins expanding with higher pricing and lower commodity costs and a mix shift favoring cheaper packages, such as cans over higher cost finished goods. We estimate SG&A expenses will remain flat as a percentage of sales.

► On an effective tax rate of 26.6%, versus 2009's 24%, and slightly lower interest expense, we see EPS of $1.82, up from 2009's $1.60, which excludes restructuring and license charges. After several years' absence and upon completion of its transaction with Coca-Cola, CCE plans to repurchase approximately $1 billion of shares within the following 18 months, and pay an annual dividend of $0.50 per share.

Investment Rationale/Risk

► In February 2010, Coca-Cola Co. agreed to acquire CCE's North America bottling business for $10 and one new CCE share for each existing CCE share. In turn, CCE will purchase Coca-Cola Co.'s bottling operations in Norway and Sweden for $822 million and have the right to acquire its 83% equity stake in its German bottling operations for fair value 18 to 36 months after the close of the deal. Coca-Cola Co. and CCE anticipate that the proposed transaction will close in the fourth quarter of 2010. We like the deal for CCE shareholders, as the new business will be higher growth with higher profitability, but we see the shares as fully valued.

► Risks to our recommendation and target price include failure to consummate the proposed transaction, sustained turmoil in the European economy and credit markets, and more rapid commodity cost inflation than we expect. In terms of corporate governance, the board of directors is controlled by insiders and affiliated outsiders, which we view unfavorably.

► Our 12-month target price of $31 is based on forward P/E of 15.5X our 2011 EPS estimate of $2.00, in line with the peer average.

Qualitative Risk Assessment

LOW	MEDIUM	HIGH

Our risk assessment for Coca-Cola Enterprises reflects our view of the relatively stable nature of the company's end markets, its strong cash flow, and its relationship with corporate partner Coca-Cola Company.

Quantitative Evaluations

S&P Quality Ranking B-

D	C	B-	B	B+	A-	A	A+

Relative Strength Rank WEAK

12
LOWEST = 1 HIGHEST = 99

Revenue/Earnings Data

Revenue (Million $)

	1Q	2Q	3Q	4Q	Year
2010	4,968	5,884	--	--	--
2009	5,050	5,909	5,569	5,117	21,645
2008	4,892	5,935	5,743	5,237	21,807
2007	4,567	5,665	5,405	5,299	20,936
2006	4,333	5,467	5,218	4,786	19,804
2005	4,196	5,128	4,895	4,487	18,706

Earnings Per Share ($)

2010	0.21	0.69	E0.53	E0.23	E1.82
2009	0.13	0.64	0.50	0.22	1.48
2008	0.02	-6.52	0.44	-2.99	-9.05
2007	0.03	0.56	0.55	0.32	1.46
2006	0.03	0.71	0.44	-3.59	-2.41
2005	0.10	0.70	0.40	-0.12	1.08

Fiscal year ended Dec. 31. Next earnings report expected: Late October. EPS Estimates based on S&P Operating Earnings; historical GAAP earnings are as reported.

Dividend Data (Dates: mm/dd Payment Date: mm/dd/yy)

Amount ($)	Date Decl.	Ex-Div. Date	Stk. of Record	Payment Date
0.080	10/27	11/24	11/27	12/10/09
0.090	02/16	03/10	03/12	03/26/10
0.090	04/26	06/09	06/11	06/24/10
0.090	07/26	09/08	09/10	09/23/10

Dividends have been paid since 1986. Source: Company reports.

Please read the Required Disclosures and Analyst Certification on the last page of this report.

The **McGraw·Hill** Companies

Coca-Cola Enterprises Inc.

STANDARD &POOR'S

Business Summary August 04, 2010

CORPORATE OVERVIEW. Coca-Cola Enterprises is the world's largest bottler of Coca-Cola beverage products. The Coca-Cola Company (KO 49, Strong Buy) owns about 34% of the company's common stock. CCE's product line also includes other nonalcoholic beverages, such as still and sparkling waters, juices, isotonics and teas. In 2009, the company sold approximately 41 billion bottles and cans (or 1.9 billion cases) throughout its territories, representing about 16% of KO's worldwide volume. More than 90% of this volume consisted of beverages produced and sold under licenses from KO and its affiliates and joint ventures. CCE also distributes Dr Pepper and several other beverage brands.

Based on net operating revenues in 2009, North America accounted for 70% of the total, unchanged from 2008, and Europe for 30%. CCE operates in parts of 46 states in the U.S., the District of Columbia, the U.S. Virgin Islands, all 10 Canadian provinces, and portions of Europe that include Belgium, France, the U.K., Luxembourg, Monaco, and The Netherlands. At December 31, 2009, CCE's bottling territories encompassed an aggregate population of 421 million people. The company's five leading brands in North America in 2009 were Coca-Cola, Diet Coke, Sprite, Dasani, and Dr Pepper, while the five leading

brands in Europe were Coca-Cola, Diet Coke/Coca-Cola Light, Coca-Cola Zero, Fanta and Capri-Sun.

During 2009, the company's package mix (based on wholesale physical case volume) in North America was as follows: 58.0% cans, 41.0% PET plastic and 1.0% glass and other. In Europe, the package mix was as follows: 39.5% cans, 45.0% PET plastic and 15.5% glass and other.

In addition to concentrates, sweeteners, juices and finished product, CCE purchases carbon dioxide, PET preforms, glass and plastic bottles, cans, closures, packaging such as plastic bags in cardboard boxes, and other packaging materials. The beverage agreements with The Coca-Cola Co. provide that all authorized containers, closures, cases, cartons and other packages, and labels for the products of The Coca-Cola Co. must be purchased from manufacturers approved by The Coca-Cola Co.

Company Financials Fiscal Year Ended Dec. 31

Per Share Data ($)	2009	2008	2007	2006	2005	2004	2003	2002	2001	2000
Tangible Book Value	NM	NM	NM	NM	NM	NM	NM	NM	6.25	6.67
Cash Flow	3.60	-6.90	3.64	-0.28	3.27	3.52	3.88	3.35	3.08	3.48
Earnings	1.48	-9.05	1.46	-2.41	1.08	1.26	1.48	1.07	-0.05	0.54
S&P Core Earnings	1.54	0.83	1.45	-2.34	1.01	1.19	1.22	0.78	-0.34	NA
Dividends	0.30	0.28	0.24	0.24	0.16	0.16	0.16	0.16	0.12	0.16
Payout Ratio	20%	NM	16%	NM	15%	13%	11%	15%	NM	30%
Prices:High	21.53	26.99	27.09	22.49	23.92	29.34	23.30	24.50	23.90	30.25
Prices:Low	9.70	7.25	19.78	18.83	18.52	18.45	16.85	15.94	13.46	14.00
P/E Ratio:High	15	NM	19	NM	22	23	16	23	NM	56
P/E Ratio:Low	7	NM	14	NM	17	15	11	15	NM	26

Income Statement Analysis (Million $)										
Revenue	21,645	21,807	20,936	19,804	18,706	18,158	17,330	16,889	15,700	14,750
Operating Income	2,684	2,510	2,537	2,439	2,475	2,504	2,674	2,409	1,954	2,387
Depreciation	1,043	1,050	1,067	1,012	1,044	1,068	1,097	1,045	1,353	1,261
Interest Expense	574	587	629	633	633	619	607	662	753	791
Pretax Income	963	-6,901	841	-2,118	790	818	972	705	-150	333
Effective Tax Rate	24.1%	NM	15.4%	NM	34.9%	27.1%	30.5%	29.9%	NM	29.1%
Net Income	731	-4,394	711	-1,143	514	596	676	494	-19.0	236
S&P Core Earnings	760	405	708	-1,110	478	563	563	356	-147	NA

Balance Sheet & Other Financial Data (Million $)										
Cash	1,057	722	170	184	107	155	80.0	68.0	284	294
Current Assets	5,170	4,583	4,092	3,691	3,395	3,264	3,000	2,844	2,876	2,631
Total Assets	16,416	15,589	24,046	23,225	25,357	26,354	25,700	24,375	23,719	22,162
Current Liabilities	4,588	5,074	5,343	3,818	3,846	3,431	3,941	3,455	4,522	3,094
Long Term Debt	7,804	7,247	7,391	9,218	9,165	10,523	10,552	11,236	10,365	10,348
Common Equity	859	-31.0	5,689	4,526	5,643	5,378	4,365	3,310	2,783	2,790
Total Capital	9,406	8,324	19,048	17,801	19,914	21,139	19,882	19,122	17,521	17,956
Capital Expenditures	916	981	938	882	914	946	1,099	1,029	972	1,181
Cash Flow	1,774	-3,344	1,178	-131	1,558	1,664	1,771	1,536	1,331	1,494
Current Ratio	1.1	0.9	0.8	1.0	0.9	1.0	0.8	0.8	0.6	0.9
% Long Term Debt of Capitalization	83.0	87.1	38.8	51.8	46.0	49.8	53.1	58.8	59.2	57.6
% Net Income of Revenue	3.4	NM	3.3	NM	2.7	3.3	3.9	2.9	NM	1.6
% Return on Assets	4.6	NM	3.0	NM	2.0	2.3	2.7	2.1	NM	1.1
% Return on Equity	NM	NM	13.9	NM	9.3	12.2	17.6	16.1	NM	8.2

Data as orig reptd.; bef. results of disc opers/spec. items. Per share data adj. for stk. divs.; EPS diluted. E-Estimated. NA-Not Available. NM-Not Meaningful. NR-Not Ranked. UR-Under Review.

Office: 2500 Windy Ridge Parkway, Atlanta, GA 30339.
Telephone: 770-989-3000.
Website: http://www.cokecce.com
Chrmn & CEO: J.F. Brock, III

EVP & CFO: B.W. Douglas, III
SVP & General Counsel: J.R. Parker, Jr.
SVP & CIO: E. Sezer
Chief Acctg Officer & Cntlr: S.D. Patterson

Investor Contact: T. Erickson (770-989-3110)
Board Members: J. Bennink, J. F. Brock, III, C. Darden, M. J. Herb, L. P. Humann, J. Hunter, O. H. Ingram, II, D. A. James, T. H. Johnson, S. Labarge, V. Morali, C. R. Welling, P. A. Wood

Founded: 1944
Domicile: Delaware
Employees: 70,000

The McGraw·Hill Companies

Cognizant Technology Solutions Corp

STANDARD &POOR'S

S&P Recommendation BUY ★★★★☆	**Price** $67.96 (as of Oct 22, 2010)	**12-Mo. Target Price** $75.00	**Investment Style** Large-Cap Growth

GICS Sector Information Technology
Sub-Industry IT Consulting & Other Services

Summary This company offers full life-cycle solutions to complex software development and maintenance problems.

Key Stock Statistics (Source S&P, Vickers, company reports)

52-Wk Range	$68.29– 38.37	S&P Oper. EPS 2010**E**	2.27	Market Capitalization(B)	$20.449	Beta	1.11
Trailing 12-Month EPS	$1.98	S&P Oper. EPS 2011**E**	2.48	Yield (%)	Nil	S&P 3-Yr. Proj. EPS CAGR(%)	17
Trailing 12-Month P/E	34.3	P/E on S&P Oper. EPS 2010**E**	29.9	Dividend Rate/Share	Nil	S&P Credit Rating	NA
$10K Invested 5 Yrs Ago	$30,164	Common Shares Outstg. (M)	300.9	Institutional Ownership (%)	93		

Price Performance

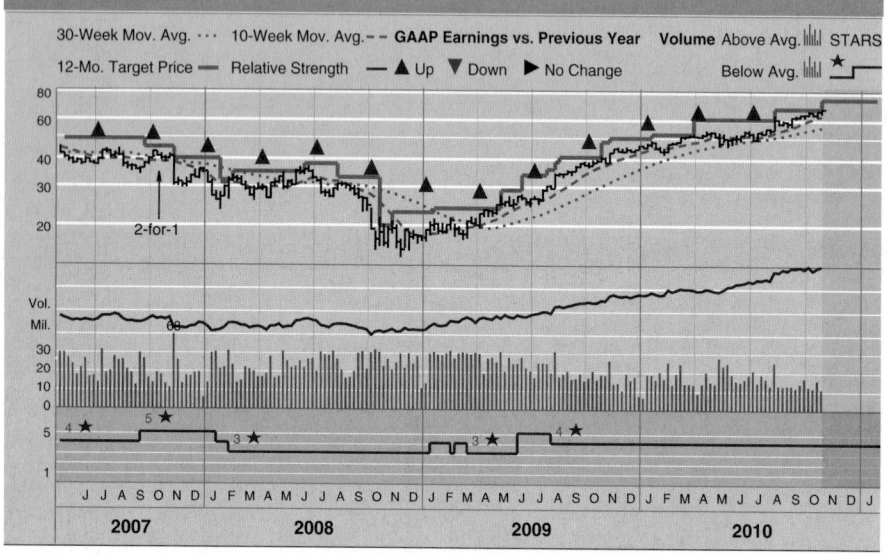

- 30-Week Mov. Avg. ··· · 10-Week Mov. Avg. — ◦ — **GAAP Earnings vs. Previous Year** Volume Above Avg. ▐▊▍ STARS
- 12-Mo. Target Price — Relative Strength — ▲ Up ▼ Down ▶ No Change   Below Avg. ▪▪▪ ★

2007   2008   2009   2010

Options: ASE, CBOE, P, Ph

Analysis prepared by **Dylan Cathers** on October 22, 2010, when the stock traded at **$68.05**.

Highlights

► We look for revenue growth of 36% in 2010 and 17% in 2011. The company is seeing growth in financial services (over 42% of revenues in the June quarter), benefiting from merger and acquisition integration work, as well as initiatives to improve costs and efficiencies. This theme continues through most of the company's verticals. Importantly, CTSH is seeing interest in more discretionary projects; application development rose 22% sequentially in the second quarter.

► We expect operating margins, including stock option expense, to narrow in 2010. We think that the improving economic backdrop will bring a resumption of wage inflation (at a roughly 14% pace in India, lower in onshore locations) and an increase in employee attrition. Partially offsetting these negatives will likely be higher utilization rates, a slight improvement in the pricing environment, and greater leverage. Lastly, the rupee/U.S. dollar exchange rate is less favorable than a year ago, but CTSH has hedged much of its exposure for this year.

► We estimate EPS of $2.27 for 2010, rising to $2.48 in 2011.

Investment Rationale/Risk

► We view CTSH shares favorably, given what we see as the company's strong balance sheet, with nearly $3.50 per share in cash and no debt, and its U.S. incorporation. Also, we think CTSH's revenue growth will be faster than that of many peers, and we believe it has done a good job moving into high-growth verticals. We think an increasing portion of companies' IT spending budgets will be spent overseas, as their needs for assistance in cost reduction actions, regulatory compliance and acquisition integration grow.

► Risks to our recommendation and target price include increasing competition in offshore outsourcing, with consequent margin pressures; rising wages of Indian employees; appreciation of the rupee; and immigration restrictions that could affect personnel. Our corporate governance concerns center around a classified board of directors and a "poison pill" that is in place.

► We apply a slight peer premium P/E of 30.2X to our 2011 EPS estimate to arrive at our 12-month target price of $75. At that level, the stock's P/E-to-growth ratio would be about 1.8X, assuming an expected three-year growth rate of 17%.

Qualitative Risk Assessment

LOW	MEDIUM	HIGH

Our risk assessment reflects what we see as CTSH's strong balance sheet, steady cash inflows, and rapid revenue growth, offset by intense competition in the IT services peer group from companies domiciled in India as well as multinationals.

Quantitative Evaluations

S&P Quality Ranking   B+

D	C	B-	B	B+	A-	A	A+

Relative Strength Rank   STRONG

82

LOWEST = 1   HIGHEST = 99

Revenue/Earnings Data

Revenue (Million $)

	1Q	2Q	3Q	4Q	Year
2010	959.7	1,105	--	--	--
2009	745.9	776.6	853.5	902.7	3,279
2008	643.1	685.4	734.7	753.0	2,816
2007	460.3	516.5	558.8	600.0	2,136
2006	285.5	336.8	377.5	424.4	1,424
2005	181.7	211.7	235.5	256.9	885.8

Earnings Per Share ($)

	1Q	2Q	3Q	4Q	Year
2010	0.49	0.56	E0.60	E0.62	E2.27
2009	0.38	0.47	0.45	0.47	1.78
2008	0.34	0.35	0.38	0.38	1.44
2007	0.25	0.27	0.32	0.32	1.15
2006	0.16	0.19	0.20	0.23	0.78
2005	0.11	0.13	0.14	0.20	0.57

Fiscal year ended Dec. 31. Next earnings report expected: Early November. EPS Estimates based on S&P Operating Earnings; historical GAAP earnings are as reported.

Dividend Data

No cash dividends have been paid.

Cognizant Technology Solutions Corp

STANDARD &POOR'S

Business Summary October 22, 2010

CORPORATE OVERVIEW. Cognizant Technology Solutions began operations in 1994 as an in-house technology development center for Dun & Bradstreet Corp. and its operating units. In its June 1998 IPO, 2,917,000 common shares were sold at $10 each.

The company's objective is to be a leading provider of full life-cycle e-business and application development projects, take full responsibility for on-going management of a client's software systems, and help clients move legacy transformation projects through to completion. The company's solutions include application development and integration, application management, and re-engineering services.

Applications development services are provided using a full life-cycle application development approach in which the company assumes total start to finish responsibility and accountability for analysis, design, implementation, testing and integration of systems, or through cooperative development, in which CTSH employees work with the customer's in-house IT personnel. In either case, the company's on-site team members work closely with end users

of the application to develop specifications and define requirements.

CTSH applications management services seeks to ensure that a customer's core operational systems are free of defects and responsive to end-users' changing needs. The company is often able to introduce product and process enhancements and improve service levels.

Through its re-engineering services, the company works with customers to migrate systems based on legacy computing environments to newer, open systems-based platforms and client/server architectures, often in response to the more stringent demands of e-business. CTSH's re-engineering tools automate many processes required to implement advanced client/server technologies.

Company Financials Fiscal Year Ended Dec. 31

Per Share Data ($)	2009	2008	2007	2006	2005	2004	2003	2002	2001	2000
Tangible Book Value	8.02	6.05	4.42	3.60	2.44	1.61	0.98	0.62	0.42	0.29
Cash Flow	2.07	1.69	1.33	0.89	0.64	0.41	0.26	0.17	0.12	0.07
Earnings	1.78	1.44	1.15	0.78	0.57	0.35	0.21	0.14	0.09	0.07
S&P Core Earnings	1.78	1.44	1.15	0.78	0.51	0.30	0.16	0.09	0.07	NA
Dividends	Nil	Nil	Nil	Nil	Nil	Nil	Nil	Nil	Nil	Nil
Payout Ratio	Nil	Nil	Nil	Nil	Nil	Nil	Nil	Nil	Nil	Nil
Prices:High	46.61	37.10	47.78	41.25	26.24	21.47	12.40	6.38	4.48	6.01
Prices:Low	17.26	14.38	29.44	24.26	17.79	9.80	4.28	2.70	1.48	2.02
P/E Ratio:High	26	26	42	53	46	61	59	47	49	83
P/E Ratio:Low	10	10	26	31	31	28	20	20	16	28

Income Statement Analysis (Million $)	2009	2008	2007	2006	2005	2004	2003	2002	2001	2000
Revenue	3,279	2,816	2,136	1,424	886	587	368	229	178	137
Operating Income	708	591	435	293	199	134	84.2	106	42.0	30.6
Depreciation	89.4	74.8	53.9	34.2	21.4	16.4	11.9	7.84	6.37	4.51
Interest Expense	NA	Nil	Nil	Nil	Nil	Nil	Nil	Nil	Nil	Nil
Pretax Income	637	515	414	278	185	122	72.2	45.1	35.4	28.2
Effective Tax Rate	16.0%	16.4%	15.5%	16.2%	10.3%	17.9%	20.6%	23.4%	37.4%	37.4%
Net Income	535	431	350	233	166	100	57.4	34.6	22.2	17.7
S&P Core Earnings	534	431	350	233	148	85.1	42.4	23.0	16.3	NA

Balance Sheet & Other Financial Data (Million $)	2009	2008	2007	2006	2005	2004	2003	2002	2001	2000
Cash	1,399	763	670	266	197	293	194	126	85.0	62.0
Current Assets	2,308	1,468	1,242	1,040	663	454	278	176	117	88.2
Total Assets	3,338	2,375	1,838	1,326	870	573	361	231	145	110
Current Liabilities	647	388	341	250	156	115	62.6	41.5	21.7	26.7
Long Term Debt	NA	Nil	Nil	Nil	Nil	Nil	Nil	Nil	Nil	Nil
Common Equity	2,653	1,966	1,468	1,073	714	454	274	165	98.8	66.1
Total Capital	2,653	1,973	1,483	1,073	714	458	298	190	123	82.8
Capital Expenditures	76.6	169	182	105	71.8	46.6	30.0	22.3	15.0	10.7
Cash Flow	624	506	404	267	188	117	69.3	42.4	28.5	17.7
Current Ratio	3.6	3.8	3.7	4.2	4.3	3.9	4.4	4.2	5.4	3.3
% Long Term Debt of Capitalization	Nil	Nil	Nil	Nil	Nil	Nil	Nil	Nil	Nil	Nil
% Net Income of Revenue	16.3	15.3	16.4	16.3	18.8	17.1	15.6	15.1	12.5	12.9
% Return on Assets	18.7	20.5	22.1	21.2	23.1	21.4	19.4	18.4	17.4	19.8
% Return on Equity	23.2	25.1	27.6	26.0	28.5	27.6	26.1	26.2	26.9	31.7

Data as orig reptd.; bef. results of disc opers/spec. items. Per share data adj. for stk. divs.; EPS diluted. E-Estimated. NA-Not Available. NM-Not Meaningful. NR-Not Ranked. UR-Under Review.

Office: 500 Glenpointe Ctr W Ste, Teaneck, NJ 07666-6821.
Telephone: 201-801-0233.
Website: http://www.cognizant.com
Chrmn: J. Klein

Pres & CEO: F. D'Souza
Vice Chrmn: L. Narayanan
COO, CFO, Chief Acctg Officer & Treas: G.J. Coburn
SVP, Secy & General Counsel: S.E. Schwartz

Investor Contact: G. Coburn (201-678-2712)
Board Members: M. Breakiron-Evans, F. D'Souza, J. N. Fox, Jr., R. W. Howe, J. Klein, L. Narayanan, R. E. Weissman, T. M. Wendel

Founded: 1988
Domicile: Delaware
Employees: 78,400

The McGraw-Hill Companies

Colgate-Palmolive Co

STANDARD & POOR'S

S&P Recommendation BUY ★★★★☆	**Price** $76.84 (as of Oct 22, 2010)	**12-Mo. Target Price** $86.00	**Investment Style** Large-Cap Growth

GICS Sector Consumer Staples
Sub-Industry Household Products

Summary This major consumer products company markets oral, personal and household care, and pet nutrition products in more than 200 countries and territories.

Key Stock Statistics (Source S&P, Vickers, company reports)

52-Wk Range	$87.39–73.12	S&P Oper. EPS 2010**E**	4.77	Market Capitalization(B)	$37.344	Beta	0.50
Trailing 12-Month EPS	$4.19	S&P Oper. EPS 2011**E**	5.15	Yield (%)	2.76	S&P 3-Yr. Proj. EPS CAGR(%)	9
Trailing 12-Month P/E	18.3	P/E on S&P Oper. EPS 2010**E**	16.1	Dividend Rate/Share	$2.12	S&P Credit Rating	AA-
$10K Invested 5 Yrs Ago	$16,651	Common Shares Outstg. (M)	486.0	Institutional Ownership (%)	75		

Price Performance

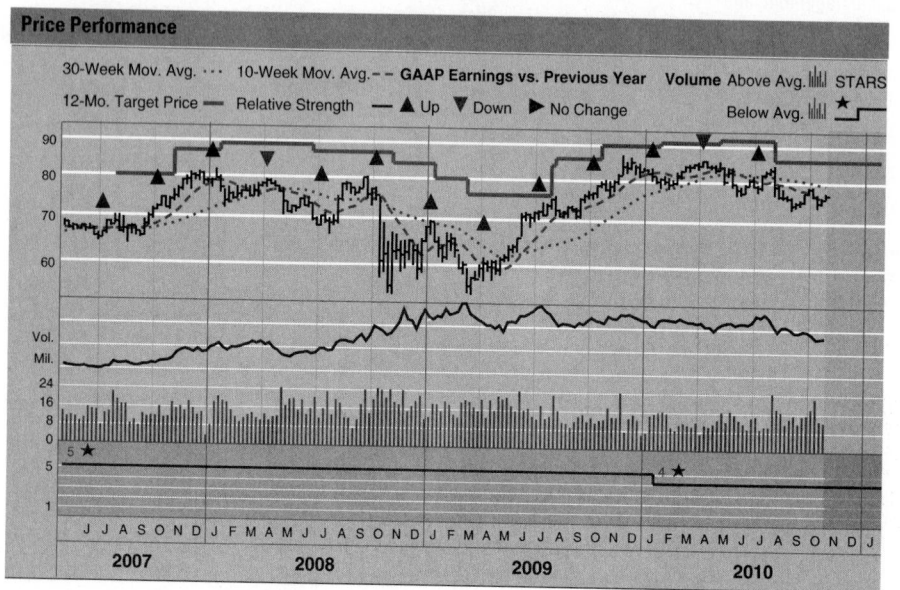

30-Week Mov. Avg. ··· 10-Week Mov. Avg.‑ ‑ **GAAP Earnings vs. Previous Year** Volume Above Avg. STARS
12-Mo. Target Price — Relative Strength — ▲ Up ▼ Down ▶ No Change Below Avg.

Options: ASE, CBOE, P

Analysis prepared by **Tom Graves, CFA** on August 05, 2010, when the stock traded at **$ 77.19**.

Highlights

► In 2010, we look for sales to increase about 4%, to $15.9 billion. This includes a projected double-digit percentage increase for the Greater Asia/Africa segment. For 2009, sales were flat, including a negative 6.5% foreign exchange effect.

► We look for CL's gross margin to widen somewhat in 2010. Also, we anticipate that SG&A will increase as a percentage of sales, but that the extent of the rise will be limited by efforts to reduce overhead costs.

► Our 2010 EPS estimate of $4.77 excludes a first-quarter charge of $0.52 a share resulting from an accounting change related to the transition to hyperinflationary accounting in Venezuela. However, our 2010 EPS estimate does include a projected net negative impact of $0.12 a share from other items related to Venezuela, including the translation of Venezuela results at a lower exchange rate, partly offset by an $0.11 first-quarter gain related to balance sheet remeasurement and accrued taxes. For 2011, we estimate EPS of $5.15.

Investment Rationale/Risk

► Our Buy opinion reflects our view that the current stock price does not fully reflect what we see as CL's above-industry-average growth prospects. We expect the company to continue to invest in R&D and marketing, with more resources to be allocated to faster-growing markets. Recent changes in the Venezuelan bolivar are expected to negatively affect 2010 results.

► Risks to our recommendation and target price include intensified competition in the global oral care market, unfavorable currency translation, difficulties in remitting funds from some countries, and low consumer acceptance of new products.

► Our 12-month target price of $86 reflects a blend of three valuation models. Our DCF model assumes a blended WACC of 8.8% and a terminal growth rate of 3%, in arriving at an intrinsic value of $90. We believe the shares should trade at a premium to peers, and we apply a 18.2X P/E to our 2010 EPS estimate, for a value of about $87. Our historical analysis uses a P/E of 17.3X, below a 10-year average, to value the stock at about $83.

Qualitative Risk Assessment

LOW	MEDIUM	HIGH

Our risk assessment reflects that demand for household and personal care products is generally static, and not affected by changes in the economy or geopolitical factors. This is partially offset by the mature and competitive nature of these industries.

Quantitative Evaluations

S&P Quality Ranking A+

D	C	B-	B	B+	A-	A	A+

Relative Strength Rank MODERATE

32

LOWEST = 1   HIGHEST = 99

Revenue/Earnings Data

Revenue (Million $)

	1Q	2Q	3Q	4Q	Year
2010	3,829	3,814	--	--	--
2009	3,503	3,745	3,998	4,081	15,327
2008	3,713	3,965	3,988	3,664	15,330
2007	3,214	3,405	3,528	3,642	13,790
2006	2,871	3,014	3,144	3,209	12,238
2005	2,743	2,838	2,912	2,905	11,397

Earnings Per Share ($)

	1Q	2Q	3Q	4Q	Year
2010	0.69	1.15	E1.16	E1.22	E4.77
2009	0.97	1.07	1.12	1.21	4.37
2008	0.87	0.92	0.94	0.94	3.66
2007	0.89	0.76	0.77	0.77	3.20
2006	0.59	0.51	0.63	0.73	2.46
2005	0.53	0.62	0.63	0.65	2.43

Fiscal year ended Dec. 31. Next earnings report expected: Late October. EPS Estimates based on S&P Operating Earnings; historical GAAP earnings are as reported.

Dividend Data (Dates: mm/dd Payment Date: mm/dd/yy)

Amount ($)	Date Decl.	Ex-Div. Date	Stk. of Record	Payment Date
0.440	01/07	01/21	01/25	02/16/10
0.530	02/04	04/22	04/26	05/14/10
0.530	07/08	07/22	07/26	08/13/10
0.530	10/14	10/21	10/25	11/15/10

Dividends have been paid since 1895. Source: Company reports.

Please read the Required Disclosures and Analyst Certification on the last page of this report.

The McGraw-Hill Companies

Colgate-Palmolive Co

STANDARD &POOR'S

Business Summary August 05, 2010

CORPORATE OVERVIEW. Colgate-Palmolive Co. is a leading global consumer products company that operates in the oral, personal, and household care, and pet food markets. Its products are marketed in more than 200 countries and territories worldwide. Sales of oral, personal, and home care products accounted for 86% of total worldwide sales in 2009. The balance of revenues was derived from the sale of pet foods. The company's oral care products include toothbrushes, toothpaste and pharmaceutical products for oral health professionals. CL's personal care products include bar and liquid soaps, shampoos, conditioners, deodorants, antiperspirants, and shave products. The home care division produces major brands such as Palmolive and Ajax soaps. Oral, personal and home care sales outside of North America accounted for 67% of total sales in 2009. The geographic breakdown of total oral, personal and home care sales in 2009 were: North America 22%, Latin America 33%, Europe/South Pacific 25% and Greater Asia/Africa 20%.

CORPORATE STRATEGY. CL follows a closely defined business strategy to develop and increase market leadership in key product categories. These categories are prioritized based on their capacity to maximize the use of the organization's core competencies and strong global equities and to deliver sustainable long-term growth. Operationally, CL is organized along geographic lines, with specific regional management teams having responsibility for the financial results in each region. On an ongoing basis, management focuses on a variety of key indicators to monitor business health and performance, including: market share; sales (including volume, pricing and foreign exchange components); gross profit margins; operating profits, net income; and EPS. CL also focuses on measures to optimize the management of working capital, capital expenditures, cash flow, and return on capital.

To enhance its global leadership position in its core businesses, in December 2004, CL commenced a four-year restructuring and business-building program. It involved: a 12% workforce reduction, the closing of a third of CL's factories, an increased focus on faster-growing markets and new product innovations, and more efficient spending on marketing. The program cost $775.5 million after taxes through 2008 and was finalized as of December 31, 2008. The company estimated that it would generate annual savings of $350 million to $375 million.

Company Financials Fiscal Year Ended Dec. 31

Per Share Data ($)	2009	2008	2007	2006	2005	2004	2003	2002	2001	2000
Tangible Book Value	NM	NM	NM	NM	NM	NM	NM	NM	NM	NM
Cash Flow	4.98	4.26	3.76	3.06	2.97	2.86	3.15	2.65	2.40	2.32
Earnings	4.37	3.66	3.20	2.46	2.43	2.33	2.46	2.19	1.89	1.70
S&P Core Earnings	4.48	3.51	3.22	2.42	2.21	2.26	2.31	2.00	1.71	NA
Dividends	1.72	1.56	1.40	1.25	1.11	0.96	0.90	0.72	0.68	0.63
Payout Ratio	39%	43%	44%	51%	46%	41%	37%	33%	36%	37%
Prices:High	87.39	81.98	81.27	67.08	57.15	59.04	60.99	58.86	64.75	66.75
Prices:Low	54.51	54.36	63.75	53.41	48.25	42.89	48.56	44.05	48.50	40.50
P/E Ratio:High	20	22	25	27	24	25	25	27	34	39
P/E Ratio:Low	12	15	20	22	20	18	20	20	26	24

Income Statement Analysis (Million $)

	2009	2008	2007	2006	2005	2004	2003	2002	2001	2000
Revenue	15,327	15,330	13,790	12,238	11,397	10,584	9,903	9,294	9,428	9,358
Operating Income	4,004	3,673	3,108	2,674	2,613	2,540	2,467	2,333	2,198	2,132
Depreciation	351	348	334	329	329	328	316	297	336	410
Interest Expense	88.0	115	173	159	143	124	124	151	192	200
Pretax Income	3,538	2,925	2,564	2,002	2,134	2,050	2,042	1,870	1,709	1,600
Effective Tax Rate	32.3%	33.1%	29.6%	32.4%	34.1%	32.9%	30.4%	31.1%	30.6%	31.4%
Net Income	2,291	1,957	1,737	1,353	1,351	1,327	1,421	1,288	1,147	1,064
S&P Core Earnings	2,320	1,848	1,718	1,306	1,207	1,262	1,309	1,152	1,011	NA

Balance Sheet & Other Financial Data (Million $)

	2009	2008	2007	2006	2005	2004	2003	2002	2001	2000
Cash	641	567	451	490	341	320	265	168	173	213
Current Assets	3,810	3,710	3,619	3,301	2,757	2,740	2,497	2,228	2,203	2,347
Total Assets	11,134	9,979	10,112	9,138	8,507	8,673	7,479	7,087	6,985	7,252
Current Liabilities	3,599	2,953	3,163	3,469	2,743	2,731	2,445	2,149	2,124	2,244
Long Term Debt	3,182	3,585	3,508	2,720	2,918	3,090	2,685	3,211	2,812	2,537
Common Equity	3,116	1,922	2,308	1,188	1,380	971	594	27.3	505	1,115
Total Capital	6,439	5,711	5,882	4,441	5,106	4,845	4,028	4,050	4,139	4,453
Capital Expenditures	575	684	583	476	389	348	302	344	340	367
Cash Flow	2,612	2,276	2,043	1,682	1,653	1,629	1,736	1,563	1,461	1,453
Current Ratio	1.2	1.3	1.1	1.0	1.0	1.0	1.0	1.0	1.0	1.0
% Long Term Debt of Capitalization	49.4	62.8	57.4	61.3	57.1	63.8	66.7	79.3	67.9	57.0
% Net Income of Revenue	15.0	12.8	12.6	11.1	11.9	12.5	14.4	13.9	12.2	11.4
% Return on Assets	21.7	19.5	17.8	15.3	15.7	16.4	19.5	18.3	16.1	14.5
% Return on Equity	94.3	97.6	91.2	118.5	99.5	166.2	457.2	475.7	139.0	80.8

Data as orig reptd.; bef. results of disc opers/spec. items. Per share data adj. for stk. divs.; EPS diluted. E-Estimated. NA-Not Available. NM-Not Meaningful. NR-Not Ranked. UR-Under Review.

Office: 300 Park Avenue, New York, NY 10022.
Telephone: 212-310-2000.
Email: investor_relations@colpal.com
Website: http://www.colgate.com

Chrmn, Pres & CEO: I.M. Cook
EVP & CFO: P. Alton
SVP, Secy & General Counsel: A.D. Hendry
Chief Acctg Officer & Cntlr: D.J. Hickey

Treas: E. Paik
Investor Contact: B. Thompson (212-310-3072)
Board Members: P. Alton, J. T. Cahill, I. M. Cook, H. D. Gayle, E. M. Hancock, J. Jimenez, D. W. Johnson, R. J. Kogan, D. Lewis, J. P. Reinhard, S. I. Sadove

Founded: 1806
Domicile: Delaware
Employees: 38,100

The McGraw-Hill Companies

Comcast Corp

STANDARD &POOR'S

S&P Recommendation	STRONG SELL ★ ★ ★ ★ ★	Price $19.46 (as of Oct 22, 2010)	12-Mo. Target Price $16.00	Investment Style Large-Cap Blend

GICS Sector Consumer Discretionary
Sub-Industry Cable & Satellite

Summary With about 23.2 million subscribers, this company is the largest U.S. cable multiple system operator (MSO), as well as a provider of cable programming content.

Key Stock Statistics (Source S&P, Vickers, company reports)

52-Wk Range	$20.56– 13.95	S&P Oper. EPS 2010**E** 1.23	Market Capitalization(B) $54.432	Beta	0.96
Trailing 12-Month EPS	$1.28	S&P Oper. EPS 2011**E** 1.34	Yield (%) 1.95	S&P 3-Yr. Proj. EPS CAGR(%)	9
Trailing 12-Month P/E	15.2	P/E on S&P Oper. EPS 2010**E** 15.8	Dividend Rate/Share $0.38	S&P Credit Rating	BBB
$10K Invested 5 Yrs Ago	$11,324	Common Shares Outstg. (M) 2,806.6	Institutional Ownership (%) 60		

Price Performance

30-Week Mov. Avg. ··· 10-Week Mov. Avg. – – **GAAP Earnings vs. Previous Year** Volume Above Avg. STARS
12-Mo. Target Price — Relative Strength — ▲ Up ▼ Down ► No Change Below Avg.

Options: ASE, CBOE, P, Ph

Analysis prepared by **Tuna N. Amobi, CFA, CPA** on July 30, 2010, when the stock traded at **$ 19.57**.

Highlights

➤ We expect consolidated revenues to advance about 5% in 2010, to $37.1 billion, and 4% in 2011, to $38.5 billion. This should reflect further penetration of bundled customers, higher pricing on advanced video services, a growing customer base of small and medium-size businesses, stronger contributions from the regional and news networks, and a rebound in local ad revenues. Also, the programming unit should reflect affiliate fee increases and higher national ad revenues. Conversely, we anticipate some moderation in subscriber growth (with basic subscriber losses), and increased promotional pricing for residential customers.

➤ We assume relatively moderate margin expansion, as further declines in direct operating costs (phone and data), and further investments in content, technology and wireless initiatives, are partly offset by higher programming, marketing and customer service expenses.

➤ We estimate annual EBITDA growth of about 5.0%, to more than $14.4 billion in 2010 and $15.1 billion in 2011. After D&A and interest expense, we see operating EPS of $1.23 in 2010 and $1.34 in 2011, noting plans to complete about $3 billion of remaining share buybacks by 2012.

Investment Rationale/Risk

➤ In July, the company reported what we saw as somewhat encouraging 2010 second quarter results, and affirmed a likely completion of its pending deal for NBCU this year. Beyond potential risks with merger execution, however, we see lingering regulatory uncertainties for the industry at large, amid concerns with potential reclassification of broadband (Title II). After a related court ruling in the company's network management case against the FCC, we remain wary of potentially onerous regulations that could have some adverse investment (and competitive) implications. Also, we note potential governance issues on dual class shares and voting control by the Roberts family.

➤ Risks to our recommendation and target price include potential upside on the NBCU deal; stronger-than-expected share gains from the telcos and satellite TV providers; potential upside on the SME and wireless broadband segments; and a dividend hike.

➤ Our 12-month target price of $16 implies about 5.3X 2010E EV/EBITDA, or nearly $2,800 per cable subscriber, reflecting potential downside on the highlighted risk factors, while noting the stock's recent 2.0% dividend yield.

Qualitative Risk Assessment

LOW	MEDIUM	HIGH

Our risk assessment mainly reflects our view of lingering merger execution risk on the pending NBCU deal, heightened regulatory exposure and intensifying competition in relatively saturated markets, offset by economies of scale and what we see as the company's relatively sound financial condition.

Quantitative Evaluations

S&P Quality Ranking B+

D	C	B-	B	B+	A-	A	A+

Relative Strength Rank MODERATE

70

LOWEST = 1   HIGHEST = 99

Revenue/Earnings Data

Revenue (Million $)

	1Q	2Q	3Q	4Q	Year
2010	9,202	--	--	--	--
2009	8,866	8,978	8,845	9,067	35,756
2008	8,389	8,553	8,549	8,765	34,256
2007	7,388	7,712	7,781	8,014	30,895
2006	5,595	5,908	6,432	7,031	24,966
2005	5,363	5,598	5,578	5,716	22,255

Earnings Per Share ($)

2010	0.31	0.31	E0.28	E0.31	E1.23
2009	0.27	0.33	0.33	0.33	1.26
2008	0.24	0.21	0.26	0.14	0.86
2007	0.26	0.19	0.18	0.20	0.83
2006	0.15	0.13	0.31	0.14	0.70
2005	0.04	0.13	0.07	0.04	0.28

Fiscal year ended Dec. 31. Next earnings report expected: Early November. EPS Estimates based on S&P Operating Earnings; historical GAAP earnings are as reported.

Dividend Data (Dates: mm/dd Payment Date: mm/dd/yy)

Amount ($)	Date Decl.	Ex-Div. Date	Stk. of Record	Payment Date
0.095	02/23	04/05	04/07	04/28/10
0.095	05/20	07/02	07/07	07/28/10
0.095	07/28	10/04	10/06	10/27/10
0.095	10/21	01/03	01/05	01/26/11

Dividends have been paid since 2008. Source: Company reports.

Please read the Required Disclosures and Analyst Certification on the last page of this report.

Comcast Corp

Business Summary July 30, 2010

CORPORATE OVERVIEW. Comcast Corp. became the largest U.S. cable multiple system operator (MSO) after its acquisition of the former AT&T Broadband (ATTB) in November 2002. In December 2009, the company formalized a plan to assume 51% control of a joint venture comprising General Electric's (GE 16, Buy) NBC Universal, in exchange for contributing its own programming networks (valued at $7.25 billion) plus an initial cash outlay of $6.5 billion.

As of June 30, 2010, the company had nearly 23.2 million video subscribers (including 19.1 million for digital video -- with advanced services such as HD and DVR), over 16.4 million for high-speed Internet service, and 8.1 million for digital phone. The primary Cable segment (about 95% of total revenues) also includes the regional sports and news networks -- Comcast SportsNet: Philadelphia, Mid-Atlantic (Baltimore/Washington), Chicago, Sacramento, New England (Boston) and Northwest; Bay Area SportsNet (San Francisco); Cable Sports Southeast; CN8 -- The Comcast Network; and MountainWest Sports Network. The Programming segment include cable networks E! Entertainment Television, The Golf Channel, Versus, G4 and Style.

Other business interests include Comcast Spectacor (which owns the Philadelphia Flyers, the Philadelphia 76ers and two large, multipurpose arenas in Philadelphia and manages other venues); and Comcast Interactive Media (comprising Internet assets such as Comcast.net, Fancast, thePlatform and Fandango).

COMPETITIVE LANDSCAPE. In a typical market, Comcast competes with satellite TV companies DirecTV Group and DISH Network as well as large telcos such as Verizon Communications and AT&T, which are increasingly deploying fiber-based video and broadband services in head-to-head competition with cable's triple-play bundle. In a number of other markets, cable providers also compete with rural telcos as well as facilities-based overbuilders that provide video, voice and data services to residential, and in some cases, enterprise customers.

Company Financials Fiscal Year Ended Dec. 31

Per Share Data ($)	2009	2008	2007	2006	2005	2004	2003	2002	2001	2000
Tangible Book Value	NM	NM	NM	NM	NM	NM	0.24	1.05	0.99	3.27
Cash Flow	3.51	2.71	2.46	2.22	1.79	1.69	0.29	-0.17	-0.89	1.44
Earnings	1.26	0.86	0.83	0.70	0.28	0.29	-0.07	0.47	-1.03	NA
S&P Core Earnings	1.04	0.84	0.74	0.48	0.33	0.14	-0.30	Nil	Nil	Nil
Dividends	0.26	0.19	Nil	Nil	Nil	Nil	Nil	Nil	Nil	Nil
Payout Ratio	21%	22%	Nil	Nil	Nil	Nil	Nil	Nil	Nil	Nil
Prices:High	18.10	22.86	30.18	28.94	23.00	24.33	23.23	25.03	30.54	34.91
Prices:Low	11.10	NA	17.37	16.90	17.20	17.50	15.61	11.37	21.23	18.62
P/E Ratio:High	14	27	36	41	82	85	NM	NM	NM	24
P/E Ratio:Low	9	NA	21	24	61	61	NM	NM	NM	13

Income Statement Analysis (Million $)										
Revenue	NA	34,256	30,895	24,966	22,255	20,307	18,348	12,460	19,697	8,219
Operating Income	NA	12,354	10,725	9,442	8,493	7,531	6,392	3,691	1,576	2,470
Depreciation	NA	5,457	5,107	4,823	4,803	4,623	4,438	2,032	6,345	2,631
Interest Expense	2,348	2,439	2,289	2,064	1,796	1,876	2,018	884	2,341	691
Pretax Income	5,106	4,058	4,349	3,594	1,880	1,810	-137	70.0	-5,927	3,602
Effective Tax Rate	29.0%	37.8%	41.4%	37.5%	49.6%	45.6%	NM	NM	NM	40.0%
Net Income	3,638	2,547	2,587	2,235	928	970	-218	-276	-3,021	2,045
S&P Core Earnings	3,000	2,484	2,313	1,541	1,090	465	-979	792	-1,482	NA

Balance Sheet & Other Financial Data (Million $)										
Cash	721	1,254	1,061	1,239	693	452	1,550	781	558	652
Current Assets	NA	3,716	3,667	5,202	2,594	3,535	5,403	7,076	4,944	5,144
Total Assets	112,733	113,017	113,417	110,405	103,146	104,694	109,159	113,105	109,319	35,745
Current Liabilities	NA	8,939	7,952	7,440	6,269	8,635	9,654	15,383	12,489	4,042
Long Term Debt	27,940	30,178	29,828	27,992	21,682	20,093	23,835	27,957	27,528	10,517
Common Equity	42,721	40,450	41,340	41,167	40,219	41,422	41,662	38,329	38,451	28,113
Total Capital	NA	97,907	98,298	96,489	89,928	88,798	91,689	92,070	94,758	45,734
Capital Expenditures	NA	5,750	6,158	4,395	3,621	3,660	4,161	1,975	NA	1,637
Cash Flow	10,138	8,004	7,694	7,058	5,731	5,593	4,220	1,756	3,324	4,653
Current Ratio	0.4	0.4	0.5	0.7	0.4	0.4	0.6	0.5	0.4	1.3
% Long Term Debt of Capitalization	38.9	30.8	30.3	29.0	24.1	22.6	26.0	30.4	29.1	23.0
% Net Income of Revenue	NA	7.4	8.4	9.0	4.2	4.8	NM	NM	NM	24.9
% Return on Assets	3.2	2.3	2.3	2.1	0.9	0.9	NM	NM	NM	6.3
% Return on Equity	8.8	6.2	6.3	5.5	2.3	2.3	NM	NM	NM	8.4

Data as orig reptd.; bef. results of disc opers/spec. items. Per share data adj. for stk. divs.; EPS diluted. E-Estimated. NA-Not Available. NM-Not Meaningful. NR-Not Ranked. UR-Under Review.

Office: 1 Comcast Ctr, Philadelphia, PA 19103-2833.
Telephone: 215-286-1700.
Website: http://www.comcast.com
Chrmn, Pres & CEO: B.L. Roberts

Vice Chrmn: J.A. Brodsky
COO & EVP: S.B. Burke
EVP & CFO: M.J. Angelakis
SVP, Chief Acctg Officer & Cntlr: L.J. Salva

Investor Contact: M. Dooner (866-281-2100)
Board Members: S. D. Anstrom, K. J. Bacon, S. M. Bonovitz, E. D. Breen, J. A. Brodsky, J. J. Collins, J. M. Cook, G. L. Hassell, J. A. Honickman, B. L. Roberts, R. J. Roberts, J. Rodin, M. I. Sovern

Founded: 1969
Domicile: Pennsylvania
Employees: 107,000

Comerica Inc

STANDARD &POOR'S

S&P Recommendation BUY ★★★★☆

Price	12-Mo. Target Price	Investment Style
$36.26 (as of Oct 22, 2010)	$41.00	Large-Cap Value

GICS Sector Financials
Sub-Industry Diversified Banks

Summary This bank holding company, based in Dallas, operates in Michigan, California, Texas, Arizona, and Florida.

Key Stock Statistics (Source S&P, Vickers, company reports)

52-Wk Range	$45.85–26.49	S&P Oper. EPS 2010**E**	0.66	Market Capitalization(B)	$6.393	Beta	1.09
Trailing 12-Month EPS	$-0.50	S&P Oper. EPS 2011**E**	1.48	Yield (%)	0.55	S&P 3-Yr. Proj. EPS CAGR(%)	NM
Trailing 12-Month P/E	NM	P/E on S&P Oper. EPS 2010**E**	54.9	Dividend Rate/Share	$0.20	S&P Credit Rating	A-
$10K Invested 5 Yrs Ago	$7,955	Common Shares Outstg. (M)	176.3	Institutional Ownership (%)	86		

Price Performance

30-Week Mov. Avg. · · · 10-Week Mov. Avg. – – GAAP Earnings vs. Previous Year   Volume Above Avg. ▮▮▮ STARS
12-Mo. Target Price — Relative Strength ▲ Up ▼ Down ▶ No Change   Below Avg. ▮▮▮ ★

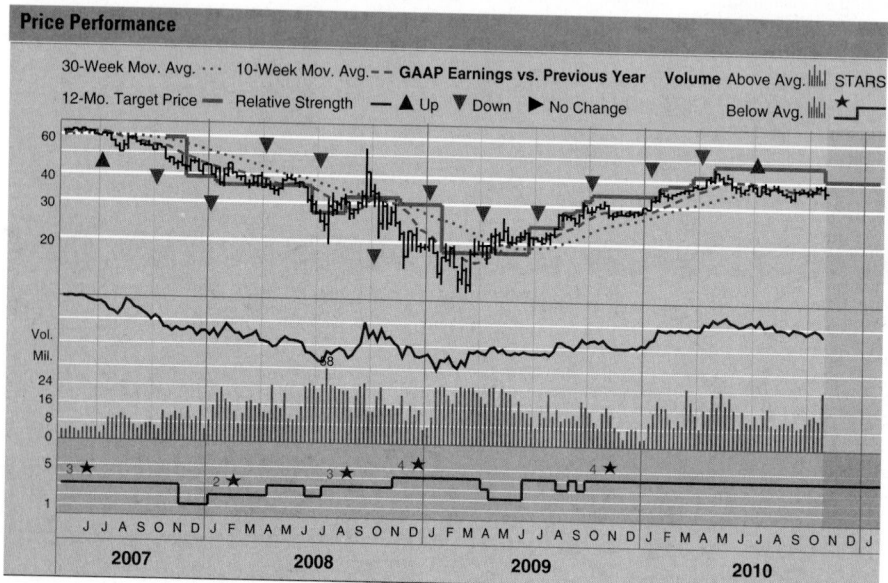

Options: ASE, CBOE, P, Ph

Qualitative Risk Assessment

LOW	MEDIUM	HIGH

Our risk assessment reflects CMA's long history of profitability and relatively high capital ratios, tempered by exposure to the Michigan and California residential real estate markets.

Quantitative Evaluations

S&P Quality Ranking   B

D	C	B-	B	B+	A-	A	A+

Relative Strength Rank   WEAK

22

LOWEST = 1   HIGHEST = 99

Revenue/Earnings Data

Revenue (Million $)

	1Q	2Q	3Q	4Q	Year
2010	670.0	670.0	--	--	--
2009	762.0	866.0	819.0	685.0	3,155
2008	1,100	979.0	975.0	890.0	3,944
2007	1,104	1,158	1,182	1,174	4,618
2006	967.0	1,048	1,088	1,174	4,277
2005	817.0	874.0	951.0	1,026	3,668

Earnings Per Share ($)

2010	-0.57	0.39	E0.33	E0.33	E0.66
2009	-0.16	-0.11	-0.10	-0.41	-0.78
2008	0.73	0.37	0.18	0.01	1.29
2007	1.19	1.25	1.17	0.77	4.40
2006	1.26	1.19	1.20	1.16	4.81
2005	1.16	1.28	1.41	1.25	5.11

Fiscal year ended Dec. 31. Next earnings report expected: NA. EPS Estimates based on S&P Operating Earnings; historical GAAP earnings are as reported.

Highlights

▶ The 12-month target price for CMA has recently been changed to $41.00 from $47.00. The Highlights section of this Stock Report will be updated accordingly.

Investment Rationale/Risk

▶ The Investment Rationale/Risk section of this Stock Report will be updated shortly. For the latest News story on CMA from MarketScope, see below.

▶ 10/20/10 11:03 am ET ... S&P MAINTAINS BUY RECOMMENDATION ON SHARES OF COMERICA INC (CMA 34.99****): Q3 EPS of $0.33, vs a $0.10 loss, misses our $0.34 EPS estimate, on lower than expected loan demand. We reduce our '10 EPS estimate to $0.66 from $0.67. Non-performing loans increased 6% from Q2 vs. improving results at many peers, a negative in our view. On our higher provision forecast for '11, we trim our EPS estimate to $1.48 from $2.27. We also cut our target price by $6 to $41, based on a slight discount to peers 1.2X our $33.85 estimate of year-end tangible book value per share. We continue to see CMA as undervalued relative to peers on this metric. /E. Oja

Dividend Data (Dates: mm/dd Payment Date: mm/dd/yy)

Amount ($)	Date Decl.	Ex-Div. Date	Stk. of Record	Payment Date
0.050	11/17	12/11	12/15	01/01/10
0.050	01/26	03/11	03/15	04/01/10
0.050	04/27	06/11	06/15	07/01/10
0.050	07/27	09/13	09/15	10/01/10

Dividends have been paid since 1936. Source: Company reports.

Comerica Inc

Business Summary July 22, 2010

CORPORATE OVERVIEW. Comerica is a Dallas-headquartered bank holding company that operates banking units in Michigan, California, Texas, Arizona and Florida. It also has international banking subsidiaries in Canada and Mexico.

Operations are divided into three major lines of business: the Business Bank, the Retail Bank (formerly known as Small Business and Personal Financial Services), and Wealth & Institutional Management. The Business Bank is primarily comprised of middle market, commercial real estate, national dealer services, global finance, large corporate, leasing, financial services, and technology and life sciences. This business segment offers various products and services, including commercial loans and lines of credit, deposits, cash management, capital market products, international trade finance, letters of credit, foreign exchange management services and loan syndication services.

CORPORATE STRATEGY. Comerica has positioned itself to deliver financial services in its four primary geographic markets: Midwest & Other, West, Texas, and Florida.

CMA's goal is to deliver attractive returns to its shareholders over time by exporting its expertise to higher-growth markets, continuing its investments to grow the Retail Bank and Wealth & Institutional Management, building and enhancing customer relationships, and improving risk management processes.

MARKET PROFILE. As of June 30, 2009, which is the latest available FDIC branch-level data, CMA had 436 branches and $40.2 billion in deposits. Almost 59% of deposits were concentrated in Michigan, where CMA had 231 branches, about $23.7 billion in deposits, and a deposit market share of about 14.5%, ranking first. A year earlier, CMA ranked second in Michigan. In California, CMA had 96 branches, 13 more than a year earlier, and $11.4 billion in deposits, down $1.8 billion from a year before, and a deposit market share of about 1.4%, ranking 11th. In Texas, CMA had 86 branches, more than $4.6 billion in deposits, and a deposit market share of about 1.0%, ranking 11th. This was up from a year earlier, when CMA's market share in Texas was 0.75%, ranking 16th. CMA also has 13 offices in Arizona and 10 offices in Florida.

Company Financials Fiscal Year Ended Dec. 31

Per Share Data ($)	2009	2008	2007	2006	2005	2004	2003	2002	2001	2000
Tangible Book Value	32.26	32.57	34.12	32.82	33.01	29.85	29.20	28.31	27.15	23.94
Earnings	-0.78	1.29	4.40	4.81	5.11	4.36	3.75	3.40	3.88	4.63
S&P Core Earnings	-0.72	0.86	4.48	4.71	4.90	4.27	3.72	3.30	3.27	NA
Dividends	0.20	0.20	2.56	2.36	2.20	2.08	2.00	1.92	1.76	1.60
Payout Ratio	NM	16%	58%	49%	43%	48%	53%	56%	45%	35%
Prices:High	32.30	54.00	63.89	60.10	63.38	63.80	56.34	66.09	65.15	61.13
Prices:Low	11.72	15.05	39.62	50.12	53.17	50.45	37.10	35.20	44.02	32.94
P/E Ratio:High	NM	42	15	12	12	15	15	19	17	13
P/E Ratio:Low	NM	12	9	10	10	12	10	10	11	7

Income Statement Analysis (Million $)	2009	2008	2007	2006	2005	2004	2003	2002	2001	2000
Net Interest Income	1,567	1,815	2,003	1,983	1,956	1,810	1,926	2,132	2,102	1,659
Tax Equivalent Adjustment	8.00	6.00	3.00	NA	4.00	3.00	3.00	4.00	4.00	4.00
Non Interest Income	1,050	893	881	855	942	857	837	819	784	827
Loan Loss Provision	1,082	686	212	37.0	-47.0	64.0	377	635	236	145
% Expense/Operating Revenue	63.0%	66.2%	58.6%	59.0%	57.4%	55.9%	53.6%	51.3%	53.9%	53.6%
Pretax Income	-115	271	988	1,127	1,279	1,110	953	882	1,111	1,151
Effective Tax Rate	NM	21.8%	31.0%	30.6%	32.7%	31.8%	30.6%	31.9%	36.1%	34.9%
Net Income	16.0	212	682	782	861	757	661	601	710	749
% Net Interest Margin	2.72	3.02	3.66	3.79	4.06	3.86	3.95	4.55	4.61	4.54
S&P Core Earnings	-107	131	694	766	826	744	657	584	587	NA

Balance Sheet & Other Financial Data (Million $)	2009	2008	2007	2006	2005	2004	2003	2002	2001	2000
Money Market Assets	4,843	2,510	36.0	2,632	1,159	3,230	4,013	2,446	1,079	165
Investment Securities	7,416	9,201	6,296	3,989	5,399	7,173	8,502	5,499	5,370	2,843
Commercial Loans	32,147	38,488	38,271	35,924	33,707	31,540	32,153	33,732	32,660	28,001
Other Loans	9,029	11,247	12,472	11,507	9,540	9,303	7,274	8,549	8,536	8,060
Total Assets	59,263	67,548	62,331	58,001	53,013	51,766	52,592	53,301	50,732	41,985
Demand Deposits	15,871	11,701	27,181	29,151	15,666	15,164	14,104	16,335	12,596	6,815
Time Deposits	7,923	17,817	17,097	15,776	26,765	25,772	27,359	25,440	24,974	20,353
Long Term Debt	11,060	15,053	8,821	5,949	3,961	4,286	4,801	5,216	5,503	8,089
Common Equity	4,878	5,023	5,126	5,153	5,068	5,105	5,110	4,947	4,807	3,757
% Return on Assets	0.0	0.3	1.1	1.4	1.6	1.5	1.2	1.2	1.4	1.9
% Return on Equity	0.3	4.2	13.3	15.3	16.9	14.8	13.1	12.3	15.4	21.0
% Loan Loss Reserve	2.3	1.5	1.1	1.0	1.2	-1.6	2.0	1.9	-1.6	1.5
% Loans/Deposits	106.3	120.4	110.1	105.6	101.9	99.8	99.3	101.2	109.7	132.7
% Equity to Assets	7.8	7.8	8.5	9.2	9.7	9.8	9.5	9.4	9.0	8.7

Data as orig reptd.; bef. results of disc opers/spec. items. Per share data adj. for stk. divs.; EPS diluted. E-Estimated. NA-Not Available. NM-Not Meaningful. NR-Not Ranked. UR-Under Review.

Office: 1717 Main St, Dallas, TX 75201-4612.
Telephone: 214-462-6831.
Website: http://www.comerica.com
Chrmn, Pres & CEO: R.W. Babb, Jr.

EVP & CFO: B. Acton
EVP, Secy & General Counsel: J.W. Bilstrom
EVP & CIO: J.R. Beran
SVP & Chief Acctg Officer: M.S. Carr

Investor Contact: D.P. Persons (313-222-2840)
Board Members: R. W. Babb, Jr., J. F. Cordes, R. A. Cregg, K. T. DeNicola, J. P. Kane, R. Lindner, A. A. Piergallini, R. S. Taubman, R. M. Turner, Jr., N. G. Vaca

Founded: 1849
Domicile: Delaware
Employees: 9,330

Computer Sciences Corp

STANDARD &POOR'S

S&P Recommendation STRONG BUY ★★★★★

Price	12-Mo. Target Price	Investment Style
$49.79 (as of Oct 22, 2010)	$56.00	Large-Cap Blend

GICS Sector Information Technology
Sub-Industry Data Processing & Outsourced Services

Summary This leading computer services company provides consulting, systems integration and outsourcing services.

Key Stock Statistics (Source S&P, Vickers, company reports)

52-Wk Range	$58.36–39.61	S&P Oper. EPS 2011**E**	5.33	Market Capitalization(B)	$7.687	Beta	1.03
Trailing 12-Month EPS	$5.33	S&P Oper. EPS 2012**E**	5.66	Yield (%)	NA	S&P 3-Yr. Proj. EPS CAGR(%)	11
Trailing 12-Month P/E	9.3	P/E on S&P Oper. EPS 2011**E**	9.3	Dividend Rate/Share	NA	S&P Credit Rating	A-
$10K Invested 5 Yrs Ago	$11,052	Common Shares Outstg. (M)	154.4	Institutional Ownership (%)	85		

Price Performance

30-Week Mov. Avg. · · · 10-Week Mov. Avg. – – GAAP Earnings vs. Previous Year   Volume Above Avg. ▮▮▮ STARS
12-Mo. Target Price — Relative Strength   ▲ Up ▼ Down ► No Change   Below Avg. ▮▮▮ ★

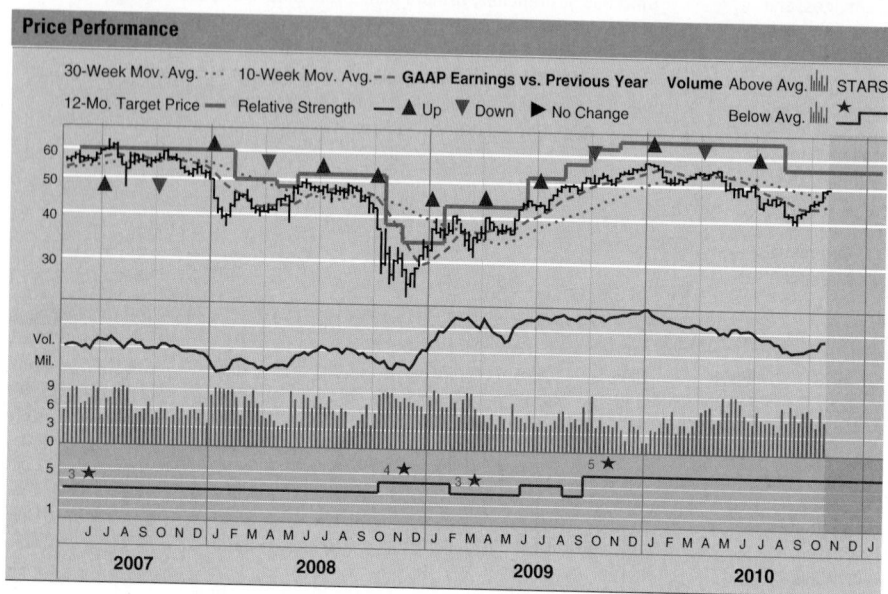

Options: ASE, CBOE, P, Ph

Analysis prepared by **Dylan Cathers** on August 17, 2010, when the stock traded at **$ 42.28**.

Highlights

► We expect revenue growth of 4.5% in FY 11 (Mar.) and 5.0% in FY 12. Despite our concerns about spending levels by the U.S. government, we think demand for IT services will remain healthy, particularly within the health care, intelligence, logistics systems support and cyber security areas. Although the procurement process remains extended, the pipeline of opportunities is strong, with about $19 billion of awards expected during FY 11. We believe the managed services sector is providing steady growth, as customers seek greater cost efficiencies. We expect some improvement within the business solutions & services segment. We note that contract size has recently been shrinking, a trend that we think will continue until there is greater certainty in the economy.

► We expect operating margins to widen again in FY 11. We see a lower cost base, including more offshore workers, tighter G&A controls, and facilities reductions offsetting increased bid activity, expenses for early-stage contracts, and investments in the business.

► For FY 11, we expect EPS of $5.33, increasing to $5.66 in FY 12.

Investment Rationale/Risk

► Our strong buy recommendation on the shares is based on valuation. We believe CSC is well positioned to take advantage of certain of the Obama administration's areas of emphasis, including health care, transportation, infrastructure, and cyber security. We had some concerns about the company's pension obligations, but it recently announced that it made a $200 million contribution and agreed to freeze its U.K. defined benefit plan. A quarterly dividend was recently initiated.

► Risks to our recommendation and target price include increased competition for large long-term contracts in the IT infrastructure and outsourcing arena, further terminations of contracts in the commercial segment, and ongoing shareholder litigation against CSC. We also have concerns regarding corporate governance, including the combination of the chairman, president and CEO roles.

► Our 12-month target price of $56 is based on a slight peer-discount P/E of 10.7X using our calendar 2010 EPS estimate of $5.24. Our peer group is comprised of other U.S.-based multinational IT outsourcing companies.

Qualitative Risk Assessment

LOW	MEDIUM	HIGH

Our risk assessment reflects the highly competitive nature of the IT consulting and outsourcing market, offset by our view of CSC's strong balance sheet and the stability afforded the company by the numerous long-term contracts it has signed with customers.

Quantitative Evaluations

S&P Quality Ranking   B+

D	C	B-	B	B+	A-	A	A+

Relative Strength Rank   STRONG

78

LOWEST = 1   HIGHEST = 99

Revenue/Earnings Data

Revenue (Million $)

	1Q	2Q	3Q	4Q	Year
2011	3,942	--	--	--	--
2010	3,898	4,041	3,953	4,236	16,128
2009	4,437	4,239	3,952	4,112	16,740
2008	3,838	4,017	4,160	4,484	16,500
2007	3,561	3,609	3,641	4,046	14,857
2006	3,583	3,573	3,577	3,884	14,616

Earnings Per Share ($)

2011	0.91	E1.17	E1.50	E1.75	E5.33
2010	0.86	1.40	1.36	1.66	5.28
2009	0.79	2.95	1.06	2.51	7.31
2008	0.61	0.43	1.05	1.15	3.20
2007	-0.31	0.51	0.62	1.42	2.16
2006	0.58	0.53	0.88	1.08	3.07

Fiscal year ended Mar. 31. Next earnings report expected: Mid November. EPS Estimates based on S&P Operating Earnings; historical GAAP earnings are as reported.

Dividend Data (Dates: mm/dd Payment Date: mm/dd/yy)

Amount ($)	Date Decl.	Ex-Div. Date	Stk. of Record	Payment Date
0.150	05/19	06/11	06/15	07/15/10
0.150	08/10	09/07	09/09	10/15/10

Dividends have been paid since 2010. Source: Company reports.

Please read the Required Disclosures and Analyst Certification on the last page of this report.

STANDARD &POOR'S

Computer Sciences Corp

Business Summary August 17, 2010

CORPORATE OVERVIEW. Computer Sciences offers what it believes is a broad array of services to clients in the global commercial and government markets. The company specializes in the application of complex information technology (IT) to achieve the strategic objectives of its customers. Offerings include IT and business process outsourcing, and IT and professional services.

Outsourcing involves operating all or a portion of a customer's technology infrastructure, including systems analysis, applications development, network operations, desktop computing, and data center management. CSC also provides business process outsourcing, which involves managing key functions for clients such as claims processing, credit checking, logistics, and customer call centers.

IT and professional services includes systems integration, consulting, and professional services. Systems integration encompasses designing, developing, implementing, and integrating complete information systems. Consulting

and professional services includes advising clients on the strategic acquisition and utilization of IT, and on business strategy, security, modeling, engineering, and business process re-engineering. CSC also licenses sophisticated software systems for health care and financial services markets, and provides a broad array of end-to-end e-business solutions to meet the needs of large commercial and government clients.

The company provides services to clients in global commercial industries and to the U.S. federal government. In the global commercial segment, offerings are marketed to clients in a wide variety of industries. In the U.S. federal government market, CSC provides traditional systems integration and outsourcing for complex project management and technical services.

Company Financials Fiscal Year Ended Mar. 31

Per Share Data ($)	2010	2009	2008	2007	2006	2005	2004	2003	2002	2001
Tangible Book Value	13.44	8.25	6.35	19.51	23.85	21.71	15.44	11.78	11.58	9.26
Cash Flow	12.49	15.08	9.26	8.95	9.42	8.56	8.29	6.95	7.02	5.17
Earnings	5.28	7.31	3.20	2.16	3.07	2.59	2.75	2.54	2.01	1.37
S&P Core Earnings	5.19	6.24	2.95	2.14	3.00	2.59	2.68	1.84	1.48	0.80
Dividends	Nil	Nil	Nil	Nil	Nil	Nil	Nil	Nil	Nil	Nil
Payout Ratio	Nil	Nil	Nil	Nil	Nil	Nil	Nil	Nil	Nil	Nil
Calendar Year	2009	2008	2007	2006	2005	2004	2003	2002	2001	2000
Prices:High	58.36	50.52	63.76	60.39	59.90	58.00	44.99	53.47	66.71	99.88
Prices:Low	31.11	23.93	46.95	46.23	42.31	38.07	26.52	24.30	28.99	58.25
P/E Ratio:High	11	7	20	28	20	22	16	21	33	73
P/E Ratio:Low	6	3	15	21	14	15	10	10	14	43

Income Statement Analysis (Million $)

	2010	2009	2008	2007	2006	2005	2004	2003	2002	2001
Revenue	16,128	16,740	16,500	14,857	14,616	14,059	14,768	11,347	11,426	10,524
Operating Income	2,359	2,396	2,205	2,211	2,149	1,845	1,968	1,609	1,497	1,302
Depreciation	1,116	1,186	1,032	1,162	1,188	1,146	1,038	858	858	649
Interest Expense	252	261	106	175	104	157	170	143	155	106
Pretax Income	1,038	949	918	607	821	715	747	612	497	330
Effective Tax Rate	NA	NM	40.7%	35.9%	29.7%	30.6%	30.5%	28.0%	30.7%	29.4%
Net Income	817	1,115	545	389	577	496	519	440	344	233
S&P Core Earnings	803	954	502	385	565	495	507	319	254	137

Balance Sheet & Other Financial Data (Million $)

	2010	2009	2008	2007	2006	2005	2004	2003	2002	2001
Cash	2,784	2,297	699	1,050	1,291	1,010	610	300	149	185
Current Assets	8,422	7,707	6,923	6,706	6,306	5,690	4,867	4,088	3,304	3,204
Total Assets	16,455	15,619	15,775	13,731	12,943	12,634	11,804	10,433	8,611	8,175
Current Liabilities	4,122	4,016	5,590	5,260	4,141	3,878	3,253	2,987	2,708	3,589
Long Term Debt	3,494	4,173	2,506	1,412	1,377	1,303	2,306	2,205	1,873	1,029
Common Equity	6,446	5,510	5,462	5,886	6,772	6,495	5,504	4,606	3,624	3,215
Total Capital	10,017	9,683	7,968	7,298	8,149	7,798	7,810	6,811	5,497	4,245
Capital Expenditures	578	699	877	686	827	855	725	638	672	897
Cash Flow	1,933	2,301	1,576	1,551	1,765	1,642	1,558	1,298	1,202	882
Current Ratio	2.0	1.9	1.2	1.3	1.5	1.5	1.5	1.4	1.2	0.9
% Long Term Debt of Capitalization	34.9	43.1	31.5	19.4	16.9	16.7	29.5	32.4	34.1	24.3
% Net Income of Revenue	5.1	6.7	3.3	2.6	3.9	3.5	3.5	3.9	3.0	2.2
% Return on Assets	5.1	7.1	3.7	2.9	4.5	4.1	4.7	4.6	4.1	3.3
% Return on Equity	13.7	20.3	9.6	6.3	8.7	8.3	10.3	10.7	10.1	7.5

Data as orig reptd.; bef. results of disc opers/spec. items. Per share data adj. for stk. divs.; EPS diluted. E-Estimated. NA-Not Available. NM-Not Meaningful. NR-Not Ranked. UR-Under Review.

Office: 3170 Fairview Park Drive, Falls Church, VA 22042.
Telephone: 703-876-1000.
Email: investorrelations@csc.com
Website: http://www.csc.com

Chrmn, Pres & CEO: M.W. Laphen
CFO: M.J. Mancuso
Chief Acctg Officer & Cntlr: D.G. DeBuck
Secy & General Counsel: W.L. Deckelman, Jr.

Investor Contact: B. Lackey (310-615-1700)
Board Members: I. W. Bailey, II, D. J. Barram, S. L. Baum, R. F. Chase, J. R. Haberkorn, M. W. Laphen, F. W. McFarlan, C. S. Park, T. H. Patrick

Founded: 1959
Domicile: Nevada
Employees: 94,000

The McGraw-Hill Companies

Compuware Corp

STANDARD &POOR'S

S&P Recommendation SELL ★ ★ ☆ ☆ ☆

Price $9.92 (as of Oct 22, 2010)	**12-Mo. Target Price** $9.00	**Investment Style** Large-Cap Blend

GICS Sector Information Technology
Sub-Industry Application Software

Summary This company provides software products and professional services designed to increase the productivity of information systems departments.

Key Stock Statistics (Source S&P, Vickers, company reports)

52-Wk Range	$10.39– 6.79	S&P Oper. EPS 2011**E**	0.45	Market Capitalization(B)	$2.215	Beta	1.25
Trailing 12-Month EPS	$0.44	S&P Oper. EPS 2012**E**	0.60	Yield (%)	Nil	S&P 3-Yr. Proj. EPS CAGR(%)	8
Trailing 12-Month P/E	22.6	P/E on S&P Oper. EPS 2011**E**	22.0	Dividend Rate/Share	Nil	S&P Credit Rating	NR
$10K Invested 5 Yrs Ago	$12,573	Common Shares Outstg. (M)	223.3	Institutional Ownership (%)	81		

Price Performance

30-Week Mov. Avg. ···· 10-Week Mov. Avg. - - GAAP Earnings vs. Previous Year Volume Above Avg. ▮▮▮ STARS
12-Mo. Target Price — Relative Strength — ▲ Up ▼ Down ► No Change Below Avg. ▮▮ ★

Options: CBOE, P

Qualitative Risk Assessment

LOW	MEDIUM	HIGH

Our risk assessment reflects our concern about the maturity of CPWR's core businesses. Its newer initiatives have been slow to bear fruit, in our opinion. Absent a meaningful pickup in revenue growth, we expect future earnings growth to be driven by ongoing cost reductions and share repurchases.

Quantitative Evaluations

S&P Quality Ranking NR

D	C	B-	B	B+	A-	A	A+

Relative Strength Rank STRONG

93

LOWEST = 1   HIGHEST = 99

Highlights

► The 12-month target price for CPWR has recently been changed to $9.00 from $7.00. The Highlights section of this Stock Report will be updated accordingly.

Investment Rationale/Risk

► The Investment Rationale/Risk section of this Stock Report will be updated shortly. For the latest News story on CPWR from MarketScope, see below.

► 10/22/10 11:56 am ET ... S&P MAINTAINS SELL RECOMMENDATION ON SHARES OF COMPUWARE (CPWR 9.98**): Sep-Q EPS of $0.12, vs. $0.12, beats our $0.11 estimate. Revenues rose 3.6% to $226M, in line with our forecast. Growth was led by its performance monitoring solutions, which rose 26%. We see stronger demand for these products, given the growing interest in cloud computing. While the mainframe business remains weak, we think it will stabilize with the introductions of new mainframe models. We raise our FY 11 (Mar.) EPS estimate by $0.05 to $0.45, FY 12's by $0.15 to $0.60, and our target price by $2 to $9. However, with the shares above our target price, our opinion is sell. /J.Yin-CFA

Revenue/Earnings Data

Revenue (Million $)

	1Q	2Q	3Q	4Q	Year
2011	206.5	--	--	--	--
2010	214.4	217.9	229.9	230.0	892.2
2009	298.6	269.9	268.7	253.4	1,090
2008	279.4	302.0	309.3	338.9	1,230
2007	296.3	288.5	315.2	313.0	1,213
2006	297.3	292.7	305.9	309.5	1,205

Earnings Per Share ($)

2011	0.06	E0.12	E0.14	E0.15	E0.45
2010	0.21	0.12	0.11	0.16	0.60
2009	0.13	0.08	0.14	0.20	0.55
2008	Nil	0.13	0.13	0.23	0.47
2007	0.08	0.07	0.11	0.21	0.45
2006	0.06	0.06	0.10	0.15	0.37

Fiscal year ended Mar. 31. Next earnings report expected: Late October. EPS Estimates based on S&P Operating Earnings; historical GAAP earnings are as reported.

Dividend Data

No cash dividends have been paid.

Compuware Corp

Business Summary July 28, 2010

CORPORATE OVERVIEW. Originally founded as a professional services company, Compuware provides software, maintenance and professional services intended to increase the productivity of the information technology (IT) departments of businesses. The company has two main product lines: mainframe products and distributed products. CPWR's mainframe software products help customers maintain their IBM OS/390 and z/Series IT infrastructure. Key mainframe products include File-AID, Xpeditor, Hiperstation, Abend-AID and Strobe. These products facilitate application analysis, testing, defect detection and remediation, fault management, file and data management. Mainframe product revenues accounted for 49% of total revenue in FY 10 (Mar.).

CPWR's distributed software products help customers maximize the performance of their corporate IT infrastructure, which include multiple hardware, software and network platforms. The company's distributed products support requirements management (Changepoint), application development (Uniface), and application performance analysis (Vantage). Distributed product revenue accounted for 21% of total revenue in FY 10.

CPWR launched its Compuware 2.0 initiative in FY 09 with the main objective of delivering value-added high end-to-end application performance to meet

the growing and ever-more critical demand from enterprises that application systems deliver value to their business. As part of this initiative, the company acquired Gomez in FY 10 for $295 million in cash. Gomez is a leading provider of web application performance services, which enable organizations to test and monitor web applications from outside their firewall. We believe this acquisition complements CPWR's Vantage products. To better focus on the faster growth, higher margined segment of the market, the company has divested its Quality and DevPartner software products.

CPWR also provides applications services, which are marketed under the brand name "Covisint." Covisint provides a secure, collaborative platform that enables trading partners, customers, and vendors to share vital business information and process transactions across disparate systems. Application services revenue accounted for about 4.5% of total revenue in FY 10, up from 3.2% in FY 09.

Company Financials Fiscal Year Ended Mar. 31

Per Share Data ($)	2010	2009	2008	2007	2006	2005	2004	2003	2002	2001
Tangible Book Value	1.24	2.09	1.95	2.57	3.33	3.15	3.11	2.93	2.60	2.02
Cash Flow	0.79	0.67	0.58	0.70	0.51	0.34	0.27	0.41	-0.40	0.60
Earnings	0.60	0.55	0.47	0.45	0.37	0.20	0.13	0.27	-0.66	0.32
S&P Core Earnings	0.39	0.49	0.43	0.41	0.33	0.12	0.03	0.14	-0.15	0.17
Dividends	Nil	Nil	Nil	Nil	Nil	Nil	Nil	Nil	Nil	Nil
Payout Ratio	Nil	Nil	Nil	Nil	Nil	Nil	Nil	Nil	Nil	Nil
Calendar Year	2009	2008	2007	2006	2005	2004	2003	2002	2001	2000
Prices:High	8.95	11.91	12.56	9.55	9.99	8.95	6.52	14.00	14.50	37.81
Prices:Low	5.18	5.08	7.32	6.02	5.51	4.35	3.22	2.35	6.25	5.63
P/E Ratio:High	15	22	27	NM	27	45	50	52	NM	NM
P/E Ratio:Low	9	9	16	NM	15	22	25	9	NM	NM

Income Statement Analysis (Million $)										
Revenue	892	1,090	1,230	1,213	1,205	1,232	1,265	1,375	1,729	2,010
Operating Income	184	220	224	188	198	143	90.5	188	264	296
Depreciation	45.0	30.4	32.8	55.0	50.2	56.4	55.2	53.8	98.2	104
Interest Expense	NA	NA	31.3	Nil	Nil	Nil	Nil	6.10	7.43	31.3
Pretax Income	209	213	180	193	191	106	56.0	156	-245	192
Effective Tax Rate	NA	34.4%	25.5%	18.1%	25.3%	28.0%	11.0%	34.0%	NM	38.0%
Net Income	141	140	134	158	143	76.5	49.8	103	-245	119
S&P Core Earnings	93.3	124	124	143	126	46.1	9.72	51.2	-55.3	62.2

Balance Sheet & Other Financial Data (Million $)										
Cash	150	278	286	261	612	498	455	319	233	53.3
Current Assets	705	859	919	921	1,445	1,358	1,143	1,050	1,063	1,004
Total Assets	2,013	1,875	2,019	2,029	2,511	2,478	2,234	2,123	1,994	2,279
Current Liabilities	613	562	645	529	545	578	493	469	556	569
Long Term Debt	NA	Nil	Nil	Nil	Nil	Nil	Nil	Nil	Nil	140
Common Equity	914	881	927	1,132	1,579	1,516	1,414	1,332	1,170	1,377
Total Capital	914	905	955	1,167	1,605	1,516	1,516	1,418	1,332	1,170	1,538
Capital Expenditures	9.58	17.9	10.5	18.6	14.5	134	74.6	225	90.4	39.8
Cash Flow	186	170	167	213	193	133	105	157	-147	223
Current Ratio	1.2	1.5	1.4	1.7	2.6	2.3	2.3	2.2	1.9	1.8
% Long Term Debt of Capitalization	Nil	Nil	Nil	Nil	Nil	Nil	Nil	Nil	Nil	9.1
% Net Income of Revenue	15.8	12.8	10.9	13.0	11.9	6.2	3.9	7.5	NM	5.9
% Return on Assets	7.2	7.2	6.6	7.0	5.7	3.2	2.3	5.0	NM	5.1
% Return on Equity	15.7	15.5	13.1	11.7	9.2	5.2	3.6	8.2	NM	9.2

Data as orig reptd.; bef. results of disc opers/spec. items. Per share data adj. for stk. divs.; EPS diluted. E-Estimated. NA-Not Available. NM-Not Meaningful. NR-Not Ranked. UR-Under Review.

Office: One Campus Martius, Detroit, MI 48226-5099.
Telephone: 313-227-7300.
Email: investor.relations@compuware.com
Website: http://www.compuware.com

Chrmn & CEO: P. Karmanos, Jr.
Pres & COO: R.C. Paul
EVP, CFO, Chief Acctg Officer & Treas: L.L. Fournier
EVP & Chief Admin Officer: D.A. Knobblock

CTO: P.A. Czarnik
Investor Contact: L. Elkin (248-737-7345)
Board Members: D. W. Archer, G. S. Bedi, W. O. Grabe, W. R. Halling, P. Karmanos, Jr., F. A. Nelson, G. Price, W. J. Prowse, G. S. Romney, R. Szygenda

Founded: 1973
Domicile: Michigan
Employees: 4,336

The McGraw-Hill Companies

ConAgra Foods Inc.

STANDARD &POOR'S

S&P Recommendation **BUY** ★★★★☆	Price $22.95 (as of Oct 22, 2010)	12-Mo. Target Price $24.00	Investment Style Large-Cap Value

GICS Sector Consumer Staples
Sub-Industry Packaged Foods & Meats

Summary This company is one of the largest U.S. packaged food processors.

Key Stock Statistics (Source S&P, Vickers, company reports)

52-Wk Range	$26.32–20.55	S&P Oper. EPS 2011**E**	1.84	Market Capitalization(B)	$10.092	Beta	0.75
Trailing 12-Month EPS	$1.57	S&P Oper. EPS 2012**E**	1.98	Yield (%)	4.01	S&P 3-Yr. Proj. EPS CAGR(%)	7
Trailing 12-Month P/E	14.6	P/E on S&P Oper. EPS 2011**E**	12.5	Dividend Rate/Share	$0.92	S&P Credit Rating	BBB
$10K Invested 5 Yrs Ago	$11,759	Common Shares Outstg. (M)	439.7	Institutional Ownership (%)	71		

Price Performance

30-Week Mov. Avg. · · · · 10-Week Mov. Avg. – – **GAAP Earnings vs. Previous Year** Volume Above Avg. STARS
12-Mo. Target Price — Relative Strength — ▲ Up ▼ Down ► No Change Below Avg.

Options: ASE, CBOE, P

Analysis prepared by **Tom Graves, CFA** on August 20, 2010, when the stock traded at **$ 21.41.**

Highlights

▸ For the company as currently constituted, we look for FY 11 (May) revenue from continuing operations to increase about 3% from the $12.1 billion reported for FY 10. Earlier, in FY 09, when reported sales totaled $12.7 billion, there was a 53rd week.

▸ Although we expect FY 11 profit margins to be bolstered by cost reduction efforts, we have become more wary of the raw material cost environment. Before some possible special items, we estimate FY 11 EPS from continuing operations of $1.88, up from about $1.70 for FY 10, which excludes a net negative impact of about $0.03 a share from special items in FY 10.

▸ In February 2010, CAG announced that its board of directors had approved a $500 million share repurchase authorization with no expiration date. In FY 10's fourth quarter, CAG repurchased about four million shares. Repurchase authorization of about $400 million remained. Also, in FY 11, we expect capital expenditures to total about $525 million, with part of this offset by some insurance proceeds.

Investment Rationale/Risk

▸ Asset sales by ConAgra since 2003 have generated total pretax proceeds of more than $4 billion. Also, CAG's reported earnings have included a variety of special items, including asset sale gains, restructuring charges, and impairment charges.

▸ Risks to our recommendation and target price include competitive pressures in CAG's businesses, the potential for increased commodity cost inflation, and the company's ability to generate interest income and achieve cost savings and efficiency targets.

▸ With the divestiture of the commodity trading and merchandising business, we anticipate increased profit stability and visibility from a re-shaped ConAgra, and we expect the stock to be accorded a higher P/E valuation than it would have otherwise been the case. Our 12-month target price of $24 reflects our view that the stock should receive a P/E that is at a discount to what we expect, on average, from a group of other packaged food stocks. CAG shares recently had an indicated dividend yield of about 3.7%.

Qualitative Risk Assessment

LOW	MEDIUM	HIGH

Our risk assessment reflects the relatively stable nature of the company's end markets, and what we view as relatively strong expected cash flows.

Quantitative Evaluations

S&P Quality Ranking A-

D	C	B-	B	B+	A-	A	A+

Relative Strength Rank MODERATE

48

LOWEST = 1   HIGHEST = 99

Revenue/Earnings Data

Revenue (Million $)

	1Q	2Q	3Q	4Q	Year
2011	2,818	--	--	--	--
2010	2,886	3,100	3,031	3,063	12,079
2009	3,066	3,252	3,125	3,298	12,731
2008	2,956	3,511	3,528	3,078	11,606
2007	2,689	3,089	2,918	3,333	12,028
2006	2,700	3,026	2,879	2,975	11,579

Earnings Per Share ($)

2011	0.32	E0.50	E0.51	E0.49	E1.84
2010	0.37	0.53	0.49	0.27	1.67
2009	0.23	0.38	0.43	0.39	1.42
2008	0.23	0.50	0.63	-0.43	1.06
2007	0.21	0.39	0.37	0.38	1.35
2006	0.63	0.24	0.18	0.10	1.15

Fiscal year ended May 31. Next earnings report expected: Late December. EPS Estimates based on S&P Operating Earnings; historical GAAP earnings are as reported.

Dividend Data (Dates: mm/dd Payment Date: mm/dd/yy)

Amount ($)	Date Decl.	Ex-Div. Date	Stk. of Record	Payment Date
0.200	12/03	01/27	01/29	03/02/10
0.200	04/01	04/28	04/30	06/02/10
0.200	07/21	07/28	07/30	09/01/10
0.230	09/21	10/27	10/29	12/01/10

Dividends have been paid since 1976. Source: Company reports.

The McGraw·Hill Companies

STANDARD &POOR'S

ConAgra Foods Inc.

Business Summary August 20, 2010

CORPORATE OVERVIEW. ConAgra Foods is one of the largest food companies in North America. The company's continuing operations businesses are now being presented in two reporting segments: consumer foods, which provided 66% of total sales in FY 10 (May); and commercial foods (34%). In June 2008, CAG sold its trading and merchandising segment (12% of FY 07 sales), which was treated as a discontinued operation for FY 08 and FY 09.

The consumer foods segment included branded, private label and customized food products. CAG's brands include Hunt's, Healthy Choice, Chef Boyardee, Peter Pan, Wesson, Blue Bonnet, Orville Redenbacher's, Slim Jim, PAM, Swiss Miss, Van Camp's, Banquet, Marie Callender's, Hebrew National, Egg Beaters, and Reddi-wip. In FY 10, what CAG calls Speciality Foods accounted for 36% of segment sales, while Convenient Meals represented 34%, Snacks accounted for 16%, and Meal Enhancers represented 14%.

CAG's commercial foods segment includes branded foods and ingredients, which are sold principally to foodservice, food manufacturing, and industrial customers. This segment's primary products include specialty potato products, milled grain ingredients, a variety of vegetable products, seasonings, blends, and flavors. Products are sold under brands such as ConAgra Mills, Lamb Weston, and Spicetec. In FY 10, what CAG calls Specialty Potatoes accounted for 56% of segment sales, while Milled Products represented 35%.

In FY 10, CAG's largest customer, Wal-Mart Stores, Inc., and its affiliates, accounted for about 18% of consolidated net sales.

CORPORATE STRATEGY. In recent years, CAG has been pursuing an acquisition and divestiture strategy, which has included shifting its focus toward its core branded and value-added food products, while exiting commodity-related businesses.

Company Financials Fiscal Year Ended May 31

Per Share Data ($)	2010	2009	2008	2007	2006	2005	2004	2003	2002	2001
Tangible Book Value	1.12	0.89	2.14	0.73	0.79	0.47	0.41	NM	NM	NM
Cash Flow	2.40	2.12	1.66	2.10	1.74	1.95	2.16	2.30	2.39	2.30
Earnings	1.67	1.42	1.06	1.35	1.15	1.27	1.50	1.58	1.47	1.33
S&P Core Earnings	1.57	1.20	1.05	1.29	0.91	1.14	1.39	1.42	1.27	1.20
Dividends	NA	0.75	0.72	0.72	1.08	1.03	0.98	NA	0.88	0.79
Payout Ratio	NA	53%	68%	53%	94%	81%	65%	NA	60%	59%
Calendar Year	2009	2008	2007	2006	2005	2004	2003	2002	2001	2000
Prices:High	23.67	24.87	27.73	28.35	30.24	29.65	26.41	27.65	26.00	26.19
Prices:Low	14.00	13.52	22.81	18.85	19.99	25.38	17.75	20.90	17.50	15.06
P/E Ratio:High	14	18	26	21	26	23	18	18	18	20
P/E Ratio:Low	8	10	22	14	17	20	12	14	12	11

Income Statement Analysis (Million $)										
Revenue	12,079	12,731	11,606	12,028	11,579	14,567	14,522	19,839	27,630	27,194
Operating Income	1,572	1,519	1,317	1,577	1,184	1,618	1,735	1,123	2,144	2,026
Depreciation	327	319	297	346	311	351	352	392	474	499
Interest Expense	160	268	467	226	307	341	275	276	402	423
Pretax Income	1,107	984	746	1,050	906	1,133	1,151	1,276	1,268	1,104
Effective Tax Rate	NA	34.3%	30.5%	34.8%	34.2%	41.5%	30.9%	34.2%	38.1%	38.2%
Net Income	747	646	519	684	596	663	796	840	785	682
S&P Core Earnings	697	547	512	657	470	589	740	750	668	612

Balance Sheet & Other Financial Data (Million $)										
Cash	953	243	141	735	332	208	589	629	158	198
Current Assets	3,960	3,337	6,082	5,006	4,790	4,524	5,145	6,060	6,434	7,363
Total Assets	11,738	11,073	13,683	11,836	11,970	12,792	14,230	15,071	15,496	16,481
Current Liabilities	2,036	1,575	3,651	2,681	2,965	2,389	3,002	3,803	4,313	6,936
Long Term Debt	3,226	3,461	3,387	3,420	3,155	4,349	5,281	5,570	5,919	4,635
Common Equity	4,929	4,721	5,337	4,583	4,650	4,859	4,840	4,622	4,308	3,983
Total Capital	8,416	8,234	8,739	8,003	7,805	9,209	10,120	10,192	10,227	8,618
Capital Expenditures	483	442	490	425	263	453	352	390	531	560
Cash Flow	1,074	965	815	1,030	907	1,014	1,148	1,232	1,259	1,181
Current Ratio	1.9	2.1	1.7	1.9	1.6	1.9	1.7	1.6	1.5	1.1
% Long Term Debt of Capitalization	38.3	42.0	38.7	42.7	40.4	47.2	52.2	54.7	57.9	53.8
% Net Income of Revenue	6.2	5.1	4.5	5.7	5.1	4.6	5.5	4.2	2.8	2.5
% Return on Assets	6.6	5.2	4.1	5.7	4.8	4.9	5.4	5.5	4.9	4.8
% Return on Equity	15.5	12.9	10.5	14.8	12.5	13.7	16.8	18.8	18.9	19.9

Data as orig reptd.; bef. results of disc opers/spec. items. Per share data adj. for stk. divs.; EPS diluted. E-Estimated. NA-Not Available. NM-Not Meaningful. NR-Not Ranked. UR-Under Review.

Office: One ConAgra Drive, Omaha, NE 68102-5001.
Telephone: 402-240-4000.
Website: http://www.conagrafoods.com
Chrmn: S.F. Goldstone

Pres & CEO: G.M. Rodkin
EVP & CFO: J.F. Gehring
EVP, Secy & General Counsel: C.R. Batcheler
SVP & Treas: S.E. Messel

Investor Contact: C.W. Klinefelter (402-595-4154)
Board Members: M. C. Bay, S. G. Butler, S. F. Goldstone, J. A. Gregor, R. Johri, W. G. Jurgensen, R. H. Lenny, R. A. Marshall, G. M. Rodkin, A. J. Schindler, K. E. Stinson

Founded: 1919
Domicile: Delaware
Employees: 24,400

The McGraw·Hill Companies

ConocoPhillips

STANDARD &POOR'S

S&P Recommendation BUY ★★★★☆

Price $61.67 (as of Oct 22, 2010)	
12-Mo. Target Price $66.00	
Investment Style Large-Cap Blend	

GICS Sector Energy
Sub-Industry Integrated Oil & Gas

Summary Formerly Phillips Petroleum, ConocoPhillips is the fourth largest integrated oil company in the world, and the second largest in the U.S.

Key Stock Statistics (Source S&P, Vickers, company reports)

52-Wk Range	$61.88– 46.63	S&P Oper. EPS 2010**E**	6.35	Market Capitalization(B)	$91.479	Beta	1.13
Trailing 12-Month EPS	$6.30	S&P Oper. EPS 2011**E**	7.36	Yield (%)	3.57	S&P 3-Yr. Proj. EPS CAGR(%)	36
Trailing 12-Month P/E	9.8	P/E on S&P Oper. EPS 2010**E**	9.7	Dividend Rate/Share	$2.20	S&P Credit Rating	A
$10K Invested 5 Yrs Ago	$12,314	Common Shares Outstg. (M)	1,483.4	Institutional Ownership (%)	73		

Price Performance

- 30-Week Mov. Avg. · · · · 10-Week Mov. Avg. – – GAAP Earnings vs. Previous Year   Volume Above Avg. STARS
- 12-Mo. Target Price — Relative Strength — ▲ Up ▼ Down ▶ No Change   Below Avg. ★

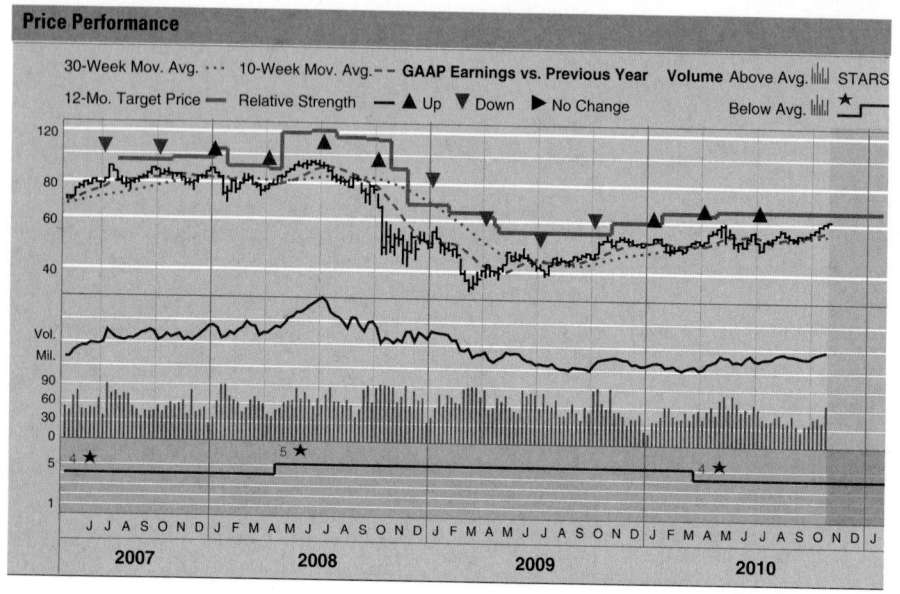

Analysis prepared by **Tina J. Vital** on July 30, 2010, when the stock traded at **$ 55.47.**

Options: ASE, CBOE, P, Ph

Highlights

➤ Second-quarter oil and gas production (excluding Lukoil) declined 7.4%, to 1.73 million boe per day, below our estimate, reflecting impacts of higher oil prices on international production contracts, field declines and maintenance activities. Compounded by asset sales, we look for production (excluding Lukoil) to drop about 3% in 2010, before rising 2%-3% per year during 2012-14 driven by heavy oil expansions, such as the relatively low-cost Canadian SAGD portfolio.

➤ Demand fell with the economic slowdown, and refiners cut throughputs and initiated cost reductions in 2009. However, so far in 2010, fuel demand has improved, and light-heavy crude differentials and U.S. refining margins have widened. As of July, we project U.S. Gulf Coast 3-2-1 crack spreads will widen 9% in 2010 and 3% in 2011.

➤ First-half 2010 operating EPS excluded net special gains of $1.03 related to dispositions and impairments. We expect after-tax operating earnings to rise 89% in 2010 and 16% in 2011 on stronger prices and margins due to improved global demand.

Investment Rationale/Risk

➤ COP is reshaping its portfolio to focus on higher growth and profit upstream assets. In April 2010, COP said it would not participate in a new refinery project with Saudi Aramco, and in July, it canceled a refinery upgrade at Wilhelmshaven, Germany. The company plans to sell $10 billion of assets over the next two years and use some proceeds to pay down debt. In March 2010, COP said 60%-80% of the targeted divestment would come from North America E&P, and 20%-40% from downstream assets. COP plans to sell its 20% equity stake in Lukoil for about $8.7 billion plus $1 billion in dividends, and has agreed to sell its 9.03% stake in Syncrude to Sinopec for $4.65 billion.

➤ Risks to our recommendation and target price include unfavorable changes in economic, industrial and operating conditions, including COP's ability to organically replace its reserves; geopolitical risk; and operational risk.

➤ Blending our DCF ($56 per share, assuming a WACC of 8.9% and a terminal growth rate of 3%) and relative market valuations, our 12-month target price is $66, which represents an expected enterprise value of about 5.2X our 2011 EBITDA estimate, in line with peers.

Qualitative Risk Assessment

LOW	MEDIUM	HIGH

Our risk assessment reflects our view of the company's diversified and solid business profile in volatile, cyclical and capital-intensive segments of the energy industry. While COP has a history of aggressive acquisition activity, we believe its earnings stability is good and its corporate governance practices are sound.

Quantitative Evaluations

S&P Quality Ranking   B

D	C	B-	**B**	B+	A-	A	A+

Relative Strength Rank   STRONG

78

LOWEST = 1   HIGHEST = 99

Revenue/Earnings Data

Revenue (Million $)

	1Q	2Q	3Q	4Q	Year
2010	41,601	42,269	--	--	--
2009	30,741	35,448	40,173	42,979	149,341
2008	54,883	71,411	70,044	44,504	240,842
2007	41,320	47,370	46,062	52,685	187,437
2006	46,906	47,149	48,076	41,519	183,650
2005	37,631	41,808	48,745	51,258	179,442

Earnings Per Share ($)

	1Q	2Q	3Q	4Q	Year
2010	1.40	2.77	E1.58	E1.64	E6.35
2009	0.56	0.87	1.00	0.81	3.24
2008	2.62	3.50	3.39	-21.37	-11.16
2007	2.12	0.18	2.23	2.71	7.22
2006	2.34	3.09	2.31	1.91	9.66
2005	2.06	2.21	2.68	2.69	9.63

Fiscal year ended Dec. 31. Next earnings report expected: Late October. EPS Estimates based on S&P Operating Earnings; historical GAAP earnings are as reported.

Dividend Data (Dates: mm/dd Payment Date: mm/dd/yy)

Amount ($)	Date Decl.	Ex-Div. Date	Stk. of Record	Payment Date
0.500	02/12	02/18	02/22	03/01/10
0.550	03/24	05/20	05/24	06/01/10
0.550	07/14	07/20	08/02	09/01/10
0.550	10/06	10/27	10/29	12/01/10

Dividends have been paid since 1934. Source: Company reports.

Please read the Required Disclosures and Analyst Certification on the last page of this report.

The McGraw·Hill Companies

ConocoPhillips

Business Summary July 30, 2010

CORPORATE OVERVIEW. On August 30, 2002, Phillips Petroleum and Conoco merged, creating ConocoPhillips (COP). Today, we estimate COP is the second largest publicly integrated oil company in the U.S., based on a blend of its oil and gas reserves and production capacity. COP operates in six segments: exploration and production (E&P; 25% of 2009 sales, 61% of 2009 net income); refining and marketing (R&M; 72%, 1%); midstream (3%, 5%); 20% stake in the Russian oil company Lukoil (NA; 28%); chemicals (NA; 4%); and emerging businesses. In July 2010, COP agreed to sell its interest in Lukoil in phases, to either Lukoil or on the open market; deal closure expected by the end of 2011.

Including Lukoil, and its share of equity affiliates, net oil and gas production rose 2.4% in 2009, to 2.29 million barrels of oil equivalent per day (boe/d), reflecting new international developments in the U.K., Russia, China, Canada, Vietnam and Norway, plus less unplanned downtime. Proved oil and gas reserves (including Lukoil, bitumen, synthetic oil, and equity affiliates) rose 3.5%, to 10.33 billion barrels (61% liquids, 77% developed), in 2009.

Using data from John S. Herold, we estimate COP's three-year (2006-08) finding and development costs at $30.58 per boe, above the peer average; three-year proved acquisition costs at $10.50 per boe, above the peer average; three-year reserve replacement costs at $17.16 per boe, above the peer average; and its three-year reserve replacement at 173%, above the peer average. We estimate COP's 2009 organic reserve replacement at 70%.

As of December 31, 2009, COP owned or had interests in 12 U.S. refineries (net crude throughput capacity of 2.0 million barrels per day, b/d), four European refineries (610,000 b/d), and one refinery in Malaysia (61,000 b/d). At year-end 2009, fuel was sold through wholesale and retail operations in the U.S. (under Phillips 66, Conoco, and 76 brands) and Europe (under the JET and Coop brand).

Company Financials Fiscal Year Ended Dec. 31

Per Share Data ($)	2009	2008	2007	2006	2005	2004	2003	2002	2001	2000
Tangible Book Value	39.03	34.15	36.40	29.69	25.49	18.53	12.85	9.91	14.07	10.77
Cash Flow	9.48	-3.86	12.54	14.19	12.63	8.49	5.90	5.31	5.14	5.94
Earnings	3.24	-11.16	7.22	9.66	9.63	5.79	3.53	0.74	2.79	3.63
S&P Core Earnings	3.36	4.96	7.49	9.59	9.72	5.88	3.43	0.64	2.60	NA
Dividends	1.91	1.88	1.64	1.44	1.18	0.90	0.82	0.74	0.70	0.68
Payout Ratio	59%	NM	23%	15%	12%	15%	23%	101%	25%	19%
Prices:High	57.44	95.96	90.84	74.89	71.48	45.61	33.02	32.05	34.00	35.00
Prices:Low	34.12	41.27	61.59	54.90	41.40	32.15	26.80	22.02	25.00	17.97
P/E Ratio:High	18	NM	13	8	7	8	9	44	12	10
P/E Ratio:Low	11	NM	9	6	4	6	8	30	9	5

Income Statement Analysis (Million $)	2009	2008	2007	2006	2005	2004	2003	2002	2001	2000
Revenue	149,341	240,842	187,437	183,650	179,442	135,076	104,196	56,748	26,868	21,113
Operating Income	NA	36,158	31,164	37,433	24,691	17,033	11,866	4,571	8,393	5,528
Depreciation, Depletion and Amortization	9,346	11,116	8,740	7,284	4,253	3,798	3,485	4,446	1,391	1,179
Interest Expense	1,289	935	1,801	1,087	497	546	864	614	391	422
Pretax Income	10,032	-3,523	23,359	28,409	23,580	14,401	8,337	2,164	3,302	3,769
Effective Tax Rate	50.8%	NM	48.7%	45.0%	42.0%	43.5%	44.9%	67.0%	50.2%	50.6%
Net Income	4,858	-16,998	11,891	15,550	13,640	8,107	4,593	714	1,643	1,862
S&P Core Earnings	5,032	7,569	12,317	15,442	13,753	8,241	4,697	618	1,533	NA

Balance Sheet & Other Financial Data (Million $)	2009	2008	2007	2006	2005	2004	2003	2002	2001	2000
Cash	542	755	1,456	817	2,214	1,387	490	307	142	149
Current Assets	21,167	20,843	24,735	25,066	19,612	15,021	11,192	10,903	4,363	2,606
Total Assets	152,588	142,865	177,757	164,781	106,999	92,861	82,455	76,836	35,217	20,509
Current Liabilities	23,695	21,780	26,882	26,431	21,359	15,586	14,011	12,816	4,542	3,492
Long Term Debt	31,912	32,754	26,583	23,091	10,758	14,370	16,340	19,267	9,295	7,272
Common Equity	62,467	55,165	88,983	82,646	52,731	42,723	34,366	29,517	14,340	6,093
Total Capital	97,348	107,186	137,757	106,939	76,137	68,583	60,113	57,796	27,650	15,259
Capital Expenditures	10,861	19,099	11,791	15,596	11,620	9,496	6,169	4,388	3,085	2,022
Cash Flow	14,204	-5,882	20,631	22,834	17,893	11,905	8,078	5,160	3,034	3,041
Current Ratio	0.9	1.0	0.9	0.9	0.9	1.0	0.8	0.9	1.0	0.7
% Long Term Debt of Capitalization	Nil	30.6	19.3	21.6	14.1	21.0	27.2	33.3	33.6	47.7
% Return on Assets	3.3	NM	6.9	11.4	13.6	9.2	5.8	1.3	5.9	10.4
% Return on Equity	NA	NM	13.9	23.0	28.6	21.0	14.4	3.3	16.1	35.0

Data as orig reptd.; bef. results of disc opers/spec. items. Per share data adj. for stk. divs.; EPS diluted. E-Estimated. NA-Not Available. NM-Not Meaningful. NR-Not Ranked. UR-Under Review.

Office: 600 N Dairy Ashford St, Houston, TX 77079-1175.
Telephone: 281-293-1000.
Website: http://www.conocophillips.com
Chrmn & CEO: J.J. Mulva

Pres: J.A. Carrig
SVP & CFO: J.W. Sheets
SVP & Chief Admin Officer: E.L. Batchelder
SVP & Chief Acctg Officer: R.C. Berney

Investor Contact: G. Russell (212-207-1996)
Board Members: R. L. Armitage, R. H. Auchinleck, J. E. Copeland, Jr., K. M. Duberstein, R. R. Harkin, H. McGraw, III, J. J. Mulva, R. A. Niblock, H. Norvik, W. K. Reilly, B. S. Shackouls, V. J. Tschinkel, K. C. Turner, W. E. Wade, Jr.

Founded: 1917
Domicile: Delaware
Employees: 30,000

Consolidated Edison Inc.

STANDARD &POOR'S

S&P Recommendation HOLD ★★★☆☆

Price	**12-Mo. Target Price**	**Investment Style**
$49.12 (as of Oct 22, 2010)	$48.00	Large-Cap Value

GICS Sector Utilities
Sub-Industry Multi-Utilities

Summary This electric and gas utility holding company serves parts of New York, New Jersey and Pennsylvania.

Key Stock Statistics (Source S&P, Vickers, company reports)

52-Wk Range	$49.36–40.55	S&P Oper. EPS 2010**E**	3.36	Market Capitalization(B)	$13.883	Beta	0.32
Trailing 12-Month EPS	$3.38	S&P Oper. EPS 2011**E**	3.47	Yield (%)	4.85	S&P 3-Yr. Proj. EPS CAGR(%)	5
Trailing 12-Month P/E	14.5	P/E on S&P Oper. EPS 2010**E**	14.6	Dividend Rate/Share	$2.38	S&P Credit Rating	A-
$10K Invested 5 Yrs Ago	$14,289	Common Shares Outstg. (M)	282.6	Institutional Ownership (%)	40		

Price Performance

30-Week Mov. Avg. · · · 10-Week Mov. Avg. - - GAAP Earnings vs. Previous Year Volume Above Avg. STARS
12-Mo. Target Price — Relative Strength — ▲ Up ▼ Down ► No Change Below Avg.

Options: ASE, CBOE, P, Ph

Analysis prepared by **Justin McCann** on October 14, 2010, when the stock traded at **$ 48.20**.

Highlights

➤ We expect operating EPS in 2010 to increase nearly 9% from 2009's $3.09, which was up 3% from 2008's $3.00. Operating EPS in the first half of 2010 reflected the benefit of rate increases and relatively flat interest expense, partially offset by new issuances of common stock and long-term debt, higher depreciation and operation and maintenance expenses, and the slowdown in the New York City economy.

➤ For the second half of 2010, we expect earnings to benefit from abnormally warm summer weather. For 2011, we expect operating EPS to grow approximately 3% from anticipated results in 2010, reflecting both rate increases and a gradual recovery in the New York City economy, partially offset by the impact of new stock and long-term debt issuances.

➤ On September 16, 2010, the New York Public Service Commission authorized Con Edison of New York (CENY) annual natural gas rate increases of $47.1 million, $47.9 million and $46.7 million for the three-year period beginning October 1, 2010. In March 2010, CENY was authorized annual electric rate increases of $420 million for the three-year period through March 31, 2013.

Investment Rationale/Risk

➤ The stock is up approximately 6% year to date. This follows a 16.7% gain in 2009, with a nearly 40% rebound from its 2009 low. We believe the rebound reflected the expectation and then the realization of additional rate increases, the appeal of the above-peer dividend yield, and the recovery in the broader market. We think the stock was hurt earlier by the impacts of the financial crisis, the slowdown in the economy, the sharp drop in the stock market, and the expected dilutive effect of new equity issuances, as well as the lingering negative political and regulatory environment that resulted from a prolonged power outage three summers ago.

➤ Risks to our recommendation and target price include extended weakness in ED's service territory economy, unfavorable regulatory rulings, and/or a sharp decline in the utility sector.

➤ We believe the shares will be supported by a dividend yield (recently 4.9%) that is above the industry average (approximately 4.6%). We believe the dividend will continue to be increased at an annual rate of slightly less than 1%. Our 12-month target price is $48, reflecting a premium-to-peers P/E multiple of 13.8X our EPS estimate for 2011.

Qualitative Risk Assessment

LOW	MEDIUM	HIGH

Our risk assessment reflects our view of the company's strong and steady cash flows from regulated electric and gas utility operations, its solid balance sheet and A- credit rating, a relatively healthy economy in its service territory, and a historically supportive regulatory environment.

Quantitative Evaluations

S&P Quality Ranking B+

D	C	B-	B	B+	A-	A	A+

Relative Strength Rank MODERATE

52

LOWEST = 1   HIGHEST = 99

Revenue/Earnings Data

Revenue (Million $)

	1Q	2Q	3Q	4Q	Year
2010	3,462	3,017	--	--	--
2009	3,423	2,845	3,489	3,273	13,032
2008	3,577	3,149	3,858	2,999	13,583
2007	3,357	2,956	3,579	3,228	13,120
2006	3,317	2,555	3,441	2,824	12,137
2005	2,801	2,406	3,375	3,108	11,690

Earnings Per Share ($)

	1Q	2Q	3Q	4Q	Year
2010	0.81	0.64	E1.20	E0.71	E3.36
2009	0.66	0.55	1.22	0.73	3.14
2008	1.10	1.02	0.66	0.58	3.36
2007	0.99	0.58	1.15	0.76	3.46
2006	0.74	0.51	0.92	0.78	2.95
2005	0.75	0.48	1.17	0.59	2.99

Fiscal year ended Dec. 31. Next earnings report expected: Early November. EPS Estimates based on S&P Operating Earnings; historical GAAP earnings are as reported.

Dividend Data (Dates: mm/dd Payment Date: mm/dd/yy)

Amount ($)	Date Decl.	Ex-Div. Date	Stk. of Record	Payment Date
0.595	01/21	02/12	02/17	03/15/10
0.595	04/15	05/10	05/12	06/15/10
0.595	07/15	08/16	08/18	09/15/10
0.595	10/21	11/15	11/17	12/15/10

Dividends have been paid since 1885. Source: Company reports.

Please read the Required Disclosures and Analyst Certification on the last page of this report.

The **McGraw-Hill** Companies

Consolidated Edison Inc.

Business Summary October 14, 2010

CORPORATE OVERVIEW. Consolidated Edison is a holding company with electric and gas utilities serving a territory that includes New York City (except part of Queens), most of Westchester County, southeastern New York state, northern New Jersey, and northeastern Pennsylvania. Although the company also has some competitive subsidiaries that participate in energy-related businesses, we expect the two regulated utilities to provide substantially all of ED's earnings over the next few years.

MARKET PROFILE. The company's principal business operations are Con Edison of New York's regulated electric, gas and steam utility operations, and Orange and Rockland Utilities' (O&R) regulated electric and gas utility operations. In 2009, electric revenues accounted for 63.8% of consolidated sales (63.4% in 2008); gas revenues 14.9% (15.4%); non-utility revenues 16.2% (16.0%); and steam revenues 5.1% (5.2%). At December 31, 2009, the distribution system of Consolidated Edison Company of New York had about 36,769 miles of overhead distribution lines and around 95,627 miles of underground distribution lines. The distribution system of O&R had about 3,764 miles of overhead distribution lines, and 1,696 miles of underground distribution lines.

The company's Con Edison of New York (CENY) unit provides electric service

(76.5% of CENY's operating revenues in 2009) to about 3.3 million customers and gas service (16.9%) to around 1.1 million customers in New York City and Westchester County. It also provides steam service (6.6%) in parts of Manhattan to around 1,760 customers (mostly large office buildings, apartment houses and hospitals). Most of the electricity sold by CENY in 2009 was purchased under firm power contracts (primarily with non-utility generators) or through the wholesale electricity market administered by the New York Independent System Operator (NYISO). We expect this to continue for the foreseeable future.

The company's O&R unit provides electric and gas service in southeastern New York and adjacent areas of eastern Pennsylvania, and electric service in areas of New Jersey adjacent to its New York service territory. In 2009, electric sales accounted for 72.8% of operating revenues, and gas sales for the remaining 27.2%.

Company Financials Fiscal Year Ended Dec. 31

Per Share Data ($)	2009	2008	2007	2006	2005	2004	2003	2002	2001	2000
Tangible Book Value	34.96	37.05	34.83	32.13	30.69	29.86	29.09	25.40	24.23	23.50
Earnings	3.14	3.36	3.46	2.95	2.99	2.32	2.36	3.13	3.21	2.74
S&P Core Earnings	3.23	1.19	2.99	2.54	2.54	1.78	1.66	0.50	0.66	NA
Dividends	2.36	2.34	2.32	2.30	2.28	2.26	2.24	2.22	2.20	2.18
Payout Ratio	75%	70%	67%	78%	76%	97%	95%	71%	69%	80%
Prices:High	46.35	49.30	52.90	49.28	49.29	45.59	46.02	45.40	43.37	39.50
Prices:Low	32.56	34.11	43.10	41.17	41.10	37.23	36.55	32.65	31.44	26.19
P/E Ratio:High	15	15	15	17	16	20	20	15	14	14
P/E Ratio:Low	10	10	12	14	14	16	15	10	10	10

Income Statement Analysis (Million $)										
Revenue	13,032	13,583	13,120	12,137	11,690	9,758	9,827	8,482	9,634	9,431
Depreciation	791	717	645	621	584	551	529	495	526	586
Maintenance	NA	NA	NA	NA	NA	NA	353	387	430	458
Fixed Charges Coverage	3.10	3.14	3.49	2.97	3.19	2.64	3.13	3.25	3.46	3.06
Construction Credits	23.0	16.0	18.0	12.0	16.0	43.0	27.0	14.0	9.00	8.00
Effective Tax Rate	33.6%	36.2%	31.8%	34.6%	34.6%	33.1%	37.5%	35.6%	38.9%	34.0%
Net Income	868	922	925	738	732	549	525	680	696	596
S&P Core Earnings	893	329	800	635	621	421	370	106	141	NA

Balance Sheet & Other Financial Data (Million $)										
Gross Property	27,921	25,993	24,698	23,028	21,467	20,394	19,294	18,000	16,630	17,021
Capital Expenditures	2,179	2,318	1,928	1,847	1,617	1,359	1,292	1,216	1,104	986
Net Property	22,464	20,874	19,914	18,445	17,112	16,106	15,225	13,330	12,136	11,786
Capitalization:Long Term Debt	10,081	9,462	7,846	8,537	7,641	6,807	6,769	6,206	5,542	5,447
Capitalization:% Long Term Debt	49.6	49.4	46.4	51.6	51.1	49.1	51.3	50.3	48.3	48.8
Capitalization:Preferred	Nil	Nil	Nil	Nil	Nil	Nil	Nil	Nil	250	250
Capitalization:% Preferred	Nil	Nil	Nil	Nil	Nil	Nil	Nil	Nil	2.18	2.24
Capitalization:Common	10,249	9,698	9,076	8,004	7,310	7,054	6,423	5,921	5,690	5,471
Capitalization:% Common	50.4	50.6	53.6	48.4	48.9	50.9	48.7	48.0	49.6	49.0
Total Capital	21,061	24,159	21,430	20,677	18,637	17,626	16,406	15,037	13,835	13,602
% Operating Ratio	88.8	91.6	89.4	89.5	90.3	90.3	88.8	74.1	88.1	117.8
% Earned on Net Property	8.8	8.1	9.6	7.1	7.0	5.9	6.4	8.3	9.4	8.8
% Return on Revenue	6.7	6.8	7.1	6.1	6.3	5.6	5.3	8.0	7.2	6.3
% Return on Invested Capital	7.3	5.3	6.9	6.6	6.7	5.9	7.3	7.8	8.3	7.7
% Return on Common Equity	8.7	9.8	11.0	9.4	10.0	7.9	8.5	11.5	12.2	10.7

Data as orig reptd.; bef. results of disc opers/spec. items. Per share data adj. for stk. divs.; EPS diluted. E-Estimated. NA-Not Available. NM-Not Meaningful. NR-Not Ranked. UR-Under Review.

Office: 4 Irving Place, New York, NY 10003-3502.
Telephone: 212-460-4600.
Email: corpcom@coned.com
Website: http://www.coned.com

Chrmn, Pres & CEO: K. Burke
SVP & CFO: R.N. Hoglund
Chief Acctg Officer & Cntlr: R. Muccilo
Treas: S. Sanders

Secy: C. Sobin
Board Members: K. Burke, V. A. Calarco, G. Campbell, Jr., G. J. Davis, M. J. Del Giudice, E. Futter, J. F. Hennessy, III, S. Hernandez-Pinero, J. F. Killian, E. R. McGrath, M. W. Ranger, L. F. Sutherland

Founded: 1884
Domicile: New York
Employees: 15,541

CONSOL Energy Inc.

STANDARD &POOR'S

| S&P Recommendation **HOLD** ★★★★★ | Price $39.03 (as of Oct 22, 2010) | 12-Mo. Target Price $45.00 | Investment Style Large-Cap Blend |

GICS Sector Energy
Sub-Industry Coal & Consumable Fuels

Summary This major producer of high-bituminous coal and coalbed methane gas is the second largest U.S. coal producer based on annual production, with coal reserves of 4.5 billion tons.

Key Stock Statistics (Source S&P, Vickers, company reports)

52-Wk Range	$58.00– 31.08	S&P Oper. EPS 2010E	2.82	Market Capitalization(B)	$8.813	Beta	1.37
Trailing 12-Month EPS	$2.04	S&P Oper. EPS 2011E	4.16	Yield (%)	1.02	S&P 3-Yr. Proj. EPS CAGR(%)	20
Trailing 12-Month P/E	19.1	P/E on S&P Oper. EPS 2010E	13.8	Dividend Rate/Share	$0.40	S&P Credit Rating	BB
$10K Invested 5 Yrs Ago	$12,372	Common Shares Outstg. (M)	225.8	Institutional Ownership (%)	88		

Price Performance

- 30-Week Mov. Avg. · · · 10-Week Mov. Avg. - - GAAP Earnings vs. Previous Year Volume Above Avg. STARS
- 12-Mo. Target Price — Relative Strength — ▲ Up ▼ Down ▶ No Change Below Avg. ★

Analysis prepared by **Mathew Christy, CFA** on October 14, 2010, when the stock traded at **$ 40.14**.

Highlights

➤ Including the recently acquired Appalachian natural gas assets from Dominion Resources, we expect 2010 revenues to rise nearly 14%. Our 2010 estimate is based on a 6.7% advance in coal volumes along with a 3.5% estimated increase in the average per ton price realization, which we believe will be about $60.50. In 2011, we look for sales to rise more than 16%, led by increases in coal pricing and volumes and natural gas production.

➤ We think that the operating margin will widen by nearly three percentage points in 2010 on greater productivity and operating leverage from higher volumes and increased pricing. Our forecast is also based on a slight decline in production costs per ton in 2010. In 2011, we see wider operating margins due mainly to higher operating leverage resulting from better pricing and volumes.

➤ Assuming greater interest expense and more shares outstanding, we estimate EPS of $2.82 for 2010 and $4.16 for 2011.

Investment Rationale/Risk

➤ We believe CNX's results will benefit from a recovery in global coal demand during 2010. We note that coal inventories at U.S. utilities recently declined from an all-time high due to above-average summer temperatures. In addition, our belief is based on our forecast for increased demand for metallurgical coal. Although we view positively CNX's recent acquisition of Dominion Resources' natural gas assets, which we believe will lead to improved overall results and a more diverse company, we see limited upside to our $45 target price.

➤ Risks to our recommendation and target price include lower-than-expected coal pricing, reduced productivity, increased supply costs, slower-than-forecast U.S. economic activity, and acquisition integration risks.

➤ Our 12-month target price of $45 is based on relative valuation analysis. We apply an EV/EBITDA multiple of about 7.3X to our 2010 EBITDA estimate. This multiple is above that of coal and natural gas peers, reflecting our view of CNX's size and relatively low-cost coal and natural gas production.

Qualitative Risk Assessment

| LOW | MEDIUM | **HIGH** |

Our risk assessment reflects the cyclical nature of the coal market, our view of unfavorable corporate governance practices concerning takeover defenses, and the heavily regulated nature of the industry and its utilities end market, notwithstanding expected benefits from the pricing cycle and a growing market share.

Quantitative Evaluations

S&P Quality Ranking B

| D | C | B- | **B** | B+ | A- | A | A+ |

Relative Strength Rank MODERATE

| 61 |

LOWEST = 1 HIGHEST = 99

Revenue/Earnings Data

Revenue (Million $)

	1Q	2Q	3Q	4Q	Year
2010	1,218	1,264	--	--	--
2009	1,195	1,031	1,069	1,214	4,509
2008	951.1	1,200	1,137	1,198	4,486
2007	890.1	938.8	847.7	888.9	3,565
2006	944.3	884.4	808.4	907.2	3,544
2005	792.7	795.2	862.4	927.2	3,378

Earnings Per Share ($)

2010	0.54	0.29	E0.66	E0.91	E2.82
2009	1.08	0.62	0.48	0.77	2.95
2008	0.41	0.54	0.49	0.97	2.40
2007	0.61	0.83	-0.03	0.04	1.45
2006	0.67	0.57	0.27	0.69	2.20
2005	0.41	0.22	2.02	0.47	3.13

Fiscal year ended Dec. 31. Next earnings report expected: Late October. EPS Estimates based on S&P Operating Earnings; historical GAAP earnings are as reported.

Dividend Data (Dates: mm/dd Payment Date: mm/dd/yy)

Amount ($)	Date Decl.	Ex-Div. Date	Stk. of Record	Payment Date
0.100	10/23	11/02	11/04	11/20/09
0.100	01/29	02/05	02/09	02/19/10
0.100	04/30	05/06	05/10	05/20/10
0.100	07/30	08/11	08/13	08/23/10

Dividends have been paid since 1999. Source: Company reports.

Options: ASE, CBOE, P, Ph

The **McGraw·Hill** Companies

CONSOL Energy Inc.

STANDARD &POOR'S

Business Summary October 14, 2010

CORPORATE OVERVIEW. Through expansion projects and acquisitions, CONSOL Energy has grown from a single fuel mining company formed in 1860 into a multi-energy producer of coal and natural gas. CNX produces high Btu coal and natural gas, two fuels that collectively generate two-thirds of all U.S. electric power, from reserves located mainly east of the Mississippi River.

The coal segment (CNX Coal) has 16 active mining complexes in the U.S., and sells steam coal to power generators and metallurgical coal to metal and coke producers. The company had an estimated 4.5 billion tons of proven and probable coal reserves at the end of 2009, nearly all of which was located east of the Mississippi River. About 62% of CNX's reserves are found in Northern Appalachia, with 18% in the Midwest, 14% in Central Appalachia, 4% in the western U.S., and 2% in western Canada. In addition, about 12% of reserves are metallurgical quality, while 88% are steam coal grade reserves. The company is a major fuel supplier to the electric power industry in the northeast quadrant of the U.S. Coal produced at CNX's mines is transported to customers via railroad cars, barges, trucks and conveyor belts, or by a combination of such methods. In 2009, the company sold 58.1 million produced tons of coal, down from 66.1 million tons in 2008. Approximately 90% of coal produced in 2009 was sold under contracts with terms of one year or more. The average sales price per produced ton sold in 2009 was $58.42, versus $48.76 in 2008 while no customer accounted for more than 10% of revenue in 2008.

CONSOL also operates a gas-fired electric generating facility in a joint venture with Allegheny Energy Supply Company, LLC and the 83%-owned CNX Gas. The 88-megawatt facility is located in southwest Virginia and was opened in June 2002. The facility is used for meeting peak load demands and uses coalbed methane gas produced by the company.

Company Financials Fiscal Year Ended Dec. 31

Per Share Data ($)	2009	2008	2007	2006	2005	2004	2003	2002	2001	2000
Tangible Book Value	9.86	8.10	6.77	5.84	5.54	2.59	NM	1.03	2.23	1.62
Cash Flow	5.37	4.53	3.24	3.80	4.54	2.17	1.40	1.74	2.71	2.24
Earnings	2.95	2.40	1.45	2.20	3.13	0.64	-0.05	0.08	1.17	0.68
S&P Core Earnings	3.03	2.13	1.02	1.88	2.05	0.69	0.04	0.03	0.98	NA
Dividends	0.40	0.40	0.31	0.28	0.28	0.28	0.28	0.42	0.56	0.56
Payout Ratio	14%	17%	21%	13%	9%	44%	NM	NM	48%	83%
Prices:High	53.50	119.10	74.18	49.09	39.91	21.95	13.40	14.16	21.24	14.00
Prices:Low	22.47	18.50	29.15	28.07	18.58	10.12	7.28	4.90	9.15	4.97
P/E Ratio:High	18	50	51	22	13	35	NM	NM	18	21
P/E Ratio:Low	8	8	20	13	6	16	NM	NM	8	7

Income Statement Analysis (Million $)	2009	2008	2007	2006	2005	2004	2003	2002	2001	2000
Revenue	4,509	4,486	3,565	3,544	3,378	2,690	2,157	2,138	2,298	2,095
Operating Income	1,180	1,008	628	743	511	308	181	222	347	534
Depreciation	441	394	329	296	262	280	242	263	243	250
Interest Expense	31.4	36.2	45.4	25.1	27.3	31.4	34.5	46.2	57.6	55.0
Pretax Income	788	726	429	551	655	82.6	-33.5	-40.4	240	107
Effective Tax Rate	28.1%	33.1%	31.7%	20.4%	9.83%	NM	NM	NM	23.6%	NM
Net Income	540	442	268	409	581	115	-12.6	11.7	184	107
S&P Core Earnings	555	391	190	349	381	125	6.95	3.70	154	NA

Balance Sheet & Other Financial Data (Million $)	2009	2008	2007	2006	2005	2004	2003	2002	2001	2000
Cash	65.6	139	41.7	224	341	6.42	6.51	11.5	16.6	8.20
Current Assets	941	984	683	914	998	470	471	623	566	578
Total Assets	7,725	7,370	6,208	5,663	5,088	4,196	4,319	4,293	3,895	3,866
Current Liabilities	1,429	1,512	1,016	740	804	705	825	814	934	953
Long Term Debt	423	468	489	493	438	426	442	488	231	301
Common Equity	1,786	1,462	1,214	984	1,025	469	291	162	352	254
Total Capital	2,447	2,143	1,866	1,612	1,557	895	733	650	583	555
Capital Expenditures	920	1,062	743	659	523	411	291	295	214	143
Cash Flow	981	837	597	705	843	396	230	275	427	357
Current Ratio	0.7	0.7	0.7	1.2	1.2	0.7	0.6	0.8	0.6	0.6
% Long Term Debt of Capitalization	17.3	21.9	26.2	30.6	28.2	47.6	60.3	75.1	39.6	54.1
% Net Income of Revenue	12.0	9.9	7.5	12.1	17.2	4.3	NM	0.5	8.0	5.0
% Return on Assets	7.2	6.5	4.5	7.6	12.5	2.7	NM	NM	4.7	2.7
% Return on Equity	33.2	33.1	23.5	40.7	77.7	30.3	NM	NM	60.6	42.0

Data as orig reptd.; bef. results of disc opers/spec. items. Per share data adj. for stk. divs.; EPS diluted. E-Estimated. NA-Not Available. NM-Not Meaningful. NR-Not Ranked. UR-Under Review.

Office: 1000 Consol Energy Dr, Canonsburg, PA 15317-6506.
Telephone: 724-485-4000.
Website: http://www.consolenergy.com
Chrmn, Pres & CEO: J.B. Harvey

Vice Chrmn: J.L. Whitmire, III
COO & EVP: N.J. Deluliis
Investor Contact: W.J. Lyons
EVP, CFO & Chief Acctg Officer: W.J. Lyons

Board Members: J. E. Altmeyer, P. W. Baxter, W. E. Davis, R. K. Gupta, P. A. Hammick, D. C. Hardesty, Jr., J. B. Harvey, J. T. Mills, W. P. Powell, J. L. Whitmire, III, J. T. Williams

Founded: 1991
Domicile: Delaware
Employees: 8,012

The McGraw-Hill Companies

Constellation Brands Inc

STANDARD &POOR'S

		Price	12-Mo. Target Price	Investment Style
S&P Recommendation BUY ★★★★☆		$19.29 (as of Oct 22, 2010)	$21.00	Large-Cap Growth

GICS Sector Consumer Staples
Sub-Industry Distillers & Vintners

Summary This leading international producer and marketer of alcoholic beverages has a broad portfolio of wine, imported beer, and distilled spirits brands.

Key Stock Statistics (Source S&P, Vickers, company reports)

52-Wk Range	$19.54–14.60	S&P Oper. EPS 2011**E**	1.72	Market Capitalization(B)	$3.620	Beta	1.01
Trailing 12-Month EPS	$0.61	S&P Oper. EPS 2012**E**	1.82	Yield (%)	Nil	S&P 3-Yr. Proj. EPS CAGR(%)	7
Trailing 12-Month P/E	31.6	P/E on S&P Oper. EPS 2011**E**	11.2	Dividend Rate/Share	Nil	S&P Credit Rating	BB
$10K Invested 5 Yrs Ago	$8,619	Common Shares Outstg. (M)	211.3	Institutional Ownership (%)	84		

Price Performance

30-Week Mov. Avg. · · · 10-Week Mov. Avg. - - GAAP Earnings vs. Previous Year Volume Above Avg. STARS
12-Mo. Target Price — Relative Strength — ▲ Up ▼ Down ► No Change Below Avg. ★

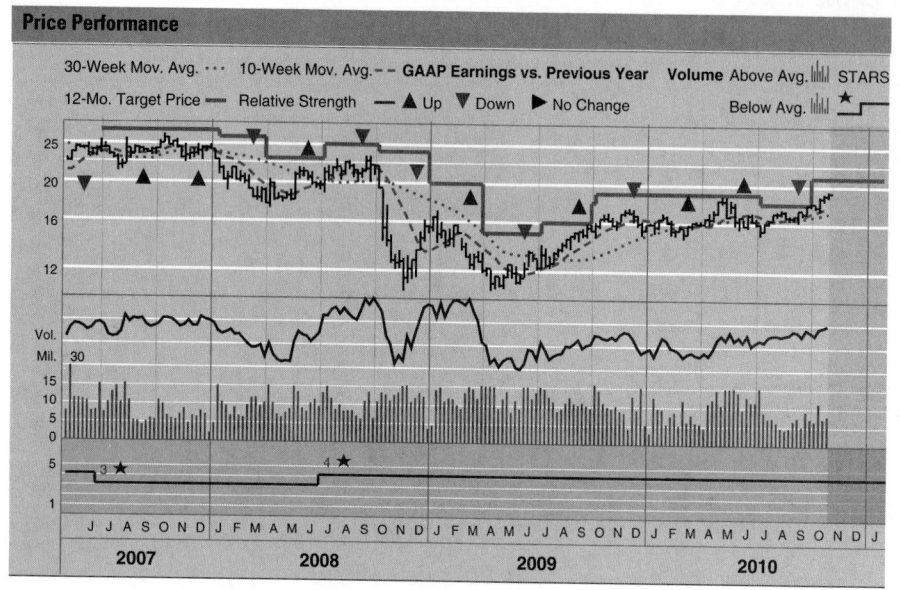

Options: ASE, CBOE, P, Ph

Analysis prepared by **Esther Y. Kwon, CFA** on October 18, 2010, when the stock traded at **$ 19.41**.

Highlights

▶ Following about an 8% sales decline in FY 10 (Feb.), on negative foreign currency translation, divestitures, and unit weakness in international markets, we see FY 11 net revenues down slightly on a tepid recovery in North America, but more than offset by divestiture of the U.K. cider business, which contributed about $100 million to net sales in FY 10. In North America, we project zero to slight growth in organic wine sales. However, we see operating margin contraction in FY 11 on higher investment spending.

▶ We expect STZ's 50/50 joint venture with Grupo Modelo to import and distribute beers, primarily top import brand Corona, to continue to face softness on market share losses, before improvement in the second half of FY 11, with equity earnings dropping about 8% in FY 11. We forecast increased pressure on earnings in the first half as marketing expenses are ramped up during the peak seasonal period.

▶ With a reduction in interest expense, and an effective tax rate of about 34% compared to just over 30% in FY 10, we estimate FY 11 EPS of $1.72, up from FY 10's operating EPS of $1.69. In April 2010, directors authorized a $300 million share repurchase program.

Investment Rationale/Risk

▶ We favorably view actions to move into higher-growth segments, divest value-priced, popular brands, and reduce debt. In December 2007, STZ completed the purchase of Fortune Brands' U.S. wine business, providing a stronger presence in the faster-growing super-premium and above segment. We look for healthy global demand for premium wines to continue over the long term. With STZ's move away from acquisitions and a focus on debt reduction, we see free cash flow of between $375 million to $425 million for FY 2011. In December 2009, a Grupo Modelo subsidiary filed a lawsuit in a dispute over marketing at its Crown Imports joint venture. While we expect this to be an overhang, we find the shares' below-peers valuation attractive.

▶ Risks to our recommendation and target price include continued pricing pressures in the U.K. and Australian wine markets, resistance to further price increases, and foreign currency risk.

▶ Our 12-month target price of $21 is based on a multiple of 12X our FY 11 EPS estimate of $1.72. We think a discount to the historical average of over 13X and current forward peer average of 15.5X is appropriate amid a backdrop of slow economic growth.

Qualitative Risk Assessment

LOW	MEDIUM	HIGH

STZ operates in an industry that we believe has demonstrated stable revenue streams. This is offset by our corporate governance concerns relating to STZ's dual class stock structure with unequal voting rights.

Quantitative Evaluations

S&P Quality Ranking B-

D	C	B-	B	B+	A-	A	A+

Relative Strength Rank STRONG

77

LOWEST = 1 HIGHEST = 99

Revenue/Earnings Data

Revenue (Million $)

	1Q	2Q	3Q	4Q	Year
2011	787.5	862.8	--	--	--
2010	791.6	876.8	987.7	708.7	3,365
2009	931.8	956.5	1,031	735.1	3,655
2008	901.2	1,168	1,406	884.4	3,773
2007	1,156	1,418	1,501	1,142	5,216
2006	1,097	1,192	1,267	1,048	4,603

Earnings Per Share ($)

2011	0.22	0.43	E0.56	E0.34	E1.72
2010	0.03	0.45	0.20	-0.23	0.45
2009	0.20	-0.11	0.38	-1.88	-1.40
2008	0.13	0.34	0.55	-3.92	-2.83
2007	0.36	0.28	0.45	0.29	1.38
2006	0.32	0.34	0.46	0.24	1.36

Fiscal year ended Feb. 28. Next earnings report expected: Early January. EPS Estimates based on S&P Operating Earnings; historical GAAP earnings are as reported.

Dividend Data

No cash dividends have been paid.

The McGraw-Hill Companies

Constellation Brands Inc

Business Summary October 18, 2010

CORPORATE OVERVIEW. Through an aggressive acquisition program over the past few years, Constellation Brands (formerly Canandaigua Brands) has become a leading international producer and marketer of alcoholic beverages in North America, Europe and Australia. With the divestiture of its value spirits business and integration of the remaining spirits business into the wine business, STZ recently restructured into three divisions -- Constellation Wines (branded wine, spirits and other), Corporate Operations and Other, and Crown Imports (imported beer).

Constellation Wines produces and markets table wines, dessert wines and sparkling wines. It is a leading producer and marketer of wine in the U.S., Canada, Australia and New Zealand, and the largest marketer of wine in the U.K. The company sells wines in the popular, premium, super-premium and ultra-premium categories. At the end of FY 10 (Feb.), the company operated 19 wineries in the U.S., eight in Australia, nine in Canada, four in New Zealand,

and one in South Africa.

STZ has developed a premium wine portfolio through acquisitions, selling 16 of the top 100 U.S. table wines in FY 10. Leading wine brands include Robert Mondavi, Franciscan Estate, Wild Horse, Simi, Toasted Head, Estancia, Clos du Bois, Blackstone, Ravenswood, Black Box, Vendange, Arbor Mist, Inniskillin, Kim Crawford, Ruffino, Nobilo, Jackson-Triggs, Alice White, Hardys, Banrock Station, Stowells, and Kumala. It also produces and sells Paul Masson Grande Amber Brandy as well as SVEDKA vodka and Black Velvet Canadian Whisky.

Company Financials Fiscal Year Ended Feb. 28

Per Share Data ($)	2010	2009	2008	2007	2006	2005	2004	2003	2002	2001
Tangible Book Value	NM	NM	NM	NM	NM	NM	NM	0.39	NM	NM
Cash Flow	1.26	-0.69	-2.07	1.95	1.86	1.59	1.39	1.42	1.08	0.95
Earnings	0.45	-1.40	-2.83	-1.38	1.36	1.19	1.03	1.10	0.79	0.65
S&P Core Earnings	0.83	-0.04	1.13	1.41	1.24	1.02	0.96	0.97	0.66	0.54
Dividends	Nil	Nil	Nil	Nil	Nil	Nil	Nil	Nil	Nil	Nil
Payout Ratio	Nil	Nil	Nil	Nil	Nil	Nil	Nil	Nil	Nil	Nil
Calendar Year	2009	2008	2007	2006	2005	2004	2003	2002	2001	2000
Prices:High	17.56	23.81	29.17	29.14	31.60	23.91	17.33	16.00	11.63	7.38
Prices:Low	10.72	10.66	18.83	23.32	21.15	14.65	10.95	10.53	6.63	5.05
P/E Ratio:High	39	NM	NM	22	23	20	17	15	15	11
P/E Ratio:Low	24	NM	NM	18	16	12	11	10	8	8

Income Statement Analysis (Million $)

	2010	2009	2008	2007	2006	2005	2004	2003	2002	2001
Revenue	3,365	3,655	3,773	5,216	4,603	4,088	3,552	2,732	2,821	2,397
Operating Income	721	711	704	895	840	689	601	470	394	315
Depreciation	156	150	160	140	128	104	82.0	60.1	51.9	44.6
Interest Expense	266	316	342	269	190	138	145	105	114	109
Pretax Income	259	-107	-441	535	477	432	344	335	230	162
Effective Tax Rate	61.7%	NM	NM	38.0%	31.8%	36.0%	36.0%	39.3%	40.0%	40.0%
Net Income	99.3	-301	-613	332	325	276	220	203	138	97.3
S&P Core Earnings	190	-10.7	243	334	288	230	199	181	115	80.7

Balance Sheet & Other Financial Data (Million $)

	2010	2009	2008	2007	2006	2005	2004	2003	2002	2001
Cash	43.5	13.1	20.5	33.5	10.9	17.6	37.1	13.8	8.96	146
Current Assets	2,589	2,535	3,199	3,023	2,701	2,734	2,071	1,330	1,231	1,191
Total Assets	8,094	8,037	10,053	9,438	7,401	7,804	5,559	3,196	3,069	2,512
Current Liabilities	1,373	1,326	1,718	1,591	1,298	1,138	1,030	585	595	427
Long Term Debt	3,277	3,971	4,649	3,715	2,516	3,205	1,779	1,192	1,293	1,307
Common Equity	2,576	1,908	2,766	3,418	2,975	2,780	2,378	1,207	956	616
Total Capital	6,041	6,423	7,950	7,607	5,862	6,375	4,344	2,544	2,412	2,056
Capital Expenditures	108	129	144	192	132	120	105	71.6	71.1	68.2
Cash Flow	249	-151	-454	467	444	370	297	263	190	142
Current Ratio	1.9	1.9	1.9	1.9	2.1	2.4	2.0	2.3	2.1	2.8
% Long Term Debt of Capitalization	54.3	61.8	58.5	48.8	42.9	50.3	41.0	46.8	53.6	63.6
% Net Income of Revenue	3.0	NM	NM	6.4	7.1	6.8	6.2	7.4	4.9	4.1
% Return on Assets	1.2	NM	NM	3.9	4.3	4.1	5.0	6.5	4.9	4.0
% Return on Equity	4.4	NM	NM	10.2	11.0	10.3	12.1	18.5	17.5	17.1

Data as orig reptd.; bef. results of disc opers/spec. items. Per share data adj. for stk. divs.; EPS diluted. E-Estimated. NA-Not Available. NM-Not Meaningful. NR-Not Ranked. UR-Under Review.

Office: 207 High Point Drive, Building 100, Victor, NY 14564.
Telephone: 585-678-7100.
Website: http://www.cbrands.com
Chrmn: R. Sands

Pres & CEO: R. Sands
EVP, CFO & Chief Acctg Officer: R.P. Ryder
EVP & Chief Admin Officer: W.K. Wilson
EVP & General Counsel: T.J. Mullin

Investor Contact: P. Yahn-Urlaub (585-218-3838)
Board Members: J. Fowden, B. A. Fromberg, J. K. Hauswald, J. A. Locke, III, R. Sands, R. Sands, P. L. Smith, M. Zupan

Founded: 1972
Domicile: Delaware
Employees: 6,000

Constellation Energy Group Inc.

STANDARD &POOR'S

S&P Recommendation HOLD ★★★★★

Price	12-Mo. Target Price	Investment Style
$31.38 (as of Oct 22, 2010)	$39.00	Large-Cap Blend

GICS Sector Utilities
Sub-Industry Independent Power Producers & Energy Traders

Summary This company, the largest wholesale power supplier in the U.S. and the parent of Baltimore Gas and Electric, closed on a major joint venture agreement with Electricite de France in late 2009.

Key Stock Statistics (Source S&P, Vickers, company reports)

52-Wk Range	$38.73–28.21	S&P Oper. EPS 2010**E**	3.35	Market Capitalization(B)	$6.338	Beta	1.05
Trailing 12-Month EPS	$23.88	S&P Oper. EPS 2011**E**	3.40	Yield (%)	3.06	S&P 3-Yr. Proj. EPS CAGR(%)	-1
Trailing 12-Month P/E	1.3	P/E on S&P Oper. EPS 2010**E**	9.4	Dividend Rate/Share	$0.96	S&P Credit Rating	BBB-
$10K Invested 5 Yrs Ago	$6,939	Common Shares Outstg. (M)	202.0	Institutional Ownership (%)	73		

Price Performance

30-Week Mov. Avg. · · · ·   10-Week Mov. Avg. – – –   **GAAP Earnings vs. Previous Year**   Volume Above Avg. ▮▮▮ STARS
12-Mo. Target Price —   Relative Strength —   ▲ Up ▼ Down ▶ No Change   Below Avg. ▮▮▮ ★

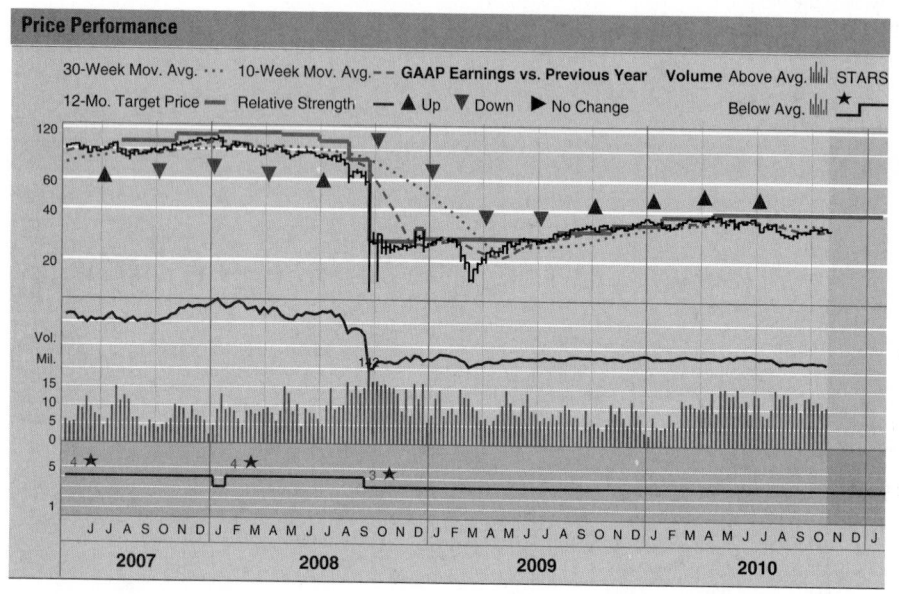

Options: ASE, CBOE, P, Ph

Analysis prepared by **Justin McCann** on September 16, 2010, when the stock traded at **$ 31.44**.

Highlights

➤ Excluding net one-time charges of $0.83, we expect operating EPS in 2010 to remain essentially flat with 2009's $3.36, which excluded net one-time gains of $18.33 primarily related to the transaction with Electricite de France. Operating EPS in the first half of 2010 were aided by higher generation earnings and sharply improved retail power margins in the first quarter. This was partially offset by the impact of severe winter storms at Baltimore Gas & Electric.

➤ For the second half of 2010 and for 2011, we expect earnings to be restricted by the ongoing weakness in power markets. However, we believe this will be largely offset by reduced operating expenses. CEG is seeking to purchase generation assets in New England, where it has significant obligations for power demand.

➤ We believe the $4.5 billion joint venture agreement with Electricite de France, which was completed in November 2009, has long-term strategic value given the potential for the upgrading and expansion of nuclear facilities in the U.S. We believe the most critical near-term impact of the transaction was the strengthening of the company's liquidity position.

Investment Rationale/Risk

➤ The stock is down about 10% year to date, hurt, in our view, by the extended weakness in the power markets. This follows a 40% gain in 2009, driven by the substantial strengthening of CEG's balance sheet and liquidity, and the transaction with Electricite de France. CEG had initially sought to be acquired, given a severe liquidity crisis brought about by the adverse effects of sharply higher commodity prices on its derivative assets and liabilities, collateral requirements and counterparty credit exposures.

➤ Risks to our recommendation and target price include prolonged weakness in the economy and power markets, and a sharp decline in the average P/E multiple of the group as a whole.

➤ While the transaction with Electricite de France valued CEG's assets at nearly twice the $4.7 billion ($26.50 a share) that was offered in the terminated acquisition with MidAmerican Energy, the transaction was an asset sale and not a purchase of CEG shares. With the 50% cut in its dividend in February 2009, CEG realized annual savings of about $190 million. Our 12-month target price of $39 represents a discount-to-peers P/E of 11.5X our EPS forecast for 2011.

Qualitative Risk Assessment

LOW	MEDIUM	HIGH

Our risk assessment reflects our view that the stability of earnings provided by CEG's regulated electric and gas utility operations is more than offset by the cyclical and volatile earnings of the unregulated merchant energy business, including power generation, energy, and energy-related marketing and trading.

Quantitative Evaluations

S&P Quality Ranking   **B**

D	C	B-	B	B+	A-	A	A+

Relative Strength Rank   **WEAK**

25

LOWEST = 1   HIGHEST = 99

Revenue/Earnings Data

Revenue (Million $)

	1Q	2Q	3Q	4Q	Year
2010	3,587	3,310	--	--	--
2009	4,303	3,864	4,028	3,404	15,599
2008	4,827	5,077	5,324	4,926	19,818
2007	5,111	4,876	5,856	5,349	21,193
2006	4,859	4,379	5,393	4,644	19,285
2005	3,630	3,549	4,922	5,159	17,132

Earnings Per Share ($)

2010	0.95	0.36	E0.80	E0.41	E3.35
2009	-0.62	0.04	0.69	21.96	22.18
2008	0.81	0.95	-1.26	-7.75	-7.34
2007	1.08	0.64	1.37	1.42	4.51
2006	0.56	0.41	1.69	1.46	4.12
2005	0.67	0.66	1.02	1.04	3.38

Fiscal year ended Dec. 31. Next earnings report expected: Early November. EPS Estimates based on S&P Operating Earnings; historical GAAP earnings are as reported.

Dividend Data (Dates: mm/dd Payment Date: mm/dd/yy)

Amount ($)	Date Decl.	Ex-Div. Date	Stk. of Record	Payment Date
0.240	01/22	03/08	03/10	04/01/10
0.240	05/28	06/08	06/10	07/01/10
0.240	07/23	09/08	09/10	10/01/10
0.240	10/22	12/08	12/10	01/03/11

Dividends have been paid since 1910. Source: Company reports.

Please read the Required Disclosures and Analyst Certification on the last page of this report.

The McGraw-Hill Companies

Constellation Energy Group Inc.

STANDARD &POOR'S

Business Summary September 16, 2010

CORPORATE OVERVIEW. Constellation Energy is the largest U.S. wholesale power seller and the biggest competitive supplier of electricity to large commercial and industrial customers. It is also the holding company for Baltimore Gas & Electric Company, a regulated utility.

IMPACT OF MAJOR DEVELOPMENTS. On November 6, 2009, Constellation Energy completed a transaction (agreed to on December 17, 2008) with EDF Development, Inc., a wholly owned subsidiary of Electricite de France, which has the largest and most modern nuclear capacity in the world, in which EDF acquired a 49.99% interest in CEG's nuclear business for $4.5 billion. The agreement was announced on the same day that CEG and MidAmerican Energy Holdings, a privately held subsidiary of Berkshire Hathaway, announced that they had jointly agreed to terminate their merger agreement of September 19, 2008. The agreement with EDF (84%-owned by the French state and with a 9.5% stake in CEG) included an immediate $1 billion cash investment in the form of nonconvertible preferred stock, which was surrendered to CEG upon the completion of the transaction and credited against the $4.5 billion purchase price. EDF also provided CEG with a two-year asset put option to sell to EDF non-nuclear generation assets with a value of up to $2 billion, and a $600 million interim backstop liquidity facility that would remain available until either six months after the investment agreement or, if earlier, receipt of all the regulatory approvals related to the transfer of the non-nuclear generation as-

sets. While the asset sale transaction received the approval of federal and state regulators, it did not require the approval of shareholders.

Under the terms of the September 19, 2008, merger agreement that was terminated on December 17, 2008, MidAmerican had agreed to purchase all of the outstanding shares of CEG for $4.7 billion in cash, or $26.50 a share. The announcement of that agreement followed several days of unprecedented volatility in CEG shares, which reflected, we believe, investor fears that the company would risk bankruptcy if it were unable to access the liquidity it needed for its commodities-trading business. Upon the signing of that agreement, CEG received $1 billion from MidAmerican in the form of preferred equity yielding 8.0%. Under the provisions of the termination agreement, these preferred shares were converted into a $1 billion note at 14% interest, maturing on December 31, 2009. MidAmerican also received about 20 million shares of CEG common stock (about 9.9%), as well as a termination fee of $175 million and an additional $418 million for common stock that could not be issued due to regulatory limits.

Company Financials Fiscal Year Ended Dec. 31

Per Share Data ($)	2009	2008	2007	2006	2005	2004	2003	2002	2001	2000
Tangible Book Value	40.14	15.08	27.46	24.66	26.76	25.99	23.81	22.71	23.44	20.88
Earnings	22.18	-7.34	4.51	4.12	3.38	3.40	2.85	3.20	0.52	2.30
S&P Core Earnings	-0.40	-7.77	4.26	3.93	3.31	3.33	2.66	1.75	0.34	NA
Dividends	0.96	1.91	1.74	1.51	1.34	1.14	1.04	0.96	0.48	1.68
Payout Ratio	4%	NM	39%	37%	40%	34%	36%	30%	92%	73%
Prices:High	36.55	107.97	104.29	70.20	62.60	44.90	39.61	32.38	50.14	52.06
Prices:Low	15.05	13.00	68.78	50.55	43.01	35.89	25.17	19.30	20.90	27.06
P/E Ratio:High	2	NM	23	17	19	13	14	10	96	23
P/E Ratio:Low	1	NM	15	12	13	11	9	6	40	12

Income Statement Analysis (Million $)										
Revenue	15,599	19,818	21,193	19,285	17,132	12,550	9,703	4,703	3,928	3,879
Depreciation	1,258	560	558	524	542	526	479	481	419	470
Maintenance	NA	NA	NA	NA	NA	NA	NA	NA	NA	NA
Fixed Charges Coverage	3.29	2.52	4.96	4.01	3.50	3.40	3.12	2.90	3.01	3.12
Construction Credits	NA	NA	NA	NA	NA	NA	NA	NA	NA	NA
Effective Tax Rate	39.9%	NM	33.9%	31.9%	25.2%	22.6%	36.2%	37.1%	31.5%	40.0%
Net Income	4,443	-1,314	822	749	607	589	476	526	82.4	345
S&P Core Earnings	-81.3	-1,391	777	714	594	578	444	290	54.9	NA

Balance Sheet & Other Financial Data (Million $)										
Gross Property	12,535	15,729	14,513	13,680	14,403	14,315	13,580	12,354	11,862	10,442
Capital Expenditures	1,530	1,934	1,296	963	760	704	658	850	1,318	1,079
Net Property	8,454	10,717	9,767	9,222	10,067	10,087	9,602	7,957	7,700	6,644
Capitalization:Long Term Debt	5,004	5,289	4,851	4,222	4,559	5,003	5,229	4,804	2,903	3,349
Capitalization:% Long Term Debt	36.5	62.4	47.6	47.8	48.1	51.4	55.8	55.4	43.0	51.5
Capitalization:Preferred	Nil	Nil	Nil	Nil	Nil	Nil	Nil	Nil	Nil	Nil
Capitalization:% Preferred	Nil	Nil	Nil	Nil	Nil	Nil	Nil	Nil	Nil	Nil
Capitalization:Common	8,697	3,181	5,340	4,609	4,916	4,727	4,141	3,862	3,844	3,153
Capitalization:% Common	63.5	37.6	52.4	52.2	51.9	48.6	44.2	44.6	57.0	48.5
Total Capital	13,833	9,211	11,849	10,419	10,720	11,105	10,833	10,083	8,271	7,943
% Operating Ratio	110.9	94.7	95.6	94.7	94.5	92.2	91.6	87.2	78.3	84.3
% Earned on Net Property	13.5	9.4	14.3	13.1	10.5	17.0	17.1	17.8	5.0	13.3
% Return on Revenue	28.5	NM	3.9	3.9	3.5	4.7	4.9	11.2	2.1	8.9
% Return on Invested Capital	NM	9.4	9.7	11.4	9.2	9.0	8.2	9.8	10.5	8.2
% Return on Common Equity	74.8	NM	16.5	15.7	12.6	13.3	11.9	13.6	2.3	11.2

Data as orig reptd.; bef. results of disc opers/spec. items. Per share data adj. for stk. divs.; EPS diluted. E-Estimated. NA-Not Available. NM-Not Meaningful. NR-Not Ranked. UR-Under Review.

Office: 100 Constellation Way, Baltimore, MD 21202-3142.
Telephone: 410-470-2800.
Website: http://www.constellation.com
Chrmn, Pres & CEO: M.A. Shattuck, III

Vice Chrmn, COO & EVP: M.J. Wallace
SVP & CFO: J.W. Thayer
SVP, Secy & General Counsel: C.A. Berardesco
Chief Acctg Officer & Cntlr: B.P. Wright

Investor Contact: K. Hadlock (410-864-6440)
Board Members: A. C. Berzin, J. T. Brady, D. Camus, J. R. Curtiss, F. A. Hrabowski, III, N. Lampton, R. J. Lawless, M. A. Shattuck, III, J. L. Skolds, M. D. Sullivan, M. J. Wallace, Y. C. de Balmann

Founded: 1906
Domicile: Maryland
Employees: 7,200

The McGraw-Hill Companies

Corning Inc

STANDARD &POOR'S

S&P Recommendation BUY ★★★★☆	**Price** $18.60 (as of Oct 22, 2010)	**12-Mo. Target Price** $22.00	**Investment Style** Large-Cap Blend

GICS Sector Information Technology
Sub-Industry Electronic Components

Summary GLW, once an old-line housewares company, is now a leading maker of glass substrates used by the electronics industry and fiber optic equipment used by the telecommunications industry.

Key Stock Statistics (Source S&P, Vickers, company reports)

52-Wk Range	$21.10–14.14	S&P Oper. EPS 2010E	2.11	Market Capitalization(B)	$29.046	Beta	1.37
Trailing 12-Month EPS	$1.97	S&P Oper. EPS 2011E	2.15	Yield (%)	1.08	S&P 3-Yr. Proj. EPS CAGR(%)	9
Trailing 12-Month P/E	9.4	P/E on S&P Oper. EPS 2010E	8.8	Dividend Rate/Share	$0.20	S&P Credit Rating	BBB+
$10K Invested 5 Yrs Ago	$10,422	Common Shares Outstg. (M)	1,561.6	Institutional Ownership (%)	76		

Price Performance

30-Week Mov. Avg. · · · 10-Week Mov. Avg. - - GAAP Earnings vs. Previous Year   Volume Above Avg. STARS
12-Mo. Target Price — Relative Strength — ▲ Up ▼ Down ▶ No Change   Below Avg. ★

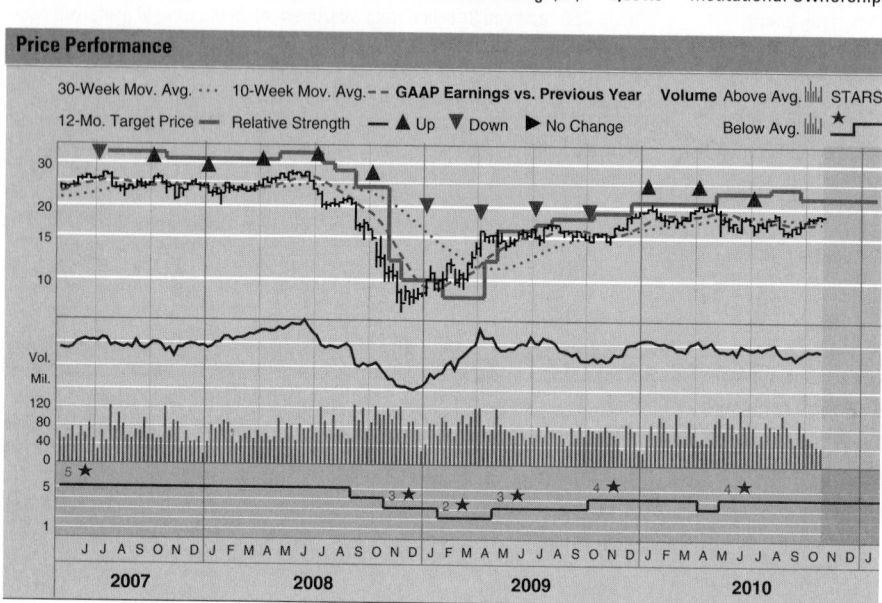

Options: ASE, CBOE, P, Ph

Analysis prepared by **Todd Rosenbluth** on September 15, 2010, when the stock traded at **$ 17.22**.

Highlights

➤ We expect GLW's sales to advance 24% in 2010, after a 9% decline in 2009. We believe improved global consumer spending led to a recovery in the previously hard-hit display segment, and we see this continuing as economies in the U.S. and China improve, despite lower capacity utilization by certain customers. We look for the environmental segment to also recover on increased demand for its automotive and diesel-related products, although the telecom segment is likely to lag the U.S. economy.

➤ We believe gross margins bottomed at 27% in the first quarter of 2009. We forecast an average of 47% in 2010 and 48% in 2011, up from 39% in 2009. We expect the high-margin display segment to improve, as glass volumes rise, even as investment in next-generation technology increases and industry capacity utilization rates are slightly reduced. Despite higher R&D, we see operating margin expansion in 2010.

➤ We expect equity earnings and a minuscule tax rate to support net income in 2010. We look for EPS to grow to $2.11 in 2010 and to $2.15 in 2011, when taxes should be much higher.

Investment Rationale/Risk

➤ Demand for GLW's LCD glass and for end-product TVs remained strong in the first half of 2010, which we think will support continued sales growth. We expect that improvement in display volume and growth in environmental operations will result in wider margins in 2010 and 2011. We think recent cost reductions and what we consider to be a sound balance sheet provide additional investment merits. Following strong second-quarter results, we believe GLW remains undervalued.

➤ Risks to our recommendation and target price include weaker-than-expected demand for flat panel displays in China, worsening pricing on display technologies products, and lackluster demand for products at the telecom unit.

➤ GLW recently traded at a P/E multiple of about 8X, a sizable discount to telecom equipment peers we cover. Our 12-month target price of $22 is based on a multiple of 10X our 2011 EPS estimate, a narrower discount to peers, as we believe that while growth is relatively modest, GLW fundamentals have improved. The recent dividend yield was about 1.2%.

Qualitative Risk Assessment

LOW	MEDIUM	HIGH

Our risk assessment reflects Corning's exposure to intense competition in its major businesses, offset by its market leadership and positive cash flow, and our view of its strong balance sheet.

Quantitative Evaluations

S&P Quality Ranking B

D	C	B-	B	B+	A-	A	A+

Relative Strength Rank MODERATE

61

LOWEST = 1   HIGHEST = 99

Revenue/Earnings Data

Revenue (Million $)

	1Q	2Q	3Q	4Q	Year
2010	1,553	1,712	--	--	--
2009	989.0	1,395	1,479	1,532	5,395
2008	1,617	1,692	1,555	1,084	5,948
2007	1,307	1,418	1,553	1,582	5,860
2006	1,262	1,261	1,282	1,369	5,174
2005	1,050	1,141	1,188	1,200	4,579

Earnings Per Share ($)

2010	0.52	0.58	E0.52	E0.49	E2.11
2009	0.01	0.39	0.41	0.47	E1.31
2008	0.64	2.01	0.49	0.16	3.32
2007	0.20	0.30	0.38	0.45	1.34
2006	0.16	0.32	0.27	0.41	1.16
2005	0.17	0.11	0.13	-0.02	0.38

Fiscal year ended Dec. 31. Next earnings report expected: Late October. EPS Estimates based on S&P Operating Earnings; historical GAAP earnings are as reported.

Dividend Data (Dates: mm/dd Payment Date: mm/dd/yy)

Amount ($)	Date Decl.	Ex-Div. Date	Stk. of Record	Payment Date
0.050	02/03	02/24	02/26	03/31/10
0.050	04/29	05/26	05/28	06/30/10
0.050	07/21	08/26	08/30	09/30/10
0.050	10/06	11/15	11/17	12/17/10

Dividends have been paid since 2007. Source: Company reports.

Please read the Required Disclosures and Analyst Certification on the last page of this report.

The **McGraw-Hill** Companies

Corning Inc

STANDARD
&POOR'S

Business Summary September 15, 2010

CORPORATE OVERVIEW. Corning (GLW) is a maker of high-technology fiber optics for the global telecom industry and high-performance glass components for the personal computer and television manufacturing industries. Results are reported in the following primary business segments: display technologies (49% of sales in the first half of 2010), telecommunications (25%), environmental technologies (12%), life sciences (7%), and specialty materials and other (7%).

PRIMARY BUSINESS DYNAMICS. The display technologies segment manufactures glass substrates for active matrix liquid crystal displays (LCDs), which are used primarily in notebook computers, flat panel desktop monitors, and LCD televisions. Large substrates (Generation 5 and higher) allow LCD manufacturers to produce larger and a greater number of panels from each substrate. The larger size leads to economies of scale for LCD manufacturers and has enabled lower display prices for consumers, which may continue in the future. During 2009, volume was improved from the recent lows of late 2008 due to TV sales growth in China, Europe and North America, and improvement in the supply chain. Volume more than doubled sequentially in the second quarter of 2009, but was up only 4% in the third quarter and 3% in the fourth quarter. During the second quarter of 2010, volumes rose more than 10% from a strong first quarter, but we expect some pressure in the second

half of 2010 as capacity utilization at key customers slows. Strong demand helped support GLW's gross margin expansion in 2009 and the first half of 2010.

The telecom segment produces optical fiber and cable, and hardware and equipment products including cable assemblies, fiber optic hardware and components. We believe demand for fiber-to-the-premise products, which had a 13% sales increase in the second half of 2009, from the first half of 2009, was being driven by demand from China. We believe sales growth for the telecom segment will lag the economic recovery, but are encouraged by gains achieved in the second quarter of 2010.

The environmental technologies segment includes solutions for emissions and pollution control. Although sales are to the emission control systems manufacturers, substrates and filters are also required by the automotive and diesel engine manufacturers following new regulations in the U.S., Europe and Japan.

Company Financials Fiscal Year Ended Dec. 31

Per Share Data ($)	2009	2008	2007	2006	2005	2004	2003	2002	2001	2000
Tangible Book Value	9.57	8.49	5.97	4.43	3.43	2.38	2.65	2.14	3.39	3.56
Cash Flow	1.79	3.76	1.72	1.56	0.71	-1.20	0.23	-1.04	-4.74	1.34
Earnings	1.28	3.32	1.34	1.16	0.38	-1.57	-0.18	-1.85	-5.89	0.46
S&P Core Earnings	1.31	3.29	1.33	1.17	0.34	-1.03	-0.37	-1.89	-3.11	NA
Dividends	0.20	0.20	0.10	Nil	Nil	Nil	Nil	Nil	0.12	0.24
Payout Ratio	16%	6%	7%	Nil	Nil	Nil	Nil	Nil	NM	52%
Prices:High	19.55	28.07	27.25	29.61	21.95	13.89	12.34	11.15	72.19	113.29
Prices:Low	8.97	7.36	18.12	17.50	10.61	9.29	3.34	1.10	6.92	34.33
P/E Ratio:High	15	8	20	26	58	NM	NM	NM	NM	NM
P/E Ratio:Low	7	2	14	15	28	NM	NM	NM	NM	NM

Income Statement Analysis (Million $)	2009	2008	2007	2006	2005	2004	2003	2002	2001	2000
Revenue	5,395	5,948	5,860	5,174	4,579	3,854	3,090	3,164	6,272	7,127
Operating Income	1,435	1,894	1,869	1,489	1,284	892	386	21.0	805	1,929
Depreciation	792	695	607	591	512	523	517	661	1,080	765
Interest Expense	82.0	90.0	101	76.0	116	141	154	179	153	107
Pretax Income	1,934	2,851	2,233	2,421	1,170	-1,137	-550	-2,604	-5,963	840
Effective Tax Rate	NM	NM	3.58%	22.9%	49.4%	NM	NM	NM	NM	48.4%
Net Income	2,008	5,257	2,150	1,855	585	-2,185	-223	-1,780	-5,498	410
S&P Core Earnings	2,048	5,200	2,134	1,865	520	-1,442	-463	-1,947	-2,908	NA

Balance Sheet & Other Financial Data (Million $)	2009	2008	2007	2006	2005	2004	2003	2002	2001	2000
Cash	3,583	2,816	3,516	1,157	1,342	1,009	833	1,471	1,037	138
Current Assets	5,521	4,619	5,294	4,798	3,860	3,281	2,694	3,825	4,107	4,634
Total Assets	21,295	19,256	15,215	13,065	11,175	9,710	10,752	11,548	12,793	17,526
Current Liabilities	1,539	2,052	2,512	2,319	2,216	2,336	1,553	1,680	1,994	1,949
Long Term Debt	1,930	1,527	1,527	1,514	1,696	1,789	2,214	2,668	3,963	4,461	3,966
Common Equity	15,543	13,443	9,496	7,246	5,609	3,752	5,379	4,536	5,414	10,633
Total Capital	17,599	15,034	11,077	8,987	7,441	6,059	8,168	8,713	10,001	14,808
Capital Expenditures	890	1,921	1,262	1,182	1,553	857	366	357	1,800	1,525
Cash Flow	2,800	5,952	2,757	2,446	1,097	-1,662	294	-1,247	-4,418	1,175
Current Ratio	3.6	2.3	2.1	2.1	1.7	1.4	1.7	2.3	2.1	2.4
% Long Term Debt of Capitalization	11.0	10.2	13.7	18.9	24.0	36.5	32.7	45.5	44.6	26.8
% Net Income of Revenue	37.2	88.4	36.7	35.9	12.8	NM	NM	NM	NM	5.7
% Return on Assets	9.9	30.5	15.2	15.3	5.6	NM	NM	NM	NM	3.4
% Return on Equity	13.9	45.8	25.7	29.1	12.5	NM	NM	NM	NM	6.2

Data as orig reptd.; bef. results of disc opers/spec. items. Per share data adj. for stk. divs.; EPS diluted. E-Estimated. NA-Not Available. NM-Not Meaningful. NR-Not Ranked. UR-Under Review.

Office: One Riverfront Plaza, Corning, NY 14831-0001.
Telephone: 607-974-9000.
Email: info@corning.com
Website: http://www.corning.com

Chrmn & CEO: W.P. Weeks
Pres & COO: P.F. Volanakis
Vice Chrmn & CFO: J.B. Flaws
EVP & Chief Admin Officer: K.P. Gregg

EVP & CTO: J.A. Miller, Jr.
Board Members: J. S. Brown, J. A. Canning, Jr., R. F. Cummings, Jr., J. B. Flaws, G. Gund, C. M. Gutierrez, K. M. Landgraf, J. O'Connor, D. Rieman, H. O. Ruding, D. Smithburg, H. E. Tookes, II, P. F. Volanakis, W. P. Weeks, M. S. Wrighton

Founded: 1851
Domicile: New York
Employees: 23,500

Costco Wholesale Corp

STANDARD &POOR'S

S&P Recommendation	HOLD ★★★★★	Price $64.03 (as of Oct 22, 2010)	12-Mo. Target Price $67.00	Investment Style Large-Cap Blend

GICS Sector Consumer Staples
Sub-Industry Hypermarkets & Super Centers

Summary This company operates about 570 membership warehouses in the U.S., Puerto Rico, Canada, the U.K., Taiwan, Japan, Korea, Mexico and Australia.

Key Stock Statistics (Source S&P, Vickers, company reports)

52-Wk Range	$65.46– 53.41	S&P Oper. EPS 2011**E**	3.30	Market Capitalization(B)	$27.682	Beta	0.69
Trailing 12-Month EPS	$2.92	S&P Oper. EPS 2012**E**	3.55	Yield (%)	1.28	S&P 3-Yr. Proj. EPS CAGR(%)	11
Trailing 12-Month P/E	21.9	P/E on S&P Oper. EPS 2011**E**	19.4	Dividend Rate/Share	$0.82	S&P Credit Rating	A+
$10K Invested 5 Yrs Ago	$14,178	Common Shares Outstg. (M)	432.3	Institutional Ownership (%)	78		

Price Performance

30-Week Mov. Avg. · · · 10-Week Mov. Avg. - - **GAAP Earnings vs. Previous Year** Volume Above Avg. STARS
12-Mo. Target Price — Relative Strength — ▲ Up ▼ Down ► No Change Below Avg. ★

Options: ASE, CBOE, P, Ph

Analysis prepared by **Joseph Agnese** on October 07, 2010, when the stock traded at **$ 64.70**.

Highlights

➤ We see net revenues increasing 6.0% to $82.6 billion in FY 11 (Aug.) from $77.9 billion in FY 10, reflecting a same-store sales rise of 4%, excluding fuel and foreign exchange rates, and square footage growth of about 4.5% (reflecting the expected opening of 29 new clubs). We believe comparable store sales will be driven mostly by increased traffic as average basket sizes are negatively impacted by the company's competitively priced offerings, despite an improved food inflation environment and increased discretionary spending in a more stable economic environment.

➤ We project that margins will widen in FY 11, reflecting increased sales leverage and rising demand for discretionary goods, partially offset by higher employee health care and benefit costs. We see pre-opening expenses rising as the company increases new club store openings, and we project higher net interest income due to increased investment income.

➤ We estimate that FY 11 EPS will rise 11% to $3.30 from FY 10 operating EPS of $2.92, excluding one-time charges.

Investment Rationale/Risk

➤ We expect COST to increase its market share in the near term, as we see it pricing aggressively as it maintains a strong value proposition and a relatively upscale product mix that appeals to a more affluent customer base. We think the company is well positioned to generate long term earnings growth due to new store expansion and what we view as a strong balance sheet.

➤ Risks to our recommendation and target price include a slowdown in sales due to weakness in the economy, more difficult foreign currency comparisons, and increased cannibalization from new store expansion.

➤ We believe the stock's valuation will be supported by increased traffic and average transaction gains as consumers continue to seek value as they increase discretionary goods purchases in a more stable economic environment. We apply a P/E of 18.8X to our FY 12 EPS estimate of $3.55, a 34% premium compared to the S&P 500, versus a 28% five-year median premium to the S&P 500, but a 8.3% discount to its five-year median P/E, to arrive at our 12-month target price of $67.

Qualitative Risk Assessment

LOW	MEDIUM	HIGH

Our risk assessment for Costco Wholesale incorporates our view of its strong balance sheet, its market leadership position, and our expectation that consistent earnings and dividend growth will continue.

Quantitative Evaluations

S&P Quality Ranking A-

D	C	B-	B	B+	A-	A	A+

Relative Strength Rank MODERATE

63

LOWEST = 1 HIGHEST = 99

Revenue/Earnings Data

Revenue (Million $)

	1Q	2Q	3Q	4Q	Year
2010	17,299	18,742	17,780	24,125	77,946
2009	16,395	16,843	15,806	22,378	71,422
2008	15,810	16,960	16,614	23,100	72,483
2007	14,152	15,112	14,659	20,477	64,400
2006	12,933	14,059	13,284	19,875	60,151
2005	11,578	12,658	11,997	16,702	52,935

Earnings Per Share ($)

2010	0.60	0.67	0.68	0.97	2.92
2009	0.60	0.55	0.48	0.85	2.47
2008	0.59	0.74	0.67	0.90	2.89
2007	0.51	0.54	0.49	0.83	2.37
2006	0.45	0.62	0.49	0.75	2.30
2005	0.40	0.62	0.43	0.73	2.18

Fiscal year ended Aug. 31. Next earnings report expected: Early December. EPS Estimates based on S&P Operating Earnings; historical GAAP earnings are as reported.

Dividend Data (Dates: mm/dd Payment Date: mm/dd/yy)

Amount ($)	Date Decl.	Ex-Div. Date	Stk. of Record	Payment Date
0.180	01/28	02/10	02/12	02/26/10
0.205	04/22	05/05	05/07	05/21/10
0.205	07/19	08/04	08/06	08/20/10
0.205	10/07	10/27	10/29	11/12/10

Dividends have been paid since 2004. Source: Company reports.

Please read the Required Disclosures and Analyst Certification on the last page of this report.

STANDARD &POOR'S

Costco Wholesale Corp

Business Summary October 07, 2010

CORPORATE OVERVIEW. Costco Wholesale (formerly Costco Companies, Inc., and prior to that, Price/Costco, Inc.) began the pioneering "I can get it for you wholesale" membership warehouse concept in 1976, in San Diego, CA. The company operated 573 warehouses worldwide as of September 2010, mainly in the U.S. and Canada (including 32 stores operated through a joint venture in Mexico). COST also operates an e-commerce Web site, costco.com.

A typical warehouse format averages about 143,000 sq. ft. Floor plans are designed for economy and efficiency in the use of selling space, in the handling of merchandise, and in the control of inventory. Merchandise is generally stored on racks above the sales floor, and is displayed on pallets containing large quantities of each item, reducing the labor required for handling and stocking. Specific items in each product line are limited to fast-selling models, sizes and colors. COST carries an average of about 4,000 stock keeping units (SKUs) per warehouse, well below the 45,000 to 60,000 SKUs of a typical discount store or supermarket. By using a membership format, and strictly controlling entrances and exits, the company limits inventory losses (shrinkage) to well below the average of discount competitors.

COST has two primary types of memberships: Gold Star (individual) and Business members. Individual memberships are available to employees of federal, state and local governments; financial institutions; corporations; utility and transportation companies; public and private educational institutions; and other organizations. Gold Star membership is $50 annually. There were 22.5 million Gold Star memberships as of September 2010, up from 21.5 million as of September 2009.

Businesses, including individuals with retail sales or business licenses, may become Business members by paying an annual $50 fee, with add-on membership cards available for an annual fee of $40. As of September 2010, there were 5.8 million Business memberships, compared to 5.7 million in September 2009. Executive memberships, available for a $100 annual fee, offer business and individual members savings on services such as merchant credit card processing and small business loans, as well as a 2% annual reward, up to a maximum of $500 annually, on qualified purchases. Executive members made up approximately one third of the primary membership base in FY 10 (Aug.), up from 29% and 26% in FY 09 and FY 08, respectively.

Company Financials Fiscal Year Ended Aug. 31

Per Share Data ($)	2010	2009	2008	2007	2006	2005	2004	2003	2002	2001
Tangible Book Value	24.82	23.27	21.08	19.73	19.78	18.80	16.48	14.33	12.51	10.71
Cash Flow	4.70	4.12	4.36	3.60	3.37	3.13	2.74	2.32	2.17	1.90
Earnings	2.92	2.47	2.89	2.37	2.30	2.18	1.85	1.53	1.48	1.29
S&P Core Earnings	2.91	2.53	2.89	2.37	2.30	2.12	1.76	1.40	1.32	1.12
Dividends	0.77	0.68	0.61	0.55	0.49	0.43	0.20	Nil	Nil	Nil
Payout Ratio	26%	28%	21%	23%	21%	20%	11%	Nil	Nil	Nil
Prices:High	65.46	61.25	75.23	72.68	57.94	51.21	50.46	39.02	46.90	46.38
Prices:Low	53.41	38.17	30.70	51.52	46.00	39.48	35.05	27.00	27.09	29.83
P/E Ratio:High	22	25	26	31	25	23	27	26	32	36
P/E Ratio:Low	18	15	11	22	20	18	19	18	18	23

Income Statement Analysis (Million $)										
Revenue	77,946	71,422	72,483	64,400	60,151	52,935	48,107	42,546	38,763	34,797
Operating Income	2,817	2,522	2,622	2,189	2,146	1,969	1,827	1,567	1,494	1,312
Depreciation	795	728	653	566	515	478	441	391	342	301
Interest Expense	111	108	103	64.1	12.6	34.4	36.7	36.9	29.1	32.0
Pretax Income	2,054	1,714	1,999	1,710	1,751	1,549	1,401	1,158	1,138	1,003
Effective Tax Rate	NA	36.6%	35.8%	36.7%	37.0%	31.4%	37.0%	37.8%	38.5%	40.0%
Net Income	1,303	1,086	1,283	1,083	1,103	1,063	882	721	700	602
S&P Core Earnings	1,300	1,114	1,283	1,082	1,104	1,044	837	660	624	525

Balance Sheet & Other Financial Data (Million $)										
Cash	4,749	3,727	3,275	2,780	1,511	2,063	2,823	1,545	806	603
Current Assets	11,708	10,337	9,462	9,324	8,232	8,086	7,269	5,712	4,631	3,882
Total Assets	23,815	21,979	20,682	19,607	17,495	16,514	15,093	13,192	11,620	10,090
Current Liabilities	10,063	9,281	8,874	8,582	7,819	6,609	6,171	5,011	4,450	4,112
Long Term Debt	2,141	2,135	2,206	2,108	215	711	994	1,290	1,211	859
Common Equity	10,829	10,018	9,192	8,623	9,143	8,881	7,625	6,555	5,694	4,883
Total Capital	13,071	12,319	11,480	10,801	9,422	9,650	8,922	8,181	7,025	5,858
Capital Expenditures	1,055	1,250	1,599	1,386	1,213	995	706	811	1,039	1,448
Cash Flow	2,098	1,814	1,936	1,649	1,619	1,541	1,323	1,112	1,042	903
Current Ratio	1.2	1.1	1.1	1.1	1.1	1.2	1.2	1.1	1.0	0.9
% Long Term Debt of Capitalization	16.4	17.3	19.2	19.5	2.3	7.4	11.1	15.8	17.2	14.7
% Net Income of Revenue	1.7	1.5	1.8	1.7	1.8	2.0	1.8	1.7	1.8	1.7
% Return on Assets	5.7	5.1	6.4	5.8	6.5	6.7	6.2	5.8	6.4	6.4
% Return on Equity	12.5	11.3	14.4	12.2	12.2	12.9	12.4	11.8	13.2	13.2

Data as orig reptd.; bef. results of disc opers/spec. items. Per share data adj. for stk. divs.; EPS diluted. E-Estimated. NA-Not Available. NM-Not Meaningful. NR-Not Ranked. UR-Under Review.

Office: 999 Lake Dr Ste, Issaquah, WA 98027.
Telephone: 425-313-8100.
Email: investor@costco.com
Website: http://www.costco.com

Chrmn: J.H. Brotman
Pres & COO: W.C. Jelinek
CEO: J.D. Sinegal
Investor Contact: R.A. Galanti (425-313-8203)

EVP & CFO: R.A. Galanti
Board Members: J. H. Brotman, B. S. Carson, S. Decker, R. D. DiCerchio, D. J. Evans, R. A. Galanti, W. H. Gates, H. E. James, W. C. Jelinek, R. M. Libenson, J. W. Meisenbach, C. Munger, J. Raikes, J. S. Ruckelshaus, J. D. Sinegal

Founded: 1976
Domicile: Washington
Employees: 147,000

The McGraw·Hill Companies

Coventry Health Care Inc.

STANDARD &POOR'S

S&P Recommendation	HOLD ★★★☆☆	Price $23.54 (as of Oct 22, 2010)	12-Mo. Target Price $24.00	Investment Style Large-Cap Growth

GICS Sector Health Care
Sub-Industry Managed Health Care

Summary This national managed health care company operates health plans, insurance companies, network rental/managed care services companies, and workers' compensation services companies.

Key Stock Statistics (Source S&P, Vickers, company reports)

52-Wk Range	$27.27– 16.61	S&P Oper. EPS 2010**E**	3.15	Market Capitalization(B)	$3.493	Beta	1.93
Trailing 12-Month EPS	$1.89	S&P Oper. EPS 2011**E**	2.60	Yield (%)	Nil	S&P 3-Yr. Proj. EPS CAGR(%)	9
Trailing 12-Month P/E	12.5	P/E on S&P Oper. EPS 2010**E**	7.5	Dividend Rate/Share	Nil	S&P Credit Rating	BBB-
$10K Invested 5 Yrs Ago	$3,997	Common Shares Outstg. (M)	148.4	Institutional Ownership (%)	90		

Price Performance

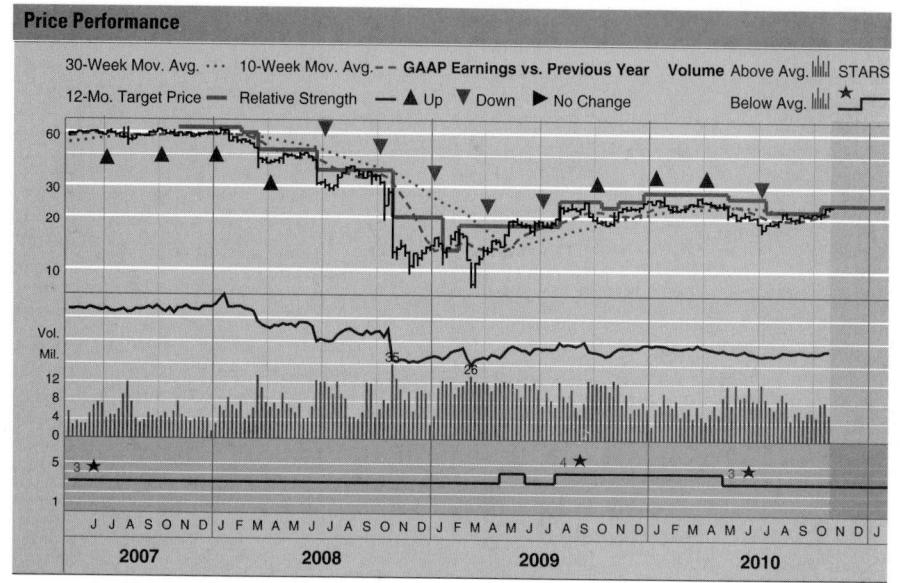

30-Week Mov. Avg. ··· 10-Week Mov. Avg. – – GAAP Earnings vs. Previous Year Volume Above Avg. STARS
12-Mo. Target Price — Relative Strength — ▲ Up ▼ Down ▶ No Change Below Avg. ★

Options: ASE, CBOE, P, Ph

Analysis prepared by **Phillip M. Seligman** on October 05, 2010, when the stock traded at **$ 20.98**.

Highlights

▶ We expect revenues to fall 17.5% in 2010, to slightly under $11.5 billion, reflecting CVH's exit from its Medicare Advantage (MA; Medicare health plan) Private Fee-for-Service (PFFS) business, lower MA premium rates, and 70,000 fewer Medicare Part D (drug plan) members. We also expect 25,000 more Medicaid, 40,000 more MA coordinated care plan, and 270,000 additional commercial members by year-end from acquisitions, partly offset by low single digit losses from the existing commercial book.

▶ We project medical costs will drop 380 basis points (bps) as a percentage of total premiums (MLR; medical loss ratio), on cost control, higher prices, the exit from PFFS and favorable prior-year claims reserve development, including the release of PFFS reserves. We expect the SG&A cost ratio to rise 140 bps, on PFFS-related costs CVH still has to eliminate and health care reform-related investments.

▶ We estimate EPS of $3.15 in 2010 before a one-time charge, versus 2009's $2.14. We look for $2.60 in 2011, before reserve development, which adds about $0.90 (as of June 30), including $0.35 tied to PFFS, to our 2010 estimate.

Investment Rationale/Risk

▶ We think CVH has made solid turnaround progress, noting its cost management focus, improved underwriting, and diversity. However, we believe CVH faces more challenges under health care reform than some peers, given its focus on individual and small group plans, many with MLRs well below health care reform's required floor. We think CVH has room to add attractive benefits, but needs to expand meaningfully to achieve improved SG&A cost efficiencies to help compensate for the higher MLRs. In this regard, we are positive on its recent acquisition of Mercy Health Plans, which adds 150,000 commercial and 30,000 MA members to its Midwest region. We expect CVH to seek more acquisitions, and we believe the $1 billion in deployable cash it expects by mid-2011, partly on the freeing up of capital supporting PFFS, will give it financial flexibility.

▶ Risks to our recommendation and target price include intensified competition, sharply higher medical costs, and a weak economy.

▶ Our 12-month target price of $24 is based on a below-peers forward P/E of 7.5X applied to our 2010 EPS estimate.

Qualitative Risk Assessment

LOW	MEDIUM	HIGH

Our risk assessment reflects CVH's increasingly diversified operations and its January 2005 acquisition of First Health, which we think provided good growth prospects. Even so, we think competition amid the soft economy and our view of rising unemployment will take a toll on commercial enrollment, but we see gains in Medicare and Medicaid enrollment.

Quantitative Evaluations

S&P Quality Ranking   B+

D	C	B-	B	B+	A-	A	A+

Relative Strength Rank   STRONG
82
LOWEST = 1   HIGHEST = 99

Revenue/Earnings Data

Revenue (Million $)

	1Q	2Q	3Q	4Q	Year
2010	2,859	2,868	--	--	--
2009	3,574	3,537	3,444	3,428	13,904
2008	2,941	2,978	2,975	3,020	11,914
2007	2,237	2,332	2,523	2,788	9,880
2006	1,939	1,945	1,909	1,941	7,734
2005	1,565	1,653	1,674	1,719	6,611

Earnings Per Share ($)

	1Q	2Q	3Q	4Q	Year
2010	0.66	0.01	E0.66	E0.64	E3.15
2009	0.30	0.13	0.68	0.74	2.14
2008	0.81	0.55	0.58	0.60	2.54
2007	0.76	0.96	1.08	1.18	3.98
2006	0.74	0.84	0.92	0.97	3.47
2005	0.73	0.79	0.81	0.77	3.10

Fiscal year ended Dec. 31. Next earnings report expected: Early November. EPS Estimates based on S&P Operating Earnings; historical GAAP earnings are as reported.

Dividend Data

No cash dividends have been paid.

Please read the Required Disclosures and Analyst Certification on the last page of this report.

The **McGraw-Hill** Companies

Coventry Health Care Inc.

STANDARD &POOR'S

Business Summary October 05, 2010

CORPORATE OVERVIEW. Coventry Health Care is a diversified national managed care company. It traditionally offered individual and employer groups a full range of commercial risk products, including health maintenance organization (HMO), preferred provider organization (PPO) and point-of service (POS) products. Through its January 2005 acquisition of First Health Group (FH), it gained a nationwide provider network and high-margin, fee-based service businesses, such as network rental, clinical programs, workers' compensation administration, Medicaid health care management services, and pharmacy benefit management. CVH also gained additional PPO members, including the Federal Employee Health Benefit program, the largest employer-sponsored group health program in the U.S., and an administrative services only (ASO, or non-risk) product for large employers with locations in several states that self-insure. Starting in 2007, CVH combined the enrollment of its existing business with that of FH.

As of June 30, 2010, the company had a total of 3,250,000 members (versus 3,586,000 at December 31, 2009), excluding standalone Medicare prescription drug program members.

The Health Plan division is comprised of Health Plan Commercial Risk members (1,522,000, versus 1,418,000), Health Plan Commercial ASO (657,000, versus 685,000), Medicare Advantage Coordinated Care Plans (192,000, versus 186,000), and Medicaid Risk (413,000, versus 402,000). Health Plan Commercial Risk membership includes the Individual business (under 65 years of age).

Other medical membership consists of other National ASO (466,000, versus 564,000). In the ASO businesses, CVH offers management services and access to its provider networks to employers that self-insure their employee health benefits. The Other National ASO membership includes active National Accounts and Federal Employees Health Benefits Plan (FEHBP) administrative services business. Medicare Part D (Prescription Drug Program) had 1,631,000 members (versus 1,683,000). The Medicare Advantage Private Fee-for-Service (PFFS) program had 329,000 members when it ended as of December 31, 2009.

Company Financials Fiscal Year Ended Dec. 31

Per Share Data ($)	2009	2008	2007	2006	2005	2004	2003	2002	2001	2000
Tangible Book Value	4.81	1.28	1.15	5.92	3.21	6.60	4.57	2.85	2.89	2.31
Cash Flow	NA	3.54	4.89	4.17	3.63	2.61	1.97	1.24	0.72	0.60
Earnings	2.14	2.54	3.98	3.47	3.10	2.48	1.83	1.06	0.55	0.41
S&P Core Earnings	2.09	2.69	3.98	3.47	3.01	2.41	1.80	1.03	0.52	NA
Dividends	Nil	Nil	Nil	Nil	Nil	Nil	Nil	Nil	Nil	Nil
Payout Ratio	Nil	Nil	Nil	Nil	Nil	Nil	Nil	Nil	Nil	Nil
Prices:High	25.78	63.89	64.00	61.88	60.31	36.20	29.46	16.89	12.22	13.31
Prices:Low	7.97	9.44	48.78	44.33	34.21	24.66	10.80	8.67	5.78	3.06
P/E Ratio:High	12	25	16	18	19	15	16	16	22	32
P/E Ratio:Low	4	4	12	13	11	10	6	8	11	7

Income Statement Analysis (Million $)	2009	2008	2007	2006	2005	2004	2003	2002	2001	2000
Revenue	13,904	11,914	9,880	7,734	6,611	5,312	4,535	3,577	3,147	2,605
Operating Income	NA	770	1,075	954	878	514	384	220	117	81.1
Depreciation	NA	150	143	113	86.2	17.6	18.2	18.9	25.9	27.0
Interest Expense	84.9	96.4	73.1	52.4	58.4	14.3	15.1	13.4	Nil	Nil
Pretax Income	505	606	995	896	799	527	393	226	135	102
Effective Tax Rate	37.5%	37.0%	37.1%	37.5%	37.3%	36.0%	36.4%	35.5%	38.0%	39.9%
Net Income	315	382	626	560	502	337	250	146	83.5	61.3
S&P Core Earnings	308	404	627	560	485	328	245	143	78.5	NA

Balance Sheet & Other Financial Data (Million $)	2009	2008	2007	2006	2005	2004	2003	2002	2001	2000
Cash	1,419	1,123	1,101	1,371	392	418	253	187	312	256
Current Assets	NA	2,410	1,847	2,134	1,326	973	534	424	579	507
Total Assets	8,167	7,727	7,159	5,665	4,895	2,341	1,982	1,643	1,451	1,239
Current Liabilities	NA	2,026	1,750	1,652	1,270	932	855	801	752	632
Long Term Debt	1,599	1,902	1,662	750	760	171	171	175	Nil	Nil
Common Equity	3,713	3,431	3,301	2,953	2,555	1,212	929	646	689	662
Total Capital	NA	5,551	5,193	3,704	3,315	1,383	1,099	821	689	662
Capital Expenditures	NA	69.4	61.3	72.6	71.4	15.0	13.4	13.0	11.9	16.0
Cash Flow	NA	532	769	673	588	355	268	164	109	88.4
Current Ratio	1.2	1.2	1.1	1.3	1.0	1.0	0.6	0.5	0.8	0.8
% Long Term Debt of Capitalization	30.1	34.3	33.5	20.3	22.9	12.3	15.5	21.3	Nil	Nil
% Net Income of Revenue	2.3	3.2	6.3	7.2	7.6	6.3	5.5	4.1	2.7	2.4
% Return on Assets	4.0	5.1	9.8	10.6	13.9	15.6	13.8	9.4	6.2	5.3
% Return on Equity	8.8	11.4	20.0	20.3	26.6	31.5	31.8	21.8	13.0	10.7

Data as orig reptd.; bef. results of disc opers/spec. items. Per share data adj. for stk. divs.; EPS diluted. E-Estimated. NA-Not Available. NM-Not Meaningful. NR-Not Ranked. UR-Under Review.

Office: 6705 Rockledge Drive, Bethesda, MD 20817.
Telephone: 301-581-0600.
Email: investor-relations@cvty.com
Website: http://www.coventryhealth.com

Chrmn & CEO: A.F. Wise
EVP & General Counsel: T.C. Zielinski
SVP & Cntlr: J.J. Ruhlmann
SVP & CIO: M. Fitzpatrick

CFO & Treas: J.J. Stelben
Board Members: J. Ackerman, L. D. Crandall, L. N. Kugelman, D. Mendelson, R. W. Moorhead, III, M. A. Stocker, J. R. Swedish, E. E. Tallett, A. F. Wise

Founded: 1986
Domicile: Delaware
Employees: 14,400

The McGraw-Hill Companies

CSX Corp

STANDARD &POOR'S

S&P Recommendation BUY ★★★★☆

Price	**12-Mo. Target Price**	**Investment Style**
$61.18 (as of Oct 22, 2010)	$66.00	Large-Cap Value

GICS Sector Industrials
Sub-Industry Railroads

Summary CSX operates a major U.S. rail network, transporting bulk commodities, industrial products and intermodal containers over its network of approximately 21,000 route miles.

Key Stock Statistics (Source S&P, Vickers, company reports)

52-Wk Range	$62.00–41.81	S&P Oper. EPS 2010**E**	3.98	Market Capitalization(B)	$22.893	Beta	1.22
Trailing 12-Month EPS	$3.71	S&P Oper. EPS 2011**E**	4.35	Yield (%)	1.70	S&P 3-Yr. Proj. EPS CAGR(%)	15
Trailing 12-Month P/E	16.5	P/E on S&P Oper. EPS 2010**E**	15.4	Dividend Rate/Share	$1.04	S&P Credit Rating	BBB-
$10K Invested 5 Yrs Ago	$30,718	Common Shares Outstg. (M)	374.2	Institutional Ownership (%)	72		

Price Performance

30-Week Mov. Avg. · · · 10-Week Mov. Avg. - - GAAP Earnings vs. Previous Year   Volume Above Avg. STARS
12-Mo. Target Price — Relative Strength — ▲ Up ▼ Down ▶ No Change   Below Avg.

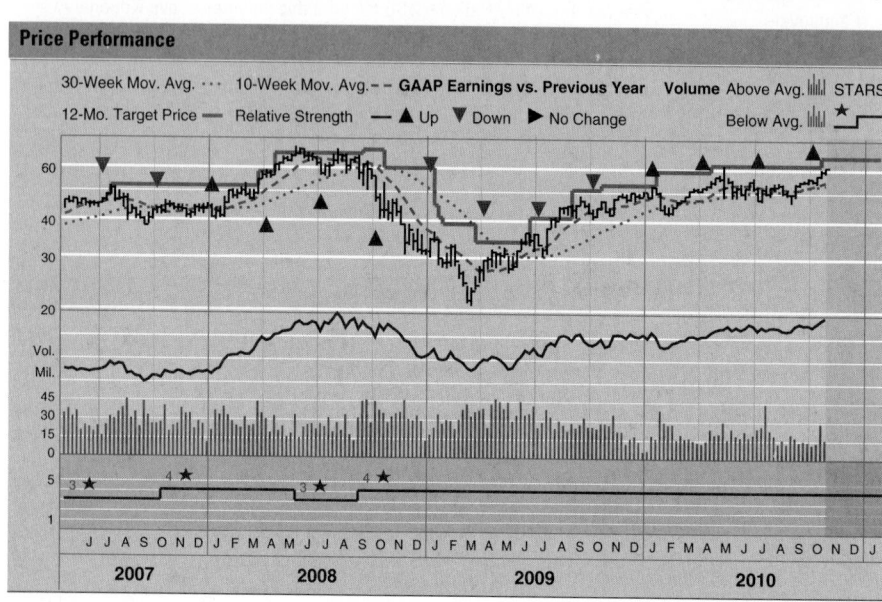

Options: ASE, CBOE, P, Ph

Analysis prepared by **Kevin Kirkeby** on October 20, 2010, when the stock traded at **$ 59.17**.

Highlights

▶ Following an expected 15% increase during 2010, we look for revenue growth at CSX to slow to about 5% in 2011. We see volumes rising almost 4%, with the remainder from price and mix. This is based on S&P's forecast for a gradually improving economy, and our view that inventory rebuilding will be a much smaller contributor to the overall increase in railroad carloadings. For CSX, the increase in carloadings will be driven, in our view, by a resumption in domestic thermal coal shipments, as well as further gains in intermodal containers.

▶ Margins should widen fractionally in 2011 due to the increased volumes and ongoing efforts to limit cost increases. However, we anticipate that labor costs will rise due to increases in health care expenses and a resumption in bonus accruals. We also think the equipment remaining in storage at this point of the volume recovery is the least efficient, in terms of capacity and fuel usage.

▶ Our EPS estimate for 2010 of $3.98 excludes $0.05 in net charges. Our estimate does not factor in additional stock buybacks, despite $650 million remaining under its current authorization as of September 2010.

Investment Rationale/Risk

▶ We believe CSX will benefit from economic recovery in the U.S., given its role in transporting many of the basic materials required in manufacturing and construction, including coal and scrap used by steel mills. We also think the recession forced a more intense focus on operating efficiencies, which should support wider margins during a period of rising volumes. In our view, a valuation above the historical average is warranted as we weigh CSX's solid cash flow generation and recovery in volumes against elevated regulatory risk.

▶ Risks to our opinion and target price include greater-than-expected regulatory oversight, and renewed softness in export coal shipments that we believe generate wider margins than most other shipments.

▶ Our discounted cash flow model, assuming a 10.9% cost of equity and a 3.5% terminal growth rate, derives an intrinsic value of about $63. Applying an enterprise value-to-EBITDA multiple of 8.3X, which is modestly above the midpoint of the historical range, to our four-quarter forward EBITDA forecast, we derive a value approaching $69. Blending these models, we arrive at our 12-month target price of $66.

Qualitative Risk Assessment

LOW	**MEDIUM**	HIGH

Our risk assessment reflects what we believe is CSX's exposure to economic cycles, freight demand and pricing, offset by its consistently positive cash flow generation and diverse customer base.

Quantitative Evaluations

S&P Quality Ranking   B+

D	C	B-	B	**B+**	A-	A	A+

Relative Strength Rank   STRONG

84

LOWEST = 1   HIGHEST = 99

Revenue/Earnings Data

Revenue (Million $)

	1Q	2Q	3Q	4Q	Year
2010	2,491	2,663	2,666	--	--
2009	2,247	2,185	2,289	2,320	9,041
2008	2,713	2,907	2,961	2,674	11,255
2007	2,422	2,530	2,501	2,577	10,030
2006	2,331	2,421	2,418	2,396	9,566
2005	2,108	2,166	2,125	2,219	8,618

Earnings Per Share ($)

2010	0.78	1.07	1.08	E1.01	E3.98
2009	0.64	0.72	0.74	0.77	2.87
2008	0.85	0.93	0.94	0.63	3.34
2007	0.52	0.71	0.67	0.86	2.74
2006	0.53	0.83	0.71	0.75	2.82
2005	0.34	0.37	0.36	0.52	1.59

Fiscal year ended Dec. 31. Next earnings report expected: Mid January. EPS Estimates based on S&P Operating Earnings; historical GAAP earnings are as reported.

Dividend Data (Dates: mm/dd Payment Date: mm/dd/yy)

Amount ($)	Date Decl.	Ex-Div. Date	Stk. of Record	Payment Date
0.240	02/10	02/24	02/26	03/15/10
0.240	05/05	05/26	05/31	06/15/10
0.240	07/14	08/27	08/31	09/15/10
0.260	09/29	11/26	11/30	12/15/10

Dividends have been paid since 1922. Source: Company reports.

CSX Corp

STANDARD &POOR'S

Business Summary October 20, 2010

CORPORATE OVERVIEW. CSX operates the largest rail network in the eastern U.S., with a 21,000-mile rail network linking commercial markets in 23 states and two Canadian provinces, and owns companies providing intermodal and rail-to-truck transload services. In 1997, the company purchased a 42% stake in Conrail, bringing CSX's system into New York City, Boston, Philadelphia and Buffalo; in 2004, CSX gained direct ownership and control of Conrail's New York Central Lines. With these routes, the company was able to offer shippers broader geographic coverage, access more ports, and expand its share of north-south traffic.

MARKET PROFILE. We consider railroads to be a mature industry, and expect 2.0% annualized U.S. rail tonnage growth between 2009 and 2020. We believe CSX's growth opportunities are slightly ahead of the industry average, as we see above-average future growth in intermodal traffic, but average prospects in coal and chemicals shipments. We believe growth in CSX's intermodal business, representing 13% of 2009 revenue, will be above the peer average. This, in our view, will be driven by the overall level of economic activity and population density in the Eastern markets it serves. Its initiatives, like the National Gateway project, are designed to capitalize on highway congestion along a key East Coast freight corridors, by converting truck traffic over to rail containers. Still, as evidenced in 2009, these types of intermodal shipments,

having a length of haul under 750 miles, are more susceptible to price competition from trucks than transcontinental moves.

Coal accounted for 30% of 2009 revenues. Most of this traffic originates from the Appalachian coal fields and is primarily delivered to power utilities. We expect CSX's domestic coal tonnage to experience average growth as its customers balance the high sulfur content of coal against using natural gas or other fuel alternatives. Coal shipments directed to export markets is expected to be more volatile than the domestic business, and be somewhat correlated to exchange rate fluctuations. CSX's merchandise freight provided 48% of freight revenues in 2009, and includes chemical, forest products, metals, and agricultural products. We believe this business is sensitive to U.S. GDP trends, and faces average long-term volume growth prospects. We think automotive freight, at 6% of revenues in 2009, has an average volume growth outlook. Following the sharp reduction in 2009, we see production improving steadily in 2010 and beyond, as the average age of vehicles in use rises and consumer finances improve.

Company Financials Fiscal Year Ended Dec. 31

Per Share Data ($)	2009	2008	2007	2006	2005	2004	2003	2002	2001	2000
Tangible Book Value	22.32	20.44	21.14	20.42	18.25	15.77	15.01	14.52	14.32	14.13
Cash Flow	5.17	5.55	4.71	4.67	3.41	2.55	1.94	2.62	2.16	2.76
Earnings	2.87	3.34	2.74	2.82	1.59	0.94	0.44	1.10	0.69	0.44
S&P Core Earnings	2.88	3.41	2.74	2.57	1.60	0.90	0.66	0.85	0.59	NA
Dividends	0.88	0.77	0.54	0.63	0.22	0.20	0.20	0.20	0.40	0.60
Payout Ratio	31%	23%	20%	22%	14%	21%	45%	18%	58%	136%
Prices:High	50.80	70.70	51.88	38.30	25.80	20.23	18.15	20.70	20.65	16.72
Prices:Low	20.70	30.01	33.50	24.29	18.45	14.40	12.75	12.55	12.41	9.75
P/E Ratio:High	18	21	19	14	16	22	41	19	30	38
P/E Ratio:Low	7	9	12	9	12	15	29	11	18	22

Income Statement Analysis (Million $)	2009	2008	2007	2006	2005	2004	2003	2002	2001	2000
Revenue	9,041	11,255	10,030	9,566	8,618	8,020	7,793	8,152	8,110	8,191
Operating Income	3,193	3,667	3,112	2,837	2,345	1,730	1,269	1,776	1,579	1,405
Depreciation	908	904	883	867	833	730	643	649	622	600
Interest Expense	558	519	417	392	423	435	418	445	518	543
Pretax Income	1,761	2,146	1,932	1,841	1,036	637	265	723	448	656
Effective Tax Rate	35.4%	36.4%	36.5%	28.8%	30.5%	34.4%	28.7%	35.4%	34.6%	13.9%
Net Income	1,137	1,365	1,226	1,310	720	418	189	467	293	565
S&P Core Earnings	1,142	1,392	1,228	1,194	729	405	280	363	249	NA

Balance Sheet & Other Financial Data (Million $)	2009	2008	2007	2006	2005	2004	2003	2002	2001	2000
Cash	1,090	745	714	461	309	859	368	264	618	684
Current Assets	2,570	2,391	2,491	2,672	2,372	2,987	1,903	1,789	2,074	2,046
Total Assets	27,036	26,288	25,534	25,129	24,232	24,581	21,760	20,951	20,801	20,491
Current Liabilities	1,865	2,404	2,671	2,522	2,979	3,317	2,210	2,454	3,303	3,280
Long Term Debt	7,895	7,512	6,470	5,362	5,093	6,234	6,886	6,519	5,839	5,810
Common Equity	8,846	8,048	8,685	9,863	8,918	7,858	7,569	7,091	7,060	6,017
Total Capital	16,868	21,816	21,272	21,335	20,093	20,071	18,207	17,177	16,520	15,211
Capital Expenditures	1,447	1,740	1,773	1,639	1,136	1,030	1,059	1,080	930	913
Cash Flow	2,045	2,269	2,109	2,177	1,553	1,148	832	1,116	915	1,165
Current Ratio	1.4	1.0	0.9	1.1	0.8	0.9	0.9	0.7	0.6	0.6
% Long Term Debt of Capitalization	46.8	34.4	30.4	25.1	25.3	31.1	37.8	38.0	35.3	38.2
% Net Income of Revenue	12.6	12.1	12.2	13.7	8.4	5.2	2.4	5.7	3.6	6.9
% Return on Assets	4.3	5.3	4.8	5.3	2.9	1.8	0.9	2.2	1.4	2.7
% Return on Equity	13.5	16.3	13.9	14.0	8.6	5.4	2.6	6.6	4.2	9.6

Data as orig reptd.; bef. results of disc opers/spec. items. Per share data adj. for stk. divs.; EPS diluted. E-Estimated. NA-Not Available. NM-Not Meaningful. NR-Not Ranked. UR-Under Review.

Office: 500 Water Street , Jacksonville , FL 32202.
Telephone: 904-359-3200.
Website: http://www.csx.com
Chrmn, Pres & CEO: M.J. Ward

COO & EVP: D.A. Brown
EVP & CFO: O. Munoz
SVP, Secy & General Counsel: E.M. Fitzsimmons
Chief Acctg Officer & Cntlr: C.T. Sizemore

Investor Contact: D. Baggs (904-359-4812)
Board Members: D. M. Alvarado, A. Behring, J. B. Breaux, P. L. Carter, S. T. Halverson, E. J. Kelly, III, G. H. Lamphere, J. D. McPherson, T. O'Toole, D. M. Ratcliffe, D. J. Shepard, M. J. Ward

Founded: 1978
Domicile: Virginia
Employees: 30,088

Cummins Inc.

STANDARD &POOR'S

S&P Recommendation	STRONG BUY ★★★★★	Price $93.63 (as of Oct 22, 2010)	12-Mo. Target Price $112.00	Investment Style Large-Cap Value

GICS Sector Industrials
Sub-Industry Construction & Farm Machinery & Heavy Trucks

Summary This leading manufacturer of truck engines also makes stand-by power equipment and industrial filters.

Key Stock Statistics (Source S&P, Vickers, company reports)

52-Wk Range	$94.87–42.10	S&P Oper. EPS 2010**E**	5.30	Market Capitalization(B)	$18.342	Beta	1.98
Trailing 12-Month EPS	$3.84	S&P Oper. EPS 2011**E**	6.53	Yield (%)	1.12	S&P 3-Yr. Proj. EPS CAGR(%)	17
Trailing 12-Month P/E	24.4	P/E on S&P Oper. EPS 2010**E**	17.7	Dividend Rate/Share	$1.05	S&P Credit Rating	BBB+
$10K Invested 5 Yrs Ago	$51,309	Common Shares Outstg. (M)	195.9	Institutional Ownership (%)	92		

Price Performance

- 30-Week Mov. Avg. · · · ·
- 10-Week Mov. Avg. – –
- **GAAP Earnings vs. Previous Year**
- Volume Above Avg. STARS
- 12-Mo. Target Price —
- Relative Strength —
- ▲ Up ▼ Down ▶ No Change
- Below Avg.

Options: ASE, CBOE, P, Ph

Analysis prepared by **Jim Corridore** on August 04, 2010, when the stock traded at **$81.49**.

Highlights

▶ We expect revenues to rise about 20% in 2010. North American truck engine sales were weak in the first half of 2010, but should pick up in the back half on pent-up demand and as customers become more comfortable with new engines being sold to meet more stringent EPA emissions regulations. We expect strong growth in engine sales in India, China, and Brazil, fueled by GDP growth and infrastructure projects in those regions. CMI has issued sales forecasts of 25% growth in engines, 30% growth in components, 20% growth in power generation, and 25% growth in its distribution segment. We think these forecasts are achievable.

▶ CMI has forecast EBIT margins of 12% for 2010, versus 6.3% in 2009. We think it can achieve this target, benefiting from cost reductions, a recent pullback in raw material and energy costs, and strong improvements in productivity at several of its plants. We also expect top-line growth to aid EBIT margins on fixed cost leverage and better capacity utilization.

▶ We estimate that operating EPS will improve to $5.30 in 2010, from $2.49 in 2009. For 2011, we forecast EPS of $6.53.

Investment Rationale/Risk

▶ For the long term, with over 50% of sales derived from outside North America, CMI should benefit from its leading edge technology in truck engines, which should help gain market share in emerging market countries and infrastructure-related power generation equipment. We think CMI will continue to use technology and its strong balance sheet to increase market share. Though visibility into the timing of the recovery is uncertain, we expect improving investor sentiment on good economic news.

▶ Risks to our recommendation and target price include weaker-than-projected demand in the truck manufacturing and/or power generation markets; slower-than-anticipated economic growth and/or industrial production; adverse forex volatility; and, lower-than-estimated savings from expense reduction initiatives.

▶ Our 12-month target price of $112 values the shares at 17X our 2011 EPS estimate of $6.53, toward the higher end of CMI's five-year historical P/E range of 4.3X-19.4X EPS, reflecting our view that we are near the start of a new earnings upcycle that we think will last for several years.

Qualitative Risk Assessment

LOW	MEDIUM	HIGH

Our risk assessment reflects the highly cyclical nature of the North America medium (class 5-7) and heavy-duty (class 8) truck markets and significant pension and post-retirement benefit obligations, offset by a geographically diverse mix of business and the low leverage of CMI's balance sheet.

Quantitative Evaluations

S&P Quality Ranking

D	C	B-	**B**	B+	A-	A	A+

B

Relative Strength Rank

STRONG

82

LOWEST = 1   HIGHEST = 99

Revenue/Earnings Data

Revenue (Million $)

	1Q	2Q	3Q	4Q	Year
2010	2,478	3,208	--	--	--
2009	2,439	2,431	2,530	3,400	10,800
2008	3,474	3,887	3,693	3,288	14,342
2007	2,817	3,343	3,372	3,516	13,048
2006	2,678	2,842	2,809	3,033	11,362
2005	2,208	2,490	2,467	2,753	9,918

Earnings Per Share ($)

2010	0.75	1.25	E1.45	E1.85	E5.30
2009	0.04	0.28	0.48	1.36	2.16
2008	0.97	1.49	1.17	0.45	4.08
2007	0.71	1.06	0.92	1.00	3.70
2006	0.68	1.10	0.84	0.94	3.55
2005	0.49	0.71	0.73	0.83	2.75

Fiscal year ended Dec. 31. Next earnings report expected: Early November. EPS Estimates based on S&P Operating Earnings; historical GAAP earnings are as reported.

Dividend Data (Dates: mm/dd Payment Date: mm/dd/yy)

Amount ($)	Date Decl.	Ex-Div. Date	Stk. of Record	Payment Date
0.175	02/09	02/17	02/19	03/01/10
0.175	05/11	05/19	05/21	06/01/10
0.263	07/13	08/19	08/23	09/01/10
0.263	10/19	11/18	11/22	12/01/10

Dividends have been paid since 1948. Source: Company reports.

Cummins Inc.

STANDARD &POOR'S

Business Summary August 04, 2010

CORPORATE OVERVIEW. This global equipment company makes and services diesel and natural gas engines, electric power generation systems and engine-related component products.

Cummins (CMI), founded in 1919, has long-standing relationships with many of the customers it serves, including Chrysler LLC, Daimler AG, Volvo AB, PACCAR Inc., International Truck and Engine Corp. (a unit of Navistar), CNH Global N.V., Komatsu, Scania AB, Ford Motor Corp., and Volkswagen. CMI has over 500 company-owned and independent distributor locations and about 5,200 dealer locations in over 190 countries and territories. CMI's key markets are the on-highway, construction, and general industrial markets.

The company believes that its competitive strengths include a group of leading brand names, alliances it has established with customers and partners, its global presence (international sales accounted for 52% of total sales in 2009), and its leading technology. In particular, Cummins' technology addresses the

reduction of diesel engine emissions. CMI's engines met the EPA's heavy-duty on-highway emission standards that went into effect in January 2010.

The engine segment (49% of sales in 2009) manufactures and markets a broad range of diesel and natural-gas powered engines under the Cummins brand name for the heavy- and medium-duty truck, bus, recreational vehicle (RV), light-duty automotive, agricultural, construction, mining, marine, oil and gas, rail and governmental equipment markets. CMI manufactures engines with displacements from 1.4 to 91 liters and horsepower ranging from 31 to 3,500. In addition, it provides new parts and service, as well as remanufactured parts and engines, through its extensive distribution network.

Company Financials Fiscal Year Ended Dec. 31

Per Share Data ($)	2009	2008	2007	2006	2005	2004	2003	2002	2001	2000
Tangible Book Value	16.04	13.48	14.20	11.12	7.56	5.18	2.79	2.42	4.06	5.05
Cash Flow	3.80	5.44	5.15	4.96	4.54	3.38	1.75	1.79	0.85	1.62
Earnings	2.16	4.08	3.70	3.55	2.75	1.85	0.34	0.52	-0.67	-0.05
S&P Core Earnings	2.21	3.20	3.73	3.62	2.85	2.00	0.40	-0.39	-1.44	NA
Dividends	0.70	0.60	0.43	0.33	0.30	0.30	0.30	0.30	0.30	0.30
Payout Ratio	32%	15%	12%	9%	11%	16%	88%	58%	NM	NM
Prices:High	51.65	75.98	71.73	34.80	23.47	21.17	13.08	12.57	11.38	12.50
Prices:Low	18.34	17.70	28.16	22.17	15.90	12.03	5.43	4.90	7.00	6.77
P/E Ratio:High	24	19	19	10	9	11	38	24	NM	NM
P/E Ratio:Low	8	4	8	6	6	7	16	10	NM	NM

Income Statement Analysis (Million $)	2009	2008	2007	2006	2005	2004	2003	2002	2001	2000
Revenue	10,800	14,342	13,048	11,362	9,918	8,438	6,296	5,853	5,681	6,597
Operating Income	887	1,382	1,221	1,287	1,058	696	316	327	304	479
Depreciation	326	314	290	296	295	272	223	219	231	240
Interest Expense	35.0	60.0	59.0	96.0	109	113	101	82.0	87.0	86.0
Pretax Income	640	1,251	1,169	1,083	798	432	80.0	57.0	-129	3.00
Effective Tax Rate	24.4%	30.9%	32.6%	29.9%	27.1%	13.0%	15.0%	NM	NM	NM
Net Income	428	801	739	715	550	350	54.0	79.0	-102	8.00
S&P Core Earnings	438	631	744	729	570	380	62.8	-61.4	-221	NA

Balance Sheet & Other Financial Data (Million $)	2009	2008	2007	2006	2005	2004	2003	2002	2001	2000
Cash	1,120	503	697	935	840	690	195	298	92.0	62.0
Current Assets	5,003	4,713	4,815	4,488	3,916	3,273	2,130	1,982	1,635	1,830
Total Assets	8,816	8,491	8,195	7,465	6,885	6,527	5,126	4,837	4,335	4,500
Current Liabilities	2,432	2,639	2,711	2,399	2,218	2,197	1,391	1,329	970	1,223
Long Term Debt	637	629	555	647	1,213	1,299	1,380	1,290	1,206	1,032
Common Equity	3,773	3,277	3,409	2,802	1,864	2,802	949	841	1,025	1,336
Total Capital	4,657	4,139	4,257	3,703	3,302	4,309	2,452	2,223	2,314	2,440
Capital Expenditures	310	543	353	249	186	151	111	90.0	206	228
Cash Flow	752	1,069	1,029	1,011	845	622	277	298	129	248
Current Ratio	2.1	1.8	1.8	1.9	1.8	1.5	1.5	1.5	1.7	1.5
% Long Term Debt of Capitalization	13.7	15.1	13.0	17.5	36.7	30.1	56.3	58.0	52.1	42.3
% Net Income of Revenue	4.0	5.6	5.7	6.3	5.5	4.1	0.9	1.3	NM	0.1
% Return on Assets	4.9	9.6	9.4	10.0	8.2	6.0	1.1	1.7	NM	0.2
% Return on Equity	12.2	24.0	23.8	30.6	33.7	14.9	6.0	8.7	NM	0.6

Data as orig reptd.; bef. results of disc opers/spec. items. Per share data adj. for stk. divs.; EPS diluted. E-Estimated. NA-Not Available. NM-Not Meaningful. NR-Not Ranked. UR-Under Review.

Office: 500 Jackson Street, PO Box 3005, Columbus, IN 47202-3005.
Telephone: 812-377-5000.
Email: investor_relations@cummins.com
Website: http://www.cummins.com

Chrmn & CEO: T.M. Solso
Pres & COO: N.T. Linebarger
CFO: P.J. Ward
CTO: J. Wall

Chief Acctg Officer & Cntlr: M.L. Hunt
Investor Contact: D.A. Cantrell (812-377-3121)
Board Members: R. J. Bernhard, F. R. Chang-Diaz, S. B. Dobbs, R. Herdman, A. Herman, N. T. Linebarger, W. I. Miller, G. R. Nelson, T. M. Solso, C. Ware

Founded: 1919
Domicile: Indiana
Employees: 34,900

The McGraw-Hill Companies

CVS Caremark Corp

STANDARD &POOR'S

S&P Recommendation	**STRONG BUY** ★★★★★	Price	12-Mo. Target Price	Investment Style
		$31.36 (as of Oct 22, 2010)	$38.00	Large-Cap Blend

GICS Sector Consumer Staples
Sub-Industry Drug Retail

Summary This company is a leading operator of retail drug stores and pharmacy benefit management services in the U.S.

Key Stock Statistics (Source S&P, Vickers, company reports)

52-Wk Range	$37.82–26.84	S&P Oper. EPS 2010E	2.70	Market Capitalization(B)	$42.594
Trailing 12-Month EPS	$2.61	S&P Oper. EPS 2011E	3.10	Yield (%)	1.12
Trailing 12-Month P/E	12.0	P/E on S&P Oper. EPS 2010E	11.6	Dividend Rate/Share	$0.35
$10K Invested 5 Yrs Ago	$12,485	Common Shares Outstg. (M)	1,358.2	Institutional Ownership (%)	83

Beta	0.85
S&P 3-Yr. Proj. EPS CAGR(%)	12
S&P Credit Rating	BBB+

Price Performance

30-Week Mov. Avg. · · · 10-Week Mov. Avg. – – GAAP Earnings vs. Previous Year Volume Above Avg.||||| STARS
12-Mo. Target Price — Relative Strength — ▲ Up ▼ Down ▶ No Change Below Avg.|||||

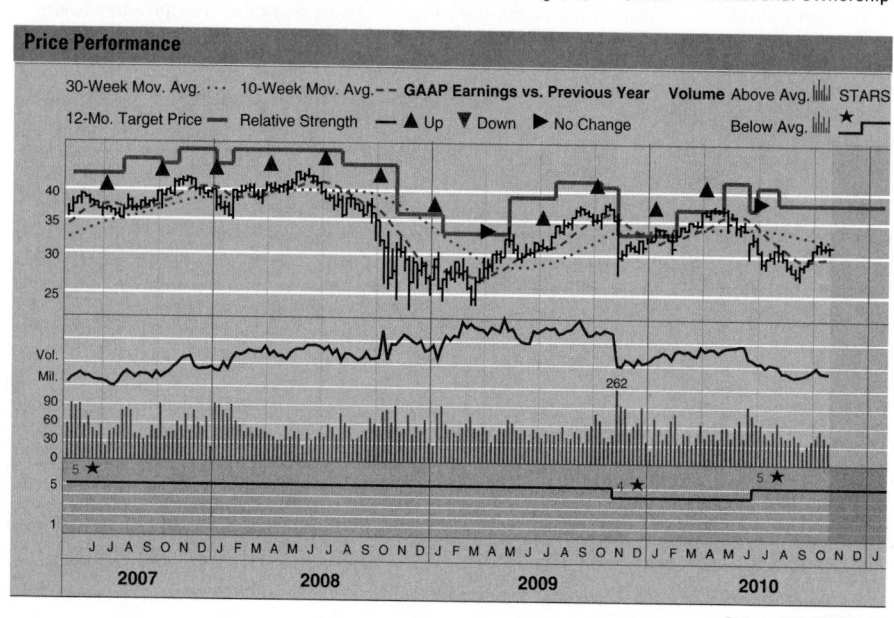

Options: ASE, CBOE, P, Ph

Analysis prepared by **Joseph Agnese** on July 29, 2010, when the stock traded at **$ 30.77.**

Highlights

▶ We expect total sales in 2010 to decline 0.5%, to $98.3 billion, from $98.7 billion in 2009, reflecting strong retail drug store market share gains and about 2.0% net new square footage growth, partially offset by significant client losses in the pharmacy benefit management (PBM) business segment. Our estimate assumes retail drug-store same-store sales growth of approximately 3%.

▶ We see margins widening in 2010, reflecting significant accretion from the turnaround of ac-quired drug stores versus a dilutive impact in 2009, and reduced investment costs for expan-sion of in-store health clinics. We expect retail business margin benefits to be partially offset by negative sales leverage in the PBM segment due to significant client losses and with the renegotiation of a large federal employee con-tract entering a less profitable contract year.

▶ With strength in the retail drug store business partially offset by weaker PBM business, we estimate that 2010 operating EPS will rise 4.2%, to $2.70 (excluding amortization of intangibles), from operating EPS of $2.59 in 2009 (before amortization of intangibles).

Investment Rationale/Risk

▶ CVS is an experienced consolidator, and we have confidence in its ability to realize signifi-cant long-term synergies from recent drug store acquisitions. However, we expect earn-ings growth in 2010 to be pressured by ongoing weakness in its PBM business. Despite poor visibility in regard to the near-term outlook for its PBM services, we believe the valuation will be supported by its strong market share posi-tions.

▶ Risks to our recommendation and target price include decreased drug reimbursement from federal and state governments, as well as con-tinued deterioration in demand for PBM ser-vices.

▶ Due to our expectation for modest earnings growth in 2010 as strong earnings generation from the retail drug store business offsets weak PBM profitability, we believe the stock should trade in line with its three-year P/E ratio dis-count when compared to the S&P 500. Assum-ing that the shares trade at 12.2X, a 16% dis-count to the forward P/E ratio of the S&P 500, applied to our 2011 EPS estimate of $3.10, we arrive at our 12-month target price of $38.

Qualitative Risk Assessment

LOW	**MEDIUM**	HIGH

Our risk assessment reflects our view of the company's leadership position and strong market share position in the relatively stable U.S. retail drug industry, offset by acquisition integration risk and the growth of non-traditional competitors.

Quantitative Evaluations

S&P Quality Ranking   A+

D	C	B-	B	B+	A-	A	**A+**

Relative Strength Rank   MODERATE

49

LOWEST = 1   HIGHEST = 99

Revenue/Earnings Data

Revenue (Million $)

	1Q	2Q	3Q	4Q	Year
2010	23,760	2,401	--	--	--
2009	23,394	24,871	24,642	25,822	98,729
2008	21,326	21,140	20,863	24,142	87,472
2007	13,189	20,703	20,495	21,942	76,330
2006	9,979	10,561	11,207	12,066	43,814
2005	9,182	9,122	8,970	9,732	37,006

Earnings Per Share ($)

2010	0.55	0.60	E0.64	E0.82	E2.70
2009	0.51	0.60	0.71	0.74	2.56
2008	0.51	0.56	0.56	0.65	2.27
2007	0.43	0.47	0.45	0.55	1.92
2006	0.39	0.40	0.33	0.49	1.60
2005	0.35	0.33	0.30	0.48	1.45

Fiscal year ended Dec. 31. Next earnings report expected: Early November. EPS Estimates based on S&P Operating Earnings; historical GAAP earnings are as reported.

Dividend Data (Dates: mm/dd Payment Date: mm/dd/yy)

Amount ($)	Date Decl.	Ex-Div. Date	Stk. of Record	Payment Date
0.088	01/12	01/20	01/22	02/02/10
0.088	03/10	04/21	04/23	05/04/10
0.088	07/07	07/20	07/22	08/02/10
0.088	09/22	10/20	10/22	11/02/10

Dividends have been paid since 1916. Source: Company reports.

Please read the Required Disclosures and Analyst Certification on the last page of this report.

The **McGraw·Hill** Companies

CVS Caremark Corp

STANDARD &POOR'S

Business Summary July 29, 2010

CORPORATE OVERVIEW. CVS Caremark Corporation operates one of the largest drug store chains and pharmacy benefit managers in the U.S., based on revenues, net income and store count. Drug stores offer prescription drugs and a wide assortment of general merchandise, including OTC drugs, beauty products and cosmetics, film and photo finishing services, seasonal merchandise, greeting cards and convenience foods. Pharmacy benefit management offerings include mail order pharmacy service, specialty pharmacy services, plan design and administration, formulary management and claims processing.

MARKET PROFILE. CVS operated about 7,000 stores as of December 2009, in 41 states and the District of Columbia. As of December 2009, the company had stores in 91 of the top 100 U.S. drug store markets, holding the number one or number two market share in 68 of these markets, and 75% of all markets in which it operates. It filled more than 615 million prescriptions in 2009, accounting for about 18% of the U.S. retail pharmacy market. Pharmacy operations are critical to CVS's success, in our view, accounting for 68% of retail store sales in 2009. Payments by third-party managed care providers under

prescription drug plans accounted for 97% of pharmacy sales in 2009. CVS's pharmacy benefit management (PBM) business generated $51.1 billion of sales in 2009, or 48% of total company sales (excluding intersegment eliminations). The company's specialty pharmacy business operates 49 retail specialty pharmacy stores and 18 specialty mail order pharmacies.

CORPORATE STRATEGY. Through its retail and PBM services, the company plans to benefit from favorable industry trends, which include an aging U.S. population, increased generic drug utilization, the discovery of new drugs, growth of specialty pharmacy services, and health care reform. CVS's long-term strategy focuses on expanding its retail drug store business in high-growth markets and increasing the size and product offerings of its PBM business. Historically, the company has grown, in large part, through acquisitions.

Company Financials Fiscal Year Ended Dec. 31

Per Share Data ($)	2009	2008	2007	2006	2005	2004	2003	2002	2001	2000
Tangible Book Value	NM	NM	NM	6.29	6.77	4.98	5.98	5.05	4.45	4.11
Cash Flow	3.52	3.13	2.71	2.45	2.14	1.69	1.46	1.25	0.88	1.26
Earnings	2.56	2.27	1.92	1.60	1.45	1.10	1.03	0.88	0.50	0.92
S&P Core Earnings	2.56	2.27	1.92	1.61	1.41	1.06	0.98	0.80	0.41	NA
Dividends	0.30	0.26	0.23	0.16	0.15	0.13	0.12	0.12	0.12	0.12
Payout Ratio	12%	11%	12%	10%	10%	12%	11%	13%	23%	13%
Prices:High	38.27	44.29	42.60	36.14	31.60	23.67	18.78	17.85	31.88	30.22
Prices:Low	23.74	23.19	30.45	26.06	22.02	16.87	10.92	11.52	11.45	13.88
P/E Ratio:High	15	20	22	23	22	22	18	20	64	33
P/E Ratio:Low	9	10	16	16	15	15	11	13	23	15

Income Statement Analysis (Million $)

	2009	2008	2007	2006	2005	2004	2003	2002	2001	2000
Revenue	98,729	87,472	76,330	43,814	37,006	30,594	26,588	24,182	22,241	20,088
Operating Income	7,827	7,343	5,970	3,175	2,609	1,952	1,765	1,517	1,091	1,619
Depreciation	1,389	1,274	1,095	733	589	497	342	310	321	297
Interest Expense	530	558	492	216	111	58.3	48.0	50.4	61.0	79.3
Pretax Income	5,913	5,537	4,359	2,226	1,909	1,396	1,376	1,156	710	1,243
Effective Tax Rate	37.3%	39.6%	39.5%	38.5%	35.8%	34.2%	38.4%	38.0%	41.8%	40.0%
Net Income	3,708	3,344	2,637	1,369	1,225	919	847	717	413	746
S&P Core Earnings	3,708	3,330	2,623	1,365	1,171	869	785	635	323	NA

Balance Sheet & Other Financial Data (Million $)

	2009	2008	2007	2006	2005	2004	2003	2002	2001	2000
Cash	1,091	1,352	1,084	531	513	392	843	700	236	337
Current Assets	17,537	16,526	14,149	10,392	8,393	7,920	6,497	5,982	5,454	4,937
Total Assets	61,641	60,960	54,722	20,570	15,283	14,547	10,543	9,645	8,628	7,950
Current Liabilities	12,300	13,490	10,766	7,001	4,584	4,859	3,489	3,106	3,066	2,964
Long Term Debt	8,756	8,057	8,350	2,870	1,594	1,926	753	1,076	810	537
Common Equity	35,768	34,383	31,163	9,704	8,109	6,759	6,022	4,991	4,306	4,037
Total Capital	46,665	46,333	43,048	12,788	9,925	8,913	6,817	6,318	12,706	4,869
Capital Expenditures	2,548	2,180	1,805	1,769	1,495	1,348	1,122	1,109	714	695
Cash Flow	5,097	4,604	3,717	2,088	1,800	1,401	1,189	1,012	719	1,028
Current Ratio	1.4	1.2	1.3	1.5	1.8	1.6	1.9	1.9	1.8	1.7
% Long Term Debt of Capitalization	18.8	17.4	19.4	22.4	16.1	21.6	11.0	17.0	63.8	11.0
% Net Income of Revenue	3.8	3.8	3.5	3.1	3.3	3.0	3.2	3.0	1.9	3.7
% Return on Assets	6.1	5.8	7.0	7.6	8.2	7.3	8.4	7.8	5.0	9.8
% Return on Equity	10.6	10.2	12.8	15.2	16.3	14.4	15.4	15.1	9.6	19.7

Data as orig reptd.; bef. results of disc opers/spec. items. Per share data adj. for stk. divs.; EPS diluted. E-Estimated. NA-Not Available. NM-Not Meaningful. NR-Not Ranked. UR-Under Review.

Office: One CVS Drive, Woonsocket, RI 02895-6184.
Telephone: 401-765-1500.
Email: investorinfo@cvs.com
Website: http://www.cvs.com

Chrmn & CEO: T.M. Ryan
Pres & COO: L.J. Merlo
EVP & CFO: D.M. Denton
EVP & General Counsel: D.A. Sgarro

SVP, Chief Acctg Officer & Cntlr: L.K. Daniels
Investor Contact: N.R. Christal (914-722-4704)
Board Members: E. M. Banks, C. D. Brown, II, D. W. Dorman, M. L. Heard, W. H. Joyce, L. J. Merlo, J. Millon, T. Murray, C. L. Piccolo, S. Z. Rosenberg, T. M. Ryan, R. J. Swift, K. E. Williams

Founded: 1892
Domicile: Delaware
Employees: 295,000

Danaher Corp

STANDARD &POOR'S

S&P Recommendation	BUY ★★★★☆	Price $43.18 (as of Oct 22, 2010)	12-Mo. Target Price $50.00	Investment Style Large-Cap Growth

GICS Sector Industrials
Sub-Industry Industrial Machinery

Summary This company is a leading maker of tools, including Sears Craftsman hand tools, and process/environmental controls and telecommunications equipment.

Key Stock Statistics (Source S&P, Vickers, company reports)

52-Wk Range	$81.40–19.72	S&P Oper. EPS 2010**E**	2.32	Market Capitalization(B)	$28.180	Beta	0.83
Trailing 12-Month EPS	$1.92	S&P Oper. EPS 2011**E**	2.78	Yield (%)	0.19	S&P 3-Yr. Proj. EPS CAGR(%)	24
Trailing 12-Month P/E	22.5	P/E on S&P Oper. EPS 2010**E**	18.6	Dividend Rate/Share	$0.08	S&P Credit Rating	A+
$10K Invested 5 Yrs Ago	$17,467	Common Shares Outstg. (M)	652.6	Institutional Ownership (%)	72		

Price Performance

30-Week Mov. Avg. · · ·   10-Week Mov. Avg. - -   **GAAP Earnings vs. Previous Year**   Volume Above Avg. ılıl   STARS
12-Mo. Target Price —   Relative Strength —   ▲ Up ▼ Down ▶ No Change   Below Avg. ılıl   ★

2-for-1

Options: ASE, CBOE, P, Ph

Analysis prepared by **Efraim Levy, CFA** on October 22, 2010, when the stock traded at **$ 43.18.**

Highlights

➤ S&P Economics expects U.S. and global growth in 2010. We expect revenues to rise 16% in 2010, aided by acquisitions and global economic growth. We expect further sales gains in 2011 and see net income rising in both years.

➤ We see streamlining activities aiding margins, partly offset by narrower margins at acquired businesses. Our EPS estimates include most restructuring charges as part of ongoing operations. EPS also includes about $0.03 per share accretion (adjusted for a 2-for-1 stock split) from the recently closed AB SCIEX acquisition, but does not include an estimated $0.075 of one-time acquisition-related costs.

➤ For the long term, we look for sales increases to be driven by internal growth, supplemented by acquisitions. We anticipate that a steady flow of new and enhanced products, as well as greater sales of traditional tool lines, will aid comparisons. We expect margins to widen over time, as DHR consolidates acquisitions and likely benefits from higher capacity utilization, productivity gains, and cost-cutting efforts. In addition, the company has targeted acquisitions of companies with gross margins above 50%.

Investment Rationale/Risk

➤ Our buy opinion is based on our forecast for improving global economic activity. In addition, we view DHR's balance sheet as strong. Based on several valuation measures, the shares trade at a premium to some peers, which we believe reflects DHR's wider net margins and faster growth. Its earnings quality appears high to us, as we expect free cash flow in 2010 and 2011 to exceed net income. We view positively DHR's 10 million share buyback program.

➤ Risks to our recommendation and target price include slowing demand for DHR's products, and unfavorable changes in foreign exchange rates. Also, we are concerned about some of Danaher's corporate governance practices, particularly its classified board of directors with staggered terms, which may allow certain policies to be entrenched longer despite shareholders' possible desire to change them.

➤ Our 12-month target price of $50 is derived by applying a multiple of 18X to our 2011 EPS estimate of $2.78, reflecting relative historical multiples, peer multiples, and brighter prospects for global GDP. Our 2010 EPS forecast includes about $0.04 of dilution from the creation of a tools joint venture with Cooper Industries.

Qualitative Risk Assessment

LOW	MEDIUM	HIGH

Our risk assessment reflects our view of favorable growth prospects in most of the company's markets, good corporate leadership, and a solid balance sheet, offset by corporate governance issues.

Quantitative Evaluations

S&P Quality Ranking   A+

D	C	B-	B	B+	A-	A	A+

Relative Strength Rank   STRONG

75

LOWEST = 1   HIGHEST = 99

Revenue/Earnings Data

Revenue (Million $)

	1Q	2Q	3Q	4Q	Year
2010	3,092	3,311	--	--	--
2009	2,628	2,674	2,751	3,133	11,185
2008	3,029	3,284	3,208	3,177	12,697
2007	2,556	2,671	2,731	3,141	11,026
2006	2,144	2,350	2,443	2,660	9,596
2005	1,826	1,929	1,966	2,264	7,985

Earnings Per Share ($)

2010	0.45	0.53	E0.60	E0.68	E2.32
2009	0.36	0.45	0.52	0.40	1.73
2008	0.42	0.55	0.56	0.46	1.96
2007	0.39	0.48	0.52	0.49	1.86
2006	0.34	0.49	0.42	0.50	1.74
2005	0.29	0.35	0.35	0.39	1.38

Fiscal year ended Dec. 31. Next earnings report expected: Late October. EPS Estimates based on S&P Operating Earnings; historical GAAP earnings are as reported.

Dividend Data (Dates: mm/dd Payment Date: mm/dd/yy)

Amount ($)	Date Decl.	Ex-Div. Date	Stk. of Record	Payment Date
0.040	02/24	03/24	03/26	04/30/10
2-for-1	05/12	06/14	05/25	06/11/10
0.020	05/12	06/23	06/25	07/30/10
0.020	09/14	09/22	09/24	10/29/10

Dividends have been paid since 1993. Source: Company reports.

Please read the Required Disclosures and Analyst Certification on the last page of this report.

The **McGraw·Hill** Companies

Danaher Corp

Business Summary October 22, 2010

CORPORATE OVERVIEW. Danaher Corp. is a leading maker of hand tools and process and environmental controls. The company has four reporting segments: professional instrumentation (39% of 2009 sales), industrial technologies (24%), tools and components (9%), and medical technologies, formerly included in professional instrumentation (28%).

The professional instrumentation segment offers professional and technical customers various products and services that are used in connection with the performance of their work.

The industrial technologies segment manufactures products and sub-systems that are typically incorporated by original equipment manufacturers (OEMs) into various end-products and systems, as well as by customers and systems integrators into production and packaging lines.

The tools and components segment encompasses one strategic line of business -- mechanics' hand tools, and four focused niche businesses -- Delta Consolidated Industries, Hennessy Industries, Jacobs Chuck Manufacturing Company, and Jacobs Vehicle Systems.

Sales in 2009 by geographic destination were: U.S. 48%, Europe 29%, Asia/Australia 14%, and other regions 9%.

CORPORATE STRATEGY. The company seeks to expand revenues through a combination of internal growth and acquisitions. We expect the company to continue its tradition of successful acquisition integrations. During 2009, the company bought 15 businesses for an aggregate purchase price of $704 million, versus 17 businesses for about $423 million in 2008, and 12 businesses in 2007 for approximately $3.6 billion.

In November 2007, as part of its acquisition strategy, the company purchased Tektronix Inc. for about $2.8 billion, including debt. Tektronix is a supplier of test, measurement and monitoring products, with about $1.1 billion in annual sales.

In May 2006, the company purchased Sybron Dental Specialties Inc. for about $2 billion, including the assumption of debt. Sybron manufactures a broad range of equipment for the dental industry and had about $650 million in revenues in its fiscal year ended September 30, 2005.

Company Financials Fiscal Year Ended Dec. 31

Per Share Data ($)	2009	2008	2007	2006	2005	2004	2003	2002	2001	2000
Tangible Book Value	NM	NM	NM	NM	NM	NM	0.50	0.00	NM	0.14
Cash Flow	1.11	2.46	2.25	2.06	1.64	1.38	1.04	0.94	0.78	0.81
Earnings	1.73	1.96	1.86	1.74	1.38	1.15	0.84	0.75	0.50	0.56
S&P Core Earnings	1.66	1.87	1.86	1.74	1.35	1.10	0.78	0.60	0.42	NA
Dividends	0.07	0.06	0.06	0.04	0.03	0.03	0.03	0.02	0.02	0.02
Payout Ratio	4%	3%	3%	2%	2%	2%	4%	3%	4%	3%
Prices:High	38.28	44.10	44.61	37.64	29.20	29.45	23.09	18.87	17.17	17.45
Prices:Low	23.87	23.60	34.56	27.02	24.16	21.91	14.89	13.15	10.98	9.11
P/E Ratio:High	22	23	24	22	21	26	27	25	34	31
P/E Ratio:Low	14	12	19	16	18	19	18	18	22	16

Income Statement Analysis (Million $)	2009	2008	2007	2006	2005	2004	2003	2002	2001	2000
Revenue	11,185	12,697	11,026	9,596	7,985	6,889	5,294	4,577	3,782	3,778
Operating Income	2,037	2,350	2,055	1,719	1,446	1,253	957	824	750	702
Depreciation	342	339	268	217	177	156	133	130	178	150
Interest Expense	123	130	110	79.8	44.9	55.0	59.0	43.7	25.7	29.2
Pretax Income	1,425	1,749	1,637	1,446	1,234	1,058	797	657	476	523
Effective Tax Rate	19.2%	24.7%	25.9%	22.4%	27.3%	29.5%	32.6%	29.4%	37.5%	38.0%
Net Income	1,152	1,318	1,214	1,122	898	746	537	464	298	324
S&P Core Earnings	1,105	1,243	1,215	1,121	876	715	491	373	249	NA

Balance Sheet & Other Financial Data (Million $)	2009	2008	2007	2006	2005	2004	2003	2002	2001	2000
Cash	1,722	393	239	318	316	609	1,230	810	707	177
Current Assets	5,221	4,187	4,050	3,395	2,945	2,919	2,942	2,387	1,875	1,474
Total Assets	19,595	17,458	17,472	12,864	9,163	8,494	6,890	6,029	4,820	4,032
Current Liabilities	2,761	2,745	2,900	2,460	2,269	2,202	1,380	1,265	1,017	1,019
Long Term Debt	2,889	2,553	3,396	2,423	858	926	1,284	1,197	1,119	714
Common Equity	11,630	9,809	9,086	6,645	5,080	4,620	3,647	3,010	2,229	1,942
Total Capital	14,563	12,428	12,481	9,068	5,938	5,545	4,931	4,207	3,348	2,656
Capital Expenditures	189	194	162	138	121	116	80.3	65.4	80.6	88.5
Cash Flow	1,493	1,657	1,482	1,339	1,075	902	670	594	476	474
Current Ratio	1.9	1.5	1.4	1.4	1.3	1.3	2.1	1.9	1.8	1.4
% Long Term Debt of Capitalization	19.8	20.5	27.2	26.7	14.4	16.7	26.0	28.5	33.4	26.9
% Net Income of Revenue	10.3	10.4	11.0	11.7	11.2	10.8	10.1	10.1	7.9	8.6
% Return on Assets	6.2	7.5	8.0	10.2	10.2	9.7	8.3	8.6	6.7	9.2
% Return on Equity	10.7	14.0	15.4	19.1	18.5	18.0	16.1	17.7	14.3	17.8

Data as orig reptd.; bef. results of disc opers/spec. items. Per share data adj. for stk. divs.; EPS diluted. E-Estimated. NA-Not Available. NM-Not Meaningful. NR-Not Ranked. UR-Under Review.

Office: 2099 Pennsylvania Ave NW Fl 12, Washington, DC 20006-1813.
Telephone: 202-828-0850.
Email: ir@danaher.com
Website: http://www.danaher.com

Chrmn: S.M. Rales
Pres & CEO: H.L. Culp, Jr.
EVP & CFO: D.L. Comas
SVP & Chief Acctg Officer: R.S. Lutz

SVP & General Counsel: J.P. Graham
Board Members: M. M. Caplin, H. L. Culp, Jr., D. J. Ehrlich, L. Hefner, W. G. Lohr, Jr., M. P. Rales, S. M. Rales, J. T. Schwieters, A. G. Spoon, E. A. Zerhouni

Founded: 1969
Domicile: Delaware
Employees: 46,600

Darden Restaurants Inc.

STANDARD &POOR'S

S&P Recommendation HOLD ★★★☆☆

Price	**12-Mo. Target Price**	**Investment Style**
$46.87 (as of Oct 22, 2010)	$47.00	Large-Cap Growth

GICS Sector Consumer Discretionary
Sub-Industry Restaurants

Summary This restaurant company operates the Red Lobster, Olive Garden, Bahama Breeze and Seasons 52 chains, as well as the LongHorn Steakhouse and Capital Grille chains, which it acquired in October 2007.

Key Stock Statistics (Source S&P, Vickers, company reports)

52-Wk Range	$49.01–29.94	S&P Oper. EPS 2011**E**	3.33	Market Capitalization(B)	$6.488	Beta	0.94
Trailing 12-Month EPS	$2.97	S&P Oper. EPS 2012**E**	3.81	Yield (%)	2.73	S&P 3-Yr. Proj. EPS CAGR(%)	11
Trailing 12-Month P/E	15.8	P/E on S&P Oper. EPS 2011**E**	14.1	Dividend Rate/Share	$1.28	S&P Credit Rating	BBB
$10K Invested 5 Yrs Ago	$16,733	Common Shares Outstg. (M)	138.4	Institutional Ownership (%)	83		

Price Performance

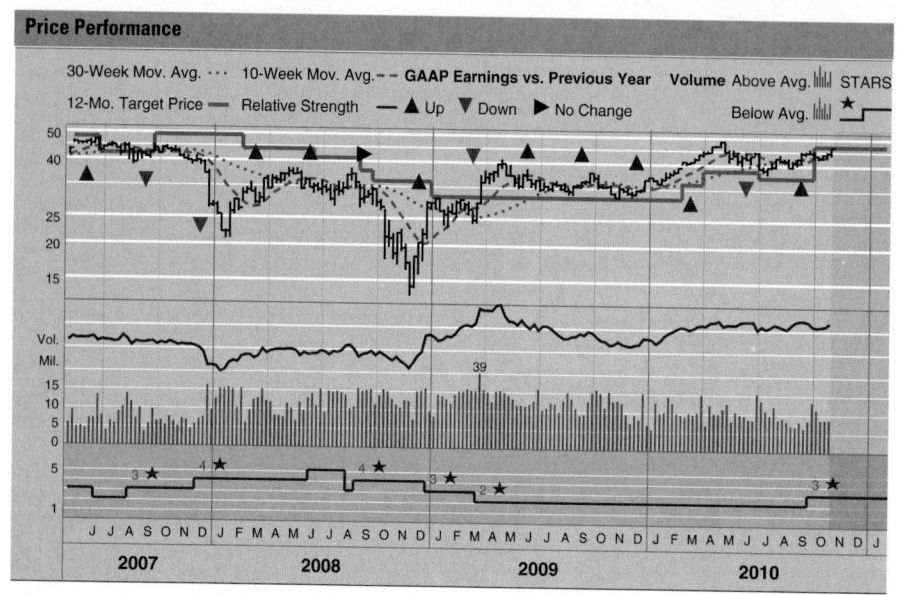

30-Week Mov. Avg. · · · 10-Week Mov. Avg. — **GAAP Earnings vs. Previous Year** Volume Above Avg. STARS
12-Mo. Target Price — Relative Strength — ▲ Up ▼ Down ► No Change Below Avg. ★

Options: ASE, CBOE, P, Ph

Analysis prepared by **Erik Kolb** on September 27, 2010, when the stock traded at **$ 43.61.**

Qualitative Risk Assessment

LOW	**MEDIUM**	HIGH

DRI competes in the casual dining industry, and we believe that its Red Lobster and Olive Garden concepts have among the strongest brand name recognition in the industry. However, the casual dining segment over-expanded in recent years, in our opinion, with an industry consolidation being accelerated by the recession. A slow recovery for the industry is likely.

Quantitative Evaluations

S&P Quality Ranking A

D	C	B-	B	B+	A-	**A**	A+

Relative Strength Rank STRONG

76

LOWEST = 1 HIGHEST = 99

Revenue/Earnings Data

Revenue (Million $)

	1Q	2Q	3Q	4Q	Year
2011	1,807	--	--	--	--
2010	1,734	1,641	1,874	1,864	7,113
2009	1,774	1,669	1,799	1,976	7,218
2008	1,468	1,522	1,811	1,826	6,627
2007	1,360	1,298	1,450	1,460	5,567
2006	1,409	1,325	1,474	1,414	5,721

Earnings Per Share ($)

2011	0.80	E0.78	E0.89	E0.86	E3.33
2010	0.67	0.43	0.95	0.81	2.86
2009	0.58	0.42	0.78	0.87	2.65
2008	0.58	0.30	0.80	0.72	2.55
2007	0.62	0.45	0.79	0.67	2.53
2006	0.53	0.35	0.67	0.62	2.16

Fiscal year ended May 31. Next earnings report expected: Mid December. EPS Estimates based on S&P Operating Earnings; historical GAAP earnings are as reported.

Dividend Data (Dates: mm/dd Payment Date: mm/dd/yy)

Amount ($)	Date Decl.	Ex-Div. Date	Stk. of Record	Payment Date
0.250	12/17	01/06	01/08	02/01/10
0.250	03/23	04/07	04/09	05/03/10
0.320	06/23	07/07	07/09	08/02/10
0.320	09/21	10/06	10/08	11/01/10

Dividends have been paid since 1995. Source: Company reports.

Highlights

► In FY 11 (May), we expect DRI to increase its restaurant base by about 4%. We think traffic is likely to be up slightly despite the sluggish economy, as we think pricing remains attractive. All told, we see comparable sales increasing about 2.0% to 3.0%. We see total sales increasing 3.0% to 4.0%. Capital expenditures supporting the restaurant expansion are likely to range from $475 million to $525 million.

► We look for flat margins overall. Although Darden has contracted for various commodities to various dates into FY 11, we remain concerned about the availability and cost of seafood. Interest expenses should decline somewhat, reflecting lower debt balances. The company expects its effective income tax rate to rise to 27.0%, from 25.1% in FY 10. We estimate EPS will increase to $3.33 from $2.86 in FY 09.

► For FY 12, we project revenues will increase 5.0% to 6.0%. We expect restaurant operating margins to narrow slightly, including a small increase in food costs. Partly offset by higher overhead as incentive compensation rises and delayed maintenance spending is accelerated, we see EPS of $3.81 in FY 12.

Investment Rationale/Risk

► We have a relatively positive view of DRI's restaurants relative to other peers in the casual dining segment, and think same store sales will slightly outpace the average over the next six to 12 months. However, this industry remains highly competitive and given our current economic concerns, we expect customers to remain extremely sensitive to price. Recent results for Red Lobster were relatively weak, but we think this was primarily a pricing issue, and, thus far, fallout from the Gulf oil spill appears to be minimal.

► Risks to our recommendation and target price include an unexpected acceleration in food cost inflation. Also, consumers may be less resilient than we expect, leading to lower traffic than we anticipate, possibly exacerbated by higher unemployment and ongoing economic uncertainty.

► Our 12-month target price of $47 is based on our relative P/E analysis. We apply a multiple of 14.0X to our FY11 EPS estimate of $3.33, a multiple that is well within the range for DRI's peer group.

Please read the Required Disclosures and Analyst Certification on the last page of this report.

The McGraw-Hill Companies

Darden Restaurants Inc.

Business Summary September 27, 2010

CORPORATE OVERVIEW. With systemwide sales from continuing operations of more than $7.1 billion in FY 10 (May), Darden Restaurants is the world's largest publicly held casual dining restaurant company. As of May 30, 2010, it operated 1,824 restaurants in the U.S. and Canada, including 694 Red Lobster units, 723 Olive Garden units, 331 LongHorn Steakhouse locations, and 76 other restaurants divided among The Capital Grille, Bahama Breeze, and Seasons 52 chains.

Olive Garden is the U.S. market share leader among casual dining Italian food restaurants. FY 09 systemwide sales (latest available) grew 7.9%, to $3.3 billion (including a 53rd week). Same-restaurant sales increased 0.3%, compared to 4.9% in FY 08. Average restaurant sales were $4.8 million. The average check per person was $15.50 to $16.00 in FY 09.

Red Lobster, founded by William Darden in 1968, is the largest U.S. casual dining seafood-specialty restaurant operator. Systemwide sales totaled $2.62 billion in FY 09, down 0.2% from FY 08. Average restaurant sales were $3.8 million in FY 09, down from $3.9 million in FY 08. Same-store sales fell 2.2% in FY 09,

following a 1.1% increase in FY 08. The average check per person was $19.00 to $19.50.

On October 1, 2007, DRI acquired RARE Hospitality International, Inc., in a cash tender offer for all RARE common shares at $38.15 per share, or total consideration of $1.41 billion in cash. Financing was obtained under a $1.2 billion senior interim credit facility and a $700 million senior revolver. Most members of RARE management agreed to join DRI in roles generally similar to those they had at RARE.

RARE operations included the LongHorn Steakhouse chain. Total sales increased 3.6% in FY 09. Annual sales per restaurant in FY 09 dipped slightly to $2.8 million from $2.9 million in FY 08. Same-store sales decreased 5.6%, following on a 1.1% decline in FY 08.

Company Financials Fiscal Year Ended May 31

Per Share Data ($)	2010	2009	2008	2007	2006	2005	2004	2003	2002	2001
Tangible Book Value	5.92	3.89	2.45	7.57	8.20	8.25	7.86	7.03	6.56	5.66
Cash Flow	4.97	4.61	4.19	3.88	3.57	3.08	2.60	2.43	2.20	1.85
Earnings	2.86	2.65	2.55	2.53	2.16	1.78	1.36	1.31	1.30	1.06
S&P Core Earnings	2.82	2.56	2.54	2.53	2.10	1.68	1.27	1.18	1.16	0.97
Dividends	NA	0.72	0.46	0.40	0.08	0.08	0.08	0.05	0.05	0.05
Payout Ratio	NA	27%	18%	16%	4%	4%	6%	4%	4%	5%
Calendar Year	2009	2008	2007	2006	2005	2004	2003	2002	2001	2000
Prices:High	41.21	37.83	47.60	44.43	39.53	28.54	23.01	29.76	24.98	18.00
Prices:Low	23.32	13.21	26.90	32.91	25.78	18.48	16.50	18.00	12.67	8.29
P/E Ratio:High	14	14	19	18	18	16	17	23	19	17
P/E Ratio:Low	8	5	11	13	12	10	12	14	10	8

Income Statement Analysis (Million $)										
Revenue	7,113	7,218	6,627	5,567	5,721	5,278	5,003	4,655	4,369	4,021
Operating Income	945	895	878	774	757	685	636	588	563	479
Depreciation	301	275	238	200	221	213	210	198	166	147
Interest Expense	93.9	118	35.2	40.7	43.1	43.1	43.7	44.1	37.8	31.5
Pretax Income	544	513	515	531	483	424	340	348	363	301
Effective Tax Rate	NA	27.5%	28.2%	29.0%	29.9%	31.4%	31.9%	33.2%	34.5%	34.6%
Net Income	407	372	370	377	338	291	231	232	238	197
S&P Core Earnings	402	360	367	378	330	274	214	208	212	181

Balance Sheet & Other Financial Data (Million $)										
Cash	249	62.9	43.2	30.2	42.3	42.8	36.7	48.6	153	61.8
Current Assets	678	555	468	545	378	407	346	326	450	328
Total Assets	5,247	5,025	4,731	2,881	3,010	2,938	2,780	2,665	2,530	2,218
Current Liabilities	1,255	1,096	1,136	1,074	1,026	1,045	683	640	601	554
Long Term Debt	1,409	1,632	1,634	492	495	350	653	658	663	518
Common Equity	1,894	1,606	1,409	1,115	1,230	1,273	1,246	1,196	1,129	1,035
Total Capital	3,528	3,238	3,043	1,633	1,815	1,738	2,075	2,005	1,909	1,644
Capital Expenditures	432	535	429	345	338	329	354	423	318	355
Cash Flow	708	646	608	578	560	504	441	430	404	344
Current Ratio	0.5	0.5	0.4	0.5	0.4	0.4	0.5	0.5	0.7	0.6
% Long Term Debt of Capitalization	39.9	50.4	53.6	30.1	27.3	20.2	31.5	32.8	34.7	31.5
% Net Income of Revenue	5.7	5.2	5.6	6.8	5.9	5.5	4.6	5.0	5.4	4.9
% Return on Assets	7.9	7.6	9.7	12.8	11.4	10.2	8.5	8.9	10.0	9.4
% Return on Equity	23.3	24.7	29.5	31.6	27.0	23.7	19.0	20.0	22.0	19.7

Data as orig reptd.; bef. results of disc opers/spec. items. Per share data adj. for stk. divs.; EPS diluted. E-Estimated. NA-Not Available. NM-Not Meaningful. NR-Not Ranked. UR-Under Review.

Office: 5900 Lake Ellenor Drive, Orlando, FL 32809-4634.
Telephone: 407-245-4000.
Email: irinfo@darden.com
Website: http://www.darden.com

Chrmn & CEO: C. Otis, Jr.
Pres & COO: A.H. Madsen
Investor Contact: C.B. Richmond (407-245-4000)
SVP, CFO & Chief Acctg Officer: C.B. Richmond

SVP, Secy & General Counsel: T.M. Sebastian
Board Members: L. L. Berry, O. C. Donald, C. J. Fraleigh, V. D. Harker, D. H. Hughes, C. A. Ledsinger, Jr., W. M. Lewis, Jr., A. H. Madsen, C. McGillicuddy, III, C. Otis, Jr., M. D. Rose, M. Sastre

Founded: 1968
Domicile: Florida
Employees: 174,079

DaVita Inc

STANDARD &POOR'S

S&P Recommendation BUY ★★★★☆

Price	12-Mo. Target Price	Investment Style
$71.65 (as of Oct 22, 2010)	$74.00	Large-Cap Growth

GICS Sector Health Care
Sub-Industry Health Care Services

Summary This company is one of the largest worldwide providers of integrated dialysis services for patients suffering from chronic kidney failure.

Key Stock Statistics (Source S&P, Vickers, company reports)

52-Wk Range	$72.96–52.71	S&P Oper. EPS 2010**E**	4.36	Market Capitalization(B)	$7.351	Beta		0.28
Trailing 12-Month EPS	$4.20	S&P Oper. EPS 2011**E**	4.60	Yield (%)	Nil	S&P 3-Yr. Proj. EPS CAGR(%)		12
Trailing 12-Month P/E	17.1	P/E on S&P Oper. EPS 2010**E**	16.4	Dividend Rate/Share	Nil	S&P Credit Rating		BB-
$10K Invested 5 Yrs Ago	$14,834	Common Shares Outstg. (M)	102.6	Institutional Ownership (%)	94			

Price Performance

30-Week Mov. Avg. · · · · 10-Week Mov. Avg. ‑ ‑ GAAP Earnings vs. Previous Year Volume Above Avg. ▌▍▎ STARS
12-Mo. Target Price — Relative Strength — ▲ Up ▼ Down ▶ No Change Below Avg. ▌▍▎ ★

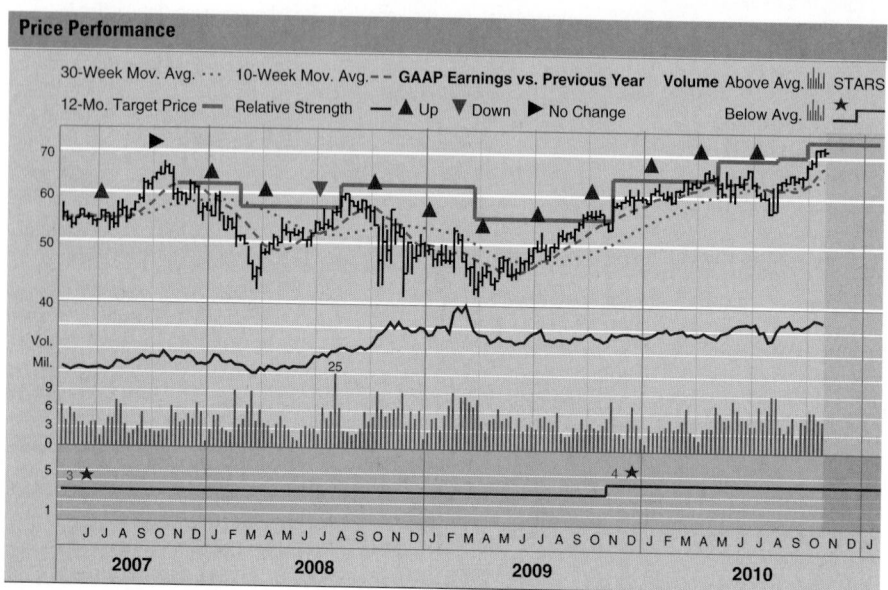

Options: CBOE, P, Ph

Analysis prepared by **Steven Silver** on September 24, 2010, when the stock traded at **$ 68.08.**

Highlights

➤ We see sales rising 4% in 2010 and 5% in 2011, reflecting an aging U.S. population, stable demand for dialysis services, and contributions from acquired dialysis centers. However, we see per treatment revenues being pressured over the near term by more conservative physician utilization among higher risk patients, and by a less favorable shift in payer mix toward Medicare and Medicaid from commercial payers for patients who have lost insurance due to continued high unemployment.

➤ We forecast a very slight decline in gross margin in 2010 on increases in center operating and Heparin costs. We see a modest rise in bad debt as a percentage of sales leading to a lesser decline in EBITDA margins. For 2011, we look for a rise in gross margins, as patient care costs should decline as a percentage of sales. We look for G&A expenses and bad debt to be essentially flat, all relative to sales, leading to a rise in EBITDA margins in 2011.

➤ We estimate operating EPS of $4.36 in 2010 and $4.60 in 2011. We assume approximately 105 million shares outstanding for both 2010 and 2011.

Investment Rationale/Risk

➤ We believe dialysis provider fundamentals are favorable, and view DVA as well positioned to make new acquisitions to expand its patient base and drive efficiencies through economies of scale. We see DVA as increasingly dependent on commercial pricing, which is sharply above Medicare rates, for its profits, and expect the company to secure long-term contracts with managed care companies, which we expect to stabilize its revenue environment. Although we anticipate some near-term impacts from Medicare's recently released bundling rules, we expect DVA to benefit over the long term from more favorable pricing on medicines used in its dialysis treatment operations.

➤ Risks to our recommendation and target price include risk of restrictions over EPO utilization, unfavorable Medicare rule changes, heightened competition, and reduced reimbursement.

➤ Our 12-month target price of $74 assumes a 16X multiple of our 2011 EPS estimate and an 8.2X EV/EBITDA multiple of our 2011 EBITDA estimate, modest discounts to DVA's historical averages to reflect greater regulatory uncertainty.

Qualitative Risk Assessment

LOW	**MEDIUM**	HIGH

Our risk assessment reflects our view of stable demand for dialysis services, driven by a rising senior population in the U.S., offset by DVA's dependence on third-party payments, including Medicare and Medicaid.

Quantitative Evaluations

S&P Quality Ranking B+

D	C	B-	B	**B+**	A-	A	A+

Relative Strength Rank STRONG

72

LOWEST = 1   HIGHEST = 99

Revenue/Earnings Data

Revenue (Million $)

	1Q	2Q	3Q	4Q	Year
2010	1,559	1,587	--	--	--
2009	1,448	1,519	1,574	1,568	6,109
2008	1,345	1,407	1,447	1,461	5,660
2007	1,278	1,313	1,318	1,355	5,264
2006	1,163	1,208	1,237	1,273	4,881
2005	578.6	617.1	644.9	1,133	2,974

Earnings Per Share ($)

2010	1.04	1.03	E1.13	E1.13	E4.36
2009	0.92	1.02	1.06	1.06	4.06
2008	0.80	0.90	0.89	0.94	3.53
2007	0.72	1.17	0.88	0.79	3.55
2006	0.55	0.61	0.88	0.70	2.73
2005	0.50	0.49	0.49	0.54	1.99

Fiscal year ended Dec. 31. Next earnings report expected: Early November. EPS Estimates based on S&P Operating Earnings; historical GAAP earnings are as reported.

Dividend Data

No cash dividends have been paid.

Please read the Required Disclosures and Analyst Certification on the last page of this report.

The McGraw-Hill Companies

DaVita Inc

Business Summary September 24, 2010

CORPORATE OVERVIEW. Da Vita is a leading U.S. provider of dialysis and re-lated services for patients suffering from chronic kidney failure, also known as end stage renal disease (ESRD). As of December 31, 2009, DVA provided dialysis and ancillary services to about 118,000 patients through a network of 1,530 outpatient dialysis facilities in 43 states. In addition, the company provid-ed acute inpatient dialysis services at over 700 hospitals.

As a result of DVA's growth through acquisitions, it became highly leveraged, in our opinion. Since a management overhaul in 1999, the company has imple-mented a new strategy focusing on improving operations and restructuring the balance sheet. In 2005, DVA acquired 492 centers through the Gambro ac-quisition, as well as 12 independent centers. The company also opened 13 new centers.

In 2009, the company acquired 19 centers, developed 78 new centers, and

closed eight. As of year end, it owned 1,530 centers outright, and provided ad-ministrative services to 17 third-party owned centers. Average revenue per treatment in 2009 was $340, up 1.8% from 2008 ($334).

Hemodialysis uses an artificial kidney, called a dialyze, to remove certain tox-ins, fluids and salt from the patient's blood, together with a machine to control external blood flow and to monitor certain vital signs of the patient. Peritoneal dialysis uses the patient's peritoneal (abdominal) cavity to eliminate fluid and toxins. In 2009, outpatient hemodialysis, peritoneal dialysis and hospital inpa-tient dialysis accounted for 84%, 11% and 5% of total treatments, respectively.

Company Financials Fiscal Year Ended Dec. 31

Per Share Data ($)	2009	2008	2007	2006	2005	2004	2003	2002	2001	2000
Tangible Book Value	NM	NM	NM	NM	NM	NM	NM	NM	NM	NM
Cash Flow	6.26	5.43	5.36	4.37	3.14	3.00	2.20	1.85	1.56	1.03
Earnings	4.06	3.53	3.55	2.73	1.99	2.16	1.66	1.52	1.01	0.13
S&P Core Earnings	4.06	3.53	3.48	2.73	1.89	2.07	1.59	1.41	0.89	NA
Dividends	Nil	Nil	Nil	Nil	Nil	Nil	Nil	Nil	Nil	Nil
Payout Ratio	Nil	Nil	Nil	Nil	Nil	Nil	Nil	Nil	Nil	Nil
Prices:High	61.97	60.23	67.44	60.70	53.90	41.10	26.94	17.63	16.33	11.88
Prices:Low	41.21	40.96	50.75	46.70	38.87	25.23	12.77	12.67	9.33	1.38
P/E Ratio:High	15	17	19	22	27	19	16	12	16	85
P/E Ratio:Low	10	12	14	17	20	12	8	8	9	10

Income Statement Analysis (Million $)	2009	2008	2007	2006	2005	2004	2003	2002	2001	2000
Revenue	6,109	5,660	5,264	4,881	2,974	2,299	2,016	1,855	1,651	1,486
Operating Income	1,167	1,069	1,046	911	607	510	461	456	423	291
Depreciation	229	201	193	173	120	86.7	74.7	64.7	105	112
Interest Expense	186	229	257	277	140	52.4	66.8	71.6	71.7	117
Pretax Income	758	656	628	512	353	376	296	325	250	45.0
Effective Tax Rate	36.7%	35.9%	39.2%	36.4%	35.0%	37.2%	38.1%	39.8%	41.8%	62.2%
Net Income	423	374	382	289	207	222	176	187	136	16.9
S&P Core Earnings	423	374	374	289	197	213	167	175	118	NA

Balance Sheet & Other Financial Data (Million $)	2009	2008	2007	2006	2005	2004	2003	2002	2001	2000
Cash	566	446	487	310	432	252	61.7	96.5	36.7	31.2
Current Assets	2,303	2,128	1,976	1,709	1,654	869	605	545	475	398
Total Assets	7,558	7,286	6,944	6,492	6,280	2,512	1,946	1,776	1,663	1,597
Current Liabilities	1,047	1,163	1,087	1,112	990	442	363	293	299	250
Long Term Debt	3,532	3,618	3,684	3,730	4,085	1,322	1,117	1,311	811	974
Common Equity	2,135	1,952	1,732	1,246	851	523	307	70.3	504	349
Total Capital	6,158	5,808	5,733	5,224	5,100	2,048	1,563	1,474	1,359	1,342
Capital Expenditures	275	318	272	263	161	128	100	103	51.2	41.1
Cash Flow	652	575	575	463	327	309	250	251	242	129
Current Ratio	2.2	1.8	1.8	1.5	1.7	2.0	1.7	1.9	1.6	1.6
% Long Term Debt of Capitalization	57.4	60.5	66.2	71.4	80.1	64.6	71.4	89.0	59.7	72.5
% Net Income of Revenue	6.9	6.6	7.3	5.9	7.0	9.7	8.7	10.1	8.3	1.1
% Return on Assets	5.7	5.3	5.7	4.5	4.7	10.0	9.4	10.9	8.4	0.1
% Return on Equity	20.7	20.3	25.6	27.6	30.2	53.6	93.2	65.1	32.0	5.0

Data as orig reptd.; bef. results of disc opers/spec. items. Per share data adj. for stk. divs.; EPS diluted. E-Estimated. NA-Not Available. NM-Not Meaningful. NR-Not Ranked. UR-Under Review.

Office: 1551 Wewatta Street, Denver, CO 80202.
Telephone: 303-405-2100.
Email: ir@davita.com
Website: http://www.davita.com

Chrmn & CEO: K.J. Thiry
COO: D. Kogod
SVP & CFO: L. Borgen
Chief Acctg Officer & Cntlr: J.K. Hilger

Secy & General Counsel: K.M. Rivera
Investor Contact: L. Zumwalt (800-310-4872)
Board Members: P. M. Arway, C. G. Berg, W. W. Brittain, Jr., P. J. Diaz, P. T. Grauer, J. M. Nehra, W. Roper, K. J. Thiry, R. J. Valine

Founded: 1994
Domicile: Delaware
Employees: 34,000

Dean Foods Co

STANDARD & POOR'S

S&P Recommendation HOLD ★★★★★	**Price** $9.97 (as of Oct 22, 2010)	**12-Mo. Target Price** $10.00	**Investment Style** Large-Cap Blend

GICS Sector Consumer Staples
Sub-Industry Packaged Foods & Meats

Summary This leading U.S. dairy processor and distributor was formed in December 2001 when Suiza Foods, the largest U.S. dairy, acquired Dean Foods and adopted the Dean Foods name.

Key Stock Statistics (Source S&P, Vickers, company reports)

52-Wk Range	$18.79–9.38	S&P Oper. EPS 2010**E**	0.98	Market Capitalization(B)	$1.816	Beta	0.65
Trailing 12-Month EPS	$1.03	S&P Oper. EPS 2011**E**	1.08	Yield (%)	Nil	S&P 3-Yr. Proj. EPS CAGR(%)	NA
Trailing 12-Month P/E	9.7	P/E on S&P Oper. EPS 2010**E**	10.2	Dividend Rate/Share	Nil	S&P Credit Rating	BB-
$10K Invested 5 Yrs Ago	$3,969	Common Shares Outstg. (M)	182.1	Institutional Ownership (%)	85		

Price Performance

- 30-Week Mov. Avg. ···· 10-Week Mov. Avg. – – GAAP Earnings vs. Previous Year Volume Above Avg. STARS
- 12-Mo. Target Price — Relative Strength ▲ Up ▼ Down ▶ No Change Below Avg. ★

Options: CBOE, P, Ph

Analysis prepared by **Tom Graves, CFA** on August 23, 2010, when the stock traded at **$ 10.16**.

Highlights

➤ In 2010, we look for net sales to increase about 8% from the $11.2 billion reported for 2009, largely due to the pass-through of higher dairy costs, especially for conventional milk. However, we expect profit margins to be adversely affected by pricing pressure, and we expect some consumer trade-down to less expensive dairy products. We think that much of the revenue decline reported for 2009 reflected the pass-through of lower commodity costs to DF's customers.

➤ Following a recent credit agreement revision, we expect that interest expense in the second half of 2010 will be higher than it was in the first half. For the full year, before special items, we estimate diluted EPS of $0.98, on about 5% more shares outstanding, compared with $1.59 in 2009, which was before a negative impact of about $0.21 from some special items. In 2011, we look for an EPS increase to $1.08.

➤ In May 2009, DF received net proceeds of about $445 million in connection with the public sale of some 25.4 million common shares. Proceeds were used to repay debt.

Investment Rationale/Risk

➤ In the future, we expect that Dean Foods will aim for clear cost leadership in the fluid milk industry, through a focus on such areas as product standardization and sourcing, facility network optimization, improved productivity, and lower distribution costs. We expect that there will be some related investment costs. In July 2009, DF acquired a European provider of soy-based beverage and food products.

➤ Risks to our recommendation and target price include the possibility that commodity costs, milk prices, and consumer spending on dairy products will be more unfavorable than we expect, and that competitive conditions will be more difficult than anticipated.

➤ Our 12-month target price of $10 represents a P/E discount to what we expect, on average, from a group of other food stocks. This reflects, in part, our view that recent profits at DF were disappointing, and that the profit outlook has weakened. Also, we have concerns about price competition, and we view DF as more weighted toward being a commodity-type business than some other food companies. DF does not pay a quarterly dividend to common shareholders.

Qualitative Risk Assessment

LOW	MEDIUM	HIGH

Our risk assessment reflects our view of DF's leading position in the U.S. milk market, and our expectation of future free cash flow. However, milk prices can be volatile, and some products are likely to enjoy stronger demand and growth than others.

Quantitative Evaluations

S&P Quality Ranking B

D	C	B-	B	B+	A-	A	A+

Relative Strength Rank WEAK

17

LOWEST = 1   HIGHEST = 99

Revenue/Earnings Data

Revenue (Million $)

	1Q	2Q	3Q	4Q	Year
2010	2,972	2,955	--	--	--
2009	2,703	2,681	2,774	3,001	11,158
2008	3,077	3,103	3,195	3,080	12,455
2007	2,630	2,844	3,117	3,232	11,822
2006	2,509	2,478	2,518	2,594	10,099
2005	2,562	2,603	2,647	2,695	10,506

Earnings Per Share ($)

	1Q	2Q	3Q	4Q	Year
2010	0.23	0.25	E0.21	E0.25	E0.98
2009	0.48	0.38	0.27	0.27	1.38
2008	0.21	0.31	0.24	0.43	1.21
2007	0.47	0.21	0.05	0.24	0.95
2006	0.37	0.53	0.54	0.56	2.01
2005	0.43	0.52	0.43	0.49	1.78

Fiscal year ended Dec. 31. Next earnings report expected: Early November. EPS Estimates based on S&P Operating Earnings; historical GAAP earnings are as reported.

Dividend Data

A special cash dividend of $15 a share was paid in April 2007.

The McGraw·Hill Companies

Dean Foods Co

Business Summary August 23, 2010

CORPORATE OVERVIEW. Dean Foods Co. is a leading U.S. processor and distributor of milk and other dairy products. In December 2001, Suiza Foods Corp., the largest U.S. dairy, acquired Dean Foods Co. Suiza subsequently changed its name to Dean Foods Co. The company has grown partly through an acquisition strategy and by realizing regional economies of scale and operating efficiencies by consolidating manufacturing and distribution operations. Some of DF's products are sold under licensed brand names.

In 2010, DF changed its presentation of business segments. Fresh Dairy Direct-Morningstar is DF's largest segment (about 84% of consolidated net sales in the first half of 2010), and includes more than 90 manufacturing facilities. Its products include milk, ice cream, cultured dairy products, creamers, ice cream mix and other dairy products, which are distributed under regional brands such as Country Fresh, Dean's, Garelick Farms, Mayfield and Oak Farms, as well as familiar local brands and private labels. Products are delivered through what the company believes to be one of the most extensive refrigerated direct-store-delivery (DSD) systems in the U.S., as well as through customer warehouse delivery systems.

DF's WhiteWave-Alpro segment (about 16% of net sales) includes the WhiteWave business, which manufactures and sells a variety of nationally branded soy, dairy and dairy-related products, such as Horizon Organic milk and other dairy products, Silk soymilk and cultured soy products, The Organic Cow dairy products, International Delight coffee creamers, and LAND O LAKES creamers and fluid dairy products.

DF's Alpro business manufactures and sells branded soy beverages and soy-based food products across Europe under the Alpro and Provamel brand names. In July 2009, DF acquired the Alpro division of Vandemoortele N.V. for about EUR315 million, excluding transaction costs, Alpro had net sales of about EUR260 million in 2008. Also, with its Hero/WhiteWave joint venture, which was formed in 2008, DF expanded into the chilled fruit-based beverage area with the introduction of Fruit2Day. DF's partner in the joint venture is Hero Group, a producer of international fruit and infant nutrition brands Hero and Beech-Nut. The Hero joint venture reduced WhiteWave-Morningstar operating profit by $12.5 million in 2009.

DF has decided to sell its Rachel's business operations, which provide dairy-related products primarily in the U.K. Rachel's, which we believe had net sales of about $23 million in 2010's first half, was previously part of the WhiteWave-Alpro segment. It has been reclassified as discontinued operations.

Company Financials Fiscal Year Ended Dec. 31

Per Share Data ($)	2009	2008	2007	2006	2005	2004	2003	2002	2001	2000
Tangible Book Value	NM	NM	NM	NM	NM	NM	NM	NM	NM	NM
Cash Flow	2.85	2.74	2.64	3.63	3.22	1.58	3.41	2.71	2.44	2.35
Earnings	1.38	1.21	0.95	2.01	1.78	1.78	2.27	1.77	1.23	1.27
S&P Core Earnings	1.45	1.15	0.92	2.00	1.66	1.58	1.85	1.57	0.91	NA
Dividends	Nil	Nil	Nil	Nil	Nil	Nil	Nil	Nil	Nil	Nil
Payout Ratio	Nil	Nil	Nil	Nil	Nil	Nil	Nil	Nil	Nil	Nil
Prices:High	22.09	29.23	50.50	43.55	42.10	38.00	33.75	27.03	24.16	17.48
Prices:Low	15.74	11.20	24.11	34.66	31.60	28.25	24.60	18.05	14.00	12.00
P/E Ratio:High	16	24	53	22	24	21	15	15	20	14
P/E Ratio:Low	11	9	25	17	18	16	11	10	11	9

Income Statement Analysis (Million $)										
Revenue	11,158	12,455	11,822	10,099	10,506	10,822	9,185	8,991	6,230	5,756
Operating Income	939	869	810	903	867	919	889	856	542	524
Depreciation	9.64	236	232	228	221	224	192	174	155	145
Interest Expense	246	310	322	195	169	205	195	231	135	147
Pretax Income	380	300	214	456	439	462	574	421	231	234
Effective Tax Rate	40.0%	38.3%	39.2%	38.5%	37.9%	38.3%	38.0%	36.4%	36.3%	38.4%
Net Income	240	185	130	280	272	285	356	268	116	114
S&P Core Earnings	252	175	126	278	254	253	288	236	79.2	NA

Balance Sheet & Other Financial Data (Million $)										
Cash	47.6	36.0	32.6	31.1	25.1	27.6	47.1	45.9	78.3	31.0
Current Assets	1,629	1,481	1,532	1,379	1,477	1,596	1,401	1,311	1,482	818
Total Assets	7,844	7,040	7,033	6,770	7,051	7,756	6,993	6,582	6,732	3,780
Current Liabilities	1,479	1,427	933	1,337	1,137	1,106	1,170	1,268	1,175	700
Long Term Debt	4,229	4,174	5,271	2,872	3,329	3,116	2,611	3,140	3,556	1,809
Common Equity	1,352	558	51.3	1,809	1,872	2,661	2,543	1,643	1,476	599
Total Capital	5,596	5,201	5,781	5,186	5,688	6,308	5,542	5,077	5,313	3,047
Capital Expenditures	268	257	241	237	307	356	292	242	137	137
Cash Flow	495	421	362	508	494	509	548	442	270	259
Current Ratio	1.3	1.0	1.6	1.0	1.3	1.4	1.2	1.0	1.3	1.2
% Long Term Debt of Capitalization	75.6	80.3	99.0	55.4	58.5	49.4	47.1	61.8	66.9	59.3
% Net Income of Revenue	2.2	1.5	1.1	2.8	2.6	2.6	3.9	3.0	1.9	1.9
% Return on Assets	3.2	2.6	1.9	4.1	3.7	3.9	5.2	4.0	2.2	3.5
% Return on Equity	25.2	60.7	14.0	15.1	12.0	11.0	17.0	17.2	11.1	19.2

Data as orig reptd.; bef. results of disc opers/spec. items. Per share data adj. for stk. divs.; EPS diluted. E-Estimated. NA-Not Available. NM-Not Meaningful. NR-Not Ranked. UR-Under Review.

Office: 2711 North Haskell Avenue, Suite 3400, Dallas, TX 75204.
Telephone: 214-303-3400.
Website: http://www.deanfoods.com
Chrmn: G.L. Engles

Pres, CEO & COO: J. Scalzo
EVP & CFO: J.F. Callahan, Jr.
EVP, Secy & General Counsel: S.J. Kemps
SVP & Chief Acctg Officer: S. Mara

Investor Contact: B. Sievert (214-303-3437)
Board Members: T. C. Davis, G. L. Engles, S. L. Green, J. S. Hardin, Jr., J. Hill, W. Mailloux, J. R. Muse, H. M. Nevares, J. L. Turner, D. A. Wright

Founded: 1925
Domicile: Delaware
Employees: 27,157

Deere & Co

STANDARD &POOR'S

S&P Recommendation BUY ★★★★☆

Price	**12-Mo. Target Price**	**Investment Style**
$77.25 (as of Oct 22, 2010)	$82.00	Large-Cap Blend

GICS Sector Industrials
Sub-Industry Construction & Farm Machinery & Heavy Trucks

Summary Deere, the world's biggest producer of farm equipment, is also a large maker of construction machinery and lawn and garden equipment.

Key Stock Statistics (Source S&P, Vickers, company reports)

52-Wk Range	$77.72– 45.19	S&P Oper. EPS 2010E	4.35	Market Capitalization(B)	$32.743	Beta	1.57
Trailing 12-Month EPS	$2.77	S&P Oper. EPS 2011E	5.05	Yield (%)	1.55	S&P 3-Yr. Proj. EPS CAGR(%)	23
Trailing 12-Month P/E	27.9	P/E on S&P Oper. EPS 2010E	17.8	Dividend Rate/Share	$1.20	S&P Credit Rating	B+
$10K Invested 5 Yrs Ago	$29,819	Common Shares Outstg. (M)	423.9	Institutional Ownership (%)	72		

Price Performance

Analysis prepared by **Michael W. Jaffe** on August 19, 2010, when the stock traded at **$ 65.54**.

Highlights

➤ After being hampered for several quarters by the very soft global economy, revenues started to pick up in the second quarter of FY 10 (Oct). Based on our outlook for a continuation of these more favorable demand trends, we expect revenues in FY 11 to increase by 9%. We see these forecasted gains being driven by an ongoing recovery of global economies, and its likely impact on the markets that DE serves, including an expected increase in crop prices. We see a resultant upturn in U.S. farm cash receipts boosting demand for agricultural equipment, and better residential construction markets lifting demand for construction equipment. We see these factors outweighing some likely ongoing sluggishness in European equipment markets.

➤ We project wider margins in FY 11, on our outlook for improving business trends. We also see DE being aided by incremental benefits from its cost cuts of the past couple of years.

➤ Our FY 11 EPS estimate compares with an FY 10 forecast which excludes $0.30 a share of second quarter charges related to the enactment of U.S. health care legislation. Operating EPS were $2.84 in FY 09.

Investment Rationale/Risk

➤ Following a sharp downturn in its business between late 2008 and late 2009, we believe better economic trends are allowing most of Deere's end markets to start recoveries, although recent uncertainties across Europe pose a challenge. We see these conditions bringing an extended upturn in DE's operating results. Based on these factors and our valuation model, we believe the stock is undervalued.

➤ Risks to our recommendation and target price include a resumed downturn in the global economy, a further decline in crop prices and farm equipment spending, and larger-than-expected loan provisions in the credit segment.

➤ The stock recently traded at about 13X our calendar 2011 EPS forecast of $5.12. We believe it is undervalued, as this falls slightly below the low end of DE's typical valuation during the second year of business recoveries, which we see taking place over the coming year. Based on these views, our 12-month target price is $82, or 16X our calendar 2011 forecast, which is in the bottom half of DE's typical valuation at this stage of its business cycle, to account for global economic uncertainties.

Qualitative Risk Assessment

| LOW | MEDIUM | HIGH |

Our risk assessment reflects Deere's leading position in many of the markets it serves, and a balance sheet that typically carries large cash balances. On the other hand, the company's businesses are highly cyclical.

Quantitative Evaluations

S&P Quality Ranking A-

| D | C | B- | B | B+ | A- | A | A+ |

Relative Strength Rank STRONG 84
LOWEST = 1 HIGHEST = 99

Revenue/Earnings Data

Revenue (Million $)

	1Q	2Q	3Q	4Q	Year
2010	4,835	7,131	6,837	--	--
2009	5,146	6,748	5,884	5,334	23,112
2008	5,201	8,097	7,739	7,401	28,438
2007	4,425	6,883	6,634	6,141	24,082
2006	4,202	6,562	6,267	5,118	22,148
2005	4,127	6,621	6,005	5,177	21,931

Earnings Per Share ($)

2010	0.57	1.28	1.44	E0.76	E4.35
2009	0.48	1.11	0.99	-0.53	2.06
2008	0.83	1.74	1.32	0.81	4.70
2007	0.52	1.36	1.32	0.94	4.00
2006	0.47	1.09	0.93	0.60	3.08
2005	0.45	1.22	0.79	0.48	2.94

Fiscal year ended Oct. 31. Next earnings report expected: Late November. EPS Estimates based on S&P Operating Earnings; historical GAAP earnings are as reported.

Dividend Data (Dates: mm/dd Payment Date: mm/dd/yy)

Amount ($)	Date Decl.	Ex-Div. Date	Stk. of Record	Payment Date
0.280	12/02	12/29	12/31	02/01/10
0.280	02/24	03/29	03/31	05/03/10
0.300	05/26	06/28	06/30	08/02/10
0.300	08/25	09/28	09/30	11/01/10

Dividends have been paid since 1937. Source: Company reports.

Deere & Co

Business Summary August 19, 2010

CORPORATE OVERVIEW. Deere & Co. is the world's largest maker of farm tractors and combines, and a leading producer of construction equipment. During FY 09 (Oct.), the company derived 37% of its equipment sales outside of North America.

Effective May 1, 2009, DE combined its agricultural equipment and commercial and consumer equipment segments to form the agriculture and turf division. This streamlining action was an attempt by Deere to act on global market opportunities, leverage its global scale, optimize global product line results, standardize processes, share resources and reduce costs.

The agricultural and turf segment (78% of FY 09 revenues; 8.0% operating margin) makes tractors, combines, and cotton and sugar cane harvesters; tillage, seeding and soil preparation machinery; and hay and forage equipment for the global farming industry. It also manufactures and distributes equipment

and service parts for commercial and residential uses. These products include small tractors for lawn, garden, commercial and utility purposes; lawn mowers; golf course equipment; utility vehicles; landscape and irrigation equipment; and other outdoor products.

The construction and forestry segment (11%; -3.2%) manufactures and distributes a broad range of machines and service parts used in construction, earth moving, material handling and timber harvesting. Products include backhoe loaders; crawler dozers and loaders; four-wheel-drive loaders; excavators; motor graders; articulated dump trucks; landscape loaders; skid-steer loaders; and log skidders, feller bunchers, harvesters and related attachments.

Company Financials Fiscal Year Ended Oct. 31

Per Share Data ($)	2009	2008	2007	2006	2005	2004	2003	2002	2001	2000
Tangible Book Value	8.61	12.19	13.17	13.92	12.13	10.93	5.91	4.75	6.57	7.78
Cash Flow	4.12	6.61	5.64	4.55	4.23	4.00	2.62	2.17	1.39	2.40
Earnings	2.06	4.70	4.00	3.08	2.94	2.78	1.32	0.67	-0.14	1.03
S&P Core Earnings	2.81	3.55	4.22	3.25	3.02	2.84	1.54	-0.19	-0.82	NA
Dividends	1.12	1.06	0.91	0.78	0.61	0.53	0.44	0.44	0.44	0.44
Payout Ratio	54%	23%	23%	22%	21%	19%	33%	66%	NM	43%
Prices:High	56.87	94.89	93.74	50.70	37.21	37.47	33.71	25.80	23.06	24.81
Prices:Low	24.51	28.50	45.12	33.45	28.50	28.36	18.78	18.75	16.75	15.16
P/E Ratio:High	28	20	23	14	13	13	26	39	NM	24
P/E Ratio:Low	12	6	11	9	10	10	14	28	NM	15

Income Statement Analysis (Million $)	2009	2008	2007	2006	2005	2004	2003	2002	2001	2000
Revenue	23,112	28,438	24,082	22,148	21,931	19,986	15,535	13,947	13,293	13,137
Operating Income	2,731	4,774	4,571	3,883	3,553	2,976	2,231	1,696	1,274	2,102
Depreciation	873	829	744	691	636	621	631	725	718	648
Interest Expense	NA	1,163	1,151	1,018	761	592	1,257	637	766	676
Pretax Income	1,334	3,164	2,676	2,195	2,162	2,115	980	578	-46.3	779
Effective Tax Rate	34.5%	35.1%	33.0%	33.8%	33.1%	33.5%	34.4%	44.7%	NM	37.7%
Net Income	874	2,053	1,822	1,453	1,447	1,406	643	319	-64.0	486
S&P Core Earnings	1,187	1,556	1,917	1,534	1,483	1,430	743	-94.8	-385	NA

Balance Sheet & Other Financial Data (Million $)	2009	2008	2007	2006	2005	2004	2003	2002	2001	2000
Cash	3,690	1,834	3,902	3,504	4,708	3,428	4,616	3,004	1,206	419
Current Assets	29,124	27,837	27,840	27,987	27,530	23,040	19,370	16,919	16,191	14,678
Total Assets	41,133	38,735	38,576	34,720	33,637	28,754	26,258	23,768	22,663	20,469
Current Liabilities	12,549	14,927	15,605	12,790	11,494	7,612	7,679	7,667	9,340	8,792
Long Term Debt	3,073	13,899	11,798	11,584	11,739	11,090	10,404	8,950	6,561	4,764
Common Equity	4,819	6,533	7,156	7,565	6,825	6,350	2,834	1,797	3,992	4,302
Total Capital	7,891	20,603	19,137	19,214	18,564	17,441	13,238	10,772	10,566	9,141
Capital Expenditures	1,308	1,608	1,023	766	513	364	310	359	491	427
Cash Flow	1,747	2,882	2,566	2,145	2,083	2,027	1,275	1,045	654	1,133
Current Ratio	2.3	1.9	NA	2.2	2.4	3.0	2.5	2.2	1.7	1.7
% Long Term Debt of Capitalization	38.9	67.5	61.6	60.3	63.2	63.6	78.6	83.1	62.1	52.1
% Net Income of Revenue	3.8	7.2	7.5	6.6	6.6	7.0	4.2	2.4	NM	3.8
% Return on Assets	2.2	5.3	4.9	4.3	4.6	5.1	2.6	1.4	NM	2.6
% Return on Equity	15.4	30.0	24.7	20.2	22.0	30.6	27.8	11.8	NM	11.6

Data as orig reptd.; bef. results of disc opers/spec. items. Per share data adj. for stk. divs.; EPS diluted. E-Estimated. NA-Not Available. NM-Not Meaningful. NR-Not Ranked. UR-Under Review.

Office: One John Deere Place, Moline, IL 61265-8098.
Telephone: 309-765-8000.
Email: stockholder@deere.com
Website: http://www.deere.com

Chrmn & CEO: S.R. Allen
SVP, CFO & Chief Acctg Officer: J.M. Field
SVP & CTO: J.H. Gilles
SVP & General Counsel: J.R. Jenkins

Treas: J.A. Davlin
Investor Contact: M. Ziegler (309-765-4491)
Board Members: S. R. Allen, C. C. Bowles, V. D. Coffman, C. O. Holliday, Jr., D. Jain, C. Jones, J. Milberg, R. B. Myers, T. H. Patrick, A. L. Peters, D. B. Speer

Founded: 1837
Domicile: Delaware
Employees: 51,262

Dell Inc

STANDARD & POOR'S

S&P Recommendation SELL ★ ★ ★ ★ ★

Price	12-Mo. Target Price	Investment Style
$14.59 (as of Oct 22, 2010)	$11.00	Large-Cap Growth

GICS Sector Information Technology
Sub-Industry Computer Hardware

Summary This company is one of the world's 10 leading manufacturers of personal computers. Dell also offers server and storage products and provides IT services.

Key Stock Statistics (Source S&P, Vickers, company reports)

52-Wk Range	$17.52–11.34	S&P Oper. EPS 2011E	1.29	Market Capitalization(B)	$28.364	Beta	1.36
Trailing 12-Month EPS	$0.79	S&P Oper. EPS 2012E	1.40	Yield (%)	Nil	S&P 3-Yr. Proj. EPS CAGR(%)	10
Trailing 12-Month P/E	18.5	P/E on S&P Oper. EPS 2011E	11.3	Dividend Rate/Share	Nil	S&P Credit Rating	A-
$10K Invested 5 Yrs Ago	$4,551	Common Shares Outstg. (M)	1,944.7	Institutional Ownership (%)	70		

Price Performance

30-Week Mov. Avg. · · · · 10-Week Mov. Avg. – – GAAP Earnings vs. Previous Year   Volume Above Avg. STARS
12-Mo. Target Price — Relative Strength — ▲ Up ▼ Down ► No Change   Below Avg.

2007   2008   2009   2010

Options: ASE, CBOE, P, Ph

Analysis prepared by **Thomas W. Smith, CFA** on September 22, 2010, when the stock traded at **$ 12.55**.

Highlights

▶ We project revenues will rise 18% in FY 11 (Jan.) and 5% in FY 12, reflecting a rebound in demand for computers, plus acquisitions. On August 16, 2010, the company agreed to acquire data storage technology provider 3PAR Inc. (PAR 33, NR) for an enterprise value of about $1.15 billion. However, rival Hewlett-Packard (HPQ 39, Buy) joined the bidding and prevailed with a price near $2.35 billion on September 2. Dell received a $72 million deal break-up payment from 3PAR, which should help offset expenses from the extended bargaining.

▶ We see potential for overall margin improvement in FY 11 and FY 12 as higher volumes, a richer product mix, and potential savings from improved supply chain management outweigh pressure on PC selling prices. On September 16, Dell announced plans to open a major manufacturing facility in Chengdu, in western China, and to expand existing operations in Xiamen, China.

▶ We estimate FY 11 operating EPS of $1.29, excluding restructuring and acquisition-related expenses. For FY 12, we estimate operating EPS of $1.40. Share buybacks should help per-share results.

Investment Rationale/Risk

▶ We believe that DELL's multi-year effort to move into new markets was enhanced with the addition of the Perot Systems service operations in November 2009. However, the bidding for storage provider 3PAR suggests to us that key acquisitions to expand in the data center area may prove expensive, or that prime targets might go to rivals, which would hinder DELL's growth strategies. While a cyclical rebound in PC unit demand that we project to continue into 2011 should aid margins ahead, we also see near-term headwinds from price competition in consumer PCs. Overall, we view the shares as overvalued, based on our P/E analysis.

▶ Risks to our recommendation and target price include the potential for stronger PC market share and margin performance than we project. Acquisitions might prove more affordable than we estimate.

▶ Applying a target multiple of 8X, a discount to Information Technology Sector peers in the S&P 500 Index and toward the low end of DELL's historical range, to our 12-month forward operating EPS estimate of $1.33, we arrive at our 12-month target price of $11.

Qualitative Risk Assessment

LOW	MEDIUM	HIGH

Our risk assessment reflects our view of Dell's economies of scale and strong execution in asset management, offset by what we see as competitive pressures on product design and pricing, industry cyclicality, and a shift to greater reliance on retail partners around the world.

Quantitative Evaluations

S&P Quality Ranking B+

D	C	B-	B	B+	A-	A	A+

Relative Strength Rank STRONG

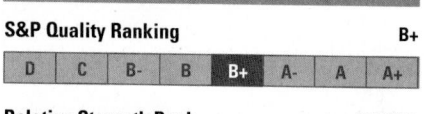

83

LOWEST = 1   HIGHEST = 99

Revenue/Earnings Data

Revenue (Million $)

	1Q	2Q	3Q	4Q	Year
2011	14,874	15,534	--	--	--
2010	12,342	12,764	12,896	14,900	52,902
2009	16,077	16,434	15,162	13,428	61,101
2008	14,722	14,776	15,646	15,989	61,133
2007	14,320	14,211	14,419	14,470	57,420
2006	13,386	13,428	13,911	15,183	55,908

Earnings Per Share ($)

2011	0.17	0.28	E0.32	E0.35	E1.29
2010	0.15	0.24	0.17	0.17	0.73
2009	0.38	0.31	0.37	0.18	1.25
2008	0.34	0.31	0.34	0.31	1.31
2007	0.34	0.21	0.27	0.32	1.14
2006	0.37	0.41	0.25	0.43	1.46

Fiscal year ended Jan. 31. Next earnings report expected: Mid November. EPS Estimates based on S&P Operating Earnings; historical GAAP earnings are as reported.

Dividend Data

No cash dividends have been paid.

Dell Inc

Business Summary September 22, 2010

CORPORATE OVERVIEW. Dell Inc. is a key player in the personal computer markets. It was number two in global PC unit shipments in 2009, with about a 13.1% market share according to IDC, up from 10.5% over the past decade, but below 2005's 18.2%. In 2009, DELL was number two by unit shipments in the U.S. market, with about a 24.5% market share.

The majority of DELL's sales are from PCs (56% of FY 10 (Jan.) total revenue), with 25% from Desktop PCs and 31% from Mobility. Other categories include Software and Peripherals (18%), Servers and Networking (11%), Services (11%), and Storage (4%). Within the PC category, sales of Mobility (mainly notebook PCs) are rising faster than sales of Desktop PCs. Revenue from notebooks pulled approximately even with desktop revenue for the first time in the FY 08 third quarter, and we expect notebooks to lead in the future.

Broken out by global segment, Large Enterprise represented 27% of DELL's FY 10 total revenue (30% in FY 09), Public 27% (25%), Small and Medium Business 23% (24%), and Consumer 23% (21%).

The customer base is broad, with no single customer accounting for 10% of sales in FY 10 or the prior two fiscal years. The company is expanding in rapid-growth emerging markets including Brazil, Russia, India and China (BRIC), and DELL's revenue from the BRIC countries rose 4% in FY 10 despite slow conditions in global computer hardware markets. Revenues derived from outside the U.S. represented 47% of total revenue in FY 10, near the 48% level in FY 09. About 70% of the company's long-lived assets were located in the U.S at the end of FY 10.

IMPACT OF MAJOR DEVELOPMENTS. In January 2007, Michael Dell reassumed his role as CEO, while retaining his duties as chairman of the board. We are encouraged by this development, as we think it will reinvigorate the corporate culture and streamline the decision-making process.

Company Financials Fiscal Year Ended Jan. 31

Per Share Data ($)	2010	2009	2008	2007	2006	2005	2004	2003	2002	2001
Tangible Book Value	NM	0.95	1.03	1.60	1.77	2.61	2.46	1.89	1.80	2.16
Cash Flow	1.16	1.64	1.58	1.34	1.62	1.32	1.11	0.88	0.54	0.90
Earnings	0.73	1.25	1.31	1.14	1.46	1.18	1.01	0.80	0.46	0.81
S&P Core Earnings	0.73	1.23	1.28	1.13	1.03	0.88	0.68	0.49	0.28	0.58
Dividends	NA	Nil	Nil	Nil	Nil	Nil	Nil	Nil	Nil	Nil
Payout Ratio	Nil	Nil	Nil	Nil	Nil	Nil	Nil	Nil	Nil	Nil
Calendar Year	2009	2008	2007	2006	2005	2004	2003	2002	2001	2000
Prices:High	17.26	26.04	30.77	30.77	42.30	42.57	37.18	31.06	31.32	59.69
Prices:Low	7.84	8.72	21.61	21.61	28.62	31.14	22.59	21.90	16.01	16.25
P/E Ratio:High	24	21	23	27	29	36	37	39	68	74
P/E Ratio:Low	11	7	16	19	20	26	22	27	35	20

Income Statement Analysis (Million $)										
Revenue	52,902	61,101	61,133	57,420	55,908	49,205	41,444	35,404	31,168	31,888
Operating Income	3,620	4,193	4,344	3,541	4,740	4,588	3,807	3,055	2,510	3,008
Depreciation	852	769	599	471	393	334	263	211	239	240
Interest Expense	160	93.0	45.0	45.0	28.0	16.0	14.0	17.0	29.0	47.0
Pretax Income	2,024	3,324	3,856	3,345	4,574	4,445	3,724	3,027	1,731	3,194
Effective Tax Rate	29.2%	25.5%	22.8%	22.8%	21.9%	31.5%	29.0%	29.9%	28.0%	30.0%
Net Income	1,433	2,478	2,947	2,583	3,572	3,043	2,645	2,122	1,246	2,236
S&P Core Earnings	1,432	2,445	2,871	2,563	2,494	2,227	1,806	1,356	781	1,602

Balance Sheet & Other Financial Data (Million $)										
Cash	11,008	9,092	7,972	9,546	7,042	4,747	4,317	4,232	3,641	4,910
Current Assets	24,245	20,151	19,880	19,939	17,706	16,897	10,633	8,924	7,877	9,491
Total Assets	33,652	26,500	27,561	25,635	23,109	23,215	19,311	15,470	13,535	13,435
Current Liabilities	18,960	14,859	18,526	17,791	15,927	14,136	10,896	8,933	7,519	6,543
Long Term Debt	3,417	1,898	362	569	504	505	505	506	520	509
Common Equity	5,641	4,271	3,735	4,328	4,129	6,485	6,280	4,873	4,694	5,622
Total Capital	9,058	6,169	4,191	5,008	4,633	6,990	6,785	5,379	5,214	6,131
Capital Expenditures	367	440	831	896	728	525	329	305	303	482
Cash Flow	2,285	3,247	3,546	3,054	3,965	3,377	2,908	2,333	1,485	2,476
Current Ratio	1.3	1.4	1.1	1.1	1.1	1.2	1.0	1.0	1.0	1.5
% Long Term Debt of Capitalization	37.7	30.8	8.6	11.4	10.9	7.2	7.4	9.4	10.0	8.3
% Net Income of Revenue	2.7	4.1	4.8	4.5	6.4	6.2	6.4	6.0	4.0	7.0
% Return on Assets	4.8	9.2	11.1	10.6	15.4	14.3	15.2	14.6	9.2	18.0
% Return on Equity	28.9	61.9	73.1	61.1	67.3	47.7	47.4	44.4	24.2	40.9

Data as orig reptd.; bef. results of disc opers/spec. items. Per share data adj. for stk. divs.; EPS diluted. E-Estimated. NA-Not Available. NM-Not Meaningful. NR-Not Ranked. UR-Under Review.

Office: One Dell Way, Round Rock, TX 78682.
Telephone: 512-338-4400.
Email: investor_relations_fulfillment@dell.com
Website: http://www.dell.com

Chrmn & CEO: M.S. Dell
COO & CTO: J.W. Clarke
SVP & CFO: B.T. Gladden
SVP, Secy & General Counsel: L.P. Tu

Chief Acctg Officer: T.W. Sweet
Investor Contact: L.A. Tyson (512-723-1130)
Board Members: J. W. Breyer, D. J. Carty, M. S. Dell, W. H. Gray, III, J. C. Lewent, T. W. Luce, III, K. S. Luft, A. J. Mandl, S. Narayen, S. A. Nunn, R. Perot, Jr.

Founded: 1984
Domicile: Delaware
Employees: 96,000

Denbury Resources Inc.

STANDARD &POOR'S

S&P Recommendation BUY ★★★★☆

Price $17.07 (as of Oct 22, 2010)	**12-Mo. Target Price** $21.00	**Investment Style** Large-Cap Growth

GICS Sector Energy
Sub-Industry Oil & Gas Exploration & Production

Summary This independent oil and gas company acquires, develops, exploits and produces oil and gas in the U.S., primarily in Mississippi and the Barnett Shale in Texas. DNR owns the largest reserves of CO2 used for tertiary oil recovery east of the Mississippi River.

Key Stock Statistics (Source S&P, Vickers, company reports)

52-Wk Range	$19.48– 12.51	S&P Oper. EPS 2010**E**	1.11	Market Capitalization(B)	$6.816	Beta	1.25
Trailing 12-Month EPS	$0.88	S&P Oper. EPS 2011**E**	0.76	Yield (%)	Nil	S&P 3-Yr. Proj. EPS CAGR(%)	-21
Trailing 12-Month P/E	19.4	P/E on S&P Oper. EPS 2010**E**	15.4	Dividend Rate/Share	Nil	S&P Credit Rating	BB
$10K Invested 5 Yrs Ago	$17,304	Common Shares Outstg. (M)	399.3	Institutional Ownership (%)	96		

Price Performance

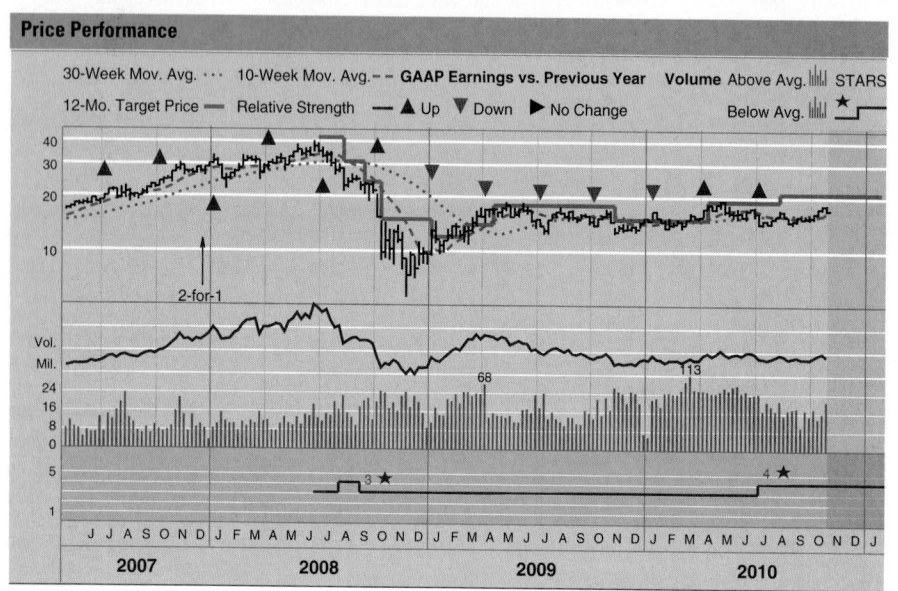

30-Week Mov. Avg. · · · 10-Week Mov. Avg. - - ▬ GAAP Earnings vs. Previous Year   Volume Above Avg. ▮▮▮ STARS
12-Mo. Target Price ▬ Relative Strength ▬ ▲ Up ▼ Down ► No Change   Below Avg. ▮▮▮ ★

Options: ASE, CBOE, P, Ph

Analysis prepared by **Michael Kay** on August 16, 2010, when the stock traded at **$ 15.47**.

Highlights

➤ DNR has ramped up activity at Bakken Shale, where it holds about 300,000 net acres. DNR is shifting capex from the gas-rich Haynesville Shale to the oilier Bakken play, where it will run 4 rigs in the second half of 2010. With DNR's completion of the acquisition of Encore Acquisition Company (EAC) and $900 million in non-core asset sales, we see remaining 2010 production averaging 70.8 MBOE/day, up 36%. We see a 14% production boost in 2011 and DNR sees a 10%-20% production CAGR at tertiary fields through 2015 on existing project inventory. DNR has repositioned its portfolio, and we expect a focus on execution going forward.

➤ DNR will drill 25-35 operated wells at Bakken in 2010, will ramp to 5 rigs in early 2011, and is currently producing 4,518 BOE/day. DNR sees a total resource potential of 350 MMBOE on its acreage. DNR has set 2010's capex at $1.06 billion, above cash flow forecasts, with 39% slated for tertiary floods and 19% for Bakken.

➤ DNR posted a 2009 loss per share of $0.25 ($0.94 non-cash charge). We see EPS of $1.11 ($0.20 asset sale gain and $0.39 non-cash gain) in 2010 and $0.76 in 2011 on production and price gains.

Investment Rationale/Risk

➤ In March, DNR closed its acquisition of EAC for $4.5 billion, including $1.6 billion in debt, $830 in cash, and the issuance of about 134 million new shares. The acquisition more than doubles DNR's production and reserve base and adds a new core region in the Rockies. EAC's enhanced recovery program in the Rockies should complement DNR's Gulf Coast tertiary operations, and we view positively its entry into the Bakken Shale and acquired acreage in Haynesville Shale. We expect DNR to use $900 million in Permian Basin asset sale proceeds to cover a capex shortfall and pay debt. DNR plans to sell its general partner interest in Encore Energy Partners LP (ENP), purchased in the EAC acquisition.

➤ Risks to our opinion and target price include a sustained decline in oil and gas prices, and inability to replace reserves at a reasonable cost.

➤ Our 12-month target price of $21 blends a ratio of 8.5X enterprise value to 2011 EBITDA forecasts, our proved NAV projection of $27 and above-peer metrics on significant tertiary oil potential, a strong Bakken Shale position, and complementary Haynesville acreage.

Qualitative Risk Assessment

LOW	MEDIUM	HIGH

Our risk assessment reflects the company's operations in a capital-intensive industry that derives value from producing commodities whose price is very volatile.

Quantitative Evaluations

S&P Quality Ranking   B

D	C	B-	B	B+	A-	A	A+

Relative Strength Rank   MODERATE

59

LOWEST = 1   HIGHEST = 99

Revenue/Earnings Data

Revenue (Million $)

	1Q	2Q	3Q	4Q	Year
2010	335.4	492.7	--	--	--
2009	171.2	214.4	225.0	269.5	880.1
2008	317.3	416.6	405.6	222.6	1,361
2007	174.2	222.5	253.5	321.8	972.0
2006	178.9	193.3	192.0	167.3	731.5
2005	113.4	128.0	141.9	177.2	560.4

Earnings Per Share ($)

2010	0.32	0.34	E0.12	E0.16	E1.11
2009	-0.07	-0.35	0.11	0.01	-0.30
2008	0.29	0.45	0.63	0.18	1.54
2007	0.07	0.25	0.27	0.42	1.00
2006	0.19	0.18	0.24	0.23	0.82
2005	0.13	0.17	0.16	0.24	0.70

Fiscal year ended Dec. 31. Next earnings report expected: Early November. EPS Estimates based on S&P Operating Earnings; historical GAAP earnings are as reported.

Dividend Data

No cash dividends have been paid.

Please read the Required Disclosures and Analyst Certification on the last page of this report.

The McGraw-Hill Companies

Denbury Resources Inc.

STANDARD &POOR'S

Business Summary August 16, 2010

CORPORATE OVERVIEW. Denbury Resources, Inc. (DNR) engages in the acquisition, development, operation and exploitation of oil and natural gas properties in the Gulf Coast region of the U.S., primarily in Louisiana, Mississippi, Alabama and Texas, and the Rocky Mountains. DNR is the largest oil and natural gas operator in Mississippi and also owns the rights to a natural source of carbon dioxide (CO_2) reserves that it uses for injection in its tertiary oil recovery operations. In March 2010, DNR acquired Encore Acquisition Company (EAC) for $4.5 billion, including $1.6 billion in debt, $830 in cash and the issuance of about 134 million new shares.

With the completion of the EAC acquisition, DNR has more than doubled its proved reserve base. As of December 31, 2009, DNR had estimated proved reserves (including tertiary-related reserves) of 428 MMBOE. This compares to estimated proved reserves of 250.5 MMBOE, of which 71% consisted of crude oil and 58% was proved developed, at year-end 2008.

CORPORATE STRATEGY. After a year of repositioning its portfolio in 2009, with the acquisition of Encore, the purchase of two additional enhanced oil recovery fields (Conroe and Hastings) and the sale of 100% of its Barnett Shale assets, DNR is now positioned to execute on its plan of tertiary oil growth, in our view. DNR added a new core area with EAC's enhanced oil recovery projects in the Rockies, where it sees significant similarities to its own fields, and now

has one of the largest positions in the prolific Bakken Oil Shale and added acreage at Haynesville Shale, one of the hottest onshore domestic reservoirs. DNR sees a 10%-20% production compound annual growth rate (CAGR) on tertiary flood fields through 2015. For 2010, DNR sees tertiary oil production of 27,000 bbls/day. Also, the company has issued pro-forma production guidance of around 76.7 MBOE/day for 2010, on a capital budget of $1.06 billion. DNR expects to sell about 8.5 MBOE/day in production from its interest in Encore Energy Partners LP (ENP).

DNR has invested over $2 billion in the last two years to expand its CO_2 pipeline network from Louisiana to Texas and to implement and expand additional tertiary floods, as part of its strategic plan. If oil prices remain at their current levels, DNR believes most of this can be funded with internally generated cash flow, but if needed, it can tap into other resources. DNR's biggest project during this period will be the construction of the $700 million Green Pipeline, a CO_2 pipeline that was completed around year-end 2009. DNR believes this project will create the backbone for a CO_2 gathering and distribution system in the southern Gulf Coast region.

Company Financials Fiscal Year Ended Dec. 31

Per Share Data ($)	2009	2008	2007	2006	2005	2004	2003	2002	2001	2000
Tangible Book Value	6.89	7.50	5.75	4.61	3.20	2.40	1.94	1.71	1.65	1.17
Cash Flow	0.66	2.42	1.77	1.42	1.11	0.79	0.67	0.65	0.63	0.96
Earnings	-0.30	1.54	1.00	0.82	0.70	0.36	0.24	0.22	0.28	0.77
S&P Core Earnings	-0.30	1.54	1.00	0.82	0.68	0.35	0.23	0.21	0.27	NA
Dividends	Nil	Nil	Nil	Nil	Nil	Nil	Nil	Nil	Nil	Nil
Payout Ratio	Nil	Nil	Nil	Nil	Nil	Nil	Nil	Nil	Nil	Nil
Prices:High	18.84	40.32	30.56	18.30	12.86	7.33	3.56	2.99	3.08	2.88
Prices:Low	9.61	5.59	12.98	11.79	6.18	3.32	2.55	1.55	1.46	0.91
P/E Ratio:High	NM	26	31	22	18	20	15	14	11	4
P/E Ratio:Low	NM	4	13	14	9	9	10	7	5	1

Income Statement Analysis (Million $)										
Revenue	880	1,361	972	732	560	383	333	285	266	179
Operating Income	NA	699	636	482	393	254	276	190	156	124
Depreciation, Depletion and Amortization	238	222	193	149	98.8	97.5	94.7	94.2	71.3	36.2
Interest Expense	47.4	32.6	51.2	23.6	18.0	19.5	23.2	26.8	22.3	15.3
Pretax Income	-122	624	393	330	248	122	80.2	70.3	81.4	74.9
Effective Tax Rate	38.5%	37.8%	35.7%	38.6%	32.9%	32.3%	32.7%	33.4%	30.5%	NM
Net Income	-75.2	388	253	202	166	82.4	53.9	46.8	56.6	142
S&P Core Earnings	-75.2	388	253	202	161	79.7	49.8	43.9	53.8	NA

Balance Sheet & Other Financial Data (Million $)										
Cash	20.6	17.1	60.1	53.9	165	33.0	24.2	23.9	23.5	22.3
Current Assets	256	415	240	183	299	173	108	128	103	98.0
Total Assets	4,270	3,590	2,771	2,140	1,505	993	983	895	790	457
Current Liabilities	394	386	265	200	154	82.9	127	95.9	79.9	38.8
Long Term Debt	1,301	853	675	514	379	0.23	298	345	335	199
Common Equity	1,972	1,840	1,404	1,106	734	542	421	374	353	216
Total Capital	3,279	3,126	2,432	1,856	1,284	639	788	790	707	415
Capital Expenditures	1,463	1,086	834	826	379	178	147	156	172	75.4
Cash Flow	163	610	446	352	265	180	149	141	128	178
Current Ratio	0.7	1.1	0.9	0.9	1.9	2.1	0.9	1.3	1.3	2.5
% Long Term Debt of Capitalization	Nil	27.3	32.6	27.7	29.6	0.0	37.8	43.6	47.4	47.9
% Return on Assets	NM	12.2	10.3	11.1	13.3	8.3	5.7	5.6	9.1	40.1
% Return on Equity	NA	23.9	20.2	22.0	26.1	17.1	13.7	12.9	19.8	98.6

Data as orig reptd.; bef. results of disc opers/spec. items. Per share data adj. for stk. divs.; EPS diluted. E-Estimated. NA-Not Available. NM-Not Meaningful. NR-Not Ranked. UR-Under Review.

Office: 5100 Tennyson Pkwy Ste 1200, Plano, TX 75024-7164.
Telephone: 972-673-2000.
Website: http://www.denbury.com
Co-Chrmn: W.F. Wettstein

Co-Chrmn: G. Roberts
Pres & COO: R.T. Evans
CEO: P. Rykhoek
SVP, CFO & Treas: M.C. Allen

Investor Contact: L. Burkes (972-673-2166)
Board Members: M. L. Beatty, M. B. Decker, R. G. Greene, D. I. Heather, G. L. McMichael, G. Roberts, R. Stein, W. F. Wettstein

Founded: 1951
Domicile: Delaware
Employees: 830

DENTSPLY International Inc

STANDARD &POOR'S

S&P Recommendation HOLD ★★★☆☆

Price	**12-Mo. Target Price**	**Investment Style**
$32.63 (as of Oct 22, 2010)	$34.00	Large-Cap Growth

GICS Sector Health Care
Sub-Industry Health Care Supplies

Summary This company is a designer, developer, manufacturer and marketer of a broad range of products for the dental market.

Key Stock Statistics (Source S&P, Vickers, company reports)

52-Wk Range	$38.15–27.76	S&P Oper. EPS 2010E	1.91	Market Capitalization(B)	$4.660	Beta	1.01
Trailing 12-Month EPS	$1.85	S&P Oper. EPS 2011E	2.10	Yield (%)	0.61	S&P 3-Yr. Proj. EPS CAGR(%)	9
Trailing 12-Month P/E	17.6	P/E on S&P Oper. EPS 2010E	17.1	Dividend Rate/Share	$0.20	S&P Credit Rating	NA
$10K Invested 5 Yrs Ago	$12,972	Common Shares Outstg. (M)	142.8	Institutional Ownership (%)	86		

Price Performance

30-Week Mov. Avg. · · · · 10-Week Mov. Avg. – – – **GAAP Earnings vs. Previous Year** Volume Above Avg. STARS
12-Mo. Target Price — Relative Strength — ▲ Up ▼ Down ▶ No Change Below Avg.

Options: CBOE, P, Ph

Analysis prepared by **Phillip M. Seligman** on August 06, 2010, when the stock traded at **$ 31.01**.

Highlights

▶ We forecast 2010 net sales, excluding precious metal content, rising about 3% from 2009's $2.0 billion. One driver we see is easy comparisons, since performance in 2009 was hurt by U.S. economic softness, channel destocking and softer European dental markets. Other revenue enhancers include improved growth in international markets, relative strength in the consumable lines and specialty products, acquisitions, and new product. However, we see a stronger U.S. dollar tempering reported results.

▶ We expect gross margins to be flat with 2009 levels, assuming the unfavorable product mix that pressured first-half margins is offset by better fixed cost absorption, higher pricing and an improved product mix in the second half. We expect SG&A costs to expand by 10 basis points as a percentage of sales, despite cost improvements, on the company's plans to invest in key growth opportunities.

▶ We estimate operating EPS of $1.91 in 2010, versus 2009's $1.84 before $0.01 of net one-time costs. We project $2.10 in 2011.

Investment Rationale/Risk

▶ We are encouraged by XRAY's view of signs of improvement in certain geographies and product categories, such as chairside consumables, dental implants and orthodontics. But the company also cited areas of continued weakness, such as the overall U.S. market, where it has been realizing negative comparisons due to equipment promotions in 2009, and the lab market, which we think should eventually improve as a result of pent-up demand from the recession. Nonetheless, long-term fundamentals of the dental products business look favorable to us, given aging populations in developed countries and rising standards of living in developing countries. Meanwhile, we view cash flow as healthy, providing financial flexibility.

▶ Risks to our recommendation and target price include intensified competition and persistent weakness in dental care in the U.S. and Europe.

▶ Applying a multiple of 18X to our 2010 EPS estimate, a discount to XRAY's historical mid-point, given recent groupwide valuation compression, we derive our 12-month target price of $34.

Qualitative Risk Assessment

LOW	MEDIUM	HIGH

Our risk assessment reflects XRAY's long-term trend of relative earnings stability and its broad product and geographic diversification, which we believe limits the impact of competition. We also believe XRAY's relatively low long-term debt to capitalization ratio provides some degree of protection from financial difficulties.

Quantitative Evaluations

S&P Quality Ranking A-

D	C	B-	B	B+	A-	A	A+

Relative Strength Rank MODERATE

61

LOWEST = 1   HIGHEST = 99

Revenue/Earnings Data

Revenue (Million $)

	1Q	2Q	3Q	4Q	Year
2010	545.9	565.1	--	--	--
2009	507.0	553.2	531.0	568.7	2,160
2008	560.8	594.9	530.0	508.1	2,194
2007	472.9	507.4	488.1	541.5	2,010
2006	431.0	472.4	435.7	471.3	1,811
2005	407.0	444.8	416.0	447.4	1,715

Earnings Per Share ($)

	1Q	2Q	3Q	4Q	Year
2010	0.41	0.49	E0.46	E0.51	E1.91
2009	0.41	0.47	0.45	0.50	1.83
2008	0.45	0.52	0.44	0.47	1.87
2007	0.38	0.42	0.42	0.45	1.68
2006	0.31	0.37	0.31	0.42	1.41
2005	0.30	0.36	-0.39	Nil	0.28

Fiscal year ended Dec. 31. Next earnings report expected: Late October. EPS Estimates based on S&P Operating Earnings; historical GAAP earnings are as reported.

Dividend Data (Dates: mm/dd Payment Date: mm/dd/yy)

Amount ($)	Date Decl.	Ex-Div. Date	Stk. of Record	Payment Date
0.050	02/10	03/24	03/26	04/06/10
0.050	05/11	06/23	06/25	07/08/10
0.050	07/28	09/27	09/29	10/07/10
0.050	09/30	12/27	12/29	01/07/11

Dividends have been paid since 1994. Source: Company reports.

Please read the Required Disclosures and Analyst Certification on the last page of this report.

The **McGraw·Hill** Companies

DENTSPLY International Inc

STANDARD &POOR'S

Business Summary August 06, 2010

CORPORATE OVERVIEW. Dentsply International, Inc. (XRAY) was created by a merger of a predecessor Dentsply International Inc. and Gendex Corp. in 1993. The predecessor Dentsply, founded in 1899, manufactured and distributed artificial teeth, dental equipment and dental consumable products. Gendex, founded in 1983, manufactured dental x-ray equipment and handpieces. In early 2004, the company divested the dental X-ray equipment business. Dentsply believes it is the world's largest developer and manufacturer of a broad range of products for the dental market.

Dental consumables (35% of net sales in 2009 and 34% in 2008, excluding precious metal content) include dental sundries, such as dental anesthetics, prophylaxis paste, dental sealants, impression materials, restorative materials, bone grafting materials, tooth whiteners, and topical fluoride; and small equipment products, such as high and low speed handpieces, intraoral curing light systems, dental diagnostic systems, and ultrasonic scalers and polishers.

Dental laboratory products (17%; 18%) are used in dental laboratories in the preparation of dental appliances. Products include dental prosthetics, including artificial teeth, precious metal dental alloys, dental ceramics, crown and bridge materials, computer aided machining (CAM) ceramics systems, and porcelain furnaces.

Dental specialty products (45%; 45%) include specialized treatment products, such as endodontic (root canal) instruments and materials, implants and related products, bone grafting materials, and orthodontic appliances and accessories.

In addition to the U.S., Dentsply conducts its business in over 120 foreign countries, principally through its foreign subsidiaries. In 2009 and 2008, net sales, excluding precious metal content, to customers outside the U.S., including export sales, accounted for approximately 62% and 62%, respectively, of net sales.

During 2009 and 2008, one customer, Henry Schein Incorporated, a dental distributor, accounted for 11% and 11%, respectively, of the company's net sales.

Company Financials Fiscal Year Ended Dec. 31

Per Share Data ($)	2009	2008	2007	2006	2005	2004	2003	2002	2001	2000
Tangible Book Value	2.93	1.39	2.07	1.39	1.52	1.17	NM	NM	NM	1.13
Cash Flow	2.26	2.25	2.00	1.71	0.59	1.58	1.34	1.20	1.11	0.91
Earnings	1.83	1.87	1.67	1.41	0.28	1.28	1.05	0.93	0.77	0.64
S&P Core Earnings	1.84	1.92	1.72	1.41	0.20	1.21	0.95	0.84	0.60	NA
Dividends	0.20	0.19	0.17	0.15	0.13	0.11	0.10	0.09	0.09	0.09
Payout Ratio	11%	10%	10%	10%	45%	8%	9%	10%	12%	13%
Prices:High	36.80	47.06	47.84	33.76	29.22	28.42	23.70	21.75	17.34	14.46
Prices:Low	21.80	22.85	29.44	26.07	25.37	20.88	16.05	15.63	10.83	7.71
P/E Ratio:High	20	25	29	24	NM	22	22	24	23	22
P/E Ratio:Low	12	12	18	18	NM	16	15	17	14	12

Income Statement Analysis (Million $)	2009	2008	2007	2006	2005	2004	2003	2002	2001	2000
Revenue	2,160	2,194	2,010	1,810	1,715	1,694	1,571	1,514	1,129	890
Operating Income	453	469	416	370	356	352	317	298	238	205
Depreciation	65.2	56.6	50.3	47.4	50.6	49.3	45.7	43.9	54.3	41.4
Interest Expense	21.9	32.5	23.8	10.8	17.8	25.1	26.1	29.2	21.7	10.2
Pretax Income	363	355	358	315	71.0	274	251	221	185	152
Effective Tax Rate	24.5%	20.1%	27.5%	28.9%	36.1%	23.3%	32.4%	33.0%	34.4%	33.5%
Net Income	274	284	260	224	45.4	210	170	148	121	101
S&P Core Earnings	276	292	265	223	32.0	198	153	134	94.6	NA

Balance Sheet & Other Financial Data (Million $)	2009	2008	2007	2006	2005	2004	2003	2002	2001	2000
Cash	450	204	169	65.1	435	506	164	25.7	33.7	15.4
Current Assets	1,218	950	982	718	1,030	1,056	727	541	484	325
Total Assets	3,088	2,830	2,676	2,181	2,407	2,798	2,446	2,087	1,798	867
Current Liabilities	445	360	312	311	741	405	338	366	359	168
Long Term Debt	387	424	482	367	270	780	790	770	724	110
Common Equity	1,832	1,588	1,516	1,274	1,242	1,444	1,122	836	610	520
Total Capital	2,294	2,152	2,060	1,694	1,555	2,283	1,964	1,634	1,366	651
Capital Expenditures	56.5	76.4	64.2	50.6	45.3	56.3	76.6	3.31	49.3	28.4
Cash Flow	339	340	310	271	96.0	260	216	192	176	142
Current Ratio	2.7	2.6	3.1	2.3	1.4	2.6	2.2	1.5	1.4	1.9
% Long Term Debt of Capitalization	16.9	19.7	23.4	21.7	17.4	34.2	40.2	47.1	53.0	16.8
% Net Income of Revenue	12.7	12.9	12.9	12.4	2.6	12.4	10.8	9.8	10.8	11.4
% Return on Assets	9.3	10.3	10.7	9.7	1.7	8.0	7.5	7.6	9.1	11.7
% Return on Equity	16.0	18.3	18.6	17.8	3.4	16.4	17.3	20.5	21.5	20.4

Data as orig reptd.; bef. results of disc opers/spec. items. Per share data adj. for stk. divs.; EPS diluted. E-Estimated. NA-Not Available. NM-Not Meaningful. NR-Not Ranked. UR-Under Review.

Office: 221 W Philadelphia St, York, PA, USA 17405-0872.
Telephone: 717-845-7511.
Email: investor@dentsply.com
Website: http://www.dentsply.com

Chrmn & CEO: B.W. Wise
Pres & COO: C.T. Clark
Investor Contact: W.R. Jellison (717-849-4243)
SVP, CFO & Chief Acctg Officer: W.R. Jellison

CTO: S.R. Jeffries
Board Members: M. C. Alfano, E. K. Brandt, P. H. Cholmondeley, M. Coleman, W. F. Hecht, L. A. Jones, F. J. Lunger, J. L. Miclot, J. C. Miles, II, B. W. Wise

Founded: 1983
Domicile: Delaware
Employees: 9,300

The McGraw-Hill Companies

Devon Energy Corp

STANDARD &POOR'S

S&P Recommendation	BUY ★★★★☆	Price $65.23 (as of Oct 22, 2010)	12-Mo. Target Price $76.00	Investment Style Large-Cap Blend

GICS Sector Energy
Sub-Industry Oil & Gas Exploration & Production

Summary Devon Energy is one of the largest independent oil and gas exploration and production companies in the U.S.

Key Stock Statistics (Source S&P, Vickers, company reports)

52-Wk Range	$76.79–58.58	S&P Oper. EPS 2010**E**	6.18	Market Capitalization(B)	$28.375	Beta	1.07
Trailing 12-Month EPS	$6.89	S&P Oper. EPS 2011**E**	6.02	Yield (%)	0.98	S&P 3-Yr. Proj. EPS CAGR(%)	-14
Trailing 12-Month P/E	9.5	P/E on S&P Oper. EPS 2010**E**	10.6	Dividend Rate/Share	$0.64	S&P Credit Rating	BBB+
$10K Invested 5 Yrs Ago	$11,691	Common Shares Outstg. (M)	435.0	Institutional Ownership (%)	78		

Price Performance

30-Week Mov. Avg. ··· 10-Week Mov. Avg. – – GAAP Earnings vs. Previous Year Volume Above Avg. STARS
12-Mo. Target Price — Relative Strength ▲ Up ▼ Down ▶ No Change Below Avg. ★

Options: ASE, CBOE, P

Analysis prepared by **Michael Kay** on October 08, 2010, when the stock traded at **$66.69**.

Highlights

➤ In late 2009, DVN began to reposition itself as a pure-play onshore E&P entity. Production growth is expected at Barnett Shale, where DVN is the largest producer, the Cana-Woodford Shale, and Jackfish Canadian oil sands, partly offsetting natural gas declines elsewhere from asset sales. DVN will spend $2.3-$2.5 billion on shale plays in 2010, and $588-$636 million on oil sands. We forecast a 4% production decline in 2010, on divestitures, but see 7%-9% growth through 2014. DVN sees 8% growth from onshore in 2010. In 2010, DVN plans to drill 425 wells at Barnett, 115 at Washakie in Wyoming, 85 at Woodford Shale, 100 at Cana-Woodford Shale, and 100 at Wolf-berry in the Permian Basin.

➤ After asset sales, DVN will focus 83%, or over $4 billion, of capex on liquids-rich activity. DVN has added rigs at the liquids-rich Wolfberry field and several prospects in the Rockies.

➤ On higher prices, we see EPS of $6.18 in 2010 (with $0.41 non-cash gain in first half), and $6.02 in 2011, up from $3.89 in 2009. DVN sees 2010 capex of $4.9-$5.3 billion for 2010, up from $3.3 billion in 2009. In May, DVN announced a $3.5 billion share repurchase program.

Investment Rationale/Risk

➤ DVN has sold close to $10 billion in assets from the deepwater GOM, the GOM shelf, Brazil, and Azerbaijan (pending close), and we expect af-ter-tax proceeds near $8 billion. Remaining as-set sales are expected by year end at other mi-nor properties. Proceeds are expected to fund onshore drilling, buyback shares, and reduce debt. Through 2011, DVN plans to spend $2.1 billion of proceeds on onshore projects. Also, DVN recently formed a JV with BP plc in the Kirby Oil Sands adjacent to its Jackfish project. DVN is adding acreage at Kirby, Cana-Woodford, and Permian Basin. We view DVN's repositioning as a high-growth onshore E&P company positively and believe its stock price does not reflect its growth potential.

➤ Risks to our opinion and target price include negative changes in economic, industry, and operating conditions.

➤ At 11X our 2011 EPS estimate and 4.6X EV to 2011 EBITDA, DVN trades at a discount to large-cap E&P peers and our $76 proved re-serve NAV estimate, which, blended with rela-tive metrics, gives us a 12-month target price of $76. With limited debt and no liquidity concerns, we see upside potential at current levels.

Qualitative Risk Assessment

LOW	MEDIUM	HIGH

Our risk assessment reflects our view of its position as a large independent exploration and production company in a highly capital-intensive industry that derives value from producing crude oil and natural gas -- commodities with very volatile prices.

Quantitative Evaluations

S&P Quality Ranking   B

D	C	B-	B	B+	A-	A	A+

Relative Strength Rank   MODERATE

39

LOWEST = 1   HIGHEST = 99

Revenue/Earnings Data

Revenue (Million $)

	1Q	2Q	3Q	4Q	Year
2010	2,600	2,232	--	--	--
2009	1,900	1,822	2,098	2,251	8,015
2008	3,763	4,763	4,386	2,453	15,365
2007	2,473	2,929	2,763	3,197	11,362
2006	2,684	2,589	2,696	2,609	10,578
2005	2,351	2,468	2,704	3,218	10,741

Earnings Per Share ($)

2010	2.40	0.79	E1.26	E1.34	E6.18
2009	-8.74	0.42	0.86	1.25	-6.20
2008	1.45	1.31	5.63	-15.46	-6.95
2007	1.27	1.82	1.43	2.45	6.97
2006	1.56	1.92	1.57	1.26	6.29
2005	1.14	1.38	1.63	2.14	6.26

Fiscal year ended Dec. 31. Next earnings report expected: Early November. EPS Estimates based on S&P Operating Earnings; historical GAAP earnings are as reported.

Dividend Data (Dates: mm/dd Payment Date: mm/dd/yy)

Amount ($)	Date Decl.	Ex-Div. Date	Stk. of Record	Payment Date
0.160	12/02	03/11	03/15	03/31/10
0.160	03/03	06/11	06/15	06/30/10
0.160	06/09	09/13	09/15	09/30/10
0.160	09/14	12/13	12/15	12/31/10

Dividends have been paid since 1993. Source: Company reports.

Please read the Required Disclosures and Analyst Certification on the last page of this report.

The **McGraw·Hill** Companies

Devon Energy Corp

STANDARD &POOR'S

Business Summary October 08, 2010

CORPORATE OVERVIEW. Devon Energy Corp. (DVN) is an independent exploration and production company primarily engaged in the exploration, development and production of oil and natural gas; the acquisition of producing properties; the transportation of oil, natural gas and natural gas liquids (NGLs); and the processing of natural gas.

DVN's operations are focused in the U.S. and Canada. So far in 2010, DVN has entered into transactions to sell over $9 billion in assets, mainly in the GOM, Brazil and Azerbaijan, transforming the company into a pure-play onshore North American E&P company. After recent asset dispositions, U.S. activities are concentrated in four regions: the Mid-Continent, the Permian Basin, the Rocky Mountains, and onshore areas of the Gulf Coast. Canadian operations are located in the provinces of Alberta, British Columbia and Saskatchewan. DVN also has marketing and midstream operations that perform various activities to support its oil and gas operations.

CORPORATE STRATEGY. DVN recently raised it 2010 capex budget to between $4.9-$5.3 billion, up from $4.4-$4.8 billion, for North American onshore properties, which will be the main focus once asset sales are completed. DVN will

spend 47% of its budget on shale plays, 12% on oil sands, 23% on conventional plays and 18% on other unconventional plays. The budget reflects the recently formed $500 million Kirby oil sands joint venture.

The Barnett Shale, among the largest onshore natural gas fields in North America, is DVN's most important asset, and DVN is the largest producer there with over 1 Bcfe/day. In Johnson County, Barnett's core, DVN holds 119,000 net acres. In 2010, DVN plans to drill 425 wells in Barnett, up from 336 in 2009. DVN estimates it holds a resource potential of 18 Tcfe in Barnett. In the Cana-Woodford Shale in Oklahoma, DVN holds a net acreage position of 118,000. DVN plans to drill 100 wells at the play in 2010, up from 41 last year. DVN estimates it holds a resource potential of 7 Tcfe in Cana-Woodford. At the Haynesville Shale, DVN holds about 110,000 net acres and plans to drill 25 wells in 2010, up from nine wells in 2009. DVN believes it holds a resource potential of 7 Tcfe in Haynesville.

Company Financials Fiscal Year Ended Dec. 31

Per Share Data ($)	2009	2008	2007	2006	2005	2004	2003	2002	2001	2000
Tangible Book Value	21.58	NA	35.31	26.09	20.31	16.30	11.50	3.20	4.32	11.03
Cash Flow	13.13	1.15	13.32	11.73	10.87	8.95	8.10	4.04	3.54	5.37
Earnings	-6.20	-6.95	6.97	6.29	6.26	4.38	4.00	0.16	0.17	2.75
S&P Core Earnings	-6.09	-7.24	6.99	6.29	6.01	4.30	3.99	0.47	0.09	NA
Dividends	0.64	NA	0.56	0.45	0.30	0.20	0.10	0.10	0.10	0.10
Payout Ratio	NM	NA	8%	7%	5%	5%	3%	63%	59%	4%
Prices:High	75.05	NA	94.75	74.75	70.35	41.64	29.40	26.55	33.38	32.37
Prices:Low	38.55	NA	62.80	48.94	36.48	25.90	21.23	16.94	15.28	15.69
P/E Ratio:High	NM	NA	14	12	11	10	7	NM	NM	12
P/E Ratio:Low	NM	NA	9	8	6	6	5	NM	NM	6

Income Statement Analysis (Million $)										
Revenue	7,631	15,365	11,362	10,578	10,741	9,189	7,352	4,316	3,075	2,784
Operating Income	NA	-153	7,380	6,938	7,290	6,038	4,589	2,403	2,350	2,094
Depreciation, Depletion and Amortization	8,516	3,595	2,858	2,442	2,191	2,290	1,793	1,211	876	693
Interest Expense	349	329	532	421	533	475	504	533	220	154
Pretax Income	-4,526	-4,033	4,224	4,012	4,552	3,293	2,245	-134	84.0	1,142
Effective Tax Rate	39.2%	23.7%	25.5%	29.6%	35.6%	33.6%	22.9%	NM	35.7%	36.0%
Net Income	-2,753	-3,079	3,146	2,823	2,930	2,186	1,731	59.0	54.0	730
S&P Core Earnings	-2,671	-3,210	3,144	2,815	2,801	2,136	1,715	147	22.9	NA

Balance Sheet & Other Financial Data (Million $)										
Cash	646	379	1,736	739	1,606	2,119	1,273	292	193	228
Current Assets	2,992	2,684	3,914	3,212	4,206	3,583	2,364	1,064	1,081	934
Total Assets	29,686	31,908	41,456	35,063	30,273	29,736	27,162	16,225	13,184	6,860
Current Liabilities	3,802	3,135	3,657	4,645	2,934	3,100	2,071	1,042	919	629
Long Term Debt	5,847	5,661	7,928	5,568	5,957	7,031	8,635	7,562	6,589	2,049
Common Equity	15,570	17,060	22,005	17,441	14,999	13,673	11,055	4,652	3,258	3,276
Total Capital	22,849	26,400	34,972	28,660	26,362	25,505	24,061	14,842	11,990	5,953
Capital Expenditures	4,879	9,375	6,158	7,551	4,090	3,103	2,587	3,426	5,326	1,280
Cash Flow	5,763	511	5,994	5,255	5,111	4,466	3,514	1,260	920	1,414
Current Ratio	0.8	0.9	1.1	0.7	1.4	1.2	1.1	1.0	1.2	1.5
% Long Term Debt of Capitalization	25.6	21.4	23.9	19.4	22.6	27.6	35.9	51.0	55.0	34.4
% Return on Assets	NM	NM	8.2	8.6	9.7	7.7	8.0	NM	0.5	11.3
% Return on Equity	NM	NM	15.9	17.4	20.3	17.6	21.9	NM	1.3	24.9

Data as orig reptd.; bef. results of disc opers/spec. items. Per share data adj. for stk. divs.; EPS diluted. E-Estimated. NA-Not Available. NM-Not Meaningful. NR-Not Ranked. UR-Under Review.

Office: 20 N Broadway, Oklahoma City, OK 73102-8260.
Telephone: 405-235-3611.
Website: http://www.devonenergy.com
Chrmn: J.L. Nichols

Pres & CEO: J. Richels
EVP & CFO: J.A. Agosta
EVP & General Counsel: L.C. Taylor
SVP & Chief Acctg Officer: D.J. Heatly

Investor Contact: V. White (405-552-4526)
Board Members: R. H. Henry, J. A. Hill, M. Kanovsky, J. T. Mitchell, R. A. Mosbacher, Jr., J. L. Nichols, D. C. Radtke, M. P. Ricciardello, J. Richels

Founded: 1988
Domicile: Delaware
Employees: 5,400

DeVry Inc

STANDARD &POOR'S

S&P Recommendation HOLD ★★★★☆

Price	**12-Mo. Target Price**	**Investment Style**
$45.15 (as of Oct 22, 2010)	$50.00	Large-Cap Growth

GICS Sector Consumer Discretionary
Sub-Industry Education Services

Summary DeVry offers career-oriented degree programs, preparatory coursework for the CPA and CFA exams, and medical, veterinary, and nursing education.

Key Stock Statistics (Source S&P, Vickers, company reports)

52-Wk Range	$74.36–36.34	S&P Oper. EPS 2011E	4.40	Market Capitalization(B)	$3.194	Beta	0.39
Trailing 12-Month EPS	$3.87	S&P Oper. EPS 2012E	4.95	Yield (%)	0.44	S&P 3-Yr. Proj. EPS CAGR(%)	12
Trailing 12-Month P/E	11.7	P/E on S&P Oper. EPS 2011E	10.3	Dividend Rate/Share	$0.20	S&P Credit Rating	NA
$10K Invested 5 Yrs Ago	$22,128	Common Shares Outstg. (M)	70.7	Institutional Ownership (%)	85		

Price Performance

30-Week Mov. Avg. · · · · 10-Week Mov. Avg. – – GAAP Earnings vs. Previous Year   Volume Above Avg. STARS
12-Mo. Target Price — Relative Strength   — ▲ Up ▼ Down ► No Change   Below Avg. ★

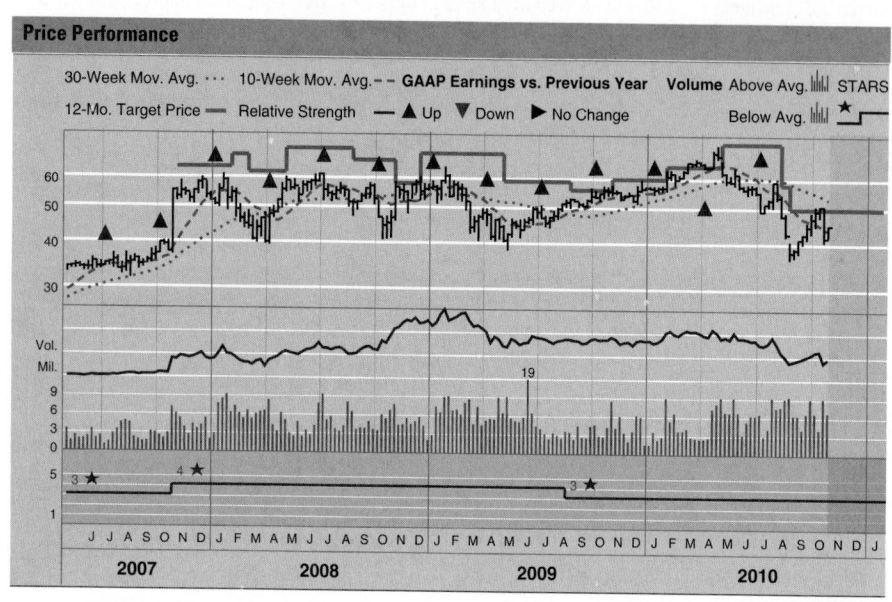

Options: CBOE, P, Ph

Analysis prepared by **Michael W. Jaffe** on August 17, 2010, when the stock traded at **$ 38.91**.

Highlights

➤ We think revenues will rise 14% in FY 11 (Jun.), on our outlook for growth in demand for DV's programs (particularly in the Business, Technology and Management segment), more campus openings, and tuition increases. We see these factors outweighing lower projected average tuition per student, on a likely higher proportion of part-time students and students taking fewer courses per semester. We also see growth being slowed somewhat by capacity constraints at Ross University, delays being experienced in the review process for a planned Ross University clinical education center in Freeport, Grand Bahama, and caution on the part of students considering Freeport.

➤ We forecast relatively flat margins in FY 11. We see margins being aided by the greater overall demand we forecast for DV's programs, and by ongoing attention to cost controls. We think these factors will be mostly offset by challenges recently being faced at Ross University.

➤ We also expect bad debt expense to remain within DV's historical range of 2.5% to 3%, as we think the favorable earnings potential of careers addressed by the company's programs boosts the loan repayment ability of graduates.

Investment Rationale/Risk

➤ DeVry continues to see solid overall demand for its programs. We are also positive about the September 2008 purchase of the Carrington Colleges Group (formerly U.S. Education), as we like DV's ongoing strategy of moving away from its previous dominant focus on technology programs. Yet, on some recent operating and regulatory challenges at several schools, and uncertainties from proposed regulations related to debt service-to-income ratios of graduates (where schools could be cut off from federal aid), we find DV shares near a fair valuation.

➤ Risks to our recommendation and target price include a major impact from proposed new industry regulations and weaker trends in DV's primary areas of education.

➤ The stock recently traded at 9X our calendar 2011 forecast of $4.67, which we think is a deserved premium to DV's peer group. We are positive on DV's prospects, and think its performance will be more consistent than most peers. Yet, DV also faces various issues that recently emerged at certain of its schools. After also factoring in regulatory issues, we apply a multiple of 10.7X to our calendar 2011 EPS estimate, for a 12-month target price of $50.

Qualitative Risk Assessment

LOW	MEDIUM	HIGH

Our risk assessment reflects DV's operating struggles for a few years in the middle part of the decade and high levels of regulatory scrutiny being given to for-profit educators, offset by what we consider positive turnaround initiatives.

Quantitative Evaluations

S&P Quality Ranking   **B**

D	C	B-	B	B+	A-	A	A+

Relative Strength Rank   **WEAK**

20

LOWEST = 1   HIGHEST = 99

Revenue/Earnings Data

Revenue (Million $)

	1Q	2Q	3Q	4Q	Year
2010	431.1	473.0	504.4	506.7	1,915
2009	303.7	369.6	391.9	396.2	1,461
2008	250.3	273.7	291.0	276.8	1,092
2007	219.2	235.6	245.8	232.8	933.5
2006	196.8	209.9	220.2	216.4	843.3
2005	188.4	194.5	201.9	196.5	781.3

Earnings Per Share ($)

2010	0.76	1.00	1.12	0.99	3.87
2009	0.48	0.59	0.70	0.51	2.28
2008	0.37	0.49	0.53	0.34	1.73
2007	0.29	0.23	0.32	0.22	1.07
2006	0.07	0.15	0.22	0.17	0.61
2005	0.04	0.08	0.17	0.09	0.38

Fiscal year ended Jun. 30. Next earnings report expected: Late October. EPS Estimates based on S&P Operating Earnings; historical GAAP earnings are as reported.

Dividend Data (Dates: mm/dd Payment Date: mm/dd/yy)

Amount ($)	Date Decl.	Ex-Div. Date	Stk. of Record	Payment Date
0.100	11/11	12/09	12/11	01/07/10
0.100	05/18	06/11	06/15	07/08/10

Dividends have been paid since 2007. Source: Company reports.

Please read the Required Disclosures and Analyst Certification on the last page of this report.

The McGraw-Hill Companies

DeVry Inc

Business Summary August 17, 2010

CORPORATE OVERVIEW. DeVry offers associate, undergraduate and graduate degree programs through its DeVry University institute. It also operates Becker Professional Education, which provides preparatory coursework for certification exams in accounting and finance; Ross University, which offers medical and veterinary education; Chamberlain College of Nursing, which offers nursing programs; Carrington Colleges Group (formerly U.S. Education; purchased in September 2008, for $290 million in cash), which operates Carrington College and Carrington College California in the western U.S. (names changed from Apollo College and Western Career College, respectively, on June 30), offering certificate and associate degree programs in health care; Fanor (now DeVry Brazil; 82% stake purchased on April 1, 2009, for $40.4 million in cash), a post-secondary education provider in Brazil; and Advanced Academics, which provides online secondary education to school districts throughout the U.S.

In August 2009, DV reported that it had reorganized its operating structure into four segments: Business, Technology and Management (comprised of DeVry University), Medical and Healthcare (Ross University, Chamberlain College of Nursing, and Carrington Colleges Group), Professional Education (Becker Professional Education), and Other Educational Services (Advanced Academics

and Fanor); as of October 1, 2010, DV was combining its Other Educational Services units into a segment with Becker and DeVry's international business development effort. In FY 09 (Jun.), the Business, Technology and Management segment accounted for 68% of DV's revenues and 51% of operating profits; Medical and Healthcare schools accounted for 25% of revenues and 37% of operating profits; and the Professional Education segment contributed 6% and 12%, respectively. The remaining 2% and a small loss were derived from the Other Educational segment.

CORPORATE STRATEGY. In an effort to boost its appeal, DV offers weekend classes, compressed and accelerated course schedules, technology-assisted delivery options for classroom-based courses, and online programs. In FY 01, DV began to operate DeVry University Centers, which are smaller than its campus facilities and more conveniently located for working adults.

Company Financials Fiscal Year Ended Jun. 30

Per Share Data ($)	2010	2009	2008	2007	2006	2005	2004	2003	2002	2001
Tangible Book Value	6.62	2.96	5.40	4.13	2.96	2.06	1.53	0.45	3.94	2.95
Cash Flow	4.73	2.98	2.28	1.69	1.29	1.19	1.62	1.45	1.42	1.27
Earnings	3.87	2.28	1.73	1.07	0.61	0.38	0.82	0.87	0.95	0.82
S&P Core Earnings	3.86	2.34	1.76	0.89	0.61	0.29	0.77	0.83	0.91	0.79
Dividends	0.20	0.16	0.12	0.10	Nil	Nil	Nil	Nil	Nil	Nil
Payout Ratio	5%	7%	7%	9%	Nil	Nil	Nil	Nil	Nil	Nil
Prices:High	74.36	64.69	61.57	59.97	28.75	24.84	32.38	30.15	34.76	40.25
Prices:Low	36.34	38.19	39.25	26.10	18.50	15.45	13.00	15.90	12.10	22.75
P/E Ratio:High	19	28	36	56	47	65	39	35	37	49
P/E Ratio:Low	9	17	23	24	30	41	16	18	13	28

Income Statement Analysis (Million $)										
Revenue	1,915	1,461	1,092	933	843	781	785	680	648	568
Operating Income	473	2,994	206	132	116	101	139	128	144	128
Depreciation	62.2	50.5	39.7	44.0	48.1	57.6	55.6	40.3	33.5	32.0
Interest Expense	1.59	2.78	0.52	4.78	10.2	9.05	7.80	1.28	0.81	0.40
Pretax Income	413	237	172	105	57.5	34.7	81.4	86.5	111	95.9
Effective Tax Rate	NA	30.2%	27.1%	27.4%	25.1%	23.1%	28.6%	29.3%	39.4%	39.8%
Net Income	280	166	126	76.2	43.1	26.7	58.1	61.1	67.1	57.8
S&P Core Earnings	279	170	128	63.5	42.8	20.2	54.6	58.4	64.4	55.8

Balance Sheet & Other Financial Data (Million $)										
Cash	323	225	220	129	131	162	160	123	78.9	49.7
Current Assets	500	385	326	219	228	242	209	170	118	88.6
Total Assets	1,628	1,434	1,018	844	872	910	884	857	468	392
Current Liabilities	344	392	211	166	211	187	156	139	104	94.4
Long Term Debt	NA	20.0	Nil	0.01	65.0	175	215	275	Nil	Nil
Common Equity	1,179	927	756	642	565	508	478	416	354	285
Total Capital	1,184	999	778	660	642	704	711	704	354	285
Capital Expenditures	131	74.0	62.8	38.6	25.3	42.9	42.8	43.8	85.9	74.6
Cash Flow	342	216	165	120	91.2	84.3	114	101	101	89.8
Current Ratio	1.5	1.0	1.6	1.3	1.1	1.3	1.3	1.2	1.1	0.9
% Long Term Debt of Capitalization	Nil	2.0	Nil	0.0	10.1	24.8	30.2	39.1	Nil	Nil
% Net Income of Revenue	14.6	11.3	11.5	8.2	5.1	3.4	7.4	9.0	10.4	10.2
% Return on Assets	18.3	13.5	13.5	8.9	4.8	3.0	6.7	9.2	15.6	16.1
% Return on Equity	26.6	19.7	18.0	12.6	8.0	5.4	13.0	15.9	21.0	22.7

Data as orig reptd.; bef. results of disc opers/spec. items. Per share data adj. for stk. divs.; EPS diluted. E-Estimated. NA-Not Available. NM-Not Meaningful. NR-Not Ranked. UR-Under Review.

Office: 1 Tower Ln Ste 1000, Oakbrook Terrace, IL 60181-4624.
Telephone: 630-571-7700.
Website: http://www.devryinc.com
Chrmn: H.T. Shapiro

Pres & CEO: D. Hamburger
SVP, CFO, Chief Acctg Officer & Treas: R.M. Gunst
SVP, Secy & General Counsel: G.S. Davis
SVP & CIO: E.P. Dirst

Investor Contact: J. Bates (630-574-1949)
Board Members: D. S. Brown, C. Curran, D. Hamburger, D. R. Huston, W. T. Keevan, L. Logan, J. A. McGee, L. W. Pickrum, F. Ruiz, H. T. Shapiro, R. L. Taylor

Founded: 1931
Domicile: Delaware
Employees: 12,117

Diamond Offshore Drilling Inc.

STANDARD &POOR'S

S&P Recommendation SELL ★★☆☆☆	**Price** $69.51 (as of Oct 22, 2010)	**12-Mo. Target Price** $61.00	**Investment Style** Large-Cap Blend

GICS Sector Energy
Sub-Industry Oil & Gas Drilling

Summary This company provides offshore contract drilling services to the oil and gas industry, and owns one of the world's largest fleets of semisubmersible rigs.

Key Stock Statistics (Source S&P, Vickers, company reports)

52-Wk Range	$108.51– 54.70	S&P Oper. EPS 2010**E**	7.02	Market Capitalization(B)	$9.664	Beta	0.82
Trailing 12-Month EPS	$8.31	S&P Oper. EPS 2011**E**	6.72	Yield (%)	0.72	S&P 3-Yr. Proj. EPS CAGR(%)	-18
Trailing 12-Month P/E	8.4	P/E on S&P Oper. EPS 2010**E**	9.9	Dividend Rate/Share	$0.50	S&P Credit Rating	A-
$10K Invested 5 Yrs Ago	$17,779	Common Shares Outstg. (M)	139.0	Institutional Ownership (%)	97		

Price Performance

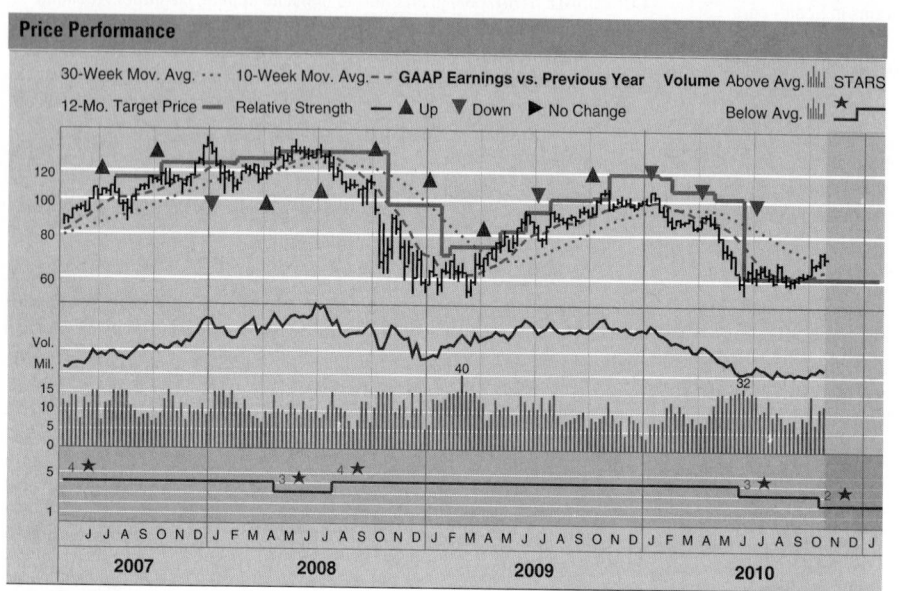

30-Week Mov. Avg. · · · · 10-Week Mov. Avg. – – – GAAP Earnings vs. Previous Year Volume Above Avg. ▮▮▮ STARS
12-Mo. Target Price — Relative Strength — ▲ Up ▼ Down ▶ No Change Below Avg. ▮▮▮ ★

Options: ASE, CBOE, P

Qualitative Risk Assessment

LOW	MEDIUM	**HIGH**

Our risk assessment reflects DO's exposure to volatile crude oil and natural gas prices, capital spending decisions made by its oil and gas producing customers, risks associated with operating in frontier regions, and an uncertain domestic regulatory regime.

Quantitative Evaluations

S&P Quality Ranking B

D	C	B-	**B**	B+	A-	A	A+

Relative Strength Rank MODERATE

67

LOWEST = 1 HIGHEST = 99

Highlights

▶ The STARS recommendation for DO has recently been changed to 2 (sell) from 3 (hold). The Highlights section of this Stock Report will be updated accordingly.

Investment Rationale/Risk

▶ The Investment Rationale/Risk section of this Stock Report will be updated shortly. For the latest News story on DO from MarketScope, see below.

▶ 10/21/10 11:17 am ET ... S&P MAINTAINS SELL OPINION ON SHARES OF DIAMOND OFFSHORE DRILLING (DO 68.47**): Q3 EPS of $1.43, vs. $2.62, is $0.01 below our estimate. Results were led by weaker dayrates and utilization for high-specification floaters. While the deepwater market appears to be rebounding in international markets, we remain concerned about prospects for midwater units. On the call, DO also echoed industry concerns that the U.S. Gulf will not recover until the permit process improves. Updating, we cut our '10 EPS estimate $0.09 to $7.02, and lower '11's by $0.12 to $6.72. On net asset value model and relative metrics, we keep our target price at $61. The shares yield 5%. /S. Glickman

Revenue/Earnings Data

Revenue (Million $)

	1Q	2Q	3Q	4Q	Year
2010	859.7	822.6	--	--	--
2009	885.7	946.4	908.4	890.8	3,631
2008	786.1	954.4	900.4	903.2	3,544
2007	608.2	648.9	644.0	666.7	2,568
2006	447.7	512.2	514.5	578.2	2,053
2005	258.8	283.4	310.5	368.3	1,221

Earnings Per Share ($)

	1Q	2Q	3Q	4Q	Year
2010	2.09	1.61	E1.43	E1.89	E7.02
2009	2.51	2.79	2.62	1.98	9.89
2008	2.09	2.99	2.23	2.11	9.43
2007	1.64	1.81	1.48	1.19	6.12
2006	1.06	1.27	1.19	1.60	5.12
2005	0.23	0.31	0.60	0.78	1.91

Fiscal year ended Dec. 31. Next earnings report expected: Late October. EPS Estimates based on S&P Operating Earnings; historical GAAP earnings are as reported.

Dividend Data (Dates: mm/dd Payment Date: mm/dd/yy)

Amount ($)	Date Decl.	Ex-Div. Date	Stk. of Record	Payment Date
.75 Spl.	07/22	07/29	08/02	09/01/10
0.125	07/22	07/29	08/02	09/01/10
.775 Spl.	10/21	10/28	11/01	12/01/10
0.125	10/21	10/28	11/01	12/01/10

Dividends have been paid since 1997. Source: Company reports.

Please read the Required Disclosures and Analyst Certification on the last page of this report.

The McGraw-Hill Companies

Diamond Offshore Drilling Inc.

STANDARD &POOR'S

Business Summary September 20, 2010

CORPORATE OVERVIEW. Diamond Offshore Drilling is engaged in contract drilling of offshore oil and gas wells, with a focus on deepwater drilling. As of January 2010, the company owned 47 mobile offshore drilling rigs: 32 semi-submersible rigs, 14 jackup rigs, and one drillship. The rigs operated in the Gulf of Mexico (GOM), the U.K. North Sea, South America, Africa, Australia and Southeast Asia. About 66% of 2009 revenues came from outside the United States. DO served 47 customers in 2009, with Petrobras accounting for 15% of total revenues.

Semisubmersible rigs, or floaters (87% of 2009 contract drilling revenues and 90% of segment operating income), operate in a semisubmerged position, afloat off the bottom, with the lower hull 55 ft. to 90 ft. below the water line, and the upper deck well above the surface. Floaters are typically anchored in position, but three company floaters are held in position by computer-controlled thrusters (dynamically positioned, or DP). Of DO's 33 floaters, 14 are high specification rigs (39%, 43%) capable of working in harsh environments

and water depths of up to 7,500 ft. The other 19 semisubmersibles (48%, 47%) operate in maximum water depths of 4,000 ft.

Jackup rigs (13%, 10%) are mobile, self-elevating drilling platforms equipped with legs that are lowered to the ocean floor until a foundation is established to support the rig. DO's 14 jackup rigs are used extensively for drilling in water depths from 20 ft. to 350 ft. The principal market for the jackups is the GOM, where seven of them are located.

Drillships, typically self-propelled, are positioned over a drillsite through the use of either an anchoring or DP system. The company owns one drillship, the Ocean Clipper, operating offshore Brazil.

Company Financials Fiscal Year Ended Dec. 31

Per Share Data ($)	2009	2008	2007	2006	2005	2004	2003	2002	2001	2000
Tangible Book Value	26.11	24.09	20.72	17.95	14.38	12.64	12.91	13.68	13.74	12.86
Cash Flow	12.38	11.49	7.79	6.54	3.14	1.33	0.98	1.71	2.35	1.50
Earnings	9.89	9.43	6.12	5.12	1.91	-0.06	-0.37	0.47	1.31	0.53
S&P Core Earnings	9.85	9.41	6.07	5.13	1.84	-0.07	-0.35	0.30	1.15	NA
Dividends	0.50	4.13	0.50	0.50	0.38	0.25	0.44	0.50	0.50	0.50
Payout Ratio	5%	44%	8%	10%	20%	NM	NM	106%	38%	94%
Prices:High	108.78	147.77	149.30	97.90	71.97	40.47	23.80	34.99	45.65	47.94
Prices:Low	53.30	54.52	73.50	62.26	37.91	20.00	17.06	17.30	22.83	26.50
P/E Ratio:High	11	16	24	19	38	NM	NM	74	35	90
P/E Ratio:Low	5	6	12	12	20	NM	NM	37	17	50

Income Statement Analysis (Million $)	2009	2008	2007	2006	2005	2004	2003	2002	2001	2000
Revenue	3,631	3,544	2,568	2,053	1,221	815	681	753	885	659
Operating Income	NA	2,233	1,454	1,141	510	213	138	229	395	203
Depreciation, Depletion and Amortization	346	287	235	201	184	179	176	177	170	146
Interest Expense	49.6	10.1	28.5	24.1	41.8	30.3	23.9	23.6	26.2	10.3
Pretax Income	1,868	1,848	1,247	966	356	-3.53	-54.2	96.2	272	111
Effective Tax Rate	26.3%	29.0%	32.1%	26.9%	27.0%	NM	NM	35.0%	33.3%	34.8%
Net Income	1,376	1,311	847	707	260	-7.24	-48.4	62.5	182	72.3
S&P Core Earnings	1,371	1,308	841	707	250	-10.5	-45.5	36.9	157	NA

Balance Sheet & Other Financial Data (Million $)	2009	2008	2007	2006	2005	2004	2003	2002	2001	2000
Cash	777	737	639	826	843	266	610	813	1,147	862
Current Assets	1,723	1,467	1,265	1,482	1,282	1,196	835	1,034	1,427	1,101
Total Assets	6,264	4,939	4,341	4,133	3,607	3,379	3,135	3,259	3,503	3,080
Current Liabilities	413	509	453	334	269	614	100	118	335	123
Long Term Debt	1,495	503	507	964	978	709	928	924	921	857
Common Equity	3,631	3,349	2,877	2,320	1,853	1,626	1,680	1,808	1,853	1,768
Total Capital	5,130	4,311	3,778	3,284	3,276	2,705	2,993	3,107	3,150	2,941
Capital Expenditures	1,362	667	647	551	294	89.2	209	274	269	324
Cash Flow	1,723	1,598	1,082	907	444	172	127	240	352	218
Current Ratio	4.2	2.9	2.8	4.4	4.8	1.9	8.4	8.7	4.3	8.9
% Long Term Debt of Capitalization	29.2	11.7	14.9	29.4	29.8	26.2	31.0	29.8	29.2	29.1
% Return on Assets	24.6	28.3	20.0	18.3	7.5	NM	NM	1.8	5.5	2.5
% Return on Equity	39.4	42.1	32.6	33.9	15.0	NM	NM	3.4	10.0	4.0

Data as orig reptd.; bef. results of disc opers/spec. items. Per share data adj. for stk. divs.; EPS diluted. E-Estimated. NA-Not Available. NM-Not Meaningful. NR-Not Ranked. UR-Under Review.

Office: 15415 Katy Freeway, Houston, TX 77094-1803.
Telephone: 281-492-5300.
Website: http://www.diamondoffshore.com
Chrmn: J.S. Tisch

Pres & CEO: L.R. Dickerson
SVP & CFO: G.T. Krenek
SVP, Secy & General Counsel: W.C. Long
Chief Acctg Officer & Cntlr: B.G. Gordon

Investor Contact: L. Van Dyke (281-492-5370)
Board Members: J. R. Bolton, L. R. Dickerson, C. L. Fabrikant, P. G. Gaffney, II, E. Grebow, H. C. Hofmann, A. L. Rebell, J. S. Tisch, R. S. Troubh

Founded: 1989
Domicile: Delaware
Employees: 5,500

The McGraw·Hill Companies

DIRECTV

STANDARD &POOR'S

| S&P Recommendation | HOLD ★★★★★ | Price $42.72 (as of Oct 22, 2010) | 12-Mo. Target Price $40.00 | Investment Style Large-Cap Blend |

GICS Sector Consumer Discretionary
Sub-Industry Cable & Satellite

Summary As the larger of the two major satellite TV providers -- with over 18.8 million subscribers across the U.S., and 7.7 million in Latin America (including Brazil, Mexico and the PanAmericana regions) -- DIRECTV merged with Liberty Media Entertainment in November 2009.

Key Stock Statistics (Source S&P, Vickers, company reports)

52-Wk Range	$43.28– 25.16	S&P Oper. EPS 2010E	2.28	Market Capitalization(B)	$38.475	Beta	0.84
Trailing 12-Month EPS	$1.52	S&P Oper. EPS 2011E	2.83	Yield (%)	Nil	S&P 3-Yr. Proj. EPS CAGR(%)	20
Trailing 12-Month P/E	28.1	P/E on S&P Oper. EPS 2010E	18.7	Dividend Rate/Share	Nil	S&P Credit Rating	BBB-
$10K Invested 5 Yrs Ago	$30,406	Common Shares Outstg. (M)	900.6	Institutional Ownership (%)	84		

Price Performance

30-Week Mov. Avg. ··· 10-Week Mov. Avg. - - GAAP Earnings vs. Previous Year   Volume Above Avg. STARS
12-Mo. Target Price — Relative Strength — ▲ Up ▼ Down ▶ No Change   Below Avg. ★

Options: ASE, CBOE, P, Ph

Analysis prepared by **Tuna N. Amobi, CFA, CPA** on August 24, 2010, when the stock traded at **$ 37.61**.

Highlights

> We project DTV U.S. gross subscriber addition of about 4.0 million and 4.2 million for 2010 and 2011, respectively, mainly on gains across the direct sales and independent retail channels, and relatively strong contributions from telco partners. Assuming stable average monthly churn of 1.5%-1.6%, we see 500,000 and 600,000 in the respective years, reaching over 19.6 million subscribers by the end of 2011.

> Factoring in solid subscriber growth at the DTV Latin America unit, higher ARPU on advanced HD DVR services, and improved advertising outlook, we expect consolidated revenue growth of 12% and 11% in 2010 and 2011, to over $24.1 billion and $26.8 billion, respectively.

> Further margin expansion should reflect some retention/upgrade cost control, versus higher SAC and programming costs. We see consolidated EBITDA up 21% and 14% in 2010 and 2011, respectively, to $6.3 billion and $7.2 billion. After D&A and interest expense, we forecast EPS of $2.28 and $2.83 in the respective years, with continued share buybacks.

Investment Rationale/Risk

> Despite some notable deceleration of 2010 first half subscriber growth and tentative full year guidance for DTV U.S., we are encouraged by continued solid momentum at the Latin America unit. We believe DTV recently enhanced its corporate governance structure following the elimination of dual-class shares in the wake of a recent reduction of John Malone's voting stake. An ongoing strategic review could offer some operating and capitalization blueprints following the Liberty Entertainment merger. We see ample financial flexibility, noting DTV's plans to tap the capital markets toward a 2.5X debt/ EBITDA leverage target by 2011.

> Risks to our recommendation and target price include uncertainties with the strategic review, and ratcheted pay TV competition on bundled offerings from cable and telco providers.

> Our 12-month target price is $40, derived by using a 7.1X multiple on our 2010 estimate EV/ EBITDA, and $2,500 per subscriber, which we see as ample relative to DISH Network (DISH 18, Hold). DTV recently had about $1.7 billion of foreign net operating loss carryforwards.

Qualitative Risk Assessment

| LOW | MEDIUM | HIGH |

Our risk assessment reflects what we view as ample financial flexibility, and a projected acceleration of free cash flow, offset by increased competition from cable operators' bundled offerings.

Quantitative Evaluations

S&P Quality Ranking B-

| D | C | B- | B | B+ | A- | A | A+ |

Relative Strength Rank MODERATE

67

LOWEST = 1   HIGHEST = 99

Revenue/Earnings Data

Revenue (Million $)

	1Q	2Q	3Q	4Q	Year
2010	5,608	--	--	--	--
2009	4,901	5,218	5,465	5,981	21,565
2008	4,591	4,807	4,981	5,314	19,693
2007	3,908	4,135	4,327	4,876	17,246
2006	3,386	3,520	3,667	4,183	14,756
2005	3,148	3,188	3,233	3,596	13,165

Earnings Per Share ($)

	1Q	2Q	3Q	4Q	Year
2010	0.59	0.60	E0.53	E0.60	E2.28
2009	0.20	0.40	0.38	-0.03	0.95
2008	0.32	0.40	0.33	0.31	1.36
2007	0.27	0.36	0.27	0.30	1.19
2006	0.17	0.36	0.30	0.29	1.12
2005	-0.03	0.10	0.07	0.09	0.22

Fiscal year ended Dec. 31. Next earnings report expected: Early November. EPS Estimates based on S&P Operating Earnings; historical GAAP earnings are as reported.

Dividend Data

No cash dividends have been paid since 1997.

DIRECTV

Business Summary August 24, 2010

CORPORATE OVERVIEW. The DIRECTV Group (formerly Hughes Electronics) is a leading provider of direct broadcast satellite (DBS) television service, providing hundreds of digital video and audio channels to nearly 18.6 million monthly subscribers in the U.S., and a selection of local and international programming to almost 6.7 million subscribers in Latin America -- mostly through Sky Brazil (74% equity stake), Sky Mexico (41%) and PanAmericana (100%), including Venezuela, Puerto Rico and Argentina. DTV distributes its services mainly through direct sales and retail channels, and through co-branding partnerships with three of the four RBOCs.

In November 2009, DTV completed its merger with Liberty Entertainment (LEI), and named Michael White, retiring CEO of PepsiCo International, as its CEO effective January 1, 2010.

CORPORATE STRATEGY. DTV offers almost 160 national HD channels (which it plans to expand to nearly 200 after the recently successful launch of its D12 satellite), and local HD covering nearly 90% of U.S. TV homes. DTV also aims for differentiation on plans to launch new features such as whole-home functionality (including multi-room viewing) and broadband connectivity (for VOD,

TV and multi-media applications), as well as a search functionality, a movie service, and three 3D TV channels. DTV also offers NFL Sunday Ticket sports programming -- with a contract through the 2014 season. In February 2010, the new CEO articulated some key priorities (including multi-platform access, customer service and international expansion), and expects completion of the board's ongoing strategic review by spring.

In July 2008, DTV acquired 180 Connect Inc., a major installation service provider, which it estimates fulfills 15%-20% of its work orders. In June 2007, DTV and DISH Network unveiled distribution pacts to offer WiMax-based wireless high-speed broadband service from Clearwire, which in turn will offer their DBS video services, with both DBS companies offering data, video and voice services in CLWR's markets starting in 2007. Earlier, in 2004, DTV divested assets such as Hughes Networks Systems and PanAmSat, and DTV Latin America emerged from a bankruptcy reorganization.

Company Financials Fiscal Year Ended Dec. 31

Per Share Data ($)	2009	2008	2007	2006	2005	2004	2003	2002	2001	2000
Tangible Book Value	NM	NM	0.92	1.10	2.17	1.61	4.36	2.76	NM	4.20
Cash Flow	3.61	3.44	2.59	1.93	0.83	-0.16	0.27	0.88	0.50	0.73
Earnings	0.95	1.36	1.19	1.12	0.22	-0.77	-0.27	-0.21	-0.55	-0.34
S&P Core Earnings	0.98	1.35	1.18	1.05	0.20	-0.96	-0.32	-0.78	-0.86	NA
Dividends	Nil	Nil	Nil	Nil	Nil	Nil	Nil	Nil	Nil	Nil
Payout Ratio	Nil	Nil	Nil	Nil	Nil	Nil	Nil	Nil	Nil	Nil
Prices:High	34.25	29.10	27.73	25.57	17.01	18.81	16.91	17.55	28.00	46.67
Prices:Low	18.81	19.40	20.73	13.28	13.17	14.70	9.40	8.00	11.50	21.33
P/E Ratio:High	36	21	23	23	77	NM	NM	NM	NM	NM
P/E Ratio:Low	20	14	17	12	60	NM	NM	NM	NM	NM

Income Statement Analysis (Million $)										
Revenue	NA	19,693	17,246	14,756	13,165	11,360	9,372	8,935	8,262	7,288
Operating Income	NA	5,029	4,145	3,274	1,441	-1,281	617	668	390	594
Depreciation	NA	2,320	1,684	1,034	853	838	755	1,067	1,148	948
Interest Expense	423	360	286	246	238	132	156	336	196	218
Pretax Income	1,834	2,471	2,388	542	480	-1,734	-478	-140	-990	-816
Effective Tax Rate	45.1%	35.0%	39.5%	NM	36.1%	NM	NM	NM	NM	NM
Net Income	942	1,515	1,434	1,420	305	-1,056	-375	-213	-614	-355
S&P Core Earnings	976	1,498	1,410	1,336	279	-1,312	-439	-862	-923	NA

Balance Sheet & Other Financial Data (Million $)										
Cash	2,605	2,005	1,098	2,499	3,701	2,830	1,720	1,129	700	1,508
Current Assets	NA	4,044	3,146	4,556	6,096	4,771	10,356	3,656	3,341	4,154
Total Assets	18,260	16,539	15,063	15,141	15,630	14,324	18,978	17,885	19,210	19,279
Current Liabilities	NA	3,585	3,434	3,323	2,828	2,695	5,840	3,203	4,407	2,691
Long Term Debt	6,500	6,267	3,347	3,395	3,405	2,410	2,435	2,390	989	1,292
Common Equity	2,911	4,853	6,302	6,681	7,940	7,507	9,631	9,063	9,574	10,830
Total Capital	NA	11,205	10,227	10,138	11,395	9,965	12,305	12,590	13,339	14,941
Capital Expenditures	NA	2,229	2,692	1,754	889	1,023	444	566	799	939
Cash Flow	3,582	3,835	3,118	2,455	1,158	-218	380	808	438	496
Current Ratio	0.9	1.1	0.9	1.4	2.2	1.8	1.8	1.1	0.8	1.5
% Long Term Debt of Capitalization	59.5	55.9	32.7	33.5	29.9	24.2	19.8	19.0	7.4	8.6
% Net Income of Revenue	NA	7.7	8.3	9.6	2.3	NM	NM	NM	NM	NM
% Return on Assets	5.4	9.6	9.5	9.2	2.0	NM	NM	NM	NM	NM
% Return on Equity	24.3	27.2	22.1	19.4	3.9	NM	NM	NM	NM	NM

Data as orig reptd.; bef. results of disc opers/spec. items. Per share data adj. for stk. divs.; EPS diluted. E-Estimated. NA-Not Available. NM-Not Meaningful. NR-Not Ranked. UR-Under Review.

Office: 2230 E Imperial Hwy, El Segundo, CA 90245-3531.
Telephone: 310-964-5000.
Website: http://www.directv.com
Chrmn, Pres & CEO: M.D. White

COO: M.W. Palkovic
EVP & CFO: P.T. Doyle
EVP, Chief Admin Officer & General Counsel: L.D. Hunter
EVP & CTO: R.C. Pontual

Investor Contact: J. Rubin (212-462-5200)
Board Members: N. R. Austrian, R. F. Boyd, Jr., S. A. DiPiazza, Jr., C. R. Lee, P. A. Lund, N. S. Newcomb, M. D. White

Founded: 1977
Domicile: Delaware
Employees: 23,300

Discover Financial Services Inc

STANDARD &POOR'S

S&P Recommendation	**STRONG BUY** ★★★★★	Price $17.41 (as of Oct 22, 2010)	12-Mo. Target Price $21.00	Investment Style Large-Cap Growth

GICS Sector Financials
Sub-Industry Consumer Finance

Summary This leading U.S. credit card issuer and payment services company offers credit and prepaid cards and provides payment processing services to merchants and financial institutions.

Key Stock Statistics (Source S&P, Vickers, company reports)

52-Wk Range	$17.94– 12.11	S&P Oper. EPS 2010E	1.08	Market Capitalization(B)	$9.481	Beta	1.61
Trailing 12-Month EPS	$1.20	S&P Oper. EPS 2011E	1.99	Yield (%)	0.46	S&P 3-Yr. Proj. EPS CAGR(%)	12
Trailing 12-Month P/E	14.5	P/E on S&P Oper. EPS 2010E	16.1	Dividend Rate/Share	$0.08	S&P Credit Rating	BBB-
$10K Invested 5 Yrs Ago	NA	Common Shares Outstg. (M)	544.6	Institutional Ownership (%)	87		

Price Performance

30-Week Mov. Avg. · · · 10-Week Mov. Avg. – – **GAAP Earnings vs. Previous Year** Volume Above Avg. | STARS
12-Mo. Target Price — Relative Strength — ▲ Up ▼ Down ▶ No Change Below Avg. |

Options: ASE, CBOE, P

Analysis prepared by **Rafay Khalid, CFA** on September 20, 2010, when the stock traded at **$ 16.00**.

Highlights

▶ We expect total revenue growth of 41% in FY 10 (Nov.), excluding one-time legal settlement revenue, and up 3% in FY 11. Our outlook reflects our view for an increase in average managed loans in the Discover credit card business. We see net interest margins of 9.14% in FY 10 and 9.30% FY 11, versus 9.48% in FY 09. On September 17, DFS agreed to acquire The Student Loan Corporation (STU $29.91, NR) for $600 million or $30 per share.

▶ We believe DFS's loss provisions will decline in FY 10 and FY 11, given our outlook for managed charge-offs to be below many industry peers. We note that DFS's managed charge-off rate in FY 09 was 8.0%, and below the industry average of 9.8%. We see expenses on an absolute dollar basis increasing in FY 10 and FY 11, reflecting our expectation for higher employee compensation costs. However, expenses as a percentage of total revenues, should decline to 31.3% in FY 10 and 31.0% in FY 11, from 46.5% in FY 09.

▶ We see operating EPS of $1.08 in FY 10 and $1.99 in FY 11, compared to operating EPS of $1.64 in FY 09. We assume an effective tax rate of 39.4% in FY 10 and 39.7% in FY 11.

Investment Rationale/Risk

▶ We believe DFS's managed charge-offs will continue to be below peers in FY 10 and FY 11, reflecting what we see as its conservative customer base and solid credit risk management. In addition, we think the company's judgmental decision process will help strengthen its risk management system, as it adds a human element to the traditional computer-generated system. We see Diners Club International increasing its contribution to the company's payment transaction volume, as we forecast international expansion, increasing global acceptance, and the creation of new partnerships.

▶ Risks to our recommendation and target price include a significant increase in U.S. unemployment levels, a rapid decline in consumer spending, and an increase in loan loss provisions.

▶ Our 12-month target price of $21 is based on a three-year historical premium book value ratio of 1.55X our FY 2011 book value per share estimate of $13.64. We believe this premium to the historical basis is warranted, reflecting what we see as below-industry charge-offs, and growth in the loan portfolio and payment transaction volume.

Qualitative Risk Assessment

LOW	**MEDIUM**	HIGH

Our risk assessment reflects what we see as solid business fundamentals and an increasing merchant base, tempered by DFS's exposure to consumer spending habits and the U.S. economy.

Quantitative Evaluations

S&P Quality Ranking NR

D	C	B-	B	B+	A-	A	A+

Relative Strength Rank STRONG

78

LOWEST = 1 HIGHEST = 99

Revenue/Earnings Data

Revenue (Million $)

	1Q	2Q	3Q	4Q	Year
2010	2,105	2,065	2,100	--	--
2009	2,006	1,939	2,149	1,892	7,986
2008	1,638	1,457	1,557	2,305	6,957
2007	1,506	1,575	1,601	1,752	6,434
2006	--	--	--	--	6,211
2005	--	--	--	--	--

Earnings Per Share ($)

2010	-0.22	0.33	0.47	E0.50	E1.08
2009	0.25	0.43	1.07	0.60	2.39
2008	0.50	0.42	0.37	0.92	2.20
2007	0.55	0.44	0.42	-0.18	1.23
2006	--	0.72	0.51	0.39	1.89
2005	--	--	--	--	--

Fiscal year ended Nov. 30. Next earnings report expected: Mid December. EPS Estimates based on S&P Operating Earnings; historical GAAP earnings are as reported.

Dividend Data (Dates: mm/dd Payment Date: mm/dd/yy)

Amount ($)	Date Decl.	Ex-Div. Date	Stk. of Record	Payment Date
0.020	12/17	12/29	12/31	01/21/10
0.020	03/16	03/30	04/01	04/22/10
0.020	06/16	07/02	07/07	07/22/10
0.020	09/15	10/05	10/07	10/21/10

Dividends have been paid since 2007. Source: Company reports.

Please read the Required Disclosures and Analyst Certification on the last page of this report.

The **McGraw·Hill** Companies

Discover Financial Services Inc

**STANDARD
&POOR'S**

Business Summary September 20, 2010

CORPORATE OVERVIEW. Discover Financial Services (DFS), formerly a business segment of Morgan Stanley, is a credit card issuer and electronic payment services company. DFS offers credit and prepaid cards and other financial products and services to qualified customers in the United States, and provides payment processing and related services to merchants and financial institutions across the globe. DFS manages its operations through two business segments: Direct Banking and Payments Services. The Direct Banking segment is the major contributor to the company, in terms of income before income taxes. The Payments Services segment is modestly profitable but continues to comprise a growing portion of DFS's income stream.

The Direct Banking segment offers Discover Card-branded credit cards issued to more than 50 million individuals and small businesses over the Discover Network, which is the company's proprietary credit card network in the United States. The segment also includes DFS's other consumer products and services businesses, including prepaid and other consumer lending and deposit products offered primarily through the company's Discover Bank subsidiary. The company entered the debit card business in 2006, allowing banks to offer Discover-branded debit cards.

In addition to credit cards, DFS offers installment loan products, including personal loans and student loans. It offers installment loan products to existing

cardmembers as well as to new customers. DFS accepts applications for installment loans online, by phone or by mail.

DFS offers money market accounts and certificates of deposit directly to its cardmembers using proprietary models to execute targeted statement insert, e-mail, and direct mail campaigns. Aside from direct-to-consumer deposits, DFS obtains deposits through third-party securities brokers that offer DFS's certificates of deposit to their customers. DFS uses deposits to finance its credit card and installment loan businesses. In the long-term, it expects to increase its direct-to-consumer deposit business.

The Payment Services segment includes the Discover network, PULSE and the Diners Club International business. PULSE, an automated teller machine (ATM), debit and electronic funds transfer network, serves more than 4,400 financial institutions and includes more than 289,000 ATMs, as well as point-of-sale terminals nationwide. The Diners Club International network is in over 185 countries. Diners Club International's 79 licensees issues credit cards and provide card acceptance services.

Company Financials Fiscal Year Ended Nov. 30

Per Share Data ($)	2009	2008	2007	2006	2005	2004	2003	2002	2001	2000
Tangible Book Value	12.48	11.37	10.98	NA	NA	NA	NA	NA	NA	NA
Earnings	2.39	2.20	1.23	1.89	NA	NA	NA	NA	NA	NA
S&P Core Earnings	0.10	1.00	1.23	2.26	1.21	NA	NA	NA	NA	NA
Dividends	0.12	0.24	0.06	Nil	NA	NA	NA	NA	NA	NA
Payout Ratio	5%	11%	5%	NA	NA	NA	NA	NA	NA	NA
Prices:High	17.36	19.87	32.17	NA	NA	NA	NA	NA	NA	NA
Prices:Low	4.73	6.59	14.81	NA	NA	NA	NA	NA	NA	NA
P/E Ratio:High	7	9	26	NA	NA	NA	NA	NA	NA	NA
P/E Ratio:Low	2	3	12	NA	NA	NA	NA	NA	NA	NA

Income Statement Analysis (Million $)	2009	2008	2007	2006	2005	2004	2003	2002	2001	2000
Net Interest Income	1,894	1,405	1,506	1,459	NA	NA	NA	NA	NA	NA
Tax Equivalent Adjustment	NA	NA	NA	NA	NA	NA	NA	NA	NA	NA
Non Interest Income	4,841	4,264	3,546	3,539	NA	NA	NA	NA	NA	NA
Loan Loss Provision	2,362	1,596	950	756	NA	NA	NA	NA	NA	NA
% Expense/Operating Revenue	33.4%	NA	49.0%	55.5%	NA	NA	NA	NA	NA	NA
Pretax Income	2,150	1,658	945	1,467	924	1,219	NA	NA	NA	NA
Effective Tax Rate	39.8%	35.9%	37.7%	31.8%	37.5%	36.3%	NA	NA	NA	NA
Net Income	1,294	1,063	589	1,001	578	776	NA	NA	NA	NA
% Net Interest Margin	4.74	NA	NA	NA	NA	NA	NA	NA	NA	NA
S&P Core Earnings	47.2	485	587	1,078	578		NA	NA	NA	NA

Balance Sheet & Other Financial Data (Million $)	2009	2008	2007	2006	2005	2004	2003	2002	2001	2000
Money Market Assets	1,350	9,378	8,416	Nil	NA	NA	NA	NA	NA	NA
Investment Securities	5,035	1,228	526	86.0	NA	NA	NA	NA	NA	NA
Commercial Loans	404	466	234	111	NA	NA	NA	NA	NA	NA
Other Loans	19,826	24,751	23,720	21,707	NA	NA	NA	NA	NA	NA
Total Assets	46,021	39,892	37,376	32,403	26,944	NA	NA	NA	NA	NA
Demand Deposits	64.5	78.4	82.0	86.0	NA	NA	NA	NA	NA	NA
Time Deposits	32,029	28,452	24,644	21,042	NA	NA	NA	NA	NA	NA
Long Term Debt	1,804	1,330	2,134	1,706	NA	NA	NA	NA	NA	NA
Common Equity	7,277	5,916	5,599	5,425	4,600	NA	NA	NA	NA	NA
% Return on Assets	3.0	2.8	1.8	NM	NA	NA	NA	NA	NA	NA
% Return on Equity	19.6	18.5	10.4	NM	NA	NA	NA	NA	NA	NA
% Loan Loss Reserve	8.0	NA	3.8	3.5	NA	NA	NA	NA	NA	NA
% Loans/Deposits	80.6	NA	96.8	NM	NA	NA	NA	NA	NA	NA
% Equity to Assets	15.4	14.9	17.1	NM	NA	NA	NA	NA	NA	NA

Data as orig reptd.; bef. results of disc opers/spec. items. Per share data adj. for stk. divs.; EPS diluted. 2006 data pro forma; bal. sheet as of Feb. 28 '07. E-Estimated. NA-Not Available. NM-Not Meaningful. NR-Not Ranked. UR-Under Review.

Office: 2500 Lake Cook Road, Riverwoods, IL 60015.
Telephone: 224-405-0900.
Website: http://www.discover.com
Chrmn & CEO: D.W. Nelms

Pres & COO: R.C. Hochschild
EVP, CFO & Treas: R.A. Guthrie
EVP, Secy & General Counsel: K.M. Corley
SVP, Chief Acctg Officer & Cntlr: M.A. Zaeske

Board Members: J. S. Aronin, M. K. Bush, G. Case, R. M. Devlin, C. A. Glassman, R. H. Lenny, T. G. Maheras, M. H. Moskow, D. W. Nelms, E. F. Smith, L. A. Weinbach

Founded: 1960
Domicile: Delaware
Employees: 10,500

The McGraw-Hill Companies

Discovery Communications Inc

STANDARD &POOR'S

S&P Recommendation **STRONG BUY** ★★★★★	Price $43.73 (as of Oct 22, 2010)	12-Mo. Target Price $55.00	Investment Style Large-Cap Growth

GICS Sector Consumer Discretionary
Sub-Industry Broadcasting & Cable TV

Summary This pure-play cable networks company, with brands such as Discovery, Animal Planet and TLC, is a leading global provider of non-fiction entertainment through 115 networks in 180 countries broadcasting in 35 languages.

Key Stock Statistics (Source S&P, Vickers, company reports)

52-Wk Range	$44.39– 26.64	S&P Oper. EPS 2010E	1.87	Market Capitalization(B)	$5.960	Beta	1.26
Trailing 12-Month EPS	$1.24	S&P Oper. EPS 2011E	2.26	Yield (%)	Nil	S&P 3-Yr. Proj. EPS CAGR(%)	20
Trailing 12-Month P/E	35.3	P/E on S&P Oper. EPS 2010E	23.4	Dividend Rate/Share	Nil	S&P Credit Rating	NA
$10K Invested 5 Yrs Ago	NA	Common Shares Outstg. (M)	284.6	Institutional Ownership (%)	NM		

Price Performance

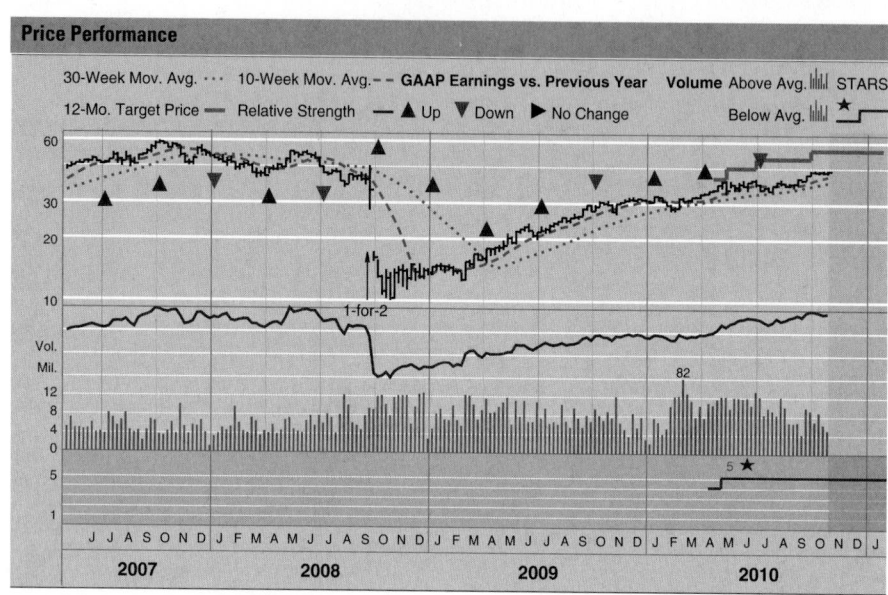

- 30-Week Mov. Avg. · · · ·
- 10-Week Mov. Avg. – –
- **GAAP Earnings vs. Previous Year**
- Volume Above Avg. ▨ STARS
- 12-Mo. Target Price —
- Relative Strength —
- ▲ Up ▼ Down ▶ No Change
- Below Avg. ▨ ★

Options: CBOE, Ph

Analysis prepared by **Tuna N. Amobi, CFA, CPA** on September 22, 2010, when the stock traded at **$ 43.28.**

Highlights

▶ We expect consolidated revenues to advance about 7% in 2010 (ex- Discovery Kids, Animal Planet, Japan and Travel Channel), to nearly $3.8 billion, and then 6.5% in 2011, to $4.1 billion -- assuming double-digit growth in U.S. and, to a greater extent, international advertising revenues, and mid- to high single digit growth in worldwide affiliate fees. Conversely, we see continuing challenges in 2010 resulting in further sharp declines for the relatively small commerce and education businesses, improving to a relatively modest gain in 2011.

▶ We anticipate continued significant margin expansion across both the U.S. and international networks -- with potentially significant upside still ahead for the latter division, as it further benefits from increased operating leverage on restructuring actions.

▶ After modestly higher operating expenses (programming and SG&A), we see 15% and 9% adjusted EBITDA growth in 2010 and 2011, respectively, to nearly $1.7 billion and over $1.8 billion, and after D&A, interest expense and taxes, EPS of $1.87 and $2.26 -- with some share buybacks under a new $1 billion plan.

Investment Rationale/Risk

▶ DISCA's stronger-than-expected 2010 second quarter results reflected a global ad rebound, as the company exploits a ratings resurgence across its core networks -- coming off a strong upfront season for its domestic channels (including the imminent Oprah Winfrey Network). With a strong management team and an asset portfolio providing enhanced business and geographic diversification, we see the company as well positioned for above-average growth in earnings and free cash flow through economic cycles. We note DISCA's strong balance sheet -- with financial flexibility enhanced by a recent $3 billion debt refinancing.

▶ Risks to our recommendation and target price include a weaker-than-expected macroeconomic rebound, a sharp U.S. ratings decline, uncertainties with OWN and The Hub rebranding, potential governance issues on multiple classes of shares, and currency exposure.

▶ We see nearly $1.6 billion of free cash in 2010 and 2011 combined (after modest capex). Our 12-month target price is $55, on 14X 2011E EV/ EBITDA and 1.3X P/E-to-growth, warranted premiums to peers and the S&P 500, in our view.

Qualitative Risk Assessment

LOW	MEDIUM	HIGH

Our risk assessment reflects the company's leading position as a provider of niche programming with global appeal, combined with business and geographic diversification and a strong balance sheet, offset by some concerns with the corporate governance framework, such as the company's multi-class stock structure.

Quantitative Evaluations

S&P Quality Ranking NR

D	C	B-	B	B+	A-	A	A+

Relative Strength Rank STRONG

71

LOWEST = 1 HIGHEST = 99

Revenue/Earnings Data

Revenue (Million $)

	1Q	2Q	3Q	4Q	Year
2010	879.0	963.0	--	--	--
2009	817.0	881.0	854.0	964.0	3,516
2008	189.3	194.5	845.0	904.0	3,443
2007	173.9	177.2	177.9	178.2	707.2
2006	153.6	165.8	169.9	198.9	688.1
2005	174.3	178.0	167.9	174.3	694.5

Earnings Per Share ($)

2010	0.39	0.25	E0.48	E0.51	E1.87
2009	0.28	0.43	0.22	0.36	1.30
2008	0.24	0.32	0.31	0.25	0.85
2007	0.14	0.52	0.06	-1.22	-0.48
2006	0.08	0.10	-0.54	0.04	-0.32
2005	0.12	0.02	Nil	0.08	0.24

Fiscal year ended Dec. 31. Next earnings report expected: Early November. EPS Estimates based on S&P Operating Earnings; historical GAAP earnings are as reported.

Dividend Data

No cash dividends have been paid.

Discovery Communications Inc

Business Summary September 22, 2010

CORPORATE OVERVIEW. Discovery Communications, Inc. (DISCA) is a leading global media and entertainment company (and a pure-play cable networks operator) reaching 368 million households and over 1.5 billion total subscribers, through 115 networks in 173 countries broadcasting in 35 languages. DISCA primarily provides nonfiction programming through networks such as Discovery Channel, TLC, Animal Planet, Science Channel, Planet Green, Investigation Discovery and HD Theater. DISCA also provides consumer and educational products and services, and owns a portfolio of digital media services (e.g., HowStuffWorks.com).

In 2009, revenues and adjusted EBITDA contributions from the company's three divisions were: US Networks, 61% and 72%, respectively; International Networks, 34% and 27%; and Commerce, Education and Other, 5% and 1%. Three networks (Discovery Channel, TLC and Animal Planet) account for about 78% of U.S. revenues. Total revenues are mostly derived from distribution fees (50% of 2009 revenues) and advertising (39%) -- the latter comprising 52% and 29% of U.S. and international revenues, respectively.

CORPORATE STRATEGY. To modernize its underdeveloped networks, DISCA rebranded Discovery Home Channel as Planet Green (April 2007) and Discov-

ery Times Channel as ID: Investigation Discovery (November 2007). It has also decided to rebrand the Discovery Health Channel as OWN: The Oprah Winfrey Network (announced in January 2008); and Discovery Kids as The Hub (January 2010). Domestically, DISCA focuses on improving the visibility and image of some of its less profitable networks through 50/50 joint ventures with known brands such as Hasbro Inc. and Oprah Winfrey -- with The Hub and OWN set for launch in 2010 and 2011, respectively.

In January 2010, as part of a three-member consortium that also includes Sony Corp. and IMAX Corp., the company announced plans for a joint venture to launch a linear 3D television channel in 2011. Meanwhile, the company also wants to get onto new distribution platforms such as brand-aligned Web properties, mobile devices and broadband channels. Internationally, growth is mostly focused on new subscription contracts and boosting the company's advertising business (which lacks the strength it has in the U.S.).

Company Financials Fiscal Year Ended Dec. 31

Per Share Data ($)	2009	2008	2007	2006	2005	2004	2003	2002	2001	2000
Tangible Book Value	NM	NM	NA	17.66	17.42	NM	NM	NM	NA	NA
Cash Flow	1.68	3.35	NA	0.16	0.78	1.02	0.12	-0.30	NA	NA
Earnings	1.30	0.85	-0.48	-0.32	0.24	0.48	-0.38	-0.78	NA	NA
S&P Core Earnings	0.89	0.85	0.24	0.34	0.18	0.44	-0.40	NA	NA	NA
Dividends	Nil	Nil	NA	Nil	Nil	Nil	Nil	Nil	NA	NA
Payout Ratio	Nil	Nil	NA	Nil	Nil	Nil	Nil	Nil	NA	NA
Prices:High	32.69	53.66	NA	33.92	32.60	NA	NA	NA	NA	NA
Prices:Low	12.46	10.02	NA	25.62	27.02	NA	NA	NA	NA	NA
P/E Ratio:High	25	63	NA	NM	NM	NA	NA	NA	NA	NA
P/E Ratio:Low	10	12	NA	NM	NM	NA	NA	NA	NA	NA

Income Statement Analysis (Million $)

	2009	2008	2007	2006	2005	2004	2003	2002	2001	2000
Revenue	3,516	3,443	707	688	695	631	506	539	NA	NA
Operating Income	NA	1,965	NA	56.2	74.2	94.6	72.2	89.0	NA	NA
Depreciation	155	804	67.7	67.9	76.4	77.6	70.5	67.3	NA	NA
Interest Expense	250	258	NA	Nil	Nil	Nil	72.2	64.8	NA	NA
Pretax Income	1,031	754	-9.23	-2.07	82.1	101	-34.5	-141	NA	NA
Effective Tax Rate	45.8%	46.7%	NM	NM	59.5%	34.6%	NM	NM	NA	NA
Net Income	560	274	-68.4	-46.0	33.3	66.1	-52.4	-109	NA	NA
S&P Core Earnings	378	274	34.1	46.1	24.2	62.2	-54.4	NA	NA	NA

Balance Sheet & Other Financial Data (Million $)

	2009	2008	2007	2006	2005	2004	2003	2002	2001	2000
Cash	623	100	209	155	250	34.4	8.60	NA	NA	NA
Current Assets	1,680	1,109	372	317	400	212	131	NA	NA	NA
Total Assets	10,965	10,484	5,866	5,871	5,819	5,565	5,397	NA	NA	NA
Current Liabilities	790	1,070	120	122	89.9	109	60.6	NA	NA	NA
Long Term Debt	3,457	3,331	NA	Nil	Nil	Nil	Nil	NA	NA	NA
Common Equity	6,206	5,534	4,494	4,549	4,575	4,347	4,260	NA	NA	NA
Total Capital	9,763	9,325	4,494	5,724	5,707	5,431	5,313	NA	NA	NA
Capital Expenditures	57.0	102	47.1	77.5	90.5	49.3	25.9	56.4	NA	NA
Cash Flow	715	1,078	-0.66	21.9	110	144	18.1	-41.7	NA	NA
Current Ratio	2.1	1.0	3.1	2.6	4.5	2.0	2.2	NA	NA	NA
% Long Term Debt of Capitalization	35.6	36.4	Nil	Nil	Nil	Nil	Nil	Nil	NA	NA
% Net Income of Revenue	15.9	8.0	NM	NM	4.8	10.5	NM	NM	NA	NA
% Return on Assets	5.2	3.4	NM	NM	0.6	1.2	NM	NM	NA	NA
% Return on Equity	9.5	5.5	NM	NM	0.7	1.5	NM	NM	NA	NA

Data as orig reptd.; bef. results of disc opers/spec. items. Per share data adj. for stk. divs.; EPS diluted. E-Estimated. NA-Not Available. NM-Not Meaningful. NR-Not Ranked. UR-Under Review.

Office: 1 Discovery Pl, Silver Spring, MD 20910-3354.
Telephone: 240-662-2000.
Website: http://www.discoveryholdingcompany.com
Chrmn: J.S. Hendricks

Pres & CEO: D. Zaslav
COO & EVP: P. Liguori
EVP, CFO & Treas: B.E. Singer
EVP & Chief Acctg Officer: T.R. Colan

Board Members: R. R. Beck, R. R. Bennett, P. A. Gould, J. S. Hendricks, L. Kramer, J. C. Malone, R. J. Miron, S. A. Miron, M. L. Robison, J. Wargo, D. Zaslav

Founded: 2005
Domicile: Delaware
Employees: 4,400

Walt Disney Co (The)

STANDARD &POOR'S

S&P Recommendation BUY ★★★★☆	**Price** $34.97 (as of Oct 22, 2010)	**12-Mo. Target Price** $42.00	**Investment Style** Large-Cap Growth

GICS Sector Consumer Discretionary
Sub-Industry Movies & Entertainment

Summary This media and entertainment conglomerate has diversified global operations in theme parks, filmed entertainment, television broadcasting and merchandise licensing.

Key Stock Statistics (Source S&P, Vickers, company reports)

52-Wk Range	$37.98– 27.01	S&P Oper. EPS 2010**E**	2.25	Market Capitalization(B)	$66.884	Beta		1.16
Trailing 12-Month EPS	$2.08	S&P Oper. EPS 2011**E**	2.44	Yield (%)	1.00	S&P 3-Yr. Proj. EPS CAGR(%)		9
Trailing 12-Month P/E	16.8	P/E on S&P Oper. EPS 2010**E**	15.5	Dividend Rate/Share	$0.35	S&P Credit Rating		A
$10K Invested 5 Yrs Ago	NA	Common Shares Outstg. (M)	1,912.6	Institutional Ownership (%)	68			

Price Performance

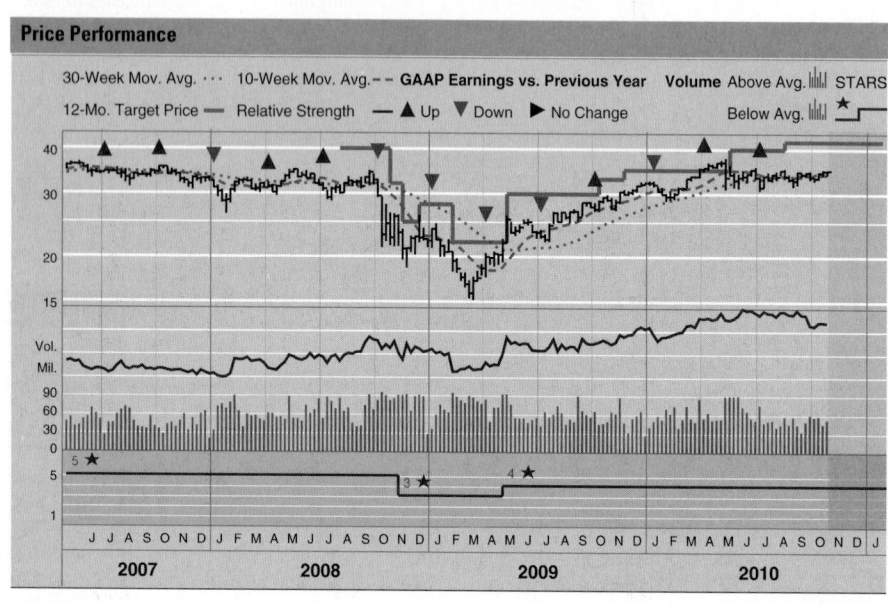

30-Week Mov. Avg. · · · · 10-Week Mov. Avg. – – GAAP Earnings vs. Previous Year Volume Above Avg. ılıl STARS
12-Mo. Target Price — Relative Strength — ▲ Up ▼ Down ▶ No Change Below Avg. ılıl ★

Options: ASE, CBOE, P, Ph

Analysis prepared by **Tuna N. Amobi, CFA, CPA** on August 11, 2010, when the stock traded at **$ 34.45**.

Highlights

▶ Including the December 2009 Marvel acquisition, we expect FY 10 (Sep.) and FY 11 consolidated revenues to advance 6.5% and 6.0%, to about $38.5 billion and $40.8 billion, respectively, with broad-based contributions from the cable networks (ESPN, Disney Channel, ABC Family), theme parks and resorts (Disney World, Disneyland), broadcasting (ABC network and stations), filmed entertainment (Disney, Pixar, Marvel) and consumer products (licensing, retail stores, publishing) businesses.

▶ After recent restructuring measures, we expect improved operating leverage to drive some margin expansion over the next two years (with further licensing and publishing of Marvel titles), against increased theme parks discounts and pension/other employee benefit costs in FY 10, higher TV programming costs, and further investments in the interactive space (video games, mobile/online).

▶ After interest expense, and an effective tax rate of about 37%, we forecast EPS of $2.25 and $2.44 for FY 10 and FY 11, respectively. As of early August, DIS had repurchased nearly 61 million shares -- entirely offsetting the shares recently issued toward the Marvel acquisition.

Investment Rationale/Risk

▶ We think DIS's encouraging results for the first nine months of FY 10 (Sep.) showed broad-based improvements across the core businesses -- while reaffirming potentially compelling cross-platform upside from the Marvel acquisition. Despite a relatively measured pace of recovery in the domestic theme parks' attendance, we see potential FY 11 catalysts including a healthy TV ad rebound, a growing stream of local broadcast TV retransmission revenues, and a resurgent film studio -- recently buoyed by Toy Story 3 and Alice in Wonderland, as well as Marvel's Iron Man 2. We believe DIS's strong balance sheet provides ample financial flexibility for "tuck-in" acquisitions, further share buybacks and a possible dividend increase.

▶ Risks to our recommendation and target price include a slower-than-expected economic and consumer spending rebound; geopolitical disruptions affecting the theme parks; and inherent volatility of film results.

▶ Our 12-month target price of $42 is derived from our sum-of-the-parts valuation analysis, reflecting relative enterprise values for the various business segments. The dividend recently offered a yield of about 1.0%.

Qualitative Risk Assessment

LOW	MEDIUM	HIGH

Our risk assessment reflects the strength of the company's content-oriented media and entertainment brands, counterbalanced by relatively high exposure to cyclical advertising-related and theme park businesses.

Quantitative Evaluations

S&P Quality Ranking A

D	C	B-	B	B+	A-	A	A+

Relative Strength Rank MODERATE

51

LOWEST = 1 HIGHEST = 99

Revenue/Earnings Data

Revenue (Million $)

	1Q	2Q	3Q	4Q	Year
2010	9,739	8,580	10,002	--	--
2009	9,599	8,087	8,956	9,867	36,149
2008	10,452	8,710	9,236	9,445	37,843
2007	9,581	7,954	9,045	8,930	35,510
2006	8,854	8,027	8,620	8,784	34,285
2005	8,666	7,829	7,715	7,734	31,944

Earnings Per Share ($)

2010	0.44	0.48	0.67	E0.63	E2.25
2009	0.45	0.33	0.51	0.47	1.76
2008	0.63	0.58	0.66	0.40	2.28
2007	0.79	0.43	0.58	0.44	2.24
2006	0.37	0.37	0.53	0.36	1.64
2005	0.33	0.31	0.39	0.20	1.24

Fiscal year ended Sep. 30. Next earnings report expected: Mid November. EPS Estimates based on S&P Operating Earnings; historical GAAP earnings are as reported.

Dividend Data (Dates: mm/dd Payment Date: mm/dd/yy)

Amount ($)	Date Decl.	Ex-Div. Date	Stk. of Record	Payment Date
0.350	12/02	12/10	12/14	01/19/10

Dividends have been paid since 1957. Source: Company reports.

Please read the Required Disclosures and Analyst Certification on the last page of this report.

The **McGraw·Hill** Companies

Walt Disney Co (The)

Business Summary August 11, 2010

CORPORATE OVERVIEW. The Walt Disney Co. is a leading media conglomerate with key operations in theme parks, television, filmed entertainment and merchandise licensing. Theme Parks and Resorts (29% of FY 09 (Sep.) revenues) includes the company's best-known assets: Disney World and Disneyland parks in Orlando, FL, and Anaheim, CA, respectively; the Disney Cruise Line; Euro Disney, Paris (39%-owned); and Hong Kong Disneyland (43%-owned), which opened in September 2005. The company plans to open another park in mainland China (Shanghai) by 2014.

Media Networks (45% of revenues) includes the ABC broadcast network; 10 TV stations; and cable networks ESPN (80%-owned), The Disney Channel and ABC Family. In November 2006, DIS sold its 39.5% stake in the E! cable network to Comcast for $1.23 billion. Studio entertainment (17% of revenues) includes the film, television and home video businesses under the Walt Disney, Touchstone and Miramax brands. Consumer products (7% of revenues) includes merchandise licensing, children's book publishing, video game development, as well as over 200 retail stores in North America, over 100 in Europe, and over 50 in Japan. Interactive (2%) primarily includes the video games production businesses, web sites and online virtual worlds.

CORPORATE STRATEGY. As a content-oriented company, DIS's top strategic priorities include creativity and innovation, international expansion (including theme parks and DIS channels), and leveraging new technology applications. Under CEO Robert Iger, we see senior management aggressively exploring new avenues to offer its branded content, characters and entertainment franchises across newer digital platforms (broadband, wireless/mobile -- including iTunes, iPhone and iPad -- as well as video games).

In July 2010, DIS agreed to acquire Playdom, an online social gaming platform, for up to $763 million, as well as Tapulous, a developer of mobile games/apps (for an undisclosed price). Also in July, DIS agreed to sell Miramax to private parties for about $660 million. In April 2008, DIS set a slate of 10 new animated films (from Disney and Pixar) to be released through 2012 -- after a 2006 restructuring that sharply pared down the annual film output (to 10 live-action/animation films plus two to three Touchstone titles), with a focus on Disney-branded films.

Company Financials Fiscal Year Ended Sep. 30

Per Share Data ($)	2009	2008	2007	2006	2005	2004	2003	2002	2001	2000
Tangible Book Value	5.27	4.18	3.15	3.10	3.24	3.15	2.01	1.78	3.99	2.24
Cash Flow	2.63	3.09	3.08	2.40	1.93	1.69	1.17	1.11	0.89	1.48
Earnings	1.76	2.28	2.24	1.64	1.24	1.12	0.65	0.60	0.11	0.57
S&P Core Earnings	1.58	2.16	1.97	1.70	1.27	1.04	0.49	0.29	0.21	NA
Dividends	0.35	0.35	0.31	0.27	0.24	0.21	0.21	0.21	0.21	0.57
Payout Ratio	20%	15%	14%	16%	19%	19%	32%	35%	191%	37%
Prices:High	32.75	35.02	36.79	34.89	29.99	28.41	23.80	25.17	34.80	43.88
Prices:Low	15.14	18.60	30.68	23.77	22.89	20.88	14.84	13.48	15.50	26.00
P/E Ratio:High	19	15	16	21	24	25	37	42	NM	77
P/E Ratio:Low	9	8	14	14	18	19	23	22	NM	46

Income Statement Analysis (Million $)										
Revenue	36,149	37,843	35,510	34,285	31,944	30,752	27,061	25,329	25,269	25,402
Operating Income	7,328	8,986	8,272	6,914	5,446	5,258	3,790	3,426	4,586	5,043
Depreciation	1,631	1,582	1,491	1,436	1,339	1,210	1,077	1,042	1,754	2,195
Interest Expense	645	774	593	592	605	629	666	453	417	558
Pretax Income	5,658	7,402	7,725	5,447	3,987	3,739	2,254	2,190	1,283	2,633
Effective Tax Rate	36.2%	36.1%	37.2%	34.7%	31.1%	32.0%	35.0%	38.9%	82.5%	61.0%
Net Income	3,307	4,427	4,674	3,374	2,569	2,345	1,338	1,236	120	920
S&P Core Earnings	2,975	4,209	4,091	3,500	2,635	2,201	1,006	606	458	NA

Balance Sheet & Other Financial Data (Million $)										
Cash	3,417	3,001	3,670	2,411	1,723	2,042	1,583	1,239	618	842
Current Assets	11,889	11,666	11,314	9,562	8,845	9,369	8,314	7,849	7,029	10,007
Total Assets	63,117	62,497	60,928	59,998	53,158	53,902	49,988	50,045	43,699	45,027
Current Liabilities	8,934	11,591	11,391	10,210	9,168	11,059	8,669	7,819	6,219	8,402
Long Term Debt	11,495	11,351	11,892	10,843	10,157	9,395	10,643	12,467	8,940	6,959
Common Equity	33,734	32,323	30,753	31,820	26,210	26,081	23,791	23,445	22,672	24,100
Total Capital	48,126	47,368	45,218	46,657	40,045	39,224	37,574	38,943	34,724	34,248
Capital Expenditures	1,753	1,586	1,566	1,299	1,823	1,427	1,049	1,086	1,795	2,013
Cash Flow	4,938	6,009	6,165	4,810	3,908	3,555	2,415	2,278	1,874	3,115
Current Ratio	1.3	1.0	1.0	0.9	1.0	0.8	1.0	1.0	1.1	1.2
% Long Term Debt of Capitalization	23.9	24.0	26.2	23.2	25.4	24.0	28.3	32.0	25.7	20.3
% Net Income of Revenue	9.2	11.7	13.1	9.8	8.0	7.6	4.9	4.9	0.5	3.6
% Return on Assets	5.3	7.2	7.7	6.0	4.8	4.5	2.7	2.6	0.3	2.1
% Return on Equity	10.0	14.0	14.9	11.6	9.8	9.4	5.7	5.4	0.5	4.1

Data as orig reptd.; bef. results of disc opers/spec. items. Per share data adj. for stk. divs.; EPS diluted. E-Estimated. NA-Not Available. NM-Not Meaningful. NR-Not Ranked. UR-Under Review.

Office: 500 South Buena Vista Street, Burbank, CA 91521.
Telephone: 818-560-1000.
Website: http://www.disney.com
Chrmn: J. Pepper, Jr.

Pres & CEO: R.A. Iger
EVP & CFO: J.A. Rasulo
EVP & Treas: C.M. McCarthy
EVP, Secy & General Counsel: A.N. Braverman

Investor Contact: L. Singer (818-560-6601)
Board Members: S. E. Arnold, J. E. Bryson, J. S. Chen, J. L. Estrin, R. A. Iger, S. P. Jobs, F. H. Langhammer, A. B. Lewis, M. Lozano, R. W. Matschullat, J. Pepper, Jr., S. Sandberg, O. Smith

Founded: 1936
Domicile: Delaware
Employees: 144,000

Dominion Resources Inc.

STANDARD &POOR'S

S&P Recommendation	HOLD ★★★★★	Price $44.51 (as of Oct 22, 2010)	12-Mo. Target Price $45.00	Investment Style Large-Cap Blend

GICS Sector Utilities
Sub-Industry Multi-Utilities

Summary This energy holding company's principal subsidiaries are Virginia Electric & Power Co. and Consolidated Natural Gas.

Key Stock Statistics (Source S&P, Vickers, company reports)

52-Wk Range	$45.12–34.00	S&P Oper. EPS 2010E	3.40	Market Capitalization(B)	$26.222	Beta	0.60
Trailing 12-Month EPS	$4.22	S&P Oper. EPS 2011E	3.55	Yield (%)	4.11	S&P 3-Yr. Proj. EPS CAGR(%)	4
Trailing 12-Month P/E	10.6	P/E on S&P Oper. EPS 2010E	13.1	Dividend Rate/Share	$1.83	S&P Credit Rating	A-
$10K Invested 5 Yrs Ago	$14,383	Common Shares Outstg. (M)	589.1	Institutional Ownership (%)	58		

Price Performance

30-Week Mov. Avg. ···   10-Week Mov. Avg. - -   **GAAP Earnings vs. Previous Year**   Volume Above Avg. ‖‖‖ STARS
12-Mo. Target Price —   Relative Strength —   ▲ Up ▼ Down ▶ No Change   Below Avg. ‖‖‖ ★

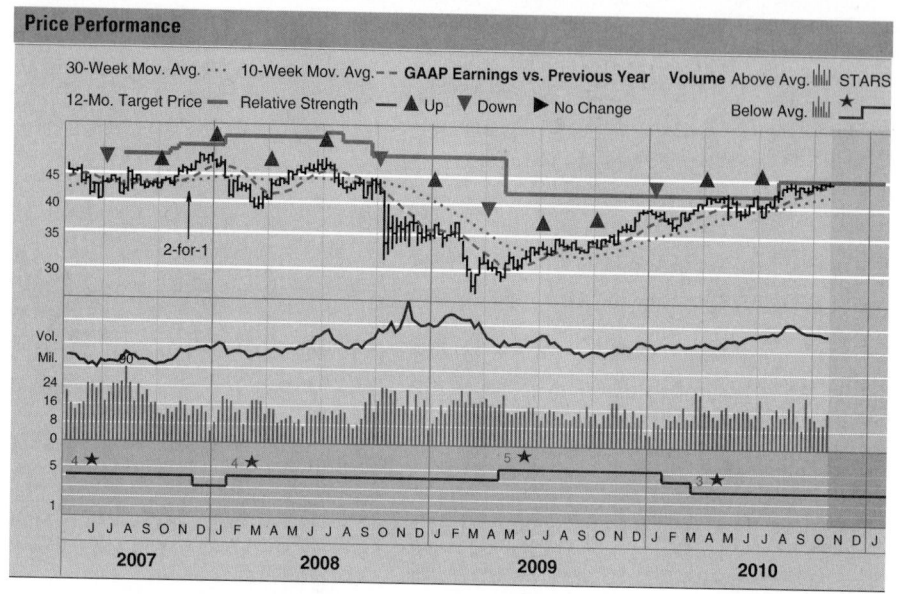

Analysis prepared by **Christopher B. Muir** on August 02, 2010, when the stock traded at **$ 43.20.**

Options: ASE, CBOE, P, Ph

Highlights

▶ We think revenues will drop 6.9% in 2010, due to lower revenues from both unregulated electric and regulated operations. We expect revenues to be hurt by the continued weak economic conditions in the company's service territories, partly offset by a full year of service related to the Cove Point LNG expansion and the USA Storage projects. We see utility revenues falling 4.8% and nonutility revenues declining 9.0%. In 2011, we expect revenues to climb 4.0%.

▶ We forecast operating margins of 26.7% in 2010 and 27.3% in 2011, versus 24.0% in 2009, on lower per-revenue fuel costs and operations & maintenance expenses, partly offset by higher per-revenue operating taxes. We project pretax profit margins of 22.2% in 2010 and 22.1% in 2011, up from 19.0% in 2009. We believe pretax margins will be helped by higher non-operating income and lower interest costs.

▶ Our 2010 recurring EPS estimate, excluding net nonrecurring gains of $1.79, is $3.40, up 3.3% from 2009's $3.29, which excludes $0.81 net non-recurring charges. Our 2011 EPS forecast is $3.55, an increase of 4.4%.

Investment Rationale/Risk

▶ We like D's continued focus on its core businesses. However, we are somewhat disappointed by the recently implemented rate case settlement that provides for no change in base rates through 2013. D's targeted dividend payout ratio of 60%-65%, up from 53.1% in 2009, by the end of 2012 means that dividends should grow slightly faster than earnings. We have a favorable view of the company's planned expansion of its wind generation operations, as well as its various other expansion and growth projects.

▶ Risks to our recommendation and target price include sharply lower electric prices, sharply higher interest rates, and a weaker economy.

▶ The stock recently traded at about 12X our 2011 EPS estimate, a slight discount to multi-utility peers. Our 12-month target price of $45 is 12.7X our 2011 EPS estimate, close to our peer target. Our valuation factors in our view of D's slightly above average dividend growth, average EPS growth, and slightly levered balance sheet relative to peers.

Qualitative Risk Assessment

LOW	MEDIUM	HIGH

Our risk assessment reflects our view of Dominion's relatively large capitalization and balanced sources of earnings, which include low-risk regulated electric and gas distribution and pipeline operations, offset by higher-risk energy marketing businesses.

Quantitative Evaluations

S&P Quality Ranking   B+

D	C	B-	B	B+	A-	A	A+

Relative Strength Rank   MODERATE

45

LOWEST = 1   HIGHEST = 99

Revenue/Earnings Data

Revenue (Million $)

	1Q	2Q	3Q	4Q	Year
2010	4,168	3,333	--	--	--
2009	4,778	3,450	3,648	3,255	15,131
2008	4,389	3,452	4,231	4,173	16,290
2007	4,661	3,730	3,589	3,694	15,674
2006	4,951	3,548	4,016	3,967	16,482
2005	4,736	3,646	4,564	5,095	18,041

Earnings Per Share ($)

	1Q	2Q	3Q	4Q	Year
2010	0.54	2.98	E1.04	E0.64	E3.40
2009	0.42	0.76	1.00	-0.01	2.17
2008	1.18	0.52	0.87	0.60	3.16
2007	0.68	-0.56	3.63	0.52	4.13
2006	0.78	0.24	0.93	0.28	2.23
2005	0.63	0.49	0.02	0.38	1.50

Fiscal year ended Dec. 31. Next earnings report expected: Early November. EPS Estimates based on S&P Operating Earnings; historical GAAP earnings are as reported.

Dividend Data (Dates: mm/dd Payment Date: mm/dd/yy)

Amount ($)	Date Decl.	Ex-Div. Date	Stk. of Record	Payment Date
0.458	12/17	02/24	02/26	03/20/10
0.458	05/18	05/26	05/28	06/20/10
0.458	07/21	08/25	08/27	09/20/10
0.458	10/22	11/24	11/29	12/20/10

Dividends have been paid since 1925. Source: Company reports.

Please read the Required Disclosures and Analyst Certification on the last page of this report.

The McGraw-Hill Companies

Dominion Resources Inc.

STANDARD &POOR'S

Business Summary August 02, 2010

CORPORATE OVERVIEW. Dominion Resources is a fully integrated gas and electric holding company. The company operates in three primary segments: Virginia Power, Energy, and Generation. The Virginia Power segment (20.5% of 2009 operating segment revenue) operates regulated electric transmission and distribution business in Virginia and northeastern North Carolina. The Generation segment (55.4%) is involved in generation for the electric utility and merchant power along with energy marketing and risk management activities. The Energy segment (17.2%) operates a regulated natural gas distribution company in Ohio, regulated gas transmission pipeline and storage operations, and regulated LNG operations. The Energy segment includes a producer services business, which engages in natural gas supply aggregation, gas transportation, market-based storage services, and gas trading and marketing.

CORPORATE STRATEGY. D focuses its efforts mainly on the Northeast, Mid-Atlantic and Midwest regions of the U.S. D believes that focusing on its core businesses will reduce earnings volatility and help to grow EPS at rates above 6% annually after 2010. It has a proactive risk management strategy, and has entered into commodity derivative agreements to hedge against commodity price risks.

MARKET PROFILE. As of December 31, 2009, D had total power generation capacity of 27,501 MW, with 16,442 MW of utility generation, 1,861 MW of utility power purchase agreements, and 9,204 MW of merchant generation. The generation unit's production was 76.6% baseload. The Virginia Power segment served a total of 2.41 million regulated electric customers. Additionally, it had 1.8 million unregulated customer accounts (25% electricity, 37% natural gas and 38% products and services). The Energy segment serves 320,535 gas sales and 988,071 gas transportation customers in Ohio and has about 12,000 miles of natural gas transmission, gathering and storage pipelines, 942 Bcf of storage capacity, and 1.3 trillion cubic feet equivalent of proved gas and oil reserves. This division also operates a liquefied natural gas (LNG) terminal at Cove Point, MD, which was recently expanded to a sendout capacity of 1.8 Bcfd with a storage capacity of 14.6 Bcf.

Company Financials Fiscal Year Ended Dec. 31

Per Share Data ($)	2009	2008	2007	2006	2005	2004	2003	2002	2001	2000
Tangible Book Value	11.92	10.05	9.21	11.45	8.79	16.37	9.60	9.09	7.85	7.10
Earnings	2.17	3.16	4.13	2.22	1.50	1.91	1.49	2.41	1.08	0.88
S&P Core Earnings	2.12	2.97	0.50	2.21	1.47	1.90	1.58	1.92	0.66	NA
Dividends	1.75	1.58	2.25	0.35	1.34	1.30	1.29	1.29	1.29	1.29
Payout Ratio	81%	50%	54%	16%	89%	68%	87%	54%	120%	147%
Prices:High	39.79	48.50	49.38	42.22	43.49	34.43	32.97	33.53	35.00	33.97
Prices:Low	27.15	31.26	39.84	34.36	33.26	30.39	25.87	17.70	27.57	17.41
P/E Ratio:High	18	15	12	19	29	18	22	14	33	39
P/E Ratio:Low	13	10	10	15	22	16	17	7	26	20

Income Statement Analysis (Million $)										
Revenue	15,131	16,290	15,674	16,482	18,041	13,972	12,078	10,218	10,558	9,260
Depreciation	1,319	1,191	1,368	1,606	1,412	1,305	1,216	1,258	1,245	1,176
Maintenance	NA	NA	NA	NA	NA	NA	NA	NA	NA	NA
Fixed Charges Coverage	3.14	4.23	4.82	3.42	2.63	3.09	2.63	3.15	2.02	1.99
Construction Credits	NA	NA	Nil	Nil	Nil	Nil	Nil	Nil	Nil	Nil
Effective Tax Rate	31.9%	32.4%	39.5%	37.0%	36.0%	35.6%	38.6%	33.3%	40.5%	30.5%
Net Income	1,287	1,836	2,705	1,563	1,034	1,264	949	1,362	544	415
S&P Core Earnings	1,256	1,729	324	1,555	1,010	1,254	1,004	1,088	331	NA

Balance Sheet & Other Financial Data (Million $)										
Gross Property	39,036	35,448	33,331	43,575	42,063	38,663	37,107	32,631	33,105	31,011
Capital Expenditures	3,817	3,519	3,972	4,052	1,683	1,451	2,138	2,828	1,224	1,385
Net Property	25,592	23,274	21,352	29,382	28,940	26,716	25,850	20,257	18,681	14,849
Capitalization:Long Term Debt	15,738	15,213	13,492	15,048	14,910	15,764	16,033	13,714	12,119	10,486
Capitalization:% Long Term Debt	58.5	60.2	58.9	53.8	58.9	58.0	60.3	57.3	58.1	58.3
Capitalization:Preferred	Nil	Nil	Nil	Nil	Nil	Nil	Nil	Nil	Nil	509
Capitalization:% Preferred	Nil	Nil	Nil	Nil	Nil	Nil	Nil	Nil	Nil	2.83
Capitalization:Common	11,185	10,077	9,406	12,913	10,397	11,426	10,538	10,213	8,368	6,992
Capitalization:% Common	41.5	39.8	41.1	46.2	41.1	42.0	39.7	42.7	40.1	38.9
Total Capital	28,061	29,427	27,179	33,842	30,291	32,689	31,134	28,136	24,811	20,955
% Operating Ratio	86.7	82.9	75.9	85.3	89.7	85.6	83.7	78.5	85.6	80.5
% Earned on Net Property	10.8	16.4	21.9	11.5	8.8	10.3	10.6	21.4	10.6	11.9
% Return on Revenue	8.5	11.3	17.3	9.5	5.7	9.0	7.9	13.3	5.2	4.5
% Return on Invested Capital	8.2	9.5	12.7	8.1	6.4	6.5	6.5	8.5	7.2	10.7
% Return on Common Equity	12.1	18.2	24.2	13.4	9.5	11.5	9.1	14.7	7.1	7.1

Data as orig reptd.; bef. results of disc opers/spec. items. Per share data adj. for stk. divs.; EPS diluted. E-Estimated. NA-Not Available. NM-Not Meaningful. NR-Not Ranked. UR-Under Review.

Office: 120 Tredegar Street, Richmond, VA 23219.
Telephone: 804-819-2000.
Email: investor_relations@domres.com
Website: http://www.dom.com

Chrmn, Pres & CEO: T.F. Farrell, II
EVP & CFO: M.F. McGettrick
SVP & Chief Admin Officer: S.A. Rogers
SVP & Treas: G.S. Hetzer

SVP & General Counsel: J.F. Stutts
Investor Contact: J. O'Hare (804-819-2156)
Board Members: W. P. Barr, P. W. Brown, G. A. Davidson, Jr., T. F. Farrell, II, J. W. Harris, R. S. Jepson, Jr., M. J. Kington, M. A. McKenna, F. S. Royal, R. H. Spilman, Jr., D. A. Wollard

Founded: 1909
Domicile: Virginia
Employees: 17,900

The McGraw-Hill Companies

R.R. Donnelley & Sons Co

STANDARD &POOR'S

S&P Recommendation HOLD ★★★★★

Price $18.40 (as of Oct 22, 2010)

12-Mo. Target Price $21.00

Investment Style Large-Cap Value

GICS Sector Industrials
Sub-Industry Commercial Printing

Summary R.R. Donnelley, the largest U.S. commercial printer, specializes in the production of catalogs, inserts, magazines, books, directories, and financial and computer documentation.

Key Stock Statistics (Source S&P, Vickers, company reports)

52-Wk Range	$23.20– 14.87	S&P Oper. EPS 2010E	1.70	Market Capitalization(B)	$3.796	Beta	2.01
Trailing 12-Month EPS	$0.36	S&P Oper. EPS 2011E	2.00	Yield (%)	5.65	S&P 3-Yr. Proj. EPS CAGR(%)	5
Trailing 12-Month P/E	51.1	P/E on S&P Oper. EPS 2010E	10.8	Dividend Rate/Share	$1.04	S&P Credit Rating	BBB
$10K Invested 5 Yrs Ago	$6,641	Common Shares Outstg. (M)	206.3	Institutional Ownership (%)	89		

Price Performance

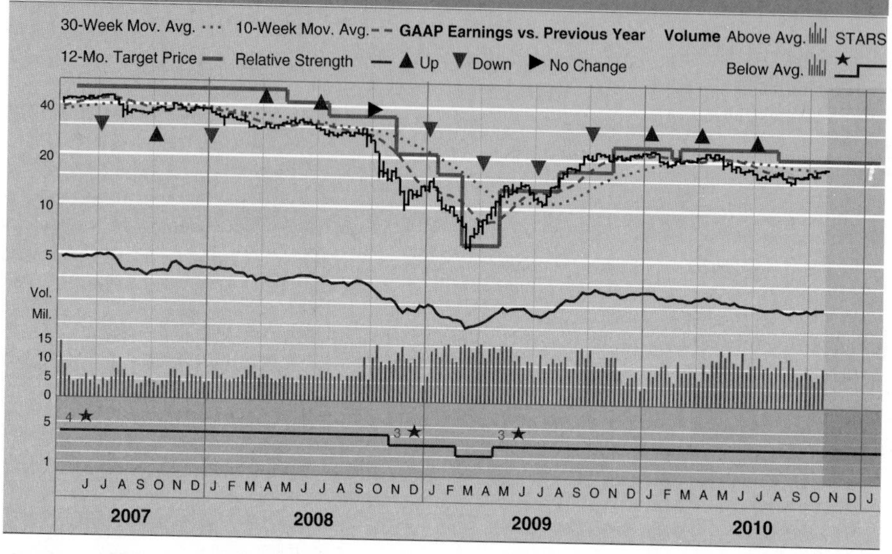
30-Week Mov. Avg. ··· 10-Week Mov. Avg. - - GAAP Earnings vs. Previous Year Volume Above Avg. STARS
12-Mo. Target Price — Relative Strength — ▲ Up ▼ Down ► No Change Below Avg.
40
20
10
5
Vol.
Mil.
15
10
5
0
5
1
J J A S O N D J F M A M J J A S O N D J F M A M J J A S O N D J F M A M J J A S O N D J
2007
2008
2009
2010

Options: CBOE, P, Ph

Analysis prepared by **Jim Corridore** on August 10, 2010, when the stock traded at **$ 17.88**.

Highlights

- We forecast that revenues will rise 3%-5% this year (excluding revenues from Bowne & Co., which RRD recently agreed to acquire) reflecting some improvement in the economies in the U.S. and Europe, RRD's main end-markets, which account for about 77% and 12% of revenues, respectively. We think most of the growth in 2010 will come in the second half of the year, and we expect meaningful growth in Europe to lag that of the U.S. by about six months. RRD expects to generate $600-$650 million in free cash in 2010, after generating $1.4 billion in 2009.
- We expect improving revenues along with the benefits of restructurings to modestly boost operating margins in 2010. We also expect productivity increases and cost synergies from recent acquisitions. Operating margins in 2009 were impacted by the effect of leveraging fixed costs over a smaller revenue base.
- We see 2010 operating EPS of $1.70, versus 2009 operating EPS of $1.44. For 2011, we see EPS of $2.00.

Investment Rationale/Risk

- We expect RRD to gain market share by leveraging its geographic and product breadth, but we think its business model is undergoing a long-term secular shift as electronic media reduces the demand for financial and other printing. We see headwinds from what we view as a highly leveraged balance sheet and digestion of recent acquisitions. However, we think improving investor sentiment on the overall U.S. economy will likely lend support to the shares if the U.S. economy starts to show growth.
- Risks to our recommendation and target price include substantially higher raw material costs, negative forex translation charges, further sharp deterioration in the company's end-markets, and a greater-than-expected increase in the amount of information disseminated electronically, which would lead to lower publishing demand.
- Our 12-month target price of $21 values the shares at 10.5X our 2011 EPS estimate of $2.00, toward the low end of RRD's five-year historical P/E range, reflecting our concerns about the maturation of RRD's business segments and high balance sheet risk.

Qualitative Risk Assessment

LOW | **MEDIUM** | HIGH

Our risk assessment reflects economies of scale that the company realizes as the largest U.S. commercial printer in a fragmented print industry, offset by industry pricing pressure and the increasingly electronic nature of communication.

Quantitative Evaluations

S&P Quality Ranking B-

D | C | **B-** | B | B+ | A- | A | A+

Relative Strength Rank MODERATE

70

LOWEST = 1 HIGHEST = 99

Revenue/Earnings Data

Revenue (Million $)

	1Q	2Q	3Q	4Q	Year
2010	2,415	2,409	--	--	--
2009	2,456	2,356	2,463	2,583	9,857
2008	2,997	2,924	2,865	2,796	11,582
2007	2,793	2,796	2,910	3,088	11,587
2006	2,267	2,274	2,309	2,467	9,317
2005	1,927	1,932	2,184	2,388	8,430

Earnings Per Share ($)

2010	0.25	0.42	E0.45	E0.53	E1.70
2009	0.07	0.12	0.06	-0.39	-0.13
2008	0.85	0.68	0.80	-3.35	-0.91
2007	0.63	-0.32	0.80	-1.37	-0.22
2006	0.52	0.57	0.75	-0.01	1.84
2005	0.50	0.44	0.59	-1.09	0.44

Fiscal year ended Dec. 31. Next earnings report expected: Early November. EPS Estimates based on S&P Operating Earnings; historical GAAP earnings are as reported.

Dividend Data (Dates: mm/dd Payment Date: mm/dd/yy)

Amount ($)	Date Decl.	Ex-Div. Date	Stk. of Record	Payment Date
0.260	10/28	11/09	11/12	12/01/09
0.260	01/07	01/20	01/22	03/01/10
0.260	04/14	04/27	04/29	06/01/10
0.260	07/21	08/03	08/05	09/01/10

Dividends have been paid since 1911. Source: Company reports.

Please read the Required Disclosures and Analyst Certification on the last page of this report.
Redistribution or reproduction is prohibited without written permission. Copyright ©2010 The McGraw-Hill Companies, Inc.

The McGraw-Hill Companies

R.R. Donnelley & Sons Co

Business Summary August 10, 2010

CORPORATE OVERVIEW. R.R. Donnelly & Sons (RRD) is the largest printing company in North America, serving customers in the publishing, health care, advertising, retail, telecommunications, technology, financial services and other industries. The company provides solutions in long- and short-run commercial printing, direct mail, financial printing, print fulfillment, forms and labels, logistics, digital printing, call centers, transactional print-and-mail, print management, online services, digital photography, color services, and content and database management.

The company has two reportable segments: U.S. Print and Related Services, and International. R.R. Donnelley management changed its reportable segments in the third quarter of 2007 to reflect changes in management reporting structure and the manner in which management assesses information for decision-making purposes.

The U.S. Print and Related Services segment (75% of revenues in 2009 and 2008) consists of the following U.S. businesses: magazine, catalog and retail,

which includes print services to consumer magazine and catalog publishers as well as retailers; book, which serves the consumer, religious, educational and specialty book and telecommunications sectors; directories, which serves the printing needs of yellow and white pages directory publishers; logistics, which delivers company and third-party printed products and distributes time-sensitive and secure material, and performs warehousing and fulfillment services; direct mail, which offers content creation, database management, printing, personalization finishing and distribution services to direct marketing companies; financial print; direct mail; and short-run commercial print, which provides print and print related services to a diversified customer base.

Company Financials Fiscal Year Ended Dec. 31

Per Share Data ($)	2009	2008	2007	2006	2005	2004	2003	2002	2001	2000
Tangible Book Value	NM	NM	NM	0.54	NM	3.81	5.14	4.51	3.92	5.89
Cash Flow	2.60	2.02	2.52	3.96	2.40	5.07	4.43	4.32	3.41	5.34
Earnings	-0.13	-0.91	-0.22	1.84	0.44	0.88	1.54	1.24	0.21	2.17
S&P Core Earnings	0.01	0.61	1.48	1.97	1.27	1.20	1.18	0.18	-0.65	NA
Dividends	1.04	1.04	1.04	1.04	1.04	1.04	1.02	0.98	0.94	0.90
Payout Ratio	NM	NM	NM	57%	NM	118%	66%	79%	NM	41%
Prices:High	22.78	38.19	45.25	36.00	38.27	35.37	30.15	32.10	31.90	27.50
Prices:Low	5.54	9.53	32.59	28.50	29.54	27.62	16.94	18.50	24.30	19.00
P/E Ratio:High	NM	NM	NM	20	87	40	20	26	NM	13
P/E Ratio:Low	NM	NM	NM	15	67	31	11	15	NM	9

Income Statement Analysis (Million $)										
Revenue	9,857	11,582	11,587	9,317	8,430	7,156	4,787	4,755	5,298	5,764
Operating Income	1,288	1,761	1,752	1,420	1,295	952	617	686	722	891
Depreciation	579	617	598	463	425	771	329	352	379	390
Interest Expense	245	241	231	139	111	85.9	50.4	62.8	71.2	89.6
Pretax Income	93.1	-269	91.4	601	332	357	208	176	74.9	434
Effective Tax Rate	123.0%	NM	NM	32.6%	71.5%	26.0%	15.3%	19.1%	66.6%	38.5%
Net Income	-27.3	-192	-48.4	403	95.6	265	177	142	25.0	267
S&P Core Earnings	1.17	129	322	430	275	243	136	21.3	-78.3	NA

Balance Sheet & Other Financial Data (Million $)										
Cash	499	324	443	211	367	642	60.8	60.5	48.6	60.9
Current Assets	2,961	3,281	3,521	2,517	2,622	2,601	1,000	866	940	1,206
Total Assets	8,748	9,494	12,087	9,636	9,374	8,554	3,189	3,152	3,400	3,914
Current Liabilities	2,040	2,487	2,765	1,612	1,814	1,487	884	955	984	1,191
Long Term Debt	2,983	3,203	3,602	2,359	2,365	1,581	752	753	881	739
Common Equity	2,134	2,319	3,907	4,125	3,724	3,987	983	915	888	1,233
Total Capital	5,144	5,783	8,382	7,087	6,686	6,144	1,970	1,882	1,982	2,205
Capital Expenditures	195	323	482	374	471	265	203	242	273	237
Cash Flow	534	425	550	866	521	1,036	506	495	404	657
Current Ratio	1.5	1.3	1.3	1.6	1.4	1.7	1.1	0.9	1.0	1.0
% Long Term Debt of Capitalization	58.0	55.4	43.0	33.3	35.4	25.7	38.2	40.0	44.5	33.5
% Net Income of Revenue	NM	NM	NM	4.3	1.1	3.7	3.7	3.0	0.5	4.6
% Return on Assets	NM	NM	NM	4.2	1.1	4.5	5.5	4.4	0.7	6.9
% Return on Equity	NM	NM	NM	10.3	2.5	10.7	18.6	15.8	2.4	22.5

Data as orig reptd.; bef. results of disc opers/spec. items. Per share data adj. for stk. divs.; EPS diluted. E-Estimated. NA-Not Available. NM-Not Meaningful. NR-Not Ranked. UR-Under Review.

Office: 111 S Wacker Dr, Chicago, IL 60606-4302.
Telephone: 312-326-8000.
Email: investor.info@rrd.com
Website: http://www.rrdonnelley.com

Chrmn: S.M. Wolf
Pres & CEO: T.J. Quinlan, III
COO: J.R. Paloian
EVP & CFO: M.W. McHugh

EVP, Secy & General Counsel: S.S. Bettman
Investor Contact: D. Leib (312-326-7710)
Board Members: L. A. Chaden, J. Hamilton, S. M. Ivey, T. S. Johnson, J. C. Pope, T. J. Quinlan, III, M. T. Riordan, O. R. Sockwell, Jr., S. M. Wolf

Founded: 1864
Domicile: Delaware
Employees: 56,800

Dover Corp

STANDARD &POOR'S

S&P Recommendation BUY ★★★★☆

Price	12-Mo. Target Price	Investment Style
$53.18 (as of Oct 22, 2010)	$60.00	Large-Cap Growth

GICS Sector Industrials
Sub-Industry Industrial Machinery

Summary This company manufactures a broad range of specialized industrial products and sophisticated manufacturing equipment.

Key Stock Statistics (Source S&P, Vickers, company reports)

52-Wk Range	$55.50–37.28	S&P Oper. EPS 2010E	3.37	Market Capitalization(B)	$9.927	Beta	1.27
Trailing 12-Month EPS	$2.57	S&P Oper. EPS 2011E	3.79	Yield (%)	2.07	S&P 3-Yr. Proj. EPS CAGR(%)	11
Trailing 12-Month P/E	20.7	P/E on S&P Oper. EPS 2010E	15.8	Dividend Rate/Share	$1.10	S&P Credit Rating	A
$10K Invested 5 Yrs Ago	$15,519	Common Shares Outstg. (M)	186.7	Institutional Ownership (%)	86		

Price Performance

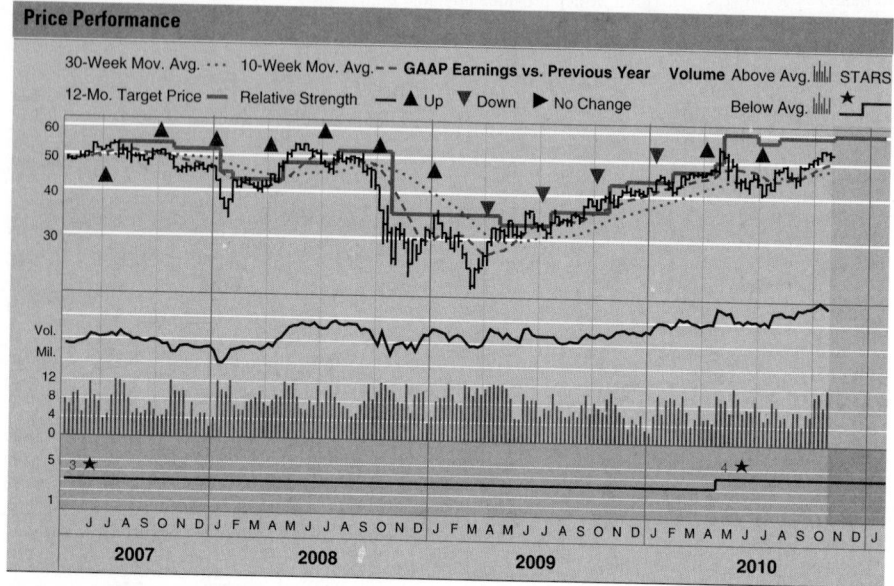

30-Week Mov. Avg. · · · · 10-Week Mov. Avg. – – **GAAP Earnings vs. Previous Year** Volume Above Avg. STARS
12-Mo. Target Price — Relative Strength — ▲ Up ▼ Down ▶ No Change Below Avg. ★

Options: CBOE, P, Ph

Qualitative Risk Assessment

LOW	MEDIUM	HIGH

Our risk assessment reflects the company's acquisition strategy, its model of operating numerous different businesses as stand-alone entities, its strategic shift to manage numerous aspects of the business using a more top-down approach, and exposure to several cyclical end markets.

Quantitative Evaluations

S&P Quality Ranking A-

D	C	B-	B	B+	A-	A	A+

Relative Strength Rank MODERATE
65
LOWEST = 1   HIGHEST = 99

Highlights

▶ The 12-month target price for DOV has recently been changed to $60.00 from $59.00. The Highlights section of this Stock Report will be updated accordingly.

Investment Rationale/Risk

▶ The Investment Rationale/Risk section of this Stock Report will be updated shortly. For the latest News story on DOV from MarketScope, see below.

▶ 10/22/10 12:47 pm ET ... S&P MAINTAINS BUY RECOMMENDATION ON SHARES OF DOVER CORP (DOV 52.9****): Excluding a $0.20 tax benefit, DOV reports Q3 EPS of $0.98, vs. $0.58, $0.16 ahead of our estimate on better-than-expected margins and revenue growth of about 26%. We view favorably the strong quarterly operating margin of 15.8% and believe this is representative of management's ongoing procurement and other strategies, a trend we expect to continue. On higher forecasted sales and margins, we increase our '10 and '11 EPS estimates by $0.24 each to $3.37 and $3.79, respectively. We also raise our target price by $1 to $60 on our higher forecasts and revised valuation analyses. /M.Christy, CFA

Revenue/Earnings Data

Revenue (Million $)

	1Q	2Q	3Q	4Q	Year
2010	1,583	1,787	--	--	--
2009	1,379	1,390	1,500	1,507	5,776
2008	1,865	2,011	1,966	1,727	7,569
2007	1,780	1,859	1,844	1,860	7,226
2006	1,500	1,650	1,647	1,715	6,512
2005	1,383	1,525	1,556	1,614	6,078

Earnings Per Share ($)

	1Q	2Q	3Q	4Q	Year
2010	0.65	0.91	E0.82	E0.83	E3.37
2009	0.33	0.54	0.58	0.55	1.99
2008	0.77	0.98	1.01	0.91	3.67
2007	0.67	0.85	0.88	0.86	3.22
2006	0.64	0.77	0.77	0.76	2.94
2005	0.47	0.59	0.65	0.61	2.32

Fiscal year ended Dec. 31. Next earnings report expected: Late October. EPS Estimates based on S&P Operating Earnings; historical GAAP earnings are as reported.

Dividend Data (Dates: mm/dd Payment Date: mm/dd/yy)

Amount ($)	Date Decl.	Ex-Div. Date	Stk. of Record	Payment Date
0.260	11/05	11/25	11/30	12/15/09
0.260	02/11	02/24	02/28	03/15/10
0.260	05/06	05/26	05/31	06/15/10
0.275	08/05	08/27	08/31	09/15/10

Dividends have been paid since 1947. Source: Company reports.

Please read the Required Disclosures and Analyst Certification on the last page of this report.

The McGraw-Hill Companies

STANDARD & POOR'S

Dover Corp

Business Summary August 03, 2010

CORPORATE OVERVIEW. Dover Corporation (DOV) is a diversified manufacturer of a broad range of specialized industrial products and manufacturing equipment. The company has evolved largely through acquisitions, with 85 deals costing approximately $4.3 billion completed between January 2000 and December 2009. There are four operating segments: Industrial Products, Engineered Systems, Fluid Management and Electronic Technologies.

Industrial Products (28% of 2009 sales, with 8.6% operating margin) manufactures a diverse mix of equipment and components for use in the waste handling, bulk transport and automotive service industries. Its two sub-units are Material Handling and Mobile Equipment. Major units include Paladin, PDQ Manufacturing, Heil Environmental, Rotary Lift, Heil Trailer International, Chief Automotive, and Marathon Equipment.

Engineered Systems (32%, 12.2%) manufactures food equipment (refrigeration systems, display cases, walk-in coolers, etc.) and packaging machinery. It is composed of two primary sub-groups -- Product Identification and Engineered Products. The food equipment businesses (Hill Phoenix and Unified Brands)

sell to the institutional and commercial foodservice markets. The packaging machinery businesses sell to the beverage and food processing industries.

Fluid Management (22%, 20.4%) manufactures products primarily for the oil and gas, automotive fueling, fluid handling, engineered components, material handling and chemical equipment industries. This segment consists of two primary sub-units -- Energy and Fluid Solutions.

Electronic Technologies (18%, 8.1%) manufactures an array of specialized electronic, electromechanical and plastic components for OEMs in multiple end markets, including hearing aids, telecom, defense and aerospace electronics, and life sciences. It also supplies ATM hardware and software for retail applications and financial institutions, and chemical proportioning and dispensing systems for janitorial/sanitation applications.

Company Financials Fiscal Year Ended Dec. 31

Per Share Data ($)	2009	2008	2007	2006	2005	2004	2003	2002	2001	2000
Tangible Book Value	NM	NM	NM	NM	NM	2.16	2.71	2.66	1.97	1.79
Cash Flow	3.37	5.05	4.43	3.92	3.18	2.78	2.14	1.83	1.89	3.60
Earnings	1.99	3.67	3.22	2.94	2.32	2.00	1.40	1.04	0.82	2.61
S&P Core Earnings	2.00	3.55	3.28	2.98	2.25	1.92	1.31	0.90	0.68	NA
Dividends	1.02	0.90	0.77	0.71	0.66	0.62	0.57	0.54	0.52	0.48
Payout Ratio	51%	25%	24%	24%	28%	31%	41%	52%	63%	18%
Prices:High	43.10	54.57	54.59	51.92	42.11	44.13	40.45	43.55	43.55	54.38
Prices:Low	21.79	23.39	44.34	40.30	34.11	35.12	22.85	23.54	26.40	34.13
P/E Ratio:High	22	15	17	18	18	22	29	42	53	21
P/E Ratio:Low	11	6	14	14	15	18	16	23	32	13

Income Statement Analysis (Million $)	2009	2008	2007	2006	2005	2004	2003	2002	2001	2000
Revenue	5,776	7,569	7,226	6,512	6,078	5,488	4,413	4,184	4,460	5,401
Operating Income	918	1,311	1,220	1,113	876	773	595	503	518	1,047
Depreciation	258	261	245	202	176	161	151	161	219	203
Interest Expense	116	96.0	89.0	77.0	72.2	61.3	62.2	70.0	91.2	97.5
Pretax Income	492	946	888	823	644	552	372	270	238	772
Effective Tax Rate	24.4%	26.6%	26.4%	26.7%	26.3%	25.9%	23.3%	21.7%	30.0%	31.0%
Net Income	372	695	653	603	474	409	285	211	167	533
S&P Core Earnings	373	672	667	613	460	392	267	182	138	NA

Balance Sheet & Other Financial Data (Million $)	2009	2008	2007	2006	2005	2004	2003	2002	2001	2000
Cash	938	827	602	374	191	358	370	295	177	187
Current Assets	2,523	2,614	2,544	2,272	1,976	2,150	1,850	1,658	1,655	1,975
Total Assets	7,808	7,867	8,070	7,627	6,573	5,792	5,134	4,437	4,602	4,892
Current Liabilities	969	1,238	1,681	1,434	1,207	1,356	911	697	819	1,605
Long Term Debt	1,825	1,861	1,452	1,480	1,344	753	1,004	1,030	1,033	632
Common Equity	4,084	3,793	3,946	3,811	3,330	3,119	2,743	2,395	2,520	2,442
Total Capital	5,944	5,968	5,714	5,656	5,046	4,168	3,980	3,561	3,656	3,141
Capital Expenditures	120	176	174	195	152	107	96.4	102	167	198
Cash Flow	630	956	898	805	650	570	437	372	386	737
Current Ratio	2.7	2.1	1.5	1.6	1.6	1.6	2.0	2.4	2.0	1.2
% Long Term Debt of Capitalization	30.7	31.2	25.4	26.2	26.6	18.1	25.2	28.9	28.3	20.1
% Net Income of Revenue	6.4	9.2	9.0	9.3	7.8	7.5	6.5	5.0	3.7	9.9
% Return on Assets	4.8	8.7	8.3	8.5	7.7	7.5	6.0	4.7	3.5	11.8
% Return on Equity	9.4	18.0	16.8	16.9	14.7	14.0	11.1	8.6	6.7	23.8

Data as orig reptd.; bef. results of disc opers/spec. items. Per share data adj. for stk. divs.; EPS diluted. E-Estimated. NA-Not Available. NM-Not Meaningful. NR-Not Ranked. UR-Under Review.

Office: 3005 Highland Parkway, Suite 200, Downers Grove, IL 60515.
Telephone: 630-541-1540.
Website: http://www.dovercorporation.com
Chrmn: R.W. Cremin

Pres & CEO: R.A. Livingston
CFO: B.M. Cerepak
Chief Acctg Officer & Cntlr: R.T. McKay, Jr.
Investor Contact: P.E. Goldberg (212-922-1640)

Board Members: D. H. Benson, R. W. Cremin, J. P. Ergas, P. T. Francis, K. C. Graham, J. L. Koley, R. A. Livingston, R. K. Lochridge, B. G. Rethore, M. B. Stubbs, M. A. Winston

Founded: 1947
Domicile: Delaware
Employees: 29,300

The McGraw-Hill Companies

Dow Chemical Co (The)

STANDARD &POOR'S

S&P Recommendation HOLD ★★★☆☆

Price	12-Mo. Target Price	Investment Style
$30.20 (as of Oct 22, 2010)	$30.00	Large-Cap Blend

GICS Sector Materials
Sub-Industry Diversified Chemicals

Summary Dow Chemical, the largest U.S. chemical company, provides chemical, plastic and agricultural products and services to many consumer markets.

Key Stock Statistics (Source S&P, Vickers, company reports)

52-Wk Range	$32.05– 22.42	S&P Oper. EPS 2010**E**	1.75	Market Capitalization(B)	$35.028	Beta	2.25
Trailing 12-Month EPS	$1.62	S&P Oper. EPS 2011**E**	2.25	Yield (%)	1.99	S&P 3-Yr. Proj. EPS CAGR(%)	20
Trailing 12-Month P/E	18.6	P/E on S&P Oper. EPS 2010**E**	17.3	Dividend Rate/Share	$0.60	S&P Credit Rating	BBB-
$10K Invested 5 Yrs Ago	$8,485	Common Shares Outstg. (M)	1,159.9	Institutional Ownership (%)	67		

Price Performance

30-Week Mov. Avg. · · ·   10-Week Mov. Avg. – –   **GAAP Earnings vs. Previous Year**   Volume Above Avg. |||| STARS
12-Mo. Target Price —   Relative Strength —   ▲ Up ▼ Down ▶ No Change   Below Avg. |||| ★

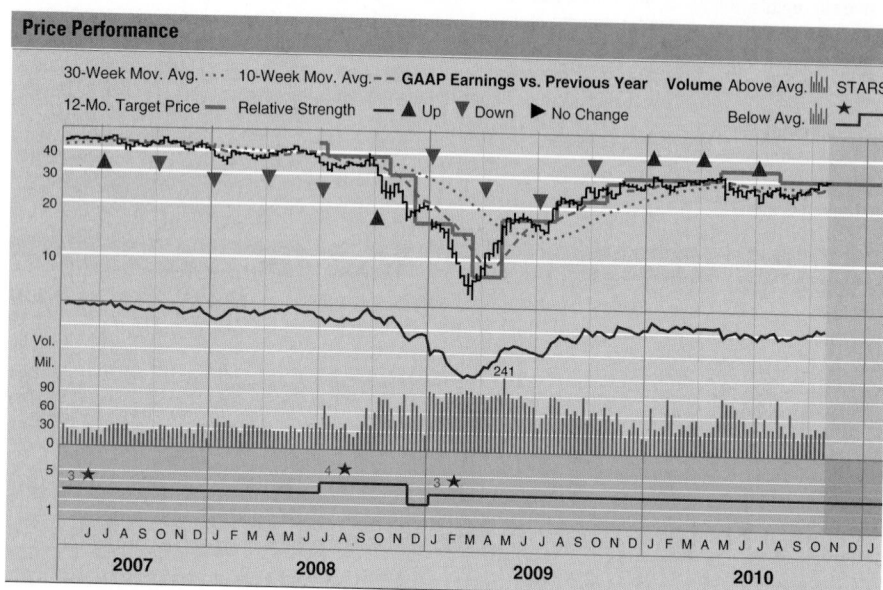

Options: ASE, CBOE, P, Ph

Analysis prepared by **Richard O'Reilly, CFA** on September 22, 2010, when the stock traded at **$ 27.36**.

Highlights

▶ We expect sales of about $53 billion in 2010 as global economic conditions have rebounded this year, led by growth in emerging markets and a recovery in the U.S., resulting in favorable volumes and price comparisons against weak 2009 levels. In mid-June 2010, Dow sold its Styron division (annual sales of about $3.7 billion, including styrenics).

▶ We see some slowing in volume growth in the second half of 2010 for most specialty products and coatings lines (up a combined 13% in the first half). Industry commodity plastic prices have declined since the first quarter, but caustic soda prices are continuing to recover. Following a 54% increase in the first half, feedstock costs are likely to remain above comparable 2009 levels. Recent equity profits were back to pre-recession levels and we see this continuing for the rest of 2010.

▶ We expect restructuring actions to reduce annual costs by over $1 billion in 2010, while synergies from Rohm & Haas have surpassed a $1.3 billion rate this year. Reported EPS in 2009 includes much greater interest expense and restructuring and merger-related charges.

Investment Rationale/Risk

▶ We view the April 2009 purchase of Rohm & Haas for $16.2 billion as positive for DOW for the long term, as less cyclical specialty products now account for about 60% of annual revenues, up from 51% in 2008. We also note that less cyclical products will now represent a larger percentage of profits.

▶ Risks to our recommendation and target price include slower-than-expected U.S. and global economies, increased global industry capacity, rising energy costs, unplanned production outages, and an inability to achieve integration savings. We note that while the purchase of Rohm & Haas greatly increased debt and leverage, Dow has been successful in repaying and refinancing much of the merger debt.

▶ To reflect higher balance sheet risk, we base our 12-month target price of $30 on a historical mid-cycle P/E of about 13X, applied to an annualized earnings rate of $2.25 that we believe the company, as currently constituted, will achieve in 2011.

Qualitative Risk Assessment

LOW	MEDIUM	HIGH

Our risk assessment reflects our view of the highly leveraged post-merger balance sheet and integration risks and the cyclical nature of the commodity chemical industry, partly offset by Dow's diverse business and geographic sales mix and manufacturing integration.

Quantitative Evaluations

S&P Quality Ranking B

D	C	B-	**B**	B+	A-	A	A+

Relative Strength Rank STRONG

81

LOWEST = 1   HIGHEST = 99

Revenue/Earnings Data

Revenue (Million $)

	1Q	2Q	3Q	4Q	Year
2010	13,417	13,618	--	--	--
2009	9,041	11,322	12,046	12,466	44,875
2008	14,824	16,380	15,411	10,899	57,514
2007	12,432	13,265	13,589	14,227	53,513
2006	12,020	12,509	12,359	12,236	49,124
2005	11,679	11,450	11,261	11,917	46,307

Earnings Per Share ($)

2010	0.41	0.50	E0.35	E0.42	E1.75
2009	0.03	-0.57	-0.64	0.08	0.22
2008	0.99	0.81	0.46	-1.68	0.62
2007	1.00	1.07	0.24	0.49	2.99
2006	1.24	1.05	0.53	1.00	3.82
2005	1.39	1.30	0.82	1.14	4.64

Fiscal year ended Dec. 31. Next earnings report expected: Late October. EPS Estimates based on S&P Operating Earnings; historical GAAP earnings are as reported.

Dividend Data (Dates: mm/dd Payment Date: mm/dd/yy)

Amount ($)	Date Decl.	Ex-Div. Date	Stk. of Record	Payment Date
0.150	12/10	12/29	12/31	01/29/10
0.150	02/11	03/29	03/31	04/30/10
0.150	05/13	06/28	06/30	07/30/10
0.150	09/09	09/28	09/30	10/29/10

Dividends have been paid since 1911. Source: Company reports.

Please read the Required Disclosures and Analyst Certification on the last page of this report.

The McGraw-Hill Companies

STANDARD &POOR'S

Dow Chemical Co (The)

Business Summary September 22, 2010

CORPORATE OVERVIEW. Dow Chemical is the largest U.S. chemical company. Foreign operations accounted for 68% of 2009 sales.

Electronic and specialty materials (9% of sales and 17% of profits in 2009) consists of photoresists, coatings, CMP slurries and pads, and plating products for electronics; water and process solutions (ion exchange resins, membranes); biocides; cellulosics; and home and personal care ingredients. The segment also includes results of the Dow Corning joint venture. Coatings and infrastructure (9%, 6%) includes coatings materials (acrylics, opaque polymers, rheology modifiers, surfactants, and solvents), building and construction products (STYROFOAM insulation products, weather barrier products, foams, sealants, roofing adhesives, and solar shingle), and adhesives.

Performance systems (13%, 11%) consists of automotive products (engineering plastics, adhesives, films, foams, and fluids); elastomers, resins, films, and plastic additives; polyolefins and flame retardants for wire and cable insulation; and polyurethanes foams and systems. Performance products (20%, 19%) consists of amines; epoxy resins and intermediates (phenol and acetone); glycols, surfactants, and fluids (lubricants, heat transfer, deicing, and coolants); polyurethanes (isocyanates, propylene oxide/glycol, polyols); solvents; acrylic acid and methyl methacrylate; and custom manufacturing.

Dow AgroSciences (10%, 10%) is a leading global maker of herbicides (Clincher, Starane), insecticides (Lorsban, Sentricon termite colony elimination system, Tracer) and fungicides for crop protection and industrial/commercial pest control. It also provides crop seeds (Mycogen), traits (Herculex) and value-added grains.

The company, a major producer of basic plastics (23%, 28%), is the world's largest producer of polyethylene; it also makes polypropylene and offers technology licensing (UNIPOL for polyethylene and polypropylene). In June 2010, Dow sold its polystyrene and polycarbonate and compounds businesses. Basic Chemicals (6%, 2%) includes chlor-alkali (chlorine, caustic soda, ethylene dichloride and vinyl chloride), chlorinated solvents, and ethylene oxide/glycol, used primarily as raw materials in the manufacture of customer products, and technology licensing (Meteor for ethylene oxide/glycol). The hydrocarbons and energy business (10%, 7%) procures fuels and raw materials and produces ethylene, propylene, aromatics, styrene, and power and steam.

Company Financials Fiscal Year Ended Dec. 31

Per Share Data ($)	2009	2008	2007	2006	2005	2004	2003	2002	2001	2000
Tangible Book Value	NM	10.05	17.00	14.50	12.14	9.01	5.79	4.19	7.59	10.78
Cash Flow	2.90	2.86	5.09	5.83	6.83	5.12	3.93	4.57	1.55	4.14
Earnings	0.22	0.62	2.99	3.82	4.64	2.93	1.88	-0.44	-0.46	2.22
S&P Core Earnings	-0.28	0.05	2.82	3.73	4.04	2.34	1.58	-1.41	-1.43	NA
Dividends	0.60	1.68	1.64	1.50	1.34	1.34	1.34	1.34	1.30	1.16
Payout Ratio	NM	271%	55%	39%	29%	46%	71%	NM	NM	52%
Prices:High	29.50	43.42	47.96	45.15	56.75	51.34	42.00	37.00	39.67	47.17
Prices:Low	5.89	14.93	38.89	33.00	40.18	36.35	24.83	23.66	25.06	23.00
P/E Ratio:High	NM	70	16	12	12	18	22	NM	NM	21
P/E Ratio:Low	NM	24	13	9	9	12	13	NM	NM	10

Income Statement Analysis (Million $)										
Revenue	44,875	57,514	53,513	49,124	46,307	40,161	32,632	27,609	27,805	23,008
Operating Income	4,443	4,482	5,903	6,675	7,437	5,466	3,922	2,925	2,953	3,462
Depreciation	2,827	2,108	2,031	1,954	2,134	2,088	1,903	1,825	1,815	1,315
Interest Expense	1,571	745	669	689	702	747	828	774	733	460
Pretax Income	469	1,321	4,229	4,972	6,399	3,796	1,751	-622	-613	2,401
Effective Tax Rate	NM	50.5%	29.4%	23.2%	27.8%	23.1%	NM	NM	NM	34.3%
Net Income	538	579	2,887	3,724	4,535	2,797	1,739	-405	-417	1,513
S&P Core Earnings	-312	29.0	2,734	3,638	3,956	2,236	1,462	-1,295	-1,303	NA

Balance Sheet & Other Financial Data (Million $)										
Cash	2,846	2,800	1,737	2,910	3,838	3,192	2,434	1,573	264	304
Current Assets	19,560	16,060	18,654	17,209	17,404	15,890	13,002	11,681	10,308	9,260
Total Assets	65,937	45,474	48,801	45,581	45,934	45,885	41,891	39,562	35,515	27,645
Current Liabilities	13,106	13,108	12,445	10,601	10,663	10,506	9,534	8,856	8,125	7,873
Long Term Debt	19,152	8,042	7,581	8,036	10,186	12,629	12,763	12,659	10,266	5,365
Common Equity	16,555	13,511	19,389	17,065	15,324	12,270	9,175	7,626	9,993	9,186
Total Capital	41,358	22,868	29,238	27,465	27,241	26,649	23,438	21,645	21,376	15,848
Capital Expenditures	2,396	2,339	2,075	1,775	1,597	1,333	1,100	1,623	1,587	1,349
Cash Flow	3,053	2,687	4,918	5,678	6,669	4,885	3,642	1,420	1,398	2,828
Current Ratio	1.5	1.2	1.5	1.6	1.6	1.5	1.4	1.3	1.3	1.2
% Long Term Debt of Capitalization	46.3	35.2	25.9	30.4	37.4	47.4	54.5	58.5	48.0	33.9
% Net Income of Revenue	1.2	1.0	5.4	7.6	9.8	7.0	5.3	NM	NM	6.6
% Return on Assets	1.0	1.2	6.1	8.1	9.9	6.4	4.3	NM	NM	5.7
% Return on Equity	3.6	3.5	15.8	23.0	32.9	26.1	20.7	NM	NM	17.3

Data as orig reptd.; bef. results of disc opers/spec. items. Per share data adj. for stk. divs.; EPS diluted. E-Estimated. NA-Not Available. NM-Not Meaningful. NR-Not Ranked. UR-Under Review.

Office: 2030 Dow Center, Midland, MI 48674.
Telephone: 989-636-1000.
Website: http://www.dow.com
Chrmn, Pres & CEO: A.N. Liveris

COO: N. Parakh
EVP & CFO: W.H. Weideman
EVP & CTO: W.F. Banholzer
EVP, Secy & General Counsel: C.J. Kalil

Investor Contact: H. Ungerleider (989-636-1463)
Board Members: A. A. Allemang, J. K. Barton, J. A. Bell, J. M. Fettig, B. H. Franklin, J. B. Hess, A. N. Liveris, P. Polman, D. H. Reilley, J. M. Ringler, R. G. Shaw, P. G. Stern

Founded: 1897
Domicile: Delaware
Employees: 52,195

The McGraw-Hill Companies

D.R. Horton Inc.

STANDARD &POOR'S

S&P Recommendation SELL ★ ★ ☆ ☆ ☆

Price $10.61 (as of Oct 22, 2010)	**12-Mo. Target Price** $9.50	**Investment Style** Large-Cap Blend

GICS Sector Consumer Discretionary
Sub-Industry Homebuilding

Summary This company is one of the largest homebuilders in the U.S., based on number of homes sold and its nationwide presence.

Key Stock Statistics (Source S&P, Vickers, company reports)

52-Wk Range	$15.44– 9.41	S&P Oper. EPS 2010**E**	0.80	Market Capitalization(B)	$3.377	Beta	1.01
Trailing 12-Month EPS	$0.13	S&P Oper. EPS 2011**E**	0.65	Yield (%)	1.41	S&P 3-Yr. Proj. EPS CAGR(%)	12
Trailing 12-Month P/E	81.6	P/E on S&P Oper. EPS 2010**E**	13.3	Dividend Rate/Share	$0.15	S&P Credit Rating	BB-
$10K Invested 5 Yrs Ago	$3,797	Common Shares Outstg. (M)	318.3	Institutional Ownership (%)	88		

Price Performance

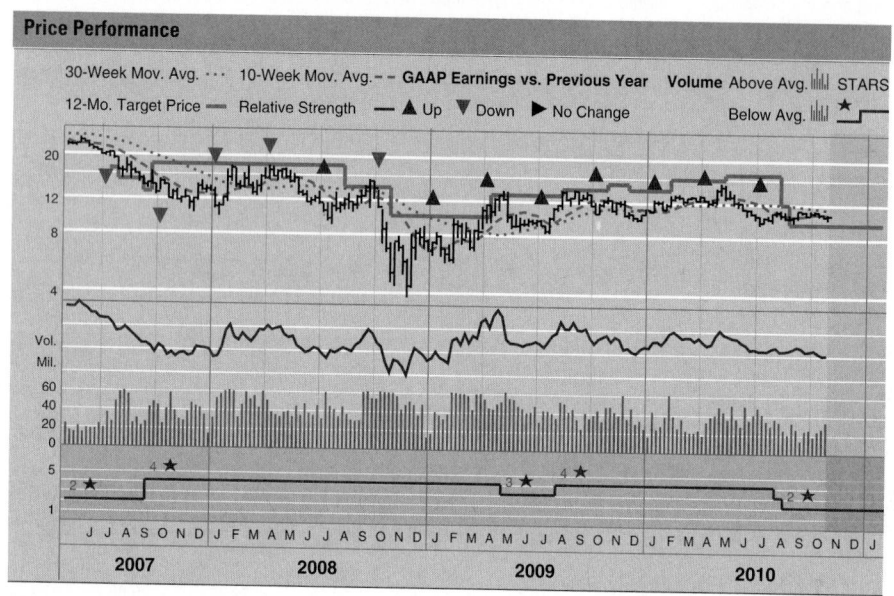

30-Week Mov. Avg. · · · 10-Week Mov. Avg. - - **GAAP Earnings vs. Previous Year** Volume Above Avg. STARS
12-Mo. Target Price — Relative Strength — ▲ Up ▼ Down ▶ No Change Below Avg.

Options: ASE, CBOE, P, Ph

Analysis prepared by **Kenneth M. Leon, CPA** on August 20, 2010, when the stock traded at **$ 10.43**.

Qualitative Risk Assessment

LOW	MEDIUM	**HIGH**

Our risk assessment reflects DHI's exposure to an extended downturn in the housing market, partly offset by its focus on reducing debt with free cash flow from operations. As the largest U.S. homebuilder, DHI has scale advantages to reduce labor and material costs, but a slow recovery in the housing market may impair earnings and cash flow growth.

Quantitative Evaluations

S&P Quality Ranking B+

D	C	B-	B	**B+**	A-	A	A+

Relative Strength Rank WEAK

25

LOWEST = 1   HIGHEST = 99

Revenue/Earnings Data

Revenue (Million $)

	1Q	2Q	3Q	4Q	Year
2010	1,132	913.5	1,401	--	--
2009	918.0	778.0	932.9	1,029	3,658
2008	1,708	1,624	1,464	1,782	6,646
2007	3,172	2,598	2,658	2,868	11,297
2006	2,903	3,598	3,668	4,883	15,051
2005	2,520	2,877	3,370	5,097	13,864

Earnings Per Share ($)

2010	0.56	0.04	0.16	E0.01	E0.80
2009	-0.20	-0.34	-0.45	-0.73	-1.72
2008	-0.41	-4.14	-1.26	-2.53	-8.34
2007	0.35	0.16	-2.62	-0.16	-2.27
2006	0.98	1.11	0.93	0.88	3.90
2005	0.76	0.92	1.17	1.77	4.62

Fiscal year ended Sep. 30. Next earnings report expected: Late November. EPS Estimates based on S&P Operating Earnings; historical GAAP earnings are as reported.

Dividend Data (Dates: mm/dd Payment Date: mm/dd/yy)

Amount ($)	Date Decl.	Ex-Div. Date	Stk. of Record	Payment Date
0.038	11/20	12/02	12/04	12/15/09
0.038	02/02	02/11	02/16	02/25/10
0.038	04/30	05/12	05/14	05/24/10
0.038	08/03	08/12	08/16	08/26/10

Dividends have been paid since 1997. Source: Company reports.

Highlights

➤ Following a 45% sales decline in FY 09 (Sep.), we forecast growth of 7% in FY 10 and 9% in FY 11 as the housing market slowly recovers. DHI realized a sequential decrease in contract backlog from $1.1 billion as of September 30, 2009, to $884 million at year end, which we attribute to seasonality. Backlog rose to $1.3 billion as of the end of the March quarter, but slipped to $954 million at the end of the June quarter due, we believe, to the now expired federal tax credit.

➤ We think net new orders and contract backlog will decline in the second half of 2010 as demand for new housing likely weakens ahead. However, we estimate that DHI's homebuilding gross margin will improve to 17.3% in FY 10 and to 17.6% in FY 11, from 13.1% in FY 09. DHI realized peak gross margins of 24% in FY 06.

➤ Along with wider gross margins, we believe DHI will also manage SG&A costs as a percentage of total revenues at the 11% to 12% level in FY 10 and FY 11, below FY 09's 14.5%. We forecast operating EPS of $0.80 for FY 10, including one-time tax benefits, and $0.65 for FY 11.

Investment Rationale/Risk

➤ DHI is one of the largest U.S. homebuilders, and we see low mortgage rates raising affordability in its target market for first-time buyers. With a balance sheet we view as strong ($1.7 billion in cash), we believe the company can be opportunistic in making new land acquisitions to expand new home communities. However, DHI's growth may stall as we see weak demand driven by high unemployment and low buyer confidence in the housing market.

➤ Risks to our recommendation and target price include the possibility of an improving economy and better employment data. An increase in demand from first-time homebuyers would benefit the company more than many peers since it concentrates primarily on this category.

➤ Our 12-month target price of $9.50 reflects a narrower risk premium on a target price-to-book multiple slightly above 1.1X applied to our forward book value estimate of $8.25. Our target multiple is near the historical low range for DHI and near peers, despite its strong cash position and operating scale advantages.

D.R. Horton Inc.

Business Summary August 20, 2010

CORPORATE OVERVIEW. D.R. Horton was founded in 1978 by Donald Horton, now chairman. In 1992, it went public to gain broader access to capital markets, which has helped fuel its subsequent growth beyond its base in the Dallas/Fort Worth area. With operating divisions in 26 states and 72 markets, D.R. Horton is the largest domestic homebuilder by number of homes closed in FY 09 (Sep.), and the most geographically diversified.

The company was the first U.S. builder to sell 50,000 homes in a single year (FY 05), and it aims to be the first to eclipse the 100,000 unit mark, although market conditions may have pushed back that target into 2011 or 2012. By emphasizing entry level and first-time move-up buyers, it targets the broadest segments of the population. In FY 09, DHI closed on 16,703 homes with an average closing sales price of approximately $213,400, compared to $233,500 in FY 08 and $253,000 in FY 07. DHI's homes are among the most affordable of all public builders.

CORPORATE STRATEGY. Most of D.R. Horton's growth in the past 15 to 20 years has been the result of organic initiatives, in our opinion. Generally, the company has established satellite operations in new markets located in rela-

tively close proximity to existing markets. We think the company has been successful at quickly ramping up volumes in these satellite operations -- often at the expense of smaller competitors -- aided by materials purchasing agreements struck at the regional level and relatively favorable access to capital markets.

Complementing this organic growth has been an aggressive takeover program, with close to 20 acquisitions since DHI went public. Most of these deals have occurred in new markets in an effort to either create a platform for future growth in a locale or to expand an existing satellite operation there. The majority of these acquisitions have been focused on a single market and have been asset-based transactions, rather than purchases of companies. However, in 2002, DHI bought Schuler Homes for about $1.8 billion, in a deal that increased its revenue base about 25%.

Company Financials Fiscal Year Ended Sep. 30

Per Share Data ($)	2009	2008	2007	2006	2005	2004	2003	2002	2001	2000
Tangible Book Value	7.07	8.90	17.64	18.75	15.28	10.87	7.93	5.77	4.83	3.81
Cash Flow	-1.64	-8.17	-2.06	4.10	4.87	3.24	2.16	1.54	1.24	0.94
Earnings	-1.72	-8.34	-2.27	3.90	4.62	3.08	2.05	1.44	1.10	0.84
S&P Core Earnings	-1.72	-8.18	-1.29	3.90	4.61	3.07	2.04	1.44	1.16	NA
Dividends	0.15	0.33	0.60	0.44	0.31	0.22	0.14	0.10	0.06	0.05
Payout Ratio	NM	NM	NM	11%	7%	7%	7%	7%	5%	5%
Prices:High	13.90	17.95	31.13	41.66	42.82	31.41	22.69	14.58	11.17	7.81
Prices:Low	5.72	3.79	10.15	19.52	26.83	18.47	8.48	8.02	5.83	3.00
P/E Ratio:High	NM	NM	NM	11	9	10	11	10	10	9
P/E Ratio:Low	NM	NM	NM	5	6	6	4	6	5	4

Income Statement Analysis (Million $)										
Revenue	3,658	6,646	11,297	15,051	13,864	10,841	8,728	6,739	4,456	3,654
Operating Income	-457	-2,474	-420	2,036	2,402	1,430	1,049	693	480	339
Depreciation	25.7	53.2	64.4	61.7	52.8	49.6	41.8	32.8	31.2	22.0
Interest Expense	198	240	328	55.0	21.2	9.30	12.6	11.5	14.1	15.8
Pretax Income	-552	-2,632	-951	1,987	2,379	1,583	1,008	648	408	309
Effective Tax Rate	NM	NM	25.1%	37.9%	38.2%	38.4%	37.9%	37.5%	37.5%	38.0%
Net Income	-545	-2,634	-712	1,233	1,471	975	626	405	255	192
S&P Core Earnings	-545	-2,582	-404	1,233	1,463	969	622	406	267	NA

Balance Sheet & Other Financial Data (Million $)										
Cash	1,923	1,356	275	588	1,150	518	583	104	239	72.5
Current Assets	6,517	7,101	10,137	13,202	10,995	7,709	6,151	4,912	3,266	2,383
Total Assets	6,757	7,710	11,556	14,821	12,515	8,985	7,279	6,018	3,652	2,695
Current Liabilities	823	1,510	2,127	3,591	3,288	1,627	1,297	1,091	691	474
Long Term Debt	2,969	2,968	3,746	4,861	3,660	3,032	2,665	2,636	1,884	1,344
Common Equity	2,260	2,834	5,587	6,453	5,360	3,961	3,031	2,270	1,250	970
Total Capital	5,477	6,410	9,644	11,419	9,224	7,159	5,832	4,927	3,143	2,319
Capital Expenditures	6.20	6.60	39.8	83.3	68.2	55.2	48.7	39.8	33.4	19.6
Cash Flow	-520	-2,580	-648	1,295	1,523	1,025	668	437	286	214
Current Ratio	7.9	4.7	4.8	3.7	3.3	4.7	4.7	4.5	4.7	5.0
% Long Term Debt of Capitalization	54.2	46.3	39.1	42.6	39.7	42.4	45.7	53.5	59.9	58.0
% Net Income of Revenue	NM	NM	NM	8.2	10.6	8.9	7.2	6.0	5.7	5.2
% Return on Assets	NM	NM	NM	9.0	13.7	12.0	9.4	8.4	8.0	7.6
% Return on Equity	NM	NM	NM	20.9	31.5	27.9	23.6	23.0	23.0	21.7

Data as orig reptd.; bef. results of disc opers/spec. items. Per share data adj. for stk. divs.; EPS diluted. E-Estimated. NA-Not Available. NM-Not Meaningful. NR-Not Ranked. UR-Under Review.

Office: 301 Commerce St Ste 500, Fort Worth, TX 76102-4178.
Telephone: 817-390-8200.
Website: http://www.drhorton.com
Chrmn: D.R. Horton

Pres, Vice Chrmn & CEO: D.J. Tomnitz
EVP, CFO & Chief Acctg Officer: B.W. Wheat
Investor Contact: S.H. Dwyer (817-390-8200)
EVP & Treas: S.H. Dwyer

Board Members: B. S. Anderson, M. R. Buchanan, M. W. Hewatt, D. R. Horton, B. G. Scott, D. J. Tomnitz, B. W. Wheat

Founded: 1978
Domicile: Delaware
Employees: 2,926

Dr Pepper Snapple Group Inc

STANDARD &POOR'S

S&P Recommendation	HOLD ★★★☆☆	Price $35.89 (as of Oct 22, 2010)	12-Mo. Target Price $40.00	Investment Style Large-Cap Growth

GICS Sector Consumer Staples
Sub-Industry Soft Drinks

Summary Spun off from Cadbury Schweppes in May 2008, DPS is the third largest marketer, bottler and distributor of non-alcoholic beverages in North America.

Key Stock Statistics (Source S&P, Vickers, company reports)

52-Wk Range	$40.24– 25.57	S&P Oper. EPS 2010E	2.46	Market Capitalization(B)	$8.573	Beta	0.97
Trailing 12-Month EPS	$2.12	S&P Oper. EPS 2011E	2.79	Yield (%)	2.79	S&P 3-Yr. Proj. EPS CAGR(%)	10
Trailing 12-Month P/E	16.9	P/E on S&P Oper. EPS 2010E	14.6	Dividend Rate/Share	$1.00	S&P Credit Rating	BBB
$10K Invested 5 Yrs Ago	NA	Common Shares Outstg. (M)	238.9	Institutional Ownership (%)	92		

Price Performance

- 30-Week Mov. Avg. · · · 10-Week Mov. Avg. - - GAAP Earnings vs. Previous Year   Volume Above Avg. STARS
- 12-Mo. Target Price — Relative Strength — ▲ Up ▼ Down ► No Change   Below Avg. ★

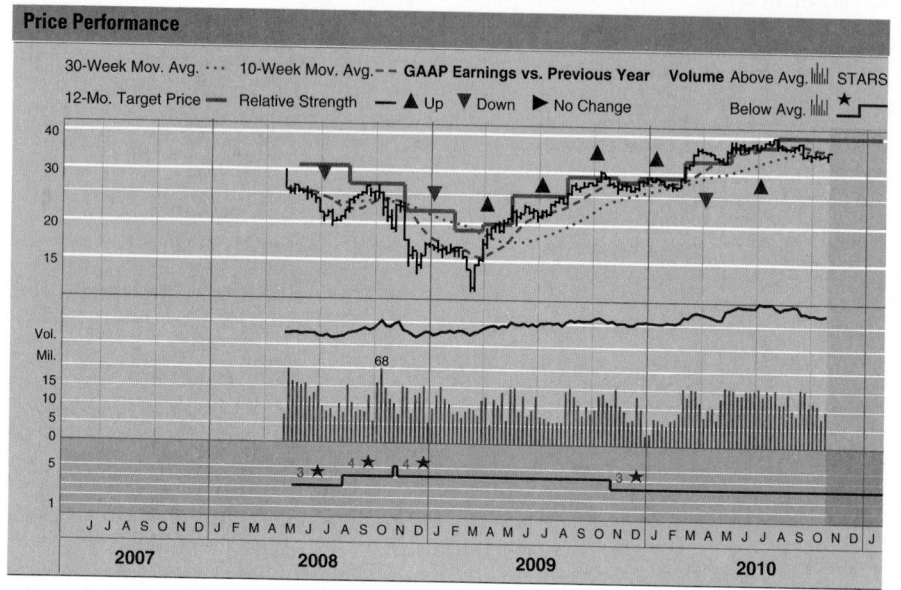

Options: CBOE, P, Ph

Analysis prepared by **Esther Y. Kwon, CFA** on August 03, 2010, when the stock traded at **$ 37.65**.

Highlights

➤ In 2010, we forecast revenue growth of approximately 3% from 2009's $5.5 billion, as we expect modest price increases and slight volume increases on flavored carbonated soft drink share gains. We think growth will continue to be driven by single serve wins in fountain and continued expansion of the cold drink program, with the placement of an additional 35,000 units on top of last year's nearly 36,000 units.

➤ We look for operating margin expansion in 2010, as the first year of inclusion of PepsiCo's $900 million payment over 25 years helps offset increased depreciation and start-up costs of the Victorville facility. While we expect an incremental $30 million in additional advertising and marketing expense in the back half of 2010, we see about $10 million in transportation cost savings from the new facility during that time.

➤ On fewer shares outstanding, we project 2010 EPS of $2.46, up from 2009 operating EPS of $1.97. In November 2009, directors authorized the repurchase of up to $200 million of stock over the next three years and a $0.15 per share quarterly dividend. In February 2010, they authorized an additional $800 million, and in May, boosted the quarterly payment to $0.25.

Investment Rationale/Risk

➤ We think DPS will have more difficulty expanding margins in the near term as favorable commodity cost benefits are lapped, manufacturing margins are hurt by initial rampup costs at its new Victorville, CA, production and distribution center, and higher oil prices likely squeeze bottling operation profits. In addition, while we still expect DPS's flavored carbonated brands to outperform the industry, we see tough comparisons on the annualization of the addition of Crush volumes.

➤ Risks to our recommendation and target price include more rapid commodity cost inflation than expected, consumer reluctance to accept new products, and unfavorable weather conditions in the company's markets.

➤ Our 12-month target price of $40 is derived from our peer multiple analysis. We apply a 14.4X multiple to our 2011 EPS estimate of $2.79, approximately a 10% discount to our blended peer average multiple of bottling and concentrate companies.

Qualitative Risk Assessment

LOW	MEDIUM	HIGH

Our risk assessment for Dr Pepper Snapple Group reflects our view of the relatively stable nature of the company's end markets and its strong cash flow generation ability.

Quantitative Evaluations

S&P Quality Ranking   NR

D	C	B-	B	B+	A-	A	A+

Relative Strength Rank   MODERATE

34

LOWEST = 1   HIGHEST = 99

Revenue/Earnings Data

Revenue (Million $)

	1Q	2Q	3Q	4Q	Year
2010	1,248	1,519	--	--	--
2009	1,260	1,481	1,434	1,356	5,531
2008	1,295	1,545	1,494	1,376	5,710
2007	1,269	1,543	1,535	1,401	5,748
2006	990.0	990.0	1,378	1,378	4,735
2005	--	--	--	--	3,205

Earnings Per Share ($)

	1Q	2Q	3Q	4Q	Year
2010	0.35	0.74	E0.69	E0.66	E2.46
2009	0.52	0.62	0.59	0.45	2.18
2008	0.38	0.42	0.41	-2.44	-1.23
2007	--	0.54	--	0.54	1.79
2006	--	--	--	--	--
2005	--	--	--	--	--

Fiscal year ended Dec. 31. Next earnings report expected: Early November. EPS Estimates based on S&P Operating Earnings; historical GAAP earnings are as reported.

Dividend Data (Dates: mm/dd Payment Date: mm/dd/yy)

Amount ($)	Date Decl.	Ex-Div. Date	Stk. of Record	Payment Date
0.150	11/20	12/17	12/21	01/08/10
0.150	02/03	03/18	03/22	04/09/10
0.250	05/19	06/17	06/21	07/09/10
0.250	08/11	09/16	09/20	10/08/10

Dividends have been paid since 2010. Source: Company reports.

Please read the Required Disclosures and Analyst Certification on the last page of this report.

The McGraw-Hill Companies

Dr Pepper Snapple Group Inc

Business Summary August 03, 2010

CORPORATE OVERVIEW. Dr Pepper Snapple Group is the third largest marketer, bottler and distributor of non-alcoholic beverages in North America and the leading flavored carbonated soft drink (CSD) company in the United States. Its CSD brands include Dr Pepper, 7UP, Sunkist, A&W, Canada Dry, Crush, Schweppes, Squirt and Penafiel. Its non-CSD brands include Snapple, Mott's, Hawaiian Punch and Clamato. The company also distributes FIJI mineral water and AriZona tea. A small portion of bottling group sales comes from fees paid by private label owners and others for bottling beverages and other products, with 87% of manufactured volumes related to company brands and the remainder to third-party and private-label products. Some 72% of Dr Pepper volumes are distributed through PepsiCo and Coca-Cola bottlers affiliated with Pepsi Bottling Group and Coca-Cola Enterprises Inc., the two largest customers of the beverages concentrate segment, accounting for 25% and 23% of net sales in 2009.

The company has three main operating segments: beverage concentrates (19.2% of 2009 sales, with an operating profit margin of 64.3%), finished goods (74.3% of sales, with a 13.9% operating margin), and Latin America beverages (6.5%, with a 15.1% operating margin).

In 2009, DPS generated 90% of its sales in the United States, 4% in Canada, and 6% in Mexico and the Caribbean.

CORPORATE STRATEGY. DPS's growth strategies include leveraging key brands through line extensions, such as launching Snapple super premium teas and antioxidant waters with functional benefits through its Snapple line. DPS is also targeting opportunities in high growth and high margin categories, including ready to drink teas, energy drinks and other functional beverages, and plans to increase its presence in higher margin channels and packages. These channels include convenience stores, vending machines and small independent retail outlets, most often offering higher margin single-serve packages. With the lackluster economy and continuing high unemployment, however, Standard & Poor's remains cautious on this segment, which is particularly sensitive to changes in discretionary income. The company may also selectively enter into distribution agreements for high growth, third-party brands that can use DPS's bottling and distribution network.

In addition, DPS plans to continue to acquire regional bottling companies to broaden geographic coverage. Management believes the integrated model of brand ownership with bottling capabilities best aligns the economic interests of all parties involved. Finally, the company is targeting improvements in operating efficiencies as it integrates recent bottling acquisitions and reduces distribution costs.

Company Financials Fiscal Year Ended Dec. 31

Per Share Data ($)	2009	2008	2007	2006	2005	2004	2003	2002	2001	2000
Tangible Book Value	NM	NM	NM	NA	NA	NA	NA	NA	NA	NA
Cash Flow	2.92	-0.56	2.19	NA	NA	NA	NA	NA	NA	NA
Earnings	2.18	-1.23	1.79	NA	NA	NA	NA	NA	NA	NA
S&P Core Earnings	2.15	1.51	1.76	1.92	NA	NA	NA	NA	NA	NA
Dividends	0.15	Nil	NA	NA	NA	NA	NA	NA	NA	NA
Payout Ratio	7%	Nil	NA	NA	NA	NA	NA	NA	NA	NA
Prices:High	30.65	30.00	NA	NA	NA	NA	NA	NA	NA	NA
Prices:Low	11.83	13.45	NA	NA	NA	NA	NA	NA	NA	NA
P/E Ratio:High	14	NM	NA	NA	NA	NA	NA	NA	NA	NA
P/E Ratio:Low	5	NM	NA	NA	NA	NA	NA	NA	NA	NA

Income Statement Analysis (Million $)	2009	2008	2007	2006	2005	2004	2003	2002	2001	2000
Revenue	5,531	5,710	5,748	4,735	3,205	3,065	NA	NA	NA	NA
Operating Income	1,235	1,134	1,113	1,152	959	953	NA	NA	NA	NA
Depreciation	207	169	100	139	79.0	84.0	NA	NA	NA	NA
Interest Expense	243	241	250	257	210	177	NA	NA	NA	NA
Pretax Income	870	-373	774	808	808	716	NA	NA	NA	NA
Effective Tax Rate	36.2%	NM	41.2%	36.9%	39.7%	37.7%	NA	NA	NA	NA
Net Income	555	-312	455	510	487	446	NA	NA	NA	NA
S&P Core Earnings	549	385	446	487	NA	NA	NA	NA	NA	NA

Balance Sheet & Other Financial Data (Million $)	2009	2008	2007	2006	2005	2004	2003	2002	2001	2000
Cash	280	214	100	35.0	28.0	NA	NA	NA	NA	NA
Current Assets	1,279	1,237	1,179	1,632	1,331	NA	NA	NA	NA	NA
Total Assets	8,776	8,638	9,598	9,346	7,433	NA	NA	NA	NA	NA
Current Liabilities	854	801	2,764	1,691	1,136	NA	NA	NA	NA	NA
Long Term Debt	2,960	3,505	1,999	3,084	2,858	NA	NA	NA	NA	NA
Common Equity	3,187	2,607	2,922	3,250	2,426	NA	NA	NA	NA	NA
Total Capital	6,147	6,112	6,245	7,042	5,688	NA	NA	NA	NA	NA
Capital Expenditures	317	304	230	158	44.0	71.0	NA	NA	NA	NA
Cash Flow	744	-143	555	649	566	530	NA	NA	NA	NA
Current Ratio	1.5	1.5	0.4	1.0	1.2	NA	NA	NA	NA	NA
% Long Term Debt of Capitalization	48.2	57.3	32.0	43.8	50.3	Nil	NA	NA	NA	NA
% Net Income of Revenue	10.0	NM	7.9	10.8	15.2	14.6	NA	NA	NA	NA
% Return on Assets	6.4	NM	NA	6.1	NA	NA	NA	NA	NA	NA
% Return on Equity	19.2	NM	NA	18.0	NA	NA	NA	NA	NA	NA

Data as orig reptd.; bef. results of disc opers/spec. items. Per share data adj. for stk. divs.; EPS diluted. Pro forma data in 2007. E-Estimated. NA-Not Available. NM-Not Meaningful. NR-Not Ranked. UR-Under Review.

Office: 5301 Legacy Drive, Plano, TX 75024.
Telephone: 972-673-7000.
Website: http://www.drpeppersnapplegroup.com
Chrmn: W.R. Sanders

Pres & CEO: L.D. Young
EVP & CFO: M.M. Ellen
EVP, Secy & General Counsel: J.L. Baldwin, Jr.
SVP, Chief Acctg Officer & Cntlr: A.A. Stephens

Investor Contact: A. Noormohamed (972-673-6050)
Board Members: J. L. Adams, T. D. Martin, P. H. Patsley, R. G. Rogers, W. R. Sanders, J. L. Stahl, M. A. Szostak, M. Weinstein, L. D. Young

Founded: 2007
Domicile: Delaware
Employees: 19,000

DTE Energy Co

STANDARD &POOR'S

S&P Recommendation HOLD ★★★☆☆

Price	12-Mo. Target Price
$46.93 (as of Oct 22, 2010)	$48.00

GICS Sector Utilities
Sub-Industry Multi-Utilities

Summary This diversified energy company is involved in the development and management of energy-related businesses and services nationwide.

Key Stock Statistics (Source S&P, Vickers, company reports)

52-Wk Range	$49.06– 36.65	S&P Oper. EPS 2010E	3.58	Market Capitalization(B)	$7.921	Beta		0.67
Trailing 12-Month EPS	$3.53	S&P Oper. EPS 2011E	3.78	Yield (%)	4.77	S&P 3-Yr. Proj. EPS CAGR(%)		9
Trailing 12-Month P/E	13.3	P/E on S&P Oper. EPS 2010E	13.1	Dividend Rate/Share	$2.24	S&P Credit Rating		BBB
$10K Invested 5 Yrs Ago	$14,489	Common Shares Outstg. (M)	168.8	Institutional Ownership (%)	60			

Price Performance

30-Week Mov. Avg. · · · 10-Week Mov. Avg. – – **GAAP Earnings vs. Previous Year** Volume Above Avg. STARS
12-Mo. Target Price — Relative Strength — ▲ Up ▼ Down ► No Change Below Avg. ★

Options: ASE, Ph

Analysis prepared by **Justin McCann** on July 22, 2010, when the stock traded at **$ 47.61**.

Qualitative Risk Assessment

LOW	MEDIUM	HIGH

Our risk assessment reflects a balance between the steady cash flow that we expect from the regulated utilities, which operate within a generally supportive regulatory environment, and most of the unregulated operations, which continue to contribute a significant portion of DTE's consolidated cash flow. While we expect DTE to benefit from the modification of Michigan's Electric Choice program, we remain concerned about the weak outlook for the state's economy.

Quantitative Evaluations

S&P Quality Ranking   B+

D	C	B-	B	B+	A-	A	A+

Relative Strength Rank   MODERATE

35

LOWEST = 1   HIGHEST = 99

Highlights

► We expect operating EPS in 2010 to increase about 12% from 2009's $3.30, which excluded $0.06 of net one-time charges. Operating EPS in 2009, which advanced more than 13% from 2008's $2.90, benefited from an electric rate increase, lower fuel and purchased power costs, tax credits, and strong results from the non-utility operations, partially offset by a decline in electric demand and higher pension costs.

► For 2010, we expect operating EPS to be aided by rate increases at MichCon Gas and Detroit Edison, and higher coke sales to a revitalized steel industry. EPS in the first quarter of 2010 was aided $0.04 by a lower tax rate. In January 2010, the Michigan Public Service Commission (MPSC) authorized Detroit Edison an electric rate increase of $217 million (4.8%). The MPSC order maintained the allowed return on equity at 11%. Longer term, we expect EPS growth to be largely driven by an expanded rate base resulting from DTE's capital investment program.

► Under the energy reform package that the governor of Michigan signed into law in October 2008, the state's electric choice program was modified and a 12-month deadline for the resolution of utility rate cases was established.

Investment Rationale/Risk

► The stock is up more than 7% year to date. This follows a 22% gain in 2009, and reflects, in our view, the company's improved earnings outlook. We see long-term benefits from the energy legislation that modified Michigan's electric choice program and assured a more efficient rate case process, but we expect the stock to stabilize around its current level over the near term. We think the stock was badly hurt in early 2009 by the weak economy in Detroit and turmoil in the financial markets.

► Risks to our recommendation and target price include a slower-than-expected recovery in the financial markets and the Michigan economy, as well as a sharp decrease in the average P/E of the peer group as a whole.

► The dividend recently yielded 4.5%, in line with the recent peer average. While the stock could remain volatile in the current market, we believe the dividend should provide some support for the shares. With a payout ratio at 57% of our operating EPS estimate for 2010, we expect DTE to keep the dividend at its current level. Our 12-month target price is $48, reflecting an approximate peer P/E of 12.9X our operating EPS estimate for 2010.

Revenue/Earnings Data

Revenue (Million $)

	1Q	2Q	3Q	4Q	Year
2010	2,453	1,792	--	--	--
2009	2,255	1,688	1,961	2,121	8,014
2008	2,570	2,251	2,338	2,170	9,329
2007	2,463	1,692	2,140	2,211	8,506
2006	2,635	1,895	2,196	2,296	9,022
2005	2,309	1,941	2,060	2,712	9,022

Earnings Per Share ($)

2010	1.38	0.51	E0.93	E0.88	E3.58
2009	1.09	0.51	0.92	0.72	3.24
2008	1.23	0.17	1.03	0.80	3.23
2007	0.54	1.99	0.92	1.17	4.62
2006	0.76	-0.18	1.07	0.81	2.45
2005	0.72	0.19	0.17	2.18	3.27

Fiscal year ended Dec. 31. Next earnings report expected: Late October. EPS Estimates based on S&P Operating Earnings; historical GAAP earnings are as reported.

Dividend Data (Dates: mm/dd Payment Date: mm/dd/yy)

Amount ($)	Date Decl.	Ex-Div. Date	Stk. of Record	Payment Date
0.530	12/03	12/17	12/21	01/15/10
0.530	02/04	03/18	03/22	04/15/10
0.530	05/07	06/17	06/21	07/15/10
0.560	07/29	09/16	09/20	10/15/10

Dividends have been paid since 1909. Source: Company reports.

Please read the Required Disclosures and Analyst Certification on the last page of this report.

The McGraw-Hill Companies

DTE Energy Co

STANDARD &POOR'S

Business Summary July 22, 2010

CORPORATE OVERVIEW. DTE Energy, formed on January 1, 1996, is the holding company for The Detroit Edison Company and Michigan Consolidated Gas (MichCon), regulated electric and gas utilities serving customers within the state of Michigan, and three non-utility operations engaged in a variety of energy-related businesses in various portions of the United States. The electric utility business accounted for 58.8% of consolidated revenues in 2009; the gas utility business 22.0%; and the non-utility operations 19.2%.

MARKET PROFILE. Detroit Edison is a regulated electric utility serving approximately 2.1 million customers in southeastern Michigan. In 2009, residential customers accounted for 40.0% of the utility's revenues; commercial customers 37.4%; industrial customers 16.0%; and other 6.6%; and wholesale 2.6%. With its high percentage of commercial and industrial customers, the utility had been hurt by the state's Customer Choice program, losing about 3% of retail sales in 2009 and 2008, 4% in 2007, 6% in 2006, 12% in 2005, and 18% in 2004. Recent energy legislation in Michigan and orders by the Michigan Public Service Commission (MPSC) placed a 10% cap on the total potential migration. When market conditions are favorable, Detroit Edison will sell excess power into the wholesale market. The utility's generating capability is heavily

dependent on the availability of coal, and the majority of its coal needs are obtained through long-term contracts, with the remainder purchased through short-term agreements or purchases in the spot market.

MichCon is a regulated natural gas utility serving about 1.2 million residential, commercial and industrial customers in the state of Michigan. It also has subsidiaries involved in the gathering and transmission of natural gas in northern Michigan, and operates one of the largest natural gas distribution and transmission systems in the U.S., with connections to interstate pipelines providing access to most of the major natural gas producing regions in the Gulf Coast, Mid-Continent and Canadian regions. The company purchases its natural gas supplies on the open market through a diversified portfolio of supply contracts, and, given its storage capacity, should be able to meet its supply requirements.

Company Financials Fiscal Year Ended Dec. 31

Per Share Data ($)	2009	2008	2007	2006	2005	2004	2003	2002	2001	2000
Tangible Book Value	25.39	23.99	23.22	21.02	20.88	20.01	19.05	14.61	16.06	28.15
Earnings	3.24	3.23	4.62	2.45	3.27	2.55	2.85	3.83	2.14	3.27
S&P Core Earnings	3.84	1.69	1.55	2.88	2.13	1.97	3.22	2.80	2.09	NA
Dividends	2.12	2.12	2.12	2.08	2.06	2.06	2.06	2.06	2.06	2.06
Payout Ratio	65%	66%	46%	85%	63%	81%	72%	54%	96%	63%
Prices:High	44.96	45.34	54.74	49.24	48.31	45.49	49.50	47.70	47.13	41.31
Prices:Low	23.32	27.82	43.96	38.77	41.39	37.88	34.00	33.05	33.13	28.44
P/E Ratio:High	14	14	12	20	15	18	17	12	22	13
P/E Ratio:Low	7	9	10	16	13	15	12	9	15	9

Income Statement Analysis (Million $)										
Revenue	8,014	9,329	8,506	9,022	9,022	7,114	7,041	6,749	7,849	5,597
Depreciation	954	899	932	1,014	869	744	687	759	795	758
Maintenance	NA	NA	NA	NA	NA	NA	NA	NA	NA	NA
Fixed Charges Coverage	2.40	2.35	1.55	1.82	1.21	1.35	1.49	2.00	2.04	2.42
Construction Credits	NA	NA	NA	NA	NA	NA	NA	NA	NA	NA
Effective Tax Rate	31.6%	35.2%	31.5%	NM	NM	NM	24.0%	NM	NM	1.89%
Net Income	532	526	787	437	576	443	480	632	329	468
S&P Core Earnings	631	275	266	512	374	344	542	463	322	NA

Balance Sheet & Other Financial Data (Million $)										
Gross Property	20,588	20,065	18,809	19,224	18,660	18,011	17,679	17,862	17,067	13,162
Capital Expenditures	1,035	1,373	1,299	1,403	1,065	904	751	984	1,096	749
Net Property	12,431	12,231	11,408	11,451	10,830	10,491	10,324	9,813	9,543	7,387
Capitalization:Long Term Debt	7,370	7,741	6,971	7,474	7,080	7,606	7,669	7,785	7,928	4,062
Capitalization:% Long Term Debt	54.0	56.4	54.4	56.1	55.1	57.8	59.2	63.0	63.0	50.3
Capitalization:Preferred	Nil	Nil	Nil	Nil	Nil	Nil	Nil	Nil	Nil	Nil
Capitalization:% Preferred	Nil	Nil	Nil	Nil	Nil	Nil	Nil	Nil	Nil	Nil
Capitalization:Common	6,278	5,995	5,853	5,849	5,769	5,548	5,287	4,565	4,657	4,015
Capitalization:% Common	46.0	43.6	45.6	43.9	44.9	42.2	40.8	37.0	37.0	49.7
Total Capital	14,357	15,833	14,804	14,950	14,468	13,429	14,256	13,434	14,063	9,878
% Operating Ratio	87.7	91.0	95.2	91.2	96.1	93.4	91.1	82.8	86.3	85.3
% Earned on Net Property	10.0	9.5	6.8	7.4	8.9	8.1	7.2	11.4	8.2	11.4
% Return on Revenue	6.6	5.6	9.3	4.8	6.4	6.2	6.8	9.4	4.2	8.4
% Return on Invested Capital	7.4	5.8	3.1	5.4	6.0	6.1	7.5	9.1	8.9	8.1
% Return on Common Equity	8.7	8.9	13.5	7.5	10.2	8.2	9.7	13.8	7.6	11.8

Data as orig reptd.; bef. results of disc opers/spec. items. Per share data adj. for stk. divs.; EPS diluted. E-Estimated. NA-Not Available. NM-Not Meaningful. NR-Not Ranked. UR-Under Review.

Office: One Energy Plaza, Detroit, MI 48226-1279.
Telephone: 313-235-4000.
Email: shareholdersvcs@dteenergy.com
Website: http://www.dteenergy.com

Chrmn: A.F. Earley, Jr.
Pres & CEO: G.M. Anderson
EVP & CFO: D.E. Meador
SVP & General Counsel: B.D. Peterson

SVP & CIO: L. Ellyn
Investor Contact: L. Muschong (313-235-8505)
Board Members: G. M. Anderson, L. Bauder, D. A. Brandon, A. F. Earley, Jr., W. F. Fountain, A. D. Gilmour, F. M. Hennessey, J. E. Lobbia, G. J. McGovern, E. A. Miller, M. A. Murray, C. W. Pryor, Jr., J. Robles, Jr., R. G. Shaw, J. H. Vandenberghe

Founded: 1995
Domicile: Michigan
Employees: 10,244

Duke Energy Corp

STANDARD &POOR'S

S&P Recommendation HOLD ★★★☆☆

Price	**12-Mo. Target Price**	**Investment Style**
$17.78 (as of Oct 22, 2010)	$18.00	Large-Cap Value

GICS Sector Utilities
Sub-Industry Electric Utilities

Summary DUK provides service to 3.9 million electric customers in North Carolina, South Carolina, Indiana, Ohio and Kentucky, and 500,000 gas customers in Kentucky and Ohio.

Key Stock Statistics (Source S&P, Vickers, company reports)

52-Wk Range	$18.08– 15.47	S&P Oper. EPS 2010**E**	1.35	Market Capitalization(B)	$23.447	Beta	0.44
Trailing 12-Month EPS	$0.52	S&P Oper. EPS 2011**E**	1.40	Yield (%)	5.51	S&P 3-Yr. Proj. EPS CAGR(%)	6
Trailing 12-Month P/E	34.2	P/E on S&P Oper. EPS 2010**E**	13.2	Dividend Rate/Share	$0.98	S&P Credit Rating	A-
$10K Invested 5 Yrs Ago	NA	Common Shares Outstg. (M)	1,318.7	Institutional Ownership (%)	48		

Price Performance

30-Week Mov. Avg. · · ·   10-Week Mov. Avg. – –   **GAAP Earnings vs. Previous Year**   **Volume** Above Avg. �‖⁙‖   STARS
12-Mo. Target Price —   Relative Strength —   ▲ Up ▼ Down ▶ No Change   Below Avg. ⁙‖⁙ ★

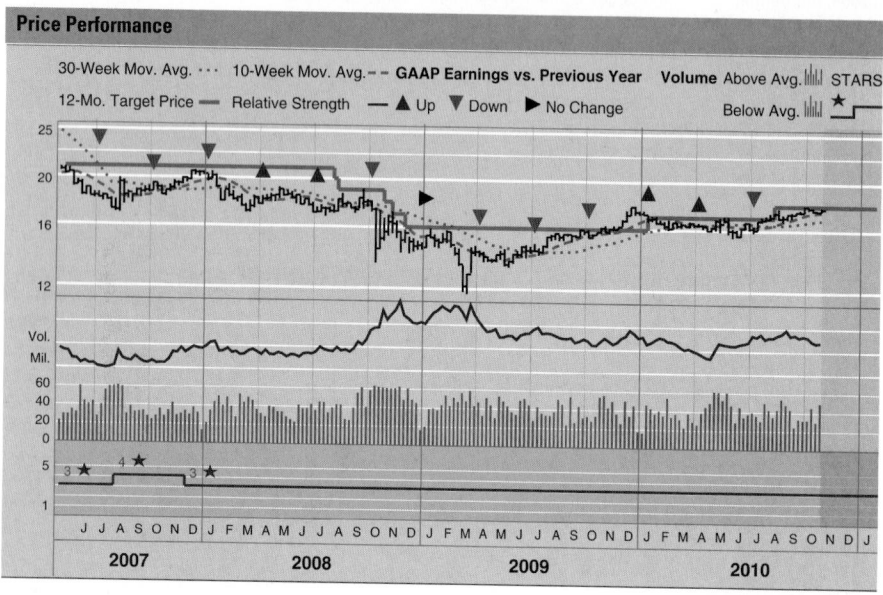

Options: ASE, CBOE, P, Ph

Analysis prepared by **Christopher B. Muir** on August 13, 2010, when the stock traded at **$ 17.15**.

Highlights

► We expect revenues to rise 7.4% in 2010, as lower industrial volumes and the weak economy are more than offset by rate increases in multiple jurisdictions. At the unregulated power unit, we see lower prices, offset by increased availability. In 2011, we expect additional rate hikes at the utility and a slower decline in industrial sales to lead to a 3.0% revenue increase.

► We forecast operating margins of 23.3% for 2010, up from 21.9% in 2009, as we see lower per-revenue operations & maintenance expenses and operating taxes partly offset by higher per-revenue depreciation costs. We see operating margins rising to 23.5% in 2011. We project pretax margins of 20.7% for 2010 and 21.0% in 2011, versus 18.8% in 2009, with higher non-operating income being partly offset by higher interest expense in 2010.

► Assuming an effective tax rate of 36.2%, we estimate 2010 operating EPS, excluding net nonrecurring charges of $0.53, of $1.35, up 13% from 2009 operating EPS of $1.20, which excludes $0.37 of net nonrecurring charges. We see 2011 EPS rising 3.7%, to $1.40.

Investment Rationale/Risk

► We believe DUK's investments in its regulated business will allow its rate base to grow faster than depreciation, providing it with opportunities to raise rates. DUK's planned investments in its commercial renewable portfolio should complement its existing generating assets. We also like DUK's higher-growth Carolina service territories. While we view positively recent developments at the company, we would not add to positions.

► Risks to our recommendation and target price include lower electric margins, a greater-than-expected rise in interest rates, and unfavorable commodity price trends.

► DUK recently traded at 12.2X our 2011 EPS estimate, about even with its electric utility peers. Our 12-month target price of $18 is 12.8X our 2011 EPS projection, a small discount to our peer target. In our view, this valuation is warranted by what we see as slower-than-peers earnings growth, but a stronger-than-peers balance sheet. We also believe that DUK's relatively high dividend payout ratio will limit its ability to grow dividends faster than peers.

Qualitative Risk Assessment

LOW	MEDIUM	HIGH

Our risk assessment reflects DUK's large market capitalization and a balanced portfolio of businesses that include lower-risk regulated electric and gas utility services, partly offset by higher-risk unregulated businesses, which contribute less than 25% of the company's earnings.

Quantitative Evaluations

S&P Quality Ranking   B

D	C	B-	**B**	B+	A-	A	A+

Relative Strength Rank   MODERATE
45
LOWEST = 1   HIGHEST = 99

Revenue/Earnings Data

Revenue (Million $)

	1Q	2Q	3Q	4Q	Year
2010	3,594	3,287	--	--	--
2009	3,312	2,913	3,396	3,110	12,731
2008	3,337	3,229	3,508	3,133	13,207
2007	3,035	2,966	3,688	3,031	12,443
2006	3,106	3,865	4,143	4,070	15,184
2005	5,328	5,274	3,028	3,116	16,746

Earnings Per Share ($)

	1Q	2Q	3Q	4Q	Year
2010	0.34	-0.17	E0.43	E0.28	E1.35
2009	0.27	0.22	0.09	0.26	0.82
2008	0.37	0.27	0.17	0.21	1.01
2007	0.27	0.24	0.48	0.21	1.20
2006	0.50	0.34	0.60	0.31	1.70
2005	0.88	0.32	0.96	0.43	2.61

Fiscal year ended Dec. 31. Next earnings report expected: Early November. EPS Estimates based on S&P Operating Earnings; historical GAAP earnings are as reported.

Dividend Data (Dates: **mm/dd** Payment Date: **mm/dd/yy**)

Amount ($)	Date Decl.	Ex-Div. Date	Stk. of Record	Payment Date
0.240	10/20	11/10	11/13	12/16/09
0.240	01/06	02/10	02/12	03/16/10
0.240	05/06	05/19	05/21	06/16/10
0.245	06/22	08/11	08/13	09/16/10

Dividends have been paid since 1926. Source: Company reports.

The McGraw-Hill Companies

Duke Energy Corp

STANDARD &POOR'S

Business Summary August 13, 2010

CORPORATE OVERVIEW. Duke provides electric and gas utility services, sells wholesale power, and has investments in various South American generation plants. Its Franchised Electric and Gas (E&G) segment generates, transmits, distributes and sells electricity in central and western North Carolina, western South Carolina, southwestern Ohio, central, north central and southern Indiana, and northern Kentucky. The Commercial Power segment owns, operates and manages power plants and engages in the wholesale marketing and procurement of electric power, fuel and emission allowances related to these plants as well as other contractual positions. The International Energy segment (IE) owns, operates and manages power generation facilities, and engages in sales and marketing of electric power and natural gas outside the U.S. The Other segment includes unallocated corporate costs and investments in other businesses.

Franchised Electric and Gas serves about 4 million electric customers over 50,000 square miles in North Carolina, South Carolina, Indiana, Ohio and Kentucky, and about 500,000 gas customers in Kentucky and Ohio, and owns generating assets totaling 26,957 MW (49% coal; 20% natural gas, oil or other; 19% nuclear; and 12% hydro) as of December 2009. Electric sales in 2009 were 30% residential, 32% commercial, 26% industrial and 11% other.

The Power segment consists of 8,005 MW, mostly supporting regulated operations in Ohio. There are 5,813 MW located in Ohio, 690 MW in Pennsylvania, 640 MW in Illinois, 480 MW in Indiana, 212 MW in Texas, and 170 MW in Wyoming. Commercial Power's fuel mix includes 47% natural gas, 44% coal, 3% fuel oil, and 6% wind. The IE segment primarily consists of power generation (4,053 MW) in Central and South America.

CORPORATE STRATEGY. In recent years, Duke has focused on utility spending in an effort to increase its rate base, which can lead to rate increases. The Power segment has focused on increasing renewable generation assets, and IE aims to take advantage of any opportunities that may arise. In June 2009, IE purchased the remaining 24% of its Aguaytia Integrated Energy Project subsidiary in Peru. We expect capital spending to be close to $5.0 billion annually through 2013, with almost all of the spending at the regulated businesses. We expect debt levels to rise during this period.

Company Financials Fiscal Year Ended Dec. 31

Per Share Data ($)	2009	2008	2007	2006	2005	2004	2003	2002	2001	2000
Tangible Book Value	12.84	12.25	12.55	13.54	13.65	12.54	10.74	12.51	14.11	11.21
Earnings	0.82	1.01	1.20	1.70	2.61	1.27	-1.13	1.22	2.56	2.38
S&P Core Earnings	1.11	0.82	1.20	1.22	1.80	1.29	1.24	-1.10	1.01	2.29	NA
Dividends	0.94	0.90	0.86	0.95	1.17	1.10	1.10	1.10	1.10	1.10
Payout Ratio	115%	89%	70%	56%	45%	87%	NM	90%	43%	46%
Prices:High	17.94	20.60	21.30	34.50	30.55	26.16	21.57	40.00	47.74	45.22
Prices:Low	11.72	13.50	16.91	26.94	24.37	18.85	12.21	16.42	32.22	22.88
P/E Ratio:High	22	20	17	20	12	21	NM	33	19	19
P/E Ratio:Low	14	13	14	16	9	15	NM	13	13	10

Income Statement Analysis (Million $)										
Revenue	12,731	13,207	12,720	15,184	16,746	22,503	22,529	15,663	59,503	49,318
Depreciation	1,656	1,670	1,746	2,049	1,728	1,851	1,803	1,571	1,336	1,167
Maintenance	NA	NA	NA	NA	NA	NA	NA	NA	NA	NA
Fixed Charges Coverage	3.88	3.72	4.03	2.77	2.91	2.40	1.96	2.46	5.33	4.25
Construction Credits	NA	NA	NA	NA	NA	NA	NA	NA	53.0	63.0
Effective Tax Rate	41.4%	32.6%	31.8%	28.8%	29.5%	27.5%	NM	35.1%	33.1%	32.9%
Net Income	1,063	1,279	1,522	2,019	2,533	1,232	-1,005	1,034	1,994	1,776
S&P Core Earnings	1,423	1,041	1,551	2,131	1,249	1,199	-994	908	1,777	NA

Balance Sheet & Other Financial Data (Million $)										
Gross Property	55,362	50,304	46,056	58,330	40,574	46,806	47,157	48,677	39,464	34,615
Capital Expenditures	4,557	4,922	3,125	3,381	2,309	2,055	2,470	4,924	5,930	5,634
Net Property	37,950	34,036	31,110	41,447	29,200	33,506	34,986	36,219	28,415	24,469
Capitalization:Long Term Debt	16,113	13,250	9,498	18,118	14,547	16,932	20,622	21,629	13,728	12,425
Capitalization:% Long Term Debt	42.6	38.7	30.9	41.0	46.9	50.5	59.8	58.9	51.5	54.7
Capitalization:Preferred	Nil	Nil	Nil	Nil	Nil	134	134	157	234	247
Capitalization:% Preferred	Nil	Nil	Nil	Nil	Nil	0.40	0.39	0.43	0.88	1.09
Capitalization:Common	21,750	20,988	21,199	26,102	16,439	16,441	13,748	14,944	12,689	10,056
Capitalization:% Common	57.4	61.3	69.1	59.0	53.1	49.1	39.8	40.7	47.6	44.2
Total Capital	38,905	39,666	35,790	52,203	36,988	40,375	40,490	43,644	33,393	29,225
% Operating Ratio	85.3	85.5	86.0	87.6	89.6	88.6	85.4	87.1	95.0	94.3
% Earned on Net Property	7.3	7.8	6.9	9.0	11.5	8.9	NM	7.6	15.5	16.8
% Return on Revenue	8.4	9.7	12.0	13.3	15.1	5.5	NM	6.6	3.4	3.6
% Return on Invested Capital	5.8	5.7	4.7	7.5	11.1	7.0	8.7	6.3	10.5	11.2
% Return on Common Equity	5.0	6.1	6.4	9.5	15.3	8.1	NM	7.4	17.4	18.4

Data as orig reptd.; bef. results of disc opers/spec. items. Per share data adj. for stk. divs.; EPS diluted. E-Estimated. NA-Not Available. NM-Not Meaningful. NR-Not Ranked. UR-Under Review.

Office: 526 South Church Street, Charlotte, NC 28202-1904.
Telephone: 704-594-6200.
Website: http://www.duke-energy.com
Chrmn, Pres & CEO: J.E. Rogers, Jr.

EVP & CIO: A.R. Mullinax
SVP, Chief Acctg Officer & Cntlr: S.K. Young
Investor Contact: S.G. De May ()
SVP & Treas: S.G. De May

Board Members: W. Barnet, III, G. A. Bernhardt, M. G. Browning, D. R. DiMicco, J. H. Forsgren, Jr., A. M. Gray, J. H. Hance, Jr., E. J. Reinsch, J. T. Rhodes, J. E. Rogers, Jr., P. R. Sharp

Founded: 1917
Domicile: Delaware
Employees: 18,680

The McGraw-Hill Companies

Dun & Bradstreet Corp (The)

STANDARD &POOR'S

S&P Recommendation HOLD ★★★★☆

Price	$75.22 (as of Oct 22, 2010)
12-Mo. Target Price	$78.00
Investment Style	Large-Cap Growth

GICS Sector Industrials
Sub-Industry Research & Consulting Services

Summary This company is a worldwide provider of business information and related decision support services and commercial receivables management services.

Key Stock Statistics (Source S&P, Vickers, company reports)

52-Wk Range	$84.95– 65.34	S&P Oper. EPS 2010**E**	5.55	Market Capitalization(B)	$3.765
Trailing 12-Month EPS	$4.65	S&P Oper. EPS 2011**E**	5.94	Yield (%)	1.86
Trailing 12-Month P/E	16.2	P/E on S&P Oper. EPS 2010**E**	13.6	Dividend Rate/Share	$1.40
$10K Invested 5 Yrs Ago	$11,975	Common Shares Outstg. (M)	50.1	Institutional Ownership (%)	85

Beta	0.52
S&P 3-Yr. Proj. EPS CAGR(%)	6
S&P Credit Rating	A-

Price Performance

- 30-Week Mov. Avg. ···· 10-Week Mov. Avg. – – **GAAP Earnings vs. Previous Year** Volume Above Avg. STARS
- 12-Mo. Target Price — Relative Strength — ▲ Up ▼ Down ► No Change Below Avg. ★

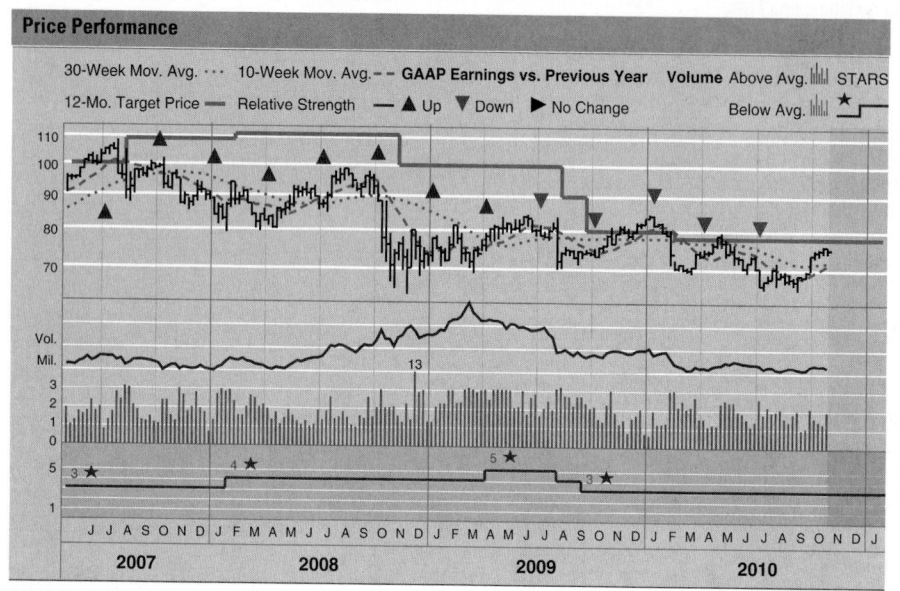

Analysis prepared by **Rafay Khalid, CFA** on September 03, 2010, when the stock traded at **$ 68.40**.

Options: Ph

Highlights

➤ We forecast sales increases of 4% in 2010 and 8% in 2011. We believe International division sales will advance 24% in 2010, on our view of strength in emerging markets and our outlook for incremental revenues from the recently acquired D&B Australia Holdings. But we expect slightly negative revenues in the North America division this year, reflecting our outlook for cautious spending by corporations and small businesses in the key U.S. market.

➤ We expect higher expenses in 2010 and 2011, primarily stemming from the company's two-year technology investment program. While this program will cost $110 million to $130 million over the two years, we forecast significant business productivity improvements that should help lower expenses in the long term. In addition, we forecast higher amortization and merger expenses related to the D&B Australia acquisition in 2010. As a result, we see operating margins declining to 26.8% in 2010, followed by 27.0% in 2011.

➤ Our operating EPS estimates are $5.55 for 2010 and $5.94 for 2011, excluding one-time items. This compares to operating EPS of $5.42 in 2009.

Investment Rationale/Risk

➤ We believe DNB's North American business will remain weak in 2010, as we project a slow recovery in employment and corporate profits in the U.S. and therefore expect DNB's customers to maintain tight budgets. We also see continued weakness among small businesses. We see DNB continuing to increase its presence internationally through investments, joint ventures and partnerships. We also expect the company to continue deploying free cash flow toward acquisitions, stock repurchases and dividends.

➤ Risks to our recommendation and target price include a stronger U.S. dollar depressing overseas profits, a deteriorating outlook for DNB's U.K. operations, and an inability by DNB to realize operating efficiencies from the company's business rationalization program.

➤ Our 12-month target price of $78 is based on a historical low P/E ratio of 13.2X our 2011 EPS forecast. We believe this multiple is warranted based on our outlook for a challenging economic recovery in the company's key U.S. market and investment in a two-year technology program.

Qualitative Risk Assessment

LOW	MEDIUM	HIGH

Our risk assessment reflects DNB's global business database and proprietary identification system, which we think provides a competitive advantage, and its notable record of long-term EPS growth, notwithstanding a slightly uncertain regulatory outlook for its ability to collect and use data.

Quantitative Evaluations

S&P Quality Ranking B+

D	C	B-	B	B+	A-	A	A+

Relative Strength Rank MODERATE

59

LOWEST = 1   HIGHEST = 99

Revenue/Earnings Data

Revenue (Million $)

	1Q	2Q	3Q	4Q	Year
2010	397.2	397.3	--	--	--
2009	407.4	416.9	399.0	463.7	1,687
2008	414.7	427.7	409.2	474.7	1,726
2007	379.0	380.8	374.7	464.7	1,599
2006	367.2	367.4	359.2	437.5	1,531
2005	341.3	351.7	341.6	409.0	1,444

Earnings Per Share ($)

2010	0.92	1.11	E1.12	E1.90	E5.55
2009	1.93	1.43	1.02	1.61	5.99
2008	1.05	1.51	1.18	1.85	5.58
2007	0.86	1.44	0.93	1.68	4.90
2006	0.75	0.79	0.72	1.46	3.70
2005	0.73	0.67	0.46	1.32	3.19

Fiscal year ended Dec. 31. Next earnings report expected: Late October. EPS Estimates based on S&P Operating Earnings; historical GAAP earnings are as reported.

Dividend Data (Dates: mm/dd Payment Date: mm/dd/yy)

Amount ($)	Date Decl.	Ex-Div. Date	Stk. of Record	Payment Date
0.350	02/04	03/01	03/03	03/18/10
0.350	05/04	05/26	05/28	06/16/10
0.350	08/04	08/27	08/31	09/15/10
0.350	10/19	11/24	11/29	12/13/10

Dividends have been paid since 2007. Source: Company reports.

Dun & Bradstreet Corp (The)

STANDARD &POOR'S

Business Summary September 03, 2010

CORPORATE OVERVIEW. Dun & Bradstreet (DNB) is a leading worldwide provider of business information and related decision support services. DNB believes it has the world's largest global business database, with over 150 million business records.

DNB operates its business through four customer solution sets: Risk Management Solutions (64% of 2009) (Risk Management includes Supply Management as of January 1, 2008), Sales and Marketing Solutions (29%), and Internet Solutions (7%). Sales in North America accounted for 78% of 2009 revenues, while the remaining 22% came from DNB's overseas presence, including strategic partner relationships and minority equity investments.

Risk Management Solutions helps clients extend commercial credit, set credit limits, and determine total credit risk exposure. It aims to help clients increase cash flow and profitability while minimizing operational, credit, and regulatory risk. Within this customer solution set, DNB offers traditional and what it considers value-added products. Traditional products consist of reports from DNB's database used primarily for making decisions about new credit applications. Value-added products generally support automated decision making and portfolio management through the use of scoring and integrated software solutions.

The Supply Management Solutions set helps customers understand their supplier base, rationalize their supplier rosters, leverage buying power, minimize supply-related risks, and identify and evaluate new sources of supply. Starting in January 2008, DNB started managing its Supply Management business as part of its Risk Management Solutions business.

Sales and Marketing Solutions helps customers conduct market segmentation, maintain updated customer relationship management systems, and offers client profiling, prospect selection and marketing list development. Traditional products generally consist of marketing lists, labels and customized data files used by DNB's customers in their direct mail and marketing activities. Value-added products primarily include decision making and customer information management solutions.

Internet Solutions represents the results of Hoover's, Inc., which DNB acquired in 2003, and AllBusiness.com. Hoover's provides information on public and private companies, primarily to senior executives and sales professionals, using a proprietary database.

Company Financials Fiscal Year Ended Dec. 31

Per Share Data ($)	2009	2008	2007	2006	2005	2004	2003	2002	2001	2000
Tangible Book Value	NM	NM	NM	NM	NM	NM	NM	NM	NM	NM
Cash Flow	7.14	5.93	5.19	4.21	3.71	3.54	3.15	2.96	3.02	2.25
Earnings	5.99	5.58	4.90	3.70	3.19	2.90	2.30	1.87	1.88	0.90
S&P Core Earnings	5.69	4.28	4.66	3.69	2.83	2.14	1.97	0.63	0.07	NA
Dividends	1.36	1.20	1.00	Nil	Nil	Nil	Nil	Nil	Nil	Nil
Payout Ratio	23%	22%	20%	Nil	Nil	Nil	Nil	Nil	Nil	Nil
Prices:High	84.95	98.90	108.45	84.98	68.00	60.80	50.81	43.40	36.90	27.00
Prices:Low	68.97	64.00	81.50	65.03	54.90	47.85	32.31	28.26	20.99	13.00
P/E Ratio:High	14	18	22	23	21	21	22	23	20	30
P/E Ratio:Low	12	11	17	18	17	16	14	15	11	14

Income Statement Analysis (Million $)										
Revenue	1,687	1,726	1,599	1,531	1,444	1,414	1,386	1,276	1,309	1,418
Operating Income	546	521	469	461	431	398	373	371	344	355
Depreciation	58.1	19.6	17.9	33.3	36.1	47.3	64.0	84.2	94.5	111
Interest Expense	45.7	47.4	28.3	20.3	21.1	18.9	18.6	19.5	16.4	8.60
Pretax Income	434	440	428	389	355	341	281	238	260	174
Effective Tax Rate	25.8%	29.1%	31.8%	37.7%	37.7%	37.9%	37.8%	39.6%	38.9%	44.9%
Net Income	319	310	293	241	221	212	175	143	153	73.6
S&P Core Earnings	302	238	278	240	197	156	151	48.5	6.51	NA

Balance Sheet & Other Financial Data (Million $)										
Cash	223	164	176	138	305	336	239	192	145	70.1
Current Assets	760	696	718	645	759	762	731	614	580	539
Total Assets	1,749	1,586	1,659	1,360	1,613	1,636	1,625	1,528	1,431	1,424
Current Liabilities	859	908	910	806	1,029	714	736	718	663	743
Long Term Debt	962	904	725	459	0.10	300	300	300	300	Nil
Common Equity	-746	-856	-440	-399	77.6	54.2	48.4	-18.8	-20.9	-51.0
Total Capital	230	53.7	288	62.4	77.7	354	348	281	280	251
Capital Expenditures	9.20	11.8	13.7	11.6	5.70	12.1	11.0	15.8	16.2	24.1
Cash Flow	378	329	311	274	257	259	239	228	248	185
Current Ratio	0.9	0.8	0.8	0.8	0.7	1.1	1.0	0.9	0.9	0.7
% Long Term Debt of Capitalization	Nil	NM	251.4	NM	0.1	84.7	86.1	106.7	107.0	Nil
% Net Income of Revenue	18.9	17.9	18.3	15.7	15.3	15.0	12.6	11.2	11.7	5.2
% Return on Assets	NA	19.1	19.4	16.2	13.6	13.0	11.1	9.6	10.7	4.9
% Return on Equity	NA	NM	NM	NM	335.7	412.9	1179.1	NM	NM	NM

Data as orig reptd.; bef. results of disc opers/spec. items. Per share data adj. for stk. divs.; EPS diluted. E-Estimated. NA-Not Available. NM-Not Meaningful. NR-Not Ranked. UR-Under Review.

Office: 103 J F K Pkwy, Short Hills, NJ 07078-2708.
Telephone: 973-921-5500.
Website: http://www.dnb.com
Chrmn, Pres & CEO: S. Mathew

SVP & CFO: A.G. Konidaris
SVP, Secy & General Counsel: J.S. Hurwitz
Chief Admin Officer: E.A. Conti
CTO & CIO: W.S. Hauck, III

Investor Contact: R. Veldran (973-921-5863)
Board Members: A. A. Adams, J. W. Alden, C. J. Coughlin, J. N. Fernandez, J. J. Judge, S. Mathew, S. E. Peterson, M. R. Quinlan, N. Seligman, M. J. Winkler

Founded: 2000
Domicile: Delaware
Employees: 5,000

The McGraw-Hill Companies

E. I. du Pont de Nemours and Co

STANDARD &POOR'S

S&P Recommendation	**SELL** ★★★★★	Price $46.83 (as of Oct 22, 2010)	12-Mo. Target Price $38.00	Investment Style Large-Cap Value

GICS Sector Materials
Sub-Industry Diversified Chemicals

Summary This broadly diversified company is the second largest U.S. chemicals manufacturer.

Key Stock Statistics (Source S&P, Vickers, company reports)

52-Wk Range	$47.50–31.02	S&P Oper. EPS 2010**E**	2.90	Market Capitalization(B)	$42.452	Beta	1.40
Trailing 12-Month EPS	$3.43	S&P Oper. EPS 2011**E**	3.00	Yield (%)	3.50	S&P 3-Yr. Proj. EPS CAGR(%)	8
Trailing 12-Month P/E	13.7	P/E on S&P Oper. EPS 2010**E**	16.1	Dividend Rate/Share	$1.64	S&P Credit Rating	A
$10K Invested 5 Yrs Ago	$14,891	Common Shares Outstg. (M)	906.5	Institutional Ownership (%)	64		

Price Performance

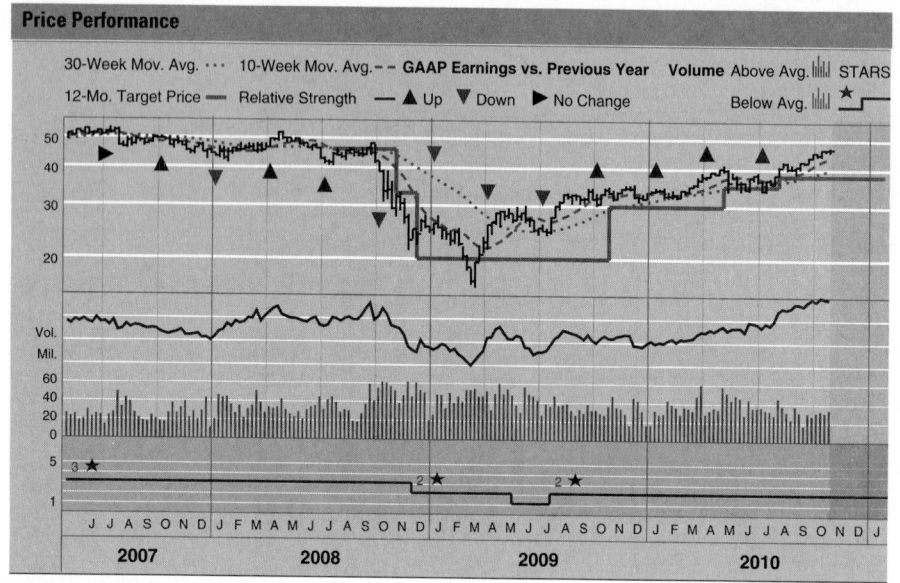

30-Week Mov. Avg. · · · 10-Week Mov. Avg. – – GAAP Earnings vs. Previous Year Volume Above Avg. STARS
12-Mo. Target Price — Relative Strength — ▲ Up ▼ Down ▶ No Change Below Avg. ★

Options: ASE, CBOE, P, Ph

Analysis prepared by **Richard O'Reilly, CFA** on July 28, 2010, when the stock traded at **$ 40.73.**

Highlights

➤ We expect sales to rise about 15% in 2010, including the 25% increase reported for the first half, reflecting recovering global demand in DD's chemicals and materials segments and higher average selling prices (including pass-throughs of changes in metal and commodity prices). We expect raw material and energy costs for the rest of 2010 to increase modestly faster than the 3% pace of the second quarter.

➤ We think the agriculture segment's sales will grow about 10% in 2010, resulting in margin expansion despite increased expected seasonal losses in the second half. Pharmaceutical profits are projected to decline about 55% in 2010 as a result of the April expiration of U.S. patents for Cozaar/Hyzaar.

➤ We expect DD to achieve $400 million of productivity gains this year, following the $1.1 billion of cost savings in 2009. Pension expense will likely rise by $0.32 a share in 2010, and currency impacts should be unfavorable in the second half, in our view, following a $0.13 headwind in the first half. We expect the effective tax rate in the second half to be higher than in the comparable 2009 period.

Investment Rationale/Risk

➤ Our sell opinion on the shares is based on valuation. While DD reported better-than-expected EPS for the second quarter of 2010, aided by a recovery in demand and cost reductions, we expect it to continue to face headwinds from much lower pharmaceutical profits beginning in 2010.

➤ Risks to our opinion and target price include better than expected global industrial activity, lower raw material costs than we assume, a greater increase in market share for corn seeds, and an ability to more quickly and successfully develop and launch new products.

➤ The stock recently traded at a multiple of 14X our 2010 EPS estimate of $2.90, just below the P/E of a group of peer diversified chemical companies. Based on our 2010 EPS estimate and assuming a 13X P/E multiple, 12% below peers due to the challenging conditions we foresee, including lower pharmaceutical profits beginning in 2010, our 12-month target price is $38.

Qualitative Risk Assessment

LOW	**MEDIUM**	HIGH

Our risk assessment reflects the company's diverse business and geographic sales mix and its leadership positions in key products, offset by the cyclical nature of the chemical industry and the volatility of raw material costs.

Quantitative Evaluations

S&P Quality Ranking B

D	C	B-	**B**	B+	A-	A	A+

Relative Strength Rank STRONG

76

LOWEST = 1   HIGHEST = 99

Revenue/Earnings Data

Revenue (Million $)

	1Q	2Q	3Q	4Q	Year
2010	8,844	9,080	--	--	--
2009	6,871	6,858	5,961	6,419	27,328
2008	8,575	8,837	7,297	5,820	31,836
2007	7,845	7,875	6,675	6,983	29,378
2006	7,394	7,442	6,309	6,276	27,421
2005	7,431	7,511	5,870	5,827	26,639

Earnings Per Share ($)

	1Q	2Q	3Q	4Q	Year
2010	1.24	1.26	E0.25	E0.25	E2.90
2009	0.54	0.46	0.45	0.48	1.92
2008	1.31	1.18	0.40	-0.70	2.20
2007	1.01	1.04	0.56	0.60	3.22
2006	0.88	1.04	0.52	0.94	3.38
2005	0.96	1.01	-0.09	0.16	2.07

Fiscal year ended Dec. 31. Next earnings report expected: NA. EPS Estimates based on S&P Operating Earnings; historical GAAP earnings are as reported.

Dividend Data (Dates: mm/dd Payment Date: mm/dd/yy)

Amount ($)	Date Decl.	Ex-Div. Date	Stk. of Record	Payment Date
0.410	01/27	02/10	02/12	03/12/10
0.410	04/28	05/12	05/14	06/11/10
0.410	07/22	08/11	08/13	09/10/10
0.410	10/21	11/10	11/15	12/14/10

Dividends have been paid since 1904. Source: Company reports.

Please read the Required Disclosures and Analyst Certification on the last page of this report.

The McGraw-Hill Companies

E. I. du Pont de Nemours and Co

Business Summary July 28, 2010

E.I. du Pont de Nemours and Company, the second largest domestic chemicals producer, has made several major changes in recent years, including expanding its life sciences businesses (now crop pesticides and nutrition). Foreign sales accounted for 62% of the total in 2009.

The Agricultural and Nutrition segment (32% of sales in 2009, and 37% of pretax operating income) consists of Pioneer Hi-Bred (56% of segment sales in 2009), the world's largest seed company, including corn (68% of sales) and soybeans; DuPont is also a major global supplier of crop protection chemicals (29%). The segment also includes nutrition and health (including the Solae soy business and food packaging products) and microbial diagnostic testing products. Segment sales rose 4% in 2009, including 17% in seeds, and profits climbed 13%.

The Electronic and Communication Technologies segment (7%, 3%) includes electronic and advanced display materials and products (photoresins, slurries, films, laminants), and flexographic printing and proofing systems.

Performance Chemicals (18%, 16%) is the world's largest maker of titanium dioxide pigments (44% of sales) used in coatings and paper, a leading produc-

er of fluorochemicals (refrigerants, blowing agents, aerosols) and fluoropolymers (Teflon resins and coatings), and makes specialty and intermediate chemicals.

The Performance Coatings unit (13%, 2%) is one of the largest global auto paint suppliers (including OEM and refinish markets) and also provides industrial and powder coatings, and inks for digital printing.

Performance Materials (21%, 3%) includes engineering polymers and elastomers for auto, electrical, consumer and industrial uses; packaging and industrial polymers and films; and polyester films.

Safety & Protection (11%, 8%) consists of Kevlar and Nomex aramid fibers and Tyvek and Sontara nonwovens for industrial, packaging, building, textile, military, and personal safety uses; solid surfaces (Corian products); and safety consulting services.

Company Financials Fiscal Year Ended Dec. 31

Per Share Data ($)	2009	2008	2007	2006	2005	2004	2003	2002	2001	2000
Tangible Book Value	2.53	2.26	6.64	4.56	4.24	6.25	4.63	4.54	7.30	4.50
Cash Flow	3.57	3.79	4.70	4.49	3.45	3.11	2.58	3.35	5.83	3.96
Earnings	1.92	2.20	3.22	3.38	2.07	1.77	0.99	1.84	4.15	2.19
S&P Core Earnings	1.69	0.74	2.93	2.98	1.98	2.00	1.14	0.40	-1.04	NA
Dividends	1.64	1.64	1.52	1.48	1.46	1.40	1.40	1.40	1.40	1.40
Payout Ratio	85%	75%	47%	44%	71%	79%	141%	76%	34%	64%
Prices:High	35.62	52.49	53.90	49.68	54.90	49.39	46.00	49.80	49.88	74.00
Prices:Low	16.05	21.32	42.25	38.52	37.60	39.88	38.60	35.02	32.64	38.19
P/E Ratio:High	19	24	17	15	27	28	46	27	12	34
P/E Ratio:Low	8	10	13	11	18	23	39	19	8	17

Income Statement Analysis (Million $)										
Revenue	27,328	31,836	29,378	27,421	26,639	27,340	26,996	24,006	24,726	28,268
Operating Income	4,246	4,796	4,269	3,612	3,507	3,574	3,176	4,263	4,130	5,244
Depreciation	1,503	1,444	1,371	1,384	1,358	1,347	1,584	1,515	1,754	1,860
Interest Expense	408	425	430	460	518	362	347	359	590	810
Pretax Income	2,184	2,391	3,743	3,329	3,558	1,442	143	2,124	6,844	3,447
Effective Tax Rate	19.0%	15.9%	20.0%	5.89%	41.3%	NM	NM	8.71%	36.0%	31.1%
Net Income	1,755	2,007	2,988	3,148	2,053	1,780	1,002	1,841	4,328	2,314
S&P Core Earnings	1,543	677	2,713	2,768	1,965	2,008	1,132	398	-1,087	NA

Balance Sheet & Other Financial Data (Million $)										
Cash	6,137	3,704	1,436	1,893	1,851	3,536	3,298	4,143	5,848	1,617
Current Assets	17,288	15,311	13,160	12,870	12,422	15,211	18,462	13,459	14,801	11,656
Total Assets	38,185	36,209	34,131	31,777	33,250	35,632	37,039	34,621	40,319	39,426
Current Liabilities	9,390	9,710	8,541	7,940	7,463	7,939	13,043	7,096	8,067	9,255
Long Term Debt	9,528	7,638	5,955	6,013	6,783	5,548	4,301	5,647	5,350	6,658
Common Equity	6,978	6,888	10,899	9,185	8,670	11,140	9,544	8,826	14,215	13,062
Total Capital	17,179	15,330	18,335	16,145	17,346	19,001	15,087	18,755	24,916	22,442
Capital Expenditures	1,308	1,978	1,585	1,532	1,340	1,232	1,713	1,280	1,494	1,925
Cash Flow	3,248	3,441	4,349	4,532	3,411	3,117	2,576	3,346	6,072	4,164
Current Ratio	1.8	1.6	1.5	1.6	1.7	1.9	1.4	1.9	1.8	1.3
% Long Term Debt of Capitalization	55.5	49.8	32.5	37.2	39.1	29.2	28.5	30.1	21.5	29.7
% Net Income of Revenue	6.4	6.3	10.2	11.5	7.7	6.5	3.7	7.7	17.5	8.2
% Return on Assets	4.7	5.7	9.1	9.7	6.0	4.9	2.8	4.9	10.9	5.8
% Return on Equity	25.3	22.6	29.7	35.2	20.6	17.1	10.8	15.9	31.7	17.9

Data as orig reptd.; bef. results of disc opers/spec. items. Per share data adj. for stk. divs.; EPS diluted. Beginning in 2008, revenues include other income. E-Estimated. NA-Not Available. NM-Not Meaningful. NR-Not Ranked. UR-Under Review.

Office: 1007 Market Street, Wilmington, DE 19898.
Telephone: 302-774-1000.
Email: info@dupont.com
Website: http://www.dupont.com

Chrmn & CEO: E.J. Kullman
EVP, CFO & Chief Acctg Officer: N.C. Fanandakis
SVP, CSO & CTO: D. Muzyka
SVP & General Counsel: T.L. Sager

Treas: S.M. Stalnecker
Investor Contact: K. Fletcher (800-441-7515)
Board Members: S. W. Bodman, III, R. H. Brown, R. A. Brown, B. Collomb, C. J. Crawford, A. M. Cutler, J. T. Dillon, M. A. Hewson, L. D. Juliber, E. J. Kullman, W. K. Reilly, E. I. du Pont, II

Founded: 1802
Domicile: Delaware
Employees: 58,000

Eastman Chemical Co

STANDARD &POOR'S

S&P Recommendation BUY ★★★★☆

Price	12-Mo. Target Price	Investment Style
$78.60 (as of Oct 22, 2010)	**$84.00**	Large-Cap Value

GICS Sector Materials
Sub-Industry Diversified Chemicals

Summary This global company manufactures and markets chemicals, fibers and polyester plastics used in consumer and industrial products.

Key Stock Statistics (Source S&P, Vickers, company reports)

52-Wk Range	$80.22– 51.10	S&P Oper. EPS 2010**E**	**7.00**	Market Capitalization(B)	**$5.678**	Beta	**1.87**
Trailing 12-Month EPS	**$4.32**	S&P Oper. EPS 2011**E**	**7.25**	Yield (%)	**2.24**	S&P 3-Yr. Proj. EPS CAGR(%)	**15**
Trailing 12-Month P/E	**18.2**	P/E on S&P Oper. EPS 2010**E**	**11.2**	Dividend Rate/Share	**$1.76**	S&P Credit Rating	**BBB**
$10K Invested 5 Yrs Ago	**$19,575**	Common Shares Outstg. (M)	**72.2**	Institutional Ownership (%)	**80**		

Price Performance

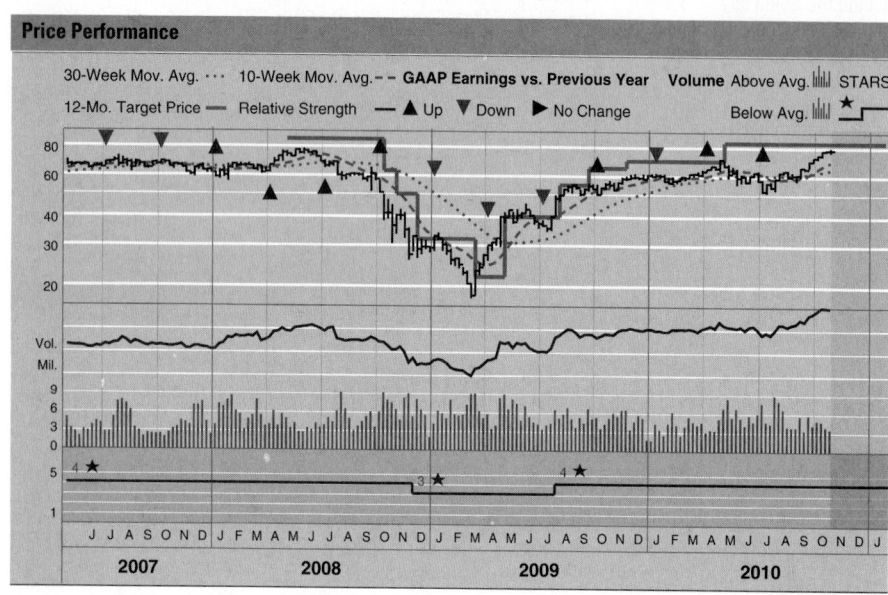

- 30-Week Mov. Avg. · · ·
- 10-Week Mov. Avg. – –
- **GAAP Earnings vs. Previous Year**
- Volume Above Avg.
- STARS
- 12-Mo. Target Price —
- Relative Strength —
- ▲ Up ▼ Down ► No Change
- Below Avg.

Options: ASE, CBOE, P, Ph

Analysis prepared by **Richard O'Reilly, CFA** on September 21, 2010, when the stock traded at **$ 71.35**.

Highlights

➤ We expect sales to increase 30% and profits to improve greatly in 2010, reflecting increased overall demand for the first full year since 2007. We expect EMN to retain a majority of the $200 million in cost savings achieved in 2009, and raw material and energy costs to be lower in the second half.

➤ We project record annual profits for the fibers and coatings & adhesives segments in 2010 and much greater profits in specialty plastics. We expect a new copolyester resin to turn profitable in 2011. We expect the polyester resin business to have a much smaller loss in 2010, including breakeven second half results, aided by the improved operations at the U.S. plant that was expanded by 50% in late 2008.

➤ We expect increased interest expense in 2010, in part due to reduced capitalized interest, but we believe the effective tax rate will be about 33.5%, down from 37.6% in 2009. Our EPS estimate for 2010 includes a projected $0.20 insurance recovery in the third quarter related to an unplanned plant outage earlier in the year.

Investment Rationale/Risk

➤ Our buy opinion reflects our favorable outlook for EMN's business. The company recently boosted its EPS guidance for 2010 and the unprofitable polyester (PET) resin business is under review for possible divestiture. We expect the coatings, specialty plastics and fibers segments (over 80% of annual profits) to grow over the long term, aided by new capacity in specialty polyesters and acetate tow.

➤ Risks to our recommendation and target price include reduced demand for the company's production, unplanned production outages and interruptions, possible greater-than-estimated asbestos liabilities, and higher-than-expected raw material costs, and an inability to eliminate losses in the PET business.

➤ We expect EMN to again generate free cash flow in 2010, as much as the $320 million of 2009, and we believe the dividend, which recently provided an above-average yield of 2.4%, is secure. Applying a peer P/E multiple of 11.5X to our 2011 EPS estimate of $7.25 results in our 12-month target price of $84.

Qualitative Risk Assessment

LOW	**MEDIUM**	HIGH

Our risk assessment reflects the diverse business and geographic sales mix of the company, offset by the cyclical nature of the chemicals industry and the volatility of raw material costs.

Quantitative Evaluations

S&P Quality Ranking   **B**

D	C	B-	**B**	B+	A-	A	A+

Relative Strength Rank   **STRONG**

87

LOWEST = 1   HIGHEST = 99

Revenue/Earnings Data

Revenue (Million $)

	1Q	2Q	3Q	4Q	Year
2010	1,564	1,724	--	--	--
2009	1,129	1,253	1,337	1,328	5,047
2008	1,727	1,834	1,819	1,346	6,726
2007	1,795	1,895	1,813	1,737	6,830
2006	1,803	1,929	1,966	1,752	7,450
2005	1,762	1,752	1,816	1,729	7,059

Earnings Per Share ($)

2010	1.37	2.02	E2.25	E1.33	E7.00
2009	0.03	0.89	1.38	-0.44	1.85
2008	1.45	1.49	1.33	-0.03	4.32
2007	0.91	1.22	0.24	1.25	3.83
2006	1.27	1.37	1.15	1.12	4.91
2005	2.00	2.51	1.50	0.81	6.81

Fiscal year ended Dec. 31. Next earnings report expected: Late October. EPS Estimates based on S&P Operating Earnings; historical GAAP earnings are as reported.

Dividend Data (Dates: mm/dd Payment Date: mm/dd/yy)

Amount ($)	Date Decl.	Ex-Div. Date	Stk. of Record	Payment Date
0.440	12/03	12/10	12/14	01/04/10
0.440	02/18	03/11	03/15	04/01/10
0.440	05/06	06/10	06/14	07/01/10
0.440	08/05	09/09	09/13	10/01/10

Dividends have been paid since 1994. Source: Company reports.

Eastman Chemical Co

Business Summary September 21, 2010

CORPORATE OVERVIEW. Eastman Chemical Co. is a large global maker of a broad range of chemicals, plastics and fibers. International operations accounted for 45% of sales in 2009. It reports results in five segments.

The coatings, adhesive, specialty polymers and inks segment (24% of 2009 sales, operating profits of $227 million) is a leading supplier of alcohols and solvents used in coatings (50% of segment sales), resins and dispersions (35%), and specialty polymers (15%) used in adhesives.

Performance chemicals and intermediates (26%, $63 million) includes oxo chemicals, acetyls, plasticizers and glycols used for polymers, photographic and home care products, agricultural chemicals and pharmaceutical intermediates; and additives for food and beverage ingredients. The segment also included contract ethylene sales of $28 million under a supply agreement related to a former polyethylene business. About 65% of annual segment sales is generated in North America.

In the fibers business (20%, $296 million), EMN is one of the world's two largest suppliers of acetate cigarette filter tow (annual capacity of 402 million lbs. at end of 2009) and the leader in acetate yarn. The company projects global growth in demand for filter tow of 1%-2% annually through 2012, with Asia and Eastern Europe having the fastest growth rates. The business also includes acetyl chemicals (acetate flake, acetic anhydride).

The performance polymers segment (14%, loss of $66 million) consists of poly-ethylene terephthalate (PET) resins and various intermediates. EMN in 2006 was the world's largest producer of polyester plastics, consisting of poly-ethylene terephthalate (PET), used for packaging applications and beverage containers such as soft-drink bottles, with annual PET capacity of 3.3 billion lbs. at year-end 2006. In 2007, EMN decided to close or sell its unprofitable polyester production sites outside the U.S.; in December 2007, it sold its two facilities in Latin America (sales of $413 million in 2007 and a loss of $127 million, including a restructuring charge of $115 million). EMN in late March 2008 sold its remaining two European plants (sales of $542 million in 2007) and reported as discontinued operations beginning in late 2007). Eastman's domestic operations had sales of $936 million in 2008 and a loss of $54 million. In early 2007, EMN completed the start-up of a new U.S. plant with annual capacity of 770 million lbs. using new Integer technology. EMN has closed 880 million lbs. of higher-cost domestic capacity and in late 2008 expanded the new plant by 50%. Integer now accounts for about 65% of EMN's U.S. PET capacity of 1.76 billion lbs.

Company Financials Fiscal Year Ended Dec. 31

Per Share Data ($)	2009	2008	2007	2006	2005	2004	2003	2002	2001	2000
Tangible Book Value	15.67	15.52	26.63	20.42	15.85	10.70	9.00	9.06	9.92	15.64
Cash Flow	5.44	7.68	6.97	8.64	10.50	6.23	1.22	6.18	3.33	9.36
Earnings	1.85	4.32	3.83	4.91	6.81	2.18	-3.54	1.02	-2.33	3.94
S&P Core Earnings	1.78	3.30	3.79	4.42	5.63	2.23	-3.45	0.26	-3.06	NA
Dividends	1.76	1.76	1.76	1.76	1.76	1.76	1.76	1.76	1.76	1.76
Payout Ratio	95%	41%	46%	36%	26%	81%	NM	173%	NM	45%
Prices:High	61.95	78.29	72.44	61.29	61.80	58.17	39.57	49.55	55.65	54.75
Prices:Low	17.76	25.87	57.54	47.30	44.10	38.00	27.56	34.53	29.03	33.63
P/E Ratio:High	33	18	19	12	9	27	NM	49	NM	14
P/E Ratio:Low	10	6	15	10	6	17	NM	34	NM	9

Income Statement Analysis (Million $)										
Revenue	5,047	6,726	6,830	7,450	7,059	6,580	5,800	5,320	5,384	5,292
Operating Income	800	805	929	981	1,092	696	590	610	755	989
Depreciation	274	256	264	308	304	322	367	397	435	418
Interest Expense	85.0	106	113	80.0	100	115	124	128	140	135
Pretax Income	226	429	470	576	783	64.0	-381	84.0	-297	452
Effective Tax Rate	39.8%	23.5%	31.7%	29.0%	28.9%	NM	NM	5.95%	NM	33.0%
Net Income	136	328	321	409	557	170	-273	79.0	-179	303
S&P Core Earnings	131	252	316	368	459	173	-266	20.4	-236	NA

Balance Sheet & Other Financial Data (Million $)										
Cash	793	387	888	939	524	325	558	77.0	66.0	101
Current Assets	1,735	1,423	2,293	2,422	1,924	1,768	2,010	1,529	1,458	1,523
Total Assets	5,515	5,281	6,009	6,173	5,773	5,872	6,230	6,273	6,086	6,550
Current Liabilities	800	832	1,122	1,059	1,051	1,099	1,477	1,224	958	1,258
Long Term Debt	1,604	1,442	1,613	1,589	1,621	2,061	2,089	2,054	2,143	1,914
Common Equity	1,513	1,553	2,082	2,029	1,612	1,184	1,913	1,271	1,378	1,812
Total Capital	3,117	3,008	3,917	3,618	3,550	3,455	4,318	3,809	3,973	4,333
Capital Expenditures	310	634	518	389	343	248	230	427	234	226
Cash Flow	399	584	585	717	861	492	94.0	476	256	721
Current Ratio	2.2	1.7	2.0	2.3	1.8	1.6	1.4	1.2	1.5	1.2
% Long Term Debt of Capitalization	51.5	47.9	42.4	43.9	45.7	59.7	48.4	53.9	53.9	44.2
% Net Income of Revenue	2.7	4.9	4.7	5.5	7.9	2.6	NM	1.5	NM	5.7
% Return on Assets	2.5	5.8	5.3	6.8	9.6	2.8	NM	1.3	NM	4.7
% Return on Equity	8.9	18.1	15.6	22.5	39.8	15.3	NM	6.0	NM	17.0

Data as orig reptd.; bef. results of disc opers/spec. items. Per share data adj. for stk. divs.; EPS diluted. E-Estimated. NA-Not Available. NM-Not Meaningful. NR-Not Ranked. UR-Under Review.

Office: 200 S Wilcox Dr, Kingsport, TN, USA 37660-5147.
Telephone: 423-229-2000.
Website: http://www.eastman.com
Chrmn: J.B. Ferguson

Pres & CEO: J.P. Rogers
SVP & CFO: C.E. Espeland
SVP & Chief Admin Officer: N.P. Sneed
SVP & CTO: G.W. Nelson

Investor Contact: G. Riddle (212-835-1620)
Board Members: G. E. Anderson, M. P. Connors, S. R. Demeritt, J. B. Ferguson, R. M. Hernandez, R. Hornbaker, L. M. Kling, H. L. Lance, T. H. McLain, D. W. Raisbeck, J. P. Rogers

Founded: 1920
Domicile: Delaware
Employees: 10,000

Eastman Kodak Co

STANDARD & POOR'S

S&P Recommendation	HOLD ★★★☆☆	Price	12-Mo. Target Price	Investment Style
		$3.93 (as of Oct 22, 2010)	$6.00	Large-Cap Value

GICS Sector Consumer Discretionary
Sub-Industry Photographic Products

Summary This multinational company provides imaging technology products and services to the photographic and graphic communications markets worldwide.

Key Stock Statistics (Source S&P, Vickers, company reports)

52-Wk Range	$9.08–3.26	S&P Oper. EPS 2010**E**	-0.04	Market Capitalization(B)	$1.056	Beta	1.48
Trailing 12-Month EPS	$1.06	S&P Oper. EPS 2011**E**	0.08	Yield (%)	Nil	S&P 3-Yr. Proj. EPS CAGR(%)	NM
Trailing 12-Month P/E	3.7	P/E on S&P Oper. EPS 2010**E**	NM	Dividend Rate/Share	Nil	S&P Credit Rating	B-
$10K Invested 5 Yrs Ago	$1,932	Common Shares Outstg. (M)	268.7	Institutional Ownership (%)	89		

Price Performance

30-Week Mov. Avg. · · · · 10-Week Mov. Avg. - - - **GAAP Earnings vs. Previous Year** Volume Above Avg. ▐▐ STARS
12-Mo. Target Price — Relative Strength — ▲ Up ▼ Down ▶ No Change Below Avg. ▐▐ ★

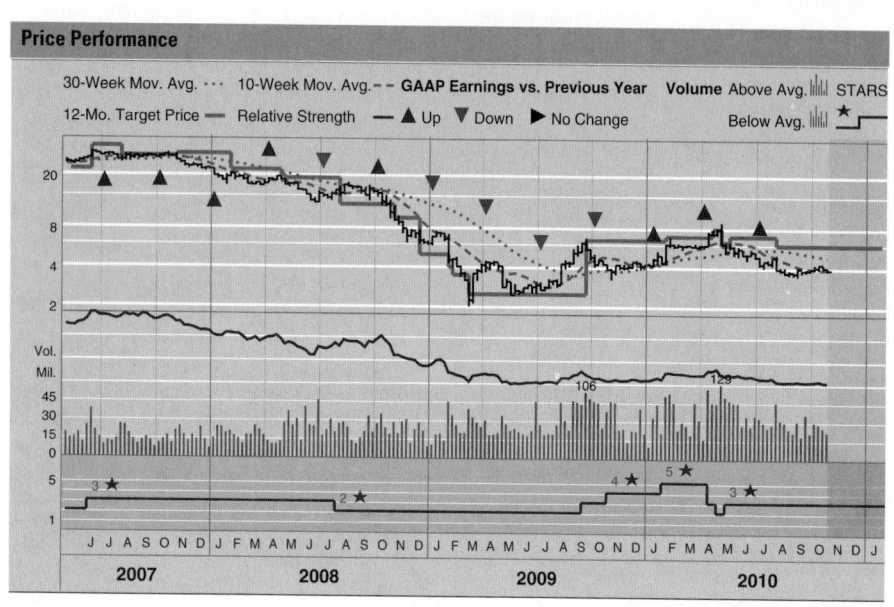

Analysis prepared by **Erik Kolb** on July 29, 2010, when the stock traded at **$ 4.01**.

Options: ASE, CBOE, P, Ph

Highlights

➤ After a 19% net sales decline in 2009, we estimate a 0.2% fall in 2010 to $7.59 billion, and we see a 0.4% increase in 2011 to $7.61 billion. We think EK's consumer digital imaging group has made modest progress, partly on sales of inkjet printers and kiosk products, but first half results indicate that the group may well be unprofitable in the near term. Elsewhere, we see a 16% decline at the film, photofinishing and entertainment segment, and a 0.3% increase in graphic communications. While we anticipate double-digit decreases for traditional film sales in coming quarters, we think the pace of declines will moderate compared to last year. In 2012, we see 3.1% growth.

➤ We see EK, after cutting 4,150 (17%) positions in 2009, along with other cost structure improvements, posting EBITDA margins in 2010 of 10.1%, up from 7.4% in 2009. We see further improvement to 11.6% in 2012.

➤ We project a $0.04 a share loss in 2010, compared to an $0.87 a share loss in 2009, on a 21% higher share count after a recent warrant placement with KKR. We forecast EPS of $0.08 in 2011 and $0.63 in 2012.

Investment Rationale/Risk

➤ Although first quarter results benefited from intellectual property revenues, these are non-recurring, and we are concerned that declining film sales will hurt core cash flow and stifle future investments, especially in the consumer products arena. EK has made notable progress in its shift toward a more digitally focused product line after completing a four-year, $3.4 billion restructuring program, but while sales are rebounding from their worst levels, we nonetheless expect the consumer inkjet segment to remain unprofitable through 2011.

➤ Risks to our recommendation and target price include a faster-than-anticipated decline in demand for traditional film product offerings, greater-than-forecast pricing pressure for digital products, successful new product launches, and decreases in market share.

➤ To arrive at our 12-month target price of $6.00, we apply a multiple of about 16X to a blend of our 2011 and 2012 EPS estimates, roughly in line with peers.

Qualitative Risk Assessment

LOW	MEDIUM	HIGH

Our risk assessment is based on the company's ongoing shift toward digital photography. While we think EK has made progress in this endeavor, we are concerned about competitive threats and margin declines in this space.

Quantitative Evaluations

S&P Quality Ranking B-

D	C	B-	B	B+	A-	A	A+

Relative Strength Rank WEAK

16

LOWEST = 1 HIGHEST = 99

Revenue/Earnings Data

Revenue (Million $)

	1Q	2Q	3Q	4Q	Year
2010	1,933	1,569	--	--	--
2009	1,477	1,766	1,781	2,582	7,606
2008	2,093	2,485	2,405	2,433	9,416
2007	2,080	2,468	2,533	3,220	10,301
2006	2,889	3,360	3,204	3,821	13,274
2005	2,832	3,686	3,553	4,197	14,268

Earnings Per Share ($)

	1Q	2Q	3Q	4Q	Year
2010	0.40	-0.62	E-0.30	E0.05	E-0.04
2009	-1.34	-0.71	-0.41	1.36	-0.87
2008	-0.40	-0.67	0.35	-0.49	0.19
2007	-0.61	-0.53	0.11	0.28	-0.71
2006	-1.04	-0.98	-0.13	0.06	-2.09
2005	-0.49	-0.49	-3.62	-0.47	-5.05

Fiscal year ended Dec. 31. Next earnings report expected: Late October. EPS Estimates based on S&P Operating Earnings; historical GAAP earnings are as reported.

Dividend Data

Dividends were suspended following the October 2008 payment.

Please read the Required Disclosures and Analyst Certification on the last page of this report.

The McGraw-Hill Companies

Eastman Kodak Co

STANDARD
&POOR'S

Business Summary July 29, 2010

CORPORATE OVERVIEW. Eastman Kodak provides imaging technology products and services to the photographic and graphic communications markets. In 2009, the consumer digital products group accounted for 37.9% of net sales from continuing operations, compared to 34.4% in 2008, while film, photofinishing and entertainment represented 27.4% (29.7%), graphic communications 34.7% (35.8%), and other activities 0.0% (0.1%).

The consumer digital imaging group is a global provider of digital photography products and services for consumer markets. Offerings include digital products such as digital cameras and digital picture frames, retail printing, online imaging services, imaging sensors, and all-in-one printers. Kodak holds top three market shares in categories such as digital still cameras, retail printing, and digital picture frames. EK's strategy in this segment is to extend picture taking, picture search/organizing, creativity, sharing and printing to bring innovative new experiences to consumers.

The film, photofinishing and entertainment group is composed of traditional photographic products and services used to create motion pictures, and for consumer, professional and industrial imaging applications. The company manufactures and markets films and one-time-use and re-loadable film cameras.

The graphic communications group serves a variety of customers in the creative, in-plant, data center, commercial printing, packaging, newspaper, and digital service bureau market segments with a range of software, media, and hardware products that provide customers with a variety of solutions for prepress equipment, workflow software, digital and traditional printing, document scanning, and multi-vendor IT services.

Through the years, EK has engaged in extensive and productive efforts in research and development. R&D expenses totaled $356 million (4.7% of sales) in 2009, compared to $478 million (5.1% of sales) in 2008, $535 million (5.2% of sales) in 2007, $578 million (5.5%) in 2006, and $739 million (6.5%) in 2005. The company also holds a portfolio of patents in several areas important to its business.

Company Financials Fiscal Year Ended Dec. 31

Per Share Data ($)	2009	2008	2007	2006	2005	2004	2003	2002	2001	2000
Tangible Book Value	NM	NM	4.77	NM	NM	6.57	5.53	6.27	6.71	8.56
Cash Flow	0.64	-0.83	2.02	2.55	-0.18	3.88	3.72	5.52	3.42	7.48
Earnings	-0.87	0.19	-0.71	-2.09	-5.05	0.28	0.83	2.72	0.26	4.59
S&P Core Earnings	-1.68	-2.30	-1.58	-2.65	-4.93	-0.42	0.53	0.44	-1.86	NA
Dividends	Nil	0.50	0.50	0.50	0.50	0.50	1.15	1.80	1.77	1.76
Payout Ratio	Nil	263%	NM	NM	NM	179%	139%	68%	NM	38%
Prices:High	7.66	22.03	30.20	30.91	35.19	34.74	41.08	38.48	49.95	67.50
Prices:Low	2.01	5.93	21.42	18.93	20.77	24.25	20.39	25.58	24.40	35.31
P/E Ratio:High	NM	NM	NM	NM	NM	NM	49	15	19	15
P/E Ratio:Low	NM	NM	NM	NM	NM	NM	25	10	9	8

Income Statement Analysis (Million $)										
Revenue	7,606	9,416	10,301	13,274	14,268	13,517	13,317	12,835	13,234	13,994
Operating Income	541	537	1,002	1,600	1,493	1,638	1,685	2,898	1,923	3,103
Depreciation	427	494	785	1,331	1,402	1,030	830	818	919	889
Interest Expense	119	108	113	262	211	168	148	173	219	178
Pretax Income	-117	-89.0	-256	-346	-762	-92.0	196	946	97.0	2,132
Effective Tax Rate	NM	NM	NM	NM	NM	NM	NM	16.1%	33.0%	34.0%
Net Income	-233	54.0	-205	-600	-1,455	81.0	238	793	76.0	1,407
S&P Core Earnings	-451	-647	-453	-757	-1,419	-119	149	127	-541	NA

Balance Sheet & Other Financial Data (Million $)										
Cash	2,024	2,145	2,976	1,469	1,665	1,255	1,250	569	448	251
Current Assets	4,303	5,004	6,053	5,557	5,781	5,648	5,455	4,534	4,683	5,491
Total Assets	7,714	9,960	13,659	14,320	14,921	14,737	14,818	13,369	13,362	14,212
Current Liabilities	2,896	3,462	4,446	4,971	5,489	4,990	5,307	5,377	5,354	6,215
Long Term Debt	1,129	1,252	1,289	2,714	2,764	1,852	2,302	1,164	1,666	1,166
Common Equity	18.0	1,742	3,029	1,388	1,967	3,811	3,264	2,777	2,894	3,428
Total Capital	1,149	2,263	4,318	4,102	4,731	5,663	5,566	3,941	4,560	4,655
Capital Expenditures	152	254	259	379	472	460	506	577	743	945
Cash Flow	172	-233	580	731	-53.0	1,111	1,068	1,611	995	2,296
Current Ratio	1.5	1.5	1.4	1.1	1.1	1.1	1.0	0.8	0.9	0.9
% Long Term Debt of Capitalization	98.3	55.6	29.9	66.2	58.4	32.7	41.4	29.5	36.5	25.0
% Net Income of Revenue	NM	0.6	NM	NM	NM	NM	1.8	6.2	0.6	10.1
% Return on Assets	NM	0.5	NM	NM	NM	NM	1.7	5.9	0.6	9.8
% Return on Equity	NM	2.3	NM	NM	NM	NM	7.9	27.9	2.4	38.3

Data as orig reptd.; bef. results of disc opers/spec. items. Per share data adj. for stk. divs.; EPS diluted. E-Estimated. NA-Not Available. NM-Not Meaningful. NR-Not Ranked. UR-Under Review.

Office: 343 State Street, Rochester, NY 14650.
Telephone: 585-724-4000.
Website: http://www.kodak.com
Chrmn & CEO: A.M. Perez

Pres & COO: P.J. Faraci
EVP & CFO: F.S. Sklarsky
SVP & General Counsel: J.P. Haag
CTO: T.R. Taber

Investor Contact: A.P. McCorvey
Board Members: R. S. Braddock, H. Y. Chen, A. H. Clammer, T. M. Donahue, M. Hawley, W. H. Hernandez, D. Lebda, D. L. Lee, K. P. Legg, D. Lewis, W. G. Parrett, A. M. Perez, J. Seligman, D. F. Strigl, L. D. Tyson

Founded: 1880
Domicile: New Jersey
Employees: 20,250

The McGraw-Hill Companies

Eaton Corp

STANDARD &POOR'S

S&P Recommendation	BUY ★★★★☆	Price $87.87 (as of Oct 22, 2010)	12-Mo. Target Price $95.00	Investment Style Large-Cap Blend

GICS Sector Industrials
Sub-Industry Industrial Machinery

Summary This diversified industrial manufacturer's products include electrical systems and components for power management, truck transmissions and fluid power systems, and services for industrial, mobile and aircraft equipment.

Key Stock Statistics (Source S&P, Vickers, company reports)

52-Wk Range	$88.50– 60.03	S&P Oper. EPS 2010E	5.54	Market Capitalization(B)	$14.745	Beta	1.40
Trailing 12-Month EPS	$4.62	S&P Oper. EPS 2011E	6.41	Yield (%)	2.64	S&P 3-Yr. Proj. EPS CAGR(%)	9
Trailing 12-Month P/E	19.0	P/E on S&P Oper. EPS 2010E	15.9	Dividend Rate/Share	$2.32	S&P Credit Rating	A-
$10K Invested 5 Yrs Ago	$17,486	Common Shares Outstg. (M)	167.8	Institutional Ownership (%)	79		

Price Performance

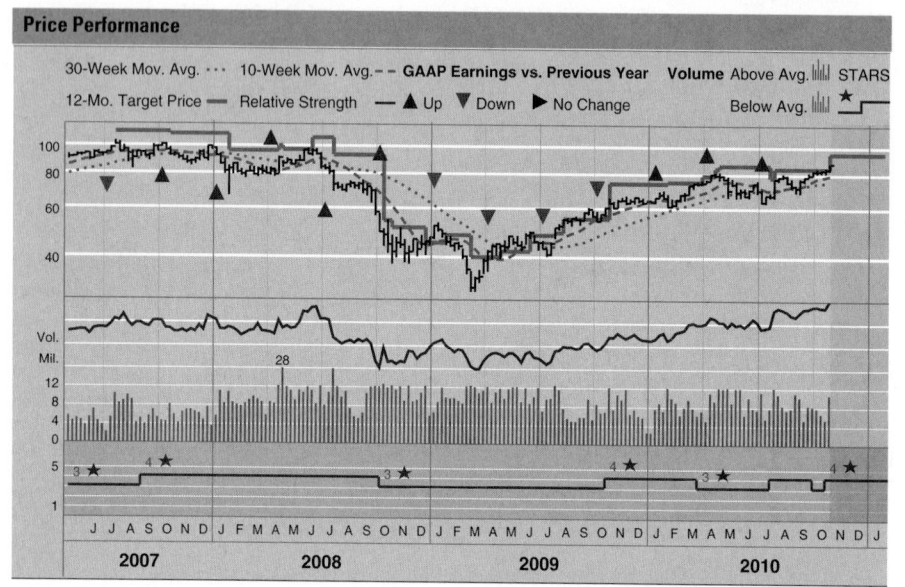

30-Week Mov. Avg. · · · 10-Week Mov. Avg. - - GAAP Earnings vs. Previous Year Volume Above Avg. STARS
12-Mo. Target Price — Relative Strength — ▲ Up ▼ Down ► No Change Below Avg. ★

Options: ASE, CBOE, P, Ph

Qualitative Risk Assessment

LOW	MEDIUM	HIGH

Our risk assessment reflects our view that ETN has good geographic and product diversification, offset by the highly cyclical nature of the company's various end markets, and significant pension and other post-retirement benefit obligations.

Quantitative Evaluations

S&P Quality Ranking   A-

D	C	B-	B	B+	A-	A	A+

Relative Strength Rank   STRONG

83

LOWEST = 1   HIGHEST = 99

Revenue/Earnings Data

Revenue (Million $)

	1Q	2Q	3Q	4Q	Year
2010	3,103	3,378	--	--	--
2009	2,813	2,901	3,028	3,131	11,873
2008	3,496	4,279	4,114	3,487	15,376
2007	3,153	3,248	3,298	3,374	13,033
2006	2,991	3,162	3,115	3,102	12,370
2005	2,654	2,834	2,789	2,838	11,115

Earnings Per Share ($)

	1Q	2Q	3Q	4Q	Year
2010	0.91	1.33	E1.34	E1.62	E5.54
2009	-0.30	0.17	1.14	1.25	2.27
2008	1.62	2.04	1.87	0.98	6.50
2007	1.53	1.60	1.59	1.67	6.38
2006	1.35	1.63	1.39	1.59	5.97
2005	1.19	1.37	1.30	1.38	5.23

Fiscal year ended Dec. 31. Next earnings report expected: NA. EPS Estimates based on S&P Operating Earnings; historical GAAP earnings are as reported.

Highlights

► The STARS recommendation for ETN has recently been changed to 4 (buy) from 3 (hold) and the 12-month target price has recently been changed to $95.00 from $84.00. The Highlights section of this Stock Report will be updated accordingly.

Investment Rationale/Risk

► The Investment Rationale/Risk section of this Stock Report will be updated shortly. For the latest News story on ETN from MarketScope, see below.

► 10/20/10 01:24 pm ET ... S&P RAISES RECOMMENDATION ON SHARES OF EATON CORP TO BUY FROM HOLD (ETN 86.4****): Adjusted for acquisition-related costs, Q3 EPS of $1.60, vs. $1.14, is $0.26 ahead of our estimate, on greater-than-expect sales growth of 18% and margins. We are positively surprised not only with the robust bookings in the quarter, but also strong margin performance, especially in regard to sales that remain below peak levels. We think both portend improved results in future periods, and we raise our '10 EPS estimate by $0.59 to $5.54 and '11's by $0.84 to $6.41. We also raise our target price $11 to $95 on higher estimates and revised valuation analyses. / M.Christy-CFA

Dividend Data (Dates: mm/dd Payment Date: mm/dd/yy)

Amount ($)	Date Decl.	Ex-Div. Date	Stk. of Record	Payment Date
0.500	10/28	11/05	11/09	11/27/09
0.500	01/27	02/04	02/08	02/26/10
0.500	04/28	05/06	05/10	05/28/10
0.580	07/21	08/05	08/09	08/27/10

Dividends have been paid since 1923. Source: Company reports.

Please read the Required Disclosures and Analyst Certification on the last page of this report.

The McGraw·Hill Companies

Eaton Corp

STANDARD &POOR'S

Business Summary October 06, 2010

CORPORATE OVERVIEW. Eaton Corp., a diversified industrial equipment and parts manufacturer with $11.9 billion in revenues in 2009, conducts business through six business segments.

ETN separates its electrical product results into two units -- Electrical Americas (29% of 2009 sales with 15.3% operating margins excluding one-time items) and Electrical Rest of World (21%, 6.7%). The two units make a wide range of power distribution and control equipment, such as switchboards, circuit boards, circuit breakers, starters, AC and DC Uninterruptible Power Systems (UPS) and power management software. They also produce electronic sensors that control industrial machinery, as well as electricity quality-monitoring systems. Both units' primary competitors include GE, Germany-based Siemens and Schneider Electric. Demand for ETN's electrical equipment and components mainly reflects the health of the non-residential, power quality, industrial, residential construction and telecom industries.

The Hydraulics segment (14%; 3.2%) makes products including, but not limited to, pumps, motors, valves, cylinders, hydraulic power units, control and sensing products, fluid conveyance products, hoses and assemblies. The principal markets for the segment's products include various energy industries, and the marine, agriculture, construction, mining, forestry, utilities, material handling, automotive, machine tool, metals and entertainment industries.

The Aerospace segment (13%; 16%) is a global provider of pumps, motors, hydraulic power units and other equipment, valves, cylinders, hoses and fittings, control and sensing products, fluid conveyance products, sensors, actuators and other products used in the aviation industry. The segment's products are sold to after-market customers as well as to manufacturers of commercial and military aviation products.

ETN's Truck unit (12%; 2.7%) is the world's largest maker of medium- and heavy-duty truck transmissions. The unit's products include transmissions and transmission components such as drive trains, clutches, gearboxes and shafts along with brake clutch products. The segment's primary competitors are Germany-based ZF Friedrichshafen AG and Wabco. Demand for ETN's truck components is mainly driven by the health of the medium- and heavy-duty truck market.

Company Financials Fiscal Year Ended Dec. 31

Per Share Data ($)	2009	2008	2007	2006	2005	2004	2003	2002	2001	2000
Tangible Book Value	NM	NM	NM	2.30	0.09	3.46	3.14	NM	0.29	NM
Cash Flow	5.69	10.15	9.50	8.80	8.08	6.67	5.18	4.49	3.78	5.05
Earnings	2.27	6.50	6.38	5.97	5.23	4.13	2.56	1.96	1.20	2.50
S&P Core Earnings	2.90	6.09	6.86	6.45	5.40	4.15	2.43	0.99	-0.18	NA
Dividends	2.00	2.00	1.72	1.48	1.24	1.08	0.92	0.88	0.88	0.88
Payout Ratio	88%	31%	27%	24%	24%	26%	36%	45%	74%	35%
Prices:High	67.06	98.14	104.12	79.98	72.69	72.64	54.70	44.34	40.72	43.28
Prices:Low	30.02	37.69	71.91	62.37	56.65	52.74	33.01	29.55	27.56	28.75
P/E Ratio:High	30	15	16	13	14	18	21	23	34	17
P/E Ratio:Low	13	6	11	10	11	13	13	15	23	11

Income Statement Analysis (Million $)	2009	2008	2007	2006	2005	2004	2003	2002	2001	2000
Revenue	11,873	15,376	13,033	12,370	11,115	9,817	8,061	7,209	7,299	8,309
Operating Income	1,281	1,847	1,646	1,487	1,468	1,287	984	870	703	1,013
Depreciation	573	592	469	434	409	400	394	353	355	364
Interest Expense	150	157	147	104	90.0	78.0	87.0	104	142	177
Pretax Income	303	1,128	1,041	989	996	781	508	399	278	552
Effective Tax Rate	NM	6.47%	7.88%	7.79%	19.2%	17.0%	24.0%	29.6%	39.2%	34.2%
Net Income	383	1,055	959	912	805	648	386	281	169	363
S&P Core Earnings	488	989	1,031	985	832	651	367	141	-25.0	NA

Balance Sheet & Other Financial Data (Million $)	2009	2008	2007	2006	2005	2004	2003	2002	2001	2000
Cash	773	530	646	114	110	85.0	61.0	75.0	112	82.0
Current Assets	4,524	4,795	4,767	4,408	3,578	3,182	3,093	2,457	2,387	2,571
Total Assets	16,282	16,655	13,430	11,417	10,218	9,075	8,223	7,138	7,646	8,180
Current Liabilities	2,689	3,745	3,659	3,407	2,968	2,262	2,126	1,734	1,669	2,107
Long Term Debt	3,349	3,190	3,417	1,774	1,830	Nil	1,651	1,887	2,252	2,447
Common Equity	6,777	6,317	5,172	4,106	3,778	3,606	3,117	2,302	2,475	2,410
Total Capital	10,172	9,776	7,604	5,880	5,608	3,606	4,768	4,752	5,307	4,857
Capital Expenditures	195	448	354	360	363	330	2,733	228	295	386
Cash Flow	956	1,647	1,428	1,346	1,214	1,048	780	634	524	727
Current Ratio	1.7	1.3	1.3	1.3	1.2	1.4	1.5	1.4	1.4	1.2
% Long Term Debt of Capitalization	32.9	31.7	32.0	30.2	32.6	Nil	34.6	39.7	42.4	50.4
% Net Income of Revenue	3.2	6.9	7.4	7.4	7.2	6.6	4.8	3.9	2.3	4.4
% Return on Assets	2.3	7.0	7.7	8.4	8.3	7.5	5.0	3.8	2.1	4.4
% Return on Equity	5.9	18.4	20.7	23.1	21.8	19.3	14.2	11.8	6.9	14.4

Data as orig reptd.; bef. results of disc opers/spec. items. Per share data adj. for stk. divs.; EPS diluted. E-Estimated. NA-Not Available. NM-Not Meaningful. NR-Not Ranked. UR-Under Review.

Office: Eaton Center 1111 Superior Ave, Cleveland, OH 44114-2584.
Telephone: 216-523-5000.
Website: http://www.eaton.com
Chrmn, Pres & CEO: A.M. Cutler

EVP & CTO: L. Jonsson
EVP & General Counsel: M.M. McGuire
SVP, Chief Acctg Officer & Cntlr: B.K. Rawot
SVP & Secy: T.E. Moran

Investor Contact: B. Hartman (216-523-4501)
Board Members: T. M. Bluedorn, C. M. Connor, M. J. Critelli, A. M. Cutler, C. E. Golden, E. Green, A. E. Johnson, N. C. Lautenbach, D. L. McCoy, G. R. Page, G. L. Tooker

Founded: 1916
Domicile: Ohio
Employees: 70,000

eBay Inc

STANDARD &POOR'S

S&P Recommendation	HOLD ★★★★★	Price	12-Mo. Target Price	Investment Style
		$28.07 (as of Oct 22, 2010)	$30.00	Large-Cap Growth

GICS Sector Information Technology
Sub-Industry Internet Software & Services

Summary EBAY owns one of the world's most popular e-commerce destinations, which bears its name, as well as PayPal, an online payments company, 30% of Skype, an Internet communications business, and other online business interests.

Key Stock Statistics (Source S&P, Vickers, company reports)

52-Wk Range	$28.44–19.06	S&P Oper. EPS 2010E	1.32	Market Capitalization(B)	$36.832	Beta	1.61
Trailing 12-Month EPS	$1.90	S&P Oper. EPS 2011E	1.60	Yield (%)	Nil	S&P 3-Yr. Proj. EPS CAGR(%)	18
Trailing 12-Month P/E	14.8	P/E on S&P Oper. EPS 2010E	21.3	Dividend Rate/Share	Nil	S&P Credit Rating	NA
$10K Invested 5 Yrs Ago	$7,144	Common Shares Outstg. (M)	1,312.2	Institutional Ownership (%)	77		

Price Performance

- 30-Week Mov. Avg. · · · 10-Week Mov. Avg. – – **GAAP Earnings vs. Previous Year** Volume Above Avg. STARS
- 12-Mo. Target Price — Relative Strength — ▲ Up ▼ Down ▶ No Change Below Avg. ★

Options: ASE, CBOE, P, Ph

Qualitative Risk Assessment

LOW	MEDIUM	HIGH

Our risk assessment reflects our view that the company operates in fast-changing areas and faces notable competition. Over the past few years, we have viewed EBAY's quarterly results, financial outlook, strategic decisions and management changes as disappointing at times. This is only partially offset by our view of EBAY as a well established leader in the Internet segment, with a business model that we see as attractive, and a strong balance sheet.

Quantitative Evaluations

S&P Quality Ranking B+

D	C	B-	B	B+	A-	A	A+

Relative Strength Rank STRONG

92

LOWEST = 1   HIGHEST = 99

Revenue/Earnings Data

Revenue (Million $)

	1Q	2Q	3Q	4Q	Year
2010	2,196	2,215	--	--	--
2009	2,021	2,098	2,238	2,371	8,727
2008	2,192	2,196	2,118	2,036	8,541
2007	1,768	1,418	1,889	2,181	7,672
2006	1,390	1,411	1,449	1,720	5,970
2005	1,032	1,086	1,106	1,329	4,552

Earnings Per Share ($)

2010	0.30	0.31	E0.33	E0.39	E1.32
2009	0.28	0.25	0.27	1.02	1.83
2008	0.34	0.35	0.38	0.29	1.36
2007	0.27	0.27	-0.69	0.39	0.25
2006	0.17	0.17	0.20	0.25	0.79
2005	0.19	0.21	0.18	0.20	0.78

Fiscal year ended Dec. 31. Next earnings report expected: NA. EPS Estimates based on S&P Operating Earnings; historical GAAP earnings are as reported.

Dividend Data

No cash dividends have been paid.

Highlights

➤ The STARS recommendation for EBAY has recently been changed to 3 (hold) from 4 (buy) and the 12-month target price has recently been changed to $30.00 from $27.00. The Highlights section of this Stock Report will be updated accordingly.

Investment Rationale/Risk

➤ The Investment Rationale/Risk section of this Stock Report will be updated shortly. For the latest News story on EBAY from MarketScope, see below.

➤ 10/22/10 01:58 pm ET ... S&P DOWNGRADES SHARES OF EBAY TO HOLD FROM BUY, ON VALUATION (EBAY 27.9***): The stock is now relatively close to our 12-month target price of $30, and we do not necessarily foresee outperformance over the next 12 months. We were encouraged by the company's recently provided Q3 results and Q4 guidance, reflecting continuing strength from Payments. However, the Marketplaces unit, which accounts for more than 60% of revenues, continues to notably lag in multiple ways, as growth remains a significant challenge. We are encouraged by a new $2 billion buyback program and $1.5 billion bond offering, but see the company's valuation as largely full. /S.Kessler

eBay Inc

STANDARD &POOR'S

Business Summary September 15, 2010

CORPORATE OVERVIEW. eBay operates the world's largest online trading community. As of June 2010, the marketplaces segment had 91.8 million active users (compared with 88.4 million a year earlier) and in the second quarter of 2010 they accounted for total gross merchandise volume (including vehicles) of $14.7 billion ($13.4 billion). Following acquisitions in recent years, the company also owns Bill Me Later (online payments), PayPal (online payments), Rent.com (apartment and home rentals), Shopping.com (comparison shopping), 30% of Skype (Internet communications), StubHub (online ticket sales), and Gmarket (Asia-focused e-commerce). As of June 2010, PayPal had 87.2 million active registered accounts (75.4 million). In November 2009, EBAY sold 70% of Skype to a group of investors in a transaction valuing the business at $2.75 billion. In August 2010, Skype filed to proceed with an IPO.

EBAY and its affiliates have websites directed toward the following geographies: Argentina, Australia, Austria, Belgium, Brazil, Canada, China, France, Germany, Hong Kong, India, Ireland, Italy, Malaysia, Mexico, the Netherlands, New Zealand, the Philippines, Poland, Singapore, South Korea, Spain, Sweden, Switzerland, Taiwan, Thailand, Turkey, the U.K. and Vietnam. In December 2006, EBAY announced it would contribute its China operations to a joint venture with Internet portal and wireless services company TOM Online.

EBAY owns a 49% stake in the venture, which was created in February 2007. In May 2010, EBAY and Gmarket's founder announced a joint venture to expand Gmarket's offerings in Japan and Singapore.

CORPORATE STRATEGY. EBAY's stated goal is to become the world's most efficient and abundant marketplace by expanding its community of users, delivering value to buyers and sellers, creating a global marketplace, and providing a faster, easier and safer trading experience. EBAY has increasingly employed acquisitions to fulfill the aforementioned goal, with a focus on international expansion and offering more choices and services to its buyers and sellers. In our view, PayPal was an extremely successful acquisition because it dramatically enhanced the user experience. Moreover, the combination accelerated the benefits the companies already derived from the Network Effect (whereby a product/service becomes more valuable to its users as its number of users increases), in our opinion.

Company Financials Fiscal Year Ended Dec. 31

Per Share Data ($)	2009	2008	2007	2006	2005	2004	2003	2002	2001	2000
Tangible Book Value	5.30	2.59	3.90	2.69	2.21	2.73	2.23	1.46	1.11	0.93
Cash Flow	2.45	1.90	0.69	1.17	1.05	0.75	0.46	0.28	0.16	0.08
Earnings	1.83	1.36	0.25	0.79	0.78	0.57	0.34	0.21	0.08	0.04
S&P Core Earnings	1.01	1.36	1.26	0.79	0.61	0.43	0.21	0.04	-0.00	NA
Dividends	Nil	Nil	Nil	Nil	Nil	Nil	Nil	Nil	Nil	Nil
Payout Ratio	Nil	Nil	Nil	Nil	Nil	Nil	Nil	Nil	Nil	NM
Prices:High	25.80	33.53	40.73	47.86	58.89	59.21	32.40	17.71	18.19	31.88
Prices:Low	9.91	10.91	28.60	22.83	30.78	31.30	16.88	12.21	7.11	6.69
P/E Ratio:High	14	25	NM	61	75	NM	95	83	NM	NM
P/E Ratio:Low	5	8	NM	29	39	NM	50	57	NM	NM

Income Statement Analysis (Million $)	2009	2008	2007	2006	2005	2004	2003	2002	2001	2000
Revenue	8,727	8,541	7,672	5,970	4,552	3,271	2,165	1,214	749	431
Operating Income	2,649	2,845	2,606	1,968	1,820	1,313	828	431	227	74.6
Depreciation	811	711	602	545	378	254	159	76.6	86.6	38.1
Interest Expense	NA	8.04	16.6	5.92	3.48	8.88	4.31	1.49	2.85	3.37
Pretax Income	2,879	2,184	751	1,547	1,549	1,128	662	398	163	78.0
Effective Tax Rate	17.0%	18.5%	53.6%	27.2%	30.2%	30.5%	31.3%	36.7%	49.1%	42.0%
Net Income	2,389	1,779	348	1,126	1,082	778	447	250	90.4	48.3
S&P Core Earnings	1,325	1,779	1,739	1,126	853	589	270	52.2	-4.04	NA

Balance Sheet & Other Financial Data (Million $)	2009	2008	2007	2006	2005	2004	2003	2002	2001	2000
Cash	4,944	3,353	5,984	2,663	1,314	1,330	1,382	1,109	524	202
Current Assets	8,460	6,287	7,123	4,971	3,183	2,911	2,146	1,468	884	675
Total Assets	18,408	15,592	15,366	13,494	11,789	7,991	5,820	4,124	1,679	1,182
Current Liabilities	3,642	3,705	3,100	2,518	1,485	1,085	647	386	180	137
Long Term Debt	NA	Nil	Nil	Nil	Nil	0.08	124	13.8	12.0	11.4
Common Equity	13,788	11,084	11,705	10,905	10,048	6,728	4,896	3,556	1,429	1,014
Total Capital	13,788	11,084	11,705	10,905	10,264	6,868	5,139	3,715	1,479	1,038
Capital Expenditures	567	566	454	515	338	293	365	139	57.4	49.8
Cash Flow	3,200	2,490	950	1,670	1,460	1,032	606	326	177	86.3
Current Ratio	2.3	1.7	2.3	2.0	2.1	2.7	3.3	3.8	4.9	4.9
% Long Term Debt of Capitalization	Nil	Nil	Nil	Nil	Nil	NM	2.4	0.4	0.8	1.1
% Net Income of Revenue	27.4	20.8	4.5	18.9	23.8	23.8	20.7	20.6	12.1	11.2
% Return on Assets	14.1	11.5	2.4	8.9	10.9	11.3	9.1	8.6	6.3	4.5
% Return on Equity	19.2	15.6	3.1	10.7	12.9	13.4	10.6	10.0	7.4	5.2

Data as orig reptd.; bef. results of disc opers/spec. items. Per share data adj. for stk. divs.; EPS diluted. E-Estimated. NA-Not Available. NM-Not Meaningful. NR-Not Ranked. UR-Under Review.

Office: 2145 Hamilton Ave, San Jose, CA 95125-5905.
Telephone: 408-376-7400.
Email: investor_relations@ebay.com
Website: http://www.ebay.com

Chrmn: P.M. Omidyar
Pres & CEO: J.J. Donahoe
SVP & CFO: R.H. Swan
SVP & CTO: M. Carges

SVP, Secy & General Counsel: M.R. Jacobson
Investor Contact: T. Ford (408-376-7205)
Board Members: F. D. Anderson, M. L. Andreessen, E. Barnholt, S. D. Cook, J. J. Donahoe, W. C. Ford, Jr., D. G. Lepore, D. M. Moffett, P. M. Omidyar, R. T. Schlosberg, III, T. J. Tierney

Founded: 1995
Domicile: Delaware
Employees: 16,400

The McGraw-Hill Companies

Ecolab Inc.

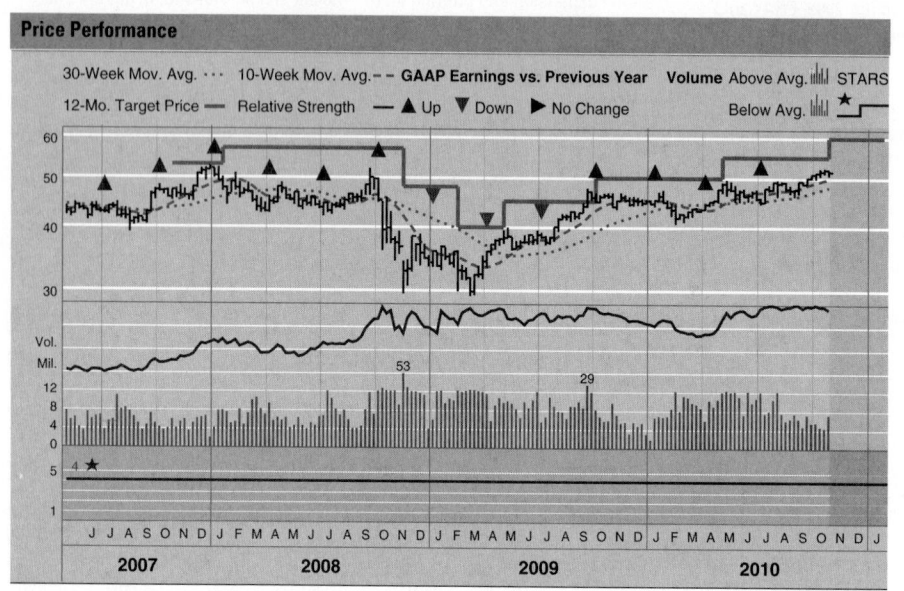

STANDARD &POOR'S

S&P Recommendation BUY ★★★★☆	Price $51.56 (as of Oct 22, 2010)	12-Mo. Target Price $60.00	Investment Style Large-Cap Growth

GICS Sector Materials
Sub-Industry Specialty Chemicals

Summary This company is the leading worldwide marketer of cleaning, sanitizing, and maintenance products and services for the hospitality, institutional, and industrial markets.

Key Stock Statistics (Source S&P, Vickers, company reports)

52-Wk Range	$52.46–40.66	S&P Oper. EPS 2010E	2.25	Market Capitalization(B)	$12.029	Beta	0.70
Trailing 12-Month EPS	$2.03	S&P Oper. EPS 2011E	2.50	Yield (%)	1.20	S&P 3-Yr. Proj. EPS CAGR(%)	10
Trailing 12-Month P/E	25.4	P/E on S&P Oper. EPS 2010E	22.9	Dividend Rate/Share	$0.62	S&P Credit Rating	A
$10K Invested 5 Yrs Ago	$16,779	Common Shares Outstg. (M)	233.3	Institutional Ownership (%)	81		

Price Performance

Analysis prepared by **Richard O'Reilly, CFA** on October 19, 2010, when the stock traded at **$ 50.89**.

Options: CBOE, P, Ph

Highlights

➤ We expect sales to grow about 6% this year, followed by a 7% rise in 2011. We see organic sales resuming growth in 2010, as end markets stabilize, aided by benefits from new products and customers, continuing expansion of the sales force, and forecasted price increases of 1%-2%, while exchange rates should be a headwind in the second half.

➤ We look for the domestic Kay, food & beverage, and health care units to continue to expand in 2010 and institutional and pest elimination sales to rebound. We believe international sales will continue to grow, including a modest gain in Europe, which fell in 2009. We project that operating margins will widen slightly, helped by the expected sales gain, a full year benefit fom restructuring actions since early 2009, and modestly lower raw material and delivery costs, despite increasing sales force and market development spending and greater pension costs.

➤ We assume an effective tax rate of 30.4%, down from 31.7% in 2009. Our EPS estimate for 2010 excludes a $0.02 charge related to devaluation of the Venezuelan currency. EPS for 2009 includes restructuring charges of $0.24.

Investment Rationale/Risk

➤ We expect ECL to post renewed sales growth and achieve continued EPS gains in coming periods, as key global end markets such as food service and lodging are stabilizing.

➤ Risks to our recommendation and target price include unexpected slowdowns in the hospitality, travel, food, and foodservice industries, an inability to continue to successfully introduce new products and services, and higher-than-projected raw material and delivery costs.

➤ The stock has historically traded at a higher P/E multiple than the S&P 500, owing to investors' willingness to pay a premium for growth and stability, in our opinion. We believe a steady grower such as ECL will be sought by investors as the economy continues to improve, and we think the shares offer solid upside potential. Our 12-month target price of $60 is 24X our 2011 EPS forecast of $2.50, in line with its historical average premium, and a P/E-to-growth (PEG) multiple of 2.4X applied to the 10% EPS gains we see for the next few years. The dividend has been raised for 18 consecutive years, a record we expect to be extended.

Qualitative Risk Assessment

LOW	MEDIUM	HIGH

Our risk assessment reflects the company's leading share positions in its core businesses, the relatively stable nature of its end markets and customers, and our view of its strong balance sheet and cash generation. The stock's S&P Quality Ranking of A+, the highest possible, indicates a superior 10-year historical record of earnings and dividend growth.

Quantitative Evaluations

S&P Quality Ranking A+

D	C	B-	B	B+	A-	A	A+

Relative Strength Rank MODERATE

54

LOWEST = 1   HIGHEST = 99

Revenue/Earnings Data

Revenue (Million $)

	1Q	2Q	3Q	4Q	Year
2010	1,432	1,520	--	--	--
2009	1,348	1,442	1,546	1,565	5,901
2008	1,458	1,570	1,626	1,483	6,138
2007	1,254	1,362	1,413	1,440	5,470
2006	1,120	1,226	1,279	1,271	4,896
2005	1,070	1,159	1,165	1,142	4,535

Earnings Per Share ($)

2010	0.40	0.55	E0.65	E0.63	E2.25
2009	0.24	0.41	0.60	0.48	1.74
2008	0.41	0.55	0.50	0.33	1.80
2007	0.35	0.44	0.46	0.45	1.70
2006	0.30	0.36	0.43	0.34	1.43
2005	0.27	0.31	0.38	0.27	1.23

Fiscal year ended Dec. 31. Next earnings report expected: Late October. EPS Estimates based on S&P Operating Earnings; historical GAAP earnings are as reported.

Dividend Data (Dates: mm/dd Payment Date: mm/dd/yy)

Amount ($)	Date Decl.	Ex-Div. Date	Stk. of Record	Payment Date
0.155	12/03	12/11	12/15	01/15/10
0.155	02/26	03/05	03/09	04/15/10
0.155	05/06	06/11	06/15	07/15/10
0.155	08/06	09/17	09/21	10/15/10

Dividends have been paid since 1936. Source: Company reports.

Please read the Required Disclosures and Analyst Certification on the last page of this report.

The **McGraw·Hill** Companies

Ecolab Inc.

STANDARD &POOR'S

Business Summary October 19, 2010

CORPORATE OVERVIEW. Ecolab is a global supplier of cleaning, sanitizing, and maintenance products and services for hospitality, institutional, and industrial markets. In the U.S. cleaning and sanitizing business (45% of 2009 sales, 63% of profits), the institutional division (25% of 2009 total sales) is the leading provider of cleaners and sanitizers for warewashing, on-premise laundry, kitchen cleaning, food safety and general housekeeping, product dispensing equipment and dishwashing racks and related kitchen sundries to the foodservice, lodging and health care industries. It also provides pool and spa treatment products. In addition, the division includes professional janitorial products (detergents, floor care, disinfectants, odor control) sold under the Airkem brand name.

The Kay division (5%) is the largest supplier of cleaning and sanitizing products (surface cleaners, degreasers, sanitizers and hand care products) for the quick-service restaurant, convenience store and food retail markets. The Food and Beverage division (9%) offers cleaning and sanitizing products and services to farms, dairy plants, food and beverage processors, and pharmaceutical plants; and water treatment products to institutional, laundry and food and beverage, and processing markets for boilers, cooling and waste treatment systems.

ECL also sells health care products (skin care, disinfectants, sterilants, surgical drapes, and fluid control products; 4%) under the Ecolab and Microtek names; textile care products (1%) for large institutional and commercial laundries; and vehicle care products (soaps, polishes, wheel treatments) for rental, fleet and retail car washes (1%).

Other U.S. services (8%, 8%) include institutional and commercial pest elimination and prevention services (6%) and GCS Services, a provider of commercial kitchen equipment repair and maintenance services (2%). ECL bought GCS Service in 1998, and has added to this business through small acquisitions; this business had operating losses for the seven years through 2009.

The International business (47%, 29%) provides services similar to those offered in the U.S. to Canada (3%) and about 71 countries in Europe (31%), Latin America (4%), and the Asia/Pacific region (9%). The institutional and food & beverage businesses constitute a larger portion of the international business compared to the U.S.

Company Financials Fiscal Year Ended Dec. 31

Per Share Data ($)	2009	2008	2007	2006	2005	2004	2003	2002	2001	2000
Tangible Book Value	1.16	NM	1.33	1.67	2.00	1.33	1.14	0.83	0.41	1.77
Cash Flow	3.13	3.14	2.85	2.48	2.22	2.13	1.93	1.67	1.35	1.35
Earnings	1.74	1.80	1.70	1.43	1.23	1.19	1.06	0.81	0.73	0.79
S&P Core Earnings	1.77	1.52	1.69	1.46	1.24	1.10	0.98	0.64	0.61	NA
Dividends	0.57	0.53	0.48	0.42	0.36	0.33	0.30	0.28	0.26	0.25
Payout Ratio	33%	29%	28%	29%	29%	28%	28%	34%	36%	31%
Prices:High	47.88	52.35	52.78	46.40	37.15	35.59	27.92	25.20	22.09	22.84
Prices:Low	29.27	29.56	37.01	33.64	30.68	26.12	23.08	18.27	14.25	14.00
P/E Ratio:High	28	29	31	32	30	30	26	31	30	29
P/E Ratio:Low	17	16	22	24	25	22	22	23	20	18

Income Statement Analysis (Million $)	2009	2008	2007	2006	2005	2004	2003	2002	2001	2000
Revenue	5,901	6,138	5,470	4,896	4,535	4,185	3,762	3,404	2,355	2,264
Operating Income	1,095	1,073	978	880	799	786	713	656	482	471
Depreciation	334	335	291	269	257	247	230	223	163	148
Interest Expense	67.5	70.8	58.9	51.3	49.8	45.3	45.3	43.9	28.4	24.6
Pretax Income	620	651	616	567	498	489	448	354	306	338
Effective Tax Rate	32.5%	31.2%	30.7%	35.0%	35.9%	36.5%	38.1%	39.6%	38.4%	38.3%
Net Income	417	448	427	369	319	310	277	214	188	209
S&P Core Earnings	424	378	424	376	322	283	260	167	157	NA

Balance Sheet & Other Financial Data (Million $)	2009	2008	2007	2006	2005	2004	2003	2002	2001	2000
Cash	73.6	66.7	137	484	104	71.2	85.6	49.2	41.8	44.0
Current Assets	1,814	1,691	1,717	1,854	1,422	1,279	1,150	1,016	930	601
Total Assets	5,021	4,757	4,723	4,419	3,797	3,716	3,229	2,878	2,525	1,714
Current Liabilities	1,250	1,442	1,518	1,503	1,119	940	851	866	828	532
Long Term Debt	869	799	600	557	519	Nil	604	540	512	234
Common Equity	2,001	1,572	1,936	1,680	1,649	1,563	1,295	1,100	880	757
Total Capital	2,878	2,376	2,536	2,237	2,169	1,563	1,900	1,639	1,393	991
Capital Expenditures	253	327	362	288	269	276	212	213	158	150
Cash Flow	752	783	718	637	576	558	507	437	351	357
Current Ratio	1.5	1.2	1.1	1.2	1.3	1.4	1.4	1.2	1.1	1.1
% Long Term Debt of Capitalization	30.2	33.7	23.7	24.9	23.9	Nil	31.8	32.9	36.8	23.6
% Net Income of Revenue	7.1	7.3	7.8	7.5	7.0	7.4	7.4	6.3	8.0	9.2
% Return on Assets	8.5	9.5	9.3	9.0	8.5	8.9	9.1	7.9	8.9	12.6
% Return on Equity	23.4	25.6	23.6	22.1	19.7	21.7	23.2	21.6	23.0	27.5

Data as orig reptd.; bef. results of disc opers/spec. items. Per share data adj. for stk. divs.; EPS diluted. E-Estimated. NA-Not Available. NM-Not Meaningful. NR-Not Ranked. UR-Under Review.

Office: 370 North Wabasha Street, Saint Paul, MN 55102-1390.
Telephone: 651-292-2233.
Email: investor.info@ecolab.com
Website: http://www.ecolab.com

Chrmn, Pres & CEO: D.M. Baker, Jr.
SVP & CTO: L.L. Berger
CFO: S.L. Fritze
Chief Acctg Officer & Cntlr: J.J. Corkrean

Secy & General Counsel: J.J. Seifert
Investor Contact: M.J. Monahan (651-293-2809)
Board Members: D. M. Baker, Jr., B. Beck, L. S. Biller, J. A. Grundhofer, A. J. Higgins, J. W. Johnson, J. W. Levin, R. L. Lumpkins, C. S. O'Hara, V. J. Reich, J. J. Zillmer

Founded: 1924
Domicile: Delaware
Employees: 25,931

The McGraw-Hill Companies

Edison International

STANDARD &POOR'S

S&P Recommendation BUY ★★★★☆

Price	12-Mo. Target Price	Investment Style
$35.99 (as of Oct 22, 2010)	$39.00	Large-Cap Blend

GICS Sector Utilities
Sub-Industry Electric Utilities

Summary EIX is the holding company for Southern California Edison. Other businesses include electric power generation, financial investments, and real estate development.

Key Stock Statistics (Source S&P, Vickers, company reports)

52-Wk Range	$36.72–30.37	S&P Oper. EPS 2010E	3.35	Market Capitalization(B)	$11.726	Beta	0.73
Trailing 12-Month EPS	$3.64	S&P Oper. EPS 2011E	3.20	Yield (%)	3.50	S&P 3-Yr. Proj. EPS CAGR(%)	-6
Trailing 12-Month P/E	9.9	P/E on S&P Oper. EPS 2010E	10.7	Dividend Rate/Share	$1.26	S&P Credit Rating	BBB-
$10K Invested 5 Yrs Ago	$10,162	Common Shares Outstg. (M)	325.8	Institutional Ownership (%)	74		

Price Performance

30-Week Mov. Avg. · · · 10-Week Mov. Avg. − − GAAP Earnings vs. Previous Year   Volume Above Avg. STARS
12-Mo. Target Price — Relative Strength   — ▲ Up ▼ Down ► No Change   Below Avg.

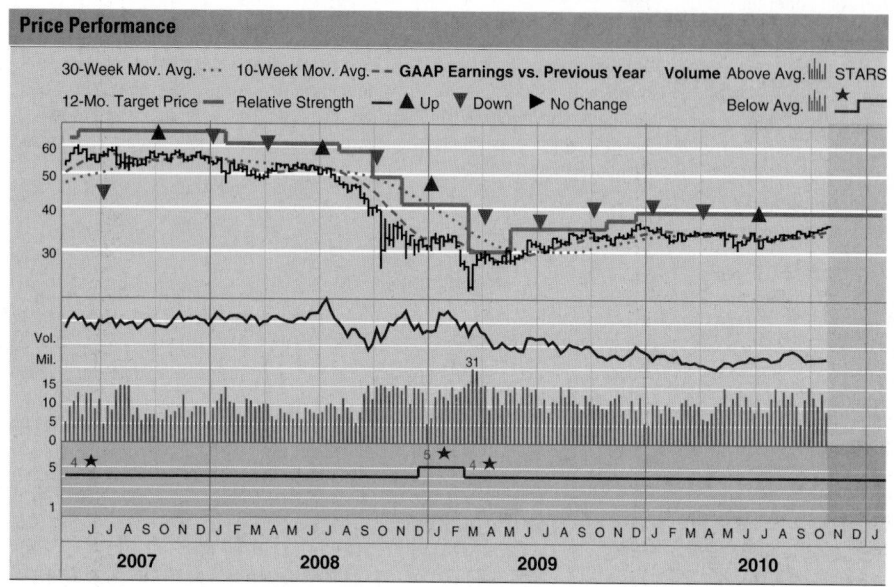

Options: ASE, CBOE, P

Analysis prepared by **Justin McCann** on August 26, 2010, when the stock traded at **$ 33.78**.

Highlights

► Excluding $0.33 of net one-time gains, we expect operating EPS in 2010 to increase about 3% from 2009's $3.25, which excluded net one-time charges of $0.66. In the first half of 2010, operating EPS was down $0.14 from the $1.58 in the first half of 2009. The decline primarily reflected sharply lower earnings at Edison Mission Energy (EME), as it completed substantially all of its planned 2010 maintenance for its coal fleet during the second quarter.

► For full-year 2010, we expect operating earnings to be relatively flat or down at EME, but for this to be more than offset by higher earnings at Southern California Edison (SCE), reflecting rate increases under a three-year program approved in 2009. Over the next few years, we see SCE's earnings growth being driven by its five-year $18 - $21.5 billion infrastructure development plan, which is expected to result in annual rate base growth of 8% to 11% through 2014.

► EIX has estimated that it would cost about $1.2 billion to retrofit all of its coal plants in Illinois so as to meet the state's future sulfur dioxide emission standards. It has not yet determined which individual coal plants it will decide to retrofit or which, if any, it would shut down.

Investment Rationale/Risk

► The shares are down about 3% year to date. The decline in 2010 reflects, we think, the continuing weakness in the power markets, while the rebound in 2009 (when the stock rose 8.3%) was likely driven by the approval of rate increases for SCE, a favorable settlement with the IRS, and the broader market recovery. We believe EIX is well positioned for a recovery in the economy and power markets, and that the stock is undervalued at a recent discount-to-peers multiple of 10.1X our EPS estimate for 2010, and remains attractive for total return potential.

► Risks to our recommendation and target price include extended weakness in the economy and power markets, a sharp drop in the P/E of the electric utility sector, and the potential for unfavorable regulatory or legislative actions.

► The recent yield from the dividend was about 3.7%. While this is still below the level of peers (recently about 4.9%), we believe it provides a base for an attractive total return over the next 12 months. Our 12-month target price is $39, reflecting a discount-to-peers P/E of approximately 12.2X our 2011 EPS estimate.

Qualitative Risk Assessment

LOW	MEDIUM	HIGH

Our risk assessment reflects our view that the strong and steady earnings and cash flow we expect from the regulated Southern California Edison utility, with its large and expanding service territory and generally supportive regulatory environment, is partially offset by the cyclical and volatile earnings of the unregulated independent power operations of Edison Mission Group.

Quantitative Evaluations

S&P Quality Ranking   **B**

D	C	B-	B	B+	A-	A	A+

Relative Strength Rank   **MODERATE**

58

LOWEST = 1   HIGHEST = 99

Revenue/Earnings Data

Revenue (Million $)

	1Q	2Q	3Q	4Q	Year
2010	2,810	2,741	--	--	--
2009	2,812	2,834	3,664	3,050	12,361
2008	3,113	3,477	4,295	3,228	14,112
2007	2,912	3,047	3,942	3,211	13,113
2006	2,751	3,001	3,802	3,067	12,622
2005	2,446	2,649	3,783	2,975	11,852

Earnings Per Share ($)

2010	0.70	1.05	E1.23	E0.68	E3.35
2009	0.75	-0.03	1.22	0.65	2.60
2008	0.92	0.79	1.31	0.66	3.68
2007	1.00	0.28	1.40	0.65	3.32
2006	0.56	0.53	1.39	0.80	3.28
2005	0.59	0.55	1.31	0.90	3.34

Fiscal year ended Dec. 31. Next earnings report expected: Early November. EPS Estimates based on S&P Operating Earnings; historical GAAP earnings are as reported.

Dividend Data (Dates: mm/dd Payment Date: mm/dd/yy)

Amount ($)	Date Decl.	Ex-Div. Date	Stk. of Record	Payment Date
0.315	12/10	12/29	12/31	01/31/10
0.315	02/25	03/29	03/31	04/30/10
0.315	04/22	06/28	06/30	07/31/10
0.315	09/02	09/28	09/30	10/31/10

Dividends have been paid since 2004. Source: Company reports.

Please read the Required Disclosures and Analyst Certification on the last page of this report.

The McGraw·Hill Companies

Edison International

STANDARD & POOR'S

Business Summary August 26, 2010

CORPORATE OVERVIEW. Edison International (EIX) is the holding company for the regulated Southern California Edison (SCE) utility and several non-regulated subsidiaries. The principal non-utility companies, held by Edison Mission Group (EMG), are Edison Mission Energy (EME), an independent power-er producer that also conducts price risk management and energy trading activities, and Edison Capital, which holds equity investments in energy and infrastructure projects. In 2009, SCE accounted for 80.6% of EIX's consolidated revenues, the non-utility power generation business 19.2%, and financial services and other operations 0.2%. The utility's retail operations are regulated by the California Public Utilities Commission (CPUC), while its wholesale operations fall under the oversight of the Federal Energy Regulatory Commission (FERC).

CORPORATE STRATEGY. The company seeks to establish a balanced approach for growth, dividends, and balance sheet strength. It has taken steps

to rebalance its capital structure and to further reduce its debt, and is working to reduce administration expenses in the non-utility companies and to establish a multi-year productivity effort at the utility. SCE is working on new projects that should expand its transmission and distribution systems, and has scheduled the installment of advanced electricity meters with more than 5 million customer accounts by the end of 2012. Given the weakness in the economy and power markets, it has also worked to manage the liquidity of its independent power business through disciplined cost cutting initiatives. However, to diversify EME's concentration in coal-fired generation, it is also making selective investments in renewable energy projects.

Company Financials Fiscal Year Ended Dec. 31

Per Share Data ($)	2009	2008	2007	2006	2005	2004	2003	2002	2001	2000
Tangible Book Value	30.06	28.99	25.92	23.65	20.30	18.56	13.86	11.59	8.10	7.43
Earnings	2.60	3.68	3.32	3.28	3.34	0.68	2.37	3.46	7.36	-5.84
S&P Core Earnings	2.73	2.93	3.26	3.28	3.35	0.60	2.45	2.81	6.78	NA
Dividends	1.24	1.23	1.17	1.10	1.02	1.05	Nil	Nil	Nil	1.11
Payout Ratio	48%	33%	35%	34%	31%	154%	Nil	Nil	Nil	NM
Prices:High	36.72	55.70	60.26	47.15	49.16	32.52	22.07	19.60	16.12	30.00
Prices:Low	23.09	26.73	42.76	37.90	30.43	21.24	10.57	7.80	6.25	14.13
P/E Ratio:High	14	15	18	14	15	48	9	6	2	NM
P/E Ratio:Low	9	7	13	12	9	31	4	2	1	NM

Income Statement Analysis (Million $)	2009	2008	2007	2006	2005	2004	2003	2002	2001	2000
Revenue	12,361	14,112	13,113	12,622	11,852	10,199	12,135	11,488	11,436	11,717
Depreciation	1,538	1,419	1,264	1,181	1,061	1,022	1,184	1,030	973	1,933
Maintenance	NA	NA	NA	NA	NA	NA	NA	NA	NA	NA
Fixed Charges Coverage	3.33	3.42	3.38	3.18	3.28	2.20	1.73	1.91	3.38	-0.98
Construction Credits	NA	NA	NA	NA	NA	NA	NA	NA	NA	NA
Effective Tax Rate	NM	31.5%	27.4%	32.3%	26.4%	NM	21.5%	25.6%	40.7%	NM
Net Income	856	1,215	1,100	1,083	1,108	226	779	1,135	2,402	-1,943
S&P Core Earnings	894	955	1,065	1,082	1,111	199	808	921	2,211	NA

Balance Sheet & Other Financial Data (Million $)	2009	2008	2007	2006	2005	2004	2003	2002	2001	2000
Gross Property	35,265	31,932	29,248	25,090	24,775	23,214	24,674	23,264	22,396	25,737
Capital Expenditures	3,282	2,824	2,826	2,536	1,868	1,733	1,288	1,590	933	1,488
Net Property	27,113	24,343	22,309	20,269	18,588	17,397	20,288	15,170	14,427	17,903
Capitalization:Long Term Debt	11,344	11,857	9,931	10,016	9,552	9,807	12,221	12,915	14,007	13,660
Capitalization:% Long Term Debt	53.5	55.5	54.0	56.5	59.1	61.3	69.4	74.4	81.1	85.0
Capitalization:Preferred	Nil	Nil	Nil	Nil	Nil	Nil	9.00	Nil	Nil	Nil
Capitalization:% Preferred	Nil	Nil	Nil	Nil	Nil	Nil	0.05	Nil	Nil	Nil
Capitalization:Common	9,841	9,517	8,444	7,709	6,615	6,049	5,383	4,437	3,272	2,420
Capitalization:% Common	46.5	44.5	46.0	43.5	40.9	37.8	30.6	25.6	18.9	15.0
Total Capital	21,820	27,485	23,980	23,415	21,854	21,688	24,246	23,786	24,163	21,609
% Operating Ratio	80.7	86.4	84.6	84.7	80.7	80.6	75.2	82.8	93.2	86.4
% Earned on Net Property	8.9	10.8	13.1	12.8	6.9	6.6	9.1	16.0	36.9	NM
% Return on Revenue	6.9	8.6	8.8	8.6	9.3	2.2	6.4	9.9	21.0	NM
% Return on Invested Capital	11.6	7.7	9.4	10.2	12.2	10.4	14.9	10.9	4.8	7.8
% Return on Common Equity	8.8	13.5	13.6	15.1	17.1	3.8	15.9	29.4	84.4	NM

Data as orig reptd.; bef. results of disc opers/spec. items. Per share data adj. for stk. divs.; EPS diluted. E-Estimated. NA-Not Available. NM-Not Meaningful. NR-Not Ranked. UR-Under Review.

Office: 2244 Walnut Grove Avenue, Rosemead, CA 91770-3714.
Telephone: 877-379-9515.
Website: http://www.edison.com
Chrmn, Pres & CEO: T.F. Craver, Jr.

EVP, CFO & Treas: W.J. Scilacci, Jr.
EVP & General Counsel: R.L. Adler
Secy: B.E. Mathews
Investor Contact: S. Cunningham (877-379-9515)

Board Members: J. S. Bindra, V. C. Chang, F. A. Cordova, T. F. Craver, Jr., C. B. Curtis, B. M. Freeman, L. G. Nogales, R. L. Olson, J. M. Rosser, R. T. Schlosberg, III, T. C. Sutton, W. B. White

Founded: 1886
Domicile: California
Employees: 19,244

Electronic Arts Inc

**STANDARD
&POOR'S**

S&P Recommendation	**STRONG SELL** ★☆☆☆☆	**Price** $15.61 (as of Oct 22, 2010)	**12-Mo. Target Price** $14.00	**Investment Style** Large-Cap Growth

GICS Sector Information Technology
Sub-Industry Home Entertainment Software

Summary This company produces entertainment software for PCs, home video game consoles, and mobile gaming devices.

Key Stock Statistics (Source S&P, Vickers, company reports)

52-Wk Range	$20.24– 14.06	S&P Oper. EPS 2011**E**	-0.69	Market Capitalization(B)	$5.156	Beta	1.36
Trailing 12-Month EPS	$-1.06	S&P Oper. EPS 2012**E**	-0.22	Yield (%)	Nil	S&P 3-Yr. Proj. EPS CAGR(%)	NM
Trailing 12-Month P/E	NM	P/E on S&P Oper. EPS 2011**E**	NM	Dividend Rate/Share	Nil	S&P Credit Rating	NA
$10K Invested 5 Yrs Ago	$2,850	Common Shares Outstg. (M)	330.3	Institutional Ownership (%)	87		

Price Performance

30-Week Mov. Avg. · · · · 10-Week Mov. Avg. - - **GAAP Earnings vs. Previous Year** Volume Above Avg. STARS
12-Mo. Target Price — Relative Strength — ▲ Up ▼ Down ▶ No Change Below Avg. ★

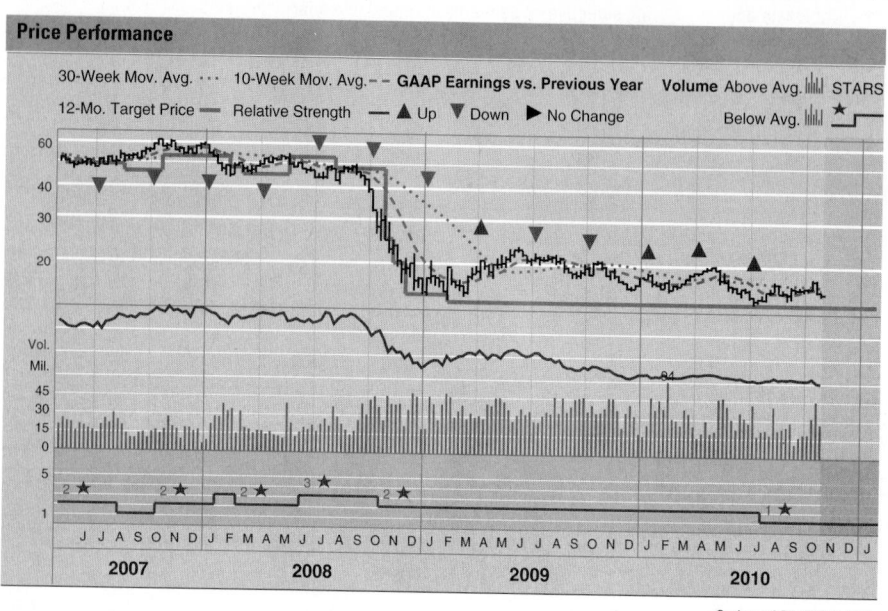

Options: ASE, CBOE, P, Ph

Analysis prepared by **Jim Yin, CFA** on October 19, 2010, when the stock traded at **$ 15.54**.

Highlights

▶ We see revenues falling 7.4% in FY 11 (Mar.), following a 13% decline in FY 10. Although we expect the economy to recover in 2010, we believe several factors will depress sales. We think consumer spending will remain weak given weak job growth. Despite the introductions of new motion-detection controllers for Xbox 360 and PlayStation 3, sales of video game consoles continue to decline. We see a shift in consumer buying behavior, resulting in a greater focus on top-selling titles. We believe this trend will hurt ERTS's sales due to the maturity of some of its games.

▶ We forecast a gross margin of 56% in FY 11, up from 49% in FY 10, reflecting a larger percentage of sales being downloaded digitally. We see operating expenses declining as a percentage of revenues as a result of a staff reduction that occurred in the second half of FY 10. We project that FY 11 operating margins will improve to -11%, from -15% in FY 10.

▶ We estimate a loss per share of $0.69 in FY 11, compared to a $2.08 loss in FY 10. We believe losses will diminish in FY 11 as the company reduces its operating expenses and curbs development of non-profitable games.

Investment Rationale/Risk

▶ Our strong sell recommendation reflects our view of weak consumer spending and deteriorating industry fundamentals. We think consumers, in addition to buying fewer titles, are focusing their purchases on top-rated games. As a result, development costs on these titles have increased significantly. We believe most of the revenue growth is in mobile games, which we think have lower barriers to entry than console games. We also believe some of ERTS's key franchises have been losing their appeal.

▶ Risks to our recommendation and target price include a stronger-than-expected economic recovery, stronger consumer spending, and further cost reductions.

▶ Our 12-month target price of $14 is based on a blend of our discounted cash flow (DCF) and enterprise value (EV) to sales analyses. Our DCF model assumes a 12.8% weighted average cost of capital and 3% terminal growth, yielding an intrinsic value of $14. We also derive a value of $14 based on an EV/sales multiple of 0.9X our FY 11 revenue estimate, a discount to the industry average of 1.1X due to ERTS's lack of profitability.

Qualitative Risk Assessment

LOW	MEDIUM	**HIGH**

Our risk assessment takes into account weak consumer spending, the volatile nature of the home entertainment software industry, and our view of a decline in the sales of video game consoles.

Quantitative Evaluations

S&P Quality Ranking B+

D	C	B-	B	**B+**	A-	A	A+

Relative Strength Rank **WEAK**

18

LOWEST = 1　　　　HIGHEST = 99

Revenue/Earnings Data

Revenue (Million $)

	1Q	2Q	3Q	4Q	Year
2011	815.0	--	--	--	--
2010	644.0	788.0	1,243	979.0	3,654
2009	804.0	894.0	1,654	860.0	4,212
2008	395.0	640.0	1,503	1,127	3,665
2007	413.0	784.0	1,281	613.0	3,091
2006	365.0	675.0	1,270	641.0	2,951

Earnings Per Share ($)

	1Q	2Q	3Q	4Q	Year
2011	0.29	E-0.70	E-0.05	E-0.22	E-0.69
2010	-0.72	-1.21	-0.25	0.09	-2.08
2009	-0.52	-0.97	-2.00	-0.13	-3.40
2008	-0.42	-0.62	-0.10	-0.29	-1.45
2007	-0.26	0.07	0.50	-0.08	0.24
2006	-0.19	0.16	0.83	-0.05	0.75

Fiscal year ended Mar. 31. Next earnings report expected: Early November. EPS Estimates based on S&P Operating Earnings; historical GAAP earnings are as reported.

Dividend Data

No cash dividends have been paid.

Electronic Arts Inc

Business Summary October 19, 2010

CORPORATE OVERVIEW. ERTS is one of the largest third-party developers of video games, which can be played on a variety of platforms including Sony PlayStation, Microsoft Xbox 360, Nintendo Wii, personal computers, and mobile devices. ERTS owns many of today's most popular video game franchises, including Madden NFL, The Sims, and Need for Speed. The company organizes its business into four labels: EA SPORTS, EA Games, EA Play, and EA Interactive. Each label operates with dedicated studio and marketing teams.

ERTS publishes titles across all major platforms, including consoles, PCs, and handheld gaming devices. The company has a diversified video game portfolio. In FY 10 (Mar.), the company produced 48 titles for mobile devices, 22 titles for Xbox 360, 21 for PlayStation 3, 19 for Nintendo Wii, 16 for PCs, and 16 for Nintendo DS. No title accounted for more than 10% of its total revenue in FY 10.

ERTS publishes and distributes games in over 35 countries throughout the world. Sales in North America were $2.0 billion in FY 10, or 55% of total revenue, while international revenue accounted for $1.6 billion, or 45%.

MARKET PROFILE. Video game sales grew at a low-teens compound annual growth rate (CAGR) from 2004 to 2008. However, sales declined about 10% in 2009 due to the economic recession. Although the economy is recovering, we expect video game sales to remain weak given the lack of job growth. We also think that most of the growth will be in mobile games, which have much lower barriers to entry than console games because they have lower design requirements such as graphic display. Thus, we expect pricing pressure to be more intense in this market segment. International Development Group (IDG), an independent research firm, forecasts that the annual sales of video game software in North America, Europe, and Japan will decline from $27.7 billion in 2008 to an estimated $16.7 billion in 2013 due to the shift in the consumer buying behavior. Thus, we believe future growth opportunity will come mostly from casual gamers rather than "hardcore" gamers, who already devote a large portion of their leisure time to playing video games.

Company Financials Fiscal Year Ended Mar. 31

Per Share Data ($)	2010	2009	2008	2007	2006	2005	2004	2003	2002	2001
Tangible Book Value	4.34	6.52	9.19	9.93	8.29	10.66	8.52	11.62	3.92	3.33
Cash Flow	-1.49	-2.81	-0.85	0.70	1.05	1.82	2.12	2.79	0.74	0.22
Earnings	-2.08	-3.40	-1.45	0.24	0.75	1.59	1.87	1.09	0.36	-0.04
S&P Core Earnings	-2.03	-2.51	-1.22	0.24	0.49	1.35	1.59	0.82	0.10	-0.25
Dividends	Nil	Nil	Nil	Nil	Nil	Nil	Nil	Nil	Nil	Nil
Payout Ratio	Nil	Nil	Nil	Nil	Nil	Nil	Nil	Nil	Nil	Nil
Calendar Year	2009	2008	2007	2006	2005	2004	2003	2002	2001	2000
Prices:High	23.76	58.35	61.62	59.85	71.16	63.71	52.89	36.22	33.46	28.97
Prices:Low	14.24	14.79	46.27	39.99	47.45	43.38	23.76	24.74	17.25	12.25
P/E Ratio:High	NM	NM	NM	NM	95	40	28	33	94	NM
P/E Ratio:Low	NM	NM	NM	NM	63	27	13	23	49	NM

Income Statement Analysis (Million $)										
Revenue	3,654	4,212	3,665	3,091	2,951	3,129	2,957	2,482	1,725	1,322
Operating Income	-352	-128	-60.0	204	454	759	863	629	267	42.1
Depreciation	192	189	186	147	95.0	75.0	77.5	91.6	111	69.7
Interest Expense	NA	Nil	Nil	Nil	Nil	Nil	Nil	Nil	Nil	Nil
Pretax Income	-706	-855	-507	138	389	725	797	461	148	-13.4
Effective Tax Rate	4.11%	NM	NM	47.8%	37.8%	30.5%	27.5%	30.9%	31.0%	NM
Net Income	-677	-1,088	-454	76.0	236	504	577	317	102	-11.1
S&P Core Earnings	-660	-805	-382	76.0	153	425	482	239	28.0	-68.2

Balance Sheet & Other Financial Data (Million $)										
Cash	1,996	2,520	3,016	1,712	1,402	1,410	2,151	951	804	477
Current Assets	2,585	3,120	3,925	3,597	3,012	3,706	2,911	1,911	1,153	819
Total Assets	4,646	4,678	6,059	5,146	4,386	4,370	3,401	2,360	1,699	1,379
Current Liabilities	1,574	1,136	1,299	1,026	869	828	722	571	453	340
Long Term Debt	NA	Nil	Nil	Nil	Nil	Nil	Nil	Nil	Nil	Nil
Common Equity	2,729	3,134	4,339	4,032	3,408	3,498	2,678	1,785	1,243	1,034
Total Capital	2,729	3,176	4,339	4,040	3,449	3,509	2,678	1,789	1,246	1,039
Capital Expenditures	305	115	84.0	178	123	126	89.6	59.1	51.5	120
Cash Flow	-485	-899	-268	223	331	579	655	409	212	58.6
Current Ratio	1.6	2.8	3.0	3.5	3.5	4.5	4.0	3.3	2.5	2.4
% Long Term Debt of Capitalization	Nil	Nil	Nil	Nil	Nil	Nil	Nil	Nil	Nil	Nil
% Net Income of Revenue	NM	NM	NM	2.5	8.0	16.1	19.5	12.8	5.9	NM
% Return on Assets	NM	NM	NM	1.6	5.4	12.9	20.0	15.6	6.6	NM
% Return on Equity	NM	NM	NM	2.0	6.8	16.3	25.9	20.9	8.9	NM

Data as orig reptd.; bef. results of disc opers/spec. items. Per share data adj. for stk. divs.; EPS diluted. E-Estimated. NA-Not Available. NM-Not Meaningful. NR-Not Ranked. UR-Under Review.

Office: 209 Redwood Shores Parkway, Redwood City, CA 94065-1175.
Telephone: 650-628-1500.
Email: investorrelations@ea.com
Website: http://www.ea.com

Chrmn: L.F. Probst, III
CEO: J. Riccitiello
COO: J. Schappert
EVP & CFO: E.F. Brown

SVP & Chief Acctg Officer: K.A. Barker
Investor Contact: J. Brown (650-628-7922)
Board Members: L. S. Coleman, Jr., J. T. Huber, G. M. Kusin, G. B. Laybourne, G. Maffei, V. Paul, L. F. Probst, III, J. Riccitiello, R. Simonson, L. J. Srere

Founded: 1982
Domicile: Delaware
Employees: 7,800

El Paso Corp

STANDARD &POOR'S

S&P Recommendation HOLD ★★★☆☆

Price	12-Mo. Target Price	Investment Style
$13.18 (as of Oct 22, 2010)	$14.00	Large-Cap Value

GICS Sector Energy
Sub-Industry Oil & Gas Storage & Transportation

Summary This provider of natural gas and related energy products owns North America's largest natural gas pipeline system and is a leading independent natural gas producer.

Key Stock Statistics (Source S&P, Vickers, company reports)

52-Wk Range	$13.45– 8.94	S&P Oper. EPS 2010E	0.99	Market Capitalization(B)	$9.279	Beta	1.08
Trailing 12-Month EPS	$1.19	S&P Oper. EPS 2011E	1.09	Yield (%)	0.30	S&P 3-Yr. Proj. EPS CAGR(%)	-5
Trailing 12-Month P/E	11.1	P/E on S&P Oper. EPS 2010E	13.3	Dividend Rate/Share	$0.04	S&P Credit Rating	BB
$10K Invested 5 Yrs Ago	$12,265	Common Shares Outstg. (M)	704.0	Institutional Ownership (%)	77		

Price Performance

30-Week Mov. Avg. · · ·   10-Week Mov. Avg. – –   GAAP Earnings vs. Previous Year   Volume Above Avg. ▯▯▮ STARS
12-Mo. Target Price —   Relative Strength —   ▲ Up ▼ Down ▶ No Change   Below Avg. ▯▯▮ ★

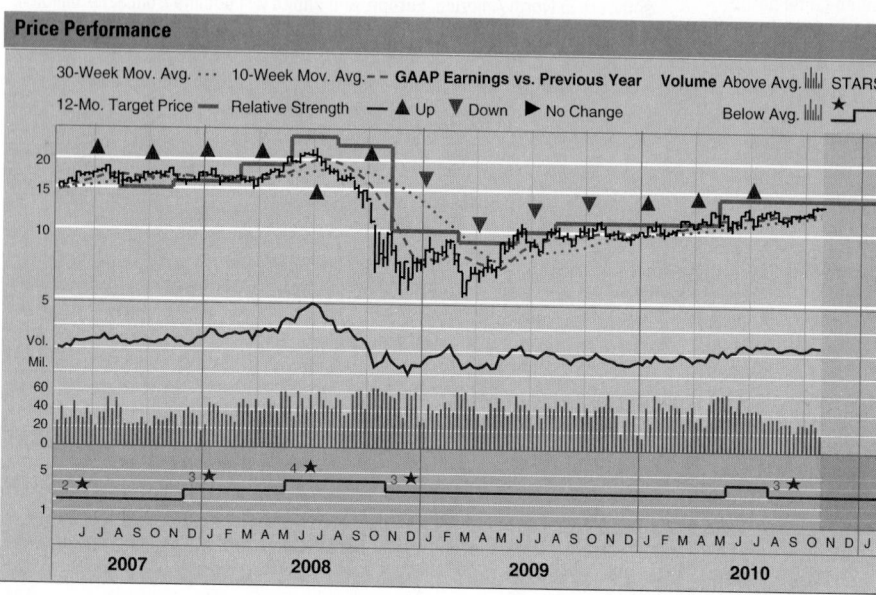

Options: ASE, CBOE, P

Analysis prepared by **Michael Kay** on August 26, 2010, when the stock traded at **$ 11.48**.

Highlights

➤ EP's pipeline segment is benefiting from several recent expansion projects, including the Medicine Bow expansion, the High Plains Pipeline, the Carthage expansion and the Totem Gas Storage project. EP has earmarked $8 billion for pipeline growth projects, with $1 billion in projects expected to be in service by year-end 2010, on time and on budget. In E&P, we see spending at low-risk onshore plays in the Haynesville Shale, Cotton Valley, and the Eagle Ford Shale. EP is ramping up to five rigs at Haynesville, where production is expected to reach 130 MMcfe/d by year end.

➤ EP expects $300 million-$500 million of asset sales in 2010. E&P capex is budgeted near $1 billion in 2010, with 50% earmarked for Haynesville and Eagle Ford development. Production in 2010 is ahead of forecast.

➤ We see a 9% EBITDA decline and a 23% drop in operating EPS in 2010, to $0.99, on more shares and lower E&P hedges, and EPS of $1.09 in 2011 on a 4% production boost. We think liquidity fears have eased following asset sales, debt offerings, and a new revolver. EP received FERC approval for the Ruby project in April, and we expect asset dropdowns to El Paso Pipelines.

Investment Rationale/Risk

➤ We think EP's risk profile has risen but that growth prospects expanded with its sharpened E&P focus. It is focusing on the high-return Haynesville and Eagle Ford plays, and on exploration in Brazil and Egypt. We see a difficult E&P market in 2010, but forecast lower costs per unit and start-ups boosting pipeline results. We believe recent project financing for the Ruby project has removed funding worries that had been hanging over EP shares. In our view, the success of Ruby is based on EP's ability to build it on time and on budget, and to secure financing and contract capacity at favorable rates. EP has formed a new midstream business, focused on Haynesville.

➤ Risks to our recommendation and target price include lower natural gas prices and weaker-than-expected economic conditions.

➤ We are positive on EP's pipeline franchise, and we see improving E&P prospects given its entry into attractive plays, but we are cautious on natural gas prices. Our 12-month target price of $14 is based on our sum-of-the-parts valuation, using a 7X enterprise value-to-2011 EBITDA multiple for the pipeline segment and NAV of $11 for the E&P segment.

Qualitative Risk Assessment

LOW	MEDIUM	HIGH

Our risk assessment reflects EP's increased focus on volatile exploration and production (E&P) activities and our view of its highly leveraged balance sheet, given the capital intensity of its operations. Partly offsetting these risks is EP's involvement in regulated pipelines.

Quantitative Evaluations

S&P Quality Ranking B-

D	C	B-	B	B+	A-	A	A+

Relative Strength Rank MODERATE

69

LOWEST = 1   HIGHEST = 99

Revenue/Earnings Data

Revenue (Million $)

	1Q	2Q	3Q	4Q	Year
2010	1,401	1,018	--	--	--
2009	1,484	973.0	981.0	1,193	4,631
2008	1,269	1,153	1,598	1,343	5,363
2007	1,022	1,198	1,166	1,262	4,648
2006	1,337	1,089	942.0	913.0	4,281
2005	1,108	1,184	768.0	957.0	4,017

Earnings Per Share ($)

2010	0.51	0.21	E0.22	E0.22	E0.99
2009	-1.41	0.11	0.08	0.36	-0.83
2008	0.33	0.25	0.58	-2.43	-1.24
2007	-0.08	0.22	0.20	0.20	0.57
2006	0.42	0.19	0.15	-0.30	0.72
2005	0.18	-0.34	-0.51	-0.45	-1.13

Fiscal year ended Dec. 31. Next earnings report expected: Early November. EPS Estimates based on S&P Operating Earnings; historical GAAP earnings are as reported.

Dividend Data (Dates: mm/dd Payment Date: mm/dd/yy)

Amount ($)	Date Decl.	Ex-Div. Date	Stk. of Record	Payment Date
0.010	02/24	03/03	03/05	04/01/10
0.010	04/01	06/02	06/04	07/01/10
0.010	07/21	09/01	09/03	10/01/10
0.010	10/14	12/01	12/03	01/03/11

Dividends have been paid since 1992. Source: Company reports.

Please read the Required Disclosures and Analyst Certification on the last page of this report.

The McGraw-Hill Companies

El Paso Corp

STANDARD &POOR'S

Business Summary August 26, 2010

CORPORATE OVERVIEW. Founded in 1928, El Paso Corp. originally served as a regional natural gas pipeline company that ultimately expanded geographically and into complementary business lines. By 2001, its total assets exceeded $44 billion and included natural gas production, power generation, trading operations and its traditional natural gas pipeline businesses. In late 2001 through 2003, various industry and company-specific events led to a substantial decline in EP's fundamentals. In late 2003, EP announced a long-term business strategy principally focused on core pipeline and production businesses. During the past several years, EP has sold off non-core assets to reduce debt and improve liquidity.

PRIMARY BUSINESS DYNAMICS. Operations are conducted through two primary segments: Pipelines; and Exploration and Production. EP also has smaller Marketing and Power segments.

The Pipelines segment is the largest U.S. owner of interstate natural gas pipelines, and owns or has interests in 42,000 miles of pipeline, with seven separate, wholly or majority owned pipeline systems, and four partially owned systems. The division also has 230 Bcf of natural gas storage capacity, and a liquefied natural gas terminal at Elba Island, GA, with 933 Mmcf of daily send-out capacity. Each pipeline system and storage facility operates under the Federal Energy Regulatory Commission (FERC).

EP's strategy in this segment is to expand systems into new markets while leveraging existing assets; recontract or contract available or expiring capacity and resolve open rate cases; leverage its coast-to-coast scale economies; and invest in maintenance and pipeline integrity projects to maintain the value and ensure the safety of its pipeline systems and assets. During 2009, EP placed several pipeline expansion projects into service, obtained a 50% partner on its Ruby project and secured financing for a portion of its remaining pipeline backlog. EP sees 2010 pipeline capex of $2.9 billion; it has a backlog of growth projects and plans to place three more projects in service by the end of 2010. A majority of capex is slated for the anticipated construction of the Ruby pipeline project.

Company Financials Fiscal Year Ended Dec. 31

Per Share Data ($)	2009	2008	2007	2006	2005	2004	2003	2002	2001	2000
Tangible Book Value	3.50	4.70	6.47	6.00	3.38	4.68	5.36	11.70	17.65	15.25
Cash Flow	3.47	0.50	2.25	2.09	0.61	0.45	0.99	0.21	2.76	4.82
Earnings	-0.83	-1.24	0.57	0.72	-1.13	-1.25	-1.03	-2.30	0.13	2.44
S&P Core Earnings	-0.79	-1.46	0.54	0.69	-1.07	-0.84	-0.68	-1.95	-0.37	NA
Dividends	0.16	0.18	0.16	0.16	0.16	0.16	0.16	0.87	0.85	0.82
Payout Ratio	NM	NM	28%	22%	NM	NM	NM	NM	NM	34%
Prices:High	11.37	22.47	18.56	16.39	14.16	11.85	10.30	46.89	75.30	74.25
Prices:Low	5.22	5.32	13.71	11.80	9.30	6.57	3.33	4.39	36.00	30.31
P/E Ratio:High	NM	NM	33	23	NM	NM	NM	NM	NM	30
P/E Ratio:Low	NM	NM	24	16	NM	NM	NM	NM	NM	12

Income Statement Analysis (Million $)	2009	2008	2007	2006	2005	2004	2003	2002	2001	2000
Revenue	4,631	5,363	4,648	4,281	4,017	5,874	6,711	12,194	57,475	21,950
Operating Income	NA	3,579	2,904	1,427	934	2,386	2,907	2,872	4,391	2,155
Depreciation	2,990	1,205	1,176	1,047	1,121	1,088	1,207	1,405	1,359	589
Interest Expense	1,008	914	1,044	1,228	1,389	1,632	1,839	1,400	1,155	538
Pretax Income	-873	-1,034	664	523	-991	-777	-1,200	-1,567	466	1,012
Effective Tax Rate	45.7%	NM	33.4%	NM	NM	NM	NM	NM	39.1%	28.3%
Net Income	-539	-823	436	531	-702	-802	-616	-1,289	67.0	582
S&P Core Earnings	-543	-1,021	375	471	-696	-531	-401	-1,096	-194	NA

Balance Sheet & Other Financial Data (Million $)	2009	2008	2007	2006	2005	2004	2003	2002	2001	2000
Cash	641	1,024	285	537	2,132	2,117	1,429	1,591	1,139	688
Current Assets	2,008	3,051	1,712	7,167	6,185	5,632	8,922	11,924	12,659	10,076
Total Assets	22,505	23,668	24,579	27,261	31,838	31,383	37,084	46,224	48,171	27,445
Current Liabilities	2,686	3,243	2,413	6,151	5,712	4,572	7,074	10,350	13,565	10,467
Long Term Debt	13,391	12,818	12,483	13,260	17,054	18,608	20,722	19,727	14,109	6,574
Common Equity	2,456	3,285	4,530	3,436	2,639	3,439	4,474	8,377	9,356	3,569
Total Capital	18,004	17,979	19,485	18,396	21,850	23,358	25,196	31,680	31,012	14,623
Capital Expenditures	2,810	2,757	2,495	2,164	1,718	1,782	2,452	3,716	4,079	1,336
Cash Flow	2,414	345	1,575	1,541	392	286	591	116	1,426	1,171
Current Ratio	0.8	0.9	0.7	1.2	1.1	1.2	1.3	1.2	0.9	1.0
% Long Term Debt of Capitalization	Nil	71.3	64.1	72.1	78.1	79.7	82.2	62.3	45.5	45.0
% Net Income of Revenue	NM	NM	9.4	12.4	NM	NM	NM	NM	0.1	2.7
% Return on Assets	NM	NM	1.7	1.8	NM	NM	NM	NM	0.1	2.6
% Return on Equity	NA	NM	10.0	16.3	NM	NM	NM	NM	0.8	17.9

Data as orig reptd.; bef. results of disc opers/spec. items. Per share data adj. for stk. divs.; EPS diluted. E-Estimated. NA-Not Available. NM-Not Meaningful. NR-Not Ranked. UR-Under Review.

Office: El Paso Building, 1001 Louisiana Street, Houston, TX 77002.
Telephone: 713-420-2600.
Email: investorrelations@epenergy.com
Website: http://www.elpaso.com

Chrmn, Pres & CEO: D.L. Foshee
COO: B. Neskora
EVP & CFO: J.R. Sult
EVP & Chief Admin Officer: S.B. Ortenstone

EVP & General Counsel: R.W. Baker
Investor Contact: B. Connery (713-420-5855)
Board Members: J. Braniff, D. W. Crane, D. L. Foshee, R. W. Goldman, A. W. Hall, Jr., T. R. Hix, F. P. McClean, T. J. Probert, S. J. Shapiro, J. M. Talbert, R. F. Vagt, J. L. Whitmire, III

Founded: 1928
Domicile: Delaware
Employees: 5,344

The McGraw-Hill Companies

EMC Corp

STANDARD &POOR'S

S&P Recommendation STRONG BUY ★★★★★

Price	12-Mo. Target Price	Investment Style
$21.44 (as of Oct 22, 2010)	$25.00	Large-Cap Blend

GICS Sector Information Technology
Sub-Industry Computer Storage & Peripherals

Summary This company is one of the world's largest suppliers of enterprise storage systems. It owns 80% of VMware, the largest provider of server virtualization software.

Key Stock Statistics (Source S&P, Vickers, company reports)

52-Wk Range	$21.83–16.12	S&P Oper. EPS 2010E	0.90	Market Capitalization(B)	$44.027	Beta	0.95
Trailing 12-Month EPS	$0.70	S&P Oper. EPS 2011E	1.05	Yield (%)	Nil	S&P 3-Yr. Proj. EPS CAGR(%)	13
Trailing 12-Month P/E	30.6	P/E on S&P Oper. EPS 2010E	23.8	Dividend Rate/Share	Nil	S&P Credit Rating	A-
$10K Invested 5 Yrs Ago	$15,615	Common Shares Outstg. (M)	2,053.5	Institutional Ownership (%)	79		

Price Performance

30-Week Mov. Avg. ··· 10-Week Mov. Avg. – – GAAP Earnings vs. Previous Year Volume Above Avg. |ılıl STARS
12-Mo. Target Price — Relative Strength — ▲ Up ▼ Down ► No Change Below Avg. |ılıl ★

Options: ASE, CBOE, P, Ph

Analysis prepared by **Jim Yin, CFA** on August 19, 2010, when the stock traded at **$ 18.61.**

Highlights

➤ We expect revenues to increase 19% in 2010, following a 5.7% decline in 2009, reflecting an improving IT spending environment amid an economic recovery. We think the Information Infrastructure business will grow 15% in 2010 due to pent-up demand. We also think demand is being driven by content digitization as more documents are stored electronically. We believe revenues from its VMware Virtual Infrastructure business will rise 39% in 2010, reflecting companies' urgency to cut costs in their data center operations.

➤ We look for overall gross margins of 58% in 2010, up from 55% in 2009, due to faster growth in the virtual infrastructure business unit, which has higher gross margins. We believe expenses will decrease as a percentage of revenues in 2010 due to better economies of scale and cost savings from restructuring. We project that operating margins will widen to 14.8% in 2010, from 10.1% in 2009.

➤ We forecast EPS of $0.88 in 2010, up from $0.53 in 2009. These include $0.32 and $0.36 of stock-based compensation, amortization of intangibles and restructuring charges in 2010 and 2009, respectively.

Investment Rationale/Risk

➤ Our strong buy recommendation reflects improving end-user demand. Besides a stronger economy, we think demand for data storage will be driven by increased usage of video and electronic record keeping. As a result of stronger demand, we think the pricing environment will remain favorable near term. We believe EMC will also benefit from the growth in the virtualization server market. We think this market segment will grow 20% per year for the next three years, as companies modernize their data center infrastructure. We are also positive on the company's cost reductions, and we see operating margins expanding in 2010.

➤ Risks to our recommendation and target price include a weaker-than-expected economic recovery, lower corporate IT spending, increased competition, unfavorable foreign currency exchange due to a rapid rise in the U.S. dollar, and a significant loss in market share.

➤ Our 12-month target price of $25 is based on our DCF analysis. Our DCF model assumes an 11% weighted average cost of capital, 16.5% operating margins, a 9.0% revenue growth rate for the next 10 years, and 3% terminal growth.

Qualitative Risk Assessment

LOW	MEDIUM	HIGH

Our risk assessment reflects our view that EMC is a market leader, generates consistent free cash flow, and has a strong balance sheet. However, we see the storage segment as somewhat cyclical, highly competitive, and often typified by pricing pressure.

Quantitative Evaluations

S&P Quality Ranking B

D	C	B-	B	B+	A-	A	A+

Relative Strength Rank STRONG

71

LOWEST = 1   HIGHEST = 99

Revenue/Earnings Data

Revenue (Million $)

	1Q	2Q	3Q	4Q	Year
2010	3,891	4,024	--	--	--
2009	3,151	3,257	3,518	4,100	14,026
2008	3,470	3,674	3,716	4,017	14,876
2007	2,975	3,125	3,300	3,831	13,230
2006	2,551	2,575	2,815	3,215	11,155
2005	2,243	2,345	2,366	2,710	9,664

Earnings Per Share ($)

2010	0.18	0.20	E0.22	E0.30	E0.90
2009	0.10	0.10	0.14	0.19	0.53
2008	0.13	0.18	0.20	0.14	0.64
2007	0.15	0.16	0.23	0.24	0.77
2006	0.12	0.12	0.13	0.18	0.54
2005	0.11	0.12	0.17	0.06	0.47

Fiscal year ended Dec. 31. Next earnings report expected: Late October. EPS Estimates based on S&P Operating Earnings; historical GAAP earnings are as reported.

Dividend Data

No cash dividends have been paid.

Please read the Required Disclosures and Analyst Certification on the last page of this report.

The **McGraw-Hill** Companies

EMC Corp

Business Summary August 19, 2010

CORPORATE OVERVIEW. EMC is a leading provider of data storage solutions for enterprises and government entities around the world. The company's products and services are used in conjunction with a variety of computing platforms that support key business processes, including transaction processing, data warehousing, electronic commerce and content management. Due to the growing complexity of its customers' infrastructure, EMC not only helps customers manage and secure their vast and ever-increasing quantities of information, but also automate their data centers and reduce their operational costs.

The company divides its operations into two major businesses, Information Infrastructure and VMware Virtual Infrastructure. Information Infrastructure business is comprised of three reporting segments - Information Storage, Content Management and Archiving and RSA Information Security. The company offers a wide range of storage systems designed to fulfill customers' needs in terms of performance, functionality, scalability, data availability and cost. Its key product line, Symmetrix, can scale to hundreds of thousands of terabytes of storage and 10s of millions of IOPS (input/output per second) supporting hundreds of thousands of virtual machines in a single federated stor-

age infrastructure. EMC also has other product lines - CLARiiON, Celerra, and Centera - that target the mid-tier and the low end of the markets. Information Storage accounted for 76% of total revenues in 2009. Sales in this business unit fell 8.3% in 2009, reflecting lower IT spending, in particular for hardware. Content Management and Archiving helps companies manage, backup, and restore their data, while RSA Information Security helps to safeguard the integrity and confidentiality of information throughout its lifecycle. Revenues from these two business units accounted 9.6% of total revenues in 2009.

VMware Virtual Infrastructure provides software solutions that help companies cut costs in their data center operations. Virtualization software can reduce the number of servers by consolidating many different types of workloads and operating systems onto virtual environments, thus enabling servers to run multiple applications. Revenues from its VMware Virtual Infrastructure business unit grew 7.7% in 2009, and accounted for 14% of total revenues.

Company Financials Fiscal Year Ended Dec. 31

Per Share Data ($)	2009	2008	2007	2006	2005	2004	2003	2002	2001	2000
Tangible Book Value	2.51	2.37	2.42	4.39	3.20	3.22	3.19	3.05	3.31	3.72
Cash Flow	1.05	0.92	1.02	0.87	0.73	0.61	0.45	0.24	0.07	1.02
Earnings	0.53	0.64	0.77	0.54	0.47	0.36	0.22	-0.05	-0.23	0.79
S&P Core Earnings	0.54	0.63	0.73	0.55	0.35	0.21	0.04	-0.23	-0.33	NA
Dividends	Nil	Nil	Nil	Nil	Nil	Nil	Nil	Nil	Nil	Nil
Payout Ratio	Nil	Nil	Nil	Nil	Nil	Nil	Nil	Nil	Nil	Nil
Prices:High	18.44	18.60	25.47	14.75	15.09	15.80	14.66	17.97	82.00	104.94
Prices:Low	9.61	8.25	12.74	9.44	11.10	9.24	5.98	3.67	10.01	47.50
P/E Ratio:High	35	29	33	27	32	44	67	NM	NM	NM
P/E Ratio:Low	18	13	17	17	24	26	27	NM	NM	NM

Income Statement Analysis (Million $)	2009	2008	2007	2006	2005	2004	2003	2002	2001	2000
Revenue	14,026	14,876	13,230	11,155	9,664	8,229	6,237	5,438	7,091	8,873
Operating Income	2,595	2,459	2,302	2,170	2,222	1,716	988	310	355	2,774
Depreciation	1,073	561	530	764	640	616	521	654	655	517
Interest Expense	183	73.8	72.9	34.1	7.99	7.52	3.03	11.4	11.3	14.6
Pretax Income	1,375	1,703	2,060	1,390	1,652	1,185	571	-296	-577	2,441
Effective Tax Rate	18.4%	18.4%	18.4%	11.7%	31.4%	26.5%	13.1%	NM	NM	27.0%
Net Income	1,088	1,346	1,666	1,227	1,133	871	496	-119	-508	1,782
S&P Core Earnings	1,124	1,312	1,569	1,241	839	504	84.2	-477	-720	NA

Balance Sheet & Other Financial Data (Million $)	2009	2008	2007	2006	2005	2004	2003	2002	2001	2000
Cash	6,695	6,807	6,127	1,828	2,322	1,477	1,869	1,687	2,129	1,983
Current Assets	10,538	10,665	10,053	6,521	6,574	4,831	4,687	4,217	4,923	6,100
Total Assets	26,812	23,875	22,285	18,566	16,790	15,423	14,093	9,590	9,890	10,628
Current Liabilities	5,148	5,218	4,408	3,881	3,674	2,949	2,547	2,042	2,179	2,114
Long Term Debt	3,100	3,450	3,450	3,450	127	128	130	Nil	Nil	14.5
Common Equity	15,550	13,042	12,521	10,326	12,065	11,523	10,885	7,226	7,601	8,177
Total Capital	18,650	17,038	16,448	13,776	12,368	11,793	11,015	7,226	7,601	8,494
Capital Expenditures	412	696	699	718	601	371	369	391	889	858
Cash Flow	2,161	1,907	2,196	1,992	1,773	1,488	1,017	535	147	2,299
Current Ratio	2.1	2.0	2.3	1.7	1.8	1.6	1.8	2.1	2.3	2.9
% Long Term Debt of Capitalization	16.6	20.3	21.4	25.0	1.0	1.1	1.2	Nil	Nil	0.2
% Net Income of Revenue	7.8	9.1	12.6	11.0	11.7	10.6	8.0	NM	NM	20.1
% Return on Assets	4.3	5.8	5.8	6.9	7.0	5.9	4.2	NM	NM	20.0
% Return on Equity	7.5	10.5	14.6	11.0	9.6	7.8	5.5	NM	NM	27.1

Data as orig reptd.; bef. results of disc opers/spec. items. Per share data adj. for stk. divs.; EPS diluted. E-Estimated. NA-Not Available. NM-Not Meaningful. NR-Not Ranked. UR-Under Review.

Office: 176 South Street, Hopkinton, MA 01748-2230.
Telephone: 508-435-1000.
Email: emc_ir@emc.com
Website: http://www.emc.com

Chrmn, Pres & CEO: J.M. Tucci
EVP & CFO: D.I. Goulden
EVP & General Counsel: P.T. Dacier
SVP & CTO: J.M. Nick

SVP & Chief Acctg Officer: M.A. Link
Board Members: M. W. Brown, R. L. Cowen, M. J. Cronin, G. Deegan, J. S. DiStasio, J. R. Egan, E. F. Kelly, W. B. Priem, P. L. Sagan, D. N. Strohm, J. M. Tucci

Founded: 1979
Domicile: Massachusetts
Employees: 43,200

Emerson Electric Co.

STANDARD &POOR'S

S&P Recommendation HOLD ★★★☆☆

Price $54.51 (as of Oct 22, 2010)	**12-Mo. Target Price** $52.00

Investment Style Large-Cap Blend

GICS Sector Industrials
Sub-Industry Electrical Components & Equipment

Summary This company designs and supplies product technology and delivers engineering services and solutions to a wide range of industrial, commercial and consumer markets around the world.

Key Stock Statistics (Source S&P, Vickers, company reports)

52-Wk Range	$55.00–37.45	S&P Oper. EPS 2010E	2.67	Market Capitalization(B)	$41.014	Beta	1.22
Trailing 12-Month EPS	$2.54	S&P Oper. EPS 2011E	3.26	Yield (%)	2.46	S&P 3-Yr. Proj. EPS CAGR(%)	9
Trailing 12-Month P/E	21.5	P/E on S&P Oper. EPS 2010E	20.4	Dividend Rate/Share	$1.34	S&P Credit Rating	A
$10K Invested 5 Yrs Ago	$18,196	Common Shares Outstg. (M)	752.4	Institutional Ownership (%)	72		

Price Performance

30-Week Mov. Avg. · · · 10-Week Mov. Avg. - - GAAP Earnings vs. Previous Year Volume Above Avg. STARS
12-Mo. Target Price — Relative Strength — ▲ Up ▼ Down ► No Change Below Avg.

Options: ASE, CBOE, P, Ph

Analysis prepared by **Mathew Christy, CFA** on September 09, 2010, when the stock traded at **$ 50.24**.

Highlights

► We expect EMR's sales to increase more than 4% in FY 10 (Sep.), as weakness in its Process Management and Industrial Automation segments mostly offsets acquisition-related growth and higher expected sales in other segments. Our forecast also assumes lower orders and declining backlogs in EMR's later-cycle businesses, weighing down the positive effects of greater demand and inventory restocking in its shorter-cycle businesses. For FY 11, we see revenues increasing about 11%, on better results across EMR's operations as well as acquisitions.

► We think operating margins will improve in FY 10, as lower operating leverage in some business units and raw material cost inflation are more than offset by the company's efforts to realign costs to address the decline in demand and lower production rates across its businesses. For FY 11, we project that operating margins will widen further as sales and production rates improve.

► With taxes at a projected effective rate of about 30% in FY 10 and 28% in FY 11, we estimate EPS of $2.67 for FY 10 and $3.26 for FY 11.

Investment Rationale/Risk

► We continue to view positively the recent improvement in the trailing three-month order growth rate, with robust orders across EMR's business units, despite the negative effects of currency in the June quarter. We think the improvement stems partly from a general strengthening in the economy and increased end-market demand. However, we see limited upside potential for the shares from recent levels.

► Risks to our recommendation and target price include weaker-than-expected global economic growth, softer industrial, energy and electronics markets, and potential value-diminishing acquisitions.

► Our 12-month target price of $52 represents a blend of two valuation metrics. Our discounted cash flow model, which assumes a 3% perpetuity growth rate and a 10.1% discount rate, indicates an intrinsic value of $54. Our relative valuation applies a 16.1X multiple, ahead of the peer average, to our forward 12-month EPS estimate, indicating a $51 value.

Qualitative Risk Assessment

LOW	MEDIUM	HIGH

Our risk assessment reflects the cyclical nature of several of the company's major end markets, its acquisition strategy, and corporate governance practices that we view as unfavorable versus peers. This is offset by our view of its strong competitive position in major product categories.

Quantitative Evaluations

S&P Quality Ranking   A

D	C	B-	B	B+	A-	A	A+

Relative Strength Rank   **STRONG**

71

LOWEST = 1   HIGHEST = 99

Revenue/Earnings Data

Revenue (Million $)

	1Q	2Q	3Q	4Q	Year
2010	5,011	5,144	5,641	--	--
2009	5,415	5,087	5,091	5,322	20,915
2008	5,520	6,023	6,568	6,696	24,807
2007	5,051	5,513	5,874	6,134	22,572
2006	4,548	4,852	5,217	5,516	20,133
2005	3,970	4,227	4,465	4,643	17,305

Earnings Per Share ($)

2010	0.56	0.55	0.78	E0.79	E2.67
2009	0.60	0.49	0.51	0.67	2.27
2008	0.65	0.75	0.82	0.88	3.11
2007	0.55	0.61	0.72	0.78	2.66
2006	0.48	0.52	0.59	0.65	2.24
2005	0.35	0.42	0.43	0.51	1.70

Fiscal year ended Sep. 30. Next earnings report expected: Early November. EPS Estimates based on S&P Operating Earnings; historical GAAP earnings are as reported.

Dividend Data (Dates: mm/dd Payment Date: mm/dd/yy)

Amount ($)	Date Decl.	Ex-Div. Date	Stk. of Record	Payment Date
0.335	11/03	11/10	11/13	12/10/09
0.335	02/02	02/10	02/12	03/10/10
0.335	05/04	05/12	05/14	06/10/10
0.335	08/03	08/11	08/13	09/10/10

Dividends have been paid since 1947. Source: Company reports.

Please read the Required Disclosures and Analyst Certification on the last page of this report.

The McGraw-Hill Companies

Emerson Electric Co.

STANDARD & POOR'S

Business Summary September 09, 2010

CORPORATE OVERVIEW. Emerson Electric is an industrial conglomerate operating more than 60 diverse businesses in five primary business segments: Process Management, Industrial Automation, Network Power, Climate Technologies, and Appliance and Tools.

The company's Process Management segment, which accounted for 29.8% of FY 09 (Sep.) total sales and 38.8% of operating profits, and had 17.1% operating margins, produces process management software and systems, analytical instrumentation, valves, control systems for measurement and control of fluid flow, and integrated solutions for process and industrial applications. In FY 09, 33% of segment sales were made within the U.S., 22% in Europe, 23% in Asia, and 22% elsewhere. Segment sales are mainly conducted via a direct sales force while segment brands include Emerson Process Management, AMS Suite, Baumann, Bettis, Bristol, PlantWeb, CSI, DeltaV, and Fisher, to name a few.

The Industrial Automation segment (17.7%, 12.9%, 9.6%) primarily makes industrial motors and drives, transmissions, alternators and controls for automated equipment. Products in this segment are sold predominantly to manufacturing firms via a direct sales force or independent resellers. Geographic distribution of segment sales: 39% U.S., 39% Europe, 13% Asia, and 9% other regions. Segment brands include Emerson Industrial Automation, Appleton, Trident, McGill, and ASCO.

The Network Power segment (25.6%, 20.6%, 10.6%) mainly makes power systems and precision cooling products used in computer, telecommunications and Internet infrastructure sold mainly to utility companies. In FY 09, 39% of segment sales were generated in the U.S., 17% in Europe, 33% in Asia, and 11% elsewhere. Product distribution is mainly through Emerson's direct sales force in Europe and Asia and independent resellers domestically. Segment brands include Emerson Network Power, Aperture, ASCO Power Technologies, Astec, Liebert, Netsure and Stratos.

The Climate Technologies segment (15.3%, 14.4%, 12.4%) makes home and building thermostats and compressors (cooling components used in air conditioning units and refrigerators). Geographic distribution of FY 09 segment sales: 56% U.S., 15% Europe, 18% Asia, and 11% other regions. Segment brands: Emerson Climate Technologies, Computer Process Controls, Dixell, and Emerson Retail Services.

Company Financials Fiscal Year Ended Sep. 30

Per Share Data ($)	2009	2008	2007	2006	2005	2004	2003	2002	2001	2000
Tangible Book Value	0.44	2.25	2.99	2.67	2.34	2.36	1.81	0.99	1.11	1.27
Cash Flow	3.13	3.92	3.47	3.04	2.41	4.37	1.84	1.90	2.07	2.44
Earnings	2.27	3.11	2.66	2.24	1.70	1.49	1.21	1.26	1.20	1.65
S&P Core Earnings	2.08	2.94	2.67	2.24	1.70	1.49	1.13	0.94	0.88	NA
Dividends	1.32	1.20	1.05	0.89	0.83	0.80	0.79	0.78	0.77	0.72
Payout Ratio	58%	39%	39%	40%	49%	54%	65%	62%	64%	44%
Prices:High	43.71	58.72	59.05	45.21	38.92	35.44	32.50	33.04	39.63	39.88
Prices:Low	24.39	29.26	41.26	36.78	30.35	28.11	21.89	20.87	22.02	20.25
P/E Ratio:High	19	19	22	20	23	24	27	26	33	24
P/E Ratio:Low	11	9	16	16	18	19	18	17	18	12

Income Statement Analysis (Million $)	2009	2008	2007	2006	2005	2004	2003	2002	2001	2000
Revenue	20,915	24,807	22,572	20,133	17,305	15,615	13,958	13,824	15,480	15,545
Operating Income	3,710	4,639	4,174	3,676	3,150	2,842	2,497	2,443	2,988	3,219
Depreciation	651	638	656	607	562	557	534	541	708	678
Interest Expense	244	244	261	225	243	234	246	250	304	288
Pretax Income	2,417	3,591	3,107	2,684	2,149	3,704	1,414	1,565	1,589	2,178
Effective Tax Rate	28.7%	31.7%	31.3%	31.3%	33.8%	16.1%	28.4%	32.3%	35.0%	34.7%
Net Income	1,724	2,454	2,136	1,845	1,422	3,109	1,013	1,060	1,032	1,422
S&P Core Earnings	1,580	2,321	2,145	1,846	1,424	1,250	951	784	753	NA

Balance Sheet & Other Financial Data (Million $)	2009	2008	2007	2006	2005	2004	2003	2002	2001	2000
Cash	1,560	1,777	1,008	810	1,233	1,346	696	381	356	281
Current Assets	7,653	9,331	8,065	7,330	6,837	6,416	5,500	4,961	5,320	5,483
Total Assets	19,763	21,040	19,680	18,672	17,227	16,361	15,194	14,545	15,046	15,164
Current Liabilities	4,956	6,573	5,546	5,374	4,931	4,339	3,417	4,400	5,379	5,219
Long Term Debt	3,998	3,297	3,372	3,128	3,128	3,136	3,733	2,990	2,256	2,248
Common Equity	8,555	9,113	8,772	7,848	7,400	12,266	6,460	5,741	6,114	10,248
Total Capital	12,553	13,131	12,144	10,976	10,528	15,402	10,193	8,731	8,370	12,496
Capital Expenditures	531	714	681	601	518	400	337	384	554	692
Cash Flow	2,375	3,092	2,792	2,452	1,984	3,666	1,547	1,601	1,740	2,101
Current Ratio	1.5	1.4	1.5	1.4	1.4	1.5	1.6	1.1	1.0	1.1
% Long Term Debt of Capitalization	31.9	25.1	27.8	28.5	29.7	20.4	36.6	34.2	26.9	18.0
% Net Income of Revenue	8.2	9.9	9.5	9.2	8.2	19.9	7.3	7.7	6.7	9.2
% Return on Assets	8.5	12.1	11.1	10.3	8.5	19.7	6.8	7.2	6.8	9.9
% Return on Equity	19.5	27.4	25.7	24.1	19.4	26.1	16.6	17.9	16.5	14.5

Data as orig reptd.; bef. results of disc opers/spec. items. Per share data adj. for stk. divs.; EPS diluted. E-Estimated. NA-Not Available. NM-Not Meaningful. NR-Not Ranked. UR-Under Review.

Office: 8000 West Florissant Avenue, St Louis, MO 63136.
Telephone: 314-553-2000.
Website: http://www.emersonelectric.com
Chrmn & CEO: D.N. Farr

Pres & COO: E.L. Monser
Vice Chrmn: W.J. Galvin
SVP & CFO: F.J. Dellaquila
SVP, Secy & General Counsel: F.L. Steeves

Investor Contact: C. Tucker (314-553-2197)
Board Members: C. A. Boersig, A. A. Busch, III, D. N. Farr, C. G. Fernandez, W. J. Galvin, A. F. Golden, H. Green, R. Horton, W. R. Johnson, V. R. Loucks, Jr., J. B. Menzer, C. A. Peters, J. W. Prueher, R. L. Ridgway, R. L. Stephenson

Founded: 1890
Domicile: Missouri
Employees: 129,000

Entergy Corp.

S&P Recommendation BUY ★★★★☆

Price $73.73 (as of Oct 25, 2010)	**12-Mo. Target Price** $88.00	**Investment Style** Large-Cap Blend

GICS Sector Utilities
Sub-Industry Electric Utilities

Summary This electric utility holding company serves 2.6 million customers in Arkansas, Louisiana, Mississippi, and Texas and has non-utility, nuclear operations in several states.

Key Stock Statistics (Source S&P, Vickers, company reports)

52-Wk Range	$84.44– 70.35	S&P Oper. EPS 2010**E**	7.10	Market Capitalization(B)	$13.774	Beta	0.71
Trailing 12-Month EPS	$7.04	S&P Oper. EPS 2011**E**	6.95	Yield (%)	4.50	S&P 3-Yr. Proj. EPS CAGR(%)	2
Trailing 12-Month P/E	10.5	P/E on S&P Oper. EPS 2010**E**	10.4	Dividend Rate/Share	$3.32	S&P Credit Rating	BBB
$10K Invested 5 Yrs Ago	$12,813	Common Shares Outstg. (M)	186.8	Institutional Ownership (%)	83		

Price Performance

30-Week Mov. Avg. ··· 10-Week Mov. Avg. -- **GAAP Earnings vs. Previous Year** Volume Above Avg. ▮▮▮ STARS
12-Mo. Target Price — Relative Strength — ▲ Up ▼ Down ► No Change Below Avg. ▮▮▮ ★

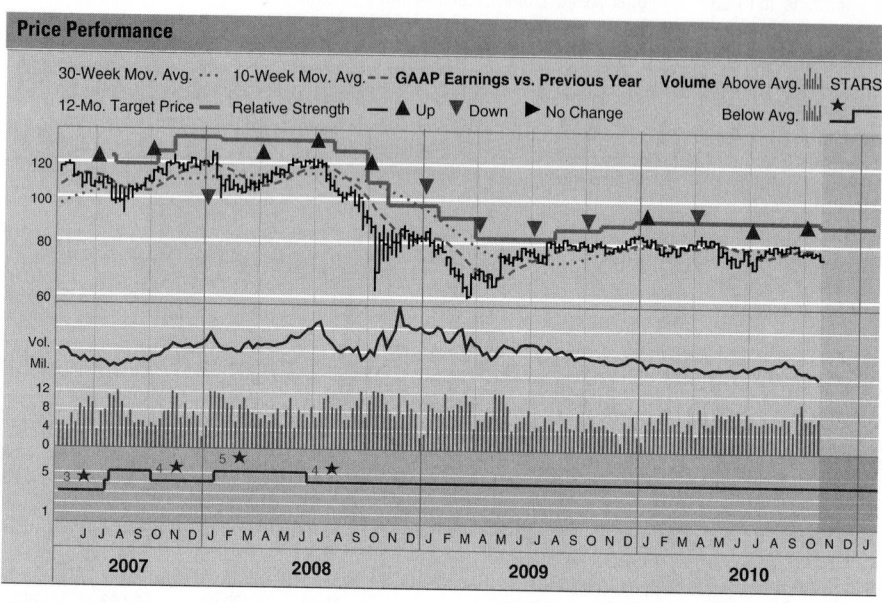

Options: ASE, CBOE, P, Ph

Analysis prepared by **Justin McCann** on October 25, 2010, when the stock traded at **$ 73.99**.

Highlights

➤ Excluding potential one-time charges of $0.45, we expect operating EPS in 2010 to increase about 6% from 2009's $6.67. Operating EPS in the first nine months of 2010 was aided by the abnormally warm weather and fewer shares, partially offset by planned and unplanned plant outages, and increased fuel and operating costs. We expect EPS in 2011 to decline due to ongoing weakness in the power markets and an assumed return to normal weather.

➤ After the cancellation of its planned spin-off of non-utility nuclear assets, and the equally owned joint venture that would have been formed with the spun-off company, ETR plans to deploy its capital in a disciplined manner as it balances the needs of its utility and non-utility businesses. ETR has estimated a total potential charge of $0.40 to $0.45 a share connected to the write-off of the costs incurred in 2010 related to the spin-off and its cancellation.

➤ Although the Vermont legislature voted against the approval of a 20-year license extension for the Vermont Yankee nuclear plant beyond its 2012 expiration, the possible extension approval for the plant, which supplies about 30% of Vermont's power, could still be obtained in 2011.

Investment Rationale/Risk

➤ The stock is down about 9% year to date. This follows an essentially flat performance in 2009 and reflects, we believe, the ongoing weakness in the economy and power markets, as well as the volatility in the utility sector. Since it had been anticipated, we do not think the stock was hurt by the cancellation of the planned spin-off of ETR's non-utility nuclear operations. Also, the announcement coincided with Entergy's declaration of a 10% increase in its dividend and its recommitment to its previously announced $750 million share buyback program.

➤ Risks to our recommendation and target price include a sharp drop in the margins of ETR's non-regulated operations, unanticipated problems with its nuclear facilities, and a decline in the average P/E of the group as a whole.

➤ With the decline in the shares, along with the 10% increase in the dividend (effective with the June payment), the recent yield was 4.5%. While slightly below the electric utility average of about 4.7%, it was roughly in line with utility holding companies with large wholesale power operations. Our 12-month target price is $88, an approximate peers' P/E multiple of about 12.7X our 2011 EPS estimate.

Qualitative Risk Assessment

LOW	MEDIUM	HIGH

Our risk assessment reflects the steady cash flow we expect from most of the regulated utilities and the nuclear operations, offset by uncertainties related to the recovery of the economy and the wholesale power markets.

Quantitative Evaluations

S&P Quality Ranking   A

D	C	B-	B	B+	A-	A	A+

Relative Strength Rank   WEAK

18

LOWEST = 1   HIGHEST = 99

Revenue/Earnings Data

Revenue (Million $)

	1Q	2Q	3Q	4Q	Year
2010	2,759	2,863	3,332	--	--
2009	2,789	2,521	2,937	2,499	10,746
2008	2,865	3,264	3,964	3,001	13,094
2007	2,600	2,769	3,289	2,825	11,484
2006	2,568	2,629	3,255	2,481	10,932
2005	2,323	2,710	3,130	2,652	10,106

Earnings Per Share ($)

	1Q	2Q	3Q	4Q	Year
2010	1.12	1.65	2.63	E1.31	E7.10
2009	1.19	1.14	2.32	1.64	6.30
2008	1.56	1.37	2.41	0.89	6.23
2007	1.03	1.32	2.30	0.96	5.60
2006	0.93	1.27	1.83	1.32	5.36
2005	0.79	1.33	1.65	0.59	4.40

Fiscal year ended Dec. 31. Next earnings report expected: Early February. EPS Estimates based on S&P Operating Earnings; historical GAAP earnings are as reported.

Dividend Data (Dates: mm/dd Payment Date: mm/dd/yy)

Amount ($)	Date Decl.	Ex-Div. Date	Stk. of Record	Payment Date
0.750	10/30	11/09	11/12	12/01/09
0.750	01/29	02/09	02/11	03/01/10
0.830	04/05	05/10	05/12	06/01/10
0.830	07/30	08/10	08/12	09/01/10

Dividends have been paid since 1988. Source: Company reports.

Please read the Required Disclosures and Analyst Certification on the last page of this report.

The McGraw-Hill Companies

Entergy Corp.

Business Summary October 25, 2010

CORPORATE OVERVIEW. Entergy is an integrated energy company primarily engaged in electric power production and retail electric distribution operations. It owns and operates power plants with about 30,000 megawatts (MW) of electric generating capacity, and is the second largest nuclear power generator in the U.S. As the holding company for Entergy Arkansas, Entergy Gulf States Louisiana, Entergy Louisiana, Entergy Mississippi, Entergy New Orleans, and Entergy Texas. Entergy Corp. provides electricity to 2.7 million U.S. retail customers. ETR also owns System Energy Resources, which has a 90% interest in the Grand Gulf 1 nuclear plant. The non-utility nuclear business owns and operates five nuclear plants (located in New York, Massachusetts and Vermont), which sell power mainly to wholesale customers.

IMPACT OF MAJOR DEVELOPMENTS. On April 5, 2009, Entergy announced that it was canceling its plan (initially announced on November 5, 2007) to spin off to shareholders the company's non-utility nuclear business into a company that would have been named Enexus Energy Corp. It was also canceling its plan to form an equally owned joint venture with the spun-off company that would have been involved in the operation of the new company's nuclear assets and which would have offered ancillary nuclear services to third parties. These services will continue to be provided by Entergy's nuclear business. The cancellation followed the rejection (announced on March 25, 2009) of the spinoff by the New York Public Service Commission, which made its decision based on the strong concerns of the commission's staff related to potential problems that could arise due to the financial condition of the company to be spun off.

Hurricanes Katrina and Rita in 2005 caused catastrophic damage to large portions of ETR's service territories in Louisiana, Mississippi and Texas, including the effect of extensive flooding in and around greater New Orleans. As of December 31, 2009, Entergy had received $317 million on its Katrina and Rita insurance claims, and had substantially completed its insurance recoveries related to Hurricanes Katrina and Rita.

On May 8, 2007, Entergy New Orleans emerged from Chapter 11 bankruptcy. This followed the approval of the company's plan of reorganization by the U.S. Bankruptcy Court for the Eastern District of Louisiana. The utility had filed for Chapter 11 reorganization in September 2005, soon after the devastation caused by Hurricane Katrina. Under the reorganization plan, all creditors would be fully compensated.

Company Financials Fiscal Year Ended Dec. 31

Per Share Data ($)	2009	2008	2007	2006	2005	2004	2003	2002	2001	2000
Tangible Book Value	43.55	40.08	38.76	38.59	35.49	36.43	36.38	33.61	33.74	31.83
Earnings	6.30	6.23	5.60	5.36	4.40	3.93	3.42	2.64	3.13	2.97
S&P Core Earnings	6.72	5.64	5.74	5.54	4.49	3.99	3.70	2.14	2.21	NA
Dividends	3.00	3.00	2.58	2.16	2.16	1.89	1.60	1.34	1.28	1.22
Payout Ratio	48%	48%	46%	40%	49%	48%	47%	51%	41%	41%
Prices:High	86.61	127.48	125.00	94.03	79.22	68.67	57.24	46.85	44.67	43.88
Prices:Low	59.87	61.93	89.60	66.78	64.48	50.64	42.26	32.12	32.56	15.94
P/E Ratio:High	14	20	22	18	18	17	17	18	14	15
P/E Ratio:Low	10	10	16	12	15	13	12	12	10	5

Income Statement Analysis (Million $)	2009	2008	2007	2006	2005	2004	2003	2002	2001	2000
Revenue	10,746	13,094	11,484	10,932	10,106	10,124	9,195	8,305	9,621	10,016
Depreciation	1,083	1,031	1,132	888	856	896	851	839	721	785
Maintenance	NA	NA	NA	NA	NA	NA	NA	NA	NA	NA
Fixed Charges Coverage	4.17	3.92	3.49	3.36	3.69	3.54	2.66	2.23	2.25	2.83
Construction Credits	92.8	69.8	67.8	63.8	75.1	65.3	75.9	57.0	48.0	56.0
Effective Tax Rate	34.0%	33.1%	30.7%	28.1%	36.6%	28.2%	37.6%	32.1%	38.5%	40.3%
Net Income	1,231	1,221	1,135	1,133	969	933	813	623	727	711
S&P Core Earnings	1,311	1,108	1,162	1,171	961	922	856	487	495	NA

Balance Sheet & Other Financial Data (Million $)	2009	2008	2007	2006	2005	2004	2003	2002	2001	2000
Gross Property	40,503	38,591	36,302	33,366	32,437	32,055	31,181	32,964	32,403	29,865
Capital Expenditures	1,872	2,435	1,578	1,586	1,458	1,411	1,569	1,580	1,380	1,494
Net Property	23,637	22,660	21,194	19,651	19,426	18,915	18,561	20,657	20,597	18,501
Capitalization:Long Term Debt	10,706	11,174	9,728	8,809	8,838	7,034	7,498	7,458	7,536	8,014
Capitalization:% Long Term Debt	54.5	57.4	54.3	50.8	53.2	44.5	45.2	47.6	49.1	52.2
Capitalization:Preferred	311	311	311	345	Nil	365	334	359	361	335
Capitalization:% Preferred	1.60	1.60	1.70	1.99	Nil	2.31	2.01	2.29	2.35	2.18
Capitalization:Common	8,613	7,967	7,863	8,198	7,761	8,400	8,773	7,839	7,456	7,003
Capitalization:% Common	43.9	41.0	44.0	47.2	46.8	53.2	52.8	50.1	48.6	45.6
Total Capital	20,342	26,343	24,625	23,531	22,399	21,266	21,805	20,355	19,399	19,095
% Operating Ratio	84.6	87.2	87.1	88.7	63.3	87.6	89.4	85.8	88.6	89.0
% Earned on Net Property	9.9	10.4	10.3	9.2	9.3	8.8	8.1	5.8	8.1	8.6
% Return on Revenue	11.5	9.3	9.9	10.4	9.6	9.2	8.8	7.5	7.6	7.1
% Return on Invested Capital	9.1	7.3	7.7	7.0	6.6	6.5	2.4	7.7	7.6	7.1
% Return on Common Equity	14.9	15.4	14.1	14.2	11.7	10.6	9.5	7.8	9.7	9.6

Data as orig reptd.; bef. results of disc opers/spec. items. Per share data adj. for stk. divs.; EPS diluted. E-Estimated. NA-Not Available. NM-Not Meaningful. NR-Not Ranked. UR-Under Review.

Office: 639 Loyola Ave, New Orleans, LA 70113-3125.
Telephone: 504-576-4000.
Website: http://www.entergy.com
Chrmn & CEO: J.W. Leonard

COO & EVP: M.T. Savoff
EVP & CFO: L.P. Denault
EVP & Chief Admin Officer: R.K. West
EVP, Secy & General Counsel: R.D. Sloan

Investor Contact: N. Morovich (504-576-5506)
Board Members: M. S. Bateman, W. Blount, G. W. Edwards, A. Herman, D. C. Hintz, J. W. Leonard, S. L. Levenick, S. C. Myers, J. R. Nichols, W. A. Percy, II, W. J. Tauzin, S. V. Wilkinson

Founded: 1989
Domicile: Delaware
Employees: 15,181

EOG Resources Inc.

STANDARD &POOR'S

| S&P Recommendation | BUY ★★★★☆ | Price $97.31 (as of Oct 22, 2010) | 12-Mo. Target Price $121.00 | Investment Style Large-Cap Growth |

GICS Sector Energy
Sub-Industry Oil & Gas Exploration & Production

Summary One of the largest independent exploration and production companies in the world, this U.S. company focuses on onshore natural gas production in North America.

Key Stock Statistics (Source S&P, Vickers, company reports)

52-Wk Range	$114.95–80.37	S&P Oper. EPS 2010**E**	1.98	Market Capitalization(B)	$24.665	Beta	0.93
Trailing 12-Month EPS	$2.30	S&P Oper. EPS 2011**E**	4.24	Yield (%)	0.64	S&P 3-Yr. Proj. EPS CAGR(%)	-17
Trailing 12-Month P/E	42.3	P/E on S&P Oper. EPS 2010**E**	49.1	Dividend Rate/Share	$0.62	S&P Credit Rating	A-
$10K Invested 5 Yrs Ago	$16,322	Common Shares Outstg. (M)	253.5	Institutional Ownership (%)	94		

Price Performance

30-Week Mov. Avg. · · · 10-Week Mov. Avg. – – **GAAP Earnings vs. Previous Year** Volume Above Avg. STARS
12-Mo. Target Price — Relative Strength — ▲ Up ▼ Down ▶ No Change Below Avg. ★

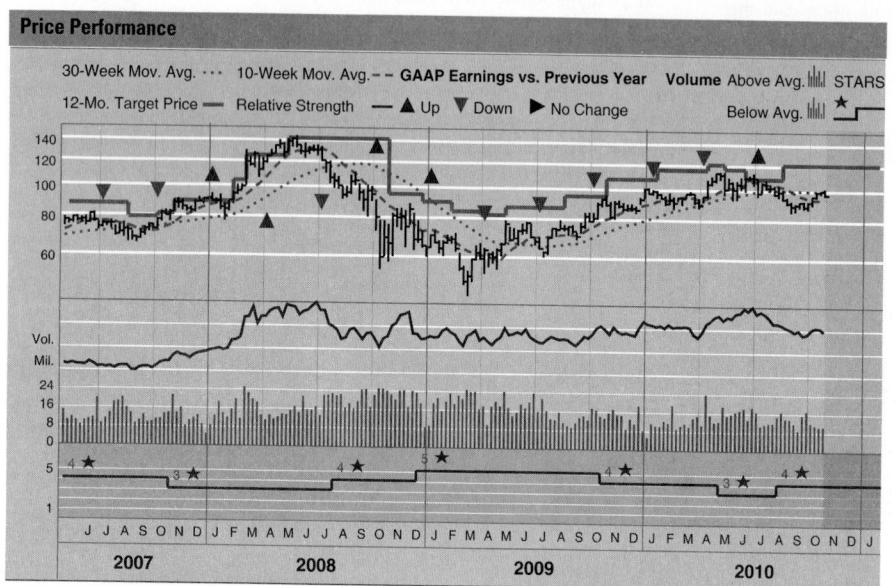

Options: ASE, CBOE, P, Ph

Analysis prepared by **Michael Kay** on September 07, 2010, when the stock traded at **$ 89.16.**

Highlights

► In 2010, EOG plans to sharpen its focus on unconventional crude oil, shifting its portfolio mix to a heavier liquids weighting to limit exposure to natural gas volatility. It sees stronger returns in Bakken and Barnett Shale Combo horizontal oil prospects versus those at deepwater plays or Canadian oil sands. EOG recently announced a discovery in the Eagle Ford Shale, where it sees a resource potential of 900 MMBOE and operates five rigs, with plans for an average of 14 rigs in 2011. In the Bakken, EOG operates 12 drilling rigs on its 580,000 net acres. We see a possible JV at Marcellus acreage. We see production growth of 13% in 2010 and 18% in 2011.

► EOG recently stated a goal of raising the liquids weighting of its production portfolio, targeting 47% liquids growth in 2010. On lower costs, EOG estimates its Bakken, Barnett, Haynesville and Marcellus plays offer stronger returns relative to others.

► After 2009 EPS of $1.80 (with a non-cash derivative loss of $1.20), we see EPS of $1.98 in 2010 on higher production and prices, and $4.24 in 2011. EOG plans 2010 capex of $5.6 billion, higher than we expected, and plans to divest $1 billion to $1.5 billion of non-core gas assets.

Investment Rationale/Risk

► EOG has focused capex on organic production growth at plays such as the Haynesville, Marcellus and Barnett Shales and the Bakken Oil Shale. We think expertise in horizontal drilling and technology will aid onshore production growth at promising new oil plays in the Barnett Shale, Niobrara in the Rockies and Eagle Ford, and we expect a competitive advantage when searching for new potential resources. Over the next three years, EOG plans to emphasize oil growth, moderate gas drilling, limit activity in Trinidad, and enter a possible horizontal project in China. Unlike others, EOG can shift its focus from liquids to natural gas should fundamentals require.

► Risks to our recommendation and target price include adverse changes in economic conditions, lower oil and gas prices, increased costs, and difficulty replacing reserves.

► We blend our NAV estimate of $120 with DCF ($125; WACC 10%, terminal growth 3%) and above-peer relative metrics, warranted, in our view, by EOG's strong production growth potential, positive earnings and cash flow momentum, and financial flexibility, to arrive at our 12-month target price of $121.

Qualitative Risk Assessment

| LOW | MEDIUM | HIGH |

Our risk assessment is based on EOG's participation in a very competitive, capital-intensive and cyclical industry, partly offset by our view of its significant net acreage position, active drilling program, and history of relatively low operating costs.

Quantitative Evaluations

S&P Quality Ranking   B+

| D | C | B- | B | B+ | A- | A | A+ |

Relative Strength Rank   MODERATE

40

LOWEST = 1   HIGHEST = 99

Revenue/Earnings Data

Revenue (Million $)

	1Q	2Q	3Q	4Q	Year
2010	1,363	1,321	--	--	--
2009	1,158	861.0	1,007	1,761	4,787
2008	1,101	1,875	3,220	1,105	6,529
2007	875.2	1,055	990.5	1,251	4,191
2006	1,085	919.1	968.3	932.5	3,904
2005	688.2	783.9	934.5	1,214	3,620

Earnings Per Share ($)

	1Q	2Q	3Q	4Q	Year
2010	0.47	0.24	E0.49	E0.83	E1.98
2009	0.63	-0.07	0.02	1.58	2.17
2008	0.96	0.71	6.20	1.85	9.72
2007	0.88	1.24	0.82	1.44	4.37
2006	1.73	1.34	1.21	0.96	5.24
2005	0.83	1.02	1.40	1.88	5.13

Fiscal year ended Dec. 31. Next earnings report expected: Early November. EPS Estimates based on S&P Operating Earnings; historical GAAP earnings are as reported.

Dividend Data (Dates: mm/dd Payment Date: mm/dd/yy)

Amount ($)	Date Decl.	Ex-Div. Date	Stk. of Record	Payment Date
0.145	12/15	01/13	01/15	01/29/10
0.155	02/09	04/14	04/16	04/30/10
0.155	04/29	07/14	07/16	07/30/10
0.155	09/09	10/13	10/15	10/29/10

Dividends have been paid since 1990. Source: Company reports.

Please read the Required Disclosures and Analyst Certification on the last page of this report.

The McGraw·Hill Companies

EOG Resources Inc.

Business Summary September 07, 2010

CORPORATE OVERVIEW. EOG Resources, Inc. (EOG), a Delaware corporation organized in 1985, together with its subsidiaries, explores for, develops, produces and markets natural gas and crude oil primarily in major producing basins in the U.S., Canada, offshore Trinidad, the U.K. North Sea, and other select regions.

Proved oil and gas reserves rose 24%, to 10.8 trillion cubic feet equivalent (Tcfe; 83% natural gas, 54% developed), in 2009. EOG had 76% of reserves classified as proved developed at year-end 2008, exhibiting the addition of significant undeveloped acreage for future drilling inventory. Also, we estimate EOG has exhibited a three-year reserve CAGR (compound annual growth rate) of 17%. About 75% of EOG's 2009 proved reserves were in the U.S., 16% in Canada, and 9% in Trinidad. We estimate EOG's 2009 organic reserve replacement at 313%, and reserve replacement cost at $1.18 per Mcf. This compares to a three-year reserve replacement of 270% and three-year reserve replacement cost of $2.15 per Mcf. Oil and gas production rose 7%, to 2.118 billion cubic feet equivalent (Bcfe) per day (78% natural gas), in 2009. Production growth came from a 21% boost in oil volumes due to the development of EOG's Bakken properties, compared to a 2% rise in natural gas production.

CORPORATE STRATEGY. One of the largest independent exploration and pro-

duction companies in the world, EOG has focused on onshore natural gas operations, primarily in the U.S. and Canada. Substantial portions of its reserves are in long-lived fields with well established production characteristics.

In the U.S., EOG has interests in the Barnett Shale play of the Fort Worth Basin; the Upper Gulf Coast area covering East Texas, Louisiana and Mississippi; the Permian Basin; the Rocky Mountain area, including the Uinta Basin, Williston Basin and Bakken play in North Dakota; the Mid-Continent area; South Texas and the Gulf of Mexico; and the Marcellus Shale in Pennsylvania.

In Canada, EOG operates through its subsidiary, EOG Resources Canada, Inc. (EOGRC), with operations focused in the Southeast Alberta/Southwest Saskatchewan shallow natural gas trends; the Pembina/Highvale area of Central Alberta; the Grand Prairie/Wapiti area of Northwest Alberta; the Waskada area in Southwest Manitoba; and the Horn River Basin in northeastern British Columbia.

Company Financials Fiscal Year Ended Dec. 31

Per Share Data ($)	2009	2008	2007	2006	2005	2004	2003	2002	2001	2000
Tangible Book Value	39.59	36.11	28.68	22.76	17.21	11.97	8.95	6.64	6.47	5.27
Cash Flow	9.53	15.79	9.27	8.56	7.81	4.69	3.73	2.02	3.32	3.17
Earnings	2.17	9.72	4.37	5.24	5.13	2.58	1.83	0.33	1.65	1.12
S&P Core Earnings	0.79	9.39	4.37	5.21	5.08	2.54	1.77	0.26	1.60	NA
Dividends	0.57	0.47	0.33	0.22	0.15	0.12	0.09	0.08	0.08	0.07
Payout Ratio	26%	5%	8%	4%	3%	5%	5%	25%	5%	6%
Prices:High	101.76	144.99	91.63	86.91	82.00	38.25	23.76	22.08	27.75	28.34
Prices:Low	45.03	54.42	59.21	56.31	32.05	21.23	17.85	15.01	12.90	6.84
P/E Ratio:High	47	15	21	17	16	15	13	68	17	25
P/E Ratio:Low	21	6	14	11	6	8	10	46	8	6

Income Statement Analysis (Million $)										
Revenue	3,820	6,529	4,191	3,904	3,620	2,271	1,745	1,095	1,655	1,490
Operating Income	NA	5,144	2,802	1,895	1,992	979	697	648	1,181	697
Depreciation, Depletion and Amortization	1,855	1,520	1,213	817	654	504	442	398	392	370
Interest Expense	101	51.7	76.1	43.2	62.5	63.1	58.7	59.7	45.1	61.0
Pretax Income	872	3,747	1,631	1,913	1,965	926	654	120	631	634
Effective Tax Rate	37.3%	35.0%	33.2%	32.0%	35.9%	32.5%	33.1%	27.2%	36.9%	37.3%
Net Income	547	2,437	1,090	1,300	1,260	625	437	87.2	399	397
S&P Core Earnings	199	2,353	1,083	1,281	1,238	605	412	62.4	376	NA

Balance Sheet & Other Financial Data (Million $)										
Cash	686	331	54.2	218	644	21.0	4.44	9.85	2.51	20.2
Current Assets	1,840	2,108	1,292	1,350	1,563	587	396	395	272	394
Total Assets	18,119	15,951	12,089	9,402	7,753	5,799	4,749	3,814	3,414	3,001
Current Liabilities	1,346	1,765	1,474	1,255	1,172	632	477	276	311	370
Long Term Debt	2,760	1,860	1,185	733	859	1,078	1,109	1,145	856	859
Common Equity	9,998	9,015	6,985	5,547	4,217	2,847	2,098	1,524	1,495	1,234
Total Capital	12,795	13,688	10,246	7,846	6,298	4,925	4,125	3,478	3,050	2,580
Capital Expenditures	3,503	5,195	3,679	2,819	1,725	1,417	1,204	714	974	603
Cash Flow	2,402	3,956	2,296	2,106	1,906	1,118	868	474	780	756
Current Ratio	1.4	1.2	0.9	1.1	1.3	0.9	0.8	1.4	0.9	1.1
% Long Term Debt of Capitalization	21.6	13.6	14.5	9.3	13.6	21.9	26.9	32.9	28.1	33.3
% Return on Assets	3.2	17.4	10.1	15.2	18.6	11.8	10.2	2.4	12.4	14.1
% Return on Equity	5.8	30.5	17.3	26.4	35.5	24.9	23.4	5.0	28.4	34.8

Data as orig reptd.; bef. results of disc opers/spec. items. Per share data adj. for stk. divs.; EPS diluted. E-Estimated. NA-Not Available. NM-Not Meaningful. NR-Not Ranked. UR-Under Review.

Office: 1111 Bagby, Sky Lobby 2, Houston, TX 77002.
Telephone: 713-651-7000.
Email: ir@eogresources.com
Website: http://www.eogresources.com

Chrmn & CEO: M.G. Papa
COO: G.L. Thomas
SVP & General Counsel: F.J. Plaeger, II
CFO: T.K. Driggers

Chief Admin Officer: P.L. Edwards
Investor Contact: M.A. Baldwin (713-651-6364)
Board Members: G. A. Alcorn, C. R. Crisp, J. C. Day, M. G. Papa, H. L. Steward, D. F. Textor, F. G. Wisner

Founded: 1985
Domicile: Delaware
Employees: 2,100

E TRADE Financial Corporation

STANDARD & POOR'S

| S&P Recommendation | HOLD ★★★★☆ | Price $14.04 (as of Oct 22, 2010) | 12-Mo. Target Price $16.00 | Investment Style Large-Cap Growth |

GICS Sector Financials
Sub-Industry Investment Banking & Brokerage

Summary This company provides online discount brokerage, mortgage and banking services, primarily to retail customers.

Key Stock Statistics (Source S&P, Vickers, company reports)

52-Wk Range	$19.90–11.15	S&P Oper. EPS 2010**E**	0.08	Market Capitalization(B)	$3.099	Beta	2.10
Trailing 12-Month EPS	$-5.20	S&P Oper. EPS 2011**E**	0.97	Yield (%)	Nil	S&P 3-Yr. Proj. EPS CAGR(%)	NM
Trailing 12-Month P/E	NM	P/E on S&P Oper. EPS 2010**E**	NM	Dividend Rate/Share	Nil	S&P Credit Rating	CCC+
$10K Invested 5 Yrs Ago	$785	Common Shares Outstg. (M)	220.7	Institutional Ownership (%)	65		

Price Performance

30-Week Mov. Avg. · · · 10-Week Mov. Avg. - - GAAP Earnings vs. Previous Year   Volume Above Avg. STARS
12-Mo. Target Price — Relative Strength — ▲ Up ▼ Down ► No Change   Below Avg.

Options: ASE, CBOE, P, Ph

Analysis prepared by **Royal F. Shepard, CFA** on October 22, 2010, when the stock traded at **$14.14**.

Highlights

➤ We believe ETFC has done well to recapitalize its balance sheet following what we think was a disastrous foray into the mortgage business. It is now in the process of winding down its loan book and deposit base, which should allow it to refocus on its core retail investor segment. Problems at ETFC's bank have not driven away brokerage clients, which continue to increase as banking client accounts decline. In the near-term, an industry slowdown in trading volume may reduce commission fees. Also, low interest rates will likely keep pressure on net interest income until short-term rates rise, which we do not expect until at least mid-2011.

➤ Non-performing loans remain elevated relative to gross loans outstanding, and charge-offs, while declining, remain high. Loan loss provisions should continue to decline through 2011 as ETFC's loan portfolio declines, providing an earnings catalyst. ETFC currently maintains a 7.41% Tier-1 ratio, above its stated goal of 6%.

➤ We project EPS of $0.08 in 2010 and $0.97 in 2011, assuming a return to more normal market conditions and lower loan losses.

Investment Rationale/Risk

➤ We see relative strength in ETFC's brokerage business beginning to offset the overhang from its remaining mortgage assets. While we believe new account growth has lagged that of its online brokerage competitors, we think its balance sheet restructuring will raise confidence. We are encouraged that the growth of home equity loans in the special mention category has slowed. It appears to us that ETFC's home equity loan deterioration has reached a plateau. In the meantime, ETFC expanded the amount of customer assets, as of September 30, by 9% over a year ago. We expect any excess cash balances to be invested in new trading platforms for retail and institutional clients.

➤ Risks to our opinion and target price include greater-than-expected declines in retail trading volume and client assets, and larger write-downs in the remaining mortgage portfolio.

➤ Our 12-month target price of $16 is based on a 0.8X multiple applied to our projection for the company's book value, a discount to peer valuations.

Qualitative Risk Assessment

| LOW | MEDIUM | **HIGH** |

Our risk assessment reflects our concerns about significant industry volatility and ETFC's exposure to residential mortgage and home equity loans, partially offset by our view of its strong client relationships.

Quantitative Evaluations

S&P Quality Ranking   C

| D | **C** | B- | B | B+ | A- | A | A+ |

Relative Strength Rank   WEAK

24

LOWEST = 1   HIGHEST = 99

Revenue/Earnings Data

Revenue (Million $)

	1Q	2Q	3Q	4Q	Year
2010	536.5	534.0	--	--	--
2009	497.3	620.9	575.3	529.1	2,217
2008	529.1	532.3	377.7	486.4	1,926
2007	645.0	663.5	321.2	-2,008	-378.0
2006	598.4	611.4	581.8	628.9	2,420
2005	417.4	387.7	419.8	478.9	1,704

Earnings Per Share ($)

	1Q	2Q	3Q	4Q	Year
2010	-0.20	0.12	E0.03	E0.13	E0.08
2009	-4.10	-2.20	-6.70	-0.40	-11.80
2008	-2.00	-2.40	-6.00	-5.00	-15.90
2007	3.90	3.70	-1.40	-39.80	-34.00
2006	3.30	3.60	3.40	4.00	14.40
2005	2.70	2.90	2.90	3.10	11.60

Fiscal year ended Dec. 31. Next earnings report expected: Late October. EPS Estimates based on S&P Operating Earnings; historical GAAP earnings are as reported.

Dividend Data (Dates: mm/dd Payment Date: mm/dd/yy)

Amount ($)	Date Decl.	Ex-Div. Date	Stk. of Record	Payment Date
1-for-10 REV.	--	06/02	--	06/02/10

Source: Company reports.

The McGraw-Hill Companies

E TRADE Financial Corporation

Business Summary October 22, 2010

CORPORATE OVERVIEW. E Trade Financial Corporation is one of the industry's leading online financial services concerns. The company provides online discount brokerage and banking services, primarily to retail customers. Although most of the company's business is done over the Internet, ETFC also serves customers through branches, automated and live telephone service, and Internet-enabled wireless devices. Retail customers can move money electronically between brokerage, banking and lending accounts. As of December 31, 2009, ETFC had about 4.5 million total retail accounts.

Brokerage customers can buy and sell stocks, bonds, options, futures, and over 7,000 non-proprietary mutual funds. Customers can also obtain streaming quotes and charts, access real-time market commentary and research reports, and perform personalized portfolio tracking. Brokerage customers can obtain margin loans collateralized by their securities. The company uses sophisticated proprietary transaction-enabling technology to automate traditionally labor-intensive transactions. The brokerage business continues to be the primary point of introduction for the majority of ETFC's customers, which are typically self-directed investors.

Through its Banking segment, the company has historically offered residential mortgage products, home equity loans and home equity lines of credit (HELOCs). However, in view of the housing-led recession, ETFC made the decision to exit all loan origination channels in 2008.

In late 2003, the Banking segment began sweeping Brokerage customer money market balances into an FDIC-insured Sweep Deposit Account (SDA) product, which lowered its cost of funds. At the end of 2009, ETFC had $12.5 billion in the SDA product, up from $4.3 billion at the end of 2003. ETFC's loan portfolio consists of first mortgages, the majority of which are adjustable-rate, home equity lines of credit, second mortgage loan products, and consumer loans for RVs, marine, automobile, and credit card loans. Going forward, we expect the asset composition of this segment to change significantly as ETFC completes its restructuring plan announced in September 2007 and realigns its focus on its core retail business.

Company Financials Fiscal Year Ended Dec. 31

Per Share Data ($)	2009	2008	2007	2006	2005	2004	2003	2002	2001	2000
Tangible Book Value	6.70	4.70	10.10	38.70	20.70	45.80	37.30	26.80	25.40	44.30
Cash Flow	-10.80	-14.30	-31.00	16.06	13.55	10.70	5.53	12.00	-2.76	3.66
Earnings	-11.80	-15.90	-34.00	14.40	11.60	9.20	5.50	3.00	-8.10	-0.60
S&P Core Earnings	-11.80	-14.50	-32.60	13.30	8.80	6.60	2.70	2.70	-8.60	NA
Dividends	Nil	Nil	Nil	Nil	Nil	Nil	Nil	Nil	Nil	Nil
Payout Ratio	Nil	Nil	Nil	Nil	Nil	Nil	Nil	Nil	Nil	Nil
Prices:High	29.00	54.80	260.80	277.60	217.10	154.00	129.10	126.40	153.75	342.50
Prices:Low	5.90	7.90	31.50	188.10	105.30	95.10	36.50	28.10	40.70	66.56
P/E Ratio:High	NM	NM	NM	19	19	17	23	42	NM	NM
P/E Ratio:Low	NM	NM	NM	13	9	10	7	9	NM	NM

Income Statement Analysis (Million $)

	2009	2008	2007	2006	2005	2004	2003	2002	2001	2000
Commissions	548	516	694	625	459	350	337	302	407	739
Interest Income	1,833	2,470	3,570	2,775	1,650	1,146	893	946	1,160	960
Total Revenue	1,291	3,128	2,978	3,840	2,537	2,077	2,009	1,903	2,062	1,973
Interest Expense	855	1,202	2,133	1,527	853	558	532	609	832	630
Pretax Income	-1,835	-1,279	-2,178	929	676	514	310	194	-310	104
Effective Tax Rate	548.0%	36.7%	33.8%	32.5%	34.0%	31.6%	36.2%	43.9%	NM	81.8%
Net Income	-1,298	-809	-1,442	627	446	351	203	107	-271	19.2
S&P Core Earnings	-1,297	-742	-1,378	580	339	247	101	96.1	-291	NA

Balance Sheet & Other Financial Data (Million $)

	2009	2008	2007	2006	2005	2004	2003	2002	2001	2000
Total Assets	47,366	48,538	56,846	53,739	44,568	31,033	26,049	21,534	18,172	17,317
Cash Items	5,067	5,051	1,778	1,212	844	940	921	2,223	1,601	301
Receivables	3,827	2,791	7,179	7,636	7,174	3,035	2,298	1,500	2,139	6,543
Securities Owned	13,358	10,862	11,385	13,922	12,565	12,589	9,876	8,702	4,726	985
Securities Borrowed	Nil	Nil	Nil	Nil	Nil	Nil	Nil	Nil	Nil	NA
Due Brokers & Customers	5,234	3,753	5,515	7,825	7,316	3,619	3,696	2,792	2,700	6,056
Other Liabilities	33,177	35,090	38,033	NA	NA	NA	NA	NA	NA	NA
Capitalization:Debt	5,206	7,104	10,469	7,166	6,189	586	695	907	605	3,336
Capitalization:Equity	3,750	2,592	2,829	4,196	3,400	2,228	1,918	1,506	1,571	1,857
Capitalization:Total	8,956	9,696	13,298	11,363	9,589	2,814	2,614	2,412	2,175	5,192
% Return on Revenue	NM	NM	NM	20.7	68.4	18.0	11.8	5.4	NM	1.6
% Return on Assets	NM	NM	NM	1.3	1.2	1.2	0.9	0.5	NM	0.2
% Return on Equity	NM	NM	NM	16.5	15.9	16.9	11.9	7.0	NM	1.2

Data as orig reptd.; bef. results of disc opers/spec. items. Per share data adj. for stk. divs.; EPS diluted. Total net revenues reported in quarterly table. E-Estimated. NA-Not Available. NM-Not Meaningful. NR-Not Ranked. UR-Under Review.

Office: 135 East 57th Street, New York, NY 10022.
Telephone: 646-521-4300.
Email: ir@etrade.com
Website: http://www.etrade.com

Chrmn: R. Druskin
Vice Chrmn: S.H. Willard
CEO: S.J. Freiberg
COO, EVP & CIO: G. Framke

EVP, CFO & Chief Acctg Officer: B.P. Nolop
Board Members: R. Druskin, R. D. Fisher, S. J. Freiberg, K. C. Griffin, F. W. Kanner, M. K. Parks, C. C. Raffaeli, L. E. Randall, J. L. Sclafani, J. M. Velli, D. L. Weaver, S. H. Willard

Founded: 1982
Domicile: Delaware
Employees: 3,084

EQT Corp

STANDARD &POOR'S

S&P Recommendation **BUY** ★★★★☆

Price	12-Mo. Target Price	Investment Style
$37.42 (as of Oct 22, 2010)	$46.00	Large-Cap Growth

GICS Sector Energy
Sub-Industry Oil & Gas Exploration & Production

Summary This energy company focuses on natural gas production, transmission and distribution, and energy management services.

Key Stock Statistics (Source S&P, Vickers, company reports)

52-Wk Range	$47.43–32.23	S&P Oper. EPS 2010E	1.55	Market Capitalization(B)	$5.580	Beta	0.77
Trailing 12-Month EPS	$1.29	S&P Oper. EPS 2011E	2.08	Yield (%)	2.35	S&P 3-Yr. Proj. EPS CAGR(%)	19
Trailing 12-Month P/E	29.0	P/E on S&P Oper. EPS 2010E	24.1	Dividend Rate/Share	$0.88	S&P Credit Rating	BBB
$10K Invested 5 Yrs Ago	$11,393	Common Shares Outstg. (M)	149.1	Institutional Ownership (%)	80		

Price Performance

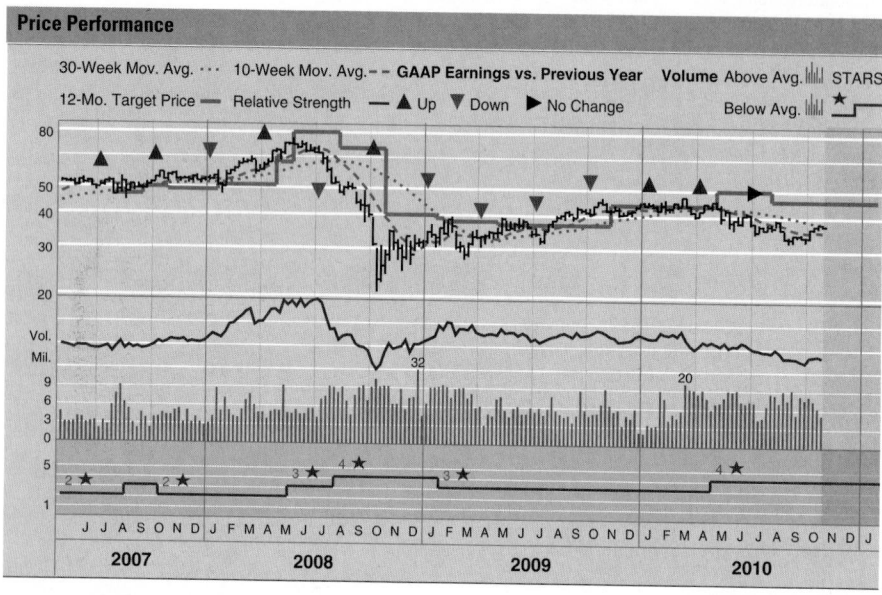

- 30-Week Mov. Avg. · · · 10-Week Mov. Avg. - - - GAAP Earnings vs. Previous Year Volume Above Avg. STARS
- 12-Mo. Target Price — Relative Strength — ▲ Up ▼ Down ▶ No Change Below Avg. ★

Options: ASE, CBOE, P, Ph

Analysis prepared by **Christopher B. Muir** on August 03, 2010, when the stock traded at **$ 38.20**.

Highlights

➤ We expect 2010 revenues to rise 2.9%, driven by higher average realized commodity prices during the year at EQT's exploration and production business. We see revenues from these unregulated businesses rising 14%, helped by higher volumes. In 2011, we forecast revenues will rise 13% as we anticipate slightly rising commodity prices and increasing volumes. We see unregulated revenues rising 11% next year.

➤ We anticipate that 2010 operating margins will rise to 35.5%, from 30.2%, on wider gross margins, lower production costs, and lower per-revenue operations and maintenance expenses, partly offset by higher depreciation & depltion and administrative costs. We see pretax margins rising to 26.2%, from 22.1%, as we expect higher interest expense and higher non-operating income. We expect operating and pretax margins in 2011 of 38.8% and 32.5%, respectively.

➤ Assuming an effective income tax rate of 34.4%, we project 2010 operating EPS of $1.55, up 14% from $1.36, excluding $0.17 of net nonrecurring charges, in 2009. Our 2011 EPS estimate is $2.08, up 34%.

Investment Rationale/Risk

➤ We like EQT's horizontal drilling program, which includes re-entry wells into existing fields. We believe results have been positive in the program so far. We expect EQT to use cash generated by recent non-core asset sales for additional investment in E&P operations. Much of the company's expansion has been in the Huron shale, but we think it also has opportunities and has shown good early results in the Berea Sandstone wells, in the Devonian shale re-entry wells, and in the Marcellus shale.

➤ Risks to our opinion and target price include lower-than-expected E&P production growth, energy prices and utility income, as well as higher-than-expected interest rates.

➤ EQT's shares recently traded at 18.5X our 2011 EPS estimate, a 30% premium to gas distribution peers. Our 12-month target price of $46 is 22.1X our 2011 EPS estimate, an even larger premium. We believe the premium is warranted by our expectation for superior EPS growth driven by EQT's unregulated businesses, partly offset by the riskier nature of its unregulated businesses.

Qualitative Risk Assessment

LOW	MEDIUM	HIGH

Our risk assessment is based on our view that the company's riskier exploration and production and energy marketing operations are balanced by its regulated gas businesses.

Quantitative Evaluations

S&P Quality Ranking B+

D	C	B-	B	B+	A-	A	A+

Relative Strength Rank MODERATE

51

LOWEST = 1   HIGHEST = 99

Revenue/Earnings Data

Revenue (Million $)

	1Q	2Q	3Q	4Q	Year
2010	436.6	257.5	--	--	--
2009	469.4	238.0	218.4	344.0	1,270
2008	535.4	334.0	297.8	408.9	1,576
2007	456.6	293.2	226.8	384.8	1,361
2006	430.1	251.2	232.8	353.8	1,268
2005	401.3	230.2	229.4	392.9	1,254

Earnings Per Share ($)

	1Q	2Q	3Q	4Q	Year
2010	0.65	0.20	E0.25	E0.47	E1.55
2009	0.55	0.20	0.02	0.42	1.19
2008	0.57	0.42	0.73	0.26	2.00
2007	0.46	0.87	0.27	0.49	2.10
2006	0.59	0.36	0.26	0.56	1.77
2005	0.60	0.47	0.37	0.65	2.09

Fiscal year ended Dec. 31. Next earnings report expected: Late October. EPS Estimates based on S&P Operating Earnings; historical GAAP earnings are as reported.

Dividend Data (Dates: mm/dd Payment Date: mm/dd/yy)

Amount ($)	Date Decl.	Ex-Div. Date	Stk. of Record	Payment Date
0.220	01/20	02/10	02/12	03/01/10
0.220	04/21	05/05	05/07	06/01/10
0.220	07/14	08/04	08/06	09/01/10
0.220	10/20	11/03	11/05	12/01/10

Dividends have been paid since 1950. Source: Company reports.

EQT Corp

STANDARD &POOR'S

Business Summary August 03, 2010

CORPORATE OVERVIEW. EQT Corp. (formerly Equitable Resources Inc.; name changed in February 2009) is a vertically integrated energy company operating through three business segments: EQT Production (EP), EQT Midstream (EM) and EQT Distribution (ED). The EP unit (36% of 2009 operating income before unallocated expenses) is engaged in exploration and production of natural gas and oil, chiefly in the Appalachian Basin. The EM unit (45%) provides gathering, processing, transmission and storage services to EP and independent third parties. Its transmission system is located throughout north central West Virginia and southwestern Pennsylvania, and its gas gathering assets are located in Kentucky, West Virginia, Virginia and Pennsylvania. The ED unit (19%) operates a regulated natural gas utility in southwestern Pennsylvania and a small gathering system in Pennsylvania, and provides off-system sales activities.

CORPORATE STRATEGY. The ED unit is focused on earning a competitive return on its asset base through regulatory mechanisms and operational efficiency. ED believes it can achieve earnings growth by establishing a reputation for excellent customer service, effectively managing its capital spending, improving the efficiency of its work force through superior work management, and continuing to leverage technology throughout its operations. In 2008, ED

filed a base rate case and agreed to a settlement of the rate case that requested a $38 million increase in revenues. In January 2009, the settlement was approved by an administrative law judge.

The EP unit's business strategy is to focus on increased drilling and development in the Appalachian basin. EP also plans to create additional reserve potential through emerging development investments. To achieve maximum value from its existing assets, EP drills multilateral and stacked multilateral horizontal wells, refracs existing wells and drills re-entry wells where low pressured vertical shale wells were previously drilled.

The EM unit's strategy focuses on building a long-term growth platform to facilitate the development of EP's growing reserve base in the Huron play, and provides opportunities to sell capacity to third parties by connecting wells to existing midstream infrastructure in an effort to fill existing capacity.

Company Financials Fiscal Year Ended Dec. 31

Per Share Data ($)	2009	2008	2007	2006	2005	2004	2003	2002	2001	2000
Tangible Book Value	16.43	15.67	11.52	7.78	2.96	6.75	7.33	5.83	6.18	4.86
Cash Flow	2.68	3.06	2.99	2.59	2.94	2.88	3.40	1.72	1.70	1.54
Earnings	1.19	2.00	2.10	1.77	2.09	2.22	1.37	1.18	1.15	0.80
S&P Core Earnings	1.20	2.08	1.45	1.79	1.59	1.33	1.35	1.11	1.09	NA
Dividends	0.88	0.88	0.88	0.87	0.82	0.72	0.49	0.34	0.31	0.29
Payout Ratio	74%	44%	42%	49%	39%	32%	35%	28%	27%	37%
Prices:High	46.80	76.14	56.75	44.48	41.18	30.59	21.71	18.78	20.25	16.69
Prices:Low	27.39	20.71	39.26	31.59	27.89	21.05	17.22	14.34	13.00	8.06
P/E Ratio:High	39	38	27	25	20	14	16	16	18	21
P/E Ratio:Low	23	10	19	18	13	9	13	12	11	10

Income Statement Analysis (Million $)	2009	2008	2007	2006	2005	2004	2003	2002	2001	2000
Revenue	1,270	1,576	1,361	1,268	1,254	1,192	1,047	1,069	1,764	1,652
Operating Income	NA	602	432	470	445	388	380	352	328	312
Depreciation	196	137	110	100	93.5	83.1	78.1	69.4	73.2	97.8
Interest Expense	112	58.4	54.4	47.1	44.4	49.2	45.8	38.8	41.1	75.7
Pretax Income	254	411	402	326	412	424	257	235	240	163
Effective Tax Rate	38.1%	37.7%	35.9%	33.7%	37.2%	33.7%	31.9%	33.0%	36.6%	35.0%
Net Income	157	256	257	216	259	280	174	151	152	106
S&P Core Earnings	158	266	177	219	197	168	170	141	143	NA

Balance Sheet & Other Financial Data (Million $)	2009	2008	2007	2006	2005	2004	2003	2002	2001	2000
Cash	NA	Nil	81.7	Nil	75.0	Nil	37.3	17.7	92.6	52.0
Current Assets	695	927	742	701	1,097	653	550	430	613	615
Total Assets	5,957	5,330	3,937	3,257	3,342	3,197	2,940	2,437	2,519	2,456
Current Liabilities	613	1,043	1,519	1,080	2,092	1,015	703	552	612	877
Long Term Debt	1,949	1,249	754	754	763	618	681	586	396	413
Common Equity	2,151	2,050	1,097	946	354	875	965	779	846	694
Total Capital	4,100	3,304	2,252	2,038	1,142	1,990	2,118	1,728	1,621	1,370
Capital Expenditures	952	1,344	777	405	276	202	222	218	133	124
Cash Flow	353	392	367	316	352	363	430	220	225	204
Current Ratio	1.1	0.9	0.5	0.6	0.5	0.6	0.8	0.8	1.0	0.7
% Long Term Debt of Capitalization	Nil	37.8	33.5	37.0	66.9	31.0	32.2	33.9	24.4	30.1
% Net Income of Revenue	12.4	16.2	18.9	17.0	20.6	23.5	16.6	14.1	8.6	6.4
% Return on Assets	2.8	5.5	7.2	6.5	7.9	9.1	6.5	6.1	6.1	5.0
% Return on Equity	NA	16.2	25.2	33.2	42.1	30.4	19.9	18.5	19.7	15.9

Data as orig reptd.; bef. results of disc opers/spec. items. Per share data adj. for stk. divs.; EPS diluted. E-Estimated. NA-Not Available. NM-Not Meaningful. NR-Not Ranked. UR-Under Review.

Office: EQT Plaza 625 Liberty Avenue, Suite 1700, Pittsburgh, PA 15222.
Telephone: 412-553-5700.
Website: http://www.eqt.com
Chrmn: M.S. Gerber

Pres, CEO & COO: D.L. Porges
SVP & CFO: P.P. Conti
Chief Acctg Officer & Cntlr: T.Z. Bone
Secy: K.L. Sachse

Investor Contact: P.J. Kane (412-553-7833)
Board Members: V. A. Bailey, P. G. Behrman, A. B. Cary, Jr., M. S. Gerber, B. S. Jeremiah, G. L. Miles, Jr., D. L. Porges, J. E. Rohr, D. S. Shapira, S. A. Thorington, L. T. Todd, Jr.

Founded: 1926
Domicile: Pennsylvania
Employees: 1,800

The McGraw-Hill Companies

Equifax Inc.

STANDARD &POOR'S

S&P Recommendation HOLD ★★★☆☆

Price	**12-Mo. Target Price**	**Investment Style**
$32.72 (as of Oct 22, 2010)	$35.00	Large-Cap Growth

GICS Sector Industrials
Sub-Industry Research & Consulting Services

Summary This company is a leading worldwide source of consumer and commercial credit information.

Key Stock Statistics (Source S&P, Vickers, company reports)

52-Wk Range	$36.63– 27.21	S&P Oper. EPS 2010E	2.32	Market Capitalization(B)	$4.091	Beta	1.15
Trailing 12-Month EPS	$1.94	S&P Oper. EPS 2011E	2.50	Yield (%)	0.49	S&P 3-Yr. Proj. EPS CAGR(%)	10
Trailing 12-Month P/E	16.9	P/E on S&P Oper. EPS 2010E	14.1	Dividend Rate/Share	$0.16	S&P Credit Rating	BBB+
$10K Invested 5 Yrs Ago	$9,148	Common Shares Outstg. (M)	125.0	Institutional Ownership (%)	76		

Price Performance

30-Week Mov. Avg. · · · 10-Week Mov. Avg. - - GAAP Earnings vs. Previous Year   Volume Above Avg. STARS
12-Mo. Target Price — Relative Strength — ▲ Up ▼ Down ▶ No Change   Below Avg.

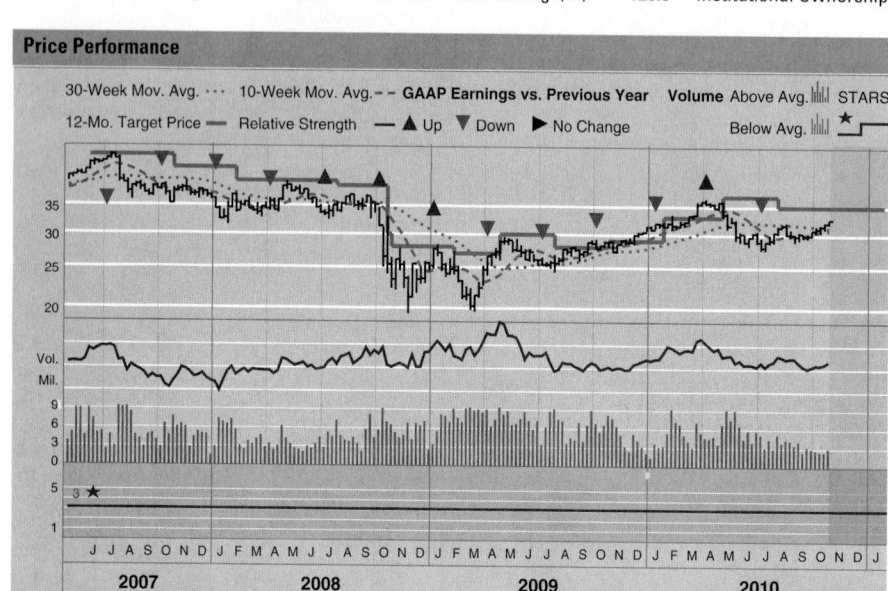

Options: ASE, P, Ph

Analysis prepared by **Zaineb Bokhari** on August 16, 2010, when the stock traded at **$ 30.05**.

Highlights

➤ We expect organic growth for many of EFX's domestic credit- and mortgage-related offerings to remain challenged by prevailing economic conditions, but see TALX and Latin America as drivers in 2010. We project operating revenues of $1.84 billion, aided by the acquisitions of IXI and Rapid Reporting Verification (both completed in the fourth quarter 2009), partly offset by the divestiture of Direct Marketing Services. We forecast sales growth of approximately 6% for 2011.

➤ EFX flattened and realigned its organizational structure, yielding cost savings, and we expect the company to continue to focus on fine-tuning existing operations, cut costs, and pay down debt as it seeks to preserve and grow operating margins. We see modestly wider operating margins in 2010 and 2011 as sales growth likely resumes, helped by contributions from acquired and organic product initiatives.

➤ We expect interest expenses to track debt levels after recent acquisition activity, but see some decline as EFX pays down debt. We estimate operating EPS of $2.32 in 2010 (before acquisition-related intangibles), rising to $2.50 in 2011.

Investment Rationale/Risk

➤ International markets have offered attractive avenues for growth, in our view, particularly in Latin America. We see this being negatively impacted, however, by currency fluctuations and weakness in Europe. EFX's largest and most profitable segment, U.S. Consumer Information Solutions, has been in decline since late 2007, but we expect this to slow in 2010, helped by acquisition and stabilization in the broader economy. We look for a rising contribution from TALX, but expect this to limit near-term operating margin expansion from expense reductions. We are optimistic about settlement and analytical tools and services, which we consider to be counter-cyclical.

➤ Risks to our recommendation and target price include increasing competition from the other major credit bureaus and data providers. We are also concerned about sharp deterioration in EFX's U.S. Consumer information solutions segments as well as in international markets.

➤ Our 12-month target price of $35 is derived by applying a 14.0X P/E multiple, within the three-year average range for EFX shares of 10.5X-16.0X, to our 2011 EPS estimate.

Qualitative Risk Assessment

LOW	MEDIUM	HIGH

Our risk assessment reflects our view that a majority of the company's domestic operations have exposure to consumer financial services. We are also concerned global economic conditions, particularly in Europe, offset by our positive outlook for the company's Latin American operations, which we see expanding faster than its domestic operations.

Quantitative Evaluations

S&P Quality Ranking B+

D	C	B-	B	B+	A-	A	A+

Relative Strength Rank MODERATE

66

LOWEST = 1   HIGHEST = 99

Revenue/Earnings Data

Revenue (Million $)

	1Q	2Q	3Q	4Q	Year
2010	461.3	460.7	--	--	--
2009	452.9	455.4	451.9	464.3	1,825
2008	503.1	501.9	484.1	446.6	1,936
2007	405.1	454.5	492.5	490.9	1,843
2006	374.0	387.7	394.6	390.0	1,546
2005	343.4	363.4	375.3	361.3	1,443

Earnings Per Share ($)

2010	0.44	0.45	E0.59	E0.59	E2.32
2009	0.43	0.47	0.47	0.47	1.83
2008	0.50	0.54	0.56	0.50	2.09
2007	0.54	0.51	0.48	0.49	2.02
2006	0.48	0.53	0.61	0.50	2.12
2005	0.44	0.47	0.47	0.48	1.86

Fiscal year ended Dec. 31. Next earnings report expected: Late October. EPS Estimates based on S&P Operating Earnings; historical GAAP earnings are as reported.

Dividend Data (Dates: mm/dd Payment Date: mm/dd/yy)

Amount ($)	Date Decl.	Ex-Div. Date	Stk. of Record	Payment Date
0.040	11/06	11/20	11/24	12/15/09
0.040	02/05	02/18	02/22	03/15/10
0.040	05/07	05/21	05/25	06/15/10
0.040	08/17	08/23	08/25	09/15/10

Dividends have been paid since 1914. Source: Company reports.

Equifax Inc.

Business Summary August 16, 2010

CORPORATE OVERVIEW. Equifax is one of three global providers of consumer and commercial credit information. Equifax collects, organizes and manages credit, financial, demographic and marketing information regarding individuals and businesses, which the company collects from various sources. These sources include financial or credit granting institutions (which provide accounts receivable information), government organizations and consumers. The company maintains information in proprietary databases regarding consumers and businesses worldwide. EFX amasses and processes this data using proprietary systems, and makes the data available to customers in various formats.

Products and services include consumer credit information, information database management, marketing information, business credit information, decisioning and analytical tools, and identity verification services that enable businesses to make informed decisions about extending credit or providing services, managing portfolio risk, and developing marketing strategies. According to the company, EFX allows consumers to manage and protect their financial affairs through products that the company sells directly to individuals using the Internet.

Equifax derived 82% of operating revenue from North America in 2009, up from 80% in 2008. The U.S. accounted for 75% of operating revenues in 2009, up from 73% in 2008, while EFX's Canadian Consumer business accounted for 7% of total revenues in 2009 (unchanged from 2008). The company's largest segment, U.S. Consumer Information Solutions (45% of revenues in 2009, down from 46% in 2008), includes Consumer Information Solutions (credit information regarding individuals; 29% of 2009 revenues, down from 31% in 2008), Mortgage Reporting Solutions (credit loan origination information; 5%, 4%), Credit Marketing Services (6%, 7%) and Direct Marketing Services (5%, 5%). The company sold its Direct Marketing business in mid 2010. Other North American operating segments include Personal Solutions (credit information sales to consumers; 8%, 8%) and Commercial Solutions (credit information concerning businesses; 4%, 4%). TALX, acquired in May 2007 (employment, income verification and human resources outsourcing services) accounted for just under 19% of revenues in 2009 (16%).

Company Financials Fiscal Year Ended Dec. 31

Per Share Data ($)	2009	2008	2007	2006	2005	2004	2003	2002	2001	2000
Tangible Book Value	NM	NM	NM	NM	NM	NM	NM	NM	NM	NM
Cash Flow	3.07	2.60	2.48	2.76	2.49	2.39	2.00	1.96	1.61	2.77
Earnings	1.83	2.09	2.02	2.12	1.86	1.78	1.31	1.39	0.84	1.68
S&P Core Earnings	1.83	1.90	2.02	2.07	1.88	1.59	1.18	1.04	0.52	NA
Dividends	0.16	0.16	0.16	0.16	0.15	0.11	0.08	0.08	0.25	0.37
Payout Ratio	9%	8%	8%	8%	8%	6%	6%	6%	29%	22%
Prices:High	31.64	39.95	46.30	41.64	39.00	28.46	27.59	31.30	38.76	36.50
Prices:Low	19.63	19.38	35.22	30.15	26.97	22.60	17.84	18.95	18.60	19.88
P/E Ratio:High	17	19	23	20	21	16	21	23	46	22
P/E Ratio:Low	11	9	17	14	14	13	14	14	22	12

Income Statement Analysis (Million $)	2009	2008	2007	2006	2005	2004	2003	2002	2001	2000
Revenue	1,825	1,936	1,843	1,546	1,443	1,273	1,225	1,109	1,139	1,966
Operating Income	591	560	548	519	504	459	438	432	420	604
Depreciation	159	66.3	62.0	82.8	82.2	81.1	95.3	80.5	106	149
Interest Expense	57.0	71.3	58.5	31.9	35.6	34.9	39.6	41.2	47.8	76.0
Pretax Income	357	412	431	420	396	388	286	317	205	385
Effective Tax Rate	32.6%	32.3%	35.3%	33.6%	36.5%	38.1%	36.5%	39.0%	41.7%	40.8%
Net Income	234	273	273	275	247	237	179	191	117	228
S&P Core Earnings	234	247	273	268	248	211	162	146	73.6	NA

Balance Sheet & Other Financial Data (Million $)	2009	2008	2007	2006	2005	2004	2003	2002	2001	2000
Cash	103	58.2	81.6	67.8	37.5	52.1	39.3	30.5	33.2	89.4
Current Assets	417	354	425	345	280	300	286	286	358	605
Total Assets	3,551	3,260	3,524	1,791	1,832	1,557	1,553	1,507	1,423	2,070
Current Liabilities	492	318	547	582	295	457	355	428	276	426
Long Term Debt	991	1,187	1,165	174	464	399	663	691	694	994
Common Equity	1,601	1,312	1,399	838	820	524	372	221	244	384
Total Capital	2,606	2,715	2,842	1,083	1,410	961	1,079	938	1,026	1,467
Capital Expenditures	70.7	111	119	52.0	17.2	16.5	14.6	12.8	13.0	37.1
Cash Flow	393	339	335	357	329	318	274	272	224	377
Current Ratio	0.9	1.1	0.8	0.6	1.0	0.7	0.8	0.7	1.3	1.4
% Long Term Debt of Capitalization	38.0	43.7	41.0	16.1	32.9	41.5	61.5	73.7	67.6	67.7
% Net Income of Revenue	12.8	14.1	14.8	17.8	17.1	18.6	14.6	17.2	10.3	11.6
% Return on Assets	6.9	8.0	10.3	15.2	14.5	15.3	11.7	13.1	7.1	11.7
% Return on Equity	16.1	20.1	24.4	33.1	36.7	53.0	60.3	82.4	37.4	76.1

Data as orig reptd.; bef. results of disc opers/spec. items. Per share data adj. for stk. divs.; EPS diluted. E-Estimated. NA-Not Available. NM-Not Meaningful. NR-Not Ranked. UR-Under Review.

Office: 1550 Peachtree St NW, Atlanta, GA 30309.
Telephone: 404-885-8000.
Email: investor@equifax.com
Website: http://www.equifax.com

Chrmn & CEO: R.F. Smith
COO: A.S. Bodea
SVP, Chief Acctg Officer & Cntlr: N.M. King
CFO: L. Adrean

Secy: D.C. Arvidson
Board Members: J. E. Copeland, Jr., R. D. Daleo, W. W. Driver, Jr., M. L. Feidler, L. P. Humann, S. S. Marshall, J. A. McKinley, Jr., R. F. Smith, M. B. Templeton

Founded: 1913
Domicile: Georgia
Employees: 6,600

Equity Residential

STANDARD &POOR'S

S&P Recommendation	HOLD ★★★★★	Price $50.83 (as of Oct 22, 2010)	12-Mo. Target Price $48.00	Investment Style Large-Cap Value

GICS Sector Financials
Sub-Industry Residential REITS

Summary This equity real estate investment trust owns and operates a nationally diversified portfolio of apartment properties.

Key Stock Statistics (Source S&P, Vickers, company reports)

52-Wk Range	$52.20–27.54	S&P FFO/Sh. 2010E	2.20	Market Capitalization(B)	$14.408	Beta	1.29
Trailing 12-Month FFO/Share	NA	S&P FFO/Sh. 2011E	2.30	Yield (%)	2.66	S&P 3-Yr. FFO/Sh. Proj. CAGR(%)	-5
Trailing 12-Month P/FFO	NA	P/FFO on S&P FFO/Sh. 2010E	23.1	Dividend Rate/Share	$1.35	S&P Credit Rating	BBB+
$10K Invested 5 Yrs Ago	$16,847	Common Shares Outstg. (M)	283.5	Institutional Ownership (%)	92		

Price Performance

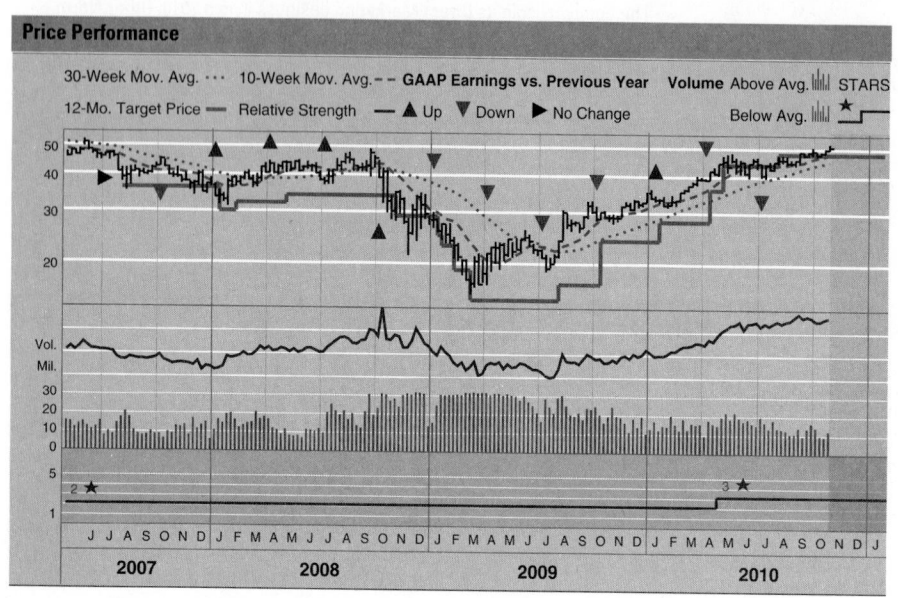

- 30-Week Mov. Avg. · · · 10-Week Mov. Avg. - - GAAP Earnings vs. Previous Year   Volume Above Avg. STARS
- 12-Mo. Target Price — Relative Strength ▲ Up ▼ Down ▶ No Change   Below Avg.   ★

Options: ASE, CBOE, Ph

Analysis prepared by **Royal F. Shepard, CFA** on August 04, 2010, when the stock traded at **$ 46.82**.

Highlights

► We think higher occupancy levels will lead to improved pricing power in the second half of 2010. During the second quarter, EQR increased average occupancy 150 basis points, to 95.1%. In our estimation, rents on new leases will begin to exceed expiring contracts during the third quarter. On a same-property basis, we estimate rental revenues will remain about flat for all of 2010, before rebounding 2%-3% in 2011.

► We expect EQR to take advantage of depressed markets conditions to increase its 2010 investment in property acquisitions. In the first half, the trust acquired eight properties at an aggregate purchase price of $849.4 million. For the full year, the trust has budgeted $1.25 billion for new purchases. Due to a decline in construction costs, EQR could also accelerate its investment in new development projects. As of June 30, 2010, it had five communities under way at a total budgeted cost of $615 million.

► We forecast 2010 FFO of $2.20 per share, excluding gains from debt buybacks or asset sales. Our outlook reflects improving rental rates as leases roll over and an increased contribution from acquisitions, partially offset by higher operating costs and real estate taxes.

Investment Rationale/Risk

► We like EQR's long-term focus on coastal markets, which we believe have favorable demographic trends. We think a gradually improving economic environment will begin to increase operating results by the second half of 2010, including higher effective rents on lease renewals. We expect that an active acquisition program will also begin to contribute to earnings by 2011. Recently at about 21X our 2010 FFO per share outlook, EQR is trading close to apartment REIT peers.

► Risks to our recommendation and target price include slower-than-anticipated job growth, increased competition from excess inventories of unsold single-family homes and condominiums, and a decline in property values due to investor demand.

► Our 12-month target price of $48 is based on a multiple of 21.8X our 2010 FFO per share estimate of $2.10, a modest premium to peers. We arrive at intrinsic value of $47 based on our estimate of net asset value using recent market transactions and a 5.5% one-year cash return.

Qualitative Risk Assessment

LOW	MEDIUM	HIGH

Our risk assessment reflects our view that EQR is one of the largest, most diversified residential REITs and has below-average financial leverage and strong coverage of fixed charges.

Quantitative Evaluations

S&P Quality Ranking   B+

D	C	B-	B	B+	A-	A	A+

Relative Strength Rank   MODERATE

70

LOWEST = 1   HIGHEST = 99

Revenue/FFO Data

Revenue (Million $)

	1Q	2Q	3Q	4Q	Year
2010	488.7	510.9	--	--	--
2009	515.1	505.2	492.8	483.0	1,944
2008	507.4	525.6	536.9	533.3	2,103
2007	483.2	507.2	522.6	528.1	2,038
2006	470.5	490.6	511.5	517.9	1,990
2005	461.6	478.9	495.5	518.9	1,955

FFO Per Share ($)

	1Q	2Q	3Q	4Q	Year
2010	0.52	0.58	E0.56	E0.57	E2.20
2009	0.57	0.63	0.56	0.46	2.12
2008	0.59	0.64	0.65	0.29	2.18
2007	0.55	0.60	0.58	0.67	2.39
2006	0.56	0.61	0.62	0.49	2.27
2005	0.74	0.56	0.56	0.66	2.52

Fiscal year ended Dec. 31. Next earnings report expected: Late October. FFO Estimates based on S&P Funds From Operations Est..

Dividend Data (Dates: mm/dd Payment Date: mm/dd/yy)

Amount ($)	Date Decl.	Ex-Div. Date	Stk. of Record	Payment Date
0.338	11/30	12/17	12/21	01/08/10
0.338	03/02	03/11	03/15	04/09/10
0.338	06/08	06/16	06/18	07/09/10
0.338	09/10	09/16	09/20	10/08/10

Dividends have been paid since 1993. Source: Company reports.

Equity Residential

Business Summary August 04, 2010

CORPORATE OVERVIEW. Equity Residential is one of the largest publicly held owners of multi-family properties. Structured as a real estate investment trust (REIT), it owns, manages and operates properties through its 93.4% interest in its operating limited partnership. At December 31, 2009, EQR owned or had interests in 495 multi-family properties with 137,007 units in 23 states. The trust adopted its current name in May 2002.

During 2006, EQR sold a majority of its ranch style properties, leaving a focus on garden and mid-rise/high-rise assets. Garden-style properties have two or three floors, while mid-rise/high-rise properties have more than three floors. At the end of December 2009, the trust's largest geographic markets as measured by net operating income were the Washington DC/N. Virginia (10.1%) market, New York Metro Area (9.5%), South Florida (9.2%), Boston (8.4%), and Los Angeles (7.9%). Average occupancy during the fourth quarter of 2009 was 94.0%, just behind 94.2% for the same period in 2008.

MARKET PROFILE. The U.S. housing market is highly fragmented and is broadly characterized by two types of housing units, multifamily and single-family. At the end of 2009, the U.S. Census Bureau estimated that there were 130.6 million housing units in the country, an increase of 0.9% from 2008. Partially due to the high fragmentation, and the fact that residents have the option of either being owners or tenants (renters), the housing market can be highly competitive. Main demand drivers for apartments are household formation and employment growth. We estimate 0.5 million new households were formed in 2009. Supply is created by new housing unit construction, which could consist of single-family homes, or multifamily apartment buildings or condominiums. We estimate that 0.55 million housing units were started in 2009, down about 39% from 2008. Multifamily housing starts, for structures with more than 5 units, dropped significantly more, declining about 63%.

With apartment tenants on relatively short leases compared to those of commercial and industrial properties, we believe apartment REITs are generally more sensitive to changes in market conditions than REITs in other property categories. Results could be hurt by new construction that adds new space in excess of actual demand. Trends in home price affordability also affect both rent levels and the level of new construction, since the relative price attractiveness of owning versus renting is an important factor in consumer decision making.

Company Financials Fiscal Year Ended Dec. 31

Per Share Data ($)	2009	2008	2007	2006	2005	2004	2003	2002	2001	2000
Tangible Book Value	17.28	17.55	17.79	18.58	16.65	15.28	15.43	15.57	16.20	20.82
Earnings	-0.02	0.09	0.23	0.20	0.51	0.37	0.43	0.78	1.36	1.67
S&P Core Earnings	0.05	0.10	0.21	0.20	0.51	0.34	0.41	0.72	1.38	NA
Dividends	1.64	1.93	1.87	1.79	1.74	1.73	1.73	1.73	1.68	1.58
Payout Ratio	NM	NM	NM	NM	NM	NM	NM	222%	124%	94%
Prices:High	36.38	49.00	56.46	61.50	42.17	36.75	30.30	30.96	30.45	28.63
Prices:Low	15.68	21.27	33.79	38.84	30.70	26.65	23.12	21.55	24.80	19.34
P/E Ratio:High	NM	NM	NM	NM	83	99	70	40	22	17
P/E Ratio:Low	NM	NM	NM	NM	60	72	54	28	18	12

Income Statement Analysis (Million $)	2009	2008	2007	2006	2005	2004	2003	2002	2001	2000
Rental Income	1,933	2,092	2,029	1,981	1,944	1,878	1,809	1,970	2,075	1,960
Mortgage Income	Nil	Nil	Nil	Nil	Nil	Nil	Nil	Nil	8.79	11.2
Total Income	1,944	2,103	2,038	1,990	1,955	1,890	1,823	1,994	2,171	2,030
General Expenses	821	890	883	881	925	870	802	841	924	812
Interest Expense	504	489	495	436	391	349	333	343	361	388
Provision for Losses	Nil	Nil	Nil	Nil	Nil	Nil	Nil	Nil	Nil	Nil
Depreciation	582	591	588	563	508	484	444	462	457	450
Net Income	8.27	40.9	93.0	101	152	135	212	302	474	555
S&P Core Earnings	13.3	26.4	58.3	59.5	98.5	74.5	86.4	194	374	NA

Balance Sheet & Other Financial Data (Million $)	2009	2008	2007	2006	2005	2004	2003	2002	2001	2000
Cash	193	891	71.0	260	88.8	83.5	49.6	540	449	417
Total Assets	15,418	16,535	15,690	15,062	14,099	12,645	11,467	11,811	12,236	12,264
Real Estate Investment	18,465	18,690	18,333	17,235	16,597	14,864	12,874	13,046	13,016	12,591
Loss Reserve	Nil	Nil	Nil	Nil	Nil	Nil	Nil	Nil	Nil	Nil
Net Investment	14,588	15,129	15,163	14,217	13,709	12,264	10,578	10,934	11,297	11,239
Short Term Debt	602	863	680	921	NA	NA	NA	334	699	Nil
Capitalization:Debt	8,790	9,638	8,829	7,136	7,032	5,642	4,836	5,050	5,044	5,706
Capitalization:Equity	4,839	4,789	4,853	5,498	4,891	4,436	4,345	4,251	4,447	4,436
Capitalization:Total	14,223	14,954	14,929	13,432	12,850	10,714	10,452	10,858	11,094	11,938
% Earnings & Depreciation/Assets	3.7	3.9	4.4	4.5	4.9	5.1	5.6	6.4	7.6	8.3
Price Times Book Value:High	2.1	2.8	3.2	3.3	2.5	1.7	1.5	1.4	1.9	1.4
Price Times Book Value:Low	0.9	1.2	1.9	2.1	1.8	1.7	1.5	1.4	1.5	0.9

Data as orig reptd.; bef. results of disc opers/spec. items. Per share data adj. for stk. divs.; EPS diluted. E-Estimated. NA-Not Available. NM-Not Meaningful. NR-Not Ranked. UR-Under Review.

Office: Two North Riverside Plaza, Chicago, IL 60606.
Telephone: 312-474-1300.
Email: investorrelations@eqrworld.com
Website: http://www.equityresidential.com

Chrmn: S.F. Zell
Pres & CEO: D.J. Neithercut
Vice Chrmn: G.A. Spector
COO: D.S. Santee

EVP & CFO: M.J. Parrell
Investor Contact: M. McKenna
Trustees: J. W. Alexander, C. L. Atwood, L. W. Bynoe, J. E. Neal, D. J. Neithercut, M. Shapiro, G. A. Spector, B. J. White, S. F. Zell

Founded: 1993
Domicile: Maryland
Employees: 4,100

Exelon Corp

STANDARD &POOR'S

S&P Recommendation BUY ★★★★☆

Price	12-Mo. Target Price	Investment Style
$42.00 (as of Oct 22, 2010)	$49.00	Large-Cap Blend

GICS Sector Utilities
Sub-Industry Electric Utilities

Summary Exelon, the holding company for Philadelphia-based PECO Energy and Chicago-based ComEd, is the largest nuclear operator in the U.S.

Key Stock Statistics (Source S&P, Vickers, company reports)

52-Wk Range	$51.98–16.78	S&P Oper. EPS 2010**E**	3.98	Market Capitalization(B)	$27.762	Beta		0.64
Trailing 12-Month EPS	$3.82	S&P Oper. EPS 2011**E**	4.14	Yield (%)	5.00	S&P 3-Yr. Proj. EPS CAGR(%)		-1
Trailing 12-Month P/E	11.0	P/E on S&P Oper. EPS 2010**E**	10.6	Dividend Rate/Share	$2.10	S&P Credit Rating		BBB
$10K Invested 5 Yrs Ago	$9,752	Common Shares Outstg. (M)	661.0	Institutional Ownership (%)	63			

Price Performance

30-Week Mov. Avg. · · · ·   10-Week Mov. Avg. – – · **GAAP Earnings vs. Previous Year** Volume Above Avg. ▮▮▮ STARS
12-Mo. Target Price — Relative Strength — ▲ Up ▼ Down ▶ No Change Below Avg. ▮▮▮ ★

Options: ASE, CBOE, P, Ph

Analysis prepared by **Justin McCann** on July 23, 2010, when the stock traded at **$ 41.80**.

Highlights

► Excluding net one-time charges of $0.19, we expect operating EPS in 2010 to decline about 3% from 2009's $4.12. Operating EPS of $1.99 in the first half of 2010 was down $0.25 from the year-earlier period, largely due to lower generating margins. However, this was partially offset by the benefit of the abnormally hot weather and 95% capacity at the nuclear facilities.

► For full year 2010, we believe the projected decline in EPS will reflect the extended weakness in the economy and power markets, partially offset by an estimated $350 million decline in O&M expenses. While EPS in 2011 should be aided by higher margin power contracts with PECO Energy, we expect a slower than previously expected recovery in the power markets.

► After the termination of its acquisition offer to the shareholders of NRG Energy (NRG 22, Buy), we do not expect EXC to initiate another merger attempt in the current environment. It intends to seek internally generated growth and is working to develop a plan for an independent transmission company, and is also planning to add 1,300 to 1,500 megawatts of new nuclear capacity through upgrades at its existing plants.

Investment Rationale/Risk

► Although the stock is down about 14% year to date, we think EXC is well positioned for an eventual recovery in the power markets, and that the shares are undervalued at 10.5X our EPS estimate for 2010. In addition to the ongoing weakness in the economy and the power markets, the decline has reflected, in our view, the change in the political environment that has made the passage of a Climate Bill with Cap and Trade provisions (which would be of decided benefit to Exelon) much less likely.

► Risks to our opinion and target price include an extended recession, sharply reduced wholesale power margins, and a drop in the average peer P/E of the sub-industry.

► The recent dividend yield was about 5.0%, which is slightly above the average yield of electric utility peers primarily involved in power distribution, and well above that of other utility holding companies with major operations in the wholesale power markets. Our 12-month target price is $49, a discount-to-peers P/E of 12.3X our EPS estimate for 2010. Given Exelon's leading position in the nuclear power industry, we believe the stock is attractive for total return potential.

Qualitative Risk Assessment

LOW	MEDIUM	HIGH

Our risk assessment reflects our view of Exelon's strong and steady cash flow from the regulated PECO Energy and ComEd utilities, as well as the healthy earnings and cash flow from very profitable but higher-risk power generating and energy marketing operations.

Quantitative Evaluations

S&P Quality Ranking   B+

D	C	B-	B	B+	A-	A	A+

Relative Strength Rank   WEAK

28

LOWEST = 1   HIGHEST = 99

Revenue/Earnings Data

Revenue (Million $)

	1Q	2Q	3Q	4Q	Year
2010	4,461	4,398	--	--	--
2009	4,722	4,141	4,339	4,116	17,318
2008	4,517	4,622	5,228	4,493	18,859
2007	4,829	4,501	5,032	4,554	18,916
2006	3,861	3,697	4,401	3,696	15,655
2005	3,561	3,484	4,473	3,838	15,357

Earnings Per Share ($)

	1Q	2Q	3Q	4Q	Year
2010	1.13	0.67	E1.11	E0.88	E3.98
2009	1.08	0.99	1.14	0.88	4.09
2008	0.88	1.13	1.06	1.04	4.10
2007	1.01	1.03	1.15	0.84	4.03
2006	0.59	0.95	-0.07	0.89	2.35
2005	0.77	0.76	1.07	-1.19	1.40

Fiscal year ended Dec. 31. Next earnings report expected: Late October. EPS Estimates based on S&P Operating Earnings; historical GAAP earnings are as reported.

Dividend Data (Dates: mm/dd Payment Date: mm/dd/yy)

Amount ($)	Date Decl.	Ex-Div. Date	Stk. of Record	Payment Date
0.525	10/28	11/10	11/13	12/10/09
0.525	01/26	02/11	02/16	03/10/10
0.525	04/27	05/12	05/14	06/10/10
0.525	07/27	08/12	08/16	09/10/10

Dividends have been paid since 1902. Source: Company reports.

Please read the Required Disclosures and Analyst Certification on the last page of this report.

The McGraw·Hill Companies

Exelon Corp

STANDARD &POOR'S

Business Summary July 23, 2010

CORPORATE OVERVIEW. Exelon Corp. was formed in October 2000 through the acquisition by Philadelphia-based PECO Energy of Chicago-based Unicom Corp. The company, along with its subsidiaries, is engaged in the energy delivery, generation and other businesses. Exelon operates in three business segments: Generation, PECO, and ComEd (Commonwealth Edison). Segment contributions to consolidated net income in 2009 were: Generation, $2,122 million ($2,278 million in 2008); ComEd, $374 million ($201 million); PECO, $353 million ($325 million), and other, a loss of $142 million (a loss of $67 million).

IMPACT OF MAJOR DEVELOPMENTS. On July 21, 2009, Exelon terminated its unsolicited offer to acquire all of the outstanding common shares of NRG Energy (NRG 22, Buy), one of the leading competitive wholesale power generators in the United States, with net generating capacity of 24,315 megawatts as

of December 31, 2008. The termination immediately followed NRG shareholder rejection of directors proposed by Exelon to the NRG board, as well as the expansion of that board. The original proposal, made on October 19, 2008, had offered a fixed exchange ratio of 0.485 of an EXC share for each NRG share. However, on July 2, 2009, Exelon increased its offer by 12.4% to a fixed exchange ratio of 0.545 of an EXC share for each NRG share. If the attempted merger had been completed, the combined company would have been the largest power company in the U.S. in terms of assets, market capitalization, enterprise value and generating capacity.

Company Financials Fiscal Year Ended Dec. 31

Per Share Data ($)	2009	2008	2007	2006	2005	2004	2003	2002	2001	2000
Tangible Book Value	15.06	12.58	11.86	11.08	8.48	7.10	5.77	4.26	4.51	3.18
Earnings	4.09	4.10	4.03	2.35	1.40	2.75	1.20	2.58	2.20	1.44
S&P Core Earnings	4.33	3.32	3.92	3.49	3.01	2.79	1.74	1.64	1.49	NA
Dividends	2.10	2.02	1.76	2.00	1.60	1.53	0.96	0.88	0.91	0.46
Payout Ratio	51%	49%	44%	85%	114%	56%	80%	34%	41%	32%
Prices:High	58.98	92.13	86.83	63.62	57.46	44.90	33.31	28.50	35.13	35.50
Prices:Low	38.41	41.23	58.74	51.13	41.77	30.92	23.04	18.92	19.38	16.50
P/E Ratio:High	14	22	22	27	41	16	28	11	16	25
P/E Ratio:Low	9	10	15	22	30	11	19	7	9	11

Income Statement Analysis (Million $)	2009	2008	2007	2006	2005	2004	2003	2002	2001	2000
Revenue	17,318	18,859	18,916	15,655	15,357	14,515	15,812	14,955	15,140	7,499
Depreciation	2,601	2,308	1,520	1,487	1,334	1,305	1,126	1,340	1,449	458
Maintenance	NA	NA	NA	NA	NA	NA	NA	NA	NA	NA
Fixed Charges Coverage	7.08	5.88	6.03	5.19	4.88	3.94	2.19	3.56	2.98	2.94
Construction Credits	NA	NA	NA	NA	NA	NA	NA	NA	NA	Nil
Effective Tax Rate	38.8%	32.7%	34.7%	43.1%	49.8%	27.5%	29.4%	37.4%	39.7%	27.3%
Net Income	2,706	2,717	2,726	1,590	951	1,841	793	1,670	1,416	907
S&P Core Earnings	2,865	2,197	2,656	2,358	2,035	1,865	1,142	1,062	962	NA

Balance Sheet & Other Financial Data (Million $)	2009	2008	2007	2006	2005	2004	2003	2002	2001	2000
Gross Property	36,364	34,055	31,964	30,025	29,853	28,711	27,578	25,904	21,526	19,886
Capital Expenditures	3,273	3,117	2,674	2,418	2,165	1,921	1,954	2,150	2,041	752
Net Property	27,341	25,813	24,153	22,775	21,981	21,482	20,630	17,134	13,742	12,936
Capitalization:Long Term Debt	11,472	12,679	12,052	11,998	11,760	12,235	13,576	14,580	13,492	14,398
Capitalization:% Long Term Debt	47.6	53.5	54.3	54.6	56.3	56.5	61.5	65.3	62.1	66.6
Capitalization:Preferred	Nil	Nil	Nil	Nil	Nil	Nil	Nil	Nil	Nil	Nil
Capitalization:% Preferred	Nil	Nil	Nil	Nil	Nil	Nil	Nil	Nil	Nil	Nil
Capitalization:Common	12,640	11,047	10,137	9,973	9,125	9,423	8,503	7,742	8,230	7,215
Capitalization:% Common	52.4	46.6	45.7	45.4	43.7	43.5	38.5	34.7	37.9	33.4
Total Capital	25,166	24,074	27,270	27,395	25,964	26,463	26,724	26,325	26,341	26,352
% Operating Ratio	82.5	78.9	83.0	80.3	80.5	81.1	82.2	73.1	83.9	80.5
% Earned on Net Property	17.9	21.2	19.9	15.7	12.5	16.3	11.4	21.3	25.2	17.0
% Return on Revenue	15.6	14.4	14.4	10.2	6.2	12.7	5.0	11.2	9.4	12.1
% Return on Invested Capital	14.1	15.1	13.5	12.1	11.4	10.3	10.2	10.2	9.8	9.8
% Return on Common Equity	22.9	25.7	27.1	16.7	10.2	20.5	9.8	21.1	18.3	20.2

Data as orig reptd.; bef. results of disc opers/spec. items. Per share data adj. for stk. divs.; EPS diluted. E-Estimated. NA-Not Available. NM-Not Meaningful. NR-Not Ranked. UR-Under Review.

Office: 10 S Dearborn St, Chicago, IL 60603-2300.
Telephone: 312-394-7398.
Website: http://www.exeloncorp.com
Chrmn & CEO: J.W. Rowe

Pres & COO: C.M. Crane
EVP & Chief Admin Officer: R.A. Gillis
SVP & CFO: M.F. Hilzinger
SVP & Secy: B.G. Wilson

Investor Contact: C.M. Patterson (312-394-7234)
Board Members: J. A. Canning, Jr., M. W. D'Alessio, N. DeBenedictis, B. DeMars, N. A. Diaz, S. L. Gin, R. B. Greco, P. L. Joskow, R. W. Mies, J. M. Palms, W. C. Richardson, T. J. Ridge, J. W. Rogers, Jr., J. W. Rowe, S. D. Steinour, D. Thompson

Founded: 1887
Domicile: Pennsylvania
Employees: 19,329

The McGraw-Hill Companies

Expedia Inc

STANDARD
&POOR'S

S&P Recommendation	SELL ★★☆☆☆	Price $28.28 (as of Oct 22, 2010)	12-Mo. Target Price $26.00	Investment Style Large-Cap Blend

GICS Sector Consumer Discretionary
Sub-Industry Internet Retail

Summary Expedia is one of the world's largest online travel-services companies. Businesses include Expedia, Hotels.com, Hotwire and TripAdvisor.

Key Stock Statistics (Source S&P, Vickers, company reports)

52-Wk Range	$29.85–18.30	S&P Oper. EPS 2010**E**	1.45	Market Capitalization(B)	$7.322	Beta	2.24
Trailing 12-Month EPS	$1.34	S&P Oper. EPS 2011**E**	1.70	Yield (%)	0.99	S&P 3-Yr. Proj. EPS CAGR(%)	24
Trailing 12-Month P/E	21.1	P/E on S&P Oper. EPS 2010**E**	19.5	Dividend Rate/Share	$0.28	S&P Credit Rating	BBB-
$10K Invested 5 Yrs Ago	$14,579	Common Shares Outstg. (M)	284.5	Institutional Ownership (%)	80		

Price Performance

30-Week Mov. Avg. ··· 10-Week Mov. Avg. - - **GAAP Earnings vs. Previous Year** **Volume** Above Avg. STARS
12-Mo. Target Price — Relative Strength — ▲ Up ▼ Down ► No Change Below Avg.

Options: ASE, CBOE, P, Ph

Analysis prepared by **Scott H. Kessler** on September 27, 2010, when the stock traded at **$ 29.13.**

Highlights

➤ We believe EXPE is among the worldwide leaders in the Internet travel segment and will benefit from the continuing migration of associated purchases online. While we have concerns related to global economic uncertainty and substantial exposure to Europe (where currency uncertainties are notable), we think revenues will increase 9% in 2010 and 8% in 2011, given what we see as intact secular growth trends and likely market share gains.

➤ We estimate that annual operating income before amortization (OIBA) and net margins bottomed in 2006, partly due to considerable sales and marketing expenses and technology investments, which yielded benefits into 2008. We expect cost-cutting and expense-containment efforts to aid 2010 margins, offset somewhat by spending on sales and marketing.

➤ EXPE had $1.1 billion in cash and short-term investments as of June 2010, and $895 million of long-term debt. In February 2010, the company announced its first dividend. In the first quarter of 2009, EXPE repaid a tapped $650 million credit facility.

Investment Rationale/Risk

➤ We recently lowered our recommendation on the shares to sell, from hold, based on valuation. We believe EXPE has some of the Internet's best-known travel franchises (including Expedia, Hotels.com and TripAdvisor), some well-positioned and strong international operations, and a healthy domestic business. We also think it has done a good job over the past few quarters of seizing upon opportunities and executing relatively well. We believe EXPE is well positioned to benefit from favorable secular trends, but that it faces challenges including weakened consumer and business spending, a maturing online travel market in the U.S., and significant competition worldwide. We view the shares as overvalued at recent levels.

➤ Risks to our opinion and target price include notable strengthening of global or domestic consumer sentiment or spending, and decreasing competitive and/or pricing pressures.

➤ Our discounted cash flow model assumes a weighted average cost of capital of 11.3%, annual free cash flow growth averaging 13% over the next five years, and a perpetuity growth rate of 3%. These inputs yield an intrinsic value of $26, which is our 12-month target price.

Qualitative Risk Assessment

LOW	MEDIUM	HIGH

Our risk assessment reflects what we believe is a maturing online travel market in the U.S., an intensely competitive landscape, and relatively low barriers to entry.

Quantitative Evaluations

S&P Quality Ranking NR

D	C	B-	B	B+	A-	A	A+

Relative Strength Rank STRONG

78

LOWEST = 1 HIGHEST = 99

Revenue/Earnings Data

Revenue (Million $)

	1Q	2Q	3Q	4Q	Year
2010	717.9	834.0	--	--	--
2009	635.7	769.8	852.4	697.5	2,955
2008	687.8	795.1	833.3	620.8	2,937
2007	550.5	689.9	759.6	665.3	2,665
2006	493.9	598.5	613.9	531.3	2,238
2005	485.1	555.0	584.1	494.8	2,119

Earnings Per Share ($)

2010	0.20	0.40	E0.52	E0.34	E1.45
2009	0.14	0.14	0.40	0.35	1.03
2008	0.17	0.33	0.33	-9.60	-8.63
2007	0.11	0.30	0.32	0.22	0.94
2006	0.06	0.27	0.17	0.20	0.70
2005	0.12	--	0.23	0.07	0.65

Fiscal year ended Dec. 31. Next earnings report expected: Late October. EPS Estimates based on S&P Operating Earnings; historical GAAP earnings are as reported.

Dividend Data (Dates: mm/dd Payment Date: mm/dd/yy)

Amount ($)	Date Decl.	Ex-Div. Date	Stk. of Record	Payment Date
0.070	02/11	03/09	03/11	03/31/10
0.070	04/29	05/25	05/27	06/17/10
0.070	07/26	08/24	08/26	09/16/10

Dividends have been paid since 2010. Source: Company reports.

Please read the Required Disclosures and Analyst Certification on the last page of this report.

Expedia Inc

STANDARD &POOR'S

Business Summary September 27, 2010

CORPORATE OVERVIEW. Expedia, Inc. leverages its portfolio of brands to target a broad range of travelers interested in different travel options. EXPE provides a wide selection of travel products and services, from simple discounted travel to more complex luxury trips. The company's offerings primarily include airline tickets, hotel reservations, car rentals, cruise arrangements, and destination services.

The company's localized Expedia-branded websites (focused on the U.S., as well as Australia, Austria, Canada, Denmark, France, Germany, Ireland, Italy, Japan, the Netherlands, New Zealand, Norway, Spain, Sweden, and the U.K.) offer a large variety of travel products and services. Expedia websites also serve as the travel channel on MSN.com. Expedia Corporate Travel is a full-service travel management firm available to corporate travelers in the U.S., Canada, China, and Europe. Hotels.com provides a multitude of lodging options to travelers, from traditional hotels, to vacation rentals. Part of Hotels.com's strategy is to position itself as a hotel expert offering premium content about lodging properties. These businesses are planning to provide other travel products and services. Hotwire.com is a discount travel website that offers deals to travelers willing to make purchases without knowing certain itinerary details such as brand, time of departure, and hotel address. eLong (LONG 20, NR) is a majority-owned online travel services company based in and focused on China (see below for more details).

TripAdvisor is an online travel content destination, with search and directory features, guidebook reviews, and user opinions. We believe TripAdvisor is an extremely valuable asset, not only because we believe it constitutes the Internet's largest and most active travel-related social networking property, but also because it diversifies EXPE operations away from transactions and into media and advertising. Expansion in China has been a major focus of TripAdvisor, with entry into the market in April 2009 with the launch of DaoDao.com (a localized reviews and community website for Chinese travelers), and acquisition of Kuxun.cn (the second-largest online travel-related website in China) in late 2009.

In December 2004, IAC/InterActiveCorp (IACI 27, Hold) announced a plan to spin off what became EXPE. In August 2005, EXPE was spun off as a separate publicly traded company.

Company Financials Fiscal Year Ended Dec. 31

Per Share Data ($)	2009	2008	2007	2006	2005	2004	2003	2002	2001	2000
Tangible Book Value	NM	NM	NM	NM	NM	NA	NA	NA	NA	NA
Cash Flow	1.29	-8.13	1.38	1.40	1.82	NA	NA	NA	NA	NA
Earnings	1.03	-8.63	0.94	0.70	0.65	0.37	NA	NA	NA	NA
S&P Core Earnings	1.08	-2.48	0.94	0.79	0.69	0.48	0.27	0.26	-1.04	NA
Dividends	Nil	Nil	Nil	Nil	Nil	NA	NA	NA	NA	NA
Payout Ratio	Nil	Nil	Nil	Nil	Nil	NA	NA	NA	NA	NA
Prices:High	27.51	31.88	35.28	27.55	27.50	NA	NA	NA	NA	NA
Prices:Low	6.31	6.00	19.97	12.87	18.49	NA	NA	NA	NA	NA
P/E Ratio:High	27	NM	38	39	42	NA	NA	NA	NA	NA
P/E Ratio:Low	6	NM	21	18	28	NA	NA	NA	NA	NA

Income Statement Analysis (Million $)

	2009	2008	2007	2006	2005	2004	2003	2002	2001	2000
Revenue	2,955	2,937	2,665	2,238	2,119	1,843	2,340	1,499	NA	NA
Operating Income	751	713	666	648	678	397	364	257	NA	NA
Depreciation	140	146	137	249	407	157	104	61.4	NA	NA
Interest Expense	84.2	72.0	52.9	17.3	Nil	7.45	2.90	NA	NA	NA
Pretax Income	458	-2,515	497	385	414	219	256	209	NA	NA
Effective Tax Rate	33.7%	NM	40.9%	36.2%	44.9%	40.0%	38.0%	39.4%	NA	NA
Net Income	300	-2,518	296	245	229	131	111	76.7	NA	NA
S&P Core Earnings	315	-722	296	275	244	163	92.3	34.2	-98.1	NA

Balance Sheet & Other Financial Data (Million $)

	2009	2008	2007	2006	2005	2004	2003	2002	2001	2000
Cash	688	758	634	853	297	232	882	NA	NA	NA
Current Assets	1,225	1,199	1,046	1,183	590	569	1,680	NA	NA	NA
Total Assets	5,937	5,894	8,295	8,269	7,757	7,803	8,755	NA	NA	NA
Current Liabilities	1,835	1,566	1,774	1,400	1,438	1,515	825	NA	NA	NA
Long Term Debt	895	1,545	1,085	500	Nil	NA	NA	NA	NA	NA
Common Equity	2,683	2,328	4,818	5,904	5,734	5,820	7,554	NA	NA	NA
Total Capital	3,645	4,115	6,316	6,835	6,174	8,171	7,554	NA	NA	NA
Capital Expenditures	92.0	160	86.7	92.6	52.3	53.4	46.2	46.5	NA	NA
Cash Flow	377	-2,372	433	494	636	320	215	138	NA	NA
Current Ratio	0.7	0.8	0.6	0.8	0.4	0.4	2.0	NA	NA	NA
% Long Term Debt of Capitalization	24.6	37.5	17.2	7.3	Nil	Nil	Nil	Nil	NA	NA
% Net Income of Revenue	10.1	NM	11.1	10.9	10.8	7.1	4.8	5.1	NA	NA
% Return on Assets	5.1	NM	3.6	3.1	2.6	1.8	NA	NA	NA	NA
% Return on Equity	12.0	NM	5.5	4.2	3.3	2.1	NA	NA	NA	NA

Data as orig reptd.; bef. results of disc opers/spec. items. Per share data adj. for stk. divs.; EPS diluted. E-Estimated. NA-Not Available. NM-Not Meaningful. NR-Not Ranked. UR-Under Review.

Office: 333 108th Ave NE, Bellevue, WA 98004-5703.
Telephone: 425-679-7200.
Website: http://www.expedia.com
Chrmn: B. Diller

Pres & CEO: D. Khosrowshahi
Vice Chrmn: V.A. Kaufman
COO: W. Crawford
EVP & CFO: M.B. Adler

Investor Contact: S. Haas (425-679-7852)
Board Members: A. G. Battle, B. Diller, J. L. Dolgen, W. R. Fitzgerald, C. A. Jacobson, V. A. Kaufman, P. Kern, D. Khosrowshahi, J. C. Malone, D. C. Marriott, J. Miller, J. A. Tazon

Founded: 1996
Domicile: Delaware
Employees: 7,960

Expeditors International of Washington Inc

S&P Recommendation	BUY ★★★★★	Price	12-Mo. Target Price	Investment Style
		$49.57 (as of Oct 22, 2010)	$54.00	Large-Cap Growth

GICS Sector Industrials
Sub-Industry Air Freight & Logistics

Summary This company is a global air and ocean freight forwarder and customs broker.

Key Stock Statistics (Source S&P, Vickers, company reports)

52-Wk Range	$49.79–31.27	S&P Oper. EPS 2010E	1.53	Market Capitalization(B)	$10.518	Beta	0.76
Trailing 12-Month EPS	$1.29	S&P Oper. EPS 2011E	2.05	Yield (%)	0.81	S&P 3-Yr. Proj. EPS CAGR(%)	16
Trailing 12-Month P/E	38.4	P/E on S&P Oper. EPS 2010E	32.4	Dividend Rate/Share	$0.40	S&P Credit Rating	NA
$10K Invested 5 Yrs Ago	$18,155	Common Shares Outstg. (M)	212.2	Institutional Ownership (%)	88		

Price Performance

30-Week Mov. Avg. · · · 10-Week Mov. Avg. - - GAAP Earnings vs. Previous Year   Volume Above Avg.||||| STARS
12-Mo. Target Price — Relative Strength — ▲ Up ▼ Down ► No Change   Below Avg.||||| ★

Options: ASE, CBOE, P, Ph

Analysis prepared by **Jim Corridore** on August 04, 2010, when the stock traded at **$ 44.26**.

Highlights

➤ We expect 2010 net revenues to rise about 35%, after falling 27% in 2009. Net revenue growth in 2010 should benefit from overall improving volumes in the early stages of a global economic recovery. In addition, EXPD should see better pricing in air and ocean freight. We look for Europe and Asia to lag the recovery in the U.S. by about six months. Volumes and pricing in the U.S. showed strong improvement in the first half and should continue to strengthen in the second half of 2010, in our view.

➤ We project margins in 2010 to be helped by improving volumes and continued reductions in ocean and air transportation rates, reflecting new ocean freight capacity that has recently come on line, as well as excess ocean and air shipping capacity. We think continued legal costs related to a Department of Justice investigation into potential anti-competitive practices, as well as some pressure on SG&A expenses, will partially offset the benefits.

➤ We forecast 2010 EPS of $1.53, which would represent 38% growth over 2009 EPS of $1.11. For 2011, we see EPS rising 34%, to $2.05.

Investment Rationale/Risk

➤ While the overall logistics sector is likely to see a recovery in volumes related to some strengthening in the U.S. and global economies, we believe EXPD's diversified revenue base, geographical reach and shipping mode will allow it to outperform peers. A debt-free balance sheet and what we view as strong long-term earnings and cash flow growth potential are additional positives. We also expect improved investor sentiment for EXPD and other logistics stocks on good economic news that points to improvement in the U.S. economy.

➤ Risks to our recommendation and target price include any worsening of the global economy. We also see management's communication style, in which it mainly answers questions through 8-K filings, as a risk, in that it may not allow investors to react quickly enough to potentially important news. The company could be hit with a large judgment related to the current Department of Justice investigation into anti-competitive practices.

➤ Our 12-month target price of $54 values the stock at about 26X our 2011 EPS estimate of $2.05, compared to a five-year historical P/E range of 21.5X-55.0X EPS.

Qualitative Risk Assessment

LOW	MEDIUM	HIGH

Our risk assessment reflects that EXPD operates in a highly cyclical industry and is exposed to currency and global economic risk. We see its communication style as an additional risk. However, we think EXPD has a diversified stream of air, ocean, and customs businesses, and we also believe the balance sheet is strong, with no debt and a relatively large amount of cash.

Quantitative Evaluations

S&P Quality Ranking A+

D	C	B-	B	B+	A-	A	A+

Relative Strength Rank STRONG

85

LOWEST = 1   HIGHEST = 99

Revenue/Earnings Data

Revenue (Million $)

	1Q	2Q	3Q	4Q	Year
2010	1,201	1,517	--	--	--
2009	912.7	895.4	1,037	1,247	4,092
2008	1,307	1,454	1,565	1,307	5,634
2007	1,119	1,259	1,411	1,447	5,235
2006	1,025	1,129	1,230	1,242	4,626
2005	825.2	928.0	1,046	1,102	3,902

Earnings Per Share ($)

	1Q	2Q	3Q	4Q	Year
2010	0.28	0.42	E0.37	E0.46	E1.53
2009	0.27	0.25	0.27	0.32	1.11
2008	0.30	0.32	0.39	0.36	1.37
2007	0.27	0.30	0.34	0.32	1.21
2006	0.24	0.25	0.29	0.28	1.06
2005	0.17	0.20	0.25	0.36	0.98

Fiscal year ended Dec. 31. Next earnings report expected: Early November. EPS Estimates based on S&P Operating Earnings; historical GAAP earnings are as reported.

Dividend Data (Dates: mm/dd Payment Date: mm/dd/yy)

Amount ($)	Date Decl.	Ex-Div. Date	Stk. of Record	Payment Date
0.190	11/03	11/27	12/01	12/15/09
0.200	05/06	05/27	06/01	06/15/10

Dividends have been paid since 1993. Source: Company reports.

Please read the Required Disclosures and Analyst Certification on the last page of this report.

Expeditors International of Washington Inc

STANDARD &POOR'S

Business Summary August 04, 2010

CORPORATE OVERVIEW. With an international network supporting the movement and strategic positioning of goods, Expeditors International of Washington is engaged in the business of providing global logistics services to customers diversified in terms of industry specialization and geographic location. In each of its U.S. offices, and in many international offices, the company acts as a customs broker, and also provides additional services, including distribution management, vendor consolidation, cargo insurance, purchase order management, and customized logistics information. EXPD does not compete for domestic freight, overnight courier, or small parcel business, and does not own aircraft or steamships. The company has historically pursued a strategy emphasizing organic growth supplemented by strategic acquisitions. As of February 2010, EXPD had a network of 182 full-service offices, 64 satellite locations, and four international service centers located on six continents.

Shipments of computer components, other electronic equipment, housewares, sporting goods, machine parts and toys comprise a significant percentage of the company's business. Import customers include computer retailers and distributors of consumer electronics, department store chains, clothing and shoe wholesalers. Historically, no single customer has accounted for over 5% of revenues.

Air freight services accounted for 45% of total revenues in 2009. EXPD typically acts either as a freight consolidator (purchasing cargo space on airlines and reselling it to customers at lower rates than the airline would charge customers directly), or as an agent for the airlines (receiving shipments from suppliers, and consolidating and forwarding them to the airlines). Shipments are usually characterized by a high value-to-weight ratio, a need for rapid delivery, or both. The company estimates that its average air freight consolidation weighs 3,500 lbs. to 4,500 lbs. Because shipping by air is relatively expensive compared with ocean transportation, air shipments are generally categorized by a high value-to-weight ratio, the need for rapid delivery, or both.

The company's strategy to not own aircraft is based on its view that the ownership of aircraft would subject EXPD to undue business risks, including large capital outlays, increased fixed operating costs, problems of fully utilizing aircraft and competition with airlines. EXPD relies on commercial aircraft to transport its shipments.

Company Financials Fiscal Year Ended Dec. 31

Per Share Data ($)	2009	2008	2007	2006	2005	2004	2003	2002	2001	2000
Tangible Book Value	7.26	6.38	5.69	4.95	4.21	3.70	2.98	2.49	2.01	1.76
Cash Flow	1.30	1.56	1.39	1.27	1.12	0.82	0.67	0.62	0.55	0.48
Earnings	1.11	1.37	1.21	1.06	0.98	0.71	0.56	0.52	0.45	0.38
S&P Core Earnings	1.11	1.37	1.21	1.06	0.85	0.59	0.46	0.44	0.39	NA
Dividends	0.38	0.32	0.28	0.22	0.15	0.11	0.08	0.06	0.04	0.04
Payout Ratio	34%	23%	23%	21%	15%	16%	14%	12%	10%	9%
Prices:High	38.10	49.92	54.46	58.32	36.37	29.20	20.42	17.22	16.48	15.03
Prices:Low	23.86	24.05	38.31	32.83	23.59	17.85	14.81	12.47	10.49	8.16
P/E Ratio:High	34	36	45	55	37	41	36	33	37	40
P/E Ratio:Low	21	18	32	31	24	25	26	24	24	21

Income Statement Analysis (Million $)	2009	2008	2007	2006	2005	2004	2003	2002	2001	2000
Revenue	4,092	5,634	5,235	4,626	3,902	3,318	2,625	2,297	1,653	1,695
Operating Income	427	515	463	411	337	268	211	194	170	150
Depreciation	40.0	41.6	40.0	35.4	32.3	26.7	24.4	22.7	23.5	22.5
Interest Expense	0.50	0.18	Nil	0.20	0.31	0.04	0.19	0.18	0.52	0.43
Pretax Income	403	500	450	396	320	250	196	178	154	133
Effective Tax Rate	40.3%	39.4%	40.0%	40.6%	29.6%	35.4%	36.4%	36.8%	37.0%	37.7%
Net Income	240	301	269	235	219	156	122	113	97.2	83.0
S&P Core Earnings	240	301	269	235	187	130	98.4	92.7	83.8	NA

Balance Sheet & Other Financial Data (Million $)	2009	2008	2007	2006	2005	2004	2003	2002	2001	2000
Cash	927	742	575	511	464	409	296	212	219	169
Current Assets	1,788	1,573	1,535	1,342	1,202	1,046	762	605	511	523
Total Assets	2,324	2,101	2,069	1,822	1,566	1,364	1,041	880	688	662
Current Liabilities	708	670	770	709	613	524	392	356	274	230
Long Term Debt	NA	Nil	Nil	Nil	Nil	Nil	Nil	Nil	Nil	Nil
Common Equity	1,553	1,366	1,227	1,070	914	807	646	524	415	362
Total Capital	1,561	1,430	1,299	1,113	954	840	649	524	415	362
Capital Expenditures	34.7	59.7	82.8	141	90.8	66.2	20.7	81.4	37.4	25.6
Cash Flow	282	343	309	271	251	183	146	135	121	106
Current Ratio	2.5	2.4	2.0	1.9	2.0	2.0	1.9	1.7	1.9	2.3
% Long Term Debt of Capitalization	Nil	Nil	Nil	Nil	Nil	Nil	Nil	Nil	Nil	Nil
% Net Income of Revenue	5.9	5.3	5.1	5.1	5.6	4.7	4.6	4.9	5.9	4.9
% Return on Assets	10.9	14.4	13.8	13.9	14.9	13.0	12.7	14.3	14.4	13.9
% Return on Equity	16.5	23.2	23.4	23.6	25.4	21.5	20.9	24.0	25.0	25.8

Data as orig reptd.; bef. results of disc opers/spec. items. Per share data adj. for stk. divs.; EPS diluted. E-Estimated. NA-Not Available. NM-Not Meaningful. NR-Not Ranked. UR-Under Review.

Office: 1015 Third Avenue, Seattle, WA 98104-1190.
Telephone: 206-674-3400.
Website: http://www.expeditors.com
Chrmn & CEO: P.J. Rose

Pres & COO: R. Gates
SVP & Cntlr: C.J. Lynch
SVP & CIO: J.S. Musser
CFO & Chief Acctg Officer: B.S. Powell

Investor Contact: R.J. Gates (206-674-3400)
Board Members: M. A. Emmert, R. Gates, D. P. Kourkoumelis, M. J. Malone, J. W. Meisenbach, P. J. Rose, L. Wang, R. R. Wright

Founded: 1979
Domicile: Washington
Employees: 12,010

The McGraw-Hill Companies

Express Scripts Inc

S&P Recommendation **STRONG BUY** ★★★★★	Price $49.00 (as of Oct 22, 2010)	12-Mo. Target Price $63.00	Investment Style Large-Cap Growth

GICS Sector Health Care
Sub-Industry Health Care Services

Summary This company offers prescription benefits and disease state management services.

Key Stock Statistics (Source S&P, Vickers, company reports)

52-Wk Range	$54.00–37.75	S&P Oper. EPS 2010**E**	2.50	Market Capitalization(B)	$26.578	Beta	0.87
Trailing 12-Month EPS	$1.75	S&P Oper. EPS 2011**E**	3.13	Yield (%)	Nil	S&P 3-Yr. Proj. EPS CAGR(%)	25
Trailing 12-Month P/E	28.0	P/E on S&P Oper. EPS 2010**E**	19.6	Dividend Rate/Share	Nil	S&P Credit Rating	BBB
$10K Invested 5 Yrs Ago	$30,750	Common Shares Outstg. (M)	542.4	Institutional Ownership (%)	92		

Price Performance

30-Week Mov. Avg. · · · 10-Week Mov. Avg. – – **GAAP Earnings vs. Previous Year** Volume Above Avg. STARS
12-Mo. Target Price — Relative Strength — ▲ Up ▼ Down ► No Change Below Avg. ★

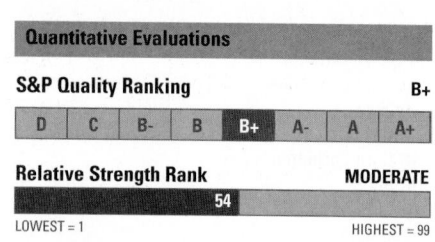

Options: ASE, CBOE, P

Analysis prepared by **Herman B. Saftlas** on August 19, 2010, when the stock traded at **$45.56**.

Highlights

➤ We forecast that revenues will surge by more than 82% to over $45.1 billion, on gains from new accounts and the December 1, 2009, acquisition of WellPoint's (WLP 51, Buy) NextRx PBM unit, which had $17.2 billion in revenues in 2008. In addition, new accounting under the renewed U.S. Department of Defense contract, which took effect in November 2009, will add $8 billion annually to revenues and $8 billion to cost of goods, thereby affecting gross margins but not gross profit dollars.

➤ We expect EBITDA per adjusted script to grow only modestly in 2010, reflecting the low mail-order penetration rate of the NextRx accounts. We forecast that ratio will continue to expand afterward, as synergies are realized and ESRX transitions more NextRx members to mail-order. We also expect interest costs to decline, assuming it reduces debt, given $2 billion in operating cash flow it expects to realize in 2010.

➤ Our 2010 non-GAAP EPS estimate, before $0.15 in amortization and one-time costs, is $2.50, versus 2009's $1.74 (adjusted for the 2-for-1 split effective June 8, 2010), before $0.24 in amortization and one-time costs. We look for EPS of $3.13 for 2011.

Investment Rationale/Risk

➤ We are encouraged by ESRX's acquisition of NextRx, which we see boosting claims volumes by almost 50%. We believe NextRx will improve ESRX's economies of scale and clout with drugmakers. Before transaction costs and intangibles amortization, the deal was accretive from the start, and upon 12-18 months integration, ESRX sees it adding over $1 billion to EBITDA. Moreover, we think a strong generic drug launch cycle that we see through 2015, and opportunities presented by health care reform, will provide healthy long-term earnings growth for ESRX and its PBM peers. We believe the strengths NextRx brings to ESRX and ESRX's history of saving clients' money should enable it to easily hold its own in the competitive PBM space.

➤ Risks to our recommendation and target price include increased government oversight of the PBM industry, loss of key clients, and problems integrating NextRx.

➤ We derive our 12-month target price of $63 by applying a multiple of 25X to our 2010 EPS estimate, above the company's historical average.

Qualitative Risk Assessment

LOW	MEDIUM	HIGH

Our risk assessment reflects our view of rising drug demand, and the company's improving financial performance and healthy operating cash flow. However, we believe intense competition and increased government regulation of pharmacy benefits managers (PBMs), which we view as likely, could result in changes to industry conditions.

Quantitative Evaluations

S&P Quality Ranking B+

D	C	B-	B	B+	A-	A	A+

Relative Strength Rank MODERATE

54

LOWEST = 1   HIGHEST = 99

Revenue/Earnings Data

Revenue (Million $)

	1Q	2Q	3Q	4Q	Year
2010	11,144	1,289	--	--	--
2009	5,423	5,503	5,619	8,203	24,749
2008	5,491	5,530	5,451	5,506	21,978
2007	4,540	4,600	4,519	4,694	18,274
2006	4,380	4,421	4,330	4,529	17,660
2005	3,839	3,944	3,848	4,635	16,266

Earnings Per Share ($)

	1Q	2Q	3Q	4Q	Year
2010	0.47	0.56	E0.65	E0.71	E2.50
2009	0.43	0.37	0.36	0.40	1.56
2008	0.35	0.38	0.41	0.42	1.55
2007	0.24	0.29	0.28	0.33	1.14
2006	0.18	0.19	0.21	0.27	0.84
2005	0.14	0.17	0.17	0.19	0.67

Fiscal year ended Dec. 31. Next earnings report expected: Late October. EPS Estimates based on S&P Operating Earnings; historical GAAP earnings are as reported.

Dividend Data (Dates: mm/dd Payment Date: mm/dd/yy)

Amount ($)	Date Decl.	Ex-Div. Date	Stk. of Record	Payment Date
2-for-1	05/05	06/08	05/21	06/07/10

Source: Company reports.

Express Scripts Inc

Business Summary August 19, 2010

CORPORATE OVERVIEW. Express Scripts is one of the largest U.S. pharmacy benefits managers (PBMs). Its PBM services (94.8% of 2009 revenue, versus 93.6% in 2008) include retail network pharmacy management, home delivery services, specialty pharmacy services patient care contact centers, benefit plan design and consultation, drug formulary management, compliance and therapy management programs, and various other programs.

Clients include health insurers, third-party administrators, employers, union-sponsored benefit plans, government health programs, office-based oncologists, renal dialysis clinics, ambulatory surgery centers, primary care physicians and others. In November 2009, it implemented a new contract with the U.S. Dept. of Defense (DoD). While it has provided services to the DoD since 2003, this new contract combines the pharmacy network services, home delivery, and specialty pharmacy, as well as additional services.

Through its Emerging Markets Services (EM) segment, it provides services including distribution of pharmaceuticals and medical supplies to providers and clinics, distribution of fertility pharmaceuticals requiring special handling or packaging, distribution of sample units to physicians, verification of practitioner licensure, healthcare account administration, and implementation of consumer-directed healthcare solutions. During 2009, 5.2% of its revenue was derived from EM services, compared to 6.4% during 2008.

Revenues are generated primarily from the delivery of prescription drugs through 60,000 contracted retail pharmacies, three home delivery fulfillment pharmacies, and eight specialty drug pharmacies, as of December 31, 2009. Revenues from the delivery of prescription drugs to members represented 98.8% of revenues in 2009, versus 98.7% in 2008. Revenues from services, such as the administration of some clients' retail pharmacy networks, medication counseling services, specialty distribution services, and sample fulfillment and sample accountability services comprised the remainder.

The five largest clients accounted for 23.7% of revenues in 2009, compared to 18.2% in 2008. In 2009, ESRX processed 404.3 million network pharmacy claims, 41.8 million home delivery and specialty pharmacy claims and 3.2 million other (patient assistance program, limited distribution network and EM) claims, versus 379.6 million, 41.9 million and 3.2 million, respectively, in 2008.

Company Financials Fiscal Year Ended Dec. 31

Per Share Data ($)	2009	2008	2007	2006	2005	2004	2003	2002	2001	2000
Tangible Book Value	NM	NM	NM	NM	NM	NM	NM	NM	NM	NM
Cash Flow	1.72	1.74	1.32	1.01	0.81	0.56	0.48	0.45	0.32	0.12
Earnings	1.56	1.55	1.14	0.84	0.67	0.45	0.40	0.32	0.20	-0.02
S&P Core Earnings	1.57	1.56	1.12	0.84	0.65	0.43	0.38	0.30	0.18	NA
Dividends	Nil	Nil	Nil	Nil	Nil	Nil	Nil	Nil	Nil	Nil
Payout Ratio	Nil	Nil	Nil	Nil	Nil	Nil	Nil	Nil	Nil	Nil
Prices:High	44.94	39.55	37.20	23.75	22.70	10.15	9.43	8.24	7.68	6.69
Prices:Low	21.38	24.19	16.16	14.70	9.13	7.29	5.79	4.83	4.36	1.78
P/E Ratio:High	29	26	33	28	34	23	24	26	39	NM
P/E Ratio:Low	14	16	14	18	14	16	15	15	22	NM

Income Statement Analysis (Million $)										
Revenue	24,749	21,978	18,274	17,660	16,266	15,115	13,295	12,261	9,329	6,787
Operating Income	1,668	1,390	1,177	925	727	563	503	454	317	279
Depreciation	110	97.7	97.5	101	84.0	70.0	54.0	82.0	80.1	78.6
Interest Expense	194	77.6	108	95.7	37.0	41.7	41.4	42.2	34.2	47.9
Pretax Income	1,309	1,214	945	740	615	451	405	330	208	-4.47
Effective Tax Rate	36.9%	35.8%	36.5%	35.9%	35.0%	38.3%	38.2%	38.2%	39.9%	NM
Net Income	826	780	600	474	400	278	251	204	125	-8.02
S&P Core Earnings	837	784	592	474	389	270	239	192	115	NA

Balance Sheet & Other Financial Data (Million $)										
Cash	1,070	539	437	131	478	166	396	191	178	53.2
Current Assets	4,144	2,044	1,968	1,772	2,257	1,443	1,560	1,394	1,213	998
Total Assets	11,931	5,509	5,256	5,108	5,493	3,600	3,409	3,207	2,500	2,277
Current Liabilities	5,457	2,722	2,475	2,429	2,394	1,813	1,626	1,544	1,246	1,116
Long Term Debt	2,493	1,340	1,760	1,270	1,401	412	455	563	346	396
Common Equity	3,552	1,078	696	1,125	1,465	1,196	1,194	1,003	832	705
Total Capital	7,384	2,732	2,735	2,395	2,866	1,608	1,649	1,565	1,178	1,102
Capital Expenditures	149	85.8	75.0	66.8	60.0	51.5	53.1	61.3	57.3	80.2
Cash Flow	914	877	698	575	484	348	305	286	205	70.6
Current Ratio	0.8	0.8	0.8	0.7	0.9	0.8	1.0	0.9	1.0	0.9
% Long Term Debt of Capitalization	33.8	49.1	64.4	53.0	48.9	25.6	27.6	35.9	29.4	36.0
% Net Income of Revenue	3.3	3.6	3.3	2.7	2.5	1.8	1.9	1.7	1.3	NM
% Return on Assets	9.5	14.5	11.6	8.9	8.8	7.9	7.6	7.1	5.2	NM
% Return on Equity	35.7	87.9	65.9	36.6	30.1	23.3	22.8	22.2	16.3	NM

Data as orig reptd.; bef. results of disc opers/spec. items. Per share data adj. for stk. divs.; EPS diluted. E-Estimated. NA-Not Available. NM-Not Meaningful. NR-Not Ranked. UR-Under Review.

Office: 1 Express Way, Saint Louis, MO 63121-1824.
Telephone: 314-996-0900.
Email: investor.relations@express-scripts.com
Website: http://www.express-scripts.com

Chrmn, Pres & CEO: G. Paz
COO & EVP: P. McNamee
EVP & CFO: J.L. Hall
EVP & General Counsel: K.J. Ebling

SVP & CIO: G. Wimberly
Investor Contact: D. Myers (314-810-3115)
Board Members: G. Benanav, F. J. Borelli, M. Breen, N. J. LaHowchic, T. P. MacMahon, F. Mergenthaler, W. Myers, Jr., J. O. Parker, Jr., G. Paz, S. K. Skinner, S. Sternberg, B. Toan

Founded: 1986
Domicile: Delaware
Employees: 14,270

Exxon Mobil Corp

STANDARD &POOR'S

| S&P Recommendation | **STRONG BUY** ★★★★★ | Price $66.34 (as of Oct 22, 2010) | 12-Mo. Target Price $79.00 | Investment Style Large-Cap Blend |

GICS Sector Energy
Sub-Industry Integrated Oil & Gas

Summary XOM, formed through the merger of Exxon and Mobil in late 1999, is the world's largest publicly owned integrated oil company.

Key Stock Statistics (Source S&P, Vickers, company reports)

52-Wk Range	$76.54– 55.94	S&P Oper. EPS 2010E	5.97	Market Capitalization(B)	$337.790	Beta	0.49
Trailing 12-Month EPS	$5.18	S&P Oper. EPS 2011E	6.72	Yield (%)	2.65	S&P 3-Yr. Proj. EPS CAGR(%)	21
Trailing 12-Month P/E	12.8	P/E on S&P Oper. EPS 2010E	11.1	Dividend Rate/Share	$1.76	S&P Credit Rating	AAA
$10K Invested 5 Yrs Ago	$13,292	Common Shares Outstg. (M)	5,091.8	Institutional Ownership (%)	48		

Price Performance

- 30-Week Mov. Avg. ···10-Week Mov. Avg. -- GAAP Earnings vs. Previous Year   Volume Above Avg. |||| STARS
- 12-Mo. Target Price — Relative Strength — ▲ Up ▼ Down ▶ No Change   Below Avg. |||| ★

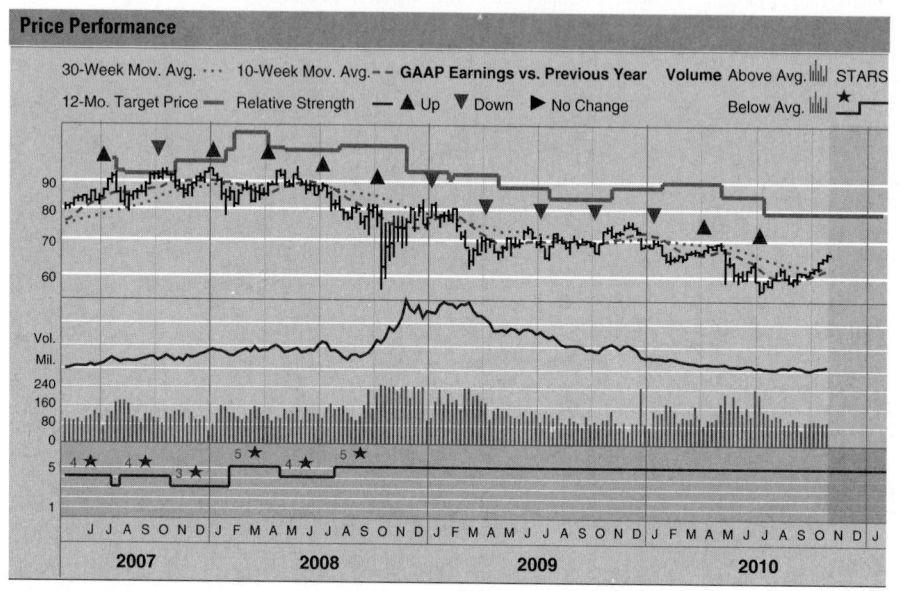

Options: ASE, CBOE, P, Ph

Analysis prepared by **Tina J. Vital** on September 03, 2010, when the stock traded at **$ 61.23.**

Highlights

➤ XOM is slated to start up 12 major projects during 2010-12 in Qatar, the U.S., the U.K., Canada, Australia, Russia, Angola, and Nigeria, and 42 thereafter. We look for oil and gas production to rise about 8% in 2010, to about 4.25 million boe per day, on contributions from XTO, and over 3% per annum between 2009 and 2013. We see minimal near-term impact to XOM's production from the Gulf oil spill (about 6% of XOM's output is from the Gulf of Mexico), but drilling on new Gulf of Mexico projects will see delays (such as Hoover Diana and Hadrian).

➤ While we expect global refining industry conditions to remain pressured through 2016, we see signs that U.S. refining margins are widening on improved fuel demand and reduced operating costs. As of July 2010, S&P Equity projected U.S. Gulf Coast 3-2-1 crack spreads to widen about 9% in 2010 and 3% in 2011. Further, XOM has a history of continuously rationalizing its refinery units, and we view the company as the low-cost leader among peers.

➤ We estimate that after-tax operating earnings will rise 51% in 2010 and 17% in 2011, on increased production and an improved economic outlook.

Investment Rationale/Risk

➤ XOM has enjoyed a superior degree of earnings and dividend growth and stability (as evidenced by its S&P Quality Ranking of A+). We believe the company will benefit from "big-pocket" upstream growth opportunities in the deepwater, liquefied natural gas (LNG), onshore unconventional, and ventures with state-owned oil companies. We think XOM's advanced technology permits project development in a timely and cost-efficient manner. In addition, we see its upstream E&P business benefiting from a strong pipeline of long-lived resources, and the downstream unit should benefit over the long term from its complex refineries, which offer feedstock and product flexibility.

➤ Risks to our recommendation and target price include deterioration in economic, industry, and operating conditions, such as difficulty replacing reserves and increased production costs.

➤ Blending our discounted cash flow ($83 per share, assuming a WACC of 6.7% and terminal growth of 3%) and relative market valuations, our 12-month target price is $79, representing an expected enterprise value of 6.1X our 2011 EBITDA estimate, a premium to U.S. supermajor oil peers.

Qualitative Risk Assessment

| **LOW** | MEDIUM | HIGH |

Our risk assessment reflects our view of the company's diversified and strong business profile in volatile, cyclical, and capital-intensive segments of the energy industry. We consider ExxonMobil's earnings stability and corporate governance practices to be above average.

Quantitative Evaluations

S&P Quality Ranking A+

| D | C | B- | B | B+ | A- | A | **A+** |

Relative Strength Rank MODERATE

69

LOWEST = 1   HIGHEST = 99

Revenue/Earnings Data

Revenue (Million $)

	1Q	2Q	3Q	4Q	Year
2010	90,251	92,486	--	--	--
2009	64,028	74,457	82,260	89,841	310,586
2008	116,854	138,072	137,737	84,696	477,359
2007	87,223	98,350	102,337	116,642	404,552
2006	86,317	96,024	96,268	86,858	377,635
2005	82,051	88,568	100,717	99,662	370,680

Earnings Per Share ($)

2010	1.33	1.60	E1.45	E1.55	E5.97
2009	0.92	0.81	0.98	1.27	3.98
2008	2.03	2.22	2.86	1.55	8.69
2007	1.62	1.83	1.70	2.14	7.28
2006	1.37	1.72	1.77	1.76	6.62
2005	1.22	1.20	1.58	1.71	5.71

Fiscal year ended Dec. 31. Next earnings report expected: Late October. EPS Estimates based on S&P Operating Earnings; historical GAAP earnings are as reported.

Dividend Data (Dates: mm/dd Payment Date: mm/dd/yy)

Amount ($)	Date Decl.	Ex-Div. Date	Stk. of Record	Payment Date
0.420	10/28	11/09	11/12	12/10/09
0.420	01/27	02/08	02/10	03/10/10
0.440	04/28	05/11	05/13	06/10/10
0.440	07/28	08/11	08/13	09/10/10

Dividends have been paid since 1882. Source: Company reports.

Exxon Mobil Corp

STANDARD &POOR'S

Business Summary September 03, 2010

CORPORATE OVERVIEW. In late 1999, the FTC allowed Exxon and Mobil to re-unite, creating Exxon Mobil Corp. ExxonMobil's businesses include oil and natural gas exploration and production (8% of 2009 sales; 81% of 2009 segment earnings); refining and marketing (83%; 8%); chemicals (9%; 11%); and other operations, such as electric power generation, coal and minerals.

Including non-consolidated equity interest, proved oil and gas reserves remained steady at 23.0 billion barrels of oil equivalent (boe; 51% petroleum liquids which included oil sands, 67% developed) in 2009. Oil and gas production rose 0.3%, to 3.93 million boe per day (61% petroleum liquids), in 2009. Using data from John S. Herold, we estimate XOM's three-year (2006-2008) reserve replacement at 128%, above the peer average; three-year finding and development cost at $8.68 per boe, below the peer average; proved acquisition costs at $0.44 per boe, below the peer average; and its reserve replacement costs at $7.63 per boe, below the peer average.

At year-end 2009, the company had an ownership interest in 37 refineries with 6.23 million barrels per day (b/d) of atmospheric distillation capacity (U.S. 32%, Europe 28%, Asia Pacific 27%, Canada 8%, and Middle East/Latin America/Other 5%).

MANAGEMENT. We believe XOM is one of the best managed companies in the energy sector. In January 2006, Lee R. Raymond retired, and Rex W. Tillerson became chairman and CEO. We expect Mr. Tillerson to benefit from the strategic plans made by Mr. Raymond, and we see Mr. Tillerson's diplomatic skills as playing an important role in enhancing those plans.

Company Financials Fiscal Year Ended Dec. 31

Per Share Data ($)	2009	2008	2007	2006	2005	2004	2003	2002	2001	2000
Tangible Book Value	23.39	22.70	22.62	19.87	18.13	15.90	13.69	11.13	10.74	10.21
Cash Flow	6.44	11.08	9.48	8.89	7.34	5.38	4.50	2.84	3.32	3.43
Earnings	3.98	8.69	7.28	6.62	5.71	3.89	3.15	1.61	2.18	2.27
S&P Core Earnings	4.36	8.64	7.40	6.75	5.72	4.01	3.03	1.52	2.03	NA
Dividends	1.66	1.55	1.37	1.28	1.14	1.06	0.98	0.92	0.91	0.88
Payout Ratio	42%	18%	19%	19%	20%	27%	31%	57%	42%	39%
Prices:High	82.73	96.12	95.27	79.00	65.96	52.05	41.13	44.58	45.84	47.72
Prices:Low	61.86	56.51	69.02	56.42	49.25	39.91	31.58	29.75	35.01	34.94
P/E Ratio:High	21	11	13	12	12	13	13	28	21	21
P/E Ratio:Low	16	7	9	9	9	10	10	18	16	15

Income Statement Analysis (Million $)										
Revenue	310,586	477,359	404,552	377,635	370,680	298,035	246,738	204,506	213,488	232,748
Operating Income	NA	78,669	156,810	150,107	59,255	45,639	32,230	23,280	29,602	33,309
Depreciation, Depletion and Amortization	11,917	12,379	12,250	11,416	10,253	9,767	9,047	8,310	7,944	8,130
Interest Expense	548	673	957	957	654	496	638	207	398	293	589
Pretax Income	34,777	81,750	71,479	68,453	60,231	42,017	32,660	17,719	24,688	27,493
Effective Tax Rate	43.5%	44.7%	41.8%	40.8%	38.7%	37.9%	33.7%	36.7%	36.5%	40.3%
Net Income	19,280	45,220	40,610	39,500	36,130	25,330	20,960	11,011	15,105	15,990
S&P Core Earnings	21,109	44,959	41,250	40,263	36,164	26,089	20,214	10,418	14,042	NA

Balance Sheet & Other Financial Data (Million $)										
Cash	10,862	32,007	34,500	32,848	28,671	18,531	10,626	7,229	6,547	7,081
Current Assets	55,235	72,266	85,963	75,777	73,342	60,377	45,960	38,291	35,681	40,399
Total Assets	233,323	228,052	242,082	219,015	208,335	195,256	174,278	152,644	143,174	149,000
Current Liabilities	52,061	49,100	58,312	48,817	46,307	42,981	38,386	33,175	30,114	38,191
Long Term Debt	6,761	7,025	7,183	6,645	6,220	5,013	4,756	6,655	7,099	7,280
Common Equity	110,569	112,965	121,762	113,844	111,186	101,756	89,915	74,597	73,161	70,757
Total Capital	123,037	144,274	156,126	141,340	138,284	131,813	118,171	100,504	99,444	97,709
Capital Expenditures	22,491	19,318	15,387	15,462	13,839	11,986	12,859	11,437	9,989	8,446
Cash Flow	31,197	57,599	52,860	50,916	46,383	35,097	30,007	19,321	23,049	24,120
Current Ratio	1.1	1.5	1.5	1.6	1.6	1.4	1.2	1.2	1.2	1.1
% Long Term Debt of Capitalization	Nil	4.9	4.6	4.7	4.4	3.8	4.0	6.6	7.1	7.5
% Return on Assets	8.4	19.2	17.6	18.5	17.9	13.7	12.8	7.4	10.3	10.9
% Return on Equity	NA	38.5	34.5	35.1	33.9	26.4	25.5	14.9	21.0	23.8

Data as orig reptd.; bef. results of disc opers/spec. items. Per share data adj. for stk. divs.; EPS diluted. E-Estimated. NA-Not Available. NM-Not Meaningful. NR-Not Ranked. UR-Under Review.

Office: 5959 Las Colinas Blvd, Irving, TX 75039-2298.
Telephone: 972-444-1000.
Website: http://www.exxonmobil.com
Chrmn, Pres & CEO: R.W. Tillerson

SVP, CFO & Treas: D. Humphreys
Chief Acctg Officer & Cntlr: P.T. Mulva
Secy: D.S. Rosenthal
General Counsel: S.J. Balagia

Board Members: M. J. Boskin, P. Brabeck-Letmathe, L. R. Faulkner, J. S. Fishman, K. C. Frazier, W. W. George, M. C. Nelson, S. J. Palmisano, S. S. Reinemund, R. W. Tillerson, E. E. Whitacre, Jr.

Founded: 1870
Domicile: New Jersey
Employees: 80,700

The McGraw·Hill Companies

Family Dollar Stores Inc.

STANDARD &POOR'S

S&P Recommendation **STRONG BUY** ★★★★★

Price	12-Mo. Target Price	Investment Style
$45.42 (as of Oct 22, 2010)	$58.00	Large-Cap Blend

GICS Sector Consumer Discretionary
Sub-Industry General Merchandise Stores

Summary This company operates a chain of over 6,700 retail discount stores in 44 states across the U.S.

Key Stock Statistics (Source S&P, Vickers, company reports)

52-Wk Range	$46.43–27.15	S&P Oper. EPS 2011**E**	3.20	Market Capitalization(B)	$6.024	Beta	0.20
Trailing 12-Month EPS	$2.62	S&P Oper. EPS 2012**E**	3.65	Yield (%)	1.37	S&P 3-Yr. Proj. EPS CAGR(%)	16
Trailing 12-Month P/E	17.3	P/E on S&P Oper. EPS 2011**E**	14.2	Dividend Rate/Share	$0.62	S&P Credit Rating	NA
$10K Invested 5 Yrs Ago	$22,638	Common Shares Outstg. (M)	132.6	Institutional Ownership (%)	93		

Price Performance

30-Week Mov. Avg. · · · 10-Week Mov. Avg. – – GAAP Earnings vs. Previous Year Volume Above Avg. STARS
12-Mo. Target Price — Relative Strength — ▲ Up ▼ Down ▶ No Change Below Avg.

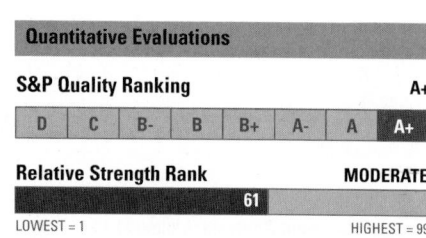

Options: ASE, CBOE, P, Ph

Analysis prepared by **Jason N. Asaeda** on October 11, 2010, when the stock traded at **$ 46.23**.

Highlights

➤ We expect net sales to reach $8.6 billion in FY 11 (Aug.). We look for growth to be driven by a same-store sales increase of about 6%, as well as an accelerated pace of expansion and an aggressive store remodel program. We see FDO attracting cost-conscious consumers with its value-priced assortment of everyday necessities, and planned improvements in the quality and packaging of private-label consumables. The company also plans to open 300 new stores in FY 11, up from 150 in FY 10, and to renovate 600 to 800 existing stores.

➤ We expect sales to be weighted toward lower-margin consumables and foresee higher freight costs and incremental expenses in support of new stores, store renovations, and longer store operating hours. However, we see opportunity for operating margins to widen modestly on lower markdowns and shrinkage, reflecting effective inventory management, increased penetration of private-label goods, higher initial mark-ups through global sourcing, and expense leverage off of projected same-store sales growth.

➤ Factoring in likely share buybacks, we see EPS of $3.20 in FY 11 ($2.75 in calendar 2010).

Investment Rationale/Risk

➤ We recently raised our recommendation on the shares to strong buy, from buy, based on valuation. With FDO reporting that its core lower-income customers are shopping close to need, we expect average customer transaction value to remain relatively flat over the near term. However, we believe the company is positioned well to drive higher customer traffic and to increase customers' shopping frequency with its growing food assortment and new easier-to-shop store layout. Longer term, we look for FDO to focus on tailoring product assortments by store to drive higher sales productivity. We also view the company's finances and balance sheet as healthy, and expect FDO to generate free cash that it can use, in part, for new store openings and share buybacks.

➤ Risks to our recommendation and target price include sales shortfalls due to changes in consumer confidence, spending habits and buying preferences; merchandise availability; and increased promotional activity by competitors.

➤ Our 12-month target price of $58 reflects a forward P/E multiple of 18.2X, FDO's 10-year historical average, applied to our FY 11 EPS estimate.

Qualitative Risk Assessment

LOW	**MEDIUM**	HIGH

Our risk assessment reflects FDO's S&P Quality Ranking of A+ for growth and stability of earnings and dividends; and our view of a healthy balance sheet and strong cash flow generation. We also believe demand for the company's merchandise is generally stable and not affected by changes in the economy, except for more discretionary categories.

Quantitative Evaluations

S&P Quality Ranking   A+

D	C	B-	B	B+	A-	A	**A+**

Relative Strength Rank   MODERATE

61

LOWEST = 1   HIGHEST = 99

Revenue/Earnings Data

Revenue (Million $)

	1Q	2Q	3Q	4Q	Year
2010	1,823	2,090	1,997	1,957	7,867
2009	1,754	1,992	1,843	1,811	7,401
2008	1,683	1,833	1,702	1,766	6,984
2007	1,600	1,947	1,655	1,632	6,834
2006	1,511	1,736	1,570	1,578	6,395
2005	1,380	1,587	1,428	1,430	5,825

Earnings Per Share ($)

2010	0.49	0.81	0.77	0.56	2.62
2009	0.42	0.60	0.62	0.43	2.07
2008	0.37	0.45	0.46	0.38	1.66
2007	0.36	0.60	0.40	0.26	1.62
2006	0.32	0.35	0.37	0.21	1.26
2005	0.32	0.48	0.32	0.18	1.30

Fiscal year ended Aug. 31. Next earnings report expected: Early January. EPS Estimates based on S&P Operating Earnings; historical GAAP earnings are as reported.

Dividend Data (Dates: mm/dd Payment Date: mm/dd/yy)

Amount ($)	Date Decl.	Ex-Div. Date	Stk. of Record	Payment Date
0.135	11/18	12/11	12/15	01/15/10
0.155	01/21	03/11	03/15	04/15/10
0.155	04/16	06/11	06/15	07/15/10
0.155	08/26	09/13	09/15	10/15/10

Dividends have been paid since 1976. Source: Company reports.

Please read the Required Disclosures and Analyst Certification on the last page of this report.

The McGraw-Hill Companies

Family Dollar Stores Inc.

STANDARD &POOR'S

Business Summary October 11, 2010

CORPORATE OVERVIEW. Family Dollar Stores Inc. (FDO) operates a chain of over 6,700 retail discount stores in 44 states. The company describes its typical customer as a woman in her mid-40s who is the head of her household and has an annual income of under $30,000. Family Dollar stores carry an assortment of hardlines and softlines priced from under $1 to $10 and are operated on a self-service basis, with limited advertising support and promotional activity. The once cash-only stores now accept PIN-based debit card payments in most locations. Food stamp and credit card acceptance is also being rolled out. In our view, broader tender options offer the company an opportunity to improve its share of customer wallet as shopping is more convenient and available cash does not limit basket size.

Store inventory is comprised of both regularly available merchandise, which provides consistency in product offerings, and a frequently changing selection of brands and products that FDO acquires through closeouts and manufacturer overruns at discounted wholesale prices. Low product costs and store overhead enable the company to sell its value-priced merchandise profitably.

PRIMARY BUSINESS DYNAMICS. FDO's primary growth drivers are same-store sales and chain expansion. In FY 10 (Aug.), same-store sales rose 4.8%, reflecting flat average customer transaction value and higher customer traffic, as measured by the company in number of register transactions. In our opinion, FDO is attracting customers with an expanded assortment of consumables and "treasure hunt" items that add an element of excitement and interest to the shopping experience. The company has also increased its marketing efforts to emphasize the value and shopping convenience it offers.

While core customers are spending more per store visit, they are also shopping less often due to macroeconomic concerns. However, we think FDO is gaining incremental business from middle-income customers trading down from higher-priced retailers for everyday basics. In the company's view, the economic downturn hurt low income consumers first and the hardest, and is now impacting higher-income consumers.

Company Financials Fiscal Year Ended Aug. 31

Per Share Data ($)	2010	2009	2008	2007	2006	2005	2004	2003	2002	2001
Tangible Book Value	NA	10.38	8.98	8.19	8.04	8.64	8.13	7.61	6.66	5.57
Cash Flow	3.88	3.21	2.72	2.59	2.13	1.99	2.10	1.94	1.69	1.49
Earnings	2.62	2.07	1.66	1.62	1.26	1.30	1.53	1.43	1.25	1.10
S&P Core Earnings	NA	2.07	1.66	1.71	1.44	1.21	1.45	1.39	1.22	1.08
Dividends	0.58	0.52	0.48	0.44	0.40	0.36	0.32	0.28	0.25	0.23
Payout Ratio	22%	25%	29%	27%	31%	28%	21%	20%	20%	21%
Prices:High	46.43	35.00	32.50	35.42	30.91	35.25	39.66	44.13	37.25	31.35
Prices:Low	27.15	24.02	14.62	17.95	21.57	19.40	25.09	25.46	23.75	18.38
P/E Ratio:High	18	17	20	22	24	27	26	31	30	29
P/E Ratio:Low	10	12	9	11	17	15	16	18	19	17

Income Statement Analysis (Million $)										
Revenue	7,867	7,401	6,984	6,834	6,395	5,825	5,282	4,750	4,163	3,665
Operating Income	748	617	515	532	452	458	512	478	419	366
Depreciation	172	160	150	144	135	115	97.9	88.3	77.0	67.7
Interest Expense	13.3	14.1	15.4	17.0	13.1	Nil	Nil	Nil	Nil	Nil
Pretax Income	564	451	362	382	311	343	414	390	342	298
Effective Tax Rate	NA	35.4%	35.6%	36.4%	37.3%	36.5%	36.6%	36.5%	36.5%	36.5%
Net Income	358	291	233	243	195	218	263	247	217	190
S&P Core Earnings	NA	291	233	257	223	202	250	241	213	186

Balance Sheet & Other Financial Data (Million $)										
Cash	503	445	159	87.0	79.7	105	150	207	220	21.8
Current Assets	1,660	1,599	1,344	1,537	1,419	1,355	1,225	1,156	1,056	807
Total Assets	2,982	2,843	2,662	2,624	2,523	2,410	2,167	1,986	1,755	1,400
Current Liabilities	1,054	1,060	1,069	1,130	986	895	714	595	531	390
Long Term Debt	250	250	250	250	250	Nil	Nil	Nil	Nil	Nil
Common Equity	1,422	1,440	1,254	1,175	1,208	2,187	1,360	1,533	1,245	959
Total Capital	1,672	1,690	1,555	1,494	1,537	2,274	1,454	1,612	1,314	1,009
Capital Expenditures	212	155	168	132	192	229	218	220	187	163
Cash Flow	530	451	383	387	330	332	361	336	294	257
Current Ratio	1.6	1.5	1.3	1.4	1.4	1.5	1.7	1.9	2.0	2.1
% Long Term Debt of Capitalization	15.0	14.8	16.1	16.7	16.2	Nil	Nil	Nil	Nil	Nil
% Net Income of Revenue	4.6	3.9	3.3	3.5	3.1	3.7	5.0	5.2	5.2	5.2
% Return on Assets	12.3	10.6	8.8	9.4	7.9	9.4	12.7	13.2	13.8	14.3
% Return on Equity	25.0	21.6	19.2	20.3	8.9	10.6	19.7	17.8	18.9	21.6

Data as orig reptd.; bef. results of disc opers/spec. items. Per share data adj. for stk. divs.; EPS diluted. E-Estimated. NA-Not Available. NM-Not Meaningful. NR-Not Ranked. UR-Under Review.

Office: 10401 Monroe Rd, Matthews, NC 28105.
Telephone: 704-847-6961.
Website: http://www.familydollar.com
Chrmn & CEO: H.R. Levine

Pres & COO: R.J. Kelly
SVP & CFO: K.T. Smith
SVP & Chief Acctg Officer: C.M. Sowers
SVP, Secy & General Counsel: J.C. Snyder, Jr.

Investor Contact: K.F. Rawlins (704-849-7496)
Board Members: M. R. Bernstein, P. L. Davies, S. A. Decker, E. C. Dolby, G. A. Eisenberg, H. R. Levine, G. R. Mahoney, Jr., J. G. Martin, H. Morgan, D. Pond

Founded: 1959
Domicile: Delaware
Employees: 47,000

Fastenal Company

STANDARD &POOR'S

S&P Recommendation	**STRONG BUY** ★★★★★	Price	12-Mo. Target Price	Investment Style
		$52.90 (as of Oct 22, 2010)	$74.00	Large-Cap Growth

GICS Sector Industrials
Sub-Industry Trading Companies & Distributors

Summary This company distributes fasteners and other industrial and construction supplies through about 2,450 stores throughout the U.S. and in a few foreign countries.

Key Stock Statistics (Source S&P, Vickers, company reports)

52-Wk Range	$56.65– 34.41	S&P Oper. EPS 2010E	1.84	Market Capitalization(B)	$7.799	Beta	0.95
Trailing 12-Month EPS	$1.66	S&P Oper. EPS 2011E	2.30	Yield (%)	1.55	S&P 3-Yr. Proj. EPS CAGR(%)	30
Trailing 12-Month P/E	31.9	P/E on S&P Oper. EPS 2010E	28.8	Dividend Rate/Share	$0.82	S&P Credit Rating	NA
$10K Invested 5 Yrs Ago	$16,672	Common Shares Outstg. (M)	147.4	Institutional Ownership (%)	84		

Price Performance

30-Week Mov. Avg. · · · 10-Week Mov. Avg. – – **GAAP Earnings vs. Previous Year** Volume Above Avg. STARS
12-Mo. Target Price — Relative Strength — ▲ Up ▼ Down ▶ No Change Below Avg.

Options: ASE, CBOE, P

Analysis prepared by **Michael W. Jaffe** on October 14, 2010, when the stock traded at **$ 52.38.**

Highlights

➤ We forecast sales to increase 19% in 2011. Sales were very soft in 2009, limited by the very weak U.S. economy. However, we believe that early signs of economic growth allowed FAST's sales to start a recovery in the first nine months of 2010, and we expect this trend to continue. We see most of the expected near-term growth coming from its manufacturing client base. We also look for FAST's top line to be assisted by the planned resumption of a more normalized pace of store openings in 2010's second half, market share gains, and expanded product offerings.

➤ We expect FAST's sales details to shift in coming periods, under its current strategy (announced in July 2007) of slowing its rate of store growth while increasing the size of the sales staff at its stores.

➤ We look for wider net margins in 2011, on the improvement that we expect in sales trends. We also see margins benefiting from FAST's likely ongoing focus on controlling operating expenses, assisted in part by a higher proportion of variable costs under its revised business model.

Investment Rationale/Risk

➤ We expect FAST's business to continue its recent revival over the coming year. Sales to manufacturing customers have rebounded very solidly in recent quarters, while non-residential construction sales are taking longer to bounce back, but have shown what we see as early signs of revival. We are also very positive about FAST's longer-term outlook under its new business strategy of larger sales staffs and fewer store openings. Combined with valuation considerations, we view FAST as undervalued.

➤ Risks to our recommendation and target price include a resumption of a downturn in the U.S. economy, and unsuccessful results from the company's change in business strategy.

➤ The shares recently traded about 23X our 2011 EPS estimate, a large premium to the S&P 500, but at the low end of FAST's typical valuation as it moves further into economic recoveries. Given our outlook for an ongoing rebound in the company's business, and our very positive views of its mid-2007 strategy change and its management effort, we think a higher P/E multiple is merited. Our 12-month target price is $74, or just over 32X our 2011 EPS forecast.

Qualitative Risk Assessment

LOW	**MEDIUM**	HIGH

Our risk assessment for FAST reflects our view of its consistent generation of solid levels of free cash flow, a healthy balance sheet with no long-term debt, and a very well run business model, with a strong focus on growth and cost controls. This is offset by the cyclical nature of FAST's business and uncertainties in its mid-2007 change in business model, to one with less store unit growth and larger sales staffs.

Quantitative Evaluations

S&P Quality Ranking A

D	C	B-	B	B+	A-	**A**	A+

Relative Strength Rank MODERATE

51

LOWEST = 1   HIGHEST = 99

Revenue/Earnings Data

Revenue (Million $)

	1Q	2Q	3Q	4Q	Year
2010	520.8	571.2	603.8	--	--
2009	489.3	474.9	489.3	476.8	1,930
2008	566.2	604.2	625.0	545.0	2,340
2007	489.2	519.7	533.8	519.2	2,062
2006	431.7	458.8	470.1	448.7	1,809
2005	353.8	383.3	402.2	384.0	1,523

Earnings Per Share ($)

2010	0.38	0.47	0.51	E0.48	E1.84
2009	0.33	0.29	0.32	0.30	1.24
2008	0.46	0.51	0.49	0.42	1.88
2007	0.36	0.40	0.41	0.38	1.55
2006	0.32	0.34	0.36	0.30	1.32
2005	0.25	0.29	0.31	0.26	1.10

Fiscal year ended Dec. 31. Next earnings report expected: Mid January. EPS Estimates based on S&P Operating Earnings; historical GAAP earnings are as reported.

Dividend Data (Dates: mm/dd Payment Date: mm/dd/yy)

Amount ($)	Date Decl.	Ex-Div. Date	Stk. of Record	Payment Date
0.400	01/18	02/10	02/15	02/26/10
0.420	07/12	08/18	08/20	09/03/10

Dividends have been paid since 1991. Source: Company reports.

Please read the Required Disclosures and Analyst Certification on the last page of this report.

The **McGraw-Hill** Companies

Fastenal Company

STANDARD &POOR'S

Business Summary October 14, 2010

CORPORATE OVERVIEW. Fastenal, which sells industrial and construction supplies, began operations in 1967, with a plan to supply threaded fasteners in small- to medium-size cities. It later changed its business plan to include some sites in large cities. At the end of 2009, FAST had 2,369 stores in all 50 states, Puerto Rico, Canada, Mexico, Singapore, China, Malaysia, Hungary and the Netherlands (2,153 in the U.S.), up 2.5% from 2,311 sites a year earlier. The company's store count had grown to 2,453 at September 30, 2010. FAST distributes products to its store sites from 14 distribution centers, with 11 located throughout the U.S., two in Canada and one in Mexico. Threaded fasteners accounted for 45% of 2009 sales (46% in 2008).

The company offered 10 product lines at the end of 2009. Its original product line now consists of about 410,000 different types of threaded fasteners and supplies. Other product lines offered include 136,000 different types of tools and equipment; 251,000 different cutting tool blades and abrasives; 64,000 types of fluid transfer components and accessories for hydraulic and pneumatic power, plumbing, and heating, ventilating and air-conditioning; 18,000 types of material handling, storage and packaging products; 16,000 kinds of janitorial supplies, chemicals and paint; 25,000 types of electrical supplies;

34,000 welding supply items; 30,000 different safety supplies; and 12,000 types of metals, alloys and materials. FAST sells mostly to customers in the manufacturing market for both OEMs and maintenance and repair operations, and to construction markets. Its construction customers serve general construction, electrical, plumbing, sheet metal, and road contractor markets.

Most products sold are made by other companies. No supplier accounted for over 5% of FAST's 2009 purchases. No customer accounts for a significant portion of total sales.

COMPETITIVE LANDSCAPE. Fastenal's business is highly competitive. Competition includes both large distributors located primarily in large cities and smaller distributors located in many of the cities in which the company has stores. FAST believes that the principal competitive factors affecting the markets for its products are customer service, price and convenience.

Company Financials Fiscal Year Ended Dec. 31

Per Share Data ($)	2009	2008	2007	2006	2005	2004	2003	2002	2001	2000
Tangible Book Value	8.07	7.68	6.76	6.10	5.19	4.51	3.80	3.30	2.80	2.37
Cash Flow	1.51	2.14	1.79	1.54	1.29	1.02	0.69	0.60	0.56	0.61
Earnings	1.24	1.88	1.55	1.32	1.10	0.86	0.56	0.50	0.46	0.53
S&P Core Earnings	1.24	1.91	1.55	1.32	1.10	0.86	0.55	0.45	0.47	NA
Dividends	0.72	0.79	0.44	0.40	0.31	0.20	0.11	0.03	0.02	0.02
Payout Ratio	58%	42%	28%	30%	28%	23%	19%	5%	5%	4%
Prices:High	42.28	56.48	52.94	49.32	41.96	32.25	25.50	21.68	18.25	18.33
Prices:Low	25.87	30.08	33.05	33.18	25.54	21.94	13.76	13.31	11.73	8.92
P/E Ratio:High	34	30	30	37	38	37	46	44	40	34
P/E Ratio:Low	21	16	21	25	23	26	25	27	26	17

Income Statement Analysis (Million $)										
Revenue	1,930	2,340	2,062	1,809	1,523	1,238	995	905	818	746
Operating Income	337	498	414	354	297	231	156	131	127	141
Depreciation	40.1	39.3	37.4	33.5	29.0	23.6	20.4	16.9	15.0	11.8
Interest Expense	NA	Nil	Nil	Nil	Nil	Nil	Nil	Nil	Nil	Nil
Pretax Income	297	451	378	321	269	208	136	121	114	131
Effective Tax Rate	38.0%	38.0%	38.4%	38.0%	38.0%	37.1%	38.3%	38.3%	38.3%	38.6%
Net Income	184	280	233	199	167	131	84.1	74.8	70.7	80.7
S&P Core Earnings	185	284	233	199	167	131	82.6	68.5	70.3	NA

Balance Sheet & Other Financial Data (Million $)										
Cash	189	86.7	57.4	33.9	70.1	74.5	95.6	51.4	68.5	32.7
Current Assets	982	975	881	768	649	538	454	396	341	293
Total Assets	1,330	1,304	1,163	1,039	890	1,308	652	559	475	402
Current Liabilities	120	148	138	104	91.5	71.2	60.9	47.1	40.6	36.6
Long Term Debt	NA	Nil	Nil	Nil	Nil	Nil	Nil	Nil	Nil	Nil
Common Equity	1,191	1,142	1,010	922	784	684	577	504	425	359
Total Capital	1,191	1,156	1,025	935	798	699	591	516	435	366
Capital Expenditures	52.5	95.3	55.8	77.6	65.9	52.7	50.2	42.7	45.3	36.7
Cash Flow	224	319	270	233	196	155	105	91.8	85.1	92.5
Current Ratio	8.2	6.6	6.4	7.4	7.1	7.6	7.5	8.4	8.4	8.0
% Long Term Debt of Capitalization	Nil	Nil	Nil	Nil	Nil	Nil	Nil	Nil	Nil	Nil
% Net Income of Revenue	9.6	12.0	11.3	11.0	11.0	10.6	8.5	8.3	8.6	10.8
% Return on Assets	14.0	22.7	21.1	20.6	20.0	10.9	13.9	14.5	16.0	22.4
% Return on Equity	15.8	26.0	24.1	23.3	22.7	20.8	15.6	16.1	17.9	25.2

Data as orig reptd.; bef. results of disc opers/spec. items. Per share data adj. for stk. divs.; EPS diluted. E-Estimated. NA-Not Available. NM-Not Meaningful. NR-Not Ranked. UR-Under Review.

Office: 2001 Theurer Boulevard, Winona, MN 55987-0978.
Telephone: 507-454-5374.
Email: info@fastenal.com
Website: http://www.fastenal.com

Chrmn: R.A. Kierlin
Pres & CEO: W.D. Oberton
COO: J.C. Jansen
EVP, CFO, Chief Acctg Officer & Treas: D.L. Florness

Board Members: M. J. Ancius, M. J. Dolan, M. M. Gostomski, R. A. Kierlin, H. L. Miller, W. D. Oberton, S. A. Satterlee, S. M. Slaggie, R. K. Wisecup

Founded: 1968
Domicile: Minnesota
Employees: 12,045

The McGraw-Hill Companies

Federated Investors Inc.

STANDARD &POOR'S

S&P Recommendation HOLD ★★★☆☆

Price $24.11 (as of Oct 22, 2010)	**12-Mo. Target Price** $25.00	**Investment Style** Large-Cap Growth

GICS Sector Financials
Sub-Industry Asset Management & Custody Banks

Summary This leading U.S. investment management company has a strong market share in money market products.

Key Stock Statistics (Source S&P, Vickers, company reports)

52-Wk Range	$28.31– 20.01	S&P Oper. EPS 2010**E**	1.57	Market Capitalization(B)	$2.485	Beta	0.74
Trailing 12-Month EPS	$1.91	S&P Oper. EPS 2011**E**	1.72	Yield (%)	3.98	S&P 3-Yr. Proj. EPS CAGR(%)	-4
Trailing 12-Month P/E	12.6	P/E on S&P Oper. EPS 2010**E**	15.4	Dividend Rate/Share	$0.96	S&P Credit Rating	NA
$10K Invested 5 Yrs Ago	$9,261	Common Shares Outstg. (M)	103.1	Institutional Ownership (%)	74		

Price Performance

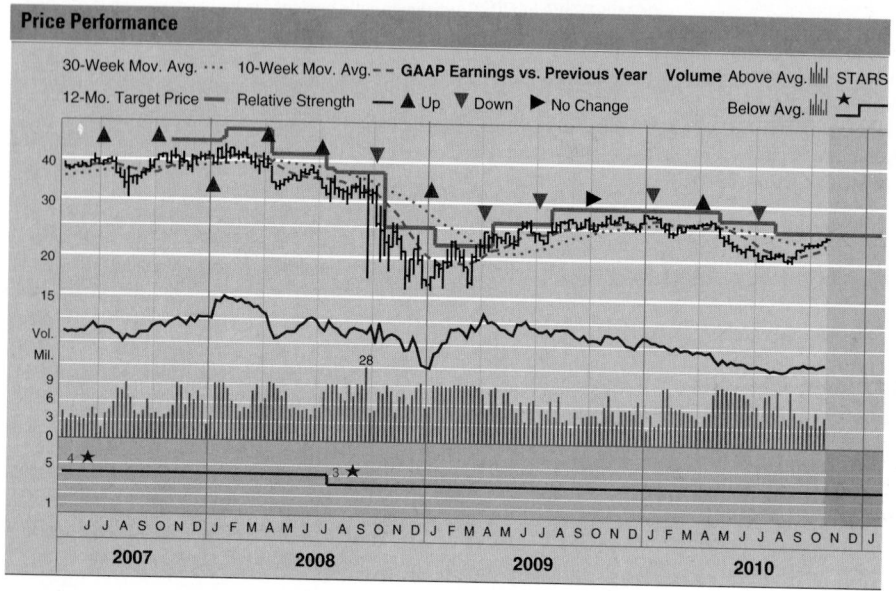

30-Week Mov. Avg. ··· 10-Week Mov. Avg.- - **GAAP Earnings vs. Previous Year** Volume Above Avg. STARS
12-Mo. Target Price — Relative Strength — ▲ Up ▼ Down ▶ No Change Below Avg. ★

Options: ASE, CBOE

Analysis prepared by **Matthew Albrecht** on July 26, 2010, when the stock traded at **$ 20.95.**

Highlights

▶ After having benefited from volatility in the markets during the financial crisis as money market and ultra-short-term bond products saw strong flows from investors, ultra-low rates have investors looking elsewhere for yield. After peaking in early 2009, money market assets have steadily declined. Equity strategies have also seen redemptions this year as market volatility and economic uncertainty has investors spooked, by our estimation. Fixed income funds have continued to attract investor dollars, but remain a small part of FII's overall asset mix. We think the firm's greatest challenge remains its ability to retain client assets in its equity and bond products as risk appetites grow. The company has pursued small acquisitions to broaden its lineup. We expect continued pressure on management fee rates due to an unfavorable asset mix and fee waivers.

▶ We think marketing and distribution costs associated with growth in the managed asset base that pressured margins over the past two years will begin to abate in 2010. Despite an increase in compensation accruals on a relative basis, the pretax margin should expand.

▶ We see earnings $1.57 in 2010 and $1.72 in 2011.

Investment Rationale/Risk

▶ We view a discounted valuation on the shares relative to peers as appropriate, given the firm's focus on lower-margined money market funds. We view favorably the company's direct sales force and strong relationships with wholesalers and intermediaries in our valuation. We also like moves to increase FII's exposure to fixed income and equity funds, which should help margins. We have a positive view of the company's common share repurchase program, which should help EPS results.

▶ Risks to our recommendation and target price include increased competition, lower short-term interest rates, and weaker equity fund performance. From a corporate governance perspective, we would like to see a greater percentage of independent directors on the board.

▶ Low interest rates have investors withdrawing money market assets, and while the asset mix has improved, results are likely to sag this year. The stock recently traded at about 13.4X our 2010 EPS estimate. Our 12-month target price of $25 is equal to 16.1X our forward 12-month earnings estimate of $1.55, a discount to peers.

Qualitative Risk Assessment

LOW	MEDIUM	HIGH

Our risk assessment reflects the company's relatively narrow product offering and significant competition from larger, more diversified fund management companies.

Quantitative Evaluations

S&P Quality Ranking A-

D	C	B-	B	B+	A-	A	A+

Relative Strength Rank MODERATE

70

LOWEST = 1   HIGHEST = 99

Revenue/Earnings Data

Revenue (Million $)

	1Q	2Q	3Q	4Q	Year
2010	233.0	231.5	--	--	--
2009	310.6	306.9	293.6	264.8	1,176
2008	305.7	310.3	305.9	301.8	1,224
2007	264.4	276.5	286.0	300.3	1,128
2006	238.8	236.4	243.9	259.7	978.9
2005	205.4	220.7	241.4	241.8	909.2

Earnings Per Share ($)

2010	0.38	0.46	E0.35	E0.38	E1.57
2009	0.34	0.52	0.56	0.51	1.92
2008	0.55	0.55	0.56	0.54	2.20
2007	0.50	0.54	0.57	0.52	2.12
2006	0.43	0.44	0.43	0.51	1.80
2005	0.07	0.35	0.61	0.48	1.51

Fiscal year ended Dec. 31. Next earnings report expected: Late October. EPS Estimates based on S&P Operating Earnings; historical GAAP earnings are as reported.

Dividend Data (Dates: mm/dd Payment Date: mm/dd/yy)

Amount ($)	Date Decl.	Ex-Div. Date	Stk. of Record	Payment Date
1.26 Spl.	01/28	02/03	02/05	02/12/10
0.240	01/28	02/03	02/05	02/12/10
0.240	04/22	05/05	05/07	05/14/10
0.240	07/22	08/04	08/06	08/13/10

Dividends have been paid since 1998. Source: Company reports.

Please read the Required Disclosures and Analyst Certification on the last page of this report.

STANDARD &POOR'S

Federated Investors Inc.

Business Summary July 26, 2010

CORPORATE OVERVIEW. A leading provider of investment management products and related financial services, Federated Investors (FII) has been in the mutual fund business for more than 40 years. The company is one of the largest mutual fund managers in the United States, based on assets under management. Assets under management totaled $389.3 billion at the end of 2009, down from $407 billion at the end of 2008.

Federated manages assets across a wide range of asset categories, including increasing participation in fast-growing areas such as equity and international investments. It is among the industry leaders in money market funds, based on assets under management, and offers one of the industry's most comprehensive product lines. Assets under management by class at the end of 2009 included money market (80% of total), equity (8%), fixed income (9%) and liquidation portfolios (3%). By product type, mutual funds represented about 85% of total assets under management, with the balance held in separately managed accounts and liquidation portfolios.

CORPORATE STRATEGY. Over the past several years, Federated has added

several investment professionals and strengthened its equity and fixed-income product portfolio, in our opinion. The company has more than 170 investment professionals, which includes portfolio managers, analysts and traders. The company ended 2007 with 148 mutual funds and various separately managed accounts. FII has managed institutional separate accounts since 1973, and is focused on growing its managed account business for high-net-worth individuals with investable equity assets of $100,000 or more.

Federated believes that it benefits from a developing industry trend toward intermediary-assisted sales (sales of mutual fund products through a financial intermediary), driven by the wide array of options now available to investors, and by a need for financial planning advice that has resulted from a recent increase in the average household's financial assets.

Company Financials Fiscal Year Ended Dec. 31

Per Share Data ($)	2009	2008	2007	2006	2005	2004	2003	2002	2001	2000
Tangible Book Value	NM	NM	0.53	0.39	1.59	1.36	2.05	1.46	0.79	0.86
Cash Flow	2.21	2.44	2.37	2.07	1.75	1.79	1.95	1.90	1.65	1.40
Earnings	1.92	2.20	2.12	1.80	1.51	1.62	1.71	1.74	1.44	1.27
S&P Core Earnings	1.91	2.23	2.16	1.80	1.67	1.70	1.67	1.69	1.46	NA
Dividends	0.96	0.93	0.81	0.69	0.58	0.41	0.30	0.22	0.22	0.14
Payout Ratio	50%	42%	38%	38%	38%	26%	17%	12%	15%	11%
Prices:High	28.31	45.01	43.35	40.17	38.11	33.79	31.90	36.18	32.80	31.69
Prices:Low	16.10	15.80	30.31	29.56	26.99	26.72	23.85	23.43	23.31	12.46
P/E Ratio:High	15	20	20	22	25	21	19	21	23	25
P/E Ratio:Low	8	7	14	16	18	16	14	13	16	10

Income Statement Analysis (Million $)										
Income Interest	NA	NA	NA	NA	NA	NA	NA	NA	9.74	19.0
Income Other	1,176	1,224	1,128	979	909	847	823	711	706	662
Total Income	1,176	1,224	1,128	979	909	847	823	711	716	681
General Expenses	847	863	770	694	634	530	531	399	388	394
Interest Expense	5.71	5.20	5.40	8.19	17.9	21.0	4.71	4.79	29.7	34.2
Depreciation	23.8	24.5	25.6	24.1	24.0	19.0	20.6	19.2	26.0	15.8
Net Income	197	222	217	191	163	179	191	204	173	155
S&P Core Earnings	191	225	222	191	181	188	187	199	175	NA

Balance Sheet & Other Financial Data (Million $)										
Cash	90.5	45.4	146	119	246	258	234	151	73.5	150
Receivables	10.7	24.0	37.3	23.3	45.8	33.8	38.3	31.2	32.6	36.9
Cost of Investments	31.5	13.2	25.9	16.2	38.4	2.10	1.53	1.00	4.60	85.3
Total Assets	912	847	841	810	897	955	879	530	432	705
Loss Reserve	Nil	Nil	Nil	Nil	Nil	Nil	Nil	Nil	0.32	0.09
Short Term Debt	21.0	51.1	Nil	Nil	Nil	Nil	Nil	Nil	Nil	14.3
Capitalization:Debt	119	157	63.0	113	160	285	328	59.2	55.0	394
Capitalization:Equity	528	423	574	529	540	458	396	341	237	148
Capitalization:Total	662	613	667	671	723	767	744	416	299	583
Price Times Book Value:High	NM	NM	81.8	103	24.0	24.8	15.6	24.8	41.5	36.7
Price Times Book Value:Low	NM	NM	57.2	76.0	17.0	19.6	11.6	16.0	29.5	14.5
Cash Flow	221	246	243	215	187	198	212	223	199	171
% Expense/Operating Revenue	72.0	70.5	68.3	71.7	71.7	65.1	65.1	56.7	58.4	62.9
% Earnings & Depreciation/Assets	25.1	29.1	29.4	25.2	20.2	19.5	25.3	46.4	35.0	24.8

Data as orig reptd.; bef. results of disc opers/spec. items. Per share data adj. for stk. divs.; EPS diluted. E-Estimated. NA-Not Available. NM-Not Meaningful. NR-Not Ranked. UR-Under Review.

Office: Federated Investors Tower, 1001 Liberty Avenue, Pittsburgh, PA 15222-3779.
Telephone: 412-288-1900.
Email: investors@federatedinv.com
Website: http://www.federatedinvestors.com

Chrmn: J.F. Donahue
Pres & CEO: J.C. Donahue
Vice Chrmn: G.J. Ceresino
Vice Chrmn, EVP, Secy & General Counsel: J.W. McGonigle

CFO & Treas: T.R. Donahue
Investor Contact: R. Hanley (412-288-1920)
Board Members: L. E. Auriana, G. J. Ceresino, J. C. Donahue, J. F. Donahue, M. J. Farrell, D. M. Kelly, J. W. McGonigle, J. L. Murdy, E. G. O'Connor

Founded: 1955
Domicile: Pennsylvania
Employees: 1,368

FedEx Corp.

STANDARD &POOR'S

S&P Recommendation	**STRONG BUY** ★★★★★	Price $88.86 (as of Oct 22, 2010)	12-Mo. Target Price $113.00	Investment Style Large-Cap Growth

GICS Sector Industrials
Sub-Industry Air Freight & Logistics

Summary This company provides guaranteed domestic and international air express, residential and business ground package delivery, heavy freight and logistics services.

Key Stock Statistics (Source S&P, Vickers, company reports)

52-Wk Range	$97.75– 69.78	S&P Oper. EPS 2011**E**	5.35	Market Capitalization(B)	$27.959	Beta	1.20
Trailing 12-Month EPS	$4.39	S&P Oper. EPS 2012**E**	6.86	Yield (%)	0.54	S&P 3-Yr. Proj. EPS CAGR(%)	15
Trailing 12-Month P/E	20.2	P/E on S&P Oper. EPS 2011**E**	16.6	Dividend Rate/Share	$0.48	S&P Credit Rating	BBB
$10K Invested 5 Yrs Ago	$10,296	Common Shares Outstg. (M)	314.6	Institutional Ownership (%)	78		

Price Performance

30-Week Mov. Avg. · · · 10-Week Mov. Avg. – – GAAP Earnings vs. Previous Year Volume Above Avg. ⅏ STARS

12-Mo. Target Price — Relative Strength — ▲ Up ▼ Down ▶ No Change Below Avg. ⅏ ★

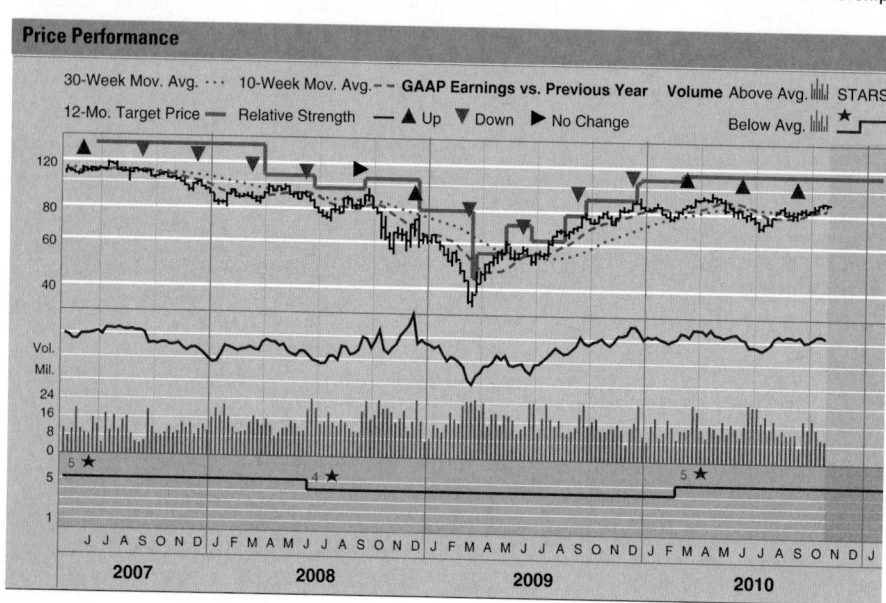

Options: ASE, CBOE, P, PH

Analysis prepared by **Jim Corridore** on September 21, 2010, when the stock traded at **$ 83.61**.

Qualitative Risk Assessment

LOW	MEDIUM	HIGH

Our risk assessment reflects our view of the company's strong and stable balance sheet, healthy cash flow generation, and strong earnings growth potential amid the inherent cyclicality of its business.

Quantitative Evaluations

S&P Quality Ranking B+

D	C	B-	B	**B+**	A-	A	A+

Relative Strength Rank MODERATE

62

LOWEST = 1 HIGHEST = 99

Revenue/Earnings Data

Revenue (Million $)

	1Q	2Q	3Q	4Q	Year
2011	9,457	--	--	--	--
2010	8,009	8,596	8,701	9,428	34,734
2009	9,970	9,538	8,137	7,852	35,497
2008	9,199	9,451	9,437	9,866	37,953
2007	8,545	8,926	8,592	9,151	35,214
2006	7,707	8,090	8,003	8,494	32,294

Earnings Per Share ($)

	1Q	2Q	3Q	4Q	Year
2011	1.20	E1.34	E1.23	E1.58	E5.35
2010	0.58	1.10	0.76	1.33	3.76
2009	1.23	1.58	0.31	-2.82	0.31
2008	1.23	1.54	1.26	-0.78	3.60
2007	1.53	1.64	1.35	1.96	6.48
2006	1.10	1.53	1.38	1.82	5.83

Fiscal year ended May 31. Next earnings report expected: Mid December. EPS Estimates based on S&P Operating Earnings; historical GAAP earnings are as reported.

Highlights

➤ We see FY 11 (May) revenues rising 12%, aided by global GDP improvement. We think FedEx Ground is likely to benefit from the exit of DHL from the U.S. business. We see Express revenues in FY 11 up 14%, Ground up 9%, and Freight up 11%. FDX announced a 5.9% rate increase for calendar 2010, and while we think it will have trouble fully passing it through, we think the company will be aggressive in pushing though rate increases as contracts expire.

➤ FDX recently announced a plan to combine and restructure its two freight operations, which should drive improving profitability in this segment. We believe improving volumes are likely to aid capacity utilization and productivity. Partly offsetting this should be rising personnel costs at Ground due to changes related to disputes over the independent contractor model. In addition, FDX faces pension cost headwinds and rising maintenance costs to bring idled planes back into service. Reinstatement of bonuses and 401k matching should lead to higher compensation expense.

➤ We forecast FY 11 EPS of $5.35, up 42% from operating EPS of $3.76 in FY 10. For FY 12, we see a 28% increase, to $6.86.

Investment Rationale/Risk

➤ We think that an improving U.S. and global economy is likely to lead to increased volumes across FDX's entire network, and improved capacity utilization should drive margin expansion in FY 11. We think the stock will benefit from increased investor interest in logistics stocks on concrete signs of economic improvement. We are encouraged by volume improvement, which we think signals that the economic recovery is starting to gain traction. As we expect that over the next three to five years EPS is likely to increase faster than the overall market, we think the shares deserve to trade at a premium valuation to the S&P 500.

➤ Risks to our recommendation and target price include a possible price war on excess industry capacity. If recent challenges to the company's independent contractor model are successful, or attempts to overturn the U.S. Railway Labor Act come to fruition, the company would likely incur higher labor costs.

➤ Our 12-month target price of $113 values the shares at 21X our FY 11 EPS estimate of $5.35, in the middle of the company's five-year historical P/E range of 13.7X-27.6X.

Dividend Data (Dates: mm/dd Payment Date: mm/dd/yy)

Amount ($)	Date Decl.	Ex-Div. Date	Stk. of Record	Payment Date
0.110	11/20	12/10	12/14	01/04/10
0.110	02/15	03/09	03/11	04/01/10
0.120	06/07	06/15	06/17	07/01/10
0.120	08/23	09/08	09/10	10/01/10

Dividends have been paid since 2002. Source: Company reports.

Please read the Required Disclosures and Analyst Certification on the last page of this report.

The McGraw·Hill Companies

FedEx Corp.

Business Summary September 21, 2010

CORPORATE OVERVIEW. FedEx Corp. provides global time-definite air express services for packages, documents and freight in more than 220 countries, and ground-based delivery of small packages in North America. In addition, the company offers expedited critical shipment delivery, customs brokerage solutions, less-than-truckload (LTL) freight transportation, and customized logistics. In February 2004, FDX paid $2.4 billion in cash for Kinko's, which operates about 1,200 copy centers that also provide business services. This business was subsequently renamed FedEx Office.

CORPORATE STRATEGY. The company intends to leverage and extend the FedEx brand and to provide customers with seamless access to its entire portfolio of integrated transportation services. Sales and marketing activities are coordinated among operating companies. Advanced information technology makes it convenient for customers to use the full range of FedEx services and provides a single point of contact for customers to access shipment tracking, customer service and invoicing information. The company intends to continue to operate independent express, ground and freight networks, but has increased its emphasis on having the individual business units work together to compete more effectively.

Company Financials Fiscal Year Ended May 31

Per Share Data ($)	2010	2009	2008	2007	2006	2005	2004	2003	2002	2001
Tangible Book Value	36.98	36.15	35.92	29.73	28.39	22.36	17.45	21.03	18.38	16.20
Cash Flow	10.01	6.64	9.84	12.20	10.83	9.48	7.28	7.20	6.89	6.35
Earnings	3.76	0.31	3.60	6.48	5.83	4.72	2.76	2.74	2.39	1.99
S&P Core Earnings	3.55	-0.16	2.77	6.32	5.60	4.48	2.61	1.38	0.95	0.44
Dividends	0.44	0.40	0.36	0.36	0.32	0.28	0.22	0.20	Nil	Nil
Payout Ratio	12%	129%	10%	6%	5%	6%	8%	7%	Nil	Nil
Calendar Year	2009	2008	2007	2006	2005	2004	2003	2002	2001	2000
Prices:High	92.59	99.46	121.42	120.01	105.82	100.92	78.05	61.35	53.48	49.85
Prices:Low	34.02	53.90	89.01	96.50	76.81	64.84	47.70	42.75	33.15	30.56
P/E Ratio:High	25	NM	34	19	18	21	28	22	22	25
P/E Ratio:Low	9	NM	25	15	13	14	17	16	14	15

Income Statement Analysis (Million $)	2010	2009	2008	2007	2006	2005	2004	2003	2002	2001
Revenue	34,734	35,497	37,953	35,214	32,294	29,363	24,710	22,487	20,607	19,629
Operating Income	3,974	3,926	4,903	5,018	4,564	3,933	3,250	2,822	2,804	2,347
Depreciation	1,958	1,975	1,946	1,742	1,550	1,462	1,375	1,351	1,364	1,276
Interest Expense	71.0	156	182	136	142	160	136	118	139	144
Pretax Income	1,894	677	2,016	3,215	2,899	2,313	1,319	1,338	1,160	928
Effective Tax Rate	NA	85.5%	44.2%	37.3%	37.7%	37.4%	36.5%	38.0%	37.5%	37.0%
Net Income	1,184	98.0	1,125	2,016	1,806	1,449	838	830	725	584
S&P Core Earnings	1,117	-49.6	868	1,966	1,733	1,376	790	415	286	130

Balance Sheet & Other Financial Data (Million $)	2010	2009	2008	2007	2006	2005	2004	2003	2002	2001
Cash	1,952	2,292	1,539	1,569	1,937	1,039	1,046	538	331	121
Current Assets	7,284	7,116	7,244	6,629	6,464	5,269	4,970	3,941	3,665	3,449
Total Assets	24,902	24,244	25,633	24,000	22,690	20,404	19,134	15,385	13,812	13,340
Current Liabilities	4,645	4,524	5,368	5,428	5,473	4,734	4,732	3,335	2,942	3,250
Long Term Debt	1,668	1,930	1,506	2,662	1,592	2,427	2,837	1,709	1,800	1,900
Common Equity	13,811	13,626	14,526	12,656	11,511	9,588	8,036	7,288	6,545	5,900
Total Capital	15,741	16,209	16,534	16,215	14,470	13,221	12,054	9,879	8,944	8,256
Capital Expenditures	2,816	2,459	2,947	2,882	2,518	2,236	1,271	1,511	1,615	1,893
Cash Flow	3,142	2,073	3,071	3,758	3,356	2,911	2,213	2,181	2,089	1,860
Current Ratio	1.6	1.6	1.4	1.2	1.2	1.1	1.1	1.2	1.2	1.1
% Long Term Debt of Capitalization	10.6	11.9	8.7	16.4	11.0	18.3	23.5	17.2	20.1	23.0
% Net Income of Revenue	3.4	0.3	3.0	5.7	5.6	4.9	3.4	3.7	3.5	3.0
% Return on Assets	4.8	0.4	4.5	8.6	8.4	7.3	4.9	5.7	5.3	4.7
% Return on Equity	8.6	0.7	8.3	16.7	17.1	16.4	10.9	11.8	11.7	10.9

Data as orig reptd.; bef. results of disc opers/spec. items. Per share data adj. for stk. divs.; EPS diluted. E-Estimated. NA-Not Available. NM-Not Meaningful. NR-Not Ranked. UR-Under Review.

Office: 942 South Shady Grove Road, Memphis, TN 38120-4117.
Telephone: 901-818-7500.
Website: http://www.fedex.com
Chrmn, Pres & CEO: F.W. Smith

COO & EVP: K. Dixon
Investor Contact: A.B. Graf, Jr. (901-818-7388)
EVP & CFO: A.B. Graf, Jr.
EVP, Secy & General Counsel: C.P. Richards

Board Members: J. L. Barksdale, J. A. Edwardson, J. R. Hyde, III, S. A. Jackson, S. R. Loranger, G. W. Loveman, S. C. Schwab, F. W. Smith, J. I. Smith, D. P. Steiner, P. S. Walsh

Founded: 1971
Domicile: Delaware
Employees: 141,000

Fidelity National Information Services Inc

STANDARD & POOR'S

S&P Recommendation BUY ★★★★☆

Price	**12-Mo. Target Price**	**Investment Style**
$28.60 (as of Oct 22, 2010)	$34.00	Large-Cap Growth

GICS Sector Information Technology
Sub-Industry Data Processing & Outsourced Services

Summary This company is a leading provider of core processing services and products to financial institutions.

Key Stock Statistics (Source S&P, Vickers, company reports)

52-Wk Range	$30.78–21.62	S&P Oper. EPS 2010**E**	1.98	Market Capitalization(B)	$10.850	Beta		0.62
Trailing 12-Month EPS	$0.59	S&P Oper. EPS 2011**E**	2.35	Yield (%)	0.70	S&P 3-Yr. Proj. EPS CAGR(%)		12
Trailing 12-Month P/E	48.5	P/E on S&P Oper. EPS 2010**E**	14.4	Dividend Rate/Share	$0.20	S&P Credit Rating		BB
$10K Invested 5 Yrs Ago	NA	Common Shares Outstg. (M)	379.4	Institutional Ownership (%)	73			

Price Performance

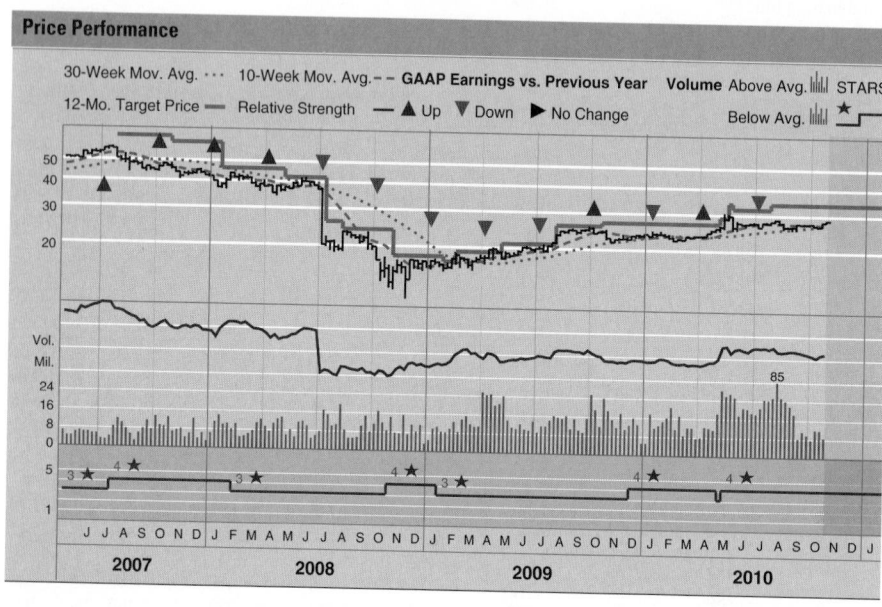

30-Week Mov. Avg. · · · · 10-Week Mov. Avg. – – **GAAP Earnings vs. Previous Year** Volume Above Avg. STARS
12-Mo. Target Price — Relative Strength — ▲ Up ▼ Down ▶ No Change Below Avg.

Options: ASE, CBOE, P, Ph

Analysis prepared by **Zaineb Bokhari** on July 22, 2010, when the stock traded at **$27.80**.

Highlights

➤ We expect revenues to rise 38% in 2010, to about $5.2 billion, aided by the October 2009 acquisition of Metavante; we see modest organic growth. We are optimistic about the scale and heft the purchase added to FIS, and we expect ample opportunity to cross-sell add-on services to the large combined base of core processing customers. While we look for near-term organic growth to be fairly modest, we think the company is gaining share and stands to benefit as the global economy eventually recovers. We project sales growth of 4% in 2011.

➤ We look for wider operating margins 2010 and 2011, reflecting internal cost containment, post-acquisition scale benefits and the anticipated achievement of targeted annual cost synergies, the majority of which are expected to be realized in 2010. We project higher interest expense after the issuance of new debt and refinancing of existing term loans. Much of the proceeds will be used to fund a $2.5 billion share buyback.

➤ Our 2010 adjusted EPS estimate is $1.98, and we see a rise to $2.35 in 2011. Our estimates exclude projected M&A and restructuring charges and purchase price amortization.

Investment Rationale/Risk

➤ We expect FIS to continue its cost-cutting efforts as it targets efficiencies after its purchase of Metavante. The purchase has sharply boosted revenue growth comparisons, but we see pro forma growth remaining modest. Existing contracts should allow FIS to generate the vast majority of revenues on a recurring basis and new core deals should drive a ramp-up in revenues as clients "go live." We are concerned about higher debt levels after FIS executes a leveraged recapitalization to buy back shares through a Dutch auction tender offer. Despite this, we see the shares as attractively valued at recent levels, and note the company's strong year-to-date adjusted cash flow, and projected earnings accretion after the share repurchase.

➤ Risks to our recommendation and target price include ongoing consolidation among financial services clients, which could lead to business loss or disruption. We are also concerned about higher interest expense after a recent debt issuance to fund a large share buyback.

➤ We apply a 15X multiple to our forward 12-month EPS estimate of $2.26 to derive our 12-month target price of $34, comparable to the recent peer mean.

Qualitative Risk Assessment

LOW	**MEDIUM**	HIGH

Our risk assessment reflects the company's exposure to the financial services industry and ongoing acquisition integration risks, offset by the high base of recurring revenue from the company's transaction processing business. We see higher debt levels ahead after a recent debt issuance.

Quantitative Evaluations

S&P Quality Ranking NR

D	C	B-	B	B+	A-	A	A+

Relative Strength Rank MODERATE

60

LOWEST = 1 HIGHEST = 99

Revenue/Earnings Data

Revenue (Million $)

	1Q	2Q	3Q	4Q	Year
2010	1,250	1,286			
2009	797.8	834.8	850.7	1,301	3,770
2008	1,291	1,339	893.8	862.0	3,446
2007	1,124	1,176	1,168	1,330	4,758
2006	900.9	1,022	1,081	1,129	4,133
2005	262.5	276.0	282.8	295.9	1,117

Earnings Per Share ($)

2010	0.25	0.24	E0.51	E0.65	E1.98
2009	0.18	0.31	0.35	-0.15	0.42
2008	0.35	0.38	0.24	0.26	0.61
2007	0.30	0.75	1.02	0.55	2.60
2006	0.23	0.34	0.41	0.39	1.37
2005	0.34	0.40	0.36	0.57	1.66

Fiscal year ended Dec. 31. Next earnings report expected: Late October. EPS Estimates based on S&P Operating Earnings; historical GAAP earnings are as reported.

Dividend Data (Dates: mm/dd Payment Date: mm/dd/yy)

Amount ($)	Date Decl.	Ex-Div. Date	Stk. of Record	Payment Date
0.050	02/04	03/12	03/16	03/30/10
0.050	04/20	06/14	06/16	06/30/10
0.050	07/20	09/14	09/16	09/30/10
0.050	10/20	12/15	12/17	12/31/10

Dividends have been paid since 2006. Source: Company reports.

Please read the Required Disclosures and Analyst Certification on the last page of this report.

The McGraw-Hill Companies

STANDARD &POOR'S

Fidelity National Information Services Inc

Business Summary July 22, 2010

CORPORATE OVERVIEW. Fidelity National Information Services, Inc. (FIS) was formed via the combination, on February 1, 2006, of the information processing subsidiary of Fidelity National Financial (FNF), a leading provider of title and specialty insurance, and Certegy, a provider of card and check processing services. As a result of the combination, the company became a leading provider of technology solutions, processing services, and information-based services to the financial industry. Until 2008, FIS operated in two main business segments: Transaction Processing Services (TPS) and Lender Processing Services (LPS). On July 2, 2008, FIS completed the spin-off of Lender Processing Services to shareholders. In October 2009, FIS acquired Metavante Technologies in a stock transaction valued at $4.2 billion. After these transactions, FIS served more than 14,000 financial institution customers in more than 100 countries.

The company's segments were recast in late 2008 as Financial Solutions, Payment Solutions and International. The Financial Solutions segment includes products and services that address the core processing needs of clients such as banks, credit unions, commercial and automotive lenders, and independent community banks. Core processing solutions include applications used to process deposits, loans, and other central services provided to customers of a financial institution. Channel solutions, which include applications that improve customer interaction are also included in this segment. These include

customer-facing channels through which customers access an institution's products and services, such as ATMs, and the Internet, as well as call centers. Other solutions offered include decision management solutions, which aid in the management of accounts throughout their lifecycle, applications that support wholesale and commercial banking, and assist in the evaluation and management of auto loans. Other solutions offered through this segment support risk management and fraud detection, branch automation and compliance. In 2009, the Financial Solutions segment accounted for almost 33% of total revenues, comparable to 2008.

Through its Payment Solutions segment, FIS offers payment and electronic funds services to banks, credit unions and other financial institutions. Segment offerings include: debit and electronic funds transfer processing, Internet banking and bill payment, merchant processing, item processing, credit card production and activation, fraud management, check authorization and pre-paid card management and administration services. Revenues from this segment comprised 46% of 2009 revenues, up from 45% in 2008.

Company Financials Fiscal Year Ended Dec. 31

Per Share Data ($)	2009	2008	2007	2006	2005	2004	2003	2002	2001	2000
Tangible Book Value	NM	NM	NM	NM	3.53	0.55	NA	NA	NA	NA
Cash Flow	2.03	2.03	4.04	3.66	2.48	2.40	NA	NA	NA	NA
Earnings	0.42	0.61	2.60	1.37	1.66	0.92	NA	NA	NA	NA
S&P Core Earnings	0.42	0.70	1.72	1.37	0.98	0.94	1.00	NA	NA	NA
Dividends	0.20	0.20	0.20	0.20	Nil	Nil	NA	NA	NA	NA
Payout Ratio	48%	33%	8%	15%	Nil	Nil	NA	NA	NA	NA
Prices:High	26.00	43.83	57.80	42.62	NA	NA	NA	NA	NA	NA
Prices:Low	15.20	11.15	39.99	33.50	NA	NA	NA	NA	NA	NA
P/E Ratio:High	62	72	22	31	NA	NA	NA	NA	NA	NA
P/E Ratio:Low	36	18	15	24	NA	NA	NA	NA	NA	NA

Income Statement Analysis (Million $)

	2009	2008	2007	2006	2005	2004	2003	2002	2001	2000
Revenue	3,770	3,446	4,758	4,133	1,117	1,040	1,945	654	418	NA
Operating Income	833	710	1,030	1,025	248	227	518	116	64.4	NA
Depreciation	434	276	284	434	51.9	47.4	144	18.6	9.45	NA
Interest Expense	134	148	201	193	12.8	12.9	2.83	2.32	1.33	NA
Pretax Income	156	179	813	409	174	168	362	106	53.8	NA
Effective Tax Rate	33.4%	32.2%	37.0%	36.7%	39.5%	37.0%	38.8%	37.3%	40.9%	NA
Net Income	101	117	510	259	106	106	207	58.2	31.0	NA
S&P Core Earnings	101	135	338	259	196	189	200	NA	NA	NA

Balance Sheet & Other Financial Data (Million $)

	2009	2008	2007	2006	2005	2004	2003	2002	2001	2000
Cash	431	221	355	212	138	86.7	100	56.5	NA	NA
Current Assets	1,666	1,180	1,830	1,301	445	409	503	260	NA	NA
Total Assets	13,998	7,490	9,795	7,631	972	922	2,371	556	NA	NA
Current Liabilities	1,235	852	1,254	881	234	290	370	168	NA	NA
Long Term Debt	3,017	2,409	4,275	2,948	228	274	10.5	18.9	NA	NA
Common Equity	8,309	3,538	3,781	3,548	459	300	1,904	295	NA	NA
Total Capital	11,772	6,212	8,194	6,892	716	614	1,958	392	NA	NA
Capital Expenditures	52.5	76.7	114	122	63.6	40.9	57.3	3.35	0.50	NA
Cash Flow	486	393	795	693	157	153	351	76.8	40.5	NA
Current Ratio	1.4	1.4	1.5	1.5	1.9	1.4	1.4	1.6	NA	NA
% Long Term Debt of Capitalization	25.6	37.3	51.3	42.8	31.8	44.6	0.5	4.8	Nil	NA
% Net Income of Revenue	2.7	3.4	10.7	6.3	9.4	10.2	10.6	8.9	7.4	NA
% Return on Assets	0.9	1.4	5.9	4.4	11.1	12.4	14.1	NA	NA	NA
% Return on Equity	1.7	3.2	14.8	12.2	27.5	37.7	18.8	NA	NA	NA

Data as orig reptd.; bef. results of disc opers/spec. items. Per share data adj. for stk. divs.; EPS diluted. E-Estimated. NA-Not Available. NM-Not Meaningful. NR-Not Ranked. UR-Under Review.

Office: 601 Riverside Avenue, Jacksonville, FL 32204.
Telephone: 904-854-5000.
Website: http://www.fisglobal.com
Chrmn: W.P. Foley, II

Pres & CEO: F.R. Martire
COO & EVP: G. Norcross
EVP & CFO: M.D. Hayford
EVP, Secy & General Counsel: M.L. Gravelle

Board Members: W. P. Foley, II, T. M. Hagerty, K. W. Hughes, D. K. Hunt, S. A. James, F. R. Martire, R. N. Massey, J. Neary

Founded: 2001
Domicile: Georgia
Employees: 31,000

The McGraw-Hill Companies

Fifth Third Bancorp

STANDARD &POOR'S

| S&P Recommendation | **STRONG BUY** ★★★★★ | Price $12.86 (as of Oct 22, 2010) | 12-Mo. Target Price $16.00 | Investment Style Large-Cap Blend |

GICS Sector Financials
Sub-Industry Regional Banks

Summary This diversified financial services company based in Cincinnati operates about 1,300 branches in Ohio, Michigan, and several other states.

Key Stock Statistics (Source S&P, Vickers, company reports)

52-Wk Range	$15.95– 8.76	S&P Oper. EPS 2010E	0.53	Market Capitalization(B)	$10.241	Beta	2.20
Trailing 12-Month EPS	$-0.35	S&P Oper. EPS 2011E	1.27	Yield (%)	0.31	S&P 3-Yr. Proj. EPS CAGR(%)	29
Trailing 12-Month P/E	NM	P/E on S&P Oper. EPS 2010E	24.3	Dividend Rate/Share	$0.04	S&P Credit Rating	BBB
$10K Invested 5 Yrs Ago	$3,957	Common Shares Outstg. (M)	796.3	Institutional Ownership (%)	74		

Price Performance

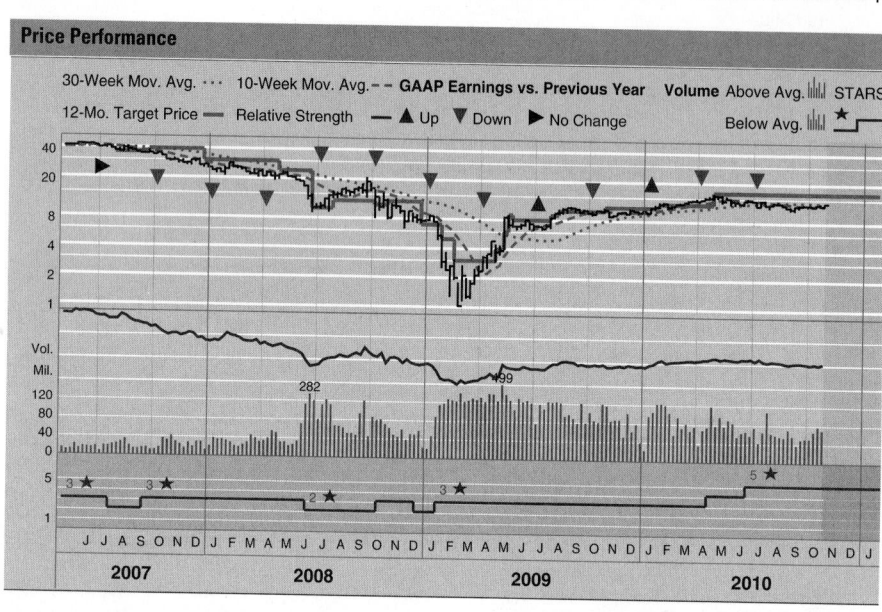

30-Week Mov. Avg. · · · · 10-Week Mov. Avg. – – GAAP Earnings vs. Previous Year   Volume Above Avg. STARS
12-Mo. Target Price — Relative Strength — ▲ Up ▼ Down ▶ No Change   Below Avg.

Options: ASE, CBOE, P, Ph

Analysis prepared by **Erik Oja** on August 09, 2010, when the stock traded at **$ 12.91**.

Highlights

► For 2010, we expect fee income, excluding gains and losses, of $2.1 billion, down from $2.5 billion in 2009, a year that included two quarters of payment processing revenues. Excluding this from 2009, we see fee income in 2010 down 6.1%, largely a reflection of a projected decline in mortgage banking and deposit service charges. However, we forecast a 6.0% increase in net interest income to $3.55 billion in 2010, on falling deposit costs, which should outweigh declining loan balances. We expect loan demand to pick up in late 2010, but we project 2011 net interest income growth of 0.5%, on some margin compression.

► We expect net chargeoffs and loan loss provisions to decline each quarter in 2010 and 2011. Our 2010 net chargeoff forecast is $1.85 billion, and our 2011 forecast is $1.00 billion, both down from $2.58 billion in 2009. We look for loan loss provisions to fall much faster than net charge-offs, given FITB's higher-than-peers allowance level, and also from the improving U.S. economy. Our provisions forecasts are $1.31 billion for 2010, and $600 million for 2011.

► We see EPS of $0.60 in 2010, $1.27 in 2011, and $1.43 for 2012.

Investment Rationale/Risk

► Second-quarter results showed continuing improvements in loan credit quality, and stability in FITB's higher-than-peers capital levels, by our analysis. We think FITB should be able to generate enough internal capital in the rest of 2010 to continue to raise capital levels by year-end. We believe this, combined with FITB's relatively high cash levels, should strictly limit the size of any further equity offering that may be needed to pay off FITB's TARP obligation. However, our recommendation is based on our view that FITB has a balance sheet that is stronger than many of its large regional banking peers in terms of a large allowance for loan losses, relatively high capital and a large and stable base of core deposits. We also think financial reform will affect FITB much less than larger banking peers. Finally, we view the shares, on a price to tangible book basis, as undervalued.

► Risks to our recommendation and target price include worsening unemployment and declining loan growth.

► Our 12-month target price of $16 represents 1.6X our $10 forecast of year-end 2010 tangible book value, and 12.6X our 2011 EPS estimate, both in line with peers.

Qualitative Risk Assessment

| LOW | **MEDIUM** | HIGH |

We have a positive view of the many steps that FITB has taken over the past year to rebuild capital levels and credit quality, which offset numerous credit challenges in the company's Florida and Michigan loan portfolios.

Quantitative Evaluations

S&P Quality Ranking   B+

| D | C | B- | B | **B+** | A- | A | A+ |

Relative Strength Rank   MODERATE

| 59 |
LOWEST = 1   HIGHEST = 99

Revenue/Earnings Data

Revenue (Million $)

	1Q	2Q	3Q	4Q	Year
2010	1,770	1,736	--	--	--
2009	1,875	3,762	2,020	1,794	9,450
2008	2,311	1,929	2,265	2,048	8,554
2007	2,108	2,202	2,251	2,048	8,479
2006	2,015	2,132	2,196	1,765	8,108
2005	1,752	1,850	1,905	1,988	7,495

Earnings Per Share ($)

	1Q	2Q	3Q	4Q	Year
2010	-0.09	0.16	E0.22	E0.24	E0.53
2009	-0.04	1.15	-0.20	-0.20	0.67
2008	0.54	-0.37	-0.14	-3.82	-3.94
2007	0.65	0.69	0.61	0.07	1.99
2006	0.65	0.69	0.68	0.12	2.12
2005	0.72	0.75	0.71	0.60	2.77

Fiscal year ended Dec. 31. Next earnings report expected: Late October. EPS Estimates based on S&P Operating Earnings; historical GAAP earnings are as reported.

Dividend Data (Dates: mm/dd Payment Date: mm/dd/yy)

Amount ($)	Date Decl.	Ex-Div. Date	Stk. of Record	Payment Date
0.010	12/15	12/29	12/31	01/21/10
0.010	03/16	03/29	03/31	04/22/10
0.010	06/15	06/28	06/30	07/22/10
0.010	09/21	09/28	09/30	10/21/10

Dividends have been paid since 1952. Source: Company reports.

Please read the Required Disclosures and Analyst Certification on the last page of this report.

STANDARD &POOR'S

Fifth Third Bancorp

Business Summary August 09, 2010

CORPORATE OVERVIEW. Fifth Third Bancorp (FITB) is now divided into four segments: commercial banking, branch banking, consumer lending, and investment advisors. Processing solutions, which was sold on June 30, 2009, had been a fifth segment until that date.

Commercial banking provides a comprehensive range of financial services and products to large and middle-market businesses, governments and professional customers. In addition to traditional lending and depository offerings, commercial banking products and services include cash management, foreign exchange and international trade finance, derivatives and capital markets services, asset-based lending, real estate finance, public finance, commercial leasing, and syndicated finance.

Branch banking offers depository and loan products, such as checking and savings accounts, home equity lines of credit, credit cards, and loans for automobiles and other personal financing needs, plus products designed to meet the specific needs of small businesses, including cash management services.

Consumer lending includes mortgage and home equity lending activities and

other indirect lending activities. Mortgage and home equity lending activities include the origination, retention and servicing of mortgage and home equity loans or lines of credit, sales and securitizations of those loans or pools of loans or lines of credit and all associated hedging activities. Other indirect lending activities include loans to consumers through dealers and federal and private student education loans.

Investment advisers provides a full range of investment alternatives for individuals, companies and not-for-profit organizations. Primary services include trust, asset management, retirement plans and custody. Fifth Third Securities, Inc., an indirect wholly owned subsidiary, offers full-service retail brokerage services to individual clients and broker dealer services to the institutional marketplace. Fifth Third Asset Management, Inc., an indirect wholly owned subsidiary, provides asset management services and also advises a proprietary family of mutual funds, Fifth Third Funds.

Company Financials Fiscal Year Ended Dec. 31

Per Share Data ($)	2009	2008	2007	2006	2005	2004	2003	2002	2001	2000
Tangible Book Value	9.26	7.87	11.11	13.78	12.72	13.33	13.46	13.12	13.09	10.50
Earnings	0.67	-3.94	1.99	2.12	2.77	2.68	2.97	2.76	1.86	1.83
S&P Core Earnings	-0.87	-2.36	2.19	2.14	2.78	2.69	2.84	2.56	1.63	NA
Dividends	0.04	0.04	1.70	1.58	1.46	1.31	1.13	0.98	0.83	0.70
Payout Ratio	6%	NM	85%	75%	53%	49%	38%	36%	45%	38%
Prices:High	11.20	28.58	43.32	41.57	48.12	60.00	62.15	69.70	64.77	60.88
Prices:Low	1.01	6.32	24.82	35.86	35.04	45.32	47.05	55.26	45.69	29.33
P/E Ratio:High	17	NM	22	20	17	22	21	25	35	33
P/E Ratio:Low	2	NM	12	17	13	17	16	20	25	16

Income Statement Analysis (Million $)	2009	2008	2007	2006	2005	2004	2003	2002	2001	2000
Net Interest Income	3,354	3,514	3,009	2,873	2,965	3,012	2,905	2,700	2,433	1,470
Tax Equivalent Adjustment	19.0	22.0	24.0	26.0	31.0	36.0	39.0	39.5	45.5	93.0
Non Interest Income	4,782	2,870	2,494	1,657	2,461	2,502	2,399	2,047	1,626	1,013
Loan Loss Provision	3,543	4,560	628	343	330	268	399	247	236	89.0
% Expense/Operating Revenue	47.0%	55.5%	55.3%	67.1%	53.6%	53.5%	46.0%	51.9%	57.7%	45.1%
Pretax Income	767	-2,664	1,537	1,627	2,208	2,237	2,547	2,432	1,653	1,275
Effective Tax Rate	3.91%	NM	30.0%	27.2%	29.8%	31.8%	31.6%	31.2%	33.3%	32.3%
Net Income	737	-2,113	1,076	1,184	1,549	1,525	1,722	1,635	1,101	863
% Net Interest Margin	3.32	3.54	3.36	3.06	3.23	3.48	3.62	3.96	3.82	3.77
S&P Core Earnings	-617	-1,301	1,183	1,191	1,555	1,529	1,650	1,513	965	NA

Balance Sheet & Other Financial Data (Million $)	2009	2008	2007	2006	2005	2004	2003	2002	2001	2000
Money Market Assets	355	1,191	171	187	117	77.0	55.0	312	225	198
Investment Securities	18,568	13,088	11,032	12,218	22,471	25,474	29,402	25,828	20,748	15,827
Commercial Loans	44,805	50,479	40,412	36,114	33,214	30,601	28,242	22,614	10,839	12,382
Other Loans	28,225	30,877	39,841	39,485	38,024	29,207	25,493	23,314	30,709	13,570
Total Assets	113,380	119,764	110,962	100,669	105,225	94,456	91,143	80,894	71,026	45,857
Demand Deposits	39,346	29,113	36,179	36,908	39,020	37,288	31,899	11,139	10,595	5,604
Time Deposits	44,959	49,500	39,266	32,472	13,656	20,938	25,196	41,069	35,259	25,344
Long Term Debt	10,507	13,585	12,857	12,558	15,227	13,983	9,063	8,179	7,030	4,034
Common Equity	9,888	7,836	9,152	10,013	9,437	8,915	8,516	8,466	7,630	4,891
% Return on Assets	0.6	NM	1.0	1.2	1.6	1.6	2.0	2.2	1.6	2.0
% Return on Equity	8.3	NM	11.2	12.2	16.9	17.3	20.3	20.3	15.4	19.2
% Loan Loss Reserve	4.9	3.3	1.1	1.0	1.0	1.2	1.4	1.4	1.4	1.4
% Loans/Deposits	91.1	107.0	106.8	108.8	105.6	103.7	94.9	94.4	95.4	85.6
% Equity to Assets	7.6	7.4	9.1	9.4	9.2	9.5	9.9	10.6	10.2	10.3

Data as orig reptd.; bef. results of disc opers/spec. items. Per share data adj. for stk. divs.; EPS diluted. E-Estimated. NA-Not Available. NM-Not Meaningful. NR-Not Ranked. UR-Under Review.

Office: Fifth Third Center, 38 Fountain Square Plaza, Cincinnati, OH 45263.
Telephone: 800-972-3030.
Website: http://www.53.com
Pres & CEO: K.T. Kabat

COO & EVP: G.D. Carmichael
EVP & CFO: D.T. Poston
EVP, Chief Admin Officer, Secy & General Counsel: Reynolds
EVP & CIO: R. Dury

Investor Contact: C.G. Marshall
Board Members: D. F. Allen, U. L. Bridgeman, Jr., E. L. P.L. Brumback, J. P. Hackett, G. R. Heminger, J. D. Hoover, W. M. Isaac, K. T. Kabat, M. D. Livingston, H. G. Meijer, J. J. Schiff, Jr., D. S. Taft, M. C. Williams

Founded: 1862
Domicile: Ohio
Employees: 20,998

The McGraw-Hill Companies

FirstEnergy Corp.

STANDARD & POOR'S

S&P Recommendation BUY ★★★★☆

Price	12-Mo. Target Price	Investment Style
$37.52 (as of Oct 22, 2010)	$45.00	Large-Cap Blend

GICS Sector Utilities
Sub-Industry Electric Utilities

Summary This electric utility holding company, which serves about 4.5 million customers in portions of Ohio, Pennsylvania and New Jersey, has agreed to acquire Allegheny Energy.

Key Stock Statistics (Source S&P, Vickers, company reports)

52-Wk Range	$47.77–33.57	S&P Oper. EPS 2010E	3.60	Market Capitalization(B)	$11.437	Beta	0.54
Trailing 12-Month EPS	$2.92	S&P Oper. EPS 2011E	3.98	Yield (%)	5.86	S&P 3-Yr. Proj. EPS CAGR(%)	-4
Trailing 12-Month P/E	12.9	P/E on S&P Oper. EPS 2010E	10.4	Dividend Rate/Share	$2.20	S&P Credit Rating	BBB-
$10K Invested 5 Yrs Ago	$9,918	Common Shares Outstg. (M)	304.8	Institutional Ownership (%)	73		

Price Performance

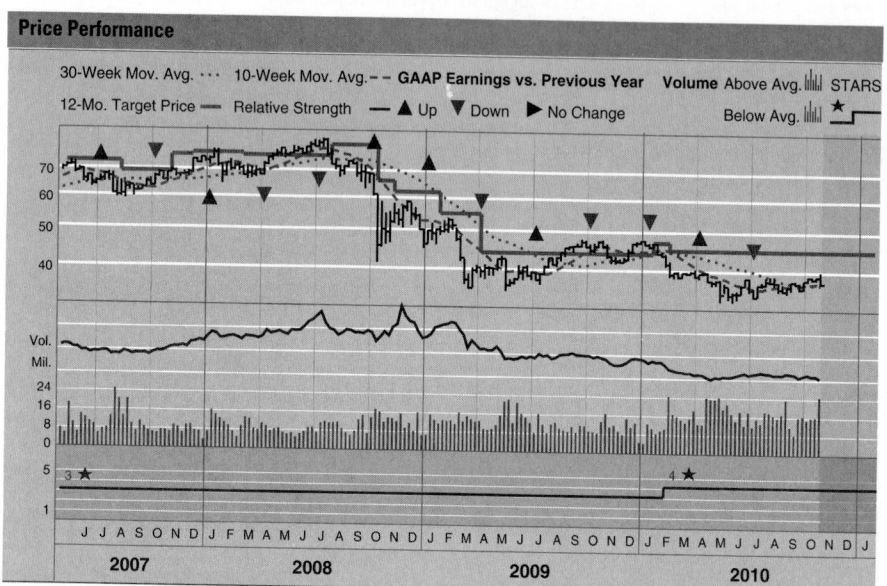

- 30-Week Mov. Avg. · · · · 10-Week Mov. Avg. - - - **GAAP Earnings vs. Previous Year** **Volume** Above Avg. |||| STARS
- 12-Mo. Target Price — Relative Strength — ▲ Up ▼ Down ► No Change Below Avg. |||| ★

Options: ASE, CBOE, P, Ph

Analysis prepared by **Justin McCann** on August 04, 2010, when the stock traded at **$37.76**.

Highlights

- Pending required approvals, the proposed acquisition of Allegheny Energy (AYE 23, Buy) would result in a 35% increase in FE's customer base and a 70% increase in its generating capacity. We believe it would be accretive to earnings 12 months after its completion. We see potential synergies of about $180 million by the end of the first year and $350 million by the second, with about half occurring in the competitive generation business.

- Excluding $0.25 of one-time charges, we expect 2010 operating EPS to decline about 4% from 2009's $3.77 (excluding $0.46 of net one-time charges). Operating results in the first half of 2010 were hurt by lower revenues at the utilities due to the weak economy, and by higher fuel and purchased power costs.

- For full-year 2010, we expect results to benefit from a full year of the Ohio rate increases, and the late June return of the Davis-Besse nuclear plant. However, we believe this will be more than offset by the reduced level of regulatory transition charges for FE's CEI subsidiary. For 2011, we expect EPS to benefit from a gradual improvement in the economy and power markets, and lower purchased power costs.

Investment Rationale/Risk

- Although the stock has declined about 17% year to date, we believe that with an above-peers yield from the dividend (recently 5.7%), the shares are attractive for above-average total return potential. The shares have been hurt, in our view, by the weakness in the economy and power markets, and concerns that the planned merger could encounter difficulties during the regulatory approval process. While there is a risk, we think it has been overblown and believe that the merger would strengthen FE's position in an eventual recovery in the economy and power markets.

- Risks to our recommendation and target price include the possibility of the planned Allegheny merger being delayed or terminated, and/or extended weakness in the power markets.

- While we do not expect dividend increases during the economic slowdown, we believe the company will still target future annual increases of 4% to 5%. The targeted growth rate is above both the industry's expected dividend growth rate and FE's own expected long-term EPS growth rate of 3% to 4%. Our 12-month target price of $45 reflects a discount-to-peers multiple of 11.3X our 2011 EPS estimate.

Qualitative Risk Assessment

LOW	MEDIUM	HIGH

Our risk assessment reflects the strong and steady cash flow we expect from the company's regulated electric utility subsidiaries; its low-cost baseload power generation in Ohio and Pennsylvania; its low-risk transmission distribution operations in New Jersey and Pennsylvania; and its rate certainty in Ohio. This is partially offset by the company's below-average production performance from nuclear operations and our view of its high level of debt and environmental spending.

Quantitative Evaluations

S&P Quality Ranking   A-

D	C	B-	B	B+	A-	A	A+

Relative Strength Rank   **WEAK**

28

LOWEST = 1   HIGHEST = 99

Revenue/Earnings Data

Revenue (Million $)

	1Q	2Q	3Q	4Q	Year
2010	3,299	3,128	--	--	--
2009	3,334	3,271	3,408	2,954	12,967
2008	3,277	3,245	3,904	3,201	13,627
2007	2,973	3,109	3,641	3,079	12,802
2006	2,705	2,751	3,365	2,680	11,501
2005	2,813	2,900	3,588	2,892	11,989

Earnings Per Share ($)

	1Q	2Q	3Q	4Q	Year
2010	0.51	0.87	E1.16	E0.81	E3.60
2009	0.39	1.36	0.77	0.78	3.29
2008	0.90	0.85	1.54	1.09	4.38
2007	0.92	1.10	1.34	0.87	4.22
2006	0.67	0.93	1.40	0.84	3.82
2005	0.42	0.54	1.01	0.67	2.65

Fiscal year ended Dec. 31. Next earnings report expected: Late October. EPS Estimates based on S&P Operating Earnings; historical GAAP earnings are as reported.

Dividend Data (Dates: mm/dd Payment Date: mm/dd/yy)

Amount ($)	Date Decl.	Ex-Div. Date	Stk. of Record	Payment Date
0.550	12/15	02/03	02/05	03/01/10
0.550	03/16	05/05	05/07	06/01/10
0.550	07/20	08/04	08/06	09/01/10
0.550	09/21	11/03	11/05	12/01/10

Dividends have been paid since 1930. Source: Company reports.

Please read the Required Disclosures and Analyst Certification on the last page of this report.

The McGraw-Hill Companies

FirstEnergy Corp.

STANDARD &POOR'S

Business Summary August 04, 2010

CORPORATE OVERVIEW. FirstEnergy (FE) is a diversified energy company involved in the generation, transmission and distribution of electricity as well as energy management and related services. The company operates primarily through two core business segments: Regulated Services, which is comprised of seven electric utility operating companies and provides transmission and distribution services, and Power Supply Management Services, which owns and operates the generation assets and wholesale purchase of electricity, energy management and other energy-related services. In 2009, the electric utilities accounted for 92.9% of consolidated revenues, and the unregulated businesses 7.1%.

IMPACT OF MAJOR DEVELOPMENTS. On February 11, 2010, FirstEnergy announced a definitive merger agreement with Allegheny Energy, Inc. (AYE 21, Buy) a Pennsylvania-headquartered electric utility holding company serving 1.6 million customers in portions of Pennsylvania, Maryland, Virginia and West Virginia. Under the terms of the transaction (which would include the assumption of approximately $3.8 billion of Allegheny net debt), Allegheny shareholders would receive 0.667 of a share of FirstEnergy for each AYE share. The companies expect that they will obtain all of the required shareholder and regulatory approvals by April 2011. Assuming the transaction is completed, FE shareholders would have an approximate 73% interest in the combined company and AYE shareholders 27%.

MARKET PROFILE. FirstEnergy's utility subsidiaries serve approximately 4.5 million customers within an area of 36,100 square miles in Ohio, Pennsylvania and New Jersey. As of December 31, 2009, the company's power generating facilities had demonstrated net capacity of 13,970 megawatts (MW) of electricity, with coal plants accounting for approximately 54.2% of the total; nuclear 29.0%; oil and natural gas peaking units 11.6%; hydroelectric 3.3%; and other 1.9%.

Company Financials Fiscal Year Ended Dec. 31

Per Share Data ($)	2009	2008	2007	2006	2005	2004	2003	2002	2001	2000
Tangible Book Value	9.79	8.88	11.06	9.83	9.63	7.70	6.55	4.11	6.04	11.42
Earnings	3.29	4.38	4.22	3.82	2.65	2.66	1.39	2.33	2.84	2.69
S&P Core Earnings	3.00	3.28	3.80	3.71	2.56	2.77	1.61	1.69	2.36	NA
Dividends	2.20	2.20	2.00	1.80	1.67	1.50	1.50	1.50	1.13	1.50
Payout Ratio	67%	50%	47%	47%	63%	56%	108%	64%	40%	56%
Prices:High	53.63	84.00	74.98	61.70	53.36	43.41	38.90	39.12	36.98	32.13
Prices:Low	35.26	41.20	57.77	47.75	37.70	35.24	25.82	24.85	25.10	18.00
P/E Ratio:High	16	19	18	16	20	16	28	17	13	12
P/E Ratio:Low	11	9	14	13	14	13	19	11	9	7

Income Statement Analysis (Million $)	2009	2008	2007	2006	2005	2004	2003	2002	2001	2000
Revenue	12,967	13,627	12,802	11,501	11,989	12,453	12,307	12,152	7,999	7,029
Depreciation	736	789	1,657	1,457	1,870	1,756	1,282	1,106	890	934
Maintenance	NA	NA	NA	NA	NA	NA	NA	NA	NA	NA
Fixed Charges Coverage	2.46	4.02	3.95	3.78	3.39	3.25	1.88	2.25	2.85	2.71
Construction Credits	NA	NA	NA	NA	NA	NA	NA	24.5	35.5	27.1
Effective Tax Rate	19.8%	36.7%	40.3%	38.7%	46.3%	43.4%	49.0%	44.5%	42.0%	38.6%
Net Income	1,006	1,342	1,309	1,258	873	874	422	686	655	599
S&P Core Earnings	920	1,005	1,177	1,211	841	911	492	496	546	NA

Balance Sheet & Other Financial Data (Million $)	2009	2008	2007	2006	2005	2004	2003	2002	2001	2000
Gross Property	30,561	28,544	25,731	24,722	23,790	22,892	22,374	21,231	20,589	12,839
Capital Expenditures	2,203	2,888	1,633	1,315	1,208	846	856	998	852	588
Net Property	19,164	17,723	15,383	14,667	13,998	13,478	13,269	12,680	12,428	7,575
Capitalization:Long Term Debt	11,908	9,100	8,869	8,535	8,339	10,348	9,789	12,680	12,508	6,552
Capitalization:% Long Term Debt	58.2	52.3	49.7	48.6	47.1	53.7	53.1	62.0	62.8	58.5
Capitalization:Preferred	Nil	Nil	Nil	Nil	184	335	352	Nil	Nil	Nil
Capitalization:% Preferred	Nil	Nil	Nil	Nil	1.04	1.74	1.91	Nil	Nil	Nil
Capitalization:Common	8,559	8,283	8,977	9,035	9,188	8,589	8,289	7,120	7,399	4,653
Capitalization:% Common	41.8	47.7	50.3	51.4	51.9	44.6	45.0	38.0	37.2	41.5
Total Capital	22,299	19,546	20,517	20,310	20,437	21,597	20,608	21,360	22,852	13,540
% Operating Ratio	87.4	85.4	84.9	84.3	89.0	87.3	90.4	86.6	50.8	37.8
% Earned on Net Property	10.2	16.7	18.7	18.2	15.0	16.5	11.2	17.4	16.8	18.1
% Return on Revenue	7.8	9.8	10.2	10.9	7.3	7.0	3.4	5.6	8.2	8.5
% Return on Invested Capital	8.7	10.2	10.1	9.6	7.3	7.4	6.5	7.4	21.8	32.0
% Return on Common Equity	12.0	15.6	14.5	13.8	9.8	10.4	5.5	9.5	10.9	13.0

Data as orig reptd.; bef. results of disc opers/spec. items. Per share data adj. for stk. divs.; EPS diluted. E-Estimated. NA-Not Available. NM-Not Meaningful. NR-Not Ranked. UR-Under Review.

Office: 76 South Main Street, Akron, OH 44308-1890.
Telephone: 800-736-3402.
Website: http://www.firstenergycorp.com
Chrmn: G.M. Smart

Pres & CEO: A.J. Alexander
EVP & CFO: M.T. Clark
EVP & General Counsel: L.L. Vespoli
Chief Acctg Officer & Cntlr: H.L. Wagner

Investor Contact: R.E. Seeholzer (800-736-3402)
Board Members: P. T. Addison, A. J. Alexander, M. Anderson, C. Cartwright, W. T. Cottle, R. B. Heisler, Jr., E. J. Novak, Jr., C. A. Rein, G. M. Smart, W. M. Taylor, J. T. Williams

Founded: 1996
Domicile: Ohio
Employees: 13,379

The **McGraw·Hill** Companies

First Horizon National Corp

STANDARD &POOR'S

S&P Recommendation BUY ★★★★☆

Price	12-Mo. Target Price	Investment Style
$9.93 (as of Oct 22, 2010)	$14.00	Large-Cap Blend

GICS Sector Financials
Sub-Industry Regional Banks

Summary Memphis, Tennessee-based First Horizon National Corp. owns First Tennessee Bank and First Horizon Home Loan Corporation, and has assets of $26.3 billion.

Key Stock Statistics (Source S&P, Vickers, company reports)

52-Wk Range	$15.40– 9.64	S&P Oper. EPS 2010**E**	0.11	Market Capitalization(B)	$2.310	Beta		0.56
Trailing 12-Month EPS	$-0.34	S&P Oper. EPS 2011**E**	0.44	Yield (%)	Nil	S&P 3-Yr. Proj. EPS CAGR(%)		NM
Trailing 12-Month P/E	NM	P/E on S&P Oper. EPS 2010**E**	90.3	Dividend Rate/Share	Nil	S&P Credit Rating		BBB-
$10K Invested 5 Yrs Ago	$3,722	Common Shares Outstg. (M)	232.6	Institutional Ownership (%)	74			

Price Performance

30-Week Mov. Avg. · · · · 10-Week Mov. Avg. – – **GAAP Earnings vs. Previous Year** Volume Above Avg. STARS
12-Mo. Target Price — Relative Strength — ▲ Up ▼ Down ► No Change Below Avg. ★

Options: P, Ph

Qualitative Risk Assessment

LOW	MEDIUM	HIGH

Our risk assessment reflects FHN's ongoing recovery from credit losses, offset by its relatively high capital levels and good prospects for fee income growth.

Quantitative Evaluations

S&P Quality Ranking B+

D	C	B-	B	B+	A-	A	A+

Relative Strength Rank WEAK

11

LOWEST = 1   HIGHEST = 99

Highlights

➤ The 12-month target price for FHN has recently been changed to $14.00 from $14.00. The Highlights section of this Stock Report will be updated accordingly.

Investment Rationale/Risk

➤ The Investment Rationale/Risk section of this Stock Report will be updated shortly. For the latest News story on FHN from MarketScope, see below.

➤ 10/15/10 11:08 am ET ... S&P MAINTAINS BUY RECOMMENDATION ON SHARES OF FIRST HORIZON NATIONAL CORP (FHN 10.49****): Q3 EPS of $0.07, vs. a loss per share of $0.19, misses our EPS estimate of $0.09 on higher than expected tax rate, which offset a lower than expected loan loss provision and higher than expected net interest income. On these results, and our lower provision estimate for Q4, we raise our '10 EPS estimate to $0.11 from $0.10. We see FHN's progress on balance sheet and credit quality improvements as on track, but recognize that national foreclosure issue raise risks. We keep our $14 target price, based on a premium to peers 2.1X our year-end tangible book value estimate. /E. Oja

Revenue/Earnings Data

Revenue (Million $)

	1Q	2Q	3Q	4Q	Year
2010	467.8	468.4	471.4	--	--
2009	669.4	547.8	540.2	246.2	2,226
2008	925.5	814.5	688.4	669.6	3,098
2007	866.4	875.2	786.1	638.5	3,166
2006	731.0	913.6	930.4	921.0	3,496
2005	728.3	781.8	867.0	862.9	3,240

Earnings Per Share ($)

2010	-0.09	Nil	0.07	E0.11	E0.11
2009	-0.36	-0.54	-0.19	-0.30	-1.40
2008	-0.05	-0.10	-0.54	-0.28	-0.99
2007	0.47	0.14	-0.09	-1.70	-1.18
2006	0.03	0.70	0.45	0.51	3.06
2005	0.72	0.68	0.76	0.74	2.90

Fiscal year ended Dec. 31. Next earnings report expected: Mid January. EPS Estimates based on S&P Operating Earnings; historical GAAP earnings are as reported.

Dividend Data (Dates: mm/dd Payment Date: mm/dd/yy)

Amount ($)	Date Decl.	Ex-Div. Date	Stk. of Record	Payment Date
Stk.	01/20	03/10	03/12	04/01/10
Stk.	04/20	06/09	06/11	07/01/10
Stk.	07/20	09/08	09/10	10/01/10
Stk.	10/20	12/08	12/10	01/01/11

Source: Company reports.

First Horizon National Corp

Business Summary July 19, 2010

CORPORATE OVERVIEW. First Horizon National (formerly First Tennessee National) is a Memphis, TN-based regional bank. FHN is one of the 40 largest bank holding companies in the U.S. in terms of asset size, with $26.1 billion in assets at December 31, 2009. FHN provides diversified financial services through five business segments. Three of the segments reflect the common activities and operations of aggregated business segments across the various delivery channels: regional banking, capital markets, and mortgage banking. National specialty lending consists of traditional consumer and construction lending activities in national markets outside of FHN's Tennessee-based market footprint. These operations were mostly discontinued in 2008, but the wind-down process could take years. During 2009, 61.7% of revenues came from fee income, versus 62.5% in 2008.

FHN has 202 financial center bank branch locations in three states: 191 branches in 17 Tennessee counties, including all of the major metropolitan areas of the state; two branches in Georgia; and nine branches in Mississippi. FHN was in the top 20 nationally in mortgage loan originations and the top 15 in mortgage loan servicing, at December 31, 2007 (latest available data), as reported by Inside Mortgage Finance.

CORPORATE STRATEGY. Beginning in 2007, and continuing throughout 2008, FHN conducted a review of business practices with the goal of improving overall profitability and productivity. In order to redeploy capital to higher-return businesses, origination through national construction lending operations was discontinued. FHN sold the national mortgage origination and servicing platforms, including servicing on $19.1 billion of unpaid principal balance; and the sale of most of the First Horizon Bank branches outside of the bank's Tennessee-based market footprint was completed.

In the first quarter of 2008, FHN revised its business segments to better align with its strategic direction, representing a focus on its regional banking franchise and capital markets business. To implement this change, the prior retail/commercial banking segment was split into its major components with the national portions of consumer lending and construction lending assigned to a new national specialty lending segment that better reflects the ongoing winding down of these businesses. Additionally, correspondent banking was shifted from retail/commercial banking to the capital markets segment to better represent the complementary nature of these businesses. To reflect its geographic focus, the remaining portions of the retail/commercial banking segment now represent the new regional banking segment.

Company Financials Fiscal Year Ended Dec. 31

Per Share Data ($)	2009	2008	2007	2006	2005	2004	2003	2002	2001	2000
Tangible Book Value	8.64	8.23	12.67	14.42	12.89	12.50	11.40	10.11	8.71	8.32
Earnings	-1.40	-0.99	-1.18	3.06	2.90	3.00	3.07	2.45	2.13	1.50
S&P Core Earnings	-1.38	-1.15	-0.83	1.66	2.66	2.78	2.70	2.11	1.53	NA
Dividends	Nil	0.34	1.53	1.53	1.48	1.38	1.10	0.89	0.77	0.75
Payout Ratio	Nil	NM	NM	50%	51%	46%	36%	36%	36%	50%
Prices:High	13.98	19.04	38.56	36.54	38.01	41.28	41.15	34.79	31.81	24.87
Prices:Low	6.19	3.84	14.98	31.48	29.51	34.61	30.19	25.25	23.02	13.52
P/E Ratio:High	NM	NM	NM	12	13	14	13	14	15	17
P/E Ratio:Low	NM	NM	NM	10	10	12	10	10	11	9

Income Statement Analysis (Million $)	2009	2008	2007	2006	2005	2004	2003	2002	2001	2000
Net Interest Income	776	895	941	997	984	856	806	753	686	598
Tax Equivalent Adjustment	1.60	1.35	0.69	NA	1.17	1.10	1.26	1.50	2.10	2.60
Non Interest Income	1,234	1,491	861	1,233	1,400	1,342	1,638	1,550	1,321	1,068
Loan Loss Provision	880	1,080	273	83.1	67.7	48.3	86.7	92.2	93.5	67.4
% Expense/Operating Revenue	77.2%	69.4%	102.3%	78.2%	70.1%	68.4%	67.1%	71.3%	67.7%	75.5%
Pretax Income	-421	-350	-316	338	645	667	719	558	494	337
Effective Tax Rate	NM	NM	NM	25.8%	31.6%	31.9%	34.2%	32.5%	33.2%	31.0%
Net Income	-257	-193	-175	251	441	454	473	376	330	233
% Net Interest Margin	3.06	2.95	2.82	2.93	3.08	3.62	3.78	4.33	4.27	3.73
S&P Core Earnings	-316	-244	-128	261	423	438	434	337	248	NA

Balance Sheet & Other Financial Data (Million $)	2009	2008	2007	2006	2005	2004	2003	2002	2001	2000
Money Market Assets	1,692	1,926	2,898	3,415	3,629	NA	NA	NA	NA	NA
Investment Securities	2,694	3,125	3,033	3,890	2,912	2,681	2,470	2,700	2,526	2,839
Commercial Loans	7,159	7,864	8,435	8,338	9,899	7,730	6,904	5,723	5,598	5,327
Other Loans	10,965	13,414	13,669	13,767	10,702	8,698	7,087	5,622	4,685	4,912
Total Assets	26,069	31,022	37,015	37,918	36,579	29,772	24,507	23,823	20,617	18,555
Demand Deposits	4,394	3,957	5,055	5,448	10,027	4,995	4,540	5,149	4,010	2,847
Time Deposits	10,473	10,285	11,977	14,766	13,411	14,788	11,140	10,564	9,596	9,342
Long Term Debt	2,891	4,768	6,825	6,132	3,733	2,617	1,117	1,074	3,066	3,119
Common Equity	2,209	2,497	2,136	2,462	2,312	2,041	1,850	1,691	1,478	1,384
% Return on Assets	NM	NM	NM	0.7	1.3	1.7	2.0	1.7	1.7	1.3
% Return on Equity	NM	NM	NM	10.4	20.3	23.1	26.7	23.8	23.0	17.7
% Loan Loss Reserve	5.0	4.0	1.5	0.9	0.8	0.7	0.9	0.9	1.1	1.2
% Loans/Deposits	121.9	149.4	118.7	123.6	106.8	109.2	108.2	102.7	100.6	98.2
% Equity to Assets	8.2	6.8	6.1	6.5	6.6	7.2	7.3	7.1	7.3	7.1

Data as orig reptd.; bef. results of disc opers/spec. items. Per share data adj. for stk. divs.; EPS diluted. E-Estimated. NA-Not Available. NM-Not Meaningful. NR-Not Ranked. UR-Under Review.

Office: 165 Madison Avenue, Memphis, TN 38103.
Telephone: 901-523-4444.
Website: http://www.fhnc.com
Chrmn: M.D. Rose

Pres & CEO: D.B. Jordan
EVP & CFO: W.C. Losch, III
EVP & Chief Acctg Officer: J.F. Keen
EVP & Treas: T.C. Adams, Jr.

Investor Contact: D. Miller (901-523-4162)
Board Members: R. B. Carter, M. A. Emkes, J. Haslam, III, D. B. Jordan, R. Martin, V. R. Palmer, C. V. Reed, M. D. Rose, W. B. Sansom, L. Yancy, III

Founded: 1968
Domicile: Tennessee
Employees: 5,731

First Solar Inc

STANDARD &POOR'S

S&P Recommendation	HOLD ★★★☆☆	Price $145.55 (as of Oct 22, 2010)	12-Mo. Target Price $153.00	Investment Style Large-Cap Blend

GICS Sector Information Technology
Sub-Industry Semiconductors

Summary This company produces solar modules using a proprietary thin film semiconductor technology.

Key Stock Statistics (Source S&P, Vickers, company reports)

52-Wk Range	$158.14–98.71	S&P Oper. EPS 2010**E**	7.24	Market Capitalization(B)	$12.453	Beta	1.60
Trailing 12-Month EPS	$7.28	S&P Oper. EPS 2011**E**	8.05	Yield (%)	Nil	S&P 3-Yr. Proj. EPS CAGR(%)	5
Trailing 12-Month P/E	20.0	P/E on S&P Oper. EPS 2010**E**	20.1	Dividend Rate/Share	Nil	S&P Credit Rating	NA
$10K Invested 5 Yrs Ago	NA	Common Shares Outstg. (M)	85.6	Institutional Ownership (%)	65		

Price Performance

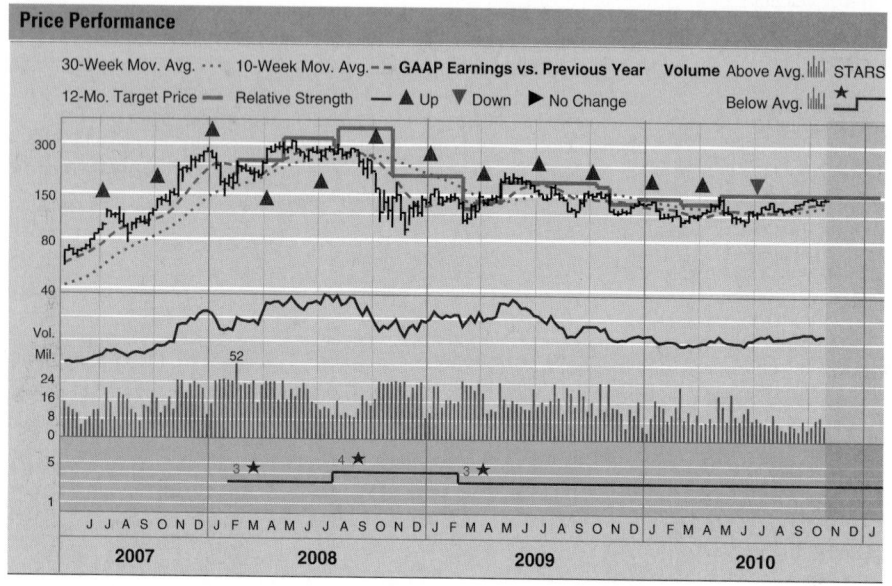

30-Week Mov. Avg. · · · 10-Week Mov. Avg. - - GAAP Earnings vs. Previous Year Volume Above Avg. STARS
12-Mo. Target Price — Relative Strength ▲ Up ▼ Down ► No Change Below Avg. ★

Options: ASE, CBOE

Analysis prepared by **Angelo Zino** on August 03, 2010, when the stock traded at **$ 126.14**.

Qualitative Risk Assessment

LOW	MEDIUM	**HIGH**

Our risk assessment reflects our view of the highly competitive nature of First Solar's business, the relatively early stages of the business cycle for alternative energy sources, and a high degree of execution risk in the company's aggressive capacity expansion plans. We also have concerns that a substantial amount of the company's common stock is held by the estate of John T. Walton and affiliates, which have considerable control over operation of the company's business.

Quantitative Evaluations

S&P Quality Ranking NR

D	C	B-	B	B+	A-	A	A+

Relative Strength Rank MODERATE

68

LOWEST = 1 HIGHEST = 99

Highlights

➤ We expect sales to increase 23% in 2010 and 40% in 2011, following a 66% rise in 2009, on higher solar module volume and greater revenue from the systems business. For the long term, we see higher volume from capacity expansion offset somewhat by lower prices, partly due to lower government subsidies and aggressive competition from China-based silicon module makers. We think FSLR continues to generate new orders, and we believe utility pipelines will develop into substantial volume.

➤ We forecast gross margins of 45% in 2010 and 37% in 2011, versus 51% in 2009, as lower selling prices are only partly offset by higher volume and reduced manufacturing costs. In addition, we see a greater percentage of sales coming from FSLR's lower-margin systems business. We think FSLR can lower its cost per watt from $0.76 currently to $0.65 by 2012, through greater scale and efficiencies. FSLR's modules had a conversion efficiency ratio of 11.2% as of June 30.

➤ We believe FSLR has plans to grow capacity to 1.34 gigawatts (GW) by year end and to 2.12 GW by the end of 2011, from 1.23 GW in 2009, as it expands production primarily in Malaysia.

Investment Rationale/Risk

➤ We believe FSLR continues to see broadening demand from utility companies for ownership of large solar systems, especially as project financing continues to improve. However, we expect FSLR's margins to trend downward, given competitive forces as well as a further shift to the lower-margin systems business, which we estimate will reach $1 billion in sales for 2011. Despite FSLR's high exposure to the German market, we think the company is diversifying its geographic exposure, and we view positively its rising presence in the U.S. Although we expect it to gain share, we think FSLR's goal of 30% market share by 2014 is overly optimistic.

➤ Risks to our recommendation and target price include potential inefficient execution of FSLR's aggressive capacity expansion plan, and falling prices.

➤ Our 12-month target price of $153 is based on a multiple of 19.0X our 2011 EPS projection, above peers. We believe FSLR merits a premium valuation, based on our view of the company as a leader in bringing out a solar energy product with low production costs. Also, we view FSLR's balance sheet and margins as considerably stronger than peers.

Revenue/Earnings Data

Revenue (Million $)

	1Q	2Q	3Q	4Q	Year
2010	568.0	587.9	--	--	--
2009	418.2	525.9	480.9	641.3	2,066
2008	196.9	267.0	348.7	433.7	1,246
2007	66.95	77.22	159.0	200.8	504.0
2006	13.62	27.86	40.79	52.70	135.0
2005	8.53	9.37	16.59	13.58	48.06

Earnings Per Share ($)

2010	2.00	1.84	E1.66	E1.74	E7.24
2009	1.99	2.11	1.79	1.65	7.53
2008	0.57	0.85	1.20	1.61	4.24
2007	0.07	0.58	0.58	0.77	2.03
2006	-0.12	-0.05	0.07	0.12	0.07
2005	-0.02	-0.01	0.03	-0.14	-0.13

Fiscal year ended Dec. 31. Next earnings report expected: Late October. EPS Estimates based on S&P Operating Earnings; historical GAAP earnings are as reported.

Dividend Data

No cash dividends have been paid.

First Solar Inc

STANDARD &POOR'S

Business Summary August 03, 2010

CORPORATE OVERVIEW. First Solar designs and manufactures solar modules using a proprietary thin film semiconductor technology. The company's solar modules employ a thin layer of cadmium telluride semiconductor material to convert sunlight into electricity. In less than three hours, FSLR is able to transform a two foot by four foot sheet of glass into a complete solar module, using about 1% of the semiconductor material needed to produce crystalline silicon solar modules. Its production process eliminates the multiple supply chain operators, and expensive and time-consuming batch processing steps that are used to make a crystalline silicon solar module. In 2009, the company derived 86% of its revenues from customers headquartered in the European Union (primarily Germany, which accounted for 65% of FSLR's revenues).

As of year-end 2009, FSLR manufactured its solar modules and conducted its research and development activities at production lines in locations including Perrysburg, OH , Frankfurt/Oder, Germany, and Kulim, Malaysia. During 2009, FSLR produced 1.1 gigawatts of solar modules, including 311 megawatts in the fourth quarter. We believe FSLR currently has plans to grow capacity from 1,228 megawatts in 2009 to 1,337 megawatts in 2010, 2,005 megawatts in 2011,

and 2,117 megawatts in 2012. FSLR intends to add eight new lines in Malaysia during 2010, with production to begin in the first half of 2011.

CORPORATE STRATEGY. FSLR aims to reduce PV system costs in three primary areas: module manufacturing, Balance of System (BoS) costs (costs unrelated to the module, including inverters, mounting hardware, grid interconnection equipment, wiring and other devices, and installation labor costs), and cost of capital. FSLR's manufacturing costs totaled $0.84 per watt in 2009's fourth quarter, down 14% from the year-earlier level. The company's average manufacturing cost for the full year was $0.87 per watt, versus $1.08 in 2008, a 19% reduction. We believe FSLR's cost lead advantage will allow it to be the first solar-module manufacturer to offer a product that competes on a non-subsidized basis with the price of retail electricity in key markets in North America, Europe and Asia.

Company Financials Fiscal Year Ended Dec. 31

Per Share Data ($)	2009	2008	2007	2006	2005	2004	2003	2002	2001	2000
Tangible Book Value	28.14	18.12	13.54	5.69	NM	NA	NA	NA	NA	NA
Cash Flow	9.05	4.99	2.35	0.21	-0.07	-0.34	-0.74	NA	NA	NA
Earnings	7.53	4.24	2.03	0.07	-0.13	-0.39	-0.78	NA	NA	NA
S&P Core Earnings	7.53	4.24	2.03	0.06	-0.09	NA	NA	NA	NA	NA
Dividends	Nil	Nil	Nil	Nil	Nil	Nil	NA	NA	NA	NA
Payout Ratio	Nil	Nil	Nil	Nil	Nil	Nil	NA	NA	NA	NA
Prices:High	207.51	317.00	283.00	30.00	NA	NA	NA	NA	NA	NA
Prices:Low	100.90	85.28	27.54	20.00	NA	NA	NA	NA	NA	NA
P/E Ratio:High	28	75	NM	NM	NA	NA	NA	NA	NA	NA
P/E Ratio:Low	13	20	NM	NM	NA	NA	NA	NA	NA	NA

Income Statement Analysis (Million $)										
Revenue	2,066	1,246	504	135	48.1	13.5	3.21	NA	NA	NA
Operating Income	832	501	162	13.0	-1.41	-14.8	-22.6	NA	NA	NA
Depreciation	130	61.5	24.8	10.2	3.38	1.94	1.50	NA	NA	NA
Interest Expense	5.26	7.39	6.07	4.36	0.42	0.10	3.97	NA	NA	NA
Pretax Income	686	464	156	9.18	-6.55	-16.8	-28.0	NA	NA	NA
Effective Tax Rate	6.73%	24.9%	NM	56.7%	NM	NA	NA	NA	NA	NA
Net Income	640	348	158	3.97	-6.55	-16.8	-28.0	NA	NA	NA
S&P Core Earnings	640	348	158	3.97	-6.55	NA	NA	NA	NA	NA

Balance Sheet & Other Financial Data (Million $)										
Cash	785	792	637	308	17.0	3.77	NA	NA	NA	NA
Current Assets	1,351	1,077	803	389	26.6	12.3	NA	NA	NA	NA
Total Assets	3,350	2,115	1,371	579	102	41.8	NA	NA	NA	NA
Current Liabilities	395	382	186	52.1	33.9	5.35	NA	NA	NA	NA
Long Term Debt	146	164	68.9	61.1	28.6	13.7	NA	NA	NA	NA
Common Equity	2,653	1,513	1,097	411	13.1	22.6	NA	NA	NA	NA
Total Capital	2,828	1,712	1,166	523	41.7	36.3	NA	NA	NA	NA
Capital Expenditures	280	459	242	153	42.5	7.73	14.9	NA	NA	NA
Cash Flow	770	410	183	14.2	-3.18	-14.8	-26.5	NA	NA	NA
Current Ratio	3.4	2.8	4.3	7.5	0.8	2.3	NA	NA	NA	NA
% Long Term Debt of Capitalization	5.2	9.6	5.9	11.7	68.5	37.7	NA	NA	NA	NA
% Net Income of Revenue	31.0	28.0	31.4	2.9	NM	NM	NM	NA	NA	NA
% Return on Assets	23.4	20.0	16.2	1.2	NM	NM	NA	NA	NA	NA
% Return on Equity	30.7	26.7	21.0	1.9	NM	NA	NA	NA	NA	NA

Data as orig reptd.; bef. results of disc opers/spec. items. Per share data adj. for stk. divs.; EPS diluted. E-Estimated. NA-Not Available. NM-Not Meaningful. NR-Not Ranked. UR-Under Review.

Office: 350 West Washington Street, Suite 600, Tempe, AZ 85281.
Telephone: 602-414-9300.
Email: info@firstsolar.com
Website: http://www.firstsolar.com

Chrmn: M.J. Ahearn
Pres: B. Sohn
CEO: R.J. Gillette
EVP, Secy & General Counsel: M.E. Gustafsson

CFO: J. Meyerhoff
Investor Contact: L. Polizzotto (602-414-9315)
Board Members: M. J. Ahearn, R. J. Gillette, C. Kennedy, J. F. Nolan, J. T. Presby, P. H. Stebbins, M. T. Sweeney, J. H. Villarreal

Founded: 1999
Domicile: Delaware
Employees: 4,700

The McGraw·Hill Companies

Fiserv Inc

STANDARD &POOR'S

S&P Recommendation HOLD ★★★☆☆	Price $55.65 (as of Oct 22, 2010)	12-Mo. Target Price $54.00	Investment Style Large-Cap Growth

GICS Sector Information Technology
Sub-Industry Data Processing & Outsourced Services

Summary This company provides account processing and integrated information management systems for financial institutions. In December 2007, it acquired CheckFree Corp. for $4.4 billion.

Key Stock Statistics (Source S&P, Vickers, company reports)

52-Wk Range	$55.88– 44.80	S&P Oper. EPS 2010E	4.05	Market Capitalization(B)	$8.353	Beta	1.08
Trailing 12-Month EPS	$3.12	S&P Oper. EPS 2011E	4.35	Yield (%)	Nil	S&P 3-Yr. Proj. EPS CAGR(%)	9
Trailing 12-Month P/E	17.8	P/E on S&P Oper. EPS 2010E	13.7	Dividend Rate/Share	Nil	S&P Credit Rating	BBB-
$10K Invested 5 Yrs Ago	$13,113	Common Shares Outstg. (M)	150.1	Institutional Ownership (%)	82		

Price Performance

30-Week Mov. Avg. ··· 10-Week Mov. Avg. – – GAAP Earnings vs. Previous Year Volume Above Avg. STARS
12-Mo. Target Price — Relative Strength — ▲ Up ▼ Down ► No Change Below Avg. ★

Options: ASE, CBOE, Ph

Analysis prepared by **Scott H. Kessler** on August 04, 2010, when the stock traded at **$ 50.36.**

Highlights

➤ Adjusted net revenues declined 13% in 2009, reflecting an unfavorable spending backdrop, offset somewhat by market share gains and cross-selling efforts. We see uncertainties related to continuing challenges and consolidation in the financial services segment, but are encouraged by notable recurring revenues. We expect a 1% gain in 2010 adjusted net revenues and a 2% increase for 2011.

➤ Historically, FISV has used free cash flow to make acquisitions intended to broaden its offerings and customer base. Acquisitions once accounted for about 50% of FISV's revenue growth. However, in recent years FISV has de-emphasized acquisitions and focused on cross-selling and margin-improvement efforts.

➤ In December 2007, FISV acquired CheckFree Corp. for $4.4 billion. We believe CheckFree notably expanded FISV's offerings, technology, and customer base, and will contribute to material market share gains. In January 2008, FISV sold Fiserv Health for $721 million. In July 2008, FISV sold 51% of its insurance unit for $510 million of after-tax proceeds.

Investment Rationale/Risk

➤ Notwithstanding FISV's substantial exposure to financial services, which has increased on a percentage basis in recent years, we believe its size and footprint, diversified customer base, and considerable recurring revenues are appealing. We also think the recent financial crisis could prove beneficial for new opportunities, especially as FISV pursues international business.

➤ Risks to our recommendation and target price include weaker demand than we expect for financial services technology offerings, segment consolidation negatively affecting existing contracts or new business prospects, and sustained weakness in internal growth rates.

➤ Comparisons to the P/E and P/E-to-growth rate multiples of data processing companies in the S&P 1500 yield a price of $50. Our DCF model (including assumptions of a discount rate of 9.7%, average growth of 10% over the next five years, and a terminal growth rate of 3%) leads to an intrinsic value calculation of $62. Weighting these considerations results in our 12-month target price of $54.

Qualitative Risk Assessment

LOW	MEDIUM	HIGH

Our risk assessment reflects our view of FISV's notable size, market position and flexible balance sheet, offset by what we consider its relatively modest internal growth rate and active acquisition strategy.

Quantitative Evaluations

S&P Quality Ranking   B+

D	C	B-	B	B+	A-	A	A+

Relative Strength Rank   MODERATE

67

LOWEST = 1   HIGHEST = 99

Revenue/Earnings Data

Revenue (Million $)

	1Q	2Q	3Q	4Q	Year
2010	1,008	1,022	--	--	--
2009	1,044	1,032	992.0	1,062	4,077
2008	1,310	1,295	1,080	1,061	4,739
2007	1,219	1,180	1,174	1,110	3,922
2006	1,097	1,093	1,157	1,198	4,544
2005	973.1	996.4	1,012	1,078	4,059

Earnings Per Share ($)

2010	0.80	0.85	E0.99	E1.11	E4.05
2009	0.65	0.73	0.80	0.83	3.04
2008	0.59	0.60	0.45	0.45	2.12
2007	0.66	0.62	0.72	0.54	2.42
2006	0.64	0.63	0.63	0.61	2.49
2005	0.71	0.59	0.58	0.80	2.68

Fiscal year ended Dec. 31. Next earnings report expected: Late October. EPS Estimates based on S&P Operating Earnings; historical GAAP earnings are as reported.

Dividend Data

No cash dividends have been paid.

Fiserv Inc

STANDARD &POOR'S

Business Summary August 04, 2010

CORPORATE OVERVIEW. At the end of 2006, Fiserv made some adjustments to its operating segments. Most notably, it created a new insurance services unit, which included the old health plan management services segment, and insurance operations that were previously classified in the financial institutions segment.

In December 2007, the company bought CheckFree Corp., entering the electronic payments area. In January 2008, FISV sold Fiserv Health, and most of its health-related businesses. In July 2008, FISV sold a majority stake of its insurance segment. In 2009, FISV sold its loan fulfillment services business and the balance of its investment support services business.

The financial segment (accounting for 47% of revenues in 2009 and 43% in 2008) provides solutions to thousands of financial institutions, including banks, credit unions, leasing and finance companies, and savings institutions. Many offerings are sold as an integrated suite to clients, and could include core processing (allowing for account servicing and management information

functionality for banks, thrifts and credit unions), lending and item processing (providing for the clearing of paper and imaged checks), payments processing (enabling FISV clients to provide their customers with services such as home-banking and bill payment offerings), and a variety of industry-specific products and services.

In December 2007, FISV acquired CheckFree for $4.4 billion, and thus created the Payments unit (53%, 46%). The segment's financial e-commerce products enable consumers to review bank accounts and receive and pay bills electronically. In 2009, the business processed 1.3 billion transactions and delivered 320 million electronic bills. We believe the CheckFree acquisition has bolstered FISV's base of offerings, technology and customers, and we see notable cross-selling potential.

Company Financials Fiscal Year Ended Dec. 31

Per Share Data ($)	2009	2008	2007	2006	2005	2004	2003	2002	2001	2000
Tangible Book Value	NM	NM	NM	NM	NM	0.96	NM	2.60	2.60	2.18
Cash Flow	4.90	2.85	2.88	3.62	3.62	2.94	2.48	2.09	1.86	1.33
Earnings	3.04	2.12	2.42	2.49	2.68	2.00	1.61	1.37	1.09	0.93
S&P Core Earnings	3.04	2.47	2.42	2.50	2.28	1.91	1.47	1.26	1.00	NA
Dividends	Nil	Nil	Nil	Nil	Nil	Nil	Nil	Nil	Nil	Nil
Payout Ratio	Nil	Nil	Nil	Nil	Nil	Nil	Nil	Nil	Nil	Nil
Prices:High	50.91	56.80	59.85	53.60	46.89	41.01	40.77	47.24	44.61	42.75
Prices:Low	29.46	27.75	44.16	40.29	36.33	32.20	27.23	22.50	29.08	16.21
P/E Ratio:High	17	27	25	21	17	21	25	34	41	46
P/E Ratio:Low	10	13	18	16	14	16	17	16	27	17

Income Statement Analysis (Million $)	2009	2008	2007	2006	2005	2004	2003	2002	2001	2000
Revenue	4,077	4,739	3,922	4,544	4,059	3,730	3,034	2,569	1,890	1,654
Operating Income	1,234	1,046	836	943	925	845	704	734	501	429
Depreciation	333	119	78.0	199	179	185	172	141	148	70.1
Interest Expense	220	260	76.0	41.0	27.8	24.9	22.9	17.8	12.1	22.1
Pretax Income	746	625	661	710	818	641	516	436	347	300
Effective Tax Rate	36.6%	44.6%	38.3%	37.6%	37.5%	38.4%	39.0%	39.0%	40.0%	41.0%
Net Income	473	346	408	443	511	395	315	266	208	177
S&P Core Earnings	473	403	408	443	435	377	288	246	191	NA

Balance Sheet & Other Financial Data (Million $)	2009	2008	2007	2006	2005	2004	2003	2002	2001	2000
Cash	363	232	309	185	184	516	203	227	136	98.9
Current Assets	1,277	2,145	4,204	963	844	3,806	2,681	2,427	1,982	2,649
Total Assets	8,378	9,331	11,846	6,208	6,040	8,383	7,214	6,439	5,322	5,586
Current Liabilities	1,161	2,047	3,754	619	626	759	2,866	2,398	1,791	2,320
Long Term Debt	3,382	3,850	5,405	747	595	505	699	483	343	335
Common Equity	3,026	2,594	2,467	2,426	2,466	2,564	2,200	1,828	1,605	1,252
Total Capital	6,667	6,974	7,933	3,173	3,227	3,204	2,990	2,357	1,948	1,622
Capital Expenditures	198	199	160	187	165	161	143	142	68.0	73.0
Cash Flow	761	465	486	642	691	580	487	407	356	247
Current Ratio	1.1	1.1	1.1	1.6	1.4	5.0	0.9	1.0	1.1	1.1
% Long Term Debt of Capitalization	50.7	55.2	66.5	23.6	18.4	15.8	23.4	20.5	17.6	20.7
% Net Income of Revenue	11.6	7.3	10.4	9.8	12.6	10.6	10.4	10.4	11.0	10.7
% Return on Assets	5.3	3.3	4.5	7.2	7.1	5.1	4.6	4.5	3.8	3.2
% Return on Equity	16.8	13.7	16.7	18.1	20.3	16.6	15.6	15.5	14.6	15.1

Data as orig reptd.; bef. results of disc opers/spec. items. Per share data adj. for stk. divs.; EPS diluted. E-Estimated. NA-Not Available. NM-Not Meaningful. NR-Not Ranked. UR-Under Review.

Office: 255 Fiserv Drive, Brookfield, WI 53045-5815.
Telephone: 262-879-5000.
Email: general_info@fiserv.com
Website: http://www.fiserv.com

Chrmn: D.F. Dillon
Pres & CEO: J. Yabuki
EVP, CFO, Chief Acctg Officer & Treas: T.J. Hirsch
EVP, Secy & General Counsel: C.W. Sprague

EVP & CIO: M. Goebel
Investor Contact: D. Banks (262-879-5055)
Board Members: D. F. Dillon, D. P. Kearney, P. J. Kight, G. J. Levy, D. J. O'Leary, G. M. Renwick, K. M. Robak, D. R. Simons, T. Wertheimer, J. Yabuki

Founded: 1984
Domicile: Wisconsin
Employees: 20,000

The McGraw·Hill Companies

FLIR Systems Inc

STANDARD
&POOR'S

S&P Recommendation HOLD ★★★★☆

Price $26.85 (as of Oct 25, 2010)	**12-Mo. Target Price** $29.00

Investment Style
Large-Cap Growth

GICS Sector Information Technology
Sub-Industry Electronic Equipment Manufacturers

Summary This company designs, manufactures, and markets thermal imaging and broadcast camera systems for use in commercial and government markets.

Key Stock Statistics (Source S&P, Vickers, company reports)

52-Wk Range	$33.35– 24.00	S&P Oper. EPS 2010**E**	1.56	Market Capitalization(B)	$4.245	Beta	0.97
Trailing 12-Month EPS	$1.47	S&P Oper. EPS 2011**E**	1.80	Yield (%)	Nil	S&P 3-Yr. Proj. EPS CAGR(%)	11
Trailing 12-Month P/E	18.3	P/E on S&P Oper. EPS 2010**E**	17.2	Dividend Rate/Share	Nil	S&P Credit Rating	NR
$10K Invested 5 Yrs Ago	$24,138	Common Shares Outstg. (M)	158.1	Institutional Ownership (%)	92		

Price Performance

30-Week Mov. Avg. · · · 10-Week Mov. Avg. – – GAAP Earnings vs. Previous Year   Volume Above Avg. STARS
12-Mo. Target Price — Relative Strength — ▲ Up ▼ Down ► No Change   Below Avg. ★

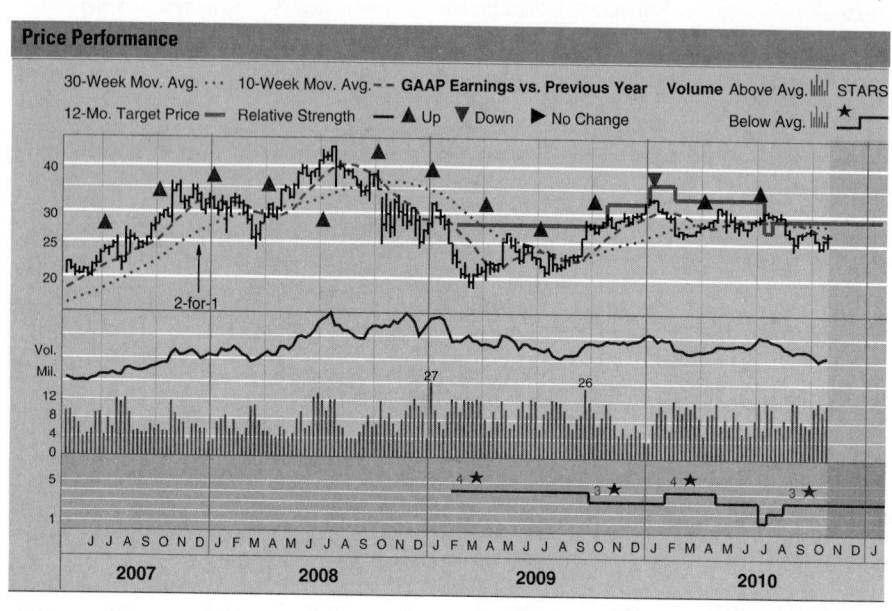

Options: ASE, CBOE, P, Ph

Analysis prepared by **Dylan Cathers** on October 25, 2010, when the stock traded at **$ 26.88**.

Highlights

➤ We are lifting our revenue growth estimates to account for the acquisitions of Raymarine and ICx Technologies. We now look for growth of 21% and 18.5% in 2010 and 2011, respectively, compared with our prior 13.5% and 12.5% forecasts. We have concerns about demand from the government segment over the near term, given the spending constraints the various agencies are under and what we believe are extended procurement cycles. Still, overseas governments will likely remain solid sources of demand. Within Commercial Systems, some important verticals are likely to be soft, but we are generally positive on areas such as security and surveillance.

➤ We expect operating margins to decline in 2010 and 2011, partially reflecting the addition of the lower-margin acquisitions. Also adversely affecting margins should be an unfavorable mix shift within government systems, but we note this business provides FLIR with its highest margins. Additionally, we think cost controls and improving leverage will be offset by a shift towards lower- and mid-priced cameras.

➤ We estimate EPS of $1.56 for 2010 and $1.80 for 2011.

Investment Rationale/Risk

➤ Our hold recommendation is based on valuation. We believe FLIR has a profitable business model, good growth opportunities, and a solid balance sheet. However, we think that sales may be erratic during the next few quarters. Our forecasts reflect risks we see related to government spending, contract wins, and the traction of growth for commercial applications. We believe that extracting value from the recent Raymarine Holdings acquisition will be challenging in the near term, but we are more positive on the recent ICx Technologies acquisition, which should expand their portfolio of offerings to the important government market.

➤ Risks to our recommendation and target price include a sharper-than-anticipated decrease in military spending on infrared related technology, formidable competition, economic headwinds, and financial and integration risks.

➤ Our 12-month target price of $29 is based on our relative valuation analysis. We arrive at our target price using a roughly peer-average P/E ratio of 16.1X our 2011 EPS estimate, which is towards the low end of FLIR's range of 14X-44X over the past four years.

Qualitative Risk Assessment

LOW	**MEDIUM**	HIGH

Our risk assessment reflects the uncertainty of government spending on infrared-related technologies balanced by the long nature of government contracts, helping to reduce business risk. The company carries long-term debt, but has also exhibited healthy profitability and cash flows that we think balances the financial risk.

Quantitative Evaluations

S&P Quality Ranking   B+

D	C	B-	B	**B+**	A-	A	A+

Relative Strength Rank   MODERATE

37

LOWEST = 1   HIGHEST = 99

Revenue/Earnings Data

Revenue (Million $)

	1Q	2Q	3Q	4Q	Year
2010	287.3	331.1	--	--	--
2009	272.0	278.0	285.6	311.6	1,147
2008	236.9	261.0	276.7	302.4	1,077
2007	161.4	184.3	191.1	242.6	779.4
2006	117.3	138.6	133.2	185.9	575.0
2005	108.3	131.0	113.0	156.3	508.6

Earnings Per Share ($)

2010	0.35	0.37	E0.37	E0.45	E1.56
2009	0.33	0.35	0.38	0.37	1.45
2008	0.24	0.29	0.35	0.41	1.28
2007	0.18	0.19	0.23	0.30	0.89
2006	0.09	0.14	0.18	0.26	0.66
2005	0.10	0.16	0.11	0.22	0.58

Fiscal year ended Dec. 31. Next earnings report expected: NA. EPS Estimates based on S&P Operating Earnings; historical GAAP earnings are as reported.

Dividend Data

No cash dividends have been paid.

FLIR Systems Inc

Business Summary October 25, 2010

CORPORATE OVERVIEW. A leading infrared technology company, FLIR Systems, Inc. (FLIR) uses its expertise in product design, infrared imagers, optics, lasers, image processing, systems integration and other technologies, to develop and produce sophisticated thermal and multi-sensor imaging systems used in various applications in commercial, industrial, and government markets. In addition to offering a variety of systems configurations to suit customer's requirements, the company also sells more general, commercial applications.

FLIR's business is organized by three divisions (from largest to smallest based on percentage of 2009 sales): Government Systems (57%), Thermography (25%), Commercial Vision Systems (18%).

The Government Systems division is focused on government contracts and markets where high performance is required. Products are often customized for specific applications, and frequently incorporate additional sensors, including visible light cameras, low light cameras, laser rangefinders, laser illuminators and laser designators. These products are used in applications such as surveillance, force protection, drug interdiction, search and rescue, special operations and target designation. Prices range from $30,000 for hand-held and fixed security systems to over $1 million for advanced stabilized laser designation systems.

The Thermography division sells products for commercial and industrial applications where imaging and temperature together are required, and include specialized cameras with analytical and image processing capabilities to less expensive cameras for less demanding applications. Prices for these cameras range from $3,000 to $150,000.

The Commercial Vision Systems division is focused on emerging commercial markets for infrared imaging technology where the primary need is to see at night or in adverse conditions. The company notes that demand from markets, such as commercial security and automotive, has grown rapidly as the cost of infrared technology has declined. CVS products range in price from under $2,000 for an OEM imaging core to more than $450,000 for a high definition airborne electronic news gathering broadcast system.

Company Financials Fiscal Year Ended Dec. 31

Per Share Data ($)	2009	2008	2007	2006	2005	2004	2003	2002	2001	2000
Tangible Book Value	5.65	3.95	2.88	1.51	1.18	0.85	1.13	1.13	0.67	0.11
Cash Flow	1.69	1.50	1.02	0.92	0.77	0.53	0.39	0.33	0.26	-0.14
Earnings	1.45	1.28	0.89	0.66	0.58	0.47	0.32	0.29	0.20	-0.23
S&P Core Earnings	1.45	1.28	0.89	0.66	0.51	0.38	0.27	0.19	0.16	NA
Dividends	Nil	Nil	Nil	Nil	Nil	Nil	Nil	Nil	Nil	Nil
Payout Ratio	Nil	Nil	Nil	Nil	Nil	Nil	Nil	Nil	Nil	Nil
Prices:High	33.35	45.49	36.43	17.02	18.18	16.67	9.25	7.44	6.19	2.41
Prices:Low	18.81	23.68	14.81	10.73	10.23	8.74	5.13	3.42	0.52	0.38
P/E Ratio:High	23	36	41	26	31	35	29	26	31	NM
P/E Ratio:Low	13	19	17	16	18	19	16	12	3	NM

Income Statement Analysis (Million $)	2009	2008	2007	2006	2005	2004	2003	2002	2001	2000
Revenue	1,147	1,077	779	575	509	483	312	261	214	186
Operating Income	390	324	218	158	142	124	69.8	56.4	44.8	-1.11
Depreciation	42.4	40.0	25.9	20.6	15.6	14.8	6.26	6.20	7.50	9.72
Interest Expense	6.88	8.99	10.2	8.96	7.92	8.09	4.86	1.68	9.42	12.0
Pretax Income	340	295	191	133	122	99.9	63.8	48.9	28.7	-22.3
Effective Tax Rate	32.4%	30.9%	28.5%	23.9%	25.7%	28.4%	30.0%	15.0%	9.77%	NM
Net Income	230	204	137	101	90.8	71.5	44.7	41.6	25.9	-26.1
S&P Core Earnings	231	204	137	101	78.4	57.6	38.4	27.6	20.5	NA

Balance Sheet & Other Financial Data (Million $)	2009	2008	2007	2006	2005	2004	2003	2002	2001	2000
Cash	422	289	204	139	107	121	198	46.6	15.5	11.9
Current Assets	971	812	656	486	406	367	382	174	140	122
Total Assets	1,485	1,244	1,024	798	694	619	450	234	185	167
Current Liabilities	178	172	166	170	90.1	88.7	70.3	52.6	71.0	56.5
Long Term Debt	58.0	190	227	207	206	205	204	Nil	Nil	75.5
Common Equity	1,204	840	623	399	369	313	165	172	105	29.0
Total Capital	1,262	1,036	833	608	586	519	369	172	105	105
Capital Expenditures	41.9	27.6	44.1	43.0	34.0	13.9	14.6	6.60	4.24	7.28
Cash Flow	273	244	163	121	106	86.3	51.0	47.8	33.4	-16.3
Current Ratio	5.5	4.7	4.0	2.9	4.5	4.1	5.4	3.3	2.0	2.2
% Long Term Debt of Capitalization	4.6	18.4	25.0	34.0	35.2	39.6	55.4	Nil	Nil	72.2
% Net Income of Revenue	20.1	18.9	17.5	17.5	17.8	14.8	14.3	15.9	12.1	NM
% Return on Assets	16.9	18.0	15.0	13.6	13.7	13.4	13.1	19.8	14.7	NM
% Return on Equity	22.5	27.8	26.8	26.7	26.6	29.9	26.5	30.0	38.7	NM

Data as orig reptd.; bef. results of disc opers/spec. items. Per share data adj. for stk. divs.; EPS diluted. E-Estimated. NA-Not Available. NM-Not Meaningful. NR-Not Ranked. UR-Under Review.

Office: 27700 SW Parkway Ave Ste A, Wilsonville, OR 97070-8238.
Telephone: 503-498-3547.
Email: investor@flir.com
Website: http://www.flir.com

Chrmn, Pres & CEO: E. Lewis
SVP, Secy & General Counsel: W.W. Davis
Investor Contact: A.L. Trunzo (503-498-3547)

Board Members: J. D. Carter, W. W. Crouch, E. Lewis, A. L. MacDonald, M. T. Smith, J. W. Wood, Jr., S. E. Wynne

Founded: 1978
Domicile: Oregon
Employees: 2,079

Flowserve Corp.

STANDARD &POOR'S

S&P Recommendation	**STRONG BUY** ★★★★★	Price	12-Mo. Target Price	Investment Style
		$114.18 (as of Oct 22, 2010)	$135.00	Large-Cap Growth

GICS Sector Industrials
Sub-Industry Industrial Machinery

Summary This company is a global manufacturer of industrial pumps and related equipment for the chemical, oil & gas, and power industries.

Key Stock Statistics (Source S&P, Vickers, company reports)

52-Wk Range	$119.83–81.35	S&P Oper. EPS 2010**E**	8.00	Market Capitalization(B)	$6.387	Beta	1.60
Trailing 12-Month EPS	$7.08	S&P Oper. EPS 2011**E**	9.75	Yield (%)	1.02	S&P 3-Yr. Proj. EPS CAGR(%)	8
Trailing 12-Month P/E	16.1	P/E on S&P Oper. EPS 2010**E**	14.3	Dividend Rate/Share	$1.16	S&P Credit Rating	BB+
$10K Invested 5 Yrs Ago	$35,200	Common Shares Outstg. (M)	55.9	Institutional Ownership (%)	86		

Price Performance

30-Week Mov. Avg. · · · · 10-Week Mov. Avg. - - GAAP Earnings vs. Previous Year Volume Above Avg. STARS
12-Mo. Target Price — Relative Strength — ▲ Up ▼ Down ► No Change Below Avg.

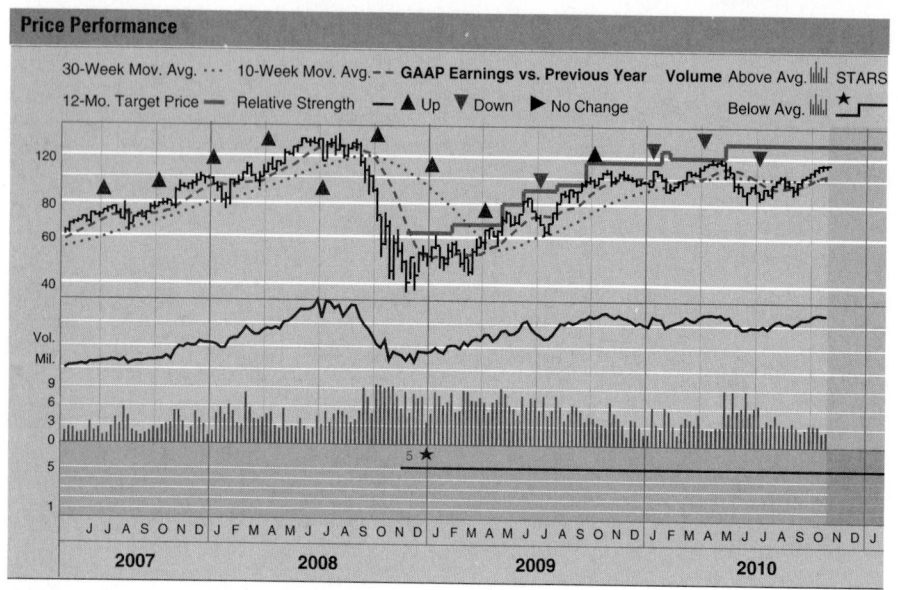

Analysis prepared by **Stewart Scharf** on August 06, 2010, when the stock traded at **$ 101.69**.

Highlights

➤ We expect sales to fall in the high single-digits in 2010, but see a sequential rebound into 2011, driven by growth in developing regions. Although customers remain cautious, we see postponed projects gradually resuming as global markets recover, with further strength in the aftermarket business. Bookings should rise as demand picks up in the oil & gas, chemical, and power sectors.

➤ We forecast gross margins in 2010 will expand from 36.5% in 2009, based on cost savings from realignments and a greater mix of aftermarket products, which should offset competitive pricing. We see slightly wider adjusted EBITDA margins (18% in 2009), with FLS continuing to focus on cost-cutting initiatives as it optimizes certain non-strategic facilities. A stronger U.S. dollar mainly against the euro should continue to negatively impact earnings.

➤ We project a higher effective tax rate for 2010 of about 28%, and we see operating EPS of $8.00 (before about $0.26 of realignment costs and a $0.15 charge due to the devaluation of the Venezuelan Bolivar), then we forecast $9.75 for 2011.

Investment Rationale/Risk

➤ Our strong buy recommendation is based on our valuation metrics, our favorable perception of FLS's strong balance sheet and diversified business model, and signs of increased bidding activity for certain large projects.

➤ Risks to our recommendation and target price include significant delays and/or project cancellations, especially in the oil & gas sector; a shortage of skilled labor; geopolitical issues in developing regions; a weak euro and other currencies; and, problems with internal controls over financial reporting.

➤ The shares trade at about 13X our 2010 EPS estimate, a near 25% discount to our projected P/E for S&P's Industrial Machinery group, which we attribute to FLS's cyclical project business and exposure to volatile markets. Our DCF model, which assumes a terminal growth rate of 4.0% and a weighted average cost of capital of 12.5%, indicates intrinsic value of about $125. Our relative metrics, including enterprise value to EBITDA and P/E-to-EPS growth, suggest a value of $145. Blending these methods, we arrive at our 12-month target price of $135.

Qualitative Risk Assessment

LOW	MEDIUM	HIGH

Our risk assessment reflects the company's exposure to cyclical end markets and its foreign exchange swings based on its significant proportion of foreign sales. We think these factors are offset by its leading position in many markets, significant aftermarket business, strong cash flows, and favorable leverage ratio.

Quantitative Evaluations

S&P Quality Ranking   B

D	C	B-	B	B+	A-	A	A+

Relative Strength Rank   STRONG

                                79

LOWEST = 1   HIGHEST = 99

Revenue/Earnings Data

Revenue (Million $)

	1Q	2Q	3Q	4Q	Year
2010	958.9	961.1	--	--	--
2009	1,025	1,090	1,051	1,199	4,365
2008	993.3	1,158	1,154	1,169	4,473
2007	803.4	930.7	919.2	1,109	3,763
2006	653.9	752.9	770.8	883.5	3,061
2005	616.1	691.2	649.5	738.5	2,695

Earnings Per Share ($)

2010	1.42	1.62	E2.15	E2.35	E8.00
2009	1.64	1.92	2.07	1.96	7.59
2008	1.53	2.13	2.04	2.03	7.74
2007	0.59	1.11	1.10	1.67	4.47
2006	0.32	0.58	0.49	0.58	2.00
2005	0.05	0.33	0.08	0.36	0.82

Fiscal year ended Dec. 31. Next earnings report expected: Late October. EPS Estimates based on S&P Operating Earnings; historical GAAP earnings are as reported.

Dividend Data (Dates: mm/dd Payment Date: mm/dd/yy)

Amount ($)	Date Decl.	Ex-Div. Date	Stk. of Record	Payment Date
0.270	11/23	12/21	12/23	01/06/10
0.290	02/24	03/22	03/24	04/07/10
0.290	05/18	06/28	06/30	07/14/10
0.290	08/12	09/28	09/30	10/14/10

Dividends have been paid since 2007. Source: Company reports.

Options: ASE, CBOE, Ph

Please read the Required Disclosures and Analyst Certification on the last page of this report.

The McGraw-Hill Companies

Flowserve Corp.

Business Summary August 06, 2010

CORPORATE OVERVIEW. Flowserve Corp., which was formed through the 1997 merger of Durco International Inc. and BW/IP, Inc., is one of the world's leading providers of fluid motion and control products and services. Customers use fluid motion and control products to regulate the movement of liquids or gases through processing systems in their facilities. As of January 1, 2010, in an effort to drive business growth and further leverage its operations, FLS combined its pump and flow solutions divisions into a new Flow Solutions Group (FSG), which will be reported in two segments: FSG Engineered Product division (highly engineered pump product operations of former pump division and all the mechanical seal operations of former flow solutions division) and FSG Industrial Product division (general purpose pump operations of former pump division). Pump systems and components are produced at 30 plants worldwide. FLS manufactures over 150 different pump models, ranging from simple fractional horsepower industrial pumps to high horsepower engineered pumps (over 30,000 horsepower). Aftermarket services through the company's global network are provided in 78 service centers in 30 countries.

Principal markets for the company's products are oil & gas (36% of bookings in 2009), general industrial (19%), chemical (18%), power generation (20%) and water treatment (7%). On a geographic basis, 2009 revenue broke down as follows: North America 32%; Europe 25%; Middle East and Africa 15%; Asia Pacific 19%; and Latin America 9%.

The FSG Engineered Product division (55% of sales in the first half of 2010; includes inter-segment sales) manufactures engineered pumps, vertical circulation and other pumps, seals, repair and service, and integrated solutions primarily used by companies in the oil & gas, power and water treatment (desalination) markets. Seals are used on a variety of rotating equipment, including pumps, mixers, compressors, steam turbines and other specialty equipment. The FSG Industrial Product division (21% of sales) manufactures industrial, water and vertical turbine pumps for the oil & gas, water and general industrial sectors. The Flow Control division (27%) provides manual valves, control valves, nuclear valves, actuators, and other aftermarket parts and services for the power generation, oil & gas, chemical and general industrial markets. These products are typically utilized within a flow control system to control the flow of liquids or gases.

The company hedges its cash flows but not its profit and loss statement, creating a headwind as the U.S. dollar strengthens against the euro.

Company Financials Fiscal Year Ended Dec. 31

Per Share Data ($)	2009	2008	2007	2006	2005	2004	2003	2002	2001	2000
Tangible Book Value	14.68	7.56	5.42	0.47	NM	NM	NM	NM	NM	NM
Cash Flow	9.29	9.12	5.82	3.30	2.07	1.68	2.36	2.29	2.29	1.91
Earnings	7.59	7.74	4.47	2.00	0.82	0.36	0.96	1.16	0.42	0.40
S&P Core Earnings	7.72	7.44	4.39	2.14	0.87	0.41	0.95	0.82	-0.08	NA
Dividends	1.08	1.00	0.60	Nil	Nil	Nil	Nil	Nil	Nil	Nil
Payout Ratio	14%	13%	13%	Nil	Nil	Nil	Nil	Nil	Nil	Nil
Prices:High	108.85	145.45	102.74	61.06	39.75	28.18	22.93	35.09	33.30	23.50
Prices:Low	43.23	37.18	48.73	39.63	23.69	18.64	10.40	7.58	18.70	10.56
P/E Ratio:High	14	19	23	31	48	78	24	30	79	59
P/E Ratio:Low	6	5	11	20	29	52	11	7	45	26

Income Statement Analysis (Million $)	2009	2008	2007	2006	2005	2004	2003	2002	2001	2000
Revenue	4,365	4,473	3,763	3,061	2,695	2,638	2,404	2,251	1,918	1,538
Operating Income	785	675	488	296	260	229	260	274	204	204
Depreciation	95.4	79.1	77.7	71.0	69.9	73.2	77.6	65.3	73.9	57.0
Interest Expense	40.0	51.3	60.1	65.7	74.1	81.0	84.2	92.9	118	70.3
Pretax Income	585	590	360	187	83.3	59.6	73.8	92.1	25.6	23.2
Effective Tax Rate	26.8%	25.0%	29.0%	39.1%	44.5%	66.2%	28.4%	34.4%	36.2%	34.0%
Net Income	428	442	256	114	46.2	20.2	52.9	60.4	16.4	15.3
S&P Core Earnings	435	425	252	122	48.9	22.5	52.4	42.7	-3.30	NA

Balance Sheet & Other Financial Data (Million $)	2009	2008	2007	2006	2005	2004	2003	2002	2001	2000
Cash	654	472	371	67.0	92.9	63.8	53.5	49.3	21.5	42.3
Current Assets	2,499	2,332	1,897	1,303	1,071	1,050	1,091	1,031	898	898
Total Assets	4,249	4,024	3,520	2,869	2,576	2,634	2,801	2,608	2,052	2,110
Current Liabilities	1,458	1,608	1,250	884	695	708	633	492	417	434
Long Term Debt	539	546	550	557	653	658	880	1,056	996	1,111
Common Equity	1,796	1,368	1,293	1,021	832	870	821	756	411	305
Total Capital	2,368	1,924	1,856	1,577	1,485	1,528	1,701	1,811	1,407	1,416
Capital Expenditures	108	127	89.0	73.5	49.3	45.2	28.8	30.9	35.2	27.7
Cash Flow	523	522	333	185	116	93.3	130	126	90.2	72.3
Current Ratio	1.7	1.5	1.5	1.5	1.5	1.5	1.7	2.1	2.2	2.1
% Long Term Debt of Capitalization	22.8	28.3	29.6	35.3	44.0	43.0	51.7	58.3	70.8	78.5
% Net Income of Revenue	9.8	9.9	6.8	3.7	1.7	0.8	2.2	2.7	0.9	1.0
% Return on Assets	10.3	11.7	8.0	4.2	1.8	0.8	2.0	2.6	0.8	1.0
% Return on Equity	27.1	33.3	22.1	12.2	5.4	2.4	6.9	10.4	4.6	5.0

Data as orig reptd.; bef. results of disc opers/spec. items. Per share data adj. for stk. divs.; EPS diluted. E-Estimated. NA-Not Available. NM-Not Meaningful. NR-Not Ranked. UR-Under Review.

Office: 5215 N O Connor Blvd Ste 2300, Irving, TX, USA 75039-3726.
Telephone: 972-443-6500.
Website: http://www.flowserve.com
Chrmn: J.O. Rollans

Pres & CEO: M.A. Blinn
SVP, CFO, Chief Acctg Officer & Cntlr: R.J. Guiltinan, Jr.
SVP & Chief Admin Officer: M.D. Dailey
SVP & Treas: D.P. Freeman

Investor Contact: P. Fehlman (972-443-6517)
Board Members: M. A. Blinn, G. J. Delly, R. Fix, J. R. Friedery, J. E. Harlan, M. F. Johnston, R. J. Mills, C. M. Rampacek, J. O. Rollans, W. C. Rusnack, K. E. Sheehan

Founded: 1912
Domicile: New York
Employees: 15,000

Fluor Corp.

STANDARD &POOR'S

S&P Recommendation **BUY** ★★★★☆	Price $49.47 (as of Oct 22, 2010)	12-Mo. Target Price $57.00	Investment Style Large-Cap Blend

GICS Sector Industrials
Sub-Industry Construction & Engineering

Summary Fluor is one of the world's largest engineering, procurement, and construction companies, with 72% of its backlog derived from outside the U.S.

Key Stock Statistics (Source S&P, Vickers, company reports)

52-Wk Range	$55.47–39.77	S&P Oper. EPS 2010**E**	3.30	Market Capitalization(B)	$8.843	Beta	1.30
Trailing 12-Month EPS	$3.33	S&P Oper. EPS 2011**E**	3.60	Yield (%)	1.01	S&P 3-Yr. Proj. EPS CAGR(%)	4
Trailing 12-Month P/E	14.9	P/E on S&P Oper. EPS 2010**E**	15.0	Dividend Rate/Share	$0.50	S&P Credit Rating	A-
$10K Invested 5 Yrs Ago	$16,935	Common Shares Outstg. (M)	178.8	Institutional Ownership (%)	82		

Price Performance

30-Week Mov. Avg. · · · 10-Week Mov. Avg. – – GAAP Earnings vs. Previous Year Volume Above Avg. ||||| STARS
12-Mo. Target Price — Relative Strength — ▲ Up ▼ Down ► No Change Below Avg. ||||| ★

Options: ASE, CBOE, P, Ph

Analysis prepared by **Stewart Scharf** on October 19, 2010, when the stock traded at **$ 48.85**.

Highlights

➤ We expect revenues to decline at least 5% in 2010, based on delays in the full release of major projects as customers reduce spending levels. However, we believe double-digit revenue growth will return in 2011, as industrial markets gradually recover. We still believe quarterly results will be lumpy, due to timing issues and customer cautiousness, but see favorable long-term trends as FLR ramps up its mining business, while bookings should strengthen for oil & gas, infrastructure, and government projects.

➤ In our view, gross margins will narrow in 2010, as more lower-margin mining projects replace oil & gas projects in the backlog, and competitive pressures persist. We expect operating margins to narrow somewhat to about 5.5%, as higher compensation and severance costs offset cost controls. Operating margins should expand in 2011 on well-controlled operating expenses.

➤ We forecast a slightly lower effective tax rate of about 34% for 2010, and estimate operating EPS of $3.30 (before $0.90 charge). We project a 9% rise to $3.60 for 2011.

Investment Rationale/Risk

➤ Our buy recommendation is based on our valuation models, along with our view of FLR's favorable long-term prospects, especially in the Americas and Asia Pacific, and its strong balance sheet. Despite customer uncertainty, we see stronger bookings as customers gradually resuming long-term capital investment plans.

➤ Risks to our recommendation and target price include additional project delays and cancellations based on challenging market conditions, labor shortages, negative foreign currency effect, credit market issues, sharply lower oil prices, and timing issues for new awards.

➤ Our 12-month target price of $57 is derived from a blend of our relative and discounted cash flow (DCF) metrics. Based on various relative metrics, we use a premium-to-peers P/E of 15X our 2011 EPS estimate, reflecting FLR's strong global prospect list and diversified business model, resulting in a value of $54. Our DCF model, which assumes a 3.5% terminal growth rate and an 8.3% weighted average cost of capital, suggests the stock's intrinsic value is $60.

Qualitative Risk Assessment

LOW	MEDIUM	HIGH

Our risk assessment reflects tight credit markets, and project delays and cancellations, along with geopolitical issues as more projects are in unstable regions of the world. This is offset by our view of FLR's strong balance sheet, modest debt levels, and diverse project mix and customer base.

Quantitative Evaluations

S&P Quality Ranking
B+

D	C	B-	B	B+	A-	A	A+

Relative Strength Rank
MODERATE

40

LOWEST = 1   HIGHEST = 99

Revenue/Earnings Data

Revenue (Million $)

	1Q	2Q	3Q	4Q	Year
2010	4,919	5,152	--	--	--
2009	5,798	5,293	5,420	5,479	21,990
2008	4,807	5,574	5,674	6,072	22,326
2007	3,642	4,222	4,155	4,712	16,691
2006	3,625	3,456	3,364	3,633	14,079
2005	2,860	2,920	3,419	3,963	13,161

Earnings Per Share ($)

	1Q	2Q	3Q	4Q	Year
2010	0.76	0.87	E0.95	E0.72	E3.30
2009	1.12	0.93	0.89	0.82	3.75
2008	0.75	1.13	1.01	1.04	3.93
2007	0.47	0.52	0.51	1.42	2.93
2006	0.50	0.37	0.16	0.45	1.48
2005	0.28	-0.10	0.76	0.37	1.31

Fiscal year ended Dec. 31. Next earnings report expected: Early November. EPS Estimates based on S&P Operating Earnings; historical GAAP earnings are as reported.

Dividend Data (Dates: mm/dd Payment Date: mm/dd/yy)

Amount ($)	Date Decl.	Ex-Div. Date	Stk. of Record	Payment Date
0.125	10/30	12/02	12/04	01/05/10
0.125	02/04	03/03	03/05	04/02/10
0.125	05/06	06/02	06/04	07/02/10
0.125	08/05	09/01	09/03	10/04/10

Dividends have been paid since 1974. Source: Company reports.

Please read the Required Disclosures and Analyst Certification on the last page of this report.

The McGraw-Hill Companies

Fluor Corp.

STANDARD &POOR'S

Business Summary October 19, 2010

CORPORATE OVERVIEW. Fluor Corp. is one of the world's largest engineering, procurement, construction and maintenance companies. It has five principal operating segments. The Oil and Gas segment provides services to oil, gas, refining, chemical, polymer and petrochemical customers. Industrial and Infrastructure provides EPC services to businesses, including industrial, commercial, telecommunications, mining and technology. Global Services provides operations and maintenance support, and equipment and outsourcing, through TRS Staffing Solutions. Government Services provides support services to the federal government and other government entities. In the Power segment, Fluor provides a full range of services to the gas fueled, solid fueled, renewables, nuclear and plant betterment markets.

Contributions to revenues and operating profits in 2009 were as follows: Oil and Gas, 54% of revenues and operating profits of $730 million; Industrial and Infrastructure, 22% and $140 million; Global Services, 9.4% and $140 million; Government, 9.0% and $117 million; and Power, 5.9% and $124 million.

FLR received new awards of $18.5 billion in 2009, down 26% from a year earlier. In the second quarter of 2010, new awards climbed 38% to nearly $9.4 billion, year to year.

Total backlog of $30.2 billion at June 30, 2010, slipped 2% from a year earlier but rose nearly 18% sequentially. During 2009, FLR removed $5.3 billion from its backlog, including $2.1 billion in the first quarter from a canceled Kuwait refinery project. The backlog at June 30, 2010, was divided by segment as follows: Oil and Gas $10.2 billion (34% of total backlog), down 35% from a year earlier; Industrial and Infrastructure $16.1 billion (53%), up 65%; Global Services $2.1 billion (7%), up 16%; Government $635 million (2%), down 35%, and Power $1.1 billion (4%), down 58%. Backlog by geographic region was: U.S. 28%; the Americas 26%; Europe, Africa and the Middle East 32%; and Asia-Pacific (including Australia) 14%. Backlog includes a long cycle of larger projects that tend to take three to five years to complete, versus earlier smaller projects, which had an 18-to-36 month cycle. Historically, the backlog burn rate has been 60% to 65%, with FLR projecting about 60% for 2010. As of June 30, 2010, FLR's percentage of fixed price work in its backlog had increased to 29%, from 21% at 2009 year end (near 30% at 2008 year end), with most in infrastructure and power, while oil and gas is primarily cost reimbursable.

Company Financials Fiscal Year Ended Dec. 31

Per Share Data ($)	2009	2008	2007	2006	2005	2004	2003	2002	2001	2000
Tangible Book Value	17.99	14.23	12.39	9.39	8.92	7.45	6.26	5.38	4.79	9.98
Cash Flow	4.79	4.82	3.74	2.18	1.91	1.68	1.61	1.55	1.26	2.69
Earnings	3.75	3.93	2.93	1.48	1.31	1.13	1.12	1.07	0.81	0.66
S&P Core Earnings	3.86	3.49	2.93	1.50	1.31	1.04	1.17	0.90	0.57	NA
Dividends	0.50	0.50	0.40	0.22	0.32	0.32	0.32	0.32	0.32	0.50
Payout Ratio	13%	13%	14%	15%	24%	28%	29%	30%	40%	76%
Prices:High	58.62	101.37	86.08	51.93	39.55	27.60	20.41	22.48	31.60	24.25
Prices:Low	30.21	28.60	37.61	36.76	25.06	18.05	13.33	10.03	15.60	11.97
P/E Ratio:High	16	26	29	35	30	25	18	21	39	37
P/E Ratio:Low	8	7	13	25	19	16	12	9	19	18

Income Statement Analysis (Million $)										
Revenue	21,990	22,326	16,691	14,079	13,161	9,380	8,806	9,959	8,972	9,970
Operating Income	1,305	1,160	755	504	396	370	344	332	258	451
Depreciation	182	163	147	126	104	91.9	79.7	78.0	71.9	312
Interest Expense	10.1	11.9	24.0	23.0	16.3	15.4	10.1	8.93	25.0	26.3
Pretax Income	1,137	1,114	649	382	300	281	268	261	185	142
Effective Tax Rate	35.5%	35.4%	17.8%	31.0%	24.1%	33.6%	33.0%	34.8%	31.1%	29.8%
Net Income	685	720	533	263	227	187	180	170	128	99.8
S&P Core Earnings	700	640	533	267	226	171	188	143	90.2	NA

Balance Sheet & Other Financial Data (Million $)										
Cash	2,291	2,108	1,714	976	789	605	497	753	573	69.4
Current Assets	5,122	4,669	4,060	3,324	3,108	2,723	2,214	1,941	1,851	1,448
Total Assets	7,178	6,424	5,796	4,875	4,574	3,970	3,449	3,142	3,091	3,653
Current Liabilities	3,301	3,163	2,860	2,406	2,339	1,764	1,829	1,756	1,811	1,620
Long Term Debt	17.7	17.7	325	187	92.0	348	44.7	17.6	17.6	17.6
Common Equity	3,306	2,671	2,274	1,730	1,631	1,336	1,082	884	789	1,609
Total Capital	3,461	2,689	2,292	1,918	1,723	1,683	1,126	901	807	1,627
Capital Expenditures	233	300	284	274	213	104	79.2	63.0	148	284
Cash Flow	867	884	680	390	331	279	259	248	200	412
Current Ratio	1.6	1.5	1.4	1.4	1.3	1.5	1.2	1.1	1.0	0.9
% Long Term Debt of Capitalization	0.5	0.7	0.8	9.8	5.3	20.7	4.0	2.0	2.2	1.1
% Net Income of Revenue	3.1	3.2	3.2	1.9	1.7	2.0	2.0	1.7	1.4	1.0
% Return on Assets	10.1	11.8	10.0	5.6	5.3	5.0	5.4	5.4	4.4	2.3
% Return on Equity	22.9	29.1	26.6	15.7	15.3	15.4	18.3	20.3	18.0	6.3

Data as orig reptd.; bef. results of disc opers/spec. items. Per share data adj. for stk. divs.; EPS diluted. E-Estimated. NA-Not Available. NM-Not Meaningful. NR-Not Ranked. UR-Under Review.

Office: 6700 Las Colinas Blvd, Irving, TX 75039-2902.
Telephone: 469-398-7000.
Email: investor@fluor.com
Website: http://www.fluor.com

Chrmn & CEO: A.L. Boeckmann
COO: D.T. Seaton
SVP, CFO & Chief Acctg Officer: D.M. Steuert
SVP, Secy & General Counsel: C.M. Hernandez

Chief Admin Officer: G.C. Gilkey
Investor Contact: K. Lockwood (469-398-7220)
Board Members: I. Adesida, P. K. Barker, R. T. Berkery, A. L. Boeckmann, H. P. Eberhart, P. J. Fluor, J. T. Hackett, K. Kresa, D. R. O'Hare, J. W. Prueher, N. H. Sultan, S. H. Woolsey

Founded: 1924
Domicile: Delaware
Employees: 36,152

FMC Corp.

STANDARD &POOR'S

S&P Recommendation **HOLD** ★★★☆☆	Price $70.18 (as of Oct 22, 2010)	12-Mo. Target Price $65.00	Investment Style Large-Cap Value

GICS Sector Materials
Sub-Industry Diversified Chemicals

Summary This company is a diversified producer of industrial, specialty and agricultural chemicals.

Key Stock Statistics (Source S&P, Vickers, company reports)

52-Wk Range	$71.47–49.53	S&P Oper. EPS 2010**E**	4.70	Market Capitalization(B)	$5.087	Beta	1.04
Trailing 12-Month EPS	$3.16	S&P Oper. EPS 2011**E**	5.10	Yield (%)	0.71	S&P 3-Yr. Proj. EPS CAGR(%)	10
Trailing 12-Month P/E	22.2	P/E on S&P Oper. EPS 2010**E**	14.9	Dividend Rate/Share	$0.50	S&P Credit Rating	BBB+
$10K Invested 5 Yrs Ago	$28,437	Common Shares Outstg. (M)	72.5	Institutional Ownership (%)	97		

Price Performance

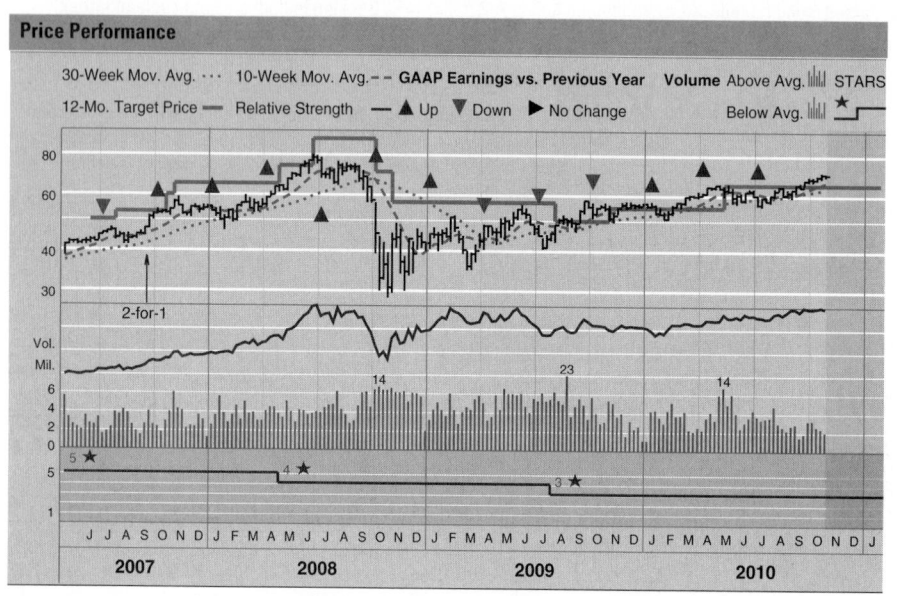

Options: ASE, CBOE, P, Ph

Analysis prepared by **Richard O'Reilly, CFA** on August 11, 2010, when the stock traded at **$61.11**.

Highlights

➤ We expect operating EPS of $4.70 in 2010, versus the depressed $4.15 of 2009. We believe industrial chemicals profits, which fell 55% in 2009 largely on lower volumes, will rise almost 30% in 2010, as some recovery in demand, especially for soda ash and peroxygens due to stronger glass, paper and pulp markets, and much lower raw material costs, outweigh lower prices for soda ash exports and peroxygens. Profits in the third quarter will be limited by costs arising from an unplanned outage at the soda ash facility.

➤ Specialty chemicals profits should increase 20% in 2010, on expected sales growth in biopolymers and a recovery in lithium volumes. We look for profits for the pesticide unit to grow in the mid-single digits, reflecting sales increases in most regions on new product introductions, limited by increased development spending.

➤ We see interest expense in 2010 increasing to about $42 million, from $27 million in 2009. Pension expense should also be greater, but we expect the effective tax rate to be about 30%, down from 30.8% in 2009.

Investment Rationale/Risk

➤ Our hold opinion is based on our belief the shares are about fairly valued. We project a rebound in EPS in 2010 on further profit gains in pesticides and specialty chemicals. Industrial chemicals should show some recovery in profitability, reflecting a recovery in demand and lower raw material costs. We believe FMC's balance sheet and cash flow will allow it to make bolt-on acquisitions in the specialty businesses while continuing stock buybacks.

➤ Risks to our recommendation and target price include higher-than-expected raw material and energy costs, unplanned production outages and interruptions, adverse weather conditions, adverse economic conditions in Brazil (17% of annual sales), and the company's inability to maintain or increase industrial chemicals selling prices and receive approvals for new specialty chemical and pesticide products.

➤ Based on our 2010 estimates, the stock trades at P/E and cash flow multiples at discounts to those of comparable-sized chemical companies. Our 12-month target price of $65 is based on a multiple of 12.7X our 2011 EPS estimate, a typical historical discount to the company's peer group.

Qualitative Risk Assessment

LOW	MEDIUM	HIGH

Our risk assessment reflects the company's diversified product mix and leading domestic market positions in many product lines, offset by the cyclical nature of the industrial chemicals business and geographic exposure to the Brazilian farm economy.

Quantitative Evaluations

S&P Quality Ranking B-

D	C	B-	B	B+	A-	A	A+

Relative Strength Rank MODERATE **68**

LOWEST = 1   HIGHEST = 99

Revenue/Earnings Data

Revenue (Million $)

	1Q	2Q	3Q	4Q	Year
2010	756.5	776.8	--	--	--
2009	690.5	700.3	713.3	722.1	2,826
2008	750.2	806.6	820.8	737.7	3,115
2007	674.1	657.9	626.6	674.3	2,633
2006	594.1	592.3	572.2	588.4	2,347
2005	552.4	565.5	510.0	522.2	2,150

Earnings Per Share ($)

	1Q	2Q	3Q	4Q	Year
2010	1.13	1.16	E1.05	E1.03	E4.70
2009	1.00	1.01	0.46	0.88	3.37
2008	1.31	1.20	1.13	0.69	4.35
2007	0.71	0.19	0.54	0.60	2.02
2006	0.48	0.44	0.49	0.43	1.84
2005	0.46	0.43	-0.04	0.57	1.42

Fiscal year ended Dec. 31. Next earnings report expected: Late October. EPS Estimates based on S&P Operating Earnings; historical GAAP earnings are as reported.

Dividend Data (Dates: mm/dd Payment Date: mm/dd/yy)

Amount ($)	Date Decl.	Ex-Div. Date	Stk. of Record	Payment Date
0.125	12/18	12/29	12/31	01/21/10
0.125	02/19	03/29	03/31	04/15/10
0.125	04/27	06/28	06/30	07/15/10
0.125	07/23	09/28	09/30	10/21/10

Dividends have been paid since 2006. Source: Company reports.

Please read the Required Disclosures and Analyst Certification on the last page of this report.

The McGraw-Hill Companies

FMC Corp.

STANDARD &POOR'S

Business Summary August 11, 2010

CORPORATE OVERVIEW. FMC Corp. concentrates solely on its chemicals businesses, consisting of pesticides, and industrial and specialty chemicals. International operations provided 65% of 2009 sales; Brazil alone accounted for 17% of sales.

Industrial chemicals accounted for 36% of sales and 17% of profits in 2009. FMC is North America's largest producer of natural soda ash (about 55% of annual sales) and a large producer of peroxygens (15%, consisting of hydrogen peroxide and specialties), and is a major European producer of phosphates, peroxygens, zeolites, silicates, and sulfur derivatives through Foret, S.A. (30%). The segment had posted three years of substantial earnings growth after its cyclical low in 2003, before easing in 2007 as higher raw material costs more than offset increased sales. Profits more than doubled in 2008 on higher selling prices and improved power markets in Europe, but fell 55% in 2009 on lower volumes due to the recession. The company in early May 2010 said it was exploring strategic alternatives for its phosphorus business.

Agricultural products (37%, 54%) consist of insecticides, herbicides, and

fungicides for crop protection and pest control. The segment achieved its seventh consecutive year of record profits in 2009, growing 18%, although sales eased 1%. Insecticides (including Founce, Furadan and Capture) account for about 48% of annual sales; almost 80% of segment sales are derived outside the U.S. Herbicide sales (45%) have grown significantly over the past several years. FMC's herbicides primarily target niche uses and include two product lines (sulfentrazone and carfentrazone) introduced in the late 1990s.

In the specialty chemicals segment (27%, 29%), FMC BioPolymer (about 77% of segment sales) is the world's leading producer of carrageenan, alginate, and microcrystalline cellulose (over 50% share), used for pharmaceutical ingredients, food stabilizers and thickeners, and personal care and household products. FMC believes that carrageenan and microcrystalline cellulose are growing faster than the overall food ingredients market.

Company Financials Fiscal Year Ended Dec. 31

Per Share Data ($)	2009	2008	2007	2006	2005	2004	2003	2002	2001	2000
Tangible Book Value	11.00	9.19	15.24	11.17	10.53	9.55	6.12	3.94	1.64	4.99
Cash Flow	5.10	5.75	3.49	3.50	3.21	4.19	2.33	2.68	-2.79	5.79
Earnings	3.37	4.35	2.02	1.84	1.42	2.35	0.56	1.01	-4.93	2.81
S&P Core Earnings	3.58	3.42	1.79	1.99	0.97	2.22	0.30	0.40	-4.94	NA
Dividends	0.50	0.48	0.41	0.36	Nil	Nil	Nil	Nil	Nil	Nil
Payout Ratio	15%	11%	20%	20%	Nil	Nil	Nil	Nil	Nil	Nil
Prices:High	58.13	80.23	59.00	38.99	31.94	25.25	17.43	21.15	42.00	38.59
Prices:Low	34.90	28.53	35.63	25.87	21.63	16.48	7.11	11.45	22.83	23.03
P/E Ratio:High	17	18	29	21	23	11	31	21	NM	14
P/E Ratio:Low	10	7	18	14	15	7	13	11	NM	8

Income Statement Analysis (Million $)	2009	2008	2007	2006	2005	2004	2003	2002	2001	2000
Revenue	2,826	3,115	2,633	2,347	2,150	2,051	1,921	1,853	1,943	3,926
Operating Income	577	656	507	461	416	363	321	306	323	565
Depreciation	127	106	114	132	136	134	125	119	132	189
Interest Expense	27.2	38.6	41.4	42.0	62.3	80.9	96.1	73.0	63.0	99.7
Pretax Income	310	472	195	153	201	135	40.9	89.9	-471	227
Effective Tax Rate	17.1%	26.6%	14.9%	NM	41.0%	NM	NM	19.4%	NM	19.9%
Net Income	247	330	157	145	111	176	39.8	69.1	-306	177
S&P Core Earnings	261	259	139	157	75.9	166	21.4	27.4	-307	NA

Balance Sheet & Other Financial Data (Million $)	2009	2008	2007	2006	2005	2004	2003	2002	2001	2000
Cash	76.6	52.4	75.5	166	206	212	57.0	364	23.4	25.1
Current Assets	1,488	1,433	1,194	1,068	1,067	1,073	1,010	1,176	820	1,330
Total Assets	3,136	2,976	2,733	2,735	2,740	2,978	2,829	2,872	2,477	3,746
Current Liabilities	709	759	751	702	659	820	728	875	1,079	1,400
Long Term Debt	588	593	420	524	640	822	1,033	1,036	652	872
Common Equity	1,133	903	1,064	1,056	1,026	942	654	406	219	800
Total Capital	1,744	1,561	1,542	1,638	1,717	1,816	1,736	1,487	915	1,720
Capital Expenditures	161	175	115	116	93.5	85.4	87.0	83.9	146	240
Cash Flow	374	436	271	277	247	310	164	188	-175	366
Current Ratio	2.1	1.9	1.6	1.5	1.6	1.3	1.4	1.3	0.8	0.9
% Long Term Debt of Capitalization	33.7	38.0	27.2	32.0	37.3	45.3	59.5	69.7	71.2	50.7
% Net Income of Revenue	8.7	10.6	6.0	6.2	5.2	8.6	2.1	3.7	NM	4.5
% Return on Assets	8.1	11.5	5.7	5.3	3.9	6.0	1.4	2.6	NM	4.6
% Return on Equity	24.2	33.5	15.0	13.9	11.3	22.0	7.0	22.1	NM	23.0

Data as orig reptd.; bef. results of disc opers/spec. items. Per share data adj. for stk. divs.; EPS diluted. E-Estimated. NA-Not Available. NM-Not Meaningful. NR-Not Ranked. UR-Under Review.

Office: 1735 Market St, Philadelphia, PA 19103-7597.
Telephone: 215-299-6000.
Email: investor-info@fmc.com
Website: http://www.fmc.com

Chrmn, Pres & CEO: P.R. Brondeau
COO: M.A. Douglas
SVP & CFO: W.K. Foster
Chief Acctg Officer & Cntlr: G.R. Wood

Treas: T.C. Deas, Jr.
Investor Contact: B. Arndt (215-299-6266)
Board Members: P. R. Brondeau, P. A. Buffler, G. P. D'Aloia, C. S. Greer, D. A. Kempthorne, E. J. Mooney, P. J. Norris, R. C. Pallash, E. Sosa, V. R. Volpe, Jr.

Founded: 1884
Domicile: Delaware
Employees: 4,800

The McGraw-Hill Companies

FMC Technologies Inc

STANDARD &POOR'S

S&P Recommendation BUY ★★★★☆	**Price** $72.30 (as of Oct 22, 2010)	**12-Mo. Target Price** $82.00	**Investment Style** Large-Cap Growth

GICS Sector Energy
Sub-Industry Oil & Gas Equipment & Services

Summary This company is a leading provider of oilfield services capital equipment, particularly for subsea equipment used in deepwater energy exploration and development.

Key Stock Statistics (Source S&P, Vickers, company reports)

52-Wk Range	$76.54–46.16	S&P Oper. EPS 2010**E**	**2.91**	Market Capitalization(B)	**$8.677**	Beta	1.30
Trailing 12-Month EPS	$3.06	S&P Oper. EPS 2011**E**	**3.10**	Yield (%)	**Nil**	S&P 3-Yr. Proj. EPS CAGR(%)	14
Trailing 12-Month P/E	23.6	P/E on S&P Oper. EPS 2010**E**	**24.8**	Dividend Rate/Share	**Nil**	S&P Credit Rating	NA
$10K Invested 5 Yrs Ago	NA	Common Shares Outstg. (M)	**120.0**	Institutional Ownership (%)	**91**		

Price Performance

30-Week Mov. Avg. · · · 10-Week Mov. Avg. – – GAAP Earnings vs. Previous Year Volume Above Avg. STARS
12-Mo. Target Price — Relative Strength ▲ Up ▼ Down ▶ No Change Below Avg.

Options: ASE, P, Ph

Analysis prepared by **Stewart Glickman, CFA** on September 13, 2010, when the stock traded at **$ 67.07**.

Highlights

➤ Energy Production Systems backlog at the end of June 2010 was $2.6 billion, up from $2.3 billion at the end of December, with subsea backlog comprising the vast majority ($2.3 billion). While new order flow into backlog may be choppy this year, we think the recent recovery in crude oil prices to above $70 per barrel raises the likelihood of improved order flow. The book-to-bill ratio at Energy Production Systems rose to 1.16 in the second quarter, after averaging 0.73 in 2009, but we forecast a pullback in the remainder of the year, yielding a value of 1.03 in 2010. The revised U.S. deepwater drilling moratorium (now due to expire on November 30) may delay U.S.-bound ordering activity, on fears that the moratorium will be extended further.

➤ FTI generated Energy Production Systems margins of 15.7% in the second quarter, which we do not view as sustainable given a tightening supply chain, but we still project operating margins of about 13.5% in the second half of 2010, and 14.0% in 2011.

➤ We project EPS of $2.91 in 2010 rising to $3.10 in 2011.

Investment Rationale/Risk

➤ Based on data from RigLogix, we see the arrival of 15 newbuild floaters in the remainder of 2010, and 28 more in 2011, which should buoy demand for related subsea equipment. The current U.S. deepwater drilling moratorium adds some near-term uncertainty to this schedule, to the extent that these rigs are slated for work in the U.S. Gulf of Mexico; we also see near-term risk to FTI from its North American surface control business, given chronically weak natural gas prices. Long term, however, we expect the moratorium to be lifted, and we view FTI as a prime beneficiary of a secular trend toward deepwater development.

➤ Risks to our recommendation and target price include reduced subsea activity, lower energy prices, unexpected contract cancellations, appreciation of the U.S. dollar; and an extended U.S. deepwater drilling moratorium.

➤ Our DCF model, assuming free cash flow growth of 12%, terminal growth of 3%, and a WACC of 11%, shows intrinsic value of $94. Applying premium multiples of 13X enterprise value to estimated 2010 EBITDA and 15X projected 2010 cash flow, and blending these values with our DCF model, our 12-month target price is $82.

Qualitative Risk Assessment

LOW	MEDIUM	HIGH

Our risk assessment reflects the company's exposure to crude oil and natural gas prices and capital spending decisions by oil and gas producers, and its commitment to technological innovation in oilfield services, offset in part by a longer-term trend towards deepwater development.

Quantitative Evaluations

S&P Quality Ranking   B+

D	C	B-	B	B+	A-	A	A+

Relative Strength Rank   STRONG

78

LOWEST = 1   HIGHEST = 99

Revenue/Earnings Data

Revenue (Million $)

	1Q	2Q	3Q	4Q	Year
2010	1,050	1,013	--	--	--
2009	1,053	1,104	1,088	1,160	4,405
2008	1,294	1,454	1,128	1,205	4,551
2007	979.9	1,153	1,136	1,364	4,615
2006	826.6	949.2	938.3	1,077	3,791
2005	681.6	812.5	776.1	956.5	3,227

Earnings Per Share ($)

2010	0.80	0.78	E0.64	E0.69	E2.91
2009	0.56	0.84	0.73	0.75	2.87
2008	0.62	0.81	0.72	0.74	2.72
2007	0.45	0.55	0.60	0.70	2.30
2006	0.34	0.45	0.44	0.47	1.51
2005	Nil	0.21	0.33	0.22	0.75

Fiscal year ended Dec. 31. Next earnings report expected: Late October. EPS Estimates based on S&P Operating Earnings; historical GAAP earnings are as reported.

Dividend Data

No cash dividends have been paid.

Please read the Required Disclosures and Analyst Certification on the last page of this report.

The **McGraw·Hill** Companies

FMC Technologies Inc

Business Summary September 13, 2010

CORPORATE OVERVIEW. FMC Technologies is a global provider of high technology solutions for the energy industry. The company designs, manufactures and services advanced systems and products such as subsea production and processing systems, surface wellhead production systems, high pressure fluid control equipment, measurement solutions, and marine loading systems for the oil & gas industry. Operations are separated into two reportable segments: Energy Production Systems, and Energy Processing Systems. Together, these two segments comprise Energy Systems. Approximately 23% of total 2009 revenues were derived in the United States, followed by Norway, with 21%. In July 2008, the company spun off its former FoodTech and Airport Systems segments to John Bean Technologies (JBT 18, Not Ranked), rendering the remainder of FTI as a pure-play energy services company that specializes in capital equipment. These former segments are now classified under discontinued operations.

The Energy Production Systems segment (84% of 2009 revenues, and 83% of 2009 segment operating profits) is a global leader in production systems that control the flow of oil and gas from producing wells. Approximately 70% of this segment's revenue base is derived from sales of subsea systems. Subsea systems are placed on the seafloor, and are used to control the flow of oil or gas from the reservoir to a host facility (such as floating production facility, a fixed platform, or an onshore facility). Many systems that the company provides are used in exploration, development and production of crude oil and

natural gas reserves located in deepwater environments, with water depths greater than 1,000 ft. The remaining 30% of this segment's revenue base is derived from surface production systems. The company is also involved in subsea separation systems, which helps to separate the flow of oil, gas and water more efficiently. Lastly, FTI is advancing the development of subsea processing, an emerging technology in the industry, which would enable separation at the seabed and thus be more cost-efficient for customers. This technology was introduced commercially in the North Sea in 2007.

The Energy Processing Systems segment (16%, 17%) designs, manufactures and supplies technologically advanced high pressure valves and fittings for oilfield services customers. FTI also builds and supplies liquid and gas measurement and transportation equipment and systems to customers involved in upstream, midstream and downstream operations. Products include the WECO/Chiksan line of flowline products, which pump fracturing fluids into a well during the well servicing process, or that pump cement during the completion of new wells. Other product lines include flow meters, fluid loading and transfer systems, material handling systems, and blending and transfer systems.

Company Financials Fiscal Year Ended Dec. 31

Per Share Data ($)	2009	2008	2007	2006	2005	2004	2003	2002	2001	2000
Tangible Book Value	5.31	3.78	5.79	5.18	3.82	3.45	1.81	1.40	0.55	0.14
Cash Flow	3.61	3.22	2.85	2.01	1.21	1.30	1.01	0.85	0.75	0.91
Earnings	2.87	2.72	2.30	1.51	0.75	0.84	0.57	0.48	0.30	0.46
S&P Core Earnings	2.91	2.52	2.20	1.49	0.56	0.58	0.51	0.27	0.17	NA
Dividends	Nil	Nil	Nil	Nil	Nil	Nil	Nil	Nil	Nil	NA
Payout Ratio	Nil	Nil	Nil	Nil	Nil	Nil	Nil	Nil	Nil	NA
Prices:High	59.56	83.18	67.78	35.95	22.11	17.25	12.30	11.92	11.24	NA
Prices:Low	23.35	20.27	27.57	21.69	14.31	10.99	8.97	7.15	5.50	NA
P/E Ratio:High	21	31	29	24	29	21	22	25	37	NA
P/E Ratio:Low	8	7	12	14	19	13	16	15	18	NA

Income Statement Analysis (Million $)										
Revenue	4,405	4,551	4,615	3,791	3,227	2,768	2,307	2,072	1,928	1,875
Operating Income	NA	596	524	375	198	174	174	154	149	165
Depreciation	93.0	64.9	73.4	70.8	65.9	63.5	57.7	48.6	57.8	59.1
Interest Expense	9.50	1.50	21.5	11.8	9.00	Nil	10.1	14.1	14.1	18.8
Pretax Income	518	506	465	299	165	160	108	92.5	63.5	78.4
Effective Tax Rate	30.0%	30.0%	33.7%	28.3%	34.1%	26.4%	28.8%	28.3%	38.0%	22.8%
Net Income	361	353	308	212	106	117	75.6	64.1	39.4	60.5
S&P Core Earnings	366	327	294	208	78.3	81.3	68.3	36.1	21.6	NA

Balance Sheet & Other Financial Data (Million $)										
Cash	461	340	130	79.5	153	124	29.0	32.4	28.0	12.0
Current Assets	2,226	2,444	2,104	1,690	1,428	1,217	949	813	755	740
Total Assets	3,510	3,586	3,211	2,488	2,096	1,894	1,591	1,363	1,438	1,408
Current Liabilities	1,679	1,963	1,785	1,208	1,058	995	845	728	681	613
Long Term Debt	392	472	122	213	253	160	201	175	194	250
Common Equity	1,103	696	1,022	886	706	669	442	322	418	379
Total Capital	1,504	1,181	1,151	1,107	965	835	650	502	616	629
Capital Expenditures	110	165	203	139	91.8	50.2	65.2	68.1	67.6	NA
Cash Flow	454	418	381	282	172	180	133	113	97.2	120
Current Ratio	1.3	1.3	1.2	1.4	1.3	1.2	1.1	1.1	1.1	1.2
% Long Term Debt of Capitalization	26.2	40.0	10.6	19.2	26.2	19.2	30.9	34.9	31.5	39.7
% Net Income of Revenue	8.2	7.8	6.7	5.6	3.3	4.2	3.3	3.1	2.0	3.2
% Return on Assets	10.2	10.4	10.8	9.2	5.3	6.7	5.1	4.6	2.8	NA
% Return on Equity	40.2	41.1	32.2	26.7	15.4	20.7	19.8	16.8	7.5	NA

Data as orig reptd.; bef. results of disc opers/spec. items. Per share data adj. for stk. divs.; EPS diluted. E-Estimated. NA-Not Available. NM-Not Meaningful. NR-Not Ranked. UR-Under Review.

Office: 1803 Gears Rd, Houston, TX 77067-4003.
Telephone: 281-591-4000.
Website: http://www.fmctechnologies.com
Chrmn & CEO: P.D. Kinnear

Pres & COO: J.T. Gremp
EVP & CFO: W.H. Schumann, III
Chief Admin Officer: M.J. Scott
CTO: B.D. Beitler

Investor Contact: R. Cherry (281-591-4560)
Board Members: M. R. Bowlin, P. Burguieres, C. M. Devine, T. Enger, C. S. Farley, T. Hamilton, P. D. Kinnear, E. J. Mooney, J. H. Netherland, Jr., R. A. Pattarozzi, J. M. Ringler, E. de Carvalho Filho

Founded: 2000
Domicile: Delaware
Employees: 10,400

Ford Motor Co

STANDARD &POOR'S

S&P Recommendation	BUY ★★★★☆	Price	12-Mo. Target Price	Investment Style
		$13.95 (as of Oct 22, 2010)	$16.00	Large-Cap Value

GICS Sector Consumer Discretionary
Sub-Industry Automobile Manufacturers

Summary As the world's third largest producer of cars and trucks, Ford also has automotive financing and insurance operations.

Key Stock Statistics (Source S&P, Vickers, company reports)

52-Wk Range	$14.57– 6.81	S&P Oper. EPS 2010E	1.68	Market Capitalization(B)	$46.990	Beta		2.54
Trailing 12-Month EPS	$1.68	S&P Oper. EPS 2011E	1.87	Yield (%)	Nil	S&P 3-Yr. Proj. EPS CAGR(%)		33
Trailing 12-Month P/E	8.3	P/E on S&P Oper. EPS 2010E	8.3	Dividend Rate/Share	Nil	S&P Credit Rating		B+
$10K Invested 5 Yrs Ago	$17,698	Common Shares Outstg. (M)	3,439.3	Institutional Ownership (%)	61			

Price Performance

30-Week Mov. Avg. ···   10-Week Mov. Avg. --   GAAP Earnings vs. Previous Year   Volume Above Avg. STARS

12-Mo. Target Price —   Relative Strength —   ▲ Up ▼ Down ▶ No Change   Below Avg.   ★

Options: ASE, CBOE, P, Ph

Analysis prepared by **Efraim Levy, CFA** on October 12, 2010, when the stock traded at **$ 13.66**.

Highlights

▶ We see Ford's total revenues rising 10% in 2010, due to gains in the U.S., China, and most non-European regions. European sales should be restrained in the aftermath of various governments' scrappage programs that stimulated demand in 2009. Automotive sales should increase 13%. The financial services segment has historically been an important contributor to sales and earnings, and we expect it to be more profitable in 2010 than in 2009.

▶ Margins should benefit from improved volume, more efficient capacity utilization, and cost-cutting efforts, partly offset by higher raw material costs. In our view, Ford's brand benefited because it did not tap government financial aid, and various new products. In addition, we believe Ford has taken advantage of Toyota's difficulties. However, we expect these benefits to diminish over time.

▶ The decision to terminate the Mercury brand should help Ford revive the Lincoln brand. We see Ford's revised contracts with the UAW enhancing profitability by about $2.5 billion a year starting in 2010. The agreements include unprecedented union givebacks in terms of benefits and work rules, customized to Ford's needs.

Investment Rationale/Risk

▶ We think Ford's president and CEO has made a noticeable positive difference in the company's improvement efforts. Also, we have become more confident in Ford's ability to bring successful vehicles to market -- one of the company's most important challenges, in our view -- and we also see progress in bolstering the company's image. However, we think competitive and economic challenges remain.

▶ Risks to our opinion and target price include increased competition, less-than-expected demand and production, weaker-than-projected financial services income, and an unfavorable shift in cash balances. As for corporate governance, we are concerned about Ford family members having greater voting rights than other shareholders.

▶ As of December 31, 2009, total stockholders' equity was negative. The stock recently traded at a price-to-sales (P/S) multiple below that of Ford's largest Japanese peers. In light of our view that the worst may be over for Ford, but some risk to demand remains, and based on historical and peer comparative P/E multiples, our 12-month target price is $13.

Qualitative Risk Assessment

LOW	MEDIUM	HIGH

Our risk assessment reflects the highly cyclical nature of Ford's markets and our view of the current and long-term challenges it faces, including weak industry demand, intensifying competition, high fixed and legacy costs, and a weak but improving balance sheet.

Quantitative Evaluations

S&P Quality Ranking   C

D	C	B-	B	B+	A-	A	A+

Relative Strength Rank   STRONG

83

LOWEST = 1   HIGHEST = 99

Revenue/Earnings Data

Revenue (Million $)

	1Q	2Q	3Q	4Q	Year
2010	31,566	31,300	--	--	--
2009	24,778	27,189	30,892	35,449	118,308
2008	43,513	38,600	32,100	29,200	139,300
2007	43,019	44,200	41,100	44,100	172,455
2006	41,055	41,965	37,110	40,318	160,123
2005	45,136	44,548	40,856	46,549	177,089

Earnings Per Share ($)

2010	0.50	0.61	E0.40	E0.26	E1.68
2009	-0.60	0.69	0.29	0.25	0.86
2008	0.05	-3.88	-0.06	-2.46	-6.41
2007	-0.15	0.30	-0.19	-1.33	-1.40
2006	-0.64	-0.14	-2.79	-2.98	-6.72
2005	0.58	0.47	-0.16	0.21	1.14

Fiscal year ended Dec. 31. Next earnings report expected: Early November. EPS Estimates based on S&P Operating Earnings; historical GAAP earnings are as reported.

Dividend Data

No cash dividends have been paid since 2006.

Please read the Required Disclosures and Analyst Certification on the last page of this report.

The McGraw-Hill Companies

Ford Motor Co

STANDARD &POOR'S

Business Summary October 12, 2010

CORPORATE OVERVIEW. Ford is the world's third largest motor vehicle manufacturer. It produces cars and trucks, and many of the vehicles' plastic, glass and electronic components, and replacement parts. It also owns a 11% stake in Mazda Motor Corp. Financial services include Ford Motor Credit (automotive financing and insurance) and American Road Insurance Co.

In recent years, Ford's margins have been pressured by an increase in competition -- primarily from Asian companies -- and a shift away from the more profitable large pickup truck and SUV segments to smaller, less profitable crossover utility vehicles (CUVs). However, in 2009, competitors' bankruptcy filings and its own new products helped it gain market share, in our view.

CORPORATE STRATEGY. Challenged by a shrinking U.S. market share and more recently by lower industry volume, the company has announced restructuring plans in recent years in an attempt to lower its costs. Also, even as global demand begins what we expect to be a multi-year uptrend, the company has worked to prune it product portfolio to focus on its Ford and Lincoln brands. Most recently, the company announced plans to discontinue production of Mercury brand vehicles.

The company sold its Volvo unit to China's Zhejiang Geely Holding Group Co. Ltd. for $1.8 billion in the third quarter of 2010.

The company's business and product portfolio has changed several times in recent years, as Ford sought to optimize its financial health and performance. In December 2005, Ford sold its Hertz Corp. unit for about $15 billion, including around $5.6 billion in cash proceeds. We believe the sale diluted EPS in 2006, as Hertz had contributed $0.16 per share to EPS in 2004 and $0.19 in the first nine months of 2005, according to company estimates. In 1999, the company acquired the car operations of AB Volvo for $6.45 billion. In 2000, Ford acquired Land Rover from BMW Group for $1.9 billion. In June 2008, the company sold Jaguar and Land Rover to Tata Motors for $2.3 billion, but used about $600 million of the proceeds to fund the Jaguar and Land Rover pension plans. In late 2008, the company reduced its stake in Mazda from 33% to 13.8% (now 11%).

Company Financials Fiscal Year Ended Dec. 31

Per Share Data ($)	2009	2008	2007	2006	2005	2004	2003	2002	2001	2000
Tangible Book Value	NM	NM	0.70	NM	3.68	4.60	2.30	NM	NM	6.10
Cash Flow	2.91	2.49	5.26	-6.71	7.62	9.12	8.31	8.45	5.78	13.46
Earnings	0.86	-6.41	-1.40	-6.72	1.14	1.80	0.50	0.15	-3.02	3.59
S&P Core Earnings	0.84	-7.69	-0.94	-5.58	0.64	1.80	1.03	-1.16	-4.56	NA
Dividends	Nil	Nil	Nil	0.35	0.40	0.40	0.40	0.40	1.05	2.30
Payout Ratio	Nil	Nil	Nil	NM	35%	22%	80%	NM	NM	64%
Prices:High	10.37	8.79	9.70	9.48	14.75	17.34	17.33	18.23	31.42	57.25
Prices:Low	1.50	1.01	6.65	1.06	7.57	12.61	6.58	6.90	14.70	21.69
P/E Ratio:High	12	NM	NM	NM	13	10	35	NM	NM	16
P/E Ratio:Low	2	NM	NM	NM	7	7	13	NM	NM	6

Income Statement Analysis (Million $)										
Revenue	118,300	139,300	172,455	160,123	177,089	171,652	164,196	163,420	162,412	170,064
Operating Income	10,935	16,199	21,189	8,286	21,052	24,945	24,770	25,034	22,941	34,530
Depreciation	6,931	20,329	13,158	16,453	14,042	13,052	14,297	15,177	15,922	14,849
Interest Expense	1,515	9,682	10,927	8,783	7,643	7,071	7,690	8,824	10,848	10,902
Pretax Income	3,008	-14,303	-3,746	-15,051	1,996	4,853	1,370	953	-7,584	8,234
Effective Tax Rate	2.29%	NM	NM	NM	NM	19.3%	9.85%	31.7%	NM	32.9%
Net Income	2,694	-14,580	-2,764	-12,615	2,228	3,634	921	284	-5,453	5,410
S&P Core Earnings	2,631	-17,458	-1,866	-10,472	1,146	3,637	1,905	-2,202	-8,266	NA

Balance Sheet & Other Financial Data (Million $)										
Cash	31,696	15,181	50,031	50,366	39,082	33,018	33,642	30,521	15,028	16,490
Total Assets	194,850	218,328	279,264	278,554	269,476	292,654	304,594	289,357	276,543	284,421
Long Term Debt	114,727	90,534	107,478	144,373	94,428	106,540	119,751	125,806	121,430	99,560
Total Debt	132,441	154,196	168,530	172,049	154,332	172,973	179,804	167,892	168,009	166,229
Common Equity	-7,820	-17,311	5,628	-3,465	12,957	16,045	11,651	5,590	7,786	18,610
Capital Expenditures	4,561	6,696	6,022	6,848	7,517	6,745	7,749	7,278	7,008	8,348
Cash Flow	9,625	5,648	10,394	-12,615	16,270	16,686	15,218	15,446	10,454	20,244
% Return on Assets	1.3	NM	NM	NM	0.8	1.2	0.3	0.1	NM	2.0
% Return on Equity	NM	NM	NM	NM	15.4	26.2	10.7	4.0	NM	23.3
% Long Term Debt of Capitalization	106.0	111.7	93.9	106.0	82.9	82.2	87.5	87.8	87.2	78.3

Data as orig reptd.; bef. results of disc opers/spec. items. Per share data adj. for stk. divs.; EPS diluted. E-Estimated. NA-Not Available. NM-Not Meaningful. NR-Not Ranked. UR-Under Review.

Office: 1 American Rd, Dearborn, MI 48126-2798.
Telephone: 313-322-3000.
Website: http://www.ford.com
Chrmn & COO: W.C. Ford, Jr.

Pres & CEO: A.R. Mulally
EVP & CFO: L.W. Booth
CTO: G. Schmidt
Chief Acctg Officer & Cntlr: R.L. Shanks

Investor Contact: L. Heck (313-594-0613)
Board Members: S. G. Butler, K. A. Casiano, A. F. Earley, Jr., E. B. Ford, II, W. C. Ford, Jr., R. A. Gephardt, J. H. Hance, Jr., I. O. Hockaday, Jr., R. A. Manoogian, E. R. Marram, A. R. Mulally, H. A. Neal, G. L. Shaheen, J. L. Thornton

Founded: 1903
Domicile: Delaware
Employees: 198,000

The McGraw-Hill Companies

Forest Laboratories Inc.

S&P Recommendation	BUY ★★★★☆	Price	12-Mo. Target Price	Investment Style
		$33.92 (as of Oct 22, 2010)	$38.00	Large-Cap Growth

GICS Sector Health Care
Sub-Industry Pharmaceuticals

Summary This company develops and makes branded and generic ethical drug products, sold primarily in the U.S., Puerto Rico, and Western and Eastern Europe.

Key Stock Statistics (Source S&P, Vickers, company reports)

52-Wk Range	$33.95– 24.17	S&P Oper. EPS 2011**E**	3.85	Market Capitalization(B)	$9.686	Beta	0.68
Trailing 12-Month EPS	$2.13	S&P Oper. EPS 2012**E**	4.10	Yield (%)	Nil	S&P 3-Yr. Proj. EPS CAGR(%)	6
Trailing 12-Month P/E	15.9	P/E on S&P Oper. EPS 2011**E**	8.8	Dividend Rate/Share	Nil	S&P Credit Rating	NA
$10K Invested 5 Yrs Ago	$9,331	Common Shares Outstg. (M)	285.5	Institutional Ownership (%)	98		

Price Performance

30-Week Mov. Avg. · · · 10-Week Mov. Avg. – – **GAAP Earnings vs. Previous Year** Volume Above Avg. STARS
12-Mo. Target Price — Relative Strength — ▲ Up ▼ Down ▶ No Change Below Avg. ★

Options: ASE, CBOE, P, Ph

Qualitative Risk Assessment

LOW	MEDIUM	HIGH

Our risk assessment reflects our view of the company's recent legal victory against generic challengers to its important Lexapro patent. We also think its R&D pipeline shows much promise. However, Forest's relatively small size among big pharma competitors and our view of its somewhat limited product line are significant risk factors.

Quantitative Evaluations

S&P Quality Ranking **B**

D	C	B-	B	B+	A-	A	A+

Relative Strength Rank **STRONG**

84

LOWEST = 1   HIGHEST = 99

Highlights

▶ The 12-month target price for FRX has recently been changed to $38.00 from $35.00. The Highlights section of this Stock Report will be updated accordingly.

Investment Rationale/Risk

▶ The Investment Rationale/Risk section of this Stock Report will be updated shortly. For the latest News story on FRX from MarketScope, see below.

▶ 10/19/10 12:02 pm ET ... S&P REITERATES BUY OPINION ON SHARES OF FOREST LABORATORIES (FRX 33.26****): Q2 operating EPS of $1.00, versus $0.85, was $0.07 ahead of our estimate, on better than expected sales growth of 7.7%, and tight control over operating costs. We continue to view FRX as an expanding R&D pipeline story, with about a dozen new projects under development. Key opportunities, in our opinion, include Daxas and aclidinium for COPD, ceftaroline novel antibiotic, and linaclotide for chronic constipation. We are raising our target price by $3 to $38, applying a discount-to-peers P/E of 9.9X to our $3.85 EPS estimate for FY '11 (Mar), raised from $3.73. /H. Saftlas

Revenue/Earnings Data

Revenue (Million $)

	1Q	2Q	3Q	4Q	Year
2011	1,060	1,080	--	--	--
2010	1,008	1,013	1,065	1,050	4,193
2009	947.9	972.8	972.4	951.9	3,845
2008	928.3	919.0	998.2	990.9	3,718
2007	816.3	847.0	893.0	885.4	3,442
2006	711.8	736.5	757.8	756.3	2,962

Earnings Per Share ($)

2011	0.39	1.00	E0.96	E0.94	E3.85
2010	0.87	0.61	0.69	0.07	2.25
2009	0.79	0.80	0.62	0.31	2.52
2008	0.83	0.71	0.96	0.55	3.06
2007	0.62	0.75	0.78	-0.75	1.41
2006	0.62	0.59	0.57	0.28	2.08

Fiscal year ended Mar. 31. Next earnings report expected: Late January. EPS Estimates based on S&P Operating Earnings; historical GAAP earnings are as reported.

Dividend Data

No cash dividends have been paid.

Forest Laboratories Inc.

Business Summary September 14, 2010

CORPORATE OVERVIEW. Forest Laboratories is a leading producer of niche-oriented branded and generic prescription pharmaceuticals. Most of Forest's products were developed in collaboration with licensing partners. Product sales accounted for 93% of total revenues in FY 10 (Mar.), contract revenues for 5%, and other income for 2%.

Lexapro antidepressant is FRX's single most important product. A single enanitomer version of Celexa (an older, off-patent FRX antidepressant), Lexapro is an advanced selective serotonin reuptake inhibitor (SSRI) indicated for both depression and generalized anxiety disorder. Lexapro had sales of $2.3 billion in FY 10, unchanged from FY 09. As of March 2010, Lexapro's share of the branded antidepressant market was estimated at about 11%. FRX in-licensed Lexapro from H. Lundbeck A/S, a Danish drug firm. FRX's Lexapro's patent expires in March 2012.

FRX's second most important product is Namenda (licensed from Merz Pharmaceuticals of Germany), a treatment for moderate to severe Alzheimer's disease. Sales of Namenda were $1.1 billion in FY 10, up from $949 million in FY 09. As of March 2010, Namenda was estimated to account for about 34% of the Alzheimer's prescription drug market.

The company's third largest drug is Benicar, an antihypertensive co-promoted with Sankyo. FRX booked income of about $192 million from Benicar in FY 10, down from $196 million in FY 09. In January 2008, FRX launched Bystolic, a novel beta blocker antihypertensive that was in-licensed from Mylan Laboratories. Bystolic had sales of $179 million in FY 10, up from $69 million in FY 09. Other products include Tiazac antihypertensive, Aerobid asthma drug, Campral for alcohol addiction, Combunox for severe pain, and other drugs.

COMPETITIVE LANDSCAPE. The U.S. antidepressant drug market totaled about $11 billion in 2009, based on estimates by Standard & Poor's. We expect this market to shrink in terms of dollar sales over the coming years, reflecting the impact of inexpensive generic versions of many patent-expired branded antidepressants. Pfizer's Zoloft antidepressant lost patent protection in 2006, and Wyeth's patent on Effexor antidepressant expired in 2008. Generics now largely comprise previously branded Prozac and Paxil antidepressant markets.

Company Financials Fiscal Year Ended Mar. 31

Per Share Data ($)	2010	2009	2008	2007	2006	2005	2004	2003	2002	2001
Tangible Book Value	14.58	11.94	10.19	8.93	7.69	8.21	8.03	5.66	3.75	2.60
Cash Flow	2.50	2.84	3.34	1.55	2.20	2.32	2.01	1.80	1.06	0.71
Earnings	2.25	2.52	3.06	1.41	2.08	2.25	1.95	1.66	0.91	0.59
S&P Core Earnings	2.26	2.53	3.01	1.41	1.97	2.15	1.85	1.58	0.74	0.47
Dividends	Nil	Nil	Nil	Nil	Nil	Nil	Nil	Nil	Nil	Nil
Payout Ratio	Nil	Nil	Nil	Nil	Nil	Nil	Nil	Nil	Nil	Nil
Calendar Year	2009	2008	2007	2006	2005	2004	2003	2002	2001	2000
Prices:High	32.76	42.76	57.97	54.70	45.21	78.81	63.23	54.99	41.60	35.33
Prices:Low	18.37	19.23	34.89	36.18	32.46	36.10	41.85	32.12	23.25	14.34
P/E Ratio:High	15	17	19	39	22	35	32	33	46	60
P/E Ratio:Low	8	8	11	26	16	16	21	19	26	24

Income Statement Analysis (Million $)	2010	2009	2008	2007	2006	2005	2004	2003	2002	2001
Revenue	4,112	3,845	3,718	3,442	2,962	3,114	2,650	2,207	1,567	1,181
Operating Income	1,027	989	1,179	754	701	1,164	929	833	490	318
Depreciation	76.5	96.5	86.7	45.4	40.7	25.4	22.2	51.6	54.6	43.3
Interest Expense	NA	Nil	Nil	Nil	Nil	Nil	Nil	Nil	Nil	Nil
Pretax Income	951	971	1,210	709	870	1,185	937	821	470	299
Effective Tax Rate	28.2%	20.9%	20.0%	35.9%	18.5%	29.2%	21.5%	24.2%	28.1%	28.0%
Net Income	682	768	968	454	709	839	736	622	338	215
S&P Core Earnings	686	771	953	454	673	800	697	589	272	170

Balance Sheet & Other Financial Data (Million $)	2010	2009	2008	2007	2006	2005	2004	2003	2002	2001
Cash	3,322	2,581	1,777	1,353	1,323	1,619	2,131	1,556	893	506
Current Assets	4,579	3,786	2,908	2,423	2,207	2,708	2,916	2,255	1,195	884
Total Assets	6,224	5,197	4,525	3,653	3,120	3,705	3,863	2,918	1,952	1,447
Current Liabilities	980	818	611	628	421	564	605	564	325	224
Long Term Debt	NA	Nil	Nil	Nil	Nil	Nil	Nil	Nil	Nil	Nil
Common Equity	4,890	4,115	3,715	3,025	2,698	3,132	3,256	2,352	1,625	1,222
Total Capital	4,890	4,115	3,716	3,026	2,699	3,141	3,258	2,354	1,627	1,223
Capital Expenditures	32.3	40.6	34.9	30.0	55.0	89.0	102	79.6	36.4	30.9
Cash Flow	759	864	1,055	500	749	864	758	674	393	258
Current Ratio	4.7	4.6	4.8	3.9	5.2	4.8	4.8	4.0	3.7	4.0
% Long Term Debt of Capitalization	Nil	Nil	Nil	Nil	Nil	Nil	Nil	Nil	Nil	Nil
% Net Income of Revenue	16.6	20.0	26.0	13.5	24.3	26.9	27.8	28.2	21.6	18.2
% Return on Assets	NA	15.8	23.7	13.4	20.8	22.2	21.7	25.5	19.9	16.7
% Return on Equity	NA	19.6	28.7	15.9	24.3	26.3	26.2	31.3	23.7	20.4

Data as orig reptd.; bef. results of disc opers/spec. items. Per share data adj. for stk. divs.; EPS diluted. E-Estimated. NA-Not Available. NM-Not Meaningful. NR-Not Ranked. UR-Under Review.

Office: 909 3rd Ave, New York, NY 10022-4748.
Telephone: 212-421-7850.
Email: investor.relations@frx.com
Website: http://www.frx.com

Chrmn & CEO: H. Solomon
Pres & COO: L.S. Olanoff
SVP, CFO & Chief Acctg Officer: F.I. Perier, Jr.
Secy: H.S. Weinstein

Investor Contact: F.J. Murdolo (212-224-6714)
Board Members: N. Basgoz, W. J. Candee, III, G. S. Cohan, D. L. Goldwasser, K. E. Goodman, L. S. Olanoff, L. Salans, H. Solomon, P. J. Zimetbaum

Founded: 1956
Domicile: Delaware
Employees: 5,200

Fortune Brands Inc.

STANDARD &POOR'S

S&P Recommendation HOLD ★★★☆☆

Price	**12-Mo. Target Price**	**Investment Style**
$56.05 (as of Oct 22, 2010)	$48.00	Large-Cap Blend

GICS Sector Consumer Discretionary
Sub-Industry Housewares & Specialties

Summary This diversified holding company has interests in consumer businesses that include home improvement, spirits, and golf-related products.

Key Stock Statistics (Source S&P, Vickers, company reports)

52-Wk Range	$59.40– 37.05	S&P Oper. EPS 2010E	2.94	Market Capitalization(B)	$8.540	Beta	1.64
Trailing 12-Month EPS	$2.85	S&P Oper. EPS 2011E	3.39	Yield (%)	1.36	S&P 3-Yr. Proj. EPS CAGR(%)	12
Trailing 12-Month P/E	19.7	P/E on S&P Oper. EPS 2010E	19.1	Dividend Rate/Share	$0.76	S&P Credit Rating	BBB-
$10K Invested 5 Yrs Ago	$8,315	Common Shares Outstg. (M)	152.4	Institutional Ownership (%)	77		

Price Performance

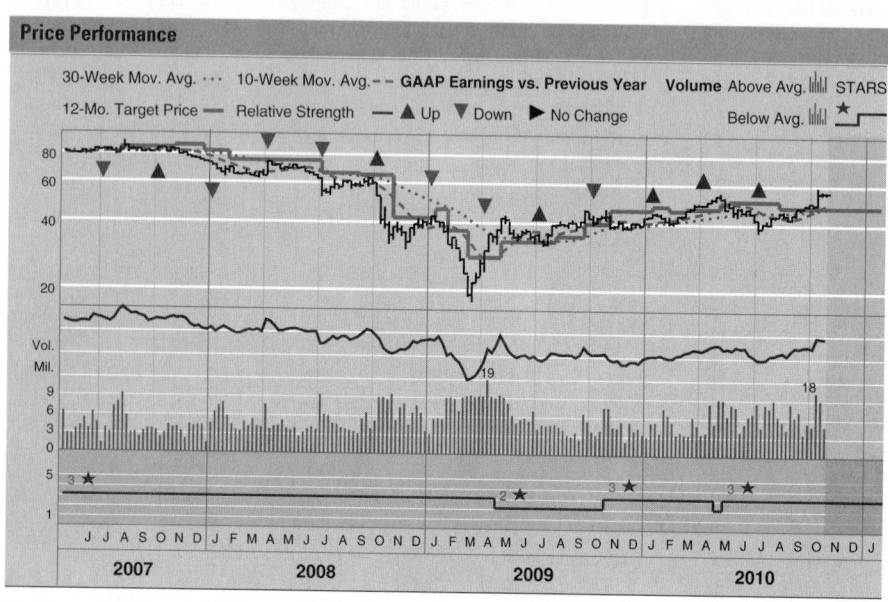

30-Week Mov. Avg. · · · · 10-Week Mov. Avg. – – **GAAP Earnings vs. Previous Year** Volume Above Avg. STARS
12-Mo. Target Price — Relative Strength — ▲ Up ▼ Down ▶ No Change Below Avg. ★

Options: ASE, CBOE, P, Ph

Analysis prepared by **Esther Y. Kwon, CFA** on August 03, 2010, when the stock traded at **$ 44.49.**

Highlights

► For 2010, our sales growth forecast of 5% assumes that the home remodeling and golf markets in the U.S. bottomed in 2009 after two to three years of revenue declines. Even the Spirits business has not been immune to weakness in consumer discretionary spending in the U.S. and other major markets. In 2009, total company sales declined 12%, including a negative foreign currency impact, with all segments down: Spirits -1%; Home & Security -20%; and Golf -11%. We think that, for the most part, FO appears to be holding its market shares overall.

► We look for a partial recovery in the operating margin in 2010 on better sales leverage and continued strong cost control. We are concerned about possible renewed commodity cost pressures later in 2010. In 2009, the operating margin, before restructuring charges, narrowed 310 basis points (which followed 2008's almost 300 bps decline), as worsening operating leverage offset benefits from restructuring programs and moderating commodity costs.

► Our 2010 EPS estimate is $2.94, up from operating EPS of $2.43 in 2009 and operating EPS of $3.79 in 2008. For 2011, we forecast EPS of $3.39.

Investment Rationale/Risk

► Our Hold opinion reflects our view that the stock price adequately reflects FO's near-term outlook. We remain concerned about the magnitude and sustainability of a recovery in consumer spending and the continuing low level of recovery in the home repair and remodeling business in the U.S. Due to the early termination in August 2008 of FO's Absolut Vodka distribution agreement, FO no longer reports non-cash recognition of about $27 million in annual deferred gains. In April 2009, FO announced a reduction in its quarterly dividend to $0.19 a share, from $0.44.

► Risks to our recommendation and target price include a delayed recovery in consumer spending in the U.S. and other major markets and weak consumer acceptance of new products.

► Our 12-month target price of $48 is based on our historical P/E analysis. We apply a forward P/E of approximately 14X, which is the average over the last four years, to our 2011 EPS estimate of $3.39.

Qualitative Risk Assessment

LOW	**MEDIUM**	HIGH

FO's businesses -- spirits, golf and home & security (primarily for the remodeling market) -- are usually less cyclical than many other consumer-related businesses. However, the depth of the economic downturn in the U.S. and in many major international markets has significantly affected FO's results.

Quantitative Evaluations

S&P Quality Ranking B+

D	C	B-	B	**B+**	A-	A	A+

Relative Strength Rank **STRONG**

87

LOWEST = 1 HIGHEST = 99

Revenue/Earnings Data

Revenue (Million $)

	1Q	2Q	3Q	4Q	Year
2010	1,499	1,771	--	--	--
2009	1,338	1,617	1,593	1,658	6,205
2008	1,711	1,967	1,922	1,628	7,105
2007	1,909	2,293	2,145	2,215	8,563
2006	2,017	2,257	2,219	2,277	8,769
2005	1,518	1,783	1,802	1,959	7,061

Earnings Per Share ($)

2010	0.47	1.48	E0.83	E0.65	E2.94
2009	0.05	0.66	0.82	0.08	1.60
2008	0.69	0.17	2.01	-1.83	1.07
2007	0.78	1.47	1.33	1.22	4.79
2006	1.15	1.63	0.98	1.65	5.42
2005	0.95	1.22	0.52	1.17	3.87

Fiscal year ended Dec. 31. Next earnings report expected: Late October. EPS Estimates based on S&P Operating Earnings; historical GAAP earnings are as reported.

Dividend Data (Dates: mm/dd Payment Date: mm/dd/yy)

Amount ($)	Date Decl.	Ex-Div. Date	Stk. of Record	Payment Date
0.190	01/26	02/08	02/10	03/01/10
0.190	04/27	05/10	05/12	06/01/10
0.190	07/26	08/09	08/11	09/01/10
0.190	09/28	11/08	11/10	12/01/10

Dividends have been paid since 1905. Source: Company reports.

Please read the Required Disclosures and Analyst Certification on the last page of this report.

The **McGraw-Hill** Companies

Fortune Brands Inc.

Business Summary August 03, 2010

CORPORATE OVERVIEW. Fortune Brands is a holding company with subsidiaries that produce spirits, home and security products, and golf products.

Spirits (formerly Spirits & Wine) (37% of total sales and 81% of operating company contributions before corporate expenses and asset impairment and restructuring charges in 2009) are sold through the Beam Global Spirits & Wine subsidiary. Leading brands include Jim Beam bourbon whiskey, DeKuyper cordials, Gilbey's gin, Kamchatka vodka, and Maker's Mark bourbon. Principal markets are the U.S., the U.K., Spain, Germany, and Australia, with markets outside the U.S. accounting for about 45% of the segment's sales.

In July 2005, the company acquired various spirits and wine brands from Pernod Ricard, which in turn were acquired by Pernod from Allied Domecq PLC. This transaction more than doubled the sales of FO's Spirits & Wine segment. In 2007, the U.S. wine businesses were sold; we believe they had annualized sales of about $225 million. In August 2008, Pernod Ricard, which purchased the Absolut Vodka brand earlier in 2008, agreed to pay FO $230 million for an early termination of FO's distribution agreement for Absolut and other brands. Also, Pernod Ricard agreed to sell the Cruzan Rum brand, already distributed by FO, to FO for $103 million.

Major units of FO's Home & Security products segment (45%, 15%) include MasterBrand Cabinets, Moen, Master Lock, Waterloo and Therma-Tru. While we believe that more of the segment's sales go into the remodeling market than the new housing market, the segment has been affected by the recent, deeply depressed housing market.

Golf products (18%, 4%) operations are conducted through Acushnet, a leading producer of golf balls (Titleist, Pinnacle), golf shoes (FootJoy), golf clubs (Cobra, Titleist), and golf gloves. Other products include bags, carts, dress and athletic shoes, socks and accessories.

In 2009, net sales by geographic region for FO, based on country of destination, were the United States, with 69% of net sales, Canada 7%, the United Kingdom 3%, Australia 4%, Spain 3% and all other 14%.

Company Financials Fiscal Year Ended Dec. 31

Per Share Data ($)	2009	2008	2007	2006	2005	2004	2003	2002	2001	2000
Tangible Book Value	NM	NM	NM	NM	NM	NM	NM	NM	2.06	0.89
Cash Flow	3.27	2.74	6.58	7.37	5.35	6.70	5.14	4.57	3.89	0.63
Earnings	1.60	1.07	4.79	5.42	3.87	5.23	3.86	3.41	2.49	-0.88
S&P Core Earnings	1.68	1.66	4.62	5.47	3.73	4.58	3.79	3.14	2.38	NA
Dividends	1.01	1.72	1.62	1.50	1.38	1.26	1.14	1.02	0.97	0.93
Payout Ratio	63%	161%	34%	28%	36%	24%	30%	30%	39%	NM
Prices:High	46.77	74.44	90.80	85.96	96.18	80.50	71.80	57.86	40.54	33.25
Prices:Low	17.67	30.24	72.13	68.45	73.50	66.10	40.60	36.85	28.38	19.19
P/E Ratio:High	29	70	19	16	25	15	19	17	16	NM
P/E Ratio:Low	11	28	15	13	19	13	11	11	11	NM

Income Statement Analysis (Million $)	2009	2008	2007	2006	2005	2004	2003	2002	2001	2000
Revenue	6,205	7,105	8,563	8,769	7,061	7,321	6,215	5,678	5,679	5,845
Operating Income	974	1,313	1,712	1,777	1,715	1,374	1,142	1,011	870	938
Depreciation	255	263	280	298	224	221	193	179	219	237
Interest Expense	216	237	294	332	159	87.9	73.8	74.1	96.8	134
Pretax Income	283	188	1,120	1,209	926	1,086	884	756	492	38.9
Effective Tax Rate	12.8%	47.6%	30.9%	25.7%	35.0%	26.1%	32.7%	28.3%	19.2%	NM
Net Income	243	165	750	830	582	784	579	526	386	-138
S&P Core Earnings	255	255	722	837	559	684	567	484	367	NA

Balance Sheet & Other Financial Data (Million $)	2009	2008	2007	2006	2005	2004	2003	2002	2001	2000
Cash	417	163	204	183	93.6	165	105	15.4	48.7	20.9
Current Assets	3,872	3,468	3,781	3,930	3,193	2,642	2,282	1,903	1,970	2,265
Total Assets	12,371	12,092	13,957	14,668	13,202	7,884	7,445	5,822	5,301	5,764
Current Liabilities	1,464	1,190	2,094	2,515	2,818	2,036	2,134	1,515	1,258	2,040
Long Term Debt	4,413	4,689	4,374	5,035	4,890	1,240	1,243	200	950	1,152
Common Equity	5,092	4,692	5,680	4,722	3,639	3,203	2,712	2,305	2,094	2,127
Total Capital	9,519	9,393	11,138	11,458	9,788	5,207	4,664	2,983	3,444	3,343
Capital Expenditures	158	176	267	266	222	242	194	194	207	227
Cash Flow	497	421	1,029	1,128	805	1,005	772	704	605	99.0
Current Ratio	2.7	2.9	1.8	1.6	1.1	1.3	1.1	1.3	1.6	1.1
% Long Term Debt of Capitalization	46.4	49.9	38.7	43.9	50.0	23.8	26.6	6.7	27.6	34.5
% Net Income of Revenue	3.9	2.3	8.7	9.5	8.2	10.7	9.3	9.3	6.8	NM
% Return on Assets	2.0	1.3	5.2	6.0	5.5	10.2	8.7	9.5	7.0	NM
% Return on Equity	5.0	3.2	14.4	19.9	17.2	26.5	23.1	23.9	18.3	NM

Data as orig reptd.; bef. results of disc opers/spec. items. Per share data adj. for stk. divs.; EPS diluted. E-Estimated. NA-Not Available. NM-Not Meaningful. NR-Not Ranked. UR-Under Review.

Office: 520 Lake Cook Rd, Deerfield, IL 60015-5611.
Telephone: 847-484-4400.
Email: investorrelations@fortunebrands.com
Website: http://www.fortunebrands.com

Chrmn & CEO: B.A. Carbonari
SVP & CFO: C.P. Omtvedt
SVP & Treas: M. Hausberg
SVP, Secy & General Counsel: M.A. Roche

Cntlr: E.A. Wiertel
Board Members: B. A. Carbonari, R. A. Goldstein, A. F. Hackett, P. Leroy, A. D. MacKay, A. M. Tatlock, D. M. Thomas, R. V. Waters, III, N. H. Wesley, P. M. Wilson

Founded: 1904
Domicile: Delaware
Employees: 24,248

Franklin Resources Inc

STANDARD & POOR'S

| S&P Recommendation HOLD ★★★☆☆ | Price $115.87 (as of Oct 22, 2010) | 12-Mo. Target Price $109.00 | Investment Style Large-Cap Growth |

GICS Sector Financials
Sub-Industry Asset Management & Custody Banks

Summary This company is one of the world's largest asset managers, serving retail, institutional and high-net-worth clients.

Key Stock Statistics (Source S&P, Vickers, company reports)

52-Wk Range	$121.90–84.00	S&P Oper. EPS 2010E	6.26	Market Capitalization(B)	$26.081	Beta	1.49
Trailing 12-Month EPS	$6.29	S&P Oper. EPS 2011E	7.06	Yield (%)	0.76	S&P 3-Yr. Proj. EPS CAGR(%)	28
Trailing 12-Month P/E	18.4	P/E on S&P Oper. EPS 2010E	18.5	Dividend Rate/Share	$0.88	S&P Credit Rating	AA-
$10K Invested 5 Yrs Ago	$14,834	Common Shares Outstg. (M)	225.1	Institutional Ownership (%)	51		

Price Performance

30-Week Mov. Avg. · · · 10-Week Mov. Avg. – – GAAP Earnings vs. Previous Year   Volume Above Avg. ▮▮▮ STARS
12-Mo. Target Price — Relative Strength — ▲ Up ▼ Down ▶ No Change   Below Avg. ▮▮▮ ★

Options: ASE, CBOE, P, Ph

Analysis prepared by **Matthew Albrecht** on August 02, 2010, when the stock traded at **$ 104.40**.

Highlights

➤ Assets under management have rebounded from their March 2009 lows, boosted by net asset inflows and equity market gains. A general improvement in the mix of assets should allow the management fee rate to recover over time. Net flows remain strongest into fixed income funds, but recent trends suggest the worst of the equity outflows have subsided. We note, however, that BEN's strong international presence likely exposes it to more risk than peers due to currency fluctuations. A return to investment gains, compared to losses, in the past few quarters, has helped results, but performance fee income will likely remain weak. Considering easier comparisons, we think higher average asset balances will help revenues advance nearly 40% in FY 10 (Sep.) before 10% growth in FY 11.

➤ Top-line growth should allow for margin improvement in FY 10 and FY 11. Reduced headcount versus prior-year levels should help lower compensation accruals, but improving asset flows will likely keep underwriting and distribution costs elevated in the near term.

➤ We see EPS of $6.26 in FY 10 and $7.06 in FY 11, aided by share repurchases.

Investment Rationale/Risk

➤ We think BEN is one of the best-managed asset gatherers, and we think its balance sheet is characterized by limited debt and ample cash on hand. We have a favorable view of its strong operating free cash flow and diversification. We think the earnings power of the firm has rebounded, taking into account strong relative fund performance, a return to positive net flows from clients, and severe cost cutting.

➤ Risks to our recommendation and target price include potential depreciation in global equity, bond and currency markets that would materially hinder growth in assets under management and inflows.

➤ The shares recently traded at 15.8X our FY 10 EPS estimate, in line with the multiples of comparable peers, but a discount to the stock's historical multiple. Our 12-month target price of $109 is equal to about 16X our forward 12-month earnings estimate of $6.81, a discount to its historical multiple to reflect its international exposure at a time when the U.S. dollar is strengthening and European markets face headwinds.

Qualitative Risk Assessment

| LOW | MEDIUM | HIGH |

Our risk assessment reflects our view of the company's strong operating margins, well-capitalized balance sheet and international exposure, offset by concerns about uneven client flow trends and recent declines in relative investment performance.

Quantitative Evaluations

S&P Quality Ranking B+

| D | C | B- | B | B+ | A- | A | A+ |

Relative Strength Rank STRONG

78

LOWEST = 1   HIGHEST = 99

Revenue/Earnings Data

Revenue (Million $)

	1Q	2Q	3Q	4Q	Year
2010	1,377	1,413	1,534	--	--
2009	969.3	912.3	1,074	1,239	4,194
2008	1,686	1,504	1,522	1,321	6,032
2007	1,428	1,509	1,640	1,629	6,206
2006	1,181	1,255	1,317	1,297	5,051
2005	986.0	1,051	1,110	1,163	4,310

Earnings Per Share ($)

2010	1.54	1.56	1.58	E1.59	E6.26
2009	0.52	0.48	1.29	1.60	3.87
2008	2.12	1.54	1.71	1.28	6.67
2007	1.67	1.73	1.86	1.76	7.03
2006	1.21	0.74	1.41	1.49	4.86
2005	0.92	0.85	1.00	1.28	4.06

Fiscal year ended Sep. 30. Next earnings report expected: Late October. EPS Estimates based on S&P Operating Earnings; historical GAAP earnings are as reported.

Dividend Data (Dates: mm/dd Payment Date: mm/dd/yy)

Amount ($)	Date Decl.	Ex-Div. Date	Stk. of Record	Payment Date
0.220	12/18	12/29	12/31	01/08/10
0.220	03/16	03/29	03/31	04/09/10
0.220	06/15	06/28	06/30	07/09/10
0.220	09/16	09/28	09/30	10/08/10

Dividends have been paid since 1981. Source: Company reports.

Please read the Required Disclosures and Analyst Certification on the last page of this report.

The McGraw·Hill Companies

Franklin Resources Inc

Business Summary August 02, 2010

CORPORATE OVERVIEW. Franklin Resources is one of the largest U.S. money managers, with $523.4 billion in assets under management at the end of FY 09 (Sep.), up from $507.3 billion at the end of FY 08. At the end of FY 09, equity-based investments accounted for 47% of assets under management, fixed income investments 33%, hybrid funds 19%, and money funds 1%. We think that a decline in the dollar relative to other major currencies would aid BEN, due to the high percentage of assets invested globally. Conversely, the company's results may be challenged by a rising U.S. dollar relative to major currencies. At the end of FY 09, about 26% of assets under management were held by investors domiciled outside the U.S.

The company's sponsored investment products are distributed under five distinct names: Franklin, Templeton, Mutual Series, Bissett and Fiduciary. The Franklin family of funds is best known for its bond funds, although it includes a range of equity and balanced products. The Templeton family of funds is known for its global investment strategies and value style. Mutual Series funds are primarily known for their value-oriented equity focus. The Bissett family of mutual funds operates in Canada, and serves a broad range of clients, primarily institutions. We are impressed with BEN's broad range of investment products, but we think the company lacks a compelling roster of growth equity products.

The company generates the majority of its revenue from investment management and related services provided to its retail and institutional mutual funds, and to its institutional, high net-worth and separately managed accounts. Investment management and related services include fund administration, shareholder services, transfer agency, underwriting, distribution, custodial, trustee, and other fiduciary services. Investment management fees depend on the level of client assets under management, and it earns higher revenues and income from equity assets, generally, and a shift in assets from equity to fixed income or balanced funds reduces revenue. Underwriting and distribution fees consist of sales charges and commissions derived from sales of sponsored investment products and distribution fees. It also generates fees from investment management services for high net worth individuals and families through Fiduciary Trust.

Company Financials Fiscal Year Ended Sep. 30

Per Share Data ($)	2009	2008	2007	2006	2005	2004	2003	2002	2001	2000
Tangible Book Value	24.54	21.72	21.49	18.57	14.39	12.23	9.31	8.69	7.23	7.37
Cash Flow	4.66	7.57	7.82	5.86	5.02	3.51	2.67	2.35	2.79	3.13
Earnings	3.87	6.67	7.03	4.86	4.06	2.78	1.97	1.65	1.91	2.28
S&P Core Earnings	3.96	6.77	6.64	4.72	3.97	2.47	1.70	1.56	1.61	NA
Dividends	0.83	0.75	0.57	0.36	0.40	0.33	0.29	0.28	0.26	0.24
Payout Ratio	21%	11%	8%	7%	10%	12%	15%	17%	14%	11%
Prices:High	116.39	129.08	145.59	114.98	98.86	71.45	52.25	44.48	48.30	45.63
Prices:Low	37.11	45.52	108.46	80.16	63.56	46.85	29.99	27.90	30.85	24.63
P/E Ratio:High	30	19	21	24	24	26	27	27	25	20
P/E Ratio:Low	10	7	15	16	16	17	15	17	16	11

Income Statement Analysis (Million $)	2009	2008	2007	2006	2005	2004	2003	2002	2001	2000
Income Interest	Nil	Nil	Nil	NA	NA	NA	NA	NA	NA	NA
Income Other	Nil	Nil	Nil	NA	NA	NA	NA	NA	NA	NA
Total Income	4,194	6,032	6,206	5,051	4,310	3,438	2,624	2,519	2,355	2,340
General Expenses	2,991	3,933	4,138	3,417	3,004	NA	NA	NA	NA	NA
Interest Expense	3.77	15.8	23.2	29.2	34.0	30.7	19.9	12.3	10.6	14.0
Depreciation	181	215	199	215	17.5	NA	NA	NA	NA	200
Net Income	897	1,588	1,773	1,268	1,058	702	503	433	485	562
S&P Core Earnings	917	1,612	1,674	1,229	1,033	622	432	410	407	NA

Balance Sheet & Other Financial Data (Million $)	2009	2008	2007	2006	2005	2004	2003	2002	2001	2000
Cash	5,269	2,528	3,584	3,613	3,152	2,917	1,054	981	569	746
Receivables	NA	1,062	1,106	711	549	444	441	393	603	693
Cost of Investments	NA	916	1,065	NA	1,566	NA	NA	NA	NA	NA
Total Assets	9,468	9,177	9,943	9,500	8,894	8,228	6,971	6,423	6,266	4,042
Loss Reserve	Nil	Nil	Nil	NA	Nil	NA	NA	NA	NA	NA
Short Term Debt	NA	13.3	420	168	169	NA	0.29	7.80	NA	NA
Capitalization:Debt	NA	118	162	628	1,208	1,196	1,109	595	566	294
Capitalization:Equity	7,632	7,074	7,332	6,685	5,684	5,107	4,310	4,267	3,978	2,965
Capitalization:Total	NA	7,416	7,750	7,620	7,204	6,615	5,622	5,037	4,544	3,260
Price Times Book Value:High	4.7	5.9	6.8	6.2	6.9	NA	5.5	5.1	NA	NA
Price Times Book Value:Low	1.5	2.1	5.2	4.3	4.4	NA	3.2	3.2	NA	NA
Cash Flow	1,078	1,803	1,972	1,483	1,075	885	680	616	709	762
% Expense/Operating Revenue	71.3	65.2	66.7	67.7	70.1	NA	NA	NA	NA	NA
% Earnings & Depreciation/Assets	11.6	18.9	20.3	16.1	12.6	NA	NA	NA	NA	NA

Data as orig reptd.; bef. results of disc opers/spec. items. Per share data adj. for stk. divs.; EPS diluted. E-Estimated. NA-Not Available. NM-Not Meaningful. NR-Not Ranked. UR-Under Review.

Office: One Franklin Parkway, Building 970 1st Floor, San Mateo, CA 94403.
Telephone: 650-312-2000.
Website: http://www.franklintempleton.com
Chrmn: C.B. Johnson

Pres & CEO: G.E. Johnson
Vice Chrmn: R.H. Johnson, Jr.
COO & EVP: J.J. Bolt
EVP, CFO, Chief Acctg Officer & Treas: K.A. Lewis

Board Members: S. H. Armacost, C. Crocker, J. R. Hardiman, F. W. Hellman, C. B. Johnson, G. E. Johnson, R. H. Johnson, Jr., T. H. Kean, C. Ratnathicam, P. M. Sacerdote, L. Stein, A. M. Tatlock

Founded: 1947
Domicile: Delaware
Employees: 7,745

Freeport-McMoran Copper & Gold Inc.

STANDARD &POOR'S

S&P Recommendation HOLD ★★★☆☆

Price	12-Mo. Target Price
$96.07 (as of Oct 25, 2010)	$95.00

GICS Sector Materials
Sub-Industry Diversified Metals & Mining

Summary FCX is the world's second largest copper producer and a major producer of gold and molybdenum.

Key Stock Statistics (Source S&P, Vickers, company reports)

52-Wk Range	$100.34– 56.71	S&P Oper. EPS 2010E	8.38	Market Capitalization(B)	$45.195
Trailing 12-Month EPS	$7.85	S&P Oper. EPS 2011E	9.24	Yield (%)	2.08
Trailing 12-Month P/E	12.2	P/E on S&P Oper. EPS 2010E	11.5	Dividend Rate/Share	$2.00
$10K Invested 5 Yrs Ago	$23,667	Common Shares Outstg. (M)	470.4	Institutional Ownership (%)	76

Beta	1.85
S&P 3-Yr. Proj. EPS CAGR(%)	16
S&P Credit Rating	BBB-

Price Performance

30-Week Mov. Avg. ··· 10-Week Mov. Avg. ‑‑ **GAAP Earnings vs. Previous Year** Volume Above Avg. STARS
12-Mo. Target Price — Relative Strength — ▲ Up ▼ Down ► No Change Below Avg.

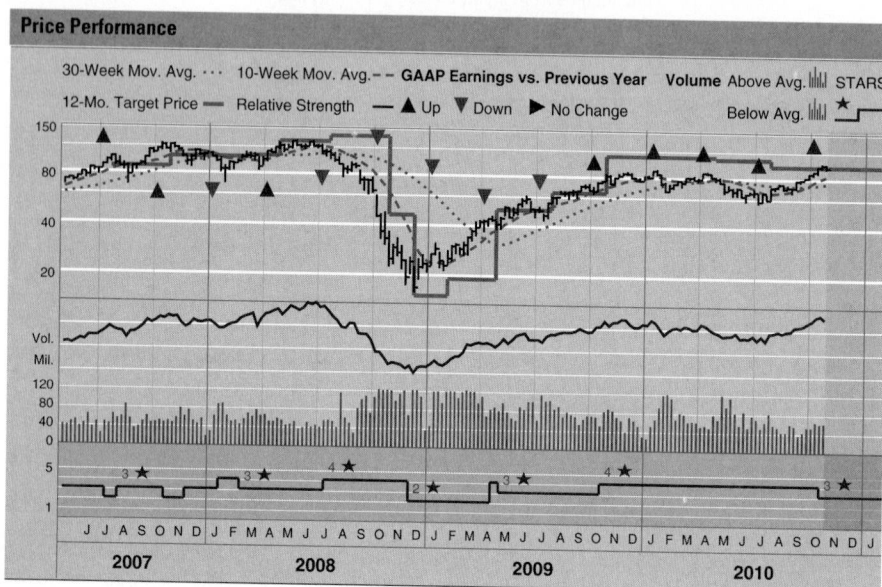

Options: ASE, CBOE, P, Ph

Analysis prepared by **Leo J. Larkin** on October 18, 2010, when the stock traded at **$ 96.49**.

Highlights

► We think that higher copper and gold prices will offset reduced output of both metals and permit a 7.5% sales gain in 2010, versus a decline of 15.5% in 2009. The estimated increase also reflects a rise in the price and production of molybdenum. Our copper price outlook is based on our forecast for a rebound in global copper demand from 2009's depressed levels and a gradual decline in metal exchange inventories. Our estimate for higher copper demand is based on the IHS Global Insight forecast for world economic growth of 3.7% in 2010, versus a decrease of 1.8% in 2009. Our expectation for a higher gold price in 2010 assumes continued low short-term interest rates worldwide and currency volatility.

► We look for an increase in operating profit in 2010, benefiting mostly from higher prices. After interest expense and taxes and with more shares outstanding, we project operating EPS of $6.91 in 2010, versus 2009's EPS of $5.86.

► For the long term, we expect earnings and reserves to increase on a secular rise in copper demand, a higher gold price and expansions at existing mines.

Investment Rationale/Risk

► In the long term, we think rising secular demand for durable goods in China and India, along with less rapid increases in the supply of copper, will support generally higher prices, sales, earnings and reserves. We believe that the depletion of existing mines will offset production from new mines and keep copper supply tight over the course of the business cycle. We think FCX, as the world's second largest copper producer, is well positioned to capitalize on rising demand and prices for copper with expansion projects in Africa and further development of existing mines. Also, we see EPS being aided on a projected rise in the gold price and a rebound in the price of molybdenum. But, with FCX recently trading in line with our target price, we would not add to positions.

► Risks to our opinion and target price include a decline in the price of copper in 2011 instead of the increase we project.

► Our 12-month target price of $95 assumes that FCX will trade at 11.6X our 2011 EPS estimate, which is toward the low end of the stock's historical range of the past 10 years, and a small premium to the P/E we apply to other base metal companies.

Qualitative Risk Assessment

LOW	MEDIUM	HIGH

Our risk assessment reflects the company's exposure to cyclical demand for copper and gold, along with sizable debt incurred in the merger with Phelps Dodge. However, we think FCX's large share of the global copper market acts as an offset.

Quantitative Evaluations

S&P Quality Ranking B-

D	C	B-	B	B+	A-	A	A+

Relative Strength Rank STRONG
89
LOWEST = 1   HIGHEST = 99

Revenue/Earnings Data

Revenue (Million $)

	1Q	2Q	3Q	4Q	Year
2010	4,363	3,864	5,152	--	--
2009	2,602	3,684	4,144	4,610	15,040
2008	5,672	5,441	4,616	2,067	17,796
2007	2,303	5,807	5,066	4,184	16,939
2006	1,086	1,426	1,636	1,642	5,791
2005	803.1	902.9	983.3	1,490	4,179

Earnings Per Share ($)

2010	2.00	1.40	2.49	E2.49	E8.38
2009	0.11	1.38	2.07	1.97	5.86
2008	2.64	2.24	1.31	-36.76	-29.72
2007	2.02	2.62	1.85	1.07	7.41
2006	1.23	1.74	1.67	1.99	6.63
2005	0.70	0.91	0.86	2.19	4.67

Fiscal year ended Dec. 31. Next earnings report expected: Late January. EPS Estimates based on S&P Operating Earnings; historical GAAP earnings are as reported.

Dividend Data (Dates: mm/dd Payment Date: mm/dd/yy)

Amount ($)	Date Decl.	Ex-Div. Date	Stk. of Record	Payment Date
0.150	12/29	01/13	01/15	02/01/10
0.150	03/25	04/13	04/15	05/01/10
0.300	06/24	07/13	07/15	08/01/10
0.300	09/29	10/13	10/15	11/01/10

Dividends have been paid since 2010. Source: Company reports.

Please read the Required Disclosures and Analyst Certification on the last page of this report.

The McGraw·Hill Companies

Freeport-McMoran Copper & Gold Inc.

STANDARD &POOR'S

Business Summary October 18, 2010

CORPORATE OVERVIEW. Freeport-McMoRan Copper & Gold is the world's second largest copper producer and is a major producer of gold and molybdenum. FCX has producing mines located in Indonesia, North America, South America and Africa.

Copper production totaled 4.1 billion pounds in 2009, versus 4.0 billion pounds in 2008; and gold production totaled 2.7 million oz., versus 1.3 million oz. in 2008. Molybdenum production was 54 million pounds in 2009, versus 73 million pounds in 2008.

In 2009, North America accounted for 28% of copper output, versus 36% in 2008; South America 34%, versus 37% in 2008; Indonesia 34% versus 27%; and Africa 4% versus 0%.

At year-end 2009, consolidated proven and probable reserves totaled 104.2 billion pounds of copper, 37.2 million ounces of gold, and 2.59 billion pounds of molybdenum. Some 33% of FCX's copper reserves were in Indonesia, about 33% were in South America, 26% were in North America and some 8% were in Africa. About 96% of FCX's gold reserves were in Indonesia, with the balance located in South America. Some 80% of molybdenum reserves are primarily in North America, with the remaining in South America.

Company Financials Fiscal Year Ended Dec. 31

Per Share Data ($)	2009	2008	2007	2006	2005	2004	2003	2002	2001	2000
Tangible Book Value	13.71	4.43	28.56	6.83	3.98	0.36	4.23	NM	NM	NM
Cash Flow	7.81	-25.02	10.03	7.33	5.38	1.96	2.52	2.67	2.49	2.09
Earnings	5.86	-29.72	7.41	6.63	4.67	0.85	1.07	0.89	0.53	0.26
S&P Core Earnings	6.00	-14.14	7.41	6.63	4.63	0.48	1.03	0.84	0.49	NA
Dividends	Nil	1.81	1.25	1.25	1.25	0.85	0.27	Nil	Nil	Nil
Payout Ratio	Nil	NM	17%	19%	27%	100%	25%	Nil	Nil	Nil
Prices:High	87.35	127.24	120.20	72.20	56.35	44.90	46.74	20.83	17.15	21.44
Prices:Low	21.16	15.70	48.85	43.10	31.52	27.76	16.01	9.95	8.31	6.75
P/E Ratio:High	15	NM	16	11	12	53	44	23	32	82
P/E Ratio:Low	4	NM	7	7	7	33	15	11	16	26

Income Statement Analysis (Million $)										
Revenue	15,040	17,796	16,939	5,791	4,179	2,372	2,212	1,910	1,839	1,869
Operating Income	7,736	-4,711	7,801	3,096	2,429	823	1,054	901	827	778
Depreciation	1,137	1,782	1,246	228	252	206	231	260	284	284
Interest Expense	586	706	660	75.6	132	148	197	171	174	205
Pretax Income	5,841	-13,294	6,133	2,826	2,037	574	584	450	359	273
Effective Tax Rate	39.5%	NM	39.1%	42.5%	44.9%	57.6%	57.9%	54.6%	56.6%	58.4%
Net Income	2,749	-11,067	2,942	1,457	995	202	197	168	113	77.0
S&P Core Earnings	2,595	-5,396	2,672	1,381	919	77.7	167	123	70.8	NA

Balance Sheet & Other Financial Data (Million $)										
Cash	2,656	872	1,626	907	764	551	464	7.84	7.59	7.97
Current Assets	7,433	5,233	5,903	2,151	2,022	1,460	1,100	638	548	569
Total Assets	25,871	23,271	40,661	5,390	5,550	5,087	4,718	4,192	4,212	3,951
Current Liabilities	3,002	3,158	3,869	972	1,369	698	632	538	628	634
Long Term Debt	6,330	7,284	7,180	661	1,003	1,874	2,076	1,961	2,133	1,988
Common Equity	6,259	2,083	14,259	1,345	743	63.6	776	-83.2	-246	-312
Total Capital	17,118	16,643	33,953	4,119	3,971	4,189	3,925	3,514	3,464	3,204
Capital Expenditures	1,587	2,708	1,755	251	143	141	139	188	167	292
Cash Flow	3,664	-9,559	3,980	1,624	1,186	363	401	391	360	323
Current Ratio	2.5	1.7	1.5	2.2	1.5	2.1	1.7	1.2	0.9	0.9
% Long Term Debt of Capitalization	37.0	43.8	26.9	16.0	25.2	44.7	52.9	55.8	61.6	62.0
% Net Income of Revenue	18.3	NM	17.4	25.2	23.8	8.5	8.9	8.8	6.1	4.1
% Return on Assets	11.2	NM	11.9	26.6	18.7	4.1	4.4	4.0	2.8	1.9
% Return on Equity	66.0	NM	35.0	133.7	231.7	37.3	49.0	NM	NM	NM

Data as orig reptd.; bef. results of disc opers/spec. items. Per share data adj. for stk. divs.; EPS diluted. E-Estimated. NA-Not Available. NM-Not Meaningful. NR-Not Ranked. UR-Under Review.

Office: 333 North Central Avenue, Phoenix, AZ 85004.
Telephone: 602-366-8100.
Email: ir@fmi.com
Website: http://www.fcx.com

Chrmn: J.R. Moffett
Pres & CEO: R.C. Adkerson
Vice Chrmn: B.M. Rankin, Jr.
Investor Contact: K.L. Quirk

EVP, CFO & Treas: K.L. Quirk
Board Members: R. C. Adkerson, R. J. Allison, Jr., R. A. Day, G. J. Ford, H. D. Graham, Jr., C. C. Krulak, B. L. Lackey, J. C. Madonna, D. E. McCoy, J. R. Moffett, B. M. Rankin, Jr., S. H. Siegele

Founded: 1987
Domicile: Delaware
Employees: 28,567

The **McGraw-Hill** Companies

Frontier Communications Corp

STANDARD & POOR'S

S&P Recommendation BUY ★★★★☆

Price	12-Mo. Target Price	Investment Style
$8.79 (as of Oct 22, 2010)	$9.00	Large-Cap Value

GICS Sector Telecommunication Services
Sub-Industry Integrated Telecommunication Services

Summary After acquiring wireline assets from Verizon Communications in mid-2010 that more than doubled its size, Frontier provides wireline communications services including voice services to 6 million customers in rural areas and small and medium-sized cities in the U.S.

Key Stock Statistics (Source S&P, Vickers, company reports)

52-Wk Range	$8.91 – 6.96	S&P Oper. EPS 2010E	0.57	Market Capitalization(B)	$8.720	Beta		0.80
Trailing 12-Month EPS	$0.42	S&P Oper. EPS 2011E	0.52	Yield (%)	8.53	S&P 3-Yr. Proj. EPS CAGR(%)		4
Trailing 12-Month P/E	20.9	P/E on S&P Oper. EPS 2010E	15.4	Dividend Rate/Share	$0.75	S&P Credit Rating		BB
$10K Invested 5 Yrs Ago	$9,500	Common Shares Outstg. (M)	992.0	Institutional Ownership (%)	19			

Price Performance

- 30-Week Mov. Avg. · · · ·
- 10-Week Mov. Avg. – – –
- **GAAP Earnings vs. Previous Year**
- Volume Above Avg. ▮▮▮ STARS
- 12-Mo. Target Price —
- Relative Strength —
- ▲ Up ▼ Down ▶ No Change
- Volume Below Avg. ▮▮▮ ★

Options: CBOE, P, Ph

Analysis prepared by **Todd Rosenbluth** on August 06, 2010, when the stock traded at **$ 7.60**.

Highlights

➤ We look for FTR to generate revenue of $3.6 billion in 2010, following the July acquisition of wireline assets from Verizon Communications that we expect to add $1.8 billion to revenues. In 2011, we expect revenues of $5.45 billion. In both legacy Frontier markets and in the acquired assets, we see pressure on voice services from access line losses, but we look for partial offsets from DSL and video penetration. We expect Frontier to have some success in new properties with service bundles.

➤ We expect the integration of the new assets to take some time, pushing EBITDA margins in the second half of 2010 down to 48%, from 53% in the first half, although we look for expansion to 50% in 2011. We expect benefits from work force cuts and billing integration, but we see this being offset by increased promotional activities for introductory service bundles and weakness in higher-margin voice services.

➤ We expect higher interest costs related to the merger. We forecast EPS of $0.57 in 2010 and $0.52 in 2011, before certain one-time merger-related expenses.

Investment Rationale/Risk

➤ We believe FTR generates sufficient cash flow to support its recently reduced dividend, and we view the Verizon asset combination favorably. We think FTR will have opportunities for cost savings, broadband growth and deleveraging, although we see risks given expected pressure on margins as it will need to spend to retain and expand its voice and broadband customer base. We believe FTR has a strong track record in small deal integration and in generating high revenues per household.

➤ Risks to our recommendation and target price include failure to smoothly integrate the Verizon assets in a timely manner; not retaining customers in legacy and acquired markets; and a further dividend reduction.

➤ Our 12-month target price of $9 is based on an EV/EBITDA multiple of 6.1X, in line with mid-size wireline telecom peers and down slightly from historical levels to reflect risks. At our target price, FTR's dividend yield of 8.3%, even following the recent reduction, would be above average.

Qualitative Risk Assessment

LOW	**MEDIUM**	HIGH

Our risk assessment for Frontier Communications reflects the rural, less competitive nature of its operations, and what we see as the strong and stable cash flow that supports its dividend policy, offset by sensitivity to the U.S. economy and the company's acquisition strategy.

Quantitative Evaluations

S&P Quality Ranking — B-

D	C	**B-**	B	B+	A-	A	A+

Relative Strength Rank — STRONG

78

LOWEST = 1   HIGHEST = 99

Revenue/Earnings Data

Revenue (Million $)

	1Q	2Q	3Q	4Q	Year
2010	519.9	516.1	--	--	--
2009	538.0	532.1	526.8	521.0	2,118
2008	569.2	562.6	557.9	547.4	2,237
2007	556.2	578.8	575.8	577.2	2,288
2006	506.9	506.9	507.2	504.4	2,025
2005	537.2	531.8	537.4	556.1	2,162

Earnings Per Share ($)

2010	0.14	0.11	E0.11	E0.11	E0.57
2009	0.12	0.09	0.17	0.01	0.38
2008	0.14	0.15	0.15	0.11	0.57
2007	0.21	0.12	0.14	0.18	0.65
2006	0.13	0.29	0.16	0.20	0.78
2005	0.11	0.13	0.11	0.23	0.59

Fiscal year ended Dec. 31. Next earnings report expected: Early November. EPS Estimates based on S&P Operating Earnings; historical GAAP earnings are as reported.

Dividend Data (Dates: mm/dd Payment Date: mm/dd/yy)

Amount ($)	Date Decl.	Ex-Div. Date	Stk. of Record	Payment Date
0.250	10/28	12/07	12/09	12/31/09
0.250	02/17	03/05	03/09	03/31/10
0.250	05/12	06/07	06/09	06/30/10
0.188	07/29	09/07	09/09	09/30/10

Dividends have been paid since 2004. Source: Company reports.

Please read the Required Disclosures and Analyst Certification on the last page of this report.

Frontier Communications Corp

STANDARD &POOR'S

Business Summary August 06, 2010

CORPORATE OVERVIEW. Frontier Communications (formerly Citizens Communications) provides wireline services to rural areas and small and medium-sized towns and cities across the country including in Arizona, California, New York and West Virginia. As of June 2010, FTR was an incumbent local exchange carrier (ILEC) with 2 million access lines (down 6% from a year earlier) and 647,000 DSL customers (50% penetration of residential customers).

In July 2010, FTR completed a combination of wireline assets that were spun out by Verizon Communications in a stock and debt assumption deal valued originally at $8.6 billion. We believe the agreed-on price was then equal to a fair 4.5X trailing EBITDA multiple. The Verizon properties, in 14 states, included 4.0 million access lines, and 1.06 million DSL and FiOS customers as of June 2010. On a pro forma basis, the combined company would have had $6 billion in revenues during 2009. FTR, which expects $500 million in expense savings largely in the second year following closing, issued new stock and assumed $3.5 billion of debt to complete the deal.

CORPORATE STRATEGY. In the first half of 2010, FTR focused on expanding by providing rural local residential phone customers with enhanced services as well as long distance, DSL and satellite video to offset access line pressure. FTR also had 180,000 satellite TV customers, which led to a 4% increase in the average monthly customer revenue per access line in the 12 months ended June 2010, to $70.27. In the second half of 2010, we expect FTR to increase its promotional activities in both legacy assets and the newly acquired ones to drive higher non-voice service penetration. In addition, we look for FTR to invest to expand broadband availability in the acquired assets to increase its pool of potential customers.

COMPETITIVE LANDSCAPE. While we believe FTR faced challenges from cable telephony and wireless that led to its 6.3% access line erosion in the 12 months ended June 2010, we are encouraged that the rate of loss slowed from 7.1% in the 12 months ended March 2009. We believe this bodes well as Verizon assets lost 11.2% of their access lines in the 12 months ended June 2010. In new and old markets, FTR competes with cable providers such as Time Warner and Comcast, which began to offer telephony services in 2006. As of late 2009, approximately 73% of FTR's legacy operating territory faced cable telephony competition.

Company Financials Fiscal Year Ended Dec. 31

Per Share Data ($)	2009	2008	2007	2006	2005	2004	2003	2002	2001	2000
Tangible Book Value	NM	NM	NM	NM	NM	NM	NM	NM	NM	4.09
Cash Flow	1.93	2.34	2.30	2.25	2.26	2.09	2.37	-0.24	2.08	1.30
Earnings	0.38	0.57	0.65	0.78	0.59	0.23	0.42	-2.93	-0.28	-0.15
S&P Core Earnings	0.45	0.46	0.52	0.64	0.59	0.19	0.68	-2.89	-0.58	NA
Dividends	1.00	1.00	1.00	1.00	1.00	0.50	Nil	Nil	Nil	Nil
Payout Ratio	NM	175%	154%	128%	169%	NM	Nil	Nil	Nil	Nil
Prices:High	8.87	12.94	16.05	14.95	14.05	14.80	13.40	11.52	15.88	19.00
Prices:Low	5.32	6.35	12.03	11.97	12.08	11.37	8.81	2.51	8.20	12.50
P/E Ratio:High	23	23	25	19	24	62	32	NM	NM	NM
P/E Ratio:Low	14	11	19	15	20	47	21	NM	NM	NM

Income Statement Analysis (Million $)	2009	2008	2007	2006	2005	2004	2003	2002	2001	2000
Revenue	2,118	2,237	2,288	2,025	2,162	2,193	2,445	2,669	2,457	1,802
Operating Income	NA	1,214	1,251	1,121	1,149	1,148	1,173	1,179	927	549
Depreciation	476	562	546	476	542	573	595	756	632	388
Interest Expense	378	363	384	336	339	379	423	478	386	194
Pretax Income	193	289	343	390	285	85.5	189	-1,238	-78.7	-44.0
Effective Tax Rate	36.2%	36.8%	37.4%	35.0%	29.6%	15.6%	35.5%	NM	NM	NM
Net Income	121	183	215	254	200	72.2	122	-823	-63.9	-40.1
S&P Core Earnings	139	146	171	206	201	57.7	198	-811	-164	NA

Balance Sheet & Other Financial Data (Million $)	2009	2008	2007	2006	2005	2004	2003	2002	2001	2000
Cash	359	164	226	1,041	266	167	584	393	57.7	31.2
Current Assets	680	468	524	1,273	542	450	896	1,201	2,533	2,263
Total Assets	6,878	6,889	7,256	6,791	6,412	6,668	7,689	8,147	10,554	6,955
Current Liabilities	393	383	446	426	617	418	536	771	1,567	992
Long Term Debt	4,794	4,722	4,739	4,461	3,999	4,267	4,397	5,159	5,736	3,264
Common Equity	339	519	998	1,058	1,042	1,362	1,415	1,172	1,946	1,720
Total Capital	5,140	5,245	6,446	6,033	5,366	5,629	6,259	6,468	8,112	5,474
Capital Expenditures	256	288	316	269	268	276	278	469	531	537
Cash Flow	597	744	761	730	742	645	717	-67.5	568	348
Current Ratio	1.7	1.2	1.2	3.0	0.9	1.1	1.7	1.6	1.6	2.3
% Long Term Debt of Capitalization	93.3	90.0	82.6	73.9	74.5	75.8	70.2	79.8	70.7	59.6
% Net Income of Revenue	5.7	8.2	9.4	12.5	9.3	3.3	5.0	NM	NM	NM
% Return on Assets	1.8	2.6	3.1	3.8	3.1	1.0	1.5	NM	NM	NM
% Return on Equity	28.2	24.1	20.9	24.2	16.7	5.2	9.4	NM	NM	NM

Data as orig reptd.; bef. results of disc opers/spec. items. Per share data adj. for stk. divs.; EPS diluted. E-Estimated. NA-Not Available. NM-Not Meaningful. NR-Not Ranked. UR-Under Review.

Office: 3 High Ridge Park, Stamford, CT 06905-1390.
Telephone: 203-614-5600.
Email: citizens@cnz.com
Website: http://www.frontier.com

Chrmn, Pres & CEO: M.A. Wilderotter
COO & EVP: D.J. McCarthy
EVP & CFO: D.R. Shassian
EVP & General Counsel: K.Q. Abernathy

SVP & Chief Acctg Officer: R.J. Larson
Board Members: L. T. Barnes, Jr., P. C. Bynoe, J. Finard, E. D. Fraioli, W. M. Kraus, P. D. Reeve, H. L. Schrott, L. D. Segil, M. Shapiro, D. H. Ward, M. Wick, III, M. A. Wilderotter

Founded: 1927
Domicile: Delaware
Employees: 5,403

GameStop Corp.

STANDARD & POOR'S

S&P Recommendation	BUY ★★★★☆	Price $19.13 (as of Oct 22, 2010)	12-Mo. Target Price $26.00	Investment Style Large-Cap Growth

GICS Sector Consumer Discretionary
Sub-Industry Computer & Electronics Retail

Summary This company is the largest U.S. video game and PC entertainment software specialty retailer, and operates over 6,000 stores worldwide.

Key Stock Statistics (Source S&P, Vickers, company reports)

52-Wk Range	$26.05–17.12	S&P Oper. EPS 2011**E**	2.63	Market Capitalization(B)	$2.876	Beta		1.10
Trailing 12-Month EPS	$2.37	S&P Oper. EPS 2012**E**	2.60	Yield (%)	Nil	S&P 3-Yr. Proj. EPS CAGR(%)		8
Trailing 12-Month P/E	8.1	P/E on S&P Oper. EPS 2011**E**	7.3	Dividend Rate/Share	Nil	S&P Credit Rating		NA
$10K Invested 5 Yrs Ago	$11,223	Common Shares Outstg. (M)	150.4	Institutional Ownership (%)	NM			

Price Performance

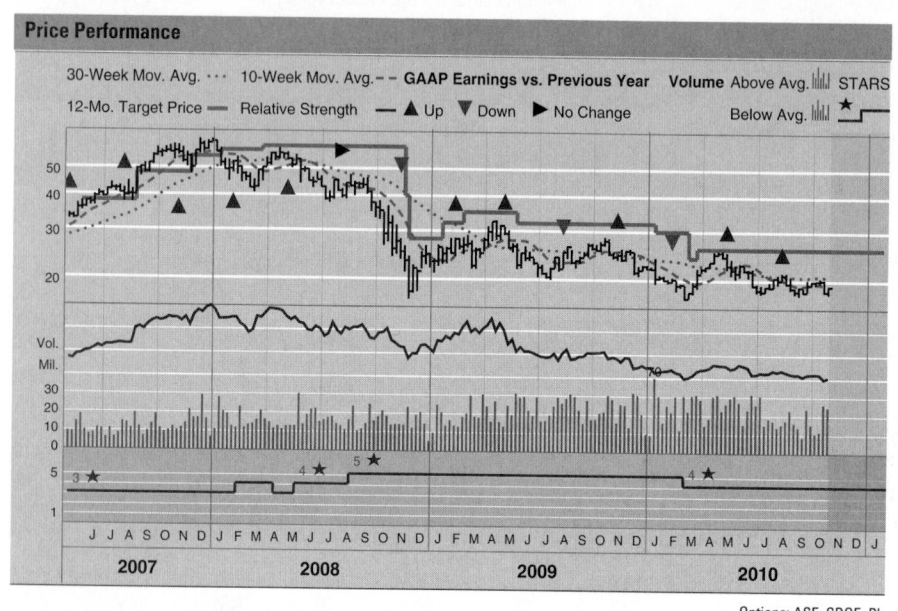

30-Week Mov. Avg. ··· 10-Week Mov. Avg. –– **GAAP Earnings vs. Previous Year** Volume Above Avg. ▮▮▮ STARS
12-Mo. Target Price — Relative Strength ▲ Up ▼ Down ▶ No Change Below Avg. ▮▮▮ ★

Options: ASE, CBOE, Ph

Analysis prepared by **Michael Souers** on August 25, 2010, when the stock traded at **$ 18.42.**

Highlights

➤ We see FY 11 (Jan.) revenues rising 5.1%, following a 3.1% advance in FY 10. We expect this growth to be driven by the opening of about 300 net new stores worldwide and a 1% increase in comp-store sales. We continue to project that GME's used game business will thrive in the current challenging economic environment, and also expect a strong lineup of new software in calendar 2010. We look for price cuts on next-generation consoles to stem recent declines of hardware sales, although we do expect a sales decline for this category.

➤ We forecast that gross margins will widen modestly in FY 11 on an expected shift in product mix to new and used software from hardware following a significant ramp-up in the installed base. We see operating margins widening slightly, as gross margin improvement is only partially offset by the de-leveraging of SG&A expenses due to a meager comp-store sales gain.

➤ After a significant decrease in GME's diluted share count, we project FY 11 EPS of $2.63, a 16% increase from the $2.27 the company earned in FY 10, excluding debt extinguishment expense. We see FY 12 EPS of $2.60.

Investment Rationale/Risk

➤ We think the video game industry continues to benefit from a growth cycle unprecedented in strength, and we expect near-term earnings growth from GME despite weakness in consumer spending. Long term, we believe the electronic game industry will benefit from hardware platform technology evolution, a growing used video game market, and broadening demographic appeal, but we have concerns that online gaming will take some share from the retail market. Nonetheless, we consider the shares' valuation to be compelling, with GME recently trading at about 7X our FY 12 EPS estimate, a significant discount to the S&P 500.

➤ Risks to our opinion and target price include a slowdown in consumer spending, inventory shortages, an inability to successfully manage new store openings or merger integration, the threat of online gaming emerging as a viable alternative for gamers, and corporate governance issues including the existence of a non-shareholder-approved "poison pill."

➤ Our 12-month target price of $26, 10X our FY 12 EPS estimate, is based on our DCF analysis, which assumes a weighted average cost of capital of 10.6% and terminal growth of 2.0%.

Qualitative Risk Assessment

LOW	**MEDIUM**	HIGH

Our risk assessment reflects the company's leading market share position, offset by industry cyclicality, as growth is partly dependent on the timing of new hardware and software releases.

Quantitative Evaluations

S&P Quality Ranking B+

D	C	B-	B	**B+**	A-	A	A+

Relative Strength Rank WEAK

25

LOWEST = 1   HIGHEST = 99

Revenue/Earnings Data

Revenue (Million $)

	1Q	2Q	3Q	4Q	Year
2011	2,083	1,799	--	--	--
2010	1,981	1,739	1,835	3,524	9,078
2009	1,814	1,804	1,696	3,492	8,806
2008	1,279	1,338	1,611	2,866	7,094
2007	1,040	963.4	1,012	2,304	5,319
2006	474.7	415.9	534.2	1,667	3,092

Earnings Per Share ($)

	1Q	2Q	3Q	4Q	Year
2011	0.48	0.26	E0.40	E1.50	E2.63
2010	0.42	0.23	0.31	1.29	2.25
2009	0.37	0.34	0.28	1.39	2.38
2008	0.15	0.34	0.31	1.14	1.75
2007	0.08	0.02	0.09	0.81	1.00
2006	0.10	0.07	-0.02	0.55	0.81

Fiscal year ended Jan. 31. Next earnings report expected: Mid November. EPS Estimates based on S&P Operating Earnings; historical GAAP earnings are as reported.

Dividend Data

No cash dividends have been paid.

GameStop Corp.

Business Summary August 25, 2010

CORPORATE OVERVIEW. GameStop is the world's largest retailer of video game products and PC entertainment software. The company sells new and used video game hardware, video game software and accessories, as well as PC entertainment software, related accessories and other merchandise. As of January 30, 2010, GameStop operated 6,450 stores in the U.S., Australia, Canada and Europe, primarily under the names GameStop and EB Games. Of the total store count, 4,429 stores are located in the U.S., with the remaining 2,021 located internationally.

In October 2005, GameStop acquired close peer Electronics Boutique Holding Corp., which essentially doubled the company's market share in video game retailing. In November 2008, GME purchased Micromania, the leading retailer of video and computer games in France, with 332 locations.

MARKET PROFILE. According to NPD Group, Inc., a market research firm, the

U.S. electronic games industry generated approximately $20 billion in 2009, and, according to the International Development Group, retail sales of video game hardware and software and PC entertainment software totaled $17.5 billion in Europe. The NPD Group also estimated that video game retail sales were approximately $1.8 billion in Canada in 2009. The Entertainment Software Association (ESA) estimates that 65% of all American head of households play video or computer games, and that the average game player is 35 years old. We believe that trends such as hardware platform technology evolution and a broadening demographic appeal will continue to propel growth in this industry.

Company Financials Fiscal Year Ended Jan. 31

Per Share Data ($)	2010	2009	2008	2007	2006	2005	2004	2003	2002	2001
Tangible Book Value	3.26	1.17	2.80	NM	NM	2.19	2.41	2.02	NM	NM
Cash Flow	3.22	3.24	2.54	1.69	1.34	0.85	0.77	0.62	0.47	0.14
Earnings	2.25	2.38	1.75	1.00	0.81	0.53	0.53	0.44	0.09	-0.17
S&P Core Earnings	2.25	2.33	1.75	1.00	0.76	0.92	0.47	0.37	0.09	NA
Dividends	NA	Nil	Nil	Nil	Nil	Nil	Nil	Nil	Nil	Nil
Payout Ratio	NA	Nil	Nil	Nil	Nil	Nil	Nil	Nil	Nil	Nil
Calendar Year	2009	2008	2007	2006	2005	2004	2003	2002	2001	2000
Prices:High	32.82	62.29	63.77	29.21	19.21	11.76	9.52	12.15	NA	NA
Prices:Low	20.02	16.91	24.95	15.57	9.27	7.19	3.75	4.46	NA	NA
P/E Ratio:High	15	26	36	29	24	22	18	28	NA	NA
P/E Ratio:Low	9	7	14	16	12	14	7	10	NA	NA

Income Statement Analysis (Million $)										
Revenue	9,078	8,806	7,094	5,319	3,092	1,843	1,579	1,353	1,121	757
Operating Income	801	825	632	450	273	163	133	110	64.4	27.8
Depreciation	164	145	130	110	66.7	37.0	28.9	22.6	30.3	22.0
Interest Expense	43.2	50.5	61.6	84.7	37.9	2.16	0.66	1.37	19.6	23.0
Pretax Income	589	634	441	254	160	98.9	105	87.7	14.6	-17.8
Effective Tax Rate	36.2%	37.2%	34.6%	37.8%	37.0%	38.4%	39.7%	40.2%	52.4%	NM
Net Income	377	398	288	158	101	60.9	63.5	52.4	6.96	-12.0
S&P Core Earnings	377	390	288	158	94.1	53.2	55.6	44.1	6.76	NA

Balance Sheet & Other Financial Data (Million $)										
Cash	905	578	857	652	402	171	205	232	80.8	8.70
Current Assets	2,127	1,818	1,795	1,440	1,121	424	473	416	237	138
Total Assets	4,955	4,513	3,776	3,350	3,015	915	899	804	607	510
Current Liabilities	1,656	1,563	1,261	1,087	888	314	284	247	206	140
Long Term Debt	447	546	574	844	963	24.3	Nil	Nil	400	385
Common Equity	2,723	2,300	1,862	1,376	1,115	543	594	549	-3.99	-20.6
Total Capital	3,170	2,845	2,437	2,220	2,091	588	612	554	399	367
Capital Expenditures	164	183	176	134	111	98.3	63.0	39.5	20.5	25.1
Cash Flow	541	543	419	268	167	97.9	92.4	75.0	37.3	10.0
Current Ratio	1.3	1.2	1.4	1.3	1.3	1.4	1.7	1.7	1.2	1.0
% Long Term Debt of Capitalization	14.1	19.2	23.6	38.0	46.1	4.1	Nil	Nil	100.2	105.0
% Net Income of Revenue	4.2	4.5	4.1	3.0	3.3	3.3	4.0	3.9	0.6	NM
% Return on Assets	8.0	9.6	8.1	5.0	5.0	6.7	7.5	7.4	1.2	NM
% Return on Equity	15.0	19.1	17.8	12.7	12.2	10.7	11.1	19.2	NM	NM

Data as orig reptd.; bef. results of disc opers/spec. items. Per share data adj. for stk. divs.; EPS diluted. E-Estimated. NA-Not Available. NM-Not Meaningful. NR-Not Ranked. UR-Under Review.

Office: 625 Westport Pkwy, Grapevine, TX 76051-6740.
Telephone: 817-424-2000.
Email: investorrelations@gamestop.com
Website: http://www.gamestop.com

Chrmn: D.A. Dematteo
Pres: T.D. Bartel
CEO: J.P. Raines
EVP & CFO: R.A. Lloyd

SVP & Chief Acctg Officer: T.W. Crawford
Investor Contact: M. Hodges (817-424-2000)
Board Members: J. L. Davis, D. A. Dematteo, S. Koonin, L. Riggio, M. N. Rosen, S. M. Shern, S. Steinberg, G. R. Szczepanski, E. A. Volkwein, L. S. Zilavy

Founded: 1994
Domicile: Delaware
Employees: 59,000

Gannett Co Inc.

STANDARD &POOR'S

S&P Recommendation HOLD ★★★☆☆	**Price** $12.18 (as of Oct 22, 2010)	**12-Mo. Target Price** $14.00	**Investment Style** Large-Cap Blend

GICS Sector Consumer Discretionary
Sub-Industry Publishing

Summary Gannett publishes 82 daily U.S. newspapers, more than 600 non-daily publications in the U.S., and more than 200 U.K. titles, and operates 23 TV stations in the U.S.

Key Stock Statistics (Source S&P, Vickers, company reports)

52-Wk Range	$19.69–9.53	S&P Oper. EPS 2010**E**	2.41	Market Capitalization(B)	$2.906	Beta	2.46
Trailing 12-Month EPS	$2.28	S&P Oper. EPS 2011**E**	2.45	Yield (%)	1.31	S&P 3-Yr. Proj. EPS CAGR(%)	4
Trailing 12-Month P/E	5.3	P/E on S&P Oper. EPS 2010**E**	5.1	Dividend Rate/Share	$0.16	S&P Credit Rating	BB
$10K Invested 5 Yrs Ago	$2,360	Common Shares Outstg. (M)	238.6	Institutional Ownership (%)	95		

Price Performance

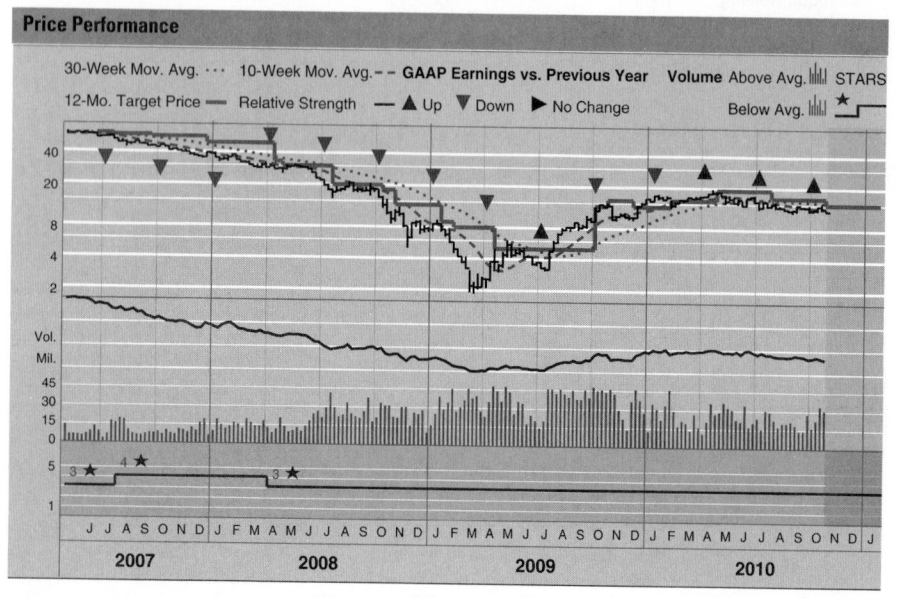

30-Week Mov. Avg. ··· 10-Week Mov. Avg. - - **GAAP Earnings vs. Previous Year** Volume Above Avg. |||| STARS
12-Mo. Target Price — Relative Strength — ▲ Up ▼ Down ▶ No Change Below Avg. |||| ★

Options: ASE, CBOE, P, Ph

Analysis prepared by **Joseph Agnese** on October 18, 2010, when the stock traded at **$12.54**.

Highlights

► We look for the contraction in print publishing revenues to continue into 2011, although at a slower rate, given a more stable economic environment in the U.S. and weak ad demand in the U.K., and we see classified advertising continuing to migrate online. We project broadcast revenue growth to moderate in 2011 after expected significant benefits in 2010 from easy comparisons and benefits from the Winter Olympics and the mid-term U.S. elections. Overall, we expect revenues to rise 1.0% in 2011, following contraction of about 2.2% in 2010. GCI has taken preemptive action to deal with weakening demand, including unpaid furloughs and reducing hard copy circulation for some subscribers, but is expanding 24/7 digital channels.

► We forecast EBIT margins will remain relatively flat at about 19% in 2011. We see the benefits of staff and cost reduction initiatives and lower newsprint usage offset by higher newsprint pricing and negative operating leverage from lower revenues.

► We see 2011 EPS of $2.45, up slightly from our operating EPS estimate of $2.41 in 2010, which excludes facility closures, asset impairments and workforce restructurings.

Investment Rationale/Risk

► We remain concerned by what we see as a secular decline in newspaper advertising, especially as only about 16.5% of the company's revenues in 2009 were from digital operations. We also expect a negative secular trend to continue to negatively impact classified advertising. On a positive note, with strong operating cash flow and a high free cash flow/equity yield, we think there is long-term value in what we see as GCI's strong free cash flow generating capabilities.

► Risks to our recommendation and target price include weaker-than-expected U.S. GDP, lower audience ratings at network-affiliated TV stations, and a weakening of the British pound versus the U.S. dollar.

► Our 12-month target price of $14 is derived by applying an enterprise value-to-EBITDA ratio of 5.5X, near the low end of its historical range, to our 2011 EBITDA estimate of $1.3 billion. We believe a historically low valuation multiple is appropriate given unfavorable impacts from a weak cyclical market and the significant negative secular challenges we believe the company is facing.

Qualitative Risk Assessment

LOW	MEDIUM	HIGH

Our risk assessment reflects a highly competitive and weak advertising environment along with significant industry upheaval as consumers increasingly opt to get their news online and for free. This is only partly offset, in our view, by GCI's strong free cash flow and profitability as well as its relatively low cost of capital.

Quantitative Evaluations

S&P Quality Ranking B+

D	C	B-	B	B+	A-	A	A+

Relative Strength Rank WEAK

13

LOWEST = 1   HIGHEST = 99

Revenue/Earnings Data

Revenue (Million $)

	1Q	2Q	3Q	4Q	Year
2010	1,322	1,365	1,312	--	--
2009	1,378	1,413	1,337	1,485	5,613
2008	1,677	1,718	1,637	1,735	6,768
2007	1,871	1,928	1,756	1,897	7,439
2006	1,883	2,028	1,915	2,208	8,033
2005	1,768	1,911	1,865	2,055	7,599

Earnings Per Share ($)

2010	0.49	0.73	0.42	E0.80	E2.41
2009	0.34	0.30	0.31	0.56	1.51
2008	0.84	-10.03	0.69	0.69	-29.11
2007	0.90	1.24	1.01	1.06	4.17
2006	0.99	1.31	1.11	1.51	4.90
2005	1.03	1.34	1.13	1.44	4.92

Fiscal year ended Dec. 31. Next earnings report expected: Early February. EPS Estimates based on S&P Operating Earnings; historical GAAP earnings are as reported.

Dividend Data (Dates: mm/dd Payment Date: mm/dd/yy)

Amount ($)	Date Decl.	Ex-Div. Date	Stk. of Record	Payment Date
0.040	10/28	12/09	12/11	01/04/10
0.040	02/24	03/03	03/05	04/01/10
0.040	05/04	06/02	06/04	07/01/10
0.040	07/27	09/08	09/10	10/01/10

Dividends have been paid since 1929. Source: Company reports.

Please read the Required Disclosures and Analyst Certification on the last page of this report.

The McGraw-Hill Companies

Gannett Co Inc.

Business Summary October 18, 2010

CORPORATE OVERVIEW. Gannett Co. is the largest newspaper publisher in the U.S. The company publishes newspapers, operates broadcasting stations, runs Web sites in connection with its newspaper and broadcast operations, and is engaged in marketing, commercial printing, a newswire service, data services, and news programming.

The newspaper publishing segment (74% of 2009 revenues) consists of the operations of 82 daily newspapers and about 600 non-daily publications. The segment includes the publication of USA TODAY, the nation's largest selling daily newspaper. The company's strategy for non-daily publications is to target these products at communities of interest, defined by geography, demographics or lifestyle. In the U.K., the company is the second largest regional publisher via its wholly owned subsidiary, Newsquest plc, generating $563 million in 2009 revenues. Newspaper publishing revenues are derived principally from the sale of advertising (67% of 2009 publishing revenues), circulation revenues (27%) and commercial printing revenues (6.0%). Within the advertising category, revenues were derived from retail (52%), national (18%) and classified (31%) advertising.

In 2008, with the purchase of a controlling interest in Careerbuilder, GCI began reporting a separate digital segment (10% of 2009 revenues). The segment al-

so includes PointRoll, an Internet ad services business, Planet Discover, a provider of local, integrated online search and advertising technology, commercial printing, newswire, marketing and data services operations. GCI's Online Internet Audience in January 2010 was 27.3 million unique visitors, about 13% of the Internet audience as measured by comScore Media Metrix.

The broadcast segment (11% of 2009 revenues) consists of 23 network-affiliated TV stations, including 12 NBC, six CBS, three ABC affiliates and two MyNetworkTV affiliates, and Captivate Network, a national news and entertainment network that delivers programming and full-motion video advertising through video screens located in office tower elevators across North America. The principal sources of GCI's television revenues are: local advertising focusing on the immediate geographic area of the stations; national advertising, compensation paid by the networks for carrying commercial network programs; advertising on the stations' Web sites; and payments by advertisers to television stations for other services, such as the production of advertising material. Captivate derives its revenue principally from national advertising.

Company Financials Fiscal Year Ended Dec. 31

Per Share Data ($)	2009	2008	2007	2006	2005	2004	2003	2002	2001	2000
Tangible Book Value	NM	NM	NM	NM	NM	NM	NM	NM	NM	NM
Cash Flow	2.53	-27.96	5.38	6.07	6.24	6.14	5.30	5.13	4.78	4.99
Earnings	1.51	-29.11	4.17	4.90	4.92	4.92	4.46	4.31	3.12	3.63
S&P Core Earnings	1.54	-0.17	4.01	4.86	4.43	4.45	4.23	3.70	2.39	NA
Dividends	0.16	1.60	1.42	1.20	1.12	1.04	0.98	0.94	0.90	0.86
Payout Ratio	11%	NM	34%	24%	23%	21%	22%	22%	29%	24%
Prices:High	15.99	39.00	63.50	64.97	82.41	91.38	89.63	79.90	71.14	81.56
Prices:Low	1.85	5.00	34.34	51.65	58.37	78.84	66.70	62.76	53.00	48.38
P/E Ratio:High	11	NM	15	13	17	19	20	19	23	22
P/E Ratio:Low	1	NM	8	11	12	16	15	15	17	13

Income Statement Analysis (Million $)	2009	2008	2007	2006	2005	2004	2003	2002	2001	2000
Revenue	5,613	6,768	7,439	8,033	7,599	7,381	6,711	6,422	6,344	6,222
Operating Income	1,101	1,477	2,005	2,275	2,322	2,392	2,213	2,149	2,034	2,190
Depreciation	243	262	282	277	274	244	232	215	444	376
Interest Expense	176	191	260	288	211	141	139	146	222	219
Pretax Income	576	-1,715	1,449	1,719	1,818	1,995	1,840	1,765	1,371	1,609
Effective Tax Rate	33.6%	NM	32.7%	32.5%	33.4%	34.0%	34.2%	34.3%	39.4%	39.6%
Net Income	355	-1,783	976	1,161	1,211	1,317	1,211	1,160	831	972
S&P Core Earnings	363	-40.6	939	1,151	1,092	1,191	1,150	998	638	NA

Balance Sheet & Other Financial Data (Million $)	2009	2008	2007	2006	2005	2004	2003	2002	2001	2000
Cash	98.8	99.0	77.3	94.3	163	136	67.2	90.4	141	193
Current Assets	1,049	1,246	1,343	1,532	1,462	1,371	1,223	1,133	1,178	1,302
Total Assets	7,148	7,797	15,888	16,224	15,743	15,399	14,706	13,733	13,096	12,980
Current Liabilities	900	1,153	962	1,117	1,096	1,005	962	959	1,128	1,174
Long Term Debt	3,062	3,817	4,098	5,210	5,438	4,608	3,835	4,547	5,080	5,748
Common Equity	1,604	1,056	9,017	8,382	7,571	8,164	8,423	6,912	5,736	5,103
Total Capital	4,888	5,083	13,832	14,319	13,897	13,685	13,094	12,138	11,319	11,126
Capital Expenditures	67.7	165	171	201	263	280	281	275	325	351
Cash Flow	598	-6,385	1,258	1,438	1,486	1,561	1,443	1,375	1,275	1,348
Current Ratio	1.2	1.1	1.4	1.4	1.3	1.4	1.3	1.2	1.0	1.1
% Long Term Debt of Capitalization	Nil	75.1	29.6	36.4	39.1	33.7	29.3	37.5	44.9	51.7
% Net Income of Revenue	6.3	NM	13.1	14.4	15.9	17.8	18.0	18.1	13.1	15.6
% Return on Assets	NA	NM	6.1	7.3	7.8	8.8	8.5	8.6	6.4	8.8
% Return on Equity	NA	NM	11.2	14.6	15.4	15.9	15.8	18.3	15.3	20.0

Data as orig reptd.; bef. results of disc opers/spec. items. Per share data adj. for stk. divs.; EPS diluted. E-Estimated. NA-Not Available. NM-Not Meaningful. NR-Not Ranked. UR-Under Review.

Office: 7950 Jones Branch Dr, McLean, VA 22107-0910.
Telephone: 703-854-6000.
Email: gcishare@gannett.com
Website: http://www.gannett.com

Chrmn & CEO: C. Dubow
Pres, COO & CFO: G.C. Martore
SVP, Secy & General Counsel: T.A. Mayman
Chief Acctg Officer & Cntlr: G.R. Gavagan

Treas: M.A. Hart
Investor Contact: J. Heinz (703-854-6917)
Board Members: C. Dubow, H. Elias, A. H. Harper, J. J. Louis, M. Magner, S. K. McCune, D. M. McFarland, D. E. Shalala, N. Shapiro, K. H. Williams

Founded: 1906
Domicile: Delaware
Employees: 35,000

Gap Inc. (The)

STANDARD &POOR'S

S&P Recommendation	HOLD ★★★☆☆	Price $19.15 (as of Oct 22, 2010)	12-Mo. Target Price $22.00	Investment Style Large-Cap Blend

GICS Sector Consumer Discretionary
Sub-Industry Apparel Retail

Summary This specialty apparel retailer operates Gap, Banana Republic and Old Navy stores, offering casual clothing to moderate, upscale and value-oriented market segments.

Key Stock Statistics (Source S&P, Vickers, company reports)

52-Wk Range	$26.34– 16.62	S&P Oper. EPS 2011E	1.78	Market Capitalization(B)	$11.852	Beta	1.17
Trailing 12-Month EPS	$1.76	S&P Oper. EPS 2012E	1.92	Yield (%)	2.09	S&P 3-Yr. Proj. EPS CAGR(%)	8
Trailing 12-Month P/E	10.9	P/E on S&P Oper. EPS 2011E	10.8	Dividend Rate/Share	$0.40	S&P Credit Rating	BB+
$10K Invested 5 Yrs Ago	$12,856	Common Shares Outstg. (M)	618.9	Institutional Ownership (%)	66		

Price Performance

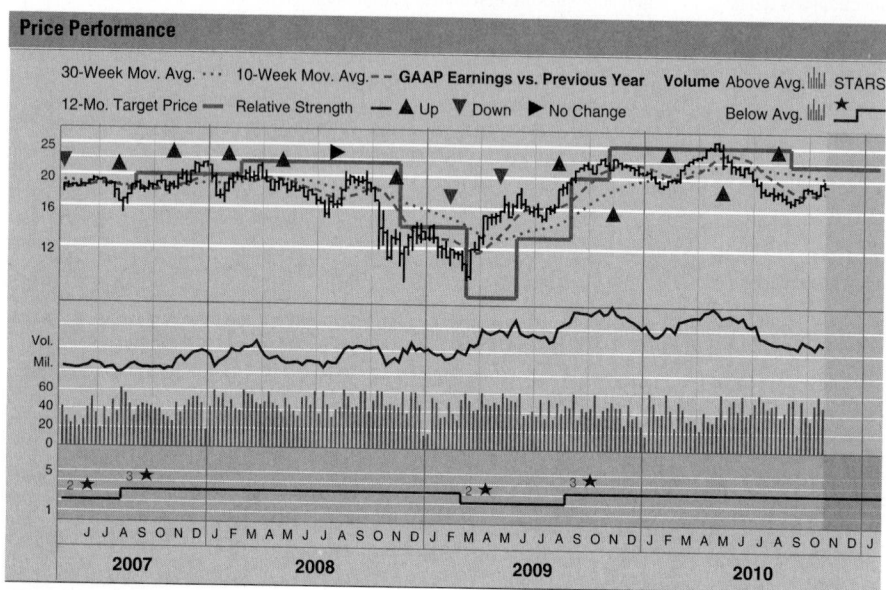

30-Week Mov. Avg. · · · 10-Week Mov. Avg. – – GAAP Earnings vs. Previous Year Volume Above Avg. ‖‖ STARS
12-Mo. Target Price — Relative Strength — ▲ Up ▼ Down ▶ No Change Below Avg. ‖‖ ★

Options: ASE, CBOE, P, Ph

Analysis prepared by **Marie Driscoll, CFA** on August 30, 2010, when the stock traded at **$ 17.03.**

Highlights

➤ We are encouraged by Old Navy's turnaround, but we expect increased competition for Banana Republic and continued lackluster top-line results at Gap NA and Gap International to mitigate consolidated gains in FY 11 (Jan.)

➤ We look for flat sales in FY 11 as a flat comp and a 3% contraction in store square footage, primarily at the Gap brand are offset by e-commerce gains, new business initiatives and international expansion. For FY 12 we look for 5% sales growth benefiting from e-commerce, the new brands Athleta and Piperlime, and international platforms.

➤ We see 40 bps gross margin expansion in FY 11 to 40.7%, reflecting April quarter gains. With a flat July quarter gross margin and promotional pricing pressure expected in the second half, we do not expect further gains on this line item until October FY 12, when we see another 10 bps. We see a 40 bps decline in the SG&A expense ratio in FY 11 and 10 bps in FY 12 despite increased marketing, resulting in a projected 13.5% and 13.8% EBIT margin for FY 11 and FY 12 respectively.

Investment Rationale/Risk

➤ Comp momentum slowed to +1% in the July quarter from April quarter's +4% as Gap NA merchandise misses and weakening apparel spending drove a -3% comp; the comp was +3% at both Old Navy and Banana Republic. GPS is pursuing a number of aggressive growth initiatives in FY 11 that we see providing profitable long term growth. Most promising, in our view, is international expansion. Its brands should be available in 80 countries by yearend either via online or franchise operations.

➤ Risks to our recommendation and target price include significantly worse than expected same-store sales trends, a substantially slower than expected global economic recovery, and a resulting further slowdown in consumer spending on discretionary purchases.

➤ Our 12-month target price of $22 assumes that GPS will trade at about 11.5X our FY 12 EPS estimate, about a 10% discount to GPS's two-year average forward P/E and its specialty apparel retail peers. GPS had $1.4 billion of cash on its balance sheet in July, and the dividend was increased 18% to $0.40 annually in February.

Qualitative Risk Assessment

LOW	MEDIUM	HIGH

Our risk assessment reflects our view of GPS's strong cash flow and balance sheet, offset by weakness at the Gap brand.

Quantitative Evaluations

S&P Quality Ranking A

D	C	B-	B	B+	A-	A	A+

Relative Strength Rank MODERATE

47

LOWEST = 1   HIGHEST = 99

Revenue/Earnings Data

Revenue (Million $)

	1Q	2Q	3Q	4Q	Year
2011	3,329	3,317	--	--	--
2010	3,127	3,245	3,589	4,236	14,197
2009	3,384	3,499	3,561	4,082	14,526
2008	3,549	3,685	3,854	4,675	15,763
2007	3,441	3,716	3,856	4,930	15,943
2006	3,626	3,716	3,860	4,821	16,023

Earnings Per Share ($)

	1Q	2Q	3Q	4Q	Year
2011	0.45	0.36	E0.46	E0.52	E1.78
2010	0.31	0.33	0.44	0.51	1.58
2009	0.34	0.32	0.35	0.34	1.34
2008	0.25	0.32	0.30	0.35	1.09
2007	0.28	0.15	0.23	0.27	0.93
2006	0.31	0.30	0.24	0.39	1.24

Fiscal year ended Jan. 31. Next earnings report expected: NA. EPS Estimates based on S&P Operating Earnings; historical GAAP earnings are as reported.

Dividend Data (Dates: mm/dd Payment Date: mm/dd/yy)

Amount ($)	Date Decl.	Ex-Div. Date	Stk. of Record	Payment Date
0.085	11/18	01/04	01/06	01/27/10
0.100	02/25	04/05	04/07	04/28/10
0.100	05/19	07/02	07/07	07/28/10
0.100	09/28	10/08	10/13	10/27/10

Dividends have been paid since 1976. Source: Company reports.

Please read the Required Disclosures and Analyst Certification on the last page of this report.

The McGraw-Hill Companies

Gap Inc. (The)

STANDARD & POOR'S

Business Summary August 30, 2010

CORPORATE OVERVIEW. Gap, Inc. is a specialty retailer that operates stores selling casual apparel, accessories, and personal care products for men, women and children. As of January 30, 2010, it operated 3,095 stores: 1,152 Gap North America; 576 Banana Republic North America; 1,039 Old Navy North America; and 328 international locations, with 38.8 million sq. ft. of total retail space.

MARKET PROFILE. GPS participates in the men's, women's and children's apparel market, which generated approximately $189 billion at U.S. retail in 2009 (a 5.2% decline from 2008), according to ND Fashionworld consumer estimated data. The apparel market is fragmented, with national brands marketed by 20 companies accounting for about 30% of total apparel sales, and the remaining 70% comprised of smaller and/or private label "store" brands. The market is mature, in our view, with demand largely mirroring population growth, and fashion trends accounting for a modicum of incremental volume. Deflationary pricing pressure is a function of channel competition and pro-

duction steadily moving offshore to low-cost producers in India, Asia and China, in our view. S&P forecasts a 2% increase in 2010 apparel sales.

COMPETITIVE LANDSCAPE. By channel, specialty stores account for the largest share of apparel sales, at 31% in 2009, according to NPD. Mass merchants (e.g., Wal-mart and Target) came in second, at 22%, and department stores came in third, at 14%, down from 19% in 2003. National chains (e.g., Sears and JC Penney) captured 13% of 2009 apparel sales, and off-price retailers (e.g., TJX and Ross Stores) were at 8%. Factory outlets, direct and e-mail pure plays and other captured the remaining 12%. GPS is the largest U.S. specialty retailer, with an estimated 20% of the channel's volume.

Company Financials Fiscal Year Ended Jan. 31

Per Share Data ($)	2010	2009	2008	2007	2006	2005	2004	2003	2002	2001
Tangible Book Value	6.96	6.04	11.50	9.58	6.33	5.73	5.33	4.12	3.48	3.43
Cash Flow	2.51	2.25	1.89	1.57	1.93	1.79	1.71	1.43	0.93	1.67
Earnings	1.58	1.34	1.09	0.93	1.24	1.21	1.09	0.54	-0.01	1.00
S&P Core Earnings	1.58	1.34	1.09	0.93	1.15	1.13	1.03	0.50	-0.10	0.86
Dividends	0.34	0.34	0.32	0.20	0.09	0.09	0.09	0.09	0.09	0.09
Payout Ratio	22%	22%	29%	22%	7%	7%	8%	17%	NM	9%
Calendar Year	2009	2008	2007	2006	2005	2004	2003	2002	2001	2000
Prices:High	23.36	21.89	22.02	21.39	22.70	25.72	23.47	17.14	34.98	53.75
Prices:Low	9.56	9.41	15.20	15.91	15.90	18.12	12.01	8.35	11.12	18.50
P/E Ratio:High	15	16	20	23	18	21	22	32	NM	54
P/E Ratio:Low	6	7	14	17	13	15	11	15	NM	18

Income Statement Analysis (Million $)										
Revenue	14,197	14,526	15,763	15,943	16,023	16,267	15,854	14,455	13,848	13,674
Operating Income	2,484	2,199	1,984	1,701	2,370	2,705	2,543	1,794	1,148	2,035
Depreciation	573	651	635	530	625	620	664	781	810	590
Interest Expense	6.00	9.00	36.0	49.0	45.0	167	234	249	109	74.9
Pretax Income	1,816	1,584	1,406	1,264	1,793	1,872	1,683	801	242	1,382
Effective Tax Rate	39.3%	39.0%	38.3%	38.5%	37.9%	38.6%	38.8%	40.4%	NM	36.5%
Net Income	1,102	967	867	778	1,113	1,150	1,030	477	-7.76	877
S&P Core Earnings	1,102	967	867	776	1,033	1,073	978	439	-89.1	760

Balance Sheet & Other Financial Data (Million $)										
Cash	2,573	1,715	1,939	2,644	2,987	7,139	2,261	3,389	1,036	409
Current Assets	4,664	4,005	4,086	5,029	5,239	6,304	6,689	5,740	3,045	2,648
Total Assets	7,985	7,564	7,838	8,544	8,821	10,048	10,343	9,902	7,591	7,013
Current Liabilities	2,131	2,158	2,433	2,272	1,942	2,242	2,492	2,727	2,056	2,799
Long Term Debt	NA	Nil	50.0	188	513	1,886	2,487	2,896	1,961	780
Common Equity	4,891	4,387	4,274	5,174	5,425	4,936	4,783	3,658	3,010	2,928
Total Capital	4,891	4,437	4,324	5,362	5,938	6,822	7,270	6,554	4,971	3,708
Capital Expenditures	334	431	682	572	600	442	272	303	940	1,859
Cash Flow	1,757	1,618	1,502	1,308	1,738	1,770	1,694	1,258	803	1,468
Current Ratio	2.2	1.9	1.7	2.2	2.7	2.8	2.7	2.1	1.5	0.9
% Long Term Debt of Capitalization	Nil	Nil	1.2	3.5	8.6	27.6	34.2	44.2	39.5	21.0
% Net Income of Revenue	7.8	6.7	5.5	4.9	6.9	7.1	6.5	3.3	NM	6.4
% Return on Assets	14.2	12.6	10.6	9.0	11.8	11.1	10.2	5.4	NM	14.4
% Return on Equity	23.8	22.3	18.4	14.7	21.5	24.0	24.4	14.3	NM	34.0

Data as orig reptd.; bef. results of disc opers/spec. items. Per share data adj. for stk. divs.; EPS diluted. E-Estimated. NA-Not Available. NM-Not Meaningful. NR-Not Ranked. UR-Under Review.

Office: 2 Folsom St, San Francisco, CA 94105-1205.
Telephone: 650-952-4400 .
Email: investor_relations@gap.com
Website: http://www.gapinc.com

Chrmn & CEO: G.K. Murphy
COO: A. Peck
EVP, CFO & Chief Acctg Officer: S.L. Simmons
EVP & CIO: J.T. Keiser

SVP & Secy: M. Banks
Investor Contact: E. Price (415-427-2360)
Board Members: A. D. Bellamy, D. De Sole, R. J. Fisher, W. S. Fisher, B. L. Martin, J. P. Montoya, G. K. Murphy, M. A. Shattuck, III, K. Tsang, K. C. Youngblood

Founded: 1969
Domicile: Delaware
Employees: 135,000

The McGraw-Hill Companies

General Dynamics Corp

STANDARD &POOR'S

S&P Recommendation HOLD ★★★☆☆	Price $64.50 (as of Oct 22, 2010)	12-Mo. Target Price $70.00	Investment Style Large-Cap Growth

GICS Sector Industrials
Sub-Industry Aerospace & Defense

Summary General Dynamics is the world's fifth largest military contractor and also one of the world's biggest makers of corporate jets.

Key Stock Statistics (Source S&P, Vickers, company reports)

52-Wk Range	$79.00– 55.46	S&P Oper. EPS 2010**E**	6.73	Market Capitalization(B)	$24.534	Beta	1.25
Trailing 12-Month EPS	$6.25	S&P Oper. EPS 2011**E**	7.00	Yield (%)	2.60	S&P 3-Yr. Proj. EPS CAGR(%)	6
Trailing 12-Month P/E	10.3	P/E on S&P Oper. EPS 2010**E**	9.6	Dividend Rate/Share	$1.68	S&P Credit Rating	A
$10K Invested 5 Yrs Ago	$12,193	Common Shares Outstg. (M)	380.4	Institutional Ownership (%)	79		

Price Performance

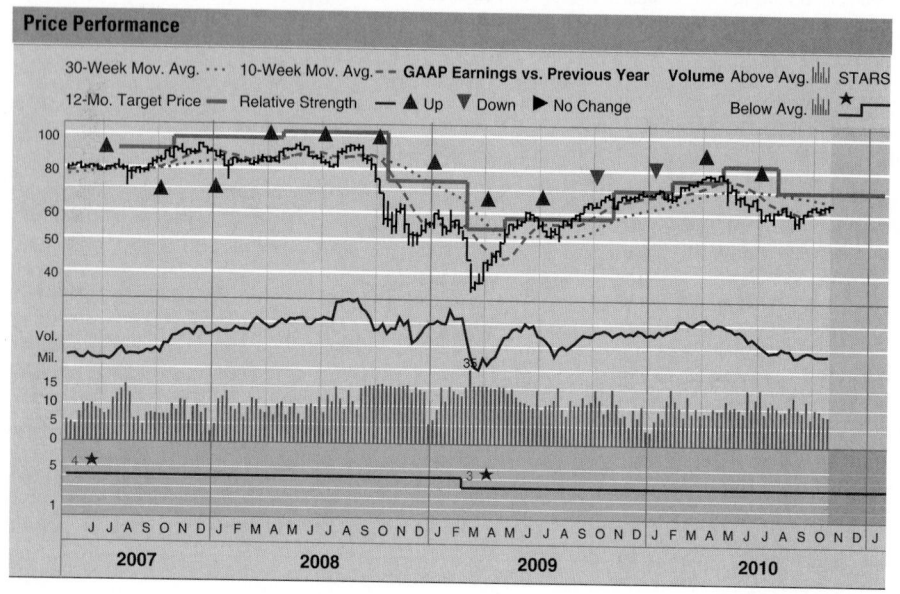

30-Week Mov. Avg. · · · · 10-Week Mov. Avg. - - **GAAP Earnings vs. Previous Year** Volume Above Avg. ▏▏▎ STARS
12-Mo. Target Price — Relative Strength — ▲ Up ▼ Down ▶ No Change Below Avg. ▏▏▎

Options: ASE, CBOE, Ph

Analysis prepared by **Richard Tortoriello** on August 10, 2010, when the stock traded at **$ 63.27**.

Highlights

▶ We project a 5% revenue increase in 2010, with strong growth in Information Systems & Technology (9% projected) and Aerospace (7%), moderate growth in Marine (about 5% each), and a slight decline in Combat Systems. We see growth in IS&T driven by cyber security initiatives; intelligence, surveillance & reconnaissance (ISR); and other IT initiatives. We see Aerospace benefiting from an increase in service demand for business jets. We see Marine growth driven by the Virginia Class submarine, with the Pentagon increasing production from one to two submarines a year in 2011. Finally, we see slightly lower MRAP and Stryker demand in Combat Systems.

▶ We see operating margins of 11.9% in 2010, up from 11.5% in 2009, on increased Aerospace margins due to increased volume and a mix shift toward services. GD has the highest margins of the defense contractors under our coverage, partly due to Aerospace, but also due to good execution, in our view.

▶ We project EPS of $6.73 in 2010 and $7.00 in 2011. GD generated $6.37 in free cash flow per share in 2009, and we look for free cash flow above net income in 2010.

Investment Rationale/Risk

▶ Although we see modest improvement in Aerospace in 2010, we continue to see results driven increasingly by GD's defense businesses. We see GD benefiting from growth in Marine, due to funding for new Virginia Class submarines and DDG 1000 destroyers, and moderate long-term growth in Combat Systems and IS&T, but we view the longer-term outlook for U.S. defense budget growth as cloudy, on ballooning overall budget deficits and shifting military priorities. We see GD valuations as below average, on a historical basis.

▶ Risks to our recommendation and target price include the potential for cuts in military budgets and failure of GD to perform well on existing contracts or to win new contracts, as well as greater-than-expected deterioration in GD's business jet backlog.

▶ Our 12-month target price of $70 is based on an enterprise value to estimated 2011 EBITDA multiple of 6.5X, below GD's 20-year historical average of 8X. Given our view of U.S. defense budget pressure, we view a below average multiple as appropriate for the shares.

Qualitative Risk Assessment

LOW	MEDIUM	HIGH

Our risk assessment for GD is based on the company's long-term record of consistent earnings and dividend growth, as reflected in its S&P Quality Ranking of A+. In addition, we note the company's conservative capitalization, with a debt-to-total capital ratio of 20% as of June 2010.

Quantitative Evaluations

S&P Quality Ranking A+

D	C	B-	B	B+	A-	A	A+

Relative Strength Rank MODERATE

51

LOWEST = 1   HIGHEST = 99

Revenue/Earnings Data

Revenue (Million $)

	1Q	2Q	3Q	4Q	Year
2010	7,750	8,104	--	--	--
2009	8,264	8,100	7,719	7,898	31,981
2008	7,005	7,303	7,140	7,852	29,300
2007	6,300	6,591	6,834	7,515	27,240
2006	5,546	5,934	6,069	6,514	24,063
2005	4,819	5,214	5,380	5,831	21,244

Earnings Per Share ($)

	1Q	2Q	3Q	4Q	Year
2010	1.54	1.68	E1.71	E1.81	E6.73
2009	1.53	1.61	1.54	1.58	6.20
2008	1.42	1.60	1.59	1.62	6.22
2007	1.07	1.27	1.34	1.42	5.10
2006	0.95	1.03	1.08	1.13	4.20
2005	0.85	0.85	0.92	1.00	3.63

Fiscal year ended Dec. 31. Next earnings report expected: Late October. EPS Estimates based on S&P Operating Earnings; historical GAAP earnings are as reported.

Dividend Data (Dates: mm/dd Payment Date: mm/dd/yy)

Amount ($)	Date Decl.	Ex-Div. Date	Stk. of Record	Payment Date
0.380	12/02	01/13	01/15	02/05/10
0.420	03/03	04/07	04/09	05/07/10
0.420	06/02	06/30	07/02	08/06/10
0.420	08/04	10/06	10/08	11/12/10

Dividends have been paid since 1979. Source: Company reports.

Please read the Required Disclosures and Analyst Certification on the last page of this report.

The McGraw·Hill Companies

General Dynamics Corp

STANDARD &POOR'S

Business Summary August 10, 2010

CORPORATE OVERVIEW. General Dynamics is the world's sixth largest defense contractor and the second largest maker of corporate jets by revenues. The company conducts business through four segments.

Information Systems & Technology (IS&T; 34% of sales and 31% of operating profits in 2009) primarily makes sophisticated electronics for land-, sea- and air-based weapons systems. Customers also include federal civilian agencies and commercial customers. The segment was created in 1998, and has grown through numerous acquisitions and internal development. The group's three principal markets are tactical and strategic mission systems (primarily secure communications systems), information technology and mission services, and intelligence mission systems, which provides specialized intelligence, surveillance and reconnaissance equipment and services, as well as cybersecurity offerings. In 2009, 71% of revenues were from the U.S. government, 9% from international defense, and the remainder from commercial customers.

Combat Systems (30% of sales and 33% of operating profit) makes, repairs and supports wheeled and tracked armored vehicles and munitions. Product lines include wheeled armored combat and tactical vehicles; main battle tanks and tracked infantry vehicles; guns and ammunition-handling systems;

ammunition and ordnance; chemical, biological and explosion detection systems; and drive train components and spare parts. Reflecting the U.S. Army's desire to transform itself into a highly agile fighting force, demand is expected to slow for tanks, but to accelerate for its various wheeled combat vehicles. Major current programs include the M1 Abrams tank (upgrade programs) and the Stryker wheeled combat vehicle.

Aerospace (16% and 19%) makes the well known Gulfstream business jet. Based on revenues, Gulfstream is the world's second-largest corporate jet maker, slightly behind Canada-based Bombardier. Textron's Cessna division, France's Dassault Aviation and Hawker Beechcraft Corp. are also significant competitors. Gulfstream sells business jets primarily to the high end of the market. In 2008, Gulfstream introduced the ultra-large, ultra-long-range G650 and the super-mid-size G250, which GD says offers the largest cabin, longest range and fastest speed in its class. The G250 is scheduled for service entry in 2011 and the G650 in 2012. Both aircraft met first flight milestones in 2009.

Company Financials Fiscal Year Ended Dec. 31

Per Share Data ($)	2009	2008	2007	2006	2005	2004	2003	2002	2001	2000
Tangible Book Value	NM	NM	0.46	0.25	1.40	NM	NM	2.81	1.92	3.22
Cash Flow	7.65	6.97	5.78	5.16	4.48	3.57	3.20	3.14	2.99	2.80
Earnings	6.20	6.22	5.10	4.20	3.63	2.99	2.50	2.59	2.33	2.24
S&P Core Earnings	6.08	5.16	4.90	4.08	3.34	2.81	2.34	1.62	1.57	NA
Dividends	1.49	1.34	1.10	0.66	0.78	0.70	0.63	0.59	0.55	0.51
Payout Ratio	24%	22%	22%	16%	22%	23%	25%	23%	24%	23%
Prices:High	70.84	95.13	94.55	77.98	61.14	54.99	45.40	55.59	48.00	39.50
Prices:Low	35.28	47.81	70.61	56.68	48.80	42.48	25.00	36.63	30.25	18.13
P/E Ratio:High	11	15	19	19	17	18	18	21	21	18
P/E Ratio:Low	6	8	14	13	13	14	10	14	13	8

Income Statement Analysis (Million $)										
Revenue	31,981	29,300	27,240	24,063	21,244	19,178	16,617	13,829	12,163	10,356
Operating Income	4,237	3,954	3,391	3,009	2,539	2,173	1,744	1,795	1,756	1,555
Depreciation	562	301	278	384	342	232	277	213	271	226
Interest Expense	171	133	131	101	154	157	98.0	45.0	56.0	60.0
Pretax Income	3,513	3,604	3,047	2,527	2,100	1,785	1,372	1,584	1,424	1,262
Effective Tax Rate	31.5%	31.2%	31.7%	32.3%	30.1%	32.6%	27.3%	33.6%	33.8%	28.6%
Net Income	2,407	2,478	2,080	1,710	1,468	1,203	997	1,051	943	901
S&P Core Earnings	2,362	2,054	1,999	1,663	1,354	1,130	931	658	636	NA

Balance Sheet & Other Financial Data (Million $)										
Cash	2,263	1,621	3,155	1,604	2,331	976	860	328	442	177
Current Assets	13,249	11,950	12,298	9,880	9,173	7,287	6,394	5,098	4,893	3,551
Total Assets	31,077	28,373	25,733	22,376	19,591	17,544	16,183	11,731	11,069	7,987
Current Liabilities	10,371	10,360	9,164	7,824	6,907	5,374	5,616	4,582	4,579	2,901
Long Term Debt	3,159	3,113	2,118	2,774	2,781	3,291	3,296	718	724	162
Common Equity	12,423	10,053	11,768	9,827	8,145	7,189	5,921	5,199	4,528	3,820
Total Capital	16,287	13,265	13,886	12,601	10,926	10,480	9,217	5,917	5,252	3,982
Capital Expenditures	385	490	474	334	279	266	224	264	356	288
Cash Flow	2,969	2,779	2,358	2,094	1,810	1,435	1,274	1,264	1,214	1,127
Current Ratio	1.3	1.2	1.3	1.3	1.3	1.4	1.1	1.1	1.1	1.2
% Long Term Debt of Capitalization	19.4	23.5	15.3	22.0	25.5	31.4	35.8	12.1	13.8	4.1
% Net Income of Revenue	7.5	8.5	7.6	7.1	6.9	6.3	6.0	7.6	7.8	8.7
% Return on Assets	8.1	9.2	8.6	8.1	7.9	7.1	7.1	9.2	9.9	11.4
% Return on Equity	21.4	22.7	19.3	19.0	19.1	18.4	17.9	21.6	22.6	25.8

Data as orig reptd.; bef. results of disc opers/spec. items. Per share data adj. for stk. divs.; EPS diluted. E-Estimated. NA-Not Available. NM-Not Meaningful. NR-Not Ranked. UR-Under Review.

Office: 2941 Fairview Park Dr Ste 100, Falls Church, VA 22042-4513.
Telephone: 703-876-3000.
Website: http://www.generaldynamics.com
Chrmn, Pres & CEO: J.L. Johnson

SVP & CFO: L.H. Redd
SVP, Secy & General Counsel: G.S. Gallopoulos
Chief Admin Officer: W. Oliver
CTO: G.J. DeMuro

Investor Contact: A. Gilliland (703-876-3748)
Board Members: N. D. Chabraja, J. S. Crown, W. P. Fricks, J. L. Johnson, G. Joulwan, P. G. Kaminski, J. M. Keane, L. L. Lyles, W. A. Osborn, R. Walmsley

Founded: 1899
Domicile: Delaware
Employees: 91,700

The McGraw·Hill Companies

General Electric Co

STANDARD &POOR'S

S&P Recommendation BUY ★★★★☆	**Price** $16.06 (as of Oct 22, 2010)	**12-Mo. Target Price** $20.00	**Investment Style** Large-Cap Blend

GICS Sector Industrials
Sub-Industry Industrial Conglomerates

Summary This conglomerate sells products ranging from jet engines and gas turbines to consumer appliances, railroad locomotives and medical equipment. It also owns NBC Universal, and is a leading provider of consumer and commercial financing.

Key Stock Statistics (Source S&P, Vickers, company reports)

52-Wk Range	$19.70–13.75	S&P Oper. EPS 2010E	1.12	Market Capitalization(B)	$171.648	Beta	1.63
Trailing 12-Month EPS	$0.92	S&P Oper. EPS 2011E	1.25	Yield (%)	2.99	S&P 3-Yr. Proj. EPS CAGR(%)	10
Trailing 12-Month P/E	17.5	P/E on S&P Oper. EPS 2010E	14.3	Dividend Rate/Share	$0.48	S&P Credit Rating	AA+
$10K Invested 5 Yrs Ago	$5,754	Common Shares Outstg. (M)	10,691.2	Institutional Ownership (%)	50		

Price Performance

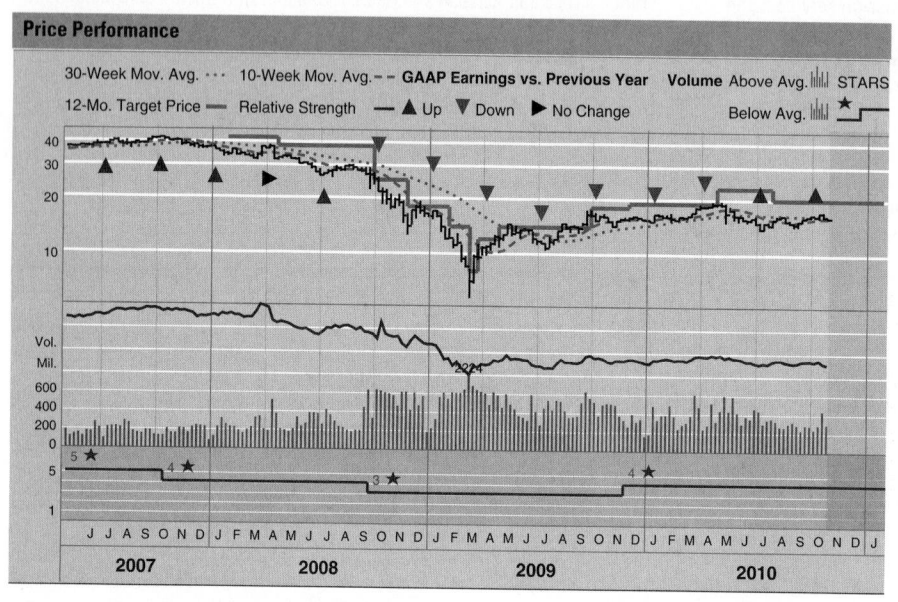

30-Week Mov. Avg. · · · 10-Week Mov. Avg. - - GAAP Earnings vs. Previous Year Volume Above Avg. STARS
12-Mo. Target Price — Relative Strength — ▲ Up ▼ Down ▶ No Change Below Avg. ★

Options: ASE, CBOE, P, Ph

Analysis prepared by **Richard Tortoriello** on October 15, 2010, when the stock traded at **$16.16**.

Highlights

➤ We estimate a 4% sales decline this year, after a 14% drop in 2009, due to the global recession and credit crisis. We see 2010 results reflecting a 5% decline at Capital Finance, as GE continues to reduce its exposure to this segment, a 7% decline at Energy Infrastructure and a 4% decline at Technology Infrastructure, on continued weakness in long order-cycle businesses, such as gas turbines, wind power, and locomotives. We project a 1% revenue increase at Home & Busines Solutions, on modest economic improvement and easy year-to-year comparisons, and an 8% rise at NBC Universal. We are modeling 3% revenue growth in 2011.

➤ We see significant segment operating margin improvement in 2010, to about 11.5%, from 9.8% in 2009, on strong improvements in Capital Finance, Energy, and Home and Business solutions. We project a further increase, to 12.5%, in 2011.

➤ We estimate EPS of $1.12 in 2010, rising to $1.25 in 2011. GE expects to generate $14 to $15 billion in industrial cash flow in 2010. It raised its dividend by 20% in July, to $0.44 annually, and restarted its share repurchase program.

Investment Rationale/Risk

➤ We see the following trends supporting our view of stock price appreciation over the next 12 months: order increases in GE's industrial businesses (equipment orders rose 17% in the second quarter and 9% in the third); an anticipated reduction in loan losses at Capital Finance, due to financial market improvement and restructuring by GE (loan loss metrics improved significantly in the third quarter); global demand for health care imaging products; and increasing commercial air traffic. Given this backdrop, we view current below-historical-average valuations for GE as attractive.

➤ Risks to our recommendation and target price include the potential that the economy fails to continue to recover from the previous recession, as well as greater-than-anticipated credit losses at Capital Finance.

➤ Our 12-month target price of $20 reflects an enterprise value to estimated 2010 EBITDA multiple of 7X. This level is slightly below a recent peer average of about 8X (which includes diversified industrial companies in our coverage universe, excluding GE).

Qualitative Risk Assessment

LOW	MEDIUM	HIGH

Our risk assessment reflects our view of GE's long-term record of earnings, cash flow and dividends, which we attribute to good management of a diversified portfolio of profitable businesses, offset by recent financial market turmoil, which has caused GE to access the capital markets.

Quantitative Evaluations

S&P Quality Ranking A-

D	C	B-	B	B+	A-	A	A+

Relative Strength Rank WEAK

29

LOWEST = 1   HIGHEST = 99

Revenue/Earnings Data

Revenue (Million $)

	1Q	2Q	3Q	4Q	Year
2010	36,605	37,444	35,888	--	--
2009	38,411	39,082	37,799	41,438	156,783
2008	42,243	46,891	47,234	46,213	182,515
2007	39,200	42,384	42,534	48,588	172,738
2006	37,370	39,243	40,286	44,621	163,391
2005	39,409	40,960	41,580	40,705	149,702

Earnings Per Share ($)

2010	0.21	0.30	0.29	E0.32	E1.12
2009	0.26	0.25	0.22	0.28	1.03
2008	0.44	0.54	0.45	0.36	1.78
2007	0.44	0.52	0.50	0.68	2.20
2006	0.40	0.48	0.48	0.64	1.99
2005	0.33	0.41	0.43	0.55	1.72

Fiscal year ended Dec. 31. Next earnings report expected: Late January. EPS Estimates based on S&P Operating Earnings; historical GAAP earnings are as reported.

Dividend Data (Dates: mm/dd Payment Date: mm/dd/yy)

Amount ($)	Date Decl.	Ex-Div. Date	Stk. of Record	Payment Date
0.100	12/15	12/23	12/28	01/25/10
0.100	02/12	02/25	03/01	04/26/10
0.100	06/11	06/17	06/21	07/26/10
0.120	07/23	09/16	09/20	10/25/10

Dividends have been paid since 1899. Source: Company reports.

Please read the Required Disclosures and Analyst Certification on the last page of this report.

The McGraw-Hill Companies

General Electric Co

STANDARD &POOR'S

Business Summary October 15, 2010

CORPORATE OVERVIEW. This multi-industry, heavy-equipment, media and financing giant does business through five segments: Energy Infrastructure, Technology Infrastructure, NBC Universal, Capital Finance, and Home & Business Solutions. Revenue by geographic region in 2009: U.S. 46%, Europe 24%, Pacific Basin 13%, Americas 8%, Middle East and Africa 6%, and Other 3%.

The Energy Infrastructure segment (26% of segment sales and 39% of segment operating profits in 2009) consists of GE's Energy and Oil & Gas businesses. Major products include gas turbines and generators, wind turbines, solar technology, integrated coal gasification systems, water treatment solutions for industrial and municipal water systems, and nuclear power plants, through joint ventures with Hitachi and Toshiba (the Energy business line); surface and subsea drilling and production systems, equipment for floating production platforms, compressors, turbines, turboexpanders, and pressure control equipment (Oil & Gas). GE provides extensive aftermarket services for its equipment.

Technology Infrastructure (25% of sales and 37% of operating profits) includes the Healthcare, Aviation, Enterprise Solutions and Transportation business lines. Healthcare makes and services a wide variety of medical imaging products, including X-ray, digital mammography, computed tomography, mag-

netic resonance and molecular imaging technologies. Aviation primarily makes and services jet engines for commercial and military aircraft. Enterprise Solutions offers integrated solutions using sensors for temperature, pressure, moisture, gas and flow rate, and non-destructive testing inspection equipment. In March 2010, GE sold its security and life safety solutions business to United Technologies. Transportation makes and services locomotives, motors and electrical drive systems for a variety of industries, and gearing technology for applications such as wind turbines.

NBC Universal (10%, 12%) principally Provides broadcast network television services within the U.S.; the production of live and recorded TV programs; the production and distribution of motion pictures; the operation of TV broadcasting stations; the ownership of several cable/satellite networks around the work; the operation of theme parks; and a variety of digital media activities. In December 2009, GE agreed to contribute NBCU to a joint venture with Comcast (see below).

Company Financials Fiscal Year Ended Dec. 31

Per Share Data ($)	2009	2008	2007	2006	2005	2004	2003	2002	2001	2000
Tangible Book Value	4.06	0.75	2.38	2.52	2.64	2.55	2.40	1.76	2.34	2.32
Cash Flow	1.55	2.92	3.21	2.90	2.53	2.39	2.24	2.11	2.11	2.04
Earnings	1.03	1.78	2.20	1.99	1.72	1.59	1.55	1.51	1.41	1.27
S&P Core Earnings	1.03	1.57	2.07	1.90	1.66	1.54	1.41	1.10	0.98	NA
Dividends	0.61	1.24	1.15	1.03	0.91	0.82	0.77	0.73	0.66	0.57
Payout Ratio	59%	70%	52%	52%	53%	52%	50%	48%	47%	45%
Prices:High	17.52	38.52	42.15	38.49	37.34	37.75	32.42	41.84	53.55	60.50
Prices:Low	5.73	12.58	33.90	32.06	32.67	28.88	21.30	21.40	28.50	41.65
P/E Ratio:High	17	22	19	19	22	24	21	28	38	48
P/E Ratio:Low	6	7	15	16	19	18	14	14	20	33

Income Statement Analysis (Million $)

	2009	2008	2007	2006	2005	2004	2003	2002	2001	2000
Revenue	156,783	182,515	172,738	163,391	149,702	152,363	134,187	131,698	125,913	129,853
Operating Income	17,022	57,897	69,594	53,972	46,840	40,262	36,792	35,431	38,200	38,329
Depreciation	5,557	11,492	10,278	9,158	8,538	8,385	6,956	5,998	7,089	7,736
Interest Expense	1,478	26,209	23,787	19,286	15,187	11,907	10,432	10,216	11,062	11,720
Pretax Income	10,344	19,782	27,514	25,528	23,115	21,034	20,194	19,217	20,049	18,873
Effective Tax Rate	NM	5.32%	15.0%	15.5%	16.7%	16.7%	21.4%	19.6%	27.8%	30.3%
Net Income	11,218	18,089	22,468	20,666	18,275	16,593	15,589	15,133	14,128	12,735
S&P Core Earnings	10,780	15,939	21,155	19,701	17,548	16,138	14,195	11,038	9,889	NA

Balance Sheet & Other Financial Data (Million $)

	2009	2008	2007	2006	2005	2004	2003	2002	2001	2000
Cash	124,200	12,300	17,578	14,275	9,011	150,864	133,388	125,772	110,099	99,534
Current Assets	445,634	463,602	451,859	391,095	383,745	358,286	294,775	271,784	239,691	204,324
Total Assets	781,000	797,800	795,337	697,239	673,342	750,330	647,483	575,244	495,023	437,006
Current Liabilities	167,284	236,074	236,228	215,266	200,471	206,280	176,530	181,827	198,904	156,112
Long Term Debt	510,200	330,067	319,015	260,804	212,281	213,161	170,004	140,632	79,806	82,132
Common Equity	117,300	104,700	115,559	112,314	109,354	110,284	79,180	63,706	54,824	50,492
Total Capital	633,300	448,263	454,722	394,867	346,019	354,242	267,611	222,328	148,975	146,250
Capital Expenditures	8,634	16,010	17,870	16,650	14,441	13,118	9,767	13,351	15,520	13,967
Cash Flow	16,475	29,506	32,746	29,824	26,813	24,978	22,545	21,131	21,217	20,471
Current Ratio	2.7	2.0	1.9	1.8	1.9	1.7	1.7	1.5	1.2	1.3
% Long Term Debt of Capitalization	80.6	73.6	70.2	66.0	61.3	60.2	63.5	63.3	53.6	56.2
% Net Income of Revenue	7.2	9.9	13.2	12.8	12.2	10.8	11.6	11.5	11.2	9.8
% Return on Assets	1.4	2.3	3.0	3.0	2.6	2.4	2.5	2.8	3.0	3.0
% Return on Equity	10.1	16.4	19.7	18.6	16.6	17.5	21.8	25.5	26.8	27.4

Data as orig reptd; bef. results of disc opers/spec. items. Per share data adj. for stk. divs.; EPS diluted. E-Estimated. NA-Not Available. NM-Not Meaningful. NR-Not Ranked. UR-Under Review.

Office: 3135 Easton Tpke, Fairfield, CT 06828-0001.
Telephone: 203-373-2211.
Website: http://www.ge.com
Chrmn & CEO: J.R. Immelt

SVP & Treas: K.A. Cassidy
SVP, Secy & General Counsel: B.B. Denniston, III
CFO: K.S. Sherin
Chief Acctg Officer & Cntlr: J.S. Miller

Investor Contact: D. Janki
Board Members: W. G. Beattie, J. I. Cash, Jr., W. M. Castell, A. M. Fudge, S. Hockfield, J. R. Immelt, A. Jung, A. G. Lafley, R. W. Lane, R. S. Larsen, R. B. Lazarus, J. J. Mulva, S. A. Nunn, R. S. Penske, R. J. Swieringa, J. S. Tisch, D. A. Warner, III

Founded: 1892
Domicile: New York
Employees: 304,000

The **McGraw·Hill** Companies

General Mills Inc.

STANDARD &POOR'S

S&P Recommendation STRONG BUY ★★★★★	**Price** $37.30 (as of Oct 22, 2010)	**12-Mo. Target Price** $41.00	**Investment Style** Large-Cap Blend

GICS Sector Consumer Staples
Sub-Industry Packaged Foods & Meats

Summary This company is a major producer of packaged consumer food products, including Big G cereals and Betty Crocker desserts/baking mixes.

Key Stock Statistics (Source S&P, Vickers, company reports)

52-Wk Range	$38.98– 32.24	S&P Oper. EPS 2011**E**	2.48	Market Capitalization(B)	$23.883	Beta	0.20
Trailing 12-Month EPS	$2.32	S&P Oper. EPS 2012**E**	2.65	Yield (%)	3.00	S&P 3-Yr. Proj. EPS CAGR(%)	8
Trailing 12-Month P/E	16.1	P/E on S&P Oper. EPS 2011**E**	15.0	Dividend Rate/Share	$1.12	S&P Credit Rating	BBB+
$10K Invested 5 Yrs Ago	$17,763	Common Shares Outstg. (M)	640.3	Institutional Ownership (%)	74		

Price Performance

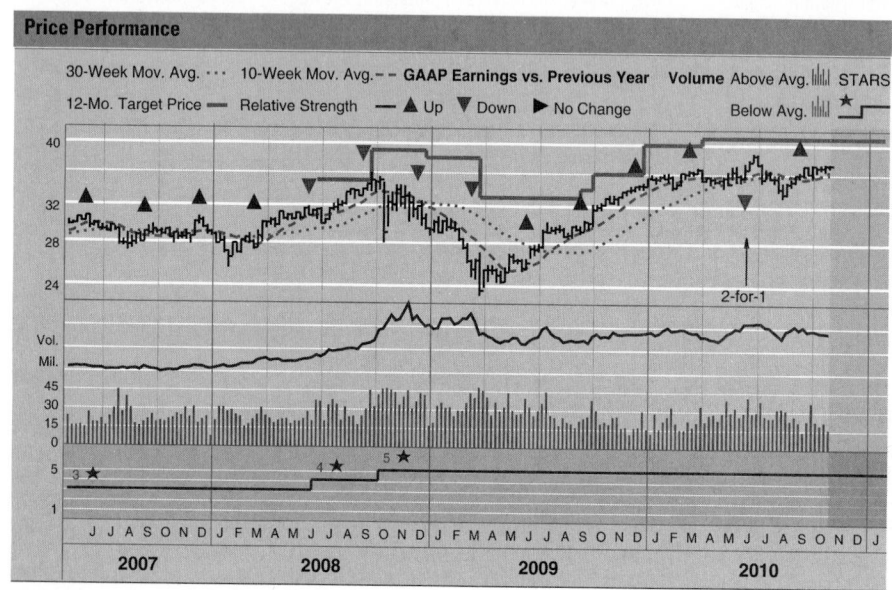

30-Week Mov. Avg. ···· 10-Week Mov. Avg. – – **GAAP Earnings vs. Previous Year** Volume Above Avg. STARS
12-Mo. Target Price — Relative Strength — ▲ Up ▼ Down ► No Change Below Avg. ★

2-for-1

2007 2008 2009 2010

Options: ASE, CBOE, P, Ph

Analysis prepared by **Tom Graves, CFA** on September 23, 2010, when the stock traded at **$ 36.36**.

Highlights

➤ In FY 11 (May), we look for net sales to increase modestly from $14.8 billion reported for FY 10, bolstered by marketing support and new products. We expect GIS to face profit margin pressure from higher retiree costs and increased input costs. However, we look for productivity gains and the absence of about $0.04 of costs related to debt repurchase to bolster FY 11 profit comparisons.

➤ Before some special items, but including about $0.03 of restructuring costs, we estimate FY 11 EPS of $2.48 (based on about 2% fewer shares outstanding), up from $2.30 in FY 10 (adjusted for a recent 2-for-1 stock split), which excludes a net negative impact of about $0.06 per share from some special items. Our FY 11 estimate excludes a favorable commodity mark-to-market impact of about $0.06 in FY 11's first quarter. For FY 12, we estimate EPS of $2.65. Also, in FY 11's first quarter, GIS repurchased 21 million common shares for a total of $788 million.

➤ Looking ahead, we expect GIS's demographic focus to include multi-cultural consumers, older adults, and the millennial generation. In developing international markets, we look for rising incomes and changing lifestyles to help GIS.

Investment Rationale/Risk

➤ We expect GIS's important U.S. Retail segment to benefit from consumers eating at home. Also, we generally like the company's brand strength, which we think will provide some protection from competitive pressure presented by less expensive private label products. We believe that GIS has opportunities to bolster long-term profit margins through a focus on areas such as manufacturing and spending efficiency, global sourcing, and sales mix. We look for GIS to continue to generate free cash flow, with a portion being used for dividends and stock repurchases.

➤ Risks to our recommendation and target price include competitive pressures, disappointing consumer acceptance of new products, higher-than-expected commodity cost inflation, and an inability to achieve sales and earnings growth forecasts.

➤ Our split-adjusted 12-month target price of $41 reflects about a 14% P/E premium to what we project on average for a group of other packaged food stocks, based on our calendar 2011 EPS estimates. Also, with a 14% dividend increase announced in June 2010, GIS shares recently had an indicated yield of 3.0%.

Qualitative Risk Assessment

LOW	MEDIUM	HIGH

Our risk assessment reflects the relatively stable nature of the company's end markets, strong cash flows, and an S&P Quality Ranking of A, which reflects the second highest ranking for historical earnings and dividend growth.

Quantitative Evaluations

S&P Quality Ranking A

D	C	B-	B	B+	A-	A	A+

Relative Strength Rank MODERATE

48

LOWEST = 1 HIGHEST = 99

Revenue/Earnings Data

Revenue (Million $)

	1Q	2Q	3Q	4Q	Year
2011	3,533	--	--	--	--
2010	3,519	4,078	3,629	3,570	14,797
2009	3,497	4,011	3,537	3,646	14,691
2008	3,072	3,703	3,406	3,471	13,652
2007	2,860	3,467	3,054	3,061	12,442
2006	2,662	3,273	2,860	2,845	11,640

Earnings Per Share ($)

	1Q	2Q	3Q	4Q	Year
2011	0.70	E0.77	E0.60	E0.48	E2.48
2010	0.63	0.83	0.49	0.31	2.24
2009	0.40	0.55	0.43	0.54	1.90
2008	0.40	0.57	0.62	0.26	1.85
2007	0.37	0.54	0.37	0.31	1.59
2006	0.32	0.49	0.34	0.31	1.45

Fiscal year ended May 31. Next earnings report expected: NA. EPS Estimates based on S&P Operating Earnings; historical GAAP earnings are as reported.

Dividend Data (Dates: mm/dd Payment Date: mm/dd/yy)

Amount ($)	Date Decl.	Ex-Div. Date	Stk. of Record	Payment Date
0.490	03/15	04/08	04/12	05/03/10
2-for-1	05/03	06/09	05/28	06/08/10
0.280	06/28	07/08	07/12	08/02/10
0.280	09/27	10/06	10/11	11/01/10

Dividends have been paid since 1898. Source: Company reports.

Please read the Required Disclosures and Analyst Certification on the last page of this report.

The McGraw-Hill Companies

General Mills Inc.

Business Summary September 23, 2010

CORPORATE OVERVIEW. General Mills (GIS) is one of the largest U.S. producers of ready-to-eat breakfast cereals, and a leading producer of other well-known packaged consumer foods. The U.S. Retail segment, which accounted for 70% of net sales in FY 10 (May), includes cereals, refrigerated yogurt, soup, dry dinners, vegetables, dough products, baking products, snacks, and organic products. The Bakeries and Foodservice segment (12%) includes products sold to distributors, convenience stores, restaurant operators and cafeterias. The International segment (18%) includes products manufactured in the U.S. for export, mainly to Caribbean and Latin American markets, as well as products manufactured for sale to GIS international joint ventures.

Cereal brands include Cheerios, Wheaties, Lucky Charms, Total, Golden Grahams, Chex, Kix, and Fiber One. Other consumer packaged food products include baking mixes (e.g., Betty Crocker, Bisquick); dry dinners; Progresso ready-to-serve soups, Green Giant canned and frozen vegetables; snacks; Pillsbury refrigerated and frozen dough products, frozen pizza; Yoplait refrigerated yogurt; Haagen-Dazs ice cream; and Cascadian Farm and Muir Glen

organic products. Some products may be marketed under licensing arrangements with other parties. GIS also has a grain merchandising operation that holds inventories carried at fair market value, and uses derivatives to hedge its net inventory position and minimize its market exposures.

During FY 10, Wal-Mart Stores, Inc., and affiliates accounted for 23% of GIS's consolidated net sales.

GIS joint ventures include a 50% equity interest in Cereal Partners Worldwide (CPW), a joint venture with Nestle S.A. that manufactures and markets cereal products outside the U.S. and Canada; and a 50% equity interest in Haagen-Dazs Japan, Inc., which manufactures, distributes and markets Haagen-Dazs ice cream products and frozen novelties.

Company Financials Fiscal Year Ended May 31

Per Share Data ($)	2010	2009	2008	2007	2006	2005	2004	2003	2002	2001
Tangible Book Value	NM	NM	NM	NM	NM	NM	NM	NM	NM	NM
Cash Flow	2.91	2.56	2.53	2.30	2.00	2.06	1.89	1.70	1.11	1.52
Earnings	2.24	1.90	1.85	1.59	1.45	1.54	1.38	1.22	0.68	1.14
S&P Core Earnings	2.09	1.44	1.65	1.52	1.36	1.09	1.22	0.87	0.28	0.90
Dividends	NA	0.86	0.78	0.72	0.67	0.62	0.55	0.55	0.55	0.55
Payout Ratio	NA	41%	42%	42%	46%	40%	40%	45%	81%	48%
Calendar Year	2009	2008	2007	2006	2005	2004	2003	2002	2001	2000
Prices:High	36.04	36.01	30.76	29.62	26.95	24.98	24.83	25.87	26.43	22.66
Prices:Low	23.19	25.50	27.09	23.53	22.34	21.51	20.72	18.69	18.63	14.69
P/E Ratio:High	16	19	17	19	19	16	18	21	39	20
P/E Ratio:Low	10	14	15	15	15	14	15	15	28	13

Income Statement Analysis (Million $)										
Revenue	14,797	14,691	13,652	12,442	11,640	11,244	11,070	10,506	7,949	7,078
Operating Income	3,095	2,727	2,687	2,515	2,420	2,435	2,442	2,290	1,569	1,392
Depreciation	457	454	459	418	424	443	399	365	296	223
Interest Expense	402	417	422	427	427	488	537	589	445	223
Pretax Income	2,306	2,025	1,917	1,704	1,631	1,904	1,583	1,377	700	1,015
Effective Tax Rate	NA	35.6%	32.5%	32.9%	33.2%	34.9%	33.4%	33.4%	34.1%	34.5%
Net Income	1,531	1,304	1,295	1,144	1,090	1,240	1,055	917	461	665
S&P Core Earnings	1,429	988	1,142	1,089	1,024	863	931	652	189	512

Balance Sheet & Other Financial Data (Million $)										
Cash	673	750	674	417	647	573	751	703	975	64.1
Current Assets	3,480	3,535	3,620	3,054	3,176	3,055	3,215	3,179	3,437	1,408
Total Assets	17,679	17,875	19,042	18,184	18,207	18,066	18,448	18,227	16,540	5,091
Current Liabilities	3,769	3,606	4,856	5,845	6,138	4,184	2,757	3,444	5,747	2,209
Long Term Debt	5,269	5,755	4,349	3,218	2,415	4,255	7,410	7,516	5,591	2,221
Common Equity	5,403	5,175	6,216	5,319	5,772	5,676	5,248	4,175	3,576	52.2
Total Capital	11,024	11,680	12,261	11,109	11,145	12,915	14,730	13,652	9,727	2,696
Capital Expenditures	650	563	522	460	360	414	628	711	506	308
Cash Flow	1,988	1,758	1,754	1,562	1,514	1,683	1,454	1,282	757	888
Current Ratio	0.9	1.0	0.8	0.5	0.5	0.7	1.2	0.9	0.6	0.6
% Long Term Debt of Capitalization	47.8	49.3	35.4	28.9	21.7	32.9	50.3	55.1	57.5	82.4
% Net Income of Revenue	10.3	8.9	9.5	9.2	9.4	11.0	9.5	8.7	5.8	9.4
% Return on Assets	8.6	7.1	7.0	6.3	6.0	6.8	5.8	5.3	4.3	13.8
% Return on Equity	28.9	22.9	22.5	20.6	18.7	22.7	22.4	23.7	25.4	NM

Data as orig reptd.; bef. results of disc opers/spec. items. Per share data adj. for stk. divs.; EPS diluted. E-Estimated. NA-Not Available. NM-Not Meaningful. NR-Not Ranked. UR-Under Review.

Office: 1 General Mills Blvd, Minneapolis, MN 55426-1348.
Telephone: 763-764-7600.
Website: http://www.generalmills.com
Chrmn & CEO: K.J. Powell

EVP & CFO: D.L. Mulligan
EVP, Secy & General Counsel: R.A. Palmore
CTO: P.C. Erickson
Chief Acctg Officer & Cntlr: R.O. Lund

Investor Contact: K. Wenker (800-245-5703)
Board Members: B. H. Anderson, R. K. Clark, P. Danos, W. T. Esrey, R. V. Gilmartin, J. R. Hope, H. G. Miller, H. M. Ochoa-Brillembourg, S. Odland, K. J. Powell, L. E. Quam, M. D. Rose, R. L. Ryan, D. A. Terrell

Founded: 1928
Domicile: Delaware
Employees: 33,000

Genuine Parts Co

STANDARD &POOR'S

S&P Recommendation	**STRONG BUY** ★★★★★	Price	12-Mo. Target Price	Investment Style
		$47.49 (as of Oct 22, 2010)	$53.00	Large-Cap Blend

GICS Sector Consumer Discretionary
Sub-Industry Distributors

Summary This company is a leading wholesale distributor of automotive replacement parts, industrial parts and supplies, and office products.

Key Stock Statistics (Source S&P, Vickers, company reports)

52-Wk Range	$48.43–34.91	S&P Oper. EPS 2010E	2.93	Market Capitalization(B)	$7.485	Beta	0.73
Trailing 12-Month EPS	$2.87	S&P Oper. EPS 2011E	3.26	Yield (%)	3.45	S&P 3-Yr. Proj. EPS CAGR(%)	12
Trailing 12-Month P/E	16.6	P/E on S&P Oper. EPS 2010E	16.2	Dividend Rate/Share	$1.64	S&P Credit Rating	NA
$10K Invested 5 Yrs Ago	$13,536	Common Shares Outstg. (M)	157.6	Institutional Ownership (%)	69		

Price Performance

- 30-Week Mov. Avg. · · ·
- 10-Week Mov. Avg. - -
- GAAP Earnings vs. Previous Year
- Volume Above Avg.
- STARS
- 12-Mo. Target Price —
- Relative Strength —
- ▲ Up ▼ Down ► No Change
- Volume Below Avg.
- ★

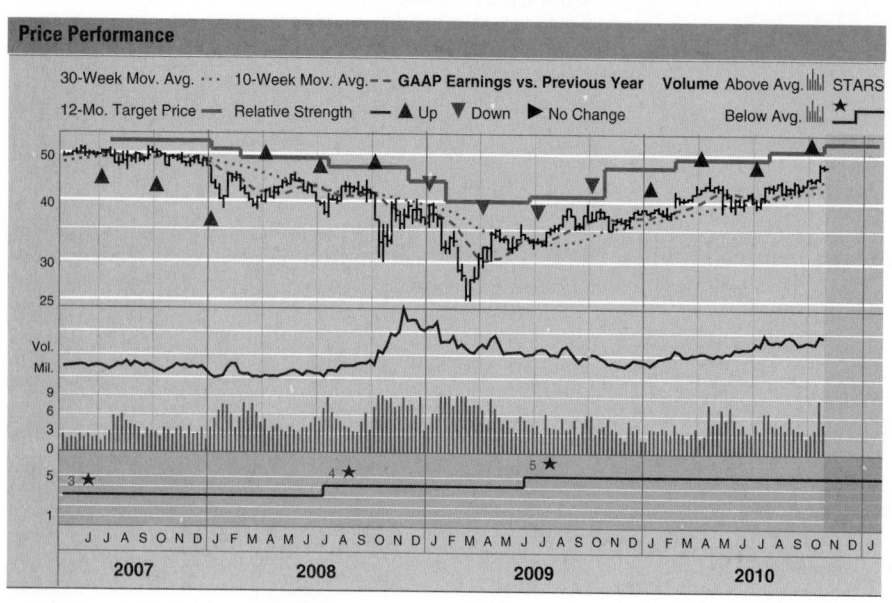

Options: ASE, P, Ph

Analysis prepared by **Efraim Levy, CFA** on October 18, 2010, when the stock traded at **$ 47.97.**

Highlights

▶ We forecast a sales increase of 10.6% for 2010, as we think most segments will enjoy sales growth in the second half of the year as the U.S. economy expands. Margins should benefit from higher volume and cost-cutting efforts, despite price pressures, but we do not see a repeat of fourth quarter 2009 LIFO (last-in-first-out) inventory accounting benefits. We see further sales and margin gains in 2011.

▶ We expect long-term prospects for GPC's auto parts segment to be enhanced by the rising number of and increasing complexity of vehicles. The median vehicle age in the U.S. is currently more than nine years. We believe GPC will benefit from an expanding market share, as long-term industry consolidation continues to drive out smaller participants. We also think GPC will use its distribution strength to leverage sales of acquired parts companies.

▶ We think the company's solid balance sheet, low debt and strong cash flow provide the ability and resources to help accelerate earnings growth over the long term. We see GPC using cash flow to repurchase shares, invest in the business, make modest-sized acquisitions, and increase the dividend.

Investment Rationale/Risk

▶ Based on our 2010 EPS estimate, the stock's recent P/E of about 16.4X is below the average for peers, as depressed peer earnings increased the group average P/E. In normal economic conditions, we think a premium for GPC is warranted by the company's greater earnings stability. We view GPC as financially strong. Earnings quality appears high to us, and an above-average dividend yield adds to GPC's total return potential.

▶ Risks to our recommendation and target price include weaker-than-expected demand for the company's products and a slower-than-anticipated improvement in operating margins.

▶ Our 12-month target price of $53 is based on a weighted blend of our relative valuation and discounted cash flow (DCF) metrics. On a relative basis, we apply a multiple of about 15.5X to our 2011 EPS estimate of $3.26, reflecting historical and peer comparisons, leading to a value of $50.50. Our DCF model, which assumes a weighted average cost of capital of 9.0%, a compound annual growth rate of 1.5% over the next 15 years, and a terminal growth rate of 3%, calculates an intrinsic value of about $56.

Qualitative Risk Assessment

LOW	MEDIUM	HIGH

Our risk assessment reflects GPC's long-term record of rising sales and earnings and what we view as strong corporate leadership and a healthy balance sheet.

Quantitative Evaluations

S&P Quality Ranking — A

D	C	B-	B	B+	A-	A	A+

Relative Strength Rank — STRONG

73

LOWEST = 1   HIGHEST = 99

Revenue/Earnings Data

Revenue (Million $)

	1Q	2Q	3Q	4Q	Year
2010	2,602	2,847	2,951	--	--
2009	2,445	2,535	2,607	2,471	10,058
2008	2,739	2,873	2,882	2,520	11,015
2007	2,649	2,770	2,798	2,627	10,843
2006	2,554	2,662	2,700	2,543	10,458
2005	2,342	2,476	2,556	2,410	9,783

Earnings Per Share ($)

	1Q	2Q	3Q	4Q	Year
2010	0.63	0.78	0.83	E0.68	E2.93
2009	0.56	0.65	0.67	0.62	2.50
2008	0.75	0.81	0.81	0.55	2.92
2007	0.71	0.76	0.76	0.75	2.98
2006	0.66	0.70	0.71	0.70	2.76
2005	0.61	0.63	0.63	0.63	2.50

Fiscal year ended Dec. 31. Next earnings report expected: Mid February. EPS Estimates based on S&P Operating Earnings; historical GAAP earnings are as reported.

Dividend Data (Dates: mm/dd Payment Date: mm/dd/yy)

Amount ($)	Date Decl.	Ex-Div. Date	Stk. of Record	Payment Date
0.400	11/16	12/02	12/04	01/04/10
0.410	02/15	03/03	03/05	04/01/10
0.410	04/19	06/09	06/11	07/01/10
0.410	08/16	09/08	09/10	10/01/10

Dividends have been paid since 1948. Source: Company reports.

Please read the Required Disclosures and Analyst Certification on the last page of this report.

The McGraw-Hill Companies

Genuine Parts Co

Business Summary October 18, 2010

CORPORATE OVERVIEW. Genuine Parts is the leading independent U.S. distributor of automotive replacement parts. It operates 58 NAPA warehouse distribution centers in the U.S., about 1,000 company-owned jobbing stores, three Rayloc auto parts rebuilding plants, four Balkamp distribution centers, two Altrom import parts distribution centers, and 16 heavy vehicle parts distribution centers and facilities. It also has operations in Canada and Mexico. The company has been expanding via a combination of internal growth and acquisitions.

The automotive parts segment (52% of 2009 revenues, 55% of profits) serves about 5,800 NAPA Auto Parts stores, including about 1,000 company-owned stores, selling to garages, service stations, car and truck dealers, fleet operators, leasing companies, bus and truck lines, etc.

The industrial parts segment (29%, 23%) distributes around three million industrial replacement parts and related supply items, including bearings, power transmission equipment replacement parts, including hydraulic and pneumatic products, material handling components, agricultural and irrigation equipment, and related items from locations in the U.S. and Canada.

Through S. P. Richards Co., the office products group (16%, 18%) distributes more than 40,000 office product items, including information processing supplies and office furniture, machines and supplies to office suppliers, from facilities in the U.S. and Canada.

The EIS electrical/electronics materials group (3%, 4%) was formed via the 1998 acquisition of EIS, Inc., for $200 million. EIS is a wholesale distributor of material and supplies to the electrical and electronic industries.

The U.S. accounted for almost 89% of sales in 2009. Canada contributed nearly 11%, and Mexico represented less than 1%.

Company Financials Fiscal Year Ended Dec. 31

Per Share Data ($)	2009	2008	2007	2006	2005	2004	2003	2002	2001	2000
Tangible Book Value	15.42	13.58	15.86	4.82	15.21	14.21	12.95	11.88	10.97	10.50
Cash Flow	3.07	3.46	3.49	3.18	2.87	2.61	2.42	2.50	2.21	2.72
Earnings	2.50	2.92	2.98	2.76	2.50	2.25	2.03	2.10	1.71	2.20
S&P Core Earnings	2.47	2.54	2.98	2.76	2.40	2.22	1.95	1.80	1.53	NA
Dividends	1.60	1.56	1.46	1.35	1.25	1.20	1.18	1.16	1.14	1.10
Payout Ratio	64%	53%	49%	49%	50%	53%	58%	55%	67%	50%
Prices:High	39.82	46.28	51.68	48.34	46.64	44.32	33.75	38.80	37.94	26.69
Prices:Low	24.93	29.92	46.00	40.00	40.75	32.03	27.20	27.10	23.91	18.25
P/E Ratio:High	16	16	17	18	19	20	17	18	22	12
P/E Ratio:Low	10	10	15	14	16	14	13	13	14	8

Income Statement Analysis (Million $)	2009	2008	2007	2006	2005	2004	2003	2002	2001	2000
Revenue	10,058	11,015	10,843	10,458	9,783	9,097	8,449	8,259	8,221	8,370
Operating Income	761	889	926	870	804	698	641	676	656	739
Depreciation	90.4	88.7	87.7	73.4	65.5	62.2	69.0	70.2	85.8	92.3
Interest Expense	27.9	31.7	31.3	31.6	29.6	Nil	Nil	Nil	Nil	Nil
Pretax Income	644	768	822	771	709	636	572	606	496	647
Effective Tax Rate	38.0%	38.1%	37.8%	38.3%	38.3%	37.8%	38.1%	39.3%	40.1%	40.4%
Net Income	400	475	506	475	437	396	354	368	297	385
S&P Core Earnings	395	414	506	475	420	388	339	316	265	NA

Balance Sheet & Other Financial Data (Million $)	2009	2008	2007	2006	2005	2004	2003	2002	2001	2000
Cash	337	67.8	232	136	189	135	15.4	20.0	85.8	27.7
Current Assets	4,033	3,871	4,053	3,835	3,807	3,633	3,418	3,336	3,146	3,019
Total Assets	5,005	4,786	4,774	4,497	4,772	4,455	4,116	4,020	4,207	4,142
Current Liabilities	1,408	1,287	1,548	1,199	1,249	1,133	1,017	1,070	919	988
Long Term Debt	500	500	250	500	500	500	625	675	836	771
Common Equity	2,621	2,324	2,717	2,550	2,694	2,544	2,312	2,130	2,345	2,261
Total Capital	3,129	2,893	3,033	3,111	3,408	3,212	3,100	2,950	3,287	3,154
Capital Expenditures	142	105	116	126	85.7	72.1	73.9	64.8	41.9	71.1
Cash Flow	490	564	594	549	503	458	423	438	383	478
Current Ratio	2.9	3.0	2.6	3.2	3.0	3.2	3.4	3.1	3.4	3.1
% Long Term Debt of Capitalization	16.0	17.3	8.2	16.1	14.7	15.6	20.2	22.9	25.4	24.4
% Net Income of Revenue	4.0	4.3	4.7	4.5	4.5	4.3	4.2	4.4	3.6	4.6
% Return on Assets	8.2	10.0	10.9	10.3	9.5	9.2	8.6	8.9	7.1	9.5
% Return on Equity	16.2	18.9	19.2	18.1	16.7	16.3	15.9	16.4	12.9	17.4

Data as orig reptd.; bef. results of disc opers/spec. items. Per share data adj. for stk. divs.; EPS diluted. E-Estimated. NA-Not Available. NM-Not Meaningful. NR-Not Ranked. UR-Under Review.

Office: 2999 Cir 75 Pkwy, Atlanta, GA 30339.
Telephone: 770-953-1700.
Website: http://www.genpt.com
Chrmn, Pres & CEO: T. Gallagher

Vice Chrmn, EVP, CFO & Chief Acctg Officer: J.W. Nix
COO: M.D. Orr
SVP & Treas: F.M. Howard
SVP & Secy: C.B. Yancey

Board Members: M. B. Bullock, J. E. Douville, T. Gallagher, G. C. Guynn, J. D. Johns, M. M. Johns, J. H. Lanier, R. C. Loudermilk, Jr., W. B. Needham, J. W. Nix, L. L. Prince, G. W. Rollins

Founded: 1928
Domicile: Georgia
Employees: 29,000

Genworth Financial Inc

STANDARD &POOR'S

S&P Recommendation	**BUY** ★★★★☆	Price $13.38 (as of Oct 22, 2010)	12-Mo. Target Price $17.00	Investment Style Large-Cap Blend

GICS Sector Financials
Sub-Industry Multi-line Insurance

Summary This insurance holding company serves lifestyle protection, retirement income, investment and mortgage insurance needs around the world.

Key Stock Statistics (Source S&P, Vickers, company reports)

52-Wk Range	$19.36–8.37	S&P Oper. EPS 2010**E**	1.09	Market Capitalization(B)	$6.547	Beta	3.34
Trailing 12-Month EPS	$0.58	S&P Oper. EPS 2011**E**	1.70	Yield (%)	Nil	S&P 3-Yr. Proj. EPS CAGR(%)	60
Trailing 12-Month P/E	23.1	P/E on S&P Oper. EPS 2010**E**	12.3	Dividend Rate/Share	Nil	S&P Credit Rating	BBB
$10K Invested 5 Yrs Ago	$4,554	Common Shares Outstg. (M)	489.3	Institutional Ownership (%)	88		

Price Performance

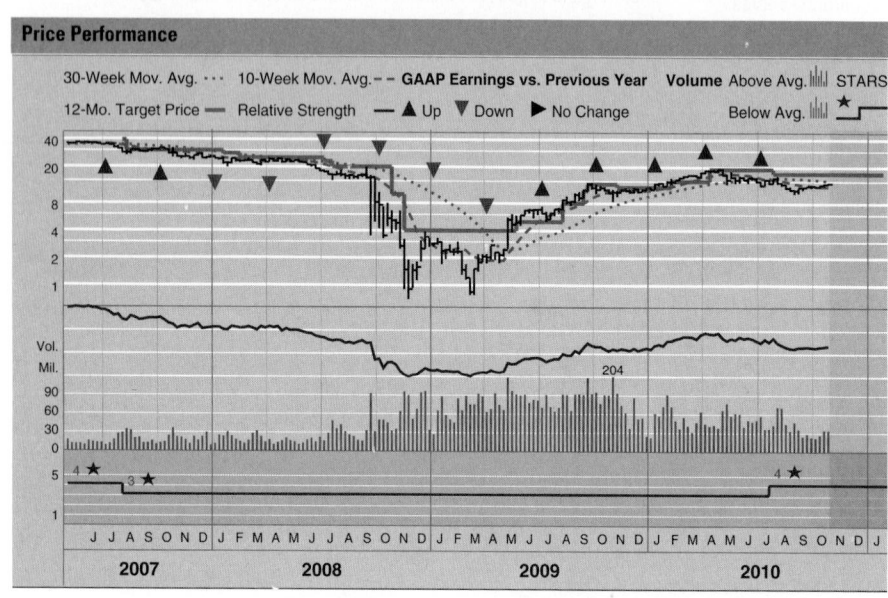

30-Week Mov. Avg. · · · 10-Week Mov. Avg. – – **GAAP Earnings vs. Previous Year**   Volume Above Avg. STARS
12-Mo. Target Price — Relative Strength — ▲ Up ▼ Down ► No Change   Below Avg.

Options: ASE, CBOE, P, Ph

Analysis prepared by **Bret Howlett** on October 22, 2010, when the stock traded at **$ 13.38**.

Highlights

➤ We forecast GNW's earnings will increase in the double-digits in 2011, on lower losses at U.S. Mortgage Insurance (MI), strong earnings growth in Intentional MI, and improved Wealth Management net flows. We expect GNW to deploy a large amount of excess liquidity in the debt markets, which will boost investment income. We believe Retirement and Protection earnings will benefit from higher account values due to the rise in the market. We believe life insurance earnings will increase considerably as easy comps, better pricing in the long-term care business, and lower deferred acquisition cost (DAC) amortization are only partially offset by higher funding costs and lower persistency in term life.

➤ We forecast U.S. MI will turn a profit in 2011 due to strong new business growth and lower delinquencies. We expect robust International earnings on the improving housing markets in Canada and Australia. We project modest growth in Lifestyle Protection earnings due to the recovery in the European economy.

➤ We forecast operating EPS of $1.09 for 2010, and EPS of $1.70 for 2011. Our estimates exclude realized investment gains or losses.

Investment Rationale/Risk

➤ Our buy recommendation reflects the steep discount that GNW currently trades at relative to peers and our belief that the stock's valuation does not reflect the company's improving fundamentals and strengthened financial position. We are growing increasingly confident that U.S. MI will return to profitability by mid 2011. We believe better results in Retirement and Protection and International MI will boost GNW's ROE to the high single-digits by next year. While we believe GNW's capital and liquidity positions are weak versus peers, its financial position has improved with better credit markets and capital raises. We think GNW's top-line trends will generally improve in 2011, but sales should be weak in interest sensitive product areas.

➤ Risks to our recommendation and target price include a continued low interest rate environment; increased investment portfolio risks; high concentrations of product line sales associated with certain third parties; and, a prolonged slowdown in the housing market.

➤ Our 12-month target price of $17 is about 0.7X our 2010 book value per share estimate -- below the stock's historical average multiple.

Qualitative Risk Assessment

LOW	MEDIUM	**HIGH**

Our risk assessment reflects the significant exposure of the mortgage insurance business to the volatile U.S. housing market. In addition, we think GNW is vulnerable to investment losses and has a weaker capital position than peers, but its financial health has recently improved. Our assessment also reflects our view of the lower return on equity prospects for GNW's life insurance subsidiaries.

Quantitative Evaluations

S&P Quality Ranking NR

D	C	B-	B	B+	A-	A	A+

Relative Strength Rank MODERATE

58

LOWEST = 1   HIGHEST = 99

Revenue/Earnings Data

Revenue (Million $)

	1Q	2Q	3Q	4Q	Year
2010	2,421	2,410	--	--	--
2009	1,734	2,483	2,391	2,461	9,069
2008	2,753	2,398	2,168	2,629	9,948
2007	2,710	2,765	2,875	2,775	11,125
2006	2,625	2,754	2,804	2,846	11,029
2005	2,611	2,610	2,628	2,655	10,504

Earnings Per Share ($)

	1Q	2Q	3Q	4Q	Year
2010	0.36	0.08	E0.29	E0.34	E1.09
2009	-1.08	-0.11	0.04	0.08	-0.88
2008	0.27	-0.25	-0.60	-0.74	-1.32
2007	0.69	0.70	0.76	0.41	2.58
2006	0.69	0.68	0.65	0.81	2.83
2005	0.65	0.60	0.64	0.64	2.52

Fiscal year ended Dec. 31. Next earnings report expected: Late October. EPS Estimates based on S&P Operating Earnings; historical GAAP earnings are as reported.

Dividend Data

The most recent payment was $0.10 a share in October 2008.

Genworth Financial Inc

Business Summary October 22, 2010

CORPORATE OVERVIEW. Genworth Financial, Inc., carved out from General Electric (GE) in May 2004, is a U.S. insurance company with an expanding international presence. As of February 2010, GNW had operations in 25 countries and offered products and services to over 15 million consumers. The company believed it was one of the largest providers of private mortgage insurance outside the U.S. based on new insurance written. In addition, GNW believed that in the U.S. it was the largest individual provider of long-term care insurance, and also one of the largest providers of mortgage insurance, based on new insurance written. GNW was a leading provider of fixed immediate annuities in 2008, but lost a considerable amount of market share in 2009, mainly given capital constraints at the company.

The company conducts its business through three major segments. The Retirement and Protection segment (62% of 2009 total revenues, 63% of 2008 total revenues) is comprised of wealth management (3.1%, 3.0%); retirement income (13%, 11%); life insurance (16%, 14%); and long-term care (30%, 35%). The International segment (28%, 28%) consists of the company's international

mortgage insurance business in Canada, Australia and Europe, in addition to proposals for other target countries for mortgage insurance. The segment also includes lifestyle protection, which provides payment protection insurance intended to help consumers meet their payment obligations in the event of illness, involuntary unemployment, disability or death. The third segment is U.S. Mortgage Insurance (9.1%, 8.0%), which facilitates home ownership by enabling borrowers to buy homes with low down payment mortgages. These products also help financial institutions manage their capital efficiently by reducing the capital required for low down payment mortgages. The company also has a Corporate and Other segment (0.2%, 0.2%), which includes unallocated corporate income and expenses, results of a small, non-core business, and most interest and other financing expenses.

Company Financials Fiscal Year Ended Dec. 31

Per Share Data ($)	2009	2008	2007	2006	2005	2004	2003	2002	2001	2000
Tangible Book Value	20.77	15.71	10.98	24.20	24.51	21.69	20.18	NA	NA	NA
Operating Earnings	NA	NA	NA	NA	NA	NA	NA	NA	NA	NA
Earnings	-0.88	-1.32	2.58	2.83	2.52	2.34	1.82	NA	NA	NA
S&P Core Earnings	0.44	1.45	3.04	2.92	2.52	2.29	1.96	NA	NA	NA
Dividends	Nil	0.40	0.37	0.32	0.27	0.07	NA	NA	NA	NA
Relative Payout	Nil	NM	14%	11%	11%	3%	NA	NA	NA	NA
Prices:High	13.68	25.57	37.16	36.47	35.25	27.84	NA	NA	NA	NA
Prices:Low	0.78	0.70	23.26	31.00	25.72	18.75	NA	NA	NA	NA
P/E Ratio:High	NM	NM	14	13	14	12	NA	NA	NA	NA
P/E Ratio:Low	NM	NM	9	11	10	8	NA	NA	NA	NA

Income Statement Analysis (Million $)

	2009	2008	2007	2006	2005	2004	2003	2002	2001	2000
Life Insurance in Force	673,719	677	670	NA	NA	NA	NA	NA	NA	NA
Premium Income:Life A & H	NA	NA	NA	NA	NA	NA	6,252	NA	NA	NA
Premium Income:Casualty/Property.	NA	NA	NA	NA	NA	NA	Nil	NA	NA	NA
Net Investment Income	3,033	3,730	4,135	3,837	3,536	3,648	2,928	NA	NA	NA
Total Revenue	9,069	9,948	11,125	11,029	10,504	11,057	9,775	11,229	11,101	10,226
Pretax Income	-792	-942	1,606	1,918	1,798	1,638	1,263	1,791	1,821	1,851
Net Operating Income	NA	NA	NA	NA	NA	NA	NA	NA	NA	NA
Net Income	-460	-572	1,154	1,324	1,221	1,145	892	1,380	1,231	1,275
S&P Core Earnings	198	624	1,359	1,369	1,221	1,126	956	NA	NA	NA

Balance Sheet & Other Financial Data (Million $)

	2009	2008	2007	2006	2005	2004	2003	2002	2001	2000
Cash & Equivalent	5,693	8,064	3,864	3,222	2,608	2,125	1,630	1,569	881	NA
Premiums Due	17,332	17,212	16,483	NA	NA	NA	NA	NA	NA	NA
Investment Assets:Bonds	49,752	42,871	55,154	55,448	53,791	52,424	50,081	NA	NA	NA
Investment Assets:Stocks	159	234	366	NA	367	374	387	NA	NA	NA
Investment Assets:Loans	8,902	10,096	10,604	9,985	8,908	7,275	6,794	NA	NA	NA
Investment Assets:Total	63,515	60,612	70,800	68,573	66,548	65,176	61,749	72,080	62,977	NA
Deferred Policy Costs	7,341	7,786	7,034	NA	5,586	5,020	4,421	NA	NA	NA
Total Assets	108,187	107,201	114,315	110,871	105,292	103,878	100,216	117,357	103,998	NA
Debt	8,014	8,849	7,558	3,921	3,336	3,042	3,016	NA	NA	NA
Common Equity	12,276	8,926	13,478	13,330	13,310	12,866	12,258	16,752	14,165	NA
Combined Loss-Expense Ratio	243.0	198.0	93.0	49.0	48.0	50.0	51.0	39.0	50.0	42.0
% Return on Revenue	NM	NM	10.4	12.0	11.6	10.4	9.1	12.3	11.1	12.5
% Return on Equity	NM	NM	8.6	2.2	9.3	8.0	6.0	8.9	NA	NA
% Investment Yield	5.2	6.0	5.9	5.7	5.4	5.2	5.4	5.9	12.4	NA

Data as orig reptd.; bef. results of disc opers/spec. items. Per share data adj. for stk. divs.; EPS diluted. E-Estimated. NA-Not Available. NM-Not Meaningful. NR-Not Ranked. UR-Under Review.

Office: 6620 West Broad Street, Richmond, VA 23230.
Telephone: 804-281-6000.
Email: investorinfo@genworth.com
Website: http://www.genworth.com

Chrmn, Pres & CEO: M.D. Fraizer
SVP & CFO: P.B. Kelleher
SVP, Secy & General Counsel: L. Roday
SVP & CIO: S.J. McKay

Chief Acctg Officer & Cntlr: A.R. Corbin
Investor Contact: C. English (804-662-2614)
Board Members: S. W. Alesio, W. H. Bolinder, M. D. Fraizer, N. J. Karch, J. R. Kerrey, R. J. Lavizzo-Mourey, C. B. Mead, T. E. Moloney, J. A. Parke, J. Riepe

Founded: 2003
Domicile: Delaware
Employees: 6,000

Genzyme Corp

STANDARD &POOR'S

S&P Recommendation	HOLD ★★★☆☆	Price $72.45 (as of Oct 22, 2010)	12-Mo. Target Price $81.00	Investment Style Large-Cap Growth

GICS Sector Health Care
Sub-Industry Biotechnology

Summary This biopharmaceutical concern, whose leading product is the Gaucher disease drug Cerezyme, has rejected a $69 a share takeover bid from Sanofi-Aventis.

Key Stock Statistics (Source S&P, Vickers, company reports)

52-Wk Range	$73.15– 45.39	S&P Oper. EPS 2010**E**	1.43	Market Capitalization(B)	$18.463
Trailing 12-Month EPS	$-0.30	S&P Oper. EPS 2011**E**	3.90	Yield (%)	Nil
Trailing 12-Month P/E	NM	P/E on S&P Oper. EPS 2010**E**	50.7	Dividend Rate/Share	Nil
$10K Invested 5 Yrs Ago	$10,310	Common Shares Outstg. (M)	254.8	Institutional Ownership (%)	99

Beta	0.35
S&P 3-Yr. Proj. EPS CAGR(%)	18
S&P Credit Rating	A-

Price Performance

30-Week Mov. Avg. · · ·   10-Week Mov. Avg.– –   **GAAP Earnings vs. Previous Year**   Volume Above Avg.▐▌▌ **STARS**
12-Mo. Target Price—   Relative Strength —   ▲ Up ▼ Down ▶ No Change   Below Avg.▐▌ ★

Options: ASE, CBOE, P, Ph

Analysis prepared by **Steven Silver** on October 22, 2010, when the stock traded at **$ 72.23**.

Highlights

➤ We expect 2010 revenues to decline 4%, to $4.3 billion, as GENZ has been slow in resuming normal shipment of Cerezyme and Fabrazyme until late in the year, following the temporary 2009 shutdown of GENZ's key manufacturing plant. We look for revenue growth of 20% in 2011, to $5.15 billion. After several prior delays, we are encouraged by the June 2010 FDA approval of large-scale produced Myozyme (called Lumizyme). We have a positive outlook for the potential successor to Cerezyme, eliglustat tartrate (GENZ-112638), in Phase III study.

➤ We expect 2010 and 2011 adjusted operating margins of 15% and 31%, respectively, versus 2009's 13%. We look for margins to recover as production and drug availability to meet full patient demand revert toward historical levels, and we see a new initiative to realign operating costs that included reductions in force boosting operational cash flows to fund capital investments and share repurchases.

➤ Our 2010 and 2011 adjusted EPS estimates of $1.43 and $3.90, respectively, include previously withheld amortization of intangible assets and other one-time items, upon the company's revision of its adjusted EPS figures.

Investment Rationale/Risk

➤ We continue to expect Sanofi-Aventis (SNY 35, Buy) to raise its rejected $69 a share bid to acquire GENZ. While we view GENZ's manufacturing issues that have raised regulatory oversight and hastened new competition as an overhang, we see potential for the company to attract additional acquisition interest. In our view, GENZ has a diverse product roster and a promising pipeline, led by Campath, in Phase III study for multiple sclerosis and which has shown robust data to date and potential for once-yearly treatment, in-licensed Phase III cholesterol-lowering drug mipomersen, and large-scale production of Myozyme.

➤ Risks to our recommendation and target price include failure to consummate an acquisition of the company, further manufacturing issues limiting drug production and ability to meet patient demand, clinical or regulatory setbacks to GENZ pipeline candidates, and failure to maintain a leading market share for key products.

➤ Our 12-month target price of $81 is 20.7X our 2011 adjusted EPS estimate of $3.90, 1.15X our projected three-year growth rate for GENZ, a premium to sector peers given our view of enhanced acquisition prospects.

Qualitative Risk Assessment

LOW	MEDIUM	**HIGH**

Our risk assessment reflects our view that Genzyme's manufacturing facility challenges underscore the complexity inherent in producing biologic drugs. Although we view GENZ's portfolio of therapeutic products and diagnostic businesses as diverse, new entrants to the Gaucher disease treatment market could mitigate the benefits of product diversity.

Quantitative Evaluations

S&P Quality Ranking   B

D	C	B-	**B**	B+	A-	A	A+

Relative Strength Rank   MODERATE

67

LOWEST = 1   HIGHEST = 99

Revenue/Earnings Data

Revenue (Million $)

	1Q	2Q	3Q	4Q	Year
2010	1,074	1,079	--	--	--
2009	1,149	1,229	1,058	1,081	4,516
2008	1,100	1,171	1,160	1,174	4,605
2007	883.2	933.4	960.2	1,037	3,814
2006	730.8	793.4	808.6	854.2	3,187
2005	630.0	668.1	708.1	728.7	2,735

Earnings Per Share ($)

	1Q	2Q	3Q	4Q	Year
2010	-0.43	-0.01	E0.42	E0.81	E1.43
2009	0.70	0.68	0.06	0.09	1.54
2008	0.52	0.25	0.42	0.31	1.50
2007	0.57	0.51	0.58	0.29	1.74
2006	0.37	0.49	0.06	-1.02	-0.06
2005	0.36	0.46	0.43	0.39	1.65

Fiscal year ended Dec. 31. Next earnings report expected: NA. EPS Estimates based on S&P Operating Earnings; historical GAAP earnings are as reported.

Dividend Data

No cash dividends have been paid.

Genzyme Corp

Business Summary October 22, 2010

CORPORATE OVERVIEW. Genzyme develops, manufactures and markets therapeutic drugs focused on rare diseases. Its leading product is Cerezyme, an enzyme replacement therapy (ERT) for Gaucher disease, a debilitating genetic disorder that causes fatigue, anemia and bone erosion. In 2009, Cerezyme sales declined by 36% to $793 million, due to an inventory shortfall caused by the mid-2009 Allston plant closure. Cerezyme's patents expire in 2013. Phase III studies of a potential successor, orally dosed eliglustat tartrate (GENZ-112638), are ongoing.

Leading GENZ's renal division is Renagel, which reduces elevated serum phosphorus levels in kidney dialysis patients, and Renvela, a buffered form launched in 2008, which generated $707 million in 2009 sales (up 4% over 2008). In November 2009, studies on an advanced phosphate binder intended as a successor to Renvela failed to outperform Renvela and were discontinued. Key Renagel/Renvela patents expire around 2014.

Also in GENZ's ERT unit is Fabrazyme, approved for Fabry disease, a rare genetic disorder in which patients are unable to metabolize lipids. Fabrazyme

sales were $430 million in 2009, down 13% from 2008 due to the 2009 Allston plant outage. Myozyme, approved for treating Pompe disease, an often fatal progressive neuromuscular disorder that afflicts an estimated 10,000 patients worldwide, generated 2009 sales of $325 million, up 10% from 2008's $296 million, despite production constraints. Production was approved at 4000 liter scale in Europe in February 2009, but FDA delays in approving the larger production scales (called Lumizyme) led GENZ to move production to a European facility. FDA approved this material in June 2010. Biosurgery unit sales are led by Synvisc, and its single-injection version Synvisc-One, injectable biomaterials to treat knee osteoarthritis, which generated $329 million in 2009 sales, 25% higher than in 2008. Mozobil, in GENZ's transplant unit, was designed to improve stem cell transplant procedure outcomes, and is approved in the U.S. and Europe for patients with non-Hodgkin's lymphoma and multiple myeloma.

Company Financials Fiscal Year Ended Dec. 31

Per Share Data ($)	2009	2008	2007	2006	2005	2004	2003	2002	2001	2000
Tangible Book Value	14.93	15.70	13.73	10.91	7.99	8.11	6.31	NM	6.10	4.05
Cash Flow	3.21	2.79	2.92	2.00	2.67	1.24	0.41	1.16	0.75	0.91
Earnings	1.54	1.50	1.74	-0.06	1.65	0.37	0.42	0.81	0.19	0.68
S&P Core Earnings	1.54	1.50	1.94	0.32	1.23	-0.03	-0.26	0.59	0.02	NA
Dividends	Nil	Nil	Nil	Nil	Nil	Nil	Nil	Nil	Nil	Nil
Payout Ratio	Nil	Nil	Nil	Nil	Nil	Nil	Nil	Nil	Nil	Nil
Prices:High	73.75	83.97	76.90	75.34	77.82	59.14	52.45	58.55	64.00	51.88
Prices:Low	47.09	57.61	58.71	54.64	55.15	40.67	28.45	15.64	34.34	19.84
P/E Ratio:High	48	56	44	NM	47	NM	NM	72	NM	77
P/E Ratio:Low	31	38	34	NM	33	NM	NM	19	NM	29

Income Statement Analysis (Million $)										
Revenue	4,516	4,605	3,814	3,187	2,735	2,201	1,714	1,080	982	752
Operating Income	1,083	1,303	1,183	913	915	717	463	318	380	-185
Depreciation	456	375	338	541	285	205	160	96.0	118	41.2
Interest Expense	NA	23.4	26.7	15.5	19.6	38.2	26.6	17.8	23.2	14.2
Pretax Income	544	623	732	-63.1	641	222	2.82	207	56.5	-179
Effective Tax Rate	22.3%	32.8%	34.9%	NM	29.2%	63.7%	NM	27.3%	93.1%	51.9%
Net Income	422	421	480	-16.8	441	86.5	-67.6	151	3.88	85.9
S&P Core Earnings	423	420	535	90.4	326	-6.61	-61.0	125	5.25	NA

Balance Sheet & Other Financial Data (Million $)										
Cash	1,050	974	947	492	292	481	293	373	167	136
Current Assets	2,803	2,516	2,609	1,990	1,665	1,634	1,323	1,100	721	605
Total Assets	10,061	8,937	8,302	7,191	6,879	6,069	5,005	3,556	3,225	2,499
Current Liabilities	1,080	914	1,502	651	550	624	392	275	243	167
Long Term Debt	21.6	23.2	717	810	816	811	1,415	600	600	454
Common Equity	7,684	7,335	6,613	5,661	5,150	4,380	2,936	2,586	2,280	1,750
Total Capital	7,684	7,331	6,727	6,481	6,301	5,417	4,558	3,268	2,961	2,329
Capital Expenditures	662	598	413	334	19.2	187	260	220	171	72.6
Cash Flow	879	796	818	524	726	292	92.9	247	122	127
Current Ratio	2.8	2.8	1.7	3.1	3.0	2.6	3.4	4.0	3.0	3.6
% Long Term Debt of Capitalization	Nil	1.7	1.7	12.5	12.9	15.0	30.1	18.4	20.3	31.1
% Net Income of Revenue	9.4	9.1	12.6	NM	16.1	3.9	NM	14.0	0.4	11.4
% Return on Assets	4.5	4.9	6.2	NM	6.8	1.6	NM	4.4	0.2	4.0
% Return on Equity	5.6	6.0	7.8	NM	9.3	2.4	NM	6.2	0.1	5.5

Data as orig reptd.; bef. results of disc opers/spec. items. Per share data adj. for stk. divs.; EPS diluted. E-Estimated. NA-Not Available. NM-Not Meaningful. NR-Not Ranked. UR-Under Review.

Office: 500 Kendall St, Cambridge, MA 02142-1108.
Telephone: 617-252-7570.
Email: information@genzyme.com
Website: http://www.genzyme.com

Chrmn, Pres & CEO: H.A. Termeer
COO & EVP: D.P. Meeker
EVP & CFO: M.S. Wyzga
EVP & Secy: P. Wirth

SVP & CSO: A.E. Smith
Investor Contact: P. Flanigan (617-768-6563)
Board Members: D. A. Berthiaume, R. J. Bertolini, G. K. Boudreaux, S. J. Burakoff, R. J. Carpenter, C. L. Cooney, V. J. Dzau, E. J. Ende, D. Fenton, C. McGillicuddy, III, R. F. Syron, H. A. Termeer, R. V. Whitworth

Founded: 1991
Domicile: Massachusetts
Employees: 12,000

Gilead Sciences Inc

STANDARD & POOR'S

S&P Recommendation **BUY** ★★★★☆	Price $39.11 (as of Oct 22, 2010)	12-Mo. Target Price $45.00	Investment Style Large-Cap Growth

GICS Sector Health Care
Sub-Industry Biotechnology

Summary This biopharmaceutical company is engaged in the discovery, development and commercialization of treatments to fight viral, bacterial and fungal infections.

Key Stock Statistics (Source S&P, Vickers, company reports)

52-Wk Range	$49.50–31.73	S&P Oper. EPS 2010E	3.51	Market Capitalization(B)	$32.799	Beta	0.40
Trailing 12-Month EPS	$3.30	S&P Oper. EPS 2011E	3.75	Yield (%)	Nil	S&P 3-Yr. Proj. EPS CAGR(%)	13
Trailing 12-Month P/E	11.9	P/E on S&P Oper. EPS 2010E	11.1	Dividend Rate/Share	Nil	S&P Credit Rating	NA
$10K Invested 5 Yrs Ago	$17,146	Common Shares Outstg. (M)	838.6	Institutional Ownership (%)	90		

Price Performance

30-Week Mov. Avg. · · · · 10-Week Mov. Avg. – – – GAAP Earnings vs. Previous Year   Volume Above Avg. STARS
12-Mo. Target Price — Relative Strength — ▲ Up ▼ Down ► No Change   Below Avg.

Options: ASE, CBOE, P, Ph

Analysis prepared by **Steven Silver** on October 21, 2010, when the stock traded at **$ 38.39**.

Highlights

► We see 2010 revenues of $7.9 billion, which would mark a 13% increase over 2009, and we forecast 5% growth in 2011 to about $8.3 billion. We expect near-term revenue growth to reflect higher Medicaid rebates and other effects from U.S. health care reform legislation, before GILD benefits from more patients under coverage by 2014. We view favorably GILD's expanding U.S. HIV drug market share, with an 85% share of all HIV patient adds and positive market trends for HIV patient diagnosis and earlier initiation of anti-viral treatment.

► We forecast operating margins, including stock option expense, between 51% and 52% in 2010 and 2011, and see potential for long-term margin expansion should GILD successfully commercialize its wholly owned HIV "Quad Pill," which is in Phase III study, and other Truvada-based combination drugs. We expect GILD to invest in new growth assets, including a broad early-stage program in Hepatitis C, but we believe it is disciplined in managing expenses.

► Our EPS estimates are $3.51 for 2010 and $3.75 for 2011. As of September 30, 2010 GILD had 845 million diluted shares outstanding and $5.1 billion in cash.

Investment Rationale/Risk

► Despite near-term headwinds to GILD's core HIV franchise due to exposure to U.S. health care reform, which affects approximately 50% of its U.S. anti-viral business as well as concerns over HIV patent expirations late in the decade, we view GILD as a core long-term biotech holding, and consider its valuation attractive. We are encouraged by progress of next-generation combination HIV drugs to possibly extend its market leading HIV franchise. We see GILD as well funded to aggressively repurchase shares and to finance acquisitions of early-stage growth assets to diversify revenues. However, we believe recent diversification efforts in building a cardiovascular unit have fallen short of expectations.

► Risks to our recommendation and target price include a slowdown in GILD's HIV product sales from competition or patent challenges, and failure to advance next-generation HIV therapies or complementary business units.

► Our 12-month target price of $45 is 12X our 2011 EPS estimate, a discount to GILD's long-term growth rate, reflecting near-term regulatory headwinds and long-term patent uncertainty.

Qualitative Risk Assessment

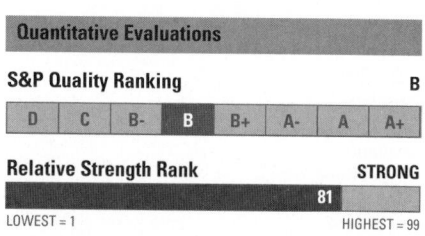

| LOW | MEDIUM | HIGH |

Our risk assessment reflects Gilead's dependence on the growth of its anti-HIV drug portfolio. Also, the company operates in a highly competitive market, and failure to successfully commercialize future pipeline candidates could diminish future growth expectations.

Quantitative Evaluations

S&P Quality Ranking B

| D | C | B- | B | B+ | A- | A | A+ |

Relative Strength Rank STRONG

81

LOWEST = 1   HIGHEST = 99

Revenue/Earnings Data

Revenue (Million $)

	1Q	2Q	3Q	4Q	Year
2010	2,086	1,927	--	--	--
2009	1,530	1,647	1,801	2,032	7,011
2008	1,258	1,278	1,371	1,428	5,336
2007	1,028	1,048	1,059	1,095	4,230
2006	692.9	685.3	748.7	899.2	3,026
2005	430.4	495.3	493.5	609.3	2,028

Earnings Per Share ($)

	1Q	2Q	3Q	4Q	Year
2010	0.92	0.79	E0.83	E0.89	E3.51
2009	0.63	0.61	0.72	E0.80	E2.82
2008	0.51	0.46	0.53	0.60	2.10
2007	0.43	0.42	0.42	0.41	1.68
2006	0.28	0.28	-0.06	-1.81	-1.30
2005	0.17	0.21	0.19	0.29	0.86

Fiscal year ended Dec. 31. Next earnings report expected: NA. EPS Estimates based on S&P Operating Earnings; historical GAAP earnings are as reported.

Dividend Data

No cash dividends have been paid.

Please read the Required Disclosures and Analyst Certification on the last page of this report.

The McGraw-Hill Companies

Gilead Sciences Inc

Business Summary October 21, 2010

CORPORATE OVERVIEW. Gilead Sciences (GILD) focuses on the research, development and marketing of anti-infective medications, with a primary focus on treatments for HIV.

Truvada has been GILD's sales leader, with 2009 sales of $2.49 billion in 2009, 18% above 2008. Truvada, approved in 2004, is a once-daily combination tablet formulated with previous-generation drugs Viread and Emtriva. Emtriva was the lead product of Triangle Pharmaceuticals, acquired in 2003. Viread was approved in 2001 to treat HIV patients who had become resistant to other reverse transcriptase inhibitors, as well as naive patients in front-line treatment settings. Viread sales rose 7% to $668 million in 2009, with most of its current use in treating hepatitis B.

In late 2004, GILD and Bristol-Myers Squibb (BMY) partnered on a combination tablet with Truvada and BMY's Sustiva. The formulation, marketed as Atripla, was launched in July 2006. GILD books Atripla sales and then pays BMY its 37% share for the Sustiva portion of the drug, which GILD counts as

cost of goods on its financial statements. Atripla generated 2009 sales of $2.38 billion, up 51% from 2008, and surpassed Truvada for the first time in the fourth quarter of 2009. Atripla received EU approval in December 2007 and began to be launched in 2008. Atripla was available in all five of the largest European markets, after a mid-2009 launch in France.

Hepsera was approved for treatment of chronic hepatitis B in the U.S. and EU in September 2002 and March 2003, respectively. Hepsera sales declined 20% in 2009 to $271 million, due to increased use of Viread in this indication. AmBisome is a liposomal formulation of amphotericin B, an antifungal agent that attacks a broad variety of life-threatening fungal infections. AmBisome is also approved to treat cryptococcal meningitis in AIDS patients. Sales were $299 million in 2009, roughly flat compared with 2008.

Company Financials Fiscal Year Ended Dec. 31

Per Share Data ($)	2009	2008	2007	2006	2005	2004	2003	2002	2001	2000
Tangible Book Value	5.38	4.56	3.71	1.97	3.30	2.09	1.17	0.72	0.58	0.47
Cash Flow	3.05	2.15	1.71	-1.24	0.90	0.51	-0.06	0.10	0.08	-0.04
Earnings	2.82	2.10	1.68	-1.30	0.86	0.50	-0.09	0.09	0.06	-0.06
S&P Core Earnings	2.81	2.10	1.67	-1.29	0.78	0.39	-0.17	0.01	-0.14	NA
Dividends	Nil	Nil	Nil	Nil	Nil	Nil	Nil	Nil	Nil	Nil
Payout Ratio	Nil	Nil	Nil	Nil	Nil	Nil	Nil	Nil	Nil	Nil
Prices:High	53.28	57.63	47.90	35.00	28.26	19.55	17.65	10.00	9.21	7.38
Prices:Low	40.62	35.60	30.96	26.24	15.20	12.88	7.81	6.52	3.11	2.70
P/E Ratio:High	19	27	29	NM	33	39	NM	NM	NM	NM
P/E Ratio:Low	14	17	18	NM	18	26	NM	NM	NM	NM

Income Statement Analysis (Million $)										
Revenue	7,011	5,336	4,230	3,026	2,028	1,325	868	467	234	196
Operating Income	3,802	2,741	2,201	1,683	1,148	656	361	95.4	-106	-40.3
Depreciation	213	51.7	36.9	47.3	36.8	24.4	20.9	14.4	14.7	12.0
Interest Expense	69.7	12.1	13.5	20.4	0.44	7.35	21.9	13.9	14.0	Nil
Pretax Income	3,502	2,726	2,261	-644	1,158	656	-168	73.4	55.3	-41.9
Effective Tax Rate	25.0%	26.5%	29.0%	NM	30.0%	31.5%	NM	1.77%	7.48%	NM
Net Income	2,636	2,011	1,615	-1,190	814	449	-72.0	72.1	51.2	-43.1
S&P Core Earnings	2,630	2,008	1,610	-1,188	737	354	-133	8.55	-108	NA

Balance Sheet & Other Financial Data (Million $)										
Cash	3,905	3,240	1,172	937	2,324	1,254	707	942	583	513
Current Assets	4,813	4,300	3,028	2,429	3,092	1,850	1,266	1,184	708	594
Total Assets	9,699	7,019	5,835	4,086	3,765	2,156	1,555	1,288	795	678
Current Liabilities	1,872	1,221	736	764	455	253	186	105	80.1	58.2
Long Term Debt	1,322	1,300	1,301	1,300	241	0.23	345	595	250	252
Common Equity	6,505	4,152	3,460	1,816	3,028	1,871	1,003	571	452	351
Total Capital	7,827	5,672	4,772	3,169	3,277	1,871	1,348	1,166	703	603
Capital Expenditures	230	115	78.7	105	2,226	51.4	38.6	17.6	26.3	15.6
Cash Flow	2,849	2,063	1,652	-1,143	851	474	-51.1	86.5	65.9	-31.1
Current Ratio	3.4	3.5	4.1	3.2	6.8	7.3	6.8	11.3	8.8	10.2
% Long Term Debt of Capitalization	16.9	22.9	27.2	41.0	7.3	NM	25.6	51.0	35.6	41.8
% Net Income of Revenue	37.6	37.7	38.2	NM	40.1	33.9	NM	15.4	21.9	NM
% Return on Assets	31.5	31.3	32.6	NM	27.5	24.2	NM	6.9	6.9	NM
% Return on Equity	49.5	52.8	61.2	NM	33.2	31.3	NM	14.1	12.7	NM

Data as orig reptd.; bef. results of disc opers/spec. items. Per share data adj. for stk. divs.; EPS diluted. E-Estimated. NA-Not Available. NM-Not Meaningful. NR-Not Ranked. UR-Under Review.

Office: 333 Lakeside Drive, Foster City, CA 94404.
Telephone: 650-574-3000.
Email: investor_relations@gilead.com
Website: http://www.gilead.com

Chrmn & CEO: J.C. Martin
Pres & COO: J.F. Milligan
EVP & CSO: N.W. Bischofberger
EVP & Secy: G.H. Alton

SVP, CFO & Chief Acctg Officer: R.L. Washington
Investor Contact: S. Hubbard (650 522-5715)
Board Members: P. Berg, J. F. Cogan, V. E. Davignon, J. M. Denny, C. A. Hills, K. E. Lofton, J. W. Madigan, J. C. Martin, G. E. Moore, N. G. Moore, R. J. Whitley, G. E. Wilson, P. Wold-Olsen

Founded: 1987
Domicile: Delaware
Employees: 3,852

Goldman Sachs Group Inc (The)

**STANDARD
&POOR'S**

S&P Recommendation	HOLD ★★★★★	Price $157.76 (as of Oct 22, 2010)	12-Mo. Target Price $176.00	Investment Style Large-Cap Growth

GICS Sector Financials
Sub-Industry Investment Banking & Brokerage

Summary Goldman Sachs is one of the world's leading investment banking and securities companies.

Key Stock Statistics (Source S&P, Vickers, company reports)

52-Wk Range	$186.41–129.50	S&P Oper. EPS 2010**E**	12.93	Market Capitalization(B)	$81.344	Beta	1.43
Trailing 12-Month EPS	$17.56	S&P Oper. EPS 2011**E**	17.15	Yield (%)	0.89	S&P 3-Yr. Proj. EPS CAGR(%)	-4
Trailing 12-Month P/E	9.0	P/E on S&P Oper. EPS 2010**E**	12.2	Dividend Rate/Share	$1.40	S&P Credit Rating	A
$10K Invested 5 Yrs Ago	$13,871	Common Shares Outstg. (M)	515.6	Institutional Ownership (%)	67		

Price Performance

30-Week Mov. Avg. · · · · 10-Week Mov. Avg. – – 12-Mo. Target Price — Relative Strength — **GAAP Earnings vs. Previous Year** ▲ Up ▼ Down ▶ No Change **Volume** Above Avg. STARS Below Avg. ★

Options: ASE, CBOE, P, Ph

Analysis prepared by **Robert McMillan** on October 19, 2010, when the stock traded at **$ 159.25.**

Highlights

➤ We think recent market volatility and continued weakness in global economies suggest that we are in the midst of a bumpy recovery. Trading results are likely to be uneven in the current environment, but better demand for M&A advice should offset trading weakness. Strength in the lower-margin debt underwriting business should help offset weakness in the equity underwriting business. We look for net revenues to decline about 11% in 2010 before advancing 13% in 2011.

➤ GS accrued compensation at 43% of net revenues in the first three quarters of 2010; a similar rate in the fourth quarter would allow for margin expansion in 2010. We see the compensation ratio expanding in 2011, but remaining below historical levels. We expect non-compensation costs to vary with activity levels, but the pretax margin will likely contract in 2010, weighed down by GS's SEC settlement and the U.K. bonus tax, before rising in 2011.

➤ We expect EPS of $12.93 in 2010 and $17.15 in 2011, although we acknowledge poor earnings visibility due to uncertainties regarding regulations and the sustainability of the economic recovery.

Investment Rationale/Risk

➤ While the company has settled the SEC fraud charges concerning the structuring and marketing of a CDO tied to subprime mortgages, we think Goldman remains vulnerable to civil suits by investors. Still, the settlement has helped reduce some overhang on the shares, and we have upgraded our opinion to hold, from sell. We believe the company must continue to assure clients that it holds employees to the highest ethical standards in a business that depends on relationships. Uncertainty regarding the impact of new regulations remains, and their specific impacts will be difficult to determine until rules are written and implemented, which may take several years.

➤ Risks to our recommendation and target price include stock and bond market depreciation, rising interest rates, widening credit spreads, and stricter regulations.

➤ Our 12-month target price of $176 is equal to 1.2X our projection for the company's book value per share at the end of 2011, which is below the stock's historical valuation.

Qualitative Risk Assessment

LOW	MEDIUM	HIGH

Our risk assessment reflects our view of the company's global footprint and strong client relationships, offset by industry cyclicality, GS's high leverage ratio, litigation, and proposed new government regulations.

Quantitative Evaluations

S&P Quality Ranking A-

D	C	B-	B	B+	A-	A	A+

Relative Strength Rank MODERATE

66

LOWEST = 1   HIGHEST = 99

Revenue/Earnings Data

Revenue (Million $)

	1Q	2Q	3Q	4Q	Year
2010	15,776	16,063	1,809	--	--
2009	11,880	15,189	13,682	10,922	51,673
2008	18,629	17,643	13,625	3,682	53,579
2007	22,280	20,351	23,803	21,534	87,968
2006	17,246	18,002	15,979	18,126	69,353
2005	9,964	8,949	12,333	12,145	43,391

Earnings Per Share ($)

	1Q	2Q	3Q	4Q	Year
2010	5.59	0.78	2.98	E3.58	E12.93
2009	3.39	4.93	5.25	8.20	22.13
2008	3.23	4.58	1.81	-4.97	4.47
2007	6.67	4.93	1.81	7.01	24.73
2006	5.08	4.78	3.26	6.59	19.69
2005	2.94	1.71	3.25	3.35	11.21

Fiscal year ended Dec. 31. Next earnings report expected: Late January. EPS Estimates based on S&P Operating Earnings; historical GAAP earnings are as reported.

Dividend Data (Dates: mm/dd Payment Date: mm/dd/yy)

Amount ($)	Date Decl.	Ex-Div. Date	Stk. of Record	Payment Date
0.350	01/21	02/26	03/02	03/30/10
0.350	04/20	05/27	06/01	06/29/10
0.350	07/20	08/30	09/01	09/29/10
0.350	10/19	11/30	12/02	12/30/10

Dividends have been paid since 1999. Source: Company reports.

Please read the Required Disclosures and Analyst Certification on the last page of this report.

The McGraw-Hill Companies

STANDARD &POOR'S

Goldman Sachs Group Inc (The)

Business Summary October 19, 2010

CORPORATE OVERVIEW. Goldman Sachs (GS) is a global investment banking, securities and investment management firm that provides a wide range of services to corporations, financial institutions, governments and high-net-worth individuals. GS operates through three core businesses: Trading and Principal Investments, Investment Banking, and Asset Management and Securities Services.

The Trading and Principal Investments business (76% of 2009 net revenues) facilitates customer transactions with a diverse group of corporations, financial institutions, governments and individuals, and takes proprietary positions through market making in, and trading of, fixed income and equity products, currencies, commodities and derivatives. The activities of the Trading and Principal Investments business can be grouped under three segments: Fixed Income, Currency and Commodities (FICC); Equities; and Principal Investments. The FICC business makes markets in and trades interest rate and credit products, mortgage-backed securities, loans and other asset-backed securities, currencies and commodities. The Equities business makes markets in, trades, and acts as a specialist for, equities and equity-related products. It

generates commissions from executing and clearing client transactions on major stock, options and futures exchanges worldwide through its Equities customer franchise and clearing activities.

The Principal Investments business primarily represents net revenues from corporate and real estate merchant banking investments. These revenues derive from four primary sources -- returns on corporate and real estate investments, its investment in the convertible preferred stock of Sumitomo Mitsui Financial Group, Inc. (SMFG), its investment in the ordinary shares of Industrial and Commercial Bank of China Limited (ICBC), and overrides. Overrides represent net revenues from the increased share of the income and gains derived from GS's merchant banking funds when the return on a fund's investments exceeds certain threshold returns.

Company Financials Fiscal Year Ended Dec. 31

Per Share Data ($)	2009	2008	2007	2006	2005	2004	2003	2002	2001	2000
Tangible Book Value	108.32	104.56	101.62	119.66	52.15	52.14	45.73	40.18	38.30	34.15
Cash Flow	25.66	7.24	27.68	20.78	12.22	9.90	6.97	5.20	5.39	6.94
Earnings	22.13	4.47	24.73	19.69	11.21	8.92	5.87	4.03	4.26	6.00
S&P Core Earnings	22.20	4.40	24.76	19.72	11.12	8.63	5.26	3.30	3.60	NA
Dividends	1.52	1.40	1.40	1.30	1.00	1.00	0.74	0.48	0.48	0.48
Payout Ratio	7%	31%	6%	7%	9%	11%	13%	12%	11%	8%
Prices:High	193.60	215.05	250.70	206.70	134.99	110.88	100.78	97.25	120.00	133.63
Prices:Low	59.13	47.41	157.38	124.23	94.75	83.29	61.02	58.57	63.27	65.50
P/E Ratio:High	9	27	10	10	12	12	17	24	28	22
P/E Ratio:Low	3	6	6	6	8	9	10	15	15	11

Income Statement Analysis (Million $)	2009	2008	2007	2006	2005	2004	2003	2002	2001	2000
Commissions	4,797	5,179	12,286	10,140	6,689	5,941	4,317	3,273	3,020	2,307
Interest Income	13,907	35,633	45,968	35,186	21,250	11,914	10,751	11,269	16,620	17,396
Total Revenue	51,673	53,579	87,968	69,353	43,391	29,839	23,623	22,854	31,138	33,000
Interest Expense	6,500	31,357	41,981	31,688	18,153	8,888	7,600	8,868	15,327	16,410
Pretax Income	19,829	2,336	17,604	14,560	8,273	6,676	4,445	3,253	3,696	5,020
Effective Tax Rate	32.5%	0.60%	34.1%	34.5%	32.0%	31.8%	32.4%	35.0%	37.5%	38.9%
Net Income	13,385	2,322	11,599	9,537	5,626	4,553	3,005	2,114	2,310	3,067
S&P Core Earnings	12,196	2,009	11,419	9,416	5,560	4,406	2,693	1,737	1,949	NA

Balance Sheet & Other Financial Data (Million $)	2009	2008	2007	2006	2005	2004	2003	2002	2001	2000
Total Assets	848,942	884,547	1,119,796	838,201	706,804	531,379	403,799	355,574	312,218	289,760
Cash Items	74,954	122,404	131,821	87,283	61,666	52,544	36,802	25,211	29,043	21,002
Receivables	257,839	271,359	425,596	312,355	75,381	52,545	36,377	28,938	33,463	159,019
Securities Owned	342,402	338,325	452,595	416,687	238,043	183,880	160,719	129,775	108,885	95,260
Securities Borrowed	15,207	17,060	28,624	22,208	23,331	19,394	17,528	12,238	81,579	40,211
Due Brokers & Customers	113,634	254,043	318,453	223,874	188,318	161,221	109,028	95,590	97,297	82,148
Other Liabilities	33,855	23,216	38,907	31,866	13,830	10,360	8,144	6,002	7,129	11,116
Capitalization:Debt	185,085	168,220	164,174	122,842	100,007	80,696	57,482	38,711	31,016	31,395
Capitalization:Equity	63,757	47,898	39,700	32,686	26,252	25,079	21,632	19,003	18,231	16,530
Capitalization:Total	255,799	232,589	206,974	189,521	128,009	105,775	79,114	57,714	49,247	47,925
% Return on Revenue	25.9	4.3	13.1	13.8	13.0	15.3	12.7	9.3	7.4	9.3
% Return on Assets	1.5	0.2	1.1	1.2	0.9	1.0	0.8	0.6	0.8	1.1
% Return on Equity	24.0	4.7	32.0	31.9	21.9	19.5	14.8	11.4	13.3	23.0

Data as orig reptd.; bef. results of disc opers/spec. items. Per share data adj. for stk. divs.; EPS diluted. Prior to 2009, fiscal year ended November 30. E-Estimated. NA-Not Available. NM-Not Meaningful. NR-Not Ranked. UR-Under Review.

Office: 85 Broad Street, New York, NY 10004.
Telephone: 212-902-1000.
Email: gs-investor-relations@gs.com
Website: http://www.gs.com

Chrmn & CEO: L.C. Blankfein
Pres & COO: G.D. Cohn
EVP & CFO: D.A. Viniar
EVP & Secy: E.E. Stecher

EVP & Secy: G.K. Palm
Investor Contact: J. Andrews (212-357-2674)
Auditor: PricewaterhouseCoopers
Board Members: L. C. Blankfein, J. H. Bryan, G. D. Cohn, C. Dahlback, S. Friedman, W. W. George, J. A. Johnson, L. D. Juliber, L. N. Mittal, J. J. Schiro, H. L. Scott, Jr.

Founded: 1869
Domicile: Delaware
Employees: 30,067

The McGraw·Hill Companies

Goodrich Corp

STANDARD &POOR'S

S&P Recommendation	BUY ★★★★☆	Price $80.49 (as of Oct 22, 2010)	12-Mo. Target Price $90.00	Investment Style Large-Cap Value

GICS Sector Industrials
Sub-Industry Aerospace & Defense

Summary This company is one of the world's largest providers of equipment, parts and services to the large commercial, regional, business and military jet markets.

Key Stock Statistics (Source S&P, Vickers, company reports)

52-Wk Range	$82.18– 53.57	S&P Oper. EPS 2010**E**	4.39	Market Capitalization(B)	$10.084	Beta	1.25
Trailing 12-Month EPS	$4.07	S&P Oper. EPS 2011**E**	5.25	Yield (%)	1.44	S&P 3-Yr. Proj. EPS CAGR(%)	9
Trailing 12-Month P/E	19.8	P/E on S&P Oper. EPS 2010**E**	18.3	Dividend Rate/Share	$1.16	S&P Credit Rating	BBB+
$10K Invested 5 Yrs Ago	$20,345	Common Shares Outstg. (M)	125.3	Institutional Ownership (%)	89		

Price Performance

30-Week Mov. Avg. · · · 10-Week Mov. Avg. – – **GAAP Earnings vs. Previous Year** Volume Above Avg. STARS
12-Mo. Target Price — Relative Strength — ▲ Up ▼ Down ▶ No Change Below Avg. ★

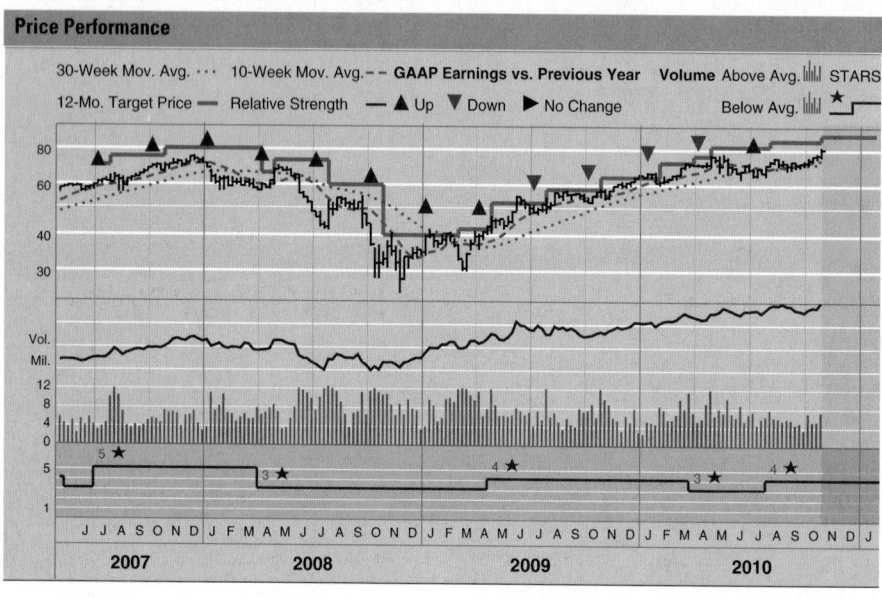

Options: ASE, CBOE, P, Ph

Qualitative Risk Assessment

LOW	MEDIUM	HIGH

Our risk assessment is based in part on GR's S&P Quality Ranking of B+ (average), which reflects its uneven earnings and dividend record of the past 10 years. We also take into account GR's long-term debt-to-capital ratio of 40% as of June 2010, which is slightly above average for peers in the aerospace & defense sub-industry.

Quantitative Evaluations

S&P Quality Ranking B+

D	C	B-	B	B+	A-	A	A+

Relative Strength Rank STRONG

81

LOWEST = 1 HIGHEST = 99

Revenue/Earnings Data

Revenue (Million $)

	1Q	2Q	3Q	4Q	Year
2010	1,695	1,718	--	--	--
2009	1,696	1,700	1,648	1,642	6,686
2008	1,745	1,849	1,772	1,695	7,062
2007	1,589	1,622	1,602	1,668	6,392
2006	1,424	1,483	1,436	1,535	5,878
2005	1,276	1,353	1,371	1,398	5,397

Earnings Per Share ($)

2010	0.86	1.24	E1.25	E1.04	E4.39
2009	1.35	1.15	1.12	0.83	4.43
2008	1.21	1.44	1.33	1.35	5.33
2007	0.78	0.98	1.10	1.05	3.89
2006	1.59	0.64	0.80	0.78	3.80
2005	0.46	0.51	0.49	0.51	1.97

Fiscal year ended Dec. 31. Next earnings report expected: Late October. EPS Estimates based on S&P Operating Earnings; historical GAAP earnings are as reported.

Highlights

► The 12-month target price for GR has recently been changed to $90.00 from $86.00. The Highlights section of this Stock Report will be updated accordingly.

Investment Rationale/Risk

► The Investment Rationale/Risk section of this Stock Report will be updated shortly. For the latest News story on GR from MarketScope, see below.

► 10/21/10 02:08 pm ET ... S&P REITERATES BUY RECOMMENDATION ON SHARES OF GOODRICH (GR 79.2****): Q3 EPS of $1.25, vs. $1.12, is $0.10 above our view, as sales rose 6%, in line with our estimate. Operating margins rose 150 bps to 17.3%, on increases from all 3 segments. We are reducing our '10 EPS estimate by $0.09 to $4.39, on an expected $0.18 Q4 debt-redemption charge, but increase '11's by $0.10 to $5.25, on GR's outlook for '11 aftermarket and OEM sales growth. We raise our 12-month target price by $4 to $90, on our revised '11 EBITDA estimate. We see GR benefitting from continued strong execution and positive OEM production and commercial aftermarket growth trends. /R.Tortoriello

Dividend Data (Dates: mm/dd Payment Date: mm/dd/yy)

Amount ($)	Date Decl.	Ex-Div. Date	Stk. of Record	Payment Date
0.270	02/16	02/25	03/01	04/01/10
0.270	04/20	05/27	06/01	07/01/10
0.270	07/16	08/30	09/01	10/01/10
0.290	10/12	11/29	12/01	12/30/10

Dividends have been paid since 1939. Source: Company reports.

Please read the Required Disclosures and Analyst Certification on the last page of this report.

The McGraw-Hill Companies

Goodrich Corp

Business Summary August 03, 2010

CORPORATE OVERVIEW. Goodrich Corp., a global aircraft components maker and services provider, is also a leading supplier of systems and products to the global defense and aerospace markets. Operations are divided into three segments.

Nacelles and Interior Systems (35% of revenues and 49% of operating profits in 2009) manufactures products and provides maintenance, repair and overhaul associated with aircraft engines, including thrust reversers, cowlings, nozzles and their components (a nacelle is the structure that surrounds an aircraft engine and includes all of the foregoing items), and aircraft interior products, including evacuation slides, aircraft crew and ejection seats, and cargo and lighting systems. N&IS's largest customers include Airbus, Boeing, Rolls-Royce and global airlines. Primary competitors in this market include Aircelle (a subsidiary of SAFRAN), GE, and Spirit Aerosystems.

Actuation and Landing Systems (38% and 25%) provides systems, components and related services pertaining to aircraft taxi, takeoff, flight control, landing and stopping, as well as engine components, including fuel delivery systems and rotating assemblies. Key products include aircraft wheels, brakes, and brake control systems; landing gear; flight control actuation systems; power transmission systems; turbine fuel technologies; and turbomachinery products. A&LS and Messier-Dowty (a division of France-based SAFRAN) each control about 50% of the global landing gear market. Other competitors in-

clude Honeywell (wheels and brakes), Meggitt Aircraft Braking Systems, Messier-Bugati (wheels and brakes), Parker Hannifin (actuation, fuel systems), and United Technologies (actuation).

The unit is also a major global provider of aircraft maintenance, repair and overhaul (MRO) services. A&LS's MRO customers mostly comprise the world's major airlines and aircraft leasing companies. Primary aircraft maintenance competitors include TIMCO Aviation Services, SIA Engineering Co., Singapore Technologies and Lufthansa Technik.

Electronic Systems (27% and 26%) produces a wide array of systems and components that provide flight performance measurements, flight management information, engine controls, fuel controls, electrical power systems, and safety data, as well as reconnaissance and surveillance systems. Key products include aircraft sensor systems; fuel and utility systems; de-icing systems; aerospace hoists/winches; intelligence, reconnaissance and surveillance systems; power systems; and engine controls. Competitors include Honeywell, Thales, United Technologies, and BAE Systems.

Company Financials Fiscal Year Ended Dec. 31

Per Share Data ($)	2009	2008	2007	2006	2005	2004	2003	2002	2001	2000
Tangible Book Value	5.63	2.42	7.15	1.31	NM	NM	NM	NM	4.66	3.48
Cash Flow	6.49	7.00	5.48	5.78	3.79	3.18	2.18	3.31	3.28	4.39
Earnings	4.43	5.33	3.89	3.80	1.97	1.30	0.33	1.57	1.65	2.68
S&P Core Earnings	5.03	4.21	3.77	3.94	2.10	1.57	0.42	0.42	0.41	NA
Dividends	1.02	0.93	0.83	1.00	0.80	0.80	0.80	0.88	1.10	1.10
Payout Ratio	23%	17%	21%	26%	41%	62%	242%	56%	67%	41%
Prices:High	65.93	71.14	75.74	47.45	45.82	33.90	30.30	34.45	44.50	43.13
Prices:Low	29.95	25.11	44.97	37.15	30.11	26.60	12.20	14.17	15.91	21.56
P/E Ratio:High	15	13	19	12	23	26	92	22	27	16
P/E Ratio:Low	7	5	12	10	15	20	37	9	10	8

Income Statement Analysis (Million $)	2009	2008	2007	2006	2005	2004	2003	2002	2001	2000
Revenue	6,686	7,062	6,392	5,878	5,397	4,725	4,383	3,910	4,185	4,364
Operating Income	1,200	1,313	1,086	886	759	636	515	586	666	830
Depreciation	249	212	205	240	226	223	219	184	174	193
Interest Expense	121	117	130	126	131	143	163	117	118	129
Pretax Income	784	967	717	462	375	199	61.3	259	271	443
Effective Tax Rate	26.5%	30.3%	30.8%	NM	31.8%	21.7%	37.2%	36.0%	34.8%	35.4%
Net Income	563	674	496	481	244	156	38.5	166	177	286
S&P Core Earnings	629	532	482	499	260	189	48.6	44.9	44.7	NA

Balance Sheet & Other Financial Data (Million $)	2009	2008	2007	2006	2005	2004	2003	2002	2001	2000
Cash	811	370	406	201	251	298	378	150	85.8	77.5
Current Assets	4,414	3,668	3,549	3,008	2,425	2,357	2,087	2,008	1,921	3,080
Total Assets	8,741	7,483	7,534	6,901	6,454	6,218	5,890	5,990	4,638	5,718
Current Liabilities	1,613	1,841	1,743	1,633	1,615	1,565	1,401	1,554	1,159	2,147
Long Term Debt	2,008	1,410	1,563	1,722	1,742	1,899	2,137	2,254	1,432	1,590
Common Equity	2,921	2,091	2,579	1,977	1,473	1,343	1,194	933	1,361	1,227
Total Capital	4,976	3,564	4,313	3,756	3,215	3,276	3,330	3,187	2,808	2,819
Capital Expenditures	169	285	283	257	216	152	125	107	191	148
Cash Flow	812	885	701	721	470	379	258	349	351	479
Current Ratio	2.7	2.0	2.0	1.8	1.5	1.5	1.5	1.3	1.7	1.4
% Long Term Debt of Capitalization	40.4	39.6	36.2	45.8	54.2	58.0	64.2	70.7	51.0	56.4
% Net Income of Revenue	8.4	9.5	7.8	8.2	4.5	3.3	0.9	4.2	4.2	6.6
% Return on Assets	6.9	9.0	6.9	7.2	3.8	2.6	0.6	3.0	3.6	5.3
% Return on Equity	22.5	28.8	21.8	27.9	17.3	12.3	3.6	14.5	13.7	22.7

Data as orig reptd.; bef. results of disc opers/spec. items. Per share data adj. for stk. divs.; EPS diluted. E-Estimated. NA-Not Available. NM-Not Meaningful. NR-Not Ranked. UR-Under Review.

Office: Four Coliseum Centre, Charlotte, NC 28217-4578.
Telephone: 704-423-7000.
Website: http://www.goodrich.com
Chrmn, Pres & CEO: M.O. Larsen

EVP & CFO: S.E. Kuechle
Chief Admin Officer & General Counsel: T.G. Linnert
CTO: J. Witowski
Chief Acctg Officer & Cntlr: S. Cottrill

Investor Contact: P. Gifford (704-423-5517)
Board Members: C. Corvi, D. C. Creel, G. A. Davidson, Jr., H. E. DeLoach, Jr., J. W. Griffith, W. R. Holland, J. P. Jumper, M. O. Larsen, L. W. Newton, D. E. Olesen, A. M. Rankin, Jr.

Founded: 1912
Domicile: New York
Employees: 24,000

The McGraw-Hill Companies

Goodyear Tire & Rubber Co

STANDARD &POOR'S

S&P Recommendation BUY ★★★★☆

Price	**12-Mo. Target Price**	**Investment Style**
$11.74 (as of Oct 22, 2010)	$15.00	Large-Cap Blend

GICS Sector Consumer Discretionary
Sub-Industry Tires & Rubber

Summary GT is the largest U.S. manufacturer of tires, and one of the biggest worldwide. Operations also include rubber and plastic products and chemicals.

Key Stock Statistics (Source S&P, Vickers, company reports)

52-Wk Range	$18.23–9.10	S&P Oper. EPS 2010**E**	0.59	Market Capitalization(B)	$2.852	Beta	2.71
Trailing 12-Month EPS	$0.66	S&P Oper. EPS 2011**E**	1.44	Yield (%)	Nil	S&P 3-Yr. Proj. EPS CAGR(%)	NM
Trailing 12-Month P/E	17.8	P/E on S&P Oper. EPS 2010**E**	19.9	Dividend Rate/Share	Nil	S&P Credit Rating	BB-
$10K Invested 5 Yrs Ago	$8,632	Common Shares Outstg. (M)	242.9	Institutional Ownership (%)	79		

Price Performance

30-Week Mov. Avg. · · · · 10-Week Mov. Avg. – – **GAAP Earnings vs. Previous Year** Volume Above Avg. STARS
12-Mo. Target Price — Relative Strength — ▲ Up ▼ Down ▶ No Change Below Avg. ★

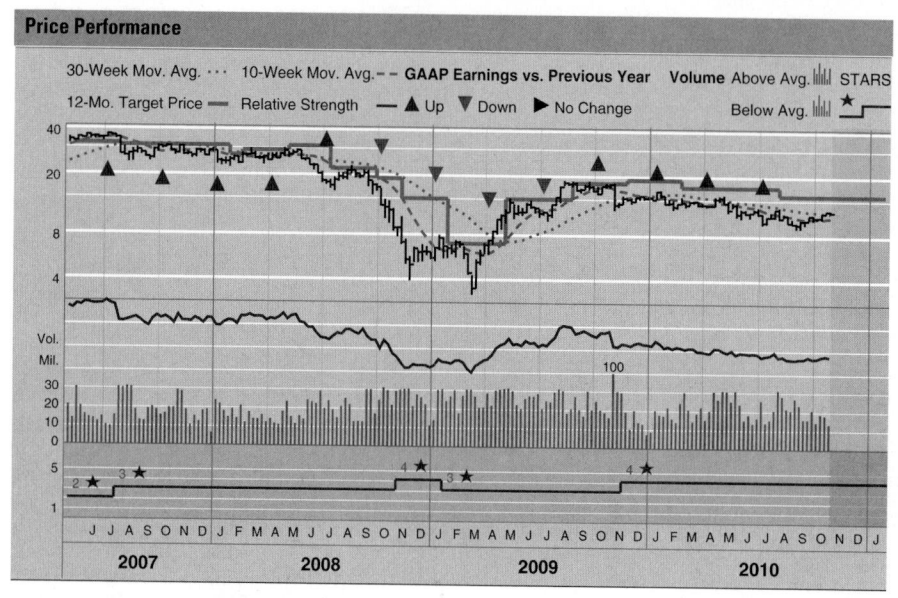

Options: ASE, CBOE, P, Ph

Analysis prepared by **Efraim Levy, CFA** on August 05, 2010, when the stock traded at **$ 11.48**.

Highlights

➤ A weak global economy, sharp vehicle production cuts, and reduced miles driven in key markets reduced Goodyear's sales in 2009. In contrast, we expect global vehicle production to rise in 2010, although regions and segments will change at varying rates and spur a return to profitability for Goodyear. We look for higher volume and increased prices to drive sales 15% higher in 2010 and 13% higher in 2011. First-quarter results were limited by some timing issues that benefited the 2009 fourth quarter.

➤ Margins in 2010 should be aided by higher selling prices, greater capacity utilization, and improved mix as well as by past and present expense reductions from restructuring activities, offset by higher raw materials costs, including oil, that we expect in the second half of the year. Pension costs should be lower, but interest expense should rise. We see reductions in higher-cost plant capacity and a shift to Asia-based production leading to savings.

➤ We expect GT to save $100 million on an annualized basis now that the courts have approved the transfer of union health care benefits to union responsibility. We expect additional savings from restructuring actions.

Investment Rationale/Risk

➤ GT has been extending its debt maturities, and we see a $350 million convertible debt offering helping liquidity, as should $833 million of net proceeds from the May 2007 equity issuance. While we have increased confidence in GT's near-term liquidity, we regard liquidity challenges from debt and employee retirement obligations as matters of concern for the long term. There is no long-term debt due in 2010. We note that our 2010 EPS estimate excludes a $0.41 per share charge resulting from the Venezuelan currency devaluation.

➤ Risks to our recommendation and target price include an increase in GT's need for cash, weaker-than-anticipated demand for tires, lower-than-expected cost savings, an inability to achieve expected price increases, and higher-than-projected raw material costs.

➤ Although we expect profits in 2010, with sharply higher projected capital spending, we forecast negative free cash flow, even before cash contributions to fund GT's pension plan. Applying a P/E multiple of about 10.4X, based on historical levels and peer multiples, to our 2010 estimate of $1.44, we derive our 12-month target price of $15.

Qualitative Risk Assessment

LOW	MEDIUM	HIGH

Our risk assessment reflects the highly cyclical nature of the company's markets as well as the current and long-term challenges that we believe GT faces given its highly leveraged balance sheet, intensifying competition, high fixed costs, and legacy costs.

Quantitative Evaluations

S&P Quality Ranking   C

D	C	B-	B	B+	A-	A	A+

Relative Strength Rank   MODERATE

67

LOWEST = 1   HIGHEST = 99

Revenue/Earnings Data

Revenue (Million $)

	1Q	2Q	3Q	4Q	Year
2010	4,270	4,528	--	--	--
2009	3,536	3,943	4,385	4,437	16,301
2008	4,942	5,239	5,172	4,135	19,488
2007	4,499	4,921	5,064	5,160	19,644
2006	4,856	5,142	5,284	4,976	20,258
2005	4,767	4,992	5,030	4,934	19,723

Earnings Per Share ($)

2010	-0.19	0.12	E0.11	E0.10	E0.59
2009	-1.38	-0.92	0.30	0.44	-1.55
2008	0.60	0.31	0.13	-1.37	-0.32
2007	-0.61	0.14	0.67	0.26	0.66
2006	0.37	0.01	-0.27	-2.02	-1.86
2005	0.35	0.34	0.70	-0.23	1.21

Fiscal year ended Dec. 31. Next earnings report expected: Late October. EPS Estimates based on S&P Operating Earnings; historical GAAP earnings are as reported.

Dividend Data

Dividends were last paid in 2002.

The McGraw·Hill Companies

STANDARD &POOR'S

Goodyear Tire & Rubber Co

Business Summary August 05, 2010

CORPORATE OVERVIEW. Goodyear Tire & Rubber is the largest U.S. manufacturer of tires, and one of the largest worldwide. Operations also include rubber and plastic products and chemicals. GT holds the leading market share in North America, Latin America, China and India.

With the sale of substantially all of its engineered products business in July 2007, the results of that segment have been classified as discontinued operations.

In February 2008, Goodyear formed a new strategic business unit, Europe, Middle East and Africa (EMEA). These regions collectively had about $7.2 billion in revenues in 2007, making the unit the second largest, after North America, in terms of sales. The company began reporting the new segment results in the 2008 first quarter.

CORPORATE STRATEGY. The company achieved more than $2.5 billion in aggregate cost savings from 2006 through 2009 through a four-point plan. Sources of savings included continuous improvement in processes, increased low-cost country sourcing, high-cost capacity reductions and reduced SG&A

expenses, including ongoing savings from the master labor agreement with the United Steel Workers. In February 2010, GT announced plans for an additional $1.0 billion in savings over the next three years.

The company sometimes uses joint ventures to facilitate the growth of its business. In 1999, GT and Sumitomo Rubber Industries (SRI) completed a global alliance that again made GT the world's leading tire manufacturer. GT created a European joint venture with SRI. GT and SRI owned 75% and 25%, respectively, of both the North American and European joint ventures. In Japan, the ownership ratio is reversed.

GT and Pacific Dunlop Ltd. participate in equally owned joint ventures in South Pacific Tyres, an Australian partnership, and South Pacific Tyres N.Z. Ltd., a New Zealand company.

Company Financials Fiscal Year Ended Dec. 31

Per Share Data ($)	2009	2008	2007	2006	2005	2004	2003	2002	2001	2000
Tangible Book Value	NM	0.74	8.58	NM	NM	NM	NM	NM	14.06	18.49
Cash Flow	1.08	2.42	3.25	1.95	4.16	3.87	-0.62	-3.01	2.71	4.22
Earnings	-1.55	-0.32	0.66	-1.86	1.21	0.63	-4.58	-6.62	-1.27	0.26
S&P Core Earnings	-0.60	-1.48	1.15	-0.88	2.61	0.84	-3.32	-8.16	-3.09	NA
Dividends	Nil	Nil	Nil	Nil	Nil	Nil	Nil	0.48	1.02	1.20
Payout Ratio	Nil	Nil	Nil	Nil	Nil	Nil	Nil	NM	NM	NM
Prices:High	18.84	30.10	36.90	21.35	18.59	15.01	8.19	28.85	32.10	31.63
Prices:Low	3.17	3.93	21.40	9.75	11.24	7.06	3.35	6.50	17.37	15.60
P/E Ratio:High	NM	NM	56	NM	15	24	NM	NM	NM	NM
P/E Ratio:Low	NM	NM	32	NM	9	11	NM	NM	NM	NM

Income Statement Analysis (Million $)

	2009	2008	2007	2006	2005	2004	2003	2002	2001	2000
Revenue	16,301	19,488	19,644	20,258	19,723	18,370	15,119	13,850	14,147	14,417
Operating Income	900	1,434	1,677	1,256	1,706	1,457	-549	915	916	1,173
Depreciation	636	660	614	675	630	629	693	603	637	630
Interest Expense	311	397	566	451	411	369	296	241	292	283
Pretax Income	-357	186	464	-113	584	381	-655	37.9	-273	92.3
Effective Tax Rate	NM	112.4%	55.0%	NM	42.8%	54.6%	NM	NM	NM	20.0%
Net Income	-375	-77.0	139	-330	239	115	-802	-1,106	-204	40.3
S&P Core Earnings	-150	-355	253	-157	522	142	-584	-1,362	-495	NA

Balance Sheet & Other Financial Data (Million $)

	2009	2008	2007	2006	2005	2004	2003	2002	2001	2000
Cash	1,922	1,894	3,654	3,899	2,178	1,968	1,565	947	959	253
Current Assets	7,225	8,340	10,172	10,179	8,680	8,632	6,988	5,227	5,255	5,467
Total Assets	14,410	15,226	17,191	17,029	15,627	16,533	15,006	13,147	13,513	13,568
Current Liabilities	4,095	4,779	4,664	4,666	4,811	5,113	3,686	4,071	3,327	4,226
Long Term Debt	4,167	4,132	4,329	6,563	4,742	449	4,826	2,989	3,204	2,350
Common Equity	735	1,022	2,850	-758	73.0	72.8	-13.1	651	2,864	3,503
Total Capital	5,857	6,550	8,456	7,015	5,910	1,774	5,639	4,380	6,855	6,698
Capital Expenditures	746	1,049	739	671	634	519	375	458	435	614
Cash Flow	261	583	753	345	869	744	-109	-503	433	671
Current Ratio	1.8	1.8	2.2	2.2	1.8	1.7	1.9	1.3	1.6	1.3
% Long Term Debt of Capitalization	71.2	62.6	51.2	93.6	80.2	25.3	85.6	68.2	46.7	35.1
% Net Income of Revenue	NM	NM	0.7	NM	1.2	0.6	NM	NM	NM	0.3
% Return on Assets	NM	NM	0.8	NM	1.5	0.7	NM	NM	NM	0.3
% Return on Equity	NM	NM	13.3	NM	325.2	565.5	NM	NM	NM	1.1

Data as orig reptd.; bef. results of disc opers/spec. items. Per share data adj. for stk. divs.; EPS diluted. E-Estimated. NA-Not Available. NM-Not Meaningful. NR-Not Ranked. UR-Under Review.

Office: 1144 East Market Street, Akron, OH, USA 44316-0001.
Telephone: 330-796-2121.
Email: goodyear.investor.relations@goodyear.com
Website: http://www.goodyear.com

Chrmn, Pres, CEO & COO: R.J. Kramer
Pres: J.C. Szulc
EVP & CFO: D.R. Wells
SVP & CTO: J. Kihn

SVP, Secy & General Counsel: D.L. Bialosky
Investor Contact: G. Dooley (330-796-6704)
Board Members: J. C. Boland, J. A. Firestone, P. S. Hellman, R. J. Kramer, W. A. McCollough, D. Morrison, R. O'Neal, S. D. Peterson, S. A. Streeter, G. C. Sullivan, T. H. Weidemeyer, M. R. Wessel

Founded: 1898
Domicile: Ohio
Employees: 69,000

The McGraw-Hill Companies

Google Inc

STANDARD &POOR'S

S&P Recommendation	**STRONG BUY** ★★★★★	Price $612.53 (as of Oct 22, 2010)	12-Mo. Target Price $700.00	Investment Style Large-Cap Growth

GICS Sector Information Technology
Sub-Industry Internet Software & Services

Summary As the world's largest Internet company, Google specializes in online search and advertising.

Key Stock Statistics (Source S&P, Vickers, company reports)

52-Wk Range	$629.51– 433.63	S&P Oper. EPS 2010E	25.61	Market Capitalization(B)	$149.380	Beta	1.14
Trailing 12-Month EPS	$24.62	S&P Oper. EPS 2011E	30.23	Yield (%)	Nil	S&P 3-Yr. Proj. EPS CAGR(%)	19
Trailing 12-Month P/E	24.9	P/E on S&P Oper. EPS 2010E	23.9	Dividend Rate/Share	Nil	S&P Credit Rating	NA
$10K Invested 5 Yrs Ago	$18,021	Common Shares Outstg. (M)	318.7	Institutional Ownership (%)	79		

Price Performance

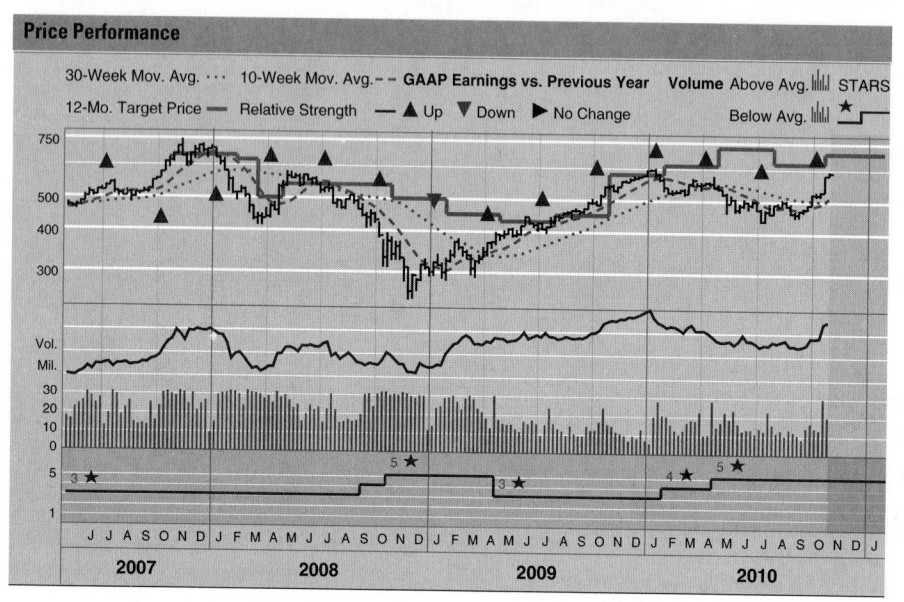

- 30-Week Mov. Avg. · · ·
- 10-Week Mov. Avg. - -
- **GAAP Earnings vs. Previous Year**
- Volume Above Avg. STARS
- 12-Mo. Target Price —
- Relative Strength
- ▲ Up ▼ Down ► No Change
- Below Avg. ★

Options: ASE, CBOE, P, Ph

Analysis prepared by **Scott H. Kessler** on October 19, 2010, when the stock traded at **$ 611.86.**

Highlights

► We believe gross revenues will rise 22% in 2010 and 15% in 2011, benefiting from more spending on Internet advertising, the appeal of search advertising, international expansion, and increasing traction for display and mobile advertising. We think GOOG continues to face challenges in some businesses and believe uncertain economies pose difficulties, but we see it as relatively well positioned.

► The pro forma operating margin improved in 2009, reflecting less reliance on large content partners and a relatively new focus on cost containment. We project these margins will rise from around 40% in 2010 to 42% in 2012, reflecting scale benefits and continuing investments in expansion and R&D. Although revenues have been adversely affected by currency fluctuations, we believe a relatively new hedging program has aided profits.

► Our EPS estimates include notable expenses related to stock-based compensation. In July 2010, GOOG announced the proposed acquisition of ITA Software, a provider of airline travel data, information and solutions, for $700 million, to enhance its travel search offerings.

Investment Rationale/Risk

► We believe competitive pressures and concerns about GOOG's size/power could detract from revenue growth. Nonetheless, its business model has been resilient, in our view. We are constructive on efforts to broaden its offerings, especially with Web applications (Apps) and mobile services, but we believe, in some cases ,GOOG paid excessive amounts to do so. In November 2006, GOOG acquired YouTube for $1.8 billion in stock, and in March 2008 it purchased DoubleClick for $3.2 billion.

► Risks to our opinion and target price include possible market share losses, new offerings or partnerships that do not succeed or continue as some expect, and challenges related to legal/regulatory issues.

► Inputs in our DCF model include a WACC of 10.8%, five-year average annual FCF growth of 15%, and a perpetuity growth rate of 3%, and yields an intrinsic value of about $700, which is our 12-month target price. GOOG generates billions of dollars in annual FCF and recently had $33 billion in cash/marketable securities and $2 billion in short-term debt.

Qualitative Risk Assessment

LOW	MEDIUM	HIGH

Our risk assessment reflects what we see as the Internet segment's emerging nature and relatively low barriers to entry, significant and mounting competition, substantial and increasing investment and related new offerings, and our view of somewhat lacking corporate governance practices.

Quantitative Evaluations

S&P Quality Ranking NR

D	C	B-	B	B+	A-	A	A+

Relative Strength Rank STRONG

92

LOWEST = 1   HIGHEST = 99

Revenue/Earnings Data

Revenue (Million $)

	1Q	2Q	3Q	4Q	Year
2010	6,775	6,820	7,286	--	--
2009	5,509	5,523	5,945	6,674	23,651
2008	5,186	5,367	5,541	5,701	21,796
2007	3,664	3,872	4,231	4,827	16,594
2006	2,254	2,456	2,690	3,206	10,605
2005	1,257	1,385	1,578	1,919	6,139

Earnings Per Share ($)

	1Q	2Q	3Q	4Q	Year
2010	6.06	5.71	6.72	E7.12	E25.61
2009	4.49	4.66	5.13	6.13	20.41
2008	4.12	3.92	4.06	1.21	13.31
2007	3.18	2.93	3.38	3.79	13.29
2006	1.95	2.33	2.36	3.29	9.94
2005	1.29	1.19	1.32	1.22	5.02

Fiscal year ended Dec. 31. Next earnings report expected: Late January. EPS Estimates based on S&P Operating Earnings; historical GAAP earnings are as reported.

Dividend Data

No cash dividends have been paid.

Google Inc

Business Summary October 19, 2010

CORPORATE OVERVIEW. Google is a global technology company whose stated mission is to organize the world's information and make it universally accessible and useful. GOOG has amassed and maintains what we believe is the Internet's largest index of information (consisting of billions of items, including Web pages, images and videos), and makes most of it freely accessible and usable to anyone with online access. GOOG's websites are a leading Internet destination, and its brand is one of the most recognized in the world. International sources contributed 52% of revenues in the second quarter of 2010 and 53% in second quarter of 2009.

GOOG's advertising program, called AdWords, enables advertisers to present online ads when users are searching for related information. Advertisers employ GOOG's tools to create text-based ads, bid on keywords that trigger display of their ads, and set daily spending budgets. Ads are ranked for presenta-

tion based on the maximum cost per click set by the advertiser, click-through rates, and other factors used to determine ad relevance. This process is designed to favor the most relevant ads. GOOG's AdSense technology enables Google Network websites to provide targeted ads from AdWords advertisers.

Advertising accounted for 97% of revenues in the second quarters of 2010 and 2009. Google websites accounted for 67% of second-quarter revenues in 2010 and 2009, and Google Network websites contributed 30% of revenues in both periods.

Company Financials Fiscal Year Ended Dec. 31

Per Share Data ($)	2009	2008	2007	2006	2005	2004	2003	2002	2001	2000
Tangible Book Value	95.44	71.09	63.67	49.02	31.20	10.25	7.66	NA	NA	NA
Cash Flow	25.19	18.01	16.36	11.79	5.90	1.93	0.75	0.53	0.09	NA
Earnings	20.41	13.31	13.29	9.94	5.02	1.46	0.51	0.45	0.04	-0.22
S&P Core Earnings	20.21	15.54	13.18	9.92	4.68	1.85	0.40	0.44	NA	NA
Dividends	Nil	Nil	Nil	Nil	Nil	Nil	NA	NA	NA	NA
Payout Ratio	Nil	Nil	Nil	Nil	Nil	Nil	NA	NA	NA	NA
Prices:High	625.99	697.37	747.24	513.00	446.21	201.60	NA	NA	NA	NA
Prices:Low	282.75	247.30	437.00	331.55	172.57	85.00	NA	NA	NA	NA
P/E Ratio:High	31	52	56	52	89	NM	NA	NA	NA	NA
P/E Ratio:Low	14	19	33	33	34	NM	NA	NA	NA	NA

Income Statement Analysis (Million $)	2009	2008	2007	2006	2005	2004	2003	2002	2001	2000
Revenue	23,651	21,796	16,594	10,605	6,139	3,189	1,466	440	86.4	19.1
Operating Income	9,836	8,219	6,052	3,550	2,274	970	393	204	21.0	NA
Depreciation	1,524	1,492	968	572	257	129	50.2	18.0	10.0	NA
Interest Expense	NA	Nil	1.30	0.26	0.78	0.86	1.93	2.57	1.76	NA
Pretax Income	8,381	5,854	5,674	4,011	2,142	650	347	185	10.1	-14.7
Effective Tax Rate	22.2%	27.8%	26.0%	23.3%	31.6%	38.6%	69.5%	46.1%	30.6%	Nil
Net Income	6,520	4,227	4,204	3,077	1,465	399	106	99.7	6.99	-14.7
S&P Core Earnings	6,458	4,933	4,170	3,071	1,366	503	103	97.4	NA	NA

Balance Sheet & Other Financial Data (Million $)	2009	2008	2007	2006	2005	2004	2003	2002	2001	2000
Cash	24,485	15,846	14,219	11,244	8,034	2,132	1,712	146	33.6	19.1
Current Assets	29,167	20,178	17,289	13,040	9,001	2,693	560	232	NA	NA
Total Assets	40,497	31,768	25,336	18,473	10,272	3,313	2,492	286	84.5	46.9
Current Liabilities	2,747	2,302	2,036	1,305	745	340	235	89.5	NA	NA
Long Term Debt	NA	Nil	Nil	Nil	Nil	Nil	NA	6.50	NA	NA
Common Equity	36,004	28,239	22,690	17,040	9,419	2,929	2,181	130	NA	NA
Total Capital	36,004	28,251	22,690	17,080	9,454	2,929	603	178	50.2	27.2
Capital Expenditures	810	2,358	2,403	1,903	838	319	177	37.2	13.1	NA
Cash Flow	8,045	5,719	5,172	3,649	1,722	528	156	118	17.0	NA
Current Ratio	10.6	8.8	8.5	10.0	12.1	7.9	2.4	2.6	NA	NA
% Long Term Debt of Capitalization	Nil	Nil	Nil	Nil	Nil	Nil	Nil	3.7	Nil	NA
% Net Income of Revenue	27.6	19.4	25.3	29.0	23.9	12.5	7.2	22.7	8.1	NM
% Return on Assets	18.1	14.8	19.1	21.4	21.6	19.1	18.2	NA	NA	NA
% Return on Equity	20.3	16.6	21.1	23.3	23.7	23.0	31.4	NA	NA	NA

Data as orig reptd.; bef. results of disc opers/spec. items. Per share data adj. for stk. divs.; EPS diluted. E-Estimated. NA-Not Available. NM-Not Meaningful. NR-Not Ranked. UR-Under Review.

Office: 1600 Amphitheatre Parkway, Mountain View, CA 94043.
Telephone: 650-253-0000.
Email: info@google.com
Website: http://www.google.com

Chrmn & CEO: E.E. Schmidt
COO: U. Holzle
SVP & CFO: P. Pichette
SVP, Secy & General Counsel: D. Drummond

CTO: S. Brin
Investor Contact: M. Shim (650-253-7663)
Board Members: S. Brin, J. Doerr, J. L. Hennessy, A. Mather, P. S. Otellini, L. Page, E. E. Schmidt, K. Shriram, S. M. Tilghman

Employees: 19,835

Grainger (W W) Inc.

STANDARD & POOR'S

S&P Recommendation **BUY** ★★★★★☆	Price $122.61 (as of Oct 22, 2010)	12-Mo. Target Price $140.00	Investment Style Large-Cap Blend

GICS Sector Industrials
Sub-Industry Trading Companies & Distributors

Summary Grainger is the largest global distributor of industrial and commercial supplies, such as hand tools, electric motors, light bulbs, and janitorial items.

Key Stock Statistics (Source S&P, Vickers, company reports)

52-Wk Range	$126.05– 92.87	S&P Oper. EPS 2010E	6.65	Market Capitalization(B)	$8.700	Beta	0.93
Trailing 12-Month EPS	$6.36	S&P Oper. EPS 2011E	7.60	Yield (%)	1.76	S&P 3-Yr. Proj. EPS CAGR(%)	17
Trailing 12-Month P/E	19.3	P/E on S&P Oper. EPS 2010E	18.4	Dividend Rate/Share	$2.16	S&P Credit Rating	AA+
$10K Invested 5 Yrs Ago	$20,719	Common Shares Outstg. (M)	71.0	Institutional Ownership (%)	72		

Price Performance

30-Week Mov. Avg. · · · 10-Week Mov. Avg. — **GAAP Earnings vs. Previous Year** Volume Above Avg. ⅉⅉⅉ STARS
12-Mo. Target Price — Relative Strength — ▲ Up ▼ Down ▶ No Change Below Avg. ⅉⅉⅉ ★

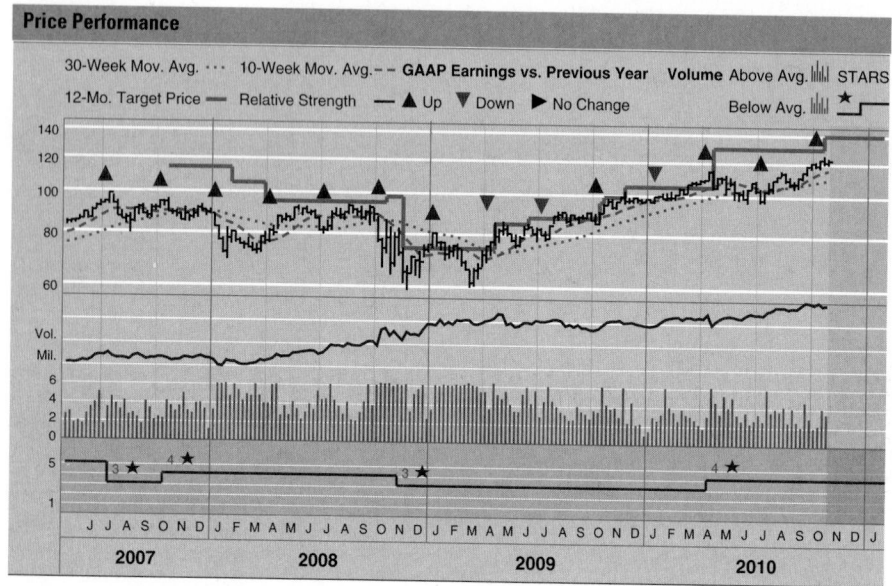

Analysis prepared by **Stewart Scharf** on October 15, 2010, when the stock traded at **$ 121.56**.

Options: ASE, CBOE, P, Ph

Highlights

➤ We expect sales to advance over 14% (near 10% organic growth) in 2010, with high single digit growth likely in 2011, driven by strength in heavy and light manufacturing, and a rebound in the retail and commercial markets in the U.S. We expect government and contractor sales to remain soft near term before gradually recovering, while growth should continue in Canada in heavy manufacturing, oil & gas, mining and forestry. Additionally, we believe acquisitions and strength in Mexico, India and China will drive emerging markets.

➤ We look for gross margin expansion in 2010 from 41.8% in 2009, with further expansion in 2011, as increased volume and higher prices offset a negative mix due to more volume discounts for large customers. We believe EBITDA margins will continue to widen from our 14% projection for 2010 (13% in 2009), as well controlled operating costs outweigh higher payroll and benefits costs.

➤ For 2010, we forecast a higher effective tax rate of about 40%, and operating EPS of $6.65 (before a $0.15 net benefit), increasing 14% in 2011 to $7.60.

Investment Rationale/Risk

➤ Our buy opinion is based on our view of improving global market trends as economic conditions gradually improve, while our valuation metrics also indicate upside potential. In our view, GWW will continue to gain market share via organic growth and product line expansion, and acquisitions in emerging regions, targeting more small to mid-size customers and overseas ventures.

➤ Risks to our recommendation and target price include another significant downturn in industrial production and non-farm payrolls; a negative impact from entering new markets; loss of customers; and a stronger U.S. dollar mainly versus the Canadian dollar.

➤ Our 12-month target price of $140 is based on a blend of our relative and DCF analyses. Based on price-to-EBITDA and P/E-to-EPS growth ratios, we believe GWW deserves an above historical P/E multiple of 17.8X our 2011 EPS estimate, which leads to a value of $135. Our DCF-based model, assuming a 3.5% terminal growth rate and an 8.3% weighted average cost of capital, indicates intrinsic value of $145.

Qualitative Risk Assessment

LOW	MEDIUM	HIGH

Our risk assessment reflects uncertain economic conditions, pricing pressures, and possible facilities disruptions or shutdowns. This is offset by GWW's S&P Quality Ranking of A+, which indicates the highest and most consistent level of earnings and dividend growth.

Quantitative Evaluations

S&P Quality Ranking A+

D	C	B-	B	B+	A-	A	A+

Relative Strength Rank MODERATE

66

LOWEST = 1   HIGHEST = 99

Revenue/Earnings Data

Revenue (Million $)

	1Q	2Q	3Q	4Q	Year
2010	1,672	1,784	1,899	--	--
2009	1,465	1,533	1,590	1,634	6,222
2008	1,661	1,757	1,839	1,593	6,850
2007	1,547	1,601	1,659	1,612	6,418
2006	1,419	1,483	1,520	1,462	5,884
2005	1,335	1,373	1,428	1,391	5,527

Earnings Per Share ($)

2010	1.31	1.73	2.07	E1.63	E6.65
2009	1.25	1.21	1.88	1.27	5.62
2008	1.43	1.43	1.79	1.39	6.04
2007	1.17	1.21	1.29	1.28	4.94
2006	0.93	1.02	1.16	1.13	4.24
2005	0.79	0.89	0.97	1.13	3.78

Fiscal year ended Dec. 31. Next earnings report expected: Late January. EPS Estimates based on S&P Operating Earnings; historical GAAP earnings are as reported.

Dividend Data (Dates: mm/dd Payment Date: mm/dd/yy)

Amount ($)	Date Decl.	Ex-Div. Date	Stk. of Record	Payment Date
0.460	10/28	11/05	11/09	12/01/09
0.460	01/27	02/04	02/08	03/01/10
0.540	04/28	05/06	05/10	06/01/10
0.540	07/28	08/05	08/09	09/01/10

Dividends have been paid since 1965. Source: Company reports.

Please read the Required Disclosures and Analyst Certification on the last page of this report.

The McGraw·Hill Companies

Grainger (W W) Inc.

Business Summary October 15, 2010

CORPORATE OVERVIEW. W.W. Grainger distributes facilities maintenance and other industrial and commercial supplies, including pumps, tools, motors, and electrical and safety products. The company holds a 4% share of the estimated $140 billion North American facilities maintenance market. As of September 30, 2010, it had 609 branches and multiple websites. Starting in 2006, the company began reporting its Canadian branch-based business as a separate segment: Acklands-Grainger. The branch-based business segment consists mainly of 410 U.S. traditional branch stores, 168 Canadian branches, and 11 Will Call Express branches, as well as 21 stores in Mexico, five stores in Columbia (opened in the third quarter of 2010), three stores in Puerto Rico, and one branch each in China and Panama. In the third quarter of 2010, GWW closed two U.S. branches while opening four in Canada. In the second quarter, it closed two U.S. branches and one in Mexico, following 11 U.S. branch closings in the first quarter. Six Will Call Express locations in China were closed in the fourth quarter of 2009, along with five U.S. branches. These Express branches sell company-made -- as well as third-party -- industrial supplies via in-store catalogs and Internet services. GWW estimates China's current market for facilities maintenance supplies at $38 billion, and projects that it will exceed $70 billion by 2014.

In 2009, the U.S. branch-based unit accounted for 87% of sales and had a pre-tax return on invested capital (ROIC) of 34.8%. The Acklands unit accounted for 10% of sales, with ROIC of 11.5%. Other businesses (Japan, Mexico, India, China and Panama) accounted for 2.6% of sales. In June 2010, GWW formed Grainger Colombia, an 80%-owned joint venture with an affiliate of Torhefe S.A., a distributor of maintenance, repair and operating (MRO) supplies in Colombia.

Sales in 2009 broke down approximately as follows: 16% heavy manufacturing, 20% commercial, 19% government, 13% contractor, 9% light manufacturing, 8% retail/wholesale, 4% reseller, 4% agriculture and mining, and 7% other.

GWW's 2010 catalog offered 307,000 facilities maintenance and other products, up 32% from 2009. Approximately 24% of sales in 2009 consisted of private label items. Through Grainger.com, customers can access more than 600,000 products. E-commerce sales in 2009 accounted for nearly 24% of the total.

In the first quarter of 2010, GWW incurred a $0.15 per share charge related to new health care legislation. In the first nine months of 2010, the company recorded a $0.24 per share benefit due to a change in paid time off policy in the U.S., which the company projects will total about $0.30 for the full year.

Company Financials Fiscal Year Ended Dec. 31

Per Share Data ($)	2009	2008	2007	2006	2005	2004	2003	2002	2001	2000
Tangible Book Value	25.06	24.35	23.47	23.40	23.47	20.89	18.43	16.92	15.51	14.67
Cash Flow	7.41	7.52	6.25	5.35	4.85	4.06	3.28	3.30	2.73	3.01
Earnings	5.62	6.04	4.94	4.24	3.78	3.13	2.46	2.50	1.84	2.05
S&P Core Earnings	5.34	6.13	4.94	4.26	3.65	2.96	2.36	2.29	1.87	NA
Dividends	1.78	1.55	1.34	1.11	0.92	0.79	0.74	0.72	0.70	0.67
Payout Ratio	32%	26%	27%	26%	24%	25%	30%	29%	38%	33%
Prices:High	102.54	93.99	98.60	79.95	72.45	66.99	53.30	59.40	48.99	56.88
Prices:Low	59.95	58.86	68.77	60.60	51.65	45.00	41.40	39.20	29.51	24.31
P/E Ratio:High	18	16	20	19	19	21	22	24	27	28
P/E Ratio:Low	11	10	14	14	14	14	17	16	16	12

Income Statement Analysis (Million $)	2009	2008	2007	2006	2005	2004	2003	2002	2001	2000
Revenue	6,222	6,850	6,418	5,884	5,527	5,050	4,667	4,644	4,754	4,977
Operating Income	799	906	782	679	617	525	463	467	461	426
Depreciation	148	117	111	101	98.1	85.6	76.1	75.9	83.7	90.6
Interest Expense	8.77	15.8	4.37	1.93	1.86	4.39	6.02	6.16	10.7	24.4
Pretax Income	707	773	682	603	533	445	381	398	297	332
Effective Tax Rate	39.1%	38.5%	38.4%	36.4%	35.0%	35.5%	40.4%	40.8%	41.3%	41.8%
Net Income	430	475	420	383	346	287	227	235	175	193
S&P Core Earnings	399	482	420	385	336	272	217	213	177	NA

Balance Sheet & Other Financial Data (Million $)	2009	2008	2007	2006	2005	2004	2003	2002	2001	2000
Cash	460	396	134	361	545	429	403	209	169	63.4
Current Assets	2,132	2,144	1,801	1,862	1,998	1,755	1,633	1,485	1,393	1,483
Total Assets	3,726	3,513	3,094	3,046	3,108	2,810	2,625	2,437	2,331	2,460
Current Liabilities	777	762	826	706	727	662	707	586	554	747
Long Term Debt	438	488	4.90	4.90	4.90	Nil	4.90	120	118	125
Common Equity	2,227	2,034	2,098	2,178	2,289	2,068	1,845	1,668	1,603	1,537
Total Capital	2,718	2,543	27,720	2,189	2,301	2,072	1,850	1,787	1,723	1,663
Capital Expenditures	141	169	189	128	112	128	74.1	134	100	65.5
Cash Flow	555	592	531	484	444	372	303	311	258	284
Current Ratio	2.7	2.8	2.2	2.6	2.7	2.6	2.3	2.5	2.5	2.0
% Long Term Debt of Capitalization	16.1	19.2	NM	0.2	0.2	Nil	0.3	6.7	6.9	7.5
% Net Income of Revenue	6.9	6.9	6.6	6.5	6.3	5.7	4.9	5.1	3.7	3.9
% Return on Assets	11.9	14.4	13.7	12.5	11.7	10.6	9.0	9.9	7.3	7.7
% Return on Equity	20.2	23.0	19.7	17.2	15.9	14.7	12.9	14.4	11.1	12.8

Data as orig reptd.; bef. results of disc opers/spec. items. Per share data adj. for stk. divs.; EPS diluted. E-Estimated. NA-Not Available. NM-Not Meaningful. NR-Not Ranked. UR-Under Review.

Office: 100 Grainger Pkwy, Lake Forest, IL 60045.
Telephone: 847-535-1000.
Website: http://www.grainger.com
Chrmn, Pres & CEO: J.T. Ryan

SVP & CFO: R.L. Jadin
SVP & General Counsel: J.L. Howard
Chief Acctg Officer & Cntlr: G.S. Irving
Secy: C.L. Kogl

Investor Contact: W.D. Chapman (847-535-0881)
Board Members: B. P. Anderson, W. H. Gantz, V. A. Hailey, W. Hall, S. L. Levenick, J. W. McCarter, Jr., N. S. Novich, M. J. Roberts, G. L. Rogers, J. T. Ryan, E. S. Santi, J. D. Slavik

Founded: 1927
Domicile: Illinois
Employees: 18,000

Halliburton Co

STANDARD &POOR'S

S&P Recommendation **HOLD** ★★★☆☆	Price $34.18 (as of Oct 22, 2010)	12-Mo. Target Price $37.00	Investment Style Large-Cap Growth

GICS Sector Energy
Sub-Industry Oil & Gas Equipment & Services

Summary This leading oilfield services company provides products and services to the global energy industry.

Key Stock Statistics (Source S&P, Vickers, company reports)

52-Wk Range	$35.89–21.10	S&P Oper. EPS 2010**E**	1.90	Market Capitalization(B)	$31.185	Beta	1.50
Trailing 12-Month EPS	$1.62	S&P Oper. EPS 2011**E**	2.44	Yield (%)	1.05	S&P 3-Yr. Proj. EPS CAGR(%)	30
Trailing 12-Month P/E	21.1	P/E on S&P Oper. EPS 2010**E**	18.0	Dividend Rate/Share	$0.36	S&P Credit Rating	A
$10K Invested 5 Yrs Ago	$12,731	Common Shares Outstg. (M)	912.4	Institutional Ownership (%)	78		

Price Performance

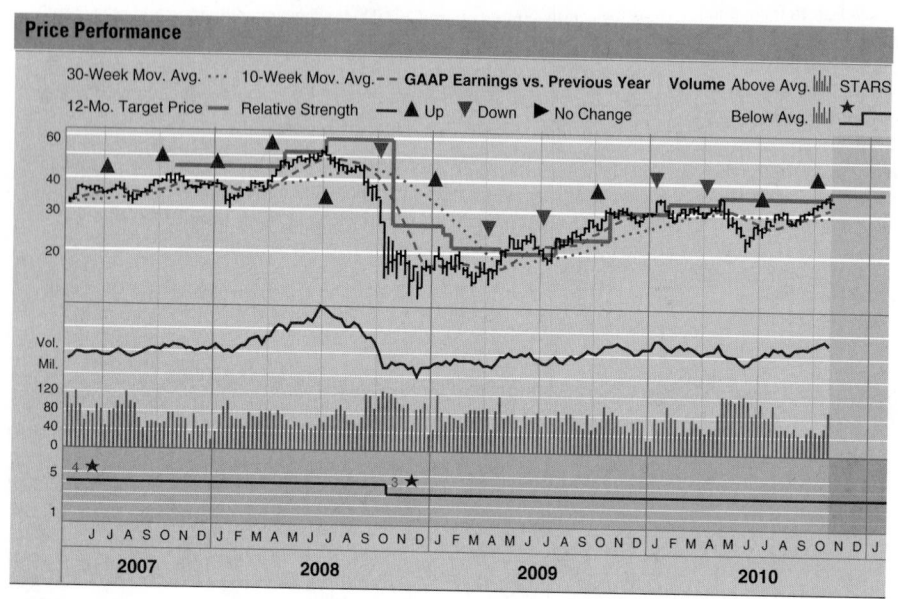

- 30-Week Mov. Avg. · · · · 10-Week Mov. Avg. - - - **GAAP Earnings vs. Previous Year** Volume Above Avg. ▉▍▐ **STARS**
- 12-Mo. Target Price — Relative Strength — ▲ Up ▼ Down ▶ No Change Below Avg. ▏▌▎ ★

Options: ASE, CBOE, P, Ph

Qualitative Risk Assessment

LOW	MEDIUM	**HIGH**

Our risk assessment reflects HAL's exposure to volatile crude oil and natural gas prices, leverage to the North American oilfield services market, and political risk associated with operating in frontier regions such as West Africa and the Middle East. A partial offset is HAL's strong number two position in oilfield services.

Quantitative Evaluations

S&P Quality Ranking   **B**

D	C	B-	**B**	B+	A-	A	A+

Relative Strength Rank   **STRONG**

76

LOWEST = 1   HIGHEST = 99

Revenue/Earnings Data

Revenue (Million $)

	1Q	2Q	3Q	4Q	Year
2010	3,761	4,387	4,665	--	--
2009	113.5	3,494	3,588	3,686	14,675
2008	4,029	4,487	4,853	4,910	18,279
2007	3,422	3,735	3,928	4,179	15,264
2006	5,184	5,545	5,831	6,016	22,576
2005	4,938	5,163	5,095	5,798	20,994

Earnings Per Share ($)

	1Q	2Q	3Q	4Q	Year
2010	0.23	0.52	0.53	E0.61	E1.90
2009	0.42	0.29	0.29	0.27	1.28
2008	0.64	0.68	-0.02	0.87	2.17
2007	0.52	0.63	0.79	0.74	2.66
2006	0.45	0.48	0.58	0.65	2.16
2005	0.36	0.38	0.48	1.04	2.27

Fiscal year ended Dec. 31. Next earnings report expected: Late January. EPS Estimates based on S&P Operating Earnings; historical GAAP earnings are as reported.

Highlights

- ▶ The 12-month target price for HAL has recently been changed to $37.00 from $35.00. The Highlights section of this Stock Report will be updated accordingly.

Investment Rationale/Risk

- ▶ The Investment Rationale/Risk section of this Stock Report will be updated shortly. For the latest News story on HAL from MarketScope, see below.

- ▶ 10/18/10 12:59 pm ET ... S&P MAINTAINS HOLD OPINION ON SHARES OF HALLIBURTON (HAL 34.07***): Q3 EPS from cont. ops. of $0.58, before $0.05 of 1X charges, vs. $0.29, is $0.13 above our est. Onshore No America drove the gains. Still, the shares are down about 5% today, which we attribute to a more tepid near-term outlook for intl. ops., where margin gains are more likely to be volume-driven, not price-driven. We think intl. start-up costs continue to weigh on short-term results, but set the stage for long-term gains. We lift our '10 EPS est by $0.22 to $1.90, and '11's $0.13 to $2.44. On DCF model and relative metrics, we lift our target price by $2 to $37. /S.Glickman

Dividend Data (Dates: mm/dd Payment Date: mm/dd/yy)

Amount ($)	Date Decl.	Ex-Div. Date	Stk. of Record	Payment Date
0.090	11/09	12/01	12/03	12/23/09
0.090	02/10	02/26	03/02	03/23/10
0.090	05/19	05/27	06/01	06/22/10
0.090	07/16	08/30	09/01	09/21/10

Dividends have been paid since 1947. Source: Company reports.

Halliburton Co

Business Summary July 30, 2010

CORPORATE OVERVIEW. Halliburton is a leading global provider of oilfield services to the energy industry, and until April 2007, provided engineering and construction expertise to energy, industrial and governmental customers. In 2006, HAL was comprised of two main business units: the Energy Services Group (ESG), and the KBR unit. In April 2007, HAL effected the complete separation of KBR via a split-off of its 135.6 million share stake in KBR in exchange for HAL shares. Under the transaction, HAL exchanged its stake in KBR for about 85.3 million shares of HAL which were retired as treasury stock in early April. Following the separation, HAL was transformed into a pure-play oilfield services company. In the second half of 2007, the company reorganized its four ESG operating segments into two new segments: Completion & Production (51% of 2009 revenues excluding KBR, and 46% of 2009 operating income excluding KBR), and Drilling & Evaluation (49%, 54%). Results from the former KBR segment have been reclassified under discontinued operations. Geographically, HAL generated 39% of its total 2009 revenues from North America, followed by Europe/CIS/West Africa (27%), Middle East/Asia (20%) and Latin America (14%). Approximately 63% of HAL's North American revenues in 2009 were derived from C&P activity.

CORPORATE STRATEGY. Subsequent to the split-off, with HAL's financial

obligations to KBR for the Barracuda-Caratinga project and the Foreign Corrupt Practices Act (FCPA) investigations limited by terms of the Master Separation Agreement with KBR, we view HAL's exposure to such issues as reduced. While we expect HAL to defend its strong market position in North America, we believe that future capital expenditures will increasingly flow to the Eastern Hemisphere, which we see as growing faster in the long term. In 2007, HAL moved its corporate headquarters to Dubai, from Houston, which we view as symbolic of the growing importance of the Eastern Hemisphere to company operations.

UPCOMING CATALYSTS. Geographically, North America remains the dominant source of revenue for HAL, and is the primary driver for the Completion & Production segment. However, results in the Drilling & Evaluation segment are likely to be increasingly drawn from overseas, in our view, given expectations that offshore rig demand will show the strongest growth outside of North America.

Company Financials Fiscal Year Ended Dec. 31

Per Share Data ($)	2009	2008	2007	2006	2005	2004	2003	2002	2001	2000
Tangible Book Value	8.46	NA	8.72	6.61	5.46	3.55	2.14	3.25	4.65	3.90
Cash Flow	2.31	2.99	3.27	2.66	2.76	1.01	0.98	0.18	1.26	0.77
Earnings	1.28	2.17	2.66	2.16	2.27	0.44	0.39	-0.40	0.64	0.21
S&P Core Earnings	1.29	2.10	2.64	2.12	2.11	0.37	0.34	-0.52	0.33	NA
Dividends	0.36	0.36	0.35	0.30	0.25	0.25	0.25	0.25	0.25	0.25
Payout Ratio	28%	17%	13%	14%	11%	57%	64%	NM	39%	119%
Prices:High	32.00	55.38	41.95	41.99	34.89	20.85	13.60	10.83	24.63	27.59
Prices:Low	14.68	12.80	27.65	26.33	18.59	12.90	8.60	4.30	5.47	16.13
P/E Ratio:High	25	26	16	19	15	48	35	NM	38	NM
P/E Ratio:Low	11	6	10	12	8	30	22	NM	9	NM

Income Statement Analysis (Million $)	2009	2008	2007	2006	2005	2004	2003	2002	2001	2000
Revenue	14,675	18,279	15,264	22,576	20,994	20,466	16,271	12,572	13,046	11,856
Operating Income	NA	4,703	4,029	3,875	2,972	1,291	1,191	363	1,615	789
Depreciation, Depletion and Amortization	931	738	583	527	504	509	518	505	531	503
Interest Expense	297	160	154	175	207	229	139	113	147	146
Pretax Income	1,682	3,163	3,460	3,449	2,492	651	612	-228	954	335
Effective Tax Rate	30.8%	38.3%	26.2%	33.2%	3.17%	37.0%	38.2%	NM	40.3%	38.5%
Net Income	1,154	1,961	2,524	2,272	2,357	385	339	-346	551	188
S&P Core Earnings	1,161	1,893	2,505	2,220	2,181	320	299	-445	287	NA

Balance Sheet & Other Financial Data (Million $)	2009	2008	2007	2006	2005	2004	2003	2002	2001	2000
Cash	3,394	1,124	2,235	4,379	2,391	2,808	1,815	1,107	290	231
Current Assets	8,638	7,411	7,573	11,183	9,327	9,962	7,919	5,560	5,573	5,568
Total Assets	16,538	14,385	13,135	16,820	15,010	15,796	15,463	12,844	10,966	10,103
Current Liabilities	2,889	2,781	2,411	4,727	4,437	7,064	6,542	3,272	2,908	3,826
Long Term Debt	3,824	2,586	2,627	2,786	2,813	3,593	3,415	1,181	1,403	1,049
Common Equity	8,728	7,725	6,866	7,376	6,372	3,932	2,547	3,558	4,752	5,618
Total Capital	13,331	10,330	9,587	10,609	9,330	7,633	6,062	4,810	6,196	6,705
Capital Expenditures	1,864	1,824	1,583	891	651	575	515	764	797	578
Cash Flow	2,085	2,699	3,107	2,799	2,861	894	857	159	1,082	691
Current Ratio	3.0	2.7	3.1	2.4	2.1	1.4	1.2	1.7	1.9	1.5
% Long Term Debt of Capitalization	28.8	26.9	27.4	26.3	30.2	47.1	56.3	24.6	22.6	15.6
% Return on Assets	7.5	14.3	16.9	14.3	15.3	2.5	2.4	NM	5.2	1.9
% Return on Equity	14.0	26.9	35.4	33.1	45.7	14.4	11.1	NM	12.7	3.7

Data as orig reptd.; bef. results of disc opers/spec. items. Per share data adj. for stk. divs.; EPS diluted. E-Estimated. NA-Not Available. NM-Not Meaningful. NR-Not Ranked. UR-Under Review.

Office: 3000 N Sam Houston Pkwy E, Houston, TX 77072.
Telephone: 281-575-3000.
Email: investors@haliburton.com
Website: http://www.halliburton.com

Chrmn, Pres & CEO: D.J. Lesar
EVP & CFO: M.A. McCollum
EVP & General Counsel: A.O. Cornelison, Jr.
SVP & Treas: C.W. Nunez

SVP & Secy: S.D. Williams
Investor Contact: C. Garcia (713-759-2688)
Board Members: A. Bennett, J. R. Boyd, M. Carroll, N. K. Dicciani, S. M. Gillis, J. T. Hackett, A. S. Jum'ah, D. J. Lesar, R. A. Malone, J. Martin, D. L. Reed

Founded: 1919
Domicile: Delaware
Employees: 51,000

Harley-Davidson Inc.

STANDARD &POOR'S

S&P Recommendation SELL ★ ★ ☆ ☆ ☆

Price	12-Mo. Target Price	Investment Style
$31.32 (as of Oct 22, 2010)	$28.00	Large-Cap Growth

GICS Sector Consumer Discretionary
Sub-Industry Motorcycle Manufacturers

Summary This leading maker of heavyweight motorcycles also produces a line of motorcycle parts and accessories.

Key Stock Statistics (Source S&P, Vickers, company reports)

52-Wk Range	$36.13–21.26	S&P Oper. EPS 2010E	1.29	Market Capitalization(B)	$7.376	Beta	2.32
Trailing 12-Month EPS	$-0.11	S&P Oper. EPS 2011E	1.77	Yield (%)	1.28	S&P 3-Yr. Proj. EPS CAGR(%)	81
Trailing 12-Month P/E	NM	P/E on S&P Oper. EPS 2010E	24.3	Dividend Rate/Share	$0.40	S&P Credit Rating	BBB
$10K Invested 5 Yrs Ago	$7,117	Common Shares Outstg. (M)	235.5	Institutional Ownership (%)	84		

Price Performance

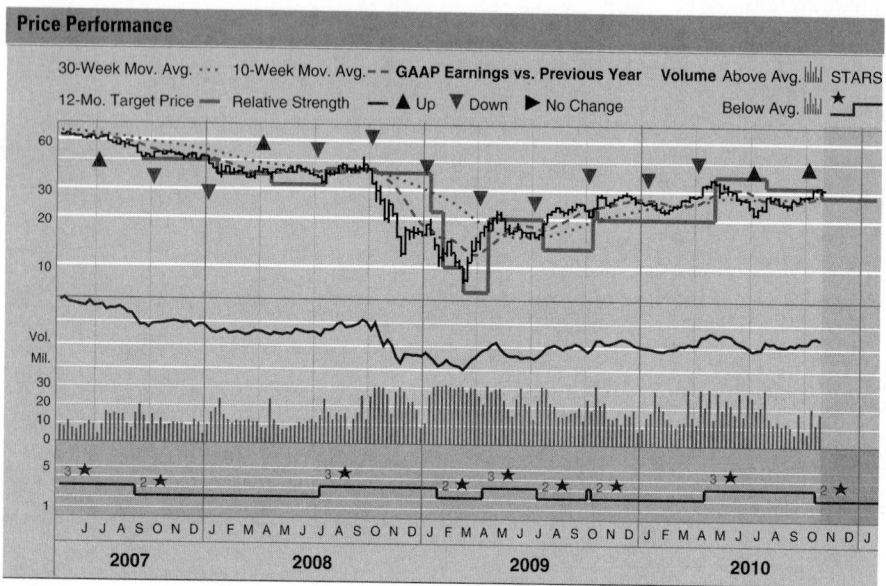

30-Week Mov. Avg. · · · 10-Week Mov. Avg. - - GAAP Earnings vs. Previous Year Volume Above Avg. STARS
12-Mo. Target Price — Relative Strength — ▲ Up ▼ Down ► No Change   Below Avg.

Options: ASE, CBOE, P, Ph

Qualitative Risk Assessment

LOW	MEDIUM	HIGH

Our risk assessment reflects our view that HOG's market leadership position and strong brand will help offset the prospect that an aging U.S. population will limit future domestic demand for motorcycles.

Quantitative Evaluations

S&P Quality Ranking A-

D	C	B-	B	B+	A-	A	A+

Relative Strength Rank STRONG

79

LOWEST = 1   HIGHEST = 99

Highlights

► The STARS recommendation for HOG has recently been changed to 2 (sell) from 3 (hold) and the 12-month target price has recently been changed to $28.00 from $32.00. The Highlights section of this Stock Report will be updated accordingly.

Investment Rationale/Risk

► The Investment Rationale/Risk section of this Stock Report will be updated shortly. For the latest News story on HOG from MarketScope, see below.

► 10/19/10 10:30 am ET ... S&P LOWERS OPINION ON SHARES OF HARLEY-DAVIDSON TO SELL FROM HOLD (HOG 31.47**): Q3 EPS of $0.40 from continuing operations, vs. $0.24, is above our $0.32 estimate. Although HOG reported a 1.9% net revenue decline, slightly lower than we expected, gross profit margins were better than expected, aided by an improving product mix. HDFS income was $51M (33% of total operating income). We think Q4 gross margins will be weaker than previously expected, and we are also lowering our revenue estimates. We cut our '10 EPS estimate to $1.29 from $1.32, and reduce our target price to $28 from $32, based on our updated peer analysis. /EKolb

Revenue/Earnings Data

Revenue (Million $)

	1Q	2Q	3Q	4Q	Year
2010	1,207	1,309	1,260	--	--
2009	1,383	1,260	1,246	893.7	4,782
2008	1,306	1,573	1,423	1,293	5,594
2007	1,179	1,620	1,541	1,386	5,727
2006	1,285	1,377	1,636	1,503	5,801
2005	1,235	1,333	1,431	1,342	5,342

Earnings Per Share ($)

	1Q	2Q	3Q	4Q	Year
2010	0.29	0.59	0.40	ENil	E1.29
2009	0.55	0.14	0.24	-0.63	0.30
2008	0.79	0.95	0.71	0.34	2.79
2007	0.74	1.14	1.07	0.78	3.74
2006	0.86	0.91	1.20	0.97	3.93
2005	0.77	0.84	0.96	0.84	3.41

Fiscal year ended Dec. 31. Next earnings report expected: Late January. EPS Estimates based on S&P Operating Earnings; historical GAAP earnings are as reported.

Dividend Data (Dates: mm/dd Payment Date: mm/dd/yy)

Amount ($)	Date Decl.	Ex-Div. Date	Stk. of Record	Payment Date
0.100	12/10	12/17	12/21	12/31/09
0.100	02/11	02/19	02/23	03/05/10
0.100	04/24	06/01	06/03	06/18/10
0.100	09/16	09/29	10/01	10/15/10

Dividends have been paid since 1993. Source: Company reports.

Harley-Davidson Inc.

STANDARD &POOR'S

Business Summary July 21, 2010

CORPORATE OVERVIEW. Harley-Davidson is a leading supplier of heavy-weight motorcycles (engine displacement exceeding about 651 cubic centimeters). The company also sells motorcycle parts, accessories, clothing and collectibles, and has a sizable financial services business.

HOG manufactures five families of Harley-Davidson brand motorcycles: Sportster, Dyna, Softail, Touring and VRSC. In 2010, the engines in these product lines ranged in size from 883 cc to 1800 cc. The company's 2010 model year line-up includes 34 models of Harley-Davidson heavyweight motorcycles, with domestic manufacturer's suggested retail prices ranging from $6,595 to $20,195. In 2010, HOG was offering some limited-edition custom motorcycles having suggested retail prices ranging from $24,995 to $33,495. In 2009, HOG shipped 223,023 Harley-Davidson brand motorcycles, down from 303,479 in 2008 and 330,619 in 2007. HOG shipped 5,572 Buell motorcycles in 2009 before shuttering the brand, down from 13,119 in 2008 and 11,513 in 2007.

CORPORATE STRATEGY. We expect the company to focus both on current owners of HOG motorcycles and on potential new customers. We believe that many purchasers of a new Harley-Davidson motorcycle previously owned a HOG bike. We expect HOG's marketing focus to include international markets, where we project that HOG's opportunities for growth are stronger than they are in the U.S. In 2009, HOG's international sales totaled about $1.38 billion (32% of total sales), up from $1.75 billion (31%) in 2008.

HOG has in the past earned sizable profits from financial services it provides to independent dealers and to retail customers of those dealers. During 2009, Harley-Davidson Financial Services financed 48.8% of the new Harley-Davidson motorcycles retailed by independent dealers in the United States, as compared to 53.5% in 2008.

In August 2008, HOG completed its acquisition of 100% of MV Agusta Group, an Italian motorcycle manufacturer, for total consideration of $109 million. In 2007, MVAG shipped 5,819 motorcycles. HOG did not disclose how many units MVAG shipped in 2008. Then, in October 2009, HOG announced it intends to divest the brand to focus on its "single-brand strategy".

Company Financials Fiscal Year Ended Dec. 31

Per Share Data ($)	2009	2008	2007	2006	2005	2004	2003	2002	2001	2000
Tangible Book Value	8.86	8.49	16.32	10.46	11.05	10.73	9.63	7.21	5.64	4.47
Cash Flow	1.36	3.83	4.55	4.87	4.25	3.72	3.18	2.48	1.93	1.56
Earnings	0.30	2.79	3.74	3.93	3.41	3.00	2.50	1.90	1.43	1.13
S&P Core Earnings	0.54	2.57	3.76	3.95	3.44	2.98	2.51	1.85	1.34	NA
Dividends	0.40	1.29	1.06	0.81	0.63	0.41	0.20	0.14	0.12	0.10
Payout Ratio	133%	46%	28%	21%	18%	13%	8%	7%	8%	9%
Prices:High	30.00	48.05	74.03	75.87	62.49	63.75	52.51	57.25	55.99	50.63
Prices:Low	7.99	11.54	44.37	47.86	44.40	45.20	35.01	42.60	32.00	29.53
P/E Ratio:High	NM	NA	17	19	18	21	21	30	39	45
P/E Ratio:Low	NM	4	12	12	13	15	14	22	22	26

Income Statement Analysis (Million $)	2009	2008	2007	2006	2005	2004	2003	2002	2001	2000
Revenue	4,782	5,594	5,727	5,801	5,342	5,015	4,624	4,091	3,363	2,906
Operating Income	695	1,441	1,721	1,431	1,676	1,576	1,346	1,059	816	648
Depreciation	246	242	204	214	206	214	197	176	153	133
Interest Expense	21.7	141	81.5	Nil	Nil	Nil	Nil	Nil	Nil	Nil
Pretax Income	179	1,034	1,448	1,624	1,488	1,379	1,166	886	673	549
Effective Tax Rate	60.5%	36.7%	35.5%	35.8%	35.5%	35.5%	34.7%	34.5%	35.0%	36.6%
Net Income	70.6	655	934	1,043	960	890	761	580	438	348
S&P Core Earnings	128	604	940	1,048	969	881	763	564	411	NA

Balance Sheet & Other Financial Data (Million $)	2009	2008	2007	2006	2005	2004	2003	2002	2001	2000
Cash	1,670	594	405	897	1,046	1,612	1,323	796	635	420
Total Assets	9,156	7,829	5,657	5,532	5,255	5,483	4,923	3,861	3,118	2,436
Long Term Debt	600	2,176	980	87.0	1,000	800	670	380	380	355
Total Debt	NA	3,915	2,100	87.0	1,205	1,295	794	763	597	445
Common Equity	2,108	2,116	2,375	2,757	3,084	3,218	2,958	2,233	1,756	1,406
Capital Expenditures	117	232	242	220	198	214	227	324	204	204
Cash Flow	317	897	1,138	1,257	1,165	1,104	958	756	591	481
% Return on Assets	0.8	9.7	16.7	19.3	17.9	17.1	17.3	16.6	15.8	15.3
% Return on Equity	3.3	29.2	36.4	35.7	30.5	28.8	29.3	29.1	27.7	27.1
% Long Term Debt of Capitalization	Nil	50.7	29.2	3.1	23.6	19.7	17.8	14.4	17.6	20.2

Data as orig reptd.; bef. results of disc opers/spec. items. Per share data adj. for stk. divs.; EPS diluted. E-Estimated. NA-Not Available. NM-Not Meaningful. NR-Not Ranked. UR-Under Review.

Office: 3700 W Juneau Ave, Milwaukee, WI 53208.
Telephone: 414-342-4680.
Email: investor_relations@harley-davidson.com
Website: http://www.harley-davidson.com

Chrmn: B.K. Allen
Pres & CEO: K.E. Wandell
SVP & CFO: J. Olin
Chief Acctg Officer: M.R. Kornetzke

Treas: J.D. Thomas
Investor Contact: T.E. Bergmann (414-342-4680)
Board Members: B. K. Allen, J. Anderson, R. I. Beattie, M. F. Brooks, G. H. Conrades, J. C. Green, D. James, S. Levinson, N. T. Linebarger, G. L. Miles, Jr., J. A. Norling, K. E. Wandell, J. Zeitz

Founded: 1903
Domicile: Wisconsin
Employees: 7,900

The McGraw-Hill Companies

Harman International Industries Inc.

STANDARD &POOR'S

S&P Recommendation HOLD ★★★☆☆	Price $34.33 (as of Oct 22, 2010)	12-Mo. Target Price $35.00	Investment Style Large-Cap Growth

GICS Sector Consumer Discretionary
Sub-Industry Consumer Electronics

Summary This company manufactures and markets high-fidelity audio products and electronic systems targeted at OEM, consumer and professional markets.

Key Stock Statistics (Source S&P, Vickers, company reports)

52-Wk Range	$53.36– 28.10	S&P Oper. EPS 2011**E**	1.61	Market Capitalization(B)	$2.387	Beta	2.01
Trailing 12-Month EPS	$2.25	S&P Oper. EPS 2012**E**	2.09	Yield (%)	Nil	S&P 3-Yr. Proj. EPS CAGR(%)	25
Trailing 12-Month P/E	15.3	P/E on S&P Oper. EPS 2011**E**	21.3	Dividend Rate/Share	Nil	S&P Credit Rating	BB
$10K Invested 5 Yrs Ago	$3,377	Common Shares Outstg. (M)	69.5	Institutional Ownership (%)	NM		

Price Performance

30-Week Mov. Avg. · · · · 10-Week Mov. Avg. – – GAAP Earnings vs. Previous Year   Volume Above Avg. STARS
12-Mo. Target Price — Relative Strength — ▲ Up ▼ Down ► No Change   Below Avg.

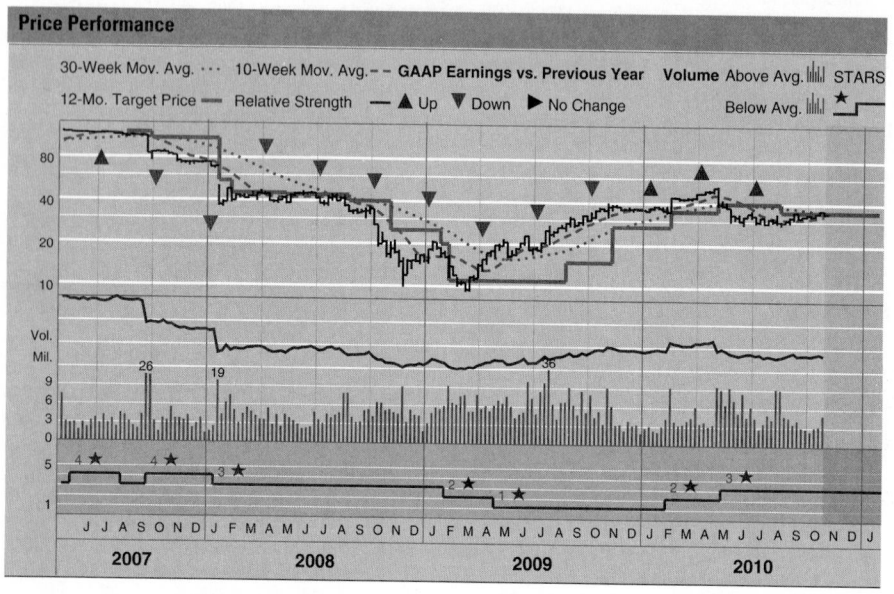

Options: ASE, CBOE, P, Ph

Analysis prepared by **Michael Souers** on October 07, 2010, when the stock traded at **$ 33.43**.

Highlights

► We see FY 11 (Jun.) revenues rising 6.9%, following a 17% advance in FY 10. We see this increase being driven by an uptick in automotive sales and market share gains. In addition, HAR has captured several audio and infotainment awards, which should lead to sales growth over the next several years. Offsetting these positive drivers is a weak global economy, which we expect to pressure consumer spending over the near to medium term.

► HAR has identified $400 million of cost savings across engineering, sourcing and manufacturing, and we expect these efforts to be ongoing. In FY 11, given our outlook for increasing revenues, we see the substantial cost-cutting leading to a significant widening of operating margins.

► After taxes at 30.0% and a slightly higher diluted share count, we project FY 11 EPS of $1.61, a significant improvement from the $0.85 the company earned in FY 10, excluding $0.34 a share of goodwill impairment and restructuring charges. We project EPS of $2.09 in FY 12.

Investment Rationale/Risk

► We think HAR's plans to sharply reduce costs have paid off handsomely, and we expect much-improved operating margins as a result. In addition, we think HAR's selection by Toyota to provide infotainment systems for its vehicles sold in Europe is a potentially major boon for future sales. Nevertheless, we continue to project a weak global economic recovery, with only modest improvement in automotive sales over the next couple of years. The shares recently traded at about 16X our FY 12 EPS estimate, a premium to the S&P 500; we think this premium is merited by the company's potential for vast operating margin improvement over the medium term.

► Risks to our recommendation and target price include higher-than-anticipated research and development costs; a double-dip recession, which would adversely impact automotive sales and overall consumer spending; and unfavorable foreign currency translation.

► We derive our 12-month target price of $35 from our discounted cash flow analysis. Our model assumes a weighted average cost of capital of 10.0% and a terminal growth rate of 3.0%.

Qualitative Risk Assessment

LOW	MEDIUM	HIGH

Our risk assessment reflects HAR's customer concentration in the automotive segment and sensitivity to the cyclical automobile industry, only partly offset by our view of its strong balance sheet.

Quantitative Evaluations

S&P Quality Ranking   B

D	C	B-	B	B+	A-	A	A+

Relative Strength Rank   MODERATE
48
LOWEST = 1   HIGHEST = 99

Revenue/Earnings Data

Revenue (Million $)

	1Q	2Q	3Q	4Q	Year
2010	748.4	928.3	837.0	850.7	3,364
2009	869.2	755.9	598.3	667.7	2,891
2008	947.0	1,066	1,033	1,067	4,113
2007	825.5	931.7	882.8	911.1	3,551
2006	754.7	832.7	801.5	859.1	3,248
2005	691.7	788.6	742.6	808.0	3,031

Earnings Per Share ($)

	1Q	2Q	3Q	4Q	Year
2010	-0.17	0.19	0.21	0.26	0.50
2009	0.40	-5.41	-1.14	-1.05	-7.19
2008	0.55	0.68	-0.06	0.54	1.73
2007	0.85	1.22	1.07	1.58	4.72
2006	0.79	1.07	0.94	0.95	3.75
2005	0.48	0.92	0.90	1.01	3.31

Fiscal year ended Jun. 30. Next earnings report expected: Late October. EPS Estimates based on S&P Operating Earnings; historical GAAP earnings are as reported.

Dividend Data

Dividends were suspended following the March 2009 payment.

Harman International Industries Inc.

Business Summary October 07, 2010

CORPORATE OVERVIEW. Harman International Industries (HAR) has three main operating segments: Automotive (73% of FY 10 (Jun.) sales), Professional (16%) and Consumer (11%). Within Automotive, HAR designs, manufactures and markets audio, electronic and infotainment systems to be installed as original equipment by automotive manufacturers. Infotainment systems are a combination of information and entertainment components that may include or control GPS navigation, traffic information, voice-activated telephone and climate control, rear seat entertainment, wireless Internet access, hard disk recording, MP3 playback, and high-end branded audio systems. Brand names include JBL, Infinity, Mark Levinson, Harmon/Kardon, Logic 7, Lexicon and Becker. Customers include Audi/Volkswagen, BMW, Daimler, Chrysler, Toyota/Lexus, Hyundai, Porsche, Land Rover, PSA Peugeot Citroen and Jaguar. HAR also produces an infotainment system for Harley-Davidson motorcycles. HAR believes its competitive position is enhanced by the company's technical expertise in designing and integrating acoustics, navigation, speech recognition and human-machine interfaces into complete infotainment systems uniquely adapted to the specific requirements of each automotive model.

HAR's Professional segment designs, manufactures and markets an extensive range of loudspeakers, power amplifiers, digital signal processors, microphones, headphones and mixing consoles used by audio professionals in concert halls, stadiums, airports, houses of worship and other public spaces. HAR's products were used at such venues as the 2008 Beijing Olympics and the 2009 Presidential Inauguration. Products are marketed globally under a number of brand names including JBL, AKG, Crown, Soundcraft, Lexicon, Mark Levinson, Revel, DigiTech, dbx and Studer.

In the Consumer segment, HAR makes audio, video and electronic systems for home, mobile and multimedia applications. Mobile products include an array of aftermarket systems to deliver audio entertainment and navigation in vehicles. Products for multimedia applications are primarily focused on enhancing sound for Apple's iPods and iPhones, computers, headphones and MP3 players. Brands include AKG, Harman/Kardon, Infinity, JBL, Mark Levinson and Selenium.

Company Financials Fiscal Year Ended Jun. 30

Per Share Data ($)	2010	2009	2008	2007	2006	2005	2004	2003	2002	2001
Tangible Book Value	14.80	12.87	15.44	16.71	12.82	10.74	9.43	6.66	5.04	4.33
Cash Flow	2.31	-4.68	4.18	6.64	5.66	4.99	3.80	2.85	2.00	1.48
Earnings	0.50	-7.19	1.73	4.72	3.75	3.31	2.27	1.55	0.85	0.48
S&P Core Earnings	0.65	-3.50	1.79	4.75	3.75	3.28	2.27	1.51	0.76	0.41
Dividends	NA	0.04	0.05	0.05	0.05	0.05	0.05	0.05	0.05	0.05
Payout Ratio	Nil	NM	3%	1%	1%	2%	2%	3%	6%	10%
Prices:High	53.36	40.33	73.75	125.13	115.85	130.45	131.74	75.35	32.65	23.31
Prices:Low	28.10	9.17	9.87	69.48	74.65	68.54	66.12	26.15	19.09	11.64
P/E Ratio:High	NM	NM	43	27	31	39	58	49	38	49
P/E Ratio:Low	NM	NM	6	15	20	21	29	17	22	24

Income Statement Analysis (Million $)	2010	2009	2008	2007	2006	2005	2004	2003	2002	2001
Revenue	3,364	2,891	4,113	3,551	3,248	3,031	2,711	2,229	1,826	1,717
Operating Income	263	-31.2	351	514	527	470	360	255	181	138
Depreciation	128	147	152	127	130	119	106	88.5	78.1	67.2
Interest Expense	30.2	15.3	21.2	1.50	13.0	10.5	17.2	22.6	22.4	25.0
Pretax Income	49.1	-520	124	382	376	335	228	142	80.2	45.1
Effective Tax Rate	NA	NM	13.8%	18.4%	32.4%	30.6%	30.6%	26.0%	28.2%	28.2%
Net Income	35.2	-423	108	314	255	233	158	105	57.5	32.4
S&P Core Earnings	45.8	-206	111	316	256	231	158	102	51.5	27.3

Balance Sheet & Other Financial Data (Million $)	2010	2009	2008	2007	2006	2005	2004	2003	2002	2001
Cash	646	591	223	106	292	291	378	148	116	2.75
Current Assets	1,674	1,511	1,439	1,233	1,249	1,183	1,204	968	877	709
Total Assets	2,556	2,492	2,827	2,509	2,355	2,187	1,989	1,704	1,480	1,162
Current Liabilities	863	744	907	816	869	729	662	487	433	350
Long Term Debt	364	629	427	57.7	179	331	388	498	470	Nil
Common Equity	1,135	974	1,340	1,510	1,228	1,061	875	656	527	423
Total Capital	1,499	1,603	1,767	1,568	1,410	1,392	1,263	1,154	999	424
Capital Expenditures	60.0	79.9	139	175	131	176	135	116	114	88.1
Cash Flow	163	-275	260	441	385	352	264	194	136	99.6
Current Ratio	1.9	2.0	1.6	1.5	1.4	1.6	1.8	2.0	2.0	2.0
% Long Term Debt of Capitalization	24.3	39.2	24.2	3.7	12.7	23.8	30.7	43.2	47.1	Nil
% Net Income of Revenue	1.1	NM	2.6	8.8	7.9	7.7	5.8	4.7	3.1	1.9
% Return on Assets	1.4	NM	4.0	12.9	11.2	11.2	8.6	6.6	4.4	2.8
% Return on Equity	3.3	NM	7.6	22.8	22.3	24.1	20.6	17.8	12.1	7.1

Data as orig reptd.; bef. results of disc opers/spec. items. Per share data adj. for stk. divs.; EPS diluted. E-Estimated. NA-Not Available. NM-Not Meaningful. NR-Not Ranked. UR-Under Review.

Office: 400 Atlantic St Ste 1500, Stamford, CT 06901.
Telephone: 203-328-3500.
Website: http://www.harman.com
Chrmn, Pres & CEO: D.C. Paliwal

EVP & CFO: H.K. Parker
EVP & CTO: S. Lawande
EVP, Secy & General Counsel: T.A. Suko
Chief Acctg Officer: J. Peter

Investor Contact: S.B. Robinson (202-393-1101)
Board Members: B. F. Carroll, H. Einsmann, R. K. Gupta, A. M. Korologos, J. Liu, E. H. Meyer, D. C. Paliwal, K. M. Reiss, H. S. Runtagh, G. G. Steel

Founded: 1980
Domicile: Delaware
Employees: 9,816

Harris Corp

STANDARD &POOR'S

S&P Recommendation BUY ★★★★☆

Price	12-Mo. Target Price	Investment Style
$43.80 (as of Oct 22, 2010)	$53.00	Large-Cap Growth

GICS Sector Information Technology
Sub-Industry Communications Equipment

Summary This company focuses on communications equipment for voice, data and video applications for commercial and governmental customers.

Key Stock Statistics (Source S&P, Vickers, company reports)

52-Wk Range	$54.50–37.44	S&P Oper. EPS 2011E	4.64	Market Capitalization(B)	$5.652	Beta	0.95
Trailing 12-Month EPS	$4.28	S&P Oper. EPS 2012E	NA	Yield (%)	2.28	S&P 3-Yr. Proj. EPS CAGR(%)	9
Trailing 12-Month P/E	10.2	P/E on S&P Oper. EPS 2011E	9.4	Dividend Rate/Share	$1.00	S&P Credit Rating	BBB+
$10K Invested 5 Yrs Ago	NA	Common Shares Outstg. (M)	129.0	Institutional Ownership (%)	85		

Price Performance

30-Week Mov. Avg. · · · ·   10-Week Mov. Avg. – – –   **GAAP Earnings vs. Previous Year**   Volume Above Avg. STARS
12-Mo. Target Price —   Relative Strength —   ▲ Up   ▼ Down   ▶ No Change   Below Avg. ★

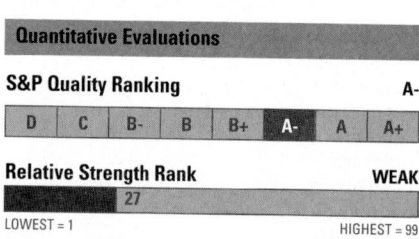

Options: ASE, CBOE, P, Ph

Analysis prepared by **Todd Rosenbluth** on August 17, 2010, when the stock traded at **$ 44.50**.

Highlights

➤ We forecast revenues of $6.0 billion in FY 11 (Jun.), up from $5.2 billion the year before, supported by an acquisition. Pressure on the RF Communications segment waned beginning in the FY 10 second quarter, and orders for tactical radios for U.S. military agencies have picked up, which we think should spur growth in segment sales in FY 11. Meanwhile, we see more modest growth for the government communications segment as key projects are completed and newer ones are begun.

➤ Following improvement in gross margins in FY 10, we look for a slight decline in FY 11 to 35% due to lower pricing for new contracts and a shift in product mix toward lower-margin products. Despite continued investment in R&D, we see the operating margin widening to 19% due to integration of a recent merger.

➤ We estimate operating EPS of $4.64 in FY 11, up from FY 10 results even with a modest increase in interest costs. FY 09 results included a $1.37 asset impairment charge for Stratex, which has since been spun off.

Investment Rationale/Risk

➤ Visibility into the company's order demand for its radios has improved, and we believe revenues and earnings will grow in FY 11. We think long-term trends favor growth in HRS's core segments, as local and federal government agencies focus on improving the technological capabilities of their communications systems, although new government spending might be limited in the near term by budgetary issues. We believe HRS has a strong balance sheet and can support its recent acquisitions. With the shares having fallen since the reporting of what we consider strong fiscal fourth-quarter earnings, we view HRS as undervalued.

➤ Risks to our recommendation and target price include reduced funding for U.S. government contracts, lower capital spending by service operators, and delays or missed contract orders.

➤ Based on projected 9% EPS growth over the next three years and a slight discount to communications and defense peers P/E of about 11.5X our FY 11 EPS estimate, we arrive at our 12-month target price of $53.

Qualitative Risk Assessment

LOW	MEDIUM	HIGH

With most of the company's sales coming from federal governments and government agencies, we believe HRS is exposed to uneven sales patterns and fixed-price contract risks, which may affect profitability. However, we think HRS's balance sheet and competitive position are strong.

Quantitative Evaluations

S&P Quality Ranking   A-

D	C	B-	B	B+	A-	A	A+

Relative Strength Rank   WEAK

27

LOWEST = 1   HIGHEST = 99

Revenue/Earnings Data

Revenue (Million $)

	1Q	2Q	3Q	4Q	Year
2010	1,203	1,218	1,330	1,456	5,206
2009	1,173	1,333	1,205	1,294	5,005
2008	1,231	1,318	1,330	1,433	5,311
2007	946.8	1,016	1,072	1,208	4,243
2006	759.7	841.6	881.1	992.4	3,475
2005	669.4	737.2	772.1	821.9	3,001

Earnings Per Share ($)

2010	0.79	1.06	1.26	1.16	4.28
2009	0.89	1.06	1.02	-0.64	2.35
2008	0.73	0.83	0.78	0.91	3.26
2007	0.60	0.67	1.52	0.63	3.43
2006	0.36	0.22	0.52	0.61	1.71
2005	0.29	0.33	0.40	0.44	1.46

Fiscal year ended Jun. 30. Next earnings report expected: Late October. EPS Estimates based on S&P Operating Earnings; historical GAAP earnings are as reported.

Dividend Data (Dates: mm/dd Payment Date: mm/dd/yy)

Amount ($)	Date Decl.	Ex-Div. Date	Stk. of Record	Payment Date
0.220	02/26	03/04	03/08	03/18/10
0.220	04/23	05/27	06/01	06/11/10
0.250	08/30	09/03	09/08	09/17/10
0.250	10/22	11/17	11/19	12/03/10

Dividends have been paid since 1941. Source: Company reports.

Please read the Required Disclosures and Analyst Certification on the last page of this report.

The McGraw·Hill Companies

STANDARD
&POOR'S

Harris Corp

Business Summary August 17, 2010

CORPORATE OVERVIEW. Harris Corp. is an international communications equipment company that focuses on providing product, system and service solutions for commercial and governmental customers including communications networks, antennas, aviation electronics, and handheld radios. The company operates in three main business segments: government communications systems, RF communications (which includes the tactical handheld radios and now includes the wireless systems business recently acquired from Tyco Electronics) and broadcast communications.

PRIMARY BUSINESS DYNAMICS. The government communications systems (GCS) segment, which contributed 52% of revenues in FY 10 (Jun.), conducts advanced research studies and produces, integrates and supports highly reliable, net-centric communications and information technology that solve the mission-critical challenges of the company's defense, intelligence and civilian U.S. government customers. The government segment has a diverse portfolio of more than 300 programs. During the fourth quarter of FY 10, revenues stemmed from a weather program for the National Oceanic and Atmospheric Administration, the Modernization of Enterprise Terminals program for the U.S. Army and the Joint Strike Fighter program for the DoD, but this was offset by the near completion of the 2010 census. During the fourth quarter of FY 10, new business included an information technology contract with the Air Na-

tional Guard and health care related contracts with the U.S. Department of Veterans Affairs. The Multimax business, acquired in 2007, is part of this segment.

The RF Communications segment (40% of revenues) supplies secure wireless voice and data communications products, systems and networks to the U.S. DoD and other federal and state agencies, and foreign government defense agencies. The segment offers a line of secure tactical radio products and systems for person-transportable, mobile, strategic fixed-site and shipboard applications used by military personnel. As of March 2009, orders on a fiscal year to date basis were down 37% from a year earlier, hurt by what HRS said was a delay in two major orders -- one from the U.S. Army and the other from the Iraq Ministry of Defense. Since then, however, orders improved inside and outside the U.S., signaling that the delays were in the past. In the June 2010 quarter, tactical radio orders amounted to $711 million, 1.5X its revenues, including Falcon III radios.

Company Financials Fiscal Year Ended Jun. 30

Per Share Data ($)	2010	2009	2008	2007	2006	2005	2004	2003	2002	2001
Tangible Book Value	2.48	0.20	2.69	NM	3.90	5.79	7.96	7.21	7.05	6.82
Cash Flow	5.59	3.68	4.46	4.75	2.53	1.94	1.36	0.87	1.04	0.75
Earnings	4.32	2.35	3.26	3.43	1.71	1.46	0.94	0.45	0.63	0.16
S&P Core Earnings	4.28	3.14	3.19	2.74	1.74	1.43	0.90	0.31	0.28	-0.45
Dividends	0.88	0.80	0.60	0.44	0.32	0.24	0.20	0.16	0.10	0.10
Payout Ratio	20%	34%	18%	13%	19%	16%	21%	36%	16%	63%
Prices:High	54.50	48.25	66.71	66.94	49.78	45.78	34.58	19.74	19.35	18.50
Prices:Low	40.24	26.11	27.56	45.85	37.69	26.94	18.92	12.68	12.05	10.40
P/E Ratio:High	13	21	20	20	29	31	37	44	31	NM
P/E Ratio:Low	9	11	8	13	22	18	20	28	19	65

Income Statement Analysis (Million $)	2010	2009	2008	2007	2006	2005	2004	2003	2002	2001
Revenue	5,206	5,005	5,311	4,243	3,475	3,001	2,519	2,093	1,876	1,955
Operating Income	1,105	972	958	676	505	393	264	142	153	167
Depreciation	166	178	164	135	98.4	71.4	55.1	56.4	55.1	79.7
Interest Expense	72.1	52.8	55.8	41.1	36.5	24.0	24.5	24.9	26.7	34.8
Pretax Income	840	485	638	661	381	298	180	90.1	125	72.4
Effective Tax Rate	NA	35.6%	31.6%	28.9%	37.5%	32.2%	30.2%	34.0%	34.0%	70.4%
Net Income	562	312	444	480	238	202	126	59.5	82.6	21.4
S&P Core Earnings	556	417	435	382	243	199	120	40.8	36.5	-60.5

Balance Sheet & Other Financial Data (Million $)	2010	2009	2008	2007	2006	2005	2004	2003	2002	2001
Cash	455	285	392	409	181	378	644	466	278	250
Current Assets	1,996	1,859	2,047	1,829	1,428	1,318	1,554	1,358	1,154	1,222
Total Assets	4,735	4,465	4,559	4,406	3,142	2,457	2,226	2,080	1,859	1,960
Current Liabilities	1,043	1,110	995	1,638	752	590	543	496	426	460
Long Term Debt	1,177	1,177	832	409	700	401	401	402	283	384
Common Equity	2,190	1,869	2,274	1,904	1,662	1,439	1,279	1,188	1,150	1,115
Total Capital	3,367	3,046	3,466	2,701	2,390	1,867	1,683	1,590	1,433	1,500
Capital Expenditures	190	98.7	113	88.8	102	75.0	66.4	73.0	45.9	55.2
Cash Flow	727	490	609	616	336	274	181	116	138	101
Current Ratio	1.9	1.7	2.1	1.1	1.9	2.2	2.9	2.7	2.7	2.7
% Long Term Debt of Capitalization	34.9	38.6	24.0	15.1	29.3	21.5	23.9	25.3	19.8	25.6
% Net Income of Revenue	10.8	6.2	8.4	11.3	6.8	6.7	5.0	2.8	4.4	1.1
% Return on Assets	12.2	6.9	9.9	12.7	8.5	8.6	5.8	3.0	4.3	1.0
% Return on Equity	27.7	15.1	21.3	26.9	15.3	14.9	10.2	5.1	7.3	1.7

Data as orig reptd.; bef. results of disc opers/spec. items. Per share data adj. for stk. divs.; EPS diluted. E-Estimated. NA-Not Available. NM-Not Meaningful. NR-Not Ranked. UR-Under Review.

Office: 1025 W. NASA Boulevard, Melbourne, FL 32919.
Telephone: 321-727-9100.
Website: http://www.harris.com
Chrmn, Pres & CEO: H.L. Lance

COO & EVP: D.R. Pearson
SVP & CFO: G.L. McArthur
CTO: R.K. Buchanan
Chief Acctg Officer: L.A. Schwartz

Investor Contact: P. Padgett (321-727-9383)
Board Members: T. A. Dattilo, T. D. Growcock, L. Hay, III, K. L. Katen, S. P. Kaufman, L. F. Kenne, H. L. Lance, D. B. Rickard, J. C. Stoffel, G. T. Swienton, H. E. Tookes, II

Founded: 1916
Domicile: Delaware
Employees: 15,800

The McGraw·Hill Companies

Hartford Financial Services Group Inc. (The)

STANDARD &POOR'S

S&P Recommendation BUY ★★★★☆	Price $23.95 (as of Oct 22, 2010)	12-Mo. Target Price $29.00	Investment Style Large-Cap Blend

GICS Sector Financials
Sub-Industry Multi-line Insurance

Summary One of the largest U.S. multi-line insurance holding companies, Hartford is a leading writer of property and casualty insurance.

Key Stock Statistics (Source S&P, Vickers, company reports)

52-Wk Range	$30.46– 18.81	S&P Oper. EPS 2010E	2.30	Market Capitalization(B)	$10.642
Trailing 12-Month EPS	$0.29	S&P Oper. EPS 2011E	4.00	Yield (%)	0.84
Trailing 12-Month P/E	82.6	P/E on S&P Oper. EPS 2010E	10.4	Dividend Rate/Share	$0.20
$10K Invested 5 Yrs Ago	$3,644	Common Shares Outstg. (M)	444.3	Institutional Ownership (%)	82

Beta	3.03
S&P 3-Yr. Proj. EPS CAGR(%)	31
S&P Credit Rating	BBB

Price Performance

30-Week Mov. Avg. · · · 10-Week Mov. Avg. - - GAAP Earnings vs. Previous Year Volume Above Avg. STARS
12-Mo. Target Price — Relative Strength — ▲ Up ▼ Down ▶ No Change Below Avg.

Options: ASE, CBOE, P, Ph

Analysis prepared by **Bret Howlett** on July 28, 2010, when the stock traded at **$22.85.**

Highlights

▸ We believe sales and flows will be below peers at HIG's life unit in 2010, and we expect the company to lose market share in several product areas, most notably annuities. In our view, HIG's life franchise was damaged following the financial crisis and we think sales will be hurt by recent product price increases and re-designs. However, we forecast double-digit earnings growth in the life unit, absent accounting charges, improved distribution, and solid growth of traditional life products. We believe the bright spot for HIG is its retirement segment, and we forecast strong 401(k), mutual fund and employee benefit sales.

▸ We forecast premiums in HIG's P&C unit to decline slightly due to heightened competition, reduced exposures, partially offset by solid premium growth at specialty property. We believe earnings in P&C will be down on a deterioration in the combined ratio. Our forecasts assume personal lines written premiums will fall 1%, small commercial lines premiums 1%, and middle-market commercial lines premiums 2%.

▸ We forecast operating EPS of $2.73 in 2010 and $4.00 in 2011. Our estimates exclude realized investment gains or losses.

Investment Rationale/Risk

▸ Our buy recommendation reflects the sizable discount HIG currently trades at versus peers, which we believe will narrow due to the company's improving fundamentals. We believe HIG's balance sheet has stabilized and investment losses have likely peaked and should continue to decline. Also, we view positively the improvement in HIG's life subsidiary's risk-based capital ratio, its repayment of TARP funds, and lower unrealized losses. While we believe HIG's life unit's results will generally be below peers, we think this is overly discounted in the share price. We also think the rebound in financial markets has reduced the likelihood of adverse accounting charges. We believe HIG will benefit from the stability of its P&C franchise, and we expect improvements in many of its life businesses in 2010.

▸ Risks to our recommendation and target price include deteriorating claim trends, increased premium price competition, a significant worsening in the credit quality of HIG's investment portfolio, and a downturn in the equity markets.

▸ Our 12-month target price of $29 assumes the shares will trade at about 0.7X our 2010 book value estimate, below the peer average.

Qualitative Risk Assessment

LOW	MEDIUM	HIGH

Our risk assessment reflects our view of HIG's vulnerability to further credit writedowns, especially considering its sizable holdings of lower quality CMBS. Our assessment also reflects the potential dilution of shares stemming from the capital infusion from Allianz, and exposure to the equity markets. This is partially offset by the earnings stability of HIG's P&C operations and the company's overall improved capital position.

Quantitative Evaluations

S&P Quality Ranking B-

D	C	B-	B	B+	A-	A	A+

Relative Strength Rank MODERATE

56

LOWEST = 1   HIGHEST = 99

Revenue/Earnings Data

Revenue (Million $)

	1Q	2Q	3Q	4Q	Year
2010	6,319	3,336	--	--	--
2009	5,394	7,637	5,230	6,440	24,701
2008	1,544	7,503	-393.0	565.0	9,219
2007	6,759	7,660	5,823	5,674	25,916
2006	6,543	4,971	7,407	7,579	26,500
2005	6,002	6,064	7,307	7,710	27,083

Earnings Per Share ($)

	1Q	2Q	3Q	4Q	Year
2010	-0.42	0.14	E0.90	E0.98	E2.30
2009	-3.77	-0.06	-0.79	1.19	-2.93
2008	0.46	1.73	-8.74	-2.71	-8.99
2007	2.71	1.96	2.68	1.88	9.24
2006	2.34	1.52	2.39	2.42	8.69
2005	2.21	1.98	1.76	1.51	7.44

Fiscal year ended Dec. 31. Next earnings report expected: Early November. EPS Estimates based on S&P Operating Earnings; historical GAAP earnings are as reported.

Dividend Data (Dates: mm/dd Payment Date: mm/dd/yy)

Amount ($)	Date Decl.	Ex-Div. Date	Stk. of Record	Payment Date
0.050	02/18	02/25	03/01	04/01/10
0.050	05/20	05/27	06/01	07/01/10
0.050	07/22	08/30	09/01	10/01/10
0.050	10/21	11/29	12/01	01/03/11

Dividends have been paid since 1996. Source: Company reports.

Please read the Required Disclosures and Analyst Certification on the last page of this report.

The McGraw·Hill Companies

Hartford Financial Services Group Inc. (The)

STANDARD &POOR'S

Business Summary July 28, 2010

CORPORATE OVERVIEW. Hartford Financial Services Group (HIG) is a multi-line insurer and one of the largest providers of investment, life insurance and property and casualty insurance products in the U.S. Revenues totaled $24.2 billion in 2009 (up from $9.2 billion in 2008). HIG's P&C operations reported operating revenues (excluding realized investment losses) of $11.5 billion, while the life insurance unit reported operating revenues of $15.2 billion.

HIG's property-casualty operation provides a wide range of commercial, personal, specialty and reinsurance coverages. It constitutes one of the largest U.S. property-casualty insurance organizations, and is the endorsed provider of automobile and homeowners coverages to members of AARP. Earned premiums of $9.9 billion in 2009 were derived from personal lines (41%), small commercial lines (26%), middle-market commercial lines (21%), and specialty commercial (12%).

HIG's life insurance operations are conducted by Hartford Life. Total assets under management increased to $330 billion in 2009, from $298 billion in 2008 The Retail Investment Products Group generated revenues of $2.8 billion (24% of total life revenues in 2009, excluding investment income) and provides an array of investment and savings products to individual investors, including annuities, mutual funds, 401(k) plans and 529 college savings plans. Group Benefits generated $4.7 billion of revenues (40%) and offers short- and long-term disability insurance, group life and accident insurance and other specialty products to employers. The Individual Life segment generated revenues of $1.3 billion (11%) and offers an array of life insurance, including variable universal life, universal life, whole life and term life insurance. The Institutional Solutions Group generated revenues of $1.3 billion (11%) and provides customized wealth creation and financial protection solutions for institutions, corporations and high net worth individuals. The Retirement Plans Group generated revenues of $632 million (5%) and provides retirement plans for corporate clients and non-profit organizations. The International unit generated $1.0 billion of revenues (8%), but has mostly suspended offering variable annuities.

Company Financials Fiscal Year Ended Dec. 31

Per Share Data ($)	2009	2008	2007	2006	2005	2004	2003	2002	2001	2000
Tangible Book Value	66.44	26.18	55.69	53.12	45.05	42.58	34.80	35.31	29.87	32.88
Operating Earnings	NA	NA	NA	NA	NA	NA	-0.93	4.96	3.00	4.29
Earnings	-2.93	-8.99	9.24	8.69	7.44	7.20	-0.33	3.97	2.27	4.36
S&P Core Earnings	0.90	4.11	11.27	8.98	7.62	6.52	-1.15	4.27	2.22	NA
Dividends	0.20	1.91	2.03	1.70	1.17	1.13	1.09	1.05	1.01	0.97
Relative Payout	NM	NM	22%	20%	16%	16%	NM	26%	44%	22%
Prices:High	29.59	87.88	106.23	94.03	89.49	69.57	59.27	70.24	71.15	80.00
Prices:Low	3.33	4.16	83.00	79.24	65.35	52.73	31.64	37.25	45.50	29.38
P/E Ratio:High	NM	NM	11	11	12	10	NM	18	31	18
P/E Ratio:Low	NM	NM	9	9	9	7	NM	9	20	7

Income Statement Analysis (Million $)										
Life Insurance in Force	1,018,728	968,723	906,890	920,964	764,293	853,184	704,369	629,028	534,489	585,582
Premium Income:Life A & H	14,424	15,503	15,619	15,023	14,359	13,566	11,891	4,884	4,903	4,565
Premium Income:Casualty/Property.	NA	NA	NA	NA	NA	NA	8,805	8,114	7,266	6,975
Net Investment Income	7,219	-6,005	5,359	6,515	8,231	5,162	3,233	2,953	2,850	2,674
Total Revenue	24,701	9,219	25,916	26,500	27,083	22,693	18,733	15,907	15,147	14,703
Pretax Income	-1,728	-4,591	4,005	3,602	2,985	2,523	-550	1,068	354	1,418
Net Operating Income	NA	NA	NA	NA	NA	NA	-253	1,250	724	962
Net Income	-887	-2,749	2,949	2,745	2,274	2,138	-91.0	1,000	549	974
S&P Core Earnings	313	1,290	3,598	2,839	2,335	1,936	-315	1,078	538	NA

Balance Sheet & Other Financial Data (Million $)										
Cash & Equivalent	2,142	1,811	2,011	1,424	1,273	1,148	462	377	353	227
Premiums Due	3,404	3,604	3,681	3,675	6,360	6,178	9,043	7,706	2,432	6,874
Investment Assets:Bonds	71,153	65,112	81,657	80,755	76,440	75,100	61,263	48,889	40,046	34,492
Investment Assets:Stocks	33,542	32,278	38,777	31,132	25,495	14,466	565	917	1,349	1,056
Investment Assets:Loans	8,112	8,677	7,471	5,369	3,747	2,662	2,512	2,934	3,317	3,610
Investment Assets:Total	25,556	118,531	131,086	119,173	106,935	94,408	65,847	54,530	46,689	40,669
Deferred Policy Costs	10,686	13,248	11,742	10,268	9,702	8,509	7,599	6,689	6,420	5,305
Total Assets	307,717	287,583	360,361	326,710	285,557	259,735	225,853	182,043	181,238	171,532
Debt	6,632	7,033	3,951	3,762	4,048	4,308	4,613	4,064	3,377	3,105
Common Equity	14,905	9,268	19,204	18,876	15,325	14,238	11,639	10,734	9,013	7,464
Combined Loss-Expense Ratio	90.4	90.7	90.8	89.3	93.2	95.3	98.0	99.2	112.4	102.4
% Return on Revenue	NM	NM	11.4	10.4	8.4	9.4	NM	6.3	3.6	6.6
% Return on Equity	NM	NM	15.5	16.1	15.4	16.5	NM	10.1	6.7	15.1
% Investment Yield	5.9	NM	4.3	5.8	8.2	6.4	5.4	5.8	6.5	6.7

Data as orig reptd.; bef. results of disc opers/spec. items. Per share data adj. for stk. divs.; EPS diluted. E-Estimated. NA-Not Available. NM-Not Meaningful. NR-Not Ranked. UR-Under Review.

Office: 1 Hartford Plz, Hartford, CT 06155-0001.
Telephone: 860-547-5000.
Website: http://www.thehartford.com
Chrmn, Pres & CEO: L.E. McGee

EVP & CFO: C.J. Swift
EVP & General Counsel: A.J. Kreczko
SVP, Chief Acctg Officer & Cntlr: B.A. Bombara
SVP & Secy: R.A. Anzaldua

Investor Contact: R. Costello (860-547-8480)
Board Members: R. B. Allardice, III, T. Fetter, P. G. Kirk, Jr., L. E. McGee, K. Mikells, M. G. Morris, T. A. Renyi, C. B. Strauss, H. P. Swygert

Founded: 1810
Domicile: Delaware
Employees: 28,000

The McGraw-Hill Companies

Hasbro Inc.

STANDARD &POOR'S

S&P Recommendation HOLD ★★★☆☆	**Price** $46.00 (as of Oct 22, 2010)	**12-Mo. Target Price** $50.00

GICS Sector Consumer Discretionary
Sub-Industry Leisure Products

Summary This large toy company has brands that include Monopoly, Playskool and Tonka, as well as various items related to categories such as Star Wars and Pokemon.

Key Stock Statistics (Source S&P, Vickers, company reports)

52-Wk Range	$48.78– 26.82	S&P Oper. EPS 2010E	2.75	Market Capitalization(B)	$6.432	Beta	0.97
Trailing 12-Month EPS	$2.87	S&P Oper. EPS 2011E	3.00	Yield (%)	2.17	S&P 3-Yr. Proj. EPS CAGR(%)	10
Trailing 12-Month P/E	16.0	P/E on S&P Oper. EPS 2010E	16.7	Dividend Rate/Share	$1.00	S&P Credit Rating	BBB
$10K Invested 5 Yrs Ago	$27,136	Common Shares Outstg. (M)	139.8	Institutional Ownership (%)	81		

Price Performance

30-Week Mov. Avg. ···   10-Week Mov. Avg. - -   **GAAP Earnings vs. Previous Year**   Volume Above Avg. STARS
12-Mo. Target Price —   Relative Strength —   ▲ Up ▼ Down ▶ No Change   Below Avg. ★

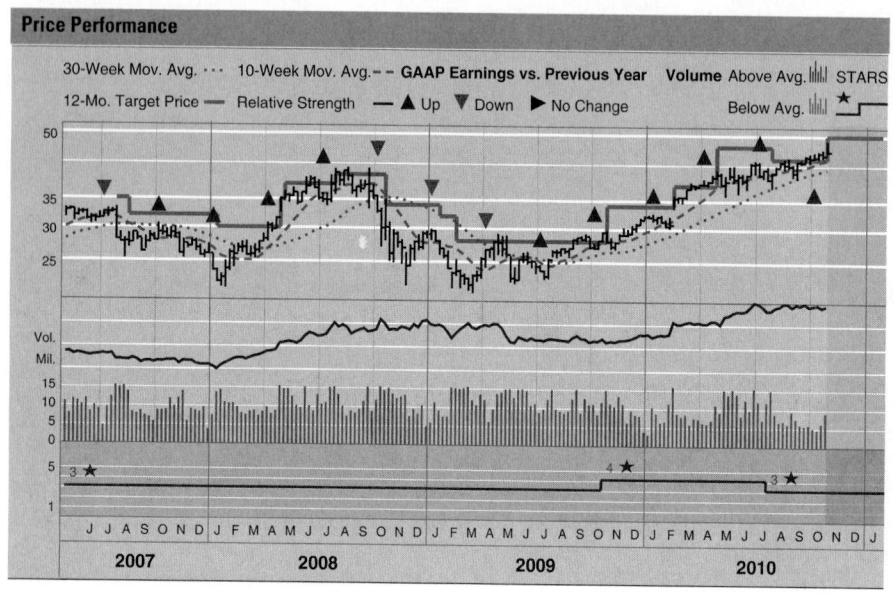

Options: ASE, CBOE, P, Ph

Analysis prepared by **Jason N. Asaeda** on October 22, 2010, when the stock traded at **$ 45.68.**

Highlights

➤ We look for net revenues to reach $4.15 billion in 2010 and $4.37 billion in 2011. While we think macroeconomic headwinds will limit consumer discretionary spending, we believe toy sales will hold up better than many other areas. Positive momentum in core brands such as Nerf and Playskool, as well as new product introductions, particularly in board games, bode well, in our view. We expect HAS to benefit in 2011 from toy sales related to Transformers 3, which is scheduled for theatrical release in July 2011. We also view The Hub, the company's newly launched children's and family television network with Discovery Communications, as an incremental revenue opportunity.

➤ We forecast operating margins will widen 90 basis points in 2010 to 15.4%, supported by an improved product mix and lower royalty and amortization expenses, partially offset by investments in product development and other growth initiatives. We see operating margins of 15.6% in 2011.

➤ Excluding a one-time $0.14 tax benefit in 2010, we estimate EPS of $2.75 and $3.00 in 2010 and 2011, respectively.

Investment Rationale/Risk

➤ We think HAS is well positioned to boost its market share in the toy category, particularly as the company increases its use of technology in offerings, and makes toys more interactive. However, given the weakened economy, we think near-term consumer spending habits are less certain. We believe HAS has strong cash flow and an improved balance sheet, which should enable the company to continue its ongoing share repurchase program. Although we view positively the recent Discovery Communications joint venture, we think it will be $0.25-$0.30 dilutive to 2010 EPS.

➤ Risks to our recommendation and target price include more store closings and tight inventory management at toy retailers, weaker than expected consumer spending, poorly received new toy introductions, and increased competition in the consumer electronic toy category from larger consumer electronics manufacturers.

➤ Our 12-month target price of $50 applies a multiple of 16.7X, modestly below HAS's historical average, but roughly in line with toy industry peer averages, to our 2011 EPS forecast.

Qualitative Risk Assessment

LOW	MEDIUM	HIGH

Our risk assessment takes into account our view of HAS's strong market share position and healthy balance sheet, offset by intense industry rivalry and the concentrated buying power of U.S. toy retailers.

Quantitative Evaluations

S&P Quality Ranking A-

D	C	B-	B	B+	A-	A	A+

Relative Strength Rank MODERATE

61

LOWEST = 1   HIGHEST = 99

Revenue/Earnings Data

Revenue (Million $)

	1Q	2Q	3Q	4Q	Year
2010	672.4	737.8	1,313	--	--
2009	621.3	792.2	1,279	1,375	4,068
2008	704.2	784.3	1,302	1,231	4,022
2007	625.3	691.4	1,223	1,298	3,838
2006	468.2	527.8	1,039	1,116	3,151
2005	454.9	572.4	988.1	1,072	3,088

Earnings Per Share ($)

2010	0.40	0.30	1.10	E1.10	E2.75
2009	0.14	0.26	0.99	1.09	2.48
2008	0.25	0.25	0.89	0.62	2.00
2007	0.19	0.03	0.95	0.84	1.97
2006	-0.03	0.07	0.58	0.62	1.29
2005	-0.02	0.13	0.47	0.48	1.09

Fiscal year ended Dec. 31. Next earnings report expected: Early February. EPS Estimates based on S&P Operating Earnings; historical GAAP earnings are as reported.

Dividend Data (Dates: mm/dd Payment Date: mm/dd/yy)

Amount ($)	Date Decl.	Ex-Div. Date	Stk. of Record	Payment Date
0.200	12/03	01/29	02/02	02/16/10
0.250	02/04	04/29	05/03	05/17/10
0.250	05/20	07/29	08/02	08/16/10
0.250	09/30	10/28	11/01	11/15/10

Dividends have been paid since 1981. Source: Company reports.

Please read the Required Disclosures and Analyst Certification on the last page of this report.

The McGraw·Hill Companies

Hasbro Inc.

STANDARD &POOR'S

Business Summary October 22, 2010

CORPORATE OVERVIEW. Hasbro is a worldwide leader in children's and family leisure time and entertainment products and services, including the design, manufacture and marketing of games and toys ranging from traditional to high-tech. Some of the company's widely recognized core brands, both internationally and in the U.S., are Playskool, Tonka, Super Soaker, Milton Bradley, Parker Brothers, Tiger And Wizards of the Coast. Offerings in the games segment include traditional board games, hand-held electronic, trading card, plug and play and DVD games, as well as electronic learning aids and puzzles. Toy offerings include boys' action figures, vehicles and playsets, girls' toys, electronic toys, plush products, preschool toys and infant products, children's consumer electronics, electronic interactive products and toy related specialty products.

Part of HAS's growth strategy includes licensing, which has been successful in the past for HAS. In 2008, revenues generated from the sale of Star Wars products produced under its license with Lucas Licensing and Lucasfilm represented approximately 7.8% of total company revenues. In January 2006, HAS completed a licensing agreement with Marvel Entertainment, Inc. to produce action figures and other toys and games based on their library of intel-

lectual property, including Spiderman and the Fantastic 4. Products related to this license began shipping late in 2006, with full ramp-up realized in 2007. In 2008, Marvel accounted for 5.7% of revenues and Transformers for 9.5% (latest available).

MARKET PROFILE. According to the NPD Group, a leading consumer and retail information provider, retail sales in the U.S. toy industry were $21.47 billion in 2009, a decline of only 0.8% despite the difficult economic conditions that affected the industry. This compares to a 1.0% rise in U.S. HAS sales for 2009.

We think certain HAS subcategories will continue to performed well, contributing to market share gains. In 2009, Boys' toys rose approximately 36% to $1.5 billion, and Girls' toys increased 1.9% to $1.3 million. Excluding HAS's international sales, we estimate that the company had approximately a 12% market share in the U.S. toy industry in 2009.

Company Financials Fiscal Year Ended Dec. 31

Per Share Data ($)	2009	2008	2007	2006	2005	2004	2003	2002	2001	2000
Tangible Book Value	4.12	2.50	2.95	3.34	3.61	3.01	1.32	0.08	NM	NM
Cash Flow	3.64	3.05	2.86	2.35	2.20	1.75	2.37	0.95	1.66	0.69
Earnings	2.48	2.00	1.97	1.29	1.09	0.96	0.98	0.43	0.35	-0.82
S&P Core Earnings	2.51	1.91	1.96	1.29	1.02	0.90	0.93	0.44	0.19	NA
Dividends	0.80	0.76	0.60	0.60	0.45	0.33	0.21	0.12	0.12	0.24
Payout Ratio	32%	39%	30%	35%	30%	22%	12%	28%	34%	NM
Prices:High	32.57	41.68	33.49	27.69	22.35	23.33	22.63	17.30	18.44	18.94
Prices:Low	21.14	21.57	25.25	17.00	17.75	16.90	11.23	9.87	10.31	8.38
P/E Ratio:High	13	21	17	21	21	24	23	40	53	NM
P/E Ratio:Low	9	11	13	13	16	18	11	23	29	NM

Income Statement Analysis (Million $)	2009	2008	2007	2006	2005	2004	2003	2002	2001	2000
Revenue	4,068	4,022	3,838	3,151	3,088	2,998	3,139	2,816	2,856	3,787
Operating Income	776	660	686	523	491	439	509	309	435	268
Depreciation	181	166	157	147	180	146	240	89.3	226	264
Interest Expense	61.6	47.1	34.6	27.5	30.5	31.7	52.5	77.5	104	114
Pretax Income	530	441	462	341	311	260	244	104	96.2	-226
Effective Tax Rate	29.2%	30.5%	28.0%	32.6%	31.8%	24.6%	28.3%	27.9%	36.8%	NM
Net Income	375	307	333	230	212	196	175	75.1	60.8	-145
S&P Core Earnings	379	293	332	230	199	184	166	79.1	33.8	NA

Balance Sheet & Other Financial Data (Million $)	2009	2008	2007	2006	2005	2004	2003	2002	2001	2000
Cash	636	630	774	715	942	725	521	495	233	127
Current Assets	2,045	1,714	1,888	1,718	1,830	1,718	1,509	1,432	1,369	1,580
Total Assets	3,897	3,169	3,237	3,097	3,301	3,241	3,163	3,143	3,369	3,828
Current Liabilities	816	800	888	906	911	1,149	930	967	759	1,240
Long Term Debt	1,132	710	710	495	496	303	687	857	1,166	1,168
Common Equity	1,595	1,391	1,385	1,538	1,723	1,640	1,405	1,191	1,353	1,327
Total Capital	2,727	2,107	2,095	2,033	2,219	1,942	2,092	2,049	2,519	2,495
Capital Expenditures	104	117	91.5	82.1	70.6	79.2	63.1	58.7	50.0	125
Cash Flow	556	473	490	377	392	342	415	164	287	120
Current Ratio	2.5	2.1	2.1	1.9	2.0	1.5	1.6	1.5	1.8	1.3
% Long Term Debt of Capitalization	41.5	33.7	33.8	24.3	22.3	15.6	32.8	41.8	46.3	46.8
% Net Income of Revenue	9.2	7.6	8.7	7.3	6.9	6.5	5.6	2.7	2.1	NM
% Return on Assets	10.6	9.6	10.5	7.2	6.5	6.1	5.6	2.3	1.7	NM
% Return on Equity	25.1	22.1	22.8	14.1	12.6	12.9	13.5	5.9	4.5	NM

Data as orig reptd.; bef. results of disc opers/spec. items. Per share data adj. for stk. divs.; EPS diluted. E-Estimated. NA-Not Available. NM-Not Meaningful. NR-Not Ranked. UR-Under Review.

Office: 1027 Newport Ave, Pawtucket, RI, USA 02861-2500.
Telephone: 401-431-8697.
Website: http://www.hasbro.com
Chrmn: A.J. Verrecchia

Pres & CEO: B. Goldner
COO: D.D. Hargreaves
SVP, CFO & Chief Acctg Officer: D. Thomas
SVP & Treas: M.R. Trueb

Investor Contact: K.A. Warren (401-727-5401)
Board Members: B. L. Anderson, A. R. Batkin, F. J. Biondi, Jr., K. A. Bronfin, J. M. Connors, Jr., M. W. Garrett, L. Gersh, B. Goldner, J. M. Greenberg, A. G. Hassenfeld, T. A. Leinbach, E. M. Philip, A. J. Verrecchia

Founded: 1926
Domicile: Rhode Island
Employees: 5,800

The McGraw-Hill Companies

HCP Inc

STANDARD &POOR'S

S&P Recommendation **HOLD** ★★★☆☆	Price $36.37 (as of Oct 22, 2010)	12-Mo. Target Price $39.00	Investment Style Large-Cap Value

GICS Sector Financials
Sub-Industry Specialized REITS

Summary This equity-oriented real estate investment trust, based in California, has direct or joint venture investments in health care-related facilities across the U.S.

Key Stock Statistics (Source S&P, Vickers, company reports)

52-Wk Range	$38.05– 26.70	S&P FFO/Sh. 2010E	2.13	Market Capitalization(B)	$11.277	Beta	1.37
Trailing 12-Month FFO/Share	NA	S&P FFO/Sh. 2011E	2.27	Yield (%)	5.11	S&P 3-Yr. FFO/Sh. Proj. CAGR(%)	-1
Trailing 12-Month P/FFO	NA	P/FFO on S&P FFO/Sh. 2010E	17.1	Dividend Rate/Share	$1.86	S&P Credit Rating	BBB
$10K Invested 5 Yrs Ago	$17,251	Common Shares Outstg. (M)	310.1	Institutional Ownership (%)	85		

Price Performance

30-Week Mov. Avg. · · · · 10-Week Mov. Avg. – – GAAP Earnings vs. Previous Year Volume Above Avg. STARS
12-Mo. Target Price — Relative Strength — ▲ Up ▼ Down ▶ No Change Below Avg.

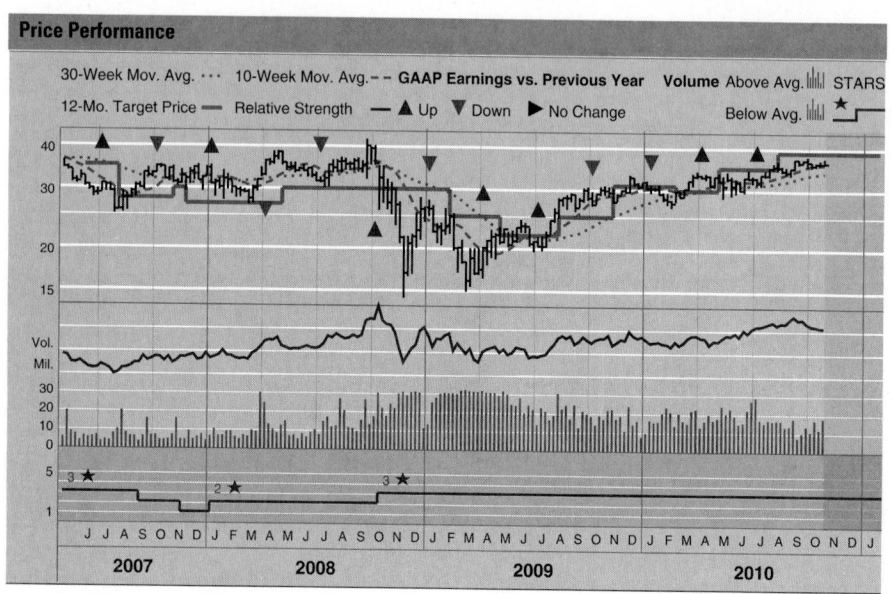

Options: CBOE

Analysis prepared by **Robert McMillan** on August 05, 2010, when the stock traded at **$ 35.44**.

Highlights

▶ We believe HCP has assembled a portfolio of health care properties that is well diversified in terms of asset type, geography, and tenant base. With its core focus on senior housing, we think HCP will benefit from increased demand driven by the aging baby boomer population.

▶ Following a 1% rise in 2009, we see revenue growth in HCP's need-based businesses advancing 2.2% in 2010. During the second quarter of 2010, net operating income advanced 5.9%; growth in net operating income in senior housing (+4.9%), skilled nursing (+1.2%), medical office buildings (+2.4%) and life sciences (+8.5%) was complemented by the hospital portfolio (+14.0%), which is being re-invigorated by new operators at certain facilities. We think expense management and general rate increases will help the company improve metrics in the senior housing portfolio, the largest of HCP's five sectors. We see management focusing on acquisitions in the life sciences and medical office building sectors.

▶ We forecast per-share funds from operations (FFO) of $2.13 for 2010 and $2.27 for 2011.

Investment Rationale/Risk

▶ We like the predictable nature of HCP's long-term, needs-oriented businesses, and believe the stock correlates less with macroeconomic trends than most other REITs. Amid economic uncertainty, we favor what we see as HCP's stable revenue stream with minimal short-term lease expirations and an improving balance sheet. Although the portfolio has been resilient during the recent recessionary environment, we do not see rapid growth as the economy rebounds, unless management significantly accelerates acquisition activities.

▶ Risks to our recommendation and target price include a faster-than-expected decline in senior housing occupancy, and a decrease in government reimbursement rates.

▶ The stock recently traded at 16.7X trailing 12-month FFO per share. Our 12-month target price of $39 is 18.0X our forward four-quarter FFO per share estimate of $2.16, a reasonable (albeit lofty) multiple relative to recent historical levels that we use given HCP's portfolio and operating performance. We expect a modest widening of the valuation multiple to be driven by continued improvement in operating results.

Qualitative Risk Assessment

LOW	MEDIUM	HIGH

Our risk assessment reflects HCP's position as a major and diversified owner of health care-related properties.

Quantitative Evaluations

S&P Quality Ranking B+

D	C	B-	B	B+	A-	A	A+

Relative Strength Rank MODERATE

44

LOWEST = 1   HIGHEST = 99

Revenue/FFO Data

Revenue (Million $)

	1Q	2Q	3Q	4Q	Year
2010	295.9	303.0	--	--	--
2009	251.6	267.3	255.3	383.4	1,157
2008	252.2	251.4	269.9	263.3	1,026
2007	223.8	223.2	262.5	273.1	982.5
2006	126.5	127.5	130.2	234.9	619.1
2005	108.4	118.5	124.4	127.7	477.3

FFO Per Share ($)

2010	0.54	E0.52	E0.51	E0.54	E2.13
2009	0.56	0.55	0.52	0.36	1.50
2008	0.55	0.51	0.71	0.48	2.25
2007	0.50	0.58	0.52	0.54	2.14
2006	0.53	0.47	0.50	0.35	1.82
2005	0.44	0.47	0.50	0.48	1.89

Fiscal year ended Dec. 31. Next earnings report expected: Early November. FFO Estimates based on S&P Funds From Operations Est..

Dividend Data (Dates: mm/dd Payment Date: mm/dd/yy)

Amount ($)	Date Decl.	Ex-Div. Date	Stk. of Record	Payment Date
0.460	10/29	11/05	11/09	11/24/09
0.465	02/01	02/09	02/11	02/23/10
0.465	04/22	04/29	05/03	05/18/10
0.465	07/29	08/05	08/09	08/24/10

Dividends have been paid since 1985. Source: Company reports.

Please read the Required Disclosures and Analyst Certification on the last page of this report.

The McGraw·Hill Companies

HCP Inc

STANDARD
&POOR'S

Business Summary August 05, 2010

CORPORATE OVERVIEW. HCP Inc. is a self-administered real estate investment trust (REIT) that invests exclusively in health care real estate throughout the U.S. At December 31, 2009, HCP's investment in properties leased to third parties totaled about $10 billion, representing 575 properties, including 30 properties accounted for as direct financing leases. The trust primarily generates revenue by leasing properties under long-term leases. Most of HCP's rents and other earned income from leases are received under triple-net leases or leases that provide for a substantial recovery of operating expenses.

CORPORATE STRATEGY. HCP's investment strategy is based on three principles: opportunistic investing, portfolio diversification, and a balance sheet that we view as conservative. The trust completes real estate transactions when they are expected to drive profitable growth and create long-term stockholder value. Another key to HCP's strategy is maintaining a diversified portfolio of health care-related real estate. The trust believes that diversification within the health care industry reduces the likelihood that a single event will materially harm its business. This allows HCP to take advantage of opportunities in different markets, based on individual market dynamics. We view HCP as one

of the most diversified health care REITs in terms of geography, property type and tenant base. Its largest tenants are Brookdale Senior Living, Sunrise Senior Living, Tenet Healthcare, HCA, Inc., and HCR ManorCare. During 2009, HCP had one tenant (Sunrise; 11%) that accounted for more than 10% of revenues.

HCP's senior housing portfolio (30%) consisted of interests in 256 senior housing facilities including independent living facilities, assisted living facilities and continuing care retirement communities, which cater to different segments of the elderly population based on their needs. Services provided by HCP's operators or tenants in these facilities are primarily paid for by the residents directly or through private insurance and are less reliant on government reimbursement programs such as Medicaid and Medicare.

Company Financials Fiscal Year Ended Dec. 31

Per Share Data ($)	2009	2008	2007	2006	2005	2004	2003	2002	2001	2000
Tangible Book Value	17.22	17.18	14.50	12.47	7.82	8.41	8.82	8.46	8.62	8.55
Earnings	0.25	0.77	0.67	0.57	1.02	1.03	0.94	0.97	0.89	1.07
S&P Core Earnings	0.49	0.65	0.67	0.57	1.02	1.02	0.94	0.96	0.88	NA
Dividends	1.84	1.82	1.78	1.70	1.68	1.67	1.66	1.63	1.55	1.10
Payout Ratio	NM	NM	NM	NM	165%	162%	177%	169%	174%	103%
Prices:High	33.45	42.16	42.11	37.84	28.92	29.67	25.85	22.54	19.52	15.22
Prices:Low	14.93	14.26	25.11	25.12	23.13	20.00	16.53	17.90	14.63	11.53
P/E Ratio:High	NM	55	63	66	28	29	27	23	22	14
P/E Ratio:Low	NM	19	37	44	23	19	18	19	16	11

Income Statement Analysis (Million $)										
Rental Income	886	962	836	557	452	389	349	332	311	307
Mortgage Income	Nil	Nil	Nil	Nil	Nil	Nil	Nil	Nil	Nil	23.0
Total Income	1,157	1,026	983	619	477	429	400	360	332	330
General Expenses	264	268	257	137	91.1	79.3	63.4	51.1	43.3	41.0
Interest Expense	299	348	357	213	107	89.1	90.7	78.0	78.5	86.7
Provision for Losses	Nil	Nil	Nil	Nil	Nil	Nil	Nil	Nil	Nil	Nil
Depreciation	320	315	274	144	107	87.0	79.1	75.7	84.1	72.6
Net Income	90.4	204	161	107	159	158	155	137	121	113
S&P Core Earnings	136	155	140	85.5	138	136	118	112	94.5	NA

Balance Sheet & Other Financial Data (Million $)										
Cash	112	57.6	133	764	69.9	81.1	228	41.2	30.2	81.2
Total Assets	12,210	11,850	12,522	10,013	3,597	3,103	3,036	2,748	2,431	2,399
Real Estate Investment	10,246	10,186	9,979	7,463	3,856	3,351	2,992	2,796	2,535	2,389
Loss Reserve	Nil	Nil	Nil	Nil	Nil	Nil	Nil	Nil	Nil	Nil
Net Investment	9,185	9,358	9,250	6,867	3,242	2,816	2,506	2,371	2,195	2,101
Short Term Debt	NA	NA	NA	NA	NA	NA	NA	NA	NA	4.30
Capitalization:Debt	5,656	5,685	7,027	4,318	1,837	1,242	1,407	1,334	358	1,155
Capitalization:Equity	5,495	4,916	3,819	3,009	1,115	1,134	1,155	1,006	972	870
Capitalization:Total	11,615	10,751	11,954	7,774	3,386	2,783	2,965	2,686	1,674	2,339
% Earnings & Depreciation/Assets	3.4	4.3	3.9	3.6	7.9	8.0	8.1	8.2	8.5	7.6
Price Times Book Value:High	1.9	2.5	2.9	3.0	3.7	3.5	2.9	2.7	2.3	1.8
Price Times Book Value:Low	0.9	0.8	1.7	2.0	3.0	2.4	1.9	2.1	1.7	1.3

Data as orig reptd.; bef. results of disc opers/spec. items. Per share data adj. for stk. divs.; EPS diluted. E-Estimated. NA-Not Available. NM-Not Meaningful. NR-Not Ranked. UR-Under Review.

Office: 3760 Kilroy Airport Way Ste 300, Long Beach, CA 90806-6862.
Telephone: 562-733-5100.
Email: investorrelations@hcpi.com
Website: http://www.hcpi.com

Chrmn, Pres, CEO & COO: J.F. Flaherty, III
EVP & CFO: T.M. Herzog
EVP, Secy & General Counsel: J.A. Gonzalez-Pita
SVP & Chief Acctg Officer: S.A. Anderson

Investor Contact: T.M. Herzog
Board Members: J. F. Flaherty, III, C. N. Garvey, D. B. Henry, L. E. Martin, M. D. McKee, H. M. Messmer, Jr., P. L. Rhein, K. B. Roath, R. M. Rosenberg, J. P. Sullivan

Founded: 1985
Domicile: Maryland
Employees: 142

Health Care REIT Inc.

STANDARD &POOR'S

S&P Recommendation BUY ★★★★☆

Price	12-Mo. Target Price	Investment Style
$50.90 (as of Oct 22, 2010)	$50.00	Large-Cap Value

GICS Sector Financials
Sub-Industry Specialized REITS

Summary This REIT invests in health care facilities, including senior housing, specialty care, and medical office buildings.

Key Stock Statistics (Source S&P, Vickers, company reports)

52-Wk Range	$51.37– 38.42	S&P FFO/Sh. 2010E	3.18	Market Capitalization(B)	$6.343	Beta	0.93
Trailing 12-Month FFO/Share	NA	S&P FFO/Sh. 2011E	3.37	Yield (%)	5.42	S&P 3-Yr. FFO/Sh. Proj. CAGR(%)	7
Trailing 12-Month P/FFO	NA	P/FFO on S&P FFO/Sh. 2010E	16.0	Dividend Rate/Share	$2.76	S&P Credit Rating	BBB-
$10K Invested 5 Yrs Ago	$19,906	Common Shares Outstg. (M)	124.6	Institutional Ownership (%)	80		

Price Performance

30-Week Mov. Avg. · · · 10-Week Mov. Avg. – – GAAP Earnings vs. Previous Year   Volume Above Avg. | STARS
12-Mo. Target Price — Relative Strength — ▲ Up ▼ Down ▶ No Change   Below Avg. | ★

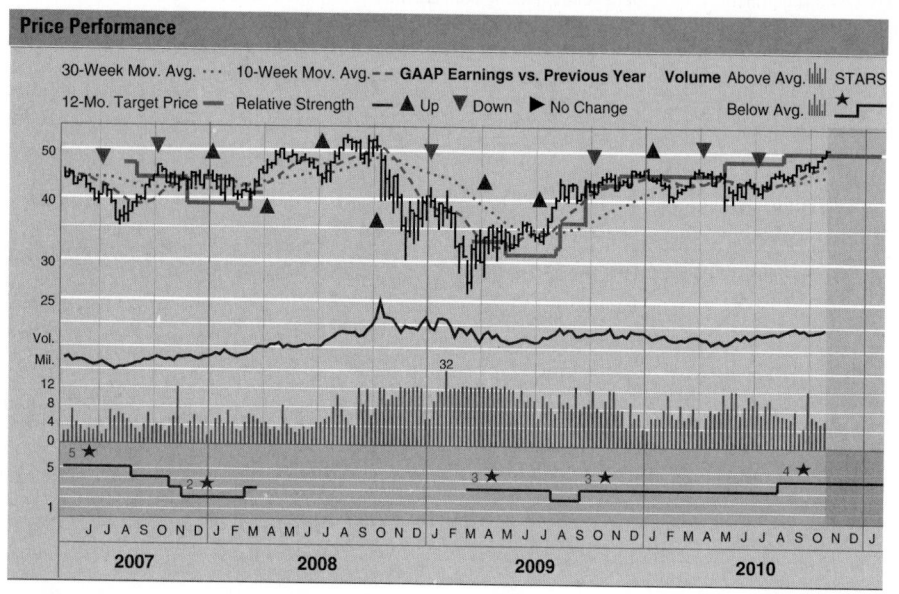

Options: CBOE, Ph

Analysis prepared by **Robert McMillan** on August 09, 2010, when the stock traded at **$ 45.50**.

Highlights

▶ We believe HCN has assembled a portfolio of health care properties that is well diversified in terms of asset type, geography, and tenant base. With its core focus on senior housing, we think HCN will benefit from increased demand driven by the aging baby boomer population.

▶ Despite a rebounding economy, we do not anticipate a material pick-up in organic growth. HCN's diverse portfolio, which is dominated by needs-based facilities, was resilient during the recession. After rising 8.6% in 2009, we see revenues advancing 15.7% in 2010, driven by stabilizing trends among the facilities operators at HCN's properties as well as acquisitions. During the second quarter, same-space revenues advanced in its skilled nursing facilities (+2.5%) and hospitals (+2.0%), but declined in the senior housing facilities (-2.5% on rent deferrals); occupancy levels in the medical office building portfolio improved to 92.6% at the end of the second quarter from 90.8% a year earlier. We are also encouraged by management's focus on increasing the proportion of its revenues derived from private payers.

▶ We forecast per-share funds from operations (FFO) of $3.18 in 2010, and $3.37 in 2011.

Investment Rationale/Risk

▶ We like the predictable nature of HCN's long-term triple net lease revenue stream, and believe the stock correlates less with macroeconomic trends than most other REITs. Amid economic uncertainty, we favor HCN's stable revenue stream with minimal short-term lease expirations, solid balance sheet, and a relatively secure dividend payout.

▶ Risks to our opinion and target price include a slower-than-expected economic recovery, and decreased government reimbursement rates.

▶ The stock recently traded at about 14.6X trailing 12-month FFO per share. Our 12-month target price of $50 is about 15.2X our forward four-quarter FFO estimate of $3.30, a modest multiple by historical standards, but reasonable, we believe, given HCN's portfolio and operating performance. We expect a modest widening of the valuation multiple to be driven by continued improvement in operating results. Further, we also view management's plan to make accretive acquisitions while also attempting to reduce leverage as a positive factor in our valuation.

Qualitative Risk Assessment

LOW	MEDIUM	HIGH

Our risk assessment reflects HCN's position as an owner of a large and diversified portfolio of health care-related properties that are leased under long-term contracts and provide what we see as a steady and predictable stream of income.

Quantitative Evaluations

S&P Quality Ranking   A-

D	C	B-	B	B+	A-	A	A+

Relative Strength Rank   STRONG

75

LOWEST = 1   HIGHEST = 99

Revenue/FFO Data

Revenue (Million $)

	1Q	2Q	3Q	4Q	Year
2010	152.8	162.1	--	--	--
2009	139.3	139.5	142.9	147.3	569.0
2008	127.8	133.1	143.2	147.1	551.0
2007	110.4	117.7	124.4	133.5	486.0
2006	76.01	78.64	80.39	87.79	322.8
2005	65.84	66.05	71.99	77.97	281.9

FFO Per Share ($)

2010	0.51	0.74	E0.81	E0.82	E3.18
2009	0.81	0.80	0.77	0.44	2.53
2008	0.81	0.87	0.86	0.83	3.38
2007	0.76	0.78	0.79	0.80	3.16
2006	0.71	0.74	0.73	0.77	2.86
2005	0.72	0.36	0.77	0.76	2.65

Fiscal year ended Dec. 31. Next earnings report expected: Early November. FFO Estimates based on S&P Funds From Operations Est..

Dividend Data (Dates: mm/dd Payment Date: mm/dd/yy)

Amount ($)	Date Decl.	Ex-Div. Date	Stk. of Record	Payment Date
0.680	10/29	11/05	11/09	11/20/09
0.680	01/28	02/04	02/08	02/19/10
0.680	04/29	05/06	05/10	05/20/10
0.690	07/29	08/05	08/09	08/20/10

Dividends have been paid since 1971. Source: Company reports.

Please read the Required Disclosures and Analyst Certification on the last page of this report.

The McGraw-Hill Companies

Health Care REIT Inc.

Business Summary August 09, 2010

CORPORATE OVERVIEW. Health Care REIT is a self-administered equity REIT that invests in health care facilities offering skilled nursing, assisted living, medical office buildings, independent living, and specialty care services. HCN's investments are primarily real estate property leased to operators under long-term operating leases or financed with operators under long-term mortgages.

As of December 31, 2009, HCN had real estate investments totaling more than $6 billion, consisting of 590 properties in 39 states. As of December 31, 2009, HCN's portfolio included 179 assisted living facilities, 214 skilled nursing facilities, 50 independent living/continuing care retirement communities, 118 medical office buildings, and 29 hospitals.

An assisted living facility is a combination of housing, personalized supportive services, and health care designed to meet the needs of those who require help with the activities of daily living. Skilled nursing facilities provide inpatient skilled nursing and personal care services as well as rehabilitative, restorative and transitional medical services. Specialty care facilities include acute care hospitals, long-term acute care hospitals, and other specialty care hospitals. Medical office buildings are office and clinical facilities designed for the use of physicians and other health care professionals.

CORPORATE STRATEGY. HCN invests mainly in long-term care facilities managed by experienced operators, and diversifies its investment portfolio by operator and by geographic location. Each facility, which includes the land, building, improvements and related rights owned by HCN is leased to an operator pursuant to a long-term operating lease. In order to better diversify the risk of any one facility, a large percentage of HCN's leased properties is subject to master leases. The leases generally cover multiple facilities under one lease and have a fixed term of 12 to 15 years and contain one or more five to 15-year renewal options. The tenants are required to repair, rebuild and maintain the leased properties. The leases for HCN's medical office buildings are generally structured as long-term gross leases, where HCN is responsible for all or a portion of the property operating expenses.

Company Financials Fiscal Year Ended Dec. 31

Per Share Data ($)	2009	2008	2007	2006	2005	2004	2003	2002	2001	2000
Tangible Book Value	27.64	27.07	24.26	27.04	19.85	24.23	20.43	19.20	18.57	19.04
Earnings	1.22	1.35	1.26	1.32	1.06	1.38	1.44	1.47	1.52	1.91
S&P Core Earnings	1.22	1.35	1.26	1.32	1.06	1.38	1.41	1.46	1.51	NA
Dividends	2.72	2.70	2.28	2.28	2.88	2.46	2.39	2.34	2.34	2.34
Payout Ratio	NM	NM	182%	NM	NM	173%	163%	159%	154%	122%
Prices:High	46.74	53.98	48.55	43.02	39.20	40.88	36.10	31.82	26.40	19.25
Prices:Low	25.86	30.14	35.08	32.80	31.15	27.70	24.84	24.02	16.06	13.81
P/E Ratio:High	38	40	39	33	37	30	25	22	17	10
P/E Ratio:Low	21	22	28	25	29	20	17	16	11	7

Income Statement Analysis (Million $)										
Rental Income	520	501	450	300	253	226	177	134	99.0	88.3
Mortgage Income	40.9	40.1	25.8	18.8	24.0	22.8	20.8	26.5	31.3	41.1
Total Income	569	551	486	323	282	251	201	163	135	135
General Expenses	95.6	91.2	75.1	27.1	17.2	16.6	11.5	9.67	8.08	7.41
Interest Expense	106	131	135	94.8	80.1	72.0	54.1	41.1	32.0	34.6
Provision for Losses	23.3	0.01	Nil	1.00	1.20	1.20	2.87	1.00	1.00	1.00
Depreciation	157	156	146	93.1	80.0	73.0	51.1	39.3	30.2	22.7
Net Income	162	150	125	104	79.2	84.9	75.7	67.4	60.8	68.1
S&P Core Earnings	140	127	100	82.0	57.4	71.9	62.4	54.4	46.8	NA

Balance Sheet & Other Financial Data (Million $)										
Cash	35.5	23.4	30.3	36.2	36.2	19.8	125	9.55	9.83	2.84
Total Assets	6,367	6,193	5,214	4,281	2,972	2,550	2,183	1,594	1,270	1,157
Real Estate Investment	6,764	6,463	5,498	4,477	3,131	2,667	2,153	1,643	1,301	1,180
Loss Reserve	5.18	7.50	7.41	7.41	6.46	5.26	7.83	4.96	6.86	5.86
Net Investment	6,081	5,854	5,013	4,123	2,850	2,442	1,992	1,524	1,214	1,121
Short Term Debt	12.2	39.7	70.3	71.7	2.60	6.28	45.8	0.40	12.6	10.0
Capitalization:Debt	2,402	2,824	2,634	2,126	1,498	1,180	967	676	479	420
Capitalization:Equity	3,508	2,922	2,074	1,640	1,154	1,052	1,029	770	608	549
Capitalization:Total	6,210	6,046	5,048	4,107	2,929	2,515	2,117	1,574	1,236	1,128
% Earnings & Depreciation/Assets	5.1	5.4	6.1	5.4	5.7	6.6	6.7	7.5	7.5	7.5
Price Times Book Value:High	1.7	2.0	2.0	1.6	2.0	1.1	1.7	1.7	1.4	1.0
Price Times Book Value:Low	0.9	1.1	1.4	1.2	1.6	1.1	1.2	1.3	0.9	0.7

Data as orig reptd.; bef. results of disc opers/spec. items. Per share data adj. for stk. divs.; EPS diluted. E-Estimated. NA-Not Available. NM-Not Meaningful. NR-Not Ranked. UR-Under Review.

Office: One Seagate Ste 1500, Toledo, OH 43604-1541.
Telephone: 419-247-2800.
Website: http://www.hcreit.com
Chrmn, Pres & CEO: G.L. Chapman

Vice Chrmn: F.S. Klipsch
EVP & CFO: S.A. Estes
EVP & General Counsel: J.H. Miller
SVP & Treas: M.A. Crabtree

Investor Contact: S.A. Estes (419-247-2800)
Board Members: W. C. Ballard, Jr., P. C. Borra, G. L. Chapman, T. J. Derosa, J. H. Donahue, P. J. Grua, F. S. Klipsch, S. M. Oster, J. R. Otten, R. S. Trumbull

Founded: 1970
Domicile: Delaware
Employees: 217

Heinz (H J) Co

STANDARD &POOR'S

S&P Recommendation	BUY ★★★★☆	Price $49.55 (as of Oct 22, 2010)	12-Mo. Target Price $51.00	Investment Style Large-Cap Blend

GICS Sector Consumer Staples
Sub-Industry Packaged Foods & Meats

Summary This company produces a wide variety of food products worldwide, primarily condiments, convenience meals and snacks.

Key Stock Statistics (Source S&P, Vickers, company reports)

52-Wk Range	$49.80– 39.69	S&P Oper. EPS 2011E	3.04	Market Capitalization(B)	$15.773	Beta	0.56
Trailing 12-Month EPS	$2.79	S&P Oper. EPS 2012E	3.27	Yield (%)	3.63	S&P 3-Yr. Proj. EPS CAGR(%)	7
Trailing 12-Month P/E	17.8	P/E on S&P Oper. EPS 2011E	16.3	Dividend Rate/Share	$1.80	S&P Credit Rating	BBB
$10K Invested 5 Yrs Ago	$16,338	Common Shares Outstg. (M)	318.3	Institutional Ownership (%)	66		

Price Performance

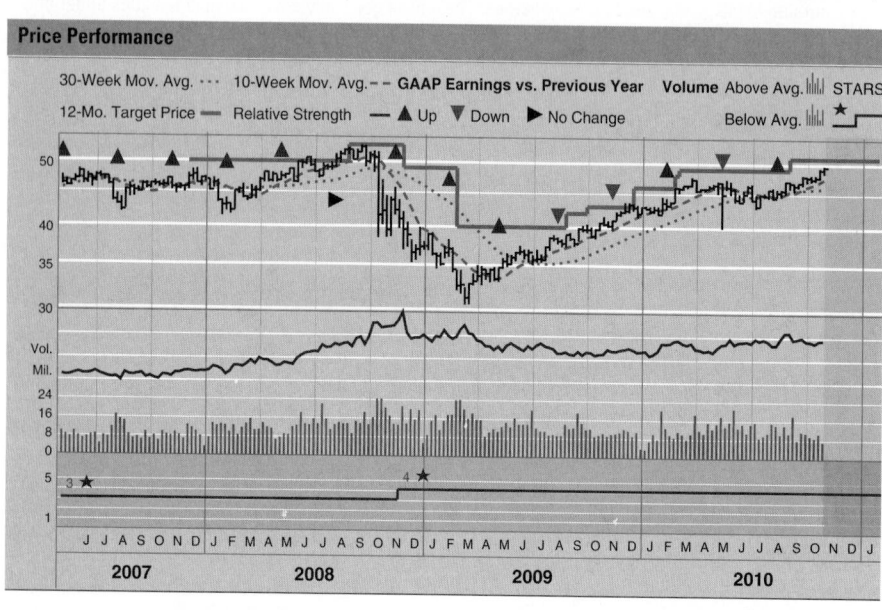

30-Week Mov. Avg. · · · 10-Week Mov. Avg. – – GAAP Earnings vs. Previous Year Volume Above Avg. STARS
12-Mo. Target Price — Relative Strength — ▲ Up ▼ Down ▶ No Change Below Avg.

Options: ASE, CBOE, P

Analysis prepared by **Tom Graves, CFA** on August 25, 2010, when the stock traded at **$ 46.05**.

Highlights

▶ We look for FY 11 (Apr.) net sales to rise modestly from the $10.5 billion reported for FY 10, with a majority of HNZ's net external sales again coming from outside the U.S. Including China, what HNZ calls emerging markets produced 15% of HNZ's total sales in FY 10. HNZ said that a pending acquisition of a manufacturer of soy sauces and fermented bean curd in China would increase its annual sales in China to about $300 million. HNZ expects emerging markets to produce as much as 25% of sales by 2016.

▶ We think HNZ's market share will be bolstered in FY 11 by marketing activity and product innovation. We see the FY 11 commodity cost picture for HNZ as mixed, but we think profit margins will be bolstered by productivity gains. All told, we estimate FY 11 EPS from continuing operations of $3.03, up from the $2.87 reported for FY 10. For FY 11, we estimate EPS of $3.27.

▶ In FY 11, if currency exchange rates stay near recent levels, we anticipate at least a modest adverse impact on HNZ's reported EPS.

Investment Rationale/Risk

▶ Our buy recommendation reflects our view that the stock will receive support from HNZ's above-average dividend yield, and what we see as some underlying strength in HNZ's business. We expect that HNZ's strategy will include a focus on innovation investments in its core brands, growth in emerging markets, reducing or controlling costs, and leveraging the company's global scale.

▶ Risks to our recommendation and target price include competitive product and pricing pressures, adverse currency fluctuations, raw material cost inflation, and unfavorable consumer acceptance of new products.

▶ Our 12-month target price of $51 reflects our view that the shares should trade at about 17X our estimated calendar 2010 EPS of $2.98, or about a 12% target P/E premium to what we expect, on average, for a group of other packaged food stocks. HNZ shares recently had an indicated dividend yield of 3.9%, after a 7.1% increase in the quarterly dividend effective with the July payment.

Qualitative Risk Assessment

LOW	MEDIUM	HIGH

Our risk assessment for H. J. Heinz reflects the relatively stable nature of the company's end markets, our view of its strong cash flow, and corporate governance practices that we believe are favorable relative to peers.

Quantitative Evaluations

S&P Quality Ranking B+

D	C	B-	B	B+	A-	A	A+

Relative Strength Rank MODERATE

61

LOWEST = 1   HIGHEST = 99

Revenue/Earnings Data

Revenue (Million $)

	1Q	2Q	3Q	4Q	Year
2011	2,481	--	--	--	--
2010	2,442	2,647	2,682	2,725	10,495
2009	2,583	2,613	2,415	2,538	10,148
2008	2,248	2,523	2,611	2,688	10,071
2007	2,060	2,232	2,295	2,414	9,002
2006	2,110	2,339	2,187	2,400	8,643

Earnings Per Share ($)

2011	0.75	E0.80	E0.86	E0.63	E3.04
2010	0.68	0.76	0.83	0.60	2.87
2009	0.72	0.87	0.76	0.76	2.90
2008	0.72	0.71	0.68	0.61	2.63
2007	0.58	0.59	0.66	0.55	2.38
2006	0.45	0.50	0.40	Nil	1.29

Fiscal year ended Apr. 30. Next earnings report expected: Late November. EPS Estimates based on S&P Operating Earnings; historical GAAP earnings are as reported.

Dividend Data (Dates: mm/dd Payment Date: mm/dd/yy)

Amount ($)	Date Decl.	Ex-Div. Date	Stk. of Record	Payment Date
0.420	11/11	12/18	12/22	01/10/10
0.420	03/10	03/22	03/24	04/10/10
0.450	05/27	06/22	06/24	07/10/10
0.450	08/31	09/20	09/22	10/10/10

Dividends have been paid since 1911. Source: Company reports.

Please read the Required Disclosures and Analyst Certification on the last page of this report.

The McGraw·Hill Companies

Heinz (H J) Co

Business Summary August 25, 2010

CORPORATE OVERVIEW. Although largely known for its familiar ketchup, H.J. Heinz boasts many other branded food products, ranging from Ore-Ida frozen potatoes to Weight Watchers frozen dinners. In FY 10 (Apr.), the North American Consumer Products segment represented 30% of sales from continuing operations, while Europe accounted for 32%, Asia/Pacific for 19%, U.S. Foodservice for 14%, and the rest of the world for 5%. In FY 10, one customer, Wal-Mart Stores Inc., accounted for 11% of sales.

The company's revenues are generated via the manufacture and sale of products in the following categories: ketchup and sauces (42% of FY 10 sales); meals and snacks (41%); infant/nutrition (11%); and other products (6%). Brands or trademarks utilized by HNZ include Heinz, Classico, Weight Watchers (licensed), Smart Ones, Boston Market (licensed), and Ore-Ida.

HNZ's top 15 brands generated 70% of the company's sales in FY 10, with Heinz-branded products showing growth of 5.4%.

CORPORATE STRATEGY. In FY 10, emerging markets accounted for 30% of HNZ's total reported sales growth and 15% of HNZ's total sales. Excluding the impacts of foreign currency exchange rate fluctuations and acquisitions and divestitures, nearly all of HNZ's FY 10 sales growth came from emerging markets.

Growth in emerging markets in FY 10 was led by higher sales of Complan and Glucon D nutritional beverages in India, ABC products in Indonesia, and Heinz Ketchup and infant feeding products in Russia.

IMPACT OF MAJOR DEVELOPMENTS. In June 2010, HNZ said that had signed an agreement to acquire Foodstar, a manufacturer of soy sauces and fermented bean curd in China, from Transpac Industrial Holdings Ltd., a private equity holding company, and various Transpac Funds. HNZ said that the acquisition of Foodstar would increase HNZ's annual sales in China to about $300 million, and enable HNZ to enter China's fast-growing retail soy sauce market. HNZ said that the purchase price consists of a cash payment at closing of $165 million and an earn-out potentially payable in 2014 based on the performance of the business. The completion of the proposed acquisition was subject to regulatory approval in China.

Company Financials Fiscal Year Ended Apr. 30

Per Share Data ($)	2010	2009	2008	2007	2006	2005	2004	2003	2002	2001
Tangible Book Value	NM	NM	NM	NM	NM	NM	NM	NM	NM	NM
Cash Flow	3.83	3.76	3.49	3.88	2.07	2.82	2.86	2.17	3.22	2.26
Earnings	2.88	2.90	2.63	2.38	1.29	2.08	2.20	1.57	2.36	1.41
S&P Core Earnings	2.82	2.55	2.26	2.36	1.72	2.29	2.11	1.43	1.99	1.31
Dividends	1.68	1.66	1.52	1.20	1.14	1.10	1.08	1.61	1.55	1.45
Payout Ratio	58%	57%	58%	50%	88%	53%	49%	88%	65%	102%
Calendar Year	2009	2008	2007	2006	2005	2004	2003	2002	2001	2000
Prices:High	43.75	53.00	53.00	46.75	39.13	40.61	36.82	43.48	47.94	48.00
Prices:Low	30.51	35.26	35.26	33.42	33.64	34.53	28.90	29.60	36.90	30.81
P/E Ratio:High	15	18	20	20	30	20	17	24	20	34
P/E Ratio:Low	11	12	13	14	26	17	13	16	16	22

Income Statement Analysis (Million $)										
Revenue	10,495	10,148	10,071	9,002	8,643	8,912	8,415	8,237	9,431	9,430
Operating Income	1,852	1,765	1,847	1,946	1,377	1,607	1,613	1,389	1,892	1,282
Depreciation	303	272	279	500	264	252	234	215	302	299
Interest Expense	296	340	333	333	316	232	212	224	294	333
Pretax Income	1,290	1,296	1,218	1,124	693	1,059	1,169	869	1,279	673
Effective Tax Rate	NA	28.8%	30.6%	29.6%	36.2%	30.5%	33.3%	36.1%	34.8%	26.5%
Net Income	914	923	845	792	443	736	779	555	834	495
S&P Core Earnings	897	812	725	784	587	809	747	500	702	458

Balance Sheet & Other Financial Data (Million $)										
Cash	554	373	618	653	445	1,084	1,180	802	207	139
Current Assets	3,051	2,945	3,326	3,019	2,704	3,646	3,611	3,284	3,374	3,117
Total Assets	10,076	9,664	10,565	10,033	9,738	10,578	9,877	9,225	10,278	9,035
Current Liabilities	2,175	2,063	2,670	2,505	2,018	2,587	2,469	1,926	2,509	3,655
Long Term Debt	4,568	5,076	4,406	4,414	4,357	4,122	4,538	4,776	4,643	3,015
Common Equity	1,891	1,220	1,888	2,280	2,049	2,614	8,841	2,876	1,719	1,374
Total Capital	6,531	6,701	7,013	7,256	7,045	7,359	13,797	8,252	7,197	4,642
Capital Expenditures	278	292	302	245	231	241	232	154	213	411
Cash Flow	1,217	1,195	1,123	1,291	707	988	1,013	770	1,136	794
Current Ratio	1.4	1.4	1.3	1.2	1.3	1.4	1.5	1.7	1.3	0.9
% Long Term Debt of Capitalization	69.9	75.8	62.8	60.8	61.8	56.0	32.9	57.9	64.5	64.9
% Net Income of Revenue	8.7	9.1	8.4	8.8	5.1	8.3	9.3	6.7	8.8	5.2
% Return on Assets	NA	9.1	8.2	8.0	4.4	7.2	8.2	5.7	8.6	5.5
% Return on Equity	NA	59.4	45.3	34.0	19.0	26.3	8.9	17.9	53.9	33.3

Data as orig reptd.; bef. results of disc opers/spec. items. Per share data adj. for stk. divs.; EPS diluted. E-Estimated. NA-Not Available. NM-Not Meaningful. NR-Not Ranked. UR-Under Review.

Office: 1 Ppg Pl, Pittsburgh, PA 15222-5415.
Telephone: 412-456-5700.
Website: http://www.heinz.com
Chrmn, Pres & CEO: W.R. Johnson

EVP & CFO: A.B. Winkleblack
EVP & General Counsel: T.N. Bobby
SVP & CIO: K.L. Alber
CSO: F.K. Dow

Investor Contact: M.R. Nollen
Board Members: C. E. Bunch, L. S. Coleman, Jr., J. G. Drosdick, E. E. Holiday, W. R. Johnson, C. Kendle, D. R. O'Hare, N. Peltz, D. H. Reilley, L. C. Swann, T. J. Usher, M. Weinstein

Founded: 1869
Domicile: Pennsylvania
Employees: 29,600

Helmerich & Payne Inc.

STANDARD &POOR'S

S&P Recommendation **BUY** ★★★★☆	Price $41.57 (as of Oct 22, 2010)	12-Mo. Target Price $49.00	Investment Style Large-Cap Blend

GICS Sector Energy
Sub-Industry Oil & Gas Drilling

Summary Helmerich & Payne, Inc. is the holding company for Helmerich & Payne International Drilling Company, an international drilling contactor.

Key Stock Statistics (Source S&P, Vickers, company reports)

52-Wk Range	$49.13–32.34	S&P Oper. EPS 2010**E**	2.50	Market Capitalization(B)	$4.399	Beta	1.01
Trailing 12-Month EPS	$1.16	S&P Oper. EPS 2011**E**	2.98	Yield (%)	0.58	S&P 3-Yr. Proj. EPS CAGR(%)	-12
Trailing 12-Month P/E	35.8	P/E on S&P Oper. EPS 2010**E**	16.6	Dividend Rate/Share	$0.24	S&P Credit Rating	NA
$10K Invested 5 Yrs Ago	$16,955	Common Shares Outstg. (M)	105.8	Institutional Ownership (%)	88		

Price Performance

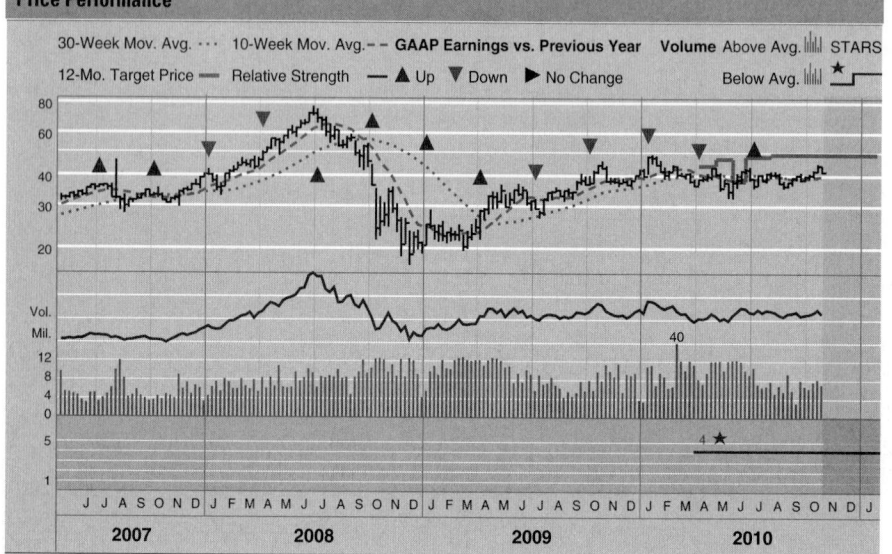

30-Week Mov. Avg. · · · 10-Week Mov. Avg. – – GAAP Earnings vs. Previous Year Volume Above Avg. STARS
12-Mo. Target Price — Relative Strength — ▲ Up ▼ Down ► No Change Below Avg.

Options: ASE, CBOE, P, Ph

Analysis prepared by **Michael Kay** on October 15, 2010, when the stock traded at **$ 44.08**.

Highlights

➤ We believe HP, with among the best utilization (76%) levels in the land drilling segment, has gained pricing power despite rig oversupply. On rising operator spending, specifically in U.S. shale plays, we think HP's FlexRigs saw a pick-up in activity in FY 10 (Sep.), while older rigs became idle or were retired. With the overhaul of its U.S. fleet near completion, we believe HP will market its FlexRigs more aggressively internationally. HP sees an average of 110 rigs on term contracts in 2010, 78 in 2011 and 42 in 2012, but we see these contracts rolling over to lower dayrates, exposing HP to the weaker spot market. HP is seeing a demand pickup in the Bakken and Eagle Ford shales.

➤ In July, Venezuela state oil company PDVSA seized HP's 11 rigs after a year-long dispute over pending payments. Venezuela said it will pay book value for the assets and agree to a price in negotiations with HP.

➤ We estimate that revenue declined 5% in FY 10, on a 16% drop in dayrates, and will rise 10% in FY 11. But we see rigs coming off contracts, partly offsetting better utilization forecasts. We see EPS of $2.50 for FY 10, rising to $2.98 in FY 11. HP projects 2010 capex of $350 million.

Investment Rationale/Risk

➤ HP employs a strategy to develop a premium land rig fleet, and with the expected completion of 15 new HP FlexRigs, 90% (209 rigs) of its U.S. land fleet will have been upgraded for over $3 billion. HP's rig utilization has held up stronger than many peers, as weaker demand has adversely affected older, less efficient conventional rigs. As a result, we estimate HP sees about a 25% premium in dayrates versus peers. HP has done well to gain market share, in our view, as customers prefer the efficiency of its rigs that are capable of horizontal drilling and faster drilling times versus conventional rigs. HP announced 19 newbuilds in FY 10; four are completed and 15 are under construction. We think HP is better positioned than many peers for an eventual recovery in drilling.

➤ Risks to our recommendation and target price include lower than expected dayrates or utilization; political risk; and, cost inflation.

➤ On above-peer multiples of 6X projected FY 11 EBITDA, 20X estimated FY 11 EPS, and 8X estimated FY 11 cash flows, our 12-month target price is $49. We apply a premium valuation on our view of a top-tier rig fleet, balance sheet, EPS and cash flow growth projections.

Qualitative Risk Assessment

LOW	MEDIUM	**HIGH**

Our risk assessment reflects HP's sensitivity to volatile crude oil and natural gas prices, capital spending decisions made by its oil and gas producing customers, and project management risk associated with a large newbuild program. Partially offsetting these risks is HP's high percentage of rigs committed to long-term contracts.

Quantitative Evaluations

S&P Quality Ranking   B

D	C	B-	**B**	B+	A-	A	A+

Relative Strength Rank   MODERATE

50

LOWEST = 1   HIGHEST = 99

Revenue/Earnings Data

Revenue (Million $)

	1Q	2Q	3Q	4Q	Year
2010	399.8	439.7	483.4	--	--
2009	623.8	520.3	387.8	362.2	1,894
2008	456.7	473.6	522.5	583.7	2,037
2007	386.4	372.5	421.3	449.5	1,630
2006	255.4	290.8	319.8	358.8	1,225
2005	174.7	185.5	207.4	233.2	800.7

Earnings Per Share ($)

2010	0.59	0.44	0.60	E0.70	E2.50
2009	1.36	0.99	0.50	0.48	3.32
2008	1.02	0.96	1.18	1.18	4.34
2007	1.06	1.02	1.09	1.10	4.27
2006	0.48	0.61	0.75	0.93	2.77
2005	0.39	0.22	0.29	0.34	1.23

Fiscal year ended Sep. 30. Next earnings report expected: Mid November. EPS Estimates based on S&P Operating Earnings; historical GAAP earnings are as reported.

Dividend Data (Dates: mm/dd Payment Date: mm/dd/yy)

Amount ($)	Date Decl.	Ex-Div. Date	Stk. of Record	Payment Date
0.050	03/03	05/12	05/14	06/01/10
0.060	06/02	08/11	08/13	09/01/10
0.060	09/01	11/10	11/15	12/01/10

Dividends have been paid since 1959. Source: Company reports.

Please read the Required Disclosures and Analyst Certification on the last page of this report.

The McGraw-Hill Companies

Helmerich & Payne Inc.

STANDARD &POOR'S

Business Summary October 15, 2010

CORPORATE OVERVIEW. Helmerich & Payne, Inc. is the holding company for Helmerich & Payne International Drilling Company, an international drilling contactor with land and offshore operations in the United States, South America, Mexico, Trinidad and Africa. It specializes in deep drilling in major gas producing basins of the U.S., and in drilling for oil and gas in remote international areas. Contract drilling operations comprised nearly all of the company's revenue base (99% of FY 09 (Sep.) revenues). The remaining 1% of FY 09 total revenues was derived mainly from its real estate operations. HP generated about 59% of FY 09 consolidated revenues from its 10 largest customers, including BP plc, Devon Energy, Occidental Oil and Gas Corp. and PDVSA (the national oil company of Venezuela).

The company's contract drilling operations are principally comprised of three operating segments. The U.S. Land Drilling segment (77% of total FY 09 external sales, and 92% of segment operating income) operated 201 land rigs at the end of September 2009, up from 185 a year earlier. As of December 2009, 190 rigs were of FlexRig design, while the remainder were highly mobile or conventional rigs. Average rig utilization in this segment in FY 09 was 68%, down from 96% in FY 08. Average rig revenue per day was $28,168 in FY 09, up 15%

over FY 08, while the average rig margin per day rose 16%, to $16,194.

The U.S. Offshore Platform segment (10% of total FY 09 revenues, and 9% of segment operating income), operated 9 platform rigs in FY 09. Average utilization was 90% in FY 09, versus 75% in FY 08, while the average dayrate was up 4%, to $48,674. The average rig margin per day rose 23%, to $21,288.

The International Drilling segment (13% of total FY 09 revenues, -1% of segment operating income) operated 39 land rigs. In Venezuela, HP's 11 rigs were seized in early July by the government, which has stated it will pay book value for the assets and agree to a price in negotiations with HP. HP has rigs in Ecuador, Colombia, Argentina and other areas. Average rig utilization was 71%, down from 83% in FY 08. Average rig revenue per day fell 22%, to $29,220, while the average margin per day fell 76%, to $3,121.

Company Financials Fiscal Year Ended Sep. 30

Per Share Data ($)	2009	2008	2007	2006	2005	2004	2003	2002	2001	2000
Tangible Book Value	25.48	NA	17.54	13.30	10.39	9.06	9.15	8.95	10.30	9.56
Cash Flow	5.53	6.32	5.66	3.73	2.15	0.97	0.99	1.14	2.28	1.93
Earnings	3.32	4.34	4.27	2.77	1.23	0.05	0.18	0.54	1.42	0.82
S&P Core Earnings	3.25	4.02	3.54	2.60	0.93	-0.19	0.12	0.33	1.33	NA
Dividends	0.20	NA	0.18	0.17	0.17	0.16	0.16	0.15	0.15	0.15
Payout Ratio	6%	NA	4%	6%	13%	NM	91%	29%	11%	18%
Prices:High	46.24	NA	46.25	40.24	32.81	17.13	16.40	21.62	29.37	22.41
Prices:Low	19.50	NA	22.72	21.26	15.68	11.97	11.30	11.73	11.70	9.88
P/E Ratio:High	14	NA	11	15	27	NM	94	40	21	27
P/E Ratio:Low	6	NA	5	8	13	NM	65	22	8	12

Income Statement Analysis (Million $)										
Revenue	1,894	2,037	1,630	1,225	801	621	515	482	827	631
Operating Income	813	891	720	511	275	167	129	154	312	219
Depreciation, Depletion and Amortization	236	211	146	102	96.3	94.4	82.5	61.4	87.3	111
Interest Expense	13.5	18.7	10.1	6.64	12.6	12.7	12.3	0.98	Nil	3.08
Pretax Income	586	717	690	448	215	8.72	32.5	94.3	237	140
Effective Tax Rate	39.7%	35.6%	36.4%	34.4%	40.7%	50.0%	45.0%	43.0%	39.2%	41.2%
Net Income	354	462	449	294	128	4.36	17.9	53.7	144	82.3
S&P Core Earnings	347	428	372	277	98.5	-19.2	11.9	32.7	135	NA

Balance Sheet & Other Financial Data (Million $)										
Cash	141	122	89.2	82.5	289	65.3	38.2	46.9	123	108
Current Assets	523	691	499	429	500	246	198	179	331	265
Total Assets	4,161	3,588	2,885	2,135	1,663	1,407	1,416	1,227	1,365	1,259
Current Liabilities	302	309	227	265	89.5	59.9	88.6	72.9	121	78.9
Long Term Debt	420	475	445	445	175	200	200	200	100	50.0	50.0
Common Equity	2,683	2,265	1,816	1,480	1,130	914	917	879	977	956
Total Capital	3,785	3,220	2,624	1,925	1,577	1,309	1,299	1,110	1,172	1,162
Capital Expenditures	881	706	894	529	86.8	89.0	246	312	275	132
Cash Flow	590	672	595	395	224	98.8	100	115	232	193
Current Ratio	1.7	2.2	2.2	1.6	5.6	4.1	2.2	2.5	2.7	3.4
% Long Term Debt of Capitalization	11.1	14.8	17.0	9.1	12.7	15.3	15.4	9.0	4.3	4.3
% Return on Assets	9.1	14.3	17.9	15.5	8.3	0.3	1.4	4.2	11.0	6.9
% Return on Equity	14.3	22.6	27.3	22.5	12.0	0.5	2.0	5.8	15.8	9.1

Data as orig reptd.; bef. results of disc opers/spec. items. Per share data adj. for stk. divs.; EPS diluted. E-Estimated. NA-Not Available. NM-Not Meaningful. NR-Not Ranked. UR-Under Review.

Office: 1437 S Boulder Ave, Tulsa, OK, USA 74119-3623.
Telephone: 918-742-5531.
Website: http://www.hpinc.com
Chrmn: W.H. Helmerich, III

Pres: J.D. Helmerich
Pres & CEO: H. Helmerich
EVP, Chief Admin Officer, Secy & General Counsel: S.R. Mackey
CFO: J.P. Tardio

Board Members: W. L. Armstrong, III, R. A. Foutch, H. Helmerich, W. H. Helmerich, III, P. Marshall, L. F. Rooney, III, E. B. Rust, Jr., J. D. Zeglis

Founded: 1920
Domicile: Delaware
Employees: 5,384

The McGraw-Hill Companies

Hershey Co (The)

S&P Recommendation	**SELL** ★ ★ ☆ ☆ ☆	Price $49.91 (as of Oct 22, 2010)	12-Mo. Target Price $43.00	Investment Style Large-Cap Growth

GICS Sector Consumer Staples
Sub-Industry Packaged Foods & Meats

Summary Hershey is a major producer of chocolate and confectionery products.

Key Stock Statistics (Source S&P, Vickers, company reports)

52-Wk Range	$52.10– 35.05	S&P Oper. EPS 2010**E**	2.55	Market Capitalization(B)	$8.306	Beta	0.26
Trailing 12-Month EPS	$2.10	S&P Oper. EPS 2011**E**	2.74	Yield (%)	2.56	S&P 3-Yr. Proj. EPS CAGR(%)	11
Trailing 12-Month P/E	23.8	P/E on S&P Oper. EPS 2010**E**	19.6	Dividend Rate/Share	$1.28	S&P Credit Rating	A
$10K Invested 5 Yrs Ago	$9,716	Common Shares Outstg. (M)	227.1	Institutional Ownership (%)	75		

Price Performance

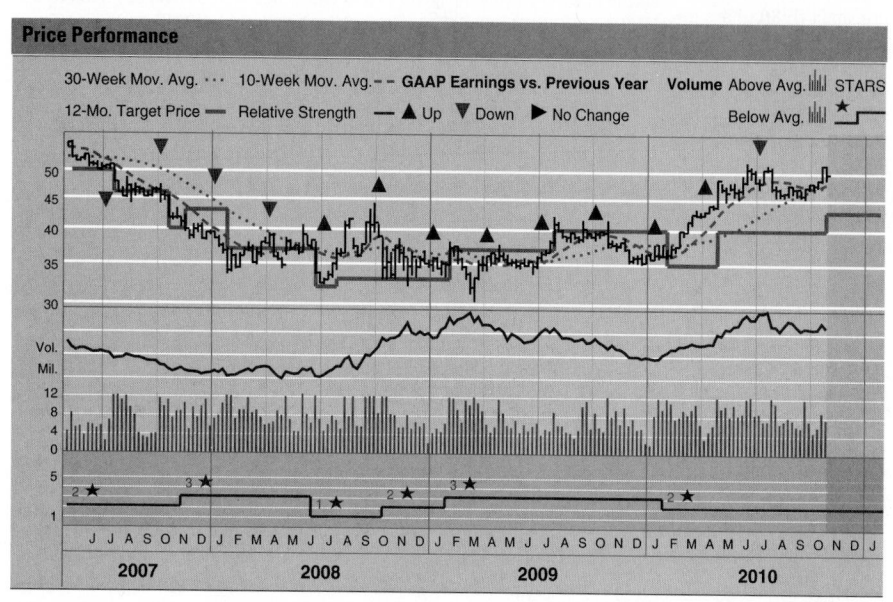

30-Week Mov. Avg. · · ·   10-Week Mov. Avg. - -   **GAAP Earnings vs. Previous Year**   Volume Above Avg. ▏▍▌ STARS
12-Mo. Target Price ——   Relative Strength —   ▲ Up ▼ Down ▶ No Change   Below Avg. ▏▍▌ ★

Options: ASE, CBOE, P, Ph

Highlights

▶ The 12-month target price for HSY has recently been changed to $43.00 from $40.00. The Highlights section of this Stock Report will be updated accordingly.

Investment Rationale/Risk

▶ The Investment Rationale/Risk section of this Stock Report will be updated shortly. For the latest News story on HSY from MarketScope, see below.

▶ 10/21/10 12:34 pm ET ... S&P REITERATES SELL OPINION ON SHARES OF HERSHEY CO. (HSY 49.77**): Before special items, Q3 EPS of $0.79, vs. $0.73, is $0.02 above our estimate. We are raising our '10 EPS forecast to $2.55 from $2.52, and increasing '11's projection to $2.74 from $2.70. We think Kraft's (KFT 32***) acquisition of Cadbury will heighten competitive environment in candy industry, and limit international expansion opportunities. But with more favorable EPS outlook, we lift our 12-month target price for HSY to $43, which reflects a P/E premium to what we expect from a group of other packaged food stocks. HSY has an indicated dividend yield of about 2.6%. /TGraves-CFA

Qualitative Risk Assessment

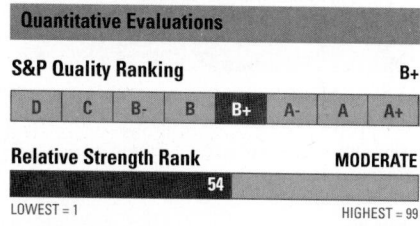

LOW	MEDIUM	HIGH

Our risk assessment reflects what we see as the relative stability of Hershey's primary end markets, the strength of its U.S. business, and the strength of its balance sheet and cash flow.

Quantitative Evaluations

S&P Quality Ranking   B+

D	C	B-	B	B+	A-	A	A+

Relative Strength Rank   MODERATE

54

LOWEST = 1   HIGHEST = 99

Revenue/Earnings Data

Revenue (Million $)

	1Q	2Q	3Q	4Q	Year
2010	1,408	1,233	--	--	--
2009	1,236	1,171	1,484	1,407	5,299
2008	1,160	1,105	1,490	1,377	5,133
2007	1,153	1,052	1,399	1,342	4,947
2006	1,140	1,052	1,416	1,337	4,944
2005	1,126	988.5	1,368	1,353	4,836

Earnings Per Share ($)

2010	0.64	0.20	E0.77	E0.61	E2.55
2009	0.33	0.31	0.71	0.55	1.90
2008	0.28	0.18	0.54	0.36	1.36
2007	0.40	0.01	0.27	0.24	0.93
2006	0.50	0.41	0.78	0.65	2.34
2005	0.47	0.39	0.48	0.70	1.99

Fiscal year ended Dec. 31. Next earnings report expected: Late October. EPS Estimates based on S&P Operating Earnings; historical GAAP earnings are as reported.

Dividend Data (Dates: mm/dd Payment Date: mm/dd/yy)

Amount ($)	Date Decl.	Ex-Div. Date	Stk. of Record	Payment Date
0.320	02/02	02/23	02/25	03/15/10
0.320	05/04	05/21	05/25	06/15/10
0.320	08/03	08/23	08/25	09/15/10
0.320	10/05	11/22	11/24	12/15/10

Dividends have been paid since 1930. Source: Company reports.

Please read the Required Disclosures and Analyst Certification on the last page of this report.

Hershey Co (The)

STANDARD &POOR'S

Business Summary July 28, 2010

CORPORATE OVERVIEW. The Hershey Co. produces and distributes a variety of chocolate, confectionery and grocery products. The company's brands include Hershey's, Kisses and Reese's.

CORPORATE STRATEGY. In June 2010, HSY announced a project called Next Century as part of its efforts to create an enhanced supply chain and cost structure. The project is expected to include a plant expansion in West Hershey, and investment in distribution and administrative facilities located in Hershey, PA. In July 2010, HSY estimated that the Next Century program would incur pretax charges of $140 million to $170 million from 2010-12, including $120 million to $150 million in realignment charges and about $20 million in start-up costs. We expect that the cash portion of the total charge would be about $95 million to $110 million, including start-up costs. Total capital expenditures related to the program were expected to be $250 million to $300 million. At the conclusion of the program, in 2014, we look for ongoing annual savings to have reached about $60 million to $80 million.

In February 2007, HSY announced a supply chain transformation program that was completed in 2009's fourth quarter. In 2009, HSY took $0.27 a share of charges related to the program. Since inception, total charges for the program amounted to $620.1 million (pretax), including $85 million of non-cash pension settlement charges. In July 2010, HSY said that except for possible non-cash pension settlement charges, it did not expect any significant charges related to the program in 2010. HSY estimated total program savings through 2009 at $160 million, with total ongoing annual savings from the program of $175 million to $185 million expected to be achieved by the end of 2010. Under the program, HSY expected to significantly increase manufacturing capacity utilization by reducing the number of its production lines; outsource the production of low-value-added items; and construct a production facility in Mexico. HSY planned to invest a portion of these savings in strategic growth initiatives.

We expect that HSY's strategy will include focus on, and advertising support for, core brands that have provided about 60% of U.S. sales.

In 2009, 14.3% of HSY's net sales were from businesses outside the U.S., down slightly from 14.4% in 2008. Longer term, we expect international expansion to include a focus on emerging markets in Asia, particularly India and China, Mexico, and selected markets in South America.

Company Financials Fiscal Year Ended Dec. 31

Per Share Data ($)	2009	2008	2007	2006	2005	2004	2003	2002	2001	2000
Tangible Book Value	0.10	NM	NM	0.18	1.63	2.03	3.29	3.55	2.65	2.57
Cash Flow	2.68	2.11	2.27	3.17	2.96	3.17	2.44	2.17	1.44	1.84
Earnings	1.90	1.36	0.93	2.34	1.99	2.30	1.76	1.46	0.75	1.21
S&P Core Earnings	2.13	1.22	1.14	2.26	1.94	2.23	1.73	1.37	0.94	NA
Dividends	1.19	1.19	1.14	1.03	0.93	0.84	0.72	0.63	0.58	0.54
Payout Ratio	63%	87%	122%	44%	47%	36%	41%	43%	78%	45%
Prices:High	42.25	44.32	56.75	57.65	67.37	56.75	39.33	39.75	35.08	33.22
Prices:Low	30.27	32.10	38.21	48.20	52.49	37.28	30.35	28.23	27.56	18.88
P/E Ratio:High	22	33	61	25	34	25	22	27	47	27
P/E Ratio:Low	16	24	41	21	26	16	17	19	37	16

Income Statement Analysis (Million $)										
Revenue	5,299	5,133	4,947	4,944	4,836	4,429	4,173	4,120	4,557	4,221
Operating Income	1,039	941	1,047	1,207	1,175	1,092	992	904	812	799
Depreciation	178	171	311	200	218	190	181	178	190	176
Interest Expense	91.3	105	119	116	89.5	66.5	63.5	60.7	71.5	81.0
Pretax Income	671	492	340	877	773	836	733	638	344	547
Effective Tax Rate	35.0%	36.7%	37.1%	36.2%	36.2%	29.3%	36.6%	36.7%	39.7%	38.8%
Net Income	436	311	214	559	493	591	465	404	207	335
S&P Core Earnings	488	279	264	540	482	573	455	377	258	NA

Balance Sheet & Other Financial Data (Million $)										
Cash	254	37.1	129	97.1	67.2	54.8	115	298	134	32.0
Current Assets	1,385	1,345	1,427	1,418	1,409	1,182	1,132	1,264	1,168	1,295
Total Assets	3,675	3,635	4,247	4,158	4,295	3,798	3,583	3,481	3,247	3,448
Current Liabilities	911	1,270	1,619	1,454	1,518	1,285	586	547	606	767
Long Term Debt	1,503	1,506	1,280	1,248	943	691	968	852	877	878
Common Equity	760	318	593	683	1,021	1,089	1,280	1,372	1,147	1,175
Total Capital	2,263	1,860	2,084	2,218	2,364	2,109	2,626	2,572	2,280	2,353
Capital Expenditures	126	263	190	183	181	182	219	133	160	138
Cash Flow	614	482	525	759	711	781	646	581	398	511
Current Ratio	1.5	1.1	0.9	1.0	0.9	0.9	1.9	2.3	1.9	1.7
% Long Term Debt of Capitalization	66.4	81.0	61.4	56.3	39.9	32.7	36.9	33.1	38.5	37.3
% Net Income of Revenue	8.2	6.1	4.3	11.3	10.2	13.3	11.1	9.8	4.5	7.9
% Return on Assets	11.9	7.9	5.1	13.3	12.2	16.0	13.2	12.0	6.2	9.8
% Return on Equity	80.9	68.4	33.6	65.8	45.7	46.4	35.1	32.0	17.8	29.4

Data as orig reptd.; bef. results of disc opers/spec. items. Per share data adj. for stk. divs.; EPS diluted. E-Estimated. NA-Not Available. NM-Not Meaningful. NR-Not Ranked. UR-Under Review.

Office: 100 Crystal A Drive, Hershey, PA 17033-9790.
Telephone: 717-534-4200.
Website: http://www.hersheys.com
Chrmn: J.E. Nevels

Pres & CEO: D.J. West
COO: T.L. O'Day
SVP & CFO: H. Alfonso
SVP, Secy & General Counsel: B.H. Snyder

Investor Contact: M.K. Pogharian (717-534-7556)
Board Members: P. M. Arway, R. F. Cavanaugh, C. A. Davis, J. E. Nevels, T. J. Ridge, D. L. Shedlarz, D. J. West, L. S. Zimmerman

Founded: 1894
Domicile: Delaware
Employees: 13,700

The McGraw·Hill Companies

Hess Corp

STANDARD &POOR'S

S&P Recommendation	**BUY** ★★★★☆	Price $63.25 (as of Oct 22, 2010)	12-Mo. Target Price $77.00	Investment Style Large-Cap Blend

GICS Sector Energy
Sub-Industry Integrated Oil & Gas

Summary This integrated oil and natural gas company has exploration and production activities worldwide, and markets refined petroleum products on the U.S. East Coast.

Key Stock Statistics (Source S&P, Vickers, company reports)

52-Wk Range	$66.49– 48.70	S&P Oper. EPS 2010**E**	4.91	Market Capitalization(B)	$20.773	Beta	0.99
Trailing 12-Month EPS	$4.93	S&P Oper. EPS 2011**E**	6.08	Yield (%)	0.63	S&P 3-Yr. Proj. EPS CAGR(%)	44
Trailing 12-Month P/E	12.8	P/E on S&P Oper. EPS 2010**E**	12.9	Dividend Rate/Share	$0.40	S&P Credit Rating	BBB
$10K Invested 5 Yrs Ago	$16,815	Common Shares Outstg. (M)	328.4	Institutional Ownership (%)	79		

Price Performance

30-Week Mov. Avg. ··· 10-Week Mov. Avg. — — **GAAP Earnings vs. Previous Year**   **Volume** Above Avg. ▮▮▮ STARS
12-Mo. Target Price — Relative Strength — ▲ Up ▼ Down ► No Change   Below Avg. ▮▮▮ ★

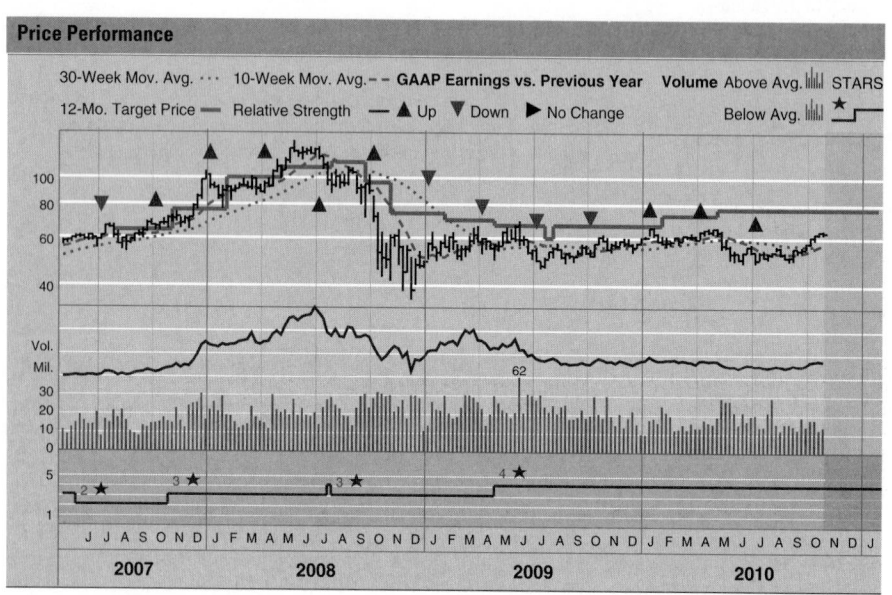

Analysis prepared by **Tina J. Vital** on August 02, 2010, when the stock traded at **$ 55.54**.

Options: ASE, CBOE, Ph

Qualitative Risk Assessment

LOW	**MEDIUM**	HIGH

Our risk assessment reflects HES's diversified business profile in volatile, cyclical, and capital-intensive segments of the energy industry. While we see risk from its investments in politically troubled locales, we think offsets include its improved, relatively low cost structure in exploration and production.

Quantitative Evaluations

S&P Quality Ranking   B+

D	C	B-	B	**B+**	A-	A	A+

Relative Strength Rank   STRONG

80

LOWEST = 1   HIGHEST = 99

Revenue/Earnings Data

Revenue (Million $)

	1Q	2Q	3Q	4Q	Year
2010	9,305	7,756	--	--	--
2009	6,915	6,751	7,270	8,678	29,569
2008	10,667	11,717	11,398	7,383	41,165
2007	7,319	7,421	7,451	9,456	31,647
2006	7,159	6,718	7,035	7,155	28,067
2005	4,956	4,963	5,769	7,059	22,747

Earnings Per Share ($)

2010	1.65	1.15	E1.10	E1.18	E4.91
2009	-0.18	0.31	1.05	1.10	2.27
2008	2.34	2.76	2.37	-0.23	7.24
2007	1.17	1.75	1.23	1.59	5.74
2006	2.21	1.79	0.94	1.13	6.07
2005	0.71	0.92	0.87	1.44	3.98

Fiscal year ended Dec. 31. Next earnings report expected: Late October. EPS Estimates based on S&P Operating Earnings; historical GAAP earnings are as reported.

Highlights

► Contributions from the Shenzi in the Gulf of Mexico and the Valhall field in Norway helped boost second quarter oil and gas production by 2%, to 415,000 boe per day. However, we look for less than 1% growth in 2010, reflecting a strategic asset trade with Shell. With about 16% of its oil and gas production from the deepwater Gulf of Mexico, we expect a drilling moratorium to cut 2011 Gulf of Mexico volumes, with little (if any) impact in 2010.

► While we expect global refining industry conditions to remain pressured through 2016, we see signs that U.S. refining margins are widening on improved demand and reduced operating costs. HES's refining operations incurred a loss in the second quarter reflecting that its Port Reading facility was shut down for 41 days. As of July 2010, we expect U.S. Gulf Coast 3-2-1 crack spreads to widen 9% in 2010 and 3% in 2011.

► First half operating EPS excluded net special gains of $0.16 related to asset sales. We project that after-tax operating earnings will increase 117% in 2010 and 24% in 2011, on improved demand and unit costs.

Investment Rationale/Risk

► We expect HES's earnings to be driven by its exploration & production business, which is oil-focused, and this should benefit over the long term from our forecast for higher crude oil prices. The company continues to rationalize its portfolio. So far in 2010, HES sold certain U.K. North Sea natural gas assets, expanded its interest in the Norwegian North Sea, agreed to acquire American Oil & Gas to enhance its Bakken oil play, and entered into a Paris Basin shale oil partnership with Toreador. We believe increased spending has improved HES's exploration success, and drilling continues on the Northwest Shelf of Australia.

► Risks to our recommendation and target price include deterioration in economic and industry conditions, and the company's potential inability to replace oil and gas reserves.

► Blending our discounted cash flow ($90 per share, assuming a WACC of 9.2% and terminal growth of 3%) with relative market valuations leads to our 12-month target price of $77, at an expected enterprise value multiple of 4.7X our 2011 EBITDA estimate, a premium to the peer average.

Dividend Data (Dates: mm/dd Payment Date: mm/dd/yy)

Amount ($)	Date Decl.	Ex-Div. Date	Stk. of Record	Payment Date
0.100	12/02	12/17	12/21	01/04/10
0.100	03/03	03/11	03/15	03/31/10
0.100	06/02	06/14	06/16	06/30/10
0.100	09/08	09/16	09/20	09/30/10

Dividends have been paid since 1922. Source: Company reports.

Hess Corp

Business Summary August 02, 2010

CORPORATE OVERVIEW. Hess Corp. (HES; formerly Amerada Hess Corp.) has two operating segments: Exploration and Production (24% of 2009 revenues; 89% of net income), and Marketing and Refining (76%; 11%). Business is conducted in the U.S. (83% of 2009 revenues; 21% of proved reserves), Europe (6%; 30%), Africa (6%; 23%), and Asia and elsewhere (5%; 26%). As of May 2009, the Hess family owned about 11% of the common shares.

Oil and gas production rose 7% in 2009, to 408,000 barrels of oil equivalent (boe) per day (72% crude oil and natural gas liquids (NGLs)). Net proved oil and gas reserves rose 0.35%, to 1.44 billion boe (59% developed; 67% crude oil and NGLs). Using data from John S. Herold, an oil industry consultant, we estimate HES's three-year (2006-08) average proved acquisition costs at $5.66 per boe, below the peer average; its three-year finding and development costs at $18.81 per boe, below the peer average; its three-year reserve replacement costs at $16.60 per boe, below the peer average; and its three-year reserve replacement at 190%, slightly above the peer average. We estimate HES's 2009 organic reserve replacement rate at 92% (103% overall).

As December 31, 2009, about 24% of the company's oil and NGL production and 13% of its natural gas production were from U.S. operations: onshore in the Williston Basin of North Dakota and in the Permian Basin in Texas, and offshore in the Gulf of Mexico, which included Shenzi (HES 28%), Llano (50%), Conger (38%), Baldpate (50%), Hack Wilson (25%), and Penn State (50%) fields.

HES's refining earnings are mainly derived from its 50% ownership in the refining joint venture HOVENSA, formed in October 1998 with a subsidiary of Petroleos de Venezuela S.A. (PdVSA) in the U.S. Virgin Islands. Refining operations at HOVENSA consist of crude units (500,000 b/d), a fluid catalytic cracker (150,000 b/d), and a delayed coker (58,000 b/d). In addition, HES owns and operates a 70,000 b/d fluid catalytic cracking facility in Port Reading, NJ, to produce gasoline and heating oil.

As of year-end 2009, HOVENSA had a long-term supply contract with PdVSA to purchase 115,000 b/d of Venezuelan Merey heavy crude oil. PdVSA also supplies 155,000 b/d of Venezuelan Masa medium gravity crude oil to HOVENSA under a long-term supply contract. The remaining crude oil requirements are purchased mainly under contracts of one year or less from third parties, and through spot purchases on the open market. After sales of refined products by HOVENSA to third parties, the company purchases 50% of HOVENSA's remaining production at market prices.

Company Financials Fiscal Year Ended Dec. 31

Per Share Data ($)	2009	2008	2007	2006	2005	2004	2003	2002	2001	2000
Tangible Book Value	37.50	34.31	26.67	21.77	16.61	14.34	13.62	12.17	14.70	14.59
Cash Flow	9.19	13.86	10.99	9.80	7.11	6.18	5.61	4.17	7.04	6.43
Earnings	2.27	7.24	5.74	6.07	3.98	3.17	1.72	-0.83	3.42	3.79
S&P Core Earnings	2.21	7.12	5.83	5.38	3.78	3.06	1.75	-1.28	3.25	NA
Dividends	0.40	0.30	0.40	0.40	0.40	0.40	0.40	0.40	0.40	0.20
Payout Ratio	18%	4%	7%	7%	10%	13%	23%	NM	12%	5%
Prices:High	69.74	137.00	105.85	56.45	47.50	31.30	19.07	28.23	30.13	25.42
Prices:Low	46.33	35.50	45.96	37.62	25.94	17.75	13.71	16.47	17.92	15.94
P/E Ratio:High	31	19	18	9	12	10	11	NM	9	7
P/E Ratio:Low	20	5	8	6	7	6	8	NM	5	4

Income Statement Analysis (Million $)	2009	2008	2007	2006	2005	2004	2003	2002	2001	2000
Revenue	29,614	41,165	31,647	28,067	22,747	16,733	14,480	12,093	13,413	11,993
Operating Income	NA	7,207	5,259	4,812	2,967	2,769	2,127	2,382	2,399	2,264
Depreciation, Depletion and Amortization	2,254	2,154	1,678	1,224	1,025	970	1,053	1,320	967	714
Interest Expense	360	267	306	201	224	241	293	269	194	162
Pretax Income	1,522	4,700	3,704	4,040	2,226	1,558	781	-51.0	1,438	1,672
Effective Tax Rate	47.0%	49.8%	50.5%	52.6%	44.2%	37.7%	40.2%	NM	36.4%	38.8%
Net Income	740	2,360	1,832	1,916	1,242	970	467	-218	914	1,023
S&P Core Earnings	720	2,320	1,865	1,657	1,131	888	468	-339	870	NA

Balance Sheet & Other Financial Data (Million $)	2009	2008	2007	2006	2005	2004	2003	2002	2001	2000
Cash	1,362	908	607	383	315	877	518	197	37.0	312
Current Assets	7,987	7,332	6,926	5,848	5,290	4,335	3,186	2,756	3,946	4,115
Total Assets	29,419	28,908	26,131	22,404	19,115	16,312	13,983	13,262	15,369	10,274
Current Liabilities	6,850	7,730	8,024	6,739	6,447	4,697	2,669	2,553	3,718	3,538
Long Term Debt	4,319	3,812	3,918	3,745	3,759	3,785	3,868	4,976	5,283	1,985
Common Equity	13,528	12,307	9,774	8,111	6,272	5,583	5,326	8,498	4,907	3,883
Total Capital	17,995	18,360	16,054	13,955	11,446	10,566	10,352	14,518	11,301	6,378
Capital Expenditures	2,918	4,438	3,578	3,844	2,341	1,521	1,358	1,404	2,501	938
Cash Flow	2,994	4,514	3,510	3,096	2,219	1,892	1,515	1,102	1,881	1,737
Current Ratio	1.2	1.0	0.9	0.9	0.8	0.9	1.2	1.1	1.1	1.2
% Long Term Debt of Capitalization	24.0	20.8	24.4	26.8	32.8	35.8	37.4	34.3	46.7	31.1
% Return on Assets	2.6	8.6	7.5	9.2	7.0	6.4	3.4	NM	7.1	11.4
% Return on Equity	5.7	21.4	20.5	26.0	20.1	16.9	9.7	NM	20.8	29.6

Data as orig reptd.; bef. results of disc opers/spec. items. Per share data adj. for stk. divs.; EPS diluted. E-Estimated. NA-Not Available. NM-Not Meaningful. NR-Not Ranked. UR-Under Review.

Office: 1185 Avenue Of The Americas, New York, NY 10036.
Telephone: 212-997-8500.
Email: investorrelations@hess.com
Website: http://www.hess.com

Chrmn & CEO: J.B. Hess
SVP, CFO & Chief Acctg Officer: J.P. Rielly
SVP & General Counsel: T.B. Goodell
CTO: S. Heck

Treas: R. Biglin
Investor Contact: J.R. Wilson (212-536-8940)
Board Members: S. W. Bodman, III, N. F. Brady, J. B. Hess, G. P. Hill, E. E. Holiday, T. H. Kean, R. J. Lavizzo-Mourey, C. G. Matthews, J. H. Mullin, III, F. A. Olson, F. B. Walker, R. N. Wilson, E. H. von Metzsch

Founded: 1920
Domicile: Delaware
Employees: 13,300

Hewlett-Packard Co

STANDARD &POOR'S

S&P Recommendation	**STRONG BUY** ★★★★★	Price	12-Mo. Target Price	Investment Style
		$42.87 (as of Oct 22, 2010)	$54.00	Large-Cap Blend

GICS Sector Information Technology
Sub-Industry Computer Hardware

Summary This leading maker of computer products, including printers, servers and PCs, has a large service and support network.

Key Stock Statistics (Source S&P, Vickers, company reports)

52-Wk Range	$54.75–37.32	S&P Oper. EPS 2010**E**	4.51	Market Capitalization(B)	$97.218	Beta	1.08
Trailing 12-Month EPS	$3.59	S&P Oper. EPS 2011**E**	5.15	Yield (%)	0.75	S&P 3-Yr. Proj. EPS CAGR(%)	14
Trailing 12-Month P/E	11.9	P/E on S&P Oper. EPS 2010**E**	9.5	Dividend Rate/Share	$0.32	S&P Credit Rating	A
$10K Invested 5 Yrs Ago	$16,187	Common Shares Outstg. (M)	2,267.7	Institutional Ownership (%)	79		

Price Performance

30-Week Mov. Avg. · · · · 10-Week Mov. Avg. – – **GAAP Earnings vs. Previous Year** **Volume** Above Avg. STARS
12-Mo. Target Price — Relative Strength — ▲ Up ▼ Down ▶ No Change Below Avg. ★

Options: ASE, CBOE, P, Ph

Analysis prepared by **Thomas W. Smith, CFA** on October 12, 2010, when the stock traded at **$ 41.38**.

Highlights

➤ We estimate revenue will grow about 9.7% in FY 10 (Oct.) and 6.0% in FY 11, reflecting a cyclical upturn in demand for information technology goods and services. On September 30, the company announced that Leo Apoteker, a former CEO of software rival SAP AG (SAP 52 Hold), would become CEO and president effective November 1. On September 13, the company agreed to acquire security and compliance software provider ArcSight (ARST 43 NR) for about $1.5 billion in cash, subject to customary closing conditions. On September 27, HPQ closed its acquisition of data storage technology provider 3PAR in a deal valued at approximately $2.35 billion.

➤ We expect operating margins, excluding acquisition and restructuring charges, to widen in FY 10 and FY 11, based on higher volumes and cost reduction efforts.

➤ We estimate operating EPS, excluding restructuring charges and pending acquisitions, of $4.51 for FY 10 and $5.15 for FY 11. Directors authorized an additional $10 billion for share buybacks on August 30, which we believe will support per-share results.

Investment Rationale/Risk

➤ We believe that HPQ has the potential to gain market share in PCs, servers, printers, and IT services. We think new management can maintain product development and cost-cutting strategies. Acquisitions are helping to broaden the product line and create more comprehensive data center solutions. Deals have been made in the networking, storage, security, and mobile operating system areas in FY 10. We view the valuation as compelling, based on our P/E analysis.

➤ Risks to our recommendation and target price include potential problems closing and integrating acquisitions. The arrival of new top leadership poses transition challenges. Costs for acquisitions and share buybacks could limit financial flexibility. Demand for computer hardware could weaken.

➤ We apply a target multiple near 10.5X, in the lower half of the seven-year historical range for HPQ and a discount to the recent average for Information Technology sector companies in the S&P 500, to our FY 11 operating EPS estimate of $5.15 to arrive at our 12-month target price of $54.

Qualitative Risk Assessment

LOW	MEDIUM	HIGH

Our risk assessment reflects the intensely price competitive environment in the computer hardware industry and potential integration risk from planned and completed acquisitions, balanced by our view of the company's broad worldwide customer base and its successful efforts in reducing its cost structure.

Quantitative Evaluations

S&P Quality Ranking   B+

D	C	B-	B	B+	A-	A	A+

Relative Strength Rank   MODERATE

46

LOWEST = 1   HIGHEST = 99

Revenue/Earnings Data

Revenue (Million $)

	1Q	2Q	3Q	4Q	Year
2010	31,177	30,849	30,729	--	--
2009	28,807	27,383	27,585	30,777	114,552
2008	28,467	28,262	28,032	33,603	118,364
2007	25,082	25,534	25,377	28,293	104,286
2006	22,659	22,554	21,890	24,555	91,658
2005	21,454	21,570	20,759	22,913	86,696

Earnings Per Share ($)

2010	0.96	0.91	0.75	E1.28	E4.51
2009	0.75	0.71	0.69	0.99	3.14
2008	0.80	0.81	0.80	0.84	3.25
2007	0.55	0.65	0.80	0.81	2.68
2006	0.42	0.66	0.48	0.60	2.18
2005	0.32	0.33	0.03	0.14	0.82

Fiscal year ended Oct. 31. Next earnings report expected: Mid November. EPS Estimates based on S&P Operating Earnings; historical GAAP earnings are as reported.

Dividend Data (Dates: mm/dd Payment Date: mm/dd/yy)

Amount ($)	Date Decl.	Ex-Div. Date	Stk. of Record	Payment Date
0.080	11/19	12/14	12/16	01/06/10
0.080	01/28	03/15	03/17	04/07/10
0.080	05/20	06/14	06/16	07/07/10
0.080	07/29	09/13	09/15	10/06/10

Dividends have been paid since 1965. Source: Company reports.

Please read the Required Disclosures and Analyst Certification on the last page of this report.

The McGraw-Hill Companies

Hewlett-Packard Co

Business Summary October 12, 2010

CORPORATE OVERVIEW. Hewlett-Packard provides personal computers, printers, enterprise server and storage technology, and a wide range of related products and services to individual and enterprise customers worldwide. Revenues in FY 09 (Oct.) came approximately 68% from products and 32% from services, including financing services.

Ongoing work force restructurings have enabled HPQ to develop a global delivery structure that has improved margins by taking advantage of low-cost technical expertise. The cost and efficiency campaign had been led by former NCR Corp. CEO Mark Hurd, who was named CEO and president of HPQ effective April 1, 2005. In addition, Mr. Hurd took over the chairman's role in late September 2006. Mr. Hurd resigned from the company on August 6, 2010, following an internal investigation that found violations of HPQ's Standards of Business Conduct. On September 30, the company announced that Leo Apoteker, a former CEO of software rival SAP AG (SAP 52 Hold), would become CEO and president effective November 1.

The breadth of the company's customer base is illustrated by the nearly 64% of FY 09 revenues that came from outside the U.S. Further, no single customer, nor any single country other than the U.S., accounted for more than 10% of sales in FY 09.

The company reports in seven segments. Three segments accounting for about 46% of sales are often grouped together as HP Enterprise Business (formerly the Technology Solutions Group). These include Enterprise Storage and Servers, representing approximately 13% of FY 09 sales, Services 30%, and HP Software 3%. Other segments include the Personal Systems Group, representing about 31% of FY 09 sales, the Imaging and Printing Group 21%, HP Financial Services 2%, and Corporate Investments less than 1%.

Company Financials Fiscal Year Ended Oct. 31

Per Share Data ($)	2009	2008	2007	2006	2005	2004	2003	2002	2001	2000
Tangible Book Value	0.34	NM	4.91	6.57	6.04	6.06	6.08	5.35	7.20	7.30
Cash Flow	5.10	4.56	3.67	3.00	1.63	1.93	1.65	0.48	1.01	2.37
Earnings	3.14	3.25	2.68	2.18	0.82	1.15	0.83	-0.37	0.32	1.73
S&P Core Earnings	3.14	2.97	2.56	2.10	0.74	0.94	0.65	-0.65	0.16	NA
Dividends	0.32	0.32	0.32	0.32	0.32	0.32	0.32	0.32	0.32	0.32
Payout Ratio	10%	10%	12%	15%	39%	28%	39%	NM	100%	18%
Prices:High	52.95	50.98	53.48	41.70	30.25	26.28	23.90	24.12	37.95	77.75
Prices:Low	25.39	28.23	38.15	28.37	18.89	16.08	14.18	10.75	12.50	29.13
P/E Ratio:High	17	16	20	19	37	23	29	NM	NM	45
P/E Ratio:Low	8	9	14	13	23	14	17	NM	NM	17

Income Statement Analysis (Million $)	2009	2008	2007	2006	2005	2004	2003	2002	2001	2000
Revenue	114,552	118,364	104,286	91,658	86,696	79,905	73,061	56,588	45,226	48,782
Operating Income	15,798	14,196	11,773	9,372	7,520	7,017	6,713	4,570	3,192	5,257
Depreciation	4,773	3,367	2,705	2,353	2,344	2,395	2,527	2,119	1,369	1,368
Interest Expense	259	467	289	249	334	247	277	212	234	233
Pretax Income	9,415	10,473	9,177	7,191	3,543	4,196	2,888	-1,052	702	4,625
Effective Tax Rate	18.6%	20.5%	20.9%	13.8%	32.3%	16.7%	12.1%	NM	11.1%	23.0%
Net Income	7,660	8,329	7,264	6,198	2,398	3,497	2,539	-923	624	3,561
S&P Core Earnings	7,659	7,598	6,913	5,992	2,150	2,886	1,983	-1,635	285	NA

Balance Sheet & Other Financial Data (Million $)	2009	2008	2007	2006	2005	2004	2003	2002	2001	2000
Cash	13,334	10,246	11,293	16,400	13,911	12,663	14,188	11,192	4,197	3,415
Current Assets	52,539	51,728	47,402	48,264	43,334	42,901	40,996	36,075	21,305	23,244
Total Assets	114,799	113,331	88,699	81,981	77,317	76,138	74,708	70,710	32,584	34,009
Current Liabilities	43,003	52,939	39,260	2,490	31,460	28,588	26,630	24,310	13,964	15,197
Long Term Debt	13,980	7,676	4,997	2,490	3,392	4,623	6,494	6,035	3,729	3,402
Common Equity	40,517	38,942	38,526	38,144	37,176	37,564	37,746	36,262	13,953	14,209
Total Capital	54,497	49,292	43,523	40,634	40,568	42,187	44,240	42,297	17,682	17,611
Capital Expenditures	3,695	2,990	3,040	2,536	1,995	2,126	1,995	1,710	1,527	1,737
Cash Flow	12,433	11,696	9,969	8,551	4,742	5,892	5,066	1,196	1,993	4,929
Current Ratio	1.2	1.0	1.2	1.3	1.4	1.5	1.5	1.5	1.5	1.5
% Long Term Debt of Capitalization	25.7	15.4	11.5	6.1	8.4	11.0	14.7	14.3	21.1	19.3
% Net Income of Revenue	6.7	7.0	7.0	6.8	2.8	4.4	3.5	NM	1.4	7.3
% Return on Assets	6.7	8.3	8.5	7.8	3.1	4.6	3.5	NM	1.9	10.3
% Return on Equity	19.3	21.5	19.0	16.5	6.4	9.3	6.9	NM	4.4	21.9

Data as orig reptd.; bef. results of disc opers/spec. items. Per share data adj. for stk. divs.; EPS diluted. E-Estimated. NA-Not Available. NM-Not Meaningful. NR-Not Ranked. UR-Under Review.

Office: 3000 Hanover Street, Palo Alto, CA 94304-1112.
Telephone: 650-857-1501.
Website: http://www.hp.com
CEO & CFO: C.A. Lesjak

EVP & Chief Admin Officer: P.J. Bocian
EVP & CTO: S.V. Robison
EVP & General Counsel: M.J. Holston
EVP & CIO: R.D. Mott

Investor Contact: B. Humphries (650-857-3342)
Board Members: M. L. Andreessen, L. T. Babbio, Jr., S. Baldauf, R. L. Gupta, J. H. Hammergren, J. Hyatt, J. R. Joyce, R. L. Ryan, L. S. Salhany, G. Thompson
Founded: 1939
Domicile: Delaware
Employees: 304,000

Home Depot Inc. (The)

STANDARD &POOR'S

S&P Recommendation	HOLD ★★★☆☆	Price	12-Mo. Target Price	Investment Style
		$31.48 (as of Oct 22, 2010)	$31.00	Large-Cap Blend

GICS Sector Consumer Discretionary
Sub-Industry Home Improvement Retail

Summary HD operates a chain of over 2,200 retail warehouse-type stores, selling a wide variety of home improvement products for the do-it-yourself and home remodeling markets.

Key Stock Statistics (Source S&P, Vickers, company reports)

52-Wk Range	$37.03–24.47	S&P Oper. EPS 2011E	1.91	Market Capitalization(B)	$52.424	Beta		0.68
Trailing 12-Month EPS	$1.75	S&P Oper. EPS 2012E	2.11	Yield (%)	3.00	S&P 3-Yr. Proj. EPS CAGR(%)		11
Trailing 12-Month P/E	18.0	P/E on S&P Oper. EPS 2011E	16.5	Dividend Rate/Share	$0.95	S&P Credit Rating		BBB+
$10K Invested 5 Yrs Ago	$9,148	Common Shares Outstg. (M)	1,665.3	Institutional Ownership (%)	71			

Price Performance

30-Week Mov. Avg. · · · · 10-Week Mov. Avg. – – – GAAP Earnings vs. Previous Year Volume Above Avg. STARS
12-Mo. Target Price — Relative Strength — ▲ Up ▼ Down ► No Change Below Avg.

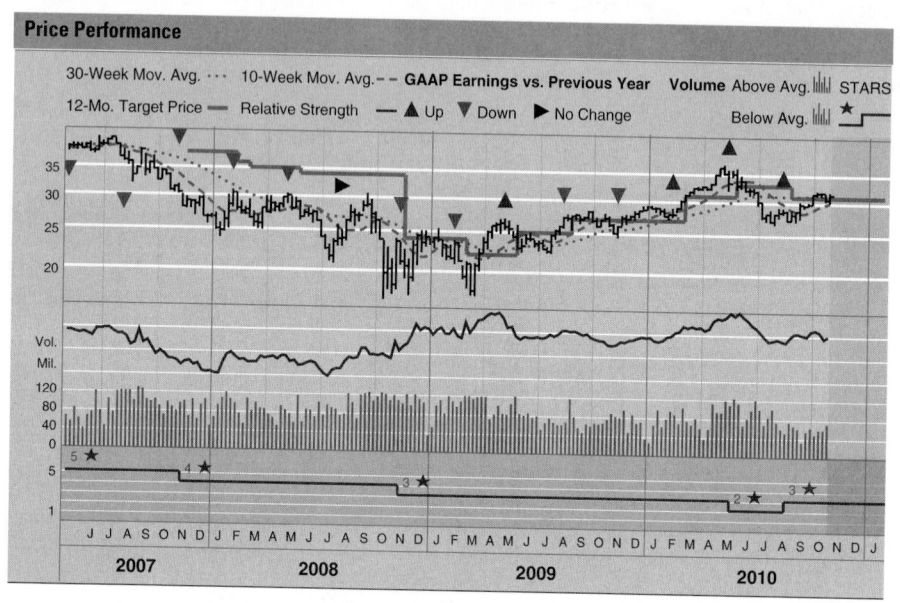

Options: ASE, CBOE, P, Ph

Analysis prepared by **Michael Souers** on August 19, 2010, when the stock traded at **$ 28.15.**

Highlights

➤ We expect retail sales to increase 2.7% in FY 11 (Jan.), following a 7.2% decline in FY 10. We see this rise reflecting 5 to 10 net new retail store additions, including international store openings, and a 2% to 3% increase in same-store sales. We project a slow recovery in the housing market in calendar 2010, and we expect the tightening of consumer credit to also adversely affect near-term sales for home improvement retailers, particularly on big-ticket remodeling projects.

➤ We see FY 11 operating margins widening 70 basis points, driven by a rational pricing environment, continued tight expense control, supply chain benefits from the recent investment in rapid deployment centers, and an improving mix. We also expect the projected increase in same-store-sales will leverage fixed expenses modestly, given HD's stringent cost control.

➤ Excluding a $0.02 charge due to a revaluation of a loan, we project FY 11 EPS of $1.91, a 15% increase from the $1.66 the company earned in FY 10, excluding $0.11 in store rationalization charges and a writedown of the company's investment in HD Supply. We see FY 12 EPS of $2.11.

Investment Rationale/Risk

➤ We expect the housing market to recover gradually over the coming year and believe HD will reap rewards from an accelerated focus on customer service. Favorable demographic trends, such as the aging of houses and low interest rates, should help support home remodeling efforts over the long term. However, although we favor HD's strong balance sheet and abundant free cash flow generation, we remain concerned that the recovery in housing will take much longer than widely anticipated. Following a sharp recent selloff, we think the shares are fairly valued trading at under 14X our FY 12 EPS estimate, a modest premium to the S&P 500 and at a slight premium to key peer Lowe's (LOW 21, Hold).

➤ Risks to our recommendation and target price include a rapid recovery in consumer spending; a greater-than-expected improvement in the housing market; and favorable currency movements.

➤ Our 12-month target price of $31, which is equal to about 15X our FY 12 EPS estimate, is derived from our DCF model, which assumes a weighted average cost of capital of 9.6% and a terminal growth rate of 3.0%.

Qualitative Risk Assessment

LOW	MEDIUM	HIGH

Our risk assessment for Home Depot reflects our view of ample opportunities for growth in the professional market domestically and the retail business overseas, and an S&P Quality Ranking of A. This is partially offset by the cyclical nature of the home improvement retail industry, which is reliant on economic growth.

Quantitative Evaluations

S&P Quality Ranking A

D	C	B-	B	B+	A-	A	A+

Relative Strength Rank MODERATE

54

LOWEST = 1   HIGHEST = 99

Revenue/Earnings Data

Revenue (Million $)

	1Q	2Q	3Q	4Q	Year
2011	16,863	19,410	--	--	--
2010	16,175	19,071	16,361	14,569	66,176
2009	17,907	20,990	17,784	14,607	71,288
2008	21,585	22,184	18,961	17,659	77,349
2007	21,461	26,026	23,085	20,265	90,837
2006	18,973	22,305	20,744	19,489	81,511

Earnings Per Share ($)

	1Q	2Q	3Q	4Q	Year
2011	0.43	0.72	E0.49	E0.25	E1.91
2010	0.30	0.66	0.41	0.18	1.55
2009	0.21	0.71	0.45	-0.03	1.37
2008	0.53	0.71	0.59	0.40	2.27
2007	0.70	0.90	0.73	0.46	2.79
2006	0.57	0.82	0.72	0.60	2.72

Fiscal year ended Jan. 31. Next earnings report expected: Mid November. EPS Estimates based on S&P Operating Earnings; historical GAAP earnings are as reported.

Dividend Data (Dates: mm/dd Payment Date: mm/dd/yy)

Amount ($)	Date Decl.	Ex-Div. Date	Stk. of Record	Payment Date
0.236	02/23	03/09	03/11	03/25/10
0.236	05/20	06/01	06/03	06/17/10
0.236	08/19	08/31	09/02	09/16/10

Dividends have been paid since 1987. Source: Company reports.

Please read the Required Disclosures and Analyst Certification on the last page of this report.

The McGraw·Hill Companies

Home Depot Inc. (The)

STANDARD &POOR'S

Business Summary August 19, 2010

CORPORATE OVERVIEW. Home Depot is the world's largest home improvement retailer, with $66 billion in revenues in FY 10 (Jan.). At January 31, 2010, HD operated 2,244 Home Depot stores (179 in Canada, 79 in Mexico and 10 in China). In January 2009, the company announced the planned closing of 34 EXPO Design Centers, five Yardbirds stores in California, and two THD Design Centers as part of HD's continued focus on its core business.

Home Depot stores average approximately 105,000 sq. ft., plus 24,000 sq. ft. of garden center and storage space. They stock 30,000 to 40,000 items, including brand name and proprietary items. Home Depot stores serve three primary customer groups: Do-It-Yourself (DIY) customers, typically homeowners who complete their own projects and installations; Do-It-For-Me (DIFM) customers, usually homeowners who purchase materials and hire third parties to complete the project and/or installation; and Professional customers, consisting of professional remodelers, general contractors, repairpeople and tradespeople. By product group, plumbing, electrical and kitchen (30% of FY 10 revenues) represented HD's largest source of revenue, followed by hardware and seasonal (29%), building materials, lumber and millwork (22%) and paint and flooring (19%).

CORPORATE STRATEGY. We believe HD is in a period of transition after years of expanding rapidly. We expect Home Depot to confront a rapidly saturating domestic market by accelerating its expansion efforts abroad. Domestically, HD is increasing its focus on service and customer retention as a means to gain market share.

At the end of 2006, Home Depot acquired The Home Way, a Chinese home improvement retailer, including 12 stores in six cities. We expect HD to either exit the Chinese market in FY 11 or embark on an aggressive expansion of stores over the next several years.

In August 2007, Home Depot closed the sale of HD Supply for $8.3 billion, recognizing a $4 million loss, net of tax. In connection with the sale, it purchased a 12.5% equity interest in the newly formed HD Supply for $325 million, but has since completely written down this investment over the past two years due to asset impairment.

Company Financials Fiscal Year Ended Jan. 31

Per Share Data ($)	2010	2009	2008	2007	2006	2005	2004	2003	2002	2001
Tangible Book Value	10.73	9.81	9.75	11.81	11.12	9.54	9.56	8.39	7.53	6.32
Cash Flow	2.62	2.43	3.19	3.65	3.45	2.85	2.35	1.95	1.62	1.35
Earnings	1.55	1.37	2.27	2.79	2.72	2.26	1.88	1.56	1.29	1.10
S&P Core Earnings	1.61	1.43	2.27	2.79	2.68	2.19	1.78	1.46	1.18	1.01
Dividends	0.90	0.90	0.68	0.68	0.40	0.33	0.26	0.21	0.17	0.16
Payout Ratio	58%	58%	30%	24%	15%	15%	14%	13%	13%	15%
Calendar Year	2009	2008	2007	2006	2005	2004	2003	2002	2001	2000
Prices:High	29.44	31.08	42.01	43.95	43.98	44.30	37.89	52.60	53.73	70.00
Prices:Low	17.49	17.05	25.57	32.85	34.56	32.34	20.10	23.01	30.30	34.69
P/E Ratio:High	19	23	19	16	16	20	20	41	43	64
P/E Ratio:Low	11	12	11	12	13	14	11	18	24	32

Income Statement Analysis (Million $)										
Revenue	66,176	71,288	77,349	90,837	81,511	73,094	64,816	58,247	53,553	45,738
Operating Income	6,755	7,093	9,032	11,435	10,942	9,245	7,922	6,733	5,696	4,792
Depreciation	1,806	1,783	1,702	1,762	1,579	1,319	1,076	903	764	601
Interest Expense	676	644	742	427	143	70.0	62.0	37.0	28.0	21.0
Pretax Income	3,982	3,590	6,620	9,308	9,282	7,912	6,843	5,872	4,957	4,217
Effective Tax Rate	34.2%	35.6%	36.4%	38.1%	37.1%	36.8%	37.1%	37.6%	38.6%	38.8%
Net Income	2,620	2,312	4,210	5,761	5,838	5,001	4,304	3,664	3,044	2,581
S&P Core Earnings	2,721	2,418	4,210	5,761	5,751	4,843	4,067	3,414	2,780	2,364

Balance Sheet & Other Financial Data (Million $)										
Cash	1,427	525	457	614	793	506	2,826	2,188	2,477	167
Current Assets	13,900	13,362	14,674	18,000	15,346	14,190	13,328	11,917	10,361	7,777
Total Assets	40,877	41,164	44,324	52,263	44,482	38,907	34,437	30,011	26,394	21,385
Current Liabilities	10,363	11,153	12,706	12,931	12,901	10,529	9,554	8,035	6,501	4,385
Long Term Debt	8,662	9,667	10,983	11,237	2,302	1,807	545	1,049	1,022	1,318
Common Equity	19,393	17,777	17,714	25,030	26,909	24,158	22,407	19,802	18,082	15,004
Total Capital	29,075	28,794	28,982	36,272	29,713	25,976	23,461	20,853	19,105	16,334
Capital Expenditures	966	1,847	3,558	3,542	3,881	3,948	3,508	2,749	3,393	3,558
Cash Flow	4,426	4,095	5,912	7,523	7,417	6,320	5,380	4,567	3,808	3,182
Current Ratio	1.3	1.2	1.2	1.4	1.2	1.3	1.4	1.5	1.6	1.8
% Long Term Debt of Capitalization	29.8	33.1	38.2	31.8	8.7	7.8	3.5	6.1	6.4	9.2
% Net Income of Revenue	4.0	3.2	5.4	6.3	7.2	6.8	6.6	6.3	5.7	5.6
% Return on Assets	6.4	5.4	8.7	11.9	14.0	13.6	13.4	13.0	12.7	13.4
% Return on Equity	14.1	13.0	19.7	22.2	22.9	21.5	20.4	19.3	18.4	18.9

Data as orig reptd.; bef. results of disc opers/spec. items. Per share data adj. for stk. divs.; EPS diluted. E-Estimated. NA-Not Available. NM-Not Meaningful. NR-Not Ranked. UR-Under Review.

Office: 2455 Paces Ferry Rd, N.W., Atlanta, GA 30339-1834.
Telephone: 770-433-8211.
Website: http://www.homedepot.com
Chrmn & CEO: F.S. Blake

Pres: A. Campbell
COO: M.D. Powers
EVP, CFO & Chief Acctg Officer: C.B. Tome
EVP, Secy & General Counsel: J.A. VanWoerkom

Investor Contact: D. Dayhoff (770-384-2666)
Board Members: F. D. Ackerman, D. H. Batchelder, F. S. Blake, A. Bousbib, G. D. Brenneman, A. P. Carey, A. M. Codina, B. G. Hill, K. L. Katen

Founded: 1978
Domicile: Delaware
Employees: 317,000

The McGraw·Hill Companies

Honeywell International Inc.

STANDARD &POOR'S

| S&P Recommendation **BUY** ★★★★☆ | Price $47.26 (as of Oct 22, 2010) | 12-Mo. Target Price $52.00 | Investment Style Large-Cap Value |

GICS Sector Industrials
Sub-Industry Aerospace & Defense

Summary The world's largest maker of cockpit controls, small jet engines and climate control equipment, HON also makes industrial materials and automotive products.

Key Stock Statistics (Source S&P, Vickers, company reports)

52-Wk Range	$48.63– 35.60	S&P Oper. EPS 2010E	2.54	Market Capitalization(B)	$36.495	Beta	1.36
Trailing 12-Month EPS	$2.80	S&P Oper. EPS 2011E	2.80	Yield (%)	2.56	S&P 3-Yr. Proj. EPS CAGR(%)	5
Trailing 12-Month P/E	16.9	P/E on S&P Oper. EPS 2010E	18.6	Dividend Rate/Share	$1.21	S&P Credit Rating	A
$10K Invested 5 Yrs Ago	$16,175	Common Shares Outstg. (M)	772.2	Institutional Ownership (%)	81		

Price Performance

30-Week Mov. Avg. ···   10-Week Mov. Avg. - - GAAP Earnings vs. Previous Year   Volume Above Avg. ▮▮▮ STARS

12-Mo. Target Price — Relative Strength ▲ Up ▼ Down ▶ No Change   Below Avg. ▮▮▮ ★

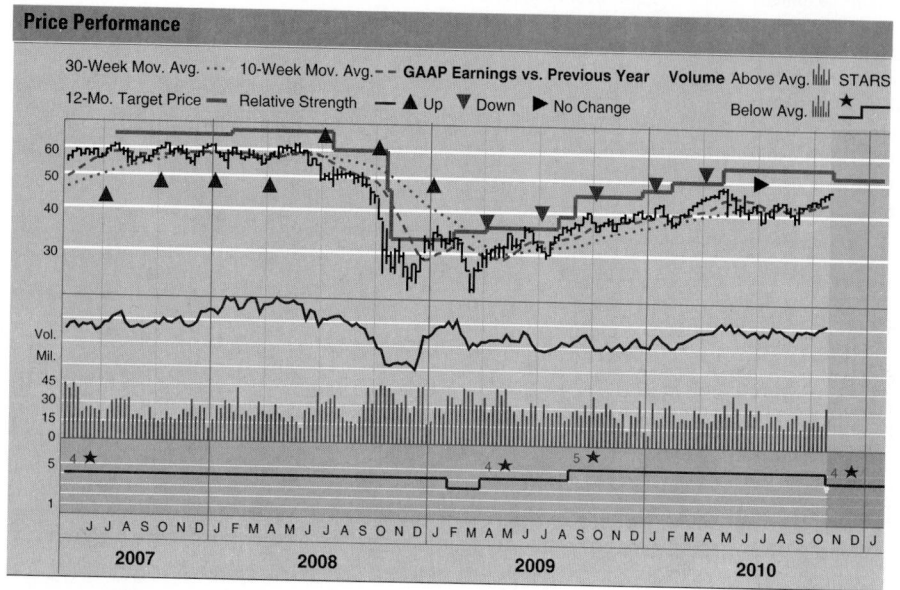

Options: ASE, CBOE, P, Ph

Qualitative Risk Assessment

| LOW | MEDIUM | HIGH |

Our risk assessment reflects what we believe is above-average exposure to market movements, economic cycles, currency fluctuations, and raw material costs. This is offset by our view of HON's strong balance sheet and its ability to generate significant amounts of cash.

Quantitative Evaluations

S&P Quality Ranking B+

| D | C | B- | B | B+ | A- | A | A+ |

Relative Strength Rank STRONG

75

LOWEST = 1   HIGHEST = 99

Revenue/Earnings Data

Revenue (Million $)

	1Q	2Q	3Q	4Q	Year
2010	7,776	8,161	--	--	--
2009	7,570	7,566	7,700	8,072	30,908
2008	8,895	9,674	9,275	8,712	36,556
2007	8,041	8,538	8,735	9,275	34,589
2006	7,241	7,898	7,952	8,276	31,367
2005	6,453	7,026	6,899	7,275	27,653

Earnings Per Share ($)

	1Q	2Q	3Q	4Q	Year
2010	0.50	0.60	E0.64	E0.80	E2.54
2009	0.54	0.60	0.80	0.91	2.85
2008	0.85	0.96	0.97	0.97	3.76
2007	0.66	0.78	0.81	0.91	3.16
2006	0.51	0.63	0.66	0.72	2.51
2005	0.42	0.33	0.51	0.61	1.86

Fiscal year ended Dec. 31. Next earnings report expected: Late October. EPS Estimates based on S&P Operating Earnings; historical GAAP earnings are as reported.

Highlights

▶ The STARS recommendation for HON has recently been changed to 4 (buy) from 5 (strong buy) and the 12-month target price has recently been changed to $52.00 from $55.00. The Highlights section of this Stock Report will be updated accordingly.

Investment Rationale/Risk

▶ The Investment Rationale/Risk section of this Stock Report will be updated shortly. For the latest News story on HON from MarketScope, see below.

▶ 10/22/10 11:37 am ET ... S&P DOWNGRADES RECOMMENDATION ON SHARES OF HONEY-WELL TO BUY FROM STRONG BUY (HON 46.87****): Q3 EPS of $0.64, vs. $0.80, is $0.02 below our estimate but $0.02 above Street. Sales rose 9%, above our 7% estimate. Margins met our view, but restructuring cost was well above our expectations. HON sees a $300-$400M additional pension headwind in '11, and although we are raising our '10 EPS estimate by $0.02 to $2.54, we are lowering '11's by $0.20 to $2.80. We also trim our 12-month target price by $3 to $52. We continue to see HON as performing well amid a cyclical upturn in aerospace and the global economy, but see more modest upside earnings momentum than previously. /R.Tortoriello

Dividend Data (Dates: mm/dd Payment Date: mm/dd/yy)

Amount ($)	Date Decl.	Ex-Div. Date	Stk. of Record	Payment Date
0.303	10/30	11/18	11/20	12/10/09
0.303	02/11	02/17	02/19	03/10/10
0.303	04/26	05/18	05/20	06/10/10
0.303	07/30	08/18	08/20	09/10/10

Dividends have been paid since 1887. Source: Company reports.

Please read the Required Disclosures and Analyst Certification on the last page of this report.

The McGraw-Hill Companies

Honeywell International Inc.

STANDARD &POOR'S

Business Summary August 06, 2010

CORPORATE OVERVIEW. Honeywell International Inc., an aerospace and industrial conglomerate with $32 billion in estimated 2010 revenues, conducts business through four operating segments. HON generated about 51% of sales from products sold outside of the U.S. in 2009, primarily in Europe, Canada, Asia, and Latin America. Sales to the U.S. government accounted for 14% of total sales in 2009.

The Aerospace segment (35% of 2009 revenues and 45% of operating profits) makes a variety of products for commercial and military aircraft, including cockpit controls and other avionics, flight safety systems, auxiliary power units, environmental controls, electric power systems, inertial sensors, lighting, and wheels and brakes. It is also a leading maker of jet engines for regional and business jet manufacturers, and makes space and military products and subsystems. The Aerospace segment is also a major player in the estimated $103 billion global aircraft maintenance, repair, and overhaul (MRO) industry, and distributes aircraft hardware.

HON's Automation and Control Solutions segment (41% of revenues and 37% of operating profits) is a leading global producer of environmental and combustion controls, sensing controls, security and life safety products and services, scanning and mobility products (e.g., bar code scanners), and process automation and building solutions and services for homes, buildings, and industrial facilities. Building solutions and services include energy management, security and asset management, building information services, and HVAC and building control.

The Specialty Materials segment (13% and 14%) makes specialty chemicals and fibers. Products include resins, fluorine products, specialty films and additives, advanced fibers and composites, intermediates, specialty chemicals, electronic materials and chemicals, and catalysts, absorbents, and equipment and technologies for the petrochemical and refining industries. HON sells its industrial materials primarily to the petrochemical, food, pharmaceutical, and electronic packaging industries.

The Transportation Systems segment (11% and 4%) consists of a portfolio of brand name car care products, such as FRAM filters, Prestone antifreeze, Autolite spark plugs, and Simoniz car waxes. The unit is also a leading manufacturer of turbochargers for passenger cars and commercial vehicles and braking products.

Company Financials Fiscal Year Ended Dec. 31

Per Share Data ($)	2009	2008	2007	2006	2005	2004	2003	2002	2001	2000
Tangible Book Value	NM	NM	NM	0.09	1.95	4.70	4.46	2.52	3.45	4.71
Cash Flow	4.12	4.97	4.24	3.59	2.74	2.24	2.25	0.53	1.02	3.28
Earnings	2.85	3.76	3.16	2.51	1.86	1.49	1.56	-0.27	-0.12	2.05
S&P Core Earnings	2.68	2.14	3.15	2.62	1.83	1.42	1.57	0.15	-0.26	NA
Dividends	1.21	1.10	1.00	0.91	1.03	0.75	0.75	0.75	0.75	0.75
Payout Ratio	42%	29%	32%	36%	55%	50%	48%	NM	NM	37%
Prices:High	41.55	62.99	62.29	45.77	39.50	38.46	33.50	40.95	53.90	60.50
Prices:Low	23.06	23.24	43.14	35.24	32.68	31.23	20.20	18.77	22.15	32.13
P/E Ratio:High	15	17	20	18	21	26	21	NM	NM	30
P/E Ratio:Low	8	6	14	14	18	21	13	NM	NM	16

Income Statement Analysis (Million $)	2009	2008	2007	2006	2005	2004	2003	2002	2001	2000
Revenue	30,908	36,556	34,589	31,367	27,653	25,601	23,103	22,274	23,652	25,023
Operating Income	4,339	5,444	4,561	3,855	3,178	2,350	2,513	2,573	1,085	3,794
Depreciation	957	903	837	794	697	650	595	671	926	995
Interest Expense	459	482	456	374	356	331	335	344	405	481
Pretax Income	2,978	3,801	3,321	2,798	2,323	1,680	1,647	-945	-422	2,398
Effective Tax Rate	26.5%	26.6%	26.4%	25.7%	31.9%	23.8%	18.0%	NM	NM	30.8%
Net Income	2,153	2,792	2,444	2,078	1,581	1,281	1,344	-220	NA	1,659
S&P Core Earnings	2,027	1,590	2,445	2,168	1,554	1,225	1,363	119	-207	NA

Balance Sheet & Other Financial Data (Million $)	2009	2008	2007	2006	2005	2004	2003	2002	2001	2000
Cash	2,801	2,065	1,829	1,224	1,234	3,586	2,950	2,021	1,393	1,196
Current Assets	13,936	13,263	13,685	12,304	11,962	12,820	11,523	10,195	9,894	10,661
Total Assets	36,004	35,490	33,805	30,941	32,294	31,062	29,344	27,559	24,226	25,175
Current Liabilities	11,147	12,289	11,941	10,135	10,430	8,739	6,783	6,574	6,220	7,214
Long Term Debt	6,246	5,865	5,419	3,909	3,082	4,069	4,961	4,719	4,731	3,941
Common Equity	8,954	7,187	9,222	9,720	11,254	11,252	7,243	8,925	9,170	9,707
Total Capital	16,218	13,750	15,375	13,981	14,839	15,718	12,520	14,063	14,776	14,821
Capital Expenditures	609	884	767	733	684	629	655	671	876	853
Cash Flow	3,110	3,695	3,281	2,872	2,278	1,931	1,939	451	827	2,654
Current Ratio	1.3	1.1	1.2	1.2	1.1	1.5	1.7	1.6	1.6	1.5
% Long Term Debt of Capitalization	38.5	42.7	35.2	28.0	20.8	25.9	39.6	33.6	32.0	26.6
% Net Income of Revenue	7.0	7.6	7.0	6.6	5.7	5.0	5.8	NM	NM	6.6
% Return on Assets	6.0	8.1	7.5	6.5	5.0	4.2	4.7	NM	NM	6.8
% Return on Equity	26.7	34.0	25.8	20.3	14.0	11.7	21.1	NM	NM	18.1

Data as orig reptd.; bef. results of disc opers/spec. items. Per share data adj. for stk. divs.; EPS diluted. E-Estimated. NA-Not Available. NM-Not Meaningful. NR-Not Ranked. UR-Under Review.

Office: 101 Columbia Rd, Morristown, NJ 07960-4640.
Telephone: 973-455-2000.
Website: http://www.honeywell.com
Chrmn & CEO: D.M. Cote

COO: K. Mikkilineni
SVP & CFO: D.J. Anderson
SVP & General Counsel: K. Adams
Chief Acctg Officer & Cntlr: K.A. Winters

Investor Contact: M. Grainger (973-455-2222)
Board Members: G. M. Bethune, K. Burke, J. Chico Pardo, D. M. Cote, D. S. Davis, L. F. Deily, C. R. Hollick, G. Paz, B. T. Sheares, M. W. Wright

Founded: 1920
Domicile: Delaware
Employees: 122,000

Hormel Foods Corp

STANDARD &POOR'S

S&P Recommendation HOLD ★★★☆☆

Price	**12-Mo. Target Price**	**Investment Style**
$45.05 (as of Oct 22, 2010)	$44.00	Large-Cap Blend

GICS Sector Consumer Staples
Sub-Industry Packaged Foods & Meats

Summary This company is a leading processor of branded, convenience meat products (primarily pork) for the consumer market.

Key Stock Statistics (Source S&P, Vickers, company reports)

52-Wk Range	$45.62–36.02	S&P Oper. EPS 2010**E**	2.88	Market Capitalization(B)	$6.000	Beta	0.40
Trailing 12-Month EPS	$2.79	S&P Oper. EPS 2011**E**	2.95	Yield (%)	1.86	S&P 3-Yr. Proj. EPS CAGR(%)	7
Trailing 12-Month P/E	16.2	P/E on S&P Oper. EPS 2010**E**	15.6	Dividend Rate/Share	$0.84	S&P Credit Rating	A
$10K Invested 5 Yrs Ago	$15,715	Common Shares Outstg. (M)	133.2	Institutional Ownership (%)	30		

Price Performance

30-Week Mov. Avg. · · · ·   10-Week Mov. Avg. – – ·   **GAAP Earnings vs. Previous Year**   Volume Above Avg. |||| STARS
12-Mo. Target Price —   Relative Strength —   ▲ Up   ▼ Down   ► No Change   Below Avg. |||| ★

Analysis prepared by **Tom Graves, CFA** on September 17, 2010, when the stock traded at **$ 44.27**.

Options: Ph

Highlights

► In FY 11 (Oct.), we look for revenues to rise about 2% from the $7.1 billion that we project for FY 10, which we expect will have an extra week in the fiscal year. We think that sales growth in FY 10 has been bolstered by the inclusion of the new MegaMex Foods joint venture.

► We estimate that FY 11 EPS will increase about 2%, to $2.95, from the $2.88 that we forecast for FY 10, which excludes a negative impact of $0.10 from special items in FY 10's second quarter. We think that near-term EPS comparisons may be limited by higher hog costs (above the average of FY 10's first half).

► In September 2010, the MegaMex joint venture entered into a definitive agreement to acquire Don Miguel Foods Corp., a provider of branded frozen and fresh flavored appetizers, snacks and handheld items. The transaction was expected to close in October 2010. In FY 10's third quarter, HRL repurchased 0.6 million shares of HRL common stock under a pair of buyback authorizations. At quarter's end, authorization remained to repurchase 4.8 million shares.

Investment Rationale/Risk

► As of July 25, 2010, HRL had cash and equivalents totaling $376.9 million. We think that the company will be looking for opportunities to make strategic acquisitions. Over time, we expect HRL to be able to increase the importance of non-U.S. sales, including a larger presence in some Asian markets. As a producer of protein products, including the Spam brand, HRL should have opportunities to benefit from rising incomes and changing lifestyles in some developing markets, in our view.

► Risks to our recommendation and target price include weaker-than-expected demand, market share losses to private label competition, and higher-than-expected turkey feed costs.

► We think the company is well positioned for long-term growth, with profitability expected to benefit as higher-margin, value-added products become a larger part of its business. Our 12-month target price of $44 is based on a P/E multiple about 7% below a historical median for HRL shares. An 11% increase in HRL's quarterly dividend became effective with the February 2010 payment. Based on the current quarterly rate, the indicated yield was recently 1.9%.

Qualitative Risk Assessment

LOW	MEDIUM	HIGH

Our risk assessment reflects our view of HRL's relatively strong balance sheet, offset by the company's sensitivity to changes in commodity costs.

Quantitative Evaluations

S&P Quality Ranking   A+

D	C	B-	B	B+	A-	A	A+

Relative Strength Rank   MODERATE

48

LOWEST = 1   HIGHEST = 99

Revenue/Earnings Data

Revenue (Million $)

	1Q	2Q	3Q	4Q	Year
2010	1,727	1,700	1,730	--	--
2009	1,689	1,595	1,574	1,675	6,534
2008	1,621	1,594	1,678	1,862	6,755
2007	1,504	1,505	1,520	1,664	6,193
2006	1,416	1,365	1,407	1,557	5,745
2005	1,271	1,310	1,355	1,478	5,414

Earnings Per Share ($)

2010	0.82	0.57	0.63	E0.76	E2.88
2009	0.60	0.59	0.57	0.77	2.53
2008	0.64	0.56	0.38	0.50	2.08
2007	0.54	0.49	0.38	0.73	2.17
2006	0.50	0.48	--	0.64	2.05
2005	0.46	0.40	0.37	0.59	1.82

Fiscal year ended Oct. 31. Next earnings report expected: Late November. EPS Estimates based on S&P Operating Earnings; historical GAAP earnings are as reported.

Dividend Data (Dates: mm/dd Payment Date: mm/dd/yy)

Amount ($)	Date Decl.	Ex-Div. Date	Stk. of Record	Payment Date
0.210	11/24	01/20	01/23	02/15/10
0.210	03/22	04/14	04/17	05/15/10
0.210	05/24	07/21	07/24	08/15/10
0.210	09/28	10/20	10/23	11/15/10

Dividends have been paid since 1928. Source: Company reports.

Please read the Required Disclosures and Analyst Certification on the last page of this report.

The McGraw-Hill Companies

Hormel Foods Corp

STANDARD &POOR'S

Business Summary September 17, 2010

CORPORATE OVERVIEW. Probably best known for its ubiquitous Spam, Hormel Foods is a diversified producer of consumer foods. Founded in 1891 as George A. Hormel & Company, the company got its start as a processor of meat products, principally pork. Over the years, it has expanded its business both internally and through acquisitions. In our view, although pork and turkey remain the major raw material for Hormel products, the company has emphasized for several years the manufacture and distribution of branded, consumer packaged items over the commodity fresh meat business closely associated with its business of the past.

The company operates under the grocery products, refrigerated foods, Jennie-O Turkey Store, specialty foods, and other business segments. The grocery product segment (14% of FY 09 (Oct.) revenues and 28% of operating income) primarily processes, markets and sells shelf-stable food products predominately in the retail market. The refrigerated foods segment (52%; 40%) primarily processes, markets and sells branded and unbranded pork and beef products for the retail, food service, and fresh product customer markets. Jennie-O Turkey Store (19%; 15%) primarily processes, markets and sells branded and unbranded turkey products for the retail, food service and fresh product customer markets. The specialty foods segment (11%; 12%) packages

and sells various sugar and sugar substitute products, salt and pepper products, liquid portion products, and other products. The "other" segment (4%; 5%) manufactures, markets and sells company products internationally.

CORPORATE STRATEGY. We expect the company to look to strategic acquisitions as a prospective use of cash. Effective February 1, 2010, HRL completed the acquisition of the Country Crock chilled side dish line. In June 2008, the company acquired Boca Grande Foods, Inc., a manufacturer and distributor of liquid portion products in Georgia. In December 2006, HRL acquired Pro vena Foods, a provider of pepperoni and pasta to pizza makers and packaged food manufacturers. In November 2006, the company acquired Sag's Products, a processor and marketer of branded, premium gourmet sausages and specialty cooked meats. In March 2006, HRL acquired Valley Fresh, a manufacturer of canned ready-to-eat chicken products and a distributor of pre-cooked chicken products. Also, in 2009, HRL formed a 50/50 joint venture. known as MegaMex Foods, LLC, to market Mexican foods in the U.S.

Company Financials Fiscal Year Ended Oct. 31

Per Share Data ($)	2009	2008	2007	2006	2005	2004	2003	2002	2001	2000
Tangible Book Value	10.20	9.20	8.31	8.04	6.77	6.43	5.36	5.41	4.45	5.64
Cash Flow	3.47	2.92	3.08	2.92	2.64	2.33	1.96	1.94	1.95	1.67
Earnings	2.53	2.08	2.17	2.05	1.82	1.65	1.33	1.35	1.30	1.20
S&P Core Earnings	2.26	1.88	2.15	2.10	1.88	1.61	1.22	1.10	1.23	NA
Dividends	0.76	0.74	0.60	0.56	0.52	0.45	0.42	0.39	0.37	0.35
Payout Ratio	30%	36%	28%	27%	29%	27%	32%	29%	28%	29%
Prices:High	40.46	42.77	41.82	39.09	35.44	32.11	27.49	28.20	27.35	20.97
Prices:Low	29.16	24.81	30.04	31.88	29.16	24.90	19.93	20.02	17.00	13.63
P/E Ratio:High	16	21	19	19	19	19	21	21	21	17
P/E Ratio:Low	12	12	14	16	16	15	15	15	13	11

Income Statement Analysis (Million $)										
Revenue	6,534	6,755	6,193	5,745	5,414	4,780	4,200	3,910	4,124	3,675
Operating Income	659	624	611	567	534	448	393	394	390	328
Depreciation	127	115	127	121	115	94.8	88.0	83.2	90.2	65.9
Interest Expense	28.0	28.0	27.7	25.6	27.7	27.1	31.9	31.4	28.0	14.9
Pretax Income	525	458	470	431	405	365	289	294	285	264
Effective Tax Rate	34.7%	37.6%	35.7%	33.5%	37.4%	36.5%	35.8%	35.6%	36.0%	35.6%
Net Income	343	286	302	286	253	232	186	189	182	170
S&P Core Earnings	307	258	300	294	263	225	171	155	173	NA

Balance Sheet & Other Financial Data (Million $)										
Cash	385	155	150	172	170	289	98.0	310	186	107
Current Assets	1,575	1,438	1,232	1,142	1,041	1,029	824	962	883	711
Total Assets	3,692	3,616	3,394	3,060	2,822	2,534	2,393	2,220	2,163	1,642
Current Liabilities	685	781	665	585	583	464	442	410	420	343
Long Term Debt	350	350	350	350	350	362	395	410	462	146
Common Equity	2,123	2,008	1,885	1,803	1,575	1,399	1,253	1,115	993	874
Total Capital	2,473	2,358	2,235	2,153	1,925	1,765	1,659	1,525	1,455	1,020
Capital Expenditures	92.0	126	126	142	107	80.4	67.1	64.5	77.1	100
Cash Flow	470	400	429	407	369	326	274	273	273	236
Current Ratio	2.3	1.8	1.9	2.0	1.8	2.2	1.9	2.3	2.1	2.1
% Long Term Debt of Capitalization	14.2	14.9	15.6	16.3	18.2	20.5	23.8	26.9	31.8	14.3
% Net Income of Revenue	5.3	4.2	4.8	5.0	4.7	4.8	4.4	4.8	4.4	4.6
% Return on Assets	9.4	8.2	9.3	9.7	9.5	9.4	8.1	8.6	9.6	10.2
% Return on Equity	16.6	14.7	16.3	16.8	17.0	17.5	15.7	18.0	19.5	19.9

Data as orig reptd.; bef. results of disc opers/spec. items. Per share data adj. for stk. divs.; EPS diluted. E-Estimated. NA-Not Available. NM-Not Meaningful. NR-Not Ranked. UR-Under Review.

Office: 1 Hormel Place, Austin, MN 55912-3680.
Telephone: 507-437-5611.
Website: http://www.hormel.com
Chrmn, Pres & CEO: J.M. Ettinger

SVP & CFO: J.H. Feragen
SVP & General Counsel: J.W. Cavanaugh
Chief Acctg Officer & Cntlr: J.N. Sheehan
Treas: R.G. Gentzler

Investor Contact: K.C. Jones (507-437-5248)
Board Members: T. K. Crews, J. M. Ettinger, J. H. Feragen, S. Marvin, J. L. Morrison, E. A. Murano, R. C. Nakasone, S. K. Nestegard, R. D. Pearson, D. A. Pippins, H. C. Smith, J. G. Turner

Founded: 1891
Domicile: Delaware
Employees: 18,600

The McGraw-Hill Companies

Hospira Inc

STANDARD & POOR'S

S&P Recommendation BUY ★★★★☆

Price	12-Mo. Target Price	Investment Style
$59.39 (as of Oct 22, 2010)	$63.00	Large-Cap Growth

GICS Sector Health Care
Sub-Industry Health Care Equipment

Summary Hospira was spun off from Abbott Laboratories in May 2004, and provides a variety of hospital products, including injectable generic drugs, pumps, and syringes.

Key Stock Statistics (Source S&P, Vickers, company reports)

52-Wk Range	$59.75–44.44	S&P Oper. EPS 2010E	3.42	Market Capitalization(B)	$9.937	Beta	0.71
Trailing 12-Month EPS	$2.63	S&P Oper. EPS 2011E	4.05	Yield (%)	Nil	S&P 3-Yr. Proj. EPS CAGR(%)	13
Trailing 12-Month P/E	22.6	P/E on S&P Oper. EPS 2010E	17.4	Dividend Rate/Share	Nil	S&P Credit Rating	BBB+
$10K Invested 5 Yrs Ago	$15,507	Common Shares Outstg. (M)	167.3	Institutional Ownership (%)	84		

Price Performance

30-Week Mov. Avg. ···· 10-Week Mov. Avg. - - GAAP Earnings vs. Previous Year — Volume Above Avg. STARS
12-Mo. Target Price — Relative Strength — ▲ Up ▼ Down ▶ No Change — Below Avg. ★

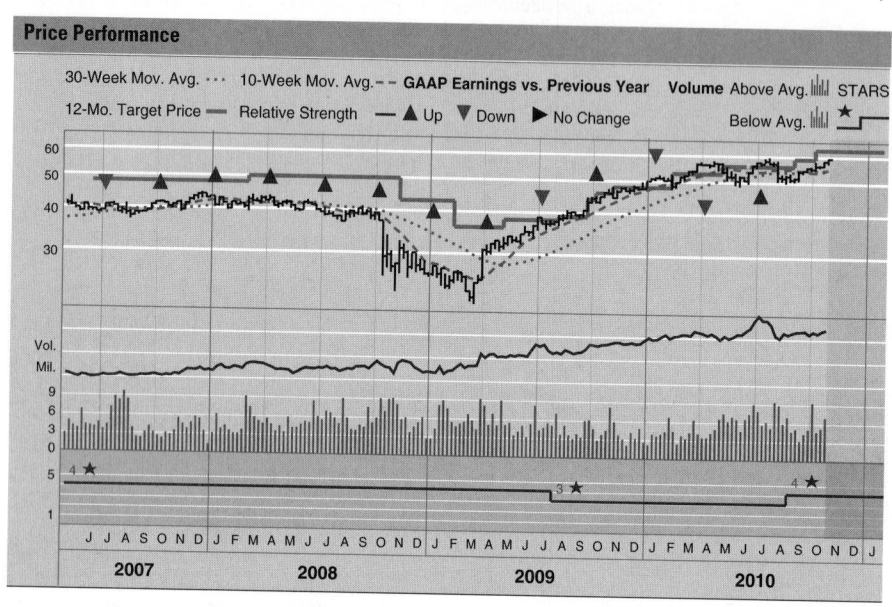

Options: ASE, CBOE, P, Ph

Analysis prepared by **Steven Silver** on September 29, 2010, when the stock traded at **$57.57**.

Highlights

➤ We expect revenues to increase about 5% in 2010 as increased Oxaliplatin revenues early in the year are mostly offset by soft results from the medical management business. We look for sales to increase about 10% in 2011 as new product growth accelerates, led by expected generics for cancer drugs Taxotere and Gemzar, and as the medical management business benefits from resumed shipments of the Symbiq pump, currently on hold, and expanded sales of Plum infusion pumps amid a recall of Baxter's Colleague pump.

➤ We project a modest increase in operating expenses as a percentage of sales in 2010, as savings from Project Fuel (HSP's new cost optimization program) only partly offset increases in R&D spending. We look for HSP to gradually transition to higher-margin products, particularly in its medication management systems business. We expect operating margins to widen to 21.5% in 2010, up more than 200 basis points over 2009, reflecting the impact of Project Fuel. We project such margins rising to 22% in 2011.

➤ We see operating EPS of $3.42 in 2010 and $4.05 in 2011, excluding restructuring charges.

Investment Rationale/Risk

➤ Our buy recommendation reflects a positive outlook for HSP to benefit from its emphasis on strategic assets and operational efficiency under Project Fuel. In addition, we expect steady, though gradually slower, growth in the medication management systems business, from a solid pipeline of new products that launched in 2009, as well as increased international sales. We see unappreciated potential in its biogeneric portfolio, where HSP, with its partner Stada, launched its first biogeneric (a generic EPO with trade name Retacrit) in Europe in the first quarter of 2008, and a second, Nivestim, for chemotherapy-induced neutropenia, in mid-2010.

➤ Risks to our recommendation and target price include failure to gain approval or slower-than-anticipated approval for injectable drugs and biogenerics, lower-than-anticipated drug pricing, and a decrease in demand for medication delivery products.

➤ Our 12-month target price of $63 applies a 15.5X multiple to our 2011 EPS estimate of $4.05, in line with HSP's historical average forward P/E multiple, reflecting our view of solid growth prospects.

Qualitative Risk Assessment

LOW	MEDIUM	HIGH

Our risk assessment reflects HSP's broad product portfolio, which reduces dependence on any one product category. We see stable demand for hospital products, given our belief that demand for hospital services will remain strong. However, we see minimal growth overall for this industry.

Quantitative Evaluations

S&P Quality Ranking NR

D	C	B-	B	B+	A-	A	A+

Relative Strength Rank MODERATE

70

LOWEST = 1 — HIGHEST = 99

Revenue/Earnings Data

Revenue (Million $)

	1Q	2Q	3Q	4Q	Year
2010	1,008	968.2	--	--	--
2009	859.7	956.9	1,008	1,055	3,879
2008	888.7	901.6	925.5	913.7	3,630
2007	782.8	869.4	838.0	946.1	3,436
2006	664.3	629.9	646.6	706.5	2,689
2005	662.1	618.5	656.6	646.2	2,627

Earnings Per Share ($)

2010	0.84	0.49	E0.70	E0.92	E3.42
2009	1.03	0.16	0.71	0.58	2.48
2008	0.41	0.43	0.51	0.65	1.99
2007	-0.19	0.20	0.37	0.47	0.85
2006	0.49	0.34	0.35	0.30	1.48
2005	0.49	0.44	0.37	0.16	1.46

Fiscal year ended Dec. 31. Next earnings report expected: Late October. EPS Estimates based on S&P Operating Earnings; historical GAAP earnings are as reported.

Dividend Data

No cash dividends have been paid.

Please read the Required Disclosures and Analyst Certification on the last page of this report.

The McGraw-Hill Companies

Hospira Inc

Business Summary September 29, 2010

CORPORATE OVERVIEW. Hospira (HSP) was created on May 3, 2004, as a spinoff from Abbott Laboratories. HSP provides medication delivery systems and specialty pharmaceuticals to hospitals, clinics, and physicians. The legal separation to become a standalone company was completed in the second quarter of 2006.

Hospira has operations in the Americas (79% of 2009 revenues); Europe, the Middle East, and Africa (14%); and Asia-Pacific (7%), and operates 13 manufacturing facilities domestically and internationally.

Operating segments include specialty injectable pharmaceuticals -- including specialty injectables and biogenerics (2009 sales of $2.07 billion, 53% of sales); medication management systems -- principally infusion pumps as well as related software and services ($658.7 million, 17%); and other pharmaceuticals -- encompassing large volume I.V. solutions, nutritionals and contract

manufacturing services ($701.2 million, 18%), with the balance of sales from other devices. Major competitors include Baxter International, Bedford Laboratories (a divisions of Boehringer Ingelheim), Fresenius Medical Care AG, Sandoz, Teva Pharmaceuticals, and CareFusion.

The specialty injectable pharmaceuticals division provides over 200 generic injectable drugs available in a wide array of dosages and formulations. Therapeutic areas of focus include cardiovascular, anesthesia, anti-infectives, analgesics, and other. We expect HSP to market a generic version of cancer drug Taxotere by 2011, following a favorable court ruling over the drug's patents in September 2010.

Company Financials Fiscal Year Ended Dec. 31

Per Share Data ($)	2009	2008	2007	2006	2005	2004	2003	2002	2001	2000
Tangible Book Value	5.96	1.28	NM	8.03	7.57	5.74	NM	NA	NA	NA
Cash Flow	3.77	3.55	2.32	2.45	2.42	2.84	NA	NA	NA	NA
Earnings	2.48	1.99	0.85	1.48	1.46	1.92	1.65	NA	NA	NA
S&P Core Earnings	2.58	1.89	0.79	1.45	1.35	1.31	1.46	NA	NA	NA
Dividends	Nil	Nil	Nil	Nil	Nil	Nil	NA	NA	NA	NA
Payout Ratio	Nil	Nil	Nil	Nil	Nil	Nil	NA	NA	NA	NA
Prices:High	51.40	44.00	44.64	47.99	45.10	34.86	NA	NA	NA	NA
Prices:Low	21.21	23.00	33.60	31.15	28.35	24.02	NA	NA	NA	NA
P/E Ratio:High	21	22	53	32	31	18	NA	NA	NA	NA
P/E Ratio:Low	9	12	40	21	19	13	NA	NA	NA	NA

Income Statement Analysis (Million $)										
Revenue	3,879	3,630	3,436	2,689	2,627	2,645	2,624	2,603	2,514	2,348
Operating Income	878	836	763	506	493	509	506	512	555	552
Depreciation	230	252	235	157	156	146	146	134	123	133
Interest Expense	106	124	145	31.0	28.3	18.8	Nil	NA	NA	NA
Pretax Income	385	408	188	324	322	412	359	352	390	421
Effective Tax Rate	NM	21.3%	27.2%	26.9%	26.8%	26.7%	27.5%	30.0%	30.0%	29.5%
Net Income	404	321	137	237	236	302	260	247	273	297
S&P Core Earnings	422	304	128	233	217	206	231	187	NA	NA

Balance Sheet & Other Financial Data (Million $)										
Cash	946	484	241	322	521	200	Nil	NA	NA	NA
Current Assets	2,526	2,149	1,841	1,523	1,561	1,198	1,075	982	1,029	NA
Total Assets	5,503	5,074	5,085	2,848	2,789	2,343	2,250	2,154	2,133	NA
Current Liabilities	882	1,048	794	606	596	536	360	411	373	NA
Long Term Debt	1,707	1,834	2,243	702	695	699	Nil	NA	NA	NA
Common Equity	2,624	1,776	1,745	1,361	1,328	984	1,453	1,334	1,461	NA
Total Capital	4,355	3,636	3,980	2,066	2,027	1,687	1,453	1,334	1,461	NA
Capital Expenditures	159	164	211	235	256	229	197	191	200	199
Cash Flow	615	573	372	393	392	447	406	380	396	430
Current Ratio	2.9	2.1	2.3	2.5	2.6	2.2	3.0	2.4	2.8	NA
% Long Term Debt of Capitalization	39.2	50.5	55.6	34.0	34.3	41.4	Nil	Nil	Nil	Nil
% Net Income of Revenue	10.4	8.8	4.0	8.8	9.0	11.4	9.9	9.5	10.9	12.7
% Return on Assets	7.6	6.3	3.5	8.4	9.2	13.1	11.8	11.5	NA	NA
% Return on Equity	18.4	18.2	8.8	17.6	20.4	24.7	18.7	17.7	NA	NA

Data as orig reptd.; bef. results of disc opers/spec. items. Per share data adj. for stk. divs.; EPS diluted. E-Estimated. NA-Not Available. NM-Not Meaningful. NR-Not Ranked. UR-Under Review.

Office: 275 North Field Drive, Lake Forest, IL 60045.
Telephone: 224-212-2000.
Website: http://www.hospira.com
Chrmn & CEO: C.B. Begley

COO: T.C. Kearney
SVP & CFO: T.E. Werner
SVP & CSO: S. Ramachandra
SVP, Secy & General Counsel: B.J. Smith

Investor Contact: K. King (224-212-2711)
Board Members: I. W. Bailey, II, C. B. Begley, B. L. Bowles, C. Curran, R. W. Hale, J. J. Sokolov, J. C. Staley, M. F. Wheeler, H. von Prondzynski

Founded: 2003
Domicile: Delaware
Employees: 13,500

Host Hotels & Resorts Inc

STANDARD &POOR'S

S&P Recommendation	HOLD ★★★★★	Price $16.21 (as of Oct 22, 2010)	12-Mo. Target Price $17.00	Investment Style Large-Cap Value

GICS Sector Financials
Sub-Industry Specialized REITS

Summary This real estate investment trust owns a portfolio of luxury and upper-upscale full-service hotels.

Key Stock Statistics (Source S&P, Vickers, company reports)

52-Wk Range	$17.09–9.64	S&P FFO/Sh. 2010E	0.68	Market Capitalization(B)	$10.795	Beta	2.31
Trailing 12-Month FFO/Share	NA	S&P FFO/Sh. 2011E	0.85	Yield (%)	0.25	S&P 3-Yr. FFO/Sh. Proj. CAGR(%)	3
Trailing 12-Month P/FFO	NA	P/FFO on S&P FFO/Sh. 2010E	23.8	Dividend Rate/Share	$0.04	S&P Credit Rating	BB-
$10K Invested 5 Yrs Ago	$11,392	Common Shares Outstg. (M)	665.9	Institutional Ownership (%)	96		

Price Performance

30-Week Mov. Avg. ···   10-Week Mov. Avg. -- ▪ GAAP Earnings vs. Previous Year   Volume Above Avg. ▮▮▮ STARS
12-Mo. Target Price —   Relative Strength —   ▲ Up ▼ Down ► No Change   Below Avg. ▮▮▮ ★

Options: ASE, CBOE, P, Ph

Analysis prepared by **Royal F. Shepard, CFA** on October 13, 2010, when the stock traded at **$15.95**.

Highlights

➤ We think occupancy levels could rise about 450 basis points at HST's hotels in 2010, to about 70.5%, boosted by a recent uptick in transient as well as group bookings. In our view, pricing is beginning to recover, and we expect it to gain more traction in 2011. HST's ancillary revenues, including food and beverage service, could take longer to rebound due to tight corporate spending. All told, we forecast a 6% increase in 2010 revenue per available room (RevPAR), followed by a 5% gain in 2011.

➤ In our estimation, acquisition activity could move to the forefront in 2011. During the third quarter, HST completed three transactions for $430 million. As distressed owners look to capitalize on improving industry conditions, we expect HST to remain aggressive in looking for new investment opportunities. We expect new investments to be funded partly through a continuous equity offering program.

➤ We expect improved room pricing to widen profit margins in 2011 and forecast an operating margin of 8.9%, up from 6.2% estimate for 2010. Our 2011 FFO estimate is $0.85, up from $0.68 in 2010, and does not include any impact from expected acquisition activity.

Investment Rationale/Risk

➤ For the industry, we think overall revenue growth began to expand in the third quarter of 2010, a trend we expect to continue in 2011. In our view, HST is well positioned to eventually increase profits, given its high-quality portfolio and strong capital-raising efforts. As a result of recent debt refinancings, we believe HST has the liquidity to consider new investments, including acquisitions. We also expect a gradual upturn in operating margins, as room rates rebound toward more historical levels. Over the next twelve months, we expect HST's performance to mirror industry trends and hotel REIT peers.

➤ Risks to our recommendation and target price include a slower than expected recovery in demand for business and leisure travel, in conjunction with any slowing momentum in the economic recovery.

➤ Our 12-month target price of $17 is based on a multiple of 20.0X our 2010 FFO estimate of $0.85 a share, a moderate premium to hotel REIT peers, based on our view of HST's strong financial position.

Qualitative Risk Assessment

LOW	MEDIUM	HIGH

Our risk assessment reflects the highly cyclical nature of the lodging industry, offset by what we view as the advantages of HST's large and well diversified portfolio.

Quantitative Evaluations

S&P Quality Ranking B-

D	C	B-	B	B+	A-	A	A+

Relative Strength Rank STRONG

80

LOWEST = 1   HIGHEST = 99

Revenue/FFO Data

Revenue (Million $)

	1Q	2Q	3Q	4Q	Year
2010	823.0	1,114	1,006	--	--
2009	882.0	1,064	912.0	1,336	4,126
2008	1,058	1,417	1,168	1,634	5,278
2007	1,031	1,385	1,201	1,809	5,437
2006	840.0	1,195	1,119	1,734	4,888
2005	802.0	976.0	831.0	1,272	3,881

FFO Per Share ($)

2010	0.08	0.23	0.11	E0.25	E0.68
2009	0.10	0.12	0.11	0.18	0.52
2008	0.33	0.56	0.31	0.53	1.74
2007	0.30	0.48	0.38	0.75	1.91
2006	0.27	0.39	0.28	0.44	1.53
2005	0.19	0.22	0.19	0.35	1.15

Fiscal year ended Dec. 31. Next earnings report expected: Mid February. FFO Estimates based on S&P Funds From Operations Est..

Dividend Data (Dates: mm/dd Payment Date: mm/dd/yy)

Amount ($)	Date Decl.	Ex-Div. Date	Stk. of Record	Payment Date
0.250	09/14	11/04	11/06	12/18/09
0.010	03/16	03/29	03/31	04/15/10
0.010	06/18	06/28	06/30	07/15/10
0.010	09/16	09/28	09/30	10/15/10

Dividends have been paid since 2005. Source: Company reports.

Please read the Required Disclosures and Analyst Certification on the last page of this report.

Host Hotels & Resorts Inc

Business Summary October 13, 2010

CORPORATE OVERVIEW. Host Hotels & Resorts operates as a self-managed and self-administered real estate investment trust (REIT). At December 31, 2009, HST owned a portfolio consisting of 110 luxury and upper-upscale hotels containing approximately 61,000 rooms. HST's hotels operate under a number of well known brands, including Marriott, Ritz-Carlton, Hyatt, Sheraton, Swissotel, Four Seasons, Hilton, Fairmont and Westin. Seventy-five of the company's properties were operated under the Marriott brand name. HST also holds a minority interest in a joint venture that owns 11 hotels in Europe with approximately 3,500 rooms. HST is geographically diversified, with hotels in most of the major metropolitan areas. The company's locations primarily include central business districts of major cities, airport areas, and resort/conference destinations.

HST's hotel revenue has traditionally experienced moderate seasonality, with a greater percentage of revenue falling in the second and fourth quarters. In addition, the fourth quarter reflects 16 or 17 weeks of results, versus 12 weeks in each of the first three fiscal quarters.

MARKET PROFILE. Our U.S. outlook for 2010 is for hotel room demand to rebound about 5% after declining 5.8% in 2009, based on statistics from Smith Travel Research. We see business demand, including both transient and group travel, picking up 7% to 9% after falling about 12% in 2009. Domestic leisure travel did not decline nearly as much in 2009, but we expect high unemployment to continue to crimp demand in 2010. Overseas tourist arrivals in the U.S. in 2009 were down about 9%, and in 2010, we see a pickup in demand only in the low to mid single-digits.

The number of available room nights in 2009 increased 3.2%, reflecting construction and redevelopment projects already financed before the financial crisis. For 2010, we see room night supply increasing a smaller 2.3%. The room occupancy rate fell 8.6% in 2009, to a rate of 55.1%, indicative of severe, near depressionary levels, by our analysis. For 2010, the smaller increase in supply and higher demand that we expect should lead to a rise in occupancy to approximately 55.5% to 56.0%.

Room rates, which tend to lag movement in occupancy, declined 8.8% in 2009 and are likely to dip slightly in 2010, in our estimation. RevPAR, which fell 16.7% in 2009, should drop a further 3.0% in 2010, based on our occupancy and room rate forecasts.

Company Financials Fiscal Year Ended Dec. 31

Per Share Data ($)	2009	2008	2007	2006	2005	2004	2003	2002	2001	2000
Tangible Book Value	9.43	10.32	10.22	9.83	NM	5.64	5.57	4.87	4.77	5.50
Earnings	-0.43	0.71	1.01	0.60	0.30	-0.31	-0.92	-0.24	0.09	0.64
S&P Core Earnings	-0.38	0.70	0.92	0.57	0.27	-0.31	-0.95	-0.25	0.09	NA
Dividends	0.25	0.65	0.80	0.71	0.41	0.10	Nil	Nil	0.78	0.86
Payout Ratio	NM	92%	79%	118%	137%	NM	Nil	Nil	NM	106%
Prices:High	12.20	18.81	28.98	25.79	19.24	17.40	12.33	12.25	13.95	12.93
Prices:Low	3.08	4.77	16.55	18.77	15.46	11.16	6.07	7.50	6.22	8.00
P/E Ratio:High	NM	26	29	43	64	NM	NM	NM	NM	20
P/E Ratio:Low	NM	7	16	31	52	NM	NM	NM	NM	13

Income Statement Analysis (Million $)										
Rental Income	107	120	120	119	111	106	100	101	126	1,390
Mortgage Income	Nil	Nil	Nil	Nil	Nil	Nil	Nil	Nil	Nil	Nil
Total Income	4,158	5,278	5,426	4,888	3,881	3,640	3,448	3,680	3,754	1,473
General Expenses	3,398	3,955	4,007	3,665	2,936	2,812	2,765	2,823	2,821	337
Interest Expense	379	341	422	450	443	483	523	498	492	465
Provision for Losses	Nil	Nil	Nil	Nil	Nil	Nil	Nil	Nil	Nil	Nil
Depreciation	662	582	517	459	368	354	367	372	378	331
Net Income	-242	402	550	309	138	-64.0	-225	-29.0	53.0	159
S&P Core Earnings	-224	386	490	276	98.0	-106	-267	-65.0	20.0	NA

Balance Sheet & Other Financial Data (Million $)										
Cash	1,642	508	553	524	225	416	838	627	608	566
Total Assets	12,555	11,951	11,812	11,808	8,245	8,421	8,592	8,316	8,338	8,396
Real Estate Investment	14,974	15,038	14,288	13,897	10,382	9,924	9,511	9,193	8,828	8,599
Loss Reserve	Nil	Nil	Nil	Nil	Nil	Nil	Nil	Nil	Nil	Nil
Net Investment	10,231	10,739	10,588	10,584	7,434	7,274	7,085	7,031	6,999	7,110
Short Term Debt	Nil	410	261	268	NA	NA	NA	NA	148	54.0
Capitalization:Debt	5,837	5,542	5,364	5,610	5,370	5,523	3,976	5,638	5,929	5,743
Capitalization:Equity	6,092	5,420	5,344	5,125	2,176	2,058	1,797	1,271	1,270	1,225
Capitalization:Total	12,187	11,239	11,021	11,045	7,932	8,126	6,112	7,471	7,748	7,649
% Earnings & Depreciation/Assets	3.4	8.3	9.0	7.6	6.0	3.4	1.7	4.1	5.2	5.9
Price Times Book Value:High	1.3	1.8	2.8	2.6	NM	3.1	2.2	2.5	2.9	2.4
Price Times Book Value:Low	0.3	0.5	1.6	1.9	NM	2.0	1.1	1.5	1.3	1.5

Data as orig reptd.; bef. results of disc opers/spec. items. Per share data adj. for stk. divs.; EPS diluted. E-Estimated. NA-Not Available. NM-Not Meaningful. NR-Not Ranked. UR-Under Review.

Office: 6903 Rockledge Drive, Bethesda, MD 20817.
Telephone: 240-744-5121.
Website: http://www.hosthotels.com
Chrmn: R.E. Marriott

Pres & CEO: W.E. Walter
EVP & CFO: L.K. Harvey
EVP, Secy & General Counsel: E.A. Abdoo
Investor Contact: G.J. Larson (240-744-5120)

Board Members: R. M. Baylis, W. W. Brittain, Jr., T. C. Golden, A. M. Korologos, R. E. Marriott, J. B. Morse, Jr., G. Smith, W. E. Walter

Founded: 1927
Domicile: Maryland
Employees: 186

Block (H&R) Inc.

STANDARD &POOR'S

S&P Recommendation HOLD ★★★☆☆

Price $10.78 (as of Oct 22, 2010)	**12-Mo. Target Price** $15.00	**Investment Style** Large-Cap Blend

GICS Sector Consumer Discretionary
Sub-Industry Specialized Consumer Services

Summary This diversified company provides a wide range of financial products and services, including income tax preparation, business, consulting, and retail banking services.

Key Stock Statistics (Source S&P, Vickers, company reports)

52-Wk Range	$23.23– 10.13	S&P Oper. EPS 2011**E**	1.49	Market Capitalization(B)	$3.326	Beta	0.57
Trailing 12-Month EPS	$1.42	S&P Oper. EPS 2012**E**	1.59	Yield (%)	5.57	S&P 3-Yr. Proj. EPS CAGR(%)	4
Trailing 12-Month P/E	7.6	P/E on S&P Oper. EPS 2011**E**	7.2	Dividend Rate/Share	$0.60	S&P Credit Rating	BBB
$10K Invested 5 Yrs Ago	$5,184	Common Shares Outstg. (M)	308.5	Institutional Ownership (%)	93		

Price Performance

30-Week Mov. Avg. · · · · 10-Week Mov. Avg. – – **GAAP Earnings vs. Previous Year** **Volume** Above Avg. ▉▉ STARS
12-Mo. Target Price — Relative Strength — ▲ Up ▼ Down ▶ No Change Below Avg. ▉▉ ★

Options: ASE, CBOE, P, Ph

Analysis prepared by **Erik Kolb** on October 11, 2010, when the stock traded at **$ 13.82.**

Highlights

▶ After a 5.1% total revenue decline in FY 10 (Apr.), we see roughly flat revenues in FY 11. HRB has been under pressure of late as potential filers, feeling pressured by job and economic uncertainty, have increasingly opted for DIY and e-filing options. Specifically, we see 1.1% growth in the tax service business offset by a 1.5% decline in business services. We are encouraged to hear HRB's goals of reducing early season customer losses and increasing digital competitiveness. However, at this point, we are awaiting signs of improvement. In FY 12, we see trends remaining relatively stable, and expect revenues to increase fractionally.

▶ We think the operating margin will remain flat at 20.2% in FY 11, reflecting our projection for a slightly lower cost of sales margin, but for other expenses to largely offset this. In FY 12, we see positive cost trends, and forecast the operating margin will reach 21.0%.

▶ We project EPS from continuing operations of $1.49 in FY 11, following FY 10's $1.43. In 2009, HRB authorized $2 billion of share repurchases through FY 12. Our FY 12 EPS estimate is $1.59.

Investment Rationale/Risk

▶ We think HRB is increasing its focus on its core tax preparer business, which we view positively given its strong market share position in that business. We also view favorably HRB's efforts to drive growth in the expert-filer demographic. However, in a difficult macroeconomic environment, we see increased risk from e-filing trends and competition from independents offering lower-priced services. We believe management made progress toward narrowing its organizational focus through the May 2008 sale of Option One and the November 2008 sale of its H&R Block Financial Advisors business, but think further work may be required. HRB's last CEO and other high-level executives departed in 2010, raising some concerns regarding the company's near-term direction.

▶ Risks to our recommendation and target price include increased competition and ongoing litigation.

▶ We derive our 12-month target price of $15 by applying a 10.0X multiple, slightly below peers and HRB's historical five-year range given the near-term risks we see, to our FY 11 estimate.

Qualitative Risk Assessment

LOW	MEDIUM	**HIGH**

Despite HRB's leading tax preparer position in its market, our risk assessment reflects uncertainty surrounding a pending IRS ruling regarding a case on refund anticipation loan products. We are also concerned about internal accounting control issues, which, in 2006, caused HRB to restate almost three years of results.

Quantitative Evaluations

S&P Quality Ranking B

D	C	B-	**B**	B+	A-	A	A+

Relative Strength Rank WEAK

6

LOWEST = 1   HIGHEST = 99

Revenue/Earnings Data

Revenue (Million $)

	1Q	2Q	3Q	4Q	Year
2011	274.5	--	--	--	--
2010	275.5	326.1	934.9	2,338	3,874
2009	271.9	351.5	993.5	2,467	4,084
2008	381.2	434.8	972.6	2,615	4,404
2007	342.8	396.1	931.2	2,351	4,021
2006	615.0	605.0	1,157	2,496	4,873

Earnings Per Share ($)

	1Q	2Q	3Q	4Q	Year
2011	-0.40	E-0.41	E0.16	E2.14	E1.49
2010	-0.39	-0.38	0.16	2.10	1.46
2009	-0.39	-0.40	0.20	2.09	1.53
2008	-0.39	-0.42	0.03	2.11	1.39
2007	-0.36	-0.38	0.07	1.81	1.15
2006	-0.08	-0.25	0.04	1.77	1.47

Fiscal year ended Apr. 30. Next earnings report expected: Early December. EPS Estimates based on S&P Operating Earnings; historical GAAP earnings are as reported.

Dividend Data (Dates: mm/dd Payment Date: mm/dd/yy)

Amount ($)	Date Decl.	Ex-Div. Date	Stk. of Record	Payment Date
0.150	11/30	12/09	12/12	01/04/10
0.150	02/22	03/09	03/11	04/01/10
0.150	05/05	06/08	06/10	07/01/10
0.150	07/29	09/08	09/10	10/01/10

Dividends have been paid since 1962. Source: Company reports.

Please read the Required Disclosures and Analyst Certification on the last page of this report.

The McGraw·Hill Companies

Block (H&R) Inc.

Business Summary October 11, 2010

CORPORATE OVERVIEW. H&R Block (HRB) provides various financial products and services, which the company believes are complementary. In FY 10 (Apr.), Tax Services accounted for 76.8% of revenues and 110.6% of profits, Business Services 22.2% and 7.5%, and the corporate division accounted for 1.0% and -18.0%.

The Tax Services division served about 23.2 million clients in FY 10 vs. 24.0 million in FY 09 and 24.6 million in FY 08. HRB's revenues related directly to the RAL program totaled $146.2 million in FY 10 or 3.8% of consolidated revenues. There were 11,506 company-owned and franchised U.S. H&R Block offices at April 30, 2010. In addition, HRB offers tax preparation services at hundreds of H&R Block Premium offices for more complex returns. International operations are located primarily in Australia, and Canada, with combined company owned and franchise offices numbering 1,643 at April 30, 2010. Tax Services also offers online tax preparation, tax preparation software, and guarantee programs.

HRB also provides wealth management, accounting, tax and consulting services, and tax, and capital market services.

MARKET PROFILE. HRB's largest segment, Tax Services, competes with other tax service chains, professional CPA/accounting firms, "mom and pop" local tax service providers and do-it-yourselfers DIYers). In addition, HRB and some other online tax service product providers participate in the Free Filing Alliance, which offers free online federal return preparation with no income limitations. We believe HRB competes successfully by offering many services at what customers believe is an acceptable price-to-value relationship. These services include: the convenience of the largest retail tax office network in the U.S.; a "Peace of Mind" Guarantee" (POM) whereby HRB commits to representing its clients if they are audited by the IRS, and assuming the cost of additional taxes resulting from errors attributable to an HRB tax professional; "Refund Anticipation Loans" and "Refund Anticipation Checks" and a service whereby DIYers using HRB's online service can have an HRB tax professional check their returns and receive the POM guarantee. By offering increased value, HRB has been able to raise its rates 5%-7% annually since 2002.

Company Financials Fiscal Year Ended Apr. 30

Per Share Data ($)	2010	2009	2008	2007	2006	2005	2004	2003	2002	2001
Tangible Book Value	0.72	0.51	NM	0.74	1.90	1.64	1.41	1.69	0.73	0.67
Cash Flow	1.78	1.90	1.83	1.62	2.05	2.43	2.42	2.02	1.57	2.61
Earnings	1.47	1.53	1.39	1.15	1.47	1.88	1.95	1.58	1.16	0.76
S&P Core Earnings	1.52	1.53	1.40	1.15	1.53	1.76	1.85	1.44	1.07	0.73
Dividends	NA	0.56	0.53	0.49	0.54	0.39	0.39	0.35	0.29	0.27
Payout Ratio	NA	37%	38%	42%	37%	21%	20%	22%	25%	35%
Calendar Year	2009	2008	2007	2006	2005	2004	2003	2002	2001	2000
Prices:High	23.27	27.97	24.95	25.75	30.00	30.50	27.89	26.75	23.19	12.38
Prices:Low	13.73	15.00	17.57	19.80	22.99	22.08	17.64	14.50	9.16	6.73
P/E Ratio:High	16	18	18	22	20	16	14	17	20	16
P/E Ratio:Low	9	10	13	17	16	12	9	9	8	9

Income Statement Analysis (Million $)

	2010	2009	2008	2007	2006	2005	2004	2003	2002	2001
Revenue	3,874	4,084	4,404	4,021	4,873	4,420	4,206	3,780	3,318	3,002
Operating Income	865	963	871	810	128	215	1,411	240	987	913
Depreciation	105	122	146	150	192	184	172	162	155	206
Interest Expense	90.6	1.65	243	46.9	49.1	62.4	84.6	92.6	116	243
Pretax Income	784	839	745	636	827	1,018	1,164	987	717	473
Effective Tax Rate	NA	38.9%	39.0%	41.1%	40.7%	37.5%	39.5%	41.2%	39.4%	41.5%
Net Income	489	513	454	374	490	636	704	580	434	277
S&P Core Earnings	506	514	458	374	509	593	665	527	400	268

Balance Sheet & Other Financial Data (Million $)

	2010	2009	2008	2007	2006	2005	2004	2003	2002	2001
Cash	1,804	1,655	729	1,254	1,088	1,617	1,617	1,337	617	326
Current Assets	2,649	2,571	2,382	3,454	2,824	3,071	2,961	2,747	2,245	2,271
Total Assets	5,234	5,360	5,623	7,499	5,989	5,539	5,380	4,604	4,231	4,122
Current Liabilities	2,321	2,398	3,096	5,176	2,893	2,209	2,472	1,897	1,880	1,988
Long Term Debt	1,060	1,107	1,032	520	418	923	546	822	868	871
Common Equity	1,441	1,406	988	1,414	2,148	1,976	1,897	1,664	1,369	1,174
Total Capital	2,554	2,546	2,131	1,934	2,565	2,899	2,443	2,486	2,238	2,045
Capital Expenditures	90.5	97.9	106	161	251	209	128	151	112	90.0
Cash Flow	594	635	600	525	682	820	876	742	590	482
Current Ratio	1.1	1.1	0.8	0.7	1.0	1.4	1.2	1.4	1.2	1.1
% Long Term Debt of Capitalization	41.5	43.5	48.4	26.9	16.3	31.8	22.3	33.1	38.8	42.6
% Net Income of Revenue	12.6	12.6	10.3	9.3	12.4	14.3	16.7	21.4	13.1	9.2
% Return on Assets	9.2	9.3	6.9	5.6	8.5	11.8	13.9	13.1	10.4	5.6
% Return on Equity	34.4	42.9	37.8	21.0	23.9	33.5	39.6	38.2	34.2	23.1

Data as orig reptd.; bef. results of disc opers/spec. items. Per share data adj. for stk. divs.; EPS diluted. E-Estimated. NA-Not Available. NM-Not Meaningful. NR-Not Ranked. UR-Under Review.

Office: 1 H&R Block Way, Kansas City, MO 64105.
Telephone: 816-854-3000.
Email: investorrelations@hrblock.com
Website: http://www.hrblock.com

Chrmn: R.C. Breeden
Pres & CEO: A. Bennett
SVP & CIO: R. Agar
CFO & Chief Acctg Officer: J. Brown

Secy: A.J. Somora
Investor Contact: S. Dudley (816-854-4505)
Board Members: A. Bennett, R. C. Breeden, W. C. Cobb, R. A. Gerard, L. J. Lauer, D. B. Lewis, B. C. Rohde, T. D. Seip, L. E. Shaw, Jr., C. Wood

Founded: 1946
Domicile: Missouri
Employees: 110,400

Hudson City Bancorp Inc

STANDARD &POOR'S

S&P Recommendation	BUY ★★★★☆	Price $11.53 (as of Oct 22, 2010)	12-Mo. Target Price $15.00	Investment Style Large-Cap Blend

GICS Sector Financials
Sub-Industry Thrifts & Mortgage Finance

Summary Hudson City Bancorp, through Hudson City Savings Bank, operates over 100 branches in the New York metropolitan area. It caters to high median household income counties and focuses on jumbo mortgage loan funding, largely through time deposits.

Key Stock Statistics (Source S&P, Vickers, company reports)

52-Wk Range	$14.75– 11.35	S&P Oper. EPS 2010**E**	1.11	Market Capitalization(B)	$6.072	Beta	0.61
Trailing 12-Month EPS	$1.14	S&P Oper. EPS 2011**E**	1.14	Yield (%)	5.20	S&P 3-Yr. Proj. EPS CAGR(%)	5
Trailing 12-Month P/E	10.1	P/E on S&P Oper. EPS 2010**E**	10.4	Dividend Rate/Share	$0.60	S&P Credit Rating	NA
$10K Invested 5 Yrs Ago	$11,584	Common Shares Outstg. (M)	526.6	Institutional Ownership (%)	59		

Price Performance

30-Week Mov. Avg. ··· 10-Week Mov. Avg. – – GAAP Earnings vs. Previous Year Volume Above Avg. STARS
12-Mo. Target Price — Relative Strength ▲ Up ▼ Down ▶ No Change Below Avg.

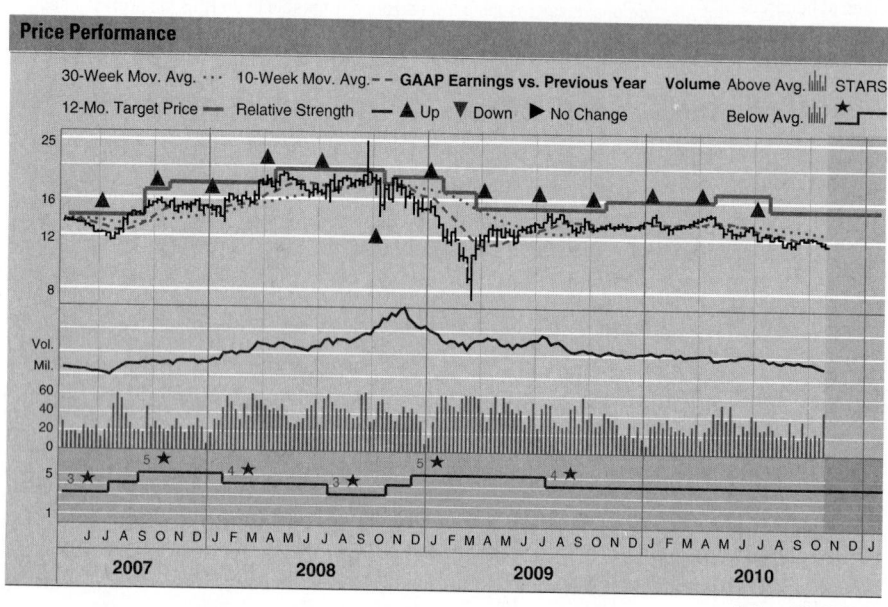

Options: ASE, CBOE, Ph

Analysis prepared by **Rafay Khalid, CFA** on October 20, 2010, when the stock traded at **$ 11.67**.

Highlights

▸ We forecast revenues will increase 7% in 2010, versus 34% in 2009, on our view of 6% loan growth. But we see flat loan growth in 2011 due to a lack of qualified borrowers and increasing competition in the jumbo loan market. As a result, we see revenues decreasing 2% in 2011. We expect the net interest margin to decline to 2.07% and 2.02% in 2010 and 2011, respectively, from 2.21% in 2009. Our forecast assumes that the low mortgage interest rate environment will continue for the rest of 2010 and in 2011.

▸ We look for HCBK's efficiency ratio to remain among the best in the industry, at 19.6% in 2010 and 18.2% in 2011. While we see full-year 2010 loss provisions increasing to $190 million, we expect quarterly provisions will gradually decline during 2010. We note that loss provisions increased to 0.68% of total loans as of September 2010, up from 0.44% as of December 2009. We see charge-offs rising through 2010, largely due to the more lengthy default and foreclosure process associated with lower loan-to-value mortgages.

▸ We forecast EPS of $1.11 in 2010 and $1.14 in 2011, compared to $1.07 in 2009.

Investment Rationale/Risk

▸ We think HCBK's avoidance of subprime, option adjustable rate mortgages and high loan-to-value products will enable the company to weather the difficult housing market better than competitors. In our opinion, HCBK has adequate capital to continue pursuing its risk-averse growth strategy, based on its tangible equity to assets ratio of 9.28% as of September 2010. We believe the new financial legislation will have little or no financial impact on the company, reflecting what we view as HCBK's conservative business operations.

▸ Risks to our opinion and target price include greater-than-expected job losses in the New York City metropolitan area, competition significantly increasing in the jumbo loan market, and severe deterioration in prime loans.

▸ Our 12-month target price of $15 is based on a on a historical average tangible book value ratio of 1.2X our 2011 tangible book value per share forecast of $12.52. We believe this historical average is warranted, reflecting what we see as an improving economic recovery environment.

Qualitative Risk Assessment

LOW	MEDIUM	HIGH

Our risk assessment reflects our view of the solid credit quality of HCBK's loan portfolio and its history of profitability. While the company operates in a highly competitive and fragmented industry, companies in the industry tend to produce relatively stable financial results.

Quantitative Evaluations

S&P Quality Ranking A

D	C	B-	B	B+	A-	A	A+

Relative Strength Rank WEAK

18

LOWEST = 1 HIGHEST = 99

Revenue/Earnings Data

Revenue (Million $)

	1Q	2Q	3Q	4Q	Year
2010	767.9	750.8	--	--	--
2009	725.6	754.4	746.7	748.7	2,975
2008	615.5	648.8	683.5	714.0	2,662
2007	481.2	513.3	550.3	590.0	2,135
2006	361.0	385.6	423.7	449.0	1,621
2005	257.5	280.5	315.2	333.8	1,187

Earnings Per Share ($)

2010	0.30	0.29	E0.25	E0.26	E1.11
2009	0.26	0.26	0.27	0.28	1.07
2008	0.18	0.22	0.25	0.25	0.90
2007	0.13	0.14	0.15	0.16	0.58
2006	0.13	0.13	0.13	0.13	0.53
2005	0.11	0.11	0.13	0.13	0.48

Fiscal year ended Dec. 31. Next earnings report expected: NA. EPS Estimates based on S&P Operating Earnings; historical GAAP earnings are as reported.

Dividend Data (Dates: mm/dd Payment Date: mm/dd/yy)

Amount ($)	Date Decl.	Ex-Div. Date	Stk. of Record	Payment Date
0.150	01/20	02/03	02/05	03/02/10
0.150	04/21	05/03	05/05	05/28/10
0.150	07/21	08/03	08/05	08/27/10
0.150	10/20	11/03	11/05	11/30/10

Dividends have been paid since 1999. Source: Company reports.

Please read the Required Disclosures and Analyst Certification on the last page of this report.

The **McGraw·Hill** Companies

Hudson City Bancorp Inc

**STANDARD
&POOR'S**

Business Summary October 20, 2010

CORPORATE OVERVIEW. New Jersey-based Hudson City Bancorp, Inc. (HCBK), a community- and consumer-oriented retail savings bank holding company, offers traditional deposit products, residential real estate mortgage loans and consumer loans. In addition, HCBK purchases mortgages, mortgage-backed securities, securities issued by the U.S. government and government-sponsored agencies and other investments permitted by applicable laws and regulations. HCBK is the holding company of its only subsidiary, Hudson City Savings Bank. The company's revenues are derived principally from interest on mortgage loans & mortgage-backed securities and interest & dividends on investment securities. The bank's primary sources of funds are customer deposits, borrowings, scheduled amortization and prepayments of mortgage loans and mortgage-backed securities, maturities and calls of investment securities and funds provided by operations.

PRIMARY BUSINESS DYNAMICS. As of December 31, 2009, HCBK had total loans of $31.8 billion. Hudson's loan portfolio primarily consists of one-to-four family residential first mortgage loans. HCBK's first mortgage loans totaled $30.8 billion as of December 31, 2009, representing 97% of the total loan port-

folio. HCBK's loan portfolio also includes multi-family and commercial mortgage loans, construction loans and consumer and other loans, which primarily consist of fixed-rate second mortgage loans and home equity credit lines. The company does not originate or purchase subprime loans, negative amortization loans or option adjustable rate mortgage loans.

CORPORATE STRATEGY. HCBK seeks to continue its growth by focusing on the origination and purchase of mortgage loans, while purchasing mortgage-backed securities and investment securities as a supplement. It intends to fund its growth with customer deposits and borrowed funds. The company aims to increase customer deposits by continuing to offer desirable products at competitive rates and by opening new branch offices. HCBK continues to focus on high median household income counties, in line with its jumbo mortgage loan and consumer deposit business model.

Company Financials Fiscal Year Ended Dec. 31

Per Share Data ($)	2009	2008	2007	2006	2005	2004	2003	2002	2001	2000
Tangible Book Value	10.55	9.77	9.22	8.54	8.83	2.35	2.18	2.14	2.03	2.04
Earnings	1.07	0.90	0.58	0.53	0.48	0.40	0.35	0.32	0.21	0.16
S&P Core Earnings	1.07	0.89	0.58	0.53	0.47	0.39	0.34	0.31	0.20	NA
Dividends	0.59	0.60	0.33	0.30	0.27	0.22	0.16	0.11	0.07	0.03
Payout Ratio	55%	67%	57%	57%	56%	54%	47%	34%	35%	21%
Prices:High	15.89	25.05	16.08	14.09	12.61	12.79	12.00	6.71	4.14	3.16
Prices:Low	7.46	13.28	11.45	11.90	10.09	9.79	5.79	4.04	2.72	1.97
P/E Ratio:High	15	28	28	27	26	32	35	21	20	19
P/E Ratio:Low	7	15	20	22	21	24	17	13	13	12

Income Statement Analysis (Million $)										
Net Interest Income	1,243	942	647	613	562	485	401	388	287	254
Loan Loss Provision	138	19.5	4.80	Nil	0.07	0.79	0.90	1.50	1.88	2.13
Non Interest Income	33.6	8.50	7.27	6.29	5.27	16.6	5.34	5.95	4.69	4.54
Non Interest Expenses	266	198	168	159	128	118	103	93.5	81.8	79.0
Pretax Income	874	733	482	461	442	382	327	301	208	177
Effective Tax Rate	39.7%	39.2%	38.6%	37.3%	37.6%	37.4%	36.6%	36.3%	35.3%	35.3%
Net Income	527	446	296	289	276	239	207	192	135	115
% Net Interest Margin	2.21	1.96	1.64	1.96	2.35	3.66	2.65	3.10	2.87	2.90
S&P Core Earnings	529	440	294	287	272	235	204	186	128	NA

Balance Sheet & Other Financial Data (Million $)										
Total Assets	60,268	54,163	44,424	35,507	28,075	20,146	17,033	14,145	11,427	9,380
Loans	31,721	29,441	24,198	19,069	15,037	11,328	8,766	6,932	5,932	4,841
Deposits	24,578	18,464	15,153	13,416	11,383	11,477	10,454	9,139	7,913	6,604
Capitalization:Debt	29,975	30,225	24,141	16,966	11,350	7,150	5,150	3,600	2,150	650
Capitalization:Equity	5,339	4,949	4,611	4,930	5,201	1,403	1,329	1,316	1,289	1,465
Capitalization:Total	35,314	35,174	28,752	21,896	16,551	8,553	6,479	4,916	3,439	2,115
% Return on Assets	0.9	0.9	0.7	0.9	1.1	1.3	1.3	1.5	1.3	1.3
% Return on Equity	10.3	9.3	6.2	5.7	8.4	17.5	15.7	14.7	9.8	7.8
% Loan Loss Reserve	0.4	0.2	0.1	0.2	0.2	0.2	0.2	0.4	0.4	0.5
% Risk Based Capital	21.0	21520.0	24.8	31.0	41.3	17.5	7.5	26.8	32.0	43.0
Price Times Book Value:High	1.5	2.6	1.1	1.6	1.4	5.4	5.5	3.1	2.0	1.5
Price Times Book Value:Low	0.7	1.4	0.8	1.4	1.1	4.2	2.7	1.9	1.3	0.9

Data as orig reptd.; bef. results of disc opers/spec. items. Per share data adj. for stk. divs.; EPS diluted. E-Estimated. NA-Not Available. NM-Not Meaningful. NR-Not Ranked. UR-Under Review.

Office: 80 W Century Rd, Paramus, NJ, USA 07652-1405.
Telephone: 201-967-1900.
Website: http://www.hcbk.com
Chrmn, Pres & CEO: R.E. Hermance, Jr.

COO, EVP & Chief Acctg Officer: D.J. Salamone
EVP & CFO: J.C. Kranz
SVP, Treas & Secy: V.A. Olszewski
Investor Contact: S. Munhall (201-967-8290)

Board Members: M. W. Azzara, W. G. Bardel, S. A. Belair, V. H. Bruni, W. J. Cosgrove, C. E. Golding, R. E. Hermance, Jr., D. O. Quest, D. J. Salamone, J. G. Sponholz

Founded: 1868
Domicile: Delaware
Employees: 1,552

Humana Inc.

STANDARD &POOR'S

S&P Recommendation **BUY** ★★★★☆	Price $56.97 (as of Oct 22, 2010)	12-Mo. Target Price $58.00	Investment Style Large-Cap Growth

GICS Sector Health Care
Sub-Industry Managed Health Care

Summary This company provides a broad range of managed health care services to more than 10.3 million individuals.

Key Stock Statistics (Source S&P, Vickers, company reports)

52-Wk Range	$57.14– 35.78	S&P Oper. EPS 2010**E**	6.39	Market Capitalization(B)	$9.641	Beta	1.08
Trailing 12-Month EPS	$6.78	S&P Oper. EPS 2011**E**	5.50	Yield (%)	Nil	S&P 3-Yr. Proj. EPS CAGR(%)	-2
Trailing 12-Month P/E	8.4	P/E on S&P Oper. EPS 2010**E**	8.9	Dividend Rate/Share	Nil	S&P Credit Rating	BBB-
$10K Invested 5 Yrs Ago	$12,404	Common Shares Outstg. (M)	169.2	Institutional Ownership (%)	91		

Price Performance

30-Week Mov. Avg. · · · · 10-Week Mov. Avg. – – · Earnings vs. Previous Year   Volume Above Avg. STARS
12-Mo. Target Price — Relative Strength — ▲ Up ▼ Down ► No Change   Below Avg. ★

Options: ASE, CBOE, Ph

Analysis prepared by **Phillip M. Seligman** on October 05, 2010, when the stock traded at **$ 50.22**.

Highlights

➤ We see operating revenues (premium, fee and other revenues, but not investment income) rising to over $33.7 billion in 2010, from $30.7 billion in 2009. Drivers we see include 255,000 more Medicare Advantage (MA; Medicare health plan) members by year end, but 215,000 fewer Medicare Part D standalone drug program members, 210,000 fewer fully insured commercial members and 120,000 fewer self-funded commercial members, and no change in Medicaid and TRICARE enrollment.

➤ We believe companywide medical costs will rise 60 basis points (bps) to 83.4% of premium revenues (MCR; medical cost ratio) in 2010. We see the impact of the reduced MA premium rate and more people covered via COBRA (temporary health plan continuation for laid-off workers) partly offset by favorable prior-year claims reserve development. We expect SG&A costs to decline 40 bps to 13.5% of operating revenue, on scale efficiencies and cost control.

➤ We project operating EPS of $6.39 (including an estimated $0.23 charge for the planned March 2011 TRICARE exit and $0.28 for additional Medicare growth initiatives) in 2010, versus $6.15 in 2009. We look for $5.50 in 2011.

Investment Rationale/Risk

➤ We believe HUM has the size, scale and flexibility to adjust to the reduced MA premium rates and the MCR floor requirements of health care reform. Moreover, as long as current and prospective members view HUM's MA plans as more attractive than rivals' or traditional Medicare, we think they will continue to expand. Meanwhile, we are encouraged that HUM has been making progress transitioning some PFFS members to its higher-margin HMOs and PPOs prior to the 2011 end of PFFS in non-rural geographies, and has developed a network-PFFS product to attract PFFS members who might otherwise leave. We are also positive on its new joint venture with Cigna (CI 36, Buy), which could augment MA enrollment, and one with Wal-Mart Stores (WMT 54, Strong Buy), which could add to its Medicare Part D enrollment.

➤ Risks to our recommendation and target price include intensified competition, a medical cost spike, and MA rate cuts.

➤ Our 12-month target price of $58 assumes a multiple of 9X applied to our 2010 EPS estimate. The slightly below-peer multiple reflects significant dependence on government business.

Qualitative Risk Assessment

LOW	MEDIUM	**HIGH**

Our risk assessment reflects HUM's heavy reliance on Medicare Advantage (MA) for growth. We also believe that intense competition will continue to limit commercial enrollment growth.

Quantitative Evaluations

S&P Quality Ranking B+

D	C	B-	B	**B+**	A-	A	A+

Relative Strength Rank STRONG

86

LOWEST = 1   HIGHEST = 99

Revenue/Earnings Data

Revenue (Million $)

	1Q	2Q	3Q	4Q	Year
2010	8,441	8,653	--	--	--
2009	7,712	7,899	7,717	7,633	30,960
2008	6,960	7,351	7,148	7,488	28,946
2007	6,205	6,427	6,320	6,339	25,290
2006	4,704	5,407	5,650	5,655	21,417
2005	3,887	3,546	3,821	3,663	14,418

Earnings Per Share ($)

	1Q	2Q	3Q	4Q	Year
2010	1.52	2.00	E1.70	E0.62	E6.39
2009	1.22	1.67	1.78	1.48	6.15
2008	0.47	1.24	1.09	1.03	3.83
2007	0.42	1.28	1.78	1.43	4.91
2006	0.50	0.53	0.95	0.92	2.90
2005	0.54	0.51	0.30	0.39	1.87

Fiscal year ended Dec. 31. Next earnings report expected: Early November. EPS Estimates based on S&P Operating Earnings; historical GAAP earnings are as reported.

Dividend Data

No cash dividends have been paid since 1993.

Please read the Required Disclosures and Analyst Certification on the last page of this report.

The **McGraw·Hill** Companies

Humana Inc.

STANDARD &POOR'S

Business Summary October 05, 2010

CORPORATE OVERVIEW. Humana is one of the largest managed care organizations, with medical membership of 10,274,300 (8,480,300 excluding Medicare Prescription Drug Program (PDP) enrollment) as of June 30, 2010, versus 10,283,300 (8,355,500) at December 31, 2009.

The Commercial segment consists of members enrolled in products marketed to employer groups and individuals, including fully insured medical (1,702,500 versus 1,839,500), administrative services only (ASO; 1,582,600 versus 1,571,000), and specialty (7,297,000 versus 7,200,100). Fully insured medical members (20.0% of total premium and fee revenues in 2009) are in health maintenance organizations (HMOs), which require members to use only doctors in their networks and generally reimburse providers on a capitated basis, and in preferred provider organizations (PPOs), which allow members the option to go to doctors outside of the network, with the members paying a portion of the provider's fees. ASO products (1.3%), which include HMOs, PPOs and consumer-directed health plans, are offered to employers that self-insure their employee health plans. Specialty products (3.1%) include dental, group and individual life, and short-term disability.

The Government segment consists of Medicare Advantage (MA; HMO:

634,800 versus 591,900; PPO: 618,300 versus 352,400; private fee-for-service; PFFS: 479,300 versus 564,200; and ASO: 28,700 versus none); Medicare PDP (1,793,400 versus 1,927,900); Medicaid (404,600 versus 401,700), and the Dept. of Defense health program, TRICARE (fully insured: 1,759,800 versus 1,756,000; ASO: 1,270,900 versus 1,278,400).

In 2009, MA revenues were $16.4 billion (53.9% of premium and fee revenues) and Medicare PDP revenues were $3.4 billion (11.2%). As of April 2008 (latest available), MA plans included 14 local HMOs, 41 local PPOs, a regional PPO in 25 states, and private fee-for-service (PFFS) programs in 50 states. HUM also offered the Medicare Prescription Drug Program in 50 states.

The Medicaid unit (2.1%) has contracts in Puerto Rico and Florida.

HUM's current TRICARE South Region contract (fully insured: 11.3%; administrative services fees: 0.3%) covers beneficiaries in 10 states.

Company Financials Fiscal Year Ended Dec. 31

Per Share Data ($)	2009	2008	2007	2006	2005	2004	2003	2002	2001	2000
Tangible Book Value	20.80	12.99	13.91	10.46	7.41	7.52	6.54	5.09	4.33	3.43
Cash Flow	NA	5.13	6.00	3.79	2.68	2.45	2.20	1.57	1.67	1.42
Earnings	6.15	3.83	4.91	2.90	1.87	1.72	1.41	0.85	0.70	0.54
S&P Core Earnings	6.08	4.14	4.87	2.64	1.99	1.55	1.23	0.87	0.63	NA
Dividends	Nil	Nil	Nil	Nil	Nil	Nil	Nil	Nil	Nil	Nil
Payout Ratio	Nil	Nil	Nil	Nil	Nil	Nil	Nil	Nil	Nil	Nil
Prices:High	46.20	88.10	81.50	68.24	55.70	31.02	23.39	17.45	15.63	15.81
Prices:Low	18.57	22.33	51.00	41.08	28.92	15.20	8.68	9.78	8.38	4.75
P/E Ratio:High	8	23	17	24	30	18	17	21	22	29
P/E Ratio:Low	3	6	10	14	15	9	6	12	12	9

Income Statement Analysis (Million $)										
Revenue	30,960	28,946	25,290	21,417	14,418	13,104	12,226	11,261	10,195	10,395
Operating Income	NA	1,293	1,543	974	590	415	489	384	114	171
Depreciation	NA	220	185	149	129	118	127	121	162	147
Interest Expense	106	80.3	68.9	63.1	39.3	23.2	17.4	17.0	25.0	29.0
Pretax Income	1,602	993	1,289	762	422	416	345	210	183	114
Effective Tax Rate	35.1%	34.8%	35.3%	36.0%	26.9%	32.7%	33.6%	32.0%	36.1%	21.1%
Net Income	1,040	647	834	487	308	280	229	143	117	90.0
S&P Core Earnings	1,027	699	826	443	330	252	200	145	104	NA

Balance Sheet & Other Financial Data (Million $)										
Cash	1,614	1,970	5,676	1,740	732	580	931	721	651	2,067
Current Assets	NA	8,396	8,733	7,333	4,206	3,596	3,321	2,795	2,623	2,499
Total Assets	14,153	13,042	12,879	10,127	6,870	5,658	5,293	4,600	4,404	4,167
Current Liabilities	NA	5,184	5,792	5,192	3,220	2,327	2,265	2,390	2,307	2,665
Long Term Debt	1,678	1,937	1,688	1,269	514	637	643	340	315	Nil
Common Equity	5,776	4,457	4,029	3,054	2,474	2,090	1,836	1,606	1,508	1,374
Total Capital	NA	6,394	5,717	4,323	2,988	2,727	2,479	1,946	1,823	1,374
Capital Expenditures	NA	262	239	193	166	114	101	112	115	135
Cash Flow	NA	868	1,018	636	437	398	356	264	279	237
Current Ratio	1.8	1.6	1.5	1.4	1.3	1.5	1.5	1.2	1.1	0.9
% Long Term Debt of Capitalization	22.5	30.3	29.5	29.4	17.2	23.3	25.9	17.5	17.3	Nil
% Net Income of Revenue	3.4	2.2	3.3	2.3	2.1	102.6	1.9	1.3	1.2	0.9
% Return on Assets	7.7	5.0	7.3	5.7	4.9	5.1	4.5	3.2	2.7	2.0
% Return on Equity	20.3	15.3	23.5	17.5	13.5	14.3	13.3	9.2	8.2	6.8

Data as orig reptd.; bef. results of disc opers/spec. items. Per share data adj. for stk. divs.; EPS diluted. E-Estimated. NA-Not Available. NM-Not Meaningful. NR-Not Ranked. UR-Under Review.

Office: 500 W Main St, Louisville, KY 40202-4268.
Telephone: 502-580-1000.
Website: http://www.humana.com
Chrmn, Pres & CEO: M.B. McCallister

COO: J.E. Murray
SVP, CFO & Treas: J.H. Bloem
SVP & General Counsel: C.M. Todoroff
SVP & CIO: B.J. Goodman

Investor Contact: R.C. Nethery (502-580-3644)
Board Members: F. A. D'Amelio, W. R. Dunbar, K. J. Hilzinger, D. A. Jones, Jr., M. B. McCallister, W. J. McDonald, W. E. Mitchell, D. B. Nash, J. J. O'Brien, M. T. Peterson, W. A. Reynolds

Founded: 1964
Domicile: Delaware
Employees: 28,100

Huntington Bancshares Inc

STANDARD &POOR'S

S&P Recommendation	BUY ★★★★★	Price	12-Mo. Target Price	Investment Style
		$5.69 (as of Oct 22, 2010)	$7.00	Large-Cap Blend

GICS Sector Financials
Sub-Industry Regional Banks

Summary This regional bank holding company has over 600 banking offices in Ohio, Michigan, Indiana, Pennsylvania, Kentucky, and West Virginia.

Key Stock Statistics (Source S&P, Vickers, company reports)

52-Wk Range	$7.40–3.50	S&P Oper. EPS 2010E	0.25	Market Capitalization(B)	$4.079	Beta	1.68
Trailing 12-Month EPS	$-0.82	S&P Oper. EPS 2011E	0.51	Yield (%)	0.70	S&P 3-Yr. Proj. EPS CAGR(%)	NA
Trailing 12-Month P/E	NM	P/E on S&P Oper. EPS 2010E	22.8	Dividend Rate/Share	$0.04	S&P Credit Rating	BB+
$10K Invested 5 Yrs Ago	$3,150	Common Shares Outstg. (M)	716.9	Institutional Ownership (%)	63		

Price Performance

30-Week Mov. Avg. · · · 10-Week Mov. Avg. − − GAAP Earnings vs. Previous Year Volume Above Avg. ılıl STARS
12-Mo. Target Price — Relative Strength — ▲ Up ▼ Down ► No Change   Below Avg. ılıl ★

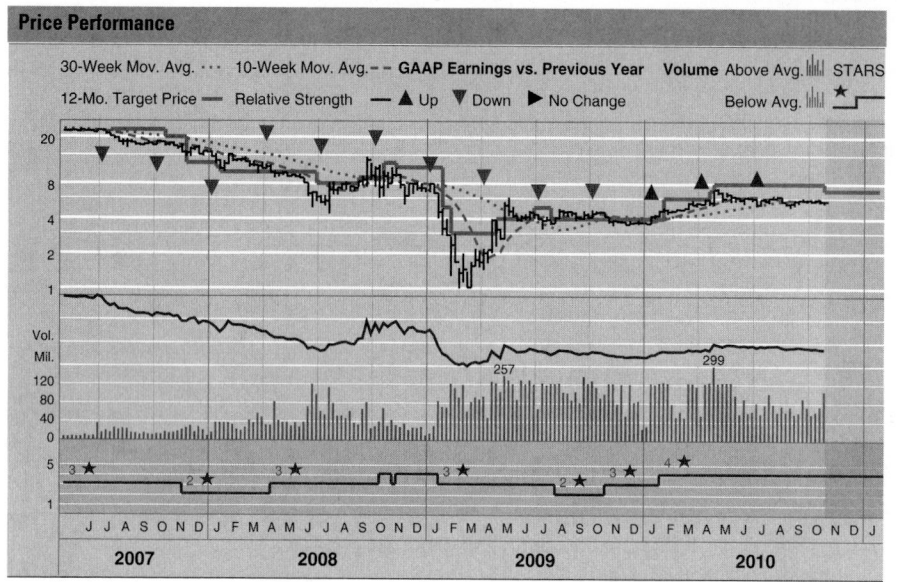

Options: CBOE, Ph

Qualitative Risk Assessment

LOW	MEDIUM	HIGH

Our risk assessment reflects HBAN's Midwestern lending exposure, offset by our view of its recently strengthened capital position, and prospects for improving credit metrics.

Quantitative Evaluations

S&P Quality Ranking B-

D	C	B-	B	B+	A-	A	A+

Relative Strength Rank WEAK

26

LOWEST = 1   HIGHEST = 99

Revenue/Earnings Data

Revenue (Million $)

	1Q	2Q	3Q	4Q	Year
2010	787.6	805.3	--	--	--
2009	809.1	829.0	809.9	795.9	3,244
2008	971.2	933.1	853.6	729.6	3,505
2007	689.1	698.7	1,056	985.0	3,420
2006	624.3	684.9	636.9	685.5	2,632
2005	544.2	558.5	581.6	589.8	2,274

Earnings Per Share ($)

2010	0.01	0.03	E0.10	E0.11	E0.25
2009	-6.79	-0.40	-0.33	-0.56	-6.14
2008	0.35	0.25	0.17	-1.20	-0.44
2007	0.40	0.34	0.38	-0.65	0.25
2006	0.45	0.46	0.65	0.37	1.92
2005	0.41	0.45	0.47	0.44	1.77

Fiscal year ended Dec. 31. Next earnings report expected: Late October. EPS Estimates based on S&P Operating Earnings; historical GAAP earnings are as reported.

Highlights

► The 12-month target price for HBAN has recently been changed to $7.00 from $8.00. The Highlights section of this Stock Report will be updated accordingly.

Investment Rationale/Risk

► The Investment Rationale/Risk section of this Stock Report will be updated shortly. For the latest News story on HBAN from MarketScope, see below.

► 10/21/10 03:37 pm ET ... S&P MAINTAINS BUY RECOMMENDATION ON SHARES OF HUNT-INGTON BANCSHARES (HBAN 5.6****): Q3 EPS of $0.10, vs. a loss per share of $0.33, misses our $0.11 EPS estimate, on a higher than expected loan loss provision and noninterest expenses. However, the decline of the provision, and improvement in credit quality was faster than most peers. On Q3 results, we lower our '10 EPS estimate to $0.25 from $0.26. On our lower credit cost estimates for '11, we raise our '11 EPS estimate to $0.51 from $0.49. On our analysis of relative valuation multiples, we lower our target price to $7, down $1, based on a slight premium to peers 13.7X our '11 EPS estimate. /E.Oja

Dividend Data (Dates: mm/dd Payment Date: mm/dd/yy)

Amount ($)	Date Decl.	Ex-Div. Date	Stk. of Record	Payment Date
0.010	01/20	03/16	03/18	04/01/10
0.010	04/19	06/15	06/17	07/01/10
0.010	07/21	09/15	09/17	10/01/10
0.010	10/20	12/16	12/20	01/03/11

Dividends have been paid since 1912. Source: Company reports.

Huntington Bancshares Inc

Business Summary August 16, 2010

CORPORATE OVERVIEW. Huntington Bancshares Inc. (HBAN) is a multi-state diversified financial holding company focused on the Midwest region of the United States. It provides full-service commercial and consumer banking services, mortgage banking services, automobile financing, equipment leasing, investment management, trust services, and brokerage services. The company also offers insurance services.

The regional banking line of business provides traditional banking products and services to consumer, small business and commercial customers located in its eight operating regions within the six states of Ohio, Pennsylvania, Michigan, West Virginia, Indiana and Kentucky. It provides these services through a banking network of 600 branches, over 1,300 ATMs, along with Internet and telephone banking channels. It also provides certain services outside of these six states, including mortgage banking and equipment leasing. Each region is further divided into retail and commercial banking units.

As of June 30, 2009, based on the most recent FDIC data, HBAN operated 624 branches, including 349 branches in its home state of Ohio. In Ohio, HBAN had

$25.8 billion in deposits, a nearly 11% deposit market share, and a number three ranking in the state. In Michigan, HBAN had 121 branches, $6.4 billion in deposits, a 3.93% deposit market share, ranking eighth. In Pennsylvania, HBAN had 60 offices, $2.7 billion in deposits, ranking 19th.

IMPACT OF MAJOR DEVELOPMENTS. During 2009, HBAN completed several transactions to increase equity capital. In the third quarter of 2009, HBAN completed an offering of 109.5 million shares of its common stock at $4.20 per share, or $460.1 million in aggregate gross proceeds. In the second quarter of 2009, HBAN completed an offering of 103.5 million shares of its common stock at $3.60 per share, or $372.6 million in aggregate gross proceeds. Also, during 2009, HBAN completed three separate discretionary equity issuance programs, issuing a total of 92.7 million new shares of common stock worth a total of $345.8 million.

Company Financials Fiscal Year Ended Dec. 31

Per Share Data ($)	2009	2008	2007	2006	2005	2004	2003	2002	2001	2000
Tangible Book Value	4.07	6.27	7.14	10.12	11.41	10.02	8.99	8.95	6.77	9.43
Earnings	-6.14	-0.44	0.25	1.92	1.77	1.71	1.67	1.49	0.71	1.32
S&P Core Earnings	-1.25	-0.52	0.32	1.95	1.73	1.66	1.56	0.67	0.60	NA
Dividends	0.04	0.04	1.06	1.00	0.85	0.75	0.67	0.64	0.72	0.74
Payout Ratio	NM	NM	NM	52%	48%	44%	40%	43%	101%	56%
Prices:High	8.00	14.87	24.14	24.97	25.41	25.38	22.55	21.77	19.28	21.82
Prices:Low	1.00	4.37	13.50	22.56	20.97	20.89	17.78	16.00	12.63	12.52
P/E Ratio:High	NM	NM	97	13	14	15	14	15	27	17
P/E Ratio:Low	NM	NM	54	12	12	12	11	11	18	9

Income Statement Analysis (Million $)										
Net Interest Income	1,424	1,532	1,302	1,019	962	911	849	984	996	942
Tax Equivalent Adjustment	11.5	20.2	19.3	16.0	13.4	NA	9.68	5.21	6.35	8.31
Non Interest Income	1,006	707	706	634	640	803	1,064	680	509	494
Loan Loss Provision	2,075	1,057	644	65.2	81.3	55.1	164	227	309	90.5
% Expense/Operating Revenue	166.0%	57.0%	62.5%	60.0%	60.5%	65.5%	64.3%	50.6%	67.4%	61.7%
Pretax Income	-3,678	-296	22.6	514	544	553	524	589	173	460
Effective Tax Rate	NM	NM	NM	10.3%	24.2%	27.8%	26.4%	38.4%	NM	28.6%
Net Income	-3,094	-114	75.2	461	412	399	386	363	179	328
% Net Interest Margin	3.11	3.25	3.36	3.29	3.33	3.33	3.49	4.19	4.02	3.73
S&P Core Earnings	-662	-190	96.8	467	405	388	360	165	152	NA

Balance Sheet & Other Financial Data (Million $)										
Money Market Assets	403	419	1,965	551	105	960	138	86.6	118	143
Investment Securities	8,588	4,384	4,500	4,363	4,527	4,239	4,929	3,411	2,862	4,107
Commercial Loans	20,577	23,639	22,308	12,354	10,845	10,303	9,486	9,336	10,415	8,887
Other Loans	14,731	16,553	17,746	13,799	13,627	13,257	11,590	11,619	11,187	11,723
Total Assets	51,555	54,312	54,697	35,329	32,765	32,565	30,484	27,579	28,500	28,599
Demand Deposits	12,797	9,560	5,372	3,616	3,390	3,392	2,987	3,074	3,741	3,505
Time Deposits	27,697	32,466	32,371	21,432	19,020	17,376	15,500	14,425	16,446	16,272
Long Term Debt	3,803	6,871	6,955	4,513	4,597	6,227	6,808	3,304	3,039	3,338
Common Equity	3,648	5,349	5,949	3,014	2,594	2,538	2,275	2,304	2,416	2,366
% Return on Assets	NM	NM	0.2	1.4	1.3	1.3	1.3	1.3	0.6	1.1
% Return on Equity	NM	NM	1.7	16.6	16.0	16.6	17.3	15.4	7.5	14.4
% Loan Loss Reserve	4.0	2.2	1.4	1.0	-0.7	1.1	1.6	1.7	1.8	1.4
% Loans/Deposits	90.9	108.3	105.4	105.5	171.3	114.5	115.2	122.8	110.1	105.0
% Equity to Assets	8.5	10.4	10.0	8.2	7.8	7.6	7.7	8.4	8.4	7.9

Data as orig reptd.; bef. results of disc opers/spec. items. Per share data adj. for stk. divs.; EPS diluted. E-Estimated. NA-Not Available. NM-Not Meaningful. NR-Not Ranked. UR-Under Review.

Office: 41 S High St, Columbus, OH 43287.
Telephone: 614-480-8300.
Website: http://www.huntington.com
Chrmn, Pres & CEO: S.D. Steinour

COO, CTO & CIO: Z. Afzal
EVP, CFO & Treas: D.R. Kimble
EVP, Secy & General Counsel: R.A. Cheap
EVP & Cntlr: D.S. Anderson

Investor Contact: D.R. Kimble (614-480-5676)
Board Members: D. M. Casto, III, A. B. Crane, M. J. Endres, J. B. Gerlach, Jr., D. J. Hilliker, D. P. Lauer, J. A. Levy, W. J. Lhota, G. P. Mastroianni, R. W. Neu, D. L. Porteous, K. H. Ransier, W. R. Robertson, S. D. Steinour

Founded: 1966
Domicile: Maryland
Employees: 10,272

Illinois Tool Works Inc.

STANDARD & POOR'S

S&P Recommendation **BUY** ★★★★☆

Price	12-Mo. Target Price	Investment Style
$46.94 (as of Oct 25, 2010)	$51.00	Large-Cap Growth

GICS Sector Industrials
Sub-Industry Industrial Machinery

Summary This diversified manufacturer operates a portfolio of about 840 industrial and consumer businesses throughout the world.

Key Stock Statistics (Source S&P, Vickers, company reports)

52-Wk Range	$52.72–40.33	S&P Oper. EPS 2010E	3.04	Market Capitalization(B)	$23.635	Beta	1.08
Trailing 12-Month EPS	$3.25	S&P Oper. EPS 2011E	3.34	Yield (%)	2.90	S&P 3-Yr. Proj. EPS CAGR(%)	10
Trailing 12-Month P/E	14.4	P/E on S&P Oper. EPS 2010E	15.4	Dividend Rate/Share	$1.36	S&P Credit Rating	A+
$10K Invested 5 Yrs Ago	$13,104	Common Shares Outstg. (M)	503.5	Institutional Ownership (%)	81		

Price Performance

30-Week Mov. Avg. · · · · 10-Week Mov. Avg. - - GAAP Earnings vs. Previous Year   Volume Above Avg. STARS

12-Mo. Target Price — Relative Strength — ▲ Up ▼ Down ► No Change   Below Avg.

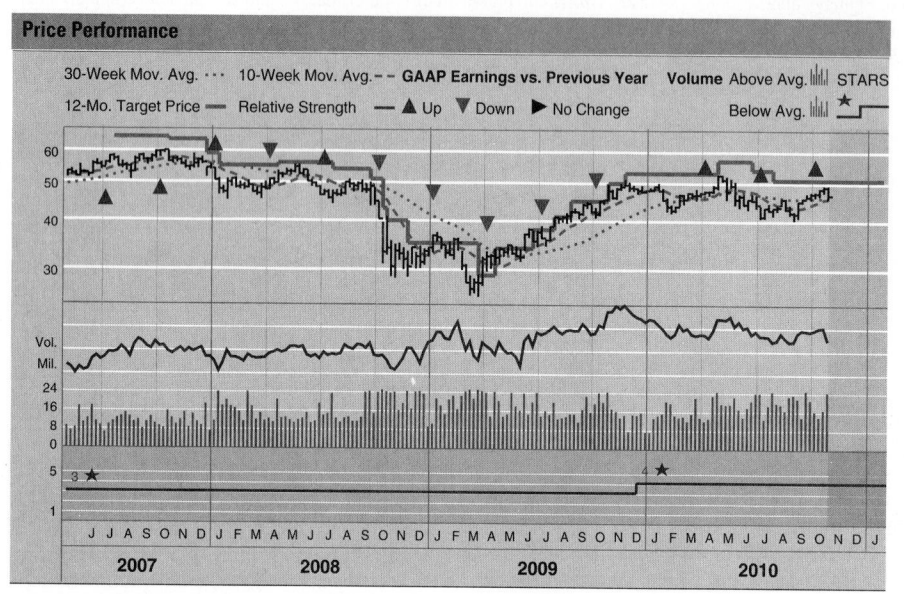

Options: ASE, CBOE, Ph

Analysis prepared by **Mathew Christy, CFA** on October 25, 2010, when the stock traded at **$ 47.04**.

Highlights

► After a decline of nearly 19% in 2009, we expect that revenue will increase nearly 14% in 2010, based on better economic conditions along with the positive benefits of acquisitions. In addition, we believe that ITW's early-cycle businesses will have larger gains relative to the remainder of the business, and we expect the company to benefit from better industrial activity, higher demand, and some inventory restocking. For 2011, we see revenue advancing more than 9% on continued growth in the industrial economy and as a result of acquisitions.

► Following the nearly four percentage point decline in the operating margin in 2009, we believe that margins will improve this year due mainly to better operating leverage and production rates along with benefits associated with cost-cutting initiatives. In 2011, we project that operating margins will be somewhat lower as compared to 2010 results.

► Assuming taxes at an effective rate between 29% and 32% in 2010 and 2011, we forecast EPS of $3.04 and $3.34 for the respective years.

Investment Rationale/Risk

► Following the weak results in 2009 due to the global recession, revenues have been improving sequentially as the global economy recovers and global industrial activity improves. (S&P forecasts economic growth for 2010 and 2011.) We look for ITW to benefit from higher industrial-related demand, acquisitions, and marginal benefits from an expected increase in automotive build rates. We view the shares as attractive, recently trading at about 13.9X our 2011 EPS estimate, below the peer average, versus a 10% historical premium.

► Risks to our recommendation and target price include lower-than-expected industrial activity and/or capital spending; acquisition execution risk; and, a significant slowing of construction activity and/or automotive markets.

► Our 12-month target price of $51 represents a blend of two valuation metrics. Our discounted cash flow model, which assumes 3% growth in perpetuity and a 9.6% weighted average cost of capital, indicates intrinsic value of about $53. In terms of relative valuation, we apply a target multiple of about 15X, ahead of peers, to our 2011 EPS estimate, suggesting a value of $50.

Qualitative Risk Assessment

LOW	MEDIUM	HIGH

Our risk assessment reflects an S&P Quality Ranking of A, a balance sheet that we see as strong with a relatively low level of debt, and free cash flow that has averaged about 121% of net income over the past 10 years.

Quantitative Evaluations

S&P Quality Ranking **A**

D	C	B-	B	B+	A-	A	A+

Relative Strength Rank **MODERATE**

43

LOWEST = 1   HIGHEST = 99

Revenue/Earnings Data

Revenue (Million $)

	1Q	2Q	3Q	4Q	Year
2010	3,606	4,076	4,018	--	--
2009	2,914	3,393	3,580	3,757	13,877
2008	4,139	4,570	4,148	3,678	15,869
2007	3,759	4,160	4,094	4,244	16,171
2006	3,297	3,579	3,538	3,641	14,055
2005	3,074	3,296	3,258	3,294	12,922

Earnings Per Share ($)

2010	0.58	0.83	0.83	E0.78	E3.04
2009	-0.06	0.36	0.60	E0.80	1.93
2008	0.57	1.01	0.85	0.54	3.04
2007	0.71	0.90	0.89	0.87	3.28
2006	0.65	0.81	0.78	0.77	3.01
2005	0.53	0.65	0.72	0.71	2.60

Fiscal year ended Dec. 31. Next earnings report expected: Late January. EPS Estimates based on S&P Operating Earnings; historical GAAP earnings are as reported.

Dividend Data (Dates: mm/dd Payment Date: mm/dd/yy)

Amount ($)	Date Decl.	Ex-Div. Date	Stk. of Record	Payment Date
0.310	10/30	12/29	12/31	01/12/10
0.310	02/12	03/29	03/31	04/13/10
0.310	05/07	06/28	06/30	07/13/10
0.340	08/06	09/28	09/30	10/13/10

Dividends have been paid since 1933. Source: Company reports.

Illinois Tool Works Inc.

STANDARD
&POOR'S

Business Summary October 25, 2010

CORPORATE OVERVIEW. Illinois Tool Works (ITW) operates about 840 consumer and industrial businesses in 57 countries in a highly decentralized structure that places responsibility on managers at the lowest level possible, in an attempt to focus each business unit on the needs of particular customers. Each business unit manager is held strictly accountable for the results of his or her individual business.

CORPORATE STRATEGY. ITW is diversified not only by customer and industry, but also by geographic region, with about 57.5% of revenues derived from overseas. At the end of 2009, ITW diversified its business segmentation beyond its former four reporting segments and now reports on the basis of eight reportable segments -- Industrial Packaging, Power Systems & Electronics, Transportation, Construction Products, Food Equipment, Decorative Surfaces, Polymers & Fluids and All Other.

The Industrial Packaging segment (13.7% of revenues and 6.4% of operating income in 2009; 4.7% operating profit margin) produces steel, plastic and paper products used for bundling, shipping and protecting transported goods. In 2009, major markets served were primary metals (20%), general industrial (29%), construction (10%) and food and beverage (12%).

The Power Systems & Electronics segment (11.6% and 15.6%; 13.4%) pro-

duces equipment and consumables associated with specialty power conversion, metallurgy, welding, and electronics. In 2009, this segment primarily served the general industrial (46%), electronics (16%) and construction (7%) markets.

The Transportation segment (14.9% and 11%; 7.4%) produces components, fasteners, fluids, fillers and putties, truck parts services, and polymers for transportation-related applications. In 2009, this segment primarily served the automotive original equipment manufacturers (56%) and auto aftermarket (28%).

The Construction Products segment (11% and 7.1%; 6.4%) produces fasteners and related fastening tools for wood applications; anchors, fasteners and related tools for concrete and wood applications; metal plate truss components and related equipment and software; and packaged hardware fasteners, anchors and other products for retail. In 2009, this segment primarily served the residential (47%), commercial (26%), and renovation (24%) construction markets.

Company Financials Fiscal Year Ended Dec. 31

Per Share Data ($)	2009	2008	2007	2006	2005	2004	2003	2002	2001	2000
Tangible Book Value	4.43	2.78	7.37	6.94	6.89	7.59	8.22	6.90	5.42	4.82
Cash Flow	3.06	3.71	4.22	3.79	3.26	2.78	2.18	2.01	1.94	2.25
Earnings	1.93	3.04	3.28	3.01	2.60	2.20	1.69	1.51	1.31	1.58
S&P Core Earnings	2.12	2.84	3.27	3.03	2.60	2.13	1.63	1.38	1.13	NA
Dividends	1.24	1.18	0.98	0.92	0.61	0.52	0.47	0.45	0.42	0.38
Payout Ratio	64%	39%	30%	30%	23%	24%	28%	30%	32%	24%
Prices:High	51.16	55.59	60.00	53.54	47.32	48.35	42.35	38.90	36.00	34.50
Prices:Low	25.60	28.50	45.60	41.54	39.25	36.46	27.28	27.52	24.58	24.75
P/E Ratio:High	27	18	18	18	18	22	25	26	27	22
P/E Ratio:Low	13	9	14	14	15	17	16	18	19	16

Income Statement Analysis (Million $)										
Revenue	13,877	15,869	16,171	14,055	12,922	11,731	10,036	9,468	9,293	9,984
Operating Income	2,060	2,690	3,147	2,865	2,558	2,410	1,940	1,812	1,692	1,977
Depreciation	569	351	523	444	383	353	307	306	386	413
Interest Expense	165	152	102	85.6	87.0	69.2	70.7	68.5	68.1	72.4
Pretax Income	1,214	2,191	2,581	2,445	2,182	1,999	1,576	1,434	1,231	1,478
Effective Tax Rate	20.1%	27.8%	29.3%	29.8%	31.5%	33.0%	34.0%	35.0%	34.8%	35.2%
Net Income	969	1,583	1,826	1,718	1,495	1,340	1,040	932	802	958
S&P Core Earnings	1,064	1,476	1,818	1,729	1,493	1,299	1,009	851	691	NA

Balance Sheet & Other Financial Data (Million $)										
Cash	1,319	743	828	590	370	667	1,684	1,058	282	151
Current Assets	5,675	5,924	6,166	5,206	4,112	4,322	4,783	3,879	3,163	3,329
Total Assets	16,082	15,213	15,526	13,880	11,446	11,352	11,193	10,623	9,822	9,603
Current Liabilities	2,836	4,876	2,960	2,637	2,001	1,851	1,489	1,567	1,518	1,818
Long Term Debt	2,915	1,244	2,299	956	958	921	920	1,460	1,267	1,549
Common Equity	8,808	7,663	9,351	9,018	7,547	7,628	7,874	6,649	6,041	5,401
Total Capital	11,733	9,022	11,501	9,973	8,505	8,549	8,795	8,109	7,308	6,950
Capital Expenditures	247	355	353	301	293	283	258	271	257	314
Cash Flow	1,538	1,935	2,349	2,162	1,878	1,693	1,347	1,238	1,189	1,371
Current Ratio	2.0	1.2	2.1	2.0	2.1	2.3	3.2	2.5	2.1	1.8
% Long Term Debt of Capitalization	24.8	13.8	16.8	9.6	11.3	10.8	10.5	18.0	17.3	22.3
% Net Income of Revenue	7.0	10.0	11.3	12.2	11.6	11.4	10.4	9.8	8.6	9.6
% Return on Assets	6.2	10.3	12.4	13.6	13.1	11.9	9.5	9.1	8.3	10.3
% Return on Equity	11.8	18.6	19.9	20.7	19.7	17.3	14.3	14.7	14.0	18.8

Data as orig reptd.; bef. results of disc opers/spec. items. Per share data adj. for stk. divs.; EPS diluted. E-Estimated. NA-Not Available. NM-Not Meaningful. NR-Not Ranked. UR-Under Review.

Office: 3600 W. Lake Avenue, Glenview, IL 60026-5811.
Telephone: 847-724-7500.
Website: http://www.itw.com
Chrmn & CEO: D.B. Speer

SVP & CFO: R.D. Kropp
SVP, Secy & General Counsel: J.H. Wooten, Jr.
Chief Acctg Officer: R.J. Scheuneman
Investor Contact: J. Brooklier (847-657-4104)

Board Members: M. D. Brailsford, S. M. Crown, D. H. Davis, Jr., R. C. McCormack, R. S. Morrison, J. Skinner, D. H. Smith, Jr., D. B. Speer, P. B. Strobel, K. M. Warren, A. D. Williams

Founded: 1912
Domicile: Delaware
Employees: 59,000

Integrys Energy Group Inc

STANDARD &POOR'S

S&P Recommendation STRONG SELL ★☆☆☆☆	**Price** $53.39 (as of Oct 22, 2010)	**12-Mo. Target Price** $40.00	**Investment Style** Large-Cap Blend

GICS Sector Utilities
Sub-Industry Multi-Utilities

Summary This utility holding company serves about 485,000 regulated electric and 1,674,000 regulated gas customers. The company also operates an unregulated retail marketing business.

Key Stock Statistics (Source S&P, Vickers, company reports)

52-Wk Range	$53.92–34.20	S&P Oper. EPS 2010E	3.33	Market Capitalization(B)	$4.123	Beta	0.92
Trailing 12-Month EPS	$2.63	S&P Oper. EPS 2011E	3.48	Yield (%)	5.09	S&P 3-Yr. Proj. EPS CAGR(%)	11
Trailing 12-Month P/E	20.3	P/E on S&P Oper. EPS 2010E	16.0	Dividend Rate/Share	$2.72	S&P Credit Rating	A-
$10K Invested 5 Yrs Ago	$13,362	Common Shares Outstg. (M)	77.2	Institutional Ownership (%)	56		

Price Performance

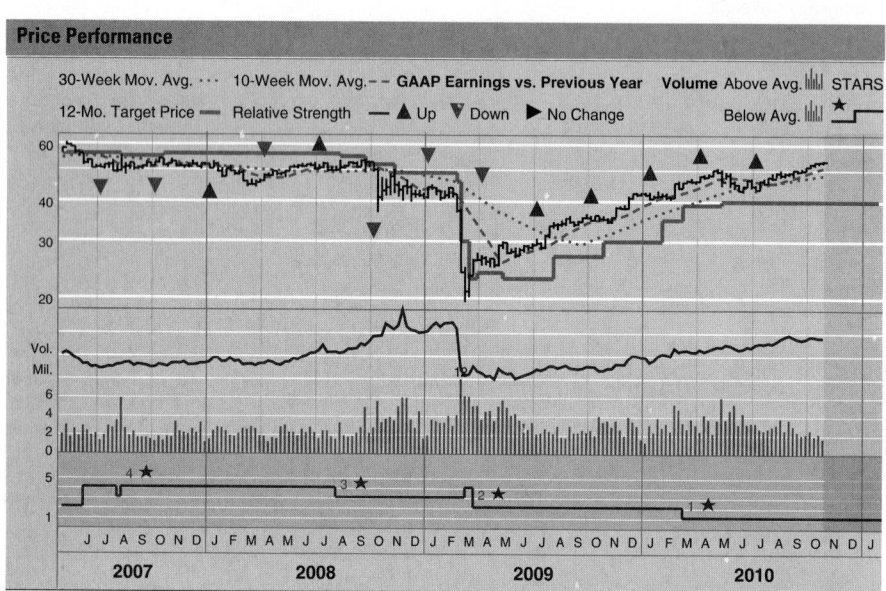

30-Week Mov. Avg. · · · 10-Week Mov. Avg. – – **GAAP Earnings vs. Previous Year** Volume Above Avg. STARS
12-Mo. Target Price — Relative Strength — ▲ Up ▼ Down ► No Change Below Avg. ★

Options: P, Ph

Analysis prepared by **Christopher B. Muir** on August 23, 2010, when the stock traded at **$ 49.03**.

Highlights

➤ We see 2010 revenues falling 22.8%. We see utility revenues falling 2.5%, reflecting lower gas prices and lower gas volumes. We estimate a 43% decline in unregulated revenues, reflecting the scaling back of the company's unregulated operations. In 2011, we see revenues rising 2.3% due to higher utility and slightly higher unregulated revenues.

➤ We forecast operating margins of 8.1% for 2010 and 8.4% for 2011, versus 2009's 5.6%, as we see lower per-revenue fuel costs partly offset by higher per-revenue non-fuel operating expenses. Margins are being helped as the company scales back lower margin unregulated operations. Our pretax profit margin estimates are 6.7% for 2010 and 7.6% for 2011, versus 2009's 4.5%, as we see lower interest expense, partly offset by lower non-operating income.

➤ Our 2010 EPS estimate, excluding net charges of $0.37, is $3.33, up 27% from 2009's $2.63, which excluded net charges of $3.59. We see EPS of $3.48 in 2011, up 20%, helped by lower interest costs. Excluding mark-to-market gains and losses, we see EPS of $3.05 in 2010, versus $2.60 in 2009.

Investment Rationale/Risk

➤ We think TEG has made some good acquisitions of late, and recently completed scaling back its unregulated businesses. As a result, TEG has substantially higher cash balances due to the return of capital, which we think will be used to maintain its dividend as well as to lower debt. TEG also said it would consider stock repurchases with any excess cash. However, we think it will take TEG until 2018 to lower its 100%-plus 2009 payout ratio to about 55%, a level in line with the multi-utility peer average, assuming 5% EPS growth from a 2011 base and no dividend growth.

➤ Risks to our recommendation and target price include greater-than-expected economic activity, merger savings and share repurchases, and lower-than-expected interest rates.

➤ TEG recently traded at 14X our 2011 EPS estimate, a 14% premium to its multi-utility peers. Our 12-month target price of $40 is 11.5X our 2011 EPS estimate, a 10% discount to our average peer forecast. We think the discounted valuation is warranted by the absence of dividend growth and the near peer average earnings growth we see.

Qualitative Risk Assessment

LOW	MEDIUM	HIGH

Our risk assessment reflects what we see as a balanced portfolio of operations, which includes lower risk gas and electric utility businesses as well as higher risk unregulated retail energy marketing services.

Quantitative Evaluations

S&P Quality Ranking **B**

D	C	B-	B	B+	A-	A	A+

Relative Strength Rank **MODERATE**

65

LOWEST = 1   HIGHEST = 99

Revenue/Earnings Data

Revenue (Million $)

	1Q	2Q	3Q	4Q	Year
2010	1,903	1,015	--	--	--
2009	3,201	1,428	1,298	1,574	7,500
2008	3,989	3,417	3,223	3,418	14,048
2007	2,747	2,362	2,123	3,062	10,292
2006	1,996	1,475	1,555	1,865	6,891
2005	1,462	1,328	1,757	2,391	6,826

Earnings Per Share ($)

2010	0.64	1.01	E0.57	E0.73	E3.33
2009	-2.35	0.45	0.63	0.30	-0.96
2008	1.77	-0.31	-0.77	0.27	1.58
2007	2.01	-0.53	0.14	1.19	2.48
2006	1.44	0.97	0.63	0.50	3.50
2005	1.62	0.62	1.25	0.53	4.11

Fiscal year ended Dec. 31. Next earnings report expected: Early November. EPS Estimates based on S&P Operating Earnings; historical GAAP earnings are as reported.

Dividend Data (Dates: mm/dd Payment Date: mm/dd/yy)

Amount ($)	Date Decl.	Ex-Div. Date	Stk. of Record	Payment Date
0.680	02/16	02/24	02/26	03/20/10
0.680	04/15	05/26	05/28	06/19/10
0.680	07/16	08/27	08/31	09/20/10
0.680	10/14	11/26	11/30	12/20/10

Dividends have been paid since 1940. Source: Company reports.

Please read the Required Disclosures and Analyst Certification on the last page of this report.

The McGraw-Hill Companies

Integrys Energy Group Inc

Business Summary August 23, 2010

CORPORATE OVERVIEW. Integrys Energy Group (TEG) is a holding company with regulated and unregulated business units. As of December 31, 2009, the company's subsidiaries were organized in three operating segments: electric utility, gas utility, and Integrys Energy Services, Inc. (ESI). A holding company and other segment includes operations that do not fit into the other segments, including nonutility operations of the regulated utilities. In 2009, ESI was the largest contributor to TEG's revenues, at 53%, although we expect this contribution to decline in 2010 as a result of the sale of part of the business. The electric utility segment contributed 17%, while the gas utility segment contributed 30%.

The electric utility segment includes the electric operations of Wisconsin Public Service Corporation (WPSC) and Upper Peninsula Power Company (UPPCO). The gas utility segment includes the gas operations of WPSC, Michigan Gas Utilities Corporation (MGUC), Minnesota Energy Resources Corporation (MERC), The Peoples Gas Light and Coke Company (PGL); and North Shore Gas Company (NSG). Integrys Energy Services is an unregulated subsidiary that operates electric generation facilities and energy marketing operations and provides energy generation and management services.

IMPACT OF MAJOR DEVELOPMENTS. On February 25, 2009, TEG announced that it intended to either fully or partially divest its ESI segment, or reduce its size, risk and financial requirements in response to increased collateral requirements. On January 20, 2010, TEG said it had achieved the objectives of its reorganization and decided to retain its retail marketing business. TEG reduced the invested capital at ESI from approximately $1 billion to $300 million as of April 30, 2010, and the invested capital for the segment's nonregulated energy marketing business segment is expected to be insignificant by December 31, 2010. TEG said it expects the remaining retail business to contribute about 16% of its 2011 EPS and for that segment to increase its earnings at a rate of 6% to 8%, faster than the 3% to 4% growth that we expect at the utility. The retail segment is also planning to reduce its scope to focus on the northeastern quadrant of the US. Longer term, ESI will be a smaller segment that requires significantly less capital, parental guarantees and overall financial liquidity.

Company Financials Fiscal Year Ended Dec. 31

Per Share Data ($)	2009	2008	2007	2006	2005	2004	2003	2002	2001	2000
Tangible Book Value	29.10	28.22	29.97	28.36	31.69	29.12	27.25	24.48	22.91	20.42
Earnings	-0.96	1.58	2.48	3.50	4.11	4.07	3.24	3.42	2.74	2.53
S&P Core Earnings	2.43	0.73	2.49	3.58	2.86	3.82	3.12	1.48	0.99	NA
Dividends	2.72	2.68	2.50	2.28	2.24	2.20	2.16	2.12	2.08	2.04
Payout Ratio	NM	170%	101%	62%	55%	54%	67%	62%	76%	81%
Prices:High	45.10	53.92	60.63	57.75	60.00	50.53	46.80	42.68	36.80	39.00
Prices:Low	19.44	36.91	48.10	47.39	47.67	43.50	36.80	30.47	31.00	22.63
P/E Ratio:High	NM	34	24	16	15	12	14	12	13	15
P/E Ratio:Low	NM	23	19	13	12	11	11	9	11	9

Income Statement Analysis (Million $)	2009	2008	2007	2006	2005	2004	2003	2002	2001	2000
Revenue	7,500	14,048	10,292	6,891	6,826	4,891	4,321	2,675	2,676	1,952
Depreciation	231	235	195	106	142	107	138	98.0	86.6	99.8
Maintenance	NA	NA	NA	NA	NA	NA	NA	NA	NA	73.0
Fixed Charges Coverage	3.22	2.11	2.57	2.85	3.80	4.31	3.55	3.97	2.32	2.14
Construction Credits	NA	NA	NA	NA	NA	NA	NA	NA	NA	4.46
Effective Tax Rate	978.8%	29.6%	32.2%	23.3%	20.7%	16.1%	22.0%	18.5%	5.83%	8.23%
Net Income	-73.7	122	181	152	148	153	114	109	77.6	67.0
S&P Core Earnings	186	56.4	179	152	111	144	103	47.1	28.2	NA

Balance Sheet & Other Financial Data (Million $)	2009	2008	2007	2006	2005	2004	2003	2002	2001	2000
Gross Property	7,792	7,483	7,066	3,961	3,099	3,308	3,065	3,186	2,979	2,716
Capital Expenditures	444	533	393	342	414	290	176	229	249	191
Net Property	4,945	4,773	4,464	2,535	2,044	2,003	1,829	1,610	1,464	1,351
Capitalization:Long Term Debt	2,446	2,339	2,316	1,338	918	866	923	926	829	761
Capitalization:% Long Term Debt	46.1	43.0	41.7	46.6	41.3	42.0	47.9	53.7	53.7	58.4
Capitalization:Preferred	Nil	Nil	Nil	Nil	Nil	Nil	Nil	Nil	Nil	Nil
Capitalization:% Preferred	Nil	Nil	Nil	Nil	Nil	Nil	Nil	Nil	Nil	Nil
Capitalization:Common	2,859	3,100	3,236	1,534	1,304	1,114	1,003	798	716	543
Capitalization:% Common	53.9	57.0	58.3	53.4	58.7	58.0	52.1	46.3	46.3	41.6
Total Capital	5,420	5,911	6,085	2,970	2,317	2,062	2,024	1,816	1,635	1,428
% Operating Ratio	95.1	98.6	97.3	97.0	98.2	96.7	97.8	95.3	96.2	94.5
% Earned on Net Property	9.3	5.5	10.5	10.9	9.2	9.9	7.4	9.8	7.6	8.6
% Return on Revenue	NM	0.9	1.8	2.2	2.2	3.1	2.6	4.1	2.9	3.4
% Return on Invested Capital	8.3	4.8	7.7	9.4	25.0	18.6	9.3	10.1	9.1	9.1
% Return on Common Equity	NM	3.8	7.5	10.5	13.3	14.5	12.8	14.5	12.3	12.4

Data as orig reptd.; bef. results of disc opers/spec. items. Per share data adj. for stk. divs.; EPS diluted. E-Estimated. NA-Not Available. NM-Not Meaningful. NR-Not Ranked. UR-Under Review.

Office: 130 East Randolph Drive, Chicago, IL 60601.
Telephone: 312-228-5400.
Email: investor@integrysgroup.com
Website: http://www.integrysgroup.com

Chrmn, Pres & CEO: C.A. Schrock
SVP & CFO: J.P. O'Leary
VP & Treas: B.A. Johnson
VP, Secy & Chief Lgl Officer: B.J. Wolf

Investor Contact: S.P. Eschbach (312-228-5408)
Board Members: K. E. Bailey, R. A. Bemis, W. J. Brodsky, A. J. Budney, Jr., P. S. Cafferty, E. Carnahan, R. C. Gallagher, K. M. Hasselblad-Pascale, J. W. Higgins, J. L. Kemerling, M. E. Lavin, W. F. Protz, Jr., C. A. Schrock

Founded: 1883
Domicile: Wisconsin
Employees: 5,025

Intel Corp

STANDARD &POOR'S

S&P Recommendation BUY ★★★★☆

Price	12-Mo. Target Price	Investment Style
$19.83 (as of Oct 22, 2010)	$22.00	Large-Cap Growth

GICS Sector Information Technology
Sub-Industry Semiconductors

Summary This company is the world's largest manufacturer of microprocessors, the central processing units of PCs, and also produces other semiconductor products.

Key Stock Statistics (Source S&P, Vickers, company reports)

52-Wk Range	$24.37–17.60	S&P Oper. EPS 2010**E**	1.99	Market Capitalization(B)	$110.441	Beta	1.16
Trailing 12-Month EPS	$1.86	S&P Oper. EPS 2011**E**	1.86	Yield (%)	3.18	S&P 3-Yr. Proj. EPS CAGR(%)	15
Trailing 12-Month P/E	10.7	P/E on S&P Oper. EPS 2010**E**	10.0	Dividend Rate/Share	$0.63	S&P Credit Rating	A+
$10K Invested 5 Yrs Ago	$9,729	Common Shares Outstg. (M)	5,568.0	Institutional Ownership (%)	63		

Price Performance

30-Week Mov. Avg. · · · · 10-Week Mov. Avg. - - ▬ GAAP Earnings vs. Previous Year Volume Above Avg. STARS
12-Mo. Target Price ▬ Relative Strength ▬ ▲ Up ▼ Down ► No Change Below Avg. ★

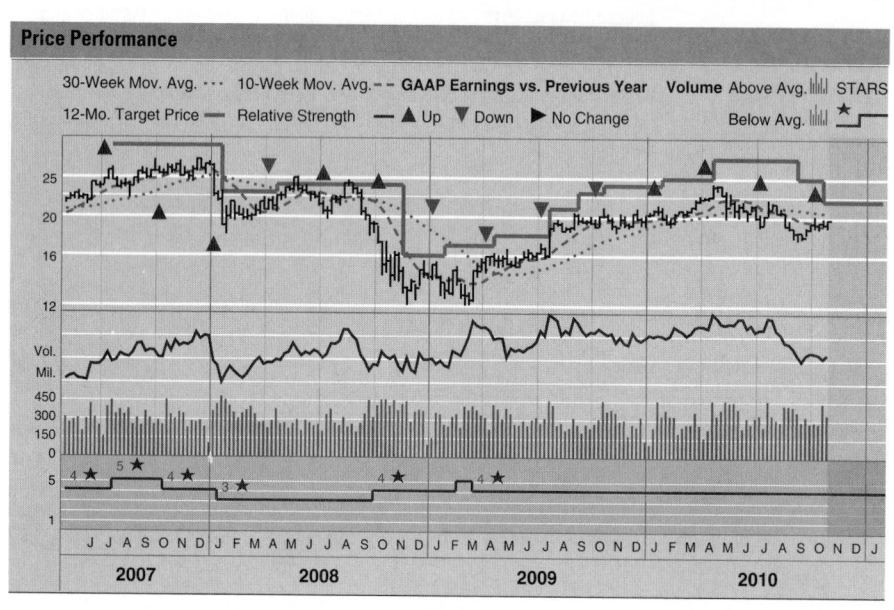

Options: ASE, CBOE, P, Ph

Analysis prepared by **Clyde Montevirgen** on October 14, 2010, when the stock traded at **$ 19.30**.

Highlights

➤ We think sales will rise 8% in 2011, after a projected 24% increase in 2010. Although we see some inventory digestion over the near-term, we believe IT spending, driven by Microsoft Windows 7, aging computers and bandwidth-consuming applications for PCs and servers will provide healthy demand for microprocessors. Laptop sales growth should balance desktop weakness and support top-line advances, in our view. We expect Intel's 32 nanometer (nm) and 22 nm chips to outperform competitors' offerings, which should lead to market share gains in higher-end segments, helping preserve average selling prices. Furthermore, we see INTC's Atom processor providing additional growth opportunities.

➤ We see gross margins narrowing to 62% in 2011 from 66% seen in 2010, as higher startup costs for implementation of its 22 nm processes offset lower chip costs and an improving sales mix. Also assuming higher expenses for compensation and headcount, we think operating margins will fall to 31% in 2011 from 37% during 2010.

➤ Our EPS projections include company-guided gains/losses and a 30% effective tax rate.

Investment Rationale/Risk

➤ We think Intel has the best competitive position in our semiconductor coverage universe, a solid balance sheet, and strong free cash flows, while carrying lower business and financial risks than most other chipmakers. As demand improves and after Intel ramps up new production lines, which should yield leading-technology chips and cost benefits, we see the company in an even better competitive position, with a larger market share in higher-end segments, and new market opportunities with Atom. With the share price reflecting relative multiples that are at a notable discount to the broader industry and their historical average, we see multiples expanding and the share price appreciating.

➤ Risks to our recommendation and target price include lower-than-expected demand for PCs, accelerated ASP erosion, and less-than-anticipated traction for INTC's latest chips.

➤ Our 12-month target price of $22 is based on our P/E analysis. We apply a P/E multiple of 12X, which reflects our view of INTC's relative growth, return on equity, and risk compared to the chip industry, to our 2011 EPS estimate.

Qualitative Risk Assessment

LOW	MEDIUM	HIGH

Our risk assessment reflects Intel's exposure to the sales cycles of the semiconductor industry and demand trends for personal computers, offset by its large size, long corporate history, and its low debt levels compared to peers.

Quantitative Evaluations

S&P Quality Ranking B+

D	C	B-	B	B+	A-	A	A+

Relative Strength Rank MODERATE

45

LOWEST = 1   HIGHEST = 99

Revenue/Earnings Data

Revenue (Million $)

	1Q	2Q	3Q	4Q	Year
2010	10,299	10,765	11,102	--	--
2009	7,145	8,024	9,389	10,569	35,127
2008	9,673	9,470	10,217	8,226	37,586
2007	8,852	8,680	10,090	10,712	38,334
2006	8,940	8,009	8,739	9,694	35,382
2005	9,434	9,231	9,960	10,201	38,826

Earnings Per Share ($)

2010	0.43	0.51	0.52	E0.54	E1.99
2009	0.12	-0.07	0.33	0.40	0.77
2008	0.25	0.28	0.35	0.04	0.92
2007	0.28	0.22	0.30	0.38	1.18
2006	0.23	0.15	0.22	0.26	0.86
2005	0.35	0.33	0.32	0.40	1.40

Fiscal year ended Dec. 31. Next earnings report expected: Mid January. EPS Estimates based on S&P Operating Earnings; historical GAAP earnings are as reported.

Dividend Data (Dates: mm/dd Payment Date: mm/dd/yy)

Amount ($)	Date Decl.	Ex-Div. Date	Stk. of Record	Payment Date
0.158	01/22	02/03	02/07	03/01/10
0.158	03/19	05/05	05/07	06/01/10
0.158	07/22	08/04	08/07	09/01/10
0.158	09/24	11/03	11/07	12/01/10

Dividends have been paid since 1992. Source: Company reports.

Please read the Required Disclosures and Analyst Certification on the last page of this report.

The McGraw·Hill Companies

Intel Corp

Business Summary October 14, 2010

CORPORATE OVERVIEW. Intel Corp. is the world's largest semiconductor chipmaker based on revenue and unit shipments, and is well known for its dominant market share in microprocessors for personal computers (PCs). The microprocessor is the central processing unit of the computer system, and acts like "the brain" of the computer. The company also sells chipsets, which it refers to as "the nervous system" in a PC or computing device, sending data between the microprocessor and input, display, and storage devices.

The company has three main operating segments: PC Client Group (PCGG), Data Center Group (DCG), and Other Intel Architecture (Other IA).

The PC Client Group (75% of 2009 total sales) makes microprocessors and related chipsets for the notebook, netbook, and desktop segments. This segment also includes motherboards designed for desktop and wireless connectivity products.

The Data Center Group (18%) makes products, including microprocessors, chipsets, motherboards, and wired connectivity devices, that are used in servers, storage, workstations, and other applications that are used in the data center and for cloud computing.

The Other Intel Architecture segments (4%) includes the company's smaller

businesses such as the Embedded and Communications Group, which makes scalable microprocessors and chipsets for various embedded applications, the Ultra-Mobility Group, which offers processors an chipsets for mobile Internet devices, and the Digital Home Group, which produces products for use in various consumer electronics devices.

CORPORATE STRATEGY. Intel's stated mission is to be the pre-eminent supplier of silicon chips and platform solutions to the worldwide digital economy. Shipping over 80% of total microprocessors in 2009, the company is a clear share leader in the worldwide microprocessor market. Although INTC has a sizable lead over competitors, runner-up Advanced Micro Devices (AMD), with about a 20% market share, has effectively increased its presence over the past couple of years. In 2005, when Intel was focusing on creating faster microprocessors, AMD went in a different direction and focused on creating chips that were not only fast but also power efficient, a quality that became increasingly attractive to enterprises with large energy bills and to laptop customers facing short battery lives, among others.

Company Financials Fiscal Year Ended Dec. 31

Per Share Data ($)	2009	2008	2007	2006	2005	2004	2003	2002	2001	2000
Tangible Book Value	6.59	6.18	6.51	5.70	5.46	5.57	5.26	4.74	4.59	4.67
Cash Flow	1.67	1.72	1.98	1.65	2.15	1.91	1.62	1.25	1.13	2.20
Earnings	0.77	0.92	1.18	0.86	1.40	1.16	0.85	0.46	0.19	1.51
S&P Core Earnings	0.94	0.96	1.18	0.77	1.22	0.99	0.83	0.35	0.11	NA
Dividends	0.56	0.55	0.45	0.40	0.32	0.16	0.08	0.08	0.08	0.07
Payout Ratio	73%	60%	38%	47%	23%	14%	9%	17%	42%	4%
Prices:High	21.27	26.34	27.99	26.63	28.84	34.60	34.51	36.78	38.59	75.81
Prices:Low	12.05	12.06	18.75	16.75	21.94	19.64	14.88	12.95	18.96	29.81
P/E Ratio:High	28	29	24	31	21	30	41	80	NM	50
P/E Ratio:Low	16	13	16	19	16	17	18	28	NM	20

Income Statement Analysis (Million $)	2009	2008	2007	2006	2005	2004	2003	2002	2001	2000
Revenue	35,127	37,586	38,334	35,382	38,826	34,209	30,141	26,764	26,539	33,726
Operating Income	13,691	14,283	13,643	10,861	16,685	15,019	13,225	9,746	8,923	15,339
Depreciation	5,052	4,619	4,798	4,654	4,595	4,889	5,070	5,344	6,469	4,835
Interest Expense	1.00	8.00	15.0	1,202	19.0	50.0	62.0	84.0	56.0	35.0
Pretax Income	5,704	7,686	9,166	7,068	12,610	10,417	7,442	4,204	2,183	15,141
Effective Tax Rate	23.4%	31.2%	23.9%	28.6%	31.3%	27.8%	24.2%	25.9%	40.9%	30.4%
Net Income	4,369	5,292	6,976	5,044	8,664	7,516	5,641	3,117	1,291	10,535
S&P Core Earnings	5,325	5,521	6,978	4,518	7,555	6,374	5,467	2,332	740	NA

Balance Sheet & Other Financial Data (Million $)	2009	2008	2007	2006	2005	2004	2003	2002	2001	2000
Cash	13,920	11,843	15,363	6,598	7,324	8,407	7,971	7,404	7,970	2,976
Current Assets	21,157	19,871	23,885	18,280	21,194	24,058	22,882	18,925	17,633	21,150
Total Assets	53,095	50,715	55,651	48,368	48,314	48,143	47,143	44,224	44,395	47,945
Current Liabilities	7,591	7,818	8,571	8,514	9,234	8,006	6,879	6,595	6,570	8,650
Long Term Debt	2,049	1,886	1,980	1,848	2,106	703	936	929	1,050	707
Common Equity	41,704	39,088	42,762	36,752	36,182	38,579	37,846	35,468	35,830	37,322
Total Capital	43,753	41,020	45,153	38,865	38,991	40,137	40,264	37,629	37,825	39,295
Capital Expenditures	4,515	5,197	5,000	5,779	5,818	3,843	3,656	4,703	7,309	6,674
Cash Flow	9,421	9,911	11,774	9,698	13,259	12,405	10,711	8,461	7,760	15,370
Current Ratio	2.8	2.5	2.8	2.1	2.3	3.0	3.3	2.9	2.7	2.4
% Long Term Debt of Capitalization	4.7	4.6	4.4	4.8	5.4	1.8	2.3	2.5	2.8	1.8
% Net Income of Revenue	12.4	14.1	18.2	14.3	22.3	22.0	18.7	11.6	4.9	31.2
% Return on Assets	8.4	10.0	13.4	10.4	18.0	15.8	12.3	7.0	2.8	23.0
% Return on Equity	10.8	12.9	17.6	13.8	23.2	19.7	15.4	8.7	3.5	30.1

Data as orig reptd.; bef. results of disc opers/spec. items. Per share data adj. for stk. divs.; EPS diluted. E-Estimated. NA-Not Available. NM-Not Meaningful. NR-Not Ranked. UR-Under Review.

Office: 2200 Mission College Boulevard, Santa Clara, CA 95054-1549.
Telephone: 408-765-8080.
Website: http://www.intc.com
Chrmn: J.E. Shaw

Pres & CEO: P.S. Otellini
EVP & Chief Admin Officer: A. Bryant
SVP, CFO & Chief Acctg Officer: S.J. Smith
SVP & General Counsel: A.D. Melamed

Investor Contact: R. Gallegos (408-765-5374)
Board Members: C. Barshefsky, S. Decker, J. J. Donahoe, R. E. Hundt, P. S. Otellini, J. Plummer, D. S. Pottruck, J. E. Shaw, F. D. Yeary, D. B. Yoffie

Founded: 1968
Domicile: Delaware
Employees: 79,800

IntercontinentalExchange Inc

STANDARD &POOR'S

S&P Recommendation **BUY** ★★★★☆	Price $116.84 (as of Oct 22, 2010)	12-Mo. Target Price $134.00	Investment Style Large-Cap Growth

GICS Sector Financials
Sub-Industry Specialized Finance

Summary ICE is a fully electronic marketplace that offers exchange-based and over-the-counter trading of a variety of energy and soft commodity products.

Key Stock Statistics (Source S&P, Vickers, company reports)

52-Wk Range	$129.53–92.18	S&P Oper. EPS 2010**E**	5.89	Market Capitalization(B)	$8.651	Beta	1.28
Trailing 12-Month EPS	$5.03	S&P Oper. EPS 2011**E**	6.28	Yield (%)	Nil	S&P 3-Yr. Proj. EPS CAGR(%)	15
Trailing 12-Month P/E	23.2	P/E on S&P Oper. EPS 2010**E**	19.8	Dividend Rate/Share	Nil	S&P Credit Rating	NA
$10K Invested 5 Yrs Ago	NA	Common Shares Outstg. (M)	74.0	Institutional Ownership (%)	90		

Price Performance

30-Week Mov. Avg. · · · 10-Week Mov. Avg. - - **GAAP Earnings vs. Previous Year**   Volume Above Avg. ▌▌▌ STARS
12-Mo. Target Price — Relative Strength — ▲ Up ▼ Down ► No Change   Below Avg. ▌▌▌ ★

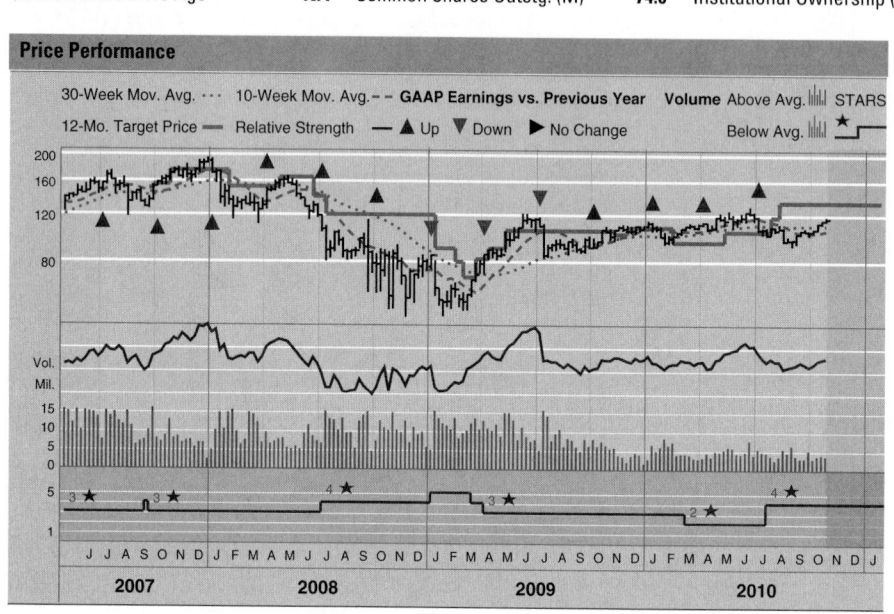

Options: ASE, CBOE, P, Ph

Analysis prepared by **Rafay Khalid, CFA** on August 27, 2010, when the stock traded at **$ 96.72**.

Highlights

► We forecast revenue growth of 18% in 2010 and 7% in 2011. We think trading volumes in both years will improve versus 2009, but remain below historical levels. In 2010, we foresee volume growth, driven by strength in the popular U.K.-based oil futures contracts and the U.S. derivatives business. We also see additional revenues from the new credit default swap clearing business and the recently acquired Climate Exchange Plc.

► We project that total expenses as a percentage of sales will decline to 40.1% in 2010 and 39.2% in 2011, reflecting our outlook for tighter control over expenses, especially selling, general, and administrative expense. As a result, we forecast operating margins will increase to 59.9% in 2010 and 60.8% in 2011, from 51.5% in 2009.

► We estimate operating EPS of $5.89 this year and see $6.28 in 2011, excluding one-time items. This compares to operating EPS of $4.50 in 2009, also excluding one-time items. We assume a 34% effective tax rate in our 2010 and 2011 EPS forecasts.

Investment Rationale/Risk

► In the short term, we believe ICE has an advantage over competitors in the credit default swap clearing business, as we see its platform generating higher trading volumes. We think the recently acquired Climate Exchange will be accretive to EPS in 2011, on our outlook for leveraging the company's existing resources. While we see a recovery in trading volumes during 2010 and 2011, we believe they will remain below historical levels.

► Risks to our recommendation and target price include greater-than-expected competition in the credit default swap clearing business, a significant decline in trading volumes, regulation of position limits on derivatives contracts, and a slowdown in the macroeconomic environment.

► Our 12-month target price of $134 is based on a historical average multiple of 21.4X our 2011 EPS projection. We believe the historical average is warranted as we forecast a gradual recovery in trading volumes.

Qualitative Risk Assessment

LOW	MEDIUM	**HIGH**

Our risk assessment reflects the volatility of energy product trading volumes, recent acquisition activity in the sector, and a changing regulatory environment.

Quantitative Evaluations

S&P Quality Ranking   NR

D	C	B-	B	B+	A-	A	A+

Relative Strength Rank   STRONG

76

LOWEST = 1   HIGHEST = 99

Revenue/Earnings Data

Revenue (Million $)

	1Q	2Q	3Q	4Q	Year
2010	281.6	296.2	--	--	--
2009	231.6	250.4	256.3	256.6	994.8
2008	207.2	197.2	201.4	207.3	813.1
2007	126.6	136.7	151.7	159.3	574.3
2006	73.59	73.59	94.66	95.26	313.8
2005	31.83	37.53	45.24	41.26	155.9

Earnings Per Share ($)

	1Q	2Q	3Q	4Q	Year
2010	1.36	1.36	E1.51	E1.51	E5.89
2009	0.98	0.97	1.18	1.13	4.27
2008	1.29	1.19	1.04	0.67	4.17
2007	0.80	0.75	0.93	0.90	3.39
2006	0.33	0.52	0.73	0.81	2.40
2005	0.17	-0.13	0.05	-0.48	0.39

Fiscal year ended Dec. 31. Next earnings report expected: Early November. EPS Estimates based on S&P Operating Earnings; historical GAAP earnings are as reported.

Dividend Data

No cash dividends have been paid.

The McGraw-Hill Companies

IntercontinentalExchange Inc

STANDARD &POOR'S

Business Summary August 27, 2010

CORPORATE OVERVIEW. IntercontinentalExchange, Inc. operates a fully electronic marketplace offering exchange-based and over-the-counter (OTC) trading of a variety of energy products, and is the leading global exchange for soft commodities. The company's primary products include futures contracts for Brent crude oil and West Texas Intermediate crude oil, OTC trading of Henry Hub natural gas contracts, and various soft commodity futures. ICE provides trading for financial settlement and contracts for physical delivery of the underlying commodity. In addition, the company provides clearing services for credit default swaps.

ICE was formed in May 2000 to provide a platform for OTC energy trading. In June 2001, the company acquired the International Petroleum Exchange (IPE), which was mainly a floor-based futures exchange. In early 2002, the company introduced the industry's first cleared OTC contract through its partnership with LCH.Clearnet. In April 2005, ICE closed the IPE trading floor and moved to an entirely electronic marketplace. In January 2007, ICE acquired the New York Board of Trade (NYBOT) for approximately $1.1 billion. NYBOT, which has been renamed ICE Futures U.S., is a leading soft commodity exchange for products such as sugar, coffee, cocoa, orange juice, pulp and cotton, as well as several financial products.

In 2009, ICE derived approximately 89% of its revenue from transaction fees associated with trading its products on its exchange and OTC platforms. ICE generates a majority of its trading commissions from a relatively small amount of crude, gas oil, and North American power futures and OTC contracts. The remaining 11% of 2009 revenues is dominated by the market data business. This business provides various data products covering the company's energy futures, OTC markets, agricultural commodities, equity indexes, and currencies.

COMPETITIVE LANDSCAPE. ICE's principal competitor in the energy market is the New York Mercantile Exchange (NYMEX). In August 2008, NYMEX merged with the Chicago Mercantile Exchange. ICE also faces global competition from a number of natural gas and power exchanges and OTC brokers. We believe competition is based on a number of factors, including the depth and liquidity of markets, transaction costs, reliability, and clearing and settlement support.

Company Financials Fiscal Year Ended Dec. 31

Per Share Data ($)	2009	2008	2007	2006	2005	2004	2003	2002	2001	2000
Tangible Book Value	3.15	NM	NM	6.42	2.82	2.56	NA	NA	NA	NA
Cash Flow	5.50	5.03	3.85	2.63	1.04	0.73	0.72	0.89	NA	NA
Earnings	4.27	4.17	3.39	2.40	0.39	0.41	0.37	0.37	NA	NA
S&P Core Earnings	4.26	4.31	3.30	2.39	0.82	0.32	0.18	NA	NA	NA
Dividends	Nil	Nil	Nil	Nil	Nil	NA	NA	NA	NA	NA
Payout Ratio	Nil	Nil	Nil	Nil	Nil	NA	NA	NA	NA	NA
Prices:High	121.93	193.87	194.92	113.85	44.21	NA	NA	NA	NA	NA
Prices:Low	50.10	49.69	108.15	36.00	26.00	NA	NA	NA	NA	NA
P/E Ratio:High	29	46	57	47	NM	NA	NA	NA	NA	NA
P/E Ratio:Low	12	12	32	15	NM	NA	NA	NA	NA	NA

Income Statement Analysis (Million $)										
Revenue	995	813	574	314	156	108	93.7	125	NA	NA
Operating Income	617	556	397	218	91.1	49.4	38.3	65.3	NA	NA
Depreciation	91.4	62.3	32.7	13.7	15.1	17.0	19.3	14.4	NA	NA
Interest Expense	22.9	19.6	18.6	0.23	0.61	0.14	0.08	0.40	NA	NA
Pretax Income	494	474	358	213	60.0	33.7	19.9	25.4	NA	NA
Effective Tax Rate	36.4%	36.4%	32.9%	32.6%	32.6%	34.7%	32.7%	33.8%	NA	NA
Net Income	316	301	241	143	40.4	21.9	13.4	34.7	NA	NA
S&P Core Earnings	315	311	234	143	43.8	17.0	9.81	NA	NA	NA

Balance Sheet & Other Financial Data (Million $)										
Cash	554	287	280	204	32.6	89.2	56.9	NA	NA	NA
Current Assets	19,460	12,553	1,142	341	164	100	106	NA	NA	NA
Total Assets	21,885	14,960	2,796	493	266	208	215	NA	NA	NA
Current Liabilities	18,968	12,312	911	37.9	26.4	34.4	17.9	NA	NA	NA
Long Term Debt	209	336	184	Nil	Nil	Nil	NA	NA	NA	NA
Common Equity	2,400	2,006	1,477	454	233	221	186	NA	NA	NA
Total Capital	2,741	2,544	1,770	454	238	221	186	NA	NA	NA
Capital Expenditures	24.4	30.5	43.3	12.4	8.61	1.70	1.61	14.8	NA	NA
Cash Flow	407	363	273	157	55.5	38.9	39.3	49.1	NA	NA
Current Ratio	1.0	1.0	1.3	9.0	6.2	2.9	5.9	NA	NA	NA
% Long Term Debt of Capitalization	7.6	13.2	10.4	Nil	Nil	Nil	Nil	Nil	NA	NA
% Net Income of Revenue	31.8	37.0	41.9	45.5	25.9	20.3	14.3	27.8	NA	NA
% Return on Assets	1.7	3.4	14.6	37.7	NM	10.4	NA	NA	NA	NA
% Return on Equity	14.3	17.3	24.9	41.6	NM	13.1	NA	NA	NA	NA

Data as orig reptd.; bef. results of disc opers/spec. items. Per share data adj. for stk. divs.; EPS diluted. E-Estimated. NA-Not Available. NM-Not Meaningful. NR-Not Ranked. UR-Under Review.

Office: 2100 RiverEdge Parkway, Atlanta, GA 30328.
Telephone: 770-857-4700.
Email: ir@theice.com
Website: http://www.theice.com

Chrmn & CEO: J.C. Sprecher
Pres & COO: C.A. Vice
SVP, CFO & Chief Acctg Officer: S.A. Hill
SVP & CTO: E.D. Marcial

SVP, Secy & General Counsel: J.H. Short
Investor Contact: K. Loeffler (770-857-4726)
Board Members: C. R. Crisp, J. Forneri, F. W. Hatfield, T. F. Martell, C. C. McCarthy, R. Reid, F. V. Salerno, F. W. Schneider, J. C. Sprecher, J. Sprieser, V. Tese

Founded: 2000
Domicile: Delaware
Employees: 826

International Business Machines Corp

STANDARD &POOR'S

S&P Recommendation BUY ★★★★☆

Price	12-Mo. Target Price	Investment Style
$139.67 (as of Oct 22, 2010)	$160.00	Large-Cap Growth

GICS Sector Information Technology
Sub-Industry IT Consulting & Other Services

Summary IBM's global capabilities include information technology services, software, computer hardware equipment, fundamental research, and related financing.

Key Stock Statistics (Source S&P, Vickers, company reports)

52-Wk Range	$143.03–116.00	S&P Oper. EPS 2010E	11.45	Market Capitalization(B)	$176.163	Beta	0.72
Trailing 12-Month EPS	$11.00	S&P Oper. EPS 2011E	12.60	Yield (%)	1.86	S&P 3-Yr. Proj. EPS CAGR(%)	12
Trailing 12-Month P/E	12.7	P/E on S&P Oper. EPS 2010E	12.2	Dividend Rate/Share	$2.60	S&P Credit Rating	A+
$10K Invested 5 Yrs Ago	$18,185	Common Shares Outstg. (M)	1,261.3	Institutional Ownership (%)	59		

Price Performance

30-Week Mov. Avg. · · · 10-Week Mov. Avg. – – 12-Mo. Target Price — Relative Strength — **GAAP Earnings vs. Previous Year** ▲ Up ▼ Down ► No Change Volume Above Avg. STARS Below Avg.

Options: ASE, CBOE, P, Ph

Analysis prepared by **Thomas W. Smith, CFA** on October 19, 2010, when the stock traded at **$138.24**.

Highlights

▶ We expect revenues to rise about 4.7% this year and 4.8% in 2011, reflecting an improving global economy. Despite a slowing pace for new service signings in the third quarter, signings for the fourth quarter are off to a good start. The services order backlog stood at $134 billion at the end of September 2010, providing some earnings visibility, in our opinion. We see growth in IBM's Software segment, partly reflecting acquisitions. New server products launched in September should boost Systems and Technology segment sales into 2011.

▶ We look for gross margins to widen to 46.0% in 2010 and to 46.6% in 2011, from 45.7% in 2009, on ongoing cost reduction efforts and an improved sales mix. We think pretax margins will expand as well. Effective tax rates should benefit from more international business.

▶ We estimate EPS of $11.45 for 2010 and $12.60 for 2011. The company spent about $3.7 billion on share repurchases in the third quarter of 2010, and we expect share buybacks to bolster EPS going forward. A dividend yield recently near 2% adds appeal.

Investment Rationale/Risk

▶ IBM's results should benefit from relatively strong revenue growth in emerging markets and improved profitability in more mature markets, by our analysis. We see a gradual widening of margins reflecting cost containment and more software in the product mix. We expect per share results to benefit from lower effective tax rates as business shifts overseas, and from share buybacks.

▶ Risks to our recommendation and target price include pricing pressure and other competitive risks, the potential for product transitions to go less smoothly than we project, and the potential for antitrust and other lawsuits to hamper results.

▶ Our 12-month target price of $160 reflects a target P/E of 14X, which is toward the middle of the recent five-year historical range for IBM, applied to our 2010 EPS estimate of $11.45. Our target P/E is lower than the P/E for Information Technology Sector companies in the S&P 500 Index based on 2010 earnings estimates. We view the stock's valuation as attractive, given IBM's economies of scale and relatively steady earnings performance.

Qualitative Risk Assessment

LOW	MEDIUM	HIGH

Our risk assessment reflects what we view as IBM's competitively positioned solutions offerings, global market presence, and significant economies of scale, offset by what we see as an intensely competitive pricing environment.

Quantitative Evaluations

S&P Quality Ranking A

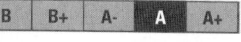

D	C	B-	B	B+	A-	A	A+

Relative Strength Rank MODERATE

62

LOWEST = 1   HIGHEST = 99

Revenue/Earnings Data

Revenue (Million $)

	1Q	2Q	3Q	4Q	Year
2010	25,857	23,724	24,272	--	--
2009	21,711	23,250	23,566	27,230	95,758
2008	24,502	26,820	25,302	27,006	103,630
2007	22,029	23,772	24,119	28,866	98,786
2006	20,659	21,890	22,617	26,257	91,424
2005	22,908	22,270	21,529	24,427	91,134

Earnings Per Share ($)

2010	1.97	2.61	2.82	E4.05	E11.45
2009	1.70	2.32	2.40	3.59	10.01
2008	1.65	1.98	2.05	3.28	8.93
2007	1.21	1.55	1.68	2.80	7.18
2006	1.08	1.30	1.45	2.30	6.06
2005	0.85	1.14	0.94	2.01	4.91

Fiscal year ended Dec. 31. Next earnings report expected: Mid January. EPS Estimates based on S&P Operating Earnings; historical GAAP earnings are as reported.

Dividend Data (Dates: mm/dd Payment Date: mm/dd/yy)

Amount ($)	Date Decl.	Ex-Div. Date	Stk. of Record	Payment Date
0.550	10/27	11/06	11/10	12/10/09
0.550	01/26	02/08	02/10	03/10/10
0.650	04/27	05/06	05/10	06/10/10
0.650	07/27	08/06	08/10	09/10/10

Dividends have been paid since 1916. Source: Company reports.

Please read the Required Disclosures and Analyst Certification on the last page of this report.

The McGraw·Hill Companies

International Business Machines Corp

STANDARD &POOR'S

Business Summary October 19, 2010

CORPORATE OVERVIEW. With a corporate history dating back to 1911, International Business Machines has grown to be a major contributor to each major category that comprises the total information technology market: hardware, software, and services. The company is a leading server vendor, among the largest software vendors (behind Microsoft Corp.), and has the largest global services organization.

The company strives for innovation as a means of product differentiation, and had a research and development budget of $5.8 billion in 2009, down from $6.3 billion in 2008, which represents about 6.1% of revenue for each year. IBM reports being awarded over 4,900 patents in 2009, more than any other company.

The company operates in over 170 countries. The global scope of operations is reflected in the mix of revenue sources in 2009, with the Americas representing about 42%, EMEA 34%, Asia Pacific 22%, and an OEM category 2%. Regional revenue performance was strongest in Asia Pacific in 2009. The company's revenue from the so-called BRIC countries (Brazil, Russia, India and China) grew 1% in 2009.

CORPORATE STRATEGY. IBM has evolved from being a computer hardware vendor to a systems, services and software company that focuses on integrated solutions. While computer hardware (included in the Systems and Technology segment) accounted for about 17% of sales in 2009 (19% of sales in 2008), IBM has emphasized -- through acquisitions and investments -- services and software. These areas serving adjacent markets to hardware have gained momentum as IBM leverages its ability to offer total solutions to customers. IBM's focus on higher value added segments such as services, at 58% of 2009 sales (57% of 2008 sales), and software 23% (21%) resulted in these areas together representing almost 81% of revenue in 2009. Global financing represented approximately 2% (3%) of 2009 revenues, and is primarily used to leverage IBM's financial structuring and portfolio management, and to expand the customer base.

Company Financials Fiscal Year Ended Dec. 31

Per Share Data ($)	2009	2008	2007	2006	2005	2004	2003	2002	2001	2000
Tangible Book Value	NM	NM	8.72	8.93	13.97	11.86	12.36	10.84	12.96	11.08
Cash Flow	13.73	12.49	10.22	9.39	8.10	7.82	7.01	5.61	7.08	6.95
Earnings	10.01	8.93	7.18	6.06	4.91	4.94	4.34	3.07	4.35	4.44
S&P Core Earnings	9.43	6.04	6.94	5.88	3.93	4.06	3.00	0.08	1.33	NA
Dividends	2.15	1.90	1.50	1.10	0.78	0.70	0.63	0.59	0.55	0.51
Payout Ratio	21%	21%	21%	18%	16%	14%	15%	19%	13%	11%
Prices:High	132.85	130.93	121.46	97.88	99.10	100.43	94.54	126.39	124.70	134.94
Prices:Low	81.76	69.50	88.77	72.73	71.85	90.82	73.17	54.01	83.75	80.06
P/E Ratio:High	13	15	17	16	20	20	22	41	29	30
P/E Ratio:Low	8	8	12	12	15	18	17	18	19	18

Income Statement Analysis (Million $)

	2009	2008	2007	2006	2005	2004	2003	2002	2001	2000
Revenue	95,757	103,630	98,786	91,424	91,134	96,293	89,131	81,186	85,866	88,396
Operating Income	23,660	21,680	18,765	16,912	14,564	15,890	14,790	11,175	14,115	16,147
Depreciation	4,994	4,930	4,405	4,983	5,188	4,915	4,701	4,379	4,820	4,513
Interest Expense	402	1,477	1,431	278	220	139	145	145	238	717
Pretax Income	18,138	16,715	14,489	13,317	12,226	12,028	10,874	7,524	10,953	11,534
Effective Tax Rate	26.0%	26.2%	28.1%	29.3%	34.6%	29.8%	30.0%	29.1%	29.5%	29.8%
Net Income	13,425	12,334	10,418	9,416	7,994	8,448	7,613	5,334	7,723	8,093
S&P Core Earnings	12,648	8,340	10,072	9,116	6,395	6,923	5,270	111	2,302	NA

Balance Sheet & Other Financial Data (Million $)

	2009	2008	2007	2006	2005	2004	2003	2002	2001	2000
Cash	13,974	12,907	16,146	10,656	13,686	10,570	7,647	5,975	6,393	3,722
Current Assets	48,935	49,004	53,177	44,660	45,661	46,970	44,998	41,652	42,461	43,880
Total Assets	109,022	109,524	120,431	103,234	105,748	109,183	104,457	96,484	88,313	88,349
Current Liabilities	36,002	42,435	44,310	40,091	35,152	39,798	37,900	34,550	35,119	36,406
Long Term Debt	21,932	22,689	23,039	13,780	15,425	14,828	16,986	19,986	15,963	18,371
Common Equity	22,637	13,465	28,470	28,506	33,098	29,747	27,864	22,782	23,614	20,624
Total Capital	44,687	45,096	51,509	42,286	48,523	44,575	44,850	42,768	39,577	38,995
Capital Expenditures	3,447	4,171	4,630	4,362	3,842	4,368	4,393	4,753	5,660	5,616
Cash Flow	18,419	17,264	14,823	14,399	13,182	13,363	12,314	9,713	12,533	12,586
Current Ratio	1.4	1.2	1.2	1.1	1.3	1.2	1.2	1.2	1.2	1.2
% Long Term Debt of Capitalization	49.1	71.6	44.7	32.6	31.7	33.3	37.9	46.7	40.3	47.1
% Net Income of Revenue	14.0	11.9	10.6	10.3	8.8	8.8	8.5	6.6	9.0	9.2
% Return on Assets	12.3	10.7	9.3	9.0	7.4	7.9	7.6	5.7	8.7	9.2
% Return on Equity	74.4	58.8	36.6	30.6	24.7	29.3	30.1	23.1	35.1	39.7

Data as orig reptd.; bef. results of disc opers/spec. items. Per share data adj. for stk. divs.; EPS diluted. E-Estimated. NA-Not Available. NM-Not Meaningful. NR-Not Ranked. UR-Under Review.

Office: 1 New Orchard Road, Armonk, NY 10504-1722.
Telephone: 914-499-1900.
Website: http://www.ibm.com
Chrmn, Pres & CEO: S.J. Palmisano

SVP & CFO: M. Loughridge
SVP & General Counsel: R.C. Weber
CTO: R.C. Adkins
Treas: M.J. Schroeter

Investor Contact: T.S. Shaughnessy (914-499-1900)
Board Members: A. J. Belda, C. P. Black, W. R. Brody, K. I. Chenault, M. L. Eskew, S. A. Jackson, A. N. Liveris, W. J. McNerney, Jr., T. Nishimuro, J. W. Owens, S. J. Palmisano, J. E. Spero, S. Taurel, L. H. Zambrano

Founded: 1910
Domicile: New York
Employees: 399,409

The **McGraw-Hill** Companies

International Flavors & Fragrances Inc.

STANDARD & POOR'S

S&P Recommendation **BUY** ★★★★☆	Price $49.80 (as of Oct 22, 2010)	12-Mo. Target Price $56.00	Investment Style Large-Cap Growth

GICS Sector Materials
Sub-Industry Specialty Chemicals

Summary This leading producer of flavors and fragrances, used in a wide variety of consumer goods, derives over 70% of annual sales from operations outside the U.S.

Key Stock Statistics (Source S&P, Vickers, company reports)

52-Wk Range	$51.77–37.74	S&P Oper. EPS 2010**E**	3.25	Market Capitalization(B)	$3.977	Beta	0.92
Trailing 12-Month EPS	$2.91	S&P Oper. EPS 2011**E**	3.50	Yield (%)	2.17	S&P 3-Yr. Proj. EPS CAGR(%)	8
Trailing 12-Month P/E	17.1	P/E on S&P Oper. EPS 2010**E**	15.3	Dividend Rate/Share	$1.08	S&P Credit Rating	BBB
$10K Invested 5 Yrs Ago	$16,855	Common Shares Outstg. (M)	79.9	Institutional Ownership (%)	80		

Price Performance

- 30-Week Mov. Avg.
- 10-Week Mov. Avg.
- **GAAP Earnings vs. Previous Year**
- Volume Above Avg.
- STARS
- 12-Mo. Target Price
- Relative Strength
- ▲ Up ▼ Down ► No Change
- Below Avg.

Options: CBOE

Analysis prepared by **Richard O'Reilly, CFA** on August 09, 2010, when the stock traded at **$ 47.62**.

Highlights

➤ We expect sales in 2010 to increase by about 11%, aided by modest impact from favorable currency exchange rates in the first half, following a 3% decline in 2009, which included a 3% impact from unfavorable exchange rates and slowdowns in domestic and European consumer markets earlier in the year. Sales in local currency rose 15% in the first half of 2010, including strong gains for fine fragrances and ingredients, and some benefit from customer restocking. We believe IFF continues to gain share with major customers in 2010, based on a high win rate of new business.

➤ We forecast a gross margin of about 41.5% in 2010, aided by a decline in raw material and freight costs, up from 40.2% in 2009, which reflected lower sales of high-margin fine fragrances and higher input costs.

➤ We expect a decline in interest expense in 2010, on lower debt and in the absence of a $4 million charge in the 2009 first quarter for the settlement of an interest rate swap. We project a 27.5% effective tax rate for 2010, down from 2009. Reported EPS for 2009 included $0.23 of special and restructuring charges.

Investment Rationale/Risk

➤ We have a buy opinion on the shares partly based on valuation. We expect the company to be helped in 2010 by a high win rate of new business, especially in flavors, and some benefit of customer restocking, although currency exchange rates should turn into a headwind in the second half. We believe IFF has strong cash flows and ample liquidity.

➤ Risks to our recommendation and target price include increased economic and political uncertainties in global markets, greater currency fluctuations, an inability to maintain close relationships with customers, lack of customers' success in new product launches, and unexpected increases in raw material costs.

➤ The shares, with a dividend yield of about 2.3%, recently traded at about 14.4X our 2010 EPS estimate, a discount to industry peers. We think the stock will outperform the S&P 500 over the next 12 months, reflecting what we see as a favorable EPS outlook for 2010 and 2011. Assuming a P/E multiple of 16X, similar to peers, our 12-month target price is $56. The dividend was recently raised 8%.

Qualitative Risk Assessment

LOW	MEDIUM	HIGH

Our risk assessment reflects our view of the stable nature of the company's businesses and end markets, and its leadership product positions, offset by a somewhat concentrated customer base.

Quantitative Evaluations

S&P Quality Ranking A-

D	C	B-	B	B+	A-	A	A+

Relative Strength Rank MODERATE

57

LOWEST = 1   HIGHEST = 99

Revenue/Earnings Data

Revenue (Million $)

	1Q	2Q	3Q	4Q	Year
2010	653.9	665.8	--	--	--
2009	599.6	568.3	612.6	585.6	2,326
2008	596.6	636.1	617.5	539.1	2,389
2007	566.1	573.7	583.3	553.5	2,277
2006	511.4	530.5	539.1	514.3	2,095
2005	523.1	515.6	493.1	461.7	1,993

Earnings Per Share ($)

2010	0.80	0.84	E0.81	E0.74	E3.25
2009	0.60	0.60	0.66	0.59	2.46
2008	0.69	0.83	0.73	0.62	2.87
2007	0.69	0.87	0.67	0.58	2.82
2006	0.58	0.67	0.70	0.53	2.48
2005	0.55	0.60	0.72	0.16	2.04

Fiscal year ended Dec. 31. Next earnings report expected: Early November. EPS Estimates based on S&P Operating Earnings; historical GAAP earnings are as reported.

Dividend Data (Dates: mm/dd Payment Date: mm/dd/yy)

Amount ($)	Date Decl.	Ex-Div. Date	Stk. of Record	Payment Date
0.250	12/08	12/17	12/21	01/06/10
0.250	03/09	03/22	03/24	04/07/10
0.250	04/27	06/21	06/23	07/07/10
0.270	07/27	09/20	09/22	10/06/10

Dividends have been paid since 1956. Source: Company reports.

Please read the Required Disclosures and Analyst Certification on the last page of this report.

International Flavors & Fragrances Inc.

STANDARD
&POOR'S

Business Summary August 09, 2010

CORPORATE OVERVIEW. International Flavors & Fragrances, founded in 1909, is a leading global maker of products used by other manufacturers to enhance the aromas and tastes of consumer products.

IFF receives more than 70% of its sales outside the U.S. In 2009, North America contributed 26% of sales; Europe 35%; Latin America 15%; and Asia-Pacific 24%.

Fragrance products accounted for 54% of sales and 45% of operating profits in 2009. Fragrances are used in the manufacture of soaps, detergents, cosmetic creams, lotions and powders, lipsticks, after shave lotions, deodorants, hair preparations, air fresheners, perfumes and colognes and other consumer products. Most major U.S. companies in these industries are IFF customers. Cosmetics (including perfumes and toiletries) and household products (soaps and detergents) are the two largest customer groups.

Flavor products account for IFF's remaining sales and profits. Flavors are sold principally to the food, beverage and other industries for use in consumer products such as soft drinks, candies, cake mixes, desserts, prepared foods,

dietary foods, dairy products, drink powders, pharmaceuticals, oral care products, alcoholic beverages and tobacco. Two of the largest customers for flavor products are major U.S. producers of prepared foods and beverages.

By category, 46% of sales in 2009 were from flavor compounds, 25% functional fragrances (for personal care and household products, including soaps, detergents, and fabric care), 17% fine fragrances and beauty care (perfumes, colognes, hair care and toiletries), and 12% ingredients.

The company uses both synthetic and natural ingredients in its compounds. IFF manufactures most of the synthetic ingredients, of which a substantial portion (45% in 2008) is sold to others. It has had a consistent commitment to R&D spending, spending 8% to 9% of annual revenues on research and development activities for each of the three years through 2009. R&D is conducted in 33 laboratories in 26 countries.

Company Financials Fiscal Year Ended Dec. 31

Per Share Data ($)	2009	2008	2007	2006	2005	2004	2003	2002	2001	2000
Tangible Book Value	0.21	NM	NM	1.78	1.54	1.28	NM	NM	NM	NM
Cash Flow	3.46	3.82	3.77	3.46	3.07	3.01	2.77	2.72	2.47	1.90
Earnings	2.46	2.87	2.82	2.48	2.04	2.05	1.83	1.84	1.20	1.22
S&P Core Earnings	2.45	2.29	2.75	2.35	2.04	1.82	1.70	1.37	0.70	NA
Dividends	1.00	0.96	0.88	0.77	0.73	0.69	0.63	0.60	0.60	1.52
Payout Ratio	41%	33%	31%	31%	36%	33%	34%	33%	50%	125%
Prices:High	42.58	48.01	54.75	49.88	42.90	43.20	36.61	37.45	31.69	37.94
Prices:Low	24.96	24.72	45.71	32.53	31.19	32.77	29.18	26.05	19.75	14.69
P/E Ratio:High	17	17	19	20	21	21	20	20	26	31
P/E Ratio:Low	10	9	16	13	15	16	16	14	16	12

Income Statement Analysis (Million $)										
Revenue	2,326	2,389	2,277	2,095	1,993	2,034	1,902	1,809	1,844	1,463
Operating Income	443	452	452	421	382	433	415	396	409	322
Depreciation	78.5	76.0	82.8	89.7	91.9	91.0	86.7	84.5	123	69.3
Interest Expense	61.8	74.0	41.5	25.5	24.0	24.0	28.5	37.0	70.4	25.1
Pretax Income	277	281	329	313	246	281	252	266	188	184
Effective Tax Rate	29.3%	18.1%	24.8%	27.7%	21.6%	30.2%	31.5%	34.0%	38.2%	33.2%
Net Income	196	230	247	227	193	196	173	176	116	123
S&P Core Earnings	195	183	241	214	193	174	161	131	68.5	NA

Balance Sheet & Other Financial Data (Million $)										
Cash	80.1	179	152	115	273	32.6	12.1	14.9	48.5	129
Current Assets	1,128	1,161	1,190	1,080	1,191	961	903	867	896	1,019
Total Assets	2,645	2,762	2,727	2,479	2,638	2,363	2,307	2,233	2,268	2,489
Current Liabilities	484	451	539	447	1,203	400	526	359	560	1,179
Long Term Debt	935	1,154	1,060	791	131	669	690	1,007	939	417
Common Equity	772	573	617	873	915	910	743	575	524	631
Total Capital	1,707	1,727	1,677	1,665	1,047	1,579	1,433	1,582	1,508	1,152
Capital Expenditures	66.8	85.4	65.6	58.3	93.4	70.6	6.40	81.8	52.0	60.7
Cash Flow	274	306	330	316	285	287	259	260	239	192
Current Ratio	2.3	2.6	2.2	2.4	1.0	2.4	1.7	2.4	1.6	0.9
% Long Term Debt of Capitalization	54.8	66.8	63.2	47.5	12.5	42.4	48.2	63.7	62.3	36.2
% Net Income of Revenue	8.4	9.6	10.9	10.8	9.7	9.6	9.1	9.7	6.3	8.4
% Return on Assets	7.3	8.4	9.1	8.9	7.7	8.4	7.6	7.8	4.9	6.3
% Return on Equity	29.1	38.6	33.2	26.0	21.1	23.7	26.2	32.0	20.1	16.5

Data as orig reptd.; bef. results of disc opers/spec. items. Per share data adj. for stk. divs.; EPS diluted. E-Estimated. NA-Not Available. NM-Not Meaningful. NR-Not Ranked. UR-Under Review.

Office: 521 West 57th Street, New York, NY 10019-2960.
Telephone: 212-765-5500.
Email: investor.relations@iff.com
Website: http://www.iff.com

Chrmn & CEO: D.D. Tough
Pres: B.M. Tansky
EVP & CFO: K.C. Berryman
SVP, Secy & General Counsel: D.M. Meany

Treas: C.D. Weller
Investor Contact: M. DeVeau (212-708-7164)
Board Members: M. H. Adame, M. V. Bottoli, L. B. Buck, J. M. Cook, R. W. Ferguson, Jr., P. A. Georgescu, A. A. Herzan, H. W. Howell, Jr., K. M. Hudson, A. C. Martinez, D. D. Tough

Founded: 1909
Domicile: New York
Employees: 5,400

International Game Technology

STANDARD &POOR'S

S&P Recommendation STRONG SELL ★☆☆☆☆	**Price** $14.81 (as of Oct 22, 2010)	**12-Mo. Target Price** $13.00	**Investment Style** Large-Cap Growth

GICS Sector Consumer Discretionary
Sub-Industry Casinos & Gaming

Summary This company is a leading maker of gaming machines and proprietary software systems for gaming machine networks.

Key Stock Statistics (Source S&P, Vickers, company reports)

52-Wk Range	$21.94– 13.65	S&P Oper. EPS 2010**E**	0.85	Market Capitalization(B)	$4.415	Beta	1.60
Trailing 12-Month EPS	$0.54	S&P Oper. EPS 2011**E**	0.93	Yield (%)	1.62	S&P 3-Yr. Proj. EPS CAGR(%)	5
Trailing 12-Month P/E	27.4	P/E on S&P Oper. EPS 2010**E**	17.4	Dividend Rate/Share	$0.24	S&P Credit Rating	BBB
$10K Invested 5 Yrs Ago	$6,130	Common Shares Outstg. (M)	298.1	Institutional Ownership (%)	86		

Price Performance

30-Week Mov. Avg. · · · 10-Week Mov. Avg. - - **GAAP Earnings vs. Previous Year** Volume Above Avg. ▥ STARS
12-Mo. Target Price — Relative Strength — ▲ Up ▼ Down ▶ No Change Below Avg. ▥ ★

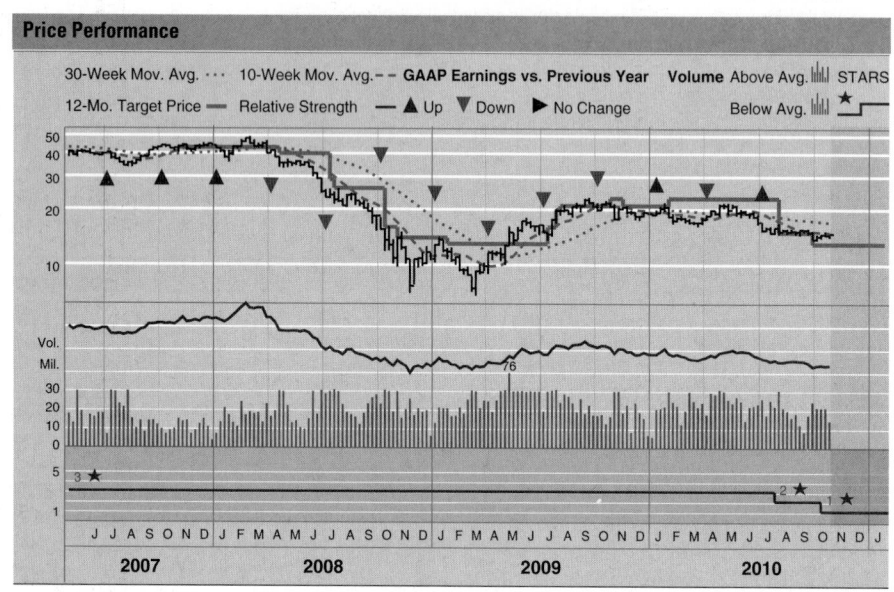

Options: ASE, CBOE

Analysis prepared by **Esther Y. Kwon, CFA** on October 14, 2010, when the stock traded at **$ 14.77**.

Highlights

▸ In FY 10 (Sep.), we see revenues decreasing about 6% after about a 16% drop in FY 09, as a slight pickup in spending by operators to re-fresh stale floors is more than offset by lower sales of units for new casino openings. We ex-pect gaming operations to decline at a greater rate than product sales as IGT loses share to its competitors in this arena. In FY 11, we project a recovery in revenue growth to over 6%.

▸ On reduced materials costs and a greater mix of higher-margin non-machine product sales, we see product gross margins expanding to over 51% and gaming gross margins of about 61% in FY 10. On restructuring benefits, we forecast R&D expenses to decline slightly from FY 09 levels, but see SG&A costs down about 18%. Overall, we project operating margin ex-pansion of over 400 basis points and EPS of $0.85 in FY 10, versus operating EPS of $0.87 in FY 11, we forecast EPS of $0.93.

▸ In May 2009, IGT issued $850 million of convert-ible notes due May 2014 and entered into hedg-ing transactions on its common stock and sepa-rate warrant transactions with hedge counter-parties. These actions may affect share count depending on the stock price.

Investment Rationale/Risk

▸ We are concerned about market share losses and revenue declines in gross gaming revenues at casino operator customers, which we think may result in purchasing delays or price com-petition among equipment manufacturers. There has also been excessive management turnover at IGT, which we think will make a turnaround more difficult. Effective April 1, 2009, former director Patti Hart, who has held several high level positions at technology companies, was named president and CEO, replacing T.J. Matthews. While we believe IGT has done a good job of reducing expenses, we think the majority of those benefits have been realized and believe it will have to invest more aggres-sively in R&D to catch up to competitors.

▸ Risks to our recommendation and target price include prospects for growth from new or ex-panded gaming markets becoming more favor-able than we expect.

▸ Our 12-month target price of $13 reflects a P/E at a discount to peers. We see limited near-term positive catalysts for the shares, given market share losses, new management, and reservations about the speed and scope of de-veloping demand for new equipment.

Qualitative Risk Assessment

LOW	MEDIUM	HIGH

Our risk assessment reflects the company's industry-leading position as a supplier of gaming machines. We expect the company to generate free cash flow, with at least some of it used for stock repurchases. This is offset by our projection that IGT will continue to spend heavily on research and development and our view that growth prospects depend on regulatory factors and technology changes, including the legalization of gaming markets.

Quantitative Evaluations

S&P Quality Ranking B+

D	C	B-	B	B+	A-	A	A+

Relative Strength Rank WEAK

23

LOWEST = 1   HIGHEST = 99

Revenue/Earnings Data

Revenue (Million $)

	1Q	2Q	3Q	4Q	Year
2010	515.7	494.4	489.7	--	--
2009	601.6	475.7	522.1	514.6	2,114
2008	645.8	573.2	677.4	632.2	2,529
2007	642.3	609.7	706.5	662.9	2,621
2006	616.2	644.4	612.4	638.7	2,512
2005	641.2	551.0	579.6	607.6	2,379

Earnings Per Share ($)

2010	0.25	Nil	0.32	E0.20	E0.85
2009	0.22	0.13	0.22	-0.07	0.51
2008	0.36	0.22	0.35	0.18	1.10
2007	0.35	0.38	0.41	0.38	1.51
2006	0.34	0.35	0.33	0.33	1.34
2005	0.33	0.26	0.32	0.30	1.20

Fiscal year ended Sep. 30. Next earnings report expected: Early November. EPS Estimates based on S&P Operating Earnings; historical GAAP earnings are as reported.

Dividend Data (Dates: mm/dd Payment Date: mm/dd/yy)

Amount ($)	Date Decl.	Ex-Div. Date	Stk. of Record	Payment Date
0.060	12/15	12/24	12/29	01/15/10
0.060	03/02	03/12	03/16	04/09/10
0.060	06/08	06/18	06/22	07/09/10
0.060	08/24	09/02	09/07	10/08/10

Dividends have been paid since 2003. Source: Company reports.

Please read the Required Disclosures and Analyst Certification on the last page of this report.

The McGraw-Hill Companies

International Game Technology

Business Summary October 14, 2010

CORPORATE OVERVIEW. International Game Technology (IGT) is a leading maker of gaming machines. In addition to selling machines, IGT's business includes the placement of machines from which it receives recurring revenues.

In FY 09 (Sep.), 44% of IGT revenues came from product sales, compared to 47% in FY 08, with the remainder from gaming operations, including progressive systems.

Product sales in FY 09 included the sale of 53,600 machines, down from 72,700 machines in FY 08 and 105,900 in FY 07. FY 09 sales included 25,900 for North America versus 35,000 and 43,000 in FY 08 and FY 07, respectively. Shipments to international markets totaled 27,700, down from 37,700 machines in FY 08 and 62,900 in FY 07. International sales may include some lower-priced machines with relatively low-value prizes. In addition to machines for casinos, IGT has made video gaming terminals (VGTs) for government-sponsored programs, including lotteries.

IGT's gaming operations segment includes the placement of games in both casinos and government-sponsored gaming markets, under a variety of recurring revenue pricing arrangements, including wide-area progressive systems, standalone participation and flat fee, equipment leasing and rental, as well as hybrid pricing or premium products that include a product sale and a recurring fee.

CORPORATE STRATEGY. In FY 09, IGT's research and development spending totaled $211.8 million (about 10.0% of revenues), down from $223.0 million (8.8%) in FY 08, and up from $202.2 million (7.7%) in FY 07. We expect that the company's ability to develop successful machines and games, with features that appeal to gamblers and casinos, will be a significant factor in the amount of product sales it has.

During the next few years, we expect a shift toward sales or licensing of server-based games to become more evident, creating opportunities for increased IGT revenues from sales or licensing of replacement machines or games for use in such locations as U.S. casinos.

Company Financials Fiscal Year Ended Sep. 30

Per Share Data ($)	2009	2008	2007	2006	2005	2004	2003	2002	2001	2000
Tangible Book Value	NM	NM	0.29	2.06	1.56	1.98	1.42	0.55	0.40	NM
Cash Flow	1.45	2.03	2.30	1.99	1.78	1.56	1.45	1.23	0.91	0.67
Earnings	0.51	1.10	1.51	1.34	1.20	1.18	1.07	0.80	0.70	0.50
S&P Core Earnings	0.54	1.20	1.47	1.33	1.15	1.11	1.02	0.79	0.67	NA
Dividends	0.33	0.57	0.52	0.50	0.48	0.30	0.18	Nil	Nil	Nil
Payout Ratio	64%	51%	34%	37%	40%	25%	16%	Nil	Nil	Nil
Prices:High	23.30	49.41	48.79	46.76	34.63	47.12	37.00	20.03	17.99	12.34
Prices:Low	6.81	7.03	33.57	30.12	24.20	28.22	18.05	11.94	8.93	4.36
P/E Ratio:High	46	45	32	35	29	40	35	25	26	25
P/E Ratio:Low	13	6	22	22	20	24	17	15	13	9

Income Statement Analysis (Million $)	2009	2008	2007	2006	2005	2004	2003	2002	2001	2000
Revenue	2,114	2,529	2,621	2,512	2,379	2,485	2,128	1,848	1,199	1,004
Operating Income	713	947	1,066	960	886	964	800	646	315	343
Depreciation	277	286	266	235	222	150	134	146	63.3	54.4
Interest Expense	125	102	77.6	50.8	58.1	90.5	117	117	102	102
Pretax Income	238	591	805	747	681	653	599	110	339	245
Effective Tax Rate	37.4%	42.0%	36.9%	36.6%	35.9%	34.2%	37.3%	NM	37.0%	36.0%
Net Income	149	343	508	474	437	430	375	277	214	157
S&P Core Earnings	159	371	493	470	415	405	357	273	204	NA

Balance Sheet & Other Financial Data (Million $)	2009	2008	2007	2006	2005	2004	2003	2002	2001	2000
Cash	168	266	261	295	289	765	1,316	424	364	245
Current Assets	1,234	1,470	1,287	1,376	1,437	1,510	2,078	1,195	968	814
Total Assets	4,388	4,557	4,168	3,903	3,864	3,873	4,185	3,316	1,923	1,624
Current Liabilities	624	737	692	1,247	1,218	560	945	511	371	259
Long Term Debt	2,170	2,247	1,503	200	200	792	1,146	971	985	992
Common Equity	967	909	1,453	2,042	1,906	1,977	1,687	1,433	296	96.6
Total Capital	3,142	3,156	2,956	2,242	2,106	2,768	2,833	2,413	1,281	1,088
Capital Expenditures	257	298	344	311	239	211	30.8	33.8	34.7	18.5
Cash Flow	426	628	774	709	659	580	509	423	277	211
Current Ratio	2.0	2.0	1.9	1.1	1.2	2.7	2.2	2.3	2.6	3.1
% Long Term Debt of Capitalization	69.2	71.2	50.9	8.9	9.5	28.6	40.4	40.3	76.9	91.1
% Net Income of Revenue	7.1	13.6	19.4	18.9	18.3	17.3	17.6	15.0	17.8	15.6
% Return on Assets	3.3	7.9	12.6	12.2	11.3	10.7	10.0	10.6	12.1	9.3
% Return on Equity	15.9	29.0	29.1	24.0	22.5	23.5	24.1	32.0	109.0	92.6

Data as orig reptd.; bef. results of disc opers/spec. items. Per share data adj. for stk. divs.; EPS diluted. E-Estimated. NA-Not Available. NM-Not Meaningful. NR-Not Ranked. UR-Under Review.

Office: 9295 Prototype Drive, Reno, NV 89521.
Telephone: 775-448-7777.
Website: http://www.igt.com
Chrmn: P.G. Satre

Pres & CEO: P.S. Hart
COO: E.P. Tom
EVP, CFO, Chief Acctg Officer & Treas: P.W. Cavanaugh
EVP & CTO: C.J. Satchell

Board Members: P. L. Alves, J. Chaffin, G. Creed, P. S. Hart, R. A. Mathewson, T. J. Matthews, R. J. Miller, D. E. Roberson, V. L. Sadusky, P. G. Satre
Founded: 1980
Domicile: Nevada
Employees: 5,100

International Paper Co

STANDARD &POOR'S

S&P Recommendation	BUY ★★★★☆	Price $23.68 (as of Oct 22, 2010)	12-Mo. Target Price $31.00	Investment Style Large-Cap Value

GICS Sector Materials
Sub-Industry Paper Products

Summary This company is a leading worldwide producer and distributor of printing papers and packaging products.

Key Stock Statistics (Source S&P, Vickers, company reports)

52-Wk Range	$29.25– 19.33	S&P Oper. EPS 2010**E**	1.90	Market Capitalization(B)	$10.349	Beta	2.32
Trailing 12-Month EPS	$0.47	S&P Oper. EPS 2011**E**	2.50	Yield (%)	2.11	S&P 3-Yr. Proj. EPS CAGR(%)	46
Trailing 12-Month P/E	50.4	P/E on S&P Oper. EPS 2010**E**	12.5	Dividend Rate/Share	$0.50	S&P Credit Rating	BBB
$10K Invested 5 Yrs Ago	$9,913	Common Shares Outstg. (M)	437.0	Institutional Ownership (%)	84		

Price Performance

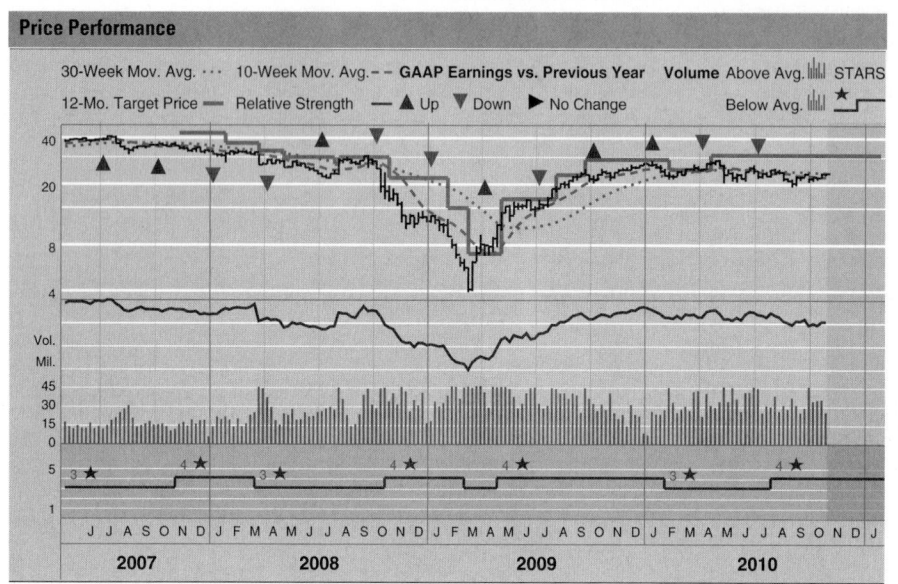

Options: ASE, CBOE, P, Ph

Analysis prepared by **Stuart J. Benway, CFA** on July 30, 2010, when the stock traded at **$ 24.20**.

Highlights

➤ We forecast sales in 2010 to increase 5%-8%. Volume in the industrial and consumer packaging businesses should improve along with renewed growth in the economy. We also expect prices to rise significantly after falling for much of 2009. Demand for printing papers is likely to be helped by replenishment of depleted inventories.

➤ We project operating margins from continuing operations to widen moderately in 2010 to 8.2%, from 6.3% in 2009. IP is continuing to find opportunities for cost reduction, especially in its packaging business, and capacity is likely to be better utilized. We also expect higher prices to add to margin gains, although higher input costs could offset some off this improvement. Pension expense is projected to rise again, but interest costs should decline.

➤ We see operating EPS of $1.90 in 2010 up from $0.88 earned in 2009, excluding unusual items. In our view, profits appear to be well on their way to recovery at IP, and we look for solid growth again in 2011 with EPS projected at $2.50.

Investment Rationale/Risk

➤ IP has made many moves in recent years aimed at focusing on faster-growing regions and higher-return businesses. The company has investments and joint ventures in Brazil, China, and Russia that we believe will contribute meaningfully to earnings as the economy recovers. Cost synergies from the major linerboard acquisition are also being realized and debt levels have been reduced.

➤ Risks to our recommendation and target price include a lack of further economic recovery, worse-than-projected demand and pricing trends for uncoated paper and packaging, and the failure of new ventures to achieve targeted returns.

➤ Our discounted cash flow model, which assumes a 9.0% weighted average cost of capital, reduced capital expenditures over the next several years, and a 2.5% terminal growth rate, calculates intrinsic value of $30. A peer group of paper stocks was recently trading at 12.9X 2011 EPS estimates. Applying this valuation to our 2011 EPS estimate for IP, we derive a value of $32. Our 12-month target price of $31 is an equal blend of these two metrics.

Qualitative Risk Assessment

LOW	MEDIUM	HIGH

IP operates in a cyclical and capital-intensive industry and is affected by changes in industrial production, interest rates, and economic growth. However, it is one of the largest companies in the sector, and has greater economies of scale than many of its competitors.

Quantitative Evaluations

S&P Quality Ranking   B

D	C	B-	B	B+	A-	A	A+

Relative Strength Rank   MODERATE

60

LOWEST = 1   HIGHEST = 99

Revenue/Earnings Data

Revenue (Million $)

	1Q	2Q	3Q	4Q	Year
2010	5,807	6,121	--	--	--
2009	5,668	5,802	5,919	5,977	23,366
2008	5,668	5,807	6,808	6,546	24,829
2007	5,217	5,291	5,541	5,841	21,890
2006	5,668	6,270	5,867	5,324	21,995
2005	6,011	5,916	6,036	6,134	24,097

Earnings Per Share ($)

	1Q	2Q	3Q	4Q	Year
2010	-0.38	0.22	E0.77	E0.67	E1.90
2009	0.61	0.32	0.87	-0.24	1.55
2008	0.35	0.54	0.35	-1.08	0.17
2007	1.02	0.46	0.52	0.80	2.81
2006	0.14	0.24	0.23	4.53	2.65
2005	0.22	0.19	1.48	-0.17	1.74

Fiscal year ended Dec. 31. Next earnings report expected: Late October. EPS Estimates based on S&P Operating Earnings; historical GAAP earnings are as reported.

Dividend Data (Dates: mm/dd Payment Date: mm/dd/yy)

Amount ($)	Date Decl.	Ex-Div. Date	Stk. of Record	Payment Date
0.025	01/12	02/11	02/16	03/15/10
0.125	04/26	05/13	05/17	06/15/10
0.125	07/13	08/12	08/16	09/15/10
0.125	10/12	11/12	11/16	12/15/10

Dividends have been paid since 1946. Source: Company reports.

Please read the Required Disclosures and Analyst Certification on the last page of this report.

The McGraw-Hill Companies

International Paper Co

STANDARD &POOR'S

Business Summary July 30, 2010

CORPORATE OVERVIEW. International Paper is the world's largest paper and forest products company. We believe its market share is about 25% in uncoated free sheet (UFS), used in copiers and for envelopes and forms, giving it the number-two position in that major category. It is the largest linerboard producer, used to make corrugated boxes, with an estimated 30% of the market. It also manufactures bleached paperboard used to package cosmetics, food, beverages, and pharmaceuticals, and is the second-largest boxboard producer in the U.S.

IMPACT OF MAJOR DEVELOPMENTS. On March 17, 2008, International Paper agreed to acquire the corrugated packaging business of Weyerhaeuser for $6 billion in cash and closed the deal on August 4, 2008. Because the transaction was a purchase of assets rather than stock, IP said that it would realize a tax benefit with a net present value of approximately $1.4 billion. This business had sales in 2007 of $5.2 billion and EBITDA of $670 million. IP originally expected to generate $400 million of synergies on an annual basis after three years but reached that target in the first 12 months. These savings have come from reduced overhead, improved logistics, greater efficiency, and better customer mix. The deal gives IP just under a 30% share of the North American corrugated packaging market. We think the move is a good strategic fit for IP,

and it is reducing debt from the acquisition faster than initially expected.

MARKET PROFILE. IP operates in a highly cyclical and capital-intensive industry. Demand for the company's products is dependent on a number of factors, including industrial non-durable goods production, consumer spending, commercial printing and advertising activity, white collar employment levels, and movements in currency exchange rates. Historical prices for paper and wood products have been volatile, and, despite its size, IP has had only a limited direct influence over the timing and extent of price changes for its products. Pricing is significantly affected by the relationship between supply and demand, and supply is mainly influenced by fluctuations in available manufacturing capacity. Technology seems to be having an impact on paper demand, especially in uncoated free sheet, where demand has grown more slowly than the economy in recent years. We doubt the trend is likely to improve in the near term considering the weakness in the worldwide economy.

Company Financials Fiscal Year Ended Dec. 31

Per Share Data ($)	2009	2008	2007	2006	2005	2004	2003	2002	2001	2000
Tangible Book Value	8.62	5.01	14.08	11.10	6.75	6.69	6.01	4.31	7.78	11.89
Cash Flow	4.99	0.19	5.31	4.99	4.38	4.19	4.07	3.90	1.51	4.28
Earnings	1.55	0.17	2.81	2.65	1.74	0.98	0.66	0.61	-2.37	0.82
S&P Core Earnings	1.68	0.12	2.45	1.13	1.67	0.84	0.51	0.92	-2.25	NA
Dividends	0.32	1.00	1.00	1.00	1.00	1.00	1.00	1.00	1.00	1.00
Payout Ratio	21%	588%	36%	38%	57%	102%	152%	164%	NM	122%
Prices:High	27.79	33.77	41.57	37.98	42.59	45.01	43.32	46.20	43.31	60.00
Prices:Low	3.93	10.20	31.05	30.69	26.97	37.12	33.09	31.35	30.70	26.31
P/E Ratio:High	18	NM	15	14	24	46	66	76	NM	73
P/E Ratio:Low	3	NM	11	12	15	38	50	51	NM	32

Income Statement Analysis (Million $)										
Revenue	23,366	24,829	21,890	21,995	24,097	25,548	25,179	24,976	26,363	28,180
Operating Income	3,139	2,717	2,796	2,609	3,228	3,251	3,293	3,576	3,305	5,432
Depreciation	1,472	1,347	1,086	1,158	1,376	1,565	1,644	1,587	1,870	1,916
Interest Expense	702	572	483	651	593	743	766	783	929	791
Pretax Income	1,150	235	1,654	3,188	586	746	346	371	-1,265	497
Effective Tax Rate	40.8%	68.9%	25.1%	59.3%	NM	27.6%	NM	NM	NM	23.5%
Net Income	663	70.0	1,215	1,282	859	478	315	295	-1,142	142
S&P Core Earnings	720	55.0	1,058	539	819	402	242	444	-1,091	NA

Balance Sheet & Other Financial Data (Million $)										
Cash	1,892	1,144	905	1,624	1,641	2,596	2,363	1,074	1,224	1,198
Current Assets	7,551	7,360	6,735	8,637	7,409	9,319	9,337	7,738	8,312	10,455
Total Assets	25,548	28,252	24,159	24,034	28,771	34,217	35,525	33,792	37,158	42,109
Current Liabilities	4,012	4,755	3,842	4,641	4,844	4,872	6,803	4,579	5,374	7,413
Long Term Debt	8,729	11,246	6,620	6,531	11,023	14,132	13,450	13,042	14,262	14,453
Common Equity	6,023	5,508	8,672	10,839	8,351	8,254	8,237	7,374	10,291	12,034
Total Capital	14,984	16,215	18,172	19,816	20,311	25,631	25,085	25,435	29,804	32,541
Capital Expenditures	534	1,002	1,288	1,009	1,155	1,262	1,166	1,009	1,049	1,352
Cash Flow	2,135	78.0	2,301	2,440	2,235	2,043	1,959	1,882	728	2,058
Current Ratio	1.9	1.6	1.8	1.9	1.5	1.9	1.4	1.7	1.5	1.4
% Long Term Debt of Capitalization	58.3	69.3	41.7	33.0	54.3	55.1	53.6	51.3	47.9	44.4
% Net Income of Revenue	2.8	0.3	5.6	5.8	3.6	1.9	1.3	1.2	NM	0.5
% Return on Assets	2.5	0.3	5.0	4.9	2.7	1.4	0.9	0.8	NM	0.4
% Return on Equity	13.0	1.0	14.6	13.4	10.3	5.8	4.0	3.3	NM	1.3

Data as orig reptd.; bef. results of disc opers/spec. items. Per share data adj. for stk. divs.; EPS diluted. E-Estimated. NA-Not Available. NM-Not Meaningful. NR-Not Ranked. UR-Under Review.

Office: 6400 Poplar Ave, Memphis, TN 38197-0198.
Telephone: 901-419-7000.
Email: comm@ipaper.com
Website: http://www.internationalpaper.com

Chrmn & CEO: J.V. Faraci
SVP & CFO: T.S. Nicholls
SVP, Secy & General Counsel: M.A. Smith
SVP & CIO: J.N. Balboni

CTO: T.S. Joseph
Investor Contact: T.A. Cleves (901-419-7566)
Board Members: D. J. Bronczek, L. L. Elsenhans, J. V. Faraci, S. G. Gibara, S. J. Mobley, J. L. Townsend, III, J. F. Turner, W. G. Walter, A. Weisser, J. S. Whisler

Founded: 1898
Domicile: New York
Employees: 56,100

The McGraw-Hill Companies

Interpublic Group of Companies Inc. (The)

STANDARD &POOR'S

S&P Recommendation BUY ★★★★☆	**Price** $10.43 (as of Oct 22, 2010)	**12-Mo. Target Price** $11.00	**Investment Style** Large-Cap Blend

GICS Sector Consumer Discretionary
Sub-Industry Advertising

Summary Interpublic is one of the world's largest organizations of advertising agencies and marketing communications companies.

Key Stock Statistics (Source S&P, Vickers, company reports)

52-Wk Range	$12.25– 5.71	S&P Oper. EPS 2010E	0.48	Market Capitalization(B)	$5.098	Beta		1.65
Trailing 12-Month EPS	$0.30	S&P Oper. EPS 2011E	0.57	Yield (%)	Nil	S&P 3-Yr. Proj. EPS CAGR(%)		12
Trailing 12-Month P/E	34.8	P/E on S&P Oper. EPS 2010E	21.7	Dividend Rate/Share	Nil	S&P Credit Rating		BB
$10K Invested 5 Yrs Ago	$10,087	Common Shares Outstg. (M)	488.8	Institutional Ownership (%)	96			

Price Performance

30-Week Mov. Avg. · · · 10-Week Mov. Avg. - - **GAAP Earnings vs. Previous Year** Volume Above Avg. STARS
12-Mo. Target Price — Relative Strength — ▲ Up ▼ Down ► No Change Below Avg. ★

Options: ASE, CBOE, Ph

Analysis prepared by **Joseph Agnese** on August 02, 2010, when the stock traded at **$ 9.33**.

Highlights

➤ The contraction in global advertising showed continued signs of easing in the second quarter of 2010, with U.S. organic revenues climbing 13.6% and an overall rise in organic revenues of 8.5%. Favorable foreign exchange rates boosted sales by 1.1%. Despite weakness in the U.K. and continental Europe, with organic sales down 7.6% and 1.0%, respectively, in the second quarter, sequential results continued to improve. We expect favorable client marketing trends to continue in the auto, financial services and retail sectors, although we expect weakness in the technology and telecom sectors, resulting in overall 2010 revenue growth of 5.3% to $6.35 billion.

➤ We expect margins to widen in 2010 due to improved sales leverage and easier comparisons. While we see headcount rising throughout 2010, we look for year-to-year comparisons to be favorable, reflecting significant reductions taken throughout 2009. Additionally, we see savings from reduced rent costs and severance expenses.

➤ We estimate EPS of $0.48 for 2010, up significantly from $0.19 in 2009.

Investment Rationale/Risk

➤ Advertising fundamentals improved in the first half of 2010, with significant increases in demand from the auto, financial services and retail sectors, despite contraction in Europe. With a more stable macro-economic environment expected in the U.S. going forward, we look for increased client marketing budgets to continue to benefit earnings growth into 2011. However, we believe risks remain high as visibility regarding a recovery in international markets remains poor and could offset some of the benefits we are expecting in the U.S.

➤ Risks to our recommendation and target price include unexpected business losses, unfavorable forex impacts, a slower-than-expected U.S. economic recovery, and higher-than-expected severance expenses or professional fees.

➤ Our 12-month target price of $11 is derived by applying an enterprise value/EBITDA multiple of 7.0X to our 2011 EBITDA estimate of approximately $880 million. This reflects a modest premium to peers and the historical average reflecting potential significant EPS benefits we see from a more favorable economic environment.

Qualitative Risk Assessment

LOW	MEDIUM	HIGH

Our risk assessment reflects our view of a highly competitive advertising industry, and economic cyclicality associated with advertising spending, offset by what we see as a moderately conservative balance sheet structure and structural improvements in profitability for IPG.

Quantitative Evaluations

S&P Quality Ranking B-

D	C	B-	B	B+	A-	A	A+

Relative Strength Rank STRONG

79

LOWEST = 1   HIGHEST = 99

Revenue/Earnings Data

Revenue (Million $)

	1Q	2Q	3Q	4Q	Year
2010	1,341	1,618	--	--	--
2009	1,325	1,474	1,427	1,801	6,028
2008	1,485	1,836	1,740	1,902	6,963
2007	1,359	1,653	1,560	1,983	6,554
2006	1,327	1,533	1,454	1,877	6,191
2005	1,328	1,611	1,440	1,896	6,274

Earnings Per Share ($)

2010	-0.15	0.15	E0.10	E0.30	E0.48
2009	-0.16	0.04	0.03	0.24	0.18
2008	-0.15	0.17	0.08	0.39	0.52
2007	-0.29	0.24	-0.06	0.31	0.26
2006	-0.43	0.09	-0.03	0.11	-0.20
2005	-0.36	0.01	-0.25	-0.10	-0.70

Fiscal year ended Dec. 31. Next earnings report expected: Late October. EPS Estimates based on S&P Operating Earnings; historical GAAP earnings are as reported.

Dividend Data

No cash dividends have been paid since 2002.

Please read the Required Disclosures and Analyst Certification on the last page of this report.

The **McGraw·Hill** Companies

Interpublic Group of Companies Inc. (The)

STANDARD &POOR'S

Business Summary August 02, 2010

CORPORATE OVERVIEW. The Interpublic Group of Companies, along with its subsidiaries, is one of the world's largest advertising and marketing services companies, made up of communication agencies around the world that deliver custom marketing solutions to clients. These agencies cover the spectrum of marketing disciplines and specialties, from traditional services such as consumer advertising and direct marketing, to emerging services such as mobile and search engine marketing.

The company generates revenue from planning, creating and placing advertising in various media and from planning and executing other communications or marketing programs. IPG also receives commissions from clients for planning and supervising work done by outside contractors in the physical preparation of finished print advertisements and the production of TV and radio commercials and other forms of advertising. In addition, IPG derives revenue in a number of other ways, including the planning and placement in media of advertising produced by unrelated advertising agencies, the creation and publication of brochures, billboards, point of sale materials and direct marketing pieces for clients, the planning and carrying out of specialized marketing research, public relations campaigns, and creating and managing special events at which client products are featured.

IPG has two reportable segments: the McCann Worldgroup unit, comprised of

Draftfcb, Lowe, Momentum, McCann Healthcare, media agencies and other standalone agencies, and the Constituent Management Group (CMG), which is made up of the bulk of IPG's specialist marketing service offerings. Draftfcb was formed from the merger of two IPG companies in 2006, and is focused on consumer advertising and behavioral, data-driven direct marketing. Lowe is a creative advertising agency operating in the world's largest advertising markets. McCann Worldgroup is a marketing communications company that consists of McCann Erickson Advertising, MRM Worldwide for relationship marketing and digital expertise, Momentum for experiential marketing, and McCann Healthcare for health care communications, as well as various other brands.

Mediabrands was installed in recent years to oversee all media operations in order to align the company's media networks with its global brand agencies. Also, in recent years the company has focused on making strategic investments, including a number of acquisitions in Brazil, India, Russia, and China, or "BRIC" countries.

Company Financials Fiscal Year Ended Dec. 31

Per Share Data ($)	2009	2008	2007	2006	2005	2004	2003	2002	2001	2000
Tangible Book Value	NM	NM	NM	NM	NM	NM	NM	NM	NM	NM
Cash Flow	0.52	0.85	0.63	0.21	-0.30	-0.91	-0.90	0.83	-0.36	1.99
Earnings	0.18	0.52	0.26	-0.20	-0.70	-1.36	-1.43	0.26	-1.37	1.15
S&P Core Earnings	0.21	0.51	0.29	-0.18	-0.62	-0.82	-0.84	0.36	-0.60	NA
Dividends	Nil	Nil	Nil	Nil	Nil	Nil	Nil	0.38	0.38	0.37
Payout Ratio	Nil	Nil	Nil	Nil	Nil	Nil	Nil	146%	NM	32%
Prices:High	7.77	10.47	13.94	12.83	13.80	17.31	16.50	34.98	47.44	57.69
Prices:Low	3.08	2.57	7.91	7.79	9.08	10.47	7.20	9.85	18.25	32.69
P/E Ratio:High	43	20	54	NM	NM	NM	NM	NM	NM	50
P/E Ratio:Low	17	5	30	NM	NM	NM	NM	NM	NM	28

Income Statement Analysis (Million $)										
Revenue	6,028	6,963	6,554	6,191	6,274	6,387	5,863	6,204	6,727	5,626
Operating Income	681	780	547	341	156	589	719	762	1,113	1,096
Depreciation	170	173	177	174	169	185	204	218	372	263
Interest Expense	156	212	237	219	182	172	173	146	165	109
Pretax Income	234	475	243	2.00	-173	-261	-330	271	-519	672
Effective Tax Rate	38.6%	33.0%	24.2%	NM	NM	NM	NM	51.8%	NM	40.7%
Net Income	121	295	168	-36.7	-272	-545	-553	99.5	-505	359
S&P Core Earnings	104	265	150	-75.8	-265	-363	-325	136	-217	NA

Balance Sheet & Other Financial Data (Million $)										
Cash	2,506	2,275	2,083	1,957	2,192	1,970	2,006	933	935	748
Current Assets	7,638	7,488	7,686	7,209	7,497	7,637	7,350	6,322	6,467	6,026
Total Assets	12,263	12,125	12,458	11,864	11,945	12,272	12,235	11,794	11,515	10,238
Current Liabilities	6,906	6,877	7,121	6,663	6,857	7,563	6,625	7,090	6,434	6,106
Long Term Debt	1,638	1,787	2,044	2,249	2,183	Nil	2,192	1,818	2,481	1,505
Common Equity	1,973	1,951	1,807	1,416	1,047	1,345	2,721	2,100	2,384	2,046
Total Capital	4,667	4,517	4,376	4,236	4,178	1,773	5,356	3,988	4,953	3,637
Capital Expenditures	67.1	138	148	128	141	194	160	183	268	202
Cash Flow	264	441	317	89.3	-129	-380	-349	317	-133	622
Current Ratio	1.1	1.1	1.1	1.1	1.1	1.0	1.1	0.9	1.0	1.0
% Long Term Debt of Capitalization	Nil	39.5	46.7	53.1	52.3	Nil	40.9	45.6	50.1	41.4
% Net Income of Revenue	2.0	4.2	2.6	NM	NM	NM	NM	1.6	NM	6.4
% Return on Assets	NA	2.4	1.4	NM	NM	NM	NM	0.9	NM	3.7
% Return on Equity	NA	14.2	10.4	NM	NM	NM	NM	5.1	NM	18.8

Data as orig reptd.; bef. results of disc opers/spec. items. Per share data adj. for stk. divs.; EPS diluted. E-Estimated. NA-Not Available. NM-Not Meaningful. NR-Not Ranked. UR-Under Review.

Office: 1114 Avenue Of The Americas, New York, NY 10036.
Telephone: 212-704-1200.
Website: http://www.interpublic.com
Chrmn & CEO: M.I. Roth

EVP & CFO: F. Mergenthaler
SVP, Chief Acctg Officer & Cntlr: C.F. Carroll
SVP & Treas: E.T. Johnson
SVP, Secy & General Counsel: N.J. Camera

Investor Contact: J. Leshne (212-704-1439)
Board Members: R. K. Brack, Jr., J. E. Carter-Miller, J. M. Considine, R. A. Goldstein, H. J. Greeniaus, M. J. Guilfoile, W. T. Kerr, M. I. Roth, D. M. Thomas

Founded: 1902
Domicile: Delaware
Employees: 40,000

The **McGraw·Hill** Companies

Intuitive Surgical Inc

STANDARD &POOR'S

S&P Recommendation	HOLD ★★★☆☆	Price $265.84 (as of Oct 22, 2010)	12-Mo. Target Price $290.00	Investment Style Large-Cap Blend

GICS Sector Health Care
Sub-Industry Health Care Equipment

Summary This company has developed the da Vinci Surgical System, which uses advanced robotics and computerized visualization technology for minimally invasive surgeries.

Key Stock Statistics (Source S&P, Vickers, company reports)

52-Wk Range	$393.92– 243.10	S&P Oper. EPS 2010**E**	8.75	Market Capitalization(B)	$10.446	Beta	1.75
Trailing 12-Month EPS	$8.41	S&P Oper. EPS 2011**E**	10.25	Yield (%)	Nil	S&P 3-Yr. Proj. EPS CAGR(%)	25
Trailing 12-Month P/E	31.6	P/E on S&P Oper. EPS 2010**E**	30.4	Dividend Rate/Share	Nil	S&P Credit Rating	NA
$10K Invested 5 Yrs Ago	$38,135	Common Shares Outstg. (M)	39.3	Institutional Ownership (%)	88		

Price Performance

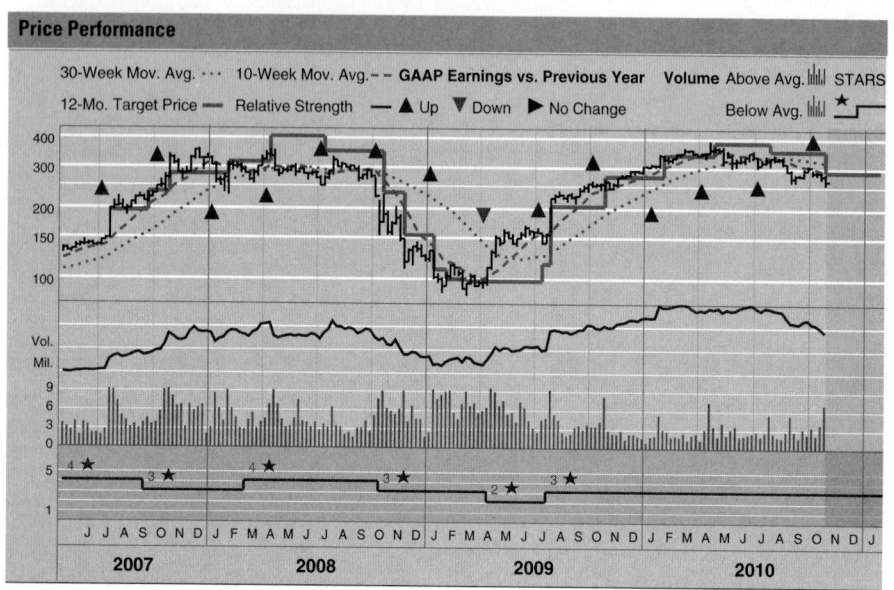

30-Week Mov. Avg. ···· 10-Week Mov. Avg. – – **GAAP Earnings vs. Previous Year** Volume Above Avg. STARS
12-Mo. Target Price — Relative Strength — ▲ Up ▼ Down ▶ No Change Below Avg.

Options: ASE, CBOE, Ph

Qualitative Risk Assessment

LOW	MEDIUM	HIGH

Our risk assessment reflects risks that we see as specific to a maker of medical devices such as ISRG, including those associated with protecting its intellectual property rights, compliance with regulations of U.S. and foreign health agencies, and legal liability for injury that may result from use of the company's products, such as inappropriate or "off-label" use.

Quantitative Evaluations

S&P Quality Ranking   B-

D	C	B-	B	B+	A-	A	A+

Relative Strength Rank   WEAK

11

LOWEST = 1   HIGHEST = 99

Highlights

▶ The 12-month target price for ISRG has recently been changed to $290.00 from $355.00. The Highlights section of this Stock Report will be updated accordingly.

Investment Rationale/Risk

▶ The Investment Rationale/Risk section of this Stock Report will be updated shortly. For the latest News story on ISRG from MarketScope, see below.

▶ 10/20/10 04:43 pm ET ... S&P MAINTAINS HOLD RECOMMENDATION ON SHARES OF INTUITIVE SURGICAL (ISRG 259.45***): Q3 EPS of $2.14 vs. $1.64 is $0.07 below our view, partly on lower revenue than we expected. While instrument and systems sales grew strongly year/year, they declined slightly sequentially, vs. year-earlier growth. We are positive on ISRG's push into new procedures, which would help reduce its reliance on prostatectomies, the growth of which has slowed in the U.S. Meantime, ISRG faces a challenging capital equipment market in Europe. We cut our '10 EPS est $0.05 to $8.75, '11's by $0.15 to $10.25, and target price by $65 to $290, on narrower P/E premium to medical device group. /P.Seligman

Revenue/Earnings Data

Revenue (Million $)

	1Q	2Q	3Q	4Q	Year
2010	328.6	350.7	344.4	--	--
2009	188.4	260.6	280.1	323.0	1,052
2008	118.2	219.2	236.0	231.6	874.9
2007	114.2	140.3	156.9	189.5	600.8
2006	77.26	87.03	95.83	112.6	372.7
2005	41.61	52.76	60.87	72.10	227.3

Earnings Per Share ($)

	1Q	2Q	3Q	4Q	Year
2010	2.12	2.19	2.14	E2.31	E8.75
2009	0.72	1.62	1.64	1.95	5.93
2008	1.12	1.28	1.44	1.27	5.12
2007	0.62	0.79	1.04	1.24	3.70
2006	0.38	0.44	0.45	0.62	1.89
2005	0.25	0.40	0.55	1.31	2.51

Fiscal year ended Dec. 31. Next earnings report expected: Late January. EPS Estimates based on S&P Operating Earnings; historical GAAP earnings are as reported.

Dividend Data

No cash dividends have been paid.

Intuitive Surgical Inc

STANDARD &POOR'S

Business Summary July 27, 2010

Intuitive Surgical (ISRG) has designed the da Vinci Surgical System, a product that incorporates advanced robotics and computerized visualization technologies to improve the ability of surgeons to perform complex, minimally invasive procedures. As of 2009 year end, the company had an installed base of 1,395 da Vinci Surgical Systems, and surgeons using the company's technology had successfully completed about 205,000 surgical procedures of various types, including urologic, gynecologic, cardiothoracic and general surgery.

The da Vinci Surgical System consists of a surgeon's console, a patient-side cart, a high performance vision system, and proprietary wristed instruments. By placing computer-enhanced technology between the surgeon and patient, ISRG believes da Vinci lets surgeons perform better surgery in a manner never before experienced. The system translates a surgeon's natural hand movements on instrument controls on a console into corresponding micro-movements of instruments positioned inside the patient through small puncture incisions (ports). It gives a surgeon the intuitive control, range of motion, fine tissue manipulation capability, and 3-D visualization characteristics of open surgery, while simultaneously allowing use of the small ports of minimally invasive surgery. During 2009, surgeons using ISRG products performed

about 90,000 prostatectomy procedures and 69,000 hysterectomy procedures worldwide.

Intuitive's strategy is targeted at establishing Intuitive surgery as the standard for complex surgical procedures and many other procedures. Over time, the company hopes to broaden the number of procedures performed using the da Vinci Surgical System and to educate surgeons and hospitals about the benefits of Intuitive surgery.

The da Vinci System is covered by over 290 U.S. patents and 300 foreign patents that are licensed or owned by the company. The manufacture, marketing, and use of Class II medical devices such as the da Vinci System is governed by extensive regulations administered by the FDA, which we think act as significant barriers to entry by competitors.

Company Financials Fiscal Year Ended Dec. 31

Per Share Data ($)	2009	2008	2007	2006	2005	2004	2003	2002	2001	2000
Tangible Book Value	35.59	28.07	19.61	12.55	8.64	4.83	3.87	3.46	4.14	4.86
Cash Flow	6.82	5.74	4.04	2.15	2.64	0.82	-0.23	-0.80	-0.76	-1.42
Earnings	5.93	5.12	3.70	1.89	2.51	0.67	-0.41	-1.02	-0.94	-1.56
S&P Core Earnings	5.93	5.31	3.70	1.89	2.14	0.39	-0.57	-1.10	-1.14	NA
Dividends	Nil	Nil	Nil	Nil	Nil	Nil	Nil	Nil	Nil	Nil
Payout Ratio	Nil	Nil	Nil	Nil	Nil	Nil	Nil	Nil	Nil	Nil
Prices:High	309.09	357.98	359.59	139.50	124.79	40.60	18.61	22.50	29.56	38.13
Prices:Low	84.86	110.35	86.20	85.63	35.69	15.08	7.34	11.20	6.00	10.75
P/E Ratio:High	52	70	97	74	50	61	NM	NM	NM	NM
P/E Ratio:Low	14	22	23	45	14	23	NM	NM	NM	NM

Income Statement Analysis (Million $)	2009	2008	2007	2006	2005	2004	2003	2002	2001	2000
Revenue	1,052	875	601	373	227	139	91.7	72.0	51.7	26.6
Operating Income	412	336	220	117	73.6	26.3	-7.73	-16.3	-17.3	-20.7
Depreciation	34.6	25.1	13.0	10.0	4.86	5.10	4.15	3.89	3.12	1.60
Interest Expense	NA	Nil	Nil	Nil	0.02	0.09	0.20	0.20	0.27	0.40
Pretax Income	396	335	237	120	73.8	24.2	-9.62	-18.4	-16.7	-18.5
Effective Tax Rate	41.3%	39.1%	39.1%	40.0%	NM	3.00%	NM	NM	NM	NM
Net Income	233	204	145	72.0	94.1	23.5	-9.62	-18.4	-16.7	-18.5
S&P Core Earnings	233	212	145	72.0	80.1	13.6	-13.6	-20.0	-20.3	NA

Balance Sheet & Other Financial Data (Million $)	2009	2008	2007	2006	2005	2004	2003	2002	2001	2000
Cash	1,172	902	427	34.4	5.51	5.77	11.3	17.6	10.5	22.7
Current Assets	847	704	610	374	209	177	152	78.6	89.2	104
Total Assets	1,810	1,475	1,040	672	502	354	315	91.6	100	112
Current Liabilities	203	165	132	80.7	58.0	38.4	34.2	26.1	21.3	19.8
Long Term Debt	NA	Nil	Nil	Nil	Nil	Nil	0.70	1.84	0.77	1.86
Common Equity	1,537	1,267	889	590	443	315	279	63.7	78.3	90.7
Total Capital	1,537	1,267	889	590	443	315	280	65.5	79.1	92.6
Capital Expenditures	53.4	62.5	20.3	15.9	30.1	22.4	2.53	5.79	5.53	3.56
Cash Flow	267	229	158	82.1	99.0	28.6	-5.47	-14.5	-13.6	-16.9
Current Ratio	8.4	4.3	4.6	4.6	3.6	4.6	4.4	3.0	4.2	5.2
% Long Term Debt of Capitalization	Nil	Nil	Nil	Nil	Nil	Nil	0.2	2.8	1.0	2.0
% Net Income of Revenue	22.1	23.4	24.1	19.3	41.4	16.9	NM	NM	NM	NM
% Return on Assets	14.2	16.3	16.9	12.3	22.0	7.0	NM	NM	NM	NM
% Return on Equity	16.6	19.0	19.6	14.0	24.9	7.9	NM	NM	NM	NM

Data as orig reptd.; bef. results of disc opers/spec. items. Per share data adj. for stk. divs.; EPS diluted. E-Estimated. NA-Not Available. NM-Not Meaningful. NR-Not Ranked. UR-Under Review.

Office: 1266 Kifer Rd, Sunnyvale, CA, USA 94086-5304.
Telephone: 408-523-2100 .
Email: ir@intusurg.com
Website: http://www.intuitivesurgical.com

Chrmn: L.M. Smith
Pres & CEO: G.S. Guthart
SVP, CFO & Chief Acctg Officer: M.L. Mohr
SVP & General Counsel: M.J. Meltzer

Cntlr: J.J. Skoglund
Board Members: R. Duggan, G. S. Guthart, E. H. Halvorson, A. M. Johnson, A. J. Levy, F. D. Loop, H. E. Rubash, L. M. Smith, G. J. Stalk, Jr.

Founded: 1995
Domicile: Delaware
Employees: 1,263

Intuit Inc

STANDARD &POOR'S

S&P Recommendation **HOLD** ★★★☆☆	Price $47.21 (as of Oct 22, 2010)	12-Mo. Target Price $45.00	Investment Style Large-Cap Growth

GICS Sector Information Technology
Sub-Industry Application Software

Summary This company develops and markets small business accounting and management, tax preparation and personal finance software.

Key Stock Statistics (Source S&P, Vickers, company reports)

52-Wk Range	$47.90–28.79	S&P Oper. EPS 2011E	2.13	Market Capitalization(B)	$14.991	Beta	0.77
Trailing 12-Month EPS	$1.77	S&P Oper. EPS 2012E	2.45	Yield (%)	Nil	S&P 3-Yr. Proj. EPS CAGR(%)	15
Trailing 12-Month P/E	26.7	P/E on S&P Oper. EPS 2011E	22.2	Dividend Rate/Share	Nil	S&P Credit Rating	BBB
$10K Invested 5 Yrs Ago	$20,820	Common Shares Outstg. (M)	317.5	Institutional Ownership (%)	89		

Price Performance

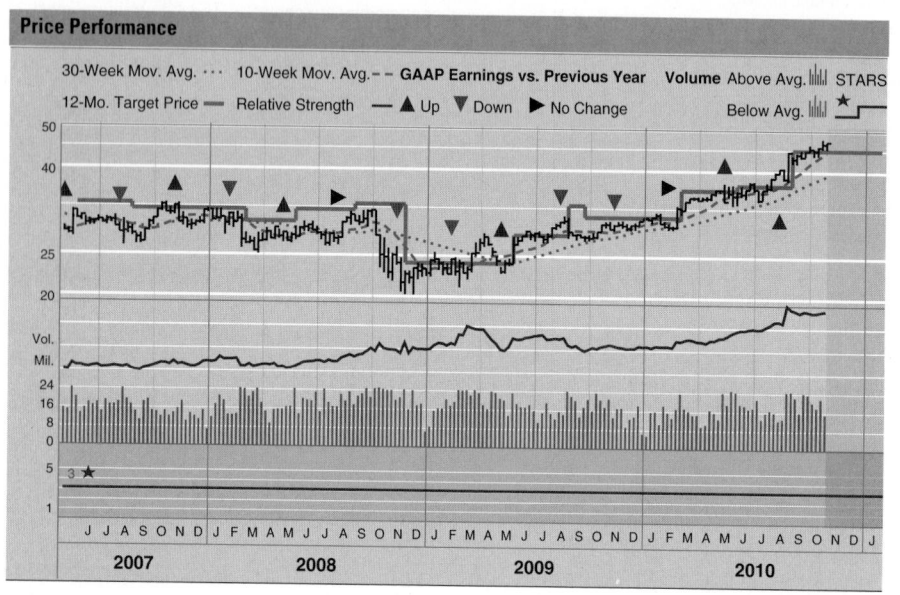

30-Week Mov. Avg. ··· 10-Week Mov. Avg. - - **GAAP Earnings vs. Previous Year** **Volume** Above Avg. STARS
12-Mo. Target Price — Relative Strength — ▲ Up ▼ Down ▶ No Change Below Avg. ★

Options: ASE, CBOE, P, Ph

Analysis prepared by **Zaineb Bokhari** on August 24, 2010, when the stock traded at **$ 42.68**.

Highlights

▶ We estimate that sales will rise 11% in FY 11 (Jul.), to $3.8 billion, driven mainly by organic growth and aided modestly by acquisitions including Medfusion (May 2010). We forecast 13% sales growth for INTU's consumer tax business, supported by rising usage of online consumer tax preparation offerings. We expect small business segment sales to increase nearly 11%, with QuickBooks sales projected to rise 10%, supported by growth in INTU's online offering even as the economic backdrop limits new business formation. We look for sales to advance 10% in FY 12.

▶ We expect INTU to continue to exercise cost discipline, but we see FY 11 non-GAAP operating margins widening modestly as INTU absorbs the recent acquisitions. Organically, we believe the company will benefit from selective hiring and data center consolidation, but we see ongoing investment in R&D, marketing, and infrastructure. We anticipate further modest margin expansion in FY 12.

▶ We estimate operating EPS of $2.13 for FY 11, excluding amortization and acquisition-related expense but including projected stock-based compensation expense of approximately $0.27.

Investment Rationale/Risk

▶ We expect INTU's small business segment to see improving growth as economic conditions continue to stabilize. While there are modest signs of new business formation, we see INTU having success through cross-sales and from its online channel. INTU's tax franchise is less sensitive to the economy, and we see the company continuing to outpace the market with projected growth of 11%. We expect recent acquisitions to help drive growth, and are encouraged by recent gains in its user base for its online financial offerings.

▶ Risks to our recommendation and target price include increased competition in the consumer tax market and a material worsening of the economic environment leading to elevated losses in INTU's small business segments. We are also concerned about potential acquisition-integration issues.

▶ Our 12-month target price of $45 is 21.0X our FY 11 operating EPS estimate, near the average three-year P/E multiple highs that we calculate for the stock, reflecting our view of share gains in INTU's consumer tax and small business franchises.

Qualitative Risk Assessment

LOW	MEDIUM	HIGH

Our risk assessment reflects our view of the company's strong market position within the consumer and professional tax segments and its solid balance sheet. However, this is tempered by our concern about the potential for a slowdown in the company's small business segment (excluding acquisitions) if the economy weakens considerably.

Quantitative Evaluations

S&P Quality Ranking   B+

D	C	B-	B	B+	A-	A	A+

Relative Strength Rank   STRONG

79

LOWEST = 1   HIGHEST = 99

Revenue/Earnings Data

Revenue (Million $)

	1Q	2Q	3Q	4Q	Year
2010	474.0	837.0	1,607	537.0	3,455
2009	481.4	791.0	1,434	475.8	3,183
2008	444.9	834.9	1,313	478.2	3,071
2007	350.5	750.6	1,139	432.7	2,673
2006	304.1	742.7	952.6	342.9	2,342
2005	266.0	662.6	849.5	301.8	2,038

Earnings Per Share ($)

2010	-0.21	0.26	1.78	-0.15	1.66
2009	-0.16	0.26	1.47	-0.22	1.35
2008	-0.14	0.34	1.33	-0.19	1.33
2007	-0.17	0.40	1.04	-0.19	1.25
2006	-0.17	0.43	0.84	-0.06	1.05
2005	-0.11	0.39	0.81	-0.06	1.00

Fiscal year ended Jul. 31. Next earnings report expected: Mid November. EPS Estimates based on S&P Operating Earnings; historical GAAP earnings are as reported.

Dividend Data

No cash dividends have been paid.

Intuit Inc

Business Summary August 24, 2010

CORPORATE OVERVIEW. Intuit is a leading provider of accounting, financial management, personal finance and tax software for consumers and small businesses. The company's flagship products include QuickBooks, TurboTax, Lacerte and Quicken. In FY 09 (Jul.), the company had four main product categories, which contained seven segments. The company's Small Business Group includes the Financial Management Solutions (formerly QuickBooks), Employee Management Solutions (formerly Payroll) and Payment Solutions (formerly Payments) segments. Its Tax Products group includes the Consumer Tax and Accounting Professional segments; other segments include Financial Institutions and Other Businesses.

Financial Management Solutions (which accounted for 18% of total net revenues in FY 09) includes products and services that provide bookkeeping capabilities and business management tools. INTU offers QuickBooks Simple Start for very small, less complex businesses; QuickBooks Pro for slightly larger businesses and QuickBooks Pro for Mac; QuickBooks Premier, to support businesses that need advanced accounting capabilities and business planning tools; and QuickBooks Enterprise Solutions, designed for mid-sized companies. INTU also offers an online version of QuickBooks and Premier and Enterprise versions that cater to specific industries, including Manufacturing, Wholesale, Retail, Non-Profit, Contractor, and Professional Services.

Employee Management Solutions (11%) consists of solutions including outsourced payroll services QuickBooks Payroll in different varieties and QuickBooks Online Payroll, for use with QuickBooks Online Edition. Direct deposit and electronic tax payment and filing services are available with some of these offerings for additional fees. The Payment Solutions (9%) segment includes credit card, debit card, electronic benefits, check guarantee and gift card processing, Web-based transaction processing services for online merchants as well as customer service, charge-back retrieval and support, and fraud and loss prevention screening.

The Consumer Tax (31%) segment is centered on TurboTax. TurboTax software enables individuals and small businesses to prepare and file income tax returns using computers. TurboTax for the Web allows individuals to prepare tax returns online. Versions of TurboTax Premier software are designed to address the special income tax needs of different types of users, including investors, those planning for retirement, and rental property owners. Electronic tax filing services are also provided.

Company Financials Fiscal Year Ended Jul. 31

Per Share Data ($)	2010	2009	2008	2007	2006	2005	2004	2003	2002	2001
Tangible Book Value	2.07	1.35	0.32	0.66	3.41	3.61	2.75	3.44	4.02	4.15
Cash Flow	2.45	2.19	1.97	1.51	1.34	1.31	1.03	0.81	0.30	-0.09
Earnings	1.66	1.35	1.33	1.25	1.05	1.00	0.79	0.82	0.16	-0.24
S&P Core Earnings	1.66	1.35	1.22	1.19	1.04	0.86	0.61	0.41	NA	-0.32
Dividends	NA	Nil	Nil	Nil	Nil	Nil	Nil	Nil	Nil	Nil
Payout Ratio	Nil	Nil	Nil	Nil	Nil	Nil	Nil	Nil	Nil	Nil
Prices:High	47.90	31.29	32.00	33.10	35.98	27.97	26.63	26.95	27.52	23.69
Prices:Low	29.00	21.07	20.18	26.14	23.99	18.62	17.92	16.65	17.26	11.31
P/E Ratio:High	29	23	24	26	34	28	34	33	NM	NM
P/E Ratio:Low	17	16	15	21	23	19	23	20	NM	NM

Income Statement Analysis (Million $)

	2010	2009	2008	2007	2006	2005	2004	2003	2002	2001
Revenue	3,455	3,183	3,071	2,673	2,342	2,038	1,868	1,651	1,358	1,261
Operating Income	1,119	957	891	773	677	659	561	461	343	265
Depreciation	256	275	216	135	104	118	97.0	76.5	59.9	59.9
Interest Expense	61.0	51.2	52.3	27.1	Nil	Nil	Nil	Nil	Nil	Nil
Pretax Income	815	653	698	696	610	556	453	393	84.9	-96.5
Effective Tax Rate	NA	31.4%	35.2%	36.1%	38.0%	32.6%	30.0%	33.0%	17.9%	NM
Net Income	539	447	451	443	377	375	317	263	69.8	-97.1
S&P Core Earnings	538	446	414	422	372	323	245	172	-0.77	-129

Balance Sheet & Other Financial Data (Million $)

	2010	2009	2008	2007	2006	2005	2004	2003	2002	2001
Cash	1,622	1,347	828	255	180	83.8	27.2	1,207	452	535
Current Assets	2,295	1,968	1,774	1,952	1,817	1,614	1,517	1,669	1,995	2,148
Total Assets	5,198	4,826	4,667	4,252	2,770	2,716	2,696	2,790	2,963	2,962
Current Liabilities	1,221	1,084	1,467	1,160	1,016	1,003	857	796	733	788
Long Term Debt	998	998	1,000	998	15.4	17.5	5.77	29.3	14.6	12.4
Common Equity	2,821	2,556	2,073	2,035	1,738	1,695	1,822	1,965	2,216	2,170
Total Capital	3,819	3,556	3,079	3,034	1,754	1,713	1,828	1,994	2,230	2,182
Capital Expenditures	130	182	306	105	44.6	38.2	52.3	50.4	42.6	77.1
Cash Flow	795	722	667	538	482	493	414	340	130	-37.2
Current Ratio	1.9	1.8	1.2	1.7	1.8	1.6	1.8	2.1	2.7	2.7
% Long Term Debt of Capitalization	26.1	28.1	32.5	32.9	0.9	1.0	0.3	1.5	0.7	0.6
% Net Income of Revenue	15.6	14.1	14.7	16.6	16.1	18.4	17.0	15.9	5.1	NM
% Return on Assets	10.8	9.4	10.1	24.1	13.8	13.8	11.6	9.2	2.4	NM
% Return on Equity	20.1	19.3	22.0	23.5	22.0	21.3	16.7	12.6	3.2	NM

Data as orig reptd.; bef. results of disc opers/spec. items. Per share data adj. for stk. divs.; EPS diluted. E-Estimated. NA-Not Available. NM-Not Meaningful. NR-Not Ranked. UR-Under Review.

Office: 2700 Coast Ave, Mountain View, CA 94043-1140.
Telephone: 650-944-6000.
Email: investor_relations@intuit.com
Website: http://www.intuit.com

Chrmn: W.V. Campbell
Pres & CEO: B.D. Smith
SVP & CFO: R.N. Williams
SVP, Secy & General Counsel: L.A. Fennell

Chief Acctg Officer & Cntlr: J.P. Hank
Investor Contact: K. Patel (650-944-3560)
Board Members: D. H. Batchelder, C. W. Brody, W. V. Campbell, S. D. Cook, D. B. Greene, M. R. Hallman, S. N. Johnson, E. A. Kangas, D. D. Powell, B. D. Smith

Founded: 1984
Domicile: Delaware
Employees: 7,700

Invesco Ltd

STANDARD &POOR'S

S&P Recommendation BUY ★★★★☆

Price	12-Mo. Target Price	Investment Style
$22.11 (as of Oct 25, 2010)	$26.00	Large-Cap Blend

GICS Sector Financials
Sub-Industry Asset Management & Custody Banks

Summary This diversified investment manager offers an array of investment options to individuals and institutions through offices around the world.

Key Stock Statistics (Source S&P, Vickers, company reports)

52-Wk Range	$24.00–16.37	S&P Oper. EPS 2010**E**	1.31	Market Capitalization(B)	$10.350	Beta	1.75
Trailing 12-Month EPS	$0.79	S&P Oper. EPS 2011**E**	1.64	Yield (%)	1.99	S&P 3-Yr. Proj. EPS CAGR(%)	33
Trailing 12-Month P/E	28.0	P/E on S&P Oper. EPS 2010**E**	16.9	Dividend Rate/Share	$0.44	S&P Credit Rating	BBB+
$10K Invested 5 Yrs Ago	$20,675	Common Shares Outstg. (M)	468.1	Institutional Ownership (%)	84		

Price Performance

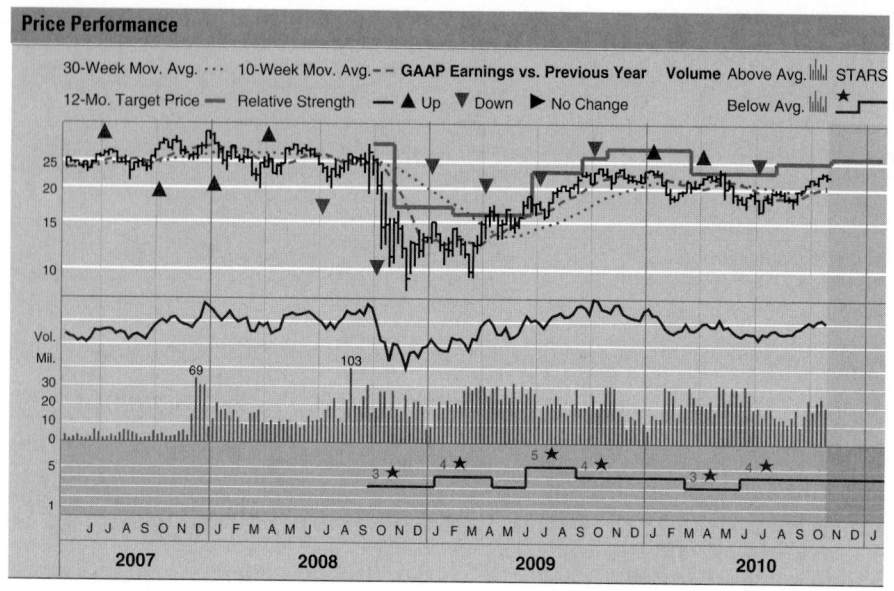

- 30-Week Mov. Avg. · · ·
- 10-Week Mov. Avg. – –
- **GAAP Earnings vs. Previous Year**
- Volume Above Avg.
- STARS
- 12-Mo. Target Price —
- Relative Strength
- ▲ Up ▼ Down ► No Change
- Below Avg.

Highlights

▶ The 12-month target price for IVZ has recently been changed to $26.00 from $25.00. The Highlights section of this Stock Report will be updated accordingly.

Investment Rationale/Risk

▶ The Investment Rationale/Risk section of this Stock Report will be updated shortly. For the latest News story on IVZ from MarketScope, see below.

▶ 10/25/10 01:15 pm ET ... S&P REITERATES BUY RECOMMENDATION ON SHARES OF INVESCO (IVZ 22.18****): IVZ posts adjusted Q3 EPS of $0.39, vs. $0.27, above our $0.31 estimate, driven by higher fees, but inflows were weak. We think IVZ's shift in asset allocation toward equities bodes well for AUMs and inflows. We believe IVZ has the flexibility to increase its adjusted operating margin to 40% in '11 on cost-savings from its acquisition of Morgan Stanley's unit (MS 25, Hold). We raise our '10 estimate to $1.31 from $1.18 and '11's to $1.64 from $1.54 on expected margin improvement. We lift our target price by $1 to $26, 16X our revised '11 EPS estimate, a slight premium to peers. / B.Howlett

Qualitative Risk Assessment

LOW	**MEDIUM**	HIGH

Our risk assessment reflects our view of the company's strong market share, broad product base and improving investment performance, offset by economic and industry cyclicality, the firm's bias toward equity products, and recent relative fund underperformance.

Quantitative Evaluations

S&P Quality Ranking   NR

D	C	B-	B	B+	A-	A	A+

Relative Strength Rank   MODERATE

66

LOWEST = 1   HIGHEST = 99

Revenue/Earnings Data

Revenue (Million $)

	1Q	2Q	3Q	4Q	Year
2010	719.1	787.0	--	--	--
2009	548.6	625.1	705.8	747.8	2,627
2008	910.4	935.6	827.2	634.4	3,308
2007	900.2	979.0	976.6	1,023	3,879
2006	584.1	588.1	587.1	655.3	2,415
2005	537.8	547.8	536.2	551.4	2,173

Earnings Per Share ($)

	1Q	2Q	3Q	4Q	Year
2010	0.22	0.09	E0.39	E0.38	E1.31
2009	0.08	0.18	0.24	0.25	0.76
2008	0.39	0.41	0.33	0.08	1.21
2007	0.38	0.43	0.41	0.43	1.64
2006	0.26	0.30	0.26	0.40	1.20
2005	0.18	0.18	0.18	-0.02	0.52

Fiscal year ended Dec. 31. Next earnings report expected: NA. EPS Estimates based on S&P Operating Earnings; historical GAAP earnings are as reported.

Dividend Data (Dates: mm/dd Payment Date: mm/dd/yy)

Amount ($)	Date Decl.	Ex-Div. Date	Stk. of Record	Payment Date
0.103	01/27	02/19	02/23	03/10/10
0.110	04/28	05/20	05/24	06/09/10
0.110	07/27	08/19	08/23	09/09/10
0.110	10/25	11/17	11/19	12/08/10

Dividends have been paid since 1995. Source: Company reports.

Business Summary July 28, 2010

CORPORATE OVERVIEW. Invesco is an independent global investment management company that provides an array of investment choices for retail, institutional and high-net-worth clients around the globe. It is incorporated under the laws of Bermuda, and it is headquartered in Atlanta, Georgia. Prior to May 2007, the company was called AMVESCAP PLC, formed through the 1997 merger of Invesco and AIM. Through its subsidiaries, it offers equity, fixed income, and alternative strategies to investors domiciled throughout the world. Assets under management (AUM) totaled $423 billion at December 31, 2009, up from $357 billion at year-end 2008. Retail assets accounted for 49% of AUM, institutional assets were 48% of the total, and assets in the private wealth management unit accounted for the remaining 3%. Clients domiciled in the U.S. accounted for 61% of AUM at the end of 2009, U.K. clients owned 20%, and clients in Canada, Europe, and Asia each represented less than 10% of assets.

The company distributes its products utilizing a number of brands through various distribution channels. Its retail products are distributed through Invesco AIM in the U.S., Invesco Trimark in Canada, Invesco Perpetual in the U.K., Invesco in Europe and Asia, and PowerShares for exchange traded funds (ETFs). Retail products are primarily distributed through third parties, including broker-dealers, retirement platforms, financial advisors and insurance companies. Its assets in China are managed through its joint-venture called Invesco Great Wall. It offers a full array of investment options, including money market, fixed income, balanced, equity and alternative fund choices.

Its institutional clients are served throughout the world through Invesco and Invesco AIM. It offers a range of products, including equities, fixed income, real estate, financial structures and absolute return strategies. Private equity options are offered through W.L. Ross & Co. A global salesforce distributes products and provides service to clients around the world. Clients include public entities, corporate, union, non-profit, endowments, foundations, and financial institutions.

Invesco's private wealth management services are offered through Atlantic Trust. It provides high-net-worth individuals with personalized service, including financial counseling, estate planning, asset allocation, investment management, private equity, trust, custody and other services. It had offices in 20 countries at December 31, 2009.

Company Financials Fiscal Year Ended Dec. 31

Per Share Data ($)	2009	2008	2007	2006	2005	2004	2003	2002	2001	2000
Tangible Book Value	NA	NM	NM	NM	NM	NM	NM	NM	NM	NM
Cash Flow	NA	1.33	1.85	1.37	0.76	-0.60	0.80	0.89	1.27	1.65
Earnings	0.76	1.21	1.64	1.20	0.52	-0.84	-0.08	0.06	0.54	1.22
Dividends	0.31	0.52	0.37	0.36	0.33	0.32	0.37	0.36	0.30	0.46
Payout Ratio	40%	43%	23%	30%	63%	NM	NM	NM	56%	38%
Prices:High	24.07	31.40	32.25	25.04	15.92	17.33	18.16	31.80	48.00	61.19
Prices:Low	9.33	8.35	26.10	15.46	11.15	9.62	7.65	7.62	16.20	20.60
P/E Ratio:High	32	3	20	21	31	NM	NM	NM	89	51
P/E Ratio:Low	12	1	16	13	21	NM	NM	NM	30	17

Income Statement Analysis (Million $)										
Revenue	2,627	3,308	3,879	2,415	2,173	1,158	1,158	1,345	1,620	1,629
Operating Income	NA	795	1,058	853	595	-63.3	362	427	591	591
Depreciation	NA	47.6	64.1	67.6	94.5	45.6	200	210	206	110
Interest Expense	NA	76.9	71.3	81.3	85.1	44.1	48.3	52.6	55.9	51.6
Pretax Income	358	657	1,244	755	360	-138	36.4	102	280	446
Effective Tax Rate	41.5%	35.9%	28.7%	35.0%	40.7%	NM	NM	83.5%	44.8%	35.3%
Net Income	323	482	674	490	212	-173	-17.3	16.9	155	289

Balance Sheet & Other Financial Data (Million $)										
Cash	972	658	1,130	924	1,957	369	393	424	209	466
Current Assets	NA	2,379	4,194	3,497	2,706	1,385	1,297	1,150	785	1,152
Total Assets	10,910	9,757	12,925	9,292	7,578	3,907	4,110	4,138	4,432	4,296
Current Liabilities	NA	2,103	3,641	3,582	2,523	1,253	1,070	1,139	641	764
Long Term Debt	746	862	1,276	973	1,212	683	730	596	844	960
Common Equity	6,913	5,690	6,591	4,270	3,613	1,863	2,232	2,283	2,282	2,103
Total Capital	NA	7,458	8,988	5,248	4,872	2,590	2,993	2,918	3,126	3,063
Capital Expenditures	NA	84.1	36.7	37.7	38.2	27.6	36.6	54.6	68.0	62.0
Cash Flow	NA	529	738	558	307	-128	183	227	361	399
Current Ratio	1.4	1.1	1.2	1.0	1.1	1.1	1.2	1.0	1.2	1.5
% Long Term Debt of Capitalization	Nil	11.6	14.2	18.5	24.9	26.4	24.4	20.4	27.0	31.3
% Net Income of Revenue	12.3	14.6	17.4	20.3	9.8	NM	NM	1.3	9.6	17.7
% Return on Assets	NA	5.9	5.3	5.8	2.8	NM	NM	0.7	3.6	9.4
% Return on Equity	NA	7.8	10.6	12.4	5.9	NM	NM	0.7	7.1	22.7

Data as orig reptd.; bef. results of disc opers/spec. items. Per share data adj. for stk. divs.; EPS diluted. Prior to 2005 balance sheet and income statement in pounds. E-Estimated. NA-Not Available. NM-Not Meaningful. NR-Not Ranked. UR-Under Review.

Office: 1555 Peachtree St, NE Ste 1800, Atlanta, GA 30309.
Telephone: 404-479-1095.
Email: jordan.krugman@invesco.com
Website: http://www.invesco.com

Chrmn: R.D. Adams
Pres & CEO: M.L. Flanagan
CFO: L.M. Starr
Chief Admin Officer: C.D. Meadows

Chief Acctg Officer & Cntlr: D.A. Hartley
Investor Contact: J. Krugman (404-439-4605)
Board Members: R. D. Adams, J. Banham, J. R. Canion, M. L. Flanagan, B. F. Johnson, III, D. Kessler, E. P. Lawrence, J. T. Presby, J. I. Robertson, P. A. Wood

Founded: 1935
Domicile: Bermuda
Employees: 4,890

Iron Mountain Inc

STANDARD &POOR'S

S&P Recommendation	HOLD ★★★★★	Price $22.61 (as of Oct 22, 2010)	12-Mo. Target Price $23.00	Investment Style Large-Cap Growth

GICS Sector Industrials
Sub-Industry Diversified Support Services

Summary This company provides information protection and storage services.

Key Stock Statistics (Source S&P, Vickers, company reports)

52-Wk Range	$28.49–19.93	S&P Oper. EPS 2010E	1.12	Market Capitalization(B)	$4.556	Beta	0.97
Trailing 12-Month EPS	$0.84	S&P Oper. EPS 2011E	1.22	Yield (%)	NA	S&P 3-Yr. Proj. EPS CAGR(%)	11
Trailing 12-Month P/E	26.9	P/E on S&P Oper. EPS 2010E	20.2	Dividend Rate/Share	NA	S&P Credit Rating	BB-
$10K Invested 5 Yrs Ago	$9,181	Common Shares Outstg. (M)	201.5	Institutional Ownership (%)	93		

Price Performance

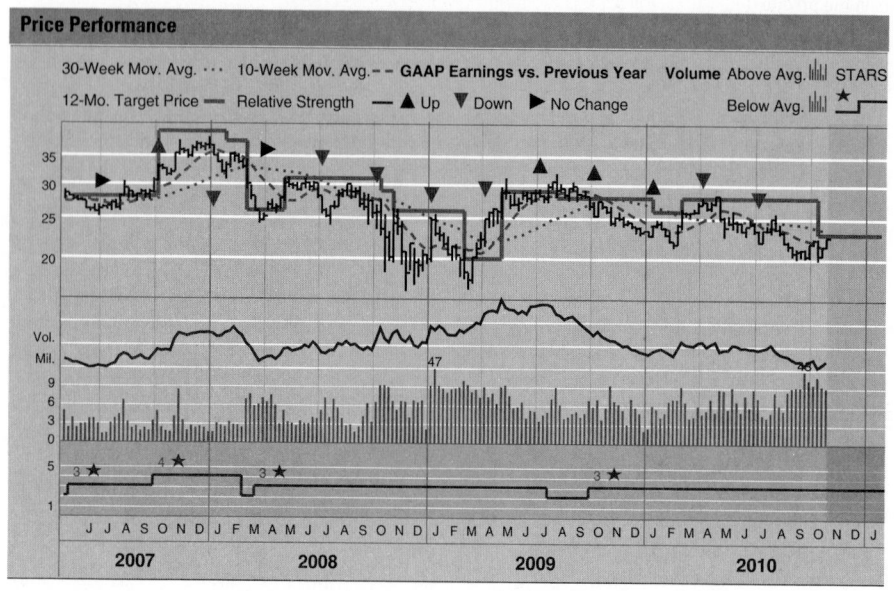

30-Week Mov. Avg. ··· 10-Week Mov. Avg. - - **GAAP Earnings vs. Previous Year** Volume Above Avg. STARS
12-Mo. Target Price — Relative Strength — ▲ Up ▼ Down ▶ No Change Below Avg. ★

Options: CBOE, P, Ph

Analysis prepared by **Dylan Cathers** on October 06, 2010, when the stock traded at **$ 20.45.**

Qualitative Risk Assessment

LOW	MEDIUM	HIGH

Our risk assessment reflects our view of IRM's diversified and significant recurring revenue base, offset by notable and increasing competition and a substantial amount of debt on its balance sheet.

Quantitative Evaluations

S&P Quality Ranking B

D	C	B-	B	B+	A-	A	A+

Relative Strength Rank MODERATE

54

LOWEST = 1   HIGHEST = 99

Revenue/Earnings Data

Revenue (Million $)

	1Q	2Q	3Q	4Q	Year
2010	776.5	779.8	--	--	
2009	723.4	746.0	764.9	779.3	3,014
2008	749.4	768.9	784.3	752.6	3,055
2007	632.5	668.7	701.8	727.0	2,730
2006	563.7	581.6	595.6	609.5	2,350
2005	501.4	511.9	526.5	538.4	2,078

Earnings Per Share ($)

	1Q	2Q	3Q	4Q	Year
2010	0.13	0.20	E0.28	E0.33	E1.12
2009	0.14	0.43	0.21	0.30	1.08
2008	0.17	0.18	0.06	0.01	0.40
2007	0.17	0.19	0.25	0.14	0.76
2006	0.13	0.19	0.13	0.18	0.64
2005	0.11	0.13	0.18	0.15	0.57

Fiscal year ended Dec. 31. Next earnings report expected: Late October. EPS Estimates based on S&P Operating Earnings; historical GAAP earnings are as reported.

Dividend Data (Dates: mm/dd Payment Date: mm/dd/yy)

Amount ($)	Date Decl.	Ex-Div. Date	Stk. of Record	Payment Date
0.063	02/25	03/23	03/25	04/15/10
0.063	06/04	06/23	06/25	07/15/10
0.063	09/15	09/24	09/28	10/15/10

Dividends have been paid since 2010. Source: Company reports.

Highlights

▶ We expect a somewhat improving demand environment to lead to sales growth of 4.5% in 2010, but we look for a decline to 3.0% in 2011. We think that weakness within the core services business in North America will remain for the next couple of quarters, given weak economic activity in general. We note that some verticals are being particularly weighed down, including legal services. Sales of complementary services, however, should increase at a slightly faster pace, despite soft project activity and subscription rates. We also see elongated sales cycles and high levels of destructions adversely affecting growth next year. Over the long term, we think revenue growth will be helped by a rigorous regulatory environment, as well as selective acquisitions, such as the recent purchase of Mimosa Systems.

▶ We expect solid operating margin gains in 2010 and 2011, as increased operational efficiencies, lower costs and improved pricing should partly offset weak sales of higher-margin services.

▶ Excluding one-time items, operating EPS was $0.96 in 2009. In 2010, we look for EPS of $1.12, improving to $1.22 in 2011.

Investment Rationale/Risk

▶ Our hold opinion is based on valuation. We believe IRM's brand and customer base are competitive advantages for the long term. Further, we take a positive view of the company's recent initiation of a $0.25 per year dividend. Nonetheless, we think still weak recycled paper prices and higher levels of destructions (which adversely affects growth in storage) will limit sales and earnings growth. In addition, we continue to have concerns about a longer sales cycle and weak demand in the difficult, but improving, economic environment.

▶ Risks to our recommendation and target price include slower growth in corporate storage spending than we project, lower-than-expected recycled paper prices, further deterioration in overseas markets, and less favorable foreign currency rates.

▶ Our 12-month target price of $23 is based on our P/E analysis. We use a peer-premium multiple of 18.9X our 2011 EPS estimate. While we believe the stability of IRM's business merits a peer-premium valuation, our P/E ratio is near a four-year low for the company reflecting what we believe are poor long-term revenue growth prospects.

Please read the Required Disclosures and Analyst Certification on the last page of this report.

The McGraw·Hill Companies

Iron Mountain Inc

STANDARD &POOR'S

Business Summary October 06, 2010

CORPORATE OVERVIEW. We view Iron Mountain as the global leader in information protection and storage services. IRM helps organizations reduce related costs and risks. Specifically, the company offers records-management and data protection solutions, and helps address information challenges including rising storage costs, litigation, regulatory compliance, and disaster recovery.

Revenues are generated by providing storage for a variety of information media formats, core records management services, data and recovery offerings, information destruction services, and an expanding menu of complementary products and services to a diverse customer base. Core services, which are highly recurring in nature, primarily consist of the collection, handling, and transportation of stored records and information. In 2009, IRM's storage and core service revenues represented about 88% of total revenues.

As of year-end 2009, IRM had more than 140,000 corporate clients around the world, including more than 97% of the Fortune 1000 and over 93% of the FTSE 1000. The company provides services in 38 countries and operates over 1,000 records management facilities. The share of international contributions to IRM's revenue in 2009 was flat versus 2008 at 32%, but it has crept up to 32% from 28% in 2005.

The customer base is diversified by industry, with commercial, legal, banking, health care, accounting, financial, entertainment and government organizations all represented. Further, no single customer represented more than 2% of revenue for 2009 or either of the three prior years.

CORPORATE STRATEGY. Primary growth drivers include increasing revenues from existing customers, adding new clients, introducing new products and services (such as secure shredding, electronic vaulting and digital archiving), and acquisitions.

Company Financials Fiscal Year Ended Dec. 31

Per Share Data ($)	2009	2008	2007	2006	2005	2004	2003	2002	2001	2000
Tangible Book Value	NM	NM	NM	NM	NM	NM	NM	NM	NM	NM
Cash Flow	2.64	1.83	1.99	1.71	1.54	1.31	1.12	0.91	0.64	0.57
Earnings	1.08	0.40	0.76	0.64	0.57	0.48	0.43	0.35	-0.17	-0.14
S&P Core Earnings	1.08	0.40	0.69	0.61	0.55	0.46	0.43	0.33	-0.17	NA
Dividends	Nil	Nil	Nil	Nil	Nil	Nil	Nil	Nil	Nil	Nil
Payout Ratio	Nil	Nil	Nil	Nil	Nil	Nil	Nil	Nil	Nil	Nil
Prices:High	32.04	37.13	38.85	29.91	30.06	23.39	18.06	15.20	13.54	11.65
Prices:Low	16.91	16.71	25.05	22.64	17.77	17.22	13.44	8.95	9.37	8.22
P/E Ratio:High	30	93	51	47	52	49	41	44	NM	NM
P/E Ratio:Low	16	42	33	35	31	36	31	26	NM	NM

Income Statement Analysis (Million $)	2009	2008	2007	2006	2005	2004	2003	2002	2001	2000
Revenue	3,014	3,055	2,730	2,350	2,078	1,818	1,501	1,319	1,171	986
Operating Income	868	791	699	611	575	507	441	364	302	257
Depreciation	319	291	249	214	192	164	135	110	154	127
Interest Expense	230	237	229	195	184	186	150	137	135	118
Pretax Income	333	225	223	224	197	167	157	120	-8.13	-18.0
Effective Tax Rate	33.2%	63.6%	30.9%	41.8%	41.4%	41.7%	42.5%	41.1%	NM	NM
Net Income	221	82.0	153	129	114	94.2	84.6	67.0	-32.2	-24.9
S&P Core Earnings	221	82.4	139	122	110	91.9	83.4	63.5	-31.7	NA

Balance Sheet & Other Financial Data (Million $)	2009	2008	2007	2006	2005	2004	2003	2002	2001	2000
Cash	447	278	133	45.4	53.4	31.9	74.7	56.3	21.4	6.20
Current Assets	1,211	976	822	680	554	501	472	367	309	237
Total Assets	6,847	6,357	6,308	5,210	4,766	4,442	3,892	3,231	2,860	2,659
Current Liabilities	815	730	766	639	592	515	585	428	359	314
Long Term Debt	3,211	3,207	3,213	2,606	2,504	2,439	1,974	1,662	1,461	1,314
Common Equity	2,141	1,803	1,795	1,553	1,370	1,219	1,066	945	886	924
Total Capital	5,397	5,050	5,389	4,444	4,105	3,877	3,262	2,748	2,459	2,320
Capital Expenditures	313	387	386	382	272	232	204	197	197	169
Cash Flow	540	373	402	343	306	258	219	177	121	102
Current Ratio	1.5	1.3	1.1	1.1	0.9	1.0	0.8	0.9	0.9	0.8
% Long Term Debt of Capitalization	59.5	63.5	64.2	58.6	61.0	62.9	60.5	60.5	59.4	56.6
% Net Income of Revenue	7.3	2.7	5.6	5.5	5.5	5.2	5.6	5.1	NM	NM
% Return on Assets	3.4	1.3	2.7	2.6	2.5	2.3	2.4	2.2	NM	NM
% Return on Equity	11.2	4.6	9.1	8.8	8.8	8.2	8.4	7.3	NM	NM

Data as orig reptd.; bef. results of disc opers/spec. items. Per share data adj. for stk. divs.; EPS diluted. E-Estimated. NA-Not Available. NM-Not Meaningful. NR-Not Ranked. UR-Under Review.

Office: 745 Atlantic Ave, Boston, MA 02111-2717.
Telephone: 617-535-4766.
Website: http://www.ironmountain.com
Chrmn: C.R. Reese

Pres & CEO: R.T. Brennan
EVP, CFO & Chief Acctg Officer: B.P. McKeon
EVP & CIO: T. Tsolakis
SVP, Secy & General Counsel: E.W. Cloutier

Investor Contact: S.P. Golden (617-535-4766)
Board Members: C. H. Bailey, C. R. Boden, R. T. Brennan, K. P. Dauten, P. F. Deninger, P. Halvorsen, M. W. Lamach, A. D. Little, C. R. Reese, V. J. Ryan, L. A. Tucker, A. J. Verrecchia

Founded: 1951
Domicile: Delaware
Employees: 20,100

ITT Corp

STANDARD &POOR'S

S&P Recommendation	**STRONG BUY** ★★★★★	Price $48.51 (as of Oct 22, 2010)	12-Mo. Target Price $63.00	Investment Style Large-Cap Growth

GICS Sector Industrials
Sub-Industry Aerospace & Defense

Summary This company is a diversified industrial manufacturer of advanced technology products.

Key Stock Statistics (Source S&P, Vickers, company reports)

52-Wk Range	$57.99– 42.05	S&P Oper. EPS 2010**E**	4.23	Market Capitalization(B)	$8.897	Beta	1.12
Trailing 12-Month EPS	$3.48	S&P Oper. EPS 2011**E**	4.53	Yield (%)	2.06	S&P 3-Yr. Proj. EPS CAGR(%)	16
Trailing 12-Month P/E	13.9	P/E on S&P Oper. EPS 2010**E**	11.5	Dividend Rate/Share	$1.00	S&P Credit Rating	BBB+
$10K Invested 5 Yrs Ago	$9,390	Common Shares Outstg. (M)	183.4	Institutional Ownership (%)	78		

Price Performance

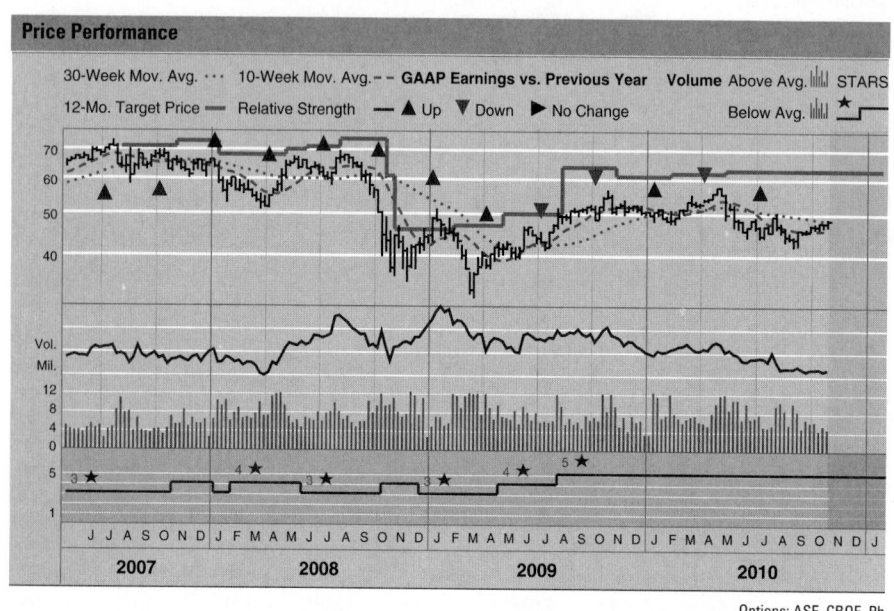

30-Week Mov. Avg. ···· 10-Week Mov. Avg. ‒‒ **GAAP Earnings vs. Previous Year** Volume Above Avg. STARS
12-Mo. Target Price — Relative Strength — ▲ Up ▼ Down ► No Change Below Avg.

Options: ASE, CBOE, Ph

Analysis prepared by **Efraim Levy, CFA** on August 06, 2010, when the stock traded at **$ 45.76**.

Highlights

► We expect U.S. GDP to rise in 2010, with ITT also benefiting from increased global sales. We see ITT's sales advancing 3% for the year, with the motion & flow control segment showing the strongest annual growth, followed by fluid technology. We expect the defense segment to be down for the year before rising in 2011 as some programs wind down. We expect all three segments to post sales gains in 2011 and overall sales to rise by mid-single digits.

► We think operating margins in 2010 will benefit from revenue growth and cost-cutting actions, despite asbestos-related costs. The recent acquisition of Godwin Pumps should be dilutive to 2010 EPS but accretive in 2011. We see higher tax rates, as well as higher pension and retirement expense, reducing profits. Our $4.23 EPS forecast excludes restructuring charges.

► Although we view the company's balance sheet and cash flow as strong, ITT has said it will focus on liquidity and temporarily cut back on share buybacks and acquisition activity. Longer term, we expect the company to post 8% to 10% average annual revenue growth, reflecting new products, expanded markets and potential acquisitions.

Investment Rationale/Risk

► We believe strong cash flow will support a modest cash dividend, debt reduction, share buybacks, and strategic acquisitions. The cash dividend was recently increased, and we expect the dividend payment to rise on an annual basis. With its long-term debt below 27% of total capitalization, which is in line with key peers, we see ITT's balance sheet as solid.

► Risks to our recommendation and target price include reduced demand at ITT's operating segments, competitive price pressures, and slower-than-expected economic growth. While we do not consider the company's expected asbestos obligations to be material, there is a risk that obligations will be greater than expected.

► Our 12-month target price of $63 is based on relative and DCF metrics. Applying a multiple of about 15X, reflecting peer and historical comparisons, to our 2010 EPS estimate of $4.23 leads to a value of $63. Our discounted cash flow model, which assumes a weighted average cost of capital of 11.5%, compound annual growth of 3.5% over the next 15 years, and a terminal growth rate of 3.0%, also generates intrinsic value of $63.

Qualitative Risk Assessment

LOW	MEDIUM	HIGH

Our risk assessment reflects our view of ITT's favorable growth prospects in most of the markets it serves and our view of its strong management team and solid balance sheet. This is offset by our outlook for U.S. defense spending growth, which we think may slow in coming years.

Quantitative Evaluations

S&P Quality Ranking A-

D	C	B-	B	B+	A-	A	A+

Relative Strength Rank MODERATE

54

LOWEST = 1   HIGHEST = 99

Revenue/Earnings Data

Revenue (Million $)

	1Q	2Q	3Q	4Q	Year
2010	2,636	2,739	--	--	--
2009	2,557	2,780	2,698	2,870	10,905
2008	2,806	3,064	2,879	2,945	11,695
2007	2,070	2,223	2,181	2,529	9,003
2006	1,792	1,964	2,001	2,051	7,808
2005	1,776	1,874	1,828	1,950	7,427

Earnings Per Share ($)

2010	0.79	1.22	E1.03	E1.19	E4.23
2009	1.01	1.10	0.36	1.06	3.54
2008	0.93	1.22	1.20	0.96	4.23
2007	0.74	1.08	0.92	0.70	3.44
2006	0.55	0.72	0.75	0.65	2.67
2005	0.65	0.70	0.79	-0.48	1.67

Fiscal year ended Dec. 31. Next earnings report expected: Early November. EPS Estimates based on S&P Operating Earnings; historical GAAP earnings are as reported.

Dividend Data (Dates: mm/dd Payment Date: mm/dd/yy)

Amount ($)	Date Decl.	Ex-Div. Date	Stk. of Record	Payment Date
0.250	02/22	03/01	03/03	04/01/10
0.250	05/11	05/19	05/21	07/01/10
0.250	08/09	08/25	08/27	10/01/10
0.250	10/12	11/09	11/12	01/01/11

Dividends have been paid since 1996. Source: Company reports.

ITT Corp

Business Summary August 06, 2010

CORPORATE OVERVIEW. ITT Corp. (name changed from ITT Industries in July 2006) is primarily a producer of defense electronics and fluid technology products.

Fluid technology products (31% of 2009 sales) include pumps, valves, heat exchangers, mixers and fluid measuring instruments and controls for residential, agricultural, commercial, municipal and industrial applications. The fluid technology segment became the world's largest pump manufacturer (formerly third largest) following its 1997 acquisition of Goulds Pumps, Inc.

Defense electronics and services (58%) are sold to the military and to government agencies. Products include traffic control systems, jamming devices that guard military planes against radar guided missiles, digital combat radios, night vision devices, radar, satellite instruments and other.

Motion & flow control products (11%) include switches and valves for industrial and aerospace applications, products for the marine and leisure markets, and fluid handling materials such as tubing systems and connectors for vari-

ous automotive and industrial markets for the transportation industry.

CORPORATE STRATEGY. The company seeks to expand revenues through a combination of internal growth and acquisitions. We expect the company to continue its history of successful acquisition integrations.

At the same time, ITT plans to divest operations that do not fit its strategic goals or provide adequate returns. A recent example is the 2007 divestiture of the switch components operations, which accounted for about half of the electronics segment's 2006 revenues.

We expect the company to increase revenues via new products, expanded markets and acquisitions.

Company Financials Fiscal Year Ended Dec. 31

Per Share Data ($)	2009	2008	2007	2006	2005	2004	2003	2002	2001	2000
Tangible Book Value	NM	NM	NM	1.72	1.38	NM	0.78	NM	NM	NM
Cash Flow	5.13	5.74	4.45	3.58	2.71	3.37	3.08	2.94	2.37	2.59
Earnings	3.54	4.23	3.44	2.67	1.67	2.32	2.08	2.03	1.20	1.47
S&P Core Earnings	3.51	2.65	3.35	2.74	2.28	2.13	1.94	0.69	-0.18	NA
Dividends	0.85	0.70	0.56	0.55	0.36	0.34	0.32	0.30	0.30	0.30
Payout Ratio	24%	17%	16%	21%	22%	15%	15%	15%	25%	20%
Prices:High	56.95	69.73	73.44	58.73	58.05	43.36	37.70	35.43	26.00	19.81
Prices:Low	31.94	34.75	56.30	45.34	40.24	35.52	25.06	22.90	17.78	11.19
P/E Ratio:High	16	16	21	22	35	19	18	17	22	13
P/E Ratio:Low	9	8	16	17	24	15	12	11	15	8

Income Statement Analysis (Million $)

	2009	2008	2007	2006	2005	2004	2003	2002	2001	2000
Revenue	10,905	11,695	9,003	7,808	7,427	6,764	5,627	4,985	4,676	4,829
Operating Income	1,519	1,566	1,229	1,024	985	871	559	706	707	695
Depreciation	293	278	185	172	197	199	188	171	213	202
Interest Expense	99.5	141	115	86.2	75.0	50.4	Nil	68.8	85.5	93.1
Pretax Income	825	1,088	898	727	448	610	531	509	333	420
Effective Tax Rate	21.2%	28.7%	29.6%	31.3%	29.8%	28.3%	26.3%	25.3%	35.0%	37.0%
Net Income	651	775	633	500	314	438	391	380	217	265
S&P Core Earnings	644	485	616	512	429	400	364	129	-31.7	NA

Balance Sheet & Other Financial Data (Million $)

	2009	2008	2007	2006	2005	2004	2003	2002	2001	2000
Cash	1,216	965	1,840	937	451	263	414	202	121	88.7
Current Assets	4,256	4,064	4,930	3,348	2,772	2,329	2,106	1,701	1,459	1,506
Total Assets	11,129	10,480	11,553	7,430	7,063	7,277	5,938	5,390	4,508	4,611
Current Liabilities	2,616	4,031	5,456	2,759	2,560	2,446	1,687	1,730	1,897	2,233
Long Term Debt	1,431	468	3,566	500	516	543	461	492	456	408
Common Equity	3,878	3,060	3,945	3,362	2,723	2,343	1,848	1,137	1,376	1,211
Total Capital	5,309	3,541	4,637	3,863	3,240	2,886	2,309	1,630	1,832	1,620
Capital Expenditures	272	249	239	177	179	165	154	153	174	181
Cash Flow	943	1,054	818	671	511	636	579	551	430	466
Current Ratio	1.6	1.0	0.9	1.2	1.1	1.0	1.2	1.0	0.8	0.7
% Long Term Debt of Capitalization	27.0	13.3	10.9	13.0	15.9	18.8	20.0	30.2	24.9	25.2
% Net Income of Revenue	6.0	6.6	7.0	6.4	4.2	6.5	6.9	7.6	4.6	5.5
% Return on Assets	6.0	7.0	6.7	6.9	4.4	6.6	6.9	7.7	4.8	5.8
% Return on Equity	18.8	22.1	18.6	16.1	12.4	20.9	26.2	30.2	16.8	22.9

Data as orig reptd.; bef. results of disc opers/spec. items. Per share data adj. for stk. divs.; EPS diluted. E-Estimated. NA-Not Available. NM-Not Meaningful. NR-Not Ranked. UR-Under Review.

Office: 1133 Westchester Ave, White Plains, NY 10604-3516.
Telephone: 914-641-2000.
Website: http://www.itt.com
Chrmn, Pres & CEO: S.R. Loranger

SVP & CFO: D.L. Ramos
Treas: C. Ostrowski
Secy: B.M. Fealing
General Counsel: F.R. Jimenez

Investor Contact: P.J. Milligan
Board Members: C. J. Crawford, A. Day, R. English, C. A. Gold, R. F. Hake, J. J. Hamre, P. J. Kern, A. Lambert, S. R. Loranger, F. T. MacInnis, S. N. Mohapatra, L. S. Sanford, M. I. Tambakeras, I. Vasello

Founded: 1920
Domicile: Indiana
Employees: 40,200

Jabil Circuit Inc

STANDARD &POOR'S

S&P Recommendation BUY ★★★★☆	**Price** $14.18 (as of Oct 22, 2010)	**12-Mo. Target Price** $16.00	**Investment Style** Large-Cap Growth

GICS Sector Information Technology
Sub-Industry Electronic Manufacturing Services

Summary This company manufactures circuit board assemblies for international OEMs in the computing, peripheral, storage, communications, networking and industrial markets.

Key Stock Statistics (Source S&P, Vickers, company reports)

52-Wk Range	$18.49– 10.17	S&P Oper. EPS 2011**E**	1.80	Market Capitalization(B)	$3.084	Beta	1.97
Trailing 12-Month EPS	$0.78	S&P Oper. EPS 2012**E**	2.00	Yield (%)	1.97	S&P 3-Yr. Proj. EPS CAGR(%)	27
Trailing 12-Month P/E	18.2	P/E on S&P Oper. EPS 2011**E**	7.9	Dividend Rate/Share	$0.28	S&P Credit Rating	BB+
$10K Invested 5 Yrs Ago	$5,149	Common Shares Outstg. (M)	217.5	Institutional Ownership (%)	83		

Price Performance

30-Week Mov. Avg. · · · · 10-Week Mov. Avg. - - **GAAP Earnings vs. Previous Year** Volume Above Avg. STARS
12-Mo. Target Price — Relative Strength — ▲ Up ▼ Down ▶ No Change Below Avg. ★

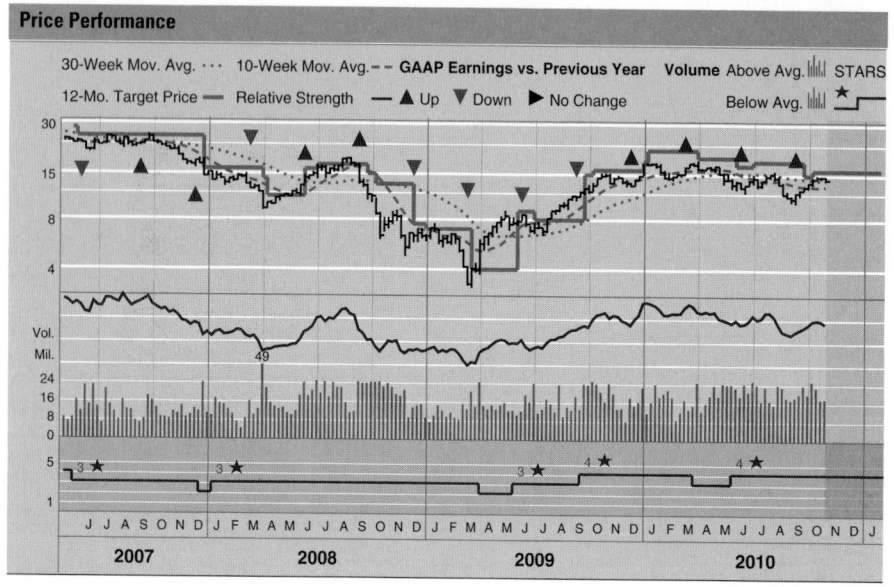

Analysis prepared by **Thomas W. Smith, CFA** on October 01, 2010, when the stock traded at **$ 14.30**.

Options: ASE, CBOE, P, Ph

Highlights

▶ We forecast an 18% revenue increase for FY 11 (Aug.), and a 9% rise in FY 12, reflecting our projection of a recovery for the electronic manufacturing services (EMS) industry from a deep downturn. We see the potential for new business wins and a continued push into low-cost geographies helping sales. While JBL benefits from providing end-to-end solutions to a well-diversified customer base, we believe some rivals have even greater scale efficiencies.

▶ We expect margins to continue to widen in FY 11, aided by rising volumes and by savings from restructuring activities. Capital expenditures rose in FY 10 to support new programs, but we project capital spending to be stable to slightly lower in FY 11 as some projects are completed. A focus on higher-margin product lines should also aid margins.

▶ On an operating basis excluding restructuring-related charges, but including stock option expense that we see at about $0.34 in FY 11 and $0.37 in FY 12, we estimate EPS of $1.80 in FY 11 and $2.00 for FY 12.

Investment Rationale/Risk

▶ We think that an economic upturn through FY 12 will lead to better results for the company. We believe a push by the company to diversify its business mix away from lower-margin consumer business will aid margins. Cost savings from restructurings should also help. However, we believe that the boost in capital expenditures creates some risk. Overall, we view these volatile shares as attractively valued in the context of an industry upturn that we project.

▶ Risks to our recommendation and target price include smaller market share gains than we project, slower and more costly implementation of new contracts and facilities than we expect, and less smooth restructuring than we foresee.

▶ We apply a price-to-book multiple of 1.9X, which is toward the low end of the 10-year historical range for JBL, to our estimate of tangible book value per share of $8.40 to derive a valuation near $16. Applying a peer-based target P/E of 9X to our FY 11 operating EPS estimate of $1.80 results in a similar valuation and, blending these measures, we arrive at our 12-month target price of $16.

Qualitative Risk Assessment

LOW	MEDIUM	**HIGH**

Our risk assessment reflects our view of the historically volatile nature of the electronic manufacturing services industry as well as what we see as the company's relatively high exposure to fluctuations in commodity prices.

Quantitative Evaluations

S&P Quality Ranking B-

D	C	**B-**	B	B+	A-	A	A+

Relative Strength Rank MODERATE

57

LOWEST = 1   HIGHEST = 99

Revenue/Earnings Data

Revenue (Million $)

	1Q	2Q	3Q	4Q	Year
2010	3,088	3,005	3,456	3,861	13,409
2009	3,383	2,887	2,615	2,800	11,685
2008	3,368	3,059	3,088	3,265	12,780
2007	3,224	2,935	3,002	3,130	12,291
2006	2,404	2,315	2,592	2,954	10,265
2005	1,833	1,716	1,938	2,037	7,524

Earnings Per Share ($)

2010	0.13	0.14	0.24	0.27	0.78
2009	-1.34	-4.19	-0.14	0.03	-5.63
2008	0.30	-0.12	0.19	0.28	0.65
2007	0.20	0.07	0.03	0.06	0.35
2006	0.37	0.32	0.30	-0.22	0.77
2005	0.27	0.22	0.29	0.34	1.12

Fiscal year ended Aug. 31. Next earnings report expected: Late December. EPS Estimates based on S&P Operating Earnings; historical GAAP earnings are as reported.

Dividend Data (Dates: mm/dd Payment Date: mm/dd/yy)

Amount ($)	Date Decl.	Ex-Div. Date	Stk. of Record	Payment Date
0.070	01/22	02/11	02/16	03/01/10
0.070	04/14	05/13	05/17	06/01/10
0.070	07/22	08/13	08/16	09/01/10
0.070	10/21	11/10	11/15	12/01/10

Dividends have been paid since 2006. Source: Company reports.

Jabil Circuit Inc

STANDARD &POOR'S

Business Summary October 01, 2010

CORPORATE OVERVIEW. Jabil Circuit provides electronic manufacturing services (EMS), working with customers in a variety of industries at facilities around the world. Among the many services the company offers are design and engineering, component selection and procurement, automated assembly, product testing, parallel global production, enclosure services, systems assembly, direct order fulfillment, and aftermarket services.

The company reports in three operating segments: Electronic Manufacturing Services (EMS) represented 58% of sales in FY 09 (Aug.), Consumer represented 36%, and Aftermarket Services (AMS) represented 6%. Within the EMS segment, industry sectors served include Automotive, at 3% of FY 09 total sales, Computing and Storage 11%, Instrumentation and Medical 19%, Networking 17%, Telecommunications 6%, and Other 2%. Within the Consumer segment, Display represented 4% of FY 09 total sales, Mobility 20%, and Peripherals 12%. Notably among trends within the company's focus, revenue from the Mobility operations revived to 20% in FY 09, after a dip to 12% in FY 08

and 16% in FY 07, almost rising back to the level of 21% set in FY 06.

In FY 09, Cisco Systems and Research in Motion were the only customers accounting for more than 10% of sales, with Cisco at 13% (16% of FY 08 sales) and Research in Motion at 12% (under 10% of FY 08 sales). Among other large customers are Hewlett-Packard, which accounted for 11% of FY 08 sales, Nokia Corp., IBM, EchoStar, NetApp, Royal Philips Electronics, and Pace PLC. In FY 09, the five largest customers represented 43% of sales, and 50 customers accounted for 90% of JBL's revenues. Overall, we believe the company faces some risk from reliance on large customer accounts. However, this is typical within the EMS industry, and we think the company has made some progress in broadening its customer base over the past three years.

Company Financials Fiscal Year Ended Aug. 31

Per Share Data ($)	2010	2009	2008	2007	2006	2005	2004	2003	2002	2001
Tangible Book Value	NA	6.15	6.90	5.97	8.26	8.22	7.29	6.06	6.63	6.43
Cash Flow	NA	-4.22	1.99	1.51	1.71	2.18	1.89	1.32	1.11	1.35
Earnings	0.78	-5.63	0.65	0.35	0.77	1.12	0.81	0.21	0.17	0.59
S&P Core Earnings	0.90	-0.73	0.64	0.35	0.77	0.64	0.59	0.04	NA	0.46
Dividends	0.28	0.28	0.28	0.28	0.14	Nil	Nil	Nil	Nil	Nil
Payout Ratio	36%	NM	43%	80%	18%	Nil	Nil	Nil	Nil	Nil
Prices:High	18.49	17.91	18.78	27.86	43.70	39.00	32.40	31.66	26.79	40.99
Prices:Low	10.17	3.10	4.77	14.27	22.01	21.80	19.18	21.20	11.13	14.00
P/E Ratio:High	24	NM	29	80	57	35	40	NM	NM	69
P/E Ratio:Low	13	NM	7	41	29	19	24	NM	65	24

Income Statement Analysis (Million $)	2010	2009	2008	2007	2006	2005	2004	2003	2002	2001
Revenue	13,409	11,685	12,780	12,291	10,265	7,524	6,253	4,729	3,545	4,331
Operating Income	643	457	582	494	522	507	439	369	296	353
Depreciation	NA	292	276	240	199	220	222	224	188	155
Interest Expense	80.3	82.3	94.3	86.1	23.5	24.8	19.4	17.0	13.1	5.86
Pretax Income	247	-1,005	157	94.5	225	276	198	37.0	44.8	166
Effective Tax Rate	NA	NM	16.0%	22.6%	26.9%	16.1%	15.5%	NM	22.4%	28.7%
Net Income	169	-1,165	134	73.2	165	232	167	43.0	34.7	119
S&P Core Earnings	195	-152	131	73.9	165	134	122	8.12	-0.11	93.4

Balance Sheet & Other Financial Data (Million $)	2010	2009	2008	2007	2006	2005	2004	2003	2002	2001
Cash	744	876	773	664	774	796	621	700	641	431
Current Assets	4,503	3,677	4,139	3,666	3,679	2,686	2,183	2,094	1,588	1,447
Total Assets	6,217	5,318	7,032	6,295	5,412	4,077	3,329	3,245	2,548	2,358
Current Liabilities	3,455	2,686	3,048	2,991	2,701	1,568	1,159	1,263	593	505
Long Term Debt	1,019	1,037	1,100	760	330	327	305	297	355	362
Common Equity	1,578	1,435	2,716	2,443	2,294	2,135	1,819	1,588	1,507	1,414
Total Capital	2,779	2,677	3,832	3,226	2,632	2,462	2,125	1,905	1,903	1,813
Capital Expenditures	NA	292	338	302	280	257	218	117	85.5	309
Cash Flow	NA	-873	410	313	363	452	389	267	223	274
Current Ratio	1.3	1.4	1.4	1.2	1.4	1.7	1.9	1.7	2.7	2.9
% Long Term Debt of Capitalization	36.7	38.7	28.7	23.6	12.5	13.3	14.4	15.6	18.6	20.0
% Net Income of Revenue	1.3	NM	1.1	0.6	1.6	3.1	2.7	0.9	1.0	2.7
% Return on Assets	2.9	NM	2.0	1.3	3.5	6.3	5.1	1.5	1.4	5.4
% Return on Equity	11.2	NM	5.2	3.1	7.4	11.7	9.8	2.8	2.4	8.8

Data as orig reptd.; bef. results of disc opers/spec. items. Per share data adj. for stk. divs.; EPS diluted. E-Estimated. NA-Not Available. NM-Not Meaningful. NR-Not Ranked. UR-Under Review.

Office: 10560 Dr. Martin Luther King Jr. Street North, St. Petersburg, FL 33716.
Telephone: 727-577-9749.
Email: investor_relations@jabil.com
Website: http://www.jabil.com

Chrmn: W.D. Morean
Pres & CEO: T.L. Main
Vice Chrmn: T.A. Sansone
COO: M.T. Mondello

CFO & Chief Acctg Officer: F.I. Alexander
Investor Contact: B. Walters (727-803-3349)
Board Members: M. S. Lavitt, T. L. Main, W. D. Morean, L. J. Murphy, F. A. Newman, S. Raymund, T. A. Sansone, D. Stout, K. A. Walters

Founded: 1969
Domicile: Delaware
Employees: 61,000

Jacobs Engineering Group Inc.

STANDARD &POOR'S

S&P Recommendation	**STRONG BUY** ★★★★★	Price $39.21 (as of Oct 22, 2010)	12-Mo. Target Price $53.00	Investment Style Large-Cap Growth

GICS Sector Industrials
Sub-Industry Construction & Engineering

Summary This company provides engineering, construction and maintenance services to private industry and federal government agencies on a worldwide basis.

Key Stock Statistics (Source S&P, Vickers, company reports)

52-Wk Range	$50.68– 33.70	S&P Oper. EPS 2010**E**	2.60	Market Capitalization(B)	$4.930	Beta	1.37
Trailing 12-Month EPS	$1.98	S&P Oper. EPS 2011**E**	3.00	Yield (%)	Nil	S&P 3-Yr. Proj. EPS CAGR(%)	3
Trailing 12-Month P/E	19.8	P/E on S&P Oper. EPS 2010**E**	15.1	Dividend Rate/Share	Nil	S&P Credit Rating	NA
$10K Invested 5 Yrs Ago	$13,083	Common Shares Outstg. (M)	125.7	Institutional Ownership (%)	77		

Price Performance

30-Week Mov. Avg. · · · 10-Week Mov. Avg. – – GAAP Earnings vs. Previous Year   Volume Above Avg. STARS
12-Mo. Target Price — Relative Strength — ▲ Up ▼ Down ► No Change   Below Avg.

2007   2008   2009   2010

Options: ASE, CBOE, Ph

Analysis prepared by **Stewart Scharf** on October 12, 2010, when the stock traded at **$ 39.60**.

Highlights

➤ We believe revenue declined in the low double digits in FY 10 (Sep.), as backlog continued to be hurt by soft customer spending levels, especially in field services. However, we see modest revenue growth resuming in FY 11, as we see improving global market trends leading to a resurgence in orders, especially for upstream oil & gas projects, driven by the oil sands in Canada. We also expect more infrastructure and building projects, while JEC targets acquisitions in the Middle East, China and India.

➤ We think gross margins narrowed to near 13% in FY 10, from 13.7% in FY 09, driven by competitive pricing pressures in the private sector. Margins should begin to improve sequentially during FY 11, due to a better backlog mix, while we believe operating margins will expand on increased global engineering work at low-cost centers (mainly in India), and other cost control efforts.

➤ We expect the effective tax rate to remain near 36% during FY 11, with FY 10 operating EPS of $2.60 (before a $0.48 litigation charge and a $0.04 office closing charge), advancing 15%, to $3.00, in FY 11.

Investment Rationale/Risk

➤ We base our strong buy opinion on our valuation metrics, along with the company's diversified customer and geographic base, and relationship-based business model, which focuses on relatively small, lower-risk projects rather than the competitively bid large lump-sum projects that are the industry standard. Also, the company's balance sheet remains strong.

➤ Risks to our recommendation and target price include a prolonged global economic downturn; project delays or cancellations based on customer liquidity issues or sharply lower oil prices; an inability to outsource skilled labor overseas; and a lack of acquisition opportunities.

➤ Our discounted cash flow (DCF) model suggests an intrinsic value of $58, assuming a perpetuity growth rate of 4% and a weighted average cost of capital (WACC) of about 13%. Based on relative metrics, and JEC's risk averse business model, we apply an above-peer and market P/E of 16X to our FY 11 EPS estimate, resulting in a value of $48. Blending these metrics, we arrive at our 12-month target price of $53.

Qualitative Risk Assessment

LOW	**MEDIUM**	HIGH

Our risk assessment reflects the cyclical nature of the company's various markets, its growth-by-acquisition strategy, changes in global political conditions, timing issues related to new awards, and fluctuations in interest rates and foreign currencies. These factors are offset by what we see as JEC's strong cash position and virtually no debt.

Quantitative Evaluations

S&P Quality Ranking B+

D	C	B-	B	**B+**	A-	A	A+

Relative Strength Rank MODERATE

49

LOWEST = 1   HIGHEST = 99

Revenue/Earnings Data

Revenue (Million $)

	1Q	2Q	3Q	4Q	Year
2010	2,478	2,587	2,508	--	--
2009	3,233	2,975	2,707	2,553	11,467
2008	2,472	2,665	2,919	3,197	11,252
2007	2,019	2,092	2,084	2,280	8,474
2006	1,683	1,832	1,926	1,979	7,421
2005	1,283	1,383	1,449	1,519	5,635

Earnings Per Share ($)

2010	0.58	0.62	0.15	E0.73	E2.60
2009	0.94	0.88	0.76	0.63	3.21
2008	0.79	0.80	0.87	0.92	3.38
2007	0.51	0.55	0.61	0.68	2.35
2006	0.36	0.37	0.42	0.49	1.64
2005	0.28	0.31	0.34	0.36	1.29

Fiscal year ended Sep. 30. Next earnings report expected: Mid November. EPS Estimates based on S&P Operating Earnings; historical GAAP earnings are as reported.

Dividend Data

No cash dividends have been paid since 1984.

Please read the Required Disclosures and Analyst Certification on the last page of this report.

The McGraw-Hill Companies

Jacobs Engineering Group Inc.

STANDARD &POOR'S

Business Summary October 12, 2010

CORPORATE OVERVIEW. Jacobs Engineering focuses on providing a broad range of technical, professional and construction services to a large number of industrial, commercial and governmental clients worldwide. The company offers project services; consulting services; operations and maintenance services; and construction services via offices primarily in North America, Europe, Asia and Australia. In November 2007, the company was moved into the S&P 500 Index from S&P's MidCap 400 Index.

In FY 09 (Sep.), revenues by sector were: refining (downstream), 35%; national government (environmental, defense and NASA), 21%; chemicals, 11%; pharmaBio (pharmaceutical and biotech), 8%; oil and gas (upstream), 8%; infrastructure, 8%; buildings, 5%; and pulp and paper, high tech, food and consumer products, 4%. The higher-margin technical professional services component accounted for 48% of revenues and 54% of backlog in FY 09, with the balance derived from field services (construction). As of July 2, 2010, backlog was $13.5 billion ($7.8 billion technical professional), down 8% sequentially and 15% from $15.8 billion a year earlier. Approximately $1.9 billion was removed from backlog due to project cancellations during FY 09 ($200 million from professional services), following $2.4 billion in FY 08. The company generally realizes about 60% to 65% of its backlog as revenues during any 12-month period. However, JEC believes about 52% of the backlog will be realized as revenues in FY 10. About 36% of revenues was generated from operations outside of the U.S in FY 09, including 19% in Europe and 14% in Canada.

Project services include the engineering and design of process plants and high-technology facilities. Construction services offers traditional field services to private and public sector clients. Operations and maintenance services include all tasks required to keep a process plant in day-to-day operation.

In FY 09, revenues derived from agencies of the U.S. government accounted for over 20% of the total, up from 16.8% in FY 08. Cost-reimbursable projects accounted for 85% of the FY 09 total, down slightly from 86% in FY 08. Fixed-price contracts accounted for 14%, while guaranteed maximum price was 1%.

At the end of FY 09, the company's pension plans were underfunded by $312 million, up from $234 million a year earlier.

Company Financials Fiscal Year Ended Sep. 30

Per Share Data ($)	2009	2008	2007	2006	2005	2004	2003	2002	2001	2000
Tangible Book Value	13.19	10.28	8.42	7.36	5.10	4.04	4.00	2.73	2.55	2.15
Cash Flow	3.90	3.97	2.85	2.04	1.70	1.44	1.45	1.31	1.16	0.86
Earnings	3.21	3.38	2.35	1.64	1.29	1.13	1.14	0.99	0.81	0.48
S&P Core Earnings	3.01	3.08	2.38	1.68	1.16	1.02	0.91	0.75	0.53	NA
Dividends	Nil	Nil	Nil	Nil	Nil	Nil	Nil	Nil	Nil	Nil
Payout Ratio	Nil	Nil	Nil	Nil	Nil	Nil	Nil	Nil	Nil	Nil
Prices:High	54.71	103.29	99.62	46.64	34.71	24.11	24.97	21.45	18.92	12.30
Prices:Low	30.16	26.00	38.25	33.90	22.33	18.43	17.48	13.05	10.56	6.55
P/E Ratio:High	17	31	42	29	27	21	22	22	24	25
P/E Ratio:Low	9	8	16	21	17	16	15	13	13	14

Income Statement Analysis (Million $)										
Revenue	11,467	11,252	8,474	7,421	5,635	4,594	4,616	4,556	3,957	3,419
Operating Income	707	716	498	350	288	232	232	207	183	165
Depreciation	86.3	73.1	55.7	48.3	46.4	34.2	35.4	35.1	38.9	40.1
Interest Expense	2.92	4.41	8.00	7.50	6.47	3.57	3.25	7.50	11.7	11.4
Pretax Income	625	657	449	305	236	198	197	169	138	81.3
Effective Tax Rate	36.0%	36.0%	36.0%	35.5%	36.0%	35.0%	35.0%	35.0%	36.5%	37.3%
Net Income	400	421	287	197	151	129	128	110	87.8	51.0
S&P Core Earnings	374	383	290	202	136	118	102	82.3	57.5	NA

Balance Sheet & Other Financial Data (Million $)										
Cash	1,034	604	613	434	240	100	126	48.5	49.3	65.8
Current Assets	2,818	2,750	2,278	1,818	1,337	1,084	970	975	946	851
Total Assets	4,429	4,278	3,389	2,854	2,354	2,071	1,671	1,674	1,557	1,384
Current Liabilities	1,296	1,577	1,276	1,041	785	686	611	740	701	684
Long Term Debt	0.74	55.7	40.0	77.7	89.6	78.8	17.8	85.7	164	147
Common Equity	2,626	2,245	1,844	1,423	1,141	1,005	842	690	592	496
Total Capital	2,650	2,386	1,884	1,508	1,237	1,089	865	781	761	648
Capital Expenditures	55.5	115	64.6	54.0	43.9	37.1	25.8	37.2	28.8	44.4
Cash Flow	486	494	343	245	197	163	163	145	127	91.1
Current Ratio	2.2	1.7	1.8	1.7	1.7	1.6	1.6	1.3	1.4	1.2
% Long Term Debt of Capitalization	NM	2.3	2.1	5.2	7.2	7.2	2.1	11.0	21.6	22.7
% Net Income of Revenue	3.5	3.7	3.3	2.7	2.7	2.8	2.8	2.4	2.2	1.5
% Return on Assets	9.2	11.0	9.1	7.5	6.8	6.9	7.7	6.8	6.0	3.9
% Return on Equity	16.4	20.6	17.5	15.2	14.1	14.0	16.7	17.1	16.1	10.8

Data as orig reptd.; bef. results of disc opers/spec. items. Per share data adj. for stk. divs.; EPS diluted. E-Estimated. NA-Not Available. NM-Not Meaningful. NR-Not Ranked. UR-Under Review.

Office: 1111 South Arroyo Parkway, Pasadena, CA, USA 91105.
Telephone: 626-578-3500.
Website: http://www.jacobs.com
Chrmn: N. Watson

Pres & CEO: C.L. Martin
EVP, CFO, Chief Admin Officer & Treas: J. Prosser, Jr.
SVP, Chief Acctg Officer & Cntlr: N.G. Thawerbhoy
SVP & General Counsel: W.C. Markley, III

Investor Contact: J.W. Prosser, Jr. (626-578-6803)
Board Members: J. R. Bronson, J. F. Coyne, R. C. Davidson, Jr., E. V. Fritzky, J. P. Jumper, C. L. Martin, B. Montoya, T. M. Niles, P. Robertson, N. Watson, L. F. levinson

Founded: 1957
Domicile: Delaware
Employees: 53,200

The McGraw-Hill Companies

Janus Capital Group Inc

STANDARD &POOR'S

S&P Recommendation BUY ★★★★☆	**Price** $10.73 (as of Oct 22, 2010)	**12-Mo. Target Price** $14.00	**Investment Style** Large-Cap Blend

GICS Sector Financials
Sub-Industry Asset Management & Custody Banks

Summary Janus is an investment management company focused on equity growth and quantitative strategies.

Key Stock Statistics (Source S&P, Vickers, company reports)

52-Wk Range	$15.72– 8.63	S&P Oper. EPS 2010E	0.70	Market Capitalization(B)	$1.971	Beta	2.69
Trailing 12-Month EPS	$0.60	S&P Oper. EPS 2011E	0.87	Yield (%)	0.37	S&P 3-Yr. Proj. EPS CAGR(%)	NM
Trailing 12-Month P/E	17.9	P/E on S&P Oper. EPS 2010E	15.3	Dividend Rate/Share	$0.04	S&P Credit Rating	BB+
$10K Invested 5 Yrs Ago	$7,267	Common Shares Outstg. (M)	183.7	Institutional Ownership (%)	100		

Price Performance

30-Week Mov. Avg. · · · 10-Week Mov. Avg. - - GAAP Earnings vs. Previous Year   Volume Above Avg. STARS
12-Mo. Target Price — Relative Strength   ▲ Up ▼ Down ► No Change   Below Avg. ★

Options: CBOE, P, Ph

Analysis prepared by **Rafay Khalid, CFA** on October 22, 2010, when the stock traded at **$ 10.83**.

Highlights

▶ We think strong relative fund performance at JNS will attract client assets once general investor sentiment improves. Right now, the firm's growth equity is seeing outflows while its fixed income and value offerings are still seeing strong sales trends. Performance at its INTECH quant subsidiary has appeared to rebound while outflows have slowed, suggesting an improving trend there too. We also expect the company will benefit from improved distribution channels and increased penetration of the institutional market. Higher average assets under management and a more favorable asset mix should help revenues grow 18% in 2010 and 12% in 2011.

▶ We expect compensation accruals to remain above historical levels in 2010, before falling on a relative basis in 2011. Cost-cutting measures have already helped reduce non-compensation expenses, and a modest decline in the accrual rate in 2010 should allow pretax margins to rebound above 20% during the year. Interest costs should also continue to decrease, and seed investment losses have abated.

▶ We project EPS of $0.70 in 2010 and $0.87 in 2011.

Investment Rationale/Risk

▶ As of September 2010, 42%, 86% and 91% of firm-wide mutual funds were in the top half of their categories on a one-, three- and five-year total return basis, respectively, and we think consistently strong relative fund performance has attracted client assets. We believe investors prefer growth products and we see solid fund performance from the company in an improving investment environment. While we think caution is warranted as the company is less diversified than many peers, an improved economic outlook and a gradual recovery in equity markets brighten our view, and our recommendation is buy.

▶ Risks to our recommendation and target price include potential equity and bond market depreciation, and increased competition. We are concerned about Janus's corporate governance practices, as we see a need for a higher proportion of independent directors.

▶ Our 12-month target price of $14 is based on a historical average P/E ratio of 16.2X our 2011 EPS estimate. We believe this historical average is warranted, reflecting what we see as an improving economic recovery environment.

Qualitative Risk Assessment

LOW	MEDIUM	HIGH

Our risk assessment reflects the company's lack of product diversification, previous regulatory issues, and turnover of investment personnel.

Quantitative Evaluations

S&P Quality Ranking   B-

D	C	B-	B	B+	A-	A	A+

Relative Strength Rank   MODERATE

30

LOWEST = 1   HIGHEST = 99

Revenue/Earnings Data

Revenue (Million $)

	1Q	2Q	3Q	4Q	Year
2010	246.9	249.3	--	--	--
2009	170.3	200.2	227.6	250.6	848.7
2008	281.2	304.2	275.4	177.1	1,038
2007	247.9	273.0	284.6	311.5	1,117
2006	256.1	254.6	250.1	265.9	1,027
2005	239.0	229.3	237.5	247.3	953.1

Earnings Per Share ($)

	1Q	2Q	3Q	4Q	Year
2010	0.17	0.17	E0.18	E0.18	E0.70
2009	0.02	0.10	0.05	-5.22	-5.22
2008	0.24	0.40	0.16	0.05	0.86
2007	0.20	0.28	0.29	0.30	1.07
2006	0.17	0.15	0.15	0.19	0.66
2005	0.09	0.12	0.15	0.05	0.40

Fiscal year ended Dec. 31. Next earnings report expected: Late October. EPS Estimates based on S&P Operating Earnings; historical GAAP earnings are as reported.

Dividend Data (Dates: mm/dd Payment Date: mm/dd/yy)

Amount ($)	Date Decl.	Ex-Div. Date	Stk. of Record	Payment Date
0.040	04/29	05/12	05/14	05/28/10

Dividends have been paid since 2000. Source: Company reports.

Please read the Required Disclosures and Analyst Certification on the last page of this report.

The McGraw·Hill Companies

Janus Capital Group Inc

STANDARD &POOR'S

Business Summary October 22, 2010

CORPORATE OVERVIEW. Janus Capital Group, a global asset management company, was created through the January 1, 2003, merger of Janus Capital Corp. into its parent company, Stilwell Financial Inc., which had been spun off from Kansas City Southern Industries in July 2000 via a stock offering. The company had total assets under management of $159.7 billion at the end of 2009, up from $123.5 billion at the end of 2008. The company distributes its products through one global distribution network directly to investors, and through advisers and financial intermediaries.

Wholly owned Janus Capital Management focuses on growth equities, and uses both fundamental and quantitative investment research. It also offers core, international, specialty fixed-income, and money market products. Its largest funds include Janus Fund (JANSX), Janus Worldwide (JAWWX) and Janus Twenty (JAVLX).

The company owns 89.5% (and is in the process of upping its stake to 92%,

per contractual obligations with the founders) of Enhanced Investment Technologies, LLC (INTECH), which focuses on mathematically driven equity investing strategies. INTECH's assets under management totaled $48.0 billion at the end of 2009, up from $7.3 billion at the end of 2002. INTECH, which manages assets for large institutions and endowments, seeks to achieve long-term returns that outperform a passive index, while controlling risks and trading costs.

JNS owns about 80% of Perkins Investment Management LLC (formerly Perkins, Wolf, McDonnell and Co.), which focuses on value investing and sub-advises a number of Janus's small- and mid-cap value products.

Company Financials Fiscal Year Ended Dec. 31

Per Share Data ($)	2009	2008	2007	2006	2005	2004	2003	2002	2001	2000
Tangible Book Value	NM	NM	NM	NM	0.88	1.43	1.00	NM	NM	3.50
Cash Flow	-4.38	1.04	1.21	0.93	0.64	0.99	4.46	0.70	1.93	3.30
Earnings	-5.22	0.86	1.07	0.66	0.40	0.73	4.17	0.38	1.31	2.90
S&P Core Earnings	0.49	1.10	1.05	0.61	0.42	0.32	1.60	0.42	1.18	NA
Dividends	0.04	0.04	0.04	0.04	0.04	0.04	0.04	0.05	0.04	0.01
Payout Ratio	NM	5%	4%	6%	10%	5%	1%	13%	3%	NM
Prices:High	16.06	36.88	37.08	24.20	20.59	17.90	19.00	29.24	46.63	54.50
Prices:Low	3.73	5.18	19.35	15.50	12.75	12.60	9.46	8.97	18.20	30.75
P/E Ratio:High	NM	43	35	37	51	25	5	77	36	19
P/E Ratio:Low	NM	6	18	23	32	17	2	24	14	11

Income Statement Analysis (Million $)	2009	2008	2007	2006	2005	2004	2003	2002	2001	2000
Revenue	849	1,038	1,117	1,027	953	1,011	995	1,145	1,556	2,248
Operating Income	NA	362	375	267	224	264	396	441	872	1,118
Depreciation	NA	28.8	24.9	47.1	50.1	60.4	67.6	72.3	131	81.2
Interest Expense	74.0	75.5	58.8	32.3	28.6	38.4	60.5	57.8	34.8	7.70
Pretax Income	-750	216	330	237	176	272	895	320	620	1,202
Effective Tax Rate	0.84%	31.9%	35.3%	34.5%	38.6%	33.9%	NM	72.6%	35.1%	35.5%
Net Income	-757	138	192	134	87.8	170	956	84.7	302	664
S&P Core Earnings	83.1	178	189	124	92.5	74.1	367	92.4	276	NA

Balance Sheet & Other Financial Data (Million $)	2009	2008	2007	2006	2005	2004	2003	2002	2001	2000
Cash	432	408	691	560	553	527	1,223	161	237	364
Current Assets	NA	584	954	925	1,004	1,065	1,466	346	478	641
Total Assets	2,530	3,337	3,564	3,538	3,629	3,768	4,332	3,322	3,392	1,581
Current Liabilities	NA	157	227	186	268	155	301	185	881	196
Long Term Debt	792	1,106	1,128	537	262	378	769	856	400	Nil
Common Equity	1,022	1,608	1,724	2,306	2,581	2,735	2,661	1,508	1,363	1,058
Total Capital	NA	2,752	3,272	3,261	3,283	3,553	3,997	3,097	2,466	1,342
Capital Expenditures	NA	20.1	16.7	17.0	23.6	26.5	23.9	16.3	34.3	107
Cash Flow	-729	167	217	181	138	230	1,023	157	433	745
Current Ratio	3.4	3.7	4.2	5.0	3.7	6.9	4.9	1.9	0.5	3.3
% Long Term Debt of Capitalization	43.7	41.2	39.3	16.5	8.0	10.6	19.2	27.6	16.2	Nil
% Net Income of Revenue	NM	13.3	17.2	13.0	9.2	16.8	96.1	7.4	19.4	29.5
% Return on Assets	NM	4.0	5.4	3.7	2.4	4.2	25.0	2.5	12.2	47.2
% Return on Equity	NM	8.3	9.5	5.5	3.3	6.3	45.9	5.9	25.0	70.9

Data as orig reptd.; bef. results of disc opers/spec. items. Per share data adj. for stk. divs.; EPS diluted. E-Estimated. NA-Not Available. NM-Not Meaningful. NR-Not Ranked. UR-Under Review.

Office: 151 Detroit St, Denver, CO 80206-4928.
Telephone: 303-333-3863.
Website: http://www.janus.com
Chrmn: S.L. Scheid

CEO: R.M. Weil
COO, SVP & CTO: G.S. Batejan
EVP, CFO, Chief Acctg Officer & Treas: G.A. Frost
EVP, Chief Admin Officer, Secy & General Counsel: K.D. Howes

Board Members: T. K. Armour, P. F. Balser, G. A. Cox, J. Diermeier, J. Fredericks, D. R. Gatzek, L. E. Kochard, R. T. Parry, J. Patton, L. H. Rowland, G. S. Schafer, S. L. Scheid, R. J. Skidelskiy, R. M. Weil

Founded: 1998
Domicile: Delaware
Employees: 1,126

The McGraw·Hill Companies

JDS Uniphase Corp

STANDARD &POOR'S

S&P Recommendation HOLD ★★★☆☆

Price	12-Mo. Target Price	Investment Style
$11.58 (as of Oct 22, 2010)	$13.00	Large-Cap Blend

GICS Sector Information Technology
Sub-Industry Communications Equipment

Summary This company manufactures fiber optic products and communications test and measurement solutions.

Key Stock Statistics (Source S&P, Vickers, company reports)

52-Wk Range	$13.95– 5.35	S&P Oper. EPS 2011E	0.43	Market Capitalization(B)	$2.566	Beta	2.30
Trailing 12-Month EPS	$-0.28	S&P Oper. EPS 2012E	0.65	Yield (%)	Nil	S&P 3-Yr. Proj. EPS CAGR(%)	17
Trailing 12-Month P/E	NM	P/E on S&P Oper. EPS 2011E	26.9	Dividend Rate/Share	Nil	S&P Credit Rating	NA
$10K Invested 5 Yrs Ago	$7,027	Common Shares Outstg. (M)	221.6	Institutional Ownership (%)	67		

Price Performance

- 30-Week Mov. Avg. ···· 10-Week Mov. Avg. -- **GAAP Earnings vs. Previous Year** Volume Above Avg. STARS
- 12-Mo. Target Price — Relative Strength — ▲ Up ▼ Down ► No Change Below Avg.

Options: ASE, CBOE, P, Ph

Analysis prepared by **Ari Bensinger** on September 16, 2010, when the stock traded at **$ 12.07**.

Highlights

► Following a 6% increase in FY 10 (Jun.), we see sales advancing 26% in FY 11, to $1.7 billion, reflecting higher demand for optical communication and test measurement products, as well as $165 million in additional revenue from the May 2010 Network Solutions Division (NSD) acquisition. We see several catalysts ahead, including the implementation of emerging technologies such as LTE and DOCSIS3.0 and an industry 40G upgrade cycle.

► We expect FY 11 gross margins to widen 160 basis points, to 46%, on a favorable product mix and lean manufacturing initiatives, partly offset by higher component expediting fees. Despite increased NSD transition costs, we believe JDSU will manage costs prudently, and we see FY 11 operating expenses rising at a slower rate than sales.

► We think JDSU can meet its 11% to 14% operating margin target range by its FY 11 second quarter. Overall, we estimate FY 11 EPS of $0.43, including $0.20 of projected stock option expense, up from the $0.22 EPS registered in FY 10, which excludes $0.50 of non-recurring items, mostly related to acquired technology amortization expense.

Investment Rationale/Risk

► Industry fundamentals are strong, in our view, as telecom carriers need to upgrade their networks to address a rapid increase in network bandwidth demand. We also are encouraged by JDSU's cost management progress, which is leading to a material ramp in profitability margins, as evidenced by our forecast for earnings growth of 95% and 51% during FY 11 and FY 12, respectively. Even so, based on our valuation analysis, we think the current stock price appropriately reflects the potential operating leverage that we see in JDSU's business model.

► Risks to our recommendation and target price include a prolonged downturn in telecom spending, market share losses, and slower-than-expected margin improvement.

► Our 12-month target price of $13 translates to an enterprise value to EBITDA ratio of 17X and 3X book value, valuation multiples that are in line with the peer mean. On a P/E basis, our target price equates to 30X our FY 11 EPS estimate of $0.43 (including $0.20 of stock option expense), above peers, warranted, in our view, by the potential earnings ramp that we see occurring over the next two years.

Qualitative Risk Assessment

LOW	MEDIUM	HIGH

Our risk assessment reflects the highly competitive nature of the communications equipment industry, and the company's dependence on telecom carrier spending, which tends to be uneven due to the uncertain timing of network projects and upgrades.

Quantitative Evaluations

S&P Quality Ranking   C

D	C	B-	B	B+	A-	A	A+

Relative Strength Rank   MODERATE

34

LOWEST = 1   HIGHEST = 99

Revenue/Earnings Data

Revenue (Million $)

	1Q	2Q	3Q	4Q	Year
2010	297.8	342.9	332.3	390.9	1,364
2009	380.7	357.0	280.6	276.1	1,294
2008	356.7	399.2	383.9	390.3	1,530
2007	318.1	366.3	361.7	350.7	1,397
2006	258.3	312.9	314.9	318.2	1,204
2005	194.5	180.5	166.3	170.9	712.2

Earnings Per Share ($)

2010	-0.14	-0.09	-0.05	0.01	-0.27
2009	-0.08	-3.28	-0.39	-0.27	-4.02
2008	-0.03	0.09	-0.03	-0.13	-0.10
2007	-0.08	0.10	-0.07	-0.08	-0.12
2006	-0.32	-0.24	0.02	-0.24	-0.72
2005	-0.16	-0.24	-0.24	-0.80	-1.44

Fiscal year ended Jun. 30. Next earnings report expected: Early November. EPS Estimates based on S&P Operating Earnings; historical GAAP earnings are as reported.

Dividend Data

No cash dividends have been paid.

The McGraw-Hill Companies

JDS Uniphase Corp

STANDARD &POOR'S

Business Summary September 16, 2010

CORPORATE OVERVIEW. JDS Uniphase supplies optical components, as well as communications test and measurement solutions for the communications market. The company also leverages its optical science capabilities on non-communications applications, offering products for display, security, medical environmental instrumentation, decorative, aerospace and defense applications.

The company operates in three principal segments: communications test and measurement (47% of FY 09 (Jun.) revenue); communications and commercial optical products (37%); and advanced optical technologies (16%).

PRIMARY BUSINESS DYNAMICS. The communications test and measurement segment provides instruments, software, systems and services that help communications equipment manufacturers and service providers accelerate the deployment of broadband networks and services from the core of the network to the home, including deployment over fiber to the curb, node or premise and digital networks. Solutions focus primarily on lab and production test platforms, field test instrumentation and software, and network and service as-

surance systems.

The communications and commercial optical product group supplies the basic building blocks for fiber optic networks, which enable the rapid transmission of large amounts of data over long distances via light waves through fiber optic components, modules and subsystems. Transmission products include optical transceivers, optical transponders, and their supporting components such as modulators and source lasers. Transport products primarily consist of amplifiers and reconfigurable optical add/drop multiplexers (ROADMs) and their supporting components such as pump lasers, passive devices, and array waveguides. The segment also offers a broad portfolio of lasers used by customers in markets and applications such as biotechnology and graphics imaging, remote sensing, and materials processing and precision machining.

Company Financials Fiscal Year Ended Jun. 30

Per Share Data ($)	2010	2009	2008	2007	2006	2005	2004	2003	2002	2001
Tangible Book Value	2.19	2.44	2.73	2.80	2.72	5.76	7.12	7.92	11.44	22.24
Cash Flow	0.35	-3.35	0.55	0.48	-0.46	-1.11	-0.32	-4.82	-42.21	-370.58
Earnings	-0.27	-4.02	-0.10	-0.12	-0.72	-1.44	-0.64	-5.28	-52.00	-411.20
S&P Core Earnings	-0.32	-0.52	-0.12	-0.21	-0.88	-2.24	-2.56	-7.84	-32.88	-175.60
Dividends	NA	Nil	Nil	Nil	Nil	Nil	Nil	Nil	Nil	Nil
Payout Ratio	Nil	Nil	Nil	Nil	Nil	Nil	Nil	Nil	Nil	Nil
Prices:High	13.95	8.75	15.33	17.99	34.40	26.08	47.08	37.68	82.72	519.50
Prices:Low	7.66	2.21	2.01	12.41	13.93	10.56	22.72	19.84	12.64	40.96
P/E Ratio:High	NM	NM	NM	NM	NM	NM	NM	NM	NM	NM
P/E Ratio:Low	NM	NM	NM	NM	NM	NM	NM	NM	NM	NM

Income Statement Analysis (Million $)										
Revenue	1,364	1,294	1,530	1,397	1,204	712	636	676	1,098	3,233
Operating Income	93.7	39.8	87.6	36.8	-107	-83.9	-58.5	-306	-374	-62.5
Depreciation	137	145	145	128	57.4	61.3	55.9	79.2	1,645	5,542
Interest Expense	24.3	7.70	8.80	7.10	27.7	Nil	Nil	Nil	Nil	Nil
Pretax Income	-57.2	-869	-19.3	-24.3	-152	-255	-128	-920	-8,501	-56,494
Effective Tax Rate	NA	NM	NM	NM	NM	NM	NM	NM	NM	NM
Net Income	-59.7	-866	-21.7	-26.3	-151	-261	-113	-934	-8,738	-56,122
S&P Core Earnings	-69.4	-111	-27.5	-45.7	-181	-394	-446	-1,399	-5,534	-23,966

Balance Sheet & Other Financial Data (Million $)										
Cash	568	685	874	363	365	511	328	242	412	763
Current Assets	1,075	1,108	1,429	1,661	1,805	1,588	1,866	1,515	1,857	3,036
Total Assets	1,704	1,670	2,906	3,025	3,065	2,080	2,422	2,138	3,005	12,245
Current Liabilities	351	310	445	348	422	240	350	423	483	848
Long Term Debt	267	325	427	808	900	467	465	Nil	5.50	12.8
Common Equity	909	861	1,817	1,736	1,584	1,335	1,571	1,671	2,471	10,706
Total Capital	1,176	1,186	2,267	2,544	2,484	1,802	2,063	1,699	2,519	11,392
Capital Expenditures	41.4	54.7	51.7	75.7	67.2	35.8	66.4	47.2	133	732
Cash Flow	77.5	-722	123	102	-93.8	-200	-56.7	-855	-7,093	-50,580
Current Ratio	3.1	3.6	3.2	4.8	4.3	6.6	5.3	3.6	3.8	3.6
% Long Term Debt of Capitalization	22.7	27.4	18.8	31.8	36.2	25.9	22.5	Nil	0.2	0.1
% Net Income of Revenue	NM	NM	NM	NM	NM	NM	NM	NM	NM	NM
% Return on Assets	NM	NM	NM	NM	NM	NM	NM	NM	NM	NM
% Return on Equity	NM	NM	NM	NM	NM	NM	NM	NM	NM	NM

Data as orig reptd.; bef. results of disc opers/spec. items. Per share data adj. for stk. divs.; EPS diluted. E-Estimated. NA-Not Available. NM-Not Meaningful. NR-Not Ranked. UR-Under Review.

Office: 430 North McCarthy Boulevard, Milpitas, CA 95035.
Telephone: 408-546-5000.
Email: investor.relations@jdsu.com
Website: http://www.jdsu.com

Chrmn: M.A. Kaplan
Pres & CEO: T.H. Waechter
Vice Chrmn: K.J. Kennedy
Investor Contact: D. Vellequette (408-546-4445)

EVP & CFO: D. Vellequette
Board Members: R. E. Belluzzo, H. L. Covert, Jr., B. D. Day, P. A. Herscher, M. Jabbar, M. A. Kaplan, K. J. Kennedy, R. T. Liebhaber, C. S. Skrzypczak, T. H. Waechter

Founded: 1979
Domicile: Delaware
Employees: 4,700

The **McGraw·Hill** Companies

Johnson Controls Inc.

STANDARD &POOR'S

S&P Recommendation **STRONG BUY** ★★★★★	Price $34.18 (as of Oct 22, 2010)	12-Mo. Target Price $42.00	Investment Style Large-Cap Blend

GICS Sector Consumer Discretionary
Sub-Industry Auto Parts & Equipment

Summary This company supplies building controls and energy management systems, automotive seating, and batteries.

Key Stock Statistics (Source S&P, Vickers, company reports)

52-Wk Range	$35.77–23.62	S&P Oper. EPS 2010**E**	1.97	Market Capitalization(B)	$23.014	Beta	1.79
Trailing 12-Month EPS	$2.03	S&P Oper. EPS 2011**E**	2.44	Yield (%)	1.52	S&P 3-Yr. Proj. EPS CAGR(%)	6
Trailing 12-Month P/E	16.8	P/E on S&P Oper. EPS 2010**E**	17.4	Dividend Rate/Share	$0.52	S&P Credit Rating	BBB
$10K Invested 5 Yrs Ago	$17,088	Common Shares Outstg. (M)	673.3	Institutional Ownership (%)	78		

Price Performance

- 30-Week Mov. Avg. · · · · 10-Week Mov. Avg. – – – **GAAP Earnings vs. Previous Year** Volume Above Avg. ⅢⅢ STARS
- 12-Mo. Target Price — Relative Strength — ▲ Up ▼ Down ► No Change Below Avg. ⅢⅢ ★

3-for-1

Options: ASE, CBOE, Ph

Analysis prepared by **Efraim Levy, CFA** on October 13, 2010, when the stock traded at **$ 32.40**.

Highlights

► In 2010, we look for vehicle sales and production in the U.S. and outside Europe to increase; Europe is likely to be weaker in the absence of 2009's government stimulus programs. We believe revenues in FY 10 (Sep.) advanced at an upper teens pace, led by rebounding automotive and battery contributions. Total revenues in FY 11 should rise 10%. Over the long term, we see the building efficiency unit benefiting from new customers, as outsourcing trends persist and the backlog of orders for installed systems continues to rise. Auto interior sales should benefit from increased business with non-U.S. manufacturers and emerging market growth.

► We see operating margins improving in FY 11 on stronger domestic and foreign demand, benefits from restructuring activities, and a reduction in restructuring costs. Partly offsetting could be pricing pressures from customers, and increases in some raw material costs.

► From depressed levels of FY 09, we see a rebound in EPS in FY 10 to $1.97, and a further 24% advance to $2.44 in FY 11. We expect to see more acquisition activity during the next 12 months as well as an increase in the dividend payout ratio.

Investment Rationale/Risk

► We expect JCI's long-term sales and earnings growth to exceed that of peers, and for the company to show greater earnings stability, aided by its diversification in geography, products and customers. The stock's P/E multiple was recently above that of the S&P 500, based on our calendar 2010 estimates. We view the balance sheet as strong, with long-term debt generally at 20% to 36% of capitalization over the past decade.

► Risks to our recommendation and target price include lower-than-expected demand, especially for automotive parts, higher-than-anticipated raw material costs, and less-than-expected acquisition synergies and restructuring savings.

► Applying a P/E multiple of 15.5X, toward the high end of its historical range, to our FY 11 EPS estimate of $2.44 results in a value of about $38. Our DCF model, which assumes a weighted average cost of capital of 9.5%, a compound annual growth rate of 17% over the next 15 years, and a terminal growth rate of 3.0%, leads to intrinsic value of about $46. Our 12-month target price of $42 is based on a weighted blend of these two metrics.

Qualitative Risk Assessment

LOW	MEDIUM	HIGH

Our risk assessment reflects our view of favorable growth prospects in the building controls markets that JCI serves and what we see as a strong management team and healthy balance sheet, offset by the challenges faced by its automotive operations.

Quantitative Evaluations

S&P Quality Ranking   A

D	C	B-	B	B+	A-	A	A+

Relative Strength Rank   STRONG

88

LOWEST = 1   HIGHEST = 99

Revenue/Earnings Data

Revenue (Million $)

	1Q	2Q	3Q	4Q	Year
2010	8,408	8,317	8,540	--	--
2009	7,336	6,315	6,979	7,867	28,497
2008	9,484	9,406	9,865	9,307	38,062
2007	8,210	8,492	8,911	9,011	34,624
2006	7,528	8,167	8,390	8,150	32,235
2005	6,618	6,899	7,062	6,900	27,479

Earnings Per Share ($)

2010	0.52	0.40	0.61	E0.57	E1.97
2009	-1.02	-0.32	0.26	0.47	-0.57
2008	0.39	0.48	0.73	0.03	1.63
2007	0.28	0.44	0.66	0.77	2.16
2006	0.29	0.28	0.57	0.62	1.75
2005	0.28	0.09	0.44	0.50	1.30

Fiscal year ended Sep. 30. Next earnings report expected: Late October. EPS Estimates based on S&P Operating Earnings; historical GAAP earnings are as reported.

Dividend Data (Dates: mm/dd Payment Date: mm/dd/yy)

Amount ($)	Date Decl.	Ex-Div. Date	Stk. of Record	Payment Date
0.130	11/18	12/09	12/11	01/04/10
0.130	01/27	03/10	03/12	04/02/10
0.130	05/18	06/09	06/11	07/02/10
0.130	07/28	09/08	09/10	10/04/10

Dividends have been paid since 1887. Source: Company reports.

Please read the Required Disclosures and Analyst Certification on the last page of this report.

The **McGraw·Hill** Companies

Johnson Controls Inc.

STANDARD &POOR'S

Business Summary October 13, 2010

CORPORATE OVERVIEW. Johnson Controls, founded in 1885, is a leading manufacturer of automotive interior systems, automotive batteries and automated building control systems. It also provides facility management services for commercial buildings.

The automotive interior segment manufactures interior products and systems, including complete seats and seating components for North American and European car and light-truck manufacturers. The segment has grown rapidly in recent years, gaining contracts to produce seats formerly manufactured in-house by automakers, and expanding in Europe. Seating accounted for 42% of sales in FY 09 (Sep.).

The power solutions unit, the largest automotive battery operation in North America, makes lead-acid batteries primarily for the automotive replacement market and for OEMs. Batteries accounted for about 14% of FY 09 sales, and the unit is expanding operations in Europe.

The building efficiency (formerly called controls) segment manufactures, installs and services controls and control systems, principally for nonresidential

buildings, which are used for temperature and energy management, and fire safety and security maintenance. The segment also includes custom engineering, installation and servicing of process control systems and a growing facilities management business. Building efficiency sales accounted for 44% of FY 09 revenues. As of March 2010, JCI had an unearned backlog of building systems and services contracts totaling $4.4 billion.

Government building trends promoting facility management outsourcing and energy efficiency programs are creating additional opportunities, in our view.

Ford, GM and Daimler were the company's three largest customers in FY 09. We expect the share of revenues from the three U.S.-based customers (Ford, GM and Chrysler) to shrink as the company grows its sales outside the U.S. and with non-domestic customers expanding in the U.S.

Company Financials Fiscal Year Ended Sep. 30

Per Share Data ($)	2009	2008	2007	2006	2005	2004	2003	2002	2001	2000
Tangible Book Value	2.77	3.63	3.38	1.10	3.52	1.93	1.27	0.74	1.17	0.61
Cash Flow	0.68	2.93	3.38	2.95	2.41	2.48	2.17	1.97	1.77	1.79
Earnings	-0.57	1.63	2.16	1.75	1.30	1.41	1.20	1.06	0.85	0.85
S&P Core Earnings	-0.50	1.39	2.16	1.74	1.31	1.42	1.16	0.89	0.70	NA
Dividends	0.52	0.63	0.33	0.37	0.33	0.30	0.24	0.22	0.21	0.19
Payout Ratio	NM	39%	15%	21%	26%	21%	20%	21%	24%	22%
Prices:High	28.34	36.52	44.46	30.00	25.07	21.33	19.37	15.53	13.78	10.85
Prices:Low	8.35	13.65	28.09	22.12	17.52	16.52	11.96	11.52	8.66	7.64
P/E Ratio:High	NM	22	21	17	19	15	16	15	16	13
P/E Ratio:Low	NM	8	13	13	13	12	10	11	10	9

Income Statement Analysis (Million $)										
Revenue	28,497	38,062	34,624	32,235	27,479	26,553	22,646	20,103	18,427	17,155
Operating Income	1,214	2,744	2,527	2,184	1,913	1,918	1,720	1,639	1,477	1,427
Depreciation	745	783	732	705	636	617	558	517	516	462
Interest Expense	255	270	277	248	121	111	114	122	129	128
Pretax Income	-318	1,324	1,607	1,138	1,003	1,212	1,058	1,006	867	856
Effective Tax Rate	NM	24.2%	18.7%	5.54%	20.4%	26.0%	31.0%	34.6%	38.7%	39.6%
Net Income	-338	979	1,295	1,033	757	818	683	600	478	472
S&P Core Earnings	-293	833	1,292	1,025	764	818	650	497	385	NA

Balance Sheet & Other Financial Data (Million $)										
Cash	761	384	674	293	171	170	136	262	375	276
Current Assets	9,826	10,676	10,872	9,264	7,139	6,377	5,620	4,946	4,544	4,277
Total Assets	23,983	25,318	24,105	21,921	16,144	15,091	13,127	11,165	9,912	9,428
Current Liabilities	8,716	9,810	9,920	8,146	6,841	6,602	5,584	4,806	4,580	4,510
Long Term Debt	3,168	3,201	3,255	4,166	1,578	1,631	1,777	1,827	1,395	1,315
Common Equity	9,121	9,411	8,907	7,355	6,058	5,206	4,164	3,396	2,862	2,447
Total Capital	12,490	12,890	11,290	11,650	7,831	7,106	6,260	5,515	4,588	3,891
Capital Expenditures	647	807	828	711	664	862	664	496	622	547
Cash Flow	407	1,762	2,027	1,738	1,394	1,434	1,234	1,110	985	924
Current Ratio	1.1	1.1	1.1	1.1	1.0	1.0	1.0	1.0	1.0	0.9
% Long Term Debt of Capitalization	25.2	24.8	28.8	35.8	20.1	22.9	28.4	33.1	30.4	33.8
% Net Income of Revenue	NM	2.6	3.7	3.2	2.8	3.1	3.0	3.0	2.6	2.8
% Return on Assets	NM	4.0	5.6	5.4	4.9	5.8	5.6	5.7	4.9	5.2
% Return on Equity	NM	10.7	15.9	15.4	13.4	17.4	17.9	18.9	17.7	20.2

Data as orig reptd.; bef. results of disc opers/spec. items. Per share data adj. for stk. divs.; EPS diluted. E-Estimated. NA-Not Available. NM-Not Meaningful. NR-Not Ranked. UR-Under Review.

Office: 5757 N. Green Bay Avenue, Milwaukee, WI 53209-4408.
Telephone: 414-524-1200.
Website: http://www.johnsoncontrols.com
Chrmn, Pres & CEO: S.A. Roell

EVP, CFO & Chief Acctg Officer: R.B. McDonald
Treas: F.A. Voltolina
Secy & General Counsel: J.D. Okarma
Investor Contact: G.Z. Ponczak (414-524-1200)

Board Members: D. P. Abney, D. W. Archer, R. L. Barnett, N. A. Black, R. A. Cornog, R. Goodman, J. Joerres, W. H. Lacy, S. J. Morcott, E. C. Reyes-Retana, S. A. Roell

Founded: 1900
Domicile: Wisconsin
Employees: 130,000

Johnson & Johnson

STANDARD &POOR'S

S&P Recommendation HOLD ★★★★★	Price $63.81 (as of Oct 22, 2010)	12-Mo. Target Price $65.00	Investment Style Large-Cap Growth

GICS Sector Health Care
Sub-Industry Pharmaceuticals

Summary This company is a leader in the pharmaceutical, medical device and consumer products industries.

Key Stock Statistics (Source S&P, Vickers, company reports)

52-Wk Range	$66.20–56.86	S&P Oper. EPS 2010**E**	4.75	Market Capitalization(B)	$175.761	Beta	0.56
Trailing 12-Month EPS	$4.84	S&P Oper. EPS 2011**E**	5.00	Yield (%)	3.39	S&P 3-Yr. Proj. EPS CAGR(%)	5
Trailing 12-Month P/E	13.2	P/E on S&P Oper. EPS 2010**E**	13.4	Dividend Rate/Share	$2.16	S&P Credit Rating	AAA
$10K Invested 5 Yrs Ago	$11,465	Common Shares Outstg. (M)	2,754.4	Institutional Ownership (%)	63		

Price Performance

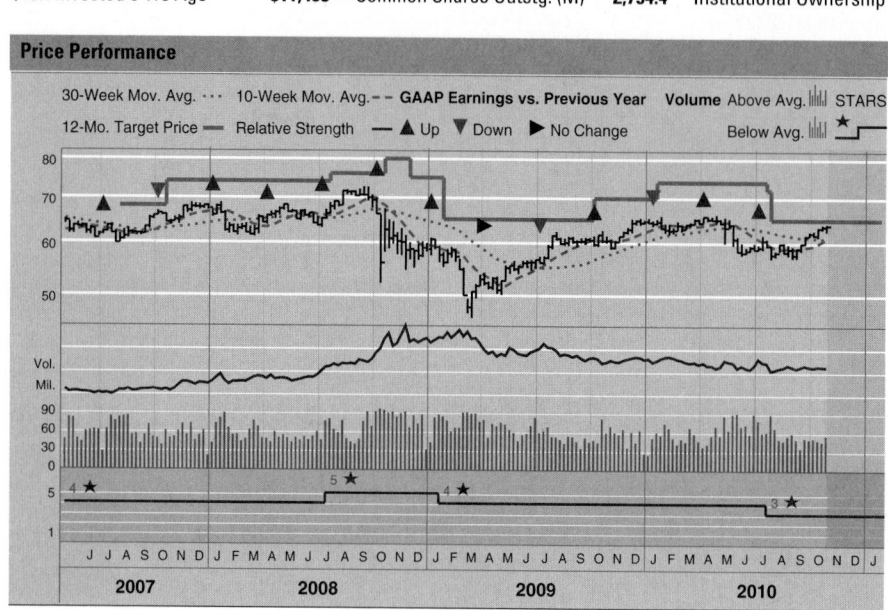

30-Week Mov. Avg. · · · 10-Week Mov. Avg. – – GAAP Earnings vs. Previous Year Volume Above Avg. STARS
12-Mo. Target Price — Relative Strength — ▲ Up ▼ Down ► No Change Below Avg. ★

Options: ASE, CBOE, P, Ph

Analysis prepared by **Herman B. Saftlas** on October 20, 2010, when the stock traded at **$ 63.29.**

Highlights

➤ We expect revenues in 2011 to advance modestly from the $62 billion that we estimate for 2010. We see gains in the orthopedics, diabetes care, Ethicon and diagnostics lines, helped by new products and greater market penetration, especially in emerging markets. We also expect modest growth in the pharmaceutical sector, with projected gains in Simponi, Stelara and Prezista more than offsetting generic erosion in older lines. Impacted by recent OTC product recalls and plant shutdowns, we think consumer product sales in 2011 will rise, helped plant remediation measures.

➤ We look for gross margins to hold relatively steady in the 70% area that we project for 2010. Despite pressures from U.S. healthcare reform and austerity pricing in Europe, we expect operating margins to benefit from cost streamlining measures. The planned acquisition of Crucell is expected to dilute earnings by $0.03-$0.05 a share in 2011.

➤ After a projected effective tax rate similar to the 22% that we project for 2010, we forecast 2011 operating EPS of $5.00, up from the $4.75 that we estimate for 2010.

Investment Rationale/Risk

➤ We believe JNJ's diversified sales base across drugs, medical devices and consumer products, along with its decentralized business model, has served it well in the past, and should continue to do so in the years ahead. In our view, JNJ's recent vaccine, aesthetics and biosurgical products acquisitions are part of a strategy to diversify into new long-term opportunities in the face of challenging prospects in drugs. The vaccines business should also be augmented with the planned acquisition of Crucell NV. Cost restructurings augur well for the future, in our opinion. We also see promise in the R&D pipeline.

➤ Risks to our recommendation and target price include faster-than-expected generic erosion in several drug lines, an inability to sustain growth in the device area, possible pipeline disappointments, and adverse foreign exchange.

➤ Our 12-month target price of $65 applies a P/E multiple of 13X to our 2011 EPS estimate, a valuation that is near JNJ's average multiple in recent years. Our DCF analysis also shows intrinsic value of $65, assuming a 9.6% WACC and 1% terminal growth.

Qualitative Risk Assessment

LOW	MEDIUM	HIGH

Our risk assessment reflects our belief that JNJ has products that are largely immune from economic cycles, has modest reliance on any single product category or customer for sustained growth, and enjoys competitive advantages owing to its large financial resources, business scale and global sales capabilities.

Quantitative Evaluations

S&P Quality Ranking A+

D	C	B-	B	B+	A-	A	A+

Relative Strength Rank MODERATE

57

LOWEST = 1   HIGHEST = 99

Revenue/Earnings Data

Revenue (Million $)

	1Q	2Q	3Q	4Q	Year
2010	15,631	15,330	--	--	--
2009	15,026	15,239	15,081	16,551	61,897
2008	16,194	16,450	15,921	15,182	63,747
2007	15,037	15,131	14,970	15,957	61,095
2006	12,992	13,363	13,287	13,682	53,324
2005	12,832	12,762	12,310	12,610	50,514

Earnings Per Share ($)

2010	1.62	1.23	E1.23	E1.02	E4.75
2009	1.26	1.15	1.20	0.79	4.40
2008	1.26	1.17	1.17	0.97	4.57
2007	0.88	1.05	0.88	0.82	3.63
2006	1.10	0.95	0.94	0.74	3.73
2005	0.97	0.89	0.87	0.73	3.46

Fiscal year ended Dec. 31. Next earnings report expected: NA. EPS Estimates based on S&P Operating Earnings; historical GAAP earnings are as reported.

Dividend Data (Dates: mm/dd Payment Date: mm/dd/yy)

Amount ($)	Date Decl.	Ex-Div. Date	Stk. of Record	Payment Date
0.490	01/04	02/19	02/23	03/09/10
0.540	04/22	05/27	06/01	06/15/10
0.540	07/19	08/27	08/31	09/14/10
0.540	10/21	11/26	11/30	12/14/10

Dividends have been paid since 1944. Source: Company reports.

The McGraw·Hill Companies

Johnson & Johnson

STANDARD
&POOR'S

Business Summary October 20, 2010

CORPORATE OVERVIEW. Johnson & Johnson ranks as one of the largest and most diversified health care firms, with products spanning across the pharmaceutical and medical device industries. The company is also a major participant in the global consumer products business, and, in December 2006, purchased the consumer products unit of Pfizer for $16.6 billion. International sales accounted for about 50% of 2009 sales.

The pharmaceutical segment (36% of 2009 sales) includes products in therapeutic areas including anti-infective, anti-psychotic, cardiovascular, contraceptive, dermatology, gastrointestinal, hematology, immunology, neurology, oncology, pain management, urology and virology. Principal pharmaceutical products include Procrit/Eprex (sales of $2.2 billion in 2009), Remicade ($4.3 billion), Floxin/Levaquin ($1.6 billion), Aciphex/Pariet ($1.1 billion), and Concerta ($1.3 billion). The U.S. patent on Risperdal expired in June 2008, and the patent on Topamax expired in March 2009.

The medical devices and diagnostics segment (38%) sells a wide range of products, including Ethicon's wound care, surgical sports medicine and women's health care products; Cordis's circulatory disease management products; Lifescan's blood glucose monitoring products; Ortho-Clinical Diagnostic's professional diagnostic products; Depuy's orthopaedic joint reconstruction and spinal products; and Vistakon's disposable contact lenses.

The consumer segment (26%) primarily sells personal care products, including nonprescription drugs, adult skin and hair care products, baby care products, oral care products, first aid products, women's health products, and nutritional products. Major brands include Band-Aid Brand Adhesive Bandages, Imodium A-D antidiarrheal, Johnson's Baby line of products, Neutrogena skin and hair care products, and Tylenol pain reliever.

Company Financials Fiscal Year Ended Dec. 31

Per Share Data ($)	2009	2008	2007	2006	2005	2004	2003	2002	2001	2000
Tangible Book Value	7.04	5.35	5.13	3.67	8.64	6.72	5.17	4.53	4.97	4.15
Cash Flow	5.39	5.57	4.59	4.57	4.20	3.58	3.01	2.67	2.35	2.23
Earnings	4.40	4.57	3.63	3.73	3.46	2.84	2.40	2.16	1.84	1.70
S&P Core Earnings	4.22	4.17	3.61	3.65	3.38	2.77	2.26	1.99	1.66	NA
Dividends	1.93	1.80	1.62	1.46	1.28	1.10	0.93	0.80	0.70	0.62
Payout Ratio	44%	39%	45%	39%	37%	39%	39%	37%	38%	36%
Prices:High	65.41	72.76	68.75	69.41	69.99	64.25	59.08	65.89	60.97	52.97
Prices:Low	46.25	52.06	59.72	56.65	59.76	49.25	48.05	41.40	40.25	33.06
P/E Ratio:High	15	16	19	19	20	23	25	31	33	31
P/E Ratio:Low	11	11	16	15	17	17	20	19	22	19

Income Statement Analysis (Million $)										
Revenue	61,897	63,747	61,095	53,324	50,514	47,348	41,862	36,298	33,004	29,139
Operating Income	19,550	19,001	17,990	15,886	15,464	14,987	12,740	11,340	9,490	7,992
Depreciation	2,774	2,832	2,777	2,177	2,093	2,124	1,869	1,662	1,605	1,515
Interest Expense	451	582	426	63.0	54.0	187	207	160	153	146
Pretax Income	15,755	16,929	13,283	14,587	13,656	12,838	10,308	9,291	7,898	6,622
Effective Tax Rate	22.2%	23.5%	20.4%	24.2%	23.8%	33.7%	30.2%	29.0%	28.2%	27.5%
Net Income	12,266	12,949	10,576	11,053	10,411	8,509	7,197	6,597	5,668	4,800
S&P Core Earnings	11,779	11,832	10,534	10,814	10,161	8,263	6,785	6,052	5,090	NA

Balance Sheet & Other Financial Data (Million $)										
Cash	19,425	12,809	9,315	4,084	16,138	12,884	9,523	7,596	8,941	6,013
Current Assets	39,541	34,377	29,945	22,975	31,394	27,320	22,995	19,266	18,473	15,450
Total Assets	94,682	84,912	80,954	70,556	58,025	53,317	48,263	40,556	38,488	31,321
Current Liabilities	21,731	20,852	19,837	19,161	12,635	13,927	13,448	11,449	8,044	7,140
Long Term Debt	8,223	8,120	7,074	2,014	2,017	2,565	2,955	2,022	2,217	2,037
Common Equity	50,588	42,511	43,319	61,266	37,871	31,813	26,869	22,697	24,233	18,808
Total Capital	60,235	52,063	51,886	42,651	40,099	34,781	30,604	25,362	26,943	21,100
Capital Expenditures	2,365	3,066	2,942	2,666	2,632	2,175	2,262	2,099	1,731	1,646
Cash Flow	15,040	15,781	13,353	13,230	12,504	10,633	9,066	8,259	7,273	6,315
Current Ratio	1.8	1.7	1.5	1.2	2.5	2.0	1.7	1.7	2.3	2.2
% Long Term Debt of Capitalization	13.7	15.6	13.6	4.7	5.0	7.4	9.7	8.0	8.2	9.7
% Net Income of Revenue	19.8	20.3	17.3	20.7	20.6	18.0	17.2	18.2	17.2	16.5
% Return on Assets	13.7	15.6	14.9	17.1	18.7	16.8	16.2	16.7	15.6	15.9
% Return on Equity	26.4	30.2	20.2	19.8	29.9	29.0	29.0	28.1	25.4	27.4

Data as orig reptd.; bef. results of disc opers/spec. items. Per share data adj. for stk. divs.; EPS diluted. E-Estimated. NA-Not Available. NM-Not Meaningful. NR-Not Ranked. UR-Under Review.

Office: One Johnson & Johnson Plaza, New Brunswick, NJ 08933.
Telephone: 732-524-0400.
Website: http://www.jnj.com
Chrmn & CEO: W.C. Weldon

COO: A. Shetty
CFO: D.J. Caruso
CSO: T.J. Torphy
Chief Acctg Officer & Cntlr: S.J. Cosgrove

Investor Contact: L. Mehrotra (732-524-6491)
Board Members: M. S. Coleman, J. G. Cullen, I. E. Davis, I. E. Davis, M. M. Johns, S. L. Lindquist, A. M. Mulcahy, L. F. Mullin, W. D. Perez, C. Prince, III, D. Satcher, W. C. Weldon

Founded: 1887
Domicile: New Jersey
Employees: 114,000

JPMorgan Chase & Co

STANDARD &POOR'S

S&P Recommendation **STRONG BUY** ★★★★★	Price $37.70 (as of Oct 22, 2010)	12-Mo. Target Price $47.00	Investment Style Large-Cap Value

GICS Sector Financials
Sub-Industry Other Diversified Financial Services

Summary This leading global financial services company has assets of $2.1 trillion and operations in more than 50 countries.

Key Stock Statistics (Source S&P, Vickers, company reports)

52-Wk Range	$48.20– 35.16	S&P Oper. EPS 2010E	4.00	Market Capitalization(B)	$149.487	Beta	1.13
Trailing 12-Month EPS	$3.59	S&P Oper. EPS 2011E	4.21	Yield (%)	0.53	S&P 3-Yr. Proj. EPS CAGR(%)	25
Trailing 12-Month P/E	10.5	P/E on S&P Oper. EPS 2010E	9.4	Dividend Rate/Share	$0.20	S&P Credit Rating	A+
$10K Invested 5 Yrs Ago	$12,083	Common Shares Outstg. (M)	3,965.2	Institutional Ownership (%)	73		

Price Performance

- 30-Week Mov. Avg. · · · 10-Week Mov. Avg. – – GAAP Earnings vs. Previous Year Volume Above Avg. STARS
- 12-Mo. Target Price — Relative Strength — ▲ Up ▼ Down ► No Change Below Avg.

Options: ASE, CBOE, P, Ph

Analysis prepared by **Erik Oja** on October 19, 2010, when the stock traded at **$ 37.71**.

Highlights

▶ Third-quarter investment banking and principal transactions results were better then we had expected, and were in line with the second quarter. Core fee income, excluding gains and losses, fell only 0.7% from strong second-quarter levels. However, for all of 2010, we expect core fee income of $44.9 billion, down from $47.3 billion in 2009, due to a fall-off in investment banking. For 2011, we forecast core fee income will rise 3.8%. We see net interest income of $51.5 billion in 2010, up slightly from $51.2 billion in 2009. We expect revenues to rise 0.2% in 2010, and 0.1% in 2011.

▶ Third-quarter net chargeoffs fell to $4.945 billion, from $5.714 billion in the second quarter, and $7.910 billion in the first, which was a record level for JPM. We expect 2010 net chargeoffs of $21.6 billion, down slightly from 2009's nearly $23 billion. Our loan loss provisioning forecast for 2010 is $17.1 billion, down sharply from 2009's $32.0 billion; for 2011, we see $15.1 billion. Declining loan loss provisions will be the major drivers of earnings growth for JPM in 2010 and 2011, in our view.

▶ We estimate EPS of $4.00 for 2010 and $4.21 for 2011.

Investment Rationale/Risk

▶ JPM's strong third-quarter revenue and credit results were overshadowed, in our view, by a developing industry-wide issue of hastily completed foreclosures, which we believe could, at worst, completely halt most foreclosures. Though JPM is currently free from the allegations of fraud and incomplete paperwork seen at a major peer, and is carefully reviewing all 115,000 foreclosures in progress, we think there is a possibility that this issue may widen. However, we believe that this is unlikely, and that JPM's rapid pace of credit quality improvements, combined with a potential for net interest income growth once loan demand picks up, should more than offset the foreclosure issue.

▶ Risks to our recommendation and target price include legal and regulatory risk, unexpected further turmoil in the credit markets, and a slower-than-expected economic recovery.

▶ Our 12-month target price of $47 is based on a premium-to-peers 1.65X our $28.50 projection of JPM's year-end tangible book value per share, reflecting our view that JPM's credit quality and balance sheet are stronger than large banking peers. Our target price equals a peer-equivalent 11.2X our 2011 EPS estimate of $4.21.

Qualitative Risk Assessment

LOW	MEDIUM	HIGH

Our risk assessment reflects our view of the company's well-reserved balance sheet, diversified lines of business and strong capital ratios. We believe JPM's diversity in its geographic presence and product offerings provides significant protection from a local or regional downturn.

Quantitative Evaluations

S&P Quality Ranking B+

D	C	B-	B	B+	A-	A	A+

Relative Strength Rank WEAK

21

LOWEST = 1 HIGHEST = 99

Revenue/Earnings Data

Revenue (Million $)

	1Q	2Q	3Q	4Q	Year
2010	30,806	28,133	26,928	--	--
2009	29,584	29,502	30,145	26,401	115,632
2008	26,763	26,634	23,069	25,025	101,491
2007	29,486	30,082	16,112	28,104	116,353
2006	23,477	24,175	24,957	26,693	99,302
2005	19,054	18,691	21,048	21,109	79,902

Earnings Per Share ($)

	1Q	2Q	3Q	4Q	Year
2010	0.74	1.09	1.01	E1.08	E4.00
2009	0.40	0.28	0.80	0.74	2.24
2008	0.68	0.54	-0.06	-0.28	0.84
2007	1.34	1.20	0.97	0.86	4.38
2006	0.86	0.98	0.90	1.26	3.82
2005	0.63	0.28	0.71	0.76	2.38

Fiscal year ended Dec. 31. Next earnings report expected: Mid January. EPS Estimates based on S&P Operating Earnings; historical GAAP earnings are as reported.

Dividend Data (Dates: mm/dd Payment Date: mm/dd/yy)

Amount ($)	Date Decl.	Ex-Div. Date	Stk. of Record	Payment Date
0.050	12/08	01/04	01/06	01/31/10
0.050	03/16	04/01	04/06	04/30/10
0.050	05/18	07/01	07/06	07/31/10
0.050	09/21	10/04	10/06	10/31/10

Dividends have been paid since 1827. Source: Company reports.

Please read the Required Disclosures and Analyst Certification on the last page of this report.

The **McGraw·Hill** Companies

JPMorgan Chase & Co

STANDARD &POOR'S

Business Summary October 19, 2010

CORPORATE OVERVIEW. JPMorgan Chase's operations are divided into six major business lines: Investment Banking, Retail Financial Services (RFS), Card Services (CS), Commercial Banking (CB), Treasury & Securities Services (TSS), and Asset Management (AM), as well as a Corporate/Private Equity segment.

JPM is one of the world's leading investment banks, with clients consisting of corporations, financial institutions, governments, and institutional investors worldwide. Its products and services include advising on corporate strategy and structure, equity and debt capital raising, sophisticated risk management, research, market making in cash securities and derivative instruments and prime brokerage and research.

RFS includes Home Finance, Consumer & Small Business Banking, Auto & Education Finance and Insurance. At year-end 2009, RFS had over 5,100 bank branches and 15,400 ATMs.

CS had over 145 million cards in circulation and $163 billion in managed loans as of December 31, 2009. CS offers a wide variety of products to satisfy the needs of its card members, including cards issued on behalf of many well-known partners, such as major airlines, hotels, universities, retailers, and other financial institutions.

CB provides lending, treasury services, investment banking and investment management services to corporations, municipalities, financial institutions and not-for-profit entities.

TSS offers transaction, investment and information services to support the needs of corporations, issuers and institutional investors worldwide. TSS reported assets under custody of $14.9 trillion in 2009, up 13% from 2008.

AM provides investment management to retail and institutional investors, financial intermediaries and high-net-worth families and individuals globally. Assets under management rose by 10% in 2009 to $1.25 trillion.

Company Financials Fiscal Year Ended Dec. 31

Per Share Data ($)	2009	2008	2007	2006	2005	2004	2003	2002	2001	2000
Tangible Book Value	26.45	19.27	18.77	16.11	15.88	14.77	14.77	15.82	12.54	12.95
Earnings	2.24	0.84	4.38	3.82	2.38	1.55	3.24	0.80	0.81	2.86
S&P Core Earnings	2.28	0.67	4.44	3.88	2.76	2.25	3.12	0.65	0.34	NA
Dividends	0.53	1.52	1.44	1.36	1.36	1.36	1.36	1.36	1.34	1.23
Payout Ratio	24%	NM	33%	34%	57%	88%	42%	170%	165%	43%
Prices:High	47.47	50.63	53.25	49.00	40.56	43.84	38.26	39.68	57.33	67.17
Prices:Low	14.96	19.69	40.15	37.88	32.92	34.62	20.13	15.26	29.04	32.38
P/E Ratio:High	21	60	12	12	17	28	12	50	71	23
P/E Ratio:Low	7	23	9	9	14	22	6	19	36	11

Income Statement Analysis (Million $)

	2009	2008	2007	2006	2005	2004	2003	2002	2001	2000
Net Interest Income	51,152	38,779	26,406	21,242	19,831	16,761	12,337	11,526	10,802	9,512
Tax Equivalent Adjustment	330	579	377	NA	269	NA	NA	NA	NA	NA
Non Interest Income	49,282	28,937	44,802	17,959	34,702	26,336	19,473	16,525	17,382	23,193
Loan Loss Provision	32,015	20,979	6,864	3,270	3,483	NA	NA	4,331	3,185	1,377
% Expense/Operating Revenue	52.1%	60.0%	58.6%	97.7%	66.5%	85.6%	73.0%	81.2%	82.7%	69.8%
Pretax Income	16,067	2,773	22,805	19,886	12,215	6,194	10,028	2,519	2,566	8,733
Effective Tax Rate	27.5%	NM	32.6%	31.4%	30.6%	27.9%	33.0%	34.0%	33.0%	34.4%
Net Income	11,652	3,699	15,365	13,649	8,483	4,466	6,719	1,663	1,719	5,727
% Net Interest Margin	3.12	2.87	2.39	2.16	2.19	2.27	2.10	2.09	1.99	1.87
S&P Core Earnings	8,861	2,409	15,563	13,852	9,802	6,456	6,439	1,290	698	NA

Balance Sheet & Other Financial Data (Million $)

	2009	2008	2007	2006	2005	2004	2003	2002	2001	2000
Money Market Assets	606,532	713,098	662,306	506,262	432,358	390,168	329,739	314,110	265,875	293,429
Investment Securities	480,020	329,943	169,634	172,022	128,578	149,675	109,328	126,834	105,537	117,494
Commercial Loans	204,175	111,654	238,210	188,372	150,111	135,067	83,097	91,548	104,864	119,460
Other Loans	429,283	610,080	281,164	294,755	269,037	267,047	136,421	124,816	112,580	96,590
Total Assets	2,031,989	2,175,052	1,562,147	1,351,520	1,198,942	1,157,248	770,912	758,800	693,575	715,348
Demand Deposits	204,003	210,899	135,748	140,443	143,075	136,188	79,465	82,029	76,974	62,713
Time Deposits	734,364	790,681	604,980	498,345	411,916	385,268	247,027	222,724	216,676	216,652
Long Term Debt	266,318	270,683	197,878	117,358	119,886	105,718	54,782	45,190	44,172	47,788
Common Equity	157,213	134,945	123,221	115,790	107,072	105,314	45,145	41,297	40,090	40,818
% Return on Assets	0.6	0.2	1.1	1.1	0.7	0.5	0.9	0.2	0.2	0.8
% Return on Equity	8.0	2.9	12.9	12.2	8.0	5.9	15.4	4.0	4.1	15.2
% Loan Loss Reserve	5.0	3.1	1.8	1.5	1.7	1.8	2.1	2.5	2.1	1.7
% Loans/Deposits	67.5	73.8	72.6	75.6	75.5	77.1	67.2	71.0	74.0	77.3
% Equity to Assets	6.9	6.9	8.2	8.7	9.0	7.8	5.7	5.6	5.7	5.4

Data as orig reptd.; bef. results of disc opers/spec. items. Per share data adj. for stk. divs.; EPS diluted. E-Estimated. NA-Not Available. NM-Not Meaningful. NR-Not Ranked. UR-Under Review.

Office: 270 Park Ave, New York, NY 10017-2070.
Telephone: 212-270-6000.
Website: http://www.jpmorganchase.com
Chrmn & CEO: J. Dimon

Pres: C. Berquo
Vice Chrmn: S.D. Black
Vice Chrmn: M. Breuer
COO & CTO: P. Cherasia

Investor Contact: J. Bates (212-270-7318)
Board Members: S. D. Black, C. C. Bowles, M. Breuer, S. B. Burke, D. M. Cote, J. S. Crown, J. Dimon, E. Futter, W. H. Gray, III, L. P. Jackson, Jr., D. C. Novak, L. R. Raymond, A. Wallace, W. C. Weldon

Founded: 1823
Domicile: Delaware
Employees: 222,316

The **McGraw·Hill** Companies

Juniper Networks Inc

STANDARD &POOR'S

S&P Recommendation HOLD ★★★★★	**Price** $31.94 (as of Oct 22, 2010)	**12-Mo. Target Price** $32.00	**Investment Style** Large-Cap Blend

GICS Sector Information Technology
Sub-Industry Communications Equipment

Summary This company provides Internet Protocol networking products and services, with an emphasis on telecom routing solutions.

Key Stock Statistics (Source S&P, Vickers, company reports)

52-Wk Range	$32.84– 22.25	S&P Oper. EPS 2010E	1.04	Market Capitalization(B)	$16.606	Beta	1.48
Trailing 12-Month EPS	$0.75	S&P Oper. EPS 2011E	1.20	Yield (%)	Nil	S&P 3-Yr. Proj. EPS CAGR(%)	17
Trailing 12-Month P/E	42.6	P/E on S&P Oper. EPS 2010E	30.7	Dividend Rate/Share	Nil	S&P Credit Rating	NR
$10K Invested 5 Yrs Ago	$13,726	Common Shares Outstg. (M)	519.9	Institutional Ownership (%)	94		

Price Performance

- 30-Week Mov. Avg. · · · ·   10-Week Mov. Avg. – –   **GAAP Earnings vs. Previous Year**   Volume Above Avg. STARS
- 12-Mo. Target Price —   Relative Strength —   ▲ Up ▼ Down ▶ No Change   Below Avg. ★

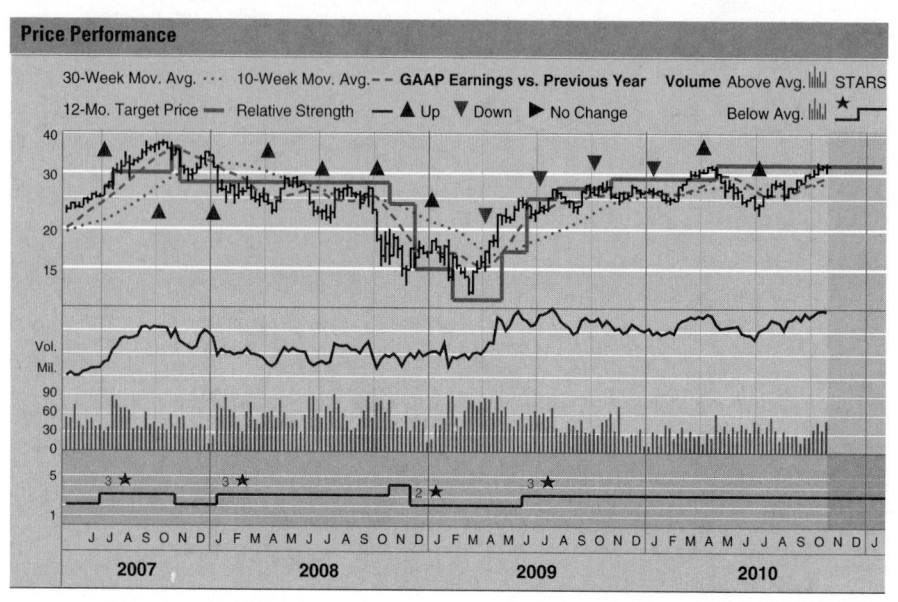

Options: ASE, CBOE, P, Ph

Analysis prepared by **Ari Bensinger** on October 20, 2010, when the stock traded at **$ 32.18**.

Highlights

▶ Following an estimated 21% increase in 2010, we see sales advancing 15% in 2011, on continued strong demand for carrier network infrastructure products, as well as increased market penetration in the enterprise sector. We are optimistic about recent portfolio enhancements and new product introductions, specifically the new MX3D edge router.

▶ We foresee 2011 gross margins narrowing modestly, to 67%, as a favorable product mix shift is outweighed by industry pricing pressure. Despite aggressive R&D investment, in part to support new data center and wireless packet transport projects, we believe JNPR will manage 2011 costs prudently, and we expect operating expenses to rise at a slower pace than sales.

▶ We see 2011 operating margins at the 24% level. After interest income and an effective tax rate of 31%, we look for 2011 operating EPS of $1.20, up from the $1.04 that we forecast for 2010. Our estimates include projected stock option expense of $0.23 and $0.24 for 2010 and 2011, respectively.

Investment Rationale/Risk

▶ We are encouraged by the company's increased customer traction in the newly entered enterprise market, and we believe new product upgrades will help boost carrier sales. We see the continued rapid increase in IP traffic acting as a strong underlying growth driver for the networking industry. Even so, we think the shares, recently trading above peers on P/E and price-to-sales metrics, adequately reflect the solid growth opportunity we see for JNPR.

▶ Risks to our recommendation and target price include a prolonged decline in carrier spending, routing market share losses, and slower-than-expected sales traction in the enterprise sector.

▶ Our 12-month target price of $32 represents a multiple of 27X our 2011 EPS estimate of $1.20 and 4X our 2011 sales forecast of $4.6 billion, valuation metrics that are above peers, warranted, we believe, by JNPR's strong position in the fast-growing IP networking sector. Using our three-year earnings growth estimate of 17%, our target price represents a forward P/E-to-growth (PEG) ratio of 1.6X, in line with the industry average.

Qualitative Risk Assessment

LOW	MEDIUM	**HIGH**

Our risk assessment reflects the highly competitive nature of the telecommunications equipment industry and execution risks related to the company's expansion into the enterprise market.

Quantitative Evaluations

S&P Quality Ranking   **B**

D	C	B-	**B**	B+	A-	A	A+

Relative Strength Rank   **STRONG**

77

LOWEST = 1   HIGHEST = 99

Revenue/Earnings Data

Revenue (Million $)

	1Q	2Q	3Q	4Q	Year
2010	912.6	978.3	--	--	--
2009	764.2	786.4	823.9	941.5	3,316
2008	822.9	879.0	947.0	923.5	3,572
2007	626.9	664.9	735.1	809.2	2,836
2006	566.7	567.5	573.6	595.8	2,304
2005	449.1	493.0	546.4	575.5	2,064

Earnings Per Share ($)

2010	0.30	0.24	E0.26	E0.30	E1.04
2009	-0.01	0.03	0.16	0.24	0.42
2008	0.20	0.22	0.27	0.25	0.93
2007	0.11	0.15	0.15	0.22	0.62
2006	0.13	-2.13	0.10	0.12	-1.76
2005	0.13	0.15	0.14	0.17	0.59

Fiscal year ended Dec. 31. Next earnings report expected: Late October. EPS Estimates based on S&P Operating Earnings; historical GAAP earnings are as reported.

Dividend Data

No cash dividends have been paid.

Juniper Networks Inc

STANDARD &POOR'S

Business Summary October 20, 2010

CORPORATE OVERVIEW. Juniper Networks, founded in 1996, makes secure Internet Protocol (IP) networking solutions that are designed to address the needs at the core and at the edge of the network, and for wireless access. The company's core product is IP backbone routers for service providers. The acquisition of NetScreen in 2004 added a broad family of network security solutions aimed at enterprises, service providers, and government entities.

The service provider sector remains the core market for JNPR, accounting for 66% of total revenue in 2009, versus 72% in the prior year. However, the enterprise market is becoming an increasingly important growth market for the company, representing 34% of 2009 sales, up from 28% in the prior year. JNPR enjoys good customer diversification, having sold its products to all of the 100 largest service providers in the world. AT&T accounted for 10% of sales during 2009.

During 2009, international revenue represented 49% of total sales, down from 51% and 53% in 2008 and 2007, respectively. Operations are organized into three operating segments: infrastructure, service layer technologies (SLT), and service.

PRIMARY BUSINESS DYNAMICS. The infrastructure segment (74% of total sales in 2009) primarily offers scalable router products that are used to control and direct network traffic from the core, through the edge, aggregation and the customer premise equipment level. The company has experienced an increased demand for infrastructure products due to the adoption and expansion of IP networks as a result of peer-to-peer interaction, increased broadband usage, video, and IP television.

Infrastructure products include the M-series and T-series routers, geared to service providers, offering carrier class reliability and scalability. The M-series can be deployed at the edge of operator networks, in small and medium core networks. The MX-Series addresses the Carrier Ethernet market. The T-series and TX Matrix are primarily designed for core IP infrastructures. Other product platforms include E-series and J-series (wireless routers, developed through JNPR's joint venture with Ericsson). The EX-series, introduced in early 2008, extends JNPR's product portfolio for routers to the Ethernet switches. Products run on JNPR's JUNOS Internet software, and are differentiated from their competition in that they also feature the company's high-performance, ASIC-based packet forwarding technology.

Company Financials Fiscal Year Ended Dec. 31

Per Share Data ($)	2009	2008	2007	2006	2005	2004	2003	2002	2001	2000
Tangible Book Value	4.14	4.26	3.09	4.08	3.04	2.89	1.48	1.18	2.36	1.87
Cash Flow	0.50	1.23	0.96	-1.46	0.82	0.52	0.27	-0.16	0.42	0.53
Earnings	0.42	0.93	0.62	-1.76	0.59	0.25	0.10	-0.34	-0.04	0.43
S&P Core Earnings	0.45	0.96	0.60	-0.27	0.26	0.12	-0.06	-0.51	-0.38	NA
Dividends	Nil	Nil	Nil	Nil	Nil	Nil	Nil	Nil	Nil	Nil
Payout Ratio	Nil	Nil	Nil	Nil	Nil	Nil	Nil	Nil	Nil	Nil
Prices:High	28.74	33.30	37.95	22.63	27.65	31.25	19.38	23.01	145.00	244.50
Prices:Low	12.43	3.29	17.21	12.09	19.65	18.75	6.88	4.15	8.90	48.83
P/E Ratio:High	68	36	61	NM	47	NM	NM	NM	NM	NM
P/E Ratio:Low	30	14	28	NM	33	NM	NM	NM	NM	NM

Income Statement Analysis (Million $)										
Revenue	3,316	3,572	2,836	2,304	2,064	1,336	701	547	887	674
Operating Income	661	876	610	496	595	376	141	42.2	205	249
Depreciation	148	167	193	173	139	145	70.0	63.0	148	34.8
Interest Expense	NA	2.90	1.70	3.59	3.93	5.38	39.1	55.6	61.4	52.7
Pretax Income	481	729	511	-897	502	219	59.0	-115	16.5	230
Effective Tax Rate	53.6%	29.8%	29.3%	NM	29.5%	38.0%	33.6%	NM	NM	35.8%
Net Income	225	512	361	-1,001	354	136	39.2	-120	-13.4	148
S&P Core Earnings	239	527	353	-156	156	65.9	-25.6	-180	-122	NA

Balance Sheet & Other Financial Data (Million $)										
Cash	2,175	2,192	1,956	1,596	918	713	396	194	607	563
Current Assets	2,879	2,816	2,555	2,522	1,818	1,414	691	681	1,126	1,349
Total Assets	7,530	7,187	6,885	7,368	8,027	7,000	2,411	2,615	2,390	2,103
Current Liabilities	1,376	1,057	1,380	763	627	503	291	242	242	216
Long Term Debt	NA	Nil	Nil	400	400	Nil	558	942	1,150	1,120
Common Equity	5,930	5,901	5,354	6,115	6,900	5,993	1,562	1,431	997	730
Total Capital	5,933	5,901	5,354	6,515	7,300	5,993	2,120	2,373	2,147	1,850
Capital Expenditures	153	165	147	102	98.2	63.2	19.4	36.1	241	35.0
Cash Flow	265	679	554	-828	493	281	109	-56.6	134	183
Current Ratio	2.3	2.7	1.9	3.3	2.9	2.8	2.4	2.8	4.6	6.2
% Long Term Debt of Capitalization	Nil	Nil	Nil	6.1	5.5	Nil	26.3	39.7	53.6	60.5
% Net Income of Revenue	6.8	14.3	12.7	NM	17.2	10.2	5.6	NM	NM	22.0
% Return on Assets	3.1	7.3	5.1	NM	4.7	2.9	1.6	NM	NM	11.3
% Return on Equity	3.8	9.1	6.3	NM	5.5	3.6	2.6	NM	NM	24.9

Data as orig reptd.; bef. results of disc opers/spec. items. Per share data adj. for stk. divs.; EPS diluted. E-Estimated. NA-Not Available. NM-Not Meaningful. NR-Not Ranked. UR-Under Review.

Office: 1194 North Mathilda Avenue, Sunnyvale, CA 94089-1206.
Telephone: 408-745-2000.
Email: investor-relations@juniper.net
Website: http://www.juniper.net

Chrmn & Pres: S.G. Kriens
Vice Chrmn & CTO: P. Sindhu
CEO: K.R. Johnson
COO: M.J. Rose

EVP & CFO: R.M. Denholm
Board Members: B. Calderoni, M. B. Cranston, K. R. Johnson, S. G. Kriens, J. M. Lawrie, W. F. Meehan, III, D. Schlotterbeck, S. Sclavos, P. Sindhu, B. Stensrud

Founded: 1996
Domicile: Delaware
Employees: 7,231

The McGraw-Hill Companies

Kellogg Co

STANDARD &POOR'S

| S&P Recommendation | HOLD ★★★☆☆ | Price $49.55 (as of Oct 22, 2010) | 12-Mo. Target Price $53.00 | Investment Style Large-Cap Growth |

GICS Sector Consumer Staples
Sub-Industry Packaged Foods & Meats

Summary Kellogg is a leading producer of ready-to-eat cereal, and also sells convenience foods such as cookies, crackers, cereal bars, fruit snacks, and frozen waffles.

Key Stock Statistics (Source S&P, Vickers, company reports)

52-Wk Range	$56.00–47.28	S&P Oper. EPS 2010E	3.29	Market Capitalization(B)	$18.718	Beta	0.47
Trailing 12-Month EPS	$3.27	S&P Oper. EPS 2011E	3.65	Yield (%)	3.27	S&P 3-Yr. Proj. EPS CAGR(%)	7
Trailing 12-Month P/E	15.2	P/E on S&P Oper. EPS 2010E	15.1	Dividend Rate/Share	$1.62	S&P Credit Rating	BBB+
$10K Invested 5 Yrs Ago	$12,281	Common Shares Outstg. (M)	377.8	Institutional Ownership (%)	81		

Price Performance

- 30-Week Mov. Avg. · · ·   10-Week Mov. Avg. – –   GAAP Earnings vs. Previous Year   Volume Above Avg. STARS
- 12-Mo. Target Price —   Relative Strength —   ▲ Up ▼ Down ▶ No Change   Below Avg. ★

Options: CBOE, Ph

Highlights

▶ The STARS recommendation for K has recently been changed to 3 (hold) from 4 (buy) and the 12-month target price has recently been changed to $53.00 from $55.00. The Highlights section of this Stock Report will be updated accordingly.

Investment Rationale/Risk

▶ The Investment Rationale/Risk section of this Stock Report will be updated shortly. For the latest News story on K from MarketScope, see below.

▶ 10/21/10 12:03 pm ET ... S&P LOWERS OPINION ON SHARES OF KELLOGG CO. TO HOLD FROM BUY (K 50.27***): After disappointing sales and profit guidance, we expect K to report, on Nov. 2, Q3 EPS of $0.90 (lowered from our previous estimate of $0.93), vs. year-ago $0.94. In cereal category, we expect more sales softness, and margin pressure from promotional activity than we had anticipated. We see earlier cereal recall by the company hurting. We are reducing our '10 EPS estimate to $3.29 from $3.40, and '11's projection to $3.65 from $3.77. We are lowering our 12-month target price to $53 from $55, which reflects our view that the shares should trade closer to a peer group target P/E. / TGraves-CFA

Qualitative Risk Assessment

| LOW | MEDIUM | HIGH |

Our risk assessment for Kellogg Company reflects the relatively stable nature of the company's end markets, what we consider its strong balance sheet and cash flow, and corporate governance practices that we think are favorable versus peers.

Quantitative Evaluations

S&P Quality Ranking   A+

| D | C | B- | B | B+ | A- | A | A+ |

Relative Strength Rank   WEAK

24

LOWEST = 1   HIGHEST = 99

Revenue/Earnings Data

Revenue (Million $)

	1Q	2Q	3Q	4Q	Year
2010	3,318	3,062	--	--	--
2009	3,169	3,229	3,277	2,900	12,575
2008	3,258	3,343	3,288	2,933	12,822
2007	2,963	3,015	3,004	2,794	11,776
2006	2,727	2,774	2,822	2,584	10,907
2005	2,572	2,587	2,623	2,394	10,177

Earnings Per Share ($)

	1Q	2Q	3Q	4Q	Year
2010	1.09	0.79	E0.90	E0.51	E3.29
2009	0.84	0.92	0.94	0.46	3.16
2008	0.81	0.82	0.89	0.47	2.98
2007	0.80	0.75	0.76	0.44	2.76
2006	0.68	0.67	0.70	0.45	2.51
2005	0.61	0.62	0.66	0.47	2.36

Fiscal year ended Dec. 31. Next earnings report expected: Late October. EPS Estimates based on S&P Operating Earnings; historical GAAP earnings are as reported.

Dividend Data (Dates: mm/dd Payment Date: mm/dd/yy)

Amount ($)	Date Decl.	Ex-Div. Date	Stk. of Record	Payment Date
0.375	02/19	02/26	03/02	03/15/10
0.375	04/23	05/27	06/01	06/15/10
0.375	04/23	05/27	06/01	06/15/10
0.405	07/23	08/30	09/01	09/15/10

Dividends have been paid since 1923. Source: Company reports.

The McGraw-Hill Companies

Kellogg Co

STANDARD &POOR'S

Business Summary August 19, 2010

CORPORATE OVERVIEW. Kellogg Co., incorporated in 1922, is a leading producer of ready-to-eat cereal. The company has expanded its operations to include convenience food products such as Pop-Tarts toaster pastries, Eggo frozen waffles, Nutri-Grain cereal bars, and Rice Krispies Treats squares.

With the 2001 acquisition of the Keebler Foods Co., the company also markets cookies, crackers and other convenience food products under brand names such as Keebler, Cheez-It, Murray and Famous Amos, and manufactures private label cookies, crackers and other products.

Sales contributions by geographic region in 2009 were: North America 68%, Europe 19%, Latin America 8%, and Asia Pacific 6%.

In 2009, cereal sold through North American retail channels represented 24% of total net sales, while international cereal sales represented 26%. Other

sales categories included North American retail snacks (32%), North American frozen and specialty channels (11%), and international convenience foods (6%).

In 2009, Kellogg's top five customers accounted for about 34% of net sales collectively, and about 44% of U.S. net sales. Kellogg's largest customer, Wal-Mart Stores, Inc., and its affiliates, accounted for about 21% of consolidated net sales during 2009.

Kellogg's expenditures for research and development were about $181 million in both 2009 and 2008.

Company Financials Fiscal Year Ended Dec. 31

Per Share Data ($)	2009	2008	2007	2006	2005	2004	2003	2002	2001	2000
Tangible Book Value	NM	NM	NM	NM	NM	NM	NM	NM	NM	1.21
Cash Flow	4.16	3.96	3.69	3.39	3.30	3.15	2.83	2.60	2.26	2.16
Earnings	3.16	2.98	2.76	2.51	2.36	2.14	1.92	1.75	1.18	1.45
S&P Core Earnings	3.08	2.48	2.74	2.62	2.29	2.10	1.86	1.24	0.77	NA
Dividends	1.43	1.30	1.49	1.14	1.06	1.01	1.01	1.01	1.01	1.00
Payout Ratio	45%	44%	54%	45%	45%	47%	53%	58%	86%	69%
Prices:High	54.10	58.51	56.89	50.95	46.99	45.32	38.57	37.00	34.00	32.00
Prices:Low	35.64	40.32	48.68	42.41	42.35	37.00	27.85	29.02	24.25	20.75
P/E Ratio:High	17	20	21	20	20	21	20	21	29	22
P/E Ratio:Low	11	14	18	17	18	17	15	17	21	14

Income Statement Analysis (Million $)	2009	2008	2007	2006	2005	2004	2003	2002	2001	2000
Revenue	12,575	12,822	11,776	10,907	10,177	9,614	8,812	8,304	8,853	6,955
Operating Income	2,542	2,431	2,347	2,119	2,142	2,091	1,917	1,857	1,640	1,367
Depreciation	384	375	372	353	392	410	373	348	439	291
Interest Expense	295	314	324	307	300	309	371	391	352	138
Pretax Income	1,684	1,633	1,547	1,471	1,425	1,366	1,170	1,144	804	868
Effective Tax Rate	28.3%	29.7%	28.7%	31.7%	31.2%	34.8%	32.7%	37.0%	40.1%	32.3%
Net Income	1,212	1,148	1,103	1,004	980	891	787	721	482	588
S&P Core Earnings	1,182	955	1,093	1,047	953	875	763	510	312	NA

Balance Sheet & Other Financial Data (Million $)	2009	2008	2007	2006	2005	2004	2003	2002	2001	2000
Cash	334	255	524	411	219	417	141	101	2,318	204
Current Assets	2,558	2,521	2,717	2,427	2,197	2,122	1,797	1,763	1,902	1,607
Total Assets	11,200	10,946	11,397	10,714	10,575	10,790	10,231	10,219	10,369	4,896
Current Liabilities	2,288	3,552	4,044	4,020	3,163	2,846	2,766	3,015	2,208	2,493
Long Term Debt	4,835	4,068	3,276	3,053	3,703	3,893	4,265	4,519	5,619	709
Common Equity	2,272	1,448	2,526	2,069	2,284	2,257	1,443	895	871	898
Total Capital	7,111	5,816	6,443	5,122	5,986	6,150	5,709	5,415	6,491	1,607
Capital Expenditures	377	461	472	453	374	279	247	254	277	231
Cash Flow	1,596	1,523	1,475	1,357	1,372	1,301	1,160	1,069	921	878
Current Ratio	1.1	0.7	0.7	0.6	0.7	0.7	0.7	0.6	0.9	0.6
% Long Term Debt of Capitalization	68.0	69.9	50.9	59.6	61.9	63.3	74.7	83.5	86.6	44.1
% Net Income of Revenue	9.6	9.0	9.4	9.2	9.6	9.3	8.9	8.7	5.4	8.5
% Return on Assets	11.0	10.3	10.0	9.4	9.3	8.5	7.7	7.0	6.3	12.1
% Return on Equity	65.2	57.8	48.0	46.1	43.2	48.1	67.3	81.6	54.5	68.7

Data as orig reptd.; bef. results of disc opers/spec. items. Per share data adj. for stk. divs.; EPS diluted. E-Estimated. NA-Not Available. NM-Not Meaningful. NR-Not Ranked. UR-Under Review.

Office: One Kellogg Sq, Battle Creek, MI, USA 49016-3599.
Telephone: 269-961-2000.
Website: http://www.kelloggcompany.com
Chrmn: J.M. Jenness

Pres & CEO: A.D. MacKay
COO & EVP: J.A. Bryant
SVP & CFO: R. Dissinger
SVP & CIO: B.S. Rice

Investor Contact: J. Wittenberg (269-961-9089)
Board Members: J. A. Bryant, B. S. Carson, J. T. Dillon, G. Gund, J. M. Jenness, D. A. Johnson, D. R. Knauss, A. M. Korologos, A. D. MacKay, R. M. Rebolledo, S. K. Speirn, R. A. Steele, J. L. Zabriskie

Founded: 1906
Domicile: Delaware
Employees: 30,949

KeyCorp

STANDARD & POOR'S

S&P Recommendation BUY ★★★★☆

Price	**12-Mo. Target Price**	**Investment Style**
$8.30 (as of Oct 22, 2010)	$10.00	Large-Cap Value

GICS Sector Financials
Sub-Industry Regional Banks

Summary Cleveland-based KeyCorp is one of the nation's largest bank-based financial services companies, with assets of $94.2 billion as of June 30, 2010.

Key Stock Statistics (Source S&P, Vickers, company reports)

52-Wk Range	$9.84– 5.29	S&P Oper. EPS 2010**E**	0.28	Market Capitalization(B)	$7.306	Beta	0.64
Trailing 12-Month EPS	$-0.89	S&P Oper. EPS 2011**E**	0.61	Yield (%)	0.48	S&P 3-Yr. Proj. EPS CAGR(%)	NM
Trailing 12-Month P/E	NM	P/E on S&P Oper. EPS 2010**E**	29.6	Dividend Rate/Share	$0.04	S&P Credit Rating	BBB+
$10K Invested 5 Yrs Ago	$3,135	Common Shares Outstg. (M)	880.3	Institutional Ownership (%)	80		

Price Performance

30-Week Mov. Avg. ··· 10-Week Mov. Avg.-- **GAAP Earnings vs. Previous Year**   Volume Above Avg. ▐▐ STARS
12-Mo. Target Price — Relative Strength — ▲ Up ▼ Down ► No Change   Below Avg. ▐▐ ★

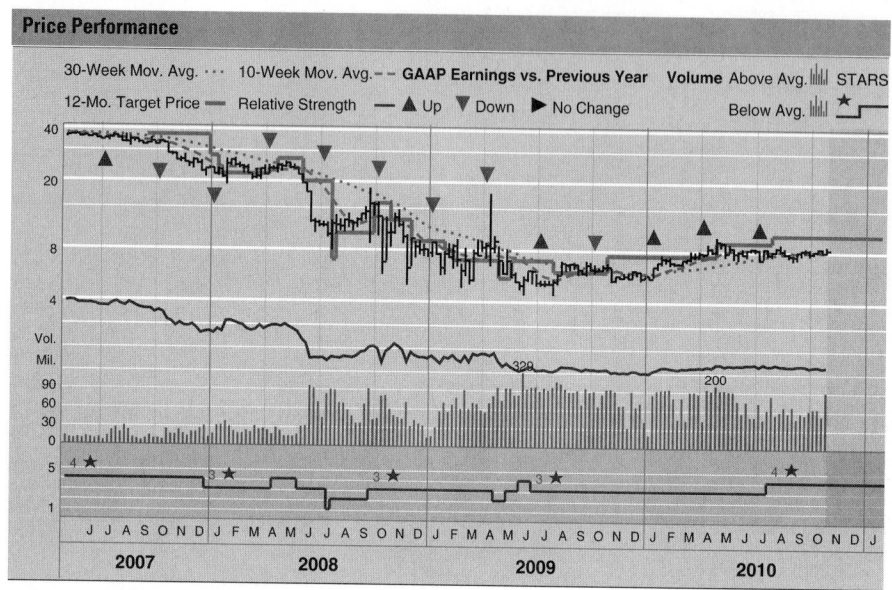

Options: ASE, CBOE, P, Ph

Analysis prepared by **Erik Oja** on July 26, 2010, when the stock traded at **$ 8.34**.

Highlights

➤ We forecast that KEY's total loan portfolio will contract 10.5% in 2010, following a 23.2% decline in 2009, reflecting net chargeoffs, weak loan demand, and the exit portfolio. We expect total interest-earning assets to fall by a lesser amount in both years, due to KEY's purchases of investment securities. Due to Q2 and expected Q3 run-offs of higher-cost CD's, we look for a year-end 2010 net interest margin of 3.20% in 2010, versus 3.00 in the fourth quarter of 2009. We expect net interest income to rise 2.1% in 2010, and 1.1% in 2011. Our estimate is for a modest increase in core fee income in 2010, reflecting a pickup in fee-driven businesses. Our 2010 core revenue growth forecast is 1.5%.

➤ New nonperforming loans totaled only $73 million in the second quarter, the lowest level in years, likely signaling a longer-term trend of credit quality improvements. Also, loan loss allowances are well above peers, at 130.3% of June 30 nonperforming loans. On the above, and our expectations for credit quality improvements, we forecast loan loss provisions of $865 million for 2010 and $390 million for 2011, down from $3.2 billion from 2009.

➤ We estimate EPS of $0.13 for 2010 and $0.40 for 2011.

Investment Rationale/Risk

➤ KEY's commercial lending credit quality improved across the board in the second quarter. Our view that much of the nonperforming, or borderline nonperforming assets have been recognized and charged-off or sold off, leads to our expectation that KEY's net chargeoffs will decline in each of the foreseeable quarters. Also, KEY's higher than peers allowance should lead to meaningful declines of provisions. Also, we expect a near-term driver of earnings from a higher net interest margin, due to large run-offs of higher priced CD's. An intermediate-term boost to earnings may come from additional improvements in KEY's non-interest expenses, which are still among the highest of major U.S. banks. Finally, we see KEY as relatively inexpensive, trading at only 0.97X June 30 tangible book value per share of $8.10.

➤ Risks to our recommendation and target price include a weaker-than-expected economic recovery.

➤ Our 12-month target price of $10 is based on a below-peers multiple of 1.15X our year-end 2010 tangible book value per share estimate of $8.60. This equates to 25X our 2011 EPS estimate of $0.40, a higher than peers multiple.

Qualitative Risk Assessment

LOW	**MEDIUM**	HIGH

Our risk assessment is medium, on our positive view of recent improvements to KEY's credit quality and capital levels.

Quantitative Evaluations

S&P Quality Ranking   B-

D	C	**B-**	B	B+	A-	A	A+

Relative Strength Rank   **MODERATE**

49

LOWEST = 1   HIGHEST = 99

Revenue/Earnings Data

Revenue (Million $)

	1Q	2Q	3Q	4Q	Year
2010	1,342	1,353	--	--	--
2009	1,524	1,709	1,322	1,402	5,798
2008	1,882	1,435	1,620	1,562	6,434
2007	2,022	2,044	1,872	1,935	7,621
2006	1,732	1,872	1,932	1,971	7,507
2005	1,565	1,602	1,705	1,823	6,695

Earnings Per Share ($)

2010	-0.11	0.06	E0.19	E0.15	E0.28
2009	-1.09	-0.69	-0.50	-0.29	-2.27
2008	0.55	-2.70	-0.07	-1.12	-3.35
2007	0.89	0.85	0.57	0.06	2.38
2006	0.66	0.75	0.74	0.76	2.91
2005	0.64	0.70	0.67	0.72	2.73

Fiscal year ended Dec. 31. Next earnings report expected: NA. EPS Estimates based on S&P Operating Earnings; historical GAAP earnings are as reported.

Dividend Data (Dates: mm/dd Payment Date: mm/dd/yy)

Amount ($)	Date Decl.	Ex-Div. Date	Stk. of Record	Payment Date
0.010	11/19	11/27	12/01	12/15/09
0.010	01/14	02/26	03/02	03/15/10
0.010	05/20	05/27	06/01	06/15/10
0.010	07/16	08/27	08/31	09/15/10

Dividends have been paid since 1963. Source: Company reports.

Please read the Required Disclosures and Analyst Certification on the last page of this report.

The McGraw·Hill Companies

KeyCorp

STANDARD &POOR'S

Business Summary July 26, 2010

CORPORATE OVERVIEW. KEY owns KeyBank, located in Ohio, New York, Washington, Oregon, Maine, Colorado, Indiana, Utah, Idaho, Vermont, Alaska, Michigan, Florida and Kentucky. The company has two business groups: Community Banking and National Banking.

The Community Banking segment, which generated 57% of total revenues in the final quarter of 2009, houses Regional Banking and Commercial Banking.

National Banking generated about 43% of total revenues in the last quarter of 2009, and houses Real Estate Capital and Corporate Banking Services, Equipment Finance, Institutional and Capital Markets, and Consumer Finance. In October 2008, KEY's Consumer Finance unit discontinued retail and floor-plan financing of marine and recreational vehicles. In September 2009, this unit discontinued education lending, which had accounted for about 5% of loans outstanding.

MARKET PROFILE. As of June 30, 2009 (latest available FDIC data), KEY had 996 branches and $67.4 billion in deposits, with about 56% of its deposits and 46% of its branches concentrated in Ohio and New York. In Ohio, KEY had 233 branches, $22.1 billion of deposits, and a deposit market share of about 9.4%, ranking fourth. In New York, KEY had 228 branches, $15.7 billion of deposits, and a deposit market share of about 1.9%, ranking 11th. In Washington State, KEY had 151 branches, $9.7 billion of deposits, and a deposit market share of about 8.6%, ranking second. In Oregon, KEY had 66 branches, $3.7 billion of deposits, and a deposit market share of about 7.0%, ranking sixth. In Maine, KEY had 61 branches, $2.8 billion of deposits, and a deposit market share of 6.0%, ranking second. In Indiana, KEY had 64 branches, $2.9 billion of deposits, and a deposit market share of about 3.1%, ranking eighth. In Colorado, KEY had 51 branches, $2.6 billion of deposits, and a deposit market share of about 3.0%, which ranks sixth. In addition, KEY had a number three ranking in Idaho, a number four market ranking in Vermont, and a number three ranking in Alaska. Finally, KEY had offices in Utah and Michigan, with a small presence in Kentucky, Florida and Connecticut.

Company Financials Fiscal Year Ended Dec. 31

Per Share Data ($)	2009	2008	2007	2006	2005	2004	2003	2002	2001	2000
Tangible Book Value	7.84	11.87	16.39	15.99	15.05	13.91	13.87	13.34	11.85	12.39
Earnings	-2.27	-3.35	2.38	2.91	2.73	2.30	2.12	2.27	0.37	2.30
S&P Core Earnings	-2.14	-2.54	2.12	2.93	2.72	2.41	2.12	2.10	0.43	NA
Dividends	0.09	1.00	1.46	1.38	1.30	1.24	1.22	1.20	1.18	1.12
Payout Ratio	NM	NM	61%	47%	48%	54%	58%	53%	NM	49%
Prices:High	9.82	27.23	39.90	38.63	35.00	34.50	29.41	29.40	29.25	28.50
Prices:Low	4.40	4.99	21.04	32.90	30.10	28.23	22.31	20.98	20.49	15.56
P/E Ratio:High	NM	NM	17	13	13	15	14	13	79	12
P/E Ratio:Low	NM	NM	9	11	11	12	11	9	55	7

Income Statement Analysis (Million $)

	2009	2008	2007	2006	2005	2004	2003	2002	2001	2000
Net Interest Income	2,380	2,409	2,769	2,815	2,790	2,637	2,725	2,749	2,825	2,730
Tax Equivalent Adjustment	26.0	436	99.0	103	121	94.0	71.0	120	45.0	28.0
Non Interest Income	2,003	1,805	2,264	2,126	2,077	1,742	1,749	1,763	1,690	2,222
Loan Loss Provision	3,159	1,835	529	150	143	185	501	553	1,350	490
% Expense/Operating Revenue	81.1%	68.2%	64.5%	62.4%	64.5%	62.8%	60.3%	57.3%	64.5%	58.6%
Pretax Income	-2,298	-1,134	1,221	1,643	1,588	1,388	1,242	1,312	259	1,517
Effective Tax Rate	NM	NM	22.9%	27.4%	28.9%	31.3%	27.3%	25.6%	39.4%	33.9%
Net Income	-1,287	-1,468	941	1,193	1,129	954	903	976	157	1,002
% Net Interest Margin	2.83	2.16	3.46	3.67	3.69	3.64	3.80	3.97	3.81	3.69
S&P Core Earnings	-1,497	-1,143	840	1,198	1,125	1,006	898	896	179	NA

Balance Sheet & Other Financial Data (Million $)

	2009	2008	2007	2006	2005	2004	2003	2002	2001	2000
Money Market Assets	1,209	1,280	1,056	Nil	Nil	NA	NA	NA	NA	NA
Investment Securities	18,153	9,988	7,860	NA	NA	NA	NA	NA	NA	NA
Commercial Loans	41,409	54,835	52,705	48,306	39,291	43,276	36,189	36,612	38,063	39,610
Other Loans	17,361	21,669	18,118	17,520	20,078	25,188	26,522	25,845	25,246	27,295
Total Assets	93,287	104,531	99,983	92,337	93,126	90,739	84,487	85,202	80,938	87,270
Demand Deposits	38,756	35,676	38,663	13,553	13,335	11,581	11,175	10,630	23,128	9,076
Time Deposits	26,815	29,584	24,436	45,563	45,430	39,683	39,683	38,716	21,667	39,573
Long Term Debt	11,558	14,995	11,957	14,533	13,939	14,846	15,294	16,865	15,842	15,404
Common Equity	7,942	7,408	7,746	7,703	7,598	7,117	6,969	6,835	6,155	6,623
% Return on Assets	NM	NM	1.0	1.3	1.2	1.1	1.1	1.2	0.2	1.2
% Return on Equity	NM	NM	12.2	15.6	15.3	13.5	13.1	15.0	2.5	15.4
% Loan Loss Reserve	4.3	2.5	1.7	1.4	1.4	1.7	2.2	2.3	2.7	1.5
% Loans/Deposits	89.6	112.2	111.8	117.5	118.9	118.4	123.3	126.6	138.0	137.5
% Equity to Assets	7.8	7.4	8.0	8.3	8.0	8.0	8.1	7.8	7.6	7.6

Data as orig reptd.; bef. results of disc opers/spec. items. Per share data adj. for stk. divs.; EPS diluted. E-Estimated. NA-Not Available. NM-Not Meaningful. NR-Not Ranked. UR-Under Review.

Office: 127 Public Square, Cleveland, OH 44114-1306.
Telephone: 216-689-6300.
Website: http://www.key.com
Chrmn, Pres & CEO: H. Meyer, III

Vice Chrmn & Chief Admin Officer: T.C. Stevens
EVP & CFO: J.B. Weeden
EVP & Chief Acctg Officer: R.L. Morris
EVP & Treas: J.M. Vayda

Board Members: W. G. Bares, E. P. Campbell, J. A. Carrabba, C. Cartwright, A. M. Cutler, H. J. Dallas, B. R. Gile, R. A. Gillis, K. L. Manos, L. E. Martin, E. R. Menasce, H. Meyer, III, B. R. Sanford, B. R. Snyder, E. W. Stack, T. C. Stevens

Founded: 1849
Domicile: Ohio
Employees: 16,698

Kimberly-Clark Corp

STANDARD &POOR'S

S&P Recommendation HOLD ★★★☆☆

Price	**12-Mo. Target Price**	**Investment Style**
$66.56 (as of Oct 22, 2010)	$67.00	Large-Cap Blend

GICS Sector Consumer Staples
Sub-Industry Household Products

Summary This leading consumer products company's global tissue, personal care and health care brands include Huggies, Pull-Ups, Kotex, Depend, Kleenex, and Scott.

Key Stock Statistics (Source S&P, Vickers, company reports)

52-Wk Range	$67.24– 58.25	S&P Oper. EPS 2010**E**	4.82	Market Capitalization(B)	$27.244	Beta	0.43
Trailing 12-Month EPS	$4.69	S&P Oper. EPS 2011**E**	5.15	Yield (%)	3.97	S&P 3-Yr. Proj. EPS CAGR(%)	8
Trailing 12-Month P/E	14.2	P/E on S&P Oper. EPS 2010**E**	13.8	Dividend Rate/Share	$2.64	S&P Credit Rating	A
$10K Invested 5 Yrs Ago	$14,058	Common Shares Outstg. (M)	409.3	Institutional Ownership (%)	73		

Price Performance

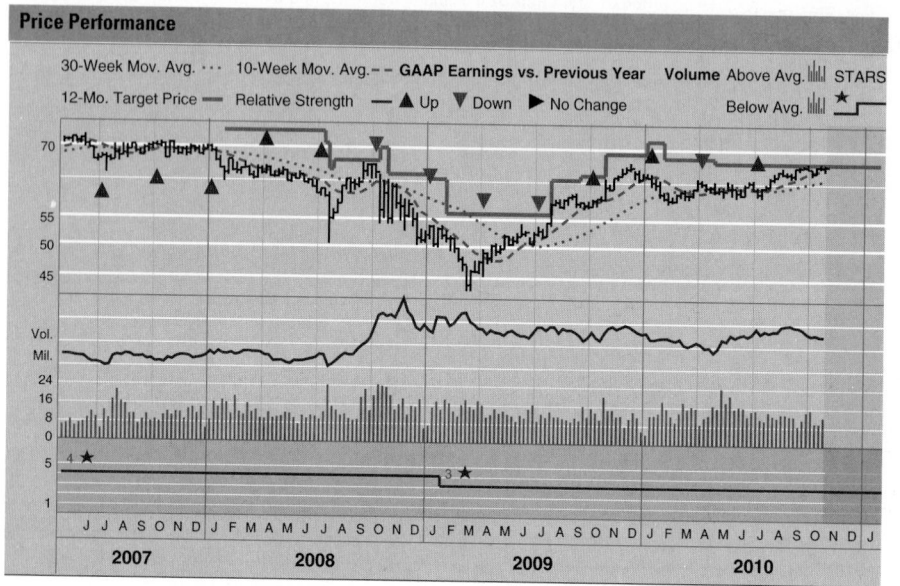

30-Week Mov. Avg. ···· 10-Week Mov. Avg. -- GAAP Earnings vs. Previous Year   Volume Above Avg. ▌▌▌ STARS
12-Mo. Target Price — Relative Strength   ▲ Up ▼ Down ▶ No Change   Below Avg. ▌▌▌ ★

Options: ASE, CBOE, P

Analysis prepared by **Mark S. Basham** on July 27, 2010, when the stock traded at **$ 64.64**.

Highlights

➤ For 2010, we forecast a sales gain of 4% to 5%, with currency providing a small positive contribution and 1% coming from acquisitions made in 2009. We look for higher growth from developing and emerging markets than developed markets, and we forecast that the slowest-growing segment will be Consumer Tissue.

➤ Excluding expenses associated with cost reduction programs, we look for the operating margin in 2010 to be about 50 basis points lower. We think benefits from earlier restructuring programs will be outweighed by higher commodity costs and marketing spending. Cost savings under the FORCE program were somewhat larger than anticipated in the first half, and pension expense has been lower than in 2009.

➤ Our 2010 operating EPS estimate is $4.82. EPS was $4.74 in 2009, excluding costs from the June 2009 plan to streamline the organization. For 2011, we see revenues rising about 4%, again with higher growth in developing markets. On flat operating margins, but lower net interest expense and a slightly lower tax rate, we estimate EPS will rise to $5.15 in 2011.

Investment Rationale/Risk

➤ We think continuing intense competition in developed countries and in consumer tissue and personal care categories will somewhat offset KMB's efforts to support sales growth by expanding in non-traditional categories for the company and focusing on certain developing markets. Also, while we saw substantial moderation of commodity cost pressures in mid-2009, some costs, particularly pulp, have begun to rise again. However, we have started to see more benefits from the strategic cost reduction program begun in late 2005 and other cost containment programs.

➤ Risks to our recommendation and target price include increased promotional activity in the consumer paper category, higher commodity costs, a lack of product innovation, unfavorable foreign currency shifts, and decreased consumer acceptance of KMB's products.

➤ Our 12-month target price of $67 is based on a blend of our historical and relative analyses. Our historical analysis suggests a value of $68, using a P/E toward the low end of the 10-year range applied to our 2010 operating EPS forecast. Our peer analysis applies a discount to the group average, implying a value of $66.

Qualitative Risk Assessment

LOW	MEDIUM	HIGH

Our risk assessment reflects the generally static demand for household and personal care products, which is usually not affected by changes in the economy or geopolitical factors.

Quantitative Evaluations

S&P Quality Ranking   A

D	C	B-	B	B+	A-	**A**	A+

Relative Strength Rank   MODERATE
44
LOWEST = 1   HIGHEST = 99

Revenue/Earnings Data

Revenue (Million $)

	1Q	2Q	3Q	4Q	Year
2010	4,835	4,857	--	--	--
2009	4,493	4,727	4,913	4,982	19,115
2008	4,813	5,006	4,998	4,598	19,415
2007	4,385	4,502	4,621	4,758	18,266
2006	4,068	4,161	4,210	4,307	16,747
2005	3,906	3,987	4,001	4,009	15,903

Earnings Per Share ($)

	1Q	2Q	3Q	4Q	Year
2010	0.92	1.20	E1.23	E1.25	E4.82
2009	0.98	0.97	1.40	1.17	4.52
2008	1.04	1.01	0.99	1.01	4.06
2007	0.98	1.00	1.04	1.07	4.09
2006	0.60	0.82	0.79	1.05	3.25
2005	0.93	0.88	0.68	0.82	3.31

Fiscal year ended Dec. 31. Next earnings report expected: Late October. EPS Estimates based on S&P Operating Earnings; historical GAAP earnings are as reported.

Dividend Data (Dates: mm/dd Payment Date: mm/dd/yy)

Amount ($)	Date Decl.	Ex-Div. Date	Stk. of Record	Payment Date
0.600	11/18	12/02	12/04	01/05/10
0.660	02/23	03/03	03/05	04/05/10
0.660	04/29	06/02	06/04	07/02/10
0.660	08/02	09/08	09/10	10/04/10

Dividends have been paid since 1935. Source: Company reports.

Please read the Required Disclosures and Analyst Certification on the last page of this report.

The McGraw-Hill Companies

Kimberly-Clark Corp

Business Summary July 27, 2010

CORPORATE OVERVIEW. Kimberly-Clark, best known for brands such as Kleenex, Scott, Huggies and Kotex, sells consumer and other products in more than 150 countries. After operating as a broadly diversified enterprise, KMB made a major transition since the early 1990s, transforming itself into a global consumer products company. The company further developed its health care business through the acquisitions of Technol Medical Products, Ballard Medical Products, and Safeskin Corp. Reflecting more than 30 strategic acquisitions and 20 strategic divestitures since 1992, KMB has become a leading global manufacturer of tissue, personal care and health care products, manufactured in 38 countries. In 2004, KMB distributed to its shareholders all of the outstanding shares of Neenah Paper, Inc., which was formed in 2004 to facilitate the spin-off of KMB's U.S. fine paper and technical paper businesses and its Canadian pulp mills.

KMB classifies its business into four reportable global segments: Personal Care; Consumer Tissue; K-C Professional & Other; and Health Care. In 2009, Personal Care contributed 44% of sales and 55% of segment operating profits; Consumer Tissue 33% and 23%; K-C Professional & Other 16% and 14%; and Health Care 7% and 8%.

In 2009, sales by geographic region were: U.S. 51%; Canada 3%; Europe 16%; and Asia, Latin America and other 30%. Wal-Mart Stores, Inc. is KMB's single largest customer, accounting for about 13% of net sales in 2009, following 14% of net sales in 2008 and in 2007 and about 13% in 2006.

CORPORATE STRATEGY. In mid-2003, KMB introduced a new strategic plan called the Global Business Plan (GBP), which involves prioritizing growth opportunities and applying greater financial discipline to KMB's global operations. The annual goals established by the GBP are: top-line growth of 3%-5%; EPS growth in the mid- to high single digits; an operating margin improvement of 40 to 50 basis points; capital spending of 5%-6% of net sales; an ROIC improvement of 40 to 50 basis points; and dividend increases in the high single digits to the low double digits. On average, in the 2004 through 2007 period, we believe KMB met or exceeded all these goals but an operating margin improvement, which was adversely affected by unusually high inflationary cost pressures. Also, under the GBP, capital allocation focused on more targeted expansion activity and an increased emphasis on innovation and cost reduction.

Company Financials Fiscal Year Ended Dec. 31

Per Share Data ($)	2009	2008	2007	2006	2005	2004	2003	2002	2001	2000
Tangible Book Value	4.40	2.45	5.92	7.10	6.22	8.13	8.21	6.65	7.10	7.04
Cash Flow	6.40	5.91	5.90	5.34	5.08	5.32	4.80	4.60	1.39	4.55
Earnings	4.52	4.06	4.09	3.25	3.31	3.55	3.33	3.24	3.02	3.34
S&P Core Earnings	4.81	3.57	4.09	3.32	3.32	3.56	3.35	2.74	2.49	NA
Dividends	2.40	2.32	2.12	1.96	1.80	1.60	1.36	1.20	1.12	1.08
Payout Ratio	53%	57%	52%	60%	54%	45%	41%	37%	37%	32%
Prices:High	67.03	69.69	72.79	68.58	68.29	69.00	59.30	66.79	72.19	73.25
Prices:Low	43.05	50.27	63.79	56.59	55.60	56.19	42.92	45.30	52.06	42.00
P/E Ratio:High	15	17	18	21	21	19	18	21	24	22
P/E Ratio:Low	10	12	16	17	17	16	13	14	17	13

Income Statement Analysis (Million $)										
Revenue	19,115	19,415	18,266	16,747	15,903	15,083	14,348	13,566	14,524	13,982
Operating Income	3,846	3,414	3,553	3,034	3,155	3,358	3,158	3,170	3,162	3,203
Depreciation	783	775	806	933	844	800	746	707	740	673
Interest Expense	275	318	283	220	190	163	168	182	192	222
Pretax Income	2,740	2,455	2,488	2,064	2,106	2,328	2,153	2,411	2,319	2,622
Effective Tax Rate	27.2%	25.2%	21.6%	22.7%	20.8%	20.8%	23.9%	27.7%	27.8%	28.9%
Net Income	1,884	1,698	1,823	1,500	1,581	1,770	1,694	1,686	1,610	1,801
S&P Core Earnings	2,004	1,497	1,820	1,533	1,581	1,777	1,708	1,424	1,329	NA

Balance Sheet & Other Financial Data (Million $)										
Cash	798	364	762	361	364	594	291	495	405	207
Current Assets	5,864	5,813	6,097	5,270	4,783	4,962	4,438	4,274	3,922	3,790
Total Assets	19,182	18,074	18,440	17,067	16,303	17,018	16,780	15,586	15,008	14,480
Current Liabilities	4,923	4,752	4,929	5,016	4,643	4,537	3,919	4,038	4,168	4,574
Long Term Debt	5,844	4,882	4,394	3,069	3,352	3,021	3,301	3,398	2,962	Nil
Common Equity	5,696	3,878	5,224	6,097	5,558	6,630	6,766	5,650	5,647	5,767
Total Capital	11,540	10,852	11,476	9,981	9,878	10,859	10,366	10,158	9,923	7,036
Capital Expenditures	848	906	989	972	710	535	878	871	1,100	1,170
Cash Flow	2,667	2,473	2,629	2,432	2,425	2,571	2,440	2,393	740	2,474
Current Ratio	1.2	1.2	1.2	1.1	1.0	1.1	1.1	1.1	0.9	0.8
% Long Term Debt of Capitalization	50.6	44.9	38.3	30.8	33.9	27.8	31.8	33.4	29.9	Nil
% Net Income of Revenue	9.9	8.8	10.0	9.0	9.9	11.7	11.8	12.4	11.1	12.9
% Return on Assets	10.1	9.3	10.3	9.0	9.5	10.5	10.5	11.0	10.9	13.2
% Return on Equity	39.4	37.3	32.2	25.7	25.9	26.4	27.3	29.8	28.2	33.2

Data as orig reptd.; bef. results of disc opers/spec. items. Per share data adj. for stk. divs.; EPS diluted. E-Estimated. NA-Not Available. NM-Not Meaningful. NR-Not Ranked. UR-Under Review.

Office: P.O. Box 619100, Dallas, TX 75261-9100.
Telephone: 972-281-1200.
Website: http://www.kimberly-clark.com
Chrmn, Pres & CEO: T.J. Falk

SVP & CFO: M.A. Buthman
Chief Acctg Officer & Cntlr: M.T. Azbell
Secy: J.W. Wesley
Investor Contact: M.D. Masseth (972-281-1478)

Board Members: J. R. Alm, D. Beresford, J. F. Bergstrom, A. E. Bru, R. W. Decherd, T. J. Falk, M. C. Jemison, J. M. Jenness, N. J. Karch, I. C. Read, L. J. Rice, M. J. Shapiro, G. C. Sullivan

Founded: 1872
Domicile: Delaware
Employees: 56,000

Kimco Realty Corp

S&P Recommendation HOLD ★★★☆☆

Price $17.33 (as of Oct 22, 2010)	**12-Mo. Target Price** $17.00

Investment Style Large-Cap Blend

GICS Sector Financials
Sub-Industry Retail REITS

Summary This real estate investment trust is one of the largest U.S. owners and operators of neighborhood and community shopping centers.

Key Stock Statistics (Source S&P, Vickers, company reports)

52-Wk Range	$17.49–11.54	S&P FFO/Sh. 2010E	1.15	Market Capitalization(B)	$7.033	Beta	1.82
Trailing 12-Month FFO/Share	NA	S&P FFO/Sh. 2011E	1.22	Yield (%)	3.69	S&P 3-Yr. FFO/Sh. Proj. CAGR(%)	-13
Trailing 12-Month P/FFO	NA	P/FFO on S&P FFO/Sh. 2010E	15.1	Dividend Rate/Share	$0.64	S&P Credit Rating	BBB+
$10K Invested 5 Yrs Ago	$7,751	Common Shares Outstg. (M)	405.8	Institutional Ownership (%)	86		

Price Performance

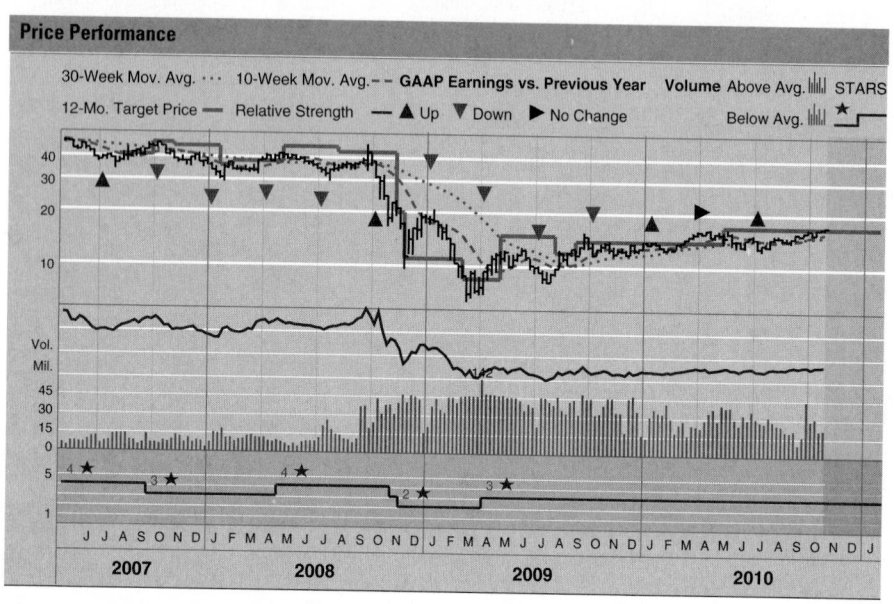

30-Week Mov. Avg. · · · 10-Week Mov. Avg. – – **GAAP Earnings vs. Previous Year** Volume Above Avg. | STARS
12-Mo. Target Price — Relative Strength — ▲ Up ▼ Down ▶ No Change Below Avg. | ★

Options: ASE, CBOE, P, Ph

Analysis prepared by **Robert McMillan** on July 29, 2010, when the stock traded at **$ 15.14.**

Highlights

➤ We expect the trust to continue to benefit from what we view as a successful strategy of operating neighborhood and community shopping centers in North America and expanding into high-growth international markets via joint ventures. After rising 3.7% in 2009, total revenues should advance 8.4% in 2010, by our analysis, on higher rents at established properties as well as acquisition activity.

➤ Operating trends appear to be stabilizing. The lease rate in KIM's total U.S portfolio rose to 92.8% at the end of the 2010 second quarter, from about 92.3% a year earlier. We believe that improving retailer sentiment will generate increased demand for new as well as existing space, which, on top of limited new construction will help results in 2010. Rents on new and renewal leases in the U.S. declined 1.6% during the second quarter. We also see continued growth in Canada and Latin America (driven in part by Walt-Mart's continued expansion) as well as acquisitions helping KIM's long-term growth.

➤ We project FFO per share of $1.15 for 2010 and $1.22 in 2011.

Investment Rationale/Risk

➤ We believe that KIM, one of the largest owners and operators of neighborhood and community shopping centers in the U.S. with a broad array of established relationships, will generate above-average rent growth in the long term. Near term, though, we think an expected drop in development stemming from the weak economy and credit crunch will restrict the shares.

➤ Risks to our recommendation and target price include slower-than-expected growth in retailer expansion and rental rates, higher-than-expected retailer bankruptcies, and a sharp drop in development activities.

➤ The shares recently traded at about 12.1X trailing 12-month FFO per share. Our 12-month target price of $17 is equal to 15.0X our forward 12-month FFO estimate of $1.13. We believe the stock has been volatile over the past year due, in part, to concerns about the effect of a soft economy on KIM's business. We think the valuation multiple will expand over time as KIM shows that its core portfolio, anchored by long-term leases, continues to grow. KIM's December 2009 equity offering, although dilutive, eased our concerns about the trust's liquidity.

Qualitative Risk Assessment

LOW	MEDIUM	HIGH

Our risk assessment reflects our view of KIM's strong fundamentals, healthy credit quality, and diversified customer base. We also believe KIM's diversity in its geographic presence helps provide significant protection from a local or regional downturn.

Quantitative Evaluations

S&P Quality Ranking A-

D	C	B-	B	B+	A-	A	A+

Relative Strength Rank STRONG

79

LOWEST = 1 HIGHEST = 99

Revenue/FFO Data

Revenue (Million $)

	1Q	2Q	3Q	4Q	Year
2010	239.5	227.7	--	--	--
2009	208.0	203.3	205.5	227.3	844.3
2008	190.5	199.9	208.6	213.6	824.7
2007	158.3	170.8	210.3	179.7	750.6
2006	138.1	147.9	150.7	157.3	653.0
2005	129.3	126.7	129.6	137.0	580.6

FFO Per Share ($)

	1Q	2Q	3Q	4Q	Year
2010	0.31	0.26	E0.24	E0.27	E1.15
2009	0.43	0.31	0.30	0.75	0.82
2008	0.64	0.66	0.37	0.04	2.02
2007	0.78	0.71	0.57	0.53	2.59
2006	0.53	0.54	0.56	0.58	2.21
2005	0.53	0.54	0.56	0.55	2.00

Fiscal year ended Dec. 31. Next earnings report expected: Early November. FFO Estimates based on S&P Funds From Operations Est..

Dividend Data (Dates: mm/dd Payment Date: mm/dd/yy)

Amount ($)	Date Decl.	Ex-Div. Date	Stk. of Record	Payment Date
0.160	11/04	12/30	01/04	01/15/10
0.160	07/27	01/01	10/05	10/15/10
0.160	02/03	03/31	04/05	04/15/10
0.160	05/05	06/29	07/01	07/15/10

Dividends have been paid since 1992. Source: Company reports.

Please read the Required Disclosures and Analyst Certification on the last page of this report.

Kimco Realty Corp

Business Summary July 29, 2010

Kimco Realty specializes in the acquisition, development and management of shopping centers that it believes are well located and have strong growth potential. At the end of 2009, KIM had interests in 1,915 properties, totaling approximately 176.9 million square feet of gross leasable area (GLA) located in 45 states, Canada, Mexico, Puerto Rico, Brazil, Chile and Peru. The trust's ownership interests in real estate consist of its consolidated portfolio and portfolios in which it owns an economic interest, such as properties in its investment management programs, where it partners with institutional investors and also retains management.

The trust's investment objective has been to increase cash flow, current income, and, consequently, the value of its existing portfolio of properties, and to seek continued growth through the strategic re-tenanting, renovation and expansion of its existing centers, and through the selective acquisition of established income-producing real estate properties and properties requiring significant re-tenanting and redevelopment. These properties are mainly located in neighborhood and community shopping centers in geographic regions in which KIM currently operates.

For KIM as well as other retail-oriented REITs, we believe that location and the financial health and growth of its retail tenants are among the most important factors affecting the success of its portfolio. KIM's neighborhood and community shopping center properties are designed to attract local area customers and typically are anchored by a discount department store, a supermarket or a drugstore tenant offering day-to-day necessities rather than high-priced luxury items. The trust seeks to reduce operating and leasing risks through diversification achieved by the geographic distribution of its properties and a large tenant base. As of December 31, 2009, no single neighborhood and community shopping center accounted for more than 1.2% of the trust's annualized base rental revenues or more than 1.0% of its total shopping center GLA; the five largest tenants were The Home Depot (3.3% of KIM's annualized base rental revenues, including the proportionate share of base rental revenues from properties in which KIM has less than a 100% economic interest), TX Companies (2.6%), Sears Holdings (2.5%), Walt-Mart (2.2%) and Kohl's (2.0%).

Company Financials Fiscal Year Ended Dec. 31

Per Share Data ($)	2009	2008	2007	2006	2005	2004	2003	2002	2001	2000
Tangible Book Value	11.96	14.66	15.40	13.24	9.70	9.17	8.87	8.04	7.95	7.26
Earnings	-0.15	0.69	1.33	1.36	1.40	1.19	1.04	1.10	1.08	0.96
S&P Core Earnings	-0.15	0.69	1.33	1.36	1.40	1.18	1.03	1.08	1.07	NA
Dividends	0.72	0.24	1.52	1.38	1.27	1.16	1.10	1.05	0.98	0.91
Payout Ratio	NM	35%	114%	101%	91%	97%	105%	96%	91%	95%
Prices:High	20.90	47.80	53.60	47.13	33.35	29.64	22.93	16.94	17.03	14.92
Prices:Low	6.33	9.56	33.74	32.02	25.90	19.77	15.13	12.98	13.58	10.92
P/E Ratio:High	NM	69	40	35	24	25	22	15	16	16
P/E Ratio:Low	NM	14	25	24	18	17	14	12	13	11

Income Statement Analysis (Million $)										
Rental Income	787	759	682	594	523	517	480	451	469	459
Mortgage Income	Nil	Nil	14.2	18.8	NA	NA	NA	NA	NA	NA
Total Income	787	825	751	653	581	517	480	451	469	466
General Expenses	111	118	104	164	128	111	104	9.15	89.7	138
Interest Expense	210	213	214	173	128	108	103	86.9	89.4	92.1
Provision for Losses	Nil	Nil	Nil	Nil	Nil	Nil	Nil	Nil	Nil	Nil
Depreciation	228	204	190	141	106	102	86.2	76.7	74.2	71.1
Net Income	-4.05	225	362	343	334	282	247	249	237	205
S&P Core Earnings	-51.3	178	342	333	322	268	222	227	209	NA

Balance Sheet & Other Financial Data (Million $)										
Cash	122	136	87.5	1,616	1,018	757	581	36.0	93.8	19.1
Total Assets	10,162	9,397	9,098	7,869	5,535	4,747	4,604	3,757	3,385	3,171
Real Estate Investment	8,882	7,819	7,325	6,002	4,560	4,877	4,137	3,399	3,201	3,112
Loss Reserve	Nil	Nil	Nil	Nil	Nil	Nil	Nil	Nil	Nil	Nil
Net Investment	7,539	6,659	6,348	5,195	3,820	4,242	3,569	2,882	2,748	2,720
Short Term Debt	380	186	281	209	NA	NA	570	147	123	4.60
Capitalization:Debt	4,054	4,371	3,936	3,378	2,397	1,860	1,585	1,430	1,205	1,321
Capitalization:Equity	4,852	3,974	3,894	3,366	2,387	2,236	2,135	1,906	1,889	1,703
Capitalization:Total	9,172	8,691	8,279	7,170	4,907	4,203	3,820	3,431	3,103	3,039
% Earnings & Depreciation/Assets	2.3	4.6	6.5	7.2	8.5	8.2	8.0	9.1	9.5	8.9
Price Times Book Value:High	1.7	3.3	3.5	3.6	3.4	3.2	2.6	2.1	2.1	2.1
Price Times Book Value:Low	0.5	0.7	2.2	2.4	2.7	2.2	1.7	1.6	1.7	1.5

Data as orig reptd.; bef. results of disc opers/spec. items. Per share data adj. for stk. divs.; EPS diluted. E-Estimated. NA-Not Available. NM-Not Meaningful. NR-Not Ranked. UR-Under Review.

Office: 3333 New Hyde Park Road, New Hyde Park, NY 11042-0020.
Telephone: 800-285-4626.
Email: ir@kimcorealty.com
Website: http://www.kimcorealty.com

Chrmn: M. Cooper
Pres, Vice Chrmn & CEO: D.B. Henry
COO & EVP: M.V. Pappagallo
EVP, CFO & Treas: G.G. Cohen

EVP & Chief Admin Officer: B.M. Pooley
Investor Contact: B. Pooley (866-831-4297)
Board Members: M. Cooper, P. E. Coviello, R. G. Dooley, J. Grills, D. B. Henry, F. P. Hughes, F. Lourenso, R. B. Saltzman

Founded: 1966
Domicile: Maryland
Employees: 640

King Pharmaceuticals Inc.

STANDARD &POOR'S

| **S&P Recommendation** HOLD ★★★☆☆ | **Price** $14.16 (as of Oct 22, 2010) | **12-Mo. Target Price** $14.00 | **Investment Style** Large-Cap Blend |

GICS Sector Health Care
Sub-Industry Pharmaceuticals

Summary In mid-October 2011, Pfizer entered into a definitive agreement to acquire the company for some $3.6 billion in cash, equal to $14.25 per KG common share.

Key Stock Statistics (Source S&P, Vickers, company reports)

52-Wk Range	$14.18– 7.18	S&P Oper. EPS 2010**E**	0.68	Market Capitalization(B)	$3.535	Beta	0.80
Trailing 12-Month EPS	$0.35	S&P Oper. EPS 2011**E**	0.75	Yield (%)	Nil	S&P 3-Yr. Proj. EPS CAGR(%)	5
Trailing 12-Month P/E	40.5	P/E on S&P Oper. EPS 2010**E**	20.8	Dividend Rate/Share	Nil	S&P Credit Rating	BB
$10K Invested 5 Yrs Ago	$9,472	Common Shares Outstg. (M)	249.7	Institutional Ownership (%)	92		

Price Performance

Options: ASE, CBOE, P, Ph

Analysis prepared by **Herman B. Saftlas** on October 14, 2010, when the stock traded at **$ 14.16**.

Highlights

▸ We see revenues declining about 16% in 2010, primarily reflecting projected generic erosion in Skelaxin, and increased competitive pressures in the Thrombin JMI, Levoxyl and Avinza lines. However, we see strong growth in newer pain products that came with the Alpharma acquisition, such as Embeda abuse-deterrent morphine pain drug, and animal health sales. Sales in the Flector pain patch and Meridian auto-injector device lines will likely be modestly higher, in our opinion.

▸ We look for gross margins close to 2009's 67%, with benefits from manufacturing efficiencies and other merger synergies roughly offsetting the projected lower volume. However, we expect the SG&A and R&D cost ratios to rise sharply, on higher new product costs. Depreciation should be relatively flat, but interest costs are expected to decline, by our analysis.

▸ After a projected effective tax rate of about 39%, up from 2009's 37.1%, we forecast cash EPS of $0.68 for 2010, down from $1.10 in 2009, excluding goodwill amortization. We project an improvement in EPS, to $0.75 in 2011.

Investment Rationale/Risk

▸ On October 12, 2010, global pharmaceutical leader Pfizer (PFE 17.7****) announced that it had entered into a definitive agreement with King to acquire all of KG's outstanding common shares for $14.25 in cash, equal to a total acquisition cost of $3.6 billion. We view this as an attractive price for KG holders, representing a 40% premium from KG's closing price on October 11, and a 46% premium to the one-month average closing price as of the same date. Directors of both firms have approved the combination. The merger, which is subject to customary terms, is expected to be completed late in the fourth quarter of 2010, or early in the first quarter of 2011.

▸ Risks to our opinion and target price include the failure to complete the planned merger with Pfizer. Business risks for KG also include possible R&D setbacks.

▸ Our 12-month target price of $14 closely approximates the $14.25 per share cash acquisition bid that Pfizer has offered for the shares. We expect the merger to be consummated as planned either in late 2010, or early 2011.

Qualitative Risk Assessment

| LOW | MEDIUM | HIGH |

Our risk assessment reflects King Pharmaceuticals' reliance on in-licensing drugs from other companies and on aggressive marketing for its sales growth. KG recently lost patent protection on its key Skelaxin drug, and faces increased competitive pressures in other lines. We think the purchase of Alpharma made strategic sense, but we see KG facing further execution risk in integrating that acquisition.

Quantitative Evaluations

S&P Quality Ranking B-

| D | C | B- | B | B+ | A- | A | A+ |

Relative Strength Rank STRONG 97

LOWEST = 1   HIGHEST = 99

Revenue/Earnings Data

Revenue (Million $)

	1Q	2Q	3Q	4Q	Year
2010	380.9	370.9	--	--	--
2009	429.1	445.0	463.4	439.1	1,777
2008	432.0	396.9	388.5	347.7	1,565
2007	516.0	542.7	544.9	533.3	2,137
2006	484.2	499.7	491.7	512.9	1,989
2005	368.6	462.9	518.0	423.3	1,773

Earnings Per Share ($)

2010	0.02	0.07	E0.20	E0.17	E0.68
2009	-0.04	0.15	0.17	0.09	0.37
2008	0.36	0.18	0.35	-2.25	-1.37
2007	0.48	0.26	-0.17	0.18	0.75
2006	0.21	0.46	0.37	0.15	1.19
2005	0.28	0.08	0.50	-0.39	0.48

Fiscal year ended Dec. 31. Next earnings report expected: Early November. EPS Estimates based on S&P Operating Earnings; historical GAAP earnings are as reported.

Dividend Data

No cash dividends have been paid.

King Pharmaceuticals Inc.

STANDARD & POOR'S

Business Summary October 14, 2010

CORPORATE OVERVIEW. King Pharmaceuticals is a vertically integrated branded drug company. A key part of its business strategy consists of the acquisition of drugs being divested by large global pharmaceutical companies. To date, King has successfully acquired and commercialized more than 35 branded products, and has introduced several product line extensions. In late December 2008, KG completed the acquisition of Alpharma Inc. for $1.6 billion in cash.

Revenues from King's branded pharmaceuticals accounted for about 63% of total revenues in 2009; Meridian Medical Technologies (a maker of auto-injectors) 14%; animal health products 20%, and royalties from licensed drugs, contract manufacturing and other 3%.

King's largest selling drug is Skelaxin (sales of $401 million in 2009), a muscle relaxant indicated for the relief of discomforts associated with acute, painful musculoskeletal conditions. Other key neuroscience products include Avinza ($131 million), a once-daily, extended-release formulation of morphine sulfate for severe pain; and Flector Patch ($139 million), a topical non-steroidal, anti-inflammatory patch for the treatment of acute pain due to minor strains, sprains and contusions.

Other important pharmaceutical products consist of Thrombin-JMI ($183 million), a drug used to control minor bleeding during surgery; Altace ($36 million), an off-patent heart drug used to treat hypertension and congestive heart failure; and Levoxyl ($71 million), a treatment for thyroid disorders. Other drugs include Sonata anti-insomnia agent, Bicillin anti-infective, Synercid injectable antibiotic; and Intall multi-dose inhaler asthma treatment. Impacted by generic erosion, sales of Altace fell 79% in 2009. Sales of Levoxyl declined 28%.

The Meridian Medical Technologies division markets auto-injectors, which are pre-filled, pen-like devices that allow patients or caregivers to automatically inject precise drug dosages.

KG markets its branded drugs to general/family practitioners, internal medicine physicians, cardiologists, and hospitals across the U.S. Pursuant to a major cost restructuring put in place in 2007, the company terminated about 20% of its total work force, primarily through a reduction in sales personnel. About 61% of sales in 2009 were derived from three key drug wholesalers: McKesson Corp. (20%), Cardinal/Bindley (27%), and AmerisourceBergen Corp. (14%).

Company Financials Fiscal Year Ended Dec. 31

Per Share Data ($)	2009	2008	2007	2006	2005	2004	2003	2002	2001	2000
Tangible Book Value	4.46	3.22	6.51	5.41	3.66	7.67	0.68	2.90	3.47	0.85
Cash Flow	1.23	-0.76	1.43	1.79	1.09	0.46	0.95	0.98	1.20	0.66
Earnings	0.37	-1.37	0.75	1.19	0.48	-0.21	0.44	0.74	0.99	0.47
S&P Core Earnings	0.38	-1.35	0.78	1.31	0.47	-0.06	0.41	0.71	0.94	NA
Dividends	Nil	Nil	Nil	Nil	Nil	Nil	Nil	Nil	Nil	Nil
Payout Ratio	Nil	Nil	Nil	Nil	Nil	Nil	Nil	Nil	Nil	Nil
Prices:High	12.45	12.60	22.25	20.00	17.99	20.62	18.13	42.13	46.05	41.63
Prices:Low	5.86	6.98	9.75	15.15	7.50	10.01	9.46	15.00	24.79	14.81
P/E Ratio:High	34	NM	30	17	37	NM	41	57	47	88
P/E Ratio:Low	16	NM	13	13	16	NM	22	20	25	31

Income Statement Analysis (Million $)										
Revenue	1,777	1,565	2,137	1,989	1,773	1,304	1,521	1,128	872	620
Operating Income	513	584	834	700	551	272	403	426	429	326
Depreciation	214	148	167	148	147	162	125	59.3	48.0	41.9
Interest Expense	88.2	8.51	8.10	9.86	11.9	12.6	13.4	12.4	12.7	37.0
Pretax Income	151	-202	251	424	178	-58.0	177	268	371	192
Effective Tax Rate	38.9%	NM	27.0%	32.0%	34.5%	NM	40.2%	31.8%	37.2%	45.4%
Net Income	92.0	-333	183	289	117	-50.6	106	183	233	105
S&P Core Earnings	93.9	-328	191	318	115	-13.1	98.4	175	222	NA

Balance Sheet & Other Financial Data (Million $)										
Cash	577	947	1,366	114	48.5	359	146	815	924	76.4
Current Assets	1,130	1,669	1,820	1,673	1,248	1,127	946	1,262	1,238	317
Total Assets	3,329	4,258	3,427	3,330	2,965	2,924	3,178	2,751	2,507	1,282
Current Liabilities	497	1,007	453	618	971	689	669	370	151	105
Long Term Debt	339	963	400	400	Nil	345	345	345	346	99.0
Common Equity	2,369	2,177	2,511	2,289	1,973	1,849	2,042	1,931	1,908	988
Total Capital	2,794	3,580	2,911	2,689	1,973	2,194	2,387	2,310	2,292	1,104
Capital Expenditures	38.8	57.5	49.6	45.8	53.3	55.1	51.2	73.6	40.2	25.1
Cash Flow	306	-185	350	436	264	111	230	242	281	147
Current Ratio	2.3	1.7	4.0	2.7	1.3	1.6	1.4	3.4	8.2	3.0
% Long Term Debt of Capitalization	12.1	26.9	13.7	14.9	Nil	15.7	14.5	14.9	15.1	9.0
% Net Income of Revenue	5.2	NM	8.6	14.5	6.6	NM	7.0	16.2	26.7	16.9
% Return on Assets	2.4	NM	5.4	9.2	4.0	NM	3.6	6.9	12.3	8.5
% Return on Equity	4.0	NM	7.6	13.5	6.1	NM	5.3	9.5	16.1	14.1

Data as orig reptd.; bef. results of disc opers/spec. items. Per share data adj. for stk. divs.; EPS diluted. E-Estimated. NA-Not Available. NM-Not Meaningful. NR-Not Ranked. UR-Under Review.

Office: .
Chrmn, Pres & CEO: B.A. Markison
Investor Contact: J.J. Howarth
CFO & Chief Acctg Officer: J. Squicciarino

Board Members: K. S. Crutchfield, E. W. Deavenport, Jr., E. M. Greetham, P. Incarnati, G. D. Jordan, B. A. Markison, R. Moyer, D. G. Rooker, D. L. Schaffer, T. G. Wood

Founded: 1993
Domicile: Tennessee
Employees: 2,600

KLA Tencor Corp

STANDARD &POOR'S

S&P Recommendation	SELL ★ ★ ★ ★ ★	Price $35.99 (as of Oct 22, 2010)	12-Mo. Target Price $28.00	Investment Style Large-Cap Growth

GICS Sector Information Technology
Sub-Industry Semiconductor Equipment

Summary This company is the world's leading manufacturer of yield monitoring and process control systems for the semiconductor industry.

Key Stock Statistics (Source S&P, Vickers, company reports)

52-Wk Range	$37.49–26.69	S&P Oper. EPS 2011**E**	3.52	Market Capitalization(B)	$6.040	Beta	1.77
Trailing 12-Month EPS	$1.23	S&P Oper. EPS 2012**E**	3.67	Yield (%)	2.78	S&P 3-Yr. Proj. EPS CAGR(%)	10
Trailing 12-Month P/E	29.3	P/E on S&P Oper. EPS 2011**E**	10.2	Dividend Rate/Share	$1.00	S&P Credit Rating	BBB
$10K Invested 5 Yrs Ago	$8,168	Common Shares Outstg. (M)	167.8	Institutional Ownership (%)	89		

Price Performance

30-Week Mov. Avg. · · · · 10-Week Mov. Avg. ‒ ‒ **GAAP Earnings vs. Previous Year** Volume Above Avg. STARS

12-Mo. Target Price — Relative Strength — ▲ Up ▼ Down ► No Change Below Avg. ★

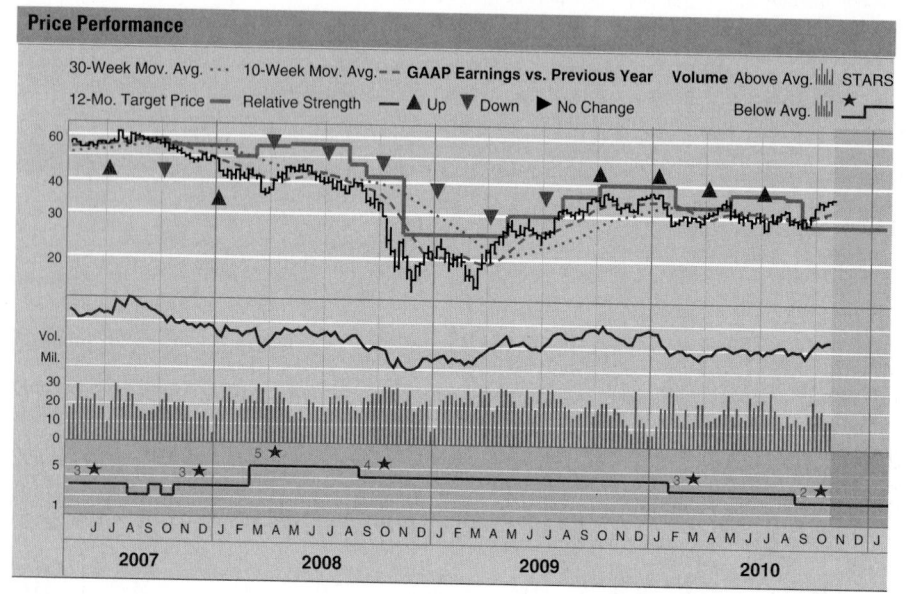

Options: ASE, CBOE, P, Ph

Analysis prepared by **Angelo Zino** on August 31, 2010, when the stock traded at **$ 28.01**.

Highlights

➤ We estimate sales will rise 42% in FY 11 (Jun.) and 1.4% in FY 12 after a 20% increase in FY 10. Although we think some leading-edge customers are moving ahead with capital investment plans, we expect KLAC's orders to slow following a significant ramp by customers in recent quarters. We think growth in its core semiconductor business continues to outpace the industry through share gain, and we see opportunities in areas such as alternative energy. We expect yield monitoring and process control systems products to fare better than other types of semiconductor equipment.

➤ We see annual gross margins of 63% in FY 11 and 64% in FY 12, compared to 55% in FY 10. We view KLAC's yield management and process control systems as only moderately susceptible to pricing pressure due to the critical value they add to semiconductor customers. We project gross and operating margins eventually surpassing previous peak levels.

➤ We estimate operating EPS of $3.52 for FY 11 and $3.67 for FY 12, versus $1.55 in FY 10, which excludes $0.32 of non-recurring charges. We view positively KLAC's leading market share position in its respective markets.

Investment Rationale/Risk

➤ Our sell recommendation reflects our expectation that customers have rebuilt inventories to more normalized levels as well as uncertain end-demand visibility. We believe monthly bookings are nearing a top and we see orders beginning to slow, as elevated customers utilization rates are likely at unsustainable levels. We view KLAC's competitive position in both inspection and metrology as strong, and we see long-term growth in yield management and process control. Long term, we think the transition to lower nanometer nodes will cause yield and defectivity challenges, which we believe will stimulate customers to increase spending.

➤ Risks to our recommendation and target price include stronger-than-projected industry sales, less competition pressuring KLAC's market share position, and a faster-than-expected global economic recovery.

➤ Our 12-month target price of $28 is based on a blend of a peer-average P/E and price-to-sales (P/S) ratio within its five-year moving average. We apply a P/E of 7.5X to our 2011 calendar year EPS estimate to obtain a $27 price. We derive a $30 price using a P/S of 2.0X our 2011 calendar year sales per share estimate.

Qualitative Risk Assessment

LOW	MEDIUM	HIGH

Our risk assessment reflects the company's exposure to the cyclicality of the semiconductor equipment industry and changes in relevant technologies, only partially offset by limited pricing pressure and our view of KLAC's strong market position, size, and financial condition.

Quantitative Evaluations

S&P Quality Ranking   B-

D	C	B-	B	B+	A-	A	A+

Relative Strength Rank   **STRONG**

83

LOWEST = 1   HIGHEST = 99

Revenue/Earnings Data

Revenue (Million $)

	1Q	2Q	3Q	4Q	Year
2010	342.7	440.4	478.3	559.4	1,821
2009	532.5	396.6	309.6	281.5	1,520
2008	693.0	635.8	602.2	590.7	2,522
2007	629.4	649.3	716.2	736.4	2,731
2006	484.3	487.7	519.7	579.0	2,071
2005	518.8	532.9	541.6	491.9	2,085

Earnings Per Share ($)

2010	0.12	0.13	0.33	0.66	1.23
2009	0.11	-2.57	-0.49	-0.15	-3.07
2008	0.46	0.45	0.61	0.43	1.95
2007	0.67	0.44	0.76	0.75	2.61
2006	0.37	0.38	0.47	0.65	1.86
2005	0.58	0.61	0.61	0.52	2.32

Fiscal year ended Jun. 30. Next earnings report expected: Late October. EPS Estimates based on S&P Operating Earnings; historical GAAP earnings are as reported.

Dividend Data (Dates: mm/dd Payment Date: mm/dd/yy)

Amount ($)	Date Decl.	Ex-Div. Date	Stk. of Record	Payment Date
0.150	11/04	11/12	11/16	12/01/09
0.150	02/04	02/11	02/16	03/01/10
0.150	05/06	05/13	05/17	06/01/10
0.250	08/05	08/12	08/16	09/01/10

Dividends have been paid since 2005. Source: Company reports.

Please read the Required Disclosures and Analyst Certification on the last page of this report.

The McGraw·Hill Companies

KLA Tencor Corp

STANDARD &POOR'S

Business Summary August 31, 2010

CORPORATE OVERVIEW. KLA-Tencor (KLAC) is the world's leading manufacturer of yield management and process monitoring systems for the semiconductor industry. Its products are also used in other industries, including the high brightness light emitting diode, data storage and photovoltaic industries.

Maximizing yields, or the number of good die (chips) per wafer, is a key goal in manufacturing integrated circuits (ICs). Higher yields increase revenues obtained for each semiconductor wafer processed. As IC line widths decrease, yields become more sensitive to microscopic-sized defects. KLAC's systems are used to improve yields by identifying defects, analyzing them to determine process problems and patterns, and facilitate corrective actions. These systems monitor subsequent results to ensure that problems have been contained. With in-line systems, corrections can be made while the wafer is still in the production line, rather than waiting for end-of-process testing and feedback.

KLAC offers a broad range of inspection and yield management. The company's wafer inspection systems include unpatterned and patterned wafer inspection tools used to find, count and characterize particles and pattern defects on wafers both in engineering applications and in-line at various stages during the semiconductor manufacturing process. KLAC's brightfield inspection systems are extremely sensitive to small defects and capture a large

range of defect types, which is critical as customers move to 32nm and smaller production.

Reticle inspection systems look for defects on the quartz plates used in copying circuit designs onto an IC during the photolithography process. Film measurement products measure a variety of optical and electrical properties of thin films. Scanning electron beam microscopes (SEMs) can measure the critical dimensions (CDs) of tiny semiconductor features. For chip manufacturing below 90nm, e-beam inspection is becoming increasingly important, not only during the research and development phase, where the highest levels of sensitivity are needed to highlight and eradicate potential design problems, but also in production, where dedicated high-speed e-beam inspection systems.

At the end of FY 10 (Jun.), KLAC's revenues by geographic region were divided as follows: United States 19% (24% in FY 10), Europe & Israel 6% (11%), Japan 13% (29%), Taiwan 38% (12%), Korea 8% (12%), and Rest of Asia 16% (12%). In FY 10, Taiwan Semiconductor Manufacturing and Intel both accounted for more than 10% of total sales.

Company Financials Fiscal Year Ended Jun. 30

Per Share Data ($)	2010	2009	2008	2007	2006	2005	2004	2003	2002	2001
Tangible Book Value	10.72	10.00	11.96	16.00	17.56	15.49	13.34	11.56	10.70	9.38
Cash Flow	1.73	2.34	2.58	3.15	2.20	2.67	1.62	1.07	1.45	2.22
Earnings	1.23	-3.07	1.95	2.61	1.86	2.32	1.21	0.70	1.10	1.93
S&P Core Earnings	1.22	-1.48	2.05	2.64	1.89	1.88	0.77	0.12	0.49	1.45
Dividends	0.60	0.60	0.60	0.48	0.48	0.12	Nil	Nil	Nil	Nil
Payout Ratio	49%	NM	31%	18%	26%	5%	Nil	Nil	Nil	Nil
Prices:High	37.41	37.71	48.35	62.67	55.03	55.00	62.82	61.25	70.58	61.00
Prices:Low	26.69	15.28	14.81	46.59	38.38	37.39	35.02	31.20	25.16	28.61
P/E Ratio:High	30	NM	25	24	30	24	52	88	64	32
P/E Ratio:Low	22	NM	8	18	21	16	29	45	23	15

Income Statement Analysis (Million $)										
Revenue	1,821	1,520	2,522	2,731	2,071	2,085	1,497	1,323	1,637	2,104
Operating Income	423	-7.00	708	699	379	653	380	201	314	512
Depreciation	87.4	124	116	109	69.4	70.9	82.9	71.4	69.6	55.6
Interest Expense	54.5	55.3	10.8	Nil	Nil	Nil	Nil	0.39	Nil	Nil
Pretax Income	291	-603	560	680	378	627	325	181	287	513
Effective Tax Rate	NA	NM	35.9%	22.1%	NM	25.0%	24.9%	24.0%	24.8%	27.2%
Net Income	212	-523	359	528	380	467	244	137	216	373
S&P Core Earnings	212	-251	379	535	386	377	156	22.4	96.5	281

Balance Sheet & Other Financial Data (Million $)										
Cash	1,534	1,330	1,579	1,711	2,326	2,195	1,876	1,488	1,334	697
Current Assets	2,835	2,399	3,036	3,253	3,543	3,203	2,192	1,806	1,619	1,897
Total Assets	3,907	3,610	4,848	4,623	4,576	3,986	3,539	2,867	2,718	2,745
Current Liabilities	772	564	950	1,073	1,002	932	912	651	687	984
Long Term Debt	746	745	745	Nil	Nil	Nil	Nil	Nil	Nil	Nil
Common Equity	2,247	2,184	2,982	3,550	3,568	3,045	2,628	2,216	2,030	1,760
Total Capital	2,992	2,930	3,726	3,550	3,573	3,055	2,628	2,216	2,030	1,760
Capital Expenditures	30.2	22.2	57.3	83.8	73.8	59.7	55.5	134	68.7	162
Cash Flow	300	-399	475	637	450	538	327	209	286	429
Current Ratio	3.7	4.3	3.2	3.0	3.5	3.4	2.4	2.8	2.4	1.9
% Long Term Debt of Capitalization	24.9	25.4	20.0	Nil	Nil	Nil	Nil	Nil	Nil	Nil
% Net Income of Revenue	11.7	NM	14.2	19.3	18.4	22.4	16.3	10.4	13.2	17.7
% Return on Assets	5.7	NM	7.6	11.5	8.8	12.4	7.6	4.9	7.9	15.1
% Return on Equity	9.6	NM	11.0	14.8	11.4	16.5	10.1	6.5	11.4	21.5

Data as orig reptd.; bef. results of disc opers/spec. items. Per share data adj. for stk. divs.; EPS diluted. E-Estimated. NA-Not Available. NM-Not Meaningful. NR-Not Ranked. UR-Under Review.

Office: 1 Technology Dr, Milpitas, CA 95035-7916.
Telephone: 408-875-3000.
Website: http://www.tencor.com
Chrmn: E. Barnholt

Pres & CEO: R.P. Wallace
EVP & CFO: M.P. Dentinger
SVP & Chief Acctg Officer: V.A. Kirloskar
SVP, Secy & General Counsel: B.M. Martin

Investor Contact: W. Lin (408-875-3000)
Board Members: R. P. Akins, E. Barnholt, R. T. Bond, B. Calderoni, J. Dickson, S. P. Kaufman, K. J. Kennedy, K. M. Patel, R. P. Wallace, D. C. Wang

Founded: 1975
Domicile: Delaware
Employees: 5,000

The **McGraw-Hill** Companies

Kohl's Corp

S&P Recommendation	BUY ★★★★★	Price $52.89 (as of Oct 22, 2010)	12-Mo. Target Price $58.00	Investment Style Large-Cap Growth

GICS Sector Consumer Discretionary
Sub-Industry Department Stores

Summary This company operates over 1,060 specialty department stores in 49 states, featuring moderately priced apparel, shoes, accessories, and products for the home.

Key Stock Statistics (Source S&P, Vickers, company reports)

52-Wk Range	$60.42– 44.07	S&P Oper. EPS 2011E	3.70	Market Capitalization(B)	$16.290	Beta	0.95
Trailing 12-Month EPS	$3.52	S&P Oper. EPS 2012E	4.30	Yield (%)	Nil	S&P 3-Yr. Proj. EPS CAGR(%)	15
Trailing 12-Month P/E	15.0	P/E on S&P Oper. EPS 2011E	14.3	Dividend Rate/Share	Nil	S&P Credit Rating	BBB+
$10K Invested 5 Yrs Ago	$11,215	Common Shares Outstg. (M)	308.0	Institutional Ownership (%)	87		

Price Performance

- 30-Week Mov. Avg. ···· 10-Week Mov. Avg. ---- GAAP Earnings vs. Previous Year   Volume Above Avg. ||||| STARS
- 12-Mo. Target Price — Relative Strength — ▲ Up ▼ Down ► No Change   Below Avg. ||||| ★

Options: ASE, CBOE, P, Ph

Analysis prepared by **Jason N. Asaeda** on August 16, 2010, when the stock traded at **$ 44.50**.

Highlights

► We expect net sales to reach $18.5 billion in FY 11 (Jan.). KSS opened 56 stores in FY 10 and plans to open 30 new stores in FY 11. We project same-store sales to rise approximately 5% in FY 11 versus the flat showing of FY 10, supported by the company's continuing efforts to inject newness into its basics-focused apparel assortments and to flow receipts more frequently in season. We also anticipate a lift in sales from 85 planned store remodels (up from 51 completed in FY 10) and size optimization, which improves apparel in-stock positions by ensuring that individual stores have inventory in the correct sizes, colors and styles.

► KSS plans to make e-commerce infrastructure investments and to increase fall marketing spending in support of growth. The company also expects to incur incremental expenses in the second half of FY 11 to notify Kohl's Charge customers of changes in late fees resulting from new credit card legislation. However, we see operating margins widening on increased penetration of private and exclusive brands as well as inventory and cost controls.

► Assuming no share buyback activity, we estimate EPS of $3.70 in FY 11.

Investment Rationale/Risk

► Our buy recommendation on the shares is based on valuation. KSS remains one of the fastest-growing department store chains, with the highest operating margin within its peer group. Over the past three years, the company's focus on more exclusive, higher-quality brands and products, lifestyle merchandising, and efforts to better tailor assortments to reflect regional market preferences have supported improving sales and margins. Despite a challenging retail environment, we believe KSS is gaining market share on the strength of its value pricing strategy, off-mall shopping convenience, targeted expansion, and a growing e-commerce business.

► Risks to our recommendation and target price include sales shortfalls due to unforeseen shifts in fashion trends and further weakening of consumer spending levels. We also see a risk of increasingly cost-conscious consumers trading down to discounters such as Wal-Mart Stores (WMT 50, Strong Buy).

► Our 12-month target price of $58 is based on a forward P/E multiple of 15.7X, KSS's five-year historical average, applied to our FY 11 EPS estimate.

Qualitative Risk Assessment

LOW	MEDIUM	HIGH

Our risk assessment reflects our view of KSS's improving sales, increasing market share in the moderate department store sector, and healthy balance sheet and cash flow, offset by uncertainty over consumer discretionary spending in light of economic conditions and debt levels.

Quantitative Evaluations

S&P Quality Ranking   B+

D	C	B-	B	B+	A-	A	A+

Relative Strength Rank   MODERATE

57

LOWEST = 1   HIGHEST = 99

Revenue/Earnings Data

Revenue (Million $)

	1Q	2Q	3Q	4Q	Year
2011	4,035	4,100	--	--	--
2010	3,638	3,806	4,051	5,682	17,178
2009	3,624	3,725	3,804	5,235	16,389
2008	3,572	3,589	3,825	5,487	16,474
2007	3,185	3,291	3,637	5,431	15,544
2006	2,743	2,888	3,119	4,652	13,402

Earnings Per Share ($)

	1Q	2Q	3Q	4Q	Year
2011	0.64	0.84	E0.63	E1.59	E3.70
2010	0.45	0.75	0.63	1.40	3.23
2009	0.49	0.77	0.52	1.10	2.88
2008	0.64	0.77	0.61	1.31	3.39
2007	0.48	0.69	0.68	1.48	3.31
2006	0.36	0.54	0.45	1.08	2.43

Fiscal year ended Jan. 31. Next earnings report expected: Mid November. EPS Estimates based on S&P Operating Earnings; historical GAAP earnings are as reported.

Dividend Data

No cash dividends have been paid.

Kohl's Corp

Business Summary August 16, 2010

CORPORATE OVERVIEW. Kohl's (KSS), with its "Expect Great Things" line, has positioned itself as a preferred shopping destination for busy women. Its traditional customers are married women aged 25 to 54. The company's stores feature easy-to-shop layouts and emphasize moderately priced exclusive and national brand family apparel and shoes, accessories, cosmetics, home furnishings, and housewares. KSS uses a "nine-box grid" merchandising strategy. Product assortments fall into three categories, "good," "better," and "best," differentiated by price and quality, and also reflect three distinct customer styles: the "classic" customer who wants a coordinated look without bending the rules; the "updated" customer who likes classic styles with a twist; and the more fashion-forward "contemporary" customer.

PRIMARY BUSINESS DYNAMICS. KSS is one of the fastest-growing retail chains in the U.S. From FY 05 through FY 10, the company increased its selling square footage at a compound annual growth rate (CAGR) of 9.7% as it expanded its store count from 637 to 1,058. KSS opened nine stores this spring and plans to open an additional 21 stores this fall, for a total of 30 new stores in FY 11.

From a merchandising standpoint, we believe KSS fell behind competitors such as J.C. Penney and Macy's in delivering newness and better quality merchandise sought by its customers in FY 04. Since then, however, we have seen the company prove itself capable of creating a more compelling sales mix by investing in new contemporary brands such as Candie's in juniors and young girls, and by entering the beauty business. KSS also responded successfully, in our view, to dress clothing trends in FY 06 with the launch of Chaps (by Ralph Lauren) in men's career casual sportswear.

In FY 07, the company filled out its contemporary apparel offerings, and expanded its most popular brands into additional product categories (e.g., Chaps into women's and boys), creating true lifestyle brands. We think these rollouts complemented KSS's ongoing efforts to capture more share of wallet among empty nesters aged 45 to 54 and single women aged 25 to 34.

Company Financials Fiscal Year Ended Jan. 31

Per Share Data ($)	2010	2009	2008	2007	2006	2005	2004	2003	2002	2001
Tangible Book Value	24.92	21.41	21.77	18.32	16.62	13.78	11.60	9.85	7.78	6.21
Cash Flow	5.17	4.65	4.80	4.47	3.42	2.95	2.43	2.41	1.93	1.48
Earnings	3.23	2.88	3.39	3.31	2.43	2.12	1.72	1.87	1.35	1.10
S&P Core Earnings	3.23	2.89	3.39	3.31	2.43	2.04	1.62	1.78	1.38	1.04
Dividends	NA	Nil	Nil	Nil	Nil	Nil	Nil	Nil	Nil	Nil
Payout Ratio	Nil	Nil	Nil	Nil	Nil	Nil	Nil	Nil	Nil	Nil
Calendar Year	2009	2008	2007	2006	2005	2004	2003	2002	2001	2000
Prices:High	60.89	56.00	79.55	75.54	58.90	54.10	65.44	78.83	72.24	66.50
Prices:Low	32.50	24.28	44.16	42.78	43.63	39.59	42.40	44.00	41.95	33.50
P/E Ratio:High	19	19	23	23	24	26	38	42	54	60
P/E Ratio:Low	10	8	13	13	18	19	25	24	31	30

Income Statement Analysis (Million $)										
Revenue	17,178	16,389	16,474	15,544	13,402	11,701	10,282	9,120	7,489	6,152
Operating Income	2,302	2,077	2,257	2,202	1,755	1,525	1,260	1,282	1,002	779
Depreciation	590	541	452	388	339	288	237	191	152	128
Interest Expense	134	140	98.7	74.4	72.1	64.1	75.2	59.4	57.4	Nil
Pretax Income	1,588	1,425	1,742	1,774	1,346	1,174	950	1,034	800	605
Effective Tax Rate	37.6%	37.9%	37.8%	37.5%	37.4%	37.8%	37.8%	37.8%	38.0%	38.5%
Net Income	991	885	1,084	1,109	842	730	591	643	496	372
S&P Core Earnings	991	885	1,084	1,109	842	703	557	608	471	349

Balance Sheet & Other Financial Data (Million $)										
Cash	2,267	676	664	620	127	117	113	90.1	107	124
Current Assets	5,485	3,700	3,724	3,401	4,266	3,643	3,025	3,284	2,464	1,922
Total Assets	13,160	11,334	10,560	9,041	9,153	7,979	6,698	6,316	4,930	3,855
Current Liabilities	2,390	1,815	1,771	1,919	1,746	1,456	1,122	1,508	880	723
Long Term Debt	2,052	2,053	2,052	1,040	1,046	1,103	1,076	1,059	1,095	803
Common Equity	7,853	6,739	6,102	5,603	5,957	4,967	4,191	3,512	2,791	2,203
Total Capital	9,905	9,112	8,416	6,887	7,221	6,367	5,504	4,743	4,001	3,090
Capital Expenditures	666	1,014	1,542	1,142	799	890	832	716	662	481
Cash Flow	1,581	1,426	1,536	1,496	1,181	1,019	828	835	648	500
Current Ratio	2.3	2.0	2.1	1.8	2.4	2.5	2.7	2.2	2.8	2.7
% Long Term Debt of Capitalization	20.7	22.5	24.4	15.7	14.5	17.3	19.5	22.3	27.4	26.0
% Net Income of Revenue	5.8	5.4	6.6	7.1	6.3	6.2	5.7	7.1	6.6	6.0
% Return on Assets	8.1	8.1	11.1	12.2	9.8	10.0	9.1	11.4	11.3	10.9
% Return on Equity	13.6	13.8	18.5	19.2	15.3	16.0	15.3	20.4	19.9	19.1

Data as orig reptd.; bef. results of disc opers/spec. items. Per share data adj. for stk. divs.; EPS diluted. E-Estimated. NA-Not Available. NM-Not Meaningful. NR-Not Ranked. UR-Under Review.

Office: N56W17000 Ridgewood Dr, Menomonee Falls, WI 53051-5660.
Telephone: 262-703-7000.
Website: http://www.kohls.com
Chrmn, Pres & CEO: K. Mansell

Investor Contact: W.S. McDonald (262-703-1893)
EVP, CFO & Chief Acctg Officer: W.S. McDonald
EVP, Secy & General Counsel: R.D. Schepp

Board Members: P. Boneparth, S. A. Burd, J. F. Herma, D. E. Jones, W. S. Kellogg, K. Mansell, F. V. Sica, P. M. Sommerhauser, S. A. Streeter, N. G. Vaca, S. E. Watson

Founded: 1986
Domicile: Wisconsin
Employees: 133,000

Kraft Foods Inc.

STANDARD &POOR'S

S&P Recommendation HOLD ★★★☆☆

Price	12-Mo. Target Price	Investment Style
$31.90 (as of Oct 22, 2010)	$32.00	Large-Cap Blend

GICS Sector Consumer Staples
Sub-Industry Packaged Foods & Meats

Summary Kraft Foods is one of the world's largest branded food and beverage companies.

Key Stock Statistics (Source S&P, Vickers, company reports)

52-Wk Range	$32.18–26.31	S&P Oper. EPS 2010E	2.02	Market Capitalization(B)	$55.635	Beta	0.57
Trailing 12-Month EPS	$2.74	S&P Oper. EPS 2011E	2.30	Yield (%)	3.64	S&P 3-Yr. Proj. EPS CAGR(%)	9
Trailing 12-Month P/E	11.6	P/E on S&P Oper. EPS 2010E	15.8	Dividend Rate/Share	$1.16	S&P Credit Rating	BBB
$10K Invested 5 Yrs Ago	$13,547	Common Shares Outstg. (M)	1,744.1	Institutional Ownership (%)	74		

Price Performance

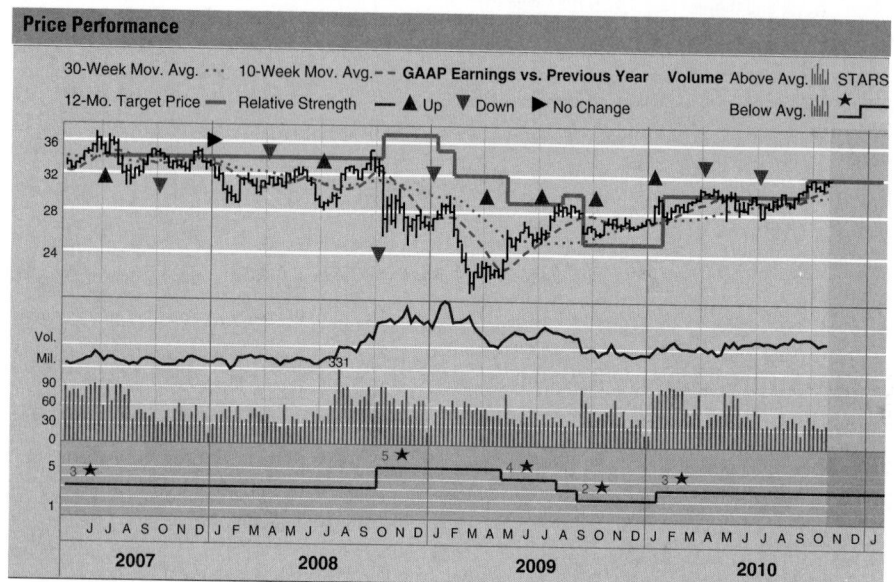

30-Week Mov. Avg. · · · · 10-Week Mov. Avg. - - GAAP Earnings vs. Previous Year Volume Above Avg. STARS
12-Mo. Target Price — Relative Strength — ▲ Up ▼ Down ▶ No Change Below Avg.

Options: ASE, CBOE, P, Ph

Analysis prepared by **Tom Graves, CFA** on October 04, 2010, when the stock traded at **$ 31.15.**

Highlights

▸ In the first half of 2010, KFT acquired ownership of British confectionery company Cadbury plc in a transaction valued at $18.5 billion. This included paying about $11 billion in cash (based on a February 2010 currency exchange rate) and issuing about 262 million KFT common shares, which increased the number of KFT shares outstanding by about 18%. KFT acquired control of Cadbury in February 2010, and owned all of Cadbury's shares as of early June. From February 2 through June 30, 2010, Cadbury provided net revenues of $3.9 billion to KFT.

▸ In September 2010, KFT estimated that the Cadbury acquisition would provide $1 billion of revenue synergies plus $750 million of cost synergies by 2013. We anticipate that total costs of the integration program will be about $1.5 billion, with roughly half in 2010.

▸ We look for KFT to have revenue of about $49 billion in 2010, including Cadbury for about 10 months. Before special items, but including some expected dilution from the Cadbury acquisition, we estimate 2010 EPS from continuing operations of $2.02. For 2011, we estimate EPS of $2.30.

Investment Rationale/Risk

▸ We see the acquisition of Cadbury offering strategic value for KFT, including the opportunity to boost its presence in developing international markets and to accelerate overall growth prospects somewhat. Various integration and acquisition-related costs are excluded from our EPS estimates. In 2009, under IFRS accounting, Cadbury had net revenues of 5.975 billion pounds (about $9.3 billion at a recent exchange rate), most of which we believe was from outside of North America. KFT's divested North American pizza business ($1.6 billion of 2009 net revenues) is being treated as a discontinued operation.

▸ Risks to our recommendation and target price include a worse than anticipated outcome to KFT's acquisition of Cadbury, more unfavorable than expected commodity costs and currency exchange rates, and market share declines.

▸ Our 12-month target price of $32 reflects our view that the stock should trade at a P/E multiple similar to what we expect from a group of other packaged food companies. KFT shares recently had an indicated dividend yield of 3.7%.

Qualitative Risk Assessment

LOW	MEDIUM	HIGH

Our risk assessment reflects the risks that we see KFT facing from competitive conditions, and other factors such as commodity costs and currency exchange rates. This is offset by the relatively stable nature of the company's end markets, by our expectation of relatively good company cash flow, and by KFT's leading market share positions.

Quantitative Evaluations

S&P Quality Ranking A-

D	C	B-	B	B+	A-	A	A+

Relative Strength Rank MODERATE

56

LOWEST = 1   HIGHEST = 99

Revenue/Earnings Data

Revenue (Million $)

	1Q	2Q	3Q	4Q	Year
2010	11,318	12,253	--	--	--
2009	9,396	10,162	9,803	11,025	40,386
2008	10,372	11,176	10,462	10,767	42,201
2007	8,586	9,205	9,054	10,396	37,241
2006	8,123	8,619	8,243	9,371	34,356
2005	8,059	8,334	8,057	9,663	34,113

Earnings Per Share ($)

2010	0.15	0.53	E0.45	E0.48	E2.02
2009	0.45	0.56	0.55	0.48	2.03
2008	0.42	0.48	0.36	0.06	1.23
2007	0.43	0.44	0.38	0.38	1.63
2006	0.61	0.41	0.45	0.38	1.85
2005	0.41	0.45	0.40	0.46	1.72

Fiscal year ended Dec. 31. Next earnings report expected: Early November. EPS Estimates based on S&P Operating Earnings; historical GAAP earnings are as reported.

Dividend Data (Dates: mm/dd Payment Date: mm/dd/yy)

Amount ($)	Date Decl.	Ex-Div. Date	Stk. of Record	Payment Date
0.290	12/17	12/28	12/30	01/13/10
0.290	03/17	03/29	03/31	04/14/10
0.290	05/18	06/28	06/30	07/14/10
0.290	08/17	09/28	09/30	10/14/10

Dividends have been paid since 2001. Source: Company reports.

The McGraw·Hill Companies

Kraft Foods Inc.

STANDARD &POOR'S

Business Summary October 04, 2010

CORPORATE OVERVIEW. Kraft Foods is one of the world's largest branded food and beverage companies. In 2009, North American business segments accounted for $23.7 billion, or approximately 59%, of total company net revenues from continuing operations. Kraft International had net revenues of $16.7 billion (41%).

Business segments include U.S. Beverages (7.6% of 2009 net revenues), U.S. Cheese (8.9%), U.S. Convenient Meals (11%), U.S. Grocery (8.6%), U.S. Snacks (12%), Canada and North America Foodservice (10%), Kraft Foods Europe (22%), and Kraft Foods Developing Markets (20%). Also, Wal-Mart Stores, Inc., and affiliates accounted for about 16% of KFT's net revenues in 2009.

At year-end 2009, Kraft had nine brands with annual revenue of at least about $1 billion each. These include Kraft cheeses, dinners and dressings; Oscar Mayer meats; Philadelphia cream cheese; Maxwell House coffee; Jacobs coffee; Nabisco cookies and crackers and its Oreo brand; Milka chocolates; and LU biscuits.

IMPACT OF MAJOR DEVELOPMENTS. In the first quarter of 2010, KFT acquired control of British confectionery company Cadbury plc for cash and stock that we value at roughly $18.5 billion. In the transaction, KFT paid about $11 billion (based on a February 2010 currency exchange rate) and issued about 262 common shares, increasing the number of shares outstanding by

about 18%. From February 2 through June 30, 2010, Cadbury provided net revenues of $3.9 billion to KFT. Also, KFT has announced agreements to divest Cadbury-related businesses in Poland and Romania.

In September 2010, KFT estimated that the Cadbury acquisition would provide $1 billion of revenue synergies plus $750 million of cost synergies by 2013. We anticipate that total costs of the integration program will be about $1.5 billion, with roughly half in 2010.

In March 2010, KFT sold assets of its North American Frozen Pizza business to Nestle USA, Inc., for total consideration of about $3.7 billion. At year-end 2009, the Frozen Pizza business did not meet criteria to be considered held-for-sale. Beginning with the first quarter of 2010, the results of the Frozen Pizza business were presented as a discontinued operation by KFT. In 2009, this business had net revenues of $1.6 billion. Other divestitures by KFT have included its Post cereal business in 2008; hot cereal assets and trademarks, which were sold in the first quarter of 2007; and its pet snacks brand and assets, which were sold in the third quarter of 2006.

Company Financials Fiscal Year Ended Dec. 31

Per Share Data ($)	2009	2008	2007	2006	2005	2004	2003	2002	2001	2000
Tangible Book Value	NM	NM	NM	NM	NM	NM	NM	NM	NM	NM
Cash Flow	2.66	1.88	2.18	2.39	2.27	2.07	2.48	2.37	2.19	2.02
Earnings	2.03	1.23	1.63	1.85	1.72	1.55	2.01	1.96	1.17	1.03
S&P Core Earnings	2.08	1.04	1.65	1.80	1.74	1.53	1.93	1.65	0.81	NA
Dividends	1.16	1.12	1.04	0.96	0.87	0.77	0.66	0.56	0.26	NA
Payout Ratio	57%	91%	64%	52%	51%	50%	33%	29%	22%	NA
Prices:High	29.84	34.97	37.20	36.67	35.65	36.06	39.40	43.95	35.57	NA
Prices:Low	20.81	24.75	29.95	27.44	27.88	29.45	26.35	32.50	29.50	NA
P/E Ratio:High	15	28	23	20	21	23	20	22	30	NA
P/E Ratio:Low	10	20	18	15	16	19	13	17	25	NA

Income Statement Analysis (Million $)										
Revenue	40,386	42,201	37,241	34,356	34,113	32,168	31,010	29,723	33,875	34,679
Operating Income	6,503	6,116	5,794	6,065	6,002	6,108	6,786	6,892	6,526	6,284
Depreciation	931	986	886	898	879	879	813	716	1,642	1,722
Interest Expense	1,260	1,272	701	510	636	666	678	854	1,437	NA
Pretax Income	4,287	2,577	3,730	4,016	4,116	3,946	5,346	5,267	3,447	3,214
Effective Tax Rate	29.4%	28.3%	30.5%	23.7%	29.4%	32.3%	34.9%	35.5%	45.4%	44.4%
Net Income	3,021	1,849	2,590	3,060	2,904	2,669	3,476	3,394	1,882	1,787
S&P Core Earnings	3,103	1,580	2,640	2,963	2,930	2,632	3,337	2,861	1,308	NA

Balance Sheet & Other Financial Data (Million $)										
Cash	2,254	1,244	567	239	316	282	514	215	162	191
Current Assets	12,454	11,366	10,737	8,254	8,153	9,722	8,124	7,456	7,006	7,152
Total Assets	66,714	63,078	67,993	55,574	57,628	59,928	59,285	57,100	55,798	52,071
Current Liabilities	11,491	11,044	17,086	10,473	8,724	9,078	7,861	7,169	8,875	7,590
Long Term Debt	18,024	18,589	12,902	7,081	8,475	9,723	11,591	10,416	13,134	15,677
Common Equity	25,876	22,200	27,295	28,555	29,593	29,911	28,530	25,832	23,478	22,755
Total Capital	44,509	41,554	45,073	39,566	44,135	45,484	45,977	41,676	41,643	38,432
Capital Expenditures	1,330	1,367	1,241	1,169	1,171	1,006	1,085	1,184	1,101	1,151
Cash Flow	3,952	2,835	3,476	3,958	3,783	3,548	4,289	4,110	3,524	3,509
Current Ratio	1.1	1.0	0.6	0.8	0.9	1.1	1.0	1.0	0.8	0.9
% Long Term Debt of Capitalization	40.5	44.7	28.6	17.9	19.2	21.4	25.2	25.0	31.5	40.8
% Net Income of Revenue	7.5	4.4	7.0	8.9	8.5	8.3	11.2	11.4	5.6	5.2
% Return on Assets	4.7	2.8	4.2	5.4	4.9	4.5	6.0	6.0	3.5	4.9
% Return on Equity	12.6	7.5	9.3	10.5	9.8	9.1	12.8	13.8	10.0	14.6

Data as orig reptd.; bef. results of disc opers/spec. items. Per share data adj. for stk. divs.; EPS diluted. E-Estimated. NA-Not Available. NM-Not Meaningful. NR-Not Ranked. UR-Under Review.

Office: Three Lakes Drive, Northfield, IL 60093.
Telephone: 847-646-2000.
Website: http://www.kraft.com
Chrmn & CEO: I. Rosenfeld

COO: D. Brearton
EVP & CFO: T.R. McLevish
EVP & General Counsel: M.S. Firestone
SVP & Treas: B. Brasier

Board Members: A. Banga, M. M. Hart, L. D. Juliber, M. **Founded:** 2000
D. Ketchum, R. A. Lerner, M. J. Mcdonald, J. C. Pope, F. **Domicile:** Virginia
G. Reynolds, I. Rosenfeld, D. C. Wright, F. G. Zarb, J. M. **Employees:** 97,000
van Boxmeer

The **McGraw·Hill** Companies

Kroger Co. (The)

STANDARD &POOR'S

S&P Recommendation	HOLD ★★★☆☆	Price $21.80 (as of Oct 22, 2010)	12-Mo. Target Price $23.00	Investment Style Large-Cap Blend

GICS Sector Consumer Staples
Sub-Industry Food Retail

Summary This supermarket operator, with about 2,500 stores in 31 states, also operates convenience stores, jewelry stores, supermarket fuel centers, and food processing plants.

Key Stock Statistics (Source S&P, Vickers, company reports)

52-Wk Range	$24.12–19.08	S&P Oper. EPS 2011**E**	1.80	Market Capitalization(B)	$13.903	Beta	0.37
Trailing 12-Month EPS	$0.02	S&P Oper. EPS 2012**E**	2.05	Yield (%)	1.93	S&P 3-Yr. Proj. EPS CAGR(%)	10
Trailing 12-Month P/E	NM	P/E on S&P Oper. EPS 2011**E**	12.1	Dividend Rate/Share	$0.42	S&P Credit Rating	BBB
$10K Invested 5 Yrs Ago	$11,716	Common Shares Outstg. (M)	637.7	Institutional Ownership (%)	81		

Price Performance

30-Week Mov. Avg. ···· 10-Week Mov. Avg. – – GAAP Earnings vs. Previous Year   Volume Above Avg. ▮▮▮ STARS
12-Mo. Target Price — Relative Strength — ▲ Up ▼ Down ▶ No Change   Below Avg. ▮▮▮ ★

Options: ASE, CBOE, P

Analysis prepared by **Joseph Agnese** on September 16, 2010, when the stock traded at **$ 21.62**.

Highlights

▶ We see sales of $82.2 billion in FY 11 (Jan.), up 7.1% from $76.7 billion in FY 10, reflecting 2.0% square footage growth, 3.0% identical-store sales gains (excluding fuel) and increased gas sales. We see the company achieving significant market share gains with a competitive pricing strategy. However, we expect sales growth to be hindered by deflationary food pressures throughout much of the year.

▶ We believe EBITDA margins will narrow as the company's pursuit of a price reduction strategy and the lack of product cost inflation offset benefits from increased sales leverage (excluding fuel), a more stable promotional spending budget, and cost-saving opportunities that we forecast in areas such as administration, labor, shrinkage and transportation. In addition, we believe merchandising, such as increased private label sales, will help the company compete against lower-priced mass merchants.

▶ After benefits from fewer shares outstanding due to an active repurchase program, we expect FY 11 EPS to increase 5.9%, to $1.80, from operating EPS of $1.70 in FY 10 (excluding $1.09 of goodwill and asset impairment charges).

Investment Rationale/Risk

▶ We believe the company is well positioned to benefit from market share gained in a weak economic environment as consumers begin to trade back up to higher-priced and wider-margin goods. We think the company will continue to gain market share due to its position as a low-priced food retailer and its strategy of boosting sales through targeted marketing, price reductions and improved service levels.

▶ Risks to our recommendation and target price include potential weakness in the economy that would cause consumers to become more price conscious, and increased price competition.

▶ Our 12-month target price of $23 is based on our P/E analysis and is supported by our EV/EBITDA valuation. Reflecting benefits we see as consumers trade up and negative impacts we see from food deflation and intensifying pricing competition, we think the shares should trade at about 11.1X our FY 12 EPS estimate of $2.05, in line with its 23% average discount to the P/E multiple of the S&P 500, leading to a projected value of $23. Our target price is supported by applying a 5.3X multiple, slightly ahead of KR's closest peers' average of 5.2X, to our FY 12 EBITDA estimate of $4.2 billion.

Qualitative Risk Assessment

LOW	MEDIUM	HIGH

Our risk assessment reflects our view of the company's diversification through multiple format offerings, strong market share positions, and potential opportunities from industry consolidation.

Quantitative Evaluations

S&P Quality Ranking   B

D	C	B-	B	B+	A-	A	A+

Relative Strength Rank   MODERATE

45

LOWEST = 1   HIGHEST = 99

Revenue/Earnings Data

Revenue (Million $)

	1Q	2Q	3Q	4Q	Year
2011	24,764	18,796	--	--	--
2010	22,789	17,728	17,662	18,554	76,733
2009	23,107	18,053	17,580	17,260	76,000
2008	20,726	16,139	16,135	17,235	70,235
2007	19,415	15,138	14,999	16,859	66,111
2006	17,948	13,865	14,021	14,720	60,553

Earnings Per Share ($)

	1Q	2Q	3Q	4Q	Year
2011	0.58	0.41	E0.32	E0.49	E1.80
2010	0.66	0.39	-1.35	0.39	0.11
2009	0.58	0.42	0.36	0.53	1.90
2008	0.47	0.42	0.37	0.48	1.69
2007	0.42	0.29	0.30	0.54	1.54
2006	0.40	0.27	0.25	0.39	1.31

Fiscal year ended Jan. 31. Next earnings report expected: Early December. EPS Estimates based on S&P Operating Earnings; historical GAAP earnings are as reported.

Dividend Data (Dates: mm/dd Payment Date: mm/dd/yy)

Amount ($)	Date Decl.	Ex-Div. Date	Stk. of Record	Payment Date
0.095	01/22	02/10	02/12	03/01/10
0.095	03/11	05/12	05/14	06/01/10
0.095	06/24	08/12	08/16	09/01/10
0.105	09/16	11/10	11/15	12/01/10

Dividends have been paid since 2006. Source: Company reports.

Please read the Required Disclosures and Analyst Certification on the last page of this report.

Kroger Co. (The)

Business Summary September 16, 2010

CORPORATE OVERVIEW. Kroger is one of the largest U.S. supermarket chains, with 2,470 supermarkets as of September 2010. The company's principal operating format is combination food and drug stores (combo stores). In addition to combo stores, KR also operates multi-department stores, marketplace stores, price-impact warehouses, convenience stores, fuel centers, jewelry stores, and food processing plants. Total food store square footage was approximately 147 million as of January 31, 2009.

Retail food stores are operated under three formats: combo stores, multi-department stores, and price-impact warehouse stores. Combo stores are considered neighborhood stores, and include many specialty departments, such as whole health sections, pharmacies, general merchandise, pet centers, and perishables, such as fresh seafood and organic produce. Combo banners include Kroger, Ralphs, King Soopers, City Market, Dillons, Smith's, Fry's, QFC, Hilander, Owen's, Jay C, Baker's, Pay Less and Gerbes.

Multi-department stores offer one-stop shopping, are significantly larger in size than combo stores, and sell a wider selection of general merchandise items, including apparel, home fashion and furnishings, electronics, automotive, toys, and fine jewelry. Multi-department formats include Fred Meyer, Fry's Marketplace, Smith's Marketplace and Kroger Marketplace. Many combination and multi-department stores include a fuel center.

Price-impact warehouse stores offer everyday low prices, plus promotions for a wide selection of grocery and health and beauty care items. Price-impact warehouse stores include Food 4 Less and Foods Co.

Company Financials Fiscal Year Ended Jan. 31

Per Share Data ($)	2010	2009	2008	2007	2006	2005	2004	2003	2002	2001
Tangible Book Value	5.72	4.48	7.07	5.61	3.04	1.85	1.18	0.36	NM	NM
Cash Flow	2.45	4.08	3.64	3.30	3.04	1.57	2.02	2.93	2.44	2.11
Earnings	0.11	1.90	1.69	1.54	1.31	-0.14	0.42	1.56	1.26	1.04
S&P Core Earnings	1.67	1.74	1.70	1.59	1.27	0.99	0.98	1.40	1.12	0.96
Dividends	0.37	0.35	0.20	Nil	Nil	Nil	Nil	Nil	Nil	Nil
Payout Ratio	NM	18%	12%	Nil	Nil	Nil	Nil	Nil	Nil	Nil
Calendar Year	2009	2008	2007	2006	2005	2004	2003	2002	2001	2000
Prices:High	26.94	30.99	31.94	24.48	20.88	19.67	19.70	23.81	27.66	27.94
Prices:Low	19.39	22.30	22.94	18.05	15.15	14.65	12.05	11.00	19.60	14.06
P/E Ratio:High	NM	16	19	16	16	NM	47	15	22	27
P/E Ratio:Low	NM	12	14	12	12	NM	29	7	16	14

Income Statement Analysis (Million $)										
Revenue	76,733	76,000	70,235	66,111	60,553	56,434	53,791	51,760	50,098	49,000
Operating Income	3,777	3,918	3,657	3,508	3,300	3,003	3,147	3,676	3,567	3,397
Depreciation	1,525	1,442	1,356	1,272	1,265	1,256	1,209	1,087	973	907
Interest Expense	502	485	474	488	510	557	604	600	648	675
Pretax Income	589	1,966	1,827	1,748	1,525	290	770	1,973	1,711	1,508
Effective Tax Rate	90.4%	36.5%	35.4%	36.2%	37.2%	NM	59.1%	37.5%	39.0%	41.6%
Net Income	70.0	1,249	1,181	1,115	958	-100	315	1,233	1,043	880
S&P Core Earnings	1,093	1,140	1,193	1,155	928	720	745	1,105	914	816

Balance Sheet & Other Financial Data (Million $)										
Cash	424	263	918	803	210	144	159	171	161	161
Current Assets	7,450	7,206	7,114	6,755	6,466	6,406	5,619	5,566	5,512	5,416
Total Assets	23,093	23,211	22,299	21,215	20,482	20,491	20,184	20,102	19,087	18,190
Current Liabilities	7,714	7,629	8,689	7,581	6,715	6,316	5,586	5,608	5,485	5,591
Long Term Debt	7,477	7,505	6,529	6,154	6,678	7,900	8,116	8,222	8,412	8,210
Common Equity	4,906	5,176	4,914	4,923	4,390	3,540	4,011	3,850	3,502	3,089
Total Capital	12,963	12,913	11,810	11,799	11,911	12,379	13,117	12,072	11,914	11,299
Capital Expenditures	2,297	2,149	2,126	1,683	1,306	1,634	2,000	1,891	2,139	1,623
Cash Flow	1,595	2,691	2,537	2,387	2,223	1,156	1,524	2,320	2,016	1,787
Current Ratio	1.0	1.0	0.8	0.9	1.0	1.0	1.0	1.0	1.0	1.0
% Long Term Debt of Capitalization	57.7	58.1	55.3	55.6	56.1	63.8	61.9	68.1	70.6	72.7
% Net Income of Revenue	0.1	1.6	1.7	1.7	1.6	NM	0.6	2.4	2.1	1.8
% Return on Assets	0.3	5.5	5.4	5.4	4.7	NM	1.6	6.3	5.6	4.9
% Return on Equity	1.4	24.8	24.0	24.0	23.9	NM	8.0	33.5	31.6	30.5

Data as orig reptd.; bef. results of disc opers/spec. items. Per share data adj. for stk. divs.; EPS diluted. E-Estimated. NA-Not Available. NM-Not Meaningful. NR-Not Ranked. UR-Under Review.

Office: 1014 Vine Street, Cincinnati, OH 45202-1100.
Telephone: 513-762-4000.
Email: investors@kroger.com
Website: http://www.kroger.com

Chrmn & CEO: D.B. Dillon
Pres & COO: W.R. McMullen
EVP, Secy & General Counsel: P.W. Heldman
SVP & CFO: J.M. Schlotman

SVP & CIO: C. Hjelm
Investor Contact: C. Fike (513-762-4969)
Board Members: R. V. Anderson, R. D. Beyer, D. B. Dillon, S. J. Kropf, J. T. Lamacchia, D. B. Lewis, W. R. McMullen, J. P. Montoya, C. R. Moore, S. M. Phillips, S. Rogel, J. A. Runde, R. Sargent, B. S. Shackouls

Founded: 1883
Domicile: Ohio
Employees: 334,000

Laboratory Corporation of America Holdings

STANDARD &POOR'S

S&P Recommendation **BUY** ★★★★☆	Price $79.16 (as of Oct 22, 2010)	12-Mo. Target Price $94.00	Investment Style Large-Cap Growth

GICS Sector Health Care
Sub-Industry Health Care Services

Summary This clinical laboratory organization offers a broad range of clinical tests through a national network of laboratories.

Key Stock Statistics (Source S&P, Vickers, company reports)

52-Wk Range	$83.00–68.48	S&P Oper. EPS 2010**E**	5.54	Market Capitalization(B)	$8.138	Beta	0.48
Trailing 12-Month EPS	$5.22	S&P Oper. EPS 2011**E**	6.15	Yield (%)	Nil	S&P 3-Yr. Proj. EPS CAGR(%)	13
Trailing 12-Month P/E	15.2	P/E on S&P Oper. EPS 2010**E**	14.3	Dividend Rate/Share	Nil	S&P Credit Rating	BBB+
$10K Invested 5 Yrs Ago	$16,050	Common Shares Outstg. (M)	102.8	Institutional Ownership (%)	99		

Price Performance

30-Week Mov. Avg. ···· 10-Week Mov. Avg. --- GAAP Earnings vs. Previous Year Volume Above Avg. ▥▥ STARS
12-Mo. Target Price — Relative Strength — ▲ Up ▼ Down ► No Change Below Avg. ▥▥ ★

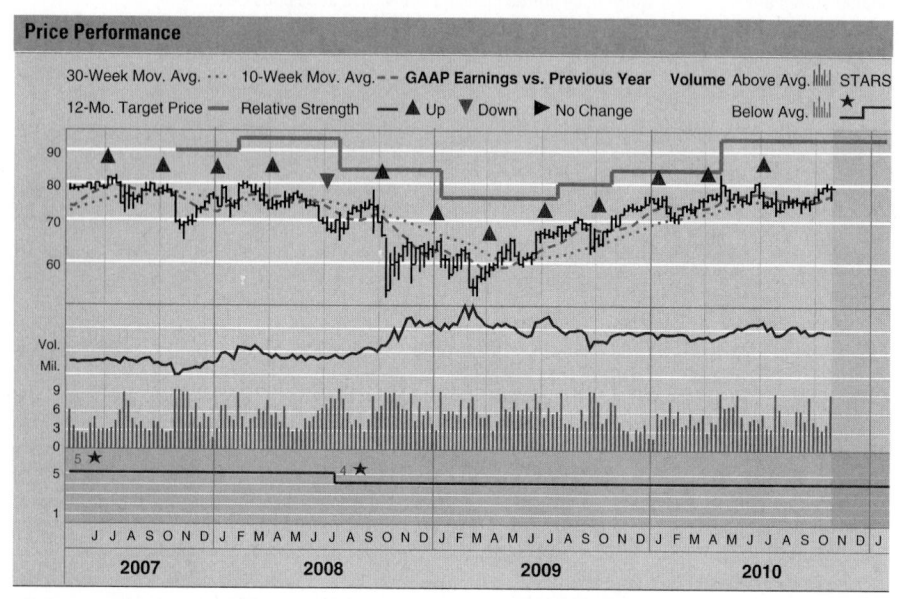

Options: ASE, CBOE, P, Ph

Analysis prepared by **Jeffrey Loo, CFA** on July 27, 2010, when the stock traded at **$ 74.02**.

Highlights

➤ We expect 2010 sales to rise 4%, to $4.89 billion, on solid growth in esoteric testing, partially offset by the adverse impact of the termination in late 2009 of two large government contracts. However, we now expect drugs-of-abuse testing volume to rebound from a soft 2009, but note it is a low-margin business. We also believe the expansion of the Empire Blue Cross Blue Shield contract in New York will aid sales growth in the second half of 2010. We expect 2010 gross margins to improve 60 basis points (bps) and operating margins to expand 90 bps on leverage and tight cost controls and improved bad debt expense.

➤ Pursuant to LH's deal with UnitedHealthcare (UNH 38, Buy), transition payments ended in 2009. LH recently received its final invoice; the final amount was approximately $120 million.

➤ LH continues to buy back shares, with 2.9 million repurchased year-to-date, following 3.9 million shares repurchased in 2009. Since 2006, LH has repurchased over $2 billion worth of stock. As of June 2010, LH had $100 million remaining on its repurchase program. We forecast EPS of $5.44 in 2010.

Investment Rationale/Risk

➤ Despite a challenging economic environment, higher unemployment levels and slower volume growth, we believe LH's core lab testing business is fundamentally sound. Although we see softness in physician office visits continuing throughout 2010, we believe LH will be able to continue to increase its esoteric testing business and will be able to supplement internal growth with acquisitions. We think the shares, recently trading at 13.7X and 12.0X our 2010 and 2011 EPS forecasts, respectively, well below historical levels, are undervalued. We also think LH will be able to maintain industry-leading margins by cutting costs and through leverage.

➤ Risks to our recommendation and target price include greater-than-expected pricing pressure, increased competition from potential physician in-sourcing for certain tests, and a significant slowdown in doctor visits.

➤ Our 12-month target price of $94 is based on a P/E-to-growth (PEG) ratio of about 1.3X, in line with peers, applied to our 2010 EPS estimate and utilizing a three-year EPS growth rate of 13%.

Qualitative Risk Assessment

LOW	MEDIUM	HIGH

Our risk assessment reflects LH's leadership position in a large, mature industry, its broad geographic service area with clients in all 50 states, and our view of its diverse and balanced payer mix.

Quantitative Evaluations

S&P Quality Ranking B+

D	C	B-	B	B+	A-	A	A+

Relative Strength Rank MODERATE

50

LOWEST = 1   HIGHEST = 99

Revenue/Earnings Data

Revenue (Million $)

	1Q	2Q	3Q	4Q	Year
2010	1,194	1,238	--	--	--
2009	1,156	1,189	1,185	1,165	4,695
2008	1,103	1,148	1,135	1,119	4,505
2007	998.7	1,043	1,021	1,006	4,068
2006	878.6	903.7	909.9	898.6	3,591
2005	799.1	853.3	852.9	822.3	3,328

Earnings Per Share ($)

	1Q	2Q	3Q	4Q	Year
2010	1.25	1.46	E1.39	E1.37	E5.54
2009	1.22	1.24	1.21	1.33	4.98
2008	1.14	0.92	1.00	1.08	4.16
2007	0.98	1.05	0.92	0.98	3.93
2006	0.76	0.87	0.81	0.81	3.24
2005	0.67	0.74	0.66	0.64	2.71

Fiscal year ended Dec. 31. Next earnings report expected: Late October. EPS Estimates based on S&P Operating Earnings; historical GAAP earnings are as reported.

Dividend Data

No cash dividends have been paid.

Please read the Required Disclosures and Analyst Certification on the last page of this report.

The McGraw-Hill Companies

Laboratory Corporation of America Holdings

STANDARD &POOR'S

Business Summary July 27, 2010

CORPORATE OVERVIEW. Laboratory Corporation of America Holdings is the second largest independent U.S. clinical laboratory. Clinical laboratory tests are used by medical professionals in routine testing, patient diagnosis, and in the monitoring and treatment of disease. As of December 2009, LH had 38 primary testing facilities and more than 1,500 service sites consisting of branches, patient service centers, and STAT laboratories that have the ability to perform certain routine tests quickly and report results to the physician immediately. The company's laboratory services involve the testing of both bodily fluids and human tissues. LH offers more than 4,400 different tests, consisting of routine tests and specialty and niche testing (esoteric). The most frequently administered routine tests include blood chemistry analyses, urinalysis, blood cell counts, pap tests, HIV tests, microbiology cultures and procedures, and alcohol and other substance abuse tests. The company's esoteric tests include testing for infectious diseases, allergies, diagnostic genetics, identity, and oncology. An average of 440,000 specimens were being processed daily as of December 2009, with routine testing results generally available within 24 hours.

The company provides testing services to a broad range of health care providers, including independent physicians, hospitals, HMOs and other managed care groups, and governmental and other institutions. During 2009, no client accounted for over 4% of net sales. Most testing services are billed to a party other than the physician or other authorized person who ordered the test. Payers other than the direct patient include insurance companies, managed care organizations, Medicare and Medicaid. Client-billed accounted for 27% of revenue in 2009 (28% in 2008), and generated an average of $34.69 ($33.65 in 2008) in revenue per requisition; patients-billed 8% (9% in 2008) and $161.76 ($165.00 in 2008); managed care clients 45% (44% in 2008) and $37.23 ($35.80 in 2008); and Medicare, Medicaid and Insurance 20% (19% in 2008) and $45.63 ($42.40 in 2008). In August 2009, LH acquired Monogram Biosciences, a provider of molecular diagnostic tests. In February 2008, LH acquired NWT, Inc., a provider of drug of abuse testing. In July 2007, LH acquired DSI Labs, expanding its operations in southwest Florida. In May 2005, the company acquired Esoterix, Inc., a provider of specialty reference testing. In February 2005, LH bought US Labs, located in Irvine, CA. In March 2004, LH purchased laboratory operations in Poughkeepsie, NY, and Atlanta, GA, from MDS Diagnostic Services.

Company Financials Fiscal Year Ended Dec. 31

Per Share Data ($)	2009	2008	2007	2006	2005	2004	2003	2002	2001	2000
Tangible Book Value	NM	NM	NM	NM	NM	1.04	0.27	2.67	0.83	0.09
Cash Flow	6.45	5.75	5.26	4.80	4.24	3.33	3.18	2.47	2.03	1.74
Earnings	4.98	4.16	3.93	3.24	2.71	2.45	2.22	1.77	1.29	0.81
S&P Core Earnings	5.00	4.04	3.89	3.21	2.53	2.25	2.04	1.56	1.15	NA
Dividends	Nil	Nil	Nil	Nil	Nil	Nil	Nil	Nil	Nil	Nil
Payout Ratio	Nil	Nil	Nil	Nil	Nil	Nil	Nil	Nil	Nil	Nil
Prices:High	76.74	80.77	82.32	74.30	55.00	50.03	37.72	52.38	45.68	45.75
Prices:Low	53.25	52.93	65.13	52.58	44.63	36.70	22.21	18.51	24.88	7.81
P/E Ratio:High	15	19	21	23	20	20	17	30	35	57
P/E Ratio:Low	11	13	17	16	16	15	10	10	19	10

Income Statement Analysis (Million $)	2009	2008	2007	2006	2005	2004	2003	2002	2001	2000
Revenue	4,695	4,505	4,068	3,591	3,328	3,085	2,939	2,508	2,200	1,919
Operating Income	1,118	1,070	989	853	785	736	671	554	472	340
Depreciation	62.6	178	161	155	150	139	136	102	104	89.6
Interest Expense	62.9	72.0	56.6	47.8	34.4	36.1	40.9	19.2	27.0	38.5
Pretax Income	885	786	802	721	641	615	540	432	332	208
Effective Tax Rate	37.2%	39.2%	40.6%	40.1%	39.7%	41.0%	40.6%	41.1%	45.0%	46.0%
Net Income	543	465	477	432	386	363	321	255	183	112
S&P Core Earnings	546	451	472	428	368	339	295	226	162	NA

Balance Sheet & Other Financial Data (Million $)	2009	2008	2007	2006	2005	2004	2003	2002	2001	2000
Cash	149	220	166	51.5	45.4	187	123	56.4	149	48.8
Current Assets	936	1,033	938	887	702	740	658	597	624	512
Total Assets	4,860	4,670	4,368	4,001	3,876	3,601	3,415	2,612	1,930	1,667
Current Liabilities	1,018	547	968	931	888	301	758	229	201	312
Long Term Debt	1,394	1,601	1,078	603	604	892	361	522	509	354
Common Equity	2,106	1,688	1,725	1,977	1,886	1,999	1,896	1,612	1,085	877
Total Capital	3,642	3,460	3,310	2,989	2,899	3,213	2,530	2,133	1,594	1,231
Capital Expenditures	115	157	143	116	93.6	95.0	83.6	74.3	88.1	55.5
Cash Flow	704	642	638	587	536	502	457	356	287	167
Current Ratio	0.9	1.9	1.0	1.0	0.8	2.5	0.9	2.6	3.1	1.6
% Long Term Debt of Capitalization	38.3	46.2	32.6	20.2	20.9	27.8	14.3	24.4	31.9	28.7
% Net Income of Revenue	11.6	10.3	11.7	12.0	11.6	11.8	10.9	10.2	8.3	5.8
% Return on Assets	11.4	10.3	11.4	11.0	10.3	10.3	10.7	11.2	10.2	6.9
% Return on Equity	28.6	27.2	25.8	22.3	19.9	18.6	18.3	18.9	18.6	14.8

Data as orig reptd.; bef. results of disc opers/spec. items. Per share data adj. for stk. divs.; EPS diluted. E-Estimated. NA-Not Available. NM-Not Meaningful. NR-Not Ranked. UR-Under Review.

Office: 358 South Main Street, Burlington, NC 27215.
Telephone: 336-229-1127.
Website: http://www.labcorp.com
Chrmn, Pres & CEO: D.P. King

COO & EVP: J.T. Boyle, Jr.
EVP, CFO, Chief Acctg Officer & Treas: W.B. Hayes
EVP & CSO: A. Conrad
SVP, Secy & General Counsel: F.S. Eberts, III

Investor Contact: S. Fleming (336-436-4879)
Board Members: K. B. Anderson, J. Belingard, D. P. King, W. E. Lane, T. P. MacMahon, R. E. Mittelstaedt, Jr., A. H. Rubenstein, M. K. Weikel, R. S. Williams

Founded: 1971
Domicile: Delaware
Employees: 28,000

Estee Lauder Companies Inc. (The)

STANDARD
&POOR'S

S&P Recommendation HOLD ★★★☆☆

Price	12-Mo. Target Price	Investment Style
$66.26 (as of Oct 22, 2010)	$63.00	Large-Cap Growth

GICS Sector Consumer Staples
Sub-Industry Personal Products

Summary This company is one of the world's leading manufacturers and marketers of skin care, makeup and fragrance products.

Key Stock Statistics (Source S&P, Vickers, company reports)

52-Wk Range	$71.29– 39.98	S&P Oper. EPS 2011**E**	3.03	Market Capitalization(B)	$7.935	Beta	1.23
Trailing 12-Month EPS	$2.38	S&P Oper. EPS 2012**E**	NA	Yield (%)	0.83	S&P 3-Yr. Proj. EPS CAGR(%)	10
Trailing 12-Month P/E	27.8	P/E on S&P Oper. EPS 2011**E**	21.9	Dividend Rate/Share	$0.55	S&P Credit Rating	A
$10K Invested 5 Yrs Ago	$20,997	Common Shares Outstg. (M)	196.8	Institutional Ownership (%)	92		

Price Performance

30-Week Mov. Avg. · · · ·   10-Week Mov. Avg. – – –   **GAAP Earnings vs. Previous Year**   **Volume** Above Avg. ▓▓▓ STARS

12-Mo. Target Price ——   Relative Strength —   ▲ Up   ▼ Down   ► No Change   Below Avg. ▓▓▓ ★

2007   2008   2009   2010

Options: ASE, CBOE, Ph

Analysis prepared by **Esther Y. Kwon, CFA** on August 16, 2010, when the stock traded at **$ 57.03**.

Highlights

► In February 2009, EL outlined a four-year strategy that builds on its strengths as a brand builder and innovator and more sharply focuses on its execution capabilities and lowering its cost bases. Elements of the plan include expanding market share; increasing non-U.S. sales; improving operating margins; cutting costs; and writing off restructuring and other one-time costs. EL shut down the global wholesale distribution of its Prescriptives Brand in January 2010.

► We look for sales to rise about 5% in FY 11 (Jun.), reflecting improvement in underlying sales and a 2% to 3% negative impact from foreign exchange. We expect international markets and the hair care and skin categories to lead growth. We also expect to a continued recovery in the segmental operating margin, despite our relatively modest sales growth forecast and increase in marketing and advertising expense. We look for most of the margin improvement to come from the restructuring and right-sizing efforts and sales mix shift (e.g., toward skin care).

► Our FY 11 EPS estimate is $3.03, versus FY 10's $2.76, excluding restructuring charges.

Investment Rationale/Risk

► Our hold recommendation reflects our view that EL's long-term growth prospects are appropriately reflected in the stock price. We are encouraged by some signs of consumer spending recovery seen since late 2009, but are concerned about how sustainable and widespread it might be. Also, EL has historically exhibited much more quarterly earnings volatility than many of the companies in our universe.

► Risks to our recommendation and target price include a prolonged decline in the economies in EL's major country markets, slow consumer acceptance of new products, and unfavorable foreign exchange translation. We also have concerns about corporate governance practices given the majority voting power of insiders.

► Our 12-month target price of $63 blends our historical and peer analyses. Our historical analysis suggests a $74 value, using a P/E at a small premium to the 10-year average applied to our calendar 2011 EPS estimate of $3.13. Our peer analysis applies a P/E of 16.4X, a premium to the peer average, valuing the stock at $51.

Qualitative Risk Assessment

LOW	MEDIUM	HIGH

Our risk assessment reflects our view of EL's market share advantage, leading brands, scale leverage, and strong balance sheet. This is partly offset by its exposure to short-term factors such as changes in the retail industry, geopolitical events, and consumer spending.

Quantitative Evaluations

S&P Quality Ranking B+

D	C	B-	B	B+	A-	A	A+

Relative Strength Rank STRONG

71

LOWEST = 1   HIGHEST = 99

Revenue/Earnings Data

Revenue (Million $)

	1Q	2Q	3Q	4Q	Year
2010	1,833	2,262	1,860	1,840	7,796
2009	1,904	2,041	1,697	1,683	7,324
2008	1,710	2,309	1,880	2,012	7,911
2007	1,594	1,991	1,691	1,762	7,038
2006	1,497	1,784	1,578	1,605	6,464
2005	1,504	1,750	1,538	1,544	6,336

Earnings Per Share ($)

2010	0.71	1.28	0.28	0.12	2.38
2009	0.26	0.80	0.14	-0.09	1.10
2008	0.20	1.14	0.46	0.61	2.40
2007	0.27	0.99	0.45	0.45	2.16
2006	0.28	0.70	0.28	0.23	1.49
2005	0.41	0.60	0.46	0.30	1.78

Fiscal year ended Jun. 30. Next earnings report expected: Late October. EPS Estimates based on S&P Operating Earnings; historical GAAP earnings are as reported.

Dividend Data (Dates: mm/dd Payment Date: mm/dd/yy)

Amount ($)	Date Decl.	Ex-Div. Date	Stk. of Record	Payment Date
0.550	11/13	11/25	11/30	12/16/09

Dividends have been paid since 1996. Source: Company reports.

Please read the Required Disclosures and Analyst Certification on the last page of this report.

The McGraw-Hill Companies

Estee Lauder Companies Inc. (The)

STANDARD & POOR'S

Business Summary August 16, 2010

CORPORATE OVERVIEW. The Estee Lauder Companies was founded in 1946 by Estee and Joseph Lauder. EL has grown into one of the world's largest manufacturers and marketers of skin care, makeup and fragrance products, sold in more than 140 countries and territories worldwide. EL has historically been a dominant player in the high-end fragrance and cosmetic categories, with brand names such as Estee Lauder, Clinique, Aramis, Prescriptives, Origins, M.A.C, Bobbi Brown, La Mer, Aveda, Stila, Jo Malone, and Bumble and Bumble. EL is also the global licensee for fragrances and cosmetics sold under the Tommy Hilfiger, Donna Karan, Michael Kors and Sean Jean brands. Each brand is distinctly positioned within the cosmetics market, according to the company.

EL reports sales and operating income by three regions. The Americas accounted for 47% of sales and 23% of profits in FY 09 (Jun.), Europe, the Middle East and Africa 35% of sales and 45% of profits, and Asia/Pacific 18% and 32%, respectively.

The skin care division (39% of FY 09 net sales) addresses various skin care needs of women and men. Products include moisturizers, creams, lotions, cleansers, sun screens and self-tanning products. The makeup division (39%) manufactures, markets and sells a full array of makeup products, including lipsticks, mascaras, foundations, eye shadows, nail polishes and powders.

The fragrance division (16%) offers a variety of fragrance products, including eau de parfum sprays and colognes, as well as lotions, powders, creams and soaps that are based on a particular fragrance. The products of the hair care division (5%) are offered mainly in salons and in freestanding retail stores and include styling products, shampoos, conditioners and finishing sprays. Other is less than 1%.

As is customary in the cosmetics industry, EL accepts returns of its products from retailers under certain conditions. In recognition of this practice and in according with generally accepted accounting principals, EL reports sales on a net basis, which is computed by deducting the amount of actual returns received and an amount established for anticipated returns from gross sales. As a percentage of gross sales, returns were 4.4% in FY 09 and in FY 08, 4.2% in FY 07 and 5.0% in FY 06.

In FY 09, Macy's, Inc. accounted for 11% of EL's accounts receivable and 12% of consolidated net sales.

Company Financials Fiscal Year Ended Jun. 30

Per Share Data ($)	2010	2009	2008	2007	2006	2005	2004	2003	2002	2001
Tangible Book Value	5.49	3.71	3.86	2.23	4.29	6.79	4.35	2.92	3.20	2.64
Cash Flow	3.70	2.39	3.66	3.16	2.41	2.64	2.45	2.01	1.46	1.82
Earnings	2.38	1.10	2.40	2.16	1.49	1.78	1.62	1.26	0.78	1.17
S&P Core Earnings	2.57	1.01	2.28	2.18	1.52	1.69	1.51	1.17	0.70	1.01
Dividends	0.55	0.55	0.55	0.50	0.40	0.40	0.30	0.20	0.20	0.20
Payout Ratio	23%	50%	23%	23%	27%	22%	19%	16%	26%	17%
Prices:High	71.29	50.57	54.75	52.31	43.60	47.50	49.34	40.20	38.80	44.35
Prices:Low	47.65	19.81	24.24	38.41	32.79	29.98	37.55	25.73	25.20	29.25
P/E Ratio:High	30	46	23	24	29	27	30	32	50	38
P/E Ratio:Low	20	18	10	18	22	17	23	20	32	25

Income Statement Analysis (Million $)										
Revenue	7,796	7,324	7,911	7,038	6,464	6,336	5,790	5,118	4,744	4,608
Operating Income	1,170	812	1,059	958	910	917	836	712	614	706
Depreciation	264	254	248	207	198	197	192	175	162	156
Interest Expense	102	75.7	66.8	38.9	23.8	13.9	27.1	8.10	9.80	12.3
Pretax Income	688	343	744	711	596	707	617	474	332	483
Effective Tax Rate	NA	33.8%	34.9%	35.9%	43.6%	41.2%	37.7%	33.9%	34.5%	36.0%
Net Income	478	218	474	449	325	406	375	320	213	307
S&P Core Earnings	516	200	450	453	332	390	351	274	171	245

Balance Sheet & Other Financial Data (Million $)										
Cash	1,121	864	402	254	369	553	612	364	547	347
Current Assets	3,121	2,913	2,787	2,239	2,177	2,303	2,199	1,845	1,928	1,739
Total Assets	5,336	5,177	5,011	4,126	3,784	3,886	3,708	3,350	3,417	3,219
Current Liabilities	1,572	1,459	1,699	1,501	1,438	1,498	1,322	1,054	960	857
Long Term Debt	1,205	1,388	1,078	1,028	432	451	462	284	404	411
Common Equity	1,965	1,640	1,653	1,199	1,622	1,693	1,733	1,424	1,462	1,352
Total Capital	3,170	3,052	2,758	2,248	2,079	2,160	2,211	2,080	2,226	2,123
Capital Expenditures	271	280	358	312	261	230	207	163	203	192
Cash Flow	742	472	722	656	523	603	567	471	351	440
Current Ratio	2.0	2.0	1.6	1.5	1.5	1.5	1.7	1.8	2.0	2.0
% Long Term Debt of Capitalization	38.0	45.5	39.1	45.7	20.8	20.9	20.9	13.6	18.1	19.4
% Net Income of Revenue	6.1	3.0	6.0	6.4	5.0	6.4	6.5	6.2	4.5	6.7
% Return on Assets	9.1	4.3	10.4	11.3	8.5	10.7	10.6	9.5	6.4	9.8
% Return on Equity	26.5	13.3	33.2	31.8	19.6	23.7	23.8	20.5	13.4	22.6

Data as orig reptd.; bef. results of disc opers/spec. items. Per share data adj. for stk. divs.; EPS diluted. E-Estimated. NA-Not Available. NM-Not Meaningful. NR-Not Ranked. UR-Under Review.

Office: 767 5th Avenue, New York, NY 10153-0023.
Telephone: 212-572-4200.
Email: irdept@estee.com
Website: http://www.elcompanies.com

Chrmn: W.P. Lauder
Pres & CEO: F. Freda
EVP, CFO & Chief Acctg Officer: R.W. Kunes
EVP & General Counsel: S.E. Moss

SVP & Secy: S.G. Smul
Investor Contact: D. D'Andrea (212-572-4384)
Board Members: C. Barshefsky, R. M. Bravo, F. Freda, P. J. Fribourg, M. Hobson, I. O. Hockaday, Jr., A. Lauder, J. Lauder, L. A. Lauder, W. P. Lauder, R. D. Parsons, B. S. Sternlicht, R. F. Zannino, L. F. de Rothschild

Founded: 1946
Domicile: Delaware
Employees: 31,200

The McGraw-Hill Companies

Leggett & Platt Inc

STANDARD &POOR'S

S&P Recommendation **SELL** ★ ★ ☆ ☆ ☆	Price $21.01 (as of Oct 22, 2010)	12-Mo. Target Price $18.00	Investment Style Large-Cap Blend

GICS Sector Consumer Discretionary
Sub-Industry Home Furnishings

Summary This company makes a broad line of bedding and furniture components and other home, office and commercial furnishings, as well as diversified products for non-furnishings markets.

Key Stock Statistics (Source S&P, Vickers, company reports)

52-Wk Range	$25.15– 17.89	S&P Oper. EPS 2010**E**	1.22	Market Capitalization(B)	$3.077	Beta	1.25
Trailing 12-Month EPS	$1.20	S&P Oper. EPS 2011**E**	1.10	Yield (%)	5.14	S&P 3-Yr. Proj. EPS CAGR(%)	15
Trailing 12-Month P/E	17.5	P/E on S&P Oper. EPS 2010**E**	17.2	Dividend Rate/Share	$1.08	S&P Credit Rating	A-
$10K Invested 5 Yrs Ago	$13,904	Common Shares Outstg. (M)	146.4	Institutional Ownership (%)	69		

Price Performance

30-Week Mov. Avg. · · · · 10-Week Mov. Avg. — — GAAP Earnings vs. Previous Year Volume Above Avg. STARS
12-Mo. Target Price — Relative Strength — ▲ Up ▼ Down ► No Change Below Avg. ★

Options: ASE, Ph

Qualitative Risk Assessment

LOW	**MEDIUM**	HIGH

Our risk assessment reflects our view of LEG's long history of profitability and strong free cash flow, offset by the steep cyclicality of its addressable markets.

Quantitative Evaluations

S&P Quality Ranking B

D	C	B-	**B**	B+	A-	A	A+

Relative Strength Rank WEAK

17

LOWEST = 1   HIGHEST = 99

Revenue/Earnings Data

Revenue (Million $)

	1Q	2Q	3Q	4Q	Year
2010	816.4	874.3	--	--	--
2009	718.1	757.4	809.9	769.7	3,055
2008	998.3	1,063	1,132	882.5	4,076
2007	1,064	1,316	1,325	1,054	4,306
2006	1,378	1,403	1,415	1,311	5,505
2005	1,301	1,310	1,349	1,340	5,299

Earnings Per Share ($)

	1Q	2Q	3Q	4Q	Year
2010	0.30	0.34	E0.31	E0.26	E1.22
2009	0.02	0.12	0.34	0.26	0.74
2008	0.23	0.25	0.29	-0.05	0.73
2007	0.31	0.30	0.36	-0.71	0.28
2006	0.33	0.45	0.45	0.38	1.61
2005	0.37	0.41	0.28	0.24	1.30

Fiscal year ended Dec. 31. Next earnings report expected: Late October. EPS Estimates based on S&P Operating Earnings; historical GAAP earnings are as reported.

Highlights

► The STARS recommendation for LEG has recently been changed to 2 (sell) from 3 (hold) and the 12-month target price has recently been changed to $18.00 from $25.00. The Highlights section of this Stock Report will be updated accordingly.

Investment Rationale/Risk

► The Investment Rationale/Risk section of this Stock Report will be updated shortly. For the latest News story on LEG from MarketScope, see below.

► 10/22/10 10:36 am ET ... S&P LOWERS OPINION ON SHARES OF LEGGETT & PLATT TO SELL FROM HOLD (LEG 20.96**): LEG posts Q3 EPS of $0.31, vs. $0.34, and below our $0.32 estimate. Sales increased 7% over last year but declined 0.9% sequentially. LEG cautions that key markets were notably weaker in Q3 and the unit pace of growth has notably subsided. We believe demand for residential furnishings has subsided after the expiration of tax purchase incentives, and we don't expect a meaningful improvement until mid-'11. We cut our '10 and '11 EPS estimates to $1.22 and $1.10, from $1.25 and $1.32, respectively. We lower our target price to $18 from $25 on updated peer comparisons. /EKolb

Dividend Data (Dates: mm/dd Payment Date: mm/dd/yy)

Amount ($)	Date Decl.	Ex-Div. Date	Stk. of Record	Payment Date
0.260	11/05	12/11	12/15	01/15/10
0.260	02/25	03/11	03/15	04/15/10
0.260	05/13	06/11	06/15	07/15/10
0.270	08/04	09/13	09/15	10/15/10

Dividends have been paid since 1939. Source: Company reports.

Please read the Required Disclosures and Analyst Certification on the last page of this report.

The **McGraw·Hill** Companies

Leggett & Platt Inc

STANDARD &POOR'S

Business Summary July 29, 2010

CORPORATE OVERVIEW. Leggett & Platt, founded in 1883, is a diversified manufacturer that conceives, designs and produces a wide range of engineered components and products that can be found in most homes, offices, retail stores and automobiles.

LEG's business is organized into five business segments. Residential Furnishings (54% of 2009 sales; 52% in 2008) consists of Bedding, Home Furniture & Consumer Products, and Fabric and Carpet Underlay. The Commercial Fixturing & Components segment (16%; 17%) consists of Fixture & Display and Office Furniture Components. Industrial Materials (15%; 16%) consists of Wire and Tubing, while Specialized Products (15%; 15%) consists of Automotive, Machinery and Commercial Vehicles.

PRIMARY BUSINESS DYNAMICS. In the past 20 years, about two-thirds of LEG's sales growth has come from acquisitions. Over the past 10 years, the average acquisition target had revenues of $15 million to $20 million, which the company believes serves to minimize the risk of any single acquisition. In 2009, LEG generated $565 million in cash from operations, down from 2007's $614 million but up from $436 million in 2008. LEG expects to use much of the excess cash to repurchase shares.

In 2007, LEG acquired three businesses in the Commercial Fixturing & Components ($20 million annual sales), Industrial Materials ($50 million) and Specialized Products ($30 million) segments. In Industrial Materials, LEG bought a maker of coated wire products, including racks for dishwashers. In Specialized Products, LEG bought a company that designs and assembles docking stations that secure computer and other electronic equipment in vehicles. In Commercial Fixturing & Components, LEG bought a company located in China that makes office furniture components.

In 2006, LEG acquired five businesses representing $75 million in annualized sales, all within the Residential Furnishings segment. The largest acquisition was a maker of rubber carpet underlay, a product type that accounts for 6% of LEG's overall revenue. In addition, the company divested five businesses in 2006 with annualized sales of about $45 million.

Company Financials Fiscal Year Ended Dec. 31

Per Share Data ($)	2009	2008	2007	2006	2005	2004	2003	2002	2001	2000
Tangible Book Value	3.06	3.72	5.73	5.72	5.55	6.38	5.62	5.36	4.81	4.61
Cash Flow	1.55	1.42	1.16	2.67	2.18	2.35	1.89	1.99	1.92	2.18
Earnings	0.74	0.73	0.28	1.61	1.30	1.45	1.05	1.17	0.94	1.32
S&P Core Earnings	0.75	0.60	0.90	1.57	1.27	1.38	1.02	1.11	0.85	NA
Dividends	1.02	1.00	0.78	0.84	0.63	0.58	0.54	0.50	0.48	0.42
Payout Ratio	138%	137%	NM	52%	48%	40%	51%	43%	51%	32%
Prices:High	21.44	24.60	24.73	27.04	29.61	30.68	23.69	27.40	24.45	22.56
Prices:Low	10.03	12.03	17.14	21.93	18.19	21.19	17.16	18.60	16.85	14.19
P/E Ratio:High	29	34	88	17	23	21	23	23	26	17
P/E Ratio:Low	14	16	61	14	14	15	16	16	18	11

Income Statement Analysis (Million $)										
Revenue	3,055	4,076	4,306	5,505	5,299	5,086	4,388	4,272	4,114	4,276
Operating Income	377	371	492	666	605	622	520	582	558	660
Depreciation	130	116	157	175	171	177	167	165	197	173
Interest Expense	37.4	48.4	58.6	56.2	46.7	45.9	46.9	42.1	58.8	66.3
Pretax Income	198	188	128	435	356	423	315	364	297	419
Effective Tax Rate	39.0%	34.6%	60.3%	30.9%	29.4%	32.5%	34.7%	35.9%	36.9%	36.9%
Net Income	118	123	51.0	300	251	285	206	233	188	264
S&P Core Earnings	118	102	161	291	245	272	202	221	169	NA

Balance Sheet & Other Financial Data (Million $)										
Cash	261	165	205	132	64.9	491	444	225	187	37.3
Current Assets	1,214	1,307	1,834	1,894	1,763	2,065	1,819	1,488	1,422	1,405
Total Assets	3,061	3,162	4,073	4,265	4,053	4,197	3,890	3,501	3,413	3,373
Current Liabilities	535	524	800	691	738	960	626	598	457	477
Long Term Debt	789	851	1,001	1,060	922	779	1,012	809	978	988
Common Equity	1,576	1,653	2,133	2,351	2,249	2,313	2,114	1,977	1,867	1,794
Total Capital	2,375	2,539	3,176	3,478	3,230	3,178	3,221	2,865	2,909	2,854
Capital Expenditures	83.0	118	149	166	164	157	137	124	128	170
Cash Flow	248	239	208	476	422	463	373	398	384	437
Current Ratio	2.3	2.5	2.3	2.7	2.4	2.2	2.9	2.5	3.1	2.9
% Long Term Debt of Capitalization	33.2	33.5	31.5	30.5	28.5	24.5	31.4	28.2	33.6	34.6
% Net Income of Revenue	3.9	3.0	1.2	5.5	4.7	5.6	4.7	5.5	4.6	6.2
% Return on Assets	3.8	3.4	1.2	7.2	6.1	7.1	5.6	6.7	5.5	8.3
% Return on Equity	7.3	6.5	2.3	13.1	11.0	12.9	10.1	12.1	10.3	15.4

Data as orig reptd.; bef. results of disc opers/spec. items. Per share data adj. for stk. divs.; EPS diluted. E-Estimated. NA-Not Available. NM-Not Meaningful. NR-Not Ranked. UR-Under Review.

Office: No. 1 Leggett Road, Carthage, MO 64836-9649.
Telephone: 417-358-8131.
Email: invest@leggett.com
Website: http://www.leggett.com

Chrmn: R.T. Fisher
Pres & CEO: D.S. Haffner
COO & EVP: K.G. Glassman
SVP & CFO: M.C. Flanigan

Chief Acctg Officer & Cntlr: W.S. Weil
Investor Contact: D.M. DeSonier (417-358-8131)
Board Members: R. E. Brunner, R. Clark, R. T. Enloe, III, R. T. Fisher, M. C. Flanigan, K. G. Glassman, R. A. Griffith, D. S. Haffner, J. W. McClanathan, J. C. Odom, M. E. Purnell, Jr., P. A. Wood

Founded: 1883
Domicile: Missouri
Employees: 18,500

Legg Mason Inc

STANDARD &POOR'S

S&P Recommendation HOLD ★★★★☆	**Investment Style** Large-Cap Growth

Price
$31.18 (as of Oct 22, 2010)

12-Mo. Target Price
$32.00

GICS Sector Financials
Sub-Industry Asset Management & Custody Banks

Summary This diversified investment manager serves individual and institutional investors through offices around the United States.

Key Stock Statistics (Source S&P, Vickers, company reports)

52-Wk Range	$34.83–24.00	S&P Oper. EPS 2011E	1.60	Market Capitalization(B)	$4.822	Beta	1.96
Trailing 12-Month EPS	$1.27	S&P Oper. EPS 2012E	2.37	Yield (%)	0.51	S&P 3-Yr. Proj. EPS CAGR(%)	25
Trailing 12-Month P/E	24.6	P/E on S&P Oper. EPS 2011E	19.5	Dividend Rate/Share	$0.16	S&P Credit Rating	BBB+
$10K Invested 5 Yrs Ago	$3,177	Common Shares Outstg. (M)	154.6	Institutional Ownership (%)	94		

Price Performance

30-Week Mov. Avg. · · · 10-Week Mov. Avg. – – GAAP Earnings vs. Previous Year Volume Above Avg. STARS
12-Mo. Target Price — Relative Strength — ▲ Up ▼ Down ► No Change Below Avg.

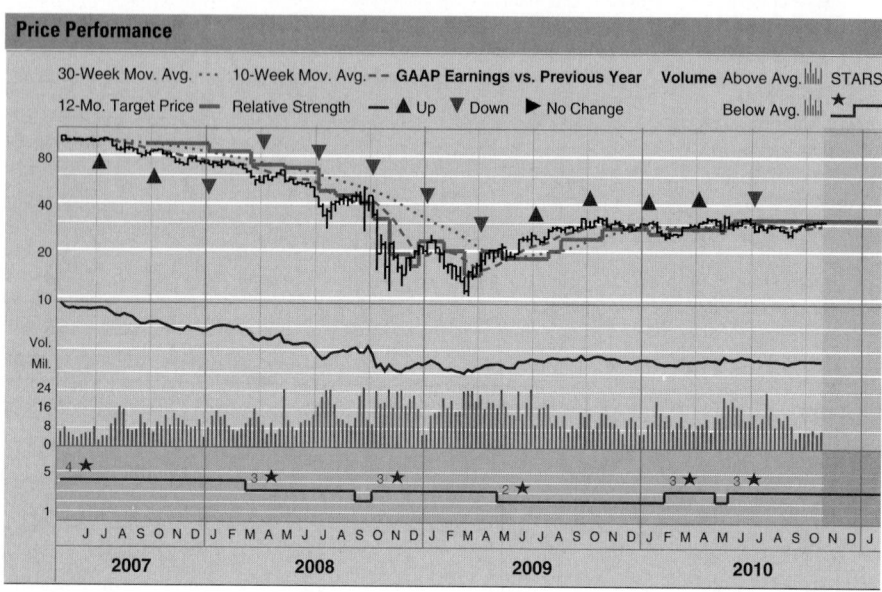

Options: ASE, CBOE, P, Ph

Analysis prepared by **Matthew Albrecht** on July 28, 2010, when the stock traded at **$ 29.07**.

Highlights

➤ We think assets under management should benefit in FY 11 (Mar.) from market appreciation, though net flows remain inconsistent. Although recent relative fund performance may be improving, particularly for some of its deep value offerings, longer-term fund track records remain challenged, and will likely prove a headwind to significant sales gains. An unfavorable asset mix favoring fixed income and money market products will likely continue to pressure the average management fee rate. LM is expanding its distribution network around the globe, but we do not anticipate a return to consistently positive flows until fund performance improves. We expect operating revenues to grow only modestly in FY 11 and then about 9% in FY 12.

➤ The distribution expense ratio remains slightly below historical levels because of poor fund sales, but will likely narrow as net flow trends improve. Head count reductions and other cost controls should help the pretax margin expand, albeit remaining below historical levels in FY 11 and FY 12.

➤ We forecast EPS of $1.60 in FY 11 and $2.37 in FY 12, helped by share repurchases.

Investment Rationale/Risk

➤ We think some of Legg Mason's flagship funds, previously hurt by a number of high-profile investments gone sour, have seen improved relative performance since equity markets bottomed in March 2009. Still, longer-term track records compare unfavorably with peers and benchmarks, although we think sales trends are improving. We believe, however, that the sale of SIV exposures has improved the outlook for LM's balance sheet and eliminated a significant overhang weighing on the stock. We think the company's outlook has improved, supported by aggressive capital management, and its discounted valuation to peers should narrow.

➤ Risks to our recommendation and target price include stock market declines, a deterioration in relative investment performance, and a rise in customer redemptions.

➤ The shares recently traded at 18.3X our FY 11 EPS estimate, in line with their historical multiples. Our 12-month target price of $32 is derived by applying a multiple of 17.9X to our forward 12-month earnings estimate of $1.79, in line with comparable peer multiples.

Qualitative Risk Assessment

LOW	MEDIUM	HIGH

Our risk assessment reflects our view of the company's strong market share and restructured balance sheet, offset by weak relative long-term investment performance and industry cyclicality.

Quantitative Evaluations

S&P Quality Ranking B+

D	C	B-	B	B+	A-	A	A+

Relative Strength Rank MODERATE

61

LOWEST = 1   HIGHEST = 99

Revenue/Earnings Data

Revenue (Million $)

	1Q	2Q	3Q	4Q	Year
2011	674.2	--	--	--	--
2010	613.1	659.9	690.5	671.4	2,635
2009	1,054	966.1	720.0	617.2	3,357
2008	1,206	1,172	1,187	1,069	4,634
2007	1,038	1,031	1,133	1,142	4,344
2006	437.7	466.4	689.0	1,052	2,645

Earnings Per Share ($)

	1Q	2Q	3Q	4Q	Year
2011	0.30	E0.35	E0.48	E0.47	E1.60
2010	0.35	0.30	0.28	0.39	1.32
2009	-0.22	-0.74	-10.55	-2.29	-13.85
2008	1.32	1.23	1.07	-1.81	1.86
2007	1.08	1.00	1.21	1.19	4.48
2006	0.93	0.75	0.77	1.04	3.30

Fiscal year ended Mar. 31. Next earnings report expected: Late October. EPS Estimates based on S&P Operating Earnings; historical GAAP earnings are as reported.

Dividend Data (Dates: mm/dd Payment Date: mm/dd/yy)

Amount ($)	Date Decl.	Ex-Div. Date	Stk. of Record	Payment Date
0.030	10/27	12/14	12/16	01/11/10
0.030	01/26	03/09	03/11	04/12/10
0.040	04/27	06/11	06/15	07/12/10
0.040	07/26	10/05	10/07	10/25/10

Dividends have been paid since 1983. Source: Company reports.

Please read the Required Disclosures and Analyst Certification on the last page of this report.

The McGraw-Hill Companies

Legg Mason Inc

Business Summary July 28, 2010

CORPORATE OVERVIEW. Legg Mason is a holding company which, through subsidiaries, is principally engaged in providing asset management and other related financial services to individuals, institutions, corporations, governments, and government agencies. At the end of FY 10 (Mar.), total assets under management were about $685 billion, up from about $632 billion a year earlier. The company operates out of offices in the U.S., the U.K. and a number of other countries worldwide. At the end of FY 10, fixed income assets represented 53% of total assets under management, equity assets 25%, and liquidity assets 22%.

Legg Mason operates through two divisions: Americas and International. Within each division, the firm provides services through individual asset managers. They each generally market their own products and services under their own brand names, and in many cases distribute retail products and services through a centralized retail distribution network. Each subsidiary primarily earns revenues by charging fees for the management of assets for clients. Fees are typically calculated as a percentage of average assets under management, and can vary with the type of account, the asset manager, and the type of client. They may also earn performance fees from certain accounts if benchmarks are met or exceeded for the particular measurement

period. Increases in assets under management can result from inflows of new assets from new and existing clients, and from appreciation of asset values. Decreases can also occur due to client redemptions and declines in the value of client assets.

The firm does business primarily through its 16 asset managers. We think LM has a diverse collection of asset management subsidiaries, which include Western Asset, Legg Mason Capital Management, Brandywine, and Permal, among others. LM's Asset Management business provides asset management services to institutional and individual clients and investment advisory services to company-sponsored investment funds. Investment products include proprietary mutual funds ranging from money market and fixed income funds to equity funds managed in a wide variety of investing styles, non-U.S. funds, and a number of unregistered, alternative investment products. LM's mutual funds group sponsors domestic and international equity, fixed income and money market mutual funds, closed-end funds, and other proprietary funds

Company Financials Fiscal Year Ended Mar. 31

Per Share Data ($)	2010	2009	2008	2007	2006	2005	2004	2003	2002	2001
Tangible Book Value	3.84	NM	NM	NM	NM	11.66	6.50	3.32	1.52	8.25
Cash Flow	2.05	-12.86	2.84	5.95	3.90	3.83	2.62	1.85	1.49	1.53
Earnings	1.32	-13.85	1.86	4.48	3.30	3.53	2.64	1.85	1.49	1.53
S&P Core Earnings	1.32	-8.12	1.86	4.48	3.25	3.41	2.57	1.63	1.35	1.44
Dividends	0.12	0.96	0.81	0.69	0.40	0.37	0.29	0.29	0.23	0.20
Payout Ratio	9%	NM	44%	15%	12%	11%	11%	15%	16%	13%
Calendar Year	2009	2008	2007	2006	2005	2004	2003	2002	2001	2000
Prices:High	33.70	75.33	110.17	140.00	129.00	73.70	56.77	38.10	37.99	40.17
Prices:Low	10.35	11.09	68.35	81.01	68.10	48.95	29.47	24.74	22.83	20.46
P/E Ratio:High	26	NM	59	31	39	21	22	21	25	26
P/E Ratio:Low	8	NM	37	18	21	14	11	13	15	13

Income Statement Analysis (Million $)										
Commissions	NA	Nil	Nil	Nil	Nil	358	344	317	331	359
Interest Income	NA	56.3	77.0	58.9	48.0	119	84.3	109	168	282
Total Revenue	2,635	3,357	4,634	4,344	2,645	2,490	2,004	1,615	1,579	1,536
Interest Expense	NA	150	83.0	71.5	52.6	80.8	63.2	87.1	127	175
Pretax Income	330	-3,156	444	1,044	703	659	472	308	253	266
Effective Tax Rate	36.0%	NM	39.7%	38.1%	39.2%	38.0%	38.5%	38.1%	39.6%	41.2%
Net Income	204	-1,948	268	646	434	408	291	191	153	156
S&P Core Earnings	204	-1,142	268	646	421	394	283	168	138	146

Balance Sheet & Other Financial Data (Million $)										
Total Assets	8,614	9,321	11,830	9,604	9,302	8,219	7,263	6,067	5,940	4,688
Cash Items	1,880	1,421	2,557	1,184	1,023	3,554	3,744	3,274	2,970	2,498
Receivables	NA	1,204	764	852	850	1,564	1,458	1,155	1,230	1,333
Securities Owned	NA	336	489	273	142	1,298	870	419	458	374
Securities Borrowed	NA	Nil	Nil	Nil	Nil	588	488	220	280	253
Due Brokers & Customers	NA	Nil	Nil	Nil	Nil	3,419	3,657	75.0	35.0	2,955
Other Liabilities	NA	NA	1,216	1,079	1,633	1,108	764	462	410	328
Capitalization:Debt	NA	2,965	1,826	1,108	1,166	811	794	787	877	219
Capitalization:Equity	5,842	4,454	6,621	6,678	5,850	2,293	1,560	1,248	1,075	917
Capitalization:Total	NA	7,679	8,802	8,229	7,016	3,104	2,354	2,035	1,952	1,136
% Return on Revenue	7.8	NM	5.8	14.9	16.4	19.2	17.5	14.7	12.3	13.3
% Return on Assets	NA	NM	2.5	6.8	5.0	5.3	4.4	3.2	2.9	3.3
% Return on Equity	NA	NM	4.1	10.2	10.7	21.2	20.7	16.4	15.4	18.7

Data as orig reptd.; bef. results of disc opers/spec. items. Per share data adj. for stk. divs.; EPS diluted. E-Estimated. NA-Not Available. NM-Not Meaningful. NR-Not Ranked. UR-Under Review.

Office: 100 International Drive, Baltimore, MD 21202-1099.
Telephone: 410-539-0000.
Website: http://www.leggmason.com
Chrmn, Pres & CEO: M.R. Fetting

EVP & Chief Admin Officer: J.A. Sullivan
SVP & General Counsel: T.P. Lemke
CFO: T.J. Murphy
Secy: T.C. Merchant

Investor Contact: A. Magleby (410-454-5246)
Board Members: H. L. Adams, R. E. Angelica, D. Beresford, J. T. Cahill, M. R. Fetting, B. Huff, J. Koerner, III, C. G. Krongard, S. C. Nuttall, N. Peltz, W. A. Reed, M. M. Richardson, K. L. Schmoke, N. J. St. George

Founded: 1899
Domicile: Maryland
Employees: 3,550

Lennar Corp

STANDARD &POOR'S

S&P Recommendation STRONG BUY ★★★★★

Price	**12-Mo. Target Price**	**Investment Style**	
$14.82 (as of Oct 22, 2010)	$19.00	Large-Cap Blend	

GICS Sector Consumer Discretionary
Sub-Industry Homebuilding

Summary Lennar, one of the largest, most geographically diversified U.S. home builders, concentrates on moderately priced homes.

Key Stock Statistics (Source S&P, Vickers, company reports)

52-Wk Range	$21.79– 11.56	S&P Oper. EPS 2010**E**	0.55	Market Capitalization(B)	$2.277	Beta	1.66
Trailing 12-Month EPS	$0.53	S&P Oper. EPS 2011**E**	1.00	Yield (%)	1.08	S&P 3-Yr. Proj. EPS CAGR(%)	20
Trailing 12-Month P/E	28.0	P/E on S&P Oper. EPS 2010**E**	26.9	Dividend Rate/Share	$0.16	S&P Credit Rating	B+
$10K Invested 5 Yrs Ago	$2,937	Common Shares Outstg. (M)	185.0	Institutional Ownership (%)	99		

Price Performance

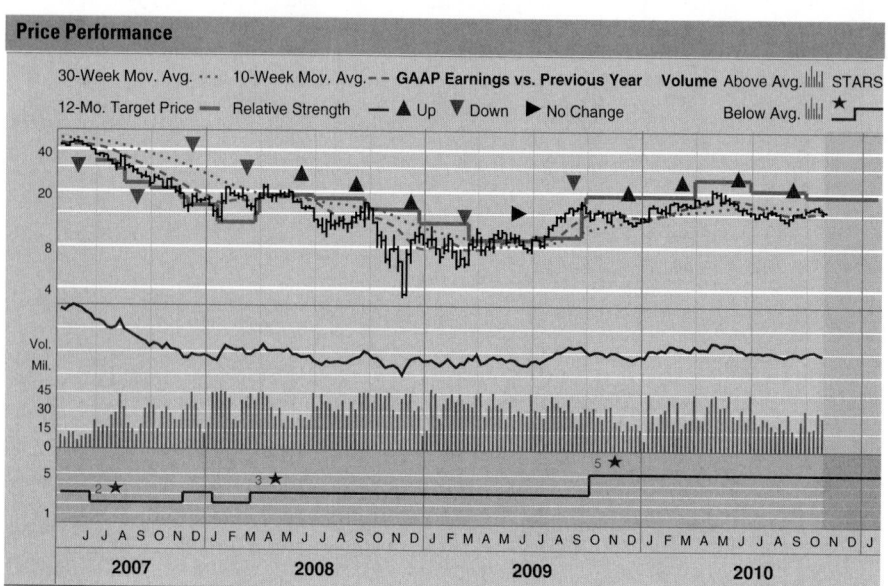

30-Week Mov. Avg. ···· 10-Week Mov. Avg.-- **GAAP Earnings vs. Previous Year** Volume Above Avg.▐▌ STARS
12-Mo. Target Price — Relative Strength — ▲ Up ▼ Down ▶ No Change Below Avg.▐▌ ★

Options: ASE, CBOE, P, Ph

Analysis prepared by **Kenneth M. Leon, CPA** on September 20, 2010, when the stock traded at **$ 15.26.**

Highlights

► Following an estimated revenue decline of 3% in FY 10 (Nov.), we project that revenues will rebound 10% in FY 11, reflecting a slow but steady recovery of the U.S. housing market. We forecast home deliveries and average selling prices will begin to stabilize from sharp declines during the housing downturn. With steady improvement in demand, we believe contract backlog will rebound in FY 11.

► LEN's newly formed Rialto Investments unit recently acquired a 40% equity interest in two portfolios of real estate loans in partnership with the FDIC for $243 million. The portfolios, with a $3 billion unpaid principal balance, consist of more than 5,500 distressed real estate loans with an initial fair value of $1.2 billion. In the third quarter, Rialto generated a $18.5 million operating profit on $38 million of revenue.

► We assume lower market risk exposure to asset impairments which should lead to sustained profitability in coming years, in our opinion. With wider margins, the company is projecting a return to profitability some time in FY 10. We estimate EPS of $0.55 for FY 10 and $1.00 for FY 11.

Investment Rationale/Risk

► We believe Lennar can achieve profitability with reduced sales incentives and lower construction costs on new scaled-down homes coming to market. In our opinion, the company can also be opportunistic in new land purchases or option land contracts with abundant land coming to market from banks that took possession of distressed or bankrupt private homebuilders. As of August 31, 2010, the company had $865 million of cash to support its working capital and debt obligations, as well as new land acquisitions.

► Risks to our recommendation and target price include prolonged housing weakness that further impairs new home purchases, higher mortgage rates, and weaker than expected demand from first-time homebuyers after the federal tax credit expiration. Rialto Investments remains a business risk with respect to market conditions and credit trends.

► Our estimated book value of $12.95 per share includes a federal tax refund. Applying a forward price-to-book value multiple of just under 1.5X, near the mid-range of other large homebuilders, our 12-month target price is $19.

Qualitative Risk Assessment

LOW	MEDIUM	HIGH

Our risk assessment reflects Lennar's exposure to the uncertainties of the housing market, where the confidence and job security of buyers is still weak and credit guidelines have tightened, partly offset by record low mortgage rates.

Quantitative Evaluations

S&P Quality Ranking B-

D	C	B-	B	B+	A-	A	A+

Relative Strength Rank WEAK

29

LOWEST = 1   HIGHEST = 99

Revenue/Earnings Data

Revenue (Million $)

	1Q	2Q	3Q	4Q	Year
2010	574.4	814.5	825.0	--	--
2009	593.1	891.9	720.7	913.7	3,119
2008	1,063	1,128	1,107	1,278	4,575
2007	2,792	2,876	2,342	2,177	10,187
2006	3,241	4,578	4,182	4,266	16,267
2005	2,406	2,933	3,498	5,030	13,867

Earnings Per Share ($)

	1Q	2Q	3Q	4Q	Year
2010	-0.04	0.21	0.16	E0.20	E0.55
2009	-0.98	-0.76	-0.97	-0.19	-2.45
2008	-0.56	-0.76	-0.56	-5.12	-7.00
2007	0.43	-1.55	-3.25	-7.92	-12.31
2006	1.58	2.00	1.30	-1.24	3.69
2005	1.17	1.55	2.06	3.54	8.17

Fiscal year ended Nov. 30. Next earnings report expected: Early January. EPS Estimates based on S&P Operating Earnings; historical GAAP earnings are as reported.

Dividend Data (Dates: mm/dd Payment Date: mm/dd/yy)

Amount ($)	Date Decl.	Ex-Div. Date	Stk. of Record	Payment Date
0.040	01/12	01/22	01/26	02/12/10
0.040	04/14	05/03	05/05	05/20/10
0.040	06/28	07/19	07/21	08/05/10
0.040	09/30	10/12	10/14	10/28/10

Dividends have been paid since 1978. Source: Company reports.

Please read the Required Disclosures and Analyst Certification on the last page of this report.

The **McGraw·Hill** Companies

Lennar Corp

Business Summary September 20, 2010

CORPORATE OVERVIEW. Lennar Corp., one of the largest homebuilders in the U.S. (based on FY 09 (Nov.) U.S. home closings), constructs homes for first-time, move-up and active adult buyers, and also provides various financial services. It takes part in all phases of planning and building, and subcontracts nearly all development and construction work. LEN sells homes primarily from models it has designed and constructed. During FY 09, these homes had an average sales price of $234,000 compared to $270,000 in FY 08. Sales incentives were down slightly to $44,800 per home for FY 09.

The financial services division provides mortgage financing, title insurance, closing services and insurance agency services for LEN homebuyers and others, and sells the loans it originates in the secondary mortgage market.

CORPORATE STRATEGY. Lennar greatly expanded its operations through the May 2000 purchase of U.S. Home Corp. (UH), and maintained an active acquisition program for several years. The company entered the North Carolina and South Carolina markets, and extended its positions in Colorado and Arizona, through the acquisition of various operations of Fortress Group in two separate transactions in late 2001 and mid-2002. It expanded its California business by acquiring Pacific Century Homes and Cambridge Homes (combined annual

deliveries of about 2,000 homes) in 2002.

In 2005, the company entered the metropolitan New York City and Boston markets by acquiring rights to develop a portfolio of properties in New Jersey facing mid-town Manhattan and waterfront properties near Boston. It also entered the Reno, NV, market through the acquisition of Barker Coleman. In addition, LEN expanded its presence in Jacksonville through the acquisition of Admiral Homes that same year.

The company had an order backlog value of $1.4 billion at the end of FY 07, which was 65% lower than the $3.98 billion a year earlier. Its backlog value was $456 million as of November 30, 2008, but rose to $545 million at May 31, 2009, and $647 million at August 31, 2009. The company ended FY 09 with a contract backlog value of $479 million, which rose to $656 million at May 31, 2010 and fell to $569 million at August 31, 2010 with the now expired tax credit easing demand.

Company Financials Fiscal Year Ended Nov. 30

Per Share Data ($)	2009	2008	2007	2006	2005	2004	2003	2002	2001	2000
Tangible Book Value	13.03	16.12	25.67	34.42	32.09	24.05	20.68	15.71	12.14	8.92
Cash Flow	-2.33	-6.69	-11.95	4.03	8.60	5.98	5.11	4.32	3.45	2.23
Earnings	-2.45	-7.00	-12.31	3.69	8.17	5.70	4.65	3.86	3.01	1.82
S&P Core Earnings	-2.45	-7.44	-12.36	3.62	8.10	5.63	4.61	3.83	2.90	NA
Dividends	0.16	0.52	0.64	0.64	0.57	0.39	0.14	0.03	0.03	0.03
Payout Ratio	NM	NM	NM	17%	7%	7%	3%	1%	1%	1%
Prices:High	17.66	22.73	56.54	66.44	68.86	57.20	50.90	31.99	24.94	19.69
Prices:Low	5.54	3.42	14.00	38.66	50.30	40.30	24.10	21.60	15.52	7.63
P/E Ratio:High	NM	NM	NM	18	8	10	11	8	8	11
P/E Ratio:Low	NM	NM	NM	10	6	7	5	6	5	4

Income Statement Analysis (Million $)										
Revenue	3,119	4,575	10,187	16,267	13,867	10,505	8,908	7,320	6,029	4,707
Operating Income	-66.8	-353	-2,626	941	2,124	1,426	1,158	1,094	868	533
Depreciation	19.9	49.8	57.0	56.5	79.6	55.6	54.5	72.4	68.7	58.5
Interest Expense	70.9	148	Nil	Nil	Nil	Nil	141	146	120	98.6
Pretax Income	-760	-566	-3,081	956	2,205	1,519	1,207	876	679	376
Effective Tax Rate	41.3%	NM	NM	36.5%	37.0%	37.8%	37.8%	37.8%	38.5%	39.0%
Net Income	-417	-1,109	-1,942	594	1,344	946	751	545	418	229
S&P Core Earnings	-417	-1,178	-1,948	582	1,331	934	744	541	404	NA

Balance Sheet & Other Financial Data (Million $)										
Cash	1,331	1,091	642	778	910	1,322	1,201	731	824	288
Current Assets	6,373	6,471	7,132	10,108	10,483	7,713	5,799	4,996	4,055	3,129
Total Assets	7,315	7,425	9,103	12,408	12,541	9,165	6,775	5,756	4,714	3,778
Current Liabilities	852	900	1,300	2,330	1,765	2,554	1,787	1,722	1,117	1,222
Long Term Debt	2,297	2,117	2,295	2,614	2,565	2,918	1,552	1,521	1,488	1,240
Common Equity	2,443	2,623	3,822	5,702	5,251	4,053	3,264	2,229	1,659	1,229
Total Capital	5,349	4,906	6,146	8,283	7,895	6,971	4,816	3,751	3,147	2,468
Capital Expenditures	NA	1.40	Nil	26.8	21.7	27.4	29.6	4.09	13.1	16.0
Cash Flow	-397	-1,059	-1,885	650	1,424	1,001	806	618	487	288
Current Ratio	7.5	7.2	5.5	4.3	5.9	3.0	3.3	2.9	3.6	2.5
% Long Term Debt of Capitalization	Nil	43.2	37.3	31.2	32.5	41.9	32.2	40.6	47.3	50.2
% Net Income of Revenue	NM	NM	NM	3.7	9.7	9.0	8.4	7.4	6.9	4.9
% Return on Assets	NA	NM	NM	4.8	12.4	11.9	12.0	10.4	9.8	7.9
% Return on Equity	NA	NM	NM	10.8	28.9	25.8	27.4	28.0	28.9	21.7

Data as orig reptd.; bef. results of disc opers/spec. items. Per share data adj. for stk. divs.; EPS diluted. E-Estimated. NA-Not Available. NM-Not Meaningful. NR-Not Ranked. UR-Under Review.

Office: 700 NW 107th Ave, Miami, FL 33172.
Telephone: 305-559-4000.
Website: http://www.lennar.com
Pres & CEO: S. Miller

COO: J.M. Jaffe
CFO: B.E. Gross
Chief Acctg Officer & Cntlr: D.M. Collins
Treas: D.J. Bessette

Investor Contact: M.H. Ames (800-741-4663)
Board Members: I. Bolotin, S. L. Gerard, T. I. Gilliam, S. W. Hudson, D. J. Kaiserman, R. K. Landon, S. Lapidus, S. Miller, D. E. Shalala, J. Sonnenfeld

Founded: 1954
Domicile: Delaware
Employees: 3,835

Leucadia National Corp

STANDARD &POOR'S

S&P Recommendation **HOLD** ★★★★☆	Price $25.10 (as of Oct 22, 2010)	12-Mo. Target Price $24.00	Investment Style Large-Cap Growth

GICS Sector Financials
Sub-Industry Multi-Sector Holdings

Summary This diversified holding company has subsidiaries engaged in manufacturing, real estate, medical product development, gaming entertainment, mining, and energy.

Key Stock Statistics (Source S&P, Vickers, company reports)

52-Wk Range	$28.37– 18.80	S&P Oper. EPS 2010E	2.00	Market Capitalization(B)	$6.107	Beta		1.72
Trailing 12-Month EPS	$0.97	S&P Oper. EPS 2011E	1.50	Yield (%)	Nil	S&P 3-Yr. Proj. EPS CAGR(%)		5
Trailing 12-Month P/E	25.9	P/E on S&P Oper. EPS 2010E	12.6	Dividend Rate/Share	Nil	S&P Credit Rating		BB+
$10K Invested 5 Yrs Ago	$12,455	Common Shares Outstg. (M)	243.3	Institutional Ownership (%)	61			

Price Performance

30-Week Mov. Avg. · · ·   10-Week Mov. Avg. – –   **GAAP Earnings vs. Previous Year**   Volume Above Avg. ▮▮▮ STARS
12-Mo. Target Price —   Relative Strength —   ▲ Up ▼ Down ▶ No Change   Below Avg. ▮▮▮ ★

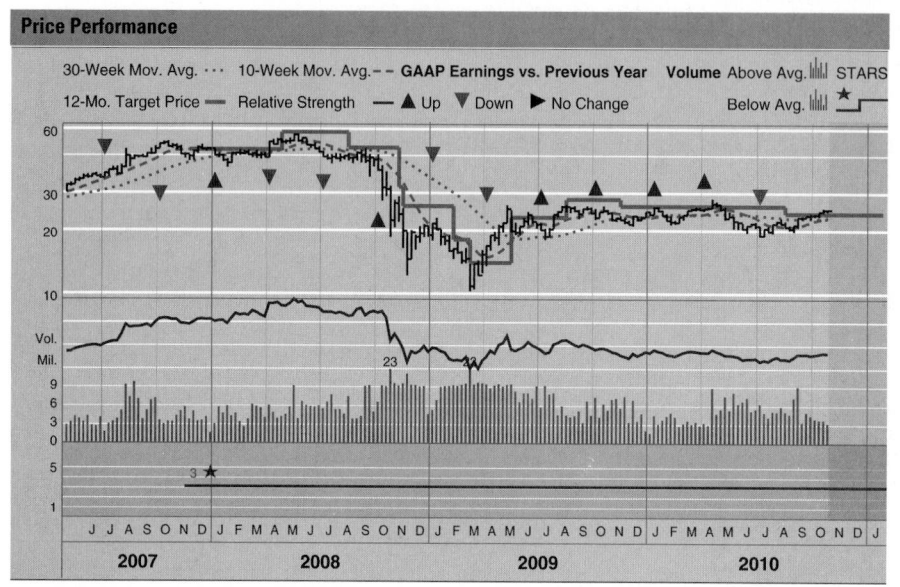

Options: ASE, CBOE, Ph

Analysis prepared by **Stuart J. Benway, CFA** on August 12, 2010, when the stock traded at **$ 21.23**.

Highlights

➤ We see revenues increasing about 30% in 2010. Sales are expected to benefit from a recovering economy, which should provide a modest boost to demand for plastics and timber. Significant interest income from an Australian mining investment is also expected to boost revenues. A weak housing market will likely hurt real estate development, and the telecommunications unit is also projected to see lower demand.

➤ Leucadia has scaled back its investments in financial entities and is working to conserve cash during this weak environment. We believe its investments in mining, auto finance and investment banking will continue to appreciate in 2010, although at a much slower pace than in 2009. Spending on medical product and energy project development should increase this year and next.

➤ Our forecast is for operating earnings of $2.00 a share in 2010, following $2.10 per share in 2009. We expect LUK to have a very uneven earnings pattern due to frequent changes in the number and types of businesses it operates, as well as changes in the value of its investments. For 2011, we project EPS of $1.50.

Investment Rationale/Risk

➤ Leucadia has a strong long-term record of increasing its book value, due, in our view, to its success in finding assets that are out of favor or are troubled, and therefore selling at a discount to their inherent value. However, this trend was disrupted in recent years due to the broad-based decline in equity markets. We expect gradual additional recovery in the company's investments in coming quarters, and LUK could accelerate acquisition activity.

➤ Risks to our recommendation and target price include reliance on the company's two top executives for most of its investment decisions, and the potential for further volatility in the value of the company's holdings due to the impact of economic uncertainty.

➤ Book value per share at Leucadia rose at a compound annual growth rate of 10.6% from 2000 through 2009, despite a sharp drop in 2008 due to the decline in the stock market. Our 12-month target price of $24 is calculated by applying a 1.30X multiple, below historical levels due to the uncertain investment environment, to our 2010 book value per share estimate of $18.65.

Qualitative Risk Assessment

LOW	**MEDIUM**	HIGH

Our risk assessment reflects the broad diversity of the company's investments and what we view as a strong management team, offset by exposure to certain development-stage businesses.

Quantitative Evaluations

S&P Quality Ranking   C

D	**C**	B-	B	B+	A-	A	A+

Relative Strength Rank   STRONG

75

LOWEST = 1   HIGHEST = 99

Revenue/Earnings Data

Revenue (Million $)

	1Q	2Q	3Q	4Q	Year
2010	374.4	412.5	--	--	--
2009	250.3	284.3	280.8	303.5	1,098
2008	324.9	337.6	251.6	166.6	1,081
2007	197.2	344.0	331.2	282.6	1,155
2006	291.6	224.4	170.2	176.4	862.7
2005	121.3	258.7	343.3	317.9	1,041

Earnings Per Share ($)

	1Q	2Q	3Q	4Q	Year
2010	0.78	-1.01	E1.25	E1.00	E2.00
2009	-0.59	1.67	1.40	-0.38	2.14
2008	-0.43	-0.76	0.37	-11.72	-11.19
2007	0.04	0.12	0.01	1.87	2.09
2006	0.37	0.17	0.02	0.03	0.60
2005	-0.03	5.23	0.22	-0.10	5.36

Fiscal year ended Dec. 31. Next earnings report expected: Early November. EPS Estimates based on S&P Operating Earnings; historical GAAP earnings are as reported.

Dividend Data

No cash dividends have been paid since 2007.

Please read the Required Disclosures and Analyst Certification on the last page of this report.

The **McGraw·Hill** Companies

Leucadia National Corp

STANDARD &POOR'S

Business Summary August 12, 2010

CORPORATE OVERVIEW. Leucadia is a diversified holding company engaged in a variety of businesses, including manufacturing, telecommunications, land-based contract oil and gas drilling, property management and services, gaming entertainment, real estate activities, medical product development, and winery operations. It also has significant investments in the common stock of two public companies that are accounted for at fair value, one of which is a full service investment bank and the other an independent auto finance company. Additionally, Leucadia owns equity interests in operating businesses and investment partnerships which are accounted for under the equity method of accounting, including a broker-dealer engaged in making markets and trading high-yield and special situation securities, an operating copper mine in Spain, a major iron ore project in Australia, and gasification projects in the United States. Revenues by major business segment in 2009 were as follows: telecommunications 38%; Idaho Timber 13%; Conwed Plastics 7%; property management and services 10%; and gaming 9%.

CORPORATE STRATEGY. Leucadia's approach to its investments is to focus on return on investment and cash flow to build long-term shareholder value. Additionally, the company continuously evaluates the retention and disposition

of its existing operations and investigates possible acquisitions of new businesses. In identifying possible acquisitions, Leucadia tends to seek assets and companies that are out of favor or troubled and, as a result, are selling substantially below the values it believes to be present. The worldwide recession, turmoil in public securities markets and lack of liquidity in the credit markets have put a strain on many businesses and caused great uncertainty about asset values in nearly all industry sectors. If these economic and market conditions continue for some time, Leucadia expects that some extraordinary investment opportunities will be available. The company has available liquidity on its balance sheet and could dispose of existing businesses or investments if additional internal liquidity is needed to take advantage of investment opportunities. We expect the composition of Leucadia's assets to change continuously as certain businesses are divested and others are acquired.

Company Financials Fiscal Year Ended Dec. 31

Per Share Data ($)	2009	2008	2007	2006	2005	2004	2003	2002	2001	2000
Tangible Book Value	17.62	10.87	24.66	17.72	16.87	17.32	10.04	8.78	7.05	7.26
Cash Flow	2.46	-10.91	2.26	0.75	6.11	1.71	0.81	1.02	0.49	0.82
Earnings	2.14	-11.19	2.09	0.60	5.36	0.70	0.46	0.91	0.39	0.69
S&P Core Earnings	2.07	-11.27	2.06	NA	4.69	0.05	0.42	1.05	0.27	NA
Dividends	Nil	Nil	0.25	0.25	0.13	0.13	0.08	0.08	0.08	0.08
Payout Ratio	Nil	Nil	12%	42%	2%	18%	18%	9%	21%	12%
Prices:High	26.47	56.90	52.67	32.62	24.64	23.50	15.40	13.42	11.90	12.50
Prices:Low	10.26	12.19	26.52	23.26	16.20	15.02	10.86	9.21	8.77	6.88
P/E Ratio:High	12	NM	25	54	5	34	34	15	31	18
P/E Ratio:Low	5	NM	13	39	3	21	24	10	22	10

Income Statement Analysis (Million $)										
Revenue	1,098	1,081	1,155	863	1,041	2,262	556	242	375	715
Operating Income	-46.3	-156	58.1	222	396	366	75.2	10.7	151	243
Depreciation	86.4	65.4	49.8	43.6	190	233	65.7	18.7	17.5	21.4
Interest Expense	129	145	112	79.4	68.4	96.8	43.6	33.5	55.2	57.7
Pretax Income	529	-906	-79.0	172	93.0	132	42.9	13.2	53.7	193
Effective Tax Rate	1.35%	NM	708.9%	24.4%	NM	NM	NM	NM	NM	37.6%
Net Income	524	-2,579	481	130	1,224	152	84.4	153	64.8	115
S&P Core Earnings	504	-2,598	473	-9.43	1,071	5.47	77.7	177	45.7	NA

Balance Sheet & Other Financial Data (Million $)										
Cash	239	604	1,440	3,430	3,063	2,781	2,033	1,044	1,183	1,613
Current Assets	551	867	1,720	1,366	2,229	2,060	1,350	1,002	1,263	1,775
Total Assets	6,762	5,198	8,127	5,304	5,261	4,800	4,397	2,542	2,577	3,144
Current Liabilities	625	563	460	327	474	659	657	119	227	391
Long Term Debt	1,660	1,833	2,004	975	987	1,484	1,155	328	424	412
Common Equity	4,362	2,677	5,570	3,893	3,662	2,259	2,134	1,487	1,195	1,204
Total Capital	6,347	4,777	7,596	4,887	4,665	3,760	3,307	1,893	1,666	1,631
Capital Expenditures	23.6	76.1	135	111	136	97.4	84.7	NA	NA	NA
Cash Flow	610	-2,514	531	173	1,414	385	150	171	82.3	136
Current Ratio	0.9	1.5	3.7	4.2	4.7	3.1	2.1	8.4	5.6	4.5
% Long Term Debt of Capitalization	Nil	38.4	26.4	19.9	20.8	38.8	34.7	17.5	25.7	24.4
% Net Income of Revenue	47.7	NM	41.6	15.7	117.6	6.8	15.2	63.1	16.2	16.8
% Return on Assets	NA	NM	77.2	2.5	24.3	3.3	2.4	6.0	2.3	3.7
% Return on Equity	NA	NM	10.2	3.4	41.4	6.9	4.7	11.4	5.4	9.9

Data as orig reptd.; bef. results of disc opers/spec. items. Per share data adj. for stk. divs.; EPS diluted. E-Estimated. NA-Not Available. NM-Not Meaningful. NR-Not Ranked. UR-Under Review.

Office: 315 Park Ave S, New York, NY 10010.
Telephone: 212-460-1900.
Chrmn: I.M. Cumming
Pres & CEO: J.S. Steinberg

CFO: J.A. Orlando
Chief Acctg Officer & Cntlr: B.L. Lowenthal
Treas: R.J. Nittoli
Investor Contact: L.E. Ulbrandt (212-460-1900)

Board Members: I. M. Cumming, P. M. Dougan, A. J. Hirschfield, J. E. Jordan, J. C. Keil, J. C. Nichols, III, M. Sorkin, J. S. Steinberg
Founded: 1854
Domicile: New York
Employees: 3,340

Lexmark International Inc.

STANDARD &POOR'S

| **S&P Recommendation** BUY ★★★★☆ | **Price** $46.92 (as of Oct 22, 2010) | **12-Mo. Target Price** $48.00 | **Investment Style** Large-Cap Growth |

GICS Sector Information Technology
Sub-Industry Computer Storage & Peripherals

Summary Lexmark develops, manufactures and supplies laser and inkjet printers and associated consumable supplies for the office and home markets.

Key Stock Statistics (Source S&P, Vickers, company reports)

52-Wk Range	$47.35– 24.46	S&P Oper. EPS 2010**E**	4.65	Market Capitalization(B)	$3.684	Beta	1.11
Trailing 12-Month EPS	$3.17	S&P Oper. EPS 2011**E**	5.00	Yield (%)	Nil	S&P 3-Yr. Proj. EPS CAGR(%)	19
Trailing 12-Month P/E	14.8	P/E on S&P Oper. EPS 2010**E**	10.1	Dividend Rate/Share	Nil	S&P Credit Rating	NA
$10K Invested 5 Yrs Ago	$11,069	Common Shares Outstg. (M)	78.5	Institutional Ownership (%)	NM		

Price Performance

30-Week Mov. Avg. · · · 10-Week Mov. Avg. – – **GAAP Earnings vs. Previous Year** Volume Above Avg. STARS
12-Mo. Target Price — Relative Strength — ▲ Up ▼ Down ▶ No Change Below Avg.

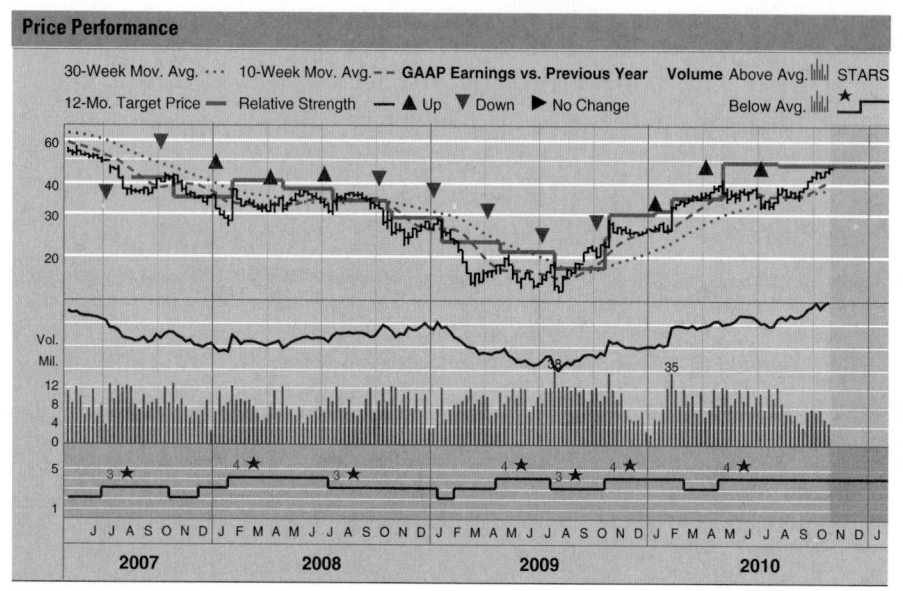

Options: ASE, CBOE, P, Ph

Analysis prepared by **Thomas W. Smith, CFA** on August 16, 2010, when the stock traded at **$ 36.33**.

Highlights

▶ We expect revenues to increase 9% in 2010 and 4% in 2011, following a 14% decline in 2009, as we project improvement in global economic conditions and a cyclical upturn for the printer industry. We see new products aiding sales in the context of very competitive printer markets.

▶ We look for operating margins to widen in 2010, based on higher volumes, a better product mix, and the benefits of ongoing restructuring plans. During the second quarter of 2010, the company closed its acquisition of Kansas-based Perceptive Software for about $280 million in cash, which adds expertise in enterprise content management software and should expand offerings of document workflow solutions aimed at particular industries, such as healthcare, education and government.

▶ We expect modest effective tax rates, reflecting shifts in the siting of operations, to aid results. We estimate operating EPS, excluding restructuring charges, of $4.65 for 2010 and $5.00 for 2011. We expect few share buybacks until the printer industry is operating on a robust level.

Investment Rationale/Risk

▶ We view LXK as attractively valued in light of new product introductions and potential cost reductions that could help earnings as a recovery in printer industry demand unfolds following a deep downturn in 2009. We think that LXK owns some important intellectual property, and should be able to expand its branded products and laser printer businesses as the economy picks up.

▶ Risks to our recommendation and target price include the possibility that competition from Hewlett-Packard (HPQ 40, Buy) and other rivals will be more than we anticipate, that savings from restructuring will come in below our estimates, and that penetration of high-growth segments will be slower than we project.

▶ Our 12-month target price of $48 is based on our P/E analysis. We apply a target multiple of 11X, which is toward the low end of a historical range for LXK to reflect the slow revenue environment we foresee, to our 12-month forward operating EPS estimate of $4.39.

Qualitative Risk Assessment

| LOW | **MEDIUM** | HIGH |

Our risk assessment reflects what we see as a difficult competitive pricing environment in the printer market, offset by our view of LXK's strides in improving its product portfolio and cost position.

Quantitative Evaluations

S&P Quality Ranking B

| D | C | B- | **B** | B+ | A- | A | A+ |

Relative Strength Rank STRONG

89

LOWEST = 1   HIGHEST = 99

Revenue/Earnings Data

Revenue (Million $)

	1Q	2Q	3Q	4Q	Year
2010	1,043	1,033	--	--	--
2009	944.1	904.6	958.0	1,073	3,880
2008	1,175	1,139	1,131	1,084	4,528
2007	1,261	1,208	1,195	1,310	4,974
2006	1,275	1,229	1,235	1,369	5,108
2005	1,358	1,283	1,216	1,365	5,222

Earnings Per Share ($)

	1Q	2Q	3Q	4Q	Year
2010	1.21	1.07	E0.98	E1.08	E4.65
2009	0.75	0.22	0.13	0.76	1.86
2008	1.07	0.89	0.42	0.23	2.69
2007	0.95	0.67	0.48	1.04	3.14
2006	0.78	0.74	0.85	0.91	3.27
2005	0.96	0.64	0.59	0.71	2.91

Fiscal year ended Dec. 31. Next earnings report expected: NA. EPS Estimates based on S&P Operating Earnings; historical GAAP earnings are as reported.

Dividend Data

No cash dividends have been paid.

Please read the Required Disclosures and Analyst Certification on the last page of this report.

The McGraw-Hill Companies

Lexmark International Inc.

STANDARD &POOR'S

Business Summary August 16, 2010

CORPORATE OVERVIEW. Lexmark shook up the printer industry with the introduction of the first desktop color printer priced under $100 with its November 1997 launch of the $99 color inkjet printer, aimed at building brand awareness and an installed base. We think LXK's competitive advantage in the past was its low cost structure and its ability to price aggressively. However, in recent years, it has been on the defensive, in our view, as peers have undercut its prices and LXK's product mix was not focused on some of the more compelling printer areas. Going forward, LXK management believes that its commitment to R&D should bear fruit and help revive unit growth and subsequently high-margin supplies sales, but we view this as a multi-year process. Starting in autumn 2008, the company began to introduce an extensive series of new laser products. Following through in 2009, some 33 new product models were introduced.

The company operates mainly in two segments -- the Printing Solutions and Services division (PSSD) and the Imaging Solutions division (ISD). Printing Solutions and Services offers mainly laser products and represented 68% of sales in 2009 (66% of 2008 sales). PSSD saw a revenue decline of 12% in 2009 compared to a decline of just 1% in 2008. Laser printer hardware unit ship-

ments decreased 21% in 2009, following a 7% decrease in 2008.

Imaging Solutions offers mainly inkjet products and represented 32% of 2009 sales (34% of 2008 sales). ISD suffered a 19% revenue decline, compared to a 22% decrease in 2008. Inkjet hardware unit shipments fell 37% in 2009 and 45% in 2008, partly because of a planned transition to a more favorable printer product mix that could potentially boost usage of associated consumable products.

Lexmark distributes to business customers via many channels, including the company's network of authorized distributors. The company distributes to consumers through retail outlets worldwide. The company also sells through alliances and OEM arrangements. One customer, Dell, accounted for 13% of revenues in 2009, the same as in 2008, and down from 14% in 2007.

Company Financials Fiscal Year Ended Dec. 31

Per Share Data ($)	2009	2008	2007	2006	2005	2004	2003	2002	2001	2000
Tangible Book Value	12.98	10.45	15.76	10.67	12.77	NM	17.46	NM	8.25	6.11
Cash Flow	4.58	4.97	5.13	5.21	4.21	5.29	4.48	3.84	2.98	2.80
Earnings	1.86	2.69	3.14	3.27	2.91	4.28	3.34	2.79	2.05	2.13
S&P Core Earnings	2.00	2.44	3.10	3.28	2.52	3.94	3.04	2.27	1.57	NA
Dividends	Nil	Nil	Nil	Nil	Nil	Nil	Nil	Nil	Nil	Nil
Payout Ratio	Nil	Nil	Nil	Nil	Nil	Nil	Nil	Nil	Nil	Nil
Prices:High	29.16	37.88	73.20	74.68	86.62	97.50	79.65	69.50	70.75	135.88
Prices:Low	14.23	22.13	32.35	44.09	39.33	76.00	56.57	41.94	40.81	28.75
P/E Ratio:High	16	14	23	23	30	23	24	25	35	64
P/E Ratio:Low	8	8	10	13	14	18	17	15	20	13

Income Statement Analysis (Million $)										
Revenue	3,880	4,528	4,974	5,108	5,222	5,314	4,755	4,356	4,143	3,807
Operating Income	573	573	564	715	692	867	743	643	525	548
Depreciation	214	203	191	201	159	135	149	138	126	91.2
Interest Expense	39.3	28.9	13.0	12.1	11.2	12.3	12.5	9.00	14.8	12.8
Pretax Income	187	276	350	459	554	746	594	496	318	396
Effective Tax Rate	22.0%	12.9%	13.9%	26.3%	35.7%	23.8%	26.0%	26.0%	13.9%	28.0%
Net Income	146	240	301	338	356	569	439	367	274	285
S&P Core Earnings	157	218	297	340	308	524	399	298	210	NA

Balance Sheet & Other Financial Data (Million $)										
Cash	1,133	973	796	551	889	1,567	1,196	498	90.7	68.5
Current Assets	2,141	2,063	2,067	1,830	2,170	3,001	2,444	1,799	1,493	1,244
Total Assets	3,354	3,265	3,121	2,849	3,330	4,124	3,450	2,808	2,450	2,073
Current Liabilities	1,192	1,258	1,497	1,324	1,234	1,468	1,183	1,099	931	979
Long Term Debt	649	649	Nil	150	150	150	149	149	149	149
Common Equity	1,014	812	1,278	1,035	1,429	2,083	1,643	1,082	1,076	777
Total Capital	1,663	1,461	1,278	1,185	1,578	2,232	1,792	1,231	1,225	926
Capital Expenditures	242	218	183	200	201	198	93.8	112	214	297
Cash Flow	360	443	492	539	515	704	588	505	399	377
Current Ratio	1.8	1.6	1.4	1.4	1.8	2.0	2.1	1.6	1.6	1.3
% Long Term Debt of Capitalization	39.0	44.4	Nil	12.6	9.5	6.7	8.3	12.1	12.2	16.1
% Net Income of Revenue	3.8	5.3	6.1	6.6	6.8	10.7	9.2	8.4	6.6	7.5
% Return on Assets	4.4	7.5	10.1	11.0	9.6	15.0	14.0	13.9	12.1	15.1
% Return on Equity	16.0	23.0	26.0	27.5	20.3	30.5	32.2	34.0	29.5	39.7

Data as orig reptd.; bef. results of disc opers/spec. items. Per share data adj. for stk. divs.; EPS diluted. E-Estimated. NA-Not Available. NM-Not Meaningful. NR-Not Ranked. UR-Under Review.

Office: 740 West New Circle Rd, Lexington, KY 40550.
Telephone: 859-232-2000.
Website: http://www.lexmark.com
Chrmn & CEO: P.J. Curlander

EVP, CFO & Chief Acctg Officer: J.W. Gamble, Jr.
Treas: B. Frost
Secy & General Counsel: R.J. Patton
Investor Contact: J. Morgan (859-232-5568)

Board Members: T. Beck, J. L. Cohon, J. E. Coleman, P. J. Curlander, W. R. Fields, R. E. Gomory, S. R. Hardis, R. Holland, Jr., M. J. Maples, J. L. Montupet, K. P. Seifert

Founded: 1990
Domicile: Delaware
Employees: 11,900

The McGraw-Hill Companies

Life Technologies Corp

STANDARD &POOR'S

S&P Recommendation **STRONG BUY** ★★★★★	Price $47.15 (as of Oct 22, 2010)	12-Mo. Target Price $68.00	Investment Style Large-Cap Growth

GICS Sector Health Care
Sub-Industry Life Sciences Tools & Services

Summary This company develops and manufactures research products and instruments for biotechnology and biopharmaceutical researchers.

Key Stock Statistics (Source S&P, Vickers, company reports)

52-Wk Range	$56.19– 41.10	S&P Oper. EPS 2010**E**	3.45	Market Capitalization(B)	$8.644	Beta	0.75
Trailing 12-Month EPS	$1.56	S&P Oper. EPS 2011**E**	3.92	Yield (%)	Nil	S&P 3-Yr. Proj. EPS CAGR(%)	14
Trailing 12-Month P/E	30.2	P/E on S&P Oper. EPS 2010**E**	13.7	Dividend Rate/Share	Nil	S&P Credit Rating	BBB-
$10K Invested 5 Yrs Ago	$13,310	Common Shares Outstg. (M)	183.3	Institutional Ownership (%)	96		

Price Performance

30-Week Mov. Avg. · · · · 10-Week Mov. Avg. - - - GAAP Earnings vs. Previous Year   Volume Above Avg. STARS
12-Mo. Target Price — Relative Strength   ▲ Up   ▼ Down   ► No Change   Below Avg.

Options: ASE, CBOE, P, Ph

Analysis prepared by **Jeffrey Loo, CFA** on August 11, 2010, when the stock traded at **$ 43.47**.

Highlights

➤ We expect sales, with a 1% adverse foreign exchange impact, to rise 9% in 2010 to $3.58 billion, and 8% in 2011 to $3.88 billion. For 2010, we look for organic sales in molecular diagnostics, driven by robust demand for genomic assays, to increase 11%; genetic systems, aided by strong sales of its SOLiD system and next-generation sequencing, to grow 6%; and Cell System sales on robust primary stem cell sales, to rise 9%. We see a rise in gross margins of 140 basis points (bps) and a 260 bps improvement in operating margins from cost savings synergies and leverage. Further, increased usage of LIFE's eCommerce platform, which currently processes 52% of transactions, should boost margins.

➤ In February, LIFE completed the sale of its ownership stake in its mass spectrometry unit, to Danaher Corporation (DHR 38, Buy), for $450 million. This unit was a joint venture with MDS Inc., with sales and income accounted for under the equity method, and provided $46 million in income in 2009. LIFE used the sales proceeds to pay down debt.

➤ We see EPS of $3.45 in 2010 and $3.92 in 2011.

Investment Rationale/Risk

➤ We think the shares, recently trading at 13.0X our 2010 EPS forecast and at a 0.93X P/E-to-growth ratio, well below historical levels, are undervalued. We believe LIFE is well positioned within its end-markets with a solid platform for expansion in high-growth markets within genomics, proteomics, and cell biology. We see continued robust growth for its next-generation sequencer, the SOLiD system, and expect it to help drive consumable sales in 2010 and 2011. We think the recently introduced SOLiD 4 with a higher throughput and lower price will gain market share and we believe the market is expanding, leading to further opportunities. LIFE also expects to release an upgrade in the second half that should further increase throughput and lower prices, in our view.

➤ Risks to our recommendation and target price include a slowdown in pharmaceutical and biotech R&D spending.

➤ Our 12-month target price of $68 is based on a 1.4X P/E-to-growth ratio, in line with peers, based on our 2010 EPS estimate and a projected growth rate of 14%.

Qualitative Risk Assessment

LOW	MEDIUM	HIGH

Our risk assessment reflects LIFE's diverse product portfolio and broad geographic client base. The life sciences industry is highly competitive, and companies need to develop new innovative products to remain viable, as technology is rapidly changing. Although life sciences is LIFE's main market, the company also sells products to the environmental, food safety, and industrial markets.

Quantitative Evaluations

S&P Quality Ranking B-

D	C	B-	B	B+	A-	A	A+

Relative Strength Rank MODERATE

39

LOWEST = 1   HIGHEST = 99

Revenue/Earnings Data

Revenue (Million $)

	1Q	2Q	3Q	4Q	Year
2010	884.9	903.7	--	--	--
2009	775.7	832.8	800.7	871.1	3,280
2008	350.2	367.8	361.4	540.6	1,620
2007	308.7	321.7	315.0	336.5	1,282
2006	309.0	313.6	311.0	329.8	1,263
2005	277.1	306.5	289.6	325.3	1,198

Earnings Per Share ($)

2010	0.48	0.58	E0.78	E0.89	E3.45
2009	0.09	0.22	0.22	0.26	0.80
2008	0.60	0.55	0.26	-0.89	0.29
2007	0.31	0.31	0.32	0.41	1.35
2006	0.18	0.18	-1.27	-1.04	-1.86
2005	0.41	0.11	0.21	0.44	1.17

Fiscal year ended Dec. 31. Next earnings report expected: Late October. EPS Estimates based on S&P Operating Earnings; historical GAAP earnings are as reported.

Dividend Data

No cash dividends have been paid.

Life Technologies Corp

Business Summary August 11, 2010

CORPORATE OVERVIEW. Life Technologies Inc. (LIFE) was formed through Invitrogen Corporation's (IVGN) $5.1 billion acquisition of Applied Biosystems Inc. (ABI) in November 2008. Prior to the transaction, IVGN had annual sales of about $1.3 billion and ABI had annual sales of about $2.2 billion. IVGN develops, manufactures and markets a broad line of tool kits and reagents, and provides other products and services, including informatics software and contract research services, used in life sciences research and the commercial manufacture of biopharmaceutical products. IVGN's revenue consisted of about 99% consumables and services and 1% instrument reagent systems. ABI develops and manufactures instrument-based systems, consumables and reagents, and software and related services for the life sciences industry, as well as for the food safety, environmental and other industrial end-markets. ABI's revenue consisted of 19% Mass Spectrometry instrument sales, 21% Instrument Reagent Systems, and 60% Consumable and Services. LIFE is now one of the largest companies within the life sciences industry based on annual revenue. LIFE's 2009 revenue breakdown was 48% molecular biology systems, 24% genetic systems, and 28% cell systems. In February 2010, LIFE sold its ownership stake in its mass spectrometry unit, to Danaher Corporation for $450 million. This unit was a joint venture with MDS Inc., with sales and income accounted for under the equity method, and provided $46 million in income in 2009.

LIFE has an extensive product portfolio offering end-to-end workflow solutions. Products primarily from IVGN's portfolio are used for sample preparation and sample processing, while ABI's instrumentation is used for detection and analysis and data interpretation. IVGN has two main units -- BioDiscovery and Cell Culture Systems. The BioDiscovery segment serves governmental and academic laboratories as well as biotechnology and pharmaceutical firms engaged in research of biological and genetic substances. The Cell Culture Systems segment primarily serves companies that are engaged in the commercialization of such substances; these concerns typically require large amounts of biologic or genetic materials or the growth media used in their manufacture. The company produces cell culture products under the GIBCO brand. These products include a variety of sera, culture media and reagents. Some of these substances are used in the manufacture of genetically engineered products, and are produced in large-scale commercial production facilities.

Company Financials Fiscal Year Ended Dec. 31

Per Share Data ($)	2009	2008	2007	2006	2005	2004	2003	2002	2001	2000
Tangible Book Value	NM	NM	NM	NM	NM	0.47	3.49	5.31	4.62	2.94
Cash Flow	3.07	1.57	2.74	-0.28	2.44	1.95	1.66	1.28	1.33	0.62
Earnings	0.80	0.29	1.35	-1.86	1.17	0.82	0.58	0.45	-1.41	-0.90
S&P Core Earnings	0.83	0.26	1.35	0.70	0.86	0.49	0.27	0.15	-1.75	NA
Dividends	Nil	Nil	Nil	Nil	Nil	Nil	Nil	Nil	Nil	Nil
Payout Ratio	Nil	Nil	Nil	Nil	Nil	Nil	Nil	Nil	Nil	Nil
Prices:High	52.97	49.00	49.58	38.33	44.25	41.00	35.47	31.35	42.97	49.75
Prices:Low	22.76	19.56	27.96	27.35	30.07	23.10	14.02	12.62	19.25	18.00
P/E Ratio:High	66	NM	37	NM	38	50	61	70	NM	NM
P/E Ratio:Low	28	NM	21	NM	26	28	24	28	NM	NM

Income Statement Analysis (Million $)	2009	2008	2007	2006	2005	2004	2003	2002	2001	2000
Revenue	3,280	1,620	1,282	1,263	1,198	1,024	778	649	629	246
Operating Income	975	431	320	286	305	284	203	172	148	35.0
Depreciation	398	133	136	162	160	147	111	87.7	287	91.8
Interest Expense	193	43.0	28.0	32.4	34.2	32.2	28.6	24.1	11.3	8.94
Pretax Income	195	154	179	-163	174	121	85.1	71.2	-137	-54.5
Effective Tax Rate	25.7%	80.6%	27.1%	NM	24.0%	26.8%	28.6%	31.2%	NM	NM
Net Income	145	30.0	130	-191	132	88.8	60.1	47.7	-148	-54.3
S&P Core Earnings	151	27.0	131	71.4	94.7	52.8	28.1	15.4	-183	NA

Balance Sheet & Other Financial Data (Million $)	2009	2008	2007	2006	2005	2004	2003	2002	2001	2000
Cash	607	336	671	367	435	198	589	547	995	431
Current Assets	1,796	1,612	1,090	798	1,151	1,332	1,287	968	1,204	672
Total Assets	9,116	8,914	3,330	3,183	3,877	3,614	3,166	2,615	2,667	2,369
Current Liabilities	1,386	1,007	234	248	512	196	126	141	127	153
Long Term Debt	2,620	3,504	1,151	1,152	1,152	1,300	1,055	672	676	179
Common Equity	4,027	3,400	1,765	1,630	2,042	1,913	1,807	1,643	1,683	1,778
Total Capital	7,128	7,542	3,019	2,883	3,335	3,367	3,023	2,427	2,525	2,194
Capital Expenditures	181	81.9	78.3	61.1	71.8	39.1	32.2	51.5	44.2	22.7
Cash Flow	556	163	266	-29.3	292	236	171	135	139	37.5
Current Ratio	1.3	1.6	4.7	3.2	2.3	6.8	10.2	6.9	9.5	4.4
% Long Term Debt of Capitalization	36.8	46.5	38.1	40.0	34.5	38.6	34.9	27.7	26.8	8.2
% Net Income of Revenue	4.4	1.9	10.2	NM	11.0	8.7	7.7	7.3	NM	NM
% Return on Assets	1.6	0.5	4.0	NM	3.5	2.6	2.1	1.8	NM	NM
% Return on Equity	3.9	1.2	7.7	NM	6.7	4.8	3.5	2.9	NM	NM

Data as orig reptd.; bef. results of disc opers/spec. items. Per share data adj. for stk. divs.; EPS diluted. E-Estimated. NA-Not Available. NM-Not Meaningful. NR-Not Ranked. UR-Under Review.

Office: 5791 Van Allen Way, Carlsbad, CA 92008-7321.
Telephone: 760-603-7200.
Website: http://www.lifetechnologies.com
Chrmn & CEO: G.T. Lucier

Pres & COO: M.P. Stevenson
CFO: D.F. Hoffmeister
CSO: B. Pollok
Chief Acctg Officer: K.A. Richard

Investor Contact: A. Clardy (760-603-7200)
Board Members: G. F. Adam, Jr., R. V. Dittamore, D. W. Grimm, B. S. Iyer, A. J. Levine, W. H. Longfield, B. G. Lorimier, G. T. Lucier, R. A. Matricaria, P. A. Peterson, W. A. Reynolds, D. C. U'Prichard

Founded: 1987
Domicile: Delaware
Employees: 9,000

STANDARD &POOR'S

Eli Lilly and Co

S&P Recommendation	HOLD ★★★☆☆	Price $35.40 (as of Oct 22, 2010)	12-Mo. Target Price $38.00	Investment Style Large-Cap Blend

GICS Sector Health Care
Sub-Industry Pharmaceuticals

Summary This leading producer of prescription drugs offers a wide range of treatments for neurological disorders, diabetes, cancer, and other conditions. The company also sells animal health products.

Key Stock Statistics (Source S&P, Vickers, company reports)

52-Wk Range	$38.08–32.02	S&P Oper. EPS 2010E	4.68	Market Capitalization(B)	$39.074	Beta	0.79
Trailing 12-Month EPS	$4.04	S&P Oper. EPS 2011E	4.45	Yield (%)	5.54	S&P 3-Yr. Proj. EPS CAGR(%)	0
Trailing 12-Month P/E	8.8	P/E on S&P Oper. EPS 2010E	7.6	Dividend Rate/Share	$1.96	S&P Credit Rating	AA-
$10K Invested 5 Yrs Ago	$8,598	Common Shares Outstg. (M)	1,103.8	Institutional Ownership (%)	79		

Price Performance

30-Week Mov. Avg. · · · · 10-Week Mov. Avg. – – GAAP Earnings vs. Previous Year Volume Above Avg. STARS
12-Mo. Target Price — Relative Strength ▲ Up ▼ Down ▶ No Change Below Avg. ★

Options: ASE, CBOE, P, Ph

Highlights

► The 12-month target price for LLY has recently been changed to $38.00 from $40.00. The Highlights section of this Stock Report will be updated accordingly.

Investment Rationale/Risk

► The Investment Rationale/Risk section of this Stock Report will be updated shortly. For the latest News story on LLY from MarketScope, see below.

► 10/21/10 10:42 am ET ... S&P REITERATES HOLD OPINION ON SHARES OF ELI LILLY (LLY 35.6***): Q3 non-GAAP EPS rose 1%, to $1.21, $0.09 above our est (largely on aggressive cost cutting). Sales rose 2%. Despite recent negative R&D news on Bydureon and teplizumab diabetes drugs, and impending patent losses, we still see positives to the LLY story, with 10 promising compounds in Phase 3 or registration, and strong sales growth projected for Japan and emerging markets. We also view LLY as a possible merger candidate. However, we are reducing our target price by $2 to $38, based on revised forward P/E and DCF assumptions. The dividend yields 5.5%. /H.Saftlas

Qualitative Risk Assessment

LOW	MEDIUM	HIGH

Our risk assessment reflects generic challenges to the company's branded patents, and drug development and regulatory risks. This is offset by our view of LLY's diverse drug portfolio, limited patent expiration exposure, and robust pipeline.

Quantitative Evaluations

S&P Quality Ranking B

D	C	B-	B	B+	A-	A	A+

Relative Strength Rank WEAK

26

LOWEST = 1   HIGHEST = 99

Revenue/Earnings Data

Revenue (Million $)

	1Q	2Q	3Q	4Q	Year
2010	5,486	5,749	--	--	--
2009	5,047	5,293	5,562	5,934	21,836
2008	4,808	5,150	5,210	5,211	20,378
2007	4,226	4,631	4,587	5,190	18,634
2006	3,715	3,867	3,864	4,245	15,691
2005	3,497	3,668	3,601	3,879	14,645

Earnings Per Share ($)

	1Q	2Q	3Q	4Q	Year
2010	1.13	1.22	E1.12	E1.05	E4.68
2009	1.20	1.06	0.86	0.83	3.94
2008	0.97	0.88	-0.43	-3.31	-1.89
2007	0.47	0.61	0.85	0.78	2.71
2006	0.77	0.76	0.80	0.12	2.45
2005	0.68	-0.23	0.73	0.66	1.83

Fiscal year ended Dec. 31. Next earnings report expected: NA. EPS Estimates based on S&P Operating Earnings; historical GAAP earnings are as reported.

Dividend Data (Dates: mm/dd Payment Date: mm/dd/yy)

Amount ($)	Date Decl.	Ex-Div. Date	Stk. of Record	Payment Date
0.490	12/14	02/10	02/12	03/10/10
0.490	04/19	05/12	05/14	06/10/10
0.490	06/21	08/11	08/13	09/10/10
0.490	10/18	11/10	11/15	12/10/10

Dividends have been paid since 1885. Source: Company reports.

Please read the Required Disclosures and Analyst Certification on the last page of this report.

The McGraw-Hill Companies

Eli Lilly and Co

STANDARD &POOR'S

Business Summary August 04, 2010

CORPORATE OVERVIEW. Eli Lilly and Co. is a leading maker of prescription drugs, offering a wide range of treatments for neurological disorders, diabetes, cancer, and other conditions. Animal health products are also sold. Foreign sales accounted for about 44% of total revenues in 2009.

LLY's largest selling drug is Zyprexa, a treatment for schizophrenia and bipolar disorder that offers clinical advantages over older antipsychotic drugs. Sales of Zyprexa totaled $4.9 billion in 2009, up from $4.7 billion in 2008. LLY also offers Symbyax, a combination of Zyprexa and Prozac, to treat bipolar depression.

In August 2004, the company launched Cymbalta, a potent antidepressant. Cymbalta works on two body chemicals involved in depression -- serotonin and norepinephrine -- while most conventional antidepressants affect only serotonin. Sales of Cymbalta climbed to $3.1 billion in 2009, from $2.7 billion in 2008, reflecting greater market penetration and expanded indications.

Endocrinology products (sales of $5.7 billion in 2009) include Humulin, a human insulin produced through recombinant DNA technology; Humalog, a

rapid-acting injectable human insulin analog; Iletin, an animal-source insulin; Actos, an oral agent for Type 2 diabetes that is manufactured by Takeda Chemical Industries of Japan and co-marketed by Lilly and Takeda; and Byetta, a treatment for Type 2 diabetes. Lilly shares in the profits from Byetta with Amylin Pharmaceuticals, co-developer of the drug. This group also includes Evista ($1.0 billion) and Forteo ($817 million) treatments for osteoporosis; and Humatrope, a recombinant human growth hormone.

Other important drugs are Gemzar, a treatment for lung cancer and pancreatic cancer (sales of $1.4 billion); Cialis, a treatment for erectile dysfunction ($1.6 billion); and Alimta, a treatment for lung cancer ($1.7 billion).

Animal health products ($1.2 billion) include cattle feed additives, antibiotics and related items.

Company Financials Fiscal Year Ended Dec. 31

Per Share Data ($)	2009	2008	2007	2006	2005	2004	2003	2002	2001	2000
Tangible Book Value	5.30	2.45	10.64	9.70	9.55	9.51	8.69	7.37	6.32	5.37
Cash Flow	5.12	-1.05	3.49	3.06	2.41	2.21	2.87	2.85	2.91	3.18
Earnings	3.94	-1.89	2.71	2.45	1.83	1.66	2.37	2.50	2.58	2.79
S&P Core Earnings	4.03	-1.38	2.78	2.90	1.85	1.42	2.09	1.96	2.17	NA
Dividends	1.96	1.88	1.70	1.60	1.52	1.42	1.34	1.24	1.12	1.04
Payout Ratio	50%	NM	63%	65%	83%	86%	57%	50%	43%	37%
Prices:High	40.78	57.52	61.00	59.24	60.98	76.95	73.89	81.09	95.00	109.00
Prices:Low	27.21	28.62	49.09	50.19	49.47	50.34	52.77	43.75	70.01	54.00
P/E Ratio:High	10	NM	23	24	33	46	31	32	37	39
P/E Ratio:Low	7	NM	18	20	27	30	22	17	27	19

Income Statement Analysis (Million $)	2009	2008	2007	2006	2005	2004	2003	2002	2001	2000
Revenue	21,836	20,378	18,634	15,691	14,645	13,858	12,583	11,078	11,543	10,862
Operating Income	7,668	6,525	5,658	4,927	4,375	4,256	4,050	3,821	4,185	3,996
Depreciation	1,298	925	855	802	726	598	548	493	455	436
Interest Expense	261	277	324	Nil	105	274	61.0	79.7	147	182
Pretax Income	5,358	-1,308	3,877	3,418	2,718	2,942	3,262	3,458	3,552	3,859
Effective Tax Rate	19.2%	NM	23.8%	22.1%	26.3%	38.5%	21.5%	21.7%	20.9%	20.8%
Net Income	4,329	-2,072	2,953	2,663	2,002	1,810	2,561	2,708	2,809	3,058
S&P Core Earnings	4,421	-1,523	3,028	3,153	2,016	1,558	2,261	2,128	2,359	NA

Balance Sheet & Other Financial Data (Million $)	2009	2008	2007	2006	2005	2004	2003	2002	2001	2000
Cash	4,498	5,926	4,831	3,109	3,007	5,365	2,756	1,946	2,702	4,115
Current Assets	12,487	12,453	12,257	9,694	10,796	12,836	8,759	7,804	6,939	7,943
Total Assets	27,461	29,213	26,788	21,955	24,581	24,867	21,678	19,042	16,434	14,691
Current Liabilities	6,568	13,110	5,268	5,086	5,716	7,594	5,551	5,064	5,203	4,961
Long Term Debt	6,609	4,616	4,594	3,494	5,764	4,492	4,688	4,358	3,132	2,634
Common Equity	9,524	6,735	13,664	11,081	11,000	10,920	9,765	8,274	7,104	8,682
Total Capital	16,141	11,771	18,545	14,638	17,459	16,032	14,453	12,632	10,236	11,407
Capital Expenditures	765	947	1,082	1,078	1,298	1,898	1,707	1,131	884	678
Cash Flow	5,627	-1,147	3,808	3,465	2,728	2,408	3,109	3,201	3,264	3,494
Current Ratio	1.9	1.0	2.3	1.9	1.9	1.7	1.6	1.5	1.3	1.6
% Long Term Debt of Capitalization	Nil	39.2	24.8	23.9	33.0	28.0	32.4	34.5	30.6	23.1
% Net Income of Revenue	19.8	NM	15.9	17.0	13.7	13.1	20.4	24.4	24.3	28.2
% Return on Assets	NA	NM	12.1	11.4	8.1	7.8	12.6	15.3	18.1	22.2
% Return on Equity	NA	NM	24.0	24.2	18.1	17.5	28.4	35.2	42.7	44.7

Data as orig reptd.; bef. results of disc opers/spec. items. Per share data adj. for stk. divs.; EPS diluted. E-Estimated. NA-Not Available. NM-Not Meaningful. NR-Not Ranked. UR-Under Review.

Office: Lilly Corporate Center, Indianapolis, IN 46285.
Telephone: 317-276-2000.
Website: http://www.lilly.com
Chrmn, Pres & CEO: J. Lechleiter

EVP & CFO: D.W. Rice
SVP & Treas: T.W. Grein
SVP & General Counsel: R.A. Armitage
SVP & Cntlr: E. O'Farrell

Investor Contact: P. Johnson (317-277-0001)
Board Members: R. Alvarez, W. Bischoff, M. L. Eskew, M. Feldstein, J. E. Fyrwald, A. G. Gilman, R. D. Hoover, K. N. Horn, J. Lechleiter, E. R. Marram, D. R. Oberhelman, F. G. Prendergast, K. P. Seifert

Founded: 1876
Domicile: Indiana
Employees: 39,337

Limited Brands Inc.

STANDARD &POOR'S

S&P Recommendation	HOLD ★★★☆☆	Price	12-Mo. Target Price	Investment Style
		$29.06 (as of Oct 22, 2010)	$30.00	Large-Cap Blend

GICS Sector Consumer Discretionary
Sub-Industry Apparel Retail

Summary This specialty retailer of women's apparel, lingerie, and personal care and beauty products operates about 3,000 specialty stores.

Key Stock Statistics (Source S&P, Vickers, company reports)

52-Wk Range	$29.95– 16.28	S&P Oper. EPS 2011E	1.78	Market Capitalization(B)	$9.380	Beta	1.71
Trailing 12-Month EPS	$2.00	S&P Oper. EPS 2012E	2.00	Yield (%)	2.06	S&P 3-Yr. Proj. EPS CAGR(%)	8
Trailing 12-Month P/E	14.5	P/E on S&P Oper. EPS 2011E	16.3	Dividend Rate/Share	$0.60	S&P Credit Rating	BB
$10K Invested 5 Yrs Ago	$18,599	Common Shares Outstg. (M)	322.8	Institutional Ownership (%)	74		

Price Performance

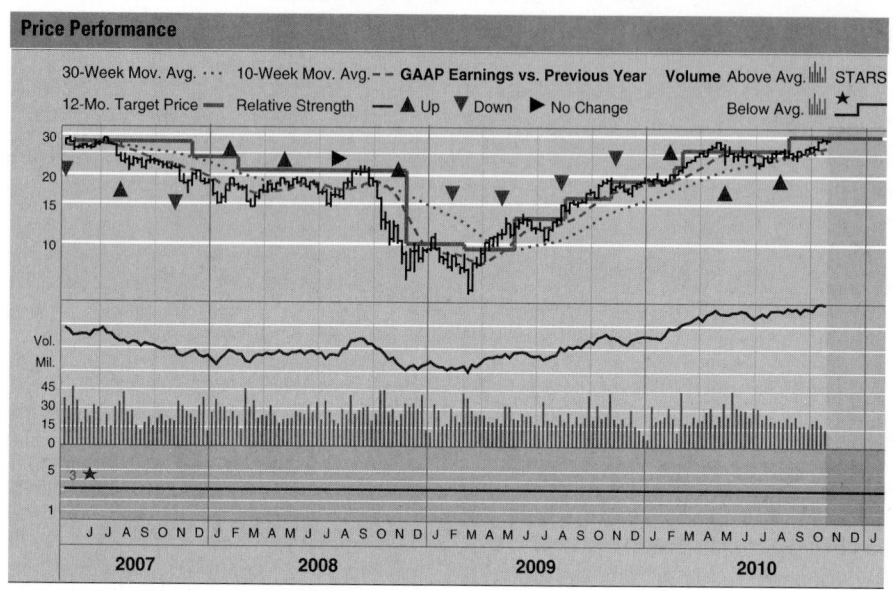

30-Week Mov. Avg. · · · 10-Week Mov. Avg. - - GAAP Earnings vs. Previous Year   Volume Above Avg. | STARS
12-Mo. Target Price — Relative Strength — ▲ Up ▼ Down ▶ No Change   Below Avg. | ★

Options: ASE, CBOE, P, Ph

Analysis prepared by **Marie Driscoll, CFA** on August 24, 2010, when the stock traded at **$ 24.84**.

Highlights

▶ We see LTD's ability to execute the retail fundamentals of 'read and react' to consumer demand, disciplined inventory and cost management along with its leading intimate apparel and personal care brands driving sales and profit gains in FY 11(Jan.) and FY 12. These strategies support improved full price selling and maintained merchandise margins. Long-term growth opportunities include potential line extensions, sub-brands, and global expansion for Victoria's Secret, Pink, and Bath & Body Works.

▶ LTD reported FY 10 (Jan.) sales of $8.63 billion, down 5% while same store sales decreased 4%. We see a 9% sales gain in FY 11 on fewer stores, a 5% comp gain and international sales. For FY 12, we look 6% sales growth.

▶ We see 220-basis points of operating margin expansion in FY 11 to 12.1%, driven by improved gross margins and modest SG&A expense leverage. We expect continued inventory management and improved merchandise margins although sourcing costs should escalate in FY 12 with higher cotton prices. We see another 20 bps in FY 12 and note LTD achieved a 200 bps EBIT margin expansion in FY 10.

Investment Rationale/Risk

▶ LTD entered the second half of FY 11 increasing August comp sales guidance to 5% to 8% from 1 to 3%, a testament to the growing brand momentum at Victoria's Secret and Pink, where comps rose 12% in the first half, despite shorter sales periods and shallower promotions. We see continued focus on cost controls while developing new concepts. La Senza (acquired in FY 08) launched LTD into the international intimate apparel market, providing a platform for further global expansion, which we believe will be important given the relative maturity of LTD's domestic retail concepts.

▶ Risks to our recommendation and target price include fashion and inventory risk, consumer spending trends, and weak same-store sales trends. With an estimated 60%+ of LTD's profits earned in the fiscal fourth quarter, we think earnings risk is heightened.

▶ We derive our $30 target price by applying LTD's historical five-year forward P/E multiple of 15X to our FY 12 EPS estimate.

Qualitative Risk Assessment

LOW	MEDIUM	HIGH

Our risk assessment reflects LTD's strong cash flow, offset by execution risk given the company's attempt to re-position its Victoria's Secret brand in an increasingly competitive marketplace.

Quantitative Evaluations

S&P Quality Ranking   B+

D	C	B-	B	B+	A-	A	A+

Relative Strength Rank   STRONG

77

LOWEST = 1   HIGHEST = 99

Revenue/Earnings Data

Revenue (Million $)

	1Q	2Q	3Q	4Q	Year
2011	1,932	2,242	--	--	--
2010	1,725	2,067	1,777	3,063	8,632
2009	1,925	2,284	1,843	2,991	9,043
2008	2,311	2,624	1,923	3,276	10,134
2007	2,077	2,454	2,115	4,025	10,671
2006	1,975	2,291	1,892	3,542	9,699

Earnings Per Share ($)

2011	0.34	0.54	E0.06	E1.12	E1.78
2010	-0.01	0.23	-0.05	1.08	1.37
2009	0.28	0.30	0.01	0.05	0.65
2008	0.13	0.30	-0.03	1.10	1.89
2007	0.25	0.28	0.06	1.08	1.68
2006	0.16	0.20	Nil	1.28	1.62

Fiscal year ended Jan. 31. Next earnings report expected: Mid November. EPS Estimates based on S&P Operating Earnings; historical GAAP earnings are as reported.

Dividend Data (Dates: mm/dd Payment Date: mm/dd/yy)

Amount ($)	Date Decl.	Ex-Div. Date	Stk. of Record	Payment Date
0.150	02/04	02/24	02/26	03/12/10
1.0 Spl.	03/15	03/31	04/05	04/19/10
0.150	05/28	06/02	06/04	06/15/10
0.150	08/16	08/25	08/27	09/10/10

Dividends have been paid since 1970. Source: Company reports.

Please read the Required Disclosures and Analyst Certification on the last page of this report.

The McGraw-Hill Companies

Limited Brands Inc.

STANDARD
&POOR'S

Business Summary August 24, 2010

CORPORATE OVERVIEW. Limited Brands (formerly The Limited) is a specialty retailer that conducts its business in two primary segments: Victoria's Secret, a women's intimate apparel, personal care products and accessories retail brand; and Bath & Body Works, a personal care and home fragrance products retail brand. At January 31, 2010, the store base consisted of 1,027 Victoria's Secret, 258 La Senza, 17 Pink, 1,655 Bath & Body Works, 11 Henri Bendel and three C.O. Bigelow locations.

Victoria's Secret (VS) is the leading specialty retailer of women's intimate apparel and beauty products, with FY 10 sales of $5.3 billion, which includes $1.4 billion at Victoria's Secret Direct, a catalog and e-commerce retailer of women's intimate and other apparel and beauty products and $424 million at La Senza. Bath & Body Works (BBW) is a specialty retailer of personal care and home fragrance products. FY 10 sales were $2.4 billion, including White Barn Candle Company.

MARKET PROFILE. The mature and fragmented U.S. women's apparel market generated about $104 billion at retail in 2009, according to NPD Fashionworld consumer estimated data. S&P forecasts that apparel sales will increase about 2% in 2010 following a 5% drop in 2009, a 4% decline in 2008 and 4% gains in 2006 and 2007, based on NPD data. For 2010, we see weak demand reflecting a weak economy with increased unemployment and deflationary pricing driving reduced apparel spending. The domestic personal care market is mature as well, with the demand function reflecting population trends in addition to the development of new categories.

Company Financials Fiscal Year Ended Jan. 31

Per Share Data ($)	2010	2009	2008	2007	2006	2005	2004	2003	2002	2001
Tangible Book Value	0.46	NM	NM	2.34	1.69	1.31	6.78	5.93	6.40	5.43
Cash Flow	2.57	1.77	2.82	2.46	2.45	2.17	1.90	1.48	1.83	1.58
Earnings	1.37	0.65	1.89	1.68	1.62	1.47	1.36	0.95	0.94	0.96
S&P Core Earnings	1.34	0.86	1.47	1.68	1.57	1.27	1.03	0.94	0.80	0.91
Dividends	0.60	0.60	0.79	0.60	0.48	0.40	0.40	0.30	0.30	0.30
Payout Ratio	49%	44%	42%	36%	30%	27%	29%	32%	32%	31%
Calendar Year	2009	2008	2007	2006	2005	2004	2003	2002	2001	2000
Prices:High	20.08	22.16	30.03	32.60	25.50	27.89	18.46	22.34	21.29	27.88
Prices:Low	5.98	6.90	16.50	21.62	18.81	17.35	10.88	12.53	9.00	14.44
P/E Ratio:High	15	34	16	19	16	19	14	24	23	29
P/E Ratio:Low	4	11	9	13	12	12	8	13	10	15

Income Statement Analysis (Million $)

	2010	2009	2008	2007	2006	2005	2004	2003	2002	2001
Revenue	8,632	9,043	10,134	10,671	9,699	9,408	8,934	8,445	9,363	10,105
Operating Income	1,255	1,095	1,232	1,492	1,285	1,360	1,246	1,148	1,025	1,148
Depreciation	393	377	352	316	299	333	28.3	276	277	272
Interest Expense	237	181	149	102	94.0	58.0	62.0	30.0	34.0	58.0
Pretax Income	641	450	1,107	1,097	960	1,116	1,166	843	968	828
Effective Tax Rate	37.3%	51.9%	37.1%	38.5%	30.3%	36.8%	38.5%	40.5%	39.8%	40.0%
Net Income	402	220	718	675	669	705	717	496	519	428
S&P Core Earnings	436	291	561	675	638	609	540	492	352	406

Balance Sheet & Other Financial Data (Million $)

	2010	2009	2008	2007	2006	2005	2004	2003	2002	2001
Cash	1,804	1,173	1,018	500	1,208	1,161	3,129	2,262	1,375	563
Current Assets	3,250	2,867	2,919	2,771	2,784	2,684	4,433	3,606	2,682	2,068
Total Assets	7,173	6,972	7,437	7,093	6,346	6,089	7,873	7,246	4,719	4,088
Current Liabilities	1,322	1,255	1,374	1,709	1,575	1,451	1,392	1,259	1,319	1,000
Long Term Debt	2,772	2,897	2,905	1,665	1,669	1,646	648	547	250	400
Common Equity	2,183	1,874	2,219	2,955	2,471	2,335	5,266	4,860	2,744	2,317
Total Capital	4,958	4,985	5,354	4,864	4,319	4,191	6,048	5,532	3,171	2,860
Capital Expenditures	202	479	749	548	480	431	293	306	337	446
Cash Flow	841	597	1,070	991	968	1,038	1,000	772	796	700
Current Ratio	2.5	2.3	2.1	1.6	1.8	1.8	3.2	2.9	2.0	2.1
% Long Term Debt of Capitalization	Nil	58.1	54.3	35.5	38.6	39.3	10.7	9.9	7.9	14.0
% Net Income of Revenue	4.7	2.4	7.1	6.3	6.9	7.5	8.0	5.9	5.5	4.2
% Return on Assets	NA	3.1	9.9	10.1	10.8	10.1	9.5	8.0	11.8	10.4
% Return on Equity	NA	10.8	27.8	24.9	27.9	18.6	14.2	13.0	20.5	19.2

Data as orig reptd.; bef. results of disc opers/spec. items. Per share data adj. for stk. divs.; EPS diluted. E-Estimated. NA-Not Available. NM-Not Meaningful. NR-Not Ranked. UR-Under Review.

Office: Three Limited Parkway, PO Box 16000, Columbus, OH 43216.
Telephone: 614-415-7000.
Website: http://www.limitedbrands.com
Chrmn & CEO: L.H. Wexner

EVP & CFO: S.B. Burgdoerfer
EVP & Chief Admin Officer: M.R. Redgrave
SVP & Secy: S.P. Fried
SVP & General Counsel: D.L. Williams

Investor Contact: T.J. Faber ()
Board Members: D. S. Hersch, J. L. Heskett, D. A. James, D. T. Kollat, W. R. Loomis, Jr., J. H. Miro, A. R. Tessler, A. S. Wexner, L. H. Wexner, R. Zimmerman

Founded: 1967
Domicile: Delaware
Employees: 92,100

The McGraw-Hill Companies

Lincoln National Corp

STANDARD &POOR'S

S&P Recommendation **BUY** ★★★★☆	Price $26.01 (as of Oct 22, 2010)	12-Mo. Target Price $33.00	Investment Style Large-Cap Value

GICS Sector Financials
Sub-Industry Life & Health Insurance

Summary This company offers annuities, life insurance, defined contribution plans, and related advisory services to affluent individuals.

Key Stock Statistics (Source S&P, Vickers, company reports)

52-Wk Range	$33.55– 20.65	S&P Oper. EPS 2010**E**	3.56	Market Capitalization(B)	$8.238
Trailing 12-Month EPS	$1.92	S&P Oper. EPS 2011**E**	4.00	Yield (%)	0.15
Trailing 12-Month P/E	13.6	P/E on S&P Oper. EPS 2010**E**	7.3	Dividend Rate/Share	$0.04
$10K Invested 5 Yrs Ago	$5,952	Common Shares Outstg. (M)	316.7	Institutional Ownership (%)	80

Beta	2.54
S&P 3-Yr. Proj. EPS CAGR(%)	11
S&P Credit Rating	A-

Price Performance

30-Week Mov. Avg. · · · 10-Week Mov. Avg. - - GAAP Earnings vs. Previous Year   Volume Above Avg. ▭ STARS
12-Mo. Target Price — Relative Strength — ▲ Up ▼ Down ▶ No Change   Below Avg. ▭ ★

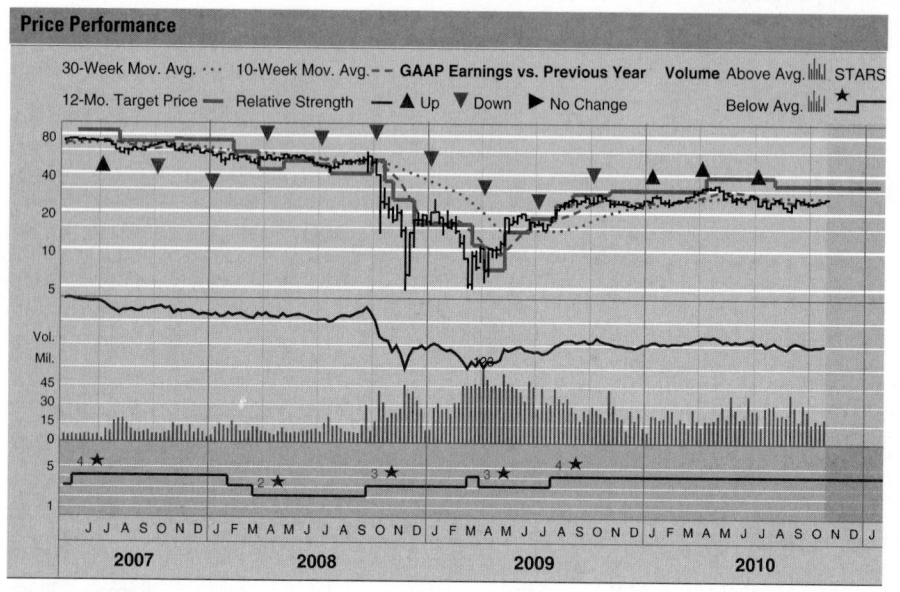

Options: ASE, CBOE, P, Ph

Analysis prepared by **Bret Howlett** on August 12, 2010, when the stock traded at **$ 22.97**.

Qualitative Risk Assessment

LOW	MEDIUM	HIGH

Our risk assessment reflects LNC's significant exposure to the equity markets and potential for elevated investment losses. We also believe the company's financial flexibility is limited relative to peers. However, we think LNC's capital position has improved substantially following equity and debt issuances, and the rebound in the financial markets. We are also encouraged that LNC repaid the government's TARP preferred investment sooner than we anticipated.

Quantitative Evaluations

S&P Quality Ranking   B

D	C	B-	B	B+	A-	A	A+

Relative Strength Rank   MODERATE

62

LOWEST = 1   HIGHEST = 99

Highlights

➤ We see operating earnings in Life Insurance increasing 6%-7% in 2010, led by solid sales of traditional life insurance and the new Moneyguard product, and higher investment income. We expect earnings in Annuities to benefit from strong sales and flows of variable annuities, as well as higher fee income. However, we forecast a sharp drop in fixed annuity sales due to the low interest rate environment. We believe product and distribution enhancements should drive modest earnings growth in Defined Contribution, although the weak macroenvironment is likely to weigh on sales.

➤ We remain cautious in our earnings outlook for the Group Protection since high unemployment should pressure enrollment levels and increase product loss ratios. However, we see strong life and dental product sales in the unit. We forecast underwriting spreads to improve in the second half of the year as mortality normalizes. We expect higher reinsurance costs and limited financing solutions to remain a headwind for the Insurance division.

➤ We forecast operating EPS of $3.56 for 2010 and $4.00 for 2011. Our estimates exclude realized investment gains or losses.

Investment Rationale/Risk

➤ Our buy recommendation is based on our belief that LNC's valuation is attractive, with the stock recently trading at a sizable discount to the group. We believe the rebound in the financial markets, the substantial amount of capital LNC raised though debt and equity offerings, and lower impairments and unrealized investment losses, have strengthened the company's financial position considerably. With over 40% of LNC's earnings derived from the equity markets, we believe the appreciation in the stock market from last year's lows has restored the core earnings power of the franchise. We expect LNC's top-line trends to improve, driven by the strength of its internal sales force, product enhancements, and partnerships with third-party distribution channels.

➤ Risks to our opinion and target price include a significant decline in equity markets, narrower-than-expected product spreads, deterioration in life insurance and annuity sales, instability in the credit markets, and investment impairments.

➤ Our 12-month target price of $33 is 0.9X LNC's projected 2010 book value (excluding FAS-115), below the historical multiple.

Revenue/Earnings Data

Revenue (Million $)

	1Q	2Q	3Q	4Q	Year
2010	2,527	2,605	--	--	--
2009	2,132	1,882	20,082	2,403	8,499
2008	2,592	2,582	2,436	2,273	9,883
2007	2,670	2,740	2,681	2,606	10,594
2006	1,417	2,496	2,487	2,658	9,063
2005	1,313	1,373	1,413	1,388	5,488

Earnings Per Share ($)

2010	0.76	0.32	E0.86	E0.96	E3.56
2009	-2.30	-0.03	0.21	0.26	-1.60
2008	1.12	0.48	0.58	-1.98	0.24
2007	1.42	1.37	1.21	0.89	4.82
2006	1.24	1.23	1.29	1.36	5.13
2005	1.01	1.13	1.30	1.28	4.72

Fiscal year ended Dec. 31. Next earnings report expected: Late October. EPS Estimates based on S&P Operating Earnings; historical GAAP earnings are as reported.

Dividend Data (Dates: mm/dd Payment Date: mm/dd/yy)

Amount ($)	Date Decl.	Ex-Div. Date	Stk. of Record	Payment Date
0.010	11/05	01/07	01/11	02/01/10
0.010	02/23	04/07	04/09	05/01/10
0.010	05/28	07/07	07/09	08/01/10
0.010	08/12	10/06	10/08	11/01/10

Dividends have been paid since 1920. Source: Company reports.

Please read the Required Disclosures and Analyst Certification on the last page of this report.

The **McGraw·Hill** Companies

Lincoln National Corp

STANDARD &POOR'S

Business Summary August 12, 2010

CORPORATE OVERVIEW. Lincoln National is a holding company with sub-sidiaries that operate multiple insurance and investment management busi-nesses. Primary operating subsidiaries include The Lincoln National Life In-surance Company, First Penn-Pacific Life Insurance Company, Lincoln Life & Annuity Company of New York, Lincoln Financial Advisors (LFA), a retail distri-bution unit, and Lincoln Financial Distributors (LFD), a wholesale distribution unit.

Following the acquisition of Jefferson-Pilot in April 2006, LNC's segments were restructured. In 2008, LNC's businesses were realigned again, and oper-ations were divided into five business segments. However, following the sale of Lincoln U.K. and Delaware Management in 2009, LNC now has three oper-ating segments: Retirement Solutions (33% of 2009 operating revenue), Insur-ance Solutions (62%), and Other Operations (5.5%).

The Retirement Solutions segment offers products through two segments: An-nuities (which accounted for 24% of operating revenues in 2009) and Defined Contribution (9.5%). LNC offers guaranteed benefit riders on some of its vari-able annuity products including the guaranteed death benefit (GDB), a guar-

anteed withdrawal benefit (GWB), and a guaranteed income benefit (GIB). The Defined Contribution segment provides employers tax-deferred retire-ment savings plans for their employees mainly through 403 (b) and 401 (k) plans. LNC offers a number of savings products including individual and group variable annuities, group fixed annuities and mutual funds. In addition, the company provides a variety of plan services including record keeping, compli-ance testing and participant education.

The Insurance Solutions segment provides products through its Life Insur-ance (44%) and Group Protection businesses (18%). The life insurance busi-ness targets the affluent market, and underwrites and sells universal life, vari-able universal life, interest-sensitive whole life, corporate-owned life insur-ance (COLI), term life insurance, and linked products such as universal life linked with long-term care benefits. The Group Protection business offers group non-medical insurance products to the employer marketplace.

Company Financials Fiscal Year Ended Dec. 31

Per Share Data ($)	2009	2008	2007	2006	2005	2004	2003	2002	2001	2000
Tangible Book Value	25.40	15.13	15.20	27.92	22.47	22.25	18.74	15.62	14.10	11.06
Operating Earnings	NA	NA	NA	NA	NA	NA	NA	2.56	3.56	3.27
Earnings	-1.60	0.24	4.82	5.13	4.72	4.09	2.85	0.49	3.13	3.19
S&P Core Earnings	3.85	1.83	4.78	5.05	4.71	3.78	4.36	1.16	3.10	NA
Dividends	0.24	1.66	1.58	1.52	1.46	1.40	1.34	1.28	1.22	1.16
Payout Ratio	NM	NM	31%	30%	31%	34%	47%	NM	39%	36%
Prices:High	28.10	59.99	74.72	66.72	54.41	50.38	41.32	53.65	52.75	56.38
Prices:Low	4.90	4.76	54.40	52.00	41.59	39.98	24.73	25.11	38.00	22.63
P/E Ratio:High	NM	NM	15	13	12	12	14	NM	17	18
P/E Ratio:Low	NM	NM	11	10	9	10	9	NM	12	7

Income Statement Analysis (Million $)

	2009	2008	2007	2006	2005	2004	2003	2002	2001	2000
Life Insurance in Force	802,900	781,400	748,200	702,600	339,100	325,700	307,800	873,595	651,900	637,100
Premium Income:Life	3,909	4,271	4,258	3,354	2,069	1,882	1,694	1,730	2,907	3,064
Premium Income:A & H	1,077	1,054	941	656	1.30	3.52	3.98	20.3	341	410
Net Investment Income	4,178	4,208	4,384	3,981	2,702	2,704	2,639	2,608	2,680	2,747
Total Revenue	8,499	9,883	10,594	9,063	5,488	5,371	5,284	4,635	6,381	6,852
Pretax Income	-521	-25.6	1,874	1,811	1,075	1,036	1,048	1.62	764	836
Net Operating Income	NA	NA	NA	NA	NA	NA	NA	474	689	639
Net Income	-415	61.8	1,321	1,316	831	732	767	91.6	606	621
S&P Core Earnings	1,074	475	1,311	1,298	831	675	782	215	600	NA

Balance Sheet & Other Financial Data (Million $)

	2009	2008	2007	2006	2005	2004	2003	2002	2001	2000
Cash & Equivalent	4,914	6,758	2,508	2,487	2,838	2,187	2,234	2,227	3,659	2,474
Premiums Due	321	481	401	356	343	233	352	213	400	297
Investment Assets:Bonds	60,818	48,935	56,276	55,853	33,443	34,701	32,769	32,767	28,346	27,450
Investment Assets:Stocks	278	288	518	701	3,391	3,399	3,319	337	471	550
Investment Assets:Loans	10,250	10,639	10,258	10,144	5,525	5,728	6,119	6,151	6,475	6,624
Investment Assets:Total	75,918	67,341	71,922	71,488	43,168	44,507	42,778	40,000	36,113	35,369
Deferred Policy Costs	9,510	11,936	9,580	8,420	4,092	3,445	3,192	2,971	2,885	3,071
Total Assets	177,433	163,136	191,435	178,494	124,788	116,219	106,745	93,133	98,001	99,844
Debt	5,050	6,758	5,168	4,116	1,333	1,083	1,459	1,512	1,336	1,457
Common Equity	10,894	7,976	11,718	71,017	6,384	6,175	5,811	5,296	5,263	4,953
% Return on Revenue	NM	0.6	12.5	14.5	15.1	13.6	14.5	2.0	9.5	9.1
% Return on Assets	NM	0.0	0.7	0.1	0.1	0.1	0.1	0.1	0.6	0.6
% Return on Equity	NM	0.6	11.1	2.3	13.2	12.2	13.8	1.7	11.9	13.5
% Investment Yield	5.9	6.2	6.1	6.8	6.1	6.8	7.1	6.9	7.5	7.7

Data as orig reptd.; bef. results of disc opers/spec. items. Per share data adj. for stk. divs.; EPS diluted. E-Estimated. NA-Not Available. NM-Not Meaningful. NR-Not Ranked. UR-Under Review.

Office: 150 N Radnor Chester Rd Ste A305, Radnor, PA 19087-5238.
Telephone: 484-583-1400.
Email: investorrelations@lnc.com
Website: http://www.lfg.com

Chrmn: W.H. Cunningham
Pres & CEO: D.R. Glass
SVP & General Counsel: N.S. Jones
CFO: F.J. Crawford

Chief Acctg Officer & Cntlr: D.N. Miller
Board Members: W. J. Avery, W. H. Cunningham, D. R. Glass, G. W. Henderson, III, E. G. Johnson, G. C. Kelly, M. L. Lachman, M. F. Mee, W. Payne, P. S. Pittard, D. A. Stonecipher, I. Tidwell

Founded: 1905
Domicile: Indiana
Employees: 8,208

Linear Technology Corp

STANDARD &POOR'S

S&P Recommendation HOLD ★★★☆☆

Price	12-Mo. Target Price	Investment Style
$30.91 (as of Oct 22, 2010)	$31.00	Large-Cap Growth

GICS Sector Information Technology
Sub-Industry Semiconductors

Summary This company manufactures high-performance linear integrated circuits.

Key Stock Statistics (Source S&P, Vickers, company reports)

52-Wk Range	$33.06–25.56	S&P Oper. EPS 2011E	2.33	Market Capitalization(B)	$6.938	Beta	1.07
Trailing 12-Month EPS	$1.91	S&P Oper. EPS 2012E	2.46	Yield (%)	2.98	S&P 3-Yr. Proj. EPS CAGR(%)	25
Trailing 12-Month P/E	16.2	P/E on S&P Oper. EPS 2011E	13.3	Dividend Rate/Share	$0.92	S&P Credit Rating	NA
$10K Invested 5 Yrs Ago	$9,777	Common Shares Outstg. (M)	224.4	Institutional Ownership (%)	95		

Price Performance

- 30-Week Mov. Avg. · · · 10-Week Mov. Avg. - - **GAAP Earnings vs. Previous Year** Volume Above Avg. STARS
- 12-Mo. Target Price — Relative Strength — ▲ Up ▼ Down ► No Change Below Avg.

Options: ASE, CBOE, P, Ph

Analysis prepared by **Clyde Montevirgen** on October 14, 2010, when the stock traded at **$ 30.69**.

Highlights

➤ We think revenues will rise 30% in FY 11 (Jun.), versus a 21% rise for FY 10. Although we anticipate slower orders over the near-term as customers adjust inventory and orders to LLTC's lower leadtimes, we believe that sales will be supported by strength in its industrial, automotive, computer and communications businesses. Generally, we think that the proliferation of semiconductors in electronic devices throughout all end markets, market share gains, and new product cycles, such as tablet computers, will aid revenue advances.

➤ We look for the gross margin to widen to 78% for FY 11 from 77% for FY 10, due largely to a more favorable sales mix and other efficiencies. However, we think capacity expansion will add business risks, and could lead to wider margin variability if revenues shift. We believe expenses will advance at a slower rate than sales, and expect the operating margin to expand to 50% from 48% during the same time frame.

➤ Our EPS projections assume an effective tax rate of around 28%, and include over $0.20 per share of stock-based compensation.

Investment Rationale/Risk

➤ Our hold opinion reflects our view of the company's solid and profitable business model, balanced by fair valuations. One of the better-run semiconductor companies, in our view, with relatively high margins, LLTC has been able to grow sales at an above industry pace through penetrating a broader range of markets, all while maintaining above-peer profitability. We believe LLTC generally offers less business risk than peers, and has more than enough cash and healthy free cash flows to reduce financial risks related to its leverage. However, with our view that operations are already highly efficient and will offer relatively less operating leverage moving forward, we see earnings growth trailing the industry's in calendar 2011.

➤ Risks to our recommendation and target price include increasing competition, higher-than-anticipated operating expenses, and worse-than-expected economic conditions.

➤ Our 12-month target price of $31 is based on a price-to-earnings multiple of around 14X, above the industry average to account for LLTC's relative growth, return on equity, and risk, applied to our calendar 2011 EPS estimate.

Qualitative Risk Assessment

LOW	MEDIUM	HIGH

Our risk assessment reflects the company's exposure to the sales cycles of the semiconductor industry. This is offset by stabilizing factors such as a high level of proprietary circuit design content, a varied customer base, diverse end markets, and wider margins than most competitors.

Quantitative Evaluations

S&P Quality Ranking A-

D	C	B-	B	B+	A-	A	A+

Relative Strength Rank MODERATE

42

LOWEST = 1   HIGHEST = 99

Revenue/Earnings Data

Revenue (Million $)

	1Q	2Q	3Q	4Q	Year
2011	388.6	--	--	--	--
2010	236.1	256.4	311.3	366.2	1,170
2009	310.4	249.2	200.9	208.0	968.5
2008	281.5	288.7	297.9	307.1	1,175
2007	292.1	267.9	255.0	268.1	1,083
2006	256.0	265.2	278.9	292.9	1,093

Earnings Per Share ($)

2011	0.59	E0.57	E0.57	E0.57	E2.33
2010	0.27	0.33	0.44	0.54	1.58
2009	0.48	0.43	0.25	0.25	1.41
2008	0.40	0.41	0.44	0.46	1.71
2007	0.37	0.34	0.32	0.36	1.39
2006	0.31	0.33	0.35	0.37	1.37

Fiscal year ended Jun. 30. Next earnings report expected: Mid January. EPS Estimates based on S&P Operating Earnings; historical GAAP earnings are as reported.

Dividend Data (Dates: mm/dd Payment Date: mm/dd/yy)

Amount ($)	Date Decl.	Ex-Div. Date	Stk. of Record	Payment Date
0.230	01/12	02/10	02/12	02/24/10
0.230	04/13	05/12	05/14	05/26/10
0.230	07/20	08/11	08/13	08/25/10
0.230	10/12	11/09	11/12	11/24/10

Dividends have been paid since 1992. Source: Company reports.

Please read the Required Disclosures and Analyst Certification on the last page of this report.

The McGraw-Hill Companies

Linear Technology Corp

STANDARD
&POOR'S

Business Summary October 14, 2010

CORPORATE OVERVIEW. Linear Technology Corp. (LLTC) designs, makes and markets a broad line of high-performance standard linear integrated circuits (ICs) that address a wide range of real-world signal processing applications. Its principal product lines include operational and high-speed amplifiers, voltage regulators, voltage references, data converters, interface circuits, and other linear circuits, including buffers, battery monitors, comparators, drivers and filters.

LLTC's products are used in a wide variety of applications, including wireless and wireline telecommunications, networking, satellite systems, notebook and desk-top PCs, computer peripherals, video/multimedia, industrial instrumentation, medical devices, and high-end consumer products such as digital cameras and MP3 players.

The company has consistently expanded its customer base throughout its history. LLTC initially served primarily an industrial customer base, with a high percentage of revenues from the military market. Since the late 1980s, new products led to growth in the PC and hand-held device markets, and commu-

nication and networking markets contributed to growth significantly in recent years. The company now sells its products to more than 15,000 original equipment manufacturers directly or through a sales distributor channel. Its largest customer in FY 09 (Jun.) was the distributor Arrow Electronics, which accounted for 12% of total revenue. No other single company comprised over 10% of sales.

Linear has fabrication plants in Camas, WA, and Milpitas, CA. The company currently produces semiconductors on six-inch diameter (150 millimeter) wafers. Processed wafers are then shipped to its assembly plant in Penang, Malaysia, or other independent assembly contractors for "back-end" functions such as separating and packaging. The chips are then sent to its Singapore facility for final testing and inspection. The process from manufacturing to final testing can take up to 16 weeks.

Company Financials Fiscal Year Ended Jun. 30

Per Share Data ($)	2010	2009	2008	2007	2006	2005	2004	2003	2002	2001
Tangible Book Value	0.11	NM	NM	NM	6.94	6.55	5.87	5.80	5.63	5.59
Cash Flow	1.78	1.63	1.93	1.56	1.53	1.53	1.17	0.88	0.74	1.39
Earnings	1.58	1.41	1.71	1.39	1.37	1.38	1.02	0.74	0.60	1.29
S&P Core Earnings	1.58	1.41	1.71	1.39	1.37	0.99	0.79	0.50	0.40	1.10
Dividends	0.90	0.86	0.78	0.66	0.50	0.36	0.28	0.21	0.17	0.13
Payout Ratio	57%	61%	46%	47%	36%	26%	27%	28%	28%	10%
Prices:High	33.06	31.07	37.77	38.84	39.35	41.67	45.09	44.80	47.50	65.13
Prices:Low	25.87	20.26	17.69	29.62	27.80	32.83	34.01	24.76	18.92	29.45
P/E Ratio:High	21	22	22	28	29	30	44	61	79	50
P/E Ratio:Low	16	14	10	21	20	24	33	33	32	23

Income Statement Analysis (Million $)										
Revenue	1,170	968	1,175	1,083	1,093	1,050	807	607	512	973
Operating Income	609	464	617	575	613	638	485	340	271	582
Depreciation	45.5	48.0	48.1	50.7	49.3	48.8	48.7	45.9	46.3	35.8
Interest Expense	75.4	52.3	57.8	12.1	Nil	Nil	Nil	Nil	Nil	Nil
Pretax Income	490	407	541	570	617	620	462	333	278	611
Effective Tax Rate	NA	23.0%	28.4%	27.8%	30.5%	30.0%	29.0%	29.0%	29.0%	30.0%
Net Income	361	314	388	412	429	434	328	237	198	427
S&P Core Earnings	361	314	388	412	429	311	253	161	132	366

Balance Sheet & Other Financial Data (Million $)										
Cash	958	869	967	156	541	323	204	136	212	321
Current Assets	1,264	1,089	1,246	861	2,077	2,007	1,832	1,776	1,728	1,728
Total Assets	1,591	1,422	1,584	1,219	2,391	2,286	2,088	2,057	1,988	2,017
Current Liabilities	583	125	175	180	237	208	203	162	169	202
Long Term Debt	767	1,406	1,700	1,700	Nil	Nil	Nil	Nil	Nil	Nil
Common Equity	39.8	-267	-434	-708	2,104	2,007	1,811	1,815	1,781	1,782
Total Capital	1,200	1,202	1,308	1,005	2,104	2,007	1,811	1,815	1,819	1,815
Capital Expenditures	38.3	39.1	35.3	62.0	69.4	62.1	20.7	6.61	17.9	128
Cash Flow	407	362	436	462	478	483	377	282	244	463
Current Ratio	2.2	8.7	7.1	4.8	8.8	9.7	9.0	11.0	10.2	8.5
% Long Term Debt of Capitalization	63.9	116.9	130.0	169.2	Nil	Nil	Nil	Nil	Nil	Nil
% Net Income of Revenue	30.9	32.4	33.0	38.0	39.2	41.3	40.7	39.0	38.6	43.9
% Return on Assets	24.0	20.9	27.7	22.8	18.3	19.8	15.8	11.7	9.9	24.3
% Return on Equity	NM	NM	NM	59.0	20.9	22.7	18.1	13.2	11.1	27.5

Data as orig reptd.; bef. results of disc opers/spec. items. Per share data adj. for stk. divs.; EPS diluted. E-Estimated. NA-Not Available. NM-Not Meaningful. NR-Not Ranked. UR-Under Review.

Office: 1630 McCarthy Boulevard, Milpitas, CA 95035-7487.
Telephone: 408-432-1900.
Website: http://www.linear.com
Chrmn: R.H. Swanson, Jr.

CEO: L. Maier
COO: A.R. McCann
Investor Contact: P. Coghlan (408-432-1900)
CFO, Chief Acctg Officer & Secy: P. Coghlan

Board Members: A. C. Agnos, J. Gordon, D. S. Lee, L. Maier, R. M. Moley, R. H. Swanson, Jr., T. S. Volpe

Founded: 1981
Domicile: Delaware
Employees: 4,191

The McGraw·Hill Companies

Lockheed Martin Corp

STANDARD &POOR'S

| **S&P Recommendation** HOLD ★★★★★ | **Price** $71.78 (as of Oct 22, 2010) | **12-Mo. Target Price** $75.00 | **Investment Style** Large-Cap Growth |

GICS Sector Industrials
Sub-Industry Aerospace & Defense

Summary This company, the world's largest military weapons manufacturer, is also a significant supplier to NASA and other non-defense government agencies. LMT receives about 93% of its revenues from global defense sales.

Key Stock Statistics (Source S&P, Vickers, company reports)

52-Wk Range	$87.19– 67.39	S&P Oper. EPS 2010**E**	6.89	Market Capitalization(B)	$26.020	Beta	1.04
Trailing 12-Month EPS	$7.90	S&P Oper. EPS 2011**E**	7.00	Yield (%)	4.18	S&P 3-Yr. Proj. EPS CAGR(%)	2
Trailing 12-Month P/E	9.1	P/E on S&P Oper. EPS 2010**E**	10.4	Dividend Rate/Share	$3.00	S&P Credit Rating	A-
$10K Invested 5 Yrs Ago	$13,175	Common Shares Outstg. (M)	362.5	Institutional Ownership (%)	88		

Price Performance

30-Week Mov. Avg. · · · · 10-Week Mov. Avg. - - - **GAAP Earnings vs. Previous Year** Volume Above Avg. STARS
12-Mo. Target Price — Relative Strength — ▲ Up ▼ Down ▶ No Change Below Avg.

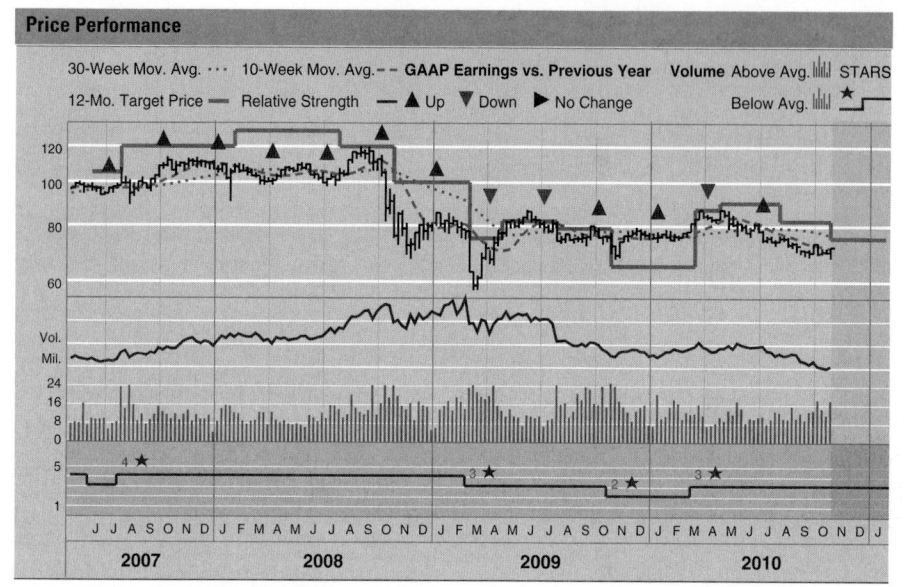

Options: ASE, CBOE, P, Ph

Qualitative Risk Assessment

| LOW | **MEDIUM** | HIGH |

Our risk assessment reflects the company's leading position in military markets and our view of a relatively health balance sheet, with $5 billion of long-term debt as of June 2010, but $3.6 billion of cash and equivalents. However, our risk evaluation also factors Lockheed's dependence on government funding, which can change with political and economic priorities.

Quantitative Evaluations

S&P Quality Ranking B+

| D | C | B- | B | **B+** | A- | A | A+ |

Relative Strength Rank MODERATE

31

LOWEST = 1 HIGHEST = 99

Revenue/Earnings Data

Revenue (Million $)

	1Q	2Q	3Q	4Q	Year
2010	10,637	11,442	--	--	--
2009	10,373	11,236	11,056	12,524	45,189
2008	9,983	11,039	10,577	11,132	42,731
2007	9,275	10,651	11,095	10,841	41,862
2006	9,214	9,961	9,605	10,840	39,620
2005	8,488	9,295	9,201	10,229	37,213

Earnings Per Share ($)

2010	1.45	1.96	E1.55	E2.00	E6.89
2009	1.68	1.88	2.07	2.17	7.78
2008	1.75	2.15	1.92	2.05	7.86
2007	1.60	1.82	1.80	1.89	7.10
2006	1.34	1.34	1.46	1.68	5.80
2005	0.83	1.02	0.96	1.29	4.10

Fiscal year ended Dec. 31. Next earnings report expected: NA. EPS Estimates based on S&P Operating Earnings; historical GAAP earnings are as reported.

Highlights

▶ The 12-month target price for LMT has recently been changed to $75.00 from $82.00. The Highlights section of this Stock Report will be updated accordingly.

Investment Rationale/Risk

▶ The Investment Rationale/Risk section of this Stock Report will be updated shortly. For the latest News story on LMT from MarketScope, see below.

▶ 10/19/10 01:13 pm ET ... S&P REITERATES HOLD OPINION ON SHARES OF LOCKHEED MARTIN (LMT 69.0***): Q3 EPS of $1.72, vs. $2.04, was $0.13 above our view, excluding a net $0.17 charge for a voluntary executive separation program. We see LMT taking aggressive steps (including the VESP) to re-align itself for the "new reality" of tight federal spending. We are reducing our '10 EPS est by $0.41 to $6.89, on VESP charge and discontinuation of PAE and EIG businesses, and '11's by $0.85 to $7.00, to reflect defense budget pressure. We also reduce our target price by $7 to $75. However, with valuations well below historical averages and a 3.7% dividend yield, our opinion is hold. / R.Tortoriello

Dividend Data (Dates: mm/dd Payment Date: mm/dd/yy)

Amount ($)	Date Decl.	Ex-Div. Date	Stk. of Record	Payment Date
0.630	01/28	02/25	03/01	03/26/10
0.630	04/22	05/27	06/01	06/25/10
0.630	06/24	08/30	09/01	09/24/10
0.750	09/23	11/29	12/01	12/31/10

Dividends have been paid since 1995. Source: Company reports.

Lockheed Martin Corp

Business Summary July 30, 2010

CORPORATE OVERVIEW. Lockheed Martin is the world's largest military weapons maker. In 2009, the company derived 85% of its net sales from the U.S. government, including the Department of Defense (DoD) as well as non-DoD agencies. Sales to foreign governments contributed 13% of net sales, with 2% of net sales to commercial and other customers. Lockheed Martin conducts business through four operating segments:

The Aeronautics segment (27% of revenues and 30% of operating profits in 2009) primarily makes fighter jets and military transport planes. Major development and production programs include the F-35 Lightning II, the F-22 Raptor, the F-16 Fighting Falcon, and the C-130J Super Hercules transport. F-22 production will be completed in 2012. In addition, LMT's "Skunk Works" research & development laboratory is well known for its advanced R&D efforts. It is currently focused on unmanned military aircraft and long-range bombers, among other initiatives.

Electronic Systems (27% and 31%) primarily makes land-, sea- and air-based missiles and missile defense systems. Other offerings include various electronic surveillance, reconnaissance, and command and control systems.

About 39% of the segment's 2009 sales came from maritime systems & sensors, with another 39% from missiles & fire control products. Major current programs include the Terminal High-Altitude Area Defense System (THAAD), the Patriot Advanced Capability (PAC-3) missile, the AEGIS Ballistic Missile Defense system, and the Littoral Combat Ship.

Space Systems (19% and 19%) mostly makes satellites, strategic and defensive missile systems and space transportation systems. Satellites include both government and commercial products. Space transportation systems include NASA's next-generation space flight systems, including the Orion crew exploration vehicle. Satellites accounted for 67% of segment sales in 2009. LMT is the prime contractor for the Space-Based Infrared System (SBIRS) missile detection program and the Advanced Extremely High Frequency (AEHF) communications system. LMT's 50/50 joint venture with Boeing, the United Launch Alliance, provides satellite launch services to the U.S. government.

Company Financials Fiscal Year Ended Dec. 31

Per Share Data ($)	2009	2008	2007	2006	2005	2004	2003	2002	2001	2000
Tangible Book Value	NM	NM	NM	NM	NM	NM	NM	NM	NM	NM
Cash Flow	9.97	9.92	9.02	7.55	5.68	4.39	3.69	2.40	2.08	1.36
Earnings	7.78	7.86	7.10	5.80	4.10	2.83	2.34	1.18	0.18	-1.05
S&P Core Earnings	8.23	4.07	6.65	5.70	4.11	3.23	2.20	-0.78	-2.29	NA
Dividends	2.34	1.83	1.47	1.25	1.05	0.91	0.58	0.44	0.44	0.44
Payout Ratio	30%	23%	21%	22%	26%	32%	25%	37%	NM	NM
Prices:High	87.06	120.30	113.74	93.24	65.46	61.77	58.95	71.52	52.98	37.58
Prices:Low	57.41	67.38	88.86	62.52	52.54	43.10	40.64	45.85	31.00	16.50
P/E Ratio:High	11	15	16	16	16	22	25	61	NM	NM
P/E Ratio:Low	7	9	13	11	13	15	17	39	NM	NM

Income Statement Analysis (Million $)	2009	2008	2007	2006	2005	2004	2003	2002	2001	2000
Revenue	45,189	42,731	41,862	39,620	37,213	35,526	31,824	26,578	23,990	25,329
Operating Income	5,062	5,494	5,032	4,198	3,242	2,624	2,585	2,507	2,366	2,582
Depreciation	859	845	819	764	705	656	609	558	823	968
Interest Expense	305	341	352	361	370	425	487	581	700	919
Pretax Income	4,284	4,702	4,368	3,592	2,616	1,664	1,532	577	188	286
Effective Tax Rate	29.4%	31.6%	30.6%	29.6%	30.2%	23.9%	31.3%	7.63%	58.0%	NM
Net Income	3,024	3,217	3,033	2,529	1,825	1,266	1,053	533	79.0	-424
S&P Core Earnings	3,198	1,666	2,844	2,486	1,830	1,448	994	-353	-989	NA

Balance Sheet & Other Financial Data (Million $)	2009	2008	2007	2006	2005	2004	2003	2002	2001	2000
Cash	2,391	2,229	2,981	1,912	2,244	1,060	1,010	2,738	912	1,505
Current Assets	12,477	10,683	10,940	10,164	10,529	8,953	9,401	10,626	10,778	11,259
Total Assets	35,105	33,434	28,926	28,231	27,744	25,554	26,175	25,758	27,654	30,349
Current Liabilities	10,703	10,542	9,871	9,553	9,428	8,566	8,893	9,821	9,689	10,175
Long Term Debt	5,052	3,563	4,303	4,405	4,784	5,104	6,072	6,217	7,422	9,065
Common Equity	4,129	2,865	9,805	6,884	7,867	7,021	6,756	5,865	6,443	7,160
Total Capital	9,181	6,428	14,108	11,289	12,651	12,125	12,828	12,082	14,857	16,961
Capital Expenditures	852	926	940	893	865	769	687	662	619	500
Cash Flow	3,878	4,062	3,852	3,293	2,530	1,922	1,662	1,091	902	544
Current Ratio	1.2	1.0	1.1	1.1	1.1	1.0	1.1	1.1	1.1	1.1
% Long Term Debt of Capitalization	55.0	55.4	30.5	39.0	37.8	42.1	47.3	51.5	50.0	53.4
% Net Income of Revenue	6.7	7.5	7.3	6.4	4.9	3.6	3.3	2.0	0.3	NM
% Return on Assets	8.8	10.3	10.6	9.0	6.8	4.9	4.0	2.0	0.3	NM
% Return on Equity	86.5	50.8	36.4	34.3	24.5	18.4	16.7	8.7	1.2	NM

Data as orig reptd.; bef. results of disc opers/spec. items. Per share data adj. for stk. divs.; EPS diluted. E-Estimated. NA-Not Available. NM-Not Meaningful. NR-Not Ranked. UR-Under Review.

Office: 6801 Rockledge Drive, Bethesda, MD 20817.
Telephone: 301-897-6000.
Website: http://www.lockheedmartin.com
Chrmn & CEO: B. Stevens

Pres & COO: C.E. Kubasik
EVP & CFO: B.L. Tanner
SVP & CTO: R.O. Johnson
SVP & General Counsel: M.R. Lavan

Board Members: E. Aldridge, Jr., N. D. Archibald, D. Burritt, J. O. Ellis, Jr., T. J. Falk, G. S. King, J. M. Loy, D. H. McCorkindale, J. W. Ralston, A. Stevens, B. Stevens
Founded: 1909
Domicile: Maryland
Employees: 140,000

Loews Corp

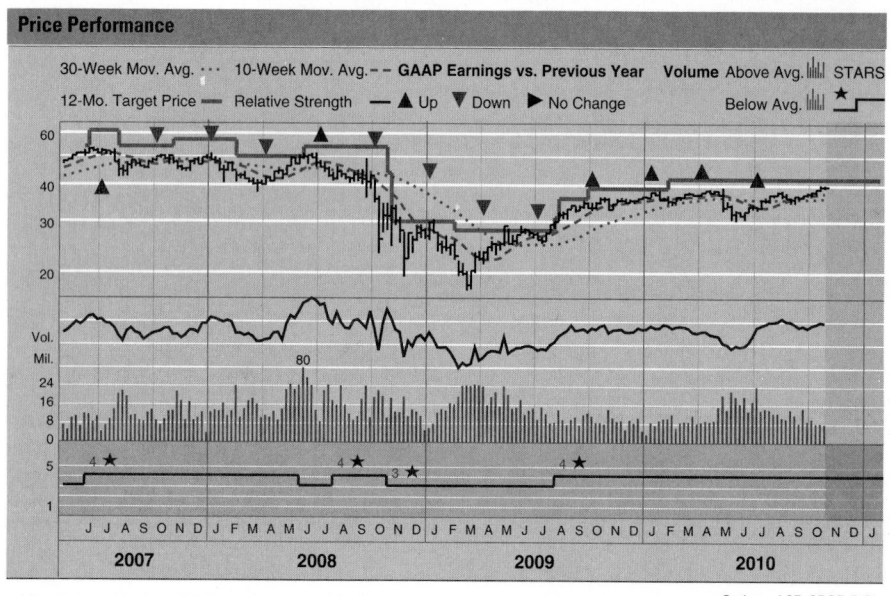

STANDARD &POOR'S

S&P Recommendation BUY ★★★★☆

Price	12-Mo. Target Price	Investment Style
$39.70 (as of Oct 22, 2010)	$42.00	Large-Cap Value

GICS Sector Financials
Sub-Industry Multi-line Insurance

Summary This conglomerate includes holdings in property/casualty insurance, offshore drilling, hotels, and natural gas pipelines.

Key Stock Statistics (Source S&P, Vickers, company reports)

52-Wk Range	$40.30–30.22	S&P Oper. EPS 2010**E**	3.75	Market Capitalization(B)	$16.605	Beta	1.25
Trailing 12-Month EPS	$3.88	S&P Oper. EPS 2011**E**	4.20	Yield (%)	0.63	S&P 3-Yr. Proj. EPS CAGR(%)	46
Trailing 12-Month P/E	10.2	P/E on S&P Oper. EPS 2010**E**	10.6	Dividend Rate/Share	$0.25	S&P Credit Rating	A
$10K Invested 5 Yrs Ago	$13,706	Common Shares Outstg. (M)	418.3	Institutional Ownership (%)	59		

Price Performance

30-Week Mov. Avg. · · · · 10-Week Mov. Avg. – – **GAAP Earnings vs. Previous Year**   **Volume** Above Avg.|ılıl| STARS

12-Mo. Target Price —— Relative Strength —— ▲ Up ▼ Down ► No Change   Below Avg.|ılıl| ★

Options: ASE, CBOE, P, Ph

Analysis prepared by **Bret Howlett** on August 10, 2010, when the stock traded at **$ 37.95.**

Highlights

➤ We see operating revenues declining 2% to 3% in 2010 at L's principal subsidiary, CNA Financial (CNA 28, Hold), on lower new business production, the continued soft P&C rate environment, but partially offset by higher investment income. We view positively CNA's solid track record of favorable reserve releases, which we believe reflects underwriting discipline. We expect the six-month moratorium on deepwater drilling in the U.S. to adversely impact Diamond Offshore (DO 65, Hold), although its robust backlog and low capital spending needs should provide solid earnings visibility. We forecast a sharp rebound in earnings at Boardwalk Pipeline, as pipeline maintenance issues are resolved and natural gas storage capacity expands.

➤ We believe better credit trends and removal of its asbestos liabilities will allow CNA to pay back L's preferred stock investment in 2010. We forecast a sizable decline in earnings at HighMount due to decreased production volumes and lower natural gas prices. We forecast a more than 10% rise in revenues at L's Hotels on higher average room rates.

➤ We forecast EPS of $3.75 for 2010 and EPS of $4.20 for 2011.

Investment Rationale/Risk

➤ Our buy recommendation is based on our forecast for improved fundamentals in most of L's subsidiaries. We believe L is undervalued based on our calculation of the net asset values of its public and private holdings. We believe a strengthening in the credit markets has considerably reduced risks related to L's investment portfolio and CNA's capital position, and we expect L to deploy excess cash by repurchasing its shares, undertaking new business ventures, and investing in the debt markets. We see the operating environment improving for CNA, and we believe the down-phase in the P&C underwriting pricing cycle should stabilize. We see L's energy subsidiaries benefiting from higher oil prices, partially offset by declining natural gas prices.

➤ Risks to our recommendation and target price include a decline in the level of oil and gas production at Diamond Offshore; higher-than-projected catastrophe losses; greater-than-expected losses in the investment portfolio; and, a slowdown in consumer spending affecting Loews Hotels.

➤ Our 12-month target price of $42 is 10.0X our 2011 EPS estimate, below historical multiples.

Qualitative Risk Assessment

LOW	**MEDIUM**	HIGH

Our risk assessment for Loews reflects exposure to investment losses from its CNA Financial subsidiary, regulatory risks, litigation risk, volatility in energy prices, and catastrophe losses. This is offset by its diversified group of holdings and substantial free cash flow.

Quantitative Evaluations

S&P Quality Ranking   **B**

D	C	B-	**B**	B+	A-	A	A+

Relative Strength Rank   **MODERATE**

66

LOWEST = 1   HIGHEST = 99

Revenue/Earnings Data

Revenue (Million $)

	1Q	2Q	3Q	4Q	Year
2010	3,713	3,486	--	--	--
2009	3,023	3,534	3,738	3,822	14,117
2008	3,612	3,922	2,970	2,743	13,247
2007	4,660	4,637	4,653	4,567	18,380
2006	4,245	4,277	4,507	4,882	17,911
2005	3,741	4,031	4,138	4,108	16,018

Earnings Per Share ($)

	1Q	2Q	3Q	4Q	Year
2010	0.99	0.87	E0.93	E0.96	E3.75
2009	-1.49	0.78	1.08	0.94	1.31
2008	0.77	1.00	-0.33	-2.20	-0.82
2007	1.19	0.96	0.76	0.71	3.64
2006	0.86	0.85	0.93	1.15	3.80
2005	0.53	0.68	0.42	0.07	1.69

Fiscal year ended Dec. 31. Next earnings report expected: Early November. EPS Estimates based on S&P Operating Earnings; historical GAAP earnings are as reported.

Dividend Data (Dates: mm/dd Payment Date: mm/dd/yy)

Amount ($)	Date Decl.	Ex-Div. Date	Stk. of Record	Payment Date
0.063	11/10	11/25	11/30	12/11/09
0.063	02/09	02/25	03/01	03/12/10
0.063	05/11	05/27	06/01	06/14/10
0.063	08/10	08/30	09/01	09/14/10

Dividends have been paid since 1967. Source: Company reports.

Please read the Required Disclosures and Analyst Certification on the last page of this report.

The McGraw·Hill Companies

Loews Corp

STANDARD
&POOR'S

Business Summary August 10, 2010

CORPORATE OVERVIEW. Loews Corp. is a holding company with interests in property/casualty insurance (CNA Financial Corp., 90% stake), hotels (Loews Hotels Holding Corp.), offshore oil and gas drilling (Diamond Offshore Drilling, Inc., 50%), exploration, production and marketing of natural gas and natural gas liquids (HighMount Exploration & Production LLC), and interstate natural gas pipelines (Boardwalk Pipeline Partners, LP, 67%).

CNA Financial Corp. (NYSE: CNA; 60% of consolidated total revenues in 2009) is an insurance holding company with subsidiaries that primarily consist of property and casualty insurance companies. The company serves small, medium and large businesses as well as associations, professionals and groups. CNA's The Loews Hotels division (2.0%) owns and/or operates 18 hotels in the U.S. and Canada. Diamond Offshore (NYSE: DO; 26%) operates 64

offshore drilling rigs that are chartered on a contract basis for fixed terms by energy exploration companies. Boardwalk Pipeline Partners (NYSE: BWP; 6.4%) owns and operates three interstate natural gas pipeline systems, Gulf Crossing Pipeline Company, Gulf South Pipeline and Texas Gas Transmission. HighMount Exploration & Production LLC (4.4%) is involved in the exploration, production and marketing of natural gas, NGLs (predominantly ethane and propane) and oil. Other activities reported consolidated revenues of $174 million in 2009.

Company Financials Fiscal Year Ended Dec. 31

Per Share Data ($)	2009	2008	2007	2006	2005	2004	2003	2002	2001	2000
Tangible Book Value	40.30	27.93	25.44	NM	NM	21.35	NM	19.88	16.23	18.28
Operating Earnings	NA	NA	NA	NA	NA	NA	NA	1.71	-2.27	1.90
Earnings	1.31	-0.82	3.64	3.80	1.69	1.88	-1.30	1.50	-0.92	3.15
S&P Core Earnings	2.39	1.57	3.76	3.65	1.49	2.17	-2.00	2.63	-2.47	NA
Dividends	0.25	0.25	0.25	0.18	0.20	0.20	0.20	0.20	0.19	0.17
Relative Payout	19%	NM	7%	5%	12%	11%	NM	13%	NM	5%
Prices:High	36.84	51.51	53.46	42.18	32.90	23.67	16.49	20.77	24.17	34.98
Prices:Low	17.40	19.39	40.21	30.42	22.35	16.36	12.75	12.50	13.68	12.75
P/E Ratio:High	28	NM	15	11	19	13	NM	14	NM	11
P/E Ratio:Low	13	NM	11	8	13	9	NM	8	NM	4

Income Statement Analysis (Million $)	2009	2008	2007	2006	2005	2004	2003	2002	2001	2000
Life Insurance in Force	NA	NA	14,090	15,652	20,548	56,645	388,968	437,751	497,732	534,781
Premium Income:Life A & H	594	611	618	641	704	901	2,275	3,382	4,351	4,549
Premium Income:Casualty/Property.	6,127	6,539	6,866	6,962	6,865	7,304	6,935	6,828	5,010	6,923
Net Investment Income	2,499	1,581	2,891	2,915	2,099	1,869	1,732	1,867	2,145	2,388
Total Revenue	14,117	13,247	18,380	17,911	16,018	15,242	16,461	17,495	19,417	21,338
Pretax Income	1,730	587	4,575	1,237	1,016	1,822	-751	1,647	-813	3,206
Net Operating Income	NA	NA	NA	NA	NA	NA	NA	1,099	-1,328	1,134
Net Income	566	-182	2,481	760	623	1,231	-468	983	-536	1,877
S&P Core Earnings	1,035	749	2,014	2,024	831	1,205	-1,112	1,594	-1,447	NA

Balance Sheet & Other Financial Data (Million $)	2009	2008	2007	2006	2005	2004	2003	2002	2001	2000
Cash & Equivalent	2,920	2,030	141	132	151	220	181	185	181	195
Premiums Due	10,212	11,672	11,677	12,423	15,314	18,807	20,468	16,601	19,453	15,302
Investment Assets:Bonds	35,816	29,451	34,663	37,570	33,381	33,502	28,781	27,434	31,191	27,244
Investment Assets:Stocks	1,007	1,185	1,347	1,309	1,107	664	888	1,121	1,646	2,683
Investment Assets:Loans	Nil	Nil	Nil	Nil	Nil	Nil	Nil	Nil	NA	NA
Investment Assets:Total	46,034	38,450	47,923	52,020	43,547	44,299	42,515	40,137	41,159	40,396
Deferred Policy Costs	1,108	1,125	1,161	1,190	1,197	1,268	2,533	2,551	2,424	2,418
Total Assets	74,070	69,857	76,079	75,325	69,548	73,750	77,881	70,520	75,251	70,877
Debt	9,475	8,187	6,900	1,230	1,627	5,980	2,032	5,652	5,920	6,040
Common Equity	16,899	13,126	17,591	15,580	-201	45,428	-729	11,235	9,649	11,191
Combined Loss-Expense Ratio	105.1	109.0	110.1	109.1	120.3	105.9	146.6	110.3	158.6	113.6
% Return on Revenue	4.0	NM	13.5	4.2	3.9	8.1	14.2	5.6	NM	8.8
% Return on Equity	3.8	NM	15.0	14.2	2.6	2.8	NM	8.1	NM	4.9
% Investment Yield	5.2	3.7	5.8	6.1	2.6	4.3	4.2	4.6	5.2	5.9

Data as orig reptd.; bef. results of disc opers/spec. items. Per share data adj. for stk. divs.; EPS diluted. E-Estimated. NA-Not Available. NM-Not Meaningful. NR-Not Ranked. UR-Under Review.

Office: 667 Madison Ave, New York, NY 10065-8087.
Telephone: 212-521-2000.
Website: http://www.loews.com
Co-Chrmn: J.M. Tisch

Co-Chrmn: A. Tisch
Pres & CEO: J.S. Tisch
SVP & CFO: P.W. Keegan
SVP, Secy & General Counsel: G.W. Garson

Investor Contact: D. Daugherty (212-521-2788)
Board Members: A. E. Berman, J. L. Bower, C. M. Diker, J. A. Frenkel, P. J. Fribourg, W. L. Harris, P. A. Laskawy, K. Miller, G. R. Scott, A. Tisch, J. S. Tisch, J. M. Tisch

Founded: 1954
Domicile: Delaware
Employees: 18,500

The McGraw-Hill Companies

Lorillard Inc

STANDARD &POOR'S

S&P Recommendation BUY ★★★★☆	**Price** $85.14 (as of Oct 25, 2010)	**12-Mo. Target Price** $94.00	**Investment Style** Large-Cap Blend

GICS Sector Consumer Staples
Sub-Industry Tobacco

Summary Lorillard is the third largest U.S. tobacco company and the leading manufacturer and marketer of menthol cigarettes.

Key Stock Statistics (Source S&P, Vickers, company reports)

52-Wk Range	$87.47–70.24	S&P Oper. EPS 2010E	6.74	Market Capitalization(B)	$12.917	Beta	0.47
Trailing 12-Month EPS	$6.18	S&P Oper. EPS 2011E	7.24	Yield (%)	5.29	S&P 3-Yr. Proj. EPS CAGR(%)	9
Trailing 12-Month P/E	13.8	P/E on S&P Oper. EPS 2010E	12.6	Dividend Rate/Share	$4.50	S&P Credit Rating	BBB-
$10K Invested 5 Yrs Ago	$23,794	Common Shares Outstg. (M)	151.7	Institutional Ownership (%)	97		

Price Performance

- 30-Week Mov. Avg. · · ·
- 10-Week Mov. Avg. - - -
- GAAP Earnings vs. Previous Year
- Volume Above Avg. ▍▍▍▍ STARS
- 12-Mo. Target Price —
- Relative Strength —
- ▲ Up ▼ Down ► No Change
- Below Avg. ▍▍▍ ★

Analysis prepared by **Esther Y. Kwon, CFA** on October 25, 2010, when the stock traded at **$ 85.78**.

Highlights

► Lorillard, formerly a division of Loews Corp., was spun off in June 2008. Its operating performance had previously been followed as a tracking stock (Loews Corp. - Carolina Group; CG).

► In 2010 and 2011, we forecast a mid-single digit percentage increase in sales from the $3.8 billion reported for 2009. We think discount brand volumes, which rose 37% in 2009, will post strong growth through 2011, offsetting some of the expansion we forecast in gross margins. While we see marketing and legal expenses rising, we look for only a modest increase in selling, general and administrative expenses on disciplined cost control. We expect operating margins to expand in 2010 and 2011.

► On higher interest expense, a reduced number of shares outstanding and an effective tax rate similar to 2009, we estimate 2010 EPS of $6.74, up from 2009 EPS of $5.76. For 2011, we forecast EPS of $7.24. In August 2010, LO's directors approved an additional share repurchase program for up to $1 billion of its common stock. As of September 30, 2010, the program had $909 million remaining.

Investment Rationale/Risk

► We view positively LO's continued market share gains for its leading brand, Newport, in both the menthol and premium categories. We believe efforts to increase its investment in this brand will result in long-term volume growth ahead of peers, less promotional activity, and higher average prices. Although we think FDA review of menthol could be an overhang on the shares, we see strong free cash flow generation as supporting the dividend, as well as share repurchase activity.

► Risks to our recommendation and target price include increasing menthol competition in the premium and deep discount segments, a slowdown in industry volume trends, and a worsening of the litigation environment.

► Applying a below recent average P/E multiple of 13X to our 2011 estimate, we arrive at our 12-month target price of $94. Our target P/E multiple is in line with the average of cigarette manufacturing peers. While we are concerned about relatively high geographic concentration and see more limited margin expansion potential, we think LO is attractive given its leadership position in the higher growth menthol cigarette market.

Qualitative Risk Assessment

LOW	MEDIUM	HIGH

Our risk assessment reflects the relatively stable revenue and income streams enjoyed by the tobacco industry, offset by significant ongoing litigation.

Quantitative Evaluations

S&P Quality Ranking NR

D	C	B-	B	B+	A-	A	A+

Relative Strength Rank STRONG

71

LOWEST = 1   HIGHEST = 99

Revenue/Earnings Data

Revenue (Million $)

	1Q	2Q	3Q	4Q	Year
2010	923.0	1,038	--	--	--
2009	767.0	1,033	953.0	932.0	3,686
2008	932.0	886.0	936.0	912.0	3,492
2007	947.3	1,055	1,044	957.0	3,281
2006	880.8	998.6	1,016	936.7	3,866
2005	--	--	--	916.0	3,640

Earnings Per Share ($)

2010	1.50	1.73	E1.66	E1.71	E6.74
2009	1.09	1.71	1.44	1.52	5.76
2008	1.00	1.25	1.38	1.53	5.15
2007	1.08	1.30	1.34	1.18	5.16
2006	0.86	1.09	1.17	1.26	4.46
2005	0.68	0.82	0.99	1.11	3.62

Fiscal year ended Dec. 31. Next earnings report expected: Late October. EPS Estimates based on S&P Operating Earnings; historical GAAP earnings are as reported.

Dividend Data (Dates: mm/dd Payment Date: mm/dd/yy)

Amount ($)	Date Decl.	Ex-Div. Date	Stk. of Record	Payment Date
1.000	02/12	02/25	03/01	03/11/10
1.000	05/20	05/27	06/01	06/11/10
1.125	08/20	08/30	09/01	09/10/10

Dividends have been paid since 2002. Source: Company reports.

The McGraw-Hill Companies

Lorillard Inc

Business Summary October 25, 2010

CORPORATE OVERVIEW. The company produces and markets cigarettes primarily in the U.S. The tobacco used in Lorillard cigarettes includes burley leaf, flue-cured tobacco grown in the U.S. and abroad, and aromatic tobacco grown primarily in Turkey and other Near Eastern countries. Through Alliance One International, Inc., Lorillard directs the purchase of more than 80% of its U.S. leaf tobacco needs. The company stores the various types and grades of its tobacco in 29 warehouses at its Danville, VA, facility. Its sole manufacturing plant, located in Greensboro, NC, has an annual production capacity of about 43 billion cigarettes, or approximately 185 million cigarettes per day. Lorillard, formerly a division of Loews Corp., was spun off in June 2008.

The company primarily sells its cigarettes to distributors that resell them to chain store organizations and government agencies. As of December 31, 2009, Lorillard had approximately 500 direct buying customers servicing more than 400,000 retail accounts. Lorillard does not sell cigarettes directly to consumers. During 2009, 2008 and 2007, sales to McLane Company, Inc. comprised 26%, 26% and 24%, respectively, of Lorillard's revenues. No other customer accounted for more than 10% of sales in any of those years.

LEGAL/REGULATORY ISSUES. Lorillard's business operations are subject to a variety of federal, state and local laws and regulations governing, among other things, the publication of health warnings on cigarette packaging, advertising and sales of tobacco products, restrictions on smoking in public places, and fire safety standards. The U.S. cigarette industry faces a number of issues that have affected and may continue to affect its operations, including substantial litigation that seeks billions of dollars of damages. As of February 22, 2010, Lorillard was a defendant in about 10,275 cases facing the industry, including approximately 7,600 Engle progeny cases.

MARKET PROFILE. According to Lorillard, industrywide cigarette shipments declined at a compound annual rate of approximately 3% from 1999 to 2009, with shipments dropping an estimated 8.6% in 2009, 3.3% in 2008, 5.0% in 2007, and 1.5% in 2006. Standard & Poor's attributes 2009's above trend decline to the significant hike in the federal excise tax on cigarettes to $1.0066 per pack from $0.6166 per pack effective April 1, 2009, to finance health insurance for children. On price increases, rising excise taxes and regulations, health concerns and proliferation of smoking bans, we expect shipments to decline at a mid-single digit rate over the next several years.

Company Financials Fiscal Year Ended Dec. 31

Per Share Data ($)	2009	2008	2007	2006	2005	2004	2003	2002	2001	2000
Tangible Book Value	0.56	3.76	6.34	NM	NM	NM	NM	NM	NA	NA
Cash Flow	5.95	5.34	NA	NA	NA	NA	8.08	NA	NA	NA
Earnings	5.76	5.15	5.16	4.46	3.62	3.15	2.76	3.50	NA	NA
S&P Core Earnings	5.81	4.91	5.31	4.46	3.63	3.13	3.31	2.92	NA	NA
Dividends	3.84	2.75	1.82	1.82	1.82	1.82	1.81	1.34	NA	NA
Payout Ratio	67%	53%	35%	41%	50%	58%	66%	38%	NA	NA
Prices:High	81.76	89.21	92.79	64.83	46.06	30.00	28.10	34.05	NA	NA
Prices:Low	52.50	53.30	64.00	43.83	28.47	22.49	17.18	16.80	NA	NA
P/E Ratio:High	14	17	18	15	13	10	10	10	NA	NA
P/E Ratio:Low	9	10	12	10	8	7	6	5	NA	NA

Income Statement Analysis (Million $)	2009	2008	2007	2006	2005	2004	2003	2002	2001	2000
Revenue	3,686	3,492	3,281	3,866	3,640	3,388	3,288	3,798	3,868	NA
Operating Income	1,671	1,465	1,392	1,352	1,156	1,041	934	NA	NA	NA
Depreciation	32.0	32.0	40.0	47.0	48.0	40.0	NA	NA	NA	NA
Interest Expense	27.0	NA	74.0	116	141	158	183	178	0.70	NA
Pretax Income	1,519	1,434	1,318	1,237	1,016	884	751	1,121	1,105	NA
Effective Tax Rate	37.6%	38.2%	35.1%	38.5%	38.6%	38.2%	37.7%	39.2%	39.0%	NA
Net Income	948	887	855	760	623	546	468	682	673	NA
S&P Core Earnings	956	845	577	417	252	184	138	117	672	NA

Balance Sheet & Other Financial Data (Million $)	2009	2008	2007	2006	2005	2004	2003	2002	2001	2000
Cash	1,384	1,191	2.00	1.50	2.50	36.0	1.90	2.20	1.70	NA
Current Assets	2,181	1,962	2,103	2,115	2,069	NA	NA	NA	NA	NA
Total Assets	2,575	2,322	2,702	2,861	2,897	2,278	2,725	2,927	2,769	NA
Current Liabilities	1,337	1,273	1,188	1,151	1,240	NA	NA	NA	NA	NA
Long Term Debt	722	Nil	424	1,230	1,627	1,871	2,032	2,438	Nil	NA
Common Equity	87.0	635	685	0.16	-201	-502	-729	-884	1,275	NA
Total Capital	809	631	1,109	1,230	1,426	1,369	1,303	1,555	1,275	NA
Capital Expenditures	51.0	44.0	51.0	29.7	31.2	50.8	56.4	51.7	41.2	NA
Cash Flow	980	919	NA	NA	NA	NA	NA	NA	NA	NA
Current Ratio	1.6	1.5	1.8	1.8	1.7	NA	NA	NA	NA	NA
% Long Term Debt of Capitalization	89.3	Nil	38.2	100.0	114.1	136.7	156.0	156.8	Nil	NA
% Net Income of Revenue	25.7	25.4	26.1	19.7	17.1	16.1	14.2	17.9	17.4	NA
% Return on Assets	38.7	36.0	30.7	26.4	22.0	19.8	16.6	23.9	NA	NA
% Return on Equity	264.1	107.7	203.4	5.4	NM	NM	NM	348.6	NA	NA

Data as orig reptd.; bef. results of disc opers/spec. items. Per share data adj. for stk. divs.; EPS diluted. Prior to June 11, 2008, data and historical prices reflect the former Loews Corp-Carolina Group. E-Estimated. NA-Not Available. NM-Not Meaningful. NR-Not Ranked. UR-Under Review.

Office: 714 Green Valley Rd, Greensboro, NC 27408-7018.
Telephone: 339-335-7000.
Email: ir@loews.com
Website: http://www.lorillard.com

Chrmn: M.L. Orlowsky
Pres & CEO: M.S. Kessler
EVP & CFO: D.H. Taylor
SVP, Chief Acctg Officer & Treas: T.R. Staab

SVP, Secy & General Counsel: R.S. Milstein
Investor Contact: P.W. Keegan (212-521-2000)
Board Members: R. C. Almon, V. W. Colbert, D. E. Dangoor, K. D. Dietz, M. S. Kessler, M. L. Orlowsky, R. W. Roedel, D. H. Taylor, N. Travis

Founded: 1969
Domicile: Delaware
Employees: 2,700

Lowe's Companies Inc.

STANDARD &POOR'S

S&P Recommendation	Price	12-Mo. Target Price	Investment Style
HOLD ★★★★★	$22.00 (as of Oct 22, 2010)	$24.00	Large-Cap Growth

GICS Sector Consumer Discretionary
Sub-Industry Home Improvement Retail

Summary This company retails building materials and supplies, lumber, hardware and appliances through more than 1,700 stores in the U.S. and Canada.

Key Stock Statistics (Source S&P, Vickers, company reports)

52-Wk Range	**$28.54–19.15**	S&P Oper. EPS 2011**E**	**1.41**	Market Capitalization(B)	**$30.872**	Beta	**1.00**
Trailing 12-Month EPS	**$1.28**	S&P Oper. EPS 2012**E**	**1.60**	Yield (%)	**2.00**	S&P 3-Yr. Proj. EPS CAGR(%)	**10**
Trailing 12-Month P/E	**17.2**	P/E on S&P Oper. EPS 2011**E**	**15.6**	Dividend Rate/Share	**$0.44**	S&P Credit Rating	**A**
$10K Invested 5 Yrs Ago	**$7,672**	Common Shares Outstg. (M)	**1,403.3**	Institutional Ownership (%)	**81**		

Price Performance

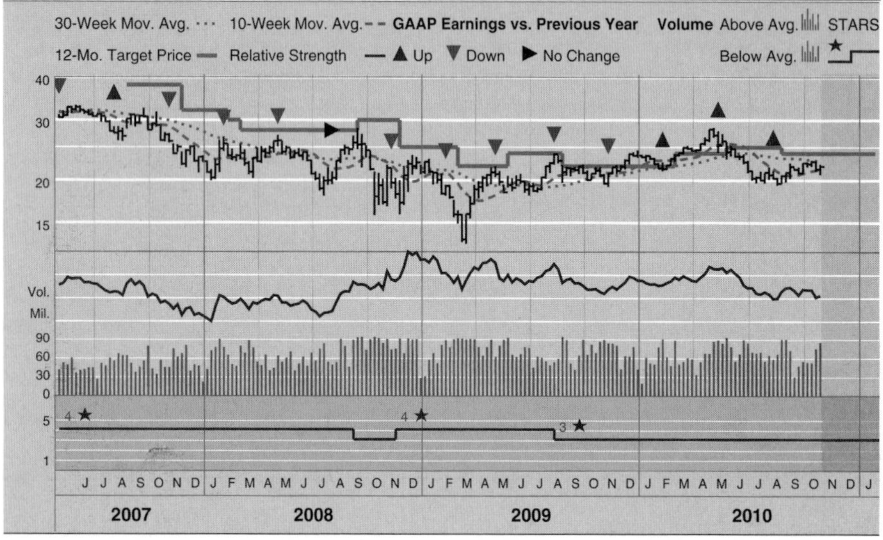
30-Week Mov. Avg.
10-Week Mov. Avg.
GAAP Earnings vs. Previous Year
Volume Above Avg.
STARS
12-Mo. Target Price
Relative Strength
Up
Down
No Change
Below Avg.
40
30
20
15
Vol.
Mil.
90
60
30
0
5
1
J J A S O N D J F M A M J J A S O N D J F M A M J J A S O N D J F M A M J J A S O N D J
2007
2008
2009
2010

Options: ASE, CBOE, P, Ph

Analysis prepared by **Michael Souers** on August 18, 2010, when the stock traded at **$ 20.55**.

Highlights

- We forecast a sales increase of 4.2% in FY 11 (Jan.), following a 2.1% decline in FY 10. We expect this rise to be driven by an estimated 40-45 net new store openings, representing a 2%-3% increase in total square footage, along with a 2% advance in same-store sales. We believe the housing market will remain under pressure throughout much of 2010, and we continue to project weak consumer spending, particularly on big-ticket home remodeling projects.
- We expect FY 11 operating margins to increase modestly, as lower sourcing costs, a rational pricing environment and improving product mix shift are only partially offset by increasing payroll expenses. We look for a slight leveraging of fixed expenses due to modest same-store sales growth.
- We project a slight increase in interest expense, an effective tax rate of 37.6%, and a 3% decline in the diluted share count, driven by share repurchases. We forecast FY 11 EPS of $1.41, a 13% increase from the $1.25 the company earned in FY 10, excluding $0.03 of charges related to the canceling of certain future store openings and an unrelated tax benefit. We see FY 12 EPS of $1.60.

Investment Rationale/Risk

- We think the aging of homes and relatively high home ownership rates are powerful long-term demographic drivers that will help mitigate the continued weakness in housing turnover we see for 2010. However, with home refinancings and home equity loans likely to be somewhat sparse in the near to medium term, we expect home remodeling activity, particularly on big projects, to remain weak. While housing turnover appears to be nearing a bottom, we do not anticipate a significant recovery in 2010. With our view of a strong balance sheet and impressive free cash flow generation, we think the shares are fairly valued despite trading at a slight premium to the S&P 500.
- Risks to our recommendation and target price include a slowdown in the economy, a spurt in long-term interest rates, and failure by LOW to execute its metro market expansion strategy.
- At about 13X our FY 12 EPS estimate, LOW shares recently traded at a slight discount to key peer Home Depot (HD 29, Hold). Our 12-month target price of $24 is derived from our discounted cash flow analysis, which assumes a weighted average cost of capital of 9.3% and a terminal growth rate of 3.0%.

Qualitative Risk Assessment

LOW | **MEDIUM** | HIGH

Our risk assessment reflects the cyclical nature of the home improvement retail industry, which is reliant on economic growth, offset by our view of ample opportunities for retail growth both domestically and abroad, and an S&P Quality Ranking of A-, reflecting LOW's long-term record of earnings and dividends.

Quantitative Evaluations

S&P Quality Ranking **A-**

D | C | B- | B | B+ | **A-** | A | A+

Relative Strength Rank **MODERATE**

41

LOWEST = 1 HIGHEST = 99

Revenue/Earnings Data

Revenue (Million $)

	1Q	2Q	3Q	4Q	Year
2011	12,388	14,361	--	--	--
2010	11,832	13,844	11,375	10,168	47,220
2009	12,009	14,509	11,728	9,984	48,230
2008	12,172	14,167	11,565	10,379	48,283
2007	11,921	13,389	11,211	10,406	46,927
2006	9,913	11,929	10,592	10,808	43,243

Earnings Per Share ($)

2011	0.34	0.58	**E**0.31	**E**0.17	**E**1.41
2010	0.32	0.51	0.23	0.14	1.21
2009	0.41	0.64	0.33	0.11	1.49
2008	0.48	0.64	0.43	0.28	1.86
2007	0.53	0.60	0.46	0.40	1.99
2006	0.37	0.52	0.41	0.44	1.73

Fiscal year ended Jan. 31. Next earnings report expected: Mid November. EPS Estimates based on S&P Operating Earnings; historical GAAP earnings are as reported.

Dividend Data (Dates: mm/dd Payment Date: mm/dd/yy)

Amount ($)	Date Decl.	Ex-Div. Date	Stk. of Record	Payment Date
0.090	11/16	01/15	01/20	02/03/10
0.090	03/22	04/19	04/21	05/05/10
0.110	05/28	07/19	07/21	08/04/10
0.110	08/20	10/18	10/20	11/03/10

Dividends have been paid since 1961. Source: Company reports.

Please read the Required Disclosures and Analyst Certification on the last page of this report.
Redistribution or reproduction is prohibited without written permission. Copyright ©2010 The McGraw-Hill Companies, Inc.

The McGraw-Hill Companies

Lowe's Companies Inc.

STANDARD &POOR'S

Business Summary August 18, 2010

CORPORATE OVERVIEW. Lowe's Companies is the world's second largest home improvement retailer, with $47 billion in revenues generated in FY 10 (Jan.). It focuses on retail do-it-yourself (DIY) customers, do-it-for-me (DIFM) customers who utilize LOW's installation services, and commercial business customers. Lowe's offers a complete line of products and services for home decorating, maintenance, repair, remodeling, and the maintenance of commercial buildings.

As of January 29, 2010, LOW operated 1,710 stores in 50 states and Canada, representing approximately 193 million sq. ft. of selling space. The company has three primary prototype stores--117,000-square-foot and 103,000-square-foot stores for larger markets and a 94,000-square-foot store format used primarily to serve smaller markets. Both prototypes include a lawn and garden center, averaging an additional 31,000 square feet for larger stores and 26,000 square feet for smaller stores. Of the total stores operating at January 29, 2010, approximately 88% were owned, including stores on leased land, while the remaining 12% were leased from unaffiliated third parties. Typical LOW stores stock more than 40,000 items, with hundreds of thousands of items available through the company's special order system.

CORPORATE STRATEGY. LOW is focusing much of its future expansion on metropolitan markets with populations of 500,000 or more. The company expected that the majority of its FY 11 expansion would be comprised of the 103,000 square-foot stores in larger markets (in place of 117,000 square-foot formats in an effort to be more cost-efficient), but it also planned to open 94,000 square-foot stores in smaller to mid-sized markets.

Lowe's opened five new stores in Canada in 2009, bringing its Canadian store count to 16, and planned to continue its expansion in FY 11. Additionally, LOW plans on expanding into Mexico, with stores expected to open in Monterrey in 2010.

Company Financials Fiscal Year Ended Jan. 31

Per Share Data ($)	2010	2009	2008	2007	2006	2005	2004	2003	2002	2001
Tangible Book Value	13.07	12.28	11.04	10.31	9.15	7.45	6.55	5.31	4.30	3.59
Cash Flow	2.40	2.54	2.77	2.73	2.44	1.92	1.68	1.32	0.98	0.79
Earnings	1.21	1.49	1.86	1.99	1.73	1.36	1.16	0.93	0.65	0.52
S&P Core Earnings	1.21	1.50	1.86	1.99	1.73	1.33	1.13	0.87	0.61	0.50
Dividends	0.36	0.34	0.18	0.11	0.08	0.06	0.06	0.04	0.04	0.04
Payout Ratio	30%	22%	10%	6%	4%	4%	5%	5%	0%	7%
Calendar Year	2009	2008	2007	2006	2005	2004	2003	2002	2001	2000
Prices:High	24.50	28.49	35.74	34.83	34.85	30.27	30.21	25.00	24.44	16.81
Prices:Low	13.00	15.76	21.01	26.15	25.36	22.95	16.69	16.25	10.94	8.56
P/E Ratio:High	20	19	19	17	20	22	26	27	38	32
P/E Ratio:Low	11	11	11	13	15	17	14	18	17	16

Income Statement Analysis (Million $)										
Revenue	47,220	48,230	48,283	46,927	43,243	36,464	30,838	26,491	22,111	18,779
Operating Income	4,959	5,333	6,071	6,314	5,715	4,878	3,959	3,186	2,332	1,811
Depreciation	1,733	1,539	1,366	1,162	1,051	920	781	645	534	409
Interest Expense	287	356	304	238	158	176	180	203	199	146
Pretax Income	2,825	3,506	4,511	4,998	4,506	3,536	2,998	2,359	1,624	1,283
Effective Tax Rate	36.9%	37.4%	37.7%	37.9%	38.5%	38.5%	37.9%	37.6%	37.0%	36.9%
Net Income	1,783	2,195	2,809	3,105	2,771	2,176	1,862	1,471	1,023	810
S&P Core Earnings	1,765	2,204	2,809	3,105	2,763	2,134	1,801	1,386	968	773

Balance Sheet & Other Financial Data (Million $)										
Cash	1,057	661	530	796	423	813	1,624	1,126	799	456
Current Assets	9,732	9,251	8,686	8,314	7,831	6,974	6,687	5,568	4,920	4,175
Total Assets	33,005	32,686	30,869	27,767	24,682	21,209	19,042	16,109	13,736	11,376
Current Liabilities	7,355	8,022	7,751	6,539	5,832	5,719	4,368	3,578	3,017	2,929
Long Term Debt	4,528	5,039	5,576	4,325	3,499	3,060	3,678	3,736	3,734	2,698
Common Equity	19,069	18,055	16,098	15,725	14,339	11,535	10,309	8,302	6,675	5,494
Total Capital	24,149	23,754	22,344	20,785	18,573	15,331	14,644	12,516	10,713	8,443
Capital Expenditures	1,799	3,322	4,010	3,916	3,379	2,927	2,444	2,362	2,199	2,332
Cash Flow	3,516	3,734	4,175	4,267	3,822	3,096	2,643	2,116	1,557	1,219
Current Ratio	1.3	1.2	1.1	1.3	1.3	1.2	1.5	1.6	1.6	1.4
% Long Term Debt of Capitalization	18.8	21.2	25.0	21.6	18.8	20.0	25.1	29.8	34.9	32.0
% Net Income of Revenue	3.8	4.6	5.8	6.6	6.4	6.0	6.0	5.6	4.6	4.3
% Return on Assets	5.4	6.9	9.6	11.9	12.1	10.9	10.6	9.9	8.2	7.9
% Return on Equity	9.6	12.9	17.7	20.7	21.4	20.0	20.0	19.6	16.8	15.9

Data as orig reptd.; bef. results of disc opers/spec. items. Per share data adj. for stk. divs.; EPS diluted. E-Estimated. NA-Not Available. NM-Not Meaningful. NR-Not Ranked. UR-Under Review.

Office: 1000 Lowes Blvd, Mooresville, NC 28117-8520.
Telephone: 704-758-1000.
Website: http://www.lowes.com
Chrmn & CEO: R.A. Niblock

Pres & COO: L.D. Stone
EVP & CFO: R.F. Hull, Jr.
SVP & Chief Acctg Officer: M.V. Hollifield
SVP, Secy & General Counsel: G.M. Keener, Jr.

Investor Contact: P. Taaffe (704-758-2033)
Board Members: R. Alvarez, D. W. Bernauer, L. L. Berry, P. C. Browning, D. E. Hudson, R. A. Ingram, R. L. Johnson, M. O. Larsen, R. K. Lochridge, R. A. Niblock, S. F. Page, O. T. Sloan, Jr.

Founded: 1952
Domicile: North Carolina
Employees: 239,000

The McGraw-Hill Companies

L-3 Communications Holdings Inc

STANDARD &POOR'S

S&P Recommendation	HOLD ★★★☆☆	Price $69.80 (as of Oct 22, 2010)	12-Mo. Target Price $82.00	Investment Style Large-Cap Blend

GICS Sector Industrials
Sub-Industry Aerospace & Defense

Summary This company is a provider of intelligence, surveillance, and reconnaissance systems; secure communications systems; aircraft modernization, training, and government services; and, other defense, intelligence, and security products.

Key Stock Statistics (Source S&P, Vickers, company reports)

52-Wk Range	$97.81– 66.11	S&P Oper. EPS 2010**E**	8.15	Market Capitalization(B)	$7.990
Trailing 12-Month EPS	$7.87	S&P Oper. EPS 2011**E**	8.60	Yield (%)	2.29
Trailing 12-Month P/E	8.9	P/E on S&P Oper. EPS 2010**E**	8.6	Dividend Rate/Share	$1.60
$10K Invested 5 Yrs Ago	$9,300	Common Shares Outstg. (M)	114.5	Institutional Ownership (%)	83

Beta	0.94
S&P 3-Yr. Proj. EPS CAGR(%)	5
S&P Credit Rating	BBB-

Price Performance

30-Week Mov. Avg. · · · 10-Week Mov. Avg. - - - **GAAP Earnings vs. Previous Year** Volume Above Avg. STARS
12-Mo. Target Price — Relative Strength — ▲ Up ▼ Down ▶ No Change Below Avg. ★

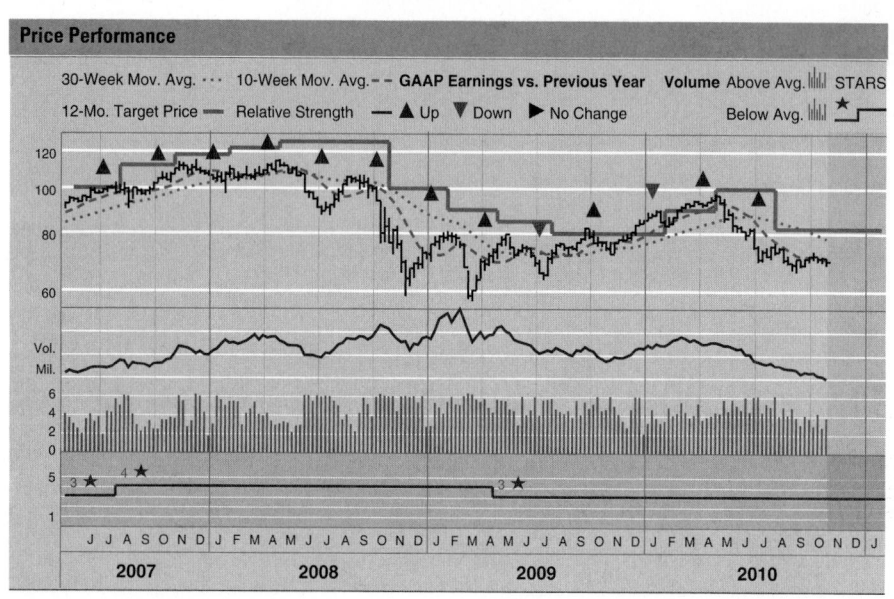

Options: ASE, CBOE, P

Analysis prepared by **Richard Tortoriello** on August 06, 2010, when the stock traded at **$ 73.61**.

Qualitative Risk Assessment

LOW	**MEDIUM**	HIGH

Our risk assessment reflects our view of LLL's strong historical record of earnings growth, offset by our view of moderately high financial leverage, and risks inherent in its dependence on government spending.

Quantitative Evaluations

S&P Quality Ranking   **A**

D	C	B-	B	B+	A-	**A**	A+

Relative Strength Rank   **WEAK**

22

LOWEST = 1   HIGHEST = 99

Revenue/Earnings Data

Revenue (Million $)

	1Q	2Q	3Q	4Q	Year
2010	3,624	3,966	--	--	--
2009	3,636	3,929	3,842	4,208	15,615
2008	3,506	3,722	3,662	4,011	14,901
2007	3,300	3,408	3,448	3,806	13,961
2006	2,904	3,083	3,105	3,385	12,477
2005	1,963	2,076	2,506	2,900	9,445

Earnings Per Share ($)

2010	1.87	1.95	E1.95	E2.38	E8.15
2009	1.66	1.90	2.12	1.93	7.61
2008	1.54	2.24	1.73	2.21	7.72
2007	1.29	1.49	1.56	1.63	5.98
2006	1.13	0.40	1.31	1.37	4.22
2005	0.86	0.99	1.11	1.24	4.20

Fiscal year ended Dec. 31. Next earnings report expected: Late October. EPS Estimates based on S&P Operating Earnings; historical GAAP earnings are as reported.

Highlights

► We project 3% revenue growth for 2010. We see this being driven primarily by C3ISR, where we are modeling an 11% increase, due to our view of high government demand for intelligence, surveillance, and reconnaissance products. We also project 4% growth for Electronic Systems (formerly called Specialized Products), on a variety of military products and systems. We expect about a 1% decline in Aircraft Modernization & Maintenance and a 3% decline in Government Services. We project a 4% revenue increase for 2011.

► We project operating margins of 11.0% for the year, up modestly from 10.6% operating margins in 2009. L-3 expects a significantly lower pension expense in 2010 versus 2009, but sees this more than offset by higher income tax expense. We project 10.9% margins in 2011.

► We forecast EPS of $8.15 for 2010, up about 9% from 2009's level, and project about 6% growth in 2011, to $8.60. We expect free cash flow (cash flow from operations less capital expenditures) per share of almost $11.00 in 2010.

Investment Rationale/Risk

► Although we think L-3's mix of defense electronics and specialized military products and government services are well matched with current military priorities, we see a pull-out of U.S. troops from Iraq (L-3 currently has significant revenue from Iraq) and our overall view of no real growth in the U.S. defense budget going forward, as preventing the shares from outperforming. We see L-3's ISR and Electronics businesses performing well, but expect continued pressure in the services areas of the business, due to tight government budgets.

► Risks to our recommendation and target price include the potential for delays and/or cuts in military budgets and failure to perform well on existing contracts or to win new business.

► Our 12-month target price of $82 is based on an enterprise value to estimated 2011 EBITDA multiple of about 6X, below the average historical multiple of 11X, but in line with multiples we are using to value other defense contractors. We believe the ongoing U.S. exit from Iraq and slower-than-historical growth at LLL warrant this multiple.

Dividend Data (Dates: mm/dd Payment Date: mm/dd/yy)

Amount ($)	Date Decl.	Ex-Div. Date	Stk. of Record	Payment Date
0.350	10/06	11/13	11/17	12/15/09
0.400	02/02	02/25	03/01	03/15/10
0.400	04/27	05/13	05/17	06/15/10
0.400	07/13	08/13	08/17	09/15/10

Dividends have been paid since 2004. Source: Company reports.

L-3 Communications Holdings Inc

STANDARD &POOR'S

Business Summary August 06, 2010

CORPORATE OVERVIEW. L-3 Communications (LLL), with $16 billion in estimated 2010 revenues, is an acquisitive maker of military and homeland security electronics, and conducts business through four operating segments.

The Command, Control, Communications, Intelligence, Surveillance, and Reconnaissance (C3ISR) business segment (20% of sales and 21% of operating income in 2009), specializes in signals intelligence (SIGINT) and communications intelligence (COMINT) products. These products provide troops the ability to collect and analyze unknown electronic signals from command centers, communications nodes and air defense systems for real-time situation awareness and response. C3ISR also provides C3 systems, networked communications systems, and secure communications products for military and other U.S. government agencies and foreign governments.

The Government Services segment (27% of sales and 24% of operating profits) provides a wide range of engineering, technical, analytical, information technology, advisory, training, logistics, and support services to the Department of Defense (DoD), Dept. of State, Dept. of Justice, U.S. Government intelligence agencies, and allied foreign governments. Major services include communication software support; high-end engineering and information systems support for command, control, communications and ISR architectures; developing and managing programs in the U.S. and internationally that focus on teaching,

training and education, logistics, strategic planning, leadership development, etc.; human intelligence support; command and control systems for maritime and expeditionary warfare; intelligence, analysis and solutions support to the DoD and U.S. government intelligence agencies; and conventional high-end enterprise IT support, systems, and services to the DoD and U.S. federal agencies.

The Aircraft Modernization & Maintenance segment (18% of sales and 15% of operating profits) provides modernization, upgrades and sustainment, maintenance and logistics support services for military and various government aircraft and other platforms. Services are sold primarily to the U.S. DoD, the Canadian Department of National Defense, and other allied foreign governments. Major products and services include aircraft and vehicle modernization, including engineering, modification, maintenance, logistics, and upgrades; aviation life-cycle management services for various military fixed and rotary wing aircraft; and aerospace and other technical services related to large fleet support.

Company Financials Fiscal Year Ended Dec. 31

Per Share Data ($)	2009	2008	2007	2006	2005	2004	2003	2002	2001	2000
Tangible Book Value	NM	NM	NM	NM	NM	NM	NM	NM	NM	NM
Cash Flow	9.46	9.16	7.53	5.30	5.46	4.27	3.52	2.96	2.37	2.25
Earnings	7.61	7.72	5.98	4.22	4.20	3.33	2.71	2.29	1.48	1.18
S&P Core Earnings	8.04	6.24	5.68	4.93	4.07	3.22	2.66	1.87	1.08	NA
Dividends	1.40	1.20	1.00	0.75	0.50	0.40	Nil	Nil	Nil	Nil
Payout Ratio	18%	16%	17%	18%	12%	12%	Nil	Nil	Nil	Nil
Prices:High	89.23	115.33	115.29	88.50	84.84	77.26	51.83	66.78	49.04	39.66
Prices:Low	57.12	58.49	79.26	66.50	64.66	49.31	34.22	40.60	30.35	17.84
P/E Ratio:High	12	15	19	21	20	23	19	29	33	33
P/E Ratio:Low	8	8	13	16	15	15	13	18	21	15

Income Statement Analysis (Million $)										
Revenue	15,615	14,901	13,961	12,477	9,445	6,897	5,062	4,011	2,347	1,910
Operating Income	1,866	1,771	1,645	1,376	1,150	868	676	530	362	297
Depreciation	218	197	196	136	153	119	95.4	75.9	87.0	74.3
Interest Expense	279	271	296	296	204	145	133	122	86.4	93.0
Pretax Income	1,386	1,462	1,183	835	798	606	437	336	191	134
Effective Tax Rate	34.3%	34.3%	35.3%	35.7%	35.1%	35.5%	35.7%	35.0%	37.1%	38.3%
Net Income	901	949	756	526	509	382	278	212	115	82.7
S&P Core Earnings	944	768	719	615	493	370	274	171	82.0	NA

Balance Sheet & Other Financial Data (Million $)										
Cash	1,016	867	780	348	394	653	135	135	361	32.7
Current Assets	5,151	4,961	4,763	3,930	3,644	2,808	1,938	1,639	1,239	830
Total Assets	14,763	14,630	14,391	13,287	11,909	7,781	6,493	5,242	3,335	2,464
Current Liabilities	2,482	2,707	2,582	2,376	1,854	1,176	924	697	524	469
Long Term Debt	4,112	4,548	4,547	4,535	4,634	2,190	2,457	1,848	1,315	1,095
Common Equity	6,565	5,836	5,989	5,306	4,491	3,800	2,574	2,202	1,214	693
Total Capital	10,770	10,462	10,857	10,069	9,325	6,067	5,108	4,123	2,599	1,788
Capital Expenditures	186	218	157	156	120	80.5	82.9	62.1	48.1	33.6
Cash Flow	1,111	1,126	952	662	661	501	373	288	202	157
Current Ratio	2.1	1.8	1.9	1.7	2.0	2.4	2.1	2.4	2.4	1.8
% Long Term Debt of Capitalization	38.2	43.4	41.8	45.0	49.7	36.1	48.1	44.8	50.6	61.3
% Net Income of Revenue	5.8	6.4	5.4	4.2	5.4	5.5	5.5	5.3	4.9	4.3
% Return on Assets	6.2	6.5	5.5	4.2	5.2	5.3	4.7	5.0	4.0	4.0
% Return on Equity	14.5	16.1	13.4	10.7	12.3	12.0	11.6	12.4	12.1	13.0

Data as orig reptd.; bef. results of disc opers/spec. items. Per share data adj. for stk. divs.; EPS diluted. E-Estimated. NA-Not Available. NM-Not Meaningful. NR-Not Ranked. UR-Under Review.

Office: 600 Third Avenue, 34th Floor, New York, NY 10016.
Telephone: 212-697-1111.
Website: http://www.l-3com.com
Chrmn, Pres & CEO: M.T. Strianese

COO: D.T. Butler, III
SVP, Secy & General Counsel: S. Post
CFO: R.G. D'Ambrosio
Chief Admin Officer: S.M. Sheridan

Investor Contact: E. Boyriven (212-850-5600)
Board Members: C. R. Canizares, T. A. Corcoran, L. Kramer, R. B. Millard, J. M. Shalikashvili, A. L. Simon, M. T. Strianese, A. H. Washkowitz, J. P. White

Founded: 1997
Domicile: Delaware
Employees: 67,000

The McGraw-Hill Companies

LSI Corp

STANDARD &POOR'S

S&P Recommendation HOLD ★★★☆☆	**Price** $4.69 (as of Oct 22, 2010)	**12-Mo. Target Price** $4.50	**Investment Style** Large-Cap Blend

GICS Sector Information Technology
Sub-Industry Semiconductors

Summary This company is a leading provider of silicon, systems and software technologies for the storage and networking markets.

Key Stock Statistics (Source S&P, Vickers, company reports)

52-Wk Range	$6.73– 3.89	S&P Oper. EPS 2010**E** 0.36	Market Capitalization(B) $3.010	Beta	1.59
Trailing 12-Month EPS	$0.23	S&P Oper. EPS 2011**E** 0.40	Yield (%) Nil	S&P 3-Yr. Proj. EPS CAGR(%)	20
Trailing 12-Month P/E	20.4	P/E on S&P Oper. EPS 2010**E** 13.0	Dividend Rate/Share Nil	S&P Credit Rating	NR
$10K Invested 5 Yrs Ago	$5,610	Common Shares Outstg. (M) 641.8	Institutional Ownership (%) 83		

Price Performance

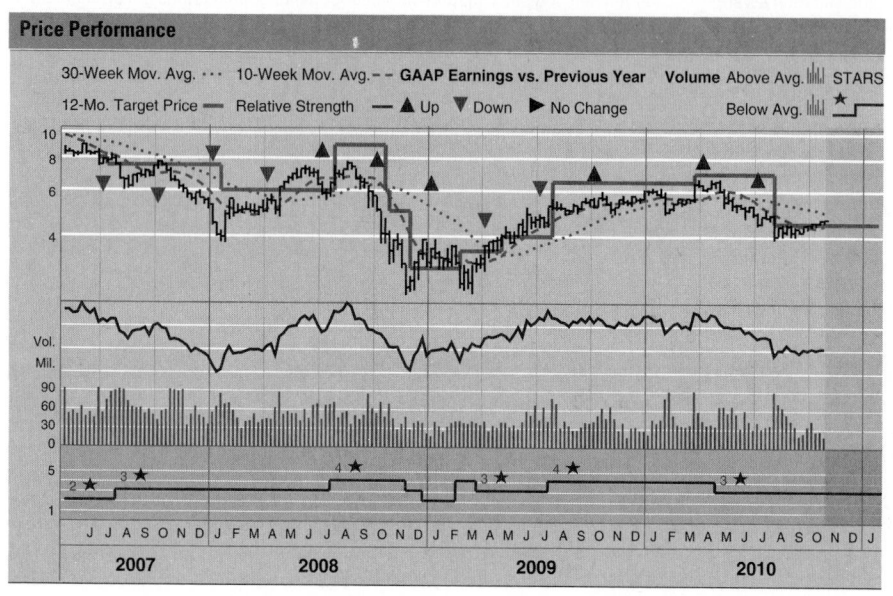

30-Week Mov. Avg. · · · · 10-Week Mov. Avg. - - **GAAP Earnings vs. Previous Year** Volume Above Avg. STARS
12-Mo. Target Price — Relative Strength — ▲ Up ▼ Down ▶ No Change Below Avg.

Options: ASE, CBOE, P, Ph

Analysis prepared by **Clyde Montevirgen** on August 02, 2010, when the stock traded at **$ 4.24**.

Highlights

➤ We project that revenues will advance 16% in 2010 and 5% in 2011. Although we believe that near-term orders will be negatively impacted by excessive inventory, we generally think that IT spending and the wireless infrastructure build-out will support longer-term growth. Also, the company is winning more designs with market-leading customers, which we see leading to market share gains and supporting top-line results as customers launch new products.

➤ We see non-GAAP gross margins of around 48% over the next several quarters as higher-margin semiconductor balance storage system sales. The company has a leaner and more flexible cost structure following a recent restructuring, and we believe LSI will be more profitable at lower sales levels. We see costs and expenses growing at a slower pace than sales, and anticipate the adjusted operating margin expanding from 9% in 2010 to 10% in 2011.

➤ Our 2011 earnings forecast includes around $0.10 per share in stock based compensation and assumes a 12% effective tax rate.

Investment Rationale/Risk

➤ Our hold recommendation reflects our view of improving fundamentals and fair valuations. We believe that LSI will manage expenses tightly as healthy demand and market share gains support sales growth. With a relatively flexible business model, LSI's free cash flow generation should improve as well, in our view, and add to the company's healthy balance sheet. We think LSI's adjusted return on equity will expand to the mid-to-high teens range, better than results in recent years. However, the anticipated growth and return metrics will still lag the industry's, in our view, and we believe LSI's stock warrants below-industry average multiples.

➤ Risks to our recommendation and target price include a slower ramp of new product sales, disruptions in the supply chain, and higher-than-expected operating expenses.

➤ Our 12-month target price of $4.50 is based on a multiple of around 11X our 2011 EPS estimate, below the industry average to reflect our view of relative earnings growth, return metrics, and business risk.

Qualitative Risk Assessment

LOW	MEDIUM	HIGH

LSI is subject to the sales cycles of the semiconductor industry and consumer electronics and data storage end markets. The company faces competition from makers of programmable logic devices as well as from many custom logic chip makers.

Quantitative Evaluations

S&P Quality Ranking C

D	C	B-	B	B+	A-	A	A+

Relative Strength Rank MODERATE

51

LOWEST = 1   HIGHEST = 99

Revenue/Earnings Data

Revenue (Million $)

	1Q	2Q	3Q	4Q	Year
2010	637.2	639.4	--	--	--
2009	482.3	520.7	578.4	637.8	2,219
2008	660.8	692.1	714.3	610.0	2,677
2007	465.4	669.9	727.4	740.9	2,604
2006	475.9	489.6	493.0	523.7	1,982
2005	450.0	481.3	481.7	506.2	1,919

Earnings Per Share ($)

	1Q	2Q	3Q	4Q	Year
2010	0.03	0.01	E0.08	E0.09	E0.36
2009	-0.16	-0.09	0.08	E0.16	-0.07
2008	-0.02	-0.02	0.02	-0.94	-0.96
2007	0.07	-0.50	-0.20	-2.88	-3.87
2006	0.03	0.13	0.11	0.14	0.42
2005	0.01	0.06	-0.19	0.09	-0.01

Fiscal year ended Dec. 31. Next earnings report expected: Late October. EPS Estimates based on S&P Operating Earnings; historical GAAP earnings are as reported.

Dividend Data

No cash dividends have been paid.

The McGraw-Hill Companies

LSI Corp

Business Summary August 02, 2010

CORPORATE OVERVIEW. LSI Corporation makes high-performance storage and networking semiconductors and storage systems that are used in end-products that create, store, consume and transport digital information. Such products include hard disk drives, solid state drives, high-speed communications systems, computer servers, storage systems and personal computers. The company operates in two segments -- semiconductors and storage systems.

LSI's semiconductor segment is focused on providing integrated circuits (ICs) for storage and networking applications, and it also generates revenues by licensing intellectual property to other entities. LSI has taken several major actions to maintain this focus, including merging with Agere Systems in 2007 to strengthen its position in storage and networking markets, divesting in businesses in which it did not benefit from scale advantages, acquiring small companies focused on its target end-markets, and selling its manufacturing operations to preserve capital and focus on product development.

The company's storage system segment sells enterprise storage systems and storage software applications that enable storage area networks. Its products are geared toward leading original equipment manufacturers (OEMs) and storage companies rather than end-users.

In 2009, the storage system segment accounted for approximately 64% of revenues, and semiconductors 36%. By market, external storage comprised around 29% of 2009's total revenues, server and storage connectivity 25%, hard disk drive and solid state drive 26%, networking 17%, and intellectual property 3%. The company believes that the served available market sizes for each can grow at compound average growth rates in the low to mid-teens.

Company Financials Fiscal Year Ended Dec. 31

Per Share Data ($)	2009	2008	2007	2006	2005	2004	2003	2002	2001	2000
Tangible Book Value	0.82	0.44	1.12	2.24	1.66	1.38	2.39	2.80	3.15	5.96
Cash Flow	0.34	-0.50	-3.48	0.62	0.36	-0.75	-0.12	0.15	-1.32	1.81
Earnings	-0.07	-0.96	-3.87	0.42	-0.01	-1.21	-0.82	-0.79	-2.84	0.70
S&P Core Earnings	-0.06	-0.68	-1.80	0.35	-0.20	-1.51	-1.33	-1.36	-3.47	NA
Dividends	Nil	Nil	Nil	Nil	Nil	Nil	Nil	Nil	Nil	Nil
Payout Ratio	Nil	Nil	Nil	Nil	Nil	Nil	Nil	Nil	Nil	Nil
Prices:High	6.14	7.97	10.68	11.81	10.75	11.50	12.90	18.60	26.10	90.38
Prices:Low	2.39	2.36	5.06	7.41	4.92	4.01	3.78	3.97	9.70	16.30
P/E Ratio:High	NM	NM	NM	28	NM	NM	NM	NM	NM	NM
P/E Ratio:Low	NM	NM	NM	18	NM	NM	NM	NM	NM	NM

Income Statement Analysis (Million $)	2009	2008	2007	2006	2005	2004	2003	2002	2001	2000
Revenue	2,219	2,677	2,604	1,982	1,919	1,700	1,693	1,817	1,785	2,738
Operating Income	181	287	168	236	283	172	171	155	-157	815
Depreciation	268	298	253	82.3	146	177	263	349	533	404
Interest Expense	21.9	34.9	31.0	24.3	25.3	25.3	30.7	52.0	44.6	41.6
Pretax Income	-131	-595	-2,475	185	20.9	-439	-284	-291	-1,030	380
Effective Tax Rate	63.5%	NM	NM	8.46%	NM	NM	NM	NM	NM	37.6%
Net Income	-47.7	-622	-2,487	170	-5.62	-464	-309	-292	-992	237
S&P Core Earnings	-45.9	-449	-1,157	140	-80.0	-582	-505	-507	-1,214	NA

Balance Sheet & Other Financial Data (Million $)	2009	2008	2007	2006	2005	2004	2003	2002	2001	2000
Cash	962	1,119	1,398	328	265	219	270	449	757	236
Current Assets	1,585	1,799	2,193	1,636	1,620	1,365	1,390	1,626	1,769	2,072
Total Assets	2,968	3,344	4,396	2,852	2,796	2,874	3,448	4,143	4,626	4,197
Current Liabilities	854	798	762	527	743	396	391	398	510	627
Long Term Debt	NA	350	718	350	350	782	866	1,241	1,336	846
Common Equity	1,461	1,441	2,485	1,896	1,628	1,618	2,042	2,300	2,480	2,498
Total Capital	1,811	2,036	3,388	2,246	1,978	2,400	2,916	3,665	3,995	3,481
Capital Expenditures	90.0	135	103	58.7	48.1	52.8	78.2	39.0	224	277
Cash Flow	220	-324	-2,234	252	141	-287	-45.8	57.0	-459	641
Current Ratio	1.9	2.3	2.9	3.1	2.2	3.4	3.6	4.1	3.5	3.3
% Long Term Debt of Capitalization	Nil	17.2	21.2	15.6	17.7	32.6	29.7	33.8	33.4	24.3
% Net Income of Revenue	NM	NM	NM	8.6	NM	NM	NM	NM	NM	8.6
% Return on Assets	NM	NM	NM	6.0	NM	NM	NM	NM	NM	6.4
% Return on Equity	NM	NM	NM	9.6	NM	NM	NM	NM	NM	10.9

Data as orig reptd.; bef. results of disc opers/spec. items. Per share data adj. for stk. divs.; EPS diluted. E-Estimated. NA-Not Available. NM-Not Meaningful. NR-Not Ranked. UR-Under Review.

Office: 1621 Barber Lane, Milpitas, CA 95035.
Telephone: 408-433-8000.
Email: investorrelations@lsil.com
Website: http://www.lsi.com

Chrmn: G. Reyes
Pres & CEO: A.Y. Talwalkar
COO: H. Thomas
EVP, CFO, Chief Admin Officer & Chief Acctg Officer: B. Look

EVP, Secy & General Counsel: J.F. Rankin
Investor Contact: S. Shah (610-712-5471)
Board Members: C. A. Haggerty, R. Hill, J. H. Miner, A. Netravali, M. J. O'Rourke, G. Reyes, M. G. Strachan, A. Y. Talwalkar, S. M. Whitney

Founded: 1980
Domicile: Delaware
Employees: 5,397

Macy's Inc

STANDARD &POOR'S

S&P Recommendation **BUY** ★★★★☆	Price $22.18 (as of Oct 22, 2010)	12-Mo. Target Price $25.00	Investment Style Large-Cap Blend

GICS Sector Consumer Discretionary
Sub-Industry Department Stores

Summary This company operates about 850 department stores under the Macy's and Bloomingdale's names.

Key Stock Statistics (Source S&P, Vickers, company reports)

52-Wk Range	$25.26– 15.34	S&P Oper. EPS 2011**E**	1.90	Market Capitalization(B)	$9.375	Beta	1.83
Trailing 12-Month EPS	$1.41	S&P Oper. EPS 2012**E**	2.25	Yield (%)	0.90	S&P 3-Yr. Proj. EPS CAGR(%)	23
Trailing 12-Month P/E	15.7	P/E on S&P Oper. EPS 2011**E**	11.7	Dividend Rate/Share	$0.20	S&P Credit Rating	BB
$10K Invested 5 Yrs Ago	$7,798	Common Shares Outstg. (M)	422.7	Institutional Ownership (%)	90		

Price Performance

30-Week Mov. Avg. · · · · 10-Week Mov. Avg. - - - **GAAP Earnings vs. Previous Year** Volume Above Avg. STARS
12-Mo. Target Price — Relative Strength — ▲ Up ▼ Down ► No Change Below Avg.

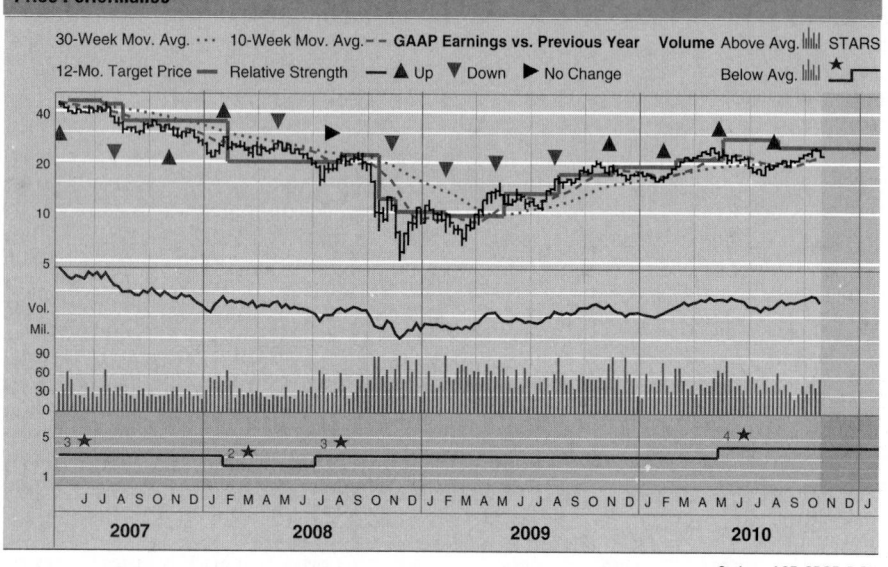

Options: ASE, CBOE, P, Ph

Analysis prepared by **Jason N. Asaeda** on August 12, 2010, when the stock traded at **$ 20.52**.

Highlights

► We project net sales will reach $24.7 billion in FY 11 (Jan.). In February 2009, M announced plans to expand nationwide "My Macy's," an initiative aimed at accelerating same-store sales growth through custom-tailoring of merchandise assortments, size ranges, marketing programs and shopping experiences to the needs of core customers surrounding each Macy's store. On expected pay off of My Macy's and other merchandising initiatives, we project same-store sales to increase about 4% in FY 11, versus FY 10's 5.3% decline. We anticipate modest square footage growth based on the company's plan to open one new Bloomingdale's store, two new Macy's stores, and to enter the off-price channel with four new Bloomingdale's Outlet stores.

► We expect operating margin expansion on sales growth in private label merchandise, disciplined inventory management, and projected cost savings of $400 million from FY 10 restructuring activity.

► Assuming no share buybacks, we see EPS of $1.90 in FY 11, up from $1.41 in FY 10, excluding division consolidation and store closing costs of $0.41 and asset impairment charges of $0.17.

Investment Rationale/Risk

► Our buy recommendation is based on valuation. In the first half of FY 11, same-store sales rose 5.2%, representing a significant improvement over the 9.3% decline in the comparable FY 10 period. We believe M's sales recovery is being supported by favorable customer response to new private/exclusive label offerings, a stronger value message in marketing, and growth in the macys.com and bloomingdales.com online businesses. We see these positive factors, coupled with increased investment in associate training, enabling the company to maintain its positive same-store sales trend in the second half of FY 11, despite tougher comparisons.

► Risks to our recommendation and target price include a loss of business due to lackluster merchandising or uncompetitive pricing. Our corporate governance concerns include the non-disclosure of specific hurdle rates for performance-based equity awards and of stock ownership by executives.

► Our 12-month target price of $25 is based on a peer-median forward P/E multiple of 12.9X, above M's 10-year historical median, applied to our FY 11 EPS estimate.

Qualitative Risk Assessment

LOW	MEDIUM	HIGH

Our risk assessment reflects merchandise localization challenges and an uncertain outlook for consumer discretionary spending, partly offset by our view of M's strong brand and geographical presence in a consolidating industry.

Quantitative Evaluations

S&P Quality Ranking B-

D	C	B-	B	B+	A-	A	A+

Relative Strength Rank MODERATE
41
LOWEST = 1   HIGHEST = 99

Revenue/Earnings Data

Revenue (Million $)

	1Q	2Q	3Q	4Q	Year
2011	5,574	5,537	--	--	--
2010	5,199	5,164	5,277	7,849	23,489
2009	5,747	5,718	5,493	7,934	24,892
2008	5,921	5,892	5,906	8,594	26,313
2007	5,930	5,995	5,886	9,159	26,970
2006	3,641	3,623	5,785	9,571	22,390

Earnings Per Share ($)

2011	0.05	0.35	E-0.01	E1.51	E1.90
2010	-0.21	0.02	-0.08	1.10	0.83
2009	-0.14	0.17	-0.10	-11.33	-11.40
2008	0.11	0.17	0.08	1.73	2.01
2007	-0.13	0.51	0.03	1.45	1.80
2006	0.36	0.84	0.89	1.23	3.16

Fiscal year ended Jan. 31. Next earnings report expected: Mid November. EPS Estimates based on S&P Operating Earnings; historical GAAP earnings are as reported.

Dividend Data (Dates: mm/dd Payment Date: mm/dd/yy)

Amount ($)	Date Decl.	Ex-Div. Date	Stk. of Record	Payment Date
0.050	02/19	03/11	03/15	04/01/10
0.050	05/14	06/11	06/15	07/01/10
0.050	08/20	09/13	09/15	10/01/10
0.050	10/22	12/13	12/15	01/03/11

Dividends have been paid since 2003. Source: Company reports.

Please read the Required Disclosures and Analyst Certification on the last page of this report.

The McGraw-Hill Companies

Macy's Inc

STANDARD
&POOR'S

Business Summary August 12, 2010

CORPORATE OVERVIEW. In February 2005, Macy's Inc. (formerly Federated Department Stores, Inc.) and The May Department Stores Co. announced merger plans. At that time, May was in need of new leadership to revive its business, and M was in the midst of a successful turnaround and on the lookout for acquisitions that would expand its presence in underserved markets. Both companies viewed the merger as a win-win proposition, as M would roll out its profit-driving merchandising, pricing, and service initiatives to May's stores, and May would extend M's presence into 15 new states.

As a result of the $17 billion May merger, which closed in August 2005, M is now the second largest U.S. department store operator in annual revenues under the Macy's and Bloomingdale's names.

CORPORATE STRATEGY. Since 2005, M has focused on three key priorities to better position its business for long-term growth: growing "better" and "affordable luxury" assortments, with an emphasis on private label merchandise; im-

proving customer perceptions of fair value in less discounted prices; and enriching the overall shopping experience. With its merger with May, the company also expanded its core Macy's brand nationwide.

Going forward, M sees an opportunity to accelerate the sales performance in about 400 former May locations that were rebranded Macy's on September 9, 2006. As part of its efforts to increase public awareness of Macy's, which contributes about 90% of the company's revenues, M changed its corporate name to Macy's, Inc. from Federated Department Stores, Inc. on June 1, 2007. On that date, the company's shares began trading under the ticker symbol "M" (replacing "FD") on the New York Stock Exchange.

Company Financials Fiscal Year Ended Jan. 31

Per Share Data ($)	2010	2009	2008	2007	2006	2005	2004	2003	2002	2001
Tangible Book Value	0.67	0.44	NM	5.56	5.34	16.55	NM	13.47	12.16	12.47
Cash Flow	3.69	-8.37	4.90	4.11	4.29	4.09	3.92	3.31	2.94	1.32
Earnings	0.83	-11.40	2.01	1.80	3.16	1.93	1.86	1.61	1.30	-0.45
S&P Core Earnings	0.86	-3.23	1.90	1.62	2.21	1.83	1.69	1.24	0.91	0.25
Dividends	0.20	0.53	0.51	0.45	0.26	0.19	Nil	Nil	Nil	Nil
Payout Ratio	24%	NM	25%	25%	8%	10%	Nil	Nil	Nil	Nil
Calendar Year	2009	2008	2007	2006	2005	2004	2003	2002	2001	2000
Prices:High	20.84	28.47	46.70	45.01	39.03	29.08	25.30	22.13	24.95	26.94
Prices:Low	6.27	5.07	24.70	32.38	27.10	21.40	11.76	11.80	13.03	10.50
P/E Ratio:High	25	NM	23	25	12	15	14	14	19	NM
P/E Ratio:Low	8	NM	12	18	9	11	6	7	10	NM

Income Statement Analysis (Million $)										
Revenue	23,489	24,892	26,313	26,970	22,390	15,630	15,264	15,435	15,651	18,407
Operating Income	2,664	2,680	3,167	2,910	3,087	2,143	2,047	2,019	1,923	2,239
Depreciation	1,210	1,278	1,304	1,265	974	743	706	676	657	727
Interest Expense	562	599	588	520	422	299	266	311	331	444
Pretax Income	507	-4,938	1,320	1,446	2,044	1,116	1,084	1,048	780	113
Effective Tax Rate	31.0%	NM	31.1%	31.7%	32.8%	38.3%	36.1%	39.1%	33.6%	NM
Net Income	350	-48,003	909	988	1,373	689	693	638	518	-184
S&P Core Earnings	362	-1,366	860	888	967	655	628	490	364	102

Balance Sheet & Other Financial Data (Million $)										
Cash	1,686	1,306	583	1,211	248	868	925	716	636	322
Current Assets	6,882	6,740	6,324	7,422	10,145	7,510	7,452	7,154	7,280	8,700
Total Assets	21,300	22,145	27,789	29,550	33,168	14,885	14,550	14,441	15,044	17,012
Current Liabilities	4,454	5,126	5,360	6,359	7,590	4,301	3,883	3,601	3,714	4,869
Long Term Debt	8,456	8,733	9,087	7,847	8,860	2,637	3,151	3,408	3,859	4,374
Common Equity	4,701	4,646	9,907	12,254	13,519	6,167	5,940	5,762	5,564	5,822
Total Capital	13,399	14,498	20,440	21,829	24,083	10,003	10,089	10,168	10,768	11,589
Capital Expenditures	355	761	994	1,317	568	467	508	568	615	742
Cash Flow	1,560	-3,525	2,213	2,253	2,347	1,432	1,399	1,314	1,175	543
Current Ratio	1.6	1.3	1.2	1.2	1.3	1.7	1.9	2.0	2.0	1.8
% Long Term Debt of Capitalization	63.1	60.2	44.5	39.0	36.8	26.4	31.2	33.5	35.8	37.7
% Net Income of Revenue	1.5	NM	3.5	3.7	6.1	4.4	4.5	4.1	3.3	NM
% Return on Assets	1.6	NM	3.2	3.2	5.7	4.7	4.8	4.2	3.4	NM
% Return on Equity	7.5	NM	8.2	7.7	13.9	11.4	11.8	11.3	9.1	NM

Data as orig reptd.; bef. results of disc opers/spec. items. Per share data adj. for stk. divs.; EPS diluted. E-Estimated. NA-Not Available. NM-Not Meaningful. NR-Not Ranked. UR-Under Review.

Office: 7 W Seventh St, Cincinnati, OH 45202.
Telephone: 513-579-7000.
Website: http://www.fds.com
Chrmn, Pres & CEO: T.J. Lundgren

Vice Chrmn: R.J. Borneo
Investor Contact: K.M. Hoguet (212-494-1602)
EVP & CFO: K.M. Hoguet
EVP, Chief Acctg Officer & Cntlr: J.A. Belsky

Board Members: S. F. Bollenbach, D. Connelly, M. Feldberg, S. Levinson, T. J. Lundgren, J. Neubauer, J. A. Pichler, J. M. Roche, C. E. Weatherup, M. C. Whittington

Founded: 1858
Domicile: Delaware
Employees: 188,000

Marathon Oil Corp

STANDARD &POOR'S

S&P Recommendation HOLD ★★★☆☆

Price	**12-Mo. Target Price**	**Investment Style**
$35.61 (as of Oct 22, 2010)	$39.00	Large-Cap Blend

GICS Sector Energy
Sub-Industry Integrated Oil & Gas

Summary As one of the largest integrated oil companies in the U.S., Marathon also has international oil and gas exploration and production operations, and domestic refining, marketing, and transportation operations.

Key Stock Statistics (Source S&P, Vickers, company reports)

52-Wk Range	$36.00– 27.64	S&P Oper. EPS 2010**E**	3.40	Market Capitalization(B)	$25.271	Beta	1.19
Trailing 12-Month EPS	$2.72	S&P Oper. EPS 2011**E**	4.83	Yield (%)	2.81	S&P 3-Yr. Proj. EPS CAGR(%)	54
Trailing 12-Month P/E	13.1	P/E on S&P Oper. EPS 2010**E**	10.5	Dividend Rate/Share	$1.00	S&P Credit Rating	BBB+
$10K Invested 5 Yrs Ago	$14,043	Common Shares Outstg. (M)	709.7	Institutional Ownership (%)	80		

Price Performance

30-Week Mov. Avg. · · · · 10-Week Mov. Avg. - - - **GAAP Earnings vs. Previous Year**   **Volume** Above Avg. ▥▥ STARS
12-Mo. Target Price — Relative Strength — ▲ Up ▼ Down ▶ No Change   Below Avg. ▥▥ ★

Options: ASE, CBOE, P, Ph

Analysis prepared by **Tina J. Vital** on August 10, 2010, when the stock traded at **$ 34.11**.

Highlights

➤ We expect a modest rise in oil and gas production in 2010, of about 1.6% to 409,000 boe per day, reflecting higher costs, turnaround activity, and asset sales. For the long term, we project MRO's oil and gas production to expand about 4% per annum between 2009 and 2013 on new international developments and emerging U.S. onshore shale plays. MRO released the Paul Romano drilling rig early at its Innsbruck prospect in the Gulf of Mexico, but the company sees little impact from the drilling moratorium on its production in 2010 or 2011.

➤ For downstream, second quarter 2010 refinery throughputs rose 20% to 1.393 million b/d on contributions from the Garyville Major Expansion start-up. With signs of improved fuel demand, as of July 2010, we project U.S. Gulf Coast 3-2-1 refining crack spreads to widen about 9% in 2010 and 3% in 2011.

➤ First half 2010 operating EPS excluded net gains of $0.08 related to asset sales, but included net gains of $0.05 related to derivatives. We expect after-tax operating earnings to rise 123% in 2010 and 42% in 2011 reflecting improved demand and cost initiatives.

Investment Rationale/Risk

➤ MRO has increased its exposure to exploration & production projects in new international regions and U.S. onshore shale plays. About 7% of its production is located in the Gulf of Mexico, but most is globally diversified (32% U.S., 40% Africa, 28% Europe). In 2008, MRO evaluated the potential separation of its E&P and refining & marketing units into two independent companies, but in 2009, MRO concluded that it was in the best interest of its shareholders to remain integrated. While we see earnings stability as an integrated business, we look for reduced contributions from refining over the next five years.

➤ Risks to our recommendation and target price include adverse economic, industry and operating conditions (including geopolitical, regulatory and environmental problems), and difficulty replacing reserves.

➤ Blending our discounted cash flow ($36 per share, assuming a WACC of 9.1% and terminal growth of 3%) and relative market valuations, our 12-month target price is $39, representing an expected enterprise value of 3.6X our 2011 EBITDA estimate, a discount to peers.

Qualitative Risk Assessment

LOW	MEDIUM	HIGH

Our risk assessment reflects our view of the company's diversified and solid business profile in volatile and cyclical segments of the energy industry. We consider MRO's earnings stability to be good, and its corporate governance practices sound.

Quantitative Evaluations

S&P Quality Ranking B+

D	C	B-	B	B+	A-	A	A+

Relative Strength Rank STRONG

71

LOWEST = 1   HIGHEST = 99

Revenue/Earnings Data

Revenue (Million $)

	1Q	2Q	3Q	4Q	Year
2010	14,657	18,574	--	--	--
2009	10,176	13,039	14,362	15,893	54,139
2008	18,100	20,617	21,841	13,064	72,128
2007	12,869	16,736	16,762	18,185	64,552
2006	16,418	18,179	16,492	13,807	64,896
2005	12,932	16,019	17,248	17,314	63,673

Earnings Per Share ($)

	1Q	2Q	3Q	4Q	Year
2010	0.64	1.00	E0.91	E0.94	E3.40
2009	0.40	0.48	0.55	0.28	1.67
2008	1.02	1.08	2.90	-0.06	4.95
2007	1.04	2.24	1.49	0.94	5.68
2006	1.07	2.04	2.26	1.53	6.87
2005	0.47	0.96	1.04	1.74	4.25

Fiscal year ended Dec. 31. Next earnings report expected: NA. EPS Estimates based on S&P Operating Earnings; historical GAAP earnings are as reported.

Dividend Data (Dates: mm/dd Payment Date: mm/dd/yy)

Amount ($)	Date Decl.	Ex-Div. Date	Stk. of Record	Payment Date
0.240	10/28	11/16	11/18	12/10/09
0.240	02/01	02/12	02/17	03/10/10
0.250	04/28	05/17	05/19	06/10/10
0.250	07/28	08/16	08/18	09/10/10

Dividends have been paid since 1991. Source: Company reports.

Please read the Required Disclosures and Analyst Certification on the last page of this report.

The McGraw·Hill Companies

Marathon Oil Corp

STANDARD &POOR'S

Business Summary August 10, 2010

CORPORATE OVERVIEW. As one of the largest integrated oil companies in the U.S., Marathon Oil (MRO; formerly USX-Marathon Group, a part of USX Corp.) is engaged in four operating segments: Exploration and Production (E&P; 15% of 2009 revenues; 67% of 2009 segment income); Oil Sands Mining (OSM; 1%; 2%), Refining, Marketing and Transportation (RM&T; 84%; 26%); and Integrated Gas (IG; less than 1%; 5%).

MRO conducts exploration in the U.S., Angola, Norway and Indonesia, and production activities in the U.S., the U.K., Norway, Ireland, Equatorial Guinea and Libya. Including synthetic crude oil (SCO), proved oil and gas reserves rose 41% to 1.68 billion barrel oil equivalent (boe; 71% developed; 73% liquids and SCO) in 2009. Conventional oil and gas net sales rose 8.4% to 400,000 boe per day (boe/d; 55% liquids; 32% U.S., 40% Africa, and 28% Europe) in 2009. Net sales of SCO production remained level at 32,000 barrels per day (b/d) in 2009. Using John S. Herold data, we estimate MRO's three-year (2006-08) finding and development costs at $35.37 per boe, above the peer average; its three-year proved acquisition costs at $13.72 per boe, above the peer average; its three-year reserve replacement costs at $22.96 per boe, above the peer average; and its three-year reserve replacement rate at 183%, in line with the peer average. Excluding oil sands, we estimate MRO's 2009 organic

reserve replacement at 48% (overall 48%).

The RM&T segment owned and operated seven refineries (436,000 b/d Garyville, LA; 212,000 b/d Catlettsburg, KY; 206,000 b/d Robinson, IL; 106,000 b/d Detroit, MI; 78,000 b/d Canton, OH; 76,000 b/d Texas City, TX; and 74,000 b/d St. Paul Park, MN) for a total throughput capacity of 1,188,000 b/d of crude oil, as of year-end 2009. MRO sourced about 78% of its refinery crude feedstock from North America, 16% from the Middle East and Africa, and 6% from other regions in 2009.

MRO terminals supplied petroleum products to private-brand marketers, as well as about 4,600 Marathon-branded retail outlets in 2009. Retail sales of gasoline and convenience store merchandise are also made through its wholly-owned subsidiary, Speedway SuperAmerica LLC (SSA), which had 1,603 retail outlets at the end of 2009 (primarily under the Speedway and SuperAmerica brand names).

Company Financials Fiscal Year Ended Dec. 31

Per Share Data ($)	2009	2008	2007	2006	2005	2004	2003	2002	2001	2000
Tangible Book Value	28.89	28.16	22.59	18.72	13.90	11.17	9.20	7.57	7.99	7.77
Cash Flow	5.35	8.00	7.91	9.30	6.14	3.57	3.53	2.80	4.12	2.69
Earnings	1.67	4.95	5.68	6.87	4.25	1.86	1.63	0.86	2.13	0.70
S&P Core Earnings	1.54	5.77	5.69	6.85	4.20	1.91	1.63	0.69	2.21	NA
Dividends	0.96	0.96	0.92	0.77	0.61	0.52	0.48	0.46	0.46	0.44
Payout Ratio	57%	19%	16%	11%	14%	28%	29%	53%	75%	63%
Prices:High	35.71	63.22	67.04	49.37	36.34	21.30	16.81	15.15	16.87	15.19
Prices:Low	20.18	19.34	41.50	31.01	17.76	15.15	9.93	9.41	12.48	10.34
P/E Ratio:High	21	13	12	7	9	11	10	18	28	22
P/E Ratio:Low	12	4	7	5	4	8	6	11	20	15

Income Statement Analysis (Million $)										
Revenue	48,546	72,128	64,552	64,896	63,673	49,598	40,963	31,464	33,019	34,487
Operating Income	NA	9,237	7,598	9,932	6,660	8,379	2,988	2,253	4,215	3,521
Depreciation, Depletion and Amortization	2,623	2,178	1,613	1,518	1,358	1,217	1,175	1,201	1,236	1,245
Interest Expense	149	50.0	290	108	145	161	238	288	196	260
Pretax Income	3,441	6,973	6,846	8,969	5,157	2,509	1,898	1,098	2,781	1,412
Effective Tax Rate	65.6%	49.4%	42.4%	44.8%	33.5%	29.0%	30.8%	35.4%	27.3%	34.1%
Net Income	1,184	3,528	3,948	4,957	3,051	1,257	1,012	536	1,318	432
S&P Core Earnings	1,092	4,112	3,953	4,949	3,013	1,290	1,014	428	1,367	NA

Balance Sheet & Other Financial Data (Million $)										
Cash	2,057	1,285	1,199	2,585	2,617	3,369	1,396	488	657	340
Current Assets	10,637	8,403	10,587	10,096	9,383	8,867	6,040	4,479	4,411	4,985
Total Assets	47,052	42,686	42,746	30,831	28,498	23,423	19,482	17,812	16,129	15,232
Current Liabilities	9,057	7,753	11,260	8,061	8,154	5,253	4,207	3,659	3,468	4,012
Long Term Debt	8,436	7,087	6,084	3,061	3,698	4,057	4,085	4,410	3,432	4,196
Common Equity	21,910	21,409	19,223	14,607	11,705	8,111	6,075	5,082	4,940	4,845
Total Capital	30,442	31,826	28,696	20,083	17,868	16,411	12,171	12,908	11,632	12,235
Capital Expenditures	6,231	7,146	4,466	3,433	2,890	2,237	1,892	1,574	1,639	1,669
Cash Flow	3,807	5,706	5,500	6,475	4,409	2,474	2,187	1,737	2,546	1,677
Current Ratio	1.2	1.1	0.9	1.3	1.2	1.7	1.4	1.2	1.3	1.2
% Long Term Debt of Capitalization	Nil	22.3	21.2	15.2	20.7	24.7	33.6	34.2	29.5	34.3
% Return on Assets	2.6	8.3	10.7	16.7	11.8	5.9	5.4	3.2	7.9	2.8
% Return on Equity	NA	17.4	23.3	37.7	30.8	17.7	18.1	10.7	22.4	9.0

Data as orig reptd.; bef. results of disc opers/spec. items. Per share data adj. for stk. divs.; EPS diluted. E-Estimated. NA-Not Available. NM-Not Meaningful. NR-Not Ranked. UR-Under Review.

Office: 5555 San Felipe St Bsmt, Houston, TX 77056-2701.
Telephone: 713-629-6600.
Website: http://www.marathon.com
Chrmn: T.J. Usher

Pres & CEO: C.P. Cazalot, Jr.
EVP & CFO: J.F. Clark
Chief Acctg Officer & Cntlr: M.K. Stewart
Treas: P.C. Reinbolt

Investor Contact: H. Thill (713-296-4140)
Board Members: G. H. Boyce, C. P. Cazalot, Jr., D. A. Daberko, W. L. Davis, S. A. Jackson, P. Lader, C. R. Lee, M. E. Phelps, D. H. Reilley, S. E. Schofield, J. W. Snow, T. J. Usher

Founded: 1901
Domicile: Delaware
Employees: 28,855

Marriott International Inc.

STANDARD &POOR'S

S&P Recommendation SELL ★★☆☆☆	**Price** $37.29 (as of Oct 22, 2010)	**12-Mo. Target Price** $29.00	**Investment Style** Large-Cap Growth

GICS Sector Consumer Discretionary
Sub-Industry Hotels, Resorts & Cruise Lines

Summary Marriott's lodging brands include nearly 3,500 properties, most of which are managed by the company or are operated by others through franchise relationships.

Key Stock Statistics (Source S&P, Vickers, company reports)

52-Wk Range	$38.15–24.39	S&P Oper. EPS 2010**E**	1.10	Market Capitalization(B)	$13.583	Beta	1.54
Trailing 12-Month EPS	$1.05	S&P Oper. EPS 2011**E**	1.25	Yield (%)	0.43	S&P 3-Yr. Proj. EPS CAGR(%)	NM
Trailing 12-Month P/E	35.5	P/E on S&P Oper. EPS 2010**E**	33.9	Dividend Rate/Share	$0.16	S&P Credit Rating	BBB
$10K Invested 5 Yrs Ago	$12,764	Common Shares Outstg. (M)	364.2	Institutional Ownership (%)	63		

Price Performance

30-Week Mov. Avg. · · · ·   10-Week Mov. Avg. – – –   **GAAP Earnings vs. Previous Year**   **Volume** Above Avg. ▦▦▦ STARS
12-Mo. Target Price —   Relative Strength —   ▲ Up ▼ Down ▶ No Change   Below Avg. ▦▦▦ ★

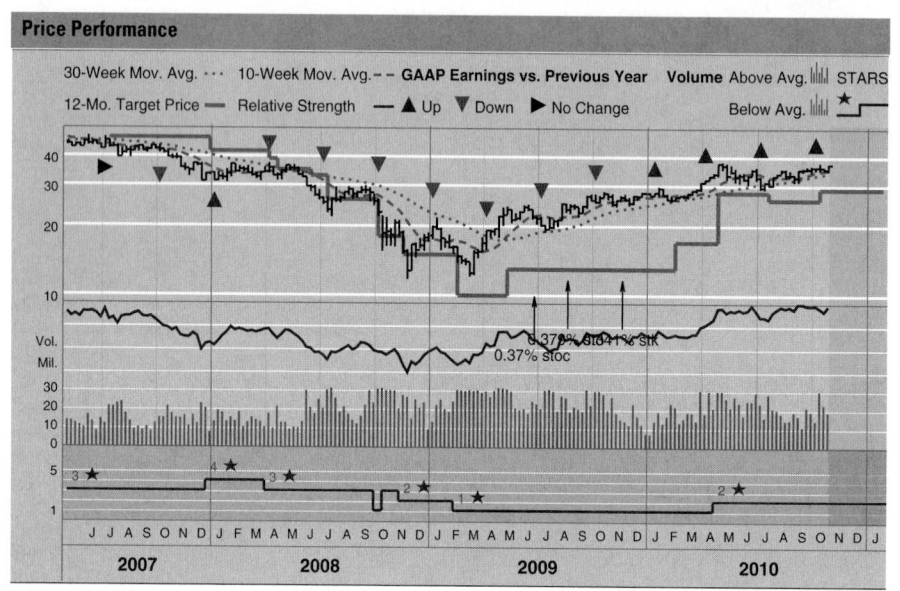

Options: ASE, CBOE, P, Ph

Analysis prepared by **Esther Y. Kwon, CFA** on October 18, 2010, when the stock traded at **$ 35.60**.

Highlights

► Global systemwide comparable RevPAR rose 8.5% in constant currencies in the third quarter of 2010 from a year earlier, due primarily to easy comparisons against a weak quarter in 2009. Comparable North American company-operated RevPAR rose 7.2% (1.9% drop in Q1 and up 7.5% in Q2), while the same measure on an international basis increased 8.5% (1.5% and 8.2%) using constant currencies.

► For 2010, we project that franchise fees, management fees, and revenues from owned hotels, all combined, will increase about 5%, due to system expansion, particularly in Asia, and 5.4% in 2011. We estimate profits from owned and operated hotels will rise approximately 40% in both 2010 and 2011. We believe timeshare operations, net of expenses and loan loss provisions, will show a $224 million profit on significant restructuring savings in 2010 and rise to $256 million in 2011.

► We estimate EBITDA of $1.04 billion and EPS of $1.10 in 2010. For 2011, we expect hotel operating profit to improve further, but see modest deterioration in timeshare profits. We estimate EBITDA will increase to $1.05 billion with EPS of $1.25.

Investment Rationale/Risk

► Our sell opinion reflects our view that global hotel industry fundamentals are likely to remain materially below pre-recession levels through at least 2012. We believe MAR's growth strategy could increase financing risks and stress its capital structure. We also think the financial health of MAR's hotel owner and franchise partners poses potential risks.

► Risks to our recommendation and target price include the prospects for a shorter and milder global economic downturn than we currently expect, raising the possibility of an earlier industry rebound. Property development could slow dramatically during this period of global financial distress, which would generally be a long-term positive.

► Our 12-month target price of $29 is based on an enterprise value of about 11X our forecast of 2011 EBITDA of approximately $1.15 billion, reflecting an EV/EBITDA discount to large market peers and the lodging group average.

Qualitative Risk Assessment

LOW	MEDIUM	HIGH

Our risk assessment reflects our view that MAR is subject not only to improving cyclical economic factors, but also to lagging weakness in industry fundamentals, with the latter outweighing the former, so that a material increase in earnings to pre-recession levels is unlikely for some time. While we expect internal cash flow to be sufficient to finance future minimum capital needs, outside capital, particularly to finance timeshare receivables, is likely to be more costly.

Quantitative Evaluations

S&P Quality Ranking   **A-**

D	C	B-	B	B+	A-	A	A+

Relative Strength Rank   **MODERATE**

LOWEST = 1   70   HIGHEST = 99

Revenue/Earnings Data

Revenue (Million $)

	1Q	2Q	3Q	4Q	Year
2010	2,630	2,771	2,648	--	--
2009	2,495	2,562	2,471	3,380	10,908
2008	2,947	3,185	2,963	3,784	12,879
2007	2,836	3,122	2,943	4,089	12,990
2006	2,705	2,891	2,703	3,861	12,160
2005	2,534	2,661	2,714	3,641	11,550

Earnings Per Share ($)

2010	0.22	0.31	0.22	E0.35	E1.10
2009	-0.06	0.10	-1.31	0.28	-0.97
2008	0.33	0.41	0.26	-0.03	0.97
2007	0.40	0.43	0.31	0.61	1.73
2006	0.38	0.43	0.33	0.51	1.65
2005	0.30	0.29	0.32	0.53	1.43

Fiscal year ended Dec. 31. Next earnings report expected: Mid February. EPS Estimates based on S&P Operating Earnings; historical GAAP earnings are as reported.

Dividend Data (Dates: mm/dd Payment Date: mm/dd/yy)

Amount ($)	Date Decl.	Ex-Div. Date	Stk. of Record	Payment Date
Stk.	11/05	11/17	11/19	12/03/09
0.040	02/04	02/17	02/19	04/09/10
0.040	05/07	05/19	05/21	06/25/10
0.040	08/05	08/17	08/19	09/17/10

Dividends have been paid since 1998. Source: Company reports.

Please read the Required Disclosures and Analyst Certification on the last page of this report.

The **McGraw-Hill** Companies

Marriott International Inc.

STANDARD & POOR'S

Business Summary October 18, 2010

CORPORATE OVERVIEW. Marriott International's lodging and timeshare businesses included 3,420 properties with 595,461 rooms or suites as of January 1, 2010. This compared with 3,178 properties with 560,681 rooms or suites as of January 2, 2009. Of the 3,420 properties, approximately 2,950 were located in the U.S.

At year-end 2009, there were 1,098 properties (280,130 rooms or suites) that MAR operated under long-term management agreements, 35 properties (9,277 rooms) that were leased and managed by MAR, and eight properties (1,785) that the company owned. With its management agreements, the company typically earns a base fee, and may receive an incentive management fee that is based on hotel profits. MAR also had 2,279 franchised properties, with 304,259 rooms, that were franchised and operated by other parties.

By brand (including franchises) as of year-end 2009, MAR's business included 545 Marriott Hotels & Resorts, Marriott Conference Centers or JW Marriott Hotels & Resorts properties; 74 Ritz-Carlton hotels; 143 Renaissance hotels; 858 Courtyard hotels; 629 Fairfield Inn properties; 256 SpringHill Suites properties; 592 Residence Inn hotels; 184 TownPlace Suites properties; two Bulgari Hotel & Resorts properties; 69 timeshare properties; and 52 residential and apartment units. Two brands for which the first properties are in planning or development are Nickelodeon Resorts by Marriott, and Edition, a global boutique hotel brand for which the company has partnered with hotelier Ian Schrager.

In 2009, MAR's North American full-service lodging segment, which included Marriott full-service and Renaissance businesses, accounted for approximately 44% of total revenues, while North American limited service accounted for 18%. In addition, international accounted for 10%, luxury 13%, and timeshare and other 14%.

The company's international presence as of year-end 2009 included: 108 properties (26,010 rooms or suites) in continental Europe, 61 in the British Isles (12,015), 114 properties (38,663) in Asia, 35 (10,433) in the Middle East or Africa, 125 (29,048) in the Americas ex-U.S., and eight (2,353) in Australia.

CORPORATE STRATEGY. In the third quarter of 2009, MAR determined that in response to difficult business conditions and a lack of consumer confidence, it would alter its timeshare strategy to stimulate sales, accelerate cash flow, and minimize future investment spending. These changes included price reductions and a cessation of most future development, and resulted in pretax charges of $752 million during the quarter.

Company Financials Fiscal Year Ended Dec. 31

Per Share Data ($)	2009	2008	2007	2006	2005	2004	2003	2002	2001	2000
Tangible Book Value	NM	NM	1.40	2.85	4.47	5.79	5.11	4.52	3.52	2.77
Cash Flow	-0.45	1.48	2.23	2.30	1.82	1.66	1.28	1.21	0.88	1.31
Earnings	-0.97	0.97	1.73	1.65	1.43	1.22	0.96	0.86	0.46	0.93
S&P Core Earnings	-0.92	0.98	1.76	1.55	1.24	0.99	0.67	0.76	0.35	NA
Dividends	0.08	0.33	0.28	0.24	0.20	0.16	0.15	0.14	0.13	0.12
Payout Ratio	NM	34%	16%	14%	14%	13%	15%	16%	28%	12%
Prices:High	28.40	37.48	51.44	47.79	35.01	31.65	23.34	22.97	24.98	21.51
Prices:Low	12.09	11.75	31.00	31.97	28.69	20.10	14.12	12.98	13.50	12.92
P/E Ratio:High	NM	39	30	29	24	26	24	27	55	23
P/E Ratio:Low	NM	12	18	19	20	16	15	15	30	14

Income Statement Analysis (Million $)										
Revenue	10,908	12,879	12,990	12,160	11,550	10,099	9,014	8,441	10,152	10,017
Operating Income	155	1,120	1,385	1,199	739	643	537	634	779	997
Depreciation	185	190	197	188	184	166	160	187	222	195
Interest Expense	118	218	184	124	106	99.0	110	86.0	109	100
Pretax Income	-418	694	1,137	997	717	654	488	471	370	757
Effective Tax Rate	15.6%	50.4%	39.0%	28.7%	13.1%	15.3%	NM	6.79%	36.2%	36.7%
Net Income	-346	359	697	717	668	594	476	439	236	479
S&P Core Earnings	-327	364	711	680	579	484	330	381	180	NA

Balance Sheet & Other Financial Data (Million $)										
Cash	115	134	332	193	203	770	229	198	817	334
Current Assets	2,851	3,368	3,572	3,314	2,010	1,946	1,235	1,744	2,130	1,415
Total Assets	7,933	8,903	8,942	8,588	8,530	8,668	8,177	8,296	9,107	8,237
Current Liabilities	2,287	2,533	2,876	2,522	1,992	2,356	1,770	2,207	1,802	1,917
Long Term Debt	2,234	2,975	2,790	1,818	1,681	836	1,391	1,553	2,815	2,016
Common Equity	1,142	1,380	1,429	2,618	3,252	4,081	3,838	3,573	3,478	3,267
Total Capital	3,440	4,366	4,219	4,436	4,944	4,929	5,398	5,232	6,293	5,283
Capital Expenditures	147	357	671	529	780	181	210	292	560	1,095
Cash Flow	-161	549	894	905	852	760	636	626	458	674
Current Ratio	1.3	1.3	1.2	1.3	1.0	0.8	0.7	0.8	1.2	0.7
% Long Term Debt of Capitalization	64.9	68.1	66.1	41.0	34.0	16.9	25.7	29.7	44.7	38.2
% Net Income of Revenue	NM	2.8	5.3	5.9	5.8	5.9	5.3	5.2	2.3	4.8
% Return on Assets	NM	4.0	7.9	8.4	7.8	7.1	5.8	5.0	2.7	6.2
% Return on Equity	NM	25.6	34.4	24.4	18.2	15.0	12.8	12.5	7.0	15.5

Data as orig reptd.; bef. results of disc opers/spec. items. Per share data adj. for stk. divs.; EPS diluted. E-Estimated. NA-Not Available. NM-Not Meaningful. NR-Not Ranked. UR-Under Review.

Office: 10400 Fernwood Road, Bethesda, MD 20817.
Telephone: 301-380-3000.
Website: http://www.marriott.com
Chrmn & CEO: J.W. Marriott, Jr.

Pres & COO: A.M. Sorenson
Vice Chrmn: J.W. Marriott, III
Vice Chrmn: W.J. Shaw
EVP, CFO & Chief Acctg Officer: C.T. Berquist

Investor Contact: T. Marder (301-380-2553)
Board Members: M. K. Bush, L. W. Kellner, D. L. Lee, J. W. Marriott, III, J. W. Marriott, Jr., G. Munoz, H. J. Pearce, S. S. Reinemund, W. M. Romney, W. J. Shaw, L. M. Small

Founded: 1971
Domicile: Delaware
Employees: 137,000

Marshall & Ilsley Corp

STANDARD &POOR'S

S&P Recommendation HOLD ★★★★★

Price $6.18 (as of Oct 22, 2010)	**12-Mo. Target Price** $8.00	**Investment Style** Large-Cap Blend

GICS Sector Financials
Sub-Industry Regional Banks

Summary This Milwaukee-based financial services company operates throughout Wisconsin, as well as in Arizona and several other states.

Key Stock Statistics (Source S&P, Vickers, company reports)

52-Wk Range	$10.66– 4.97	S&P Oper. EPS 2010**E**	-1.07	Market Capitalization(B)	$3.258	Beta	1.46
Trailing 12-Month EPS	$-1.73	S&P Oper. EPS 2011**E**	0.12	Yield (%)	0.65	S&P 3-Yr. Proj. EPS CAGR(%)	NM
Trailing 12-Month P/E	NM	P/E on S&P Oper. EPS 2010**E**	NM	Dividend Rate/Share	$0.04	S&P Credit Rating	A
$10K Invested 5 Yrs Ago	$2,141	Common Shares Outstg. (M)	527.6	Institutional Ownership (%)	74		

Price Performance

30-Week Mov. Avg. ··· 10-Week Mov. Avg. - - 12-Mo. Target Price — Relative Strength — GAAP Earnings vs. Previous Year ▲ Up ▼ Down ► No Change Volume Above Avg. Below Avg. STARS

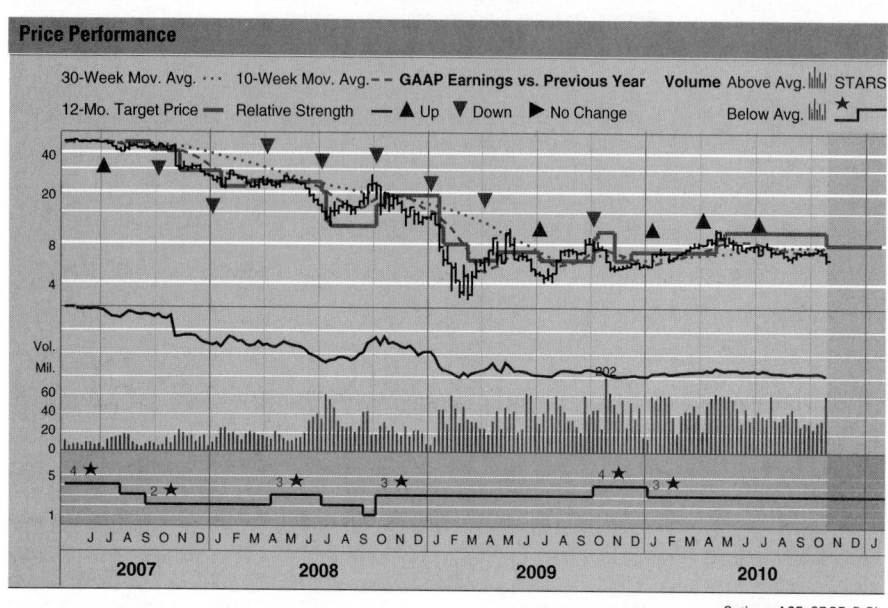

Options: ASE, CBOE, P, Ph

Highlights

► The 12-month target price for MI has recently been changed to $8.00 from $10.00. The Highlights section of this Stock Report will be updated accordingly.

Investment Rationale/Risk

► The Investment Rationale/Risk section of this Stock Report will be updated shortly. For the latest News story on MI from MarketScope, see below.

► 10/20/10 03:43 pm ET ... S&P MAINTAINS HOLD RECOMMENDATION ON SHARES OF MARSHALL & ILSLEY CORP (MI 6.25***): Q3 loss per share of $0.32, vs. a $0.68 loss, is wider than our estimate of a $0.26 loss, on a higher than expected loan loss provision, and lower than expected net interest income, partly offset by gains on securities. On Q3 results, we are widening our '10 loss per share estimate to $1.07 loss from $0.98. Though we see credit quality as stable, we were hoping for improvements. We are therefore cutting our target price by $3.00 to $8.00, and basing it on a discount to peers 1.0X our $7.85 per share year-end estimate of tangible book value. /E. Oja

Qualitative Risk Assessment

LOW	MEDIUM	HIGH

Our risk assessment reflects our view of the company's large-cap valuation and its history of profitability, offset by the risk that credit quality may suffer further from weakness in the Sunbelt and Midwest.

Quantitative Evaluations

S&P Quality Ranking B+

D	C	B-	B	B+	A-	A	A+

Relative Strength Rank WEAK

9

LOWEST = 1   HIGHEST = 99

Revenue/Earnings Data

Revenue (Million $)

	1Q	2Q	3Q	4Q	Year
2010	797.2	732.3	--	--	--
2009	820.5	895.7	830.9	773.4	3,383
2008	1,090	1,002	982.5	951.5	4,169
2007	1,386	1,438	1,474	3,873	4,398
2006	1,139	1,290	1,381	1,317	5,128
2005	895.1	975.8	1,014	1,076	3,963

Earnings Per Share ($)

	1Q	2Q	3Q	4Q	Year
2010	-0.27	-0.33	E-0.32	E-0.15	E-1.07
2009	-0.44	-0.83	-0.68	-0.54	-2.46
2008	0.56	-1.52	0.32	-7.25	-7.92
2007	0.83	0.83	0.85	-0.09	1.87
2006	0.72	0.74	0.92	0.79	3.17
2005	0.73	0.81	0.78	0.78	3.10

Fiscal year ended Dec. 31. Next earnings report expected: NA. EPS Estimates based on S&P Operating Earnings; historical GAAP earnings are as reported.

Dividend Data (Dates: mm/dd Payment Date: mm/dd/yy)

Amount ($)	Date Decl.	Ex-Div. Date	Stk. of Record	Payment Date
0.010	02/18	02/25	03/01	03/12/10
0.010	04/27	05/27	06/01	06/11/10
0.010	08/19	08/30	09/01	09/10/10
0.010	10/21	11/29	12/01	12/10/10

Dividends have been paid since 1938. Source: Company reports.

Please read the Required Disclosures and Analyst Certification on the last page of this report.

The McGraw-Hill Companies

Marshall & Ilsley Corp

STANDARD &POOR'S

Business Summary July 21, 2010

CORPORATE OVERVIEW. Marshall & Ilsley Corp. owns banking subsidiaries with operations in Wisconsin and the metropolitan areas of Phoenix and Tucson, AZ, Minneapolis/St. Paul, MN, St. Louis, MO, Las Vegas, NV, and Naples and Bonita Springs, FL. MI also owns nonbanking subsidiaries that are related or incidental to banking. The company also has other business operations that include trust services, residential mortgage banking, capital markets, brokerage and insurance, commercial leasing, commercial mortgage banking and community development investments.

PRIMARY BUSINESS DYNAMICS. In 2007, MI separated MI and Metavante Corporation into two separate publicly held companies. Warburg Pincus, a global private equity investor, invested $625 million to acquire an equity stake of 25% in Metavante Corp, while MI shareholders owned the remaining 75% of Metavante. By the terms of the deal, each share of the "old" MI was entitled to receive one share of "new" Marshall & Ilsley Corp., plus one-third of a share of Metavante Corp. MI received a cash infusion of about $1.665 billion, which may be invested, used to improve MI's capital ratios, buy back shares or increase the dividend.

Starting in the 1990s, the company made several sizable bank acquisitions, mostly in Wisconsin. Beginning in 2000, it shifted its bank acquisition focus outside Wisconsin. Between 1994 and 1998, the company acquired six Wisconsin banks, with assets totaling $9.3 billion, for $2.0 billion. In 2001 and 2002, MI acquired three banks in Minnesota and one bank in Missouri, with combined assets of $4.3 billion, for a total of $994 million. On April 3, 2006, MI closed its acquisition of Gold Banc Corp. in Kansas, with assets of $4.1 billion, for $715 million. On March 1, 2006, the company completed its acquisition of Trustcorp Financial in Missouri, with assets of $705 million, for $181 million. On December 4, 2006, MI announced the pending acquisition of United Heritage Bank of Orlando, for $217 million; this deal closed on April 2, 2007. On February 12, 2007, MI announced the acquisition of Excel Bank Corp. for $101 million, and this transaction closed July 2, 2007. MI's most recent acquisition was First Indiana Corp., for $538 million cash, on January 3, 2008.

Company Financials Fiscal Year Ended Dec. 31

Per Share Data ($)	2009	2008	2007	2006	2005	2004	2003	2002	2001	2000
Tangible Book Value	11.86	20.71	19.82	11.51	9.02	7.76	9.96	8.61	9.00	9.06
Earnings	-2.46	-7.92	1.87	3.17	3.10	2.77	2.38	2.16	1.54	1.45
S&P Core Earnings	-2.46	-2.06	1.87	3.17	2.99	2.66	2.28	2.07	1.49	NA
Dividends	0.04	1.27	1.20	1.05	0.93	0.81	0.70	0.55	0.57	0.52
Payout Ratio	NM	NM	64%	33%	30%	29%	29%	25%	37%	36%
Prices:High	13.98	29.07	51.48	49.10	47.40	44.70	38.46	32.12	32.12	31.13
Prices:Low	2.98	10.90	26.04	40.83	40.05	35.67	24.60	23.11	23.54	19.13
P/E Ratio:High	NM	NM	28	15	15	16	16	15	21	22
P/E Ratio:Low	NM	NM	14	13	13	13	10	11	15	13

Income Statement Analysis (Million $)	2009	2008	2007	2006	2005	2004	2003	2002	2001	2000
Net Interest Income	1,583	1,781	1,616	1,490	1,233	1,132	1,057	1,006	843	673
Tax Equivalent Adjustment	25.0	27.8	28.2	NA	33.3	NA	NA	32.2	31.2	31.0
Non Interest Income	816	733	729	1,906	1,704	1,411	1,194	1,089	1,020	978
Loan Loss Provision	2,315	2,038	320	50.6	44.8	38.0	63.0	74.4	54.1	30.4
% Expense/Operating Revenue	65.8%	117.8%	56.1%	63.6%	62.2%	62.7%	64.5%	61.9%	68.1%	65.4%
Pretax Income	-1,396	-2,503	711	1,196	1,090	945	758	719	501	470
Effective Tax Rate	NM	NM	30.1%	32.4%	33.3%	33.6%	28.3%	33.2%	32.6%	32.5%
Net Income	-759	-2,043	497	808	727	627	544	480	338	317
% Net Interest Margin	2.85	3.12	3.14	3.27	3.31	3.52	3.65	3.96	3.67	2.81
S&P Core Earnings	-858	-533	496	808	705	605	519	453	319	NA

Balance Sheet & Other Financial Data (Million $)	2009	2008	2007	2006	2005	2004	2003	2002	2001	2000
Money Market Assets	1,448	749	587	293	330	191	163	250	947	163
Investment Securities	7,177	7,669	7,818	7,473	6,320	6,085	5,607	5,209	4,464	5,848
Commercial Loans	12,950	14,880	26,526	23,717	19,023	16,646	14,254	6,586	10,815	9,649
Other Loans	31,268	35,105	19,770	17,917	14,866	12,810	10,896	17,011	8,480	7,938
Total Assets	57,210	63,824	59,849	56,230	46,213	40,437	34,373	32,875	27,254	26,078
Demand Deposits	7,833	6,880	6,174	6,112	5,525	15,005	4,715	4,462	3,559	3,130
Time Deposits	33,805	34,143	29,017	27,972	22,149	11,450	17,555	15,932	12,934	16,119
Long Term Debt	6,426	9,614	9,873	8,026	6,669	5,027	2,735	2,284	1,560	921
Common Equity	6,975	7,748	7,033	6,151	4,769	3,970	3,329	3,037	2,536	3,200
% Return on Assets	NM	NM	0.9	1.6	1.7	1.7	1.6	1.6	1.3	1.3
% Return on Equity	NM	NM	7.5	14.7	16.6	17.1	17.1	17.4	13.8	10.6
% Loan Loss Reserve	3.4	2.4	1.1	1.0	1.1	1.2	1.4	1.4	1.4	1.3
% Loans/Deposits	106.2	121.9	125.8	123.0	123.5	111.6	113.1	117.2	117.0	91.4
% Equity to Assets	12.2	10.9	11.4	10.7	9.9	9.8	9.5	9.2	9.0	11.9

Data as orig reptd.; bef. results of disc opers/spec. items. Per share data adj. for stk. divs.; EPS diluted. E-Estimated. NA-Not Available. NM-Not Meaningful. NR-Not Ranked. UR-Under Review.

Office: 770 N Water St, Milwaukee, WI 53202.
Telephone: 414-765-7801.
Website: http://www.micorp.com
Chrmn, Pres & CEO: M.F. Furlong

SVP & CFO: G.A. Smith
SVP, Chief Admin Officer & General Counsel: R.J. Erickson
SVP, Chief Acctg Officer & Cntlr: P.R. Justiliano
SVP & Treas: M.C. Smith

Investor Contact: D.L. Urban (414-765-7853)
Board Members: J. F. Chait, J. Daniels, Jr., M. F. Furlong, T. D. Kellner, D. J. Kuester, D. J. Lubar, K. C. Lyall, J. A. Mellowes, R. J. O'Toole, S. W. Orr, Jr., P. M. Platten, III, J. S. Shiely, G. E. Wardeberg, J. B. Wigdale

Founded: 1959
Domicile: Wisconsin
Employees: 9,410

The **McGraw-Hill** Companies

Marsh & McLennan Companies Inc.

STANDARD &POOR'S

S&P Recommendation **HOLD** ★★★★★	Price $25.19 (as of Oct 22, 2010)	12-Mo. Target Price $26.00	Investment Style Large-Cap Blend

GICS Sector Financials
Sub-Industry Insurance Brokers

Summary This global professional services concern provides risk and insurance services, investment management and consulting services through its operating companies.

Key Stock Statistics (Source S&P, Vickers, company reports)

52-Wk Range	$25.47– 20.21	S&P Oper. EPS 2010**E**	1.78	Market Capitalization(B)	$13.665	Beta	0.69
Trailing 12-Month EPS	$1.33	S&P Oper. EPS 2011**E**	2.05	Yield (%)	3.33	S&P 3-Yr. Proj. EPS CAGR(%)	13
Trailing 12-Month P/E	18.9	P/E on S&P Oper. EPS 2010**E**	14.2	Dividend Rate/Share	$0.84	S&P Credit Rating	BBB-
$10K Invested 5 Yrs Ago	$10,355	Common Shares Outstg. (M)	542.5	Institutional Ownership (%)	82		

Price Performance

30-Week Mov. Avg. · · · · 10-Week Mov. Avg. – – **GAAP Earnings vs. Previous Year** Volume Above Avg. STARS
12-Mo. Target Price — Relative Strength — ▲ Up ▼ Down ► No Change Below Avg.

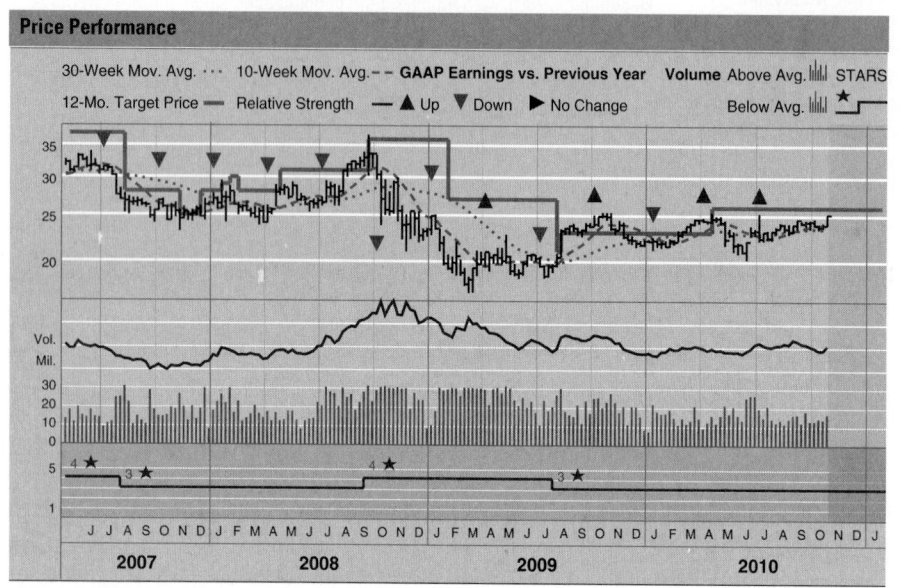

Options: ASE, CBOE, P, Ph

Analysis prepared by **Bret Howlett** on August 18, 2010, when the stock traded at **$ 23.74**.

Highlights

➤ We anticipate organic revenue growth of 2%-3% in the risk and insurance segment in 2010, driven by solid new business production, better P&C pricing in some business lines, and the favorable impact of foreign currency. We forecast 8%-10% revenue growth at Guy Carpenter due to acquisitions, strong retention, and new business wins. We estimate that consulting revenues will increase 2%-3%, boosted by strong organic growth at Oliver Wyman. Expense reductions should keep consulting margins stable. We anticipate risk and insurance operating margins increasing to 21%-22%.

➤ We expect MMC to continue its aggressive expense management, and forecast at least $100 million of cost savings in 2010. We believe MMC's financial position is strong, and estimate that the company will have at least $1.5 billion in excess cash following the Alaska settlement. We believe the company is well positioned to capitalize on M&A opportunities. We expect fiduciary income to be weak as interest rates are likely to remain low.

➤ We forecast EPS of $1.78 for 2010 and $2.05 for 2011, excluding certain one-time items and discontinued operations.

Investment Rationale/Risk

➤ While we believe MMC is making progress with its restructuring initiatives, and think it will benefit from an improved insurance pricing environment, we expect its economically sensitive consulting business to be a drag on earnings growth. MMC has been aggressively cutting costs at Mercer, Oliver Wyman and Kroll (sold in 2010), but its consulting businesses contribute nearly half of the company's revenues, and could present earnings challenges, in our view. Still, we view favorably MMC's organic growth outlook, new business production and improving customer retention rates despite a weak environment. We see considerable room for margin expansion given cost-cutting efforts, restructured operations, and top-line growth.

➤ Risks to our recommendation and target price include lower-than-expected revenue on rate increases; deteriorating client retention; lower-than-projected cost savings from restructurings and layoffs; and unfavorable legal and regulatory developments.

➤ Our 12-month target price is $26, about 14.6X our estimate of 2010 EPS, below MMC's historical multiples.

Qualitative Risk Assessment

LOW	MEDIUM	HIGH

Our risk assessment reflects the company's leading market share position, diversified businesses and global scale, offset by regulatory scrutiny and business model changes as a result of contingent commissions, and potential impairment charges related to goodwill. We believe MMC is more exposed to the weak economy than peers due to its sizable consulting businesses.

Quantitative Evaluations

S&P Quality Ranking B

D	C	B-	**B**	B+	A-	A	A+

Relative Strength Rank MODERATE

65

LOWEST = 1 HIGHEST = 99

Revenue/Earnings Data

Revenue (Million $)

	1Q	2Q	3Q	4Q	Year
2010	2,795	2,606	--	--	--
2009	2,609	2,629	2,523	2,732	10,493
2008	3,047	3,048	2,838	2,662	11,587
2007	2,812	2,819	2,794	2,925	11,350
2006	3,016	2,970	2,872	3,063	11,921
2005	3,070	2,977	2,779	2,826	11,652

Earnings Per Share ($)

2010	0.50	-0.06	E0.40	E0.50	E1.78
2009	0.35	-0.32	0.40	0.01	0.43
2008	-0.41	0.11	0.03	0.14	-0.13
2007	0.41	0.25	0.15	0.17	0.98
2006	0.43	0.31	0.32	0.39	1.45
2005	0.24	0.30	0.11	0.03	0.67

Fiscal year ended Dec. 31. Next earnings report expected: Early November. EPS Estimates based on S&P Operating Earnings; historical GAAP earnings are as reported.

Dividend Data (Dates: mm/dd Payment Date: mm/dd/yy)

Amount ($)	Date Decl.	Ex-Div. Date	Stk. of Record	Payment Date
0.200	01/20	01/27	01/29	02/16/10
0.200	03/17	04/07	04/09	05/17/10
0.200	05/20	07/07	07/09	08/16/10
0.210	09/15	10/06	10/08	11/15/10

Dividends have been paid since 1923. Source: Company reports.

Please read the Required Disclosures and Analyst Certification on the last page of this report.

Marsh & McLennan Companies Inc.

STANDARD &POOR'S

Business Summary August 18, 2010

CORPORATE OVERVIEW. Marsh & McLennan is one of the world's largest insurance brokers and provides advice and solutions in areas of risk, strategy and human capital. In 2009, total revenues exceeded $10.0 billion, with MMC providing its services in more than 100 countries.

The insurance brokerage industry has suffered in recent years from probes into bid rigging and contingent commissions. We believe settlements and corporate restructurings have improved the outlook at MMC, but ongoing legal and regulatory proceedings and uncertainty regarding implementing a new business model remain risks.

MMC operates in three main segments: risk and insurance services, risk consulting and technology, and consulting. Risk and insurance services (50% of operating segment revenues in 2009; 47% in 2008) includes insurance services, reinsurance services and risk capital holdings, risk management and consulting, insurance broking, and insurance program management. Reinsurance broking and catastrophe and financial modeling services are provided under the Guy Carpenter name. Risk consulting and technology (6% in 2009; 9% in 2008) is conducted under the Kroll name (sold in 2010). Consulting and

human resource outsourcing (44% in 2009; 45% in 2008) is offered under the Mercer and Oliver Wyman Group names.

LEGAL/REGULATORY ISSUES. In June 2010, MMC announced that its Mercer consulting subsidiary had reached a settlement of litigation brought by the Alaska Retirement Management Board (ARMB). Mercer will pay $400 million (excluding the $100 million covered by insurance), while denying any liability. We believe the $400 million settlement is a positive for MMC since it is significantly below the $2.8 billion that was sought by ARMB, and removes the uncertainty surrounding a jury trial in Alaska.

In the fourth quarter of 2009, MMC recorded a $205 million charge related to the securities and ERISA class action lawsuits filed in 2004. MMC did not admit to any liability or wrongdoing in connection with the settlement.

Company Financials Fiscal Year Ended Dec. 31

Per Share Data ($)	2009	2008	2007	2006	2005	2004	2003	2002	2001	2000
Tangible Book Value	NM	NM	0.13	NM	NM	NM	NM	NM	NM	9.47
Cash Flow	1.13	0.61	1.80	2.34	1.58	1.18	3.52	3.10	2.61	2.94
Earnings	0.43	-0.13	0.98	1.45	0.67	0.33	2.81	2.45	1.70	2.05
S&P Core Earnings	0.79	-0.12	0.86	1.30	0.38	1.11	2.29	1.60	0.91	NA
Dividends	0.80	0.80	0.76	0.68	0.68	0.99	1.18	1.09	1.03	0.95
Payout Ratio	186%	NM	71%	47%	101%	NM	42%	44%	61%	46%
Prices:High	25.46	36.82	33.90	32.73	34.25	49.69	54.97	57.30	59.03	67.84
Prices:Low	17.18	20.96	23.12	24.00	26.67	22.75	38.27	34.61	39.50	35.25
P/E Ratio:High	59	NM	35	23	51	NM	19	23	35	33
P/E Ratio:Low	40	NM	24	17	40	NM	14	14	23	17

Income Statement Analysis (Million $)	2009	2008	2007	2006	2005	2004	2003	2002	2001	2000
Revenue	10,493	11,587	11,350	11,921	11,652	12,159	11,588	10,440	9,943	10,157
Operating Income	1,394	1,561	1,586	1,946	1,386	2,073	2,887	2,633	2,283	2,179
Depreciation	365	382	442	488	490	456	391	359	520	488
Interest Expense	241	220	267	303	332	219	185	160	196	247
Pretax Income	308	79.0	847	1,219	571	450	2,335	2,133	1,590	1,955
Effective Tax Rate	16.6%	173.4%	34.8%	31.8%	33.6%	57.6%	33.0%	35.0%	37.7%	38.5%
Net Income	242	-69.0	538	818	369	176	1,540	1,365	974	1,181
S&P Core Earnings	410	-57.9	462	732	211	590	1,254	890	525	NA

Balance Sheet & Other Financial Data (Million $)	2009	2008	2007	2006	2005	2004	2003	2002	2001	2000
Cash	1,777	1,685	2,133	2,089	2,020	1,396	665	546	537	240
Current Assets	4,931	4,784	5,454	5,834	5,262	4,887	3,901	3,664	3,792	3,639
Total Assets	15,322	15,221	17,359	18,137	17,892	18,337	15,053	13,855	13,293	13,769
Current Liabilities	3,703	3,386	3,493	5,549	4,351	4,735	4,089	3,863	3,938	4,119
Long Term Debt	3,034	3,194	3,604	3,860	5,044	4,691	2,910	2,891	2,334	2,347
Common Equity	5,878	5,722	7,822	5,819	5,360	5,056	5,451	5,018	5,173	5,228
Total Capital	9,470	8,916	11,426	9,679	10,404	9,747	8,361	7,909	7,507	7,575
Capital Expenditures	305	386	378	307	345	376	436	423	433	472
Cash Flow	592	313	980	1,306	859	632	1,931	1,724	1,494	1,669
Current Ratio	1.3	1.4	1.6	1.1	1.2	1.0	1.0	0.9	1.0	0.9
% Long Term Debt of Capitalization	32.0	35.8	31.5	39.9	48.5	48.1	34.8	36.6	31.1	31.0
% Net Income of Revenue	2.3	NM	4.7	6.9	3.2	1.4	13.3	13.1	9.8	11.6
% Return on Assets	1.6	NM	3.0	4.5	2.0	1.1	10.7	10.1	7.2	8.8
% Return on Equity	4.2	NM	7.9	14.6	7.1	3.4	29.4	26.8	18.7	25.1

Data as orig reptd.; bef. results of disc opers/spec. items. Per share data adj. for stk. divs.; EPS diluted. E-Estimated. NA-Not Available. NM-Not Meaningful. NR-Not Ranked. UR-Under Review.

Office: 1166 Avenue of the Americas, New York, NY 10036-2774.
Telephone: 212-345-5000.
Email: shareowner-svcs@email.bankofny.com
Website: http://www.mmc.com

Chrmn: S.R. Hardis
Pres & CEO: B. Duperreault
EVP & CFO: V.A. Wittman
EVP & General Counsel: P.J. Beshar

SVP & Chief Admin Officer: M.A. Petrullo
Investor Contact: M.B. Bartley (212-345-5000)
Board Members: L. M. Baker, Jr., Z. W. Carter, B. Duperreault, O. Fanjul Martin, H. E. Hanway, S. R. Hardis, G. S. King, I. B. Lang, B. P. Nolop, M. D. Oken, M. Schapiro, A. Simmons

Founded: 1923
Domicile: Delaware
Employees: 52,000

Masco Corp

STANDARD &POOR'S

S&P Recommendation BUY ★★★★☆

Price	12-Mo. Target Price	Investment Style
$10.95 (as of Oct 22, 2010)	$14.00	Large-Cap Blend

GICS Sector Industrials
Sub-Industry Building Products

Summary This company is one of the world's leading makers of faucets, cabinets, coatings, and other consumer brand-name home improvement and building products.

Key Stock Statistics (Source S&P, Vickers, company reports)

52-Wk Range	$18.78– 9.94	S&P Oper. EPS 2010E	0.35	Market Capitalization(B)	$3.926
Trailing 12-Month EPS	$-0.47	S&P Oper. EPS 2011E	0.70	Yield (%)	2.74
Trailing 12-Month P/E	NM	P/E on S&P Oper. EPS 2010E	31.3	Dividend Rate/Share	$0.30
$10K Invested 5 Yrs Ago	$4,682	Common Shares Outstg. (M)	358.5	Institutional Ownership (%)	88

Beta	2.06
S&P 3-Yr. Proj. EPS CAGR(%)	53
S&P Credit Rating	BBB

Price Performance

30-Week Mov. Avg. ···· 10-Week Mov. Avg. – – GAAP Earnings vs. Previous Year   Volume Above Avg. STARS
12-Mo. Target Price — Relative Strength — ▲ Up ▼ Down ▶ No Change   Below Avg.

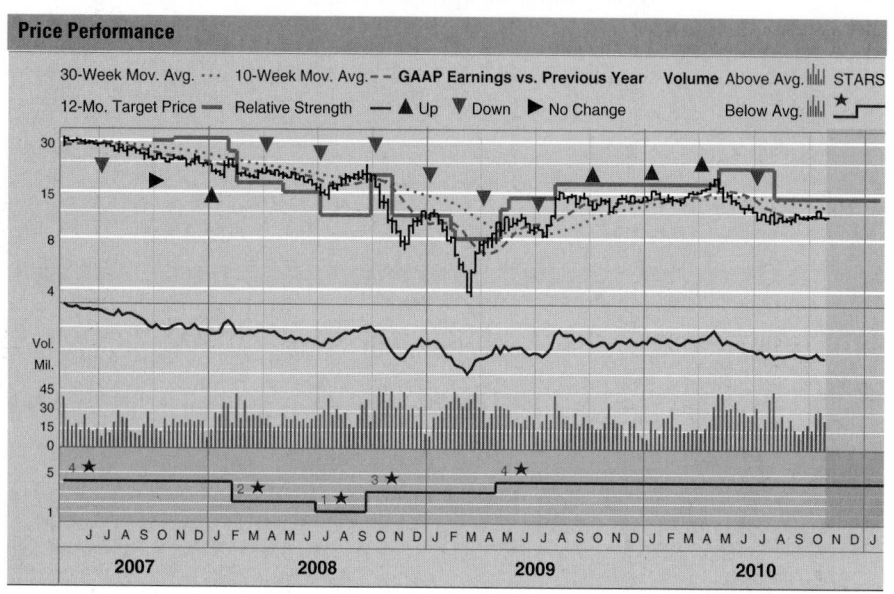

Options: ASE, CBOE, P, Ph

Analysis prepared by **Michael W. Jaffe** on August 11, 2010, when the stock traded at **$ 11.02**.

Highlights

► We expect sales to rise 3% in 2010, followed by an 8% gain in 2011. Results have weakened sharply over the past three plus years, hurt by a very soft U.S. economy and housing market, much slower big-ticket consumer spending, and economic woes in Europe. Yet, with government stimulus finally seeming to bring stabilization to housing markets, we see a modest sales upturn in 2010 and a somewhat more robust recovery in 2011. We expect the strongest sales in coming periods will be in the plumbing and decorative architectural products areas, as we see home improvement being one of the first places for spending to pick up.

► We see margins improving in both 2010 and 2011, on our better sales outlook, incremental benefits from cost-cutting efforts, and some savings from MAS's early 2010 plans to integrate its cabinet businesses into one organization (eventually expected to bring $30 million of annual savings). We see these factors outweighing a likely increase in interest charges, as notes were issued in March 2010.

► Our 2011 EPS estimate compares with a forecast for 2010 that excludes $0.12 of first half charges. Operating EPS was $0.28 in 2009.

Investment Rationale/Risk

► MAS has been hurt for an extended period by very soft U.S. housing and home improvement markets, and Europe's major economic downturn. Yet, we see MAS's business starting to revive over the next year, on an apparent economic recovery. We also think MAS was wise to sharply cut its dividend in early 2009, and its recent amendment of debt covenants puts MAS in better financial order, in our view. Our valuation model finds MAS shares undervalued.

► Risks to our recommendation and target price include a longer than expected U.S. housing downturn, and weaker than expected performance in foreign markets served by MAS.

► MAS recently traded at almost 16X our 2011 EPS forecast, in the bottom half of its valuation during its recovery from prior economic downturns. We think that valuation is too low, as we believe we are entering the early stages of a rebound in housing and home improvement markets, and that aggressive streamlining actions undertaken by MAS should eventually bring a strong earnings recovery. We set our 12-month target price at $14, 20X our 2011 EPS forecast and the higher end of its typical valuation early in business recoveries.

Qualitative Risk Assessment

LOW	MEDIUM	HIGH

Our risk assessment for Masco reflects its generation of strong levels of free cash flow during most business cycles, and what we view as a good business model. However, it also operates in a very cyclical area, as evidenced by the recent major downturn in its operating performance.

Quantitative Evaluations

S&P Quality Ranking   B-

D	C	B-	B	B+	A-	A	A+

Relative Strength Rank   WEAK

22

LOWEST = 1   HIGHEST = 99

Revenue/Earnings Data

Revenue (Million $)

	1Q	2Q	3Q	4Q	Year
2010	1,852	2,048	--	--	--
2009	1,797	2,013	2,084	1,869	7,792
2008	2,446	2,640	2,528	1,979	9,600
2007	2,865	3,148	3,059	2,698	11,770
2006	3,167	3,370	3,295	2,946	12,778
2005	2,914	3,286	3,296	3,146	12,642

Earnings Per Share ($)

2010	-0.02	0.01	E0.18	E0.06	E0.35
2009	-0.24	0.19	0.14	-0.49	-0.41
2008	0.07	0.20	0.10	-1.45	-1.08
2007	0.37	0.50	0.57	-0.39	1.06
2006	0.50	0.53	0.57	-0.48	1.15
2005	0.47	0.62	0.60	0.34	2.03

Fiscal year ended Dec. 31. Next earnings report expected: Late October. EPS Estimates based on S&P Operating Earnings; historical GAAP earnings are as reported.

Dividend Data (Dates: mm/dd Payment Date: mm/dd/yy)

Amount ($)	Date Decl.	Ex-Div. Date	Stk. of Record	Payment Date
0.075	12/09	01/06	01/08	02/08/10
0.075	03/26	04/07	04/09	05/10/10
0.075	06/25	07/07	07/09	08/09/10
0.075	09/10	10/06	10/08	11/08/10

Dividends have been paid since 1944. Source: Company reports.

Please read the Required Disclosures and Analyst Certification on the last page of this report.

The McGraw-Hill Companies

Masco Corp

STANDARD &POOR'S

Business Summary August 11, 2010

CORPORATE OVERVIEW. Masco is one of the largest U.S. makers of brand name consumer products for home improvement and new construction markets; it derives most of its revenues from the sale of faucets, kitchen and bath cabinets, plumbing supplies and architectural coatings. Operations are focused on North America (79% of 2009 sales) and Europe (most of the rest). Home Depot contributed 26% of 2009 sales (21% in 2008).

The plumbing products division (33% of 2009 sales) is a major global faucet maker. Masco revolutionized faucets in 1954 with the Delta line, and also offers the Peerless, Brizo and Newport Brass brands, among others. In addition, the division offers other bath products, including plumbing fittings and valves, bathtubs and shower enclosures, and spa items; brand names include Aqua Glass and HotSpring. The cabinets and related products division (21%) makes cabinetry for kitchen, bath, storage, home office and home entertainment applications, featuring the Kraftmaid, Tvilum-Scanbirk and Merillat brands.

Masco sells decorative architectural items (22%), including paints and stains,

and decorative bath and shower accessories. Trade names include Behr in paints and stains and Franklin Brass in bath and shower. It also supplies and installs insulation products and other building products (16%) such as gutters, fireplaces, garage doors and framing components, and sells other specialty products (7%), such as windows, patio doors and electric staple guns.

MANAGEMENT. In July 2007, Richard Manoogian, Masco's chairman and CEO, gave up his CEO duties and moved into a new post as executive chairman. Based on Mr. Manoogian's recommendation, Timothy Wadhams, Masco's senior vice president and CFO since 2001, was appointed to the CEO role. In addition, Alan Barry, Masco's president, stepped down from his post at the end of 2007, when he reached normal retirement age, with Mr. Wadhams also assuming that title.

Company Financials Fiscal Year Ended Dec. 31

Per Share Data ($)	2009	2008	2007	2006	2005	2004	2003	2002	2001	2000
Tangible Book Value	NM	NM	NM	0.54	0.88	1.54	1.36	1.31	1.30	2.78
Cash Flow	0.32	-0.41	1.71	1.76	2.66	2.56	2.00	1.85	1.02	1.84
Earnings	-0.41	-1.08	1.06	1.15	2.03	2.04	1.51	1.33	0.42	1.31
S&P Core Earnings	0.21	0.23	1.56	2.17	2.17	2.25	1.67	1.52	1.12	NA
Dividends	0.46	0.93	0.91	0.86	0.78	0.66	0.58	0.55	0.52	0.49
Payout Ratio	NM	NM	86%	75%	38%	32%	38%	41%	125%	37%
Prices:High	15.50	23.50	34.72	33.70	38.43	37.02	28.44	29.43	26.94	27.00
Prices:Low	3.64	6.82	20.89	25.85	27.15	25.88	16.59	17.25	17.76	14.50
P/E Ratio:High	NM	NM	33	29	19	18	19	22	64	21
P/E Ratio:Low	NM	NM	20	22	13	13	11	13	42	11

Income Statement Analysis (Million $)										
Revenue	7,792	9,600	11,770	12,778	12,642	12,074	10,936	9,419	8,358	7,243
Operating Income	571	780	1,419	1,700	1,881	1,944	1,738	1,683	1,309	1,295
Depreciation	254	236	241	244	241	237	244	220	269	238
Interest Expense	225	228	258	240	247	217	262	237	239	191
Pretax Income	-151	-211	770	900	1,412	1,518	1,216	1,031	301	893
Effective Tax Rate	32.5%	NM	43.6%	45.8%	36.7%	37.5%	38.1%	33.8%	34.0%	33.8%
Net Income	-140	-382	397	461	872	930	740	682	199	592
S&P Core Earnings	78.1	80.1	582	866	936	1,027	816	779	528	NA

Balance Sheet & Other Financial Data (Million $)										
Cash	1,413	1,028	922	1,958	1,964	1,256	795	1,067	312	169
Current Assets	3,451	3,300	3,808	5,115	5,123	4,402	3,804	3,950	2,627	2,308
Total Assets	9,175	9,483	10,907	12,325	12,559	12,541	12,149	12,050	9,183	7,744
Current Liabilities	1,781	1,547	1,908	3,389	2,894	2,147	2,099	1,932	1,237	1,078
Long Term Debt	3,604	3,915	3,966	3,533	3,915	4,187	3,848	4,316	3,628	3,018
Common Equity	2,817	2,846	4,025	4,471	4,848	5,596	5,456	5,294	4,120	3,426
Total Capital	6,785	7,323	7,991	8,004	9,665	9,783	9,304	9,610	7,747	6,444
Capital Expenditures	125	200	248	388	282	310	271	285	274	388
Cash Flow	114	-146	638	705	1,113	1,167	984	902	468	830
Current Ratio	1.9	2.1	2.0	1.5	1.8	2.1	1.8	2.0	2.1	2.1
% Long Term Debt of Capitalization	53.1	53.5	49.6	44.1	40.5	42.8	41.4	44.9	46.8	46.8
% Net Income of Revenue	NM	NM	3.4	3.6	6.9	7.7	6.8	7.2	2.4	8.2
% Return on Assets	NM	NM	3.4	3.7	6.9	7.5	6.1	6.5	2.3	8.2
% Return on Equity	NM	NM	9.4	9.9	17.0	16.6	13.8	14.7	5.3	18.0

Data as orig reptd.; bef. results of disc opers/spec. items. Per share data adj. for stk. divs.; EPS diluted. E-Estimated. NA-Not Available. NM-Not Meaningful. NR-Not Ranked. UR-Under Review.

Office: 21001 Van Born Road, Taylor, MI 48180.
Telephone: 313-274-7400.
Website: http://www.masco.com
Chrmn: R.A. Manoogian

Pres & CEO: T. Wadhams
COO & EVP: D.J. Demarie, Jr.
CFO & Treas: J.G. Sznewajs
Chief Acctg Officer & Cntlr: W.T. Anderson

Investor Contact: M.C. Duey (313-274-7400)
Board Members: D. W. Archer, T. G. Denomme, A. F. Earley, Jr., V. G. Istock, J. M. Losh, R. A. Manoogian, L. A. Payne, M. A. Van Lokeren, T. Wadhams

Founded: 1929
Domicile: Delaware
Employees: 35,400

Massey Energy Co

STANDARD &POOR'S

S&P Recommendation **HOLD** ★★★☆☆	Price $39.83 (as of Oct 22, 2010)	12-Mo. Target Price $42.00

GICS Sector Energy
Sub-Industry Coal & Consumable Fuels

Summary Massey Energy is the fourth largest U.S. coal producer, with an estimated 23% of production sold into the metallurgical coal markets.

Key Stock Statistics (Source S&P, Vickers, company reports)

52-Wk Range	$54.80– 25.85	S&P Oper. EPS 2010E	0.46	Market Capitalization(B)	$4.067
Trailing 12-Month EPS	$-0.16	S&P Oper. EPS 2011E	4.35	Yield (%)	0.60
Trailing 12-Month P/E	NM	P/E on S&P Oper. EPS 2010E	86.6	Dividend Rate/Share	$0.24
$10K Invested 5 Yrs Ago	$9,363	Common Shares Outstg. (M)	102.1	Institutional Ownership (%)	77

Beta	2.11
S&P 3-Yr. Proj. EPS CAGR(%)	20
S&P Credit Rating	NA

Price Performance

30-Week Mov. Avg. ···   10-Week Mov. Avg. ‑ ‑   GAAP Earnings vs. Previous Year   Volume Above Avg. STARS
12-Mo. Target Price —   Relative Strength   ▲ Up ▼ Down ▶ No Change   Below Avg. ★

Options: ASE, CBOE, P, Ph

Analysis prepared by **Mathew Christy, CFA** on October 21, 2010, when the stock traded at **$ 39.24**.

Highlights

▶ Including the operations of Cumberland Resources, we forecast that 2010 sales will rise about 17%. Our projection is based on an expected 6% increase in coal volumes from higher anticipated utility, metallurgical and industrial coal shipments. In addition, we estimate a 12% advance in average realized coal prices mainly on higher expected metallurgical coal and utility coal pricing. In 2011, we forecast a 27% increase in sales, as we look for higher volumes and overall better pricing.

▶ Following the nearly 5 percentage point decline in 2009, we project that operating margins will fall again in 2010, by 3.8 percentage points. This forecast is based on our expectation for higher absorption of fixed costs among reduced production capacity due to increased regulatory oversight and management's focus on the fallout from the Upper Big Bend mine explosion. In 2011, however, we forecast a significant rise in the operating margin, on positive operating leverage.

▶ Excluding charges and assuming tax rates of about 20.6% in 2010 and 22% in 2011, we estimate EPS of $0.46 for 2010 and $4.35 in 2011.

Investment Rationale/Risk

▶ We view positively the downward trend in thermal coal inventories at U.S. utilities over the past few months, which we attribute to higher electricity generation and coal use. We also believe a recovery in global steel production will persist, benefiting metallurgical coal producers such as MEE. However, we believe that the threat of a federal probe and/or charges following the mining accident that occurred at the Upper Big Bend mine increases the risks for lower future production, higher operating expenses, and litigation costs.

▶ Risks to our recommendation and target price include lower-than-expected coal prices, production volumes or productivity; reduced demand for metallurgical coal; adverse legislation or litigation; and the potential of a federal investigation and/or criminal negligence charges.

▶ Our 12-month target price of $42 is based on relative peer valuation analysis. We apply an EV/EBITDA multiple of 6.3X, below the peer average, to our forward 12-month EBITDA estimate, suggesting a $42 value.

Qualitative Risk Assessment

LOW	MEDIUM	**HIGH**

Our risk assessment reflects the cyclicality of the coal market, MEE's and the industry's high fixed-cost structure, the concentration of company reserves in the central Appalachian region, the heavy regulation of the industry and its utilities end market, and recent lawsuits pending against the company.

Quantitative Evaluations

S&P Quality Ranking   B

D	C	B-	**B**	B+	A-	A	A+

Relative Strength Rank   **STRONG**

94

LOWEST = 1   HIGHEST = 99

Revenue/Earnings Data

Revenue (Million $)

	1Q	2Q	3Q	4Q	Year
2010	682.8	810.2	--	--	--
2009	768.1	697.6	641.6	583.9	2,691
2008	644.6	826.8	763.3	755.0	2,990
2007	607.3	617.8	603.4	585.0	2,414
2006	559.5	556.1	555.9	548.4	2,220
2005	570.0	582.5	533.7	518.0	2,204

Earnings Per Share ($)

2010	0.38	-0.88	E-0.47	E0.59	E0.46
2009	0.51	0.24	0.19	0.28	1.22
2008	0.52	-1.16	0.64	0.63	0.68
2007	0.40	0.43	0.27	0.06	1.17
2006	0.08	0.04	0.30	0.10	0.51
2005	0.59	0.44	0.28	-2.37	-1.33

Fiscal year ended Dec. 31. Next earnings report expected: Late October. EPS Estimates based on S&P Operating Earnings; historical GAAP earnings are as reported.

Dividend Data (Dates: mm/dd Payment Date: mm/dd/yy)

Amount ($)	Date Decl.	Ex-Div. Date	Stk. of Record	Payment Date
0.060	11/09	12/15	12/17	12/31/09
0.060	02/16	03/15	03/17	03/31/10
0.060	05/18	06/14	06/16	06/30/10
0.060	08/17	09/14	09/16	09/30/10

Dividends have been paid since 2001. Source: Company reports.

The **McGraw-Hill** Companies

Massey Energy Co

STANDARD &POOR'S

Business Summary October 21, 2010

CORPORATE OVERVIEW. Massey Energy produces low-sulfur coal for electric generation, steel-making, and various industrial applications. MEE is the fifth largest U.S. coal company, by our calculation, and the largest in the central Appalachian region. It produces, processes and sells bituminous, low-sulfur coal of steam and metallurgical grades from 42 underground mines and 14 surface mines in West Virginia, Kentucky and Virginia. Its steam coal is primarily purchased by utilities and industrial clients as fuel for power plants. Its metallurgical coal is used primarily to make coke for use in the manufacture of steel. Coal tons sold declined to 36.7 million in 2009, from 40.9 million in 2008, while revenue per ton increased to $63.25, from $62.47, respectively. Average cash cost per ton was $53.06 in 2009, up from $48.57 in 2008. In 2009, approximately 99% of coal sales volumes was sold under long-term contracts.

The breakdown of tonnage sold by end market in 2009 was as follows: electric utilities, 73%; metallurgical (steel industry sector), 20%; and general industrial,

7%. In 2009, Constellation Energy Commodities Group, Inc. accounted for 19% of total produced coal revenue. The company produces coal using four distinct mining methods: underground room and pillar, underground longwall, surface, and highwall. Use of continuous miner machines in the room and pillar method of underground mining accounted for 45% of production in 2009, underground longwall mining operations provided 3% of production, surface mining accounted for 44%, and highwall 8%. MEE estimated that it had total recoverable reserves of about 2.4 billion tons as of December 31, 2009. The company projected that 61% of its reserves were comprised of coal containing less than 1% sulfur. Low-sulfur coal is vital to utility customers seeking to reduce emissions and reduce the costs of compliance with the Clean Air Act.

Company Financials Fiscal Year Ended Dec. 31

Per Share Data ($)	2009	2008	2007	2006	2005	2004	2003	2002	2001	2000
Tangible Book Value	14.67	12.13	10.17	8.60	10.26	10.16	10.05	10.73	11.55	NM
Cash Flow	4.54	3.93	4.22	3.34	1.74	3.12	2.20	2.35	2.38	3.39
Earnings	1.22	0.68	1.17	0.51	-1.33	0.18	-0.43	-0.44	-0.07	1.07
S&P Core Earnings	1.31	2.55	1.09	0.27	-1.83	0.14	-0.60	-0.33	-0.30	NA
Dividends	0.24	0.21	0.17	0.16	0.16	0.16	0.16	0.16	0.12	Nil
Payout Ratio	20%	31%	15%	31%	NM	89%	NM	NM	NM	Nil
Prices:High	44.40	95.70	37.99	44.34	57.00	36.96	21.60	22.41	28.95	13.19
Prices:Low	9.62	10.05	16.01	18.77	31.80	17.99	7.30	4.55	11.25	9.94
P/E Ratio:High	36	NM	32	87	NM	NM	NM	NM	NM	12
P/E Ratio:Low	8	NM	14	37	NM	NM	NM	NM	NM	9

Income Statement Analysis (Million $)										
Revenue	2,691	2,990	2,414	2,220	2,204	1,767	1,553	1,630	1,432	1,141
Operating Income	NA	647	433	348	426	280	179	181	191	268
Depreciation	284	269	246	231	235	225	196	208	181	171
Interest Expense	102	89.9	85.8	86.1	67.1	60.7	48.3	35.3	34.2	0.35
Pretax Income	137	60.3	130	45.0	-75.4	-5.64	-60.7	-57.5	-15.9	122
Effective Tax Rate	24.0%	6.80%	27.3%	7.57%	NM	NM	NM	NM	NM	35.5%
Net Income	104	56.2	94.1	41.6	-102	13.9	-32.3	-32.6	-5.42	78.8
S&P Core Earnings	112	211	87.6	22.8	-140	10.6	-44.8	-24.0	-22.1	NA

Balance Sheet & Other Financial Data (Million $)										
Cash	677	646	365	239	319	123	88.8	2.73	5.66	6.93
Current Assets	1,315	1,236	887	800	1,044	791	703	510	458	384
Total Assets	3,800	3,676	2,861	2,741	2,986	2,651	2,377	2,241	2,271	2,161
Current Liabilities	445	504	368	355	374	332	259	573	542	275
Long Term Debt	1,296	1,464	1,103	1,102	1,103	900	784	286	300	Nil
Common Equity	1,256	1,037	784	697	841	777	759	808	861	1,375
Total Capital	2,575	2,618	2,041	1,916	2,177	1,894	1,770	1,339	1,411	1,629
Capital Expenditures	275	737	270	298	347	347	164	135	248	205
Cash Flow	389	325	340	272	133	238	164	175	176	250
Current Ratio	3.0	2.5	2.4	2.3	2.8	2.4	2.7	0.9	0.8	1.4
% Long Term Debt of Capitalization	50.3	55.9	54.0	57.5	50.6	47.5	44.3	21.4	21.3	Nil
% Net Income of Revenue	3.9	1.9	3.9	1.9	NM	NM	NM	NM	NM	6.9
% Return on Assets	2.8	1.7	3.4	1.5	NM	NM	NM	NM	NM	3.8
% Return on Equity	9.1	6.2	12.7	5.4	NM	NM	NM	NM	NM	5.9

Data as orig reptd.; bef. results of disc opers/spec. items. Per share data adj. for stk. divs.; EPS diluted. E-Estimated. NA-Not Available. NM-Not Meaningful. NR-Not Ranked. UR-Under Review.

Office: 4 North 4th Street, Richmond, VA 23219.
Telephone: 804-788-1800.
Website: http://www.masseyenergyco.com
Chrmn & CEO: D.L. Blankenship

Pres: B.F. Phillips, Jr.
COO & SVP: J.C. Adkins
CFO: E.B. Tolbert
Chief Admin Officer: J.M. Poma

Board Members: D. L. Blankenship, J. B. Crawford, R. H. Foglesong, R. M. Gabrys, R. B. Holland, III, B. R. Inman, D. R. Moore, B. F. Phillips, Jr., S. C. Suboleski, L. J. Welty

Founded: 1912
Domicile: Delaware
Employees: 5,851

The **McGraw·Hill** Companies

MasterCard Inc

STANDARD &POOR'S

S&P Recommendation	**BUY** ★★★★☆	Price $245.15 (as of Oct 25, 2010)	12-Mo. Target Price $284.00	Investment Style Large-Cap Growth

GICS Sector Information Technology
Sub-Industry Data Processing & Outsourced Services

Summary MasterCard is a global leader in transaction processing and brand licensing providing services in over 210 countries and territories. The company has nearly 30 million acceptance locations.

Key Stock Statistics (Source S&P, Vickers, company reports)

52-Wk Range	$269.88– 191.00	S&P Oper. EPS 2010E	13.50	Market Capitalization(B)	$29.132	Beta	1.18
Trailing 12-Month EPS	$12.65	S&P Oper. EPS 2011E	15.76	Yield (%)	0.24	S&P 3-Yr. Proj. EPS CAGR(%)	15
Trailing 12-Month P/E	19.4	P/E on S&P Oper. EPS 2010E	18.2	Dividend Rate/Share	$0.60	S&P Credit Rating	NA
$10K Invested 5 Yrs Ago	NA	Common Shares Outstg. (M)	130.9	Institutional Ownership (%)	82		

Price Performance

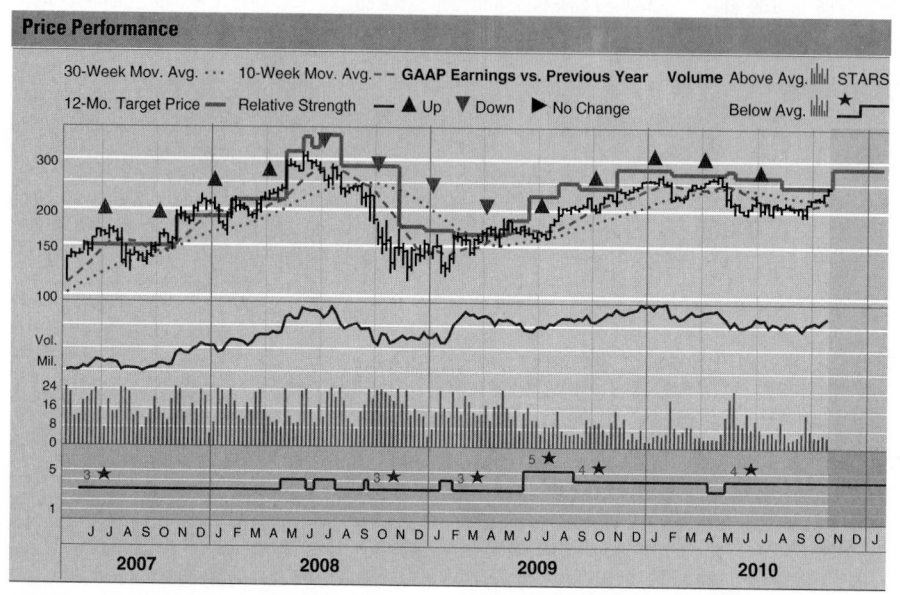

30-Week Mov. Avg. ···   10-Week Mov. Avg. - -   **GAAP Earnings vs. Previous Year**   Volume Above Avg. |lil| STARS
12-Mo. Target Price —   Relative Strength —   ▲ Up ▼ Down ► No Change   Below Avg. |lil| ★

Options: ASE, CBOE, P, Ph

Highlights

➤ The 12-month target price for MA has recently been changed to $284.00 from $244.00. The Highlights section of this Stock Report will be updated accordingly.

Investment Rationale/Risk

➤ The Investment Rationale/Risk section of this Stock Report will be updated shortly. For the latest News story on MA from MarketScope, see below.

➤ 10/25/10 10:39 am ET ... S&P MAINTAINS BUY RECOMMENDATION ON SHARES OF MASTER-CARD INC. (MA 245.02****): We raise our '11 EPS est. to $15.76 from $15.25, reflecting a recent $1B share buyback plan; we expect MA's purchase of DataCash, completed 10/22, to be EPS neutral in '11. We note that there has been considerable uncertainty related to the "Durbin amendment", part of the financial regulatory reform signed into law in July. We continue to think that the card networks will still be able to grow their business profitably, as they have in other markets that have faced regulation. We lift our target price to $284 from $244, 18X our '11 est., in historical P/E ranges for MA shares. /Z. Bokhari

Qualitative Risk Assessment

LOW	MEDIUM	HIGH

Our risk assessment reflects what we view as a dynamic market environment, offset by pending litigation risks and an evolving competitive and regulatory environment.

Quantitative Evaluations

S&P Quality Ranking   NR

D	C	B-	B	B+	A-	A	A+

Relative Strength Rank   STRONG

84

LOWEST = 1   HIGHEST = 99

Revenue/Earnings Data

Revenue (Million $)

	1Q	2Q	3Q	4Q	Year
2010	1,308	1,365	--	--	--
2009	1,156	1,280	1,364	1,298	5,099
2008	1,182	1,247	1,338	1,225	4,992
2007	915.1	997.0	1,083	1,073	4,068
2006	738.5	846.5	902.0	839.2	3,326
2005	658.2	771.9	791.6	715.9	2,938

Earnings Per Share ($)

	1Q	2Q	3Q	4Q	Year
2010	3.47	3.49	E3.28	E3.27	E13.50
2009	2.80	2.67	3.45	2.24	11.16
2008	3.38	-5.74	-1.49	1.84	-1.95
2007	1.57	1.85	2.31	2.26	8.00
2006	0.94	-2.30	1.42	0.30	0.37
2005	0.93	1.20	1.06	-0.53	2.67

Fiscal year ended Dec. 31. Next earnings report expected: Early November. EPS Estimates based on S&P Operating Earnings; historical GAAP earnings are as reported.

Dividend Data (Dates: mm/dd Payment Date: mm/dd/yy)

Amount ($)	Date Decl.	Ex-Div. Date	Stk. of Record	Payment Date
0.150	12/08	01/06	01/08	02/10/10
0.150	02/02	04/07	04/09	05/10/10
0.150	06/07	07/01	07/06	08/10/10
0.150	09/21	10/07	10/12	11/10/10

Dividends have been paid since 2006. Source: Company reports.

Please read the Required Disclosures and Analyst Certification on the last page of this report.

The **McGraw·Hill** Companies

MasterCard Inc

STANDARD &POOR'S

Business Summary August 13, 2010

CORPORATE OVERVIEW. MasterCard Incorporated (MA), a leading global payment solutions company, provides a variety of services in support of the credit, debit and related payment programs of about 23,000 financial institutions and other types of entities. MA follows a three-tiered business model as a franchisor, processor and advisor. The company, through its businesses, develops and markets payment solutions, processes payment transactions, and provides consulting services to its customers and merchants. MA manages a family of payment card brands, including MasterCard, MasterCard Electronic, Maestro, and Cirrus, which it licenses to its customers.

MasterCard generates revenues from two sources: operations fees and assessments. The company follows a "four-party" payment system, which typically involves four parties in addition to the company: the cardholder, the merchant, the issuer (the cardholder's bank) and the acquirer (the merchant's bank). Issuers typically pay operations fees and assessments, while acquirers principally pay assessments on gross dollar volume (GDV) or cards and, to a lesser extent, certain operations fees.

MA charges operations fees to its customers for providing transaction processing and other payment-related services. Operations fees include core authorization, clearing and settlement fees, cross-border and currency conversion fees, switch fees, connectivity fees and other operations fees, such as acceptance development fees, warning bulletins, holograms, fees for com-

pliance programs, and user-pay fees for a variety of transaction enhancement services. The company charges assessments based on customers' GDV of activity on the cards that carry its brands, and rates vary by region. GDV includes the aggregated dollar amount of usage (purchases, cash disbursements, balance transfers and convenience checks) on MasterCard-branded cards.

On an aggregate basis, the company processed 22.4 billion transactions (including PIN-based online transactions) during 2009, a 6.9% increase over the number of transactions processed in 2008. GDV on cards carrying the MasterCard brand, as reported by MA's customers, declined 3.3%, to approximately $2.45 trillion, in 2009. In 2009, MA's five largest customers accounted for 28% of total revenue, but no single customer exceeded 10% of total revenues. MA's revenue by geographic market is based on the location of the customer who issued the cards that are generating the revenue. Revenue generated in the U.S. contributed approximately 45.5%, 47.2% and 49.7% to net revenues in 2009, 2008 and 2007, respectively. No other country generated more than 10% of total revenues in those periods.

Company Financials Fiscal Year Ended Dec. 31

Per Share Data ($)	2009	2008	2007	2006	2005	2004	2003	2002	2001	2000
Tangible Book Value	21.42	9.56	18.79	13.90	6.99	NA	NA	NA	NA	NA
Cash Flow	12.32	-1.50	8.37	1.10	3.77	3.61	-2.71	2.40	2.96	2.48
Earnings	11.16	-1.95	8.00	0.37	2.67	2.38	-3.91	1.35	1.98	1.65
S&P Core Earnings	11.29	9.37	5.77	0.53	2.97	2.56	1.06	NA	NA	NA
Dividends	0.60	0.60	0.54	0.09	Nil	NA	NA	NA	NA	NA
Payout Ratio	5%	NM	7%	24%	Nil	NA	NA	NA	NA	NA
Prices:High	259.00	320.30	227.18	108.60	NA	NA	NA	NA	NA	NA
Prices:Low	117.06	113.05	95.30	39.00	NA	NA	NA	NA	NA	NA
P/E Ratio:High	23	NM	28	NM	NA	NA	NA	NA	NA	NA
P/E Ratio:Low	10	NM	12	NM	NA	NA	NA	NA	NA	NA

Income Statement Analysis (Million $)	2009	2008	2007	2006	2005	2004	2003	2002	2001	2000
Revenue	5,099	4,992	4,068	3,326	2,938	2,593	2,231	1,892	1,611	1,445
Operating Income	2,560	2,007	1,161	713	580	494	285	239	299	246
Depreciation	141	59.1	49.3	43.5	110	123	120	90.5	70.0	59.4
Interest Expense	115	104	57.3	61.2	70.2	69.7	62.9	9.89	9.55	9.65
Pretax Income	2,218	-383	1,671	294	407	324	-612	158	229	193
Effective Tax Rate	34.1%	NM	35.0%	82.9%	34.5%	26.5%	36.1%	26.5%	39.7%	42.5%
Net Income	1,463	-254	1,086	50.2	267	238	-391	116	142	118
S&P Core Earnings	1,471	1,230	782	72.8	297	257	107	NA	NA	NA

Balance Sheet & Other Financial Data (Million $)	2009	2008	2007	2006	2005	2004	2003	2002	2001	2000
Cash	2,880	2,247	2,970	2,484	1,282	1,138	911	872	670	NA
Current Assets	5,003	4,312	4,592	3,577	2,228	1,903	1,610	1,456	1,118	NA
Total Assets	7,470	6,476	6,260	5,082	3,701	3,265	2,901	2,261	1,486	NA
Current Liabilities	3,167	2,990	2,363	1,812	1,557	1,301	1,189	930	650	NA
Long Term Debt	21.6	19.4	150	230	229	230	230	80.1	80.1	NA
Common Equity	3,504	1,927	3,027	2,364	1,169	975	699	1,023	607	NA
Total Capital	3,533	2,026	3,253	2,665	1,403	1,209	933	1,104	687	NA
Capital Expenditures	56.6	75.6	81.6	61.2	43.9	30.5	76.3	54.2	57.9	113
Cash Flow	1,604	-195	1,135	150	377	361	-271	207	212	178
Current Ratio	1.6	1.4	1.9	2.0	1.4	1.5	1.4	1.6	1.7	NA
% Long Term Debt of Capitalization	0.6	1.0	4.6	8.8	16.4	19.0	24.6	7.3	11.7	Nil
% Net Income of Revenue	28.7	NM	26.7	1.5	9.1	9.2	NM	6.2	8.8	8.2
% Return on Assets	21.0	NM	19.2	1.1	7.7	7.7	NM	6.2	NA	NA
% Return on Equity	53.9	NM	40.3	2.8	24.9	28.5	NM	14.3	NA	NA

Data as orig reptd.; bef. results of disc opers/spec. items. Per share data adj. for stk. divs.; EPS diluted. E-Estimated. NA-Not Available. NM-Not Meaningful. NR-Not Ranked. UR-Under Review.

Office: 2000 Purchase Street, Purchase, NY 10577.
Telephone: 914-249-2000.
Website: http://www.mastercard.com
Chrmn: R.N. Haythornthwaite

Pres & CEO: A. Banga
Vice Chrmn: R.W. Selander
CFO: M. Hund-Mejean
CTO: M. Manchisi

Investor Contact: B. Gasper (914-249-4565)
Board Members: A. Banga, S. Barzi, D. R. Carlucci, S. J. Freiberg, R. N. Haythornthwaite, N. J. Karch, M. R. Olivie, J. O. Reyes, J. O. Reyes Lagunes, M. Schwartz, R. W. Selander, J. Tai, S. Tian

Founded: 1966
Domicile: Delaware
Employees: 5,500

The McGraw-Hill Companies

Mattel Inc.

STANDARD &POOR'S

S&P Recommendation HOLD ★★★☆☆	Price $23.25 (as of Oct 22, 2010)	12-Mo. Target Price $25.00	Investment Style Large-Cap Blend

GICS Sector Consumer Discretionary
Sub-Industry Leisure Products

Summary This large toy company's brands and products include Barbie dolls, Fisher-Price toys, American Girl dolls and books, and Hot Wheels.

Key Stock Statistics (Source S&P, Vickers, company reports)

52-Wk Range	$24.60– 18.41	S&P Oper. EPS 2010**E**	1.85	Market Capitalization(B)	$8.364	Beta	1.02
Trailing 12-Month EPS	$1.87	S&P Oper. EPS 2011**E**	1.95	Yield (%)	3.23	S&P 3-Yr. Proj. EPS CAGR(%)	12
Trailing 12-Month P/E	12.4	P/E on S&P Oper. EPS 2010**E**	12.6	Dividend Rate/Share	$0.75	S&P Credit Rating	BBB
$10K Invested 5 Yrs Ago	$18,639	Common Shares Outstg. (M)	359.7	Institutional Ownership (%)	91		

Price Performance

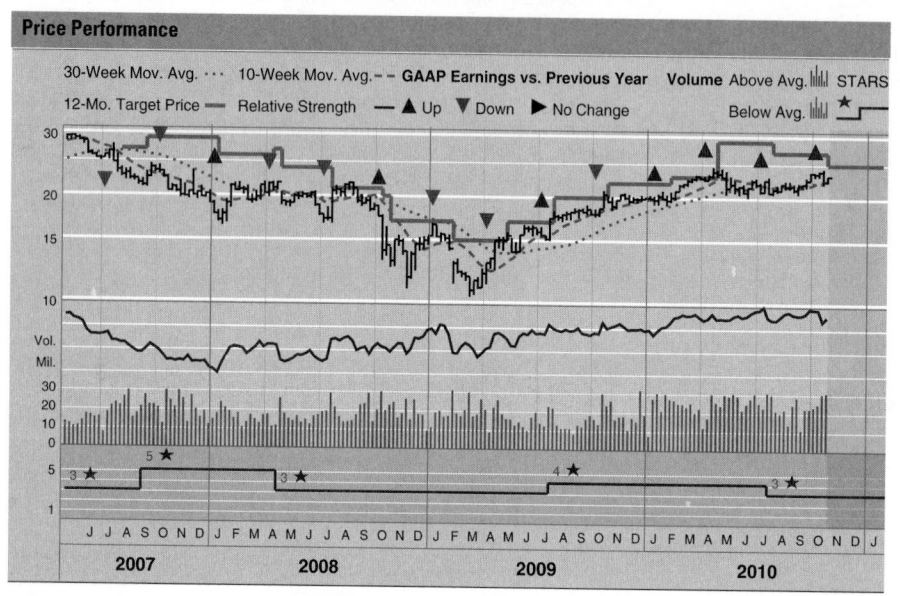

30-Week Mov. Avg. · · · 10-Week Mov. Avg. — GAAP Earnings vs. Previous Year   Volume Above Avg. STARS
12-Mo. Target Price — Relative Strength ▲ Up ▼ Down ► No Change   Below Avg. ★

Options: CBOE, P, Ph

Analysis prepared by **Jason N. Asaeda** on October 19, 2010, when the stock traded at **$ 22.71**.

Highlights

► Although we expect consumer spending to remain skittish due to high unemployment and economic uncertainty, we think conditions are generally improving and spending on toys will benefit. We look for net sales to reach $5.82 billion in 2010 and $6.05 billion 2011, with annual growth driven by momentum we see in core brands including Barbie, Disney Princess, Hot Wheels and American Girl, as well as popular entertainment properties Toy Story 3 and WWE Wrestling. We also expect top line benefit from an improving price-value offering in Fisher Price toys and new product introductions such as Monster High, Thomas and Friends and Sing-A-Ma-Jigs. We see currency translation as a headwind in 2010.

► We project annual operating margin expansion, as cost savings from MAT's Global Cost Leadership program outweigh higher royalty expense due to increased sales related to licensed products, continued external cost pressures such as higher raw material and transportation costs, and foreign exchange. Price increases should help modestly.

► We project 2010 EPS of $1.85, versus $1.46 in 2009, and 2011 EPS of $1.95.

Investment Rationale/Risk

► Our hold recommendation is based on valuation. We have confidence in MAT's portfolio of leading consumer brands and its strong cash flow, and think it is effectively handling a difficult selling environment that we see carrying into the upcoming holiday season and into 2011. We note that cost-cutting efforts have been helping the bottom line, and we think efforts to market lower price point items are well placed. We also believe the recent recall of about 10 million Fisher Price products by federal regulators carries little of the headline risk associated with the company's 2007 recall of lead-tainted toys. We see MAT taking necessary steps to remedy the situation and maintain consumer confidence in the safety of its products.

► Risks to our recommendation and target price include an uncertain toy retailing environment and the possibility of continued toy store closings, an inability to reinvigorate the top line, continued cost pressures, and a material impact from toy recalls.

► Our 12-month target price of $25 is based on a peer-median forward P/E multiple of about 13X applied to our 2011 EPS estimate.

Qualitative Risk Assessment

LOW	MEDIUM	HIGH

Our risk assessment reflects our favorable view of MAT's leading market share position and strong balance sheet, offset by our negative view of intense industry rivalry and concentrated buying power of U.S. toy retailers.

Quantitative Evaluations

S&P Quality Ranking   B+

D	C	B-	B	B+	A-	A	A+

Relative Strength Rank   MODERATE

50

LOWEST = 1   HIGHEST = 99

Revenue/Earnings Data

Revenue (Million $)

	1Q	2Q	3Q	4Q	Year
2010	880.1	1,019	1,833	--	--
2009	785.7	898.2	1,792	1,955	5,431
2008	919.3	1,112	1,946	1,940	5,918
2007	940.3	1,003	1,839	2,189	5,970
2006	793.3	957.7	1,790	2,109	5,650
2005	783.1	886.8	1,666	1,843	5,179

Earnings Per Share ($)

	1Q	2Q	3Q	4Q	Year
2010	0.07	0.14	0.78	E0.87	E1.85
2009	-0.14	0.06	0.63	0.90	1.45
2008	-0.13	0.03	0.66	0.49	1.05
2007	0.03	0.06	0.61	0.89	1.54
2006	0.08	0.10	0.62	0.75	1.53
2005	0.02	-0.23	0.55	0.69	1.01

Fiscal year ended Dec. 31. Next earnings report expected: Early February. EPS Estimates based on S&P Operating Earnings; historical GAAP earnings are as reported.

Dividend Data (Dates: mm/dd Payment Date: mm/dd/yy)

Amount ($)	Date Decl.	Ex-Div. Date	Stk. of Record	Payment Date
0.750	11/12	11/25	11/30	12/17/09

Dividends have been paid since 1990. Source: Company reports.

Please read the Required Disclosures and Analyst Certification on the last page of this report.

The McGraw-Hill Companies

Mattel Inc.

Business Summary October 19, 2010

CORPORATE OVERVIEW. Mattel markets a wide variety of toy products on a worldwide basis. Brands are grouped in the following categories: Mattel Girls & Boys Brands, Fisher-Price Brands and American Girl Brands. Mattel brands include Barbie, Polly Pocket, Disney Classics, Hot Wheels, Matchbox and Tyco R/C vehicles and playsets, Nickelodeon, Harry Potter, Yu-Gi-Oh!, Batman, Justice League, and Megaman, among others. Fisher-Price brands include Fisher-Price, Power Wheels, Sesame Street, Little People, Winnie the Pooh, Rescue Heroes, Barney, See 'N Say, Dora the Explorer, BabyGear, and View-Master. American Girl brand products are sold directly to consumers, and its children's publications are sold to certain retailers. Brand names include American Girl Today, the American Girls Collection, Just Like You and Bitty Baby.

MAT operates in the U.S. and internationally. Revenues from the international segment provided 46% of consolidated gross sales in 2009. In the international segment, the geographic breakdown was as follows: Europe, 52% of 2009 sales; Latin America, 31%; Asia Pacific, 10; and Other, 7%.

CORPORATE STRATEGY. We believe that two key elements of MAT's growth strategy are to build its brands and cut costs. With declining sales in its core Barbie brand, MAT has been focused on reinvigorating this product line, while driving growth in other key brands. To further leverage its brands, MAT also pursues licensing arrangements and strategic partnerships, which we think helps to extend its portfolio of brands into areas outside of traditional toys.

In early August 2007, MAT reported a recall of 967,000 plastic preschool toys made by a Chinese vendor because of an excessive amount of lead paint and announced that it would cut its already announced second-quarter operating income by $30 million. Two weeks afterward, MAT announced an additional recall involving die-cast cars and other toys involving magnets. Then, in early September, MAT announced a third recall of toys that contain an excessive amount of lead, including Barbie Doll accessories. MAT's 2007 third-quarter results included $40 million in charges related to the product recalls. This included a $13.3 million increase in reserves due primarily to higher product return rates, $9.1 million in reserves for subsequent product recalls and $17 million in incremental legal, advertising and administrative costs. We remain concerned, but we believe the impact on worldwide sales has been minimal and that MAT has been able to restore consumer confidence in the safety of its products. In December 2008, MAT settled litigation with 39 U.S. states, agreeing to pay $12 million related to the recalls, to be divided among the states.

Company Financials Fiscal Year Ended Dec. 31

Per Share Data ($)	2009	2008	2007	2006	2005	2004	2003	2002	2001	2000
Tangible Book Value	4.11	2.97	4.04	4.13	3.51	3.97	3.49	2.92	1.46	0.59
Cash Flow	1.93	1.51	1.97	1.98	1.44	1.79	1.63	1.47	1.31	1.00
Earnings	1.45	1.05	1.54	1.53	1.01	1.35	1.22	1.03	0.71	0.40
S&P Core Earnings	1.54	1.06	1.54	1.55	0.88	1.25	1.14	1.00	0.66	NA
Dividends	0.75	0.75	0.75	0.65	0.50	0.45	0.40	0.05	0.05	0.27
Payout Ratio	52%	71%	49%	42%	50%	33%	33%	5%	7%	67%
Prices:High	21.05	21.99	29.71	23.98	21.64	19.79	23.20	22.36	19.92	15.13
Prices:Low	10.36	10.89	18.83	14.75	14.52	15.94	18.57	15.05	13.52	8.94
P/E Ratio:High	15	21	19	16	21	15	19	22	28	38
P/E Ratio:Low	7	10	12	10	14	12	15	15	19	22

Income Statement Analysis (Million $)	2009	2008	2007	2006	2005	2004	2003	2002	2001	2000
Revenue	5,431	5,918	5,970	5,650	5,179	5,103	4,960	4,885	4,804	4,670
Operating Income	964	761	1,011	901	840	913	974	934	881	652
Depreciation	170	170	170	172	175	182	184	192	263	256
Interest Expense	71.8	81.9	71.0	79.9	76.5	77.8	80.6	114	155	153
Pretax Income	660	488	703	684	652	696	741	621	430	225
Effective Tax Rate	19.9%	22.2%	14.7%	13.3%	36.0%	17.7%	27.4%	26.8%	27.7%	24.5%
Net Income	529	380	600	593	417	573	538	455	311	170
S&P Core Earnings	555	380	601	600	359	531	502	439	288	NA

Balance Sheet & Other Financial Data (Million $)	2009	2008	2007	2006	2005	2004	2003	2002	2001	2000
Cash	1,117	618	901	1,206	998	1,157	1,153	1,267	617	232
Current Assets	2,555	2,387	2,593	2,850	2,413	2,637	2,395	2,389	2,093	1,751
Total Assets	4,781	4,675	4,805	4,956	4,372	4,756	4,511	4,460	4,541	4,313
Current Liabilities	1,061	1,260	1,570	1,583	1,463	1,727	1,468	1,649	1,597	1,502
Long Term Debt	700	750	550	636	525	400	589	640	1,021	1,242
Common Equity	2,531	2,117	2,307	2,433	2,102	2,386	2,216	1,979	1,738	1,403
Total Capital	3,281	2,915	2,857	3,069	2,627	2,786	2,805	2,619	2,759	2,645
Capital Expenditures	120	199	147	64.1	137	144	101	167	101	162
Cash Flow	699	550	770	765	592	755	721	647	573	427
Current Ratio	2.4	1.9	1.7	1.8	1.6	1.5	1.6	1.4	1.3	1.2
% Long Term Debt of Capitalization	21.3	25.7	19.3	20.7	20.0	14.4	21.0	24.4	37.0	47.0
% Net Income of Revenue	9.7	6.4	10.0	10.5	8.1	11.2	10.8	9.3	6.5	3.6
% Return on Assets	11.2	8.0	12.3	12.7	9.1	12.4	12.0	10.1	7.0	3.8
% Return on Equity	22.8	17.2	25.3	26.2	18.6	24.9	25.6	24.5	19.8	10.1

Data as orig reptd.; bef. results of disc opers/spec. items. Per share data adj. for stk. divs.; EPS diluted. E-Estimated. NA-Not Available. NM-Not Meaningful. NR-Not Ranked. UR-Under Review.

Office: 333 Continental Boulevard, El Segundo, CA 90245-5012.
Telephone: 310-252-2000.
Website: http://www.mattel.com
Chrmn & CEO: R.A. Eckert

COO: T.A. Debrowski
SVP, Chief Acctg Officer & Cntlr: H.S. Topham
SVP, Secy & General Counsel: R. Normile
CFO: K.M. Farr

Board Members: M. Dolan, R. A. Eckert, F. D. Fergusson, T. M. Friedman, D. Ng, V. M. Prabhu, A. L. Rich, R. Sargent, D. A. Scarborough, C. A. Sinclair, G. C. Sullivan, K. B. White

Founded: 1945
Domicile: Delaware
Employees: 27,000

McAfee Inc

S&P Recommendation HOLD ★★★☆☆

Price	12-Mo. Target Price	Investment Style
$47.35 (as of Oct 22, 2010)	$48.00	Large-Cap Growth

GICS Sector Information Technology
Sub-Industry Systems Software

Summary This company develops network security and management software products. Intel has agreed to acquire the company.

Key Stock Statistics (Source S&P, Vickers, company reports)

52-Wk Range	$47.44–29.53	S&P Oper. EPS 2010E	1.22	Market Capitalization(B)	$7.194	Beta	0.77
Trailing 12-Month EPS	$1.06	S&P Oper. EPS 2011E	1.45	Yield (%)	Nil	S&P 3-Yr. Proj. EPS CAGR(%)	10
Trailing 12-Month P/E	44.7	P/E on S&P Oper. EPS 2010E	38.8	Dividend Rate/Share	Nil	S&P Credit Rating	NA
$10K Invested 5 Yrs Ago	$15,474	Common Shares Outstg. (M)	151.9	Institutional Ownership (%)	93		

Price Performance

30-Week Mov. Avg. · · · 10-Week Mov. Avg. - - GAAP Earnings vs. Previous Year Volume Above Avg. STARS
12-Mo. Target Price — Relative Strength — ▲ Up ▼ Down ► No Change Below Avg. ★

Options: ASE, CBOE, P, Ph

Analysis prepared by **Jim Yin, CFA** on August 26, 2010, when the stock traded at **$ 47.05.**

Highlights

► We project revenues will increase 7.2% in 2010, compared to 21% growth in 2009. Our projection of slower revenue growth reflects our view of a sluggish recovery in spending for enterprise software. Although we project 5% growth in overall IT spending in 2010, we believe most of the growth will be in hardware. We believe MFE will continue to gain market share in the corporate business segment in 2010, but at a slower pace than in 2009. We project mid-single digit growth in the consumer business segment, based on 21% growth in PC unit sales, partially offset by lower average selling prices.

► We expect gross margins of 73% in 2010, down from 75% in 2009. We project operating expenses to decline to 61% of revenues in 2010, from 63% in 2009, due to cost synergies achieved from recent acquisitions and economies of scale. We see the operating margin staying at 12% in 2010, the same as in 2009, on higher revenues, offset by lower gross margins.

► Our EPS estimate for 2010 is $1.22, compared to $1.09 in 2009. The expected increase reflects our forecast of higher revenues.

Investment Rationale/Risk

► On August 19, Intel (INTC 18, Buy) announced it agreed to acquire MFE for $48 per share in cash, a 60% premium to the prior day's closing price. INTC plans to operate MFE as a wholly-owned subsidiary, but will incorporate its security software technology in future microprocessors. Although we believe the synergy of the two companies is minimal, we doubt another company will make a higher offer, given INTC's significant premium. With the shares trading near INTC's takeover price, we think they are fairly valued.

► Risks to our opinion and target price include failure to consummate the merger with INTC, a weaker than expected economic recovery, lower IT spending, and intense competition in the Internet security software sector as competitors broaden product offerings.

► Our 12-month target price of $48 is based on INTC's takeover bid and our view that no other bid will emerge.

Qualitative Risk Assessment

LOW	MEDIUM	HIGH

Our risk assessment reflects our view of the highly competitive security software market, rapid technological obsolescence, and a slow recovery in IT spending.

Quantitative Evaluations

S&P Quality Ranking B

D	C	B-	B	B+	A-	A	A+

Relative Strength Rank STRONG

76

LOWEST = 1   HIGHEST = 99

Revenue/Earnings Data

Revenue (Million $)

	1Q	2Q	3Q	4Q	Year
2010	502.7	489.2	--	--	--
2009	447.7	468.7	485.3	525.7	1,927
2008	369.6	396.8	409.7	424.0	1,600
2007	314.9	314.8	322.0	356.5	1,308
2006	275.2	277.6	287.1	305.2	1,145
2005	235.7	245.4	252.9	253.3	987.3

Earnings Per Share ($)

2010	0.23	0.25	E0.31	E0.43	E1.22
2009	0.34	0.18	0.23	0.34	1.09
2008	0.18	0.30	0.32	0.29	1.08
2007	0.28	0.30	0.39	0.07	1.02
2006	0.25	0.19	0.19	0.21	0.84
2005	0.21	0.25	0.13	0.23	0.82

Fiscal year ended Dec. 31. Next earnings report expected: Late October. EPS Estimates based on S&P Operating Earnings; historical GAAP earnings are as reported.

Dividend Data

No cash dividends have been paid.

Please read the Required Disclosures and Analyst Certification on the last page of this report.

The **McGraw·Hill** Companies

McAfee Inc

Business Summary August 26, 2010

CORPORATE OVERVIEW. MFE is a leading supplier of computer security software that helps home users, businesses, government agencies and service providers protect their systems and networks from potential threats around the world. The company was incorporated in 1992 as an application service provider (ASP) targeted at consumers and small to medium-sized businesses. It merged with Network General Corporation in December 1997 to become Network Associates, Inc. The company adopted its current name in June 2004, and began trading on the New York Stock Exchange under the symbol MFE.

MFE provides integrated solutions that help its customers solve problems, enhance security and reduce costs. The company's major product lines are system security, network security and vulnerability and risk management. Its system security products protect both consumer and corporate computer systems including laptops and other mobile devices from malicious attacks such as viruses and spyware. The products also safeguard sensitive data stored in mobile devices from leaking to the public that occurs through theft. MFE's mobile security offerings also limit the spread of mobile malware, inappropriate content, and unsolicited messaging.

MFE's network security products provide the same type of protection as its system security products, but are focused on the enterprise IT infrastructure. Network protection encompasses firewall, intrusion prevention, and email and data loss protection security appliances. It also includes McAfee SiteAdvisor, which warns Internet users of potential harmful websites.

MFE's vulnerability and risk management offerings help companies meet regulatory statues, resolve policy issues, conduct audits and identify risks such as non-compliant personal computers connecting to the internal network.

MFE markets its products to commercial and government customers through resellers and distributors. The top 10 distributors typically account for 30%-45% of total revenue. The two largest distributors, Ingram Micro and Tech Data Corp., together accounted for approximately 23% of total revenue in 2009. For the consumer market, MFE sells its products through original equipment manufacturers, retail stores and online. The company generated approximately 43%, 47% and 48% of its revenue outside of North America in 2009, 2008 and 2007, respectively.

Company Financials Fiscal Year Ended Dec. 31

Per Share Data ($)	2009	2008	2007	2006	2005	2004	2003	2002	2001	2000
Tangible Book Value	3.41	1.74	6.32	4.90	5.58	4.04	2.09	2.55	1.85	2.16
Cash Flow	2.17	1.86	1.53	1.27	1.20	1.65	0.75	1.03	0.04	-0.09
Earnings	1.09	1.08	1.02	0.84	0.82	1.31	0.36	0.80	-0.74	-0.74
S&P Core Earnings	1.07	1.14	1.02	0.83	0.81	0.28	0.05	0.62	-1.58	NA
Dividends	Nil	Nil	Nil	Nil	Nil	Nil	Nil	Nil	Nil	Nil
Payout Ratio	Nil	Nil	Nil	Nil	Nil	Nil	Nil	Nil	Nil	Nil
Prices:High	45.68	40.97	41.66	277.60	33.24	33.55	20.70	30.50	27.84	37.19
Prices:Low	26.65	24.72	27.74	287.10	20.35	14.90	10.42	8.14	3.56	3.25
P/E Ratio:High	42	38	41	1145	41	26	58	38	NM	NM
P/E Ratio:Low	24	23	27	23	25	11	29	10	NM	NM

Income Statement Analysis (Million $)	2009	2008	2007	2006	2005	2004	2003	2002	2001	2000
Revenue	1,927	1,600	1,308	1,145	987	911	936	1,043	834	746
Operating Income	406	348	286	210	280	146	157	257	29.9	-61.9
Depreciation	172	124	84.4	70.0	64.9	66.7	62.8	53.7	108	90.1
Interest Expense	4.90	Nil	Nil	Nil	Nil	5.32	7.54	25.1	24.7	18.2
Pretax Income	224	222	229	184	182	316	73.1	130	-91.4	-97.8
Effective Tax Rate	22.7%	22.5%	27.2%	25.1%	23.5%	28.9%	18.1%	NM	NM	NM
Net Income	173	172	167	137	139	225	59.9	128	-102	-103
S&P Core Earnings	170	181	166	136	139	37.3	9.42	102	-217	NA

Balance Sheet & Other Financial Data (Million $)	2009	2008	2007	2006	2005	2004	2003	2002	2001	2000
Cash	950	594	733	606	1,045	524	508	674	749	361
Current Assets	1,763	1,405	1,408	1,177	1,568	966	961	1,194	1,083	621
Total Assets	3,963	3,453	3,414	2,800	2,643	2,238	2,120	2,045	1,627	1,385
Current Liabilities	1,436	1,329	1,178	1,030	869	706	545	882	541	424
Long Term Debt	NA	Nil	Nil	Nil	Nil	Nil	347	356	579	396
Common Equity	2,118	1,752	1,905	1,427	1,455	1,201	888	770	445	519
Total Capital	2,118	1,752	1,905	1,427	1,455	1,201	1,236	1,126	1,061	934
Capital Expenditures	60.5	48.8	33.6	44.0	28.9	25.4	60.0	59.4	31.5	54.0
Cash Flow	346	296	251	207	204	292	123	182	5.67	-12.6
Current Ratio	4.3	1.1	1.2	1.1	1.8	1.4	1.8	1.4	2.0	1.5
% Long Term Debt of Capitalization	Nil	Nil	Nil	Nil	Nil	Nil	28.1	31.6	54.5	42.4
% Net Income of Revenue	9.0	10.8	12.8	11.9	14.1	24.7	7.2	12.3	NM	NM
% Return on Assets	4.7	5.0	5.4	5.0	5.7	10.3	2.9	7.0	NM	NM
% Return on Equity	9.0	9.4	10.0	9.5	10.5	21.5	7.2	23.1	NM	NM

Data as orig reptd.; bef. results of disc opers/spec. items. Per share data adj. for stk. divs.; EPS diluted. E-Estimated. NA-Not Available. NM-Not Meaningful. NR-Not Ranked. UR-Under Review.

Office: 3965 Freedom Circle, Santa Clara, CA 95054.
Telephone: 408-988-3832.
Email: ir@nai.com
Website: http://www.mcafee.com

Chrmn: C. Robel
Pres & CEO: D.G. DeWalt
EVP & CTO: G. Kurtz
EVP, Secy & General Counsel: M.D. Cochran

SVP & Chief Acctg Officer: K.S. Krzeminski
Investor Contact: K. Doherty (917-842-0334)
Board Members: C. Bass, T. E. Darcy, D. G. DeWalt, L. G. Denend, J. A. Miller, L. M. Norrington, D. J. O'Leary, R. W. Pangia, C. Robel, A. Zingale

Founded: 1989
Domicile: Delaware
Employees: 6,100

McCormick & Co Inc

STANDARD &POOR'S

S&P Recommendation **HOLD** ★★★☆☆	Price $43.40 (as of Oct 22, 2010)	12-Mo. Target Price $43.00	Investment Style Large-Cap Growth

GICS Sector Consumer Staples
Sub-Industry Packaged Foods & Meats

Summary This company primarily produces spices, seasonings, and flavorings for the retail food, food service, and industrial markets. Trademarks include McCormick and Lawry's.

Key Stock Statistics (Source S&P, Vickers, company reports)

52-Wk Range	$43.40– 34.09	S&P Oper. EPS 2010E	2.59	Market Capitalization(B)	$5.233	Beta	0.40
Trailing 12-Month EPS	$2.63	S&P Oper. EPS 2011E	2.75	Yield (%)	2.40	S&P 3-Yr. Proj. EPS CAGR(%)	8
Trailing 12-Month P/E	16.5	P/E on S&P Oper. EPS 2010E	16.8	Dividend Rate/Share	$1.04	S&P Credit Rating	A-
$10K Invested 5 Yrs Ago	$16,129	Common Shares Outstg. (M)	132.9	Institutional Ownership (%)	79		

Price Performance

30-Week Mov. Avg. · · · 10-Week Mov. Avg. – – GAAP Earnings vs. Previous Year   Volume Above Avg. |||| STARS
12-Mo. Target Price — Relative Strength — ▲ Up ▼ Down ► No Change   Below Avg. |||| ★

Options: Ph

Analysis prepared by **Tom Graves, CFA** on October 01, 2010, when the stock traded at **$ 41.59**.

Highlights

➤ For FY 11 (Nov.), we look for sales to increase 3% from the $3.3 billion we project for FY 10. We expect that sales to be bolstered by sales of ethnic-related and new products.

➤ We are wary that FY 11 profit margins will be restrained by higher input costs, but we think that margins will benefit from productivity improvements and sales mix. Overall, we look for an operating margin in FY 11 of 15.9%, up from the 15.6% that we project for FY 10. We think that FY 10's profitability will reflect a substantial expansion of MKC's gross margin, helped by productivity benefits, which we think will help offset some higher costs elsewhere.

➤ We estimate that FY 11 EPS will increase to $2.75, from the $2.59 that we project for FY 10, which excludes a $0.10 benefit in FY 10's third quarter from the reversal of a tax accrual. Also, MKC spent $38 million on stock repurchase in FY 11's third quarter, and said in September 2010 that it was projecting about $75 million of stock repurchase in all of FY 10. MKC has completed a buyback authorization that started in 2005, and a new $400 million repurchase program was approved in June 2010.

Investment Rationale/Risk

➤ We believe the July 2008 acquisition of Lawry's was a good fit with MKC, and we expect it to be more accretive to EPS in FY 10 than in FY 09. Also, we expect additional cost savings in FY 10 and FY 11 from MKC's Comprehensive Continuous Improvement program. We look for incremental savings of more than $45 million related to this program in FY 10.

➤ Risks to our recommendation and target price include competitive pressures in MKC's businesses, consumer acceptance of new product introductions, consumer shifts to private label, and commodity cost inflation. In terms of corporate governance, the company has a dual class capital structure with unequal voting rights, which we view unfavorably.

➤ Our 12-month target price of $43 is based on a blend of our historical and relative analyses. Our historical analysis suggests a discounted P/E of 16.7X our FY 11 EPS estimate of $2.75, for about a $46 value. Our peer analysis applies a P/E of 14.3X, a 10% to the peer average, for a $39 value. For peers, we use a mixture of small and mid-capitalization stocks in the food industry or the flavoring and/or coloring business.

Qualitative Risk Assessment

LOW	MEDIUM	HIGH

Our risk assessment reflects the relatively stable nature of the company's end markets, our view of its strong balance sheet and cash flow, and an S&P Quality Ranking of A+, which reflects historical growth of earnings and dividends.

Quantitative Evaluations

S&P Quality Ranking A+

D	C	B-	B	B+	A-	A	A+

Relative Strength Rank MODERATE

66

LOWEST = 1   HIGHEST = 99

Revenue/Earnings Data

Revenue (Million $)

	1Q	2Q	3Q	4Q	Year
2010	764.5	798.3	794.6	--	--
2009	718.5	757.3	791.7	924.5	3,192
2008	724.0	764.1	781.6	906.9	3,177
2007	652.6	687.2	716.2	860.1	2,916
2006	609.7	639.9	663.1	803.7	2,716
2005	603.6	628.6	622.7	737.1	2,592

Earnings Per Share ($)

2010	0.51	0.49	0.76	E0.93	E2.59
2009	0.44	0.38	0.57	0.88	2.27
2008	0.39	0.41	0.52	0.62	1.94
2007	0.33	0.31	0.43	0.67	1.73
2006	0.11	0.46	0.32	0.62	1.50
2005	0.26	0.31	0.35	0.65	1.56

Fiscal year ended Nov. 30. Next earnings report expected: Late January. EPS Estimates based on S&P Operating Earnings; historical GAAP earnings are as reported.

Dividend Data (Dates: mm/dd Payment Date: mm/dd/yy)

Amount ($)	Date Decl.	Ex-Div. Date	Stk. of Record	Payment Date
0.260	11/24	12/29	12/31	01/15/10
0.260	03/31	04/08	04/12	04/26/10
0.260	06/22	07/01	07/06	07/20/10
0.260	09/28	10/06	10/11	10/25/10

Dividends have been paid since 1925. Source: Company reports.

Please read the Required Disclosures and Analyst Certification on the last page of this report.

The McGraw-Hill Companies

McCormick & Co Inc

Business Summary October 01, 2010

CORPORATE OVERVIEW. Founded by Willoughby M. McCormick in 1889, Mc-Cormick & Co. is a global leader in the manufacture, marketing and distribution of spices, herbs, seasonings, specialty foods and flavors to the entire food industry. The company markets its products to retail food, foodservice and industrial markets under a number of brands, including McCormick, Lawry's, Zatarain's, Thai Kitchen, Ducros, Schwartz and Vahine.

McCormick's consumer segment, which accounted for 60% of sales and 82% of operating profits (before restructuring and impairment charges) in FY 09 (Nov.), sells spices, herbs, extracts, seasoning blends, sauces, marinades and specialty foods to the consumer food market. The industrial segment (40%, 18%) sells seasoning blends, natural spices and herbs, wet flavors, coating systems and compound flavors to multi-national food manufacturers and the food service industry, both directly and through distributors.

Sales to MKC's five largest customers in FY 09 accounted for about 30% of total sales, with the two largest customers - PepsiCo, Inc. and Wal-Mart Stores,

Inc. - each accounting for about 11% of total sales.

In FY 09, the United States accounted for 62% of total sales (58% in FY 08), Europe 21% (24%) and Other countries 17% (18%). Sales outside the United States in FY 09 were hurt by negative foreign currency translation.

MARKET PROFILE. Although we think MKC has impressive leading market shares in the relevant spices and seasonings categories of MKC's four major geographic markets (U.S., Canada, U.K. and France), there is a constant threat from private label products. While MKC itself accounts for about half of the private label business in the U.S., this business carries lower margins than MKC's branded business.

Company Financials Fiscal Year Ended Nov. 30

Per Share Data ($)	2009	2008	2007	2006	2005	2004	2003	2002	2001	2000
Tangible Book Value	NM	NM	NM	NM	NM	0.45	0.28	0.62	NM	NM
Cash Flow	2.98	2.50	2.36	2.14	2.10	2.11	1.85	1.73	1.57	1.43
Earnings	2.27	1.94	1.73	1.50	1.56	1.52	1.40	1.26	1.05	0.99
S&P Core Earnings	2.20	1.70	1.81	1.40	1.51	1.43	1.28	1.12	0.90	NA
Dividends	0.96	0.88	0.80	0.72	0.64	0.56	0.46	0.37	0.40	0.38
Payout Ratio	42%	45%	46%	48%	41%	37%	33%	29%	38%	38%
Prices:High	36.80	42.06	39.73	39.82	39.14	38.94	30.21	27.25	23.27	18.88
Prices:Low	28.08	28.21	33.89	30.09	28.95	28.60	21.71	20.70	17.00	11.88
P/E Ratio:High	16	22	23	27	25	26	22	22	22	19
P/E Ratio:Low	12	15	20	20	19	19	16	16	16	12

Income Statement Analysis (Million $)										
Revenue	3,192	3,177	2,916	2,716	2,592	2,526	2,270	2,320	2,372	2,124
Operating Income	577	496	468	429	429	402	366	353	324	287
Depreciation	94.3	73.5	83.0	86.8	74.6	72.0	65.3	66.8	73.0	61.3
Interest Expense	52.8	57.6	61.0	53.7	48.2	41.0	38.6	43.6	52.9	39.7
Pretax Income	433	356	302	270	316	308	286	257	212	204
Effective Tax Rate	30.7%	28.2%	30.4%	24.0%	30.6%	28.9%	29.1%	28.9%	29.7%	32.6%
Net Income	300	256	230	202	215	215	199	180	147	138
S&P Core Earnings	291	224	240	189	208	202	182	158	126	NA

Balance Sheet & Other Financial Data (Million $)										
Cash	56.5	38.9	46.0	49.0	30.3	70.3	25.1	47.3	31.3	23.9
Current Assets	970	968	983	899	800	864	762	725	636	620
Total Assets	3,388	3,220	2,788	2,568	2,273	2,370	2,148	1,931	1,772	1,660
Current Liabilities	818	1,034	861	780	699	773	713	673	714	1,027
Long Term Debt	875	885	574	570	464	465	449	454	454	160
Common Equity	1,335	1,055	1,085	933	800	890	755	592	463	359
Total Capital	2,225	1,988	1,669	1,575	1,293	1,386	1,226	1,046	943	523
Capital Expenditures	82.4	85.8	79.0	84.8	73.8	69.8	91.6	111	112	53.6
Cash Flow	394	329	313	289	290	287	265	247	220	199
Current Ratio	1.2	0.9	1.1	1.2	1.1	1.1	1.1	1.1	0.9	0.6
% Long Term Debt of Capitalization	39.3	44.5	34.3	37.8	35.9	33.6	36.6	43.4	48.2	30.6
% Net Income of Revenue	9.4	8.1	7.8	7.4	8.3	8.5	8.8	7.8	6.2	6.5
% Return on Assets	9.1	8.5	8.5	8.4	9.3	9.5	9.8	9.7	8.5	9.7
% Return on Equity	25.1	23.9	22.7	23.3	25.4	26.1	29.6	34.1	35.7	37.1

Data as orig reptd.; bef. results of disc opers/spec. items. Per share data adj. for stk. divs.; EPS diluted. E-Estimated. NA-Not Available. NM-Not Meaningful. NR-Not Ranked. UR-Under Review.

Office: 18 Loveton Circle, Sparks, MD 21152-6000.
Telephone: 410-771-7301.
Website: http://www.mccormick.com
Chrmn, Pres & CEO: A.D. Wilson

EVP & CFO: G.M. Stetz, Jr.
SVP, Chief Acctg Officer & Cntlr: K.A. Kelly, Jr.
SVP & Treas: P.C. Beard
SVP, Secy & General Counsel: W.G. Carpenter

Investor Contact: J. Brooks (410-771-7244)
Board Members: J. P. Bilbrey, J. T. Brady, J. Fitzpatrick, F. A. Hrabowski, III, P. Little, M. D. Mangan, M. M. Preston, G. A. Roche, W. E. Stevens, A. D. Wilson

Founded: 1889
Domicile: Maryland
Employees: 7,500

McDonald's Corp

STANDARD &POOR'S

S&P Recommendation HOLD ★★★☆☆

Price
$78.70 (as of Oct 25, 2010)

12-Mo. Target Price
$83.00

Investment Style
Large-Cap Growth

GICS Sector Consumer Discretionary
Sub-Industry Restaurants

Summary MCD is the largest fast-food restaurant company in the world, with about 32,500 restaurants in 117 countries.

Key Stock Statistics (Source S&P, Vickers, company reports)

52-Wk Range	$79.48– 58.44	S&P Oper. EPS 2010**E**	4.57	Market Capitalization(B)	$83.763	Beta	0.59
Trailing 12-Month EPS	$4.53	S&P Oper. EPS 2011**E**	4.92	Yield (%)	3.10	S&P 3-Yr. Proj. EPS CAGR(%)	7
Trailing 12-Month P/E	17.4	P/E on S&P Oper. EPS 2010**E**	17.2	Dividend Rate/Share	$2.44	S&P Credit Rating	A
$10K Invested 5 Yrs Ago	$28,295	Common Shares Outstg. (M)	1,064.3	Institutional Ownership (%)	70		

Price Performance

30-Week Mov. Avg. · · · 10-Week Mov. Avg. - - GAAP Earnings vs. Previous Year   Volume Above Avg. STARS
12-Mo. Target Price — Relative Strength — ▲ Up ▼ Down ▶ No Change   Below Avg.

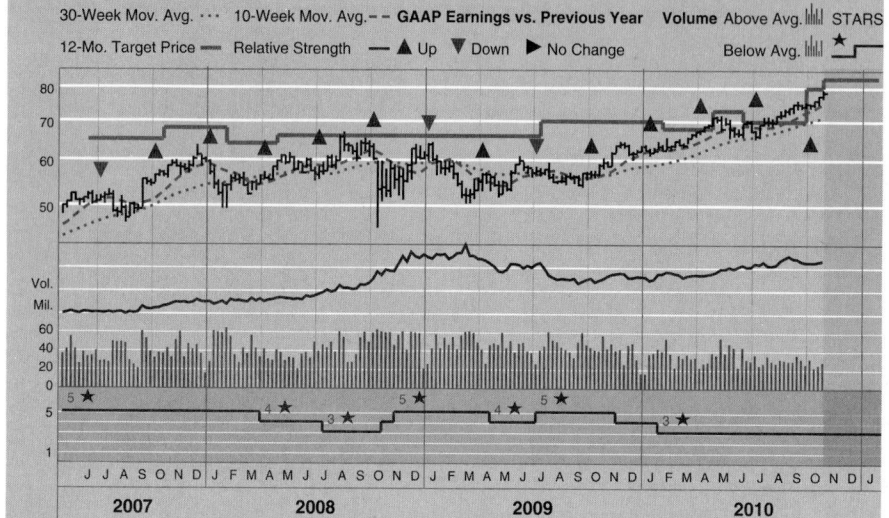

Options: ASE, CBOE, P, Ph

Analysis prepared by **Erik Kolb** on October 25, 2010, when the stock traded at **$ 78.87**.

Highlights

➤ We project that revenues in 2010 will increase about 4%, exclusive of a small positive forex effect of about 1%, which occurred primarily in the first half. We expect systemwide sales in the U.S. to be up 3%, while they are likely to climb about 4% in local currencies in Europe and 7% in Asia Pacific/Middle East/Africa. In 2011, we see a similar 4%-5% increase.

➤ We think various food and other commodity input costs will likely decrease 3% in the U.S. and 2% in Europe in 2010. While much of MCD's top-line forex exposure is naturally hedged, we expect negative forex translation effects on EPS in the fourth quarter of about $0.02, after a negative $0.02 effect in the third quarter, a neutral effect in the second quarter, and a positive $0.05 in the first.

➤ We estimate that 2010 operating EPS, aided by stock repurchases, will increase to $4.57, from $4.03 in 2009, which excluded an $0.08 non-recurring gain related to the 2007 divestiture of MCD's Latin American operations, but included several other small non-operating gains. We see EPS of $4.92 in 2011.

Investment Rationale/Risk

➤ We think expansion opportunities in international markets will help to drive growth in the coming quarters, particularly in Asia/Pacific, the Middle East, and Africa. MCD's focus on menu innovation, which has seen success with frappes and smoothes of late, is helping it to gain market share relative to peers. We also think its Dollar Menu will help to drive positive traffic trends. Although costs have been relatively contained of late, we expect a modest increase in 2011. We believe the $2.44 per share annual cash dividend adds to total return potential.

➤ Risks to our recommendation and target price include higher-than-expected food costs, poor customer acceptance of MCD's new menu offerings, and exchange rate risk in light of MCD's substantial international business.

➤ Our 12-month target price of $83 is based on a multiple of approximately 16.8X our 2011 EPS estimate of $4.92, a slight premium to the peer group average. The 2010 fourth quarter increase in the annual dividend rate to $2.44 provides a 3.2% dividend yield at recent stock prices.

Qualitative Risk Assessment

LOW	MEDIUM	HIGH

McDonald's competes in the global fast food industry, where it arguably has the most dominant brand name presence. However, results can vary widely due to fluctuations in food costs, competitive discounting, and exchange rate volatility. Our risk assessment reflects our view that global economic weakness has started to subside, although recovery prospects remain uncertain.

Quantitative Evaluations

S&P Quality Ranking   A

D	C	B-	B	B+	A-	A	A+

Relative Strength Rank   MODERATE

66

LOWEST = 1   HIGHEST = 99

Revenue/Earnings Data

Revenue (Million $)

	1Q	2Q	3Q	4Q	Year
2010	5,610	5,946	6,305	--	--
2009	5,077	5,647	6,047	5,973	22,745
2008	5,615	6,075	6,267	5,565	23,522
2007	5,293	5,839	5,901	5,754	22,787
2006	4,914	5,367	5,671	5,634	21,586
2005	4,803	5,096	5,327	5,235	20,460

Earnings Per Share ($)

2010	1.00	1.13	1.29	E1.15	E4.57
2009	0.87	0.98	1.15	1.11	4.11
2008	0.81	1.04	1.05	0.87	3.76
2007	0.63	-0.59	0.83	1.06	1.93
2006	0.46	0.56	0.67	0.61	2.30
2005	0.56	0.42	0.58	0.48	2.04

Fiscal year ended Dec. 31. Next earnings report expected: Late January. EPS Estimates based on S&P Operating Earnings; historical GAAP earnings are as reported.

Dividend Data (Dates: mm/dd Payment Date: mm/dd/yy)

Amount ($)	Date Decl.	Ex-Div. Date	Stk. of Record	Payment Date
0.550	01/22	02/25	03/01	03/15/10
0.550	05/20	05/27	06/01	06/15/10
0.550	07/22	08/30	09/01	09/16/10
0.610	09/23	11/29	12/01	12/15/10

Dividends have been paid since 1976. Source: Company reports.

Please read the Required Disclosures and Analyst Certification on the last page of this report.

The McGraw·Hill Companies

McDonald's Corp

STANDARD
&POOR'S

Business Summary October 25, 2010

CORPORATE OVERVIEW. With one of the world's most widely known brand names, McDonald's operates and franchises about 32,500 restaurants around the world. Systemwide sales totaled $72.4 billion in 2009, up from $70.7 billion in 2008.

In the U.S., the McDonald's chain leads the $160 billion quick-service restaurant industry. With U.S. systemwide sales of $31 billion, its domestic business is several times larger than its closest competitors, Burger King and Wendy's Old Fashioned Hamburgers. MCD's international segment has supplied much of its earnings growth over the past two decades, and, in 2009, contributed 53% of operating income (before corporate expenses and one-time charges). All restaurants are operated by MCD, franchisees, or affiliates under joint venture agreements.

In August 2007, the company completed the sale of its existing businesses in Brazil, Argentina, Mexico, Puerto Rico, Venezuela and 13 other countries in Latin America and the Caribbean to a developmental licensee (the Latam transaction). The company recorded impairment charges totaling approximately $1.7 billion, substantially all of which was non-cash. The charges included approximately $892 million for the difference between the net book value of the Latam business and the approximately $680 million in cash proceeds,

and $773 million in foreign currency translation losses previously included in comprehensive income.

CORPORATE STRATEGY. In 2010, the company will continue its "Plan to Win" corporate strategy that it commenced in 2003. MCD's stated operating priorities include fixing operating inadequacies in existing restaurants; taking a more integrated and focused approach to growth, with an emphasis on increasing sales, margins and returns in existing restaurants; and ensuring the correct operating structure and resources, aligned behind focusing priorities that create benefits for its customers and restaurants.

A significant part of the new corporate strategy was to de-emphasize Partner Brands concepts in order to focus on the McDonald's brand. In 2006 and 2007, MCD disposed of interests in the Chipotle Mexican Grill restaurant concept as well as the Boston Market chain, and it sold its minority interest in Pret a Manger in 2008.

Company Financials Fiscal Year Ended Dec. 31

Per Share Data ($)	2009	2008	2007	2006	2005	2004	2003	2002	2001	2000
Tangible Book Value	10.78	10.00	11.14	11.01	10.45	9.74	8.18	6.88	6.30	5.86
Cash Flow	5.21	4.78	2.87	3.29	3.05	2.73	2.08	1.59	2.08	2.20
Earnings	4.11	3.76	1.93	2.30	2.04	1.79	1.18	0.77	1.25	1.46
S&P Core Earnings	3.99	3.60	1.88	2.28	2.00	1.66	0.96	0.51	1.01	NA
Dividends	2.05	1.63	1.50	1.00	0.67	0.55	0.40	0.24	0.23	0.22
Payout Ratio	50%	43%	78%	43%	33%	31%	34%	31%	18%	15%
Prices:High	64.75	67.00	63.69	44.68	35.69	32.96	27.01	30.72	35.06	43.63
Prices:Low	50.44	45.79	42.31	31.73	27.36	24.54	12.12	15.17	24.75	26.38
P/E Ratio:High	16	18	33	19	17	18	23	40	28	30
P/E Ratio:Low	12	12	22	14	13	14	10	20	20	18

Income Statement Analysis (Million $)										
Revenue	22,745	23,522	22,787	21,586	20,460	19,065	17,141	15,406	14,870	14,243
Operating Income	7,774	7,445	6,683	5,829	5,243	4,742	3,980	3,164	3,983	4,144
Depreciation	1,216	1,162	1,145	1,250	1,250	1,201	1,148	1,051	1,086	1,011
Interest Expense	473	535	417	402	356	358	388	360	452	430
Pretax Income	6,487	6,158	3,572	4,166	3,702	3,202	2,346	1,662	2,330	2,882
Effective Tax Rate	29.8%	30.0%	34.6%	31.0%	29.7%	28.9%	35.7%	40.3%	29.8%	31.4%
Net Income	4,551	4,313	2,335	2,873	2,602	2,279	1,508	992	1,637	1,977
S&P Core Earnings	4,416	4,127	2,277	2,848	2,540	2,100	1,226	667	1,328	NA

Balance Sheet & Other Financial Data (Million $)										
Cash	1,796	2,063	1,981	2,136	4,260	1,380	493	330	418	422
Current Assets	3,416	3,518	3,582	3,625	5,850	2,858	1,885	1,715	1,819	1,662
Total Assets	30,225	28,462	29,392	29,024	29,989	27,838	25,525	23,971	22,535	21,683
Current Liabilities	2,989	2,538	4,499	3,008	4,036	3,521	2,486	2,422	2,248	2,361
Long Term Debt	10,564	10,186	7,310	8,417	8,937	8,357	9,343	9,704	8,556	7,844
Common Equity	14,034	13,383	15,280	15,458	15,146	14,202	11,982	10,281	9,488	9,204
Total Capital	24,616	24,514	23,551	24,941	25,060	23,340	22,340	20,988	19,156	18,133
Capital Expenditures	1,952	2,136	1,947	1,742	1,607	1,419	1,307	2,004	1,906	1,945
Cash Flow	5,767	5,475	3,480	4,123	3,852	3,480	2,656	2,043	2,723	2,988
Current Ratio	1.1	1.4	0.8	1.2	1.4	0.8	0.8	0.7	0.8	0.7
% Long Term Debt of Capitalization	Nil	41.6	31.0	33.7	35.7	35.8	41.8	46.2	44.7	43.3
% Net Income of Revenue	20.0	18.3	10.3	13.3	12.7	12.0	8.8	6.4	11.0	13.9
% Return on Assets	NA	NA	8.9	9.7	9.0	8.5	6.1	4.3	7.4	9.3
% Return on Equity	NA	NA	15.2	18.8	17.7	17.4	13.5	10.0	17.5	21.0

Data as orig reptd.; bef. results of disc opers/spec. items. Per share data adj. for stk. divs.; EPS diluted. E-Estimated. NA-Not Available. NM-Not Meaningful. NR-Not Ranked. UR-Under Review.

Office: McDonald's Plaza, Oak Brook, IL 60523.
Telephone: 630-623-3000.
Website: http://www.mcdonalds.com
Chrmn: A.J. McKenna

Pres & COO: D. Thompson
Vice Chrmn & CEO: J. Skinner
EVP & CFO: P.J. Bensen
EVP, Secy & General Counsel: G. Santona

Investor Contact: M.K. Shaw (630-623-7559)
Board Members: S. E. Arnold, R. A. Eckert, E. Hernandez, Jr., J. P. Jackson, R. H. Lenny, W. E. Massey, A. J. McKenna, C. D. McMillan, S. A. Penrose, J. W. Rogers, Jr., J. Skinner, R. W. Stone, M. D. White

Founded: 1948
Domicile: Delaware
Employees: 385,000

McGraw-Hill Companies Inc. (The)

STANDARD &POOR'S

S&P Recommendation `NOT RANKED`	**Price** $36.40 (as of Oct 22, 2010)	**Investment Style** Large-Cap Growth

GICS Sector Consumer Discretionary
Sub-Industry Publishing

Summary This leading information services organization serves worldwide markets in education, business, industry, other professions and government.

Key Stock Statistics (Source S&P, Vickers, company reports)

52-Wk Range	$36.94– 26.95	S&P Oper. EPS 2010E	NA	Market Capitalization(B)	$11.251	Beta		1.14
Trailing 12-Month EPS	$2.54	S&P Oper. EPS 2011E	NA	Yield (%)	2.58	S&P 3-Yr. Proj. EPS CAGR(%)		
Trailing 12-Month P/E	14.3	P/E on S&P Oper. EPS 2010E	NA	Dividend Rate/Share	$0.94	S&P Credit Rating		NR
$10K Invested 5 Yrs Ago	$8,548	Common Shares Outstg. (M)	309.1	Institutional Ownership (%)	84			

Price Performance

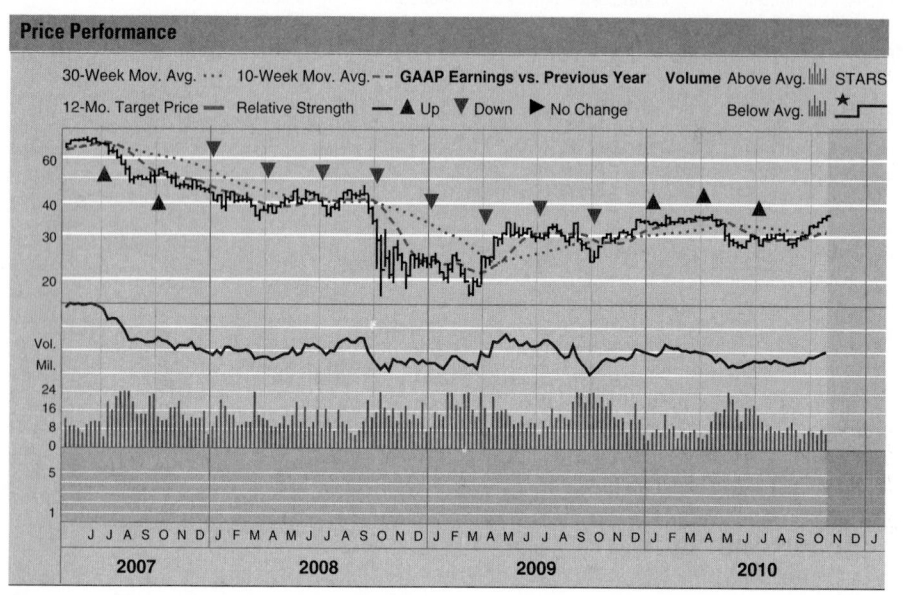

30-Week Mov. Avg. · · · 10-Week Mov. Avg. - - **GAAP Earnings vs. Previous Year** Volume Above Avg. STARS
12-Mo. Target Price — Relative Strength — ▲ Up ▼ Down ▶ No Change Below Avg.

Options: ASE, CBOE, P, Ph

Analysis prepared by **Tom Graves, CFA** on July 27, 2010, when the stock traded at **$ 30.64**.

Highlights

➤ In 2010's second quarter, MHP's total revenue was up 0.6%, year to year, and would have increased 2.7% if the divestitures of Business-Week and Vista Research were excluded. Overall segment profit was up 6.8%, helped by the absence of restructuring charges and a year-ago loss on a divestiture.

➤ In July 2010, MHP said that due to choppiness in some of its key markets, it expects to report diluted EPS for 2010 at the low end of its previous guidance range of $2.55 to $2.65. Earlier, in January, MHP directors approved the 37th consecutive annual increase in the quarterly cash dividend on MHP's common stock. MHP's quarterly dividend was increased 4.4%, to $0.235 per share, with the March 2010 payment.

➤ MHP repurchased 6.5 million of its common shares in the 2010 second quarter for $186.9 million. Authorization to repurchase 10.6 million shares remained. At June 30, 2010, MHP had cash and short-term investments of $1.145 billion, and long-term debt of $1.198 billion.

Investment Rationale/Risk

➤ In July 2010, MHP said it anticipates 2010 free cash flow (after investments and dividends) of $600 million to $650 million, down from $770 million in 2009. Pre-publication investments were expected to be $195 million to $205 million in 2010, up from $177 million in 2009. The company said it expects 2010 expenditures for property and equipment of $90 million to $100 million, up from $68.5 million in 2009, and depreciation and amortization charges of $415 million to $420 million, compared to about $436 million in 2009.

➤ MHP noted in its 2009 10-K report filed with the SEC in February 2010 that possible risk factors for the company include exposure to litigation, changes in the volume of debt securities issued in capital markets, possible loss of market share or revenue due to competition or regulation, and changes in educational funding.

➤ Standard & Poor's is a division of MHP, and provides no EPS estimates, target price or recommendation for the company.

Qualitative Risk Assessment

A Qualitative Risk Assessment is not available for this company.

Quantitative Evaluations

S&P Quality Ranking NR

D	C	B-	B	B+	A-	A	A+

Relative Strength Rank STRONG

88

LOWEST = 1 HIGHEST = 99

Revenue/Earnings Data

Revenue (Million $)

	1Q	2Q	3Q	4Q	Year
2010	1,190	1,500	--	--	--
2009	1,148	1,465	1,876	1,462	5,952
2008	1,218	1,673	2,049	1,415	6,355
2007	1,296	1,718	2,188	1,570	6,772
2006	1,141	1,528	1,993	1,594	6,255
2005	1,029	1,456	1,977	1,541	6,004

Earnings Per Share ($)

2010	0.33	0.61	--	--	--
2009	0.20	0.52	1.07	0.53	2.33
2008	0.25	0.66	1.23	0.37	2.51
2007	0.40	0.79	1.34	0.43	2.94
2006	0.20	0.60	1.06	0.56	2.40
2005	0.21	0.51	1.00	0.50	2.21

Fiscal year ended Dec. 31. Next earnings report expected: Late October. EPS Estimates based on S&P Operating Earnings; historical GAAP earnings are as reported.

Dividend Data (Dates: mm/dd Payment Date: mm/dd/yy)

Amount ($)	Date Decl.	Ex-Div. Date	Stk. of Record	Payment Date
0.225	10/28	11/23	11/25	12/10/09
0.235	01/20	02/22	02/24	03/10/10
0.235	04/28	05/24	05/26	06/10/10
0.235	07/26	08/24	08/26	09/10/10

Dividends have been paid since 1937. Source: Company reports.

McGraw-Hill Companies Inc. (The)

STANDARD &POOR'S

Business Summary July 27, 2010

CORPORATE OVERVIEW. The McGraw-Hill Companies, Inc. is a leading provider of information products and services to business, professional and education markets worldwide. The company believes that through acquisitions, new product and service development, and a strong commitment to customer service, many of its business units have grown to be leaders in their respective fields. Well known brands include Standard & Poor's and Platts.

The Financial Services segment (44% of revenues and 73% of segment operating profit in 2009) operates under the Standard & Poor's brand and provides services to investors, corporations, governments, financial institutions, investment managers and advisors globally. S&P provides independent credit ratings, credit risk evaluations, and credit ratings-related information and products. This can include analyses related to corporations, financial institutions, securitized and project financings, and local, state and sovereign governments. Also, S&P's Investment Services business provides financial data, information, indices and research.

In 2005, MHP acquired majority ownership of Crisil Limited, a leading provider

of credit ratings, financial news and risk and policy advisory services in India. In 2004, MHP acquired privately owned Capital IQ, a provider of information solutions to the global investment and financial services communities. In May 2009, MHP sold its Vista Research business to Guidepoint Global, LLC. MHP had acquired Vista, a leading provider of primary research, in 2005. In February 2007, MHP announced the sale of its mutual fund data business to Morningstar, Inc.

McGraw-Hill Education (40%, 20%) operates in in the elementary and high school, college and university, professional, international and adult education markets. In the el-hi market, MHP sells textbooks (print and digital versions) and supplementary material, and provides assessment and reporting services. In the college and university and the international market, MHP sells textbooks and other resources to higher education institutions.

Company Financials Fiscal Year Ended Dec. 31

Per Share Data ($)	2009	2008	2007	2006	2005	2004	2003	2002	2001	2000
Tangible Book Value	NM	NM	NM	1.00	2.04	2.72	2.24	0.94	0.09	0.17
Cash Flow	2.86	3.07	3.41	2.85	3.21	2.98	2.84	1.71	2.04	2.13
Earnings	2.33	2.51	2.94	2.40	2.21	1.96	1.79	1.48	0.96	1.21
S&P Core Earnings	2.29	2.29	2.89	2.38	2.05	1.80	1.44	1.15	0.60	NA
Dividends	0.90	0.88	0.82	0.73	0.66	0.60	0.54	0.51	0.49	0.47
Payout Ratio	39%	35%	28%	30%	30%	31%	30%	34%	51%	39%
Prices:High	35.24	47.13	72.50	69.25	53.97	46.06	35.00	34.85	35.44	33.84
Prices:Low	17.22	17.15	43.46	46.37	40.51	34.55	25.87	25.36	24.35	20.94
P/E Ratio:High	15	19	25	29	24	23	20	24	37	28
P/E Ratio:Low	7	7	15	19	18	18	14	17	25	17

Income Statement Analysis (Million $)										
Revenue	5,952	6,355	6,772	6,255	6,004	5,251	4,828	4,788	4,646	4,281
Operating Income	1,440	1,607	1,846	1,580	1,749	1,467	1,369	1,037	1,044	1,128
Depreciation	165	178	161	162	385	393	403	89.6	421	362
Interest Expense	76.9	75.6	40.6	13.6	5.20	5.79	7.10	22.5	55.1	52.8
Pretax Income	1,179	1,279	1,623	1,405	1,360	1,169	1,130	905	615	767
Effective Tax Rate	36.4%	37.5%	37.5%	37.2%	37.9%	35.3%	39.1%	36.3%	38.7%	38.5%
Net Income	730	799	1,014	882	844	756	688	577	377	472
S&P Core Earnings	717	729	995	874	786	694	552	446	233	NA

Balance Sheet & Other Financial Data (Million $)										
Cash	1,235	472	396	353	749	681	696	58.2	53.5	3.17
Current Assets	2,936	2,303	2,333	2,258	2,591	2,448	2,256	1,674	1,813	1,802
Total Assets	6,475	6,080	6,357	6,043	6,396	5,863	5,394	5,032	5,161	4,931
Current Liabilities	2,452	2,531	2,657	2,468	2,225	1,969	1,994	1,775	1,876	1,781
Long Term Debt	1,198	1,198	1,197	0.31	0.34	0.51	0.39	459	834	818
Common Equity	1,847	1,282	1,607	7,785	3,113	4,952	2,557	2,202	1,884	1,761
Total Capital	3,127	2,480	2,943	7,936	3,432	5,185	2,758	2,861	2,908	2,742
Capital Expenditures	68.5	106	230	127	120	139	115	70.0	117	97.7
Cash Flow	896	978	1,175	1,044	1,230	1,149	1,091	666	798	834
Current Ratio	1.2	0.9	0.9	0.9	1.2	1.2	1.1	0.9	1.0	1.0
% Long Term Debt of Capitalization	Nil	48.2	40.7	NM	0.0	0.0	0.0	16.0	28.7	29.8
% Net Income of Revenue	12.3	12.6	15.0	14.1	14.1	14.4	14.2	12.0	8.1	11.0
% Return on Assets	NA	12.8	16.3	14.2	13.8	13.5	13.2	11.3	7.5	10.4
% Return on Equity	NA	55.3	47.3	12.8	27.7	16.5	29.1	28.2	20.5	27.7

Data as orig reptd.; bef. results of disc opers/spec. items. Per share data adj. for stk. divs.; EPS diluted. E-Estimated. NA-Not Available. NM-Not Meaningful. NR-Not Ranked. UR-Under Review.

Office: 1221 Avenue Of The Americas, New York, NY 10020-1095.
Telephone: 212-512-2000.
Email: investor_relations@mcgraw-hill.com
Website: http://www.mcgraw-hill.com

Chrmn, Pres & CEO: H. McGraw, III
EVP & CFO: R.J. Bahash
EVP & General Counsel: K.M. Vittor
EVP & CIO: B.D. Marcus

SVP, Chief Acctg Officer & Cntlr: E.K. Korakis
Investor Contact: D.S. Rubin (212-512-4321)
Board Members: P. A. Armella, W. Bischoff, D. N. Daft, L. K. Lorimer, R. P. McGraw, H. McGraw, III, H. M. Ochoa-Brillembourg, M. Rake, E. B. Rust, Jr., K. L. Schmoke, S. Taurel

Founded: 1899
Domicile: New York
Employees: 21,077

The McGraw-Hill Companies

McKesson Corp

**STANDARD
&POOR'S**

| S&P Recommendation **STRONG BUY** ★★★★★ | Price $61.08 (as of Oct 22, 2010) | 12-Mo. Target Price $78.00 | Investment Style Large-Cap Blend |

GICS Sector Health Care
Sub-Industry Health Care Distributors

Summary This company (formerly McKesson HBOC) provides pharmaceutical supply management and information technologies to a broad range of health care customers.

Key Stock Statistics (Source S&P, Vickers, company reports)

52-Wk Range	$71.49– 55.82	S&P Oper. EPS 2011**E** 4.82	Market Capitalization(B)	$15.969	Beta 0.73
Trailing 12-Month EPS	$4.66	S&P Oper. EPS 2012**E** 5.35	Yield (%)	1.18	S&P 3-Yr. Proj. EPS CAGR(%) 10
Trailing 12-Month P/E	13.1	P/E on S&P Oper. EPS 2011**E** 12.7	Dividend Rate/Share	$0.72	S&P Credit Rating A-
$10K Invested 5 Yrs Ago	$14,434	Common Shares Outstg. (M) 261.5	Institutional Ownership (%)	86	

Price Performance

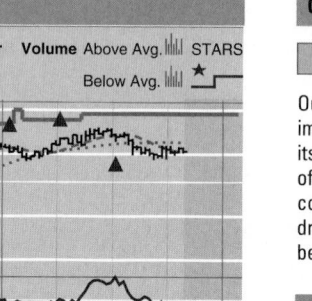

30-Week Mov. Avg. ···· 10-Week Mov. Avg. -- **GAAP Earnings vs. Previous Year** Volume Above Avg.||||| STARS
12-Mo. Target Price — Relative Strength — ▲ Up ▼ Down ► No Change Below Avg.||||| ★

Options: ASE, CBOE, P, Ph

Analysis prepared by **Herman B. Saftlas** on August 31, 2010, when the stock traded at **$ 59.05**.

Highlights

► For FY 11 (Mar.), we forecast total revenues will rise 3.4%, paced by higher revenues from branded and generic drugs (Distribution Solutions). However, we see only a 1%-2% gain for the Medical-Surgical Solutions division, well below the growth in achieved by that unit in FY 10, which was inflated by H1N1 flu vaccine volume. International sales are expected to decline due to the recent sale of an Asian Pacific subsidiary. We project 7.3% revenue growth for the Technology Solutions division, following a 2.0% rise in FY 10, as hospitals' consultations with MCK on electronic health record systems likely translate into bookings.

► We expect firmwide FY 11 operating margins to narrow slightly versus FY 10's, as the benefits from further generic drug penetration, cost controls and higher Technology Solutions sales are unlikely to compensate for the margin gains in FY 10 from the spike in flu-related sales and a favorable settlement related to MCK's 401(k) plan.

► We project FY 11 operating EPS of $4.82, versus FY 10's $4.58, excluding one-time items in both years. We look for EPS of $5.35 in FY 12.

Investment Rationale/Risk

► We believe MCK's large footprints in drugs, medical supplies and information technology will enable it to benefit strongly from cross-selling opportunities. We think its leading positions in drug distribution, med-surg supply (in the alternate site market) and pharmacy systems reinforce its cost-competitiveness, while distribution margins will continue to benefit from generic drug penetration. We also view the high-margin Technology Solutions segment as poised to gain greatly from stimulus-related spending, and we are encouraged that bookings have begun. While it may be tough for MCK to match H1N1's $0.37 a share contribution in FY 10 during FY 11, we believe its $3.3 billion cash hoard as of June 30, 2010, and healthy cash flow provide it with financial flexibility.

► Risks to our recommendation and target price include the loss of major accounts and unfavorable regulatory changes. Recent moves to cut drug spending in Canada is another risk.

► Our 12-month target price of $78 is derived by applying an approximate peer-level 14.6X P/E to our FY 12 EPS estimate of $5.35.

Qualitative Risk Assessment

| LOW | **MEDIUM** | HIGH |

Our risk assessment reflects our view of MCK's improving profitability and the rising demand for its highly profitable IT products and services, offset by our belief the company is more price competitive than peers and that future drugmaker-distributor contract negotiations might be less favorable for distributors.

Quantitative Evaluations

S&P Quality Ranking A-

| D | C | B- | B | B+ | **A-** | A | A+ |

Relative Strength Rank WEAK

25

LOWEST = 1 HIGHEST = 99

Revenue/Earnings Data

Revenue (Million $)

	1Q	2Q	3Q	4Q	Year
2011	27,450	--	--	--	--
2010	26,657	27,130	28,272	26,643	108,702
2009	26,704	26,574	27,130	26,224	106,632
2008	24,528	24,450	26,494	26,231	101,703
2007	23,315	22,386	23,111	24,165	92,977
2006	20,968	21,515	22,510	23,057	88,050

Earnings Per Share ($)

	1Q	2Q	3Q	4Q	Year
2011	1.10	E1.13	E1.22	E1.37	E4.82
2010	1.06	1.11	1.19	1.26	4.62
2009	0.83	1.17	-0.07	1.01	2.99
2008	0.77	0.83	0.68	1.05	3.32
2007	0.60	0.94	0.79	0.85	3.17
2006	0.55	0.49	0.61	0.70	2.34

Fiscal year ended Mar. 31. Next earnings report expected: Late October. EPS Estimates based on S&P Operating Earnings; historical GAAP earnings are as reported.

Dividend Data (Dates: mm/dd Payment Date: mm/dd/yy)

Amount ($)	Date Decl.	Ex-Div. Date	Stk. of Record	Payment Date
0.120	10/30	11/27	12/01	01/04/10
0.120	01/20	02/25	03/01	04/01/10
0.180	05/26	06/08	06/10	07/01/10
0.180	07/28	08/30	09/01	10/01/10

Dividends have been paid since 1995. Source: Company reports.

McKesson Corp

STANDARD
&POOR'S

Business Summary August 31, 2010

CORPORATE OVERVIEW. McKesson Corp. is a leading distributor of medical products and supplies and health care information technology products and services. Beginning in FY 08 (Mar.), MCK started reporting its results in two segments:

McKesson Distribution Solutions (MDS; 97.1% of FY 10 revenue on a pro forma basis) includes what was previously reported as Pharmaceutical Solutions and Medical-Surgical Solutions, with the exception of its Payor business. The pharmaceutical distribution unit primarily distributes ethical and proprietary drugs and health and beauty care, and focuses on three customer segments: retail independent pharmacies, retail chains, and institutions, in all 50 states and Canada. The medical-surgical distribution unit provides medical-surgical supplies, equipment, logistics and related services to alternate-site health care providers, including physicians' offices, long-term care and home care. Through its investment in Parata Systems, MDS also markets automated pharmacy systems to hospitals and retail pharmacies.

McKesson Technology Solutions (MTS; 2.9%) consists primarily of the former

Provider Technologies segment and the aforementioned Payor business. MTS delivers enterprise-wide patient care, clinical, financial, supply chain, and strategic management software solutions, pharmacy automation for hospitals, as well as connectivity, outsourcing and other services, to health care organizations throughout North America, the United Kingdom and other European countries. Its customers include hospitals, physicians, home care providers, retail pharmacies and payors.

CORPORATE STRATEGY. Distribution agreements between distributors and most drugmakers have transitioned toward a more fee-based approach, with the distributors appropriately and predictably compensated for distribution and related logistic and administrative services and data, in our opinion. MCK and its peers see over 80% of their drugmaker compensation as fixed and not dependent upon drug price inflation.

Company Financials Fiscal Year Ended Mar. 31

Per Share Data ($)	2010	2009	2008	2007	2006	2005	2004	2003	2002	2001
Tangible Book Value	9.95	4.83	10.42	9.10	13.36	12.47	12.66	10.57	9.81	8.55
Cash Flow	6.12	3.89	4.09	4.14	3.28	0.32	2.94	2.65	2.20	0.72
Earnings	4.62	2.99	3.32	3.17	2.34	-0.53	2.19	1.90	1.43	-0.15
S&P Core Earnings	4.62	4.16	3.33	3.16	2.07	1.93	1.29	1.24	0.87	-0.39
Dividends	0.48	0.48	0.24	0.24	0.24	0.24	0.24	0.24	0.24	0.24
Payout Ratio	10%	16%	7%	8%	10%	NM	11%	13%	17%	NM
Calendar Year	2009	2008	2007	2006	2005	2004	2003	2002	2001	2000
Prices:High	64.98	68.40	68.43	55.10	52.89	35.90	37.14	42.09	41.50	37.00
Prices:Low	33.13	28.27	50.80	44.60	30.13	22.61	22.61	24.99	23.40	16.00
P/E Ratio:High	14	23	21	17	23	NM	17	22	29	NM
P/E Ratio:Low	7	9	15	14	13	NM	10	13	16	NM

Income Statement Analysis (Million $)										
Revenue	108,702	106,632	101,703	92,977	88,050	80,515	69,506	57,121	50,006	42,010
Operating Income	2,400	1,951	1,736	1,553	1,425	1,260	1,216	1,134	923	454
Depreciation	474	261	231	295	266	251	232	204	208	246
Interest Expense	187	144	142	99.0	94.0	118	120	121	119	118
Pretax Income	1,864	1,064	1,457	1,297	1,158	-240	911	855	601	9.60
Effective Tax Rate	32.2%	22.7%	32.1%	25.4%	36.4%	NM	29.1%	34.3%	30.4%	NM
Net Income	1,263	823	989	968	737	-157	646	562	419	-42.7
S&P Core Earnings	1,260	1,159	991	964	650	565	380	364	255	-113

Balance Sheet & Other Financial Data (Million $)										
Cash	3,731	2,109	1,362	1,954	2,142	1,809	718	534	563	446
Current Assets	21,504	18,671	17,786	17,856	16,919	15,332	13,004	11,254	10,699	9,164
Total Assets	28,189	25,267	24,603	23,943	20,975	18,775	16,240	14,353	13,324	11,530
Current Liabilities	17,012	15,606	15,348	15,126	13,515	11,793	9,456	7,974	7,588	6,550
Long Term Debt	2,293	2,290	1,795	1,803	965	1,202	1,210	1,487	1,485	1,232
Common Equity	7,532	6,193	6,121	6,273	5,907	5,275	5,165	4,529	3,940	3,493
Total Capital	9,828	8,483	7,916	8,076	6,872	6,477	6,375	6,016	5,425	4,724
Capital Expenditures	199	195	195	126	167	140	115	116	132	159
Cash Flow	1,670	1,084	1,220	1,263	1,003	94.2	879	766	626	203
Current Ratio	1.3	1.2	1.2	1.2	1.3	1.3	1.4	1.4	1.4	1.4
% Long Term Debt of Capitalization	23.3	27.0	22.7	22.3	14.0	18.6	19.0	24.7	27.4	26.1
% Net Income of Revenue	1.2	0.8	1.0	1.0	0.8	NM	0.9	1.0	0.8	NM
% Return on Assets	4.7	3.3	4.1	4.3	3.7	NM	4.2	4.1	3.4	NM
% Return on Equity	18.4	13.4	16.0	15.9	13.2	NM	13.3	13.3	11.3	NM

Data as orig reptd.; bef. results of disc opers/spec. items. Per share data adj. for stk. divs.; EPS diluted. E-Estimated. NA-Not Available. NM-Not Meaningful. NR-Not Ranked. UR-Under Review.

Office: One Post St McKesson Plaza, San Francisco, CA 94104-5296.
Telephone: 415-983-8300.
Email: investors@mckesson.com
Website: http://www.mckesson.com

Chrmn, Pres & CEO: J.H. Hammergren
EVP & CFO: J. Campbell
EVP, CTO & CIO: R. Spratt
EVP & General Counsel: L.E. Seeger

Chief Acctg Officer & Cntlr: N.A. Rees
Investor Contact: J.C. Campbell (800-826-9360)
Board Members: A. Bryant, W. A. Budd, J. H. Hammergren, A. F. Irby, III, M. C. Jacobs, M. L. Knowles, D. M. Lawrence, E. A. Mueller, J. E. Shaw

Founded: 1994
Domicile: Delaware
Employees: 32,500

The McGraw-Hill Companies

Mead Johnson Nutrition Co

STANDARD &POOR'S

S&P Recommendation HOLD ★★★☆☆	

Price	12-Mo. Target Price	Investment Style
$59.04 (as of Oct 22, 2010)	**$52.00**	Large-Cap Blend

GICS Sector Consumer Staples
Sub-Industry Packaged Foods & Meats

Summary Mead Johnson Nutrition, split off from Bristol-Myers Squibb in 2009, is a global leader in pediatric nutrition.

Key Stock Statistics (Source S&P, Vickers, company reports)

52-Wk Range	**$59.46– 40.57**	S&P Oper. EPS 2010**E**	2.38	Market Capitalization(B)	**$12.077**	Beta		**NA**
Trailing 12-Month EPS	**$1.99**	S&P Oper. EPS 2011**E**	2.67	Yield (%)	1.52	S&P 3-Yr. Proj. EPS CAGR(%)		10
Trailing 12-Month P/E	**29.7**	P/E on S&P Oper. EPS 2010**E**	24.8	Dividend Rate/Share	$0.90	S&P Credit Rating		BBB
$10K Invested 5 Yrs Ago	**NA**	Common Shares Outstg. (M)	204.5	Institutional Ownership (%)	90			

Price Performance

- 30-Week Mov. Avg. · · · ·
- 10-Week Mov. Avg. – –
- **GAAP Earnings vs. Previous Year**
- Volume Above Avg. ▮▮▮ STARS
- 12-Mo. Target Price —
- Relative Strength —
- ▲ Up ▼ Down ► No Change
- Below Avg. ▮▮▮ ★

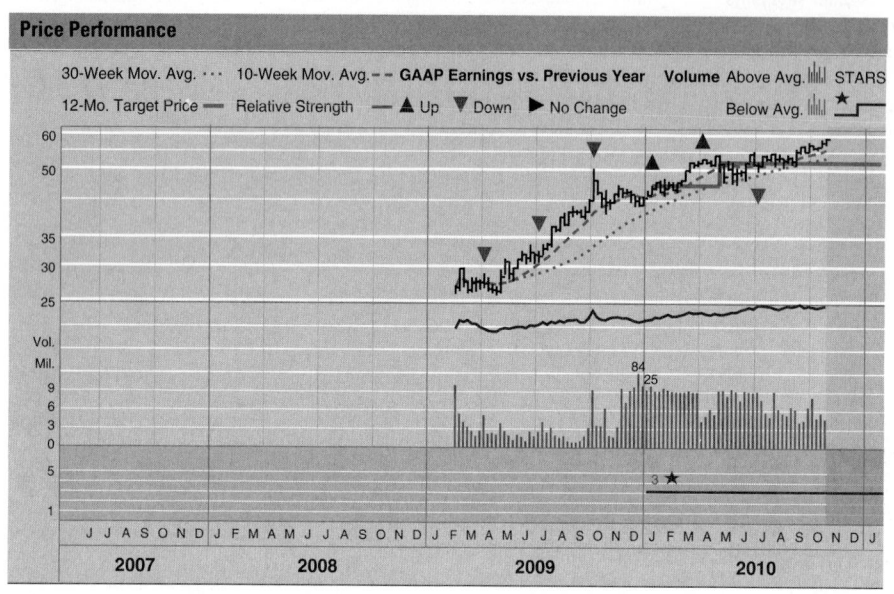

Analysis prepared by **Joseph Agnese** on August 02, 2010, when the stock traded at **$ 53.14**.

Qualitative Risk Assessment

LOW	MEDIUM	HIGH

Our risk assessment reflects our view that demand for Mead Johnson's infant formula and children's nutritional products is comparatively predictable in developed economies and growing in emerging markets. Demand in these categories has a relatively low sensitivity to changes in general economic and geopolitical conditions. This is partly offset by volatility in dairy prices.

Quantitative Evaluations

S&P Quality Ranking   NR

D	C	B-	B	B+	A-	A	A+

Relative Strength Rank   MODERATE

70

LOWEST = 1   HIGHEST = 99

Revenue/Earnings Data

Revenue (Million $)

	1Q	2Q	3Q	4Q	Year
2010	763.5	764.2	--	--	--
2009	693.0	719.3	699.8	714.4	2,827
2008	716.0	716.0	742.8	707.7	2,882
2007	615.1	615.1	673.1	673.1	2,576
2006	--	--	--	--	2,345
2005	--	--	--	--	2,202

Earnings Per Share ($)

2010	0.61	0.59	E0.60	E0.52	E2.38
2009	0.55	0.66	0.48	0.31	1.99
2008	0.77	0.67	0.60	0.23	2.32
2007	--	--	--	--	--
2006	--	--	--	--	--
2005	--	--	--	--	--

Fiscal year ended Dec. 31. Next earnings report expected: Late October. EPS Estimates based on S&P Operating Earnings; historical GAAP earnings are as reported.

Highlights

- ► In December 2009, Bristol-Myers Squibb completed an exchange offer that resulted in the split-off of MJN. This followed MJN's February 2009 initial public offering. For 2010, we look for sales to rise 8.7%, with almost all of the growth coming from the Asia/Latin America segment and a slightly positive contribution from foreign currency. Sales were down 0.7% in 2009, on negative foreign currency translation, market share losses in the North America/Europe segment, and a decrease in U.S. births.

- ► For 2010, we look for a 300 basis point decline in the operating margin, primarily due to a forecasted increase in raw material costs, additional expenses related to being an independent company and impact of changes in Venezuelan bolivar. In 2009, the operating margin improved 110 bps, with lower commodity costs more than offsetting higher expenses. We expect interest expense to decline in 2010, following a drop in 2009. For the historical periods, we use the management-provided adjusted income statements, which we think better reflect MJN's results as an independent company.

- ► Our EPS estimate is $2.38 for 2010, versus adjusted EPS of $2.23 in 2009 and $1.90 in 2008.

Investment Rationale/Risk

- ► We think the current stock price adequately reflects what we see as MJN's good long-term growth prospects, especially in Asia. The pediatric nutrition industry is projected to grow at a compound annual rate of 7% for the next few years. However, MJN's higher cost brands may not be as attractive in a weak spending environment.

- ► Risks to our recommendation and target price include consolidation of retail customers, prolonged economic downturns causing consumers to trade down to lower-priced products (including private label or store brands), rising dairy costs, changes in government programs, product quality and safety issues, high financial leverage, and unfavorable foreign exchange.

- ► Our 12-month target price of $52 is a weighted blend of our DCF and relative analyses. Our DCF model assumes an 7.7% terminal weighted average cost of capital and 3% terminal growth, to arrive at a $56 valuation. Our peer analysis assumes a premium to the average peer P/E multiple applied to our 2010 EPS estimate, to value the stock at $50.

Dividend Data (Dates: mm/dd Payment Date: mm/dd/yy)

Amount ($)	Date Decl.	Ex-Div. Date	Stk. of Record	Payment Date
0.200	12/18	12/29	12/31	01/15/10
0.225	03/17	03/22	03/24	04/01/10
0.225	06/16	06/23	06/25	07/01/10
0.225	09/16	09/22	09/24	10/01/10

Dividends have been paid since 2009. Source: Company reports.

Please read the Required Disclosures and Analyst Certification on the last page of this report.

The McGraw·Hill Companies

Mead Johnson Nutrition Co

Business Summary August 02, 2010

CORPORATE OVERVIEW. Mead Johnson Nutrition Company is a global leader in pediatric nutrition with about $2.8 billion in net sales in 2009. Its Enfa family of brands, including Enfamil infant formula, addresses a broad range of nutritional needs for infants, children and expectant and nursing mothers. MJN also markets some other brands on a local, regional or global basis. MJN's principal product categories are infant formula (63.9% of 2009 sales) and children's nutrition and other (26.1%).

MJN markets its portfolio of more than 70 products to mothers, health care professionals and retailers in more than 50 countries in Asia, North America, Latin America and Europe. MJN has two reportable segments -- Asia/Latin America (58% of sales and 60% of segment operating profits in 2009) and North America/Europe (43% and 40%). The U.S. represented 35% of revenues in 2009. Wal-Mart Stores, Inc. was MJN's largest single customer, accounting for 12% of sales in 2009.

Mead Johnson was founded in 1905 and introduced its first infant formula product in 1911. Over the years, MJN expanded to more countries and added more products. In 1967, it became a wholly owned subsidiary of Bristol-Myers Squibb Company. In February 2009, MJN completed an initial public offering of 34.5 million shares of its Class A common stock, with Bristol-Myers owning 100% of MJN's Class B common stock and over 42 million shares (55%) of its Class A common stock. Each Class B share had 10 votes per share and Class

A one vote. Bristol-Myers retained 83.1% of the outstanding shares.

In December 2009, Bristol-Myers completed an exchange offer, resulting in the split-off of MJN. This also involved the conversion of Class B shares into Class A shares, with Bristol-Myers distributing 170 million shares of Class A stock, or 83% of the outstanding shares of MJN. Subsequently, Bristol-Myers retained no share ownership in MJN.

MARKET PROFILE. There are five general stages of child development: Stage 0 (Pre-natal); Stage 1 (0-6 months old); Stage 2 (6-12 months old); Stage 3 (12 months to 3 years old); Stage 4 (3-5 years old); and Stage 5 (beyond 5 years old).

MJN produces different products for each stage. In the U.S., its business has been focused on the infant formula category (Stages 1 and 2), while outside the U.S., it sells infant formula products (Stages 1 and 2) and children's nutritional products (Stages 3, 4 and 5). In August 2009, MJN first shipped Enfagrow, nutrition tailored for toddlers, in the U.S.

Company Financials Fiscal Year Ended Dec. 31

Per Share Data ($)	2009	2008	2007	2006	2005	2004	2003	2002	2001	2000
Tangible Book Value	NM	NM	NA	NA	NA	NA	NA	NA	NA	NA
Cash Flow	2.28	2.58	NA	NA	NA	NA	NA	NA	NA	NA
Earnings	1.99	2.32	NA	NA	NA	NA	NA	NA	NA	NA
S&P Core Earnings	2.02	1.97	2.11	1.99	NA	NA	NA	NA	NA	NA
Dividends	0.40	Nil	NA	NA	NA	NA	NA	NA	NA	NA
Payout Ratio	20%	Nil	NA	NA	NA	NA	NA	NA	NA	NA
Prices:High	50.35	NA	NA	NA	NA	NA	NA	NA	NA	NA
Prices:Low	25.72	NA	NA	NA	NA	NA	NA	NA	NA	NA
P/E Ratio:High	25	NA	NA	NA	NA	NA	NA	NA	NA	NA
P/E Ratio:Low	13	NA	NA	NA	NA	NA	NA	NA	NA	NA

Income Statement Analysis (Million $)

	2009	2008	2007	2006	2005	2004	2003	2002	2001	2000
Revenue	2,827	2,882	2,576	2,345	2,202	NA	NA	NA	NA	NA
Operating Income	822	753	710	696	667	NA	NA	NA	NA	NA
Depreciation	58.9	44.1	51.0	49.5	53.8	NA	NA	NA	NA	NA
Interest Expense	95.9	43.3	NA	NA	NA	NA	NA	NA	NA	NA
Pretax Income	587	652	663	635	618	NA	NA	NA	NA	NA
Effective Tax Rate	30.1%	38.5%	35.2%	36.3%	36.0%	NA	NA	NA	NA	NA
Net Income	400	394	423	398	390	NA	NA	NA	NA	NA
S&P Core Earnings	411	394	423	398	NA	NA	NA	NA	NA	NA

Balance Sheet & Other Financial Data (Million $)

	2009	2008	2007	2006	2005	2004	2003	2002	2001	2000
Cash	561	NA	NA	NA	NA	NA	NA	NA	NA	NA
Current Assets	1,336	717	688	624	NA	NA	NA	NA	NA	NA
Total Assets	2,070	1,361	1,302	1,204	NA	NA	NA	NA	NA	NA
Current Liabilities	1,100	653	563	530	NA	NA	NA	NA	NA	NA
Long Term Debt	1,485	2,000	NA	NA	NA	NA	NA	NA	NA	NA
Common Equity	-675	-1,401	631	586	NA	NA	NA	NA	NA	NA
Total Capital	821	604	638	592	NA	NA	NA	NA	NA	NA
Capital Expenditures	95.8	81.1	78.4	68.9	56.4	NA	NA	NA	NA	NA
Cash Flow	459	438	466	441	436	NA	NA	NA	NA	NA
Current Ratio	1.2	1.1	1.2	1.2	NA	NA	NA	NA	NA	NA
% Long Term Debt of Capitalization	Nil	330.9	Nil	Nil	Nil	NA	NA	NA	NA	NA
% Net Income of Revenue	14.1	13.7	16.4	17.0	17.7	NA	NA	NA	NA	NA
% Return on Assets	NA	29.6	33.7	NA	NA	NA	NA	NA	NA	NA
% Return on Equity	NA	NM	69.5	NA	NA	NA	NA	NA	NA	NA

Data as orig reptd.; bef. results of disc opers/spec. items. Per share data adj. for stk. divs.; EPS diluted. E-Estimated. NA-Not Available. NM-Not Meaningful. NR-Not Ranked. UR-Under Review.

Office: 2701 Patriot Blvd, Glenview, IL 60026.
Telephone: 847-832-2420.
Website: http://www.meadjohnson.com
Chrmn: J.M. Cornelius

Pres & CEO: S.W. Golsby
SVP & CFO: P.G. Leemputte
SVP, Secy & General Counsel: W. P'Pool
Chief Acctg Officer & Cntlr: S.D. Burhans

Investor Contact: K. Chieger (847-804-9896)
Board Members: S. M. Altschuler, H. B. Bernick, K. A. Casiano, A. C. Catalano, J. M. Cornelius, S. W. Golsby, P. G. Ratcliffe, E. Sigal, R. S. Singer

Founded: 1905
Domicile: Delaware
Employees: 5,600

MeadWestvaco Corp

STANDARD &POOR'S

S&P Recommendation	HOLD ★★★☆☆		Price $25.14 (as of Oct 22, 2010)	12-Mo. Target Price $28.00	Investment Style Large-Cap Value

GICS Sector Materials
Sub-Industry Paper Products

Summary This company is primarily a major producer of paperboard packaging used in a variety of consumer markets.

Key Stock Statistics (Source S&P, Vickers, company reports)

52-Wk Range	$29.74–20.81	S&P Oper. EPS 2010**E**	1.35	Market Capitalization(B)	$4.294	Beta		1.76
Trailing 12-Month EPS	$1.45	S&P Oper. EPS 2011**E**	1.60	Yield (%)	3.66	S&P 3-Yr. Proj. EPS CAGR(%)		36
Trailing 12-Month P/E	17.3	P/E on S&P Oper. EPS 2010**E**	18.6	Dividend Rate/Share	$0.92	S&P Credit Rating		BBB
$10K Invested 5 Yrs Ago	$11,959	Common Shares Outstg. (M)	170.8	Institutional Ownership (%)	85			

Price Performance

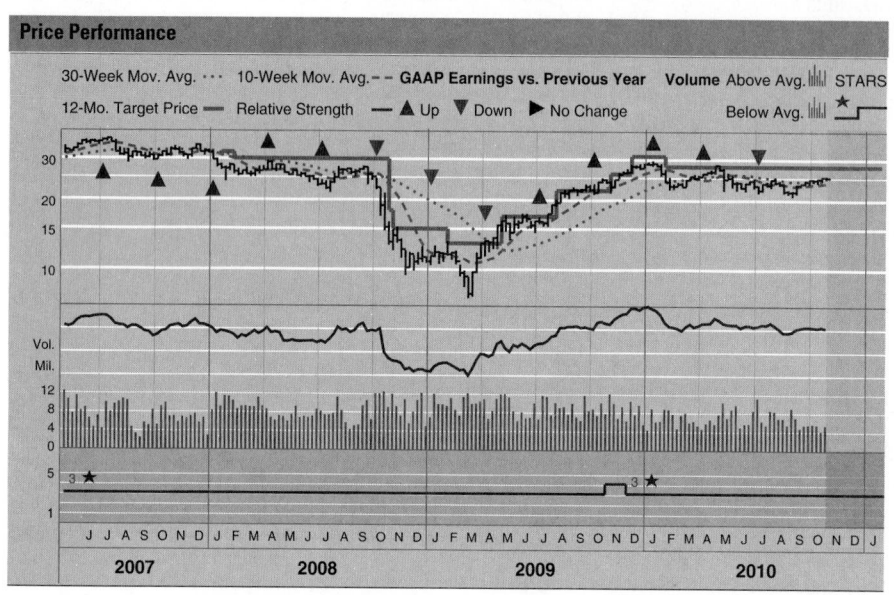

30-Week Mov. Avg. · · ·   10-Week Mov. Avg. – –   **GAAP Earnings vs. Previous Year**   Volume Above Avg. ▮▮▮ STARS
12-Mo. Target Price —   Relative Strength —   ▲ Up   ▼ Down   ▶ No Change   Below Avg. ▮▮▮ ★

Options: ASE, CBOE, P

Analysis prepared by **Stuart J. Benway, CFA** on August 09, 2010, when the stock traded at **$ 23.70.**

Highlights

➤ We expect sales to rebound by 4%-6% in 2010. Demand for media and office products is likely to be weak due to secular declines in usage for CDs, DVDs and time management products. MWV has also shut several facilities and eliminated certain product lines. However, we look for economic activity to improve moderately in 2010, which should boost demand for paperboard packaging and specialty chemicals, and growth in emerging markets should resume. Similar revenue growth is expected in 2011.

➤ We anticipate margin improvement in 2010. Weak demand in 2009 prompted management to reduce its product line and close several manufacturing facilities. We expect lower costs from reduced overhead and improved manufacturing efficiencies to boost margins in 2010. Our forecast is for operating margins to widen to 7.7% in 2010 from 5.6% in 2009.

➤ Our operating EPS forecast for 2010 is $1.35 (excluding charges), up significantly from $0.70 earned in 2009. Our 2010 estimate includes modest land sales gains, which could be significant in certain quarters. For 2011, we project EPS of $1.60.

Investment Rationale/Risk

➤ We believe that volume trends will improve in 2010 as customers rebuild inventories and new products generate market share gains. MWV's strong position in emerging markets and its moves to eliminate low-margin product lines should also aid long-term growth, by our analysis. Additionally, we think that MWV has valuable land that it will sell gradually over the long term. We believe these shares fully reflect the improved results that we project.

➤ Risks to our recommendation and target price include a weaker-than-expected global economy, softer-than-projected demand and pricing trends for MWV's packaging grades, and a renewed rise in energy and raw material costs.

➤ Our discounted cash flow model, which assumes a weighted average cost of capital of 10.0%, solid cash flow generation in 2010, and growth in perpetuity of 3%, values the shares at $30. A peer group of packaging stocks is trading at 15.7X our 2011 estimates. Applying this forward P/E to our 2011 forecast for MWV values the shares at $24. Our 12-month target price of $28 is a weighted blend of these metrics.

Qualitative Risk Assessment

LOW	MEDIUM	HIGH

MWV operates in a moderately cyclical and seasonal sector and is subject to swings in certain commodity prices. However, it has some pricing power due to its high market share, and its debt levels are low relative to many of its peers.

Quantitative Evaluations

S&P Quality Ranking B

D	C	B-	B	B+	A-	A	A+

Relative Strength Rank MODERATE

59

LOWEST = 1   HIGHEST = 99

Revenue/Earnings Data

Revenue (Million $)

	1Q	2Q	3Q	4Q	Year
2010	1,402	1,552	--	--	--
2009	1,354	1,432	1,627	1,636	6,049
2008	1,518	1,709	1,811	1,599	6,637
2007	1,552	1,706	1,796	1,852	6,906
2006	1,434	1,570	1,751	1,775	6,530
2005	1,373	1,587	1,583	1,627	6,170

Earnings Per Share ($)

2010	0.14	0.29	E0.55	E0.34	E1.35
2009	-0.46	0.72	0.74	0.29	1.30
2008	-0.05	0.33	0.26	-0.09	0.46
2007	-0.09	0.17	0.66	0.82	1.56
2006	0.02	-0.04	0.31	0.23	0.52
2005	0.08	-0.06	0.30	0.33	0.62

Fiscal year ended Dec. 31. Next earnings report expected: Late October. EPS Estimates based on S&P Operating Earnings; historical GAAP earnings are as reported.

Dividend Data (Dates: mm/dd Payment Date: mm/dd/yy)

Amount ($)	Date Decl.	Ex-Div. Date	Stk. of Record	Payment Date
0.230	11/17	11/24	11/27	12/01/09
0.230	01/25	02/02	02/04	03/01/10
0.230	04/26	05/05	05/06	06/01/10
0.230	06/29	07/29	08/02	09/01/10

Dividends have been paid since 1892. Source: Company reports.

Please read the Required Disclosures and Analyst Certification on the last page of this report.

The McGraw-Hill Companies

MeadWestvaco Corp

Business Summary August 09, 2010

CORPORATE OVERVIEW. Through a series of mergers and divestitures, Mead-Westvaco has molded itself into one of the largest producers of packaging products in the world, and it is also a major supplier of consumer and office products and specialty chemicals. The Packaging Resources segment (38% of 2009 revenues) produces bleached paperboard, coated paperboard, kraft paperboard, linerboard and saturating kraft, and packaging for consumer products including beverage and dairy, cosmetics, tobacco, pharmaceuticals, and health care products. Some of the company's major customers include Altria, Anheuser-Busch, Coca-Cola and Procter & Gamble. The Consumer Solutions segment (35%) sells a full range of consumer packaging products, including printed plastic packaging and injection-molded products used for packaging DVDs, CDs, cosmetics, and pharmaceuticals, and plastic dispensing and spraying systems for worldwide personal care, health care, fragrance, and lawn and garden markets. The Consumer and Office Products segment (16%) makes, markets and distributes school and office products, time management products, and envelopes. The Specialty Chemicals segment (8%) produces, markets and distributes specialty chemicals derived from sawdust and other by-products of the pulp and papermaking process. These chemicals include activated carbon, printing ink resins, emulsifiers used in asphalt paving, and

dyestuffs. Real estate and corporate and other accounted for 3% of sales in 2009. The company also owns about 800,000 acres of forest lands in the U.S.

MARKET PROFILE. We believe MeadWestvaco is the largest producer of paperboard, also known as folding boxboard or cartonboard, in North America, with a share of about 16%. The market is somewhat fragmented, with more than 15 companies accounting for at least a 1% share. Unlike containerboard, paperboard has a bendable quality for creasing, scoring and shaping, and usually packages single items meant for consumer purchase. It is used in a variety of consumer applications where print quality, strength and customer appeal are important. Folding carton demand is primarily driven by consumer spending and industrial production. We believe the company's market position, technical expertise and product line diversity give it a moderate level of control over pricing.

Company Financials Fiscal Year Ended Dec. 31

Per Share Data ($)	2009	2008	2007	2006	2005	2004	2003	2002	2001	2000
Tangible Book Value	12.02	9.37	13.52	14.74	14.58	18.44	19.89	20.44	17.34	23.17
Cash Flow	3.86	2.91	4.13	3.37	3.17	1.87	3.60	3.49	4.29	5.63
Earnings	1.30	0.46	1.56	0.52	0.62	-1.73	-0.01	-0.01	0.87	2.53
S&P Core Earnings	0.82	-0.68	0.21	-0.11	0.27	-2.67	-0.81	-1.37	-1.04	NA
Dividends	0.92	0.92	Nil	0.92	0.92	0.92	0.92	0.92	0.88	0.88
Payout Ratio	71%	NM	Nil	177%	148%	NM	NM	NM	101%	35%
Prices:High	29.33	31.44	36.50	30.85	34.33	34.34	29.83	36.50	32.10	34.75
Prices:Low	7.53	9.44	28.39	24.76	25.06	25.16	21.37	15.57	22.68	24.06
P/E Ratio:High	23	68	23	59	55	NM	NM	NM	37	14
P/E Ratio:Low	6	21	18	48	40	NM	NM	NM	26	10

Income Statement Analysis (Million $)										
Revenue	6,049	6,637	6,906	6,530	6,170	8,227	7,553	7,242	3,935	3,663
Operating Income	828	734	893	743	818	1,042	855	859	677	869
Depreciation	443	423	473	517	491	726	724	674	347	314
Interest Expense	204	210	219	211	208	278	291	309	208	192
Pretax Income	375	79.0	400	98.0	135	-454	-29.0	-15.0	119	404
Effective Tax Rate	40.0%	NM	28.8%	5.10%	11.9%	NM	NM	NM	25.6%	36.9%
Net Income	225	80.0	285	93.0	119	-349	-2.00	-3.00	88.2	255
S&P Core Earnings	141	-118	36.7	-22.1	50.6	-539	-164	-264	-104	NA

Balance Sheet & Other Financial Data (Million $)										
Cash	850	549	245	156	297	270	225	372	81.2	255
Current Assets	2,530	2,161	2,167	2,015	2,030	2,562	2,426	2,431	1,016	1,064
Total Assets	9,021	8,455	9,837	9,285	8,908	11,681	12,487	12,921	6,787	6,570
Current Liabilities	1,245	1,274	1,455	1,465	1,042	1,751	1,501	1,620	701	567
Long Term Debt	2,153	2,309	2,375	2,372	2,417	3,427	3,969	4,233	2,660	2,687
Common Equity	3,406	2,967	3,708	3,533	3,483	4,317	4,768	4,831	2,341	2,333
Total Capital	5,576	6,195	7,311	7,082	7,052	9,249	10,415	10,821	6,009	5,927
Capital Expenditures	224	288	347	302	305	407	393	377	290	214
Cash Flow	668	503	758	610	610	377	722	671	436	569
Current Ratio	2.0	1.7	1.5	1.4	1.9	1.5	1.6	1.5	1.4	1.9
% Long Term Debt of Capitalization	38.6	37.3	32.5	33.5	34.3	37.1	38.1	39.1	44.3	45.3
% Net Income of Revenue	3.7	1.2	4.1	1.4	1.9	NM	NM	NM	2.2	7.0
% Return on Assets	2.6	0.9	3.0	1.0	1.2	NM	NM	NM	1.3	4.4
% Return on Equity	7.1	2.4	7.9	2.7	3.1	NM	NM	NM	3.8	11.3

Data as orig reptd.; bef. results of disc opers/spec. items. Per share data adj. for stk. divs.; EPS diluted. E-Estimated. NA-Not Available. NM-Not Meaningful. NR-Not Ranked. UR-Under Review.

Office: 501 South 5th Street, Richmond, VA 23219-0501.
Telephone: 804-444-1000.
Website: http://www.meadwestvaco.com
Chrmn & CEO: J.A. Luke, Jr.

Pres: J.A. Buzzard
SVP & CFO: E.M. Rajkowski
SVP, Secy & General Counsel: W.L. Willkie, II
CTO: M.T. Watkins

Investor Contact: E.M. Rajkowski (804-327-5200)
Board Members: M. E. Campbell, T. W. Cole, Jr., J. G. Kaiser, R. B. Kelson, J. M. Kilts, S. J. Kropf, D. S. Luke, J. A. Luke, Jr., R. C. McCormack, T. H. Powers, E. M. Straw, J. L. Warner

Founded: 1846
Domicile: Delaware
Employees: 20,000

Medco Health Solutions Inc.

STANDARD &POOR'S

| S&P Recommendation | STRONG BUY ★★★★★ | Price $51.34 (as of Oct 22, 2010) | 12-Mo. Target Price $70.00 | Investment Style Large-Cap Blend |

GICS Sector Health Care
Sub-Industry Health Care Services

Summary Medco is the largest U.S. pharmacy benefit manager (PBM) in terms of revenues and script count.

Key Stock Statistics (Source S&P, Vickers, company reports)

52-Wk Range	$66.94–43.45	S&P Oper. EPS 2010E	3.38	Market Capitalization(B)	$22.264	Beta	0.46
Trailing 12-Month EPS	$2.84	S&P Oper. EPS 2011E	3.90	Yield (%)	Nil	S&P 3-Yr. Proj. EPS CAGR(%)	21
Trailing 12-Month P/E	18.1	P/E on S&P Oper. EPS 2010E	15.2	Dividend Rate/Share	Nil	S&P Credit Rating	BBB+
$10K Invested 5 Yrs Ago	$18,129	Common Shares Outstg. (M)	433.7	Institutional Ownership (%)	77		

Price Performance

- 30-Week Mov. Avg. · · · · 10-Week Mov. Avg. – – GAAP Earnings vs. Previous Year Volume Above Avg. STARS
- 12-Mo. Target Price — Relative Strength — ▲ Up ▼ Down ▶ No Change Below Avg. ★

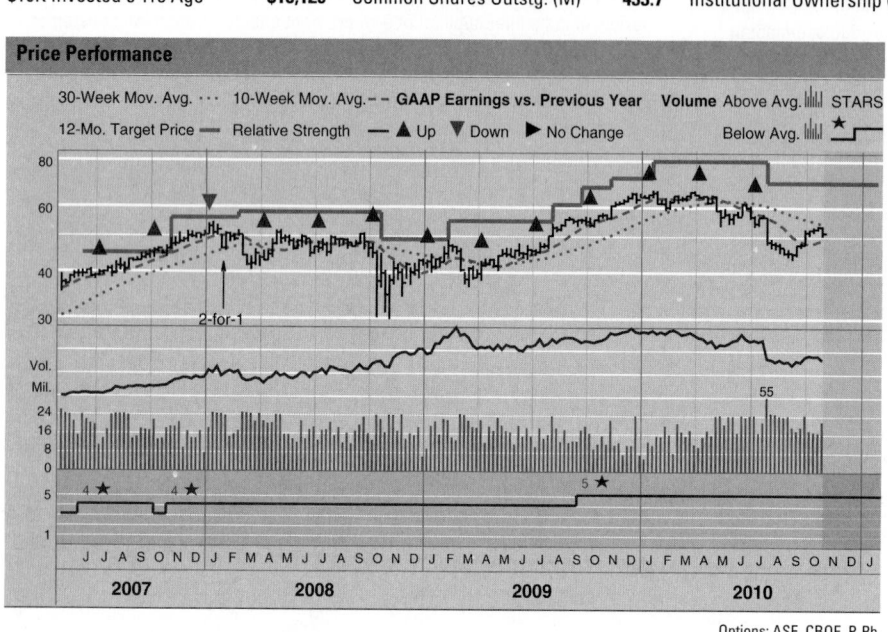

Options: ASE, CBOE, P, Ph

Analysis prepared by **Herman B. Saftlas** on July 30, 2010, when the stock traded at **$ 47.67**.

Highlights

▶ We forecast revenues will rise about 9% in 2010, to over $65 billion. Drivers we see include a 99% retention rate of existing business, net new business of $5 billion garnered so far for 2010 as of June 30, and brand-name drug price inflation. MHS expects to renew $15 billion of business in 2010. However, we see growth tempered by the weak economy and the penetration of generic drugs, which carry lower prices but wider margins than branded drugs.

▶ We expect EBITDA per adjusted prescription (one three-month mail prescription counted as three one-month retail prescriptions), a measure of PBM profitability, to increase in the low single-digits, reflecting projected higher retail volumes. The acquisition of DNA Direct in early 2010 is expected to be about $0.01 dilutive to 2010 EPS.

▶ We look for operating EPS before amortization charges of $3.38 for 2010, versus 2009's $2.79 (before a one-time state tax gain), and we see $3.90 in 2011. MHS expects cash from operations in 2010 of about $2.4 billion, which we view as providing it with significant financial flexibility.

Investment Rationale/Risk

▶ We view the fundamentals of the PBM space as bright, as health plans, governments and employers seek to control drug costs. We believe MHS has significant opportunities to expand generic drug mail penetration of its new accounts and has begun to make progress. In addition, we see the company and peers benefiting from the $102.1 billion in brand-name drugs it expects to go off-patent from 2009 to 2015. Meanwhile, we view its initiatives, including personalized medicine based on genetics, as bolstering its competitive position. In general, we believe Medco is well positioned in the PBM industry, with a record of high-quality service and competitive pricing. MHS also plans to expand PBM services in Europe through a joint venture with Celesio, a German drug distributor.

▶ Risks to our recommendation and target price include intensifying competition and more regulatory oversight.

▶ Our 12-month target price of $70 is derived by applying a peer EBITDA/share multiple of 10X to our 2011 EBITDA forecast. Applying a close-to-peers price-to-EPS before amortization ratio of 18X to our 2011 estimate also yields a $70 price.

Qualitative Risk Assessment

| LOW | MEDIUM | HIGH |

Our risk assessment reflects rising drug demand and our view of MHS's improving financial performance and declining debt leverage. However, we believe that intense competition and increased government regulation of pharmacy benefit managers, which we view as likely, could slow long-term progress in profits.

Quantitative Evaluations

S&P Quality Ranking NR

| D | C | B- | B | B+ | A- | A | A+ |

Relative Strength Rank MODERATE

| 38 |

LOWEST = 1   HIGHEST = 99

Revenue/Earnings Data

Revenue (Million $)

	1Q	2Q	3Q	4Q	Year
2010	16,311	16,408	--	--	--
2009	14,834	14,930	14,795	15,245	59,804
2008	12,963	12,775	12,559	12,961	51,258
2007	11,160	11,050	10,919	11,379	44,506
2006	10,564	10,589	10,461	10,930	42,544
2005	8,743	8,999	9,325	10,803	37,871

Earnings Per Share ($)

2010	0.67	0.77	E0.88	E0.94	E3.38
2009	0.58	0.64	0.69	0.70	2.61
2008	0.50	0.51	0.58	0.54	2.13
2007	0.47	0.38	0.39	0.38	1.63
2006	0.08	0.28	0.31	0.39	1.05
2005	0.24	0.24	0.26	0.29	1.03

Fiscal year ended Dec. 31. Next earnings report expected: Early November. EPS Estimates based on S&P Operating Earnings; historical GAAP earnings are as reported.

Dividend Data

No cash dividends have been paid.

Medco Health Solutions Inc.

STANDARD
&POOR'S

Business Summary July 30, 2010

CORPORATE OVERVIEW. Medco Health Solutions was spun off to Merck & Co. (MRK) shareholders in a tax-free transaction on August 19, 2003. The company is one of the largest U.S. pharmacy benefit managers (PBMs). It provides programs and services to clients and members of PBMs, and to physicians and pharmacies that they use.

In 2009, MHS processed about 899 million adjusted prescriptions (with one mail-order prescription is the equivalent of three retail prescriptions), compared to 796 million in 2008. Revenues and net income are derived from: rebates and discounts on prescription drugs from pharmaceutical manufacturers; competitive discounts from retail pharmacies; the negotiation of favorable client pricing, including rebate sharing terms; the shift in dispensing volumes from retail to home delivery; and the provision of services in a cost-efficient manner.

Rebates from brand-name pharmaceutical manufacturers, which are reflect-

ed as a reduction in cost of product net revenues, totaled $4,447 million in 2008, $3,561 million in 2007, and $3,417 million in 2006, with formulary rebates representing 54.7%, 50.1% and 51.9% of total rebates, respectively, and market share rebates reflecting the remainder. The increases in rebates reflect improved formulary management and patient compliance, as well as favorable pharmaceutical manufacturer rebate contract revisions, and volume from new 2008 clients, partially offset by lower rebates as a result of brand-name drug volumes that have converted to generic drugs. MHS retained about $806 million, or 18.1%, of total rebates in 2008, $547 million, or 15.4%, in 2007, and $670 million, or 19.6%, in 2006.

Company Financials Fiscal Year Ended Dec. 31

Per Share Data ($)	2009	2008	2007	2006	2005	2004	2003	2002	2001	2000
Tangible Book Value	NM	NM	NM	NM	NM	0.49	NM	NM	0.85	0.66
Cash Flow	3.60	2.98	2.33	1.69	1.63	1.56	1.31	1.07	1.08	0.94
Earnings	2.61	2.13	1.63	1.05	1.03	0.88	0.79	0.59	0.48	0.40
S&P Core Earnings	2.62	2.11	1.62	1.21	0.93	0.74	0.52	0.54	0.36	NA
Dividends	Nil	Nil	Nil	Nil	Nil	Nil	Nil	Nil	NA	NA
Payout Ratio	Nil	Nil	Nil	Nil	Nil	Nil	Nil	Nil	NA	NA
Prices:High	66.00	54.63	51.67	32.06	28.98	20.95	19.00	NA	NA	NA
Prices:Low	36.46	29.80	26.26	23.54	20.28	14.70	10.10	NA	NA	NA
P/E Ratio:High	25	26	32	31	28	24	24	NA	NA	NA
P/E Ratio:Low	14	14	16	22	20	17	13	NA	NA	NA

Income Statement Analysis (Million $)	2009	2008	2007	2006	2005	2004	2003	2002	2001	2000
Revenue	59,804	51,258	44,506	42,544	37,871	35,352	34,265	32,959	29,071	22,266
Operating Income	2,751	2,461	2,000	1,470	1,350	1,244	1,025	886	837	731
Depreciation	485	443	397	392	358	378	283	257	323	289
Interest Expense	173	234	134	65.9	73.9	Nil	Nil	73.5	Nil	Nil
Pretax Income	2,103	1,791	1,503	1,012	953	806	729	547	518	448
Effective Tax Rate	39.1%	38.4%	39.3%	37.7%	36.8%	40.3%	41.6%	41.7%	50.5%	51.6%
Net Income	1,280	1,103	912	630	602	482	426	319	257	217
S&P Core Earnings	1,284	1,092	908	726	544	404	279	287	188	NA

Balance Sheet & Other Financial Data (Million $)	2009	2008	2007	2006	2005	2004	2003	2002	2001	2000
Cash	2,548	1,002	844	818	888	1,146	638	203	16.3	NA
Current Assets	8,159	7,098	6,303	5,855	5,061	4,320	3,760	3,044	2,534	NA
Total Assets	17,916	17,011	16,218	14,388	13,703	10,542	10,263	9,714	9,252	8,915
Current Liabilities	6,348	5,798	5,129	4,827	3,761	2,645	2,605	2,370	1,809	NA
Long Term Debt	4,000	4,003	2,894	866	944	1,093	1,346	1,385	Nil	Nil
Common Equity	6,387	5,958	6,875	7,504	7,724	5,719	5,080	4,738	6,268	6,358
Total Capital	10,387	11,026	10,937	9,531	9,882	6,812	7,604	7,305	7,423	7,502
Capital Expenditures	239	287	178	151	132	98.1	125	235	322	251
Cash Flow	1,765	1,546	1,309	1,022	960	859	709	576	580	506
Current Ratio	1.3	1.2	1.2	1.2	1.3	1.6	1.4	1.3	1.4	NA
% Long Term Debt of Capitalization	38.5	36.3	26.5	9.1	9.6	16.0	17.7	19.0	Nil	Nil
% Net Income of Revenue	2.1	2.2	2.1	1.5	1.6	1.4	1.2	1.0	0.9	1.0
% Return on Assets	7.3	6.6	6.0	4.4	5.0	4.6	4.2	NA	2.8	NA
% Return on Equity	20.7	17.2	12.7	8.3	9.0	8.9	7.3	NA	4.1	NA

Data as orig reptd.; bef. results of disc opers/spec. items. Per share data adj. for stk. divs.; EPS diluted. E-Estimated. NA-Not Available. NM-Not Meaningful. NR-Not Ranked. UR-Under Review.

Office: 100 Parsons Pond Drive, Franklin Lakes, NJ 07417-2603.
Telephone: 201-269-3400.
Website: http://www.medcohealth.com
Chrmn & CEO: D.B. Snow, Jr.

Pres & COO: K.O. Klepper
SVP & CFO: R.J. Rubino
SVP, Chief Acctg Officer & Cntlr: G.R. Cappucci
SVP, Secy & General Counsel: T.M. Moriarty

Board Members: H. W. Barker, Jr., J. L. Cassis, M. Goldstein, C. M. Lillis, M. S. Potter, W. Roper, D. B. Snow, Jr., D. D. Stevens, B. J. Wilson

Founded: 1983
Domicile: Delaware
Employees: 22,850

The McGraw-Hill Companies

Medtronic Inc.

STANDARD &POOR'S

S&P Recommendation HOLD ★★★☆☆	**Price** $35.75 (as of Oct 22, 2010)	**12-Mo. Target Price** $36.00	**Investment Style** Large-Cap Growth

GICS Sector Health Care
Sub-Industry Health Care Equipment

Summary This global medical device manufacturer has leadership positions in the pacemaker, defibrillator, orthopedic, diabetes management, and other medical markets.

Key Stock Statistics (Source S&P, Vickers, company reports)

52-Wk Range	$46.66– 30.80	S&P Oper. EPS 2011**E**	3.40	Market Capitalization(B)	$38.606	Beta	0.82
Trailing 12-Month EPS	$3.16	S&P Oper. EPS 2012**E**	3.75	Yield (%)	2.52	S&P 3-Yr. Proj. EPS CAGR(%)	9
Trailing 12-Month P/E	11.3	P/E on S&P Oper. EPS 2011**E**	10.5	Dividend Rate/Share	$0.90	S&P Credit Rating	AA-
$10K Invested 5 Yrs Ago	$6,913	Common Shares Outstg. (M)	1,079.9	Institutional Ownership (%)	77		

Price Performance

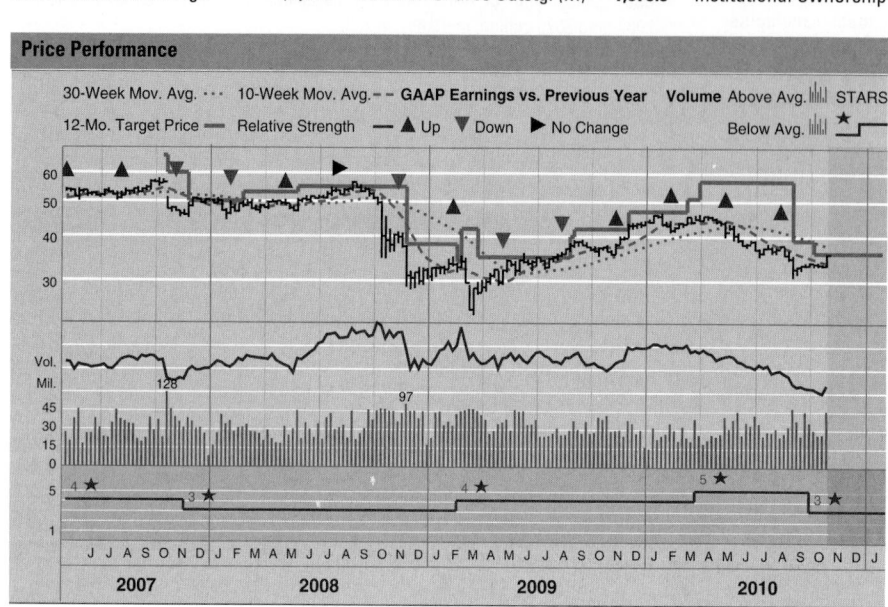

30-Week Mov. Avg. · · · · 10-Week Mov. Avg. - - - **GAAP Earnings vs. Previous Year** Volume Above Avg. STARS
12-Mo. Target Price — Relative Strength — ▲ Up ▼ Down ► No Change Below Avg. ★

Options: ASE, CBOE, P, Ph

Analysis prepared by **Phillip M. Seligman** on September 30, 2010, when the stock traded at **$ 33.58**.

Qualitative Risk Assessment

LOW	MEDIUM	HIGH

Our risk assessment reflects MDT's exposure to intensely competitive areas of the medical equipment markets, which are typically characterized by relatively short product life cycles, pricing pressures, and threat of new market entrants. However, we believe this is offset by MDT's many competitive advantages from the scale of its operations and sales force, product breadth, and what we see as its financial strength.

Quantitative Evaluations

S&P Quality Ranking A

D	C	B-	B	B+	A-	A	A+

Relative Strength Rank MODERATE

54

LOWEST = 1   HIGHEST = 99

Highlights

➤ Following weaker-than-expected July-quarter sales, MDT reduced its outlook for sales growth in constant currency to 2%-5% for FY 11 (Apr.) from 4%-7%. Taking a more conservative posture, we expect total sales to decline by 0.3%. In this regard, we look for a mid single-digit decline in the cardiac rhythm disease management (CRDM) division sales and a low single-digit decline in spine division sales, outweighing mid single-digit growth in cardiovascular sales and high single-digit growth in neuromodulation and diabetes sales. We expect revenues and earnings to be back-end loaded on new products and seasonality.

➤ We look for gross margins to widen slightly to about the high end of MDT's goal of 75.5%-76%, reflecting ongoing cost optimization efforts and assuming an improving product mix. We see R&D costs rising 30 basis points (bps) to 9.5% of sales, driven by additions to R&D head count. We expect SG&A costs to be flat with FY 10 levels as a percentage of sales, on cost control.

➤ We see FY 11 operating EPS of $3.40, including $0.06-$0.07 of acquisition-related dilution, up from $3.22 in FY 10. We forecast EPS of $3.75 for FY 12.

Investment Rationale/Risk

➤ In late September, we reduced our opinion on MDT shares to hold from strong buy. We view MDT's diversification, product pipeline, emerging market sales, cost reduction, and balance sheet positively. The dividend yield also looks attractive to us. Even so, procedure volumes remain down amid the tough economy and payor pushback, and while we think health care reform can eventually bring a lift, we view the timing as uncertain. We also see more pricing pressures ahead, though we think MDT may be able to limit their impact by improving product mix. However, the company noted market share losses in ICDs and drug-eluting stents, and recent positive news from rivals in the areas of spine and transcatheter aortic valves suggests that MDT may see other market share losses.

➤ Risks to our opinion and target price include loss of share in key markets, adverse reimbursement rate changes, and further weakness in the U.S. ICD and spinal surgery markets.

➤ Our 12-month target price of $36 is 10.5X our FY 11 EPS estimate, a discount to peers given MDT's recent and potential market share losses.

Revenue/Earnings Data

Revenue (Million $)

	1Q	2Q	3Q	4Q	Year
2011	3,773	--	--	--	--
2010	3,933	3,838	3,851	4,196	15,817
2009	3,706	3,570	3,494	3,829	14,599
2008	3,127	3,124	3,405	3,860	13,515
2007	2,897	3,075	3,048	3,280	12,299
2006	2,690	2,765	2,770	3,077	11,292

Earnings Per Share ($)

2011	0.76	E0.81	E0.85	E0.95	E3.40
2010	0.40	0.78	0.75	0.86	2.79
2009	0.66	0.51	0.65	0.11	1.93
2008	0.66	0.58	0.07	0.72	1.95
2007	0.51	0.59	0.61	0.70	2.41
2006	0.26	0.67	0.55	0.62	2.09

Fiscal year ended Apr. 30. Next earnings report expected: Late November. EPS Estimates based on S&P Operating Earnings; historical GAAP earnings are as reported.

Dividend Data (Dates: mm/dd Payment Date: mm/dd/yy)

Amount ($)	Date Decl.	Ex-Div. Date	Stk. of Record	Payment Date
0.205	12/03	01/06	01/08	01/29/10
0.205	02/18	04/07	04/09	04/30/10
0.225	06/24	07/07	07/09	07/30/10
0.225	08/25	10/06	10/08	10/29/10

Dividends have been paid since 1977. Source: Company reports.

The **McGraw·Hill** Companies

Medtronic Inc.

Business Summary September 30, 2010

CORPORATE OVERVIEW. Medtronic has leading positions in medical device categories, including cardiac rhythm management, spinal, vascular, neurology and cardiac surgery.

Cardiac rhythm disease management products (CRDM; 33% of FY 10 (Apr.) revenues) include implantable pacemakers to treat bradycardia, a condition of slow or irregular heartbeats. Some models are non-invasively programmed by a physician to adjust sensing, electrical pulse intensity, duration, rate and other factors, as well as pacers that can sense in both upper and lower heart chambers and produce appropriate impulses. In May 2005, FDA approval was received for EnRhythm, a dual-chamber pacemaker and the first pacemaker to offer an exclusive pacing mode, called Managed Ventricular Pacing, which enables the device to be programmed to minimize pacing pulses to the right ventricle.

Implantable cardioverter defibrillators (ICDs) treat abnormally fast heart beats

by monitoring the heart; when a rapid rhythm is detected, electrical impulses or shocks are delivered. Cardiac resynchronization therapy (CRT) devices synchronize contractions of multiple heart chambers. The company's InSynch ICD offers CRT for heart failure, as well as advanced defibrillation capabilities for patients also at risk for potentially lethal tachyarrhythmias that may lead to cardiac arrest. The CDRM segment also includes diagnostics and monitoring devices to record the heart's electrical activity and patient management tools, including CareLink, which enables patients to transmit data from their pacemaker, ICD or CRT-D using a portable monitor that is connected to a standard telephone line.

Company Financials Fiscal Year Ended Apr. 30

Per Share Data ($)	2010	2009	2008	2007	2006	2005	2004	2003	2002	2001
Tangible Book Value	3.35	1.95	1.62	4.56	2.98	4.26	3.18	2.21	1.10	3.53
Cash Flow	3.49	2.55	2.51	2.91	2.54	1.86	1.96	1.64	1.07	1.10
Earnings	2.79	1.93	1.95	2.41	2.09	1.48	1.60	1.30	0.80	0.85
S&P Core Earnings	3.06	2.12	2.12	2.44	2.00	1.65	1.46	1.10	0.76	0.91
Dividends	NA	0.50	0.44	0.39	0.34	0.29	0.25	0.25	0.20	0.12
Payout Ratio	NA	26%	23%	16%	16%	20%	16%	19%	25%	14%
Calendar Year	2009	2008	2007	2006	2005	2004	2003	2002	2001	2000
Prices:High	44.94	56.97	57.99	59.87	58.91	53.70	52.92	50.69	60.81	62.00
Prices:Low	24.06	28.33	44.87	42.37	48.70	43.99	42.90	32.50	36.64	32.75
P/E Ratio:High	16	30	30	25	28	36	33	39	72	61
P/E Ratio:Low	9	15	23	18	23	30	27	25	43	32

Income Statement Analysis (Million $)										
Revenue	15,817	14,599	13,515	12,299	11,292	10,055	9,087	7,665	6,411	5,552
Operating Income	5,909	5,276	4,728	4,322	4,248	3,907	3,583	3,062	2,479	2,176
Depreciation	772	699	637	583	544	463	443	408	330	297
Interest Expense	246	217	255	228	Nil	55.1	56.5	7.20	Nil	74.0
Pretax Income	3,969	2,772	2,885	3,515	3,161	2,544	2,797	2,341	1,524	1,549
Effective Tax Rate	NA	17.4%	22.7%	20.3%	19.4%	29.1%	29.9%	31.7%	35.4%	32.5%
Net Income	3,099	2,291	2,231	2,802	2,547	1,804	1,959	1,600	984	1,046
S&P Core Earnings	3,395	2,392	2,423	2,841	2,450	2,006	1,790	1,347	936	1,121

Balance Sheet & Other Financial Data (Million $)										
Cash	3,775	1,676	1,613	1,256	2,994	2,232	1,594	1,470	411	1,030
Current Assets	9,839	7,460	7,322	7,918	10,377	7,422	5,313	4,606	3,488	3,757
Total Assets	28,090	23,605	22,198	19,512	19,665	16,617	14,111	12,321	10,905	7,039
Current Liabilities	5,121	3,147	3,535	2,563	4,406	3,380	4,241	1,813	3,985	1,359
Long Term Debt	6,944	6,772	5,700	5,578	5,486	1,973	1.10	1,980	9.50	13.0
Common Equity	14,629	12,973	11,536	10,977	9,383	10,450	9,077	7,906	6,431	5,510
Total Capital	21,573	19,570	17,330	16,555	14,891	12,901	9,486	10,191	6,674	5,523
Capital Expenditures	573	498	513	573	407	452	425	380	386	440
Cash Flow	3,871	2,868	2,868	3,385	3,090	2,267	2,402	2,008	1,314	1,343
Current Ratio	1.9	2.4	2.1	3.1	2.4	2.2	1.3	2.5	0.9	2.8
% Long Term Debt of Capitalization	32.2	34.6	33.3	33.7	36.8	15.3	0.0	19.4	0.1	0.2
% Net Income of Revenue	19.6	15.7	16.5	22.8	22.6	17.9	21.6	20.9	15.3	18.8
% Return on Assets	12.0	10.0	10.7	14.3	14.0	11.7	14.8	13.8	11.0	16.5
% Return on Equity	22.6	18.7	19.8	27.5	25.7	18.5	23.1	22.3	16.5	20.9

Data as orig reptd.; bef. results of disc opers/spec. items. Per share data adj. for stk. divs.; EPS diluted. E-Estimated. NA-Not Available. NM-Not Meaningful. NR-Not Ranked. UR-Under Review.

Office: 710 Medtronic Parkway, Minneapolis, MN 55432-5604.
Telephone: 763-514-4000.
Website: http://www.medtronic.com
Chrmn & CEO: W.A. Hawkins, III

COO: H.J. Dallas
SVP, CFO & Chief Acctg Officer: G.L. Ellis
SVP & CSO: R. Kuntz
SVP, Secy & General Counsel: D.C. Findlay

Investor Contact: J. Warren (763-505-2696)
Board Members: R. H. Anderson, D. L. Calhoun, V. J. Dzau, W. A. Hawkins, III, S. A. Jackson, J. T. Lenehan, D. M. O'Leary, K. J. Powell, R. C. Pozen, J. Rosso, J. W. Schuler

Founded: 1957
Domicile: Minnesota
Employees: 43,000

MEMC Electronic Materials Inc

STANDARD &POOR'S

S&P Recommendation HOLD ★★★☆☆

Price	12-Mo. Target Price	Investment Style
$12.56 (as of Oct 22, 2010)	$13.00	Large-Cap Growth

GICS Sector Information Technology
Sub-Industry Semiconductor Equipment

Summary This company is a worldwide producer of silicon wafers used in semiconductors for microelectronic applications. It also provides silicon materials to the solar industry.

Key Stock Statistics (Source S&P, Vickers, company reports)

52-Wk Range	$16.99– 9.19	S&P Oper. EPS 2010E	0.41	Market Capitalization(B)	$2.856	Beta	1.42
Trailing 12-Month EPS	$-0.30	S&P Oper. EPS 2011E	0.84	Yield (%)	Nil	S&P 3-Yr. Proj. EPS CAGR(%)	NM
Trailing 12-Month P/E	NM	P/E on S&P Oper. EPS 2010E	30.6	Dividend Rate/Share	Nil	S&P Credit Rating	NA
$10K Invested 5 Yrs Ago	$6,382	Common Shares Outstg. (M)	227.4	Institutional Ownership (%)	89		

Price Performance

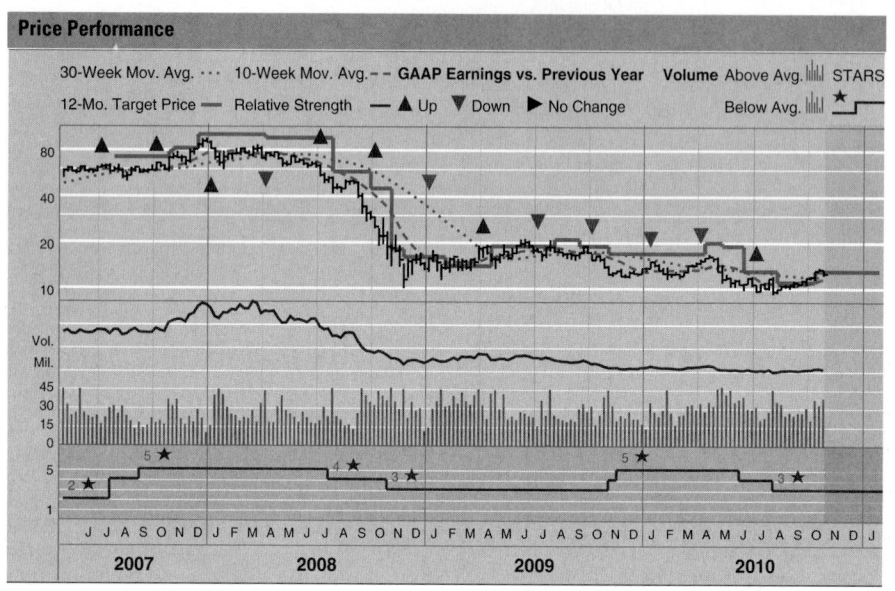

30-Week Mov. Avg. · · · 10-Week Mov. Avg. – – 30-Week Mov. Avg. ... 10-Week Mov. Avg. -- GAAP Earnings vs. Previous Year   Volume Above Avg. STARS
12-Mo. Target Price — Relative Strength — ▲ Up ▼ Down ► No Change   Below Avg. ★

Options: ASE, CBOE, P, Ph

Analysis prepared by **Angelo Zino** on October 05, 2010, when the stock traded at **$ 12.13**.

Highlights

► We see sales rising 9% in 2011 following our forecast for a 71% increase in 2010. We project that sales will be driven by WFR's semiconductor materials segment, where we anticipate gains of 71% in 2010 and 8% in 2011. Within WFR's solar materials segment, we expect sales to increase 23% in 2010 and 11% in 2011, as we see robust volume partly offset by further pricing declines. Finally, we forecast about $276 million in sales for the SunEdison business during 2010 and $300 million in 2011.

► We project an annual gross margin of 26% in 2011, versus our outlook for a 21% margin in 2010. We do not see significant solar margin expansion until 2011, when WFR should benefit from manufacturing internal wafers. However, solar wafer pricing visibility is expected to remain limited. We forecast semiconductor margins to widen, on rising volume and selling prices. We expect operating expenses, excluding restructuring costs, to comprise 16% of sales in 2010 and 2011.

► We forecast EPS of $0.41 in 2010 and $0.84 in 2011, compared to a $0.30 loss in 2009. WFR has signed long-term solar agreements with Suntech, Gintech, Conergy and Tainergy.

Investment Rationale/Risk

► We expect sales and margins to benefit from elevated semiconductor capacity utilization levels and healthy wafer starts. Given strong current demand for semiconductor wafers, we see prices increasing, which should aid margins. Although we continue to see solar pricing pressure, we expect the rate of decline to slow considerably. We look for polysilicon prices to drop to about $45/kg by the middle of 2011. We view positively WFR's solar vertical integration strategy and what we perceive as a strong balance sheet. We think WFR has been able to gain share and are encouraged by a rising SunEdison pipeline. We view WFR's financial position as superior to most peers.

► Risks to our recommendation and target price include faster expansion of industry capacity than we expect, changes in governmental policy related to alternative energy technology, a further slowdown in the global economy, and slower-than-expected growth.

► Our 12-month target price of $13 is based on a price/sales multiple of 1.3X our 2011 sales per share forecast of $9.49, above semiconductor and solar peers. However, this is below WFR's three and five year moving averages.

Qualitative Risk Assessment

LOW	MEDIUM	HIGH

Our risk assessment reflects WFR's exposure to the historical cyclicality of the semiconductor equipment industry and intense competition, partly offset by what we view as WFR's strong market position and size.

Quantitative Evaluations

S&P Quality Ranking B-

D	C	B-	B	B+	A-	A	A+

Relative Strength Rank STRONG

72

LOWEST = 1   HIGHEST = 99

Revenue/Earnings Data

Revenue (Million $)

	1Q	2Q	3Q	4Q	Year
2010	437.7	448.3	--	--	--
2009	214.0	282.9	310.0	356.7	1,164
2008	501.4	531.4	546.0	425.7	2,005
2007	440.4	472.7	472.8	535.9	1,922
2006	341.6	370.5	408.0	420.6	1,541
2005	250.9	272.3	280.7	303.4	1,107

Earnings Per Share ($)

	1Q	2Q	3Q	4Q	Year
2010	-0.04	0.06	E0.09	E0.30	E0.41
2009	0.01	0.01	-0.29	-0.03	-0.30
2008	-0.18	0.76	0.80	0.33	1.71
2007	0.58	0.70	0.65	1.62	3.56
2006	0.29	0.36	0.40	0.56	1.61
2005	0.25	0.18	0.45	0.22	1.10

Fiscal year ended Dec. 31. Next earnings report expected: NA. EPS Estimates based on S&P Operating Earnings; historical GAAP earnings are as reported.

Dividend Data

No cash dividends have been paid.

Please read the Required Disclosures and Analyst Certification on the last page of this report.

The **McGraw-Hill** Companies

MEMC Electronic Materials Inc

STANDARD &POOR'S

Business Summary October 05, 2010

CORPORATE OVERVIEW. MEMC Electronic Materials, Inc. (WFR) is a global leader in the manufacture of silicon wafers. The company designs, manufactures and provides wafers and intermediate products for use in the semiconductor, solar and related industries. WFR operates manufacturing facilities in every major semiconductor manufacturing region, including Europe, Japan, Malaysia, South Korea, Taiwan, and the U.S. Its customers include virtually all of the world's major semiconductor device manufacturers, such as the major memory, microprocessor, and applications specific integrated circuit (ASIC) manufacturers, as well as the world's largest foundries.

WFR's products include prime polish wafers, epitaxial wafers, test and monitor wafers, and silicon-on-insulator (SOI) wafers. WFR's prime wafer is a polished, highly refined, pure wafer with an ultraflat and ultraclean surface. The majority of these wafers are manufactured with a sophisticated chemical-mechanical polishing process that removes defects and leaves an extremely smooth surface. WFR's epitaxial, or epi, wafers consist of a thin silicon layer grown on the polished surface of the wafer. The epitaxial layer usually has different electrical properties from the underlying wafer, which provides customers with better isolation between circuit elements than a polished wafer, and the ability to tailor the wafer to the specific demands of the device.

WFR supplies test/monitor wafers to customers for their use in testing semiconductor manufacturing lines and processes. Although test/monitor wafers are essentially the same as prime wafers with respect to cleanliness, it has some less rigorous requirements, allowing WFR to produce some of the test/monitor wafers from the portion of the silicon ingot that does not meet customer specifications. A SOI wafer is a new type of starting material for the chip making process. SOI wafers have three layers: a thin surface layer of silicon where the transistors are formed, an underlying layer of insulating material, and a support bulk silicon wafer. Transistors built within the top silicon layer typically switch signals faster, run at lower voltages, and are much less vulnerable to signal noise from background cosmic ray particles.

Through WFR's SunEdison business, the company is a leading solar energy installer in North America, and also provides financing services under long-term power purchase arrangements and feed-in tariff arrangements. Customers pay only for the electricity output generated by the solar system installed, avoiding the significant capital outlays usually associated with solar projects.

Company Financials Fiscal Year Ended Dec. 31

Per Share Data ($)	2009	2008	2007	2006	2005	2004	2003	2002	2001	2000
Tangible Book Value	8.08	9.27	8.98	5.23	3.21	2.13	0.94	NM	NM	4.61
Cash Flow	0.25	2.15	3.90	1.91	1.35	1.22	0.68	0.09	-4.65	1.86
Earnings	-0.30	1.71	3.56	1.61	1.10	1.02	0.53	-0.17	-7.51	-0.62
S&P Core Earnings	-0.28	1.68	3.57	1.62	1.06	0.96	0.49	-0.33	-7.60	NA
Dividends	Nil	Nil	Nil	Nil	Nil	Nil	Nil	Nil	Nil	Nil
Payout Ratio	Nil	Nil	Nil	Nil	Nil	Nil	Nil	Nil	Nil	Nil
Prices:High	21.36	91.45	96.08	48.90	24.68	13.28	14.51	11.50	11.90	24.25
Prices:Low	11.32	10.00	39.51	22.60	10.70	7.33	7.00	2.25	1.05	6.25
P/E Ratio:High	NM	53	27	30	17	13	27	NM	NM	NM
P/E Ratio:Low	NM	6	11	14	7	7	13	NM	NM	NM

Income Statement Analysis (Million $)	2009	2008	2007	2006	2005	2004	2003	2002	2001	2000
Revenue	1,164	2,005	1,922	1,541	1,107	1,028	781	687	618	872
Operating Income	61.1	969	929	629	314	304	174	114	-9.69	161
Depreciation	124	103	79.3	70.3	57.2	44.1	31.0	34.2	169	173
Interest Expense	4.00	2.60	2.40	2.43	7.26	13.5	12.9	73.4	78.4	78.8
Pretax Income	-112	590	1,112	590	252	175	162	20.8	-259	-65.6
Effective Tax Rate	37.7%	33.4%	25.4%	36.4%	NM	NM	22.7%	NM	NM	NM
Net Income	-68.3	390	826	369	249	226	117	-5.07	-489	-43.4
S&P Core Earnings	-61.8	385	827	370	240	212	108	-41.9	-529	NA

Balance Sheet & Other Financial Data (Million $)	2009	2008	2007	2006	2005	2004	2003	2002	2001	2000
Cash	719	1,137	1,316	528	126	92.3	96.9	166	107	94.8
Current Assets	1,250	1,454	1,590	900	436	390	365	364	264	410
Total Assets	3,558	2,940	2,887	1,766	1,148	1,010	727	632	549	1,891
Current Liabilities	509	473	444	258	225	216	244	286	222	324
Long Term Debt	379	26.1	25.6	29.4	34.8	116	59.3	161	145	943
Common Equity	2,169	2,085	2,035	1,167	711	443	194	-24.7	-9.74	366
Total Capital	2,620	2,146	2,096	1,235	791	605	317	194	186	1,384
Capital Expenditures	253	303	276	148	163	150	85.2	22.0	7.00	57.8
Cash Flow	55.7	490	906	440	307	270	148	12.1	-324	130
Current Ratio	2.5	3.1	3.6	3.5	1.9	1.8	1.5	1.3	1.2	1.3
% Long Term Debt of Capitalization	14.5	1.2	1.2	2.4	4.4	19.2	18.7	82.9	77.8	68.1
% Net Income of Revenue	NM	19.5	43.0	24.0	22.5	22.0	14.9	NM	NM	NM
% Return on Assets	NM	13.4	35.5	25.3	22.9	26.0	17.2	NM	NM	NM
% Return on Equity	NM	19.0	51.6	39.3	43.2	71.1	138.1	NM	NM	NM

Data as orig reptd.; bef. results of disc opers/spec. items. Per share data adj. for stk. divs.; EPS diluted. E-Estimated. NA-Not Available. NM-Not Meaningful. NR-Not Ranked. UR-Under Review.

Office: 501 Pearl Drive, St. Peters, MO 63376.
Telephone: 636-474-5000.
Email: invest@memc.com
Website: http://www.memc.com

Chrmn: J.W. Marren
Pres & CEO: A.R. Chatila
SVP & CFO: T.C. Oliver
Chief Acctg Officer: D. McCarthy

Secy & General Counsel: B.D. Kohn
Investor Contact: B. Michalek (636-474-5443)
Board Members: P. Blackmore, R. J. Boehlke, A. R. Chatila, E. Hernandez, J. W. Marren, C. D. Marsh, M. McNamara, W. E. Stevens, M. Turner, Jr., J. B. Williams

Founded: 1984
Domicile: Delaware
Employees: 5,143

The **McGraw-Hill** Companies

Merck & Co Inc.

STANDARD &POOR'S

S&P Recommendation **BUY** ★★★★☆	Price $37.10 (as of Oct 22, 2010)	12-Mo. Target Price $42.00	Investment Style Large-Cap Blend

GICS Sector Health Care
Sub-Industry Pharmaceuticals

Summary This company, one of the world's largest drugmakers, acquired Schering-Plough in November 2009 for about $41 billion in cash and stock.

Key Stock Statistics (Source S&P, Vickers, company reports)

52-Wk Range	$41.56–30.29	S&P Oper. EPS 2010**E**	3.38	Market Capitalization(B)	$114.030	Beta	0.73
Trailing 12-Month EPS	$3.92	S&P Oper. EPS 2011**E**	3.80	Yield (%)	4.10	S&P 3-Yr. Proj. EPS CAGR(%)	8
Trailing 12-Month P/E	9.5	P/E on S&P Oper. EPS 2010**E**	11.0	Dividend Rate/Share	$1.52	S&P Credit Rating	AA-
$10K Invested 5 Yrs Ago	$17,504	Common Shares Outstg. (M)	3,073.6	Institutional Ownership (%)	74		

Price Performance

- 30-Week Mov. Avg. ···
- 10-Week Mov. Avg. - -
- GAAP Earnings vs. Previous Year
- Volume Above Avg.
- STARS
- 12-Mo. Target Price —
- Relative Strength —
- ▲ Up ▼ Down ► No Change
- Below Avg.

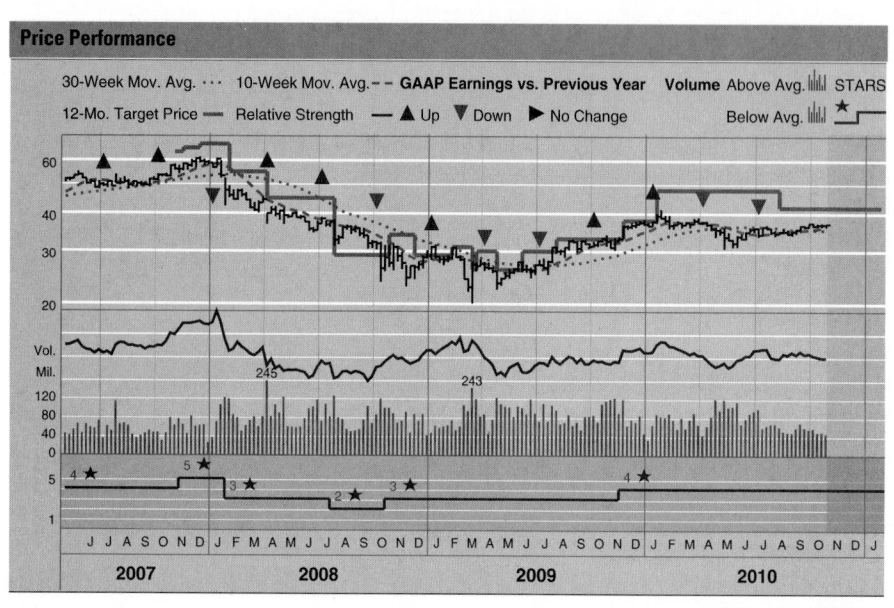

Analysis prepared by **Herman B. Saftlas** on August 04, 2010, when the stock traded at **$ 35.01**.

Options: ASE, CBOE, P, Ph

Highlights

▶ We project revenues of about $46 billion in 2010, up from 2009's $27.4 billion, with the increase reflecting the full-year inclusion of Schering-Plough (acquired in early November 2009). In our opinion, key established Merck drivers should be Singulair, Januvia/Janumet, and viral vaccines. Among Schering's products, we see gains in Nasonex and Remicade. We project relatively flat sales of Vytorin and Zetia cholesterol drugs, reflecting lingering effects of past disappointing clinical data. Sales of Cozaar/Hyzaar should decline sharply due to generic erosion, in our view.

▶ We forecast that gross margins will narrow slightly in 2010, partly reflecting the inclusion of Schering's relatively low-margin animal health and consumer products lines. The SG&A cost ratios will likely decline, helped by merger synergies and other cost-streamlining measures, but we believe that interest expense will rise sharply.

▶ After a projected adjusted tax rate of about 23%, versus 2009's 20%, we estimate 2010 non-GAAP EPS of $3.38, up from 2009's $3.25. We see further EPS progress to $3.80 in 2011.

Investment Rationale/Risk

▶ We view the November 2009 acquisition of drugmaker Schering-Plough for $41 billion in cash and stock as a major transforming event for Merck. In our opinion, this has significantly expanded and diversified Merck's revenue base ahead of impending patent expirations on Cozaar/Hyzaar and Singulair. The deal should also provide annual cost synergies of close to $3.5 billion, which should be fully realized by the end of 2012. The acquisition also beefed up Merck's R&D pipeline, which consists of over 60 projects in Phase II, Phase III and regulatory review. Key opportunities, in our opinion, include Tredaptive for atherosclerosis, and Simponi for autoimmune diseases.

▶ Risks to our opinion and target price include failure to successfully integrate Schering-Plough, uncertainties with respect to Remicade/Simponi litigation with Johnson & Johnson, and possible pipeline setbacks.

▶ Our 12-month target price of $42 applies a modest premium-to-peers P/E of 11.1X our $3.80 operating EPS estimate for 2011. The dividend, which we think may be raised over the next 12 months, recently yielded 4.3%.

Qualitative Risk Assessment

LOW	MEDIUM	HIGH

Our risk assessment reflects challenges to branded patents, new drug development, and regulatory risks. In addition, MRK's Vytorin/Zetia franchise has been affected by disappointing clinical trial results. However, we see significant synergies accruing from the recent acquisition of Schering-Plough. We also think MRK has one of the stronger R&D pipelines in the sector.

Quantitative Evaluations

S&P Quality Ranking B+

D	C	B-	B	B+	A-	A	A+

Relative Strength Rank MODERATE

48

LOWEST = 1   HIGHEST = 99

Revenue/Earnings Data

Revenue (Million $)

	1Q	2Q	3Q	4Q	Year
2010	11,422	11,346	--	--	--
2009	5,385	5,900	6,050	10,094	27,428
2008	5,822	6,052	5,944	6,032	23,850
2007	5,769	6,111	6,074	6,243	24,198
2006	5,410	5,772	5,410	6,044	22,636
2005	5,362	5,468	5,416	5,766	22,012

Earnings Per Share ($)

2010	0.10	0.24	E0.83	E0.86	E3.38
2009	0.67	0.74	1.61	2.35	5.65
2008	1.52	0.82	0.51	0.78	3.64
2007	0.78	0.77	0.70	-0.74	1.49
2006	0.69	0.69	0.43	0.22	2.03
2005	0.62	0.33	0.65	0.51	2.10

Fiscal year ended Dec. 31. Next earnings report expected: Late October. EPS Estimates based on S&P Operating Earnings; historical GAAP earnings are as reported.

Dividend Data (Dates: mm/dd Payment Date: mm/dd/yy)

Amount ($)	Date Decl.	Ex-Div. Date	Stk. of Record	Payment Date
0.380	11/24	12/11	12/15	01/08/10
0.380	02/23	03/11	03/15	04/07/10
0.380	05/26	06/11	06/15	07/08/10
0.380	07/27	09/13	09/15	10/07/10

Dividends have been paid since 1935. Source: Company reports.

Please read the Required Disclosures and Analyst Certification on the last page of this report.

The **McGraw·Hill** Companies

Merck & Co Inc.

STANDARD &POOR'S

Business Summary August 04, 2010

CORPORATE OVERVIEW. Merck & Co. is a leading global drugmaker, producing a wide range of prescription drugs in many therapeutic classes in the U.S. and abroad. Foreign operations accounted for 47% of total pharmaceutical and vaccine sales in 2009. In early November 2009, MRK acquired rival drugmaker Schering-Plough for about $41 billion in cash and stock. Schering earned $2.5 billion from operations on sales of $13.5 billion in the first three quarters of 2009.

MRK's largest-selling products include Singulair (sales of $4.7 billion in 2009), a treatment for asthma and seasonal allergic rhinitis; Cozaar/Hyzaar ($3.6 billion), treatments for high blood pressure and congestive heart failure; Fosamax ($1.1 billion), a drug for osteoporosis (a bone-thinning disease that affects postmenopausal women); and Januvia/Janumet ($2.5 billion), treatments for type 2 diabetes.

Merck is also a leading maker of vaccines, which accounted for 13% of total sales in 2009. Key vaccines include ProQuad ($1.4 billion) for measles, mumps,

rubella and chicken pox; Gardasil ($1.1 billion) for human papillomavirus, the main cause of cervical cancer; and, RotaTeq for rotavirus.

With the purchase of Schering-Plough, Merck gained total rights to Zetia -- a cholesterol therapy that works by blocking cholesterol absorption in the intestines -- as well as Vytorin, a combination pill containing both Zocor and Zetia. In 2009, Vytorin had sales of $1.7 billion ($2.4 billion in 2008), and Zetia had sales of $1.8 billion ($2.3 billion in 2008). OTC medications are offered through a venture with Johnson & Johnson. Through a venture with AstraZeneca, Merck books sales of Nexium and other drugs. In March 2010, MRK and Sanofi-Aventis announced plans to combine their animal health businesses into a new joint venture, with annual sales projected at over $5 billion.

Company Financials Fiscal Year Ended Dec. 31

Per Share Data ($)	2009	2008	2007	2006	2005	2004	2003	2002	2001	2000
Tangible Book Value	1.97	7.97	11.76	7.00	7.48	7.03	6.13	4.88	3.77	3.23
Cash Flow	6.65	4.30	2.19	3.06	2.88	3.29	3.51	3.79	3.77	3.44
Earnings	5.65	3.64	1.49	2.03	2.10	2.61	2.92	3.14	3.14	2.90
S&P Core Earnings	2.61	2.78	2.85	2.28	2.09	2.56	2.71	2.81	2.87	NA
Dividends	1.52	1.52	1.52	1.52	1.52	1.49	1.45	1.41	1.37	1.26
Payout Ratio	27%	42%	102%	75%	72%	57%	50%	45%	44%	43%
Prices:High	38.42	61.18	61.62	46.37	35.36	49.33	63.50	64.50	95.25	96.69
Prices:Low	20.05	22.82	42.35	31.81	25.50	25.60	40.57	38.50	56.80	52.00
P/E Ratio:High	7	17	41	23	17	19	22	21	30	33
P/E Ratio:Low	4	6	28	16	12	10	14	12	18	18

Income Statement Analysis (Million $)										
Revenue	27,428	23,850	24,198	22,636	22,012	22,939	22,486	51,790	47,716	40,363
Operating Income	7,081	7,854	7,779	5,955	7,567	8,074	9,912	11,361	11,192	10,686
Depreciation	2,227	1,415	1,528	2,268	1,708	1,451	1,314	1,488	1,464	1,277
Interest Expense	458	251	384	375	386	294	351	391	465	484
Pretax Income	15,292	9,808	3,492	6,342	7,486	8,129	9,220	10,428	10,693	10,133
Effective Tax Rate	14.8%	20.4%	2.73%	28.2%	36.5%	26.6%	26.7%	29.3%	29.2%	29.6%
Net Income	12,901	7,808	3,275	4,434	4,631	5,813	6,590	7,150	7,282	6,822
S&P Core Earnings	5,936	5,958	6,255	4,973	4,582	5,699	6,089	6,395	6,649	NA

Balance Sheet & Other Financial Data (Million $)										
Cash	9,605	5,486	8,231	5,915	9,585	2,879	1,201	2,243	2,144	2,537
Current Assets	28,429	19,305	15,045	15,230	21,049	13,475	11,527	14,834	12,962	13,353
Total Assets	112,090	47,196	48,351	44,570	44,846	42,573	40,588	47,561	44,007	39,910
Current Liabilities	15,751	14,319	12,258	12,723	13,304	11,744	9,570	12,375	11,544	9,710
Long Term Debt	16,075	3,943	3,916	5,551	5,126	4,692	5,096	4,879	4,799	3,601
Common Equity	59,058	18,758	18,185	17,560	17,917	17,288	15,576	18,200	16,050	14,832
Total Capital	78,316	25,118	24,903	25,517	25,449	24,387	24,588	28,008	25,686	23,454
Capital Expenditures	1,461	1,298	1,011	980	1,403	1,726	1,916	2,370	2,725	2,728
Cash Flow	15,127	9,223	4,803	6,702	6,339	7,264	7,904	8,638	8,746	8,099
Current Ratio	1.8	1.4	1.2	1.2	1.6	1.1	1.2	1.2	1.1	1.4
% Long Term Debt of Capitalization	Nil	15.5	15.7	21.8	20.1	19.2	20.7	17.4	18.7	15.4
% Net Income of Revenue	47.0	32.7	13.5	19.6	21.0	25.3	29.3	13.8	15.3	16.9
% Return on Assets	NA	16.3	7.1	9.9	10.6	14.0	15.0	15.6	17.3	18.1
% Return on Equity	NA	42.3	18.3	25.0	26.3	35.4	39.0	41.7	47.2	48.6

Data as orig reptd.; bef. results of disc opers/spec. items. Per share data adj. for stk. divs.; EPS diluted. E-Estimated. NA-Not Available. NM-Not Meaningful. NR-Not Ranked. UR-Under Review.

Office: One Merck Drive, PO Box 100, Whitehouse Station, NJ 08889-0100.
Telephone: 908-423-1000.
Website: http://www.merck.com
Chrmn & CEO: R.T. Clark

Pres: K.C. Frazier
EVP & CFO: P.N. Kellogg
EVP & General Counsel: B.N. Kuhlik
EVP & CIO: J.C. Scalet

Investor Contact: G. Bell (908-423-5185)
Board Members: L. A. Brun, T. R. Cech, R. T. Clark, T. H. Glocer, S. F. Goldstone, W. B. Harrison, Jr., H. R. Jacobson, W. N. Kelley, C. R. Kidder, R. B. Lazarus, C. E. Represas, P. F. Russo, T. Shenk, A. M. Tatlock, C. B. Thompson, W. P. Weeks, P. C. Wendell

Founded: 1891
Domicile: New Jersey
Employees: 100,000

The **McGraw-Hill** Companies

Meredith Corp

STANDARD &POOR'S

S&P Recommendation	BUY ★★★★☆	Price $35.00 (as of Oct 22, 2010)	12-Mo. Target Price $37.00	Investment Style Large-Cap Growth

GICS Sector Consumer Discretionary
Sub-Industry Publishing

Summary This company derives its earnings mainly from magazine publishing (primarily Better Homes and Gardens and Ladies' Home Journal) and ownership of 12 TV stations.

Key Stock Statistics (Source S&P, Vickers, company reports)

52-Wk Range	$38.08– 25.83	S&P Oper. EPS 2011**E**	2.61	Market Capitalization(B)	$1.272	Beta		1.65
Trailing 12-Month EPS	$2.28	S&P Oper. EPS 2012**E**	2.80	Yield (%)	2.63	S&P 3-Yr. Proj. EPS CAGR(%)		12
Trailing 12-Month P/E	15.4	P/E on S&P Oper. EPS 2011**E**	13.4	Dividend Rate/Share	$0.92	S&P Credit Rating		NA
$10K Invested 5 Yrs Ago	$8,130	Common Shares Outstg. (M)	45.4	Institutional Ownership (%)	NM			

Price Performance

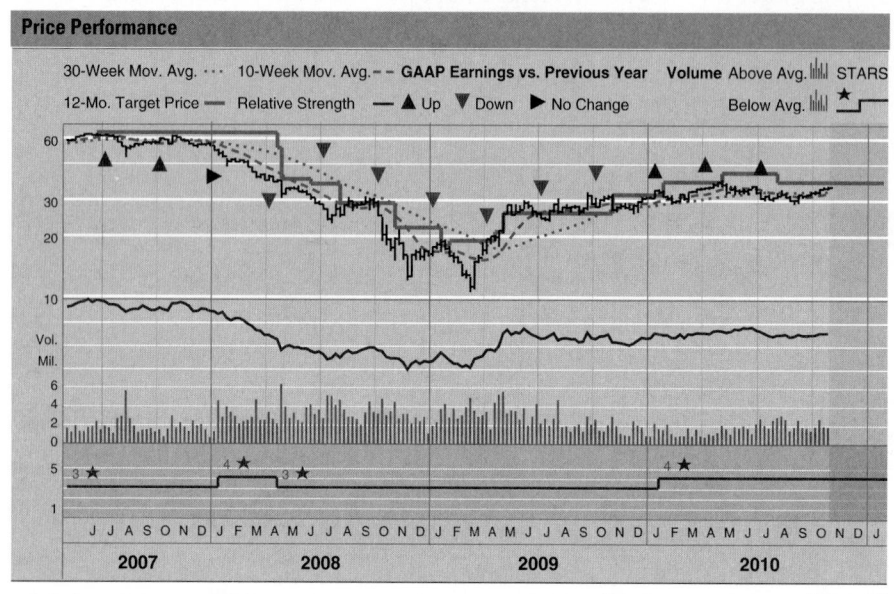

30-Week Mov. Avg. · · · 10-Week Mov. Avg. - - GAAP Earnings vs. Previous Year Volume Above Avg. STARS
12-Mo. Target Price — Relative Strength ▲ Up ▼ Down ▶ No Change Below Avg. ★

Options: ASE

Analysis prepared by **Joseph Agnese** on August 09, 2010, when the stock traded at **$ 32.66**.

Highlights

➤ Advertising revenues increased 7.5% in the second half of FY 10 (Jun.), following declines in the first half, due to an improved economic environment and easier comparisons. Despite the closing of magazines, circulation revenues increased more than 1.5% in the fourth quarter, reflecting increased newsstand prices. We project total revenues will rise 4.0%, to $1.443 billion, in FY 11, from $1.388 billion in FY 10, reflecting low single digit growth in circulation, $25 to $30 million in net political advertising revenues, improvement in non-political advertising demand, and growth in retransmission fees and in revenues from MDP's highly profitable brand licensing, video production and integrated marketing businesses.

➤ We see operating margin expansion in FY 11 due to improved sales leverage following stabilization of publishing and broadcasting advertising revenues and continued expense reductions. However, we believe margin benefits will be partially offset by less favorable raw material prices and increased pension expense.

➤ We see operating EPS rising 11%, to $2.62, in FY 11, from operating EPS of $2.25 in FY 10 (excluding one-time tax benefits).

Investment Rationale/Risk

➤ We expect MDP to continue to supplement organic growth with selective acquisitions. We also believe recent licensing deals demonstrate the company's ability to leverage its strong brands into incremental and profitable revenue streams. In addition, we see incremental revenue growth opportunities for MDP in its non-core advertising categories. However, our optimism is tempered by a difficult economic environment with poor visibility.

➤ Risks to our opinion and target price include a slower-than-expected increase in advertising spending. We also are concerned about MDP's corporate governance, as we do not believe policies such as a dual class voting structure are in the best interests of common shareholders.

➤ We believe MDP, with a more conservative debt/EBITDA ratio than peers in an unstable economic environment, should trade at a premium to the peer average enterprise value (EV)/ EBITDA multiple of 6.6X. Applying a 7.6X ratio, representing a 15% premium to peers EV/ EBITDA ratio, to our forward 12-month EBITDA estimate of $253 million yields our 12-month target price of $37.

Please read the Required Disclosures and Analyst Certification on the last page of this report.

Redistribution or reproduction is prohibited without written permission. Copyright ©2010 The McGraw-Hill Companies, Inc.

The **McGraw-Hill** Companies

Qualitative Risk Assessment

LOW	MEDIUM	HIGH

Our risk assessment reflects a highly competitive environment for advertising among publishers and other media, offset by incremental growth opportunities we see in brand licensing and integrated marketing.

Quantitative Evaluations

S&P Quality Ranking B+

D	C	B-	B	B+	A-	A	A+

Relative Strength Rank MODERATE

69

LOWEST = 1 HIGHEST = 99

Revenue/Earnings Data

Revenue (Million $)

	1Q	2Q	3Q	4Q	Year
2010	332.4	336.9	353.3	365.1	1,388
2009	370.1	361.3	337.6	345.9	1,409
2008	404.1	396.3	401.0	385.2	1,587
2007	386.4	399.4	337.6	428.5	1,616
2006	390.3	386.0	394.9	426.4	1,598
2005	288.9	294.6	305.5	332.4	1,221

Earnings Per Share ($)

2010	0.40	0.42	0.73	0.73	2.28
2009	0.42	0.39	0.55	-3.64	-2.28
2008	0.68	0.73	0.98	0.41	2.82
2007	0.62	0.73	1.08	1.01	3.44
2006	0.52	0.58	0.97	0.97	2.86
2005	0.46	0.52	0.69	0.83	2.50

Fiscal year ended Jun. 30. Next earnings report expected: Late October. EPS Estimates based on S&P Operating Earnings; historical GAAP earnings are as reported.

Dividend Data (Dates: mm/dd Payment Date: mm/dd/yy)

Amount ($)	Date Decl.	Ex-Div. Date	Stk. of Record	Payment Date
0.225	11/05	11/25	11/30	12/15/09
0.230	02/01	02/24	02/26	03/15/10
0.230	05/13	05/26	05/28	06/15/10
0.230	08/12	08/27	08/31	09/15/10

Dividends have been paid since 1930. Source: Company reports.

Meredith Corp

STANDARD
&POOR'S

Business Summary August 09, 2010

CORPORATE OVERVIEW. Meredith Corp. is a diversified media and marketing company with operations in publishing (80% of FY 10 (Jun.) revenues) and broadcasting (20%). Advertising accounted for about 56% of total revenues, followed by magazine circulation (20%) and other (23%).

The national media group focuses on the home and family market. Meredith has more than 25 subscription-based magazines, including Better Homes and Gardens, Family Circle, Ladies' Home Journal and approximately 135 special interest publications. The segment also includes book publishing, integrated marketing, a large consumer database, 30 websites, brand licensing and other related activities. Books are published under the Better Homes and Gardens trademark and under licensed trademarks such as The Home Depot books. Meredith Integrated Marketing offers integrated promotional, database management, relationship and direct marketing capabilities for corporate customers. In April 2006, Meredith acquired O'Grady Meyers (OGM), an interactive marketing services agency that specializes in online customer relationship marketing. Overall FY 10 publishing segment revenues were derived from

advertising (48%), circulation (26%) and other (27%).

The local media group consists of 12 network-affiliated TV stations, one AM radio station, related interactive media operations, and video related operations. Broadcasting affiliations consist of CBS (six stations), FOX (three), MyNetwork TV (two), and NBC (one). The segment also includes 28 websites and video related operations. Local and national advertising contributed approximately 94% of segment revenues in FY 09, and the company reports that 30% to 40% of a market's television ad revenues are generated by local news on major network-affiliated stations. The other 6% of revenues comes primarily from broadcast retransmission fees. The company negotiated a 20% increase in retransmission fees for FY 10 when most of its retransmission agreements expired at the end of FY 09.

Company Financials Fiscal Year Ended Jun. 30

Per Share Data ($)	2010	2009	2008	2007	2006	2005	2004	2003	2002	2001
Tangible Book Value	NM	NM	NM	NM	NM	NM	NM	NM	NM	NM
Cash Flow	3.18	-1.33	3.85	4.94	3.76	3.19	2.82	2.40	3.64	2.39
Earnings	2.28	-2.28	2.82	3.44	2.86	2.50	2.14	1.78	1.79	1.39
S&P Core Earnings	2.28	1.85	2.69	3.48	2.84	2.49	2.01	1.64	0.92	0.92
Dividends	0.91	0.88	0.80	0.69	0.60	0.52	0.43	0.37	0.35	0.33
Payout Ratio	40%	NM	28%	20%	20%	21%	20%	22%	20%	24%
Prices:High	38.08	33.17	55.08	63.41	57.29	54.33	55.94	50.32	47.75	38.97
Prices:Low	28.92	10.60	12.06	48.15	45.04	44.51	48.24	47.09	33.42	26.50
P/E Ratio:High	17	NM	20	18	20	22	26	28	27	28
P/E Ratio:Low	13	NM	4	14	16	18	23	26	19	19

Income Statement Analysis (Million $)

	2010	2009	2008	2007	2006	2005	2004	2003	2002	2001
Revenue	1,388	1,409	1,587	1,616	1,598	1,221	1,162	1,080	988	1,053
Operating Income	230	202	317	365	312	263	238	209	212	204
Depreciation	40.9	42.6	49.2	73.8	45.7	35.3	35.2	31.4	93.8	51.6
Interest Expense	18.6	20.8	22.4	27.2	30.2	Nil	22.7	27.8	33.2	32.9
Pretax Income	164	-155	220	263	237	209	181	149	149	116
Effective Tax Rate	NA	NM	39.1%	35.7%	39.0%	38.7%	38.7%	38.7%	38.7%	38.7%
Net Income	104	-103	134	169	145	128	111	91.1	91.4	71.3
S&P Core Earnings	104	83.4	128	171	144	127	104	83.5	46.8	47.6

Balance Sheet & Other Financial Data (Million $)

	2010	2009	2008	2007	2006	2005	2004	2003	2002	2001
Cash	48.6	27.9	37.6	39.2	30.7	29.8	58.7	22.3	28.2	36.3
Current Assets	381	340	403	453	432	304	314	268	272	291
Total Assets	1,727	1,669	2,060	2,090	2,041	1,491	1,466	1,437	1,460	1,438
Current Liabilities	438	349	443	487	464	439	371	297	307	371
Long Term Debt	250	380	410	375	515	125	225	375	385	400
Common Equity	688	609	788	833	698	652	589	501	508	448
Total Capital	988	1,053	1,337	1,375	1,338	871	912	948	985	907
Capital Expenditures	24.7	23.5	29.6	42.6	29.2	23.8	24.5	26.6	23.4	56.0
Cash Flow	145	-59.9	183	243	190	163	146	123	185	123
Current Ratio	0.9	1.0	0.9	0.9	0.9	0.7	0.8	0.9	0.9	0.8
% Long Term Debt of Capitalization	25.3	36.1	30.7	27.3	38.5	14.4	24.7	39.6	39.1	44.1
% Net Income of Revenue	7.5	NM	8.5	10.4	9.1	10.5	9.5	8.4	9.3	6.8
% Return on Assets	6.1	NM	6.5	8.2	8.2	8.7	7.6	6.3	6.3	5.0
% Return on Equity	16.0	NM	16.6	22.1	21.5	20.3	20.4	18.1	19.1	16.4

Data as orig reptd.; bef. results of disc opers/spec. items. Per share data adj. for stk. divs.; EPS diluted. E-Estimated. NA-Not Available. NM-Not Meaningful. NR-Not Ranked. UR-Under Review.

Office: 1716 Locust Street, Des Moines, IA 50309-3023.
Telephone: 515-284-3000.
Website: http://www.meredith.com
Chrmn, Pres & CEO: S.M. Lacy

Vice Chrmn: D.M. Frazier
CFO & Chief Acctg Officer: J.H. Ceryanec
Secy & General Counsel: J.S. Zieser
Investor Contact: S.V. Radia (515-284-3357)

Board Members: M. S. Coleman, J. R. Craigie, A. H. Drewes, D. M. Frazier, F. B. Henry, J. W. Johnson, S. M. Lacy, P. A. Marineau, E. E. Tallett

Founded: 1902
Domicile: Iowa
Employees: 3,225

Metlife Inc.

STANDARD &POOR'S

S&P Recommendation BUY ★★★★☆

Price	12-Mo. Target Price	Investment Style
$40.34 (as of Oct 22, 2010)	$51.00	Large-Cap Blend

GICS Sector Financials
Sub-Industry Life & Health Insurance

Summary This company is a leading publicly traded diversified U.S. life insurance and financial services concern.

Key Stock Statistics (Source S&P, Vickers, company reports)

52-Wk Range	$47.75– 32.16	S&P Oper. EPS 2010**E**	4.53	Market Capitalization(B)	$33.097	Beta	1.88
Trailing 12-Month EPS	$2.39	S&P Oper. EPS 2011**E**	5.50	Yield (%)	1.83	S&P 3-Yr. Proj. EPS CAGR(%)	25
Trailing 12-Month P/E	16.9	P/E on S&P Oper. EPS 2010**E**	8.9	Dividend Rate/Share	$0.74	S&P Credit Rating	A-
$10K Invested 5 Yrs Ago	$9,089	Common Shares Outstg. (M)	820.4	Institutional Ownership (%)	62		

Price Performance

30-Week Mov. Avg. · · ·   10-Week Mov. Avg. – –   **GAAP Earnings vs. Previous Year**   **Volume** Above Avg. ▮▮▮ STARS
12-Mo. Target Price —   Relative Strength —   ▲ Up   ▼ Down   ▶ No Change   Below Avg. ▮▮▮ ★

Options: ASE, CBOE, P

Analysis prepared by **Bret Howlett** on August 04, 2010, when the stock traded at **$ 41.68**.

Highlights

▸ We see operating earnings increasing approximately 50% in the U.S. business in 2010 on favorable underwriting, higher investment income, lower expenses and increased fee income. We expect the segment's results to be driven by strong dental, group life, term life and variable annuities sales. We forecast robust earnings growth in Retirement due to strong premium growth, solid flows across most products and increased account values. We project double-digit earnings growth in Corporate Benefits as MET gains market share in structured settlements and pension closeouts. We believe variable income should boost revenue growth substantially in 2010 as income from hedge funds and real estate JVs picks up.

▸ We forecast that International operating earnings will increase roughly 10% on growth in Latin America. We anticipate Metlife Bank's earnings being down sharply on lower mortgage refinancing activity. In Auto & Home, we belive earnings will decline 12% to 14% on a worsening of the combined ratio.

▸ We forecast operating EPS of $4.53 in 2010 and $5.50 in 2011. Our estimates exclude realized investment gains or losses.

Investment Rationale/Risk

▸ We believe MET is well positioned to capture market share given its strong capital position, scale, diverse businesses, distribution capabilities, and global reach. We believe the acquisition of Alico will significantly boost MET's International earnings and increase the company's exposure to faster growing and more profitable markets in 2011. We expect credit impairment to trend down, and we believe MET holds enough excess capital to absorb future investment losses. We believe MET is poised to generate 12% to 13% ROE in 2011 from higher new business returns, investment income growth, and a higher earnings contribution from its International segment. We expect earnings growth to be fueled by expense reduction initiatives, strong net flows in many businesses, and better investment spreads.

▸ Risks to our recommendation and target price include credit and interest rate risk; a decline in the equity markets; the potential need for additional capital; and exposure to asbestos-related liability claims.

▸ Our 12-month target price of $51 is about 1.1X our 2010 book value per share (Ex- FAS 115) projection, below MET's historical multiples.

Qualitative Risk Assessment

LOW	MEDIUM	HIGH

Our risk assessment reflects our view of the company's consistent earnings growth, strong brand identity, diversified product offerings, and geographic footprint, offset by the potential for further losses in its investment portfolio and vulnerability to declines in the equity markets.

Quantitative Evaluations

S&P Quality Ranking   B+

D	C	B-	B	B+	A-	A	A+

Relative Strength Rank   MODERATE

43

LOWEST = 1   HIGHEST = 99

Revenue/Earnings Data

Revenue (Million $)

	1Q	2Q	3Q	4Q	Year
2010	13,190	14,246	--	--	--
2009	10,216	8,266	10,238	12,341	41,058
2008	13,027	13,715	13,378	13,962	50,989
2007	12,908	13,216	13,053	13,830	53,007
2006	11,565	11,387	12,551	12,893	48,396
2005	10,257	10,961	12,012	11,546	44,776

Earnings Per Share ($)

2010	0.98	1.83	E1.14	E1.15	E4.53
2009	-0.75	-1.74	-0.79	0.35	-2.94
2008	0.84	1.26	1.42	1.15	4.55
2007	1.29	1.47	1.25	1.44	5.44
2006	0.92	0.74	1.19	1.00	3.85
2005	1.08	1.36	0.96	0.77	4.16

Fiscal year ended Dec. 31. Next earnings report expected: Late October. EPS Estimates based on S&P Operating Earnings; historical GAAP earnings are as reported.

Dividend Data (Dates: mm/dd Payment Date: mm/dd/yy)

Amount ($)	Date Decl.	Ex-Div. Date	Stk. of Record	Payment Date
0.740	10/29	11/05	11/09	12/14/09

Dividends have been paid since 2000. Source: Company reports.

Please read the Required Disclosures and Analyst Certification on the last page of this report.

The **McGraw·Hill** Companies

Metlife Inc.

STANDARD &POOR'S

Business Summary August 04, 2010

CORPORATE OVERVIEW. MetLife (MET) is one of the largest insurance and financial services companies in the U.S. The company benefits from a strong brand, a solid financial position, and a large distribution network, in our view. At the end of 2009, the MetLife distribution channel had 5,762 agents under contract in 82 agencies. According to the American Council of Life Insurers, MetLife was the largest life insurer in 2008, based on total assets. The company ranked fourth in total net life insurance premiums. As of February 2007, MetLife had access to over 71% of the world's life insurance markets, up from 36% in 2004. Formerly a mutual insurance company, MetLife demutualized and issued publicly traded stock in April 2000.

In the fourth quarter of 2009, MET realigned its U.S. Business segment. MET's U.S. Business now consists of Insurance Products, Retirement Products, Corporate Benefit Funding, and Auto & Home. Other segments include International Business, and Banking, Corporate & Other. MET's U.S. Business accounted for 83.5% of operating earnings in 2009, and the International Business segment acounted for 16.5% Corporate and other activities, including MetLife Bank operations, reported a loss of $450 million for the year.

CORPORATE STRATEGY. MET's international strategy is to establish meaningful positions in growing markets that can provide attractive margins. We see

MET focusing on building relationships and investing in growth and upgrading systems. We expect investments in Japan, Brazil, China, Hong Kong and India to add to EPS in 2010 and 2011.

IMPACT OF MAJOR DEVELOPMENTS. In February 2010, MET said it was in talks with American International Group (AIG 36, Hold) to purchase its subsidiary American Life Insurance Company (ALICO). On March 8, 2010, MET said it had reached an agreement with AIG to purchase ALICO for roughly $15.5 billion. MET will pay AIG $6.8 billion in cash and issue $8.7 billion in stock for the unit. The transaction is expected to close at the end of 2010. In 2009, ALICO's after-tax operating income was $1.5 billion, and we believe the unit's earnings would increase roughly 25% under the MET umbrella. We believe ALICO would add $0.45-$0.50 to MET's 2011 EPS. We view the deal positively for MET, as it would increase the company's footprint in faster growing insurance markets, especially in Japan. The planned acquisition would triple the size of MET's International segment.

Company Financials Fiscal Year Ended Dec. 31

Per Share Data ($)	2009	2008	2007	2006	2005	2004	2003	2002	2001	2000
Tangible Book Value	52.73	19.54	34.79	35.64	32.06	31.16	27.94	24.83	22.43	21.53
Operating Earnings	NA	NA	NA	NA	NA	NA	NA	NA	NA	NA
Earnings	-2.94	4.55	5.44	3.85	4.16	3.59	2.57	1.58	0.62	1.49
S&P Core Earnings	3.44	2.42	5.91	5.01	4.12	3.41	2.87	2.06	0.91	NA
Dividends	0.74	0.74	0.74	0.59	0.52	0.46	0.23	0.21	0.20	0.20
Payout Ratio	NM	16%	14%	15%	13%	13%	9%	13%	32%	13%
Prices:High	41.45	65.50	71.23	60.00	52.57	41.27	34.14	34.85	36.63	36.50
Prices:Low	11.37	15.72	58.48	48.00	37.29	32.30	23.51	20.60	24.70	14.25
P/E Ratio:High	NM	14	13	16	13	11	13	22	59	24
P/E Ratio:Low	NM	3	11	12	9	9	9	13	40	10

Income Statement Analysis (Million $)										
Life Insurance in Force	4,540,576	4,382,280	6,135,797	5,707,215	5,125,427	4,346,898	3,875,110	2,679,870	2,419,341	2,572,261
Premium Income:Life	17,001	16,410	19,254	18,368	17,399	15,341	14,065	13,070	11,611	11,224
Premium Income:A & H	6,546	6,523	5,666	4,991	4,489	4,016	3,537	3,052	2,744	2,377
Net Investment Income	14,838	NA	19,006	17,192	14,910	12,418	11,636	11,329	11,923	11,768
Total Revenue	41,058	50,989	53,007	49,746	44,869	39,014	36,147	33,147	31,928	31,947
Pretax Income	-4,333	5,090	6,279	4,221	4,399	3,779	2,630	1,671	739	1,416
Net Operating Income	NA	NA	NA	NA	NA	NA	NA	NA	NA	NA
Net Income	-2,286	3,510	4,280	3,105	3,139	2,708	1,943	1,155	473	953
S&P Core Earnings	2,813	1,811	4,495	3,867	3,123	2,574	2,144	1,512	697	NA

Balance Sheet & Other Financial Data (Million $)										
Cash & Equivalent	13,285	27,268	13,998	10,454	7,054	6,389	5,919	4,411	9,535	5,484
Premiums Due	16,752	16,973	14,607	14,490	12,186	6,696	7,047	7,669	6,437	8,343
Investment Assets:Bonds	227,642	188,251	242,242	243,428	230,050	176,763	167,752	140,553	115,398	112,979
Investment Assets:Stocks	3,084	3,197	6,829	5,890	4,163	2,188	1,598	1,348	3,063	2,193
Investment Assets:Loans	60,970	61,166	57,449	52,467	47,170	41,305	34,998	33,666	31,893	30,109
Investment Assets:Total	327,567	298,311	334,734	324,689	301,709	234,985	218,099	188,335	162,222	156,527
Deferred Policy Costs	19,256	20,144	21,521	20,851	19,641	14,336	12,943	11,727	11,167	10,618
Total Assets	539,314	501,678	558,562	527,715	481,645	356,808	326,841	277,385	256,898	255,018
Debt	21,708	18,617	19,834	13,759	12,022	5,944	5,703	5,690	4,884	3,516
Common Equity	33,120	23,733	35,178	33,797	29,100	22,824	21,149	17,385	16,062	16,389
% Return on Revenue	NM	6.9	8.1	6.2	7.0	6.9	5.4	3.5	1.5	3.0
% Return on Assets	NM	0.7	0.8	0.6	0.7	0.8	0.6	0.4	0.2	0.4
% Return on Equity	NM	11.9	12.0	9.4	11.8	12.3	10.1	6.9	2.9	6.3
% Investment Yield	4.7	5.3	5.8	5.5	5.6	6.8	5.7	6.5	7.5	8.0

Data as orig reptd.; bef. results of disc opers/spec. items. Per share data adj. for stk. divs.; EPS diluted. E-Estimated. NA-Not Available. NM-Not Meaningful. NR-Not Ranked. UR-Under Review.

Office: 200 Park Ave, New York, NY 10166-0188.
Telephone: 212-578-2211.
Website: http://www.metlife.com
Chrmn, Pres & CEO: C.R. Henrikson

COO & CTO: M.R. Morris
EVP & CFO: W.J. Wheeler
EVP & Chief Admin Officer: R.A. Fattori
EVP & Chief Acctg Officer: P.M. Carlson

Board Members: S. M. Burwell, E. Castro-Wright, C. W. Grise, C. R. Henrikson, R. G. Hubbard, J. M. Keane, A. F. Kelly, Jr., J. M. Kilts, C. R. Kinney, H. B. Price, D. Satcher, K. J. Sicchitano, L. C. Wang

Founded: 1999
Domicile: Delaware
Employees: 54,000

MetroPCS Communications Inc

STANDARD &POOR'S

S&P Recommendation	STRONG BUY ★★★★★	Price $10.61 (as of Oct 22, 2010)	12-Mo. Target Price $15.00	Investment Style Large-Cap Blend

GICS Sector Telecommunication Services
Sub-Industry Wireless Telecommunication Services

Summary This company provides wireless services primarily to the youth and minority markets under the brand name MetroPCS.

Key Stock Statistics (Source S&P, Vickers, company reports)

52-Wk Range	$11.24–5.52	S&P Oper. EPS 2010E	0.79	Market Capitalization(B)	$3.755	Beta	0.62
Trailing 12-Month EPS	$0.59	S&P Oper. EPS 2011E	1.05	Yield (%)	Nil	S&P 3-Yr. Proj. EPS CAGR(%)	14
Trailing 12-Month P/E	18.0	P/E on S&P Oper. EPS 2010E	13.4	Dividend Rate/Share	Nil	S&P Credit Rating	NA
$10K Invested 5 Yrs Ago	NA	Common Shares Outstg. (M)	353.9	Institutional Ownership (%)	63		

Price Performance

30-Week Mov. Avg. ··· 10-Week Mov. Avg. -- **GAAP Earnings vs. Previous Year** Volume Above Avg. |||| STARS

12-Mo. Target Price — Relative Strength — ▲ Up ▼ Down ▶ No Change   Below Avg. |||| ★

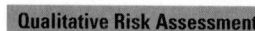

Analysis prepared by **James Moorman, CFA** on August 19, 2010, when the stock traded at **$ 8.80**.

Highlights

➤ We estimate subscriber revenue increases of 16.8% for 2010 and 12.2% for 2011, following a 28% advance in 2009, with growth driven by new, simplified pricing plans and further penetration of recently launched markets, such as Las Vegas (late March 2008), Philadelphia (July 1, 2008), Boston (February 4, 2009) and New York (February 4, 2009). We also believe that its early adoption of LTE (Long Term Evolution), a new radio platform technology, could further spur growth. However, we are concerned that adverse economic conditions could pressure net additions, and new rate plans could pressure average revenue per user (ARPU) in 2010.

➤ We see EBITDA margins on service revenue expanding to 33.2% in 2010, from 30.5% in 2009, and to 34.4% in 2011. We expect continued solid subscriber growth and a decline in churn to benefit EBITDA margins.

➤ We estimate higher depreciation charges for 2010 stemming from PCS's market launches. We see EPS of $0.79 in 2010 and $1.05 in 2011, following operating EPS of $0.49 in 2009.

Investment Rationale/Risk

➤ Our buy opinion reflects our outlook for 16% EBITDA growth in 2011, despite a competitive wireless industry. We believe that the implementation of their Wireless for All plans have contributed to a significant reduction in churn and solid subscriber growth. We expect further consolidation in the prepaid space that will eventually take pressure off of the competitive pricing. Additionally, we believe that PCS's early move into 4G with LTE could bring it an early adopter advantage and make it a potential takeout candidate. We consider PCS shares very attractive at current levels.

➤ Risks to our recommendation and target price include weaker-than-expected net customer growth, higher-than-expected churn, pressure on EBITDA margins, and debt issuance. Further, increased or prolonged pricing pressure could cause margins to deteriorate.

➤ Our 12-month target price of $15 is derived from an enterprise value-to-EBITDA multiple of 5.5X projected 2011 results, in line with the peer average. We expect the shares to be volatile.

Qualitative Risk Assessment

LOW	MEDIUM	HIGH

Our risk assessment reflects the competitive nature of the wireless market and the company's focus on the prepaid market, partly offset by our view of its relatively strong balance sheet.

Quantitative Evaluations

S&P Quality Ranking   NR

D	C	B-	B	B+	A-	A	A+

Relative Strength Rank   STRONG

73

LOWEST = 1   HIGHEST = 99

Revenue/Earnings Data

Revenue (Million $)

	1Q	2Q	3Q	4Q	Year
2010	970.5	1,013	--	--	--
2009	795.3	859.6	895.6	930.0	3,481
2008	662.4	678.8	686.7	723.6	2,752
2007	536.7	551.2	556.7	591.1	2,236
2006	329.5	368.2	396.1	453.1	1,547
2005	236.0	250.7	263.6	288.2	1,038

Earnings Per Share ($)

	1Q	2Q	3Q	4Q	Year
2010	0.06	0.22	E0.29	E0.20	E0.79
2009	0.12	0.07	0.21	0.09	0.50
2008	0.11	0.14	0.13	0.04	0.42
2007	0.11	0.17	0.15	-0.10	0.28
2006	0.04	0.06	0.08	-0.08	0.18
2005	0.26	0.47	0.03	0.05	0.62

Fiscal year ended Dec. 31. Next earnings report expected: Early November. EPS Estimates based on S&P Operating Earnings; historical GAAP earnings are as reported.

Dividend Data

No cash dividends have been paid.

MetroPCS Communications Inc

STANDARD &POOR'S

Business Summary August 19, 2010

CORPORATE OVERVIEW. Metro PCS offers digital wireless services in the U.S. under the MetroPCS brand. The company's services are based on the Code Division Multiple Access (CDMA 1xRTT) technology. PCS offers unlimited service for a flat rate to customer segments that we believe are underserved by traditional wireless carriers. The company sells handsets that are equipped with color screens, camera phones and other features to facilitate digital data transmission. In the second quarter of 2010, equipment sales accounted for 9% of total revenues, while service revenues contributed 91%. PCS provided services to roughly 7.6 million subscribers at the end of the second quarter of 2010, up from 6.3 million a year earlier.

In the second half of 2006, the company won eight licenses costing a total of $1.4 billion in Auction 66, the Advanced Wireless Services auction, covering roughly 126 million potential customers, including areas where PCS already provides service. The company expanded its coverage with launches in New York, Philadelphia, Boston and Las Vegas, and plans to build out these markets to cover 40 million POPs in 2010. In March 2008, PCS participated in the 700 MHz spectrum auction and won a license covering the Boston market for roughly $360 million.

In September 2007, PCS announced a stock-based offer to merge with Leap

Wireless (LEAP 11, Hold), a regional prepaid wireless carrier. The terms of the deal, equal to 2.75 shares of PCS for every LEAP share, originally valued LEAP at $5.5 billion, or $75 a share. In November 2007, PCS withdrew its offer. In September 2008, PCS and LEAP announced a national roaming agreement and spectrum swap. As part of the agreement, both companies also settled all outstanding litigation. We believe that consolidation in the competitive prepaid market will continue throughout 2010 and into 2011.

PRIMARY BUSINESS DYNAMICS. In the second quarter of 2010, PCS added 303,009 net subscribers, and had a monthly churn rate of 3.3% and average revenue per user (ARPU) of $39.84, down 1.7% from a year earlier. In the second and third quarters of any given year, PCS's churn rate tends to increase and customer growth slows, but this is likely to be more pronounced in 2010 due to economic issues, including less disposable income. The company's customer profile is skewed toward first-time users, with roughly 55% of its customers fitting into that category. About 90% of its subscribers use their wireless phone as their primary phone service.

Company Financials Fiscal Year Ended Dec. 31

Per Share Data ($)	2009	2008	2007	2006	2005	2004	2003	2002	2001	2000
Tangible Book Value	NM	NM	NM	NM	NA	NA	NA	NA	NA	NA
Cash Flow	1.57	1.14	0.91	0.54	1.72	0.82	0.30	1.37	-0.46	NA
Earnings	0.50	0.42	0.28	0.18	0.62	0.33	0.01	0.57	-0.48	NA
S&P Core Earnings	0.49	0.51	0.47	0.18	0.17	NA	NA	NA	NA	NA
Dividends	Nil	Nil	Nil	NA	NA	NA	NA	NA	NA	NA
Payout Ratio	Nil	Nil	Nil	NA	NA	NA	NA	NA	NA	NA
Prices:High	18.98	21.86	40.87	NA	NA	NA	NA	NA	NA	NA
Prices:Low	5.65	10.23	13.77	NA	NA	NA	NA	NA	NA	NA
P/E Ratio:High	38	52	NM	NA	NA	NA	NA	NA	NA	NA
P/E Ratio:Low	11	24	NM	NA	NA	NA	NA	NA	NA	NA

Income Statement Analysis (Million $)										
Revenue	3,481	2,752	2,236	1,547	1,038	748	451	129	NA	NA
Operating Income	NA	742	639	381	292	193	84.0	-95.9	NA	NA
Depreciation	383	255	178	135	87.9	62.2	42.4	21.5	0.21	NA
Interest Expense	270	179	202	116	58.0	19.0	11.1	6.72	10.5	16.1
Pretax Income	264	279	224	90.5	326	112	31.7	156	-45.2	-20.6
Effective Tax Rate	32.9%	46.5%	55.1%	40.6%	39.1%	42.0%	51.1%	16.4%	NA	NA
Net Income	177	149	100	53.8	199	64.9	15.5	130	-45.2	-20.6
S&P Core Earnings	175	182	164	59.5	55.2	NA	NA	NA	NA	NA

Balance Sheet & Other Financial Data (Million $)										
Cash	1,154	698	1,470	1,375	503	59.4	236	61.7	42.7	NA
Current Assets	1,491	1,044	1,733	NA	612	157	293	110	51.3	NA
Total Assets	7,386	6,422	5,806	NA	2,159	965	902	563	324	NA
Current Liabilities	797	742	580	NA	236	163	200	119	204	NA
Long Term Debt	3,626	3,058	2,986	2,596	903	171	182	41.4	48.6	NA
Common Equity	2,288	2,034	1,849	1,730	368	125	84.9	76.1	-52.9	NA
Total Capital	5,761	5,116	5,130	4,326	1,744	712	660	422	119	NA
Capital Expenditures	865	955	768	551	278	251	117	212	134	0.09
Cash Flow	560	405	271	164	265	106	43.8	150	-49.9	-21.2
Current Ratio	1.9	1.4	3.0	NA	2.6	1.0	1.5	0.9	0.3	NA
% Long Term Debt of Capitalization	61.1	59.8	58.2	NA	51.8	24.0	27.6	9.8	40.8	NA
% Net Income of Revenue	5.1	5.4	4.5	NA	19.1	8.7	4.5	110.7	NA	NA
% Return on Assets	2.6	2.4	2.0	NA	12.7	7.0	2.8	31.4	NA	NA
% Return on Equity	8.2	7.7	8.2	NA	80.5	61.7	25.6	NA	NA	NA

Data as orig reptd.; bef. results of disc opers/spec. items. Per share data adj. for stk. divs.; EPS diluted. E-Estimated. NA-Not Available. NM-Not Meaningful. NR-Not Ranked. UR-Under Review.

Office: 2250 Lakeside Boulevard, Richardson, TX 75082.
Telephone: 214-570-5800.
Website: http://www.metropcs.com
Chrmn, Pres & CEO: R.D. Linquist

COO: T.C. Keys
EVP & CFO: J.B. Carter, II
EVP, Secy & General Counsel: M.A. Stachiw
SVP, Chief Acctg Officer & Cntlr: C.B. Kornegay

Investor Contact: J. Mathias (214-570-4641)
Board Members: R. A. Anderson, W. M. Barnes, J. F. Callahan, Jr., C. C. Landry, R. D. Linquist, A. C. Patterson, J. N. Perry, Jr.

Founded: 2004
Domicile: Delaware
Employees: 3,600

The McGraw-Hill Companies

Microchip Technology Inc

STANDARD &POOR'S

S&P Recommendation	HOLD ★★★☆☆	Price $31.35 (as of Oct 22, 2010)	12-Mo. Target Price $34.00	Investment Style Large-Cap Growth

GICS Sector Information Technology
Sub-Industry Semiconductors

Summary This company supplies microcontrollers and analog and other semiconductor products for a wide variety of high-volume embedded control applications.

Key Stock Statistics (Source S&P, Vickers, company reports)

52-Wk Range	$31.99– 23.55	S&P Oper. EPS 2011E	2.10	Market Capitalization(B)	$5.829	Beta	1.12
Trailing 12-Month EPS	$1.48	S&P Oper. EPS 2012E	2.34	Yield (%)	4.38	S&P 3-Yr. Proj. EPS CAGR(%)	37
Trailing 12-Month P/E	21.2	P/E on S&P Oper. EPS 2011E	14.9	Dividend Rate/Share	$1.37	S&P Credit Rating	NA
$10K Invested 5 Yrs Ago	$12,951	Common Shares Outstg. (M)	185.9	Institutional Ownership (%)	NM		

Price Performance

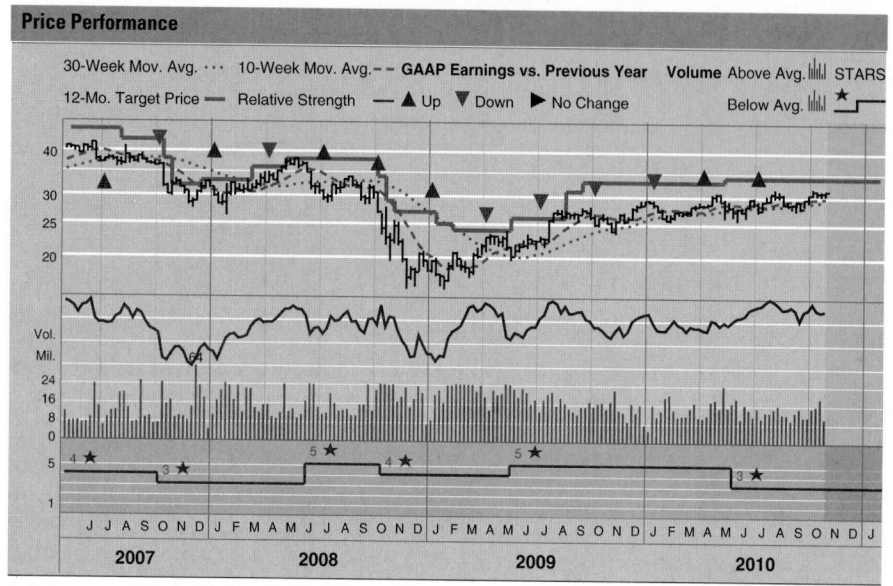

30-Week Mov. Avg. · · · · 10-Week Mov. Avg. – – **GAAP Earnings vs. Previous Year** Volume Above Avg. STARS
12-Mo. Target Price — Relative Strength — ▲ Up ▼ Down ▶ No Change Below Avg.

Options: ASE, CBOE, Ph

Analysis prepared by **Clyde Montevirgen** on August 11, 2010, when the stock traded at **$ 29.20**.

Highlights

➤ We expect sales to advance 44% in FY 11 (Mar.) after a 5% increase in FY 10. Assuming improving economic conditions and including recently acquired Silicon Storage Technology Inc. businesses, we believe sales growth will be supported by business and product cycles. We see more share gains in the 8-bit and 16-bit microcontroller (MCU) markets, as the company expands its served available market and focuses on further penetrating a wider range of end-products. We also expect MCHP's relatively small but budding analog business to grow faster than peers.

➤ We look for non-GAAP gross margins to widen to 63% in FY 11, from 56% in FY 10, reflecting higher plant utilization, cost efficiencies, and licensing revenues. Although we believe that variable expenses will rise as business conditions improve, we still expect non-GAAP operating margins to expand to about 36% in FY 11, from 26% in FY 10, reflecting benefits from operating leverage as sales rise faster than costs and expenses.

➤ Our EPS estimates assume a 14% effective tax rate and include around $0.20 per share of stock-based compensation.

Investment Rationale/Risk

➤ We believe healthy sales growth and operational efficiencies will lead to multi-year high profitability, greater free cash flow and improving return metrics. We also think MCHP, through its ability to reduce volatility in margins by effectively managing cost and expenses, has relatively less business risk than peers. Although we see earnings advancing at an above-industry pace, we believe that this is already reflected in multiples, which are trading above the industry's.

➤ Risks to our recommendation and target price include a weaker than expected recovery in MCHP's industrial and related businesses, and slower than anticipated share gains in the 8-bit and 16-bit MCU markets.

➤ Our 12-month target price of $34 is based on a weighted blend of valuation metrics. We apply a P/E multiple of 13X, above the peer average to account for its relative growth, return metrics, and risk, to our calendar 2011 EPS estimate, implying a value of $30. We also utilize a DCF model, which assumes a 10% weighted average cost of capital and a terminal growth rate of 4%, resulting in an intrinsic value of $41.

Qualitative Risk Assessment

LOW	MEDIUM	HIGH

Our risk assessment reflects the cyclicality of the semiconductor industry, offset by the company's very broad customer base and end-markets and its low cost structure.

Quantitative Evaluations

S&P Quality Ranking B+

D	C	B-	B	B+	A-	A	A+

Relative Strength Rank MODERATE

59

LOWEST = 1   HIGHEST = 99

Revenue/Earnings Data

Revenue (Million $)

	1Q	2Q	3Q	4Q	Year
2011	320.8	--	--	--	--
2010	193.0	226.7	250.1	278.0	947.7
2009	268.2	269.7	192.2	173.3	903.3
2008	264.1	258.7	252.6	260.4	1,036
2007	262.6	267.9	251.0	258.2	1,040
2006	218.5	227.3	234.9	247.2	927.9

Earnings Per Share ($)

2011	0.47	E0.53	E0.54	E0.53	E2.10
2010	0.15	0.24	0.37	0.40	1.16
2009	0.40	0.41	0.40	0.12	1.33
2008	0.36	0.27	0.38	0.40	1.40
2007	0.35	0.36	0.33	0.57	1.62
2006	0.29	0.31	0.19	0.35	1.13

Fiscal year ended Mar. 31. Next earnings report expected: Early November. EPS Estimates based on S&P Operating Earnings; historical GAAP earnings are as reported.

Dividend Data (Dates: mm/dd Payment Date: mm/dd/yy)

Amount ($)	Date Decl.	Ex-Div. Date	Stk. of Record	Payment Date
0.340	11/04	11/16	11/18	12/02/09
0.341	02/03	02/16	02/18	03/04/10
0.342	05/05	05/17	05/19	06/02/10
0.343	08/05	08/17	08/19	09/02/10

Dividends have been paid since 2002. Source: Company reports.

Microchip Technology Inc

STANDARD &POOR'S

Business Summary August 11, 2010

CORPORATE OVERVIEW. Microchip Technology Inc. (MCHP) develops and manufactures specialized chips used in a wide variety of embedded control applications. MCHP is a leading microcontroller (MCU) company, having shipped over 7 billion PIC microcontrollers since 1990. MCHP also offers a broad range of high-performance linear, mixed-signal, power management, thermal management, battery management, and interface devices, and serial EEPROMs.

Microcontrollers are low-cost components that form the brains of the vast majority of electronic devices, except for PCs. MCHP's signature products include a broad family of proprietary 8- and 16-bit field programmable microcontrollers under the PIC name, designed for applications requiring high performance, fast time-to-market, and user programmability. The company offers a comprehensive set of low-cost and easy-to-learn application development tools that let system designers program a PIC microcontroller for specific applications.

By main product line, microcontrollers provided 81.0% of sales in FY 09 (Mar.) (80.4% in FY 08), memory products 9.9% (11.6%), and analog and interface products 9.1% (8.0%). Average selling prices are relatively stable for the microcontrollers and for analog products with significant proprietary content, which is about half the analog segment. Pricing for some commodity-type products, such as EEPROMs, tend to fluctuate.

Foreign sales accounted for 75% of FY 09 net sales, similar to FY 08. By major region, FY 09 sales came from Asia (46.2%), Europe (28.5%) and the Americas (25.3%). Approximately 23% of FY 09 sales were sourced from China, including Hong Kong, and Taiwan accounted for about 10%. About 64% of net sales in FY 09 were made through distributors.

Company Financials Fiscal Year Ended Mar. 31

Per Share Data ($)	2010	2009	2008	2007	2006	2005	2004	2003	2002	2001
Tangible Book Value	7.86	5.18	5.39	9.03	7.89	6.95	6.19	5.58	5.36	4.80
Cash Flow	1.64	1.85	1.87	2.14	1.64	1.58	1.32	1.00	0.98	1.20
Earnings	1.16	1.33	1.40	1.62	1.13	1.01	0.65	0.47	0.45	0.69
S&P Core Earnings	1.16	1.35	1.48	1.62	1.05	0.89	0.47	0.30	0.28	0.57
Dividends	1.36	1.35	0.97	0.57	0.21	0.11	0.04	0.04	Nil	Nil
Payout Ratio	117%	102%	69%	35%	18%	11%	6%	9%	Nil	Nil
Calendar Year	2009	2008	2007	2006	2005	2004	2003	2002	2001	2000
Prices:High	29.56	38.37	42.46	38.56	34.98	34.88	36.50	33.99	28.29	34.39
Prices:Low	16.23	16.28	27.50	30.63	24.06	25.12	17.85	15.02	14.00	12.92
P/E Ratio:High	25	29	30	24	31	35	56	72	62	50
P/E Ratio:Low	14	12	20	19	21	25	27	32	31	19

Income Statement Analysis (Million $)

	2010	2009	2008	2007	2006	2005	2004	2003	2002	2001
Revenue	948	903	1,036	1,040	928	847	699	651	571	716
Operating Income	336	336	427	464	567	400	314	286	232	304
Depreciation	90.1	96.1	98.2	116	111	120	142	111	109	104
Interest Expense	31.2	24.3	0.75	5.42	1.97	0.94	0.25	0.49	0.57	0.75
Pretax Income	238	237	351	401	359	277	178	128	127	196
Effective Tax Rate	8.75%	NM	15.2%	11.0%	32.5%	22.9%	22.8%	22.3%	25.5%	27.2%
Net Income	217	249	298	357	242	214	137	99.7	94.8	143
S&P Core Earnings	216	253	314	357	226	190	100	63.5	58.2	117

Balance Sheet & Other Financial Data (Million $)

	2010	2009	2008	2007	2006	2005	2004	2003	2002	2001
Cash	1,214	1,390	1,325	167	565	68.7	105	53.9	281	130
Current Assets	1,611	1,743	1,718	1,085	1,119	1,075	884	609	549	372
Total Assets	2,516	2,421	2,512	2,270	2,351	1,818	1,622	1,428	1,276	1,161
Current Liabilities	203	156	191	256	609	307	270	215	168	195
Long Term Debt	341	1,149	1,150	Nil	Nil	Nil	Nil	Nil	Nil	Nil
Common Equity	1,533	991	1,036	2,004	1,726	1,486	1,321	1,179	1,076	943
Total Capital	1,874	2,192	2,208	2,013	1,741	1,510	1,351	1,212	1,107	966
Capital Expenditures	47.6	102	69.8	60.0	76.3	63.2	63.5	80.4	44.7	441
Cash Flow	307	345	396	473	353	334	279	211	204	247
Current Ratio	7.9	11.2	9.0	4.2	1.8	3.5	3.3	2.8	3.3	1.9
% Long Term Debt of Capitalization	18.2	52.4	52.1	Nil	Nil	Nil	Nil	Nil	Nil	Nil
% Net Income of Revenue	22.9	27.6	28.8	34.3	26.1	25.2	19.6	15.3	16.6	20.0
% Return on Assets	8.8	10.1	12.5	15.5	11.6	12.4	9.0	7.4	7.8	14.1
% Return on Equity	17.2	24.6	19.6	19.1	15.1	15.2	11.0	8.8	9.4	17.8

Data as orig reptd.; bef. results of disc opers/spec. items. Per share data adj. for stk. divs.; EPS diluted. E-Estimated. NA-Not Available. NM-Not Meaningful. NR-Not Ranked. UR-Under Review.

Office: 2355 West Chandler Boulevard, Chandler, AZ 85224-6199.
Telephone: 480-792-7200.
Email: ir@mail.microchip.com
Website: http://www.microchip.com

Chrmn, Pres & CEO: S. Sanghi
COO & EVP: G. Moorthy
CFO & Chief Acctg Officer: J.E. Bjornholt
CTO: S.V. Drehobl

Secy & General Counsel: K. Van Herk
Investor Contact: G. Parnell (480-792-7374)
Board Members: M. W. Chapman, L. Day, IV, A. Hugo-Martinez, W. Meyercord, S. Sanghi

Founded: 1989
Domicile: Delaware
Employees: 5,418

Micron Technology Inc.

S&P Recommendation	HOLD ★★★★★	Price $7.69 (as of Oct 22, 2010)	12-Mo. Target Price $10.00	Investment Style Large-Cap Value

GICS Sector Information Technology
Sub-Industry Semiconductors

Summary This company is a manufacturer of semiconductor memory products, including DRAM and NAND flash memory, as well as image sensors.

Key Stock Statistics (Source S&P, Vickers, company reports)

52-Wk Range	$11.40 – 6.12	S&P Oper. EPS 2011E	1.27	Market Capitalization(B)	$7.645	Beta	1.01
Trailing 12-Month EPS	$1.76	S&P Oper. EPS 2012E	NA	Yield (%)	Nil	S&P 3-Yr. Proj. EPS CAGR(%)	NM
Trailing 12-Month P/E	4.4	P/E on S&P Oper. EPS 2011E	6.1	Dividend Rate/Share	Nil	S&P Credit Rating	B
$10K Invested 5 Yrs Ago	$6,069	Common Shares Outstg. (M)	994.2	Institutional Ownership (%)	85		

Price Performance

- 30-Week Mov. Avg. · · ·   10-Week Mov. Avg. - -   **GAAP Earnings vs. Previous Year**   Volume Above Avg. ▉▉ STARS
- 12-Mo. Target Price —   Relative Strength —   ▲ Up   ▼ Down   ▶ No Change   Below Avg. ▉▉ ★

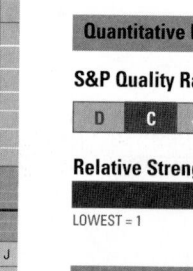

Analysis prepared by **Clyde Montevirgen** on October 11, 2010, when the stock traded at **$7.71**.

Options: ASE, CBOE, P, Ph

Highlights

▶ We forecast revenues will increase 19% in FY 11 (Aug.), after a 77% rise in FY 10. The industry dynamics for memory chips have improved over the past year, and we expect average selling prices (ASPs) for DRAM and NAND chips to fall at a more reasonable pace ahead. Although we anticipate a couple of quarters of softer demand, we expect strong bit growth over the longer term due to our projection of healthy sales of computing and consumer electronic devices. Our projection also assumes healthy shipments for NOR, which MU recently acquired from Numonyx.

▶ We expect a gross margin of 27% in FY 11, versus 32% in FY 10, largely based on lower average selling prices. Nonetheless, we believe gross margins will benefit from higher volumes, and consequent cost per bit reductions, as well as an improving sales mix of specialty DRAM chips. All told, we anticipate operating margins narrowing to 13% in FY 11, from 19% in FY 10.

▶ Our FY 11 EPS estimate includes $275 million from a patent cross-licensing agreement with Samsung. Considering MU's debt, we see interest expense continuing to weigh on profitability.

Investment Rationale/Risk

▶ With our view that Micron has the right technology to compete favorably in the memory market and to reduce cost-per-bit at a fast rate, we think its growth will beat that of competitors. We are modeling ASP deterioration and see margins taking a hit, but we expect them to be far better than those seen in recent years. The anticipated profitability should provide healthy cash flows and help strengthen the balance sheet as MU reduces debt. We see return on equity staying around historically high levels, but remaining below the industry average.

▶ Risks to our opinion and target price include worse-than-expected sales of computers and consumer electronic products, faster-than-expected capacity expansion, and lower-than-anticipated unit cost reductions.

▶ Our 12-month target price of $10 is based on a weighted blend of relative metrics. We apply a price-to-earnings multiple of 10X our calendar 2011 EPS estimate and a price-to-sales multiple of 1.0X our forward 12-month sales per share estimate. Both valuations are below peer averages to account for our view of risk and projected relative profitability.

Qualitative Risk Assessment

LOW	MEDIUM	HIGH

Micron is subject to semiconductor industry cyclicality and to sudden changes in pricing for commodity memory products. It is a relatively large semiconductor company and is the lone American survivor in the global DRAM industry, which has been consolidating in recent years.

Quantitative Evaluations

S&P Quality Ranking   C

D	C	B-	B	B+	A-	A	A+

Relative Strength Rank   MODERATE

51

LOWEST = 1   HIGHEST = 99

Revenue/Earnings Data

Revenue (Million $)

	1Q	2Q	3Q	4Q	Year
2010	1,740	1,961	2,288	2,493	8,482
2009	1,402	993.0	1,106	1,302	4,803
2008	1,535	1,359	1,498	1,449	5,841
2007	1,530	1,427	1,294	1,437	5,688
2006	1,362	1,225	1,312	1,373	5,272
2005	1,260	1,308	1,054	1,258	4,880

Earnings Per Share ($)

2010	0.23	0.39	0.92	0.30	1.76
2009	-0.91	-0.97	0.23	-0.10	-2.29
2008	-0.34	-1.01	-0.30	-0.45	-2.10
2007	0.15	-0.07	-0.29	-0.21	-0.42
2006	0.09	0.27	0.12	0.08	0.57
2005	0.23	0.17	-0.20	0.07	0.29

Fiscal year ended Aug. 31. Next earnings report expected: Late December. EPS Estimates based on S&P Operating Earnings; historical GAAP earnings are as reported.

Dividend Data

No cash dividends have been paid since 1996.

Please read the Required Disclosures and Analyst Certification on the last page of this report.

The McGraw-Hill Companies

Micron Technology Inc.

STANDARD
&POOR'S

Business Summary October 11, 2010

CORPORATE OVERVIEW. Micron Technology is a global manufacturer and marketer of dynamic random access memory (DRAM) and NAND flash memory. The company's products are used in an increasingly broad range of electronic devices, including personal computers, workstations, network servers, mobile phones, digital still cameras, MP3 players and other consumer electronics products. About 30% of FY 09 (Aug.) total sales were to the computing market. Intel accounted for 20% of the company's FY 09 sales.

The company has been in the DRAM business since 1980, and is currently one of the world's largest DRAM suppliers. DRAM products are high-density, low-cost per bit, random access memory devices that provide high-speed data storage and retrieval. Micron offers DRAM products with a variety of performance, pricing, and other characteristics. The company's DRAM products may be classified as core DRAM or specialty memory.

Micron has two segments -- memory, which includes both DRAM and NAND flash memory, and imaging. The memory segment comprised 89% of total revenues in FY 09. By memory type, DRAM sales accounted for 50% of the total in FY 09, down from 54% in the previous fiscal year, reflecting an expansion into flash memory and CMOS image sensors over the last couple of years. NAND flash memory sales comprised 39% of sales in FY 09, up from 54% in the prior year, reflecting growing market demand for memory devices that can retain memory when the power is turned off, for use in handheld electronic devices such as digital still cameras.

The imaging segment made up 11% of total revenues in FY 09. This segment's main product is the CMOS image sensor. Micron has a supply agreement to manufacture the image sensors to Aptina Imaging Corporation, which was once a wholly-owned subsidiary of Micron.

Company Financials Fiscal Year Ended Aug. 31

Per Share Data ($)	2010	2009	2008	2007	2006	2005	2004	2003	2002	2001
Tangible Book Value	NA	5.08	7.56	9.00	9.64	9.07	8.73	7.68	9.93	11.59
Cash Flow	NA	0.35	0.57	1.81	2.33	2.07	2.13	-0.10	0.45	1.00
Earnings	1.76	-2.29	-2.10	-0.42	0.57	0.29	0.24	-2.11	-1.51	-0.88
S&P Core Earnings	NA	-2.27	-1.54	-0.38	0.40	-0.12	-0.09	-2.60	-2.14	-1.06
Dividends	NA	Nil	Nil	Nil	Nil	Nil	Nil	Nil	Nil	Nil
Payout Ratio	Nil	Nil	Nil	Nil	Nil	Nil	Nil	Nil	Nil	Nil
Prices:High	11.40	10.87	8.97	14.31	18.65	14.82	18.25	15.66	39.50	49.61
Prices:Low	6.36	2.55	1.59	7.11	13.12	9.32	10.89	6.60	9.50	16.39
P/E Ratio:High	6	NM	NM	NM	33	51	76	NM	NM	NM
P/E Ratio:Low	4	NM	NM	NM	23	32	45	NM	NM	NM

Income Statement Analysis (Million $)	2010	2009	2008	2007	2006	2005	2004	2003	2002	2001
Revenue	8,482	4,803	5,841	5,688	5,272	4,880	4,404	3,091	2,589	3,936
Operating Income	3,566	673	887	1,381	1,631	1,458	1,445	133	152	138
Depreciation	NA	2,113	2,056	1,718	1,281	1,265	1,218	1,210	1,177	1,114
Interest Expense	160	138	95.0	40.0	25.0	46.9	36.0	36.5	17.1	16.7
Pretax Income	1,881	-1,944	-1,611	-168	433	199	232	-1,200	-998	-960
Effective Tax Rate	NA	NM	NM	NM	4.16%	5.34%	32.2%	NM	NM	NM
Net Income	1,850	-1,835	-1,619	-320	408	188	157	-1,273	-907	-521
S&P Core Earnings	NA	-1,819	-1,190	-290	288	-75.8	-62.2	-1,578	-1,288	-626

Balance Sheet & Other Financial Data (Million $)	2010	2009	2008	2007	2006	2005	2004	2003	2002	2001
Cash	2,913	1,485	1,362	2,192	1,431	525	486	570	398	469
Current Assets	6,333	3,344	3,779	5,234	5,101	2,926	2,639	2,037	2,119	3,138
Total Assets	14,693	11,455	13,430	14,818	12,221	8,006	7,760	7,158	7,555	8,363
Current Liabilities	2,702	1,892	1,598	2,026	1,661	979	972	993	753	687
Long Term Debt	1,648	2,674	2,451	1,987	405	1,020	1,028	997	361	445
Common Equity	8,020	4,654	6,178	7,752	8,114	5,847	5,615	5,038	6,367	7,135
Total Capital	12,176	9,738	11,503	12,371	10,115	6,902	6,685	6,035	6,727	7,599
Capital Expenditures	NA	488	2,529	3,603	1,365	1,065	1,081	822	760	1,489
Cash Flow	NA	278	437	1,398	1,689	1,453	1,375	-63.3	270	593
Current Ratio	2.3	1.8	2.4	2.6	3.1	3.0	2.7	2.1	2.8	4.6
% Long Term Debt of Capitalization	13.5	27.5	21.3	16.1	4.0	14.8	15.4	16.5	5.4	5.9
% Net Income of Revenue	21.8	NM	NM	NM	7.7	3.9	3.6	NM	NM	NM
% Return on Assets	14.2	NM	NM	NM	4.0	2.4	2.1	NM	NM	NM
% Return on Equity	29.2	NM	NM	NM	5.8	3.3	3.0	NM	NM	NM

Data as orig reptd.; bef. results of disc opers/spec. items. Per share data adj. for stk. divs.; EPS diluted. E-Estimated. NA-Not Available. NM-Not Meaningful. NR-Not Ranked. UR-Under Review.

Office: 8000 South Federal Way, Boise, ID 83707-0006.
Telephone: 208-368-4000.
Email: invrel@micron.com
Website: http://www.micron.com

Chrmn & CEO: S.R. Appleton
Pres & COO: D.M. Durcan
CFO & Chief Acctg Officer: R.C. Foster
Treas: P. Morali

Secy & General Counsel: R.W. Lewis
Investor Contact: K.A. Bedard (208-368-4400)
Board Members: T. Aoki, S. R. Appleton, J. W. Bageley, R. L. Bailey, M. Johnson, L. Mondry, R. E. Switz

Founded: 1978
Domicile: Delaware
Employees: 18,200

The McGraw-Hill Companies

Microsoft Corp

STANDARD &POOR'S

S&P Recommendation HOLD ★★★☆☆

Price	12-Mo. Target Price	Investment Style
$25.38 (as of Oct 22, 2010)	$31.00	Large-Cap Growth

GICS Sector Information Technology
Sub-Industry Systems Software

Summary Microsoft, the world's largest software company, develops PC software, including the Windows operating system and the Office application suite.

Key Stock Statistics (Source S&P, Vickers, company reports)

52-Wk Range	$31.58– 22.73	S&P Oper. EPS 2011E	2.24	Market Capitalization(B)	$219.606	Beta	1.09
Trailing 12-Month EPS	$2.10	S&P Oper. EPS 2012E	2.40	Yield (%)	2.52	S&P 3-Yr. Proj. EPS CAGR(%)	7
Trailing 12-Month P/E	12.1	P/E on S&P Oper. EPS 2011E	11.3	Dividend Rate/Share	$0.64	S&P Credit Rating	AAA
$10K Invested 5 Yrs Ago	$11,167	Common Shares Outstg. (M)	8,653.6	Institutional Ownership (%)	63		

Price Performance

30-Week Mov. Avg. · · · 10-Week Mov. Avg. – – GAAP Earnings vs. Previous Year   Volume Above Avg. ⅼⅼⅼⅼ STARS
12-Mo. Target Price — Relative Strength — ▲ Up ▼ Down ▶ No Change   Below Avg. ⅼⅼⅼⅼ ★

Options: ASE, CBOE, P, Ph

Analysis prepared by **Jim Yin, CFA** on August 12, 2010, when the stock traded at **$ 24.50**.

Highlights

➤ We expect revenues to rise 5.5% in FY 11 (Jun.), following 6.9% growth in FY 10. We see Windows and Windows Live revenue advancing 8.3% in FY 11, based on a low-teens growth rate in PC sales in the next 12 months, driven by strong consumer adoption of Windows 7 and a greater mix of premium versions. These factors should be partly offset by lower selling prices in emerging and laptop markets. We project 6.9% growth in Server and Tools revenue and 4.5% in Microsoft Business in FY 11, driven by new releases of Microsoft Office and SharePoint products. We see Entertainment and Devices division revenue increasing 23% in FY 11.

➤ We look for gross margins to narrow to 79% in FY 11, from 80% in FY 10, due mostly to higher Xbox sales, which have much lower gross margins than other MSFT businesses. We see operating margins staying at 38% in FY 11, as lower gross margins are offset by economies of scale.

➤ We estimate EPS of $2.24 in FY 11, up from $2.10 in FY 10, reflecting our forecast for higher revenues due to improving economies and new product releases.

Investment Rationale/Risk

➤ We recently lowered our recommendation on the shares to Hold, from Buy, reflecting our concern about a slowing global economy, given recent economic data. We think PC unit sales growth will moderate after rising over 20% in the first half of 2010. In addition to softer consumer demand, we believe companies may delay refreshing their aging PCs. These concerns are mitigated by several new product introductions, including Office 2010 and the next version of Xbox with its controller-free input device. We also think Bing, the company's new Web search engine, will gain market share.

➤ Risks to our recommendation and target price include lower-than-projected PC sales, a slowdown in the global economy, and further losses in the desktop operating systems market.

➤ Our 12-month target price of $31 is based on a blend of our discounted cash flow (DCF) and P/E analyses. Our DCF model assumes an 11.1% weighted average cost of capital and 3% terminal growth, yielding an intrinsic value of $34. Our P/E analysis derives a value of $28, based on an industry P/E-to-growth ratio of 1.8X, or 12.5X our FY 11 EPS estimate of $2.24.

Qualitative Risk Assessment

LOW	MEDIUM	HIGH

Our risk assessment reflects our concerns about a sluggish recovery in enterprise IT spending, market share losses in Internet search engine, and difficulties inherent in releasing new products in a timely manner, mitigated by the company's current leading market positions and financial strength.

Quantitative Evaluations

S&P Quality Ranking   B+

D	C	B-	B	B+	A-	A	A+

Relative Strength Rank   MODERATE

43

LOWEST = 1   HIGHEST = 99

Revenue/Earnings Data

Revenue (Million $)

	1Q	2Q	3Q	4Q	Year
2010	12,920	19,022	14,503	16,039	62,484
2009	15,061	16,629	13,648	13,099	58,437
2008	13,762	16,367	14,454	15,837	60,420
2007	10,811	12,542	14,398	13,371	51,122
2006	9,741	11,837	10,900	11,804	44,282
2005	9,189	10,818	9,620	10,161	39,788

Earnings Per Share ($)

2010	0.40	0.74	0.45	0.51	2.10
2009	0.48	0.47	0.33	0.34	1.62
2008	0.45	0.50	0.47	0.46	1.87
2007	0.35	0.26	0.50	0.31	1.42
2006	0.29	0.34	0.29	0.28	1.20
2005	0.23	0.32	0.23	0.34	1.12

Fiscal year ended Jun. 30. Next earnings report expected: Late October. EPS Estimates based on S&P Operating Earnings; historical GAAP earnings are as reported.

Dividend Data (Dates: mm/dd Payment Date: mm/dd/yy)

Amount ($)	Date Decl.	Ex-Div. Date	Stk. of Record	Payment Date
0.130	12/09	02/16	02/18	03/11/10
0.130	03/08	05/18	05/20	06/10/10
0.130	06/16	08/17	08/19	09/09/10
0.160	09/21	11/16	11/18	12/09/10

Dividends have been paid since 2003. Source: Company reports.

Please read the Required Disclosures and Analyst Certification on the last page of this report.

The McGraw-Hill Companies

Microsoft Corp

Business Summary August 12, 2010

CORPORATE OVERVIEW. Microsoft is the world's largest software maker, primarily as a result of its near-monopoly position in desktop operating systems and its Office productivity suite. The combination of these two strongholds poses a formidable barrier to entry for competitors, in our opinion. MSFT has used the strong cash flows from these businesses to fund research and development of other markets, including home entertainment consoles and Internet online advertising.

The company has five operating business divisions: Windows and Windows Live, Server and Tools, Online Services Business, Microsoft Business, and Entertainment and Devices.

Windows and Windows Live is responsible for the development of the Windows product family. The division generated over 80% of its revenue from OEMs pre-installing versions of Windows operating systems. Despite some market share loss to Apple and the Linux operating system in recent years, Microsoft Windows operating systems still run more than 90% of all PCs currently in use.

Server and Tools develops and markets software server products, software developer tools, services, and solutions. Windows Server-based products are

integrated server infrastructure and middleware software designed to support software applications built on the Windows Server operating system. Windows-based server products accounted for about 70% of the server market in 2009 in terms of unit shipments, according to IDC, an independent research firm.

Online Services Business is comprised of various Internet websites that offer content and personal communications services. It also includes an online advertising platform that links publishers and advertisers to their targeted audiences. In 2009, MSFT updated its Internet search engine, called Bing, and trailed in third place behind Google and Yahoo! with about a 12% market share.

Microsoft Business is comprised of the Microsoft Office system and Microsoft Dynamics business solutions. Despite the growing popularity of online software application suites such as Google Apps, Microsoft Office suite is the prevailing productivity application used in major enterprises.

Company Financials Fiscal Year Ended Jun. 30

Per Share Data ($)	2010	2009	2008	2007	2006	2005	2004	2003	2002	2001
Tangible Book Value	3.76	2.84	2.43	2.71	3.55	4.14	6.55	5.34	2.05	4.39
Cash Flow	2.40	1.90	2.07	1.57	1.28	1.20	0.86	1.05	0.80	0.83
Earnings	2.10	1.62	1.87	1.42	1.20	1.12	0.75	0.92	0.71	0.66
S&P Core Earnings	2.07	1.63	1.99	1.38	1.27	1.20	0.83	0.75	0.65	0.58
Dividends	0.52	0.50	0.43	0.39	0.34	3.32	0.16	0.08	Nil	Nil
Payout Ratio	25%	31%	23%	27%	28%	NM	21%	9%	Nil	Nil
Prices:High	31.58	31.50	35.96	37.50	30.26	28.25	30.20	30.00	35.31	38.08
Prices:Low	22.73	14.87	17.50	26.60	21.46	23.82	24.86	22.55	20.71	21.44
P/E Ratio:High	15	19	19	26	25	25	40	33	50	58
P/E Ratio:Low	11	9	9	19	18	21	33	25	29	32

Income Statement Analysis (Million $)										
Revenue	62,484	58,437	60,420	51,122	44,282	39,788	36,835	32,187	28,365	25,296
Operating Income	27,363	23,255	25,877	19,964	17,375	15,416	10,220	14,656	12,994	13,256
Depreciation	2,673	2,562	1,872	1,440	903	855	1,186	1,439	1,084	1,536
Interest Expense	151	58.0	NA	Nil	Nil	Nil	Nil	Nil	Nil	Nil
Pretax Income	25,013	19,821	23,814	20,101	18,262	16,628	12,196	14,726	11,513	11,525
Effective Tax Rate	NA	26.5%	25.8%	30.0%	31.0%	26.3%	33.0%	32.1%	32.0%	33.0%
Net Income	18,760	14,569	17,681	14,065	12,599	12,254	8,168	9,993	7,829	7,721
S&P Core Earnings	18,534	14,650	18,873	13,643	13,329	13,107	9,042	8,155	7,051	6,518

Balance Sheet & Other Financial Data (Million $)										
Cash	36,726	29,907	21,171	6,111	6,714	4,851	15,982	6,438	3,016	3,922
Current Assets	55,676	49,280	43,242	40,168	49,010	48,737	70,566	58,973	48,576	39,637
Total Assets	86,113	77,888	72,793	63,171	69,597	70,815	92,389	79,571	67,646	59,257
Current Liabilities	26,147	27,034	29,886	23,754	22,442	16,877	14,969	13,974	12,744	11,132
Long Term Debt	4,939	3,746	1.00	Nil	Nil	Nil	Nil	Nil	Nil	Nil
Common Equity	46,175	39,558	36,286	31,097	40,104	48,115	74,825	61,020	52,180	47,289
Total Capital	51,114	43,304	36,287	31,097	40,104	48,115	74,825	62,751	52,578	48,125
Capital Expenditures	1,977	3,119	3,182	2,264	1,578	812	1,109	891	770	1,103
Cash Flow	21,433	17,131	19,553	15,505	13,502	13,109	9,354	11,432	8,913	9,257
Current Ratio	2.1	1.8	1.5	1.7	2.2	2.9	4.7	4.2	3.8	3.6
% Long Term Debt of Capitalization	9.7	8.7	NM	Nil	Nil	Nil	Nil	Nil	Nil	Nil
% Net Income of Revenue	30.0	24.9	29.3	27.5	28.5	30.8	22.2	31.0	27.6	30.5
% Return on Assets	22.9	19.3	26.0	21.2	17.9	14.8	9.4	13.6	12.4	13.9
% Return on Equity	43.8	38.4	52.5	39.5	28.6	19.9	11.7	17.7	15.7	17.4

Data as orig reptd.; bef. results of disc opers/spec. items. Per share data adj. for stk. divs.; EPS diluted. E-Estimated. NA-Not Available. NM-Not Meaningful. NR-Not Ranked. UR-Under Review.

Office: 1 Microsoft Way, Redmond, WA 98052-8300.
Telephone: 425-882-8080.
Email: msft@microsoft.com
Website: http://www.microsoft.com

Chrmn: W.H. Gates, III
CEO: S.A. Ballmer
COO: B.K. Turner
SVP, Secy & General Counsel: B.L. Smith

CFO: P.S. Klein
Investor Contact: F. Brod (800-285-7772)
Board Members: S. A. Ballmer, D. Dublon, W. H. Gates, III, R. V. Gilmartin, R. Hastings, M. M. Klawe, D. F. Marquardt, C. H. Noski, H. Panke

Founded: 1975
Domicile: Washington
Employees: 89,000

Molex Inc

STANDARD &POOR'S

S&P Recommendation	BUY ★★★★☆	Price	12-Mo. Target Price	Investment Style
		$21.84 (as of Oct 22, 2010)	$27.00	Large-Cap Growth

GICS Sector Information Technology
Sub-Industry Electronic Manufacturing Services

Summary This company makes electrical and electronic devices primarily for OEMs in the computer, telecommunications, home appliance, and home entertainment industries.

Key Stock Statistics (Source S&P, Vickers, company reports)

52-Wk Range	$23.66– 17.50	S&P Oper. EPS 2011**E**	1.75	Market Capitalization(B)	$2.087	Beta		1.54
Trailing 12-Month EPS	$0.44	S&P Oper. EPS 2012**E**	1.95	Yield (%)	2.79	S&P 3-Yr. Proj. EPS CAGR(%)		28
Trailing 12-Month P/E	49.6	P/E on S&P Oper. EPS 2011**E**	12.5	Dividend Rate/Share	$0.61	S&P Credit Rating		NA
$10K Invested 5 Yrs Ago	$9,730	Common Shares Outstg. (M)	174.3	Institutional Ownership (%)	72			

Price Performance

30-Week Mov. Avg. ···· 10-Week Mov. Avg. ─ ─ **GAAP Earnings vs. Previous Year** Volume Above Avg. ⥮ STARS
12-Mo. Target Price ─ Relative Strength ▲ Up ▼ Down ▶ No Change Below Avg. ⥮ ★

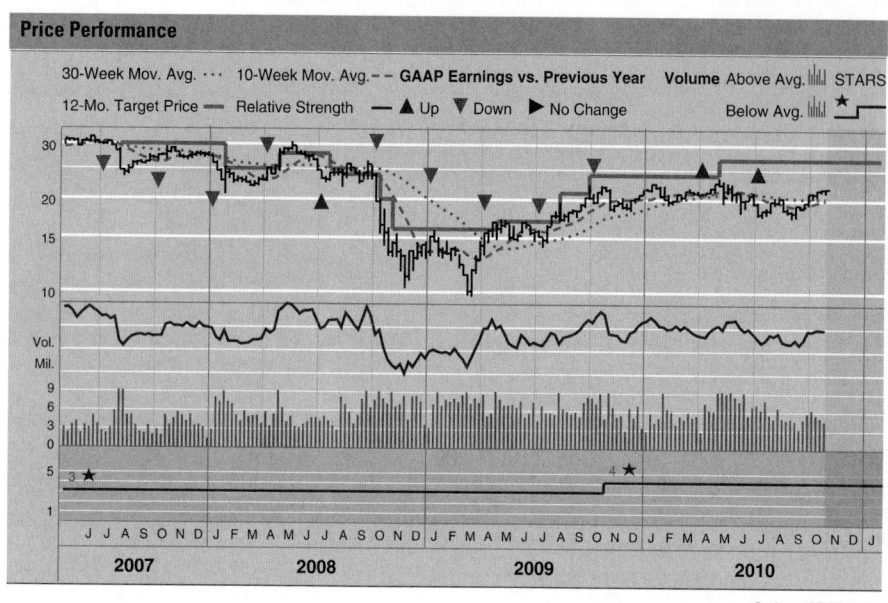

Options: CBOE, P, Ph

Analysis prepared by **Stewart Scharf** on August 06, 2010, when the stock traded at **$ 19.91**.

Highlights

▶ We expect revenues to advance close to 15% in FY 11, led by favorable order trends in tele-com, data, and consumer electronics, especial-ly for Asia/Pacific and parts of the Americas. We see a recovery in global industrial markets, driven by factory automation and alternative energy, while military and medical markets grow rapidly. We see some moderation in de-mand for automotive products in North America and Europe following incentive-driven strength.

▶ We look for gross margins to expand further in FY 11 to near 32%, from 29.6% in FY 10, on a bet-ter product mix and supply-chain cost savings, as MOLX improves its operating leverage. We expect a more than $2.5 million negative impact in the first half of FY 11 from higher copper and gold costs, as a hedge program expires at the end of FY 10. However, in our view, EBITDA margins should widen from 17.3% in FY 10, re-flecting cost savings from a restructuring pro-gram completed in late FY 10.

▶ We project a lower effective tax rate of below 30% for FY 11, and operating EPS of $1.75, and then a 11% increase to $1.95 in FY 12.

Investment Rationale/Risk

▶ Our buy recommendation on the shares is based on our valuation metrics and signs of a further sequential rebound in order rates in most sectors. We view the balance sheet as solid, while return on net assets continues to trend upward.

▶ Risks to our recommendation and target price include a significant rise in copper, gold, and plastics prices; adverse foreign exchange rates; and, a prolonged global economic down-turn. Corporate governance practices are also a concern to us, as MOLX has two classes of stock, and the board of directors consists most-ly of insiders.

▶ Based on a blend of our relative and DCF valua-tion metrics, our 12-month target price is $27. Our relative metrics, including historical aver-age price-to-sales and three-year PEG ratios, lead us to use a P/E multiple of about 14X our FY 11 EPS estimate, a modest premium to peers but below MOLX's five-year average historical forward P/E, valuing the shares at $24. Our DCF analysis, which assumes a 10.3% cost of capital (WACC) and a 3% terminal growth rate, sug-gests an intrinsic value of $30.

Qualitative Risk Assessment

LOW	**MEDIUM**	HIGH

Our risk assessment reflects the cyclicality in MOLX's global markets, price and product competition, volatile raw material costs, and fluctuating foreign currency exchange rates. However, we view the balance sheet as strong.

Quantitative Evaluations

S&P Quality Ranking B

D	C	B-	**B**	B+	A-	A	A+

Relative Strength Rank STRONG

73

LOWEST = 1   HIGHEST = 99

Revenue/Earnings Data

Revenue (Million $)

	1Q	2Q	3Q	4Q	Year
2010	674.0	729.6	756.3	847.3	3,007
2009	839.0	666.7	505.5	570.6	2,582
2008	792.6	841.6	822.3	871.9	3,328
2007	829.6	837.5	807.0	791.9	3,266
2006	659.8	697.4	720.3	783.8	2,861
2005	640.2	651.8	612.8	643.8	2,549

Earnings Per Share ($)

2010	-0.09	E0.20	0.22	0.23	0.44
2009	0.25	-0.50	-0.34	-1.27	-1.84
2008	0.29	0.33	0.28	0.29	1.19
2007	0.41	0.36	0.35	0.18	1.30
2006	0.25	0.31	0.33	0.38	1.26
2005	0.29	0.27	0.24	0.03	0.81

Fiscal year ended Jun. 30. Next earnings report expected: Late October. EPS Estimates based on S&P Operating Earnings; historical GAAP earnings are as reported.

Dividend Data (Dates: mm/dd Payment Date: mm/dd/yy)

Amount ($)	Date Decl.	Ex-Div. Date	Stk. of Record	Payment Date
0.153	12/21	12/29	12/31	01/25/10
0.153	03/16	03/29	03/31	04/26/10
0.153	06/16	06/28	06/30	07/26/10
0.153	09/15	09/28	09/30	10/25/10

Dividends have been paid since 1976. Source: Company reports.

Molex Inc

Business Summary August 06, 2010

CORPORATE OVERVIEW. Molex is the world's second largest connector maker, operating 39 plants in 16 countries, and offering more than 100,000 products.

MOLX's products include electrical and electronic devices such as terminals, cable assemblies, interconnection systems, fiber-optic interconnection systems, and mechanical and electronic switches. In FY 10 (Jun.), these products were sold to the following industries: data products (22%), telecommunications (25%), consumer products (20%), automotive (16%), industrial (14%), and other (3%). Revenues by segment were: Connector, 72%; Custom & Electrical, 28%; and Corporate and other, less than 1%.

MOLX sells primarily to original equipment manufacturers (OEMs), subcontractors and suppliers. Customers include Apple, Arrow, Cisco, Dell, Ford, General Motors, Hewlett-Packard, IBM, Motorola, Nokia, Panasonic and Research in Motion. Competitors include Tyco Electronics and Amphenol. The highly fragmented $40 billion global connector industry has grown at a compound annual rate (CAGR) of 5% over the past 25 years.

Net revenues outside the U.S. accounted for 76% of the FY 10 total. About 60% of net revenues were generated in Asia/Pacific (including 28% in China and 18% in Japan), 16% in Europe and 24% in the Americas. More than 50% of manufacturing capacity is in lower-cost regions such as Eastern Europe, Mexico and China.

At June 30, 2010, order backlog was $473 million, up 8% on a sequential basis and 87% from a year ago. New orders in the fourth quarter of FY 10 were $910 million, up 58% from a year earlier and 9% sequentially, driven by orders in the Asia/Pacific. The book-to-bill ratio remained positive at 1.07, exceeding 1.0 for the fifth straight quarter. MOLX's annual target range for new products (introduced within the past 36 months) as a percent of sales is 20% to 30%.

In the fourth quarter of FY 10, MOLX incurred a pretax restructuring charge of $26.5 million ($0.14 a share, after tax), and a pretax loss of $4.8 million ($0.02) related to unauthorized activities in Japan. In the third quarter of FY 10, MOLX incurred a $31 million pretax charge ($0.11 a share, after tax) related to alleged unauthorized loans and trading activity by an individual in a Japan subsidiary. The company projects the total fraud amount at $193 million, and has recorded a contingency liability of $166 million.

Company Financials Fiscal Year Ended Jun. 30

Per Share Data ($)	2010	2009	2008	2007	2006	2005	2004	2003	2002	2001
Tangible Book Value	10.39	10.89	12.66	10.64	11.60	10.78	10.05	9.10	8.64	8.25
Cash Flow	1.81	-0.40	2.58	2.58	2.41	2.02	2.10	1.62	1.53	2.13
Earnings	0.44	-1.84	1.19	1.30	1.26	0.81	0.92	0.44	0.39	1.03
S&P Core Earnings	0.45	-0.36	1.13	1.30	1.27	0.76	0.85	0.39	0.39	1.01
Dividends	0.61	0.61	0.45	0.30	0.23	0.15	0.10	0.10	0.10	0.10
Payout Ratio	139%	NM	38%	23%	18%	19%	11%	23%	26%	10%
Prices:High	23.66	22.41	30.61	32.34	40.10	30.00	36.10	35.12	39.61	48.00
Prices:Low	17.50	9.68	10.29	23.50	25.63	23.75	27.07	19.98	19.43	25.76
P/E Ratio:High	54	NM	26	25	32	37	39	80	NM	47
P/E Ratio:Low	40	NM	22	18	20	29	29	45	50	25

Income Statement Analysis (Million $)	2010	2009	2008	2007	2006	2005	2004	2003	2002	2001
Revenue	3,007	2,582	3,328	3,266	2,861	2,549	2,247	1,843	1,712	2,366
Operating Income	521	321	599	596	552	481	450	-120	324	498
Depreciation	239	252	252	238	215	231	228	229	224	218
Interest Expense	5.42	Nil	Nil	Nil	Nil	Nil	Nil	Nil	Nil	Nil
Pretax Income	131	-319	339	338	329	217	240	110	93.2	291
Effective Tax Rate	NA	NM	36.4%	28.8%	28.0%	28.8%	26.5%	22.5%	17.9%	30.0%
Net Income	76.9	-321	215	241	237	154	176	84.9	76.5	204
S&P Core Earnings	77.3	-62.1	205	241	238	143	164	76.1	76.7	200

Balance Sheet & Other Financial Data (Million $)	2010	2009	2008	2007	2006	2005	2004	2003	2002	2001
Cash	395	468	510	461	486	498	339	350	313	208
Current Assets	1,776	1,448	1,783	1,591	1,548	1,374	1,169	962	915	892
Total Assets	3,237	2,942	3,600	3,316	2,973	2,728	2,572	2,335	2,254	2,214
Current Liabilities	913	714	649	531	595	470	428	356	360	374
Long Term Debt	183	30.3	146	128	8.81	9.98	14.0	16.9	17.8	25.5
Common Equity	1,985	2,063	2,677	2,523	2,281	2,168	2,066	1,897	1,828	1,766
Total Capital	2,273	2,093	2,823	2,651	2,290	2,180	2,081	1,914	1,846	1,793
Capital Expenditures	229	178	235	297	277	231	190	171	172	376
Cash Flow	316	-69.4	468	479	452	385	404	314	300	422
Current Ratio	2.0	2.0	2.8	3.0	2.6	2.9	2.7	2.7	2.5	2.4
% Long Term Debt of Capitalization	8.1	1.5	5.2	4.8	0.4	0.5	0.7	0.9	1.0	1.4
% Net Income of Revenue	2.6	NM	6.5	7.4	8.3	6.1	7.8	4.6	4.5	8.6
% Return on Assets	2.5	NM	6.2	7.7	8.3	5.8	7.2	3.7	3.4	9.1
% Return on Equity	3.8	NM	8.3	10.0	10.7	7.3	8.9	4.6	4.3	11.7

Data as orig reptd.; bef. results of disc opers/spec. items. Per share data adj. for stk. divs.; EPS diluted. E-Estimated. NA-Not Available. NM-Not Meaningful. NR-Not Ranked. UR-Under Review.

Office: 2222 Wellington Court, Lisle, IL 60532.
Telephone: 630-969-4550.
Website: http://www.molex.com
Co-Chrmn: J.H. Krehbiel, Jr.

Co-Chrmn: F.A. Krehbiel
Pres & COO: L. McCarthy
Vice Chrmn & CEO: M.P. Slark
EVP, CFO & Treas: D.D. Johnson

Investor Contact: S. Martens (630-527-4344)
Board Members: M. J. Birck, M. L. Collins, A. Dhebar, E. D. Jannotta, F. L. Krehbiel, F. A. Krehbiel, J. H. Krehbiel Jr., D. L. Landsittel, J. W. Laymon, D. G. Lubin, J. S. Metcalf, R. J. Potter, M. P. Slark

Founded: 1938
Domicile: Delaware
Employees: 35,519

Molson Coors Brewing Co

STANDARD &POOR'S

S&P Recommendation	HOLD ★★★☆☆	Price	12-Mo. Target Price	Investment Style
		$48.53 (as of Oct 22, 2010)	$50.00	Large-Cap Blend

GICS Sector Consumer Staples
Sub-Industry Brewers

Summary TAP, the fifth largest brewer in the world, was formed in early 2005 via the combination of Adolph Coors Co. and Molson, Inc.

Key Stock Statistics (Source S&P, Vickers, company reports)

52-Wk Range	$51.33–38.44	S&P Oper. EPS 2010E	3.40	Market Capitalization(B)	$7.809	Beta	0.78
Trailing 12-Month EPS	$4.28	S&P Oper. EPS 2011E	3.70	Yield (%)	2.31	S&P 3-Yr. Proj. EPS CAGR(%)	8
Trailing 12-Month P/E	11.3	P/E on S&P Oper. EPS 2010E	14.3	Dividend Rate/Share	$1.12	S&P Credit Rating	BBB-
$10K Invested 5 Yrs Ago	$17,508	Common Shares Outstg. (M)	185.9	Institutional Ownership (%)	85		

Price Performance

30-Week Mov. Avg. · · · 10-Week Mov. Avg. - - GAAP Earnings vs. Previous Year Volume Above Avg. STARS
12-Mo. Target Price — Relative Strength ▲ Up ▼ Down ▶ No Change Below Avg. ★

2-for-1

2007 2008 2009 2010

Options: CBOE, P, Ph

Analysis prepared by **Esther Y. Kwon, CFA** on August 10, 2010, when the stock traded at **$ 45.89**.

Highlights

➤ In June 2008, TAP combined its U.S. operations in a joint venture with SABMiller, with accounting on an equity interest basis. By pooling breweries, distribution resources and brand marketing, the companies believe they can achieve $500 million of cost synergies annually in three years.

➤ In 2010, we see sales rising at a high single digit rate, after falling more than 35% in 2009 as a result of the joint venture. We expect continued growth for Coors Light, Blue Moon and Keystone Light in the U.S., partially offsetting volume drops for Miller brands. We look for continued pressures in the U.K. market to hurt overall sales growth and margins, but we expect improvement in Canadian operations on new product line extensions and further penetration of existing brands into new geographies. On a new $200 million cost savings plan, we look for operating margin improvement, and we forecast a high-single digit improvement in MillerCoors equity income.

➤ On an effective tax rate of 16%, compared to slightly over 1% in 2009, we estimate 2010 operating EPS of $3.40, before special items, versus 2008's adjusted $3.80.

Investment Rationale/Risk

➤ We remain concerned about raw material inflation, particularly in Canada and the U.K., where TAP has limited ability to hedge, despite recent declines in key commodities. While volumes recently improved in Canada on narrowing price gaps and new product introductions, we look for weakness in U.S. operations as Miller brand volumes remain soft and Coors Light volumes have recently turned negative. We expect U.K. results to be under pressure as sales shift to lower-margin off-premise channels, but we consider TAP's valuation -- at a discount to peers -- to be reasonable.

➤ Risks to our opinion and target price include a weakening of Coors Light volumes in the U.S. and Canada, an inability to successfully raise prices, and heightened competitive pressures, particularly in Canada. Commodity cost increases could pose additional risks. We see significant execution risk in the joint venture.

➤ Our 12-month target price of $50 is based on our P/E analysis. We apply a multiple of 13.5X, below both TAP's recent average and the beverage group multiple, to our 2011 EPS estimate.

Qualitative Risk Assessment

LOW	MEDIUM	HIGH

Our risk assessment reflects the stable revenue streams of the brewing industry, in which TAP is a major player, offset by our corporate governance concerns with respect to TAP's multi-class stock structure and its more than 50% controlling family interest.

Quantitative Evaluations

S&P Quality Ranking A-

D	C	B-	B	B+	A-	A	A+

Relative Strength Rank MODERATE

61

LOWEST = 1 HIGHEST = 99

Revenue/Earnings Data

Revenue (Million $)

	1Q	2Q	3Q	4Q	Year
2010	661.0	883.3	--	--	--
2009	559.0	798.9	853.7	820.8	3,032
2008	1,357	1,757	921.1	739.2	4,774
2007	1,229	1,676	1,685	1,600	6,191
2006	1,154	1,583	1,577	1,531	5,845
2005	1,048	1,547	1,527	1,385	5,507

Earnings Per Share ($)

2010	0.33	1.27	E1.11	E0.66	E3.40
2009	0.43	1.01	1.31	1.17	3.92
2008	0.25	0.50	0.92	0.49	2.16
2007	0.11	1.02	0.74	0.96	2.84
2006	-0.11	0.91	0.71	0.65	2.16
2005	-0.24	0.56	0.76	0.20	1.44

Fiscal year ended Dec. 31. Next earnings report expected: Early November. EPS Estimates based on S&P Operating Earnings; historical GAAP earnings are as reported.

Dividend Data (Dates: mm/dd Payment Date: mm/dd/yy)

Amount ($)	Date Decl.	Ex-Div. Date	Stk. of Record	Payment Date
0.240	11/12	11/25	11/30	12/15/09
0.240	02/11	02/24	02/26	03/15/10
0.280	05/03	05/26	05/28	06/15/10
0.280	08/05	08/27	08/31	09/15/10

Dividends have been paid since 1970. Source: Company reports.

Please read the Required Disclosures and Analyst Certification on the last page of this report.

The McGraw-Hill Companies

Molson Coors Brewing Co

Business Summary August 10, 2010

CORPORATE OVERVIEW. Molson Coors Brewing Company was formed in February 2005 by the combination of Adolph Coors Co. and Canadian brewer Molson, Inc. The transaction resulted in each Molson Class B voting share being converted to shares with 0.126 voting rights and 0.234 non-voting rights of Molson Coors stock, and each Molson Class A converted to shares with a 0.360 non-voting share of Molson Coors. In June 2008, Molson Coors and SABMiller formed a joint venture of each company's United States and Puerto Rican operations. The deal gave TAP a 50% voting and 42% economic interest.

Molson Inc. was the world's 14th largest brewer in 2004, pre-merger, with operations in Canada, Brazil and the United States. A global brewer with C$3.5 billion in gross annual sales, Molson traces its roots back to 1786, making it North America's oldest beer brand. Adolph Coors Co. was the third largest U.S. brewer, with a 10.3% share of the U.S. beer market in 2004, selling 32.7 million barrels of beer and other malt beverage products, up 3% from the level of 2003. The company was founded in 1873.

TAP has a portfolio of over 65 strategic brands, including core brands Coors Light, Molson Canadian and Carling. In Canada, brands sold include Coors Light, Canadian, Export, Molson Canadian 67, Molson Dry , Molson M,

Creemore, Rickard's Red and other Rickard's brands, Carling, and Pilsner. In the U.S., key brands sold through MillerCoors include Coors Light and Miller Lite. Premium segment brands include Coors Banquet, Miller Genuine Draft and MGD 64, while super premium brands include Miller Chill and Sparks. Below premium brands include Miller High Life, Keystone Light and Milwaukee's Best, while craft and import brands include Blue Moon, Henry Weinhard's, George Killian's Irish Red, Leinenkugel's brands, Molson brands, Foster's, Peroni Nastro Azzurro, Pilsner Urquell and Grolsch. U.K. brands include Carling, C2, Coors Light, Worthington's, While Shield, Caffrey's, Kasteel Cru and Blue Moon.

CORPORATE STRATEGY. We look favorably on TAP's strategy to gain market share in each area by cross marketing its products. We are particularly pleased with the gains we see for Coors Light in Canada, where it now has a 14% market share according to TAP, making it among the best-selling beer brands in that country.

Company Financials Fiscal Year Ended Dec. 31

Per Share Data ($)	2009	2008	2007	2006	2005	2004	2003	2002	2001	2000
Tangible Book Value	5.77	4.13	NM	NM	NM	1.72	NM	NM	12.03	12.16
Cash Flow	4.93	3.63	4.74	4.68	3.89	6.13	5.71	5.36	3.28	3.19
Earnings	3.92	2.16	2.84	2.16	1.44	2.60	2.39	2.21	1.66	1.47
S&P Core Earnings	3.74	1.03	2.53	1.87	1.07	2.13	2.10	0.77	0.68	NA
Dividends	0.92	0.76	0.64	0.64	0.64	0.41	0.41	0.41	0.40	0.36
Payout Ratio	23%	35%	23%	31%	44%	16%	17%	19%	24%	25%
Prices:High	51.33	59.51	57.70	38.50	40.00	40.06	32.41	35.08	40.59	41.16
Prices:Low	30.76	35.00	37.56	30.38	28.69	26.87	22.93	25.25	21.33	18.69
P/E Ratio:High	13	28	20	18	28	15	14	16	25	28
P/E Ratio:Low	8	16	13	15	20	10	10	11	13	13

Income Statement Analysis (Million $)	2009	2008	2007	2006	2005	2004	2003	2002	2001	2000
Revenue	3,032	4,774	6,191	5,845	5,507	4,306	4,000	3,776	2,429	2,414
Operating Income	592	874	1,099	1,097	960	609	551	535	296	295
Depreciation	187	273	346	438	393	268	244	230	121	129
Interest Expense	96.6	104	136	143	131	72.4	81.2	70.9	2.01	6.41
Pretax Income	718	515	534	472	295	308	254	257	198	170
Effective Tax Rate	NM	20.0%	0.78%	17.5%	17.0%	30.9%	31.2%	37.0%	37.9%	35.3%
Net Income	729	400	515	374	230	197	175	162	123	110
S&P Core Earnings	695	190	459	324	172	161	154	56.1	50.7	NA

Balance Sheet & Other Financial Data (Million $)	2009	2008	2007	2006	2005	2004	2003	2002	2001	2000
Cash	734	216	377	182	39.4	123	19.4	59.2	310	120
Current Assets	1,763	1,107	1,777	1,458	1,468	1,268	1,079	1,054	607	498
Total Assets	12,021	10,417	13,452	11,603	11,799	4,658	4,486	4,297	1,740	1,629
Current Liabilities	1,581	986	1,736	1,800	2,237	1,177	1,134	1,148	518	379
Long Term Debt	1,413	1,832	2,261	2,130	2,137	894	1,160	1,383	20.0	105
Common Equity	7,080	5,980	7,149	5,817	5,325	1,601	1,267	982	951	932
Total Capital	8,806	7,822	10,059	8,601	8,151	2,682	2,623	2,522	1,033	1,127
Capital Expenditures	125	231	428	446	406	212	240	240	245	154
Cash Flow	917	674	861	812	623	465	418	392	244	239
Current Ratio	1.1	1.1	1.0	0.8	0.7	1.1	1.0	0.9	1.2	1.3
% Long Term Debt of Capitalization	16.0	23.4	22.5	24.8	26.2	33.3	44.2	54.9	1.9	9.3
% Net Income of Revenue	24.1	8.4	8.3	6.4	4.2	4.6	4.4	4.3	5.1	4.5
% Return on Assets	6.5	3.4	4.1	3.2	2.8	4.3	4.0	5.4	7.3	6.9
% Return on Equity	11.2	6.1	7.9	6.7	6.7	13.7	15.5	16.7	13.1	12.4

Data as orig reptd.; bef. results of disc opers/spec. items. Per share data adj. for stk. divs.; EPS diluted. E-Estimated. NA-Not Available. NM-Not Meaningful. NR-Not Ranked. UR-Under Review.

Office: 1225 17th St, Denver, CO 80202-5534.
Telephone: 303-279-6565.
Website: http://www.molsoncoors.com
Chrmn: P.H. Coors

Pres & CEO: P.S. Swinburn
Vice Chrmn: A.T. Molson
CFO: S. Glendinning
Chief Acctg Officer & Cntlr: W.G. Waters

Investor Contact: D. Dunnewald (303-279-6565)
Board Members: F. Bellini, R. Brewer, J. E. Cleghorn, C. C. Coors, P. H. Coors, R. Hargrow, C. M. Herington, F. W. Hobbs, A. T. Molson, E. H. Molson, G. E. Molson, I. Napier, D. P. Obrien, H. S. Riley, P. S. Swinburn

Founded: 1873
Domicile: Delaware
Employees: 14,540

Monsanto Co

STANDARD &POOR'S

S&P Recommendation HOLD ★★★☆☆	**Price** $57.15 (as of Oct 22, 2010)	**12-Mo. Target Price** $55.00

Investment Style
Large-Cap Blend

GICS Sector Materials
Sub-Industry Fertilizers & Agricultural Chemicals

Summary This company is a global provider of agricultural products and integrated solutions for farmers.

Key Stock Statistics (Source S&P, Vickers, company reports)

52-Wk Range	$87.06– 44.61	S&P Oper. EPS 2011E	2.90	Market Capitalization(B)	$30.887	Beta		0.79
Trailing 12-Month EPS	$2.01	S&P Oper. EPS 2012E	NA	Yield (%)	1.96	S&P 3-Yr. Proj. EPS CAGR(%)		12
Trailing 12-Month P/E	28.4	P/E on S&P Oper. EPS 2011E	19.7	Dividend Rate/Share	$1.12	S&P Credit Rating		A+
$10K Invested 5 Yrs Ago	$20,460	Common Shares Outstg. (M)	540.5	Institutional Ownership (%)	75			

Price Performance

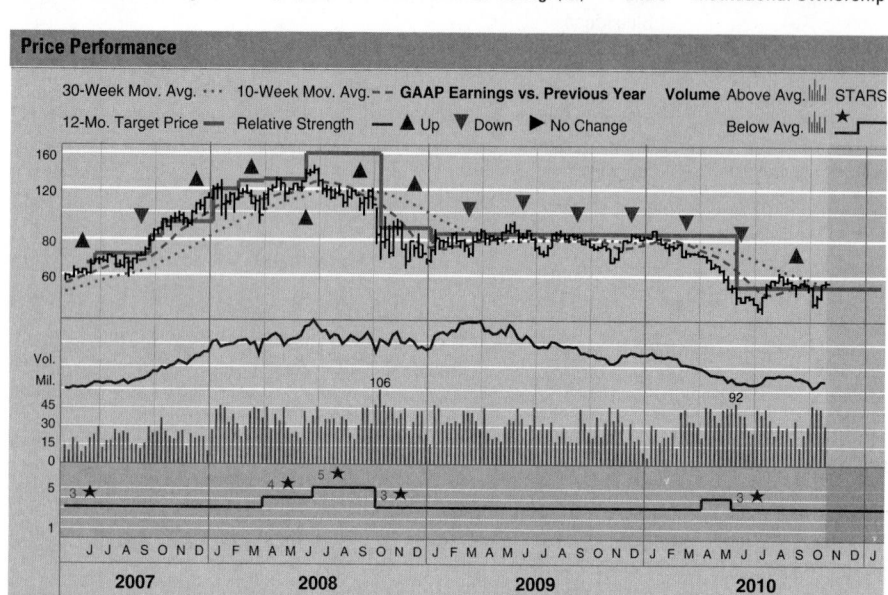

30-Week Mov. Avg. · · · · 10-Week Mov. Avg. – – **GAAP Earnings vs. Previous Year** Volume Above Avg. STARS
12-Mo. Target Price — Relative Strength — ▲ Up ▼ Down ► No Change Below Avg. ★

Options: ASE, CBOE, P

Analysis prepared by **Kevin Kirkeby** on October 12, 2010, when the stock traded at **$ 51.83.**

Highlights

➤ Following a 10% revenue decline in FY 10 (Aug.), we look for a 9% increase for FY 11. In our view, revenues will largely be driven by volume gains and a shift in mix as the latest generation of seeds are rolled out. Still, MON's strategic shift last year toward offering greater seed/trait variety and a larger number of price points will, in our view, lead to flat pricing, on average. For Roundup, we expect sales to be flat in FY 11 with volume gains balancing out lower prices after MON had to sharply cut prices during FY 10 in response to aggressive tactics by competitors.

➤ With initiatives already under way to lower production costs in its Roundup unit, we think MON will also be more aggressive in managing corporate overhead in the coming year. On this and a shift in the sales mix toward more value-added seeds, we see margins widening in FY 11. We think there is an overhang of higher-cost inventories that will pressure margins in early FY 11, but that will likely be cleared out with the spring planting season.

➤ Our EPS estimate for FY 11 of $2.90 does not include further restructuring charges, nor does it build in additional stock buybacks.

Investment Rationale/Risk

➤ MON shares trade at a valuation premium to the S&P 500, reflecting what we see as its above-average earnings growth prospects. We forecast primary contributors being the introduction of next-generation seeds, and development of its smaller product segments. Even so, we believe the combination of a highly competitive glyphosate market and increased regulatory scrutiny will offset the favorable growth prospects for its seeds/traits segment, and warrants a below-average valuation.

➤ Risks to our recommendation and target price include below peer-average yield performance from its latest seeds, expansion of antitrust investigations, continued glyphosate oversupply, and a decline in grain prices.

➤ Our DCF model, which assumes a 10.3% cost of equity and annual free cash flow growth averaging 10% for five years, slowing to 4% terminal growth thereafter, calculates intrinsic value near $61. Our relative valuation model targets a four-quarter forward P/E multiple of 17.0X, which is below the 10-year historical average, and produces a value of about $49. Blending these two metrics results in our 12-month target price of $55.

Qualitative Risk Assessment

LOW	**MEDIUM**	HIGH

Our risk assessment reflects MON's exposure to global agricultural markets and currencies, adverse weather, unfavorable legal and regulatory developments, and risks relating to the enforcement of intellectual property rights. This is offset by relatively low exposure to economic cycles and our view of consistent cash flow generation.

Quantitative Evaluations

S&P Quality Ranking B+

D	C	B-	B	**B+**	A-	A	A+

Relative Strength Rank MODERATE

61

LOWEST = 1 HIGHEST = 99

Revenue/Earnings Data

Revenue (Million $)

	1Q	2Q	3Q	4Q	Year
2010	1,697	3,890	2,962	1,953	10,502
2009	2,649	4,035	3,161	1,879	11,724
2008	2,049	3,727	3,538	2,051	11,365
2007	1,539	2,609	2,842	1,573	8,563
2006	1,405	2,200	2,348	1,391	7,344
2005	1,072	1,908	2,040	1,274	6,294

Earnings Per Share ($)

2010	-0.04	1.60	0.70	-0.26	2.01
2009	0.98	1.97	1.25	-0.43	3.78
2008	0.45	2.00	1.46	-0.32	3.59
2007	0.17	0.99	1.02	-0.52	1.66
2006	0.11	0.80	0.61	-0.25	1.27
2005	-0.24	0.68	0.08	-0.24	0.29

Fiscal year ended Aug. 31. Next earnings report expected: Mid December. EPS Estimates based on S&P Operating Earnings; historical GAAP earnings are as reported.

Dividend Data (Dates: mm/dd Payment Date: mm/dd/yy)

Amount ($)	Date Decl.	Ex-Div. Date	Stk. of Record	Payment Date
0.265	12/07	01/06	01/08	01/29/10
0.265	01/26	04/07	04/09	04/30/10
0.265	06/09	07/07	07/09	07/30/10
0.280	08/04	10/06	10/08	10/29/10

Dividends have been paid since 2001. Source: Company reports.

Monsanto Co

Business Summary October 12, 2010

CORPORATE OVERVIEW. Monsanto (MON) produces leading seed brands and develops biotechnology traits that assist farmers in controlling insects and weeds, and provides other seed companies with genetic material and biotech traits. MON's Roundup herbicides are used for agricultural, industrial and residential weed control, and are sold in more than 80 countries.

MARKET PROFILE. The company operates in two segments: agricultural productivity, and seeds and genomics. Agricultural productivity (28% of sales and 11% of gross profits in FY 10 (Aug.)) consists of MON's crop protection products (Roundup herbicide and other glyphosate products), its animal agriculture business, and the Roundup lawn and garden products. In FY 10, Roundup and other glyphosate-based herbicides accounted for 19% of total sales, down from 30% in FY 09. Patent protection for the active ingredient in Roundup herbicides expired in the U.S. in 2000. MON repositioned itself as one of the lowest cost producers, while still working to retain the higher pricing afforded a premium brand. Still, selling prices came under renewed pressure during FY 10 as global production of generic glyphosate rose. This forced MON to cut prices sharply and initiate a new round of restructuring. We think this division will contribute just 18% of sales in FY 11 as the impact of the low-er pricing offsets a partial recovery in volumes.

Seeds and genomics (72% of sales and 89% of gross profits) consists of the global seeds and related traits businesses, and technology platforms based on plant genomics, which increases the speed and power of genetic research. MON's seeds and genomics segment focuses on corn, soybeans and other oilseeds, cotton and wheat. Given the loss of patent protection for Roundup, we believe MON has focused on capturing value and profitability in its patent-protected seeds and traits business, and expanded its product line through its acquisition of Seminis in 2005 and De Ruiter in 2008, among other smaller purchases. De Ruiter is a leader in the protected-culture segment of the vegetable seeds market, where MON had little presence. Given this trend, we think that the growth and margin outlook for MON's seeds and genomics segment is superior to that of its agricultural productivity segment.

Company Financials Fiscal Year Ended Aug. 31

Per Share Data ($)	2010	2009	2008	2007	2006	2005	2004	2003	2002	2001
Tangible Book Value	NA	10.02	8.59	6.35	6.95	5.99	7.71	7.26	7.24	7.84
Cash Flow	3.10	4.77	4.61	2.61	2.25	1.21	1.37	0.56	1.12	1.61
Earnings	2.01	3.78	3.59	1.66	1.27	0.29	0.51	-0.02	0.25	0.57
S&P Core Earnings	NA	3.60	3.27	1.72	1.36	0.67	0.68	0.61	0.01	0.52
Dividends	1.06	1.01	0.77	0.48	0.39	0.33	0.27	0.25	0.24	0.23
Payout Ratio	53%	27%	21%	29%	30%	113%	53%	NM	98%	40%
Prices:High	87.06	93.35	145.80	116.25	53.49	39.93	28.22	14.45	17.00	19.40
Prices:Low	44.61	66.57	63.47	49.10	37.91	25.00	14.04	6.78	6.60	13.44
P/E Ratio:High	43	25	41	70	42	NM	55	NM	69	34
P/E Ratio:Low	22	18	18	30	30	86	28	NM	27	24

Income Statement Analysis (Million $)										
Revenue	10,502	11,724	11,365	8,563	7,344	6,294	5,457	3,373	4,673	5,462
Operating Income	2,533	4,161	3,458	2,138	1,694	1,503	1,254	768	882	1,335
Depreciation	602	548	573	527	519	488	452	302	460	554
Interest Expense	162	163	132	139	134	115	91.0	57.0	59.0	99.0
Pretax Income	1,494	2,967	2,926	1,336	1,055	261	402	-38.0	202	463
Effective Tax Rate	NA	28.5%	30.7%	30.1%	32.2%	39.8%	32.6%	NM	36.1%	35.9%
Net Income	1,105	2,098	2,007	922	698	157	271	-11.0	129	297
S&P Core Earnings	NA	1,997	1,830	951	745	363	362	317	5.45	277

Balance Sheet & Other Financial Data (Million $)										
Cash	1,485	1,956	1,613	866	1,460	525	1,037	511	428	307
Current Assets	7,172	7,883	7,609	5,084	5,461	4,644	4,931	4,962	4,424	4,797
Total Assets	17,917	17,874	17,993	12,983	11,728	10,579	9,164	9,461	8,890	11,429
Current Liabilities	3,587	3,756	4,439	3,075	2,279	2,159	1,894	1,944	1,810	2,377
Long Term Debt	1,862	1,724	1,792	1,150	1,639	1,458	1,075	1,258	851	893
Common Equity	10,099	10,056	9,374	7,503	6,680	5,613	5,258	5,156	5,180	7,483
Total Capital	12,005	11,780	11,370	8,653	8,319	7,071	6,333	6,414	6,031	8,376
Capital Expenditures	755	916	918	509	370	281	210	114	224	382
Cash Flow	1,707	2,646	2,580	1,449	1,217	645	723	291	589	851
Current Ratio	2.0	2.1	1.7	1.7	2.4	2.2	2.6	2.6	2.4	2.0
% Long Term Debt of Capitalization	15.5	14.6	15.8	13.3	19.7	20.6	17.0	19.6	14.1	10.7
% Net Income of Revenue	10.5	17.9	17.7	10.8	9.5	2.5	5.0	NM	2.8	5.4
% Return on Assets	6.2	11.7	13.0	7.5	6.3	1.6	2.9	NM	1.3	2.6
% Return on Equity	11.0	21.6	23.8	13.0	11.2	2.9	5.2	NM	2.0	4.0

Data as orig reptd.; bef. results of disc opers/spec. items. Per share data adj. for stk. divs.; EPS diluted. E-Estimated. NA-Not Available. NM-Not Meaningful. NR-Not Ranked. UR-Under Review.

Office: 800 North Lindbergh Boulevard, St. Louis, MO 63167-0001.
Telephone: 314-694-1000.
Email: info@monsanto.com
Website: http://www.monsanto.com

Chrmn, Pres & CEO: H. Grant
EVP & CFO: C.M. Casale
EVP & CTO: R.T. Fraley
SVP, Secy & General Counsel: D.F. Snively

Treas: T.D. Hartley
Investor Contact: S.L. Foster (314-694-8148)
Board Members: F. V. AtLee, III, J. W. Bachmann, D. L. Chicoine, J. Fields, H. Grant, A. H. Harper, G. S. King, C. S. McMillan, W. U. Parfet, G. H. Poste, B. Stevens

Founded: 2000
Domicile: Delaware
Employees: 27,000

Monster Worldwide Inc

STANDARD &POOR'S

S&P Recommendation BUY ★★★★☆	**Price** $14.13 (as of Oct 22, 2010)	**12-Mo. Target Price** $18.00	**Investment Style** Large-Cap Blend

GICS Sector Information Technology
Sub-Industry Internet Software & Services

Summary Monster Worldwide operates a multinational online career network. It also provides offerings to help consumers develop and direct their careers.

Key Stock Statistics (Source S&P, Vickers, company reports)

52-Wk Range	$19.10–10.01	S&P Oper. EPS 2010E	-0.05	Market Capitalization(B)	$1.834	Beta		2.16
Trailing 12-Month EPS	$0.03	S&P Oper. EPS 2011E	0.40	Yield (%)	Nil	S&P 3-Yr. Proj. EPS CAGR(%)		171
Trailing 12-Month P/E	NM	P/E on S&P Oper. EPS 2010E	NM	Dividend Rate/Share	Nil	S&P Credit Rating		NA
$10K Invested 5 Yrs Ago	$4,670	Common Shares Outstg. (M)	129.8	Institutional Ownership (%)	99			

Price Performance

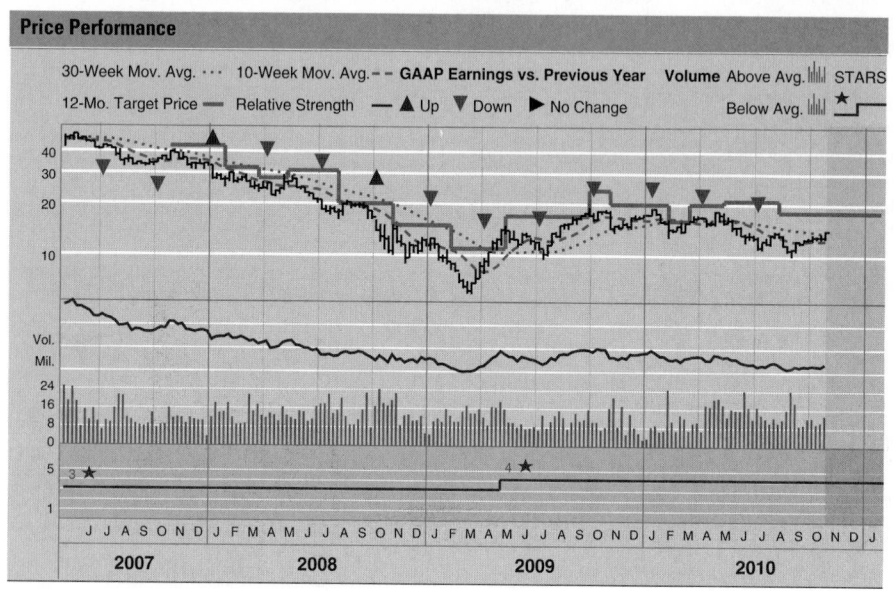

30-Week Mov. Avg. · · · 10-Week Mov. Avg. - - **GAAP Earnings vs. Previous Year** Volume Above Avg. STARS
12-Mo. Target Price — Relative Strength — ▲ Up ▼ Down ► No Change Below Avg. ★

Options: ASE, CBOE, P

Analysis prepared by **Michael W. Jaffe** on August 04, 2010, when the stock traded at **$13.84**.

Highlights

➤ We expect a 1% rise in revenues in 2010, followed by a 15% gain in 2011. Revenues have been much lower for the past two years, as U.S. labor markets have been depressed, and major downturns were also experienced in Monster's foreign markets. However, with global economies now seemingly in the midst of recoveries, we see a healthy rise in demand for MWW's services over the coming year.

➤ We see slightly narrower net margins in 2010, on the still sluggish revenue level that we forecast and a likely increase in employee salary and benefit costs (on improving trends in contract bookings). We expect margins to improve in 2011, largely on our outlook for better revenue trends. We also see margins in both years being aided by some likely incremental benefits from MWW's restructuring program, completed in mid-2009, which we believe has brought considerable cost control discipline.

➤ Our 2011 forecast compares with a 2010 forecast that excludes $0.08 a share of one-time charges in the year's first half. Our forecasts will not incorporate the planned acquisition of Yahoo! HotJobs until the deal closes (expected in 2010's third quarter).

Investment Rationale/Risk

➤ We think that a likely ongoing recovery of global economies will allow Monster's business to rebound in coming periods. We also have a positive view of MWW's pending acquisition of Yahoo! HotJobs, as we think Monster will derive a substantial benefit from having access to Yahoo's vast traffic network. Moreover, we have been impressed by MWW's aggressive actions to operate more efficiently and rein in costs. Based on these factors and our valuation model, we find the shares undervalued.

➤ Risks to our recommendation and target price include weaker-than-projected global labor markets, and less than expected success in MWW's restructuring initiatives.

➤ MWW's business is highly cyclical, as evidenced by the sharp downturn in its results over the past couple of years. Yet, it typically records growth above that of peers. On these views, we think MWW is undervalued. Our 12-month target price is $18, or 45X our 2011 EPS estimate, which is in the top half of MWW's historical range. We think that valuation is merited by our belief that MWW is poised for a strong business rebound once a labor recovery takes place.

Qualitative Risk Assessment

LOW	MEDIUM	**HIGH**

Our risk assessment reflects the cyclicality of the help wanted industry, as it strongly correlates with the economy. In addition, foreign operations carry operating and exchange rate risks.

Quantitative Evaluations

S&P Quality Ranking B-

D	C	**B-**	B	B+	A-	A	A+

Relative Strength Rank STRONG
83
LOWEST = 1   HIGHEST = 99

Revenue/Earnings Data

Revenue (Million $)

	1Q	2Q	3Q	4Q	Year
2010	215.3	214.9	--	--	--
2009	254.4	223.1	214.5	213.2	905.1
2008	366.5	354.3	332.2	290.7	1,344
2007	329.0	331.2	337.1	354.0	1,351
2006	257.0	275.2	285.9	298.6	1,117
2005	232.1	239.0	249.3	266.6	986.9

Earnings Per Share ($)

2010	-0.20	-0.02	E0.02	E0.07	E-0.05
2009	-0.09	-0.01	0.27	-0.02	0.16
2008	0.19	0.15	0.36	0.24	0.94
2007	0.30	0.21	0.25	0.36	1.13
2006	0.26	0.29	0.31	0.31	1.17
2005	0.19	0.21	0.25	0.28	0.92

Fiscal year ended Dec. 31. Next earnings report expected: Late October. EPS Estimates based on S&P Operating Earnings; historical GAAP earnings are as reported.

Dividend Data

No cash dividends have been paid.

Please read the Required Disclosures and Analyst Certification on the last page of this report.

The **McGraw·Hill** Companies

Monster Worldwide Inc

STANDARD &POOR'S

Business Summary August 04, 2010

CORPORATE OVERVIEW. Monster Worldwide is a leading online recruitment and career management services provider through its Monster.com Web site. MWW's clients range from Fortune 100 companies, to small and medium-sized enterprises and government agencies. During 2009, the company derived 45% of its revenues from its Monster Careers North America division, 40% from Monster Careers International, and 15% from its Advertising & Fees division. No client accounts for more than 5% of MWW's revenues.

Among the most visited brands on the Internet, the Monster network is designed to connect companies with qualified job seekers, offering innovative technology and services that provide greater control over the recruiting process. As of early 2010, the Monster.com network was available in about 50 countries.

Monster's job search, resume posting services and basic networking are free to the job seeker. It also offers premium career services to job seekers at a

fee, including resume writing, resume priority listing, and premium networking. MWW charges a fee to employers and human resources professionals who want to post jobs, search its resume database, and use its career site hosting and other ancillary services.

The company's Internet Advertising & Fees division provides consumers with content, services and offers, to help them manage the development and direction of their current and future careers. The majority of its services are free to users and are primarily available in North America at present, although MWW plans to expand its offerings across its global network. Revenues for the division are derived mostly from lead generation, display advertising, and products sold to consumers for a fee.

Company Financials Fiscal Year Ended Dec. 31

Per Share Data ($)	2009	2008	2007	2006	2005	2004	2003	2002	2001	2000
Tangible Book Value	1.37	0.85	3.97	3.65	1.47	0.27	0.18	2.02	2.61	5.16
Cash Flow	0.72	1.42	1.49	1.47	1.22	0.92	0.31	-0.46	1.28	1.11
Earnings	0.16	0.94	1.13	1.17	0.92	0.62	0.06	-0.96	0.61	0.53
S&P Core Earnings	0.12	1.16	1.13	1.17	0.47	0.37	-0.08	-1.48	0.10	NA
Dividends	Nil	Nil	Nil	Nil	Nil	Nil	Nil	Nil	Nil	Nil
Payout Ratio	Nil	Nil	Nil	Nil	Nil	Nil	Nil	Nil	Nil	Nil
Prices:High	19.28	32.66	54.79	59.99	42.03	34.25	29.65	48.13	68.73	94.69
Prices:Low	5.95	8.91	31.07	34.75	22.44	17.60	7.63	7.94	25.21	45.00
P/E Ratio:High	NM	35	48	51	46	55	NM	NM	NM	NM
P/E Ratio:Low	NM	9	27	30	24	28	NM	NM	NM	NM

Income Statement Analysis (Million $)										
Revenue	905	1,344	1,351	1,117	987	846	680	1,115	1,448	1,292
Operating Income	72.6	284	303	270	214	152	101	112	262	222
Depreciation	68.5	58.0	47.0	39.8	38.0	37.6	28.0	55.5	76.0	62.6
Interest Expense	1.43	NA	Nil	Nil	Nil	Nil	Nil	4.90	10.6	9.49
Pretax Income	-19.0	179	232	241	179	112	23.6	-130	125	114
Effective Tax Rate	199.9%	36.2%	36.5%	36.3%	35.8%	34.6%	69.0%	NM	46.1%	50.5%
Net Income	18.9	114	147	154	115	73.1	7.32	-107	69.0	56.9
S&P Core Earnings	14.5	141	147	154	59.2	44.0	-8.08	-165	11.4	NA

Balance Sheet & Other Financial Data (Million $)										
Cash	285	224	578	58.7	320	198	142	192	341	572
Current Assets	645	683	1,185	1,124	773	704	567	809	1,006	1,248
Total Assets	1,827	1,917	2,078	1,970	1,679	1,544	1,122	1,631	2,206	1,992
Current Liabilities	507	724	829	826	697	731	640	799	930	853
Long Term Debt	45.0	0.01	0.23	0.42	15.7	34.0	2.09	3.93	9.13	28.0
Common Equity	1,133	1,047	1,117	1,110	920	756	468	813	1,229	1,058
Total Capital	1,183	1,072	1,136	1,143	981	789	470	817	1,238	1,086
Capital Expenditures	48.7	93.6	64.1	55.6	39.8	24.3	21.6	46.7	73.6	78.9
Cash Flow	87.5	173	194	193	153	111	35.4	-51.0	145	119
Current Ratio	1.3	0.9	1.4	1.4	1.1	1.0	0.9	1.0	1.1	1.5
% Long Term Debt of Capitalization	3.8	Nil	0.0	0.0	1.6	4.3	0.4	0.5	0.7	2.6
% Net Income of Revenue	2.1	8.5	10.9	13.8	11.7	8.6	1.1	NM	4.8	4.4
% Return on Assets	1.0	5.7	7.3	8.4	7.1	5.5	0.5	NM	3.2	3.7
% Return on Equity	1.7	10.6	13.2	15.0	13.7	11.9	1.1	NM	6.0	8.2

Data as orig reptd.; bef. results of disc opers/spec. items. Per share data adj. for stk. divs.; EPS diluted. E-Estimated. NA-Not Available. NM-Not Meaningful. NR-Not Ranked. UR-Under Review.

Office: 622 Third Ave, New York, NY 10017-6707.
Telephone: 212-351-7000.
Email:
corporate.communications@monsterworldwide.com
Website: http://www.monsterworldwide.com

Chrmn, Pres & CEO: S. Iannuzzi
EVP & CFO: T.T. Yates
EVP & Chief Admin Officer: L. Poulos
EVP, Secy & General Counsel: M.C. Miller

EVP & CIO: D. Dejanovic
Investor Contact: T.T. Yates
Board Members: R. J. Chrenc, J. R. Gaulding, E. P. Giambastiani, Jr., S. Iannuzzi, C. P. McCague, J. F. Rayport, R. Tunioli, T. T. Yates

Founded: 1967
Domicile: Delaware
Employees: 5,700

The McGraw-Hill Companies

Moody's Corp.

S&P Recommendation	HOLD ★★★☆☆	Price $26.84 (as of Oct 22, 2010)	12-Mo. Target Price $23.00	Investment Style Large-Cap Growth

GICS Sector Financials
Sub-Industry Specialized Finance

Summary Moody's is a leading global credit rating, research and risk analysis concern.

Key Stock Statistics (Source S&P, Vickers, company reports)

52-Wk Range	$31.04– 18.50	S&P Oper. EPS 2010E	1.80	Market Capitalization(B)	$6.289	Beta	1.32
Trailing 12-Month EPS	$1.84	S&P Oper. EPS 2011E	1.90	Yield (%)	1.56	S&P 3-Yr. Proj. EPS CAGR(%)	4
Trailing 12-Month P/E	14.6	P/E on S&P Oper. EPS 2010E	14.9	Dividend Rate/Share	$0.42	S&P Credit Rating	BBB+
$10K Invested 5 Yrs Ago	$5,533	Common Shares Outstg. (M)	234.3	Institutional Ownership (%)	NM		

Price Performance

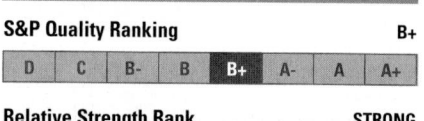

30-Week Mov. Avg. · · · 10-Week Mov. Avg. – – GAAP Earnings vs. Previous Year   Volume Above Avg. STARS
12-Mo. Target Price — Relative Strength — ▲ Up ▼ Down ► No Change   Below Avg.

2007   2008   2009   2010

Options: ASE, CBOE, P, Ph

Analysis prepared by **Royal F. Shepard, CFA** on August 13, 2010, when the stock traded at **$ 22.13**.

Highlights

► We expect a resurgence in debt issuance by U.S. corporations and financial institutions to drive revenue growth in 2010. Also, scheduled debt maturities could spark demand in the speculative grade sector. Non-U.S. demand will be more tepid, in our view, primarily due to a decline in new issuance by the European insurance and banking sectors. We project steady growth for analytical services, including risk management software. Overall, we look for a 2010 revenue increase of about 6.5%.

► Financial reform, passed by the U.S. Congress in July, will result in new rule-making and compliance standards to be implemented by the SEC. In our view, MCO will need to ramp up hiring for intensified regulatory compliance in 2010. This may include the increased documentation of ratings decisions and the use of third-party verification services where appropriate. We project about $15 million in incremental costs in 2010, increasing to an estimated $25 million in 2011.

► Our 2010 EPS estimate is $1.80, up from $1.69 in 2009. During the second quarter, MCO reactivated its $1.4 billion share repurchase program to buy back 2.8 million shares for $70 million.

Investment Rationale/Risk

► We believe MCO's credit ratings business has significant barriers to entry, which should help it maintain steady cash flow despite increased spending for regulatory compliance. We also expect growth to come from capital markets development overseas, acquisitions, and analytical services. We think the economic environment in the U.S. is beginning to improve, although the sovereign debt crisis in southern Europe could slow growth opportunities overseas. Recently passed financial reform is likely to increase regulatory scrutiny as new rules are implemented by the SEC.

► Risks to our opinion and target price include a greater-than-anticipated decline in the volume of debt issued in domestic and global capital markets, regulatory changes that increase competition, and persistently high long-term interest rates.

► Our 12-month target price of $23 is based primarily on applying an 8.0X EV/EBITDA multiple to our 2010 EBITDA estimate of $820 million. This multiple is at the low end of MCO's historical average, which we think is appropriate given an uncertain outlook for regulatory reform and potential litigation.

Qualitative Risk Assessment

LOW	MEDIUM	HIGH

Our risk assessment reflects Moody's significant market share in the high barrier-to-entry ratings industry, and what we consider the company's net positive balance sheet cash position, offset by ratings business sensitivity to higher interest rates, and the possibility of regulatory reform designed to increase competition.

Quantitative Evaluations

S&P Quality Ranking   B+

D	C	B-	B	B+	A-	A	A+

Relative Strength Rank   STRONG

78

LOWEST = 1   HIGHEST = 99

Revenue/Earnings Data

Revenue (Million $)

	1Q	2Q	3Q	4Q	Year
2010	476.6	477.8	--	--	--
2009	408.9	450.7	451.8	485.8	1,797
2008	430.7	487.6	433.4	403.7	1,755
2007	583.0	646.1	525.0	504.9	2,259
2006	440.2	511.4	495.5	590.0	2,037
2005	390.5	446.8	421.1	473.2	1,732

Earnings Per Share ($)

2010	0.47	0.51	E0.42	E0.43	E1.80
2009	0.38	0.46	0.42	0.43	1.69
2008	0.48	0.55	0.46	0.37	1.87
2007	0.62	0.95	0.51	0.49	2.58
2006	0.49	0.59	0.55	0.97	2.58
2005	0.39	0.47	0.48	0.50	1.84

Fiscal year ended Dec. 31. Next earnings report expected: Late October. EPS Estimates based on S&P Operating Earnings; historical GAAP earnings are as reported.

Dividend Data (Dates: mm/dd Payment Date: mm/dd/yy)

Amount ($)	Date Decl.	Ex-Div. Date	Stk. of Record	Payment Date
0.100	10/29	11/18	11/20	12/10/09
0.105	12/15	02/17	02/20	03/10/10
0.105	04/21	05/18	05/20	06/10/10
0.105	07/29	08/18	08/20	09/10/10

Dividends have been paid since 1934. Source: Company reports.

Please read the Required Disclosures and Analyst Certification on the last page of this report.

Moody's Corp.

STANDARD &POOR'S

Business Summary August 13, 2010

CORPORATE PROFILE. Moody's Investors Service and the Dun & Bradstreet (D&B) operating company were separated into stand-alone entities on September 30, 2000. Old D&B changed its name to Moody's Corp. (MCO), and new D&B assumed the name Dun & Bradstreet Corp. (DNB).

Moody's is a provider of credit ratings, research and analysis covering debt instruments and securities in the global capital markets, and a provider of quantitative credit assessment services, credit training services and credit process software to banks and other financial institutions. Moody's credit ratings and research help investors analyze the credit risks associated with fixed-income securities. Beyond credit rating services for issuers, Moody's provides research services, data, and analytic tools that are utilized by institutional investors and other credit and capital markets professionals.

Moody's provides ratings and credit research on governmental and commercial entities in more than 110 countries, and its customers include a wide range of corporate and governmental issuers of securities as well as institutional investors, depositors, creditors, investment banks, commercial banks, and other financial intermediaries. In 2009, 48.8% of total revenues were derived from non-U.S. markets.

Moody's operates in two reportable segments: Moody's Investors Service (MIS), and Moody's Analytics. Moody's Investors Service consists of core credit ratings services, including four ratings groups: corporate finance (34% of 2009 segment revenues), structured finance (25%), financial institutions and sovereign risk (21%), and public finance (20%). MIS revenues are derived from the originators and issuers of such transaction, typically known as an Issuer-Fee Model. The ratings groups generate revenue mainly from the assignment of credit ratings on fixed-income instruments in the debt markets.

Moody's Analytics (MA), formerly Moody's KMV, provides a variety of credit risk processing and credit risk management products for banks and investors in credit-sensitive assets in about 120 countries. In addition, MA distributes investor-oriented research and data developed by MIS as part of its credit rating business. MA estimates that more than 30,000 clients access its data and research, primarily through the Moody's research web site.

Company Financials Fiscal Year Ended Dec. 31

Per Share Data ($)	2009	2008	2007	2006	2005	2004	2003	2002	2001	2000
Tangible Book Value	NM	NM	NM	NM	0.30	0.39	NM	NM	NM	NM
Cash Flow	1.96	2.06	2.73	2.72	1.95	1.51	1.30	1.00	0.72	0.54
Earnings	1.69	1.87	2.58	2.58	1.84	1.40	1.20	0.92	0.66	0.49
S&P Core Earnings	1.69	1.85	2.61	2.26	1.83	1.35	1.12	0.85	0.64	NA
Dividends	0.40	0.38	0.32	0.28	0.20	0.15	0.09	0.07	0.11	0.28
Payout Ratio	24%	20%	12%	11%	11%	11%	8%	7%	17%	57%
Prices:High	31.79	46.36	76.09	73.29	62.50	43.86	30.43	26.20	20.55	18.09
Prices:Low	15.57	15.41	35.05	49.76	39.55	29.85	19.75	17.90	12.78	11.31
P/E Ratio:High	19	25	29	28	34	31	25	29	31	37
P/E Ratio:Low	9	8	14	19	21	21	17	20	19	23

Income Statement Analysis (Million $)

	2009	2008	2007	2006	2005	2004	2003	2002	2001	2000
Revenue	1,797	1,755	2,259	2,037	1,732	1,438	1,247	1,023	797	602
Operating Income	769	818	1,222	1,138	975	820	696	563	416	305
Depreciation	64.1	46.7	41.2	39.5	35.2	34.1	32.6	25.0	17.0	16.6
Interest Expense	44.0	73.7	62.2	15.2	21.0	16.2	21.8	21.0	16.5	3.60
Pretax Income	646	726	1,117	1,261	935	771	656	517	382	284
Effective Tax Rate	37.0%	37.0%	37.2%	40.2%	40.0%	44.9%	44.6%	44.1%	44.4%	44.2%
Net Income	402	458	702	754	561	425	364	289	212	159
S&P Core Earnings	402	452	710	662	558	413	340	269	203	NA

Balance Sheet & Other Financial Data (Million $)

	2009	2008	2007	2006	2005	2004	2003	2002	2001	2000
Cash	484	253	441	408	486	606	269	40.0	163	119
Current Assets	1,013	809	989	1,002	1,052	1,023	569	272	371	278
Total Assets	2,004	1,772	1,715	1,498	1,457	1,376	941	631	505	398
Current Liabilities	1,236	1,393	1,349	700	579	837	432	462	359	253
Long Term Debt	746	750	600	300	300	Nil	300	300	300	300
Common Equity	-596	-996	-784	167	309	318	-32.1	-327	-304	-283
Total Capital	154	-244	-184	467	609	318	268	-27.0	-4.10	17.5
Capital Expenditures	90.7	84.4	182	31.1	31.3	21.3	17.9	18.0	14.8	12.3
Cash Flow	466	504	743	793	596	459	397	314	229	175
Current Ratio	0.8	0.6	0.7	1.4	1.8	1.2	1.3	0.6	1.0	1.1
% Long Term Debt of Capitalization	484.9	NM	-326.8	64.2	49.2	Nil	112.0	NM	NM	NM
% Net Income of Revenue	22.4	26.1	31.1	37.0	32.4	29.6	29.2	28.2	26.6	26.3
% Return on Assets	21.3	26.3	43.7	51.0	39.4	36.5	46.3	50.9	47.0	47.1
% Return on Equity	NM	NM	NM	316.2	178.9	297.9	NM	NM	NM	NM

Data as orig reptd.; bef. results of disc opers/spec. items. Per share data adj. for stk. divs.; EPS diluted. E-Estimated. NA-Not Available. NM-Not Meaningful. NR-Not Ranked. UR-Under Review.

Office: 7 World Trade Center, at 250 Greenwich Street, New York, NY 10007.
Telephone: 212-553-0300.
Website: http://www.moodys.com
Chrmn & CEO: R.W. McDaniel, Jr.

EVP & CFO: L.S. Huber
SVP, Chief Acctg Officer & Cntlr: J. McCabe
SVP & General Counsel: J.J. Goggins
SVP & CIO: T. Stoupas

Investor Contact: L. Westlake (212-553-7179)
Board Members: B. L. Anderson, J. D. Duffie, R. R. Glauber, E. Kist, R. W. McDaniel, Jr., C. McGillicuddy, III, H. A. McKinnell, Jr., N. S. Newcomb, J. K. Wulff

Founded: 1998
Domicile: Delaware
Employees: 4,000

The McGraw-Hill Companies

Morgan Stanley

STANDARD &POOR'S

S&P Recommendation **HOLD** ★★★☆☆	Price $24.38 (as of Oct 25, 2010)	12-Mo. Target Price $30.00	Investment Style Large-Cap Blend

GICS Sector Financials
Sub-Industry Investment Banking & Brokerage

Summary Morgan Stanley is among the largest financial services firms in the U.S., with operations in investment banking, securities, and investment and wealth management.

Key Stock Statistics (Source S&P, Vickers, company reports)

52-Wk Range	$35.00– 22.40	S&P Oper. EPS 2010**E**	2.34	Market Capitalization(B)	$34.058	Beta	1.44
Trailing 12-Month EPS	$1.27	S&P Oper. EPS 2011**E**	3.10	Yield (%)	0.82	S&P 3-Yr. Proj. EPS CAGR(%)	40
Trailing 12-Month P/E	19.2	P/E on S&P Oper. EPS 2010**E**	10.4	Dividend Rate/Share	$0.20	S&P Credit Rating	A
$10K Invested 5 Yrs Ago	NA	Common Shares Outstg. (M)	1,397.0	Institutional Ownership (%)	72		

Price Performance

30-Week Mov. Avg. · · · 10-Week Mov. Avg. - - GAAP Earnings vs. Previous Year Volume Above Avg. STARS
12-Mo. Target Price — Relative Strength ▲ Up ▼ Down ▶ No Change Below Avg. ★

Options: ASE, CBOE, P, Ph

Analysis prepared by **Robert McMillan** on October 20, 2010, when the stock traded at **$ 25.24**.

Highlights

➤ We think he outlook for investment banking has brightened somewhat, although recent market volatility and economic weakness suggest that trading results will be uneven. We expect improved margins in the asset management business as the firm focuses on institutional clients. Also, wealth management results should continue to improve as the Morgan Stanley Smith Barney joint venture gains momentum. We think MS is on solid financial footing now, with sufficient excess capital and credit spreads on its own debt that have narrowed to near pre-crisis levels. We forecast that net revenues will rise 29% in 2010 and 11% in 2011.

➤ We expect compensation costs to decline to around 50% of net revenues in 2010 and 2011, helped by a more normal revenue stream. Non-compensation costs may rise as business volume picks up, although they should decline on a relative basis, helping the pretax margin.

➤ We project earnings of $2.34 in 2010 and $3.10 in 2011, although these estimates are clouded by the impact of new regulations, which are likely to limit the size and scope of operations and raise costs.

Investment Rationale/Risk

➤ We think the creation of the Smith Barney joint venture and its sizable brokerage force will provide some long-term revenue stability. We believe trends in the Institutional Securities segment have improved, although near-term hurdles exist, and we think a global footprint will continue to provide business opportunities. We are also encouraged that MS was able to raise funds relatively easily to repay investments under TARP and is now well capitalized, by our analysis. Still, we think the company continues to lag peers at this point in the recovery, and we view the shares as appropriately valued.

➤ Risks to our recommendation and target price include stock and bond market depreciation and widening credit spreads, as well as additional industry regulation.

➤ MS recently traded at a discount to the overall market and its historical average multiples. Our 12-month target price of $30 represents a discount to our 2011 year end book value per share projection, a discount we think is warranted given the company's mix of businesses, which are sensitive to volatility in the capital markets.

Qualitative Risk Assessment

LOW	**MEDIUM**	HIGH

Our risk assessment reflects our favorable view of the company's diversification by product and by region, offset by our concerns about corporate governance and view that certain segments lack competitive advantages.

Quantitative Evaluations

S&P Quality Ranking   B-

D	C	**B-**	B	B+	A-	A	A+

Relative Strength Rank   WEAK

17

LOWEST = 1   HIGHEST = 99

Revenue/Earnings Data

Revenue (Million $)

	1Q	2Q	3Q	4Q	Year
2010	1,367	1,603	1,754	--	--
2009	5,417	1,881	1,408	1,190	6,712
2008	21,184	16,523	16,699	1,829	62,264
2007	23,192	26,195	21,230	14,711	85,328
2006	18,119	19,062	20,055	19,473	76,551
2005	11,641	11,845	13,157	15,525	52,081

Earnings Per Share ($)

2010	1.03	0.60	0.05	E0.46	E2.34
2009	-0.57	-1.37	0.38	0.13	-0.94
2008	1.45	0.95	1.32	-2.24	1.54
2007	2.17	2.24	1.32	-3.61	2.37
2006	1.50	1.85	1.75	2.08	7.09
2005	1.23	0.86	1.09	1.69	4.81

Fiscal year ended Dec. 31. Next earnings report expected: Late January. EPS Estimates based on S&P Operating Earnings; historical GAAP earnings are as reported.

Dividend Data (Dates: mm/dd Payment Date: mm/dd/yy)

Amount ($)	Date Decl.	Ex-Div. Date	Stk. of Record	Payment Date
0.050	01/20	01/27	01/29	02/12/10
0.050	04/21	04/28	04/30	05/14/10
0.050	07/21	07/28	07/30	08/13/10
0.050	10/20	10/27	10/29	11/15/10

Dividends have been paid since 1993. Source: Company reports.

Please read the Required Disclosures and Analyst Certification on the last page of this report.

The McGraw·Hill Companies

Morgan Stanley

STANDARD &POOR'S

Business Summary October 20, 2010

CORPORATE OVERVIEW. Morgan Stanley is a global financial services firm that provides a comprehensive suite of products to a diverse group of clients and customers, including corporations, governments, financial institutions and individuals. MS currently has three operating segments: Institutional Securities, Global Wealth Management Group and Asset Management.

The Institutional Securities segment includes capital raising; financial advisory services; corporate lending; sales, trading, financing and market-making activities for equity and fixed-income securities and related products such as foreign exchange and commodities; benchmark indices and risk management analytics; research; and investment activities. The investment banking business is included in this segment, and includes capital raising activities, financial advisory services and corporate lending. This business is one of the largest in the world, ranking second globally during its fiscal year in announced mergers and acquisitions, third in initial public offerings, and 10th in global debt issuance. This segment accounted for approximately 55% of net revenues in 2009.

The Global Wealth Management Group provides brokerage and investment advisory services; financial and wealth planning services; annuity and insurance products; credit and other lending products; banking and cash management services; retirement services; and trust and fiduciary services through the 51%-owned Morgan Stanley Smith Barney joint venture with Citigroup (C 4, Buy). It provides these services to clients through a network of more than 18,000 global representatives, overseeing $1.6 trillion in client assets at the end of 2009. The segment accounted for about 40% of net revenues in 2009.

The Asset Management segment provides global asset management products and services in equity, fixed income, alternative investments and private equity to institutional clients. It had $253 billion of assets under management or supervision at the end of 2009. These totals exclude its retail asset management unit, which the company has sold to Invesco (IVZ 22, Buy). In the deal, completed in June 2010, MS gained about a 6.5% stake in Invesco. MS hopes to renew its focus on institutional asset management customers. The segment accounted for 6% of net revenues in 2009.

Company Financials Fiscal Year Ended Dec. 31

Per Share Data ($)	2009	2008	2007	2006	2005	2004	2003	2002	2001	2000
Tangible Book Value	18.38	27.24	25.75	34.89	25.23	23.93	21.52	19.43	17.36	16.91
Earnings	-0.94	1.54	2.37	7.09	4.81	4.08	3.45	2.69	3.19	4.73
S&P Core Earnings	-1.15	1.07	2.17	7.12	5.00	4.18	3.48	2.38	2.84	NA
Dividends	0.40	1.08	1.08	1.08	1.08	1.00	0.92	0.92	0.92	0.80
Payout Ratio	NM	70%	46%	15%	22%	25%	27%	34%	29%	17%
Prices:High	35.78	53.40	90.95	83.40	60.51	62.83	58.78	60.02	90.49	110.00
Prices:Low	13.10	6.71	47.25	54.52	47.66	46.54	32.46	28.80	35.75	58.63
P/E Ratio:High	NM	8	38	12	13	15	17	22	28	23
P/E Ratio:Low	NM	1	20	8	10	11	9	11	11	12

Income Statement Analysis (Million $)										
Net Interest Income	990	3,202	2,781	3,279	3,750	3,731	2,935	3,896	3,348	3,058
Non Interest Income	22,368	21,537	25,245	45,558	23,906	20,959	19,189	16,549	19,600	24,179
Loan Loss Provision	Nil	Nil	831	756	878	925	1,267	1,336	1,052	810
Non Interest Expenses	22,501	22,452	24,858	23,614	20,857	18,333	16,636	15,725	17,264	18,746
% Expense/Operating Revenue	61.8%	49.9%	96.0%	84.6%	84.2%	80.8%	79.9%	81.3%	84.6%	79.5%
Pretax Income	857	2,287	3,394	10,772	7,050	6,312	5,334	4,633	5,684	8,526
Effective Tax Rate	NM	21.0%	24.5%	30.4%	26.4%	28.6%	29.0%	35.5%	36.5%	36.0%
Net Income	1,133	1,807	2,563	7,497	5,192	4,509	3,787	2,988	3,610	5,456
% Net Interest Margin	NA	NA	NA	NA	NA	NA	5.40	5.50	5.57	6.08
S&P Core Earnings	-1,371	1,163	2,284	7,511	5,401	4,624	3,830	2,658	3,203	NA

Balance Sheet & Other Financial Data (Million $)										
Money Market Assets	168,211	140,155	126,887	174,866	174,330	123,041	78,205	76,910	54,618	50,992
Investment Securities	313,434	233,542	457,192	680,484	304,172	260,640	228,904	185,588	164,011	130,818
Earning Assets:Total Loans	7,259	6,528	11,629	24,173	23,754	21,169	20,384	24,322	20,955	21,870
Total Assets	771,462	658,812	1,045,409	1,120,645	898,523	775,410	602,843	529,499	482,628	426,794
Demand Deposits	57,114	36,673	27,186	14,872	2,629	1,117	1,264	1,441	1,741	1,589
Time Deposits	5,101	6,082	3,993	13,471	16,034	12,660	11,575	12,316	10,535	10,341
Long Term Debt	167,286	141,466	190,624	144,978	110,465	95,286	68,410	43,985	40,851	36,830
Common Equity	37,091	31,676	30,169	34,264	29,248	28,272	24,933	21,951	20,437	18,796
% Return on Assets	0.2	0.2	0.2	0.7	0.6	0.7	0.7	0.6	0.8	1.4
% Return on Equity	3.4	5.8	7.7	23.5	18.9	16.9	16.2	14.1	18.2	30.3
% Loan Loss Reserve	Nil	Nil	Nil	3.3	3.5	4.5	4.9	3.8	4.0	3.6
% Loans/Deposits	12.2	24.5	78.0	85.2	127.3	153.7	158.8	176.8	170.7	183.3
% Loans/Assets	1.0	1.1	2.1	2.3	2.7	3.0	3.9	4.5	4.7	5.4
% Equity to Assets	4.7	3.6	3.0	3.1	3.3	3.9	4.1	4.2	4.3	4.5

Data as orig reptd.; bef. results of disc opers/spec. items. Per share data adj. for stk. divs.; EPS diluted. Prior to 2009, fiscal year ended November 30. E-Estimated. NA-Not Available. NM-Not Meaningful. NR-Not Ranked. UR-Under Review.

Office: 1585 Broadway, New York, NY 10036.
Telephone: 212-761-4000.
Website: http://www.morganstanley.com
Chrmn: J.J. Mack

Pres & CEO: J. Gorman
COO: T.R. Nides
EVP & CFO: R. Porat
Chief Admin Officer: S. Barney

Investor Contact: W. Pike (212-761-0008)
Board Members: R. J. Bostock, E. B. Bowles, H. Davies, J. Gorman, J. H. Hance, Jr., N. Hirano, C. R. Kidder, J. J. Mack, D. T. Nicolaisen, H. Olayan, O. G. Sexton, L. D. Tyson

Auditor: Deloitte & Touche
Founded: 1981
Domicile: Delaware
Employees: 61,388

Motorola Inc.

STANDARD
&POOR'S

S&P Recommendation	BUY ★★★★☆	Price $7.83 (as of Oct 22, 2010)	12-Mo. Target Price $10.00	Investment Style Large-Cap Blend

GICS Sector Information Technology
Sub-Industry Communications Equipment

Summary This manufacturer of wireless and networking equipment for cable, fixed-line and wireless service providers recently announced plans to split into two independent public companies.

Key Stock Statistics (Source S&P, Vickers, company reports)

52-Wk Range	$9.36– 6.04	S&P Oper. EPS 2010E	0.26	Market Capitalization(B)	$18.274	Beta	1.70
Trailing 12-Month EPS	$0.17	S&P Oper. EPS 2011E	0.37	Yield (%)	Nil	S&P 3-Yr. Proj. EPS CAGR(%)	10
Trailing 12-Month P/E	46.1	P/E on S&P Oper. EPS 2010E	30.1	Dividend Rate/Share	Nil	S&P Credit Rating	BB+
$10K Invested 5 Yrs Ago	$3,980	Common Shares Outstg. (M)	2,333.9	Institutional Ownership (%)	81		

Price Performance

30-Week Mov. Avg. · · · ·   10-Week Mov. Avg. – –   **GAAP Earnings vs. Previous Year**   Volume Above Avg. STARS
12-Mo. Target Price —   Relative Strength —   ▲ Up ▼ Down ▶ No Change   Below Avg.

Options: ASE, CBOE, P, Ph

Analysis prepared by **James Moorman, CFA** on July 30, 2010, when the stock traded at **$ 7.50**.

Highlights

➤ Following a 27% drop in sales in 2009, we expect a slight increase of 0.5% in 2010 and then an increase of 5.2% in 2011. We look for a recovery in MOT's still large Mobile Devices unit in 2010 and a 59% increase in average selling prices to be offset by a roughly 33% decrease in volumes. We expect Mobile Devices, Home and Enterprise to see continued improvement in the second half of the year.

➤ Despite our expectations for a slight decline in revenues in 2010, we believe gross margins will improve to 36.6% in 2010, from 32% in 2009, and then be roughly flat at 36.7% in 2011. The wider margins should reflect improvements in MOT's handset manufacturing process and a focus on higher-margin smartphones. We believe that Home and Networks profitability will improve in 2010, despite the projected decline in revenues.

➤ After breakeven operating earnings in 2009, we expect EPS of $0.26 in 2010 and $0.37 in 2011, including projected stock option expense.

Investment Rationale/Risk

➤ We are encouraged by MOT's efforts to lower costs and consolidate its mobile device operations as it seeks to return the business to profitability. We believe MOT will focus more on the high-end smartphone market, which could mean lower volumes but higher selling prices and margins. We anticipate mixed operating performance in non-handset operations due in part to the economy. Management recently announced plans to split the company into two publicly traded entities in 2011 and a deal to sell the wireless network infrastructure business to Nokia Siemens Networks for $1.2 billion.

➤ Risks to our recommendation and target price include execution risks involving the handset unit, failure to successfully introduce and ship new handset products, increasing competition in the handset and smartphone markets, and a slowdown in telecom equipment capital spending.

➤ Based on a below-peers enterprise value-to-sales multiple of 1.05X our 2011 estimate, our 12-month target price is $10. We believe the shares are attractive at current levels.

Qualitative Risk Assessment

LOW	MEDIUM	HIGH

Our risk assessment reflects the company's exposure to the economic health of the telecom and broadband industries and risks related to high-volume manufacturing and distribution to service providers. This is offset by our view of MOT's strong cash balance.

Quantitative Evaluations

S&P Quality Ranking   C

D	C	B-	B	B+	A-	A	A+

Relative Strength Rank   WEAK

24

LOWEST = 1   HIGHEST = 99

Revenue/Earnings Data

Revenue (Million $)

	1Q	2Q	3Q	4Q	Year
2010	5,044	5,414	--	--	--
2009	5,371	5,497	5,453	5,723	22,044
2008	7,448	8,082	7,480	7,136	30,146
2007	9,433	8,732	8,811	9,646	36,622
2006	9,608	10,876	10,603	11,792	42,879
2005	8,161	8,825	9,424	10,433	36,843

Earnings Per Share ($)

2010	0.03	0.07	E0.08	E0.10	E0.26
2009	-0.13	-0.01	0.01	0.06	-0.05
2008	-0.09	Nil	-0.18	-1.61	-1.87
2007	-0.09	-0.02	0.02	0.05	-0.05
2006	0.26	0.54	0.29	0.21	1.30
2005	0.28	0.38	0.69	0.47	1.82

Fiscal year ended Dec. 31. Next earnings report expected: NA. EPS Estimates based on S&P Operating Earnings; historical GAAP earnings are as reported.

Dividend Data

No cash dividends have been paid since 2008.

Please read the Required Disclosures and Analyst Certification on the last page of this report.

The McGraw-Hill Companies

Motorola Inc.

Business Summary July 30, 2010

CORPORATE OVERVIEW. Motorola provides wireless and networking equipment for cable and telecom service providers. We believe all these markets are exposed to increased buyers' power due to the industry consolidation of service providers. The Mobile Devices segment (31.7% of sales in the second quarter of 2010, down from 33.3% a year earlier) manufactures wireless handsets for GSM and CDMA standards. With the sale of 160 million handsets in 2007, 100 million in 2008 and 56 million in 2009, we estimate that MOT's global handset market share declined to 13%, 6.5% and 3.7% in the respective years, from 22% in 2006. The Mobile Devices segment incurred operating losses in 2008 and 2009.

In October 2008, MOT announced efforts to revamp its handset software platforms to reduce its cost structure and better align its offerings with customer demand for both smartphones and low-end handsets; we believe this will result in a number of product cancellations. We also think this will result in further pressure on handset volumes in 2010. In early 2009, MOT announced an additional work force reduction. We also expect the company to move away from the low-end handset business and focus more on the high-end smartphone market.

The remainder of MOT's revenues come from the Home (16.3%), Enterprise Mobility (34.1%) and Networks (17.8%) segments. In the Networks segment, MOT provides infrastructure for CDMA, GSM and iDEN wireless networks. Within Enterprise Mobility, sales to the government and public safety segments remain a large percentage of the total.

COMPETITIVE LANDSCAPE. Within the handset market, we see ongoing pressure from diversified manufacturers such as Nokia and Samsung and smartphone specialists such as Apple and Research in Motion that have been gaining market share as consumers look to use their phones for data services.

Company Financials Fiscal Year Ended Dec. 31

Per Share Data ($)	2009	2008	2007	2006	2005	2004	2003	2002	2001	2000
Tangible Book Value	2.64	2.42	4.28	7.15	6.67	5.45	5.43	4.85	6.07	8.50
Cash Flow	0.28	-1.51	0.35	1.53	2.06	1.15	1.09	-0.17	-0.63	1.70
Earnings	-0.05	-1.87	-0.05	1.30	1.82	0.90	0.38	-1.09	-1.78	0.58
S&P Core Earnings	-0.08	-1.16	0.07	1.24	1.18	0.78	0.08	-0.93	-2.23	NA
Dividends	Nil	0.20	0.20	0.19	0.16	0.16	0.16	0.16	0.16	0.16
Payout Ratio	Nil	NM	NM	15%	9%	18%	42%	NM	NM	28%
Prices:High	9.45	16.20	20.91	26.30	24.99	20.89	14.40	17.12	25.13	61.54
Prices:Low	2.98	3.00	14.87	18.66	14.48	13.83	7.59	7.30	10.50	15.81
P/E Ratio:High	NM	NM	NM	20	14	23	38	NM	NM	NM
P/E Ratio:Low	NM	NM	NM	14	8	15	20	NM	NM	NM

Income Statement Analysis (Million $)										
Revenue	22,044	30,146	36,622	42,879	36,843	31,323	27,058	26,679	30,004	37,580
Operating Income	1,322	703	1,349	4,675	4,851	3,887	2,694	2,059	-2,595	4,544
Depreciation	751	829	906	558	613	659	1,667	2,108	2,552	2,522
Interest Expense	213	313	365	335	325	199	295	668	645	494
Pretax Income	-165	-2,536	-390	4,610	6,520	3,252	1,293	-3,446	-5,511	2,231
Effective Tax Rate	46.7%	NM	73.1%	29.3%	29.5%	32.6%	30.9%	NM	NM	40.9%
Net Income	-111	-4,163	-105	3,261	4,599	2,191	893	-2,485	-3,937	1,318
S&P Core Earnings	-168	-2,641	186	3,132	2,964	1,899	164	-2,084	-4,893	NA

Balance Sheet & Other Financial Data (Million $)										
Cash	7,963	6,979	8,606	15,416	14,641	10,556	7,877	6,507	6,082	3,301
Current Assets	16,032	17,363	22,222	30,975	27,869	21,082	17,907	17,134	17,149	19,885
Total Assets	25,603	27,887	34,812	38,593	35,649	30,889	32,098	31,152	33,398	42,343
Current Liabilities	8,261	10,620	12,500	15,425	12,488	10,573	9,433	9,810	9,698	16,257
Long Term Debt	3,365	4,092	3,991	2,704	3,806	4,578	7,161	7,674	8,857	4,778
Common Equity	9,775	9,525	15,447	17,142	16,673	13,331	12,689	11,239	13,691	18,612
Total Capital	13,248	13,602	20,371	19,846	20,479	17,909	19,850	18,913	22,548	24,894
Capital Expenditures	275	504	527	649	583	494	655	607	1,321	4,131
Cash Flow	640	-3,415	801	3,819	5,212	2,850	2,560	-377	-1,385	3,840
Current Ratio	1.9	1.6	1.8	2.0	2.2	2.0	1.9	1.7	1.8	1.2
% Long Term Debt of Capitalization	25.4	30.1	19.6	13.6	18.6	25.6	36.1	40.6	39.3	19.2
% Net Income of Revenue	NM	NM	NM	7.6	12.5	7.0	3.3	NM	NM	3.5
% Return on Assets	NM	NM	NM	8.8	13.8	7.0	2.8	NM	NM	3.2
% Return on Equity	NM	NM	NM	19.3	30.7	16.8	7.5	NM	NM	7.1

Data as orig reptd.; bef. results of disc opers/spec. items. Per share data adj. for stk. divs.; EPS diluted. E-Estimated. NA-Not Available. NM-Not Meaningful. NR-Not Ranked. UR-Under Review.

Office: 1303 East Algonquin Road, Schaumburg, IL 60196.
Telephone: 800-262-8509.
Email: investors@motorola.com
Website: http://www.motorola.com

Chrmn: D.W. Dorman
Co-CEO: G.Q. Brown
Co-CEO: S.K. Jha
EVP, Secy & General Counsel: A.P. Lawson

SVP & CFO: E.J. Fitzpatrick
Investor Contact: D. Lindroth (847-576-6899)
Board Members: G. Q. Brown, D. W. Dorman, W. R. Hambrecht, S. K. Jha, K. A. Meister, T. J. Meredith, S. C. Scott, III, J. R. Stengel, T. Vinciquerra, D. A. Warner, III, J. A. White, III

Founded: 1928
Domicile: Delaware
Employees: 53,000

M&T Bank Corp

STANDARD &POOR'S

S&P Recommendation BUY ★★★★☆

Price	12-Mo. Target Price	Investment Style
$74.44 (as of Oct 22, 2010)	$85.00	Large-Cap Blend

GICS Sector Financials
Sub-Industry Regional Banks

Summary This bank holding company for M&T Bank has offices in New York, Pennsylvania, Maryland, Virginia, West Virginia, New Jersey, Delaware, and Washington, DC.

Key Stock Statistics (Source S&P, Vickers, company reports)

52-Wk Range	$96.15–60.39	S&P Oper. EPS 2010**E**	5.72	Market Capitalization(B)	$8.867	Beta	0.83
Trailing 12-Month EPS	$4.63	S&P Oper. EPS 2011**E**	6.47	Yield (%)	3.76	S&P 3-Yr. Proj. EPS CAGR(%)	41
Trailing 12-Month P/E	16.1	P/E on S&P Oper. EPS 2010**E**	13.0	Dividend Rate/Share	$2.80	S&P Credit Rating	A-
$10K Invested 5 Yrs Ago	$8,481	Common Shares Outstg. (M)	119.1	Institutional Ownership (%)	75		

Price Performance

- 30-Week Mov. Avg. ···
- 10-Week Mov. Avg. ― ―
- **GAAP Earnings vs. Previous Year**
- 12-Mo. Target Price ―
- Relative Strength ―
- ▲ Up ▼ Down ► No Change
- Volume Above Avg. ⅠⅡⅠ STARS
- Below Avg. ⅠⅡⅠ ★

Options: ASE, CBOE, P, Ph

Qualitative Risk Assessment

LOW	MEDIUM	HIGH

Our risk assessment reflects the company's large-cap valuation, its history of profitability, its low chargeoff levels relative to peers, and its ability to build capital through income generation.

Quantitative Evaluations

S&P Quality Ranking　　　　　　B+

D	C	B-	B	B+	A-	A	A+

Relative Strength Rank　　　　WEAK

11

LOWEST = 1　　　　　　　　　　HIGHEST = 99

Revenue/Earnings Data

Revenue (Million $)

	1Q	2Q	3Q	4Q	Year
2010	934.1	958.3	--	--	--
2009	891.8	954.3	984.6	964.5	3,773
2008	1,197	1,089	915.1	1,016	4,217
2007	1,098	1,161	1,146	1,073	4,478
2006	1,030	1,076	1,127	1,127	4,360
2005	872.6	921.9	942.3	1,002	3,738

Earnings Per Share ($)

	1Q	2Q	3Q	4Q	Year
2010	1.17	1.46	E1.48	E1.56	E5.72
2009	0.49	0.36	0.97	1.04	2.89
2008	1.82	1.44	0.82	0.92	5.01
2007	1.57	1.95	1.83	0.60	5.95
2006	1.77	1.87	1.85	1.88	7.37
2005	1.62	1.69	1.64	1.78	6.73

Fiscal year ended Dec. 31. Next earnings report expected: NA. EPS Estimates based on S&P Operating Earnings; historical GAAP earnings are as reported.

Highlights

► The 12-month target price for MTB has recently been changed to $85.00 from $80.00. The Highlights section of this Stock Report will be updated accordingly.

Investment Rationale/Risk

► The Investment Rationale/Risk section of this Stock Report will be updated shortly. For the latest News story on MTB from MarketScope, see below.

► 10/20/10 12:02 pm ET ... S&P MAINTAINS BUY RECOMMENDATION ON SHARES OF M&T BANK (MTB 74.55****): Q3 EPS of $1.48, vs. $0.97, beat our $1.42 EPS estimate, on higher than expected mortgage banking revenues, off-setting higher than expected loan loss provisions, and lower than expected net interest income. On Q3 results, we raise our '10 EPS estimate to $5.72 from $5.66. Nonperforming loans are up 1% from Q2, a negative, in our view, but this level is still much better than peers. On a recent decline in banking valuation multiples, we reduce our target price to $85 down $5, based on a slight premium to peers 13.1X multiple on our unchanged '11 EPS estimate of $6.47. /E.Oja

Dividend Data (Dates: mm/dd Payment Date: mm/dd/yy)

Amount ($)	Date Decl.	Ex-Div. Date	Stk. of Record	Payment Date
0.700	11/17	11/27	12/01	12/31/09
0.700	02/16	02/24	02/26	03/31/10
0.700	05/19	05/27	06/01	06/30/10
0.700	08/17	08/30	09/01	09/30/10

Dividends have been paid since 1979. Source: Company reports.

Please read the Required Disclosures and Analyst Certification on the last page of this report.

The McGraw·Hill Companies

M&T Bank Corp

STANDARD
&POOR'S

Business Summary July 21, 2010

CORPORATE OVERVIEW. M&T Bank Corporation is a Buffalo, NY-based bank holding company with $68.9 billion of assets as of December 31, 2009. Its principal subsidiary is M&T Bank, a New York State chartered bank that focuses its lending on consumers and small and medium-sized businesses in the Mid-Atlantic region. It also owns M&T Bank, National Association (N.A.), a national banking association that offers selected deposit and loan products on a nationwide basis through direct mail and telephone marketing, and operates other subsidiaries that provide insurance, securities, investments, leasing, mortgage, mortgage reinsurance, real estate and other financial products and services.

Following MTB's acquisition of Allfirst Financial Inc., a bank holding company in Baltimore, MD, from Allied Irish Banks, p.l.c. (AIB) in 2003, AIB gained a 22.5% stake in MTB. As of December 31, 2009, AIB owned 22.6% of MTB's common stock. As long as AIB maintains a significant ownership in MTB, each bank will have representation on the other's board.

MARKET PROFILE. As of June 30, 2009, including the acquisition of Maryland-based Provident Bankshares Corporation, MTB had 803 branches and $46.6 billion in deposits, with about 50% of its deposits and 33% of its branches concentrated in New York. In addition, 96.8% of MTB's deposits and 92% of branches were concentrated in the three adjoining states of New York, Maryland and Pennsylvania. In New York, MTB had 266 branches, $23.5 billion in deposits, and a deposit market share of about 2.85%, ranking eighth. In Pennsylvania, MTB had 213 branches, $7.7 billion in deposits, and a deposit market share of about 2.6%, also ranking eighth. In Maryland, MTB had 258 branches, $13.9 billion in deposits, and a deposit market share of about 12.9%, ranking second. Finally, MTB has a smaller presence in the Virginia, the District of Columbia, West Virginia, Delaware and New Jersey.

Company Financials Fiscal Year Ended Dec. 31

Per Share Data ($)	2009	2008	2007	2006	2005	2004	2003	2002	2001	2000
Tangible Book Value	28.03	24.21	30.62	30.05	25.56	24.52	21.43	20.23	17.84	16.10
Earnings	2.89	5.01	5.95	7.37	6.73	6.00	4.95	5.07	3.82	3.44
S&P Core Earnings	2.89	4.63	5.87	7.36	6.64	5.97	4.95	4.60	3.40	NA
Dividends	2.80	2.80	2.60	2.25	1.75	1.60	1.20	1.05	1.00	0.62
Payout Ratio	97%	56%	44%	31%	26%	27%	24%	21%	26%	18%
Prices:High	69.89	108.53	125.13	124.98	112.50	108.75	98.98	90.05	82.11	68.42
Prices:Low	29.11	52.20	77.39	105.72	96.71	82.90	74.71	67.70	59.80	35.70
P/E Ratio:High	24	22	21	17	17	18	20	18	21	20
P/E Ratio:Low	10	10	13	14	14	14	15	13	16	10

Income Statement Analysis (Million $)	2009	2008	2007	2006	2005	2004	2003	2002	2001	2000
Net Interest Income	2,056	1,940	1,850	1,818	1,794	1,735	1,599	1,248	1,158	854
Tax Equivalent Adjustment	22.0	21.9	20.8	NA	17.3	NA	16.3	14.0	17.5	10.5
Non Interest Income	1,048	939	1,059	1,043	978	940	831	513	476	325
Loan Loss Provision	604	412	192	80.0	88.0	95.0	131	122	104	NA
% Expense/Operating Revenue	63.8%	54.4%	55.9%	54.2%	53.2%	56.7%	59.6%	51.9%	57.4%	61.6%
Pretax Income	519	740	964	1,232	1,171	1,067	851	716	584	446
Effective Tax Rate	26.8%	24.9%	32.1%	31.9%	33.2%	32.3%	32.5%	32.3%	35.2%	35.9%
Net Income	380	556	654	839	782	723	574	485	378	286
% Net Interest Margin	3.49	3.38	3.60	3.70	3.77	3.88	4.09	4.36	4.23	4.02
S&P Core Earnings	333	514	646	838	772	718	574	440	336	NA

Balance Sheet & Other Financial Data (Million $)	2009	2008	2007	2006	2005	2004	2003	2002	2001	2000
Money Market Assets	540	649	348	143	211	199	250	380	84.4	57.8
Investment Securities	7,781	7,919	8,962	7,371	8,400	8,475	7,259	3,955	3,024	3,310
Commercial Loans	28,259	27,397	25,715	23,165	23,940	22,886	20,869	14,522	14,071	13,399
Other Loans	24,047	21,963	22,637	20,042	16,614	15,758	15,169	11,415	11,117	9,571
Total Assets	68,880	65,816	64,876	57,065	55,146	52,939	49,826	33,175	31,450	28,949
Demand Deposits	13,795	8,856	9,322	8,820	9,044	9,246	10,150	5,101	4,634	4,218
Time Deposits	33,655	32,584	31,944	25,660	28,056	26,183	20,756	16,564	16,946	16,014
Long Term Debt	10,240	12,075	10,318	6,891	5,586	6,349	5,535	4,497	3,462	3,415
Common Equity	7,023	6,217	6,485	6,281	5,876	5,730	5,717	3,182	2,939	38.0
% Return on Assets	0.6	0.9	1.1	1.5	1.4	1.4	1.4	1.5	1.3	1.1
% Return on Equity	5.7	8.4	10.3	13.8	13.5	12.6	12.9	15.8	13.4	12.7
% Loan Loss Reserve	1.7	1.6	1.6	1.5	1.6	1.6	1.7	1.7	1.7	1.6
% Loans/Deposits	109.5	115.1	112.1	107.6	108.7	108.4	108.0	119.7	116.7	112.4
% Equity to Assets	9.8	9.7	10.5	10.8	10.7	11.1	10.8	9.5	9.3	8.8

Data as orig reptd.; bef. results of disc opers/spec. items. Per share data adj. for stk. divs.; EPS diluted. E-Estimated. NA-Not Available. NM-Not Meaningful. NR-Not Ranked. UR-Under Review.

Office: 1 M And T Plz, Buffalo, NY 14203-2399.
Telephone: 716-842-5445.
Email: ir@mandtbank.com
Website: http://www.mandtbank.com

Chrmn & CEO: R.G. Wilmers
Pres: M.J. Czarnecki
Vice Chrmn: J.G. Pereira
Vice Chrmn: R.E. Sadler, Jr.

Vice Chrmn: M. Pinto
Investor Contact: D.J. MacLeod (716-842-5138)
Board Members: B. D. Baird, R. J. Bennett, C. A. Bontempo, R. T. Brady, M. D. Buckley, T. J. Cunningham, III, M. J. Czarnecki, G. N. Geisel, P. W. Hodgson, R. G. King, J. G. Pereira, M. Pinto, M. R. Rich, R. E. Sadler, Jr., E. Sheehy, H. L. Washington, R. G. Wilmers

Founded: 1969
Domicile: New York
Employees: 14,226

The *McGraw-Hill* Companies

Murphy Oil Corp

STANDARD &POOR'S

S&P Recommendation	BUY ★★★★☆	Price	12-Mo. Target Price	Investment Style
		$65.39 (as of Oct 22, 2010)	$70.00	Large-Cap Blend

GICS Sector Energy
Sub-Industry Integrated Oil & Gas

Summary This international integrated oil company has exploration and production interests worldwide, and refining and marketing operations in the U.S.

Key Stock Statistics (Source S&P, Vickers, company reports)

52-Wk Range	$66.27– 48.14	S&P Oper. EPS 2010**E**	4.83	Market Capitalization(B)	$12.541	Beta	0.95
Trailing 12-Month EPS	$4.82	S&P Oper. EPS 2011**E**	5.45	Yield (%)	1.68	S&P 3-Yr. Proj. EPS CAGR(%)	21
Trailing 12-Month P/E	13.6	P/E on S&P Oper. EPS 2010**E**	13.5	Dividend Rate/Share	$1.10	S&P Credit Rating	BBB
$10K Invested 5 Yrs Ago	$16,530	Common Shares Outstg. (M)	191.8	Institutional Ownership (%)	76		

Price Performance

30-Week Mov. Avg. · · · · 10-Week Mov. Avg. - - GAAP Earnings vs. Previous Year Volume Above Avg. STARS
12-Mo. Target Price — Relative Strength ▲ Up ▼ Down ▶ No Change Below Avg. ★

Options: ASE, CBOE, P, Ph

Analysis prepared by **Tina J. Vital** on August 11, 2010, when the stock traded at **$ 53.90**.

Highlights

➤ Second quarter oil and gas production was up 33% from last year to 189,951 boe per day, on project ramp-ups. However, as we expected, second quarter volumes declined 3% from the first quarter on maintenance work in Malaysia, and we have trimmed our 2010 growth forecast to 20% reflecting unplanned downtime at Kikeh in Malaysia and project delays at Azurite in the Republic of Congo, and we expect about 16% growth for 2011. We see minimal impact on MUR's overall production from the Gulf of Mexico drilling moratorium, as reduced Gulf volumes will likely be made up elsewhere.

➤ On the downstream, we are seeing signs of improved U.S. fuel demand. As of July 2010, we look for U.S. Gulf Coast 3-2-1 crack spreads to widen by 9% in 2010 and by 3% in 2011. We expect MUR's ethanol and marketing business to post solid earnings in 2010 and 2011, and MUR is planning to expand its U.S. retail segment.

➤ First-half 2010 operating EPS excluded a net charge of $0.22 related to foreign exchange. We expect after-tax operating earnings to rise 65% in 2010 and 18% in 2011, reflecting production growth and improved economic conditions.

Investment Rationale/Risk

➤ With its oil focus and solid queue of projects, we look for MUR to benefit from our forecast for higher oil prices. While MUR's upstream operations had focused on the U.S. deepwater Gulf of Mexico, we see added growth from international prospects. In July 2010, MUR said it will exit its refining and U.K. retail business and use proceeds to reduce debt and speed up growth of upstream operations; while we like the move, we believe the market is tough to be selling refining assets. In August 2010, MUR said it signed a letter of intent to buy a partially completed ethanol plant in Hereford, TX from Panda Ethanol.

➤ Risks to our recommendation and target price include unfavorable changes to economic, industry and operating conditions, such as rising costs, or difficulty replacing oil and gas reserves.

➤ Blending our discounted cash flow ($68 per share, assuming a WACC of 9.8% and terminal growth of 3%) and relative market valuations leads to our 12-month target price of $70. This represents an expected enterprise value of about 4.5X our 2011 EBITDA estimate, a slight discount to the major oil peer average.

Qualitative Risk Assessment

LOW	MEDIUM	HIGH

Our risk assessment reflects our view of MUR's moderate financial policies and integrated operations in a volatile, cyclical, and capital-intensive segment of the energy industry. We believe its low reserve-to-production ratio limits its operating flexibility, increasing dependence on long-term projects.

Quantitative Evaluations

S&P Quality Ranking B+

D	C	B-	B	B+	A-	A	A+

Relative Strength Rank STRONG

81

LOWEST = 1 HIGHEST = 99

Revenue/Earnings Data

Revenue (Million $)

	1Q	2Q	3Q	4Q	Year
2010	5,180	5,592	--	--	--
2009	3,416	4,496	5,202	5,804	19,012
2008	6,533	8,363	8,186	4,431	27,513
2007	3,435	4,614	4,781	5,610	18,439
2006	2,991	3,799	4,153	3,364	14,307
2005	2,415	2,950	3,317	3,195	11,877

Earnings Per Share ($)

2010	0.77	1.41	E1.14	E1.29	E4.83
2009	0.37	0.84	0.98	1.66	3.85
2008	2.14	3.22	3.04	0.83	9.22
2007	0.58	1.32	1.04	1.07	4.01
2006	0.60	1.13	1.18	0.46	3.37
2005	0.60	1.85	1.18	0.82	4.46

Fiscal year ended Dec. 31. Next earnings report expected: Early November. EPS Estimates based on S&P Operating Earnings; historical GAAP earnings are as reported.

Dividend Data (Dates: mm/dd Payment Date: mm/dd/yy)

Amount ($)	Date Decl.	Ex-Div. Date	Stk. of Record	Payment Date
0.250	02/03	02/11	02/16	03/01/10
0.250	04/07	05/12	05/14	06/01/10
0.275	08/04	08/12	08/16	09/01/10
0.275	10/06	11/09	11/12	12/01/10

Dividends have been paid since 1961. Source: Company reports.

Please read the Required Disclosures and Analyst Certification on the last page of this report.

The **McGraw·Hill** Companies

Murphy Oil Corp

Business Summary August 11, 2010

CORPORATE OVERVIEW. Originally incorporated in Louisiana in 1950 as Murphy Corp., the company was reincorporated in Delaware in 1964 under the name Murphy Oil Corp. (MUR). As an international integrated oil and gas company, MUR explores for oil and gas worldwide, and has refining and marketing interests in the U.S. The company operates in two business segments: Exploration and Production (16% of 2009 revenues; 91% of segment income), and Refining and Marketing (84%; 9%).

Exploration and Production activities are conducted in the U.S. by wholly owned Murphy Exploration & Production Co - USA (Murphy Expro USA); in Malaysia, the Republic of Congo, Indonesia, Australia and Suriname by wholly owned Murphy Exploration & Production Co. - International (Murphy Expro International and its subsidiaries); in Western Canada and offshore Eastern Canada by wholly owned Murphy Oil Co. Ltd. (MOCL) and its subsidiaries; and in the U.K. North Sea and the Atlantic Margin by wholly owned Murphy Petroleum Ltd.

As of year-end 2009, U.S. producing fields (about 16% of MUR's 2009 oil and gas production) included seven in the deepwater Gulf of Mexico - including Medusa (60% interest), Habanero (33.75%), Front Runner (37.5%), Front Runner South (37.5%), Quatrain (37.5%), and Thunder Hawk (37.5%) -- and two onshore Louisiana.

MUR's operations in Canada include limited heavy oil exploration and exploitation in Western Canada, combined with its non-operated interests in legacy properties: Terra Nova (12%), Hibernia (6.5%), and Syncrude Canada Ltd. (5%). In June 2007, the company acquired the Tupper leases, a tight natural gas play in northeastern British Columbia.

In Malaysia, the company has majority interests in seven separate production-sharing contracts (PSCs) and serves as operator. In 2002, MUR made an important discovery at the Kikeh field (80%) in deepwater Block K, offshore Sabah, and added another important discovery at Kakap in 2004. In April 2010, Petronas informed MUR that offshore Blocks L and M were no longer part of Malaysia, and as a result, MUR's production-sharing contracts for these blocks with Petronas were terminated; MUR is discussing replacement production-sharing contracts covering these areas.

The company also has interests in the U.K. sector of the North Sea, offshore Ecuador, and offshore the Republic of Congo.

Company Financials Fiscal Year Ended Dec. 31

Per Share Data ($)	2009	2008	2007	2006	2005	2004	2003	2002	2001	2000
Tangible Book Value	38.22	32.73	25.99	21.37	18.38	14.16	10.27	8.41	7.99	6.72
Cash Flow	9.22	13.48	6.75	5.40	6.57	4.38	3.39	2.16	3.07	2.87
Earnings	3.85	9.22	4.01	3.37	4.46	2.66	1.63	0.53	1.82	1.69
S&P Core Earnings	3.79	8.55	4.03	3.32	3.85	2.40	1.40	0.39	1.30	NA
Dividends	1.00	0.88	0.68	0.52	0.45	0.43	0.40	0.39	0.38	0.36
Payout Ratio	26%	9%	17%	16%	10%	16%	25%	73%	21%	21%
Prices:High	65.12	101.47	85.94	60.18	57.07	43.69	34.35	24.86	21.96	17.27
Prices:Low	37.96	35.55	45.45	44.72	37.80	28.45	19.27	15.95	13.81	12.05
P/E Ratio:High	17	11	21	18	13	16	21	47	12	10
P/E Ratio:Low	10	4	11	13	8	11	12	30	8	7

Income Statement Analysis (Million $)										
Revenue	19,012	27,513	18,439	14,307	11,877	8,360	5,345	3,967	4,479	4,639
Operating Income	NA	3,640	1,845	1,514	1,854	1,110	781	492	768	723
Depreciation, Depletion and Amortization	1,028	850	523	384	397	321	328	300	229	213
Interest Expense	24.4	43.7	75.5	9.48	8.77	34.1	20.5	27.0	19.0	16.3
Pretax Income	1,277	2,850	1,237	1,028	1,372	805	419	152	506	465
Effective Tax Rate	42.0%	37.9%	38.1%	37.9%	38.9%	38.3%	28.1%	35.7%	34.6%	34.3%
Net Income	741	1,771	767	638	838	496	301	97.5	331	306
S&P Core Earnings	728	1,643	772	630	725	448	259	71.4	236	NA

Balance Sheet & Other Financial Data (Million $)										
Cash	301	666	674	543	585	536	252	165	82.7	133
Current Assets	3,376	2,846	2,887	2,107	1,839	1,629	1,039	854	599	817
Total Assets	12,827	12,205	10,536	7,446	6,369	5,458	4,713	3,886	3,259	3,134
Current Liabilities	2,182	1,888	2,109	1,311	1,287	1,205	810	718	560	745
Long Term Debt	1,353	1,026	1,516	840	610	613	1,090	863	521	525
Common Equity	7,246	6,314	5,066	4,053	3,461	2,649	1,951	1,594	1,498	1,260
Total Capital	8,699	8,183	7,526	5,498	4,685	3,263	3,463	2,784	2,322	2,014
Capital Expenditures	1,989	2,186	1,949	1,192	1,246	938	938	834	814	512
Cash Flow	1,774	2,590	1,290	1,022	1,235	818	630	398	560	519
Current Ratio	1.5	1.5	1.4	1.6	1.4	1.4	1.3	1.2	1.1	1.1
% Long Term Debt of Capitalization	15.7	12.5	20.2	15.3	13.0	18.8	31.5	31.0	22.4	26.1
% Return on Assets	6.2	15.6	8.5	9.2	14.2	9.8	7.0	2.7	10.4	11.0
% Return on Equity	11.0	31.1	16.8	17.0	27.4	21.6	17.0	6.3	24.0	26.4

Data as orig reptd.; bef. results of disc opers/spec. items. Per share data adj. for stk. divs.; EPS diluted. E-Estimated. NA-Not Available. NM-Not Meaningful. NR-Not Ranked. UR-Under Review.

Office: 200 Peach Street, El Dorado, AR 71730-7000.
Telephone: 870-862-6411.
Email: murphyoil@murphyoilcorp.com
Website: http://www.murphyoilcorp.com

Chrmn: W.C. Nolan, Jr.
Pres & CEO: D.M. Wood
EVP & General Counsel: S.A. Cosse
SVP & CFO: K.G. Fitzgerald

Chief Admin Officer: K.M. Hammock
Investor Contact: M. West (870-864-6315)
Board Members: F. W. Blue, C. P. Deming, R. A. Hermes, J. V. Kelley, R. M. Murphy, W. C. Nolan, Jr., N. E. Schmale, D. J. Smith, C. G. Theus, D. M. Wood

Founded: 1950
Domicile: Delaware
Employees: 8,369

Mylan Inc

**STANDARD
&POOR'S**

S&P Recommendation	**STRONG BUY** ★★★★★	Price $19.38 (as of Oct 22, 2010)	12-Mo. Target Price $25.00	Investment Style Large-Cap Growth

GICS Sector Health Care
Sub-Industry Pharmaceuticals

Summary This leading manufacturer of generic pharmaceuticals produces a broad range of generic drugs in varying strengths. In October 2007, Mylan acquired the generic drug division of German drugmaker Merck KGaA for some $7.0 billion in cash.

Key Stock Statistics (Source S&P, Vickers, company reports)

52-Wk Range	$23.63– 15.71	S&P Oper. EPS 2010E	1.60	Market Capitalization(B)	$5.995	Beta	0.68
Trailing 12-Month EPS	$0.25	S&P Oper. EPS 2011E	2.00	Yield (%)	Nil	S&P 3-Yr. Proj. EPS CAGR(%)	21
Trailing 12-Month P/E	77.5	P/E on S&P Oper. EPS 2010E	12.1	Dividend Rate/Share	Nil	S&P Credit Rating	BB
$10K Invested 5 Yrs Ago	$9,663	Common Shares Outstg. (M)	309.4	Institutional Ownership (%)	NM		

Price Performance

30-Week Mov. Avg. · · · 10-Week Mov. Avg. – – **GAAP Earnings vs. Previous Year** Volume Above Avg. STARS
12-Mo. Target Price — Relative Strength — ▲ Up ▼ Down ▶ No Change Below Avg.

Options: ASE, CBOE, P, Ph

Analysis prepared by **Herman B. Saftlas** on August 23, 2010, when the stock traded at **$ 17.55**.

Highlights

➤ We forecast 2010 net revenues of $5.4 billion, up from 2009's $5.1 billion. We see sales growth in 2010 driven by gains in existing lines, as well as by new products such as recently launched generic versions of Prevacid and Benzaclin. In total, MYL has some 141 ANDAs awaiting FDA review, of which 41 represent potential first-to-file opportunities with six months of marketing exclusivity. We also expect significant new product launches overseas. In the branded business, we see robust growth for EpiPen, an auto-injector treatment for potential life-threatening allergic reactions.

➤ We look for gross margins in 2010 to show modest expansion on the projected better volume and productivity enhancements. We also see tight control of SG&A costs and R&D spending, helped by ongoing merger synergies (over $350 million expected to be realized in 2010). We expect an adjusted tax rate of about 29% in 2010, down from 30% in 2009.

➤ After projected lower preferred dividend payments, we see 2010 operating EPS of $1.60, up from $1.30 in 2009. We see further EPS progress to $2.00 in 2011.

Investment Rationale/Risk

➤ We believe MYL's efforts to expand through acquisitions hold much long-term promise. In July 2010, MYL announced plans to purchase Bioniche Pharma, an Ireland-based maker of injectable drugs. Mylan expects this deal to be EPS accretive within one year after completion. Other acquisitions, such as Merck KGaA's generic business and Matrix Laboratories, have broadened MYL's geographic reach and provided access to in-house raw materials and generic biologics. We expect MYL to launch over 500 new products worldwide in 2010 and maintain that level in coming years. We see MYL as uniquely positioned to benefit from the robust growth we see for the generics market.

➤ Risks to our recommendation and target price include possible problems integrating acquisitions, as well as cash flow risks that could threaten MYL's ability to manage its heavy debt load.

➤ Our 12-month target price of $25 applies a peer multiple of 12.5X to our 2011 EPS estimate. Our DCF model, which assumes a WACC of 8% and perpetuity growth of 1%, also shows intrinsic value in the $25 area.

Qualitative Risk Assessment

LOW	**MEDIUM**	HIGH

Our risk assessment reflects risks inherent in the generic pharmaceutical business, which include the need to successfully develop generic products, obtain regulatory approvals and legally challenge branded patents. However, we believe these risks are offset by Mylan's wide and diverse generic portfolio and promising branded drugs business. We also think the acquisition of Merck KGaA's generic business holds long-term promise.

Quantitative Evaluations

S&P Quality Ranking   A-

D	C	B-	B	B+	**A-**	A	A+

Relative Strength Rank   MODERATE

63

LOWEST = 1   HIGHEST = 99

Revenue/Earnings Data

Revenue (Million $)

	1Q	2Q	3Q	4Q	Year
2010	1,292	1,369	--	--	--
2009	1,181	1,267	1,264	1,352	5,064
2008	1,074	1,203	1,657	1,203	5,138
2007	356.1	366.7	401.8	487.3	1,612
2006	323.4	298.0	311.3	324.6	1,257
2005	339.0	307.0	291.0	316.4	1,253

Earnings Per Share ($)

2010	0.20	0.16	E0.42	E0.45	E1.60
2009	0.23	0.19	-0.13	0.01	0.30
2008	-1.46	-0.03	0.45	-0.13	-1.05
2007	0.35	0.36	0.63	-0.31	0.99
2006	0.16	0.16	0.22	0.27	0.79
2005	0.30	0.18	0.13	0.14	0.74

Fiscal year ended Dec. 31. Next earnings report expected: Late October. EPS Estimates based on S&P Operating Earnings; historical GAAP earnings are as reported.

Dividend Data

Dividends were suspended in 2008.

Please read the Required Disclosures and Analyst Certification on the last page of this report.

The McGraw-Hill Companies

Mylan Inc

**STANDARD
&POOR'S**

Business Summary August 23, 2010

CORPORATE PROFILE. Mylan Laboratories is a leading manufacturer of generic pharmaceutical products in finished tablet, capsule and powder dosage forms. Generic drugs are the chemical equivalents of branded drugs, and are marketed after patents on the primary products expire. Generics are typically sold at prices significantly below those of comparable branded products.

Generics accounted for some 92% of operating revenues in 2009, with specialty products representing the balance. By geographic region, generics sales in 2009 were derived as follows: North America 45%, Europe 34%, and Asia/Pacific 21%.

MYL markets more than 900 products throughout the world. The U.S. generic division markets about 224 generic products, primarily solid oral dose drugs encompassing a wide variety of therapeutic categories. Some 25 generics are extended-release drugs. UDL Laboratories is the largest U.S. repackager of pharmaceuticals in unit dose formats, which are used primarily in hospitals, nursing homes and similar settings. Mylan Technologies develops and markets products using transdermal drug delivery systems.

IMPACT OF MAJOR DEVELOPMENTS. In October 2007, Mylan acquired a

generic drug business from German drugmaker Merck KGaA (referred to as Merck Generics) that markets several hundred products. The operation has a strong presence in key foreign generic markets, including France, Italy, the U.K., Japan, Canada and Australia. As part of this acquisition, MYL also acquired Dey, a producer of branded specialty respiratory and allergy drugs. Key Dey products are EpiPen, an auto-injector treatment for allergic reactions; and DuoNeb, a nebulized treatment for COPD.

Through its India-based Matrix Laboratories subsidiary, Mylan manufactures active pharmaceutical ingredients (APIs) for use in MYL products, as well as for third parties. Matrix ranks as one of the largest API producers in the world. Matrix also offers finished dose drugs and other products.

In July 2010, MYL announced plans to purchase Bioniche Pharma, an Ireland-based maker of injectable drugs, for $550 million in cash. Mylan expects this deal to be EPS accretive within one year after completion.

Company Financials Fiscal Year Ended Dec. 31

Per Share Data ($)	2009	2008	2007	2006	2005	2004	2003	2002	2001	2000
Tangible Book Value	NM	NM	2.75	2.76	6.03	5.30	4.39	3.97	2.97	3.00
Cash Flow	1.61	0.33	1.27	0.99	0.91	1.37	1.11	1.07	0.28	0.65
Earnings	0.30	-1.05	0.99	0.79	0.74	1.21	0.97	0.91	0.13	0.52
S&P Core Earnings	0.75	0.25	-4.50	0.78	0.64	1.05	0.89	0.84	0.40	NA
Dividends	Nil	Nil	0.24	0.12	0.10	0.08	0.08	0.07	0.07	0.07
Payout Ratio	Nil	Nil	24%	15%	14%	7%	18%	8%	55%	14%
Prices:High	19.21	15.49	22.90	25.00	21.69	26.35	28.75	16.56	16.94	14.33
Prices:Low	9.65	5.75	12.93	18.65	15.21	14.24	15.56	11.15	8.96	7.11
P/E Ratio:High	64	NM	23	25	27	36	24	17	19	NM
P/E Ratio:Low	32	NM	13	19	19	19	13	12	12	NM

Income Statement Analysis (Million $)	2009	2008	2007	2006	2005	2004	2003	2002	2001	2000
Revenue	5,064	5,138	1,612	1,257	1,253	1,375	1,269	1,104	847	790
Operating Income	1,122	1,359	586	347	321	504	452	441	209	259
Depreciation	401	422	61.5	46.8	45.1	44.3	40.6	46.1	42.4	35.7
Interest Expense	319	357	52.3	31.3	Nil	Nil	Nil	Nil	Nil	Nil
Pretax Income	227	-47.8	426	275	312	513	427	408	58.0	243
Effective Tax Rate	NM	NM	48.9%	32.8%	34.8%	34.7%	36.1%	36.3%	36.0%	36.5%
Net Income	233	-181	217	185	204	335	272	260	37.1	154
S&P Core Earnings	232	75.6	-1,156	184	175	286	247	241	113	NA

Balance Sheet & Other Financial Data (Million $)	2009	2008	2007	2006	2005	2004	2003	2002	2001	2000
Cash	408	599	1,427	518	808	687	687	617	285	303
Current Assets	3,285	3,175	2,412	1,192	1,528	1,318	1,228	1,062	879	687
Total Assets	10,802	10,410	4,254	1,871	2,136	1,875	1,745	1,617	1,466	1,341
Current Liabilities	1,718	1,545	701	265	246	174	266	175	291	87.8
Long Term Debt	4,985	5,165	1,655	685	19.3	19.1	19.9	21.9	23.3	30.6
Common Equity	3,131	2,704	1,649	4,242	2,786	2,600	1,446	1,607	1,133	1,204
Total Capital	8,130	8,443	3,390	4,948	2,830	2,642	1,479	1,646	1,175	1,253
Capital Expenditures	154	165	162	104	90.7	118	32.6	20.6	24.7	28.8
Cash Flow	495	101	279	231	249	379	313	306	79.5	190
Current Ratio	1.9	2.1	3.4	4.5	6.2	7.6	4.6	6.1	3.0	7.8
% Long Term Debt of Capitalization	61.3	61.2	48.8	13.8	0.7	0.7	1.3	1.3	2.0	2.4
% Net Income of Revenue	4.6	NM	13.5	14.7	16.2	24.3	21.5	23.6	4.4	19.5
% Return on Assets	2.2	NM	7.1	9.2	10.1	18.5	16.2	16.9	2.6	12.1
% Return on Equity	8.0	NM	17.8	5.3	7.6	14.1	19.1	17.7	3.2	13.6

Data as orig reptd.; bef. results of disc opers/spec. items. Per share data adj. for stk. divs.; EPS diluted. E-Estimated. NA-Not Available. NM-Not Meaningful. NR-Not Ranked. UR-Under Review.

Office: 1500 Corporate Dr, Canonsburg, PA 15317-8580.
Telephone: 724-514-1800.
Email: investor_relations@mylan.com
Website: http://www.mylan.com

Chrmn & CEO: R.J. Coury
Pres: H. Bresch
Vice Chrmn: R. Piatt
COO & EVP: R. Malik

EVP & CFO: J. Sheehan
Investor Contact: K. King (724-514-1800)
Board Members: W. Cameron, R. J. Coury, N. Dimick, D. J. Leech, J. Maroon, M. W. Parrish, R. Piatt, C. B. Todd, R. L. Vanderveen

Founded: 1970
Domicile: Pennsylvania
Employees: 15,500

The McGraw·Hill Companies

Nabors Industries Ltd

STANDARD &POOR'S

S&P Recommendation HOLD ★★★☆☆	**Price** $19.35 (as of Oct 22, 2010)	**12-Mo. Target Price** $19.00	**Investment Style** Large-Cap Growth

GICS Sector Energy
Sub-Industry Oil & Gas Drilling

Summary This Bermuda company is the world's largest oil and gas land drilling contractor.

Key Stock Statistics (Source S&P, Vickers, company reports)

52-Wk Range	$27.05– 15.54	S&P Oper. EPS 2010**E**	0.94	Market Capitalization(B)	$5.520	Beta	1.49
Trailing 12-Month EPS	$0.23	S&P Oper. EPS 2011**E**	1.38	Yield (%)	Nil	S&P 3-Yr. Proj. EPS CAGR(%)	-23
Trailing 12-Month P/E	84.1	P/E on S&P Oper. EPS 2010**E**	20.6	Dividend Rate/Share	Nil	S&P Credit Rating	A-
$10K Invested 5 Yrs Ago	$6,287	Common Shares Outstg. (M)	285.3	Institutional Ownership (%)	82		

Price Performance

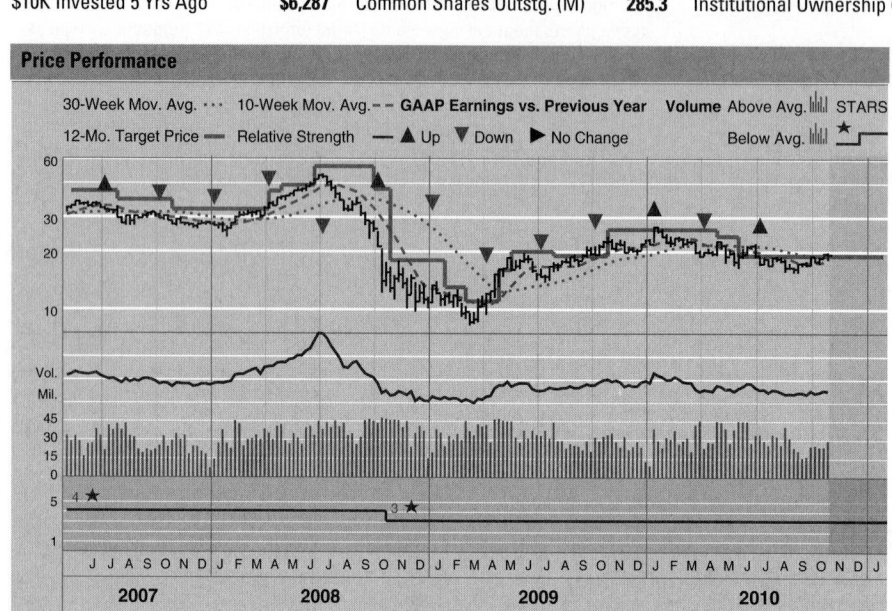

- 30-Week Mov. Avg. · · · 10-Week Mov. Avg. - - **GAAP Earnings vs. Previous Year** Volume Above Avg. STARS
- 12-Mo. Target Price — Relative Strength — ▲ Up ▼ Down ▶ No Change Below Avg.

Options: ASE, CBOE, P, Ph

Analysis prepared by **Michael Kay** on September 29, 2010, when the stock traded at **$ 18.62**.

Highlights

➤ Second-quarter cash margins fell $629 per day, to $7,788. NBR had an average of 172 working rigs, versus about 143 rigs last year. As of late July, NBR's rig count stood at 179, with four idle rigs under contract. The well servicing segment incurred greater than normal costs to bring equipment back into service during the second quarter. With a dominant position in U.S. shale, as two-thirds of its rigs are higher-spec used for horizontal drilling and one-third of its rigs are now employed in liquids-rich markets, NBR stands to further improve market share when natural gas markets strengthen. We see third quarter utilization at 55%, but continue to see challenges in pricing into 2011. NBR recently closed on the acquisition of Superior Well Services for $900 million, expanding into the pressure pumping business.

➤ International results continue to disappoint, most recently on project deferrals in Saudi Arabia and Mexico. We see opportunities in Canadian shale, but uncertainty in Alaska.

➤ We see 2010 and 2011 EPS of $0.94 and $1.38, respectively, versus 2009's of $1.30. We estimate capex reduction to $600 million in 2010, from about $1 billion in 2009.

Investment Rationale/Risk

➤ North American onshore drilling has faced challenges due to capacity additions, spending cutbacks and an overall decline in drilling activity. While we view NBR as somewhat protected by long-term contracts, an emphasis on larger operators, segment diversification and a modern fleet, we expect volatility in the sector as rig counts remain well-below 2008 levels. In our view, NBR has strong drilling prospects in unconventional plays, given technology advantages and its newbuild program. We are positive on the outlook of the pressure pumping business; however, NBR's core business has been drilling and it remains to be seen what synergies will arise.

➤ Risks to our opinion and target price include reduced oil and gas prices and dayrates; delays in rig deliveries; and cost inflation.

➤ Shares of land drillers recovered nicely in 2009, but weak dayrates and utilization (albeit rising), uncertain economies and weak natural gas fundamentals have us cautious on the sector. Blending peer-average valuations of 5.5X our 2011 EBITDA estimate, 4.5X our 2011 cash flow projection, and 14X our 2011 EPS estimate, we arrive at our 12-month target price of $19.

Qualitative Risk Assessment

LOW	MEDIUM	HIGH

Our risk assessment reflects NBR's sensitivity to commodity prices, capital spending by oil and gas producers, and the rising US rig supply. Partly offsetting these risks is NBR's diversified fleet, including overseas operations, and its leadership position in the industry.

Quantitative Evaluations

S&P Quality Ranking NR

D	C	B-	B	B+	A-	A	A+

Relative Strength Rank MODERATE

69

LOWEST = 1   HIGHEST = 99

Revenue/Earnings Data

Revenue (Million $)

	1Q	2Q	3Q	4Q	Year
2010	902.1	905.1	--	--	--
2009	1,143	867.9	791.9	834.5	3,692
2008	1,322	1,282	1,455	1,475	5,512
2007	1,277	1,128	1,226	1,309	4,941
2006	1,164	1,144	1,244	1,329	4,943
2005	783.7	786.1	893.3	1,016	3,551

Earnings Per Share ($)

	1Q	2Q	3Q	4Q	Year
2010	0.14	0.15	E0.24	E0.30	E0.94
2009	0.44	-0.68	0.10	-0.17	-0.30
2008	0.81	0.67	0.73	-0.30	1.93
2007	0.92	0.79	0.68	0.78	3.13
2006	0.79	0.77	1.02	0.97	3.40
2005	0.40	0.41	0.56	0.65	2.00

Fiscal year ended Dec. 31. Next earnings report expected: NA. EPS Estimates based on S&P Operating Earnings; historical GAAP earnings are as reported.

Dividend Data

No cash dividends have been paid.

Nabors Industries Ltd

STANDARD &POOR'S

Business Summary September 29, 2010

CORPORATE OVERVIEW. The world's largest land drilling contractor, Nabors Industries Ltd. owns a fleet of about 528 land drilling rigs. Formed as a Bermuda-exempt company in December 2001, but operating continuously in the drilling sector since the early 1900s, Nabors conducts oil, gas and geothermal land drilling operations in the lower 48 U.S. states, Alaska and Canada, and internationally, mainly in South and Central America, the Middle East and Africa. NBR actively markets 548 land drilling rigs and 557 land workover and well servicing rigs in the U.S. and approximately 172 rigs in Canada. In addition, it markets 40 platform, 13 jackup and three barge rigs in the Gulf of Mexico and international markets; these rigs provide well servicing, workover and drilling services. NBR also has a 51% ownership interest in a joint venture in Saudi Arabia, which actively markets nine rigs.

The contract drilling segment (98% of 2009 revenues) provides drilling, workover, well servicing and related services in the U.S. (including the lower 48, Alaska and offshore), Canada, and internationally. During 2009, 44% of contract drilling revenues served customers in the Lower 48, either for land drilling or land well-servicing. Well servicing and workover services are provided for existing wells where some form of artificial lift is required to bring oil to the surface. To supplement its primary business, NBR offers ancillary wellsite services, such as oilfield management, engineering, transportation, construction, maintenance, and well logging.

NBR's contract drilling business is dependent on the level of capital spending by oil and gas exploration and production companies. The decline in oil and gas prices in late 2008 led to a sharp drop in drilling activity during 2009, sending rig utilization levels and dayrates plunging. We estimate NBR's U.S. onshore rig utilization averaged 46% in 2009, versus 79% in 2008, and dayrates declined about 10%, less pronounced than the industry given NBR's contract coverage. We expect rig utilization of about 54% in 2010 and over 65% in 2011 as drilling activity improves. Internationally, NBR's business has grown significantly in the past decade. In 2009, International land drilling represented a greater percentage of operating income than U.S. land drilling. However, we see better 2010 results at U.S. land drilling offset by the decline in international activity, most notably in Saudi Arabia and Mexico. International markets are seeing a shift in focus to natural gas, the opposite of the domestic environment, causing significant downtime and lagging results.

Company Financials Fiscal Year Ended Dec. 31

Per Share Data ($)	2009	2008	2007	2006	2005	2004	2003	2002	2001	2000
Tangible Book Value	NA	15.96	14.84	11.46	10.83	8.68	7.35	6.39	5.89	5.51
Cash Flow	NA	4.24	5.01	4.77	3.04	1.84	1.36	1.06	1.59	0.94
Earnings	-0.30	1.93	3.13	3.40	2.00	0.96	0.63	0.41	1.09	0.45
Dividends	Nil	Nil	Nil	Nil	Nil	Nil	Nil	Nil	Nil	Nil
Payout Ratio	Nil	Nil	Nil	Nil	Nil	Nil	Nil	Nil	Nil	Nil
Prices:High	24.07	50.58	36.42	41.35	39.94	27.13	22.93	24.99	31.56	30.24
Prices:Low	8.25	9.72	26.00	27.26	23.10	20.01	16.10	13.07	9.00	14.06
P/E Ratio:High	NM	26	12	12	20	28	37	62	29	68
P/E Ratio:Low	NM	5	8	8	12	21	26	32	8	32

Income Statement Analysis (Million $)										
Revenue	3,692	5,512	4,941	4,943	3,551	2,394	1,880	1,466	2,121	1,327
Operating Income	NA	1,264	1,750	1,952	1,304	626	438	351	0.69	377
Depreciation, Depletion and Amortization	736	658	540	409	339	300	235	195	190	152
Interest Expense	265	91.6	63.6	46.6	44.8	48.5	70.7	67.1	60.7	35.4
Pretax Income	-235	802	1,135	1,471	874	336	175	141	542	227
Effective Tax Rate	63.5%	31.2%	21.1%	30.6%	25.8%	9.94%	NM	13.7%	35.9%	40.2%
Net Income	-85.6	551	896	1,021	649	302	192	121	348	135

Balance Sheet & Other Financial Data (Million $)										
Cash	1,091	584	767	701	565	1,253	1,532	1,331	919	551
Current Assets	NA	2,167	2,205	2,505	2,617	1,581	1,516	1,370	1,031	1,018
Total Assets	10,664	10,468	10,103	9,142	7,230	5,863	5,603	5,064	4,152	3,137
Current Liabilities	NA	1,129	1,494	854	1,352	1,199	598	751	330	279
Long Term Debt	3,941	3,888	3,306	4,004	1,252	1,202	1,986	1,615	1,568	855
Common Equity	5,168	4,692	4,514	3,537	3,758	2,929	2,490	2,158	1,858	1,806
Total Capital	NA	9,339	8,363	8,125	5,727	4,517	4,849	4,175	3,711	2,759
Capital Expenditures	1,093	1,490	2,014	1,927	907	544	353	317	701	301
Cash Flow	NA	1,209	1,436	1,430	987	603	427	317	538	288
Current Ratio	3.6	1.9	1.5	2.9	1.9	1.3	2.5	1.8	3.1	3.6
% Long Term Debt of Capitalization	43.3	41.6	39.5	49.3	21.9	26.6	41.0	38.7	42.2	31.0
% Return on Assets	NA	5.4	9.3	12.5	9.9	5.3	3.6	2.6	9.5	4.9
% Return on Equity	NM	12.0	22.3	28.0	19.4	11.2	8.3	6.0	19.0	8.3

Data as orig reptd.; bef. results of disc opers/spec. items. Per share data adj. for stk. divs.; EPS diluted. E-Estimated. NA-Not Available. NM-Not Meaningful. NR-Not Ranked. UR-Under Review.

Office: 8 Par-La-Ville Road, Hamilton, Bermuda HM08.
Telephone: 441-292-1510.
Website: http://www.nabors.com
Chrmn & CEO: E.M. Isenberg

Pres, Vice Chrmn & COO: A.G. Petrello
CFO, Chief Acctg Officer & Cntlr: R.C. Wood
Secy: M.D. Andrews
Investor Contact: D.A. Smith (281-775-8038)

Board Members: W. T. Comfort, III, E. M. Isenberg, J. V. Lombardi, J. L. Payne, A. G. Petrello, M. M. Sheinfeld, M. J. Whitman.
Founded: 1968
Domicile: Bermuda
Employees: 15,242

The McGraw-Hill Companies

Nasdaq OMX Group Inc (The)

STANDARD &POOR'S

S&P Recommendation HOLD ★★★☆☆	**Price** $20.66 (as of Oct 22, 2010)	**12-Mo. Target Price** $21.00	**Investment Style** Large-Cap Blend

GICS Sector Financials
Sub-Industry Specialized Finance

Summary This leading global exchange group delivers trading, exchange technology, securities listing, and public company services across six continents.

Key Stock Statistics (Source S&P, Vickers, company reports)

52-Wk Range	$23.11–17.18	S&P Oper. EPS 2010**E**	1.97	Market Capitalization(B)	$4.187	Beta	1.01
Trailing 12-Month EPS	$1.21	S&P Oper. EPS 2011**E**	2.18	Yield (%)	Nil	S&P 3-Yr. Proj. EPS CAGR(%)	12
Trailing 12-Month P/E	17.1	P/E on S&P Oper. EPS 2010**E**	10.5	Dividend Rate/Share	Nil	S&P Credit Rating	BBB
$10K Invested 5 Yrs Ago	$7,101	Common Shares Outstg. (M)	202.7	Institutional Ownership (%)	60		

Price Performance

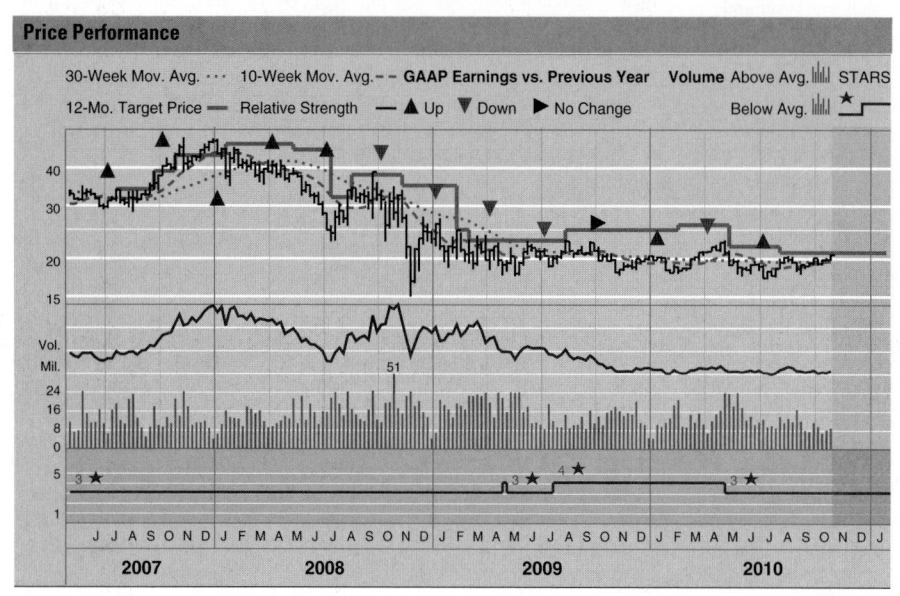

30-Week Mov. Avg. ···   10-Week Mov. Avg. --   GAAP Earnings vs. Previous Year   Volume Above Avg. STARS
12-Mo. Target Price —   Relative Strength   ▲ Up   ▼ Down   ► No Change   Below Avg.

Options: ASE, CBOE, P, Ph

Analysis prepared by **Rafay Khalid, CFA** on July 30, 2010, when the stock traded at **$ 19.46**.

Highlights

➤ We project that revenues will increase 1% in 2010, reflecting our expectation for stabilization in NDAQ's U.S. cash equities market share. We believe the company's new pricing scheme will help it gain market share and generate revenue growth in the Market Services business unit. We forecast the company's Market Technology business segment will experience growth, on our view of increasing customer orders. We see revenue growth of about 3% in 2011.

➤ We expect gross margins will widen in 2010, on our outlook for lower liquidity rebates as the company introduces a new pricing scheme. However, we project expenses on a dollar basis to increase to about $858 million in 2010 and $896 million in 2011, from $838 million in 2009. Overall, we see operating margins improving to 20.8% in 2010 and 22.2% in 2011, from 18.1% in 2009.

➤ Our operating EPS estimates are $1.97 for 2010 and $2.20 in 2011, both excluding one-time items. This compares to operating EPS of $1.83 in 2009, also excluding one-time items.

Investment Rationale/Risk

➤ We believe NDAQ has made solid progress in integrating its recent acquisitions and establishing new opportunities such as interest rate swap clearing through its subsidiary, IDCG, which has garnered significant participant interest. We expect the company to benefit financially from its initiative to introduce central clearing to all Nordic cash equity markets and diversify its revenue stream away from just cash equities. However, we are concerned about execution risk, given the large number of new initiatives the company is undertaking during 2010.

➤ Risks to our recommendation and target price include a significant decline in pricing, legislation that restricts proprietary trading, integration risk related to acquisitions, and longer-than-expected time to complete new initiatives.

➤ Our 12-month target price of $21, reflects a historical average P/E ratio of 9.7X our 2011 EPS forecast. We believe the historical average is warranted, given our outlook for a gradually improving economy.

Qualitative Risk Assessment

LOW	MEDIUM	HIGH

Our risk assessment reflects the potential volatility in results due to changes in equity trading volumes, the potential impact of future regulatory changes, and the uncertainty surrounding NDAQ's international strategy.

Quantitative Evaluations

S&P Quality Ranking   NR

D	C	B-	B	B+	A-	A	A+

Relative Strength Rank   MODERATE

65

LOWEST = 1   HIGHEST = 99

Revenue/Earnings Data

Revenue (Million $)

	1Q	2Q	3Q	4Q	Year
2010	764.0	876.0	--	--	--
2009	895.0	889.0	810.0	815.0	3,409
2008	813.8	821.5	990.3	1,024	3,649
2007	562.0	558.2	652.0	664.5	2,437
2006	396.2	411.0	402.9	447.2	1,658
2005	180.2	219.7	220.5	259.6	879.9

Earnings Per Share ($)

2010	0.28	0.46	E0.51	E0.52	E1.97
2009	0.44	0.33	0.28	0.20	1.25
2008	0.69	0.48	0.28	0.17	1.56
2007	0.14	0.39	2.41	0.57	3.46
2006	0.16	0.13	0.22	0.43	0.95
2005	0.13	0.13	0.16	0.15	0.57

Fiscal year ended Dec. 31. Next earnings report expected: Early November. EPS Estimates based on S&P Operating Earnings; historical GAAP earnings are as reported.

Dividend Data

No cash dividends have been paid.

Please read the Required Disclosures and Analyst Certification on the last page of this report.

The **McGraw-Hill** Companies

Business Summary July 30, 2010

CORPORATE OVERVIEW. Nasdaq OMX Group is a leading global exchange group that delivers trading, exchange technology, securities listing and public company services across six continents. In the U.S., it operates The Nasdaq Stock Market, the largest electronic equity securities market in the country, with 3,700 listed companies as of December 31, 2009. The company earns revenue from a number of products and services including trade execution, reselling market data, listing fees, intellectual property licensing, and corporate client services.

NDAQ's business is divided into three segments - Market Services, Issuer Services, and Market Technology. In 2009, Market Services accounted for approximately 86% of the company's revenue. This segment consists of NDAQ's U.S. and European transaction-based business, market data, and broker services. The largest portion of Market Services segment is transaction fees NDAQ receives for executing trades on its electronic platform. A smaller revenue source is the fees the company earns from aggregating and reselling trade and quote information from its systems.

Issuer Services, which accounts for about 10% of revenues, includes fees from its securities listings business and other financial products. Revenues in this segment are primarily derived from annual fees from companies whose shares are listed on the Nasdaq Stock Market, fees for listing additional shares, and fees for new listings (initial public offerings). Issuer Services also generates revenue from developing and licensing the Nasdaq brand. Market Technology made up 4% of the NDAQ's revenues in 2009. This segment offers systems solutions, which support trading, clearing and settlement, and information dissemination for a variety of instruments including equities and derivatives.

COMPETITIVE LANDSCAPE. We see NDAQ competing with other domestic exchanges, primarily the NYSE Euronext (NYX), for company listings, and competing with these exchanges, regional exchanges and electronic communication networks (ECNs) for trade execution volume. While consolidation, particularly among ECNs, has decreased the number of domestic competitors, we believe technology advancements and regulatory changes have kept the U.S. equity exchange business highly competitive. We think NDAQ competes on the basis of liquidity, speed and price in its core trade execution services. NDAQ plans to be the low price provider in the market for trade execution, and we expect it to continue offering lower listing fees than the NYSE.

Company Financials Fiscal Year Ended Dec. 31

Per Share Data ($)	2009	2008	2007	2006	2005	2004	2003	2002	2001	2000
Tangible Book Value	NM	NM	7.54	2.44	NM	NM	2.04	NA	NA	NA
Cash Flow	1.72	2.02	3.65	1.20	1.08	0.99	0.57	1.56	1.15	1.92
Earnings	1.25	1.56	3.46	0.95	0.57	-0.14	-0.68	0.40	0.35	1.34
S&P Core Earnings	1.55	1.75	1.62	0.96	0.53	-0.19	-0.69	0.31	NA	NA
Dividends	Nil	Nil	Nil	Nil	Nil	Nil	Nil	NA	NA	NA
Payout Ratio	Nil	Nil	Nil	Nil	Nil	Nil	Nil	NA	NA	NA
Prices:High	27.39	49.90	50.47	46.75	45.23	NA	NA	NA	NA	NA
Prices:Low	17.51	14.96	26.57	23.91	8.15	NA	NA	NA	NA	NA
P/E Ratio:High	22	32	15	49	79	NM	NA	NA	NA	NA
P/E Ratio:Low	14	10	8	25	14	NM	NA	NA	NA	NA

Income Statement Analysis (Million $)	2009	2008	2007	2006	2005	2004	2003	2002	2001	2000
Revenue	3,409	3,649	2,437	1,658	880	540	590	799	857	868
Operating Income	766	758	440	288	181	85.0	126	197	207	300
Depreciation	104	92.6	38.9	45.1	67.0	76.0	90.0	97.9	93.4	65.6
Interest Expense	102	86.6	72.9	91.1	20.0	11.0	19.0	19.6	9.65	NA
Pretax Income	391	524	794	212	106	2.60	-66.0	71.7	73.1	254
Effective Tax Rate	32.7%	38.6%	34.7%	40.2%	41.8%	29.3%	NM	57.3%	52.4%	41.3%
Net Income	266	320	518	128	62.0	1.80	-45.0	43.1	40.5	150
S&P Core Earnings	330	355	238	129	50.5	-15.2	-54.1	26.4	NA	NA

Balance Sheet & Other Financial Data (Million $)	2009	2008	2007	2006	2005	2004	2003	2002	2001	2000
Cash	902	793	1,325	1,950	165	58.0	149	445	522	516
Current Assets	3,454	5,435	1,682	2,313	597	406	530	697	815	718
Total Assets	10,722	12,695	2,979	3,716	2,047	815	851	1,176	1,326	1,075
Current Liabilities	2,867	5,061	411	461	325	208	238	295	294	224
Long Term Debt	1,867	2,294	118	1,493	1,185	265	265	430	289	25.0
Common Equity	4,927	4,242	2,208	1,457	253	157	27.0	137	518	765
Total Capital	7,051	7,224	2,419	3,066	1,533	452	467	705	812	805
Capital Expenditures	59.0	54.7	18.5	21.0	25.0	26.0	32.0	85.4	123	187
Cash Flow	370	412	557	172	129	77.8	45.0	131	134	216
Current Ratio	1.2	1.1	4.1	5.0	1.8	2.0	2.2	2.4	2.8	3.2
% Long Term Debt of Capitalization	26.5	31.8	4.9	50.6	77.2	58.6	56.7	60.9	35.5	3.1
% Net Income of Revenue	7.8	8.8	21.3	7.7	7.0	0.0	NM	5.4	4.7	17.3
% Return on Assets	2.3	4.1	15.5	4.4	4.3	0.0	NM	3.5	3.4	18.2
% Return on Equity	5.8	9.9	28.3	15.8	30.2	6.7	NM	13.2	6.3	26.9

Data as orig reptd.; bef. results of disc opers/spec. items. Per share data adj. for stk. divs.; EPS diluted. E-Estimated. NA-Not Available. NM-Not Meaningful. NR-Not Ranked. UR-Under Review.

Office: One Liberty Plaza, 165 Broadway, New York, NY 10006.
Telephone: 212-401-8700.
Website: http://www.nasdaq.com
Chrmn: H.F. Baldwin

Vice Chrmn: U. Backstrom
CEO: R. Greifeld
EVP & CFO: A.T. Friedman
EVP & General Counsel: E. Knight

Investor Contact: V. Palmiere (212-401-8742)
Board Members: U. Backstrom, H. F. Baldwin, M. Casey, L. Gorman, R. Greifeld, G. H. Hutchins, B. Kantola, E. Kazim, J. D. Markese, H. M. Nielsen, T. F. O'Neill, J. Riepe, M. R. Splinter, L. Wedenborn, D. L. Wince-Smith

Founded: 1979
Domicile: Delaware
Employees: 2,216

National Oilwell Varco Inc

STANDARD &POOR'S

S&P Recommendation **BUY** ★★★★☆	Price $48.59 (as of Oct 22, 2010)	12-Mo. Target Price $52.00	Investment Style Large-Cap Growth

GICS Sector Energy
Sub-Industry Oil & Gas Equipment & Services

Summary This company designs and manufactures drill rig equipment, provides downhole tools and services, and also provides supply chain integration services to the upstream oil and gas industry.

Key Stock Statistics (Source S&P, Vickers, company reports)

52-Wk Range	$49.02–32.18	S&P Oper. EPS 2010**E**	3.87	Market Capitalization(B)	$20.363	Beta	1.39
Trailing 12-Month EPS	$3.83	S&P Oper. EPS 2011**E**	3.72	Yield (%)	0.82	S&P 3-Yr. Proj. EPS CAGR(%)	4
Trailing 12-Month P/E	12.7	P/E on S&P Oper. EPS 2010**E**	12.6	Dividend Rate/Share	$0.40	S&P Credit Rating	A-
$10K Invested 5 Yrs Ago	$17,391	Common Shares Outstg. (M)	419.1	Institutional Ownership (%)	82		

Price Performance

30-Week Mov. Avg. · · · 10-Week Mov. Avg. - - GAAP Earnings vs. Previous Year Volume Above Avg. STARS
12-Mo. Target Price — Relative Strength ▲ Up ▼ Down ▶ No Change Below Avg. ★

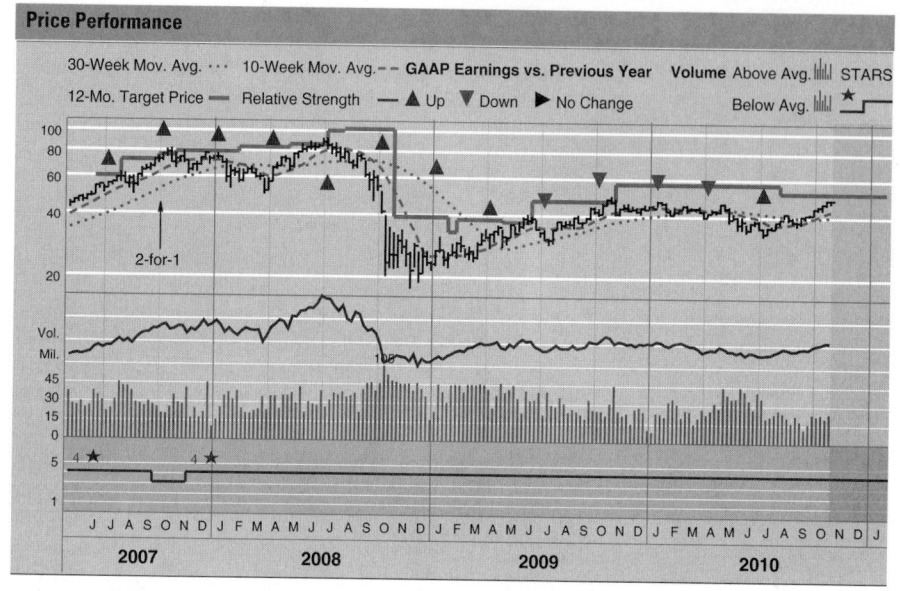

Options: ASE, CBOE, P

Analysis prepared by **Stewart Glickman, CFA** on August 03, 2010, when the stock traded at **$ 40.96**.

Highlights

► At the end of June, total backlog stood at $4.9 billion, down $0.5 billion sequentially, as second quarter new orders (net of cancellations) of $660 million were about 53% of the revenues out of backlog. We note that additions to backlog are inherently uneven. Given the amount of work slated to be done in key markets such as Brazil, and NOV's key role in the oilfield capital equipment market, we think order and thus backlog recovery is mainly a question of timing. We expect NOV to exit 2010 with a backlog of about $4.3 billion, and note that NOV anticipates Brazil tenders possibly occurring in late 2010, but more likely early 2011.

► With the rise of U.S. shale plays, which yield high service intensity, we see improved 2010 revenues in the Petroleum Services & Supplies segment. We expect cannibalization of oilfield equipment from idled rigs to drop off in 2010, and note that both shale plays and deepwater wells tend to require premium equipment, such as drill pipe, which NOV offers.

► We see revenues down 4.3% in 2010, but rising 3.2% in 2011. We see EPS of $3.87 in 2010, falling about 4% to $3.72 in 2011.

Investment Rationale/Risk

► We view NOV as an attractive play on the need for new rig equipment, particularly for deepwater and unconventional natural gas projects. While the current book of 122 rigs under construction (53 jackups, 35 semisubmersibles, and 34 drillships) implies about a 22% addition to the existing marketed fleet, we think that currently unsatisfied demand (especially for deepwater-capable equipment) will absorb most new additions. We also see potential regulatory changes to U.S. Gulf of Mexico deepwater drilling that may require new equipment.

► Risks to our opinion and target price include lower-than-expected prices for crude oil and natural gas; a slowdown in drilling activity; delays in meeting capital equipment orders; and unexpected contract cancellations.

► Our discounted cash flow (DCF) model, assuming free cash flow growth of 9%, terminal growth of 3% and a WACC of 12.8%, yields intrinsic value of $52. Applying below-peer multiples of 8X enterprise value to projected 2010 EBITDA, 11X estimated 2010 cash flow, and our DCF model, our 12-month target price is $52.

Qualitative Risk Assessment

LOW	MEDIUM	HIGH

Our risk assessment reflects NOV's exposure to volatile crude oil and natural gas prices, and capital spending decisions made by its contract driller and exploration and production customers. Offsetting these risks is what we view as NOV's leading industry position as a manufacturer of rig capital equipment.

Quantitative Evaluations

S&P Quality Ranking B+

D	C	B-	B	B+	A-	A	A+

Relative Strength Rank STRONG

88

LOWEST = 1   HIGHEST = 99

Revenue/Earnings Data

Revenue (Million $)

	1Q	2Q	3Q	4Q	Year
2010	3,032	2,941	--	--	--
2009	3,481	3,010	3,087	3,134	12,712
2008	2,685	3,324	3,612	3,810	13,431
2007	2,166	2,385	2,580	2,659	9,789
2006	1,512	1,657	1,778	2,079	7,026
2005	814.9	1,216	1,237	1,377	4,645

Earnings Per Share ($)

	1Q	2Q	3Q	4Q	Year
2010	1.01	0.96	E0.95	E0.95	E3.87
2009	1.13	0.53	0.92	0.94	3.52
2008	1.11	1.04	1.31	1.40	4.90
2007	0.78	0.90	1.02	1.05	3.76
2006	0.34	0.42	0.50	0.68	1.94
2005	0.17	0.18	0.25	0.29	0.91

Fiscal year ended Dec. 31. Next earnings report expected: Late October. EPS Estimates based on S&P Operating Earnings; historical GAAP earnings are as reported.

Dividend Data (Dates: mm/dd Payment Date: mm/dd/yy)

Amount ($)	Date Decl.	Ex-Div. Date	Stk. of Record	Payment Date
1.0 Spl.	11/17	11/30	12/02	12/16/09
0.100	02/26	03/10	03/12	03/26/10
0.100	05/13	06/09	06/11	06/25/10
0.100	08/19	09/08	09/10	09/24/10

Dividends have been paid since 2009. Source: Company reports.

Please read the Required Disclosures and Analyst Certification on the last page of this report.

The McGraw·Hill Companies

National Oilwell Varco Inc

STANDARD
&POOR'S

Business Summary August 03, 2010

CORPORATE OVERVIEW. Formerly known as National-Oilwell, this company changed its name to National Oilwell Varco (NOV) on March 14, 2005, following the completion of the merger with Varco International. NOV, a worldwide designer, manufacturer and marketer of comprehensive systems and components used in oil and gas drilling and production, as well as a provider of downhole tools and services, also provides supply chain integration services to the upstream oil and gas industry. The company estimates that more than 90% of the mobile offshore rig fleet and the majority of the world's larger land rigs (2,000 horsepower and greater) manufactured in the past 20 years use drawworks, mud pumps and other drilling components manufactured by NOV.

The company generated 2009 revenues of about $12.7 billion, and operating income of $2.3 billion, for an operating margin of approximately 18.2%. The company's Rig Technology segment ($8.1 billion of revenue in 2009, and $2.3 billion of 2009 segment operating income) designs, manufactures and sells drilling systems and components for both land and offshore drilling rigs, as well as complete land drilling and well servicing rigs. The major mechanical components include drawworks, mud pumps, power swivels, SCR houses,

solids control equipment, traveling equipment and rotary tables. Many of these components are designed specifically for applications in offshore, extended reach and deep land drilling. This equipment is installed on new rigs and is often replaced during the upgrade and refurbishment of existing rigs. As of December 31, 2009, total backlog in this segment was about $6.4 billion, down 42% from a year earlier.

The company's Petroleum Services & Supplies segment ($3.7 billion, $453 million) provides a variety of consumable goods and services used in the drilling, completion, workover and remediation of oil and gas wells, service pipelines, flowlines, and other oilfield tubular goods. Products include transfer pumps, solids control systems, drilling motors and other downhole tools, rig instrumentation systems, and mud pump consumables. Following the April 2008 acquisition of Grant Prideco, this segment now offers drill pipe and drill bits.

Company Financials Fiscal Year Ended Dec. 31

Per Share Data ($)	2009	2008	2007	2006	2005	2004	2003	2002	2001	2000
Tangible Book Value	10.93	NA	9.65	5.91	4.20	3.33	2.49	2.17	3.19	2.72
Cash Flow	4.70	5.90	4.19	2.39	1.27	0.89	0.68	0.60	0.87	0.30
Earnings	3.52	4.90	3.76	1.94	0.91	0.64	0.45	0.45	0.64	0.08
S&P Core Earnings	3.75	4.89	3.76	1.94	0.90	0.58	0.41	0.38	0.57	NA
Dividends	0.10	NA	Nil	Nil	Nil	Nil	Nil	Nil	Nil	Nil
Payout Ratio	3%	NA	Nil	Nil	Nil	Nil	Nil	Nil	Nil	Nil
Prices:High	50.17	NA	82.00	38.80	34.17	18.69	12.43	14.41	20.62	19.84
Prices:Low	22.19	NA	26.88	25.81	16.54	10.83	8.75	7.60	6.20	7.00
P/E Ratio:High	14	NA	22	20	38	29	28	32	32	NM
P/E Ratio:Low	6	NA	7	13	18	17	19	17	10	NM

Income Statement Analysis (Million $)										
Revenue	12,712	13,431	9,789	7,026	4,645	2,318	2,005	1,522	1,747	1,150
Operating Income	NA	3,419	2,198	1,280	623	213	198	159	228	97.6
Depreciation, Depletion and Amortization	490	401	153	161	115	44.0	39.2	25.0	38.9	35.0
Interest Expense	53.0	67.3	50.3	48.7	52.9	38.4	38.9	27.3	24.9	Nil
Pretax Income	2,208	2,961	2,029	1,049	430	132	117	112	168	27.0
Effective Tax Rate	33.3%	33.5%	33.3%	33.9%	32.3%	14.6%	28.9%	35.0%	38.1%	51.4%
Net Income	1,469	1,952	1,337	684	287	110	76.8	73.1	104	13.1
S&P Core Earnings	1,565	1,947	1,338	685	283	99.2	69.3	61.6	93.6	NA

Balance Sheet & Other Financial Data (Million $)										
Cash	2,622	1,543	1,842	957	209	143	74.2	118	43.2	42.5
Current Assets	9,598	9,657	7,594	4,966	2,998	1,537	1,246	1,115	909	743
Total Assets	21,532	21,399	12,115	9,019	6,679	2,599	2,243	1,969	1,472	1,279
Current Liabilities	4,174	5,624	4,027	2,665	1,187	800	452	346	277	263
Long Term Debt	876	870	738	835	836	350	594	595	300	222
Common Equity	14,113	12,637	6,661	5,024	4,194	1,296	1,090	933	868	767
Total Capital	15,111	15,728	8,026	6,283	5,428	1,767	1,753	1,592	1,188	1,006
Capital Expenditures	250	379	252	200	105	39.0	32.4	24.8	27.4	24.6
Cash Flow	1,959	2,353	1,490	845	402	154	116	98.1	143	48.2
Current Ratio	2.3	1.7	1.9	1.9	2.5	1.9	2.8	3.2	3.3	2.8
% Long Term Debt of Capitalization	5.8	5.5	9.2	13.3	15.4	19.8	33.9	37.3	25.3	22.1
% Return on Assets	6.8	11.6	12.7	8.7	6.2	4.6	3.6	4.2	7.6	1.2
% Return on Equity	11.0	20.2	22.9	14.8	10.5	9.2	7.6	8.1	12.7	1.9

Data as orig reptd.; bef. results of disc opers/spec. items. Per share data adj. for stk. divs.; EPS diluted. E-Estimated. NA-Not Available. NM-Not Meaningful. NR-Not Ranked. UR-Under Review.

Office: 7909 Parkwood Circle Dr, Houston, TX 77036-6565.
Telephone: 713-346-7500.
Email: investor.relations@natoil.com
Website: http://www.natoil.com

Chrmn, Pres & CEO: M.A. Miller, Jr.
EVP & CFO: C.C. Williams
SVP, Secy & General Counsel: D.W. Rettig
CTO: H. Kverneland

Chief Acctg Officer & Cntlr: R.W. Blanchard
Board Members: G. L. Armstrong, R. E. Beauchamp, B. A. Guill, D. Harrison, R. L. Jarvis, E. L. Mattson, M. A. Miller, Jr., J. Smisek

Founded: 1987
Domicile: Delaware
Employees: 36,802

National Semiconductor Corp

STANDARD &POOR'S

S&P Recommendation	HOLD ★★★☆☆	Price $13.17 (as of Oct 22, 2010)	12-Mo. Target Price $16.00	Investment Style Large-Cap Growth

GICS Sector Information Technology
Sub-Industry Semiconductors

Summary This company is a leading manufacturer of a broad line of semiconductors, including analog, digital and mixed-signal integrated circuits.

Key Stock Statistics (Source S&P, Vickers, company reports)

52-Wk Range	$16.00– 11.84	S&P Oper. EPS 2011E	1.26	Market Capitalization(B)	$3.155	Beta	1.12
Trailing 12-Month EPS	$1.10	S&P Oper. EPS 2012E	1.24	Yield (%)	3.04	S&P 3-Yr. Proj. EPS CAGR(%)	25
Trailing 12-Month P/E	12.0	P/E on S&P Oper. EPS 2011E	10.5	Dividend Rate/Share	$0.40	S&P Credit Rating	BBB-
$10K Invested 5 Yrs Ago	$6,091	Common Shares Outstg. (M)	239.6	Institutional Ownership (%)	89		

Price Performance

30-Week Mov. Avg. ··· 10-Week Mov. Avg. ‑‑ **GAAP Earnings vs. Previous Year** Volume Above Avg. STARS
12-Mo. Target Price — Relative Strength — ▲ Up ▼ Down ▶ No Change Below Avg.

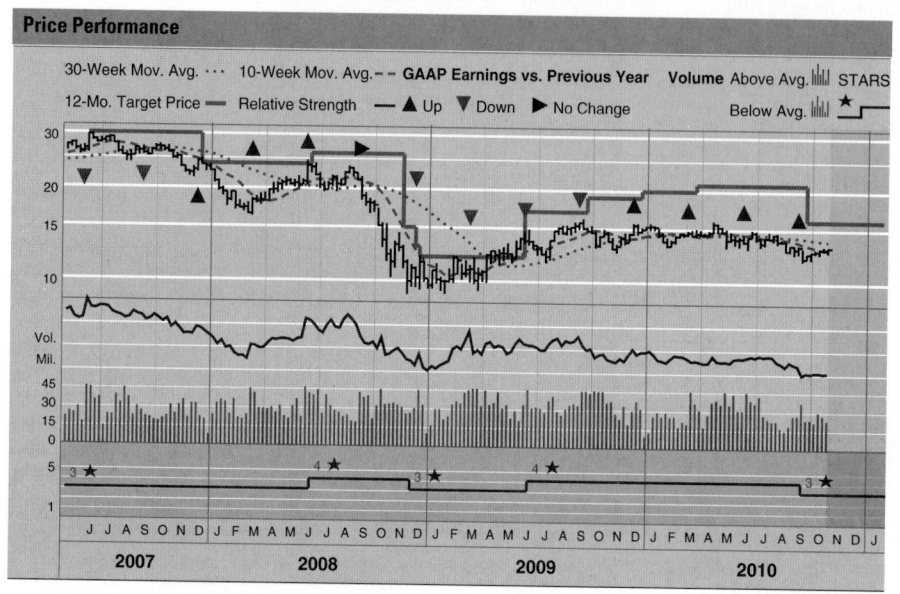

Options: ASE, CBOE, P, Ph

Analysis prepared by **Clyde Montevirgen** on September 10, 2010, when the stock traded at **$ 11.94**.

Highlights

► We expect revenues to rise 12% in FY 11 (May), after a decline of 3% in FY 10. With a renewed focus on growing sales and taking market share, NSM has cut lower-margin product lines and transformed its product portfolio, now consisting of higher-margin chips for faster-growing markets. We see power management products, new solar and light-emitting diode (LED) products and better penetration in end markets, such as wireless, supporting long-term revenue advances. But, we think economic uncertainty and rising inventory will limit growth over the near-term.

► We see gross margins widening to 69% in FY 11, from 66% in FY 10. We expect an improving sales mix, higher plant utilization and recent capacity rationalization to boost profitability in coming quarters. Although we expect expenses to rise for new product development and sales, we still look for operating margins to widen to 31% in FY 11, from 23% in FY 10, reflecting operating leverage and fewer non-recurring expenses.

► Our projections assume an effective tax rate of 30% and include stock-based compensation and restructuring-related charges.

Investment Rationale/Risk

► Our hold opinion reflects our view of sub-industry growth and fair valuation. Although we believe that the company is gaining design wins, we anticipate below-industry growth over the next few quarters as better-positioned competitors defend their market share. We also think that margins, following recent restructuring, are peaking and should ebb as orders slow. However, NSM has what we view as attractive margins, free cash flows, and return on equity. Based on these factors, we believe relative multiples should be more-or-less in line with the industry average, which is reflected in our valuation.

► Risks to our recommendation and target price include a weaker-than-anticipated economy, a worse-than-expected impact from product mix, and market share loss for NSM or its larger customers.

► Our 12-month target price of $16 is based on our price/earnings (P/E) analysis. We apply a P/E multiple of 12X, near the industry average to account for our view of NSM's relative growth, return on equity, and risks, to our calendar 2011 EPS estimate.

Qualitative Risk Assessment

LOW	MEDIUM	HIGH

NSM operates in the semiconductor industry, which tends to be cyclical. Sudden slowdowns can result from downturns in demand for electronics or from chip inventory buildup and industry overcapacity.

Quantitative Evaluations

S&P Quality Ranking B

D	C	B-	B	B+	A-	A	A+

Relative Strength Rank MODERATE

37

LOWEST = 1 HIGHEST = 99

Revenue/Earnings Data

Revenue (Million $)

	1Q	2Q	3Q	4Q	Year
2011	412.0	--	--	--	--
2010	314.4	344.6	361.9	398.5	1,419
2009	465.6	421.6	292.4	280.8	1,460
2008	471.5	499.0	453.4	462.0	1,886
2007	541.4	501.6	431.0	455.9	1,930
2006	493.8	544.0	547.7	572.6	2,158

Earnings Per Share ($)

	1Q	2Q	3Q	4Q	Year
2011	0.36	E0.33	E0.27	E0.30	E1.26
2010	0.13	0.20	0.22	0.33	0.87
2009	0.33	0.16	0.09	-0.28	0.31
2008	0.33	0.33	0.29	0.34	1.26
2007	0.35	0.27	0.22	0.28	1.12
2006	0.24	0.32	0.37	0.34	1.26

Fiscal year ended May 31. Next earnings report expected: Mid December. EPS Estimates based on S&P Operating Earnings; historical GAAP earnings are as reported.

Dividend Data (Dates: mm/dd Payment Date: mm/dd/yy)

Amount ($)	Date Decl.	Ex-Div. Date	Stk. of Record	Payment Date
0.080	12/10	12/17	12/21	01/11/10
0.080	03/11	03/18	03/22	04/12/10
0.080	06/10	06/17	06/21	07/12/10
0.100	07/14	09/16	09/20	10/12/10

Dividends have been paid since 2005. Source: Company reports.

Please read the Required Disclosures and Analyst Certification on the last page of this report.

The McGraw-Hill Companies

National Semiconductor Corp

STANDARD &POOR'S

Business Summary September 10, 2010

CORPORATE OVERVIEW. National Semiconductor Corp. designs, develops, makes and markets a wide range of semiconductor products. Leading-edge products include power management circuits, display drivers, audio and operational amplifiers, communication interface products and data conversion solutions.

The company targets a broad range of markets and applications such as wireless handsets, medical applications, displays, automotive applications, networks, test and measurement applications, industrial markets, and a broad range of portable applications. Most of its products are analog and mixed-signal integrated circuits, comprising about 91% of FY 09 (May) total revenue.

NSM recently consolidated its product line operations into one group called The Product Group, which can be further divided into four different businesses that address the power management markets including: advanced power, infrastructure power products, mobile devices power and performance power products. There are also two more business units that address the signal path area, precision signal path and high speed product, as well as a custom solutions business.

The company markets its products globally to original equipment manufacturers (OEMs) and original design manufacturers through a direct sales force. In FY 09, 60% of sales were to its top 10 customers. NSM listed two large customers, including distributors Avnet (which accounted for 15% of NSM's FY 09 sales) and Arrow (13%). Some 53% of FY 09 revenues came from distributors.

CORPORATE STRATEGY. National Semiconductor has transformed from a low to high margin company. In 1996, NSM spun off its logic, memory and discrete products (considered commodity-type components) as a separate company, Fairchild Semiconductor. The company's current expertise has been primarily in analog intensive, digital and mixed-signal complex integrated circuits; and its stated goal is to become the premier provider of high-performance, energy-efficient analog and mixed-signal solutions.

Company Financials Fiscal Year Ended May 31

Per Share Data ($)	2010	2009	2008	2007	2006	2005	2004	2003	2002	2001
Tangible Book Value	1.52	0.50	0.59	5.43	5.57	5.65	4.21	4.18	4.46	4.70
Cash Flow	1.26	0.82	1.76	1.56	1.72	1.63	1.27	0.54	0.31	1.30
Earnings	0.87	0.31	1.26	1.12	1.26	1.11	0.74	-0.09	-0.34	0.65
S&P Core Earnings	0.85	0.28	1.24	1.11	1.21	1.11	0.26	-0.59	-0.84	0.29
Dividends	0.32	0.20	0.14	0.10	0.04	Nil	Nil	Nil	Nil	Nil
Payout Ratio	37%	65%	11%	9%	3%	Nil	Nil	Nil	Nil	Nil
Calendar Year	2009	2008	2007	2006	2005	2004	2003	2002	2001	2000
Prices:High	16.20	24.75	29.69	30.93	28.75	24.35	22.63	18.65	17.55	42.97
Prices:Low	9.06	9.02	21.54	20.56	18.36	11.85	6.27	4.98	9.85	8.56
P/E Ratio:High	19	80	24	28	23	22	31	NM	NM	66
P/E Ratio:Low	10	29	17	18	15	11	8	NM	NM	13

Income Statement Analysis (Million $)										
Revenue	1,419	1,460	1,886	1,930	2,158	1,913	1,983	1,673	1,495	2,113
Operating Income	440	447	404	642	844	626	582	248	81.9	517
Depreciation	94.5	120	133	145	166	194	210	229	230	243
Interest Expense	60.3	72.7	85.5	Nil	Nil	Nil	Nil	Nil	3.90	5.00
Pretax Income	269	114	451	531	695	410	334	-23.3	-123	307
Effective Tax Rate	NA	35.5%	26.4%	29.3%	35.4%	NM	14.7%	NM	NM	19.4%
Net Income	209	73.3	332	375	449	415	285	-33.3	-122	246
S&P Core Earnings	203	66.9	326	372	433	430	102	-215	-298	108

Balance Sheet & Other Financial Data (Million $)										
Cash	1,027	700	737	829	932	867	643	802	681	818
Current Assets	1,471	1,087	1,172	1,291	1,541	1,514	1,246	1,281	1,073	1,275
Total Assets	2,275	1,963	2,149	2,202	2,511	2,504	2,280	2,245	2,289	2,362
Current Liabilities	548	276	309	300	398	285	461	367	404	472
Long Term Debt	1,001	1,227	1,415	20.6	21.1	23.0	Nil	19.9	20.4	26.0
Common Equity	426	177	197	1,749	1,926	2,062	1,681	1,706	1,781	1,768
Total Capital	1,703	1,467	1,674	1,769	1,947	2,085	1,681	1,726	1,802	1,794
Capital Expenditures	43.3	83.7	111	107	163	96.6	215	171	138	228
Cash Flow	304	193	465	520	616	610	495	195	109	489
Current Ratio	2.7	4.0	3.8	4.3	3.9	5.3	2.7	3.5	2.7	2.7
% Long Term Debt of Capitalization	58.8	83.7	84.5	1.2	1.1	1.1	Nil	1.2	1.1	1.4
% Net Income of Revenue	14.7	5.0	17.6	19.4	20.8	21.7	14.4	NM	NM	11.6
% Return on Assets	9.9	3.6	15.3	15.9	17.9	17.4	12.6	NM	NM	10.3
% Return on Equity	69.4	39.2	34.2	20.4	22.6	22.1	16.8	NM	NM	14.4

Data as orig reptd.; bef. results of disc opers/spec. items. Per share data adj. for stk. divs.; EPS diluted. E-Estimated. NA-Not Available. NM-Not Meaningful. NR-Not Ranked. UR-Under Review.

Office: 2900 Semiconductor Drive, Santa Clara, CA 95051.
Telephone: 408-721-5000.
Email: invest.group@nsc.com
Website: http://www.national.com

Chrmn, Pres & CEO: D. Macleod
SVP & CFO: L. Chew
SVP, Secy & General Counsel: T.M. DuChene
CTO: A. Bahai

Chief Acctg Officer & Cntlr: J.E. Samath
Investor Contact: R.E. DeBarr ()
Board Members: W. J. Amelio, S. R. Appleton, G. P. Arnold, R. J. Danzig, R. J. Frankenberg, D. Macleod, E. McCracken, R. McGeary, W. E. Mitchell

Founded: 1959
Domicile: Delaware
Employees: 5,800

NetApp Inc

STANDARD &POOR'S

S&P Recommendation	HOLD ★★★★★	Price	12-Mo. Target Price	Investment Style
		$51.97 (as of Oct 22, 2010)	$40.00	Large-Cap Growth

GICS Sector Information Technology
Sub-Industry Computer Storage & Peripherals

Summary This company provides storage hardware, software, and services to a variety of enterprise customers.

Key Stock Statistics (Source S&P, Vickers, company reports)

52-Wk Range	$52.42–26.89	S&P Oper. EPS 2011E	1.57	Market Capitalization(B)	$18.557	Beta	1.39
Trailing 12-Month EPS	$1.36	S&P Oper. EPS 2012E	1.69	Yield (%)	Nil	S&P 3-Yr. Proj. EPS CAGR(%)	15
Trailing 12-Month P/E	38.2	P/E on S&P Oper. EPS 2011E	33.1	Dividend Rate/Share	Nil	S&P Credit Rating	NA
$10K Invested 5 Yrs Ago	$19,611	Common Shares Outstg. (M)	357.1	Institutional Ownership (%)	93		

Price Performance

30-Week Mov. Avg. · · · 10-Week Mov. Avg. - · - GAAP Earnings vs. Previous Year   Volume Above Avg. STARS

12-Mo. Target Price — Relative Strength — ▲ Up ▼ Down ► No Change   Below Avg.

Options: ASE, CBOE, P, Ph

Analysis prepared by **Jim Yin, CFA** on August 23, 2010, when the stock traded at **$ 40.33**.

Highlights

➤ We expect revenues to rise 23% in FY 11 (Apr.), following a 15% increase in FY 10. Although the growth of the global economy has slowed considerably recently, we expect demand for data storage products to remain robust given the severity of the cutback during the downturn. We see strong demand coming from the continued trend of content digitization and increased adoption of server virtualization. We also think NTAP is gaining market share due to its presence in the network-attached storage (NAS) market, which is expected to grow faster than the overall data storage market.

➤ We project gross margins of 63% in FY 11, versus 64% in FY 10, based on our outlook for modest pricing pressure. We also think margins will be hurt by higher component costs. We believe NTAP will keep a tight control over employee head count. As a result, we see operating margins widening to 14% in FY 11, from 12% in FY 10.

➤ We estimate EPS of $1.57 for FY 11, compared to $1.13 posted in FY 10. In addition to stronger demand, we think earnings will be helped by better cost containment.

Investment Rationale/Risk

➤ Our hold recommendation is based mostly on valuation, following recent price appreciation. We think NTAP's fundamentals remain strong. Despite the financial crisis in Europe, we expect demand for data storage to remain robust due to the severity of the decline during the downturn. In addition to a modest economic recovery, we believe demand will be driven by growth of content digitization, such as record retention for compliance with government regulations. We think NTAP will gain market share with new products and stronger distribution partnerships.

➤ Risks to our recommendation and target price include a weaker-than-expected economic recovery, lower IT spending, and significant loss of market share.

➤ Our 12-month target price of $40 is based on a blend of our discounted cash flow (DCF) and enterprise value (EV)-to-sales analyses. Our DCF model assumes a weighted average cost of capital of 12% and 3% terminal growth, and yields an intrinsic value of $40. We apply an EV-to-sales multiple of 2.4X, near the company's historical average, to our FY 11 sales estimate of $4.8 billion and derive a same $40 valuation.

Qualitative Risk Assessment

LOW	MEDIUM	HIGH

Our risk assessment takes into account the historical volatility of the data storage industry and the rapid pace of technological change that typifies the industry.

Quantitative Evaluations

S&P Quality Ranking   B

D	C	B-	B	B+	A-	A	A+

Relative Strength Rank   STRONG

87

LOWEST = 1   HIGHEST = 99

Revenue/Earnings Data

Revenue (Million $)

	1Q	2Q	3Q	4Q	Year
2011	1,138	--	--	--	--
2010	838.0	910.0	1,012	1,172	3,931
2009	868.8	911.6	746.3	879.6	3,406
2008	689.2	792.2	884.0	937.7	3,303
2007	621.3	652.5	729.3	801.2	2,804
2006	448.4	483.1	537.0	598.0	2,066

Earnings Per Share ($)

2011	0.38	E0.37	E0.39	E0.42	E1.57
2010	0.15	0.27	0.30	0.40	1.13
2009	0.11	0.15	-0.23	0.23	0.26
2008	0.11	0.23	0.29	0.26	0.86
2007	0.14	0.22	0.17	0.23	0.77
2006	0.16	0.18	0.20	0.15	0.69

Fiscal year ended Apr. 30. Next earnings report expected: Mid November. EPS Estimates based on S&P Operating Earnings; historical GAAP earnings are as reported.

Dividend Data

No cash dividends have been paid.

Please read the Required Disclosures and Analyst Certification on the last page of this report.

The **McGraw·Hill** Companies

NetApp Inc

Business Summary August 23, 2010

CORPORATE OVERVIEW. NetApp Inc. (formerly known as Network Appliance) is a provider of enterprise-level storage hardware and data-management software products and services. NTAP's solutions help global enterprises meet major information technology challenges such as managing the continuing growth in the volume of data, scaling existing infrastructure, complying with regulatory regimes, and security corporate networks and information.

The NTAP family of modular and scalable networked systems provides seamless access to a full range of enterprise data for users working with a variety of platforms, including Fibre Channel (FC), network-attached storage (NAS), storage area network (SAN), and iSCSI environments, as well as online data residing in central locations. NTAP refers to this as fabric-attached storage (FAS). Products include the 200, 900, 3000 and 6000 series.

NTAP's V-Series is a network-based solution that consolidates storage arrays from different suppliers, enabling unified SAN and file access to data stored in heterogeneous FC SAN storage arrays. The V-Series family supports products from Hewlett-Packard, Hitachi and IBM.

CORPORATE STRATEGY. NearStore products focus on optimizing data protection and retention applications. This system offers an alternative to customers by providing faster data access than off-line storage at a significantly lower cost than primary storage. Offerings in this category include the Virtual Tape Library (VTL), a disk-to-disk backup appliance that appears as a tape library to a back-up software application.

The NetCache suite of solutions is designed to manage, control and improve access to Web-based information. Working with a range of software partners, NetCache provides large enterprises with the ability to manage Internet access and security. It essentially enables IT managers to control user access to information, based on profiles, actions, timing, etc.

Company Financials Fiscal Year Ended Apr. 30

Per Share Data ($)	2010	2009	2008	2007	2006	2005	2004	2003	2002	2001
Tangible Book Value	5.25	2.82	2.72	3.56	3.62	3.67	2.91	2.75	2.39	2.21
Cash Flow	1.60	0.77	1.26	1.05	0.90	0.77	0.58	0.38	0.14	0.33
Earnings	1.13	0.26	0.86	0.77	0.69	0.59	0.42	0.22	0.01	0.21
S&P Core Earnings	1.12	0.71	0.84	0.73	0.45	0.39	0.16	-0.28	-0.77	-0.52
Dividends	NA	Nil	Nil	Nil	Nil	Nil	Nil	Nil	Nil	Nil
Payout Ratio	NA	Nil	Nil	Nil	Nil	Nil	Nil	Nil	Nil	Nil
Calendar Year	2009	2008	2007	2006	2005	2004	2003	2002	2001	2000
Prices:High	34.99	27.49	40.89	41.56	34.98	34.99	26.69	27.95	74.98	152.75
Prices:Low	12.39	10.39	22.51	25.85	22.50	15.92	9.26	5.18	6.00	33.88
P/E Ratio:High	31	NM	48	54	51	59	64	NM	NM	NM
P/E Ratio:Low	11	NM	26	34	33	27	22	NM	NM	NM

Income Statement Analysis (Million $)										
Revenue	3,931	3,406	3,303	2,804	2,066	1,598	1,170	892	798	1,006
Operating Income	617	410	464	387	395	319	228	146	76.5	179
Depreciation	166	171	144	111	81.8	65.6	59.5	57.4	65.3	42.3
Interest Expense	74.1	26.9	Nil	11.6	1.28	Nil	Nil	Nil	Nil	Nil
Pretax Income	447	44.8	383	360	350	276	170	97.8	2.53	133
Effective Tax Rate	NA	NM	19.1%	17.2%	23.9%	18.3%	10.8%	21.8%	NM	43.7%
Net Income	400	86.5	310	298	266	226	152	76.5	3.03	74.9
S&P Core Earnings	398	235	303	282	175	148	59.5	-98.0	-256	-167

Balance Sheet & Other Financial Data (Million $)										
Cash	3,724	2,604	1,164	489	461	194	241	284	211	272
Current Assets	4,537	3,439	2,067	2,241	2,033	1,576	1,089	853	679	636
Total Assets	6,494	5,453	4,071	3,658	3,261	2,373	1,877	1,319	1,109	1,036
Current Liabilities	1,911	1,679	1,414	1,188	917	520	344	265	216	219
Long Term Debt	1,273	1,430	173	Nil	138	4.47	4.86	3.10	3.73	0.15
Common Equity	2,531	1,662	1,700	1,989	1,923	1,661	1,416	987	858	804
Total Capital	3,804	3,092	1,873	1,989	2,061	1,665	1,421	990	862	805
Capital Expenditures	136	290	188	166	133	93.6	48.6	61.3	284	83.7
Cash Flow	566	257	454	409	348	291	212	134	47.4	117
Current Ratio	2.4	2.1	1.5	1.9	2.2	3.0	3.2	3.2	3.2	2.9
% Long Term Debt of Capitalization	33.5	46.2	9.2	Nil	6.7	0.3	0.3	0.3	0.4	0.0
% Net Income of Revenue	10.2	2.5	9.4	10.6	12.9	14.1	13.0	8.6	0.4	7.4
% Return on Assets	6.7	1.8	8.0	8.6	9.5	10.6	9.5	6.3	0.3	9.2
% Return on Equity	19.1	5.2	16.8	15.2	14.9	14.7	12.7	8.3	0.4	11.7

Data as orig reptd.; bef. results of disc opers/spec. items. Per share data adj. for stk. divs.; EPS diluted. E-Estimated. NA-Not Available. NM-Not Meaningful. NR-Not Ranked. UR-Under Review.

Office: 495 East Java Drive, Sunnyvale, CA 94089.
Telephone: 408-822-6000.
Email: investor_relations@netapp.com
Website: http://www.netapp.com

Chrmn: D. Warmenhoven
Pres, CEO & COO: T. Georgens
Investor Contact: S. Gomo ()
EVP, CFO & Chief Acctg Officer: S. Gomo

SVP & CSO: S. Kleiman
Board Members: J. R. Allen, A. L. Earhart, T. Georgens, G. Held, N. G. Moore, T. Nevens, G. T. Shaheen, R. T. Wall, D. Warmenhoven

Founded: 1992
Domicile: Delaware
Employees: 8,333

Newell Rubbermaid Inc.

STANDARD &POOR'S

S&P Recommendation HOLD ★★★☆☆	**Price** $18.07 (as of Oct 22, 2010)	**12-Mo. Target Price** $20.00	**Investment Style** Large-Cap Value

GICS Sector Consumer Discretionary
Sub-Industry Housewares & Specialties

Summary Major product lines of this high-volume brand name consumer products concern include housewares, home furnishings, office products and hardware.

Key Stock Statistics (Source S&P, Vickers, company reports)

52-Wk Range	$18.48–13.11	S&P Oper. EPS 2010**E**	1.45	Market Capitalization(B)	$5.029	Beta	1.72
Trailing 12-Month EPS	$1.09	S&P Oper. EPS 2011**E**	1.62	Yield (%)	1.11	S&P 3-Yr. Proj. EPS CAGR(%)	10
Trailing 12-Month P/E	16.6	P/E on S&P Oper. EPS 2010**E**	12.5	Dividend Rate/Share	$0.20	S&P Credit Rating	BBB-
$10K Invested 5 Yrs Ago	$9,228	Common Shares Outstg. (M)	278.3	Institutional Ownership (%)	95		

Price Performance

30-Week Mov. Avg. · · ·   10-Week Mov. Avg. - - -   **GAAP Earnings vs. Previous Year**   Volume Above Avg. |||| STARS
12-Mo. Target Price —   Relative Strength —   ▲ Up ▼ Down ▶ No Change   Below Avg. |||| ★

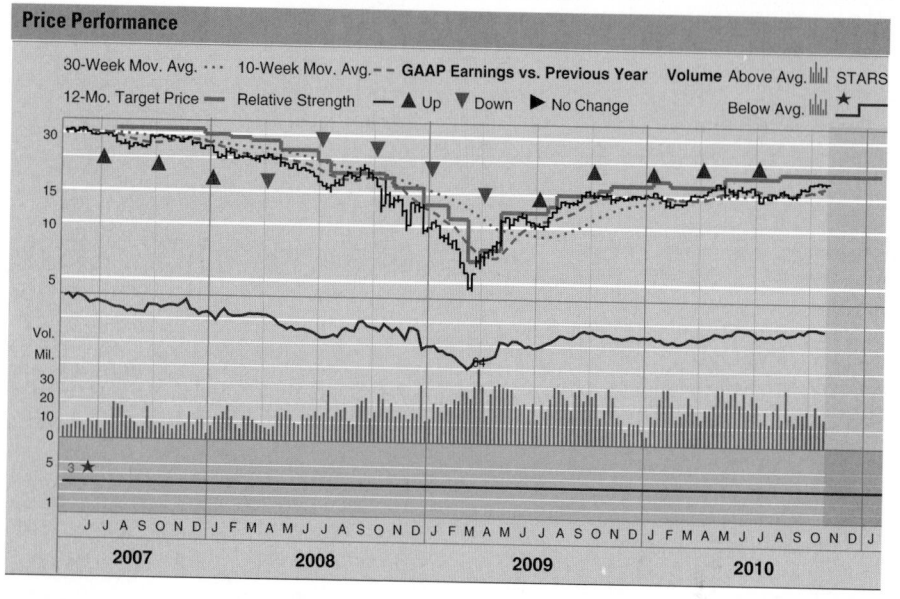

Options: ASE, CBOE, P

Analysis prepared by **Efraim Levy, CFA** on August 05, 2010, when the stock traded at **$ 16.44**.

Highlights

► Our 2010 sales growth projection is 3.2%, which assumes minimal foreign exchange impact but a continuing negative impact from 2009's planned product line exits. Using the revised 2009 segmentation, we project sales growth of 4% for Office Products, 9% for Tools, Hardware & Commercial Products, and less than 2% for Home & Family. In 2009, sales fell 14%, with negative foreign currency translation of 2% and planned product line exits of 5%.

► For 2010, we see further operating margin improvement on top of the gain achieved in 2009, excluding impairment and restructuring charges, allowing the operating margin to get close to the level in 2007. In 2009, moderation in commodity cost pressures and gross margin benefits from product line exits more than offset negative sales leverage, allowing the operating margin to rise 250 basis points. We also assume lower interest & other expenses in 2010, following a decline in 2009.

► We estimate that EPS will be $1.45 in 2010, versus 2009's operating EPS of $1.31. Our 2010 EPS estimate incorporates a $0.04 per share impact from the devaluation of the Venezuelan bolivar.

Investment Rationale/Risk

► We think the stock price adequately reflects NWL's improved longer-term growth prospects but a current difficult environment. We believe the company is poised for better innovation and efficiency. NWL has been exiting lower-margin, often resin-intensive product lines and investing in what we think are more profitable categories. In our view, NWL should be able to gain market share through better consumer research and greater product innovation.

► Risks to our recommendation and target price include poor consumer acceptance of new products, a prolonged weak consumer spending environment, a low level of cost savings from the company's reorganization program, negative currency translation, and a material increase in prices of key raw materials.

► Our 12-month target price of $20 is based on a blend of our historical and relative analyses. Our historical model uses a P/E of 13.8X our 2010 EPS estimate, a discount to the 10-year median, and arrives at a $20 value. Our relative analysis uses a near peer-average multiple for a $20 value.

Qualitative Risk Assessment

LOW	**MEDIUM**	HIGH

Our risk assessment reflects that housewares companies' products are generally affordable, low-priced goods that are usually modestly affected by swings in the economy. However, there is a greater level of import competition for commodity-type goods.

Quantitative Evaluations

S&P Quality Ranking B-

D	C	**B-**	B	B+	A-	A	A+

Relative Strength Rank MODERATE

67

LOWEST = 1 HIGHEST = 99

Revenue/Earnings Data

Revenue (Million $)

	1Q	2Q	3Q	4Q	Year
2010	1,306	1,496	--	--	--
2009	1,204	1,504	1,449	1,420	5,578
2008	1,434	1,825	1,760	1,452	6,471
2007	1,384	1,693	1,687	1,643	6,407
2006	1,343	1,634	1,586	1,638	6,201
2005	1,363	1,646	1,585	1,749	6,343

Earnings Per Share ($)

2010	0.19	0.41	E0.39	E0.29	E1.45
2009	0.12	0.37	0.28	0.20	0.97
2008	0.21	0.33	0.20	-0.93	-0.19
2007	0.23	0.51	0.61	0.36	1.72
2006	0.47	0.49	0.41	0.33	1.71
2005	0.33	0.30	0.37	0.31	1.29

Fiscal year ended Dec. 31. Next earnings report expected: Late October. EPS Estimates based on S&P Operating Earnings; historical GAAP earnings are as reported.

Dividend Data (Dates: mm/dd Payment Date: mm/dd/yy)

Amount ($)	Date Decl.	Ex-Div. Date	Stk. of Record	Payment Date
0.050	11/12	11/25	11/30	12/15/09
0.050	02/11	02/24	02/26	03/15/10
0.050	05/13	05/26	05/28	06/15/10
0.050	08/12	08/27	08/31	09/15/10

Dividends have been paid since 1946. Source: Company reports.

Please read the Required Disclosures and Analyst Certification on the last page of this report.

The McGraw-Hill Companies

Newell Rubbermaid Inc.

Business Summary August 05, 2010

CORPORATE OVERVIEW. Newell Rubbermaid is a global manufacturer and marketer of name brand consumer products and their commercial extensions, serving a wide array of retail channels including department stores, warehouse clubs, home centers, hardware stores, commercial distributors, office superstores, contract stationers, automotive stores and small superstores. As of April 2009, NWL recategorized its four business segments into three: Office Products (30% of 2009 sales, 31% of segment operating profits), Tools, Hardware & Commercial Products (27%, 33%), and Home & Family (43%, 36%). About 30% of 2009 sales were made outside the U.S. Sales to Wal-Mart Stores, Inc. and its subsidiaries amounted to about 12% of sales in 2009.

The global business units (GBUs) that formerly comprised the Cleaning, Organization & Decor segment, that is Home Products, Foodservice Products, Commercial Products and Decor, have been integrated into two of the three remaining segments. Brands include Rubbermaid, Brute, Roughneck, TakeAlongs, Levolor and Kirsch. The Rubbermaid Food & Home Products and Decor GBUs are now included in Home & Family segment. Also, the Amerock brand, which was previously part of the Tools & Hardware segment, has been integrated into the Decor GBU.

The office products segment is comprised of the following GBUs: Markers, Highlighters, Art & Office Organization, Everyday Writing & Coloring, Technology, and Fine Writing & Luxury Accessories. Brands include Sharpie, Paper-Mate, Waterman, Parker, and DYMO.

The tools & hardware business is composed of the following GBUs: Commercial Products, Construction Tools & Accessories, Industrial Products & Services, and Hardware. It sells hand tools, power tool accessories, propane torches, manual paint applicator products, cabinet hardware, and window hardware under brand names such as Irwin, Lenox, Rubbermaid Commercial Products, Technical Concepts, and BernzOmatic.

The home & family segment includes the following GBUs: Rubbermaid Consumer Products, Baby & Parenting Essentials, Decor, Culinary Lifestyles and Beauty & Style. Brand names include Rubbermaid, Graco, Aprica, Levelor, Calphalon and Goody.

Company Financials Fiscal Year Ended Dec. 31

Per Share Data ($)	2009	2008	2007	2006	2005	2004	2003	2002	2001	2000
Tangible Book Value	NM	NM	NM	NM	NM	0.84	0.84	2.21	0.44	0.97
Cash Flow	1.56	0.29	2.18	2.41	2.07	0.84	0.84	2.21	2.22	2.57
Earnings	0.97	-0.19	1.72	1.71	1.29	-0.07	-0.17	1.16	0.99	1.57
S&P Core Earnings	0.98	0.71	1.73	1.73	1.22	0.56	0.39	0.86	0.71	NA
Dividends	0.25	0.84	0.84	0.84	0.84	0.84	0.84	0.84	0.84	0.84
Payout Ratio	26%	NM	49%	49%	65%	NM	NM	72%	85%	54%
Prices:High	16.10	25.94	32.19	29.98	25.69	26.41	32.00	36.70	29.50	31.88
Prices:Low	4.51	9.13	24.22	23.25	20.50	19.05	20.27	26.11	20.50	18.25
P/E Ratio:High	17	NM	19	18	20	NM	NM	32	30	20
P/E Ratio:Low	5	NM	14	14	16	NM	NM	23	21	12

Income Statement Analysis (Million $)	2009	2008	2007	2006	2005	2004	2003	2002	2001	2000
Revenue	5,578	6,471	6,407	6,201	6,343	6,748	7,750	7,454	6,909	6,935
Operating Income	850	752	970	916	843	870	992	1,033	966	1,173
Depreciation	175	131	143	193	214	249	278	281	329	293
Interest Expense	149	147	132	155	142	130	140	111	137	130
Pretax Income	428	1.80	632	515	418	86.3	20.1	495	443	685
Effective Tax Rate	33.3%	NM	23.7%	8.58%	14.8%	NM	NM	31.7%	34.2%	38.5%
Net Income	286	-51.8	479	471	356	-19.1	-46.6	312	265	422
S&P Core Earnings	288	196	481	476	333	153	108	232	190	NA

Balance Sheet & Other Financial Data (Million $)	2009	2008	2007	2006	2005	2004	2003	2002	2001	2000
Cash	278	275	329	201	116	506	144	55.1	6.80	31.7
Current Assets	2,182	2,394	2,652	2,477	2,473	3,012	3,000	3,080	2,851	2,897
Total Assets	6,424	6,793	6,683	6,311	6,446	6,666	7,481	7,389	7,266	7,262
Current Liabilities	1,760	2,206	2,564	1,897	1,798	1,871	2,022	2,614	2,534	1,551
Long Term Debt	2,015	2,118	1,197	1,972	2,430	2,424	2,869	2,357	1,865	2,815
Common Equity	1,779	1,614	2,247	1,890	1,643	1,764	2,016	2,064	2,433	2,449
Total Capital	4,290	4,485	3,445	3,863	4,073	4,189	4,887	4,426	4,373	5,358
Capital Expenditures	153	158	157	138	92.2	122	300	252	250	317
Cash Flow	461	79.3	622	664	570	230	232	592	593	714
Current Ratio	1.2	1.1	1.0	1.3	1.4	1.6	1.5	1.2	1.1	1.9
% Long Term Debt of Capitalization	47.0	47.2	34.8	51.1	59.7	57.9	58.7	53.2	42.7	52.5
% Net Income of Revenue	5.1	NM	7.5	7.6	5.6	NM	NM	4.2	3.8	6.1
% Return on Assets	4.3	NM	7.4	7.4	5.4	NM	NM	4.3	3.6	6.0
% Return on Equity	16.8	NM	23.2	26.6	20.9	NM	NM	13.9	10.8	16.4

Data as orig reptd.; bef. results of disc opers/spec. items. Per share data adj. for stk. divs.; EPS diluted. E-Estimated. NA-Not Available. NM-Not Meaningful. NR-Not Ranked. UR-Under Review.

Office: Three Glenlake Parkway, Atlanta, GA 30328.
Telephone: 770-418-7000.
Email: investor.relations@newellco.com
Website: http://www.newellrubbermaid.com

Chrmn: M.T. Cowhig
Pres & CEO: M.D. Ketchum
EVP & CFO: J.R. Figuereo
SVP, Secy & General Counsel: J.K. Stipancich

SVP & CIO: G.C. Steele
Investor Contact: N. O'Donnell (770-418-7723)
Board Members: T. E. Clarke, S. S. Cowen, M. T. Cowhig, E. Cuthbert-Millett, D. De Sole, M. D. Ketchum, W. Marohn, C. A. Montgomery, M. Polk, S. J. Strobel, M. A. Todman, R. Viault

Founded: 1903
Domicile: Delaware
Employees: 19,500

Newmont Mining Corp

STANDARD &POOR'S

S&P Recommendation **BUY** ★★★★☆	Price $59.37 (as of Oct 22, 2010)	12-Mo. Target Price $68.00	Investment Style Large-Cap Growth

GICS Sector Materials
Sub-Industry Gold

Summary Newmont is one of the world's largest gold producers, and is also engaged in the production of copper.

Key Stock Statistics (Source S&P, Vickers, company reports)

52-Wk Range	$65.50–41.45	S&P Oper. EPS 2010E	3.51	Market Capitalization(B)	$28.777	Beta	0.46
Trailing 12-Month EPS	$3.80	S&P Oper. EPS 2011E	3.90	Yield (%)	1.01	S&P 3-Yr. Proj. EPS CAGR(%)	18
Trailing 12-Month P/E	15.6	P/E on S&P Oper. EPS 2010E	16.9	Dividend Rate/Share	$0.60	S&P Credit Rating	BBB+
$10K Invested 5 Yrs Ago	$14,147	Common Shares Outstg. (M)	484.7	Institutional Ownership (%)	83		

Price Performance

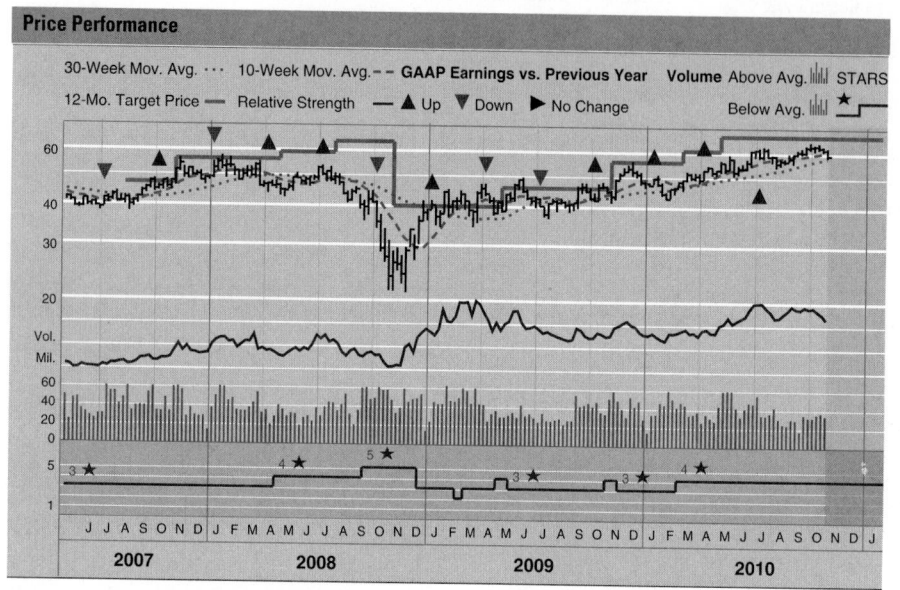

30-Week Mov. Avg. · · · 10-Week Mov. Avg. – – GAAP Earnings vs. Previous Year   Volume Above Avg. STARS
12-Mo. Target Price — Relative Strength — ▲ Up ▼ Down ▶ No Change   Below Avg.

Options: ASE, CBOE, P, Ph

Analysis prepared by **Leo J. Larkin** on August 05, 2010, when the stock traded at **$ 56.36**.

Highlights

▶ Following a sales gain of 24% in 2009, we look for a 17% rise in 2010. This year, we expect a higher average price for both gold and copper compared to 2009, and we look for higher gold production as increases from the Boddington and Batu Hijau mines should more than offset declines in Nevada and Peru. We think that copper production will slightly exceed 2009's level of 507 million pounds. We expect that continued low short-term interest rates worldwide and volatility in the world's major currencies will support another rise in the gold price in 2010. We believe that a gradual decline in metal exchange inventories and a rebound in global demand will boost the copper price.

▶ Reflecting increased gold output and increased prices for both metals, we look for higher operating profits. After interest expense, taxes, and more shares outstanding, we estimate operating EPS of $3.51 for 2010, versus operating EPS of $2.79 for 2009, which excludes unusual items totaling $0.11.

▶ Long term, we see EPS and reserves being aided by a projected rise in the price of gold, further consolidation of the industry, acquisitions, and expansion projects.

Investment Rationale/Risk

▶ We see NEM's growth prospects as more secure following a series of acquisitions in recent years. Also, with its output exposed to the spot gold price, NEM appears well positioned for a continued bull market in gold. We believe that gold will remain in a bull market for several reasons: we expect the gap between consumption and production to persist as production worldwide stagnates; we think gold and gold shares will be viewed as attractive alternative investments, given our view that financial asset returns will continue to trail the high levels seen in the late 1990s; and, we believe that currency instability will increase gold's role as a monetary reserve asset. We think shares of NEM are attractively valued, recently trading at about 14.1X our 2011 estimate.

▶ Risks to our recommendation and target price include declines in the prices of gold and copper in 2011 instead of the increases that we project.

▶ Applying a P/E multiple of 17.4X to our 2011 EPS estimate, at the low end of its historical range and at a discount to its major peer, we arrive at our 12-month target price of $68. We think a discount is warranted given our view of NEM's comparatively less robust growth profile.

Qualitative Risk Assessment

LOW	MEDIUM	HIGH

Our risk assessment reflects Newmont's exposure to the cyclical markets for copper and gold. This is offset by our view of its moderate balance sheet leverage and our expectation that the company will generate positive free cash flow on a more consistent basis.

Quantitative Evaluations

S&P Quality Ranking   B-

D	C	B-	B	B+	A-	A	A+

Relative Strength Rank   WEAK

23

LOWEST = 1   HIGHEST = 99

Revenue/Earnings Data

Revenue (Million $)

	1Q	2Q	3Q	4Q	Year
2010	2,242	2,153	--	--	--
2009	1,552	1,602	2,049	2,518	7,705
2008	1,943	1,522	1,392	1,342	6,199
2007	1,256	1,302	1,646	1,410	5,526
2006	1,132	1,293	1,102	1,460	4,987
2005	945.0	998.0	1,158	1,305	4,406

Earnings Per Share ($)

2010	1.11	0.77	E0.91	E1.01	E3.51
2009	0.40	0.35	0.79	1.14	2.68
2008	0.80	0.61	0.39	0.02	1.82
2007	0.15	-0.90	0.72	-2.03	-2.13
2006	0.46	0.34	0.59	0.47	1.86
2005	0.19	0.19	0.29	0.16	0.83

Fiscal year ended Dec. 31. Next earnings report expected: Late October. EPS Estimates based on S&P Operating Earnings; historical GAAP earnings are as reported.

Dividend Data (Dates: mm/dd Payment Date: mm/dd/yy)

Amount ($)	Date Decl.	Ex-Div. Date	Stk. of Record	Payment Date
0.100	10/28	12/04	12/08	12/29/09
0.100	02/24	03/10	03/12	03/30/10
0.100	04/23	06/11	06/15	06/29/10
0.150	07/28	09/03	09/08	09/29/10

Dividends have been paid since 1934. Source: Company reports.

Please read the Required Disclosures and Analyst Certification on the last page of this report.

The McGraw·Hill Companies

Newmont Mining Corp

STANDARD &POOR'S

Business Summary August 05, 2010

CORPORATE OVERVIEW. Newmont Mining Corp. is one of the world's largest gold producers. It has significant assets and operations in the United States, Australia, Peru, Indonesia, Ghana, Canada, Bolivia, New Zealand and Mexico. The company has two large development projects in Ghana, West Africa. Newmont is also engaged in the production of copper, principally through its Batu Hijau operation in Indonesia.

Proven and probable gold reserves totaled 91.8 million oz. at the end of 2009 using a gold price of $800 an oz., versus 85 million oz. at the end of 2008 using a gold price of $725 an oz.

At December 31, 2009 NEM's proven and probable gold reserves in North America were 30.3 million equity ounces. Outside of North America, year-end proven and probable gold reserves were 61.5 million equity ounces, including 32.9 million equity ounces in Asia Pacific, 16.8 million equity ounces in Africa and 11.8 million equity ounces in South America.

Copper reserves totaled 9.1 billion lbs. at the end of 2009, using a copper price of $2.00 per lb., versus 7.8 billion lbs. at the end of 2008, using a copper price assumption of $2.00 per lb. Equity copper sales totaled 226 million lbs. in 2009,

versus 130 million lbs. in 2008.

In 2009, 32% of Newmont's gold sales came from North America, 32% from Peru, 19% from Australia/New Zealand, 9% from Indonesia and 8% from Ghana. Equity gold sales totaled 5.22 million oz. in 2009, versus 5.18 million oz. in 2008.

As of December 31, 2009, 21% of the company's total long-lived assets were located in the U.S., 13% in Canada, 10% in Peru, 33% in Australia/New Zealand, 15% in Indonesia and 8% in Ghana.

CORPORATE STRATEGY. NEM's main strategy is to increase its portfolio of low-cost, long-life mines. In 2007's second quarter, NEM incurred a charge to eliminate its remaining gold hedges, as it anticipates higher gold prices over the longer term, and seeks to provide shareholders with maximum leverage to the price of gold.

Company Financials Fiscal Year Ended Dec. 31

Per Share Data ($)	2009	2008	2007	2006	2005	2004	2003	2002	2001	2000
Tangible Book Value	21.37	15.20	16.27	14.98	12.27	11.02	8.39	2.77	7.49	8.58
Cash Flow	4.45	3.56	-0.59	3.27	2.27	2.66	2.60	1.75	1.38	1.61
Earnings	2.68	1.82	-2.13	1.86	0.83	1.10	1.23	0.39	-0.16	-0.06
S&P Core Earnings	2.69	1.86	0.42	1.45	0.79	1.22	1.05	0.25	-0.26	NA
Dividends	0.40	0.40	0.40	0.40	0.40	0.30	0.17	0.12	0.12	0.12
Payout Ratio	15%	22%	NM	22%	48%	28%	14%	31%	NM	NM
Prices:High	56.45	57.55	56.35	62.72	53.93	50.20	50.28	32.75	25.23	28.38
Prices:Low	34.40	21.17	38.01	39.84	34.90	34.70	24.08	18.52	14.00	12.75
P/E Ratio:High	21	32	NM	34	65	46	41	84	NM	NM
P/E Ratio:Low	13	12	NM	21	42	32	20	47	NM	NM

Income Statement Analysis (Million $)										
Revenue	7,705	6,199	5,526	4,987	4,406	4,524	3,214	2,658	1,656	1,555
Operating Income	3,910	2,057	2,041	2,059	1,621	1,878	1,219	852	435	502
Depreciation	852	789	695	636	644	697	564	506	300	293
Interest Expense	120	149	155	97.0	98.0	97.6	88.6	130	86.4	79.6
Pretax Income	2,897	1,271	-353	1,627	1,068	1,102	890	268	-10.2	94.2
Effective Tax Rate	27.2%	8.89%	NM	26.1%	29.4%	25.0%	23.2%	7.43%	NM	12.1%
Net Income	1,308	829	-963	840	374	490	510	150	-23.3	-10.5
S&P Core Earnings	1,308	847	192	657	356	540	435	96.7	-52.8	NA

Balance Sheet & Other Financial Data (Million $)										
Cash	3,271	447	1,292	1,275	1,899	1,726	1,459	402	149	60.3
Current Assets	5,822	2,361	2,672	2,642	3,036	2,721	2,360	1,113	709	512
Total Assets	22,299	15,839	15,598	15,601	13,992	12,771	11,050	10,155	4,062	3,510
Current Liabilities	2,320	1,596	1,500	1,739	1,350	1,101	834	693	486	291
Long Term Debt	4,652	3,373	2,683	Nil	1,733	1,311	887	1,701	1,090	976
Common Equity	10,703	7,102	7,548	9,865	8,376	7,938	7,385	5,419	1,469	1,466
Total Capital	17,422	12,896	12,705	10,963	11,489	10,500	9,251	8,132	2,955	2,695
Capital Expenditures	1,769	1,881	1,670	1,551	1,226	718	501	300	402	378
Cash Flow	2,165	1,618	-268	1,476	1,018	1,187	1,075	652	269	283
Current Ratio	2.5	1.5	1.8	1.5	2.2	2.5	2.8	1.6	1.5	1.8
% Long Term Debt of Capitalization	26.7	26.2	21.1	Nil	15.1	12.5	9.6	20.9	40.3	36.2
% Net Income of Revenue	17.0	13.4	NM	16.8	8.5	10.8	15.9	5.7	NM	NM
% Return on Assets	6.9	5.3	NM	5.7	2.8	4.2	4.8	2.1	NM	NM
% Return on Equity	14.8	11.3	NM	9.0	4.5	6.4	8.0	4.4	NM	NM

Data as orig reptd.; bef. results of disc opers/spec. items. Per share data adj. for stk. divs.; EPS diluted. E-Estimated. NA-Not Available. NM-Not Meaningful. NR-Not Ranked. UR-Under Review.

Office: 6363 South Fiddlers Green Circle, Suite 800, Greenwood Village, CO 80111.
Telephone: 303-863-7414.
Website: http://www.newmont.com
Chrmn: V.A. Calarco

Pres & CEO: R. O'Brien
COO: B.A. Hill
EVP & CFO: R. Ball
CFO: D.B. Russell

Investor Contact: J. Seaberg (303-837-5743)
Board Members: G. A. Barton, V. A. Calarco, J. A. Carrabba, N. Doyle, V. M. Hagen, M. S. Hamson, R. J. Miller, R. O'Brien, J. B. Prescott, D. C. Roth, S. R. Thompson

Founded: 1916
Domicile: Delaware
Employees: 14,500

The **McGraw-Hill** Companies

New York Times Co (The)

STANDARD &POOR'S

S&P Recommendation HOLD ★★★☆☆	**Price** $7.68 (as of Oct 22, 2010)

12-Mo. Target Price	**Investment Style**
$8.00	Large-Cap Blend

GICS Sector Consumer Discretionary
Sub-Industry Publishing

Summary This diversified communications company publishes newspapers, operates radio and television stations, and has equity holdings in newsprint and paper mills.

Key Stock Statistics (Source S&P, Vickers, company reports)

52-Wk Range	$14.87–7.06	S&P Oper. EPS 2010E	0.63	Market Capitalization(B)	$1.114	Beta	1.52
Trailing 12-Month EPS	$0.66	S&P Oper. EPS 2011E	0.66	Yield (%)	Nil	S&P 3-Yr. Proj. EPS CAGR(%)	5
Trailing 12-Month P/E	11.6	P/E on S&P Oper. EPS 2010E	12.2	Dividend Rate/Share	Nil	S&P Credit Rating	B+
$10K Invested 5 Yrs Ago	$3,212	Common Shares Outstg. (M)	145.9	Institutional Ownership (%)	68		

Price Performance

30-Week Mov. Avg. · · · · 10-Week Mov. Avg. - - - **GAAP Earnings vs. Previous Year** Volume Above Avg. STARS
12-Mo. Target Price — Relative Strength — ▲ Up ▼ Down ▶ No Change Below Avg.

Options: ASE, CBOE, P, Ph

Analysis prepared by **Joseph Agnese** on September 23, 2010, when the stock traded at **$ 7.66**.

Highlights

▶ For full-year 2011, we expect advertising revenues to decline 0.7%, following our estimate of a 3.4% decline in 2010, as trends improve significantly on a sequential basis with clients boosting marketing budgets in a more stable economic environment. However, we see circulation revenues declining 2.3% in 2011, following our estimate of a 0.4% decrease in 2010, on lower volumes and the cycling of newsstand price increases in June 2009. In total, we look for revenues to decline 1.3% in 2011, following our estimate of a 2.3% drop in 2010.

▶ We expect the operating margin to widen slightly in 2011 after significant expansion in 2010, as a continued focus on cost reduction improves sales leverage and newsprint prices rise beginning in the 2010 third quarter. We look for interest expense to be stable as reduced borrowings are offset by higher interest rates.

▶ We estimate EPS of $0.56 in 2011, up 3.7% from our estimate of $0.54 in 2010. Our estimates include severance and pension costs, which we view as operational due to ongoing restructuring activity at NYT, but exclude one-time costs in 2010 (gain on asset sales and one-time tax charges).

Investment Rationale/Risk

▶ We believe NYT's valuation will be supported by an improving cyclical trend in advertising spending in the second half of 2010. Additionally, debt refinancing concerns were lessened in 2009 after NYT reduced its capital expenditures budget, cut costs, suspended its dividend (February 2009), entered into two private loan agreements totaling $250 million (January 2009), did a sale-leaseback on part of its headquarters space (March 2009), and announced interest in selling other assets.

▶ Risks to our recommendation and target price include contraction in the health of the New York City and Boston economies, where NYT derives most of its newspaper advertising revenues.

▶ Our 12-month target price of $8 reflects our historical and relative enterprise value/EBITDA models. Our historical model applies a multiple of 7.0X to our 2011 EBITDA estimate of $350 million, to value the stock at $8. Our relative analysis uses a multiple of 5.4X, in line with peers, to reach an $8 valuation.

Qualitative Risk Assessment

LOW	MEDIUM	HIGH

Our risk assessment reflects our view of a highly competitive advertising environment for publishers and other media.

Quantitative Evaluations

S&P Quality Ranking B-

D	C	B-	B	B+	A-	A	A+

Relative Strength Rank WEAK

15

LOWEST = 1   HIGHEST = 99

Revenue/Earnings Data

Revenue (Million $)

	1Q	2Q	3Q	4Q	Year
2010	587.9	589.6	--	--	--
2009	607.1	582.7	569.5	681.2	2,440
2008	747.9	741.9	687.0	772.1	2,949
2007	786.0	788.9	754.4	865.8	3,195
2006	799.2	819.6	739.6	931.5	3,290
2005	805.6	845.1	791.1	931.0	3,373

Earnings Per Share ($)

	1Q	2Q	3Q	4Q	Year
2010	-0.08	0.21	E0.07	E0.27	E0.63
2009	-0.52	-0.27	-0.24	0.48	0.01
2008	Nil	0.15	-0.01	0.19	-0.46
2007	0.14	0.15	0.10	0.37	0.76
2006	0.21	0.37	0.06	-4.59	-3.93
2005	0.76	0.42	0.16	0.49	1.82

Fiscal year ended Dec. 31. Next earnings report expected: Late October. EPS Estimates based on S&P Operating Earnings; historical GAAP earnings are as reported.

Dividend Data

The most recent (quarterly) payment of $0.06 a share was made in December 2008.

Please read the Required Disclosures and Analyst Certification on the last page of this report.

The McGraw-Hill Companies

New York Times Co (The)

STANDARD
&POOR'S

Business Summary September 23, 2010

CORPORATE OVERVIEW. The New York Times Company is a media company that includes newspapers, Internet businesses, a radio station, investments in paper mills and other investments. The NYT classifies its businesses into two segments, the News Media Group (about 95% of revenues) and the About Group (5%).

The News Media Group primarily consists of The New York Times, the International Herald Tribune, The Boston Globe, the Worcester Telegram & Gazette, 14 daily newspapers in Alabama, California, Florida, Louisiana, North Carolina and South Carolina, and related print and digital businesses, such as NYT.com. The majority of the News Media Group's revenue comes from advertising sold in its newspapers and other publications and on its Web sites. In 2009, revenues for the News Media Group were derived from national advertising (55%), classified (18%), retail and pre-print (25%), and other (3%). We note that as one of only three national newspapers (along with USA Today and The Wall Street Journal), the New York Times garners a disproportionate amount of its advertising from national advertisers relative to most other newspapers. According to TNS Media Intelligence, the New York Times had a

50% market share of national advertising revenue among national newspapers in 2008.

The About Group consists of the websites About.com, ConsumerSearch.com, UCompareHealthCare.com and Caloriecount.about.com. About.com provides users with information and advice on thousands of topics, and the site was one of the top 15 most visited ad supported Web sites in 2009. About.com generates revenues through display advertising relevant to adjacent content, cost-per-click advertising, and e-commerce. ConsumerSearch.com is a leading online aggregator and publisher of reviews of consumer products. UCompareHealthCare.com provides Web-based interactive tools to enable users to measure the quality of certain healthcare services. Caloriecount.about.com offers weight loss tools and nutritional information.

Company Financials Fiscal Year Ended Dec. 31

Per Share Data ($)	2009	2008	2007	2006	2005	2004	2003	2002	2001	2000
Tangible Book Value	NM	NM	1.16	0.25	NM	NM	NM	NM	NM	NM
Cash Flow	0.92	0.51	1.82	-2.76	2.81	2.94	2.95	2.93	2.48	3.65
Earnings	0.01	-0.46	0.76	-3.93	1.82	1.96	1.98	1.94	1.26	2.32
S&P Core Earnings	-0.20	-1.04	0.91	1.13	1.41	1.62	1.77	1.35	0.72	NA
Dividends	Nil	0.75	0.87	0.69	0.65	0.61	0.57	0.53	0.49	0.45
Payout Ratio	Nil	NM	114%	NM	36%	31%	29%	27%	39%	19%
Prices:High	12.75	21.14	26.90	28.98	40.90	49.23	49.06	53.00	47.98	49.88
Prices:Low	3.44	4.95	16.02	21.54	26.09	38.47	43.29	38.60	35.48	32.63
P/E Ratio:High	NM	NM	35	NM	22	25	25	27	38	21
P/E Ratio:Low	NM	NM	21	NM	14	20	22	20	28	14

Income Statement Analysis (Million $)										
Revenue	2,440	2,949	3,195	3,290	3,373	3,304	3,227	3,079	3,016	3,489
Operating Income	320	302	492	464	502	657	687	698	568	864
Depreciation	134	139	153	170	144	147	148	153	194	228
Interest Expense	83.1	50.8	59.1	50.7	49.2	44.2	44.8	48.7	51.4	64.1
Pretax Income	3.78	-71.4	185	-552	446	477	500	491	340	673
Effective Tax Rate	58.4%	NM	41.2%	NM	40.4%	38.5%	39.6%	39.0%	40.5%	40.9%
Net Income	1.56	-66.1	109	-568	266	293	303	300	202	398
S&P Core Earnings	-28.8	-149	129	164	205	242	268	208	116	NA

Balance Sheet & Other Financial Data (Million $)										
Cash	36.5	56.8	51.5	72.4	44.9	42.4	39.4	37.0	52.0	69.0
Current Assets	501	624	664	1,185	658	614	603	563	560	611
Total Assets	3,089	3,402	3,473	3,856	4,533	3,950	3,805	3,634	3,439	3,607
Current Liabilities	501	1,033	976	1,298	1,067	1,120	760	736	861	877
Long Term Debt	769	580	679	795	898	471	726	729	599	637
Common Equity	604	504	978	820	1,516	1,401	1,392	1,362	1,150	1,281
Total Capital	1,376	1,180	1,663	1,621	2,683	2,139	2,350	2,164	1,813	2,024
Capital Expenditures	51.1	167	380	332	221	154	121	161	90.4	85.3
Cash Flow	135	73.3	262	-398	409	439	450	453	396	626
Current Ratio	1.0	0.6	0.7	0.9	0.6	0.5	0.8	0.8	0.7	0.7
% Long Term Debt of Capitalization	Nil	49.1	40.8	49.1	33.5	22.0	30.9	33.7	33.0	31.5
% Net Income of Revenue	0.1	NM	3.4	NM	7.9	8.9	9.4	9.7	6.7	11.4
% Return on Assets	NA	NM	3.0	NM	6.3	7.5	8.1	8.5	5.7	11.2
% Return on Equity	NA	NM	12.1	NM	18.2	21.0	22.7	23.9	16.6	29.1

Data as orig reptd.; bef. results of disc opers/spec. items. Per share data adj. for stk. divs.; EPS diluted. E-Estimated. NA-Not Available. NM-Not Meaningful. NR-Not Ranked. UR-Under Review.

Office: 620 8th Ave, New York, NY 10018-1618.
Telephone: 212-556-1234.
Website: http://www.nytco.com
Chrmn: A.O. Sulzberger, Jr.

Pres & CEO: J.L. Robinson
Vice Chrmn: M. Golden
SVP & CFO: J.M. Follo
SVP, Chief Acctg Officer & Cntlr: R.A. Benten

Investor Contact: C.J. Mathis (212-556-1981)
Board Members: R. E. Cesan, R. E. Denham, L. Dolnick, S. W. Dryfoos, M. Golden, C. D. Greenspon, J. A. Kohlberg, D. G. Lepore, D. E. Liddle, E. R. Marram, T. T. Middelhoff, J. L. Robinson, A. O. Sulzberger, Jr., D. A. Toben

Founded: 1896
Domicile: New York
Employees: 7,665

The McGraw-Hill Companies

News Corp

STANDARD &POOR'S

S&P Recommendation BUY ★★★★☆

Price	**12-Mo. Target Price**	**Investment Style**
$14.40 (as of Oct 22, 2010)	$17.00	Large-Cap Blend

GICS Sector Consumer Discretionary
Sub-Industry Movies & Entertainment

Summary This media conglomerate owns controlling interests in some of the world's leading media and entertainment brands, including Fox (film/TV), The Wall Street Journal, SKY Italia, BSkyB, and STAR TV, as well as other newspaper and magazine businesses.

Key Stock Statistics (Source S&P, Vickers, company reports)

52-Wk Range	$17.00– 11.11	S&P Oper. EPS 2011**E**	1.11	Market Capitalization(B)	$26.246	Beta	1.48
Trailing 12-Month EPS	$0.97	S&P Oper. EPS 2012**E**	1.28	Yield (%)	1.04	S&P 3-Yr. Proj. EPS CAGR(%)	12
Trailing 12-Month P/E	14.9	P/E on S&P Oper. EPS 2011**E**	13.0	Dividend Rate/Share	$0.15	S&P Credit Rating	BBB+
$10K Invested 5 Yrs Ago	$10,406	Common Shares Outstg. (M)	2,621.2	Institutional Ownership (%)	84		

Price Performance

30-Week Mov. Avg. ··· 10-Week Mov. Avg. – – **GAAP Earnings vs. Previous Year** Volume Above Avg. ▮▮▮ STARS
12-Mo. Target Price — Relative Strength — ▲ Up ▼ Down ▶ No Change Below Avg. ▮▮▮ ★

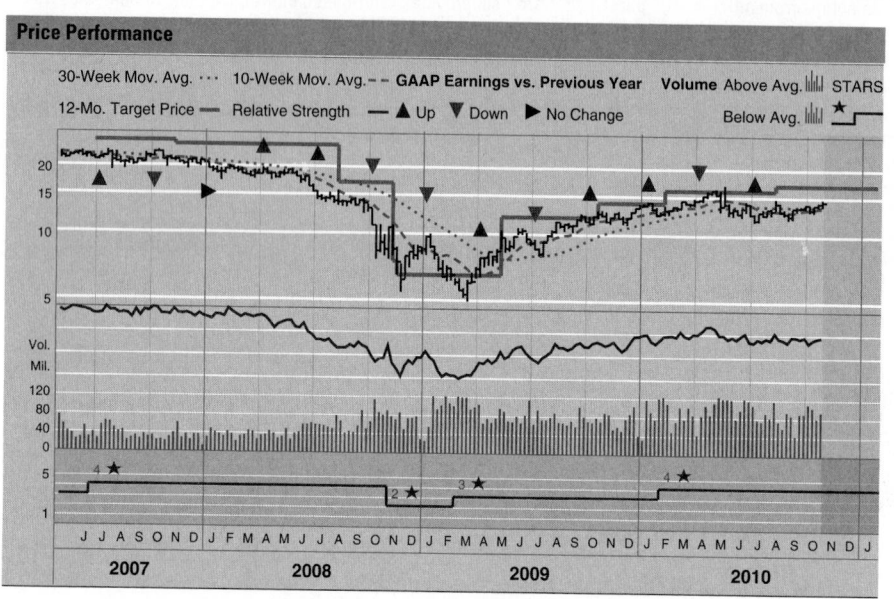

2007 2008 2009 2010

Options: ASE, CBOE, P, Ph

Analysis prepared by **Tuna N. Amobi, CFA, CPA** on August 19, 2010, when the stock traded at **$ 12.76**.

Highlights

➤ We see total revenues up about 4.0% in FY 11 (June) to $34.1 billion -- mainly on continued strong growth in affiliate and advertising revenues for the cable networks businesses. A continued ad rebound should also help the print and broadcast TV businesses -- the latter buoyed by political ads and retransmission revenues for the owned-and-operated stations. We see difficult film comparisons in FY 10 (on Avatar's record performance), versus relatively moderate growth for the Sky Italia satellite TV unit. With book publishing increasingly aided by e-book sales, and newspapers by WSJ's rising digital subscriptions, we see about 5.3% FY 11 total revenue growth, to nearly $35.9 billion.

➤ Management expects low double-digit growth in FY 11 adjusted EBIT (from over $4.4 billion in FY 10), and we project at nearly $5.0 billion -- with the cable networks contributing more than half. With further operating leverage on recent restructuring actions, we project FY 12 adjusted EBIT of nearly $5.7 billion.

➤ Including equity affiliate earnings, and after interest and taxes, we estimate operating EPS of $1.11 and $1.28 for FY 11 and FY 12, respectively.

Investment Rationale/Risk

➤ Despite mixed June quarter results, we think the company's encouraging FY 10 results and cautious FY 11 guidance reflect expectations for continued improvements across the core ads, content, and subscriptions businesses -- with trends at Sky Italia also appearing to stabilize. We see early progress in the quest for "innovative subscriptions models" for online news properties. We see ample liquidity, but note a pending non-binding offer for the remaining 61% of BSkyB which, if successful, could entail a potential cash outlay of about $11.5 billion.

➤ Risks to our recommendation and target price include a weaker-than-expected economic recovery; uncertainty with the BSkyB offer; secular hurdles for the print brands; continued challenges for the MySpace unit; a sharp decline for Fox ratings; succession and governance issues with the Murdoch family; dilutive acquisitions; and, currency exposure.

➤ Our PEG-based 12-month target price is $17, blending EV/EBITDA and P/E-to-growth analyses -- with some non-voting discount on shares (recently offering a 1.1% dividend yield) -- while noting recent cash of $8.7 billion ($3.30 a share).

Qualitative Risk Assessment

LOW	MEDIUM	HIGH

Our risk assessment reflects the company's portfolio of leading properties, with relatively balanced business and geographic diversification, combined with our view of its strong balance sheet, offset by some high cyclical ad exposure, film volatility, currency risk, and some corporate governance issues.

Quantitative Evaluations

S&P Quality Ranking   A-

D	C	B-	B	B+	A-	A	A+

Relative Strength Rank   MODERATE

69

LOWEST = 1   HIGHEST = 99

Revenue/Earnings Data

Revenue (Million $)

	1Q	2Q	3Q	4Q	Year
2010	7,199	8,684	8,785	8,110	32,778
2009	7,509	7,871	7,373	7,670	30,423
2008	7,067	8,590	8,750	8,589	32,996
2007	5,914	7,844	7,530	7,367	28,655
2006	5,682	6,665	6,198	6,782	25,327
2005	5,191	6,562	6,043	6,108	23,859

Earnings Per Share ($)

	1Q	2Q	3Q	4Q	Year
2010	0.22	0.10	0.32	0.33	0.97
2009	0.20	-2.45	1.04	-0.08	-1.29
2008	0.23	0.27	0.91	0.43	1.81
2007	0.28	0.27	0.29	0.30	1.14
2006	0.19	0.22	0.27	0.24	0.92
2005	0.22	0.14	0.14	0.23	0.73

Fiscal year ended Jun. 30. Next earnings report expected: Early November. EPS Estimates based on S&P Operating Earnings; historical GAAP earnings are as reported.

Dividend Data (Dates: mm/dd Payment Date: mm/dd/yy)

Amount ($)	Date Decl.	Ex-Div. Date	Stk. of Record	Payment Date
0.075	02/02	03/08	03/10	04/14/10
0.075	08/04	09/03	09/08	10/13/10

Dividends have been paid since 1995. Source: Company reports.

Please read the Required Disclosures and Analyst Certification on the last page of this report.

The McGraw-Hill Companies

News Corp

STANDARD &POOR'S

Business Summary August 19, 2010

CORPORATE OVERVIEW. News Corp., once a small publisher of Australian newspapers, has grown into one of the world's premier media conglomerates. In December 2004, the company moved its domicile to the U.S., followed in March 2005 by a tender offer for the public's 18% minority stake in its Fox Entertainment Group.

Key U.S. assets include Fox film studio and 20th Century Fox TV; Fox broadcast network and TV stations; Fox News, FX and regional sports networks (including FSN Ohio, FSN Florida and 40% of FSN Bay Area); HarperCollins (book publishers); the Wall Street Journal and New York Post newspapers; and an inserts business. International assets include several newspaper businesses in the U.K. and Australia (including The Times, The Sun, News of the World and The Australian); the wholly owned DBS provider SKY Italia; a 39% controlling stake in U.K. DBS provider BSkyB; a 40% stake in Sky Deutschland; and other associated entities in Asia, Australia and Latin America. About 54% of FY 10 (Jun.) revenues were derived from the U.S. and Canada, 30% from Europe, and 16% from Australasia/other.

CORPORATE STRATEGY. Over the past few years, the company has completed several strategic transactions. In June 2010, it made a non-binding offer to acquire 61% of BSkyB which it doesn't already own (for 700 pence a share), and in August 2010, NWS agreed to transfer a controlling stake in three TV channels in China, as well as its Chinese movie library, to a local private equity firm, for undisclosed terms. Earlier in December 2007, the company acquired Dow Jones for $5.7 billion. In February 2009, it divested a 38.4% stake in DIRECTV, plus three regional sports networks and $550 million of cash, in exchange for Liberty Media's 16.3% voting stake.

In 2005, the company paid about $650 million for social networking site MySpace (as part of its Fox Interactive Media unit -- also including IGN Entertainment, Scout Media, iLike and imeem. Meanwhile, with MySpace's multi-year search deal with Google set to expire in August 2010, the company has been exploring strategic alliances with other Internet companies. It provides content through online video site Hulu -- a JV of Fox, Disney's ABC and GE's NBC -- as well as other digital outlets (including Apple's iTunes and mobile content destination Mobizzo).

Company Financials Fiscal Year Ended Jun. 30

Per Share Data ($)	2010	2009	2008	2007	2006	2005	2004	2003	2002	2001
Tangible Book Value	0.96	NM	NM	2.37	1.86	1.81	1.85	NM	0.68	3.34
Cash Flow	1.42	-0.86	2.22	1.38	1.62	1.40	0.79	0.65	-2.39	-0.01
Earnings	0.97	-1.29	1.81	1.14	0.92	0.73	0.58	0.46	-2.75	0.32
S&P Core Earnings	1.06	0.53	1.39	1.00	0.83	0.66	0.52	0.51	-1.10	NA
Dividends	0.14	0.12	0.12	0.12	0.13	0.11	0.10	0.08	0.07	0.07
Payout Ratio	14%	NM	7%	11%	14%	14%	17%	17%	NM	22%
Prices:High	17.00	14.00	20.55	25.40	21.94	18.88	18.77	15.54	13.60	18.70
Prices:Low	11.61	4.95	5.43	19.00	15.17	13.94	14.57	9.33	7.54	9.80
P/E Ratio:High	18	NM	11	22	24	26	32	34	NM	58
P/E Ratio:Low	12	NM	3	17	16	19	25	20	NM	31

Income Statement Analysis (Million $)	2010	2009	2008	2007	2006	2005	2004	2003	2002	2001
Revenue	32,778	30,423	32,996	28,655	25,327	23,859	29,428	29,913	29,014	25,578
Operating Income	5,644	4,696	6,482	5,331	4,643	4,329	5,146	4,372	4,291	3,799
Depreciation	1,185	1,138	1,207	879	775	765	844	776	749	706
Interest Expense	NA	927	970	843	791	736	958	1,094	1,384	1,358
Pretax Income	3,323	-5,539	7,321	5,306	4,405	3,561	3,855	3,000	-10,959	-562
Effective Tax Rate	20.4%	NM	24.6%	34.2%	34.6%	34.3%	32.3%	25.8%	NM	NM
Net Income	2,539	-3,378	5,387	3,426	2,812	2,128	2,312	1,808	-11,962	-746
S&P Core Earnings	2,771	1,379	4,142	3,171	2,663	2,017	1,563	1,303	-2,718	NA

Balance Sheet & Other Financial Data (Million $)	2010	2009	2008	2007	2006	2005	2004	2003	2002	2001
Cash	8,709	6,540	4,662	7,654	5,783	6,470	6,217	6,746	6,337	5,615
Current Assets	NA	15,836	14,362	15,906	13,123	12,779	15,012	14,861	14,647	16,173
Total Assets	54,384	53,121	62,308	62,343	56,649	54,692	73,738	67,747	71,441	84,961
Current Liabilities	NA	10,639	9,182	7,494	6,373	6,649	10,437	9,303	11,005	9,776
Long Term Debt	13,191	12,204	13,230	12,147	11,385	10,087	12,972	14,480	15,275	23,345
Common Equity	25,113	23,224	28,623	32,922	29,874	29,377	39,387	31,834	34,101	42,050
Total Capital	39,186	39,455	48,303	51,530	46,740	44,500	59,473	53,867	54,743	70,940
Capital Expenditures	914	1,101	1,443	1,308	976	901	517	551	505	1,113
Cash Flow	3,724	-2,240	6,594	4,305	3,587	2,883	3,156	2,584	-11,213	-40.0
Current Ratio	2.0	1.5	1.6	2.1	2.1	1.9	1.4	1.6	1.3	1.7
% Long Term Debt of Capitalization	33.7	30.9	27.4	23.6	24.4	22.7	21.8	26.9	27.9	32.9
% Net Income of Revenue	7.8	NM	16.3	12.0	11.1	8.9	7.9	6.0	NM	NM
% Return on Assets	4.7	NM	8.6	5.8	5.1	4.1	3.3	2.6	NM	NM
% Return on Equity	10.5	NM	17.5	10.9	9.5	8.4	6.5	5.5	NM	NM

Data as orig reptd.; bef. results of disc opers/spec. items. Per share data adj. for stk. divs.; EPS diluted. Income and balance sheet data in Australian $ prior to 2005. E-Estimated. NA-Not Available. NM-Not Meaningful. NR-Not Ranked. UR-Under Review.

Office: 1211 Avenue Of The Americas, New York, NY 10036-8701.
Telephone: 212-852-7000.
Website: http://www.newscorp.com
Chrmn & CEO: K.R. Murdoch

Pres, Vice Chrmn & COO: C. Carey
EVP, CFO & Chief Acctg Officer: D.F. DeVoe
EVP & General Counsel: L. Jacobs
SVP & Cntlr: R. Gannon

Investor Contact: R. Nolte (212-852-7017)
Board Members: J. M. Aznar, N. Bancroft, P. L. Barnes, C. Carey, K. E. Cowley, D. F. DeVoe, V. Dinh, R. Eddington, A. S. Knight, J. Murdoch, K. R. Murdoch, L. Murdoch, T. J. Perkins, A. M. Siskind, J. L. Thornton

Founded: 1922
Domicile: Delaware
Employees: 51,000

NextEra Energy Inc

STANDARD &POOR'S

S&P Recommendation	BUY ★★★★☆		Price $55.45 (as of Oct 22, 2010)	12-Mo. Target Price $58.00	Investment Style Large-Cap Blend

GICS Sector Utilities
Sub-Industry Electric Utilities

Summary NextEra Energy, Inc. (formerly FPL Group) is the holding company for Florida Power & Light and NextEra Energy Resources.

Key Stock Statistics (Source S&P, Vickers, company reports)

52-Wk Range	$56.57– 45.29	S&P Oper. EPS 2010E	4.45	Market Capitalization(B)	$23.058	Beta	0.65
Trailing 12-Month EPS	$4.53	S&P Oper. EPS 2011E	4.58	Yield (%)	3.61	S&P 3-Yr. Proj. EPS CAGR(%)	6
Trailing 12-Month P/E	12.2	P/E on S&P Oper. EPS 2010E	12.5	Dividend Rate/Share	$2.00	S&P Credit Rating	A-
$10K Invested 5 Yrs Ago	$15,378	Common Shares Outstg. (M)	415.8	Institutional Ownership (%)	62		

Price Performance

30-Week Mov. Avg. · · · · 10-Week Mov. Avg. - - GAAP Earnings vs. Previous Year Volume Above Avg. STARS
12-Mo. Target Price — Relative Strength — ▲ Up ▼ Down ▶ No Change Below Avg.

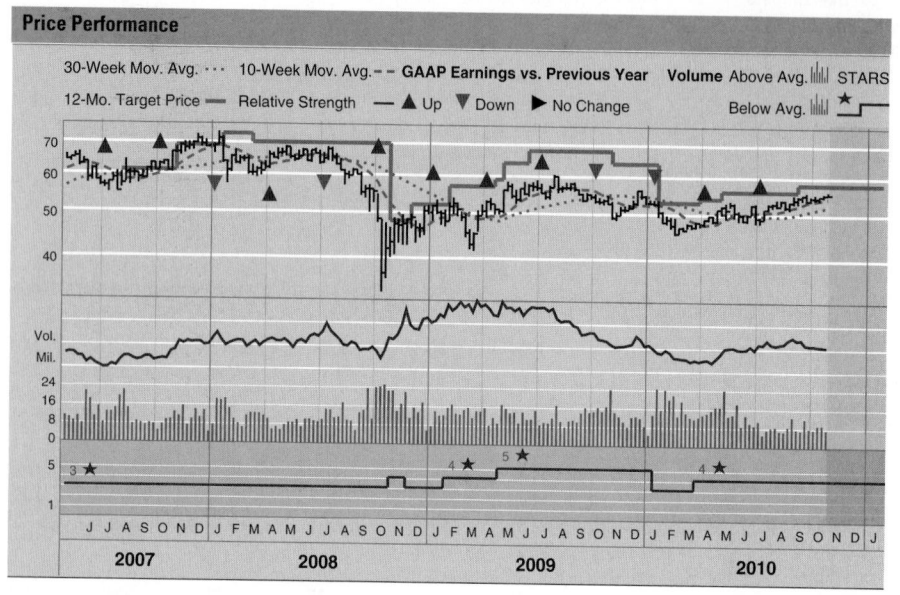

Options: ASE, CBOE, P, Ph

Analysis prepared by **Justin McCann** on September 01, 2010, when the stock traded at **$ 53.73**.

Highlights

► Excluding one-time net gains of $0.32, we expect operating EPS in 2010 to increase nearly 10% from 2009's $4.05, which excluded net one-time charges of $0.08. Operating results in the first half of 2010 benefited from very favorable weather and a modest rate increase at Florida Power & Light, partially offset by poor first quarter wind resources and higher interest expense at NextEra Energy Resources.

► We believe EPS growth in the second half of 2010 and in 2011 will be driven by new wind power investments and tax credits at NextEra Energy Resources. However, we expect the gas merchant market in Texas to remain weak. We think growth prospects at FP&L will largely reflect the timing and extent of a recovery in Florida's economy and housing market, but believe that once it has recovered, the utility will realize growth rates above the national average.

► On January 13, 2010, the Florida Public Service Commission granted FP&L a rate base increase of $75 million, far lower than the $1.04 billion increase requested. Following the announcement of the rate case ruling, FP&L announced that it would suspend projects representing about $10 billion of investment over the next five years.

Investment Rationale/Risk

► Although the stock has recovered nearly 19% from its year-to-date low, we still view it as attractive for above-average total return potential. The shares had been hurt by the far worse than expected regulatory decision on FP&L's rate increase request, but we believe that the name change of the company to NextEra Energy, Inc. will continue to direct investor focus to the growth prospects we still see for NextEra Energy Resources, driven by the expansion of its wind and solar power projects and from the tax credits provided by the passage of the federal stimulus package.

► Risks to our opinion and target price include lower-than-expected results from the NextEra Energy Resources subsidiary, prolonged weakness in the Florida economy and housing market, and a reduction in the average P/E for the electric utilities sub-industry as a whole.

► We believe the stock will benefit from the company being the national leader in wind and solar power development. We expect the company to sustain annual dividend growth of about 5% over the next few years. Our 12-month target price is $58, an approximate peers P/E of 12.7X our operating EPS estimate for 2011.

Qualitative Risk Assessment

LOW	MEDIUM	HIGH

Our risk assessment reflects our view of NextEra Energy's steady cash flows from its Florida Power & Light utility, despite the weak economy and housing market, a reduced number of customer accounts, and a much less supportive political and regulatory environment. We believe this will be complemented by the fast-growing but higher-risk cash flows from NextEra Energy Resources, its independent power subsidiary.

Quantitative Evaluations

S&P Quality Ranking A

D	C	B-	B	B+	A-	A	A+

Relative Strength Rank MODERATE

49

LOWEST = 1 HIGHEST = 99

Revenue/Earnings Data

Revenue (Million $)

	1Q	2Q	3Q	4Q	Year
2010	3,622	3,591	--	--	--
2009	3,705	3,811	4,473	3,655	15,643
2008	3,434	3,585	5,387	4,003	16,410
2007	3,075	3,929	4,575	3,683	15,263
2006	3,584	3,809	4,694	3,623	15,710
2005	2,437	2,741	3,504	3,164	11,846

Earnings Per Share ($)

2010	1.36	1.02	E1.50	E0.88	E4.45
2009	0.90	0.91	1.31	0.85	3.97
2008	0.62	0.52	1.92	1.01	4.07
2007	0.38	1.01	1.33	0.56	3.27
2006	0.64	0.60	1.32	0.67	3.23
2005	0.36	0.52	0.87	0.53	2.29

Fiscal year ended Dec. 31. Next earnings report expected: Late October. EPS Estimates based on S&P Operating Earnings; historical GAAP earnings are as reported.

Dividend Data (Dates: mm/dd Payment Date: mm/dd/yy)

Amount ($)	Date Decl.	Ex-Div. Date	Stk. of Record	Payment Date
0.500	02/12	02/24	02/26	03/15/10
0.500	05/21	06/02	06/04	06/15/10
0.500	07/30	08/25	08/27	09/15/10
0.500	10/15	11/23	11/26	12/15/10

Dividends have been paid since 1944. Source: Company reports.

Please read the Required Disclosures and Analyst Certification on the last page of this report.

The McGraw-Hill Companies

Business Summary September 01, 2010

CORPORATE OVERVIEW. NextEra Energy, Inc. (formerly FPL Group), one of the largest providers of electricity-related services in the U.S., is the holding company for Florida Power & Light Co. (FP&L), a regulated and vertically integrated utility, and NextEra Energy Resources (formerly FPL Energy), a wholesale generator of electricity with operations in 28 states and Canada.

IMPACT OF MAJOR DEVELOPMENTS. On May 21, 2010, the company changed its name from FPL Group, Inc. to NextEra Energy, Inc. The management believes that the new name, which reflects the name of its subsidiary, NextEra Energy Resources, will better reflect the company's scale as one of the largest and cleanest energy providers in North America, and is well positioned for the ongoing transition to a low-carbon economy. The ticker symbol is expected to be changed from FPL to NEE on or about June 23.

MARKET PROFILE. Florida Power & Light provides electricity to about 4.5 million customers in an area covering nearly all of Florida's eastern seaboard, as well as the southern part of the state. Electric revenues by customer class in 2009 were: residential 55%; commercial 41%; industrial 3%; wholesale, 1%; and other (including deferred, and the net change in unbilled revenues), -1%. Given its unusually low level of exposure to industrial customers, we consider the company to normally be much less vulnerable to economic downturns. However, after experiencing average annual customer growth over the previous 10 years, FP&L started to experience a slowdown in retail customer growth in 2007, as well as a decline in non-weather-related usage, and in 2009, retail customer growth was down 0.2%. We do not expect to see a recovery in this growth until there is a broader recovery in the state's economy.

Company Financials Fiscal Year Ended Dec. 31

Per Share Data ($)	2009	2008	2007	2006	2005	2004	2003	2002	2001	2000
Tangible Book Value	31.35	28.57	26.35	24.52	21.52	20.24	18.93	17.46	17.09	15.89
Earnings	3.97	4.07	3.27	3.23	2.29	2.46	2.51	2.01	2.31	2.07
S&P Core Earnings	3.73	3.84	3.04	3.00	2.06	2.17	2.21	1.52	1.83	NA
Dividends	1.89	1.78	1.64	1.50	1.42	1.30	1.20	1.16	1.12	1.08
Payout Ratio	48%	44%	50%	46%	62%	53%	48%	58%	48%	52%
Prices:High	60.61	73.75	72.77	55.57	48.11	38.05	34.04	32.66	35.81	36.50
Prices:Low	41.48	33.81	53.72	37.81	35.90	30.10	26.78	22.50	25.61	18.19
P/E Ratio:High	15	18	22	17	21	15	14	16	16	18
P/E Ratio:Low	10	8	16	12	16	12	11	11	11	9

Income Statement Analysis (Million $)	2009	2008	2007	2006	2005	2004	2003	2002	2001	2000
Revenue	15,643	16,410	15,263	15,710	11,846	10,522	9,630	8,311	8,475	7,082
Depreciation	1,947	1,579	1,261	1,185	1,285	1,198	1,105	952	983	1,032
Maintenance	NA	NA	NA	NA	NA	NA	NA	NA	NA	NA
Fixed Charges Coverage	3.16	3.43	3.18	3.30	2.87	3.26	3.95	4.52	4.51	4.55
Construction Credits	53.0	35.0	23.0	21.0	28.0	37.0	NA	NA	NA	Nil
Effective Tax Rate	16.8%	21.5%	21.9%	23.7%	23.5%	23.1%	29.2%	26.0%	32.7%	32.3%
Net Income	1,615	1,639	1,312	1,281	885	887	893	695	781	704
S&P Core Earnings	1,516	1,547	1,218	1,187	797	782	786	527	616	NA

Balance Sheet & Other Financial Data (Million $)	2009	2008	2007	2006	2005	2004	2003	2002	2001	2000
Gross Property	50,169	45,528	41,040	36,152	33,351	31,720	30,272	26,505	23,388	21,022
Capital Expenditures	5,645	4,989	1,826	1,763	1,616	1,394	1,383	1,277	1,544	1,299
Net Property	36,078	32,411	28,652	24,499	22,463	21,226	20,297	14,304	11,662	9,934
Capitalization:Long Term Debt	16,300	13,833	11,280	9,591	8,039	8,027	8,728	6,016	5,084	4,202
Capitalization:% Long Term Debt	55.7	54.2	51.2	49.1	48.6	51.6	55.6	47.4	45.8	42.9
Capitalization:Preferred	Nil	Nil	Nil	Nil	Nil	Nil	Nil	Nil	Nil	Nil
Capitalization:% Preferred	Nil	Nil	Nil	Nil	Nil	Nil	Nil	Nil	Nil	Nil
Capitalization:Common	12,967	11,681	10,735	9,930	8,499	7,537	6,967	6,688	6,015	5,593
Capitalization:% Common	44.3	45.8	48.8	50.9	51.4	48.4	44.4	52.6	54.2	57.1
Total Capital	29,836	29,745	25,836	22,953	19,615	15,645	17,850	14,444	12,629	11,442
% Operating Ratio	85.5	85.5	87.5	87.1	88.6	87.8	87.9	85.7	87.6	86.3
% Earned on Net Property	7.6	9.3	8.6	8.9	6.7	7.1	8.1	9.5	10.3	12.9
% Return on Revenue	10.3	10.0	8.6	8.2	7.5	8.4	9.3	8.4	9.2	9.9
% Return on Invested Capital	8.3	8.4	8.2	10.9	8.6	9.2	8.1	9.0	9.6	9.7
% Return on Common Equity	13.1	14.6	12.7	13.9	11.0	12.0	13.4	10.7	13.5	12.8

Data as orig reptd.; bef. results of disc opers/spec. items. Per share data adj. for stk. divs.; EPS diluted. E-Estimated. NA-Not Available. NM-Not Meaningful. NR-Not Ranked. UR-Under Review.

Office: 700 Universe Boulevard, Juno Beach, FL 33408.
Telephone: 561-694-4000.
Website: http://www.nexteraenergy.com
Chrmn & CEO: L. Hay, III

Pres & COO: J.L. Robo
EVP & CFO: A. Pimentel, Jr.
EVP & General Counsel: C.E. Sieving
Chief Acctg Officer & Cntlr: C.N. Froggatt

Investor Contact: P. Cutler (800-222-4511)
Board Members: S. S. Barrat, R. Beall, II, J. H. Brown, J. L. Camaren, K. B. Dunn, J. B. Ferguson, L. Hay, III, T. Jennings, O. D. Kingsley, Jr., R. E. Schupp, W. H. Swanson, M. H. Thaman, H. E. Tookes, II

Founded: 1984
Domicile: Florida
Employees: 15,070

Nicor Inc.

STANDARD & POOR'S

S&P Recommendation HOLD ★★★☆☆

Price $47.75 (as of Oct 22, 2010)	**12-Mo. Target Price** $47.00	**Investment Style** Large-Cap Blend

GICS Sector Utilities
Sub-Industry Gas Utilities

Summary This holding company's Nicor Gas subsidiary is one of the largest U.S. distributors of natural gas.

Key Stock Statistics (Source S&P, Vickers, company reports)

52-Wk Range	$48.47–36.69	S&P Oper. EPS 2010**E**	3.28	Market Capitalization(B)	$2.173	Beta	0.42
Trailing 12-Month EPS	$3.37	S&P Oper. EPS 2011**E**	3.31	Yield (%)	3.90	S&P 3-Yr. Proj. EPS CAGR(%)	6
Trailing 12-Month P/E	14.2	P/E on S&P Oper. EPS 2010**E**	14.6	Dividend Rate/Share	$1.86	S&P Credit Rating	AA
$10K Invested 5 Yrs Ago	$15,621	Common Shares Outstg. (M)	45.5	Institutional Ownership (%)	62		

Price Performance

30-Week Mov. Avg. · · · 10-Week Mov. Avg. – – **GAAP Earnings vs. Previous Year** Volume Above Avg. STARS
12-Mo. Target Price — Relative Strength — ▲ Up ▼ Down ▶ No Change Below Avg. ★

Options: P

Analysis prepared by **Christopher B. Muir** on August 13, 2010, when the stock traded at **$ 42.90**.

Highlights

➤ We see revenues rising 3.0% in 2010. We expect utility revenues to rise as a result of higher gas prices and customer usage, customer growth and the full year effect of a large rate hike. We project nearly flat revenues at the Tropical Shipping unit due to the economic slowdown. Revenues at the Other Energy Ventures segment should grow slowly, in our view. In 2011, we see revenues rising by 1.7%.

➤ We project operating margins of 9.2% in 2010 and 9.4% in 2011, up from 8.3% in 2008, reflecting lower per-revenue non-utility operating costs and utility operating taxes, partly offset by higher per-revenue cost of gas. We expect other expense categories to grow about as fast as revenues. We forecast pretax margins of 8.2% in 2010 and 2011, up from 7.2% in 2008, as we see higher interest expense outweighed by higher non-operating income in 2010.

➤ Assuming a small increase in the number of shares outstanding, we estimate EPS of $3.28 in 2010, up 13% from 2009's $2.89, excluding a net one-time gain of $0.09 and helped by prior-year bad debt recoveries. Our 2011 EPS projection is $3.31, up 0.9%.

Investment Rationale/Risk

➤ Our 2010 projected payout ratio of 57% is near the peer average of around 55%, and the shares recently yielded about 4.3%. GAS was granted rate increases of $69 million effective April 2009 and $11 million effective October 2009, helping boost its earnings. We think this will allow GAS to consider a resumption of dividend increases in 2011. Should economic growth in the U.S. recover, we see strong earnings growth returning to GAS's unregulated businesses.

➤ Risks to our recommendation and target price include a weak economy in GAS's service territory, higher-than-expected interest rates, and slower-than-projected growth in unregulated operations.

➤ The stock recently traded at about 13.1X our 2011 EPS estimate, a 6% discount to natural gas utility peers. Our 12-month target price of $47 equates to a multiple of 14.2X our 2011 EPS estimate, a 7% discount to our peer forecast. We think this valuation is warranted by our view of no dividend increases through the end of 2010 and relatively moderate EPS and dividend growth after 2010, partly offset by what we see as an extremely strong balance sheet.

Qualitative Risk Assessment

LOW	MEDIUM	HIGH

Our risk assessment reflects the low-risk nature of the company's main subsidiary, a regulated natural gas distribution company, slightly offset by the higher-risk nature of its much smaller competitive operations. The company benefits from being the lone delivery agent of natural gas to customers within its service territory.

Quantitative Evaluations

S&P Quality Ranking B

D	C	B-	B	B+	A-	A	A+

Relative Strength Rank MODERATE

65

LOWEST = 1 HIGHEST = 99

Revenue/Earnings Data

Revenue (Million $)

	1Q	2Q	3Q	4Q	Year
2010	1,193	425.6	--	--	--
2009	1,111	447.6	325.6	768.1	2,652
2008	1,596	699.8	440.3	1,041	3,777
2007	1,335	556.9	365.2	919.5	3,176
2006	1,319	451.3	351.1	838.2	2,960
2005	1,180	484.4	336.0	1,358	3,358

Earnings Per Share ($)

2010	1.33	0.53	E0.30	E1.13	E3.28
2009	0.96	0.50	0.30	1.21	2.98
2008	0.91	0.64	0.03	1.05	2.63
2007	1.04	0.40	0.32	1.23	2.99
2006	0.99	0.19	0.39	1.29	2.87
2005	0.99	0.75	-0.06	1.40	3.07

Fiscal year ended Dec. 31. Next earnings report expected: Early November. EPS Estimates based on S&P Operating Earnings; historical GAAP earnings are as reported.

Dividend Data (Dates: mm/dd Payment Date: mm/dd/yy)

Amount ($)	Date Decl.	Ex-Div. Date	Stk. of Record	Payment Date
0.465	11/20	12/29	12/31	02/01/10
0.465	02/19	03/29	03/31	05/01/10
0.465	04/22	06/28	06/30	08/01/10
0.465	07/22	09/28	09/30	11/01/10

Dividends have been paid since 1954. Source: Company reports.

Please read the Required Disclosures and Analyst Certification on the last page of this report.

The **McGraw-Hill** Companies

Nicor Inc.

Business Summary August 13, 2010

CORPORATE OVERVIEW. Nicor Inc. is a holding company, whose principal subsidiaries are Northern Illinois Gas Company (doing business as Nicor Gas Company), one of the nation's largest distributors of natural gas, and Tropical Shipping, a transporter of containerized freight in the Bahamas and the Caribbean region. Nicor also owns several energy-related ventures, including Nicor Services and Nicor Solutions, which provide energy-related products and services to retail markets, and Nicor Enerchange, a wholesale natural gas marketing company.

PRIMARY BUSINESS DYNAMICS. Nicor seeks earnings growth through investment in unregulated operations, including its Tropical Shipping and Other Energy Ventures segments. However, the company's main operating segment remains its regulated gas utility operations.

As of the end of 2009, Nicor Gas (68% of 2009 segment operating profits) served 2.2 million customers in a service area that covers most of northern Illinois, excluding Chicago. In 2009, gas deliveries fell to 475.9 billion cubic feet (Bcf), from 498.1 Bcf in 2008. The company has an extensive storage and transmission system that is directly connected to eight interstate pipelines, and includes eight owned underground gas storage facilities, with about 150

Bcf of annual storage capacity. In addition, Nicor Gas has about 40 Bcf of purchased storage from an affiliated party under contracts that expire between 2012 and 2013.

Nicor Gas also operates the Chicago Hub, which provides natural gas storage and transmission-related services to marketers and other gas distribution companies, but revenues are passed on directly to Nicor Gas's customers.

GAS's Tropical Shipping unit (13%) is one of the largest containerized cargo carriers in the Caribbean, with a fleet of 11 owned and four chartered vessels, with total container capacity of about 5,270 20-foot equivalent units (TEU), serving 25 ports. Total volumes shipped in 2009 were 176,600 TEU, down from 197,100 TEU in 2008 and 206,600 TEU in 2007. However, revenues per TEU remained relatively steady at $1,997 in 2009, versus $2,158 in 2008 and $1,955 in 2007.

Company Financials Fiscal Year Ended Dec. 31

Per Share Data ($)	2009	2008	2007	2006	2005	2004	2003	2002	2001	2000
Tangible Book Value	22.38	21.02	20.51	19.43	18.36	16.99	17.15	16.55	16.39	15.56
Cash Flow	7.28	6.40	6.64	6.44	6.55	5.05	5.73	6.00	6.46	4.12
Earnings	2.98	2.63	2.99	2.87	3.07	1.70	2.48	2.88	3.17	1.00
S&P Core Earnings	3.14	2.11	2.74	2.83	2.47	1.97	2.45	2.30	1.99	NA
Dividends	1.86	1.86	1.86	1.86	1.86	1.86	1.86	1.84	1.76	1.66
Payout Ratio	62%	71%	62%	65%	61%	109%	75%	64%	56%	166%
Prices:High	43.39	51.99	53.66	49.92	42.97	39.65	39.30	49.00	42.38	43.88
Prices:Low	27.50	32.35	37.80	38.72	35.50	32.04	23.70	18.09	34.00	29.38
P/E Ratio:High	15	20	18	17	14	23	16	17	13	44
P/E Ratio:Low	9	12	13	13	12	19	10	6	11	29

Income Statement Analysis (Million $)										
Revenue	2,652	3,777	3,176	2,960	3,358	2,740	2,663	1,897	2,544	2,298
Operating Income	NA	356	372	366	202	138	189	227	244	507
Depreciation	196	171	166	160	155	149	144	138	149	144
Interest Expense	38.7	40.1	38.2	49.8	48.0	41.6	37.3	38.5	44.9	48.6
Pretax Income	201	164	184	174	171	105	169	186	217	61.1
Effective Tax Rate	32.5%	27.1%	26.6%	26.3%	20.3%	28.7%	35.2%	31.0%	33.8%	23.6%
Net Income	136	120	135	128	136	75.1	110	128	144	46.7
S&P Core Earnings	143	96.2	124	127	110	87.7	108	102	90.4	NA

Balance Sheet & Other Financial Data (Million $)										
Cash	134	95.5	91.9	41.1	119	12.9	50.3	75.2	10.7	55.8
Current Assets	1,003	1,339	1,024	911	1,346	1,021	916	708	518	915
Total Assets	4,436	4,784	4,252	4,090	4,391	3,975	3,797	2,899	2,575	2,885
Current Liabilities	1,168	1,668	1,276	1,142	1,623	1,174	1,069	1,099	826	1,312
Long Term Debt	498	449	423	498	486	495	497	396	446	347
Common Equity	1,038	973	945	873	811	749	755	728	728	708
Total Capital	1,536	1,822	1,769	1,787	1,751	1,873	1,813	1,514	1,548	1,173
Capital Expenditures	220	250	173	592	202	190	181	193	186	158
Cash Flow	331	290	301	288	291	224	253	266	292	191
Current Ratio	0.9	0.8	0.8	0.8	0.8	0.9	0.9	0.6	0.6	0.7
% Long Term Debt of Capitalization	Nil	24.6	23.9	27.9	27.7	26.4	27.4	26.1	28.8	29.6
% Net Income of Revenue	5.1	3.2	4.3	4.3	4.5	2.7	4.1	6.7	5.6	2.0
% Return on Assets	2.9	2.1	3.2	3.0	11.4	7.8	3.3	4.7	5.3	1.8
% Return on Equity	NA	12.5	14.9	15.2	17.4	9.9	14.8	12.3	20.0	6.2

Data as orig reptd.; bef. results of disc opers/spec. items. Per share data adj. for stk. divs.; EPS diluted. E-Estimated. NA-Not Available. NM-Not Meaningful. NR-Not Ranked. UR-Under Review.

Office: 1844 Ferry Road, Naperville, IL 60563-9600.
Telephone: 630-305-9500.
Website: http://www.nicor.com
Chrmn, Pres & CEO: R.M. Strobel

EVP & CFO: R.L. Hawley
SVP, Secy & General Counsel: P.C. Gracey, Jr.
Chief Acctg Officer & Cntlr: K.K. Pepping
Treas: D.M. Ruschau

Investor Contact: K.D. Brunner (630-388-2529)
Board Members: R. M. Beavers, Jr., B. P. Bickner, J. H. Birdsall, III, N. R. Bobins, B. J. Gaines, R. A. Jean, D. J. Keller, R. E. Martin, G. R. Nelson, A. J. Olivera, J. E. Rau, J. C. Staley, R. M. Strobel

Founded: 1953
Domicile: Illinois
Employees: 3,900

NIKE Inc

STANDARD &POOR'S

| S&P Recommendation | BUY ★★★★★ | Price $81.92 (as of Oct 22, 2010) | 12-Mo. Target Price $90.00 | Investment Style Large-Cap Growth |

GICS Sector Consumer Discretionary
Sub-Industry Footwear

Summary NIKE is the world's leading designer and marketer of high-quality athletic footwear, athletic apparel, and accessories.

Key Stock Statistics (Source S&P, Vickers, company reports)

52-Wk Range	$83.40–60.89	S&P Oper. EPS 2011E	4.39	Market Capitalization(B)	$31.775	Beta	0.92
Trailing 12-Month EPS	$3.96	S&P Oper. EPS 2012E	4.87	Yield (%)	1.32	S&P 3-Yr. Proj. EPS CAGR(%)	8
Trailing 12-Month P/E	20.7	P/E on S&P Oper. EPS 2011E	18.7	Dividend Rate/Share	$1.08	S&P Credit Rating	A+
$10K Invested 5 Yrs Ago	$21,238	Common Shares Outstg. (M)	477.9	Institutional Ownership (%)	89		

Price Performance

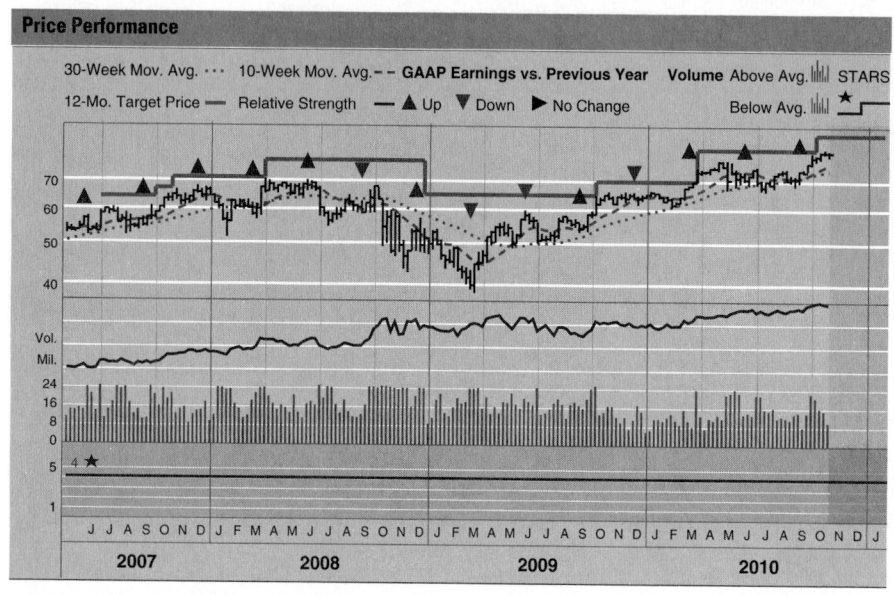

30-Week Mov. Avg. · · · · 10-Week Mov. Avg. - - GAAP Earnings vs. Previous Year   Volume Above Avg. STARS
12-Mo. Target Price — Relative Strength   ▲ Up ▼ Down ▶ No Change   Below Avg.

Options: ASE, CBOE, P, Ph

Analysis prepared by **Marie Driscoll, CFA** on September 29, 2010, when the stock traded at **$79.98**.

Highlights

➤ We expect FY 11 (May) sales growth of 9%. We see international business, direct to consumer (retail), and apparel being growth drivers for FY 11 and beyond. We think NKE's broad geographic exposure, with about 58% of sales outside the U.S., positions it well for long-term growth, but in FY 11, we see foreign currency exchange adversely impacting sales and earnings. NKE entered FY 11 with Nike brand future orders up 10%, with momentum for the August quarter to 13%, on a currency neutral basis.

➤ We see 50 bps of gross margin expansion, as NKE manages increases in raw materials, labor, and transportation costs with improved full price selling, and a more favorable merchandise and channel mix. Inventories remain in check, down 3% YOY in August. We see 50 bps of improvement in the SG&A expense ratio, benefiting from sales and global support services leverage, and fewer management layers.

➤ NKE had $5.1 billion in cash and short-term investments entering FY 11 ($9.50/share net of debt), and generates strong free cash flow. In FY 10, NKE purchased 11.3 million of its shares for $754 million, completing a $3 billion program, and a $5 billion four-year program was started.

Investment Rationale/Risk

➤ Over the past three years, NKE more than doubled its quarterly dividend and has repurchased nearly $3.6 billion worth of its shares. We see strong fundamentals and a dominant global brand with exceptional international growth opportunities supporting the share price. Moreover, NKE has launched key marketing and sales strategies designed to more closely align the company and sales with key markets. We expect NKE to pick up market share in most product categories as consumers tend to opt for established brands in uncertain environments.

➤ Risks to our recommendation and target price include a severe economic slowdown domestically and a greater-than-expected moderation in consumer spending. International risks include economic weakness, supply disruptions, and unfavorable currency fluctuations.

➤ Our 12-month target price of $90 is equal to about 19X our calendar 2011 EPS estimate of $4.67, about a 15% premium to peers and NKE's average five-year forward P/E to reflect our expectation of continued business momentum through FY 12.

Qualitative Risk Assessment

| LOW | MEDIUM | HIGH |

Our risk assessment reflects what we see as NKE's strong financial and operating metrics, offset by an increasingly competitive global marketplace and weak consumer spending in the U.S.

Quantitative Evaluations

S&P Quality Ranking   A+

| D | C | B- | B | B+ | A- | A | A+ |

Relative Strength Rank   MODERATE

69

LOWEST = 1   HIGHEST = 99

Revenue/Earnings Data

Revenue (Million $)

	1Q	2Q	3Q	4Q	Year
2011	5,175	--	--	--	--
2010	4,799	4,406	4,733	5,077	19,014
2009	5,432	4,590	4,441	4,713	19,176
2008	4,655	4,340	4,544	5,088	18,627
2007	4,194	3,822	3,927	4,383	16,326
2006	3,862	3,475	3,613	4,005	14,955

Earnings Per Share ($)

	1Q	2Q	3Q	4Q	Year
2011	1.14	E0.85	E1.14	E1.25	E4.39
2010	1.04	0.76	1.01	1.06	3.86
2009	1.03	0.80	0.50	0.70	3.03
2008	1.12	0.71	0.92	0.98	3.74
2007	0.74	0.64	0.68	0.86	2.93
2006	0.81	0.57	0.62	0.64	2.64

Fiscal year ended May 31. Next earnings report expected: Mid December. EPS Estimates based on S&P Operating Earnings; historical GAAP earnings are as reported.

Dividend Data (Dates: mm/dd Payment Date: mm/dd/yy)

Amount ($)	Date Decl.	Ex-Div. Date	Stk. of Record	Payment Date
0.270	11/19	12/03	12/07	01/04/10
0.270	02/11	03/04	03/08	04/01/10
0.270	05/17	06/03	06/07	07/01/10
0.270	08/16	09/02	09/07	10/01/10

Dividends have been paid since 1984. Source: Company reports.

The McGraw-Hill Companies

NIKE Inc

STANDARD &POOR'S

Business Summary September 29, 2010

CORPORATE OVERVIEW. Nike Inc. is the world's largest supplier of athletic footwear, with an estimated 50% of this $20 billion market (at wholesale). Sports apparel and equipment are also sold under the Nike banner, and the company's Other segment (13% of sales) houses its affiliated brands including Cole Haan, Converse, Hurley Nike Golf and Umbro.

MARKET PROFILE. Innovation, marketing and the sports cycle drive the global footwear and athletic apparel markets, in our view. Technologically superior performance products, we think, convey the idea of extraordinary ability to the wearer and are the root of the marketing campaigns aimed at lifestyle consumers (individuals attracted to a brand's attributes of an active lifestyle regardless of sports participation) while providing a basis for pricing. The global market for athletic apparel is several times as large as the footwear market, and totals over $100 billion, according to industry sources. An estimated 30% of this market consists of active sports apparel (purchased with the intent to be used in an active sport), and the remainder is lifestyle or casual wear. We see apparel representing a significant opportunity for NKE via its brand extensions and market penetration. According to NPD Fashionworld

consumer estimated data, U.S. athletic footwear sales dropped about 3.2% in 2008, to $18.6 billion, following several years of low single digit gains, and was off another 1.4% in 2009 on a 3% decline in men's and modest increases in women's and kids'. S&P projects a low single digit sales gain in 2010 for athletic footwear and apparel.

COMPETITIVE LANDSCAPE. The athletic apparel market is fragmented, providing opportunities for growing market share, in our view. Significant domestic footwear retail channels in 2009 include athletic footwear specialty shops (8% market share), sporting goods stores (6%), and discounters or mass merchants (14%). We see NKE's prowess in athletic footwear and strong brand attributes as competitive advantages that should serve the company well as it aims to capture share of the underserved women's athletic apparel market.

Company Financials Fiscal Year Ended May 31

Per Share Data ($)	2010	2009	2008	2007	2006	2005	2004	2003	2002	2001
Tangible Book Value	18.80	16.54	13.51	12.93	11.23	9.77	8.14	7.22	6.39	5.77
Cash Flow	4.66	3.74	4.36	3.51	3.17	2.72	2.22	1.83	3.51	1.44
Earnings	3.86	3.03	3.74	2.93	2.64	2.24	1.76	1.39	1.23	1.08
S&P Core Earnings	3.86	3.56	3.67	2.89	2.56	2.14	1.68	1.31	1.16	1.03
Dividends	NA	0.83	0.68	0.56	0.45	0.45	0.34	0.26	0.24	0.24
Payout Ratio	NA	27%	18%	19%	17%	20%	19%	19%	20%	22%
Calendar Year	2009	2008	2007	2006	2005	2004	2003	2002	2001	2000
Prices:High	66.62	70.60	67.93	50.60	45.77	46.22	34.27	32.14	30.03	28.50
Prices:Low	38.24	42.68	47.46	37.76	37.55	32.91	21.19	19.27	17.75	12.91
P/E Ratio:High	17	23	18	17	17	21	20	26	24	26
P/E Ratio:Low	10	14	13	13	14	15	12	16	14	12

Income Statement Analysis (Million $)

	2010	2009	2008	2007	2006	2005	2004	2003	2002	2001
Revenue	19,014	19,176	18,627	16,326	14,955	13,740	12,253	10,697	9,893	9,489
Operating Income	2,824	2,802	2,747	2,402	23,912	2,151	1,802	1,485	1,291	1,212
Depreciation	396	347	313	270	282	257	252	239	224	197
Interest Expense	6.30	40.2	67.1	Nil	Nil	39.7	40.3	42.9	47.6	58.7
Pretax Income	2,517	1,957	2,503	2,200	2,142	1,860	1,450	1,123	2,035	921
Effective Tax Rate	NA	24.0%	24.8%	32.2%	35.0%	34.9%	34.8%	34.1%	17.2%	36.0%
Net Income	1,907	1,487	1,883	1,492	1,392	1,212	946	740	1,686	590
S&P Core Earnings	1,907	1,748	1,848	1,472	1,346	1,148	897	698	632	559

Balance Sheet & Other Financial Data (Million $)

	2010	2009	2008	2007	2006	2005	2004	2003	2002	2001
Cash	5,146	3,455	2,776	1,857	954	1,388	828	634	576	304
Current Assets	10,959	9,734	8,839	8,077	7,359	6,351	5,512	4,680	4,158	3,625
Total Assets	14,419	13,250	12,443	10,688	9,870	8,794	7,892	6,714	6,443	5,820
Current Liabilities	3,364	3,277	3,322	2,584	2,623	1,999	2,009	2,015	1,836	1,787
Long Term Debt	446	437	441	Nil	Nil	687	682	552	626	436
Common Equity	9,754	8,693	7,825	7,025	6,285	5,644	4,782	3,991	3,839	3,495
Total Capital	10,207	9,130	8,267	7,026	6,286	6,332	5,464	4,543	4,465	3,931
Capital Expenditures	335	456	449	314	334	257	214	186	283	318
Cash Flow	2,302	1,834	2,196	1,761	1,674	1,469	1,198	979	1,909	787
Current Ratio	3.3	3.0	2.7	3.1	2.8	3.2	2.7	2.3	2.3	2.0
% Long Term Debt of Capitalization	4.4	4.8	5.3	Nil	Nil	10.9	12.5	12.1	14.0	11.1
% Net Income of Revenue	10.0	7.8	10.1	9.1	9.3	8.8	7.7	6.9	17.0	6.2
% Return on Assets	13.8	11.6	16.3	14.5	14.9	14.5	12.9	11.3	27.5	10.1
% Return on Equity	20.7	18.0	25.4	22.4	23.3	23.2	21.6	18.9	46.0	17.8

Data as orig reptd.; bef. results of disc opers/spec. items. Per share data adj. for stk. divs.; EPS diluted. E-Estimated. NA-Not Available. NM-Not Meaningful. NR-Not Ranked. UR-Under Review.

Office: 1 Bowerman Dr, Beaverton, OR 97005-0979.
Telephone: 503-641-6453.
Website: http://www.nikebiz.com
Chrmn: P. Knight

Pres & CEO: M.G. Parker
COO: G.M. DeStefano
CFO: D.W. Blair
Chief Acctg Officer & Cntlr: B.F. Pliska

Investor Contact: K. Hall (800-640-8007)
Board Members: J. G. Connors, J. K. Conway, T. D. Cook, R. D. DeNunzio, A. B. Graf, Jr., D. G. Houser, P. Knight, J. Lechleiter, M. G. Parker, J. A. Rodgers, O. Smith, J. R. Thompson, Jr., P. M. Wise

Founded: 1964
Domicile: Oregon
Employees: 34,400

NiSource Inc.

STANDARD &POOR'S

S&P Recommendation SELL ★ ★ ★ ★ ★

Price	12-Mo. Target Price	Investment Style
$17.71 (as of Oct 22, 2010)	$15.00	Large-Cap Value

GICS Sector Utilities
Sub-Industry Multi-Utilities

Summary NI, the third largest U.S. gas distribution utility and the fourth largest gas pipeline company, also provides electric utility services.

Key Stock Statistics (Source S&P, Vickers, company reports)

52-Wk Range	$17.96–12.83	S&P Oper. EPS 2010E	1.17	Market Capitalization(B)	$4.923
Trailing 12-Month EPS	$1.08	S&P Oper. EPS 2011E	1.25	Yield (%)	5.19
Trailing 12-Month P/E	16.4	P/E on S&P Oper. EPS 2010E	15.1	Dividend Rate/Share	$0.92
$10K Invested 5 Yrs Ago	$10,366	Common Shares Outstg. (M)	278.0	Institutional Ownership (%)	75

Beta	0.89
S&P 3-Yr. Proj. EPS CAGR(%)	9
S&P Credit Rating	BBB-

Price Performance

30-Week Mov. Avg. · · · · 10-Week Mov. Avg. – – GAAP Earnings vs. Previous Year   Volume Above Avg. ▮▮▮ STARS
12-Mo. Target Price — Relative Strength — ▲ Up ▼ Down ► No Change   Below Avg. ▮▮▮ ★

Options: ASE, CBOE, Ph

Analysis prepared by **Christopher B. Muir** on August 19, 2010, when the stock traded at **$ 16.69**.

Highlights

➤ We see 2010 revenues falling 6.2%. For the regulated utilities, we expect revenue contraction of 4.4% due to lower gas prices and declining per-customer usage as a result of customer conservation, partly offset by multiple rate increases and customer growth. We think gas transmission and storage revenues will benefit from higher short-term transportation and storage volumes, as well as a new pipeline. We see non-regulated revenues falling 20% due to lower prices, partly offset by higher volumes. We look for revenues to advance 3.0% in 2011.

➤ We expect NI to report operating margins of 14.4% in 2010 and 14.9% in 2011, versus 2009's 12.8%. We think 2010 results will reflect lower per-revenue energy costs, partly offset by higher per-revenue non-energy expenses. In 2011, we see lower per-revenue energy costs and operating taxes. We see pretax margins of 8.3% in 2010 and 8.7% in 2011, versus 7.3% in 2009. For 2010, we project higher interest expense.

➤ Our 2010 recurring EPS estimate, excluding $0.02 in nonrecurring charges, is $1.17, up 9.3% from 2009's $1.07, which excludes $0.16 of nonrecurring charges. Our 2011 forecast is $1.25, an increase of 6.8%.

Investment Rationale/Risk

➤ We view NI's utility service territory as having relatively slow, but stable, customer growth, and we see no near-term impetus for base revenue growth outside of rate increases. NI has several rate cases filed. Depreciation charges are rising as a result of capital spending programs now in place, and operations and maintenance costs have increased as a result of electric plant maintenance activities. We expect EPS growth of about 5% starting in 2010.

➤ Risks to our recommendation and target price include wider power margins, unusually cold winter weather, lower natural gas prices, and lower interest rates.

➤ The stock recently traded at 13.5X our 2011 EPS estimate, a 9% premium to multi-utility peers. Our 12-month target price of $15 is 12.0X our 2011 EPS estimate, a 6% discount to our peer target. We believe this is warranted by what we view as NI's absence of dividend growth and slightly below-average longer-term EPS growth. We do not think NI will increase its dividend until 2016, when we believe its payout ratio will be more in line with its peers.

Qualitative Risk Assessment

LOW	MEDIUM	HIGH

Our risk assessment reflects the company's reliance on fairly stable regulated sources of earnings including gas distribution, gas transmission, and electric utility services.

Quantitative Evaluations

S&P Quality Ranking   B

D	C	B-	B	B+	A-	A	A+

Relative Strength Rank   MODERATE

53

LOWEST = 1   HIGHEST = 99

Revenue/Earnings Data

Revenue (Million $)

	1Q	2Q	3Q	4Q	Year
2010	2,358	1,171	--	--	--
2009	1,685	1,268	974.7	1,685	6,649
2008	3,290	1,792	1,409	2,386	8,874
2007	2,894	1,577	1,241	2,245	7,940
2006	2,972	1,312	1,156	2,050	7,490
2005	2,683	1,356	1,165	2,695	7,899

Earnings Per Share ($)

	1Q	2Q	3Q	4Q	Year
2010	0.71	0.10	E0.01	E0.32	E1.17
2009	0.58	-0.01	-0.05	0.32	0.84
2008	0.69	0.08	0.12	0.46	1.34
2007	0.76	0.11	0.03	0.24	1.14
2006	0.63	0.08	0.10	0.33	1.14
2005	0.77	0.03	-0.02	0.24	1.04

Fiscal year ended Dec. 31. Next earnings report expected: Early November. EPS Estimates based on S&P Operating Earnings; historical GAAP earnings are as reported.

Dividend Data (Dates: mm/dd Payment Date: mm/dd/yy)

Amount ($)	Date Decl.	Ex-Div. Date	Stk. of Record	Payment Date
0.230	01/19	01/27	01/29	02/19/10
0.230	03/23	04/28	04/30	05/20/10
0.230	05/11	07/28	07/30	08/20/10
0.230	08/25	10/27	10/29	11/19/10

Dividends have been paid since 1987. Source: Company reports.

Please read the Required Disclosures and Analyst Certification on the last page of this report.

The McGraw·Hill Companies

NiSource Inc.

STANDARD &POOR'S

Business Summary August 19, 2010

CORPORATE OVERVIEW. NiSource is one of the largest U.S. natural gas distributors (measured by customers served), one of the largest owners of U.S. natural gas interstate pipelines (by route miles), and one of the largest owners of underground natural gas storage. It also provides electric utility services in northern Indiana. The company's operating divisions include Gas Distribution (41% of year end-2009 segment operating income), Gas Transmission and Storage (48%), Electric Operations (15%), and Other Operations and corporate (-4%).

Gas Distribution operations provide gas utility service to 3.3 million customers in seven states. The division owns and operates 57,785 miles of pipeline, 28,479 acres of underground storage, 90 underground storage wells and 75.8 million gallons of liquefied natural gas storage facilities. In 2009, total sales and transportation volumes were 831 MM Dth, down from 923 MM Dth in 2008. Deliveries were 32% to residential customers, 20% to commercial customers, 41% to industrial customers and 7% to off-system sales and other customers.

Gas Transmission and Storage operates 14,926 miles of interstate natural gas pipelines and 773,000 acres of underground storage systems with a capacity of about 639 billion cubic feet (Bcf). In 2009, total throughput was 1,391 MM

Dth, down 6.5% from 2008 due to decreased transportation deliveries, partly offset by the completion of projects in late 2008 and in 2009. The division has recently completed Millennium Pipeline and Hardy Storage projects and is engaged in other projects. The Millennium project is a 182-mile, 0.53 MM Dth/day pipeline across southern New York State. The 12 Bcf Hardy storage project in West Virginia became fully operational in 2009. NI said it is in the process of a potential separation of Columbia Gas into a master limited partnership structure, but we do not expect any action until the economy and financial markets improve.

NI's Northern Indiana subsidiary, NIPSCO, generates and distributes electricity for 456,835 electric utility customers. The utility owns four and operates three coal-fired plants (2,574 MW), six gas-fired units (738 MW), and two hydroelectric plants (10 MW). In 2009, the utility generated 85.2% of its electric requirements, and purchased the rest. NI has said it was considering a possible sale of this business.

Company Financials Fiscal Year Ended Dec. 31

Per Share Data ($)	2009	2008	2007	2006	2005	2004	2003	2002	2001	2000
Tangible Book Value	3.10	2.63	3.58	3.29	2.79	2.14	0.70	NM	NM	NM
Cash Flow	2.87	3.40	3.17	3.16	3.04	3.54	3.53	4.70	4.07	3.84
Earnings	0.84	1.34	1.14	1.14	1.04	1.62	1.63	2.00	1.01	1.08
S&P Core Earnings	1.18	0.83	1.09	1.13	1.20	1.62	1.67	1.43	0.32	NA
Dividends	0.92	0.92	0.92	0.92	0.92	0.92	1.10	1.16	1.16	1.08
Payout Ratio	110%	69%	78%	81%	88%	57%	67%	58%	115%	100%
Prices:High	15.82	19.82	25.43	24.80	25.50	22.82	21.97	24.99	32.55	31.50
Prices:Low	7.79	10.35	17.49	19.51	20.44	19.65	16.39	14.51	18.25	12.75
P/E Ratio:High	19	15	22	22	25	14	13	12	32	29
P/E Ratio:Low	9	8	15	17	20	12	10	7	18	12

Income Statement Analysis (Million $)										
Revenue	6,649	8,874	7,940	7,490	7,899	6,666	6,247	6,492	9,459	6,031
Operating Income	NA	1,468	1,493	880	1,520	1,072	1,116	1,203	1,009	568
Depreciation	589	567	559	549	545	510	497	574	642	374
Interest Expense	399	380	418	7,304	425	408	469	533	605	325
Pretax Income	397	555	484	484	433	671	662	680	416	298
Effective Tax Rate	41.8%	33.4%	35.6%	35.3%	34.5%	35.9%	35.4%	34.4%	44.1%	43.7%
Net Income	231	370	312	314	284	430	426	426	212	147
S&P Core Earnings	328	229	298	310	324	429	437	305	67.9	NA

Balance Sheet & Other Financial Data (Million $)										
Cash	16.4	20.6	95.4	33.1	69.4	30.1	27.3	56.2	128	193
Current Assets	2,224	3,411	2,455	2,783	3,061	2,286	2,063	1,869	2,567	4,918
Total Assets	19,272	20,032	18,005	18,157	17,959	16,988	16,624	16,897	17,374	19,697
Current Liabilities	3,150	4,583	3,393	3,821	3,843	3,602	2,609	4,177	4,729	6,893
Long Term Debt	5,988	5,944	5,594	5,146	5,271	4,917	6,075	5,448	6,214	6,148
Common Equity	4,854	4,729	5,077	5,014	4,933	4,787	4,416	4,175	3,469	3,415
Total Capital	11,504	12,223	12,234	11,775	11,866	11,448	10,490	11,581	11,515	11,483
Capital Expenditures	777	970	788	637	590	517	575	622	668	366
Cash Flow	792	937	871	863	829	940	923	1,000	854	521
Current Ratio	0.7	0.7	0.7	0.7	0.8	0.6	0.8	0.4	0.5	0.7
% Long Term Debt of Capitalization	51.9	48.6	45.7	43.7	44.4	42.9	57.9	47.0	54.0	53.5
% Net Income of Revenue	3.5	4.2	3.9	4.2	3.6	6.5	6.8	6.6	2.2	2.4
% Return on Assets	1.2	1.9	1.7	1.7	1.6	2.6	2.5	2.5	1.1	1.1
% Return on Equity	4.8	7.5	6.2	6.3	5.8	9.3	9.9	11.1	6.2	6.2

Data as orig reptd.; bef. results of disc opers/spec. items. Per share data adj. for stk. divs.; EPS diluted. E-Estimated. NA-Not Available. NM-Not Meaningful. NR-Not Ranked. UR-Under Review.

Office: 801 East 86th Avenue, Merrillville, IN, USA 46410-6272.
Telephone: 877-647-5990.
Email: questions@nisource.com
Website: http://www.nisource.com

Chrmn: I.M. Rolland
Pres & CEO: R.C. Skaggs, Jr.
EVP & CFO: S.P. Smith
EVP & General Counsel: C.J. Hightman

Chief Admin Officer & CIO: V.G. Sistovaris
Investor Contact: D.J. Vajda (877-647-5990)
Board Members: R. A. Abdoo, S. C. Beering, D. E. Foster, M. E. Jesanis, M. R. Kittrell, W. L. Nutter, D. S. Parker, I. M. Rolland, R. C. Skaggs, Jr., R. L. Thompson, C. Y. Woo

Founded: 1912
Domicile: Delaware
Employees: 7,616

The McGraw·Hill Companies

Noble Energy Inc

STANDARD &POOR'S

S&P Recommendation HOLD ★★★★☆

Price
$78.24 (as of Oct 22, 2010)

12-Mo. Target Price
$82.00

Investment Style
Large-Cap Growth

GICS Sector Energy
Sub-Industry Oil & Gas Exploration & Production

Summary This independent exploration and production company is engaged in the exploration, development and production of oil and natural gas worldwide.

Key Stock Statistics (Source S&P, Vickers, company reports)

52-Wk Range	$81.50– 56.23	S&P Oper. EPS 2010**E**	4.07	Market Capitalization(B)	$13.676	Beta	0.86
Trailing 12-Month EPS	$3.12	S&P Oper. EPS 2011**E**	4.05	Yield (%)	0.92	S&P 3-Yr. Proj. EPS CAGR(%)	-17
Trailing 12-Month P/E	25.1	P/E on S&P Oper. EPS 2010**E**	19.2	Dividend Rate/Share	$0.72	S&P Credit Rating	BBB
$10K Invested 5 Yrs Ago	$21,948	Common Shares Outstg. (M)	174.8	Institutional Ownership (%)	93		

Price Performance

30-Week Mov. Avg. · · · 10-Week Mov. Avg. – – 12-Mo. Target Price — Relative Strength — **GAAP Earnings vs. Previous Year** ▲ Up ▼ Down ► No Change **Volume** Above Avg. Below Avg. **STARS** ★

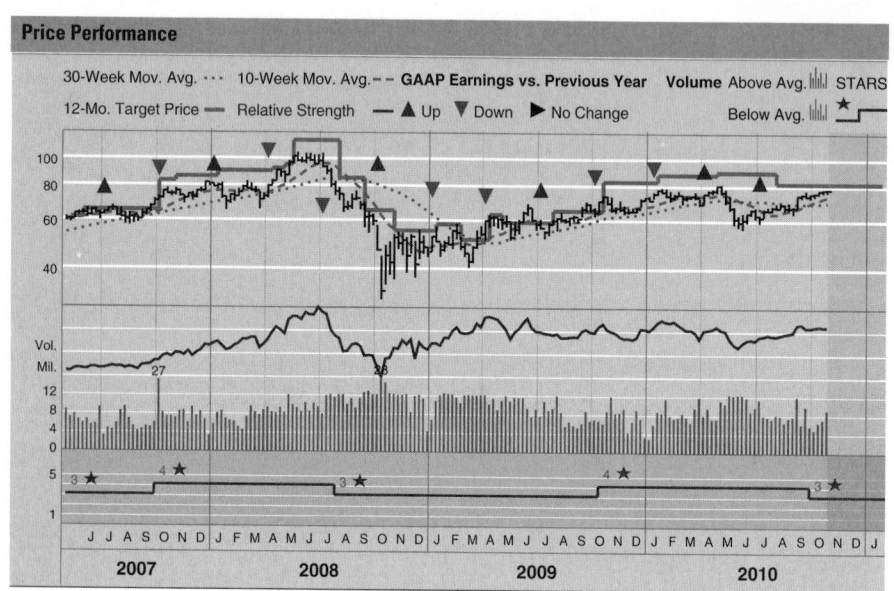

Options: ASE, CBOE, P, Ph

Analysis prepared by **Michael Kay** on October 01, 2010, when the stock traded at **$ 75.58.**

Highlights

▸ Production fell 1% in 2009 on asset sales and slower activity. In 2010, we expect oil volumes to be up more than 9% and we see strength in international gas, mainly from Israel and Equatorial Guinea (EG), offsetting a natural gas decline of 2%. We see total growth of 4% before production start-ups in 2011 boost forecasted volumes by 5%. NBL has expanded its Wattenberg field position in the Rockies DJ Basin, adding two rigs at the play where it owns 700,000 net acres with prospective for the Niobrara oil shale. We see development at the Aseng oil project in EG and the Tamar natural gas field in Israel. NBL recently lowered capex plans due to the drilling moratorium in the Gulf of Mexico.

▸ Capex plans for 2010 of $2.2 billion are up 67% from 2009. NBL's GOM Double Mountain exploration well was a dry hole and will be plugged and abandoned. We await results from Niobrara horizontal wells.

▸ Operating EPS in 2009 was $1.08. Before non-cash charges, EPS was $3.36, and we see $4.07 (with $0.56 gain) in 2010 and $4.05 in 2011, on higher prices and production, partly offset by higher operating and exploration costs.

Investment Rationale/Risk

▸ Solid exploration success with an attractive inventory of prospects and large development projects characterizes NBL's portfolio of assets, in our view. We view NBL as geographically balanced with financial flexibility, holding $1 billion in cash with low relative debt levels. NBL appears poised to translate exploration success into development at core areas. We see U.S. gas drilling projects, mainly in the Rockies, shelved in favor of high impact international targets and domestic onshore crude oil opportunities. We see potential catalysts in onshore horizontal drilling in the Niobrara oil shale and production boosts in Israel and EG. NBL's discoveries at Gunflint and Galapagos in the GOM, Tamar in Israel and Aseng in EG are expected to add over 80,000 BOE/d by 2013.

▸ Risks to our recommendation and target price include declines in oil and gas prices and production, and exploration and geographic risks.

▸ Our 12-month target price of $82 blends our proved NAV estimate ($88) with our DCF ($87; WACC 10.8%; terminal growth 3%) and above-peer relative metrics.

Qualitative Risk Assessment

LOW	MEDIUM	HIGH

Our risk assessment reflects our view of NBL's participation in the cyclical, competitive and capital-intensive exploration and production sector, and by U.S. and international oil and gas operations that carry heightened political and operational risk.

Quantitative Evaluations

S&P Quality Ranking B+

D	C	B-	B	B+	A-	A	A+

Relative Strength Rank STRONG

71

LOWEST = 1 HIGHEST = 99

Revenue/Earnings Data

Revenue (Million $)

	1Q	2Q	3Q	4Q	Year
2010	733.0	727.0	--	--	--
2009	441.0	491.0	621.0	760.0	2,313
2008	1,025	1,205	1,098	573.0	3,901
2007	742.6	794.2	813.8	921.5	3,272
2006	712.0	772.6	741.3	714.2	2,940
2005	368.2	485.4	632.1	701.0	2,187

Earnings Per Share ($)

	1Q	2Q	3Q	4Q	Year
2010	1.34	1.10	E0.78	E0.85	E4.07
2009	-1.09	-0.33	0.61	0.05	-0.75
2008	1.20	-0.84	5.37	1.72	7.58
2007	1.22	1.21	1.28	1.73	5.45
2006	1.26	-0.17	1.75	0.94	3.79
2005	0.92	0.91	0.99	1.18	4.12

Fiscal year ended Dec. 31. Next earnings report expected: Late October. EPS Estimates based on S&P Operating Earnings; historical GAAP earnings are as reported.

Dividend Data (Dates: mm/dd Payment Date: mm/dd/yy)

Amount ($)	Date Decl.	Ex-Div. Date	Stk. of Record	Payment Date
0.180	10/27	11/05	11/09	11/23/09
0.180	01/26	02/04	02/08	02/22/10
0.180	04/26	05/06	05/10	05/24/10
0.180	07/27	08/05	08/09	08/23/10

Dividends have been paid since 1975. Source: Company reports.

.The **McGraw·Hill** Companies

Noble Energy Inc

STANDARD &POOR'S

Business Summary October 01, 2010

CORPORATE OVERVIEW. Noble Energy is a large independent exploration and production concern, engaged in exploration, development, production and marketing of oil and natural gas. In the U.S., NBL operates primarily in the Rocky Mountains, Mid-Continent region and deepwater Gulf of Mexico. International operations are focused on offshore Israel and West Africa.

As of December 31, 2009, NBL had estimated proved reserves of 4.92 Bcfe, of which 64% was natural gas and 69% proved developed. This compares with estimated proved reserves of 5.18 Bcfe, 64% natural gas and 69% proved developed, at the end of 2008, a 5% decline, mostly reflecting negative price revisions. The U.S. accounted for 57% of proved reserves. NBL anticipates substantial multi-year growth in reserves beginning in 2010 as it books reserves from discoveries at Tamar (Israel), Belinda (EG), Gunflint (GOM), Galapagos (GOM), Aseng (EG) and Diega/Carmen (EG).

CORPORATE STRATEGY. We believe NBL's geographical diversification has reduced dependence on any one operating region and that NBL has successfully executed a niche strategy by agreeing to undertake nontraditional construction projects with various host countries to obtain leases in potentially lucrative hydrocarbon fields. NBL aims to achieve growth in earnings and cash flow through exploration success and the development of a high quality portfolio of assets that is balanced between U.S. and international projects. Exploration success, along with additional capex, in U.S. and international lo-

cations such as Equatorial Guinea and Israel, have resulted in solid growth in the past several years. In addition, occasional strategic acquisitions such as Patina in 2005, combined with the sale of non-core assets, have allowed NBL to enhance its asset portfolio. The result is a company with assets and capabilities in major U.S. basins coupled with a significant portfolio of international properties.

NBL has a 2010 capex budget of $2.2 billion, up from $1.3 billion in 2009, with 40% slated for major project development, 20% for exploration, and 40% for maintenance and near-term growth projects. About 55% is to be spent in the U.S. Major project development capex is expected at $1 billion, with the majority directed toward development of Galapagos in the deepwater GOM, Aseng offshore Equatorial Guinea, and Tamar offshore Israel. About $500 million is allocated to exploration, targeting an estimated 700 MMBOE of resource potential with plans to drill seven high-impact offshore wells in the deepwater GOM, Equatorial Guinea and the Mediterranean Sea. The remainder of the budget is focused on liquid-rich and emerging opportunities onshore in the U.S., as well as development projects in Israel, the North Sea and China.

Company Financials Fiscal Year Ended Dec. 31

Per Share Data ($)	2009	2008	2007	2006	2005	2004	2003	2002	2001	2000
Tangible Book Value	31.11	31.95	23.51	19.35	12.68	12.37	9.38	8.80	8.86	7.58
Cash Flow	7.45	12.17	9.65	7.27	6.61	5.26	3.47	2.62	3.64	3.72
Earnings	-0.75	7.58	5.45	3.79	4.12	2.70	0.78	0.16	1.17	1.69
S&P Core Earnings	-0.84	7.52	5.42	3.05	4.08	2.58	0.70	0.08	1.08	NA
Dividends	0.72	0.66	0.44	0.28	0.15	0.10	0.09	0.08	0.08	0.08
Payout Ratio	NM	9%	8%	7%	4%	4%	11%	52%	7%	5%
Prices:High	74.09	105.11	81.71	54.64	48.75	32.30	23.00	20.38	25.55	24.19
Prices:Low	40.33	30.89	46.04	36.14	27.78	21.33	16.19	13.33	13.75	9.59
P/E Ratio:High	NM	14	15	14	12	12	29	NM	22	14
P/E Ratio:Low	NM	4	8	9	7	8	21	NM	12	6

Income Statement Analysis (Million $)										
Revenue	2,229	3,901	3,272	2,940	2,187	1,351	1,011	1,444	1,572	1,381
Operating Income	NA	2,295	2,029	2,019	1,423	884	539	376	535	550
Depreciation, Depletion and Amortization	1,420	791	728	623	391	309	309	285	284	231
Interest Expense	84.0	69.0	130	117	87.5	48.2	47.0	47.7	26.0	31.6
Pretax Income	-264	2,061	1,368	1,096	969	516	142	42.6	225	299
Effective Tax Rate	50.4%	34.5%	31.0%	38.1%	33.3%	39.2%	36.5%	58.6%	40.5%	36.0%
Net Income	-131	1,350	944	678	646	314	89.9	17.7	134	192
S&P Core Earnings	-147	1,340	938	548	640	305	81.0	8.88	123	NA

Balance Sheet & Other Financial Data (Million $)										
Cash	1,014	1,140	660	153	110	180	62.4	15.4	73.2	23.2
Current Assets	1,678	2,158	1,569	1,069	1,176	734	478	310	352	271
Total Assets	11,807	12,384	10,831	9,589	8,878	3,443	2,843	2,730	2,480	1,879
Current Liabilities	990	1,174	1,636	1,184	1,240	665	655	472	381	325
Long Term Debt	2,008	2,241	1,851	1,801	2,031	880	776	977	837	525
Common Equity	6,157	6,309	4,809	4,114	3,231	1,460	1,074	1,009	1,010	850
Total Capital	8,165	10,724	8,644	7,673	5,262	2,524	2,013	2,188	2,024	1,492
Capital Expenditures	1,268	1,971	1,415	1,357	786	661	527	596	739	537
Cash Flow	1,289	2,141	1,672	1,301	1,036	623	399	303	418	422
Current Ratio	1.7	1.8	1.0	0.9	0.9	1.1	0.7	0.7	0.9	0.8
% Long Term Debt of Capitalization	24.6	20.9	21.4	23.5	38.6	34.9	38.6	44.6	41.4	35.2
% Return on Assets	NM	11.6	9.2	7.3	10.5	10.0	3.2	0.7	6.1	11.6
% Return on Equity	NM	24.3	51.7	18.8	27.5	24.8	8.6	1.7	14.4	25.0

Data as orig reptd.; bef. results of disc opers/spec. items. Per share data adj. for stk. divs.; EPS diluted. E-Estimated. NA-Not Available. NM-Not Meaningful. NR-Not Ranked. UR-Under Review.

Office: 100 Glenborough Drive, Houston, TX 77067.
Telephone: 281-872-3100.
Email: info@nobleenergyinc.com
Website: http://www.nobleenergyinc.com

Chrmn & CEO: C.D. Davidson
Pres & COO: D.L. Stover
SVP & CFO: K.M. Fisher
SVP, Secy & General Counsel: A.J. Johnson

Chief Acctg Officer: F. Bruning
Investor Contact: D. Larson (281-872-3100)
Board Members: J. L. Berenson, M. A. Cawley, E. F. Cox, C. D. Davidson, T. J. Edelman, E. P. Grubman, K. L. Hedrick, S. D. Urban, W. T. Van Kleef

Auditor: KPMG
Founded: 1969
Domicile: Delaware

The McGraw-Hill Companies

Nordstrom Inc.

STANDARD &POOR'S

S&P Recommendation HOLD ★★★☆☆

Price	12-Mo. Target Price	Investment Style
$36.89 (as of Oct 22, 2010)	$35.00	Large-Cap Growth

GICS Sector Consumer Discretionary
Sub-Industry Department Stores

Summary This specialty retailer of apparel and accessories, widely known for its emphasis on service, operates about 193 stores in 28 states.

Key Stock Statistics (Source S&P, Vickers, company reports)

52-Wk Range	$46.22– 28.44	S&P Oper. EPS 2011**E**	2.60	Market Capitalization(B)	$8.085
Trailing 12-Month EPS	$2.33	S&P Oper. EPS 2012**E**	2.95	Yield (%)	2.17
Trailing 12-Month P/E	15.8	P/E on S&P Oper. EPS 2011**E**	14.2	Dividend Rate/Share	$0.80
$10K Invested 5 Yrs Ago	$12,123	Common Shares Outstg. (M)	219.2	Institutional Ownership (%)	62

Beta	1.74
S&P 3-Yr. Proj. EPS CAGR(%)	18
S&P Credit Rating	BBB+

Price Performance

30-Week Mov. Avg. · · · · 10-Week Mov. Avg. - - - **GAAP Earnings vs. Previous Year** Volume Above Avg. |||| STARS
12-Mo. Target Price — Relative Strength — ▲ Up ▼ Down ► No Change Below Avg. |||| ★

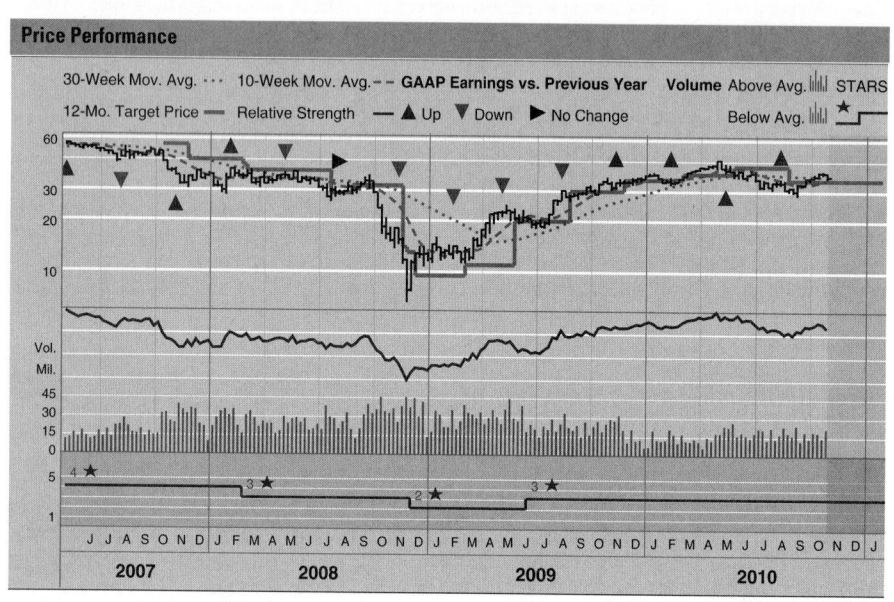

Analysis prepared by **Jason N. Asaeda** on August 17, 2010, when the stock traded at **$ 30.12**.

Options: ASE, CBOE, P, Ph

Highlights

➤ Following a 4% decline in FY 10 (Jan.), we look for same-store sales to increase about 5.5% in FY 11. We see JWN weathering the economic downturn by focusing on its most productive brands and improving the value proposition at its full-line stores. We also think the company is meeting the needs of increasingly cost-conscious shoppers through expansion of its off-price Nordstrom Rack business. JWN opened three full-line and 13 Rack stores in FY 10 and plans to open an additional three full-line and 17 Rack units in FY 11. All told, we project net sales of $9.06 billion in FY 11, versus FY 10's $8.26 billion.

➤ We look for the company, by keeping inventory aligned with sales trends, to drive merchandise margin improvement through increased full-price selling and lower markdowns. We also expect operating margins to expand, supported by cost savings initiatives, expense leverage off projected same-store sales growth, and stronger credit segment performance.

➤ Assuming no share repurchase activity, we see EPS of $2.60 in FY 11.

Investment Rationale/Risk

➤ Our hold recommendation is based on valuation. We see JWN benefiting from a return of its core higher-income customer base that had stopped shopping a year ago in response to macroeconomic concerns. We also believe that sharper opening price points and a broader offering of contemporary brands are attracting a growing number of new customers to the company's full-line stores. In addition, we see a consistent customer-focused shopping experience across JWN's store base, expansion of Nordstrom Rack, suspended share repurchases, and a disciplined approach to capital spending as underlying positives to the company.

➤ Risks to our recommendation and target price include a loss of business due to lackluster merchandising and uncompetitive pricing.

➤ Our 12-month target price of $35 blends two valuation metrics. Applying a peer-median forward P/E multiple of 12.3X to our FY 11 EPS estimate, we arrive at a $32 value. Our historical valuation uses a forward P/E multiple of 14.6X, JWN's 10-year historical median, yielding a $38 value.

Qualitative Risk Assessment

LOW	MEDIUM	HIGH

Our risk assessment reflects our view of JWN's improving sales and profit margins, increasing market share in the better department store sector, and healthy balance sheet and cash flow. This is offset by uncertainty over consumer discretionary spending in light of higher interest rates and debt levels.

Quantitative Evaluations

S&P Quality Ranking A-

D	C	B-	B	B+	A-	A	A+

Relative Strength Rank MODERATE

50

LOWEST = 1   HIGHEST = 99

Revenue/Earnings Data

Revenue (Million $)

	1Q	2Q	3Q	4Q	Year
2011	2,087	2,515	--	--	--
2010	1,792	2,232	1,963	2,640	8,627
2009	1,949	2,359	1,879	2,386	8,573
2008	1,954	2,390	1,970	2,514	8,828
2007	1,787	2,270	1,872	2,631	8,561
2006	1,654	2,106	1,666	2,296	7,723

Earnings Per Share ($)

2011	0.52	0.66	E0.50	E0.92	E2.60
2010	0.37	0.48	0.38	0.77	2.01
2009	0.54	0.65	0.33	0.31	1.83
2008	0.60	0.65	0.68	0.92	2.88
2007	0.48	0.67	0.52	0.89	2.55
2006	0.38	0.53	0.39	0.69	1.98

Fiscal year ended Jan. 31. Next earnings report expected: Mid November. EPS Estimates based on S&P Operating Earnings; historical GAAP earnings are as reported.

Dividend Data (Dates: mm/dd Payment Date: mm/dd/yy)

Amount ($)	Date Decl.	Ex-Div. Date	Stk. of Record	Payment Date
0.160	11/18	11/25	11/30	12/15/09
0.160	02/19	02/24	02/26	03/15/10
0.200	05/18	05/26	05/28	06/15/10
0.200	08/19	08/27	08/31	09/15/10

Dividends have been paid since 1971. Source: Company reports.

Please read the Required Disclosures and Analyst Certification on the last page of this report.

The McGraw-Hill Companies

Nordstrom Inc.

Business Summary August 17, 2010

CORPORATE OVERVIEW. In our view, Nordstrom (JWN) is the clear leader in the U.S. better department store sector, reflecting its focus on high-quality, differentiated merchandise; personalized customer service; and a consistent upscale shopping experience across its entire Nordstrom store base. The company derives its revenues from retail, credit and direct sales channels. JWN formerly owned Faconnable, a wholly owned wholesaler and retailer of high-quality men's, women's and boy's apparel and accessories. In FY 10 (Jan.), merchandise category sales were: women's apparel 34%; shoes 22%; men's apparel 15%; women's accessories 12%; cosmetics 11%; children's apparel 3%; and other 3%.

IMPACT OF MAJOR DEVELOPMENTS. JWN spends about $150 million annually on information technology (IT). In FY 03, the company invested in a perpetual inventory system that has enabled its merchant teams to more accurately forecast sales trends and to better track and plan store-level inventory and expenses, resulting in improved sales performance and profitability, in our

opinion. In FY 05, JWN put into place a new point of sales system that includes Personal Book, a tool that allows salespeople to tailor service to the needs of each customer by organizing and tracking customer preferences, purchases, and contact information. The company has noted that Personal Book has driven incremental sales volume.

In July 2007, JWN agreed to sell Faconnable to M1 Group, a Lebanon-based, family-owned diversified business, for $210 million. As part of the agreement, JWN will continue to buy Faconnable merchandise at historical levels for at least the next three years and will continue to offer Faconnable in Nordstrom stores. The company realized a gain of $33.9 million on the sale ($0.09 per share, after-tax), which closed in the third quarter of FY 08.

Company Financials Fiscal Year Ended Jan. 31

Per Share Data ($)	2010	2009	2008	2007	2006	2005	2004	2003	2002	2001
Tangible Book Value	6.98	5.37	4.81	7.90	7.26	6.10	5.40	4.55	4.38	4.06
Cash Flow	3.43	3.21	3.95	3.62	2.98	2.31	1.78	1.24	1.27	1.16
Earnings	2.01	1.83	2.88	2.55	1.98	1.39	0.88	0.38	0.46	0.39
S&P Core Earnings	2.01	1.84	2.80	2.55	1.93	2.62	1.67	0.62	0.80	0.83
Dividends	0.64	0.64	0.42	0.32	0.24	0.21	0.21	0.19	0.18	0.16
Payout Ratio	32%	35%	15%	13%	12%	15%	23%	50%	38%	41%
Calendar Year	2009	2008	2007	2006	2005	2004	2003	2002	2001	2000
Prices:High	38.71	40.59	59.70	51.40	39.00	23.68	17.75	13.44	11.49	17.25
Prices:Low	11.19	6.61	30.46	31.77	22.71	16.55	7.50	7.80	6.90	7.06
P/E Ratio:High	19	22	21	20	20	17	20	35	25	44
P/E Ratio:Low	6	4	11	12	11	12	9	20	15	18

Income Statement Analysis (Million $)

	2010	2009	2008	2007	2006	2005	2004	2003	2002	2001
Revenue	8,627	8,272	8,828	8,561	7,723	7,131	6,492	5,975	5,634	5,529
Operating Income	1,147	1,072	1,503	1,195	1,010	817	585	424	363	335
Depreciation	313	302	269	285	276	265	251	234	218	203
Interest Expense	141	145	71.7	62.4	45.3	85.4	91.0	86.2	73.5	63.0
Pretax Income	696	648	1,173	1,106	885	647	398	196	204	167
Effective Tax Rate	36.6%	38.1%	39.1%	38.7%	37.7%	39.2%	39.0%	47.1%	39.0%	38.9%
Net Income	441	401	715	678	551	393	243	104	125	102
S&P Core Earnings	441	403	697	677	536	373	229	83.9	107	109

Balance Sheet & Other Financial Data (Million $)

	2010	2009	2008	2007	2006	2005	2004	2003	2002	2001
Cash	795	72.0	358	403	463	361	476	208	331	25.0
Current Assets	4,054	3,217	3,361	2,742	2,874	2,572	2,455	2,073	2,055	1,813
Total Assets	6,579	5,661	5,600	4,822	4,921	4,605	4,466	4,096	4,049	3,608
Current Liabilities	2,014	1,601	1,635	1,433	1,623	1,341	1,050	870	948	951
Long Term Debt	2,257	2,214	2,236	624	628	929	1,605	1,342	1,351	1,100
Common Equity	1,572	1,210	1,115	2,169	2,093	1,789	1,634	1,372	1,314	1,229
Total Capital	4,185	3,435	3,612	2,792	2,720	2,718	3,239	2,714	2,666	2,329
Capital Expenditures	360	563	501	264	272	247	258	328	390	321
Cash Flow	754	703	984	963	828	658	494	338	342	305
Current Ratio	2.0	2.0	2.1	1.9	1.8	1.9	2.3	2.4	2.2	1.9
% Long Term Debt of Capitalization	53.9	64.5	61.9	22.3	23.1	34.2	49.5	49.4	50.7	47.2
% Net Income of Revenue	5.1	4.9	8.1	7.9	7.1	5.5	3.7	1.7	2.2	1.8
% Return on Assets	7.2	7.1	13.7	13.9	11.6	8.6	5.7	2.5	3.3	3.1
% Return on Equity	31.7	34.5	43.6	31.8	28.4	23.0	16.2	7.7	9.8	8.5

Data as orig reptd.; bef. results of disc opers/spec. items. Per share data adj. for stk. divs.; EPS diluted. E-Estimated. NA-Not Available. NM-Not Meaningful. NR-Not Ranked. UR-Under Review.

Office: 1617 6th Ave, Seattle, WA 98101-1707.
Telephone: 206-628-2111.
Email: invrelations@nordstrom.com
Website: http://www.nordstrom.com

Chrmn: E. Hernandez, Jr.
Pres & CEO: B.W. Nordstrom
EVP & CFO: M. Koppel
EVP & Chief Admin Officer: D.F. Little

EVP, Secy & General Counsel: R.B. Sari
Investor Contact: C. Holloway (206-303-3200)
Board Members: P. J. Campbell, E. Hernandez, Jr., R. G. Miller, B. W. Nordstrom, E. B. Nordstrom, P. E. Nordstrom, P. G. Satre, R. D. Walter, A. A. Winter

Founded: 1901
Domicile: Washington
Employees: 52,000

Norfolk Southern Corp

STANDARD &POOR'S

S&P Recommendation BUY ★★★★☆	Price $62.10 (as of Oct 22, 2010)	12-Mo. Target Price $67.00	Investment Style Large-Cap Blend

GICS Sector Industrials
Sub-Industry Railroads

Summary This railroad operates 21,200 route miles serving 22 eastern states, the District of Columbia, and Ontario, Canada.

Key Stock Statistics (Source S&P, Vickers, company reports)

52-Wk Range	$62.71– 45.94	S&P Oper. EPS 2010E	3.84	Market Capitalization(B)	$22.891	Beta	1.08
Trailing 12-Month EPS	$3.35	S&P Oper. EPS 2011E	4.39	Yield (%)	2.32	S&P 3-Yr. Proj. EPS CAGR(%)	10
Trailing 12-Month P/E	18.5	P/E on S&P Oper. EPS 2010E	16.2	Dividend Rate/Share	$1.44	S&P Credit Rating	BBB+
$10K Invested 5 Yrs Ago	$17,809	Common Shares Outstg. (M)	368.6	Institutional Ownership (%)	69		

Price Performance

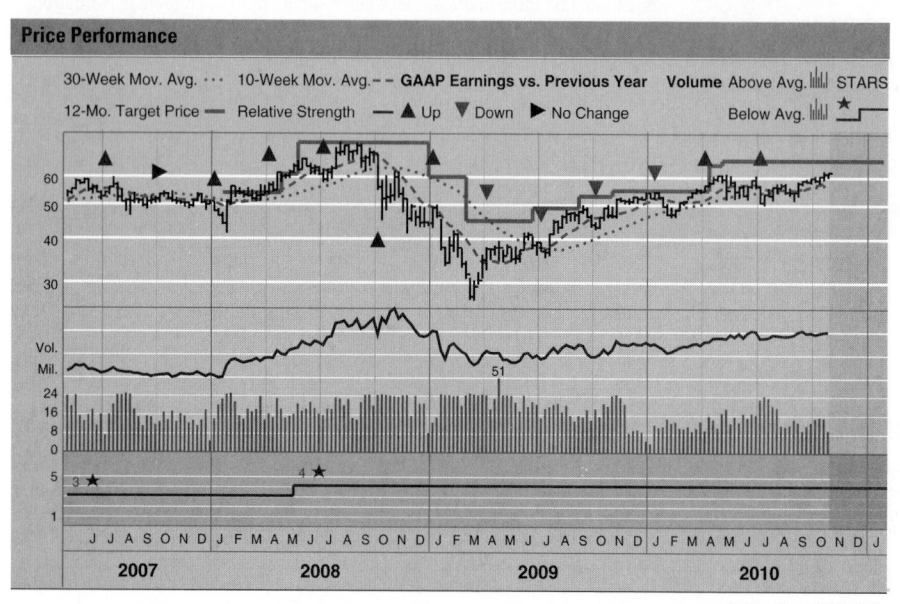

30-Week Mov. Avg. · · · 10-Week Mov. Avg. - - GAAP Earnings vs. Previous Year   Volume Above Avg. STARS
12-Mo. Target Price — Relative Strength — ▲ Up ▼ Down ▶ No Change   Below Avg.

Options: ASE, CBOE, P, Ph

Analysis prepared by **Kevin Kirkeby** on September 20, 2010, when the stock traded at **$ 58.45**.

Highlights

➤ We forecast revenue growth near 19% in 2010, based on a 12% increase in carloadings, aided by a general improvement in the economy, and a 6% rise in yield. With auto and steel production rising globally, we think volumes of metallurgical coal will stay elevated through the remainder of 2010 and into 2011. Likewise, we see NSC benefiting from added fertilizer volumes, and the opening of ethanol terminals along its network. We expect fuel surcharges to add 5% to yield this year. We expect current trends to prevail into 2011, and contribute to 2.8% volume growth and a 4.5% rise in revenues.

➤ We see the operating margin widening into 2011, on improved fixed cost coverage as volumes are forecast to rise. While we see a contractual wage hike and generally higher health-care costs, we think this will be outweighed by cost control measures and the deployment of new locomotives and higher capacity railcars. Still, we think costs will start to come back into operations in 2011 at a faster pace as excess capacity on existing train sets is filled.

➤ Our EPS forecast of $3.84 for 2010 excludes $0.07 in deferred tax charges tied to health care reform, as well as an effective tax rate of 37%.

Investment Rationale/Risk

➤ Medium-term trends in NSC's primary markets remain favorable and support rising traffic, in our opinion. We see investments in its network improving capacity on heavily trafficked lanes like the Heartland and Crescent corridors, and leading to greater conversion of truck traffic over to rail, particularly as the economy recovers and truck capacity tightens. With the economy continuing to show improvement, we believe a valuation above the historical average, and generally in line with peers, is warranted.

➤ Risks to our recommendation and target price include a slowdown in manufacturing and overall economic activity, unfavorable changes in the regulatory framework, a prolonged period of low natural gas prices that encourages utilities to use less coal in their overall fuel mix, and a slowing in export coal shipments.

➤ Blending a P/E of 16.4X our four-quarter forward EPS estimate, which is a premium to the 10-year average, with our DCF model that assumes a 10.8% cost of equity, 8% average free cash flow growth over the next five years, and a 3.5% terminal growth rate (yielding an intrinsic value of $65), we arrive at our 12-month target price of $67.

Qualitative Risk Assessment

LOW	MEDIUM	HIGH

Our risk assessment reflects what we see as NSC's exposure to economic cycles, regulations, labor costs, significant capital expenditure requirements, and challenges in maintaining system fluidity, offset by our view of a diverse customer base, historically positive free cash flow, and moderate financial leverage.

Quantitative Evaluations

S&P Quality Ranking A-

D	C	B-	B	B+	A-	A	A+

Relative Strength Rank MODERATE

69

LOWEST = 1   HIGHEST = 99

Revenue/Earnings Data

Revenue (Million $)

	1Q	2Q	3Q	4Q	Year
2010	2,238	2,430	--	--	--
2009	1,943	1,857	2,063	2,106	7,969
2008	2,500	2,765	2,894	2,502	10,661
2007	2,247	2,378	2,353	2,454	9,432
2006	2,303	2,392	2,393	2,319	9,407
2005	1,961	2,154	2,155	2,257	8,527

Earnings Per Share ($)

2010	0.68	1.04	E1.07	E0.98	E3.84
2009	0.47	0.66	0.81	0.82	2.76
2008	0.76	1.18	1.37	1.21	4.52
2007	0.71	0.98	1.02	1.02	3.68
2006	0.72	0.89	1.02	0.95	3.57
2005	0.47	1.04	0.73	0.87	3.11

Fiscal year ended Dec. 31. Next earnings report expected: Late October. EPS Estimates based on S&P Operating Earnings; historical GAAP earnings are as reported.

Dividend Data (Dates: mm/dd Payment Date: mm/dd/yy)

Amount ($)	Date Decl.	Ex-Div. Date	Stk. of Record	Payment Date
0.340	10/27	11/04	11/06	12/10/09
0.340	01/26	02/03	02/05	03/10/10
0.340	04/27	05/05	05/07	06/10/10
0.360	07/27	08/04	08/06	09/10/10

Dividends have been paid since 1901. Source: Company reports.

Please read the Required Disclosures and Analyst Certification on the last page of this report.

The McGraw-Hill Companies

Norfolk Southern Corp

STANDARD
&POOR'S

Business Summary September 20, 2010

CORPORATE OVERVIEW. Norfolk Southern provides rail transportation service in the eastern U.S., operating over 21,000 miles of road, with an extensive intermodal and coal service network and a significant general freight business, including an automotive business that is the largest in North America. NSC owns 58% of Conrail's shares, with CSX holding the remainder, and holds 50% voting rights. NSC and CSX operate separate portions of Conrail's rail routes and assets. NSC's non-rail activities include real estate and natural resources.

NSC's intermodal business represented 19% of 2009 freight revenues. Although it was the second largest contributor to revenues, intermodal was the largest category by volume at 42% of total carloads. Coal, which we believe is NSC's most profitable segment due to its unit train structure, accounted for 29% of 2009 freight revenues, and 24% of carloads. Most of this traffic, which is delivered primarily to power utilities, originates from the Appalachian coal fields. However, the company has been increasing the number of carloads it carries with origins in the Illinois Basin and the Powder River Basin. General merchandise, sensitive to U.S. GDP trends, provided 52% of freight revenues in 2009. This includes the chemicals and automotive categories, representing 13% and 7% of 2009 freight revenues, respectively. We consider NSC to have considerable exposure to the auto market since it serves 24 assembly plants, fourteen of which belong to the domestic manufacturers Ford, Chrysler and General Motors. It also provides services for Toyota, which in January 2010 initiated a large vehicle recall.

COMPETITIVE LANDSCAPE. The U.S. rail industry has an oligopoly-like structure, with over 80% of revenues generated by the four largest railroads: NSC and CSX Corp. operating on the East Coast, and Union Pacific Corp. and Burlington Northern Santa Fe Corp. operating on the West Coast. Railroads simultaneously compete for customers while cooperating by sharing assets, interfacing systems, and completing customer movements. NSC, for example, is a net payer of equipment rents as it takes on more freight originated by other carriers than it hands off to them at its major gateways. Likewise, NSC has formed separate joint ventures with Kansas City Southern and Pan Am Railways that enhance its access along certain corridors in exchange for much needed capital investments.

Company Financials Fiscal Year Ended Dec. 31

Per Share Data ($)	2009	2008	2007	2006	2005	2004	2003	2002	2001	2000
Tangible Book Value	28.06	26.23	27.12	24.19	22.66	19.98	17.83	16.71	15.78	15.17
Cash Flow	5.05	6.63	5.63	5.50	5.02	3.83	2.40	2.50	2.27	1.80
Earnings	2.76	4.52	3.68	3.57	3.11	2.31	1.05	1.18	0.94	0.45
S&P Core Earnings	2.72	4.21	3.48	3.43	2.97	2.13	0.95	0.70	0.41	NA
Dividends	1.36	1.22	0.96	0.68	0.48	0.46	0.30	0.26	0.24	0.80
Payout Ratio	49%	27%	26%	19%	15%	20%	29%	22%	26%	178%
Prices:High	54.55	75.53	59.77	57.71	45.81	36.69	24.62	26.98	24.11	22.75
Prices:Low	26.69	41.36	45.38	39.10	29.60	20.38	17.35	17.20	13.41	11.94
P/E Ratio:High	20	17	16	16	15	16	23	23	26	51
P/E Ratio:Low	10	9	12	11	10	9	17	15	14	27

Income Statement Analysis (Million $)	2009	2008	2007	2006	2005	2004	2003	2002	2001	2000
Revenue	7,969	10,661	9,432	9,407	8,527	7,312	6,468	6,270	6,170	6,159
Operating Income	2,807	3,901	3,360	3,307	2,904	2,311	1,592	1,158	1,521	1,150
Depreciation	845	804	775	750	787	609	528	515	514	517
Interest Expense	467	457	482	493	500	506	497	518	553	551
Pretax Income	1,622	2,750	2,237	2,230	1,697	1,302	586	706	553	250
Effective Tax Rate	36.3%	37.6%	34.6%	33.6%	24.5%	29.1%	29.9%	34.8%	34.5%	31.2%
Net Income	1,034	1,716	1,464	1,481	1,281	923	411	460	362	172
S&P Core Earnings	1,011	1,595	1,377	1,417	1,224	849	365	270	155	NA

Balance Sheet & Other Financial Data (Million $)	2009	2008	2007	2006	2005	2004	2003	2002	2001	2000
Cash	1,086	618	206	527	289	579	284	184	204	Nil
Current Assets	2,246	1,999	1,675	2,400	2,650	1,967	1,425	1,299	1,047	849
Total Assets	27,369	26,297	26,144	26,028	25,861	24,750	20,596	19,956	19,418	18,976
Current Liabilities	1,789	2,105	1,948	2,093	1,921	2,201	1,801	1,853	2,386	1,887
Long Term Debt	6,679	6,316	6,132	6,109	6,616	6,863	6,800	7,006	7,027	7,339
Common Equity	10,353	9,597	9,727	9,615	9,289	7,990	6,976	6,500	6,090	5,824
Total Capital	17,406	22,295	22,290	22,168	22,525	21,403	17,008	16,561	15,943	15,958
Capital Expenditures	1,299	1,558	1,341	1,178	1,025	1,041	720	689	746	731
Cash Flow	1,879	2,520	2,239	2,231	2,068	1,532	939	975	876	689
Current Ratio	1.3	1.0	0.9	1.1	1.4	0.9	0.8	0.7	0.4	0.4
% Long Term Debt of Capitalization	38.4	28.3	27.5	27.6	29.4	32.1	40.0	42.3	44.1	46.0
% Net Income of Revenue	13.0	16.1	15.5	15.7	15.0	12.6	6.4	7.3	5.9	2.8
% Return on Assets	3.9	6.5	5.6	5.7	5.1	4.1	2.0	2.3	1.9	0.9
% Return on Equity	10.4	17.8	15.1	15.7	14.8	12.3	6.1	7.3	6.1	2.9

Data as orig reptd.; bef. results of disc opers/spec. items. Per share data adj. for stk. divs.; EPS diluted. E-Estimated. NA-Not Available. NM-Not Meaningful. NR-Not Ranked. UR-Under Review.

Office: 3 Commercial Pl, Norfolk, VA 23510-2191.
Telephone: 757-629-2680.
Website: http://www.nscorp.com
Chrmn, Pres & CEO: C.W. Moorman, IV

COO & EVP: M.D. Manion
EVP & CFO: J.A. Squires
EVP & CIO: D.H. Butler
Chief Admin Officer: J.P. Rathbone

Investor Contact: M. Parkerson (757-533-4939)
Board Members: G. L. Baliles, T. D. Bell, Jr., D. A. Carp, G. R. Carter, A. D. Correll, L. Hilliard, K. N. Horn, B. M. Joyce, S. F. Leer, M. D. Lockhart, C. W. Moorman, IV, J. P. Reason

Founded: 1980
Domicile: Virginia
Employees: 28,593

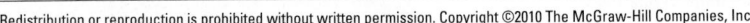

Northeast Utilities

S&P Recommendation HOLD ★★★☆☆

Price	12-Mo. Target Price	Investment Style
$30.85 (as of Oct 22, 2010)	$32.00	Large-Cap Blend

GICS Sector Utilities
Sub-Industry Electric Utilities

Summary This utility holding company, which serves Connecticut, western Massachusetts and New Hampshire, has agreed to buy NSTAR, a Boston-based utility.

Key Stock Statistics (Source S&P, Vickers, company reports)

52-Wk Range	$31.09–22.20	S&P Oper. EPS 2010**E**	1.98	Market Capitalization(B)	$5.434	Beta	0.54
Trailing 12-Month EPS	$1.74	S&P Oper. EPS 2011**E**	2.19	Yield (%)	3.32	S&P 3-Yr. Proj. EPS CAGR(%)	6
Trailing 12-Month P/E	17.7	P/E on S&P Oper. EPS 2010**E**	15.6	Dividend Rate/Share	$1.03	S&P Credit Rating	BBB
$10K Invested 5 Yrs Ago	$20,330	Common Shares Outstg. (M)	176.2	Institutional Ownership (%)	73		

Price Performance

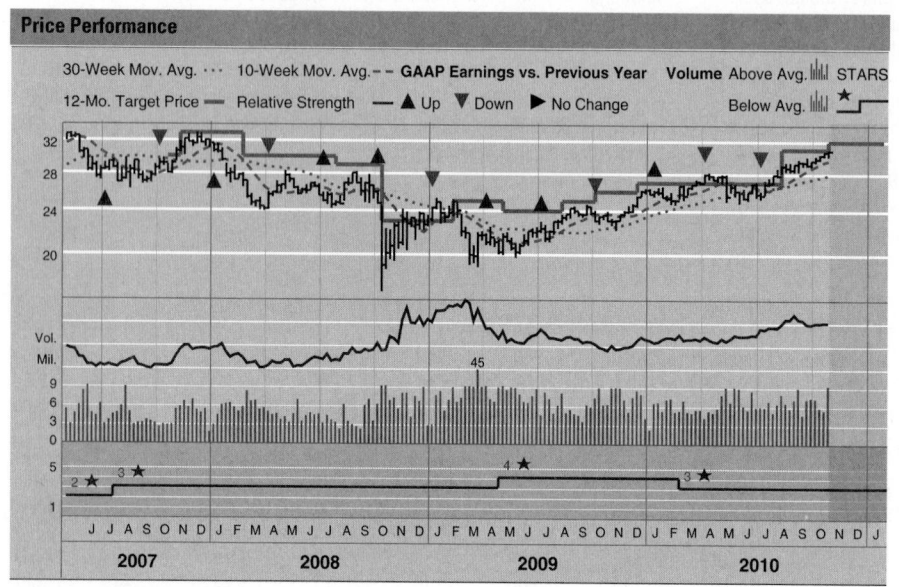

30-Week Mov. Avg. · · · 10-Week Mov. Avg. - - GAAP Earnings vs. Previous Year   Volume Above Avg. STARS
12-Mo. Target Price — Relative Strength — ▲ Up ▼ Down ► No Change   Below Avg. ★

Options: Ph

Analysis prepared by **Justin McCann** on October 20, 2010, when the stock traded at **$ 30.96**.

Highlights

➤ Subject to required approvals, the proposed merger with NSTAR (NST 40, Hold) is expected to close in the second half of 2011 and to result in one of the largest utility companies in the U.S. We believe the transaction would be accretive to combined earnings in the first year and that NST's strong balance sheet will help provide significant investment opportunities for the new company's transmission business.

➤ We expect operating EPS in 2010 to increase more than 3% from 2009's $1.91. Although results in the first half of 2010 were hurt by the mild weather in the first quarter, and higher operating costs, the second half was expected to benefit from an abnormally hot July, expectation of strong transmission results, and the rate increases implemented on July 1.

➤ We believe the regulated distribution and generating companies will earn about $1.03 a share in 2010, the transmission business about $0.95, and the competitive businesses about $0.05, with the parent company recording a loss of about $0.05. For 2011, we expect EPS to grow about 10% from anticipated results in 2010, driven by higher transmission earnings, new rate hikes, and an improved economic outlook.

Investment Rationale/Risk

➤ The stock is up approximately 19% year to date. This follows a 7.2% gain in 2009 (after a more than 35% rebound from its 2009 low), and reflects, we believe, NU's improved earnings outlook. If completed, the agreed-to merger with NST is expected to result in a nearly 20% increase in the dividend, and to eliminate the need for the previously planned 2012 equity issuance. Although we think the stock has become fairly valued for the near term, we expect it to benefit over the long term from NU's investments in its transmission system.

➤ Risks to our recommendation and target price include the possibility of the planned merger with NSTAR being delayed or terminated, a slower-than-expected recovery in the company's service territory economy, and a sharp decrease in the average peer group P/E multiple.

➤ Following the recent rise in the shares, the yield from the dividend was around 3.3%, well below the recent peer average yield of approximately 4.6%. However, the merger with NST, if approved, is expected to increase the dividend by nearly 20%. Our 12-month target price is $32, reflecting a premium-to-peers multiple of about 14.6X our EPS estimate for 2011.

Qualitative Risk Assessment

LOW	MEDIUM	HIGH

Our risk assessment reflects the steady cash flow we expect from regulated electric and gas utility operations, a generally healthy economy in most of NU's service territories, and a relatively supportive regulatory environment. It also reflects the company's exit from its nonregulated and high-risk wholesale energy marketing and energy services businesses.

Quantitative Evaluations

S&P Quality Ranking B

D	C	B-	**B**	B+	A-	A	A+

Relative Strength Rank MODERATE

63

LOWEST = 1   HIGHEST = 99

Revenue/Earnings Data

Revenue (Million $)

	1Q	2Q	3Q	4Q	Year
2010	1,339	1,111	--	--	--
2009	1,593	1,224	1,306	1,315	5,439
2008	1,520	1,325	1,507	1,448	5,800
2007	1,704	1,392	1,451	1,276	5,822
2006	2,147	1,671	1,594	1,483	6,884
2005	2,265	1,551	1,755	1,878	7,397

Earnings Per Share ($)

	1Q	2Q	3Q	4Q	Year
2010	0.49	0.41	E0.53	E0.55	E1.98
2009	0.60	0.47	0.37	0.48	1.91
2008	0.38	0.37	0.47	0.46	1.67
2007	0.50	0.30	0.32	0.47	1.58
2006	-0.13	0.09	0.67	0.19	0.82
2005	-0.91	-0.21	-0.71	-0.08	-1.74

Fiscal year ended Dec. 31. Next earnings report expected: Early November. EPS Estimates based on S&P Operating Earnings; historical GAAP earnings are as reported.

Dividend Data (Dates: mm/dd Payment Date: mm/dd/yy)

Amount ($)	Date Decl.	Ex-Div. Date	Stk. of Record	Payment Date
0.256	02/09	02/25	03/01	03/31/10
0.256	04/13	05/27	06/01	06/30/10
0.256	07/12	08/30	09/01	09/30/10
0.256	10/12	11/29	12/01	12/31/10

Dividends have been paid since 1999. Source: Company reports.

Northeast Utilities

Business Summary October 20, 2010

CORPORATE OVERVIEW. Northeast Utilities (NU) is a holding company that provides electricity and gas services through its utility subsidiaries. The company's electric subsidiaries include The Connecticut Light & Power Company, Public Service Company of New Hampshire, and Western Massachusetts Electric Company. NU distributes natural gas through its Yankee Gas Services Company subsidiary. Yankee Gas operates the largest natural gas distribution system in Connecticut. NU Enterprises Inc., the nonregulated subsidiary of NU, owns a number of competitive energy and related businesses. In 2009, the electric distribution segment accounted for 79.7% of consolidated revenues (80.9% in 2008), the transmission segment 10.6% (7.3%), the gas distribution segment 8.2% (9.9%), and the competitive businesses 1.5% (1.9%).

IMPACT OF MAJOR DEVELOPMENTS. On October 18, 2010, NU announced a definitive merger agreement with NSTAR (NST 40, Hold), a Boston-headquartered energy delivery company serving 1.1 million electric distribution customers and about 300,000 natural gas customers in Massachusetts. Under the terms of the stock-for-stock agreement, NSTAR shareholders would receive 1.312 NU shares for each NST share. Upon the completion of the transaction, it is expected that NU shareholders would have a 56% interest in the combined company, which will maintain the Northeast Utilities name, with NST holders 44%. NU's chairman, president and CEO, Charles Shivery, would become the non-executive chairman of the new company, while NST's chairman, president and CEO, Thomas May, would become president and CEO. After a period of 18 months, Mr. May would replace Mr. Shivery as chairman.

MARKET PROFILE. NU provides retail electric services in all major cities and towns in Connecticut, New Hampshire and Massachusetts. The company's electric utilities serve nearly 1.9 million customers in 419 cities and towns in Connecticut, New Hampshire and western Massachusetts. In 2009, residential customers contributed about 58% of NU's electric distribution revenues (55% in 2008); commercial customers 34% (35%); industrial customers 7% (9%); and others 1% (1%).

NU also distributes natural gas to more than 200,000 customers in 71 cities and towns in Connecticut. Residential customers, the largest user segment, contributed 48% of natural gas revenues in 2009 (45% in 2008), followed by the commercial and industrial segments, which contributed 31% (29%) and 18% (23%), respectively, while others accounted for 3% (3%).

Company Financials Fiscal Year Ended Dec. 31

Per Share Data ($)	2009	2008	2007	2006	2005	2004	2003	2002	2001	2000
Tangible Book Value	18.74	17.54	16.81	16.28	13.98	14.87	14.68	14.20	13.79	12.73
Earnings	1.91	1.67	1.58	0.82	-1.74	0.91	0.95	1.18	1.96	1.55
S&P Core Earnings	2.01	1.11	1.55	0.93	-1.59	0.96	1.13	-0.77	-3.68	NA
Dividends	0.95	0.83	0.78	0.72	0.68	0.63	0.58	0.52	0.45	0.40
Payout Ratio	50%	49%	49%	88%	NM	69%	61%	44%	23%	26%
Prices:High	26.48	31.62	33.62	28.90	21.95	20.27	20.32	20.70	24.35	24.56
Prices:Low	19.01	17.16	26.21	19.07	17.30	17.17	13.13	12.66	16.59	18.00
P/E Ratio:High	14	19	21	35	NM	22	21	18	12	16
P/E Ratio:Low	10	10	17	23	NM	19	14	11	8	12

Income Statement Analysis (Million $)	2009	2008	2007	2006	2005	2004	2003	2002	2001	2000
Revenue	5,439	5,800	5,822	6,884	7,397	6,687	6,069	5,216	6,874	5,877
Depreciation	310	279	265	445	614	528	540	667	983	515
Maintenance	234	254	212	194	200	188	232	263	259	256
Fixed Charges Coverage	2.83	2.33	2.25	1.23	-0.26	1.63	1.72	1.10	-0.24	2.00
Construction Credits	NA	NA	NA	NA	NA	NA	NA	NA	Nil	Nil
Effective Tax Rate	35.3%	28.8%	30.3%	NM	NM	30.7%	33.1%	35.1%	39.5%	43.0%
Net Income	330	261	251	126	-229	117	121	152	266	205
S&P Core Earnings	348	173	240	144	-209	122	143	-99.7	-500	NA

Balance Sheet & Other Financial Data (Million $)	2009	2008	2007	2006	2005	2004	2003	2002	2001	2000
Gross Property	11,682	10,978	9,892	8,857	8,969	8,247	7,674	7,213	7,241	10,588
Capital Expenditures	908	1,255	1,115	872	752	644	532	492	443	414
Net Property	8,840	8,208	7,230	6,242	6,417	5,864	5,430	4,728	3,822	3,547
Capitalization:Long Term Debt	5,052	4,906	4,517	4,254	4,494	4,453	4,387	4,186	4,311	2,228
Capitalization:% Long Term Debt	58.5	61.9	60.8	60.3	64.9	66.0	66.0	64.3	65.9	50.1
Capitalization:Preferred	Nil	Nil	Nil	Nil	Nil	Nil	Nil	Nil	116	Nil
Capitalization:% Preferred	Nil	Nil	Nil	Nil	Nil	Nil	Nil	Nil	1.78	Nil
Capitalization:Common	3,578	3,020	2,914	2,798	2,429	2,297	2,264	2,211	2,118	2,219
Capitalization:% Common	41.5	38.1	39.2	39.7	35.1	34.0	34.0	33.9	32.4	49.9
Total Capital	8,696	9,175	8,527	8,184	8,325	8,283	8,042	8,056	8,156	6,285
% Operating Ratio	89.5	91.6	92.6	95.4	99.3	96.1	93.8	96.2	104.0	90.9
% Earned on Net Property	8.8	7.7	8.0	3.5	NM	7.3	8.3	6.1	NM	12.4
% Return on Revenue	6.1	4.5	4.3	1.8	NM	1.7	2.0	2.9	3.9	3.5
% Return on Invested Capital	7.3	6.1	8.6	4.6	1.1	4.8	4.7	5.5	8.2	8.4
% Return on Common Equity	10.0	8.8	8.6	4.8	NM	5.1	5.4	7.0	11.9	8.9

Data as orig reptd.; bef. results of disc opers/spec. items. Per share data adj. for stk. divs.; EPS diluted. E-Estimated. NA-Not Available. NM-Not Meaningful. NR-Not Ranked. UR-Under Review.

Office: 1 Federal St Bldg 111-4, Springfield, MA 01105-1192.
Telephone: 413-785-5871.
Email: nucommunications@nu.com
Website: http://www.nu.com

Chrmn, Pres & CEO: C.W. Shivery
COO & EVP: L.J. Olivier
EVP & CFO: D.R. McHale
SVP & General Counsel: G.B. Butler

Chief Acctg Officer & Cntlr: J.S. Buth
Investor Contact: J.R. Kotkin (860-665-5154)
Trustees: R. Booth, J. S. Clarkeson, C. M. Cleveland, S. Cloud, Jr., J. G. Graham, E. T. Kennan, K. R. Leibler, R. Patricelli, C. W. Shivery, J. F. Swope, D. R. Wraase

Founded: 1927
Domicile: Massachusetts
Employees: 6,078

Northern Trust Corp

STANDARD &POOR'S

S&P Recommendation HOLD ★★★☆☆

Price	12-Mo. Target Price	Investment Style
$47.81 (as of Oct 22, 2010)	$51.00	Large-Cap Growth

GICS Sector Financials
Sub-Industry Asset Management & Custody Banks

Summary Northern Trust is a leading provider of fiduciary, asset management and private banking services.

Key Stock Statistics (Source S&P, Vickers, company reports)

52-Wk Range	$59.36–45.30	S&P Oper. EPS 2010E	2.95	Market Capitalization(B)	$11.574	Beta	0.76
Trailing 12-Month EPS	$3.05	S&P Oper. EPS 2011E	3.75	Yield (%)	2.34	S&P 3-Yr. Proj. EPS CAGR(%)	12
Trailing 12-Month P/E	15.7	P/E on S&P Oper. EPS 2010E	16.2	Dividend Rate/Share	$1.12	S&P Credit Rating	AA-
$10K Invested 5 Yrs Ago	$10,056	Common Shares Outstg. (M)	242.1	Institutional Ownership (%)	79		

Price Performance

30-Week Mov. Avg. · · · 10-Week Mov. Avg. - - **GAAP Earnings vs. Previous Year** **Volume** Above Avg. STARS
12-Mo. Target Price — Relative Strength — ▲ Up ▼ Down ► No Change Below Avg.

Options: ASE, CBOE, P, Ph

Analysis prepared by **Matthew Albrecht** on July 22, 2010, when the stock traded at **$ 46.97**.

Highlights

▶ Growth in assets under custody and management will likely remain uneven, depending on market gains and new customer wins. Securities lending-related fees have picked up somewhat, but won't reach pre-crisis levels for some time, by our estimation. Foreign exchange trading activity has picked up with global economic uncertainty, and will likely increase further once global trade picks up. Interest rates have stabilized and money market fee waivers have declined somewhat, but we don't expect growth in net interest income until the Fed hikes rates, which likely won't happen until mid-2011 at the earliest. We think revenues could decline marginally in 2010 before advancing 8% in 2011.

▶ We forecast a 7% increase in non-interest expense this year, as incentive compensation accruals increase. We expect loan charge-offs and new loan loss provisions to remain elevated because non-performing loans continue to rise relative to total loans, although marketwide credit quality has improved somewhat.

▶ We look for earnings of $3.09 in 2010 and $3.75 in 2011.

Investment Rationale/Risk

▶ We have a positive view of NTRS's product and geographic diversity. We believe the company's leading position in the affluent market will result in above peer-average revenue. We are also encouraged by the defensive positioning of its securities portfolio. We look for the net interest margin to widen once the Fed hikes rates. NTRS's investment portfolio is highly conservative and should result in limited writedowns, by our analysis. However, we think the stock's recent valuation takes into account most of the positives that we foresee.

▶ Risks to our opinion and target price include failure to generate new business from existing and new clients, a significant decline in economic activity, and adverse litigation or regulation.

▶ Over the past five years, on average, the shares have traded at about 18X NTRS's forward 12-month EPS. Our 12-month target price of $51 is equal to approximately 15X our forward 12-month EPS estimate of $3.39, a discount to the historical average to reflect the poor rate environment, NTRS's shrinking balance sheet and uncertain economic growth.

Qualitative Risk Assessment

LOW	MEDIUM	HIGH

Our risk assessment reflects what we see as solid business fundamentals and a strong customer base. We view NTRS as well diversified geographically and able to withstand an economic downturn.

Quantitative Evaluations

S&P Quality Ranking A-

D	C	B-	B	B+	A-	A	A+

Relative Strength Rank WEAK

25

LOWEST = 1   HIGHEST = 99

Revenue/Earnings Data

Revenue (Million $)

	1Q	2Q	3Q	4Q	Year
2010	981.8	1,049	--	--	--
2009	1,010	1,140	1,013	--	3,216
2008	1,204	1,434	1,314	1,373	5,678
2007	1,250	1,338	1,385	1,699	5,395
2006	1,030	1,134	1,117	1,192	4,473
2005	792.9	902.4	912.0	947.1	3,554

Earnings Per Share ($)

	1Q	2Q	3Q	4Q	Year
2010	0.65	0.82	E0.64	E0.84	E2.95
2009	0.61	0.95	0.77	0.83	3.19
2008	1.71	0.96	-0.67	1.47	3.47
2007	0.84	0.92	0.93	0.55	3.24
2006	0.74	0.76	0.74	0.77	3.00
2005	0.63	0.68	0.67	0.67	2.64

Fiscal year ended Dec. 31. Next earnings report expected: NA. EPS Estimates based on S&P Operating Earnings; historical GAAP earnings are as reported.

Dividend Data (Dates: mm/dd Payment Date: mm/dd/yy)

Amount ($)	Date Decl.	Ex-Div. Date	Stk. of Record	Payment Date
0.280	02/16	03/08	03/10	04/01/10
0.280	04/20	06/08	06/10	07/01/10
0.280	07/20	09/08	09/10	10/01/10
0.280	10/19	12/08	12/10	01/03/11

Dividends have been paid since 1896. Source: Company reports.

Please read the Required Disclosures and Analyst Certification on the last page of this report.

The McGraw-Hill Companies

STANDARD &POOR'S

Northern Trust Corp

Business Summary July 22, 2010

CORPORATE OVERVIEW. Northern Trust Corp. (NTRS) organizes its services globally around its two principal business units: Corporate and Institutional Services (C&IS) and Personal Financial Services (PFS). C&IS is a leading worldwide provider of asset servicing, asset management and related services to corporate and public entity retirement funds, foundation and endowment clients, fund managers, insurance companies and government funds. C&IS also offers a full range of commercial banking services through the bank, placing special emphasis on developing and supporting institutional relationships in two target markets: large and mid-sized corporations and financial institutions (both U.S. and non-U.S.). Asset servicing, asset management and related services encompass a full range of capabilities including: global master trust and custody, trade, settlement, and reporting; fund administration; cash management; and investment risk and performance analytical services.

In 2005, NTRS completed its acquisition of the Financial Services Group Limited (FSG) from Baring Asset Management Holdings Limited. The purchase of

FSG brought to C&IS expanded capabilities in institutional fund administration, custody, trust and related services as well as new capabilities in hedge fund and private equity administration, in our view.

PFS provides personal trust, investment management, custody and philanthropic services; financial consulting; guardianship and estate administration; qualified retirement plans; brokerage services; and private and business banking. PFS focuses on high net worth individuals and families, business owners, executives, professionals, retirees and established privately held businesses in its target markets. PFS also includes the Wealth Management Group, which provides customized products and services to meet the complex financial needs of families and individuals in the U.S. and throughout the world, with assets typically exceeding $200 million.

Company Financials Fiscal Year Ended Dec. 31

Per Share Data ($)	2009	2008	2007	2006	2005	2004	2003	2002	2001	2000
Tangible Book Value	24.20	NA	18.04	15.53	14.72	14.14	13.88	13.04	11.97	10.54
Earnings	3.19	3.47	3.24	3.00	2.64	2.26	1.89	1.97	2.11	2.08
S&P Core Earnings	3.15	3.31	3.69	3.04	2.51	2.19	1.63	1.64	1.82	NA
Dividends	1.12	1.12	1.03	0.94	0.86	0.78	0.70	0.68	0.64	0.56
Payout Ratio	35%	32%	32%	31%	33%	35%	37%	35%	30%	27%
Prices:High	66.08	88.92	83.17	61.40	55.00	51.35	48.75	62.67	82.25	92.13
Prices:Low	43.32	33.88	56.52	49.12	41.60	38.40	27.64	30.41	41.40	46.75
P/E Ratio:High	21	26	26	20	21	23	26	32	39	44
P/E Ratio:Low	14	10	17	16	16	17	15	15	20	22

Income Statement Analysis (Million $)										
Net Interest Income	NA	NA	832	730	661	561	548	602	595	569
Tax Equivalent Adjustment	40.2	49.8	62.5	64.8	60.9	54.4	52.4	48.7	52.6	53.3
Non Interest Income	NA	3,032	2,326	2,018	1,783	1,711	1,542	1,537	1,580	1,537
Loan Loss Provision	215	115	18.0	15.0	2.50	-15.0	2.50	37.5	66.5	24.0
% Expense/Operating Revenue	37.6%	32.6%	77.0%	69.6%	69.2%	65.9%	68.1%	67.2%	61.8%	62.6%
Pretax Income	1,255	1,276	1,061	1,024	888	754	631	669	732	730
Effective Tax Rate	31.2%	37.7%	31.5%	35.0%	34.2%	33.1%	32.9%	33.2%	33.4%	33.6%
Net Income	864	795	727	665	584	505	423	447	488	485
% Net Interest Margin	1.56	1.76	1.67	1.73	1.79	1.66	1.73	1.93	2.02	2.02
S&P Core Earnings	744	747	828	674	561	491	365	369	418	NA

Balance Sheet & Other Financial Data (Million $)										
Money Market Assets	13,147	16,890	25,051	16,790	16,036	13,168	9,565	9,332	10,546	5,865
Investment Securities	18,346	15,571	8,888	12,365	11,109	9,042	9,471	6,594	6,331	7,270
Commercial Loans	6,312	8,254	7,907	6,515	5,064	4,498	4,702	5,137	5,767	5,708
Other Loans	21,494	22,501	17,433	16,094	14,905	13,445	13,111	12,927	12,213	12,437
Total Assets	82,142	82,054	67,611	60,712	53,414	45,277	41,450	39,478	39,665	36,022
Demand Deposits	9,178	11,824	10,118	9,315	7,427	6,377	5,767	6,602	7,110	5,375
Time Deposits	49,103	50,582	41,095	34,505	31,093	24,681	20,503	19,460	17,909	17,453
Long Term Debt	4,666	5,359	5,721	2,421	2,791	1,340	1,341	1,284	1,485	1,356
Common Equity	6,312	6,389	4,509	3,944	3,601	3,296	3,055	2,880	2,653	2,342
% Return on Assets	1.1	1.1	1.1	1.2	3.0	1.2	1.0	1.1	1.3	1.5
% Return on Equity	15.4	14.6	17.2	17.6	42.7	15.9	14.2	16.1	19.4	21.8
% Loan Loss Reserve	1.1	0.7	0.6	0.6	0.6	0.7	0.8	0.9	0.9	0.9
% Loans/Deposits	48.5	50.9	50.5	51.6	51.8	57.8	67.8	69.3	71.9	79.5
% Equity to Assets	7.7	6.3	6.6	6.6	7.0	7.3	7.3	7.0	6.6	6.8

Data as orig reptd.; bef. results of disc opers/spec. items. Per share data adj. for stk. divs.; EPS diluted. E-Estimated. NA-Not Available. NM-Not Meaningful. NR-Not Ranked. UR-Under Review.

Office: 50 S La Salle St, Chicago, IL 60603-1003.
Telephone: 312-630-6000.
Website: http://www.northerntrust.com
Chrmn, Pres & CEO: F.H. Waddell

COO: J.R. Schreuder
EVP & Chief Admin Officer: T.P. Moen
EVP & CTO: N. Krishnamurthy
EVP, Chief Acctg Officer & Cntlr: A.B. Blake

Investor Contact: S.L. Fradkin
Board Members: L. W. Bynoe, N. D. Chabraja, S. M. Crown, D. Jain, R. W. Lane, R. C. McCormack, E. J. Mooney, J. W. Rowe, D. H. Smith, Jr., W. D. Smithburg, E. Sosa, C. A. Tribbett, III, F. H. Waddell

Founded: 1889
Domicile: Delaware
Employees: 12,400

The **McGraw-Hill** Companies

Northrop Grumman Corp

STANDARD &POOR'S

S&P Recommendation HOLD ★ ★ ★ ★ ★

Price $61.90 (as of Oct 22, 2010)	**12-Mo. Target Price** $65.00	**Investment Style** Large-Cap Blend

GICS Sector Industrials
Sub-Industry Aerospace & Defense

Summary This company is the world's third largest producer of military arms and equipment, and also has a large government IT services business.

Key Stock Statistics (Source S&P, Vickers, company reports)

52-Wk Range	$69.80– 49.63	S&P Oper. EPS 2010**E**	6.70	Market Capitalization(B)	$18.212
Trailing 12-Month EPS	$6.69	S&P Oper. EPS 2011**E**	6.50	Yield (%)	3.04
Trailing 12-Month P/E	9.3	P/E on S&P Oper. EPS 2010**E**	9.2	Dividend Rate/Share	$1.88
$10K Invested 5 Yrs Ago	$13,315	Common Shares Outstg. (M)	294.2	Institutional Ownership (%)	87

Beta	1.10
S&P 3-Yr. Proj. EPS CAGR(%)	10
S&P Credit Rating	BBB+

Price Performance

30-Week Mov. Avg. · · · 10-Week Mov. Avg. – – **GAAP Earnings vs. Previous Year** Volume Above Avg. STARS
12-Mo. Target Price — Relative Strength — ▲ Up ▼ Down ▶ No Change Below Avg.

Options: ASE, CBOE, P

Analysis prepared by **Richard Tortoriello** on August 16, 2010, when the stock traded at **$ 56.24**.

Highlights

▶ We estimate sales growth of 3% this year, following a 4.5% rise in 2009 (restated for the December 2009 sale of the TASC advisory services business). We see strong growth in Technical Services (about 10%) and Aerospace Systems (6%), and moderate growth in Electronic Systems (3%) and Shipbuilding (2.5%). We see growth driven by new contract awards in Technical Services, manned and unmanned aircraft demand in Aerospace, ISR demand for electronics, and higher aircraft carrier and submarine volume in Shipbuilding. We project 2% overall revenue growth in 2011.

▶ We expect operating margins to improve to 9.2% in 2010, from 8.7% in 2009, on significantly reduced pension expense and segment operating improvement in all segments except Electronic Systems (NOC's highest margin segment).

▶ We project EPS of $6.70 in 2010 (including the $0.73 net effect of a one-time tax benefit), and see growth to $6.50 in 2011. We expect free cash flow (cash flow from operating activities less capital expenditures) per share of about $4.50 in 2010, about even with 2009.

Investment Rationale/Risk

▶ Although NOC's funded backlog fell 7% as of year-end 2009, and was up just 1% as of the second quarter of 2010, we expect growth in Shipbuilding and Aerospace, led by the Virginia Class Submarine and various manned and unmanned aircraft programs. We also expect good results from defense electronics and cybersecurity. However, we see a ballooning U.S. budget deficit and increased social spending leading to low defense-budget growth over the long term. Along these lines, the fiscal 2010 defense budget proposes a slowing in production of several ship-building programs, including the Navy Aircraft Carrier program, for which NOC is the prime contractor.

▶ Risks to our recommendation and target price include the potential for large cuts in military budgets, and failure to perform well on existing contracts or to win new contracts.

▶ Our 12-month target price of $65 is based on an enterprise value to estimated 2011 EBITDA multiple of 6X. This multiple is below NOC's 20-year average of 8X. We believe the below-average valuation is appropriate due to our view of flat to declining U.S. defense budget growth.

Qualitative Risk Assessment

LOW	MEDIUM	HIGH

Our risk assessment reflects our view of NOC's typically strong levels of cash flow and a solid balance sheet with a relatively low level of debt. This is offset by NOC's dependence on government spending on defense, which is subject to political and budgetary considerations.

Quantitative Evaluations

S&P Quality Ranking B+

D	C	B-	B	B+	A-	A	A+

Relative Strength Rank MODERATE

56

LOWEST = 1   HIGHEST = 99

Revenue/Earnings Data

Revenue (Million $)

	1Q	2Q	3Q	4Q	Year
2010	8,610	8,826	--	--	--
2009	7,935	8,545	8,350	8,925	33,755
2008	7,724	8,628	8,381	9,154	33,887
2007	7,340	7,926	7,928	8,824	32,018
2006	7,093	7,601	7,433	8,021	30,148
2005	7,453	7,962	7,446	7,860	30,721

Earnings Per Share ($)

2010	1.51	2.34	E1.40	E1.44	E6.70
2009	1.10	1.13	1.45	1.19	4.87
2008	0.76	1.40	1.50	-7.76	-3.83
2007	1.11	1.33	1.41	1.32	5.16
2006	1.03	1.26	0.87	1.29	4.44
2005	1.08	1.00	0.80	0.92	3.81

Fiscal year ended Dec. 31. Next earnings report expected: NA. EPS Estimates based on S&P Operating Earnings; historical GAAP earnings are as reported.

Dividend Data (Dates: mm/dd Payment Date: mm/dd/yy)

Amount ($)	Date Decl.	Ex-Div. Date	Stk. of Record	Payment Date
0.430	10/19	11/25	11/30	12/12/09
0.430	02/17	02/25	03/01	03/13/10
0.470	05/19	05/27	06/01	06/12/10
0.470	07/27	08/26	08/30	09/11/10

Dividends have been paid since 1951. Source: Company reports.

Please read the Required Disclosures and Analyst Certification on the last page of this report.

The McGraw·Hill Companies

Northrop Grumman Corp

Business Summary August 16, 2010

CORPORATE OVERVIEW. This $35 billion in estimated 2010 revenues defense electronics, aerospace, and warship-making giant, conducts most of its business with the U.S. government, principally the Department of Defense. NOC also transacts with foreign governments and makes commercial sales both domestically and overseas. In January 2009, the company reorganized its reported business segments into five from a previous seven.

The Information & Services segment (24% of 2009 revenue and 20% of 2009 operating income) provides products and services in the areas of command, control, communications, computers, and intelligence (C4I); air and missile defense; airborne reconnaissance; intelligence processing; decision support systems; cybersecurity; information technology (IT); and systems engineering and integration. It consists of three business areas: Defense Systems, Intelligence Systems, and Civil Systems.

The Technical Services segment (8% of revenue and 5% of operating profit) is

a leading provider of logistics, infrastructure, and sustainment support, while also providing a wide array of technical services including training and simulation. It consists of three business areas: Systems Support, Training & Simulation, and Life Cycle Optimization & Engineering.

The Aerospace Systems segment (29% and 34%) is a developer, integrator, producer, and supporter of manned and unmanned aircraft, spacecraft, high-energy laser systems, microelectronics and other systems and subsystems critical to maintaining the nation's security and leadership in technology. It consists of four business areas: Strike & Surveillance Systems, Space Systems, Battle Management & Engagement Systems, and Advanced Programs & Technology.

Company Financials Fiscal Year Ended Dec. 31

Per Share Data ($)	2009	2008	2007	2006	2005	2004	2003	2002	2001	2000
Tangible Book Value	NM	NM	NM	NM	NM	NM	NM	NM	NM	NM
Cash Flow	7.14	-1.71	7.09	6.34	5.94	5.01	4.05	5.29	6.31	7.08
Earnings	4.87	-3.83	5.16	4.44	3.81	2.99	2.16	2.86	2.40	4.41
S&P Core Earnings	5.29	1.44	4.09	3.67	2.84	2.63	2.42	-0.95	-2.85	NA
Dividends	1.69	1.57	1.48	1.16	1.01	0.89	0.80	0.80	0.80	0.80
Payout Ratio	35%	NM	29%	26%	27%	30%	37%	28%	33%	18%
Prices:High	57.32	83.40	85.21	71.37	60.26	58.15	50.55	67.50	55.28	46.94
Prices:Low	33.81	33.96	66.23	59.10	51.10	46.91	41.50	43.60	38.20	21.31
P/E Ratio:High	12	NM	17	16	16	19	23	24	23	11
P/E Ratio:Low	7	NM	13	13	13	16	19	15	16	5

Income Statement Analysis (Million $)										
Revenue	33,755	33,887	32,018	30,148	30,721	29,853	26,206	17,206	13,558	7,618
Operating Income	3,219	3,920	3,716	3,159	2,951	2,740	1,538	1,391	1,649	1,479
Depreciation	736	708	710	705	773	734	682	525	645	381
Interest Expense	281	295	336	347	388	431	497	422	373	175
Pretax Income	2,266	-368	2,686	2,276	2,044	1,615	1,131	1,009	699	975
Effective Tax Rate	30.6%	NM	32.9%	31.2%	32.3%	32.3%	28.6%	30.9%	38.9%	35.9%
Net Income	1,573	-1,281	1,803	1,567	1,383	1,093	808	697	427	625
S&P Core Earnings	1,712	481	1,426	1,288	1,026	961	892	-223	-487	NA

Balance Sheet & Other Financial Data (Million $)										
Cash	3,275	1,504	963	1,015	1,605	1,230	342	1,412	464	319
Current Assets	8,635	7,189	6,772	6,719	7,549	6,907	5,745	15,835	4,589	2,526
Total Assets	30,252	30,197	33,373	32,009	34,214	33,361	33,009	42,266	20,886	9,622
Current Liabilities	6,985	7,424	6,432	6,753	7,974	6,223	6,361	11,373	5,132	2,688
Long Term Debt	4,191	3,443	4,268	3,992	3,881	5,116	5,410	9,398	5,033	1,605
Common Equity	12,687	11,920	17,687	16,615	16,825	16,970	15,785	14,322	7,391	3,919
Total Capital	16,969	15,363	22,285	20,957	21,651	22,942	22,067	24,209	13,443	5,800
Capital Expenditures	654	681	685	737	824	672	635	538	393	274
Cash Flow	2,309	-573	2,513	2,272	2,156	1,827	1,490	1,222	1,072	1,006
Current Ratio	1.2	1.0	1.1	1.0	0.9	1.1	0.9	1.4	0.9	0.9
% Long Term Debt of Capitalization	24.7	22.4	19.2	19.0	17.9	22.3	24.5	38.8	37.4	27.7
% Net Income of Revenue	4.7	NM	5.6	5.2	4.5	3.7	3.1	4.1	3.1	8.2
% Return on Assets	5.2	NM	5.5	4.7	4.1	3.3	2.1	2.2	2.8	6.6
% Return on Equity	12.8	NM	10.5	9.4	8.2	6.6	5.4	6.4	7.6	17.4

Data as orig reptd.; bef. results of disc opers/spec. items. Per share data adj. for stk. divs.; EPS diluted. E-Estimated. NA-Not Available. NM-Not Meaningful. NR-Not Ranked. UR-Under Review.

Office: 1840 Century Park E, Los Angeles, CA 90067-2199.
Telephone: 310-553-6262.
Email: investor_relations@mail.northrum.com
Website: http://www.northropgrumman.com

Chrmn: L.W. Coleman
Pres & CEO: W.G. Bush
CFO: J.F. Palmer
Chief Admin Officer: I.V. Ziskin

CTO: A.C. Livanos
Investor Contact: P. Gregory (310-201-1634)
Board Members: W. G. Bush, L. W. Coleman, T. B. Fargo, V. Fazio, D. E. Felsinger, S. E. Frank, B. S. Gordon, M. Kleiner, K. J. Krapek, R. B. Myers, A. L. Peters, K. W. Sharer

Founded: 1939
Domicile: Delaware
Employees: 120,700

Novell Inc

STANDARD &POOR'S

S&P Recommendation HOLD ★★★☆☆

Price	12-Mo. Target Price	Investment Style
$6.07 (as of Oct 22, 2010)	$6.50	Large-Cap Blend

GICS Sector Information Technology
Sub-Industry Systems Software

Summary This leading vendor of directory-enabled networking software has been seeking strategic alternatives since rejecting a $5.75 a share bid from a hedge fund earlier this year.

Key Stock Statistics (Source S&P, Vickers, company reports)

52-Wk Range	$6.53– 3.84	S&P Oper. EPS 2010E	0.21	Market Capitalization(B)	$2.131	Beta	0.96
Trailing 12-Month EPS	$-0.57	S&P Oper. EPS 2011E	0.17	Yield (%)	Nil	S&P 3-Yr. Proj. EPS CAGR(%)	-5
Trailing 12-Month P/E	NM	P/E on S&P Oper. EPS 2010E	28.9	Dividend Rate/Share	Nil	S&P Credit Rating	NA
$10K Invested 5 Yrs Ago	$8,163	Common Shares Outstg. (M)	351.3	Institutional Ownership (%)	70		

Price Performance

30-Week Mov. Avg. ···· 10-Week Mov. Avg.– – **GAAP Earnings vs. Previous Year** Volume Above Avg. STARS
12-Mo. Target Price — Relative Strength — ▲ Up ▼ Down ▶ No Change Below Avg.

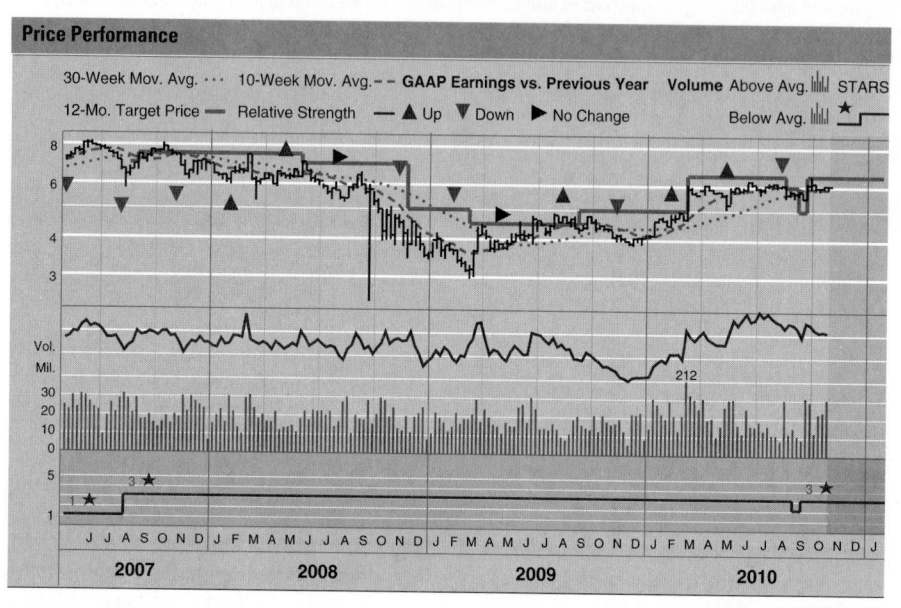

Options: ASE, CBOE, P, Ph

Analysis prepared by **Jim Yin, CFA** on September 20, 2010, when the stock traded at **$ 6.18**.

Highlights

➤ We estimate that revenues will decrease 6.8% and 2.8% in FY 10 (Oct.) and FY 11, respectively, after a 9.9% decline in FY 09. The expected decline reflects our view of a slow recovery in enterprise software and continued weakness in legacy products. We see a 5% drop in its work-group segment in FY 11. We project a 5% rise in open platform solutions revenue, as NOVL expands its presence in the Linux and open source software markets, but we expect growth in this segment to decelerate from 13% in FY 09, as NOVL adds fewer new customers.

➤ We expect gross margins to stay at 78% in both FY 10 and FY 11, the same as in FY 09. Total operating expenses should decrease as a result of further head count reductions and lower research and development expenses, partially offset by increased stock-based compensation. We project operating margins of 10.3% and 9.7% in FY 10 and FY 11, respectively.

➤ We estimate EPS of $0.21 and $0.17 in FY 10 and FY 11, respectively, compared to a loss of $0.62 in FY 09, which included $302 million of restructuring charges.

Investment Rationale/Risk

➤ Since rejecting an unsolicited $5.75 a share takeover offer from a hedge fund in March 2010, NOVL has been seeking other strategic alternatives. We think the company is in negotiation with several bidders about splitting itself into two parts and selling each part to different acquirers. We think this type of deal structure seems reasonable because potential strategic acquirers are only interested in NOVL's Linux business, while financial buyers may be interested in its legacy business because of its positive cash flows. Although we believe the takeout price could be above the current stock price, we think the potential gain is offset by the risk that a deal may fall through due to its complexity.

➤ Risks to our opinion and target price include failure to complete a merger deal, slower-than-expected growth in the Linux products, and a slowdown in the global economy.

➤ Our 12-month target price of $6.50 is based on an enterprise value/sales ratio of 1.6X, which is a blend of a takeout premium of 4.0X for the company's Linux business and 1.0X for its legacy business.

Qualitative Risk Assessment

LOW	MEDIUM	HIGH

Our risk assessment reflects the volatile market conditions in the Linux and open source software markets, the continuing decline in sales of NOVL's legacy products, and our belief that NOVL is having difficulty gaining sufficient traction in Linux to offset the decline in other businesses.

Quantitative Evaluations

S&P Quality Ranking C

D	C	B-	B	B+	A-	A	A+

Relative Strength Rank MODERATE

45

LOWEST = 1 HIGHEST = 99

Revenue/Earnings Data

Revenue (Million $)

	1Q	2Q	3Q	4Q	Year
2010	202.4	204.0	199.0	--	--
2009	214.9	215.6	216.1	215.6	862.2
2008	230.9	235.7	245.2	244.7	956.5
2007	218.4	232.4	236.8	244.9	932.5
2006	274.4	278.3	241.4	244.9	967.3
2005	290.1	297.1	290.2	320.3	1,198

Earnings Per Share ($)

2010	0.06	0.06	0.04	E0.04	E0.21
2009	0.03	0.04	0.05	-0.74	-0.62
2008	0.04	0.04	-0.04	-0.05	-0.04
2007	-0.04	Nil	-0.04	-0.03	-0.08
2006	Nil	0.01	0.03	0.06	0.02
2005	0.90	-0.04	Nil	-0.01	0.86

Fiscal year ended Oct. 31. Next earnings report expected: Early December. EPS Estimates based on S&P Operating Earnings; historical GAAP earnings are as reported.

Dividend Data

No cash dividends have been paid.

Novell Inc

STANDARD &POOR'S

Business Summary September 20, 2010

CORPORATE OVERVIEW. Novell Inc. (NOVL) is a provider of software and services that help customers manage their information technology infrastructure. The company's legacy products are based on its proprietary network operating system, NetWare. Sales of NetWare have been declining, and IDC, an independent market research firm, expects NetWare's market share of the worldwide server installed base to decrease to 0.4% in 2012 from 2.5% in 2008. Meanwhile, Linux's share is forecast to rise to 22% in 2012, from 20% in 2008.

In the past few years, NOVL has embraced and promoted Linux and open source computing. The company is the second largest provider of Linux operating systems and subsystems, capturing 30% of the market by revenue in 2008, according to IDC, up from 15% in 2005. As a result of increased use of open source software in enterprise applications, NOVL has repositioned itself as a solution provider in a mixed operating system environment that includes open source and proprietary technologies, thus reducing reliance on its legacy products, such as NetWare.

NOVL has reorganized into four product-related business units and a consulting unit. The four business unit segments are: open platform solutions, which encompasses SUSE Linux operating system; identity and security management, which helps to provide secured logon and protect information assets;

systems and resource management, which includes software to manage multiple infrastructure resources in a virtual environment; and workgroup, which helps customers to collaborate across the enterprise. This segment includes NetWare-related product revenues. In FY 09 (Oct.), the open platform solutions segment accounted for 20% of the total revenues, the identity and security management segment 18%, the systems and resource management segment 21%, and the workgroup segment 39%.

CORPORATE STRATEGY. NOVL relies on a series of alliances and partnerships to drive sales growth; its partners include IBM, HP, Dell, Intel, Oracle, SAP, AMD, CA, EMC and Adobe. NOVL believes it has created an ecosystem around it to combine its strengths with those of its partners; however, these partners are also counted among the strategic partners of many other software firms, and we doubt the partnerships provide a significant competitive advantage. In addition, NOVL's go-to market strategy embraces both a direct and indirect sales channel, with the indirect channel including independent distributors, value-added resellers, systems integrators and hardware OEMs.

Company Financials Fiscal Year Ended Oct. 31

Per Share Data ($)	2009	2008	2007	2006	2005	2004	2003	2002	2001	2000
Tangible Book Value	1.56	1.32	2.05	1.86	2.42	1.39	1.89	2.31	2.98	3.80
Cash Flow	-0.50	0.08	0.04	0.15	0.98	0.22	-0.27	-0.09	-0.53	0.39
Earnings	-0.62	-0.04	-0.08	0.02	0.86	0.08	-0.44	-0.28	-0.79	0.15
S&P Core Earnings	-0.11	0.01	-0.09	-0.02	-0.11	-0.07	-0.45	-0.47	-1.27	NA
Dividends	Nil	Nil	Nil	Nil	Nil	Nil	Nil	Nil	Nil	Nil
Payout Ratio	Nil	Nil	Nil	Nil	Nil	Nil	Nil	Nil	Nil	Nil
Prices:High	4.98	7.59	8.26	9.83	9.27	14.24	10.77	5.64	9.13	44.56
Prices:Low	2.97	2.49	5.76	5.70	4.94	5.62	2.14	1.57	2.96	4.88
P/E Ratio:High	NM	NM	NM	NM	11	NM	NM	NM	NM	33
P/E Ratio:Low	NM	NM	NM	NM	6	NM	NM	NM	NM	33

Income Statement Analysis (Million $)										
Revenue	862	957	933	967	1,198	1,166	1,105	1,134	1,040	1,162
Operating Income	136	90.7	30.4	27.8	99.3	140	52.3	103	46.1	98.2
Depreciation	40.7	40.4	40.4	47.0	56.3	53.5	61.1	68.8	86.7	81.9
Interest Expense	0.85	23.4	25.9	8.02	9.63	Nil	Nil	Nil	Nil	Nil
Pretax Income	-204	22.9	8.40	30.9	466	75.0	-55.0	-92.2	-277	70.7
Effective Tax Rate	NM	153.9%	NM	75.3%	19.2%	23.7%	NM	NM	NM	30.0%
Net Income	-215	-12.3	-26.3	7.63	377	57.2	-162	-103	-262	49.5
S&P Core Earnings	-39.5	3.64	-29.5	-8.34	-52.6	-30.8	-167	-172	-384	NA

Balance Sheet & Other Financial Data (Million $)										
Cash	983	1,068	1,080	676	811	434	752	636	705	698
Current Assets	1,281	1,386	2,154	1,761	2,009	1,535	1,031	920	1,027	1,007
Total Assets	1,903	2,269	2,854	2,450	2,762	2,292	1,568	1,665	1,904	1,712
Current Liabilities	731	900	822	686	753	693	626	592	611	455
Long Term Debt	NA	4.00	600	600	600	600	Nil	Nil	Nil	Nil
Common Equity	935	1,088	1,158	1,105	1,386	963	934	1,066	1,271	1,245
Total Capital	935	1,218	1,758	1,718	2,004	1,599	941	1,074	1,293	1,257
Capital Expenditures	22.1	37.7	25.2	26.7	30.8	27.0	39.5	27.6	33.3	57.8
Cash Flow	-174	28.1	14.1	54.6	433	84.6	-101	-34.3	-175	131
Current Ratio	1.8	1.5	2.6	2.6	2.7	2.2	1.6	1.6	1.7	2.2
% Long Term Debt of Capitalization	Nil	0.4	34.1	34.9	29.9	37.5	Nil	Nil	Nil	Nil
% Net Income of Revenue	NM	NM	NM	0.8	31.5	4.9	NM	NM	NM	4.3
% Return on Assets	NM	NM	NM	0.3	14.9	3.0	NM	NM	NM	2.7
% Return on Equity	NM	NM	NM	0.6	32.1	3.3	NM	NM	NM	3.6

Data as orig reptd.; bef. results of disc opers/spec. items. Per share data adj. for stk. divs.; EPS diluted. E-Estimated. NA-Not Available. NM-Not Meaningful. NR-Not Ranked. UR-Under Review.

Office: 404 Wyman St Ste 500, Waltham, MA 02451-1212.
Telephone: 781-464-8000.
Website: http://www.novell.com
Chrmn: R.L. Crandall

Pres & CEO: R.W. Hovsepian
SVP, CFO & Chief Acctg Officer: D.C. Russell
Investor Contact: E.M. Hennessy (781-464-8553)
CIO: J. Almandoz

Board Members: A. Aiello, Jr., F. Corrado, R. L. Crandall, G. G. Greenfield, J. H. Hamilton, R. W. Hovsepian, P. Jones, R. L. Nolan, J. W. Poduska

Founded: 1983
Domicile: Delaware
Employees: 3,600

The McGraw-Hill Companies

Novellus Systems Inc

STANDARD &POOR'S

S&P Recommendation HOLD ★★★☆☆	**Price** $27.60 (as of Oct 22, 2010)	**12-Mo. Target Price** $29.00	**Investment Style** Large-Cap Growth

GICS Sector Information Technology
Sub-Industry Semiconductor Equipment

Summary This company manufactures, markets, and services automated wafer fabrication systems for the deposition of thin films.

Key Stock Statistics (Source S&P, Vickers, company reports)

52-Wk Range	$28.90– 19.42	S&P Oper. EPS 2010**E**	2.75	Market Capitalization(B)	$2.537	Beta	1.25
Trailing 12-Month EPS	$1.41	S&P Oper. EPS 2011**E**	3.45	Yield (%)	Nil	S&P 3-Yr. Proj. EPS CAGR(%)	NM
Trailing 12-Month P/E	19.6	P/E on S&P Oper. EPS 2010**E**	10.0	Dividend Rate/Share	Nil	S&P Credit Rating	NA
$10K Invested 5 Yrs Ago	$12,591	Common Shares Outstg. (M)	91.9	Institutional Ownership (%)	95		

Price Performance

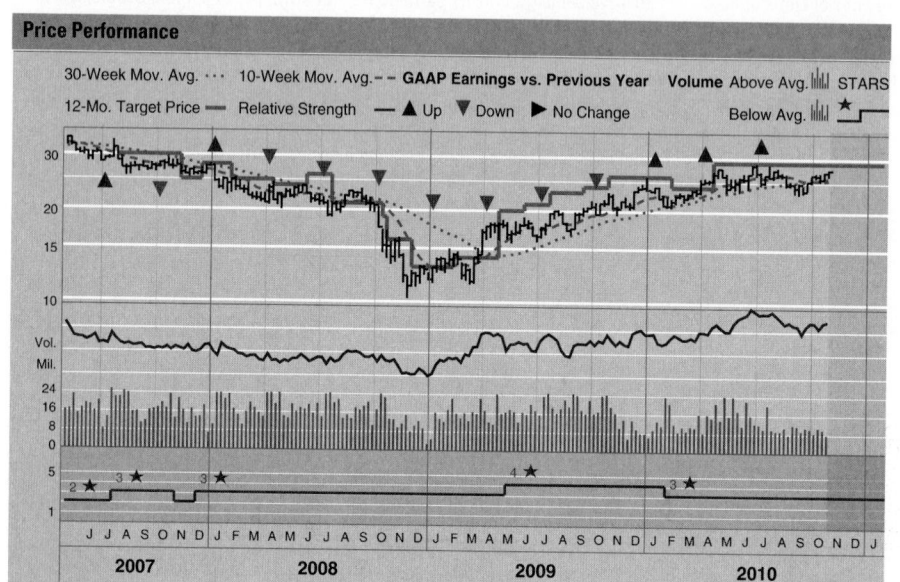

30-Week Mov. Avg. · · · · 10-Week Mov. Avg. – – GAAP Earnings vs. Previous Year Volume Above Avg. STARS
12-Mo. Target Price — Relative Strength ▲ Up ▼ Down ▶ No Change Below Avg.

2007 2008 2009 2010

Options: ASE, CBOE, P, Ph

Analysis prepared by **Angelo Zino** on September 03, 2010, when the stock traded at **$ 24.88.**

Qualitative Risk Assessment

LOW	MEDIUM	HIGH

Our risk assessment reflects the historical cyclicality of the semiconductor equipment industry, the lack of visibility in the medium term, the dynamic nature of semiconductor technology, and intense competition. We believe these risks are partially offset by our view of the company's strong market position, size, and financial condition.

Quantitative Evaluations

S&P Quality Ranking C

D	C	B-	B	B+	A-	A	A+

Relative Strength Rank MODERATE

70

LOWEST = 1 HIGHEST = 99

Revenue/Earnings Data

Revenue (Million $)

	1Q	2Q	3Q	4Q	Year
2010	276.2	321.4	--	--	--
2009	98.91	119.2	176.9	244.2	639.2
2008	314.7	257.7	250.1	188.5	1,011
2007	397.0	416.3	393.3	363.5	1,570
2006	365.9	410.1	444.0	438.5	1,659
2005	339.7	329.6	338.9	332.3	1,340

Earnings Per Share ($)

	1Q	2Q	3Q	4Q	Year
2010	0.43	0.66	E0.81	E0.81	E2.75
2009	-0.69	-0.52	-0.04	0.36	-0.88
2008	0.15	-0.02	0.01	-1.36	-1.18
2007	0.42	0.45	0.41	0.47	1.75
2006	0.18	0.42	0.57	0.34	1.49
2005	0.22	0.24	0.17	0.17	0.80

Fiscal year ended Dec. 31. Next earnings report expected: Late October. EPS Estimates based on S&P Operating Earnings; historical GAAP earnings are as reported.

Dividend Data

No cash dividends have been paid.

Highlights

➤ We anticipate sales to rise 13% in 2011 following our projection for revenues to more than double in 2010, as we think industry conditions will continue to improve. We believe the memory supply and demand balance remains healthy, and that rising end-market demand and improving customer profitability are leading to advanced technology spending by manufacturers. Although we project soft PC demand, we see sales being held up by rising demand for mobile devices and enterprise spending. We are cautious about falling memory prices but expect customers to stay profitable.

➤ We look for the annual gross margin to widen to 51% in 2011 versus our 49% forecast in 2010. Going forward, we expect gross margins to expand, driven by higher system sales from low levels and benefits from cost-cutting efforts. We look for NVLS to maintain tight cost control and refrain from significant increases to operating costs. We see operating expenses running at about 23% to 27% of sales.

➤ We project operating EPS of $2.75 in 2010, which excludes $0.04 from non-recurring charges, and $3.45 in 2011. We model a 16%-18% tax rate for both years.

Investment Rationale/Risk

➤ We think NVLS will benefit from the transition to copper processes, and see potential for share gain. We believe demand for consumer electronics continues to be driven by emerging mobile devices and new innovations such as the iPad. As a result of improving demand and relatively healthy inventory levels across the supply chain, we foresee greater spending by NAND flash memory customers and stable logic spending. Also, we expect some customers to invest more heavily in capacity expansion. We see the company's industrial segment rebounding as the economy improves, but at a sluggish pace.

➤ Risks to our recommendation and target price include a longer-than-expected semiconductor equipment downturn, weaker-than-projected global economic growth, and higher-than-expected R&D expense growth.

➤ We derive our 12-month target price of $29 based on a blend of our peer-average P/E and below historical average price-to-sales (P/S) multiples. We obtain a $27 price using a multiple of 7.8X our 2011 EPS estimate. We apply a P/S multiple of 2.0X to our 2011 sales per share estimate of $15.37 to arrive at a $31 price.

Please read the Required Disclosures and Analyst Certification on the last page of this report.

The McGraw-Hill Companies

Novellus Systems Inc

Business Summary September 03, 2010

CORPORATE OVERVIEW. Novellus is the second largest maker of deposition equipment used to deposit conductive and insulating layers on semiconductor wafers to form integrated circuits (ICs). Novellus operates in two segments, the Semiconductor Group and the Industrial Applications Group. The Semiconductor Group comprised 89% and 83% of total sales in 2009 and 2008.

NVLS's product line of deposition equipment includes chemical vapor deposition (CVD), physical vapor deposition (PVD) and electrochemical deposition (ECD), all of which are used to form the layers of wiring and insulation, known as the interconnect, of ICs. High-density plasma CVD (HDP) and plasma-enhanced CVD (PECVD) systems employ chemical plasma to deposit all of the insulating layers and some of the conductive layers on the surface of a wafer. PVD systems deposit conductive layers through a process known as sputtering, where ions of an inert gas such as argon are electrically accelerated in a high vacuum toward a target of pure metal, such as tantalum or copper. ECD systems are used to build the copper conductive layers on wafers.

Although NVLS's original tool sets established it as a leader in CVD, the company has centered its product strategy on the emergence of the copper interconnect market. Copper has lower resistance and capacitance values than

aluminum, the conductive metal generally used in ICs, offering increased speed and decreased chip size. The company's SABRE tool offers a complete solution for the deposition of copper interconnects and holds the leading market share in copper.

Surface preparation products, including photoresist strip and clean, are becoming more important with the industry's migration to copper interconnects. Surface preparation systems remove photoresist and other potential contaminants from a wafer before proceeding with the next deposition step. CMP systems polish the surface of a wafer after a deposition step to create a flat topography before moving on to subsequent manufacturing steps. Since copper is more difficult to polish and smooth than previous generation aluminum interconnects, and low-k dielectrics are much more porous than predecessors, NVLS's products in this category have become very important, in our view.

Company Financials Fiscal Year Ended Dec. 31

Per Share Data ($)	2009	2008	2007	2006	2005	2004	2003	2002	2001	2000
Tangible Book Value	10.67	11.73	11.98	12.54	11.29	11.06	12.42	12.69	13.04	11.49
Cash Flow	-0.40	-0.53	2.30	2.05	1.39	1.66	0.43	0.45	1.32	2.04
Earnings	-0.88	-1.18	1.75	1.49	0.80	1.06	-0.03	0.15	0.97	1.75
S&P Core Earnings	-0.89	-0.11	1.71	1.47	0.43	0.74	-0.42	-0.33	0.52	NA
Dividends	Nil	Nil	Nil	Nil	Nil	Nil	Nil	Nil	Nil	Nil
Payout Ratio	Nil	Nil	Nil	Nil	Nil	Nil	Nil	Nil	Nil	Nil
Prices:High	26.00	27.66	34.97	35.00	30.77	44.52	45.50	54.48	58.70	70.25
Prices:Low	11.43	10.26	25.40	22.28	20.83	22.89	24.93	19.40	25.37	24.94
P/E Ratio:High	NM	NM	20	23	38	42	NM	NM	61	40
P/E Ratio:Low	NM	NM	15	15	26	22	NM	NM	26	14

Income Statement Analysis (Million $)										
Revenue	639	1,011	1,570	1,659	1,340	1,357	925	840	1,339	1,174
Operating Income	-4.57	81.1	329	388	228	308	56.5	46.3	273	328
Depreciation	46.9	63.3	66.9	69.7	82.8	89.3	69.6	44.3	51.9	40.1
Interest Expense	2.07	7.02	6.38	4.29	3.51	2.13	0.91	1.02	1.15	2.34
Pretax Income	-69.4	-107	315	339	159	223	-15.3	22.9	209	342
Effective Tax Rate	NM	NM	32.1%	44.2%	30.6%	29.8%	NM	NM	31.0%	31.0%
Net Income	-85.2	-116	214	189	110	157	-5.03	22.9	144	236
S&P Core Earnings	-86.7	-10.0	209	186	59.8	108	-67.2	-50.7	81.6	NA

Balance Sheet & Other Financial Data (Million $)										
Cash	501	471	593	58.5	649	106	497	616	551	571
Current Assets	898	1,043	1,224	1,505	1,364	1,369	1,572	1,634	2,517	1,827
Total Assets	1,559	1,638	2,077	2,362	2,290	2,402	2,339	2,494	3,010	2,015
Current Liabilities	171	305	329	361	344	324	221	382	1,138	505
Long Term Debt	114	Nil	143	128	125	161	Nil	Nil	Nil	Nil
Common Equity	1,180	1,247	1,529	1,835	1,779	1,862	2,072	2,056	1,872	1,511
Total Capital	1,294	1,248	1,700	1,963	1,904	2,023	2,072	2,075	1,872	1,511
Capital Expenditures	11.9	17.9	33.2	39.4	44.7	31.7	31.1	26.8	80.0	68.5
Cash Flow	-38.4	-52.4	281	259	193	246	64.5	67.2	196	276
Current Ratio	5.4	3.4	3.7	4.2	4.0	4.2	7.1	4.3	2.2	3.6
% Long Term Debt of Capitalization	8.8	Nil	8.4	6.5	6.6	8.0	Nil	Nil	Nil	Nil
% Net Income of Revenue	NM	NM	13.6	11.4	8.2	11.5	NM	2.7	10.8	20.1
% Return on Assets	NM	NM	9.6	8.1	4.7	6.6	NM	0.8	5.5	16.1
% Return on Equity	NM	NM	12.7	10.5	6.0	8.0	NM	1.2	8.2	20.7

Data as orig reptd.; bef. results of disc opers/spec. items. Per share data adj. for stk. divs.; EPS diluted. E-Estimated. NA-Not Available. NM-Not Meaningful. NR-Not Ranked. UR-Under Review.

Office: 4000 North First Street, San Jose, CA 95134-1568.
Telephone: 408-943-9700.
Email: info@novellus.com
Website: http://www.novellus.com

Chrmn & CEO: R. Hill
COO: G. Addiego
CFO, Chief Acctg Officer & Cntlr: J.D. Hertz
Treas & Secy: K. Rammohan

General Counsel: A. Gottlieb
Investor Contact: R. Yim (408-943-9700)
Board Members: N. R. Bonke, Y. A. El-Mansy, R. Hill, Y. Nishi, G. G. Possley, A. D. Rhoads, W. R. Spivey, D. A. Whitaker

Founded: 1984
Domicile: California
Employees: 2,544

NRG Energy Inc

STANDARD &POOR'S

S&P Recommendation BUY ★★★★☆

Price	12-Mo. Target Price	Investment Style
$20.24 (as of Oct 22, 2010)	$27.00	Large-Cap Blend

GICS Sector Utilities
Sub-Industry Independent Power Producers & Energy Traders

Summary This wholesale power generation company owns and operates power generation facilities and sells energy, capacity and related products internationally.

Key Stock Statistics (Source S&P, Vickers, company reports)

52-Wk Range	$27.56– 20.02	S&P Oper. EPS 2010E	2.68	Market Capitalization(B)	$5.124	Beta	0.88
Trailing 12-Month EPS	$2.19	S&P Oper. EPS 2011E	2.91	Yield (%)	Nil	S&P 3-Yr. Proj. EPS CAGR(%)	-3
Trailing 12-Month P/E	9.2	P/E on S&P Oper. EPS 2010E	7.6	Dividend Rate/Share	Nil	S&P Credit Rating	BB-
$10K Invested 5 Yrs Ago	$9,691	Common Shares Outstg. (M)	253.2	Institutional Ownership (%)	NM		

Price Performance

30-Week Mov. Avg. · · · 10-Week Mov. Avg. – – GAAP Earnings vs. Previous Year   Volume Above Avg. STARS
12-Mo. Target Price — Relative Strength — ▲ Up ▼ Down ► No Change   Below Avg.

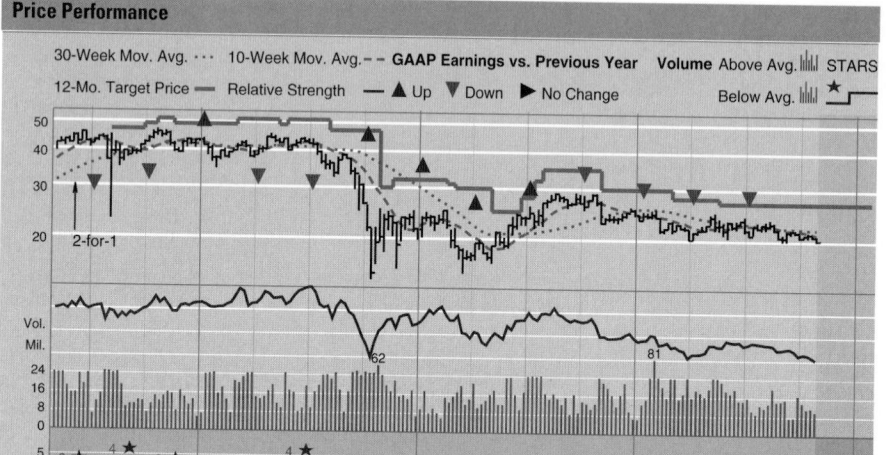

Options: ASE, CBOE, P, Ph

Analysis prepared by **Christopher B. Muir** on August 31, 2010, when the stock traded at **$ 20.32**.

Highlights

▶ We estimate a 7.0% rise in revenues for 2010, helped by higher realized prices and increased generation volumes. We believe NRG will benefit from stabilizing market conditions in the regions where it operates, which should lead to stable to slightly stronger peak wholesale prices. Higher natural gas prices in 2010 will likely make unsold capacity from baseload plants more valuable, in our view. We see 2011 revenues rising 3.5%.

▶ We forecast operating profit margins of 15.5% in 2010, up from 13.9% in 2009, on lower per-revenue cost of operations, depreciation charges, and general, administrative & develoment expenses. We see pretax margins widening to 10.7% in 2010, from 8.7% in 2009. We see lower nonoperating income partly offset by lower interest expense in 2010. In 2011, we look for operating margins of 16.2% and pretax margins of 10.9%.

▶ We estimate 2010 EPS of $2.68, down 22% from 2009's $3.45, excluding $0.05 of non-recurring charges. Our 2011 EPS forecast is $2.91, up 8.6%. Excluding mark-to-market adjustments, we see EPS of $2.68 in 2010, versus $1.80 in 2009.

Investment Rationale/Risk

▶ In May 2009, NRG purchased RRI Energy's (RRI 3, Buy) Reliant retail business for $288 million. We view the acquisition positively, as we think NRG was able to acquire the business at a very favorable price while simultaneously helping ward off what we viewed as an inadequate offer. NRG also recently agreed to purchase three power plants in California, Texas and Maine for far below the cost to build new plants. We continue to like NRG's focus on cost control, its proposed nuclear, repowering and greenfield development efforts, and its share repurchase program.

▶ Risks to our recommendation and target price include less favorable energy market conditions, difficulty refinancing maturing debt, and inability to sell certain assets.

▶ The stock recently traded at about 7X our 2011 EPS estimate, a 36% discount to independent power producer peers. Our 12-month target price of $27 is 9.3X our 2011 EPS estimate, a 35% discount to our peer target. We think the discount is appropriate given the possibility that nuclear development efforts will turn out to be more costly than projected.

Qualitative Risk Assessment

LOW	MEDIUM	HIGH

Our risk assessment is based on our view that the geographic and fuel diversity benefits of NRG's power plants offset the company's exposure to volatile natural gas and power commodity markets.

Quantitative Evaluations

S&P Quality Ranking   NR

D	C	B-	B	B+	A-	A	A+

Relative Strength Rank   WEAK

16

LOWEST = 1   HIGHEST = 99

Revenue/Earnings Data

Revenue (Million $)

	1Q	2Q	3Q	4Q	Year
2010	2,215	2,133	--	--	--
2009	1,658	2,237	2,916	2,141	8,952
2008	1,302	1,316	2,612	1,655	6,885
2007	1,310	1,548	1,786	1,382	5,989
2006	1,075	1,404	2,000	1,144	5,623
2005	597.0	579.0	762.0	770.0	2,708

Earnings Per Share ($)

2010	0.22	0.81	E1.17	E0.49	E2.68
2009	0.70	1.56	1.02	0.11	3.44
2008	0.14	-0.22	2.65	0.98	3.66
2007	0.21	0.51	0.93	0.34	1.95
2006	0.02	0.62	1.17	-0.19	1.82
2005	0.10	0.10	-0.26	0.37	0.33

Fiscal year ended Dec. 31. Next earnings report expected: Late October. EPS Estimates based on S&P Operating Earnings; historical GAAP earnings are as reported.

Dividend Data

No cash dividends have been paid.

Please read the Required Disclosures and Analyst Certification on the last page of this report.

The McGraw-Hill Companies

NRG Energy Inc

STANDARD &POOR'S

Business Summary August 31, 2010

CORPORATE OVERVIEW. NRG Energy is a competitive wholesale power generation company that owns, operates, develops and builds generating facilities. As of December 2009, the company owned interests in 44 power projects, mostly in North America, with net generating capacity of 23,475 MW. In the U.S., NRG operates plants in Texas (11,340 MW), the Northeast (7,015 MW), South Central (2,855 MW) and the West (2,150 MW), and thermal capacity (115 MW) in Delaware and Pennsylvania. Internationally, NRG owns 1,005 net MW of generation in Australia and Germany. NRG also owns another 1,021 MW in seven steam and chilled water facilities in the U.S. The sale of capacity and power from baseload power plants accounts for the majority of NRG's revenues and provides a stable source of cash flow. As of December 2009, the company's U.S. generating capacity was fueled 46% by natural gas, 32% by coal, 16% by oil, 5% by nuclear, 1% by wind, and less than 0.1% by solar. About 9% of capacity had ability to use dual or multiple fuels. By dispatch type, 25% of capacity was peaking, 37% baseload, 37% intermediate, and 1% intermittent. In 2009, 88% of NRG's MW hours produced were from coal or nuclear power plants.

CORPORATE STRATEGY. NRG is pursuing opportunities to repower existing facilities and develop new generation capacity in markets in which it currently owns assets in an initiative referred to as Repowering NRG. The program consists of the development, construction and operation of new and enhanced power generation facilities at its existing sites, with an emphasis on new baseload capacity that is supported by long-term power sales agreements and financed with limited or non-recourse project financing. The company expects to achieve improved heat rates at existing facilities, lower delivered costs of electricity, increased overall capacity, an improvement in the firm's dispatch curve, better fuel diversity, and environmental enhancements.

In September 2007, NRG filed an application with the Nuclear Regulatory Commission (NRC) to build and operate two new advanced boiling water reactors (ABWR) at its South Texas Project nuclear plant. Together, the units will have an operating capacity of 2.7 GW (or 3.0 GW if an amendment to the license is approved), if approved and built. The ABWR design has already been certified for use in the U.S. by the NRC. These new units are part of its broader Repowering NRG strategy. NRG expects the plant to cost $3,229/kW. NRG is also developing renewable and non renewable generation and has made a few small acquisitions to support its renewables efforts.

Company Financials Fiscal Year Ended Dec. 31

Per Share Data ($)	2009	2008	2007	2006	2005	2004	2003	2002	2001	2000
Tangible Book Value	15.91	15.89	9.14	8.05	9.60	11.74	9.59	NA	NA	NA
Cash Flow	7.06	5.86	4.08	3.66	1.48	2.34	0.13	NA	1.22	0.92
Earnings	3.44	3.66	1.95	1.82	0.33	0.81	0.05	NA	0.68	0.55
S&P Core Earnings	3.14	3.67	1.92	1.67	0.45	0.86	NA	NA	NA	NA
Dividends	Nil	Nil	Nil	Nil	Nil	Nil	NA	NA	NA	NA
Payout Ratio	Nil	Nil	Nil	Nil	Nil	Nil	NA	NA	NA	NA
Prices:High	29.26	45.78	47.19	29.74	24.72	18.09	NA	NA	NA	NA
Prices:Low	15.19	14.39	23.03	20.90	15.15	9.59	NA	NA	NA	NA
P/E Ratio:High	9	13	24	16	75	22	NA	NA	NA	NA
P/E Ratio:Low	4	4	12	12	46	12	NA	NA	NA	NA

Income Statement Analysis (Million $)	2009	2008	2007	2006	2005	2004	2003	2002	2001	2000
Revenue	8,952	6,885	5,989	5,623	2,708	2,361	152	2,212	2,799	2,158
Operating Income	NA	2,922	2,201	1,438	445	754	33.7	NA	NA	NA
Depreciation	1,007	649	658	593	195	308	14.8	287	212	123
Interest Expense	634	620	689	786	253	341	21.6	494	444	294
Pretax Income	1,669	1,729	946	880	120	228	10.0	-3,078	305	287
Effective Tax Rate	43.6%	41.2%	39.9%	36.9%	35.8%	28.5%	NM	5.37%	11.0%	32.3%
Net Income	942	1,016	569	555	77.0	162	10.5	-2,908	265	183
S&P Core Earnings	829	967	507	460	77.2	172	3,357	-2,781	NA	NA

Balance Sheet & Other Financial Data (Million $)	2009	2008	2007	2006	2005	2004	2003	2002	2001	2000
Cash	2,304	1,494	1,161	795	506	1,223	738	385	186	95.2
Current Assets	6,208	8,492	3,562	3,083	2,197	2,118	2,114	1,486	1,187	673
Total Assets	23,378	24,808	19,274	19,435	7,431	7,830	9,261	10,884	12,895	5,979
Current Liabilities	3,762	6,581	2,277	2,032	1,356	1,088	2,026	9,797	1,951	563
Long Term Debt	7,746	7,704	7,895	8,647	2,581	3,254	1,213	1,193	7,844	3,651
Common Equity	7,536	6,256	4,612	5,055	1,825	2,286	2,437	-696	2,237	1,462
Total Capital	16,239	16,257	14,489	15,396	5,194	6,086	3,801	7,720	10,649	5,274
Capital Expenditures	734	899	481	221	106	114	10.6	1,504	1,472	310
Cash Flow	1,916	1,610	1,172	1,098	252	470	25.2	-2,621	478	306
Current Ratio	1.7	1.3	1.6	1.5	1.6	1.9	1.0	0.2	0.6	1.2
% Long Term Debt of Capitalization	47.7	47.4	54.5	56.2	49.7	53.5	31.9	NM	74.1	69.4
% Net Income of Revenue	10.5	14.8	9.5	9.9	2.8	6.9	6.9	NM	9.5	8.5
% Return on Assets	3.9	4.6	2.7	4.1	1.0	1.9	NA	NM	2.8	3.9
% Return on Equity	13.7	18.7	11.0	14.7	2.8	6.9	NA	NM	14.3	15.5

Data as orig reptd.; bef. results of disc opers/spec. items. Per share data adj. for stk. divs.; EPS diluted. E-Estimated. NA-Not Available. NM-Not Meaningful. NR-Not Ranked. UR-Under Review.

Office: 211 Carnegie Ctr, Princeton, NJ 08540-6213.
Telephone: 609-524-4500.
Website: http://www.nrgenergy.com
Chrmn: H.E. Cosgrove

Pres & CEO: D.W. Crane
COO & EVP: M. Gutierrez
EVP & CFO: C.S. Schade
EVP & Chief Admin Officer: D.M. Wilson

Investor Contact: K. Sullivan (612-373-8875)
Board Members: K. H. Caldwell, J. F. Chlebowski, Jr., L. S. Coben, H. E. Cosgrove, D. W. Crane, S. L. Cropper, W. E. Hantke, P. W. Hobby, G. Luterman, K. A. McGinty, A. Schaumburg, H. H. Tate, Jr., T. H. Weidemeyer, W. R. Young

Founded: 1992
Domicile: Delaware

The McGraw-Hill Companies

Nucor Corp

STANDARD
&POOR'S

S&P Recommendation BUY ★★★★☆	**Price** $37.88 (as of Oct 22, 2010)	**12-Mo. Target Price** $44.00	**Investment Style** Large-Cap Blend

GICS Sector Materials
Sub-Industry Steel

Summary The largest minimill steelmaker in the U.S., Nucor has one of the most diverse product lines of any steelmaker in the Americas.

Key Stock Statistics (Source S&P, Vickers, company reports)

52-Wk Range	$50.72– 35.71	S&P Oper. EPS 2010**E**	0.49	Market Capitalization(B)	$11.953	Beta	1.10
Trailing 12-Month EPS	$0.47	S&P Oper. EPS 2011**E**	2.97	Yield (%)	3.80	S&P 3-Yr. Proj. EPS CAGR(%)	NM
Trailing 12-Month P/E	80.6	P/E on S&P Oper. EPS 2010**E**	77.3	Dividend Rate/Share	$1.44	S&P Credit Rating	A
$10K Invested 5 Yrs Ago	$15,985	Common Shares Outstg. (M)	315.6	Institutional Ownership (%)	74		

Price Performance

30-Week Mov. Avg. · · · · 10-Week Mov. Avg. - - - **GAAP Earnings vs. Previous Year** Volume Above Avg. |||| STARS
12-Mo. Target Price ⎯ Relative Strength ⎯ ▲ Up ▼ Down ▶ No Change   Below Avg. |||| ★

Options: ASE, CBOE, P, Ph

Highlights

➤ The 12-month target price for NUE has recently been changed to $44.00 from $50.00. The Highlights section of this Stock Report will be updated accordingly.

Investment Rationale/Risk

➤ The Investment Rationale/Risk section of this Stock Report will be updated shortly. For the latest News story on NUE from MarketScope, see below.

➤ 10/21/10 04:53 pm ET ... S&P REITERATES BUY OPINION ON SHARES OF NUCOR CORP (NUE 37.89****): NUE posts Q3 EPS of $0.07, vs. a $0.10 loss, on a 33% sales increase, and short of our $0.10 estimate, as severe gross margin compression offset higher than expected sales. To reflect a more conservative assumption for future gross margin, we cut our '10 estimate to $0.49 from $0.85 and reduce our '11 estimate to $2.97 from $3.59. We lower our 12-month target price to $44 from $50, to adjust for the downward revision to '11's estimate. Our projected P/E on our revised '11 estimate represents a premium to the P/E we apply to the company's peers. /L.Larkin

Qualitative Risk Assessment

LOW	MEDIUM	HIGH

Our risk assessment reflects that despite Nucor's exposure to cyclical markets such as non-residential construction, the company has a solid share of the markets in which it competes, a very low ratio of total debt to assets, and a very diverse product mix.

Quantitative Evaluations

S&P Quality Ranking B

D	C	B-	B	B+	A-	A	A+

Relative Strength Rank WEAK

21

LOWEST = 1   HIGHEST = 99

Revenue/Earnings Data

Revenue (Million $)

	1Q	2Q	3Q	4Q	Year
2010	3,655	4,196	--	--	--
2009	2,654	2,478	3,120	2,938	11,190
2008	4,974	7,091	7,448	4,151	23,663
2007	3,769	4,168	4,259	4,397	16,593
2006	3,545	3,806	3,931	3,469	14,751
2005	3,323	3,145	3,026	3,207	12,701

Earnings Per Share ($)

	1Q	2Q	3Q	4Q	Year
2010	-0.10	0.29	E0.10	E0.03	E0.49
2009	-0.60	-0.43	-0.10	0.18	-0.94
2008	1.41	1.94	2.31	0.34	5.98
2007	1.26	1.14	1.29	1.26	4.94
2006	1.21	1.45	1.68	1.35	5.68
2005	1.10	1.02	0.93	1.09	4.13

Fiscal year ended Dec. 31. Next earnings report expected: Late October. EPS Estimates based on S&P Operating Earnings; historical GAAP earnings are as reported.

Dividend Data (Dates: mm/dd Payment Date: mm/dd/yy)

Amount ($)	Date Decl.	Ex-Div. Date	Stk. of Record	Payment Date
0.360	12/02	12/29	12/31	02/11/10
0.360	02/24	03/29	03/31	05/12/10
0.360	06/03	06/28	06/30	08/11/10
0.360	09/08	09/28	09/30	11/11/10

Dividends have been paid since 1973. Source: Company reports.

Nucor Corp

Business Summary September 16, 2010

CORPORATE OVERVIEW. Nucor is the largest U.S. minimill steelmaker. In 2009, production was 14.0 million tons, and outside shipments were 12.1 million tons.

CORPORATE STRATEGY. Nucor's growth strategy involves four initiatives. The first is to optimize existing operations. The second is to make strategic acquisitions. The third involves construction of new plants and development of new technologies for markets where the company believes it has a major cost advantage. The fourth initiative is to expand globally through joint ventures that leverage new technologies.

MARKET PROFILE. The primary factors affecting demand for steel products are economic growth in general and growth in demand for durable goods in particular. The two largest end markets for steel products in the U.S. are autos and construction. In 2009, these two markets accounted for 28.3% of shipments in the U.S. market. Other end markets include appliances, containers,

machinery, and oil and gas. Distributors, also known as service centers, accounted for 20.6% of industry shipments in the U.S. market in 2009. Distributors are the largest single market for the steel industry in the U.S. Because distributors sell to a wide variety of OEMs, it is impossible to trace the final destination of much of the industry's shipments. Consequently, demand for steel from the auto, construction and other industries may be higher than the shipment data would suggest. In terms of production, the size of the U.S. market was 64.2 million tons in 2009, and Nucor's market share was 21.8%. In the U.S. market, consumption decreased at a compound annual rate (CAGR) of 7.9% from 2000 through 2009. Global steel production was 1.22 billion metric tons in 2009, versus 1.33 billion metric tons in 2008.

Company Financials Fiscal Year Ended Dec. 31

Per Share Data ($)	2009	2008	2007	2006	2005	2004	2003	2002	2001	2000
Tangible Book Value	14.88	16.72	13.18	15.56	13.80	10.84	7.45	7.43	7.07	6.87
Cash Flow	0.87	7.78	6.38	7.05	5.43	4.72	1.36	1.50	1.29	1.74
Earnings	-0.94	5.98	4.94	5.68	4.13	3.51	0.20	0.52	0.36	0.95
S&P Core Earnings	-0.94	6.19	4.94	5.68	4.09	3.49	0.15	0.46	0.33	NA
Dividends	1.41	1.59	0.63	0.40	0.30	0.24	0.20	0.19	0.17	0.15
Payout Ratio	NM	27%	13%	7%	7%	7%	100%	37%	47%	16%
Prices:High	51.08	83.56	69.93	67.55	35.11	27.74	14.70	17.54	14.13	14.11
Prices:Low	29.84	25.25	41.62	33.63	22.78	13.04	8.76	9.00	8.36	7.38
P/E Ratio:High	NM	14	14	12	9	8	73	34	39	15
P/E Ratio:Low	NM	4	8	6	6	4	44	17	23	8

Income Statement Analysis (Million $)										
Revenue	11,190	23,663	16,593	14,751	12,701	11,377	6,266	4,802	4,139	4,586
Operating Income	372	3,849	2,980	3,240	2,497	2,216	468	601	469	737
Depreciation	566	549	428	364	375	383	364	307	289	259
Interest Expense	150	135	51.1	Nil	4.20	22.4	24.6	22.9	22.0	24.1
Pretax Income	-414	3,104	2,547	2,913	2,127	1,812	90.8	310	174	478
Effective Tax Rate	42.7%	30.9%	30.7%	32.1%	33.2%	33.6%	4.51%	22.0%	35.0%	35.0%
Net Income	-294	1,831	1,472	1,758	1,310	1,121	62.8	162	113	311
S&P Core Earnings	-296	1,895	1,472	1,758	1,296	1,114	47.9	143	101	NA

Balance Sheet & Other Financial Data (Million $)										
Cash	2,242	2,355	1,576	786	1,838	779	350	219	462	491
Current Assets	5,182	6,397	5,073	4,675	4,072	3,175	1,621	1,424	1,374	1,381
Total Assets	12,572	13,874	9,826	7,885	7,139	6,133	4,492	4,381	3,759	3,722
Current Liabilities	1,227	1,854	1,582	1,450	1,256	1,066	630	592	484	558
Long Term Debt	3,080	3,086	2,250	922	922	924	904	879	460	460
Common Equity	7,391	7,929	5,113	4,826	4,280	3,456	2,342	2,323	2,201	2,131
Total Capital	10,670	11,523	7,651	5,987	5,396	4,553	3,423	3,419	2,946	2,904
Capital Expenditures	391	1,019	520	338	331	286	215	244	261	415
Cash Flow	273	2,380	1,900	2,122	1,685	1,505	427	469	402	570
Current Ratio	4.2	3.5	3.2	3.2	3.2	3.0	2.6	2.4	2.8	2.5
% Long Term Debt of Capitalization	28.9	26.8	29.4	15.4	17.1	20.3	26.4	25.7	15.6	15.9
% Net Income of Revenue	NM	7.7	8.9	11.9	10.3	9.9	1.0	3.4	2.7	6.8
% Return on Assets	NM	15.5	16.6	23.4	19.7	21.1	1.4	4.0	3.0	8.3
% Return on Equity	NM	28.1	29.6	38.6	33.9	38.7	2.7	5.1	5.2	14.2

Data as orig reptd.; bef. results of disc opers/spec. items. Per share data adj. for stk. divs.; EPS diluted. E-Estimated. NA-Not Available. NM-Not Meaningful. NR-Not Ranked. UR-Under Review.

Office: 1915 Rexford Rd, Charlotte, NC 28211-3441.
Telephone: 704-366-7000.
Email: info@nucor.com
Website: http://www.nucor.com

Chrmn, Pres & CEO: D.R. DiMicco
COO: J.J. Ferriola
EVP, CFO & Treas: J.D. Frias
Chief Acctg Officer & Cntlr: M.D. Keller

Secy: A.R. Eagle
Board Members: P. C. Browning, C. C. Daley, Jr., D. R. DiMicco, H. B. Gantt, V. F. Haynes, J. D. Hlavacek, B. L. Kasriel, C. J. Kearney, J. H. Walker

Founded: 1940
Domicile: Delaware
Employees: 20,400

NVIDIA Corp

STANDARD &POOR'S

S&P Recommendation SELL ★ ★ ★ ★ ★

Price	**12-Mo. Target Price**	**Investment Style**
$11.80 (as of Oct 22, 2010)	$9.00	Large-Cap Growth

GICS Sector Information Technology
Sub-Industry Semiconductors

Summary This company develops and markets graphics processors for personal computers, workstations and mobile devices.

Key Stock Statistics (Source S&P, Vickers, company reports)

52-Wk Range	$18.96– 8.65	S&P Oper. EPS 2011**E**	0.24	Market Capitalization(B)	$6.773	Beta	1.60
Trailing 12-Month EPS	$0.42	S&P Oper. EPS 2012**E**	0.67	Yield (%)	Nil	S&P 3-Yr. Proj. EPS CAGR(%)	28
Trailing 12-Month P/E	28.1	P/E on S&P Oper. EPS 2011**E**	49.2	Dividend Rate/Share	Nil	S&P Credit Rating	NR
$10K Invested 5 Yrs Ago	$11,083	Common Shares Outstg. (M)	574.0	Institutional Ownership (%)	74		

Price Performance

30-Week Mov. Avg. · · ·   10-Week Mov. Avg. – – **GAAP Earnings vs. Previous Year**   Volume Above Avg. |||| STARS
12-Mo. Target Price —   Relative Strength   ▲ Up ▼ Down ► No Change   Below Avg. |||| ★

Options: ASE, CBOE, P, Ph

Analysis prepared by **Clyde Montevirgen** on September 23, 2010, when the stock traded at **$ 11.67**.

Highlights

➤ We see sales rising 7% in FY 11 (Jan.) and 6% in FY 12. We think long-term drivers, such as the growth of graphics-intensive applications and healthy PC demand, remain intact, and with NVDA's strong brand recognition and new product cycles, we believe it will be able to defend its share in the highest-end of the graphics markets while expanding its served available market size. But considering economic uncertainty, increasing lower-end PC sales, and share loss in notebook graphics, we see hurdles to growth over the near-term.

➤ We believe that gross margins will widen from a projected 38% in FY 11 to 45% in FY 12 as sales of higher-end graphics chips balance pricing pressure and anticipated inventory writedowns. We expect variable expenses to rise as sales improve, but we believe R&D expenses, as a percentage of sales, will moderate following heavy investments in new products over the last couple of years. All told, we see operating margins widening from 4% in FY 11 to 12% in FY 12.

➤ We project a 17% effective tax rate and include around $0.20 per share in stock based compensation.

Investment Rationale/Risk

➤ Our sell recommendation reflects our view of overextended multiples and relatively weak fundamentals. We believe that the softening PC demand environment and anticipated market share loss in notebooks will contribute to below-industry sales growth in coming quarters. Although we see margins widening due to an improving sales mix, we still expect profitability and return on equity to remain below their historical averages. Based on these factors, we think NVDA's relative multiples should be below the historical average and closer to the industry average, which is reflected in our valuation.

➤ Risks to our opinion and target price include better than anticipated desktop sales, faster than expected inventory digestion, and market share gains.

➤ Our 12-month target price of $9 is based on our price-to-earnings (P/E) analysis. We apply a multiple of about 13X, below the historical average and around the industry average to account for its relative profitability, growth, and returns, to our FY 12 EPS estimate.

Qualitative Risk Assessment

LOW	MEDIUM	HIGH

Our risk assessment reflects the cyclicality of the semiconductor industry and of demand trends for electronics goods that benefit from advanced visual displays, and revenue volatility resulting from wins and losses of deals with big accounts.

Quantitative Evaluations

S&P Quality Ranking   B-

D	C	B-	B	B+	A-	A	A+

Relative Strength Rank   STRONG

75

LOWEST = 1   HIGHEST = 99

Revenue/Earnings Data

Revenue (Million $)

	1Q	2Q	3Q	4Q	Year
2011	1,002	811.2	--	--	--
2010	664.2	776.5	903.2	982.5	3,326
2009	1,153	892.7	897.7	481.1	3,425
2008	844.3	935.3	1,116	1,203	4,098
2007	681.8	687.5	820.6	878.9	3,069
2006	583.9	574.8	583.4	633.6	2,376

Earnings Per Share ($)

2011	0.23	-0.25	E0.11	E0.14	E0.24
2010	-0.37	-0.19	0.19	0.23	-0.12
2009	0.30	-0.22	0.11	-0.27	-0.05
2008	0.22	-0.22	0.38	0.42	1.32
2007	0.15	0.15	0.18	0.27	0.77
2006	0.12	0.14	0.12	0.18	0.55

Fiscal year ended Jan. 31. Next earnings report expected: Early November. EPS Estimates based on S&P Operating Earnings; historical GAAP earnings are as reported.

Dividend Data

No cash dividends have been paid.

NVIDIA Corp

**STANDARD
&POOR'S**

Business Summary September 23, 2010

CORPORATE OVERVIEW. NVIDIA Corp. designs, develops and markets high-performance graphics processing units (GPUs), media and communications processors (MCPs), handheld GPUs, and related software for PCs and digital entertainment platforms, ranging from professional workstations to video game consoles to handheld electronic devices. The company's products are designed to generate realistic, interactive graphics on consumer and professional computing devices. It aims to be the leading supplier of performance GPUs, MCPs and handheld GPUs.

NVDA has four major product line operating segments: the graphics processing units business, the professional solutions business (PSB), the media and communications processor (MCP) business, and the consumer product business (CPB).

Interactive 3D graphics displays are an integral part of many computing applications for workstations, consumer and commercial desktop and laptop PCs, personal digital assistants, cellular phones, and gaming consoles. NVDA's products are designed into products offered by nearly all leading PC OEMs.

The company supplied graphics chips for Microsoft's Xbox video game console, but lost to rival AMD/ATI Technologies for the GPU for the next-generation Xbox. However, the company presently supplies GPU products for Sony's PlayStation 3 video game console.

CORPORATE STRATEGY. NVDA's goal is to become the leading supplier of performance GPUs, MCPs, and handheld GPUs and application processors. The elements behind the strategy include: building award-winning and architecturally compatible graphics and media products for various platforms; targeting leading OEMs, ODMs, and system builders; sustaining technology and product leadership in graphics and media products; increasing market share; creating synergy by combining expertise in graphics and media; and using its intellectual property and resources to enter into license and development contracts.

Company Financials Fiscal Year Ended Jan. 31

Per Share Data ($)	2010	2009	2008	2007	2006	2005	2004	2003	2002	2001
Tangible Book Value	3.87	3.49	4.35	3.32	2.52	2.08	1.83	1.81	1.52	0.93
Cash Flow	0.23	0.28	1.54	0.95	0.73	0.38	0.30	0.29	0.43	0.24
Earnings	-0.12	-0.05	1.32	0.77	0.55	0.19	0.14	0.18	0.34	0.21
S&P Core Earnings	-0.25	-0.05	1.31	0.79	0.42	0.03	-0.00	-0.22	0.10	0.12
Dividends	NA	Nil	Nil	Nil	Nil	Nil	Nil	Nil	Nil	Nil
Payout Ratio	Nil	Nil	Nil	Nil	Nil	Nil	Nil	Nil	Nil	Nil
Calendar Year	2009	2008	2007	2006	2005	2004	2003	2002	2001	2000
Prices:High	18.95	34.25	39.67	25.97	12.83	9.12	9.25	24.22	23.42	14.67
Prices:Low	7.08	5.75	18.69	11.45	6.82	3.10	3.11	2.40	4.71	2.92
P/E Ratio:High	NM	NM	30	34	23	48	65	NM	68	71
P/E Ratio:Low	NM	NM	14	15	12	16	22	NM	14	14

Income Statement Analysis (Million $)

	2010	2009	2008	2007	2006	2005	2004	2003	2002	2001
Revenue	3,326	3,425	4,098	3,069	2,376	2,010	1,823	1,909	1,369	735
Operating Income	29.1	334	976	593	452	216	172	202	299	146
Depreciation	197	185	136	108	98.0	103	82.0	58.2	43.5	15.7
Interest Expense	3.32	0.41	0.05	0.02	0.07	0.16	12.0	Nil	16.2	4.85
Pretax Income	-82.3	-43.0	901	494	360	125	86.7	151	253	147
Effective Tax Rate	17.4%	NM	11.5%	9.37%	16.0%	20.0%	14.1%	39.7%	30.0%	31.9%
Net Income	-68.0	-30.0	798	448	303	100	74.4	90.8	177	100
S&P Core Earnings	-140	-30.4	798	460	230	14.6	-1.44	-104	49.4	54.7

Balance Sheet & Other Financial Data (Million $)

	2010	2009	2008	2007	2006	2005	2004	2003	2002	2001
Cash	1,728	1,255	1,809	1,118	950	670	604	1,028	791	674
Current Assets	2,481	2,168	2,889	2,032	1,549	1,305	1,053	1,352	1,234	930
Total Assets	3,586	3,351	3,748	2,675	1,915	1,629	1,399	1,617	1,503	1,017
Current Liabilities	784	779	967	639	439	421	334	379	433	110
Long Term Debt	NA	25.6	Nil	Nil	Nil	Nil	0.86	305	306	300
Common Equity	2,665	2,395	2,618	2,007	1,458	1,178	1,051	933	764	406
Total Capital	2,665	2,420	2,705	2,007	1,466	1,199	1,061	1,238	1,070	706
Capital Expenditures	77.6	408	188	145	79.6	67.3	128	63.1	97.0	36.3
Cash Flow	129	155	933	556	401	203	156	149	220	114
Current Ratio	3.2	2.8	3.0	3.2	3.5	3.1	3.2	3.6	2.8	8.4
% Long Term Debt of Capitalization	Nil	1.1	Nil	Nil	Nil	Nil	0.1	24.6	28.6	42.4
% Net Income of Revenue	NM	NM	19.5	14.6	12.7	5.0	4.1	4.8	12.9	13.4
% Return on Assets	NM	NM	24.8	19.4	17.1	6.6	4.9	5.8	14.0	16.1
% Return on Equity	NM	NM	34.5	25.6	23.0	9.0	7.5	10.7	30.2	36.9

Data as orig reptd.; bef. results of disc opers/spec. items. Per share data adj. for stk. divs.; EPS diluted. E-Estimated. NA-Not Available. NM-Not Meaningful. NR-Not Ranked. UR-Under Review.

Office: 2701 San Tomas Expressway, Santa Clara, CA 95050.
Telephone: 408-486-2000.
Email: ir@nvidia.com
Website: http://www.nvidia.com

Pres & CEO: J. Huang
COO: D. Shoquist
EVP, CFO & Chief Acctg Officer: D.L. White
EVP, Secy & General Counsel: D.M. Shannon

CSO: B. Dally
Investor Contact: M. Hara (408-486-2511)
Board Members: T. Coxe, J. C. Gaither, J. Huang, H. C. Jones, Jr., W. J. Miller, M. L. Perry, B. Seawell, M. A. Stevens

Founded: 1993
Domicile: Delaware
Employees: 5,706

The *McGraw-Hill* Companies

NYSE Euronext

STANDARD &POOR'S

S&P Recommendation `HOLD` ★★★☆☆

Price	12-Mo. Target Price	Investment Style
$30.29 (as of Oct 22, 2010)	$34.00	Large-Cap Growth

GICS Sector Financials
Sub-Industry Specialized Finance

Summary This holding company operates six cash equities exchanges and six derivatives exchanges in six countries.

Key Stock Statistics (Source S&P, Vickers, company reports)

52-Wk Range	$34.82– 22.30	S&P Oper. EPS 2010**E**	2.49	Market Capitalization(B)	$7.906	Beta		1.65
Trailing 12-Month EPS	$2.34	S&P Oper. EPS 2011**E**	2.59	Yield (%)	3.96	S&P 3-Yr. Proj. EPS CAGR(%)		11
Trailing 12-Month P/E	12.9	P/E on S&P Oper. EPS 2010**E**	12.2	Dividend Rate/Share	$1.20	S&P Credit Rating		A+
$10K Invested 5 Yrs Ago	NA	Common Shares Outstg. (M)	261.0	Institutional Ownership (%)	67			

Price Performance

- 30-Week Mov. Avg. · · · ·
- 10-Week Mov. Avg. – –
- **GAAP Earnings vs. Previous Year**
- **Volume** Above Avg. STARS
- 12-Mo. Target Price —
- Relative Strength —
- ▲ Up ▼ Down ▶ No Change
- Below Avg.

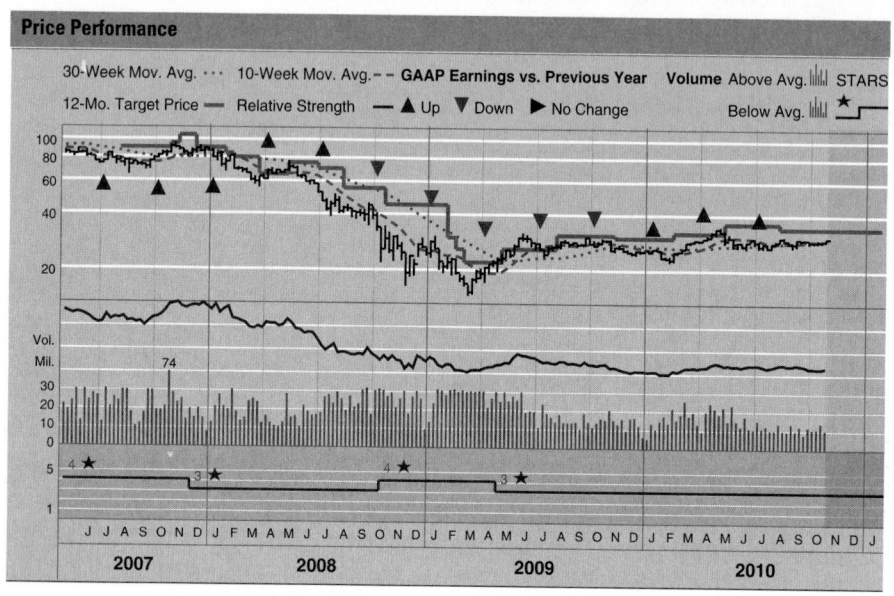

Analysis prepared by **Rafay Khalid, CFA** on August 17, 2010, when the stock traded at **$ 29.29**.

Highlights

➤ We project that revenues will increase 3.7% in 2010. Our outlook reflects our expectation for market share stabilization in the cash equities business in 2010, as the company is making significant progress reducing order execution times. In addition, we believe NYX's new initiatives will continue to generate revenue growth in 2010 and 2011. As a result, we forecast revenue growth of 3.0% in 2011.

➤ In 2010, we foresee the company's cost-cutting program helping to reduce fixed expenses, which exclude one-time items, liquidity payments, and routing fees. This should be partially offset by our forecast for an increase in other line items, such as liquidity payments and technology costs related to the new data center and other initiatives. We expect the company to keep a tight control over expenses in 2011. As a result, we see adjusted operating margins of 27.0% in 2010 and 27.6% in 2011, versus 21.4% in 2009.

➤ Our operating EPS estimates are $2.49 for 2010 and $2.59 for 2011, excluding one-time items. This compares to operating EPS of $2.04 in 2009. Our estimates assume a tax rate of 28% in 2010 and 2011.

Investment Rationale/Risk

➤ We believe NYX is taking the right steps to position itself for what we view as a globally competitive exchange environment, including initiatives such as its move to UTP-Direct, a universal trading platform; block trading in the U.S. and Europe; and the shift to the designated market maker model from the specialist model on the NYSE trading floor. We believe incentives to attract liquidity to NYX's exchanges may benefit it in the long term, once it has increased market share. However, we are concerned that NYX is still in a transition phase as more than 50% of the company's transaction volume still comes from lower-margin cash trading. We also see increased uncertainty from proposed government regulations, including stopping deposit-taking banks from proprietary trading.

➤ Risks to our recommendation and target price include execution risk related to growth initiatives, and lower than expected trading volumes.

➤ Our 12-month target price of $34 is based on a historical average P/E ratio of 13.2X our 2011 EPS forecast.

Qualitative Risk Assessment

LOW	MEDIUM	**HIGH**

Our risk assessment reflects the potential volatility in results due to changes in equity and equity options trading volumes, the impact of current and future regulatory changes, and the integration of a number of recent acquisitions.

Quantitative Evaluations

S&P Quality Ranking NR

D	C	B-	B	B+	A-	A	A+

Relative Strength Rank MODERATE

56

LOWEST = 1   HIGHEST = 99

Revenue/Earnings Data

Revenue (Million $)

	1Q	2Q	3Q	4Q	Year
2010	1,020	1,148	--	--	--
2009	1,112	1,125	1,048	1,014	4,299
2008	1,191	1,112	1,159	1,177	4,474
2007	702.0	1,078	1,198	1,180	3,602
2006	478.9	659.5	602.9	658.5	2,376
2005	282.8	262.5	301.9	301.9	1,667

Earnings Per Share ($)

2010	0.50	0.71	E0.54	E0.76	E2.49
2009	0.40	-0.70	0.48	0.66	0.84
2008	0.87	0.73	0.64	-5.08	-2.81
2007	0.43	0.62	0.97	0.59	2.70
2006	0.24	0.39	0.43	0.29	1.36
2005	--	--	0.01	-0.17	0.58

Fiscal year ended Dec. 31. Next earnings report expected: Early November. EPS Estimates based on S&P Operating Earnings; historical GAAP earnings are as reported.

Dividend Data (Dates: mm/dd Payment Date: mm/dd/yy)

Amount ($)	Date Decl.	Ex-Div. Date	Stk. of Record	Payment Date
0.300	05/01	12/11	12/15	12/31/09
0.300	12/03	03/11	03/15	03/31/10
0.300	04/29	06/11	06/15	06/30/10
0.300	07/30	09/13	09/15	09/30/10

Dividends have been paid since 2007. Source: Company reports.

Please read the Required Disclosures and Analyst Certification on the last page of this report.

The **McGraw·Hill** Companies

NYSE Euronext

Business Summary August 17, 2010

CORPORATE OVERVIEW. NYSE Euronext (NYX) is a holding company created by the combination of NYSE Group and Euronext on April 4, 2007. NYX operates the world's largest and most liquid exchange group and offers a diverse array of financial products and services. The company, which brings together six cash equities exchanges in five countries and six derivatives exchanges in six countries, offers listings, trading in cash equities, equity and interest rate derivatives, bonds and the distribution of market data. As of December 31, 2009, NYX had 3,981 combined listed companies. In addition, there were 326 new listings in 2009, and IPOs raised $87 billion on NYX's markets.

NYX generates revenue primarily from transactions, company listing fees, market data, regulatory fees, and exchange licenses. The company also records activity assessment revenue, which is a pass through netted against section 31 fee expense. We have excluded this revenue line item when examining NYX's revenue from operations. Following the combination of the NYSE with Archipelago (now NYSE Arca), transaction fees have become the largest revenue driver for NYX (69% of total revenue in 2009). Transaction revenue is generated from fees paid for trading on NYX's exchanges, and benefits from higher trading volumes. Listing fees (9.1%) include initial fees charged for

companies listing on one of NYX's exchanges and an ongoing annual listing fee. Market data is NYX's third largest revenue contributor (9.0%) and includes real time information related to price, transaction or order data of all instruments traded on the cash and derivatives markets on NYX's exchanges. We view transactional revenue as the key growth driver for NYX moving forward.

CORPORATE STRATEGY. We believe NYX is in the middle of a transformational phase as it fully integrates the NYSE Arca assets with the NYSE, transitions the NYSE from a floor-based trading system to a hybrid floor/electronic model, completes its merger with Euronext, and readies for significant regulatory and structural changes in U.S. and European equity and equity options trading. We expect the number and scope of ongoing projects and regulatory changes to likely make for uneven financial performance and difficult historical and peer comparisons over the coming quarters.

Company Financials Fiscal Year Ended Dec. 31

Per Share Data ($)	2009	2008	2007	2006	2005	2004	2003	2002	2001	2000
Tangible Book Value	NM	NM	NM	3.51	NA	NA	NA	NA	NA	NA
Cash Flow	1.99	-1.86	3.76	2.27	1.50	NA	NA	NA	NA	NA
Earnings	0.84	-2.81	2.70	1.36	0.58	NA	NA	NA	NA	NA
S&P Core Earnings	0.83	0.92	2.55	1.28	0.35	0.31	NA	NA	NA	NA
Dividends	1.20	1.15	0.75	Nil	NA	NA	NA	NA	NA	NA
Payout Ratio	143%	NM	28%	Nil	NA	NA	NA	NA	NA	NA
Prices:High	31.93	87.70	109.50	112.00	NA	NA	NA	NA	NA	NA
Prices:Low	14.52	16.33	64.26	48.62	NA	NA	NA	NA	NA	NA
P/E Ratio:High	38	NM	41	82	NA	NA	NA	NA	NA	NA
P/E Ratio:Low	17	NM	24	36	NA	NA	NA	NA	NA	NA

Income Statement Analysis (Million $)	2009	2008	2007	2006	2005	2004	2003	2002	2001	2000
Revenue	4,299	4,474	4,158	2,376	1,667	1,044	1,034	1,018	1,035	NA
Operating Income	1,104	1,403	1,228	424	3.18	130	115	56.6	53.3	NA
Depreciation	301	253	252	136	143	95.7	67.6	61.9	60.6	NA
Interest Expense	122	150	129	Nil	Nil	NA	NA	NA	NA	NA
Pretax Income	205	-645	921	328	176	NA	87.3	42.1	52.8	NA
Effective Tax Rate	NM	NM	27.5%	36.7%	47.6%	NA	41.7%	27.8%	33.6%	NA
Net Income	219	-745	643	205	90.0	NA	49.6	28.1	31.8	NA
S&P Core Earnings	215	244	609	193	54.1	42.3	NA	NA	NA	NA

Balance Sheet & Other Financial Data (Million $)	2009	2008	2007	2006	2005	2004	2003	2002	2001	2000
Cash	490	1,013	973	298	328	930	880	963	963	NA
Current Assets	1,520	2,026	2,278	1,443	1,204	1,245	1,223	1,156	1,168	NA
Total Assets	14,358	13,948	16,618	3,466	3,154	NA	1,777	1,757	1,730	NA
Current Liabilities	2,149	2,582	3,462	832	823	487	416	340	390	NA
Long Term Debt	2,166	1,787	522	Nil	Nil	NA	NA	NA	NA	NA
Common Equity	6,935	6,556	9,384	1,669	1,366	NA	952	896	882	NA
Total Capital	9,101	8,770	12,469	1,934	1,646	801	983	921	910	NA
Capital Expenditures	497	376	182	97.8	NA	84.6	68.5	113	89.0	NA
Cash Flow	520	-492	895	341	233	126	117	89.9	92.4	NA
Current Ratio	0.7	0.8	0.7	1.7	1.5	2.6	2.9	3.4	3.0	NA
% Long Term Debt of Capitalization	23.8	21.4	4.2	Nil	Nil	Nil	Nil	Nil	Nil	NA
% Net Income of Revenue	5.1	NM	15.5	8.6	5.4	2.9	4.8	2.8	3.1	NA
% Return on Assets	1.6	NM	6.4	7.2	NA	1.6	2.8	1.6	NA	NA
% Return on Equity	3.3	NM	11.6	16.6	NA	3.5	5.4	3.2	NA	NA

Data as orig reptd.; bef. results of disc opers/spec. items. Per share data adj. for stk. divs.; EPS diluted. E-Estimated. NA-Not Available. NM-Not Meaningful. NR-Not Ranked. UR-Under Review.

Office: 11 Wall Street, New York, NY 10005.
Telephone: 212-656-3000.
Website: http://www.nyse.com
Chrmn: J.M. Hessels

Pres: D. Cerutti
Vice Chrmn: M.N. Carter
CEO: D.L. Niederauer
COO: L. Leibowitz

Investor Contact: S.C. Davidson (212-656-2183)
Board Members: A. Bergen, E. L. Brown, M. N. Carter, P. M. Cloherty, G. Cox, S. M. Hefes, J. M. Hessels, D. M. McFarland, J. J. McNulty, D. L. Niederauer, R. S. Salgado, R. G. Scott, J. Tai, J. Theodore, R. W. Van Tets, B. Williamson

Founded: 2006
Domicile: Delaware
Employees: 3,367

Occidental Petroleum Corp

STANDARD &POOR'S

S&P Recommendation BUY ★★★★☆	Price $79.58 (as of Oct 22, 2010)	12-Mo. Target Price $96.00	Investment Style Large-Cap Blend

GICS Sector Energy
Sub-Industry Integrated Oil & Gas

Summary As one of the largest oil and gas companies in the U.S., OXY has global exploration and production operations. Its subsidiary, OxyChem, is one of the largest U.S. merchant marketers of chlorine and caustic soda.

Key Stock Statistics (Source S&P, Vickers, company reports)

52-Wk Range	$90.99– 72.13	S&P Oper. EPS 2010E	5.62	Market Capitalization(B)	$64.638
Trailing 12-Month EPS	$5.23	S&P Oper. EPS 2011E	7.24	Yield (%)	1.91
Trailing 12-Month P/E	15.2	P/E on S&P Oper. EPS 2010E	14.2	Dividend Rate/Share	$1.52
$10K Invested 5 Yrs Ago	$24,436	Common Shares Outstg. (M)	812.2	Institutional Ownership (%)	81

Beta	0.97
S&P 3-Yr. Proj. EPS CAGR(%)	37
S&P Credit Rating	A

Price Performance

30-Week Mov. Avg. · · · 10-Week Mov. Avg. – – GAAP Earnings vs. Previous Year   Volume Above Avg. ⣿ STARS
12-Mo. Target Price — Relative Strength   ▲ Up ▼ Down ▶ No Change   Below Avg. ⣿

Options: ASE, CBOE, P, Ph

Analysis prepared by **Tina J. Vital** on October 20, 2010, when the stock traded at **$ 81.20**.

Highlights

▶ Third quarter oil and gas production rose 6.5% to 751,000 boe per day, in line with our estimate, reflecting contributions from the Middle East and North Africa. OXY is shifting towards more oil production and is reevaluating 2011 U.S. natural gas drilling plans due to low U.S. natural gas prices. Still, we look for overall volumes to rise about 19% in 2010, averaging 767,000 boe per day, driven by fields in the U.S. (California and Permian Basin) and international regions, and about 9% annual growth between 2010 and 2014.

▶ Oil and gas cash production costs rose to $10.25 per boe in the 2010 first nine months, up from $9.37 for the full year 2009, on the expensing of injected carbon dioxide beginning in 2010; we look for fourth quarter levels to be near those of the third quarter. Chemical earnings were hurt by narrowed caustic soda margins in the 2010 first half, but we look for modest improvement in the second half of the year.

▶ We expect after-tax operating earnings to rise about 48% in 2010 and 29% in 2011, on expectations of strong production growth and widened margins on improved demand.

Investment Rationale/Risk

▶ With an oil focus and no refining, a solid pipeline of development projects, and a strong balance sheet, we expect OXY to benefit in the long term based on our forecast for higher oil prices. Oil and gas operations are the core of OXY's business, driven by strong prospects in long-lived reserves in California (with virtually no royalties) and the Permian Basin, with potential contributions from international developments in Bahrain, Oman, Libya, Argentina, and Iraq. OXY projects U.S. oil and gas production growth of about 10.9% per annum between 2010 and 2014, and international growth of 7.4% over the same period.

▶ Risks to our recommendation and target price include negative changes in economic, industry, and operating conditions, including geopolitical risk and difficulty replacing reserves.

▶ Blending our discounted cash flow valuation (which is $97 per share, assuming a WACC of 9.6% and terminal growth of 3%) and relative valuations, our 12-month target price is $96 per share, which represents an expected enterprise value of 5.6X our 2011 EBITDA estimate, a premium to the peer average.

Qualitative Risk Assessment

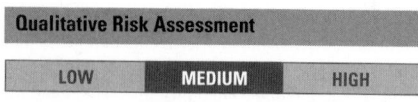

LOW	MEDIUM	HIGH

Our risk assessment reflects our view of OXY's strong business profile and modest financial risk profile. The company has a large, geographically diverse reserve base, predictable production, and substantial liquidity. However, we believe its strengths are limited by participation in volatile, competitive, and capital-intensive businesses, and a penchant for debt-financed acquisitions.

Quantitative Evaluations

S&P Quality Ranking   A-

D	C	B-	B	B+	A-	A	A+

Relative Strength Rank   MODERATE

33

LOWEST = 1   HIGHEST = 99

Revenue/Earnings Data

Revenue (Million $)

	1Q	2Q	3Q	4Q	Year
2010	4,771	4,761	4,896	--	--
2009	3,073	3,687	4,104	4,539	15,403
2008	6,020	7,116	7,060	4,021	24,217
2007	4,015	4,411	4,841	5,517	18,784
2006	4,396	4,599	4,522	4,144	17,661
2005	3,303	3,518	4,057	4,330	15,208

Earnings Per Share ($)

	1Q	2Q	3Q	4Q	Year
2010	1.32	1.31	1.47	E1.52	E5.62
2009	0.45	0.84	1.14	1.16	3.59
2008	2.20	2.79	2.78	0.55	8.33
2007	1.38	1.36	1.57	1.74	6.05
2006	1.34	1.39	1.35	1.08	5.15
2005	1.04	1.89	2.12	1.40	6.45

Fiscal year ended Dec. 31. Next earnings report expected: Late January. EPS Estimates based on S&P Operating Earnings; historical GAAP earnings are as reported.

Dividend Data (Dates: mm/dd Payment Date: mm/dd/yy)

Amount ($)	Date Decl.	Ex-Div. Date	Stk. of Record	Payment Date
0.330	02/11	03/08	03/10	04/15/10
0.380	05/06	06/08	06/10	07/15/10
0.380	07/15	09/08	09/10	10/15/10
0.380	10/14	12/08	12/10	01/15/11

Dividends have been paid since 1975. Source: Company reports.

Please read the Required Disclosures and Analyst Certification on the last page of this report.

Occidental Petroleum Corp

STANDARD &POOR'S

Business Summary October 20, 2010

CORPORATE OVERVIEW. One of the largest oil and gas companies in the U.S., Occidental Petroleum Corp. (OXY) engages in oil and gas exploration and production in three main regions: the U.S. (61% of 2009 net sales), the Middle East/North Africa (26%), and Latin America (10%). OxyChem, a wholly owned subsidiary, manufactures and markets chlor-alkali products and vinyls, and is one of the largest merchant marketers of chlorine and caustic soda in the U.S.

OXY's businesses operate in three segments: Oil and Gas (73% of 2009 net sales; 88% of 2009 earnings), Chemicals (20%; 7%), and Midstream, Marketing and Other (7%; 5%).

The Oil and Gas segment explores for, develops, produces and markets crude oil and natural gas. Oil and gas sales volumes rose 6.6%, to 643,000 boe per day (76% liquids), in 2009. Proved oil and gas reserves rose 8.3%, to 3.2 billion barrels of oil equivalent (boe; 77% developed, 73% liquids) at year-end 2009. Using data from John S. Herold, an industry research firm, we estimate OXY's three-year (2006-08) proved acquisition costs at $10.74 per boe, below the peer average; three-year finding and development costs at $27.56 per boe, above peers; three-year reserve replacement costs at $18.35, below peers; and three-year reserve replacement at 168%, below the peer average. We es-

timate OXY's 2009 overall reserve replacement at 206% (organic reserve replacement at 138%).

OxyChem manufactures and markets basic chemicals, vinyls, and performance chemicals, focused on the chlorovinyls chain beginning with chlorine. As of year-end 2009, the company owned and operated chemical plants at 22 domestic sites in the U.S., and at three international sites in Brazil, Canada and Chile. In 2009, OxyChem acquired Dow Chemical Co.'s calcium chloride operations, the world's largest.

MARKET PROFILE. OXY's oil and gas operations are focused on large, long-lived "legacy" oil and gas assets, such as those in Elk Hills in California (OXY is the number one natural gas producer in California, and the number two oil producer, as of year-end 2009) and the Permian Basin (OXY is the largest oil producer in the Permian Basin, as well as in the state of Texas, as of year-end 2009).

Company Financials Fiscal Year Ended Dec. 31

Per Share Data ($)	2009	2008	2007	2006	2005	2004	2003	2002	2001	2000
Tangible Book Value	35.82	33.69	27.63	22.84	18.69	13.30	10.25	8.35	7.53	6.45
Cash Flow	7.43	12.31	8.86	7.71	8.26	4.93	3.56	2.87	2.88	3.35
Earnings	3.59	8.33	6.05	5.15	6.45	3.25	2.06	1.54	1.59	2.13
S&P Core Earnings	3.63	8.28	5.19	4.97	5.78	3.26	2.03	1.28	1.70	NA
Dividends	1.31	1.21	0.94	NA	0.65	0.41	0.52	0.50	0.50	0.50
Payout Ratio	36%	15%	16%	NA	10%	13%	25%	33%	32%	23%
Prices:High	85.20	100.04	79.25	NA	44.90	30.38	21.49	15.38	15.55	12.78
Prices:Low	47.50	39.93	42.06	NA	27.09	20.98	13.59	11.49	10.94	7.88
P/E Ratio:High	24	12	13	NA	7	9	10	10	10	6
P/E Ratio:Low	13	5	7	NA	4	6	7	7	7	4

Income Statement Analysis (Million $)	2009	2008	2007	2006	2005	2004	2003	2002	2001	2000
Revenue	15,403	24,217	18,784	17,661	15,208	11,368	9,326	7,338	13,985	13,574
Operating Income	NA	14,652	10,044	9,664	7,860	5,573	4,281	3,119	3,638	3,826
Depreciation, Depletion and Amortization	3,117	3,267	2,356	2,042	1,485	1,303	1,177	1,012	971	901
Interest Expense	109	26.0	396	291	293	260	332	295	392	518
Pretax Income	4,845	11,468	8,660	8,012	7,365	4,389	2,884	1,662	1,892	3,196
Effective Tax Rate	39.6%	40.4%	40.5%	43.3%	27.4%	38.9%	42.5%	25.4%	29.8%	45.1%
Net Income	2,927	6,839	5,078	4,435	5,272	2,606	1,595	1,163	1,186	1,569
S&P Core Earnings	2,954	6,803	4,360	4,280	4,729	2,607	1,568	963	1,273	NA

Balance Sheet & Other Financial Data (Million $)	2009	2008	2007	2006	2005	2004	2003	2002	2001	2000
Cash	1,230	1,777	1,964	1,339	2,189	1,449	683	146	199	97.0
Current Assets	8,086	7,172	8,595	6,006	6,574	4,431	2,474	1,873	1,483	2,067
Total Assets	44,229	41,537	36,519	32,355	26,108	21,391	18,168	16,548	17,850	19,414
Current Liabilities	6,092	6,134	6,266	4,724	4,280	3,423	2,526	2,235	1,890	2,740
Long Term Debt	2,557	2,073	1,742	2,619	2,873	3,345	3,993	4,452	4,528	5,658
Common Equity	29,081	27,300	22,823	19,184	15,032	10,550	7,929	6,318	5,634	4,774
Total Capital	31,955	32,058	26,923	24,470	19,207	15,470	13,235	12,085	13,489	13,977
Capital Expenditures	5,363	9,365	3,497	3,005	2,423	1,843	1,601	1,236	1,401	952
Cash Flow	6,044	10,106	7,434	6,477	6,757	3,909	2,772	2,175	2,157	2,470
Current Ratio	1.3	1.2	1.4	1.3	1.5	1.3	1.0	0.8	0.8	0.8
% Long Term Debt of Capitalization	Nil	6.5	6.5	10.7	15.0	21.6	30.2	36.8	33.6	40.5
% Return on Assets	6.8	17.5	14.7	15.2	22.2	13.2	9.2	6.8	6.4	9.4
% Return on Equity	NA	27.3	24.2	25.9	41.2	28.2	22.4	19.5	22.8	37.8

Data as orig reptd.; bef. results of disc opers/spec. items. Per share data adj. for stk. divs.; EPS diluted. E-Estimated. NA-Not Available. NM-Not Meaningful. NR-Not Ranked. UR-Under Review.

Office: 10889 Wilshire Boulevard, Los Angeles, CA 90024-4201.
Telephone: 310-208-8800.
Email: investorrelations_newyork@oxy.com
Website: http://www.oxy.com

Chrmn & CEO: R.R. Irani
Pres & COO: S.I. Chazen
EVP & CFO: J.M. Lienert
EVP, Secy & General Counsel: D.P. de Brier

Chief Acctg Officer & Cntlr: R. Pineci
Investor Contact: C.G. Stavros (212-603-8184)
Board Members: S. Abraham, H. I. Atkins, J. S. Chalsty, S. I. Chazen, E. P. Djerejian, J. E. Feick, C. M. Gutierrez, R. R. Irani, I. W. Maloney, A. B. Poladian, R. Segovia, A. R. Syriani, R. Tomich, W. L. Weisman

Founded: 1920
Domicile: Delaware
Employees: 10,100

The McGraw·Hill Companies

Office Depot Inc

STANDARD &POOR'S

S&P Recommendation SELL ★ ★ ★ ★ ★	

Price	12-Mo. Target Price	Investment Style
$4.79 (as of Oct 25, 2010)	$4.00	Large-Cap Growth

GICS Sector Consumer Discretionary
Sub-Industry Specialty Stores

Summary Office Depot is a leading operator of office products superstores and mail order catalogs.

Key Stock Statistics (Source S&P, Vickers, company reports)

52-Wk Range	$9.19–3.36	S&P Oper. EPS 2010E	-0.05	Market Capitalization(B)	$1.322	Beta	3.29
Trailing 12-Month EPS	$-1.78	S&P Oper. EPS 2011E	-0.02	Yield (%)	Nil	S&P 3-Yr. Proj. EPS CAGR(%)	NM
Trailing 12-Month P/E	NM	P/E on S&P Oper. EPS 2010E	NM	Dividend Rate/Share	Nil	S&P Credit Rating	B
$10K Invested 5 Yrs Ago	$1,825	Common Shares Outstg. (M)	276.0	Institutional Ownership (%)	75		

Price Performance

30-Week Mov. Avg. · · · ·   10-Week Mov. Avg. - - -   **GAAP Earnings vs. Previous Year**   Volume Above Avg. ▊▊▍ STARS
12-Mo. Target Price —   Relative Strength —   ▲ Up ▼ Down ▶ No Change   Below Avg. ▏▏▏ ★

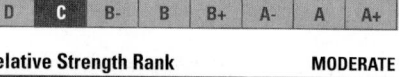

Options: ASE, CBOE, P, Ph

Analysis prepared by **Michael Souers** on July 28, 2010, when the stock traded at **$ 4.40**.

Highlights

➤ We expect sales to fall 3.0% this year, following a 16% decrease in 2009. We forecast a slight decline in same-store sales following a 14% drop in 2009, as spending conditions for consumers and small businesses remain challenging. We look for a modest decrease in sales in the U.S. contract business on weak business spending and our belief that ODP has been more selective in signing accounts in an attempt to increase profitability.

➤ We project a modest widening of gross margins in 2010, reflecting inventory optimization, a reduction in promotional activity and increased private label sales, slightly offset by a product mix shift to lower-margin goods. We expect ODP's operating margins to widen slightly on gross margin improvement and cost control, partially offset by expense de-leveraging from weak same-store sales.

➤ We estimate a net loss of $0.10 per share in 2010, a modest improvement from the $0.26 loss per share the company incurred in 2009, excluding $2.04 in charges for deferred tax asset valuation and writedowns related to store closures and other restructuring charges. We see a net loss of $0.02 in 2011.

Investment Rationale/Risk

➤ We think the loss of market share and macro-related challenges have created an overhang of uncertainty. While we believe the company has sufficient liquidity to weather a multi-year economic downturn given current credit availability and the recent cash infusion by private equity firm BC Partners ($350 million of convertible preferred stock), we do not foresee any positive catalyst for the shares. We are also concerned that the retail market for office supply stores has reached saturation levels, providing little opportunity for future growth. We think the significant share price increase from the lows set in early 2009 has been overdone, given the multitude of risks we foresee.

➤ Risks to our recommendation and target price include a greater-than-expected increase in capital spending by businesses, solid same-store sales gains in ODP's North American Retail division, and favorable currency fluctuations.

➤ Our 12-month target price of $4.00 is based on our DCF analysis, which assumes a weighted average cost of capital of 9.7% and a terminal growth rate of 3.0%.

Qualitative Risk Assessment

LOW	MEDIUM	HIGH

Our risk assessment reflects the cyclical nature of the office supply retailing industry, which is highly dependent on consumer and business spending, and the company's considerable exposure to international markets.

Quantitative Evaluations

S&P Quality Ranking   C

D	C	B-	B	B+	A-	A	A+

Relative Strength Rank   MODERATE

64

LOWEST = 1   HIGHEST = 99

Revenue/Earnings Data

Revenue (Million $)

	1Q	2Q	3Q	4Q	Year
2010	3,072	2,699	--	--	--
2009	3,225	2,824	3,029	3,066	12,144
2008	3,962	3,605	3,658	3,271	14,496
2007	4,094	3,632	3,935	3,867	15,528
2006	3,816	3,495	3,857	3,843	15,011
2005	3,703	3,364	3,493	3,719	14,279

Earnings Per Share ($)

	1Q	2Q	3Q	4Q	Year
2010	0.07	-0.07	E0.03	E-0.08	E-0.05
2009	-0.20	-0.31	-1.51	-0.28	-2.30
2008	0.25	-0.01	-0.02	-5.64	-5.42
2007	0.55	0.38	0.43	0.07	1.43
2006	0.43	0.41	0.47	0.48	1.79
2005	0.37	0.31	-0.15	0.34	0.87

Fiscal year ended Dec. 31. Next earnings report expected: Late October. EPS Estimates based on S&P Operating Earnings; historical GAAP earnings are as reported.

Dividend Data

No cash dividends have been paid.

Please read the Required Disclosures and Analyst Certification on the last page of this report.

The **McGraw·Hill** Companies

Office Depot Inc

STANDARD &POOR'S

Business Summary July 28, 2010

CORPORATE OVERVIEW. Office Depot is a global supplier of office products and services. It generated net sales of $12.1 billion in 2009 from customers and businesses of all sizes through three business segments: the North American Retail division (42% of revenues), the North American Business Solutions division (29%), and the International division (29%). Sales by product group were as follows: supplies 66%; technology 22%; and furniture and other 12%.

At January 23, 2010, ODP's North American Retail division operated 1,130 office supply stores in 46 states, the District of Columbia, Puerto Rico and Canada. North American Retail sells a broad assortment of merchandise, including brand name and private brand office supplies, business machines and computers, computer software, office furniture, and other business-related products through its chain of office supply stores. Most stores also contain a copy and print center that offers printing, reproduction, mailing, shipping, and other services. Also, ODP maintains the national availability of a PC support and network installation service that provides customers with in-home, in-office and in-store support for their technology needs. ODP plans to add approximately 20 new retail stores in North America in 2010, after closing 115 net underperforming stores in 2009 (as part of a strategic review initiated during the

fourth quarter of 2008).

ODP's North American Business Solutions division provides office supply products and services directly to businesses, selling branded and private label products by means of a dedicated sales force, through catalogs, and electronically through its Internet sites. Its direct business is tailored to serve small- to medium-sized customers, while its contract business serves the office supply needs of predominantly medium-sized to Fortune 100 customers.

ODP's International division served customers in 51 countries throughout North America, Europe, Asia and Latin America through 137 wholly owned or majority-owned stores and 195 additional stores operating under licensing and joint venture agreements as of December 31, 2009. It also participates in 100 franchised stores in South Korea, Thailand and the Middle East.

Company Financials Fiscal Year Ended Dec. 31

Per Share Data ($)	2009	2008	2007	2006	2005	2004	2003	2002	2001	2000
Tangible Book Value	2.71	4.78	6.20	5.11	6.26	6.96	5.77	6.61	5.28	4.66
Cash Flow	-1.48	-4.49	2.46	2.76	1.72	1.92	1.75	1.59	1.27	0.86
Earnings	-2.30	-5.42	1.43	1.79	0.87	1.06	0.96	0.98	0.66	0.16
S&P Core Earnings	-2.22	-0.95	1.42	1.74	0.86	1.03	0.91	0.92	0.58	NA
Dividends	Nil	Nil	Nil	Nil	Nil	Nil	Nil	Nil	Nil	Nil
Payout Ratio	Nil	Nil	Nil	Nil	Nil	Nil	Nil	Nil	Nil	Nil
Prices:High	7.84	15.54	39.66	46.52	31.76	19.50	18.50	21.96	18.70	14.88
Prices:Low	0.59	1.45	13.08	30.64	16.50	13.87	10.28	10.60	7.13	5.88
P/E Ratio:High	NM	NM	28	26	37	18	19	22	28	93
P/E Ratio:Low	NM	NM	9	17	19	13	11	11	11	37

Income Statement Analysis (Million $)	2009	2008	2007	2006	2005	2004	2003	2002	2001	2000
Revenue	12,144	14,496	15,528	15,011	14,279	13,565	12,359	11,357	11,154	11,570
Operating Income	212	266	797	998	750	799	719	707	562	433
Depreciation	224	254	282	279	268	269	248	201	199	206
Interest Expense	65.6	68.3	63.1	40.8	32.4	61.1	54.8	46.2	44.3	33.9
Pretax Income	-311	-1,578	459	727	362	461	445	479	314	92.5
Effective Tax Rate	NM	NM	13.7%	29.0%	24.3%	27.3%	32.1%	35.0%	36.0%	46.6%
Net Income	-596	-1,479	396	516	274	336	302	311	201	49.3
S&P Core Earnings	-607	-260	392	500	270	327	286	292	178	NA

Balance Sheet & Other Financial Data (Million $)	2009	2008	2007	2006	2005	2004	2003	2002	2001	2000
Cash	660	156	223	174	703	794	791	877	563	151
Current Assets	3,206	3,122	3,716	3,455	3,530	3,916	3,577	3,210	2,806	2,699
Total Assets	4,890	5,268	7,257	6,570	6,099	6,767	6,145	4,766	4,332	4,196
Current Liabilities	2,428	2,626	2,973	2,970	2,469	2,618	2,277	1,992	2,102	1,908
Long Term Debt	663	689	607	571	569	584	829	412	318	598
Common Equity	786	1,363	3,084	2,610	2,739	3,223	2,794	2,297	1,848	1,601
Total Capital	1,807	1,770	3,707	3,197	3,308	3,957	3,868	2,774	2,230	2,200
Capital Expenditures	131	369	461	343	261	391	212	202	207	268
Cash Flow	-403	-1,225	678	795	542	605	550	512	400	255
Current Ratio	1.3	1.2	1.3	1.2	1.4	1.5	1.6	1.6	1.3	1.4
% Long Term Debt of Capitalization	36.7	38.9	16.4	17.9	17.2	14.8	21.4	14.9	14.2	27.2
% Net Income of Revenue	NM	NM	2.6	3.4	1.9	2.5	2.4	2.7	1.8	0.4
% Return on Assets	NM	NM	5.7	8.1	4.2	5.2	5.5	6.8	4.7	1.2
% Return on Equity	NM	NM	13.9	19.3	9.2	11.2	11.9	15.0	11.7	2.8

Data as orig reptd.; bef. results of disc opers/spec. items. Per share data adj. for stk. divs.; EPS diluted. E-Estimated. NA-Not Available. NM-Not Meaningful. NR-Not Ranked. UR-Under Review.

Office: 6600 N Military Trl, Boca Raton, FL 33496-2434.
Telephone: 561-438-4800.
Email: investor.relations@officedepot.com
Website: http://www.officedepot.com

Chrmn & CEO: S. Odland
EVP & CFO: M.D. Newman
EVP, Secy & General Counsel: E.D. Garcia
SVP, Chief Acctg Officer & Cntlr: M.E. Hutchens

SVP & CIO: T. Toews
Investor Contact: B. Turcotte (561-438-3657)
Board Members: L. A. Ault, III, N. R. Austrian, J. Bateman, D. W. Bernauer, T. J. Colligan, M. J. Evans, D. I. Fuente, B. J. Gaines, M. M. Hart, W. Hedrick, K. Mason, S. Odland, J. S. Rubin, R. Svider

Founded: 1986
Domicile: Delaware
Employees: 41,000

Omnicom Group Inc.

S&P Recommendation BUY ★★★★☆	Price $43.23 (as of Oct 22, 2010)	12-Mo. Target Price $47.00	Investment Style Large-Cap Growth

GICS Sector Consumer Discretionary
Sub-Industry Advertising

Summary This company owns the DDB Worldwide, BBDO Worldwide and TBWA Worldwide advertising agency networks; and more than 100 marketing and specialty services firms.

Key Stock Statistics (Source S&P, Vickers, company reports)

52-Wk Range	$44.08–33.50	S&P Oper. EPS 2010**E**	2.71	Market Capitalization(B)	$13.028	Beta		1.12
Trailing 12-Month EPS	$2.56	S&P Oper. EPS 2011**E**	3.06	Yield (%)	1.85	S&P 3-Yr. Proj. EPS CAGR(%)		13
Trailing 12-Month P/E	16.9	P/E on S&P Oper. EPS 2010**E**	16.0	Dividend Rate/Share	$0.80	S&P Credit Rating		BBB+
$10K Invested 5 Yrs Ago	$11,943	Common Shares Outstg. (M)	301.4	Institutional Ownership (%)	86			

Price Performance

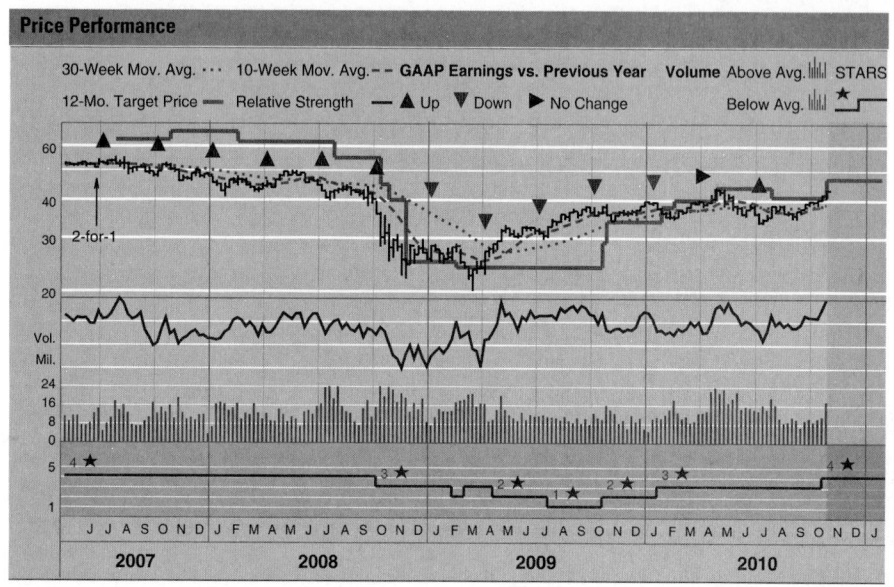

30-Week Mov. Avg. · · · 10-Week Mov. Avg. − − GAAP Earnings vs. Previous Year Volume Above Avg. |ılıl STARS
12-Mo. Target Price — Relative Strength — ▲ Up ▼ Down ▶ No Change Below Avg. |ılıl ★

2007 2008 2009 2010

Options: ASE, CBOE, P, Ph

Qualitative Risk Assessment

LOW	MEDIUM	HIGH

Our risk assessment primarily reflects a highly competitive advertising industry, partly offset by OMC's diversified geographic and product revenue sources coupled with its position as the world's largest advertising agency by revenue, and our view of its strong track record of EPS and free cash flow growth.

Quantitative Evaluations

S&P Quality Ranking   A+

D	C	B-	B	B+	A-	A	A+

Relative Strength Rank   STRONG

83

LOWEST = 1   HIGHEST = 99

Revenue/Earnings Data

Revenue (Million $)

	1Q	2Q	3Q	4Q	Year
2010	2,920	3,041	--	--	--
2009	2,747	2,871	2,838	3,266	11,721
2008	3,195	3,477	3,316	3,371	13,360
2007	2,841	3,126	3,101	3,626	12,694
2006	2,563	2,823	2,774	3,216	11,377
2005	2,403	2,616	2,523	2,939	10,481

Earnings Per Share ($)

2010	0.53	0.79	E0.58	E0.81	E2.71
2009	0.53	0.75	0.53	0.73	2.53
2008	0.65	0.96	0.69	0.88	3.17
2007	0.55	0.84	0.62	0.96	2.95
2006	0.47	0.71	0.52	0.81	2.50
2005	0.41	0.62	0.45	0.71	2.18

Fiscal year ended Dec. 31. Next earnings report expected: NA. EPS Estimates based on S&P Operating Earnings; historical GAAP earnings are as reported.

Highlights

▸ The STARS recommendation for OMC has recently been changed to 4 (buy) from 3 (hold) and the 12-month target price has recently been changed to $47.00 from $41.00. The Highlights section of this Stock Report will be updated accordingly.

Investment Rationale/Risk

▸ The Investment Rationale/Risk section of this Stock Report will be updated shortly. For the latest News story on OMC from MarketScope, see below.

▸ 10/19/10 09:33 am ET ... S&P UPGRADES OPINION ON SHARES OF OMNICOM GROUP TO BUY FROM HOLD (OMC 40.75****): OMC reports Q3 EPS of $0.57, vs. $0.53, $0.01 below our expectations. Results benefitted as revenue growth of 5.5% was stronger than we estimated on strength in Europe, despite amortization expenses higher than we projected. We believe the company is well positioned to deliver margin expansion in 2011 on improving demand and easing comparisons. Although keeping our 2010 EPS estimate of $2.71, we are raising our 2011 EPS forecast by $0.22 to $3.06 on improving environment. As a result, we are raising our 12-month target price by $8 to $41, based on our EV/EBITDA analyses. /J.Agnese

Dividend Data (Dates: mm/dd Payment Date: mm/dd/yy)

Amount ($)	Date Decl.	Ex-Div. Date	Stk. of Record	Payment Date
0.150	12/04	12/14	12/16	01/04/10
0.200	02/10	03/03	03/05	04/02/10
0.200	05/25	06/11	06/15	07/12/10
0.200	07/21	09/20	09/22	10/06/10

Dividends have been paid since 1986. Source: Company reports.

The McGraw-Hill Companies

Omnicom Group Inc.

STANDARD &POOR'S

Business Summary July 21, 2010

CORPORATE OVERVIEW. Omnicom Group, a global advertising and marketing services company, is one of the world's largest corporate communications companies. OMC is comprised of more than 1,500 subsidiary agencies, operating in over 100 countries. It operates as three independent global agency networks: the BBDO Worldwide Network, the DDB Worldwide Network, and the TBWA Worldwide Network. Each agency network has its own clients, and the networks compete with each other in the same markets.

OMC's companies provide an extensive range of services, which it groups into four disciplines: traditional media advertising (44% of 2009 revenues), customer relationship management (37%), public relations (9.2%), and specialty communications (9.1%). In 2009, the company's 10 and 100 largest clients accounted for approximately 17.8% and 50.4% of consolidated revenue, respectively. The largest client accounted for about 3.1% of 2009 revenues; no other single client accounted for more than 2.5% of revenues. Operations cover the major regions of North America, the U.K., Europe, the Middle East, Africa, Latin America, the Far East and Australia. In 2009, 53% of revenues were derived from the U.S., 22% from euro-denominated markets, 8.9% from the U.K., and 17% from other international markets.

The services in these categories include but are not limited to: advertising, brand consultancy, crisis communications, database management, digital and interactive marketing, direct marketing, directory advertising, experiential marketing, field marketing, health care communications, in-store design, investor relations, marketing research, media planning and buying, organizational communications, product placement, promotional marketing, public relations, recruitment communications, reputation consulting, retail marketing, and sports and event marketing.

In our opinion, the breadth, depth and diversity of OMC's business reduces exposure to any single industry, and to an economic reversal in any world region. It also provides the company with significant opportunities to benefit from growth in non-advertising services, such as public relations and event marketing, expenditures for which are growing faster than those for traditional advertising.

Company Financials Fiscal Year Ended Dec. 31

Per Share Data ($)	2009	2008	2007	2006	2005	2004	2003	2002	2001	2000
Tangible Book Value	NM	NM	NM	NM	NM	NM	NM	NM	NM	NM
Cash Flow	3.34	3.75	3.45	3.13	2.71	2.40	2.10	2.03	1.88	1.81
Earnings	2.53	3.17	2.95	2.50	2.18	1.94	1.80	1.72	1.35	1.37
S&P Core Earnings	2.57	3.17	2.95	2.50	2.18	1.92	1.69	1.56	1.24	NA
Dividends	0.60	0.60	0.50	0.50	0.46	0.45	0.40	0.40	0.39	0.35
Payout Ratio	24%	19%	17%	20%	21%	23%	22%	23%	29%	26%
Prices:High	39.99	50.16	55.45	53.03	45.74	44.41	43.80	48.68	49.10	50.47
Prices:Low	20.09	22.02	45.82	39.38	37.88	33.22	23.25	18.25	29.55	34.06
P/E Ratio:High	16	16	19	21	21	23	24	28	36	37
P/E Ratio:Low	8	7	16	16	17	17	13	11	22	25

Income Statement Analysis (Million $)										
Revenue	11,721	13,360	12,694	11,377	10,481	9,747	8,621	7,536	6,889	6,154
Operating Income	1,669	1,872	1,823	1,674	1,515	1,388	1,289	1,224	1,179	1,065
Depreciation	243	183	164	190	175	172	124	120	211	187
Interest Expense	122	125	107	125	78.0	51.1	57.9	45.5	72.8	76.5
Pretax Income	1,305	1,657	1,624	1,422	1,308	1,196	1,137	1,087	908	923
Effective Tax Rate	33.2%	32.8%	33.1%	32.8%	33.3%	33.1%	33.5%	34.5%	38.8%	40.0%
Net Income	793	1,000	976	864	791	724	676	643	503	499
S&P Core Earnings	796	1,000	976	866	790	715	631	584	456	NA

Balance Sheet & Other Financial Data (Million $)										
Cash	1,595	1,112	1,841	1,740	836	1,166	1,529	667	472	517
Current Assets	8,789	8,565	10,504	9,647	7,967	8,095	7,286	5,637	5,234	5,367
Total Assets	17,921	17,318	19,272	18,164	15,920	16,002	14,499	11,820	10,617	9,891
Current Liabilities	10,083	9,754	11,227	10,296	8,700	8,744	7,762	6,840	6,644	6,625
Long Term Debt	2,221	3,054	3,055	3,055	2,357	2,358	2,537	1,945	1,340	1,245
Common Equity	4,195	3,523	4,092	3,871	3,948	4,079	3,466	2,569	2,178	1,548
Total Capital	6,906	6,810	7,563	7,562	6,921	6,949	6,394	4,687	3,677	2,970
Capital Expenditures	131	212	223	178	163	160	141	117	149	150
Cash Flow	1,036	1,183	1,140	1,054	966	896	800	763	714	685
Current Ratio	0.9	0.9	0.9	0.9	0.9	0.9	0.9	0.8	0.8	0.8
% Long Term Debt of Capitalization	Nil	42.9	40.4	40.4	34.1	33.9	39.7	41.5	36.4	41.9
% Net Income of Revenue	6.8	7.5	7.7	7.6	7.5	7.4	7.8	8.5	7.3	8.1
% Return on Assets	NA	5.5	5.2	5.1	5.0	4.7	5.1	5.7	4.9	5.3
% Return on Equity	NA	26.3	24.5	22.1	19.7	18.8	22.4	27.1	27.0	32.2

Data as orig reptd.; bef. results of disc opers/spec. items. Per share data adj. for stk. divs.; EPS diluted. E-Estimated. NA-Not Available. NM-Not Meaningful. NR-Not Ranked. UR-Under Review.

Office: 437 Madison Ave Bsmt, New York, NY 10022-7000.
Telephone: 212-415-3600.
Email: IR@OmnicomGroup.com
Website: http://www.omnicomgroup.com

Chrmn: B.A. Crawford
Pres & CEO: J. Wren
Vice Chrmn: W.T. Love
Vice Chrmn: T. Love

Investor Contact: R.J. Weisenburger
Board Members: A. R. Batkin, R. C. Clark, L. S. Coleman, Jr., E. M. Cook, B. A. Crawford, S. Denison, M. A. Henning, T. Love, W. T. Love, J. R. Murphy, J. R. Purcell, L. J. Rice, G. L. Roubos, J. Wren

Founded: 1944
Domicile: New York
Employees: 63,000

ONEOK Inc.

STANDARD &POOR'S

| S&P Recommendation **STRONG BUY** ★★★★★ | Price $50.10 (as of Oct 22, 2010) | 12-Mo. Target Price $58.00 | Investment Style Large-Cap Value |

GICS Sector Utilities
Sub-Industry Gas Utilities

Summary This Oklahoma-based integrated natural gas company also has an energy marketing and trading business.

Key Stock Statistics (Source S&P, Vickers, company reports)

52-Wk Range	$50.85– 29.56	S&P Oper. EPS 2010**E**	3.11	Market Capitalization(B)	$5.332	Beta	1.08
Trailing 12-Month EPS	$3.15	S&P Oper. EPS 2011**E**	3.44	Yield (%)	3.83	S&P 3-Yr. Proj. EPS CAGR(%)	8
Trailing 12-Month P/E	15.9	P/E on S&P Oper. EPS 2010**E**	16.1	Dividend Rate/Share	$1.92	S&P Credit Rating	BBB
$10K Invested 5 Yrs Ago	$21,383	Common Shares Outstg. (M)	106.4	Institutional Ownership (%)	67		

Price Performance

- 30-Week Mov. Avg. · · ·
- 10-Week Mov. Avg. – –
- 12-Mo. Target Price —
- Relative Strength —
- GAAP Earnings vs. Previous Year
- ▲ Up ▼ Down ► No Change
- Volume Above Avg. Below Avg.
- STARS

Options: CBOE, Ph

Highlights

➤ The 12-month target price for OKE has recently been changed to $58.00 from $56.00. The Highlights section of this Stock Report will be updated accordingly.

Investment Rationale/Risk

➤ The Investment Rationale/Risk section of this Stock Report will be updated shortly. For the latest News story on OKE from MarketScope, see below.

➤ 10/22/10 09:16 am ET ... S&P MAINTAINS STRONG BUY OPINION ON SHARES OF ONEOK INC (OKE 49.2*****): OKE announces that it has authorized a $750MM share repurchase program, subject to a maximum of $300MM per year, that expires at the end of '13. We think that a total of 9MM to 11MM shares will be repurchased under the program and we believe OKE is likely to complete the program by the end of '12. We are raising our '10 EPS estimate by $0.01 to $3.11 and '12's by $0.14 to $3.44, reflecting a lower number of expected shares. We are boosting our target price by $2 to $58. We also like the dividend increase to $1.92, sooner than we anticipated. The shares are yielding 3.9%. /CMuir

Qualitative Risk Assessment

| LOW | **MEDIUM** | HIGH |

Our risk assessment reflects our view of steady cash flow from the company's regulated utility and pipeline operations, offset by unregulated trading and gathering and processing operations.

Quantitative Evaluations

S&P Quality Ranking   A-

| D | C | B- | B | B+ | **A-** | A | A+ |

Relative Strength Rank   STRONG

LOWEST = 1   78   HIGHEST = 99

Revenue/Earnings Data

Revenue (Million $)

	1Q	2Q	3Q	4Q	Year
2010	3,924	2,807	--	--	--
2009	2,790	2,228	2,365	3,729	11,112
2008	4,902	4,173	4,239	2,843	16,157
2007	3,806	2,876	2,810	3,985	13,477
2006	3,756	2,432	2,641	3,068	11,896
2005	2,707	2,081	3,192	4,696	12,676

Earnings Per Share ($)

	1Q	2Q	3Q	4Q	Year
2010	1.44	0.39	E0.39	E0.89	E3.11
2009	1.16	0.39	0.45	0.87	2.87
2008	1.36	0.40	0.55	0.65	2.95
2007	1.36	0.31	0.13	0.98	2.79
2006	1.17	0.65	0.21	0.66	2.68
2005	0.92	0.16	0.41	2.32	3.73

Fiscal year ended Dec. 31. Next earnings report expected: Early November. EPS Estimates based on S&P Operating Earnings; historical GAAP earnings are as reported.

Dividend Data (Dates: mm/dd Payment Date: mm/dd/yy)

Amount ($)	Date Decl.	Ex-Div. Date	Stk. of Record	Payment Date
0.440	01/20	01/27	01/29	02/12/10
0.440	04/22	04/28	04/30	05/14/10
0.460	07/15	07/28	07/30	08/13/10
0.480	10/21	10/27	10/29	11/12/10

Dividends have been paid since 1939. Source: Company reports.

ONEOK Inc.

Business Summary August 19, 2010

CORPORATE OVERVIEW. ONEOK is an integrated energy company engaged in gas marketing and trading, transportation and storage, gathering and processing, natural gas liquids and gas utility distribution. The distribution segment is the largest gas utility in Kansas and Oklahoma and the third largest in Texas.

PRIMARY BUSINESS DYNAMICS. OKE derives earnings from geographically diverse operations in various segments of the energy and utility sectors. Utility operations include the Distribution segment (24% of total 2009 operating income, or $210 million). Non-utility reporting segments include Energy Services (15%, $76 million) and ONEOK Partners, L.P. (OKS) (61%, $645 million).

The Distribution segment serves nearly 2.1 million natural gas utility customers in Oklahoma, Kansas and Texas. We think the regulatory environment appears productive in all the states in which the company operates. In June 2009, Oklahoma Natural Gas (ONG) filed for a base rate increase of $66.1 million, which includes existing riders that would effectively reduce the requested rate increase to a net amount of $37.6 million. In December 2009, the company received approval to raise rates by $54.5 million including riders. Performance-based rates and a more streamlined regulatory process were approved in May 2009.

In November 2006, Kansas Gas Service (KGS) received approval for a settlement that included a $52.0 million increase. Since then, KGS has received an authorization to recover costs related to system reliability. In December 2009, KGS filed a request to become an efficiency loan program utility partner, contingent upon the commission approving a rate mechanism that would recover losses from declining sales and an energy conservation rider to recover program costs.

Texas Gas Service (TGS) files rate cases with individual municipalities in Texas and has received approvals for rate increases totaling $14.8 million since the beginning of 2006. In February 2009, TGS filed for a $3.6 million rate increase in central Texas. In June 2009, regulators approved a $1.1 million rate increase. In August 2009, the cities of the Rio Grande Valley service area approved an increase in base rates of $1.3 million. In December 2009, TGS submitted its intent to file for a $7.3 million rate increase in El Paso.

Company Financials Fiscal Year Ended Dec. 31

Per Share Data ($)	2009	2008	2007	2006	2005	2004	2003	2002	2001	2000
Tangible Book Value	11.11	10.01	8.90	10.52	11.38	13.26	10.67	20.60	19.19	37.73
Earnings	2.87	2.95	2.79	2.68	3.73	2.30	2.13	1.30	0.85	1.46
S&P Core Earnings	2.97	2.66	2.89	2.07	2.11	2.19	2.12	1.08	0.45	NA
Dividends	1.64	1.56	1.40	1.22	1.09	0.88	0.69	0.62	0.62	0.62
Payout Ratio	57%	53%	50%	46%	29%	38%	32%	48%	73%	42%
Prices:High	44.97	51.33	55.27	44.48	35.85	28.99	22.44	23.14	24.34	25.31
Prices:Low	18.10	21.56	39.26	26.35	26.30	19.69	16.00	14.62	14.17	10.88
P/E Ratio:High	16	17	20	17	10	13	11	18	29	17
P/E Ratio:Low	6	7	14	10	7	9	8	11	17	7

Income Statement Analysis (Million $)										
Revenue	11,112	16,157	13,477	11,896	12,676	5,988	2,999	2,104	6,803	6,643
Depreciation	289	244	228	236	183	189	161	148	157	143
Maintenance	NA	NA	NA	NA	NA	NA	NA	NA	NA	NA
Fixed Charges Coverage	3.06	3.61	3.31	3.53	7.16	4.79	3.50	2.54	1.67	2.26
Construction Credits	NA	NA	NA	NA	NA	NA	NA	NA	NA	NA
Effective Tax Rate	29.7%	24.4%	27.0%	26.8%	37.6%	38.2%	37.9%	39.7%	33.3%	38.6%
Net Income	305	312	305	307	403	242	214	156	104	143
S&P Core Earnings	316	281	315	237	229	231	181	71.8	8.23	NA

Balance Sheet & Other Financial Data (Million $)										
Gross Property	10,146	9,477	7,893	6,725	5,575	5,406	5,180	4,216	4,508	4,207
Capital Expenditures	791	1,473	884	376	250	264	215	0.21	342	311
Net Property	7,794	7,264	5,845	4,845	3,994	3,787	3,692	3,015	3,273	3,096
Capitalization:Long Term Debt	4,334	4,113	4,215	4,031	2,024	1,543	1,979	1,620	1,620	1,473
Capitalization:% Long Term Debt	66.3	66.3	68.2	64.5	53.0	49.0	61.4	54.3	56.1	54.6
Capitalization:Preferred	Nil	Nil	Nil	Nil	Nil	Nil	Nil	0.20	Nil	1.00
Capitalization:% Preferred	Nil	Nil	Nil	Nil	Nil	Nil	Nil	0.01	Nil	0.04
Capitalization:Common	2,207	2,088	1,969	2,216	1,795	1,606	1,241	1,365	1,266	1,226
Capitalization:% Common	33.7	33.7	31.8	35.5	47.0	51.0	38.6	45.7	43.9	45.4
Total Capital	8,048	8,171	7,667	7,755	4,423	3,793	3,635	3,461	3,385	3,082
% Operating Ratio	93.9	95.5	95.3	95.4	97.7	94.3	89.5	87.2	96.4	96.3
% Earned on Net Property	11.8	14.0	15.4	24.0	19.7	13.1	13.3	12.3	9.3	12.8
% Return on Revenue	2.8	1.9	2.3	2.6	3.2	4.0	7.1	7.4	1.5	2.2
% Return on Invested Capital	9.3	9.6	8.6	13.0	14.0	9.6	9.1	7.7	7.5	9.8
% Return on Common Equity	14.2	15.4	14.6	15.3	23.7	17.0	14.6	9.0	5.4	8.9

Data as orig reptd.; bef. results of disc opers/spec. items. Per share data adj. for stk. divs.; EPS diluted. E-Estimated. NA-Not Available. NM-Not Meaningful. NR-Not Ranked. UR-Under Review.

Office: 100 West Fifth Street, Tulsa, OK 74103.
Telephone: 918-588-7000.
Website: http://www.oneok.com
Chrmn: D.L. Kyle

Pres & CEO: J.W. Gibson
COO: R.F. Martinovich
EVP, CFO & Treas: C.L. Dinan
EVP & General Counsel: J.R. Barker

Investor Contact: D. Harrison (918-588-7950)
Board Members: J. C. Day, J. H. Edwards, W. L. Ford, J. W. Gibson, D. L. Kyle, B. H. Mackie, J. W. Mogg, P. L. Moore, G. D. Parker, E. Rodriguez, G. B. Smith, D. J. Tippeconnic

Founded: 1906
Domicile: Oklahoma
Employees: 4,758

Oracle Corp

STANDARD &POOR'S

S&P Recommendation BUY ★★★★☆

Price	12-Mo. Target Price	Investment Style
$28.99 (as of Oct 22, 2010)	$31.00	Large-Cap Growth

GICS Sector Information Technology
Sub-Industry Systems Software

Summary This leading supplier of enterprise database management systems and business applications added hardware with the 2010 acquisition of Sun Microsystems.

Key Stock Statistics (Source S&P, Vickers, company reports)

52-Wk Range	$29.24–20.65	S&P Oper. EPS 2011E	1.90	Market Capitalization(B)	$145.749	Beta	1.06
Trailing 12-Month EPS	$1.25	S&P Oper. EPS 2012E	2.10	Yield (%)	0.69	S&P 3-Yr. Proj. EPS CAGR(%)	15
Trailing 12-Month P/E	23.2	P/E on S&P Oper. EPS 2011E	15.3	Dividend Rate/Share	$0.20	S&P Credit Rating	A
$10K Invested 5 Yrs Ago	$24,013	Common Shares Outstg. (M)	5,027.1	Institutional Ownership (%)	60		

Price Performance

30-Week Mov. Avg. · · · 10-Week Mov. Avg. – – GAAP Earnings vs. Previous Year   Volume Above Avg. STARS
12-Mo. Target Price — Relative Strength — ▲ Up ▼ Down ► No Change   Below Avg.

Options: ASE, CBOE, P, Ph

Analysis prepared by **Zaineb Bokhari** on September 24, 2010, when the stock traded at **$ 26.95**.

Highlights

➤ We expect non-GAAP sales to rise nearly 28% in FY 11 (May), to $34.5 billion, including $7.6 billion of projected hardware systems and support sales gained through acquisition. We think ORCL is well positioned due to its product breadth. We see new software license sales rising 7% in FY 11, reflecting ongoing strength in database and middleware amid a gradual improvement in global economic conditions. We see 10% growth for software license updates and support, which we consider to be more stable than licenses. In FY 12, we see sales rising 8%, to about $37 billion.

➤ In view of ORCL's success in integrating past acquisitions, we expect targeted synergies from the purchase of Sun Microsystems to be achieved. We project FY 11 non-GAAP operating margins will narrow to 42%, from 46% in FY 10, reflecting a full year's impact of Sun and what we expect to be stepped-up R&D investment, and variable compensation rising with sales. We expect non-GAAP operating margins to widen modestly in FY 12, to about 43%.

➤ We estimate non-GAAP EPS of $1.90 in FY 11 and $2.10 in FY 12, excluding amortization and other items.

Investment Rationale/Risk

➤ The acquisition of Sun Microsystems has transformed ORCL into a software and systems vendor. While not without risk, we see the potential for earnings accretion as ORCL streamlines Sun's supply chain and refines its sales approach. For customers, we see benefits in the form of integrated and optimized hardware and software offerings and lower implementation risk. Execution remains key, in our view, but we are inclined to give ORCL the benefit of the doubt in view of its acquisition track record. We think successes with Exadata foreshadow long-term success with an integrated offering, and we view favorably the recent hire of Mark Hurd, former CEO of Hewlett-Packard (HPQ 41, Buy).

➤ Risks to our recommendation and target price include acquisition integration risk, pricing pressure, and adverse currency movement.

➤ We blend relative and intrinsic valuation metrics to derive our 12-month target price of $31. For our discounted cash flow model, we assume an 8% weighted average cost of capital and 2% terminal growth, which yields a value of $35. For our P/E analysis, we apply a 14.4X five-year average multiple to our FY 11 EPS estimate, resulting in a $27 value.

Qualitative Risk Assessment

LOW	MEDIUM	HIGH

Our risk assessment reflects acquisition integration risks following a series of large deals over the past few years. This is offset by our favorable view of ORCL's balance sheet, free cash flow and depth of management.

Quantitative Evaluations

S&P Quality Ranking A-

D	C	B-	B	B+	A-	A	A+

Relative Strength Rank STRONG

85

LOWEST = 1   HIGHEST = 99

Revenue/Earnings Data

Revenue (Million $)

	1Q	2Q	3Q	4Q	Year
2011	7,502	--	--	--	--
2010	5,054	5,858	6,404	9,505	26,820
2009	5,331	5,607	5,453	6,861	23,252
2008	4,529	5,313	5,349	7,239	22,430
2007	3,591	4,163	4,414	5,828	17,996
2006	2,768	3,292	3,470	4,851	14,380

Earnings Per Share ($)

	1Q	2Q	3Q	4Q	Year
2011	0.27	E0.44	E0.46	E0.60	E1.90
2010	0.22	0.29	0.23	0.46	1.21
2009	0.21	0.25	0.26	0.38	1.09
2008	0.16	0.25	0.26	0.39	1.06
2007	0.13	0.18	0.20	0.31	0.81
2006	0.10	0.15	0.14	0.24	0.64

Fiscal year ended May 31. Next earnings report expected: Mid December. EPS Estimates based on S&P Operating Earnings; historical GAAP earnings are as reported.

Dividend Data (Dates: mm/dd Payment Date: mm/dd/yy)

Amount ($)	Date Decl.	Ex-Div. Date	Stk. of Record	Payment Date
0.050	12/17	01/14	01/19	02/09/10
0.050	03/25	04/12	04/14	05/05/10
0.050	06/23	07/12	07/14	08/04/10
0.050	09/16	10/04	10/06	11/03/10

Dividends have been paid since 2009. Source: Company reports.

Please read the Required Disclosures and Analyst Certification on the last page of this report.

The McGraw·Hill Companies

Oracle Corp

Business Summary September 24, 2010

CORPORATE OVERVIEW. Oracle Corp., a leading provider of enterprise software, added hardware to its product portfolio via the acquisition of Sun Microsystems, completed on January 26, 2010. Its software business consists of new software licenses and software license updates (28% of non-GAAP revenues in FY 10 (May)), and product support (49%). The services business comprises consulting (10%), on demand (3%) and education (1%). Oracle's software products fall into two broad categories: database and middleware (68% of software revenues in FY 10), and application software. In FY 10, hardware and related support revenues comprised 9% of non-GAAP revenues; we see this rising to 22% in FY 11.

MARKET PROFILE. Enterprises scaled back spending on information technology in 2009, and we expect continued caution as the global economy stabilizes. With some exceptions, we expect developed regions outside the U.S. to recover at a pace that lags the U.S. somewhat. We also think companies that operate globally will continue to be affected by shifts in foreign exchange rates. We expect corporate spending on software to rise in 2010, likely in the low single digits, mainly due to maintenance contracts. Large enterprise software deals are sporadic and tend to be susceptible to delays and disruptions due to long sales cycles and the greater number of approvals needed to close such deals. We think the economic climate has improved from the depths of the economic crisis seen in late 2008/early 2009, but we think the specter of increased regulation and the consensus outlook for a moderate economic recovery and weak jobs growth will keep buyers cautious. We see this accruing to the benefit of technology vendors that provide solutions that support and maintain mission critical systems, including database and storage-related technology assets. We see growth in applications tied more closely to an economic recovery. We still expect visibility on large deals to be limited, and we think software vendors face intense competition and pricing pressure as they close deals.

Company Financials Fiscal Year Ended May 31

Per Share Data ($)	2010	2009	2008	2007	2006	2005	2004	2003	2002	2001
Tangible Book Value	0.29	NM	NM	NM	0.13	0.09	1.55	1.21	1.13	1.12
Cash Flow	1.66	1.48	1.34	1.03	0.79	0.63	0.55	0.49	0.45	0.50
Earnings	1.21	1.09	1.06	0.81	0.64	0.55	0.50	0.43	0.39	0.44
S&P Core Earnings	1.21	1.09	1.05	0.80	0.62	0.52	0.46	0.37	0.34	0.36
Dividends	NA	0.05	Nil	Nil	Nil	Nil	Nil	Nil	Nil	Nil
Payout Ratio	NA	5%	Nil	Nil	Nil	Nil	Nil	Nil	Nil	Nil
Calendar Year	2009	2008	2007	2006	2005	2004	2003	2002	2001	2000
Prices:High	25.11	23.62	23.31	19.75	14.51	15.51	14.03	17.50	35.00	46.47
Prices:Low	13.80	15.00	15.97	12.06	11.25	9.78	10.64	7.25	10.16	21.50
P/E Ratio:High	21	22	22	24	23	28	28	41	90	NM
P/E Ratio:Low	11	14	15	15	18	18	21	17	26	NM

Income Statement Analysis (Million $)

	2010	2009	2008	2007	2006	2005	2004	2003	2002	2001
Revenue	26,820	23,252	22,430	17,996	14,380	11,799	10,156	9,475	9,673	10,860
Operating Income	12,109	10,531	9,489	726	5,764	4,802	4,098	3,767	3,934	4,124
Depreciation	2,271	1,976	1,480	1,127	806	425	234	327	363	347
Interest Expense	754	630	24.0	343	169	135	21.0	16.0	20.0	24.0
Pretax Income	8,243	7,834	7,834	5,986	4,810	4,051	3,945	3,425	3,408	3,971
Effective Tax Rate	NA	28.6%	29.5%	28.6%	29.7%	28.8%	32.0%	32.6%	34.7%	35.5%
Net Income	6,135	5,593	5,521	4,274	3,381	2,886	2,681	2,307	2,224	2,561
S&P Core Earnings	6,135	5,593	5,481	4,224	3,237	2,750	2,459	2,049	1,923	2,119

Balance Sheet & Other Financial Data (Million $)

	2010	2009	2008	2007	2006	2005	2004	2003	2002	2001
Cash	18,469	12,624	11,043	7,020	7,605	4,802	4,138	4,737	3,095	4,449
Current Assets	27,004	18,581	18,103	12,883	11,974	8,479	11,336	9,227	8,728	8,963
Total Assets	61,578	47,416	47,268	34,572	29,029	20,687	12,763	11,064	10,800	11,030
Current Liabilities	14,691	9,149	10,029	9,387	6,930	8,063	4,272	4,158	3,960	3,917
Long Term Debt	11,510	9,237	10,234	6,235	5,735	159	163	175	298	301
Common Equity	31,199	25,090	23,025	16,919	15,012	10,837	7,995	6,320	6,117	6,278
Total Capital	45,854	35,682	34,628	24,275	21,311	12,006	8,217	6,681	6,619	6,906
Capital Expenditures	230	529	243	319	236	188	189	291	278	313
Cash Flow	8,406	7,569	7,001	5,401	4,187	3,311	2,915	2,634	2,587	2,908
Current Ratio	1.8	2.0	1.8	1.4	1.7	1.1	2.7	2.2	2.2	2.3
% Long Term Debt of Capitalization	25.1	25.9	29.7	25.7	26.9	1.3	2.0	2.6	4.5	4.4
% Net Income of Revenue	22.9	24.1	24.6	22.7	23.5	24.4	26.4	24.3	23.0	23.6
% Return on Assets	11.3	11.8	13.5	13.4	13.6	17.3	22.6	21.1	20.4	21.2
% Return on Equity	21.8	23.3	27.6	26.8	26.2	30.7	37.5	37.1	35.9	40.2

Data as orig reptd.; bef. results of disc opers/spec. items. Per share data adj. for stk. divs.; EPS diluted. E-Estimated. NA-Not Available. NM-Not Meaningful. NR-Not Ranked. UR-Under Review.

Office: 500 Oracle Parkway, Redwood Shores, CA 94065-1675.
Telephone: 650-506-7000.
Email: investor_us@oracle.com
Website: http://www.oracle.com

Chrmn: J.O. Henley
CEO: L.J. Ellison
EVP & CFO: J. Epstein
SVP, Chief Acctg Officer & Cntlr: W.C. West

SVP, Secy & General Counsel: D. Daley
Investor Contact: K. Bond (650-607-0349)
Board Members: J. S. Berg, H. R. Bingham, M. J. Boskin, S. A. Catz, B. R. Chizen, G. H. Conrades, L. J. Ellison, H. Garcia-Molina, J. O. Henley, M. V. Hurd, D. L. Lucas, N. Seligman

Founded: 1977
Domicile: Delaware
Employees: 105,000

O'Reilly Automotive Inc

STANDARD &POOR'S

S&P Recommendation	HOLD ★★★☆☆	Price	12-Mo. Target Price	Investment Style
		$54.02 (as of Oct 22, 2010)	$55.00	Large-Cap Growth

GICS Sector Consumer Discretionary
Sub-Industry Automotive Retail

Summary This company is one of the largest U.S. retailers of car parts and accessories.

Key Stock Statistics (Source S&P, Vickers, company reports)

52-Wk Range	$54.42–33.61	S&P Oper. EPS 2010E	2.85	Market Capitalization(B)	$7.496	Beta	0.43
Trailing 12-Month EPS	$2.55	S&P Oper. EPS 2011E	3.18	Yield (%)	Nil	S&P 3-Yr. Proj. EPS CAGR(%)	13
Trailing 12-Month P/E	21.2	P/E on S&P Oper. EPS 2010E	19.0	Dividend Rate/Share	Nil	S&P Credit Rating	NA
$10K Invested 5 Yrs Ago	$20,158	Common Shares Outstg. (M)	138.8	Institutional Ownership (%)	96		

Price Performance

30-Week Mov. Avg. · · · 10-Week Mov. Avg. - - GAAP Earnings vs. Previous Year Volume Above Avg. STARS
12-Mo. Target Price — Relative Strength — ▲ Up ▼ Down ► No Change Below Avg.

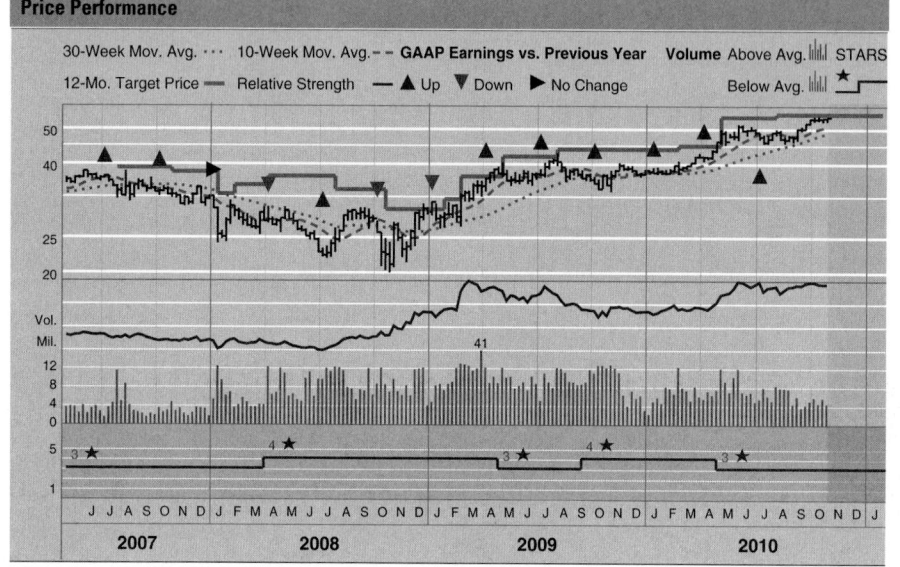

Options: ASE, CBOE, Ph

Analysis prepared by **Michael Souers** on August 02, 2010, when the stock traded at **$49.28**.

Highlights

► We look for sales to increase 9.5% in 2010, following a 36% advance in 2009, which included a full year contribution from the July 2008 acquisition of CSK Auto. We expect 2010 sales to be bolstered by the opening of about 150 net new stores and by a same-store sales increase of 6%-7%. We believe challenging macro conditions will lead consumers to defer vehicle maintenance when possible, but that industry tailwinds such as the increasing age of vehicles and a recent uptick in miles driven should support continued growth.

► We think operating margins will widen significantly in 2010, as the conversion of CSK Auto stores should drive increased cost synergies. Also, we see continued efficiency improvements from current distribution centers and increased buying power with vendors. Lastly, we expect strong comp-store growth to leverage SG&A expenses in 2010.

► Excluding a $0.10 charge related to a legal investigation over former CSK Auto practices, we forecast 2010 EPS of $2.85, a 26% increase from 2009's $2.26, which excludes $0.03 of acquisition-related charges. We see 2011 EPS of $3.18.

Investment Rationale/Risk

► We expect ORLY to outpace the industry in terms of square footage, sales and EPS growth over the next few years, and we like its dual sales strategy focused on commercial as well as retail customers. In addition, we think strong recent execution bodes well for continued market share gains in a fragmented industry. We also favor the acquisition of CSK Auto, and expect significant revenue and cost benefits to accrue over the longer term. However, despite these favorable drivers, we think the shares are fairly valued, following a strong recent rise in price, trading at over 15X our 2011 EPS estimate, a significant premium to peers.

► Risks to our recommendation and target price include an increase in new car sales and declines in miles driven. Our concerns with regard to corporate governance include ORLY's board of directors being controlled by a large percentage of insiders as well as a non-shareholder-approved "poison pill" anti-takeover plan.

► Our 12-month target price of $55 is based on our DCF model, which assumes a weighted average cost of capital of 10.3% and a terminal growth rate of 3.5%.

Qualitative Risk Assessment

LOW	MEDIUM	HIGH

Our risk assessment reflects the cyclical nature of the auto parts retailing industry. However, what we see as the company's stronger-than-average balance sheet and its large opportunity for continued domestic expansion offset the industry risk, in our opinion.

Quantitative Evaluations

S&P Quality Ranking B+

D	C	B-	B	B+	A-	A	A+

Relative Strength Rank MODERATE

66

LOWEST = 1   HIGHEST = 99

Revenue/Earnings Data

Revenue (Million $)

	1Q	2Q	3Q	4Q	Year
2010	1,280	1,381	--	--	--
2009	1,164	1,251	1,258	1,174	4,847
2008	646.2	704.4	1,111	1,115	3,577
2007	613.2	643.1	661.8	604.3	2,522
2006	536.6	591.2	597.1	558.3	2,283
2005	466.2	521.2	542.9	515.0	2,045

Earnings Per Share ($)

	1Q	2Q	3Q	4Q	Year
2010	0.70	0.71	E0.74	E0.61	E2.85
2009	0.46	0.62	0.63	0.52	2.23
2008	0.40	0.48	0.31	0.32	1.49
2007	0.42	0.45	0.46	0.35	1.67
2006	0.35	0.43	0.42	0.35	1.55
2005	0.30	0.38	0.42	0.35	1.45

Fiscal year ended Dec. 31. Next earnings report expected: Late October. EPS Estimates based on S&P Operating Earnings; historical GAAP earnings are as reported.

Dividend Data

No cash dividends have been paid.

The McGraw-Hill Companies

O'Reilly Automotive Inc

Business Summary August 02, 2010

CORPORATE OVERVIEW. O'Reilly Automotive is one of the largest specialty retailers of automotive aftermarket parts, tools, supplies, equipment and accessories in the United States, with 3,421 stores in 38 states, as of December 31, 2009. This includes the July 2008 acquisition of CSK Auto, one of the largest specialty retailers of auto parts in the Western U.S. At the time of acquisition, CSK was comprised of 1,342 stores operating under four brand names: Checker Auto Parts, Schuck's Auto Supply, Kragen Auto Parts, and Murray's Discount Auto Parts. As of December 31, 2009, ORLY had converted 405 CSK stores to O'Reilly systems, merged 41 CSK stores with existing O'Reilly locations, closed 13 stores and opened five new stores in CSK historical markets.

ORLY stores carry, on average, about 22,000 SKUs, and average approximately 7,000 total square feet in size. The company's stores carry an extensive product line of new and remanufactured automotive hard parts (alternators, starters, fuel pumps, water pumps, brake shoes and pads), maintenance items (oil, antifreeze, fluids, filters, lighting, engine additives, appearance products), accessories (floor mats, seat covers), and a complete line of autobody paint, automotive tools, and professional service equipment. Merchandise consists of nationally recognized brands and a wide variety of private label products. ORLY offers engine machining services through its stores, but does not sell tires nor does it perform automotive repairs or installations.

ORLY currently operates 21 distribution centers, in Alabama, Arkansas, California, Georgia, Indiana, Iowa, Michigan, Minnesota, Missouri, Montana, North Carolina, Oklahoma, Tennessee,Texas and Washington. Inventory management and distribution systems electronically link each of ORLY's stores to a distribution center, providing for efficient inventory control and management. The distribution system provides each of the stores with same day or overnight access to over 118,000 SKUs, many of which are hard-to-find items.

CORPORATE STRATEGY. The company has a dual market strategy, targeting do-it-yourself (DIY) customers as well as professional installers. ORLY believes this gives it a competitive advantage, allowing the company to target a larger base of consumers of automotive aftermarket parts; capitalize on existing retail and distribution infrastructure; operate profitably not only in large metropolitan markets but also in less densely populated areas, which typically attract fewer competitors; and enhance service levels to the DIY market by offering a broad selection of products and extensive product knowledge required by professional installers. In 2009, 53% of sales were to the DIY market, and 47% to professional installers. O'Reilly seeks to aggressively add new stores to achieve greater penetration in existing markets and to expand into new, contiguous ones. In 2010, ORLY plans on opening approximately 150 net new stores.

Company Financials Fiscal Year Ended Dec. 31

Per Share Data ($)	2009	2008	2007	2006	2005	2004	2003	2002	2001	2000
Tangible Book Value	13.82	11.16	13.38	11.97	10.19	8.56	7.18	6.10	5.27	4.50
Cash Flow	3.30	2.41	2.35	2.11	1.95	1.54	1.31	1.11	0.92	0.74
Earnings	2.23	1.49	1.67	1.55	1.45	1.05	0.92	0.77	0.63	0.50
S&P Core Earnings	2.23	1.48	1.67	1.55	1.27	1.97	1.67	1.39	1.15	NA
Dividends	Nil	Nil	Nil	Nil	Nil	Nil	Nil	Nil	Nil	Nil
Payout Ratio	Nil	Nil	Nil	Nil	Nil	Nil	Nil	Nil	Nil	Nil
Prices:High	42.93	32.68	38.84	38.30	32.53	23.54	22.45	18.63	19.22	13.63
Prices:Low	26.47	20.00	30.43	27.49	21.98	18.03	11.46	12.05	7.75	4.13
P/E Ratio:High	19	22	23	25	22	22	24	24	31	27
P/E Ratio:Low	12	13	18	18	15	17	12	16	12	8

Income Statement Analysis (Million $)	2009	2008	2007	2006	2005	2004	2003	2002	2001	2000
Revenue	4,847	3,577	2,522	2,283	2,045	1,721	1,512	1,312	1,092	890
Operating Income	686	462	384	347	310	245	208	175	144	65.2
Depreciation	148	117	78.9	64.9	57.2	54.3	42.4	36.9	30.5	24.8
Interest Expense	45.2	28.5	6.28	4.32	5.06	4.70	6.86	9.25	9.09	8.36
Pretax Income	497	303	307	282	251	188	160	131	107	83.2
Effective Tax Rate	38.1%	38.4%	36.9%	36.9%	34.6%	37.3%	37.5%	37.4%	37.8%	37.8%
Net Income	308	186	194	178	164	118	100	82.0	66.4	51.7
S&P Core Earnings	307	186	194	178	143	110	90.9	74.8	60.9	NA

Balance Sheet & Other Financial Data (Million $)	2009	2008	2007	2006	2005	2004	2003	2002	2001	2000
Cash	26.9	31.3	58.4	29.9	31.4	69.0	21.1	29.3	15.0	9.20
Current Assets	2,227	1,875	1,102	1,001	911	813	687	631	551	449
Total Assets	4,781	4,193	2,280	1,977	1,714	1,432	1,188	1,009	857	716
Current Liabilities	1,231	1,054	529	434	486	334	246	147	121	153
Long Term Debt	684	718	75.2	110	25.5	100	121	190	166	90.5
Common Equity	2,686	2,282	1,592	1,364	1,181	973	784	651	556	464
Total Capital	3,370	3,000	1,695	1,512	1,249	1,112	935	857	731	558
Capital Expenditures	415	342	283	229	205	173	136	102	68.5	82.0
Cash Flow	456	303	273	243	221	172	142	119	96.9	76.5
Current Ratio	1.8	1.8	2.1	2.3	1.9	2.4	2.8	4.3	4.5	2.9
% Long Term Debt of Capitalization	20.3	24.1	4.4	7.3	2.0	9.0	12.9	22.2	22.7	16.2
% Net Income of Revenue	6.3	5.2	7.7	7.8	8.0	6.8	6.6	6.2	6.1	5.8
% Return on Assets	6.9	5.8	9.1	9.6	10.4	9.1	9.1	8.8	8.4	7.8
% Return on Equity	12.4	9.6	13.1	14.2	15.3	13.3	14.0	13.6	13.0	11.9

Data as orig reptd.; bef. results of disc opers/spec. items. Per share data adj. for stk. divs.; EPS diluted. E-Estimated. NA-Not Available. NM-Not Meaningful. NR-Not Ranked. UR-Under Review.

Office: 233 S Patterson Ave, Springfield, MO 65802.
Telephone: 417-862-6708.
Website: http://www.oreillyauto.com
Chrmn: D. O'Reilly

Vice Chrmn: C.H. O'Reilly, Jr.
Vice Chrmn: L.P. O'Reilly
CEO & Co-Pres: G.L. Henslee
COO & Co-Pres: T.F. Wise

Investor Contact: T.G. McFall
Board Members: J. D. Burchfield, T. T. Hendrickson, P. R. Lederer, J. R. Murphy, D. O'Reilly, L. P. O'Reilly, C. H. O'Reilly, Jr., R. O'Reilly-Wooten, R. Rashkow

Founded: 1957
Domicile: Missouri
Employees: 44,822

Owens-Illinois Inc.

STANDARD &POOR'S

S&P Recommendation	HOLD ★★★☆☆	Price	12-Mo. Target Price	Investment Style
		$28.96 (as of Oct 22, 2010)	$33.00	Large-Cap Blend

GICS Sector Materials
Sub-Industry Metal & Glass Containers

Summary This company is a large global maker of glass bottles and containers.

Key Stock Statistics (Source S&P, Vickers, company reports)

52-Wk Range	$37.97– 24.92	S&P Oper. EPS 2010E	3.10	Market Capitalization(B)	$4.736	Beta	2.10
Trailing 12-Month EPS	$1.14	S&P Oper. EPS 2011E	3.60	Yield (%)	Nil	S&P 3-Yr. Proj. EPS CAGR(%)	13
Trailing 12-Month P/E	25.4	P/E on S&P Oper. EPS 2010E	9.3	Dividend Rate/Share	Nil	S&P Credit Rating	BB+
$10K Invested 5 Yrs Ago	$16,044	Common Shares Outstg. (M)	163.6	Institutional Ownership (%)	93		

Price Performance

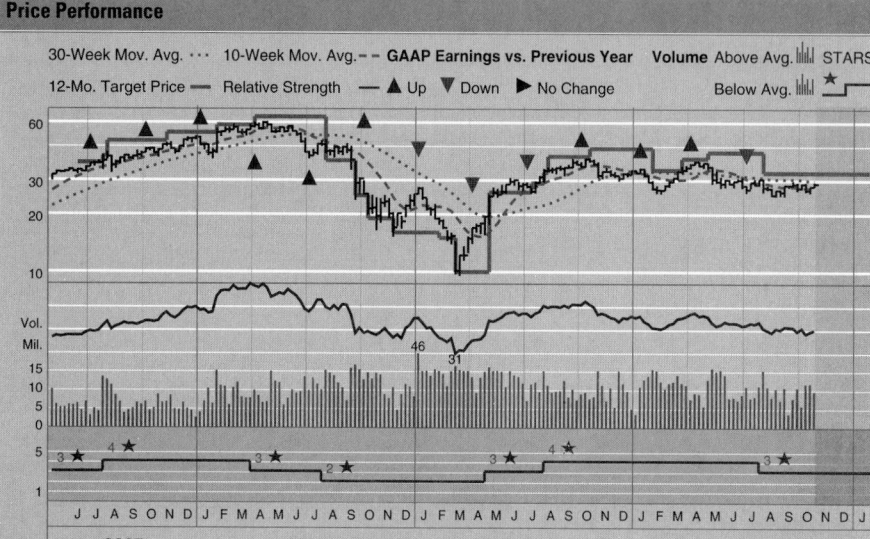

30-Week Mov. Avg. · · · 10-Week Mov. Avg. – – GAAP Earnings vs. Previous Year Volume Above Avg. STARS
12-Mo. Target Price — Relative Strength — ▲ Up ▼ Down ► No Change Below Avg. ★

Options: ASE, CBOE, P, Ph

Analysis prepared by **Stewart Scharf** on August 02, 2010, when the stock traded at **$ 27.98**.

Highlights

► We expect net sales to decline modestly in 2010, as soft glass container shipments in North America and Europe driven by weak beer demand offsets growth in South American and Asia. Additionally, sales and earnings will likely continue to be negatively impacted by a stronger U.S. dollar primarily against the euro. Sales growth should return in 2011 as markets gradually recover.

► In our view, gross margins will expand in 2010, from 21% in 2009, reflecting contractual price hikes in North America and a better product mix, which should offset slightly higher input costs. We believe operating (EBITDA) margins will expand slightly in 2010, from 19.7% in 2009, as strategic footprint initiatives and increased capacity utilization offset higher production costs. However, pension and interest expense are likely to rise.

► We forecast an effective tax rate of about 26% for 2010, and estimate operating EPS of $3.10 (before at least $0.10 of charges), advancing to $3.60 in 2011. OI expects a negative $0.10 to $0.15 per share impact from a change in the method of reporting its Venezuelan results.

Investment Rationale/Risk

► We recently lowered our recommendation on the shares to Hold, from Buy, based on our view that global markets will gradually rebound during 2010, but beer demand in North America and Europe will remain challenging. Additionally, our valuation metrics indicate the shares are fairly valued. Longer term, we expect OI to benefit from growth in emerging markets and new strategic initiatives geared toward improving its footprint.

► Risks to our recommendation and target price include a prolonged global market downturn, a stronger U.S. dollar versus the euro and the Australian dollar, another sharp rise in commodity prices, more inventory de-stocking, and fewer long-term contract extensions.

► Based on our relative valuation, we apply a multiple of near 10X our 2010 EPS estimate, a discount to other companies in S&P's Metal & Glass group as well as to our projected P/E for the S&P 500, which values the shares at $30. Our DCF model, assuming a 9.5% weighted average cost of capital and 4% terminal growth rate, derives intrinsic value of $37. Blending these metrics, we arrive at our 12-month target price of $33.

Qualitative Risk Assessment

LOW	MEDIUM	HIGH

Our risk assessment reflects ongoing asbestos claims and volatile commodity costs, offset by our view of sound corporate governance practices and an improving balance sheet.

Quantitative Evaluations

S&P Quality Ranking B-

D	C	B-	B	B+	A-	A	A+

Relative Strength Rank MODERATE

52

LOWEST = 1 HIGHEST = 99

Revenue/Earnings Data

Revenue (Million $)

	1Q	2Q	3Q	4Q	Year
2010	1,583	1,711	--	--	--
2009	1,519	1,807	1,875	1,866	7,067
2008	1,961	2,211	2,009	1,705	7,885
2007	1,684	1,997	1,928	1,957	7,567
2006	1,688	1,946	1,912	1,877	7,422
2005	1,663	1,853	1,808	1,756	7,090

Earnings Per Share ($)

	1Q	2Q	3Q	4Q	Year
2010	0.50	0.85	E1.10	E0.60	E3.10
2009	0.27	0.88	0.74	-0.95	0.95
2008	1.02	1.33	0.46	-1.38	1.48
2007	0.31	0.92	0.45	0.06	1.78
2006	0.12	0.24	0.02	-0.71	-0.32
2005	0.73	0.53	0.34	-5.86	-4.26

Fiscal year ended Dec. 31. Next earnings report expected: Late October. EPS Estimates based on S&P Operating Earnings; historical GAAP earnings are as reported.

Dividend Data

No cash dividends have been paid.

Please read the Required Disclosures and Analyst Certification on the last page of this report.

The McGraw-Hill Companies

Owens-Illinois Inc.

STANDARD &POOR'S

Business Summary August 02, 2010

CORPORATE OVERVIEW. In 2005, Owens-Illinois began operating under the name O-I as part of a transformation strategy begun in 2004 to leverage its global capabilities, broaden its market base, and focus on its core glass container business. OI believes it is the world's largest manufacturer of glass packaging products. It has 78 glass manufacturing plants and 156 furnaces in 22 countries, and has acquired 18 glass container businesses since 1990, in regions that include Europe, South America and Asia/Pacific. In 2009, geographic sales were: Europe 41%; North America 29%; South America 16%; and Asia/Pacific 13%. The company accounts for about 50% of the glass containers produced worldwide. In July 2010, OI invested $132 million in a plant in China and a joint venture in Southeast Asia.

We expect the company to focus on improving its operational and capital performance, while integrating operations in Europe. OI maintains a hedging program, with about 50% of natural gas hedged in North America. In Europe, the company enters into fixed-price contracts for 50% of its energy spend. In late 2009, OI entered into contracts with several large North American customers, which included provisions for more rapid pass-throughs of volatile commodity costs such as energy. As of mid-2010, 25% of North American volume was sold under customer contracts that include clauses for OI to quickly pass through costs. In 2009, currency translation cut sales by $344 million and operating EPS by $0.16, based on a stronger U.S. dollar mainly against the euro and the Australian dollar. However, a weaker U.S. dollar in the 2009 fourth quarter resulted in a positive $183 million effect on sales and a $0.13 boost to operating EPS, versus the year-earlier period. In the second quarter of 2010, a stronger U.S. dollar negatively impacted sales by $81 million, year to year, and operating EPS by $0.08.

In 2009, OI incurred pretax restructuring and impairment charges of $214 million ($1.07 a share, after tax), asbestos-related charges of $180 million ($1.06) and Venezuelan currency remeasurement charges of nearly $18 million ($0.10), and a non-cash tax benefit of $48 million ($0.28).

Company Financials Fiscal Year Ended Dec. 31

Per Share Data ($)	2009	2008	2007	2006	2005	2004	2003	2002	2001	2000
Tangible Book Value	NM	NM	NM	NM	NM	NM	NM	NM	NM	NM
Cash Flow	3.27	3.99	4.18	2.53	-0.99	3.91	-3.67	2.84	5.08	0.83
Earnings	0.95	1.48	1.78	-0.32	-4.26	1.00	-6.89	-0.08	2.33	-2.00
S&P Core Earnings	0.95	0.39	1.47	0.36	-0.89	1.22	0.04	-1.45	-0.92	NA
Dividends	Nil	Nil	Nil	Nil	Nil	Nil	Nil	Nil	Nil	Nil
Payout Ratio	Nil	Nil	Nil	Nil	Nil	Nil	Nil	Nil	Nil	Nil
Prices:High	39.56	60.60	50.97	22.60	27.50	23.89	15.50	19.19	10.08	24.88
Prices:Low	9.53	15.20	18.48	13.10	17.50	10.80	7.51	9.55	3.62	2.50
P/E Ratio:High	42	8	29	NM	NM	24	NM	NM	4	NM
P/E Ratio:Low	10	2	10	NM	NM	11	NM	NM	2	NM

Income Statement Analysis (Million $)										
Revenue	7,067	7,885	7,567	7,422	7,090	6,128	6,059	5,640	5,403	5,552
Operating Income	1,315	1,529	1,432	-1,100	1,297	1,185	1,175	1,281	1,173	245
Depreciation	396	431	423	469	480	436	473	428	403	413
Interest Expense	222	253	339	488	467	475	491	422	434	487
Pretax Income	325	558	507	143	-219	210	-1,091	16.6	667	-392
Effective Tax Rate	39.2%	42.4%	29.2%	NM	NM	2.81%	NM	NM	42.9%	NM
Net Income	162	252	299	-27.5	-622	172	-991	9.40	361	-270
S&P Core Earnings	161	60.3	226	55.4	-134	185	5.85	-213	-135	NA

Balance Sheet & Other Financial Data (Million $)										
Cash	813	405	448	223	247	278	163	126	156	230
Current Assets	2,797	2,445	2,695	2,433	2,282	2,401	2,122	1,887	1,987	2,082
Total Assets	8,727	7,977	9,325	9,321	9,522	10,737	9,531	9,869	10,107	10,343
Current Liabilities	2,034	2,003	2,530	2,366	1,822	1,907	1,363	1,297	1,232	1,318
Long Term Debt	3,258	2,940	3,014	4,719	5,019	5,168	5,333	5,268	5,330	5,730
Common Equity	1,538	1,041	1,735	-83.9	271	1,092	551	1,218	1,699	1,428
Total Capital	4,994	4,311	5,562	5,407	6,110	7,065	6,617	7,359	8,106	8,005
Capital Expenditures	428	362	293	320	404	437	432	496	365	481
Cash Flow	558	677	701	420	-163	586	-539	416	742	121
Current Ratio	1.4	1.2	1.1	1.0	1.3	1.3	1.6	1.5	1.6	1.6
% Long Term Debt of Capitalization	65.2	68.2	54.2	87.3	82.1	73.1	80.6	71.6	65.8	71.6
% Net Income of Revenue	2.3	3.2	4.0	NM	NM	2.8	NM	0.2	6.7	NM
% Return on Assets	1.9	2.9	3.0	NM	NM	1.7	NM	0.1	3.5	NM
% Return on Equity	12.6	18.1	33.9	NM	NM	18.3	NM	0.6	21.7	NM

Data as orig reptd.; bef. results of disc opers/spec. items. Per share data adj. for stk. divs.; EPS diluted. E-Estimated. NA-Not Available. NM-Not Meaningful. NR-Not Ranked. UR-Under Review.

Office: 1 Michael Owens Way, Perrysburg, OH 43551-2999.
Telephone: 567-336-5000.
Website: http://www.o-i.com
Chrmn, Pres & CEO: A.P. Stroucken

COO & CTO: R.E. Lachmiller
SVP & CFO: E.C. White
SVP, Secy & General Counsel: J.W. Baehren
Chief Acctg Officer: T. Caracciolo

Investor Contact: S. Sekpeh (567-336-2355)
Board Members: G. F. Colter, J. Geldmacher, P. S. Hellman, D. H. Ho, A. D. Kelly, J. J. McMackin, Jr., C. A. McNeill, Jr., H. H. Roberts, A. P. Stroucken, H. H. Wehmeier, D. K. Williams, T. L. Young

Founded: 1903
Domicile: Delaware
Employees: 22,000

The **McGraw·Hill** Companies

PACCAR Inc

STANDARD &POOR'S

S&P Recommendation	HOLD ★★★☆☆	Price $50.77 (as of Oct 22, 2010)	12-Mo. Target Price $52.00	Investment Style Large-Cap Blend

GICS Sector Industrials
Sub-Industry Construction & Farm Machinery & Heavy Trucks

Summary This heavy-duty truck manufacturer produces the well-known Peterbilt and Kenworth brand heavy-duty highway trucks.

Key Stock Statistics (Source S&P, Vickers, company reports)

52-Wk Range	$51.71– 33.45	S&P Oper. EPS 2010E	1.06	Market Capitalization(B)	$18.507	Beta	1.33
Trailing 12-Month EPS	$0.62	S&P Oper. EPS 2011E	2.20	Yield (%)	0.95	S&P 3-Yr. Proj. EPS CAGR(%)	10
Trailing 12-Month P/E	81.9	P/E on S&P Oper. EPS 2010E	47.9	Dividend Rate/Share	$0.48	S&P Credit Rating	A+
$10K Invested 5 Yrs Ago	$20,760	Common Shares Outstg. (M)	364.5	Institutional Ownership (%)	59		

Price Performance

30-Week Mov. Avg. ··· 10-Week Mov. Avg. - - GAAP Earnings vs. Previous Year Volume Above Avg. STARS
12-Mo. Target Price — Relative Strength ▲ Up ▼ Down ► No Change Below Avg. ★

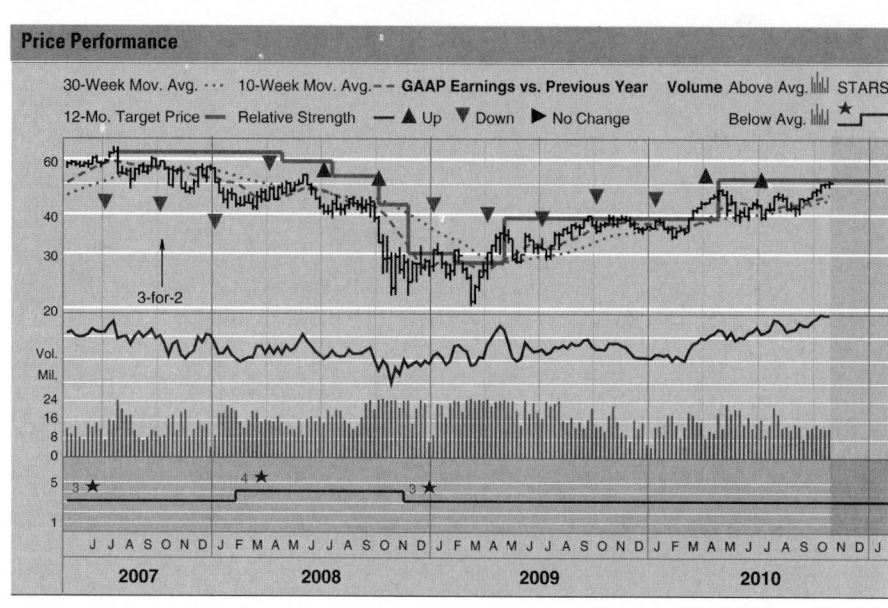

Options: ASE, CBOE, P, Ph

Analysis prepared by **Jim Corridore** on July 28, 2010, when the stock traded at **$ 45.62**.

Highlights

➤ We project truck revenues will rise about 10% in 2010 after a 48% decrease in 2009, and see finance revenues rising about 5% after a 20% decline last year. We look for the North American market for heavy trucks to start improving in mid-2010, driven by fleet owners replacing older vehicles and positioning their fleets ahead of more stringent emission standards. We expect a recovery in Europe in late 2010, lagging the North American economy by about six months.

➤ We forecast that margins within the truck division will benefit from the leverage of fixed costs over an improving revenue base as well as more efficient capacity utilization and ongoing benefits from recent cost-cutting actions. Within the financial services segment, we believe operating margins will continue to be pressured by rising provisions for credit losses and reduced finance margins.

➤ We estimate EPS of $1.06 for 2010, versus $0.31 in 2009. For 2011, we see EPS of $2.20, based on our view that the U.S. truck market should be significantly stronger.

Investment Rationale/Risk

➤ We believe weak demand in both the North American and international truck markets has likely bottomed and should begin to show improvement. Along with demand, we think earnings have also troughed and should show improvement during the next economic upcycle, though the timing of that recovery is still uncertain. We view favorably the company's ability to remain profitable in 2009 on a 48% decline in truck sales. However, the shares are already trading above the high end of their historical P/E range based on our 2011 EPS estimate, which we think will limit upside potential.

➤ Risks to our recommendation and target price include a longer duration to the economic downturn than we are currently forecasting, potential supply disruptions, foreign exchange volatility, and potential increases in raw material costs.

➤ Our 12-month target price of $52 values the shares at 24X our 2011 EPS estimate of $2.20, above the high end of PCAR's historical P/E range, reflecting our view that earnings are at a trough and should improve over the next several years.

Qualitative Risk Assessment

LOW	MEDIUM	HIGH

Our risk assessment for Paccar reflects the highly cyclical nature of the heavy-duty (Class 8) truck market, offset by our view of a strong balance sheet with a relatively low amount of manufacturing debt and a geographical sales mix that is increasingly diversified.

Quantitative Evaluations

S&P Quality Ranking   B+

D	C	B-	B	B+	A-	A	A+

Relative Strength Rank   STRONG

79

LOWEST = 1   HIGHEST = 99

Revenue/Earnings Data

Revenue (Million $)

	1Q	2Q	3Q	4Q	Year
2010	2,231	2,464	--	--	--
2009	1,985	1,846	2,000	2,240	8,087
2008	3,938	4,113	4,005	2,917	14,973
2007	3,985	3,716	3,762	3,759	15,222
2006	3,852	3,937	3,959	3,968	16,454
2005	3,422	3,555	3,541	3,426	14,057

Earnings Per Share ($)

2010	0.19	0.27	E0.29	E0.31	E1.06
2009	0.07	0.07	0.04	0.13	0.31
2008	0.79	0.86	0.82	0.31	2.78
2007	0.97	0.79	0.81	0.71	3.29
2006	0.90	0.98	1.07	1.01	3.97
2005	0.69	0.62	0.79	0.81	2.92

Fiscal year ended Dec. 31. Next earnings report expected: Late October. EPS Estimates based on S&P Operating Earnings; historical GAAP earnings are as reported.

Dividend Data (Dates: mm/dd Payment Date: mm/dd/yy)

Amount ($)	Date Decl.	Ex-Div. Date	Stk. of Record	Payment Date
0.090	12/07	02/17	02/19	03/05/10
0.090	04/20	05/17	05/19	06/07/10
0.090	07/13	08/17	08/19	09/07/10
0.120	09/14	11/17	11/19	12/06/10

Dividends have been paid since 1943. Source: Company reports.

PACCAR Inc

STANDARD
&POOR'S

Business Summary July 28, 2010

CORPORATE OVERVIEW. Originally incorporated in 1924 as the Pacific Car and Foundry Company, and tracing its roots back to the Seattle Car Manufacturing Company, PACCAR has grown into a multinational company with principal businesses that include the design, manufacture and distribution of high-quality light, medium and heavy-duty commercial trucks and related aftermarket parts. The company's heavy-duty (Class 8) diesel trucks are marketed under the Peterbilt, Kenworth, DAF and Foden names. In addition, through its Peterbilt and Kenworth divisions, PCAR competes in the North American medium-duty (Class 6/7) markets and the European light/medium (6 to 15 metric ton) commercial vehicle market with DAF cab-over-engine trucks.

In 2009, the company's truck production and related aftermarket parts distribution businesses accounted for 88% of revenues and 45% of pretax income. Segment profit margins in 2009, 2008, 2007 and 2006 were 0.96%, 8.5%, 9.7%, 1.9%, and 11.5%, respectively; in the previous cycle, during the boom years of

2000, 1999 and 1998, segment profit margins were 6.9%, 9.0% and 7.4%, respectively.

Like other big truck makers, the company aims to capitalize on a growing trend toward truck leasing and financing. The Finance Services segment accounted for 12% of 2009 revenues, but generated 55% of pretax income; it posted operating margins of 8.4%, 17%, 24%, and 26% in 2009, 2008, 2007 and 2006, respectively. In 2009, 2008, 2007, 2006 and 2005, provisions for loan losses were $104 million, $103 million, $41 million, $34 million, and $40 million, respectively.

Company Financials Fiscal Year Ended Dec. 31

Per Share Data ($)	2009	2008	2007	2006	2005	2004	2003	2002	2001	2000
Tangible Book Value	14.02	13.36	13.66	11.98	10.27	9.61	7.36	6.08	5.64	5.64
Cash Flow	2.06	4.56	4.70	5.12	3.87	3.09	2.00	1.50	0.91	1.54
Earnings	0.31	2.78	3.29	3.97	2.92	2.29	1.33	0.95	0.45	1.13
S&P Core Earnings	0.18	2.63	3.24	3.97	2.92	2.25	1.32	0.89	0.37	NA
Dividends	0.54	0.82	0.83	0.64	0.39	0.33	0.46	0.29	0.24	0.24
Payout Ratio	174%	29%	25%	16%	13%	15%	35%	30%	53%	21%
Prices:High	40.26	55.54	65.75	46.17	36.17	36.19	25.95	15.70	13.68	10.72
Prices:Low	20.38	21.96	42.15	30.12	28.13	22.05	12.37	9.09	8.44	7.16
P/E Ratio:High	NM	20	20	12	12	16	20	17	31	9
P/E Ratio:Low	NM	8	13	8	10	10	9	10	19	6

Income Statement Analysis (Million $)	2009	2008	2007	2006	2005	2004	2003	2002	2001	2000
Revenue	8,087	14,973	15,222	16,454	14,057	11,396	8,195	7,219	6,089	7,437
Operating Income	812	2,859	2,932	3,136	2,572	1,972	1,313	1,012	672	1,122
Depreciation	638	649	526	435	370	315	268	218	180	156
Interest Expense	12.8	NA	737	573	445	331	3.50	249	275	294
Pretax Income	175	1,464	1,764	2,175	1,774	1,368	806	574	255	665
Effective Tax Rate	36.1%	30.5%	30.4%	31.2%	36.1%	33.7%	34.6%	35.2%	32.0%	33.6%
Net Income	112	1,018	1,227	1,496	1,133	907	527	372	174	442
S&P Core Earnings	64.5	962	1,208	1,496	1,134	889	523	349	145	NA

Balance Sheet & Other Financial Data (Million $)	2009	2008	2007	2006	2005	2004	2003	2002	2001	2000
Cash	2,056	2,075	1,948	2,628	2,290	2,220	1,724	1,308	1,062	910
Current Assets	10,040	3,643	3,919	4,200	3,508	3,332	2,599	2,102	1,834	1,861
Total Assets	14,569	16,250	17,228	16,107	13,715	12,228	9,940	8,703	7,914	8,271
Current Liabilities	5,286	1,829	2,503	2,738	2,182	2,151	1,482	1,258	1,134	1,268
Long Term Debt	172	19.3	3,039	498	936	2,314	1,557	1,552	1,547	1,655
Common Equity	5,104	4,847	5,013	4,456	3,901	3,762	3,246	2,601	2,253	2,249
Total Capital	5,276	4,866	8,052	4,954	4,837	6,077	4,803	4,152	3,800	3,904
Capital Expenditures	971	1,550	1,267	312	300	232	111	78.8	83.9	143
Cash Flow	750	1,667	1,754	1,931	1,503	1,222	794	590	354	598
Current Ratio	1.3	2.0	1.6	1.5	1.6	1.5	1.8	1.7	1.6	1.5
% Long Term Debt of Capitalization	3.3	0.3	37.7	10.1	19.3	38.1	32.4	37.4	40.7	42.4
% Net Income of Revenue	1.4	6.8	8.1	9.1	8.1	8.0	6.4	5.2	2.9	5.9
% Return on Assets	0.7	6.1	7.4	10.0	8.7	8.2	5.6	4.5	2.1	5.5
% Return on Equity	2.3	20.7	25.9	35.8	29.6	25.9	18.0	15.3	7.7	20.3

Data as orig reptd.; bef. results of disc opers/spec. items. Per share data adj. for stk. divs.; EPS diluted. E-Estimated. NA-Not Available. NM-Not Meaningful. NR-Not Ranked. UR-Under Review.

Office: 777 106th Avenue NE, Bellevue, WA 98004-5027.
Telephone: 425-468-7400.
Website: http://www.paccar.com
Chrmn & CEO: M.C. Pigott

Pres: J. Cardillo
Vice Chrmn & CFO: T.E. Plimpton
Chief Acctg Officer & Cntlr: M.T. Barkley
Secy: J.M. D'Amato

Investor Contact: R. Easton
Board Members: A. J. Carnwath, J. Fluke, Jr., K. S. Hachigian, S. F. Page, R. T. Parry, J. M. Pigott, M. C. Pigott, T. E. Plimpton, W. G. Reed, Jr., G. M. Spierkel, W. R. Staley, C. R. Williamson

Founded: 1905
Domicile: Delaware
Employees: 15,200

The McGraw-Hill Companies

STANDARD &POOR'S

Pactiv Corp

S&P Recommendation HOLD ★★★☆☆	**Price** $33.17 (as of Oct 22, 2010)	**12-Mo. Target Price** $33.00	**Investment Style** Large-Cap Growth

GICS Sector Materials
Sub-Industry Metal & Glass Containers

Summary This company is a leading provider of specialty packaging and consumer products. In August 2010, it definitively agreed to be acquired by Reynolds Group Holdings.

Key Stock Statistics (Source S&P, Vickers, company reports)

52-Wk Range	$33.22– 21.55	S&P Oper. EPS 2010E	2.20	Market Capitalization(B)	$4.411	Beta	0.90
Trailing 12-Month EPS	$2.15	S&P Oper. EPS 2011E	2.50	Yield (%)	Nil	S&P 3-Yr. Proj. EPS CAGR(%)	3
Trailing 12-Month P/E	15.4	P/E on S&P Oper. EPS 2010E	15.1	Dividend Rate/Share	Nil	S&P Credit Rating	BBB
$10K Invested 5 Yrs Ago	$19,500	Common Shares Outstg. (M)	133.0	Institutional Ownership (%)	93		

Price Performance

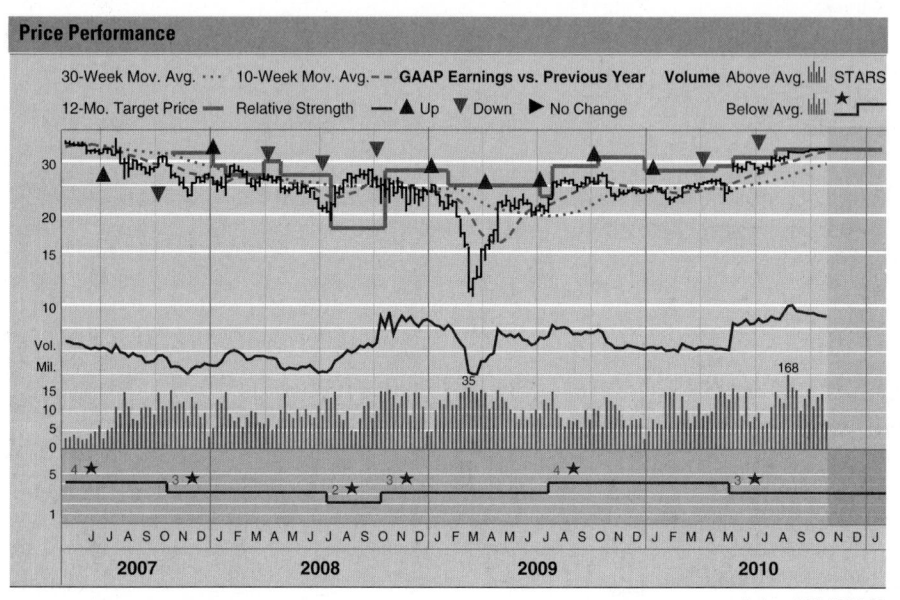

30-Week Mov. Avg. ··· 10-Week Mov. Avg. – – GAAP Earnings vs. Previous Year Volume Above Avg. STARS
12-Mo. Target Price — Relative Strength — ▲ Up ▼ Down ► No Change Below Avg.

Options: ASE, CBOE, Ph

Analysis prepared by **Stewart Scharf** on August 19, 2010, when the stock traded at **$ 32.51**.

Highlights

► We expect sales for 2010 to rise at least 8% (including 4% from the PWP acquisition), on improving demand for foodservice products and new store brand waste bags. Demand for disposable cookware, cups and cutlery, and produce packaging and trays should continue to grow.

► We look for gross margins (before $200 million of D&A), as adjusted for a change to FIFO accounting, to narrow to near 28.5% in 2010, from 33% in 2009, based on an unfavorable price/cost spread and lost volume due to sequentially falling raw material costs. We see EBITDA margins also narrowing somewhat from 2009's 22.7%, as the negative price spread and product mix and higher advertising expenses outweigh lower SG&A expenses resulting from productivity improvement programs and lower incentive compensation accruals.

► We expect a relatively steady effective tax rate of 36.5% in 2010, and we see adjusted operating EPS of $2.20 (including $0.23 of pension income and $0.05 of accretion from PWP, but before a $0.02 charge), rising 14% to $2.50 in 2011.

Investment Rationale/Risk

► Our hold opinion is based on our valuation metrics and PTV's recent agreement to be acquired for about $33 a share, along with still soft demand for Hefty consumer products and a competitive pricing environment.

► Risks to our recommendation and target price include sharp increases in resin and other commodity prices, and a loss of market share as customers continue to purchase lower-priced packaging products. Regarding corporate governance, we are somewhat concerned that the positions of chairman and CEO are held by the same person.

► Our 12-month target price of $33 is derived from a blend of our DCF and relative valuations. Our DCF model, which assumes a 3% terminal growth rate and an 8.5% weighted average cost of capital (WACC), produces an intrinsic value of $35. Based on relative metrics, we apply a multiple of 14X to our 2010 EPS estimate, a premium to peers, and arrive at a value of $31. Our target price also approximates the offering price of $33.25 per share.

Qualitative Risk Assessment

LOW	MEDIUM	HIGH

Our risk assessment reflects a customer shift to private-label products due to the soft economy, supplier and customer consolidation, pension plan costs, and volatile raw material costs. However, we believe the balance sheet is strong, and the company is generating cash for acquisitions and share buybacks.

Quantitative Evaluations

S&P Quality Ranking   B-

D	C	B-	B	B+	A-	A	A+

Relative Strength Rank   MODERATE

55

LOWEST = 1   HIGHEST = 99

Revenue/Earnings Data

Revenue (Million $)

	1Q	2Q	3Q	4Q	Year
2010	777.0	973.0	--	--	--
2009	766.0	901.0	839.0	854.0	3,360
2008	808.0	951.0	925.0	883.0	3,567
2007	677.0	828.0	872.0	876.0	3,253
2006	680.0	750.0	749.0	738.0	2,917
2005	613.0	707.0	695.0	741.0	2,756

Earnings Per Share ($)

	1Q	2Q	3Q	4Q	Year
2010	0.36	0.56	E0.58	E0.69	E2.20
2009	0.58	0.61	0.59	0.53	2.31
2008	0.27	0.49	0.40	0.52	1.67
2007	0.43	0.52	0.45	0.45	1.84
2006	0.35	0.49	0.75	0.39	1.98
2005	0.14	0.24	0.28	0.30	0.96

Fiscal year ended Dec. 31. Next earnings report expected: NA. EPS Estimates based on S&P Operating Earnings; historical GAAP earnings are as reported.

Dividend Data

No cash dividends have been paid.

The McGraw-Hill Companies

Pactiv Corp

STANDARD &POOR'S

Business Summary August 19, 2010

CORPORATE OVERVIEW. Pactiv Corp., a global supplier of specialty packaging and consumer products, derives more than 80% of its sales from markets in which it holds the No. 1 or No. 2 market share position. It operates 43 manufacturing plants in North America and one in Germany. It also has a 62.5%-owned joint venture corrugated-converting facility and a 51%-owned folding carton operation in China. In 2009, 96% of sales were generated in North America (91% in the U.S.). Wal-Mart accounted for 21% of total sales.

After discontinuing the protective and flexible packaging division during 2005, PTV operated two units: Hefty Consumer Products and Foodservice/Food Packaging. Consumer products sales accounted for 38% of total sales in 2009 ($297 million of operating income), and foodservice/food packaging 62% ($300 million). In June 2007, PTV acquired Prairie Packaging Inc., a manufacturer of disposable tableware products with sales of over $500 million, broadening its cups and cutlery business.

The company manufactures consumer products such as plastic storage bags and waste bags; foam and molded fiber disposable tableware; and disposable aluminum cookware. It sells many products under recognized brand names such as Hefty, Baggies and Kordite. Hefty products include One-Zip, Zoo Pals, Odor Block, The Gripper, Cinch Sak, Ultra Flex, Kitchen Fresh, Elegantware,

Hearty Meals, E-Z Foil and Easy Grip. The company expects new product innovations to generate $100 million in annual retail sales over the next few years. In late 2009, the company added private-label waste bags to its product mix, signing a multi-year contract with Wal-Mart to be their exclusive supplier of value waste bags.

PTV makes food packaging products for the food processing industry, including molded fiber egg cartons, foam meat trays and aluminum containers. The company also offers tableware products such as plates, bowls, cups, and takeout-service containers made from microwaveable plastic, foam, molded fiber, paperboard and aluminum.

The company estimates that a 1% change in resin costs equates to a $0.03 effect on EPS on an annualized basis, assuming no pricing actions. PTV incurred a $2.5 million ($0.02 a share) tax charge in the first quarter of 2010 related to health care legislation.

Company Financials Fiscal Year Ended Dec. 31

Per Share Data ($)	2009	2008	2007	2006	2005	2004	2003	2002	2001	2000
Tangible Book Value	NM	NM	NM	0.68	0.23	0.98	0.77	1.79	4.91	3.79
Cash Flow	3.69	3.04	3.08	3.02	1.94	2.10	2.24	2.35	2.14	1.84
Earnings	2.31	1.67	1.84	1.98	0.96	1.01	1.21	1.37	1.03	0.70
S&P Core Earnings	2.06	0.14	1.51	1.71	0.56	0.64	1.00	-0.23	-0.57	NA
Dividends	Nil	Nil	Nil	Nil	Nil	Nil	Nil	Nil	Nil	Nil
Payout Ratio	Nil	Nil	Nil	Nil	Nil	Nil	Nil	Nil	Nil	Nil
Prices:High	27.71	29.52	36.91	36.53	25.58	25.73	24.03	24.47	18.10	13.31
Prices:Low	10.62	18.97	22.79	21.50	16.50	19.80	17.55	15.35	11.26	7.50
P/E Ratio:High	12	18	20	18	27	25	20	18	18	19
P/E Ratio:Low	5	11	12	11	17	20	15	11	11	11

Income Statement Analysis (Million $)	2009	2008	2007	2006	2005	2004	2003	2002	2001	2000
Revenue	3,360	3,567	3,253	2,917	2,756	3,382	3,138	2,880	2,812	3,134
Operating Income	763	649	644	568	452	954	630	617	574	570
Depreciation	184	181	165	145	146	169	163	158	177	185
Interest Expense	94.0	108	98.0	73.0	82.0	101	96.0	96.0	107	134
Pretax Income	486	342	381	391	224	244	314	367	284	207
Effective Tax Rate	36.4%	35.1%	35.4%	29.2%	36.2%	36.9%	37.6%	39.8%	41.5%	44.0%
Net Income	308	221	244	277	143	155	195	220	165	113
S&P Core Earnings	274	18.5	200	239	82.3	96.9	160	-36.1	-91.1	NA

Balance Sheet & Other Financial Data (Million $)	2009	2008	2007	2006	2005	2004	2003	2002	2001	2000
Cash	46.0	80.0	95.0	181	172	222	140	127	41.0	26.0
Current Assets	832	785	797	838	820	1,079	982	904	740	900
Total Assets	3,574	3,692	3,765	2,758	2,820	3,741	3,706	3,412	4,060	4,341
Current Liabilities	417	333	460	549	456	984	474	501	459	512
Long Term Debt	1,275	1,345	1,574	771	869	869	1,336	1,224	1,211	1,560
Common Equity	985	640	1,226	853	820	1,083	1,061	897	1,689	1,539
Total Capital	2,276	2,000	3,032	1,753	1,802	2,209	2,617	2,282	3,502	3,595
Capital Expenditures	111	136	151	78.0	121	100	112	126	145	135
Cash Flow	492	402	409	422	289	324	358	378	342	298
Current Ratio	2.0	2.4	1.7	1.5	1.8	1.1	2.1	1.8	1.6	1.8
% Long Term Debt of Capitalization	56.0	67.3	51.9	44.0	48.2	39.3	51.1	53.6	34.6	43.4
% Net Income of Revenue	9.2	6.2	7.5	9.5	5.2	4.6	6.2	7.6	5.9	3.6
% Return on Assets	8.4	5.9	7.5	9.9	4.4	4.2	5.5	5.9	4.0	2.5
% Return on Equity	37.9	23.7	23.5	33.1	15.0	14.5	19.9	17.0	10.2	7.8

Data as orig reptd.; bef. results of disc opers/spec. items. Per share data adj. for stk. divs.; EPS diluted. E-Estimated. NA-Not Available. NM-Not Meaningful. NR-Not Ranked. UR-Under Review.

Office: 1900 West Field Court, Lake Forest, IL 60045-4828.
Telephone: 847-482-2000.
Email: investorrelations@pactiv.com
Website: http://www.pactiv.com

Chrmn, Pres & CEO: R.L. Wambold
SVP & CFO: E.T. Walters
Chief Acctg Officer & Cntlr: D.E. King
Secy & General Counsel: J.E. Doyle

Investor Contact: C. Hanneman (847-482-2429)
Board Members: L. D. Brady, II, K. D. Brookster, R. J. Darnall, M. R. Henderson, N. T. Linebarger, R. B. Porter, R. L. Wambold, N. H. Wesley

Founded: 1965
Domicile: Delaware
Employees: 12,000

Pall Corp

STANDARD &POOR'S

S&P Recommendation BUY ★★★★☆

Price	**12-Mo. Target Price**
$43.43 (as of Oct 22, 2010)	$46.00

GICS Sector Industrials
Sub-Industry Industrial Machinery

Summary This company is a leading producer of filters for the health care, aerospace, microelectronics, and other industries.

Key Stock Statistics (Source S&P, Vickers, company reports)

52-Wk Range	$44.65– 30.74	S&P Oper. EPS 2011**E**	2.50	Market Capitalization(B)	$5.019	Beta	1.15
Trailing 12-Month EPS	$2.03	S&P Oper. EPS 2012**E**	2.80	Yield (%)	1.47	S&P 3-Yr. Proj. EPS CAGR(%)	14
Trailing 12-Month P/E	21.4	P/E on S&P Oper. EPS 2011**E**	17.4	Dividend Rate/Share	$0.64	S&P Credit Rating	BBB
$10K Invested 5 Yrs Ago	$18,517	Common Shares Outstg. (M)	115.6	Institutional Ownership (%)	89		

Price Performance

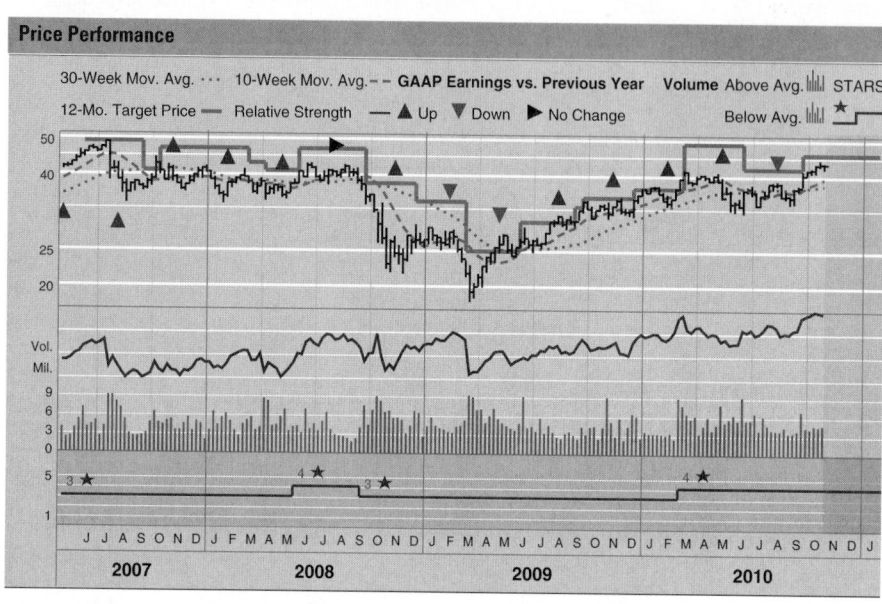

30-Week Mov. Avg. ··· 10-Week Mov. Avg. - - **GAAP Earnings vs. Previous Year** Volume Above Avg. STARS
12-Mo. Target Price — Relative Strength — ▲ Up ▼ Down ▶ No Change Below Avg. ★

Options: CBOE, Ph

Analysis prepared by **Stewart Scharf** on September 16, 2010, when the stock traded at **$ 40.13**.

Highlights

➤ We expect sales in FY 11 (Jul.) to rise at least 7% (before modest negative foreign currency effect), driven by favorable global order trends in both segments. In our view, life sciences will benefit from increased demand for biotech drugs and vaccines, while the food & beverage market is drvien by tighter regulations. The industrial segment should see strong aerospace sales and growth in machinery & equipment, and microelectronics, while energy orders pick up, and municipal water demand strengthens mainly in the U.S.

➤ We see gross margins widening to at least 50.5% in FY 11, from 50.2% in FY 10, based on absorption of manufacturing costs, a better product mix, pricing initiatives, and cost savings. In our view, operating margins (EBITDA) will expand by about 50-basis points to 20.5% in FY 11, on improved productivity and efficiencies, as PLL implements its strategic plan and information technology system.

➤ We forecast a lower effective tax rate of 27% for FY 11, and see operating EPS of $2.50 (including a $0.03 negative foreign exchange headwind), rising 12% to $2.80 in FY 12.

Investment Rationale/Risk

➤ Our buy opinion is based on signs of a pick up in global orders, and our valuation metrics. Additionally, Millipore was acquired in July 2010 by Germany-based Merck KGZaA, which we think adds to PLL's appeal as a potential takeover candidate. Also, some Millipore customers may defect to PLL.

➤ Risks to our recommendation and target price include a weaker economy, negative foreign currency translations, and a significant rise in raw material costs. We have some corporate governance concerns based on financial reporting errors that led to seven years of restated earnings, although we think internal controls are now more solid.

➤ Our relative valuation results in a value of $44 using a multiple of 17.5X our FY 11 EPS estimate, a modest premium to our projected P/E (adjusted for FY end) for S&P's Industrial Machinery sub-industry group. Our intrinsic value estimate of $48 is based on our DCF model, which assumes a terminal growth rate of 3.5% and a weighted average cost of capital of 8.5%. Blending these metrics, our 12-month target price is $46.

Qualitative Risk Assessment

LOW	MEDIUM	HIGH

Our risk assessment reflects the historically cyclical semiconductor sector, PLL's exposure to foreign markets, and a pending settlement with the IRS and other civil lawsuits related to understating tax payments, even though the SEC inquiry and restatements have been completed. Also, an IRS audit and U.S. Attorney inquiry are still pending. This is offset by our view of PLL's reduced debt levels and positive cash generation.

Quantitative Evaluations

S&P Quality Ranking B+

D	C	B-	B	B+	A-	A	A+

Relative Strength Rank STRONG

78

LOWEST = 1   HIGHEST = 99

Revenue/Earnings Data

Revenue (Million $)

	1Q	2Q	3Q	4Q	Year
2010	546.9	560.4	616.0	678.6	2,402
2009	578.0	543.3	555.9	652.0	2,329
2008	561.0	625.8	661.7	723.2	2,572
2007	499.3	544.9	559.4	646.3	2,250
2006	431.2	478.4	510.0	597.3	2,017
2005	414.7	469.5	493.5	524.5	1,902

Earnings Per Share ($)

2010	0.56	0.42	0.58	0.46	2.03
2009	0.36	0.33	0.37	0.58	1.64
2008	0.29	0.39	0.51	0.57	1.76
2007	0.13	0.36	0.40	0.57	1.03
2006	0.20	0.26	0.20	0.50	1.16
2005	0.17	0.26	0.35	0.34	1.12

Fiscal year ended Jul. 31. Next earnings report expected: Early December. EPS Estimates based on S&P Operating Earnings; historical GAAP earnings are as reported.

Dividend Data (Dates: mm/dd Payment Date: mm/dd/yy)

Amount ($)	Date Decl.	Ex-Div. Date	Stk. of Record	Payment Date
0.160	01/21	02/05	02/09	02/23/10
0.160	04/23	05/05	05/07	05/14/10
0.160	07/15	08/04	08/06	08/20/10
0.160	09/23	10/06	10/08	10/29/10

Dividends have been paid since 1974. Source: Company reports.

Please read the Required Disclosures and Analyst Certification on the last page of this report.

The McGraw-Hill Companies

Pall Corp

Business Summary September 16, 2010

CORPORATE OVERVIEW. Pall Corp. is a global producer of filters for health care, aerospace and industrial markets. Pall divides these markets into the following subsegments: Medical, BioPharmaceuticals and Food & Beverage (the Life Sciences segment), Energy & Water, Aeropower and Microelectronics (the Industrial segment). The Industrial group includes machinery and equipment, aerospace, fuels & chemicals, power generation and municipal water. System sales in the fourth quarter of FY 10 (Jul.) accounted for 12% of sales, with PLL expecting an increase to 13% to 14% of sales in FY 11, driven by double-digit system sales growth.

The Industrial segment (49% of revenues in FY 10 and $165 million of profits) makes filters and separation products for three markets. Aerospower (36% of the segment's sales) includes both commercial and military markets. Energy & Water (41%) produces filters for the aluminum, paper, automobile, oil, gas, chemical, petrochemical and power industries. Microelectronics (23%) makes products for the semiconductor, data storage and photographic film industries. Consumer electronics accounted for over 40% of segment sales in FY 10, up from 25% in 2000. Main competitors in the Energy & Water group include 3M's CUNO, General Electric's GE Infrastructure unit, Siemens's U.S. Filter, Rohm & Haas (acquired by Dow Chemical in 2009), and Parker-Hannifin. More than 90% of systems sales are in this segment. PLL sees a potential market for this group of $39 billion.

The Life Sciences segment contributed 51% of total revenues ($280 million in operating profits) in FY 10. The BioPharmaceuticals division makes filter products used in the development of drugs and vaccines, while food and beverage filters help produce yeast- and bacteria-free water. The rapidly expanding blood division offers hospitals and blood centers blood filters that reduce leukocyte (white cells) and other bloodborne viral contaminants, such as bacteria. Biopharmaceutical sales accounted for 50% of the segment's total sales in FY 10, while medical products (blood and cardiovascular filtration) accounted for 32% and food & beverage 18%. New products accounted for 30% of medical sales in FY 10. PLL projects the medical market potential size at $6.8 billion by FY 13.

In FY 10, the Western Hemisphere accounted for 33% of sales, Europe for 39%, and Asia for 28%. In FY 10, pro forma EPS was $2.12, excluding $0.48 of restructuring and other charges. Foreign currency added $0.10 to EPS.

Company Financials Fiscal Year Ended Jul. 31

Per Share Data ($)	2010	2009	2008	2007	2006	2005	2004	2003	2002	2001
Tangible Book Value	7.19	6.57	6.94	6.14	7.21	6.73	6.21	5.16	NM	6.29
Cash Flow	2.82	2.38	2.51	1.78	1.92	1.85	1.90	1.51	1.19	1.53
Earnings	2.03	1.64	1.76	1.03	1.16	1.12	1.20	0.83	0.59	0.95
S&P Core Earnings	2.11	1.55	1.67	1.05	1.22	1.13	1.16	0.70	0.42	0.83
Dividends	0.61	0.42	0.50	0.35	0.53	0.38	0.27	0.36	0.52	0.68
Payout Ratio	30%	26%	28%	34%	46%	34%	23%	43%	88%	71%
Prices:High	44.65	37.25	43.19	49.00	35.57	31.52	29.80	27.00	24.48	26.25
Prices:Low	31.84	18.20	21.61	33.23	25.26	25.21	22.00	15.01	14.68	17.50
P/E Ratio:High	22	23	25	48	31	28	25	33	41	28
P/E Ratio:Low	16	11	12	32	22	23	18	18	25	18

Income Statement Analysis (Million $)	2010	2009	2008	2007	2006	2005	2004	2003	2002	2001
Revenue	2,402	2,329	2,572	2,250	2,017	1,902	1,771	1,614	1,291	1,235
Operating Income	484	419	483	419	341	337	320	299	215	256
Depreciation	93.6	89.2	93.2	94.0	95.7	90.9	88.9	83.9	74.0	71.5
Interest Expense	14.3	36.9	50.9	56.8	23.0	26.0	20.5	24.4	14.3	16.6
Pretax Income	328	271	326	261	210	181	198	143	100.0	150
Effective Tax Rate	NA	27.8%	33.3%	51.1%	30.8%	22.2%	23.4%	27.9%	26.7%	21.5%
Net Income	241	196	217	128	145	141	152	103	73.2	118
S&P Core Earnings	250	185	205	131	153	142	148	87.4	52.1	102

Balance Sheet & Other Financial Data (Million $)	2010	2009	2008	2007	2006	2005	2004	2003	2002	2001
Cash	499	414	454	443	318	165	199	127	105	54.9
Current Assets	1,703	1,570	1,660	1,606	1,377	1,160	1,070	938	916	779
Total Assets	2,999	2,841	2,957	2,709	2,553	2,265	2,140	2,017	2,027	1,549
Current Liabilities	637	717	574	832	531	457	419	421	438	314
Long Term Debt	741	578	747	592	640	510	489	490	620	359
Common Equity	1,182	1,115	1,139	1,061	1,179	1,140	1,054	935	820	770
Total Capital	1,924	1,692	1,890	1,654	1,826	1,660	1,559	1,439	1,478	1,149
Capital Expenditures	136	133	124	97.8	96.0	86.2	61.3	62.2	69.9	77.8
Cash Flow	335	285	310	221	241	232	241	187	147	190
Current Ratio	2.7	2.2	2.9	1.9	2.6	2.5	2.6	2.2	2.1	2.5
% Long Term Debt of Capitalization	38.5	34.1	39.4	35.8	35.0	30.7	31.3	34.0	41.9	31.2
% Net Income of Revenue	10.0	8.4	8.5	5.7	7.2	7.4	8.6	6.4	5.7	9.6
% Return on Assets	8.3	6.8	7.7	4.9	6.0	6.3	7.3	5.1	4.1	7.7
% Return on Equity	21.0	17.4	19.8	11.4	12.5	12.8	15.2	11.8	9.2	15.4

Data as orig reptd.; bef. results of disc opers/spec. items. Per share data adj. for stk. divs.; EPS diluted. E-Estimated. NA-Not Available. NM-Not Meaningful. NR-Not Ranked. UR-Under Review.

Office: 25 Harbor Park Dr, Port Washington, NY 11050.
Telephone: 516-484-5400.
Email: invrel@pall.com
Website: http://www.pall.com

Chrmn, Pres & CEO: E. Krasnoff
COO: R. Perez
SVP, Secy & General Counsel: S. Marino
CFO & Treas: L. McDermott

CTO: M. Egholm
Investor Contact: J. Conenello (516-801-9850)
Board Members: A. E. Alving, D. J. Carroll, Jr., R. B. Coutts, C. W. Grise, U. Haynes, Jr., R. L. Hoffman, E. Krasnoff, D. N. Longstreet, E. W. Martin, Jr., K. L. Plourde, E. L. Snyder, E. Travaglianti

Founded: 1946
Domicile: New York
Employees: 10,400

Parker-Hannifin Corp

STANDARD &POOR'S

S&P Recommendation **BUY** ★★★★☆	Price $76.31 (as of Oct 22, 2010)	12-Mo. Target Price $88.00	Investment Style Large-Cap Blend

GICS Sector Industrials
Sub-Industry Industrial Machinery

Summary This company is a global maker of industrial pumps, valves, pneumatics, and hydraulics. Its products are used in everything from jet engines to trucks and autos and utility turbines.

Key Stock Statistics (Source S&P, Vickers, company reports)

52-Wk Range	$78.71– 52.46	S&P Oper. EPS 2011**E**	5.72	Market Capitalization(B)	$12.299	Beta	1.41
Trailing 12-Month EPS	$3.40	S&P Oper. EPS 2012**E**	5.95	Yield (%)	1.42	S&P 3-Yr. Proj. EPS CAGR(%)	22
Trailing 12-Month P/E	22.4	P/E on S&P Oper. EPS 2011**E**	13.3	Dividend Rate/Share	$1.08	S&P Credit Rating	A
$10K Invested 5 Yrs Ago	$20,251	Common Shares Outstg. (M)	161.2	Institutional Ownership (%)	81		

Price Performance

30-Week Mov. Avg. · · · · 10-Week Mov. Avg. – – **GAAP Earnings vs. Previous Year** Volume Above Avg. |ılıl| STARS
12-Mo. Target Price — Relative Strength — ▲ Up ▼ Down ► No Change   Below Avg. |ılıl| ★

[Price performance chart showing PH stock from 2007 to 2010, with a 3-for-2 split noted, volume in millions, and STARS ratings. Price scale shows 30, 40, 60, 80. Volume scale shows 4, 8, 12.]

Options: ASE, CBOE, Ph

Highlights

► The STARS recommendation for PH has recently been changed to 4 (buy) from 4 (buy) and the 12-month target price has recently been changed to $88.00 from $78.00. The Highlights section of this Stock Report will be updated accordingly.

Investment Rationale/Risk

► The Investment Rationale/Risk section of this Stock Report will be updated shortly. For the latest News story on PH from MarketScope, see below.

► 10/19/10 11:11 am ET ... S&P RAISES RECOMMENDATION ON SHARES OF PARKER-HANNIFIN TO BUY FROM HOLD (PH 75.99****): Sep-Q EPS of $1.51, vs. $0.45, were well above our $0.89 estimate, as sales rose 27%. Also, total orders rose 29% in the Sep-Q, with strength in all segments. Operating margins reached 15.5% vs. 13.9% in the Sep-Q. On results and order strength, we are raising our FY 11 EPS estimate by $1.77 to $5.72, above FY 08 (Jun) peak EPS of $5.53, and lifting FY 12's by $1.70 to $5.95. We up our 12-month target price by $10 to $88, on our revised earnings outlook. We see PH benefiting from strong execution, U.S. economic growth, and a good position in Asia and Latin America. /R.Tortoriello

Qualitative Risk Assessment

LOW	MEDIUM	HIGH

Our risk assessment reflects the highly cyclical nature of the company's industrial and aviation markets, volatile energy and materials costs, and a competitive environment. This is offset by our view of PH's favorable earnings and dividend track record, as exemplified by an S&P Quality Ranking of A-.

Quantitative Evaluations

S&P Quality Ranking A

D	C	B-	B	B+	A-	**A**	A+

Relative Strength Rank STRONG

87

LOWEST = 1   HIGHEST = 99

Revenue/Earnings Data

Revenue (Million $)

	1Q	2Q	3Q	4Q	Year
2010	2,237	2,355	2,615	2,786	9,993
2009	3,065	2,689	2,345	2,211	10,309
2008	2,787	2,829	3,183	3,347	12,146
2007	2,552	2,511	2,781	2,874	10,718
2006	2,114	2,158	2,498	2,617	9,386
2005	1,947	1,943	2,142	2,211	8,215

Earnings Per Share ($)

2010	0.45	0.64	0.94	1.35	3.40
2009	1.50	0.96	0.33	0.31	3.13
2008	1.33	1.23	1.49	1.47	5.53
2007	1.17	1.09	1.19	1.23	4.67
2006	0.79	0.71	0.97	1.03	3.52
2005	0.74	0.63	0.79	0.89	3.03

Fiscal year ended Jun. 30. Next earnings report expected: NA. EPS Estimates based on S&P Operating Earnings; historical GAAP earnings are as reported.

Dividend Data (Dates: mm/dd Payment Date: mm/dd/yy)

Amount ($)	Date Decl.	Ex-Div. Date	Stk. of Record	Payment Date
0.250	10/28	11/17	11/19	12/04/09
0.250	01/28	02/16	02/18	03/05/10
0.260	04/15	05/18	05/20	06/04/10
0.270	08/12	08/19	08/23	09/03/10

Dividends have been paid since 1949. Source: Company reports.

Please read the Required Disclosures and Analyst Certification on the last page of this report.

The **McGraw·Hill** Companies

Parker-Hannifin Corp

STANDARD &POOR'S

Business Summary August 05, 2010

CORPORATE OVERVIEW. Parker-Hannifin is one of the world's largest makers of components that control the flow of industrial fluids. It is also a major global maker of components that move and/or control the operation of a variety of machinery and equipment. In addition to motion control products, PH also produces fluid purification, fluid and fuel control, process instrumentation, air conditioning, refrigeration, electromagnetic shielding, and thermal management products and systems. PH's offerings include a wide range of valves, pumps, hydraulics, filters and related products. The company's components are used in everything from jet engines to medical devices, farm tractors and utility turbines.

Although U.S. markets still account for most of the company's revenues, PH has been expanding its overseas presence in recent years. International sales accounted for 41% of total revenue in FY 09 (Jun.), and 45% in FY 08.

PH's Industrial business (74% of FY 09 sales and 74% of segment operating earnings) makes valves, pumps, filters, seals and hydraulic components for a broad range of industries, as well as pneumatic and electromechanical components and systems. The company's industrial components are sold to manufacturers (as part of original equipment) and to end users (as replacement

parts). Replacement part sales are generally more profitable than original equipment sales. PH's industrial components are designed for both standard and custom specifications. Custom-made components are typically more profitable than standard components. The industrial business is reported as two segments: Industrial North America (36% of sales and 39% of operating profits) and Industrial International (38% and 35%). Sales through distributors account for about half of PH's total industrial business.

Aerospace (18% of sales and 26% of segment operating profits) primarily makes hydraulic, pneumatic and fuel equipment used in civilian and military airframes and jet engines. It also makes aircraft wheels and brakes for small planes and military aircraft. PH sells aircraft components to aircraft manufacturers as new equipment, and to end-users (such as airlines) as replacement parts. As with industrial components, aircraft-related replacement parts sales are generally more profitable than are original equipment sales.

Company Financials Fiscal Year Ended Jun. 30

Per Share Data ($)	2010	2009	2008	2007	2006	2005	2004	2003	2002	2001
Tangible Book Value	2.68	0.07	8.59	10.69	9.75	9.23	9.39	7.63	8.18	8.95
Cash Flow	5.63	5.32	7.43	6.45	5.07	4.50	3.34	2.57	2.37	3.53
Earnings	3.40	3.13	5.53	4.67	3.52	3.03	1.94	1.12	0.75	1.99
S&P Core Earnings	3.76	2.71	5.10	4.77	3.83	3.08	2.00	0.61	0.37	1.19
Dividends	1.01	1.00	0.84	0.69	0.61	0.52	0.51	0.49	0.48	0.47
Payout Ratio	30%	32%	15%	15%	17%	17%	26%	44%	64%	23%
Prices:High	78.71	59.36	86.91	86.56	58.67	50.82	52.28	39.87	36.59	33.40
Prices:Low	53.50	27.69	31.29	50.41	43.44	37.87	34.49	23.88	23.01	20.27
P/E Ratio:High	23	19	16	19	17	17	27	36	49	17
P/E Ratio:Low	16	9	6	11	12	12	18	21	31	10

Income Statement Analysis (Million $)	2010	2009	2008	2007	2006	2005	2004	2003	2002	2001
Revenue	9,993	10,309	12,146	10,718	9,386	8,215	7,107	6,411	6,149	5,980
Operating Income	1,232	1,196	1,773	1,513	1,263	1,100	817	639	628	836
Depreciation	363	358	325	295	281	265	253	259	282	265
Interest Expense	104	112	99.0	83.4	75.8	67.0	73.4	81.6	82.0	90.4
Pretax Income	755	681	1,327	1,159	900	756	494	297	218	534
Effective Tax Rate	NA	25.4%	28.4%	28.4%	NM	27.6%	30.0%	34.0%	40.3%	35.5%
Net Income	554	509	949	830	638	548	346	196	130	344
S&P Core Earnings	613	441	876	846	694	557	357	107	65.0	204

Balance Sheet & Other Financial Data (Million $)	2010	2009	2008	2007	2006	2005	2004	2003	2002	2001
Cash	576	188	326	173	172	336	184	246	46.0	23.7
Current Assets	3,589	3,124	4,096	3,386	3,139	2,786	2,537	2,397	2,236	2,196
Total Assets	9,910	9,856	10,387	8,441	8,173	6,899	6,257	5,986	5,733	5,338
Current Liabilities	2,205	2,006	2,183	1,925	1,681	1,336	1,260	1,424	1,360	1,413
Long Term Debt	1,414	1,840	1,952	1,087	1,059	938	954	966	1,089	857
Common Equity	4,368	4,280	5,259	4,712	4,241	3,340	2,982	2,521	2,584	2,529
Total Capital	5,873	6,393	7,374	5,913	5,419	4,314	4,015	3,508	3,750	3,518
Capital Expenditures	129	271	280	238	198	157	142	158	207	345
Cash Flow	917	866	1,274	1,125	919	813	599	455	412	609
Current Ratio	1.6	1.6	1.9	1.8	1.9	2.1	2.0	1.7	1.6	1.6
% Long Term Debt of Capitalization	24.1	28.8	26.5	18.4	19.6	21.8	23.8	27.5	29.0	24.4
% Net Income of Revenue	5.5	4.9	7.8	7.7	6.8	6.7	4.9	3.1	2.1	5.8
% Return on Assets	5.6	5.0	10.1	10.0	8.5	8.3	5.6	3.3	2.3	6.9
% Return on Equity	12.8	10.7	19.1	18.5	16.8	17.3	12.6	7.7	5.1	14.2

Data as orig reptd.; bef. results of disc opers/spec. items. Per share data adj. for stk. divs.; EPS diluted. E-Estimated. NA-Not Available. NM-Not Meaningful. NR-Not Ranked. UR-Under Review.

Office: 6035 Parkland Boulevard, Cleveland, OH 44124-4141.
Telephone: 216-896-3000.
Website: http://www.parker.com
Chrmn, Pres & CEO: D.E. Washkewicz

CFO & Chief Admin Officer: T.K. Pistell
CTO: M.C. Maxwell
Chief Acctg Officer & Cntlr: J.P. Marten
Investor Contact: P.J. Huggins (216-896-2240)

Board Members: R. G. Bohn, L. Harty, W. E. Kassling, R. J. Kohlhepp, G. Mazzalupi, K. Muller, C. M. Obourn, J. M. Scaminace, W. R. Schmitt, A. Svensson, M. I. Tambakeras, J. L. Wainscott, D. E. Washkewicz

Founded: 1924
Domicile: Ohio
Employees: 54,794

The McGraw·Hill Companies

Patterson Companies Inc

STANDARD &POOR'S

S&P Recommendation HOLD ★★★★★

Price	12-Mo. Target Price	Investment Style
$27.92 (as of Oct 22, 2010)	$30.00	Large-Cap Growth

GICS Sector Health Care
Sub-Industry Health Care Distributors

Summary This company is one of the largest distributors of dental supplies in North America and also sells veterinary supplies and rehabilitative equipment.

Key Stock Statistics (Source S&P, Vickers, company reports)

52-Wk Range	$32.84– 24.13	S&P Oper. EPS 2011**E**	1.95	Market Capitalization(B)	$3.462	Beta	0.83
Trailing 12-Month EPS	$1.85	S&P Oper. EPS 2012**E**	2.15	Yield (%)	1.43	S&P 3-Yr. Proj. EPS CAGR(%)	11
Trailing 12-Month P/E	15.1	P/E on S&P Oper. EPS 2011**E**	14.3	Dividend Rate/Share	$0.40	S&P Credit Rating	NA
$10K Invested 5 Yrs Ago	$7,060	Common Shares Outstg. (M)	124.0	Institutional Ownership (%)	71		

Price Performance

30-Week Mov. Avg. · · · 10-Week Mov. Avg. - - GAAP Earnings vs. Previous Year   Volume Above Avg. STARS
12-Mo. Target Price — Relative Strength   ▲ Up ▼ Down ▶ No Change   Below Avg.

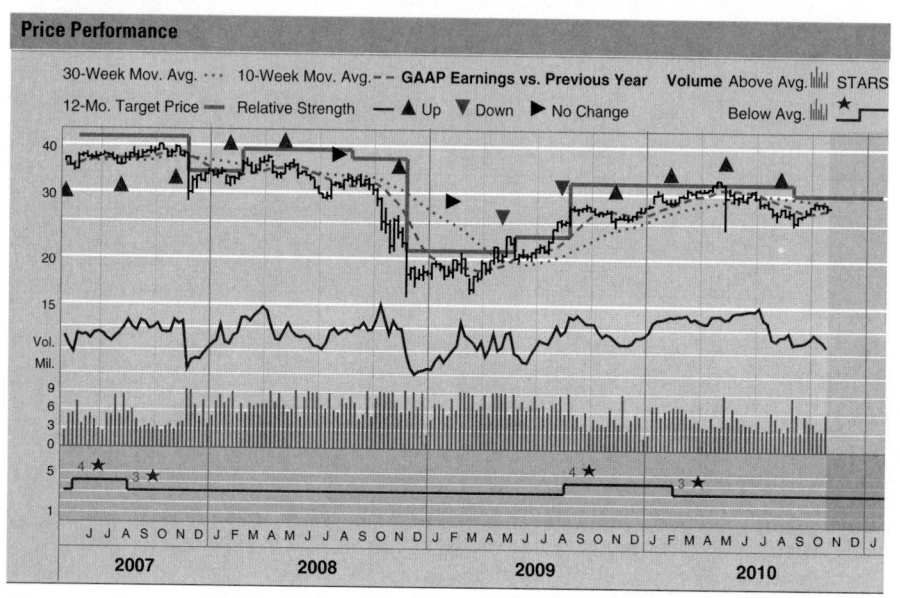

Options: CBOE, Ph

Analysis prepared by **Herman B. Saftlas** on September 01, 2010, when the stock traded at **$ 25.27**.

Highlights

▶ We project sales growth of about 6% in FY 11 (Apr.), to over $3.4 billion. We look for a slight uptick in dental consumable and equipment sales, as the market appears to have stabilized somewhat amid a still weak U.S. economy. We think basic dental equipment sales, while still soft, will benefit from dentists' need to replace aging equipment, while high-tech equipment sales benefit from their need to improve productivity. Elsewhere, we expect rehab sales growth to accelerate from FY 10 levels, with a recent acquisition in Ireland, while veterinary sales benefit slightly from a partnership with a small firm into which PDCO recently made an equity investment.

▶ We expect gross margins to widen slightly in FY 11, partly on an improved sales mix. We also assume the SG&A cost ratio will narrow modestly, on several cost-reduction initiatives and the completion of acquisition-integration efforts.

▶ We estimate EPS of $1.95 in FY 11, aided by an additional week of sales in the July quarter that should add an indicated $0.03 to the bottom line, versus FY 10's $1.78. We look for $2.15 in FY 12.

Investment Rationale/Risk

▶ PDCO appears to us to be maintaining or gaining market share in high-tech dental equipment sales, likely because dentists view its products as offering rapid rates of return on investment. Nonetheless, we believe meaningful sales growth will be dependent on promotional activities, including financing. While we expect continued weakness in basic dental equipment persisting over the next few quarters, we believe comparisons will get easier. Meanwhile, the veterinary business continues to realize better organic growth than we expected, with sales in the July 2010 quarter rising 6%. Elsewhere, we see the rehab business benefiting over time from an aging baby-boomer population and more active lifestyles, and we are encouraged by PDCO's expanding position in the global rehab market.

▶ Risks to our recommendation and target price include intensified competition and further deterioration of the economy.

▶ Our 12-month target price of $30 assumes a multiple of 15.4X our FY 11 EPS estimate of $1.95, which approximates the company's historical average P/E over the past three years.

Qualitative Risk Assessment

LOW	MEDIUM	HIGH

Our risk assessment is based on our view of PDCO's strong long-term record of earnings growth, offset by the impact that the economy and consumer confidence (both currently weak) can have on consumer demand for the services of the company's dental, medical and veterinary clients.

Quantitative Evaluations

S&P Quality Ranking   B+

D	C	B-	B	B+	A-	A	A+

Relative Strength Rank   MODERATE

35

LOWEST = 1   HIGHEST = 99

Revenue/Earnings Data

Revenue (Million $)

	1Q	2Q	3Q	4Q	Year
2011	849.8	--	--	--	--
2010	789.6	815.0	820.1	812.8	3,237
2009	743.9	759.5	811.0	779.9	3,094
2008	701.4	742.0	777.0	778.4	2,999
2007	655.5	694.3	709.5	739.1	2,798
2006	595.9	641.7	682.4	695.2	2,615

Earnings Per Share ($)

2011	0.45	E0.44	E0.52	E0.54	E1.95
2010	0.38	0.41	0.47	0.52	1.78
2009	0.39	0.40	0.45	0.46	1.69
2008	0.39	0.39	0.45	0.51	1.69
2007	0.30	0.35	0.43	0.44	1.51
2006	0.31	0.32	0.39	0.41	1.43

Fiscal year ended Apr. 30. Next earnings report expected: Mid November. EPS Estimates based on S&P Operating Earnings; historical GAAP earnings are as reported.

Dividend Data (Dates: mm/dd Payment Date: mm/dd/yy)

Amount ($)	Date Decl.	Ex-Div. Date	Stk. of Record	Payment Date
0.100	03/16	03/30	04/02	04/20/10
0.100	06/15	07/07	07/09	07/27/10
0.100	09/15	10/06	10/11	10/28/10

Dividends have been paid since 2010. Source: Company reports.

Please read the Required Disclosures and Analyst Certification on the last page of this report.

The McGraw·Hill Companies

STANDARD &POOR'S

Patterson Companies Inc

Business Summary September 01, 2010

CORPORATE OVERVIEW. Patterson Companies (formerly Patterson Dental), one of two large distributors of dental products in North America, is a full-service supplier to dentists, dental laboratories, institutions, physicians, and other health care professionals. Through the July 2001 acquisition of J.A. Webster, PDCO became the second largest U.S. distributor of companion-pet veterinary supplies. Also, through the August 2003 acquisition of AbilityOne Products Corp. (now Patterson Medical), PDCO became the largest distributor of non-wheelchair assistive products for patient rehabilitation in the U.S. and the U.K.

PDCO's Patterson Dental subsidiary, 67.0% of FY 10 (Apr.) sales, versus 70.3% in FY 09, provides a broad range of consumables (X-ray film, restorative materials, and sterilization products), advanced technology dental equipment, practice management software, and office forms and stationery. It has a 35% share of a $6 billion market.

Consumables and printed products accounted for 56.1% of dental supply sales in FY 10, slightly above FY 09's 56.0%. The company offers its own private label line of anesthetics, instruments, preventative and restorative products, as well as brand name supplies, including X-ray film, protective clothing, tooth-brushes, and other dental accessories. Printed products include insurance and billing forms, stationery, appointment books, and other stock office supply products.

PDCO offers a wide range of dental equipment, which accounted for 32.7% of dental supply sales in FY 10, down from 33.6% in FY 09. The product line includes X-ray machines, sterilizers, dental chairs, dental lights and diagnostic equipment. Two of PDCO's fastest growing product lines are the CEREC chairside ceramic dental-restorative system and digital radiography (X-ray) systems. CEREC sales slowed in FY 07 and FY 08's first half, but picked up afterward. However, sales of digital radiography systems slowed sharply in FY 08's final quarter.

Other products, which accounted for 11.2% of dental supply sales in FY 10 and 10.4% in FY 09, include software services, equipment installation and repair, dental office design, and equipment financing.

Company Financials Fiscal Year Ended Apr. 30

Per Share Data ($)	2010	2009	2008	2007	2006	2005	2004	2003	2002	2001
Tangible Book Value	3.53	1.79	1.01	3.70	2.73	1.95	0.76	3.66	2.85	2.64
Cash Flow	2.11	1.88	1.84	1.70	1.60	1.52	1.27	0.94	0.80	0.65
Earnings	1.78	1.69	1.69	1.51	1.43	1.32	1.09	0.85	0.70	0.57
S&P Core Earnings	1.78	1.69	1.69	1.51	1.39	1.30	1.08	0.84	0.70	0.57
Dividends	Nil	Nil	Nil	Nil	Nil	Nil	Nil	Nil	Nil	Nil
Payout Ratio	Nil	Nil	Nil	Nil	Nil	Nil	Nil	Nil	Nil	Nil
Calendar Year	2009	2008	2007	2006	2005	2004	2003	2002	2001	2000
Prices:High	28.34	37.78	40.08	38.28	53.85	44.20	35.75	27.56	21.03	17.25
Prices:Low	16.08	15.75	28.32	29.61	33.21	29.70	17.71	19.00	13.75	8.13
P/E Ratio:High	16	22	24	25	38	33	33	32	30	31
P/E Ratio:Low	9	9	17	20	23	22	16	22	20	14

Income Statement Analysis (Million $)

	2010	2009	2008	2007	2006	2005	2004	2003	2002	2001
Revenue	3,237	3,094	2,999	2,798	2,615	2,421	1,969	1,657	1,416	1,156
Operating Income	395	369	379	361	347	329	262	192	161	391
Depreciation	39.5	22.9	19.5	25.5	23.7	26.9	19.4	12.8	14.3	11.1
Interest Expense	25.7	30.2	0.12	14.2	13.4	15.1	9.60	0.07	0.11	0.12
Pretax Income	339	320	357	330	317	293	240	186	152	122
Effective Tax Rate	NA	37.6%	37.1%	36.8%	37.4%	37.4%	37.6%	37.6%	37.4%	37.4%
Net Income	212	200	225	208	198	184	150	116	95.3	76.5
S&P Core Earnings	212	200	225	208	194	180	147	115	95.3	76.5

Balance Sheet & Other Financial Data (Million $)

	2010	2009	2008	2007	2006	2005	2004	2003	2002	2001
Cash	341	158	308	242	224	233	287	195	126	160
Current Assets	1,134	938	985	886	847	800	778	606	529	443
Total Assets	2,423	2,129	2,076	1,940	1,912	1,685	1,589	824	718	549
Current Liabilities	348	334	466	377	410	322	264	184	198	133
Long Term Debt	525	525	525	130	210	302	480	0.13	Nil	Nil
Common Equity	1,442	1,186	1,005	1,379	1,243	1,015	802	634	514	409
Total Capital	1,967	1,250	1,660	1,563	1,502	1,363	1,325	634	514	409
Capital Expenditures	29.8	32.3	36.0	19.5	49.2	31.5	19.6	11.4	11.1	10.0
Cash Flow	252	223	244	234	222	211	169	129	110	87.6
Current Ratio	3.3	2.8	2.1	2.3	2.1	2.5	2.9	3.3	2.7	3.3
% Long Term Debt of Capitalization	26.7	42.0	33.1	8.3	14.0	22.1	36.2	Nil	Nil	Nil
% Net Income of Revenue	6.6	6.5	7.5	7.4	7.6	7.6	7.6	7.0	6.7	6.6
% Return on Assets	9.3	9.5	11.2	10.8	11.0	11.2	12.4	15.1	15.0	15.3
% Return on Equity	16.2	18.2	18.9	15.9	17.6	20.2	20.8	20.3	20.7	20.7

Data as orig reptd.; bef. results of disc opers/spec. items. Per share data adj. for stk. divs.; EPS diluted. E-Estimated. NA-Not Available. NM-Not Meaningful. NR-Not Ranked. UR-Under Review.

Office: 1031 Mendota Heights Road, St Paul, MN 55120.
Telephone: 651-686-1600.
Email: investors@pattersondental.com
Website: http://www.pattersoncompanies.com

Chrmn: P.L. Frechette
Pres & CEO: S.P. Anderson
COO: D.H. Peckskamp
EVP, CFO, Chief Acctg Officer & Treas: R.S. Armstrong

Secy & General Counsel: M.L. Levitt
Board Members: S. P. Anderson, J. D. Buck, R. E. Ezerski, P. L. Frechette, A. B. Lacy, C. Reich, E. A. Rudnick, H. C. Slavkin, B. Tyler, L. C. Vinney, J. W. Wiltz

Founded: 1877
Domicile: Minnesota
Employees: 6,890

The **McGraw-Hill** Companies

Paychex Inc

STANDARD &POOR'S

S&P Recommendation HOLD ★★★☆☆	**Price** $28.00 (as of Oct 22, 2010)	**12-Mo. Target Price** $28.00	**Investment Style** Large-Cap Growth

GICS Sector Information Technology
Sub-Industry Data Processing & Outsourced Services

Summary Paychex provides payroll accounting services to small- and medium-sized concerns throughout the U.S.

Key Stock Statistics (Source S&P, Vickers, company reports)

52-Wk Range	$32.88– 24.65	S&P Oper. EPS 2011**E**	1.38	Market Capitalization(B)	$10.127	Beta	0.82
Trailing 12-Month EPS	$1.34	S&P Oper. EPS 2012**E**	1.49	Yield (%)	4.43	S&P 3-Yr. Proj. EPS CAGR(%)	4
Trailing 12-Month P/E	20.9	P/E on S&P Oper. EPS 2011**E**	20.3	Dividend Rate/Share	$1.24	S&P Credit Rating	NA
$10K Invested 5 Yrs Ago	$8,781	Common Shares Outstg. (M)	361.7	Institutional Ownership (%)	70		

Price Performance

30-Week Mov. Avg. ···· 10-Week Mov. Avg. ── GAAP Earnings vs. Previous Year   Volume Above Avg. ▮▮▮ STARS
12-Mo. Target Price ── Relative Strength ── ▲ Up ▼ Down ▶ No Change   Below Avg. ▮▮▮ ★

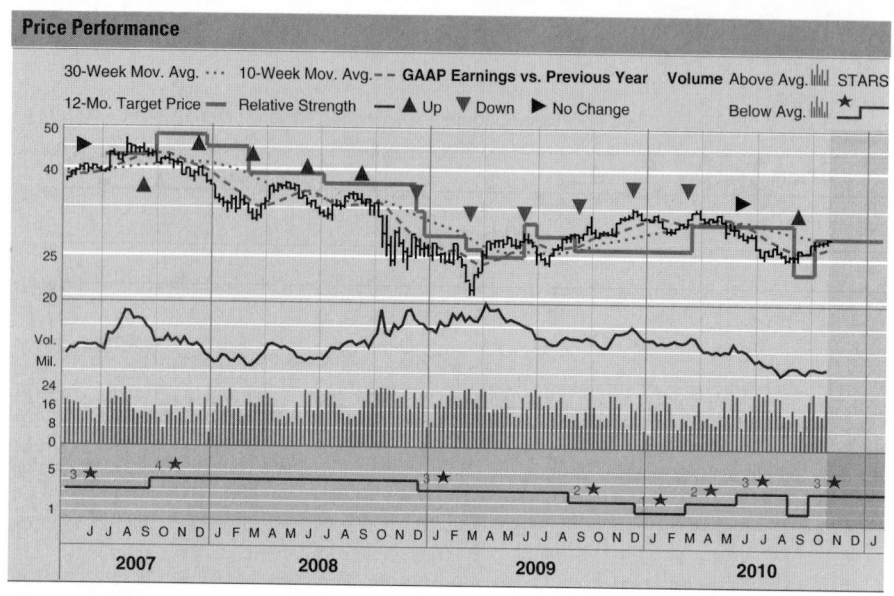

Options: ASE, CBOE, Ph

Analysis prepared by **Dylan Cathers** on September 28, 2010, when the stock traded at **$ 27.11**.

Highlights

➤ The first fiscal quarter brought another increase in average checks per client, and the pace of client losses decreased. Still, given the weakness in the employment market and the economy in general, we look for the company to continue to be affected by problems among its clients, and we look for revenue growth of 3.5% in FY 11 (May), before improving to 5% in FY 12. For the full fiscal year, we expect PAYX to experience growth of a modest 1% in its core payroll services business. We think HR services growth will return this fiscal year, and we look for a gain of about 9%. Interest on funds held for clients should remain weak due to low short-term interest rates.

➤ We think operating margins will rebound in FY 11 after narrowing in FY 10. We believe expenses from rising personnel levels, increased sales efforts, and investments in the business will be offset by solid cost controls, reduced attrition levels, improving customer retention rates, and increased checks per client.

➤ After operating EPS of $1.35 in FY 10, excluding a litigation charge, we look for EPS of $1.38 in FY 11 and $1.49 in FY 12.

Investment Rationale/Risk

➤ We recently raised our opinion on the shares to hold from strong sell. Although we think the small and mid-sized business segment that PAYX caters to will be slow to turn around, we think the worst is behind the company. There have been some improvements in PAYX's fundamentals, and we expect some traction on efforts to revitalize the sales force. We view the balance sheet as strong with no debt and over $270 million in cash. Further, we think the over 4% dividend will drive interest in the shares.

➤ Risks to our recommendation and target price stem from volatility in the small- to medium-sized business environment, and the impact of competition on pricing and margins. Automatic Data Processing (ADP 41, Buy) is the leader in the payroll processing space, and is promoting a payroll processing and tax filing software solution coupled with Microsoft's small business software. Separately, the employment environment could remain weak for an extended period of time.

➤ We arrive at our 12-month target price of $28 by applying a roughly peer-average P/E of 19.7X to our calendar 2011 EPS estimate of $1.42.

Qualitative Risk Assessment

LOW	**MEDIUM**	HIGH

Our risk assessment reflects what we see as the company's strong balance sheet and regular cash inflows, offset by the highly competitive nature of the outsourcing industry as well as the threat of new entrants into the human resources segment.

Quantitative Evaluations

S&P Quality Ranking   A

D	C	B-	B	B+	A-	**A**	A+

Relative Strength Rank   MODERATE

58

LOWEST = 1   HIGHEST = 99

Revenue/Earnings Data

Revenue (Million $)

	1Q	2Q	3Q	4Q	Year
2011	518.3	--	--	--	--
2010	500.2	496.6	507.8	496.2	2,001
2009	534.1	524.2	528.6	495.9	2,083
2008	507.1	307.8	532.2	519.2	2,066
2007	459.4	455.0	485.3	487.4	1,887
2006	403.7	399.8	430.6	440.5	1,675

Earnings Per Share ($)

	1Q	2Q	3Q	4Q	Year
2011	0.36	E0.34	E0.35	E0.33	E1.38
2010	0.34	0.35	0.31	0.32	1.32
2009	0.41	0.39	0.36	0.32	1.48
2008	0.40	0.40	0.39	0.38	1.56
2007	0.35	0.35	0.33	0.32	1.39
2006	0.30	0.30	0.30	0.32	1.22

Fiscal year ended May 31. Next earnings report expected: Mid December. EPS Estimates based on S&P Operating Earnings; historical GAAP earnings are as reported.

Dividend Data (Dates: mm/dd Payment Date: mm/dd/yy)

Amount ($)	Date Decl.	Ex-Div. Date	Stk. of Record	Payment Date
0.310	01/08	01/28	02/01	02/16/10
0.310	04/08	04/29	05/03	05/17/10
0.310	07/07	07/29	08/02	08/16/10
0.310	10/13	10/28	11/01	11/15/10

Dividends have been paid since 1988. Source: Company reports.

Please read the Required Disclosures and Analyst Certification on the last page of this report.

The **McGraw·Hill** Companies

Paychex Inc

Business Summary September 28, 2010

CORPORATE OVERVIEW. Paychex is a leading provider of payroll processing, human resources and benefits services. The company was founded in 1971, and began by serving the payroll accounting services of businesses with fewer than 200 employees. It currently has more than 100 locations and serves over 536,000 clients throughout the U.S.

The company's payroll segment prepares payroll checks, earnings statements, internal accounting records, all federal, state and local payroll tax returns, and provides collection and remittance of payroll obligations. PAYX's tax filing and payment services provide automatic tax filing and payment, preparation and submission of tax returns, plus deposit of funds with tax authorities. Employee Payment Services provides a variety of ways for businesses to pay employees.

In our opinion, PAYX has shown an ability to expand its client base and increase the use of ancillary services, which we believe will lead to consistent growth for its mainstay payroll segment.

The Human Resources/Professional Employer Organization (HRS/PEO) segment provides employee benefits, management and human resources ser-

vices. The Paychex Administrative Services (PAS) product offers businesses a bundled package that includes payroll, employer compliance, and human resource and employee benefit administration. PAYX also offers 401(k) plan services.

MARKET PROFILE. The worldwide market for HR services totaled $102.3 billion in calendar 2009, according to market researcher IDC. Between 2009 and 2014, IDC expects this area to post a compound annual growth rate (CAGR) of 4.6%, with the market in the U.S. increasing at a CAGR of 4.3% from $50.2 billion in 2009. For the more narrow U.S. payroll services market, where we believe Automatic Data Processing is the market leader, IDC sees a CAGR of 3.7% between 2009 and 2014. In contrast, in the U.S. market for business process outsourcing (BPO) services, IDC expects a CAGR of 4.9% over the same time frame.

Company Financials Fiscal Year Ended May 31

Per Share Data ($)	2010	2009	2008	2007	2006	2005	2004	2003	2002	2001
Tangible Book Value	2.54	2.30	1.91	3.87	3.12	2.40	1.88	1.55	2.43	2.00
Cash Flow	1.56	1.72	1.78	1.54	1.39	1.13	1.02	0.89	0.80	0.75
Earnings	1.32	1.48	1.56	1.39	1.22	0.97	0.80	0.78	0.73	0.68
S&P Core Earnings	1.34	1.48	1.55	1.41	1.17	0.93	0.80	0.72	0.66	0.65
Dividends	NA	1.20	0.79	0.61	0.51	0.47	0.44	0.33	0.33	0.22
Payout Ratio	NA	81%	51%	44%	42%	48%	55%	56%	45%	32%
Calendar Year	2009	2008	2007	2006	2005	2004	2003	2002	2001	2000
Prices:High	32.88	37.47	47.14	42.37	43.37	39.12	40.54	42.15	51.00	61.25
Prices:Low	20.31	23.22	35.96	32.98	28.60	28.83	23.76	20.39	28.27	24.17
P/E Ratio:High	25	25	30	30	36	40	51	54	70	90
P/E Ratio:Low	15	16	23	24	23	30	30	26	39	36

Income Statement Analysis (Million $)

	2010	2009	2008	2007	2006	2005	2004	2003	2002	2001
Revenue	2,001	2,083	2,066	1,887	1,675	1,445	1,294	1,099	955	870
Operating Income	811	891	909	775	716	596	516	444	393	700
Depreciation	86.4	85.8	80.6	73.4	66.5	62.0	82.8	43.4	29.5	26.4
Interest Expense	NA	Nil	Nil	Nil	Nil	Nil	Nil	Nil	Nil	Nil
Pretax Income	729	812	855	743	675	546	450	432	395	364
Effective Tax Rate	NA	34.3%	32.6%	30.7%	31.1%	32.5%	32.6%	32.0%	30.5%	30.0%
Net Income	477	534	576	515	465	369	303	293	275	255
S&P Core Earnings	486	533	572	537	445	353	304	272	252	243

Balance Sheet & Other Financial Data (Million $)

	2010	2009	2008	2007	2006	2005	2004	2003	2002	2001
Cash	367	492	393	79.4	137	281	219	79.9	61.9	45.8
Current Assets	4,159	4,240	4,466	4,861	4,444	3,689	3,280	3,033	2,815	2,791
Total Assets	5,226	5,127	5,310	6,247	5,549	4,379	3,950	3,691	2,953	2,907
Current Liabilities	3,742	3,702	4,037	4,237	3,838	2,942	2,722	2,588	2,023	2,144
Long Term Debt	NA	Nil	Nil	Nil	Nil	Nil	Nil	Nil	Nil	Nil
Common Equity	1,402	1,341	1,197	1,985	1,670	1,411	1,235	1,077	924	745
Total Capital	1,402	1,341	1,197	1,994	1,686	1,429	1,249	1,084	924	745
Capital Expenditures	61.3	64.7	82.3	79.0	81.1	70.7	50.6	60.2	54.4	45.3
Cash Flow	563	619	657	589	531	431	386	337	304	281
Current Ratio	1.1	1.2	1.1	1.1	1.2	1.3	1.2	1.2	1.4	1.3
% Long Term Debt of Capitalization	Nil	Nil	Nil	Nil	Nil	Nil	Nil	Nil	Nil	Nil
% Net Income of Revenue	23.8	25.6	27.9	27.3	27.8	25.5	23.4	26.7	28.7	29.3
% Return on Assets	9.2	10.2	10.0	8.7	9.1	8.9	7.9	8.8	9.4	9.5
% Return on Equity	34.8	42.0	36.6	28.2	30.2	27.9	26.2	29.3	32.6	38.7

Data as orig reptd.; bef. results of disc opers/spec. items. Per share data adj. for stk. divs.; EPS diluted. E-Estimated. NA-Not Available. NM-Not Meaningful. NR-Not Ranked. UR-Under Review.

Office: 911 Panorama Trail South, Rochester, NY 14625-2396.
Telephone: 585-385-6666.
Website: http://www.paychex.com
Chrmn: B.T. Golisano

Pres & CEO: M. Mucci
SVP, CFO, Chief Acctg Officer & Secy: J.M. Morphy
General Counsel: S.L. Schaeffer
Investor Contact: T.J. Allen (585-383-3406)

Board Members: J. G. Doody, D. J. Flaschen, B. T. Golisano, G. M. Inman, P. A. Joseph, J. J. Judge, M. Mucci, J. M. Tucci, J. M. Velli

Founded: 1979
Domicile: Delaware
Employees: 12,200

Peabody Energy Corp

STANDARD &POOR'S

S&P Recommendation **BUY** ★★★★☆

Price	12-Mo. Target Price	Investment Style
$51.04 (as of Oct 22, 2010)	$60.00	Large-Cap Blend

GICS Sector Energy
Sub-Industry Coal & Consumable Fuels

Summary BTU is the world's largest publicly traded coal company, with 9 billion tons of coal reserves. Its coal fuels about 10% of the electricity generated in the U.S. and 2% worldwide.

Key Stock Statistics (Source S&P, Vickers, company reports)

52-Wk Range	$52.73–34.89	S&P Oper. EPS 2010**E**	3.13	Market Capitalization(B)	$13.738
Trailing 12-Month EPS	$2.00	S&P Oper. EPS 2011**E**	4.50	Yield (%)	0.67
Trailing 12-Month P/E	25.5	P/E on S&P Oper. EPS 2010**E**	16.3	Dividend Rate/Share	$0.34
$10K Invested 5 Yrs Ago	NA	Common Shares Outstg. (M)	269.2	Institutional Ownership (%)	79

Beta	1.38
S&P 3-Yr. Proj. EPS CAGR(%)	8
S&P Credit Rating	BB+

Price Performance

30-Week Mov. Avg. ··· 10-Week Mov. Avg. - - GAAP Earnings vs. Previous Year   Volume Above Avg. ▯▮▮ STARS
12-Mo. Target Price — Relative Strength ▲ Up ▼ Down ► No Change   Below Avg. ▯▯▮ ★

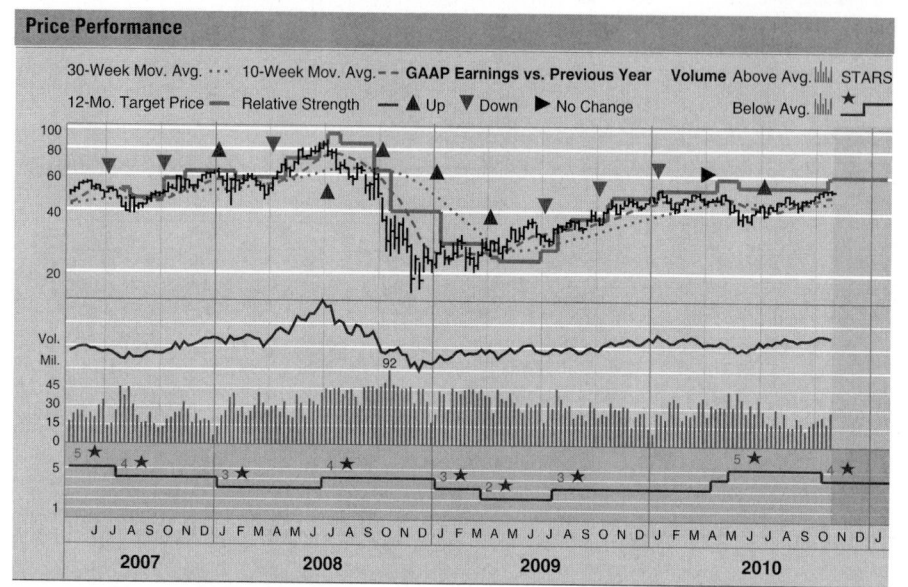

Options: ASE, CBOE, P, Ph

Analysis prepared by **Mathew Christy, CFA** on October 21, 2010, when the stock traded at **$ 51.33**.

Highlights

➤ After a nearly 5% decline in volume and a 4% decrease in pricing that led to a 9% drop in 2009 revenue, we estimate that 2010 revenue will increase more than 16% on a greater-than-2% rise in coal volumes and a nearly 14% gain in pricing. Our 2010 coal volume forecast is based on higher expected production across all of BTU's operating regions, while our pricing outlook assumes an increase in metallurgical and thermal coal pricing. For 2011, we project that revenue will advance more than 13% on further volume and pricing increases.

➤ Following a nearly seven percentage point decline in 2009's EBITDA margin, we think that higher coal volumes and pricing will lead to improved operating leverage and better overall EBITDA margins this year. Our forecast assumes that production costs per ton will increase more than 7%. For 2011, we project a further increase in BTU's EBITDA margin, mainly due to continued improvement in operating leverage.

➤ On projected effective tax rates of about 25% in both periods, we estimate EPS of $3.13 in 2010 and $4.50 in 2011.

Investment Rationale/Risk

➤ Our buy recommendation is based on our belief that thermal coal inventories at utilities will move into better balance on higher overall demand, and that metallurgical coal will remain in high demand globally, as steel production is expected to remain strong. In addition, we think BTU's focus on western U.S. and international assets increases the company's growth profile and provides direct access to Asian seaborne markets. We view BTU's valuation as compelling, with the stock recently trading at about 6.3X our 2011 EBITDA estimate, below its five-year historical average.

➤ Risks to our recommendation and target price include declines in coal and natural gas prices, lower productivity and production, higher production costs, and higher coal market inventories.

➤ Our 12-month target price of $60 is based on our relative peer valuation analysis. We apply an EV/EBITDA multiple of about 7.3X to our 2011 EBITDA per share estimate, ahead of peer multiples due to the company's size, diversity, historical valuation premium and international growth strategy.

Qualitative Risk Assessment

LOW	MEDIUM	HIGH

Our risk assessment reflects the industry's cyclicality and extensive regulation, the potential for geological difficulties with mines, transportation problems, volatility in the prices of competing fuels, and a narrow customer focus. This is offset by the company's leading market position and geographically well diversified coal holdings.

Quantitative Evaluations

S&P Quality Ranking   B+

D	C	B-	B	B+	A-	A	A+

Relative Strength Rank   STRONG

71

LOWEST = 1   HIGHEST = 99

Revenue/Earnings Data

Revenue (Million $)

	1Q	2Q	3Q	4Q	Year
2010	1,516	1,661	--	--	--
2009	1,453	1,338	1,667	1,554	6,012
2008	1,276	1,531	1,906	1,881	6,593
2007	1,365	1,322	1,494	1,212	4,575
2006	1,312	1,316	1,265	1,363	5,256
2005	1,077	1,109	1,224	1,235	4,644

Earnings Per Share ($)

2010	0.50	0.77	E0.88	E0.87	E3.13
2009	0.50	0.32	0.41	0.41	1.68
2008	0.26	0.89	1.38	1.11	3.63
2007	0.33	0.40	0.12	0.71	1.56
2006	0.48	0.57	0.53	0.65	2.23
2005	0.20	0.36	0.42	0.61	1.58

Fiscal year ended Dec. 31. Next earnings report expected: NA. EPS Estimates based on S&P Operating Earnings; historical GAAP earnings are as reported.

Dividend Data (Dates: mm/dd Payment Date: mm/dd/yy)

Amount ($)	Date Decl.	Ex-Div. Date	Stk. of Record	Payment Date
0.070	01/27	02/08	02/10	03/03/10
0.070	05/04	05/14	05/18	06/03/10
0.070	07/23	08/04	08/06	08/27/10
0.085	10/21	11/02	11/04	11/26/10

Dividends have been paid since 2001. Source: Company reports.

Peabody Energy Corp

STANDARD &POOR'S

Business Summary October 21, 2010

CORPORATE OVERVIEW. Peabody Energy Corp. (BTU) was founded in 1883 as Peabody, Daniels and Co., a retail coal supplier. BTU is currently the world's largest private sector coal company. In 2009, it produced nearly 211 million tons of coal, down from 225 million tons produced in 2008, with U.S. operations producing more than 188 million tons, or about a 17.4% share of U.S. production, by our calculation, and 21.7 million tons produced in Australia. BTU sold nearly 244 million tons of coal to 345 electricity generating and industrial plants in 23 countries. At December 31, 2009, BTU had 9 billion tons of proven and probable coal reserves. BTU owns majority interests in 28 coal operations located in the Western and Midwestern U.S. coal producing regions and in Australia. In addition, the company owns a 50% interest in Mongolian coal and mineral interests and also owns purchase rights for up to 15% of its Mongolian joint venture partner, Polo Resources Limited. It also owns a minority interest in one Venezuelan mine through a joint venture agreement. In 2009, 83% of the U.S. mining operation's coal sales were shipped from the U.S. West, and the remaining 17% from the Midwest. Most production in the West is low sulfur coal from the Powder River Basin, which has seen the fastest growth of all U.S. coal regions, according to the Energy Information Administration (EIA). In the West, the company owns and operates mines in Arizona,

Colorado, New Mexico and Wyoming. In the Midwest, BTU owns and operates mines in Illinois and Indiana.

In 2009, 81% of sales were to U.S. electricity generators, 2% to the U.S. industrial sector, and 17% to foreign customers. About 93% of 2009 coal sales were under long-term contracts, with terms ranging from one to 17 years. As of January 26, 2010, the company had 11 million to 13 million and 18 million to 20 million tons of its planned Australian production unpriced for 2010 and 2011, respectively. In the company's U.S. operations, all of the planned production in 2010 is priced, while 30% of planned production in 2011 is unpriced. In addition to its mining operations, BTU markets and trades coal and emission allowances. Total tons traded amounted to 29.4 million in 2009 as compared to 31.2 million tons in 2008. Other energy-related businesses include coalbed methane production, transportation services, and the development of coal-fueled generation plants.

Company Financials Fiscal Year Ended Dec. 31

Per Share Data ($)	2009	2008	2007	2006	2005	2004	2003	2002	2001	2000
Tangible Book Value	13.98	10.96	9.33	7.95	8.27	3.33	5.18	5.16	4.98	5.72
Cash Flow	3.17	5.31	2.91	3.63	2.76	0.88	1.26	1.57	0.96	3.12
Earnings	1.68	3.63	1.56	2.23	1.58	0.70	0.19	0.49	0.10	0.74
S&P Core Earnings	1.60	3.36	1.42	2.00	1.43	0.63	0.11	0.27	-0.03	NA
Dividends	0.25	0.24	0.24	0.24	0.17	0.13	0.11	0.10	0.05	0.05
Payout Ratio	15%	7%	15%	11%	11%	19%	59%	20%	53%	7%
Prices:High	48.21	88.69	62.55	76.29	43.48	21.70	10.75	7.69	9.51	NA
Prices:Low	20.17	16.00	36.20	32.94	18.37	9.10	6.13	4.38	5.55	NA
P/E Ratio:High	29	24	40	34	28	31	57	16	NM	NA
P/E Ratio:Low	12	4	23	15	12	13	32	9	NM	NA

Income Statement Analysis (Million $)	2009	2008	2007	2006	2005	2004	2003	2002	2001	2000
Revenue	6,012	6,593	4,575	5,256	4,644	3,632	2,829	2,717	2,027	2,670
Operating Income	NA	1,774	827	884	703	519	385	390	276	405
Depreciation	405	454	362	377	316	270	234	232	175	241
Interest Expense	201	226	237	143	103	96.8	98.5	102	89.0	198
Pretax Income	652	1,177	341	531	426	153	-3.18	78.8	29.0	153
Effective Tax Rate	29.7%	15.8%	NM	NM	0.23%	NM	NM	NM	12.9%	27.9%
Net Income	443	985	421	601	423	178	41.5	106	19.0	103
S&P Core Earnings	431	910	383	541	382	160	23.9	58.5	-5.74	NA

Balance Sheet & Other Financial Data (Million $)	2009	2008	2007	2006	2005	2004	2003	2002	2001	2000
Cash	989	450	45.3	327	503	390	118	71.2	39.0	67.7
Current Assets	2,189	1,971	1,927	1,274	1,325	1,055	683	550	527	630
Total Assets	9,955	9,822	9,668	9,514	6,852	6,179	5,280	5,140	5,151	5,209
Current Liabilities	1,312	1,856	2,187	1,368	1,023	774	632	632	684	777
Long Term Debt	2,738	3,139	3,139	3,168	1,383	1,406	1,173	982	985	1,369
Common Equity	3,756	2,904	2,520	2,339	2,178	1,725	1,132	1,081	1,040	631
Total Capital	6,508	6,061	5,975	5,735	3,902	3,526	2,742	2,599	2,590	2,613
Capital Expenditures	441	486	649	478	384	267	156	209	194	151
Cash Flow	848	1,439	783	978	739	448	276	338	194	344
Current Ratio	1.7	1.1	0.9	0.9	1.3	1.4	1.1	0.9	0.8	0.8
% Long Term Debt of Capitalization	42.1	51.9	52.5	55.2	35.4	39.9	42.8	37.8	38.0	52.4
% Net Income of Revenue	7.4	14.9	9.2	11.4	9.1	4.9	NM	3.9	0.1	3.8
% Return on Assets	4.5	10.1	4.4	7.3	6.5	3.1	NM	2.1	0.3	1.9
% Return on Equity	13.3	36.3	17.3	26.6	21.7	12.5	NM	10.0	2.3	18.0

Data as orig reptd.; bef. results of disc opers/spec. items. Per share data adj. for stk. divs.; EPS diluted. E-Estimated. NA-Not Available. NM-Not Meaningful. NR-Not Ranked. UR-Under Review.

Office: 701 Market St, St. Louis, MO 63101-1826.
Telephone: 314-342-3400.
Email: publicrelations@peabodyenergy.com
Website: http://www.peabodyenergy.com

Chrmn & CEO: G.H. Boyce
Pres: R.A. Navarre
COO & EVP: E. Ford
EVP & CFO: M.C. Crews

EVP & Chief Admin Officer: S.D. Fiehler
Investor Contact: C. Morrow (314-342-7900)
Board Members: G. H. Boyce, W. A. Coley, W. E. James, R. B. Karn, III, M. F. Keeth, H. E. Lentz, Jr., R. A. Malone, W. C. Rusnack, J. F. Turner, S. A. Van Trease, A. H. Washkowitz

Founded: 1883
Domicile: Delaware
Employees: 7,300

The McGraw-Hill Companies

J. C. Penney Company Inc.

STANDARD &POOR'S

S&P Recommendation HOLD ★★★☆☆

Price	**12-Mo. Target Price**	**Investment Style**
$32.55 (as of Oct 22, 2010)	$30.00	Large-Cap Blend

GICS Sector Consumer Discretionary
Sub-Industry Department Stores

Summary This company is the leading mall-based family department store operator in the U.S., with over 1,100 retail locations and catalog/Internet operations.

Key Stock Statistics (Source S&P, Vickers, company reports)

52-Wk Range	$36.54– 19.42	S&P Oper. EPS 2011E	1.55	Market Capitalization(B)	$7.696	Beta	1.84
Trailing 12-Month EPS	$1.27	S&P Oper. EPS 2012E	2.00	Yield (%)	2.46	S&P 3-Yr. Proj. EPS CAGR(%)	30
Trailing 12-Month P/E	25.6	P/E on S&P Oper. EPS 2011E	21.0	Dividend Rate/Share	$0.80	S&P Credit Rating	BB+
$10K Invested 5 Yrs Ago	$7,228	Common Shares Outstg. (M)	236.4	Institutional Ownership (%)	NM		

Price Performance

30-Week Mov. Avg. ···   10-Week Mov. Avg. - -   GAAP Earnings vs. Previous Year   Volume Above Avg. STARS
12-Mo. Target Price —   Relative Strength —   ▲ Up   ▼ Down   ▶ No Change   Below Avg. ★

Options: ASE, CBOE, P

Analysis prepared by **Jason N. Asaeda** on October 08, 2010, when the stock traded at **$ 31.64**.

Highlights

➤ We see net sales reaching $17.8 billion in FY 11 (Jan.), supported by a same-store sales increase of about 2%. In our view, middle-income consumers, JCP's target demographic, continue to spend cautiously due to macroeconomic concerns. However, we look for the company to achieve higher sales through the delivery of differentiated merchandise, the continued rollout of the "Sephora inside JCPenney" concept (215 locations as of July 31), and customer service initiatives such as the new JCP Rewards program.

➤ Despite the elimination of higher-margin "big book" catalog sales in FY 11, we anticipate 90 bps of operating margin improvement, to 4.7%, supported by good sell-through of "wear now" apparel at regular and promotional prices, reduced clearance sales through disciplined inventory management, well-controlled SG&A expense growth, and lower projected non-cash pension expense of $221 million versus FY 10's $298 million.

➤ Also factoring in $393 million of debt that matured in March 2010, which should reduce the company's interest expense, we see EPS rising 44% in FY 11, to $1.55.

Investment Rationale/Risk

➤ We recently lowered our recommendation on the shares to hold from buy, based on valuation. However, our near-term outlook for the company remains positive. We see quarterly same-store sales growth strengthening this fall, supported by appointment shopping events such as back-to-school and holiday promotions, the company's new Red Zone Clearance strategy, which gives customers clearer pricing on in-season merchandise, closer alignment of assortments between stores and jcpenney.com, and new marketing initiatives across traditional, online, and mobile media. We also expect the company to attract new customers with the Liz Claiborne and MNG by Mango exclusive brand launches.

➤ Risk to our recommendation and target price include sales shortfalls due to unforeseen shifts in fashion trends and cost-conscious consumers trading down to discounters such as Wal-Mart Stores (WMT 54, Strong Buy) for basic apparel and home merchandise.

➤ Our 12-month target price of $30 is based on a peer-median forward price-to-sales multiple of 0.4X applied to our FY 11 sales per share estimate of $75.

Qualitative Risk Assessment

LOW	MEDIUM	HIGH

Our risk assessment reflects our view of JCP's strong brand and increasing market share in the moderate department store sector, offset by a challenging macroeconomic environment that has led to weakening sales and profit trends in recent quarters.

Quantitative Evaluations

S&P Quality Ranking B

D	C	B-	B	B+	A-	A	A+

Relative Strength Rank STRONG

94

LOWEST = 1   HIGHEST = 99

Revenue/Earnings Data

Revenue (Million $)

	1Q	2Q	3Q	4Q	Year
2011	3,929	3,938	--	--	--
2010	3,884	3,943	4,179	5,550	17,556
2009	4,127	4,282	4,318	5,759	18,486
2008	4,350	4,391	4,729	6,390	19,860
2007	4,220	4,238	4,781	6,664	19,903
2006	4,192	3,981	4,479	6,203	18,781

Earnings Per Share ($)

2011	0.25	0.06	E0.19	E1.05	E1.55
2010	-0.11	Nil	0.11	0.83	1.07
2009	0.54	0.52	0.55	0.93	2.54
2008	1.04	0.52	1.17	1.93	4.91
2007	0.90	0.75	1.26	2.00	4.88
2006	0.63	0.46	0.94	1.92	3.83

Fiscal year ended Jan. 31. Next earnings report expected: Mid November. EPS Estimates based on S&P Operating Earnings; historical GAAP earnings are as reported.

Dividend Data (Dates: mm/dd Payment Date: mm/dd/yy)

Amount ($)	Date Decl.	Ex-Div. Date	Stk. of Record	Payment Date
0.200	12/09	01/06	01/08	02/01/10
0.200	03/26	04/07	04/09	05/03/10
0.200	05/21	07/07	07/09	08/02/10
0.200	09/17	10/06	10/08	11/01/10

Dividends have been paid since 1922. Source: Company reports.

Please read the Required Disclosures and Analyst Certification on the last page of this report.

The McGraw-Hill Companies

J. C. Penney Company Inc.

STANDARD &POOR'S

Business Summary October 08, 2010

CORPORATE OVERVIEW. In our view, JCP is the leading mall-based family department store operator, with 1,107 JCPenney stores in 49 states and Puerto Rico, as of August 13, 2010. We think the company is also adeptly addressing the needs of time-strapped shoppers with the shopping convenience afforded by its direct business, comprised of JCPenney specialty catalogs and the jcpenney.com web site, as well as its growing off-mall retail presence. JCP discontinued publishing its twice-yearly "big book" catalogs in FY 11.

CORPORATE STRATEGY. From FY 01 (Jan.) to FY 06, JCP executed a turnaround plan to improve the profitability of its JCPenney stores. The company focused on delivering competitive, fashionable merchandise assortments; developing a compelling and appealing marketing program; improving store environments; reducing its expense structure; and attracting and retaining an experienced and professional work force. In support of these objectives, JCP moved from decentralized to centralized merchandising, marketing and operating functions, and invested in a new store distribution network and in new merchandise planning, allocation and replenishment systems.

With what we view as the success of its turnaround, JCP has mapped out a new long-range plan for making JCPenney the preferred shopping choice for "Middle America," which it defines as customers aged 35 to 54 with annual household incomes of $35,000 to $85,000. Key strategies include offering styles that make an emotional connection with the customer; making it easier for the customer to shop seamlessly across store/catalog/Internet channels; creating and sustaining a customer-focused culture; and using the off-mall store format to expand the company's presence in high-potential markets. JCP sees the potential for up to 400 new stores, relocations or expansions on a long-term basis.

Company Financials Fiscal Year Ended Jan. 31

Per Share Data ($)	2010	2009	2008	2007	2006	2005	2004	2003	2002	2001
Tangible Book Value	19.49	18.09	23.93	18.97	17.20	17.92	18.54	12.04	11.46	NM
Cash Flow	3.19	4.65	6.80	6.57	5.79	3.33	2.68	3.45	3.00	0.36
Earnings	1.07	2.54	4.91	4.88	3.83	2.23	1.21	1.25	0.32	-2.29
S&P Core Earnings	1.70	1.15	4.37	4.66	3.77	2.26	1.24	0.66	0.15	-2.47
Dividends	0.80	0.80	0.72	0.50	0.50	0.50	0.50	0.50	0.50	0.50
Payout Ratio	75%	75%	15%	10%	13%	22%	41%	40%	156%	NM
Calendar Year	2009	2008	2007	2006	2005	2004	2003	2002	2001	2000
Prices:High	37.21	51.42	87.18	82.49	57.99	41.82	26.42	27.75	29.50	22.50
Prices:Low	13.71	13.95	39.98	54.18	40.26	25.29	15.57	14.07	10.50	8.63
P/E Ratio:High	35	20	18	17	15	19	22	22	92	NM
P/E Ratio:Low	13	5	8	11	11	11	13	11	33	NM

Income Statement Analysis (Million $)										
Revenue	17,556	18,486	19,860	19,903	18,781	18,424	17,786	32,347	32,004	31,846
Operating Income	1,187	1,579	2,268	2,277	1,949	1,680	1,184	1,681	1,473	873
Depreciation	495	469	426	389	372	368	394	667	717	695
Interest Expense	255	268	278	270	169	233	261	388	386	427
Pretax Income	403	910	1,723	1,792	1,444	1,020	546	584	203	-886
Effective Tax Rate	38.2%	37.7%	35.9%	36.7%	32.3%	34.6%	33.3%	36.5%	43.8%	NM
Net Income	249	567	1,105	1,134	977	667	345	371	114	-568
S&P Core Earnings	396	258	986	1,081	960	662	345	171	41.0	-650

Balance Sheet & Other Financial Data (Million $)										
Cash	3,011	2,352	2,471	2,747	3,016	4,687	2,994	2,474	2,840	944
Current Assets	6,652	6,220	6,751	6,648	6,702	8,427	6,515	8,353	8,677	7,257
Total Assets	12,581	12,011	14,309	12,673	12,461	14,127	18,300	17,867	18,048	19,742
Current Liabilities	3,249	2,794	3,338	3,492	2,762	3,447	3,754	4,159	4,499	4,235
Long Term Debt	2,999	3,505	3,505	3,010	3,444	3,464	5,114	4,940	5,179	5,448
Common Equity	4,778	4,155	5,312	4,288	4,007	4,856	5,121	6,037	5,766	5,860
Total Capital	8,170	7,659	10,280	8,504	8,738	9,638	11,756	12,701	12,539	12,843
Capital Expenditures	600	969	1,243	772	535	412	373	658	631	648
Cash Flow	744	1,036	1,531	1,523	1,349	1,023	733	1,011	802	94.0
Current Ratio	2.1	2.2	2.0	1.9	2.4	2.4	1.7	2.0	1.9	1.7
% Long Term Debt of Capitalization	36.7	45.8	34.1	41.2	39.4	35.9	43.5	38.9	41.3	42.4
% Net Income of Revenue	1.4	3.1	5.6	5.7	5.2	3.6	2.0	1.1	0.4	NM
% Return on Assets	2.0	4.3	8.2	9.0	7.3	4.1	2.0	2.1	0.1	NM
% Return on Equity	5.6	12.0	23.0	27.3	22.0	13.1	6.1	5.8	1.9	NM

Data as orig reptd.; bef. results of disc opers/spec. items. Per share data adj. for stk. divs.; EPS diluted. E-Estimated. NA-Not Available. NM-Not Meaningful. NR-Not Ranked. UR-Under Review.

Office: 6501 Legacy Drive, Plano, TX 75024-3698.
Telephone: 972-431-1000.
Website: http://www.jcpenney.net
Chrmn & CEO: M. Ullman, III

EVP & CFO: R.B. Cavanaugh
EVP & Chief Admin Officer: M.T. Theilmann
EVP, Secy & General Counsel: J.L. Dhillon
EVP & CIO: T.M. Nealon

Investor Contact: P. Sanchez (972-431-5575)
Board Members: C. C. Barrett, M. A. Burns, T. J. Engibous, K. B. Foster, G. B. Laybourne, B. Osborne, L. H. Roberts, J. G. Teruel, R. G. Turner, M. Ullman, III, M. B. West

Founded: 1902
Domicile: Delaware
Employees: 147,000

The McGraw-Hill Companies

People's United Financial Inc

STANDARD &POOR'S

S&P Recommendation STRONG BUY ★★★★★

Price $12.66 (as of Oct 25, 2010)	**12-Mo. Target Price** $20.00	**Investment Style** Large-Cap Blend

GICS Sector Financials
Sub-Industry Thrifts & Mortgage Finance

Summary This company provides a full range of banking and financial service products to individuals, corporations and municipal customers in the U.S. Northeast.

Key Stock Statistics (Source S&P, Vickers, company reports)

52-Wk Range	$17.16– 12.56	S&P Oper. EPS 2010E	0.36	Market Capitalization(B)	$4.695	Beta	0.19
Trailing 12-Month EPS	$0.22	S&P Oper. EPS 2011E	0.47	Yield (%)	4.90	S&P 3-Yr. Proj. EPS CAGR(%)	18
Trailing 12-Month P/E	57.6	P/E on S&P Oper. EPS 2010E	35.2	Dividend Rate/Share	$0.62	S&P Credit Rating	A-
$10K Invested 5 Yrs Ago	$9,610	Common Shares Outstg. (M)	370.9	Institutional Ownership (%)	75		

Price Performance

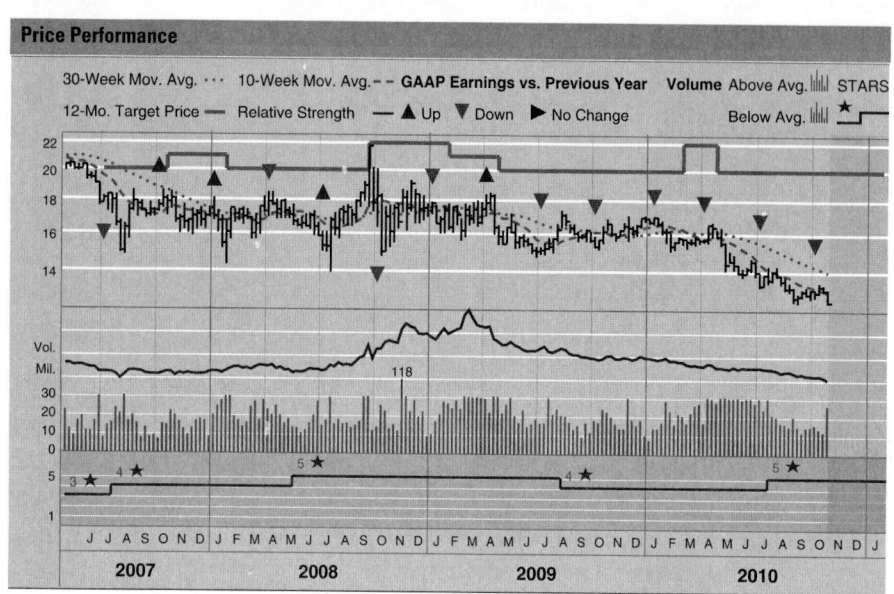

30-Week Mov. Avg. · · · · 10-Week Mov. Avg. – – GAAP Earnings vs. Previous Year   Volume Above Avg. STARS
12-Mo. Target Price — Relative Strength — ▲ Up ▼ Down ► No Change   Below Avg.

Options: ASE, CBOE, Ph

Analysis prepared by **Rafay Khalid, CFA** on October 25, 2010, when the stock traded at **$ 12.61**.

Highlights

➤ We forecast revenue growth of 12% in 2010, reflecting our outlook for a modest increase in average earning assets and a widening of the net interest margin. In addition, we believe the recently completed Financial Federal Corporation (FFC) acquisition will help boost revenue growth. FFC will continue to be managed as a separate wholly owned subsidiary. Our 2010 estimates include a net interest margin of 3.64%, up 45 basis points from 3.19% in 2009. We expect revenue growth of 7% in 2011.

➤ We see expenses increasing on a dollar basis in 2010, following the FFC acquisition. We forecast expenses as a percentage of revenues will increase to 77.9% in 2010, from 76.5% in 2009, but then decrease to 73.5% in 2011. We do not expect any special FDIC assessments in 2010. We believe loan loss provisions will continue to decline to $56 million in 2010 and $34 million in 2011, from $57 million in 2009. Our view assumes a gradual economic recovery in 2010.

➤ Our EPS forecasts are $0.36 in 2010 and $0.47 in 2011. This compares to $0.30 in 2009. Our EPS estimates assume a 32% effective tax rate.

Investment Rationale/Risk

➤ We believe the FFC acquisition gives PBCT additional exposure to the high-yielding equipment leasing business. We think the FFC deal will be accretive to the company's 2010 earnings. We view the proposed acquisitions of Smithtown Bancorp. and LSB Corp. favorably, as they should increase PBCT's market share in the Northeast region. In addition, we expect further deals to follow, as PBCT will likely continue to put its excess liquidity to work. We view the company's balance sheet as solid, given its $3.3 billion in cash and cash equivalents and $437 million of debt as of September 30, 2010.

➤ Risks to our recommendation and target price include possible integration problems related to the FFC acquisition, higher-than-expected loan loss provisions, and significant deterioration in the macroeconomic environment.

➤ Our 12-month target price of $20 is based on a historical average tangible book value ratio of 1.88X applied to our 2011 tangible book value per share forecast of $10.65.

Qualitative Risk Assessment

LOW	MEDIUM	HIGH

Our risk assessment reflects our view of the good credit quality of PBCT's loan portfolio and its history of profitability, offset by execution risk, mostly stemming from the investment of the proceeds from the company's second-step conversion.

Quantitative Evaluations

S&P Quality Ranking   **B**

D	C	B-	B	B+	A-	A	A+

Relative Strength Rank   **WEAK**

17

LOWEST = 1   HIGHEST = 99

Revenue/Earnings Data

Revenue (Million $)

	1Q	2Q	3Q	4Q	Year
2010	264.2	283.7	283.4	--	--
2009	267.4	277.2	272.1	259.2	1,076
2008	337.2	300.9	296.6	286.1	1,221
2007	193.0	233.0	239.6	226.8	892.4
2006	179.5	183.5	161.4	195.9	729.5
2005	157.2	164.3	172.7	185.5	679.7

Earnings Per Share ($)

	1Q	2Q	3Q	4Q	Year
2010	0.04	0.05	0.07	E0.11	E0.36
2009	0.08	0.08	0.08	0.08	0.30
2008	0.05	0.13	0.14	0.11	0.42
2007	0.11	0.05	0.20	0.16	0.51
2006	0.11	0.11	0.05	0.13	0.40
2005	0.10	0.10	0.11	0.11	0.42

Fiscal year ended Dec. 31. Next earnings report expected: Late January. EPS Estimates based on S&P Operating Earnings; historical GAAP earnings are as reported.

Dividend Data (Dates: mm/dd Payment Date: mm/dd/yy)

Amount ($)	Date Decl.	Ex-Div. Date	Stk. of Record	Payment Date
0.153	01/21	01/28	02/01	02/15/10
0.155	04/15	04/28	05/01	05/15/10
0.155	07/15	07/28	08/01	08/15/10
0.155	10/21	10/28	11/01	11/15/10

Dividends have been paid since 1993. Source: Company reports.

Please read the Required Disclosures and Analyst Certification on the last page of this report.

The McGraw-Hill Companies

People's United Financial Inc

Business Summary October 25, 2010

CORPORATE OVERVIEW. People's United Financial (formerly People's Bank of Connecticut), formed in 1842, is a state-chartered stock savings bank headquartered in Bridgeport, CT. As of December 31, 2009, assets totaled roughly $21.3 billion. The company offers a full range of financial services to individual, corporations, and municipal customers. In addition to traditional banking activities, People's provides specialized services tailored to specific markets, including personal, institutional and employee benefits; cash management; and municipal banking and finance. PBCT offers brokerage, financial advisory services and life insurance through its People's Securities subsidiary and Chittenden Securities; equipment financing through People's Capital and Leasing (PCLC) and Financial Federal Corp (FFC); and other insurance services through R.C. Knox and Company, Inc. and Chittenden Insurance Group, LLC. Services are delivered through a network of over 300 branches in Connecticut, Massachusetts, New Hampshire, Vermont, Maine and New York, including 79 full-service supermarket branches, 43 investment and brokerage offices, nine PCLC offices, 16 commercial banking offices, and over 400 ATMs.

PBCT has increased its residential mortgage and home equity lending activities in the contiguous markets of New York and Massachusetts. In addition, PBCT maintains a loan production office in Massachusetts, and PCLC main-

tains a sales presence in six states to support its equipment financing operations outside of New England. Within the Commercial Banking division, PBCT maintains a national credits group, which has participated in commercial loans and real estate loans to borrowers in various industries on a national scale.

PRIMARY BUSINESS DYNAMICS. As of December 31, 2009, total loans of $14.2 billion were 38% commercial real estate loans (34%); 28% commercial loans (29%); 18% residential real estate loans (versus 22% in 2008); and 16% consumer loans (15%).

As of December 31, 2009, deposits comprised 97.8% of funding costs, versus 97.5% at December 31, 2008. At year-end 2009, deposits consisted of non-interest 22% (versus 22% in 2008); low interest 45% (44%); and time deposits 33% (34%).

Company Financials Fiscal Year Ended Dec. 31

Per Share Data ($)	2009	2008	2007	2006	2005	2004	2003	2002	2001	2000
Tangible Book Value	10.68	10.87	15.06	8.68	3.98	5.53	4.55	2.83	2.82	2.61
Earnings	0.30	0.42	0.51	0.40	0.42	-0.02	0.22	0.19	0.30	0.37
S&P Core Earnings	0.29	0.37	0.51	0.41	0.41	-0.01	0.22	0.16	0.09	NA
Dividends	0.61	0.58	0.52	0.46	0.41	0.45	0.32	0.30	0.28	0.25
Payout Ratio	NM	138%	102%	115%	96%	NM	148%	158%	96%	68%
Prices:High	18.54	21.76	22.81	21.62	16.07	14.12	7.20	5.94	6.01	5.71
Prices:Low	14.72	13.92	14.78	14.29	11.43	6.88	5.13	4.37	4.37	3.47
P/E Ratio:High	62	52	45	54	38	NM	33	31	20	15
P/E Ratio:Low	49	33	29	36	27	NM	23	23	15	9

Income Statement Analysis (Million $)	2009	2008	2007	2006	2005	2004	2003	2002	2001	2000
Net Interest Income	577	636	487	382	370	327	320	351	354	385
Loan Loss Provision	57.0	26.2	8.00	3.40	8.60	13.3	48.6	77.7	101	59.9
Non Interest Income	309	303	180	175	172	155	252	251	339	290
Non Interest Expenses	685	654	439	347	343	479	436	441	441	453
Pretax Income	144	208	225	180	190	-14.2	86.9	80.4	133	166
Effective Tax Rate	29.9%	32.8%	33.6%	32.2%	33.7%	NM	26.6%	31.1%	34.8%	34.5%
Net Income	101	140	149	122	126	-5.60	63.8	55.4	86.7	108
% Net Interest Margin	3.19	3.62	4.12	3.87	3.68	3.33	2.95	3.40	4.33	4.47
S&P Core Earnings	98.4	124	147	124	124	-4.16	63.9	46.6	27.2	NA

Balance Sheet & Other Financial Data (Million $)	2009	2008	2007	2006	2005	2004	2003	2002	2001	2000
Total Assets	21,256	20,168	13,555	10,687	10,933	10,718	11,672	12,261	11,891	11,571
Loans	14,061	14,408	8,877	9,298	8,498	7,861	8,122	7,336	6,931	7,345
Deposits	15,446	14,269	8,881	9,083	9,083	8,862	8,714	8,426	7,983	7,761
Capitalization:Debt	341	368	65.4	65.3	109	122	1,162	1,165	1,478	1,824
Capitalization:Equity	5,101	5,176	4,445	1,340	1,289	1,200	1,002	940	935	882
Capitalization:Total	5,442	5,544	4,511	1,405	1,398	1,322	2,164	2,104	2,413	2,706
% Return on Assets	0.5	0.8	1.2	1.1	1.2	NM	0.5	0.5	0.7	1.0
% Return on Equity	2.0	2.9	5.2	9.3	10.1	NM	6.6	5.9	9.5	13.0
% Loan Loss Reserve	1.2	1.1	0.8	0.8	0.9	0.9	1.4	1.5	1.6	1.4
% Risk Based Capital	14.1	13400.0	33.4	16.1	16.4	16.7	13.1	12.5	12.3	11.6
Price Times Book Value:High	1.7	2.0	1.5	2.5	4.0	2.6	1.6	2.1	2.1	2.2
Price Times Book Value:Low	1.4	1.3	1.0	1.6	2.9	1.2	1.1	1.5	1.6	1.3

Data as orig reptd.; bef. results of disc opers/spec. items. Per share data adj. for stk. divs.; EPS diluted. E-Estimated. NA-Not Available. NM-Not Meaningful. NR-Not Ranked. UR-Under Review.

Office: 850 Main St, Bridgeport, CT 06604-4904.
Telephone: 203-338-7171.
Website: http://www.peoples.com
Chrmn: G.P. Carter

Pres & CEO: J.P. Barnes
COO: M.K. Vitelli
EVP & CFO: P.D. Burner
EVP & Chief Admin Officer: L.C. Powlus

Investor Contact: J. Shaw
Board Members: J. P. Barnes, C. P. Baron, G. P. Carter, J. K. Dwight, J. Franklin, E. S. Groark, J. M. Hansen, R. M. Hoyt, M. W. Richards, J. A. Thomas

Founded: 1842
Domicile: Connecticut
Employees: 4,534

Pepco Holdings Inc.

STANDARD & POOR'S

S&P Recommendation	HOLD ★★★☆☆	Price $19.41 (as of Oct 22, 2010)	12-Mo. Target Price $18.00	Investment Style Large-Cap Blend

GICS Sector Utilities
Sub-Industry Electric Utilities

Summary This energy holding company for three regulated utilities and an unregulated energy services business recently sold its Conectiv Energy power generation business.

Key Stock Statistics (Source S&P, Vickers, company reports)

52-Wk Range	$19.80– 14.34	S&P Oper. EPS 2010E	0.98	Market Capitalization(B)	$4.346	Beta	0.57
Trailing 12-Month EPS	$0.66	S&P Oper. EPS 2011E	1.25	Yield (%)	5.56	S&P 3-Yr. Proj. EPS CAGR(%)	-13
Trailing 12-Month P/E	29.4	P/E on S&P Oper. EPS 2010E	19.8	Dividend Rate/Share	$1.08	S&P Credit Rating	BBB+
$10K Invested 5 Yrs Ago	$12,323	Common Shares Outstg. (M)	223.9	Institutional Ownership (%)	54		

Price Performance

30-Week Mov. Avg. · · · 10-Week Mov. Avg. - - GAAP Earnings vs. Previous Year Volume Above Avg. STARS
12-Mo. Target Price — Relative Strength — ▲ Up ▼ Down ► No Change Below Avg.

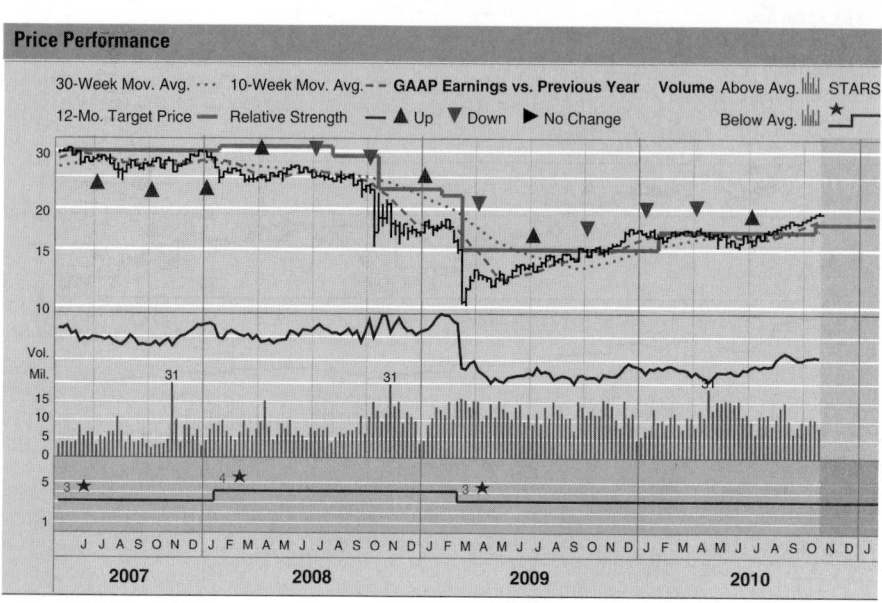

Options: Ph

Analysis prepared by **Justin McCann** on October 13, 2010, when the stock traded at **$ 19.17**.

Highlights

➤ With the sale of Conectiv Energy (completed on July 1, 2010), we believe POM's earnings volatility will be greatly reduced as the regulated utility operations are now expected to account for at least 90% of consolidated earnings.

➤ We view 2010 as a transition year for POM, and expect much stronger results in 2011. Operating EPS from continuing operations in the first half of 2010 benefited from rate increases and the more favorable weather in the second quarter. Results were also aided by higher transmission revenues due to the accrual of rate adjustments for the prior rate year. These factors were partially offset by restoration costs related to two severe storms in the first quarter. We expect the sale of Conectiv Energy to result in a one-time reported GAAP after-tax loss of $0.27 to $0.40 per share.

➤ For 2011, we expect operating EPS from continuing operations to grow more than 25% from anticipated results in 2010, driven by rate increases, a sharp decline in interest expense, and a gradual recovery in the economy. We see EPS growth over the next five years being driven by expansion of the rate base through infrastructure investments.

Investment Rationale/Risk

➤ The stock is up around 13% year to date, reflecting, in our view, the recent investor shift to the utility sector and POM's well above-peers yield from the dividend. This follows a 5.1% decline in 2009. The sale of Conectiv Energy has greatly reduced POM's exposure to the energy commodity market and its earnings volatility, in our view. We think that with the proceeds from the transaction to be used for debt reduction, POM's balance sheet and credit profile will be strengthened, eliminating the need to issue new equity through at least 2012.

➤ Risks to our recommendation and target price include much weaker than expected earnings from the unregulated Pepco Energy Services unit, unfavorable regulatory rulings, and the potential for a sharp decline in the average P/E of the group as a whole.

➤ POM believes the sale of Conectiv Energy will support its renewed commitment to the dividend, whose recent yield (around 5.6%) was still well above the average peer yield of about 4.7%. Our 12-month target price is $18, reflecting a premium-to-peers P/E of 14.4X our operating EPS estimate for 2011.

Qualitative Risk Assessment

LOW	MEDIUM	HIGH

Our risk assessment reflects our view that with the completion of the sale of Conectiv Energy, whose earnings and cash flows were highly volatile, there will be much greater financial stability, with the regulated electric transmission and distribution businesses accounting for at least 90% of earnings and cash flows.

Quantitative Evaluations

S&P Quality Ranking   B

D	C	B-	B	B+	A-	A	A+

Relative Strength Rank   MODERATE

68

LOWEST = 1   HIGHEST = 99

Revenue/Earnings Data

Revenue (Million $)

	1Q	2Q	3Q	4Q	Year
2010	2,359	1,636	--	--	--
2009	2,520	2,065	2,539	2,135	9,259
2008	2,641	2,518	3,060	2,481	10,700
2007	2,179	2,084	2,770	2,333	9,366
2006	1,952	1,917	2,590	1,905	8,363
2005	1,805	1,712	2,489	2,063	8,066

Earnings Per Share ($)

	1Q	2Q	3Q	4Q	Year
2010	0.16	0.34	E0.37	E0.11	E0.98
2009	0.21	0.11	0.56	0.19	1.06
2008	0.49	0.07	0.59	0.32	1.47
2007	0.27	0.30	0.87	0.29	1.72
2006	0.29	0.27	0.54	0.19	1.30
2005	0.24	0.34	0.90	0.43	1.91

Fiscal year ended Dec. 31. Next earnings report expected: Late October. EPS Estimates based on S&P Operating Earnings; historical GAAP earnings are as reported.

Dividend Data (Dates: mm/dd Payment Date: mm/dd/yy)

Amount ($)	Date Decl.	Ex-Div. Date	Stk. of Record	Payment Date
0.270	10/22	12/08	12/10	12/31/09
0.270	01/28	03/08	03/10	03/31/10
0.270	04/22	06/08	06/10	06/30/10
0.270	07/22	09/08	09/10	09/30/10

Dividends have been paid since 1904. Source: Company reports.

Please read the Required Disclosures and Analyst Certification on the last page of this report.

Pepco Holdings Inc.

STANDARD &POOR'S

Business Summary October 13, 2010

CORPORATE OVERVIEW. Pepco Holdings (POM) is an energy holding company involved in the power delivery business, which provides transmission and distribution of electricity and distribution of natural gas. These operations are conducted through POM's three regulated utility subsidiaries: Potomac Electric Power Company (Pepco), Delmarva Power & Light Company (DPL), and Atlantic City Electric Company (ACE). POM is also involved in the competitive energy business, but with the July 2010 sale of the bulk of Conectiv Energy, which provided non-regulated generation and the marketing and supply of electricity and natural gas, this segment of POM's operations was reduced to the energy management services provided by its Pepco Energy Services (PES) subsidiary. In 2009, the power delivery business contributed 49.3% of POM's consolidated operating revenues; PES, 24.9%; Conectiv Energy, 22.6%; and other, 0.5%.

IMPACT OF IMPORTANT DEVELOPMENTS. On July 1, 2010, the company completed the sale (announced on April 21, 2010) of its Conectiv Energy power generation business to Calpine Corporation (CPN) for $1.63 billion, after adjustments. The sale did not include Conectiv's power supply contracts, its energy hedging portfolio, and other non-core assets, which POM expects to have liquidated by the end of April 2011. The estimated $2 billion in proceeds from the sales (which includes the return of related collateral, working capital and the liquidation of the supply contracts) are expected to be used for the payment of $300 million of projected taxes, and the reduction of $1.75 billion of POM debt. With the completion of the transaction, the regulated operations are now expected to account for 90% to 95% of POM's consolidated operating income, compared to 71% in 2009.

Company Financials Fiscal Year Ended Dec. 31

Per Share Data ($)	2009	2008	2007	2006	2005	2004	2003	2002	2001	2000
Tangible Book Value	12.82	12.69	13.01	11.48	11.34	10.28	9.12	9.20	17.01	16.77
Earnings	1.06	1.47	1.72	1.30	1.91	1.47	0.63	1.61	1.50	2.96
S&P Core Earnings	1.25	1.08	1.60	1.28	1.37	1.38	0.87	1.31	1.20	NA
Dividends	0.54	0.54	1.04	1.04	1.00	1.00	1.00	0.92	1.17	1.66
Payout Ratio	51%	37%	60%	80%	52%	68%	159%	57%	78%	56%
Prices:High	18.71	29.64	30.71	26.99	24.46	21.71	20.56	23.83	24.90	27.88
Prices:Low	10.07	15.27	24.20	21.79	20.26	16.94	16.10	15.37	20.08	19.06
P/E Ratio:High	18	20	18	21	13	15	33	15	17	9
P/E Ratio:Low	9	10	14	17	11	12	26	10	13	6

Income Statement Analysis (Million $)	2009	2008	2007	2006	2005	2004	2003	2002	2001	2000
Revenue	9,259	10,700	9,366	8,363	8,066	7,222	7,271	4,325	2,503	2,624
Depreciation	391	377	366	413	423	441	422	240	171	248
Maintenance	NA	NA	NA	NA	NA	NA	NA	NA	NA	NA
Fixed Charges Coverage	1.82	2.42	2.41	2.25	2.37	2.06	1.43	2.47	3.06	4.32
Construction Credits	NA	NA	NA	NA	NA	NA	NA	NA	NA	NA
Effective Tax Rate	31.9%	35.9%	36.0%	39.4%	41.3%	40.1%	38.0%	37.1%	33.1%	49.2%
Net Income	235	300	334	248	362	259	108	211	168	352
S&P Core Earnings	279	219	311	246	259	241	147	171	130	NA

Balance Sheet & Other Financial Data (Million $)	2009	2008	2007	2006	2005	2004	2003	2002	2001	2000
Gross Property	13,717	12,926	12,307	11,820	11,384	11,045	10,747	10,625	4,367	4,339
Capital Expenditures	864	781	623	475	467	517	564	504	245	226
Net Property	8,863	8,314	7,877	7,577	7,312	7,088	6,965	6,798	2,758	2,776
Capitalization:Long Term Debt	4,947	5,378	4,735	4,367	4,885	5,128	5,373	5,122	1,722	1,985
Capitalization:% Long Term Debt	53.8	56.2	54.1	54.7	57.7	60.4	63.7	62.2	45.9	50.4
Capitalization:Preferred	Nil	Nil	Nil	Nil	Nil	Nil	63.2	111	210	90.3
Capitalization:% Preferred	Nil	Nil	Nil	Nil	Nil	Nil	0.75	1.35	5.59	2.29
Capitalization:Common	4,256	4,190	4,018	3,612	3,584	3,366	3,003	2,996	1,823	1,863
Capitalization:% Common	46.2	43.8	45.9	45.3	42.3	39.6	35.6	36.4	48.5	47.3
Total Capital	9,752	11,883	10,903	10,134	10,455	10,532	8,439	9,833	4,282	4,384
% Operating Ratio	95.8	94.4	93.7	93.2	92.4	91.6	92.6	90.3	87.1	91.9
% Earned on Net Property	5.8	9.5	10.0	9.3	12.6	11.0	18.6	16.4	27.5	16.0
% Return on Revenue	2.5	2.8	3.6	3.0	4.5	3.6	1.5	4.9	6.7	13.4
% Return on Invested Capital	5.8	5.5	6.0	6.2	8.0	6.7	8.3	6.4	9.6	11.8
% Return on Common Equity	5.6	7.3	8.8	6.9	10.5	8.1	3.4	8.7	8.9	18.4

Data as orig reptd.; bef. results of disc opers/spec. items. Per share data adj. for stk. divs.; EPS diluted. E-Estimated. NA-Not Available. NM-Not Meaningful. NR-Not Ranked. UR-Under Review.

Office: 701 Ninth Street N.W., Washington, DC 20068.
Telephone: 202-872-2000.
Email: shareholder@pepco.com
Website: http://www.pepcoholdings.com

Chrmn, Pres & CEO: J.M. Rigby
SVP & CFO: P.H. Barry
Chief Acctg Officer & Cntlr: R. Clark
Treas: K.M. McGowan

Secy: E.S. Rogers
Investor Contact: E.J. Bourscheid (202-872-2797)
Board Members: J. B. Dunn, IV, T. C. Golden, P. Harker, F. O. Heintz, B. J. Krumsiek, G. F. MacCormack, L. C. Nussdorf, P. A. Oelrich, J. M. Rigby, F. K. Ross, P. A. Schneider, L. Silverman

Founded: 1896
Domicile: Delaware
Employees: 5,110

The McGraw·Hill Companies

PepsiCo Inc

STANDARD &POOR'S

S&P Recommendation BUY ★★★★☆

Price	$65.01 (as of Oct 22, 2010)
12-Mo. Target Price	$71.00
Investment Style	Large-Cap Growth

GICS Sector Consumer Staples
Sub-Industry Soft Drinks

Summary This company is a major international producer of branded beverage and snack food products.

Key Stock Statistics (Source S&P, Vickers, company reports)

52-Wk Range	$68.11– 58.75	S&P Oper. EPS 2010**E**	4.14	Market Capitalization(B)	$103.031	Beta		0.54
Trailing 12-Month EPS	$3.97	S&P Oper. EPS 2011**E**	4.59	Yield (%)	2.95	S&P 3-Yr. Proj. EPS CAGR(%)		8
Trailing 12-Month P/E	16.4	P/E on S&P Oper. EPS 2010**E**	15.7	Dividend Rate/Share	$1.92	S&P Credit Rating		A
$10K Invested 5 Yrs Ago	$12,771	Common Shares Outstg. (M)	1,584.8	Institutional Ownership (%)	66			

Price Performance

- 30-Week Mov. Avg. · · · 10-Week Mov. Avg. - - GAAP Earnings vs. Previous Year   Volume Above Avg. STARS
- 12-Mo. Target Price — Relative Strength — ▲ Up ▼ Down ► No Change   Below Avg. ★

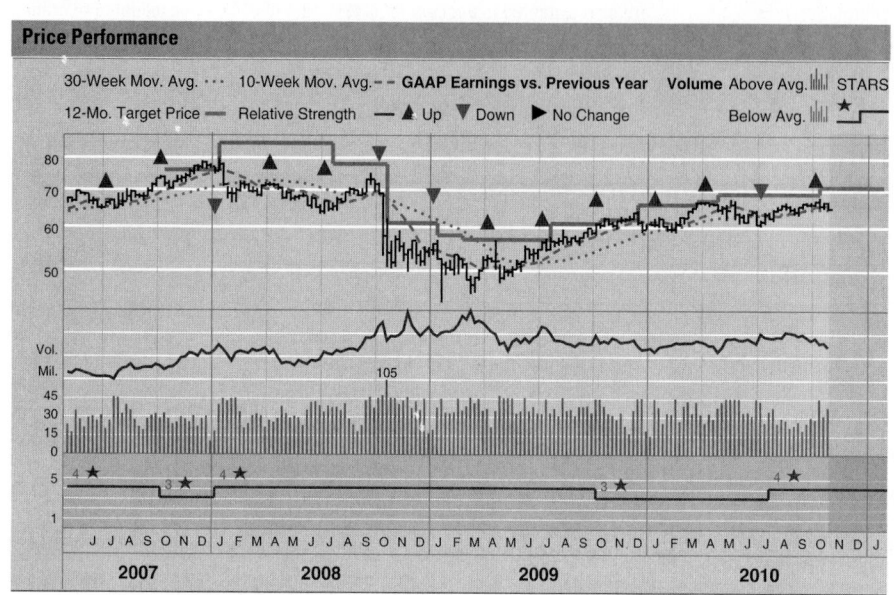

Options: ASE, CBOE, P, Ph

Analysis prepared by **Esther Y. Kwon, CFA** on October 18, 2010, when the stock traded at **$ 66.68**.

Highlights

► In 2010, we see net sales advancing more than 30% from 2009's $43.2 billion, largely on the acquisitions of anchor bottlers Pepsi Bottling Co. and PepsiAmericas, completed in February 2010. We see beverage volumes in the Americas continuing to struggle but expect better performance from Gatorade as the brand is refreshed. We also think PEP will improve sales in the convenience and gas and food service channels. For 2011, we forecast sales growth of over 6%.

► We expect operating margins to decline on investments in infrastructure and product and packaging innovation, offset somewhat by acquisition synergies, which we estimate will boost income by about $150 million, and lower commodity costs.

► On a higher tax rate of about 27%, compared to 2009's effective tax rate of 25.6%, and higher interest expense, we estimate 2010 operating EPS of $4.14, up from 2009's $3.71. In March, PEP's directors reinstated the company's share repurchase program upon the close of the bottler acquisitions, and PEP said it plans to repurchase about $4.4 billion of stock in 2010. For 2011, we see EPS of $4.59.

Investment Rationale/Risk

► We view favorably PEP's international growth opportunities and healthy cash flow growth. Although we remain cautious about sluggish Americas beverage trends, we think new product introductions and new marketing initiatives in 2010 will drive improvement, while we see exposure to stronger international markets as a potential offset. In addition to the company's leading market positions, we view PEP's product innovation strategy as trend-setting for the industry. Its focus on health and wellness should continue to drive the top line, and we look for strong returns to shareholders in the form of dividends and share repurchases.

► Risks to our recommendation and target price include unfavorable weather conditions in the company's markets and increased competitive activity. As PEP boosts its exposure to foreign markets, political and currency risks also increase.

► Our relative valuation model, derived from analysis of peer and historical P/E multiples, indicates a value of $71, which is our 12-month target price. This reflects a multiple of projected 2011 EPS below the recent historical range of 19X to 27X.

Qualitative Risk Assessment

LOW	MEDIUM	HIGH

Our risk assessment reflects the relatively stable nature of the company's end markets, its strong cash flow, leading global market positions, corporate governance practices that we view as favorable versus peers, and an S&P Quality Ranking of A+, reflecting superior long-term earnings and dividend growth.

Quantitative Evaluations

S&P Quality Ranking A+

D	C	B-	B	B+	A-	A	A+

Relative Strength Rank WEAK

28

LOWEST = 1   HIGHEST = 99

Revenue/Earnings Data

Revenue (Million $)

	1Q	2Q	3Q	4Q	Year
2010	9,368	14,801	15,514	--	--
2009	8,263	10,592	11,080	13,297	43,232
2008	8,333	10,945	11,244	12,729	43,251
2007	7,350	9,607	10,171	12,346	39,474
2006	7,205	8,599	8,950	10,383	35,137
2005	6,585	7,697	8,184	10,096	32,562

Earnings Per Share ($)

	1Q	2Q	3Q	4Q	Year
2010	0.89	0.98	1.19	E1.06	E4.14
2009	0.72	1.06	1.09	0.91	3.77
2008	0.70	1.05	0.99	0.46	3.21
2007	0.65	0.94	1.06	0.77	3.41
2006	0.60	0.80	0.88	1.06	3.34
2005	0.53	0.70	0.51	0.65	2.39

Fiscal year ended Dec. 31. Next earnings report expected: Mid February. EPS Estimates based on S&P Operating Earnings; historical GAAP earnings are as reported.

Dividend Data (Dates: mm/dd Payment Date: mm/dd/yy)

Amount ($)	Date Decl.	Ex-Div. Date	Stk. of Record	Payment Date
0.450	11/13	12/02	12/04	01/04/10
0.450	02/09	03/03	03/05	03/31/10
0.480	03/15	06/02	06/04	06/30/10
0.480	07/16	09/01	09/03	09/30/10

Dividends have been paid since 1952. Source: Company reports.

Please read the Required Disclosures and Analyst Certification on the last page of this report.

The **McGraw·Hill** Companies

PepsiCo Inc

Business Summary October 18, 2010

CORPORATE OVERVIEW. Originally incorporated in 1919, PepsiCo is a leader in the global snack and beverage industry. The company manufactures, markets and sells a variety of salty, convenient, sweet and grain-based snacks, carbonated and non-carbonated beverages, and foods. PepsiCo is organized into three business units with six reportable segments: PepsiCo Americas Foods (PAF), which includes Frito-Lay North America (FLNA), Quaker Foods North America (QFNA), and Latin America Foods (LAF); PepsiCo Beverages America (PAB), which includes PepsiCo Beverages North America and all of its Latin American beverage businesses; and PepsiCo International, which includes all of PepsiCo businesses in Europe and Asia, the Middle East and Africa (AMEA).

FLNA (31% of 2009 net revenue, 24.6% of operating profits before corporate overhead) produces the best-selling line of snack foods in the U.S., including Fritos brand corn chips, Lay's and Ruffles potato chips, Doritos and Tostitos tortilla chips, Cheetos cheese-flavored snacks, SunChips multigrain snacks, and Quaker Chewy granola bars. FLNA branded products are sold to independent distributors and retailers. Products are transported from Frito-Lay's manufacturing plants to major distribution centers, principally in company-owned trucks.

QFNA (4.4%, 33.3%) manufactures, markets and sells Cap'n Crunch and Life ready-to-eat cereals, Quaker hot cereals, Rice-A-Roni, Near East and Pasta Roni side dishes, Aunt Jemima mixes and syrups and Quaker grits.

LAF (13%, 15.9%) manufactures, markets and sells snack foods under the brands Gamesa, Doritos, Cheetos, Ruffles, Lay's and Sabritas as well as many Quaker branded products.

PAB (23%, 21.5%) manufactures or uses contract manufacturers, markets and sells beverage concentrates, fountain syrups and finished goods, under the brands Pepsi, Mountain Dew, Gatorade, 7UP (outside the U.S.), Tropicana Pure Premium, Sierra Mist, SoBe Lifewater, Tropicana juice drinks, Amp Energy, Naked juice and Izze. PBNA also manufactures, markets and sells ready-to-drink tea and coffee products through joint ventures with Lipton and Starbucks. In addition, it markets the Aquafina water brand and licenses it to its bottlers.

Company Financials Fiscal Year Ended Dec. 31

Per Share Data ($)	2009	2008	2007	2006	2005	2004	2003	2002	2001	2000
Tangible Book Value	4.95	3.36	6.80	1.93	2.17	1.96	3.82	2.37	1.90	1.91
Cash Flow	4.73	4.14	4.27	4.30	3.25	2.45	2.75	2.47	2.07	2.13
Earnings	3.77	3.21	3.41	3.34	2.39	2.41	2.05	1.85	1.47	1.48
S&P Core Earnings	3.77	2.99	3.38	3.30	2.37	2.44	2.03	1.54	1.20	NA
Dividends	1.77	1.65	1.43	1.16	1.01	0.85	0.63	0.60	0.58	0.56
Payout Ratio	47%	51%	42%	35%	42%	35%	31%	32%	39%	38%
Prices:High	64.48	79.79	79.00	65.99	60.34	55.71	48.88	53.50	50.46	49.94
Prices:Low	43.78	49.74	61.89	56.00	51.34	45.30	36.24	34.00	40.25	29.69
P/E Ratio:High	17	25	23	20	25	23	24	29	34	34
P/E Ratio:Low	12	15	18	17	21	19	18	18	27	20

Income Statement Analysis (Million $)										
Revenue	43,232	43,251	39,474	35,137	32,562	29,261	26,971	25,112	26,935	20,438
Operating Income	9,596	8,964	8,596	7,845	7,230	6,673	6,208	6,066	5,490	4,185
Depreciation	1,635	1,486	1,426	1,406	1,308	1,264	1,221	1,112	1,082	960
Interest Expense	397	329	224	239	256	167	163	178	219	221
Pretax Income	8,079	7,021	7,631	6,989	6,382	5,546	4,992	4,868	4,029	3,210
Effective Tax Rate	26.0%	26.8%	25.8%	19.3%	36.1%	24.7%	28.5%	31.9%	33.9%	32.0%
Net Income	5,946	5,142	5,658	5,642	4,078	4,174	3,568	3,313	2,662	2,183
S&P Core Earnings	5,945	4,781	5,602	5,565	4,028	4,191	3,543	2,749	2,164	NA

Balance Sheet & Other Financial Data (Million $)										
Cash	4,135	2,277	910	1,651	1,716	1,280	820	1,638	683	864
Current Assets	12,571	10,806	10,151	9,130	10,454	8,639	6,930	6,413	5,853	4,604
Total Assets	39,848	35,994	34,628	29,930	31,727	27,987	25,327	23,474	21,695	18,339
Current Liabilities	8,756	8,787	7,753	6,860	9,406	6,752	6,415	6,052	4,998	3,935
Long Term Debt	7,400	7,858	4,203	2,550	2,313	2,397	1,702	2,187	2,651	2,346
Common Equity	16,908	12,203	17,325	15,327	14,210	13,572	11,896	9,250	8,648	7,249
Total Capital	24,842	20,190	22,174	18,446	17,998	17,226	14,837	13,196	12,821	10,956
Capital Expenditures	2,128	2,446	2,430	2,068	1,736	1,387	1,345	1,437	1,324	1,067
Cash Flow	7,461	6,626	7,084	7,047	5,384	4,109	4,786	4,421	3,744	3,143
Current Ratio	1.4	1.2	1.3	1.3	1.1	1.3	1.1	1.1	1.2	1.2
% Long Term Debt of Capitalization	29.8	38.9	18.9	13.8	12.9	13.9	11.5	16.6	20.7	21.4
% Net Income of Revenue	13.8	11.9	14.3	16.1	12.5	14.3	13.2	13.2	9.9	10.7
% Return on Assets	15.7	14.6	17.5	18.3	13.7	15.7	14.6	14.7	12.5	12.2
% Return on Equity	40.9	34.8	34.6	38.2	29.4	22.3	33.3	37.0	32.8	30.9

Data as orig reptd.; bef. results of disc opers/spec. items. Per share data adj. for stk. divs.; EPS diluted. E-Estimated. NA-Not Available. NM-Not Meaningful. NR-Not Ranked. UR-Under Review.

Office: 700 Anderson Hill Road, Purchase, NY 10577.
Telephone: 914-253-2000.
Website: http://www.pepsico.com
Chrmn, Pres & CEO: I. Nooyi

COO & CFO: H.F. Johnston
SVP, Chief Acctg Officer & Cntlr: P.A. Bridgman
SVP & Treas: T. Hilado
SVP, Secy & General Counsel: L.D. Thompson

Board Members: S. Brown, I. M. Cook, D. Dublon, V. J. Dzau, R. L. Hunt, A. Ibarguen, A. C. Martinez, I. Nooyi, S. P. Rockefeller, J. J. Schiro, L. G. Trotter, D. L. Vasella **Founded:** 1916
Domicile: North Carolina
Employees: 203,000

PerkinElmer Inc.

STANDARD &POOR'S

S&P Recommendation **BUY** ★★★★☆	Price $23.43 (as of Oct 22, 2010)	12-Mo. Target Price $28.00	Investment Style Large-Cap Value

GICS Sector Health Care
Sub-Industry Life Sciences Tools & Services

Summary This diversified technology company provides advanced scientific and technical products and services worldwide to pharmaceutical and industrial markets.

Key Stock Statistics (Source S&P, Vickers, company reports)

52-Wk Range	$25.45–18.22	S&P Oper. EPS 2010**E**	1.27	Market Capitalization(B)	$2.763	Beta	0.83
Trailing 12-Month EPS	$1.15	S&P Oper. EPS 2011**E**	1.60	Yield (%)	1.20	S&P 3-Yr. Proj. EPS CAGR(%)	13
Trailing 12-Month P/E	20.4	P/E on S&P Oper. EPS 2010**E**	18.4	Dividend Rate/Share	$0.28	S&P Credit Rating	BBB
$10K Invested 5 Yrs Ago	$12,052	Common Shares Outstg. (M)	117.9	Institutional Ownership (%)	90		

Price Performance

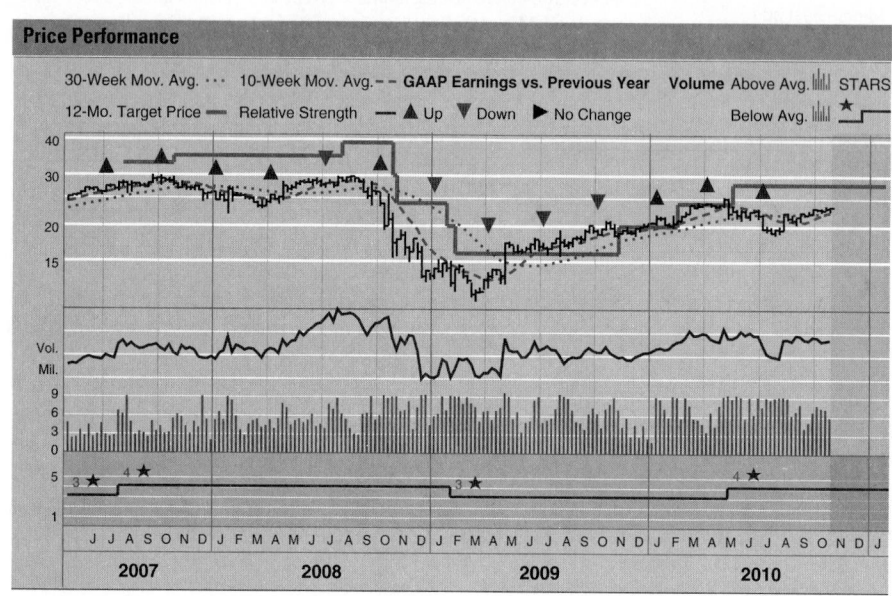

30-Week Mov. Avg. · · · 10-Week Mov. Avg. - - **GAAP Earnings vs. Previous Year** Volume Above Avg. STARS
12-Mo. Target Price — Relative Strength — ▲ Up ▼ Down ► No Change Below Avg.

Options: ASE, CBOE, Ph

Analysis prepared by **Jeffrey Loo, CFA** on September 15, 2010, when the stock traded at **$ 22.58**.

Highlights

➤ We see sales increasing 10% in 2010 and 7% in 2011, to $1.98 billion and $2.12 billion, respectively, as several of PKI's end-markets stabilize, particularly food and environmental safety. However, we continue to see only modest instrument sales within health care end-markets due to capital constraints, particularly within the pharmaceutical sector. We see robust growth of over 20% in China and India on increased adoption of pre-natal and neo-natal genetic tests, as well as expanded compliance regulations for food and water safety driving industrial sales. But we expect sales in the U.S. and Europe to remain challenging. We look for improvements of 55 and 40 basis points (bps) in operating margins in 2010 and 2011.

➤ In August 2010, PKI agreed to sell its Illumination and Detection Solutions (IDS) unit to Veritas Capital for $482 million, subject to approvals. IDS is a provider of specialty lighting and sensor components for health, environmental and security applications and has annual sales of about $300 million. PKI will account for IDS as discontinued operations.

➤ Excluding intangible amortization, we estimate operating EPS of $1.27 in 2010 and $1.60 in 2011.

Investment Rationale/Risk

➤ We believe the shares, recently trading at 14.0X our 2011 EPS forecast and at a 1.1X P/E-to-growth ratio, both slightly below peers, are undervalued. We see signs that PKI's end-markets are stabilizing, and we believe growth will be more robust than we had initially anticipated. We also believe PKI is benefiting from its years-long portfolio restructuring and strategic efforts of international expansion, significant R&D investments, and strategic acquisitions to supplement organic growth. We believe PKI's expanding geographic presence in developing countries, particularly in India and China, where it has made acquisitions and built new facilities, will benefit both its Human and Environmental Health units and enable it to increase its market share.

➤ Risks to our recommendation and target price include a greater-than-anticipated decline in instrument sales, and slowing growth in industrial end-markets.

➤ Our 12-month target price of $28 is based on our relative valuation analysis, using a 13% projected three-year EPS growth rate, our 2011 EPS estimate and a P/E-to-growth ratio of 1.35X, in line with peers.

Qualitative Risk Assessment

LOW	MEDIUM	HIGH

Our risk assessment reflects PKI's broad product mix and diverse global client base. However, the company has been actively restructuring its business units and product portfolio and pursuing acquisitions, which we believe could increase operating risks.

Quantitative Evaluations

S&P Quality Ranking B

D	C	B-	**B**	B+	A-	A	A+

Relative Strength Rank MODERATE

62

LOWEST = 1   HIGHEST = 99

Revenue/Earnings Data

Revenue (Million $)

	1Q	2Q	3Q	4Q	Year
2010	465.1	497.8	--	--	--
2009	435.2	438.3	440.5	498.3	1,812
2008	482.3	528.6	505.1	495.0	1,937
2007	402.9	437.3	435.7	511.5	1,787
2006	355.5	377.0	386.9	427.0	1,546
2005	358.2	368.0	360.0	387.7	1,474

Earnings Per Share ($)

2010	0.22	0.46	E0.21	E0.38	E1.27
2009	0.13	0.20	0.14	0.33	0.80
2008	0.20	0.27	0.37	0.29	1.06
2007	0.12	0.28	0.26	0.46	1.11
2006	0.17	0.21	0.23	0.33	0.94
2005	0.12	0.23	0.20	-0.05	0.51

Fiscal year ended Dec. 31. Next earnings report expected: Late October. EPS Estimates based on S&P Operating Earnings; historical GAAP earnings are as reported.

Dividend Data (Dates: mm/dd Payment Date: mm/dd/yy)

Amount ($)	Date Decl.	Ex-Div. Date	Stk. of Record	Payment Date
0.070	10/21	01/20	01/22	02/12/10
0.070	01/24	04/14	04/16	05/07/10
0.070	06/03	07/21	07/23	08/13/10
0.070	07/30	10/20	10/22	11/12/10

Dividends have been paid since 1965. Source: Company reports.

Please read the Required Disclosures and Analyst Certification on the last page of this report.

The **McGraw-Hill** Companies

STANDARD & POOR'S

PerkinElmer Inc.

Business Summary September 15, 2010

CORPORATE OVERVIEW. PerkinElmer is a global technology company with operations in more than 125 countries. It develops, manufactures and provides scientific instruments, consumables and services to the pharmaceutical, biomedical, environmental testing, food and consumer safety testing, and general industrial markets. Collectively, these markets are commonly referred to as the health sciences and industrial sciences markets. In 2005, PKI operated three business segments within its end markets: Life and Analytical Sciences, Optoelectronics, and Fluid Sciences. However, in 2005 and 2006, PKI divested its Fluid Sciences unit in an effort to focus on the health sciences market, which PKI believes has greater growth and profitability potential. The health sciences market includes all of the businesses in the Life and Analytical Sciences unit and the medical imaging, medical sensors and lighting business in the Optoelectronics unit. The industrial sciences market includes the remaining businesses in Optoelectronics. In 2009, PKI again realigned its business units to Human Health and Environmental Health and plans to divest its specialty lighting business, which includes xenon flashtubes, ceramic xenon light sources, and laser pump sources.

Human Health provides drug discovery, genetic screening, reagents, consumables and services. Its instruments are used for scientific research and clinical applications. For drug discovery, PKI offers a wide range of instrumentation, software and consumables, including reagents, based on its core expertise in fluorescent, chemiluminescent and radioactive labeling, and the detection of nucleic acids and proteins. For genetic screening laboratories, it provides software, reagents and analysis tools to test for various inherited disorders. For chemical analysis, the company offers analytical tools employing technologies such as molecular and atomic spectroscopy, high-pressure liquid chromatography, gas chromatography and thermal analysis.

Environmental Health unit makes products for environmental safety and security and includes digital imaging, sensor and specialty lighting components to customers in biomedical, consumer products and other specialty end-markets. PKI supplies amorphous silicon digital X-ray detectors, a technology for medical imaging and radiation therapy.

Company Financials Fiscal Year Ended Dec. 31

Per Share Data ($)	2009	2008	2007	2006	2005	2004	2003	2002	2001	2000
Tangible Book Value	NM	NM	NM	0.45	1.91	NM	NM	NM	NM	NM
Cash Flow	1.58	1.81	1.76	1.52	1.03	1.35	1.07	0.58	0.77	1.62
Earnings	0.80	1.06	1.11	0.94	0.51	0.75	0.43	-0.03	-0.01	1.32
S&P Core Earnings	0.84	0.91	1.03	0.91	0.40	0.63	0.25	-0.34	-0.68	NA
Dividends	0.28	0.28	0.28	0.28	0.28	0.28	0.28	0.28	0.28	0.28
Payout Ratio	35%	26%	25%	30%	55%	37%	65%	NM	NM	21%
Prices:High	21.09	29.95	30.00	24.17	24.02	23.28	18.71	36.30	52.31	60.50
Prices:Low	10.88	12.70	21.28	16.31	17.92	15.05	7.22	4.28	21.28	19.00
P/E Ratio:High	26	28	27	26	47	31	44	NM	NM	46
P/E Ratio:Low	14	12	19	17	35	20	17	NM	NM	14

Income Statement Analysis (Million $)

	2009	2008	2007	2006	2005	2004	2003	2002	2001	2000
Revenue	1,812	1,937	1,787	1,546	1,474	1,687	1,535	1,505	1,330	1,695
Operating Income	261	287	249	221	229	253	211	131	196	263
Depreciation	91.8	88.3	78.0	69.2	67.0	76.2	80.2	76.6	80.5	79.1
Interest Expense	17.2	25.2	15.3	9.16	74.3	38.0	Nil	Nil	Nil	Nil
Pretax Income	131	147	151	151	66.7	137	80.9	-8.55	34.2	144
Effective Tax Rate	29.0%	14.4%	11.5%	21.5%	0.19%	28.2%	32.0%	NM	NM	40.4%
Net Income	92.7	126	134	118	66.5	98.3	55.0	-4.14	-0.62	86.1
S&P Core Earnings	96.7	109	124	114	53.8	81.3	31.2	-43.1	-71.3	NA

Balance Sheet & Other Financial Data (Million $)

	2009	2008	2007	2006	2005	2004	2003	2002	2001	2000
Cash	180	179	203	199	502	208	202	317	138	126
Current Assets	884	831	843	745	999	748	766	991	997	893
Total Assets	3,064	2,935	2,949	2,510	2,693	2,576	2,608	2,836	2,919	2,260
Current Liabilities	496	516	548	477	495	446	452	698	708	718
Long Term Debt	558	509	516	152	243	365	544	614	598	583
Common Equity	1,629	1,568	1,575	1,578	1,651	1,460	1,349	1,252	1,364	728
Total Capital	2,187	2,077	2,159	1,730	1,894	1,825	1,893	1,866	1,962	1,312
Capital Expenditures	31.7	43.3	47.0	44.5	25.1	19.0	16.6	37.8	88.7	70.6
Cash Flow	185	214	212	188	134	174	135	72.4	79.9	165
Current Ratio	1.8	1.6	1.5	1.6	2.0	1.7	1.7	1.4	1.4	1.2
% Long Term Debt of Capitalization	25.5	24.5	23.9	8.8	12.8	20.0	28.7	32.9	30.5	44.5
% Net Income of Revenue	5.1	6.5	7.5	7.7	4.5	5.8	3.6	NM	NM	5.1
% Return on Assets	3.1	4.3	4.9	4.5	2.5	3.8	2.0	NM	NM	4.3
% Return on Equity	5.8	8.0	8.5	7.3	4.3	7.0	4.2	NM	NM	13.5

Data as orig reptd.; bef. results of disc opers/spec. items. Per share data adj. for stk. divs.; EPS diluted. E-Estimated. NA-Not Available. NM-Not Meaningful. NR-Not Ranked. UR-Under Review.

Office: 940 Winter St, Waltham, MA 02451-1457.
Telephone: 781-663-6900.
Website: http://www.perkinelmer.com
Chrmn, Pres & CEO: R. Friel

SVP, CFO & Chief Acctg Officer: F.A. Wilson
SVP & CSO: D.R. Marshak
SVP, Secy & General Counsel: J.S. Goldberg
Treas: S. Delahunt

Board Members: R. Friel, N. A. Lopardo, A. P. Michas, J. C. Mullen, V. L. Sato, G. Schmergel, K. J. Sicchitano, P. J. Sullivan, G. R. Tod

Founded: 1947
Domicile: Massachusetts
Employees: 8,200

The McGraw-Hill Companies

Pfizer Inc

STANDARD &POOR'S

S&P Recommendation **BUY** ★★★★☆	Price $17.50 (as of Oct 22, 2010)	12-Mo. Target Price $19.00	Investment Style Large-Cap Blend

GICS Sector Health Care
Sub-Industry Pharmaceuticals

Summary The world's largest pharmaceutical company, Pfizer produces a wide range of drugs across a broad therapeutic spectrum. In October 2009, PFE acquired rival drugmaker Wyeth for some $68 billion in cash and stock.

Key Stock Statistics (Source S&P, Vickers, company reports)

52-Wk Range	$20.36– 14.00	S&P Oper. EPS 2010E	2.20	Market Capitalization(B)	$140.670	Beta	0.70
Trailing 12-Month EPS	$1.06	S&P Oper. EPS 2011E	2.28	Yield (%)	4.11	S&P 3-Yr. Proj. EPS CAGR(%)	5
Trailing 12-Month P/E	16.5	P/E on S&P Oper. EPS 2010E	8.0	Dividend Rate/Share	$0.72	S&P Credit Rating	AA
$10K Invested 5 Yrs Ago	$10,463	Common Shares Outstg. (M)	8,038.3	Institutional Ownership (%)	69		

Price Performance

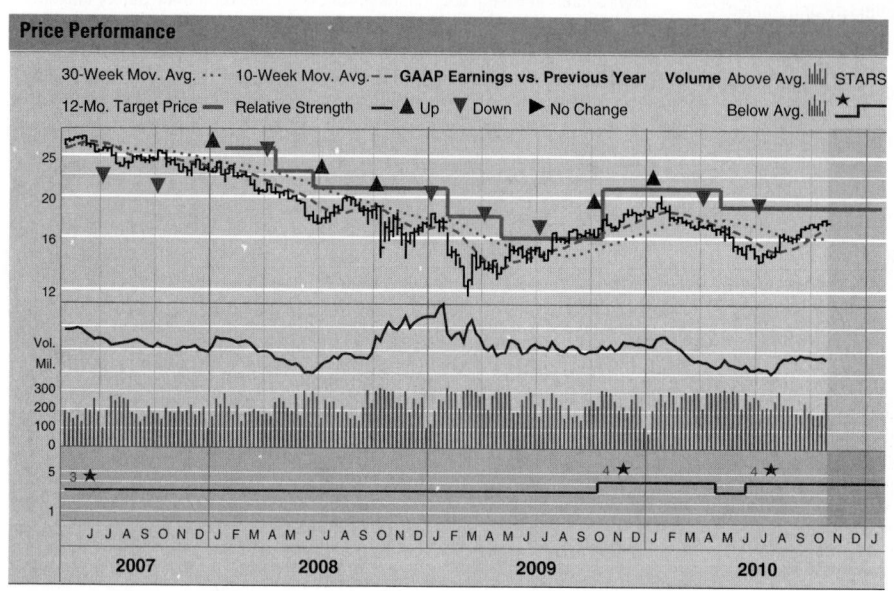

30-Week Mov. Avg. · · · 10-Week Mov. Avg. – – GAAP Earnings vs. Previous Year Volume Above Avg. STARS
12-Mo. Target Price — Relative Strength — ▲ Up ▼ Down ▶ No Change Below Avg.

Options: ASE, CBOE, P, Ph

Analysis prepared by **Herman B. Saftlas** on October 13, 2010, when the stock traded at **$ 17.73**.

Qualitative Risk Assessment

LOW	MEDIUM	HIGH

Our risk assessment reflects PFE's leading position in the global pharmaceutical market, which we believe affords important competitive operating and financial advantages. While we believe PFE's 2009 acquisition of Wyeth will bolster sales and margins ahead of major patent expirations in 2011, we remain uncertain whether PFE will be able to realize all of its key strategic objectives from the deal.

Quantitative Evaluations

S&P Quality Ranking B+

D	C	B-	B	B+	A-	A	A+

Relative Strength Rank MODERATE

58

LOWEST = 1 HIGHEST = 99

Highlights

► We project sales (excluding the planned acquisition of King Pharmaceuticals) of $66 billion in 2011, down from $68 billion that we estimate for 2010. The decline should largely reflect anticipated generic erosion in Lipitor, whose U.S. patent expires in October 2011. We also project declines in the Norvasc, Xalatan and Effexor lines, primarily due to increased generic competition as well. On the plus side, we see growth in newer products such as Lyrica neuropathic pain drug, Enbrel treatment for rheumatoid arthritis and Prevnar vaccines. We also look for modest growth in animal health and consumer product lines.

► We forecast 2011 adjusted gross margins close to the 81% that we estimate for 2010, supported by productivity efficiencies. We also see improvement in SG&A and R&D cost ratios, driven by aggressive cost streamlining measures. Net interest expense should also be somewhat lower, in our opinion.

► After a projected effective tax rate in 2011 of about 30.0%, versus an estimated 30.4% in 2010, we see adjusted operating EPS increasing to $2.28, from $2.20 that we forecast for 2010.

Investment Rationale/Risk

► In October 2010, PFE agreed to acquire specialty drugmaker King Pharmaceuticals (KG 14 Hold) for $3.6 billion in cash ($3.3 billion net of KG's cash), equal to $14.25 per KG share, subject to approvals. We view KG's portfolio of novel pain treatments, and large animal health division, as a good strategic fit with PFE, with future growth of these products expected to accelerate via an expanded sales force. We see especially strong potential for KG's pain patch and abuse deterrent pain products. PFE expects KG to be accretive to EPS by $0.02 annually in 2011 and 2012, and by $0.03-$0.04 in 2013-2015, on $200 million in cost synergies.

► Risks to our recommendation and target price include an inability to achieve planned synergies from Wyeth and King, and possible pipeline setbacks.

► Our 12-month target price of $19 applies a below-peers multiple of 8.3X to our 2011 EPS estimate. Our target price is also close to our calculation of intrinsic value, derived from our DCF model, which assumes slowing cash flow growth over the next few years, a WACC of 9.3%, and a terminal growth rate of 1%.

Revenue/Earnings Data

Revenue (Million $)

	1Q	2Q	3Q	4Q	Year
2010	16,750	17,327	--	--	--
2009	10,867	10,984	11,621	16,537	50,009
2008	11,848	12,129	11,973	12,346	48,296
2007	12,474	11,084	11,990	12,870	48,418
2006	11,747	11,741	12,280	12,603	48,371
2005	13,091	12,425	12,189	13,592	51,298

Earnings Per Share ($)

2010	0.25	0.31	E0.51	E0.48	E2.20
2009	0.40	0.33	0.43	0.10	1.23
2008	0.41	0.41	0.33	0.03	1.19
2007	0.48	0.19	0.12	0.40	1.18
2006	0.55	0.31	0.44	0.21	1.52
2005	0.04	0.47	0.22	0.37	1.09

Fiscal year ended Dec. 31. Next earnings report expected: NA. EPS Estimates based on S&P Operating Earnings; historical GAAP earnings are as reported.

Dividend Data (Dates: mm/dd Payment Date: mm/dd/yy)

Amount ($)	Date Decl.	Ex-Div. Date	Stk. of Record	Payment Date
0.160	10/22	11/04	11/06	12/01/09
0.180	12/14	02/03	02/05	03/02/10
0.180	04/22	05/05	05/07	06/01/10
0.180	06/24	08/04	08/06	09/01/10

Dividends have been paid since 1901. Source: Company reports.

Pfizer Inc

Business Summary October 13, 2010

CORPORATE OVERVIEW. Pfizer stands out above its peers in the $780 billion global pharmaceutical sector, in our opinion. Growth over the past 10 years was largely augmented by two major acquisitions -- Warner-Lambert Co. in 2000 and Pharmacia Corp. in 2003 -- as well as by in-licensed products. The business was significantly further expanded with the acquisition of Wyeth in October 2009.

Pfizer's drug portfolio is unmatched in terms of breadth and depth in the global drug market, by our analysis. Principal cardiovasculars include Lipitor, the world's largest-selling cholesterol-lowering agent as well as the biggest drug in any therapeutic category in 2009 (sales of $11.4 billion in 2009), antihypertensives such as off-patent Norvasc ($2.0 billion), and Caduet ($548 million), a combination of Lipitor and Norvasc. Key central nervous system medicines include Lyrica, a treatment for nerve pain and epileptic seizures ($2.8 billion); and Geodon, an antipsychotic ($1.0 billion). Infectious disease drugs consist of Zyvox ($1.1 billion), a treatment for severe bacterial infections, and Vfend ($743 million), an anti-fungal. Foreign sales accounted for 57% of total revenues in 2009.

Other key drugs sold include Celebrex COX-2 inhibitor for arthritis and pain (sales of $2.4 billion); Viagra for male erectile dysfunction ($1.9 billion); Xalatan/Xalcom, for glaucoma ($1.7 billion); Detrol and LA/Detrol, treatments for in-

continence ($1.2 billion); Sutent ($964 million) for kidney and other cancers; Genotropin ($887 million), a human growth hormone; and Chantix ($700 million) for smoking cessation. The animal health division ($2.8 billion) offers one of the largest-selling and broadest product lines in the field. Principal products include feed additives, vaccines, antibiotics, antihelmintics, and other veterinary products.

MARKET PROFILE. The dollar value of the global drug market is projected to grow about 4%-6% in 2010, from $837 billion in 2009 (in constant currency), according to IMS Health. Worldwide pharmaceutical industry growth from 2009 through 2014 is expected to expand at a CAGR (compound annual growth rate) of 5%-8%, based on IMS projections. Key drivers should be strong growth projected for worldwide emerging markets, and continued strong patient demand for cost-effective pharmaceutical therapies. These factors will likely more than offset the negative effects of patent expiration losses, and tighter reimbursement in major developed markets, by our analysis. Sales in both North America and Europe are expected to grow 3%-5% in 2010, according to IMS.

Company Financials Fiscal Year Ended Dec. 31

Per Share Data ($)	2009	2008	2007	2006	2005	2004	2003	2002	2001	2000
Tangible Book Value	NM	2.71	4.93	3.65	1.91	1.48	0.85	3.04	2.64	2.26
Cash Flow	1.90	1.94	1.93	2.24	1.84	2.16	0.78	1.64	1.39	0.74
Earnings	1.23	1.19	1.18	1.52	1.09	1.49	0.22	1.47	1.22	0.59
S&P Core Earnings	1.35	1.42	1.14	1.53	1.02	1.45	0.29	1.35	1.09	NA
Dividends	0.80	1.28	1.16	0.96	0.76	0.68	0.60	0.52	0.44	0.36
Payout Ratio	65%	108%	98%	63%	70%	46%	273%	35%	36%	61%
Prices:High	18.99	24.24	27.73	28.60	29.21	38.89	36.92	42.46	46.75	49.25
Prices:Low	11.62	14.26	22.24	22.16	20.27	21.99	27.90	25.13	34.00	30.00
P/E Ratio:High	15	20	23	19	27	26	NM	29	38	83
P/E Ratio:Low	9	12	19	15	19	15	NM	17	28	51

Income Statement Analysis (Million $)

	2009	2008	2007	2006	2005	2004	2003	2002	2001	2000
Revenue	50,009	48,296	48,418	48,371	51,298	52,516	45,188	32,373	32,259	29,574
Operating Income	21,268	21,925	19,983	19,575	20,501	22,117	17,061	13,436	12,147	9,758
Depreciation	4,757	5,090	5,200	5,293	5,576	5,093	4,078	1,036	1,068	968
Interest Expense	1,233	562	440	488	488	359	290	279	432	401
Pretax Income	10,827	9,694	9,278	13,028	11,534	14,007	3,263	11,796	10,329	5,781
Effective Tax Rate	20.3%	17.0%	11.0%	15.3%	29.7%	19.0%	49.7%	22.1%	24.8%	35.4%
Net Income	8,621	8,026	8,213	11,024	8,094	11,332	1,639	9,181	7,752	3,718
S&P Core Earnings	9,377	9,538	7,963	11,048	7,588	11,030	2,147	8,441	6,862	NA

Balance Sheet & Other Financial Data (Million $)

	2009	2008	2007	2006	2005	2004	2003	2002	2001	2000
Cash	25,969	23,731	25,475	1,827	2,247	1,808	1,520	1,878	1,036	1,099
Current Assets	61,670	43,076	46,849	46,949	41,896	39,694	29,741	24,781	18,450	17,187
Total Assets	212,949	111,148	115,268	114,837	117,565	123,684	116,775	46,356	39,153	33,510
Current Liabilities	37,225	27,009	21,835	21,389	28,448	26,458	23,657	18,555	13,640	11,981
Long Term Debt	43,218	7,963	7,314	5,546	6,347	7,279	5,755	3,140	2,609	1,123
Common Equity	89,953	57,483	64,917	71,217	65,458	68,085	65,158	19,950	18,293	16,076
Total Capital	133,691	66,640	80,134	84,919	82,214	88,189	84,370	23,454	21,354	17,579
Capital Expenditures	1,205	1,701	1,880	2,050	2,106	2,601	2,641	1,758	2,203	2,191
Cash Flow	13,376	13,113	13,409	16,317	13,661	16,417	5,710	10,217	8,820	4,686
Current Ratio	1.7	1.6	2.2	2.2	1.5	1.5	1.3	1.3	1.4	1.4
% Long Term Debt of Capitalization	Nil	11.6	9.1	6.5	7.7	8.3	6.8	13.4	12.2	6.4
% Net Income of Revenue	17.2	16.6	17.0	22.8	15.8	21.6	3.6	28.4	24.0	12.6
% Return on Assets	NA	7.1	7.1	9.5	6.7	9.4	2.0	21.5	21.3	11.5
% Return on Equity	NA	13.1	12.1	16.1	12.1	17.0	3.8	48.0	45.1	24.8

Data as orig reptd.; bef. results of disc opers/spec. items. Per share data adj. for stk. divs.; EPS diluted. E-Estimated. NA-Not Available. NM-Not Meaningful. NR-Not Ranked. UR-Under Review.

Office: 235 East 42nd Street, New York, NY 10017-5703.
Telephone: 212-733-2323.
Website: http://www.pfizer.com
Chrmn & CEO: J.B. Kindler

COO & CFO: F.A. D'Amelio
SVP, Chief Acctg Officer & Cntlr: L.V. Cangialosi
SVP, Secy & General Counsel: A.W. Schulman
CSO: M. Ehlers

Investor Contact: J. Davis (212-733-0717)
Board Members: D. A. Ausiello, M. S. Brown, M. A. Burns, R. N. Burt, W. D. Cornwell, F. D. Fergusson, W. H. Gray, III, C. J. Horner, S. N. Johnson, J. M. Kilts, J. B. Kindler, G. A. Lorch, J. P. Mascotte, S. W. Sanger, W. C. Steere, Jr.

Founded: 1849
Domicile: Delaware
Employees: 116,500

PG&E Corp

STANDARD &POOR'S

S&P Recommendation HOLD ★★★☆☆	**Price** $47.66 (as of Oct 22, 2010)	**12-Mo. Target Price** $47.00	**Investment Style** Large-Cap Blend

GICS Sector Utilities
Sub-Industry Multi-Utilities

Summary This energy holding company is the parent of Pacific Gas & Electric Co., which serves northern and central California.

Key Stock Statistics (Source S&P, Vickers, company reports)

52-Wk Range	$48.34– 34.95	S&P Oper. EPS 2010**E**	3.43	Market Capitalization(B)	$18.623	Beta		0.33
Trailing 12-Month EPS	$3.08	S&P Oper. EPS 2011**E**	3.71	Yield (%)	3.82	S&P 3-Yr. Proj. EPS CAGR(%)		8
Trailing 12-Month P/E	15.5	P/E on S&P Oper. EPS 2010**E**	13.9	Dividend Rate/Share	$1.82	S&P Credit Rating		BBB+
$10K Invested 5 Yrs Ago	$15,880	Common Shares Outstg. (M)	390.8	Institutional Ownership (%)	66			

Price Performance

30-Week Mov. Avg. ···· 10-Week Mov. Avg. ‑‑ **GAAP Earnings vs. Previous Year** Volume Above Avg. STARS
12-Mo. Target Price — Relative Strength — ▲ Up ▼ Down ▶ No Change Below Avg. ★

Options: ASE, CBOE, P

Analysis prepared by **Justin McCann** on October 18, 2010, when the stock traded at **$ 47.34**.

Highlights

► Excluding one-time charges of $0.16, we expect operating EPS in 2010 to grow nearly 7% from 2009's $3.21, which excluded a one-time net loss of $0.01. In the first half of 2010, operating EPS was driven by higher electric revenues resulting from Pacific Gas & Electric's (PG&E) pre-approved rate base transmission and generation investments, and through the realization of energy efficiency incentive revenues.

► Operating EPS for full-year 2010 should reflect the final year of PG&E's four-year general rate case, which authorized a net 4.5% increase in electric and gas rates. We expect operating EPS in 2011 to rise approximately 7% from anticipated results in 2010. The utility is expected to receive a final decision for the 2011 general rate case in the fourth quarter of 2010.

► On October 15, 2010, the California Public Utility Commission appointed an independent panel to look for any systemic problems within PG&E that could have led to the explosion of a gas pipeline on September 9, 2010, in San Bruno, California. On September 13, 2010, the utility announced that it was establishing a $100 million fund for the victims of the explosion that killed 8 people and destroyed 37 homes.

Investment Rationale/Risk

► The stock is up about 6% year to date, reflecting, we believe, the recent rebound in the utility sector. This follows an increase of 15% in 2009, which underperformed PCG's gas utility peers, but outperformed its electric utility peers. With the authorized decoupling of Pacific Gas & Electric's revenues from electric demand (so as to promote energy efficiencies), earnings are not impacted by the decline in demand. Over the next 12 months, we expect the stock to trade at a modest discount to PCG's peers (based on our EPS estimates for 2011).

► Risks to our recommendation and target price include a much worse-than-expected earnings performance, and/or a major decline in the average P/E multiple of the peer group.

► The recent yield from the dividend was around 3.9%, below the peer yield for combined electric and gas utilities of about 4.5%. However, with the projected dividend payout ratio at 53% of our operating EPS estimate for 2010 being below the peer ratio of 59%, we believe PCG has the financial flexibility for additional increases in the payment. Our 12-month target price is $47, reflecting an approximate peers P/E of 12.7X our EPS estimate for 2011.

Qualitative Risk Assessment

LOW	MEDIUM	HIGH

Our risk assessment reflects our view of the company's strong and steady cash flow from the regulated Pacific Gas & Electric subsidiary, its much improved balance sheet and credit profile, a healthy economy in its service territory, and a greatly improved regulatory environment.

Quantitative Evaluations

S&P Quality Ranking B

D	C	B-	**B**	B+	A-	A	A+

Relative Strength Rank MODERATE

58

LOWEST = 1   HIGHEST = 99

Revenue/Earnings Data

Revenue (Million $)

	1Q	2Q	3Q	4Q	Year
2010	3,475	3,232	--	--	--
2009	3,431	3,194	3,235	3,539	13,399
2008	3,733	3,578	3,674	3,643	14,628
2007	3,356	3,187	3,279	3,415	13,237
2006	3,148	3,017	3,168	3,206	12,539
2005	2,669	2,498	2,804	3,732	11,703

Earnings Per Share ($)

2010	0.66	0.86	E0.99	E0.74	E3.43
2009	0.65	1.02	0.83	0.71	3.20
2008	0.62	0.80	0.83	0.97	3.22
2007	0.71	0.74	0.77	0.56	2.78
2006	0.60	0.65	1.09	0.43	2.76
2005	0.54	0.70	0.62	0.49	2.34

Fiscal year ended Dec. 31. Next earnings report expected: Late October. EPS Estimates based on S&P Operating Earnings; historical GAAP earnings are as reported.

Dividend Data (Dates: mm/dd Payment Date: mm/dd/yy)

Amount ($)	Date Decl.	Ex-Div. Date	Stk. of Record	Payment Date
0.420	12/17	12/29	12/31	01/15/10
0.455	02/19	03/29	03/31	04/15/10
0.455	06/16	06/28	06/30	07/15/10
0.455	09/15	09/28	09/30	10/15/10

Dividends have been paid since 2005. Source: Company reports.

Please read the Required Disclosures and Analyst Certification on the last page of this report.

The McGraw-Hill Companies

PG&E Corp

Business Summary October 18, 2010

CORPORATE OVERVIEW. PG&E Corporation (PCG) is an energy-based holding company that conducts its business through Pacific Gas and Electric Company (PG&E), a public utility operating in northern and central California. The utility's business consists of four main operational units: electricity and natural gas distribution, electricity generation, gas transmission, and electricity transmission. The utility is primarily regulated by the California Public Utilities Commission (CPUC) and the Federal Energy Regulatory Commission (FERC).

CORPORATE STRATEGY. To support anticipated customer growth and the improvement of its existing services, Pacific Gas & Electric plans to make major capital additions to its infrastructure. The utility is also devoting substantial resources to the building and expansion of its transmission lines, which has become the fastest-growing part of its business. It has proposed constructing additional gas and electric transmission arteries so as to create access to new supplies of renewable energy and new sources of natural gas. California law requires its electric utilities to purchase 30% of their power from renewable resources by 2017. In addition to maintaining its ongoing investment in its existing hydroelectric and nuclear facilities, the company brought into service a new state-of-the-art power plant in 2009, and expects to bring into operation two more during the third and fourth quarters of 2010. The three plants are expected to generate enough power for approximately 950,000 homes.

MARKET PROFILE. PG&E's electricity and gas distribution network covers 70,000 square miles and 47 of the 58 counties in California. The utility served approximately 5.1 million electricity distribution customers and about 4.3 million natural gas distribution customers as of December 31, 2009. In 2009, commercial customers accounted for about 39% of electricity deliveries, residential 36%, industrial 17%, and agricultural and other 8%. Transport-only customers accounted for about 62% of natural gas deliveries in 2009, residential 27%, and commercial 11%. As of December 31, 2009, the company had $42.7 billion of total assets.

Company Financials Fiscal Year Ended Dec. 31

Per Share Data ($)	2009	2008	2007	2006	2005	2004	2003	2002	2001	2000
Tangible Book Value	27.69	25.97	25.80	20.89	19.67	20.60	10.11	8.92	11.87	8.74
Earnings	3.20	3.22	2.78	2.76	2.34	8.97	1.96	-0.15	2.99	-9.18
S&P Core Earnings	3.65	1.91	2.53	2.64	2.45	9.00	2.05	-1.08	1.59	NA
Dividends	1.68	1.56	1.44	1.32	1.23	Nil	Nil	Nil	Nil	1.20
Payout Ratio	52%	48%	52%	48%	53%	Nil	Nil	Nil	Nil	NM
Prices:High	45.80	45.68	52.17	48.17	40.10	34.46	27.98	23.75	20.94	31.81
Prices:Low	34.50	26.67	42.58	36.25	31.83	25.90	11.69	8.00	6.50	17.00
P/E Ratio:High	14	14	19	17	17	4	14	NM	7	NM
P/E Ratio:Low	11	8	15	13	14	3	6	NM	2	NM

Income Statement Analysis (Million $)	2009	2008	2007	2006	2005	2004	2003	2002	2001	2000
Revenue	13,399	14,628	13,237	12,539	11,703	11,080	10,435	12,495	22,959	26,232
Depreciation	1,947	1,863	1,770	1,709	1,735	1,497	1,222	1,309	1,068	3,659
Maintenance	NA	NA	NA	NA	NA	NA	NA	NA	NA	NA
Fixed Charges Coverage	3.34	3.21	3.03	3.09	3.48	2.75	2.23	2.94	2.48	3.01
Construction Credits	NA	NA	NA	NA	NA	NA	NA	NA	NA	NA
Effective Tax Rate	27.4%	26.4%	34.9%	35.9%	37.6%	39.2%	36.7%	NM	35.8%	NM
Net Income	1,220	1,184	1,006	991	904	3,820	791	-57.0	1,090	-3,324
S&P Core Earnings	1,391	720	940	972	974	3,828	830	-404	580	NA

Balance Sheet & Other Financial Data (Million $)	2009	2008	2007	2006	2005	2004	2003	2002	2001	2000
Gross Property	43,080	39,833	36,584	34,214	32,030	30,509	29,222	31,179	33,012	28,469
Capital Expenditures	3,958	3,628	2,769	2,402	1,804	1,559	1,698	3,032	2,665	1,758
Net Property	28,892	26,261	23,656	21,785	19,955	18,989	18,107	16,928	19,167	16,591
Capitalization:Long Term Debt	11,460	10,786	10,005	8,885	9,794	8,311	9,924	11,590	9,527	5,516
Capitalization:% Long Term Debt	52.6	53.5	53.9	53.2	57.5	49.0	70.2	76.2	68.8	63.5
Capitalization:Preferred	Nil	Nil	Nil	Nil	Nil	Nil	Nil	Nil	Nil	Nil
Capitalization:% Preferred	Nil	Nil	Nil	Nil	Nil	Nil	Nil	Nil	Nil	Nil
Capitalization:Common	10,333	9,377	8,553	7,811	7,240	8,633	4,215	3,613	4,322	3,172
Capitalization:% Common	47.4	46.5	46.1	46.8	42.5	51.0	29.8	23.8	31.2	36.5
Total Capital	22,521	23,654	21,710	19,642	20,238	20,596	15,122	16,786	15,668	10,536
% Operating Ratio	86.3	87.4	88.1	87.6	87.8	102.2	80.4	67.2	90.3	84.1
% Earned on Net Property	8.3	9.1	9.3	10.1	10.1	38.4	14.6	31.2	15.0	34.7
% Return on Revenue	9.1	8.1	7.6	7.9	7.7	34.5	7.6	NM	4.7	NM
% Return on Invested Capital	8.9	8.4	8.6	8.7	7.3	15.6	13.9	22.8	16.7	29.1
% Return on Common Equity	12.4	13.2	12.3	13.2	11.4	59.5	20.2	NM	29.1	NM

Data as orig reptd.; bef. results of disc opers/spec. items. Per share data adj. for stk. divs.; EPS diluted. E-Estimated. NA-Not Available. NM-Not Meaningful. NR-Not Ranked. UR-Under Review.

Office: One Market Spear Tower, Suite 2400, San Francisco, CA 94105-1126.
Telephone: 415-267-7000.
Email: invrel@pg-corp.com
Website: http://www.pgecorp.com

Chrmn, Pres & CEO: P.A. Darbee
SVP & CFO: K.M. Harvey
SVP & General Counsel: H. Park
Chief Acctg Officer & Cntlr: D.B. Mistry

Treas: N. Bijur
Investor Contact: L.Y. Cheng (415-267-7070)
Board Members: D. R. Andrews, L. Chew, C. L. Cox, P. A. Darbee, M. C. Herringer, R. H. Kimmel, R. Meserve, F. E. Miller, R. G. Parra, B. L. Rambo, B. L. Williams

Founded: 1995
Domicile: California
Employees: 19,425

Philip Morris International Inc

S&P Recommendation **BUY** ★★★★☆	Price **$58.13** (as of Oct 22, 2010)	12-Mo. Target Price **$61.00**	Investment Style Large-Cap Blend

GICS Sector Consumer Staples
Sub-Industry Tobacco

Summary This company, comprising the international operations spun off by Altria in early 2008, is the largest publicly traded manufacturer and marketer of tobacco products.

Key Stock Statistics (Source S&P, Vickers, company reports)

52-Wk Range	$58.78– 42.94	S&P Oper. EPS 2010E	3.82	Market Capitalization(B)	$106.545	Beta	0.84
Trailing 12-Month EPS	$3.69	S&P Oper. EPS 2011E	4.24	Yield (%)	4.40	S&P 3-Yr. Proj. EPS CAGR(%)	10
Trailing 12-Month P/E	15.8	P/E on S&P Oper. EPS 2010E	15.2	Dividend Rate/Share	$2.56	S&P Credit Rating	A
$10K Invested 5 Yrs Ago	NA	Common Shares Outstg. (M)	1,832.9	Institutional Ownership (%)	70		

Price Performance

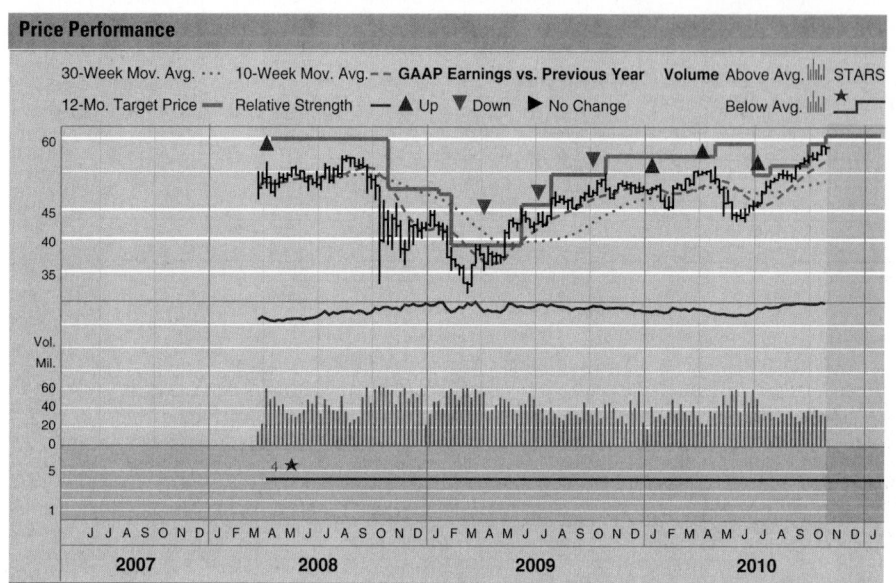

- 30-Week Mov. Avg. ···
- 10-Week Mov. Avg. —
- **GAAP Earnings vs. Previous Year**
- Volume Above Avg. STARS
- 12-Mo. Target Price —
- Relative Strength — ▲ Up ▼ Down ▶ No Change
- Below Avg.

Options: ASE, CBOE, Ph

Analysis prepared by **Esther Y. Kwon, CFA** on October 22, 2010, when the stock traded at **$ 57.88**.

Highlights

➤ For 2010, we see net revenue rising about 7% on positive pricing. In 2011, we project revenues to climb 8%, boosted somewhat by foreign exchange. With growing health concerns, smoking bans and higher taxes, we look for a mid- single digit percentage decline in consumption in Western Europe, offset by low single digit or faster growth in emerging markets. While we still see some downtrading persisting in Greece, Spain and Germany, we believe these negative trends will moderate and be offset by growth in other countries, such as Indonesia, Korea, and Russia.

➤ After embarking on an extensive three-year cost reduction program, which we calculate will widen operating margins on net savings of about $1 billion, we expect further savings on continued rationalization of less dynamic brands offset by investments in new and existing markets in 2011. We see synergies from PM's venture in the Philippines with Fortune Tobacco, which we forecast will be accretive to earnings in 2011 after being neutral in 2010.

➤ On a 29% effective tax rate, we estimate 2010 EPS of $3.82, up about 15% from 2009 operating EPS of $3.31. For 2011, we forecast EPS of $4.24.

Investment Rationale/Risk

➤ Separated from operations in the U.S. and the regulatory and litigation risk of that market, PM will, in our view, be better positioned to innovate, tailor offerings to higher-growth emerging markets, achieve cost savings, and incentivize managers. We think PM's low penetration of markets with potentially high cigarette consumption, such as China, India and Vietnam, also provides attractive opportunities. In addition, the spinoff provided PM with currency for acquisitions. We believe its high cash flow generation is supportive of regular stock repurchases and its dividend, which yields about 4.5%.

➤ Risks to our recommendation and target price include execution risk, higher-than-expected excise taxes or regulatory constraints, greater-than-expected price competition, and commodity cost inflation.

➤ Our 12-month target price of $61 is based on a blend of comparative and historical forward P/E. Considering PM's scale, growth prospects and brand equity, we believe a premium to its domestic tobacco comparables is appropriate. We assign a multiple of 14.5X to our 2011 EPS estimate of $4.24 which is slightly above historical average.

Qualitative Risk Assessment

LOW	MEDIUM	HIGH

Our risk assessment reflects the geographic diversity of the company's operations and end-markets and its participation in a generally stable industry, producing ample free cash flow. Health concerns, excise tax increases, extensive regulation and, to some extent, litigation have limited the growth prospects for the industry, but have also kept barriers to entry high.

Quantitative Evaluations

S&P Quality Ranking NR

D	C	B-	B	B+	A-	A	A+

Relative Strength Rank STRONG

72

LOWEST = 1   HIGHEST = 99

Revenue/Earnings Data

Revenue (Million $)

	1Q	2Q	3Q	4Q	Year
2010	6,496	7,061	--	--	--
2009	5,597	6,134	6,587	6,717	25,035
2008	6,330	6,709	6,953	6,122	25,705
2007	5,549	5,835	5,916	5,498	55,096
2006	5,228	5,346	5,412	4,926	20,794
2005	--	--	--	--	20,013

Earnings Per Share ($)

	1Q	2Q	3Q	4Q	Year
2010	0.90	1.07	E1.00	E0.92	E3.82
2009	0.74	0.79	0.93	0.80	3.24
2008	0.89	0.80	1.01	0.71	3.32
2007	0.69	--	--	--	2.75
2006	--	--	--	--	--
2005	--	--	--	--	--

Fiscal year ended Dec. 31. Next earnings report expected: NA. EPS Estimates based on S&P Operating Earnings; historical GAAP earnings are as reported.

Dividend Data (Dates: mm/dd Payment Date: mm/dd/yy)

Amount ($)	Date Decl.	Ex-Div. Date	Stk. of Record	Payment Date
0.580	12/09	12/23	12/28	01/11/10
0.580	03/11	03/23	03/25	04/09/10
0.580	06/09	06/22	06/24	07/09/10
0.640	09/10	09/22	09/24	10/08/10

Dividends have been paid since 2008. Source: Company reports.

Please read the Required Disclosures and Analyst Certification on the last page of this report.

The McGraw·Hill Companies

Philip Morris International Inc

STANDARD &POOR'S

Business Summary October 22, 2010

CORPORATE OVERVIEW. Philip Morris International is the world's largest publicly traded manufacturer and marketer of tobacco products, with a 15.4% share of 2009 international market volumes, down from 15.7% in 2008 and 15.6% in 2007, according to Philip Morris estimates. Excluding China, PM's estimated market share was 26.0%, 25.8% and 25.2% in 2009, 2008 and 2007, respectively. PM sold 864.0 billion cigarettes in 2009, with the Marlboro brand contributing about 35% of total PM volume. Other brands include Merit, Parliament and Virginia Slims in the premium category; L&M and Chesterfield in the mid-price category; Bond Street, Lark, Muratti, Next, Philip Morris, and Red & White in the value category; and local brands such as A Mild, Diana, Optima, f6, Assos and Delicados.

The geographic breakdown of 2009 revenue was as follows: European Union 46.0%; Eastern Europe, Middle East & Africa 22.3%; Asia 20.0%; and Latin America and Canada 11.7%. Adjusted operating income (on revenues minus excise taxes) from the European Union was 43.9% of the company total, followed by Eastern Europe, Middle East & Africa (25.9%), Asia (23.7%), and Latin America and Canada (6.5%).

CORPORATE STRATEGY. Philip Morris International seeks to grow organically as well as through acquisitions. Using its existing brands, PM plans to introduce new packaging, new blends and other line extensions across its portfolio and in existing and new markets. It sees four major markets -- China, India, Bangladesh and Vietnam -- where it has little or no presence and which account for approximately 40% of total international cigarette consumption as opportunities. We estimate China alone accounts for about one-third of the total market. In addition, PM plans to spend about half of its R&D budget to develop next-generation products that meet consumer preferences and that could cause less harm than traditional tobacco products.

PM also plans to evaluate potential acquisitions and other business development opportunities. In September 2009, PM acquired Swedish Match South Africa for approximately $256 million, while in July 2009, it agreed to acquire Colombian cigarette manufacturer Productora Tabacalera de Colombia, Protabaco Ltda. for $452 million, with an expected close in 2010. In February 2009, it acquired Petteroes, which sells fine cut tobacco products in Norway and Sweden. Also in February 2009, PM entered into a joint venture with Swedish Match AB to develop the market for Swedish style snus and other smokeless tobacco products, outside of Sweden and the U.S.

In September 2008, PM acquired Rothmans Inc., Canada's second largest tobacco company, for C$2.0 billion.

Company Financials Fiscal Year Ended Dec. 31

Per Share Data ($)	2009	2008	2007	2006	2005	2004	2003	2002	2001	2000
Tangible Book Value	NM	NM	2.31	NA	NA	NA	NA	NA	NA	NA
Cash Flow	3.69	3.72	3.10	NA	NA	NA	NA	NA	NA	NA
Earnings	3.24	3.32	2.75	NA	NA	NA	NA	NA	NA	NA
S&P Core Earnings	3.27	3.30	2.91	2.81	NA	NA	NA	NA	NA	NA
Dividends	2.24	1.54	Nil	NA	NA	NA	NA	NA	NA	NA
Payout Ratio	69%	46%	Nil	NA	NA	NA	NA	NA	NA	NA
Prices:High	52.35	56.26	NA	NA	NA	NA	NA	NA	NA	NA
Prices:Low	32.04	33.30	NA	NA	NA	NA	NA	NA	NA	NA
P/E Ratio:High	16	17	NA	NA	NA	NA	NA	NA	NA	NA
P/E Ratio:Low	10	10	NA	NA	NA	NA	NA	NA	NA	NA

Income Statement Analysis (Million $)

	2009	2008	2007	2006	2005	2004	2003	2002	2001	2000
Revenue	25,035	25,705	55,096	20,794	20,013	17,583	NA	NA	NA	NA
Operating Income	10,922	11,174	9,685	8,664	8,352	7,235	NA	NA	NA	NA
Depreciation	853	842	748	658	527	459	NA	NA	NA	NA
Interest Expense	905	528	209	371	325	191	NA	NA	NA	NA
Pretax Income	9,243	9,937	8,572	8,226	7,641	6,478	NA	NA	NA	NA
Effective Tax Rate	29.1%	28.1%	28.9%	22.2%	24.0%	27.2%	NA	NA	NA	NA
Net Income	6,342	6,890	5,821	6,146	5,620	4,570	NA	NA	NA	NA
S&P Core Earnings	6,368	6,852	6,153	5,904	NA	NA	NA	NA	NA	NA

Balance Sheet & Other Financial Data (Million $)

	2009	2008	2007	2006	2005	2004	2003	2002	2001	2000
Cash	1,540	1,531	1,284	1,676	1,209	NA	NA	NA	NA	NA
Current Assets	14,682	14,939	14,423	11,925	10,025	NA	NA	NA	NA	NA
Total Assets	34,552	32,972	31,414	26,120	23,135	NA	NA	NA	NA	NA
Current Liabilities	11,178	10,144	8,465	6,989	6,334	NA	NA	NA	NA	NA
Long Term Debt	13,672	11,377	5,578	2,222	4,141	NA	NA	NA	NA	NA
Common Equity	5,716	7,500	14,700	14,267	10,307	NA	NA	NA	NA	NA
Total Capital	19,899	19,086	21,481	16,634	14,593	NA	NA	NA	NA	NA
Capital Expenditures	715	1,099	1,072	886	736	711	NA	NA	NA	NA
Cash Flow	7,195	7,732	6,569	6,804	6,147	5,029	NA	NA	NA	NA
Current Ratio	1.3	1.5	1.7	1.7	1.6	NA	NA	NA	NA	NA
% Long Term Debt of Capitalization	68.7	59.6	26.0	13.4	28.4	Nil	NA	NA	NA	NA
% Net Income of Revenue	25.3	26.8	10.6	29.6	28.1	26.0	NA	NA	NA	NA
% Return on Assets	18.8	21.2	NA	25.0	NA	NA	NA	NA	NA	NA
% Return on Equity	96.0	60.2	NA	50.0	NA	NA	NA	NA	NA	NA

Data as orig reptd.; bef. results of disc opers/spec. items. Per share data adj. for stk. divs.; EPS diluted. Data prior to 2008 are pro forma. E-Estimated. NA-Not Available. NM-Not Meaningful. NR-Not Ranked. UR-Under Review.

Office: 120 Park Avenue, New York, NY 10017-5592.
Telephone: 917-663-2000.
Website: http://www.pmi.com
Chrmn & CEO: L.C. Camilleri

Vice Chrmn: M. Cabiallavetta
COO: A. Calantzopoulos
EVP & CFO: H.G. Waldemer
SVP & General Counsel: D. Bernick

Board Members: H. Brown, M. Cabiallavetta, L. C. Camilleri, J. D. Fishburn, J. Li, G. MacKay, S. Marchionne, L. Noto, C. S. Slim Helu, S. M. Wolf

Founded: 1987
Domicile: Virginia
Employees: 77,300

The McGraw-Hill Companies

Pinnacle West Capital Corp

STANDARD &POOR'S

S&P Recommendation HOLD ★★★☆☆	**Price** $42.18 (as of Oct 22, 2010)	**12-Mo. Target Price** $41.00	**Investment Style** Large-Cap Value

GICS Sector Utilities
Sub-Industry Electric Utilities

Summary This utility holding company is the parent of Arizona Public Service (APS), Arizona's largest electric utility.

Key Stock Statistics (Source S&P, Vickers, company reports)

52-Wk Range	$42.68–31.08	S&P Oper. EPS 2010**E**	3.01	Market Capitalization(B)	$4.583	Beta		0.60
Trailing 12-Month EPS	$2.57	S&P Oper. EPS 2011**E**	3.05	Yield (%)	4.98	S&P 3-Yr. Proj. EPS CAGR(%)		1
Trailing 12-Month P/E	16.4	P/E on S&P Oper. EPS 2010**E**	14.0	Dividend Rate/Share	$2.10	S&P Credit Rating		BBB-
$10K Invested 5 Yrs Ago	$13,802	Common Shares Outstg. (M)	108.6	Institutional Ownership (%)	75			

Price Performance

30-Week Mov. Avg. · · · 10-Week Mov. Avg. - - **GAAP Earnings vs. Previous Year** Volume Above Avg. STARS
12-Mo. Target Price — Relative Strength — ▲ Up ▼ Down ► No Change Below Avg. ★

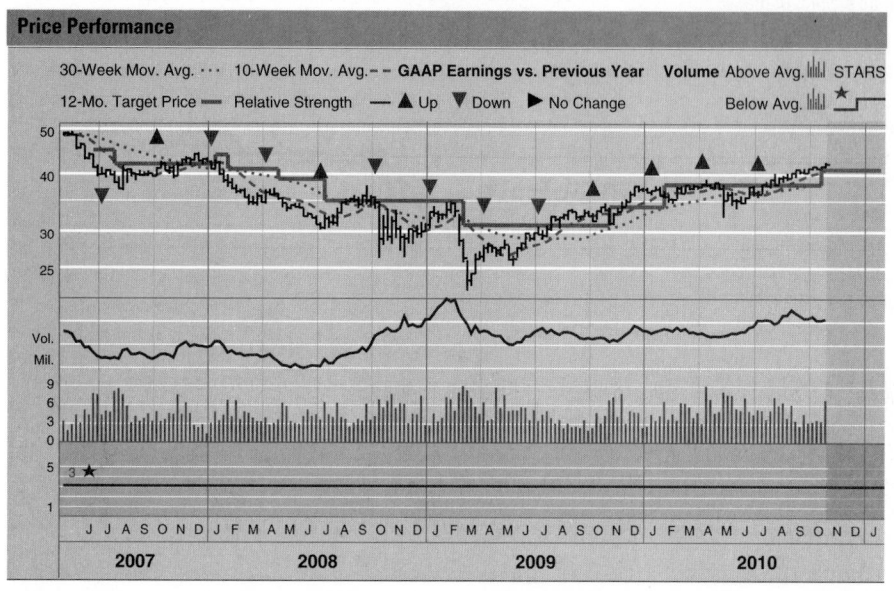

Options: P

Analysis prepared by **Justin McCann** on October 12, 2010, when the stock traded at **$ 41.04**.

Qualitative Risk Assessment

LOW	MEDIUM	HIGH

Our risk assessment reflects the steady cash flow that we project from the electric utility operations of Arizona Public Service, which has one of the fastest-growing service territories in the U.S. While the regulatory environment has often been difficult, we do not expect to see the general strength of the utility significantly impeded by regulatory rulings. This should help offset the less-predictable earnings stream from the real estate business and the power marketing and trading operations.

Quantitative Evaluations

S&P Quality Ranking   **B**

D	C	B-	B	B+	A-	A	A+

Relative Strength Rank   **MODERATE**

58

LOWEST = 1   HIGHEST = 99

Highlights

➤ Excluding net one-time charges of $0.12, we expect ongoing operating EPS in 2010 to grow nearly 30% from 2009's $2.33, which excluded $1.66 of one-time charges. Operating EPS in the first half of 2010 was aided by the electric base rate increase that was implemented for Arizona Public Service (APS) in January 2010 and by a 13% decline in its fuel and purchased power costs. This was partially offset by the unusually mild weather in April and May.

➤ For the second half of 2010, we expect earnings to reflect the benefit of the electric base rate increase and APS's cost reduction program, partially offset by the absence of the much hotter than normal third quarter in 2009. For 2011, we expect operating EPS to reflect only a modest increase over anticipated results in 2010. APS will not be able to file for a new rate increase before June 2011, with the new rates not to be implemented before the end of 2012.

➤ The company decided to restructure a significant portion of its SunCor real estate assets in 2009 due to the distressed conditions in the local real estate and credit markets. As of June 30, 2010, all of SunCor's assets had been reclassified as discontinued operations.

Investment Rationale/Risk

➤ The stock is up nearly 13% year to date. This follows a 15.6% gain in 2009, on a more than 60% rebound from its 2009 low, reflecting the expectation and ultimate authorization of a favorable regulatory ruling on APS's base rate case, the recovery in the broader market, and the well-above-peers yield (which had risen to above 9%) from the dividend, to which PNW had confirmed its commitment. We believe the stock was hurt earlier by the weak local economy and real estate market and uncertainty as to whether regulators would authorize a rate increase that would enable APS to recover the costs of its infrastructure expansion.

➤ Risks to our recommendation and target price include extended weakness in the local economy, and/or a sharp decline in the average P/E multiple of the group as a whole.

➤ The company discontinued its long-standing policy of raising the annual dividend $0.10 a year with the December 2007 payment. Despite the strong rebound in the shares, the yield from the dividend (recently at 5.1%) was still above peers (4.7%). Our 12-month target price of $41 reflects a premium-to-peers multiple of 13.4X our EPS estimate for 2011.

Revenue/Earnings Data

Revenue (Million $)

	1Q	2Q	3Q	4Q	Year
2010	633.6	820.6	--	--	--
2009	625.9	836.0	1,142	693.1	3,297
2008	736.7	926.2	1,080	624.2	3,367
2007	695.1	863.4	1,206	759.1	3,524
2006	670.2	925.0	1,076	730.1	3,402
2005	585.4	755.3	955.6	691.7	2,988

Earnings Per Share ($)

2010	-0.06	0.83	E2.09	E-0.02	E3.01
2009	-1.50	0.70	1.85	-0.29	0.81
2008	-0.05	1.13	1.49	-0.46	2.12
2007	0.16	0.78	1.99	-0.03	2.96
2006	0.12	1.11	1.84	0.10	3.17
2005	0.32	0.88	0.86	0.24	2.31

Fiscal year ended Dec. 31. Next earnings report expected: Late October. EPS Estimates based on S&P Operating Earnings; historical GAAP earnings are as reported.

Dividend Data (Dates: mm/dd Payment Date: mm/dd/yy)

Amount ($)	Date Decl.	Ex-Div. Date	Stk. of Record	Payment Date
0.525	01/20	01/28	02/01	03/01/10
0.525	04/21	04/29	05/03	06/01/10
0.525	06/22	07/29	08/02	09/01/10
0.525	10/20	10/28	11/01	12/01/10

Dividends have been paid since 1993. Source: Company reports.

Please read the Required Disclosures and Analyst Certification on the last page of this report.

The McGraw·Hill Companies

Pinnacle West Capital Corp

STANDARD &POOR'S

Business Summary October 12, 2010

CORPORATE OVERVIEW. Pinnacle West Capital, formed in 1985, is the holding company for Arizona Public Service (APS), which, with about 1.1 million customers, is Arizona's largest electric utility. PNW's other major subsidiaries are APS Energy Services, which provides competitive energy services, including wholesale marketing and trading, and SunCor, which is engaged in real estate development and investment activities. In 2009, the regulated electricity segment accounted for 95.5% of PNW's consolidated revenues (compared to 94.5% in 2008); the real estate segment 3.1% (2.2%); the marketing and trading segment 0.0% (2.0%); and other 1.4% (1.3%).

MARKET PROFILE. APS provides vertically integrated retail and wholesale electric service to the entire state of Arizona, with the exception of Tucson and about 50% of the Phoenix area. In 2009, residential customers accounted for 47.5% of the utility's total electric revenues (46.4% in 2008); commercial customers 40.3% (39.4%); industrial customers 5.6% (6.0%); off-system sales 1.8% (2.8%); and other wholesale and other 4.8% (5.4%). APS has a 29.1% owned or leased interest in the Palo Verde Nuclear Generating Station's Units 1 and 3, and about 17% in Unit 2. It has a 100% interest in Units 1, 2 and 3 and a 15% interest in Units 4 and 5 of the coal-fueled Four Corners Steam Generating Station; and a 14.0% interest in Units 1, 2 and 3 of the coal-fueled Navajo Steam Generating Station (NGS). Consolidated fuel sources for APS in 2009

were: coal, 36.3% (37.4% in 2008); nuclear, 25.9% (24.2%); purchased power, 20.6% (20.3%); and gas, oil and other, 17.2% (18.1%). With APS dependent on purchased power for so much of its fuel sources, we believe that its earnings can be significantly affected by the price of natural gas and by the time lags involved in being authorized to recover the difference between its actual fuel costs and the rates the company is allowed to charge its customers.

SunCor develops residential, commercial and industrial real estate projects in Arizona, Idaho, New Mexico and Utah. The company, which had total assets of $166 million at the end of 2009, has been hurt by the impact of the housing crisis in Arizona. The decline in 2009 from total assets of $547 million at the end of 2008 was primarily due to impairment charges of $266 million and asset sales. In 2009, SunCor had operating revenues of about $103 million, compared to $75 million in 2008 and $190 million in 2007, and a net loss of about $279 million, compared to a net loss of $26 million in 2008 and net income of $24 million in 2007. Certain components of SunCor's real estate sales activities are now reported as discontinued operations.

Company Financials Fiscal Year Ended Dec. 31

Per Share Data ($)	2009	2008	2007	2006	2005	2004	2003	2002	2001	2000
Tangible Book Value	31.07	32.85	34.11	34.48	34.58	30.99	29.81	28.23	29.46	28.09
Earnings	0.81	2.12	2.96	3.17	2.31	2.57	2.52	2.53	3.85	3.56
S&P Core Earnings	0.54	1.76	2.71	3.00	2.00	2.15	2.43	1.65	3.00	NA
Dividends	2.10	2.10	2.10	2.03	1.93	1.83	1.73	1.63	1.53	1.43
Payout Ratio	NM	99%	71%	64%	83%	71%	68%	64%	40%	40%
Prices:High	37.96	42.92	51.67	51.00	46.68	45.84	40.48	46.68	50.70	52.69
Prices:Low	22.32	26.27	36.79	38.31	39.81	36.30	28.34	21.70	37.65	25.69
P/E Ratio:High	47	20	17	16	20	18	16	18	13	15
P/E Ratio:Low	28	12	12	12	17	14	11	9	10	7

Income Statement Analysis (Million $)										
Revenue	3,297	3,367	3,524	3,402	2,988	2,900	2,818	2,637	4,551	3,690
Depreciation	443	424	373	359	348	401	438	425	428	394
Maintenance	NA	NA	NA	NA	NA	NA	NA	NA	NA	NA
Fixed Charges Coverage	2.63	2.68	3.37	3.23	2.77	2.75	2.43	2.64	3.80	3.95
Construction Credits	15.0	18.6	21.2	14.3	11.2	4.89	14.2	NA	NA	NA
Effective Tax Rate	36.0%	23.5%	33.6%	33.0%	36.2%	35.4%	31.4%	39.1%	39.5%	42.5%
Net Income	82.0	214	299	317	223	235	231	215	327	302
S&P Core Earnings	54.6	178	273	300	193	197	223	140	255	NA

Balance Sheet & Other Financial Data (Million $)										
Gross Property	13,958	13,396	12,762	11,679	11,200	18,280	10,470	16,316	9,285	8,383
Capital Expenditures	775	954	919	738	634	538	693	896	1,041	659
Net Property	9,258	8,917	8,437	7,882	7,577	14,914	7,310	12,842	5,907	5,133
Capitalization:Long Term Debt	3,371	3,032	3,127	3,233	2,608	2,585	2,898	2,882	2,673	1,955
Capitalization:% Long Term Debt	50.4	46.8	47.0	48.4	43.2	46.7	50.6	51.8	51.7	45.1
Capitalization:Preferred	Nil	Nil	Nil	Nil	Nil	Nil	Nil	Nil	Nil	Nil
Capitalization:% Preferred	Nil	Nil	Nil	Nil	Nil	Nil	Nil	Nil	Nil	Nil
Capitalization:Common	3,316	3,446	3,532	3,446	3,425	2,950	2,830	2,686	2,499	2,383
Capitalization:% Common	49.6	53.2	53.0	51.6	56.8	53.3	49.4	48.2	48.3	54.9
Total Capital	6,994	7,881	7,902	7,905	7,259	6,763	7,057	6,777	6,237	5,481
% Operating Ratio	83.5	86.2	86.7	85.6	82.4	85.8	86.6	81.7	89.9	87.7
% Earned on Net Property	6.4	6.1	7.6	8.0	6.8	3.4	6.8	4.2	24.6	13.6
% Return on Revenue	2.5	6.3	8.5	9.3	7.5	8.1	8.2	8.2	7.2	8.2
% Return on Invested Capital	8.0	5.9	6.2	7.2	8.0	6.9	6.2	7.7	7.9	8.2
% Return on Common Equity	2.4	6.1	8.6	9.2	7.0	8.1	8.4	8.3	13.4	13.2

Data as orig reptd.; bef. results of disc opers/spec. items. Per share data adj. for stk. divs.; EPS diluted. E-Estimated. NA-Not Available. NM-Not Meaningful. NR-Not Ranked. UR-Under Review.

Office: 400 N 5th St Frnt, Phoenix, AZ 85004-3903.
Telephone: 602-250-1000.
Website: http://www.pinnaclewest.com
Chrmn, Pres & CEO: D.E. Brandt

EVP, Secy & General Counsel: D.P. Falck
SVP & CFO: J.R. Hatfield
Chief Acctg Officer & Cntlr: D.R. Danner
Treas: L.R. Nickloy

Investor Contact: R. Hickman (602-250-5668)
Board Members: E. N. Basha, Jr., D. E. Brandt, S. Clark-Johnson, D. A. Cortese, M. L. Gallagher, P. Grant, R. A. Herberger, Jr., D. E. Klein, H. S. Lopez, K. L. Munro, B. J. Nordstrom, W. D. Parker

Founded: 1920
Domicile: Arizona
Employees: 7,200

The McGraw-Hill Companies

Pioneer Natural Resources Co

STANDARD
&POOR'S

S&P Recommendation **BUY** ★★★★☆	Price $72.61 (as of Oct 22, 2010)	12-Mo. Target Price $87.00	Investment Style Large-Cap Blend

GICS Sector Energy
Sub-Industry Oil & Gas Exploration & Production

Summary This company explores for and produces oil and natural gas in the U.S., Canada and Africa.

Key Stock Statistics (Source S&P, Vickers, company reports)

52-Wk Range	$74.49–39.13	S&P Oper. EPS 2010**E**	3.88	Market Capitalization(B)	$8.422	Beta	1.78
Trailing 12-Month EPS	$3.94	S&P Oper. EPS 2011**E**	2.49	Yield (%)	0.11	S&P 3-Yr. Proj. EPS CAGR(%)	10
Trailing 12-Month P/E	18.4	P/E on S&P Oper. EPS 2010**E**	18.7	Dividend Rate/Share	$0.08	S&P Credit Rating	BB+
$10K Invested 5 Yrs Ago	$15,893	Common Shares Outstg. (M)	116.0	Institutional Ownership (%)	96		

Price Performance

30-Week Mov. Avg. · · · 10-Week Mov. Avg. - - **GAAP Earnings vs. Previous Year**   **Volume** Above Avg. ▍▍▍ STARS
12-Mo. Target Price — Relative Strength — ▲ Up ▼ Down ▶ No Change   Below Avg. ▍▍▍ ★

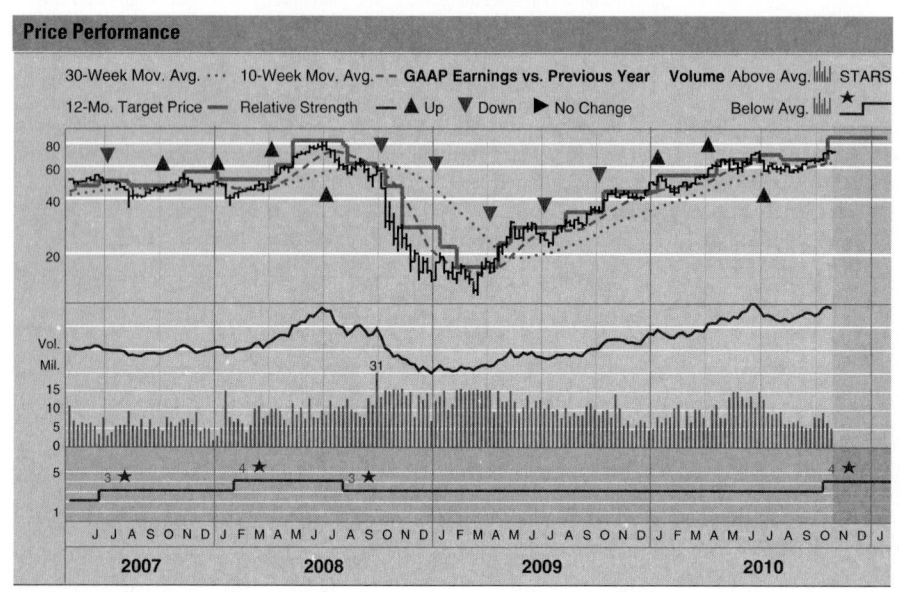

Options: ASE, CBOE, P, Ph

Analysis prepared by **Michael Kay** on October 22, 2010, when the stock traded at **$ 71.98**.

Highlights

➤ Production rose 3% in 2009, to 115 MBOE/day, despite major drilling curtailments and downtime at PXD's plant in South Africa, reflecting its slow-decline Spraberry oil field assets. PXD expects to drill 440 Spraberry wells in 2010 and boost production at a 25% compound annual rate through 2013. PXD is running 24 rigs at Spraberry and expects to ramp to 40 rigs by 2012. In South Texas, PXD has drilled eight successful horizontal wells in the Eagle Ford Shale, where PXD is running seven rigs and completing three wells. PXD expects to ramp Eagle Ford to 10 rigs and drill 70 wells in 2011; it closed on a $1.2 billion JV with India-based Reliance Industries at the play in June. We see 2010 production flat on asset sales, but we expect double-digit growth starting in 2011.

➤ For 2010, capex is budgeted at $1.2 billion. Drilling capex of $960 million is 100% oil-focused, up from $313 million in 2009 on a severely curtailed drilling program.

➤ We see EPS of $3.88 (after a $2.11 non-cash gain) in 2010 and $2.49 in 2011, as production and prices rise. This compares to a $1.66 per share operating loss in 2009 (after a $0.95 non-cash charge), as prices fell.

Investment Rationale/Risk

➤ After a lengthy restructuring, PXD is now an on-shore producer with, we believe, strong liquids production growth prospects and impending project start-ups. We see PXD focusing on core Spraberry properties and the Eagle Ford Shale in 2010, which should drive overall production growth; the oil focus of these assets is helping returns. We expect near-term asset sales at mature properties to reduce debt. In 2009, PXD severely curtailed activity at the Raton field in the Rockies and saw natural declines in the Edwards Trend in South Texas. We think investors will focus on PXD's accelerated activity at Eagle Ford, where the $1.2 billion JV with Reliance involved selling a 45% stake in 212,000 net acres, alleviating its drilling costs.

➤ Risks to our recommendation and target price include negative changes to economic, industry and operating conditions, such as rising costs or increased geopolitical risk.

➤ PXD stock has performed well in 2010 as higher oil prices and Eagle Ford success have acted as catalysts. We blend our proved reserve NAV estimate of $97 with DCF ($80; WACC 13%, terminal growth 3%) and premium relative metrics to arrive at our 12-month target price of $87.

Qualitative Risk Assessment

LOW	MEDIUM	**HIGH**

Our risk assessment reflects our view of the company's participation in a volatile and capital-intensive segment of the energy industry.

Quantitative Evaluations

S&P Quality Ranking   B

D	C	B-	**B**	B+	A-	A	A+

Relative Strength Rank   **STRONG**

83

LOWEST = 1   HIGHEST = 99

Revenue/Earnings Data

Revenue (Million $)

	1Q	2Q	3Q	4Q	Year
2010	507.8	462.1	--	--	--
2009	373.8	370.7	410.0	461.5	1,610
2008	584.2	653.3	612.2	453.4	2,277
2007	367.3	444.7	490.4	530.9	1,833
2006	396.5	413.9	432.6	389.8	1,633
2005	550.9	592.6	568.2	622.2	2,216

Earnings Per Share ($)

	1Q	2Q	3Q	4Q	Year
2010	2.08	1.18	E0.39	E0.47	E3.88
2009	-0.13	-0.82	-0.17	-0.17	-1.24
2008	1.07	1.32	-0.02	-0.54	1.86
2007	0.25	0.29	0.77	0.71	1.99
2006	-0.01	0.52	0.64	0.22	1.36
2005	0.58	0.72	0.74	1.07	3.02

Fiscal year ended Dec. 31. Next earnings report expected: Early November. EPS Estimates based on S&P Operating Earnings; historical GAAP earnings are as reported.

Dividend Data (Dates: mm/dd Payment Date: mm/dd/yy)

Amount ($)	Date Decl.	Ex-Div. Date	Stk. of Record	Payment Date
0.040	02/17	03/29	03/31	04/14/10
0.040	08/30	09/28	09/30	10/14/10

Dividends have been paid since 2004. Source: Company reports.

The **McGraw·Hill** Companies

Pioneer Natural Resources Co

STANDARD &POOR'S

Business Summary October 22, 2010

CORPORATE OVERVIEW. This independent oil and gas exploration and pro-duction company has an asset base anchored by the Spraberry oil field in West Texas, the Hugoton gas field in Kansas, the West Panhandle gas field in the Texas Panhandle, and the Raton gas field in southern Colorado. Comple-menting these areas, PXD has oil and gas exploration, development and pro-duction activities in the onshore Gulf Coast area, Alaska, South Africa and Tunisia.

As of December 31, 2009, PXD had estimated proved reserves of 898.6 MM-BOE, of which 54% consisted of crude oil and natural gas liquids, and 46% natural gas. This compares to estimated proved reserves of 959.6 MMBOE, of which 52% was natural gas, and 48% crude oil and natural gas liquids, at year-end 2008. We estimate PXD's year-end 2009 reserve life to be 19.9 years, compared to 21.5 years at the end of 2008. The decline in reserves was a re-sult of negative price revisions attributable to natural gas assets.

CORPORATE STRATEGY. PXD believes it offers significant upside potential from its exposure to oil with a large drilling inventory; an aggressive Spraberry program and early Eagle Ford Shale success. Over the next five years, PXD expects liquids production to go from 45% to 60% of its production portfolio.

On development of Eagle Ford and Spraberry, PXD is forecasting double-digit production growth between 2011 and 2015. In 2010, PXD is planning a capex budget of $1.2 billion, $960 million for drilling, with 100% allocated to oil activi-ty.

Like many operators, PXD drastically curtailed drilling activity early in 2009 due to plummeting oil and gas prices, high costs and a global economic re-cession. As costs have realigned with prices, PXD appears poised to boost rig counts, capex and activity levels in 2010, as oil prices have risen nearly 80% since early 2009. In October 2009, PXD initiated production from its most prolif-ic well at the South Coast Gas Project in Africa and drilled its first two wells in the Pierre Shale in the Rocky Mountains. At Oooguruk in Alaska's North Slope, drilling results have been better than expected. In 2009, PXD curtailed activity at the Raton field in the Rockies, given weakening returns, and we ex-pect weak activity in the Edwards Trend, where drilling is dependent on nat-ural gas prices.

Company Financials Fiscal Year Ended Dec. 31

Per Share Data ($)	2009	2008	2007	2006	2005	2004	2003	2002	2001	2000
Tangible Book Value	28.21	28.56	24.38	22.01	14.82	19.55	14.75	11.73	12.37	9.19
Cash Flow	4.74	6.66	5.40	4.17	7.01	6.96	6.63	2.32	3.27	3.82
Earnings	-1.24	1.86	1.99	1.36	3.02	2.46	3.33	0.43	1.04	1.65
S&P Core Earnings	-1.25	1.82	1.57	1.34	2.00	2.41	3.26	0.32	0.93	NA
Dividends	0.08	0.30	0.27	0.25	0.22	0.20	Nil	Nil	Nil	Nil
Payout Ratio	NM	16%	14%	18%	7%	8%	Nil	Nil	Nil	Nil
Prices:High	50.00	82.21	54.87	54.46	56.35	37.50	32.90	27.50	23.05	20.63
Prices:Low	11.88	14.03	35.51	36.43	32.91	29.27	22.76	16.10	12.62	6.75
P/E Ratio:High	NM	44	28	40	19	15	10	64	22	12
P/E Ratio:Low	NM	8	18	27	11	12	7	37	12	4

Income Statement Analysis (Million $)										
Revenue	1,610	2,277	1,833	1,633	2,216	1,833	1,299	702	847	853
Operating Income	NA	1,256	1,019	757	1,262	1,191	804	351	433	475
Depreciation, Depletion and Amortization	684	569	415	360	568	575	391	216	223	215
Interest Expense	173	154	168	107	128	103	91.4	95.8	132	162
Pretax Income	-180	448	355	309	715	479	331	54.1	108	158
Effective Tax Rate	26.7%	45.9%	31.7%	44.2%	40.8%	34.7%	NM	9.35%	3.73%	NM
Net Income	-142	221	242	172	424	313	395	49.1	104	164
S&P Core Earnings	-142	217	192	170	280	307	386	36.4	92.2	NA

Balance Sheet & Other Financial Data (Million $)										
Cash	27.4	48.3	12.2	7.03	18.8	7.26	19.3	8.49	14.3	26.2
Current Assets	616	487	765	537	624	312	205	147	256	191
Total Assets	8,867	9,163	8,617	7,355	7,329	6,647	3,952	3,455	3,271	2,954
Current Liabilities	571	695	994	887	1,033	544	430	275	228	217
Long Term Debt	2,761	2,964	2,755	1,497	2,058	2,569	1,604	1,669	1,577	1,579
Common Equity	3,643	3,582	3,043	2,985	2,217	2,832	1,760	1,375	1,285	905
Total Capital	6,404	8,083	7,028	5,654	4,276	5,927	3,376	3,052	2,876	2,512
Capital Expenditures	437	1,403	2,204	1,499	1,123	616	688	615	530	300
Cash Flow	541	790	657	532	992	888	786	265	326	379
Current Ratio	1.1	0.7	0.8	0.6	0.6	0.6	0.5	0.5	1.1	0.9
% Long Term Debt of Capitalization	43.1	36.7	39.2	26.5	48.1	43.3	47.5	54.7	54.8	62.8
% Return on Assets	NM	2.5	3.0	2.3	6.0	5.9	10.7	1.5	3.3	5.6
% Return on Equity	NM	6.7	8.0	6.6	16.8	13.6	25.2	3.7	9.5	19.6

Data as orig reptd.; bef. results of disc opers/spec. items. Per share data adj. for stk. divs.; EPS diluted. E-Estimated. NA-Not Available. NM-Not Meaningful. NR-Not Ranked. UR-Under Review.

Office: 5205 North O Connor Boulevard, Suite 200, Irving, TX 75039.
Telephone: 972-444-9001.
Email: ir@pxd.com
Website: http://www.pxd.com

Chrmn & CEO: S.D. Sheffield
Pres & COO: T.L. Dove
EVP & CFO: R.P. Dealy
EVP & General Counsel: M.S. Berg

Chief Admin Officer: L.N. Paulsen
Investor Contact: F.E. Hopkins (972-969-4065)
Board Members: T. D. Arthur, E. Buchanan, A. F. Cates, R. H. Gardner, A. Lundquist, C. E. Ramsey, Jr., S. J. Reiman, F. A. Risch, S. D. Sheffield, J. A. Watson

Founded: 1997
Domicile: Delaware
Employees: 1,888

The McGraw-Hill Companies

Pitney Bowes Inc.

STANDARD &POOR'S

S&P Recommendation	HOLD ★★★☆☆	Price $22.11 (as of Oct 22, 2010)	12-Mo. Target Price $21.00	Investment Style Large-Cap Growth

GICS Sector Industrials
Sub-Industry Office Services & Supplies

Summary PBI, the world's largest maker of mailing systems, also provides production and document management equipment and facilities management services.

Key Stock Statistics (Source S&P, Vickers, company reports)

52-Wk Range	$26.00–19.06	S&P Oper. EPS 2010E	2.17	Market Capitalization(B)	$4.570	Beta	1.01
Trailing 12-Month EPS	$1.65	S&P Oper. EPS 2011E	2.30	Yield (%)	6.60	S&P 3-Yr. Proj. EPS CAGR(%)	4
Trailing 12-Month P/E	13.4	P/E on S&P Oper. EPS 2010E	10.2	Dividend Rate/Share	$1.46	S&P Credit Rating	BBB+
$10K Invested 5 Yrs Ago	$6,630	Common Shares Outstg. (M)	206.7	Institutional Ownership (%)	84		

Price Performance

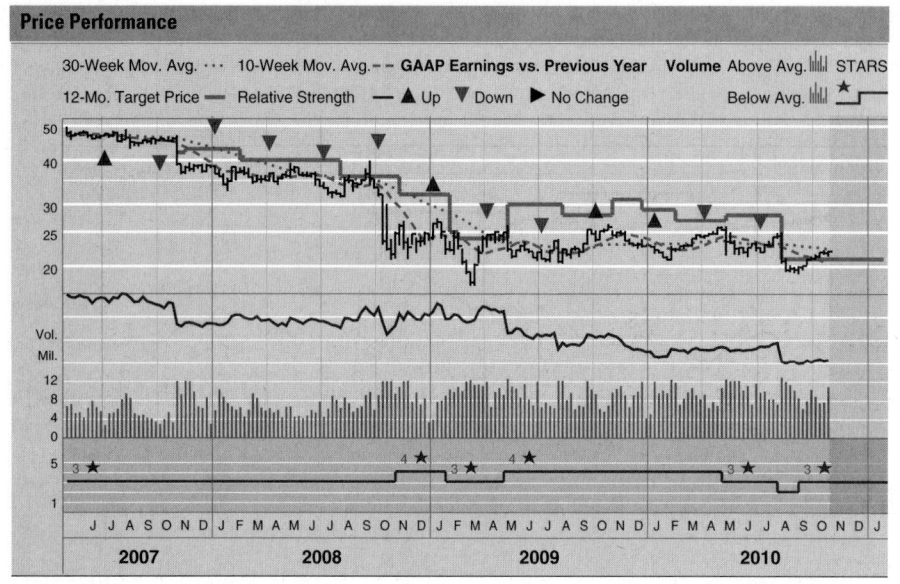

30-Week Mov. Avg. ···· 10-Week Mov. Avg. --- **GAAP Earnings vs. Previous Year** Volume Above Avg. STARS
12-Mo. Target Price — Relative Strength ▲ Up ▼ Down ▶ No Change Below Avg.

Options: CBOE, P, Ph

Analysis prepared by **Thomas W. Smith, CFA** on September 07, 2010, when the stock traded at **$19.87**.

Highlights

➤ We look for revenues to decrease 3% in 2010, and then increase 2% in 2011. The company reported soft spots in demand toward the end of the second quarter of 2010, and we believe that office products related to mail processing face a protracted recovery after a general economic downturn in 2009. New products, including the new IntelliJet 30 Printing System, should help to offset demand weakness. We believe several product partnerships are helping the company expand sales opportunities and extend its marketing reach into Asia.

➤ On December 15, 2009, the company announced a set of transformation initiatives including a cut of up to 10% of the workforce, enterprise-wide systems and common platforms, enhanced procurement processes, and more outsourcing relationships. We expect operating margins to widen in 2011 as cost savings from restructurings are more fully realized. The company has been paying down total debt in recent quarters.

➤ We estimate operating EPS, excluding restructuring charges, at $2.17 for 2010 and $2.30 for 2011.

Investment Rationale/Risk

➤ PBI has a large recurring revenue stream and a leadership position within its market, in our view. We project weak demand for office equipment to limit near-term sales potential, although we expect some synergies from acquisitions, and from new product introductions focusing on digital technology, to aid long-term growth. The cash dividend yield is near 7%, which is over twice the yield for Industrials sector peers, but we think a high payout ratio may limit financial flexibility.

➤ Risks to our recommendation and target price include a slower economic recovery and more competition in the document management outsourcing market than we project. Cash flows might weaken more than we expect in a period of slow demand.

➤ Our 12-month target price of $21 is based mainly on our P/E analysis. We apply a target P/E multiple of 9.5X, a discount to Industrials sector peers in the S&P 500 Index and toward the low end of a historical range for PBI, to reflect sluggish near-term revenue growth that we foresee, to our 12-month forward operating EPS estimate of $2.22.

Qualitative Risk Assessment

LOW	**MEDIUM**	HIGH

Our risk assessment reflects our view of PBI's steady cash flow, recurring revenue streams, consistent dividend increases and share buybacks. However, we think these factors are offset by a lackluster rate of revenue growth and integration risk associated with recent acquisitions.

Quantitative Evaluations

S&P Quality Ranking   B+

D	C	B-	B	**B+**	A-	A	A+

Relative Strength Rank   MODERATE

51

LOWEST = 1   HIGHEST = 99

Revenue/Earnings Data

Revenue (Million $)

	1Q	2Q	3Q	4Q	Year
2010	1,348	1,297	--	--	--
2009	1,380	1,378	1,357	1,454	5,569
2008	1,574	1,588	1,548	1,553	6,262
2007	1,414	1,543	1,508	1,664	6,130
2006	1,362	1,389	1,433	1,546	5,730
2005	1,318	1,360	1,356	1,458	5,492

Earnings Per Share ($)

2010	0.40	0.31	E0.52	E0.62	E2.17
2009	0.49	0.54	0.51	0.54	2.08
2008	0.58	0.63	0.48	0.45	2.13
2007	0.66	0.69	0.59	-0.32	1.63
2006	0.60	0.54	0.64	0.73	2.51
2005	0.64	0.60	0.62	0.41	2.27

Fiscal year ended Dec. 31. Next earnings report expected: Early November. EPS Estimates based on S&P Operating Earnings; historical GAAP earnings are as reported.

Dividend Data (Dates: mm/dd Payment Date: mm/dd/yy)

Amount ($)	Date Decl.	Ex-Div. Date	Stk. of Record	Payment Date
0.360	11/06	11/18	11/20	12/12/09
0.365	02/04	02/17	02/19	03/12/10
0.365	04/12	05/12	05/14	06/12/10
0.365	07/12	08/11	08/13	09/12/10

Dividends have been paid since 1934. Source: Company reports.

Please read the Required Disclosures and Analyst Certification on the last page of this report.

The McGraw-Hill Companies

Pitney Bowes Inc.

Business Summary September 07, 2010

CORPORATE OVERVIEW. In business since 1920, Pitney Bowes is a major global provider of mail processing equipment and integrated mail solutions. The company's postage meters and other offerings help business customers optimize the flow of physical and electronic mail, documents and packages. The company operates seven business units within two business groups known as Mailstream Solutions and Mailstream Services.

The Mailstream Solutions segment, which accounted for 68% of 2009 revenue (70% in 2008), is comprised of four units. The first, U.S. Mailing, includes U.S. revenue and related expenses from the sale, rental and financing of mail finishing, mail creation, shipping equipment and software, services, and payment solutions. The second, International Mailing, includes non-U.S. revenue and related expenses from activities similar to those of the first unit. The third unit, Production Mail, includes the worldwide sales, service and financing of high-speed production mail systems and sorting equipment. The fourth unit, Software, includes the worldwide sales and support services of non-equipment-based mailing and customer communication and location intelligence software.

The Mailstream Services segment (32%, 30%) is made up of three units. The first, Management Services, includes worldwide facilities management services, secure mail services, reprographic, document management, litigation support, eDiscovery and other services. The second, Mail Services, offers presort mail services and cross-border mail services. The third, Marketing Services, focuses on direct marketing campaign services, web-tools for customization of promotional mail, and other marketing consulting services.

Reviewing revenue sources by product category, Business Services is the largest area, representing 32% of 2009 revenues (31% in 2008), following by Equipment Sales 18% (20%), Support Services 13% (12%), Financing 12% (12%), Rentals 12% (12%), Software 7% (7%), and Supplies 6% (6%).

Company Financials Fiscal Year Ended Dec. 31

Per Share Data ($)	2009	2008	2007	2006	2005	2004	2003	2002	2001	2000
Tangible Book Value	NM	NM	NM	NM	NM	NM	NM	0.10	1.05	4.34
Cash Flow	3.72	3.60	3.37	4.21	3.70	3.36	3.32	2.98	3.44	3.55
Earnings	2.08	2.13	1.63	2.51	2.27	2.05	2.10	1.81	2.08	2.18
S&P Core Earnings	2.10	1.67	1.61	2.50	2.09	1.94	1.87	1.34	0.81	NA
Dividends	1.44	1.40	1.32	1.28	1.24	1.22	1.20	1.18	1.16	1.14
Payout Ratio	69%	66%	81%	51%	55%	60%	57%	65%	56%	52%
Prices:High	27.46	39.98	49.70	47.97	47.50	46.97	42.75	44.41	44.70	54.13
Prices:Low	17.62	20.83	36.40	40.18	40.34	38.88	29.45	28.55	32.00	24.00
P/E Ratio:High	13	19	30	19	21	23	20	25	21	25
P/E Ratio:Low	8	10	22	16	18	19	14	16	15	11

Income Statement Analysis (Million $)

	2009	2008	2007	2006	2005	2004	2003	2002	2001	2000
Revenue	5,569	6,262	6,130	5,730	5,492	4,957	4,577	4,410	4,122	3,881
Operating Income	1,187	1,437	1,549	1,487	1,435	1,352	1,291	1,276	1,046	1,316
Depreciation	339	307	383	363	332	307	289	264	317	321
Interest Expense	111	229	251	228	214	172	168	185	193	201
Pretax Income	693	713	661	914	867	699	721	619	766	803
Effective Tax Rate	34.7%	34.3%	42.4%	36.6%	39.3%	31.3%	31.4%	29.3%	32.9%	29.9%
Net Income	432	447	361	566	527	481	495	438	514	563
S&P Core Earnings	435	352	357	564	485	456	440	324	199	NA

Balance Sheet & Other Financial Data (Million $)

	2009	2008	2007	2006	2005	2004	2003	2002	2001	2000
Cash	427	398	440	239	244	316	294	315	232	198
Current Assets	2,971	3,033	3,320	2,919	2,742	2,693	2,513	2,553	2,557	2,627
Total Assets	8,551	8,827	9,550	8,480	10,621	9,821	8,891	8,732	8,318	7,901
Current Liabilities	2,566	3,243	3,556	2,747	2,911	3,294	2,647	3,350	3,083	2,882
Long Term Debt	4,214	3,935	3,802	4,232	3,850	3,109	3,151	2,317	2,419	2,192
Common Equity	12.8	-189	642	698	1,301	1,289	1,086	852	890	1,283
Total Capital	4,524	4,405	5,302	5,287	7,074	4,399	5,898	4,706	4,584	4,704
Capital Expenditures	167	237	265	328	292	317	286	225	256	269
Cash Flow	770	754	744	929	858	787	784	702	832	884
Current Ratio	1.2	0.9	0.9	1.1	0.9	0.8	0.9	0.8	0.8	0.9
% Long Term Debt of Capitalization	93.2	89.3	71.7	80.0	54.4	70.7	53.4	49.2	52.8	46.6
% Net Income of Revenue	7.8	7.2	5.9	9.9	11.2	9.7	10.8	9.9	12.5	14.5
% Return on Assets	5.0	4.9	4.0	5.9	5.1	5.1	5.6	5.1	6.3	7.0
% Return on Equity	NM	NM	53.9	54.9	40.7	40.5	51.1	50.3	47.3	38.7

Data as orig reptd.; bef. results of disc opers/spec. items. Per share data adj. for stk. divs.; EPS diluted. E-Estimated. NA-Not Available. NM-Not Meaningful. NR-Not Ranked. UR-Under Review.

Office: 1 Elmcroft Rd, Stamford, CT 06926-0700.
Telephone: 203-351-6858.
Email: investorrelations@pb.com
Website: http://www.pb.com

Chrmn, Pres & CEO: M. Martin
EVP & CFO: M. Monahan
EVP & General Counsel: D.J. Goldstein
EVP & CIO: G.E. Buoncontri

SVP & CTO: J.E. Wall
Investor Contact: C.F. McBride (203-351-6349)
Board Members: R. C. Adkins, L. G. Alvarado, A. M. Busquet, A. S. Fuchs, E. Green, J. H. Keyes, M. Martin, J. McFarlane, E. R. Menasce, M. I. Roth, D. L. Shedlarz, D. B. Snow, Jr., R. E. Weissman

Founded: 1920
Domicile: Delaware
Employees: 33,004

Plum Creek Timber Co Inc.

STANDARD &POOR'S

S&P Recommendation **HOLD** ★★★☆☆	Price $37.09 (as of Oct 22, 2010)	12-Mo. Target Price $42.00	Investment Style Large-Cap Blend

GICS Sector Financials
Sub-Industry Specialized REITS

Summary Plum Creek Timber Co., a real estate investment trust (REIT), is the largest private timberland owner in the United States, with more than 7 million acres of timberland in 19 states.

Key Stock Statistics (Source S&P, Vickers, company reports)

52-Wk Range	$43.75–30.71	S&P Oper. EPS 2010E	1.45	Market Capitalization(B)	$5.994	Beta	1.07
Trailing 12-Month EPS	$1.04	S&P Oper. EPS 2011E	1.60	Yield (%)	4.53	S&P 3-Yr. Proj. EPS CAGR(%)	6
Trailing 12-Month P/E	35.7	P/E on S&P Oper. EPS 2010E	25.6	Dividend Rate/Share	$1.68	S&P Credit Rating	BBB-
$10K Invested 5 Yrs Ago	$12,817	Common Shares Outstg. (M)	161.6	Institutional Ownership (%)	69		

Price Performance

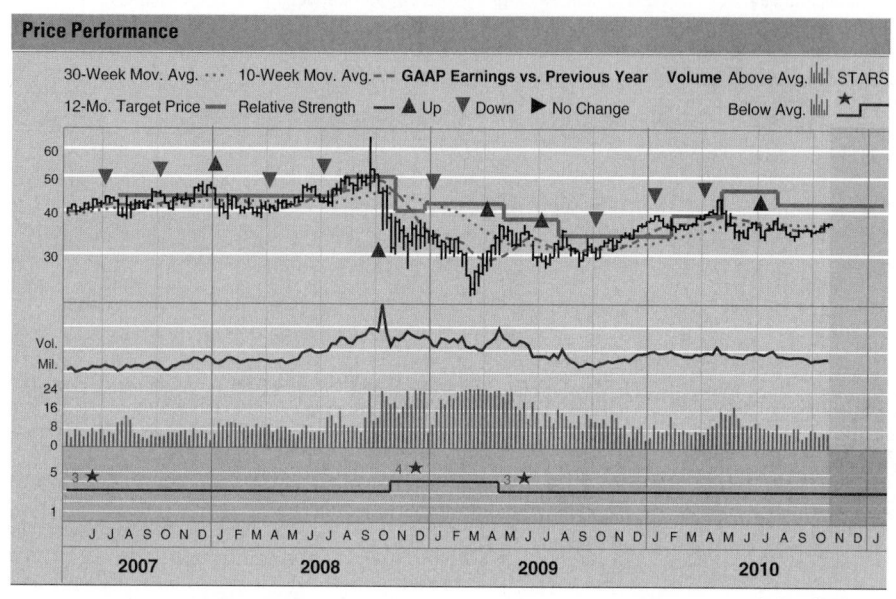

- 30-Week Mov. Avg. · · · 10-Week Mov. Avg. - - **GAAP Earnings vs. Previous Year**   **Volume** Above Avg. STARS
- 12-Mo. Target Price — Relative Strength — ▲ Up ▼ Down ► No Change   Below Avg.

Options: CBOE, P, Ph

Analysis prepared by **Stuart J. Benway, CFA** on July 28, 2010, when the stock traded at **$ 37.36**.

Highlights

- S&P projects that housing starts will rise by about 16% in 2010, followed by a nearly 50% rebound in 2011. We expect this to support increases in sawlog prices, and pulpwood demand is forecast to remain fairly strong. However, sawlog harvest levels at Plum Creek are likely to remain flat in anticipation of higher prices. Moreover, rural land sales are expected to decline due to lower sales of large tracts in Montana. Overall, we expect revenues to fall about 5% this year, before rebounding 4%-6% in 2011.

- We think that average wood product prices in 2010 will be above those of 2009, as demand from the housing market improves gradually. Margins are expected to widen in the timberland operations in 2010, and we look for a return to profitability in wood products. We see PCL capturing improved prices for its higher and better use land sales over the long term.

- Our 2010 operating EPS estimate is $1.45, and we project EPS of $1.60 for 2011. We note that the timing of real estate transactions will likely create quarterly volatility.

Investment Rationale/Risk

- We believe PCL has significant value in its land holdings, and we expect real estate to become a rising source of earnings in coming years. It plans to develop 150,000 acres of land over the next 15 years, and we estimate that these properties can be sold at high margin levels. Before year end, PCL plans to sell 70,000 acres in Montana. However, demand and prices for timber in the near term are likely to remain below historical averages due to expected sustained weakness in the housing market.

- Risks to our recommendation and target price include renewed declines in log demand and prices due to weakness in the U.S. housing market, and lower-than-projected profits on sales of higher and better use land.

- Using a sum-of-the-parts analysis, which recognizes the value of PCL's land holdings, we value the shares at $43. Our dividend discount model, which assumes a $1.68 payout in 2011, a required rate of return of 8.5%, and constant dividend growth of 4.5%, indicates that PCL has an intrinsic value of $42. Our 12-month target price of $42 is based on these two measures.

Qualitative Risk Assessment

LOW	**MEDIUM**	HIGH

Our risk assessment reflects that Plum Creek operates in a cyclical industry, with demand for its products tied to residential construction and paper manufacturing. It is subject to movements in interest rates, economic conditions and currency, and prices for its products have historically been volatile. However, it is a major landowner, and its debt levels are relatively low.

Quantitative Evaluations

S&P Quality Ranking   B

D	C	B-	**B**	B+	A-	A	A+

Relative Strength Rank   **MODERATE**

52

LOWEST = 1   HIGHEST = 99

Revenue/Earnings Data

Revenue (Million $)

	1Q	2Q	3Q	4Q	Year
2010	317.0	258.0	--	--	--
2009	470.0	272.0	294.0	258.0	1,294
2008	363.0	376.0	414.0	461.0	1,614
2007	369.0	395.0	407.0	504.0	1,675
2006	414.0	380.0	454.0	379.0	1,627
2005	400.0	358.0	427.0	391.0	1,576

Earnings Per Share ($)

2010	0.47	0.22	E0.33	E0.50	E1.45
2009	0.95	0.19	0.12	0.17	1.44
2008	0.22	0.18	0.40	0.57	1.37
2007	0.25	0.33	0.34	0.68	1.60
2006	0.50	0.34	0.51	0.39	1.74
2005	0.56	0.37	0.52	0.34	1.79

Fiscal year ended Dec. 31. Next earnings report expected: Late October. EPS Estimates based on S&P Operating Earnings; historical GAAP earnings are as reported.

Dividend Data (Dates: mm/dd Payment Date: mm/dd/yy)

Amount ($)	Date Decl.	Ex-Div. Date	Stk. of Record	Payment Date
0.420	11/03	11/12	11/16	11/30/09
0.420	02/09	02/17	02/19	03/05/10
0.420	05/04	05/12	05/14	05/28/10
0.420	08/03	08/12	08/16	08/31/10

Dividends have been paid since 1989. Source: Company reports.

Please read the Required Disclosures and Analyst Certification on the last page of this report.

The McGraw-Hill Companies

STANDARD & POOR'S

Plum Creek Timber Co Inc.

Business Summary July 28, 2010

CORPORATE OVERVIEW. Plum Creek Timber Co., a real estate investment trust (REIT), is the largest private timberland owner in the United States, with more than 7 million acres of timberlands in 19 states. In addition, the trust operates several wood products manufacturing facilities and is actively involved in land purchases and sales. The company conducts operations through four business segments: the timber operation accounted for 42% of 2009 revenues, manufacturing (19%), real estate (38%), and other (1%). The Northern Resources portion of the timber segment encompasses 3.5 million acres of timberlands, in Maine, Michigan, Montana, New Hampshire, Oregon, Vermont, Washington, West Virginia, and Wisconsin. The Southern Resources portion of the timber segment consists of 3.5 million acres of timberlands in Alabama, Arkansas, Florida, Georgia, Louisiana, Mississippi, North Carolina, Oklahoma, South Carolina, and Texas.

MARKET PROFILE. The timber industry provides raw materials and manages resources for the paper and forest products industry. Harvested logs are marketed and either as sawlogs to lumber and other wood products manufacturers or as pulplogs to pulp and paper manufacturers or producers of oriented strand board. Over time, timberlands may become more valuable for purposes other than growing timber. In these circumstances, timberlands may be sold to realize these values. There are six primary end markets for most of the tim-

ber harvested in the United States: new housing construction, home repair and remodeling, products for industrial uses, raw material for the manufacture of pulp and paper, wood fiber for energy production, and logs for export.

The demand for timber is directly related to the underlying demand for pulp and paper products, lumber, panels, and other wood products. The demand for pulp and paper is largely driven by population growth, per-capita income levels, and industry capacity. The demand for lumber and manufactured wood products is primarily affected by the level of new residential construction activity and repair and remodeling activity, which, in turn, is affected by changes in general economic and demographic factors, including population growth and interest rates for home mortgages and construction loans. The market for wood fiber used in paper production and wood products manufacturing is very diverse, with many manufacturers of various sizes. We therefore believe that Plum Creek has only limited control over the prices that it can charge for timber and wood products.

Company Financials Fiscal Year Ended Dec. 31

Per Share Data ($)	2009	2008	2007	2006	2005	2004	2003	2002	2001	2000
Tangible Book Value	NA	9.47	12.06	11.80	12.62	12.19	11.57	12.04	12.21	7.46
Cash Flow	NA	2.10	2.37	2.45	1.92	2.46	1.63	1.82	3.00	2.47
Earnings	1.44	1.37	1.60	1.74	1.79	1.84	1.04	1.26	2.58	1.91
S&P Core Earnings	1.47	1.35	1.61	1.67	1.78	1.82	1.04	1.24	2.57	NA
Dividends	1.68	1.26	1.68	1.60	1.52	1.42	1.40	1.49	2.85	2.28
Payout Ratio	117%	2%	105%	92%	85%	77%	135%	118%	110%	119%
Prices:High	38.69	65.00	48.45	40.00	39.63	39.45	30.75	31.98	30.00	29.81
Prices:Low	22.88	27.33	37.13	31.21	33.40	27.30	20.88	18.92	23.30	21.50
P/E Ratio:High	27	47	30	23	22	21	30	25	12	16
P/E Ratio:Low	16	20	23	18	19	15	20	15	9	11

Income Statement Analysis (Million $)										
Revenue	1,294	1,614	1,675	1,627	1,576	1,528	1,196	1,137	598	209
Operating Income	NA	453	558	571	561	586	410	443	305	166
Depreciation	99.0	125	134	128	113	114	107	105	55.0	38.9
Interest Expense	147	148	147	133	109	111	117	103	54.0	46.8
Pretax Income	205	206	277	328	339	366	186	235	196	132
Effective Tax Rate	NM	NM	NM	3.90%	2.30%	7.40%	NM	0.85%	NM	NM
Net Income	236	233	280	315	331	339	192	233	338	132
S&P Core Earnings	241	229	281	301	329	336	193	229	336	NA

Balance Sheet & Other Financial Data (Million $)										
Cash	299	369	240	301	395	376	260	246	193	181
Current Assets	NA	699	456	513	574	499	405	378	306	195
Total Assets	4,448	4,780	4,664	4,661	4,812	4,378	4,387	4,289	4,122	1,250
Current Liabilities	NA	307	303	281	375	184	168	155	149	180
Long Term Debt	2,728	2,807	2,376	1,617	1,524	1,853	2,031	1,839	1,667	560
Common Equity	1,466	1,572	1,901	2,089	2,325	2,240	2,119	2,222	2,247	507
Total Capital	NA	4,383	4,297	3,731	3,888	4,138	4,187	4,105	3,952	1,066
Capital Expenditures	NA	189	Nil	86.0	89.0	70.0	246	231	59.0	21.7
Cash Flow	NA	358	414	443	444	453	299	338	393	171
Current Ratio	2.8	2.3	1.5	1.8	1.5	2.7	2.4	2.4	2.1	1.1
% Long Term Debt of Capitalization	64.2	64.0	55.3	43.3	39.1	44.8	48.5	44.8	42.2	52.5
% Net Income of Revenue	18.2	14.4	16.7	19.3	21.0	22.2	16.1	20.5	56.5	63.1
% Return on Assets	5.1	4.9	6.0	6.6	7.2	7.7	4.4	5.5	11.8	10.5
% Return on Equity	15.5	13.4	14.0	14.2	14.5	15.6	8.8	10.4	28.3	25.4

Data as orig reptd.; bef. results of disc opers/spec. items. Per share data adj. for stk. divs.; EPS diluted. E-Estimated. NA-Not Available. NM-Not Meaningful. NR-Not Ranked. UR-Under Review.

Office: 999 3rd Ave Ste 4300, Seattle, WA 98104-4096.
Telephone: 206-467-3600.
Email: info@plumcreek.com
Website: http://www.plumcreek.com

Chrmn: J.F. Morgan
Pres & CEO: R.R. Holley
COO & EVP: T.M. Lindquist
SVP & CFO: D.W. Lambert

SVP, Secy & General Counsel: J.A. Kraft
Investor Contact: J. Hobbs (800-858-5347)
Board Members: R. R. Holley, R. Josephs, J. G. McDonald, R. B. McLeod, J. F. Morgan, M. F. Racicot, J. H. Scully, S. C. Tobias, M. A. White

Founded: 1989
Domicile: Delaware
Employees: 1,252

The McGraw-Hill Companies

PNC Financial Services Group Inc.

STANDARD &POOR'S

S&P Recommendation	**BUY** ★★★★☆	Price	12-Mo. Target Price	Investment Style
		$54.72 (as of Oct 22, 2010)	$61.00	Large-Cap Value

GICS Sector Financials
Sub-Industry Regional Banks

Summary This bank holding company conducts regional banking, wholesale banking and asset management in 13 eastern states, with concentration in Pennsylvania and Ohio.

Key Stock Statistics (Source S&P, Vickers, company reports)

52-Wk Range	$70.45– 48.83	S&P Oper. EPS 2010**E**	5.49	Market Capitalization(B)	$28.750	Beta	1.22
Trailing 12-Month EPS	$5.27	S&P Oper. EPS 2011**E**	6.05	Yield (%)	0.73	S&P 3-Yr. Proj. EPS CAGR(%)	7
Trailing 12-Month P/E	10.4	P/E on S&P Oper. EPS 2010**E**	10.0	Dividend Rate/Share	$0.40	S&P Credit Rating	A
$10K Invested 5 Yrs Ago	$10,759	Common Shares Outstg. (M)	525.4	Institutional Ownership (%)	80		

Price Performance

- 30-Week Mov. Avg. · · ·
- 10-Week Mov. Avg. – –
- **GAAP Earnings vs. Previous Year**
- Volume Above Avg. STARS
- 12-Mo. Target Price —
- Relative Strength —
- ▲ Up ▼ Down ▶ No Change
- Below Avg.

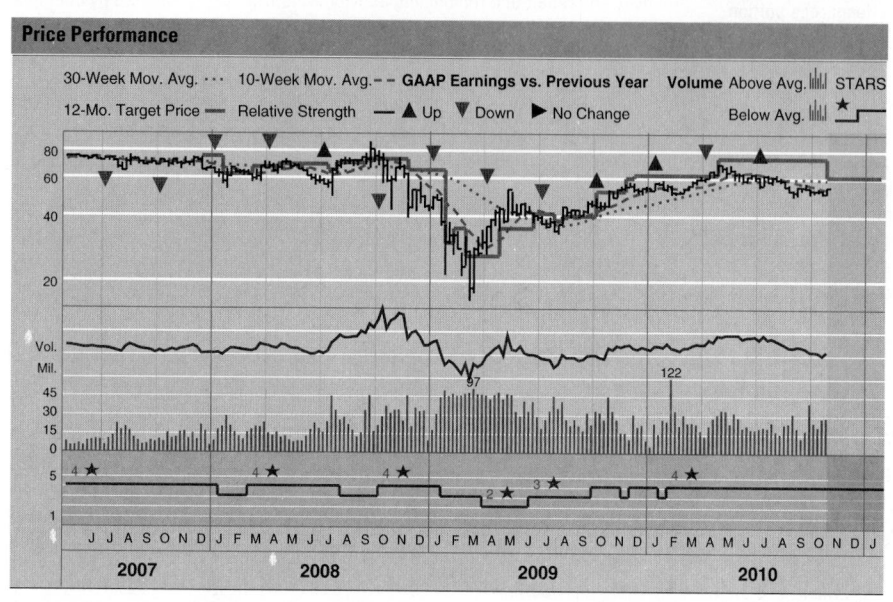

Options: ASE, CBOE, Ph

Qualitative Risk Assessment

LOW	**MEDIUM**	HIGH

Our risk assessment reflects our view of PNC's large-cap valuation and history of profitability.

Quantitative Evaluations

S&P Quality Ranking B+

D	C	B-	B	**B+**	A-	A	A+

Relative Strength Rank MODERATE

36

LOWEST = 1   HIGHEST = 99

Revenue/Earnings Data

Revenue (Million $)

	1Q	2Q	3Q	4Q	Year
2010	4,289	4,350	--	--	--
2009	4,625	4,610	4,517	5,479	19,231
2008	2,586	2,639	2,228	2,227	9,680
2007	2,306	1,721	1,757	1,634	10,083
2006	2,251	2,356	4,146	2,186	10,939
2005	1,777	1,826	2,108	2,185	7,896

Earnings Per Share ($)

2010	0.61	1.43	E1.45	E1.25	E5.49
2009	1.01	0.11	0.96	2.16	4.36
2008	1.09	1.45	0.71	-0.77	2.46
2007	1.46	1.22	1.19	0.51	4.35
2006	1.19	1.28	5.01	1.27	8.73
2005	1.24	0.98	1.14	1.20	4.55

Fiscal year ended Dec. 31. Next earnings report expected: Late October. EPS Estimates based on S&P Operating Earnings; historical GAAP earnings are as reported.

Highlights

- ➤ The 12-month target price for PNC has recently been changed to $61.00 from $74.00. The Highlights section of this Stock Report will be updated accordingly.

Investment Rationale/Risk

- ➤ The Investment Rationale/Risk section of this Stock Report will be updated shortly. For the latest News story on PNC from MarketScope, see below.

- ➤ 10/21/10 12:50 pm ET ... S&P MAINTAINS BUY RECOMMENDATION ON SHARES OF PNC FI-NANCIAL SERVICES GROUP (PNC 53.91****): Q3 EPS of $1.45, vs. $0.96, exceeds our $1.11 estimate, on a lower than expected loan loss provision. On Q3 results, we are raising our '10 EPS estimate to $5.49 from $5.15. We see credit quality, as measured by net chargeoff trends and new nonperforming loans, as stable, but improving more slowly than at many peers. However, based on Q3 results and outlook, we reiterate our '11 EPS estimate of $6.05. Based on our relative peer group analysis, we think PNC should trade at about a 10.1X multiple on our '11 estimate, which leads us to lower our target price by $13 to $61. /E. Oja

Dividend Data (Dates: mm/dd Payment Date: mm/dd/yy)

Amount ($)	Date Decl.	Ex-Div. Date	Stk. of Record	Payment Date
0.100	01/07	01/13	01/15	01/24/10
0.100	04/01	04/09	04/13	04/24/10
0.100	07/01	07/12	07/14	07/24/10
0.100	10/07	10/13	10/15	10/24/10

Dividends have been paid since 1865. Source: Company reports.

PNC Financial Services Group Inc.

STANDARD &POOR'S

Business Summary August 10, 2010

CORPORATE OVERVIEW. PNC Financial Services Group is a bank holding company that operates businesses engaged in retail banking, corporate and institutional banking, asset management, and global fund processing services. PNC currently has six primary reportable business segments: Retail Banking, Corporate and Institutional Banking, Asset Management, Residential Mortgage Banking, the Distressed Assets Portfolio (largely from NCC), and Other. Effective July 1, 2010, PNC's Global Investment Servicing unit, which until then had been PNC's seventh business segment, was sold to Bank of New York Mellon Corp (BK 26, Buy) for $2.3 billion cash.

IMPACT OF MAJOR DEVELOPMENTS. On December 31, 2008, PNC issued $7.6 billion of Fixed Rate Cumulative Perpetual Preferred Shares, Series N, and a related warrant for common stock to the U.S. Treasury under the U.S. Treasury's Troubled Asset Relief Program (TARP) Capital Purchase Program. As approved by the Federal Reserve Board, the U.S. Treasury and PNC's other

banking regulators, on February 10, 2010, PNC redeemed all 75,792 shares of Series N Preferred Stock held by the U.S. Treasury for $7.6 billion in cash.

In February 2010, PNC issued 63.9 million shares of common stock in an underwritten offering at $54 per share, resulting in a $3.4 billion increase in total shareholders' equity. Common shares outstanding were 526 million at June 30, 2010, up from 462 million at December 31, 2009.

In May 2009, PNC raised $624 million in common equity through the issuance of 15 million shares of common stock.

Company Financials Fiscal Year Ended Dec. 31

Per Share Data ($)	2009	2008	2007	2006	2005	2004	2003	2002	2001	2000
Tangible Book Value	24.50	13.13	15.55	23.02	13.98	14.55	14.22	14.78	12.19	13.37
Earnings	4.36	2.46	4.35	8.73	4.55	4.21	3.65	4.20	1.26	4.09
S&P Core Earnings	2.79	1.83	4.47	8.63	4.43	4.00	3.53	3.83	0.92	NA
Dividends	0.96	2.61	2.44	2.15	2.00	2.00	1.94	1.92	1.92	1.83
Payout Ratio	22%	106%	56%	25%	44%	48%	53%	46%	152%	45%
Prices:High	57.86	87.99	76.41	75.15	65.66	59.79	55.55	62.80	75.81	75.00
Prices:Low	16.20	39.09	63.54	61.78	49.35	48.90	41.63	32.70	51.14	36.00
P/E Ratio:High	13	36	18	9	14	14	15	15	60	18
P/E Ratio:Low	4	16	15	7	11	12	11	8	41	9

Income Statement Analysis (Million $)	2009	2008	2007	2006	2005	2004	2003	2002	2001	2000
Net Interest Income	9,083	3,823	2,915	2,245	2,154	1,969	1,996	2,197	2,262	2,164
Tax Equivalent Adjustment	36.0	36.0	27.0	25.0	33.0	NA	NA	NA	NA	18.0
Non Interest Income	7,934	3,306	3,795	6,534	4,203	3,508	3,141	3,108	2,412	2,871
Loan Loss Provision	3,930	1,517	315	124	21.0	52.0	177	309	903	136
% Expense/Operating Revenue	53.3%	62.0%	64.0%	50.5%	48.6%	68.2%	67.7%	60.8%	71.4%	60.8%
Pretax Income	3,324	1,243	2,094	4,005	1,962	1,745	1,600	1,858	564	1,848
Effective Tax Rate	27.7%	29.0%	29.9%	34.0%	30.8%	30.8%	33.7%	33.4%	33.2%	34.3%
Net Income	2,447	882	1,467	2,595	1,325	1,197	1,029	1,200	377	1,214
% Net Interest Margin	3.82	3.37	3.00	2.92	3.00	3.22	3.64	3.99	3.84	3.64
S&P Core Earnings	1,277	639	1,503	2,565	1,294	1,134	993	1,093	270	NA

Balance Sheet & Other Financial Data (Million $)	2009	2008	2007	2006	2005	2004	2003	2002	2001	2000
Money Market Assets	2,390	1,856	2,729	1,763	350	1,635	50.0	3,658	1,335	1,151
Investment Securities	56,027	43,473	30,225	31,651	23,253	18,609	16,409	17,421	15,243	7,053
Commercial Loans	61,020	99,516	39,956	27,672	26,115	19,418	15,987	22,335	23,134	28,635
Other Loans	96,523	75,973	28,363	22,433	23,821	24,077	18,093	13,115	14,840	21,966
Total Assets	269,863	291,081	138,920	101,820	91,954	79,723	68,168	66,377	69,568	69,844
Demand Deposits	44,384	43,212	19,440	16,070	14,988	12,915	11,505	9,538	10,124	8,490
Time Deposits	142,538	149,653	63,256	50,231	45,287	40,354	33,736	35,444	37,180	39,174
Long Term Debt	26,310	47,087	21,157	10,266	6,797	8,684	7,667	9,112	8,922	7,266
Common Equity	21,968	17,504	14,854	10,788	8,563	7,548	6,735	6,943	5,822	6,649
% Return on Assets	0.9	0.4	1.2	2.7	1.5	1.6	1.5	1.8	0.5	1.7
% Return on Equity	12.4	5.5	11.4	26.8	16.5	16.8	15.0	18.7	5.9	19.0
% Loan Loss Reserve	3.2	2.2	1.2	1.1	1.2	1.3	1.8	1.8	1.5	1.3
% Loans/Deposits	84.3	91.0	79.5	79.1	123.7	84.8	78.4	82.4	89.1	109.6
% Equity to Assets	7.0	7.5	10.7	10.0	9.3	9.7	10.2	9.4	8.9	9.0

Data as orig reptd.; bef. results of disc opers/spec. items. Per share data adj. for stk. divs.; EPS diluted. E-Estimated. NA-Not Available. NM-Not Meaningful. NR-Not Ranked. UR-Under Review.

Office: 249 5th Ave, 1 PNC Plz, Pittsburgh, PA 15222-2707.
Telephone: 412-762-2000.
Email: corporate.communiations@pncbank.com
Website: http://www.pnc.com

Chrmn & CEO: J.E. Rohr
Pres: J.C. Guyaux
EVP & CFO: R.J. Johnson
EVP & General Counsel: H.P. Pudlin

SVP, Chief Acctg Officer & Cntlr: S.R. Patterson
Investor Contact: W. Callihan (800-843-2206)
Board Members: R. O. Berndt, C. E. Bunch, P. W. Chellgren, K. C. James, R. B. Kelson, B. C. Lindsay, A. A. Massaro, J. G. Pepper, J. E. Rohr, D. J. Shepard, L. K. Steffes, D. F. Strigl, S. G. Thieke, T. J. Usher, G. H. Walls, Jr., H. H. Wehmeier

Founded: 1922
Domicile: Pennsylvania
Employees: 55,820

Polo Ralph Lauren Corp

STANDARD & POOR'S

S&P Recommendation	**STRONG BUY** ★★★★★	Price $94.03 (as of Oct 22, 2010)	12-Mo. Target Price $105.00	Investment Style Large-Cap Growth

GICS Sector Consumer Discretionary
Sub-Industry Apparel, Accessories & Luxury Goods

Summary This company designs, markets and distributes men's and women's clothing and other premium lifestyle products.

Key Stock Statistics (Source S&P, Vickers, company reports)

52-Wk Range	$95.98– 71.12	S&P Oper. EPS 2011E	5.11	Market Capitalization(B)	$6.115	Beta	1.55
Trailing 12-Month EPS	$5.18	S&P Oper. EPS 2012E	5.69	Yield (%)	0.43	S&P 3-Yr. Proj. EPS CAGR(%)	10
Trailing 12-Month P/E	18.2	P/E on S&P Oper. EPS 2011E	18.4	Dividend Rate/Share	$0.40	S&P Credit Rating	BBB+
$10K Invested 5 Yrs Ago	$18,276	Common Shares Outstg. (M)	95.9	Institutional Ownership (%)	NM		

Price Performance

30-Week Mov. Avg. · · · · 10-Week Mov. Avg. – – GAAP Earnings vs. Previous Year   Volume Above Avg. STARS
12-Mo. Target Price — Relative Strength   ▲ Up ▼ Down ► No Change   Below Avg. ★

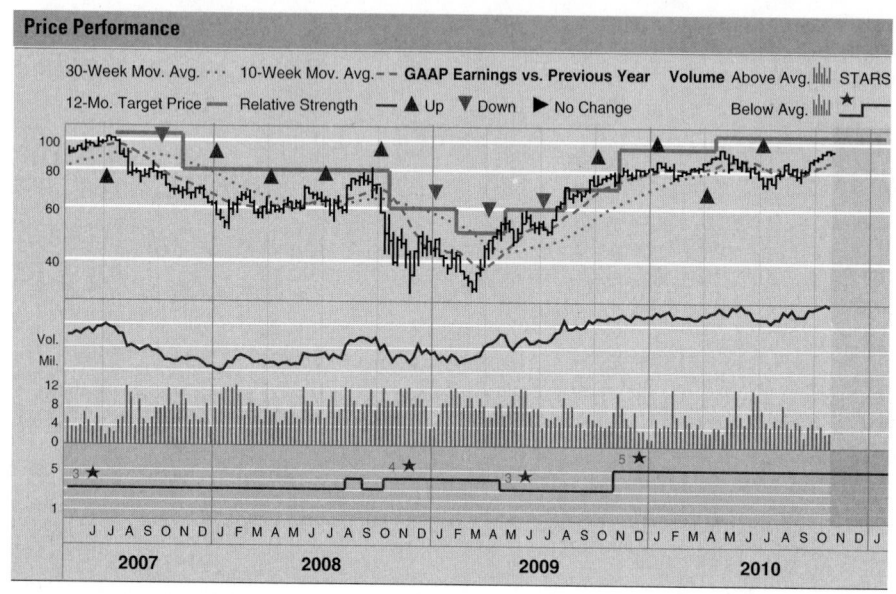

Options: ASE, CBOE, Ph

Analysis prepared by **Marie Driscoll, CFA** on August 13, 2010, when the stock traded at **$ 80.81**.

Highlights

► We believe the global luxury market has stabilized at a pre-2007 level, but is trending positively, with some aspirational shoppers cautiously nibbling. RL, however, is bucking industry dynamics, and its recently reported June quarter results speak to its healthy brand with significant global opportunities. We see incremental growth in FY 11 (Mar.), driven by further extension of the Asian business (brand sales approximate $850 million, concentrated in Japan and South Korea) as RL assumes direct control of South Korea in January 2011, the European ecommerce site launch in October, and domestically, the Lauren handbag launch at 150 better department stores.

► We estimate FY 11 sales of $5.4 billion, up 8.4%, driven by store expansion, a mid-single digit comp store gain and a 20%+ gain in ecommerce. We see retail up 12%, wholesale up 4%, and licensing revenues down 9%.

► We see the EBIT margin flat at 14.2% despite strategic investments internationally and in the direct channel as we see supply chain and sourcing initiatives and well controlled inventories (-4%, excluding the Asian increment in the June quarter) offsetting margin pressure.

Investment Rationale/Risk

► We think geographic expansion and strong brand positioning provide RL with attractive long-term growth opportunities. RL's assumption of direct control of its Southeast Asia business should better align the region with RL's global brand positioning while providing substantial long-term growth opportunities given the strong demographic underpinnings; ultimately RL seeks to have this region comprise a third of sales. As of June 2010, trailing 12-month (TTM) ROE and ROI were 18% and 35%, respectively.

► Risks to our recommendation and target price include integration risk from recent licensee acquisitions, execution risk in Asia, and a sharp decline in consumer discretionary spending. Regarding corporate governance, we are concerned that chairman, CEO and founder Ralph Lauren controls approximately 83% of the voting shares.

► Our 12-month target price of $105 is about 21X our FY 11 EPS estimate of $5.11, in line with the median five-year peer forward multiple. RL added $255 million to its existing share repurchase program, which had $319 million available at the end of the June quarter.

Qualitative Risk Assessment

LOW	**MEDIUM**	HIGH

Our risk assessment reflects our view of RL's strong balance sheet, with $865 million in cash net of debt as of April 3, 2010, offset by its exposure to the consolidating and contracting department store channel.

Quantitative Evaluations

S&P Quality Ranking   A-

D	C	B-	B	B+	**A-**	A	A+

Relative Strength Rank   **STRONG**

75
LOWEST = 1   HIGHEST = 99

Revenue/Earnings Data

Revenue (Million $)

	1Q	2Q	3Q	4Q	Year
2011	1,153	--	--	--	--
2010	1,024	1,374	1,244	1,337	4,979
2009	1,114	1,429	1,252	1,224	5,019
2008	1,070	1,299	1,270	1,241	4,880
2007	953.6	1,167	1,144	1,031	4,295
2006	751.9	964.8	995.5	971.6	3,746

Earnings Per Share ($)

	1Q	2Q	3Q	4Q	Year
2011	1.21	E1.69	E1.24	E0.97	E5.11
2010	0.76	1.75	1.10	1.13	4.73
2009	0.93	1.58	1.05	0.44	4.01
2008	0.82	1.09	1.08	1.00	3.99
2007	0.74	1.28	1.03	0.68	3.73
2006	0.48	0.97	0.84	0.58	2.87

Fiscal year ended Mar. 31. Next earnings report expected: Early November. EPS Estimates based on S&P Operating Earnings; historical GAAP earnings are as reported.

Dividend Data (Dates: mm/dd Payment Date: mm/dd/yy)

Amount ($)	Date Decl.	Ex-Div. Date	Stk. of Record	Payment Date
0.100	11/04	12/22	12/24	01/08/10
0.100	03/22	03/30	04/02	04/16/10
0.100	06/22	06/30	07/02	07/16/10
0.100	09/20	09/29	10/01	10/15/10

Dividends have been paid since 2003. Source: Company reports.

Please read the Required Disclosures and Analyst Certification on the last page of this report.

The **McGraw·Hill** Companies

Polo Ralph Lauren Corp

Business Summary August 13, 2010

CORPORATE OVERVIEW. Since its modest beginnings in men's ties in 1967, Polo Ralph Lauren has grown into one of America's leading lifestyle brands encompassing multiple permutations targeted at specific demographics, usage occasions and price points, with merchandise available at approximately 9,000 retail locations throughout the world. Licensor relationships extend the brand to fragrance, eyewear, jewelry, and an extensive home merchandise offering. All told, we believe the Polo Ralph Lauren brand generates about $12 billion at retail worldwide.

MARKET PROFILE. The domestic men's, women's and children's apparel market represented an estimated $189 billion at retail in 2009, according to NPD Fashionworld consumer estimated data. S&P forecasts a 2% to 3% increase in 2010 apparel sales, which compares with a 5% decline in 2009, a 3% drop in 2008 and 4% increases for both 2006 and 2007. The apparel market is fragmented, with national brands marketed by 20 companies accounting for about 30% of total apparel sales, and the remaining 70% comprised of smaller and/or private label "store" brands. The market is mature, and subject to pricing pressure due to channel competition and production steadily moving offshore to low-cost producers in India, Asia and China.

COMPETITIVE LANDSCAPE. By channel, specialty stores account for the largest share of apparel sales (31% in 2009, according to NPD). Mass merchants (Wal-Mart and Target) came in second, at 22%, and department stores, RL's primary channel, came in third, at 14%, down about 600 basis points since 2003. National chains (Sears and JC Penney) captured 13% of 2009 apparel sales, and off-price retailers (TJX and Ross Stores) 9%. The remaining 11% is divided among factory outlets and direct and e-mail pure plays. RL holds leading market shares in department stores with seven key department stores accounting for about 50% of its wholesale volume and Macy's the largest wholesale account at 19%. RL competes with Jones Apparel Group, Liz Claiborne and VF Corp., as well as private label offerings, which garner about a third of total apparel purchases and are an important differentiator for retailers. RL also sells directly to consumers through 350 specialty retail locations globally as of April 2010 spanning the luxury, mid-market and factory channels and at RalphLauren.com and Rugby.com.

Company Financials Fiscal Year Ended Mar. 31

Per Share Data ($)	2010	2009	2008	2007	2006	2005	2004	2003	2002	2001
Tangible Book Value	18.33	14.41	10.71	11.99	10.35	10.38	10.56	8.93	7.38	5.76
Cash Flow	6.52	5.83	5.90	5.07	4.06	2.83	2.52	2.55	2.60	1.41
Earnings	4.73	4.01	3.99	3.73	2.87	1.83	1.69	1.76	1.75	0.61
S&P Core Earnings	4.73	4.01	3.99	3.75	2.80	2.32	1.53	1.55	1.54	0.44
Dividends	0.30	0.20	0.20	0.20	0.20	0.20	Nil	Nil	Nil	Nil
Payout Ratio	6%	5%	5%	5%	7%	11%	Nil	Nil	Nil	Nil
Calendar Year	2009	2008	2007	2006	2005	2004	2003	2002	2001	2000
Prices:High	83.50	82.02	102.58	83.15	56.84	42.83	31.52	30.82	31.34	23.25
Prices:Low	31.64	31.22	60.41	45.65	34.19	27.28	19.30	16.49	17.80	12.75
P/E Ratio:High	18	20	26	22	20	23	19	18	18	38
P/E Ratio:Low	7	8	15	12	12	15	11	9	10	21

Income Statement Analysis (Million $)										
Revenue	4,979	5,019	4,880	4,295	3,746	3,305	2,650	2,439	2,364	2,226
Operating Income	898	859	860	802	663	406	377	382	393	319
Depreciation	181	184	201	145	127	104	83.2	78.6	83.9	78.6
Interest Expense	22.2	26.6	25.1	21.6	12.5	11.0	10.0	13.5	19.0	25.1
Pretax Income	689	588	644	659	516	298	266	274	276	98.0
Effective Tax Rate	NA	30.9%	34.5%	36.8%	37.7%	36.0%	35.7%	36.5%	37.5%	39.5%
Net Income	480	406	420	401	308	190	171	174	173	59.3
S&P Core Earnings	479	406	420	403	299	242	154	154	151	43.1

Balance Sheet & Other Financial Data (Million $)										
Cash	1,147	820	626	564	286	350	343	344	239	102
Current Assets	2,276	2,057	1,894	1,686	1,379	1,414	1,271	1,166	1,008	902
Total Assets	4,649	4,357	4,366	3,758	2,089	2,727	2,270	2,039	1,749	1,626
Current Liabilities	747	674	909	640	844	622	501	500	392	440
Long Term Debt	282	406	546	399	Nil	291	277	248	285	297
Common Equity	3,117	2,735	2,390	2,335	2,050	1,676	1,422	1,209	998	809
Total Capital	3,399	3,142	2,966	2,734	2,070	1,967	1,699	1,457	1,284	1,106
Capital Expenditures	201	185	217	184	159	174	123	98.7	88.0	105
Cash Flow	661	590	621	546	435	294	254	253	256	138
Current Ratio	3.1	3.1	2.1	2.6	1.6	2.3	2.5	2.3	2.6	2.1
% Long Term Debt of Capitalization	8.3	12.9	18.4	14.6	Nil	14.8	16.3	17.1	22.2	26.8
% Net Income of Revenue	9.6	8.1	8.6	9.3	8.2	5.8	6.5	7.1	7.3	2.7
% Return on Assets	10.7	9.3	10.3	11.7	12.8	7.6	7.9	9.2	10.2	3.7
% Return on Equity	16.4	15.8	17.8	18.3	16.5	12.3	13.0	15.8	19.1	7.5

Data as orig reptd.; bef. results of disc opers/spec. items. Per share data adj. for stk. divs.; EPS diluted. E-Estimated. NA-Not Available. NM-Not Meaningful. NR-Not Ranked. UR-Under Review.

Office: 650 Madison Ave, New York, NY 10022-1062.
Telephone: 212-318-7000.
Website: http://www.ralphlauren.com
Chrmn & CEO: R. Lauren

Pres & COO: R.N. Farah
SVP, CFO & Chief Acctg Officer: T.T. Travis
SVP, Secy & General Counsel: A.S. Fischer
Investor Contact: J. Hurley (212-318-7000)

Board Members: J. R. Alchin, A. H. Aronson, F. A. Bennack, Jr., J. F. Brown, R. N. Farah, J. L. Fleishman, H. Joly, R. Lauren, S. P. Murphy, J. Nemerov, R. C. Wright

Founded: 1967
Domicile: Delaware
Employees: 19,000

PPG Industries Inc.

STANDARD &POOR'S

S&P Recommendation | STRONG BUY ★★★★★ | **Price** $76.43 (as of Oct 22, 2010) | **12-Mo. Target Price** $90.00 | **Investment Style** Large-Cap Blend

GICS Sector Materials
Sub-Industry Diversified Chemicals

Summary This company is a leading manufacturer of coatings and resins, flat and fiber glass, and industrial and specialty chemicals.

Key Stock Statistics (Source S&P, Vickers, company reports)

52-Wk Range	$77.95– 55.89	S&P Oper. EPS 2010E	5.00	Market Capitalization(B)	$12.622	Beta	1.28
Trailing 12-Month EPS	$3.62	S&P Oper. EPS 2011E	5.60	Yield (%)	2.88	S&P 3-Yr. Proj. EPS CAGR(%)	10
Trailing 12-Month P/E	21.1	P/E on S&P Oper. EPS 2010E	15.3	Dividend Rate/Share	$2.20	S&P Credit Rating	BBB+
$10K Invested 5 Yrs Ago	$15,596	Common Shares Outstg. (M)	165.2	Institutional Ownership (%)	72		

Price Performance

30-Week Mov. Avg. · · · · 10-Week Mov. Avg. – - **GAAP Earnings vs. Previous Year** Volume Above Avg. STARS
12-Mo. Target Price — Relative Strength — ▲ Up ▼ Down ► No Change Below Avg. ★

Options: ASE, CBOE, Ph

Analysis prepared by **Richard O'Reilly, CFA** on October 22, 2010, when the stock traded at **$ 76.67.**

Highlights

➤ We expect sales in 2011 to rise about 8%, versus a 9% increase projected for 2010. We think the coatings, silicas, fiberglass and commodity chemicals businesses will continue to be boosted by the stronger global auto, industrial and electronics-related markets, but currency should remain a headwind in the near term.

➤ Optical products sales should continue to rebound in 2011 assuming stronger consumer spending. We forecast that margins for the coatings units will be helped by price increases designed to offset higher raw material costs seen in 2010. We expect commodity chemicals profits to be greater in late 2010 and early 2011 on favorable price comparisons, and see the fiberglass business remaining healthy on strong demand, but flat glass to stay at about breakeven on the downturn in commercial construction activity.

➤ We see the effective tax rate, before special items, staying at 27.0%. Our EPS estimate for 2010 excludes a special tax charge of $0.51.

Investment Rationale/Risk

➤ Our strong buy opinion on the shares is based on our expectation that business conditions will continue to recover in 2011. The purchase of SigmaKalon greatly expanded PPG's less capital intensive coatings business in both size and geographic diversity. We view PPG's liquidity as healthy, with the balance sheet showing more than $900 million of cash at the end of September 2010, which should allow it to consider making acquisitions in coatings while repurchasing common stock.

➤ Risks to our recommendation and target price include slower-than-projected industrial activity, unplanned production outages and interruptions, higher raw materials costs, and unexpected weakness in selling prices for commodity chemicals.

➤ Our 12-month target price of $90 assumes that the stock's forward P/E multiple, based on our EPS estimate for 2011, will expand to its historical average high level of about 16X as a result of the cyclical recovery in earnings that we foresee. The dividend was recently increased for the 39th consecutive year, and the yielded about 50% above the level of the S&P 500.

Qualitative Risk Assessment

LOW	MEDIUM	HIGH

Our risk assessment reflects the company's diversified business mix, large market shares in key products, and what we see as its healthy balance sheet, offset by the cyclical nature of the commodity chemicals business and the auto and construction-related end markets.

Quantitative Evaluations

S&P Quality Ranking B+

D	C	B-	B	B+	A-	A	A+

Relative Strength Rank STRONG

72

LOWEST = 1 HIGHEST = 99

Revenue/Earnings Data

Revenue (Million $)

	1Q	2Q	3Q	4Q	Year
2010	3,126	3,458	--	--	--
2009	2,783	3,115	3,225	3,116	12,239
2008	3,962	4,474	4,225	3,188	15,849
2007	2,917	3,173	2,823	2,874	11,206
2006	2,638	2,824	2,802	2,773	11,037
2005	2,493	2,656	2,547	2,505	10,201

Earnings Per Share ($)

2010	0.18	1.63	E1.02	E1.09	E5.00
2009	-0.68	0.89	0.96	0.85	2.03
2008	0.53	1.51	0.70	0.43	3.25
2007	1.17	1.50	1.29	1.17	4.91
2006	1.11	1.68	0.54	0.94	4.27
2005	0.55	1.34	0.92	0.68	3.49

Fiscal year ended Dec. 31. Next earnings report expected: NA. EPS Estimates based on S&P Operating Earnings; historical GAAP earnings are as reported.

Dividend Data (Dates: mm/dd Payment Date: mm/dd/yy)

Amount ($)	Date Decl.	Ex-Div. Date	Stk. of Record	Payment Date
0.540	01/21	02/17	02/19	03/12/10
0.540	04/15	05/06	05/10	06/11/10
0.550	07/15	08/06	08/10	09/10/10
0.550	10/22	11/08	11/10	12/10/10

Dividends have been paid since 1899. Source: Company reports.

PPG Industries Inc.

STANDARD
&POOR'S

Business Summary October 22, 2010

CORPORATE OVERVIEW. PPG Industries is a diversified producer of coatings, chemicals and glass products. International operations contributed 58% of sales and 47% of operating profits in 2009.

PPG Industries is one of the world's leading producers of protective and decorative coatings. Industrial coatings (25% of sales in 2009 and 13% of operating profits) is comprised of original automotive, industrial (used in appliance and industrial equipment), and packaging (container) coatings. PPG also produces adhesives and sealants for the automotive industry and metal pretreatments.

Performance coatings (34%, 46%) consists of automotive and industrial refinish coatings, aerospace coatings, marine and specialty industrial coatings, and a major North American supplier of architectural coatings (Pittsburgh, Olympic, Porter and Lucite brands). The architectural finishes business at the end of 2009 operated 400 company-owned service centers in North America and 50 stores in Australia. The company is a global supplier of aircraft coatings, sealants, and transparencies to OEM, maintenance and aftermarket customers. The European Architectural coatings (16%, 11%) segment consists of the majority of the sales of the former SigmaKalon acquired in January 2008. The coatings industry is highly competitive and consists of a few large firms

with a global presence and many smaller firms serving local or regional markets.

PPG's commodity chemicals business (10%, 13%) is the fourth largest U.S. producer of chlorine and caustic soda (used in a wide variety of industrial applications), vinyl chloride monomer (for use in polyvinyl chloride resins), calcium hypochlorite, and chlorinated solvents. These commodity chemicals are highly cyclical; PPG's volumes declined 9% in 2009, following increases of 9% and 1% in 2007 and 2008, respectively. The company's electrochemical unit (ECU) average price declined in 2009 after rising 28% in 2008.

Optical and specialty materials (8%, 20%) consists of optical resins (Transitions photochromic lenses, sun lenses, and polarized film), silica compounds, and Teslin synthetic printing sheet. A fine chemicals business was sold in late 2007 (reported as discontinued operations). The optical products business declined in 2009 from 2008, which was aided by the introduction of the newest version of Transitions in early 2008.

Company Financials Fiscal Year Ended Dec. 31

Per Share Data ($)	2009	2008	2007	2006	2005	2004	2003	2002	2001	2000
Tangible Book Value	NM	NM	55.71	7.59	8.46	10.81	7.36	3.49	9.10	8.57
Cash Flow	4.93	6.55	7.20	6.61	5.66	5.66	6.19	1.99	4.93	6.20
Earnings	2.03	3.25	4.91	4.27	3.49	3.95	2.92	-0.36	2.29	3.57
S&P Core Earnings	2.61	2.62	5.28	4.78	4.57	4.42	3.48	1.76	1.17	NA
Dividends	2.13	2.09	2.04	1.91	1.86	1.79	1.73	1.70	1.68	1.60
Payout Ratio	105%	64%	42%	45%	53%	45%	59%	NM	73%	45%
Prices:High	62.31	71.00	82.42	69.80	74.73	68.79	64.42	62.86	59.75	65.06
Prices:Low	28.16	35.94	64.01	56.53	55.64	54.81	42.61	41.39	38.99	36.00
P/E Ratio:High	31	22	17	16	21	17	22	NM	26	18
P/E Ratio:Low	14	11	13	13	16	14	15	NM	17	10

Income Statement Analysis (Million $)										
Revenue	12,239	15,849	11,206	11,037	10,201	9,513	8,756	8,067	8,169	8,629
Operating Income	1,376	1,924	1,698	1,703	1,648	1,496	1,367	1,309	1,371	1,649
Depreciation	480	546	380	380	372	388	394	398	447	447
Interest Expense	193	262	104	83.0	81.0	90.0	107	128	169	161
Pretax Income	617	908	1,243	1,060	947	1,063	843	-28.0	666	1,017
Effective Tax Rate	31.0%	31.3%	28.6%	26.2%	29.8%	30.3%	34.8%	NM	37.1%	36.3%
Net Income	336	538	815	711	596	683	500	-60.0	387	620
S&P Core Earnings	432	434	877	797	780	765	597	300	197	NA

Balance Sheet & Other Financial Data (Million $)										
Cash	1,057	1,021	2,232	455	466	709	499	117	108	111
Current Assets	5,981	6,348	7,136	4,592	4,019	4,054	3,537	2,945	2,703	3,093
Total Assets	14,240	14,698	12,629	10,021	8,681	8,932	8,424	7,863	8,452	9,125
Current Liabilities	3,577	4,210	4,661	2,787	2,349	2,221	2,139	1,920	1,955	2,543
Long Term Debt	3,044	3,009	1,201	1,155	1,169	1,184	1,339	1,699	1,699	1,810
Common Equity	3,753	3,333	4,151	3,234	3,053	3,572	2,911	2,150	3,080	3,097
Total Capital	6,968	6,923	5,649	4,673	4,420	4,997	4,475	4,044	5,453	5,578
Capital Expenditures	239	383	353	372	288	244	217	238	291	561
Cash Flow	816	1,084	1,195	1,091	968	1,071	894	338	834	1,067
Current Ratio	1.7	1.5	1.5	1.6	1.7	1.8	1.7	1.5	1.4	1.2
% Long Term Debt of Capitalization	Nil	43.5	21.3	24.7	26.4	23.7	29.9	42.0	31.2	32.4
% Net Income of Revenue	2.8	3.4	7.8	6.4	5.8	7.2	5.7	NM	4.7	7.2
% Return on Assets	NA	3.9	7.2	7.6	6.8	7.9	6.1	NM	4.4	6.9
% Return on Equity	NA	14.4	22.1	22.6	18.0	21.1	19.8	NM	12.5	20.0

Data as orig reptd.; bef. results of disc opers/spec. items. Per share data adj. for stk. divs.; EPS diluted. E-Estimated. NA-Not Available. NM-Not Meaningful. NR-Not Ranked. UR-Under Review.

Office: 1 PPG Pl, Pittsburgh, PA 15272.
Telephone: 412-434-3131.
Website: http://www.ppg.com
Chrmn & CEO: C.E. Bunch

SVP, CFO & Chief Acctg Officer: R.J. Dellinger
SVP & General Counsel: G.E. Bost, II
CTO: C.F. Kahle, II
Treas: A.S. Giga

Investor Contact: V. Morales (412-434-3740)
Board Members: J. G. Berges, C. E. Bunch, H. Grant, V. F. Haynes, M. J. Hooper, R. Mehrabian, M. H. Richenhagen, R. Ripp, T. J. Usher, D. R. Whitwam

Founded: 1883
Domicile: Pennsylvania
Employees: 39,900

PPL Corp

STANDARD &POOR'S

S&P Recommendation	HOLD ★★★★★	Price $26.91 (as of Oct 22, 2010)	12-Mo. Target Price $28.00	Investment Style Large-Cap Blend

GICS Sector Utilities
Sub-Industry Electric Utilities

Summary This holding company for PPL Utilities and a utility in the U.K. has agreed to acquire the holding company for Louisville Gas & Electric and Kentucky Utilities.

Key Stock Statistics (Source S&P, Vickers, company reports)

52-Wk Range	$33.05–23.75	S&P Oper. EPS 2010**E**	2.89	Market Capitalization(B)	$12.990	Beta	0.45
Trailing 12-Month EPS	$1.34	S&P Oper. EPS 2011**E**	2.51	Yield (%)	5.20	S&P 3-Yr. Proj. EPS CAGR(%)	16
Trailing 12-Month P/E	20.1	P/E on S&P Oper. EPS 2010**E**	9.3	Dividend Rate/Share	$1.40	S&P Credit Rating	BBB
$10K Invested 5 Yrs Ago	$10,941	Common Shares Outstg. (M)	482.7	Institutional Ownership (%)	70		

Price Performance

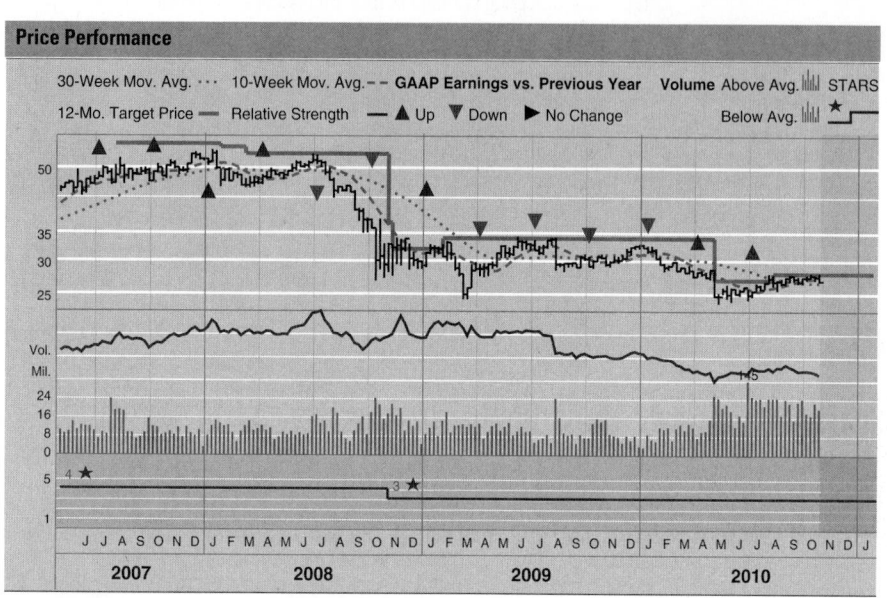

30-Week Mov. Avg. · · · 10-Week Mov. Avg. - - **GAAP Earnings vs. Previous Year** Volume Above Avg. STARS
12-Mo. Target Price — Relative Strength — ▲ Up ▼ Down ▶ No Change Below Avg.

Options: CBOE, P, Ph

Analysis prepared by **Justin McCann** on August 10, 2010, when the stock traded at **$ 26.40**.

Highlights

➤ Subject to required approvals, we expect PPL's acquisition of the holding company for the Kentucky-headquartered utilities LG&E and KU to close by the end of 2010. We expect it to be modestly dilutive in the first full year following its completion and not accretive until 2013.

➤ Excluding $0.68 of one-time charges, we expect operating EPS in 2010 to grow nearly 50% from 2009's $1.95, which was before $0.87 of net one-time charges. We expect sharply higher earnings in the power supply segment, as expired energy contracts were replaced by higher-margin contracts. We believe this will be partially offset by lower earnings from the Pennsylvania and International delivery segments. We expect the power supply segment to earn about $2.10 a share in 2010 (compared to $0.88 in 2009), the Pennsylvania delivery segment around $0.25 ($0.35), and the International delivery segment about $0.54 ($0.72).

➤ For 2011, we expect operating EPS to decline about 13% from anticipated results in 2010, largely reflecting a full year of the 103.5 million new shares issued at the end of June 2010.

Investment Rationale/Risk

➤ After a 5.3% increase in 2009, the shares are down about 18% year to date. The shares fell more than 13% during the week PPL announced its agreement to acquire the Kentucky utilities, which is not expected to be accretive until 2013. Earlier this year, the shares had been hurt, in our view, by the weakness in the power markets and by the investor shift away from utility stocks. In 2009, the stock had recovered about 22% from its year low, reflecting, we think, the recovery in the broader market and the increased market focus on the strong earnings advance projected for 2010.

➤ Risks to our recommendation and target price include potentially unfavorable regulatory rulings, significantly lower results from the unregulated operations, and a major shift in the average P/E multiple of the peer group as a whole.

➤ Our 12-month target price is $28. While we expect PPL's earnings to improve significantly in 2010, we believe the shares will continue to reflect the still depressed state of the wholesale power markets and trade at a discount-to-peers P/E of 11.2X our 2011 EPS estimate.

Qualitative Risk Assessment

LOW	MEDIUM	HIGH

Our risk assessment reflects the steady cash flow we expect from the regulated Pennsylvania and U.K. distribution segments, which operate within supportive regulatory environments. This is offset by the highly profitable but less predictable earnings and cash flow from the power supply segment, as well as the currency risks related to the U.K. and Latin American businesses.

Quantitative Evaluations

S&P Quality Ranking A-

D	C	B-	B	B+	A-	A	A+

Relative Strength Rank WEAK

27

LOWEST = 1   HIGHEST = 99

Revenue/Earnings Data

Revenue (Million $)

	1Q	2Q	3Q	4Q	Year
2010	3,033	1,503	--	--	--
2009	2,359	1,673	1,805	1,727	7,556
2008	1,526	1,024	2,981	2,513	8,044
2007	1,638	1,613	1,763	1,606	6,498
2006	1,781	1,642	1,752	1,724	6,899
2005	1,602	1,476	1,643	1,498	6,219

Earnings Per Share ($)

2010	0.66	0.22	E0.79	E0.56	E2.89
2009	0.64	0.07	0.12	0.37	1.18
2008	0.65	0.50	0.55	0.74	2.45
2007	0.58	0.63	0.72	0.57	2.63
2006	0.73	0.52	0.58	0.47	2.29
2005	0.44	0.47	0.51	0.50	1.92

Fiscal year ended Dec. 31. Next earnings report expected: Late October. EPS Estimates based on S&P Operating Earnings; historical GAAP earnings are as reported.

Dividend Data (Dates: mm/dd Payment Date: mm/dd/yy)

Amount ($)	Date Decl.	Ex-Div. Date	Stk. of Record	Payment Date
0.345	11/20	12/08	12/10	01/01/10
0.350	02/26	03/08	03/10	04/01/10
0.350	05/19	06/08	06/10	07/01/10
0.350	08/27	09/08	09/10	10/01/10

Dividends have been paid since 1946. Source: Company reports.

PPL Corp

STANDARD &POOR'S

Business Summary August 10, 2010

CORPORATE OVERVIEW. PPL Corporation is an energy and utility holding company organized into three operating segments: the supply segment, the Pennsylvania delivery segment, and the international delivery segment. PPL's subsidiaries PPL Generation and PPL EnergyPlus comprise the supply segment. These units are involved in electricity generation and marketing of electricity and other power purchases to deregulated wholesale and retail markets. The Pennsylvania delivery segment operates through its PPL Electric subsidiary, which provides electric utility services in the regulated Pennsylvania market. In October 2008, PPL completed the sale of its natural gas distribution unit PPL Gas Utilities and its propane unit Penn Fuel Propane for proceeds of $303 million.

IMPACT OF MAJOR DEVELOPMENTS. On April 28, 2010, PPL announced a definitive agreement under which it would acquire, for $7.625 billion, E.ON U.S. LLC, the parent company of Kentucky's two major utilities, Louisville Gas & Electric Company (LG&E) and Kentucky Utilities Company (KU). LG&E and KU, which have combined power generating capacity of about 8,000 megawatts (mw), provide electricity service to 941,000 customers, mostly in Kentucky, with some customers in Virginia and Tennessee. LG&E also provides natural gas delivery service to 321,000 customers in Kentucky. PPL will pay for the

transaction with $6.7 billion of cash and through the assumption of $925 million of tax-exempt debt. Including the projected tax benefits with a present value of approximately $450 million, the company has effectively valued the transaction at $7.125 billion. Subject to required approvals, the transaction is expected to close by the end of 2010.

CORPORATE STRATEGY. The company's business strategy is to achieve stable growth in the regulated delivery business. It plans to achieve long-term growth in delivery through efficient and low-cost operations while working to enhance strong customer and regulatory relations. In the unregulated supply business, PPL intends to reduce the volatility in both its cash flows and earnings and to ensure disciplined growth. The company's strategy for its electricity generation and marketing business is to build an effective risk management framework to handle energy price risk and counterparty risk. It will work to reduce risk by entering into supply contracts of varying duration, which should reflect fluctuations in demand.

Company Financials Fiscal Year Ended Dec. 31

Per Share Data ($)	2009	2008	2007	2006	2005	2004	2003	2002	2001	2000
Tangible Book Value	10.80	9.93	11.33	9.35	7.73	7.50	5.53	5.87	6.98	6.65
Earnings	1.18	2.45	2.63	2.29	1.92	1.89	2.08	1.17	0.58	1.68
S&P Core Earnings	1.23	1.86	2.61	2.33	1.87	1.74	1.95	0.79	0.90	NA
Dividends	1.38	1.34	1.22	1.10	1.21	0.82	0.77	0.68	0.53	0.53
Payout Ratio	117%	55%	47%	48%	63%	43%	37%	57%	92%	32%
Prices:High	34.42	55.23	54.58	37.34	33.68	27.08	22.17	19.98	31.18	23.06
Prices:Low	24.25	26.84	34.43	27.83	25.52	19.92	15.83	13.00	15.50	9.19
P/E Ratio:High	29	23	21	16	18	14	11	17	54	14
P/E Ratio:Low	21	11	13	12	13	11	8	11	27	5

Income Statement Analysis (Million $)	2009	2008	2007	2006	2005	2004	2003	2002	2001	2000
Revenue	7,556	8,044	6,498	6,899	6,219	5,812	5,587	5,429	5,725	5,683
Depreciation	556	551	756	446	420	412	380	367	254	261
Maintenance	NA	NA	NA	NA	NA	NA	NA	314	269	261
Fixed Charges Coverage	2.60	3.86	3.61	3.46	2.70	2.72	2.72	2.49	3.08	2.95
Construction Credits	NA	NA	NA	NA	NA	NA	NA	NA	NA	NA
Effective Tax Rate	21.8%	32.3%	20.7%	23.5%	14.0%	21.6%	18.5%	29.5%	54.4%	36.3%
Net Income	447	922	1,013	885	737	700	748	425	221	513
S&P Core Earnings	466	705	1,007	897	716	645	674	240	262	NA

Balance Sheet & Other Financial Data (Million $)	2009	2008	2007	2006	2005	2004	2003	2002	2001	2000
Gross Property	21,385	20,299	20,377	20,079	18,615	18,692	17,775	16,406	12,477	11,418
Capital Expenditures	1,225	1,429	1,685	1,394	811	703	771	648	565	460
Net Property	13,174	12,416	12,605	12,069	10,916	11,209	10,446	9,566	6,135	5,948
Capitalization:Long Term Debt	7,143	7,151	6,890	6,728	6,044	6,881	8,145	6,562	5,906	4,717
Capitalization:% Long Term Debt	55.2	57.1	54.1	55.4	57.5	61.6	71.1	74.0	75.3	69.1
Capitalization:Preferred	301	301	301	301	51.0	51.0	51.0	82.0	82.0	97.0
Capitalization:% Preferred	2.30	2.40	2.40	2.50	0.50	0.46	0.45	0.92	1.05	1.42
Capitalization:Common	5,496	5,077	5,556	5,122	4,418	4,239	3,259	2,224	1,857	2,012
Capitalization:% Common	42.5	40.5	43.5	42.1	42.0	37.9	28.5	25.1	23.7	29.5
Total Capital	12,958	14,311	14,958	14,241	12,766	13,653	13,710	11,274	9,332	6,880
% Operating Ratio	89.0	82.9	78.3	80.8	80.3	79.5	78.9	76.8	81.1	84.0
% Earned on Net Property	7.5	14.5	13.6	13.9	12.2	12.7	13.4	17.5	14.2	28.6
% Return on Revenue	5.9	11.5	15.6	12.8	11.9	12.0	13.4	7.8	3.9	9.0
% Return on Invested Capital	6.9	9.6	12.1	12.1	10.3	9.5	9.0	10.0	12.6	12.4	14.3
% Return on Common Equity	8.5	17.3	19.0	18.6	17.0	18.6	26.2	17.5	8.7	28.3

Data as orig reptd.; bef. results of disc opers/spec. items. Per share data adj. for stk. divs.; EPS diluted. E-Estimated. NA-Not Available. NM-Not Meaningful. NR-Not Ranked. UR-Under Review.

Office: 2 N 9th St, Allentown, PA, USA 18101-1170.
Telephone: 610-774-5151.
Email: invrel@pplweb.com
Website: http://www.pplweb.com

Chrmn, Pres & CEO: J.H. Miller
COO & EVP: W.H. Spence
EVP & CFO: P. Farr
SVP, Secy & General Counsel: R.J. Grey

Treas: J.E. Abel
Investor Contact: T.J. Paukovits (610-774-4124)
Board Members: F. Bernthal, J. W. Conway, E. A. Deaver, L. Goeser, S. E. Graham, S. Heydt, J. H. Miller, C. A. Rogerson, N. Von Althann, K. H. Williamson

Founded: 1920
Domicile: Pennsylvania
Employees: 10,489

The McGraw-Hill Companies

Praxair Inc.

STANDARD &POOR'S

S&P Recommendation	**HOLD** ★★★☆☆	Price $92.18 (as of Oct 22, 2010)	12-Mo. Target Price $90.00	Investment Style Large-Cap Growth

GICS Sector Materials
Sub-Industry Industrial Gases

Summary This company is the largest producer of industrial gases in North and South America, and the second largest worldwide. It also provides ceramic and metallic coatings.

Key Stock Statistics (Source S&P, Vickers, company reports)

52-Wk Range	$92.95–72.70	S&P Oper. EPS 2010**E**	4.65	Market Capitalization(B)	$28.213	Beta	0.90
Trailing 12-Month EPS	$4.33	S&P Oper. EPS 2011**E**	5.00	Yield (%)	1.95	S&P 3-Yr. Proj. EPS CAGR(%)	10
Trailing 12-Month P/E	21.3	P/E on S&P Oper. EPS 2010**E**	19.8	Dividend Rate/Share	$1.80	S&P Credit Rating	A
$10K Invested 5 Yrs Ago	$21,632	Common Shares Outstg. (M)	306.1	Institutional Ownership (%)	87		

Price Performance

30-Week Mov. Avg. · · · 10-Week Mov. Avg. – – **GAAP Earnings vs. Previous Year** Volume Above Avg. ▥▥ STARS
12-Mo. Target Price — Relative Strength — ▲ Up ▼ Down ▶ No Change Below Avg. ▥▥ ★

Analysis prepared by **Richard O'Reilly, CFA** on August 03, 2010, when the stock traded at **$ 87.80**.

Options: ASE, CBOE, Ph

Highlights

➤ We expect sales to rebound by about 12% in 2010 after a decline of 17% in 2009, on stronger global demand for industrial gases from strengthening manufacturing markets, start-ups of new projects and applications, and about 2% from favorable currency exchange rates. Underlying sales (excluding currency and the pass-through of energy costs) were 8% lower in 2009, but have increased sequentially quarterly since mid-2009.

➤ We look for Surface Technologies' sales (6% of total) to be stronger in the second half of 2010 on expected greater demand for coatings services for industrial equipment and jet engines.

➤ We forecast that operating margins in 2010 will be about 21.5%, up from the record 21.0% in 2009, on the volumes leverage and cost and productivity improvements since late 2008 and despite the adverse impact from the pass-through of higher energy costs. We expect increased interest expense in 2010 on higher average rates, and an effective tax rate of 28% in 2010, versus 27.6% in 2009. Our EPS estimate for 2010 excludes an $0.08 charge in the first quarter resulting from Venezuela currency exchange.

Investment Rationale/Risk

➤ Our hold opinion is based on valuation, as the shares were recently trading at 19X our 2010 EPS estimate of $4.65. We believe the global manufacturing sector is now showing continued sequential recovery, which should result in strengthening demand for industrial gases. The scheduled start-up through 2012 of new gases plants will also contribute to revenue growth over the next few years.

➤ Risks to our recommendation and target price include an unexpected decline in industrial activity, especially in general manufacturing and metal-related markets; higher-than-projected power and natural gas costs; and, an inability to rapidly develop and successfully introduce new products and applications for industrial gases.

➤ Our 12-month target price of $90 assumes a modest widening of the multiple to a peer-level 19.5X, reflecting our view of the company's improved EPS outlook. The quarterly dividend was raised in early 2010 for the 17th consecutive year.

Qualitative Risk Assessment

LOW	**MEDIUM**	HIGH

Our risk assessment reflects the relatively stable growth and cash flow of the industrial gases industry versus commodity chemicals, and PX's superior S&P Quality Ranking of A+, offset by the company's exposure to volatile energy costs.

Quantitative Evaluations

S&P Quality Ranking A+

D	C	B-	B	B+	A-	A	**A+**

Relative Strength Rank MODERATE

61

LOWEST = 1 · HIGHEST = 99

Revenue/Earnings Data

Revenue (Million $)

	1Q	2Q	3Q	4Q	Year
2010	2,428	2,527	--	--	--
2009	2,123	2,138	2,288	2,407	8,956
2008	2,663	2,878	2,852	2,403	10,796
2007	2,175	2,332	2,372	2,523	9,402
2006	2,026	2,076	2,099	2,123	8,324
2005	1,827	1,919	1,890	2,020	7,656

Earnings Per Share ($)

	1Q	2Q	3Q	4Q	Year
2010	1.01	1.19	E1.16	E1.21	E4.65
2009	0.93	0.96	1.04	1.09	4.01
2008	0.96	1.08	1.11	0.64	3.80
2007	0.81	0.89	0.94	0.98	3.62
2006	0.68	0.75	0.75	0.82	3.00
2005	0.59	0.63	0.33	0.67	2.22

Fiscal year ended Dec. 31. Next earnings report expected: Late October. EPS Estimates based on S&P Operating Earnings; historical GAAP earnings are as reported.

Dividend Data (Dates: mm/dd Payment Date: mm/dd/yy)

Amount ($)	Date Decl.	Ex-Div. Date	Stk. of Record	Payment Date
0.400	10/28	12/03	12/07	12/15/09
0.450	01/27	03/03	03/05	03/15/10
0.450	04/28	06/03	06/07	06/15/10
0.450	07/28	09/02	09/07	09/15/10

Dividends have been paid since 1992. Source: Company reports.

Please read the Required Disclosures and Analyst Certification on the last page of this report.

The McGraw·Hill Companies

Praxair Inc.

Business Summary August 03, 2010

CORPORATE OVERVIEW. Since its 1992 spin-off from Union Carbide Corp., Praxair Inc. (PX), the largest producer of industrial gases in North and South America, has expanded its operations more than 30 countries. Foreign sales accounted for 59% of the total in 2009, with Brazil alone providing 15%.

PX conducts its industrial gases business through four operating segments: North America (52% of sales and 56% of profits in 2009); South America (18%, 19%); Europe (14%,14%); and Asia (10%, 7%). The capital-intensive industrial gases business involves the production, distribution and sale of atmospheric gases (oxygen, nitrogen, argon and rare gases), carbon dioxide, hydrogen, helium, acetylene, and specialty and electronic gases. Atmospheric gases are produced through air separation processes, primarily cryogenic, while other gases are produced by various methods. PX also produces specialty products (sputtering targets, mechanical planarization slurries and polishing pads, and coatings) for use in semiconductor manufacturing. In addition, the business includes the construction and sale of equipment to produce industrial gases.

Industrial gases are supplied to customers through three basic methods: on-site/pipeline (24% of total 2009 sales, sold under long-term contracts), merchant (29%, with three- to five-year contracts) and packaged (31%). At the end of 2009, the company had 250 major production facilities (air separation, hydrogen and carbon dioxide plants) in North America and five major pipeline complexes; more than 50 facilities and three pipeline complexes in Europe; more than 40 plants in South America, primarily in Brazil; and more than 25 plants in Asia, mainly in China, Korea and India. S.A. White Martins is the largest producer of industrial gases in South America.

The Surface Technologies business (6%, 4%) applies metallic and ceramic coatings and powders to parts and equipment provided by customers, including aircraft engine, printing, power generation and other industrial markets, and manufactures electric arc, plasma and oxygen fuel spray equipment.

Company Financials Fiscal Year Ended Dec. 31

Per Share Data ($)	2009	2008	2007	2006	2005	2004	2003	2002	2001	2000
Tangible Book Value	10.12	6.45	9.64	8.91	7.05	6.08	6.00	4.03	7.59	3.97
Cash Flow	6.72	6.48	6.01	5.12	4.23	3.85	3.33	3.12	2.84	2.59
Earnings	4.01	3.80	3.62	3.00	2.22	2.10	1.77	1.66	1.32	1.13
S&P Core Earnings	4.62	3.60	3.55	2.99	2.16	2.02	1.67	1.38	1.04	NA
Dividends	1.60	1.50	1.20	1.00	0.72	0.60	0.46	0.38	0.34	0.31
Payout Ratio	40%	39%	33%	33%	32%	29%	26%	23%	26%	28%
Prices:High	86.07	99.74	92.12	63.70	54.31	46.25	38.26	30.56	27.96	27.47
Prices:Low	53.35	4740	57.97	50.36	41.06	34.52	25.02	22.28	18.25	15.16
P/E Ratio:High	21	26	25	21	24	22	22	18	21	24
P/E Ratio:Low	13	12	16	17	18	16	14	13	14	13

Income Statement Analysis (Million $)										
Revenue	8,956	10,796	9,402	8,324	7,656	6,594	5,613	5,128	5,158	5,043
Operating Income	2,449	2,892	2,557	2,183	1,948	1,681	1,444	1,358	1,333	1,220
Depreciation	846	850	774	696	665	578	517	483	499	471
Interest Expense	138	247	208	155	163	155	151	206	224	224
Pretax Income	1,466	1,721	1,639	1,312	1,145	959	735	726	585	493
Effective Tax Rate	11.5%	27.0%	25.6%	27.1%	32.8%	24.2%	23.7%	21.8%	23.1%	20.9%
Net Income	1,254	1,211	1,177	988	732	697	585	548	432	363
S&P Core Earnings	1,441	1,145	1,154	983	711	671	552	454	343	NA

Balance Sheet & Other Financial Data (Million $)										
Cash	45.0	32.0	17.0	36.0	173	25.0	50.0	39.0	39.0	31.0
Current Assets	2,223	2,301	2,408	2,059	2,133	1,744	1,449	1,286	1,276	1,361
Total Assets	14,317	13,054	13,382	11,102	10,491	9,878	8,305	7,401	7,715	7,762
Current Liabilities	1,813	2,979	2,650	1,758	2,001	1,875	1,117	1,100	1,194	1,439
Long Term Debt	4,757	3,709	3,364	2,981	2,926	2,876	2,661	2,510	2,725	2,641
Common Equity	5,315	4,009	5,142	4,554	3,902	3,608	3,088	2,340	2,477	2,357
Total Capital	10,476	8,551	8,506	7,757	6,828	6,709	5,944	5,014	5,363	5,156
Capital Expenditures	1,352	1,611	1,376	1,100	877	668	983	498	595	704
Cash Flow	2,100	2,061	1,951	1,684	1,397	1,275	1,102	1,031	931	834
Current Ratio	1.2	0.8	0.9	1.2	1.1	0.9	1.3	1.2	1.1	0.9
% Long Term Debt of Capitalization	45.4	43.4	39.5	38.4	42.9	42.9	44.8	50.1	50.8	51.2
% Net Income of Revenue	14.0	11.2	12.5	11.9	9.6	10.6	10.4	10.7	8.4	7.2
% Return on Assets	9.2	9.2	9.6	9.2	7.2	7.7	7.4	7.3	5.6	4.7
% Return on Equity	26.9	26.5	24.3	23.4	19.5	20.8	21.6	22.8	17.9	15.6

Data as orig reptd.; bef. results of disc opers/spec. items. Per share data adj. for stk. divs.; EPS diluted. E-Estimated. NA-Not Available. NM-Not Meaningful. NR-Not Ranked. UR-Under Review.

Office: 39 Old Ridgebury Rd, Danbury, CT 06810-5113.
Telephone: 203-837-2000.
Website: http://www.praxair.com
Chrmn, Pres & CEO: S.F. Angel

EVP & CFO: J.S. Sawyer
SVP & CTO: R.P. Roberge
SVP, Secy & General Counsel: J.T. Breedlove
Chief Acctg Officer & Treas: M.J. White

Investor Contact: E.T. Hirsch (203-837-2354)
Board Members: S. F. Angel, O. D. Bernardes, N. K. Dicciani, E. G. Galante, C. W. Gargalli, I. D. Hall, R. W. Leboeuf, L. D. McVay, W. T. Smith, R. L. Wood

Founded: 1988
Domicile: Delaware
Employees: 26,164

Precision Castparts Corp.

STANDARD &POOR'S

S&P Recommendation STRONG BUY ★★★★★	**Price** $139.52 (as of Oct 22, 2010)	**12-Mo. Target Price** $160.00	**Investment Style** Large-Cap Growth

GICS Sector Industrials
Sub-Industry Aerospace & Defense

Summary This company is a provider of complex metal components used primarily in the manufacture of jet engines and industrial gas turbines, and in the oil and gas, chemicals and automotive industries.

Key Stock Statistics (Source S&P, Vickers, company reports)

52-Wk Range	$140.63– 93.00	S&P Oper. EPS 2011**E**	7.10	Market Capitalization(B)	$19.846	Beta	1.57
Trailing 12-Month EPS	$6.42	S&P Oper. EPS 2012**E**	8.50	Yield (%)	0.09	S&P 3-Yr. Proj. EPS CAGR(%)	12
Trailing 12-Month P/E	21.7	P/E on S&P Oper. EPS 2011**E**	19.7	Dividend Rate/Share	$0.12	S&P Credit Rating	A-
$10K Invested 5 Yrs Ago	$29,323	Common Shares Outstg. (M)	142.2	Institutional Ownership (%)	89		

Price Performance

30-Week Mov. Avg. ··· 10-Week Mov. Avg. - - **GAAP Earnings vs. Previous Year** Volume Above Avg. ▮▮▮ STARS
12-Mo. Target Price — Relative Strength — ▲ Up ▼ Down ► No Change Below Avg. ▮▮▮ ★

Options: ASE, CBOE, Ph

Highlights

➤ The 12-month target price for PCP has recently been changed to $160.00 from $146.00. The Highlights section of this Stock Report will be updated accordingly.

Investment Rationale/Risk

➤ The Investment Rationale/Risk section of this Stock Report will be updated shortly. For the latest News story on PCP from MarketScope, see below.

➤ 10/21/10 11:33 am ET ... S&P MAINTAINS STRONG BUY RECOMMENDATION ON SHARES OF PRECISION CASTPARTS (PCP 138.36*****): Sep-Q EPS of $1.70, vs. $1.54, is $0.06 above our estimate, as sales rose 17%, vs. our 7% forecast. PCP sees demand for 787 pushed out 1 quarter, to begin in Mar-Q, so we lower our FY 11 (Mar) EPS estimate $0.20 to $7.10, but increase FY 12's by $0.20 to $8.50. We also raise our target price by $14 to $160, or 11X our FY 12 EBITDA estimate, on our strong sales outlook and view of cont'd cost containment. We see 3 trends supporting earnings growth: the 787 production ramp; A320, 737, and 777 production rate increases; global economic improvement aiding industrial and IGT demand. /R.Tortoriello

Qualitative Risk Assessment

LOW	MEDIUM	HIGH

Precision Castparts operates in a cyclical and capital-intensive industry and is subject to swings in commodity prices. However, due to PCP's large market share in most markets, we believe the company has significant pricing power for its products. We also consider its financial condition to be solid, including a relatively low debt level (total debt was 4% of capital as of June 2010).

Quantitative Evaluations

S&P Quality Ranking   **B**

D	C	B-	B	B+	A-	A	A+

Relative Strength Rank   **STRONG**

85

LOWEST = 1   HIGHEST = 99

Revenue/Earnings Data

Revenue (Million $)

	1Q	2Q	3Q	4Q	Year
2011	1,447	--	--	--	--
2010	1,376	1,298	1,372	1,441	5,487
2009	1,810	1,799	1,615	1,604	6,828
2008	1,660	1,727	1,697	1,791	6,852
2007	1,112	1,318	1,385	1,547	5,361
2006	854.6	874.9	864.4	952.6	3,546

Earnings Per Share ($)

	1Q	2Q	3Q	4Q	Year
2011	1.65	E1.70	E1.83	E1.92	E7.10
2010	1.70	1.54	1.61	1.66	6.50
2009	1.94	1.88	1.69	1.87	7.38
2008	1.61	1.67	1.73	1.88	6.89
2007	0.83	1.03	1.15	1.44	4.45
2006	0.58	0.60	0.67	0.74	2.57

Fiscal year ended Mar. 31. Next earnings report expected: NA.
EPS Estimates based on S&P Operating Earnings; historical GAAP earnings are as reported.

Dividend Data (Dates: mm/dd Payment Date: mm/dd/yy)

Amount ($)	Date Decl.	Ex-Div. Date	Stk. of Record	Payment Date
0.030	11/12	12/02	12/04	12/28/09
0.030	02/11	03/03	03/05	03/29/10
0.030	05/20	06/02	06/04	06/28/10
0.030	08/11	09/01	09/03	09/27/10

Dividends have been paid since 1978. Source: Company reports.

Please read the Required Disclosures and Analyst Certification on the last page of this report.

The McGraw·Hill Companies

Precision Castparts Corp.

STANDARD &POOR'S

Business Summary August 20, 2010

CORPORATE OVERVIEW. Precision Castparts, a manufacturer of jet engine and industrial gas turbine (IGT) engine components, conducts business through three operating units. The aerospace market accounted for 54% of FY 10 (Mar.) sales, power generation for 27%, and general industrial and automotive for the remaining 19%. General Electric accounted for 14% of FY 10 sales. Although no other customer accounted for more than 10% of sales, the Pratt & Whitney division of United Technologies, Rolls-Royce and Boeing are all key customers.

PCP's Investment Cast Products segment (34% and 36% of FY 10 revenues and operating earnings, respectively) includes Aerospace Structural Castings, Aerospace Airfoil Castings, IGT Castings, and the Specialty Materials and Alloys Group (SMAG). These operations manufacture investment castings for aircraft engines, IGT engines, and airframes. PCP also makes metal castings for medical prostheses, unmanned aerial vehicles, satellites, and armament systems (such as howitzers). Investment casting involves a technical, multi-step process that uses ceramic molds in the manufacture of metal components with more complex shapes, closer tolerances and finer surface finishes than parts manufactured using other casting methods. PCP is the world's largest maker of jet engine structural castings used to strengthen sections of a jet engine, and makes castings for every jet engine program in production or

under development. It is also the leading supplier of investment casts for industrial gas turbine (IGT) engines, used in power generation. The company emphasizes low-cost, high-quality products and timely delivery. SMAG principally provides metal alloys to the company's investment casting operations, as well as to other companies with investment casting or other foundry operations.

The Forged Products segment (41% and 35%) is a large maker of forged components for the aerospace and power generation markets. Forged Products segment aerospace and IGT sales are primarily derived from the same large engine customers served by the Investment Cast segment, with additional aerospace sales to manufacturers of landing gear and airframes. In addition, Forged Products manufactures high performance nickel-based alloys used to produce forged components for aerospace and non-aerospace markets, which includes products for oil and gas, chemical processing and pollution control applications.

Company Financials Fiscal Year Ended Mar. 31

Per Share Data ($)	2010	2009	2008	2007	2006	2005	2004	2003	2002	2001
Tangible Book Value	18.13	16.42	12.28	5.37	3.56	1.51	0.62	0.74	NM	NM
Cash Flow	7.60	8.37	7.81	5.27	3.30	2.53	1.73	2.28	1.37	2.23
Earnings	6.51	7.38	6.89	4.45	2.57	1.80	1.18	1.51	0.41	1.23
S&P Core Earnings	6.49	6.95	6.87	4.47	2.51	1.79	1.21	1.17	0.63	1.22
Dividends	0.12	0.12	0.12	0.11	0.06	0.06	0.06	0.06	0.06	0.06
Payout Ratio	2%	2%	2%	2%	2%	3%	5%	4%	15%	5%
Calendar Year	2009	2008	2007	2006	2005	2004	2003	2002	2001	2000
Prices:High	115.60	142.94	160.73	80.90	53.91	34.19	22.97	19.00	24.75	22.78
Prices:Low	47.71	47.08	77.51	48.80	31.15	20.68	10.61	8.43	9.00	5.92
P/E Ratio:High	18	19	23	18	21	19	19	13	61	19
P/E Ratio:Low	7	6	11	11	12	11	9	6	22	5

Income Statement Analysis (Million $)										
Revenue	5,487	6,828	6,852	5,361	3,546	2,919	2,175	2,117	2,557	2,326
Operating Income	1,576	1,739	1,639	1,086	656	517	380	390	448	401
Depreciation	155	139	128	113	99.2	97.0	88.2	82.5	101	102
Interest Expense	16.2	18.1	81.0	52.2	41.4	56.6	54.1	56.4	66.2	81.0
Pretax Income	1,411	1,578	1,463	918	513	360	212	242	135	209
Effective Tax Rate	34.4%	34.2%	33.9%	33.2%	31.6%	33.7%	35.7%	34.5%	68.6%	40.1%
Net Income	924	1,038	966	615	349	240	136	159	42.4	125
S&P Core Earnings	924	978	963	618	341	237	140	123	65.4	124

Balance Sheet & Other Financial Data (Million $)										
Cash	112	554	221	150	59.9	154	80.3	28.7	38.1	40.1
Current Assets	2,522	2,785	2,372	2,037	1,234	1,213	1,188	786	878	863
Total Assets	7,661	6,721	6,050	5,259	3,751	3,625	3,756	2,467	2,565	2,573
Current Liabilities	894	1,061	1,205	1,658	768	780	913	625	727	657
Long Term Debt	235	251	335	319	600	799	823	532	697	838
Common Equity	5,889	4,860	4,045	2,836	2,244	1,780	1,715	1,062	952	902
Total Capital	6,142	5,222	4,400	3,182	2,844	2,579	2,538	1,594	1,649	1,740
Capital Expenditures	170	205	226	222	99.2	61.7	65.5	70.5	125	90.2
Cash Flow	1,080	1,177	1,094	727	448	337	224	242	143	227
Current Ratio	2.8	2.6	2.0	1.2	1.6	1.6	1.3	1.3	1.2	1.3
% Long Term Debt of Capitalization	Nil	4.8	7.6	10.0	21.1	31.0	32.4	33.4	42.3	48.2
% Net Income of Revenue	16.9	15.2	14.1	11.5	9.8	8.2	6.2	7.5	1.7	5.4
% Return on Assets	NA	16.3	17.1	13.6	9.5	6.5	4.4	6.3	1.7	5.0
% Return on Equity	NA	23.3	28.1	24.7	17.0	13.7	9.8	15.8	4.6	14.9

Data as orig reptd.; bef. results of disc opers/spec. items. Per share data adj. for stk. divs.; EPS diluted. E-Estimated. NA-Not Available. NM-Not Meaningful. NR-Not Ranked. UR-Under Review.

Office: 4650 SW Macadam Ave Ste 400, Portland, OR 97239-4262.
Telephone: 503-417-4850.
Email: info@precastcorp.com
Website: http://www.precast.com

Chrmn, Pres & CEO: M. Donegan
SVP, CFO & Chief Acctg Officer: S.R. Hagel
SVP, Secy & General Counsel: R.A. Cooke
Treas: S.C. Blackmore

Investor Contact: W.D. Larsson
Board Members: M. Donegan, D. R. Graber, L. L. Lyles, D. J. Murphy, Jr., V. E. Oechsle, S. G. Rothmeier, U. Schmidt, R. L. Wambold, T. A. Wicks

Founded: 1949
Domicile: Oregon
Employees: 17,950

The McGraw-Hill Companies

priceline.com Inc

S&P Recommendation HOLD ★★★☆☆

Price	12-Mo. Target Price	Investment Style
$363.50 (as of Oct 22, 2010)	$350.00	Large-Cap Growth

GICS Sector Consumer Discretionary
Sub-Industry Internet Retail

Summary This company is a leading provider of online travel services, primarily in the U.S. and Europe.

Key Stock Statistics (Source S&P, Vickers, company reports)

52-Wk Range	$364.93– 154.12	S&P Oper. EPS 2010E	8.25	Market Capitalization(B)	$17.589	Beta	1.10
Trailing 12-Month EPS	$11.09	S&P Oper. EPS 2011E	10.60	Yield (%)	Nil	S&P 3-Yr. Proj. EPS CAGR(%)	22
Trailing 12-Month P/E	32.8	P/E on S&P Oper. EPS 2010E	44.1	Dividend Rate/Share	Nil	S&P Credit Rating	BBB-
$10K Invested 5 Yrs Ago	$178,888	Common Shares Outstg. (M)	48.4	Institutional Ownership (%)	100		

Price Performance

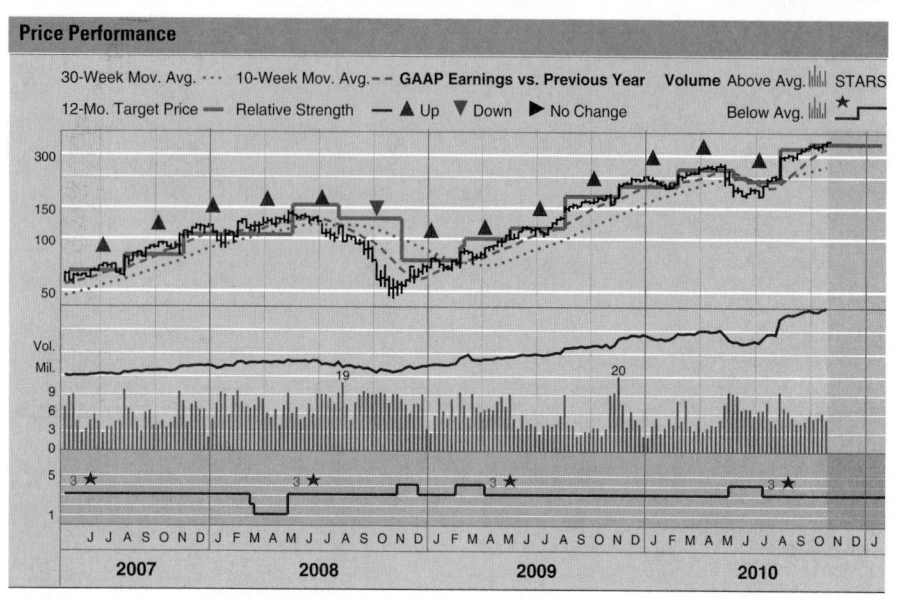

30-Week Mov. Avg. ···· 10-Week Mov. Avg. – – **GAAP Earnings vs. Previous Year** Volume Above Avg. STARS
12-Mo. Target Price — Relative Strength — ▲ Up ▼ Down ► No Change Below Avg.

Options: ASE, CBOE, P, Ph

Analysis prepared by **Scott H. Kessler** on September 26, 2010, when the stock traded at **$ 344.27**.

Highlights

▸ We estimate revenues will increase 27% in 2010 and 16% in 2011, due to market share gains, healthy volumes, and stable-to-improving pricing, offset somewhat by relative Europe-related weakness. We expect international and merchant operations to drive growth, reflecting PCLN's past acquisitions of Active Hotels and Bookings B.V., providers of Internet hotel reservation services in Europe, which have enabled the company to become an overseas leader in online hotel reservations.

▸ We believe PCLN will continue to build on its user and supplier bases in Europe, largely reflecting the benefits of efficient marketing efforts and the "network effect" (where more users beget more suppliers, etc.). In particular, we see PCLN's opaque travel offerings (where some details are not disclosed until the transaction is completed), especially in the U.S., as attractive in light of relatively high retail pricing.

▸ In March 2010, PCLN issued $575 million of convertible debt. It also announced a $500 million stock buyback, and immediately repurchased $100 million of shares. We see the company's financial position as strong and flexible.

Investment Rationale/Risk

▸ While we believe PCLN has established itself as a global leader in online travel services, we do not think it is widely known that over half of PCLN's gross bookings and revenues are derived from international businesses (mostly focused on Europe). Although we have concerns about the euro and European economies, we think positive secular trends are intact, such as a growing percentage of travel purchases being effected online. PCLN hopes it can replicate its European success in Asia, with the acquisition of Agoda. Given current conditions and uncertainties, we believe the stock is fairly valued at recent levels.

▸ Risks to our recommendation and target price include possible negative impacts from weak global economies (especially related to Europe) and leisure travel demand, and less success than we expect with regard to new offerings and/or acquisitions.

▸ Our DCF model (which assumes a WACC of 10.3%, annual free cash flow growth averaging 19% from 2010 to 2014, and a terminal growth rate of 3%) yields an intrinsic value of about $350, which is our 12-month target price.

Qualitative Risk Assessment

LOW	MEDIUM	HIGH

Our risk assessment reflects our view of a very competitive online travel segment, with relatively low barriers to entry.

Quantitative Evaluations

S&P Quality Ranking B-

D	C	B-	B	B+	A-	A	A+

Relative Strength Rank STRONG

91

LOWEST = 1   HIGHEST = 99

Revenue/Earnings Data

Revenue (Million $)

	1Q	2Q	3Q	4Q	Year
2010	584.4	767.4	--	--	--
2009	462.1	603.7	730.7	541.8	2,338
2008	403.2	514.0	561.6	406.0	1,885
2007	301.4	355.9	417.3	334.9	1,409
2006	241.9	307.7	313.5	260.1	1,123
2005	233.4	266.6	258.8	203.9	962.7

Earnings Per Share ($)

	1Q	2Q	3Q	4Q	Year
2010	1.06	2.26	E3.06	E1.86	E8.25
2009	0.53	1.38	6.42	1.55	9.88
2008	0.37	1.08	1.81	0.73	3.98
2007	-0.44	0.79	2.27	0.68	3.42
2006	-0.02	0.28	1.05	0.33	1.68
2005	0.21	0.29	3.71	0.09	4.21

Fiscal year ended Dec. 31. Next earnings report expected: Early November. EPS Estimates based on S&P Operating Earnings; historical GAAP earnings are as reported.

Dividend Data

No cash dividends have been paid.

priceline.com Inc

Business Summary September 26, 2010

CORPORATE OVERVIEW. Priceline.com is an online travel company that provides a broad range of travel services, including airline tickets, hotel rooms, car rentals, vacation packages, cruises, and destination services. PCLN offers customers a choice of purchasing certain travel services in a traditional, price-disclosed manner (retail products), or of using its proprietary Name Your Own Price service, which allows users to make offers for travel services at discounted prices (opaque products). Internationally, PCLN offers hotel room reservations in over 84 countries and 32 languages.

PCLN enables customers to make hotel reservations on a worldwide basis primarily under the Booking.com and Agoda brands internationally, and the priceline.com brand in the U.S. In the U.S., PCLN also allows users to purchase many other types of travel offerings. Interestingly, even though PCLN is best known in the U.S. for its Name Your Own Price system, 61% of its gross bookings and three-quarters of its operating income in 2009 were derived from its international (primarily European) operations. PCLN expects these

percentages to increase in 2010 and beyond.

The U.S. business consists of Name Your Own Price offerings (provided via a unique e-commerce pricing system intended to enable consumers to use the Internet to save money on products and services, while allowing sellers to generate incremental revenue and retail offerings) and retail services (whereby customers can choose specific suppliers and/or itineraries when making purchases of airline tickets and hotel and rental car reservations, and travel packages). The company has provided retail offerings since 2003, and believes that offering both opaque and retail products enables it to serve a broad array of value-conscious travelers, while providing diversified revenues.

Company Financials Fiscal Year Ended Dec. 31

Per Share Data ($)	2009	2008	2007	2006	2005	2004	2003	2002	2001	2000
Tangible Book Value	17.53	5.13	3.43	NM	0.53	0.79	3.44	3.12	3.30	NM
Cash Flow	10.68	4.86	4.24	2.41	4.70	1.03	0.56	-0.09	0.02	-10.71
Earnings	9.88	3.98	3.42	1.68	4.21	0.96	0.27	-0.54	-0.48	-11.82
S&P Core Earnings	9.91	3.99	4.19	1.70	4.13	0.53	-0.49	-2.94	-4.62	NA
Dividends	Nil	Nil	Nil	Nil	Nil	Nil	Nil	Nil	Nil	Nil
Payout Ratio	Nil	Nil	Nil	Nil	Nil	Nil	Nil	Nil	Nil	Nil
Prices:High	231.49	144.34	120.67	44.28	27.08	29.52	39.81	41.36	62.12	625.75
Prices:Low	64.95	45.15	41.80	21.06	18.20	17.42	6.78	6.30	7.88	6.38
P/E Ratio:High	23	36	35	26	6	31	NM	NM	NM	NM
P/E Ratio:Low	7	11	12	13	4	18	NM	NM	NM	NM

Income Statement Analysis (Million $)	2009	2008	2007	2006	2005	2004	2003	2002	2001	2000
Revenue	2,338	1,885	1,409	1,123	963	914	864	1,004	1,172	1,235
Operating Income	509	333	175	95.6	64.9	43.9	26.0	22.7	23.3	-40.5
Depreciation	39.2	43.2	37.5	33.4	27.3	13.5	11.5	18.3	16.6	17.4
Interest Expense	24.1	9.38	10.4	7.06	5.07	3.72	0.91	Nil	Nil	Nil
Pretax Income	442	292	145	62.1	36.5	31.3	11.9	-19.2	-7.30	-315
Effective Tax Rate	NM	33.7%	NM	NM	NM	NM	NM	NM	NM	NM
Net Income	489	193	157	74.5	193	31.5	11.9	-19.2	-7.30	-315
S&P Core Earnings	491	194	191	73.3	187	20.3	-18.6	-111	-157	NA

Balance Sheet & Other Financial Data (Million $)	2009	2008	2007	2006	2005	2004	2003	2002	2001	2000
Cash	800	463	509	424	80.3	101	93.7	85.4	115	90.6
Current Assets	1,023	624	613	503	224	273	284	170	185	131
Total Assets	1,834	1,344	1,351	1,106	754	542	338	211	262	195
Current Liabilities	409	547	695	101	71.0	74.4	49.6	65.3	87.3	79.3
Long Term Debt	36.0	Nil	Nil	569	224	224	125	Nil	Nil	Nil
Common Equity	1,322	730	579	349	369	199	149	132	147	-249
Total Capital	1,517	779	643	953	672	467	287	145	172	111
Capital Expenditures	15.1	18.3	16.0	12.9	11.0	6.94	6.58	9.13	9.42	37.3
Cash Flow	529	237	193	108	218	43.5	22.0	-3.26	0.71	-298
Current Ratio	2.5	1.1	0.9	5.0	3.1	3.7	5.7	2.6	2.1	1.7
% Long Term Debt of Capitalization	2.4	Nil	Nil	59.7	33.3	48.1	43.4	Nil	Nil	Nil
% Net Income of Revenue	20.9	10.3	11.1	6.6	20.0	3.4	1.4	NM	NM	NM
% Return on Assets	30.8	14.4	12.7	8.0	29.7	7.2	4.3	NM	NM	NM
% Return on Equity	47.7	29.6	33.5	20.8	67.2	17.2	7.4	NM	NM	NM

Data as orig reptd.; bef. results of disc opers/spec. items. Per share data adj. for stk. divs.; EPS diluted. E-Estimated. NA-Not Available. NM-Not Meaningful. NR-Not Ranked. UR-Under Review.

Office: 800 Connecticut Ave, Norwalk, CT 06854-1625.
Telephone: 203-299-8000.
Website: http://www.priceline.com
Chrmn: R.M. Bahna

Pres & CEO: J.H. Boyd
Vice Chrmn: R.J. Mylod, Jr.
COO: L. Gillingham
EVP, Secy & General Counsel: P.J. Millones

Investor Contact: D.J. Finnegan (203-299-8000)
Board Members: R. M. Bahna, H. W. Barker, Jr., J. H. Boyd, J. L. Docter, J. Epstein, J. M. Guyette, R. J. Mylod, Jr., N. B. Peretsman, C. W. Rydin

Founded: 1997
Domicile: Delaware
Employees: 2,010

Principal Financial Group Inc.

STANDARD &POOR'S

S&P Recommendation HOLD ★★★☆☆

Price	12-Mo. Target Price	Investment Style
$27.07 (as of Oct 22, 2010)	$27.00	Large-Cap Blend

GICS Sector Financials
Sub-Industry Life & Health Insurance

Summary This company offers businesses, individuals and other clients various financial products and services, including insurance, retirement and investment services.

Key Stock Statistics (Source S&P, Vickers, company reports)

52-Wk Range	$31.41–20.89	S&P Oper. EPS 2010E	2.75	Market Capitalization(B)	$8.671	Beta	2.95
Trailing 12-Month EPS	$2.02	S&P Oper. EPS 2011E	3.10	Yield (%)	1.85	S&P 3-Yr. Proj. EPS CAGR(%)	11
Trailing 12-Month P/E	13.4	P/E on S&P Oper. EPS 2010E	9.8	Dividend Rate/Share	$0.50	S&P Credit Rating	BBB
$10K Invested 5 Yrs Ago	$6,099	Common Shares Outstg. (M)	320.3	Institutional Ownership (%)	61		

Price Performance

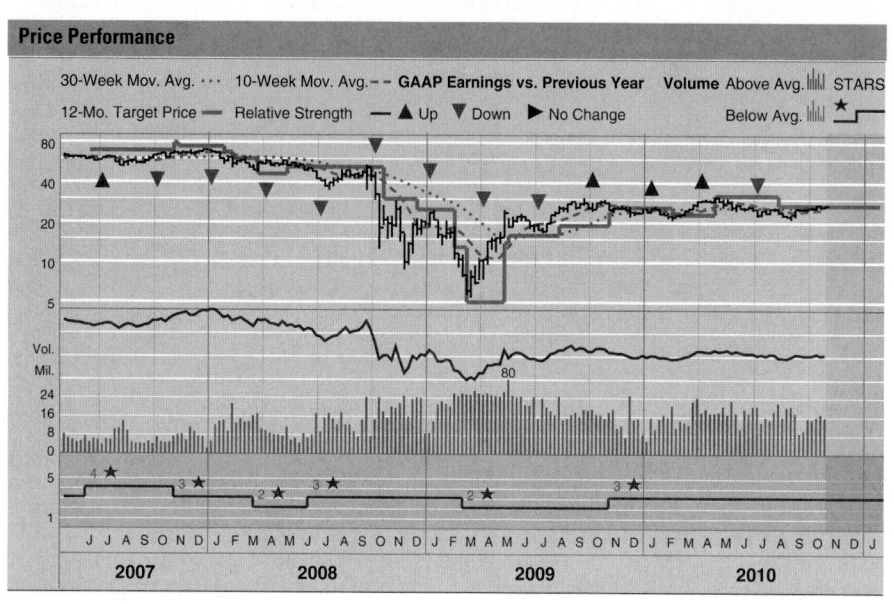

30-Week Mov. Avg. · · · · 10-Week Mov. Avg. – – **GAAP Earnings vs. Previous Year** Volume Above Avg. STARS
12-Mo. Target Price — Relative Strength — ▲ Up ▼ Down ▶ No Change Below Avg. ★

Options: CBOE

Analysis prepared by **Bret Howlett** on August 16, 2010, when the stock traded at **$ 22.81**.

Highlights

➤ We forecast a 3%-4% decline in U.S. Asset Management and Accumulation (USAMA) earnings in 2010. We expect 401(k) sales and flows to be pressured by the weak macro conditions for small businesses, higher withdrawals, and lower employee contributions and employer matching. However, the recovery in the equity markets has boosted average account values, and we expect higher fee income at USAMA. We are cautious on our outlook for Life & Health due to our forecast for sluggish sales and higher benefit ratios.

➤ We expect earnings to be up considerably at International Asset Management and Accumulation (IAMA). We believe IAMA will benefit from greater assets under management, higher investment income, and foreign currency shifts. However, PFG reduced its stake in a joint venture in Brazil, which should adversely affect earnings. We believe Global Asset Management profits will increase 20% on the improved financial markets and higher real estate associated income.

➤ We forecast operating EPS of $2.75 for 2010 and $3.10 for 2011. Our estimates exclude realized investment gains or losses.

Investment Rationale/Risk

➤ While we believe PFG's economy-sensitive businesses still face headwinds, we have become more optimistic about its prospects given the improving macro environment. Although we think multiple expansion will be held back by slow revenue growth and elevated investment losses, we believe this is reflected in PFG's shares. PFG trades at only a slight premium to the group, but we believe a premium is warranted since its businesses are less capital-intensive and typically generate a higher return on equity versus peers. PFG's exposure to commercial real estate is a concern, as we think impairments have yet to peak in this asset class. We believe future losses will be manageable, though, based on PFG's solid statutory financial position and capital raises.

➤ Risks to our recommendation and target price include a significant decline in the equity markets, narrowing margins in the company's health insurance business, outflows in its USAMA business, and deteriorating credit and economic conditions.

➤ Our 12-month target price of $27 is 1.0X our 2010 year-end book value forecast, below historical multiples.

Qualitative Risk Assessment

LOW	MEDIUM	HIGH

Our risk assessment reflects our view of PFG's significant exposure to the equity markets and potential for further investment losses, especially considering its exposure to commercial real estate. We believe PFG's capital position could come under strain if the economic environment and capital markets worsen. However, we believe PFG's financial position has improved following recent capital raises.

Quantitative Evaluations

S&P Quality Ranking B+

D	C	B-	B	B+	A-	A	A+

Relative Strength Rank MODERATE

64

LOWEST = 1   HIGHEST = 99

Revenue/Earnings Data

Revenue (Million $)

	1Q	2Q	3Q	4Q	Year
2010	2,264	2,234	--	--	--
2009	2,189	2,158	2,270	2,232	8,849
2008	2,501	2,658	2,498	2,279	9,936
2007	2,661	2,832	2,850	2,564	10,907
2006	2,402	2,460	2,450	2,559	9,871
2005	2,144	2,200	2,218	2,445	9,008

Earnings Per Share ($)

2010	0.59	0.42	E0.62	E0.71	E2.75
2009	0.43	0.52	0.57	0.44	1.98
2008	0.67	0.64	0.35	-0.03	1.63
2007	0.95	1.14	0.88	0.05	3.01
2006	1.01	0.76	0.92	0.93	3.63
2005	0.68	0.77	0.74	0.83	3.02

Fiscal year ended Dec. 31. Next earnings report expected: Early November. EPS Estimates based on S&P Operating Earnings; historical GAAP earnings are as reported.

Dividend Data (Dates: mm/dd Payment Date: mm/dd/yy)

Amount ($)	Date Decl.	Ex-Div. Date	Stk. of Record	Payment Date
0.500	10/26	11/10	11/13	12/04/09

Dividends have been paid since 2002. Source: Company reports.

The McGraw·Hill Companies

Principal Financial Group Inc.

STANDARD &POOR'S

Business Summary August 16, 2010

CORPORATE OVERVIEW. The Principal Financial Group is a leading provider of retirement savings, investment and insurance products and services, with approximately $285 billion in assets under management at December 31, 2009. The focus of the company is to provide retirement and employment products and services, specifically 401(k) plans, to small and medium-sized businesses. According to Spectrem Group, a consulting and market research firm, PFG is a leading corporate defined contributions plan provider with over 33,000 plans.

PFG's businesses are organized into five operating segments. The U.S. Asset Management and Accumulation segment (USAMA), which accounted for 43% of operating revenues excluding corporate and other in 2009, provides retirement savings and related investment products and services, and asset management operations, with a concentration on small and medium-sized businesses with fewer than 1,000 employees. At year-end 2009, USAMA account values totaled $164 billion.

The Global Asset Management segment includes Principal Global Investors and its affiliates, and focuses on providing a range of asset management services. The segment accounted for 4.6% of operating revenues excluding cor-

porate and other in 2009.

The International Asset Management and Accumulation segment (IAMA) consists of Principal International and offers retirement products and services, annuities, mutual funds and life insurance through operations in Brazil, Chile, Mexico, China, Hong Kong and India. IAMA accounted for 5.9% of operating revenues from continuing operations in 2009.

The Life and Health Insurance segment, which accounted for 47% of operating revenues from continuing operations in 2009, offers individual and group life and disability insurance, as well as group health, dental and vision insurance. The Corporate and Other segment includes, among other things, intersegment eliminations, income on capital not allocated to other segments, and the company's financing activities. The segment reported a loss of $168 million in 2009.

Company Financials Fiscal Year Ended Dec. 31

Per Share Data ($)	2009	2008	2007	2006	2005	2004	2003	2002	2001	2000
Tangible Book Value	33.18	4.41	22.35	22.24	24.14	23.67	22.12	19.32	10.59	14.89
Operating Earnings	NA	NA	NA	NA	NA	NA	NA	2.46	1.96	NA
Earnings	1.98	1.63	3.01	3.63	3.02	2.23	2.23	1.77	1.02	1.74
S&P Core Earnings	3.07	2.77	3.69	3.45	3.02	2.36	2.38	1.85	1.69	NA
Dividends	0.50	0.45	0.90	0.80	0.65	0.55	0.45	0.25	Nil	NA
Payout Ratio	25%	28%	30%	22%	22%	25%	20%	14%	Nil	NA
Prices:High	30.87	68.94	70.85	59.40	52.00	41.26	34.67	31.50	24.75	NA
Prices:Low	5.41	8.78	51.52	45.91	36.80	32.00	25.21	22.00	18.50	NA
P/E Ratio:High	16	42	24	16	17	19	16	18	24	NA
P/E Ratio:Low	3	5	17	13	12	14	11	12	18	NA

Income Statement Analysis (Million $)										
Life Insurance in Force	239,782	246,329	243,119	218,947	197,690	180,344	136,530	137,794	62,309	60,389
Premium Income:Life	1,254	1,564	1,827	1,560	1,546	1,477	1,500	1,824	2,089	1,792
Premium Income:A & H	2,496	2,646	2,808	2,745	2,429	2,233	2,135	2,058	2,033	2,205
Net Investment Income	3,401	3,994	3,967	3,618	3,361	3,227	3,420	3,305	3,395	3,172
Total Revenue	8,849	9,936	10,907	9,871	9,008	8,304	9,404	9,223	8,818	8,885
Pretax Income	746	454	1,048	1,329	1,124	882	954	666	449	872
Net Operating Income	NA	NA	NA	NA	NA	NA	NA	864	711	NA
Net Income	623	458	840	1,034	892	702	728	620	370	627
S&P Core Earnings	918	722	991	951	871	742	778	647	608	NA

Balance Sheet & Other Financial Data (Million $)										
Cash & Equivalent	2,932	3,359	2,119	2,314	2,324	1,131	2,344	1,685	1,218	940
Premiums Due	1,065	988	951	1,252	593	628	720	460	531	572
Investment Assets:Bonds	47,253	40,961	47,268	44,727	42,117	40,916	37,553	34,287	30,030	29,328
Investment Assets:Stocks	436	401	586	848	815	763	712	379	834	579
Investment Assets:Loans	12,748	12,748	13,522	12,515	12,312	12,529	14,312	11,900	11,898	12,359
Investment Assets:Total	63,937	59,107	64,365	60,367	57,583	57,012	55,578	48,996	44,773	44,403
Deferred Policy Costs	3,681	4,153	2,810	2,419	2,174	1,838	1,572	1,414	1,373	1,338
Total Assets	137,759	128,182	154,520	143,658	127,035	113,798	107,754	89,861	88,351	86,838
Debt	1,585	1,291	1,399	1,554	899	844	2,767	1,333	1,378	1,391
Common Equity	7,893	2,473	7,422	7,861	7,807	7,544	7,400	13,314	6,820	6,624
% Return on Revenue	7.0	4.6	7.7	10.5	9.9	8.5	7.7	7.0	4.2	7.1
% Return on Assets	0.5	0.3	0.6	0.8	0.7	0.6	0.7	0.7	0.4	0.8
% Return on Equity	12.0	9.3	10.6	12.8	11.4	9.4	10.4	4.6	5.7	10.5
% Investment Yield	5.5	6.7	6.4	6.1	5.9	5.8	6.5	7.0	7.8	7.9

Data as orig reptd.; bef. results of disc opers/spec. items. Per share data adj. for stk. divs.; EPS diluted. E-Estimated. NA-Not Available. NM-Not Meaningful. NR-Not Ranked. UR-Under Review.

Office: 711 High Street, Des Moines, IA 50392-9992.
Telephone: 515-247-5111.
Website: http://www.principal.com
Chrmn, Pres & CEO: L.D. Zimpleman

EVP & General Counsel: K.E. Shaff
SVP, CFO & Chief Acctg Officer: T.J. Lillis
SVP & Secy: J.N. Hoffman
SVP & Cntlr: G. Elming

Investor Contact: T. Graf (515-235-9500)
Board Members: B. J. Bernard, J. E. Carter-Miller, G. E. Costley, M. T. Dan, C. Gelatt, Jr., S. L. Helton, R. L. Keyser, A. K. Mathrani, E. E. Tallett, L. D. Zimpleman

Founded: 1998
Domicile: Delaware
Employees: 14,487

Procter & Gamble Co (The)

STANDARD &POOR'S

S&P Recommendation **BUY** ★★★★★	Price $63.40 (as of Oct 22, 2010)	12-Mo. Target Price $66.00	Investment Style Large-Cap Growth

GICS Sector Consumer Staples
Sub-Industry Household Products

Summary This leading consumer products company markets household and personal care products in more than 180 countries.

Key Stock Statistics (Source S&P, Vickers, company reports)

52-Wk Range	$64.58–39.37	S&P Oper. EPS 2011E	3.97	Market Capitalization(B)	$179.959	Beta	0.51
Trailing 12-Month EPS	$4.11	S&P Oper. EPS 2012E	NA	Yield (%)	3.04	S&P 3-Yr. Proj. EPS CAGR(%)	7
Trailing 12-Month P/E	15.4	P/E on S&P Oper. EPS 2011E	16.0	Dividend Rate/Share	$1.93	S&P Credit Rating	AA-
$10K Invested 5 Yrs Ago	$13,133	Common Shares Outstg. (M)	2,838.5	Institutional Ownership (%)	57		

Price Performance

30-Week Mov. Avg. · · · 10-Week Mov. Avg. - - GAAP Earnings vs. Previous Year   Volume Above Avg. STARS
12-Mo. Target Price — Relative Strength — ▲ Up ▼ Down ► No Change   Below Avg. ★

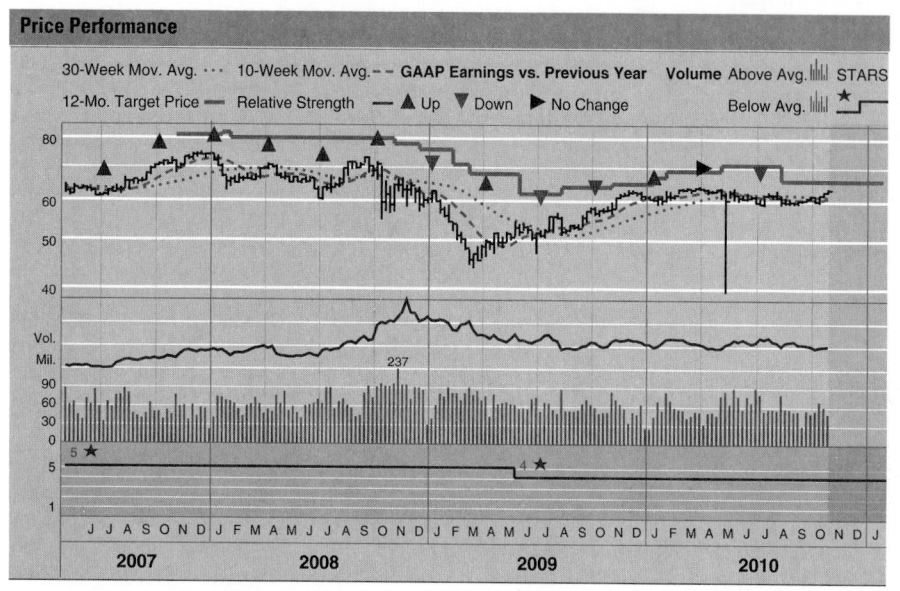

Options: ASE, CBOE, P, Ph

Analysis prepared by **Tom Graves, CFA** on October 04, 2010, when the stock traded at **$ 59.95**.

Highlights

▶ We think PG has benefited from its tiered portfolio, which offers products at different price points, from new products that command higher pricing through innovation, and from its broad geographic reach. In FY 11 (Jun.), we look for sales growth of about 4%, following a rise of 2.9% in FY 10.

▶ In FY 11, we expect a segment operating profit margin of about 15%, similar to what was reported for FY 10, as we look for higher commodity costs to at least partly offset continuing productivity gains and cost reductions. For FY 11, we estimate EPS of $3.97, up from $3.67 in FY 10, which excludes a $0.05 charge for taxation of a retiree health care subsidy, and $0.09 of charges for potential competition law fines. In FY 11, we expect year-to-year EPS comparisons to be more favorable in the second half than in the first.

▶ In the company's FY 10 annual report, PG said it expects share repurchases of $6 billion to $8 billion in FY 11, following total share repurchases of $6.0 billion in FY 10.

Investment Rationale/Risk

▶ Looking ahead, we expect PG to benefit from innovation, acquisitions and growth in new markets and categories. In our view, PG's competitive strengths in developing markets include its broad product portfolio and sizable distribution network.

▶ Risks to our recommendation and target price include heightened competition, a worsening consumer spending environment, unfavorable currency translation, greater commodity cost pressures, higher promotional spending, and slow consumer acceptance of new products.

▶ Our 12-month target price of $66 is based on a blended valuation. Our historical P/E analysis uses a multiple of about 14.6X our calendar 2011 EPS estimate of $4.12, which is below the 10-year median, while our peer analysis, based on PG's strong earnings track record and leading market share positions, uses a premium 15.8X multiple. These multiples imply values of $60 and $65, respectively. Our DCF model implies a $73 intrinsic value, assuming a blended WACC of 8.5%, and a 3% terminal growth rate. The stock recently had an indicated dividend yield of 3.2%

Qualitative Risk Assessment

LOW	MEDIUM	HIGH

Our risk assessment reflects that demand for household and personal care products is generally stable and not affected by changes in the economy or geopolitical factors, except for select categories such as fragrances.

Quantitative Evaluations

S&P Quality Ranking   A+

D	C	B-	B	B+	A-	A	A+

Relative Strength Rank   MODERATE

53

LOWEST = 1   HIGHEST = 99

Revenue/Earnings Data

Revenue (Million $)

	1Q	2Q	3Q	4Q	Year
2010	19,807	21,027	19,178	18,926	78,938
2009	21,582	20,368	18,417	18,662	79,029
2008	20,199	21,575	20,463	21,266	83,503
2007	18,785	19,725	18,694	19,272	76,476
2006	14,793	18,337	17,250	17,842	68,222
2005	13,744	14,452	14,287	14,258	56,741

Earnings Per Share ($)

2010	0.97	1.01	0.83	0.71	3.53
2009	1.03	0.94	0.83	0.80	3.58
2008	0.92	0.98	0.82	0.92	3.64
2007	0.79	0.84	0.74	0.67	3.04
2006	0.77	0.72	0.63	0.55	2.64
2005	0.73	0.74	0.63	0.56	2.66

Fiscal year ended Jun. 30. Next earnings report expected: Late October. EPS Estimates based on S&P Operating Earnings; historical GAAP earnings are as reported.

Dividend Data (Dates: mm/dd Payment Date: mm/dd/yy)

Amount ($)	Date Decl.	Ex-Div. Date	Stk. of Record	Payment Date
0.440	01/12	01/20	01/22	02/16/10
0.482	04/19	04/28	04/30	05/17/10
0.482	07/13	07/21	07/23	08/16/10
0.482	10/12	10/20	10/22	11/15/10

Dividends have been paid since 1891. Source: Company reports.

Procter & Gamble Co (The)

STANDARD
&POOR'S

Business Summary October 04, 2010

CORPORATE OVERVIEW. Procter & Gamble's business is focused on providing branded products of what it considers superior quality and value to improve the lives of the world's consumers. PG's products are sold in more than 180 countries. In FY 10 (Jun.), North America accounted for 42% of total sales, Western Europe 21%, Asia 15%, Latin America 9%, and other geographic areas 13%. PG's customers include mass merchandisers, grocery stores, membership club stores, drug stores and high-frequency stores. Sales to Wal-Mart Stores, Inc. and its affiliates represented about 16% of total FY 10 revenue. PG's top 10 customers accounted for about 32% of total unit volume.

Under U.S. accounting standards, PG has six reportable business segments: Beauty (25% of FY 10 net sales and 25% of net income from continuing operations); Grooming (10%; 13%); Health Care (15%; 17%); Snacks and Pet Care

(4%; 3%); Fabric Care and Home Care (30%; 31%); and Baby Care and Family Care (19%; 19%).

IMPACT OF MAJOR DEVELOPMENTS. In October 2005, PG acquired The Gillette Company for about $54 billion. Gillette is the world leader in the male and female grooming categories and holds the number one position worldwide in alkaline batteries and toothbrushes. We expect the acquisition to add to increased shareholder value over time through cost synergies and sales growth opportunities, following the initial two years of dilution.

Company Financials Fiscal Year Ended Jun. 30

Per Share Data ($)	2010	2009	2008	2007	2006	2005	2004	2003	2002	2001
Tangible Book Value	NM	NM	NM	NM	NM	NM	NM	0.43	NM	0.78
Cash Flow	4.53	4.50	4.54	4.30	3.56	3.30	2.90	2.41	2.11	1.85
Earnings	3.53	3.58	3.64	3.04	2.64	2.66	2.32	1.85	1.54	1.04
S&P Core Earnings	3.53	3.38	3.24	2.96	2.60	2.45	2.17	1.58	1.28	0.81
Dividends	1.80	1.64	1.45	1.28	1.15	1.03	0.93	0.82	0.76	0.70
Payout Ratio	51%	46%	40%	42%	44%	39%	40%	44%	49%	68%
Prices:High	64.58	63.48	73.81	75.18	64.73	59.70	57.40	49.97	47.38	40.86
Prices:Low	39.37	43.93	54.92	60.42	52.75	51.16	48.89	39.79	37.04	27.98
P/E Ratio:High	18	18	20	25	25	22	25	27	31	39
P/E Ratio:Low	11	12	15	20	20	19	21	22	24	27

Income Statement Analysis (Million $)										
Revenue	78,938	79,029	83,503	76,476	68,222	56,741	51,407	43,377	40,238	39,244
Operating Income	19,129	19,205	20,249	18,580	15,876	12,811	11,560	9,556	8,371	7,007
Depreciation	3,108	3,082	3,166	3,130	2,627	1,884	1,733	1,703	1,693	2,271
Interest Expense	946	1,358	1,467	1,304	1,119	834	629	561	603	794
Pretax Income	15,047	15,325	16,078	14,710	12,413	10,439	9,350	7,530	6,383	4,616
Effective Tax Rate	NA	26.3%	24.9%	29.7%	30.0%	30.5%	30.7%	31.1%	31.8%	36.7%
Net Income	10,946	11,293	12,075	10,340	8,684	7,257	6,481	5,186	4,352	2,922
S&P Core Earnings	10,730	10,467	10,575	9,917	8,420	6,552	5,922	4,313	3,486	2,165

Balance Sheet & Other Financial Data (Million $)										
Cash	2,879	4,781	3,541	5,354	6,693	6,389	5,469	5,912	3,427	2,306
Current Assets	18,782	21,905	24,515	24,031	24,329	20,329	17,115	15,220	12,166	10,889
Total Assets	128,172	134,833	143,992	138,014	135,695	61,527	57,048	43,706	40,776	34,387
Current Liabilities	24,282	30,901	30,958	30,717	19,985	25,039	22,147	12,358	12,704	9,846
Long Term Debt	21,360	20,652	23,581	23,375	35,976	12,887	12,554	11,475	11,201	9,792
Common Equity	61,439	63,099	69,494	65,354	61,457	15,994	15,752	14,606	12,072	10,309
Total Capital	91,271	95,827	104,880	102,150	111,238	33,258	32,093	29,057	25,984	22,696
Capital Expenditures	3,067	3,238	3,046	2,945	2,667	2,181	2,024	1,482	1,679	2,486
Cash Flow	14,054	14,183	15,065	13,470	11,311	9,005	8,083	6,764	5,921	5,193
Current Ratio	0.8	0.7	0.8	0.8	1.2	0.8	0.8	1.2	1.0	1.1
% Long Term Debt of Capitalization	23.4	21.6	22.5	22.9	32.3	38.7	39.1	39.5	43.1	43.1
% Net Income of Revenue	13.9	14.3	14.5	13.5	12.7	12.8	12.6	12.0	10.8	7.4
% Return on Assets	8.3	8.1	8.6	7.6	8.8	12.2	12.9	12.3	11.6	8.5
% Return on Equity	17.8	17.2	17.9	16.3	22.1	45.7	41.8	37.9	37.8	28.0

Data as orig reptd.; bef. results of disc opers/spec. items. Per share data adj. for stk. divs.; EPS diluted. E-Estimated. NA-Not Available. NM-Not Meaningful. NR-Not Ranked. UR-Under Review.

Office: One Procter & Gamble Plaza, Cincinnati, OH 45202.
Telephone: 513-983-1100.
Website: http://www.pg.com
Chrmn, Pres & CEO: R.A. McDonald

SVP, Chief Acctg Officer & Cntlr: V.L. Sheppard
SVP & Treas: T.L. List
CFO: J.R. Moeller
CTO: B. Brown

Investor Contact: M. Erceg (800-742-6253)
Board Members: A. F. Braly, K. I. Chenault, S. D. Cook, R. K. Gupta, R. A. McDonald, W. J. McNerney, Jr., J. A. Rodgers, M. A. Wilderotter, P. Woertz, E. Zedillo

Founded: 1837
Domicile: Ohio
Employees: 127,000

The McGraw-Hill Companies

Progressive Corp (The)

STANDARD &POOR'S

S&P Recommendation	HOLD ★★★☆☆	Price	12-Mo. Target Price	Investment Style
		$20.97 (as of Oct 22, 2010)	$22.00	Large-Cap Growth

GICS Sector Financials
Sub-Industry Property & Casualty Insurance

Summary One of the largest auto insurance groups in the U.S., Progressive is the largest seller of motorcycle policies and a market leader in commercial auto insurance.

Key Stock Statistics (Source S&P, Vickers, company reports)

52-Wk Range	$21.59– 15.90	S&P Oper. EPS 2010**E**	1.51	Market Capitalization(B)	$14.000	Beta	0.85
Trailing 12-Month EPS	$1.61	S&P Oper. EPS 2011**E**	1.60	Yield (%)	NA	S&P 3-Yr. Proj. EPS CAGR(%)	3
Trailing 12-Month P/E	13.0	P/E on S&P Oper. EPS 2010**E**	13.9	Dividend Rate/Share	NA	S&P Credit Rating	A+
$10K Invested 5 Yrs Ago	$8,483	Common Shares Outstg. (M)	667.6	Institutional Ownership (%)	69		

Price Performance

30-Week Mov. Avg. · · · 10-Week Mov. Avg. - - **GAAP Earnings vs. Previous Year**   **Volume** Above Avg. ▮▮▮ **STARS**
12-Mo. Target Price — Relative Strength — ▲ Up ▼ Down ► No Change   Below Avg. ▮▮▮ ★

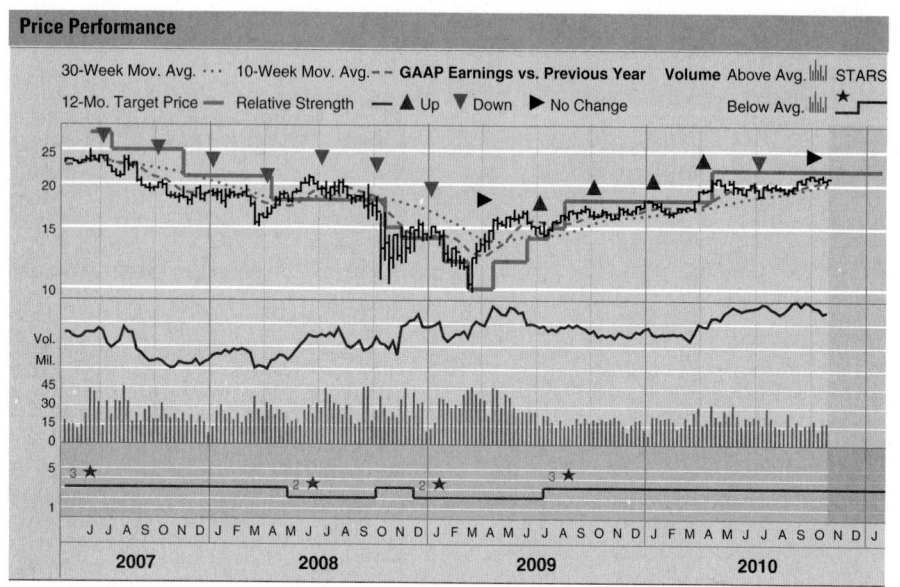

Options: ASE, CBOE, P, Ph

Analysis prepared by **Cathy A. Seifert** on July 19, 2010, when the stock traded at **$ 19.53**.

Highlights

► We believe earned premiums will rise 2% to 4% in 2010 and 4% in 2011, reflecting likely market share gains, partly offset by continued price competition. Earned premiums advanced 2.8% in 2009 and 4% in the first half of 2010, following a decline of 1.8% in 2008. We expect total operating revenue growth in 2010 to remain constrained by an expected rise in net investment income of between 2% and 3%.

► Barring a surge in catastrophe losses, we expect underwriting results to remain profitable in coming periods. Underwriting results in 2009 were aided by a 1.1% decline in loss costs, partly offset by a 1.8% rise in policy acquisition costs and other underwriting expenses. As a result, the combined (loss and expense) ratio improved to 91.6% in 2009 from 94.6% in 2008.

► We estimate operating EPS of $1.49 in 2010, rising to $1.60 in 2011, versus the $1.55 of operating EPS reported for 2009. Our estimates assume that a flat to modestly higher earned premium base and profitable underwriting results will be slightly offset by only modestly higher net investment income in coming periods, in a more challenging investment environment.

Investment Rationale/Risk

► We view PGR's technology and marketing capabilities as superior to many peers. However, at recent levels, the shares traded at a premium to most peers on both a forward price/earnings and price/tangible book value basis. We view the shares as appropriately valued. We note that PGR is still being affected by ongoing competitive pressures that we think may force PGR to lower its underwriting standards to gain market share.

► Risks to our recommendation and target price include a greater-than-expected deterioration in premium revenues, higher-than-expected claim cost inflation and erosion in claim trends, and greater-that-expected erosion in the company's investment portfolio.

► Our 12-month target price of $22 assumes that the shares will continue to trade at a premium to property-casualty insurance peers, albeit a smaller one, on a forward price-to-tangible book value basis and a forward price/earnings basis.

Qualitative Risk Assessment

LOW	MEDIUM	HIGH

Our risk assessment reflects our view of PGR's position as a leading underwriter of personal lines coverage. As primarily an auto insurer, PGR is less exposed to catastrophe losses than a number of peers, although they still pose a risk.

Quantitative Evaluations

S&P Quality Ranking   B+

D	C	B-	B	B+	A-	A	A+

Relative Strength Rank   MODERATE

49

LOWEST = 1   HIGHEST = 99

Revenue/Earnings Data

Revenue (Million $)

	1Q	2Q	3Q	4Q	Year
2010	3,666	3,686	3,770	--	--
2009	3,468	3,584	3,611	3,901	14,564
2008	3,586	3,537	2,210	3,508	12,840
2007	3,687	3,671	3,710	3,615	14,687
2006	3,661	3,708	3,724	3,694	14,786
2005	3,492	3,590	3,623	3,599	14,303

Earnings Per Share ($)

2010	0.44	0.32	0.40	E0.37	E1.51
2009	0.35	0.37	0.40	0.46	1.57
2008	0.35	0.32	-1.03	0.24	-0.10
2007	0.49	0.39	0.42	0.34	1.65
2006	0.55	0.51	0.53	0.53	2.10
2005	0.51	0.49	0.39	0.36	1.75

Fiscal year ended Dec. 31. Next earnings report expected: Early December. EPS Estimates based on S&P Operating Earnings; historical GAAP earnings are as reported.

Dividend Data (Dates: mm/dd Payment Date: mm/dd/yy)

Amount ($)	Date Decl.	Ex-Div. Date	Stk. of Record	Payment Date
0.161	12/14	01/25	01/27	02/05/10

Dividends have been paid since 2010. Source: Company reports.

The McGraw-Hill Companies

Progressive Corp (The)

Business Summary July 19, 2010

CORPORATE OVERVIEW. Progressive Corp. underwrites an array of personal and commercial lines insurance. Net written premiums totaled $14.0 billion in 2009, of which personal lines accounted for 89% and commercial and other lines 11%.

PGR's core business (90% of 2009's $12.5 billion in personal lines net premiums written) is underwriting private passenger automobile insurance. Based on year-end 2008 industry net written premium data (latest available), the company was the fourth largest private U.S. passenger auto insurer, a position that PGR believes it retained in 2009. PGR's other lines of business include recreational vehicle, motorcycle and small commercial vehicle insurance, and, to a lesser degree, commercial indemnity insurance.

Personal lines products are distributed through a network of more than 30,000, including independent agents, as well as brokers in New York and California, and strategic alliance business relationships with an array of financial institu-

tions. During 2009, 59% of total personal lines net written premiums were distributed through the agency channel (62% in 2008). Distribution through direct channels, including a toll free telephone line and the Internet, accounted for 41% of net written premiums in 2009 (38% in 2008).

PGR conducts its personal lines business in 50 states and in the District of Columbia. Commercial auto policies are written in every state except Hawaii; and not in the District of Columbia.

The commercial auto business (11% of net written premiums in 2009) writes primarily liability and physical damage insurance for automobiles and trucks owned by small businesses.

Company Financials Fiscal Year Ended Dec. 31

Per Share Data ($)	2009	2008	2007	2006	2005	2004	2003	2002	2001	2000
Tangible Book Value	9.15	6.23	7.26	9.15	7.74	6.43	5.85	4.32	3.69	3.25
Operating Earnings	NA	NA	NA	NA	NA	NA	NA	0.81	0.54	0.06
Earnings	1.57	-0.10	1.65	2.10	1.75	1.91	1.42	0.75	0.46	0.05
S&P Core Earnings	1.54	1.29	1.55	2.11	1.77	1.85	1.40	0.79	0.52	NA
Dividends	Nil	Nil	Nil	0.06	0.03	0.04	0.03	0.02	0.02	0.02
Payout Ratio	Nil	Nil	Nil	3%	2%	2%	2%	3%	5%	44%
Prices:High	18.22	21.31	25.16	30.09	31.23	24.32	21.17	15.12	12.65	9.25
Prices:Low	9.76	10.29	17.26	22.18	20.34	18.28	11.56	11.19	6.84	3.75
P/E Ratio:High	12	NM	15	14	18	13	15	20	28	NM
P/E Ratio:Low	6	NM	10	11	12	10	8	15	15	NM

Income Statement Analysis (Million $)	2009	2008	2007	2006	2005	2004	2003	2002	2001	2000
Premium Income	14,013	13,631	13,877	14,118	13,764	13,170	11,341	8,884	7,162	6,348
Net Investment Income	507	638	681	648	537	484	465	455	414	385
Other Revenue	44.0	-1,429	116	20.7	539	612	54.5	34.3	24.7	37.4
Total Revenue	14,564	12,840	14,687	14,786	14,303	13,782	11,892	9,373	7,488	6,771
Pretax Income	1,557	-222	1,693	2,433	2,059	2,451	1,860	981	588	31.8
Net Operating Income	NA	NA	NA	NA	NA	NA	NA	718	486	55.4
Net Income	1,058	-70.0	1,183	1,648	1,394	1,649	1,255	667	411	46.1
S&P Core Earnings	1,040	869	1,113	1,654	1,415	1,591	1,234	702	469	NA

Balance Sheet & Other Financial Data (Million $)	2009	2008	2007	2006	2005	2004	2003	2002	2001	2000
Cash & Equivalent	271	129	148	140	139	124	110	94.8	86.4	73.1
Premiums Due	3,020	2,697	2,730	2,932	2,906	2,669	2,351	1,959	1,497	1,567
Investment Assets:Bonds	11,563	9,559	9,185	9,959	10,222	9,084	9,133	7,713	5,949	4,784
Investment Assets:Stocks	2,072	2,266	4,598	4,149	3,279	2,621	2,751	2,004	2,050	2,012
Investment Assets:Loans	Nil	Nil	Nil	Nil	Nil	Nil	Nil	Nil	Nil	Nil
Investment Assets:Total	14,713	12,978	14,165	14,689	14,275	13,082	12,532	10,284	8,226	6,983
Deferred Policy Costs	402	414	426	441	445	432	412	364	317	310
Total Assets	19,846	18,251	18,843	19,482	18,899	17,184	16,282	13,564	11,122	10,052
Debt	2,177	2,176	2,174	1,186	1,285	1,284	1,490	1,489	1,096	749
Common Equity	5,749	4,215	4,936	6,847	6,108	5,155	5,060	3,768	3,251	2,870
Property & Casualty:Loss Ratio	70.7	73.5	71.5	66.6	68.1	65.0	67.4	70.9	73.6	83.2
Property & Casualty:Expense Ratio	20.9	21.1	21.1	19.9	87.4	19.6	18.8	20.4	21.0	21.0
Property & Casualty Combined Ratio	91.6	94.6	92.6	86.5	19.3	84.6	86.2	91.3	94.7	104.2
% Return on Revenue	7.3	NM	8.1	11.1	9.7	12.0	10.6	7.1	5.4	0.7
% Return on Equity	21.2	NM	20.1	25.4	24.8	32.4	28.4	19.3	13.4	1.6

Data as orig reptd.; bef. results of disc opers/spec. items. Per share data adj. for stk. divs.; EPS diluted. E-Estimated. NA-Not Available. NM-Not Meaningful. NR-Not Ranked. UR-Under Review.

Office: 6300 Wilson Mills Road, Mayfield Village, OH 44143.
Telephone: 440-461-5000.
Website: http://www.progressive.com
Chrmn: P.B. Lewis

Pres & CEO: G.M. Renwick
CFO: B. Domeck
Chief Acctg Officer: J.W. Basch
Treas: T.A. King

Investor Contact: P. Brennan (440-395-2370)
Board Members: S. B. Burgdoerfer, C. A. Davis, R. N. Farah, L. W. Fitt, S. R. Hardis, B. P. Healy, A. F. Kohnstamm, P. B. Lewis, N. S. Matthews, P. H. Nettles, G. M. Renwick, B. T. Sheares

Founded: 1965
Domicile: Ohio
Employees: 24,661

Progress Energy Inc.

STANDARD &POOR'S

S&P Recommendation HOLD ★★★☆☆

Price	**12-Mo. Target Price**	**Investment Style**
$44.91 (as of Oct 22, 2010)	$41.00	Large-Cap Blend

GICS Sector Utilities
Sub-Industry Electric Utilities

Summary This diversified energy company owns two electric utilities that serve approximately 3.1 million customers in North Carolina, South Carolina and Florida.

Key Stock Statistics (Source S&P, Vickers, company reports)

52-Wk Range	$45.61–36.67	S&P Oper. EPS 2010E	3.06	Market Capitalization(B)	$13.140	Beta	0.40
Trailing 12-Month EPS	$2.72	S&P Oper. EPS 2011E	3.15	Yield (%)	5.52	S&P 3-Yr. Proj. EPS CAGR(%)	2
Trailing 12-Month P/E	16.5	P/E on S&P Oper. EPS 2010E	14.7	Dividend Rate/Share	$2.48	S&P Credit Rating	BBB+
$10K Invested 5 Yrs Ago	$14,344	Common Shares Outstg. (M)	292.6	Institutional Ownership (%)	55		

Price Performance

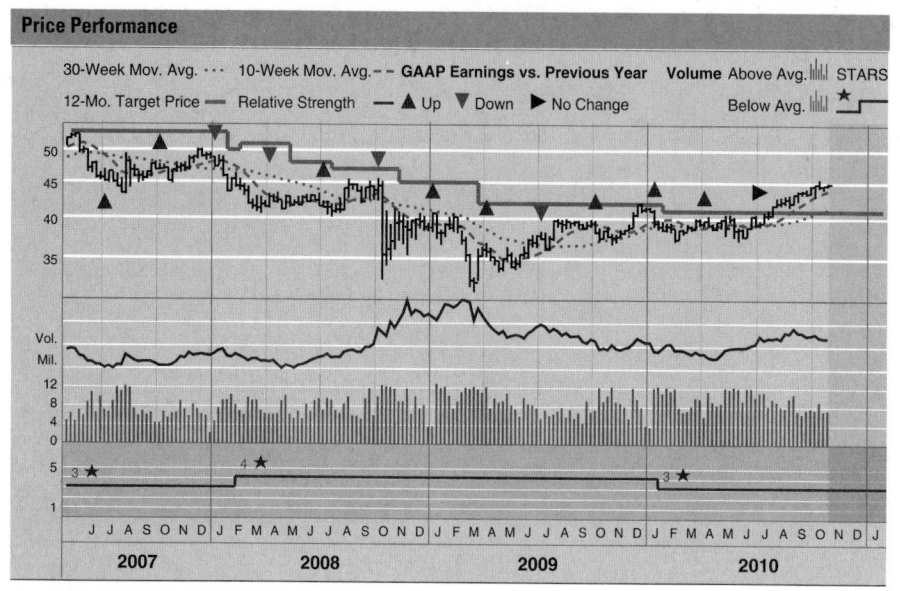

30-Week Mov. Avg. · · · 10-Week Mov. Avg. – – **GAAP Earnings vs. Previous Year** Volume Above Avg. STARS
12-Mo. Target Price — Relative Strength — ▲ Up ▼ Down ► No Change Below Avg.

Options: ASE, CBOE, Ph

Analysis prepared by **Justin McCann** on September 20, 2010, when the stock traded at **$ 43.80**.

Highlights

▸ Excluding net one-time charges of $0.09, we expect operating EPS in 2010 to increase about 1% from 2009's $3.03, which excluded net one-time charges of $0.28. Despite the rejection of a proposed rate increase for the Florida utility, operating EPS in the first half of 2010 benefited from the base rate increase it received in July 2009, as well as more favorable weather in both the Carolinas and Florida.

▸ For the second half of 2010, we expect results to reflect higher operating and purchased power costs due to a nuclear plant outage, partially offset by the benefit of the warmer than normal weather in the third quarter. For 2011, we expect earnings to benefit from a modest recovery in the Florida economy and above average customer growth in the Carolinas.

▸ On January 12, 2010, the Florida Public Service Commission rejected Progress Energy Florida's request for a $500 million base rate increase, leaving only the $132 million increase that was tentatively approved and implemented in July 2009. It also authorized an ROE of 10.5%, instead of the 12.54% requested. On June 1, 2010, the FPSC authorized the utility to seek a rate adjustment if its actual ROE fell below 9.5%.

Investment Rationale/Risk

▸ The stock is up about 6% year to date, reflecting, in our view, the rebound in the electric utility sector and the above-peers yield from the dividend (recently 5.7%). This follows a 4.6% increase in 2009. The shares had been hurt earlier this year, due, we believe, to the worse than expected regulatory decision on Progress Energy Florida's rate increase request. In addition to lower than previously anticipated revenues, the adverse decision could also have brought about a higher risk profile for the company and its cost of capital, as well as a reduction in the utility's capital expenditure plans and maintenance operations. While the 82% payout ratio on 2009 operating EPS is well above peers, we believe PGN is strongly committed to at least maintaining the current dividend.

▸ Risks to our recommendation and target price include the possibility of extended weakness in the Florida economy and housing market, as well as a sharp reduction in the average P/E for the electric utilities sub-sector as a whole.

▸ Our 12-month target price of $41 represents a premium-to-peers multiple of 13X our EPS estimate for 2011, warranted, in our view, by the well above peers yield from the dividend.

Qualitative Risk Assessment

LOW	MEDIUM	HIGH

With the higher risk synthetic fuel business having been discontinued, our risk assessment reflects the strong and steady cash flow we still forecast from the regulated utilities in the Carolinas and Florida, despite the slowdown in customer growth due to the downturn in the economy and the housing market and an unfavorable regulatory environment in Florida.

Quantitative Evaluations

S&P Quality Ranking B

D	C	B-	B	B+	A-	A	A+

Relative Strength Rank MODERATE

52

LOWEST = 1 HIGHEST = 99

Revenue/Earnings Data

Revenue (Million $)

	1Q	2Q	3Q	4Q	Year
2010	2,535	2,372	--	--	--
2009	2,442	2,312	2,824	2,307	9,885
2008	2,066	2,244	2,696	2,161	9,167
2007	2,072	2,129	2,750	2,202	9,153
2006	2,433	2,499	2,913	2,273	9,570
2005	2,198	2,333	3,097	2,578	10,108

Earnings Per Share ($)

2010	0.67	0.62	E1.31	E0.37	E3.06
2009	0.66	0.62	1.24	0.46	2.99
2008	0.58	0.77	1.18	0.44	2.96
2007	0.62	0.41	1.27	0.09	2.70
2006	0.19	0.06	0.97	0.51	2.05
2005	0.43	0.02	1.81	0.63	2.94

Fiscal year ended Dec. 31. Next earnings report expected: Early November. EPS Estimates based on S&P Operating Earnings; historical GAAP earnings are as reported.

Dividend Data (Dates: mm/dd Payment Date: mm/dd/yy)

Amount ($)	Date Decl.	Ex-Div. Date	Stk. of Record	Payment Date
0.620	12/09	01/07	01/11	02/01/10
0.620	03/17	04/08	04/12	05/03/10
0.620	05/12	07/08	07/12	08/02/10
0.620	09/17	10/06	10/11	11/01/10

Dividends have been paid since 1937. Source: Company reports.

Please read the Required Disclosures and Analyst Certification on the last page of this report.

Progress Energy Inc.

Business Summary September 20, 2010

CORPORATE OVERVIEW. Headquartered in Raleigh, NC, Progress Energy operates in retail utility markets in the southeastern U.S., and in competitive electricity, gas and other fuel markets in the eastern U.S. It is the holding company for the fully integrated regulated utilities Progress Energy Carolinas (PEC) and Progress Energy Florida (PEF), which together serve approximately 3.1 million retail electric customers. In 2009, PEC contributed about 54% of utility income (58% in 2008), and PEF 46% (42%).

CORPORATE STRATEGY. As an integrated energy company, PGN has stated that its primary focus will be on the end-use and wholesale electricity markets in its service territory and region. However, the company has experienced the adverse impact of the current economic recession and the downturns in the housing and consumer credit markets. PGN has attempted to offset this im-

pact through its ongoing cost management initiatives, and to mitigate its fuel costs through its diverse generation mix, staggered fuel contracts and hedging, as well as through supplier and transportation diversity. Despite the company's expectation of a challenging economic environment in 2010, it remains intent on enhancing its operational excellence, strengthening its financial flexibility and growth, preparing for future power generating capacity, and continuing its record of having increased its dividend for 21 consecutive years.

Company Financials Fiscal Year Ended Dec. 31

Per Share Data ($)	2009	2008	2007	2006	2005	2004	2003	2002	2001	2000
Tangible Book Value	20.69	19.15	18.33	18.09	15.94	14.48	13.78	12.43	10.58	7.48
Earnings	2.99	2.96	2.70	2.05	2.94	3.10	3.40	2.53	2.64	3.03
S&P Core Earnings	3.18	2.59	2.67	1.95	2.94	2.93	3.44	2.04	2.59	NA
Dividends	2.48	2.46	2.44	2.42	2.36	2.30	2.24	2.18	2.12	2.06
Payout Ratio	83%	83%	90%	118%	80%	74%	66%	86%	80%	68%
Prices:High	42.20	49.16	52.75	49.55	46.00	47.95	48.00	52.70	49.25	49.38
Prices:Low	31.35	32.60	43.12	40.27	40.19	40.09	37.45	32.84	38.78	28.25
P/E Ratio:High	14	17	20	24	16	15	14	21	19	16
P/E Ratio:Low	10	11	16	20	14	13	11	13	15	9

Income Statement Analysis (Million $)	2009	2008	2007	2006	2005	2004	2003	2002	2001	2000
Revenue	9,885	9,167	9,153	9,570	10,108	9,772	8,743	7,945	8,461	4,119
Depreciation	1,135	957	905	1,032	1,074	1,068	1,040	820	1,090	740
Maintenance	NA	NA	NA	NA	NA	NA	NA	NA	NA	NA
Fixed Charges Coverage	2.82	2.84	2.76	2.28	1.93	2.21	2.16	1.64	1.75	2.60
Construction Credits	163	162	17.0	7.00	13.0	6.00	7.00	8.13	18.0	20.7
Effective Tax Rate	32.2%	33.7%	32.2%	28.1%	NM	13.5%	NM	NM	NM	29.8%
Net Income	846	773	693	514	727	753	811	552	542	478
S&P Core Earnings	887	677	685	487	726	712	819	445	532	NA

Balance Sheet & Other Financial Data (Million $)	2009	2008	2007	2006	2005	2004	2003	2002	2001	2000
Gross Property	31,309	29,591	27,500	25,796	26,401	25,602	25,172	23,021	22,541	21,028
Capital Expenditures	2,295	2,333	2,201	1,423	1,286	998	1,018	2,109	1,216	950
Net Property	19,733	18,293	16,605	15,732	16,799	16,819	17,056	12,541	12,445	11,677
Capitalization:Long Term Debt	12,365	10,983	9,069	8,928	10,539	9,650	10,027	9,840	9,577	5,983
Capitalization:% Long Term Debt	56.7	55.8	51.8	51.9	56.7	55.8	57.4	59.6	61.5	52.4
Capitalization:Preferred	Nil	Nil	Nil	Nil	Nil	Nil	Nil	Nil	Nil	Nil
Capitalization:% Preferred	Nil	Nil	Nil	Nil	Nil	Nil	Nil	Nil	Nil	Nil
Capitalization:Common	9,449	8,687	8,422	8,286	8,038	7,633	7,444	6,677	6,004	5,424
Capitalization:% Common	43.3	44.2	48.2	48.1	43.3	44.2	42.6	40.4	38.5	47.6
Total Capital	22,226	19,803	17,714	17,681	19,061	18,058	18,398	17,656	17,241	13,476
% Operating Ratio	86.1	85.9	86.8	87.5	87.2	86.7	66.8	85.4	83.5	87.1
% Earned on Net Property	9.3	9.6	9.7	8.5	7.7	8.8	8.2	8.3	10.3	7.6
% Return on Revenue	8.6	8.4	7.6	5.4	7.2	7.7	9.3	6.9	6.4	11.6
% Return on Invested Capital	7.3	7.6	7.4	6.8	7.3	7.6	8.2	7.2	9.2	7.1
% Return on Common Equity	9.3	9.0	8.3	6.3	9.3	10.0	11.5	8.7	9.4	10.8

Data as orig reptd.; bef. results of disc opers/spec. items. Per share data adj. for stk. divs.; EPS diluted. E-Estimated. NA-Not Available. NM-Not Meaningful. NR-Not Ranked. UR-Under Review.

Office: 410 South Wilmington Street, Raleigh, NC 27601-1748.
Telephone: 919-546-6111.
Email: shareholder.relations@progress-energy.com
Website: http://www.progress-energy.com

Chrmn, Pres & CEO: W.D. Johnson
SVP & CFO: M.F. Mulhern
CFO: S.A. Allaire
Chief Admin Officer, Secy & General Counsel: J. McArthur

Chief Acctg Officer & Cntlr: J.M. Stone
Investor Contact: B. Drennan (919-546-7474)
Board Members: J. D. Baker, II, J. E. Bostic, Jr., H. E. DeLoach, Jr., J. B. Hyler, Jr., W. D. Johnson, R. W. Jones, W. S. Jones, M. Martinez, E. M. McKee, J. H. Mullin, III, C. W. Pryor, Jr., C. A. Saladrigas, T. M. Stone, A. C. Tollison, Jr.

Founded: 1926
Domicile: North Carolina
Employees: 11,000

ProLogis

STANDARD &POOR'S

S&P Recommendation BUY ★★★★☆

Price
$12.60 (as of Oct 22, 2010)

12-Mo. Target Price
$14.00

GICS Sector Financials
Sub-Industry Industrial REITS

Summary This real estate investment trust is a major global provider of distribution facilities to manufacturers, retailers, and transportation and third-party logistics companies across North America, Europe and Asia.

Key Stock Statistics (Source S&P, Vickers, company reports)

52-Wk Range	$15.04– 9.15	S&P FFO/Sh. 2010E	0.55	Market Capitalization(B)	$6.008	Beta	2.79
Trailing 12-Month FFO/Share	NA	S&P FFO/Sh. 2011E	0.71	Yield (%)	4.76	S&P 3-Yr. FFO/Sh. Proj. CAGR(%)	4
Trailing 12-Month P/FFO	NA	P/FFO on S&P FFO/Sh. 2010E	22.9	Dividend Rate/Share	$0.60	S&P Credit Rating	BBB-
$10K Invested 5 Yrs Ago	$3,985	Common Shares Outstg. (M)	476.8	Institutional Ownership (%)	100		

Price Performance

30-Week Mov. Avg. · · · ·   10-Week Mov. Avg. - - -   **GAAP Earnings vs. Previous Year**   Volume Above Avg. ▮▮▮▮ STARS
12-Mo. Target Price —   Relative Strength —   ▲ Up ▼ Down ▶ No Change   Below Avg. ▮▮▮ ★

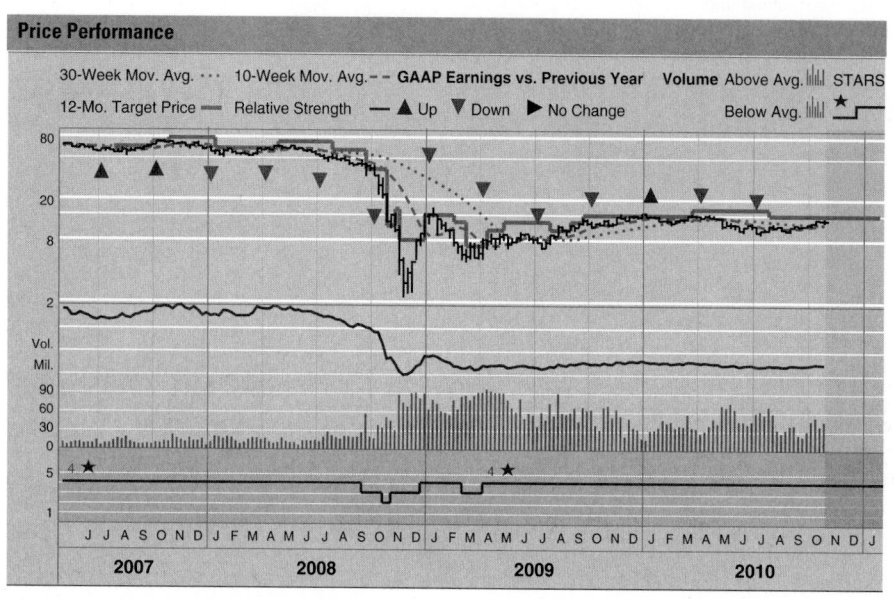

Options: ASE, CBOE, P, Ph

Analysis prepared by **Robert McMillan** on October 18, 2010, when the stock traded at **$ 12.31**.

Highlights

▶ We believe rental income, after falling 8.6% in 2008 and 78% in 2009, on softer demand for space in PLD's industrial properties, sharply lower property disposition proceeds, and fewer properties in the portfolio, will decline 19% in 2010 due to property disposition proceeds and continued portfolio re-positioning.

▶ We see a gradual rebound in global trade stimulating demand for PLD's properties; we believe inventory rebuilding by industrial companies will be a major catalyst. At the end of the 2010 second quarter, PLD's total industrial operating portfolio (including completed developments) was 89.7% leased, up from 88.7% last year. We expect re-leasing spreads, which declined 15.7% in the second quarter, to improve over the next 12-18 months. Developers, like PLD, have sharply reduced new developments over the past year, helping to limit supply, which we believe will allow rents to increase once demand recovers. We also think management's continued de-leveraging efforts will help improve the trust's risk profile.

▶ We estimate funds from operations (FFO) per share of $0.55 for 2010 and $0.71 for 2011.

Investment Rationale/Risk

▶ Long term, we see shareholders benefiting from PLD's position as one of the largest owners of global distribution facilities, which are increasingly important, in our view, to global companies looking to increase efficiency. In the short term, however, lingering concerns about PLD's debt burden may weigh on the shares.

▶ Risks to our recommendation and target price include a sharp drop in demand and rental rates for industrial space, a sharper-than-expected downturn in development activity, and higher interest rates.

▶ The stock recently traded at 19.2X PLD's trailing 12-month operating FFO per share. Our 12-month target price of $14 is about 19X our forward 12-month FFO estimate of $0.73. Although our target valuation multiple is toward the high end of recent historical levels, we think it is warranted. Over the past 12 months, PLD has significantly de-levered its balance sheet and has made efforts to re-position the portfolio for more stable long-term growth. We believe that the combination of rising demand for space and limited new construction will considerably help long-term growth.

Qualitative Risk Assessment

LOW	MEDIUM	HIGH

Our risk assessment reflects our view of PLD's position as one of the largest owners of industrial space in the world, and its broad geographic and customer diversification. Although the trust's debt burden remains heavy, we think it is manageable, with no sizable debt maturities until 2012.

Quantitative Evaluations

S&P Quality Ranking   **B**

D	C	B-	**B**	B+	A-	A	A+

Relative Strength Rank   **STRONG**

75

LOWEST = 1   HIGHEST = 99

Revenue/FFO Data

Revenue (Million $)

	1Q	2Q	3Q	4Q	Year
2010	260.0	264.0	--	--	--
2009	433.3	259.1	270.4	260.3	1,223
2008	1,637	1,515	1,122	1,388	5,599
2007	955.9	989.4	3,461	799.9	6,205
2006	571.1	687.4	580.5	624.9	2,464
2005	431.9	469.6	532.0	434.6	1,868

FFO Per Share ($)

	1Q	2Q	3Q	4Q	Year
2010	0.01	0.20	E0.20	E0.19	E0.55
2009	0.86	0.34	0.21	-0.64	0.35
2008	1.38	1.06	0.63	0.61	3.68
2007	1.25	1.16	1.41	0.79	4.61
2006	0.90	0.90	0.79	1.11	3.69
2005	0.90	0.90	0.79	0.58	2.51

Fiscal year ended Dec. 31. Next earnings report expected: Late October. FFO Estimates based on S&P Funds From Operations Est..

Dividend Data (Dates: mm/dd Payment Date: mm/dd/yy)

Amount ($)	Date Decl.	Ex-Div. Date	Stk. of Record	Payment Date
0.150	11/02	11/12	11/16	11/30/09
0.150	02/01	02/10	02/12	02/26/10
0.150	05/03	05/12	05/14	05/28/10
0.150	08/02	08/12	08/16	08/31/10

Dividends have been paid since 1994. Source: Company reports.

Please read the Required Disclosures and Analyst Certification on the last page of this report.

ProLogis

Business Summary October 18, 2010

ProLogis (formerly ProLogis Trust, and prior to that Security Capital Industrial Trust) is a real estate investment trust that owns and operates industrial distribution and facilities in North America, Europe and Asia. The trust's business strategy is to integrate international scope and expertise with a strong local presence in its markets, thereby becoming an attractive choice for its targeted customer base, the largest global users of distribution space, while achieving long-term sustainable growth in cash flow.

PLD's business is dividend into two operating segments: direct owned (66.7% of 2009 net operating income) and investment management (13.5%). In 2009, PLD discontinued its corporate distribution facilities services segment (CDFS, which represented 19.8% of 2009 net operating income); its operations were contributed to the other two segments The direct owned segment represents the direct long-term ownership of industrial and retail properties. It is involved in long-term ownership, management and leasing of industrial distribution facilities, usually adaptable for distribution and light manufacturing or assembly uses. The trust earns income from rents and reimbursement of property operating expenses from unaffiliated customers, and management fees from entities in which it has an ownership interest. At December 31, 2009, PLD's direct owned segment consisted of 1,220 properties aggregating about 196 million square feet in North America, Europe and Asia. The properties are primarily distribution properties, although it owned 27 retail properties aggregating 1 million square feet.

The investment management segment (5% of 2009 operating income) represents PLD's investment management of unconsolidated property funds and certain joint ventures and the properties they own. PLD utilizes its investment management expertise to manage the property funds and joint ventures and utilizes its leasing and property management expertise to manage the properties owned by these entities. The trust's property fund strategy allows PLD, as the manager of the property funds, to maintain and expand its market presence and customer relationships; to maintain a long-term ownership position in the properties; to earn fees for providing services to the property funds; and to earn incentive performance participation income based on the investors' returns over a specified period. As of December 31, 2009, PLD had investments in and advances to 15 property funds, totaling $1.9 billion with ownership interests ranging from 20% to 50% in investments in North America, Europe and Asia. These property funds own, on a combined basis, 1,287 distribution properties aggregating 274.2 million square feet with a total entity investment (not PLD's proportionate share) in operating properties of $19.5 billion. Also included in this segment are certain industrial joint ventures that PLD manages and that own 92 operating properties with 10.0 million square feet, all located in North America.

Company Financials Fiscal Year Ended Dec. 31

Per Share Data ($)	2009	2008	2007	2006	2005	2004	2003	2002	2001	2000
Tangible Book Value	15.27	21.27	25.44	23.09	21.08	14.82	14.35	13.96	12.94	13.53
Earnings	-0.73	-0.85	3.61	2.71	1.39	1.09	1.16	1.20	0.52	0.96
S&P Core Earnings	-0.73	-0.85	3.61	2.71	1.39	1.06	1.14	1.17	0.49	NA
Dividends	0.70	2.07	1.84	1.60	1.48	1.46	1.44	1.42	1.38	1.34
Payout Ratio	NM	NM	51%	59%	106%	134%	124%	118%	NM	140%
Prices:High	16.68	66.58	73.35	67.52	47.62	43.33	32.62	26.00	23.30	24.69
Prices:Low	4.87	2.20	51.64	46.29	36.50	27.62	23.63	20.96	19.35	17.56
P/E Ratio:High	NM	NM	20	25	34	40	28	22	45	26
P/E Ratio:Low	NM	NM	14	17	26	25	20	17	37	18

Income Statement Analysis (Million $)										
Rental Income	891	1,002	1,068	928	635	527	Nil	449	466	480
Mortgage Income	Nil	Nil	Nil	Nil	Nil	Nil	Nil	Nil	Nil	Nil
Total Income	1,223	5,599	6,205	2,464	1,868	598	734	675	574	644
General Expenses	493	4,692	4,760	1,403	1,210	224	210	91.0	83.0	78.0
Interest Expense	373	341	368	294	178	153	155	153	164	172
Provision for Losses	Nil	Nil	Nil	Nil	Nil	Nil	Nil	Nil	Nil	Nil
Depreciation	316	339	309	293	199	172	165	153	143	151
Net Income	-266	-195	987	718	318	234	251	249	128	214
S&P Core Earnings	-292	-221	962	692	292	199	208	210	86.8	NA

Balance Sheet & Other Financial Data (Million $)										
Cash	34.4	175	419	1,775	1,241	1,145	1,009	111	28.0	57.9
Total Assets	16,885	19,252	19,724	15,904	13,114	7,098	6,369	5,924	5,604	5,946
Real Estate Investment	15,216	15,706	16,579	13,954	11,875	6,334	5,854	5,396	4,588	4,689
Loss Reserve	Nil	Nil	Nil	Nil	Nil	Nil	Nil	Nil	Nil	Nil
Net Investment	13,545	14,123	15,210	12,674	10,757	5,345	5,007	4,683	4,013	4,213
Short Term Debt	Nil	Nil	Nil	Nil	Nil	Nil	Nil	222	49.3	69.7
Capitalization:Debt	7,977	11,008	9,650	7,844	6,678	3,414	2,991	2,510	2,529	2,555
Capitalization:Equity	7,637	6,075	7,086	6,049	5,138	2,752	2,586	2,486	2,276	2,236
Capitalization:Total	15,984	17,453	17,165	14,295	12,225	6,583	6,089	5,439	5,251	5,574
% Earnings & Depreciation/Assets	0.3	7.4	7.3	4.7	5.1	6.0	6.8	7.0	4.7	6.2
Price Times Book Value:High	1.1	3.1	2.9	2.9	2.3	2.9	2.3	1.9	1.8	1.8
Price Times Book Value:Low	0.3	0.1	2.0	2.0	1.7	1.9	1.6	1.5	1.5	1.3

Data as orig reptd.; bef. results of disc opers/spec. items. Per share data adj. for stk. divs.; EPS diluted. E-Estimated. NA-Not Available. NM-Not Meaningful. NR-Not Ranked. UR-Under Review.

Office: 4545 Airport Way, Denver, CO 80239-5716.
Telephone: 303-567-5000.
Email: info@prologis.com
Website: http://www.prologis.com

Chrmn: S.L. Feinberg
Pres: T.R. Antenucci
CEO: W.C. Rakowich
COO: G.A. Anderson

SVP & Chief Acctg Officer: J.S. Finnin
Investor Contact: M. Marsden (303-567-5622)
Trustees: S. L. Feinberg, G. L. Fotiades, C. N. Garvey, L. V. Jackson, D. P. Jacobs, I. F. Lyons, III, W. C. Rakowich, D. M. Steuert, A. M. Zulberti, J. A. de Barros Teixeira

Founded: 1991
Domicile: Maryland
Employees: 1,135

Prudential Financial Inc

STANDARD &POOR'S

S&P Recommendation	STRONG BUY ★★★★★	Price $52.71 (as of Oct 22, 2010)	12-Mo. Target Price $75.00	Investment Style Large-Cap Value

GICS Sector Financials
Sub-Industry Life & Health Insurance

Summary This company provides a wide range of insurance, investment management and other financial products and services to customers in the U.S. and overseas.

Key Stock Statistics (Source S&P, Vickers, company reports)

52-Wk Range	$66.80– 43.41	S&P Oper. EPS 2010E	5.95	Market Capitalization(B)	$24.510	Beta	2.49
Trailing 12-Month EPS	$8.97	S&P Oper. EPS 2011E	6.75	Yield (%)	1.33	S&P 3-Yr. Proj. EPS CAGR(%)	13
Trailing 12-Month P/E	5.9	P/E on S&P Oper. EPS 2010E	8.9	Dividend Rate/Share	$0.70	S&P Credit Rating	A
$10K Invested 5 Yrs Ago	$8,612	Common Shares Outstg. (M)	465.0	Institutional Ownership (%)	54		

Price Performance

30-Week Mov. Avg. · · · · 10-Week Mov. Avg. - - GAAP Earnings vs. Previous Year   Volume Above Avg. STARS
12-Mo. Target Price — Relative Strength — ▲ Up ▼ Down ► No Change   Below Avg. ★

Options: ASE, CBOE, Ph

Analysis prepared by **Bret Howlett** on August 16, 2010, when the stock traded at **$ 54.72.**

Qualitative Risk Assessment

LOW	MEDIUM	HIGH

Our risk assessment reflects PRU's exposure to equity markets and risk of further asset impairments on its balance sheet, especially considering its sizable holdings of commercial real estate loans and CMBS. However, we believe its financial flexibility and excess capital cushion will make future losses manageable. We also view favorably PRU's varied product offerings, geographic diversification and prominent market position.

Quantitative Evaluations

S&P Quality Ranking   NR

D	C	B-	B	B+	A-	A	A+

Relative Strength Rank   WEAK

20

LOWEST = 1   HIGHEST = 99

Highlights

► We believe retirement fundamentals are strong, and we look for a sharp increase in earnings on robust full-service sales and flows and higher account values. We believe PRU is gaining market share in variable annuities due to the attractiveness of its products, and we forecast strong sales growth. We see earnings rebounding in asset management on better proprietary investment returns and strong flows. We see slight earnings growth in PRU's insurance unit on higher investment income and in the absence of accounting charges, despite lower premiums and poor life and disability margins. Price hikes and the challenging macro environment should pressure sales.

► We expect 10%-12% international earnings growth, on strong premium growth at Gibraltar, fueled by robust sales of protection-oriented products in the bank channel. We also see strong results at Life Planner on higher sales of variable life and retirement products, expanded distribution and acquisitions, and increased agent productivity.

► We see operating EPS of $5.95 for 2010 and EPS of $6.75 for 2011. Our estimates exclude realized investment gains or losses.

Investment Rationale/Risk

► Our strong buy recommendation is based on our view of PRU's collection of high-growth businesses and its superior financial flexibility. We believe PRU will expand earnings and return on equity (ROE) at a faster rate than many peers and is well positioned to gain market share in many product areas. We expect PRU's strong financial position to allow it to deploy a considerable amount of excess capital in the credit markets, and the company could potentially execute a sizable acquisition in 2010. Also, we think PRU might resume share repurchases. We believe PRU's stock warrants a higher valuation versus many peers due to its broad business mix, distribution capabilities, and its rapidly growing international division, which will benefit from a favorable competitive landscape in Asia, in our view.

► Risks to our recommendation and target price include currency risk; reserving risks for new guaranteed minimum benefits; integration risk from acquisitions; credit risk; and exposure to equity market declines.

► Our 12-month target price is $75, or roughly 1.2X our 2011 book value (ex- FAS 115) estimate, below PRU's historical multiple, but above peers.

Revenue/Earnings Data

Revenue (Million $)

	1Q	2Q	3Q	4Q	Year
2010	9,292	11,054	--	--	--
2009	8,563	6,906	8,564	8,659	32,688
2008	7,564	7,709	7,036	6,966	29,275
2007	8,775	8,425	8,383	8,808	34,401
2006	7,850	7,373	8,408	8,857	32,488
2005	7,721	8,318	7,787	7,882	31,708

Earnings Per Share ($)

2010	1.16	1.70	E1.45	E1.50	E5.95
2009	0.01	1.22	2.36	3.82	7.66
2008	0.20	1.35	-0.24	-3.91	-2.49
2007	2.10	1.86	1.89	1.89	7.58
2006	1.39	0.92	2.24	1.85	6.37
2005	1.47	1.56	2.61	0.78	6.46

Fiscal year ended Dec. 31. Next earnings report expected: Early November. EPS Estimates based on S&P Operating Earnings; historical GAAP earnings are as reported.

Dividend Data (Dates: mm/dd Payment Date: mm/dd/yy)

Amount ($)	Date Decl.	Ex-Div. Date	Stk. of Record	Payment Date
0.700	11/10	11/20	11/24	12/18/09

Dividends have been paid since 2002. Source: Company reports.

Please read the Required Disclosures and Analyst Certification on the last page of this report.

The McGraw-Hill Companies

Prudential Financial Inc

Business Summary August 16, 2010

CORPORATE OVERVIEW. Prudential Financial is one of the largest U.S. financial services companies, with $641 billion in assets under management and $2.6 trillion in life insurance in force at year-end 2009, and customers in roughly 37 other countries.

The financial services business operates through three divisions: retirement and investments (33% of 2009 operating revenues, 33% in 2008), insurance (29%, 32%), and international insurance and investments (39%, 36%). PRU also has a corporate and other segment which reported a loss of $5 million in 2009. The insurance division consists of the individual life unit (34% of the division's 2009 operating revenues) and the group insurance unit (66%), which distributes group life, disability and related insurance products through employee and member benefit plans.

The asset management unit (14% of the division's 2009 operating revenues), the individual annuities unit (33%) and the retirement services unit (53%) comprise the retirement and investments division. International insurance and investments consists of insurance (96% of the division's 2009 operating revenues) and investments (4%). PRU distributes life insurance products to the mass affluent markets mostly in Japan and Korea through its Life Planner operations (which contributed to 62% of the division's insurance operating revenues in 2009). Additionally, the company's Life Advisor agents market insurance products to the middle class in Japan through its Gibraltar Life subsidiary (38%)

The closed block businesses represent some insurance products no longer offered, including certain participating insurance and annuity policies. At December 31, 2009, PRU had reinsurance agreements covering about 73% of the closed block policies.

CORPORATE STRATEGY. We believe PRU is focused on two prime areas of growth: international businesses and domestic retirement and savings. Prudential has made strategic acquisitions to enhance these opportunities.

Company Financials Fiscal Year Ended Dec. 31

Per Share Data ($)	2009	2008	2007	2006	2005	2004	2003	2002	2001	2000
Tangible Book Value	84.86	31.18	52.43	46.32	45.53	42.40	39.65	37.89	34.90	NA
Operating Earnings	NA	NA	NA	NA	NA	NA	NA	NA	NA	NA
Earnings	7.66	-2.49	7.58	6.37	6.46	3.45	2.06	1.36	0.07	0.82
S&P Core Earnings	10.75	2.77	6.18	5.41	4.96	1.91	1.79	1.13	NA	NA
Dividends	0.70	0.58	1.15	0.95	0.78	0.63	0.50	0.40	Nil	NA
Payout Ratio	9%	NM	15%	15%	12%	18%	24%	29%	Nil	NA
Prices:High	55.99	93.14	103.27	87.18	78.62	55.62	42.21	36.00	33.74	NA
Prices:Low	10.63	13.10	81.61	71.28	52.07	40.14	27.03	25.25	27.50	NA
P/E Ratio:High	7	NM	14	14	12	16	20	26	NM	NA
P/E Ratio:Low	1	NM	11	11	8	12	13	19	NM	NA

Income Statement Analysis (Million $)										
Life Insurance in Force	NA	NA	NA	NA	NA	NA	1,928,650	1,800,788	1,768,038	NA
Premium Income:Life	16,545	15,468	14,351	13,908	13,685	12,580	10,972	10,897	10,078	NA
Premium Income:A & H	NA	NA	NA	NA	NA	NA	806	586	515	NA
Net Investment Income	11,421	11,883	12,017	11,354	10,560	9,079	8,681	8,832	9,151	9,467
Total Revenue	32,688	29,275	34,401	32,488	31,708	28,348	27,907	26,675	27,177	26,514
Pretax Income	3,092	-1,565	4,932	4,611	4,471	3,287	1,958	64.0	-227	525
Net Operating Income	NA	NA	NA	NA	NA	NA	NA	NA	NA	NA
Net Income	3,105	-1,104	3,687	3,363	3,602	2,332	1,308	256	-170	304
S&P Core Earnings	4,810	1,189	2,899	2,675	2,580	1,022	981	650	-403	NA

Balance Sheet & Other Financial Data (Million $)										
Cash & Equivalent	32,217	33,239	13,234	10,731	9,866	10,100	9,746	11,688	20,364	19,994
Premiums Due	NA	1,558	2,119	1,958	3,548	32,790	Nil	Nil	Nil	NA
Investment Assets:Bonds	180,345	161,864	165,710	166,285	158,515	153,715	132,011	128,075	110,316	NA
Investment Assets:Stocks	25,948	24,276	26,216	24,574	18,792	4,283	6,703	2,807	2,272	NA
Investment Assets:Loans	41,530	42,817	39,384	34,626	32,811	32,761	27,621	22,094	28,299	NA
Investment Assets:Total	260,552	242,025	243,107	245,349	221,401	216,624	181,041	183,094	165,834	169,251
Deferred Policy Costs	14,578	15,126	12,339	10,863	9,438	8,847	7,826	7,031	6,868	6,751
Total Assets	480,203	445,011	485,814	454,266	417,776	401,058	321,274	292,746	293,030	298,414
Debt	21,037	20,290	14,101	11,423	8,270	7,627	5,610	4,757	5,304	14,812
Common Equity	25,195	13,422	23,457	22,892	22,763	22,344	21,292	21,330	20,453	20,692
% Return on Revenue	9.5	NM	10.7	10.4	11.4	8.2	4.7	1.0	NM	1.1
% Return on Assets	0.7	NM	0.8	0.8	0.9	0.6	0.4	0.1	NM	NA
% Return on Equity	16.1	NA	15.9	14.7	16.0	10.7	6.1	1.2	NM	NA
% Investment Yield	4.5	4.9	5.0	4.8	4.8	4.6	4.8	5.1	5.8	NA

Data as orig reptd.; bef. results of disc opers/spec. items. Per share data adj. for stk. divs.; EPS diluted. E-Estimated. NA-Not Available. NM-Not Meaningful. NR-Not Ranked. UR-Under Review.

Office: 751 Broad St, Newark, NJ 07102.
Telephone: 973-802-6000.
Email: investor.relations@prudential.com
Website: http://www.investor.prudential.com

Chrmn, Pres & CEO: J.R. Strangfeld, Jr.
Vice Chrmn: M.B. Grier
COO & EVP: E.P. Baird
EVP & CFO: R.J. Carbone

SVP & Chief Acctg Officer: P. Sayre
Board Members: T. J. Baltimore, Jr., G. M. Bethune, G. Caperton, III, G. F. Casellas, J. G. Cullen, W. H. Gray, III, M. B. Grier, J. F. Hanson, C. J. Horner, M. Hund-Mejean, K. J. Krapek, C. A. Poon, J. R. Strangfeld, Jr., J. A. Unruh

Founded: 1875
Domicile: New Jersey
Employees: 41,943

Public Storage

STANDARD &POOR'S

S&P Recommendation	HOLD ★★★★★	Price	12-Mo. Target Price	Investment Style
		$103.08 (as of Oct 22, 2010)	$108.00	Large-Cap Blend

GICS Sector Financials
Sub-Industry Specialized REITS

Summary This real estate investment trust primarily invests in self-service storage facilities (mini-warehouses), but also has commercial and industrial properties.

Key Stock Statistics (Source S&P, Vickers, company reports)

52-Wk Range	$104.35– 71.33	S&P FFO/Sh. 2010E	4.43	Market Capitalization(B)	$17.535	Beta	1.00
Trailing 12-Month FFO/Share	NA	S&P FFO/Sh. 2011E	5.45	Yield (%)	3.10	S&P 3-Yr. FFO/Sh. Proj. CAGR(%)	2
Trailing 12-Month P/FFO	NA	P/FFO on S&P FFO/Sh. 2010E	23.3	Dividend Rate/Share	$3.20	S&P Credit Rating	A-
$10K Invested 5 Yrs Ago	$18,792	Common Shares Outstg. (M)	170.1	Institutional Ownership (%)	75		

Price Performance

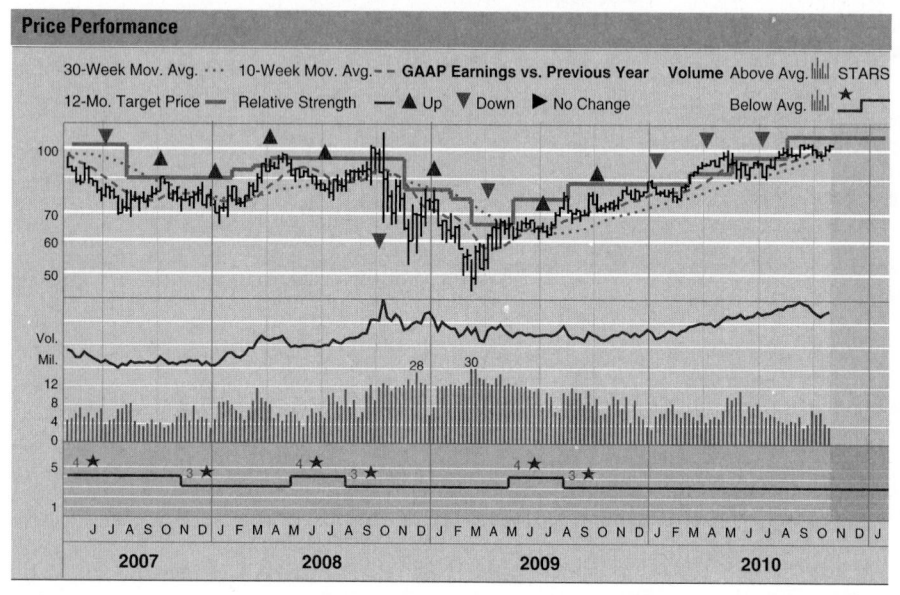

30-Week Mov. Avg. ···· 10-Week Mov. Avg. -- GAAP Earnings vs. Previous Year Volume Above Avg. STARS
12-Mo. Target Price — Relative Strength ▲ Up ▼ Down ► No Change Below Avg. ★

Options: ASE, Ph

Analysis prepared by **Robert McMillan** on August 09, 2010, when the stock traded at **$ 101.18.**

Highlights

➤ After a revenue drop of 5.6% in 2009 on the disposition of a majority stake in the Shurgard European storage business and weak demand for storage space, we expect a fractional decline in 2010, driven by continued discounting activity. We think occupancy and rent trends will improve as the year progresses on firmer demand (helped by an improving economy), which should allow management to gradually reduce discounting.

➤ Same-store domestic occupancy rose to 91.0% at the end of the second quarter, from 90.0% last year; rents per available square foot fell 1.5%, partially reflecting the need for continued discounting and promotional activity. We are encouraged that the European storage business, which weakened earlier than the U.S. business, appears to be stabilizing. Shurgard Europe's occupancy fell to 85.0% from 86.1%, but rents per occupied square foot rose 3.4%. In 2010, lower anticipated media spending should help results. Reflecting healthy liquidity and very little debt, we look for PSA to make small opportunistic property acquisitions.

➤ We estimate FFO of $4.43 ($4.22 including charges) for 2010 and $5.45 for 2011.

Investment Rationale/Risk

➤ We see PSA benefiting from its ability to continue to gain share at the expense of smaller competitors by creating customer awareness in its markets and offering an array of customer services that many small competitors cannot provide. Also, given its size versus the competition, the trust has significant pricing power, as well as the funds to launch advertising campaigns to create public awareness, which many smaller competitors cannot afford.

➤ Risks to our recommendation and target price include slower-than-expected growth in rental rates and occupancy levels, a sharp drop in moving activity, and higher interest rates.

➤ The stock recently traded at about 21.0X trailing 12-month FFO per share. Our 12-month target price of $108 is equal to 21.0X our forward four-quarter FFO estimate of $5.16. Although the valuation multiple is high relative to recent historical levels, we think it is warranted given our expectation of improved earnings as well as contributions from acquisitions and the company's huge size relative to its nearest competitors. We also consider PSA's relatively most debt burden and large cash balances as positive factors in our valuation.

Qualitative Risk Assessment

LOW	MEDIUM	HIGH

Our risk assessment reflects PSA's position as one of the largest providers of self-storage space in a consolidating industry. In our opinion, the trust has a very strong balance sheet.

Quantitative Evaluations

S&P Quality Ranking B+

D	C	B-	B	B+	A-	A	A+

Relative Strength Rank MODERATE

57

LOWEST = 1   HIGHEST = 99

Revenue/FFO Data

Revenue (Million $)

	1Q	2Q	3Q	4Q	Year
2010	398.1	410.0	--	--	--
2009	404.7	407.3	412.9	402.9	1,628
2008	462.8	428.8	443.2	428.5	1,766
2007	434.4	449.2	469.0	464.4	1,829
2006	278.5	297.9	371.4	433.9	1,382
2005	243.8	254.3	264.9	273.6	1,061

FFO Per Share ($)

	1Q	2Q	3Q	4Q	Year
2010	0.78	0.92	E1.26	E1.27	E4.43
2009	1.51	1.40	1.44	1.27	5.61
2008	1.39	1.10	1.09	1.49	5.07
2007	1.05	1.10	1.43	1.40	4.97
2006	0.94	0.99	0.77	0.89	3.57
2005	0.79	0.90	0.97	0.96	3.61

Fiscal year ended Dec. 31. Next earnings report expected: Early November. FFO Estimates based on S&P Funds From Operations Est..

Dividend Data (Dates: mm/dd Payment Date: mm/dd/yy)

Amount ($)	Date Decl.	Ex-Div. Date	Stk. of Record	Payment Date
0.650	03/01	03/11	03/15	03/31/10
0.372	05/06	06/11	06/15	06/30/10
0.800	05/06	06/11	06/15	06/30/10
0.800	08/05	09/13	09/15	09/30/10

Dividends have been paid since 2010. Source: Company reports.

Please read the Required Disclosures and Analyst Certification on the last page of this report.

The McGraw·Hill Companies

Public Storage

Business Summary August 09, 2010

Public Storage is an equity real estate investment trust that was organized as a corporation under the laws of California on July 10, 1980. At December 31, 2009, PSA operated three business segments: domestic self-storage, Europe self-storage, and commercial. In the U.S., PSA is the largest U.S. owner and operator of storage space, with direct and indirect equity investments in 2,010 self-storage facilities located in 38 states within the U.S. operating under the Public Storage name at the end of 2008. The facilities contain approximately 127 million net rentable square feet of space. The Europe self-storage business comprises PSA's 49% equity interest in Shurgard Europe which owns 187 self-storage facilities (10 million net rentable square feet of space) located in seven countries in Europe which operate under the "Shurgard Storage Centers" brand name and manages one facility located in the United Kingdom that PSA wholly owned at the end of 2009. PSA also has direct and indirect equity interests in approximately 21 million net rentable square feet of commercial space located in 11 states in the U.S. operated under the PS Business Parks and Public Storage, Inc. brands. PSA has a 41% ownership interest in PS Business Parks, Inc. (PSB: hold, $49 at the end of 2009).

PSA's growth strategies consist of improving the operating performance of stabilized existing traditional self-storage properties; acquiring additional interests in entities that own properties operated by the trust; purchasing interests in properties that are owned or operated by others; developing properties in selected markets; improving the operating performance of the containerized storage operations; and participating in the growth of PS Business Parks,

Inc as well as its European business.

The trust's storage facilities are designed to offer accessible storage space for personal and business use at a relatively low cost. Individuals usually obtain this space for storage of furniture, household appliances, personal belongings, motor vehicles, boats, campers, motorcycles and other household goods. Businesses normally employ this space for storage of excess inventory, business records, seasonal goods, equipment and fixtures. A user rents a fully enclosed space that is for the user's exclusive use and that only the user has access to on an unrestricted basis during business hours. Some storage facilities also include rentable uncovered parking areas for vehicle storage, as well as space for portable storage containers. Leases for storage facility space may be on a long-term or short-term basis, although typically spaces are rented on a month-to-month basis. Rental rates vary according to the location of the property, the size of the storage space and the length of stay. PSA's self-storage facilities generally consist of three to seven buildings containing an aggregate of between 350 and 750 storage spaces, most of which have between 25 and 400 square feet and an interior height of approximately eight to 12 feet.

Company Financials Fiscal Year Ended Dec. 31

Per Share Data ($)	2009	2008	2007	2006	2005	2004	2003	2002	2001	2000
Tangible Book Value	30.13	30.21	28.85	28.16	16.72	16.69	17.03	16.16	28.37	18.24
Earnings	3.52	4.20	1.17	0.32	1.92	1.39	1.27	1.28	1.51	1.41
S&P Core Earnings	3.52	4.20	1.15	0.32	1.91	1.38	1.25	1.26	1.48	NA
Dividends	2.20	2.20	2.00	2.00	1.85	1.80	1.80	1.80	1.69	1.48
Payout Ratio	63%	52%	171%	NM	97%	129%	142%	1%	112%	105%
Prices:High	85.10	110.00	117.16	98.05	72.02	57.64	45.81	39.29	35.15	26.93
Prices:Low	45.35	52.52	68.09	67.72	51.50	39.50	28.25	27.98	24.13	20.87
P/E Ratio:High	24	26	NM	NM	38	41	36	33	23	19
P/E Ratio:Low	13	13	NM	NM	27	28	22	24	16	15

Income Statement Analysis (Million $)	2009	2008	2007	2006	2005	2004	2003	2002	2001	2000
Rental Income	1,490	1,581	1,663	1,240	980	894	844	813	782	703
Mortgage Income	Nil	Nil	Nil	Nil	Nil	Nil	Nil	Nil	Nil	Nil
Total Income	1,628	1,766	1,829	1,382	1,061	928	875	841	835	757
General Expenses	459	644	712	585	400	349	336	311	297	273
Interest Expense	29.9	44.0	64.0	33.1	8.22	0.76	1.12	3.81	3.23	3.29
Provision for Losses	Nil	Nil	Nil	Nil	Nil	Nil	Nil	Nil	Nil	Nil
Depreciation	340	414	622	438	196	183	186	180	168	149
Net Income	843	936	458	312	450	367	335	319	324	297
S&P Core Earnings	595	710	197	44.7	247	179	157	156	183	NA

Balance Sheet & Other Financial Data (Million $)	2009	2008	2007	2006	2005	2004	2003	2002	2001	2000
Cash	764	681	245	857	329	708	205	103	49.3	89.5
Total Assets	9,806	9,936	10,643	11,198	5,552	5,205	4,968	4,844	4,626	4,514
Real Estate Investment	10,296	10,227	11,719	11,262	6,314	5,908	5,544	5,424	5,062	4,822
Loss Reserve	Nil	Nil	Nil	Nil	Nil	Nil	Nil	Nil	Nil	Nil
Net Investment	7,562	7,822	9,591	9,507	4,814	4,588	4,391	4,436	4,242	4,154
Short Term Debt	12.7	13.0	216	Nil	Nil	Nil	Nil	39.8	Nil	Nil
Capitalization:Debt	506	631	808	1,848	134	130	76.0	76.1	144	156
Capitalization:Equity	5,529	5,291	5,236	5,353	2,319	2,328	2,353	2,342	2,369	2,569
Capitalization:Total	9,581	9,710	9,270	8,785	5,205	4,989	4,722	4,675	4,508	4,413
% Earnings & Depreciation/Assets	12.0	13.1	9.8	8.9	12.0	10.8	10.6	10.5	7.1	10.2
Price Times Book Value:High	2.8	3.6	4.1	3.5	4.3	3.5	2.7	2.4	1.2	1.5
Price Times Book Value:Low	1.5	1.7	2.4	2.4	3.1	2.4	1.7	1.7	0.9	1.1

Data as orig reptd.; bef. results of disc opers/spec. items. Per share data adj. for stk. divs.; EPS diluted. E-Estimated. NA-Not Available. NM-Not Meaningful. NR-Not Ranked. UR-Under Review.

Office: 701 Western Ave, Glendale, CA 91201-2349.
Telephone: 818-244-8080.
Email: investor@publicstorage.com
Website: http://www.publicstorage.com

Chrmn: B. Hughes
Pres, Vice Chrmn & CEO: R.L. Havner, Jr.
COO & SVP: M.C. Good
SVP, CFO & Chief Acctg Officer: J. Reyes

SVP & General Counsel: S.M. Glick
Investor Contact: C. Teng (818-244-8080)
Board Members: D. V. Angeloff, J. T. Evans, T. H. Gustavson, U. P. Harkham, R. L. Havner, Jr., B. Hughes, B. W. Hughes, Jr., H. Lenkin, A. B. Poladian, G. E. Pruitt, R. P. Spogli, D. C. Staton

Founded: 1980
Domicile: Maryland
Employees: 4,900

Public Service Enterprise Group Inc

STANDARD &POOR'S

S&P Recommendation BUY ★★★★☆

Price $33.25 (as of Oct 22, 2010)	**12-Mo. Target Price** $36.00

Investment Style Large-Cap Blend

GICS Sector Utilities
Sub-Industry Multi-Utilities

Summary PEG is the holding company for Public Service Electric and Gas (PSE&G), with a service area that encompasses 70% of New Jersey.

Key Stock Statistics (Source S&P, Vickers, company reports)

52-Wk Range	$34.93–29.01	S&P Oper. EPS 2010**E**	3.17	Market Capitalization(B)	$16.823	Beta	0.54
Trailing 12-Month EPS	$3.06	S&P Oper. EPS 2011**E**	3.10	Yield (%)	4.12	S&P 3-Yr. Proj. EPS CAGR(%)	2
Trailing 12-Month P/E	10.9	P/E on S&P Oper. EPS 2010**E**	10.5	Dividend Rate/Share	$1.37	S&P Credit Rating	BBB
$10K Invested 5 Yrs Ago	$13,037	Common Shares Outstg. (M)	506.0	Institutional Ownership (%)	62		

Price Performance

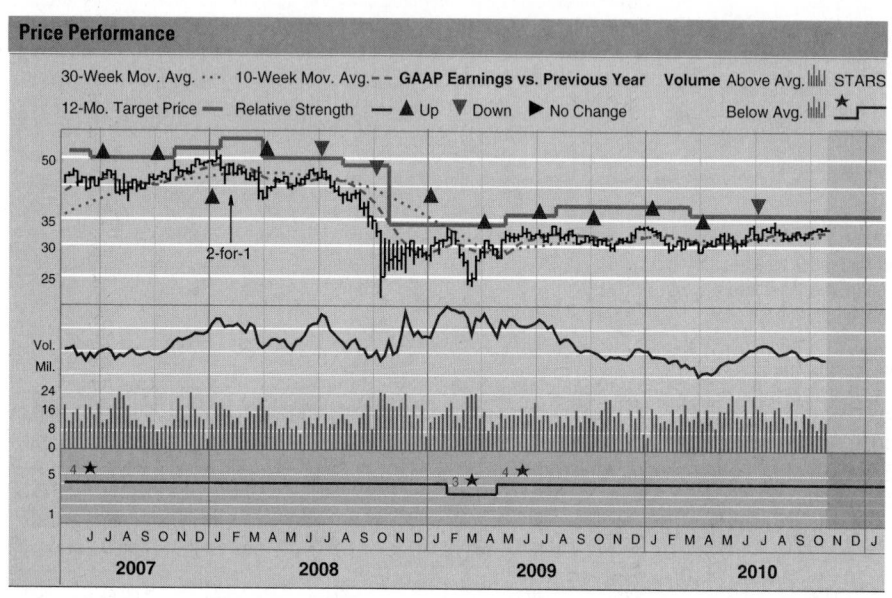

Options: ASE, CBOE, Ph

Analysis prepared by **Justin McCann** on August 31, 2010, when the stock traded at **$31.80**.

Highlights

▸ Excluding $0.08 in net one-time charges, we expect 2010 operating EPS to increase less than 2% from 2009's $3.12, which excluded a net one-time gain of $0.02. Operating EPS in the first half of 2010 was down $0.09 from the year-earlier period as the benefit of much more favorable weather was more than offset by lower pricing in the Power segment.

▸ For full-year 2010, we expect operating results to benefit from the reversal of the below normal weather in 2009. However, we believe this could be partially offset by lower earnings for the power generation business due to an unplanned 17-day outage at the Salem 1 nuclear unit. For 2011, we expect a decline in operating EPS, due to lower-margin power contracts and the ongoing weakness in the economy.

▸ PEG's Energy Holdings unit sold its interest in nine leveraged leases in 2009. The leases had a combined book value of $369 million, including seven international leases for which the IRS disallowed deductions taken in prior years. Total proceeds were about $460 million, and are being used to reduce the related tax exposure range of $360 million to $780 million. PEG plans to litigate for the recovery of these taxes.

Investment Rationale/Risk

▸ Although the stock is down more than 5% year to date (after a 14% increase in 2009), it has rebounded 10% from its 2010 low. We believe the current weakness in the shares offers an attractive buying opportunity, and we continue to recommend it for above-average total return potential over the next 12 months. Although we expect near-term earnings to be pressured by the ongoing weakness in the economy and power markets, we think the company's cost-control efforts and its effective management of its power supply operations will leave it well positioned for an economic recovery.

▸ Risks to our recommendation and target price include a decline in PEG's wholesale power margins, as well as weakness in the broader market and/or an event that would reduce the average P/E of the group as a whole.

▸ With the 3% increase effective with the March dividend payment, the recent yield was 4.3%. While this is still below the recent peer average of about 4.7%, it is roughly in line with the yields of other utility holding companies with large wholesale power operations. Our 12-month target price of $36 reflects a discount-to-peers P/E of 11.6X our EPS estimate for 2011.

Qualitative Risk Assessment

LOW	MEDIUM	HIGH

Our risk assessment reflects our view of the strong and steady cash flows from the regulated electric and gas utility operations of PSE&G, as well as the strong albeit less predictable earnings and cash flows from the non-regulated power generating operations. It also reflects what we see as a lowering of PEG's risk profile through the divestiture of non-core international investments.

Quantitative Evaluations

S&P Quality Ranking B+

D	C	B-	B	B+	A-	A	A+

Relative Strength Rank MODERATE
43
LOWEST = 1   HIGHEST = 99

Revenue/Earnings Data

Revenue (Million $)

	1Q	2Q	3Q	4Q	Year
2010	3,680	2,455	--	--	--
2009	3,921	2,561	3,039	2,886	12,406
2008	3,803	2,561	3,718	3,262	13,322
2007	3,508	2,718	3,356	3,271	12,853
2006	3,461	2,556	3,212	2,935	12,164
2005	3,310	2,442	3,376	3,472	12,430

Earnings Per Share ($)

2010	0.97	0.44	E0.98	E0.70	E3.17
2009	0.88	0.61	0.96	0.69	3.14
2008	0.85	-0.33	0.94	0.47	1.93
2007	0.64	0.56	0.96	0.44	2.59
2006	0.41	Nil	0.75	0.35	1.49
2005	0.59	0.21	0.53	0.45	1.76

Fiscal year ended Dec. 31. Next earnings report expected: Late October. EPS Estimates based on S&P Operating Earnings; historical GAAP earnings are as reported.

Dividend Data (Dates: mm/dd Payment Date: mm/dd/yy)

Amount ($)	Date Decl.	Ex-Div. Date	Stk. of Record	Payment Date
0.333	11/17	12/07	12/09	12/31/09
0.343	02/16	03/08	03/10	03/31/10
0.343	04/20	06/07	06/09	06/30/10
0.343	07/20	09/07	09/09	09/30/10

Dividends have been paid since 1907. Source: Company reports.

Please read the Required Disclosures and Analyst Certification on the last page of this report.

The McGraw-Hill Companies

Public Service Enterprise Group Inc

STANDARD & POOR'S

Business Summary August 31, 2010

CORPORATE OVERVIEW. Headquartered in Newark, NJ, Public Service Enterprise Group has three primary operating units: Public Service Electric and Gas Co. - PSE&G ($325 million of net income in 2009), Power ($1.189 billion), and Energy Holdings ($72 million). The parent company and intersegment eliminations accounted $6 million. PEG has sought to minimize its earnings and cash flow volatility through the divestiture of its international operations, and by entering into long-term contracts for most of its competitive wholesale power generation.

MARKET PROFILE. At the end of 2009, the company's New Jersey utility operations served about 2.1 million electric customers and 1.7 million natural gas customers. PSE&G earns income from the delivery of electricity and gas, with the cost of the gas passed through to ratepayers. In 2009, commercial customers accounted for 58% of total electric customers (36% of gas customers), residential 31% (60%), and industrial 11% (4%). As part of New Jersey's utility deregulation, PSE&G transferred its power generating and gas supply opera-

tions to PEG's unregulated Power division in 2000 and 2002, respectively. Based on the proximity of its plants to PSE&G's customer base, Power has been able to win competitive bids for a significant portion of the utility's electricity supply obligations. Power's generating fleet, which had 15,548 megawatts (MW) of owned generating capacity as of December 31, 2009, is concentrated in Pennsylvania and New Jersey and serves the Pennsylvania, New Jersey and Maryland Interconnection (known as PJM). Power also has plants in Texas, Connecticut and New York. In addition to its electric business, Power provides PSE&G with all of the utility's gas supply needs under a contract that was extended from March 31, 2007, to March 31, 2012, and year to year thereafter.

Company Financials Fiscal Year Ended Dec. 31

Per Share Data ($)	2009	2008	2007	2006	2005	2004	2003	2002	2001	2000
Tangible Book Value	17.09	15.22	14.23	12.23	10.79	10.71	10.42	7.39	8.47	9.60
Earnings	3.14	1.93	2.59	1.49	1.76	1.52	1.86	1.00	1.84	1.78
S&P Core Earnings	3.33	1.85	2.59	1.92	1.70	1.49	2.02	1.53	1.58	NA
Dividends	1.33	1.29	1.17	1.14	1.12	1.10	1.08	1.08	1.08	1.08
Payout Ratio	42%	67%	45%	77%	64%	73%	58%	109%	59%	61%
Prices:High	34.14	52.30	49.88	36.31	34.24	26.32	22.25	23.63	25.78	25.00
Prices:Low	23.65	22.09	32.16	29.50	24.66	19.05	16.05	10.00	18.44	12.84
P/E Ratio:High	11	27	19	24	20	17	12	24	14	14
P/E Ratio:Low	8	11	12	20	14	13	9	10	10	7

Income Statement Analysis (Million $)	2009	2008	2007	2006	2005	2004	2003	2002	2001	2000
Revenue	12,406	13,322	12,853	12,164	12,430	10,996	11,116	8,390	9,815	6,848
Depreciation	838	792	783	832	748	719	527	571	522	362
Maintenance	NA	NA	NA	NA	NA	NA	NA	NA	NA	NA
Fixed Charges Coverage	5.97	4.18	4.10	2.73	2.55	2.21	2.43	2.38	2.46	2.88
Construction Credits	NA	NA	NA	NA	NA	NA	NA	NA	NA	NA
Effective Tax Rate	39.6%	48.5%	44.5%	NM	38.7%	38.2%	35.3%	37.3%	NM	39.1%
Net Income	1,592	983	1,319	752	858	721	852	416	763	764
S&P Core Earnings	1,682	945	1,316	967	834	708	925	638	656	NA

Balance Sheet & Other Financial Data (Million $)	2009	2008	2007	2006	2005	2004	2003	2002	2001	2000
Gross Property	22,069	20,818	19,310	18,851	18,896	19,121	17,406	16,562	14,886	11,968
Capital Expenditures	1,794	1,771	1,348	1,015	1,024	1,255	1,351	1,814	2,053	959
Net Property	15,440	14,433	13,275	13,002	13,336	13,750	12,422	11,449	10,064	7,702
Capitalization:Long Term Debt	7,725	8,085	8,742	10,450	11,359	13,005	13,025	12,391	11,061	6,505
Capitalization:% Long Term Debt	46.8	51.0	54.5	60.8	65.4	69.4	70.2	75.7	72.8	60.2
Capitalization:Preferred	Nil	Nil	Nil	Nil	Nil	Nil	Nil	Nil	Nil	Nil
Capitalization:% Preferred	Nil	Nil	Nil	Nil	Nil	Nil	Nil	Nil	Nil	Nil
Capitalization:Common	8,788	7,771	7,299	6,747	6,022	5,739	5,529	3,987	4,137	4,294
Capitalization:% Common	53.2	49.0	45.5	39.2	34.6	30.6	29.8	24.3	27.2	39.8
Total Capital	17,053	19,721	20,495	21,659	21,629	23,091	22,750	19,302	18,403	13,906
% Operating Ratio	83.3	87.3	85.0	78.7	88.6	87.5	86.5	78.8	76.9	79.6
% Earned on Net Property	20.9	18.9	23.3	15.1	15.9	14.9	17.3	14.3	21.3	18.9
% Return on Revenue	12.8	7.4	10.3	6.2	6.9	6.6	7.7	5.0	7.8	11.2
% Return on Invested Capital	12.8	7.8	9.3	9.3	7.6	6.9	8.1	9.3	9.6	10.8
% Return on Common Equity	19.2	13.0	18.8	11.8	14.6	12.8	18.1	10.2	18.8	18.4

Data as orig reptd.; bef. results of disc opers/spec. items. Per share data adj. for stk. divs.; EPS diluted. E-Estimated. NA-Not Available. NM-Not Meaningful. NR-Not Ranked. UR-Under Review.

Office: 80 Park Plaza, Newark, NJ 07102-4109.
Telephone: 973-430-7000.
Email: stkserv@pseg.com
Website: http://www.pseg.com

Chrmn, Pres & CEO: R. Izzo
EVP & CFO: C.D. Dorsa
EVP & General Counsel: J. Bouknight, Jr.
Chief Acctg Officer & Cntlr: D.M. Dirisio

Secy: E.J. Biggins, Jr.
Investor Contact: K.A. Lally
Board Members: A. R. Gamper, Jr., C. K. Harper, W. V. Hickey, R. Izzo, S. A. Jackson, D. Lilley, T. A. Renyi, H. C. Shin, R. J. Swift

Founded: 1985
Domicile: New Jersey
Employees: 10,352

PulteGroup Inc

STANDARD &POOR'S

S&P Recommendation BUY ★★★★☆	**Price** $8.24 (as of Oct 22, 2010)	**12-Mo. Target Price** $13.00	**Investment Style** Large-Cap Blend

GICS Sector Consumer Discretionary
Sub-Industry Homebuilding

Summary This company became the largest U.S. homebuilder following the 2009 acquisition of rival Centex Corp.

Key Stock Statistics (Source S&P, Vickers, company reports)

52-Wk Range	$13.91– 7.70	S&P Oper. EPS 2010**E**	0.10	Market Capitalization(B)	$3.154	Beta	1.00
Trailing 12-Month EPS	$-1.14	S&P Oper. EPS 2011**E**	0.40	Yield (%)	Nil	S&P 3-Yr. Proj. EPS CAGR(%)	15
Trailing 12-Month P/E	NM	P/E on S&P Oper. EPS 2010**E**	82.4	Dividend Rate/Share	Nil	S&P Credit Rating	BB-
$10K Invested 5 Yrs Ago	$2,320	Common Shares Outstg. (M)	382.7	Institutional Ownership (%)	88		

Price Performance

30-Week Mov. Avg. · · · 10-Week Mov. Avg. - - **GAAP Earnings vs. Previous Year** Volume Above Avg. STARS
12-Mo. Target Price — Relative Strength — ▲ Up ▼ Down ► No Change Below Avg. ★

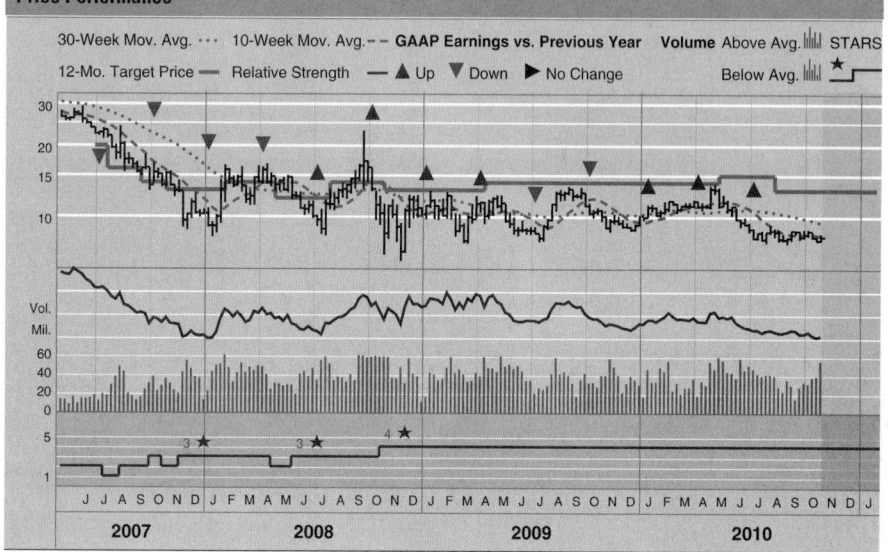

Options: ASE, CBOE, P, Ph

Analysis prepared by **Kenneth M. Leon, CPA** on August 05, 2010, when the stock traded at **$ 8.60.**

Highlights

➤ Following a sizable revenue decline in 2009 and taking into account a contract backlog of $1.6 billion, we forecast that revenues will rise 13% in 2010 and 12% in 2011, with 2010 results boosted by the Centex acquisition in August 2009. PHM reported a 21% sequential revenue increase in 2010's second quarter due to the now expired federal housing tax credit.

➤ We believe PHM, with scale advantages over peers, will gain market share as the housing market slowly recovers. In attractive markets where there is land scarcity, the addition of Centex land inventory is a positive, in our view. We estimate homebuilding gross margins will widen to 14% in 2010 and 15% in 2011, from almost 10% in 2009, excluding asset impairment charges.

➤ We see SG&A costs as a percentage of total revenue reverting to a more normalized 12% to 13% level in 2010 and 2011, compared to 17.3% in 2009. The company is targeting $440 million in cost synergies and/or operating savings from the Centex merger. We estimate EPS of $0.10 in 2010 and $0.40 in 2011, excluding one-time adjustments.

Investment Rationale/Risk

➤ In August 2009, PHM finalized the purchase of rival Centex Corp. via a stock swap valued at around $1.3 billion. We believe PHM can realize up to $300 million in operating cost savings and $100 million in interest cost savings from early debt retirements. With the companies combined, we see better sales execution and market share gains ahead.

➤ Risks to our recommendation and target price include problems integrating the Centex operations, further weakening of housing demand, a deepening recession, tighter mortgage lending, and future downward revisions of PHM's land inventory.

➤ We believe PHM has a strong balance sheet, with $2.7 billion in cash that can be used to build or acquire communities, and the company has one of the industry's largest land inventories. Our 12-month target price of $13 is derived by applying a target price-to-book multiple of just above 1.5X -- toward the middle of the historical range, and near peers -- to our forward book value per share estimate of $8.60 a share.

Qualitative Risk Assessment

LOW	MEDIUM	**HIGH**

Our risk assessment reflects risks involved in integrating the recently acquired Centex operations, which requires the combination of the home communities and the streamlining of sales and marketing and support services. While PHM enjoys greater scale post-merger, market risks remain should there be a delay in the recovery of the U.S. housing market.

Quantitative Evaluations

S&P Quality Ranking B+

D	C	B-	B	**B+**	A-	A	A+

Relative Strength Rank WEAK

20

LOWEST = 1 HIGHEST = 99

Revenue/Earnings Data

Revenue (Million $)

	1Q	2Q	3Q	4Q	Year
2010	1,020	1,306	--	--	--
2009	583.9	678.6	1,091	1,731	4,084
2008	1,442	1,619	1,565	1,644	6,263
2007	1,871	2,021	2,472	2,899	9,257
2006	2,963	3,359	3,564	4,389	14,274
2005	2,518	3,251	3,794	5,132	14,695

Earnings Per Share ($)

2010	-0.03	-0.20	E-0.03	E-0.03	E0.10
2009	-2.02	-0.74	-1.15	-0.31	-3.94
2008	-2.75	-0.62	-1.11	-1.33	-5.81
2007	-0.34	-2.01	-3.12	-3.54	-9.02
2006	1.01	0.94	0.74	-0.03	2.67
2005	0.83	1.16	1.45	2.03	5.47

Fiscal year ended Dec. 31. Next earnings report expected: Early November. EPS Estimates based on S&P Operating Earnings; historical GAAP earnings are as reported.

Dividend Data

The most recent payment, $0.04 a share, was made in early January 2009

The **McGraw·Hill** Companies

PulteGroup Inc

STANDARD &POOR'S

Business Summary August 05, 2010

CORPORATE OVERVIEW. As of 2009 year end, following the merger with Centex, the new Pulte had 882 home communities. The average selling price for company homes in 2009 was $258,000, down from $284,000 in 2008 and a high of $337,000 in 2006. The average selling price was $251,000 in the second quarter in 2010.

PHM targets buyers in nearly all home categories, but has recently concentrated its expansion efforts on affordable housing and on mature buyers (age 50 and over). In July 2001, it acquired Del Webb Corp., the leading U.S. builder of active adult communities, for a total of $1.9 billion in stock, cash, and the assumption of debt. Growth in this active adult segment and among first-time buyers, two groups that often prefer townhouses, condominiums or duplexes, helps to explain the decrease in single-family homes in PHM's product mix over the past five years.

CORPORATE STRATEGY. As of December 31, 2009, the company controlled 546,694 lots, of which 138,273 were owned and 16,421 were under option agreements. Land is generally purchased after it is properly zoned and developed or is ready for development. In addition, PHM will dispose of owned land not required in the business through sales to appropriate end users. Where

the company develops land, its engages directly in many phases of the development process, including land and site planning, and obtaining environmental and other regulatory approvals, as well as constructing roads, sewers, water and drainage facilities, and other amenities.

To assist its home sales effort, PHM offers mortgage banking and title insurance services through Pulte Mortgage and other units mainly for the benefit of its domestic home buyers, but it also services the general public. In addition, it engages in the sale of loans and related servicing rights. Mortgage underwriting, processing and closing functions are centralized in Denver, CO, and Charlotte, NC, using a mortgage operations center concept.

In December 2005, the company sold Pulte Mexico, sharply reducing its international presence, and realized cash proceeds of $131.5 million. In the fourth quarter of 2005, PHM reported these results as discontinued operations.

Company Financials Fiscal Year Ended Dec. 31

Per Share Data ($)	2009	2008	2007	2006	2005	2004	2003	2002	2001	2000
Tangible Book Value	5.54	10.59	16.35	23.82	21.49	15.95	12.13	9.41	7.64	7.51
Cash Flow	-3.76	-5.52	-8.69	2.99	5.70	4.01	2.61	1.92	1.67	1.38
Earnings	-3.94	-5.81	-9.02	2.67	5.47	3.84	2.46	1.80	1.50	1.30
S&P Core Earnings	-2.72	-5.80	-7.69	2.59	5.46	3.82	2.45	1.76	1.43	NA
Dividends	Nil	0.16	0.16	0.16	0.09	0.10	0.04	0.04	0.04	0.04
Payout Ratio	Nil	NM	NM	6%	2%	3%	2%	2%	3%	3%
Prices:High	13.59	23.24	35.56	44.70	48.23	32.50	24.71	14.94	12.56	11.25
Prices:Low	7.71	6.49	8.78	26.02	30.01	20.00	11.36	9.05	6.53	3.81
P/E Ratio:High	NM	NM	NM	17	9	8	10	8	8	9
P/E Ratio:Low	NM	NM	NM	10	5	5	5	5	4	3

Income Statement Analysis (Million $)										
Revenue	4,084	6,263	9,263	14,274	14,695	11,711	9,049	7,472	5,382	4,159
Operating Income	-262	-1,496	-1,800	2,678	244	1,587	997	746	601	429
Depreciation	54.3	74.0	83.9	83.7	62.0	46.3	40.2	29.8	32.9	14.2
Interest Expense	2.26	229	260	256	43.3	56.4	Nil	Nil	81.6	65.1
Pretax Income	-1,975	-1,683	-2,497	1,083	2,277	1,601	996	729	492	355
Effective Tax Rate	40.1%	NM	NM	36.3%	36.8%	37.6%	38.0%	39.0%	38.5%	38.5%
Net Income	-1,183	-1,473	-2,274	690	1,437	998	617	445	302	218
S&P Core Earnings	-817	-1,469	-1,939	670	1,435	993	615	436	288	NA

Balance Sheet & Other Financial Data (Million $)										
Cash	1,858	1,655	1,060	551	1,002	315	404	613	72.1	184
Current Assets	8,494	7,162	8,869	11,335	10,954	8,521	6,596	5,568	4,407	2,407
Total Assets	10,051	7,708	10,226	13,177	13,048	10,407	8,063	6,888	5,714	2,886
Current Liabilities	1,544	1,258	2,273	2,782	3,276	2,702	2,359	2,224	1,703	979
Long Term Debt	4,282	3,143	3,478	3,538	3,387	2,737	1,962	1,913	1,738	678
Common Equity	3,194	2,836	4,320	6,577	5,957	4,522	3,448	2,760	2,277	1,248
Total Capital	7,476	5,978	7,798	10,115	9,352	7,274	5,418	4,674	4,015	1,926
Capital Expenditures	39.3	18.9	70.1	98.6	88.9	75.2	39.1	NA	NA	NA
Cash Flow	-1,128	-1,399	-2,191	773	1,499	1,044	657	474	335	233
Current Ratio	3.2	3.9	3.9	4.1	3.3	3.2	2.8	2.5	2.6	2.5
% Long Term Debt of Capitalization	57.3	52.6	44.6	35.0	36.2	37.6	36.2	40.9	43.3	35.2
% Net Income of Revenue	NM	NM	NM	4.8	9.7	8.5	6.8	6.0	5.6	5.3
% Return on Assets	NM	NM	NM	5.3	12.2	10.8	8.3	7.1	7.0	8.1
% Return on Equity	NM	NM	NM	11.0	27.4	25.0	19.9	17.7	17.2	18.7

Data as orig reptd.; bef. results of disc opers/spec. items. Per share data adj. for stk. divs.; EPS diluted. E-Estimated. NA-Not Available. NM-Not Meaningful. NR-Not Ranked. UR-Under Review.

Office: 100 Bloomfield Hills Pkwy Ste 300, Bloomfield Hills, MI 48304-2950.
Telephone: 248-647-2750.
Website: http://www.pulte.com
Chrmn, Pres & CEO: R.J. Dugas, Jr.

Vice Chrmn: T.R. Eller
EVP & CFO: R.A. Cregg
SVP, Secy & General Counsel: S.M. Cook
Chief Acctg Officer & Cntlr: M.J. Schweninger

Investor Contact: C. Boyd (248-647-2750)
Board Members: B. P. Anderson, R. J. Dugas, Jr., T. R. Eller, C. W. Grise, D. J. Kelly-Ennis, D. N. McCammon, C. W. Murchison, III, P. J. O'Leary, J. J. Postl, B. W. Reznicek, T. M. Schoewe

Founded: 1969
Domicile: Michigan
Employees: 5,700

The **McGraw·Hill** Companies

QEP Resources Inc

STANDARD &POOR'S

S&P Recommendation HOLD ★★★☆☆

Price	12-Mo. Target Price	Investment Style
$31.80 (as of Oct 22, 2010)	$35.00	Large-Cap Growth

GICS Sector Energy
Sub-Industry Oil & Gas Exploration & Production

Summary This Questar spinoff is an independent oil and gas exploration and production company focused on the Rocky Mountain and Midcontinent regions of the U.S.

Key Stock Statistics (Source S&P, Vickers, company reports)

52-Wk Range	$37.00–27.90	S&P Oper. EPS 2010**E**	1.60	Market Capitalization(B)	$5.569	Beta		NA
Trailing 12-Month EPS	$2.27	S&P Oper. EPS 2011**E**	1.66	Yield (%)	NA	S&P 3-Yr. Proj. EPS CAGR(%)		NA
Trailing 12-Month P/E	14.0	P/E on S&P Oper. EPS 2010**E**	19.9	Dividend Rate/Share	NA	S&P Credit Rating		BB+
$10K Invested 5 Yrs Ago	NA	Common Shares Outstg. (M)	175.1	Institutional Ownership (%)	5			

Price Performance

- 30-Week Mov. Avg. · · ·
- 10-Week Mov. Avg. - -
- **GAAP Earnings vs. Previous Year**
- Volume Above Avg. ‖‖‖ STARS
- 12-Mo. Target Price —
- Relative Strength —
- ▲ Up ▼ Down ► No Change
- Below Avg. ‖‖‖ ★

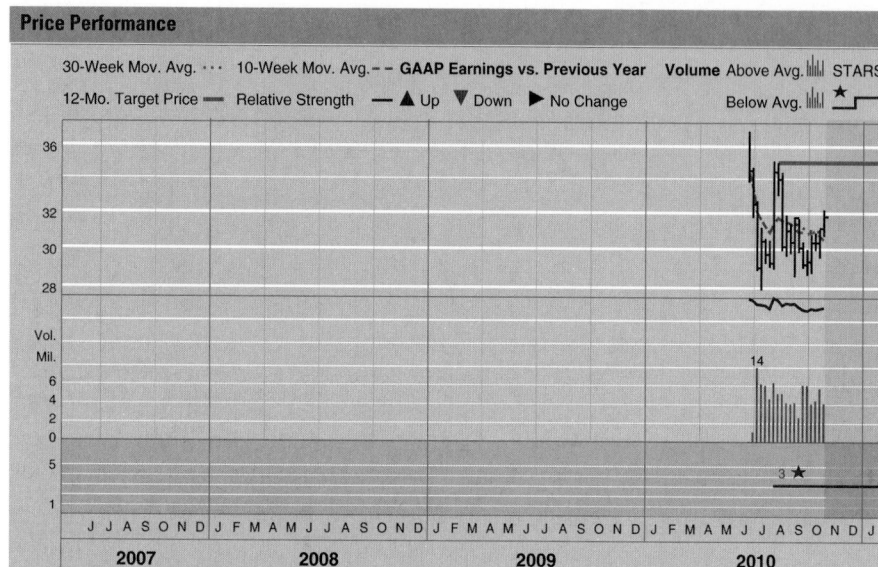

Analysis prepared by **Michael Kay** on August 03, 2010, when the stock traded at **$ 33.88**.

Highlights

▶ QEP boosted volumes by 11%, to 190 Bcfe, in 2009. Production in the first half of 2010 was up 16%, with strength in the Midcontinent region, driven by the Haynesville and Woodford Cana shales. QEP currently has seven rigs running at Haynesville, six at the Pinedale Anticline, two at Granite Wash, and one each at Woodford Cana and the Bakken Shale. We expect QEP to ramp activity for Bakken oil in the 2010 second half to lift exposure to liquids production. QEP targets 2010 production of 218-222 Bcfe, up 15%-17% from 2009, and up from previous targets as drilling efficiency improves at Haynesville.

▶ QEP sees 2010 EBITDAX (EBITDA before exploration expense) of $1,025 million, with 84% from E&P operations and the remainder from midstream field services, where we are concerned about NGL margins. QEP's 2010 capital expenditure budget of $1.34 billion allocates 78% to E&P and 22% to field services.

▶ We see 2010 EPS of $1.68 (with a $0.22 non-cash gain in the first half) and 2011 EPS of $1.66 on a 16% production increase each year. We expect capex to surpass cash flows in 2010, but the completion of two NGL plants and declining capex should bridge the gap in 2011.

Investment Rationale/Risk

▶ We recently initiated coverage with a hold opinion, as we think the shares will trade in line with E&P natural gas peers. QEP has a 92% reserve weighting toward natural gas. On June 30, 2010, QEP was spun off from Questar Corp. (STR 17, Hold) and began trading as a stand-alone E&P company, focusing onshore. This should allow for sharper focus on core E&P assets, greater capital commitment and the pursuit of growth, possibly by acquisition. We think minimal balance sheet leverage and a supportive midstream business will help support strategic growth initiatives. QEP has three-year production and reserve compound annual growth rates (CAGRs) of 13% and 19%, respectively.

▶ Risks to our recommendation and target price include a sustained decline in natural gas prices, an inability to replace reserves at a reasonable cost, and production declines.

▶ Our 12-month target price of $35 is based on our proved reserve NAV estimate of $43, blended with peer average relative metrics, including a target of 5X enterprise value to our 2011 EBITDA forecast and 5X our 2011 cash flow estimate. We see upside to NAV, but remain cautious on exposure to natural gas prices.

Qualitative Risk Assessment

LOW	MEDIUM	**HIGH**

Our risk assessment reflects QEP's operations in a capital-intensive industry that derives value from producing commodities whose price is very volatile.

Quantitative Evaluations

S&P Quality Ranking NR

D	C	B-	B	B+	A-	A	A+

Relative Strength Rank MODERATE

51

LOWEST = 1   HIGHEST = 99

Revenue/Earnings Data

Revenue (Million $)

	1Q	2Q	3Q	4Q	Year
2010	580.1	529.6	--	--	--
2009	--	--	--	--	1,973
2008	--	--	--	--	2,319
2007	--	--	--	--	1,688
2006	--	--	--	--	--
2005	--	--	--	--	--

Earnings Per Share ($)

2010	0.44	0.39	E0.35	E0.38	E1.60
2009	--	--	--	--	1.21
2008	--	--	--	--	2.90
2007	--	--	--	--	2.05
2006	--	--	--	--	--
2005	--	--	--	--	--

Fiscal year ended Dec. 31. Next earnings report expected: NA. EPS Estimates based on S&P Operating Earnings; historical GAAP earnings are as reported.

Dividend Data (Dates: mm/dd Payment Date: mm/dd/yy)

Amount ($)	Date Decl.	Ex-Div. Date	Stk. of Record	Payment Date
0.020	08/09	08/18	08/20	09/13/10

Dividends have been paid since 2010. Source: Company reports.

Please read the Required Disclosures and Analyst Certification on the last page of this report.

The **McGraw·Hill** Companies

QEP Resources Inc

STANDARD &POOR'S

Business Summary August 03, 2010

CORPORATE OVERVIEW. QEP Resources, Inc. is a leading independent natural gas and oil exploration and production company. On June 30, 2010, Questar Corporation (STR) spun off the shares of QEP Resources, Inc., creating a new publicly traded, independent natural gas and oil exploration and production company. QEP Resources is a major Rocky Mountain and Midcontinent region producer. QEP also gathers, compresses, treats and processes natural gas in its core producing areas.

As of December 31, 2009, QEP had estimated proved reserves of 2,747 Bcfe, of which 92% consisted of natural gas and 8% crude oil and liquids. This compares to estimated proved reserves of 2,218 Bcfe, of which 92% were natural gas, at year-end 2008. We estimate QEP's year-end 2009 reserve life to be 14.5 years, compared to 12.9 years at the end of 2008. We estimate QEP has grown reserves at a three-year CAGR of 19%. Production in 2009 was 189.7 Bcfe, up 11%, and we estimate a 2009 reserve replacement ratio of 379%, above peers. Total costs incurred for drilling in 2009 were $1.056 billion, down 44% on lower oil and gas prices, and we calculate a 2009 finding and development cost of $1.17 per Mcf with a three-year CAGR of $2.46 per Mcf.

CORPORATE STRATEGY. QEP intends to create value through strong growth, superior execution, and a low cost structure. QEP plans to allocate capital to projects that generate top returns; maintain a sustainable inventory of low-cost, high-margin resource plays; build contiguous acreage positions to drive efficiencies; own and operate midstream infrastructure in core areas to capture value; build gas processing plants to extract liquids from gas streams; gather, compress and treat its own production to drive down costs; and maintain a strong balance sheet and financial flexibility. QEP operates under three segments: Exploration & Production, Midstream and Marketing.

The E&P segment (84% of forecast 2010 EBITDAX) acquires, explores for, develops and produces natural gas, crude oil and natural gas liquids. QEP operates and is active in some of the most economic, high-growth domestic resources plays. As it develops acreage in these plays, QEP is forecasting 2010 and 2011 production growth of about 16% per annum. QEP plans to spend about $1 billion on E&P capex in 2010 and $860 million in 2011.

Company Financials Fiscal Year Ended Dec. 31

Per Share Data ($)	2009	2008	2007	2006	2005	2004	2003	2002	2001	2000
Tangible Book Value	NA	NA	NA	NA	NA	NA	NA	NA	NA	NA
Cash Flow	4.39	5.01	NA	NA	NA	NA	NA	NA	NA	NA
Earnings	1.21	2.90	NA	NA	NA	NA	NA	NA	NA	NA
S&P Core Earnings	NA	NA	NA	NA	NA	NA	NA	NA	NA	NA
Dividends	NA	NA	NA	NA	NA	NA	NA	NA	NA	NA
Payout Ratio	NA	NA	NA	NA	NA	NA	NA	NA	NA	NA
Prices:High	NA	NA	NA	NA	NA	NA	NA	NA	NA	NA
Prices:Low	NA	NA	NA	NA	NA	NA	NA	NA	NA	NA
P/E Ratio:High	NA	NA	NA	NA	NA	NA	NA	NA	NA	NA
P/E Ratio:Low	NA	NA	NA	NA	NA	NA	NA	NA	NA	NA

Income Statement Analysis (Million $)	2009	2008	2007	2006	2005	2004	2003	2002	2001	2000
Revenue	1,973	2,319	1,688	NA	NA	NA	NA	NA	NA	NA
Operating Income	1,163	1,280	860	NA	NA	NA	NA	NA	NA	NA
Depreciation	559	362	264	NA	NA	NA	NA	NA	NA	NA
Interest Expense	70.1	61.7	33.6	NA	NA	NA	NA	NA	NA	NA
Pretax Income	333	804	573	NA	NA	NA	NA	NA	NA	NA
Effective Tax Rate	35.3%	35.3%	36.9%	NA	NA	NA	NA	NA	NA	NA
Net Income	215	521	362	NA	NA	NA	NA	NA	NA	NA
S&P Core Earnings	294	586	421	356	258	165	121	66.2	92.1	NA

Balance Sheet & Other Financial Data (Million $)	2009	2008	2007	2006	2005	2004	2003	2002	2001	2000
Cash	Nil	NA	NA	NA	NA	NA	NA	NA	NA	NA
Current Assets	685	NA	NA	NA	NA	NA	NA	NA	NA	NA
Total Assets	6,190	NA	NA	NA	NA	NA	NA	NA	NA	NA
Current Liabilities	700	NA	NA	NA	NA	NA	NA	NA	NA	NA
Long Term Debt	999	NA	NA	NA	NA	NA	NA	NA	NA	NA
Common Equity	2,885	NA	NA	NA	NA	NA	NA	NA	NA	NA
Total Capital	4,088	NA	NA	NA	NA	NA	NA	NA	NA	NA
Capital Expenditures	NA	NA	NA	NA	NA	NA	NA	NA	NA	NA
Cash Flow	774	883	626	NA	NA	NA	NA	NA	NA	NA
Current Ratio	1.0	NA	NA	NA	NA	NA	NA	NA	NA	NA
% Long Term Debt of Capitalization	24.4	NA	NA	NA	NA	NA	NA	NA	NA	NA
% Net Income of Revenue	10.9	22.5	21.4	NA	NA	NA	NA	NA	NA	NA
% Return on Assets	NM	NA	NA	NA	NA	NA	NA	NA	NA	NA
% Return on Equity	NM	NA	NA	NA	NA	NA	NA	NA	NA	NA

Data as orig reptd.; bef. results of disc opers/spec. items. Per share data adj. for stk. divs.; EPS diluted. Pro forma data to 2009; 2009 bal. sheet as of Mar. 31, 2010. E-Estimated. NA-Not Available. NM-Not Meaningful. NR-Not Ranked. UR-Under Review.

Chrmn: K.O. Rattie
Pres & CEO: C.B. Stanley
EVP, CFO & Treas: R.J. Doleshek
Chief Acctg Officer & Cntlr: B.K. Watts

Secy: A.L. Jones

Board Members: P. S. Baker, Jr., L. R. Flury, J. A. Harmon, R. E. McKee, III, K. O. Rattie, M. W. Scoggins, C. B. Stanley

Auditor: Ernst & Young

The McGraw-Hill Companies

QLogic Corp

STANDARD &POOR'S

S&P Recommendation	HOLD ★★★☆☆	Price $16.73 (as of Oct 22, 2010)	12-Mo. Target Price $17.00	Investment Style Large-Cap Growth

GICS Sector Information Technology
Sub-Industry Computer Storage & Peripherals

Summary This company supplies storage networking and network infrastructure solutions primarily to original equipment manufacturers and distributors.

Key Stock Statistics (Source S&P, Vickers, company reports)

52-Wk Range	$22.40–14.30	S&P Oper. EPS 2011E	1.07	Market Capitalization(B)	$1.828	Beta	1.46
Trailing 12-Month EPS	$0.56	S&P Oper. EPS 2012E	1.18	Yield (%)	Nil	S&P 3-Yr. Proj. EPS CAGR(%)	8
Trailing 12-Month P/E	29.9	P/E on S&P Oper. EPS 2011E	15.6	Dividend Rate/Share	Nil	S&P Credit Rating	NA
$10K Invested 5 Yrs Ago	$11,308	Common Shares Outstg. (M)	109.3	Institutional Ownership (%)	98		

Price Performance

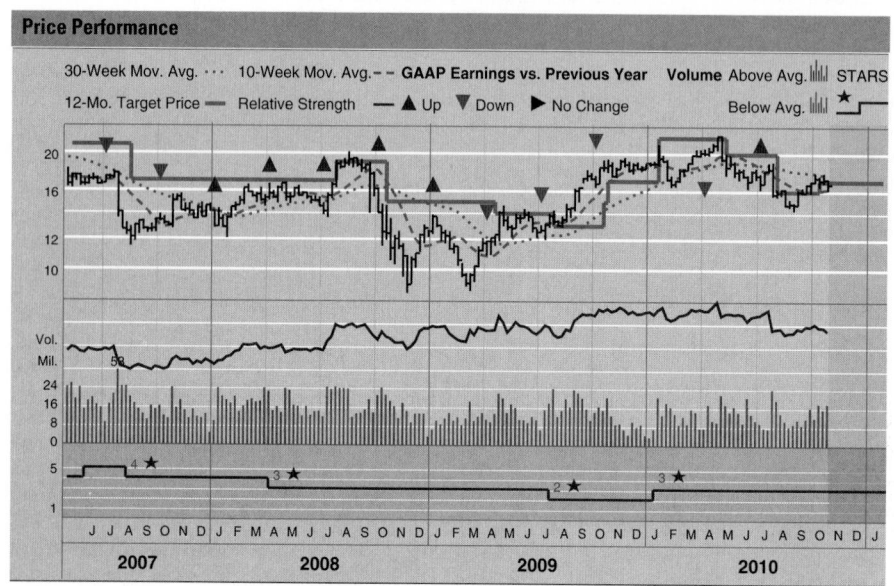

30-Week Mov. Avg. · · · 10-Week Mov. Avg. - - GAAP Earnings vs. Previous Year Volume Above Avg. STARS
12-Mo. Target Price — Relative Strength — ▲ Up ▼ Down ► No Change Below Avg.

Options: ASE, CBOE, P, Ph

Analysis prepared by **Jim Yin, CFA** on October 08, 2010, when the stock traded at **$ 17.13**.

Highlights

➤ We expect revenues to increase 8.0% in FY 11 (Mar.), following a 13% decline in FY 10. Our forecast is based on our outlook for a rebound in the data storage industry amid a modest economic recovery in 2010. We believe enterprises have underinvested in data storage and network infrastructure solutions during the downturn. We think sales will benefit from a server upgrade cycle and new products, in particular those related to Fibre Channel over Ethernet, which we think will become an emerging standard. We also believe sales will be aided by favorable foreign currency exchange due to the recent decline in the U.S. dollar.

➤ We project gross margins of 66% in FY 11, up from 64% in FY 10. We believe QLGC will keep a tight control over employee headcount in FY 11. As a result, we see operating margins widening to 23% in FY 11 from 18% in FY 10.

➤ We estimate EPS of $1.03 in FY 11, compared to $0.47 in FY 10. The increased earnings we see in FY 11 reflects our projection for higher revenues and wider operating margins.

Investment Rationale/Risk

➤ Our hold recommendation reflects our concern about slowing demand in 2011. Recent data indicate that the recovery in the global economy has decelerated due to weak consumer spending and lack of job growth. Additionally, many governments plan to implement austerity programs to control their budget deficits. Still, we see mid-single digit revenue growth in FY 12, driven by growing interest in cloud computing. We believe demand for QLGC's solutions is also driven by the emergence of Fibre Channel over Ethernet as a new standard.

➤ Risks to our recommendation and target price include a slowdown in the global economy, a rise in the U.S. dollar, lower-than-expected cost savings, and significant loss in market share.

➤ Our 12-month target price of $17 is based on a weighted blend of our discounted cash flow (DCF) and P/E analyses. Our DCF model assumes a weighted average cost of capital of 12% and 3% terminal growth, yielding an intrinsic value of $18. From our P/E analysis, we derive a value of $16, based on an industry P/E-to-growth ratio of 1.8X, or about 14X our FY 12 EPS estimate of $1.13.

Qualitative Risk Assessment

LOW	MEDIUM	HIGH

Our risk assessment reflects the volatile nature of the data storage industry and the rapid pace of technological change. Offsetting these factors is our view of the company's significant market share and strong financial position.

Quantitative Evaluations

S&P Quality Ranking B+

D	C	B-	B	B+	A-	A	A+

Relative Strength Rank MODERATE

30

LOWEST = 1   HIGHEST = 99

Revenue/Earnings Data

Revenue (Million $)

	1Q	2Q	3Q	4Q	Year
2011	142.6	--	--	--	--
2010	122.8	131.5	149.1	145.7	549.1
2009	168.4	171.2	163.7	130.6	633.9
2008	139.8	140.3	158.0	159.7	597.9
2007	136.7	145.3	157.6	147.1	586.7
2006	158.8	119.0	129.2	130.5	494.1

Earnings Per Share ($)

2011	0.22	E0.28	E0.29	E0.28	E1.07
2010	0.13	0.14	E0.31	-0.04	0.47
2009	0.24	0.20	0.24	0.16	0.85
2008	0.12	0.16	0.23	0.17	0.67
2007	0.13	0.19	0.22	0.12	0.66
2006	0.23	0.17	0.20	0.19	0.70

Fiscal year ended Mar. 31. Next earnings report expected: NA.
EPS Estimates based on S&P Operating Earnings; historical GAAP earnings are as reported.

Dividend Data

No cash dividends have been paid.

The McGraw-Hill Companies

QLogic Corp

STANDARD & POOR'S

Business Summary October 08, 2010

CORPORATE OVERVIEW. QLogic Corp. designs and develops storage networking infrastructure components sold to OEMs and distributors. QLGC produces host bus adapters (HBAs), fabric switches and management controller chips that provide the connectivity infrastructure for storage networks. The company serves customers with solutions based on various storage connectivity technologies, including Small Computer Systems Interface (SCSI), Internet SCSI (iSCSI), Fibre Channel, Fibre Channel over Ethernet (FCoE), Infiniband and intelligent Ethernet.

International revenues accounted for 52% of net revenues in FY 09 (Mar.), up from 49% in FY 08. IBM, Hewlett-Packard and Sun Microsystems each accounted for over 10% of FY 09 sales. The 10 largest customers accounted for 84% of FY 09 revenues, down from 85% in FY 08. QLGC works closely with independent hardware and software vendors, as well as with developers and integrators who create, test and evaluate complementary storage networking

products. Other key alliance partners include Cisco Systems, Dell, and EMC.

MARKET PROFILE. According to research firm IDC, growing server virtualization is driving an increase in storage area network (SAN) connectivity levels, partially offset by moderating server unit growth rates. IDC predicts worldwide HBA port shipments will increase from 4.5 million to 7.5 million between 2008 and 2013, resulting in a compound annual growth rate (CAGR) of 10.9% for the period. IDC expects single-port and multiport Fiber Channel (FC) HBA unit shipments to grow somewhat slower (a 2008-2013 CAGR of 4%), with 2013 shipments reaching 5.4 million.

Company Financials Fiscal Year Ended Mar. 31

Per Share Data ($)	2010	2009	2008	2007	2006	2005	2004	2003	2002	2001
Tangible Book Value	3.97	4.09	3.79	4.61	5.10	5.19	4.61	4.00	3.33	2.84
Cash Flow	0.81	1.22	1.01	0.83	0.81	0.92	0.77	0.62	0.44	0.42
Earnings	0.47	0.85	0.67	0.66	0.70	0.84	0.70	0.55	0.37	0.36
S&P Core Earnings	0.44	0.90	0.70	0.70	0.49	0.67	0.52	0.35	0.22	0.16
Dividends	Nil	Nil	Nil	Nil	Nil	Nil	Nil	Nil	Nil	Nil
Payout Ratio	Nil	Nil	Nil	Nil	Nil	Nil	Nil	Nil	Nil	Nil
Calendar Year	2009	2008	2007	2006	2005	2004	2003	2002	2001	2000
Prices:High	19.62	20.21	22.46	22.94	21.83	26.57	29.36	28.55	49.56	101.63
Prices:Low	8.82	8.69	11.46	15.86	14.10	10.72	16.07	9.83	8.60	19.84
P/E Ratio:High	42	24	34	35	31	32	42	52	NM	NM
P/E Ratio:Low	19	10	17	24	20	13	23	18	NM	NM

Income Statement Analysis (Million $)										
Revenue	549	634	598	587	494	572	524	441	344	358
Operating Income	146	219	190	169	196	240	214	157	99.5	132
Depreciation	40.1	48.4	48.4	27.6	17.9	15.6	14.8	14.7	13.0	10.8
Interest Expense	NA	Nil	Nil	Nil	Nil	Nil	Nil	Nil	Nil	Nil
Pretax Income	110	169	148	155	200	242	216	159	106	117
Effective Tax Rate	NA	35.6%	34.9%	31.9%	39.2%	35.0%	38.0%	35.0%	33.0%	41.2%
Net Income	55.0	109	96.2	105	122	158	134	103	70.7	68.8
S&P Core Earnings	51.7	115	100	112	85.6	126	99.4	67.0	42.1	30.5

Balance Sheet & Other Financial Data (Million $)										
Cash	376	343	321	544	125	166	157	138	76.1	128
Current Assets	489	482	471	697	819	940	854	748	587	490
Total Assets	751	780	811	971	938	1,026	929	817	670	571
Current Liabilities	82.4	93.3	86.7	94.5	78.4	68.8	60.8	66.7	51.0	47.8
Long Term Debt	NA	Nil	Nil	Nil	Nil	Nil	Nil	Nil	Nil	Nil
Common Equity	583	627	666	875	859	956	868	751	619	524
Total Capital	583	627	666	877	859	958	868	751	619	524
Capital Expenditures	24.5	30.7	30.0	31.7	28.3	25.7	22.3	15.7	14.5	16.7
Cash Flow	95.1	157	145	133	140	173	149	118	83.7	79.6
Current Ratio	5.9	5.2	5.4	7.4	10.5	13.7	14.0	11.2	11.5	10.3
% Long Term Debt of Capitalization	Nil	Nil	Nil	Nil	Nil	Nil	Nil	Nil	Nil	Nil
% Net Income of Revenue	10.0	17.2	16.1	18.0	24.7	27.6	25.5	23.5	20.5	19.2
% Return on Assets	7.2	13.7	10.8	11.0	12.4	16.1	15.3	13.9	11.4	14.2
% Return on Equity	9.1	16.8	12.5	12.2	13.4	17.3	16.5	15.1	12.4	15.6

Data as orig reptd.; bef. results of disc opers/spec. items. Per share data adj. for stk. divs.; EPS diluted. E-Estimated. NA-Not Available. NM-Not Meaningful. NR-Not Ranked. UR-Under Review.

Office: 26650 Aliso Viejo Pkwy, Aliso Viejo, CA 92656-2674.
Telephone: 949-389-6000.
Website: http://www.qlogic.com
Chrmn & CEO: H.K. Desai

COO: P. Mulligan
SVP, CFO & Chief Acctg Officer: S. Biddiscombe
Secy & General Counsel: M.L. Hawkins
Investor Contact: J.D. Herbert (949-389-6343)

Board Members: J. S. Birnbaum, H. K. Desai, J. R. Fiebiger, B. S. Iyer, K. B. Lewis, S. Mercer, G. Wells, B. Zeitler

Founded: 1992
Domicile: Delaware
Employees: 1,038

QUALCOMM Inc

STANDARD &POOR'S

S&P Recommendation **BUY** ★★★★☆	Price $44.18 (as of Oct 22, 2010)	12-Mo. Target Price $52.00	Investment Style Large-Cap Growth

GICS Sector Information Technology
Sub-Industry Communications Equipment

Summary This company focuses on developing products and services based on its advanced wireless broadband technology.

Key Stock Statistics (Source S&P, Vickers, company reports)

52-Wk Range	$49.80–31.63	S&P Oper. EPS 2010E	1.86	Market Capitalization(B)	$70.918	Beta	0.97
Trailing 12-Month EPS	$1.90	S&P Oper. EPS 2011E	1.93	Yield (%)	1.72	S&P 3-Yr. Proj. EPS CAGR(%)	11
Trailing 12-Month P/E	23.3	P/E on S&P Oper. EPS 2010E	23.8	Dividend Rate/Share	$0.76	S&P Credit Rating	NA
$10K Invested 5 Yrs Ago	$10,543	Common Shares Outstg. (M)	1,605.2	Institutional Ownership (%)	79		

Price Performance

30-Week Mov. Avg. · · · 10-Week Mov. Avg. - - GAAP Earnings vs. Previous Year   Volume Above Avg. ▮▮▮ STARS
12-Mo. Target Price ── Relative Strength ── ▲ Up ▼ Down ► No Change   Below Avg. ▮▮▮ ★

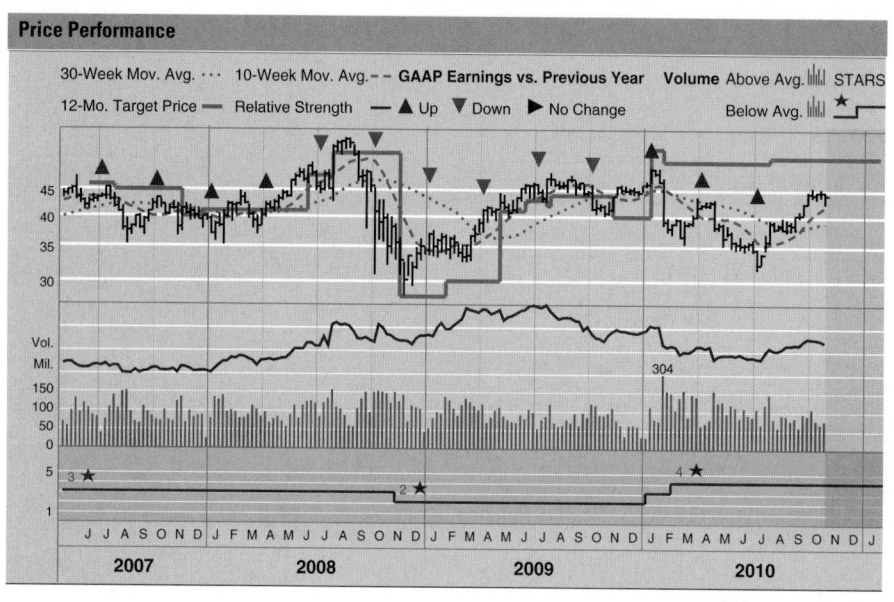

Options: ASE, CBOE, P, Ph

Analysis prepared by **James Moorman, CFA** on July 23, 2010, when the stock traded at **$ 38.91**.

Highlights

➤ We forecast a 4.8% revenue increase for FY 10 (Sep.) and a 6.3% increase for FY 11, following a 6.5% decline in FY 09. We believe that pressure on QCOM's chipset pricing is starting to abate following a period of decline due to competition and product mix. While we see stronger growth for its royalty business, we look for this to be tempered by a lower overall royalty rate.

➤ We expect growth in the WCDMA handset market, which supports QCOM's high-margin royalty business. We believe this will help maintain margins, but we are concerned about the effect of price declines as more growth comes from emerging markets and royalty rates decrease. We look for gross margins to decline slightly to 68.3% in FY 10 but then increase to 68.9% in FY 11, versus 69.5% in FY 09, as handset and chipset sales begin to reaccelerate with growth in the smartphone segment.

➤ We estimate that operating EPS will increase to $1.86 in FY 10 and $1.93 in FY 11, following $1.52 in FY 09.

Investment Rationale/Risk

➤ We believe QCOM will see increasing chipset sales throughout the coming year as the economy begins to improve and with rapid growth in the smartphone market. We also believe that the popularity of QCOM's Snapdragon chipset will give it an advantage as media-centric wireless devices become more popular. QCOM has a strong balance sheet, in our view, and should continue to generate sizable cash flow, but we are moderately concerned about handset and chipset pricing. With our view of upside potential in the share price, our recommendation is buy.

➤ Risks to our recommendation and target price include weaker demand in the replacement rate for more advanced CDMA handsets; lower selling prices for handsets and chipsets; and a slower recovery in orders to shore up low inventory levels.

➤ Applying a multiple of 27X to our FY 11 EPS estimate -- a premium to peers, reflecting QCOM's above-average margins and cash flow generation -- we arrive at our 12-month target price of $52.

Qualitative Risk Assessment

LOW	**MEDIUM**	HIGH

We believe QCOM's intellectual property rights and strong service provider relations give it a solid position in its industry. With our view of its healthy cash flow, we think the company's cash balance can support potentially weaker demand from customers and litigation risks related to its CDMA patents.

Quantitative Evaluations

S&P Quality Ranking   B

D	C	B-	**B**	B+	A-	A	A+

Relative Strength Rank   MODERATE

66

LOWEST = 1   HIGHEST = 99

Revenue/Earnings Data

Revenue (Million $)

	1Q	2Q	3Q	4Q	Year
2010	2,670	2,663	2,706	--	--
2009	2,517	2,455	2,753	2,690	10,416
2008	2,440	2,606	2,762	3,334	11,142
2007	2,019	2,221	2,325	2,306	8,871
2006	1,741	1,834	1,951	1,999	7,526
2005	1,390	1,365	1,358	1,560	5,673

Earnings Per Share ($)

2010	0.50	0.46	0.47	E0.43	E1.86
2009	0.20	-0.18	0.44	0.49	0.95
2008	0.46	0.47	0.45	0.52	1.90
2007	0.38	0.43	0.47	0.67	1.95
2006	0.36	0.34	0.37	0.36	1.44
2005	0.30	0.31	0.33	0.32	1.26

Fiscal year ended Sep. 30. Next earnings report expected: Early November. EPS Estimates based on S&P Operating Earnings; historical GAAP earnings are as reported.

Dividend Data (Dates: mm/dd Payment Date: mm/dd/yy)

Amount ($)	Date Decl.	Ex-Div. Date	Stk. of Record	Payment Date
0.170	01/07	02/24	02/26	03/26/10
0.190	04/05	05/26	05/28	06/25/10
0.190	07/08	08/25	08/27	09/24/10
0.190	10/04	11/22	11/24	12/22/10

Dividends have been paid since 2003. Source: Company reports.

QUALCOMM Inc

Business Summary July 23, 2010

CORPORATE OVERVIEW. QUALCOMM Inc. is comprised of the following operating segments: CDMA technology (QCT), technology licensing (QTL), wireless and Internet (QWI), and strategic initiatives (QSI). The equipment and services unit, mostly in QCT, accounted for about 65% of total sales in the third quarter of FY 10 (Sep.), providing integrated circuits and system software solutions to top wireless handset and infrastructure manufacturers. QCOM uses a fabless business model, employing several independent semiconductor foundries to manufacture its semiconductor products. Approximately 103 million model station modem (MSM) integrated circuits were sold during the third quarter of FY 10, compared to approximately 94 million a year earlier. QCOM expects to sell between 106 million and 111 million MSM circuits in the fourth quarter of FY 10.

The license and royalty fee segment (QTL) accounted for about 35% of total sales, with 79% operating margins. QCOM holds a number of patents related to CDMA, and derives royalties from licensing its technology. Royalties are paid when manufacturers earn revenue from the sale of CDMA-based equipment, including CDMA and WCDMA handsets made by customers Samsung, LG Electronics, Motorola, and others. QCOM expects 23% growth in CDMA and WCDMA handsets in calendar 2010, mostly from WCDMA handsets.

QCOM estimated that the average selling price of a handset was between $202 and $208 in FY 09, and projected it to decline to between $184 and $188 in FY 10, limiting the growth of its royalty revenues.

LEGAL/REGULATORY ISSUES. QCOM has been involved in various legal issues involving patents on its chipsets and competitors' chipsets. The company's multiple disputes with Nokia included litigation over Nokia's obligation to pay royalties for the use of certain of QCOM's patents. Without a license contract with QCOM, Nokia had opted to cancel its CDMA-related handset division. However, in July 2008, QCOM and Nokia signed a new 15-year agreement covering various second, third and fourth-generation technology standards that we believe keeps QCOM's royalty pipeline active beyond supporting current handset offerings. In addition to a lump-sum cash payment that helped boost fourth-quarter FY 08 revenues by $580 million, Nokia returned to being a royalty customer of QCOM in late FY 08.

Company Financials Fiscal Year Ended Sep. 30

Per Share Data ($)	2009	2008	2007	2006	2005	2004	2003	2002	2001	2000
Tangible Book Value	9.44	8.05	8.82	7.37	6.43	5.69	4.54	2.77	2.82	3.14
Cash Flow	1.33	2.18	2.18	1.60	1.38	1.13	0.62	0.47	-0.14	0.57
Earnings	0.95	1.90	1.95	1.44	1.26	1.03	0.51	0.22	-0.36	0.43
S&P Core Earnings	1.64	2.05	1.86	1.40	1.03	0.83	0.74	0.34	-0.68	NA
Dividends	0.66	0.60	0.52	0.42	0.32	0.19	0.09	Nil	Nil	Nil
Payout Ratio	69%	32%	27%	29%	25%	18%	17%	Nil	Nil	Nil
Prices:High	48.72	56.88	47.72	53.01	46.60	44.99	27.43	26.67	44.69	100.00
Prices:Low	32.64	28.16	35.23	32.76	32.08	26.67	14.79	11.61	19.16	25.75
P/E Ratio:High	51	30	24	37	37	44	54	NM	NM	NM
P/E Ratio:Low	34	15	18	23	25	26	29	NM	NM	NM

Income Statement Analysis (Million $)	2009	2008	2007	2006	2005	2004	2003	2002	2001	2000
Revenue	10,416	11,142	8,871	7,526	5,673	4,880	3,971	3,040	2,680	3,197
Operating Income	3,880	4,200	3,266	2,962	2,586	2,266	1,684	1,068	877	1,105
Depreciation	635	456	383	272	200	163	180	394	320	244
Interest Expense	24.0	22.0	Nil	Nil	3.00	2.00	30.7	25.7	10.2	4.92
Pretax Income	2,076	3,826	3,626	3,156	2,809	2,313	1,285	461	-426	1,197
Effective Tax Rate	23.3%	17.4%	8.90%	21.7%	23.7%	25.4%	35.6%	22.0%	NM	44.0%
Net Income	1,592	3,160	3,303	2,470	2,143	1,725	827	360	-531	670
S&P Core Earnings	2,744	3,407	3,148	2,397	1,733	1,395	610	274	-512	NA

Balance Sheet & Other Financial Data (Million $)	2009	2008	2007	2006	2005	2004	2003	2002	2001	2000
Cash	11,069	6,411	6,581	5,721	6,548	5,982	4,561	2,795	2,283	1,772
Current Assets	12,570	11,723	8,821	7,049	7,791	7,227	5,949	3,941	3,055	2,730
Total Assets	27,445	24,563	18,495	15,208	12,479	10,820	8,822	6,510	5,747	6,063
Current Liabilities	2,813	2,291	2,258	1,422	1,070	894	808	675	521	472
Long Term Debt	187	142	Nil	Nil	Nil	Nil	123	94.3	Nil	Nil
Common Equity	20,316	17,944	15,835	13,406	11,119	9,664	7,599	5,392	4,890	5,516
Total Capital	20,316	18,087	15,835	13,406	11,119	9,664	7,722	5,530	4,896	5,563
Capital Expenditures	761	1,397	818	685	576	332	231	142	114	163
Cash Flow	2,227	3,616	3,686	2,742	2,343	1,888	1,007	754	-211	914
Current Ratio	4.5	5.1	3.9	5.0	7.3	8.1	7.4	5.8	5.9	5.8
% Long Term Debt of Capitalization	0.9	0.8	Nil	Nil	Nil	Nil	1.6	1.7	Nil	Nil
% Net Income of Revenue	15.3	28.4	37.2	32.8	37.8	35.3	20.8	11.8	NM	21.0
% Return on Assets	6.1	14.7	19.6	17.8	18.4	17.6	10.8	5.9	NM	12.6
% Return on Equity	8.3	18.7	22.5	20.1	20.6	20.0	12.7	7.1	NM	16.0

Data as orig reptd.; bef. results of disc opers/spec. items. Per share data adj. for stk. divs.; EPS diluted. E-Estimated. NA-Not Available. NM-Not Meaningful. NR-Not Ranked. UR-Under Review.

Office: 5775 Morehouse Drive, San Diego, CA 92121-1714.
Telephone: 858-587-1121.
Email: ir@qualcomm.com
Website: http://www.qualcomm.com

Chrmn & CEO: P.E. Jacobs
Pres: S.R. Altman
EVP, CFO & Chief Acctg Officer: W.E. Keitel
EVP & CTO: R. Padovani

EVP, Secy & General Counsel: D.J. Rosenberg
Investor Contact: J. Gilbert (858-658-4813)
Board Members: B. T. Alexander, S. M. Bennett, D. G. Cruickshank, R. V. Dittamore, T. Horton, I. M. Jacobs, P. E. Jacobs, R. E. Kahn, S. Lansing, D. A. Nelles, B. Scowcroft, M. I. Stern

Founded: 1985
Domicile: Delaware
Employees: 16,100

Quanta Services Inc.

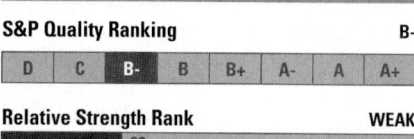
STANDARD &POOR'S

S&P Recommendation BUY ★★★★☆

Price	12-Mo. Target Price	Investment Style
$19.40 (as of Oct 22, 2010)	**$23.00**	Large-Cap Blend

GICS Sector Industrials
Sub-Industry Construction & Engineering

Summary This company provides specialized contracting services, offering end-to-end network solutions to the electric power, gas, telecommunications and cable television industries.

Key Stock Statistics (Source S&P, Vickers, company reports)

52-Wk Range	$23.34– 16.75	S&P Oper. EPS 2010**E**	0.94	Market Capitalization(B)	$4.085	Beta	1.18
Trailing 12-Month EPS	$0.79	S&P Oper. EPS 2011**E**	1.22	Yield (%)	Nil	S&P 3-Yr. Proj. EPS CAGR(%)	25
Trailing 12-Month P/E	24.6	P/E on S&P Oper. EPS 2010**E**	20.6	Dividend Rate/Share	Nil	S&P Credit Rating	NR
$10K Invested 5 Yrs Ago	$17,275	Common Shares Outstg. (M)	211.0	Institutional Ownership (%)	89		

Price Performance

30-Week Mov. Avg. · · · 10-Week Mov. Avg. – – **GAAP Earnings vs. Previous Year**   Volume Above Avg. ▯▮▯ STARS

12-Mo. Target Price — Relative Strength — ▲ Up ▼ Down ► No Change   Below Avg. ▯▮▯ ★

Options: ASE, CBOE, P, Ph

Analysis prepared by **Mathew Christy, CFA** on August 11, 2010, when the stock traded at **$ 18.68**.

Highlights

► We see revenues in 2010 advancing about 20% on some organic sales growth, but mainly due to the acquisition of Price Gregory. Our estimates are also based on PWR's 12-month backlog of $2.7 billion, and total backlog of $5.8 billion, as of June 30, reflecting recent major contract wins, including Northeast Utilities, Nebraska Public Power and Light, Duke Power, and renewable energy contracts. In addition, we base our estimates on continued contract wins, such as National Grid and the recent Teanaway Solar Reserve. In 2011, we estimate revenues will increase 16%.

► For both 2010 and 2011, we estimate that PWR's gross margin will increase compared to the 17.9% rate posted in 2009, as older lower priced contracts are completed. We also believe that the company will show overall improvement in the operating margin in both years due to greater operating leverage over higher sales, along with cost savings associated with recent acquisitions.

► With an expected 39% effective tax rate in both years, we estimate EPS of $0.94 for 2010 and $1.22 for 2011.

Investment Rationale/Risk

► Following lower overall results in 2009 due to reduced capital spending by customers and the recession, we believe 2010 results will increase due to favorable acquisitions and better customer spending levels. In addition, we view positively the long-term trend toward higher spending to maintain and upgrade aging transmission and distribution networks. Although we continue to see regulatory constraints subduing spending, we think the shares are attractively valued at about 7.5X our 2010 EBITDA estimate.

► Risks to our recommendation and target price include lower-than-expected capital spending by utilities and gas, telecommunications and cable companies, and an economic downturn.

► Our 12-month target price of $23 is based on a blend of valuation metrics. Our discounted cash flow model, which assumes a 3% perpetuity growth rate and a 10.9% discount rate, indicates a $24 intrinsic value. In terms of relative valuation, we apply an EV/EBITDA multiple of 8.4X to our 2010 EBITDA estimate, ahead of peers due to PWR's historical premium valuation, implying a value of $22.

Qualitative Risk Assessment

LOW	MEDIUM	HIGH

Our risk assessment reflects PWR's dependence on just a few industries, the erratic spending patterns of the company's major customers, the lack of minimum service volumes in most contracts, the ability of customers to terminate agreements on short notice, the volatility of the storm restoration service business, and the large portion of revenue derived from fixed-price agreements.

Quantitative Evaluations

S&P Quality Ranking   B-

D	C	B-	B	B+	A-	A	A+

Relative Strength Rank   WEAK

29

LOWEST = 1   HIGHEST = 99

Revenue/Earnings Data

Revenue (Million $)

	1Q	2Q	3Q	4Q	Year
2010	748.3	870.5	--	--	--
2009	738.5	813.4	780.8	985.4	3,318
2008	844.4	960.9	1,053	921.5	3,780
2007	574.9	557.6	655.9	879.0	2,656
2006	496.5	514.1	528.5	592.0	2,131
2005	372.5	439.3	523.3	523.5	1,859

Earnings Per Share ($)

	1Q	2Q	3Q	4Q	Year
2010	0.11	0.16	E0.31	E0.34	E0.94
2009	0.11	0.17	0.32	0.21	0.81
2008	0.14	0.22	0.29	0.24	0.88
2007	0.23	0.17	0.30	0.18	0.87
2006	0.07	0.14	0.17	-0.26	0.15
2005	-0.04	0.03	0.11	0.15	0.25

Fiscal year ended Dec. 31. Next earnings report expected: Early November. EPS Estimates based on S&P Operating Earnings; historical GAAP earnings are as reported.

Dividend Data

No cash dividends have been paid.

Quanta Services Inc.

Business Summary August 11, 2010

CORPORATE OVERVIEW. Quanta Services, Inc. (PWR) is a provider of special-ty contracting services that designs, installs and maintains the infrastructure and networks for four primary areas: electric power, natural gas, telecommu-nications and cable television, and fiber optic licensing and leasing. PWR had over 14,600 employees in 2009, of which approximately 37% were covered by collective bargaining agreements, primarily with the International Brother-hood of Electrical Workers (IBEW). The company believes it is the largest contractor serving the transmission and distribution sector of the U.S. electric utility industry. The electric power infrastructure segment (64% of PWR's 2009 revenues) installs, repairs and maintains electric power distribution networks and transmission lines. The natural gas and pipeline segment (17%) provides design, installation, repair, and maintenance services for natural gas distribu-tion and transmission networks. The telecommunications and cable network segment (19%) designs, installs and maintains fiber optic, coaxial and copper cable for video, data and voice transmission, and builds wireless communica-tions towers and installs switching systems for telecommunications carriers. The fiber optic licensing and leasing segment (less than 1%) designs, pro-cures, constructs, maintains, and licenses fiber optic networks in select mar-kets in the U.S.

MARKET PROFILE. During the recent economic downturn, we believe the lack of available credit dampened demand dynamics and spending levels. For in-stance, several large telecom customers, including Verizon and AT&T, slowed spending on their fiber optic build-out initiatives such as fiber to the premises (FTTP) and fiber to the node (FTTN) in 2009, while the utility industry reduced or deferred capital expenditures that were slated for 2009. However, we think that longer-term demand for infrastructure services in the electric, gas, tele-com and cable industries is powered by the need to maintain and upgrade networks, while keeping costs low by outsourcing these services to third par-ties. Due to the Energy Policy Act of 2005 and the American Recovery and Reinvestment Act of 2009, which both promote investment in aging U.S. ener-gy infrastructure, we expect many utilities to continue spending on the up-grade of their power transmission and distribution networks. In addition, we see improving spending levels in 2010, as a result of the economic recovery.

Company Financials Fiscal Year Ended Dec. 31

Per Share Data ($)	2009	2008	2007	2006	2005	2004	2003	2002	2001	2000
Tangible Book Value	7.08	5.87	4.01	3.36	2.67	2.34	2.35	3.05	2.79	2.76
Cash Flow	1.43	1.39	1.24	0.63	0.73	0.45	0.23	-1.41	2.10	2.12
Earnings	0.81	0.88	0.87	0.15	0.25	-0.08	-0.30	-2.26	1.10	1.42
S&P Core Earnings	0.84	0.88	0.88	0.88	0.61	0.26	-0.09	-0.30	-1.91	0.83	NA
Dividends	Nil	Nil	Nil	Nil	Nil	Nil	Nil	Nil	Nil	Nil
Payout Ratio	Nil	Nil	Nil	Nil	Nil	Nil	Nil	Nil	Nil	Nil
Prices:High	25.80	35.39	33.42	20.05	14.97	9.52	9.87	18.90	37.50	63.13
Prices:Low	15.84	10.56	18.66	12.24	7.18	4.83	2.80	1.75	9.94	17.92
P/E Ratio:High	32	40	38	NM	60	NM	NM	NM	34	44
P/E Ratio:Low	20	12	21	NM	29	NM	NM	NM	9	13

Income Statement Analysis (Million $)										
Revenue	3,318	3,780	2,656	2,131	1,859	1,627	1,643	1,751	2,015	1,793
Operating Income	375	403	250	189	124	70.2	83.1	71.6	273	308
Depreciation	126	114	74.7	56.2	55.4	60.4	60.1	60.6	79.4	57.3
Interest Expense	11.3	17.5	21.5	26.8	23.9	25.1	31.8	35.9	36.1	25.7
Pretax Income	234	282	167	65.1	52.2	-12.6	-53.1	-194	157	200
Effective Tax Rate	30.0%	40.8%	20.5%	73.2%	43.4%	NM	NM	NM	45.4%	47.0%
Net Income	162	167	133	17.5	29.6	-9.19	-35.0	-174	85.8	106
S&P Core Earnings	168	167	134	74.1	30.3	-10.2	-33.9	-96.4	64.5	NA

Balance Sheet & Other Financial Data (Million $)										
Cash	700	438	407	384	304	266	180	27.9	6.29	17.3
Current Assets	1,583	1,381	1,305	991	831	700	676	529	577	602
Total Assets	4,117	3,555	3,388	1,639	1,555	1,460	1,466	1,365	2,043	1,874
Current Liabilities	496	452	757	334	258	221	199	212	242	253
Long Term Debt	127	144	144	414	450	464	501	386	500	491
Common Equity	3,109	2,658	2,185	729	704	663	663	612	1,207	1,069
Total Capital	3,241	2,803	2,430	1,143	1,154	1,128	1,164	1,153	1,801	1,560
Capital Expenditures	165	186	128	48.5	42.6	39.0	35.9	49.5	85.0	89.6
Cash Flow	288	281	208	73.7	85.0	51.2	25.1	-114	164	162
Current Ratio	3.2	3.1	1.7	3.0	3.2	3.2	3.4	2.5	2.4	2.4
% Long Term Debt of Capitalization	3.9	5.1	5.9	36.2	39.0	41.2	43.0	33.5	27.8	31.5
% Net Income of Revenue	4.9	4.4	5.0	0.8	1.6	NM	NM	NM	4.3	5.9
% Return on Assets	4.2	4.8	5.3	1.1	2.0	NM	NM	NM	4.4	7.0
% Return on Equity	5.6	6.9	9.1	2.4	4.3	NM	NM	NM	7.5	11.5

Data as orig reptd.; bef. results of disc opers/spec. items. Per share data adj. for stk. divs.; EPS diluted. E-Estimated. NA-Not Available. NM-Not Meaningful. NR-Not Ranked. UR-Under Review.

Office: 1360 Post Oak Boulevard, Suite 2100, Houston, TX 77056.
Telephone: 713-629-7600.
Email: headquarters@quantaservices.com
Website: http://www.quantaservices.com

Chrmn & CEO: J.R. Colson
Pres & COO: J.F. O'Neil, III
CFO: J. Haddox
Chief Admin Officer: D.B. Miller

Chief Acctg Officer: D.A. Jensen
Investor Contact: K. Dennard (713-529-6600)
Board Members: J. R. Ball, J. R. Colson, J. M. Conaway, R. R. DiSibio, V. D. Foster, B. Fried, L. Golm, W. F. Jackman, B. Ranck, J. R. Wilson, P. Wood, III

Founded: 1997
Domicile: Delaware
Employees: 14,673

Quest Diagnostics Inc

STANDARD &POOR'S

S&P Recommendation BUY ★★★★☆	**Price** $49.03 (as of Oct 22, 2010)	**12-Mo. Target Price** $60.00	**Investment Style** Large-Cap Growth

GICS Sector Health Care
Sub-Industry Health Care Services

Summary This company provides diagnostic testing, information and services to physicians, hospitals, managed care organizations, employers and government agencies.

Key Stock Statistics (Source S&P, Vickers, company reports)

52-Wk Range	$62.83– 40.80	S&P Oper. EPS 2010**E**	3.98	Market Capitalization(B)	$8.689	Beta	0.51
Trailing 12-Month EPS	$3.95	S&P Oper. EPS 2011**E**	4.36	Yield (%)	0.82	S&P 3-Yr. Proj. EPS CAGR(%)	12
Trailing 12-Month P/E	12.4	P/E on S&P Oper. EPS 2010**E**	12.3	Dividend Rate/Share	$0.40	S&P Credit Rating	BBB+
$10K Invested 5 Yrs Ago	$10,731	Common Shares Outstg. (M)	177.2	Institutional Ownership (%)	70		

Price Performance

30-Week Mov. Avg. · · ·   10-Week Mov. Avg. – –   **GAAP Earnings vs. Previous Year**   Volume Above Avg. STARS
12-Mo. Target Price —   Relative Strength —   ▲ Up ▼ Down ▶ No Change   Below Avg. ★

Options: ASE, CBOE, Ph

Analysis prepared by **Jeffrey Loo, CFA** on October 22, 2010, when the stock traded at **$ 48.25.**

Highlights

▶ We see 2010 sales off 2%, to $7.3 billion, amid a challenging employment environment, resulting in fewer patient visits. We believe physician office visits in the first nine months of 2010 declined 3% to 5%, and we see only a modest recovery in the fourth quarter. We expect growth to pick up steadily in 2011, and we look for a 4% sales increase to $7.6 billion. We see a continued increase in esoteric testing and tests per requisition, resulting in higher revenue per requisition, and we believe drugs-of-abuse testing volume has stabilized and should increase as the economy recovers. We see gross margins narrowing by 60 basis points (bps) in 2010 but expanding by 30 bps in 2011. DGX is ramping up its sales force to focus on its esoteric tests offering, but we see DGX maintaining its cost structure following years of cost cutting. We see operating margins falling 30 bps in 2010 before rising 50 bps in 2011.

▶ DGX has been a prolific acquirer, and we believe the current environment may present attractive opportunities. In October, DGX's directors approved a $250 million stock buyback.

▶ Our 2010 and 2011 EPS estimates are $3.98 and $4.36, respectively.

Investment Rationale/Risk

▶ We believe the shares are attractive, recently trading at 12.0X and 10.9X our 2010 and 2011 EPS estimates, respectively, well below historical levels. Although we have some concerns about economic challenges leading to slowing volume, we think DGX's core lab testing business is fundamentally sound and will be able to maintain stable growth and margin expansion through improved efficiency and cost cutting. Further, DGX has been successful in renewing managed care contracts, and we do not see significant pricing pressure over the next two years. We see two important metrics -- revenue per requisition and tests per requisition -- continuing to increase. We believe diagnostic testing remains an essential health care service and believe health care reform will benefit the lab industry through increased utilization, partially offset by lower reimbursement rates.

▶ Risks to our recommendation and target price include a greater-than-expected slowdown in physician office visits.

▶ Our 12-month target price of $60 is based on a P/E-to-growth ratio of about 1.15X applied to our 2011 EPS estimate, and assumes a three-year EPS growth rate of 12%, in line with peers.

Qualitative Risk Assessment

LOW	MEDIUM	HIGH

Our risk assessment reflects our view of DGX's leadership position in the large and mature diagnostic testing industry, the company's broad geographic service area, its diverse and balanced payor mix, and the growing recognition of the importance and significance of diagnostic testing.

Quantitative Evaluations

S&P Quality Ranking B+

D	C	B-	B	B+	A-	A	A+

Relative Strength Rank MODERATE

33

LOWEST = 1   HIGHEST = 99

Revenue/Earnings Data

Revenue (Million $)

	1Q	2Q	3Q	4Q	Year
2010	1,806	1,875	--	--	--
2009	1,808	1,902	1,897	1,848	7,455
2008	1,785	1,838	1,827	1,800	7,249
2007	1,526	1,641	1,767	1,770	6,705
2006	1,553	1,583	1,583	1,549	6,269
2005	1,319	1,378	1,372	1,435	5,504

Earnings Per Share ($)

	1Q	2Q	3Q	4Q	Year
2010	0.89	1.07	E0.97	E0.90	E3.98
2009	0.89	1.00	1.02	0.97	3.88
2008	0.72	0.83	0.81	0.87	3.23
2007	0.55	0.73	0.77	0.79	2.84
2006	0.77	0.78	0.82	0.77	3.14
2005	0.64	0.72	0.66	0.64	2.66

Fiscal year ended Dec. 31. Next earnings report expected: NA. EPS Estimates based on S&P Operating Earnings; historical GAAP earnings are as reported.

Dividend Data (Dates: mm/dd Payment Date: mm/dd/yy)

Amount ($)	Date Decl.	Ex-Div. Date	Stk. of Record	Payment Date
0.100	12/09	01/05	01/07	01/22/10
0.100	02/11	04/01	04/06	04/20/10
0.100	05/06	07/01	07/06	07/20/10
0.100	08/11	09/30	10/04	10/19/10

Dividends have been paid since 2004. Source: Company reports.

Please read the Required Disclosures and Analyst Certification on the last page of this report.

The **McGraw·Hill** Companies

Quest Diagnostics Inc

STANDARD
&POOR'S

Business Summary October 22, 2010

CORPORATE OVERVIEW. Quest Diagnostics is the largest independent U.S. clinical lab operator. The clinical lab market is estimated to be about a $45 billion market, with hospital-based labs accounting for about 60% of the market, independent commercial labs, such as DGX, accounting for 33%, and physician-office labs the rest. DGX offers a broad range of clinical laboratory testing services used by physicians in the detection, diagnosis, and treatment of diseases and other medical conditions. Tests range from routine (such as blood cholesterol tests) to highly complex esoteric (such as gene-based testing and molecular diagnostics testing). At the end of 2008, DGX had a network of 35 principal laboratories throughout the U.S., 150 smaller "rapid response" (STAT) laboratories, and over 2,100 patient service centers, along with facilities in Mexico, Puerto Rico and England. In 2008, DGX started providing clinical lab services in India.

In 2009, DGX processed approximately 148 million requisitions (physician testing requests) annually. Routine testing and anatomic pathology generated 70% of net sales in 2009 (68% in 2008), esoteric testing 20% (20% in 2008), clinical trials and risk assessment services from LabOne (acquired in November 2005) 8% (9%), and 3% from overseas operations. Routine tests measure important health parameters such as the function of the kidney, heart, liver, thyroid and other organs. Esoteric tests are performed less frequently than routine tests, and/or require more sophisticated equipment and materials, professional hands-on attention, and more highly skilled personnel. As a result, they are generally priced substantially higher than routine tests.

Company Financials Fiscal Year Ended Dec. 31

Per Share Data ($)	2009	2008	2007	2006	2005	2004	2003	2002	2001	2000
Tangible Book Value	NM	NM	NM	NM	NM	NM	NM	NM	NM	NM
Cash Flow	5.26	4.58	4.06	4.24	3.51	3.12	2.79	2.31	1.70	1.27
Earnings	3.88	3.23	2.84	3.14	2.66	2.35	2.06	1.62	0.94	0.56
S&P Core Earnings	3.83	3.29	2.85	3.17	2.57	2.13	1.80	1.42	0.83	NA
Dividends	0.40	0.40	0.40	0.39	0.26	0.30	Nil	Nil	Nil	Nil
Payout Ratio	10%	12%	14%	12%	10%	13%	Nil	Nil	Nil	Nil
Prices:High	62.83	59.95	58.63	64.69	54.80	48.41	37.50	48.07	37.88	36.56
Prices:Low	42.36	38.66	47.98	48.59	44.32	35.94	23.68	24.55	18.30	7.28
P/E Ratio:High	16	19	21	21	21	21	18	30	40	66
P/E Ratio:Low	11	12	17	15	17	15	11	15	19	13

Income Statement Analysis (Million $)	2009	2008	2007	2006	2005	2004	2003	2002	2001	2000
Revenue	7,455	7,249	6,705	6,269	5,504	5,127	4,738	4,108	3,628	3,421
Operating Income	1,600	1,508	1,350	1,325	1,144	1,060	950	724	559	452
Depreciation	257	265	238	197	176	169	154	131	148	134
Interest Expense	147	185	186	96.5	61.4	57.9	59.8	53.7	70.5	120
Pretax Income	1,228	1,051	939	1,057	930	854	755	557	343	210
Effective Tax Rate	37.5%	36.8%	38.2%	38.6%	39.2%	39.3%	39.9%	39.5%	43.4%	45.7%
Net Income	730	632	554	626	546	499	437	322	184	105
S&P Core Earnings	719	644	556	632	531	456	377	279	162	NA

Balance Sheet & Other Financial Data (Million $)	2009	2008	2007	2006	2005	2004	2003	2002	2001	2000
Cash	534	254	168	150	92.1	73.3	155	96.8	122	171
Current Assets	1,679	1,497	1,374	1,191	1,069	931	996	824	877	981
Total Assets	8,564	8,404	8,566	5,661	5,306	4,204	4,301	3,324	2,931	2,865
Current Liabilities	1,059	1,225	1,288	1,151	1,101	1,044	724	636	659	955
Long Term Debt	2,937	3,078	3,377	1,239	1,255	724	1,029	797	820	761
Common Equity	3,990	3,605	3,324	3,019	2,763	2,289	2,397	1,769	1,336	1,031
Total Capital	7,119	6,873	6,911	4,258	4,018	3,013	3,426	2,565	2,156	1,793
Capital Expenditures	167	213	219	193	224	176	175	155	149	116
Cash Flow	987	897	792	823	722	668	591	454	332	239
Current Ratio	1.6	1.2	1.1	1.0	1.0	0.9	1.4	1.3	1.3	1.0
% Long Term Debt of Capitalization	41.3	44.8	48.9	29.1	31.2	24.0	30.0	31.0	38.0	42.4
% Net Income of Revenue	9.8	8.7	8.3	10.0	9.9	9.7	9.2	7.8	5.1	3.1
% Return on Assets	8.6	7.5	7.8	11.4	11.5	11.7	11.5	10.3	6.3	3.7
% Return on Equity	19.2	18.3	17.5	21.6	21.6	21.3	20.9	20.8	15.5	11.1

Data as orig reptd.; bef. results of disc opers/spec. items. Per share data adj. for stk. divs.; EPS diluted. E-Estimated. NA-Not Available. NM-Not Meaningful. NR-Not Ranked. UR-Under Review.

Office: Three Giralda Farms, Madison, NJ 07940.
Telephone: 973-520-2700.
Email: investor@questdiagnostics.com
Website: http://www.questdiagnostics.com

Chrmn, Pres & CEO: S.N. Mohapatra
COO: W.R. Simmons
SVP & CFO: R.A. Hagemann
SVP & General Counsel: M.E. Prevoznik

Chief Acctg Officer & Cntlr: T.F. Bongiorno
Investor Contact: L. Park (973-520-2900)
Board Members: J. C. Baldwin, J. K. Britell, W. F. Buehler, R. Haggerty, S. N. Mohapatra, G. M. Pfeiffer, D. C. Stanzione, G. Wilensky, J. Ziegler

Founded: 1967
Domicile: Delaware
Employees: 43,000

Qwest Communications International Inc.

STANDARD
&POOR'S

S&P Recommendation HOLD ★★★★★	Price $6.46 (as of Oct 22, 2010)	12-Mo. Target Price $6.00	Investment Style Large-Cap Blend

GICS Sector Telecommunication Services
Sub-Industry Integrated Telecommunication Services

Summary This company, which provides telecommunications services, primarily serving customers in 14 western and midwestern U.S. states, has agreed to be acquired by peer CenturyLink in a stock-based deal, subject to necessary approvals.

Key Stock Statistics (Source S&P, Vickers, company reports)

52-Wk Range	$6.49– 3.42	S&P Oper. EPS 2010E	0.39	Market Capitalization(B)	$11.236	Beta	0.81
Trailing 12-Month EPS	$0.25	S&P Oper. EPS 2011E	NA	Yield (%)	4.95	S&P 3-Yr. Proj. EPS CAGR(%)	5
Trailing 12-Month P/E	25.8	P/E on S&P Oper. EPS 2010E	16.6	Dividend Rate/Share	$0.32	S&P Credit Rating	BB
$10K Invested 5 Yrs Ago	$19,137	Common Shares Outstg. (M)	1,739.3	Institutional Ownership (%)	94		

Price Performance

30-Week Mov. Avg. ···   10-Week Mov. Avg. - - **GAAP Earnings vs. Previous Year**   Volume Above Avg. STARS
12-Mo. Target Price —   Relative Strength —   ▲ Up ▼ Down ► No Change   Below Avg. ★

Options: ASE, CBOE, P, Ph

Analysis prepared by **Todd Rosenbluth** on August 05, 2010, when the stock traded at **$ 5.64.**

Highlights

► We expect Q's revenues to decline 4.3% in 2010, a lesser decrease than in 2009. We forecast downward pressure on voice services from access line losses, due to competition and still-slow housing sales, and from wholesale weakness amid prior customer consolidation. In addition, in 2010, the company will not have wireless revenues as it has migrated customers off its service. We look for broadband additions and modest gains in the enterprise segment from new contracts, particularly in the second half, to provide an offset.

► Despite revenue pressure, we look for EBITDA to narrow to only $4.34 billion, from $4.42 billion in 2009, before restructuring costs. We look for expense reductions from a smaller work force and network cost savings that we think will help outweigh pension expenses and costs to support new broadband offerings. We expect depreciation charges to be relatively flat.

► We estimate Q will generate EPS of $0.39 in 2010, with relatively stable interest expenses. Our estimates reflect a normal mid-30% effective tax rate.

Investment Rationale/Risk

► Q has agreed to be acquired by peer CenturyLink (CTL 36, Hold) in a stock-based deal, subject to necessary approvals that are expected by mid-2011. We view the offer, equal to an enterprise value/EBITDA multiple of 5X, to be fair given Q's relatively high debt leverage and access line losses. We see merger synergies and an opportunity to reduce debt leverage and the dividend payout for the combined entity, assuming a smooth closing. On a standalone basis, we think Q faces difficulty growing its cash flow, but we view its dividend as stable.

► Risks to our recommendation and target price include failure to receive approval for the planned merger, greater-than-expected line losses, and inability to access credit markets.

► Based on the terms of the proposed merger, which we expect to be completed, our 12-month target price is $6.00. Each Q share is to be exchanged for 0.1664 of a share of CTL, and we have a 12-month target price of $36 on CTL. The 5.2X enterprise value/EBITDA multiple and P/E of 15X, using a $6 price, are premiums to what we thought Q was worth, but the P/E is at only a modest premium to peers.

Qualitative Risk Assessment

LOW	MEDIUM	HIGH

Our risk assessment reflects the highly competitive nature of the industry and our view of the above-average debt load Q carries, offset by our view of steady operating cash flow that supports the dividend.

Quantitative Evaluations

S&P Quality Ranking B-

D	C	B-	B	B+	A-	A	A+

Relative Strength Rank STRONG

73

LOWEST = 1   HIGHEST = 99

Revenue/Earnings Data

Revenue (Million $)

	1Q	2Q	3Q	4Q	Year
2010	2,966	2,930	--	--	--
2009	3,173	3,090	3,054	2,994	12,311
2008	3,399	3,382	3,379	3,315	13,475
2007	3,446	3,463	3,434	3,435	13,778
2006	3,476	3,472	3,487	3,488	13,923
2005	3,449	3,470	3,504	3,480	13,903

Earnings Per Share ($)

2010	0.02	0.09	E0.09	E0.10	E0.39
2009	0.12	0.12	0.07	0.06	0.42
2008	0.09	0.11	0.09	0.11	0.39
2007	0.12	0.13	1.08	0.20	1.52
2006	0.05	0.06	0.09	0.10	0.30
2005	0.03	-0.09	-0.08	-0.27	-0.41

Fiscal year ended Dec. 31. Next earnings report expected: Late October. EPS Estimates based on S&P Operating Earnings; historical GAAP earnings are as reported.

Dividend Data (Dates: mm/dd Payment Date: mm/dd/yy)

Amount ($)	Date Decl.	Ex-Div. Date	Stk. of Record	Payment Date
0.080	12/17	02/17	02/19	03/12/10
0.080	04/15	05/19	05/21	06/11/10
0.080	08/19	09/08	09/10	09/24/10
0.080	10/21	12/01	12/03	12/17/10

Dividends have been paid since 2008. Source: Company reports.

Qwest Communications International Inc.

Business Summary August 05, 2010

CORPORATE OVERVIEW. Qwest Communications International (Q) provides telecommunications services in 14 midwestern and western states. As of June 2010, Q had 9.4 million local access lines for consumers and businesses and 2.9 million consumer broadband customers (up 4% from a year earlier), with approximately 80% of its access lines in its eight largest markets, including Denver, Portland and Seattle. In March 2004, Q began offering wireless services using Sprint's network but retained control of all marketing, customer service, pricing and promotional offerings. In May 2008, the company announced plans to switch to using Verizon Wireless as part of a service bundle, and at the end of October 2009 had migrated all customers. In the second quarter of 2010, Q's revenues were pressured in its wholesale segment (22% of overall revenues) and in the mass markets segment (41%), but revenues in the business markets segment (34%) were flat.

IMPACT OF MAJOR DEVELOPMENTS. In April 2010, Q agreed to be acquired by CenturyLink (CTL), formerly known as CenturyTel, in a stock-based transaction, including debt assumption, valued at $22 billion. CTL believes it can realize $625 million of annual synergies following closing, which is expected, subject to approvals, by mid-2011. We believe the combined entity, with approximately 17 million access lines and $20 billion in revenues, will be able to maintain its dividend payout and will have lower debt leverage than Q would have on its own. CTL's access lines were also more stable than Q's in the second quarter of 2010, helped by its broadband penetration and less competitive operating environment.

COMPETITIVE LANDSCAPE. As a standalone, we believe Q faces competitive challenges partly due to low barriers to entry and characteristics unique to the company. As of June 2010, Q's access line count was 10.5% lower than a year earlier, as wireless and to a lesser extent cable telephony substitution was intense, and we believe fewer housing sales in core markets limited new customer additions. Q competes with cable providers such as Cox Communications and Comcast, which offer broadband services and telephony products that were aggressively marketed in the past two years. To offset possible customer migration to cable, Q is offering a triple-play package of voice, data and video services through a partnership with satellite provider Direct TV (951,000 customers); 15% of its mass markets lines were subscribing to the service.

Company Financials Fiscal Year Ended Dec. 31

Per Share Data ($)	2009	2008	2007	2006	2005	2004	2003	2002	2001	2000
Tangible Book Value	NM	NM	0.32	NM	NM	NM	NM	NM	1.28	5.37
Cash Flow	1.56	1.72	2.80	1.51	1.26	0.74	1.07	-7.65	0.83	2.56
Earnings	0.42	0.39	1.52	0.30	-0.41	-1.00	-0.76	-10.48	-2.38	-0.06
S&P Core Earnings	0.38	0.07	1.58	0.25	-0.68	-0.81	-0.81	-7.38	-1.39	NA
Dividends	0.32	0.32	Nil	Nil	Nil	Nil	Nil	Nil	0.05	Nil
Payout Ratio	76%	82%	Nil	Nil	Nil	Nil	Nil	Nil	NM	Nil
Prices:High	4.87	7.07	10.45	9.22	5.95	5.00	6.15	15.19	48.19	66.00
Prices:Low	2.86	2.05	6.23	5.10	3.30	2.56	3.01	1.07	11.08	32.13
P/E Ratio:High	12	18	7	31	NM	NM	NM	NM	NM	NM
P/E Ratio:Low	7	5	4	17	NM	NM	NM	NM	NM	NM

Income Statement Analysis (Million $)										
Revenue	12,311	13,475	13,778	13,923	13,903	13,809	14,288	15,385	19,695	16,610
Depreciation	2,014	2,314	2,459	2,381	3,065	3,123	3,167	3,847	5,335	3,342
Maintenance	NA	NA	NA	NA	NA	NA	NA	NA	NA	NA
Construction Credits	NA	NA	NA	NA	NA	NA	NA	NA	NA	NA
Effective Tax Rate	26.7%	38.0%	NM	NM	NM	NM	NM	NM	NM	NM
Net Income	662	681	2,917	593	-757	-1,794	-1,313	-17,625	-3,958	-81.0
S&P Core Earnings	664	124	3,037	492	-1,154	-1,465	-1,382	-12,411	-2,327	NA

Balance Sheet & Other Financial Data (Million $)										
Gross Property	46,600	46,770	46,646	46,374	45,954	45,428	45,094	44,580	55,099	48,318
Net Property	12,299	13,045	13,671	14,579	15,568	16,853	18,149	18,995	29,977	25,583
Capital Expenditures	1,409	1,777	1,669	1,632	1,613	1,731	2,088	2,764	8,543	6,597
Total Capital	13,022	11,390	14,213	11,761	11,751	14,078	14,744	16,924	59,046	58,493
Fixed Charges Coverage	1.8	2.1	1.6	1.4	0.6	NM	NM	0.2	1.3	2.5
Capitalization:Long Term Debt	12,004	12,839	13,650	13,206	14,968	16,690	15,639	19,754	20,197	15,421
Capitalization:Preferred	Nil	Nil	Nil	Nil	Nil	Nil	Nil	Nil	Nil	Nil
Capitalization:Common	-1,178	-1,449	563	-1,445	-3,217	-2,612	-1,016	-2,830	36,655	41,304
% Return on Revenue	5.4	5.1	21.2	4.3	NM	NM	NM	NM	NM	NM
% Return on Invested Capital	13.9	14.1	31.0	15.0	8.1	NM	NM	12.4	NM	7.6
% Return on Common Equity	NM	NM	NM	NM	NM	NM	NM	NM	NM	NM
% Earned on Net Property	15.6	16.6	12.4	10.3	5.3	NM	17.5	16.9	26.4	32.9
% Long Term Debt of Capitalization	110.9	112.7	96.0	112.3	127.4	118.6	106.9	116.7	34.2	27.2
Capital % Preferred	Nil	Nil	Nil	Nil	Nil	Nil	Nil	Nil	Nil	Nil
Capitalization:% Common	-10.9	-12.7	4.0	-12.3	-27.4	-18.6	-6.9	-16.7	62.0	72.8

Data as orig reptd.; bef. results of disc opers/spec. items. Per share data adj. for stk. divs.; EPS diluted. E-Estimated. NA-Not Available. NM-Not Meaningful. NR-Not Ranked. UR-Under Review.

Office: 1801 California St, Denver, CO 80202-2658.
Telephone: 303-992-1400.
Email: investor.relations@qwest.com
Website: http://www.qwest.com

Chrmn & CEO: E.A. Mueller
COO & EVP: T.A. Taylor
EVP & CFO: J.J. Euteneuer
EVP, Chief Admin Officer & General Counsel: R. Baer

SVP, Chief Acctg Officer & Cntlr: R.W. Johnston
Board Members: C. L. Biggs, K. D. Brooksher, P. S. Hellman, R. D. Hoover, P. J. Martin, C. S. Mathews, E. A. Mueller, W. Murdy, J. L. Murley, M. J. Roberts, J. A. Unruh, A. Welters

Founded: 1983
Domicile: Delaware
Employees: 30,138

RadioShack Corp

STANDARD &POOR'S

S&P Recommendation	HOLD ★★★☆☆	Price $20.74 (as of Oct 25, 2010)	12-Mo. Target Price $26.00	Investment Style Large-Cap Blend

GICS Sector Consumer Discretionary
Sub-Industry Computer & Electronics Retail

Summary This consumer electronics retailer operates the RadioShack chain, which has about 7,000 outlets (including dealers/franchises).

Key Stock Statistics (Source S&P, Vickers, company reports)

52-Wk Range	$24.00– 16.39	S&P Oper. EPS 2010**E**	1.87	Market Capitalization(B)	$2.601	Beta	1.82
Trailing 12-Month EPS	$1.70	S&P Oper. EPS 2011**E**	2.04	Yield (%)	1.21	S&P 3-Yr. Proj. EPS CAGR(%)	8
Trailing 12-Month P/E	12.2	P/E on S&P Oper. EPS 2010**E**	11.1	Dividend Rate/Share	$0.25	S&P Credit Rating	BB
$10K Invested 5 Yrs Ago	$10,752	Common Shares Outstg. (M)	125.4	Institutional Ownership (%)	96		

Price Performance

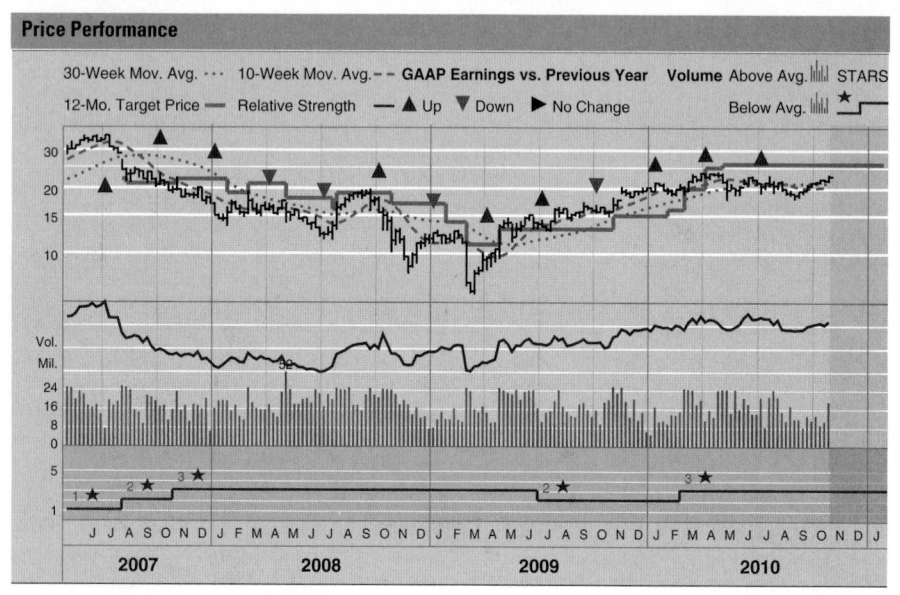

30-Week Mov. Avg. · · · 10-Week Mov. Avg. - - GAAP Earnings vs. Previous Year   Volume Above Avg. STARS
12-Mo. Target Price — Relative Strength   ▲ Up ▼ Down ▶ No Change   Below Avg.

Options: ASE, CBOE, P

Analysis prepared by **Michael Souers** on August 02, 2010, when the stock traded at **$ 21.54**.

Highlights

► We see sales increasing 3.8% in 2010, following a 1.2% advance in 2009. We expect RSH to continue to focus on increasing profitability by opportunistically closing underperforming stores and kiosks. We project a 4%-5% increase in comparable store sales, boosted by the addition of national wireless carrier T-Mobile and an improved product assortment that includes Apple's iPhone. We also look for the company to increase its focus on selling prepaid wireless handsets and airtime, and expect a sales lift from netbooks, offsetting anticipated sales declines in GPS devices, digital converter boxes and televisions.

► We expect a modest widening of operating margins, reflecting mix shift and a slight leveraging of fixed costs on solid comp-store sales growth. However, we think RSH will struggle to achieve historical gross margins due to increased competitive pressures and the company's focus on faster-moving, lower-margin categories.

► After taxes that we forecast at 38.0%, we estimate EPS of $1.80 in 2010, a 10% increase from the $1.63 the company earned in 2009. We see 2011 EPS of $1.88.

Investment Rationale/Risk

► We see the company in the late stages of its turnaround plan, which is focused on increasing average unit volume, rationalizing its cost structure, and growing profitable square footage. While RSH's CEO has extensive retail experience with turnarounds, we think the longer-term outlook for the company is uncertain, due to the highly competitive environment for electronics products. Given our view of the company's lackluster longer-term sales outlook and lack of earnings visibility, we believe the shares are fairly valued despite trading at about 11X our 2011 EPS estimate, a slight discount to peers and the S&P 500.

► Risks to our recommendation and target price include macroeconomic factors that could result in weaker-than-anticipated consumer spending levels, and competitive pressures from rivals into the wireless handset space.

► Our 12-month target price of $26, about 14X our 2011 EPS estimate, is derived from our discounted cash flow analysis. Our DCF model assumes a weighted average cost of capital of 10.3% and a terminal growth rate of 3.0%.

Qualitative Risk Assessment

LOW	MEDIUM	HIGH

The company is a relatively large player in a fragmented industry, with numerous suppliers and buyers, and a history of profitability. However, we view consumer electronics retailing as highly competitive, with numerous rivals and strong price competition.

Quantitative Evaluations

S&P Quality Ranking B+

D	C	B-	B	B+	A-	A	A+

Relative Strength Rank WEAK

27

LOWEST = 1   HIGHEST = 99

Revenue/Earnings Data

Revenue (Million $)

	1Q	2Q	3Q	4Q	Year
2010	1,042	1,011	--	--	--
2009	1,002	965.7	990.0	1,318	4,276
2008	949.0	994.9	1,022	1,259	4,225
2007	992.3	934.8	960.3	1,364	4,252
2006	1,160	1,100	1,060	1,458	4,778
2005	1,123	1,092	1,195	1,672	5,082

Earnings Per Share ($)

2010	0.39	0.41	E0.37	E0.70	E1.87
2009	0.34	0.39	0.30	0.60	1.63
2008	0.30	0.32	0.39	0.50	1.49
2007	0.31	0.34	0.34	0.77	1.74
2006	0.06	-0.02	-0.12	0.62	0.54
2005	0.34	0.33	0.75	0.40	1.81

Fiscal year ended Dec. 31. Next earnings report expected: Late October. EPS Estimates based on S&P Operating Earnings; historical GAAP earnings are as reported.

Dividend Data (Dates: mm/dd Payment Date: mm/dd/yy)

Amount ($)	Date Decl.	Ex-Div. Date	Stk. of Record	Payment Date
0.250	11/09	11/24	11/27	12/16/09

Dividends have been paid since 1987. Source: Company reports.

RadioShack Corp

STANDARD &POOR'S

Business Summary August 02, 2010

CORPORATE OVERVIEW. As of December 31, 2009, this consumer electronics retailer had 4,476 company-operated stores located through the U.S., including Puerto Rico and the U.S. Virgin Islands. RSH also had a network of 1,308 dealer/franchise stores, including 34 located outside the U.S. At the end of 2009, RSH operated 562 non-RadioShack branded kiosks, which offer product lines such as wireless phones and associated accessories. In addition, in December 2008, RadioShack acquired the remaining interest in its Mexican joint venture, RadioShack de Mexico, S.A. de C.V., RadioShack de Mexico had 204 stores and 10 dealers throughout Mexico at December 31, 2009.

Each store carries a broad assortment of electronics products, including batteries and accessories; wireless phones and communication devices such as scanners and GPS units; flat panel televisions; DVD players; direct-to-home (DTH) satellite systems; PCs; home entertainment, wireless and other computer accessories; wire, cable and connectivity products; digital cameras; and specialized products such as radio-controlled cars and other toys. RSH also provides access to third-party services, such as wireless telephone and DTH satellite activation, satellite radio service, prepaid wireless airtime and extended service plans. We believe that RSH is focusing on revamping its product offerings in order to enhance its competitive position within the consumer electronics industry. In the second half of 2005, RSH began dedicating floor space to Apple's iPod and accessories, and the company made a concerted push to sell video gaming products in 2007, another hot product category. At the end of 2009, RSH began selling Apple's iPhone in select locations, with a nationwide rollout anticipated in 2010.

In April 2009, RSH agreed with Sprint Nextel to cease the companies' arrangement to jointly operate the Sprint-branded kios. In August 2009, RSH transitioned these kiosks to multiple wireless carrier RadioShack-branded locations.

RadioShack has been conducting a test rollout of non-RadioShack branded kiosk locations in approximately 100 Target stores, with the expected completion of this test in 2010. The company has a similar arrangement with Sam's Club, and in February 2009 signed a contract extension with Sam's Club through March 2011.

Company Financials Fiscal Year Ended Dec. 31

Per Share Data ($)	2009	2008	2007	2006	2005	2004	2003	2002	2001	2000
Tangible Book Value	8.06	6.24	5.88	4.81	4.36	5.83	4.73	4.24	4.04	4.46
Cash Flow	2.36	2.26	2.57	1.48	2.65	2.70	2.31	1.97	1.41	2.38
Earnings	1.63	1.49	1.74	0.54	1.81	2.08	1.77	1.45	0.85	1.84
S&P Core Earnings	1.63	1.49	1.74	0.67	1.69	1.94	1.49	1.18	1.06	NA
Dividends	0.25	0.25	0.25	0.25	0.25	0.25	0.25	0.22	0.22	0.22
Payout Ratio	15%	17%	14%	46%	14%	12%	14%	15%	25%	12%
Prices:High	20.57	19.90	35.00	23.37	34.48	36.24	32.48	36.21	56.50	72.94
Prices:Low	6.47	8.06	16.69	13.73	20.55	26.04	18.74	16.99	20.10	35.06
P/E Ratio:High	13	13	20	43	19	17	18	25	66	40
P/E Ratio:Low	4	5	10	25	11	13	11	12	24	19

Income Statement Analysis (Million $)	2009	2008	2007	2006	2005	2004	2003	2002	2001	2000
Revenue	4,276	4,225	4,252	4,778	5,082	4,841	4,649	4,577	4,776	4,795
Operating Income	464	428	464	329	474	660	576	510	583	736
Depreciation	92.9	99.3	113	128	124	101	92.0	94.7	108	107
Interest Expense	44.1	29.9	38.8	44.3	44.5	29.6	35.7	43.4	50.8	53.9
Pretax Income	329	304	367	111	322	542	473	425	292	594
Effective Tax Rate	37.6%	36.8%	35.4%	34.1%	16.0%	37.8%	36.9%	38.0%	42.8%	38.0%
Net Income	205	192	237	73.4	270	337	299	263	167	368
S&P Core Earnings	205	192	236	92.3	251	315	252	211	200	NA

Balance Sheet & Other Financial Data (Million $)	2009	2008	2007	2006	2005	2004	2003	2002	2001	2000
Cash	908	815	510	472	224	438	635	447	401	131
Current Assets	2,016	1,792	1,567	1,600	1,627	1,775	1,667	1,707	1,714	1,818
Total Assets	2,429	2,284	1,990	2,070	2,205	2,517	2,244	1,707	2,245	2,577
Current Liabilities	654	637	748	984	986	957	858	829	826	1,232
Long Term Debt	628	732	348	346	495	507	541	591	565	303
Common Equity	1,048	817	770	654	589	922	769	729	714	812
Total Capital	1,676	1,550	1,118	1,000	1,084	1,429	1,311	1,320	1,344	1,284
Capital Expenditures	81.0	85.6	45.3	91.0	171	229	190	107	139	120
Cash Flow	298	292	350	202	394	439	391	354	270	470
Current Ratio	3.1	2.8	2.1	1.6	1.6	1.9	1.9	2.1	2.1	1.5
% Long Term Debt of Capitalization	37.5	47.3	31.1	34.6	45.7	35.5	41.3	44.8	42.1	23.6
% Net Income of Revenue	4.8	4.6	5.6	1.5	5.3	7.0	6.4	5.8	3.5	7.7
% Return on Assets	8.7	9.0	11.7	3.4	11.4	14.2	13.4	13.3	6.9	15.6
% Return on Equity	22.0	24.3	33.3	11.8	35.7	39.9	39.9	35.9	21.2	46.2

Data as orig reptd.; bef. results of disc opers/spec. items. Per share data adj. for stk. divs.; EPS diluted. E-Estimated. NA-Not Available. NM-Not Meaningful. NR-Not Ranked. UR-Under Review.

Office: 300 Radioshack Cir, Fort Worth, TX 76102-1964.
Telephone: 817-415-3011.
Email: investor.relations@radioshack.com
Website: http://www.radioshack.com

Chrmn & CEO: J.C. Day
COO: B. Bevin
EVP & CFO: J.F. Gooch
SVP & CIO: S.S. Stufflebeme

Chief Acctg Officer, Treas & Cntlr: M.O. Moad
Investor Contact: M. Salky (817-415-3189)
Board Members: F. J. Belatti, J. C. Day, D. R. Feehan, H. E. Lockhart, J. L. Messman, T. G. Plaskett, E. D. Woodbury

Founded: 1899
Domicile: Delaware
Employees: 37,000

The McGraw·Hill Companies

Range Resources Corp.

STANDARD &POOR'S

S&P Recommendation BUY ★★★★☆

Price	12-Mo. Target Price	Investment Style
$36.75 (as of Oct 22, 2010)	$44.00	Large-Cap Growth

GICS Sector Energy
Sub-Industry Oil & Gas Exploration & Production

Summary This company explores, develops and acquires oil and gas properties, primarily in the Southwest, Appalachian and Gulf Coast regions of the U.S.

Key Stock Statistics (Source S&P, Vickers, company reports)

52-Wk Range	$56.73– 32.25	S&P Oper. EPS 2010**E**	0.97	Market Capitalization(B)	$5.881	Beta	0.47
Trailing 12-Month EPS	$0.25	S&P Oper. EPS 2011**E**	1.06	Yield (%)	0.44	S&P 3-Yr. Proj. EPS CAGR(%)	-18
Trailing 12-Month P/E	NM	P/E on S&P Oper. EPS 2010**E**	37.9	Dividend Rate/Share	$0.16	S&P Credit Rating	BB
$10K Invested 5 Yrs Ago	$17,372	Common Shares Outstg. (M)	160.0	Institutional Ownership (%)	95		

Price Performance

30-Week Mov. Avg. · · · 10-Week Mov. Avg. – – GAAP Earnings vs. Previous Year   Volume Above Avg. ▧ STARS
12-Mo. Target Price — Relative Strength — ▲ Up ▼ Down ▶ No Change   Below Avg. ▨ ★

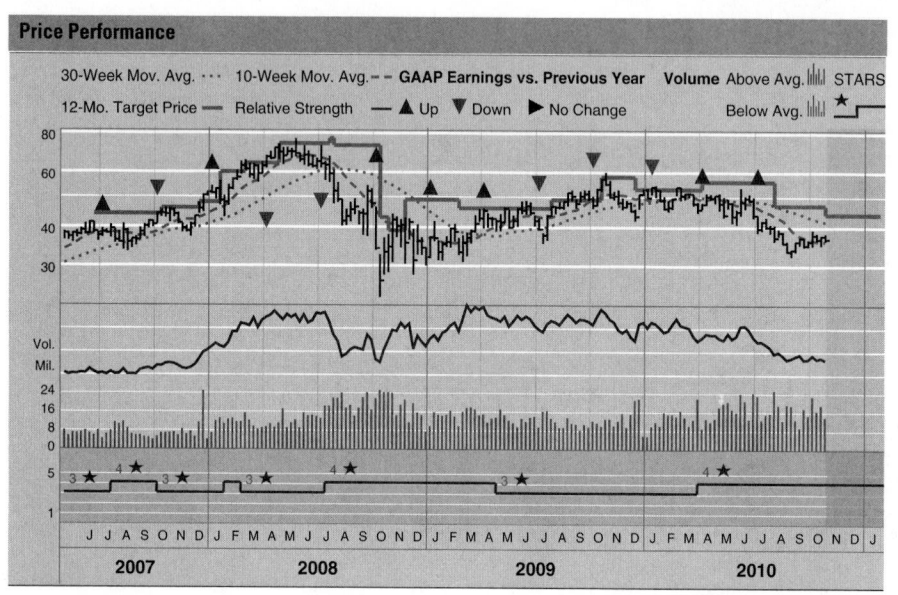

Options: ASE, CBOE, P, Ph

Qualitative Risk Assessment

LOW	MEDIUM	**HIGH**

Our risk assessment reflects the company's operations in a capital-intensive industry that is cyclical and derives value from producing a commodity whose price is very volatile.

Quantitative Evaluations

S&P Quality Ranking B+

D	C	B-	B	**B+**	A-	A	A+

Relative Strength Rank WEAK

24

LOWEST = 1   HIGHEST = 99

Revenue/Earnings Data

Revenue (Million $)

	1Q	2Q	3Q	4Q	Year
2010	348.5	224.8	--	--	--
2009	276.4	180.4	203.6	246.8	907.3
2008	205.3	150.1	622.7	344.9	1,323
2007	152.8	243.5	242.4	223.4	862.1
2006	189.2	177.6	228.9	184.1	779.7
2005	108.0	119.7	141.9	166.5	536.0

Earnings Per Share ($)

2010	0.48	0.06	E0.12	E0.16	E0.97
2009	0.21	-0.26	-0.19	-0.11	-0.35
2008	0.01	-0.23	1.81	0.60	2.22
2007	0.06	0.43	0.39	0.22	1.11
2006	0.41	0.37	0.46	0.19	1.42
2005	0.18	0.17	0.19	0.32	0.86

Fiscal year ended Dec. 31. Next earnings report expected: NA. EPS Estimates based on S&P Operating Earnings; historical GAAP earnings are as reported.

Highlights

➤ The 12-month target price for RRC has recently been changed to $44.00 from $47.00. The Highlights section of this Stock Report will be updated accordingly.

Investment Rationale/Risk

➤ The Investment Rationale/Risk section of this Stock Report will be updated shortly. For the latest News story on RRC from MarketScope, see below.

➤ 10/21/10 11:34 am ET ... S&P REITERATES BUY RECOMMENDATION ON SHARES OF RANGE RESOURCES (RRC 37.38****): RRC gives Q3 update ahead of its 10/28 release. Production of 503 MMcfe/d, up 15%, beat our forecast, as Marcellus ramps on solid drilling and new midstream build-out. RRC will redirect capex to liquids and is cutting gas drilling. About 90% of current capex is being spent at liquids plays. Despite higher production, we cut our '10 EPS view $0.11 to $0.97 (with $0.44 item) and '11's $0.24 to $1.06 on weak gas prices. On above peer multiples reflecting strong growth, and our DCF and NAV, we cut our target price $3 to $44. We see Q3 EPS of $0.12 vs. $0.26 (before items). /M.Kay

Dividend Data (Dates: mm/dd Payment Date: mm/dd/yy)

Amount ($)	Date Decl.	Ex-Div. Date	Stk. of Record	Payment Date
0.040	12/01	12/11	12/15	12/31/09
0.040	03/01	03/11	03/15	03/31/10
0.040	06/01	06/11	06/15	06/30/10
0.040	09/01	09/13	09/15	09/30/10

Dividends have been paid since 2004. Source: Company reports.

Range Resources Corp.

STANDARD &POOR'S

Business Summary July 29, 2010

CORPORATE OVERVIEW. Range Resources Corp. is an independent oil and gas company primarily engaged in acquiring, developing, exploring and producing oil and gas properties. RRC has established three core operating areas in the Appalachian, Southwestern and Gulf Coast regions of the U.S. The Southwest business unit encompasses operations in East Texas, West Texas, New Mexico, and the Mid-continent region of Oklahoma and the Texas Panhandle.

As of December 31, 2009, RRC had estimated proved reserves of 3.13 Tcfe, of which 84% was natural gas and 55% was proved developed. This compares with estimated proved reserves of 2.65 Tcfe, 83% natural gas and 62% proved developed, at the end of 2008, an 18% increase. We forecast RRC's reserve life to be 19.7 years, compared to 18.8 years at the end of 2008.

We estimate that RRC replaced 486% (405% in 2008) of production in 2009, all of it from organic drilling. We estimate finding and development costs (exclude acquisitions) in 2009 were $1.04 per Mcfe versus a three-year average of $1.83 per Mcfe. Total reserve replacement costs (including acquisitions) in 2009 were $1.04 per Mcfe, versus a three-year average of $1.88 per Mcfe.

CORPORATE STRATEGY. RRC pursues what we consider a balanced growth strategy that targets the exploitation of its inventory of development drilling lo-

cations, higher potential exploration projects, and acquisitions. RRC focuses on acquisition opportunities within its core operating areas to capitalize on regional expertise and drive down costs.

In June 2006, RRC completed the acquisition of Stroud Energy for $465.2 million, including $278 million in cash. RRC purchased 171 Bcfe of proved reserves located primarily in the Barnett Shale play of North Texas, the Cotton Valley play of East Texas and the Austin Chalk play of Central Texas. RRC has a goal of doubling production in this region over the next 12 months.

Since 2004, RRC has completed over $850 million in non-core asset sales. RRC has sold West Texas oil properties, New York gas and Ohio tight gas assets, Austin Chalk acreage and properties in the Gulf of Mexico.

IMPACT OF MAJOR DEVELOPMENTS. In February 2007, RRC completed the sale of its Austin Chalk assets acquired in the Stroud Energy transaction in 2006 for $82 million. RRC originally stated its intention to sell the assets In late July 2006, just as natural gas prices fell into a fairly steep decline, and RRC had difficulty selling the assets.

Company Financials Fiscal Year Ended Dec. 31

Per Share Data ($)	2009	2008	2007	2006	2005	2004	2003	2002	2001	2000
Tangible Book Value	15.10	15.82	11.57	9.04	5.36	4.65	3.24	2.50	3.11	2.43
Cash Flow	2.74	4.45	2.59	2.65	1.84	1.43	1.34	1.23	1.05	1.23
Earnings	-0.35	2.22	1.11	1.42	0.86	0.38	0.35	0.29	0.07	0.38
S&P Core Earnings	-0.38	2.14	1.11	1.42	0.82	0.29	0.33	0.29	0.18	NA
Dividends	0.16	0.16	0.13	0.09	0.07	0.03	Nil	Nil	Nil	Nil
Payout Ratio	NM	7%	12%	6%	8%	9%	Nil	Nil	Nil	Nil
Prices:High	60.13	76.81	51.88	31.77	28.37	14.43	6.57	3.97	4.75	4.67
Prices:Low	30.90	23.77	25.29	21.74	12.34	6.25	3.33	2.69	2.62	0.96
P/E Ratio:High	NM	35	47	22	33	38	19	14	65	12
P/E Ratio:Low	NM	11	23	15	14	16	9	9	36	3

Income Statement Analysis (Million $)	2009	2008	2007	2006	2005	2004	2003	2002	2001	2000
Revenue	907	1,323	862	780	536	321	230	195	219	188
Operating Income	NA	965	564	549	344	193	140	119	152	132
Depreciation, Depletion and Amortization	478	348	221	170	128	103	86.5	76.8	77.8	72.2
Interest Expense	117	99.8	77.7	57.6	38.8	23.1	22.2	23.2	30.7	40.0
Pretax Income	-58.7	543	266	321	177	66.8	49.4	19.3	4.99	18.6
Effective Tax Rate	8.28%	36.2%	37.2%	38.5%	37.4%	36.8%	37.4%	NM	NM	NM
Net Income	-53.9	346	167	198	111	42.2	30.9	23.8	5.05	20.2
S&P Core Earnings	-57.3	333	167	198	105	27.9	27.3	23.5	14.1	NA

Balance Sheet & Other Financial Data (Million $)	2009	2008	2007	2006	2005	2004	2003	2002	2001	2000
Cash	0.77	0.75	4.02	2.38	4.75	18.4	0.63	1.33	3.25	2.48
Current Assets	175	404	262	320	208	136	66.1	37.4	78.6	62.1
Total Assets	5,396	5,563	4,017	3,188	2,019	1,595	830	658	692	689
Current Liabilities	314	354	305	232	322	177	107	67.2	44.0	45.9
Long Term Debt	1,708	1,791	1,151	1,049	616	621	358	368	392	458
Common Equity	2,379	2,458	1,728	1,346	770	566	224	206	246	185
Total Capital	4,086	5,032	3,470	2,864	1,561	1,305	643	574	648	643
Capital Expenditures	574	918	808	517	277	175	2.62	2.82	2.33	2.26
Cash Flow	424	694	388	367	239	140	117	101	82.9	91.0
Current Ratio	0.6	1.1	0.9	1.4	0.6	0.8	0.6	0.6	1.8	1.4
% Long Term Debt of Capitalization	41.8	35.6	33.1	36.6	39.5	47.6	55.7	64.1	60.6	71.2
% Return on Assets	NM	7.2	4.7	7.6	6.1	3.5	4.2	3.5	0.7	2.8
% Return on Equity	NM	16.5	10.9	18.7	16.1	9.4	14.0	10.8	2.3	12.1

Data as orig reptd.; bef. results of disc opers/spec. items. Per share data adj. for stk. divs.; EPS diluted. E-Estimated. NA-Not Available. NM-Not Meaningful. NR-Not Ranked. UR-Under Review.

Office: 100 Throckmorton Street, Suite 1200, Fort Worth, TX 76102.
Telephone: 817-870-2601.
Website: http://www.rangeresources.com
Chrmn & CEO: J.H. Pinkerton

Pres & COO: J.L. Ventura
EVP & CFO: R.S. Manny
SVP, Secy & General Counsel: D.P. Poole
Investor Contact: R.L. Waller (817-870-2601)

Board Members: C. L. Blackburn, A. V. Dub, V. R. Eales, A. Finkelson, J. M. Funk, J. S. Linker, K. S. McCarthy, J. H. Pinkerton, J. L. Ventura

Founded: 1976
Domicile: Delaware
Employees: 787

The McGraw-Hill Companies

Raytheon Co.

STANDARD &POOR'S

S&P Recommendation	HOLD ★★★☆☆	Price $47.60 (as of Oct 22, 2010)	12-Mo. Target Price $52.00	Investment Style Large-Cap Value

GICS Sector Industrials
Sub-Industry Aerospace & Defense

Summary Raytheon, the world's sixth largest military contractor, specializes in making high-tech missiles, advanced radar systems, defense electronics, and missile-defense systems.

Key Stock Statistics (Source S&P, Vickers, company reports)

52-Wk Range	$60.10– 42.65	S&P Oper. EPS 2010**E**	4.24	Market Capitalization(B)	$17.808	Beta		0.69
Trailing 12-Month EPS	$4.18	S&P Oper. EPS 2011**E**	5.20	Yield (%)	3.15	S&P 3-Yr. Proj. EPS CAGR(%)		4
Trailing 12-Month P/E	11.4	P/E on S&P Oper. EPS 2010**E**	11.2	Dividend Rate/Share	$1.50	S&P Credit Rating		A-
$10K Invested 5 Yrs Ago	$14,508	Common Shares Outstg. (M)	374.1	Institutional Ownership (%)	76			

Price Performance

30-Week Mov. Avg. · · · 10-Week Mov. Avg. – · – **GAAP Earnings vs. Previous Year** Volume Above Avg. STARS
12-Mo. Target Price — Relative Strength — ▲ Up ▼ Down ► No Change Below Avg. ★

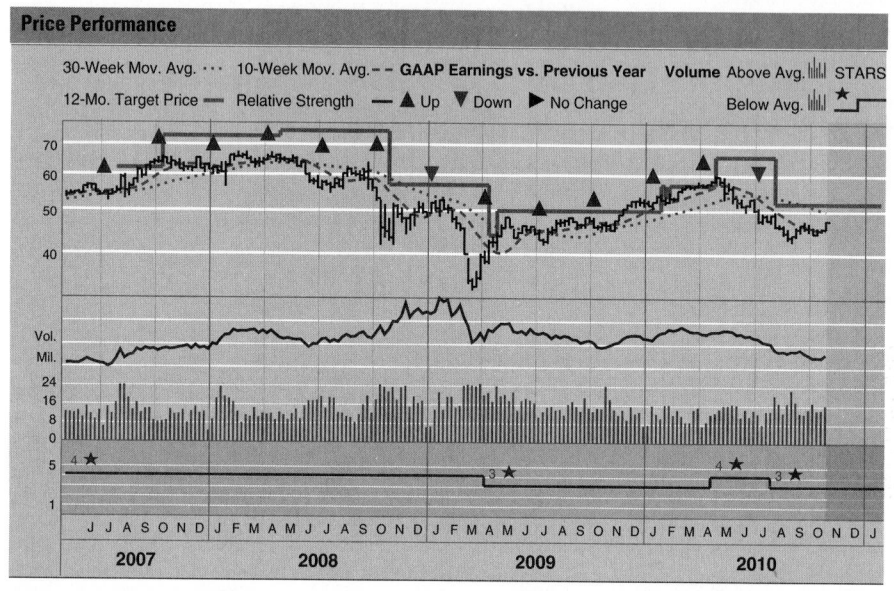

Options: ASE, CBOE, P

Analysis prepared by **Richard Tortoriello** on August 02, 2010, when the stock traded at **$ 46.89.**

Highlights

➤ We see revenue growth of 4% in 2010, driven by international orders for Patriot, classified programs, cyber warfare/security, missiles, homeland security, and training programs. International customers accounted for 30% of bookings in 2009, and we expect continued demand for international missile defense. We also project 4% revenue growth in 2011. The company had a book-to-bill ratio of 1.01 in 2009, and recorded a book-to-bill of 1.03 for the first six months of 2010. However, funded backlog declined 6% in the second quarter of 2010, and total backlog has declined slightly for each of the past five quarters.

➤ We see operating profit margins narrowing to 9.7% this year, from 12.2% in 2009, on increased pension expense (versus a pension gain in 2009) and a $395 million pre-tax charge to terminate the UK e-Borders program (which RTN believes it has performed well on).

➤ We project 2010 EPS of $4.24, including the e-Borders charge, with growth to $5.20 in 2011. We look for free cash flow (cash generated from operations less capital expenditures) per share of about $4.90 in 2010.

Investment Rationale/Risk

➤ We recently downgraded our recommendation on the shares to Hold, from Buy. Although we have a favorable view of RTN's order rates over the past few years, we are concerned that total backlog has begun to decline. We see good opportunities for RTN with U.S. and international customers for missile defense and defense electronics, but note that U.S. and European defense budgets are beginning to tighten significantly, which we believe will constrain growth at large defense contractors going forward.

➤ Risks to our recommendation and target price include the potential for delays and/or cuts in military contracts and failure to perform well on existing contracts or to win new business.

➤ Our 12-month target price of $52 is based on an enterprise value-to-EBITDA multiple of about 6X, using our 2011 EBITDA estimate of about $3.4 billion. This compares to a 20-year low EV/EBITDA multiple for RTN of 3.5X and a 20-year average of 9.0X. We believe the shares deserve a below-average valuation, due to our view of projected weak defense spending.

Qualitative Risk Assessment

LOW	MEDIUM	HIGH

Our risk assessment reflects RTN's exposure to changes in defense spending and its historically average earnings stability, offset by its relatively low long-term debt to capital ratio of 19%, as of June 2010, its leading defense contractor status, and its large project backlog.

Quantitative Evaluations

S&P Quality Ranking B+

D	C	B-	B	B+	A-	A	A+

Relative Strength Rank MODERATE

47

LOWEST = 1   HIGHEST = 99

Revenue/Earnings Data

Revenue (Million $)

	1Q	2Q	3Q	4Q	Year
2010	6,053	5,973	--	--	--
2009	5,884	6,125	6,205	6,667	24,881
2008	5,354	5,870	5,864	6,086	23,174
2007	4,928	5,419	5,355	6,000	21,301
2006	4,660	4,973	4,936	5,722	20,291
2005	4,944	5,409	5,331	6,210	21,894

Earnings Per Share ($)

	1Q	2Q	3Q	4Q	Year
2010	1.18	0.55	E1.19	E1.32	E4.24
2009	1.11	1.24	1.25	1.30	4.89
2008	0.93	1.00	1.01	1.02	3.95
2007	0.69	0.79	0.69	1.45	3.80
2006	0.61	0.61	0.59	0.81	2.46
2005	0.43	0.51	0.51	0.63	2.08

Fiscal year ended Dec. 31. Next earnings report expected: Late October. EPS Estimates based on S&P Operating Earnings; historical GAAP earnings are as reported.

Dividend Data (Dates: mm/dd Payment Date: mm/dd/yy)

Amount ($)	Date Decl.	Ex-Div. Date	Stk. of Record	Payment Date
0.310	12/09	12/30	01/04	01/28/10
0.375	03/24	04/01	04/06	04/29/10
0.375	05/27	07/01	07/06	08/12/10
0.375	09/23	10/01	10/05	11/04/10

Dividends have been paid since 1964. Source: Company reports.

Please read the Required Disclosures and Analyst Certification on the last page of this report.

The McGraw·Hill Companies

Raytheon Co.

STANDARD
&POOR'S

Business Summary August 02, 2010

CORPORATE OVERVIEW. Raytheon, with estimated 2010 revenues of $26.3 billion, is the world's sixth largest military contractor and a leading maker of missiles. It does business through six segments.

Integrated Defense Systems (20% of sales and 26% of operating profits in 2009) is a leading provider of integrated naval, air and missile defense and civil security response solutions. Customers include the U.S. Missile Defense Agency (MDA), the U.S. Armed Forces, as well as key international customers. Main product lines include seapower capability systems, focusing on the DDG-1000, the Navy's next-generation naval destroyer; national & theater security programs, including the X-band radars and missile defense systems; Patriot programs, principally the Patriot Air & Missile Defense System; and global business operations, which provides a variety of products.

Intelligence & Information Systems (12% of sales and 8% of profits) provides intelligence and information solutions specializing in ground processing, unmanned ground systems, cybersecurity solutions, homeland/civil security and other markets. About half its business is classified. Areas of focus include integrated mission support and systems engineering; intelligence data management and HUMINT operations support; information processing, information integration, and visualization systems; information security solutions; and next-generation classified systems.

Missile Systems (21% of sales and 18% of profits) makes and supports a broad range of leading-edge missile systems for the armed forces of the U.S. and other countries. Business areas include naval weapon systems, which provides defensive missiles and guided projectiles to the navies of over 30 countries; air warfare systems, with products focused on air and ground-based targets, including the Tomahawk cruise missile and AMRAAM air-to-air missile; land combat, which includes the Javelin anti-tank missile; and other programs.

Network Centric Systems (18% of sales and 21% of profits) leverages its networking, command and control, and communications capabilities to provide solutions for the U.S. military, other U.S. government customers, and international customers. Business areas include combat systems, which provides ground-based surveillance and target engagement systems; integrated communication systems; command and control systems; Thales-Raytheon Systems, a joint venture between the two companies; and operations and precision components, which provides a broad range of imaging capabilities.

Company Financials Fiscal Year Ended Dec. 31

Per Share Data ($)	2009	2008	2007	2006	2005	2004	2003	2002	2001	2000
Tangible Book Value	NM	NM	2.15	NM	NM	NM	NM	NM	NM	NM
Cash Flow	5.69	4.69	4.63	3.28	3.19	1.93	2.22	2.74	2.03	3.50
Earnings	4.89	3.95	3.80	2.46	2.08	0.99	1.29	1.85	0.01	1.46
S&P Core Earnings	5.21	2.50	4.15	3.10	2.61	1.96	1.11	-0.25	-2.68	NA
Dividends	1.24	1.12	1.02	0.96	0.86	0.80	0.80	0.80	0.80	0.80
Payout Ratio	25%	28%	27%	34%	41%	81%	62%	43%	NM	55%
Prices:High	53.84	67.49	65.94	54.17	40.57	41.89	33.97	45.70	37.44	35.81
Prices:Low	33.20	41.81	50.96	39.43	35.96	29.28	24.31	26.30	23.95	17.50
P/E Ratio:High	11	17	17	19	21	42	26	25	NM	25
P/E Ratio:Low	7	11	13	14	19	30	19	14	NM	12

Income Statement Analysis (Million $)

	2009	2008	2007	2006	2005	2004	2003	2002	2001	2000
Revenue	24,881	23,174	21,301	20,291	21,894	20,245	18,109	16,760	16,867	16,895
Operating Income	3,358	2,907	2,700	2,213	2,131	1,822	1,709	2,118	1,488	2,319
Depreciation	402	311	372	373	444	434	393	364	729	694
Interest Expense	123	129	196	273	312	418	537	497	660	736
Pretax Income	2,930	2,498	2,225	1,688	1,440	579	762	1,074	117	877
Effective Tax Rate	32.5%	33.0%	23.9%	34.4%	34.6%	24.2%	29.8%	29.7%	95.7%	43.2%
Net Income	1,936	1,674	1,693	1,107	942	439	535	755	5.00	498
S&P Core Earnings	2,064	1,059	1,848	1,392	1,180	866	460	-105	-970	NA

Balance Sheet & Other Financial Data (Million $)

	2009	2008	2007	2006	2005	2004	2003	2002	2001	2000
Cash	2,642	2,259	2,655	2,460	1,202	556	661	544	1,214	871
Current Assets	7,868	7,417	7,616	9,517	7,567	7,124	6,585	7,190	8,362	8,013
Total Assets	23,607	23,296	23,281	25,491	24,381	24,153	23,668	23,946	26,636	26,777
Current Liabilities	5,523	5,149	4,788	6,715	5,900	5,644	3,849	5,107	5,753	4,865
Long Term Debt	2,329	2,309	2,268	3,278	3,969	4,637	7,376	7,138	6,875	9,054
Common Equity	9,827	9,087	12,542	11,101	10,798	10,611	9,162	8,870	11,290	10,823
Total Capital	12,268	11,659	15,261	14,544	15,011	15,345	16,538	16,008	18,743	20,650
Capital Expenditures	280	304	313	295	75.0	363	428	458	486	431
Cash Flow	2,252	1,985	2,065	1,480	1,386	873	928	1,119	734	1,192
Current Ratio	1.4	1.4	1.6	1.4	1.3	1.3	1.7	1.4	1.5	1.6
% Long Term Debt of Capitalization	19.0	19.8	14.9	22.5	26.4	30.2	44.6	44.6	36.7	43.8
% Net Income of Revenue	7.8	7.2	8.0	5.5	4.3	2.2	3.0	4.5	0.0	2.9
% Return on Assets	8.3	7.2	19.8	4.4	3.9	1.8	2.2	3.0	0.0	1.8
% Return on Equity	20.5	15.5	14.3	10.2	8.8	4.4	5.9	7.5	0.0	4.6

Data as orig reptd.; bef. results of disc opers/spec. items. Per share data adj. for stk. divs.; EPS diluted. E-Estimated. NA-Not Available. NM-Not Meaningful. NR-Not Ranked. UR-Under Review.

Office: 870 Winter St, Waltham, MA 02451-1449.
Telephone: 781-522-3000.
Email: invest@raytheon.com
Website: http://www.raytheon.com

Chrmn & CEO: W.H. Swanson
Pres: J.R. Harbison
SVP & CFO: D.C. Wajsgras
SVP, Secy & General Counsel: J.B. Stephens

CFO: D.E. Smith
Investor Contact: M. Kaplan (781-522-5141)
Board Members: V. Clark, J. M. Deutch, S. J. Hadley, F. M. Poses, M. Ruettgers, R. L. Skates, W. R. Spivey, L. G. Stuntz, W. H. Swanson

Founded: 1928
Domicile: Delaware
Employees: 75,100

Red Hat Inc

STANDARD
&POOR'S

S&P Recommendation HOLD ★★★☆☆

Price	12-Mo. Target Price	Investment Style
$40.66 (as of Oct 22, 2010)	$40.00	Large-Cap Growth

GICS Sector Information Technology
Sub-Industry Systems Software

Summary This company is a leading provider of Linux operating system software for enterprises.

Key Stock Statistics (Source S&P, Vickers, company reports)

52-Wk Range	$41.75–25.45	S&P Oper. EPS 2011**E**	0.51	Market Capitalization(B)	$7.749	Beta	1.25
Trailing 12-Month EPS	$0.45	S&P Oper. EPS 2012**E**	0.57	Yield (%)	Nil	S&P 3-Yr. Proj. EPS CAGR(%)	20
Trailing 12-Month P/E	90.4	P/E on S&P Oper. EPS 2011**E**	79.7	Dividend Rate/Share	Nil	S&P Credit Rating	BB+
$10K Invested 5 Yrs Ago	$18,912	Common Shares Outstg. (M)	190.6	Institutional Ownership (%)	91		

Price Performance

- 30-Week Mov. Avg. · · · 10-Week Mov. Avg. – – **GAAP Earnings vs. Previous Year** Volume Above Avg. STARS
- 12-Mo. Target Price — Relative Strength — ▲ Up ▼ Down ▶ No Change Below Avg. ★

Options: CBOE, P, Ph

Analysis prepared by **Jim Yin, CFA** on October 12, 2010, when the stock traded at **$ 39.15**.

Highlights

▶ We estimate that total revenue in FY 11 (Feb.) will rise 18%, following a 15% advance in FY 10. Our revenue forecast for FY 11 is based on our projection of a low-teens increase in the unit sales of servers. We think this growth will be above the historical average due to the severity of the decline during the downturn. We also expect RHT to extend its lead in the Linux operating system market. We believe the company is gaining traction for its middleware and virtualization products, as companies need to upgrade their cloud computing infrastructure.

▶ We expect the gross margin in FY 11 to be 84%, down from 85% in FY 10. We see operating expenses increasing 12% in FY 11, as RHT improves product and service offerings, but we look for a decrease to 68% of revenues, from 71% in FY 10, due to economies of scale. We project that operating margins in FY 11 will widen to 16%, from 13% in FY 10, reflecting better operating efficiency.

▶ Our EPS forecast for FY 11 is $0.51, versus $0.45 in FY 10. The projected rise reflects our expectations for higher revenues and improved operating margins.

Investment Rationale/Risk

▶ Our hold recommendation reflects RHT's improving fundamentals. Despite concern about a slower global economy and weaker IT spending in response to the economic uncertainty, we see stronger demand for RHT's Linux products. Additionally, RHT is broadening its product offerings into middleware and virtualization software. Although we see stiffer competition in these segments than in Linux given the presence of incumbent market leaders, we believe the company will be modestly successful in expanding its presence in these areas.

▶ Risks to our recommendation and target price include a slowdown in the global economy, lower IT spending, and lack of market share gains in new markets.

▶ Our 12-month target price of $40 is based on a blend of our DCF and enterprise value (EV)-to-sales analyses. Our DCF model assumes a 12% weighted average cost of capital and a 3% terminal growth rate, yielding an intrinsic value of $40. From our EV-to-sales analysis, we derive a value of $41, based on an EV-to-sales ratio of 8.0X, a premium to the industry average of 3.1X, reflecting our view of RHT's higher growth potential.

Qualitative Risk Assessment

LOW	MEDIUM	HIGH

Our risk assessment reflects the volatility of the enterprise software sector due to rapid changes in technology and competition as a result of mergers and acquisitions.

Quantitative Evaluations

S&P Quality Ranking B-

D	C	B-	B	B+	A-	A	A+

Relative Strength Rank STRONG

82

LOWEST = 1   HIGHEST = 99

Revenue/Earnings Data

Revenue (Million $)

	1Q	2Q	3Q	4Q	Year
2011	209.1	219.8	--	--	--
2010	174.4	183.6	194.4	195.9	748.2
2009	156.6	164.4	165.3	166.2	652.6
2008	118.9	127.3	135.4	141.5	523.0
2007	84.00	99.67	105.8	111.1	400.6
2006	60.78	65.72	73.11	78.72	278.3

Earnings Per Share ($)

	1Q	2Q	3Q	4Q	Year
2011	0.12	0.12	E0.13	E0.14	E0.51
2010	0.10	0.15	0.08	0.12	0.45
2009	0.08	0.10	0.12	0.08	0.39
2008	0.08	0.09	0.10	0.10	0.36
2007	0.07	0.05	0.07	0.10	0.29
2006	0.07	0.09	0.12	0.13	0.41

Fiscal year ended Feb. 28. Next earnings report expected: Late December. EPS Estimates based on S&P Operating Earnings; historical GAAP earnings are as reported.

Dividend Data

No cash dividends have been paid.

Red Hat Inc

STANDARD &POOR'S

Business Summary October 12, 2010

CORPORATE OVERVIEW. RHT is the leading provider of Linux operating systems and subsystems, capturing 65% of the market in terms of new license and maintenance revenues in 2008, according to IDC, a technology research firm, followed by Novell (NOVL 6, Hold), with 30%. The company introduced its core operating system -- Red Hat Enterprise Linux (RHEL) -- in 2002. RHT also offers enterprise middleware software -- JBoss Enterprise Middleware. Both software packages utilize an open source software development model, which provides users and developers access to the source code and permits them to copy, modify and redistribute the software. RHT enhances the open source software and delivers the technologies and related services in the form of annual or multi-year subscriptions, which accounted for 88% of revenues in FY 10 (Feb.). The remaining 12% of revenues came from services, primarily customization, implementation and training.

CORPORATE STRATEGY. RHT is focused on increasing the adoption of RHEL by large enterprises and growing sales of services to its customers. To drive increased adoption, RHT has formed partnerships and strategic relationships with BEA, BMC Software, Computer Associates, IBM, Oracle, SAP, Sybase, Symantec, HP, Dell, Fujitsu, Fujitsu Siemens, NEC and VMware. These part-

ners and others generally contribute between 50% and 60% of bookings in any given quarter, with the balance coming from direct sales. We believe this heavy reliance on the indirect channel will enable RHT to maintain higher operating margins than would be possible with an entirely in-house sales team, but we believe this will come at the cost of control over this portion of its business.

RHT will continue to expand its capabilities through strategic acquisitions. In June 2006, the company acquired JBoss, a provider of open source middleware, and the remaining minority interest in the Indian joint venture. In 2007, RHT acquired MetaMatrix, a leading provider of enterprise data management software. In September 2008, RHT acquired Qumranet, Inc. for $107 million in cash. Qumranet is a provider of virtualization software for managing Microsoft desktops.

Company Financials Fiscal Year Ended Feb. 28

Per Share Data ($)	2010	2009	2008	2007	2006	2005	2004	2003	2002	2001
Tangible Book Value	3.01	2.87	2.94	2.06	2.12	1.54	1.79	1.73	1.76	1.88
Cash Flow	0.69	0.56	0.50	0.38	0.46	0.26	0.11	Nil	-0.35	-0.19
Earnings	0.45	0.39	0.36	0.29	0.41	0.24	0.08	-0.04	-0.71	-0.53
S&P Core Earnings	0.48	0.39	0.35	0.29	0.28	0.06	-0.37	-0.20	-0.75	-1.07
Dividends	Nil	Nil	Nil	Nil	Nil	Nil	Nil	Nil	Nil	Nil
Payout Ratio	Nil	Nil	Nil	Nil	Nil	Nil	Nil	Nil	Nil	Nil
Calendar Year	2009	2008	2007	2006	2005	2004	2003	2002	2001	2000
Prices:High	31.76	24.84	25.25	32.48	28.65	29.06	19.98	9.50	10.12	148.00
Prices:Low	12.98	7.50	18.04	13.70	10.37	11.21	4.95	3.46	2.40	5.00
P/E Ratio:High	71	64	70	NM	70	NM	NM	NM	NM	NM
P/E Ratio:Low	29	19	50	NM	25	NM	NM	NM	NM	NM

Income Statement Analysis (Million $)										
Revenue	748	653	523	401	278	196	126	90.9	78.9	103
Operating Income	155	123	103	76.1	73.5	39.5	10.1	-8.38	-17.7	-52.5
Depreciation	45.9	40.3	33.0	23.9	15.4	10.9	6.87	6.52	59.7	55.0
Interest Expense	0.16	4.80	6.25	6.02	6.12	6.44	Nil	Nil	Nil	0.35
Pretax Income	122	122	125	89.6	82.0	44.9	14.0	-6.34	-120	-86.4
Effective Tax Rate	28.2%	35.2%	38.4%	33.1%	2.84%	NM	NM	NM	NM	NM
Net Income	87.3	78.7	76.7	59.9	79.7	45.4	14.0	-6.34	-120	-86.7
S&P Core Earnings	92.9	78.7	73.5	59.9	53.1	6.25	-63.8	-34.4	-126	-176

Balance Sheet & Other Financial Data (Million $)										
Cash	761	663	990	527	268	140	545	45.3	55.5	85.2
Current Assets	1,003	891	1,192	1,007	881	385	658	120	119	180
Total Assets	1,871	1,754	2,080	1,786	1,314	1,134	1,110	390	370	505
Current Liabilities	566	447	970	300	201	139	83.6	47.1	37.0	40.7
Long Term Debt	NA	Nil	Nil	570	570	600	601	1.39	1.56	0.28
Common Equity	1,111	1,106	951	821	477	361	409	336	327	464
Total Capital	1,111	1,106	951	1,391	1,048	962	1,010	338	329	465
Capital Expenditures	28.4	24.5	41.8	22.6	16.8	14.9	13.2	6.77	6.75	11.1
Cash Flow	133	119	110	83.8	95.1	56.3	20.9	0.18	-59.8	-31.7
Current Ratio	1.8	2.0	1.2	3.4	4.4	2.8	7.9	2.6	3.2	4.4
% Long Term Debt of Capitalization	Nil	Nil	Nil	41.0	54.4	62.4	59.5	0.4	0.5	0.1
% Net Income of Revenue	11.7	12.1	14.7	15.0	28.6	23.1	11.1	NM	NM	NM
% Return on Assets	4.8	4.1	4.0	3.9	6.5	4.0	1.9	NM	NM	NM
% Return on Equity	7.9	7.7	8.7	9.2	19.0	11.8	3.8	NM	NM	NM

Data as orig reptd.; bef. results of disc opers/spec. items. Per share data adj. for stk. divs.; EPS diluted. E-Estimated. NA-Not Available. NM-Not Meaningful. NR-Not Ranked. UR-Under Review.

Office: 1801 Varsity Drive, Raleigh, NC 27606.
Telephone: 919-754-3700.
Email: investors@redhat.com
Website: http://www.redhat.com

Chrmn: H.H. Shelton
Pres & CEO: J.M. Whitehurst
EVP & CFO: C.E. Peters, Jr.
EVP, Secy & General Counsel: M.R. Cunningham

CTO: B. Stevens
Investor Contact: L. Brewton (919-754-4476)
Board Members: M. Chau, J. J. Clarke, M. A. Fox, N. K. Gupta, W. S. Kaiser, D. H. Livingstone, H. H. Shelton, J. M. Whitehurst

Founded: 1993
Domicile: Delaware
Employees: 3,200

The McGraw-Hill Companies

Regions Financial Corp

STANDARD
&POOR'S

S&P Recommendation	HOLD ★★★☆☆	Price $7.14 (as of Oct 22, 2010)	12-Mo. Target Price $9.00	Investment Style Large-Cap Value

GICS Sector Financials
Sub-Industry Regional Banks

Summary This major southeastern financial holding company has $135 billion in assets and $96 billion of deposits, with 1,774 banking offices in 16 mostly Sunbelt states, plus 325 Morgan Keegan brokerage branches.

Key Stock Statistics (Source S&P, Vickers, company reports)

52-Wk Range	$9.33– 4.61	S&P Oper. EPS 2010**E**	-0.60	Market Capitalization(B)	$8.967	Beta	1.17
Trailing 12-Month EPS	$-1.37	S&P Oper. EPS 2011**E**	0.50	Yield (%)	0.56	S&P 3-Yr. Proj. EPS CAGR(%)	NM
Trailing 12-Month P/E	NM	P/E on S&P Oper. EPS 2010**E**	NM	Dividend Rate/Share	$0.04	S&P Credit Rating	BBB-
$10K Invested 5 Yrs Ago	$2,769	Common Shares Outstg. (M)	1,255.9	Institutional Ownership (%)	64		

Price Performance

30-Week Mov. Avg. · · · · · 10-Week Mov. Avg. – – **GAAP Earnings vs. Previous Year**   Volume Above Avg. ▮▮▮ STARS
12-Mo. Target Price — Relative Strength — ▲ Up ▼ Down ► No Change   Below Avg. ▮▮▮ ★

Options: C, Ph

Analysis prepared by **Erik Oja** on July 28, 2010, when the stock traded at **$ 7.23**.

Highlights

▶ We expect net interest income to increase 2.3% in 2010, despite our expectation that loans outstanding will fall in each of the next four quarters, as we see a slight widening of the net interest margin as well as increases in the available-for-sale securities portfolio. However, we expect core fee income to decline 3.5%, as we think mortgage income peaked in 2009.

▶ Based on RF's recent trends, and our outlook for the U.S. economy and for RF's loan portfolios, we project total net charge-offs of $2.40 billion in 2010, versus $2.25 billion in 2009. Despite this elevated projection, we see two positives -- a decline in new nonperforming loans, and an allowance that stands at 91.7% of June 30 nonperforming loans, which we see as above peers. Our 2010 estimate for loan loss provisions is $2.35 billion, equal to 0.98X net charge-offs, down sharply from 2009's $3.54 billion, which was equal to 1.57X net charge-offs. For 2011, we project a sharp drop in the loan loss provision, to $790 million.

▶ We estimate a 2010 loss per share of $0.60, followed by EPS of $0.50 in 2011.

Investment Rationale/Risk

▶ Regions Financial's overall loan credit quality improved strongly in the second quarter, setting the stage, in our view, for a broad decline in net charge-offs for the rest of 2010. We expect total net charge-offs to fall in each remaining quarter of 2010, as well as in 2011, but the rate of decline will likely not be as dramatic as it was in the past three quarters, due to the uncertain pace of economic growth and employment levels. RF currently trades at just over 1.0X June 30 tangible book value per share, which we see as about in line with other banks that have a similar level of nonperforming loans (over 4.0%), as well as a tangible common equity ratio of about 6.0% (6.58% for RF).

▶ Risks to our recommendation and target price include a faster than expected decline in loan growth, and a sharp fall-off in mortgage banking and commission revenues.

▶ Our 12-month target price of $9 equates to an above-peers 18.0X our 2011 EPS estimate of $0.50, and 1.3X our estimate of RF's tangible book value per share of $6.90 for year-end 2010, about in line with banks having similar levels of capital and credit quality.

Qualitative Risk Assessment

LOW	MEDIUM	HIGH

Our risk assessment reflects our positive view of the many steps RF has taken since early 2009 to rebuild capital levels and credit quality, offset by numerous remaining credit challenges in the company's loan portfolios.

Quantitative Evaluations

S&P Quality Ranking   B-

D	C	B-	B	B+	A-	A	A+

Relative Strength Rank   MODERATE

33

LOWEST = 1   HIGHEST = 99

Revenue/Earnings Data

Revenue (Million $)

	1Q	2Q	3Q	4Q	Year
2010	2,027	1,936	--	--	--
2009	2,445	2,550	2,086	2,006	9,087
2008	1,935	2,360	2,288	2,283	9,587
2007	2,797	2,724	2,742	2,667	10,925
2006	1,666	1,756	1,806	2,529	7,756
2005	1,423	1,565	1,564	1,572	6,124

Earnings Per Share ($)

	1Q	2Q	3Q	4Q	Year
2010	-0.21	-0.28	E-0.10	ENil	E-0.60
2009	0.04	-0.28	-0.37	-0.51	-1.27
2008	0.48	0.30	0.13	-8.97	-8.03
2007	0.65	0.63	0.56	0.10	1.96
2006	0.64	0.75	0.77	0.56	2.67
2005	0.51	0.53	0.55	0.55	2.15

Fiscal year ended Dec. 31. Next earnings report expected: NA. EPS Estimates based on S&P Operating Earnings; historical GAAP earnings are as reported.

Dividend Data (Dates: mm/dd Payment Date: mm/dd/yy)

Amount ($)	Date Decl.	Ex-Div. Date	Stk. of Record	Payment Date
0.010	10/15	12/15	12/17	01/03/11

Dividends have been paid since 1968. Source: Company reports.

Please read the Required Disclosures and Analyst Certification on the last page of this report.

The **McGraw·Hill** Companies

Regions Financial Corp

Business Summary July 28, 2010

CORPORATE OVERVIEW. Regions Financial is a financial holding company that operates primarily in the southeastern U.S., with operations consisting of banking, brokerage and investment services, mortgage banking, insurance brokerage, credit life insurance, commercial accounts receivable factoring and specialty financing. RF conducts its banking operations through Regions Bank, an Alabama-chartered commercial bank that is a member of the Federal Reserve System. Banking operations also include Regions Mortgage (RMI). RMI's primary business is the origination and servicing of mortgage loans for long-term investors. RMI generally provides services in the same states in which RF has banking operations. Financial services operations include Morgan Keegan, a regional full-service brokerage and investment bank, which was acquired in 2001. Other subsidiaries include Regions Insurance Group, Inc., Regions Agency Inc., Regions Life Insurance Company, Regions Interstate Billings Service Inc., and Regions Equipment Finance Corporation, providing all lines of personal and commercial insurance, credit-related insurance products, and other financial services.

MARKET PROFILE. As of June 30, 2009, which is the latest available FDIC data, RF had 1,819 branches, down from 1,924 branches a year earlier, and $93.7 bil-

lion in deposits, up from $86.2 billion a year before. In Alabama, RF had 233 branches, $18.9 billion of deposits, and a deposit market share of about 22.7%, ranking first. In Florida, RF had 421 branches, $17.4 billion of deposits, and a deposit market share of about 4.3%, ranking fourth. In Tennessee, RF had 285 branches, $17.3 billion of deposits, and a deposit market share of about 15.5%, ranking first. In Mississippi, RF had 144 branches, $7.2 billion of deposits, and a deposit market share of about 16.3%, ranking first. In Georgia, RF had 154 branches, $6.4 billion of deposits, and a deposit market share of about 3.5%, ranking sixth. In Louisiana, RF had 125 branches, $7.3 billion of deposits, and a deposit market share of about 9.3%, ranking third. In Arkansas, RF had 102 branches, $4.6 billion of deposits, and a deposit market share of about 9.4%, ranking second. RF also had a total of 355 offices and $14.6 billion of deposits in Texas, Illinois, Missouri, Indiana, South Carolina, Kentucky, Iowa, North Carolina and Virginia.

Company Financials Fiscal Year Ended Dec. 31

Per Share Data ($)	2009	2008	2007	2006	2005	2004	2003	2002	2001	2000
Tangible Book Value	6.89	10.35	10.45	11.74	11.55	11.58	16.25	15.29	10.58	11.00
Earnings	-1.27	-8.03	1.96	2.67	2.15	2.19	2.35	2.20	1.81	1.93
S&P Core Earnings	-1.23	0.39	1.97	2.67	2.11	2.17	2.32	2.11	1.63	NA
Dividends	0.12	0.96	1.46	2.11	1.36	0.93	1.00	0.94	0.91	0.87
Payout Ratio	NM	NM	74%	79%	63%	43%	43%	43%	50%	45%
Prices:High	9.07	25.84	38.17	39.15	35.54	35.97	30.70	31.10	26.72	22.68
Prices:Low	2.35	6.41	22.84	32.37	29.16	27.26	24.16	21.95	20.84	14.83
P/E Ratio:High	NM	NM	19	15	17	16	13	14	15	12
P/E Ratio:Low	NM	NM	12	12	14	12	10	10	11	8

Income Statement Analysis (Million $)										
Net Interest Income	3,335	3,843	4,398	3,353	2,821	2,113	1,475	1,498	1,425	1,389
Tax Equivalent Adjustment	32.0	36.7	38.1	NA	NA	NA	NA	NA	NA	NA
Non Interest Income	3,032	3,021	2,864	2,054	1,832	1,591	1,373	1,207	950	641
Loan Loss Provision	3,541	2,057	555	143	165	129	122	128	165	127
% Expense/Operating Revenue	74.6%	66.4%	64.2%	61.3%	65.5%	66.5%	64.6%	65.1%	64.2%	55.2%
Pretax Income	-1,202	-5,932	2,039	1,959	1,422	1,176	912	869	718	742
Effective Tax Rate	NM	NM	31.7%	30.9%	29.6%	29.9%	28.5%	28.7%	29.1%	28.9%
Net Income	-1,031	-5,584	1,393	1,353	1,001	824	652	620	509	528
% Net Interest Margin	2.67	3.23	3.79	4.17	3.91	3.66	3.49	3.73	3.66	3.55
S&P Core Earnings	-1,225	272	1,405	1,355	983	811	647	592	458	NA

Balance Sheet & Other Financial Data (Million $)										
Money Market Assets	8,998	9,380	2,116	2,610	1,794	1,761	1,491	1,424	1,502	112
Investment Securities	24,100	18,896	17,369	18,562	11,979	12,617	9,088	8,995	7,847	8,994
Commercial Loans	21,547	23,595	20,907	24,145	14,728	15,180	9,914	10,842	9,912	9,070
Other Loans	69,127	73,823	74,472	70,360	43,677	42,556	22,501	20,144	21,225	22,402
Total Assets	142,318	146,248	141,042	143,369	84,786	84,106	48,598	47,939	45,383	43,688
Demand Deposits	23,204	18,457	18,417	20,709	13,699	11,424	5,718	5,148	5,085	4,513
Time Deposits	75,476	72,447	76,358	80,519	46,679	47,243	27,015	27,779	26,463	27,510
Long Term Debt	18,464	19,231	11,325	8,643	11,938	7,240	5,712	5,386	4,748	4,478
Common Equity	14,279	13,505	19,823	20,701	10,614	10,749	4,452	4,178	4,036	3,458
% Return on Assets	NM	NM	1.0	1.2	1.2	1.2	1.4	1.3	1.1	1.2
% Return on Equity	NM	NM	6.9	8.6	9.4	10.8	15.1	15.1	13.6	16.2
% Loan Loss Reserve	3.4	1.9	1.4	1.1	1.3	1.3	1.4	1.3	1.3	1.2
% Loans/Deposits	91.9	107.2	97.0	98.3	99.3	101.1	102.1	98.7	100.7	98.7
% Equity to Assets	9.6	11.6	14.3	13.7	12.6	11.5	8.9	8.8	8.4	7.5

Data as orig reptd.; bef. results of disc opers/spec. items. Per share data adj. for stk. divs.; EPS diluted. E-Estimated. NA-Not Available. NM-Not Meaningful. NR-Not Ranked. UR-Under Review.

Office: 1900 Fifth Avenue North, Birmingham, AL 35203.
Telephone: 205-326-5807.
Email: askus@regionsbank.com
Website: http://www.regions.com

Chrmn: E.W. Deavenport, Jr.
Pres, Vice Chrmn, CEO & COO: O.B. Hall, Jr.
EVP & CFO: D.J. Turner, Jr.
EVP & Chief Admin Officer: D.B. Edmonds

EVP, Chief Acctg Officer & Cntlr: H.B. Kimbrough, Jr.
Investor Contact: L. Underwood (205-801-0265)
Board Members: S. W. Bartholomew, Jr., G. W. Bryan, C. H. Byrd, D. J. Cooper, D. DeFosset, Jr., E. W. Deavenport, Jr., E. C. Fast, O. B. Hall, Jr., J. R. Malone, S. W. Matlock, J. E. Maupin, Jr., C. D. McCrary, J. R. Roberts, L. Styslinger, III

Founded: 1970
Domicile: Delaware
Employees: 28,509

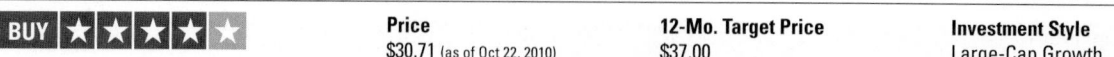

Republic Services Inc.

STANDARD &POOR'S

S&P Recommendation	**BUY** ★★★★☆	Price $30.71 (as of Oct 22, 2010)	12-Mo. Target Price $37.00	Investment Style Large-Cap Growth

GICS Sector Industrials
Sub-Industry Environmental & Facilities Services

Summary This company became the second largest U.S. provider of solid waste services in North America when it acquired Allied Waste Industries in December 2008.

Key Stock Statistics (Source S&P, Vickers, company reports)

52-Wk Range	$32.95–25.15	S&P Oper. EPS 2010E	1.75	Market Capitalization(B)	$11.762	Beta	0.91
Trailing 12-Month EPS	$0.99	S&P Oper. EPS 2011E	2.05	Yield (%)	2.61	S&P 3-Yr. Proj. EPS CAGR(%)	15
Trailing 12-Month P/E	31.0	P/E on S&P Oper. EPS 2010E	17.5	Dividend Rate/Share	$0.80	S&P Credit Rating	BBB
$10K Invested 5 Yrs Ago	$15,247	Common Shares Outstg. (M)	383.0	Institutional Ownership (%)	78		

Price Performance

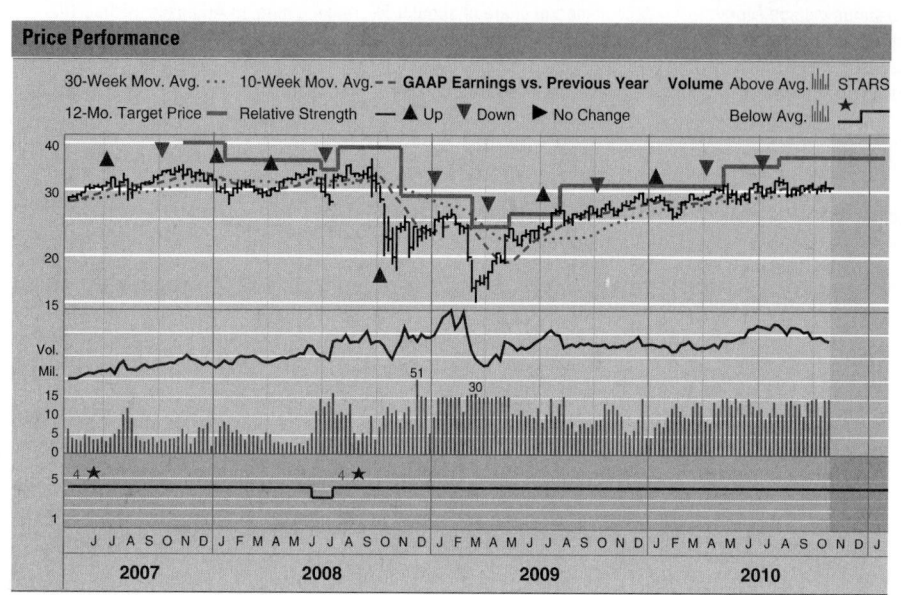

30-Week Mov. Avg. ···· 10-Week Mov. Avg. – – GAAP Earnings vs. Previous Year Volume Above Avg. STARS
12-Mo. Target Price — Relative Strength — ▲ Up ▼ Down ► No Change Below Avg. ★

Options: CBOE, Ph

Analysis prepared by **Stewart Scharf** on August 04, 2010, when the stock traded at **$ 32.39**.

Highlights

➤ We expect organic revenues to decline modestly in 2010, as 2% higher core prices and a rise in commodity recycling are offset by lower, albeit, improving volume. We look for volume growth to return in the fourth quarter, driven by sequentially recovering industrial special waste and commercial collection, and growth in landfill volumes.

➤ In our view, gross margins in 2010 will widen from 41% in 2009, driven by pricing initiatives on the collection side. We still see better MSW landfill pricing, offset somewhat by lower-margin C&D and special waste work. Adjusted EBITDA before merger-related costs should also expand to above 31%, from 30.6% in 2009, as RSG leverages its health insurance costs, focusing on safety, training and systems, and achieves at least $185 million in run-rate synergies by the end of 2010.

➤ We expect lower interest expense and a drop in the tax rate to about 42% in 2010, and we estimate operating EPS rising 18%, to $1.75 (before restructuring and merger-related costs, and a loss on the extinguishment of debt); we see a further advance to $2.05 in 2011.

Investment Rationale/Risk

➤ Our Buy opinion is based on our valuation metrics and our view of RSG's strong cash generation, balance sheet, and return on invested capital. We also expect projected synergies from the Allied Waste merger to create long-term value as RSG boosts its position in the solid waste industry.

➤ Risks to our recommendation and target price include a slower-than-expected recovery in the housing market and economy, a decline in the customer retention rate, a rapid decline in commodity recycling prices, and sharply higher fuel and commodity costs. We also have corporate governance concerns related to compensation and board issues.

➤ Our DCF model, assuming a 3.5% perpetual growth rate and a weighted average cost of capital of 7%, results in an intrinsic value of $39. We apply a premium-to-peers forward P/E of 20X to our 2010 EPS estimate, which we think is warranted, given our view of RSG's superior operating margins, strong cash position, and higher ROIC, resulting in a value of $35. Blending these metrics, our 12-month target price is $37.

Qualitative Risk Assessment

LOW	MEDIUM	HIGH

Our risk assessment reflects our view of the company's strong balance sheet and focus on cash generation mainly for debt paydowns, share buybacks and dividend payments, as well as synergies and asset divestiture gains resulting from the Allied Waste acquisition.

Quantitative Evaluations

S&P Quality Ranking B+

D	C	B-	B	**B+**	A-	A	A+

Relative Strength Rank MODERATE

34

LOWEST = 1 HIGHEST = 99

Revenue/Earnings Data

Revenue (Million $)

	1Q	2Q	3Q	4Q	Year
2010	1,958	2,066	--	--	--
2009	2,061	2,066	2,074	1,999	8,199
2008	779.2	827.5	834.0	1,244	3,685
2007	765.6	808.4	806.2	796.0	3,176
2006	737.5	779.8	787.1	766.2	3,071
2005	677.2	718.6	730.0	738.1	2,864

Earnings Per Share ($)

2010	0.17	0.42	E0.47	E0.44	E1.75
2009	0.30	0.59	0.32	0.09	1.30
2008	0.41	0.34	0.48	-0.55	0.37
2007	0.28	0.45	0.35	0.44	1.51
2006	0.31	0.35	0.39	0.34	1.38
2005	0.29	0.29	0.30	0.29	1.17

Fiscal year ended Dec. 31. Next earnings report expected: Early November. EPS Estimates based on S&P Operating Earnings; historical GAAP earnings are as reported.

Dividend Data (Dates: mm/dd Payment Date: mm/dd/yy)

Amount ($)	Date Decl.	Ex-Div. Date	Stk. of Record	Payment Date
0.190	11/02	12/30	01/04	01/15/10
0.190	02/11	03/30	04/01	04/15/10
0.190	04/29	06/29	07/01	07/15/10
0.200	07/29	09/29	10/01	10/15/10

Dividends have been paid since 2003. Source: Company reports.

Please read the Required Disclosures and Analyst Certification on the last page of this report.

The McGraw·Hill Companies

Business Summary August 04, 2010

CORPORATE OVERVIEW. Republic Services is the third largest U.S. provider of services in the non-hazardous solid waste industry. It provides collection services to commercial, industrial, municipal and residential customers through 376 collection companies in 40 states and Puerto Rico, and operates 223 transfer stations, 192 solid waste landfills and 78 recycling facilities. RSG also operates 74 landfill gas and renewable energy projects. At the end of 2009, operations were divided into five regions: eastern, central, southern, southwestern and western. Collection revenues accounted for 77% of the total at December 31, 2009 (35% residential, 40% commercial, 24% industrial and 0.4% other), while 19% was derived from net transfer and disposal revenues, and 4.2% from other. The average estimated landfill life for all of RSG's 192 landfills is 46 years. Twelve of its landfills meet the criteria for probable expansion airspace, and have an estimated remaining site life of 39 years. RSG's internalization rate at 2009 year-end was about 69%, up from 68% in 2008. The average age of the company's truck fleet is about seven years. The customer churn rate was about 7% in the second quarter of 2010. The industry tends to lag economic swings by six to nine months. About 60% of volumes are protected either through a floor contract or financial hedge.

In the second quarter of 2010, the average wholesale price of diesel fuel per gallon rose to $3.03, from $2.33 a year earlier; diesel fuel was $4.34 per gallon

at September 30, 2008. RSG notes that a $0.01 change in the price of diesel fuel changes its fuel costs by about $1.7 million on an annual basis, partially offset by a smaller change in the fuel recovery fees charged to its customers. About 50% of its revenues are tied to index-based pricing (CPI).

The company resumed its share repurchase program in late 2009, buying back $1 million of stock. About $247 million of stock remains authorized for repurchase. Since 2000, stock buybacks totaled nearly $2.3 billion (44% of shares). RSG is targeting close to $400 million in share buybacks in 2011.

In the first quarter of 2010, RSG incurred charges of $0.24 a share, with $0.22 from a loss on the extinguishment of debt. In 2009, RSG recorded a net charge of $0.18 a share, consisting mainly of a $0.19 a share gain on the disposition of assets, restructuring charges and costs to achieve synergies of $0.16 and loss on the extinguishment of debt of $0.22.

Bill Gates's investment firm, Cascade Investments LLC, owns nearly 15% of RSG's common stock.

Company Financials Fiscal Year Ended Dec. 31

Per Share Data ($)	2009	2008	2007	2006	2005	2004	2003	2002	2001	2000
Tangible Book Value	NM	NM	NM	NM	0.07	1.24	1.36	1.27	0.80	0.91
Cash Flow	3.82	2.28	3.08	2.84	2.45	2.13	1.87	1.76	1.33	1.59
Earnings	1.30	0.37	1.51	1.38	1.17	1.02	0.89	0.96	0.49	0.84
S&P Core Earnings	1.05	0.44	1.47	1.38	1.10	0.99	0.85	0.90	0.45	NA
Dividends	0.76	0.72	0.55	0.40	0.35	0.24	0.08	Nil	Nil	Nil
Payout Ratio	58%	195%	37%	29%	30%	24%	9%	Nil	Nil	Nil
Prices:High	29.82	36.52	35.00	29.47	25.56	22.65	17.39	14.84	13.93	11.67
Prices:Low	15.05	18.25	26.22	24.47	20.07	16.33	12.17	10.84	9.17	6.42
P/E Ratio:High	23	99	23	21	22	22	19	15	29	14
P/E Ratio:Low	12	49	17	18	17	16	14	11	19	8

Income Statement Analysis (Million $)										
Revenue	8,199	3,685	3,176	3,071	2,864	2,708	2,518	2,365	2,258	2,103
Operating Income	2,516	1,017	892	816	756	712	1,077	654	598	638
Depreciation	958	378	302	296	279	259	239	200	215	197
Interest Expense	596	135	97.8	95.8	81.0	76.7	78.0	77.0	80.1	81.6
Pretax Income	865	159	468	444	409	384	347	387	209	356
Effective Tax Rate	42.6%	53.6%	38.0%	37.0%	38.0%	38.0%	38.0%	38.0%	40.0%	38.0%
Net Income	495	73.8	290	280	254	238	215	240	126	221
S&P Core Earnings	400	87.8	282	280	240	229	206	225	114	NA

Balance Sheet & Other Financial Data (Million $)										
Cash	48.0	68.7	21.8	29.1	132	142	334	317	158	86.3
Current Assets	1,265	1,326	414	393	482	497	556	452	325	406
Total Assets	19,540	19,921	4,468	4,429	4,551	4,465	4,554	4,209	3,856	3,562
Current Liabilities	2,549	2,566	629	602	667	447	672	392	386	382
Long Term Debt	6,420	7,199	1,566	1,545	1,472	1,352	1,289	1,439	1,334	1,200
Common Equity	7,565	7,281	1,304	1,422	1,606	1,873	3,809	1,881	1,756	1,675
Total Capital	14,530	14,985	2,869	3,386	3,468	3,631	5,452	3,515	3,209	3,002
Capital Expenditures	826	387	293	338	329	284	273	259	249	208
Cash Flow	1,454	452	592	576	533	497	455	439	341	418
Current Ratio	0.5	0.5	0.7	0.7	0.7	1.1	0.8	1.2	0.8	1.1
% Long Term Debt of Capitalization	44.2	48.0	54.6	45.6	42.4	37.2	23.6	40.9	41.6	40.0
% Net Income of Revenue	6.0	2.0	9.1	9.1	8.9	8.8	8.6	10.1	5.6	10.5
% Return on Assets	2.5	0.6	6.5	6.2	5.6	5.3	4.9	5.9	3.4	6.5
% Return on Equity	6.7	1.7	21.3	18.5	14.6	12.6	5.7	13.2	7.3	13.9

Data as orig reptd.; bef. results of disc opers/spec. items. Per share data adj. for stk. divs.; EPS diluted. E-Estimated. NA-Not Available. NM-Not Meaningful. NR-Not Ranked. UR-Under Review.

Office: 18500 North Allied Way, Phoenix, AZ 85054.
Telephone: 480-627-2700.
Website: http://www.republicservices.com
Chrmn & CEO: J.E. O'Connor

Pres & COO: D.W. Slager
Investor Contact: T.C. Holmes
EVP & CFO: T.C. Holmes
EVP, Secy & General Counsel: M.P. Rissman

Board Members: J. W. Croghan, J. W. Crownover, W. J. Flynn, D. I. Foley, M. Larson, N. Lehmann, W. L. Nutter, J. E. O'Connor, R. A. Rodriguez, A. Sorensen, J. M. Trani, M. W. Wickham

Founded: 1996
Domicile: Delaware
Employees: 31,000

Reynolds American Inc

STANDARD
&POOR'S

S&P Recommendation BUY ★★★★☆

Price	12-Mo. Target Price	Investment Style
$62.74 (as of Oct 22, 2010)	$70.00	Large-Cap Value

GICS Sector Consumer Staples
Sub-Industry Tobacco

Summary Reynolds American, the second largest U.S. cigarette manufacturer, was formed via the mid-2004 merger of R.J. Reynolds and Brown & Williamson.

Key Stock Statistics (Source S&P, Vickers, company reports)

52-Wk Range	$63.35–36.35	S&P Oper. EPS 2010E	4.97	Market Capitalization(B)	$18.290	Beta	0.63
Trailing 12-Month EPS	$3.42	S&P Oper. EPS 2011E	5.26	Yield (%)	6.25	S&P 3-Yr. Proj. EPS CAGR(%)	6
Trailing 12-Month P/E	18.4	P/E on S&P Oper. EPS 2010E	12.6	Dividend Rate/Share	$3.92	S&P Credit Rating	BBB-
$10K Invested 5 Yrs Ago	$20,621	Common Shares Outstg. (M)	291.5	Institutional Ownership (%)	47		

Price Performance

- 30-Week Mov. Avg. · · ·
- 10-Week Mov. Avg. – –
- 12-Mo. Target Price —
- Relative Strength —
- GAAP Earnings vs. Previous Year
- ▲ Up ▼ Down ▶ No Change
- Volume Above Avg. STARS
- Below Avg. ★

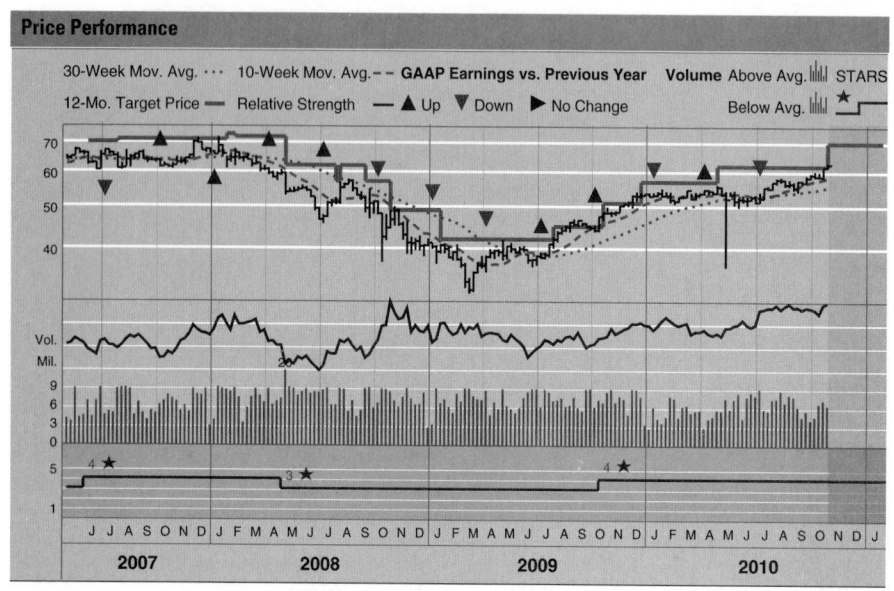

Options: ASE, CBOE, P, Ph

Analysis prepared by **Esther Y. Kwon, CFA** on October 21, 2010, when the stock traded at **$ 63.06**.

Highlights

➤ We estimate that RAI's revenues in 2010 will rise approximately 2% above last year's $8.4 billion, versus 2009's 5% drop, with a favorable product mix shift, price increases and new product introductions offset by a mid-single digit rate shipment decline. We believe growth brands Camel, Pall Mall and American Spirit, which now account for over half the company's total cigarette volume, will see gains, with other brands, including low-margin private label, suffering declines as marketing efforts remain minimal.

➤ We see continued operating margin improvement in 2010 as gross margins benefit from the rationalization of non-core brands and brand styles, higher pricing and lower promotions, while SG&A spending, excluding additional pension expense, should remain well controlled as the company benefits from cost-saving actions. We estimate savings of about $35 million in 2011 on rationalization of cigarette manufacturing facilities.

➤ In 2010, we estimate EPS of $4.97 on lower interest expense and a comparable effective tax rate of approximately 37%. For 2011, we forecast EPS of $5.26.

Investment Rationale/Risk

➤ We think leading smokeless tobacco company Conwood, which RAI acquired in mid-2006 for $3.5 billion, could continue to drive profits as higher-margin smokeless tobacco growth offsets declining cigarette sales. While we were somewhat wary of potential heightened competition from Altria's UST unit as Altria extended its price cuts on Copenhagen and Skoal to additional markets, Altria has since begun to raise prices and we expect price competition to remain manageable. We also see continued good performance from Pall Mall as consumers trade down in a weak economic environment. With an indicated dividend yield over 6%, we find the shares attractive on a total return basis.

➤ Risks to our opinion and target price include additional regulation and taxation of tobacco products, in addition to near-term pressure on trading multiples due to ongoing litigation. We also think RAI's "poison pill" anti-takeover provision is not in shareholders' best interests.

➤ Applying a multiple of 13.3X, a slight discount to the peer average and a discount to the S&P 500 staples P/E of nearly 14X, to our 2011 EPS estimate of $5.26, we arrive at a relative valuation of $70, which is our 12-month target price.

Qualitative Risk Assessment

LOW	MEDIUM	HIGH

The domestic tobacco industry typically produces stable revenue streams and strong cash flow. While the industry is involved in significant litigation, recent rulings have led to an improvement in the litigation environment.

Quantitative Evaluations

S&P Quality Ranking B+

D	C	B-	B	B+	A-	A	A+

Relative Strength Rank STRONG

74

LOWEST = 1   HIGHEST = 99

Revenue/Earnings Data

Revenue (Million $)

	1Q	2Q	3Q	4Q	Year
2010	1,986	1,113	--	--	--
2009	1,921	2,250	2,152	2,096	8,419
2008	2,057	2,339	2,272	2,177	8,845
2007	2,148	2,348	2,297	2,230	9,023
2006	1,960	2,291	2,190	2,069	8,510
2005	1,957	2,103	2,149	2,047	8,256

Earnings Per Share ($)

	1Q	2Q	3Q	4Q	Year
2010	1.02	1.17	E1.34	E1.22	E4.97
2009	0.03	1.29	1.24	0.74	3.30
2008	1.71	1.24	0.72	0.89	4.57
2007	1.11	1.10	1.21	1.01	4.43
2006	0.95	1.24	1.05	0.61	3.85
2005	0.95	0.85	0.72	0.82	3.34

Fiscal year ended Dec. 31. Next earnings report expected: Late October. EPS Estimates based on S&P Operating Earnings; historical GAAP earnings are as reported.

Dividend Data (Dates: mm/dd Payment Date: mm/dd/yy)

Amount ($)	Date Decl.	Ex-Div. Date	Stk. of Record	Payment Date
0.900	05/07	06/08	06/10	07/01/10
0.900	07/15	09/08	09/10	10/01/10
2-for-1	10/15	11/16	11/01	11/15/10
0.490	10/15	12/08	12/10	01/03/11

Dividends have been paid since 1999. Source: Company reports.

Reynolds American Inc

Business Summary October 21, 2010

CORPORATE OVERVIEW. On July 30, 2004, R.J. Reynolds Tobacco Co. (RJRT) merged with Brown & Williamson (B&W), the U.S. operations of British American Tobacco (BTI), to form a new publicly traded company, Reynolds American, Inc. Combining RJRT and B&W, the second and third largest players, RAI is the second largest U.S. cigarette manufacturer, having a combined market share of 28.3% in 2009, down slightly from 28.4% in 2008.

RAI is the parent company of RJRT, Santa Fe Natural Tobacco, which RJRT acquired in 2002, and Lane Limited, which was purchased from BTI for $400 million as part of the merger. In 2003, prior to the merger, RJRT began a significant restructuring plan, targeting cost savings of $1 billion by the end of 2005 through a significant work force reduction, asset divestitures and associated exit activities. Full integration of RJRT and B&W was expected to be completed in 2006, but realization of cost savings continued into 2007. The business combination was expected to result in approximately $600 million in annualized savings, including headcount reductions and operations consolidation, when compared with a separate entity basis.

In May 2006, RAI completed the acquisition of Conwood, the second largest manufacturer of smokeless tobacco products in the U.S., for $3.5 billion. RAI combined Conwood with its Lane Limited subsidiary into an Other Tobacco Products division in 2007. RAI's reportable segments are RJRT and Conwood.

The company's leading products are its Camel, Kool, Pall Mall, Doral and Winston brand cigarettes. The company's other brands include Salem, Misty and Capri. RAI also manages and contract manufactures cigarettes and tobacco products through its relationship with BAT affiliates.

Conwood's primary brands included Grizzly and Kodiak moist snuff.

CORPORATE STRATEGY. RAI's management has stated that its strategy is to generate sustainable earnings growth and strong cash flow in order to maximize shareholder value. To that end, RAI implemented a new portfolio strategy, designed to improve profitability, which established three categories for the combined brands of RJRT and B&W. The investment brand category, which includes premium brand Camel and value brand Pall Mall, receive the majority of resources to promote market share growth. The selective support brands, which include Kool, Winston, Salem, Capri and value brands Doral and Misty, receive limited support to optimize profitability; and the remaining brands are called non-support brands, which are managed to maximize profitability.

Company Financials Fiscal Year Ended Dec. 31

Per Share Data ($)	2009	2008	2007	2006	2005	2004	2003	2002	2001	2000
Tangible Book Value	NM	NM	NM	NM	NM	NM	NM	NM	NM	NM
Cash Flow	3.70	5.05	4.92	4.39	4.00	2.65	-20.81	3.34	4.72	4.10
Earnings	3.30	4.57	4.43	3.85	3.34	2.81	-22.04	2.32	2.24	1.73
S&P Core Earnings	4.76	3.63	4.41	3.95	3.96	3.59	2.13	1.73	1.52	NA
Dividends	3.45	3.40	3.20	1.38	2.10	0.95	1.90	1.86	1.65	1.55
Payout Ratio	105%	74%	72%	36%	63%	34%	NM	80%	74%	90%
Prices:High	54.26	72.00	71.72	67.09	51.19	40.27	30.07	35.95	31.35	25.13
Prices:Low	31.55	37.21	58.55	47.48	38.24	26.69	13.76	17.42	22.09	7.88
P/E Ratio:High	16	16	16	17	15	14	NM	15	14	15
P/E Ratio:Low	10	8	13	12	11	9	NM	8	10	5

Income Statement Analysis (Million $)										
Revenue	4,492	6,955	9,023	8,510	8,256	6,437	5,267	6,211	8,585	8,167
Operating Income	2,639	2,602	2,496	2,183	1,880	1,239	873	1,200	1,409	1,399
Depreciation	118	142	143	162	195	153	151	184	491	485
Interest Expense	251	275	338	270	113	85.0	111	147	150	168
Pretax Income	1,534	2,128	2,073	1,809	1,416	829	-3,918	683	892	748
Effective Tax Rate	37.3%	37.1%	37.0%	37.2%	30.4%	24.4%	NM	38.8%	50.2%	52.9%
Net Income	962	1,338	1,307	1,136	985	627	-3,689	418	444	352
S&P Core Earnings	1,388	1,063	1,302	1,167	1,167	800	357	313	301	NA

Balance Sheet & Other Financial Data (Million $)										
Cash	2,727	2,601	2,592	1,433	1,333	1,499	1,523	1,584	2,020	2,543
Current Assets	5,495	5,019	4,992	4,935	5,065	4,624	3,331	3,992	3,856	3,871
Total Assets	18,009	18,154	18,629	18,178	14,519	14,428	9,677	14,651	15,050	15,554
Current Liabilities	4,340	3,923	3,903	4,092	4,149	4,055	2,865	3,427	2,792	2,776
Long Term Debt	4,136	4,486	4,515	4,389	1,558	1,595	1,671	1,755	1,631	1,674
Common Equity	6,498	6,237	7,466	7,043	6,553	6,176	3,057	6,716	8,026	8,436
Total Capital	10,634	11,005	13,165	12,599	8,750	8,576	5,534	9,707	11,383	11,966
Capital Expenditures	141	113	142	136	105	92.0	70.0	111	74.0	60.0
Cash Flow	1,080	1,480	1,450	1,298	1,180	780	-3,538	602	935	837
Current Ratio	1.3	1.3	1.3	1.2	1.2	1.1	1.2	1.2	1.4	1.4
% Long Term Debt of Capitalization	38.9	40.8	34.3	34.8	17.8	18.6	30.2	18.1	14.3	14.0
% Net Income of Revenue	21.4	19.2	14.5	13.3	11.9	9.7	NM	6.7	5.2	4.3
% Return on Assets	5.3	7.3	7.1	6.9	6.8	5.2	NM	2.8	2.9	2.4
% Return on Equity	15.1	19.5	18.0	16.7	15.5	13.6	NM	5.7	5.4	4.5

Data as orig reptd.; bef. results of disc opers/spec. items. Per share data adj. for stk. divs.; EPS diluted. E-Estimated. NA-Not Available. NM-Not Meaningful. NR-Not Ranked. UR-Under Review.

Office: 401 North Main Street, Winston-Salem, NC 27102-2866.
Telephone: 336-741-2000.
Email: talktorjrt@rjrt.com
Website: http://www.reynoldsamerican.com

Chrmn, Pres & CEO: S.M. Ivey
Pres: J.B. O'Brien
EVP & CFO: T.R. Adams
EVP & General Counsel: E.J. Lambeth

SVP & Chief Acctg Officer: F.W. Smothers
Board Members: M. D. Feinstein, S. M. Ivey, L. Jobin, H. K. Koeppel, N. Mensah, L. L. Nowell, III, H. G. Powell, T. C. Wajnert, N. R. Withington, J. J. Zillmer

Auditor: KPMG, Greensboro
Founded: 1875
Domicile: Delaware
Employees: 6,550

Robert Half International Inc.

STANDARD &POOR'S

S&P Recommendation HOLD ★★★☆☆

Price	**12-Mo. Target Price**	**Investment Style**
$27.36 (as of Oct 22, 2010)	$30.00	Large-Cap Blend

GICS Sector Industrials
Sub-Industry Human Resource & Employment Services

Summary This company is the world's largest specialized provider of temporary and permanent personnel in the fields of accounting and finance.

Key Stock Statistics (Source S&P, Vickers, company reports)

52-Wk Range	$32.25– 21.16	S&P Oper. EPS 2010**E**	0.45	Market Capitalization(B)	$4.038	Beta	0.97
Trailing 12-Month EPS	$0.28	S&P Oper. EPS 2011**E**	0.80	Yield (%)	1.90	S&P 3-Yr. Proj. EPS CAGR(%)	55
Trailing 12-Month P/E	97.7	P/E on S&P Oper. EPS 2010**E**	60.8	Dividend Rate/Share	$0.52	S&P Credit Rating	NA
$10K Invested 5 Yrs Ago	$7,938	Common Shares Outstg. (M)	147.6	Institutional Ownership (%)	94		

Price Performance

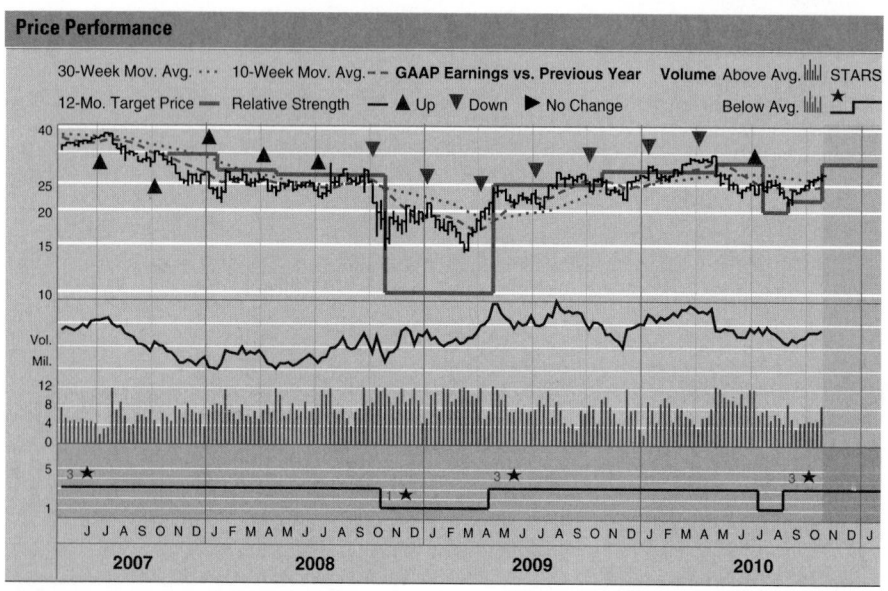

30-Week Mov. Avg. · · · 10-Week Mov. Avg. – – GAAP Earnings vs. Previous Year Volume Above Avg. ▮▮▮ STARS
12-Mo. Target Price — Relative Strength — ▲ Up ▼ Down ► No Change Below Avg. ▮▮▮ ★

Options: ASE, CBOE, Ph

Highlights

➤ The 12-month target price for RHI has recently been changed to $30.00 from $22.00. The Highlights section of this Stock Report will be updated accordingly.

Investment Rationale/Risk

➤ The Investment Rationale/Risk section of this Stock Report will be updated shortly. For the latest News story on RHI from MarketScope, see below.

➤ 10/21/10 12:48 pm ET ... S&P MAINTAINS HOLD OPINION ON SHARES OF ROBERT HALF (RHI 27.25***): Q3 EPS of $0.14, vs. $0.06, beats our forecast by $0.02, as a 13% revenue gain was stronger than we expected, with RHI seeing a pick up in demand for its services. We think RHI's operating rebound will go on for an extended period, and see it aided in the coming year by an ongoing focus of businesses on temp hirings for staffing needs. We raise our '10 EPS estimate by $0.05 to $0.45, and '11's by $0.10 to $0.80. We also lift our target price by $8 to $30, 37.5X our '11 estimate, and the high-end of RHI's valuation during a similar stage of its last business recovery. /M.Jaffe

Qualitative Risk Assessment

LOW	MEDIUM	HIGH

Our risk assessment reflects what we view as RHI's strong position in accounting and finance placements and a healthy balance sheet. This is offset by the highly cyclical nature of the company's business, which is largely dependent on the U.S. economy and the health of labor markets.

Quantitative Evaluations

S&P Quality Ranking   **B**

D	C	B-	**B**	B+	A-	A	A+

Relative Strength Rank   **STRONG**

76

LOWEST = 1   HIGHEST = 99

Revenue/Earnings Data

Revenue (Million $)

	1Q	2Q	3Q	4Q	Year
2010	737.2	769.1	--	--	--
2009	823.3	749.9	725.9	737.4	3,037
2008	1,226	1,225	1,160	989.8	4,601
2007	1,097	1,149	1,179	1,220	4,646
2006	943.9	981.8	1,028	1,060	4,014
2005	770.0	816.7	867.0	884.8	3,338

Earnings Per Share ($)

2010	0.05	0.08	E0.12	E0.16	E0.45
2009	0.06	0.03	0.06	0.09	0.24
2008	0.45	0.48	0.43	0.26	1.63
2007	0.42	0.44	0.46	0.50	1.81
2006	0.38	0.39	0.43	0.45	1.65
2005	0.29	0.33	0.37	0.37	1.36

Fiscal year ended Dec. 31. Next earnings report expected: NA. EPS Estimates based on S&P Operating Earnings; historical GAAP earnings are as reported.

Dividend Data (Dates: mm/dd Payment Date: mm/dd/yy)

Amount ($)	Date Decl.	Ex-Div. Date	Stk. of Record	Payment Date
0.120	10/27	11/23	11/25	12/15/09
0.130	02/10	02/23	02/25	03/15/10
0.130	05/06	05/21	05/25	06/15/10
0.130	07/28	08/23	08/25	09/15/10

Dividends have been paid since 2004. Source: Company reports.

Please read the Required Disclosures and Analyst Certification on the last page of this report.

The **McGraw·Hill** Companies

Robert Half International Inc.

Business Summary August 26, 2010

CORPORATE OVERVIEW. Robert Half International is the world's largest specialized staffing service in the fields of accounting and finance. In May 2002, RHI expanded its offerings to include risk consulting and internal audit services through its Protiviti unit. In 2009, the company derived 81% of its revenues from activities in temporary and consultant staffing, 6% from permanent placement staffing, and 13% from risk consulting and internal audit services. Foreign operations accounted for 29% of RHI's revenues in 2009. As of 2009 year-end, the company's staffing businesses had more than 365 offices in 42 states, the District of Columbia and 20 foreign countries, while Protiviti had more than 60 offices in 23 states and 16 foreign countries.

RHI's Accountemps temporary services division offers customers an economical means of dealing with uneven or peak work loads for accounting, tax and finance personnel. The temporary workers are employees of Accountemps, and are paid by Accountemps only when working on customer assignments. The customer pays a fixed rate for hours worked. If the client converts the temporary hire to a permanent worker, it typically pays a one-time fee for the conversion.

RHI offers permanent placement services through Robert Half Finance & Accounting, which specializes in accounting, financial, tax and banking personnel. Fees for successful permanent placements are paid only by the employer and are usually a percentage of the new employee's annual salary.

Since the early 1990s, the company has expanded into additional specialty fields. OfficeTeam, formed in 1991, provides skilled temporary and full-time administrative and office personnel. In 1992, RHI acquired Robert Half Legal (formerly The Affiliates), which places temporary and regular employees in attorney, paralegal, legal administrative and other legal support positions. In 1994, Robert Half Technology (formerly RHI Consulting) was created to concentrate on the placement of contract and full-time information technology consultants. In 1997, the company established Robert Half Management Resources (formerly RHI Management Resources) to provide senior level project professionals specializing in the accounting and finance fields. The Creative Group, which started up in 1999, provides project staffing in the advertising, marketing and Web design fields. In 2009, Accountemps provided 40% of revenues, OfficeTeam 18%, other placement businesses 29%, and Protiviti 13%.

Company Financials Fiscal Year Ended Dec. 31

Per Share Data ($)	2009	2008	2007	2006	2005	2004	2003	2002	2001	2000
Tangible Book Value	4.78	5.26	4.99	5.15	4.72	4.30	3.65	3.41	3.69	3.13
Cash Flow	0.70	2.11	2.25	2.00	1.66	1.07	0.42	0.42	1.07	1.30
Earnings	0.24	1.63	1.81	1.65	1.36	0.79	0.04	0.01	0.67	1.00
S&P Core Earnings	0.24	1.63	1.81	1.65	1.29	0.71	-0.11	-0.17	0.51	NA
Dividends	0.48	0.44	0.40	0.32	0.28	0.18	Nil	Nil	Nil	Nil
Payout Ratio	NM	27%	22%	19%	21%	23%	Nil	Nil	Nil	Nil
Prices:High	28.06	29.99	42.21	43.94	39.86	30.98	25.18	30.90	30.90	38.63
Prices:Low	14.06	14.31	24.41	29.91	23.95	20.69	11.44	11.94	18.50	12.34
P/E Ratio:High	NM	18	23	27	29	39	NM	NM	46	39
P/E Ratio:Low	NM	9	13	18	18	26	NM	NM	28	12

Income Statement Analysis (Million $)	2009	2008	2007	2006	2005	2004	2003	2002	2001	2000
Revenue	3,037	4,601	4,646	4,014	3,338	2,676	1,975	1,905	2,453	2,699
Operating Income	131	487	549	511	433	280	75.0	71.2	261	348
Depreciation	65.3	73.2	71.4	61.1	51.3	49.1	65.9	72.3	73.1	56.6
Interest Expense	0.50	5.30	4.10	Nil	Nil	Nil	Nil	Nil	Nil	Nil
Pretax Income	66.8	419	490	466	392	235	11.7	3.50	196	302
Effective Tax Rate	44.2%	40.3%	39.6%	39.3%	39.3%	40.1%	45.5%	38.0%	38.3%	38.3%
Net Income	37.3	250	296	283	238	141	6.39	2.17	121	186
S&P Core Earnings	35.1	250	296	283	224	125	-18.4	-30.2	91.1	NA

Balance Sheet & Other Financial Data (Million $)	2009	2008	2007	2006	2005	2004	2003	2002	2001	2000
Cash	366	355	310	447	458	437	377	317	347	239
Current Assets	923	1,033	1,060	1,112	1,017	916	699	643	686	672
Total Assets	1,284	1,412	1,450	1,459	1,319	1,199	980	936	994	971
Current Liabilities	367	413	448	403	337	280	189	184	177	237
Long Term Debt	1.78	1.89	3.75	3.83	2.70	2.27	2.34	2.40	2.48	2.54
Common Equity	900	984	984	1,043	971	912	789	745	806	719
Total Capital	902	986	988	1,047	974	914	791	747	808	721
Capital Expenditures	41.3	73.4	83.8	80.4	61.8	32.9	36.5	48.3	84.7	74.0
Cash Flow	103	323	368	344	289	190	72.3	74.5	194	243
Current Ratio	2.5	2.5	2.4	2.8	3.0	3.3	3.7	3.5	3.9	2.8
% Long Term Debt of Capitalization	Nil	0.2	0.4	0.4	0.3	0.2	0.3	0.3	0.3	0.4
% Net Income of Revenue	1.2	5.4	6.4	7.1	7.1	5.3	0.3	0.1	4.9	6.9
% Return on Assets	NA	17.5	20.4	20.4	18.9	12.9	0.7	0.2	12.3	21.3
% Return on Equity	NA	25.4	29.2	28.1	25.3	16.5	0.8	0.3	15.9	28.7

Data as orig reptd.; bef. results of disc opers/spec. items. Per share data adj. for stk. divs.; EPS diluted. E-Estimated. NA-Not Available. NM-Not Meaningful. NR-Not Ranked. UR-Under Review.

Office: 2884 Sand Hill Rd, Menlo Park, CA 94025-7072.
Telephone: 650-234-6000.
Website: http://www.rhi.com
Chrmn & CEO: H.M. Messmer, Jr.

Pres, Vice Chrmn & CFO: M.K. Waddell
EVP, Chief Admin Officer, Chief Acctg Officer & Treas: M.C. Buckley
EVP, Secy & General Counsel: S. Karel
CIO: K. White

Board Members: A. S. Berwick, Jr., E. W. Gibbons, H. M. Messmer, Jr., B. J. Novogradac, R. J. Pace, F. A. Richman, J. S. Schaub, M. K. Waddell

Founded: 1967
Domicile: Delaware
Employees: 166,900

Rockwell Automation Inc.

STANDARD &POOR'S

S&P Recommendation SELL ★ ★ ☆ ☆ ☆

Price	**12-Mo. Target Price**	**Investment Style**
$62.71 (as of Oct 22, 2010)	$58.00	Large-Cap Blend

GICS Sector Industrials
Sub-Industry Electrical Components & Equipment

Summary This company manufactures and develops automated industrial equipment and power generators for applications in many different manufacturing processes.

Key Stock Statistics (Source S&P, Vickers, company reports)

52-Wk Range	$63.90–39.39	S&P Oper. EPS 2010E	3.04	Market Capitalization(B)	$8.896	Beta		1.69
Trailing 12-Month EPS	$2.51	S&P Oper. EPS 2011E	3.74	Yield (%)	2.23	S&P 3-Yr. Proj. EPS CAGR(%)		30
Trailing 12-Month P/E	25.0	P/E on S&P Oper. EPS 2010E	20.6	Dividend Rate/Share	$1.40	S&P Credit Rating		A
$10K Invested 5 Yrs Ago	$13,588	Common Shares Outstg. (M)	141.9	Institutional Ownership (%)	71			

Price Performance

30-Week Mov. Avg. · · · 10-Week Mov. Avg. – – GAAP Earnings vs. Previous Year Volume Above Avg. STARS
12-Mo. Target Price — Relative Strength — ▲ Up ▼ Down ► No Change Below Avg. ★

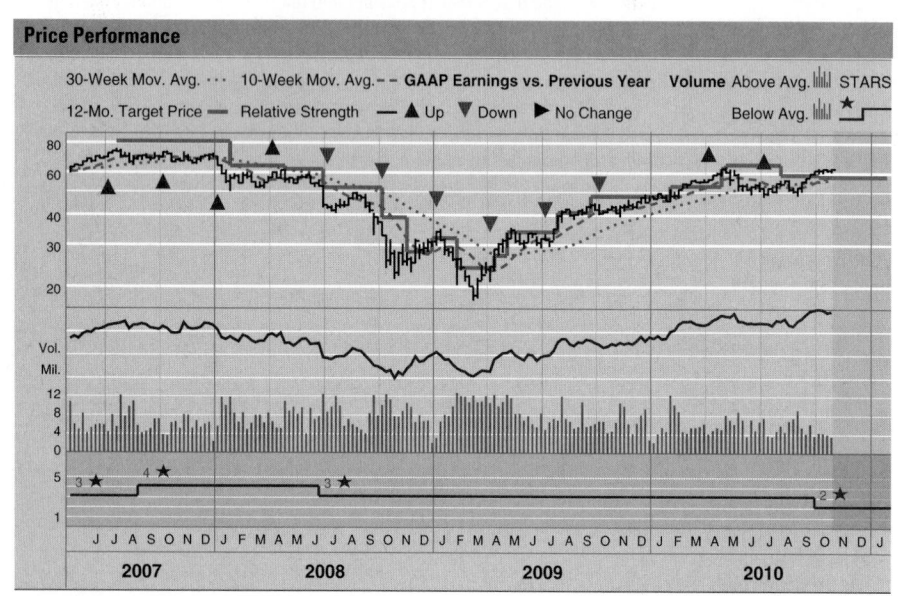

Options: ASE, CBOE, Ph

Analysis prepared by **Mathew Christy, CFA** on October 07, 2010, when the stock traded at **$ 61.87.**

Highlights

► After a 24% revenue decline in FY 09 (Sep.), we expect an increase of about 11% for FY 10, due in part to a better economic environment, with industrial production and capacity utilization both improving in recent months. Our forecast primarily reflects projected 4% sales growth at the Control Products unit, and a 28% gain for Architecture & Software sales, driven by revenue from higher maintenance, repair, and product sales, partly offset by lower project work. We believe the global economic recovery will continue, and look for FY 11 revenues to advance 13%.

► We forecast that operating margins will widen in FY 10, as the company benefits from restructuring efforts, offset somewhat by lower operating leverage expected in the controls business. In FY 11, we see operating margins expanding further on greater operating leverage and operating rates.

► Assuming effective tax rates of 20.3% for FY 10 and 25% for FY 11, and excluding earnings from discontinued operations, we project operating EPS of $3.04 for FY 10 and $3.74 for FY 11.

Investment Rationale/Risk

► Our recent downgrade to sell, from hold, is primarily based on valuation after a substantial rise in the share price since the August lows. This is despite recent gains in capacity utilization and industrial production rates, as reported by the Federal Reserve, which we think indicate increased spending on automation products. That said, we see risk in the apparent deceleration in manufacturing activity, as evidenced by recent reductions in the ISM's PMI, and we view the stock as overvalued at recent levels.

► Risks to our recommendation and target price include greater-than-expected global economic growth, higher-than-expected project spending, and a significant expansion in global manufacturing capacity.

► Our 12-month target price of $58 is based on a blend of valuation metrics. On relative peer valuation, we apply a target P/E multiple of about 17X, in line with the peer average, to our forward 12-month EPS per share estimate, resulting in a $62 value. Our discounted cash flow model, which assumes a 3% growth rate in perpetuity and a 10.7% discount rate, implies intrinsic value of $54.

Qualitative Risk Assessment

LOW	**MEDIUM**	HIGH

Our risk assessment reflects the highly cyclical end-market demand for the company's products, offset by corporate governance practices that we view favorably, and we note the company has an S&P Quality Ranking of B+, which reflects average stability in earnings and dividend growth, and low capital requirements.

Quantitative Evaluations

S&P Quality Ranking   B+

D	C	B-	B	**B+**	A-	A	A+

Relative Strength Rank   STRONG

73

LOWEST = 1   HIGHEST = 99

Revenue/Earnings Data

Revenue (Million $)

	1Q	2Q	3Q	4Q	Year
2010	1,068	1,165	1,268	--	--
2009	1,189	1,058	1,011	1,074	4,333
2008	1,332	1,407	1,475	1,484	5,698
2007	1,146	1,207	1,281	1,371	5,004
2006	1,301	1,378	1,428	1,454	5,561
2005	1,185	1,218	1,265	1,335	5,003

Earnings Per Share ($)

	1Q	2Q	3Q	4Q	Year
2010	E0.42	0.78	0.83	E0.89	E3.04
2009	0.81	0.29	0.23	0.20	1.53
2008	1.04	0.96	1.03	0.87	3.90
2007	0.76	0.65	1.07	1.07	3.53
2006	0.80	0.83	0.83	1.04	3.49
2005	0.65	0.75	0.68	0.69	2.77

Fiscal year ended Sep. 30. Next earnings report expected: Early November. EPS Estimates based on S&P Operating Earnings; historical GAAP earnings are as reported.

Dividend Data (Dates: mm/dd Payment Date: mm/dd/yy)

Amount ($)	Date Decl.	Ex-Div. Date	Stk. of Record	Payment Date
0.290	11/04	11/12	11/16	12/10/09
0.290	02/03	02/11	02/16	03/10/10
0.290	04/07	05/13	05/17	06/10/10
0.350	06/03	08/12	08/16	09/10/10

Dividends have been paid since 1948. Source: Company reports.

Rockwell Automation Inc.

**STANDARD
&POOR'S**

Business Summary October 07, 2010

CORPORATE OVERVIEW. In the early 1990s, Rockwell Automation (formerly Rockwell International) operated a broad range of manufacturing businesses. Following a series of divestitures that included the 2001 spin-off of Rockwell Collins, the 2006 divestitures of ElectroCraft Engineered Solutions, the sale of a 50% interest in Rockwell Scientific, and the 2007 divestiture of Dodge Mechanical and Reliance Electric Motors. ROK now operates two business segments: Control Products and Solutions and Architecture and Software.

The Control Products and Solutions (CS) segment accounted for 60.2% of FY 09 (Sep.) total revenues and 47% of total operating profits, with 8.4% profit margins. CS supplies industrial control products and services focused on helping customers control, monitor and improve manufacturing processes. Products include industrial controls, variable frequency drives, smart motor controls, electronic overload controls, power control and motor control centers, drive systems, custom OEM panels, information systems and systems integration. Major markets served include consumer products, food and beverage, transportation, metals, mining, pulp and paper, and oil and gas. Competitors include Emerson Electric, General Electric, and Schneider Electric.

The Architecture and Software (A&S) segment generated 39.8% of FY 09 sales and 53% of operating profits, with 14.2% operating margins. The division offers control platforms and software as well as bundled automation products for enterprise business systems, distribution and supply chains. Control offerings include controllers, electronic interface devices, communications and network products, motor control sensors, programmable logic controllers (PLCs), input/output devices, sensors, safety components, and other products used in the automation of manufacturing operations. Software product offerings include configuration and visualization software, control platforms, and other manufacturing control software. Major competitors include Siemens AG, Mitsubishi Corp, ABB Ltd, Schneider Electric, Honeywell International, and Emerson Electric. Major markets served include food and beverage, automotive, oil and gas, metals and mining, home and personal care, and life sciences.

Company Financials Fiscal Year Ended Sep. 30

Per Share Data ($)	2009	2008	2007	2006	2005	2004	2003	2002	2001	2000
Tangible Book Value	1.21	3.65	4.29	4.40	2.95	3.95	2.41	2.61	2.23	6.90
Cash Flow	2.36	4.72	4.26	4.35	3.68	2.83	2.53	2.29	5.39	4.80
Earnings	1.53	3.90	3.53	3.49	2.77	1.85	1.49	1.20	0.68	3.35
S&P Core Earnings	0.71	3.03	3.45	3.48	2.68	1.88	1.16	0.75	-0.06	NA
Dividends	1.16	1.16	1.16	0.90	0.78	0.66	0.66	0.66	0.93	1.02
Payout Ratio	76%	30%	33%	26%	28%	36%	44%	55%	137%	30%
Prices:High	49.25	69.72	75.60	799.47	63.30	49.97	36.10	22.79	49.45	54.50
Prices:Low	17.50	21.51	56.73	53.49	45.40	28.45	18.75	14.71	11.78	27.69
P/E Ratio:High	32	18	21	23	23	27	24	19	73	16
P/E Ratio:Low	11	6	16	15	16	15	13	12	17	8

Income Statement Analysis (Million $)	2009	2008	2007	2006	2005	2004	2003	2002	2001	2000
Revenue	4,333	5,698	5,004	5,561	5,003	4,411	4,104	3,909	4,279	7,151
Operating Income	520	1,021	937	1,073	944	691	543	488	1,079	1,223
Depreciation	118	122	118	154	171	187	198	206	872	276
Interest Expense	60.9	68.2	63.4	58.4	45.8	41.7	52.0	66.0	83.0	73.0
Pretax Income	274	809	789	365	737	438	299	233	168	943
Effective Tax Rate	20.5%	28.6%	27.8%	NM	29.7%	19.2%	5.69%	3.00%	25.6%	32.6%
Net Income	218	578	569	628	518	354	282	226	125	636
S&P Core Earnings	102	449	556	628	498	361	221	142	-12.0	NA

Balance Sheet & Other Financial Data (Million $)	2009	2008	2007	2006	2005	2004	2003	2002	2001	2000
Cash	644	582	624	415	464	474	226	289	121	190
Current Assets	2,135	2,437	2,382	2,188	2,187	2,026	1,736	1,775	1,697	3,206
Total Assets	4,306	4,594	4,546	4,735	4,525	4,201	3,986	4,024	4,074	6,390
Current Liabilities	947	1,303	1,745	1,293	941	864	820	966	867	1,820
Long Term Debt	905	904	406	748	748	758	764	767	922	924
Common Equity	1,316	1,689	1,743	1,918	1,649	1,861	1,587	1,609	1,600	2,669
Total Capital	2,221	2,593	2,149	2,822	2,397	2,708	2,388	2,534	2,693	3,593
Capital Expenditures	98.0	151	131	150	124	98.0	109	104	157	315
Cash Flow	336	700	687	782	690	541	480	432	997	912
Current Ratio	2.3	1.9	1.4	1.7	2.3	2.3	2.1	1.8	2.0	1.8
% Long Term Debt of Capitalization	40.7	34.9	18.9	26.5	31.2	28.0	32.0	30.3	34.2	25.7
% Net Income of Revenue	5.0	10.1	11.4	11.3	10.4	8.0	6.9	5.8	2.9	8.9
% Return on Assets	4.9	12.6	12.3	13.6	11.9	8.7	7.1	5.6	2.7	9.8
% Return on Equity	14.5	33.7	31.1	35.2	29.5	20.5	17.6	14.1	5.9	24.4

Data as orig reptd.; bef. results of disc opers/spec. items. Per share data adj. for stk. divs.; EPS diluted. E-Estimated. NA-Not Available. NM-Not Meaningful. NR-Not Ranked. UR-Under Review.

Office: 1201 S 2nd St, Milwaukee, WI 53204-2498.
Telephone: 414-382-2000.
Website: http://www.rockwellautomation.com
Chrmn, Pres & CEO: K.D. Nosbusch

COO: M. Thomas
SVP & CFO: T.D. Crandall
SVP & CTO: S. Chand
SVP, Secy & General Counsel: D.M. Hagerman

Board Members: B. C. Alewine, V. G. Istock, B. C. Johnson, W. T. McCormick, Jr., K. D. Nosbusch, D. R. Parfet, B. M. Rockwell, D. B. Speer, J. F. Toot, Jr.

Founded: 1928
Domicile: Delaware
Employees: 19,000

Rockwell Collins Inc.

STANDARD &POOR'S

S&P Recommendation **BUY** ★★★★☆	Price $61.39 (as of Oct 22, 2010)	12-Mo. Target Price $70.00	Investment Style Large-Cap Growth

GICS Sector Industrials
Sub-Industry Aerospace & Defense

Summary This company is one of the world's largest makers of military and commercial avionics and electronics, including cockpit controls, communications and navigation systems, and in-flight entertainment systems.

Key Stock Statistics (Source S&P, Vickers, company reports)

52-Wk Range	$68.04– 47.19	S&P Oper. EPS 2010**E**	3.54	Market Capitalization(B)	$9.650	Beta	1.35
Trailing 12-Month EPS	$3.42	S&P Oper. EPS 2011**E**	3.95	Yield (%)	1.56	S&P 3-Yr. Proj. EPS CAGR(%)	5
Trailing 12-Month P/E	18.0	P/E on S&P Oper. EPS 2010**E**	17.3	Dividend Rate/Share	$0.96	S&P Credit Rating	A
$10K Invested 5 Yrs Ago	$14,006	Common Shares Outstg. (M)	157.2	Institutional Ownership (%)	72		

Price Performance

- 30-Week Mov. Avg. · · ·
- 10-Week Mov. Avg. - - -
- **GAAP Earnings vs. Previous Year**
- Volume Above Avg.
- STARS
- 12-Mo. Target Price —
- Relative Strength —
- ▲ Up
- ▼ Down
- ▶ No Change
- Below Avg.
- ★

Options: ASE, CBOE, Ph

Analysis prepared by **Richard Tortoriello** on August 06, 2010, when the stock traded at **$ 57.76**.

Highlights

➤ We estimate that sales will rise about 6% in FY 10 (Sep.), following a 6% decline in FY 09, as we see significant sales growth in Government Systems (GS) partially offset by a sales decline in Commercial Systems (CS). For FY 11, we project a 6% sales gain, with increases in both CS and GS. We see CS achieving slight growth, primarily due to increased commercial and business & regional aftermarket demand, due to rising flight hours. We see GS achieving continued substantial growth on aircraft display and control systems and defense communications.

➤ We expect segment operating margins to decline to 19.2% in FY 10, from 21.4% in FY 09, and we project a rise to 20.2% in FY 11, as production volume should increase. We note that previous peak segment margins for COL have been well above 22%.

➤ We estimate EPS of $3.54 for FY 10 and $3.95 for FY 11. We project free cash flow (cash flow from operating activities less capital expenditures) of about 90% of net income in FY 10.

Investment Rationale/Risk

➤ Although we expect weak business jet OEM demand to continue to constrain earnings in FY 10 and into FY 11, we look for a bounce-back in overall aftermarket demand due to a variety of factors, including depleted inventories at airlines and a recent increase in air travel. We see the company generating returns on invested capital (ROIC) of over 25%, despite the recent economic downturn. We also see COL conserving cash for attractive acquisitions, which we think would favorably expand its market position. At the same time, we see COL's valuations below historical averages on slightly depressed earnings.

➤ Risks to our recommendation and target price include an unanticipated slowdown in the global economy, failure to gain new contracts, and operational or other missteps.

➤ Our 12-month target price of $70 is based on an enterprise value to FY 12 estimated EBITDA multiple of 10X. Over its eight-year operating history, COL has recorded EV-to-EBITDA multiples ranging from 5X to 15X. Given this stage of the economic recovery, we believe a multiple near the middle of this range is appropriate.

Qualitative Risk Assessment

LOW	MEDIUM	HIGH

Our risk assessment reflects the company's exposure to the commercial airline industry, dependence on U.S. military procurement and R&D budgets, and high fixed-cost structure, offset by what we view as a solid balance sheet and strong returns.

Quantitative Evaluations

S&P Quality Ranking   A

D	C	B-	B	B+	A-	**A**	A+

Relative Strength Rank   MODERATE

65

LOWEST = 1   HIGHEST = 99

Revenue/Earnings Data

Revenue (Million $)

	1Q	2Q	3Q	4Q	Year
2010	1,027	1,142	1,214	--	--
2009	1,058	1,138	1,084	1,190	4,470
2008	1,112	1,186	1,194	1,277	4,769
2007	993.0	1,083	1,113	1,226	4,415
2006	881.0	957.0	964.0	1,061	3,863
2005	763.0	829.0	890.0	963.0	3,445

Earnings Per Share ($)

	1Q	2Q	3Q	4Q	Year
2010	0.76	0.93	0.89	E0.96	E3.54
2009	0.95	1.03	0.91	0.84	3.73
2008	0.93	1.03	1.07	1.13	4.16
2007	0.84	0.82	0.86	0.93	3.45
2006	0.59	0.65	0.70	0.79	2.73
2005	0.50	0.52	0.56	0.62	2.20

Fiscal year ended Sep. 30. Next earnings report expected: Early November. EPS Estimates based on S&P Operating Earnings; historical GAAP earnings are as reported.

Dividend Data (Dates: mm/dd Payment Date: mm/dd/yy)

Amount ($)	Date Decl.	Ex-Div. Date	Stk. of Record	Payment Date
0.240	10/26	11/12	11/16	12/07/09
0.240	01/19	02/10	02/15	03/08/10
0.240	04/26	05/13	05/17	06/07/10
0.240	07/27	08/12	08/16	09/07/10

Dividends have been paid since 2001. Source: Company reports.

Please read the Required Disclosures and Analyst Certification on the last page of this report.

The McGraw-Hill Companies

Rockwell Collins Inc.

**STANDARD
&POOR'S**

Business Summary August 06, 2010

CORPORATE OVERVIEW. This global $4.5 billion revenue aircraft electronics (avionics) maker conducts its business through two segments: Commercial Systems (CS) and Government Systems (GS). CS (42% of revenues and 37% of segment operating earnings, and segment operating margins of 18.7% in FY 09 (Sep.)) primarily makes flight deck electronic systems. CS also provides a range of repair and overhaul services. GS (58%; 63%; 23.3%) primarily makes communication radios and cockpit displays installed in military jets. GS also makes navigation equipment embedded in guided missiles.

Commercial Systems products include integrated avionics systems, which include liquid crystal flight displays, flight management, integrated flight control, automatic flight controls, engine indications, and crew alerts; cabin electronics, including passenger connectivity and entertainment, business support systems, networks, and environmental controls; communications products and systems; navigation products and systems; situational awareness and surveillance products and systems, such as Heads-Up Guidance Systems, weather radar, and collision avoidance systems; flight deck systems, including liquid crystal, cathode ray tube, and heads-up displays; information management systems; electro-mechanical pilot controls and stabilization systems; simulation and training systems; and maintenance, repair, parts, and support

services. Customers include large commercial airplane, regional jet, and business jet makers; commercial airlines; regional airlines; fractional jet operators; and business jet operators.

Government Systems products include communications systems and products; military data link products; navigation systems and products, including radio navigation systems, global positioning systems (GPS), handheld navigation systems, and multi-mode receivers; subsystems for the flight deck that combine flight operations with navigation and guidance functions; cockpit display systems, including flat panel, helmet-mounted and other displays for fighter/attack aircraft; integrated computer systems for the Army's FCS initiative; simulation and training systems; and maintenance, repair, parts, and support services. Customers include the U.S. Department of Defense, other government agencies, civil agencies, defense contractors, and foreign ministries of defense. Products are used for airborne, ground, and shipboard applications.

Company Financials Fiscal Year Ended Sep. 30

Per Share Data ($)	2009	2008	2007	2006	2005	2004	2003	2002	2001	2000
Tangible Book Value	2.09	3.79	5.97	3.30	2.13	3.29	2.21	2.93	4.48	NA
Cash Flow	4.63	4.95	4.14	3.34	2.86	2.28	2.02	1.85	1.47	1.87
Earnings	3.73	4.16	3.45	2.73	2.20	1.67	1.43	1.28	0.72	1.35
S&P Core Earnings	3.08	3.39	3.35	2.66	2.04	1.47	0.82	0.46	NA	NA
Dividends	0.96	0.88	0.64	0.56	0.48	0.39	0.36	0.36	Nil	NA
Payout Ratio	26%	21%	19%	21%	22%	23%	25%	28%	Nil	NA
Prices:High	56.88	72.41	76.00	64.31	49.80	40.94	30.10	28.00	27.12	NA
Prices:Low	27.67	27.76	61.25	43.49	37.22	29.16	17.20	18.50	11.80	NA
P/E Ratio:High	15	17	22	24	23	25	21	22	38	NA
P/E Ratio:Low	7	7	18	16	17	17	12	14	16	NA

Income Statement Analysis (Million $)										
Revenue	4,470	4,769	4,415	3,863	3,445	2,930	2,542	2,492	2,820	2,510
Operating Income	1,029	1,090	959	776	660	539	440	427	492	492
Depreciation	144	129	118	106	119	109	105	105	131	99.0
Interest Expense	18.0	21.0	13.0	13.0	11.0	8.00	3.00	6.00	3.00	20.0
Pretax Income	867	953	843	689	547	430	368	341	224	381
Effective Tax Rate	31.5%	28.9%	30.6%	30.8%	27.6%	30.0%	29.9%	30.8%	37.9%	32.5%
Net Income	594	678	585	477	396	301	258	236	139	257
S&P Core Earnings	491	552	568	465	367	264	148	86.8	59.2	NA

Balance Sheet & Other Financial Data (Million $)										
Cash	235	175	231	144	145	196	66.0	49.0	60.0	20.0
Current Assets	2,362	2,338	2,169	1,927	1,775	1,663	1,427	1,438	1,639	1,531
Total Assets	4,645	4,144	3,750	3,278	3,140	2,874	2,591	2,560	2,628	2,628
Current Liabilities	1,359	1,740	1,459	1,324	1,177	964	901	1,043	1,135	1,073
Long Term Debt	532	228	223	245	200	201	Nil	Nil	Nil	Nil
Common Equity	1,292	1,408	1,573	1,206	939	1,133	833	987	1,110	1,086
Total Capital	1,824	1,646	1,840	1,451	1,139	1,334	833	987	1,110	1,086
Capital Expenditures	153	171	125	144	111	94.0	72.0	62.0	110	NA
Cash Flow	738	807	703	583	515	410	363	341	270	356
Current Ratio	1.7	1.3	1.5	1.5	1.5	1.7	1.6	1.4	1.4	1.4
% Long Term Debt of Capitalization	29.2	13.9	12.1	16.9	17.6	15.1	Nil	Nil	Nil	Nil
% Net Income of Revenue	13.3	14.2	13.3	12.3	11.5	10.3	10.1	9.5	4.9	10.2
% Return on Assets	13.5	17.2	16.7	14.8	13.2	11.0	10.0	9.1	5.9	NA
% Return on Equity	44.0	45.5	42.1	44.5	38.2	30.6	28.4	22.5	13.8	NA

Data as orig reptd.; bef. results of disc opers/spec. items. Per share data adj. for stk. divs.; EPS diluted. E-Estimated. NA-Not Available. NM-Not Meaningful. NR-Not Ranked. UR-Under Review.

Office: 400 Collins Rd NE, Cedar Rapids, IA 52498-0503.
Telephone: 319-295-1000.
Email: investorrelations@rockwellcollins.com
Website: http://www.rockwellcollins.com

Chrmn, Pres & CEO: C. Jones
COO: J.A. Moore
SVP & CFO: P.E. Allen
SVP & CTO: N. Mattai

SVP, Secy & General Counsel: G.R. Chadick
Investor Contact: D. Crookshank (319-295-7575)
Board Members: D. R. Beall, A. J. Carbone, C. A. Davis, M. Donegan, R. E. Eberhart, C. Jones, D. Lilley, A. J. Policano, C. L. Shavers

Founded: 2001
Domicile: Delaware
Employees: 19,300

The McGraw-Hill Companies

Roper Industries Inc.

STANDARD &POOR'S

S&P Recommendation	HOLD ★★★☆☆	Price $70.38 (as of Oct 25, 2010)	12-Mo. Target Price $78.00	Investment Style Large-Cap Growth

GICS Sector Industrials
Sub-Industry Electrical Components & Equipment

Summary This company makes high-tech industrial equipment and analytical instruments for oil and gas producers, semiconductor equipment makers, and industrial companies.

Key Stock Statistics (Source S&P, Vickers, company reports)

52-Wk Range	$72.91– 49.53	S&P Oper. EPS 2010**E**	3.25	Market Capitalization(B)	$6.628	Beta	0.75
Trailing 12-Month EPS	$2.74	S&P Oper. EPS 2011**E**	3.76	Yield (%)	0.54	S&P 3-Yr. Proj. EPS CAGR(%)	13
Trailing 12-Month P/E	25.7	P/E on S&P Oper. EPS 2010**E**	21.7	Dividend Rate/Share	$0.38	S&P Credit Rating	BBB-
$10K Invested 5 Yrs Ago	$20,324	Common Shares Outstg. (M)	94.2	Institutional Ownership (%)	94		

Price Performance

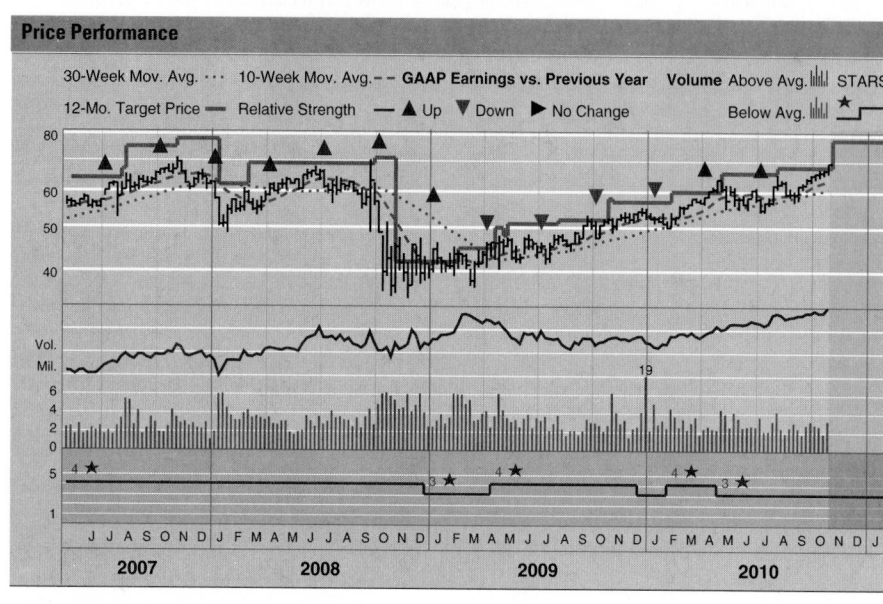

30-Week Mov. Avg. ··· 10-Week Mov. Avg.-- **GAAP Earnings vs. Previous Year** Volume Above Avg. STARS
12-Mo. Target Price — Relative Strength — ▲ Up ▼ Down ► No Change Below Avg. ★

Qualitative Risk Assessment

LOW	**MEDIUM**	HIGH

Our risk assessment reflects the company's significant proportion of rapidly growing international sales and ROP's proprietary product portfolio, offset by its acquisition strategy and corporate governance practices, which we view as unfavorable versus peers.

Quantitative Evaluations

S&P Quality Ranking   **A**

D	C	B-	B	B+	A-	**A**	A+

Relative Strength Rank   **STRONG**

LOWEST = 1   81   HIGHEST = 99

Revenue/Earnings Data

Revenue (Million $)

	1Q	2Q	3Q	4Q	Year
2010	534.4	567.1	--	--	--
2009	505.4	504.9	485.7	553.6	2,050
2008	543.0	594.4	593.1	575.9	2,306
2007	478.4	530.6	530.9	560.1	2,102
2006	382.7	425.3	427.2	465.5	1,701
2005	333.8	361.6	365.2	393.2	1,454

Earnings Per Share ($)

	1Q	2Q	3Q	4Q	Year
2010	0.62	0.74	E0.78	E0.99	E3.25
2009	0.56	0.64	0.61	0.77	2.58
2008	0.68	0.80	0.80	0.78	3.06
2007	0.56	0.66	0.70	0.77	2.68
2006	0.42	0.53	0.56	0.62	2.13
2005	0.33	0.41	0.45	0.57	1.74

Fiscal year ended Dec. 31. Next earnings report expected: Late October. EPS Estimates based on S&P Operating Earnings; historical GAAP earnings are as reported.

Highlights

► The 12-month target price for ROP has recently been changed to $78.00 from $68.00. The Highlights section of this Stock Report will be updated accordingly.

Investment Rationale/Risk

► The Investment Rationale/Risk section of this Stock Report will be updated shortly. For the latest News story on ROP from MarketScope, see below.

► 10/25/10 10:43 am ET ... S&P MAINTAINS HOLD RECOMMENDATION ON SHARES OF ROPER INDUSTRIES (ROP 71.27***): ROP reports Q3 EPS of $0.87, vs. $0.61, $0.09 ahead of our estimate on greater-than-expected revenue growth of 25% and a lower tax rate. We are increasing our '10 EPS forecast $0.11 to $3.25 and '11's by $0.23 to $3.76 on revised sales and margin forecasts and view favorably new order growth of 31% (20% organically). Although we would expect that order growth will continue, albeit at a slower pace due mainly to more normalized comparisons, we see limited upside potential to our $78 target price, which we raise $10 today on higher estimates and revised valuation analyses. /M.Christy, CFA

Dividend Data (Dates: mm/dd Payment Date: mm/dd/yy)

Amount ($)	Date Decl.	Ex-Div. Date	Stk. of Record	Payment Date
0.095	11/23	01/06	01/08	01/29/10
0.095	01/25	04/07	04/09	04/23/10
0.095	06/18	07/07	07/09	07/30/10
0.095	08/12	10/06	10/08	10/29/10

Dividends have been paid since 1992. Source: Company reports.

Please read the Required Disclosures and Analyst Certification on the last page of this report.

The McGraw-Hill Companies

Roper Industries Inc.

STANDARD & POOR'S

Business Summary August 03, 2010

CORPORATE OVERVIEW. Roper Industries is a high-tech industrial components and equipment maker that designs, manufactures and distributes energy systems and controls, scientific and industrial imaging products and software, specialty industrial technology products, and instrumentation products and services. ROP's target end markets include radio frequency (RF) applications, water and wastewater, oil and gas, research, power generation, and general industry. The company's products are broken down into four segments: Industrial Technology; Energy Systems and Controls; Scientific and Industrial Imaging; and RF Technology.

The Industrial Technology segment (26% of 2009 sales; 28% of segment operating profits; 24% operating margins) provides products and solutions for improving customer productivity. Offerings include industrial pumps, flow measurement and metering equipment, industrial valves and controls, and water meter and automatic meter reading products and systems. ROP's strategy for this segment includes global sourcing, geographic expansion, asset velocity improvements, and the capture of market-based synergies among business units.

The Energy Systems and Controls segment (22%; 21%; 22%) provides service and solutions to improve quality, safety and efficiency for customer equipment and processes, primarily in energy markets. Customers benefit from industry-leading application expertise, coupled with advanced vibration-monitoring components, turbo-machinery control systems and non-destructive testing solutions, often incorporating significant software content. The company's strategy for the segment includes focusing on expanding into new applications and increasing aftermarket revenue. About half of this segment's revenues are derived from the oil and gas industry.

The Scientific and Industrial Imaging segment (17%; 17%; 21%) provides solutions that enable global research in life and physical sciences. Key products are digital imaging cameras, spectrographic systems, electron microscope accessories, high-speed digital video equipment and image processing software. In addition, through ROP's Imaging Alliance, these businesses are working closely with internal and external sources.

The RF Technology segment (35%; 34%; 22%) provides radio frequency identification and satellite-based communications technologies that are used in toll and traffic systems and processing, security and access control, and mobile asset tracking.

Company Financials Fiscal Year Ended Dec. 31

Per Share Data ($)	2009	2008	2007	2006	2005	2004	2003	2002	2001	2000
Tangible Book Value	NM	NM	NM	NM	NM	NM	NM	NM	NM	NM
Cash Flow	3.69	3.42	3.02	3.03	2.55	1.79	1.01	1.28	1.32	1.15
Earnings	2.58	3.06	2.68	2.13	1.74	1.24	0.75	1.04	0.89	0.79
S&P Core Earnings	2.55	3.06	2.68	2.13	1.63	1.11	0.66	0.93	0.81	NA
Dividends	0.33	0.29	0.26	0.24	0.27	0.19	0.18	0.17	0.15	0.14
Payout Ratio	13%	9%	10%	11%	15%	16%	23%	16%	17%	18%
Prices:High	55.50	70.48	71.01	51.75	41.10	31.84	25.98	26.46	26.13	18.97
Prices:Low	36.82	34.85	48.40	38.32	28.28	22.33	13.18	13.63	15.50	12.00
P/E Ratio:High	22	23	26	24	24	26	35	25	30	24
P/E Ratio:Low	14	11	18	18	16	18	18	13	18	15
Income Statement Analysis (Million $)										
Revenue	2,050	2,306	2,102	1,701	1,454	970	657	627	587	504
Operating Income	511	524	470	420	336	213	124	130	126	110
Depreciation	103	33.9	31.8	82.0	71.3	41.4	16.4	15.2	27.5	22.3
Interest Expense	58.5	53.7	52.2	44.8	43.4	28.8	16.4	18.5	15.9	13.5
Pretax Income	340	436	384	293	221	134	66.3	95.7	86.4	75.9
Effective Tax Rate	29.5%	34.3%	34.8%	34.0%	30.6%	29.8%	27.5%	31.0%	35.4%	35.1%
Net Income	239	287	250	193	153	93.9	48.1	66.0	55.8	49.3
S&P Core Earnings	237	287	250	193	144	83.8	42.1	59.0	50.9	NA
Balance Sheet & Other Financial Data (Million $)										
Cash	168	178	309	69.5	53.1	129	70.2	12.4	16.2	11.4
Current Assets	871	858	951	627	498	556	381	248	233	214
Total Assets	4,328	3,972	3,453	2,995	2,522	2,366	1,515	829	762	597
Current Liabilities	478	619	668	588	506	254	161	130	104	84.5
Long Term Debt	1,041	1,034	727	727	621	855	630	312	324	235
Common Equity	2,421	2,004	1,790	1,487	1,250	1,114	656	376	324	270
Total Capital	3,575	3,271	2,739	2,384	1,995	2,095	1,336	688	647	505
Capital Expenditures	25.9	30.1	30.1	32.2	24.8	12.1	10.4	7.78	7.46	15.2
Cash Flow	343	320	282	275	224	135	64.4	81.2	83.3	71.6
Current Ratio	1.8	1.4	1.4	1.1	1.0	2.2	2.4	1.9	2.2	2.5
% Long Term Debt of Capitalization	29.1	31.6	26.6	30.5	31.1	40.8	47.2	45.3	50.0	46.5
% Net Income of Revenue	11.7	12.4	11.9	11.4	10.5	9.7	7.3	10.5	9.5	9.8
% Return on Assets	5.8	7.7	7.8	7.0	6.3	4.8	4.1	8.3	8.2	9.7
% Return on Equity	10.8	15.1	15.3	14.1	13.0	10.6	9.3	18.9	18.8	19.6

Data as orig reptd.; bef. results of disc opers/spec. items. Per share data adj. for stk. divs.; EPS diluted. E-Estimated. NA-Not Available. NM-Not Meaningful. NR-Not Ranked. UR-Under Review.

Office: 6901 Professional Pkwy E Ste 200, Sarasota, FL 34240-8473.
Telephone: 941-556-2601.
Email: investor_relations@roperind.com
Website: http://www.roperind.com

Chrmn, Pres & CEO: B.D. Jellison
CFO: J. Humphrey
Chief Acctg Officer & Cntlr: P.J. Soni
Secy & General Counsel: D.B. Liner

Board Members: D. W. Devonshire, J. F. Fort, III, B. D. Jellison, R. D. Johnson, R. E. Knowling, Jr., J. Prezzano Jr., R. F. Wallman, C. Wright
Founded: 1981
Domicile: Delaware
Employees: 7,650

The McGraw-Hill Companies

Ross Stores Inc

STANDARD &POOR'S

S&P Recommendation HOLD ★★★★☆	**Price** $57.62 (as of Oct 22, 2010)	**12-Mo. Target Price** $55.00	**Investment Style** Large-Cap Growth

GICS Sector Consumer Discretionary
Sub-Industry Apparel Retail

Summary This off-price retailer offers in-season branded apparel and other merchandise through over 1,000 stores in 27 states and Guam.

Key Stock Statistics (Source S&P, Vickers, company reports)

52-Wk Range	$58.93– 42.30	S&P Oper. EPS 2011**E**	4.25	Market Capitalization(B)	$6.941	Beta	0.72
Trailing 12-Month EPS	$4.24	S&P Oper. EPS 2012**E**	4.70	Yield (%)	1.11	S&P 3-Yr. Proj. EPS CAGR(%)	13
Trailing 12-Month P/E	13.6	P/E on S&P Oper. EPS 2011**E**	13.6	Dividend Rate/Share	$0.64	S&P Credit Rating	BBB
$10K Invested 5 Yrs Ago	$23,397	Common Shares Outstg. (M)	120.5	Institutional Ownership (%)	100		

Price Performance

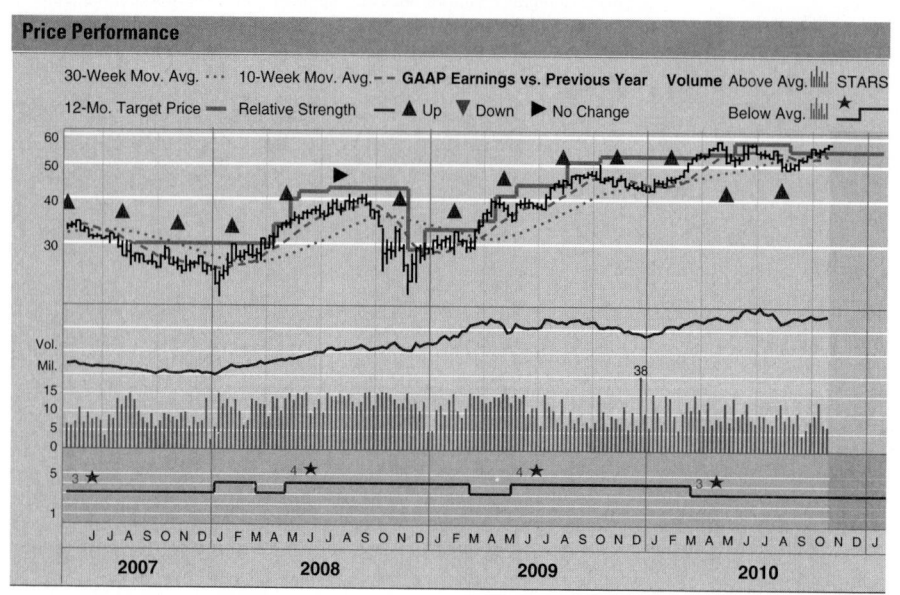

30-Week Mov. Avg. · · · 10-Week Mov. Avg. -- GAAP Earnings vs. Previous Year   Volume Above Avg. STARS
12-Mo. Target Price — Relative Strength — ▲ Up ▼ Down ► No Change   Below Avg. ★

Options: ASE, CBOE, Ph

Analysis prepared by **Jason N. Asaeda** on August 27, 2010, when the stock traded at **$ 50.95.**

Highlights

➤ We forecast a 7.5% increase in net sales for FY 11 (Jan.), following FY 10's 11% advance. We project about a 4% increase in net selling square footage based on ROST's plans to open 35 new Ross and 15 new dd's DISCOUNTS stores and closure of a handful of locations. The company opened 52 new Ross and four new dd's stores in FY 10. In a difficult macroeconomic environment, we think ROST will benefit from cost-conscious consumers trading down from higher-priced retailers for more affordable brand-name merchandise. We forecast that same-store sales will rise 4% in FY 11, on top of FY 10's 6% increase.

➤ While we expect ROST to take timely markdowns in an effort to support the inflow of new assortments, we see an overall reduction in clearance levels and higher merchandise margins as a result of improved inventory management and micro-merchandising tools. We also look for the company to exercise tight cost controls, as we anticipate operating expenses will increase with planned expansion.

➤ Factoring in planned share buybacks under ROST's new two-year $750 million repurchase authorization, we see EPS of $4.25 for FY 11.

Investment Rationale/Risk

➤ Our hold recommendation is based on valuation. We believe ROST's planned expansion of Ross Stores mainly in its top-performing markets such as Florida, and management's efforts to lift the chain's profitability with improved execution of off-price buying, bode well for company fundamentals. And with fine-tuning of merchandise offerings driving profit improvement, we view dd's DISCOUNTS as an attractive long-term growth vehicle. However, our near-term outlook for ROST is tempered by tough comparisons this fall, as well as the company's significant presence in California, where sales weakened in the second quarter.

➤ Risks to our recommendation and target price include sales shortfalls due to changes in consumer confidence, spending habits, and buying preferences; merchandise availability; and, increased promotional activity by competitors.

➤ Our 12-month target price of $55 blends two valuation metrics. Applying a peer-median forward P/E multiple of 12.4X to our FY 11 EPS estimate, we arrive at a $53 value. Our historical valuation uses a forward P/E multiple of 13.5X, ROST's 10-year historical median, yielding a $57 value.

Qualitative Risk Assessment

LOW	**MEDIUM**	HIGH

Our risk assessment reflects our view of ROST's promising new turnaround initiatives at Ross Stores, and favorable growth prospects for dd's DISCOUNTS, offset by an uncertain outlook for consumer discretionary spending.

Quantitative Evaluations

S&P Quality Ranking A+

D	C	B-	B	B+	A-	A	**A+**

Relative Strength Rank MODERATE

68

LOWEST = 1   HIGHEST = 99

Revenue/Earnings Data

Revenue (Million $)

	1Q	2Q	3Q	4Q	Year
2011	1,935	1,912	--	--	--
2010	1,692	1,769	1,744	1,980	7,184
2009	1,556	1,640	1,555	1,734	6,486
2008	1,411	1,445	1,468	1,652	5,975
2007	1,292	1,308	1,362	1,608	5,570
2006	1,124	1,172	1,237	1,411	4,944

Earnings Per Share ($)

	1Q	2Q	3Q	4Q	Year
2011	1.16	1.07	E0.83	E1.18	E4.25
2010	0.72	0.82	0.84	1.16	3.54
2009	0.60	0.54	0.44	0.76	2.33
2008	0.48	0.54	0.36	0.70	1.90
2007	0.41	0.32	0.31	0.66	1.70
2006	0.34	0.29	0.25	0.49	1.36

Fiscal year ended Jan. 31. Next earnings report expected: Mid November. EPS Estimates based on S&P Operating Earnings; historical GAAP earnings are as reported.

Dividend Data (Dates: mm/dd Payment Date: mm/dd/yy)

Amount ($)	Date Decl.	Ex-Div. Date	Stk. of Record	Payment Date
0.110	11/18	12/04	12/08	12/31/09
0.160	02/04	02/17	02/19	03/31/10
0.160	05/19	06/03	06/07	06/30/10
0.160	08/18	08/31	09/02	09/30/10

Dividends have been paid since 1994. Source: Company reports.

Please read the Required Disclosures and Analyst Certification on the last page of this report.

The McGraw·Hill Companies

Ross Stores Inc

Business Summary August 27, 2010

CORPORATE OVERVIEW. Ross Stores operated 1,036 (as of July 31, 2010) off-price retail stores that feature first-quality, in-season apparel, shoes, fragrances, and apparel-related accessories, as well as home furnishings and jewelry under the Ross (979) and dd's DISCOUNTS (57) names. Both chains target value-conscious 25 to 54 year-old men and women, with Ross targeting mainly middle-income households and dd's DISCOUNTS more moderate income households. Ross stores average 29,800 sq. ft. of selling space, and are located in 27 states (mainly warm weather) and Guam. dd's DISCOUNTS stores average 24,900 sq. ft of selling space, and are located in California, Florida, Texas and Arizona. Nearly all stores occupy leased facilities and are situated in neighborhood or strip shopping centers in heavily populated urban and suburban areas.

The company believes it derives a competitive advantage by offering a wide assortment of quality brand-name and fashion merchandise in an easy-to-shop environment at prices generally 20% to 60% below those charged by most department and specialty stores at Ross, and 20% to 70% below moderate department and discount store regular prices at dd's DISCOUNTS. Working with more than 7,700 vendors and manufacturers, ROST purchases later in the buying cycle than department and specialty stores, and can take advantage of supply/demand imbalances. The vast majority of merchandise is acquired through opportunistic purchases of cancellations and overruns. Most orders have one delivery, and generally exclude promotional and markdown allowances and return privileges, enabling buyers to obtain significant discounts on in-season purchases.

MARKET PROFILE. Apparel generated $188.5 billion at retail in the U.S. in 2009, down 5.2% from 2008, according to The NPD Group, Inc. consumer estimated data. Sales of women's apparel accounted for 55.2% of all apparel sales, followed by men's at 27.1%, and children's at 17.7%. In 2009, specialty stores accounted for approximately 30.8% of U.S. apparel sales, followed by mass merchants such as Target and Kmart at 21.6%, department stores including Nordstrom and Macy's at 13.5%, and national chains like Kohl's and JCPenney at 13.0%. ROST participates in the off-price retail channel, which gained ground last year, capturing an estimated 9.3% of U.S. apparel sales in 2009, up from 8.9% in 2008.

Company Financials Fiscal Year Ended Jan. 31

Per Share Data ($)	2010	2009	2008	2007	2006	2005	2004	2003	2002	2001
Tangible Book Value	9.39	7.74	7.23	6.53	5.80	5.22	4.99	4.15	3.45	2.91
Cash Flow	4.81	3.41	2.78	2.47	2.12	1.76	1.96	1.68	1.26	1.18
Earnings	3.54	2.33	1.90	1.70	1.36	1.13	1.47	1.26	0.96	0.91
S&P Core Earnings	3.54	2.33	1.90	1.70	1.30	1.07	1.41	1.22	0.92	0.87
Dividends	NA	0.38	0.24	0.21	0.17	0.12	0.10	0.10	0.09	0.07
Payout Ratio	NA	11%	13%	12%	12%	10%	6%	8%	9%	7%
Calendar Year	2009	2008	2007	2006	2005	2004	2003	2002	2001	2000
Prices:High	50.50	41.56	35.17	31.80	31.37	32.86	28.08	23.62	17.07	12.16
Prices:Low	28.08	21.23	24.42	22.12	22.34	20.95	16.29	15.85	8.28	6.00
P/E Ratio:High	14	18	19	19	23	29	19	19	18	13
P/E Ratio:Low	8	9	13	13	16	19	11	13	9	7

Income Statement Analysis (Million $)										
Revenue	7,184	6,486	5,975	5,570	4,944	4,240	3,921	3,531	2,987	2,709
Operating Income	885	637	542	498	436	390	451	397	308	297
Depreciation	159	142	121	108	111	94.6	76.7	66.2	49.9	44.4
Interest Expense	9.40	11.5	10.7	8.63	Nil	0.92	Nil	0.28	3.17	3.47
Pretax Income	719	495	425	398	328	279	375	330	255	249
Effective Tax Rate	38.4%	38.3%	38.6%	39.3%	39.2%	39.1%	39.1%	39.1%	39.1%	39.1%
Net Income	443	305	261	242	200	170	228	201	155	152
S&P Core Earnings	443	305	261	242	190	160	218	193	149	143

Balance Sheet & Other Financial Data (Million $)										
Cash	770	322	264	367	192	115	202	151	40.4	37.2
Current Assets	1,745	1,314	1,398	1,515	1,229	1,123	1,121	922	715	631
Total Assets	2,769	2,356	2,371	2,359	1,939	1,736	1,657	1,361	1,083	975
Current Liabilities	1,191	955	1,011	1,083	879	712	712	627	490	434
Long Term Debt	150	150	150	150	Nil	50.0	50.0	25.0	Nil	30.0
Common Equity	1,157	996	971	910	836	766	755	643	544	468
Total Capital	1,307	1,244	1,200	1,146	937	908	885	668	544	498
Capital Expenditures	158	224	236	137	176	150	147	133	86.0	82.1
Cash Flow	602	447	382	350	310	264	305	267	205	196
Current Ratio	1.5	1.4	1.4	1.4	1.4	1.6	1.6	1.5	1.5	1.5
% Long Term Debt of Capitalization	11.5	12.1	12.5	13.1	Nil	5.5	5.6	3.7	Nil	6.0
% Net Income of Revenue	6.2	4.7	4.4	4.3	4.0	4.0	5.8	5.7	5.2	5.6
% Return on Assets	17.3	12.9	11.0	11.2	10.8	9.9	15.0	16.5	15.1	15.8
% Return on Equity	41.1	31.1	27.8	27.7	24.9	22.4	32.6	33.9	30.6	32.3

Data as orig reptd.; bef. results of disc opers/spec. items. Per share data adj. for stk. divs.; EPS diluted. E-Estimated. NA-Not Available. NM-Not Meaningful. NR-Not Ranked. UR-Under Review.

Office: 4440 Rosewood Dr, Pleasanton, CA 94588-3050.
Telephone: 925-965-4400.
Email: investor.relations@ros.com
Website: http://www.rossstores.com

Chrmn: N.A. Ferber
Vice Chrmn & CEO: M. Balmuth
COO & Co-Pres: M.B. O'Sullivan
SVP, CFO & Chief Acctg Officer: J.G. Call

SVP, Secy & General Counsel: M. LeHocky
Investor Contact: B. Chaville (925-965-4289)
Board Members: M. Balmuth, K. Bjorklund, M. J. Bush, N. A. Ferber, S. D. Garrett, G. Orban, G. L. Quesnel, D. H. Seiler

Founded: 1957
Domicile: Delaware
Employees: 45,600

Rowan Companies Inc.

STANDARD & POOR'S

S&P Recommendation HOLD ★★★☆☆

Price $32.24 (as of Oct 22, 2010)

12-Mo. Target Price $30.00

Investment Style Large-Cap Value

GICS Sector Energy
Sub-Industry Oil & Gas Drilling

Summary This company performs contract oil and natural gas drilling, and builds heavy equipment and offshore drilling rigs.

Key Stock Statistics (Source S&P, Vickers, company reports)

52-Wk Range	$33.49–20.44	S&P Oper. EPS 2010E	2.48	Market Capitalization(B)	$3.696	Beta	1.60
Trailing 12-Month EPS	$2.58	S&P Oper. EPS 2011E	2.15	Yield (%)	Nil	S&P 3-Yr. Proj. EPS CAGR(%)	-17
Trailing 12-Month P/E	12.5	P/E on S&P Oper. EPS 2010E	13.0	Dividend Rate/Share	Nil	S&P Credit Rating	BBB-
$10K Invested 5 Yrs Ago	$11,144	Common Shares Outstg. (M)	114.6	Institutional Ownership (%)	90		

Price Performance

30-Week Mov. Avg. · · · 10-Week Mov. Avg. - - GAAP Earnings vs. Previous Year Volume Above Avg. STARS
12-Mo. Target Price — Relative Strength — ▲ Up ▼ Down ▶ No Change Below Avg.

Options: ASE, CBOE, P

Analysis prepared by **Stewart Glickman, CFA** on October 01, 2010, when the stock traded at **$ 30.36**.

Highlights

► The recent acquisition of three rigs under construction, previously owned by privately held Norwegian player Skeie Drilling, raises RDC's newbuild slate to seven units, from four units previously. While only two of the seven units have obtained contract commitments, we believe that because the remaining five units are all high-specification jackups (a jackup niche which enjoys utilization in excess of 90%, globally, versus standard jackups in the 70% range), RDC should obtain contracts in short order. The first uncontracted unit is due for delivery in October 2010, three more in 2011, and one in 2012.

► As of August 2010, RDC had nine jackups in the U.S. Gulf of Mexico, which has experienced some delays in the permitting process due to the U.S. drilling moratorium (slated to end on November 30). Despite the pending termination, we expect companies to move units out of the U.S. Gulf to international locations, given uncertainty over post-ban operating costs and regulations.

► We see EPS of $2.48 in 2010, declining to $2.15 in 2011 on weaker dayrates.

Investment Rationale/Risk

► We think RDC's high-spec jackup strategy offers a good value proposition to customers, enhanced by recent deep gas finds in the shallow U.S. Gulf of Mexico. While jackups in general have seen lower utilization in 2010 than in most prior years, this does not apply to high-end jackups, a niche in which RDC is a dominant player. Still, a rising supply of newbuild jackups, with 9 jackups due by the end of the year and 19 more in 2011, will likely be hard to absorb without causing pressure on leading edge dayrates.

► Risks to our recommendation and target price include lower dayrates and utilization; permitting delays in the U.S. Gulf of Mexico; shipyard delays; and risk of contract terminations at LTI.

► Our net asset valuation model, assuming terminal growth of 3% per year and a weighted average cost of capital of 11.1%, indicates that the shares have an intrinsic value of $25. Assuming relative multiples of 7X enterprise value to estimated 2011 EBITDA and 8X projected 2011 cash flow (slight premium to peers, warranted, we think, by lack of deepwater U.S. Gulf exposure) and blending these values with our NAV model, our 12-month target price is $30.

Qualitative Risk Assessment

LOW	MEDIUM	HIGH

Our risk assessment reflects RDC's exposure to volatile crude oil and natural gas prices, capital spending decisions made by its oil and gas producing customers, and risks associated with operating in frontier regions. Offsetting these risks is the company's relatively higher specification jackup rig fleet than peers.

Quantitative Evaluations

S&P Quality Ranking B

D	C	B-	B	B+	A-	A	A+

Relative Strength Rank STRONG

82

LOWEST = 1 HIGHEST = 99

Revenue/Earnings Data

Revenue (Million $)

	1Q	2Q	3Q	4Q	Year
2010	432.4	490.1	--	--	--
2009	494.8	482.2	393.4	399.8	1,770
2008	485.5	587.1	527.1	613.0	2,213
2007	465.3	507.0	502.2	623.6	2,095
2006	299.8	382.9	417.1	411.0	1,511
2005	222.4	244.6	284.4	317.4	1,069

Earnings Per Share ($)

	1Q	2Q	3Q	4Q	Year
2010	0.56	0.79	E0.53	E0.38	E2.48
2009	1.16	0.85	0.69	0.53	3.24
2008	0.88	1.06	1.00	0.81	3.77
2007	0.77	1.14	1.16	1.23	4.31
2006	0.53	0.98	0.77	0.56	2.84
2005	0.28	0.39	0.67	0.63	1.97

Fiscal year ended Dec. 31. Next earnings report expected: Early November. EPS Estimates based on S&P Operating Earnings; historical GAAP earnings are as reported.

Dividend Data

Quarterly dividends were eliminated in January 2009.

Business Summary October 01, 2010

CORPORATE OVERVIEW. Rowan Companies is a major provider of international and domestic contract drilling services, and also has manufacturing operations. As of February 2010, RDC operated 23 jackup rigs (comprised of 20 cantilever jackups and three conventional jackups), and a fleet of 29 land rigs. Of the 23 active jackups in the fleet, eight were in the Gulf of Mexico (GOM), nine were in the Middle East, two were in the North Sea, and one apiece were in West Africa, Egypt, Eastern Canada, and Mexico. RDC's jackup rigs perform both exploratory and development drilling and, in certain areas, well workover operations. Its larger jackups can drill to depths of 20,000 ft. to 30,000 ft. in maximum water depths of 250 ft. to 490 ft.

RDC conducts business via two main operations. In 2009, Drilling Services operations, which includes the offshore rigs and land rigs, contributed $1.21 billion in revenues (down 16% from 2008), and accounted for 69% of RDC's total 2009 revenues (60% offshore, 9% land). Manufacturing operations contributed $555 million in net revenues in 2009 (down 27% from 2008), accounting for the remaining 31% of total revenues. Manufacturing operations are further subdivided into two business segments. The Drilling Products and Services segment (DPS) provides equipment, parts and services for the drilling industry including jack-up rigs, rig kits and component packages. DPS generated $369 million in revenues to external customers in 2009 (after eliminations), down 25% from 2008. The Mining, Forestry and Steel Products segment (MFS),

which produces large-wheeled mining and timber equipment and related parts and carbon and alloy steel, generated $268 million in revenues to external customers in 2009, down 31% from 2008.

IMPACT OF MAJOR DEVELOPMENTS. In July 2010, RDC acquired a 48.8% stake in privately held Skeie Drilling (which was managing the construction of three high-specification N-class jackup rigs), adding to its prior 1.5% stake, by issuing 0.00574 shares of RDC stock in exchange for each Skeie share. RDC also said that upon completion, it would tender for all remaining Skeie shares. Factoring in Skeie debt and expected remaining newbuild construction costs on the rigs, we estimate that the deal implies total consideration of $1.2 billion for the three rigs, and raises RDC's share count by approximately 11%. In March 2008, the company said it would explore strategic alternatives for its LTI business, including a potential spin-off to RDC shareholders. In November 2008, however, RDC said that due to financial market and industry conditions, it would not pursue further negotiations toward sale of LTI, although it will continue to review all strategic options.

Company Financials Fiscal Year Ended Dec. 31

Per Share Data ($)	2009	2008	2007	2006	2005	2004	2003	2002	2001	2000
Tangible Book Value	27.32	23.52	20.99	16.97	14.75	12.97	11.95	12.09	11.84	11.17
Cash Flow	4.74	5.02	5.37	3.64	2.71	1.14	0.84	1.72	1.52	1.36
Earnings	3.24	3.77	4.31	2.84	1.97	0.25	-0.08	0.90	0.80	0.74
S&P Core Earnings	3.30	3.22	4.10	2.76	1.63	0.28	-0.05	-0.31	0.65	NA
Dividends	Nil	0.40	0.40	0.30	Nil	Nil	Nil	Nil	Nil	Nil
Payout Ratio	Nil	11%	9%	11%	Nil	Nil	Nil	Nil	Nil	Nil
Prices:High	27.54	47.94	46.16	48.15	39.50	27.26	26.72	27.03	33.89	34.25
Prices:Low	10.28	12.00	29.48	29.03	24.53	20.44	17.70	16.04	11.10	19.06
P/E Ratio:High	8	13	11	17	20	NM	NM	30	42	46
P/E Ratio:Low	3	3	7	10	12	NM	NM	18	14	26

Income Statement Analysis (Million $)										
Revenue	1,770	2,213	2,095	1,511	1,069	709	679	617	731	646
Operating Income	NA	843	812	555	355	152	89.0	65.1	193	170
Depreciation, Depletion and Amortization	171	141	119	90.0	81.3	95.7	86.9	78.1	68.5	58.9
Interest Expense	8.03	4.00	25.9	20.6	22.0	18.7	15.9	15.9	13.1	12.1
Pretax Income	501	654	739	493	345	42.8	-12.0	133	120	111
Effective Tax Rate	26.7%	34.6%	34.5%	35.8%	36.9%	38.4%	NM	35.0%	35.9%	36.7%
Net Income	368	428	484	317	218	26.4	-7.77	86.3	77.0	70.2
S&P Core Earnings	375	366	460	308	181	28.9	-4.74	-30.2	62.8	NA

Balance Sheet & Other Financial Data (Million $)										
Cash	640	222	284	258	676	466	58.2	179	237	193
Current Assets	1,550	1,369	1,303	1,103	1,208	815	444	470	507	483
Total Assets	5,211	4,549	3,875	3,435	2,975	2,492	2,191	2,055	1,939	1,678
Current Liabilities	568	745	496	517	341	235	150	116	201	104
Long Term Debt	788	356	420	485	550	574	569	513	438	372
Common Equity	3,110	2,660	2,348	1,874	1,620	1,409	1,137	1,132	1,108	1,053
Total Capital	3,963	3,442	3,182	2,707	2,485	2,147	1,924	1,811	1,674	1,516
Capital Expenditures	566	829	463	479	200	137	250	243	305	216
Cash Flow	539	569	603	407	299	122	79.1	164	145	129
Current Ratio	2.7	1.8	2.6	2.1	3.5	3.5	3.0	4.1	2.5	4.6
% Long Term Debt of Capitalization	19.9	10.3	13.2	17.9	22.1	26.8	29.6	28.3	26.2	24.5
% Return on Assets	7.5	10.2	13.2	9.9	8.0	1.1	NM	4.3	4.3	4.6
% Return on Equity	12.7	17.1	22.9	18.1	14.4	2.1	NM	7.7	7.1	7.9

Data as orig reptd.; bef. results of disc opers/spec. items. Per share data adj. for stk. divs.; EPS diluted. E-Estimated. NA-Not Available. NM-Not Meaningful. NR-Not Ranked. UR-Under Review.

Office: 2800 Post Oak Blvd Ste 5450, Houston, TX 77056-6189.
Telephone: 713-621-7800.
Email: ir@rowancompanies.com
Website: http://www.rowancompanies.com

Chrmn: H.E. Lentz, Jr.
Pres & CEO: W.M. Ralls
SVP, CFO & Treas: W.H. Wells
Chief Acctg Officer & Cntlr: G.M. Hatfield

Secy: M.M. Trent
Investor Contact: S.M. McLeod (713-960-7517)
Board Members: R. G. Croyle, W. T. Fox, III, G. Hearne, T. R. Hix, R. E. Kramek, F. R. Lausen, H. E. Lentz, Jr., C. B. Moynihan, P. D. Peacock, J. J. Quicke, W. M. Ralls

Founded: 1923
Domicile: Delaware
Employees: 4,846

Ryder System Inc

STANDARD &POOR'S

S&P Recommendation	**BUY** ★★★★☆	Price $44.87 (as of Oct 22, 2010)	12-Mo. Target Price $54.00	Investment Style Large-Cap Value

GICS Sector Industrials
Sub-Industry Trucking

Summary This company provides truck leasing and rental, logistics and supply chain management solutions.

Key Stock Statistics (Source S&P, Vickers, company reports)

52-Wk Range	$48.49– 31.86	S&P Oper. EPS 2010**E**	2.20	Market Capitalization(B)	$2.352	Beta	1.40
Trailing 12-Month EPS	$1.37	S&P Oper. EPS 2011**E**	2.65	Yield (%)	2.41	S&P 3-Yr. Proj. EPS CAGR(%)	14
Trailing 12-Month P/E	32.8	P/E on S&P Oper. EPS 2010**E**	20.4	Dividend Rate/Share	$1.08	S&P Credit Rating	BBB+
$10K Invested 5 Yrs Ago	$14,996	Common Shares Outstg. (M)	52.4	Institutional Ownership (%)	99		

Price Performance

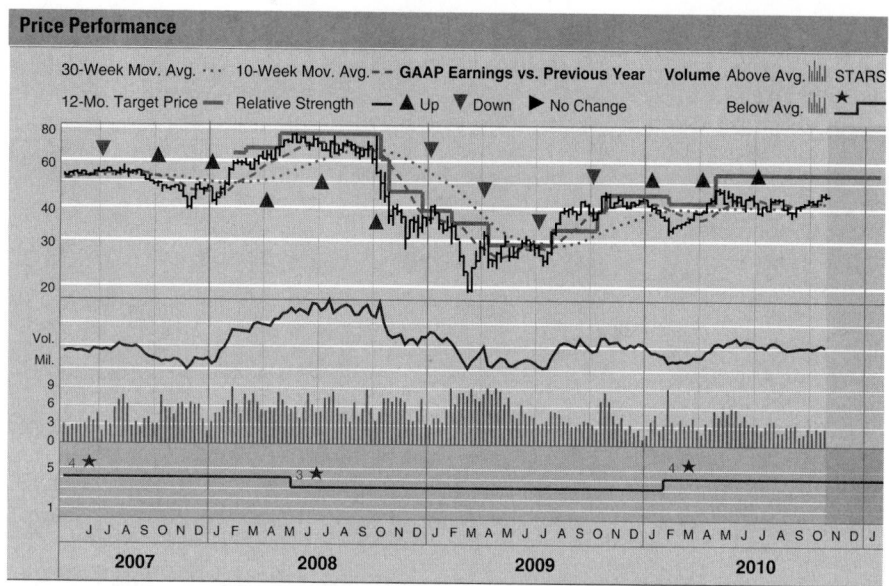

30-Week Mov. Avg. · · · · 10-Week Mov. Avg. – – – **GAAP Earnings vs. Previous Year** Volume Above Avg. STARS
12-Mo. Target Price — Relative Strength — ▲ Up ▼ Down ▶ No Change Below Avg. ★

Options: ASE, CBOE, P

Analysis prepared by **Kevin Kirkeby** on August 09, 2010, when the stock traded at **$ 44.04**.

Highlights

▸ We forecast operating revenue, excluding fuel and subcontracted transportation, in 2010 to be unchanged from 2009 as R's customers reach fleet size targets, having reduced the capacity stipulated in their contracts. Still, we expect the economy to improve over the remainder of 2010 and 2011, and believe this is already starting to be reflected in R's commercial rental unit and will broaden to its contract-based leasing and dedicated segments. Based on this outlook, we anticipate a 5% increase in operating revenues in 2011.

▸ We see margins widening in 2010 due to cost cuts and a stabilization in customer shipping schedules, allowing for more effective fleet positioning. Since prices for used equipment appear to have bottomed, we anticipate that depreciation expense will decrease in 2010, reflecting fewer revaluations to truck values. We expect variable compensation to rise as business recovers, but pension expenses will likely be lower than in 2009. These same factors will contribute to a further widening in margins during 2011, in our view.

▸ After incorporating a higher effective tax rate, our EPS forecast for 2010 is $2.08.

Investment Rationale/Risk

▸ Economic weakness has weighed upon R's leasing operations, which are contract-based and generally slower to respond to changes in the economy. However, with manufacturing plants increasing production, we see R's rental operations as a key near-term capacity supplier to companies still reluctant to commit to new trucks. We also believe the economy is improving and that R's other segments will begin to show sequential gains this year. On this, we think valuations above the 10-year average are justified.

▸ Risks to our recommendation and target price include renewed weakness in the economy and a slowing in rental activity; large increases in capacity across the truckload industry; and higher interest rates, to which R is exposed in light of its financial leverage.

▸ Our DCF model assumes an 11.8% cost of equity and terminal growth of 3.5%, and calculates intrinsic value approaching $52. Using a 0.85X multiple, which is above the historical average but not top quartile, in our price-to-invested capital model yields a $56 value. Blending these two metrics, we arrive at our 12-month target price of $54.

Qualitative Risk Assessment

LOW	**MEDIUM**	HIGH

Our risk assessment reflects our view of the company's financial leverage, exposure to low-margin businesses, and heavy capital spending needs to maintain its rental fleet, offset by its strong market position in truck leasing and what we see as steady cash flow generated by multi-year lease contracts.

Quantitative Evaluations

S&P Quality Ranking   B+

D	C	B-	B	**B+**	A-	A	A+

Relative Strength Rank   MODERATE

61

LOWEST = 1   HIGHEST = 99

Revenue/Earnings Data

Revenue (Million $)

	1Q	2Q	3Q	4Q	Year
2010	1,220	1,286	--	--	--
2009	1,174	1,212	1,254	1,247	4,887
2008	1,544	1,660	1,626	1,374	6,204
2007	1,594	1,658	1,648	1,666	6,566
2006	1,496	1,596	1,621	1,594	6,307
2005	1,316	1,390	1,491	1,545	5,741

Earnings Per Share ($)

	1Q	2Q	3Q	4Q	Year
2010	0.24	0.58	E0.65	E0.60	E2.20
2009	0.20	0.48	0.51	0.43	1.62
2008	0.96	1.10	1.25	0.19	3.52
2007	0.84	1.07	1.11	1.24	4.24
2006	0.77	1.13	1.06	1.08	4.04
2005	0.64	0.98	0.98	0.93	3.53

Fiscal year ended Dec. 31. Next earnings report expected: Late October. EPS Estimates based on S&P Operating Earnings; historical GAAP earnings are as reported.

Dividend Data (Dates: mm/dd Payment Date: mm/dd/yy)

Amount ($)	Date Decl.	Ex-Div. Date	Stk. of Record	Payment Date
0.250	02/10	02/19	02/23	03/19/10
0.250	05/14	05/21	05/25	06/15/10
0.270	07/16	08/19	08/23	09/17/10
0.270	10/20	11/18	11/22	12/17/10

Dividends have been paid since 1976. Source: Company reports.

Please read the Required Disclosures and Analyst Certification on the last page of this report.

The **McGraw·Hill** Companies

Ryder System Inc

STANDARD &POOR'S

Business Summary August 09, 2010

CORPORATE OVERVIEW. Ryder System is primarily a provider of transportation services and equipment to third parties. In 2009, the company generated over 93% of revenues in the United States and Canada, with the remainder spread across Europe, Asia and Mexico. The company serves a broad array of industries, with clients in the automotive, electronics, paper and paper products, food and beverage and retailing industries, among others. For reporting purposes, operations are divided into three segments: Fleet Management Solutions (FMS), Supply Chain Solutions (SCS), and Dedicated Contract Carriage (DCC).

FMS (68% of revenues and 68% of operating profits before eliminations and unallocated costs in 2009) provides full-service truck leasing to customers worldwide. Under a typical full-service lease, R provides customers with vehicles, maintenance, supplies and related equipment necessary for operation, while customers furnish and supervise their own drivers, as well as dispatch and exercise control over the vehicles. R leased approximately 115,100 vehicles under full-service leases at December 31, 2009. FMS also provides short-term truck rental to commercial customers that need to supplement their fleets during peak periods. About 12% of FMS revenue in 2009 was generated through commercial rentals. At December 31, 2009, the commercial rental fleet had about 27,400 units, down from about 38,400 at the end of 2005, re-

flecting the company's shift toward more longer-term, contractual portions of its business rather than the more cyclical rental market.

SCS (23%, 13%) provides logistics support and transportation along the entire supply chain for its customers. This includes managing inbound raw materials all the way through to distribution of finished goods. Services include combinations of logistics systems and information technology design, the provision of vehicles and equipment (including maintenance and drivers), warehouse and transportation management, vehicle dispatch, and just-in-time delivery. The company said that its business with auto manufacturers, as well as parts suppliers, represented about 42% of SCS revenue in 2009. We believe General Motors is one of the unit's largest customers, at 13% of SCS revenues (and 3% of total company-wide revenues). R supports 9 General Motors plants, three less than in 2008 due to facility closures as part of that company's reorganization plan. There are about $20 million included in revenues that originated from R's serving those three facilities during 2009 prior to their closure.

Company Financials Fiscal Year Ended Dec. 31

Per Share Data ($)	2009	2008	2007	2006	2005	2004	2003	2002	2001	2000
Tangible Book Value	21.93	19.95	29.32	25.48	21.81	20.65	18.09	14.97	17.51	17.43
Cash Flow	16.62	18.38	17.89	10.57	15.65	14.03	11.90	10.65	9.30	11.20
Earnings	1.62	3.52	4.24	4.04	3.53	3.28	2.12	1.80	0.31	1.49
S&P Core Earnings	1.93	1.93	3.43	3.72	3.09	2.80	2.26	0.84	-0.76	NA
Dividends	0.96	0.92	0.84	0.72	0.64	0.60	0.60	0.60	0.60	0.60
Payout Ratio	59%	26%	20%	18%	18%	18%	28%	33%	194%	40%
Prices:High	46.58	76.64	57.70	59.93	47.82	55.55	34.65	31.09	23.19	25.13
Prices:Low	19.00	27.71	38.95	39.61	32.00	33.61	20.00	21.05	16.06	14.81
P/E Ratio:High	29	22	14	15	14	17	16	17	75	17
P/E Ratio:Low	12	8	9	10	9	10	9	12	52	10

Income Statement Analysis (Million $)										
Revenue	4,887	6,204	6,566	6,307	5,741	5,150	4,802	4,776	5,006	5,337
Operating Income	1,111	1,384	1,336	1,218	1,165	1,076	905	854	798	906
Depreciation	826	844	817	743	740	706	625	552	545	580
Interest Expense	144	157	160	141	120	100	96.2	91.7	119	154
Pretax Income	144	350	405	786	357	331	212	176	30.7	141
Effective Tax Rate	37.3%	42.9%	37.4%	18.3%	36.3%	34.9%	36.2%	36.0%	39.2%	37.0%
Net Income	90.2	200	254	642	228	216	136	113	18.7	89.0
S&P Core Earnings	107	110	206	229	200	184	145	53.1	-46.3	NA

Balance Sheet & Other Financial Data (Million $)										
Cash	98.5	120	200	129	129	101	141	104	118	122
Current Assets	880	951	1,222	1,262	1,164	1,228	1,107	1,024	982	928
Total Assets	6,260	6,690	6,855	6,829	6,033	5,638	5,279	4,767	4,924	5,475
Current Liabilities	850	1,111	1,019	1,268	1,253	1,455	1,074	862	1,014	1,302
Long Term Debt	2,265	2,479	2,553	2,484	1,916	1,394	1,449	1,389	1,392	1,604
Common Equity	1,427	1,345	1,888	1,721	1,527	1,510	1,344	1,108	1,231	1,253
Total Capital	3,692	4,741	5,425	5,112	4,293	3,775	3,688	3,431	3,625	3,874
Capital Expenditures	652	1,234	1,317	1,695	1,399	1,092	725	600	657	1,289
Cash Flow	916	1,044	1,071	642	968	922	760	665	564	669
Current Ratio	1.0	0.9	1.2	1.0	0.9	0.8	1.0	1.2	1.0	0.7
% Long Term Debt of Capitalization	61.4	52.3	47.1	48.6	44.6	36.9	39.3	40.5	38.4	41.4
% Net Income of Revenue	1.9	3.2	3.9	10.2	4.0	4.2	2.8	2.4	0.4	1.7
% Return on Assets	1.4	3.0	3.7	10.0	3.9	3.9	2.7	2.3	0.4	1.6
% Return on Equity	6.5	12.4	14.1	39.5	15.0	15.1	11.1	9.6	1.5	7.2

Data as orig reptd.; bef. results of disc opers/spec. items. Per share data adj. for stk. divs.; EPS diluted. E-Estimated. NA-Not Available. NM-Not Meaningful. NR-Not Ranked. UR-Under Review.

Office: 11690 NW 105th Street, Miami, FL 33178.
Telephone: 305-500-3726.
Email: ryderforinvestor@ryder.com
Website: http://www.ryder.com

Chrmn & CEO: G.T. Swienton
Pres: R.M. Schneider
EVP & CFO: A.A. Garcia
EVP & Chief Admin Officer: G.F. Greene

EVP, Secy & General Counsel: R.D. Fatovic
Investor Contact: B. Brunn (305-500-4053)
Board Members: J. S. Beard, J. M. Berra, D. I. Fuente, L. P. Hassey, L. M. Martin, L. P. Nieto, Jr., E. A. Renna, A. J. Smith, E. F. Smith, G. T. Swienton, H. E. Tookes, II

Founded: 1933
Domicile: Florida
Employees: 22,900

Safeway Inc

STANDARD &POOR'S

S&P Recommendation	HOLD ★★★☆☆	Price $22.29 (as of Oct 22, 2010)	12-Mo. Target Price $23.00	Investment Style Large-Cap Blend

GICS Sector Consumer Staples
Sub-Industry Food Retail

Summary This major food retailer operates about 1,725 stores in the U.S. and Canada.

Key Stock Statistics (Source S&P, Vickers, company reports)

52-Wk Range	$27.04– 18.73	S&P Oper. EPS 2010E	1.54	Market Capitalization(B)	$8.310	Beta	0.72
Trailing 12-Month EPS	$-3.25	S&P Oper. EPS 2011E	1.75	Yield (%)	2.15	S&P 3-Yr. Proj. EPS CAGR(%)	14
Trailing 12-Month P/E	NM	P/E on S&P Oper. EPS 2010E	14.5	Dividend Rate/Share	$0.48	S&P Credit Rating	BBB
$10K Invested 5 Yrs Ago	$10,383	Common Shares Outstg. (M)	372.8	Institutional Ownership (%)	95		

Price Performance

30-Week Mov. Avg. · · · 10-Week Mov. Avg. – – GAAP Earnings vs. Previous Year Volume Above Avg. STARS
12-Mo. Target Price — Relative Strength — ▲ Up ▼ Down ▶ No Change Below Avg. ★

Options: ASE, CBOE, P

Qualitative Risk Assessment

LOW	MEDIUM	HIGH

Our risk assessment reflects our view of an improved shopping experience associated with new Lifestyle store remodelings. This is offset by a continued intense competitive environment as high unemployment rates and reduced consumer spending results in increased pricing pressure and trading down by consumers.

Quantitative Evaluations

S&P Quality Ranking — B-

D	C	B-	B	B+	A-	A	A+

Relative Strength Rank — MODERATE

LOWEST = 1 — 69 — HIGHEST = 99

Highlights

▶ The 12-month target price for SWY has recently been changed to $23.00 from $20.00. The Highlights section of this Stock Report will be updated accordingly.

Investment Rationale/Risk

▶ The Investment Rationale/Risk section of this Stock Report will be updated shortly. For the latest News story on SWY from MarketScope, see below.

▶ 10/14/10 12:10 pm ET ... S&P REITERATES HOLD RECOMMENDATION ON SHARES OF SAFEWAY INC (SWY 21.68***): Q3 EPS of $0.33, vs. $0.31, is $0.01 below our estimate. Results benefitted from lower interest expense and an 8.5% reduction in shares, despite a 2.0% decline in identical store sales (vs. our -0.5% estimate) and narrower margins due to price reduction efforts. Although we see decreased deflationary food pressures in 2011, we believe sales growth will continue to be restricted by weak consumer demand. As a result, we are reducing our 2011 EPS estimate $0.10 to $1.75. However, due to our updated comparative and P/E analyses, we are raising our target price by $3 to $23. /J.Agnese

Revenue/Earnings Data

Revenue (Million $)

	1Q	2Q	3Q	4Q	Year
2010	9,327	9,520	9,400	--	--
2009	9,236	9,462	9,458	12,694	40,851
2008	9,999	10,120	10,169	13,816	44,104
2007	9,322	9,823	9,785	13,356	42,286
2006	8,895	9,367	9,420	12,504	40,185
2005	8,621	8,803	8,946	12,046	38,416

Earnings Per Share ($)

2010	0.25	0.37	0.33	E0.61	E1.54
2009	0.34	0.57	0.31	-4.06	-2.66
2008	0.44	0.53	0.46	0.79	2.21
2007	0.39	0.49	0.44	0.68	1.99
2006	0.32	0.55	0.39	0.69	1.94
2005	0.29	0.30	0.27	0.39	1.25

Fiscal year ended Dec. 31. Next earnings report expected: Late February. EPS Estimates based on S&P Operating Earnings; historical GAAP earnings are as reported.

Dividend Data (Dates: mm/dd Payment Date: mm/dd/yy)

Amount ($)	Date Decl.	Ex-Div. Date	Stk. of Record	Payment Date
0.100	12/11	12/22	12/24	01/14/10
0.100	03/11	03/23	03/25	04/15/10
0.120	05/19	06/22	06/24	07/15/10
0.120	08/25	09/21	09/23	10/14/10

Dividends have been paid since 2005. Source: Company reports.

Please read the Required Disclosures and Analyst Certification on the last page of this report.

The **McGraw·Hill** Companies

Safeway Inc

STANDARD &POOR'S

Business Summary July 23, 2010

CORPORATE OVERVIEW. Safeway is one of the largest U.S. food and drug retailers, operating about 1,725 stores principally in California, Oregon, Washington, Alaska, Colorado, Arizona, Texas, the Chicago metropolitan area, and the Mid-Atlantic region in the U.S., and in British Columbia, Alberta and Manitoba/Saskatchewan in Canada. To support its store network, SWY has a network of distribution, manufacturing and food processing facilities. The company seeks to provide value to customers by maintaining high store standards while differentiating its offerings with a wide selection of high-quality produce and meat at competitive prices. The company also provides third-party gift cards, prepaid cards and sports and entertainment cards to retailers for sales to customers in North America and the U.K. through its Blackhawk subsidiary.

MARKET PROFILE. The U.S. grocery industry was a $995 billion business in 2008, according to Progressive Grocer. Supermarkets generated $547 billion, or 55% of total grocery industry sales, followed by convenience stores ($320 billion, 32%) and warehouse clubs ($107 billion, 11%). When supermarkets are

broken down by format, conventional supermarkets have the largest market share, holding 76% of the supermarket category, with $361 billion in sales. However, the natural/gourmet foods format is the fastest-growing category, holding a 6.1% market share in 2008 ($19.8 billion in sales).

With $40.2 billion in sales excluding fuel ($3.9 billion) in 2008, Safeway held about a 7.3% market share within the supermarket category and 4.0% of total grocery sales. The average size of Safeway's stores (about 46,000 square feet) exceeded the industry average (33,300 square feet). Additionally, the company's sales per square foot ($500 per square foot) is higher than the supermarket average of $465 per square foot in 2008.

Company Financials Fiscal Year Ended Dec. 31

Per Share Data ($)	2009	2008	2007	2006	2005	2004	2003	2002	2001	2000
Tangible Book Value	11.64	10.25	9.76	7.44	5.60	4.24	2.79	1.77	1.67	1.35
Cash Flow	0.18	4.83	4.40	4.16	3.32	3.24	1.57	2.91	4.29	3.77
Earnings	-2.66	2.21	1.99	1.94	1.25	1.25	-0.38	1.20	2.44	2.13
S&P Core Earnings	1.88	2.03	1.87	1.91	1.26	1.15	1.21	2.42	2.19	NA
Dividends	0.38	0.32	0.26	0.22	0.15	Nil	Nil	Nil	Nil	Nil
Payout Ratio	NM	14%	13%	11%	12%	Nil	Nil	Nil	Nil	Nil
Prices:High	24.25	34.87	38.31	35.61	26.46	25.64	25.83	46.90	61.38	62.69
Prices:Low	17.19	17.19	30.10	22.23	17.85	17.26	16.20	18.45	37.44	30.75
P/E Ratio:High	NM	16	19	18	21	21	NM	39	25	29
P/E Ratio:Low	NM	8	15	11	14	14	NM	15	15	14

Income Statement Analysis (Million $)										
Revenue	40,851	44,104	42,286	40,185	38,416	35,823	35,553	32,399	34,301	31,977
Operating Income	2,604	2,994	2,816	2,591	2,147	2,067	2,167	3,190	3,535	3,119
Depreciation	1,171	1,141	1,071	991	933	895	864	812	946	838
Interest Expense	332	371	405	396	403	411	442	369	447	457
Pretax Income	-953	1,505	1,404	1,240	849	794	141	1,320	2,095	1,867
Effective Tax Rate	NM	35.8%	36.7%	29.8%	33.9%	29.4%	NM	56.9%	40.1%	41.5%
Net Income	-1,098	965	888	871	561	560	-170	568	1,254	1,092
S&P Core Earnings	780	888	835	859	566	517	538	1,140	1,122	NA

Balance Sheet & Other Financial Data (Million $)										
Cash	472	383	278	217	373	267	175	73.7	68.5	91.7
Current Assets	3,825	3,976	4,008	3,566	3,702	3,598	3,508	4,259	3,312	3,224
Total Assets	14,964	17,485	17,651	16,274	15,757	15,377	15,097	16,047	17,463	15,965
Current Liabilities	4,238	4,499	5,136	4,601	4,264	3,792	3,464	3,936	3,883	3,780
Long Term Debt	3,874	4,184	4,658	5,037	5,605	6,124	7,072	7,522	6,712	5,822
Common Equity	4,946	6,786	6,702	5,667	4,920	4,307	3,644	3,628	5,890	5,390
Total Capital	9,330	11,729	11,614	10,821	10,748	10,894	11,139	11,727	13,100	11,721
Capital Expenditures	852	1,596	1,769	1,674	1,384	1,213	936	1,371	1,793	1,573
Cash Flow	73.7	2,106	1,960	1,862	1,494	1,455	694	1,381	2,200	1,930
Current Ratio	0.9	0.9	0.8	0.8	0.9	0.9	1.0	1.1	0.9	0.9
% Long Term Debt of Capitalization	41.5	35.7	40.1	46.5	52.2	56.2	63.5	64.1	51.2	49.7
% Net Income of Revenue	NM	2.2	2.1	2.2	1.5	1.6	NM	1.8	3.7	3.4
% Return on Assets	NM	5.5	5.2	5.4	3.6	3.7	NM	3.4	7.5	7.1
% Return on Equity	NM	14.3	14.4	16.4	12.2	14.1	NM	11.9	22.2	23.0

Data as orig reptd.; bef. results of disc opers/spec. items. Per share data adj. for stk. divs.; EPS diluted. E-Estimated. NA-Not Available. NM-Not Meaningful. NR-Not Ranked. UR-Under Review.

Office: 5918 Stoneridge Mall Road, Pleasanton, CA 94588-3229.
Telephone: 925-467-3000.
Website: http://www.safeway.com
Chrmn, Pres & CEO: S.A. Burd

EVP & CFO: R.L. Edwards
EVP & Chief Admin Officer: L.M. Renda
SVP & Chief Acctg Officer: D.F. Bond
SVP, Secy & General Counsel: R.A. Gordon

Investor Contact: M.C. Plaisance (925-467-3136)
Board Members: S. A. Burd, J. Grove, M. S. Gyani, P. M. Hazen, F. C. Herringer, K. W. Oder, A. Sarin, M. S. Shannon, W. Y. Tauscher

Founded: 1915
Domicile: Delaware
Employees: 186,000

SAIC Inc

STANDARD &POOR'S

S&P Recommendation	HOLD ★★★☆☆	Price $15.76 (as of Oct 22, 2010)	12-Mo. Target Price $16.00	Investment Style Large-Cap Value

GICS Sector Information Technology
Sub-Industry IT Consulting & Other Services

Summary This company is a provider of scientific, engineering, systems integration and technical services and solutions primarily to the U.S. government.

Key Stock Statistics (Source S&P, Vickers, company reports)

52-Wk Range	$19.76–14.87	S&P Oper. EPS 2011E	1.46	Market Capitalization(B)	$5.858	Beta	0.23
Trailing 12-Month EPS	$1.46	S&P Oper. EPS 2012E	1.51	Yield (%)	Nil	S&P 3-Yr. Proj. EPS CAGR(%)	9
Trailing 12-Month P/E	10.8	P/E on S&P Oper. EPS 2011E	10.8	Dividend Rate/Share	Nil	S&P Credit Rating	NA
$10K Invested 5 Yrs Ago	NA	Common Shares Outstg. (M)	371.7	Institutional Ownership (%)	38		

Price Performance

- 30-Week Mov. Avg. · · · 10-Week Mov. Avg. - - GAAP Earnings vs. Previous Year Volume Above Avg. STARS
- 12-Mo. Target Price — Relative Strength — ▲ Up ▼ Down ▶ No Change Below Avg.

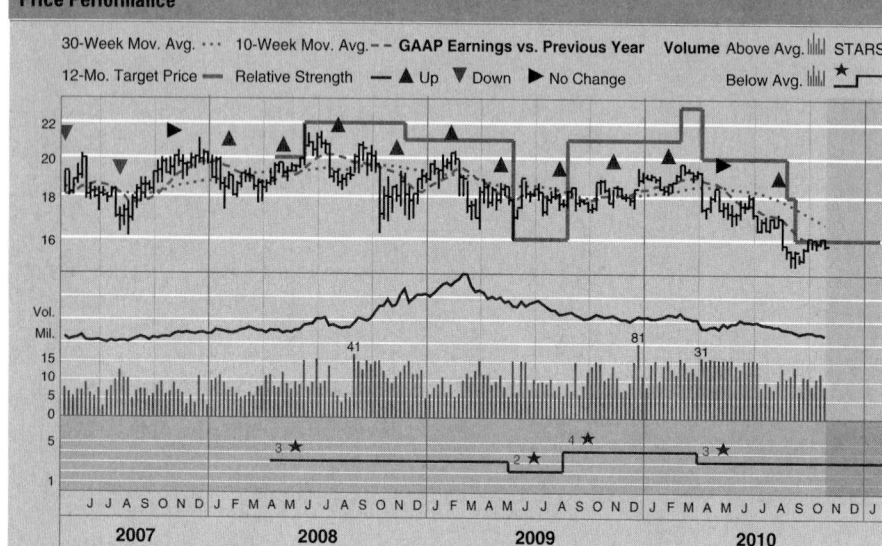

Analysis prepared by **Dylan Cathers** on September 02, 2010, when the stock traded at **$ 15.22**.

Highlights

➤ We look for revenue growth of 4.5% in FY 11 (Jan.). We expect SAI to post healthy gains in the October and January quarters, given our view of easy comparisons and an expected ramp-up of previously signed contracts. In FY 12, we anticipate growth of 6.0%, given a large pipeline of opportunities as well as a strong funded backlog, which was $5.8 billion at the end of July. However, we still believe there are a number of headwinds, most important of which is our expectation of nominal growth for spending by the Federal government in its FY 11 (Sep.) budget for defense and Federal IT. Further, we think the contract award cycle remains extended, a problem that is exacerbated by uncertainty in the contracting process and increased protest activity by competitors.

➤ We see operating margins widening slightly in FY 11. We expect increased levels of research and development, bid and proposal activity, and pricing pressures to be offset by cost reduction initiatives and the receipt of a $56 million royalty payment, which had little expense associated with it.

➤ We estimate EPS of $1.46 in FY 11, aided by share buybacks, and see $1.51 in FY 12.

Investment Rationale/Risk

➤ Although we believe the stock's valuation is reasonable, we have concerns about the next few quarters, given the tightening of expenditures on defense-related items not directly related to the troops on the ground in Afghanistan. Long term, we have some concerns about defense spending levels in general, but we are more positive on the growth prospects related to cybersecurity and intelligence, as well as energy and healthcare IT, areas that SAI is attempting to expand into.

➤ Risks to our recommendation and target price include acquisition integration risk, pricing pressures from the outsourcing arena, changes in government procurement policies, increased contract protest activity by competitors, and a slowdown in defense spending reflecting shifting Administration priorities.

➤ Our 12-month target price of $16 is based on our relative valuation analysis. We use a peer-discount multiple of 10.6X our FY 12 EPS estimate. The peer group includes companies in the IT Consulting & Other Services sub-industry that regularly compete with SAI and have significant exposure to the U.S. Department of Defense.

Qualitative Risk Assessment

LOW	MEDIUM	HIGH

Our risk assessment reflects the long-term nature of SAI's contracts, which typically provide steady cash flow, and its large cash position, offset by intense industry competition and the company's high percentage of revenue from the intelligence community and the Department of Defense.

Quantitative Evaluations

S&P Quality Ranking NR

D	C	B-	B	B+	A-	A	A+

Relative Strength Rank WEAK

26

LOWEST = 1 HIGHEST = 99

Revenue/Earnings Data

Revenue (Million $)

	1Q	2Q	3Q	4Q	Year
2011	2,685	2,794	--	--	--
2010	2,649	2,749	2,765	2,683	10,846
2009	2,369	2,555	2,631	2,518	10,070
2008	2,011	2,222	2,365	2,337	8,935
2007	1,954	2,051	2,142	2,147	8,294
2006	1,846	1,952	2,028	1,966	7,792

Earnings Per Share ($)

2011	0.30	0.42	E0.36	E0.36	E1.46
2010	0.30	0.31	0.34	0.31	1.24
2009	0.25	0.26	0.29	0.30	1.10
2008	0.18	0.24	0.26	0.24	0.93
2007	0.27	0.30	0.26	0.20	1.01
2006	0.15	0.24	0.20	0.38	0.74

Fiscal year ended Jan. 31. Next earnings report expected: Early December. EPS Estimates based on S&P Operating Earnings; historical GAAP earnings are as reported.

Dividend Data

No cash dividends have been paid.

Please read the Required Disclosures and Analyst Certification on the last page of this report.

The **McGraw·Hill** Companies

SAIC Inc

Business Summary September 02, 2010

CORPORATE OVERVIEW. Science Applications International Corporation was formed in 1969. In October 2006, it completed a reorganization merger and became a wholly owned subsidiary of SAIC, Inc., which is a publicly traded company trading under the symbol SAI.

The company provides scientific, engineering, systems integration and technical services and solutions primarily to the U.S. government, with specific emphasis on all branches of the U.S. military, the Department of Defense (DoD), the intelligence community, and the Department of Homeland Security (DoHS). It also provides these services to U.S. government, civil, state and local agencies, as well as to foreign governments and customers in select commercial markets.

SAI has three reportable segments: Government, Commercial, and Corporate and other. Government is the largest, with sales from this segment contributing 96% of the company total in FY 10 (Jan.), up slightly from FY 09. The commercial segment operates mainly in the oil and gas, utilities and life sciences verticals, providing systems integration and advanced technical services, as well as more focused offerings such as IT infrastructure and data lifecycle management.

CORPORATE STRATEGY. Acquisitions are common in the IT services industry and are particularly prevalent among the companies that cater to the DoD and other related military, defense and intelligence communities. Acquisitions are an effective way for companies to increase their breadth of offerings and gain new skills. Equally important, acquisitions have become a method for adding employees, specifically those with high security clearances.

During the past five fiscal years, SAI has made many acquisitions. In FY 08, it acquired The Benham Companies LLC, a consulting, engineering and architectural design company specializing in industrial manufacturing and facilities construction. In FY 09, it acquired Icon Systems, Inc., which designs, develops and produces laser-based systems and products for military testing, and SM Consulting, Inc, which provides various services to the government and private industries. In FY 10, it acquired R.W. Beck Group, Inc. a provider of business, engineering, energy, and infrastructure consulting services.

Company Financials Fiscal Year Ended Jan. 31

Per Share Data ($)	2010	2009	2008	2007	2006	2005	2004	2003	2002	2001
Tangible Book Value	1.94	1.84	4.03	5.17	16.28	NA	NA	NA	NA	NA
Cash Flow	1.52	1.25	1.12	1.21	0.89	0.87	1.14	0.84	0.43	4.42
Earnings	1.24	1.10	0.93	1.01	0.74	0.72	0.93	0.61	0.04	4.05
S&P Core Earnings	1.24	1.10	0.92	0.83	0.72	NA	NA	NA	NA	NA
Dividends	NA	Nil	Nil	Nil	Nil	Nil	NA	NA	NA	NA
Payout Ratio	NA	Nil	Nil	Nil	Nil	Nil	NA	NA	NA	NA
Calendar Year	2009	2008	2007	2006	2005	2004	2003	2002	2001	2000
Prices:High	20.42	21.90	21.13	21.10	NA	NA	NA	NA	NA	NA
Prices:Low	15.94	16.25	16.11	15.00	NA	NA	NA	NA	NA	NA
P/E Ratio:High	16	20	23	21	NA	NA	NA	NA	NA	NA
P/E Ratio:Low	13	15	17	15	NA	NA	NA	NA	NA	NA

Income Statement Analysis (Million $)

	2010	2009	2008	2007	2006	2005	2004	2003	2002	2001
Revenue	10,846	10,070	8,935	8,294	7,792	7,187	5,833	5,903	6,095	5,896
Operating Income	960	835	746	657	567	542	439	619	712	596
Depreciation	93.0	59.0	80.0	72.0	70.0	56.0	37.0	96.3	179	188
Interest Expense	76.0	78.0	90.0	92.0	89.0	88.0	80.0	45.0	18.1	19.6
Pretax Income	799	703	629	615	497	417	374	365	43.9	3,291
Effective Tax Rate	37.4%	36.4%	38.2%	38.0%	28.0%	31.4%	37.4%	30.4%	20.2%	37.1%
Net Income	500	447	386	369	345	272	224	247	18.2	2,059
S&P Core Earnings	485	448	382	370	334	NA	NA	NA	NA	NA

Balance Sheet & Other Financial Data (Million $)

	2010	2009	2008	2007	2006	2005	2004	2003	2002	2001
Cash	861	936	1,096	1,113	3,455	2,350	2,365	2,189	1,189	1,346
Current Assets	3,193	3,217	3,237	2,945	NA	4,986	3,928	3,505	2,586	2,901
Total Assets	5,295	5,048	4,981	4,558	6,419	6,010	5,493	4,804	4,948	6,092
Current Liabilities	1,706	1,683	1,832	1,663	NA	2,299	1,713	1,552	1,711	1,785
Long Term Debt	1,103	1,099	1,098	1,199	1,192	1,215	1,232	897	123	119
Common Equity	2,291	2,084	1,901	1,536	1,221	2,351	2,190	2,007	2,524	3,344
Total Capital	3,397	3,183	2,999	2,791	2,413	3,682	3,510	2,952	2,695	3,501
Capital Expenditures	58.0	59.0	61.0	74.0	54.0	42.0	131	43.4	127	147
Cash Flow	593	506	466	441	415	328	432	343	197	2,247
Current Ratio	1.9	1.9	1.8	1.8	NA	2.2	2.3	2.3	1.5	1.6
% Long Term Debt of Capitalization	32.5	34.5	36.6	43.0	49.4	33.0	35.1	30.4	4.6	3.4
% Net Income of Revenue	4.6	4.4	4.3	4.4	4.4	3.8	5.2	4.2	0.3	34.9
% Return on Assets	9.7	8.9	8.1	7.2	NA	4.7	6.8	5.1	0.3	39.2
% Return on Equity	22.9	22.4	22.5	17.0	NA	12.0	16.7	10.9	0.6	79.6

Data as orig reptd.; bef. results of disc opers/spec. items. Per share data adj. for stk. divs.; EPS diluted. Data for 2006 pro forma as adj.; bal. sheet & book value as of July 31, 2006; per sh. data based on adj. pro forma shs. E-Estimated. NA-Not Available. NM-Not Meaningful. NR-Not Ranked. UR-Under Review.

Office: 1710 SAIC Drive, McLean, VA 22102.
Telephone: 703-676-4300.
Website: http://www.saic.com
Chrmn: A.T. Young

CEO: W.P. Havenstein
COO: L.B. Prior, III
COO: A.J. Moraco
EVP & CFO: M.W. Sopp

Investor Contact: S. Davis (703-676-2283)
Board Members: F. A. Cordova, J. A. Drummond, T. F. Frist, III, J. J. Hamre, W. P. Havenstein, M. E. John, A. K. Jones, J. P. Jumper, H. M. Kraemer, Jr., L. C. Nussdorf, E. J. Sanderson, Jr., L. A. Simpson, A. T. Young

Founded: 1969
Domicile: Delaware
Employees: 46,200

St. Jude Medical Inc.

STANDARD &POOR'S

S&P Recommendation **BUY** ★★★★★	Price $38.83 (as of Oct 22, 2010)	12-Mo. Target Price $44.00	Investment Style Large-Cap Growth

GICS Sector Health Care
Sub-Industry Health Care Equipment

Summary This leading maker of mechanical heart valves also produces pacemakers, defibrillators, and other cardiac devices. In July 2008, it acquired EP Medsystems for $91 million in a deal that expanded its capabilities in the atrial fibrillation market.

Key Stock Statistics (Source S&P, Vickers, company reports)

52-Wk Range	$42.87– 33.92	S&P Oper. EPS 2010**E**	2.99	Market Capitalization(B)	$12.713	Beta		0.57
Trailing 12-Month EPS	$2.55	S&P Oper. EPS 2011**E**	3.20	Yield (%)	Nil	S&P 3-Yr. Proj. EPS CAGR(%)		14
Trailing 12-Month P/E	15.2	P/E on S&P Oper. EPS 2010**E**	13.0	Dividend Rate/Share	Nil	S&P Credit Rating		A
$10K Invested 5 Yrs Ago	$8,088	Common Shares Outstg. (M)	327.4	Institutional Ownership (%)	83			

Price Performance

30-Week Mov. Avg. · · ·   10-Week Mov. Avg. - - **GAAP Earnings vs. Previous Year**   Volume Above Avg. STARS
12-Mo. Target Price —   Relative Strength —   ▲ Up ▼ Down ► No Change   Below Avg.

Options: ASE, CBOE

Qualitative Risk Assessment

LOW	MEDIUM	HIGH

The company operates in a highly competitive industry characterized by relatively short product life cycles and volatile market share fluctuations. However, there are significant barriers to entry in the company's core markets, as products must obtain FDA approval prior to launch, and they require a large investment in research and development and sales effort.

Quantitative Evaluations

S&P Quality Ranking B+

D	C	B-	B	B+	A-	A	A+

Relative Strength Rank MODERATE
47
LOWEST = 1   HIGHEST = 99

Highlights

➤ The 12-month target price for STJ has recently been changed to $44.00 from $43.00. The Highlights section of this Stock Report will be updated accordingly.

Investment Rationale/Risk

➤ The Investment Rationale/Risk section of this Stock Report will be updated shortly. For the latest News story on STJ from MarketScope, see below.

➤ 10/20/10 10:40 am ET ... S&P REITERATES BUY OPINION ON SHARES OF ST. JUDE MEDICAL (STJ 38.5****): Q3 adjusted EPS of $0.72, vs. $0.59, beats our estimate by $0.05. Sales rose 6.9% on implantable cardioverter defibrillator, atrial fibrillation and neuromodulation gains. Gross margins declined on lower pacemaker margins, but the EBIT margin was above our view on well-controlled operating costs. We are positive on STJ's product development, which should improve gross margin trends, and its overseas penetration. We also think it is gaining share in several markets. We raise our '10 adjusted EPS estimate $0.08 to $2.99, '11's by $0.05 to $3.20 and our target price by $1 to $44. /P.Seligman

Revenue/Earnings Data

Revenue (Million $)

	1Q	2Q	3Q	4Q	Year
2010	1,262	1,313	--	--	--
2009	1,134	1,184	1,160	1,203	4,681
2008	1,011	1,136	1,084	1,133	4,363
2007	887.0	947.3	926.8	1,018	3,779
2006	784.4	832.9	821.3	863.8	3,302
2005	663.9	723.7	737.8	789.9	2,915

Earnings Per Share ($)

2010	0.73	0.77	E0.67	E0.73	E2.99
2009	0.58	0.63	0.48	0.57	2.26
2008	0.53	0.58	0.55	-0.56	1.10
2007	0.41	0.39	0.46	0.34	1.59
2006	0.36	0.38	0.32	0.42	1.47
2005	0.32	0.27	0.44	0.01	1.04

Fiscal year ended Dec. 31. Next earnings report expected: NA. EPS Estimates based on S&P Operating Earnings; historical GAAP earnings are as reported.

Dividend Data

No cash dividends have been paid since 1994.

The **McGraw-Hill** Companies

St. Jude Medical Inc.

STANDARD &POOR'S

Business Summary July 28, 2010

CORPORATE OVERVIEW. St. Jude Medical sells medical devices in the cardiac rhythm management (CRM), cardiac surgery, atrial fibrillation, and pain management categories. Although the company has a diversified product line, the principal driver of growth in recent years has been the CRM segment, where it sells pacemakers and defibrillators.

CRM products (59% of 2009 sales) include implantable cardioverter defibrillators (ICDs) that are used to treat hearts that beat too fast (tachycardia) by monitoring the heartbeat and delivering high energy electrical impulses to terminate ventricular tachycardia and ventricular fibrillation. ICD products include the AnalyST Accel (approved in Europe in 2009) and Current Plus and Promote Plus devices (approved in 2009) with features that provide physicians more options for customizing therapy for patients with potentially lethal heart arrhythmias and heart failure. In addition, the company's products include the Current RF (radio frequency) VR/DR (single chamber/dual chamber) ICDs and Promote RF CRT-D. These devices are available in both standard and high energy versions and feature wireless telemetry.

Also within the CRM division, pacemakers and related systems are sold to treat patients with hearts that beat too slowly (bradycardia). STJ's other pacing products include the Zephyr family of pacemakers, Victory product line as well as Team ADx pacemakers, a group comprised of the Identity ADx, Integrity ADx, and Verity ADx families of devices.

The Zephyr family of pacemakers includes automatic features to simplify device follow-up; the Victory line which includes the Victory and Victory XL family models, adding new capabilities, such as automatic P-wave and R-wave measurements with trends, lead monitoring, and automatic polarity switching. The Identity ADx family models maintain the therapeutic features of previous St. Jude Medical pacemakers, including the AF Suppression algorithm and the beat-by-beat auto capture pacing system that lets the pacemaker monitor each paced beat to verify heart stimulation. This family offers atrial tachycardia and atrial fibrillation arrhythmia diagnostics.

In 2009, STJ received both European and FDA of its Accent RF pacemaker and Anthem RF CRT-P (cardiac resynchronization therapy pacemaker). In 2010, STJ anticipates introducing an MRI compatible pacemaker outside the U.S. and intends to file an application for a U.S. trial in 2010.

Company Financials Fiscal Year Ended Dec. 31

Per Share Data ($)	2009	2008	2007	2006	2005	2004	2003	2002	2001	2000
Tangible Book Value	2.65	2.19	2.25	2.23	1.84	4.27	3.02	3.27	2.28	1.50
Cash Flow	2.88	1.63	2.08	1.92	1.38	1.34	1.12	0.96	0.74	0.65
Earnings	2.26	1.10	1.59	1.47	1.04	1.10	0.92	0.76	0.48	0.38
S&P Core Earnings	2.27	1.12	1.64	1.47	0.90	1.03	0.82	0.63	0.38	NA
Dividends	Nil	Nil	Nil	Nil	Nil	Nil	Nil	Nil	Nil	Nil
Payout Ratio	Nil	Nil	Nil	Nil	Nil	Nil	Nil	Nil	Nil	Nil
Prices:High	41.96	48.49	48.10	54.75	52.80	42.90	32.00	21.56	19.52	15.63
Prices:Low	28.86	24.98	34.90	31.20	34.48	29.90	19.38	15.26	11.11	5.91
P/E Ratio:High	19	44	30	37	51	39	35	29	41	41
P/E Ratio:Low	13	23	22	21	33	27	21	20	23	16

Income Statement Analysis (Million $)

	2009	2008	2007	2006	2005	2004	2003	2002	2001	2000
Revenue	4,681	4,363	3,779	3,302	2,915	2,294	1,933	1,590	1,347	1,179
Operating Income	1,440	1,275	1,093	945	911	672	533	445	347	326
Depreciation	213	186	176	167	130	85.8	76.7	74.9	90.3	92.3
Interest Expense	45.6	22.6	38.2	33.9	Nil	Nil	Nil	Nil	Nil	Nil
Pretax Income	1,057	631	744	721	621	537	459	373	228	177
Effective Tax Rate	26.5%	39.1%	24.9%	23.9%	36.7%	23.7%	26.0%	26.0%	24.3%	27.2%
Net Income	777	384	559	548	393	410	339	276	173	129
S&P Core Earnings	782	393	576	548	341	377	302	231	136	NA

Balance Sheet & Other Financial Data (Million $)

	2009	2008	2007	2006	2005	2004	2003	2002	2001	2000
Cash	393	136	389	79.9	535	688	461	402	148	108
Current Assets	2,560	2,080	2,128	1,690	1,941	1,863	1,492	1,114	798	705
Total Assets	6,426	5,724	5,329	4,790	4,845	3,231	2,556	1,951	1,629	1,533
Current Liabilities	1,067	1,029	1,849	676	1,534	605	510	375	322	297
Long Term Debt	1,588	1,126	182	859	177	235	352	Nil	123	295
Common Equity	3,324	3,236	2,928	2,969	2,883	2,334	1,604	1,577	1,184	941
Total Capital	5,246	4,476	3,217	3,992	3,217	2,625	2,046	1,577	1,307	1,235
Capital Expenditures	326	344	287	268	159	89.5	49.6	62.2	63.1	39.7
Cash Flow	991	570	735	715	524	496	416	351	263	221
Current Ratio	2.4	2.0	1.2	2.5	1.3	3.1	2.9	3.0	2.5	2.4
% Long Term Debt of Capitalization	30.3	25.2	5.7	21.5	5.5	8.9	17.2	Nil	9.4	23.8
% Net Income of Revenue	16.6	8.8	14.8	16.6	13.5	17.9	17.6	17.4	12.8	11.0
% Return on Assets	12.8	7.0	29.3	11.4	9.7	14.2	15.1	15.4	10.9	8.4
% Return on Equity	23.7	12.5	19.0	18.7	15.1	20.8	21.3	20.0	16.2	14.9

Data as orig reptd.; bef. results of disc opers/spec. items. Per share data adj. for stk. divs.; EPS diluted. E-Estimated. NA-Not Available. NM-Not Meaningful. NR-Not Ranked. UR-Under Review.

Office: One St Jude Medical Drive, St Paul, MN 55117-9983.
Telephone: 651-756-2000.
Website: http://www.sjm.com
Chrmn, Pres & CEO: D.J. Starks

EVP, CFO & Chief Acctg Officer: J.C. Heinmiller
Secy & General Counsel: P. Krop
Investor Contact: A. Craig (651-481-7789)
Cntlr: D. Zurbay

Board Members: J. W. Brown, R. R. Devenuti, S. M. Essig, T. H. Garrett, III, B. B. Hill, M. A. Rocca, D. J. Starks, W. L. Yarno

Founded: 1976
Domicile: Minnesota
Employees: 14,000

The McGraw·Hill Companies

salesforce.com inc

STANDARD &POOR'S

S&P Recommendation HOLD ★★★☆☆	**Price** $107.94 (as of Oct 22, 2010)	**12-Mo. Target Price** $110.00	**Investment Style** Large-Cap Growth

GICS Sector Information Technology
Sub-Industry Application Software

Summary This San Francisco-based company is a leading provider of on-demand customer relationship management applications.

Key Stock Statistics (Source S&P, Vickers, company reports)

52-Wk Range	$123.77– 56.17	S&P Oper. EPS 2011E	0.45	Market Capitalization(B)	$14.021	Beta	1.72
Trailing 12-Month EPS	$0.56	S&P Oper. EPS 2012E	0.60	Yield (%)	Nil	S&P 3-Yr. Proj. EPS CAGR(%)	3
Trailing 12-Month P/E	NM	P/E on S&P Oper. EPS 2011E	NM	Dividend Rate/Share	Nil	S&P Credit Rating	NA
$10K Invested 5 Yrs Ago	$43,985	Common Shares Outstg. (M)	129.9	Institutional Ownership (%)	91		

Price Performance

30-Week Mov. Avg. · · · · 10-Week Mov. Avg. - - **GAAP Earnings vs. Previous Year** Volume Above Avg. STARS
12-Mo. Target Price — Relative Strength — ▲ Up ▼ Down ▶ No Change Below Avg. ★

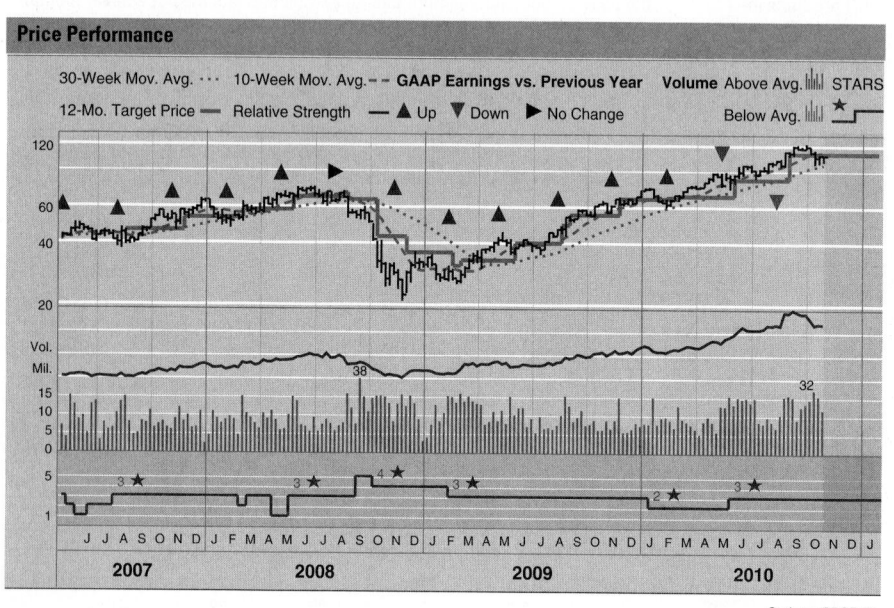

Options: CBOE, Ph

Analysis prepared by **Zaineb Bokhari** on August 25, 2010, when the stock traded at **$ 112.93**.

Highlights

➤ We see sales rising 23% in FY 11 (Jan.), to $1.6 billion, following a 21% increase in FY 10. We expect sales to be driven by a 24% rise in subscription and support sales. We think clients will manage implementations to control costs, and we look for dollar-based attrition rates to stabilize in the mid-teens due to prevailing employment trends and clients' caution about the macro-economy; we see attrition improving modestly in FY 12. We see sales advancing 20% in FY 12, to $1.9 billion.

➤ We expect gross margins to improve slightly in FY 11 as we look for professional services to decline as a percentage of revenues. We forecast operating margins of 7.5% in FY 11, versus 8.8% in FY 10. Our outlook includes higher stock-based compensation expense, which we believe will rise to $117 million in FY 11, from $89 million in FY 10. We anticipate slightly wider operating margins again in FY 12.

➤ We forecast EPS of $0.45 in FY 11, down from $0.63 in FY 10. We expect CRM's effective tax rate to remain near 41% in FY 11. We estimate EPS of $0.60 in FY 12.

Investment Rationale/Risk

➤ We remain cautious in our outlook for IT spending over the next 12 month, as we expect customer caution to prevail amid sluggish global macro-economic conditions. Nevertheless, we think new product offerings and the appeal of CRM's software-as-a-service delivery model will allow the company to post growth that exceeds that of traditional software peers. While we look for profitability to improve over time, in the near term, we see this being limited by planned investments in distribution and sales. We continue to see competitive on-demand offerings from traditional vendors in future periods, but we think CRM enjoys strong market leadership. We believe the company's on-demand model will have strong appeal in the current economic environment, but we think the shares are richly valued.

➤ Risks to our recommendation and target price include a sharp downturn in the global economy, a sharp decline in sales or bookings growth from anticipated levels, and heightened competition.

➤ Our 12-month target price of $110 applies a 7.5X enterprise value-to-sales multiple to our FY 12 sales estimate, a notable premium to peers.

Qualitative Risk Assessment

LOW	MEDIUM	HIGH

Our risk assessment reflects the company's dominance in one of the growth areas of the software market. However, we think competition from traditional software vendors, and increasingly difficult annual comparisons, may result in lower future reported growth relative to historical rates.

Quantitative Evaluations

S&P Quality Ranking NR

D	C	B-	B	B+	A-	A	A+

Relative Strength Rank MODERATE

38

LOWEST = 1   HIGHEST = 99

Revenue/Earnings Data

Revenue (Million $)

	1Q	2Q	3Q	4Q	Year
2011	376.8	394.4	--	--	--
2010	304.9	316.1	330.6	354.1	1,306
2009	247.6	263.1	276.5	289.6	1,077
2008	162.4	176.6	192.8	216.9	748.7
2007	104.7	118.1	130.1	144.2	497.1
2006	64.18	71.94	82.67	91.06	309.9

Earnings Per Share ($)

2011	0.13	0.11	E0.15	E0.06	E0.45
2010	0.15	0.17	0.16	0.16	0.63
2009	0.08	0.08	0.08	0.11	0.35
2008	0.01	0.08	0.05	0.06	0.15
2007	Nil	Nil	Nil	Nil	Nil
2006	0.04	0.04	0.11	0.05	0.24

Fiscal year ended Jan. 31. Next earnings report expected: Mid November. EPS Estimates based on S&P Operating Earnings; historical GAAP earnings are as reported.

Dividend Data

No cash dividends have been paid.

salesforce.com inc

Business Summary August 25, 2010

CORPORATE OVERVIEW. Salesforce.com is a leading provider of "on-demand" customer relationship management software. On-demand, used interchangeably with software-as-a-service (SAAS), refers to the delivery of application or programming or platform services over the Internet as needed. Under this delivery model, customers access a software provider's solutions via the Web, with minor implementation and customization and little to no on-premise installation or maintenance of software. Payment for this "service" is generally on a per-seat per-user basis over an agreed-upon term.

In our view, the delivery of software on demand offers several benefits to customers, including lower up front investment, increased vendor accountability and risk sharing, greater awareness of customer needs due to the constant feedback from customers, and flexible subscription pricing, which can be tailored to customer requirements. This model also offers benefits to the software vendor, including improved visibility into customers' needs and potentially higher customer satisfaction and retention levels. Another benefit we see is lower development and support costs arising from the use of a single version of software across a vendor's installed base. Among the drawbacks to this model for the customer is that over time, depending on the number of seats contracted for or level of usage, the ultimate cost of buying software

on-demand can become quite high and the level of customization may not always address a client's specific needs. A vendor typically incurs considerable up front cost in launching and supporting an SAAS solution. Many SAAS vendors operate at losses until they cross a certain revenue threshold. We note that Salesforce.com, in particular, had 82,400 customers at the end of July 2010, but achieved 7.5% GAAP operating margins.

CRM experienced service outages in late December 2005 and in early 2006. We believe these service issues have been largely addressed, although we note another outage took place in early January 2010. We credit the company with the transparency it provides regarding the performance, uptime, and security of its system. Since the delivery of its service over the Web is a point of differentiation, we expect the company to continue to invest in infrastructure in future quarters. The low up front cost of CRM's products has significant appeal to small- and mid-sized businesses, in our view, although the company has had notable success in selling its services to larger institutions.

Company Financials Fiscal Year Ended Jan. 31

Per Share Data ($)	2010	2009	2008	2007	2006	2005	2004	2003	2002	2001
Tangible Book Value	7.50	4.78	3.71	2.40	1.78	1.38	1.13	NA	NA	NA
Cash Flow	0.97	0.51	0.29	0.11	0.29	0.09	0.06	-0.27	-1.25	-2.31
Earnings	0.63	0.35	0.15	Nil	0.24	0.07	0.04	-0.37	-1.36	-2.38
S&P Core Earnings	0.58	0.36	0.14	Nil	0.07	-0.04	-0.02	-0.43	NA	NA
Dividends	NA	Nil	Nil	Nil	Nil	Nil	NA	NA	NA	NA
Payout Ratio	Nil	Nil	Nil	Nil	Nil	Nil	NA	NA	NA	NA
Calendar Year	2009	2008	2007	2006	2005	2004	2003	2002	2001	2000
Prices:High	74.95	75.21	65.52	44.58	36.19	22.70	NA	NA	NA	NA
Prices:Low	25.19	20.82	35.55	21.64	12.96	9.00	NA	NA	NA	NA
P/E Ratio:High	NM	NM	NM	NM	NM	NM	NA	NA	NA	NA
P/E Ratio:Low	NM	NM	NM	NM	NM	NM	NA	NA	NA	NA

Income Statement Analysis (Million $)

	2010	2009	2008	2007	2006	2005	2004	2003	2002	2001
Revenue	1,306	1,077	749	497	310	176	96.0	51.0	22.4	5.43
Operating Income	159	84.7	37.1	8.91	25.8	9.67	2.86	-7.84	-19.5	-32.7
Depreciation	53.2	21.0	16.8	12.5	6.03	3.15	2.59	2.66	2.40	0.86
Interest Expense	2.00	0.11	0.05	0.19	0.07	0.04	0.02	0.08	0.27	0.04
Pretax Income	142	85.6	46.2	12.5	28.2	9.15	4.24	-10.0	-29.0	-31.9
Effective Tax Rate	40.5%	43.9%	50.6%	78.4%	NM	13.3%	12.8%	Nil	Nil	NA
Net Income	80.7	43.4	18.4	0.48	28.5	7.35	3.51	-9.72	-28.6	-31.7
S&P Core Earnings	74.7	44.4	17.5	0.48	8.59	-3.26	-0.61	-11.4	NA	NA

Balance Sheet & Other Financial Data (Million $)

	2010	2009	2008	2007	2006	2005	2004	2003	2002	2001
Cash	1,242	698	451	252	208	119	142	16.0	11.7	NA
Current Assets	1,706	1,069	741	419	303	179	NA	30.1	18.2	NA
Total Assets	2,460	1,480	1,090	665	435	280	191	39.4	29.1	NA
Current Liabilities	908	767	606	377	235	132	NA	28.8	12.3	NA
Long Term Debt	450	4.05	Nil	0.01	0.18	0.72	Nil	NA	NA	NA
Common Equity	1,044	672	452	282	196	145	115	-56.1	-52.0	NA
Total Capital	1,507	687	461	286	199	147	115	5.42	9.47	NA
Capital Expenditures	53.9	61.1	43.6	22.1	23.4	4.31	NA	2.37	0.71	5.87
Cash Flow	124	64.4	35.2	13.0	34.5	10.5	6.11	-7.06	-26.2	-30.8
Current Ratio	1.9	1.4	1.2	1.1	1.3	1.4	NA	1.1	1.5	NA
% Long Term Debt of Capitalization	29.9	0.6	Nil	0.0	0.1	0.5	Nil	Nil	Nil	NA
% Net Income of Revenue	6.2	4.0	2.5	0.1	9.2	4.2	3.7	NM	NM	NM
% Return on Assets	4.1	3.4	2.1	0.1	8.0	4.0	NA	NA	NA	NA
% Return on Equity	9.4	7.7	5.0	0.2	16.7	14.9	NA	NM	NA	NA

Data as orig reptd.; bef. results of disc opers/spec. items. Per share data adj. for stk. divs.; EPS diluted. E-Estimated. NA-Not Available. NM-Not Meaningful. NR-Not Ranked. UR-Under Review.

Office: The Landmark @ One Market, San Francisco, CA 94105.
Telephone: 415-901-7000.
Website: http://www.salesforce.com
Chrmn & CEO: M. Benioff

EVP, CFO & Chief Acctg Officer: G.V. Smith
EVP, Secy & General Counsel: D. Schellhase
CTO: B. Pech

Board Members: M. Benioff, C. Conway, A. G. Hassenfeld, C. Ramsey, S. R. Robertson, S. Sclavos, L. J. Tomlinson, M. Webb, Jr., S. Young

Founded: 1999
Domicile: Delaware
Employees: 3,969

SanDisk Corp

STANDARD &POOR'S

S&P Recommendation HOLD ★ ★ ★ ★ ★

Price	12-Mo. Target Price	Investment Style
$37.41 (as of Oct 25, 2010)	$47.00	Large-Cap Growth

GICS Sector Information Technology
Sub-Industry Computer Storage & Peripherals

Summary This company designs, makes, and markets flash memory storage products used in a wide variety of electronic systems.

Key Stock Statistics (Source S&P, Vickers, company reports)

52-Wk Range	$50.55–19.18	S&P Oper. EPS 2010E	4.48	Market Capitalization(B)	$8.719	Beta	1.75
Trailing 12-Month EPS	$4.85	S&P Oper. EPS 2011E	4.15	Yield (%)	Nil	S&P 3-Yr. Proj. EPS CAGR(%)	20
Trailing 12-Month P/E	7.7	P/E on S&P Oper. EPS 2010E	8.4	Dividend Rate/Share	Nil	S&P Credit Rating	BB-
$10K Invested 5 Yrs Ago	$6,553	Common Shares Outstg. (M)	233.1	Institutional Ownership (%)	80		

Price Performance

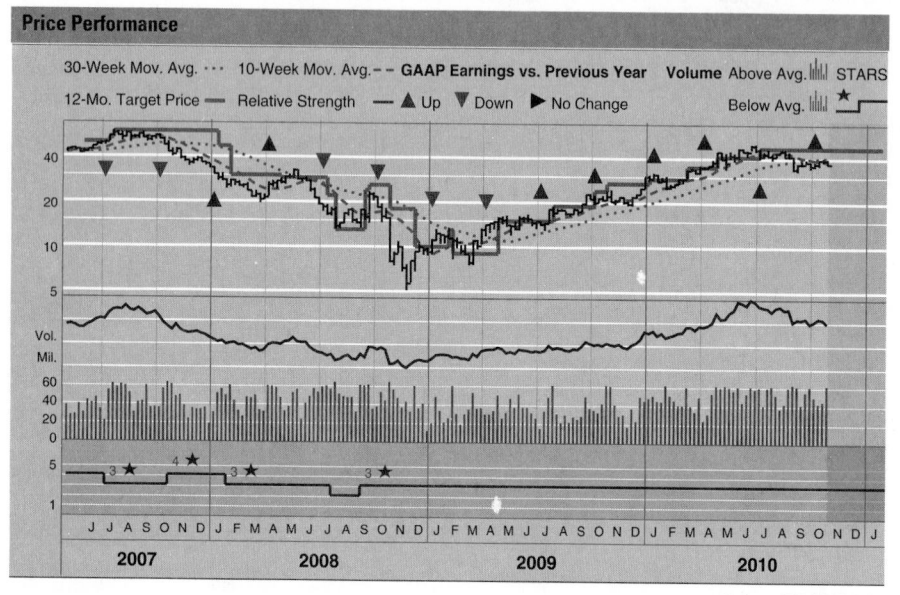

30-Week Mov. Avg. ···· 10-Week Mov. Avg. − − **GAAP Earnings vs. Previous Year** Volume Above Avg. STARS
12-Mo. Target Price — Relative Strength — ▲ Up ▼ Down ▶ No Change Below Avg. ★

Options: ASE, CBOE, P, Ph

Analysis prepared by **Angelo Zino** on October 25, 2010, when the stock traded at **$ 37.69.**

Highlights

➤ We forecast that sales will increase 9.2% in 2011, following our projection for a 34% rise in 2010, as we see growth in megabytes partially offset by average price deflation. We see demand for SNDK's products increasing at a modest pace, with growth primarily being driven by higher demand for new mobile phones. In addition, we anticipate that new product cycles in devices such as tablets and smartphones will drive the need for increased NAND flash-based storage solutions.

➤ We project an annual gross margin of 37% in 2011, versus our 43% forecast in 2010. We think SNDK will benefit from higher growth in megabytes, but we expect some pricing pressure despite a relatively healthy supply and demand picture for NAND flash memory. We see margins aided by cost reductions as the company transitions to more advanced processes. We estimate an operating margin of 25% in 2011, compared to our 31% margin outlook in 2010.

➤ We forecast GAAP EPS of $4.48 for 2010 and $4.15 for 2011. Despite higher projected unit sales, we expect profit margins to narrow in 2011, given a lower pricing environment.

Investment Rationale/Risk

➤ We see SNDK poised to benefit from new applications in flash memory, such as solid state drives, but we are wary of pricing pressure as the industry expands capacity. We believe inventory levels across the supply chain are healthy and expect end-demand to improve going forward, partly aided by new tablet devices like the iPad. We expect the mobile market to be SNDK's highest growth business, and we see the stock being supported to some extent by net cash per share of nearly $14 as of the end of September 2010. We view co-founder and COO Sanjay Mehrotra as a suitable replacement following CEO Eli Harari's announcement to retire at the end of 2010.

➤ Risks to our recommendation and target price include the potential for more aggressive price erosion than we forecast, and more weakening in end-market demand than we foresee.

➤ Our 12-month target price of $47 is based on a P/E multiple of 11.3X our 2011 EPS estimate of $4.15, near comparable semiconductor manufacturers. Our target price is supported by a price-to-sales of 2.2X our 2011 sales per share estimate of $21.75, within its five-year historical range.

Qualitative Risk Assessment

LOW	MEDIUM	HIGH

Our risk assessment reflects the volatile nature of the flash memory space, an intensifying competitive environment, and what we deem to be significant price erosion within the industry.

Quantitative Evaluations

S&P Quality Ranking B-

D	C	B-	B	B+	A-	A	A+

Relative Strength Rank WEAK

19

LOWEST = 1   HIGHEST = 99

Revenue/Earnings Data

Revenue (Million $)

	1Q	2Q	3Q	4Q	Year
2010	1,087	1,179	1,234	--	--
2009	659.5	730.6	935.2	1,242	3,567
2008	850.0	816.0	821.5	863.9	3,351
2007	786.1	827.0	1,037	1,246	3,896
2006	623.3	719.2	751.4	1,164	3,258
2005	451.0	514.9	589.6	750.6	2,306

Earnings Per Share ($)

2010	0.99	1.08	1.34	E1.07	E4.48
2009	-0.92	0.23	0.99	1.45	1.79
2008	0.08	-0.30	-0.69	-8.25	-9.19
2007	Nil	0.12	0.36	0.45	0.93
2006	0.17	0.47	0.51	-0.17	0.96
2005	0.39	0.37	0.55	0.68	2.00

Fiscal year ended Dec. 31. Next earnings report expected: Late January. EPS Estimates based on S&P Operating Earnings; historical GAAP earnings are as reported.

Dividend Data

No cash dividends have been paid.

The McGraw·Hill Companies

SanDisk Corp

Business Summary October 25, 2010

CORPORATE OVERVIEW. SanDisk Corp. (SNDK) designs, makes and markets flash storage card products used in a wide variety of consumer electronics products such as digital cameras, mobile phones, laptops, Universal Serial Bus, or USB, drives, gaming devices and MP3 players. Flash storage technology allows data to be stored in a durable, compact format that retains the digital information even after the power has been switched off. SNDK also provides high-speed and high-capacity storage solutions, known as solid-state drives, or SSDs, that can be used in lieu of hard disk drives in a variety of computing devices, including personal computers and enterprise servers.

SNDK focuses on three primary markets: mobile phones, consumer, and computing. For mobile phones, SNDK's cards are experiencing increasing demand as multimedia features such as video and Internet access become more prevalent. The company is a leading supplier of the microSD and Memory Stick Micro product lines of removable storage cards used in mobile phones.

Within the consumer market, SNDK provides flash storage products for imaging, gaming, audio/video and global positioning system (GPS). Flash storage cards are used as the film for all major brands of digital cameras. Its cards are also used to store video in solid-state digital camcorders and to store digital data in many other devices, such as maps in GPS devices.

In the computing market, SNDK sells USB flash drives that allow consumers to store computer files, pictures and music on keychain-sized devices and then transfer these files between laptops, notebooks, desktops and other devices that incorporate a USB connection. SNDK is currently developing SSDs for the mainstream notebook and desktop computer markets and it believes that SSDs will become a major application for NAND flash memory over the next several years as they are increasingly likely to replace hard disk drives.

CORPORATE STRATEGY. Most of SNDK's products are manufactured by combining NAND flash memory with a controller chip. The vast majority of its NAND flash memory supply requirements are purchased through its flash venture relationship with Toshiba Corporation, which provide the company with memory wafers. From time to time, SNDK also purchase flash memory on a foundry basis from NAND flash manufacturers including Toshiba, Samsung, and Hynix Semiconductor. SNDK typically designs its controllers in-house and has them manufactured at third-party foundries.

Company Financials Fiscal Year Ended Dec. 31

Per Share Data ($)	2009	2008	2007	2006	2005	2004	2003	2002	2001	2000
Tangible Book Value	16.85	13.76	16.94	15.31	13.41	10.78	9.32	4.54	4.93	6.40
Cash Flow	2.79	-8.00	1.97	1.61	2.34	1.62	1.12	0.40	-2.04	2.17
Earnings	1.79	-9.19	0.93	0.96	2.00	1.44	1.02	0.26	-2.19	2.06
S&P Core Earnings	1.77	-5.06	0.96	0.94	1.76	1.29	0.89	0.18	-1.05	NA
Dividends	Nil	Nil	Nil	Nil	Nil	Nil	Nil	Nil	Nil	Nil
Payout Ratio	Nil	Nil	Nil	Nil	Nil	Nil	Nil	Nil	Nil	Nil
Prices:High	31.18	33.73	59.75	79.80	65.49	36.35	43.15	14.60	24.34	84.81
Prices:Low	7.53	5.07	32.74	37.34	20.25	19.28	7.39	4.80	4.30	13.75
P/E Ratio:High	17	NM	64	83	33	25	42	57	NM	41
P/E Ratio:Low	4	NM	35	39	10	13	7	19	NM	7

Income Statement Analysis (Million $)	2009	2008	2007	2006	2005	2004	2003	2002	2001	2000
Revenue	3,567	3,351	3,896	3,258	2,306	1,777	1,080	541	366	602
Operating Income	750	-569	536	688	642	457	280	79.5	-124	141
Depreciation	231	254	246	136	65.8	38.9	23.0	21.3	20.5	15.9
Interest Expense	68.6	16.5	16.9	Nil	0.57	5.95	6.75	6.70	Nil	Nil
Pretax Income	504	-1,903	398	431	613	423	242	40.0	-442	492
Effective Tax Rate	17.6%	NM	43.9%	53.4%	37.0%	37.0%	30.2%	9.35%	NM	39.3%
Net Income	415	-2,070	218	199	386	267	169	36.2	-298	299
S&P Core Earnings	411	-1,138	225	195	339	239	149	25.7	-144	NA

Balance Sheet & Other Financial Data (Million $)	2009	2008	2007	2006	2005	2004	2003	2002	2001	2000
Cash	1,919	1,439	1,835	1,581	762	464	734	267	254	106
Current Assets	2,915	2,703	3,300	4,242	2,576	1,880	1,725	757	542	697
Total Assets	6,002	5,879	7,235	6,968	3,120	2,320	2,024	976	932	1,108
Current Liabilities	871	1,263	914	896	571	353	347	173	127	171
Long Term Debt	935	1,225	1,225	1,225	Nil	Nil	150	150	125	Nil
Common Equity	3,910	3,162	4,960	4,768	2,524	1,940	1,501	628	675	863
Total Capital	4,918	4,400	6,200	5,999	2,524	1,940	1,651	778	800	863
Capital Expenditures	59.7	184	259	176	134	126	52.5	16.6	26.2	26.6
Cash Flow	646	-1,803	464	334	452	305	192	57.6	-277	315
Current Ratio	3.4	2.1	3.6	4.7	4.5	5.3	5.0	4.4	4.3	4.1
% Long Term Debt of Capitalization	19.0	27.9	19.8	20.4	Nil	Nil	9.1	19.3	15.6	Nil
% Net Income of Revenue	11.6	NM	5.6	6.1	16.8	15.0	15.6	6.7	NM	49.6
% Return on Assets	7.0	NM	3.1	3.9	14.2	12.2	11.3	3.8	NM	33.8
% Return on Equity	11.7	NM	4.5	5.5	17.3	15.4	15.9	5.6	NM	41.6

Data as orig reptd.; bef. results of disc opers/spec. items. Per share data adj. for stk. divs.; EPS diluted. E-Estimated. NA-Not Available. NM-Not Meaningful. NR-Not Ranked. UR-Under Review.

Office: 601 McCarthy Blvd, Milpitas, CA 95035-7932.
Telephone: 408-801-1000.
Email: investor_relations@sandisk.com
Website: http://www.sandisk.com

Chrmn & CEO: E. Harari
Pres & COO: S. Mehrotra
Vice Chrmn: I. Federman
EVP & CTO: Y. Cedar

SVP, Secy & General Counsel: J. Brelsford
Investor Contact: J. Bruner
Board Members: K. A. DeNuccio, I. Federman, S. Gomo, E. Harari, E. Hartenstein, C. C. Hu, C. P. Lego, M. E. Marks, S. Mehrotra, J. D. Meindl

Founded: 1988
Domicile: Delaware
Employees: 3,267

Sara Lee Corp

STANDARD &POOR'S

S&P Recommendation HOLD ★★★☆☆

Price $14.50 (as of Oct 22, 2010)	**12-Mo. Target Price** $16.00

Investment Style Large-Cap Blend

GICS Sector Consumer Staples
Sub-Industry Packaged Foods & Meats

Summary This company is a diversified provider of branded food products such as meats, fresh and frozen baked goods, and coffee. SLE is divesting some other businesses.

Key Stock Statistics (Source S&P, Vickers, company reports)

52-Wk Range	$15.40–11.18	S&P Oper. EPS 2011E	0.87	Market Capitalization(B)	$9.602	Beta	0.79
Trailing 12-Month EPS	$0.73	S&P Oper. EPS 2012E	NA	Yield (%)	3.03	S&P 3-Yr. Proj. EPS CAGR(%)	11
Trailing 12-Month P/E	19.9	P/E on S&P Oper. EPS 2011E	16.7	Dividend Rate/Share	$0.44	S&P Credit Rating	BBB
$10K Invested 5 Yrs Ago	NA	Common Shares Outstg. (M)	662.2	Institutional Ownership (%)	76		

Price Performance

30-Week Mov. Avg. · · · 10-Week Mov. Avg. - - GAAP Earnings vs. Previous Year Volume Above Avg. STARS
12-Mo. Target Price — Relative Strength — ▲ Up ▼ Down ► No Change Below Avg.

Options: ASE, CBOE, P

Analysis prepared by **Tom Graves, CFA** on August 24, 2010, when the stock traded at **$14.74.**

Highlights

▶ SLE is in the midst of divesting various businesses in its International Household and Body Care (H&BC) segment. As of August 2010, SLE has announced transactions with divestiture sale prices totaling about 1.93 billion euros. Also, in February 2010, SLE hedged 1.6 billion euros at a euro-dollar rate of $1.35 per euro in anticipation of divestiture proceeds.

▶ We look for SLE to spend $2.5 billion to $3 billion on stock repurchases over a three-year period, including $500 million (about 36 million shares) already spent in 2010 through an accelerated share repurchase program. We expect cash sources for stock repurchases to include divestiture proceeds.

▶ In FY 11 (Jun.), from continuing operations, and before the prospective use of some divestiture proceeds, we estimate EPS of $0.87, up from $0.78 for FY 10, which excludes some special items, but includes about a $0.02 benefit from a 53rd week. Our sales estimate of about $10.8 billion for FY 11 excludes the H&BC segment, which is being treated as a discontinued operation.

Investment Rationale/Risk

▶ We look for a multi-year improvement program called Project Accelerate to incur costs, but also to lead to substantial expense savings. In August 2010, SLE said that from businesses classified as continuing operations, it expected annualized project benefits of $350 million to $400 million by the end of FY 12. Cumulative costs by the end of FY 12 were expected to total more than $300 million. We are pleased by acquisition offers that SLE has received for pieces of its H&BC business.

▶ Risks to our recommendation and target price include divestiture activity proceeding less favorably than expected, weaker-than-expected sales resulting from disappointing demand, and significantly more cost pressure than we anticipate.

▶ Our 12-month target price of $16 largely reflects a P/E multiple of about 17X applied to our calendar 2010 EPS estimate from continuing operations of $0.80, which is about a 14% premium to what we expect from a group of other food stocks. We also include between $2 and $3 a share from prospective divestiture proceeds that SLE has yet to receive. The stock recently had an indicated dividend yield of about 3.0%.

Qualitative Risk Assessment

LOW	MEDIUM	HIGH

Our risk assessment for Sara Lee reflects the relatively stable nature of the company's end markets, what we expect to be sizable cash flow from operating activities, and corporate governance practices that we view as favorable relative to peers.

Quantitative Evaluations

S&P Quality Ranking B

D	C	B-	B	B+	A-	A	A+

Relative Strength Rank MODERATE

39

LOWEST = 1   HIGHEST = 99

Revenue/Earnings Data

Revenue (Million $)

	1Q	2Q	3Q	4Q	Year
2010	2,588	2,858	2,578	2,769	10,793
2009	3,349	3,340	3,028	3,164	12,881
2008	3,054	3,408	3,243	3,507	13,212
2007	2,891	3,182	3,006	3,199	12,278
2006	3,900	2,974	3,789	4,100	15,944
2005	4,861	5,199	4,785	4,754	19,254

Earnings Per Share ($)

2010	0.27	0.43	0.04	0.17	0.92
2009	0.32	-0.02	0.24	-0.02	0.52
2008	0.28	0.25	0.33	-0.96	-0.06
2007	0.34	-0.08	0.15	0.16	0.57
2006	0.25	-0.06	0.18	-0.15	0.53
2005	0.44	0.41	0.24	-0.14	0.92

Fiscal year ended Jun. 30. Next earnings report expected: Early November. EPS Estimates based on S&P Operating Earnings; historical GAAP earnings are as reported.

Dividend Data (Dates: mm/dd Payment Date: mm/dd/yy)

Amount ($)	Date Decl.	Ex-Div. Date	Stk. of Record	Payment Date
0.110	10/29	11/27	12/01	01/08/10
0.110	01/28	02/25	03/01	04/07/10
0.110	04/28	05/27	06/01	07/08/10
0.110	06/24	09/02	09/07	10/07/10

Dividends have been paid since 1946. Source: Company reports.

Please read the Required Disclosures and Analyst Certification on the last page of this report.

The **McGraw-Hill** Companies

Sara Lee Corp

Business Summary August 24, 2010

CORPORATE OVERVIEW. Sara Lee, best known for its baked goods, also has various other branded food and non-food businesses. In North America, this includes Jimmy Dean and Hillshire Farm meat products, while outside the U.S., it includes coffee and tea. In North America, in addition to providing products to retailers, SLE provides coffee, meats and bakery products to food-service operators.

In FY 10 (Jun.), from continuing operations, before intersegment eliminations, SLE's North American Retail (e.g., packaged meat, frozen bakery products, U.S. Senseo retail coffee business) represented 26% of total sales; North American Fresh Bakery accounted for 20%; North American Foodservice 17%; International Beverage 30%; and International Bakery 7%. SLE's International Household and Body Care (H&BC) segment is being treated as a discontinued operation.

CORPORATE STRATEGY. In February 2010, SLE said that it anticipated $2.5 billion to $3 billion of stock repurchases within three years. Also, SLE said that it looked to maintain and gradually increase its current $0.44 per share annual dividend following the sale of its International Household and Body Care business, which we see SLE seeking to divest in pieces.

Related to the H&BC segment, as of August 2010, SLE had announced com-

pleted or proposed divestiture transactions amounting to a total of about 1.93 billion euros. Also, in February 2010, SLE hedged 1.6 billion euros at a euro-dollar rate of $1.35 per euro in anticipation of divestiture proceeds. Closed transactions include the air care business for 320 million euros and the Indian insecticides business for 185 million euros. Planned transactions include the global body care business for 1.275 billion euros, and the non-Indian insecticides business for 153.5 million euros. SLE said that both proposed transactions are expected to close in 2010, subject to regulatory approval. Also, SLE said in August 2010 that it is confident it will be able to successfully divest its remaining household businesses, primarily its global shoe care and Asian cleaning businesses, based on interest from various parties.

At the end of FY 10's third quarter, SLE's balance sheet included $935 million of cash equivalents. We expected SLE to be paying sizable repatriation-related taxes related to it its pending divestiture proceeds and cash balance, but we think that stock repurchases are a good use for a large part of SLE's proceeds or cash.

Company Financials Fiscal Year Ended Jun. 30

Per Share Data ($)	2010	2009	2008	2007	2006	2005	2004	2003	2002	2001
Tangible Book Value	NM	NM	NM	NM	NM	NM	NM	NM	NM	NM
Cash Flow	1.58	1.22	0.51	1.33	1.46	1.87	2.53	2.44	1.94	2.80
Earnings	0.92	0.52	-0.06	0.57	0.53	0.92	1.59	1.50	1.23	1.87
S&P Core Earnings	0.84	0.47	0.69	0.50	0.44	0.86	1.67	1.30	1.00	0.92
Dividends	0.44	0.44	0.42	0.50	0.79	0.78	0.60	0.62	0.60	0.57
Payout Ratio	48%	84%	NM	88%	149%	85%	38%	41%	48%	30%
Prices:High	15.40	12.61	16.08	18.15	19.64	25.00	24.49	23.13	23.84	24.75
Prices:Low	11.67	6.80	7.74	14.75	14.08	17.31	20.17	16.25	16.15	18.26
P/E Ratio:High	17	24	NM	32	37	27	15	15	19	13
P/E Ratio:Low	13	13	NM	26	27	19	13	11	13	10

Income Statement Analysis (Million $)										
Revenue	10,793	12,881	13,212	12,278	15,944	19,254	19,566	18,291	17,628	17,747
Operating Income	1,418	1,488	1,484	1,242	1,779	2,183	2,386	2,345	2,138	2,191
Depreciation	455	497	403	539	701	737	734	674	582	599
Interest Expense	147	170	205	265	308	290	271	276	304	270
Pretax Income	795	588	137	419	683	934	1,542	1,484	1,185	1,851
Effective Tax Rate	NA	38.1%	146.7%	NM	40.0%	21.7%	17.5%	17.7%	14.8%	13.4%
Net Income	635	364	-64.0	426	410	731	1,272	1,221	1,010	1,603
S&P Core Earnings	586	327	501	385	339	684	1,336	1,047	806	768

Balance Sheet & Other Financial Data (Million $)										
Cash	955	959	1,284	2,520	2,231	545	638	942	298	548
Current Assets	3,810	3,830	4,467	5,643	6,774	5,811	5,746	5,953	4,986	5,083
Total Assets	8,836	9,417	10,830	12,190	14,522	14,412	14,883	15,084	13,753	10,167
Current Liabilities	2,723	2,846	3,841	4,301	6,277	4,968	5,423	5,199	5,463	4,958
Long Term Debt	2,693	2,704	2,340	2,803	3,807	4,115	4,171	5,157	4,326	2,640
Common Equity	1,487	2,036	2,811	2,615	2,449	2,938	2,948	1,870	1,534	899
Total Capital	4,214	4,872	5,347	6,066	6,324	7,134	7,194	7,806	7,252	4,646
Capital Expenditures	373	357	454	529	625	538	530	746	669	532
Cash Flow	1,090	861	362	965	1,111	1,468	2,006	1,895	1,592	2,191
Current Ratio	1.4	1.4	1.2	1.3	1.1	1.2	1.1	1.1	0.9	1.0
% Long Term Debt of Capitalization	63.9	55.5	43.8	46.2	60.2	57.6	58.0	66.1	59.7	56.8
% Net Income of Revenue	5.9	2.8	NM	3.5	2.6	3.8	6.5	6.7	5.7	9.0
% Return on Assets	NA	3.6	NM	3.2	2.8	5.0	8.4	8.5	8.4	14.7
% Return on Equity	NA	15.0	NM	16.8	15.2	24.7	52.8	71.7	83.0	167.1

Data as orig reptd.; bef. results of disc opers/spec. items. Per share data adj. for stk. divs.; EPS diluted. E-Estimated. NA-Not Available. NM-Not Meaningful. NR-Not Ranked. UR-Under Review.

Office: 3500 Lacey Rd, Downers Grove, IL 60515-5424.
Telephone: 630-598-6000.
Website: http://www.saralee.com
Chrmn: J.S. Crown

CEO: M. Smits
EVP, Secy & General Counsel: B.J. Hart
SVP & CFO: M. Garvey
Chief Acctg Officer & Cntlr: J. Zyck

Investor Contact: L.M. de Kool
Board Members: C. B. Begley, C. C. Bowles, V. W. Colbert, J. S. Crown, L. T. Koellner, C. J. Lede, J. D. McAdam, I. Prosser, N. Sorensen, J. W. Ubben, J. P. Ward

Founded: 1941
Domicile: Maryland
Employees: 33,400

SCANA Corp

STANDARD &POOR'S

S&P Recommendation HOLD ★★★☆☆	**Price** $41.20 (as of Oct 22, 2010)	**12-Mo. Target Price** $37.00	**Investment Style** Large-Cap Blend

GICS Sector Utilities
Sub-Industry Multi-Utilities

Summary Through its subsidiaries, this energy-based holding company provides electric, natural gas, and telecommunications services.

Key Stock Statistics (Source S&P, Vickers, company reports)

52-Wk Range	$41.97– 33.59	S&P Oper. EPS 2010**E**	2.95	Market Capitalization(B)	$5.217	Beta	0.60
Trailing 12-Month EPS	$2.90	S&P Oper. EPS 2011**E**	3.15	Yield (%)	4.61	S&P 3-Yr. Proj. EPS CAGR(%)	6
Trailing 12-Month P/E	14.2	P/E on S&P Oper. EPS 2010**E**	14.0	Dividend Rate/Share	$1.90	S&P Credit Rating	BBB+
$10K Invested 5 Yrs Ago	$13,499	Common Shares Outstg. (M)	126.6	Institutional Ownership (%)	47		

Price Performance

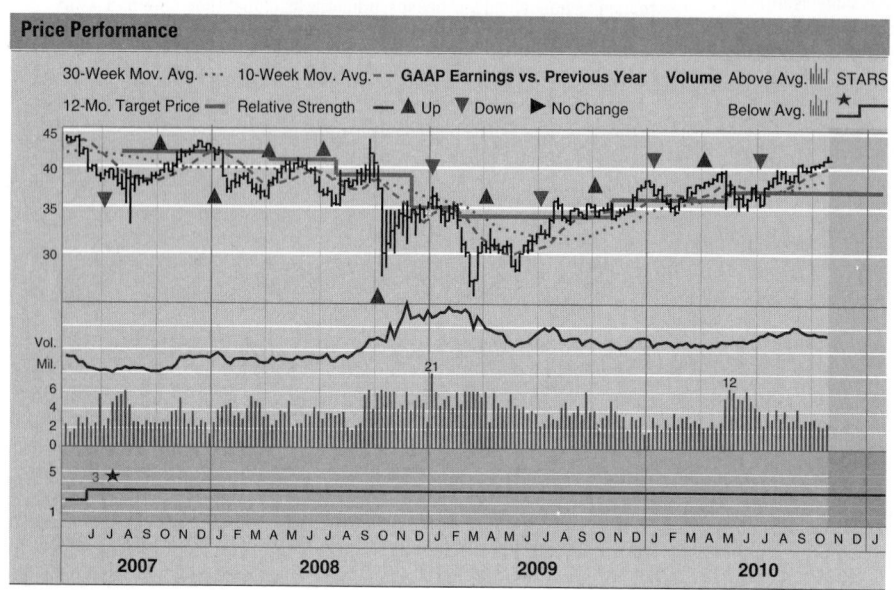

30-Week Mov. Avg. · · · 10-Week Mov. Avg. - - **GAAP Earnings vs. Previous Year** Volume Above Avg. STARS
12-Mo. Target Price — Relative Strength — ▲ Up ▼ Down ► No Change Below Avg. ★

Options: Ph

Analysis prepared by **Christopher B. Muir** on August 20, 2010, when the stock traded at **$ 38.27.**

Highlights

➤ We see 2010 revenue growth of 6.7%, stemming from stabilizing gas prices and industrial volumes, and growth in residential and commercial categories. SCG's gas and electric distribution territories should provide the utility with steady annual customer growth. In 2011, we see revenues rising 3.3% as we expect to see continuing economic improvements and rising gas prices, but we also see pressure on industrial sales.

➤ We expect operating margins of 17.3% this year rising to 18.2% in 2011, versus 16.5% in 2009. We expect lower per-revenue operating expenses in all categories in 2010 except electric fuel. For 2011, we see lower per-revenue electric fuel costs. We see pretax margins of 12.5% in 2010 and 13.7% in 2011, up from 12.2% in 2009, with 2010 affected by our expectations for higher interest expense and lower nonoperating income.

➤ Assuming an effective tax rate of 34.8% and continued upward share drift related to compensation, we estimate 2010 EPS of $2.95, up 8.1% from 2009's $2.73, excluding $0.12 in net non-recurring gains. Our 2011 EPS estimate is $3.15, up 6.8%.

Investment Rationale/Risk

➤ We think above-average population growth in SCG's service areas will provide solid opportunities for further rate and rate base increases. SCG's cash flow generation has been solid, in our view. We see the unregulated gas business in Georgia providing more growth than the regulated businesses. However, with our expectation for a 4% EPS CAGR over the next three years, we think the stock is fairly valued.

➤ Risks to our recommendation and target price include a sharp increase in interest rates, prolonged mild temperatures, unfavorable regulatory actions, and weaker-than-expected economic growth in the utility's service area.

➤ The stock recently traded at 12.1X our 2011 EPS estimate, or a small discount to its multi-utility peers. Our 12-month target price of $37 is 11.8X our 2011 estimate, an 8% discount to our peer target. We believe this valuation is warranted by what we see as a relatively strong balance sheet, offset by our expectation of slower than peers EPS growth and little improvement in the capital structure over the next three years. The dividend recently yielded 4.9%.

Qualitative Risk Assessment

LOW	MEDIUM	HIGH

We think the largely regulated nature of SCG's operations provides a stable source of cash flow and earnings. In addition, the company has a less leveraged balance sheet than peers.

Quantitative Evaluations

S&P Quality Ranking   B

D	C	B-	B	B+	A-	A	A+

Relative Strength Rank   MODERATE

53

LOWEST = 1   HIGHEST = 99

Revenue/Earnings Data

Revenue (Million $)

	1Q	2Q	3Q	4Q	Year
2010	1,428	939.0	--	--	--
2009	1,343	878.0	921.0	1,094	4,237
2008	1,533	1,218	1,266	1,301	5,319
2007	1,363	1,007	1,079	1,172	4,621
2006	1,389	944.0	1,062	1,168	4,563
2005	1,266	891.0	1,127	1,492	4,777

Earnings Per Share ($)

	1Q	2Q	3Q	4Q	Year
2010	1.03	0.43	E0.82	E0.68	E2.95
2009	0.94	0.45	0.84	0.62	2.85
2008	0.93	0.49	0.80	0.73	2.96
2007	0.73	0.47	0.79	0.75	2.74
2006	0.80	0.50	0.76	0.57	2.63
2005	0.89	0.39	0.88	0.65	2.81

Fiscal year ended Dec. 31. Next earnings report expected: Late October. EPS Estimates based on S&P Operating Earnings; historical GAAP earnings are as reported.

Dividend Data (Dates: mm/dd Payment Date: mm/dd/yy)

Amount ($)	Date Decl.	Ex-Div. Date	Stk. of Record	Payment Date
0.470	10/28	12/08	12/10	01/01/10
0.475	02/11	03/08	03/10	04/01/10
0.475	05/06	06/08	06/10	07/01/10
0.475	07/29	09/08	09/10	10/01/10

Dividends have been paid since 1946. Source: Company reports.

The McGraw-Hill Companies

SCANA Corp

STANDARD &POOR'S

Business Summary August 20, 2010

CORPORATE OVERVIEW. SCG's primary regulated operating businesses are South Carolina Electric & Gas (SCE&G), Public Service of North Carolina (PSNC), SCANA Energy, and an intrastate pipeline operation in South Carolina. As of December 31, 2009, SCE&G had 655,000 electric customers and 309,800 natural gas customers. PSNC had 472,900 gas utility customers. The company projects that its consolidated regulated base of more than 1.4 million electric and gas customers will grow 2.4% annually. The company's unregulated SCANA Energy served about 30% of the 1.5 million customers in Georgia's competitive natural gas supply market, with about 90,000 of its 455,000 gas customers receiving regulated services.

In 2009, 51% of SCG's external revenues were derived from electric operations (42% in 2008), 22% (23%) from natural gas distribution, 14% (23%) from energy marketing, and 12% (12%) from retail gas marketing. SCE&G owned 5,611 megawatt (MW) of generating plants as of December 2009. This capacity consisted of 45% coal, 29% oil/gas, 14% hydro and 11% nuclear. In 2009, 63% of SCE&G's power was generated by coal plants, 21% by nuclear, 12% by natural gas and oil, and 4% by hydroelectric.

CORPORATE STRATEGY. SCG sees reserve margins falling in its service territory over the next several years and believes that new baseload power will be needed. As a result, it plans to invest in nuclear generation to fill the gap. SCE&G submitted a joint application to the NRC on March 31, 2008, with Santee Cooper, a state-owned utility, for a combined construction and operating license (COL) that covers two nuclear units. SCE&G has said that the companies have elected to use a 1,000 MW design, which would be built at the existing VC Summer nuclear station, if the economic need still exists after the approximately three-year COL application process. If the companies decide to move ahead with the project, SCG said the first plant could be built by 2016. SCE&G operates the VC Summer nuclear station and would remain the operator for all units after completion. Financially, SCG aims to increase earnings at a rate of 4%-6% annually and maintain a dividend payout ratio in the 55%-60% range.

Company Financials Fiscal Year Ended Dec. 31

Per Share Data ($)	2009	2008	2007	2006	2005	2004	2003	2002	2001	2000
Tangible Book Value	25.84	23.86	23.33	24.32	23.28	21.69	20.77	19.61	20.90	19.51
Earnings	2.85	2.96	2.74	2.63	2.81	2.30	2.54	0.83	5.15	2.12
S&P Core Earnings	2.99	2.55	2.52	2.44	2.60	2.51	2.40	1.93	1.59	NA
Dividends	1.88	1.84	1.76	1.68	1.56	1.46	1.38	1.30	1.20	1.15
Payout Ratio	66%	62%	64%	64%	56%	63%	54%	157%	23%	54%
Prices:High	38.64	44.06	45.49	42.43	43.65	39.71	35.70	32.15	30.00	31.13
Prices:Low	26.01	27.75	32.93	36.92	36.56	32.82	28.10	23.50	24.25	22.00
P/E Ratio:High	14	15	17	16	16	17	14	39	6	15
P/E Ratio:Low	9	9	12	14	13	14	11	28	5	10
Income Statement Analysis (Million $)										
Revenue	4,237	5,319	4,621	4,563	4,777	3,885	3,416	2,954	3,451	3,433
Depreciation	347	344	324	333	510	265	238	220	224	217
Maintenance	NA	NA	NA	NA	NA	NA	558	522	482	NA
Fixed Charges Coverage	3.12	3.25	3.18	3.02	2.18	2.83	2.81	2.68	2.49	2.47
Construction Credits	NA	NA	NA	NA	3.00	26.0	11.0	NA	NA	7.00
Effective Tax Rate	32.4%	35.3%	30.0%	28.1%	NM	32.4%	32.4%	29.0%	36.1%	39.0%
Net Income	348	346	320	304	320	257	282	88.0	539	221
S&P Core Earnings	365	299	294	282	296	280	268	204	167	NA
Balance Sheet & Other Financial Data (Million $)										
Gross Property	12,602	11,645	10,650	9,954	9,540	9,181	9,025	7,777	7,215	7,413
Capital Expenditures	914	904	712	485	366	498	738	675	523	334
Net Property	9,300	8,499	7,669	7,139	6,842	6,866	6,745	5,301	4,851	5,201
Capitalization:Long Term Debt	4,483	4,361	2,879	3,067	3,062	3,301	3,340	2,999	2,812	3,016
Capitalization:% Long Term Debt	56.8	58.0	48.4	50.9	53.4	58.3	59.2	57.9	56.2	59.7
Capitalization:Preferred	Nil	113	113	114	Nil	Nil	Nil	Nil	Nil	Nil
Capitalization:% Preferred	Nil	1.50	1.90	1.89	Nil	Nil	Nil	Nil	Nil	Nil
Capitalization:Common	3,408	3,045	2,960	2,846	2,677	2,357	2,306	2,177	2,194	2,032
Capitalization:% Common	43.2	40.5	49.7	47.2	46.6	41.7	40.8	42.1	43.8	40.3
Total Capital	7,919	8,631	7,000	7,094	6,800	6,658	6,550	6,041	5,844	5,888
% Operating Ratio	87.4	90.2	89.3	89.4	88.4	87.8	87.8	83.8	93.5	88.0
% Earned on Net Property	7.9	8.8	8.5	8.6	6.4	8.9	8.5	10.1	11.3	11.0
% Return on Revenue	8.2	6.5	6.9	6.7	6.7	6.6	8.3	3.0	15.6	6.4
% Return on Invested Capital	7.5	7.3	9.8	8.8	10.9	7.6	8.8	9.9	14.2	8.7
% Return on Common Equity	10.8	11.5	11.0	11.0	12.5	10.8	12.3	4.0	25.5	10.7

Data as orig reptd.; bef. results of disc opers/spec. items. Per share data adj. for stk. divs.; EPS diluted. E-Estimated. NA-Not Available. NM-Not Meaningful. NR-Not Ranked. UR-Under Review.

Office: 1426 Main Street, Columbia, SC 29201.
Telephone: 803-217-9000.
Email: invrel@scana.com
Website: http://www.scana.com

Chrmn, Pres & CEO: W.B. Timmerman
SVP & CFO: J. Addison
SVP & General Counsel: R.T. Lindsay
Chief Acctg Officer & Cntlr: J.E. Swan, IV

Secy: G. Champion
Investor Contact: J. Winn (803-217-9240)
Board Members: B. Amick, J. A. Bennett, S. A. Decker, D. M. Hagood, J. W. Martin, III, J. M. Micali, L. M. Miller, J. W. Roquemore, M. K. Sloan, H. C. Stowe, W. B. Timmerman

Founded: 1924
Domicile: South Carolina
Employees: 5,828

Schlumberger Ltd

STANDARD &POOR'S

S&P Recommendation **STRONG BUY** ★★★★★	Price $67.77 (as of Oct 22, 2010)	12-Mo. Target Price $85.00	Investment Style Large-Cap Blend

GICS Sector Energy
Sub-Industry Oil & Gas Equipment & Services

Summary This leading oilfield services company provides equipment and technology to the oil and gas industry worldwide.

Key Stock Statistics (Source S&P, Vickers, company reports)

52-Wk Range	$73.99– 51.67	S&P Oper. EPS 2010**E**	2.94	Market Capitalization(B)	$92.787	Beta	1.27
Trailing 12-Month EPS	$2.54	S&P Oper. EPS 2011**E**	4.22	Yield (%)	1.24	S&P 3-Yr. Proj. EPS CAGR(%)	23
Trailing 12-Month P/E	26.7	P/E on S&P Oper. EPS 2010**E**	23.1	Dividend Rate/Share	$0.84	S&P Credit Rating	A+
$10K Invested 5 Yrs Ago	$17,934	Common Shares Outstg. (M)	1,369.1	Institutional Ownership (%)	69		

Price Performance

30-Week Mov. Avg. ··· 10-Week Mov. Avg. - - 12-Mo. Target Price — Relative Strength — GAAP Earnings vs. Previous Year ▲ Up ▼ Down ▶ No Change Volume Above Avg. Below Avg. STARS

Options: ASE, CBOE, P, Ph

Qualitative Risk Assessment

LOW	MEDIUM	HIGH

Our risk assessment reflects the company's exposure to volatile crude oil and natural gas prices; its dependence on capital spending decisions by its oil and gas producing customers; and political risk associated with operating in frontier regions around the world. This is offset by the company's leading industry position.

Quantitative Evaluations

S&P Quality Ranking NR

D	C	B-	B	B+	A-	A	A+

Relative Strength Rank STRONG
85
LOWEST = 1   HIGHEST = 99

Revenue/Earnings Data

Revenue (Million $)

	1Q	2Q	3Q	4Q	Year
2010	5,598	5,937	--	--	--
2009	6,000	5,528	5,430	5,744	22,702
2008	6,290	6,746	7,259	6,868	27,163
2007	5,464	5,639	5,926	6,248	23,277
2006	4,239	4,687	4,955	5,350	19,230
2005	3,159	3,429	3,698	4,023	14,309

Earnings Per Share ($)

	1Q	2Q	3Q	4Q	Year
2010	0.56	0.68	E0.70	E0.94	E2.94
2009	0.78	0.51	0.65	0.67	2.61
2008	1.06	1.16	1.25	0.95	4.42
2007	0.96	1.02	1.09	1.12	4.20
2006	0.59	0.69	0.81	0.92	3.01
2005	0.44	0.39	0.45	0.54	1.81

Fiscal year ended Dec. 31. Next earnings report expected: Late October. EPS Estimates based on S&P Operating Earnings; historical GAAP earnings are as reported.

Highlights

► The 12-month target price for SLB has recently been changed to $85.00 from $76.00. The Highlights section of this Stock Report will be updated accordingly.

Investment Rationale/Risk

► The Investment Rationale/Risk section of this Stock Report will be updated shortly. For the latest News story on SLB from MarketScope, see below.

► 10/22/10 11:41 am ET ... S&P MAINTAINS STRONG BUY OPINION ON SHARES OF SCHLUMBERGER (SLB 67.35*****): Q3 EPS of $0.70 before $0.68 of net 1X gains, vs. $0.65, is $0.07 below our est. We believe that the integration of the former Smith International is going relatively smoothly, and that SLB is likely to generate cost efficiencies and potential revenue efficiencies as a result. We think margins have room to the upside and, aside from Mexico, think international prospects look generally solid. We cut our '10 EPS estimate by $0.01 to $2.94, but lift '11's by $0.22 to $4.22. On our DCF model and higher peer multiples, we raise our 12-month target price by $9 to $85. /S. Glickman

Dividend Data (Dates: mm/dd Payment Date: mm/dd/yy)

Amount ($)	Date Decl.	Ex-Div. Date	Stk. of Record	Payment Date
0.210	01/21	02/12	02/17	04/02/10
0.210	04/22	05/28	06/02	07/02/10
0.210	07/22	08/30	09/01	10/01/10
0.210	10/21	11/29	12/01	01/07/11

Dividends have been paid since 1957. Source: Company reports.

The **McGraw-Hill** Companies

Schlumberger Ltd

Business Summary July 26, 2010

CORPORATE OVERVIEW. As a global oilfield and information services company with major activity in the energy industry, Schlumberger operates in two primary business segments: Oilfield Services (91% of 2009 revenues; 89% of 2008 revenues), and WesternGeco (9%, 11%). Oilfield Services provides exploration and production services, solutions and technology to the petroleum industry. It is managed through four geographic areas (North America, South America, Europe/CIS/Africa, and the Middle East/Asia).

The company is largely focused on international operations; North America generated only 18% of Oilfield Services' total revenues in 2009, and just 5% of the segment's 2009 pretax operating income (the latter number reflecting the extent to which the credit crisis-fueled pullback in oilfield activity hit the region). The Middle East/Asia region generated the highest operating margins in 2009, at 32.4%, with Europe/CIS/West Africa second, at 23.9%.

Operations within Oilfield Services are organized into eight technology segments: (1) wireline services, providing information technology to evaluate the reservoir, plan and monitor wells, and evaluate and monitor production; (2) drilling and measurements, including directional drilling, measurement while drilling and logging while drilling services; (3) well testing; (4) well services, which includes pressure pumping, coiled tubing, well cementing and stimulation; (5) completions, which includes gas-lift and safety valves, and a range of intelligent well completions technology and equipment; (6) artificial lift, which offers production optimization services using electric submersible pumps and

other equipment; (7) data and consulting services; and (8) Schlumberger Information Solutions. Supporting these eight technologies are 20 R&D centers.

In addition, SLB operates its WesternGeco seismic segment. WesternGeco provides worldwide comprehensive reservoir imaging, monitoring and development services, with seismic crews and data processing centers, as well as a large multiclient seismic library. Services include 3D and time-lapse (4D) seismic surveys, and multi-component surveys for delineating prospects and reservoir management.

CORPORATE STRATEGY. SLB has made a strategic focus of improving its research and development of advanced oilfield technologies, with the goal of enhancing oilfield efficiency, reducing finding and development (F&D) costs, improving productivity, maximizing reserve recovery, and increasing asset values. We believe that advanced technology will become increasingly important, as existing oilfields mature and new oilfields are developed in harsh environments and challenging geological conditions. We anticipate that most new major oilfield developments are likely to be found in the Eastern Hemisphere, given relatively lower F&D costs and higher growth reservoir potential.

Company Financials Fiscal Year Ended Dec. 31

Per Share Data ($)	2009	2008	2007	2006	2005	2004	2003	2002	2001	2000
Tangible Book Value	NA	8.85	7.23	3.84	3.63	2.54	1.87	0.70	1.14	5.87
Cash Flow	NA	5.97	5.41	4.24	2.89	1.89	1.74	-0.75	2.08	1.73
Earnings	2.61	4.42	4.20	3.01	1.81	0.85	0.41	-2.09	0.46	0.64
Dividends	0.84	0.84	0.70	0.50	0.42	0.38	0.38	0.38	0.38	0.38
Payout Ratio	32%	19%	17%	17%	23%	44%	93%	NM	82%	59%
Prices:High	71.10	111.95	114.84	74.75	51.49	34.95	28.12	31.22	41.41	44.44
Prices:Low	35.05	37.07	55.68	49.20	31.57	26.27	17.81	16.70	20.42	26.75
P/E Ratio:High	27	25	27	25	28	41	69	NM	91	70
P/E Ratio:Low	13	8	13	16	17	31	44	NM	45	42

Income Statement Analysis (Million $)										
Revenue	22,702	27,163	23,277	19,230	14,309	11,480	14,059	13,474	13,746	9,611
Operating Income	NA	8,602	7,994	6,458	4,520	2,895	2,474	-456	3,165	2,084
Depreciation, Depletion and Amortization	2,476	1,904	1,526	1,561	1,351	1,308	1,571	1,545	1,896	1,271
Interest Expense	221	247	275	235	197	272	334	368	385	276
Pretax Income	3,934	6,852	6,624	4,948	2,972	1,327	568	-2,230	1,126	959
Effective Tax Rate	19.6%	20.9%	21.9%	24.0%	22.9%	20.9%	36.9%	NM	51.1%	23.8%
Net Income	3,156	5,397	5,177	3,710	2,199	1,014	473	-2,418	522	733

Balance Sheet & Other Financial Data (Million $)										
Cash	4,616	3,692	3,169	166	191	224	234	168	178	3,040
Current Assets	NA	12,894	11,055	9,186	8,554	7,060	10,369	7,185	7,705	7,493
Total Assets	33,465	31,991	27,853	22,832	18,077	16,001	20,041	19,435	22,326	17,173
Current Liabilities	NA	8,125	7,505	6,455	5,515	4,701	6,795	6,451	6,218	3,991
Long Term Debt	4,355	3,694	3,794	4,664	3,591	3,944	6,097	6,029	6,216	3,573
Common Equity	19,229	16,862	14,876	10,420	7,592	6,117	5,881	5,606	8,378	8,295
Total Capital	NA	20,628	18,732	15,084	11,688	10,477	12,376	12,188	15,231	12,474
Capital Expenditures	2,395	3,723	3,191	2,457	1,593	1,216	1,025	1,366	2,053	1,323
Cash Flow	NA	7,301	6,703	5,271	3,550	2,322	2,044	-872	2,418	2,003
Current Ratio	1.9	1.6	1.5	1.4	1.6	1.5	1.5	1.1	1.2	1.9
% Long Term Debt of Capitalization	18.2	17.9	20.3	30.9	30.7	37.6	49.3	49.5	40.8	28.6
% Return on Assets	NA	18.0	20.4	18.1	12.9	5.6	2.4	NM	2.6	4.5
% Return on Equity	17.5	34.0	40.9	41.2	32.1	16.9	8.2	NM	6.3	9.1

Data as orig reptd.; bef. results of disc opers/spec. items. Per share data adj. for stk. divs.; EPS diluted. E-Estimated. NA-Not Available. NM-Not Meaningful. NR-Not Ranked. UR-Under Review.

Office: 5599 San Felipe St 17th Fl, Houston, TX 77056-2724.
Telephone: 713-513-2000.
Email: irsupport@slb.com
Website: http://www.slb.com

Chrmn & CEO: A. Gould
COO: P. Kibsgaard
EVP & CFO: S. Ayat
Chief Acctg Officer: H. Guild

Treas: H.S. Oyinlola
Investor Contact: M. Theobald (713-375-3535)
Board Members: P. Camus, A. Gould, A. E. Isaac, N. Kudryavtsev, A. Lajous, M. E. Marks, E. A. Moler, L. R. Reif, T. I. Sandvold, H. Seydoux

Founded: 1926
Domicile: Netherlands Antilles
Employees: 77,000

Schwab (Charles) Corp

STANDARD & POOR'S

S&P Recommendation	HOLD ★★★☆☆	Price	12-Mo. Target Price	Investment Style
		$14.98 (as of Oct 22, 2010)	$17.00	Large-Cap Blend

GICS Sector Financials
Sub-Industry Investment Banking & Brokerage

Summary This company's subsidiary, Charles Schwab & Co., is among the largest brokerage firms in the U.S., primarily serving retail clients.

Key Stock Statistics (Source S&P, Vickers, company reports)

52-Wk Range	$19.95–12.64	S&P Oper. EPS 2010**E**	0.54	Market Capitalization(B)	$17.884	Beta	1.25
Trailing 12-Month EPS	$0.42	S&P Oper. EPS 2011**E**	0.95	Yield (%)	1.60	S&P 3-Yr. Proj. EPS CAGR(%)	-7
Trailing 12-Month P/E	35.7	P/E on S&P Oper. EPS 2010**E**	27.7	Dividend Rate/Share	$0.24	S&P Credit Rating	A
$10K Invested 5 Yrs Ago	$12,064	Common Shares Outstg. (M)	1,193.9	Institutional Ownership (%)	70		

Price Performance

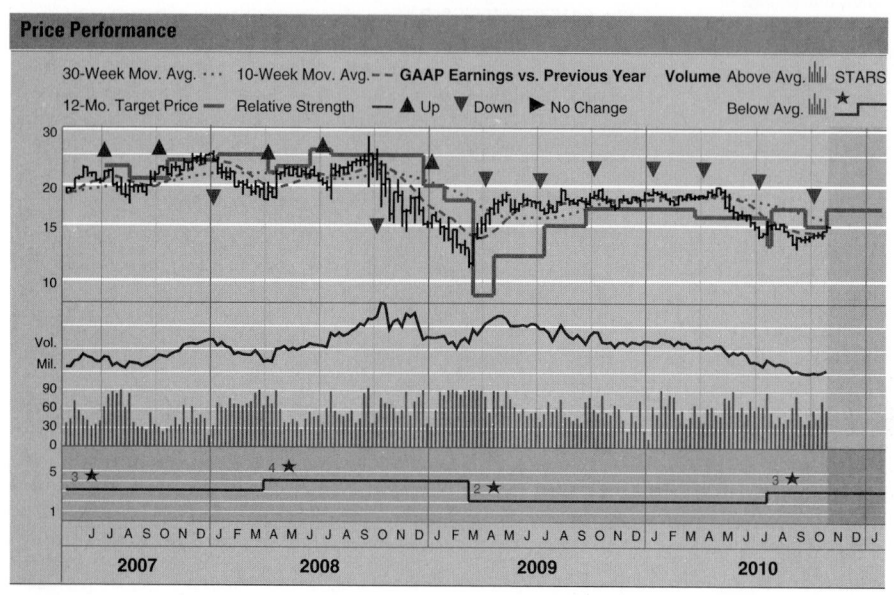

30-Week Mov. Avg. · · · 10-Week Mov. Avg. - - **GAAP Earnings vs. Previous Year** Volume Above Avg. ▦ STARS
12-Mo. Target Price — Relative Strength — ▲ Up ▼ Down ▶ No Change Below Avg. ▦ ★

Options: ASE, CBOE, P, Ph

Analysis prepared by **Robert McMillan** on October 19, 2010, when the stock traded at **$ 14.98**.

Qualitative Risk Assessment

LOW	MEDIUM	HIGH

Our risk assessment reflects our view of the company's strong competitive position, brand recognition and affluent client base, offset by industry cyclicality and our concerns about corporate governance.

Quantitative Evaluations

S&P Quality Ranking B+

D	C	B-	B	B+	A-	A	A+

Relative Strength Rank MODERATE

57

LOWEST = 1   HIGHEST = 99

Highlights

► We think revenues will inch up this year before a 17% increase in 2011. We look for asset-based fee income to decline, with higher asset balances due to new accounts and market gains outweighed by rate pressures. Commissions should also decrease as a modest uptick in activity is likely offset by lower commissions. We see net interest revenue increasing, helped by higher average interest earning assets and lower funding costs. While interest rates remain low, they seem to have stabilized somewhat, which should allow for fewer management fee waivers. SCHW continues to add clients and their assets, which should position the firm to grow revenues quickly once rates rise. An eventual move by the Fed to raise short-term rates would be immediately accretive to revenues, by our estimation.

► We expect pretax margins to contract in 2010 as the firm invests for growth. A slight reduction in compensation on a relative basis may be offset by rising advertising expenses. Other costs may decline on a relative basis, helped by cost-cutting efforts over the past year.

► We forecast EPS of $0.54 in 2010 and $0.95 in 2011.

Investment Rationale/Risk

► Although we think a premium multiple afforded the shares versus peers is appropriate, given SCHW's high proportion of recurring asset-based fees and strong brand recognition, we believe near-term challenges are likely to persist. Net interest income is not likely to improve significantly despite asset growth until the Federal Reserve raises short-term interest rates. A move to flat commissions regardless of the activity levels or assets should help the firm gain market share, although it is likely to reduce revenues in the near term. Nevertheless, we think SCHW's revenue streams are better diversified than many other discount brokers in our coverage, and are properly situated to benefit from an economic recovery.

► Risks to our recommendation and target price include a decline in trading volumes, equity market depreciation, and a delayed rise in short-term interest rates.

► Our 12-month target price of $17 is 20X our forward 12-month EPS estimate of $0.85, a premium to discount brokerage peers.

Revenue/Earnings Data

Revenue (Million $)

	1Q	2Q	3Q	4Q	Year
2010	978.0	1,080	58.00	--	--
2009	1,111	1,085	1,011	986.0	4,193
2008	1,307	1,308	1,251	1,284	5,150
2007	1,153	1,205	1,291	1,345	4,994
2006	1,054	1,093	1,066	1,096	4,309
2005	1,059	1,087	1,138	1,180	4,464

Earnings Per Share ($)

2010	Nil	0.17	0.10	E0.16	E0.54
2009	0.19	0.18	0.17	0.14	0.68
2008	0.26	0.26	0.26	0.27	1.06
2007	0.19	0.23	0.27	0.26	0.92
2006	0.19	0.19	0.21	0.37	0.69
2005	0.11	0.14	0.16	0.14	0.56

Fiscal year ended Dec. 31. Next earnings report expected: Mid January. EPS Estimates based on S&P Operating Earnings; historical GAAP earnings are as reported.

Dividend Data (Dates: mm/dd Payment Date: mm/dd/yy)

Amount ($)	Date Decl.	Ex-Div. Date	Stk. of Record	Payment Date
0.060	10/22	11/10	11/13	11/27/09
0.060	01/27	02/10	02/12	02/26/10
0.060	04/27	05/05	05/07	05/21/10
0.060	07/27	08/11	08/13	08/27/10

Dividends have been paid since 1989. Source: Company reports.

The McGraw-Hill Companies

Schwab (Charles) Corp

STANDARD &POOR'S

Business Summary October 19, 2010

CORPORATE OVERVIEW. Charles Schwab Corp. (SCHW) is a financial holding company that provides securities brokerage and related financial services through three segments, Schwab Investor Services, Schwab Institutional and Schwab Corporate and Retirement Services. Another subsidiary, Charles Schwab Investment Management, is the investment adviser for Schwab's proprietary mutual funds. In December 2007, CyberTrader, Inc., formerly a subsidiary of SCHW, which provides electronic trading and brokerage services to highly active, online traders, was merged into Schwab.

Through the Schwab Investor Services segment (65% of 2009 net revenue), the company provides retail brokerage and banking services. Through various types of brokerage accounts, Schwab offers the purchase and sale of securities, including NASDAQ, exchange-listed and other equity securities, options, mutual funds, unit investment trusts, variable annuities and fixed-income investments. At the end of 2009, the company, through subsidiaries, served nearly 10 million active client accounts, and held client assets of more than $1.4 trillion.

Through the Institutional Services segment (35%), Schwab provides custodial, trading, technology, practice management, trust asset and other support services to independent advisers. To attract and serve independent advisers, this segment has a dedicated sales force and service teams assigned to meet their needs. Institutional Services offers an array of services to help advisers establish their own independent practices, which includes access to dedicated service teams and outsourcing of back-office operations, as well as third-party firms that provide assistance with real estate, errors and omissions insurance, and company benefits. SCHW also offers a variety of educational materials and events to IAs seeking to expand their knowledge of industry issues and trends, as well as sharpen their individual expertise and practice management skills.

The Institutional Services segment also provides retirement plan services, plan administrator services, stock plan services and mutual fund clearing services, and supports the availability of Schwab proprietary mutual funds on third-party platforms. The company serves a range of employer-sponsored plans: equity compensation plans, defined contribution plans, defined benefit plans, and other investment-related benefits plans.

Company Financials Fiscal Year Ended Dec. 31

Per Share Data ($)	2009	2008	2007	2006	2005	2004	2003	2002	2001	2000
Tangible Book Value	3.89	3.03	2.76	3.63	2.71	2.57	2.56	0.55	2.58	2.69
Cash Flow	0.82	1.19	1.04	0.81	0.72	0.47	0.35	0.30	0.30	0.70
Earnings	0.68	1.06	0.92	0.69	0.56	0.30	0.35	0.07	0.06	0.51
S&P Core Earnings	0.67	1.08	0.92	0.68	0.53	0.23	0.27	-0.02	-0.09	NA
Dividends	0.24	0.22	0.20	0.14	0.09	0.07	0.05	0.04	0.04	0.04
Payout Ratio	35%	21%	22%	14%	16%	25%	14%	63%	73%	8%
Prices:High	19.87	28.75	25.72	19.49	16.14	13.92	14.20	19.00	33.00	44.75
Prices:Low	11.00	14.28	17.41	14.00	9.65	8.25	6.25	7.22	8.13	22.46
P/E Ratio:High	29	27	28	21	29	46	41	NM	NM	88
P/E Ratio:Low	16	13	19	15	17	28	18	NM	NM	44

Income Statement Analysis (Million $)	2009	2008	2007	2006	2005	2004	2003	2002	2001	2000
Commissions	996	1,080	860	785	779	936	1,207	1,206	1,355	2,294
Interest Income	1,428	1,908	2,270	2,113	1,944	1,213	970	1,186	1,857	2,589
Total Revenue	4,414	5,393	5,617	4,988	5,151	4,479	4,328	4,480	5,281	7,139
Interest Expense	221	243	623	679	687	277	241	345	928	1,352
Pretax Income	1,276	2,028	1,853	1,476	1,185	645	710	168	135	1,231
Effective Tax Rate	38.3%	39.4%	39.6%	39.6%	38.4%	35.8%	33.5%	42.3%	42.2%	41.7%
Net Income	787	1,230	1,120	891	730	414	472	97.0	78.0	718
S&P Core Earnings	779	1,247	1,117	875	678	314	357	-31.5	-131	NA

Balance Sheet & Other Financial Data (Million $)	2009	2008	2007	2006	2005	2004	2003	2002	2001	2000
Total Assets	75,431	51,675	42,286	48,992	47,351	47,133	45,866	39,705	40,464	38,154
Cash Items	27,530	20,127	15,567	15,369	17,589	21,797	24,175	24,119	22,148	14,300
Receivables	16,535	13,932	16,482	11,577	11,600	10,323	9,137	7,067	10,066	16,680
Securities Owned	23,036	15,072	8,201	6,386	6,857	5,335	4,023	1,716	1,700	1,603
Securities Borrowed	Nil	Nil	Nil	Nil	Nil	Nil	Nil	Nil	Nil	Nil
Due Brokers & Customers	28,619	21,356	22,212	22,119	25,994	28,622	29,845	27,877	27,822	26,785
Other Liabilities	40,227	25,375	15,441	21,477	NA	NA	NA	NA	NA	NA
Capitalization:Debt	1,512	883	899	388	514	585	772	642	730	770
Capitalization:Equity	5,073	4,061	3,732	5,008	4,450	4,386	4,461	4,011	4,163	4,230
Capitalization:Total	6,585	4,944	4,631	5,396	4,964	4,971	5,233	4,653	4,893	5,000
% Return on Revenue	17.8	22.8	19.9	17.9	14.2	9.2	15.1	3.0	2.0	14.8
% Return on Assets	1.2	2.6	2.5	1.8	1.5	0.9	1.1	0.2	0.2	2.0
% Return on Equity	1.2	31.6	25.6	18.8	16.5	9.4	11.1	2.4	1.9	21.1

Data as orig reptd.; bef. results of disc opers/spec. items. Per share data adj. for stk. divs.; EPS diluted. Quarterly revs. excl. interest expense. E-Estimated. NA-Not Available. NM-Not Meaningful. NR-Not Ranked. UR-Under Review.

Office: 211 Main Street, San Francisco, CA 94105.
Telephone: 415-667-7000.
Email: investor.relations@schwab.com
Website: http://www.schwab.com

Chrmn: C.R. Schwab, Jr.
Pres & CEO: W.W. Bettinger, II
EVP, CFO & Chief Acctg Officer: J.R. Martinetto
EVP, Secy & General Counsel: C.E. Dwyer

EVP & CIO: J. Hier-King
Investor Contact: R.G. Fowler (415-636-9869)
Board Members: N. H. Bechtle, W. W. Bettinger, II, P. P. Butcher, F. C. Herringer, S. T. McLin, A. Sarin, C. R. Schwab, Jr., P. A. Sneed, R. O. Walther, R. N. Wilson

Founded: 1971
Domicile: Delaware
Employees: 12,400

Scripps Networks Interactive Inc

STANDARD
&POOR'S

S&P Recommendation BUY ★★★★☆	Price $48.28 (as of Oct 22, 2010)	12-Mo. Target Price $52.00	Investment Style Large-Cap Value

GICS Sector Consumer Discretionary
Sub-Industry Broadcasting & Cable TV

Summary SNI, spun off by E.W. Scripps in 2008, is one of the leading developers of lifestyle-oriented content for television and the Internet.

Key Stock Statistics (Source S&P, Vickers, company reports)

52-Wk Range	$49.00–36.87	S&P Oper. EPS 2010E	2.01	Market Capitalization(B)	$6.280	Beta	1.12
Trailing 12-Month EPS	$2.03	S&P Oper. EPS 2011E	2.51	Yield (%)	0.62	S&P 3-Yr. Proj. EPS CAGR(%)	16
Trailing 12-Month P/E	23.8	P/E on S&P Oper. EPS 2010E	24.0	Dividend Rate/Share	$0.30	S&P Credit Rating	NA
$10K Invested 5 Yrs Ago	NA	Common Shares Outstg. (M)	166.3	Institutional Ownership (%)	67		

Price Performance

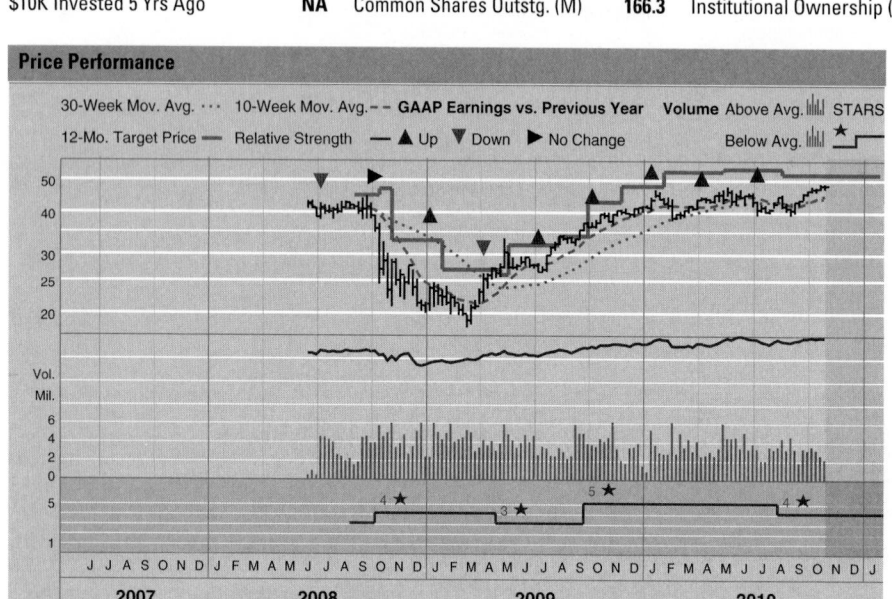

30-Week Mov. Avg. · · · · 10-Week Mov. Avg. – – GAAP Earnings vs. Previous Year   Volume Above Avg. STARS
12-Mo. Target Price —   Relative Strength —   ▲ Up ▼ Down ▶ No Change   Below Avg. ★

Options: Ph

Analysis prepared by **Erik Kolb** on August 12, 2010, when the stock traded at **$ 42.23**.

Highlights

▶ We think SNI, spun off from E.W. Scripps (SSP 5, hold) on July 1, 2008, will grow net revenues 26%, to $1.96 billion, in 2010, compared to a 2.8% pro forma revenue decline in 2009. Although the ad market is still somewhat depressed, we think it is showing significant signs of improvement, and we believe SNI will continue to fare better than most peers. Retransmission revenues should also continue to rise. Specifically, we see a 30% increase at the Lifestyle Media segment and a 11% decline at the Interactive segment. In 2011, we see 11.0% net revenue growth.

▶ We think EBITDA margins will rise to 41.5% in 2010, from 38.7% in 2009, as improving ad rates and higher affiliate fees outweigh integration expenses and the still weak Interactive segment. We also note that most of SNI's programming is low-cost due to its unscripted nature, which we think leads to better margins than most peers. In 2011, we see a 160 basis point improvement to 43.1%.

▶ Our 2010 and 2011 EPS estimates are $2.01 and $2.51, respectively, versus adjusted 2009 EPS of $1.76, which excludes various one-time charges.

Investment Rationale/Risk

▶ We view SNI's niche television networks positively, as we think they will garner attractive ratings and attention from advertisers. The focused content of SNI's networks should also generate consistent advertising from specialty retailers, which should help provide a baseline advertising level. In the near term, we see higher affiliate fees as SNI renegotiates key contracts, especially for the Food Network. We see the beleaguered Interactive Services segment improving in 2011. Given SNI's unique networks and attractive balance sheet, we think it could become an acquisition target at some point.

▶ Risks to our recommendation and target price include a greater-than-expected slowdown in advertising, a decline in ratings for SNI's television networks, and a drop in visitors resulting in lower market share for the Interactive Services segment's comparison shopping websites.

▶ Our 12-month target price of $52 is derived by applying a 10.5X enterprise value multiple, slightly higher than peers in our coverage universe, to our 2011 EBITDA estimate.

Qualitative Risk Assessment

LOW	MEDIUM	HIGH

Our risk assessment reflects SNI's leading TV properties and our view of the company's solid ratings and advertising revenue growth. This is offset by a soft advertising market and higher volatility in the Interactive Services segment.

Quantitative Evaluations

S&P Quality Ranking   NR

D	C	B-	B	B+	A-	A	A+

Relative Strength Rank   MODERATE

70

LOWEST = 1   HIGHEST = 99

Revenue/Earnings Data

Revenue (Million $)

	1Q	2Q	3Q	4Q	Year
2010	469.4	516.0	--	--	--
2009	361.2	391.3	364.5	429.7	1,541
2008	388.3	416.1	374.7	411.5	1,591
2007	332.4	367.2	344.0	397.7	1,441
2006	--	--	--	--	1,323
2005	--	--	--	--	1,002

Earnings Per Share ($)

2010	0.43	0.57	E0.40	E0.56	E2.01
2009	0.37	0.49	0.39	0.40	1.65
2008	0.41	0.33	0.35	-0.94	0.14
2007	--	0.43	0.35	-1.83	-0.72
2006	--	--	--	--	--
2005	--	--	--	--	--

Fiscal year ended Dec. 31. Next earnings report expected: Early November. EPS Estimates based on S&P Operating Earnings; historical GAAP earnings are as reported.

Dividend Data (Dates: mm/dd Payment Date: mm/dd/yy)

Amount ($)	Date Decl.	Ex-Div. Date	Stk. of Record	Payment Date
0.075	11/18	11/25	11/30	12/10/09
0.075	02/18	02/24	02/26	03/10/10
0.075	05/18	05/26	05/31	06/10/10
0.075	08/04	08/27	08/31	09/10/10

Dividends have been paid since 2008. Source: Company reports.

Please read the Required Disclosures and Analyst Certification on the last page of this report.

The **McGraw·Hill** Companies

Scripps Networks Interactive Inc

STANDARD &POOR'S

Business Summary August 12, 2010

CORPORATE OVERVIEW. Scripps Networks Interactive is a lifestyle content and Internet search company with national television networks and interactive brands. SNI manages its operations through the Lifestyle Media (formerly Scripps Networks) and Interactive Services (formerly Interactive Media) segments. Lifestyle Media includes HGTV, Food Network, DIY, Fine Living, Great American Country, a minority interest in Fox-BRV South Sports Holdings, and Internet-based businesses, including RecipeZaar.com, HGTVPro.com, and FrontDoor.com. Interactive Media includes online comparison shopping and consumer information services, including Shopzilla, BizRate and UpMyStreet.

The Lifestyle Media segment derives revenues principally from advertising sales, affiliate fees, and ancillary sales, including the sale and licensing of consumer products. Revenues from the Interactive Media segment are generated primarily from referral fees and commissions paid by merchants and ser-

vice providers for online leads generated by its websites. Lifestyle Media and Interactive Services accounted for 88% and 12% of 2009 revenue, respectively, compared 82% and 18% in 2008, 83% and 17% in 2007, 80% and 20% in 2006, and 90% and 10% in 2005.

In 2009, HGTV accounted for 45.1% of operating revenue, Food Network for 37.1%, DIY for 5.1%, Fine Living for 3.4%, GAC for 2.0%, SN Digital for 6.0%, and Travel Channel for 0.8%. In 2009, the HGTV network reached 98,700 homes, according to Nielsen; Food Network 99,200; DIY 53,200; Fine Living 56,400; GAC 58,500, and Travel Channel 95,200.

Company Financials Fiscal Year Ended Dec. 31

Per Share Data ($)	2009	2008	2007	2006	2005	2004	2003	2002	2001	2000
Tangible Book Value	NM	2.26	2.25	NA	NA	NA	NA	NA	NA	NA
Cash Flow	2.14	0.59	-0.19	NA	NA	NA	NA	NA	NA	NA
Earnings	1.65	0.14	-0.72	NA	NA	NA	NA	NA	NA	NA
S&P Core Earnings	1.68	1.63	1.11	1.44	NA	NA	NA	NA	NA	NA
Dividends	0.30	0.15	NA	NA	NA	NA	NA	NA	NA	NA
Payout Ratio	18%	107%	NA	NA	NA	NA	NA	NA	NA	NA
Prices:High	42.36	44.98	NA	NA	NA	NA	NA	NA	NA	NA
Prices:Low	18.10	20.00	NA	NA	NA	NA	NA	NA	NA	NA
P/E Ratio:High	26	NM	NA	NA	NA	NA	NA	NA	NA	NA
P/E Ratio:Low	11	NM	NA	NA	NA	NA	NA	NA	NA	NA

Income Statement Analysis (Million $)	2009	2008	2007	2006	2005	2004	2003	2002	2001	2000
Revenue	1,541	1,591	1,441	1,323	1,002	NA	NA	NA	NA	NA
Operating Income	NA	651	591	NA	NA	NA	NA	NA	NA	NA
Depreciation	81.5	73.9	86.7	101	67.0	NA	NA	NA	NA	NA
Interest Expense	2.81	14.2	15.2	54.0	37.0	NA	NA	NA	NA	NA
Pretax Income	520	309	98.7	427	343	NA	NA	NA	NA	NA
Effective Tax Rate	31.0%	62.5%	NM	28.3%	32.8%	NA	NA	NA	NA	NA
Net Income	273	23.6	-118	234	176	NA	NA	NA	NA	NA
S&P Core Earnings	278	267	183	235	NA	NA	NA	NA	NA	NA

Balance Sheet & Other Financial Data (Million $)	2009	2008	2007	2006	2005	2004	2003	2002	2001	2000
Cash	254	12.7	44.2	19.0	NA	NA	NA	NA	NA	NA
Current Assets	982	638	658	604	NA	NA	NA	NA	NA	NA
Total Assets	2,963	1,773	2,064	2,385	NA	NA	NA	NA	NA	NA
Current Liabilities	211	166	124	172	NA	NA	NA	NA	NA	NA
Long Term Debt	884	80.0	450	765	NA	NA	NA	NA	NA	NA
Common Equity	1,384	1,135	1,157	1,186	NA	NA	NA	NA	NA	NA
Total Capital	2,533	1,368	1,391	2,069	NA	NA	NA	NA	NA	NA
Capital Expenditures	90.0	77.4	NA	40.4	29.0	NA	NA	NA	NA	NA
Cash Flow	355	97.5	-31.0	335	243	NA	NA	NA	NA	NA
Current Ratio	4.7	3.8	5.3	3.5	NA	NA	NA	NA	NA	NA
% Long Term Debt of Capitalization	Nil	5.8	32.3	39.2	Nil	NA	NA	NA	NA	NA
% Net Income of Revenue	17.7	1.5	NM	17.7	17.5	NA	NA	NA	NA	NA
% Return on Assets	11.5	1.2	NM	NA	NA	NA	NA	NA	NA	NA
% Return on Equity	NA	2.2	NM	NA	NA	NA	NA	NA	NA	NA

Data as orig reptd.; bef. results of disc opers/spec. items. Per share data adj. for stk. divs.; EPS diluted. Data for 2007 pro forma; bal. sheet & book val. as of March 31, 2008. E-Estimated. NA-Not Available. NM-Not Meaningful. NR-Not Ranked. UR-Under Review.

Office: 312 Walnut Street, Cincinnati, OH 45202.
Telephone: 513-824-3200.
Website:
http://www.scrippsnetworksinteractive.com
Chrmn, Pres & CEO: K.W. Lowe

COO: R. Boehne
EVP & CTO: M.S. Hale
CFO & Chief Admin Officer: J.G. NeCastro
Chief Acctg Officer: J. Liddicoat

Board Members: J. H. Burlingame, M. R. Costa, D. A. Galloway, K. W. Lowe, J. Mohn, N. B. Paumgarten, M. M. Peirce, D. Pond, J. Sagansky, N. E. Scagliotti, R. W. Tysoe

Founded: 2007
Domicile: Ohio
Employees: 1,800

The McGraw-Hill Companies

Sealed Air Corp

STANDARD &POOR'S

S&P Recommendation **BUY** ★★★★☆	Price $23.76 (as of Oct 22, 2010)	12-Mo. Target Price $26.00	Investment Style Large-Cap Growth

GICS Sector Materials
Sub-Industry Paper Packaging

Summary This company is a leading global manufacturer of a wide range of food and protective packaging materials and systems.

Key Stock Statistics (Source S&P, Vickers, company reports)

52-Wk Range	$24.20–18.43	S&P Oper. EPS 2010**E**	1.65	Market Capitalization(B)	$3.792	Beta	1.36
Trailing 12-Month EPS	$1.43	S&P Oper. EPS 2011**E**	1.80	Yield (%)	2.19	S&P 3-Yr. Proj. EPS CAGR(%)	11
Trailing 12-Month P/E	16.6	P/E on S&P Oper. EPS 2010**E**	14.4	Dividend Rate/Share	$0.52	S&P Credit Rating	BB+
$10K Invested 5 Yrs Ago	$11,141	Common Shares Outstg. (M)	159.6	Institutional Ownership (%)	87		

Price Performance

- 30-Week Mov. Avg. ···· 10-Week Mov. Avg. --- **GAAP Earnings vs. Previous Year** Volume Above Avg. STARS
- 12-Mo. Target Price — Relative Strength — ▲ Up ▼ Down ▶ No Change Below Avg. ★

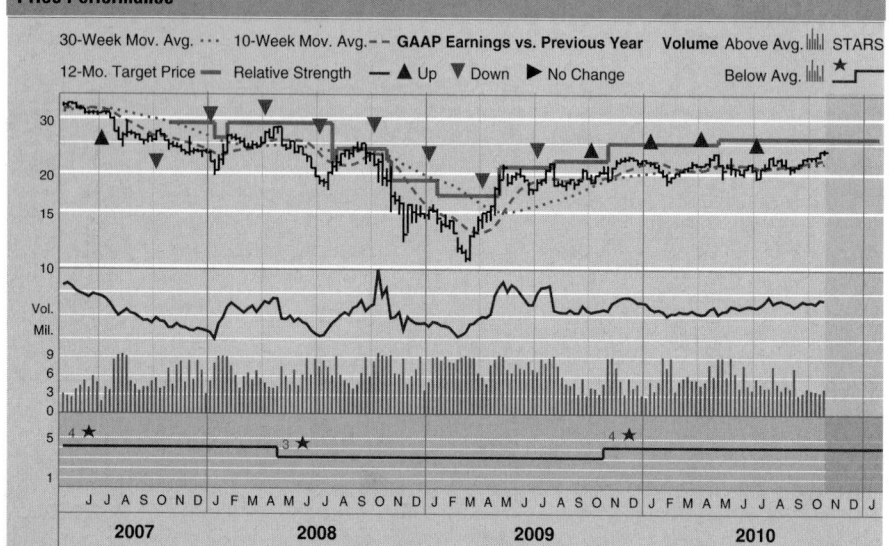

Options: CBOE, P, Ph

Analysis prepared by **Stewart Scharf** on August 03, 2010, when the stock traded at **$ 22.25**.

Highlights

▸ We expect net sales to rise about 6% (before foreign exchange) in 2010, driven by strength in developing regions and a pick-up in demand for protective packaging unit volume in the U.S. and Europe. We see favorable trends for new food packaging and solutions products in parts of Latin America and Asia/Pacific. However, we still believe consumers will dine at home more and buy lower-priced meat products, especially in Europe.

▸ We look for gross margins to widen by around 100 basis points in 2010, from 28.7% in 2009, as price hikes and contractual pricing pass-throughs offset higher resin prices, following a lag in the first half; we also see a better product mix and improving supply chain efficiencies. In our view, EBITDA margins should expand somewhat from 2009's 16.6% (excluding special charges), due to well-controlled costs and im-proved productivity resulting from SEE's global manufacturing strategy.

▸ We estimate a higher effective tax rate of about 27% for 2010, and operating EPS of $1.65 (before $0.02 of restructuring charges), advanc-ing 9% to $1.80 for 2011.

Investment Rationale/Risk

▸ Our Buy recommendation is based on our view that global markets will gradually recover into 2011. We expect the company to focus on gen-erating strong free cash and developing new technologies and innovative products, espe-cially for emerging markets. Our valuation mod-els also suggest the shares are undervalued at recent levels.

▸ Risks to our recommendation and target price include a prolonged global economic downturn, another significant increase in resin costs, a strengthening U.S. dollar, and a new "mad cow" type disease scare. We have some concern re-garding corporate governance issues, since at least one former CEO serves on the board of di-rectors.

▸ Applying a P/E of 15X to our 2010 EPS estimate - - in line with historical forward levels but at a modest premium to the S&P Paper Packaging sub-industry group multiple -- we arrive at a value of $25. Our discounted cash flow model, which assumes a perpetual growth rate of 3.5% and a weighted average cost of capital of 9%, leads to an intrinsic value of $27. Our 12-month target price of $26 is a blend of these two met-rics.

Qualitative Risk Assessment

LOW	MEDIUM	HIGH

Our risk assessment reflects challenging global markets, volatile resin costs, and food-related health issues that could lead to restrictions on imports and exports. This is offset by our view of the company's sound balance sheet and cash flow generation.

Quantitative Evaluations

S&P Quality Ranking B

D	C	B-	B	B+	A-	A	A+

Relative Strength Rank MODERATE

70

LOWEST = 1   HIGHEST = 99

Revenue/Earnings Data

Revenue (Million $)

	1Q	2Q	3Q	4Q	Year
2010	1,061	1,090	--	--	--
2009	988.5	1,028	1,080	1,146	4,243
2008	1,177	1,279	1,219	1,168	4,844
2007	1,095	1,145	1,161	1,250	4,651
2006	1,019	1,082	1,081	1,146	4,328
2005	969.8	1,020	1,020	1,076	4,085

Earnings Per Share ($)

2010	0.35	0.38	E0.45	E0.55	E1.65
2009	0.32	0.33	0.34	0.37	1.35
2008	0.33	0.34	0.05	0.26	0.99
2007	0.67	0.40	0.39	0.43	1.89
2006	0.30	0.31	0.41	0.45	1.47
2005	0.29	0.33	0.34	0.39	1.35

Fiscal year ended Dec. 31. Next earnings report expected: Late October. EPS Estimates based on S&P Operating Earnings; historical GAAP earnings are as reported.

Dividend Data (Dates: mm/dd Payment Date: mm/dd/yy)

Amount ($)	Date Decl.	Ex-Div. Date	Stk. of Record	Payment Date
0.120	02/18	03/03	03/05	03/19/10
0.120	04/13	06/02	06/04	06/18/10
0.130	07/27	09/01	09/03	09/17/10
0.130	10/14	12/01	12/03	12/17/10

Dividends have been paid since 2006. Source: Company reports.

Please read the Required Disclosures and Analyst Certification on the last page of this report.

The McGraw·Hill Companies

Sealed Air Corp

STANDARD &POOR'S

Business Summary August 03, 2010

CORPORATE OVERVIEW. Sealed Air Corp., a leading protective and specialty packaging company, expects an increasing proportion of sales to come from outside the U.S. Foreign operations (excluding Canada, with about 3%) accounted for about 50% of sales in 2009, with Europe accounting for 28% of total sales, Latin America 9.1%, and Asia/Pacific 13%.

As of the second quarter of 2007, the company realigned its segment reporting to reflect its growth strategies in core markets and new business opportunities, as it focuses on long-term global trends, including higher living standards in emerging markets, conservation and energy efficiency, convenience and longevity. The food packaging segment (43% of net sales in 2009; $252 million of operating income) focuses on industrial products and new technologies that enable food processors to package and ship fresh and processed meats and cheeses through their supply chain. Food Solutions (21%; $86 million) targets advancements in food packaging technologies that provide consumers with fresh meals from food service outlets or expanding retail cases at grocery stores. Protective Packaging (28%; $150 million) includes core packaging technologies and solutions slated for traditional industrial applications while emphasizing consumer-oriented packaging solutions. Other sales accounted for 7.5% ($12 million).

Food packaging products primarily consist of flexible materials and related

systems marketed mainly under the Cryovac trademark for a broad range of perishable food applications. The segment also manufactures polystyrene foam trays that are used by supermarkets and food processors to protect and display fresh meat, poultry and produce. The U.S. Department of Agriculture (USDA) projects increases in U.S. protein consumption. Case-ready packaging sales exceeded $480 million in 2008. The protective packaging products segment includes surface protection and other cushioning products such as air cellular packaging materials, and plastic sheets containing encapsulated air bubbles that protect products from damage during shipment, under the Bubble Wrap and Air Cap brand names. The new "Other" segment focuses on newer markets, including specialty materials for non-packaging applications such as insulation and products for value-added medical applications, as well as new ventures that include products sourced from renewable materials.

In the second quarter of 2010, SEE reported a $0.03 a share foreign currency gain related to its Venezuelan unit. In the first quarter of 2010, the company incurred a $0.6 million pretax restructuring charge ($0.01 a share, after tax). In 2009, SEE incurred restructuring and other charges of $0.09 per share.

Company Financials Fiscal Year Ended Dec. 31

Per Share Data ($)	2009	2008	2007	2006	2005	2004	2003	2002	2001	2000
Tangible Book Value	1.21	NM	NM	NM	NM	NM	NM	NM	NM	NM
Cash Flow	2.18	1.77	2.62	2.30	2.64	1.99	1.95	-1.17	1.92	2.16
Earnings	1.35	0.99	1.89	1.47	1.35	1.13	1.00	-2.15	0.61	0.97
S&P Core Earnings	1.42	1.06	1.78	1.49	1.37	1.14	1.03	1.29	0.63	NA
Dividends	0.48	0.48	0.40	0.30	Nil	Nil	Nil	Nil	Nil	Nil
Payout Ratio	36%	48%	21%	20%	Nil	Nil	Nil	Nil	Nil	Nil
Prices:High	22.99	28.32	33.87	32.88	28.32	27.45	27.24	24.20	23.55	30.94
Prices:Low	10.38	12.01	22.41	22.81	22.78	22.03	17.50	6.35	14.40	13.19
P/E Ratio:High	17	29	18	22	21	24	27	NM	39	32
P/E Ratio:Low	8	12	12	16	17	20	17	NM	24	14

Income Statement Analysis (Million $)

	2009	2008	2007	2006	2005	2004	2003	2002	2001	2000
Revenue	4,243	4,844	4,651	4,328	4,085	3,798	3,532	3,204	3,067	3,068
Operating Income	653	642	712	707	687	716	693	1,766	641	687
Depreciation	155	155	149	168	175	180	154	166	221	220
Interest Expense	155	137	150	148	150	154	134	65.3	76.4	64.5
Pretax Income	330	222	456	400	377	323	377	-392	297	413
Effective Tax Rate	26.0%	19.1%	22.6%	31.5%	32.1%	33.2%	36.2%	NM	47.3%	45.5%
Net Income	244	180	353	274	256	216	240	-309	157	225
S&P Core Earnings	254	193	333	278	259	219	192	227	111	NA

Balance Sheet & Other Financial Data (Million $)

	2009	2008	2007	2006	2005	2004	2003	2002	2001	2000
Cash	694	129	430	407	456	412	365	127	13.8	11.2
Current Assets	2,073	1,673	1,936	1,757	1,695	1,611	1,428	1,056	776	877
Total Assets	5,416	4,978	5,438	5,021	4,864	4,855	4,704	4,261	3,908	4,048
Current Liabilities	1,434	1,622	1,742	1,406	1,534	1,304	1,190	1,153	627	675
Long Term Debt	1,626	1,290	1,532	1,827	1,813	2,088	2,260	868	788	944
Common Equity	2,212	1,942	2,020	1,530	1,392	1,334	1,124	813	850	753
Total Capital	3,845	3,220	3,561	3,364	3,229	3,448	3,418	3,039	3,215	3,301
Capital Expenditures	80.3	181	211	168	96.9	103	124	91.6	146	114
Cash Flow	399	335	502	442	430	395	366	-197	322	381
Current Ratio	1.4	1.0	1.1	1.2	1.1	1.2	1.2	0.9	1.2	1.3
% Long Term Debt of Capitalization	42.3	40.1	43.0	54.3	56.1	60.5	66.1	28.6	24.5	28.6
% Net Income of Revenue	5.8	3.7	7.6	6.3	6.3	5.7	6.8	NM	5.1	7.3
% Return on Assets	4.7	3.5	6.8	5.5	5.3	4.5	5.4	NM	3.9	5.7
% Return on Equity	11.8	9.1	19.2	19.9	18.8	17.5	21.9	NM	12.7	24.7

Data as orig reptd.; bef. results of disc opers/spec. items. Per share data adj. for stk. divs.; EPS diluted. E-Estimated. NA-Not Available. NM-Not Meaningful. NR-Not Ranked. UR-Under Review.

Office: 200 Riverfront Blvd, Elmwood Park, NJ 07407-1033.
Telephone: 201-791-7600.
Website: http://www.sealedair.com
Pres & CEO: W.V. Hickey

SVP & CFO: D.H. Kelsey
Chief Acctg Officer & Cntlr: J.S. Warren
Treas: T.S. Christie
Secy & General Counsel: H.K. White

Investor Contact: A. Butler (201-703-4210)
Board Members: H. Brown, M. Chu, L. R. Codey, P. Duff, D. T. Dunphy, C. F. Farrell, Jr., W. V. Hickey, J. Kosecoff, K. P. Manning, W. J. Marino

Founded: 1996
Domicile: Delaware
Employees: 16,200

Sears Holdings Corp

S&P Recommendation SELL ★ ★ ★ ★ ★

Price	**12-Mo. Target Price**	**Investment Style**
$76.32 (as of Oct 22, 2010)	$58.00	Large-Cap Blend

GICS Sector Consumer Discretionary
Sub-Industry Department Stores

Summary Through its wholly owned Sears and Kmart subsidiaries, Sears Holdings is among the largest broadline retailers in the U.S.

Key Stock Statistics (Source S&P, Vickers, company reports)

52-Wk Range	$125.42–59.21	S&P Oper. EPS 2011**E**	2.50	Market Capitalization(B)	$8.445	Beta	1.64
Trailing 12-Month EPS	$2.44	S&P Oper. EPS 2012**E**	2.70	Yield (%)	Nil	S&P 3-Yr. Proj. EPS CAGR(%)	5
Trailing 12-Month P/E	31.3	P/E on S&P Oper. EPS 2011**E**	30.5	Dividend Rate/Share	Nil	S&P Credit Rating	BB-
$10K Invested 5 Yrs Ago	$6,269	Common Shares Outstg. (M)	110.6	Institutional Ownership (%)	87		

Price Performance

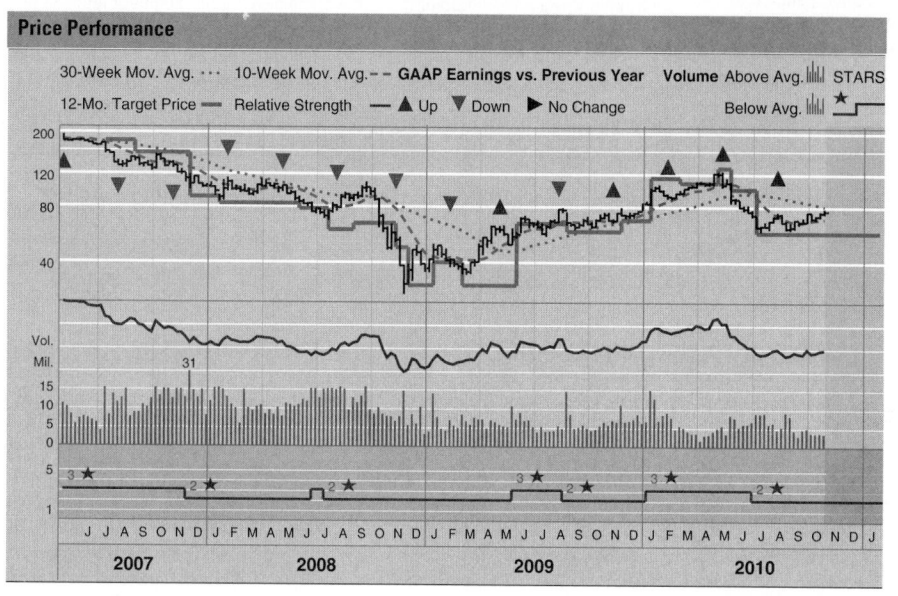

30-Week Mov. Avg. ···· 10-Week Mov. Avg. - - **GAAP Earnings vs. Previous Year** Volume Above Avg. STARS
12-Mo. Target Price — Relative Strength — ▲ Up ▼ Down ▶ No Change Below Avg. ★

Options: ASE, CBOE, P, Ph

Analysis prepared by **Jason N. Asaeda** on August 26, 2010, when the stock traded at **$ 66.00**.

Highlights

➤ We project net sales of $43.5 billion in FY 11 (Jan.). By division, we expect same-store sales to be flat at Kmart and to decline 3% at Sears. We look for Kmart to outperform Sears (domestic) on the strength of its value proposition on basic goods, a layaway program that enables cash-strapped customers to purchase higher-margin discretionary categories, and a new customer loyalty program that rewards frequent shoppers. While we believe promotional activity, new products and the federal Cash for Appliances Program supported a recovery in appliance sales during the first half of FY 11, we think a soft U.S. housing market will hurt demand for big ticket home items at Sears.

➤ We look for operating margins to narrow modestly on lower-margin appliance sales, and investments in new customer service initiatives, partially offset by inventory and cost controls, and closure of underperforming stores.

➤ Factoring in likely share buybacks, we see EPS of $2.50 in FY 11, down from FY 10's $2.71 (excluding a $44 million asset sales gain, $33 million in mark-to-market losses on Sears Canada hedge transactions, and a $131 million charge for store closings).

Investment Rationale/Risk

➤ Our sell recommendation is based on valuation. We look for SHLD to effectively manage its flow of goods, which should help keep inventories in line with demand, and to maintain a low cost structure to limit margin erosion. However, we think Kmart's food and consumables business, which we consider to be a key traffic driver, is being hurt by aggressive pricing from competitors such as Wal-Mart Stores, Inc. (WMT 51, Strong Buy). We also see downside risk for Sears given a sluggish housing recovery and what we perceive to be a lack of destination brands in fashion apparel and accessories relative to moderate-price department store peers such as J.C. Penney (JCP 21, Buy). Our corporate governance concerns include cash-only payments to directors and the non-disclosure of specific hurdle rates for performance-based equity awards.

➤ Risks to our recommendation and target price include better-than-expected sales due to faster-than-expected economic and housing recoveries.

➤ Our 12-month target price of $58 reflects SHLD's historical median forward P/E multiple of 23.1X applied to our FY 11 EPS estimate.

Qualitative Risk Assessment

LOW	MEDIUM	HIGH

Our risk assessment reflects what we consider Kmart's and Sears's long records of inconsistent sales and earnings. This is partially offset by our view of SHLD's opportunity to leverage the two units' best practices and brands to strengthen its competitive positioning.

Quantitative Evaluations

S&P Quality Ranking NR

D	C	B-	B	B+	A-	A	A+

Relative Strength Rank MODERATE

70

LOWEST = 1 HIGHEST = 99

Revenue/Earnings Data

Revenue (Million $)

	1Q	2Q	3Q	4Q	Year
2011	10,046	10,458	--	--	--
2010	10,055	10,551	10,190	13,247	44,043
2009	11,068	11,762	10,660	13,280	46,770
2008	11,702	12,239	11,548	1,507	50,703
2007	11,998	12,785	11,941	16,288	53,012
2006	7,626	13,192	12,202	16,086	49,124

Earnings Per Share ($)

2011	0.14	-0.35	E-0.98	E3.75	E2.50
2010	-0.22	-0.79	-1.09	3.74	1.99
2009	-0.42	0.50	-1.16	1.55	0.42
2008	1.40	0.51	0.01	3.21	5.70
2007	1.14	1.88	1.27	5.33	9.57
2006	0.65	0.98	0.35	4.03	6.17

Fiscal year ended Jan. 31. Next earnings report expected: Mid November. EPS Estimates based on S&P Operating Earnings; historical GAAP earnings are as reported.

Dividend Data

No cash dividends have been paid.

Please read the Required Disclosures and Analyst Certification on the last page of this report.

The **McGraw·Hill** Companies

Sears Holdings Corp

STANDARD &POOR'S

Business Summary August 26, 2010

CORPORATE OVERVIEW. Through the March 2005 merger of Kmart Holding Corp. and Sears, Roebuck and Co., which continue to operate under their separate brand names, Sears Holdings has emerged as one of the largest broadline retailers in the U.S. based on FY 09 (Jan.) reported revenues. As of July 31, 2010, the company operated 2,670 Sears-branded full line and specialty stores in the U.S. and Canada (operated by Sears Canada), and 1,309 Kmart-branded discount stores and supercenters across the U.S.

CORPORATE STRATEGY. SHLD believes it has an opportunity to leverage Kmart's off-mall locations to expand the distribution of Sears products and services at a more rapid pace and at a lower cost than Sears would have been able to accomplish on its own. The company also sees the potential for Kmart to improve its value proposition and competitive positioning through the addition of Sears-owned brands and services (cross-selling).

SHLD initially planned to convert about 400 Kmart stores to a new mid-size

store format called Sears Essentials, which combines convenience items found in Kmart stores with Sears's more destination-focused purchase categories. However, based on what we believe were disappointing results from 50 Sears Essentials stores opened during FY 06, SHLD decided to focus on its other off-mall format, Sears Grand.

In response to declining sales trends, the company is attempting to raise productivity of its Sears and Kmart businesses through aggressive closure of underperforming stores in FY 10. During the fiscal year, SHLD closed 62 Kmart and Sears full-line stores. The company recorded a charge for costs associated with store closings and severance of $131 million in FY 10.

Company Financials Fiscal Year Ended Jan. 31

Per Share Data ($)	2010	2009	2008	2007	2006	2005	2004	2003	2002	2001
Tangible Book Value	39.10	38.57	42.64	49.25	41.80	50.21	24.36	NA	NA	NA
Cash Flow	9.85	8.14	12.95	16.90	12.24	11.59	2.81	-4.02	-3.57	1.10
Earnings	1.99	0.42	5.70	9.57	6.17	11.00	2.52	-5.47	-5.24	-0.48
S&P Core Earnings	1.39	-0.99	4.44	9.24	4.53	4.51	-4.53	-6.80	-5.74	-0.55
Dividends	NA	Nil	Nil	Nil	Nil	Nil	Nil	Nil	NA	NA
Payout Ratio	Nil	Nil	Nil	Nil	Nil	Nil	Nil	NA	NA	NA
Calendar Year	2009	2008	2007	2006	2005	2004	2003	2002	2001	2000
Prices:High	86.53	114.00	195.18	182.38	163.50	119.69	34.55	NA	NA	NA
Prices:Low	34.27	26.80	98.25	114.90	84.51	22.41	12.00	NA	NA	NA
P/E Ratio:High	43	NM	34	19	26	11	14	NA	NA	NA
P/E Ratio:Low	17	NM	17	12	14	2	5	NA	NA	NA

Income Statement Analysis (Million $)

	2010	2009	2008	2007	2006	2005	2004	2003	2002	2001
Revenue	44,043	46,770	50,703	53,012	49,124	19,701	17,072	30,762	36,151	37,028
Operating Income	1,834	1,530	2,542	3,611	2,901	944	442	-1,303	-386	1,460
Depreciation	926	981	1,049	1,142	932	69.0	31.0	737	824	777
Interest Expense	265	272	286	337	322	146	105	155	418	333
Pretax Income	420	184	1,452	2,464	1,965	1,775	400	-3,286	-2,702	-378
Effective Tax Rate	29.3%	46.2%	37.9%	37.7%	36.4%	37.7%	38.0%	NM	4.26%	35.5%
Net Income	235	53.0	826	1,490	948	1,106	248	-3,262	-2,587	-244
S&P Core Earnings	165	-126	645	1,439	696	448	-405	-3,439	-2,840	-260

Balance Sheet & Other Financial Data (Million $)

	2010	2009	2008	2007	2006	2005	2004	2003	2002	2001
Cash	1,689	1,173	1,622	3,968	4,440	3,435	2,088	613	1,245	401
Current Assets	11,438	11,416	12,802	15,406	15,207	7,541	5,811	6,102	7,884	7,624
Total Assets	24,808	25,342	27,397	30,066	30,573	8,651	6,084	11,238	14,298	14,630
Current Liabilities	8,786	8,512	9,562	10,052	10,350	2,086	1,776	2,120	624	3,799
Long Term Debt	1,698	1,527	2,606	2,849	3,268	661	819	623	4,565	2,971
Common Equity	9,435	9,380	10,667	12,714	11,611	4,469	2,192	-301	3,459	6,083
Total Capital	11,615	14,168	13,586	15,563	14,879	5,130	3,011	322	8,024	9,122
Capital Expenditures	361	497	570	513	546	230	108	252	1,456	1,087
Cash Flow	1,161	1,034	1,875	2,632	1,880	1,175	279	-2,525	-1,763	533
Current Ratio	1.3	1.3	1.3	1.5	1.5	3.6	3.3	2.9	12.6	2.0
% Long Term Debt of Capitalization	14.6	10.8	19.2	18.3	22.0	12.9	27.2	NM	56.9	32.6
% Net Income of Revenue	0.5	0.1	1.6	2.8	1.9	5.6	1.5	NM	NM	NM
% Return on Assets	0.9	0.2	2.9	4.9	4.8	15.0	3.9	NM	NM	NM
% Return on Equity	2.5	0.5	7.1	12.3	11.8	33.1	12.7	NM	NM	NM

Data as orig reptd.; bef. results of disc opers/spec. items. Per share data adj. for stk. divs.; EPS diluted. E-Estimated. NA-Not Available. NM-Not Meaningful. NR-Not Ranked. UR-Under Review.

Office: 3333 Beverly Rd, Hoffman Estates, IL 60179-0001.
Telephone: 847-286-2500.
Website: http://www.searsholdings.com
Chrmn: E.S. Lampert

Pres & CEO: W.B. Johnson
SVP & CFO: M.D. Collins
SVP, Chief Acctg Officer & Cntlr: W.K. Phelan
SVP & CIO: T. Kasbe

Board Members: W. B. Johnson, W. C. Kunkler, III, E. S. Lampert, S. T. Mnuchin, A. N. Reese, E. Scott, T. J. Tisch
Founded: 1899
Domicile: Delaware
Employees: 322,000

Sempra Energy

STANDARD &POOR'S

S&P Recommendation HOLD ★★★☆☆	**Price** $53.52 (as of Oct 22, 2010)	**12-Mo. Target Price** $55.00	**Investment Style** Large-Cap Blend

GICS Sector Utilities
Sub-Industry Multi-Utilities

Summary This gas and electric utility is also engaged in unregulated power, liquefied natural gas, and international energy projects.

Key Stock Statistics (Source S&P, Vickers, company reports)

52-Wk Range	$57.18– 43.91	S&P Oper. EPS 2010E	3.80	Market Capitalization(B)	$13.265	Beta	0.59
Trailing 12-Month EPS	$3.74	S&P Oper. EPS 2011E	4.49	Yield (%)	2.91	S&P 3-Yr. Proj. EPS CAGR(%)	2
Trailing 12-Month P/E	14.3	P/E on S&P Oper. EPS 2010E	14.1	Dividend Rate/Share	$1.56	S&P Credit Rating	BBB+
$10K Invested 5 Yrs Ago	$14,753	Common Shares Outstg. (M)	247.9	Institutional Ownership (%)	66		

Price Performance

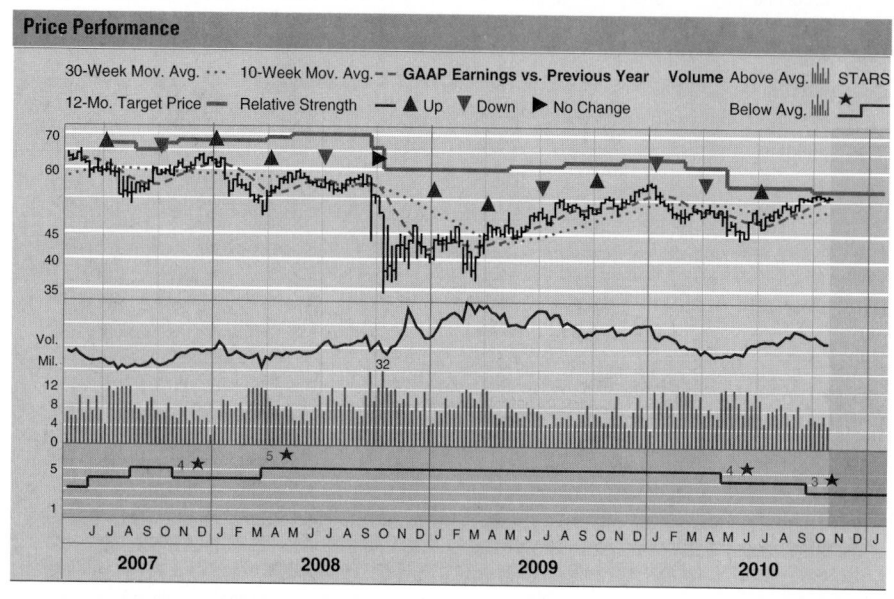

30-Week Mov. Avg. · · · 10-Week Mov. Avg. — GAAP Earnings vs. Previous Year   Volume Above Avg. STARS
12-Mo. Target Price — Relative Strength — ▲ Up ▼ Down ▶ No Change   Below Avg. ★

Options: CBOE

Analysis prepared by **Christopher B. Muir** on October 01, 2010, when the stock traded at **$ 54.16**.

Highlights

➤ We see revenues rising 13% in 2010 and 2.5% in 2011. We believe 2010 growth should accelerate due to the addition of an LNG facility that opened in late 2009, and the November 2009 completion of Rockies Express (REX)-East. We see additional projects being completed in 2010 and 2011. Rate increases at the utilities should also help revenue growth.

➤ We expect operating margins to widen to 16.8% in 2010 and 17.4% in 2011, from 16.1% in 2009, as we see lower per-revenue operations & maintenance expenses partly offset by higher per-revenue cost of gas, electric fuel, and purchased power. We see pretax margins falling to 15.0% in 2010 and 16.7% in 2011, from 20.6% in 2009, as we expect higher interest expense and lower non-operating income.

➤ We forecast 2010 operating EPS of $3.80, which excludes net nonrecurring charges of $0.41, down 21% from 2009's $4.78, which excludes net nonrecurring charges of $0.26. We see reduced contributions from the commodities trading joint venture as responsible for the decreased earnings. Our 2011 EPS forecast is $4.49, an 18% increase, helped by debt reduction and share repurchases.

Investment Rationale/Risk

➤ We view favorably SRE's plans to sell its commodities trading joint venture, as we see proceeds being used to reduce debt and repurchase shares. The joint venture has already agreed to sell the European and Asian businesses and may renegotiate the terms of the joint venture agreement to facilitate a sale of the remaining North American business. Separately, Cameron LNG and the REX-East pipeline started operating in 2009. We see growth opportunities in all of SRE's businesses.

➤ Risks to our recommendation and target price include declining wholesale power margins, potential losses from energy and metals trading, or a weaker-than-expected economy.

➤ The stock recently traded at a multiple of 11.9X our 2011 EPS estimate, a 7% discount to multi-utility peers. Our 12-month target price of $55 is about 12.3X our 2011 EPS estimate, a 3% discount to our peer P/E forecast, warranted, we believe, by SRE's prospects for slightly stronger-than-peers EPS and dividend growth beyond 2010, offset by uncertainty related to the price it could receive for its North American commodities trading joint venture.

Qualitative Risk Assessment

LOW	**MEDIUM**	HIGH

Our risk assessment reflects a balance between stable and steady earnings provided by SRE's regulated gas and electric utility operations and cyclical and volatile earnings from unregulated businesses, including power generation, energy marketing and trading, and international energy investments.

Quantitative Evaluations

S&P Quality Ranking   A-

D	C	B-	B	B+	**A-**	A	A+

Relative Strength Rank   MODERATE

46

LOWEST = 1   HIGHEST = 99

Revenue/Earnings Data

Revenue (Million $)

	1Q	2Q	3Q	4Q	Year
2010	2,534	2,008	--	--	--
2009	2,108	1,689	1,853	2,456	8,106
2008	3,270	2,503	2,692	2,293	10,758
2007	3,004	2,661	2,663	3,110	11,438
2006	3,336	2,486	2,694	3,245	11,761
2005	2,697	2,276	2,770	3,994	11,737

Earnings Per Share ($)

2010	0.42	0.89	E1.12	E0.97	E3.80
2009	1.29	0.80	1.27	1.16	4.52
2008	0.92	0.98	1.24	1.31	4.43
2007	0.86	1.06	1.24	1.10	4.26
2006	0.90	0.71	2.07	0.49	4.17
2005	0.92	0.49	0.86	1.40	3.69

Fiscal year ended Dec. 31. Next earnings report expected: Early November. EPS Estimates based on S&P Operating Earnings; historical GAAP earnings are as reported.

Dividend Data (Dates: mm/dd Payment Date: mm/dd/yy)

Amount ($)	Date Decl.	Ex-Div. Date	Stk. of Record	Payment Date
0.390	12/18	12/28	12/30	01/15/10
0.390	02/12	03/16	03/18	04/15/10
0.390	05/12	06/16	06/18	07/15/10
0.390	08/19	09/27	09/29	10/15/10

Dividends have been paid since 1998. Source: Company reports.

Sempra Energy

STANDARD
&POOR'S

Business Summary October 01, 2010

CORPORATE OVERVIEW. Sempra Energy is a holding company that operates five segments in two major divisions: California Utilities (CU) and Sempra Global. The CU division includes regulated public utilities Southern California Gas (SCG -- 36% of 2009 revenue) and San Diego Gas & Electric (SDGE -- 41%), which provide electricity and natural gas services in the Southern California. Sempra Global includes Sempra Generation (13%), which develops and operates power plants and energy infrastructure; RBS Sempra Commodities (1%), a joint venture that provides marketing and risk management services for energy products and base metals; Sempra Pipelines & Storage (6%), which operates in Mexico, the U.S. and South America; and other (3%), which primarily operates LNG receipt terminals in North America, but also includes parent organizations.

CORPORATE STRATEGY. Sempra seeks to increase EPS through faster growth in its unregulated businesses through both acquisitions and organic growth. In the utility segment, the company focuses on managing regulatory risk as well as operating and capital expenditures. Recently, SRE has focused on new construction in most of its segments. The company has recently focused on developing renewable generation initiatives. In 2008, we believe the company reduced its risk profile and enhanced its growth prospects by placing its commodities trading business into a joint venture with a partner that has a stronger credit profile, but has recently agreed to sell the entire business.

In July 2007, SRE announced a deal with the Royal Bank of Scotland (RBS 15, Hold) that placed its commodity trading business in a joint venture. At closing, on April 1, 2008, SRE received about $1 billion in cash that had been used as collateral. RBS has been forced to sell its stake in the venture by the European Commission. On February 16, 2010, the venture agreed to sell the European and Asian businesses for $1.7 billion. SRE's share of the proceeds is expected to be $1.2 billion, which it plans to use to repurchase shares and reduce debt. The venture now intends to sell the entire business rather than to seek a new partner to replace RBS. RBS Sempra sold its retail business on September 20, 2010, for $317 million and announced it might take a charge for $50 million to $150 million, indicating to us that it might not get as much as it originally expected for the remainder of the business.

Company Financials Fiscal Year Ended Dec. 31

Per Share Data ($)	2009	2008	2007	2006	2005	2004	2003	2002	2001	2000
Tangible Book Value	34.53	30.54	31.27	28.67	23.97	20.79	17.14	13.78	13.17	12.27
Cash Flow	7.66	7.17	6.86	6.70	6.25	6.59	6.12	5.68	5.35	4.76
Earnings	4.52	4.43	4.26	4.17	3.69	3.93	3.24	2.79	2.52	2.06
S&P Core Earnings	4.83	3.59	4.26	4.19	3.44	3.65	3.29	2.16	1.76	NA
Dividends	1.56	1.37	1.24	1.20	1.16	1.00	1.00	1.00	1.00	1.00
Payout Ratio	35%	31%	29%	29%	31%	25%	31%	36%	40%	49%
Prices:High	57.18	63.00	66.38	57.35	47.86	37.93	30.90	26.25	28.61	24.88
Prices:Low	36.43	34.29	50.95	42.90	35.53	29.51	22.25	15.50	17.31	16.19
P/E Ratio:High	13	14	16	14	13	10	10	9	11	12
P/E Ratio:Low	8	8	12	10	10	8	7	6	7	8

Income Statement Analysis (Million $)										
Revenue	8,106	10,758	11,438	11,761	11,737	9,410	7,887	6,020	8,029	7,143
Operating Income	NA	2,027	2,365	1,785	1,111	1,272	939	987	993	NA
Depreciation	775	687	686	657	646	621	615	596	579	563
Interest Expense	377	263	381	361	321	332	327	323	352	301
Pretax Income	1,534	1,551	1,659	1,732	971	1,113	742	721	731	699
Effective Tax Rate	27.5%	28.2%	31.6%	37.0%	4.33%	17.3%	6.33%	20.2%	29.1%	38.6%
Net Income	1,119	1,113	1,135	1,091	929	920	695	575	518	429
S&P Core Earnings	1,197	904	1,124	1,096	866	855	708	445	362	NA

Balance Sheet & Other Financial Data (Million $)										
Cash	110	507	669	920	772	419	432	455	605	637
Current Assets	2,295	2,476	11,338	12,016	13,318	8,776	7,886	7,010	4,808	6,425
Total Assets	28,512	26,400	30,091	28,949	29,213	23,643	22,009	17,757	15,156	15,612
Current Liabilities	3,888	3,612	10,394	10,349	12,157	9,082	8,348	7,247	5,524	7,467
Long Term Debt	7,462	6,646	4,655	4,704	5,002	4,371	4,199	4,487	3,840	3,468
Common Equity	9,007	7,969	8,339	7,511	6,160	4,865	3,890	2,825	2,692	2,494
Total Capital	17,394	15,980	13,852	12,694	11,480	9,734	8,807	8,202	7,474	7,093
Capital Expenditures	1,912	2,061	2,011	1,907	1,404	1,083	1,049	1,214	1,068	759
Cash Flow	1,894	1,800	1,811	1,748	1,575	1,541	1,310	1,171	1,097	992
Current Ratio	0.6	0.7	1.1	1.2	1.1	1.0	0.9	1.0	0.9	0.9
% Long Term Debt of Capitalization	43.7	41.6	33.6	37.1	43.6	44.9	47.7	54.7	51.4	54.8
% Net Income of Revenue	13.8	10.4	9.9	9.3	7.9	9.8	8.8	9.6	6.5	6.1
% Return on Assets	4.1	3.9	3.8	3.7	3.5	4.0	3.3	3.5	3.4	3.2
% Return on Equity	13.2	13.7	14.2	16.0	16.9	21.0	20.7	20.8	20.0	15.7

Data as orig reptd.; bef. results of disc opers/spec. items. Per share data adj. for stk. divs.; EPS diluted. E-Estimated. NA-Not Available. NM-Not Meaningful. NR-Not Ranked. UR-Under Review.

Office: 101 Ash Street, San Diego, CA 92101.
Telephone: 619-696-2000.
Email: investor@sempra.com
Website: http://www.sempra.com

Chrmn & CEO: D.E. Felsinger
Pres & COO: N.E. Schmale
EVP & CFO: M.A. Snell
EVP & General Counsel: J. Chaudhri

SVP, Chief Acctg Officer & Cntlr: J.A. Householder
Investor Contact: S. Davis
Board Members: J. G. Brocksmith, Jr., D. E. Felsinger, W. D. Godbold, Jr., W. D. Jones, L. T. Kuenzler, W. G. Ouchi, C. Ruiz, W. C. Rusnack, W. Rutledge, L. Schenk, N. E. Schmale

Founded: 1998
Domicile: California
Employees: 13,800

Sherwin-Williams Co (The)

STANDARD & POOR'S

S&P Recommendation	**STRONG SELL** ★☆☆☆☆	Price $72.98 (as of Oct 22, 2010)	12-Mo. Target Price $60.00	Investment Style Large-Cap Growth

GICS Sector Materials **Sub-Industry** Specialty Chemicals	**Summary** This company, the largest U.S. producer of paints, is also a major seller of wallcoverings and related products.

Key Stock Statistics (Source S&P, Vickers, company reports)

52-Wk Range	$80.53– 56.24	S&P Oper. EPS 2010**E**	4.55	Market Capitalization(B)	$7.939	Beta	0.69
Trailing 12-Month EPS	$4.06	S&P Oper. EPS 2011**E**	4.86	Yield (%)	1.97	S&P 3-Yr. Proj. EPS CAGR(%)	7
Trailing 12-Month P/E	18.0	P/E on S&P Oper. EPS 2010**E**	16.0	Dividend Rate/Share	$1.44	S&P Credit Rating	A-
$10K Invested 5 Yrs Ago	$18,668	Common Shares Outstg. (M)	108.8	Institutional Ownership (%)	71		

Price Performance

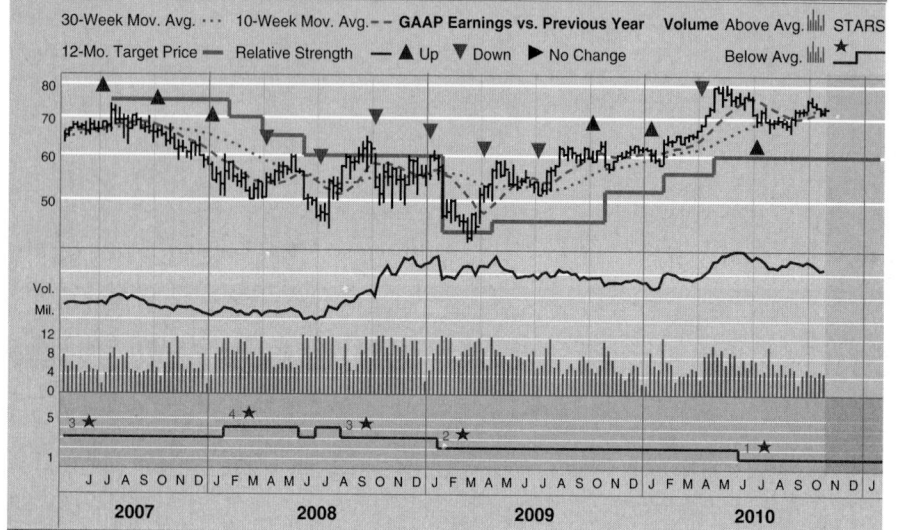

Legend: 30-Week Mov. Avg. · · · 10-Week Mov. Avg. — **GAAP Earnings vs. Previous Year** Volume Above Avg. STARS
12-Mo. Target Price — Relative Strength — ▲ Up ▼ Down ► No Change Below Avg. ★

Options: CBOE

Analysis prepared by **Michael Souers** on July 27, 2010, when the stock traded at **$ 69.68**.

Highlights

➤ We expect sales to increase 6.6% in 2010, following an 11% decline in 2009. We forecast a slight pickup in residential construction, which should positively affect architectural and do-it-yourself (DIY) sales, but we continue to see severe weakness in non-residential construction in 2010. We believe Paint Stores segment sales will increase modestly, on a projected 30-45 net new stores and a slight increase in same-store-sales.

➤ We project a slight narrowing in gross margins in 2010, as raw material cost pressure is only partially offset by improved pricing and product mix. We anticipate a 30 basis point widening in operating margins, as cost-cutting initiatives outweigh a de-leveraging of fixed expenses due to flat projected same-store sales.

➤ We project a 5% decline in share count due to SHW's active share repurchase program. Excluding a $0.10 charge for the recently passed health care legislation and an $0.08 charge related to a debt repurchase, we estimate 2010 EPS of $4.55, a 16% increase from the $3.91 the company earned in 2009, excluding a $0.13 charge. We see 2011 EPS of $4.86.

Investment Rationale/Risk

➤ We continue to have a positive outlook with regard to the company's balance sheet and generation of free cash flow. In addition, we think the ruling by the Rhode Island Supreme Court, which overturned a negative verdict against SHW over the manufacturing and selling of lead paint, makes future negative rulings far less likely. However, we remain concerned that a weak housing market and deteriorating commercial real estate market will limit sales and earnings growth over the medium term. We think the shares lack a positive near-term catalyst and are overvalued, recently trading at more than 14X our 2011 EPS estimate, a modest premium to historical averages and the S&P 500.

➤ Risks to our recommendation and target price include a significant increase in economic growth; a rapid recovery in the housing market; and declines in raw material costs, which would ease pressure on gross margins.

➤ Our 12-month target price of $60, about 12X our 2011 EPS estimate, is based on our DCF analysis, which assumes a weighted average cost of capital of 9.6% and a terminal growth rate of 3.0%.

Qualitative Risk Assessment

LOW	**MEDIUM**	HIGH

Our risk assessment for Sherwin-Williams reflects the cyclical nature of the company's business, which is reliant on new housing starts and remodeling, and lead pigment litigation risk, offset by an above-average S&P Quality Ranking of A.

Quantitative Evaluations

S&P Quality Ranking **A**

D	C	B-	B	B+	A-	**A**	A+

Relative Strength Rank **MODERATE**

37

LOWEST = 1   HIGHEST = 99

Revenue/Earnings Data

Revenue (Million $)

	1Q	2Q	3Q	4Q	Year
2010	1,565	2,143	--	--	--
2009	1,551	1,948	1,997	1,599	7,094
2008	1,782	2,230	2,269	1,700	7,980
2007	1,756	2,198	2,197	1,854	8,005
2006	1,769	2,130	2,117	1,795	7,810
2005	1,539	1,965	1,977	1,710	7,191

Earnings Per Share ($)

	1Q	2Q	3Q	4Q	Year
2010	0.30	1.64	E1.67	E0.74	E4.55
2009	0.32	1.35	1.51	0.58	3.78
2008	0.64	1.45	1.50	0.42	4.00
2007	0.83	1.52	1.55	0.80	4.70
2006	0.82	1.33	1.30	0.73	4.19
2005	0.58	1.08	1.07	0.54	3.28

Fiscal year ended Dec. 31. Next earnings report expected: NA. EPS Estimates based on S&P Operating Earnings; historical GAAP earnings are as reported.

Dividend Data (Dates: mm/dd Payment Date: mm/dd/yy)

Amount ($)	Date Decl.	Ex-Div. Date	Stk. of Record	Payment Date
0.360	02/17	02/24	02/26	03/12/10
0.360	04/20	05/19	05/21	06/04/10
0.360	07/19	08/18	08/20	09/10/10
0.360	10/20	11/17	11/19	12/03/10

Dividends have been paid since 1979. Source: Company reports.

Please read the Required Disclosures and Analyst Certification on the last page of this report.

The McGraw·Hill Companies

Sherwin-Williams Co (The)

Business Summary July 27, 2010

CORPORATE PROFILE. Sherwin-Williams develops, manufactures, distributes and sells paints, coatings and related products to professional, industrial, commercial and retail customers primarily in North and South America with additional operations in the Caribbean region, Europe and Asia. The company is structured into three reportable segments: Paint Stores, Consumer and Global Finishes.

The Paint Stores segment (60% of revenues in 2009) offers Sherwin-Williams branded architectural and industrial paints, stains and related products. Its diverse customer base includes architectural and industrial painting contractors, residential and commercial builders, property owners and managers, OEM product finishers and do-it-yourself (DIY) homeowners. In 2009, SHW opened eight net new stores, bringing the North America Paint Stores store count to 3,354. Architects, builders, designers and consumers have embraced the "green" movement, and SHW leads the industry in the sale of environmentally favorable paints and coatings.

The Consumer segment (17%) develops, manufactures and distributes architectural paints, stains, varnishes, industrial maintenance products, wood finishing products, paint applicators, corrosion inhibitors and paint-related prod-

ucts. Brands include Dutch Boy, Krylon, Minwax, Thompson's Water Seal, Purdy and Pratt & Lambert, as well as private label brands. Approximately 51% of the total sales of the Consumer Group in 2009, including inter-segment transfers, represented products sold through the Paint Stores Group.

The Global Finishes segment (23%) develops, licenses, manufactures, distributes and sells paints, stains, coatings, varnishes, industrial products, wood finishing products, applicators, aerosols, high-performance interior and exterior coatings for the automotive, aviation, fleet and heavy truck markets, OEM product finishes and related products. SHW sells these products through 539 company-operated architectural, automotive, industrial and chemical coatings branches and other operations in the United States, Argentina, Brazil, Canada, Chile, China, India, Malaysia, Mexico, Peru, Philippines, Portugal, Singapore, Uruguay and Vietnam. It also distributes these products to 19 other countries through wholly owned subsidiaries, joint ventures and licensees of technology, trademarks and tradenames.

Company Financials Fiscal Year Ended Dec. 31

Per Share Data ($)	2009	2008	2007	2006	2005	2004	2003	2002	2001	2000
Tangible Book Value	1.80	2.55	23.99	2.67	3.83	3.12	2.95	4.05	3.69	3.18
Cash Flow	5.26	5.20	5.76	5.41	4.30	3.59	3.13	2.86	2.39	0.77
Earnings	3.78	4.00	4.70	4.19	3.28	2.72	2.26	2.04	1.68	0.10
S&P Core Earnings	3.98	4.06	4.59	4.11	3.24	2.60	2.15	1.81	1.62	NA
Dividends	1.42	1.40	1.58	1.00	0.82	0.68	0.62	0.60	0.58	0.54
Payout Ratio	38%	35%	34%	24%	25%	25%	27%	29%	35%	NM
Prices:High	64.13	65.00	73.96	64.76	48.84	45.61	34.77	33.24	28.23	27.63
Prices:Low	42.19	44.51	56.75	37.40	40.47	32.95	24.42	21.75	19.73	17.13
P/E Ratio:High	17	16	16	15	15	17	15	16	17	NM
P/E Ratio:Low	11	11	12	9	12	12	11	11	12	NM

Income Statement Analysis (Million $)										
Revenue	7,094	7,980	8,005	7,810	7,191	6,114	5,408	5,185	5,067	5,212
Operating Income	875	998	1,145	1,024	898	758	690	670	599	676
Depreciation	171	143	139	146	144	126	117	116	109	109
Interest Expense	40.0	65.7	71.6	67.2	49.6	39.9	38.7	40.5	54.6	62.0
Pretax Income	623	714	913	834	656	580	523	497	424	143
Effective Tax Rate	30.0%	33.3%	32.6%	31.0%	29.2%	32.0%	36.5%	37.5%	38.0%	88.8%
Net Income	436	477	616	576	463	393	332	311	263	16.0
S&P Core Earnings	459	483	602	564	458	376	317	276	254	NA

Balance Sheet & Other Financial Data (Million $)										
Cash	69.3	26.2	27.3	469	36.0	45.9	303	164	119	2.90
Current Assets	1,770	1,909	2,070	2,450	1,891	1,782	1,715	1,506	1,507	1,552
Total Assets	4,324	4,416	4,855	4,995	4,369	4,274	3,683	3,432	3,628	3,751
Current Liabilities	1,394	1,937	2,141	2,075	1,554	1,520	1,154	1,083	1,141	1,115
Long Term Debt	783	304	293	292	487	488	503	507	504	624
Common Equity	1,491	1,606	1,461	1,559	1,696	1,475	1,174	1,300	1,319	1,472
Total Capital	2,286	1,923	2,079	2,284	2,218	2,139	1,962	1,849	1,991	2,095
Capital Expenditures	91.3	117	166	210	143	107	117	127	82.6	133
Cash Flow	607	620	755	722	607	519	449	426	372	125
Current Ratio	1.3	1.0	1.0	1.2	1.2	1.2	1.5	1.4	1.3	1.4
% Long Term Debt of Capitalization	Nil	15.7	14.0	12.8	22.0	22.8	25.6	27.4	25.3	29.8
% Net Income of Revenue	6.1	6.0	7.7	7.4	6.4	6.4	6.1	6.0	5.2	0.3
% Return on Assets	NA	10.3	12.5	12.3	10.7	9.9	9.3	8.8	7.1	0.4
% Return on Equity	NA	31.1	32.6	35.4	29.2	29.7	26.8	23.7	18.9	1.0

Data as orig reptd.; bef. results of disc opers/spec. items. Per share data adj. for stk. divs.; EPS diluted. E-Estimated. NA-Not Available. NM-Not Meaningful. NR-Not Ranked. UR-Under Review.

Office: 101 West Prospect Avenue, Cleveland, OH 44115-1075.
Telephone: 216-566-2000.
Website: http://www.sherwin-williams.com
Chrmn & CEO: C.M. Connor

Pres & COO: J.G. Morikis
SVP & CFO: S.P. Hennessy
SVP, Secy & General Counsel: L.E. Stellato
Chief Admin Officer: R.M. Weaver

Investor Contact: R.J. Wells (216-566-2244)
Board Members: A. F. Anton, J. C. Boland, C. M. Connor, D. F. Hodnik, T. G. Kadien, S. J. Kropf, G. E. McCullough, A. Mixon, III, C. E. Moll, R. K. Smucker, J. M. Stropki, Jr.

Founded: 1866
Domicile: Ohio
Employees: 29,220

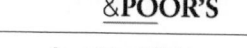

Sigma Aldrich Corporation

STANDARD &POOR'S

S&P Recommendation **BUY** ★★★★☆	Price $62.29 (as of Oct 22, 2010)	12-Mo. Target Price $74.00	Investment Style Large-Cap Growth

GICS Sector Materials
Sub-Industry Specialty Chemicals

Summary This company makes and sells a wide range of biochemicals, organic chemicals, and chromatography products.

Key Stock Statistics (Source S&P, Vickers, company reports)

52-Wk Range	$62.95– 46.50	S&P Oper. EPS 2010**E**	3.25	Market Capitalization(B)	$7.557	Beta	0.86
Trailing 12-Month EPS	$3.05	S&P Oper. EPS 2011**E**	3.51	Yield (%)	1.03	S&P 3-Yr. Proj. EPS CAGR(%)	13
Trailing 12-Month P/E	20.4	P/E on S&P Oper. EPS 2010**E**	19.2	Dividend Rate/Share	$0.64	S&P Credit Rating	A
$10K Invested 5 Yrs Ago	$20,958	Common Shares Outstg. (M)	121.3	Institutional Ownership (%)	79		

Price Performance

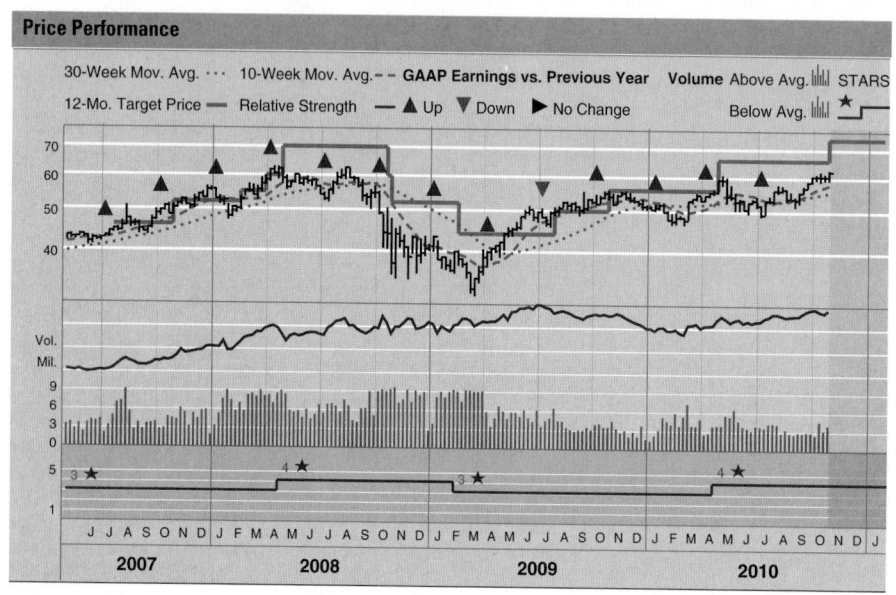

30-Week Mov. Avg. · · · ·   10-Week Mov. Avg. – –   **GAAP Earnings vs. Previous Year**   Volume Above Avg. ılıl   STARS
12-Mo. Target Price —   Relative Strength —   ▲ Up ▼ Down ► No Change   Below Avg. ılıl ★

Options: ASE, CBOE

Qualitative Risk Assessment

LOW	**MEDIUM**	HIGH

Our risk assessment reflects the stable nature of the company's laboratory chemicals business, its broad geographic sales mix, and our view of its strong balance sheet. However, SIAL's business lines are highly competitive.

Quantitative Evaluations

S&P Quality Ranking   A+

D	C	B-	B	B+	A-	A	**A+**

Relative Strength Rank   STRONG

73

LOWEST = 1   HIGHEST = 99

Revenue/Earnings Data

Revenue (Million $)

	1Q	2Q	3Q	4Q	Year
2010	572.0	554.0	--	--	--
2009	519.3	522.0	533.8	572.0	2,148
2008	569.6	580.7	540.6	509.8	2,201
2007	495.9	507.5	503.2	532.1	2,039
2006	443.1	448.5	441.4	464.5	1,798
2005	399.8	444.0	412.2	410.5	1,667

Earnings Per Share ($)

2010	0.81	1.23	E0.73	E0.77	E3.25
2009	0.68	0.68	0.70	0.75	2.80
2008	0.64	0.70	0.64	0.68	2.65
2007	0.56	0.60	0.54	0.64	2.34
2006	0.49	0.52	0.51	0.53	2.05
2005	0.54	0.46	0.47	0.42	1.88

Fiscal year ended Dec. 31. Next earnings report expected: Late October. EPS Estimates based on S&P Operating Earnings; historical GAAP earnings are as reported.

Highlights

► The 12-month target price for SIAL has recently been changed to $74.00 from $66.00. The Highlights section of this Stock Report will be updated accordingly.

Investment Rationale/Risk

► The Investment Rationale/Risk section of this Stock Report will be updated shortly. For the latest News story on SIAL from MarketScope, see below.

► 10/21/10 01:12 pm ET ... S&P REITERATES BUY OPINION ON SHARES OF SIGMA ALDRICH CORPORATION (SIAL 62.19****): Q3 adjusted EPS of $0.83, vs. $0.70, is $0.10 above our estimate. Sales including a 2% adverse forex impact, grew robust 5%, with organic sales growth in its SAFC unit up 14% and Research units up 5%. International sales were the main drivers of growth. We are also encouraged by a 60 bps rise in operating margin despite higher SG&A costs. But we see SAFC growth moderating over the next few quarters on tougher year-earlier comparisons and as Europe sales remain sluggish, particularly in pharmaceutical sector. We are upping our target price by $8 to $74, on 1.6X PEG, above peers. /J.Loo-CFA

Dividend Data (Dates: mm/dd Payment Date: mm/dd/yy)

Amount ($)	Date Decl.	Ex-Div. Date	Stk. of Record	Payment Date
0.145	11/10	11/27	12/01	12/15/09
0.160	02/10	02/25	03/01	03/15/10
0.160	05/04	05/27	06/01	06/15/10
0.160	08/10	08/30	09/01	09/15/10

Dividends have been paid since 1970. Source: Company reports.

Sigma Aldrich Corporation

Business Summary August 05, 2010

CORPORATE OVERVIEW. Sigma-Aldrich, well known for its extensive catalog business, is one of the world's largest providers of research chemicals, reagents, chromatography products, and related products.

Foreign sales accounted for 65% of the total in 2009 (65% in 2008).

SIAL distributes more than 170,000 chemical products, under the Sigma, Aldrich, Fluka and Supelco brand names, for use primarily in research and development, diagnosis of disease, and as specialty chemicals for manufacturing. About 75% of sales are to customers in the life sciences, with the remaining 25% used in high-technology applications. Customer sectors include pharmaceutical (40% of sales), academia and government (30%), chemical industry (20%), and hospitals and commercial laboratories (10%). The company itself produces about 48,000 products, accounting for 65% of 2009 (61% in 2008) net sales of chemical products. Remaining products are purchased from outside sources. The company also supplies 40,000 equipment products.

The Research Essentials unit, 19% of sales in 2009 (19% in 2008), sells biological buffers, cell culture reagents, biochemicals, chemicals, solvents, and other reagents and kits. The Research Specialties unit, 37% of sales in 2009 (37%), sells organic chemicals, biochemicals, analytical reagents, chromatography consumables, reference materials and high-purity products. The Research Biotech unit, 16% of sales in 2009 (15%), supplies immunochemical, molecular biology, cell signaling and neuroscience biochemicals and kits used in biotechnology, genomic, proteomic and other life science research applications. Sigma-Genosys (acquired in 1998) is a major maker of custom synthetic DNA products, synthetic peptides and genes to the life science product categories. SIAL believes it is the leading supplier of products used in cell signaling and neuroscience. The SAFC (Fine Chemicals) unit, 28% of sales in 2009 (29%), is a top 10 supplier of large-scale organic chemicals and biochemicals used in development and production by pharmaceutical, biotechnology, industrial and diagnostic companies. The February 2007 purchase of Epichem Group (annual sales of $40 million) greatly expanded SAFC's high technology sales.

SIAL also offers about 80,000 esoteric chemicals (less than 1% of total sales) as a special service to customers that screen them for potential applications.

Company Financials Fiscal Year Ended Dec. 31

Per Share Data ($)	2009	2008	2007	2006	2005	2004	2003	2002	2001	2000
Tangible Book Value	9.50	7.13	8.19	7.00	5.71	7.67	6.42	5.45	3.38	3.67
Cash Flow	3.55	3.42	3.07	1.37	2.54	2.19	1.83	1.72	1.41	1.24
Earnings	2.80	2.65	2.34	2.05	1.88	1.67	1.34	0.89	0.94	0.83
S&P Core Earnings	2.86	2.56	2.34	2.05	1.81	1.58	1.28	1.05	0.88	NA
Dividends	0.58	0.52	0.46	0.42	0.38	0.34	0.25	0.17	0.17	0.16
Payout Ratio	21%	20%	20%	20%	20%	20%	19%	19%	18%	19%
Prices:High	56.29	63.04	56.59	39.68	33.55	30.81	28.96	26.40	25.75	20.44
Prices:Low	31.45	34.33	37.40	31.27	27.67	26.61	20.47	19.08	18.13	10.09
P/E Ratio:High	20	24	24	19	18	18	22	30	28	25
P/E Ratio:Low	11	13	16	15	15	16	15	21	19	12

Income Statement Analysis (Million $)	2009	2008	2007	2006	2005	2004	2003	2002	2001	2000
Revenue	2,148	2,201	2,039	1,798	1,667	1,409	1,298	1,207	1,179	1,096
Operating Income	601	602	557	494	452	392	353	323	291	284
Depreciation	92.4	98.6	97.8	90.9	90.1	73.4	69.3	66.3	71.4	67.6
Interest Expense	10.0	21.0	28.9	24.0	18.1	7.20	10.1	13.8	18.2	10.2
Pretax Income	490	490	438	379	343	312	273	272	202	203
Effective Tax Rate	29.2%	30.2%	28.9%	26.9%	24.8%	25.3%	30.2%	31.4%	30.2%	31.5%
Net Income	347	342	311	277	258	233	190	187	141	139
S&P Core Earnings	354	331	310	276	249	221	180	155	133	NA

Balance Sheet & Other Financial Data (Million $)	2009	2008	2007	2006	2005	2004	2003	2002	2001	2000
Cash	373	252	238	174	98.6	169	128	52.4	37.6	31.1
Current Assets	1,384	1,309	1,283	1,113	950	893	815	695	727	714
Total Assets	2,714	2,557	2,629	2,334	2,131	1,745	1,548	1,390	1,440	1,348
Current Liabilities	742	794	635	443	461	231	257	266	398	335
Long Term Debt	100	200	207	338	283	177	176	177	178	101
Common Equity	1,686	1,379	1,617	1,411	1,233	1,212	999	882	810	859
Total Capital	1,886	1,598	1,866	1,797	1,597	1,389	1,176	1,059	987	960
Capital Expenditures	120	89.9	79.7	74.5	92.2	70.3	57.7	60.7	110	69.2
Cash Flow	439	440	409	368	348	306	260	253	212	207
Current Ratio	1.9	1.7	2.0	2.5	2.1	3.9	3.2	2.6	1.8	2.1
% Long Term Debt of Capitalization	5.3	12.5	11.1	18.8	17.7	12.8	15.0	16.7	18.0	10.5
% Net Income of Revenue	16.1	15.5	15.3	15.4	15.5	16.5	14.7	15.5	11.9	12.7
% Return on Assets	13.2	13.2	12.5	12.4	13.3	14.1	12.7	13.2	10.1	10.0
% Return on Equity	22.6	22.8	20.6	20.9	21.1	21.1	20.2	22.1	16.9	13.1

Data as orig reptd.; bef. results of disc opers/spec. items. Per share data adj. for stk. divs.; EPS diluted. E-Estimated. NA-Not Available. NM-Not Meaningful. NR-Not Ranked. UR-Under Review.

Office: 3050 Spruce Street, St. Louis, MO 63103.
Telephone: 314-771-5765.
Website: http://www.sigma-aldrich.com
Chrmn, Pres & CEO: J.P. Nagarkatti

SVP, CFO & Chief Admin Officer: R. Sachdev
SVP, Secy & General Counsel: G.L. Miller
Chief Acctg Officer & Cntlr: M.F. Kanan
Investor Contact: K.A. Richter (314-286-8004)

Board Members: R. M. Bergman, G. Church, D. R. Harvey, W. L. McCollum, J. P. Nagarkatti, A. M. Nash, S. M. Paul, J. P. Reinhard, D. D. Spatz, B. Toan

Founded: 1951
Domicile: Delaware
Employees: 7,740

Simon Property Group Inc.

STANDARD &POOR'S

S&P Recommendation	STRONG BUY ★★★★★	Price $97.69 (as of Oct 22, 2010)	12-Mo. Target Price $105.00	Investment Style Large-Cap Blend

GICS Sector Financials
Sub-Industry Retail REITS

Summary This real estate investment trust owns, develops and manages retail real estate, primarily regional malls, outlet centers and community/lifestyle centers, across the U.S.

Key Stock Statistics (Source S&P, Vickers, company reports)

52-Wk Range	$99.46– 64.20	S&P FFO/Sh. 2010E	5.38	Market Capitalization(B)	$28.605	Beta	1.71
Trailing 12-Month FFO/Share	NA	S&P FFO/Sh. 2011E	6.32	Yield (%)	2.46	S&P 3-Yr. FFO/Sh. Proj. CAGR(%)	-1
Trailing 12-Month P/FFO	NA	P/FFO on S&P FFO/Sh. 2010E	18.2	Dividend Rate/Share	$2.40	S&P Credit Rating	A-
$10K Invested 5 Yrs Ago	$17,514	Common Shares Outstg. (M)	292.8	Institutional Ownership (%)	93		

Price Performance

30-Week Mov. Avg. · · · 10-Week Mov. Avg. - - GAAP Earnings vs. Previous Year Volume Above Avg. STARS
12-Mo. Target Price — Relative Strength — ▲ Up ▼ Down ▶ No Change Below Avg. ★

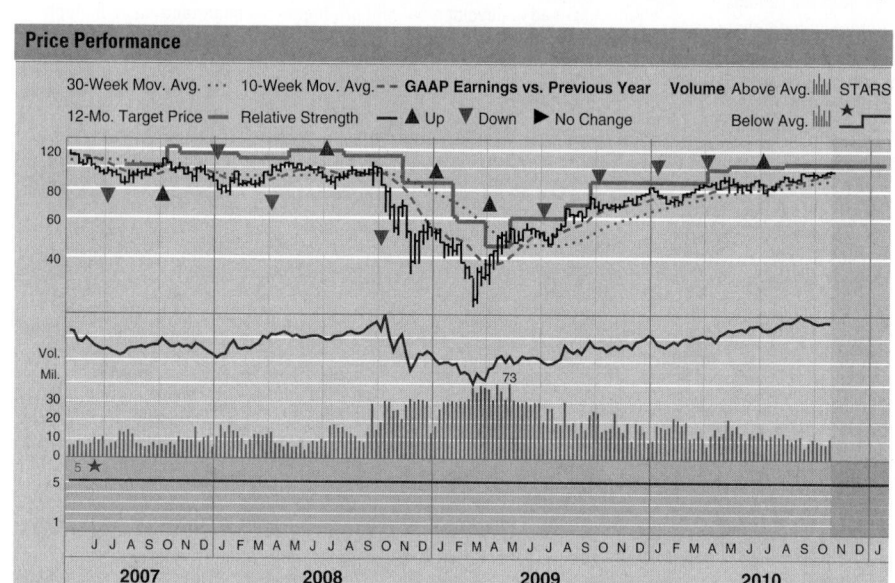

Options: ASE, CBOE, Ph

Analysis prepared by **Robert McMillan** on August 03, 2010, when the stock traded at **$ 93.53**.

Highlights

➤ We expect the trust to continue to benefit from what we view as a successful strategy of operating large and strategically located regional malls and shopping centers in major metropolitan markets.

➤ After a fractional decline in 2009, we look for total revenues to advance 3.8% in 2010 on higher rents and tenant reimbursements, as well as contributions from acquisitions. We believe that improving retailer sentiment will fuel rising demand for SPG's space. Occupancy in SPG's U.S. regional mall and premium outlet centers rose to 93.1% at the end of the second quarter from 92.3% a year earlier, while re-leasing spreads rose 1.2% during the second quarter. Occupancy levels also rose in SPG's community and lifestyle and Mills portfolios in the U.S., while they declined in the international shopping center portfolios. We think a prolonged drop in new construction activity, due in part to more stringent lending terms, as well as ongoing cost reductions, will benefit SPG.

➤ We see FFO per share of $5.38 ($5.84 excluding certain charges) in 2010 and $6.32 in 2011.

Investment Rationale/Risk

➤ We think SPG's position as one of the largest owners and managers of shopping centers in the U.S. and its established relationships with numerous retailers will allow it to continue to generate solid growth long term. We also view the geographic, customer and format diversity of SPG's portfolio and management's acquisition acumen as positive factors in our valuation.

➤ Risks to our recommendation and target price include slower-than-expected retailer expansion, higher-than-normal retailer bankruptcies, and a rise in interest rates.

➤ The shares recently traded at 15.5X our forward 12-month FFO estimate of $6.04. Our 12-month target price of $105 is equal to 17.4X this estimate. We believe the multiple will expand based on improvements in the trust's operating performance, and easing of concerns about the impact of the economy on SPG's retailer-dependent business, which is anchored by long-term leases. Although the multiple is toward the upper end of SPG's recent historical valuation range, we believe a higher valuation is warranted, given SPG's ample liquidity, which could be used for debt reduction and/or accretive acquisitions.

Qualitative Risk Assessment

LOW	MEDIUM	HIGH

Our risk assessment reflects SPG's position as one of the largest owners of shopping centers, with a diverse tenant and geographic mix and a variety of shopping center formats. The majority of SPG's customers are under long-term leases, reducing short-term volatility. Although the trust has sizable maturing debt, we think recent equity and debt offerings enhance its liquidity.

Quantitative Evaluations

S&P Quality Ranking B

D	C	B-	**B**	B+	A-	A	A+

Relative Strength Rank MODERATE

61

LOWEST = 1   HIGHEST = 99

Revenue/FFO Data

Revenue (Million $)

	1Q	2Q	3Q	4Q	Year
2010	925.1	933.6	--	--	--
2009	918.5	903.6	924.9	1,028	3,775
2008	895.3	913.5	932.2	1,029	3,783
2007	852.1	855.9	907.2	1,036	3,651
2006	787.7	798.7	818.7	927.0	3,332
2005	756.9	756.3	786.8	889.8	3,167

FFO Per Share ($)

	1Q	2Q	3Q	4Q	Year
2010	1.11	1.66	E1.35	E1.77	E5.38
2009	1.61	0.96	1.38	1.40	5.33
2008	1.46	1.49	1.61	1.86	6.42
2007	1.37	1.31	1.46	1.76	5.90
2006	1.26	1.26	1.30	1.57	5.39
2005	1.12	1.18	1.19	1.47	4.96

Fiscal year ended Dec. 31. Next earnings report expected: Early November. FFO Estimates based on S&P Funds From Operations Est..

Dividend Data (Dates: mm/dd Payment Date: mm/dd/yy)

Amount ($)	Date Decl.	Ex-Div. Date	Stk. of Record	Payment Date
0.600	10/30	11/12	11/16	12/18/09
0.600	02/05	02/11	02/16	02/26/10
0.600	04/30	05/12	05/14	05/28/10
0.600	07/30	08/13	08/17	08/31/10

Dividends have been paid since 1994. Source: Company reports.

Please read the Required Disclosures and Analyst Certification on the last page of this report.

The McGraw-Hill Companies

Simon Property Group Inc.

STANDARD & POOR'S

Business Summary August 03, 2010

CORPORATE OVERVIEW. Simon Property Group is a real estate investment trust that owns, develops, manages, leases and acquires primarily regional malls and community shopping centers. It is one of the largest owners of shopping centers in the world. As of December 31, 2009, SPG owned or held an interest in 321 income-producing properties in the United States, which consisted of 162 regional malls, 41 premium outlet centers, 67 community/lifestyle centers, 36 properties acquired in the 2007 acquisition of The Mills Corporation, and 15 other shopping centers or outlet centers in 41 states and Puerto Rico. The company also had ownership interests in 51 European shopping centers, and 10 premium outlet centers in Japan, Mexico and South Korea, as well as two shopping centers in Italy currently under development.

SPG's regional malls typically contain at least one traditional department store anchor or a combination of anchors and big box retailers with a wide variety of smaller stores located in enclosed malls connecting the anchors. Additional freestanding stores are usually located along the perimeter of the parking area. SPG's regional malls range in size from approximately 400,000 to 2.3 million square feet of gross leasable area (GLA) and contain more than 18,600 occupied stores, including approximately 710 anchors, which are mostly national retailers. SPG's premium outlet centers, ranging in size from 200,000 to 850,000 square feet of GLA, contain a wide variety of retailers located in open-air manufacturers' outlet centers near metropolitan areas .

SPG's community and lifestyle shopping centers are generally unenclosed and smaller than its regional malls. The community and lifestyle centers usu-ally range in size from approximately 100,000 to 900,000 square feet of GLA and are designed to serve a larger trade area, and typically contain at least two anchors and other tenants that are usually national retailers among the leaders in their markets. These tenants generally occupy a significant portion of the GLA of the center. The trust also owns traditional community shopping centers that focus primarily on value-oriented and convenience goods and services. These centers are normally anchored by a supermarket, discount retailer or drugstore and are designed to service a neighborhood area. The trust also owns open-air centers adjacent to its regional malls designed to take advantage of the drawing power of the mall.

The Mills portfolio, which SPG acquired in 2007 with Farallon Capital Management, consists of Mills centers, regional malls, and community centers. The Mills centers, ranging from 1.0 million to 2.3 million square feet of GLA, are located in major metropolitan areas and combine a traditional mall or outlet center format with big box retailers and entertainment uses. The Mills regional malls generally range in size from 700,000 to 1.3 million square feet of GLA and contain a wide variety of national retailers. The four community centers are adjacent to Mills centers, and contain a mix of big box and other local and national retail tenants.

Company Financials Fiscal Year Ended Dec. 31

Per Share Data ($)	2009	2008	2007	2006	2005	2004	2003	2002	2001	2000
Tangible Book Value	15.25	10.93	12.40	13.98	14.64	16.21	14.66	13.87	13.00	14.29
Earnings	1.05	1.77	2.08	2.19	1.27	1.44	1.53	1.93	0.87	1.13
S&P Core Earnings	1.05	1.87	2.20	2.19	1.12	1.44	1.55	2.07	0.97	NA
Dividends	2.70	3.60	3.36	3.04	2.80	2.60	2.40	2.18	2.08	2.02
Payout Ratio	NM	203%	162%	139%	NM	181%	157%	113%	NM	179%
Prices:High	83.82	106.43	123.96	104.08	80.97	65.87	48.59	36.95	30.97	27.13
Prices:Low	24.27	33.78	82.60	76.14	58.29	44.39	31.70	28.80	23.75	21.50
P/E Ratio:High	80	60	60	48	64	46	32	19	36	24
P/E Ratio:Low	23	19	40	35	46	31	21	15	27	19

Income Statement Analysis (Million $)	2009	2008	2007	2006	2005	2004	2003	2002	2001	2000
Rental Income	3,464	3,458	3,288	3,063	2,920	2,411	1,423	1,386	1,320	1,284
Mortgage Income	Nil	Nil	Nil	Nil	Nil	Nil	Nil	Nil	Nil	Nil
Total Income	3,775	3,783	3,651	3,332	3,167	2,642	2,314	2,186	2,045	2,013
General Expenses	1,174	1,191	1,210	856	820	675	611	788	712	674
Interest Expense	992	965	1,535	822	799	662	615	603	622	667
Provision for Losses	22.7	24.0	9.56	9.50	8.10	17.7	Nil	8.97	8.41	9.64
Depreciation	998	970	906	856	850	623	498	423	453	420
Net Income	309	464	519	563	457	450	339	1,109	201	242
S&P Core Earnings	283	423	491	486	247	301	288	371	169	NA

Balance Sheet & Other Financial Data (Million $)	2009	2008	2007	2006	2005	2004	2003	2002	2001	2000
Cash	3,958	774	502	929	929	520	536	397	255	214
Total Assets	25,948	23,597	23,606	22,084	21,131	22,070	15,685	14,905	13,794	13,911
Real Estate Investment	25,336	25,206	24,415	24,390	23,307	23,175	14,972	14,250	13,187	13,038
Loss Reserve	Nil	Nil	Nil	Nil	Nil	Nil	Nil	20.5	24.7	20.1
Net Investment	18,332	19,021	19,103	19,784	19,499	20,012	12,415	12,027	11,311	11,558
Short Term Debt	2,312	1,476	810	NA	NA	NA	1,481	940	665	1,164
Capitalization:Debt	16,318	16,567	16,409	13,711	14,106	13,044	8,786	8,606	8,176	7,904
Capitalization:Equity	4,412	2,615	2,817	3,095	3,227	3,580	2,971	2,653	2,327	2,515
Capitalization:Total	21,501	19,607	21,821	18,885	19,681	19,065	13,241	12,074	11,381	10,958
% Earnings & Depreciation/Assets	5.3	6.1	6.2	6.7	6.0	5.7	5.5	10.7	4.7	4.7
Price Times Book Value:High	5.5	9.7	10.0	7.4	5.5	4.1	3.3	2.7	2.4	1.9
Price Times Book Value:Low	1.6	3.1	6.7	5.4	4.0	2.7	2.2	2.1	1.8	1.5

Data as orig reptd.; bef. results of disc opers/spec. items. Per share data adj. for stk. divs.; EPS diluted. E-Estimated. NA-Not Available. NM-Not Meaningful. NR-Not Ranked. UR-Under Review.

Office: 225 W Washington St, Indianapolis, IN 46204-3438.
Telephone: 317-636-1600.
Website: http://www.simon.com
Chrmn & CEO: D.E. Simon

Pres & COO: R.S. Sokolov
EVP & CFO: S.E. Sterrett
EVP & Chief Admin Officer: J. Rulli
EVP & Treas: A.A. Juster

Investor Contact: S.J. Doran (317-685-7330)
Board Members: M. E. Bergstein, L. W. Bynoe, L. C. Glasscock, K. N. Horn, A. B. Hubbard, R. S. Leibowitz, D. E. Simon, H. Simon, D. C. Smith, J. A. Smith, Jr., R. S. Sokolov

Founded: 1993
Domicile: Delaware
Employees: 5,200

The **McGraw-Hill** Companies

SLM Corp

STANDARD &POOR'S

S&P Recommendation **HOLD** ★★★☆☆	Price $11.54 (as of Oct 22, 2010)	12-Mo. Target Price $13.00	Investment Style Large-Cap Growth

GICS Sector Financials
Sub-Industry Consumer Finance

Summary This company (formerly USA Education) is a leading U.S. provider of post-secondary educational financial services.

Key Stock Statistics (Source S&P, Vickers, company reports)

52-Wk Range	$13.96–9.28	S&P Oper. EPS 2010E	1.69	Market Capitalization(B)	$5.605	Beta	1.41
Trailing 12-Month EPS	$1.88	S&P Oper. EPS 2011E	1.49	Yield (%)	Nil	S&P 3-Yr. Proj. EPS CAGR(%)	18
Trailing 12-Month P/E	6.1	P/E on S&P Oper. EPS 2010E	6.8	Dividend Rate/Share	Nil	S&P Credit Rating	BBB-
$10K Invested 5 Yrs Ago	$2,182	Common Shares Outstg. (M)	485.8	Institutional Ownership (%)	100		

Price Performance

30-Week Mov. Avg. · · · 10-Week Mov. Avg. - - - GAAP Earnings vs. Previous Year Volume Above Avg. STARS
12-Mo. Target Price — Relative Strength — ▲ Up ▼ Down ▶ No Change Below Avg. ★

Options: ASE, CBOE, P

Analysis prepared by **Rafay Khalid, CFA** on October 20, 2010, when the stock traded at **$ 11.41**.

Highlights

➤ We project that the loan portfolio mix will shift toward private student loans in 2010, reflecting legislation to eliminate student loan subsidies for government-sponsored loans. As a result, we forecast that SLM's net interest margin will widen to 1.58% in 2010 from 1.05% in 2009. However, we see the net interest margin narrowing to 1.32% in 2011, as we think new legislation will negatively impact the company's origination business. On September 27, SLM agreed to acquire $28 billion of securitized federal student loans and other assets from The Student Loan Corporation, subject to approvals.

➤ We forecast that loan loss provisions will decline in both 2010 and 2011, given our outlook for lower charge-offs from improved forbearance policies. We expect that other income will decrease in 2010, after doubling in 2009, but we see an increase in 2011, on our outlook for continuing improvement in credit spreads. We see other expenses declining in 2010 and 2011, based on the company restructuring its business from origination to servicing of loans, following the passage of the new legislation.

➤ We estimate operating EPS of $1.69 for 2010 and $1.49 for 2011, compared to $0.95 in 2009.

Investment Rationale/Risk

➤ Recently, both houses of Congress passed legislation that eliminated student loan subsidies for government-sponsored loans. We believe the company will transition its primary business to focus on servicing loans instead of originating them. As a result, we think SLM, the largest provider of government-sponsored loans, will experience lower loan volumes and a decline in interest-earning assets. On a positive note, we expect SLM's run-off portfolio of government-sponsored loans to generate solid financial returns, and we see credit spreads continuing to improve in 2010, reflecting our outlook for ongoing economic recovery.

➤ Risks to our recommendation and target price include changes in government legislation that can remove subsidies for the company's loan products, loss of market share, and higher-than-expected loss provisions.

➤ Our 12-month target price of $13 is based on a P/E multiple of 8.8X our 2011 operating EPS estimate. This multiple is a discount to the historical average, reflecting what we think is a transition period in the company's business.

Qualitative Risk Assessment

LOW	MEDIUM	HIGH

Our risk assessment reflects what we see as the negative impact from new legislation, offset by our view of lower loss provisions and a potentially higher net interest margin.

Quantitative Evaluations

S&P Quality Ranking B-

D	C	B-	B	B+	A-	A	A+

Relative Strength Rank MODERATE

35

LOWEST = 1   HIGHEST = 99

Revenue/Earnings Data

Revenue (Million $)

	1Q	2Q	3Q	4Q	Year
2010	1,641	--	--	--	--
2009	1,530	1,248	1,551	1,815	6,145
2008	1,963	2,331	1,697	631.2	7,881
2007	2,466	2,495	2,119	1,270	9,171
2006	1,766	2,695	2,252	2,038	8,751
2005	1,285	1,506	1,715	2,012	6,518

Earnings Per Share ($)

	1Q	2Q	3Q	4Q	Year
2010	0.45	0.61	E0.35	E0.55	E1.69
2009	Nil	-0.31	0.26	0.71	0.71
2008	-0.28	0.50	-0.40	-0.52	-0.39
2007	0.26	1.03	-0.85	-3.98	-2.26
2006	0.34	1.52	0.60	0.02	2.63
2005	0.49	0.66	0.95	0.96	3.05

Fiscal year ended Dec. 31. Next earnings report expected: NA. EPS Estimates based on S&P Operating Earnings; historical GAAP earnings are as reported.

Dividend Data

Dividends were omitted in April 2007.

Please read the Required Disclosures and Analyst Certification on the last page of this report.

The **McGraw·Hill** Companies

SLM Corp

Business Summary October 20, 2010

CORPORATE OVERVIEW. SLM Corp., formerly USA Education Inc., is the largest U.S. private source of funding, delivery and service support for higher education loans, primarily through its participation in the Federal Family Education Loan Program (FFELP). The company's main business is to originate, acquire and hold student loans with the net interest income and gains on the sales of student loans in securitization, the primary source of earnings. The company funds its operation through student loan asset-backed securities and unsecured debt securities. SLM was chartered by an Act of Congress in 1972, but in 1996 it was rechartered as a private sector corporation and completed its privatization process in December 2004.

The company is divided into two business segments: Lending and Asset Performance Group (APG). According to the company, the SLM Lending segment manages the largest portfolio of FFELP and Private Education Loans in the student loan industry. As of December 31, 2009, the company served nearly 10 million borrowers, and managed $176 billion of student loans, of which 84% were federally insured.

PRIMARY BUSINESS DYNAMICS. There are two competing programs that divide student loans where the ultimate risk lies with the federal government: the FFELP and the Federal Direct Lending program (FDLP). FFELP loans are provided by private sector institutions, such as SLM, and are ultimately guaranteed by the U.S. Department of Education (ED). FDLP loans are funded by taxpayers and provided to borrowers directly by ED. Private Education Loans are originated by financial institutions where the lender assumes the credit risk of the borrower.

The company acquires student loans from three principal sources: SLM's Preferred Channel, which consists of the company's own brand of loans and loans originated by lenders with commitments to SLM; Consolidation Loans, which earn a lower yield than FFELP Loans due to a Consolidation Rebate Fee; and strategic acquisitions.

Company Financials Fiscal Year Ended Dec. 31

Per Share Data ($)	2009	2008	2007	2006	2005	2004	2003	2002	2001	2000
Tangible Book Value	5.62	4.37	5.93	5.90	5.13	4.81	4.55	3.08	3.59	2.54
Earnings	0.71	-0.39	-2.26	2.63	3.05	4.04	3.01	1.64	0.76	0.92
S&P Core Earnings	0.70	-0.70	-2.24	2.62	2.98	3.95	2.75	1.40	0.53	NA
Dividends	Nil	Nil	0.25	0.97	0.85	0.74	0.59	0.28	0.24	0.22
Payout Ratio	Nil	Nil	NM	37%	28%	18%	20%	17%	32%	24%
Prices:High	12.43	25.05	58.00	58.35	56.48	54.44	42.92	35.65	29.33	22.75
Prices:Low	3.11	4.19	18.68	44.65	45.56	36.43	33.73	25.67	18.63	9.27
P/E Ratio:High	18	NM	NM	22	19	13	14	22	39	25
P/E Ratio:Low	4	NM	NM	17	15	9	11	16	25	10

Income Statement Analysis (Million $)	2009	2008	2007	2006	2005	2004	2003	2002	2001	2000
Interest on:Mortgages	4,732	6,994	7,966	6,074	4,233	2,500	2,197	2,124	2,625	2,977
Interest on:Investment	26.1	276	708	503	277	233	151	87.9	373	501
Interest Expense	3,036	5,905	7,086	5,123	3,059	1,434	1,022	1,203	2,124	2,837
Guaranty Fees	Nil	Nil	Nil	Nil	Nil	Nil	Nil	Nil	Nil	Nil
Loan Loss Provision	1,119	720	1,015	287	203	111	147	117	66.0	32.1
Administration Expenses	1,255	1,357	1,529	1,346	1,138	895	808	690	708	586
Pretax Income	721	-376	-482	1,995	2,117	2,557	2,183	1,223	617	712
Effective Tax Rate	33.1%	NM	NM	41.8%	34.4%	25.1%	35.7%	35.3%	36.2%	33.1%
Net Income	482	-213	-896	1,157	1,382	1,913	1,404	792	384	465
S&P Core Earnings	330	-327	-923	1,119	1,324	1,853	1,276	664	261	NA

Balance Sheet & Other Financial Data (Million $)	2009	2008	2007	2006	2005	2004	2003	2002	2001	2000
Mortgages	144,227	145,532	125,327	97,228	83,980	66,161	51,078	43,541	42,037	38,635
Investment	7,183	4,577	6,008	5,986	4,775	3,579	5,268	4,231	5,072	5,206
Cash & Equivalent	6,070	4,070	7,582	2,621	2,499	3,395	1,652	758	715	734
Total Assets	169,985	168,768	155,565	116,136	99,339	84,094	64,611	53,175	52,874	48,792
Short Term Debt	30,897	41,933	35,947	3.50	3,810	2,208	18,735	25,619	31,065	30,464
Long Term Debt	130,546	118,225	111,098	104,559	88,119	75,915	23,211	22,242	17,285	14,911
Equity	3,903	3,284	3,659	3,795	3,226	2,937	3,564	1,833	1,507	1,250
% Return on Assets	0.3	NM	NM	1.1	1.5	2.6	2.4	1.5	0.8	1.0
% Return on Equity	13.4	NM	NM	31.9	44.1	70.4	25.8	47.4	27.8	48.2
Equity/Assets Ratio	2.1	2.1	2.7	3.3	3.4	4.4	4.6	3.1	2.7	2.1
Price Times Book Value:High	2.2	5.7	9.8	9.9	11.0	11.3	9.4	11.6	8.2	8.9
Price Times Book Value:Low	0.6	1.0	3.2	7.6	8.9	7.6	7.4	8.3	5.2	3.6

Data as orig reptd.; bef. results of disc opers/spec. items. Per share data adj. for stk. divs.; EPS diluted. E-Estimated. NA-Not Available. NM-Not Meaningful. NR-Not Ranked. UR-Under Review.

Office: 12061 Bluemont Way, Reston, VA 20190.
Telephone: 703-810-3000.
Website: http://www.salliemae.com
Chrmn: A.P. Terracciano

Chrmn: D.W. Acklie
Vice Chrmn & CEO: A.L. Lord
EVP & Treas: J.C. Clark
EVP & General Counsel: M.L. Heleen

Founded: 1972
Domicile: Delaware
Employees: 8,000

J.M. Smucker Co (The)

STANDARD &POOR'S

S&P Recommendation	BUY ★★★★☆	Price $63.03 (as of Oct 22, 2010)	12-Mo. Target Price $66.00	Investment Style Large-Cap Blend

GICS Sector Consumer Staples
Sub-Industry Packaged Foods & Meats

Summary This company's products include coffee, fruit spreads, peanut butter, shortening and oils, ice cream toppings, health and natural foods, and beverages. The Folgers coffee business was acquired in November 2008.

Key Stock Statistics (Source S&P, Vickers, company reports)

52-Wk Range	$63.75– 51.19	S&P Oper. EPS 2011**E**	4.55	Market Capitalization(B)	$7.532	Beta	0.67
Trailing 12-Month EPS	$4.18	S&P Oper. EPS 2012**E**	4.87	Yield (%)	2.54	S&P 3-Yr. Proj. EPS CAGR(%)	8
Trailing 12-Month P/E	15.1	P/E on S&P Oper. EPS 2011**E**	13.9	Dividend Rate/Share	$1.60	S&P Credit Rating	NA
$10K Invested 5 Yrs Ago	$17,206	Common Shares Outstg. (M)	119.5	Institutional Ownership (%)	72		

Price Performance

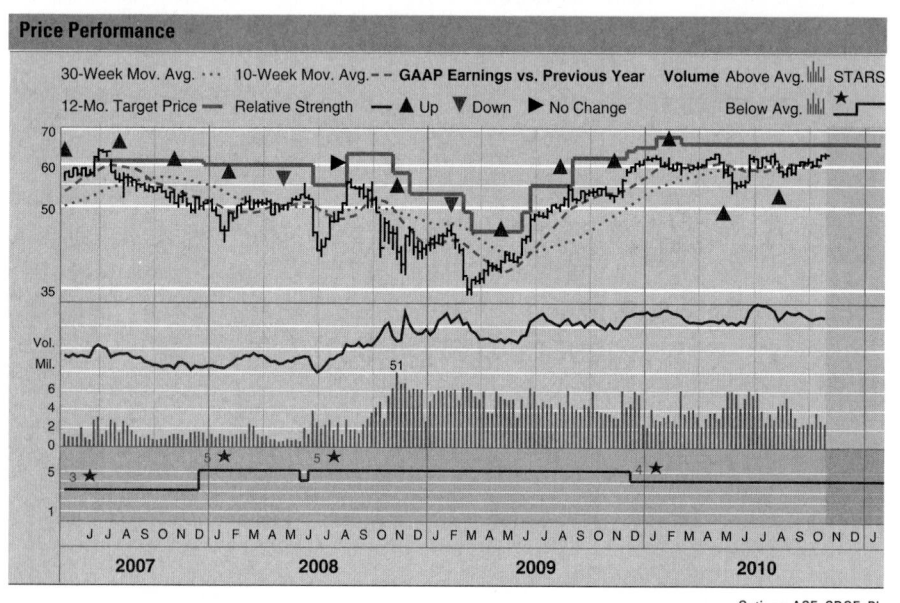

30-Week Mov. Avg. · · · · 10-Week Mov. Avg. – – **GAAP Earnings vs. Previous Year** Volume Above Avg. STARS
12-Mo. Target Price — Relative Strength — ▲ Up ▼ Down ▶ No Change Below Avg.

Options: ASE, CBOE, Ph

Analysis prepared by **Tom Graves, CFA** on August 27, 2010, when the stock traded at **$ 58.07**.

Highlights

▶ In FY 11 (Apr.), we look for SJM sales to rise about 4%. SJM's revenue base increased substantially with the 2008 acquisition of the Folgers coffee business. We expect that by the end of FY 10, the Folgers transaction resulted in one-time costs of about $100 million to $125 million, and that SJM realized $80 million of annualized synergy benefits.

▶ While we view a supply chain improvement plan that was announced in March 2010 as a decent long-term investment, we are not especially enthused by the financial outline. Over 3-to-5 years, we expect SJM to have about $190 million of restructuring charges, and we look for annual savings of about $60 million to be fully realized in FY 15.

▶ Before some special items, we estimate FY 11 EPS at $4.55, up from about $4.29 in FY 10, which excludes a net negative impact of about $0.14 a share from special items. Also, both years include an estimated $0.40 of non-cash intangible asset amortization. Excluded from our FY 11 estimate are some restructuring merger and integration costs. For FY 12, we estimate EPS of $4.87.

Investment Rationale/Risk

▶ We generally like the acquisition of the Folgers coffee business, which adds diversification and should provide economies of scale. We look for SJM's overall sales to benefit from the introduction of new or reformulated products, including items such as Crisco olive oil and reduced sugar products.

▶ Risks to our recommendation and target price include competitive pressures, commodity cost inflation, consumer acceptance of new product introductions, and SJM's ability to fully integrate and realize expected cost savings from the Folgers acquisition. We think the May 2009 adoption by SJM directors of a shareholder rights plan seemed aimed at protecting SJM's independence.

▶ Our 12-month target price of $66 reflects our view that the shares should trade at about a 5% P/E discount (based on estimated calendar 2010 EPS) to what we expect, on average, for a group of packaged food stocks. SJM shares recently had an indicated dividend yield of 2.7%, based on a quarterly dividend that was raised 14% with the June 2010 payment.

Qualitative Risk Assessment

LOW	MEDIUM	HIGH

Our risk assessment reflects the relative stability of the company's end markets, our view of its relatively strong balance sheet, and an S&P Quality Ranking of A+, which reflects S&P's appraisal of the historical growth and stability of SJM's earnings and dividends.

Quantitative Evaluations

S&P Quality Ranking   A+

D	C	B-	B	B+	A-	A	A+

Relative Strength Rank   MODERATE

53

LOWEST = 1   HIGHEST = 99

Revenue/Earnings Data

Revenue (Million $)

	1Q	2Q	3Q	4Q	Year
2011	1,047	--	--	--	--
2010	1,052	1,279	1,206	1,069	4,605
2009	663.7	843.1	1,183	1,069	3,758
2008	561.5	707.9	665.4	590.0	2,525
2007	526.5	605.0	523.1	493.5	2,148
2006	510.3	606.3	536.5	501.7	2,155

Earnings Per Share ($)

2011	0.86	E1.35	E1.22	E0.94	E4.55
2010	0.83	1.18	1.14	1.01	4.15
2009	0.77	0.94	0.68	0.80	3.12
2008	0.77	0.87	0.75	0.67	3.00
2007	0.50	0.80	0.71	0.75	2.76
2006	0.51	0.79	0.54	0.62	2.45

Fiscal year ended Apr. 30. Next earnings report expected: Late November. EPS Estimates based on S&P Operating Earnings; historical GAAP earnings are as reported.

Dividend Data (Dates: mm/dd Payment Date: mm/dd/yy)

Amount ($)	Date Decl.	Ex-Div. Date	Stk. of Record	Payment Date
0.350	10/27	11/10	11/13	12/01/09
0.350	01/28	02/10	02/12	03/01/10
0.400	04/22	05/12	05/14	06/01/10
0.400	07/19	08/11	08/13	09/01/10

Dividends have been paid since 1949. Source: Company reports.

Please read the Required Disclosures and Analyst Certification on the last page of this report.

The **McGraw·Hill** Companies

J.M. Smucker Co (The)

STANDARD &POOR'S

Business Summary August 27, 2010

CORPORATE PROFILE. From its origins in 1897, when Jerome M. Smucker first pressed cider at a mill that he opened in that year, the J. M. Smucker Co. has become a leading U.S. producer of such products as fruit spreads, peanut butter, shortening, ice cream toppings, and coffee.

In November 2008, SJM completed the acquisition of the Folgers coffee business from Procter & Gamble (PG 60, Buy). PG shareholders received about 63 million SJM shares (about 53.5% of the total shares now outstanding) in exchange for the Folgers business. The Folgers transaction was preceded by SJM paying a one-time special dividend of $5 a share to SJM shareholders of record on September 30, 2008. On a pro forma basis, Folgers would have accounted for about 42% of SJM's total sales in FY 08 (assuming $1.8 billion from the Folgers business).

SJM's U.S. retail coffee market segment (37% of FY 10 (Apr.) net sales) includes much of the Folgers business. SJM's U.S. retail consumer market segment (24%) includes such items as Smucker's fruit spreads and toppings, Jif peanut butter, and various products carrying the Hungry Jack and Smucker's

Uncrustables brands. The U.S. retail oils and baking market segment (20%) includes baking mixes, frostings, flour, private label canned milk, and oils. The special markets segment (19%) includes Canada, foodservice, natural foods (formerly beverage), and international businesses areas.

SJM's international business accounted for 9.5% of net sales in FY 10. Sales to Wal-Mart Stores, Inc. and its subsidiaries accounted for about 27% of net sales.

SJM product categories include coffee (40% of FY 10 sales), peanut butter (12%), shortening and oils (8%), fruit spreads (8%), baking mixes and frostings (6%), canned milk (5%), flour and baking ingredients (5%), portion control (3%), juices and beverages (3%), Uncrustables frozen sandwiches (3%), toppings and syrups (2%), and other (5%).

Company Financials Fiscal Year Ended Apr. 30

Per Share Data ($)	2010	2009	2008	2007	2006	2005	2004	2003	2002	2001
Tangible Book Value	NM	NM	0.98	5.75	5.52	4.61	7.10	5.58	9.32	8.27
Cash Flow	5.73	4.50	4.11	3.81	3.77	3.19	3.01	2.81	2.39	2.40
Earnings	4.15	3.12	3.00	2.76	2.45	2.26	2.21	2.02	1.24	1.23
S&P Core Earnings	4.19	2.98	2.55	2.70	2.30	2.16	2.20	1.89	1.10	1.19
Dividends	NA	1.28	1.12	1.08	1.00	0.92	0.76	0.76	0.64	0.60
Payout Ratio	NA	41%	37%	39%	41%	41%	34%	38%	52%	49%
Calendar Year	2009	2008	2007	2006	2005	2004	2003	2002	2001	2000
Prices:High	62.70	56.69	64.32	49.98	51.65	53.50	46.75	40.42	37.73	29.00
Prices:Low	34.09	37.22	46.57	37.15	43.64	40.80	33.00	28.71	22.61	15.00
P/E Ratio:High	15	18	21	18	21	24	21	20	30	24
P/E Ratio:Low	8	12	16	13	18	18	15	14	18	12

Income Statement Analysis (Million $)

Revenue	4,605	3,758	2,525	2,148	2,155	2,044	1,417	1,312	687	651
Operating Income	1,021	655	354	318	325	526	227	214	88.4	83.7
Depreciation	182	118	62.6	58.9	71.1	56.0	39.9	37.8	28.6	26.9
Interest Expense	65.2	62.5	42.1	23.4	24.0	22.6	6.37	8.75	9.21	0.78
Pretax Income	731	396	255	241	216	205	179	155	50.2	50.0
Effective Tax Rate	NA	32.9%	33.1%	34.8%	33.5%	36.2%	37.7%	38.0%	38.5%	36.6%
Net Income	494	266	170	157	143	130	111	96.3	30.9	31.7
S&P Core Earnings	495	254	144	154	134	126	111	90.5	25.9	28.9

Balance Sheet & Other Financial Data (Million $)

Cash	284	457	184	200	121	75.8	163	181	91.9	51.1
Current Assets	1,224	1,399	776	639	571	556	425	467	280	229
Total Assets	7,975	8,192	3,130	2,694	2,650	2,636	1,684	1,615	525	470
Current Liabilities	479	1,061	239	236	235	308	175	167	80.4	67.1
Long Term Debt	900	910	790	393	429	432	135	135	135	135
Common Equity	5,326	4,940	1,800	1,796	1,728	1,691	1,211	1,124	280	247
Total Capital	6,236	6,127	2,765	2,347	2,312	2,233	1,482	1,393	419	387
Capital Expenditures	137	109	76.4	57.0	63.2	87.6	100	49.5	23.5	29.4
Cash Flow	676	384	233	216	214	187	151	134	59.4	58.6
Current Ratio	2.6	1.3	3.2	2.7	2.4	1.8	2.4	2.8	3.5	3.4
% Long Term Debt of Capitalization	14.4	14.9	28.6	16.7	18.5	19.3	9.1	9.7	32.2	34.9
% Net Income of Revenue	10.7	7.1	6.8	7.3	6.7	6.4	7.9	7.3	4.5	4.9
% Return on Assets	6.1	4.7	5.9	5.9	5.4	6.0	6.7	9.0	6.1	6.8
% Return on Equity	9.6	7.9	9.5	8.9	8.4	9.0	9.5	13.7	11.6	11.3

Data as orig reptd.; bef. results of disc opers/spec. items. Per share data adj. for stk. divs.; EPS diluted. E-Estimated. NA-Not Available. NM-Not Meaningful. NR-Not Ranked. UR-Under Review.

Office: 1 Strawberry Ln, Orrville, OH 44667-0280.
Telephone: 330-682-3000.
Email: investor.relations@jmsmucker.com
Website: http://www.smuckers.com

Co-Chrmn, Pres & Co-CEO: R.K. Smucker
Co-Chrmn & Co-CEO: T. Smucker
SVP & CFO: M.R. Belgya
Chief Acctg Officer & Cntlr: J.W. Denman

Treas: D.A. Marthey
Investor Contact: S. Robinson (330-684-3440)
Board Members: V. C. Byrd, R. D. Cowan, K. W. Dindo, P. Dolan, N. L. Knight, E. V. Long, G. A. Oatey, A. Shumate, M. Smucker, R. K. Smucker, T. Smucker, W. H. Steinbrink, P. S. Wagstaff

Founded: 1897
Domicile: Ohio
Employees: 4,850

The McGraw-Hill Companies

Snap-On Inc

S&P Recommendation	HOLD ★★★☆☆	Price $50.00 (as of Oct 22, 2010)	12-Mo. Target Price $54.00	Investment Style Large-Cap Value

GICS Sector Industrials
Sub-Industry Industrial Machinery

Summary This company is the largest manufacturer and distributor of hand tools, storage units and diagnostic equipment for professional mechanics.

Key Stock Statistics (Source S&P, Vickers, company reports)

52-Wk Range	$50.11–35.25	S&P Oper. EPS 2010E	3.08	Market Capitalization(B)	$2.905	Beta	1.49
Trailing 12-Month EPS	$2.48	S&P Oper. EPS 2011E	3.64	Yield (%)	2.40	S&P 3-Yr. Proj. EPS CAGR(%)	12
Trailing 12-Month P/E	20.2	P/E on S&P Oper. EPS 2010E	16.2	Dividend Rate/Share	$1.20	S&P Credit Rating	A-
$10K Invested 5 Yrs Ago	$15,388	Common Shares Outstg. (M)	58.1	Institutional Ownership (%)	89		

Price Performance

30-Week Mov. Avg. · · · 10-Week Mov. Avg. – – **GAAP Earnings vs. Previous Year** Volume Above Avg. STARS
12-Mo. Target Price — Relative Strength — ▲ Up ▼ Down ► No Change Below Avg. ★

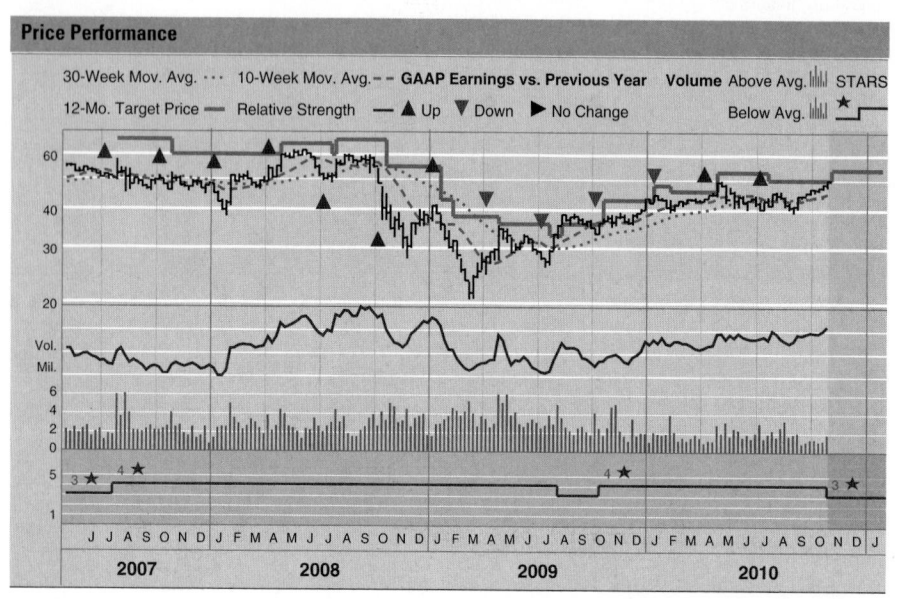

Options: ASE, Ph

Qualitative Risk Assessment

LOW	MEDIUM	HIGH

Our risk assessment is based on our view of SNA's strong brand equity and healthy balance sheet, offset by an industry categorized by intense competition. We believe an improved global supply chain and cost reduction initiatives will offset rising raw material and delivery costs.

Quantitative Evaluations

S&P Quality Ranking B+

D	C	B-	B	B+	A-	A	A+

Relative Strength Rank STRONG

81

LOWEST = 1   HIGHEST = 99

Revenue/Earnings Data

Revenue (Million $)

	1Q	2Q	3Q	4Q	Year
2010	621.6	647.6	--	--	--
2009	592.6	615.6	587.8	624.8	2,421
2008	747.0	784.4	713.8	687.5	2,935
2007	705.7	711.9	680.7	742.9	2,841
2006	593.5	624.4	599.5	656.0	2,522
2005	612.8	608.6	567.2	573.6	2,362

Earnings Per Share ($)

2010	0.63	0.78	E0.64	E0.87	E3.08
2009	0.60	0.65	0.44	0.63	2.32
2008	0.97	1.15	0.94	1.01	4.07
2007	0.66	0.90	0.70	0.99	3.23
2006	0.37	0.20	0.48	0.64	1.69
2005	0.31	0.46	0.36	0.47	1.59

Fiscal year ended Dec. 31. Next earnings report expected: Late October. EPS Estimates based on S&P Operating Earnings; historical GAAP earnings are as reported.

Highlights

➤ The STARS recommendation for SNA has recently been changed to 3 (hold) from 4 (buy) and the 12-month target price has recently been changed to $54.00 from $50.00. The Highlights section of this Stock Report will be updated accordingly.

Investment Rationale/Risk

➤ The Investment Rationale/Risk section of this Stock Report will be updated shortly. For the latest News story on SNA from MarketScope, see below.

➤ 10/22/10 02:57 pm ET ... S&P REDUCES RECOMMENDATION ON SHARES OF SNAP-ON TO HOLD FROM BUY (SNA 49.93***): SNA reports Q3 EPS of $0.80, vs. $0.44, and $0.16 ahead of our view, on greater-than-expected operating margins, and sales growth of 14%. We find positive SNA's strong performance in what historically has been a weaker seasonal quarter, and we raise our '10 EPS estimate by $0.18 to $3.08, and '11's by $0.13 to $3.64, on revised revenue and margin forecasts. That said, we believe the shares are now closer to fully valued, following the 24% advance since the August low, and we see less upside to our $54 target price, raised $4 today, on revised valuation analyses. / M.Christy,CFA

Dividend Data (Dates: mm/dd Payment Date: mm/dd/yy)

Amount ($)	Date Decl.	Ex-Div. Date	Stk. of Record	Payment Date
0.300	11/05	11/12	11/16	12/07/09
0.300	02/10	02/23	02/25	03/10/10
0.300	04/22	05/18	05/20	06/10/10
0.300	08/05	08/18	08/20	09/10/10

Dividends have been paid since 1939. Source: Company reports.

The McGraw-Hill Companies

Snap-On Inc

Business Summary July 30, 2010

CORPORATE OVERVIEW. Snap-on Inc. is a major global manufacturer and marketer of high-quality tool, diagnostic, service and equipment solutions for professional tool and equipment users under various brands and trade names. Product lines include a broad range of hand and power tools, tool storage, saws and cutting tools, pruning tools, vehicle service diagnostics equipment, vehicle service equipment, including wheel service, safety testing and collision repair equipment, vehicle service information, business management systems, equipment repair services, and other tool and equipment solutions. SNA's customers include automotive technicians, vehicle service centers, manufacturers, industrial tool and equipment users, and those involved in commercial applications such as construction, electrical and agriculture. SNA services these customers through three primary channels of distribution: the mobile dealer van channel, including the company's technical representatives; company direct sales; and non-franchise, independent distributors.

SNA has four reportable business segments. The Snap-on Tools Group, formerly the Dealer Group (42% of 2009 sales, 38% of 2008 sales) consists of SNA's business operations serving the worldwide franchised dealer van channel. The Commercial & Industrial Group (44%, 49%) provides tools, equip-

ment products and equipment repair services to industrial and commercial customers worldwide through direct, distributor and other non-franchised distribution channels. The Diagnostics & Information Group (22%, 22%) provides diagnostic equipment, vehicle service information, business management systems and other solutions for customers in the vehicle service and repair marketplace. Financial Services (2%, 3%) is a relatively new business segment, which was originated in 2004. It consists of Snap-on Credit LLC, which following the July 2009 acquisition of the 50% ownership controlled by The CIT Group became a fully controlled subsidiary, and SNA's wholly owned finance subsidiaries in international markets where SNA has dealer operations. Segment eliminations as a percentage of total sales were -10% in 2009 and -11% in 2008. In regard to global reach, nearly 41% of total sales in 2009 were outside the U.S. market, or $981 million, a decline of 22% from the year before, due largely to currency translation.

Company Financials Fiscal Year Ended Dec. 31

Per Share Data ($)	2009	2008	2007	2006	2005	2004	2003	2002	2001	2000
Tangible Book Value	4.67	2.90	3.94	0.72	8.17	9.67	8.29	6.27	6.01	6.53
Cash Flow	3.44	5.17	4.52	2.57	2.48	2.45	2.38	2.65	1.54	3.23
Earnings	2.32	4.07	3.23	1.69	1.59	1.40	1.35	1.76	0.37	2.10
S&P Core Earnings	2.35	3.31	3.15	2.07	1.56	1.35	1.31	0.92	0.09	NA
Dividends	1.20	1.20	1.11	1.08	1.00	1.00	1.00	0.97	0.96	0.94
Payout Ratio	52%	29%	34%	64%	63%	71%	74%	55%	NM	45%
Prices:High	43.88	62.21	57.81	48.65	38.71	34.67	32.38	35.15	34.40	32.44
Prices:Low	20.51	27.70	44.58	36.38	30.57	27.15	22.60	20.71	21.15	20.88
P/E Ratio:High	19	15	18	29	24	25	24	20	93	15
P/E Ratio:Low	9	7	14	22	19	19	17	12	57	10

Income Statement Analysis (Million $)										
Revenue	2,421	2,935	2,841	2,522	2,362	2,407	2,233	2,109	2,096	2,176
Operating Income	338	467	401	217	220	203	167	217	168	270
Depreciation	74.6	63.8	76.0	51.9	52.2	61.0	60.3	51.7	68.0	66.2
Interest Expense	47.7	33.8	46.0	20.6	21.7	23.0	24.4	28.7	35.5	40.7
Pretax Income	206	355	284	146	148	120	117	161	47.6	193
Effective Tax Rate	30.4%	33.2%	32.5%	31.4%	37.2%	32.1%	32.6%	36.0%	54.8%	36.1%
Net Income	134	237	189	100	92.9	81.7	78.7	103	21.5	123
S&P Core Earnings	136	193	184	123	91.6	78.3	76.6	53.9	5.49	NA

Balance Sheet & Other Financial Data (Million $)										
Cash	699	116	93.0	63.4	170	150	96.1	18.4	6.70	6.10
Current Assets	1,676	1,141	1,187	1,113	1,073	1,193	1,132	1,051	1,139	1,186
Total Assets	3,447	2,710	2,765	2,655	2,008	2,290	2,139	1,994	1,974	2,050
Current Liabilities	740	548	639	682	506	674	567	552	549	538
Long Term Debt	675	530	502	506	202	203	303	304	446	473
Common Equity	1,290	1,187	1,280	1,076	962	1,111	1,011	830	868	844
Total Capital	1,980	1,834	1,873	1,671	1,239	1,390	1,348	1,168	1,339	1,342
Capital Expenditures	64.4	73.9	62.0	50.5	40.1	38.7	29.4	45.8	53.6	57.6
Cash Flow	199	301	265	152	145	143	139	155	89.5	189
Current Ratio	2.3	2.1	1.9	1.6	2.1	1.8	2.0	1.9	2.1	2.2
% Long Term Debt of Capitalization	34.1	28.9	26.8	30.3	16.3	14.6	22.5	26.0	33.3	35.3
% Net Income of Revenue	5.5	8.1	6.6	4.0	3.9	3.4	3.5	4.9	1.0	5.7
% Return on Assets	4.4	8.7	6.9	4.3	4.3	3.7	3.8	5.2	1.1	5.9
% Return on Equity	10.8	19.2	16.0	9.8	9.0	7.7	8.5	12.9	2.4	14.7

Data as orig reptd.; bef. results of disc opers/spec. items. Per share data adj. for stk. divs.; EPS diluted. E-Estimated. NA-Not Available. NM-Not Meaningful. NR-Not Ranked. UR-Under Review.

Office: 2801 80th St, Kenosha, WI 53143-5656.
Telephone: 262-656-5200.
Website: http://www.snapon.com
Chrmn, Pres & CEO: N.T. Pinchuk

SVP & CFO: A.J. Pagliari
Chief Acctg Officer & Cntlr: C.R. Johnsen
Secy & General Counsel: I.M. Shur
Investor Contact: L. Kratcoski (262-656-6121)

Board Members: B. S. Chelberg, K. L. Daniel, R. J. Decyk, J. F. Fiedler, J. P. Holden, N. J. Jones, A. L. Kelly, W. D. Lehman, N. T. Pinchuk, E. H. Rensi, R. F. Teerlink

Founded: 1920
Domicile: Delaware
Employees: 11,000

Southern Co (The)

STANDARD &POOR'S

S&P Recommendation **HOLD** ★★★☆☆	Price $38.32 (as of Oct 22, 2010)	12-Mo. Target Price $37.00	Investment Style Large-Cap Value

GICS Sector Utilities
Sub-Industry Electric Utilities

Summary This Atlanta-based energy holding company is one of the largest producers of electricity in the U.S.

Key Stock Statistics (Source S&P, Vickers, company reports)

52-Wk Range	$38.48–30.85	S&P Oper. EPS 2010E	2.43	Market Capitalization(B)	$31.833	Beta	0.37
Trailing 12-Month EPS	$2.50	S&P Oper. EPS 2011E	2.50	Yield (%)	4.75	S&P 3-Yr. Proj. EPS CAGR(%)	3
Trailing 12-Month P/E	15.3	P/E on S&P Oper. EPS 2010E	15.8	Dividend Rate/Share	$1.82	S&P Credit Rating	A
$10K Invested 5 Yrs Ago	$14,395	Common Shares Outstg. (M)	830.7	Institutional Ownership (%)	42		

Price Performance

30-Week Mov. Avg. · · · 10-Week Mov. Avg. - - **GAAP Earnings vs. Previous Year** Volume Above Avg. STARS
12-Mo. Target Price — Relative Strength ▲ Up ▼ Down ▶ No Change Below Avg. ★

Options: ASE, CBOE, P, Ph

Analysis prepared by **Justin McCann** on July 30, 2010, when the stock traded at **$ 35.23**.

Highlights

▶ We expect operating EPS in 2010 to increase nearly 5% from 2009's $2.32, which excluded a one-time charge of $0.25. Operating earnings in 2009 were hurt by the economic slowdown in SO's service territory, particularly in the industrial sector, where electricity demand was down 11.8% for the year. Results in the first half of 2010 were aided by the weather, which was abnormally cold in the first quarter and abnormally warm in the second quarter.

▶ Operating EPS in the second half of 2010 is expected to be restricted by more shares outstanding, and by higher operating expenses, which are expected to return to more normal levels after their sharp decline in 2009. Longer term, we expect SO to realize average annual EPS growth of 4% to 6%, with the utilities seeing customer growth of about 1.7% and demand growth of around 2%. We expect SO to have total capital expenditures of about $16.4 billion in the 2010 through 2012 period.

▶ We do not expect any significant change in the company's policies with the replacement of David Ratcliffe as president (on August 1), and as chairman and CEO (on December 1) by the current COO Thomas Fanning.

Investment Rationale/Risk

▶ The stock is up nearly 10% year to date, after declining 8.8% in 2009. We believe the weakness in the housing market in SO's territory has been milder than in other areas and that with an increase in industrial activity there could be a gradual improvement in the service territory economy. Despite the attractive yield from the dividend (recently 5.0%), we believe the stock has become fully valued at its recent level. However, we expect it to trade at a premium to peers, reflecting the relative predictability of SO's earnings and dividend stream.

▶ Risks to our recommendation and target price include a severe economic downturn in the company's service territory, and a significant decline in the average P/E of the electric utility group as a whole.

▶ We expect future dividends to increase at around a 4% annual rate. With the current dividend payout ratio at 75% of our operating EPS estimate for 2010, such increases would keep payouts at the top of SO's targeted payout range of 70% to 75%. We see the shares trading at a premium-to-peers P/E of about 14.8X our EPS estimate for 2011. Our 12-month target price is $37.

Qualitative Risk Assessment

LOW	MEDIUM	HIGH

Our risk assessment reflects our view of the company's strong and steady cash flow from its regulated electric utility operations, its solid balance sheet, and a generally supportive regulatory environment, partially offset by a slowing economy in its service territories.

Quantitative Evaluations

S&P Quality Ranking A-

D	C	B-	B	B+	A-	A	A+

Relative Strength Rank MODERATE

58

LOWEST = 1   HIGHEST = 99

Revenue/Earnings Data

Revenue (Million $)

	1Q	2Q	3Q	4Q	Year
2010	4,157	4,207	--	--	--
2009	3,666	3,885	4,682	3,510	15,743
2008	3,683	4,215	5,426	3,802	17,127
2007	3,409	3,772	4,832	3,340	15,353
2006	3,063	3,592	4,549	3,152	14,356
2005	2,864	3,144	4,378	3,287	13,554

Earnings Per Share ($)

2010	0.60	0.62	E0.97	E0.27	E2.43
2009	0.18	0.60	0.99	0.31	2.07
2008	0.47	0.55	1.01	0.24	2.26
2007	0.45	0.57	1.00	0.27	2.28
2006	0.35	0.52	0.99	0.25	2.10
2005	0.43	0.52	0.97	0.21	2.14

Fiscal year ended Dec. 31. Next earnings report expected: Late October. EPS Estimates based on S&P Operating Earnings; historical GAAP earnings are as reported.

Dividend Data (Dates: mm/dd Payment Date: mm/dd/yy)

Amount ($)	Date Decl.	Ex-Div. Date	Stk. of Record	Payment Date
0.455	04/19	04/29	05/03	06/05/10
0.455	04/19	04/29	05/03	06/05/10
0.455	07/19	07/29	08/02	09/04/10
0.455	10/18	10/28	11/01	12/06/10

Dividends have been paid since 1948. Source: Company reports.

Please read the Required Disclosures and Analyst Certification on the last page of this report.

The McGraw-Hill Companies

Southern Co (The)

Business Summary July 30, 2010

CORPORATE OVERVIEW. The Southern Company is one of the largest producers of electricity in the U.S. Based in Atlanta, GA, this utility holding company has approximately 42,932 megawatts of generating capacity and provides electricity to around 4.4 million customers in the Southeast through the following integrated utilities: Alabama Power, Georgia Power, Gulf Power (located in the northwestern portion of Florida), and Mississippi Power. Savannah Electric & Power was merged into Georgia Power on July 1, 2006.

MARKET PROFILE. Southern Power Company (SPC) was formed by SO in January 2001 to own, manage and finance wholesale generating assets in the Southeast. It serves both the utility units and the wholesale power market. Energy from SPC's assets, which included 7,880 megawatts of generating capacity at the end of 2009, is marketed to wholesale customers through the Southern Company Generation and Energy Marketing unit. SPC and the utility

units enter into contracts for power purchases, sales and exchanges among themselves, as well as with other utilities in the Southeast. Although Southern Power is not subject to state regulation, it is subject to regulation by the Federal Energy Regulatory Commission.

SO is also the parent company for SouthernLINC Wireless, which provides digital, wireless communications services to SO's four utility units, as well as to non-affiliates within the Southeast. It also provides wholesale fiber optic solutions to telecommunication providers in the Southeast.

Company Financials Fiscal Year Ended Dec. 31

Per Share Data ($)	2009	2008	2007	2006	2005	2004	2003	2002	2001	2000
Tangible Book Value	18.15	17.08	16.23	15.00	14.19	13.65	12.92	11.56	10.87	15.12
Earnings	2.07	2.26	2.28	2.10	2.14	2.06	2.02	1.85	1.61	1.52
S&P Core Earnings	2.29	1.83	2.26	2.06	2.04	1.93	1.85	1.35	1.12	NA
Dividends	1.73	1.66	1.60	1.54	1.48	1.77	1.39	1.36	1.34	1.34
Payout Ratio	84%	74%	70%	72%	69%	86%	69%	74%	83%	88%
Prices:High	37.62	40.60	39.35	37.40	36.47	33.96	32.00	31.14	35.72	35.00
Prices:Low	26.48	29.82	33.16	30.48	31.14	27.44	27.00	23.22	20.89	20.38
P/E Ratio:High	18	18	17	18	17	16	16	17	22	23
P/E Ratio:Low	13	13	15	14	15	13	13	13	13	13

Income Statement Analysis (Million $)	2009	2008	2007	2006	2005	2004	2003	2002	2001	2000
Revenue	15,743	17,127	15,353	14,356	13,554	11,902	11,251	10,549	10,155	10,066
Depreciation	1,788	1,704	1,245	1,200	1,176	955	1,027	1,047	1,173	1,171
Maintenance	NA	NA	1,175	1,096	1,116	1,027	937	961	909	852
Fixed Charges Coverage	3.82	3.84	3.73	3.73	3.90	4.11	4.21	3.80	3.25	2.87
Construction Credits	200	152	106	50.0	51.0	47.0	25.0	22.0	NA	NA
Effective Tax Rate	35.3%	34.4%	31.9%	33.2%	27.2%	27.7%	29.3%	28.6%	33.3%	37.2%
Net Income	1,645	1,742	1,734	1,574	1,591	1,532	1,474	1,318	1,119	994
S&P Core Earnings	1,822	1,412	1,720	1,551	1,532	1,436	1,351	964	776	NA

Balance Sheet & Other Financial Data (Million $)	2009	2008	2007	2006	2005	2004	2003	2002	2001	2000
Gross Property	60,314	56,152	53,094	50,167	47,580	45,585	43,722	41,764	38,104	35,972
Capital Expenditures	4,670	3,961	3,545	2,994	2,370	2,110	2,002	2,717	2,617	2,225
Net Property	41,193	37,866	35,681	33,585	31,853	30,634	29,418	26,315	23,084	21,622
Capitalization:Long Term Debt	19,213	17,898	15,223	13,247	13,442	13,010	10,587	8,956	10,941	10,457
Capitalization:% Long Term Debt	56.4	57.4	55.1	53.8	55.7	55.9	52.3	50.7	57.8	49.4
Capitalization:Preferred	Nil	Nil	Nil	Nil	Nil	Nil	Nil	Nil	Nil	Nil
Capitalization:% Preferred	Nil	Nil	Nil	Nil	Nil	Nil	Nil	Nil	Nil	Nil
Capitalization:Common	14,878	13,276	12,385	11,371	10,689	10,278	9,648	8,710	7,984	10,690
Capitalization:% Common	43.6	42.6	44.9	46.2	44.3	44.1	47.7	49.3	42.2	50.6
Total Capital	35,204	37,968	34,198	31,110	30,394	29,077	25,809	22,937	24,147	26,436
% Operating Ratio	83.6	84.9	83.8	83.0	82.5	81.2	79.7	80.5	81.9	82.0
% Earned on Net Property	8.8	9.5	9.6	9.9	9.5	9.4	10.0	10.1	10.7	11.4
% Return on Revenue	10.5	10.2	11.3	11.0	11.7	12.9	13.1	12.5	11.0	9.9
% Return on Invested Capital	8.4	7.4	8.3	8.0	8.0	7.9	8.9	8.5	7.4	7.3
% Return on Common Equity	11.7	13.6	14.6	14.3	15.2	15.4	16.1	15.8	12.0	10.0

Data as orig reptd.; bef. results of disc opers/spec. items. Per share data adj. for stk. divs.; EPS diluted. E-Estimated. NA-Not Available. NM-Not Meaningful. NR-Not Ranked. UR-Under Review.

Office: 30 Ivan Allen Jr Blvd NW, Atlanta, GA 30308-3003.
Telephone: 404-506-5000.
Email: investors@southerncompany.com
Website: http://www.southernco.com

Chrmn & CEO: D.M. Ratcliffe
Pres: T.A. Fanning
COO & EVP: A.J. Topazi
EVP & CFO: A.P. Beattie

EVP & Secy: G.E. Holland, Jr.
Investor Contact: G. Kundert (404-506-5135)
Board Members: J. P. Baranco, J. A. Boscia, H. A. Clark, III, H. W. Habermeyer, Jr., V. M. Hagen, W. A. Hood, Jr., D. M. James, D. E. Klein, J. N. Purcell, D. M. Ratcliffe, W. G. Smith, Jr., S. R. Specker, L. D. Thompson

Founded: 1945
Domicile: Delaware
Employees: 26,112

Southwestern Energy Co

STANDARD &POOR'S

S&P Recommendation	BUY ★★★★☆	Price $33.91 (as of Oct 22, 2010)	12-Mo. Target Price $40.00	Investment Style Large-Cap Growth

GICS Sector Energy
Sub-Industry Oil & Gas Exploration & Production

Summary This Houston-based company is engaged in oil and gas exploration and production, natural gas gathering and marketing.

Key Stock Statistics (Source S&P, Vickers, company reports)

52-Wk Range	$52.82– 30.61	S&P Oper. EPS 2010E	1.72	Market Capitalization(B)	$11.736	Beta	0.53
Trailing 12-Month EPS	$1.64	S&P Oper. EPS 2011E	2.09	Yield (%)	Nil	S&P 3-Yr. Proj. EPS CAGR(%)	11
Trailing 12-Month P/E	20.7	P/E on S&P Oper. EPS 2010E	19.7	Dividend Rate/Share	Nil	S&P Credit Rating	BBB-
$10K Invested 5 Yrs Ago	$21,065	Common Shares Outstg. (M)	346.1	Institutional Ownership (%)	88		

Price Performance

30-Week Mov. Avg. · · · · 10-Week Mov. Avg. - - GAAP Earnings vs. Previous Year Volume Above Avg. STARS
12-Mo. Target Price — Relative Strength — ▲ Up ▼ Down ▶ No Change Below Avg.

2-for-1

Options: ASE, CBOE, Ph

Analysis prepared by **Michael Kay** on October 13, 2010, when the stock traded at **$ 34.66**.

Highlights

▶ Since SWN's discovery of the Fayetteville Shale in 2004, total annual production has risen to more than 300 Bcfe, from 54 Bcfe. Production in 2009 rose 54%, with 244 Bcfe from Fayetteville, up 81%. In 2010, on a growth target of 42% at Fayetteville, currently producing 1.5 Bcfe/day, we see production up 33%, to 400 Bcfe. SWN will allocate 70% of 2010's capex budget to Fayetteville, where it is running 24 rigs. It has begun drilling at the Marcellus Shale, with one rig, and it will run two rigs at its Haynesville Shale acreage.

▶ SWN has drilled four horizontal Marcellus wells, scheduled to have been completed in the third quarter, and sees 30-35 Marcellus wells in 2010. We view SWN as a low-cost producer, as lease operating expenses fell about 35% over the past two years on Fayetteville operations.

▶ In 2009, operating EPS was flat at $1.52, as production growth was offset by falling natural gas prices. With attractive hedges, we see EPS of $1.72 in 2010 and $2.09 in 2011, on 23% production growth. After investing $1.8 billion in 2009, SWN has set a capex budget for 2010 of $2.1 billion, above cash flows, and we expect asset sales to bridge the gap.

Investment Rationale/Risk

▶ SWN spent $1.3 billion at Fayetteville in 2009, 72% of its total capex budget, and plans $1.5 billion (70%) in 2010, providing production and reserve growth visibility. We view positively its growth prospects and low-cost operations, which we think position it well to boost earnings and cash flow. SWN holds significant leasehold acreage acquired at attractive prices due to limited attention paid to the region before 2004. We believe additional acreage at Marcellus and Haynesville should add value over the next several years. Despite weak natural gas markets, we expect SWN's top-tier production growth to be internally funded by 2011, and view its low-cost operations as attractive under current market conditions.

▶ Risks to our opinion and target price include a sustained drop in oil and gas prices and further deterioration in global economic conditions.

▶ We see production, EPS and cash flow growth, with potential upside if gas markets improve. We blend our NAV estimate of $39 with a target of 8X our 2011 EBITDA estimate, above peers, to arrive at our 12-month target price of $40. We believe the shares have been negatively impacted by SWN's aggressive spending.

Qualitative Risk Assessment

LOW	MEDIUM	HIGH

Our risk assessment reflects SWN's operations in a capital-intensive industry that is competitive and cyclical and derives value from producing a commodity whose price is very volatile.

Quantitative Evaluations

S&P Quality Ranking B

D	C	B-	B	B+	A-	A	A+

Relative Strength Rank WEAK

24

LOWEST = 1   HIGHEST = 99

Revenue/Earnings Data

Revenue (Million $)

	1Q	2Q	3Q	4Q	Year
2010	668.1	589.9	--	--	--
2009	540.8	477.5	503.0	624.5	2,146
2008	524.1	604.5	683.0	500.1	2,312
2007	284.7	270.1	297.6	402.8	1,255
2006	226.7	154.0	168.4	214.0	763.1
2005	161.1	132.5	162.1	220.7	676.3

Earnings Per Share ($)

2010	0.49	0.35	E0.42	E0.46	E1.72
2009	-1.26	0.35	0.34	0.45	-0.10
2008	0.31	0.39	0.63	0.30	1.64
2007	0.15	0.14	0.15	0.21	0.64
2006	0.17	0.11	0.10	0.10	0.48
2005	0.11	0.09	0.13	0.15	0.48

Fiscal year ended Dec. 31. Next earnings report expected: Late October. EPS Estimates based on S&P Operating Earnings; historical GAAP earnings are as reported.

Dividend Data

Cash dividends have not been paid since 2000.

Please read the Required Disclosures and Analyst Certification on the last page of this report.

The McGraw-Hill Companies

Southwestern Energy Co

STANDARD
&POOR'S

Business Summary October 13, 2010

CORPORATE OVERVIEW. Southwestern Energy Company (SWN) is primarily focused on the exploration and production of natural gas. SWN is engaged in natural gas and crude oil exploration and production (E&P) in the Arkoma Basin, Oklahoma, Texas and Pennsylvania. SWN also has natural gas gathering and marketing activities located in core market areas. Current operations are being principally focused on development of the unconventional gas reservoir located on the Arkansas side of the Arkoma Basin, the Fayetteville Shale play.

As of December 31, 2009, SWN had estimated proved reserves of 3.66 Tcfe, of which 100% was natural gas and 54% was proved developed. This compares with estimated proved reserves of 2.19 Tcfe, 100% natural gas and 62% proved developed, at the end of 2008, a 67% increase. We calculate SWN's reserve life was 12.2 years as of year-end 2009, up from 11.2 years a year earlier. We believe this is especially impressive given SWN's production growth and indicative of very strong reserve additions.

We estimate that SWN replaced 592% of production in 2009 (523% in 2008). As of the end of 2009, SWN's three-year average reserve replacement ratio was 548%. During 2009, SWN invested a total of $1.8 billion, with $1.6 billion allocated to the E&P business. Capital spending, which included $214 million (13%) for Midstream Services, focused primarily on active drilling programs in

the Fayetteville Shale (72%), East Texas (10%), the conventional Arkoma Basin (2%), Appalachian Basin (2%) and other (1%).

CORPORATE STRATEGY. SWN is focused on promoting long-term growth in the net asset value of its business. The key elements of SWN's E&P business strategy are to exploit and develop its existing asset base, control operations and costs, hedge production to stabilize cash flow, and achieve growth through new exploration and development activities.

SWN's primary business is natural gas and oil exploration, development and production, with operations primarily located in Arkansas, Oklahoma and Texas. These operations are conducted through its wholly owned subsidiaries, SEECO, Inc., and Southwestern Energy Production Company (SEPCO). Diamond M, also wholly owned, has interests in properties in the Permian Basin of Texas. DeSoto Drilling, Inc. (DDI), a wholly owned subsidiary of SEPCO, operates drilling rigs in the Fayetteville Shale play and in East Texas.

Company Financials Fiscal Year Ended Dec. 31

Per Share Data ($)	2009	2008	2007	2006	2005	2004	2003	2002	2001	2000
Tangible Book Value	6.76	7.30	4.82	4.25	3.32	1.54	1.19	0.86	0.91	0.71
Cash Flow	3.98	2.84	1.49	0.92	0.78	0.60	0.39	0.33	0.43	0.00
Earnings	-0.10	1.64	0.64	0.48	0.48	0.35	0.19	0.07	0.17	-0.23
S&P Core Earnings	-0.11	1.54	0.63	0.46	0.46	0.33	0.17	0.05	0.15	NA
Dividends	Nil	Nil	Nil	Nil	Nil	Nil	Nil	Nil	Nil	0.02
Payout Ratio	Nil	Nil	Nil	Nil	Nil	Nil	Nil	Nil	Nil	NM
Prices:High	51.33	52.69	28.50	22.14	20.90	6.93	3.19	1.91	2.04	1.30
Prices:Low	25.26	19.05	15.57	11.83	5.51	2.42	1.36	1.19	1.10	0.68
P/E Ratio:High	NM	32	45	47	44	20	17	28	12	NM
P/E Ratio:Low	NM	12	24	25	12	7	7	17	6	NM

Income Statement Analysis (Million $)

	2009	2008	2007	2006	2005	2004	2003	2002	2001	2000
Revenue	2,146	2,312	1,255	763	676	477	327	262	345	364
Operating Income	NA	1,301	969	246	246	182	97.3	111	145	112
Depreciation	1,403	414	294	151	96.2	73.7	55.9	54.0	52.9	45.9
Interest Expense	18.6	28.9	37.7	12.4	21.0	19.8	19.1	21.5	24.0	23.2
Pretax Income	-52.2	920	357	262	234	163	78.6	23.0	57.2	-74.7
Effective Tax Rate	31.4%	38.2%	38.1%	38.0%	36.7%	36.2%	35.8%	35.6%	38.3%	NM
Net Income	-35.7	568	221	163	148	104	49.8	14.3	35.3	-45.8
S&P Core Earnings	-37.0	533	217	157	143	98.6	46.6	10.3	30.8	NA

Balance Sheet & Other Financial Data (Million $)

	2009	2008	2007	2006	2005	2004	2003	2002	2001	2000
Cash	13.2	196	0.73	43.0	224	1.20	1.30	1.69	3.64	2.39
Current Assets	564	889	363	324	461	131	100	76.1	93.2	113
Total Assets	4,770	4,760	3,623	2,379	1,869	1,146	891	740	743	705
Current Liabilities	536	793	431	379	302	134	95.1	74.6	71.5	240
Long Term Debt	998	674	978	136	100	325	279	342	350	225
Common Equity	2,331	2,508	1,647	1,434	1,110	448	342	177	183	141
Total Capital	3,340	3,253	103	1,953	1,477	989	780	649	668	464
Capital Expenditures	1,780	1,756	1,519	851	454	291	167	92.1	106	75.7
Cash Flow	1,367	982	515	314	244	177	106	68.3	88.2	0.07
Current Ratio	1.1	1.1	0.8	0.9	1.5	1.0	1.1	1.0	1.3	0.5
% Long Term Debt of Capitalization	30.0	20.7	31.5	6.9	6.7	32.9	35.7	52.8	52.4	48.5
% Net Income of Revenue	NM	24.6	17.6	21.3	21.8	21.7	15.2	5.5	10.2	NM
% Return on Assets	NM	13.6	7.4	7.6	9.8	10.2	6.1	1.9	4.9	NM
% Return on Equity	NM	27.3	14.3	12.7	18.9	26.2	19.2	7.9	21.8	NM

Data as orig reptd.; bef. results of disc opers/spec. items. Per share data adj. for stk. divs.; EPS diluted. E-Estimated. NA-Not Available. NM-Not Meaningful. NR-Not Ranked. UR-Under Review.

Office: 2350 North Sam Houston Parkway East, Suite 125, Houston, TX 77032.
Telephone: 281-618-4700.
Website: http://www.swn.com
Chrmn: H.M. Korell
Pres & CEO: S.L. Mueller
EVP & CFO: G.D. Kerley
EVP, Secy & General Counsel: M.K. Boling
Chief Admin Officer & CIO: D.W. Hency
Investor Contact: B.D. Sylvester (281-618-4897)
Board Members: L. E. Epley, Jr., R. L. Howard, G. D. Kerley, H. M. Korell, V. A. Kuuskraa, K. R. Mourton, S. L. Mueller, C. E. Scharlau, A. H. Stevens
Founded: 1929
Domicile: Delaware
Employees: 1,702

Southwest Airlines Co.

STANDARD &POOR'S

S&P Recommendation	BUY ★★★★☆	Price $13.47 (as of Oct 22, 2010)	12-Mo. Target Price $17.00

GICS Sector Industrials
Sub-Industry Airlines

Summary As the fifth largest U.S. airline, Southwest offers discounted fares, primarily on shorter-haul, point-to-point flights.

Key Stock Statistics (Source S&P, Vickers, company reports)

52-Wk Range	$14.16–8.10	S&P Oper. EPS 2010E	0.78	Market Capitalization(B)	$10.048	Beta	1.08
Trailing 12-Month EPS	$0.30	S&P Oper. EPS 2011E	1.13	Yield (%)	0.13	S&P 3-Yr. Proj. EPS CAGR(%)	14
Trailing 12-Month P/E	44.9	P/E on S&P Oper. EPS 2010E	17.3	Dividend Rate/Share	$0.02	S&P Credit Rating	BBB
$10K Invested 5 Yrs Ago	$8,591	Common Shares Outstg. (M)	745.9	Institutional Ownership (%)	83		

Price Performance

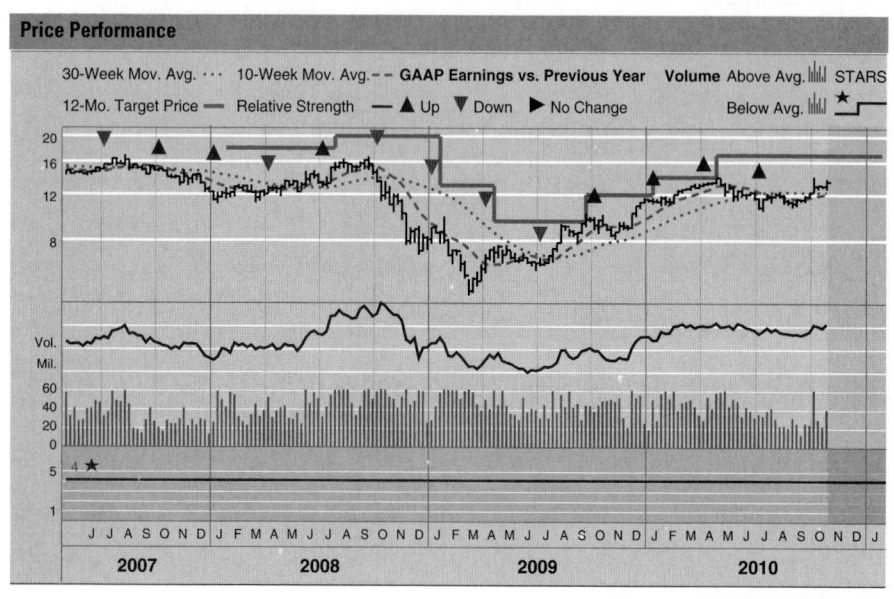

- 30-Week Mov. Avg. · · · 10-Week Mov. Avg. – – **GAAP Earnings vs. Previous Year** Volume Above Avg. STARS
- 12-Mo. Target Price — Relative Strength — ▲ Up ▼ Down ► No Change Below Avg.

2007 2008 2009 2010

Options: ASE, CBOE, P, Ph

Analysis prepared by **Jim Corridore** on October 04, 2010, when the stock traded at **$ 12.71**.

Highlights

- On September 27, LUV announced that it would acquire AirTran Holdings (AAI $7, Buy) for a total of $1.4 billion in cash and stock. Under terms of the deal, LUV would exchange $3.25 in cash and 0.321 LUV share for each AAI share. Completion of the acquisition was subject to regulatory approval and AAI shareholder approval. We look for LUV standalone revenues to rise about 17% on flat capacity, a two percentage point improvement in loads and 14% higher yields. We expect incremental revenues from the sale of assigned boarding slots, a more sophisticated revenue management system, and other ancillary revenue-generating initiatives.

- We see margins in 2010 aided by revenue and mix improvement from LUV's recent initiative to redeploy flights to more profitable markets, coupled with our view of a modest rebound in business travel demand along with stronger leisure demand. We see jet fuel costs rising about 18% in 2010.

- We estimate 2010 operating EPS of $0.85, a sharp improvement over 2009 operating EPS of $0.19 (excluding $43 million in special items). For 2011, we see EPS of $1.13.

Investment Rationale/Risk

- While LUV is straying away from its traditional business model with the proposed acquisition of AirTran, we think the benefits are likely to outweigh the risks. LUV would get about 22% larger without adding a single seat to industry-wide capacity. AAI shares a low cost culture and has a strong presence in Atlanta, a strong business travel market. While LUV is taking on additional complexity due to the addition of new plane types, we think it will be able to manage this risk to keep expenses low. We believe LUV has the balance sheet strength to be able to make this acquisition without harming its financial health.

- Risks to our recommendation and target price include a poorly integrated acquisition, a possible price war with one or more competitors, and weakening of air travel demand. We are concerned about LUV's corporate governance relating to its use of affiliated outsiders on its board of directors' nominating and compensation committees.

- Our 12-month target price of $17 values the shares at an enterprise value-to-EBITDAR (EBITDA plus aircraft rent) multiple of 8X our 2010 EBITDAR estimate, a premium to peers.

Qualitative Risk Assessment

LOW	MEDIUM	HIGH

Even though Southwest participates in the highly volatile airline industry, we think its conservative balance sheet, with low debt to total capitalization, and its track record of 37 consecutive years of profitability mitigate this risk.

Quantitative Evaluations

S&P Quality Ranking B

D	C	B-	B	B+	A-	A	A+

Relative Strength Rank STRONG

80

LOWEST = 1   HIGHEST = 99

Revenue/Earnings Data

Revenue (Million $)

	1Q	2Q	3Q	4Q	Year
2010	2,630	3,168	--	--	--
2009	2,357	2,616	2,666	2,712	10,350
2008	2,530	2,869	2,891	2,734	11,023
2007	2,198	2,583	2,588	2,492	9,861
2006	2,019	2,449	2,342	2,276	9,086
2005	1,663	1,944	1,989	1,987	7,584

Earnings Per Share ($)

2010	0.01	0.15	E0.26	E0.22	E0.78
2009	-0.12	0.12	-0.02	0.16	0.13
2008	0.05	0.44	-0.16	-0.08	0.24
2007	0.12	0.36	0.22	0.15	0.84
2006	0.07	0.40	0.06	0.07	0.61
2005	0.09	0.20	0.28	0.10	0.67

Fiscal year ended Dec. 31. Next earnings report expected: NA. EPS Estimates based on S&P Operating Earnings; historical GAAP earnings are as reported.

Dividend Data (Dates: mm/dd Payment Date: mm/dd/yy)

Amount ($)	Date Decl.	Ex-Div. Date	Stk. of Record	Payment Date
0.005	11/19	12/08	12/10	01/07/10
0.005	01/28	03/02	03/04	03/25/10
0.005	05/19	06/07	06/09	06/23/10
0.005	07/15	08/24	08/26	09/16/10

Dividends have been paid since 1976. Source: Company reports.

Southwest Airlines Co.

Business Summary October 04, 2010

CORPORATE OVERVIEW. Southwest Airlines was the largest provider of scheduled domestic passenger air travel in the U.S. in 2008. Overall, the airline ranks as the fifth largest in U.S., based on total revenue passenger miles (RPMs). At December 31, 2009, it served 68 cities in 35 states. LUV specializes in low-fare, point-to-point, short-haul, high-frequency service. Although 80% of its work force belongs to unions, the company believes that it has generally enjoyed harmonious labor relations. LUV began service to four new airports in 2009: Minneapolis-St. Paul, New York's La Guardia, Boston's Logan International, and Milwaukee International. The company expects to start service to Panama City, Florida in May 2010.

On September 27, 2010, LUV announced that it had reached an agreement to acquire AirTran Holdings, the parent company of AirTran Airlines (AAI), for $3.75 a share in cash plus 0.321 of a LUV share for each AAI share. Based on LUV's closing price on September 24, the deal was valued at $1.4 billion, or $3.4 billion including the assumption of debt and operating leases. Completion of the acquisition was subject to approval by AirTran stockholders and regulatory authorities, among other things. AirTran is a low-cost carrier based primarily in the southeast U.S. with 2009 revenues of $2.3 billion.

MARKET PROFILE. The U.S. airline industry is a $186 billion market, according to 2008 data (latest available) from the U.S. Department of Transportation. With 2008 revenues of $11.0 billion (which fell 6%, to $10.4 billion, in 2009), LUV comprised around 5.9% of total industry revenues. Southwest also has an approximate 10.3% market share when measured by RPMs, as of April 2009. Southwest was profitable in 2009 for the 37th consecutive year and was profitable throughout the industry downturn that took place after 9/11/01, with net income totaling $2.1 billion in 2001-2005. Over the same period, S&P believes the 10 largest U.S. airlines lost about $58.6 billion.

COMPETITIVE LANDSCAPE. The industry consists of about 50 mainline commercial passenger airlines, of which about 20 are considered major airlines, defined as airlines with annual revenues in excess of $1.0 billion. Major competitors include Delta Air Lines (22.2% market share, as measured by RPMs, as of April 2009), AMR Corp.'s American Airlines (17.1%), UAL Corp.'s United Airlines (13.7%), Continental (10.8%), US Airways (8.0%) and JetBlue Airways (3.6%). The U.S. airline industry is fragmented, and highly competitive. Barriers to entry are high, and there are highly entrenched competitors. Pricing is extremely competitive. Fuel costs, the second largest cost category for Southwest, have risen sharply over the past three years, although Southwest is partly protected by a fuel hedging position that we think is by far the best in the industry.

Company Financials Fiscal Year Ended Dec. 31

Per Share Data ($)	2009	2008	2007	2006	2005	2004	2003	2002	2001	2000
Tangible Book Value	7.36	6.69	10.49	8.23	8.38	7.04	6.40	5.69	5.23	4.57
Cash Flow	0.96	1.05	1.56	1.23	1.25	0.91	1.00	0.74	1.03	1.14
Earnings	0.13	0.24	0.84	0.61	0.67	0.38	0.54	0.30	0.63	0.79
S&P Core Earnings	0.12	0.23	0.83	0.60	0.62	0.30	0.48	0.23	0.61	NA
Dividends	0.02	0.02	0.02	0.02	0.02	0.02	0.02	0.02	0.01	0.01
Payout Ratio	14%	8%	2%	3%	3%	5%	3%	6%	2%	1%
Prices:High	11.78	16.77	16.96	18.20	16.95	17.06	19.69	22.00	23.32	23.32
Prices:Low	4.95	7.05	12.12	14.61	13.05	12.88	11.72	10.90	11.25	10.00
P/E Ratio:High	91	70	20	30	25	45	36	73	37	30
P/E Ratio:Low	38	29	14	24	19	34	22	36	18	13

Income Statement Analysis (Million $)										
Revenue	10,350	11,023	9,861	9,086	7,584	6,530	5,937	5,522	5,555	5,650
Operating Income	944	1,058	1,371	1,449	1,289	985	867	774	949	1,302
Depreciation	616	599	555	515	469	431	384	356	318	281
Interest Expense	165	130	119	77.0	83.0	49.0	58.0	89.3	49.3	42.3
Pretax Income	164	278	1,058	790	874	489	708	393	828	1,017
Effective Tax Rate	39.6%	36.0%	39.0%	36.8%	37.3%	36.0%	37.6%	38.6%	38.2%	38.5%
Net Income	99.0	178	645	499	548	313	442	241	511	625
S&P Core Earnings	93.2	169	635	489	504	236	385	188	486	NA

Balance Sheet & Other Financial Data (Million $)										
Cash	2,593	1,803	2,779	1,390	2,280	1,305	1,865	1,815	2,280	523
Current Assets	3,358	2,893	4,443	2,601	3,620	2,172	2,313	2,232	2,520	832
Total Assets	14,269	14,308	16,772	13,460	14,218	11,337	9,878	8,954	8,997	6,670
Current Liabilities	2,676	2,806	4,838	2,887	3,848	2,142	172	1,434	2,239	1,298
Long Term Debt	3,325	3,498	2,050	1,567	1,394	1,700	1,332	1,553	1,327	761
Common Equity	5,466	4,953	6,941	6,449	6,675	5,524	5,052	4,422	4,014	3,451
Total Capital	8,981	10,355	11,526	10,120	9,965	8,834	7,804	7,202	6,399	5,065
Capital Expenditures	585	923	1,331	1,399	1,210	1,775	1,238	603	998	1,135
Cash Flow	715	777	1,200	1,014	1,017	744	826	597	829	906
Current Ratio	1.3	1.0	0.9	0.9	0.9	1.0	13.4	1.6	1.1	0.6
% Long Term Debt of Capitalization	37.0	33.8	17.8	15.5	14.0	19.2	17.1	21.6	20.7	15.0
% Net Income of Revenue	1.0	1.6	6.5	5.5	7.2	4.8	7.4	4.4	9.2	11.1
% Return on Assets	0.7	1.2	4.3	3.6	4.3	3.0	4.7	2.7	6.5	10.1
% Return on Equity	1.9	3.0	9.6	7.6	9.0	5.9	9.3	5.7	13.7	19.9

Data as orig reptd.; bef. results of disc opers/spec. items. Per share data adj. for stk. divs.; EPS diluted. E-Estimated. NA-Not Available. NM-Not Meaningful. NR-Not Ranked. UR-Under Review.

Office: P.O. Box 36611, Dallas, TX 75235-1611.
Telephone: 214-792-4000.
Website: http://www.southwest.com
Chrmn, Pres & CEO: G.C. Kelly

CEO: J.O. Parker, Jr.
COO & EVP: M.G. Van De Ven
EVP & Secy: R. Ricks
SVP, CFO & Chief Acctg Officer: L.H. Wright

Investor Contact: L. Wright (214-792-4415)
Board Members: D. W. Biegler, D. H. Brooks, W. H. Cunningham, J. G. Denison, T. C. Johnson, G. C. Kelly, N. B. Loeffler, J. Montford, D. D. Villanueva

Founded: 1967
Domicile: Texas
Employees: 34,726

Spectra Energy Corp

STANDARD &POOR'S

S&P Recommendation BUY ★★★★☆

Price	12-Mo. Target Price	Investment Style
$23.78 (as of Oct 22, 2010)	$27.00	Large-Cap Blend

GICS Sector Energy
Sub-Industry Oil & Gas Storage & Transportation

Summary This integrated natural gas holding company is engaged in gas gathering and processing, and gas transportation and storage, in the U.S. and Canada, and has retail gas distribution to 1.3 million customers in Ontario, Canada.

Key Stock Statistics (Source S&P, Vickers, company reports)

52-Wk Range	$23.86–18.57	S&P Oper. EPS 2010E	1.55	Market Capitalization(B)	$15.410	Beta	0.89
Trailing 12-Month EPS	$1.45	S&P Oper. EPS 2011E	1.81	Yield (%)	4.21	S&P 3-Yr. Proj. EPS CAGR(%)	13
Trailing 12-Month P/E	16.4	P/E on S&P Oper. EPS 2010E	15.3	Dividend Rate/Share	$1.00	S&P Credit Rating	NA
$10K Invested 5 Yrs Ago	NA	Common Shares Outstg. (M)	648.0	Institutional Ownership (%)	65		

Price Performance

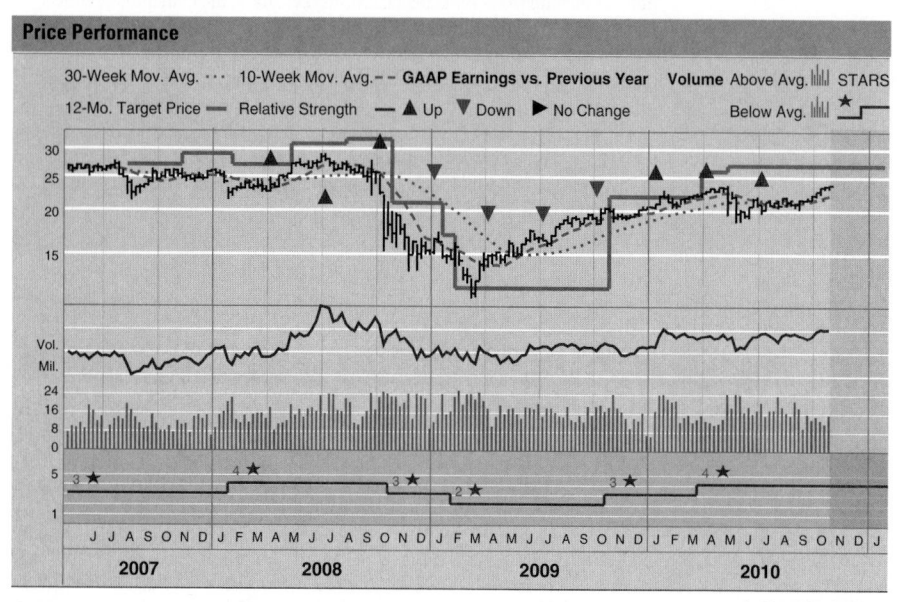

30-Week Mov. Avg. · · · · 10-Week Mov. Avg. – – GAAP Earnings vs. Previous Year Volume Above Avg. STARS
12-Mo. Target Price — Relative Strength — ▲ Up ▼ Down ► No Change Below Avg. ★

Options: ASE, CBOE, Ph

Analysis prepared by **Tanjila Shafi** on August 16, 2010, when the stock traded at **$ 21.02**.

Highlights

► We believe that 2011 earnings will benefit from the company's fee-based businesses. We expect EBIT of $2.3 billion to $2.4 billion in 2011. We see improving earnings at the company's Distribution segment, reflecting higher storage and transportation revenues. We expect its U.S. Transmission business to benefit from contributions from new projects placed into service. We see the company's Western Canada Transmission and Processing segment being aided by higher contracted volumes and revenues from expansions.

► The company has budgeted $1 billion in expansion capital expenditures for 2010 with another $0.6 billion for maintenance and upgrades of existing plants, pipelines and infrastructure. In addition, it has targeted $1 billion for expansion projects in 2011.

► SE paid a cash distribution of $0.25 per unit for the second quarter of 2010, unchanged from the previous year's second quarter distribution. For 2010, we see cash distributions of $1.00.

Investment Rationale/Risk

► Our buy recommendation is based on our view of improving fundamentals at the company's field services and U.S. transmission segments, reflecting higher volumes and prices. We believe the company's fee-based businesses and expansion projects will enhance earnings growth for the remainder of 2010 and 2011. In July, SE announced that it had entered into a definitive agreement to purchase the Bobcat Gas Storage assets and development project from privately-held Haddington Energy Partners III LP and GE (GE 15****) for $540 million. We believe that the pending acquisition will expand SE's footprint in the natural gas storage area. We are also encouraged with management's consideration to increase its quarterly distribution from its current $0.25 per share rate.

► Risks to our opinion and target price include slower natural gas production growth, lower natural gas prices, and a less favorable credit environment.

► Our 12-month target price of $27 is based on our revised 9.8X enterprise value-to-2010 EBITDA estimate, in line with its historical multiples.

Qualitative Risk Assessment

LOW	MEDIUM	HIGH

Our risk assessment reflects the company's large market capitalization and the lower risk inherent in its regulated gas transmission and distribution businesses, offset by its investments in higher-risk gas gathering and processing businesses.

Quantitative Evaluations

S&P Quality Ranking NR

D	C	B-	B	B+	A-	A	A+

Relative Strength Rank STRONG

72

LOWEST = 1 HIGHEST = 99

Revenue/Earnings Data

Revenue (Million $)

	1Q	2Q	3Q	4Q	Year
2010	1,480	1,063	--	--	--
2009	1,384	937.0	933.0	1,298	4,552
2008	1,608	1,141	1,080	1,261	5,074
2007	1,401	985.0	959.0	1,397	4,742
2006	NA	NA	NA	--	4,532
2005	--	--	--	--	4,132

Earnings Per Share ($)

2010	0.53	0.27	E0.35	E0.38	E1.55
2009	0.47	0.22	0.29	0.33	1.31
2008	0.58	0.47	0.49	0.27	1.81
2007	0.37	0.29	0.38	0.45	1.49
2006	NA	NA	NA	--	NA
2005	--	--	--	--	1.07

Fiscal year ended Dec. 31. Next earnings report expected: Early November. EPS Estimates based on S&P Operating Earnings; historical GAAP earnings are as reported.

Dividend Data (Dates: mm/dd Payment Date: mm/dd/yy)

Amount ($)	Date Decl.	Ex-Div. Date	Stk. of Record	Payment Date
0.250	01/05	02/10	02/12	03/15/10
0.250	04/26	05/12	05/14	06/14/10
0.250	07/06	08/11	08/13	09/13/10
0.250	10/19	11/09	11/12	12/13/10

Dividends have been paid since 2007. Source: Company reports.

Please read the Required Disclosures and Analyst Certification on the last page of this report.

The **McGraw·Hill** Companies

Spectra Energy Corp

Business Summary August 16, 2010

CORPORATE OVERVIEW. SE owns and operates a diversified portfolio of natural gas-related energy assets and is primarily a natural gas midstream company. The company operates in three areas of the natural gas industry: transmission and storage, distribution, and gathering and processing. SE also owns a natural gas distribution company, Union Gas, and participates in a 50%-owned joint venture, DCP Midstream.

MARKET PROFILE. The company manages its business in four segments: U.S. Transmission, Distribution, Western Canada Transmission and Processing, and Field Services.

The U.S. Transmission segment provides transportation and storage of natural gas for customers in the eastern and southeastern U.S. and the Maritime provinces of Canada. The segment had 14,300 miles of natural gas at year-end 2009. The company's largest pipeline, Texas Eastern Transmission, is 8,700 miles, has a capacity of 6.7 billion cubic feet per day (bcf/d), and has 74 bcf of storage capacity. The pipeline connects Gulf Coast gas supply to demand centers in the Northeast, as well as to the East Tennessee Natural Gas and Algonquin Gas Transmission pipelines. The Algonquin pipeline can transport 2.2 bcf/d and connects to both the Texas Eastern and Maritimes and North-

east pipelines to provide gas to areas between Boston, MA, and northern New Jersey. The East Tennessee pipeline brings gas from the Texas Eastern pipeline through eastern Tennessee as far as Roanoke, VA. The 44%-owned Gulfstream pipeline brings natural gas into the fast growing state of Florida. The Maritimes and Northeast pipeline provides Sable Island area Canadian natural gas down into the Boston area and helps to supply the Algonquin pipeline. The segment also operates other pipeline interconnection assets and storage assets.

The Distribution segment provides retail natural gas distribution in Ontario, Canada, as well as natural gas transportation and storage services to other utilities and energy market participants in Ontario, Quebec and the U.S. Union Gas is the company's regulated transmission and distribution subsidiary, serving 1.3 million customers in communities throughout Ontario. Union Gas distributes its gas through 37,300 miles of distribution pipelines and owns 3,000 miles of transmission pipelines and 156 bcf of high deliverability storage.

Company Financials Fiscal Year Ended Dec. 31

Per Share Data ($)	2009	2008	2007	2006	2005	2004	2003	2002	2001	2000
Tangible Book Value	4.91	3.53	4.60	NM	NA	NA	NA	NA	NA	NA
Cash Flow	2.24	2.72	2.31	NA	2.04	NA	NA	NA	NA	NA
Earnings	1.31	1.81	1.49	NA	1.07	NA	NA	NA	NA	NA
S&P Core Earnings	1.33	1.71	1.46	NA	NA	NA	NA	NA	NA	NA
Dividends	1.00	0.96	0.88	Nil	Nil	NA	NA	NA	NA	NA
Payout Ratio	76%	53%	59%	Nil	Nil	NA	NA	NA	NA	NA
Prices:High	20.78	29.18	30.00	29.00	NA	NA	NA	NA	NA	NA
Prices:Low	11.21	13.36	21.24	27.50	NA	NA	NA	NA	NA	NA
P/E Ratio:High	16	16	20	NA	NA	NA	NA	NA	NA	NA
P/E Ratio:Low	9	7	14	NA	NA	NA	NA	NA	NA	NA

Income Statement Analysis (Million $)	2009	2008	2007	2006	2005	2004	2003	2002	2001	2000
Revenue	4,552	5,074	4,742	4,532	4,132	13,255	10,784	NA	NA	NA
Operating Income	NA	2,061	1,967	1,804	1,697	NA	NA	NA	NA	NA
Depreciation	562	569	525	606	458	NA	NA	NA	NA	NA
Interest Expense	610	636	651	605	607	744	806	NA	NA	NA
Pretax Income	1,271	1,688	1,458	1,376	862	1,156	719	NA	NA	NA
Effective Tax Rate	27.8%	29.4%	30.4%	28.7%	41.7%	123.8%	29.2%	NA	NA	NA
Net Income	843	1,129	944	936	502	-489	404	NA	NA	NA
S&P Core Earnings	852	1,060	928	926	NA	NA	NA	NA	NA	NA

Balance Sheet & Other Financial Data (Million $)	2009	2008	2007	2006	2005	2004	2003	2002	2001	2000
Cash	196	214	94.0	299	NA	NA	NA	NA	NA	NA
Current Assets	1,429	1,450	1,379	1,625	18,601	NA	NA	NA	NA	NA
Total Assets	24,079	21,924	22,970	20,345	21,442	NA	NA	NA	NA	NA
Current Liabilities	2,495	3,044	2,422	2,358	2,052	NA	NA	NA	NA	NA
Long Term Debt	8,947	8,290	8,345	7,726	7,957	NA	NA	NA	NA	NA
Common Equity	7,665	5,540	6,857	5,639	5,225	NA	NA	NA	NA	NA
Total Capital	17,663	15,346	16,008	16,910	16,100	NA	NA	NA	NA	NA
Capital Expenditures	1,336	2,030	1,202	987	NA	NA	NA	NA	NA	NA
Cash Flow	1,441	1,698	1,469	1,542	960	NA	NA	NA	NA	NA
Current Ratio	0.6	0.5	0.6	0.7	NA	NA	NA	NA	NA	NA
% Long Term Debt of Capitalization	53.9	54.0	52.1	45.7	Nil	Nil	Nil	NA	NA	NA
% Net Income of Revenue	18.5	22.3	19.9	20.7	12.2	NM	3.8	NA	NA	NA
% Return on Assets	3.7	5.0	4.4	3.4	NA	NA	NA	NA	NA	NA
% Return on Equity	12.8	18.2	15.1	10.9	NA	NA	NA	NA	NA	NA

Data as orig reptd.; bef. results of disc opers/spec. items. Per share data adj. for stk. divs.; EPS diluted. E-Estimated. NA-Not Available. NM-Not Meaningful. NR-Not Ranked. UR-Under Review.

Office: 5400 Westheimer Court, Houston, TX 77056-5310.
Telephone: 713-627-5400 .
Website: http://www.spectraenergy.com
Chrmn: W.T. Esrey

Pres & CEO: G.L. Ebel
COO: A.N. Harris
CFO: J.P. Reddy
Chief Admin Officer: D.M. Ables

Investor Contact: J. Arensdorf (713-627-4600)
Board Members: A. A. Adams, P. Anderson, P. L. Carter, F. A. Comper, G. L. Ebel, W. T. Esrey, P. B. Hamilton, D. Hendrix, M. McShane, J. H. Netherland, Jr., M. E. Phelps

Founded: 2006
Domicile: Delaware
Employees: 5,400

Sprint Nextel Corp

STANDARD &POOR'S

S&P Recommendation	BUY ★★★★☆	Price	12-Mo. Target Price	Investment Style
		$4.85 (as of Oct 22, 2010)	$6.50	Large-Cap Value

GICS Sector Telecommunication Services
Sub-Industry Wireless Telecommunication Services

Summary This leading provider of wireless and other telecommunications services was formed in August 2005 through the merger of Sprint Corp. and Nextel Communications, Inc.

Key Stock Statistics (Source S&P, Vickers, company reports)

52-Wk Range	$5.31–2.78	S&P Oper. EPS 2010E	-0.55	Market Capitalization(B)	$14.475	Beta	1.11
Trailing 12-Month EPS	$-1.05	S&P Oper. EPS 2011E	-0.13	Yield (%)	Nil	S&P 3-Yr. Proj. EPS CAGR(%)	NA
Trailing 12-Month P/E	NM	P/E on S&P Oper. EPS 2010E	NM	Dividend Rate/Share	Nil	S&P Credit Rating	BB-
$10K Invested 5 Yrs Ago	NA	Common Shares Outstg. (M)	2,984.5	Institutional Ownership (%)	86		

Price Performance

- 30-Week Mov. Avg. ····
- 10-Week Mov. Avg. ---
- GAAP Earnings vs. Previous Year
- Volume Above Avg. / Below Avg.
- STARS
- 12-Mo. Target Price —
- Relative Strength —
- ▲ Up ▼ Down ► No Change

Options: ASE, CBOE, P, Ph

Analysis prepared by **James Moorman, CFA** on July 29, 2010, when the stock traded at **$ 4.71**.

Highlights

➤ Following 9.5% lower revenues in 2009, we expect flat revenues in 2010 and 2.3% growth in 2011, as S continues to work on maintaining its subscriber base in its wireless business (87% of projected revenues) while attracting new subscribers. We believe the company is beginning to make progress in improving its network quality and customer satisfaction and continues to see sequential quarterly improvement in subscriber losses. Within global markets, we see revenues declining roughly 9% in 2010 due to competitive pressures.

➤ We estimate total EBITDA margins of 18.1% in 2010 and 19.4% in 2011, versus 19.8% in 2009. While we believe most of the cost-cutting measures have been completed, we expect some margin improvement in 2011 as revenue growth resumes and the company benefits from its lower cost structure.

➤ We estimate operating losses per share of $0.55 in 2010 and $0.13 in 2011, following an operating loss per share of $0.36 in 2009.

Investment Rationale/Risk

➤ Our buy recommendation is largely based on valuation. In our view, the company is in a transition, trying to regain favor with customers, as competitors take market share. However, we believe S is making progress, as subscriber losses continue to decline sequentially. The company has also done a good job of continuing to bring on new and exciting handsets and smartphones to retain and draw subscribers. While we think S has more work to do in turning around its operations, we believe the shares are nonetheless attractive at recent levels.

➤ Risks to our recommendation and target price include higher capital spending to deploy new services, liquidity issues relating to declining cash flow, and increased competition from nationwide peers that could lead to delayed growth in subscriber additions.

➤ Our 12-month target price of $6.50 assumes an enterprise value of 5.5X our 2011 EBITDA estimate, slightly below larger-cap telecom peers, to reflect S's subscriber losses, and below smaller pure-play wireless carriers that we think have stronger growth prospects.

Qualitative Risk Assessment

LOW	MEDIUM	HIGH

Given that we think S is one of the weakest national wireless carriers, its free cash flow could continue to be pressured in the near term. We believe this risk is partly offset by our view of the company's strong balance sheet and operating expense reductions.

Quantitative Evaluations

S&P Quality Ranking B

D	C	B-	B	B+	A-	A	A+

Relative Strength Rank STRONG

75

LOWEST = 1   HIGHEST = 99

Revenue/Earnings Data

Revenue (Million $)

	1Q	2Q	3Q	4Q	Year
2010	8,085	8,025	--	--	--
2009	8,209	8,141	8,042	7,868	32,260
2008	9,334	9,055	8,816	8,430	35,635
2007	10,092	10,163	10,044	9,847	40,146
2006	11,548	10,014	10,496	10,444	41,028
2005	6,936	7,113	9,335	11,296	34,680

Earnings Per Share ($)

	1Q	2Q	3Q	4Q	Year
2010	-0.29	-0.25	E-0.12	E-0.10	E-0.55
2009	-0.21	-0.13	-0.17	-0.34	-0.84
2008	-0.18	-0.12	-0.11	-0.57	-0.98
2007	-0.07	0.01	0.02	-10.36	-10.31
2006	0.14	0.10	0.08	0.09	0.34
2005	0.32	0.40	0.23	0.07	0.87

Fiscal year ended Dec. 31. Next earnings report expected: Late October. EPS Estimates based on S&P Operating Earnings; historical GAAP earnings are as reported.

Dividend Data

No cash dividends have been paid since 2007.

Please read the Required Disclosures and Analyst Certification on the last page of this report.

The McGraw-Hill Companies

Sprint Nextel Corp

STANDARD &POOR'S

Business Summary July 29, 2010

CORPORATE OVERVIEW. Sprint Nextel, a leading provider of wireless and other telecommunications services, was formed in August 2005 through the merger of Sprint Corp. and Nextel Communications, Inc. The company has a balanced mix of consumer, business and government wireless customers. S spun off the local telephone business to shareholders in May 2006. As of the end of the second quarter of 2010, S provided service to roughly 48.2 million wireless subscribers, with 69% of them direct post-paid customers, while 23% were prepaid (Boost Mobile and Virgin Mobile), and 8% were wholesale customers. S also generates revenues from wireline voice and data communication services, and services to the cable multiple systems operators that use S's network and back-office capabilities.

COMPETITIVE LANDSCAPE. In most major U.S. metropolitan markets, four national carriers offer competing wireless services to customers along with some regional carriers. Wireless carriers such as S have adjusted to potential substitutes by integrating the service features into the handsets. Until recently, S had a unique service with push-to-talk service through Nextel's iDEN network, but AT&T (formerly Cingular) has launched a competing nationwide service aimed at the consumer segment, in contrast to S's dominant position with small business and enterprise firms.

Wireless services are very price elastic. For the consumer market, service rate plans have taken on new features such as $9.99 for each family member added to the account. S realized 1.85% post-paid churn in the second quarter of 2010, its best ever, but generated $55 in average revenue per user (ARPU). Pre-paid customers had a 5.61% churn rate and generated $28 in ARPU. The company has simplified its pricing with plans that include a $100 plan with unlimited voice, data, text and other features, as well as a $90 plan for unlimited voice and texting. We believe this translates to roughly $80 for unlimited voice and compares to recent offers by the other three major wireless companies of $100 for unlimited voice alone. In our view, this is a good move that will help change S's image, but we do not expect the plans to drive big changes in customer growth. S also provides a $50 unlimited prepaid plan under its Boost Mobile brand on its iDEN and CDMA networks that we believe continues to be very successful, although we believe a handset shortage limited Boost's net additions in the second quarter.

Company Financials Fiscal Year Ended Dec. 31

Per Share Data ($)	2009	2008	2007	2006	2005	2004	2003	2002	2001	2000
Tangible Book Value	NM	NM	NM	NM	0.88	3.85	14.40	11.45	11.41	13.95
Cash Flow	1.73	1.96	-7.17	3.67	3.93	2.56	3.12	4.14	2.60	4.00
Earnings	-0.84	-0.98	-10.31	0.34	0.87	-0.71	0.33	1.18	-0.16	1.45
S&P Core Earnings	-0.91	-0.66	-0.05	0.30	0.86	-0.72	1.20	1.26	-0.12	NA
Dividends	Nil	Nil	0.10	0.13	0.30	0.50	0.50	0.50	0.50	0.50
Payout Ratio	Nil	Nil	NM	37%	34%	NM	152%	42%	NM	34%
Prices:High	5.94	13.16	23.42	26.89	27.20	25.80	16.76	20.47	29.31	67.81
Prices:Low	1.83	1.35	12.96	15.92	21.57	15.74	10.22	6.65	18.50	19.63
P/E Ratio:High	NM	NM	NM	79	31	NM	51	17	NM	47
P/E Ratio:Low	NM	NM	NM	47	25	NM	31	6	NM	14

Income Statement Analysis (Million $)	2009	2008	2007	2006	2005	2004	2003	2002	2001	2000
Revenue	32,260	35,635	40,146	41,028	34,680	27,428	14,185	15,182	16,924	17,688
Operating Income	NA	7,664	10,282	12,283	10,220	8,148	4,376	4,488	4,238	5,101
Depreciation	7,416	8,396	9,023	9,592	6,269	4,720	2,519	2,645	2,449	2,267
Interest Expense	1,416	1,362	1,433	1,533	1,351	1,248	236	295	57.0	76.0
Pretax Income	-3,494	-4,060	-29,945	1,817	2,906	-1,603	434	1,453	-129	2,170
Effective Tax Rate	30.3%	NM	NM	26.9%	38.0%	NM	32.3%	28.0%	NM	40.5%
Net Income	-2,436	-2,796	-29,580	1,329	1,801	-1,012	294	1,046	-146	1,292
S&P Core Earnings	-2,632	-1,864	-155	849	1,772	-1,036	1,096	1,132	-112	NA

Balance Sheet & Other Financial Data (Million $)	2009	2008	2007	2006	2005	2004	2003	2002	2001	2000
Cash	3,924	3,719	2,440	2,061	10,665	4,556	1,635	641	134	122
Current Assets	8,593	8,344	8,661	10,304	19,092	9,975	4,378	3,327	3,485	4,512
Total Assets	55,424	58,252	64,109	97,161	102,580	41,321	21,862	23,043	24,164	23,649
Current Liabilities	6,785	6,281	9,104	9,798	14,050	6,902	2,359	4,320	6,298	5,004
Long Term Debt	20,293	20,992	20,469	21,011	Nil	15,916	2,627	2,736	3,258	3,482
Common Equity	18,095	19,605	21,999	53,131	51,937	13,521	13,372	11,814	11,704	12,343
Total Capital	39,156	47,793	51,157	84,237	52,184	29,684	17,632	16,385	16,514	17,101
Capital Expenditures	1,603	3,882	6,322	7,556	5,057	3,980	1,674	2,181	5,295	4,105
Cash Flow	4,980	5,600	-20,557	10,919	8,063	3,701	2,821	3,698	2,310	3,566
Current Ratio	1.3	1.3	1.0	1.1	1.4	1.4	1.9	0.8	0.6	0.9
% Long Term Debt of Capitalization	51.8	43.9	40.0	24.9	Nil	53.6	14.9	16.7	19.7	20.4
% Net Income of Revenue	NM	NM	NM	3.2	5.2	NM	2.1	6.9	NM	7.3
% Return on Assets	NM	NM	NM	1.3	2.5	NM	1.3	4.4	NM	5.7
% Return on Equity	NM	NM	NM	2.5	5.5	NM	2.3	8.8	NM	11.2

Data as orig reptd.; bef. results of disc opers/spec. items. Per share data adj. for stk. divs.; EPS diluted. E-Estimated. NA-Not Available. NM-Not Meaningful. NR-Not Ranked. UR-Under Review.

Office: 6200 Sprint Pkwy, Overland Park, KS 66251-6117.
Telephone: 800-829-0965.
Email: investorrelation.sprintcom@mail.sprint.com
Website: http://www.sprint.com

Chrmn: J.H. Hance, Jr.
Pres & CEO: D. Hesse
SVP & Treas: R.S. Lindahl
CFO: R.H. Brust

Chief Acctg Officer & Cntlr: R.H. Siurek
Board Members: R. R. Bennett, G. M. Bethune, L. C. Glasscock, J. H. Hance, Jr., D. Hesse, V. J. Hill, F. Ianna, S. Nilsson, W. R. Nuti, R. O'Neal

Founded: 1925
Domicile: Kansas
Employees: 40,000

The McGraw-Hill Companies

Stanley Black & Decker Inc

STANDARD &POOR'S

S&P Recommendation **HOLD** ★★★☆☆	Price $61.11 (as of Oct 22, 2010)	12-Mo. Target Price $65.00	Investment Style Large-Cap Blend

GICS Sector Consumer Discretionary
Sub-Industry Household Appliances

Summary This diversified global provider of hand tools, power tools and related accessories and systems resulted from the March 2010 merger of Stanley Works and Black & Decker.

Key Stock Statistics (Source S&P, Vickers, company reports)

52-Wk Range	$66.27– 44.60	S&P Oper. EPS 2010**E**	3.73	Market Capitalization(B)	$10.124	Beta	1.29
Trailing 12-Month EPS	$0.52	S&P Oper. EPS 2011**E**	4.49	Yield (%)	2.23	S&P 3-Yr. Proj. EPS CAGR(%)	12
Trailing 12-Month P/E	NM	P/E on S&P Oper. EPS 2010**E**	16.4	Dividend Rate/Share	$1.36	S&P Credit Rating	A
$10K Invested 5 Yrs Ago	$14,715	Common Shares Outstg. (M)	165.7	Institutional Ownership (%)	81		

Price Performance

30-Week Mov. Avg. ··· 10-Week Mov. Avg. - - **GAAP Earnings vs. Previous Year** Volume Above Avg. ▮▮▮ STARS
12-Mo. Target Price — Relative Strength — ▲ Up ▼ Down ▶ No Change Below Avg. ▮▮▮ ★

Options: P

Highlights

▸ The 12-month target price for SWK has recently been changed to $65.00 from $60.00. The Highlights section of this Stock Report will be updated accordingly.

Investment Rationale/Risk

▸ The Investment Rationale/Risk section of this Stock Report will be updated shortly. For the latest News story on SWK from MarketScope, see below.

▸ 10/20/10 11:21 am ET ... S&P MAINTAINS HOLD RECOMMENDATION ON SHARES OF STANLEY BLACK & DECKER (SWK 61.13***): Adjusted for certain items, SWK reports Q3 EPS of $0.97, vs. $0.77, and $0.18 greater than our view on better-than-expected margins, as sales of $2.4B were in line with our forecast. Looking ahead, we raise our '10 EPS estimate by $0.24 to $3.73 and '11's by $0.45 to $4.49 on Q3 results and revised sales and margin forecasts. We continue to think SWK will benefit from an improvement in the global industrial economy, but also believe there is limited upside potential to our $65 target price, which we raise by $5 on higher estimates and revised valuation analyses. / M.Christy,CFA

Qualitative Risk Assessment

LOW	MEDIUM	HIGH

Our risk assessment takes into account our positive view of SWK's strong brand names and solid competitive position, offset by our negative view of industry cyclicality.

Quantitative Evaluations

S&P Quality Ranking B+

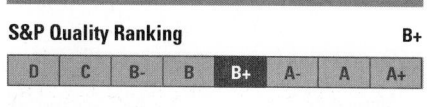

| D | C | B- | B | B+ | A- | A | A+ |

Relative Strength Rank MODERATE

51

LOWEST = 1   HIGHEST = 99

Revenue/Earnings Data

Revenue (Million $)

	1Q	2Q	3Q	4Q	Year
2010	1,262	2,366	--	--	--
2009	913.0	919.2	935.5	969.4	3,737
2008	1,097	1,154	1,120	1,086	4,426
2007	1,062	1,123	1,131	1,167	4,484
2006	968.7	1,018	1,013	1,019	4,019
2005	796.3	814.7	834.9	839.4	3,285

Earnings Per Share ($)

2010	-1.11	0.28	E0.79	E0.81	E3.73
2009	0.48	0.89	0.77	E0.72	2.82
2008	0.85	0.95	0.98	0.07	2.82
2007	0.80	1.01	1.09	1.11	4.00
2006	0.45	0.90	1.09	1.04	3.47
2005	0.78	0.77	0.89	0.75	3.18

Fiscal year ended Dec. 31. Next earnings report expected: NA. EPS Estimates based on S&P Operating Earnings; historical GAAP earnings are as reported.

Dividend Data (Dates: mm/dd Payment Date: mm/dd/yy)

Amount ($)	Date Decl.	Ex-Div. Date	Stk. of Record	Payment Date
0.330	10/16	12/02	12/04	12/15/09
0.330	02/16	03/01	03/03	03/23/10
0.340	07/16	09/01	09/03	09/21/10
0.340	10/15	12/01	12/03	12/14/10

Dividends have been paid since 1877. Source: Company reports.

Please read the Required Disclosures and Analyst Certification on the last page of this report.

The McGraw·Hill Companies

Stanley Black & Decker Inc

Business Summary August 04, 2010

CORPORATE OVERVIEW. Stanley Black & Decker, the result of the March 2010 merger of Stanley Works and Black & Decker, is a diversified global provider of hand tools, power tools and related accessories, mechanical access solutions and electronic security solutions, engineered fastening systems, and more. The company offers a broad line of hand tools and has many well-known brands. Prior to the 2010 purchase of Black & Decker, SWK's operations were classified into three business segments in 2009: Consumer Products (34.6% of 2009 sales), Industrial Tools (23.6%), and Security Solutions (41.8%).

MARKET PROFILE. In Consumer Products, SWK manufactures and markets hand tools, consumer mechanics tools and storage units, and hardware. Products are distributed directly to retailers (including home centers, mass merchants, hardware stores, and retail lumber yards) as well as third-party distributors, and include measuring instruments, hammers, knives and blades, screwdrivers, sockets and tool boxes. Among the company's brands are Stanley, FatMax, Powerlock, IntelliTools, ZAG, and National.

The Industrial Tools segment manufactures and markets professional mechanics tools and storage systems, pneumatic tools and fasteners, hydraulic tools and accessories, assembly tools and systems, and electronic measuring tools. Products are distributed primarily through third-party distributors.

Brands include Stanley, Proto, Facom, USAG, MAC, Jensen, Bostich, Virax, David White, and Rolatape.

The Security Solutions segment is a provider of access and security solutions primarily for retailers, educational and health care institutions, government, financial institutions, and commercial and industrial customers. Products include security integration systems, software, related installation and maintenance services, automatic doors, and locking mechanisms, and are sold on a direct sales basis. Brands include Stanley, Blick, Frisco Bay, PAC, ISR, WanderGuard, StanVision, Sargent and Greenleaf, BEST and Xmark.

About 58% of Stanley Works 2009 sales were made in the U.S., 9.4% in Other Americas, 13.3% in France, 13.5% in Other Europe, and 5.7% in Asia. A large portion of SWK's products in the Consumer Products and Industrial Tools segments are sold through home centers and mass merchant distribution channels in the U.S. market. Despite the significant exposure, the company has actively reduced the amount of total sales to the mass merchant channels, reducing it from 22% of consolidated sales in 2002 to less than 6% in 2009.

Company Financials Fiscal Year Ended Dec. 31

Per Share Data ($)	2009	2008	2007	2006	2005	2004	2003	2002	2001	2000
Tangible Book Value	NM	NM	NM	NM	4.59	3.56	2.65	5.05	7.05	6.59
Cash Flow	5.31	5.11	5.94	4.92	4.40	4.07	2.16	2.90	2.76	3.17
Earnings	2.82	2.82	4.00	3.47	3.18	2.85	1.14	2.10	1.81	2.22
S&P Core Earnings	2.88	2.63	4.08	3.57	3.16	2.49	1.12	1.43	1.30	NA
Dividends	1.30	1.26	1.22	1.18	1.14	1.08	1.03	0.99	0.94	0.90
Payout Ratio	46%	45%	30%	34%	36%	38%	90%	47%	52%	41%
Prices:High	53.42	52.18	64.25	54.59	51.75	49.33	37.87	52.00	46.97	31.88
Prices:Low	22.61	24.19	47.01	41.60	41.51	36.42	20.84	27.31	28.06	18.44
P/E Ratio:High	19	19	16	16	16	17	33	25	26	14
P/E Ratio:Low	8	9	12	12	13	13	18	13	16	8

Income Statement Analysis (Million $)

	2009	2008	2007	2006	2005	2004	2003	2002	2001	2000
Revenue	3,737	4,426	4,484	4,019	3,285	3,043	2,678	2,594	2,624	2,749
Operating Income	564	747	800	567	493	513	342	360	412	424
Depreciation	200	183	162	121	96.5	95.0	86.5	71.2	82.9	83.3
Interest Expense	63.7	82.0	85.2	69.3	40.4	38.6	34.2	28.5	18.9	34.6
Pretax Income	283	301	451	367	358	329	133	273	237	294
Effective Tax Rate	19.7%	25.2%	25.4%	20.8%	24.1%	27.0%	27.3%	32.1%	33.1%	33.8%
Net Income	226	225	337	291	272	240	96.7	185	158	194
S&P Core Earnings	232	211	343	299	270	209	94.7	127	113	NA

Balance Sheet & Other Financial Data (Million $)

	2009	2008	2007	2006	2005	2004	2003	2002	2001	2000
Cash	401	212	240	177	658	250	204	122	115	93.6
Current Assets	1,412	1,499	1,768	1,639	1,826	1,372	1,201	1,190	1,141	1,094
Total Assets	4,773	4,879	4,780	3,935	3,545	2,851	2,424	2,418	2,056	1,885
Current Liabilities	1,192	1,197	1,278	1,251	875	819	754	681	826	707
Long Term Debt	1,085	1,420	1,212	679	895	482	535	564	197	249
Common Equity	1,985	1,688	1,729	1,552	1,946	1,388	1,032	1,165	844	933
Total Capital	3,095	3,121	3,022	2,298	2,925	1,960	1,567	1,729	1,041	1,181
Capital Expenditures	93.4	141	65.5	59.6	53.3	47.6	31.4	37.2	55.7	59.8
Cash Flow	427	408	499	412	368	335	183	256	241	278
Current Ratio	1.2	1.3	1.4	1.3	2.1	1.7	1.6	1.7	1.4	1.5
% Long Term Debt of Capitalization	35.1	45.7	40.1	29.6	30.6	24.6	34.1	32.6	18.9	21.1
% Net Income of Revenue	6.0	5.1	7.5	7.2	8.3	7.9	3.6	7.1	6.0	7.1
% Return on Assets	4.7	4.7	7.7	7.8	8.5	9.1	4.0	8.3	8.0	10.3
% Return on Equity	12.3	13.2	20.5	19.4	14.4	19.8	8.8	16.9	20.0	20.8

Data as orig reptd.; bef. results of disc opers/spec. items. Per share data adj. for stk. divs.; EPS diluted. E-Estimated. NA-Not Available. NM-Not Meaningful. NR-Not Ranked. UR-Under Review.

Office: 1000 Stanley Drive, New Britain, CT 06053.
Telephone: 860-225-5111.
Website: http://www.stanleyblackanddecker.com/
Chrmn: N.D. Archibald

CEO: J.F. Lundgren
COO & EVP: J.M. Loree
SVP, CFO & Chief Acctg Officer: D. Allan, Jr.
SVP, Secy & General Counsel: B.H. Beatt

Investor Contact: K. White (860-827-3833)
Board Members: N. D. Archibald, J. G. Breen, G. W. Buckley, P. D. Campbell, C. M. Cardoso, V. W. Colbert, R. B. Coutts, M. A. Fernandez, B. H. Griswold, IV, E. S. Kraus, A. Luiso, J. F. Lundgren, M. M. Parrs, R. L. Ryan, L. Zimmerman

Founded: 1843
Domicile: Connecticut
Employees: 16,700

Staples Inc

STANDARD
&POOR'S

S&P Recommendation HOLD ★★★☆☆	**Price** $20.60 (as of Oct 22, 2010)	**12-Mo. Target Price** $22.00	**Investment Style** Large-Cap Growth

GICS Sector Consumer Discretionary
Sub-Industry Specialty Stores

Summary This leading operator of office products superstores has over 2,000 units in the U.S. and internationally.

Key Stock Statistics (Source S&P, Vickers, company reports)

52-Wk Range	$26.00– 17.45	S&P Oper. EPS 2011E	1.28	Market Capitalization(B)	$15.040	Beta	0.85
Trailing 12-Month EPS	$1.13	S&P Oper. EPS 2012E	1.50	Yield (%)	1.75	S&P 3-Yr. Proj. EPS CAGR(%)	12
Trailing 12-Month P/E	18.2	P/E on S&P Oper. EPS 2011E	16.1	Dividend Rate/Share	$0.36	S&P Credit Rating	BBB
$10K Invested 5 Yrs Ago	$10,278	Common Shares Outstg. (M)	730.1	Institutional Ownership (%)	88		

Price Performance

30-Week Mov. Avg. · · · 10-Week Mov. Avg. - - **GAAP Earnings vs. Previous Year** Volume Above Avg. STARS

12-Mo. Target Price — Relative Strength — ▲ Up ▼ Down ▶ No Change Below Avg. ★

Options: ASE, CBOE, P, Ph

Analysis prepared by **Michael Souers** on August 25, 2010, when the stock traded at **$18.07**.

Highlights

➤ We estimate sales growth of 2.3% in FY 11 (Jan.), following the 5.2% advance in FY 10. We expect this growth to be driven by the opening of about 40 net new stores in North America, continued international penetration, and flattish same-store sales results in North American Retail. We expect customer traffic to remain weak, but we see the average ticket rising slightly. We also project marginal improvement in the contract business as customers react to a gradual economic recovery.

➤ We expect a slight widening of gross margins in FY 11, with a growing private label business, supply chain initiatives, and lower sourcing costs. We see operating margins widening modestly, as continued cost synergies from the Corporate Express acquisition are only partially offset by a slight de-leveraging of fixed costs due to meager same-store sales gains.

➤ Following flat net interest expense and excluding integration and restructuring charges, we estimate FY 11 operating EPS of $1.28, an 11% increase from the $1.15 the company earned in FY 10, excluding integration and restructuring charges. We see FY 12 EPS of $1.50.

Investment Rationale/Risk

➤ We continue to favor SPLS's management, strong balance sheet, significant free cash flow generation and cost synergies from the Corporate Express acquisition that should accrue over the next few years. We also anticipate strong results for SPLS's North American Delivery division over the longer term, although we have been disappointed by the severity of the recent slowdown. Despite these positive drivers, we continue to think the office supply industry is extremely mature, with limited long-term growth potential. Following a recent pullback in price, we now find the shares fairly valued, trading at about 12X our FY 12 EPS estimate, a slight premium to the S&P 500.

➤ Risks to our recommendation and target price include a double-dip recession and weaker-than-expected capital spending and hiring by businesses. International risks include unfavorable currency movements and Europe debt contagion fears.

➤ Our 12-month target price of $22, about 15X our FY 12 EPS projection, is derived from our discounted cash flow model, which assumes a weighted average cost of capital of 9.6% and a terminal growth rate of 3.0%.

Qualitative Risk Assessment

LOW	MEDIUM	HIGH

Our risk assessment reflects the cyclicality of the company's business, which relies on consumer as well as business spending, and investments in emerging markets for future growth. This is offset by untapped growth areas in major domestic metro markets.

Quantitative Evaluations

S&P Quality Ranking B+

D	C	B-	B	B+	A-	A	A+

Relative Strength Rank MODERATE

46

LOWEST = 1   HIGHEST = 99

Revenue/Earnings Data

Revenue (Million $)

	1Q	2Q	3Q	4Q	Year
2011	6,058	5,534	--	--	--
2010	5,818	5,534	6,518	6,406	24,275
2009	4,885	5,075	6,951	6,174	23,084
2008	4,589	4,290	5,168	5,324	19,373
2007	4,238	3,881	4,757	5,286	18,161
2006	3,899	3,472	4,246	4,462	16,079

Earnings Per Share ($)

2011	0.26	0.18	E0.41	E0.39	E1.28
2010	0.20	0.13	0.37	0.37	1.02
2009	0.30	0.21	0.22	0.40	1.13
2008	0.29	0.21	0.38	0.47	1.38
2007	0.25	0.22	0.39	0.46	1.32
2006	0.20	0.20	0.32	0.39	1.12

Fiscal year ended Jan. 31. Next earnings report expected: Early December. EPS Estimates based on S&P Operating Earnings; historical GAAP earnings are as reported.

Dividend Data (Dates: mm/dd Payment Date: mm/dd/yy)

Amount ($)	Date Decl.	Ex-Div. Date	Stk. of Record	Payment Date
0.083	12/08	12/21	12/23	01/14/10
0.090	03/09	03/24	03/26	04/15/10
0.090	06/07	06/23	06/25	07/15/10
0.090	09/14	09/22	09/24	10/14/10

Dividends have been paid since 2004. Source: Company reports.

Please read the Required Disclosures and Analyst Certification on the last page of this report.

The **McGraw·Hill** Companies

Staples Inc

STANDARD &POOR'S

Business Summary August 25, 2010

CORPORATE OVERVIEW. Staples is the world's leading office products company, with net sales of nearly $24.3 billion in FY 10 (Jan.). Staples operates in three segments: North American Delivery (40% of total revenues in FY 10); North American Retail (39%); and International Operations (22%). Sales by product line: office supplies and services 48%; business machines and related products 32%; computers and related products 15%; and office furniture 5%.

At January 30, 2010, SPLS operated 2,243 superstores, mostly in the United States (1,555 stores) and Canada (316 stores), but also in a number of other countries, including: the U.K. (137), Germany (58), the Netherlands (47), Portugal (35), Sweden (22), China (22), Norway (21), Australia (20), Belgium (6), Argentina (2), Denmark (1) and Ireland (1).

SPLS has approximately 8,000 stock-keeping units (SKUs) stocked in each of its typical North American retail stores and approximately 15,000 SKUs stocked in its North American Delivery fulfillment centers. On Staples.com,

the company's Internet site, approximately 50,000 SKUs are available to customers.

CORPORATE STRATEGY. Staples seeks to maintain its leadership position in the office products industry by differentiating itself from the competition, delivering industry-best execution and expanding its market share. In FY 10, it added 48 new stores in North America, filling in existing markets along with expansion into untapped metro markets. A few of the new stores were stand-alone copy and print shops, which average 4,000 square feet with 1,800 SKUs in supplies. We believe significant growth opportunities remain in other metropolitan markets where SPLS has yet to venture, and we expect the company to establish a strong Midwest presence over the next several years.

Company Financials Fiscal Year Ended Jan. 31

Per Share Data ($)	2010	2009	2008	2007	2006	2005	2004	2003	2002	2001
Tangible Book Value	2.89	1.51	5.28	4.64	3.84	3.45	3.01	1.74	2.63	2.19
Cash Flow	1.79	1.90	1.92	1.78	1.56	1.33	1.03	1.01	0.73	0.42
Earnings	1.02	1.13	1.38	1.32	1.12	0.93	0.66	0.63	0.42	0.10
S&P Core Earnings	1.06	1.20	1.42	1.32	1.05	0.88	0.61	0.58	0.32	0.21
Dividends	0.33	0.33	0.22	0.17	0.17	0.13	Nil	Nil	Nil	Nil
Payout Ratio	32%	29%	16%	13%	15%	14%	Nil	Nil	Nil	Nil
Calendar Year	2009	2008	2007	2006	2005	2004	2003	2002	2001	2000
Prices:High	25.10	26.57	27.66	28.00	24.14	22.57	18.58	14.97	12.97	19.17
Prices:Low	14.35	13.57	19.69	21.08	18.64	15.79	10.49	7.79	7.35	6.83
P/E Ratio:High	25	24	20	21	22	24	28	24	31	NM
P/E Ratio:Low	14	12	14	16	17	17	16	12	17	NM

Income Statement Analysis (Million $)

	2010	2009	2008	2007	2006	2005	2004	2003	2002	2001
Revenue	24,275	23,084	19,373	18,161	16,079	14,448	13,181	11,596	10,744	10,674
Operating Income	2,019	2,094	1,975	1,802	1,617	1,405	1,081	950	768	719
Depreciation	552	549	389	339	304	279	283	267	249	231
Interest Expense	237	150	38.3	47.8	56.8	39.9	20.2	20.6	27.2	45.2
Pretax Income	1,156	1,243	1,554	1,471	1,314	1,116	778	662	431	244
Effective Tax Rate	34.5%	34.5%	36.0%	33.8%	36.5%	36.5%	37.0%	32.6%	38.5%	75.5%
Net Income	739	805	996	974	834	708	490	446	265	59.7
S&P Core Earnings	766	857	1,020	974	784	667	450	413	221	147

Balance Sheet & Other Financial Data (Million $)

	2010	2009	2008	2007	2006	2005	2004	2003	2002	2001
Cash	1,416	634	1,272	1,018	978	997	457	596	395	264
Current Assets	6,175	5,730	4,555	4,431	4,145	3,782	3,479	2,717	2,403	2,356
Total Assets	13,717	13,006	9,036	8,397	7,677	7,071	6,503	5,721	4,093	3,989
Current Liabilities	3,782	4,778	2,610	2,788	2,480	2,197	2,123	2,175	1,596	1,711
Long Term Debt	2,500	1,969	342	569	528	558	567	732	350	441
Common Equity	6,772	5,564	5,718	5,022	4,425	4,115	3,663	2,659	2,054	1,764
Total Capital	9,423	7,591	6,094	5,600	4,963	4,696	4,230	3,441	2,411	2,205
Capital Expenditures	313	378	470	528	456	335	278	265	340	450
Cash Flow	1,291	1,354	1,385	1,313	1,138	987	773	713	514	291
Current Ratio	1.6	1.2	1.8	1.6	1.7	1.7	1.6	1.2	1.5	1.4
% Long Term Debt of Capitalization	26.5	25.9	5.6	10.2	10.6	11.9	13.4	21.3	14.5	20.0
% Net Income of Revenue	3.0	3.5	5.1	5.4	5.2	4.9	3.7	3.8	2.5	0.6
% Return on Assets	5.5	7.3	11.4	12.1	11.3	10.4	8.0	9.1	6.6	1.5
% Return on Equity	12.0	14.3	18.5	20.5	19.5	18.2	15.5	18.9	13.9	3.3

Data as orig reptd.; bef. results of disc opers/spec. items. Per share data adj. for stk. divs.; EPS diluted. E-Estimated. NA-Not Available. NM-Not Meaningful. NR-Not Ranked. UR-Under Review.

Office: Five Hundred Staples Dr, Framingham , MA 01702.
Telephone: 508-253-5000.
Email: investor@staples.com
Website: http://www.staples.com

Chrmn & CEO: R. Sargent
Pres & COO: M. Miles, Jr.
EVP & CIO: B.T. Light
SVP, Chief Acctg Officer & Cntlr: C.T. Komola

SVP, Secy & General Counsel: K.A. Campbell
Investor Contact: N. Hotchkin (800-468-7751)
Board Members: B. L. Anderson, A. M. Blank, M. E. Burton, J. M. King, C. M. Meyrowitz, R. T. Moriarty, R. C. Nakasone, R. Sargent, E. A. Smith, R. E. Sulentic, V. Vishwanath, P. F. Walsh

Founded: 1985
Domicile: Delaware
Employees: 91,095

The McGraw-Hill Companies

STANDARD & POOR'S

Starbucks Corp

S&P Recommendation **SELL** ★★☆☆☆	Price $28.49 (as of Oct 22, 2010)	12-Mo. Target Price $20.00	Investment Style Large-Cap Growth

GICS Sector Consumer Discretionary
Sub-Industry Restaurants

Summary Starbucks is the leading coffee roaster and retailer of high-quality coffee products in the world, which it sells through its approximate 16,700 retail stores globally, as well as increasingly through multiple retail channels.

Key Stock Statistics (Source S&P, Vickers, company reports)

52-Wk Range	$28.61–18.69	S&P Oper. EPS 2010E	1.23	Market Capitalization(B)	$21.085	Beta	1.26
Trailing 12-Month EPS	$1.07	S&P Oper. EPS 2011E	1.42	Yield (%)	1.83	S&P 3-Yr. Proj. EPS CAGR(%)	8
Trailing 12-Month P/E	26.6	P/E on S&P Oper. EPS 2010E	23.2	Dividend Rate/Share	$0.52	S&P Credit Rating	BBB+
$10K Invested 5 Yrs Ago	$10,455	Common Shares Outstg. (M)	740.1	Institutional Ownership (%)	75		

Price Performance

30-Week Mov. Avg. · · · · 10-Week Mov. Avg. - - **GAAP Earnings vs. Previous Year** Volume Above Avg. STARS
12-Mo. Target Price — Relative Strength — ▲ Up ▼ Down ► No Change Below Avg. ★

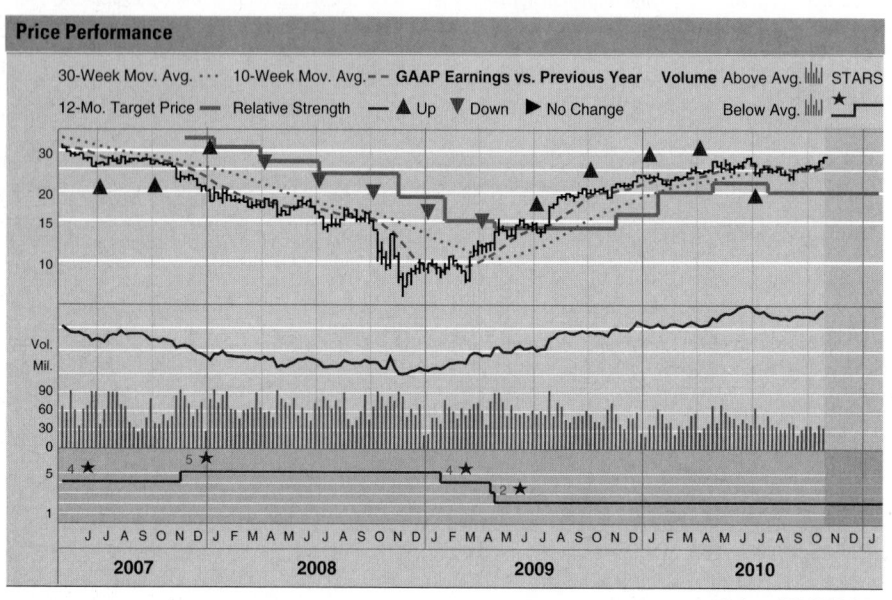

Options: ASE, CBOE, P, Ph

Analysis prepared by **Mark S. Basham** on July 23, 2010, when the stock traded at **$ 25.38**.

Highlights

➤ In FY 09 (Sep.), SBUX essentially completed a restructuring plan, which included closing stores and reduced new store openings. Savings from the closings and other cost initiatives were $590 million, $90 million more than previously estimated by SBUX. Nearly all of these savings carried over into FY 10 and beyond.

➤ For FY 10, SBUX is unveiling new product, service and store initiatives to revitalize the brand. Prominently, it has introduced VIA instant coffee, which is being rolled out through multiple channels. We expect initial results from these efforts, such as initial trial sales of VIA, the opening of 250 new stores, as well as a 53rd week, to result in an 8.2% increase in revenues. We expect operating margins to widen by about 325 basis points. Including incremental EPS of $0.04 from the 53rd week, we see EPS rising to $1.20.

➤ Assuming global economic growth remains on track, we project revenues will rise about 6% in FY 11, including the effect of opening an anticipated 500 new stores. We expect operating margins will widen further on cost leverage, and see EPS rising to $1.35.

Investment Rationale/Risk

➤ We think the company's revitalization agenda is on the right track, and the restructuring and cost cutting done in FY 09 has resulted in a material improvement in fundamentals. Despite the definite improvement we see occurring at SBUX, we think the current share price reflects a stronger U.S. economic recovery than S&P currently anticipates.

➤ Risks to our recommendation and target price include a greater than anticipated positive impact from the company's revitalization initiatives on customer traffic, as well as greater cost savings from restructuring initiatives.

➤ Our 12-month target price of $20 is largely derived from our DCF model, which assumes a weighted average cost of capital of 10.5% and reflects a substantial FY 10 cash flow increase over FY 09 levels. We also assume average annual cash flow increases of 6% through FY 20, then moderation to a perpetuity growth rate of 3%. We also use a roughly peer-average P/E of 15X our FY 11 estimate, which is reflective of SBUX's recent conservative bent in its capital structure, to derive a value of $20.

Qualitative Risk Assessment

LOW	MEDIUM	HIGH

Our risk assessment reflects uncertainties of ongoing steps to reinvigorate the Starbucks brand. We also see a threat from specialty coffee offerings by competitors. Offsetting these concerns, we think the company has significant financial strength, affording it the capacity to potentially return to moderate growth. Recent cost cutting has further bolstered the company's finances.

Quantitative Evaluations

S&P Quality Ranking B+

D	C	B-	B	B+	A-	A	A+

Relative Strength Rank STRONG

82

LOWEST = 1   HIGHEST = 99

Revenue/Earnings Data

Revenue (Million $)

	1Q	2Q	3Q	4Q	Year
2010	2,723	2,535	2,612	--	--
2009	2,615	2,333	2,404	2,422	9,775
2008	2,768	2,526	2,574	2,515	10,383
2007	2,356	2,256	2,359	2,441	9,411
2006	1,934	1,886	1,964	2,003	7,787
2005	1,590	1,519	1,602	1,659	6,369

Earnings Per Share ($)

2010	0.32	0.28	0.27	E0.31	E1.23
2009	0.09	0.03	0.20	0.20	0.52
2008	0.28	0.15	-0.01	0.01	0.43
2007	0.26	0.19	0.21	0.21	0.87
2006	0.22	0.16	0.18	0.17	0.73
2005	0.17	0.12	0.16	0.16	0.61

Fiscal year ended Sep. 30. Next earnings report expected: Early November. EPS Estimates based on S&P Operating Earnings; historical GAAP earnings are as reported.

Dividend Data (Dates: mm/dd Payment Date: mm/dd/yy)

Amount ($)	Date Decl.	Ex-Div. Date	Stk. of Record	Payment Date
0.100	03/24	04/05	04/07	04/23/10
0.130	07/21	08/02	08/04	08/20/10

Dividends have been paid since 2010. Source: Company reports.

The McGraw-Hill Companies

Starbucks Corp

Business Summary July 23, 2010

CORPORATE OVERVIEW. The Starbucks brand is nearly synonymous with specialty coffee. However, a slowing economy and over-expansion under prior management led the company, beginning in FY 08 (Sep.) under returning CEO H. Schultz, to dramatically reduce expansion and begin to evolve the brand.

The number of Starbucks retail stores fell slightly, by 45, to 16,635 at September 30, 2009, from a year earlier. However, this decline gains a somewhat different perspective when compared to the 165 stores open at the end of FY 92. Company-operated retail stores accounted for 84% of net sales in both FY 09 and FY 08. Stores are typically clustered in high-traffic, high-visibility locations in each market. In FY 08 (latest available), the retail store sales mix by product type was 76% beverages, 17% food items, 3% whole bean coffees, and 4% coffee-related hardware items.

At September 30, 2009, SBUX owned and operated 6,764 (7,238 as of September 30, 2008) of its stores in the U.S., and 2,068 (1,979) stores in international markets. It closed a net 385 company stores in FY 09, compared to a net total of 681 company-owned stores opened in FY 08.

There were also 4,364 (4,329) licensed retail stores in the U.S. and 3,439 (3,134)

in international markets at September 30, 2009. A net 340 licensed store opened in FY 09, compared to 988 opened in FY 08. Revenue from retail licensees was approximately 13% of total revenues in FY 09 (11% in FY 08). The Global Consumer Products Group and a number of foodservice accounts were 3.8% of total revenues in FY 09 (4.2% in FY 08).

IMPACT OF MAJOR DEVELOPMENTS. At the time of the January 2008 reappointment of Howard Schultz as CEO, the company outlined a five-point agenda: 1) improve the U.S. business by focusing on the customer experience and other factors affecting store operations; 2) slow the pace of U.S. expansion and close underperforming U.S. locations; 3) re-energize the Starbucks brand and create an emotional connection to the brand with customers and employees; 4) realign and streamline management and back-end functions to better support customer-focused initiatives; and 5) accelerate expansion outside the U.S. and drive profit margins higher at international operations.

Company Financials Fiscal Year Ended Sep. 30

Per Share Data ($)	2009	2008	2007	2006	2005	2004	2003	2002	2001	2000
Tangible Book Value	3.66	2.93	2.74	2.68	2.56	3.00	2.52	2.20	1.78	1.50
Cash Flow	1.24	1.17	1.51	1.25	1.06	0.85	0.66	0.55	0.45	0.48
Earnings	0.52	0.43	0.87	0.73	0.61	0.48	0.34	0.27	0.23	0.12
S&P Core Earnings	0.53	0.44	0.86	0.73	0.53	0.42	0.29	0.23	0.18	NA
Dividends	Nil	Nil	Nil	Nil	Nil	Nil	Nil	Nil	Nil	Nil
Payout Ratio	Nil	Nil	Nil	Nil	Nil	Nil	Nil	Nil	Nil	Nil
Prices:High	23.95	21.01	36.61	40.01	32.46	32.13	16.72	12.85	12.83	12.70
Prices:Low	8.12	7.06	19.89	28.72	22.29	16.45	9.81	9.22	6.73	5.78
P/E Ratio:High	46	49	42	55	53	68	50	48	56	NM
P/E Ratio:Low	16	16	23	39	37	35	29	34	29	NM

Income Statement Analysis (Million $)										
Revenue	9,775	10,383	9,411	7,787	6,369	5,294	4,076	3,289	2,649	2,169
Operating Income	1,331	1,279	1,437	1,213	1,071	854	646	504	430	334
Depreciation	535	549	491	413	367	305	259	221	177	142
Interest Expense	42.0	60.6	Nil	Nil	Nil	Nil	Nil	Nil	Nil	Nil
Pretax Income	559	460	1,056	906	796	624	436	341	289	161
Effective Tax Rate	30.1%	31.3%	36.3%	35.8%	37.9%	37.2%	38.5%	37.0%	37.3%	41.1%
Net Income	391	316	673	581	494	392	268	215	181	94.6
S&P Core Earnings	399	325	668	579	437	346	231	181	143	NA

Balance Sheet & Other Financial Data (Million $)										
Cash	666	322	281	313	174	299	201	175	113	70.8
Current Assets	2,036	1,748	1,696	1,530	1,209	1,368	924	848	594	460
Total Assets	5,577	5,673	5,344	4,429	3,514	3,328	2,730	2,293	1,851	1,493
Current Liabilities	1,581	2,190	2,156	1,936	1,227	783	609	537	445	313
Long Term Debt	549	550	550	1.96	2.87	3.62	4.35	5.08	5.79	6.48
Common Equity	3,046	2,491	2,284	2,229	2,091	2,487	2,082	1,727	1,376	1,148
Total Capital	3,595	3,059	2,834	2,230	2,094	2,537	2,120	1,754	1,406	1,180
Capital Expenditures	446	984	1,080	771	644	386	357	375	384	316
Cash Flow	926	865	1,164	994	862	697	528	436	358	367
Current Ratio	1.3	0.8	0.8	0.8	1.0	1.7	1.5	1.6	1.3	1.5
% Long Term Debt of Capitalization	15.3	18.0	19.4	0.1	0.1	0.1	0.2	0.3	0.4	0.5
% Net Income of Revenue	4.0	3.0	7.1	7.5	7.8	7.4	6.6	6.5	6.8	4.4
% Return on Assets	7.0	5.7	13.8	14.6	14.3	12.9	10.9	10.4	10.8	6.9
% Return on Equity	14.1	13.2	29.8	26.9	21.7	17.1	14.1	13.9	14.4	9.0

Data as orig reptd.; bef. results of disc opers/spec. items. Per share data adj. for stk. divs.; EPS diluted. E-Estimated. NA-Not Available. NM-Not Meaningful. NR-Not Ranked. UR-Under Review.

Office: 2401 Utah Avenue South, Seattle, WA 98134.
Telephone: 206-447-1575.
Email: investorrelations@starbucks.com
Website: http://www.starbucks.com

Chrmn, Pres & CEO: H.D. Schultz
EVP, CFO, Chief Admin Officer & Chief Acctg Officer: T. Hobson, K. R. Johnson, O. C. Lee, S. Sandberg, H. D.
Alstead
EVP, Secy & General Counsel: P.E. Boggs
SVP & CIO: S. Gillett

Board Members: B. Bass, W. W. Bradley, M. Schultz, J. G. Shennan, Jr., J. G. Teruel, M. Ullman, III, C. E. Weatherup

Founded: 1985
Domicile: Washington
Employees: 142,000

Starwood Hotels & Resorts Worldwide Inc.

S&P Recommendation	HOLD ★★★☆☆	Price $56.96 (as of Oct 22, 2010)	12-Mo. Target Price $59.00	Investment Style Large-Cap Blend

GICS Sector Consumer Discretionary
Sub-Industry Hotels, Resorts & Cruise Lines

Summary Starwood is one of the world's largest lodging companies, with over 1,000 hotels in approximately 100 countries operating under nine brands.

Key Stock Statistics (Source S&P, Vickers, company reports)

52-Wk Range	$57.60–27.66	S&P Oper. EPS 2010E	1.05	Market Capitalization(B)	$10.830	Beta	2.03
Trailing 12-Month EPS	$0.42	S&P Oper. EPS 2011E	1.37	Yield (%)	0.35	S&P 3-Yr. Proj. EPS CAGR(%)	15
Trailing 12-Month P/E	NM	P/E on S&P Oper. EPS 2010E	54.2	Dividend Rate/Share	$0.20	S&P Credit Rating	BB+
$10K Invested 5 Yrs Ago	$13,616	Common Shares Outstg. (M)	190.1	Institutional Ownership (%)	91		

Price Performance

Analysis prepared by **Esther Y. Kwon, CFA** on September 22, 2010, when the stock traded at **$ 52.09**.

Highlights

▶ With easy year-to-year RevPAR comparisons in the first half of 2010, we think the benefits of cost-cutting and restructuring undertaken in 2009 were strongly seen in first half results. Worldwide RevPAR rose 9.5%. For the second half, comparisons are not quite as easy.

▶ For 2010, we forecast systemwide RevPAR will be up 5%. We see outsized gains in the Asia/Pacific region, mixed results in Europe, and marginally higher RevPAR in North America. We forecast vacation ownership revenues will be about 6% higher. Reflecting 80-100 new hotels that HOT expects to open (with 10-20 likely to exit its portfolio), we see total revenues up 6%, including expected favorable foreign currency translation.

▶ We expect cash operating costs to rise somewhat less than revenues, owing to prior restructuring and asset writedowns, and we see operating profit up 10%. With a below historical 20% effective tax rate, we estimate EPS will increase to $1.05. For 2011, we expect costs to rise to support the growing worldwide portfolio but at a lower rate than the 6% revenue increase we forecast, resulting in EPS of $1.37.

Investment Rationale/Risk

▶ Although we do not expect the hotel industry to stage a full recovery to pre-2008 levels until some time in 2012, we believe HOT is positioned to disproportionately benefit from stronger international economies, and we expect major metropolitan markets, in which HOT has higher exposure, to outperform. Moreover, we see its premium positioning as a key differentiator. However, we believe the shares, trading at a premium to peers, already incorporate substantial prospective improvement in operating performance

▶ Risks to our recommendation and target price include the potential for industry conditions to improve at a slower rate than we currently foresee should the global economy recover later than S&P expects. Capital for some of the unfunded projects in the development pipeline may be less available under a tightening of capital market conditions.

▶ Our 12-month target price of $59 is based on an enterprise value multiple of 15X our 2011 EBITDA projection. This multiple is a premium to peers due to HOT's greater exposure to international and large metropolitan markets as well as the premium positioning of its properties.

Qualitative Risk Assessment

LOW	MEDIUM	HIGH

In our view, Starwood's financial flexibility has been substantially constrained by the current industry downturn. This was due in part to its decision to use cash and increase leverage to repurchase just over a quarter of its outstanding shares from 2006 to 2008. During 2009, it sold non-core assets and substantially reduced capital expenditures, enabling it to reduce its net debt position by almost $700 million.

Quantitative Evaluations

S&P Quality Ranking NR

D	C	B-	B	B+	A-	A	A+

Relative Strength Rank STRONG

84

LOWEST = 1 HIGHEST = 99

Revenue/Earnings Data

Revenue (Million $)

	1Q	2Q	3Q	4Q	Year
2010	1,187	1,289	--	--	--
2009	1,091	1,190	1,192	1,283	4,712
2008	1,466	1,573	1,535	1,333	5,907
2007	1,431	1,572	1,540	1,610	6,153
2006	1,441	1,505	1,461	1,572	5,979
2005	1,406	1,559	1,496	1,516	5,977

Earnings Per Share ($)

	1Q	2Q	3Q	4Q	Year
2010	0.16	0.42	E0.26	E0.31	E1.05
2009	0.04	0.78	0.20	-1.03	Nil
2008	0.42	0.57	0.62	-0.25	1.37
2007	0.56	0.67	0.61	0.74	2.57
2006	0.34	3.01	0.71	0.94	5.01
2005	0.36	0.65	0.18	0.72	1.88

Fiscal year ended Dec. 31. Next earnings report expected: Late October. EPS Estimates based on S&P Operating Earnings; historical GAAP earnings are as reported.

Dividend Data (Dates: mm/dd Payment Date: mm/dd/yy)

Amount ($)	Date Decl.	Ex-Div. Date	Stk. of Record	Payment Date
0.200	11/08	12/29	12/31	01/14/10

Dividends have been paid since 1995. Source: Company reports.

Starwood Hotels & Resorts Worldwide Inc.

Business Summary September 22, 2010

CORPORATE OVERVIEW. Starwood Hotels & Resorts (HOT) is one of the world's largest hotel companies, with owned, leased, managed or franchised hotels in approximately 100 countries. At December 31, 2009, the company's business included 992 hotels, with 298,522 rooms, vs. 942 properties with 284,800 rooms as of December 31, 2008. Of the 992 properties, 63 were wholly or majority owned, 440 were managed or operated as a joint venture, and 476 were franchised.

HOT's business includes owned, managed and franchised properties. Its brands include St. Regis (luxury full-service hotels and resorts), The Luxury Collection (luxury full-service hotels and resorts), Westin (luxury and upscale full-service hotels and resorts), Sheraton (full-service hotels and resorts), W (boutique full-service urban hotels) and Four Points (moderately priced full-service hotels). At December 31, 2009, the company's hotel business included 392 Sheratons (139,411 rooms), 165 Westins (65,521 rooms), 82 properties (14,961 rooms) in the St. Regis and Luxury Collection groups, 148 Four Points (24,930 rooms), 34 hotels (10,632 rooms) in the W chain, 105 Le Meridien properties (27,381 rooms), 39 hotels with 5,905 rooms in HOT's new boutique hotel brand, aloft, six hotels in its new green brand, element (762 rooms), and eight other hotels (1,935 rooms).

Approximately 58% of management and franchise fees in 2009 were generated outside the U.S. The company's top six domestic markets by percentage of total owned EBITDA during 2009 were: New York (9%), Hawaii (8%), Phoenix (5%), Chicago, Atlanta and San Francisco/SanMateo (4% each). The top six international markets were Canada (12%), Mexico (10%), Italy (10%), Australia (8%), Argentina (5%) and the U.K. (4%). Worldwide operating statistics for the 53 owned hotels operating in both 2008 and 2009 were: average daily rate of $199.22 in 2009, down 17.1% from $240.23 in 2008, occupancy of 64.7% vs. 71.2%, and RevPAR of $128.95, down 24.6% from $171.09.

In addition, the company had 23 vacation ownership resorts as of December 31, 2009, including 22 in operation and 17 in active sales. There were 4,826 completed units, with 206 additional units under development. A potential additional 734 units were possible, based on land owned and average unit densities in existing markets. In total and assuming 52 intervals per unit, HOT had inventory of 299,832 vacation ownership intervals.

Company Financials Fiscal Year Ended Dec. 31

Per Share Data ($)	2009	2008	2007	2006	2005	2004	2003	2002	2001	2000
Tangible Book Value	NM	NM	NM	3.31	13.59	10.73	4.55	3.57	2.35	2.50
Cash Flow	1.51	3.12	4.02	6.37	3.69	3.72	2.58	2.28	3.29	4.30
Earnings	Nil	1.37	2.57	5.01	1.88	1.72	0.51	1.20	0.73	1.96
S&P Core Earnings	0.36	1.31	2.69	4.87	1.66	1.37	0.12	0.77	0.52	NA
Dividends	0.20	0.90	0.90	0.84	0.84	0.84	0.84	0.84	0.80	0.69
Payout Ratio	NM	66%	35%	17%	45%	49%	165%	70%	110%	35%
Prices:High	37.55	56.00	75.45	68.87	65.22	59.50	37.60	39.94	40.89	37.50
Prices:Low	8.99	10.97	42.78	49.68	51.50	34.81	21.68	19.00	17.10	19.75
P/E Ratio:High	NM	41	29	14	35	35	74	33	56	19
P/E Ratio:Low	NM	8	17	10	27	20	43	16	23	10

Income Statement Analysis (Million $)	2009	2008	2007	2006	2005	2004	2003	2002	2001	2000
Revenue	4,756	5,907	6,153	5,979	5,977	5,368	4,630	4,659	3,967	4,345
Operating Income	678	1,083	1,217	1,145	1,242	1,047	1,698	1,856	1,191	1,509
Depreciation	273	323	306	306	407	431	429	222	526	481
Interest Expense	194	245	215	244	258	257	287	338	369	439
Pretax Income	-296	330	733	682	642	412	-5.00	252	200	610
Effective Tax Rate	99.0%	23.0%	25.8%	NM	34.1%	10.4%	NM	1.59%	23.0%	33.0%
Net Income	-1.00	254	543	1,115	423	369	105	246	151	401
S&P Core Earnings	65.3	241	570	1,084	376	291	27.7	157	107	NA

Balance Sheet & Other Financial Data (Million $)	2009	2008	2007	2006	2005	2004	2003	2002	2001	2000
Cash	87.0	389	358	183	897	326	508	216	157	189
Current Assets	1,491	2,166	1,824	1,810	2,283	1,683	1,245	950	897	1,048
Total Assets	8,761	9,703	9,622	9,280	12,454	12,298	11,894	12,259	12,461	12,660
Current Liabilities	2,027	2,688	2,101	2,461	2,879	2,128	1,644	2,199	1,587	1,805
Long Term Debt	2,955	3,502	3,590	1,827	2,926	3,823	4,393	4,449	5,269	5,074
Common Equity	1,824	1,621	2,076	3,008	5,211	4,788	4,326	6,357	3,756	3,851
Total Capital	4,805	5,652	5,720	4,891	8,724	9,518	9,676	11,882	10,380	10,417
Capital Expenditures	196	476	384	371	464	333	307	82.0	477	544
Cash Flow	272	577	849	1,421	830	800	534	468	677	882
Current Ratio	0.7	0.8	0.9	0.7	0.8	0.8	0.8	0.4	0.6	0.6
% Long Term Debt of Capitalization	61.5	61.9	62.8	37.4	33.5	40.2	45.4	37.4	50.8	48.7
% Net Income of Revenue	NM	4.3	8.8	18.6	7.1	6.9	NM	5.3	3.8	9.2
% Return on Assets	NM	2.6	5.8	10.2	3.4	3.1	NM	2.0	1.2	3.1
% Return on Equity	NM	13.7	21.4	27.1	8.5	8.1	NM	3.9	4.0	10.6

Data as orig reptd.; bef. results of disc opers/spec. items. Per share data adj. for stk. divs.; EPS diluted. E-Estimated. NA-Not Available. NM-Not Meaningful. NR-Not Ranked. UR-Under Review.

Office: 1111 Westchester Avenue, White Plains, NY 10604.
Telephone: 914-640-8100.
Website: http://www.starwoodhotels.com
Chrmn: B.W. Duncan

Pres & CEO: F. van Paasschen
Investor Contact: V.M. Prabhu (914-640-8100)
EVP & CFO: V.M. Prabhu
EVP, Chief Admin Officer, Secy & General Counsel: K.S. Siegel

Board Members: A. M. Aron, C. Barshefsky, T. E. Clarke, C. C. Daley, Jr., B. W. Duncan, L. Galbreath, E. C. Hippeau, S. R. Quazzo, T. O. Ryder, K. C. Youngblood, F. van Paasschen
Founded: 1969
Domicile: Maryland
Employees: 145,000

State Street Corp

STANDARD &POOR'S

S&P Recommendation **STRONG BUY** ★★★★★	Price	12-Mo. Target Price	Investment Style
	$40.40 (as of Oct 22, 2010)	$47.00	Large-Cap Growth

GICS Sector Financials
Sub-Industry Asset Management & Custody Banks

Summary This bank holding company, with about $20 trillion in assets under custody, is a leading servicer of financial assets worldwide.

Key Stock Statistics (Source S&P, Vickers, company reports)

52-Wk Range	$48.80– 32.47	S&P Oper. EPS 2010**E**	3.41	Market Capitalization(B)	$20.275	Beta	1.32
Trailing 12-Month EPS	$3.52	S&P Oper. EPS 2011**E**	3.95	Yield (%)	0.10	S&P 3-Yr. Proj. EPS CAGR(%)	7
Trailing 12-Month P/E	11.5	P/E on S&P Oper. EPS 2010**E**	11.8	Dividend Rate/Share	$0.04	S&P Credit Rating	A+
$10K Invested 5 Yrs Ago	$7,795	Common Shares Outstg. (M)	501.9	Institutional Ownership (%)	85		

Price Performance

30-Week Mov. Avg. · · · ·   10-Week Mov. Avg. - - **GAAP Earnings vs. Previous Year**   Volume Above Avg. STARS
12-Mo. Target Price —   Relative Strength —   ▲ Up ▼ Down ▶ No Change   Below Avg.

Analysis prepared by **Bret Howlett** on October 20, 2010, when the stock traded at **$ 40.45**.

Options: Ph

Highlights

➤ We expect operating revenue to advance 8%-9% in 2010 and 4%-5% in 2011, as recent acquisitions and improved servicing results outweigh lower trading service revenue. We look for assets under management to benefit from a secular shift to passive investing and ETFs, along with continued market growth . An improving asset mix should also help boost servicing and management fees. Considering our expectation for a sluggish economic recovery, we do not see interest rates rising until late 2011 at the earliest, keeping a lid on net interest income. We believe long-term favorable macro trends remain intact, including the consolidation among financial processing providers, growth in worldwide pension systems, and development of more complex investment vehicles.

➤ We think the operating margin will fall in 2010 on higher compensation costs, but revenue growth and realized efficiencies should result in wider margins in 2011.

➤ We project operating EPS of $3.41 in 2010 and $3.95 in 2011. Operating earnings exclude the accretion of the discount associated with conduits consolidated on STT's balance sheet.

Investment Rationale/Risk

➤ We believe STT is poised for double-digit earnings growth in 2011 on strong servicing fee growth, higher management fees, and cost controls. Despite the consolidation of asset conduits onto its balance sheet, we think the firm is adequately capitalized to absorb future losses. As of September 30, 2010, STT's Tier 1 common ratio stood at 13.9%, and we believe it should continue to improve based on our profitability outlook. With our view that most of STT's major risks have been removed, we look for its P/E multiple to slowly expand closer to historical levels, and we are valuing the company based on our 2011 estimated earnings.

➤ Risks to our recommendation and target price include a significant slowdown in capital markets, further securities writedowns, and further adverse litigation.

➤ Our 12-month target price is $47, or 11.9X our 2011 operating earnings estimate of $3.95. We think multiple expansion is warranted by what we view as the company's superior growth prospects compared to peers as the industry consolidates. Also, we see interest rates eventually rising, and providing another boost.

Qualitative Risk Assessment

LOW	**MEDIUM**	HIGH

Our risk assessment reflects our view of solid fundamentals coupled with a strong customer base, good diversification and healthy earnings growth, offset by lower-than-peers capital ratios and our belief that the securities book is risky.

Quantitative Evaluations

S&P Quality Ranking   A-

D	C	B-	B	B+	**A-**	A	A+

Relative Strength Rank   MODERATE

60

LOWEST = 1   HIGHEST = 99

Revenue/Earnings Data

Revenue (Million $)

	1Q	2Q	3Q	4Q	Year
2010	2,296	2,304	--	--	--
2009	2,002	2,122	2,236	2,280	8,640
2008	2,577	2,672	2,771	2,673	10,693
2007	1,696	2,740	3,165	2,479	11,818
2006	2,218	2,409	2,349	2,531	9,510
2005	1,699	1,837	1,925	2,035	7,496

Earnings Per Share ($)

2010	0.99	0.87	E0.86	E0.88	E3.41
2009	1.02	0.79	0.66	1.00	3.46
2008	1.35	1.35	1.09	0.54	4.30
2007	0.93	1.07	0.91	0.57	3.45
2006	0.84	0.68	0.83	0.91	3.26
2005	0.67	0.66	0.75	0.74	2.82

Fiscal year ended Dec. 31. Next earnings report expected: NA. EPS Estimates based on S&P Operating Earnings; historical GAAP earnings are as reported.

Dividend Data (Dates: mm/dd Payment Date: mm/dd/yy)

Amount ($)	Date Decl.	Ex-Div. Date	Stk. of Record	Payment Date
0.010	12/17	12/30	01/04	01/19/10
0.010	02/25	03/30	04/01	04/16/10
0.010	06/17	06/29	07/01	07/16/10
0.010	09/16	09/29	10/01	10/15/10

Dividends have been paid since 1910. Source: Company reports.

Please read the Required Disclosures and Analyst Certification on the last page of this report.

The McGraw-Hill Companies

State Street Corp

Business Summary October 20, 2010

CORPORATE OVERVIEW. State Street Corp. (STT) is a leading specialist in meeting the needs of institutional investors worldwide. Its customers include mutual funds, collective investment funds and other investment pools, corporate and public retirement plans, insurance companies, foundations, endowments and investment managers. STT operates in 27 countries and more than 100 geographic markets worldwide including the U.S., Australia, Austria, Belgium, Canada, the Cayman Islands, Chile, France, Germany, India, Ireland, Italy, Japan, Luxembourg, Mauritius, the Netherlands, New Zealand, China, Singapore, South Africa, South Korea, Switzerland, Taiwan, Thailand, the United Arab Emirates and the United Kingdom.

STT reports two lines of business: Investment Servicing and Investment Management. Investment Servicing provides services for U.S. mutual funds, collective investment funds and other investment pools, corporate and public retirement plans, insurance companies, foundations and endowments worldwide. Products include custody, product- and participant-level accounting, daily pricing and administration; master trust and master custody; record keeping; foreign exchange, brokerage and other trading services; securities finance; deposit and short-term investment facilities; loans and lease financ-

ing; investment manager and hedge fund manager operations outsourcing; and performance, risk and compliance analytics to support institutional investors.

Investment Management offers a broad array of services for managing financial assets, including investment management and investment research services, primarily for institutional investors worldwide. These services include passive and active U.S. and non-U.S. equity and fixed income strategies, and other related services, such as securities finance. Its exchange-traded fund (ETF)family holds onto a second place market share with nearly a quarter of industry assets under management at year-end 2009. We think the secular shift by investors to ETFs in lieu of mutual funds is a sustainable long-term trend, and STT is well positioned to increase assets under management faster than the industry average over the next few years.

Company Financials Fiscal Year Ended Dec. 31

Per Share Data ($)	2009	2008	2007	2006	2005	2004	2003	2002	2001	2000
Tangible Book Value	16.43	10.46	12.67	16.37	13.73	12.49	11.66	12.92	11.87	10.13
Earnings	3.46	4.30	3.45	3.26	2.82	2.35	2.15	3.10	1.90	1.82
S&P Core Earnings	3.84	3.73	3.47	3.30	2.80	2.30	1.41	2.01	1.83	NA
Dividends	0.04	0.95	0.88	0.80	0.72	0.64	0.56	0.48	0.41	0.35
Payout Ratio	1%	22%	26%	25%	26%	27%	26%	15%	21%	19%
Prices:High	55.87	86.55	82.53	68.56	59.80	56.90	53.63	58.36	63.93	68.40
Prices:Low	14.43	28.06	59.13	54.39	40.62	39.91	30.37	32.11	36.25	31.22
P/E Ratio:High	16	20	24	21	21	24	25	19	34	38
P/E Ratio:Low	4	7	17	17	14	17	14	10	19	17

Income Statement Analysis (Million $)	2009	2008	2007	2006	2005	2004	2003	2002	2001	2000
Net Interest Income	2,564	2,650	1,730	1,110	907	859	810	979	1,025	894
Tax Equivalent Adjustment	126	104	58.0	NA	42.0	45.0	51.0	61.0	67.0	65.0
Non Interest Income	5,935	7,747	6,599	5,201	4,566	4,074	3,925	3,421	2,782	2,665
Loan Loss Provision	Nil	Nil	Nil	Nil	Nil	-18.0	Nil	4.00	10.0	9.00
% Expense/Operating Revenue	70.2%	75.5%	77.2%	71.9%	73.8%	76.2%	76.5%	64.6%	75.3%	74.3%
Pretax Income	2,525	2,564	1,903	1,771	1,432	1,192	1,112	1,555	930	906
Effective Tax Rate	28.6%	36.0%	33.7%	38.1%	34.0%	33.1%	35.1%	34.7%	32.5%	34.3%
Net Income	1,803	1,642	1,261	1,096	945	798	722	1,015	628	595
% Net Interest Margin	2.19	2.08	1.71	1.25	1.08	1.08	1.17	1.42	1.66	1.66
S&P Core Earnings	1,822	1,549	1,269	1,107	939	782	473	658	604	NA

Balance Sheet & Other Financial Data (Million $)	2009	2008	2007	2006	2005	2004	2003	2002	2001	2000
Money Market Assets	26,780	56,548	29,841	20,699	12,039	26,829	31,694	46,342	37,991	44,083
Investment Securities	93,576	76,017	74,559	64,992	59,870	37,571	38,215	28,071	20,781	13,740
Commercial Loans	6,710	7,287	13,822	6,617	4,152	2,352	2,768	2,052	3,289	3,476
Other Loans	4,098	1,844	1,980	2,329	2,312	2,277	2,253	2,122	2,052	1,797
Total Assets	157,946	173,631	142,543	107,353	97,968	94,040	87,534	85,794	69,896	69,298
Demand Deposits	11,969	32,785	15,039	10,194	9,402	13,671	7,893	7,279	9,390	10,009
Time Deposits	78,093	79,440	80,750	55,452	50,244	41,458	39,623	38,189	29,169	27,928
Long Term Debt	8,838	4,419	3,636	2,616	2,659	2,458	2,222	1,270	1,217	1,219
Common Equity	14,491	10,721	11,299	7,252	6,367	6,159	5,747	4,787	3,845	3,262
% Return on Assets	1.1	1.0	1.0	1.1	1.0	0.9	0.8	1.3	0.9	0.9
% Return on Equity	14.2	14.9	13.6	16.1	15.1	13.4	13.7	23.5	17.7	20.1
% Loan Loss Reserve	0.7	0.2	0.1	0.2	0.3	0.4	1.2	1.5	1.1	1.1
% Loans/Deposits	9.9	9.2	15.3	13.6	10.9	8.4	10.6	9.2	13.9	13.9
% Equity to Assets	7.6	7.0	7.4	6.6	6.5	6.6	6.1	5.5	5.1	4.5

Data as orig reptd.; bef. results of disc opers/spec. items. Per share data adj. for stk. divs.; EPS diluted. E-Estimated. NA-Not Available. NM-Not Meaningful. NR-Not Ranked. UR-Under Review.

Office: 1 Lincoln St, Boston, MA 02111-2900.
Telephone: 617-786-3000.
Email: ir@statestreet.com
Website: http://www.statestreet.com

Chrmn: R.E. Logue
Pres & CEO: J.L. Hooley
EVP & CFO: E.J. Resch
EVP & Chief Admin Officer: D.C. O'Leary

EVP, Chief Acctg Officer & Cntlr: J.J. Malerba
Investor Contact: S.K. MacDonald (617-786-3000)
Board Members: K. F. Burnes, P. Coym, P. De Saint-Aignan, A. Fawcett, D. P. Gruber, L. A. Hill, J. L. Hooley, R. Kaplan, C. R. Lamantia, R. E. Logue, R. Sergel, R. L. Skates, G. L. Summe, R. E. Weissman

Founded: 1832
Domicile: Massachusetts
Employees: 27,310

Stericycle Inc

STANDARD &POOR'S

S&P Recommendation **BUY** ★★★★☆	Price $72.21 (as of Oct 22, 2010)	12-Mo. Target Price $78.00	Investment Style Large-Cap Growth

GICS Sector Industrials
Sub-Industry Environmental & Facilities Services

Summary SRCL provides medical waste collection, transportation, treatment and disposal services, and safety and compliance programs to health care companies throughout the U.S.

Key Stock Statistics (Source S&P, Vickers, company reports)

52-Wk Range	$72.88– 50.62	S&P Oper. EPS 2010E	2.45	Market Capitalization(B)	$6.160	Beta	0.22
Trailing 12-Month EPS	$2.23	S&P Oper. EPS 2011E	2.75	Yield (%)	Nil	S&P 3-Yr. Proj. EPS CAGR(%)	15
Trailing 12-Month P/E	32.4	P/E on S&P Oper. EPS 2010E	29.5	Dividend Rate/Share	Nil	S&P Credit Rating	NR
$10K Invested 5 Yrs Ago	$26,489	Common Shares Outstg. (M)	85.3	Institutional Ownership (%)	90		

Price Performance

- 30-Week Mov. Avg. · · · 10-Week Mov. Avg. - - GAAP Earnings vs. Previous Year   Volume Above Avg. STARS
- 12-Mo. Target Price — Relative Strength — ▲ Up ▼ Down ▶ No Change   Below Avg. ★

Options: CBOE, P, Ph

Analysis prepared by **Stewart Scharf** on September 30, 2010, when the stock traded at **$ 69.84**.

Highlights

► We project revenue to rise at least 16% in 2010, and expect similar growth in 2011, driven by acquisitions and increased small-quantity (SQ) volume in the Steri-Safe regulatory program. We also see large-quantity (LQ) growth aided by the ongoing adoption of the waste management service (Bio Systems) and new medical waste contracts. We project small-quantity organic growth near 10%, while domestic and international markets should advance in the mid- to high single digits.

► In our view, gross margins should expand modesty in 2010, from 47% in 2009, as price hikes, a better mix of higher-margin SQ customer accounts and stabilizing energy costs offset acquisition-related mix issues. We believe operating margins (EBITDA) will widen further from about 30.5% in 2009, on synergies from integrating acquisitions and well-controlled SG&A expenses.

► We see an effective tax rate of near 37% in 2010, and estimate operating EPS of $2.45 in 2010 (before at least $0.04 of net acquisition-related and restructuring charges), followed by a 12% advance in 2011, to $2.75.

Investment Rationale/Risk

► Our buy recommendation is based on favorable domestic and international trends in what we view as the recession-resistant medical waste business, and our view of the company's highly consistent operating model with solid cash flow generation.

► Risks to our recommendation and target price include potential new competitors, significant changes in environmental regulations for medical waste disposal, a rebound in fuel and energy costs, and problems integrating acquisitions.

► We attribute the stock's recent above-peers and S&P 500 multiple of over 28X our 2010 EPS estimate to the company's broad medical services network, its expanding market reach, and an acquisition strategy that has been accretive. Using historical and projected price-to-sales, P/E-to-three-year-EPS-growth (PEG) and price-to-EBITDA ratios, we derive a relative valuation of $76. Based on our DCF analysis, assuming 4% terminal growth and a 7.5% weighted average cost of capital, our intrinsic valuation estimate is $80. Blending these metrics, we arrive at our 12-month target price of $78.

Qualitative Risk Assessment

LOW	MEDIUM	HIGH

Our risk assessment reflects our view that the regulated medical waste industry is relatively recession resistant, debt levels are reasonable, cash flow generation is sufficient, and ROIC is strong.

Quantitative Evaluations

S&P Quality Ranking B+

D	C	B-	B	B+	A-	A	A+

Relative Strength Rank MODERATE

65

LOWEST = 1   HIGHEST = 99

Revenue/Earnings Data

Revenue (Million $)

	1Q	2Q	3Q	4Q	Year
2010	335.2	347.7	--	--	--
2009	277.1	289.3	297.8	313.5	1,178
2008	254.8	277.8	277.1	274.0	1,084
2007	211.1	232.9	237.3	251.6	932.8
2006	179.3	198.4	203.3	208.7	789.6
2005	140.6	149.2	153.2	166.6	609.5

Earnings Per Share ($)

	1Q	2Q	3Q	4Q	Year
2010	0.56	0.61	E0.64	E0.62	E2.45
2009	0.47	0.51	0.54	0.52	2.03
2008	0.35	0.44	0.45	0.45	1.68
2007	0.33	0.36	0.37	0.27	1.32
2006	0.26	0.28	0.31	0.32	1.17
2005	0.24	0.26	0.26	-0.01	0.74

Fiscal year ended Dec. 31. Next earnings report expected: Late October. EPS Estimates based on S&P Operating Earnings; historical GAAP earnings are as reported.

Dividend Data

No cash dividends have been paid.

The McGraw·Hill Companies

Stericycle Inc

STANDARD
&POOR'S

Business Summary September 30, 2010

CORPORATE OVERVIEW. Stericycle, North America's largest regulated medical waste management company, serves customers throughout the U.S., Canada, Mexico, the United Kingdom, Ireland and Argentina. In addition to waste collection, transfer and disposal, the company provides OSHA compliance services, accreditation readiness monitoring software, hospital-acquired infection monitoring software, and expired medications return services. It entered the U.K. market through the June 2004 acquisition of White Rose Environmental Ltd., and the February 2006 purchase of Sterile Technologies Group Limited (STG).

SRCL's global network includes 113 processing or processing/collection sites and 135 additional transfer, collection or combined transfer/collection sites. The company uses its network to provide the industry's broadest service offering, including medical waste collection, transportation and treatment, and related consulting, training and education services and products.

The company's two principal groups had over 471,000 customers as of June 30, 2010, including 459,000 small-quantity (SQ) medical waste generators, such as outpatient clinics, medical and dental offices, and long-term and sub-acute

care facilities; and about 12,000 large-quantity (LQ) medical waste generators, such as hospitals, blood banks and pharmaceutical manufacturers. In the U.K., the mix is over 70% LQ and near 30% SQ customers. SQ customers accounted for 63% of domestic medical waste revenues in 2009, up from 33% in 1996, with a gross margin of 46.9%, up from 21% in 1996. Foreign revenues accounted for over 22% of the total in 2009, with Europe responsible for 60% (13% of total sales).

MARKET PROFILE. SRCL estimates that annual revenues in the U.S. regulated medical waste services market are $3 billion, and about $10.5 billion globally. The company believes its global market share rose to 11.2% in 2009, from 10.3% in 2008. Waste generators outsource medical waste handling to reduce costs. Compliance issues have historically grown more complex, which has led to a shift toward more outsourcing.

Company Financials Fiscal Year Ended Dec. 31

Per Share Data ($)	2009	2008	2007	2006	2005	2004	2003	2002	2001	2000
Tangible Book Value	NM	NM	NM	NM	NM	NM	NM	NM	NM	NM
Cash Flow	2.49	2.08	1.66	1.47	0.98	1.08	0.90	0.67	0.56	0.47
Earnings	2.03	1.68	1.32	1.17	0.74	0.85	0.72	0.51	0.26	0.18
S&P Core Earnings	2.03	1.72	1.39	1.16	0.98	0.79	0.65	0.45	0.20	NA
Dividends	Nil	Nil	Nil	Nil	Nil	Nil	Nil	Nil	Nil	Nil
Payout Ratio	Nil	Nil	Nil	Nil	Nil	Nil	Nil	Nil	Nil	Nil
Prices:High	58.34	66.15	62.56	38.22	31.80	26.61	26.01	20.27	15.71	10.56
Prices:Low	44.36	46.45	36.52	28.33	21.38	20.85	16.03	12.50	6.50	3.80
P/E Ratio:High	29	39	47	33	43	31	36	40	60	59
P/E Ratio:Low	22	28	28	24	29	25	22	25	25	21

Income Statement Analysis (Million $)										
Revenue	1,178	1,084	933	790	610	516	453	402	359	324
Operating Income	365	316	272	233	191	169	144	119	102	91.4
Depreciation	40.0	34.2	31.1	27.0	21.4	21.8	17.3	15.0	25.2	23.5
Interest Expense	34.3	33.1	34.0	28.4	13.0	11.2	12.8	21.5	35.4	39.8
Pretax Income	278	239	191	173	112	129	109	75.6	36.7	23.8
Effective Tax Rate	36.5%	37.8%	38.1%	39.0%	40.0%	39.2%	39.5%	39.5%	40.1%	39.1%
Net Income	176	149	118	105	67.2	78.2	65.8	45.7	22.0	14.5
S&P Core Earnings	176	152	124	105	87.6	71.8	59.0	39.7	14.0	NA

Balance Sheet & Other Financial Data (Million $)										
Cash	16.9	10.5	18.4	13.5	7.83	7.85	7.24	8.38	12.7	2.67
Current Assets	247	224	210	219	144	115	97.7	94.4	98.0	91.0
Total Assets	2,183	1,759	1,608	1,328	1,048	834	707	667	615	598
Current Liabilities	221	180	150	142	98.8	83.2	69.0	53.8	63.4	43.1
Long Term Debt	923	754	614	443	349	190	163	224	267	345
Common Equity	846	670	714	625	522	495	408	327	233	135
Total Capital	1,846	1,571	1,453	1,174	942	743	634	610	545	551
Capital Expenditures	39.9	47.5	48.4	36.4	26.3	33.3	21.0	14.8	15.4	11.6
Cash Flow	216	183	150	132	88.6	100.0	83.0	60.7	47.3	38.0
Current Ratio	1.1	1.3	1.4	1.5	1.5	1.4	1.4	1.8	1.5	2.1
% Long Term Debt of Capitalization	50.0	48.0	42.3	37.8	37.0	25.6	25.7	36.8	49.1	62.6
% Net Income of Revenue	14.9	13.7	12.7	13.3	11.0	15.1	14.5	11.4	6.1	4.5
% Return on Assets	8.9	8.8	8.1	8.9	7.1	10.1	9.6	7.1	3.6	2.4
% Return on Equity	23.2	21.5	17.7	18.4	13.2	17.3	17.9	16.4	12.0	11.5

Data as orig reptd.; bef. results of disc opers/spec. items. Per share data adj. for stk. divs.; EPS diluted. E-Estimated. NA-Not Available. NM-Not Meaningful. NR-Not Ranked. UR-Under Review.

Office: 28161 North Keith Drive, Lake Forest, IL 60045.
Telephone: 847-367-5910.
Email: investor@stericycle.com
Website: http://www.stericycle.com

Chrmn, Pres & CEO: M.C. Miller
COO & EVP: R. Kogler
EVP, CFO & Chief Acctg Officer: F.J. ten Brink

Board Members: T. D. Brown, R. Dammeyer, W. Hall, J. T. Lord, M. C. Miller, J. Patience, J. Reid-Anderson, J. W. Schuler, R. G. Spaeth

Founded: 1989
Domicile: Delaware
Employees: 8,199

Stryker Corp

STANDARD &POOR'S

S&P Recommendation BUY ★★★★☆

Price
$51.27 (as of Oct 25, 2010)

12-Mo. Target Price
$60.00

Investment Style
Large-Cap Growth

GICS Sector Health Care
Sub-Industry Health Care Equipment

Summary This company makes specialty surgical and medical products such as orthopedic implants, endoscopic items, and hospital beds.

Key Stock Statistics (Source S&P, Vickers, company reports)

52-Wk Range	$59.72– 42.74	S&P Oper. EPS 2010E	3.30	Market Capitalization(B)	$20.351	Beta	0.90
Trailing 12-Month EPS	$3.22	S&P Oper. EPS 2011E	3.65	Yield (%)	1.17	S&P 3-Yr. Proj. EPS CAGR(%)	12
Trailing 12-Month P/E	15.9	P/E on S&P Oper. EPS 2010E	15.5	Dividend Rate/Share	$0.60	S&P Credit Rating	A+
$10K Invested 5 Yrs Ago	$12,789	Common Shares Outstg. (M)	396.9	Institutional Ownership (%)	61		

Price Performance

30-Week Mov. Avg. · · · · 10-Week Mov. Avg. – – **GAAP Earnings vs. Previous Year** Volume Above Avg. STARS
12-Mo. Target Price — Relative Strength — ▲ Up ▼ Down ▶ No Change Below Avg. ★

Options: ASE, CBOE, Ph

Analysis prepared by **Phillip M. Seligman** on October 25, 2010, when the stock traded at **$ 51.27**.

Highlights

➤ We expect sales to rise about 6.5% in 2011, to over $7.7 billion, following a 7.5% increase we see in 2010, to over $7.2 billion, led by improved med-surg sales, and new spine, hip and knee implant products. However, we see orthopedic implant growth continuing to be tempered by pricing pressures and elective procedure deferrals. SYK's European markets remain soft due to austerity measures and the company's 2009 decision to discontinue certain products, but sales declines there have begun to narrow sequentially and we expect this trend to continue. We project high single-/low-double-digit med-surg equipment sales to continue through 2011, aided by a recent acquisition and assuming order trends are sustainable.

➤ We think gross margins will continue to expand, partly on an improving product mix and higher cost absorption. We expect SG&A costs to continue to decline as a percentage of sales, on cost controls, while R&D costs continue to consume a slightly higher proportion of sales.

➤ We look for EPS of $3.65 in 2011, versus our estimate of $3.30 in 2010. Operating EPS was $2.95 in 2009.

Investment Rationale/Risk

➤ Despite U.S. hospital spending constraints, SYK appears to be realizing a strong recovery in the med-surg arena. Looking ahead, we see long-term growth opportunities for SYK's orthopedic implant segment enabled by its active R&D, demographic trends, and procedure deferrals lessening over time. Meanwhile, although orthopedic implant sales are being impacted by soft volume trends and pricing pressures, we are encouraged that volume trends appear to be improving sequentially in Europe. We expect its global hip and knee sales to improve in 2011 assuming the new hip products gain more traction and FDA approval is received for an instrument system to customize knee implants. We view SYK's cash position and cash flow as healthy, providing financial flexibility.

➤ Risks to our recommendation and target price include Medicare reimbursement rate reductions, intensified competition, and rejection of a promising product by the FDA.

➤ Our 12-month target price of $60 reflects a P/E of 16.5X our 2011 EPS estimate. In our view, Stryker's superior projected growth rate relative to peers warrants a premium valuation.

Qualitative Risk Assessment

LOW	**MEDIUM**	HIGH

Stryker operates in very competitive areas of the global medical device industry, characterized by rapid technological innovation and market share volatility. We believe the medical/surgical supplies unit may be vulnerable to reductions in hospital capital equipment spending, but we think demand for its orthopedic products is largely immune from economic cycles.

Quantitative Evaluations

S&P Quality Ranking   A+

D	C	B-	B	B+	A-	A	**A+**

Relative Strength Rank   MODERATE

59

LOWEST = 1   HIGHEST = 99

Revenue/Earnings Data

Revenue (Million $)

	1Q	2Q	3Q	4Q	Year
2010	1,799	1,758	1,768	--	--
2009	1,601	1,634	1,653	1,834	6,723
2008	1,634	1,713	1,653	1,718	6,718
2007	1,426	1,464	1,453	1,658	6,001
2006	1,321	1,328	1,294	1,463	5,406
2005	1,203	1,219	1,172	1,279	4,872

Earnings Per Share ($)

2010	0.80	0.80	0.85	E0.90	E3.30
2009	0.71	0.73	0.57	0.76	2.77
2008	0.70	0.73	0.66	0.69	2.78
2007	0.58	0.58	0.55	0.66	2.37
2006	0.36	0.52	0.46	0.55	1.89
2005	0.42	0.45	0.32	0.45	1.64

Fiscal year ended Dec. 31. Next earnings report expected: Late January. EPS Estimates based on S&P Operating Earnings; historical GAAP earnings are as reported.

Dividend Data (Dates: mm/dd Payment Date: mm/dd/yy)

Amount ($)	Date Decl.	Ex-Div. Date	Stk. of Record	Payment Date
0.150	12/03	12/28	12/30	01/29/10
0.150	02/25	03/28	03/30	04/30/10
0.150	06/21	06/28	06/30	07/30/10
0.150	09/15	09/28	09/30	10/29/10

Dividends have been paid since 1992. Source: Company reports.

Stryker Corp

STANDARD & POOR'S

Business Summary October 25, 2010

Stryker Corp. traces its origins to a business founded in 1941 by Dr. Homer H. Stryker, a leading orthopedic surgeon and the inventor of several orthopedic products. The company has significant exposure to the artificial hip, prosthetic knee and trauma product areas. International sales accounted for 36% of the total in 2009.

Orthopedic implants (61% of 2009 sales) consist of products such as hip, knee, shoulder and spinal implants, associated implant instrumentation, trauma-related products, and bone cement. Artificial joints are made of cobalt chromium, titanium alloys, ceramics, or ultra-high molecular weight polyethylene, and are implanted in patients whose natural joints have been damaged by arthritis, osteoporosis, other diseases, or injury. SYK also sells trauma-related products, used primarily in the fixation of fractures resulting from sudden injury, including internal fixation devices such as nails, plates and screws, and external fixation devices such as pins, wires and connection bars. In addition, the division sells Simplex bone cement, a material used to secure cemented implants to bone, and the OP-1 Bone Growth Device. Composed of recombinant human osteogenic protein-1 and a bioresorbable collagen matrix, the product induces the formation of new bone when implanted into existing bone, and is approved to treat long bone fractures in patients in whom use of autograft treatments has failed or is not a feasible option. In March 2009, an

FDA panel voted not to recommend the company receive broad-based marketing approval for its OP-1 putty, a new formulation of OP-1. As of April 2010, Stryker is in the process of reviewing its strategic alternatives for the use of OP-1.

The medical and surgical equipment unit (39%) operates through four units. Stryker Instruments sells powered surgical drills, saws, fixation and reaming equipment, as well as other instruments used for drilling, burring, rasping or cutting bone, wiring or pinning bone fractures, and preparing hip or knee surfaces for the placement of artificial hip or knee joints. Stryker Endoscopy offers medical video cameras, light sources, arthroscopes, laparascopes, powered surgical instruments, and disposable suction/irrigation devices. Stryker Medical produces a wide variety of specialty stretchers customized for acute care and specialty surgical facilities. Stryker Leibinger makes plate and screw systems for craniomaxillofacial surgery to repair small bones in the hands, face and head, and sells a proprietary bone substitute material, BoneSource.

Company Financials Fiscal Year Ended Dec. 31

Per Share Data ($)	2009	2008	2007	2006	2005	2004	2003	2002	2001	2000
Tangible Book Value	12.58	11.28	10.84	7.98	5.75	4.44	2.98	1.42	0.65	0.04
Cash Flow	3.74	3.25	2.79	2.69	2.34	1.78	1.71	1.30	1.09	0.97
Earnings	2.77	2.78	2.37	1.89	1.64	1.14	1.12	0.85	0.67	0.55
S&P Core Earnings	2.69	2.76	2.37	1.89	1.57	1.08	1.08	0.80	0.63	NA
Dividends	0.15	0.40	0.33	0.22	0.11	0.09	0.07	0.06	0.05	0.03
Payout Ratio	5%	14%	14%	12%	7%	8%	6%	7%	7%	5%
Prices:High	52.66	74.94	76.89	55.92	56.32	57.66	42.68	33.74	31.60	28.88
Prices:Low	30.82	35.38	54.89	39.77	39.74	40.30	29.83	21.93	21.65	12.22
P/E Ratio:High	19	27	32	30	34	51	38	40	47	52
P/E Ratio:Low	11	13	23	21	24	35	27	26	32	22

Income Statement Analysis (Million $)	2009	2008	2007	2006	2005	2004	2003	2002	2001	2000
Revenue	6,723	6,718	6,001	5,406	4,872	4,262	3,625	3,012	2,602	2,289
Operating Income	2,109	1,749	1,506	1,459	1,305	1,092	901	751	645	600
Depreciation	385	195	179	332	290	251	230	186	172	169
Interest Expense	22.4	30.5	22.2	Nil	7.70	6.80	22.6	40.3	67.9	96.6
Pretax Income	1,624	1,580	1,370	1,104	1,003	717	652	507	406	335
Effective Tax Rate	31.8%	27.4%	28.0%	29.5%	32.7%	35.0%	30.5%	31.8%	33.0%	34.0%
Net Income	1,107	1,148	987	778	675	466	454	346	272	221
S&P Core Earnings	1,075	1,141	987	779	645	441	436	324	257	NA

Balance Sheet & Other Financial Data (Million $)	2009	2008	2007	2006	2005	2004	2003	2002	2001	2000
Cash	2,955	2,196	2,411	1,415	1,057	349	65.9	37.8	50.1	54.0
Current Assets	5,851	4,979	4,905	3,534	2,870	2,143	1,398	1,151	993	997
Total Assets	9,071	7,603	7,354	5,874	4,944	4,084	3,159	2,816	2,424	2,431
Current Liabilities	1,441	1,462	1,333	1,352	1,249	1,114	850	708	533	617
Long Term Debt	Nil	Nil	Nil	Nil	184	0.70	18.8	491	721	876
Common Equity	6,595	5,407	5,379	4,191	3,252	2,752	2,155	1,498	1,056	855
Total Capital	6,595	5,568	5,524	4,191	3,436	2,753	2,174	1,989	1,777	1,731
Capital Expenditures	131	155	188	218	272	188	145	139	162	80.7
Cash Flow	1,493	1,343	1,165	1,110	965	717	683	532	444	390
Current Ratio	4.1	3.4	3.7	2.6	2.3	1.9	1.6	1.6	1.9	1.6
% Long Term Debt of Capitalization	Nil	Nil	Nil	Nil	5.4	0.0	0.9	24.7	40.6	50.6
% Net Income of Revenue	16.5	17.1	16.4	14.4	13.9	10.9	12.5	11.5	10.4	9.7
% Return on Assets	13.3	15.4	14.9	14.3	15.0	12.9	15.2	13.2	11.2	8.8
% Return on Equity	18.5	21.3	20.6	20.8	22.5	19.0	24.8	27.1	28.4	29.0

Data as orig reptd.; bef. results of disc opers/spec. items. Per share data adj. for stk. divs.; EPS diluted. E-Estimated. NA-Not Available. NM-Not Meaningful. NR-Not Ranked. UR-Under Review.

Office: 2825 Airview Blvd, Portage, MI 49002-1802.
Telephone: 269-385-2600.
Website: http://www.stryker.com
Chrmn, Pres & CEO: S.P. MacMillan

COO: L.J. Carpenter
CFO: C.R. Hartman
Chief Acctg Officer: T.M. McKinney
Treas: J. Blondia

Investor Contact: K.A. Owen (269-385-2600)
Board Members: H. E. Cox, Jr., S. M. Datar, R. F. Doliveux, R. Doliveux, D. M. Engelman, L. L. Francesconi, H. L. Lance, S. P. MacMillan, W. U. Parfet, R. E. Stryker

Founded: 1946
Domicile: Michigan
Employees: 18,582

The McGraw-Hill Companies

Sunoco Inc.

STANDARD &POOR'S

S&P Recommendation	HOLD ★★★☆☆	Price $39.20 (as of Oct 22, 2010)	12-Mo. Target Price $39.00	Investment Style Large-Cap Blend

GICS Sector Energy
Sub-Industry Oil & Gas Refining & Marketing

Summary As one of the largest independent refiners in the U.S., this company has diversified operations in refining, marketing, chemicals, logistics, and cokemaking.

Key Stock Statistics (Source S&P, Vickers, company reports)

52-Wk Range	$40.63–24.25	S&P Oper. EPS 2010E	2.29	Market Capitalization(B)	$4.726	Beta	0.61
Trailing 12-Month EPS	$-1.72	S&P Oper. EPS 2011E	2.70	Yield (%)	1.53	S&P 3-Yr. Proj. EPS CAGR(%)	NM
Trailing 12-Month P/E	NM	P/E on S&P Oper. EPS 2010E	17.1	Dividend Rate/Share	$0.60	S&P Credit Rating	BBB-
$10K Invested 5 Yrs Ago	$6,503	Common Shares Outstg. (M)	120.6	Institutional Ownership (%)	82		

Price Performance

30-Week Mov. Avg. · · · 10-Week Mov. Avg. – – GAAP Earnings vs. Previous Year Volume Above Avg. STARS
12-Mo. Target Price — Relative Strength — ▲ Up ▼ Down ► No Change Below Avg.

[Chart: price performance 2007–2010]

Options: CBOE, Ph

Analysis prepared by **Tina J. Vital** on August 02, 2010, when the stock traded at **$35.78**.

Highlights

► With the economic slowdown reducing the demand for petroleum products, refining margins narrowed in 2009. As a result, SUN shut down its Eagle Point refinery in October 2009. Refining throughputs fell 8% to 667,700 b/d in the second quarter, and we look for drop of 13% for the year 2010, reflecting reduced refining capacity due to divestments and idlings. However, we are seeing signs of improved fuel demand, and as of July 2010, S&P Equity projected that U.S. Gulf Coast 3-2-1 crack spreads would widen 9% in 2010 and 3% in 2011.

► In June 2010, SUN announced plans to spin off its SunCoke Energy unit. Subject to necessary approvals, separation is slated for the first half of 2011. We do not like the idea, as we think it will eliminate a relatively stable source of cash flow and expose SUN's earnings to volatility from its Refining segment.

► First half operating EPS excluded net special charges of $0.78 related to divestments. As we expected, the Refining segment posted a profit in the second quarter, and we expect after-tax earnings to turn positive in 2010 and 2011 on improved margins, reflecting cost initiatives after a loss in 2009 on reduced demand.

Investment Rationale/Risk

► SUN's finances had deteriorated due to poor refining conditions, but on the back of cost initiatives and signs of improved demand, we believe the worst is over. In October 2009, SUN shut its Eagle Point refinery, and in April 2010, sold its polypropylene business. SUN is optimizing its refining units, and pursuing a possible oil sands joint venture for its Toledo refinery, and is expanding its logistics operations. We believe its Retail Marketing business will provide long-term earnings stability. We expect the Logistics segment to produce steady income growth in 2010 and 2011 from its expanded asset base and the July 2010 purchase of Texon which offers state-of-the art blending capabilities.

► Risks to our recommendation and target price include unfavorable changes in economic, industry, and operating conditions that would lead to a narrowing of margins.

► A blend of our DCF ($39 per share; assuming a WACC of 6.3% and a terminal growth rate of 3%) and relative valuations leads to our 12-month target of $39. This represents an expected enterprise value of about 4.7X our 2011 EBITDA estimate, a discount to peers.

Qualitative Risk Assessment

LOW	MEDIUM	HIGH

Our risk assessment reflects the company's weakened business profile in the volatile and competitive refining industry, and diversification into retail marketing, chemicals, logistics, and cokemaking.

Quantitative Evaluations

S&P Quality Ranking B+

D	C	B-	B	B+	A-	A	A+

Relative Strength Rank STRONG

76

LOWEST = 1 HIGHEST = 99

Revenue/Earnings Data

Revenue (Million $)

	1Q	2Q	3Q	4Q	Year
2010	8,192	8,964	--	--	--
2009	6,128	7,482	8,634	8,947	31,312
2008	12,813	15,426	15,447	8,479	51,558
2007	9,305	10,764	11,497	13,162	44,728
2006	8,593	10,590	10,496	9,036	38,715
2005	7,209	7,990	9,295	9,270	33,764

Earnings Per Share ($)

	1Q	2Q	3Q	4Q	Year
2010	-0.34	1.20	E0.45	E0.20	E2.29
2009	0.05	-0.59	-2.67	-0.04	-3.16
2008	-0.50	0.70	4.70	1.74	6.63
2007	1.44	4.20	1.81	-0.08	7.43
2006	0.59	3.22	2.76	1.00	7.59
2005	0.84	1.75	2.39	2.12	7.08

Fiscal year ended Dec. 31. Next earnings report expected: Early November. EPS Estimates based on S&P Operating Earnings; historical GAAP earnings are as reported.

Dividend Data (Dates: mm/dd Payment Date: mm/dd/yy)

Amount ($)	Date Decl.	Ex-Div. Date	Stk. of Record	Payment Date
0.150	02/04	02/12	02/17	03/10/10
0.150	05/06	05/17	05/19	06/10/10
0.150	07/01	08/16	08/18	09/10/10
0.150	09/02	11/15	11/17	12/10/10

Dividends have been paid since 1904. Source: Company reports.

The McGraw·Hill Companies

Sunoco Inc.

Business Summary August 02, 2010

CORPORATE OVERVIEW. Sunoco Inc. (SUN) has been active in the petroleum industry since 1886, and conducts its business through five operating segments: Refining and Supply (39% of 2009 revenues; segment loss of $316 million); Retail Marketing (37%; income of $86 million); Chemicals (5%; income of $1 million); Logistics (15%; income of $97 million); and Coke (4%; income of $180 million).

Refining and Supply manufactures refined petroleum products and commodity petrochemicals. As of December 31, 2009, SUN owned and operated three refineries with a crude unit capacity of about 675,000 barrels per day (b/d), located in the Northeast (Marcus Hook, PA, and Philadelphia, PA) and the Mid-Continent (Toledo, OH). In June 2009, SUN sold its Tulsa refinery to Holly Corp. (HOC) for $65 million. In the 2009 fourth quarter, SUN permanently shut down all process units at its Eagle Point refinery in Westville, NJ, in response to weak demand and increased global refining capacity; SUN is exploring options for the site, including use for biofuels production. Production available for sale declined 12.1%, to 689,900 b/d, in 2009 (gasoline 49%, middle distillates 31%, residual fuels 8%, petrochemicals 4%, and other 8%).

SUN meets all of its crude oil requirements through purchases from third parties. Approximately 58% of SUN's 2009 crude oil supply came from West Africa (20% from Nigeria), 9% from the U.S., 11% from Canada, 14% from Central Asia, 5% from the North Sea, 2% from South and Central America, and 1% from lubes extracted from gasoil/naphtha intermediate feedstock. In the 2004 second half, the company began processing limited amounts of lower value high acid sweet crude oils in some of its Northeast refineries; during 2009, about 61,000 b/d of high acid crude oil was processed.

The Chemicals segment manufactures, distributes and markets commodity and intermediate petrochemicals, consisting of aromatic derivatives (cumene, phenol, acetone and bispenol-A) and polypropylene. On March 31, 2010, SUN sold its subsidiary Sunoco Chemicals, Inc. (comprised of its propylene business) to Braskern S.A. for about $350 million. SUN will retain its phenol and derivatives business.

Company Financials Fiscal Year Ended Dec. 31

Per Share Data ($)	2009	2008	2007	2006	2005	2004	2003	2002	2001	2000
Tangible Book Value	19.92	22.30	19.12	17.01	15.42	11.65	10.23	9.05	10.88	10.03
Cash Flow	1.29	11.03	11.43	11.15	10.20	9.50	4.35	1.85	4.38	4.05
Earnings	-3.16	6.63	7.43	7.59	7.08	4.04	2.02	-0.31	2.43	2.35
S&P Core Earnings	-2.36	6.23	6.74	7.63	7.56	4.19	2.13	-0.70	1.88	NA
Dividends	1.20	1.17	1.08	0.95	0.75	0.58	0.51	0.50	0.50	0.50
Payout Ratio	NM	18%	14%	13%	11%	14%	25%	NM	21%	21%
Prices:High	47.40	73.68	86.40	97.25	85.29	42.26	26.30	21.13	21.37	17.28
Prices:Low	21.45	21.30	56.68	57.50	38.10	25.26	14.84	13.51	14.56	10.97
P/E Ratio:High	NM	11	12	13	12	10	13	NM	9	7
P/E Ratio:Low	NM	3	8	8	5	6	7	NM	6	5

Income Statement Analysis (Million $)	2009	2008	2007	2006	2005	2004	2003	2002	2001	2000
Revenue	28,804	51,558	44,728	38,715	33,764	25,508	17,929	14,384	14,063	14,300
Operating Income	NA	1,988	1,835	2,049	2,078	1,501	934	313	954	948
Depreciation, Depletion and Amortization	502	515	480	459	429	818	363	329	321	298
Interest Expense	106	72.0	127	89.0	69.0	97.0	111	108	103	78.0
Pretax Income	-601	1,173	1,476	1,580	1,580	995	495	-73.0	587	596
Effective Tax Rate	59.9%	33.8%	35.1%	38.0%	38.4%	39.2%	37.0%	NM	32.2%	31.0%
Net Income	-370	776	891	979	974	605	312	-47.0	398	411
S&P Core Earnings	-277	729	808	984	1,040	626	330	-106	307	NA

Balance Sheet & Other Financial Data (Million $)	2009	2008	2007	2006	2005	2004	2003	2002	2001	2000
Cash	377	240	648	263	919	405	431	390	42.0	239
Current Assets	3,764	2,835	4,638	4,015	3,687	2,551	2,068	1,898	1,510	1,683
Total Assets	11,895	11,150	12,426	10,982	9,931	8,079	6,922	6,441	5,932	5,426
Current Liabilities	4,418	3,937	5,640	4,755	4,210	3,022	2,170	1,776	1,778	1,646
Long Term Debt	2,061	1,705	1,724	1,705	1,234	1,379	1,350	1,453	1,142	933
Common Equity	2,557	2,842	2,533	2,075	2,051	1,607	1,556	1,394	1,642	1,702
Total Capital	5,186	5,844	5,723	5,227	4,749	4,271	3,940	3,816	3,335	2,885
Capital Expenditures	899	1,286	1,179	1,019	970	832	425	385	331	465
Cash Flow	151	1,291	1,371	1,438	1,403	1,423	675	282	719	709
Current Ratio	0.9	0.7	0.8	0.8	0.9	0.8	1.0	1.1	0.8	1.0
% Long Term Debt of Capitalization	44.6	29.2	30.1	32.6	26.0	32.3	34.3	38.1	34.2	32.3
% Return on Assets	NM	6.6	7.6	9.4	10.8	8.0	4.7	NM	7.0	7.7
% Return on Equity	NM	28.9	38.7	47.5	53.3	38.3	21.2	NM	23.8	25.6

Data as orig reptd.; bef. results of disc opers/spec. items. Per share data adj. for stk. divs.; EPS diluted. E-Estimated. NA-Not Available. NM-Not Meaningful. NR-Not Ranked. UR-Under Review.

Office: 1735 Market St Ste LL, Philadelphia, PA 19103-7583.
Telephone: 215-977-3000.
Email: sunocoonline@sunocoinc.com
Website: http://www.sunocoinc.com

Chrmn, Pres & CEO: L.L. Elsenhans
SVP & CFO: B.P. MacDonald
SVP & General Counsel: S.L. Fox
CTO: V.J. Kelley

Chief Acctg Officer & Cntlr: J.P. Krott
Investor Contact: T. Harr (215-977-6764)
Investor Contact: T.P. Delaney
Board Members: C. C. Casciato, G. W. Edwards, L. L. Elsenhans, U. O. Fairbairn, R. B. Greco, J. P. Jones, III, J. G. Kaiser, J. W. Rowe, J. K. Wulff

Founded: 1886
Domicile: Pennsylvania

SunTrust Banks Inc.

STANDARD &POOR'S

S&P Recommendation	HOLD ★★★☆☆	Price $26.20 (as of Oct 22, 2010)	12-Mo. Target Price $27.00	Investment Style Large-Cap Blend

GICS Sector Financials
Sub-Industry Regional Banks

Summary STI is one of the largest regional banks in the U.S., and is concentrated primarily in Florida, Georgia, Maryland, North Carolina, South Carolina, Virginia, Tennessee, and the District of Columbia.

Key Stock Statistics (Source S&P, Vickers, company reports)

52-Wk Range	$32.02– 18.45	S&P Oper. EPS 2010**E**	-0.28	Market Capitalization(B)	$13.098	Beta	1.30
Trailing 12-Month EPS	$-1.98	S&P Oper. EPS 2011**E**	0.99	Yield (%)	0.15	S&P 3-Yr. Proj. EPS CAGR(%)	NM
Trailing 12-Month P/E	NM	P/E on S&P Oper. EPS 2010**E**	NM	Dividend Rate/Share	$0.04	S&P Credit Rating	BBB
$10K Invested 5 Yrs Ago	$4,359	Common Shares Outstg. (M)	499.9	Institutional Ownership (%)	75		

Price Performance

30-Week Mov. Avg. ··· 10-Week Mov. Avg. - - GAAP Earnings vs. Previous Year Volume Above Avg. STARS
12-Mo. Target Price — Relative Strength — ▲ Up ▼ Down ► No Change Below Avg.

Options: CBOE, P, Ph

Qualitative Risk Assessment

LOW	MEDIUM	HIGH

Our risk assessment reflects SunTrust's large-cap valuation and history of profitability, offset by exposure to possible further declines in residential and commercial lending credit quality.

Quantitative Evaluations

S&P Quality Ranking B+

D	C	B-	B	B+	A-	A	A+

Relative Strength Rank MODERATE

50

LOWEST = 1   HIGHEST = 99

Revenue/Earnings Data

Revenue (Million $)

	1Q	2Q	3Q	4Q	Year
2010	2,272	2,522	--	--	--
2009	2,851	2,765	2,433	2,372	10,420
2008	3,316	3,479	3,303	2,683	12,801
2007	3,407	3,698	3,334	3,025	13,313
2006	3,130	3,299	3,384	3,447	13,260
2005	2,470	2,614	2,829	2,973	10,886

Earnings Per Share ($)

	1Q	2Q	3Q	4Q	Year
2010	-0.46	-0.11	E0.17	E0.12	E-0.28
2009	-2.49	-0.41	-0.76	-0.64	-3.98
2008	0.82	1.53	0.88	-1.08	2.13
2007	1.44	1.89	1.18	0.01	4.55
2006	1.46	1.49	1.47	1.39	5.82
2005	1.36	1.28	1.40	1.43	5.47

Fiscal year ended Dec. 31. Next earnings report expected: Late October. EPS Estimates based on S&P Operating Earnings; historical GAAP earnings are as reported.

Highlights

➤ The 12-month target price for STI has recently been changed to $27.00 from $25.00. The Highlights section of this Stock Report will be updated accordingly.

Investment Rationale/Risk

➤ The Investment Rationale/Risk section of this Stock Report will be updated shortly. For the latest News story on STI from MarketScope, see below.

➤ 10/21/10 09:41 am ET ... S&P MAINTAINS HOLD RECOMMENDATION ON SHARES OF SUN-TRUST BANKS INC (STI 26.3***): Q3 EPS of $0.17, vs. a $0.76 loss, beats our loss per share estimate of $0.14 on all-around improvements in loan loss provision, net interest income and noninterest income. On Q3 results and our higher noninterest income forecast for Q4, we have narrowed our '10 loss per share estimate to $0.28 loss from $0.63. On a recent increase in peer multiples, we raise our target price by $2 to $27, based on a discount to peers 1.4X our year end estimate of tangible book value per share. This equals a premium to peers 27.2X multiple on our unchanged '11 EPS estimate of $0.99. /E. Oja

Dividend Data (Dates: mm/dd Payment Date: mm/dd/yy)

Amount ($)	Date Decl.	Ex-Div. Date	Stk. of Record	Payment Date
0.010	11/10	11/27	12/01	12/15/09
0.010	02/09	02/25	03/01	03/15/10
0.010	04/27	05/27	06/01	06/15/10
0.010	08/10	08/30	09/01	09/15/10

Dividends have been paid since 1985. Source: Company reports.

The McGraw-Hill Companies

SunTrust Banks Inc.

STANDARD &POOR'S

Business Summary July 26, 2010

CORPORATE OVERVIEW. SunTrust Banks Inc. has four lines of business: Retail and Commercial Banking, Corporate and Investment Banking, Household Lending, and Wealth and Investment Management.

The Retail and Commercial Banking segment generated about 45% of total segment revenues in 2009, up from 43% in 2008. Retail Banking provides lending and deposit gathering as well as other banking-related products and services to consumers and small businesses with sales up to $10 million. Commercial Banking offers financial products and services, including commercial lending, treasury management, financial risk management, and corporate bankcard services, to enterprises with sales up to $250 million.

The Corporate and Investment Banking segment (13% of revenues in 2009, up from 10% in 2008) houses the company's corporate banking, investment banking, capital markets, commercial leasing and merchant banking activities. This segment focuses on companies with sales in excess of $250 million, and concentrates on small-cap and mid-cap growth companies, raising public and

private equity, and providing merger and acquisition advisory services for investment banking.

The Household Lending segment (18% of revenues in 2009, up from 13% in 2008) offers residential mortgage products nationally through its retail, broker and correspondent channels.

The Wealth and Investment Management segment (13% of revenues in 2009, down from 14% in 2008) provides wealth management products and professional services to individual and institutional clients. The remaining 11% (in 2009) and 20% (in 2008) of segment revenues are allocated to corporate, other, treasury, and reconciling items.

Company Financials Fiscal Year Ended Dec. 31

Per Share Data ($)	2009	2008	2007	2006	2005	2004	2003	2002	2001	2000
Tangible Book Value	22.28	33.72	28.41	26.04	24.67	23.13	29.73	25.46	26.67	25.07
Earnings	-3.98	2.13	4.55	5.82	5.47	5.19	4.73	4.66	4.70	4.30
S&P Core Earnings	-2.19	1.32	4.37	5.64	5.39	5.17	4.80	4.38	4.50	NA
Dividends	0.22	2.85	2.92	2.44	2.20	2.00	1.80	1.72	1.60	1.48
Payout Ratio	NM	134%	64%	42%	40%	39%	38%	37%	34%	34%
Prices:High	30.18	70.00	94.18	85.64	75.77	76.65	71.73	70.20	72.35	68.06
Prices:Low	6.00	19.75	60.02	69.68	65.32	61.27	51.44	51.48	57.29	41.63
P/E Ratio:High	NM	33	21	15	14	15	15	15	15	16
P/E Ratio:Low	NM	7	13	12	12	12	11	11	12	10

Income Statement Analysis (Million $)	2009	2008	2007	2006	2005	2004	2003	2002	2001	2000
Net Interest Income	4,466	4,620	4,720	4,660	4,579	3,685	3,320	3,244	3,253	3,108
Tax Equivalent Adjustment	123	118	103	87.9	75.5	NA	45.0	39.5	40.8	40.4
Non Interest Income	3,511	4,010	3,186	3,519	3,162	2,646	2,179	2,187	2,003	1,767
Loan Loss Provision	4,064	2,552	683	263	177	136	314	470	275	134
% Expense/Operating Revenue	82.3%	62.6%	66.2%	59.0%	60.6%	67.3%	68.4%	61.5%	59.2%	58.0%
Pretax Income	-2,327	728	2,250	2,986	2,866	2,257	1,909	1,823	2,020	1,920
Effective Tax Rate	NM	NM	27.4%	29.1%	30.7%	30.3%	30.2%	27.0%	32.2%	32.6%
Net Income	-1,564	796	1,634	2,117	1,987	1,573	1,332	1,332	1,369	1,294
% Net Interest Margin	3.04	3.10	3.11	3.00	3.16	3.15	3.08	3.41	3.58	3.55
S&P Core Earnings	-950	463	1,542	2,045	1,957	1,570	1,351	1,253	1,310	NA

Balance Sheet & Other Financial Data (Million $)	2009	2008	2007	2006	2005	2004	2003	2002	2001	2000
Money Market Assets	5,521	11,411	11,890	3,849	4,457	3,796	3,243	2,820	3,025	2,223
Investment Securities	28,477	19,697	16,264	25,102	26,526	28,941	25,607	23,445	19,656	18,810
Commercial Loans	32,494	27,926	48,539	47,182	33,764	31,824	30,682	28,694	28,946	30,781
Other Loans	78,061	96,721	73,780	74,273	80,791	69,602	50,050	44,474	40,013	41,459
Total Assets	174,165	189,289	179,574	182,162	179,714	158,870	125,393	117,323	104,741	103,496
Demand Deposits	24,244	21,522	21,083	22,887	41,973	30,979	24,185	21,250	19,200	15,064
Time Deposits	92,059	83,754	80,787	101,134	80,081	72,382	57,004	58,456	48,337	54,469
Long Term Debt	17,490	26,812	22,957	18,993	20,779	22,127	15,314	11,880	12,661	8,945
Common Equity	17,614	19,502	17,553	17,314	16,887	15,987	9,731	16,030	15,064	14,536
% Return on Assets	NM	0.4	0.9	1.2	1.2	1.1	1.1	1.2	1.3	1.3
% Return on Equity	NM	4.6	9.2	12.3	12.1	12.2	14.4	8.6	9.3	9.2
% Loan Loss Reserve	2.7	1.9	1.0	0.8	0.5	1.0	1.1	1.1	1.2	1.2
% Loans/Deposits	93.3	112.0	100.4	107.4	171.3	104.5	106.3	101.5	108.5	106.4
% Equity to Assets	10.2	9.4	9.6	9.5	9.7	9.1	7.6	14.0	14.2	14.2

Data as orig reptd.; bef. results of disc opers/spec. items. Per share data adj. for stk. divs.; EPS diluted. E-Estimated. NA-Not Available. NM-Not Meaningful. NR-Not Ranked. UR-Under Review.

Office: 303 Peachtree St NE, Atlanta, GA 30308-3201.
Telephone: 404-588-7711.
Website: http://www.suntrust.com
Chrmn & CEO: J.M. Wells, III

Pres: W.H. Rogers, Jr.
Investor Contact: M.A. Chancy (800-568-3476)
EVP & CFO: M.A. Chancy
EVP & Chief Admin Officer: D.F. Dierker

Board Members: R. Beall, II, A. D. Correll, J. C. Crowe, B. P. Garrett, Jr., D. H. Hughes, M. Ivester, J. H. Lanier, W. A. Linnenbringer, G. G. Minor, III, L. L. Prince, F. S. Royal, T. R. Watjen, J. M. Wells, III, K. H. Williams, P. Wynn, Jr.

Founded: 1891
Domicile: Georgia
Employees: 28,001

The McGraw·Hill Companies

SUPERVALU INC.

STANDARD & POOR'S

S&P Recommendation	HOLD ★★★☆☆	Price $10.80 (as of Oct 22, 2010)	12-Mo. Target Price $11.00	Investment Style Large-Cap Blend

GICS Sector Consumer Staples
Sub-Industry Food Retail

Summary This company, one of the largest U.S. food wholesalers, is also one of the biggest supermarket retailers in the U.S.

Key Stock Statistics (Source S&P, Vickers, company reports)

52-Wk Range	$17.89– 9.67	S&P Oper. EPS 2011**E**	1.55	Market Capitalization(B)	$2.291	Beta	1.06
Trailing 12-Month EPS	$1.63	S&P Oper. EPS 2012**E**	1.57	Yield (%)	3.24	S&P 3-Yr. Proj. EPS CAGR(%)	3
Trailing 12-Month P/E	6.6	P/E on S&P Oper. EPS 2011**E**	7.0	Dividend Rate/Share	$0.35	S&P Credit Rating	BB-
$10K Invested 5 Yrs Ago	$4,150	Common Shares Outstg. (M)	212.2	Institutional Ownership (%)	88		

Price Performance

30-Week Mov. Avg. · · · ·   10-Week Mov. Avg. – –   **GAAP Earnings vs. Previous Year**   Volume Above Avg. STARS
12-Mo. Target Price —   Relative Strength —   ▲ Up   ▼ Down   ► No Change   Below Avg. ★

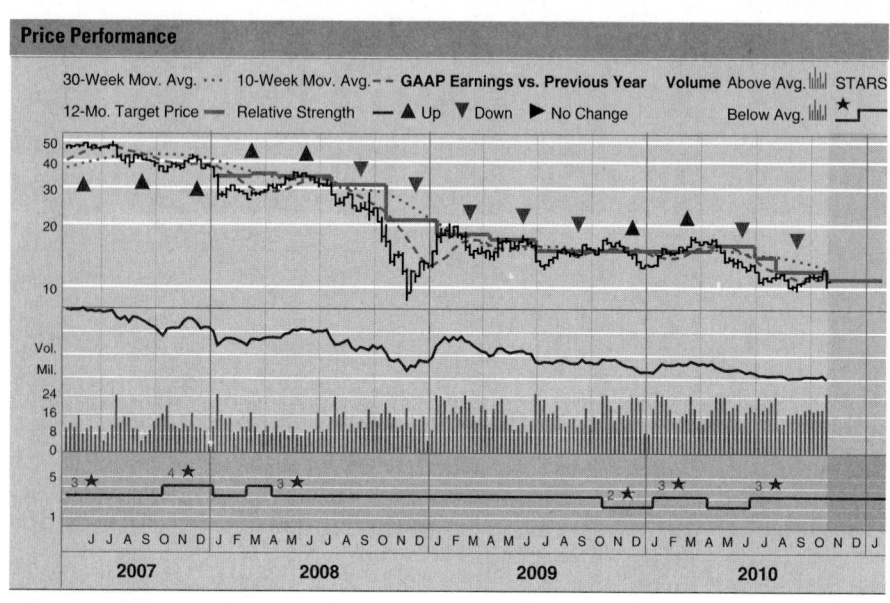

Options: CBOE, P, Ph

Highlights

➤ The 12-month target price for SVU has recently been changed to $11.00 from $12.00. The Highlights section of this Stock Report will be updated accordingly.

Investment Rationale/Risk

➤ The Investment Rationale/Risk section of this Stock Report will be updated shortly. For the latest News story on SVU from MarketScope, see below.

➤ 10/19/10 10:57 am ET ... S&P REITERATES HOLD RECOMMENDATION ON SHARES OF SUPERVALU INC (SVU 10.88***): Aug-Q operating EPS of $0.28, vs. $0.35, is $0.04 below our estimate. Results were hurt by a 6.4% decline in identical food store sales and negative sales leverage, despite more effective promotional spending. We expect turnaround of retail supermarkets to be a multiyear process with EPS growth restricted until completion. With implementation of marketing, merchandising and operational initiatives taking longer than we originally expected, we are reducing our FY 11 (Feb.) EPS estimate $0.20 to $1.55 and our target price by $1 to $11, on our comparative and EV/EBITDA analyses. /J.Agnese

Qualitative Risk Assessment

LOW	MEDIUM	HIGH

Our risk assessment reflects the intensely competitive environment in which the company operates, and threats of new entrants into its markets, partially offset by SVU's strong market share positions.

Quantitative Evaluations

S&P Quality Ranking B+

D	C	B-	B	B+	A-	A	A+

Relative Strength Rank WEAK

18

LOWEST = 1   HIGHEST = 99

Revenue/Earnings Data

Revenue (Million $)

	1Q	2Q	3Q	4Q	Year
2011	11,545	8,656	--	--	--
2010	12,715	9,461	9,216	9,205	40,597
2009	13,347	10,226	10,171	10,820	44,564
2008	13,292	10,159	10,211	10,386	44,048
2007	5,783	10,666	10,657	10,301	37,406
2006	5,972	4,556	4,695	4,640	19,864

Earnings Per Share ($)

2011	0.31	-6.94	E0.36	E0.48	E1.55
2010	0.53	0.35	0.51	0.46	1.85
2009	0.76	0.60	-13.95	-0.95	-13.51
2008	0.69	0.69	0.66	0.73	2.76
2007	0.57	0.61	0.54	0.57	2.32
2006	0.64	0.24	0.53	0.04	1.46

Fiscal year ended Feb. 28. Next earnings report expected: Mid January. EPS Estimates based on S&P Operating Earnings; historical GAAP earnings are as reported.

Dividend Data (Dates: mm/dd Payment Date: mm/dd/yy)

Amount ($)	Date Decl.	Ex-Div. Date	Stk. of Record	Payment Date
0.088	10/20	02/25	03/01	03/15/10
0.088	04/15	05/27	06/01	06/15/10
0.088	06/24	08/30	09/01	09/15/10
0.088	08/11	11/29	12/01	12/15/10

Dividends have been paid since 1936. Source: Company reports.

SUPERVALU INC.

Business Summary July 27, 2010

CORPORATE OVERVIEW. SUPERVALU, organized in 1925 as the successor to two wholesale grocery concerns established in the 1870s, has grown into the largest U.S. food distributor to supermarkets, and the second largest conventional food retailer in the U.S. Retail operations are conducted through limited assortment stores, food stores, and combination food and drug stores. As of February 2010, the company operated about 2,350 multi-format retail food stores and was the primary grocery supplier to approximately 1,940 stores in addition to its own retail operations.

CORPORATE STRATEGY. The company aims to leverage its retail food and supply chain services by benefiting from economies of scale and its low-cost supply chain network. The company operated 1,161 traditional food stores and 333 hard discount food stores as of February 2010. Traditional food store banners (Acme, Albertson's, Bristol Farms, Cub Foods, Farm Fresh, Hornbacher's, Jewel-Osco, Lucky, Shaw's, Shop 'n Save, Shoppers Food & Pharmacy and

Star Market) typically carry 40,000 to 50,000 items and average in size from 40,000 to 60,000 square feet.

Hard discount food stores include Save-A-Lot stores. The company licenses 855 Save-A-Lot stores to independent operators. Save-A-Lot food stores are typically 15,000 square feet and stock 1,400 high volume food items as well as a limited number of general merchandise items. The majority of food products offered for sale are private label products. The company positions itself to offer low prices by carrying a limited selection of the most frequently purchased goods. The majority of Save-A-Lot stores are found in small town/rural communities as opposed to urban and suburban locations.

Company Financials Fiscal Year Ended Feb. 28

Per Share Data ($)	2010	2009	2008	2007	2006	2005	2004	2003	2002	2001
Tangible Book Value	NM	NM	NM	NM	7.37	6.52	4.84	3.24	2.54	1.43
Cash Flow	6.34	-8.43	7.55	6.79	3.55	4.75	4.34	4.14	4.08	3.20
Earnings	1.85	-13.51	2.76	2.32	1.46	2.71	2.07	1.91	1.53	0.62
S&P Core Earnings	1.96	1.85	2.42	2.45	1.90	2.21	2.03	1.61	1.24	0.39
Dividends	0.61	0.69	0.66	0.64	0.60	0.58	0.57	0.56	0.55	0.54
Payout Ratio	33%	NM	24%	28%	41%	21%	27%	29%	36%	87%
Calendar Year	2009	2008	2007	2006	2005	2004	2003	2002	2001	2000
Prices:High	20.38	37.46	49.78	36.59	35.88	35.15	28.84	30.81	24.10	22.88
Prices:Low	12.13	8.59	34.46	26.14	29.55	25.70	12.60	14.75	12.60	11.75
P/E Ratio:High	11	NM	18	16	25	13	14	16	16	37
P/E Ratio:Low	7	NM	12	11	20	9	6	8	8	19

Income Statement Analysis (Million $)

	2010	2009	2008	2007	2006	2005	2004	2003	2002	2001
Revenue	40,597	44,564	44,048	37,406	19,864	19,543	20,210	19,160	20,909	23,194
Operating Income	2,243	2,682	2,788	2,058	750	936	919	870	904	860
Depreciation	957	1,077	1,030	879	311	303	302	297	341	344
Interest Expense	569	647	733	600	139	138	166	182	194	213
Pretax Income	632	-2,779	977	747	329	601	455	408	344	154
Effective Tax Rate	37.8%	NM	39.3%	39.5%	37.4%	35.8%	38.4%	37.0%	40.1%	46.8%
Net Income	393	-2,855	593	452	206	386	280	257	206	82.0
S&P Core Earnings	417	396	518	477	269	313	276	217	166	51.2

Balance Sheet & Other Financial Data (Million $)

	2010	2009	2008	2007	2006	2005	2004	2003	2002	2001
Cash	211	240	243	285	686	464	292	29.2	12.0	11.0
Current Assets	3,711	4,105	4,147	4,460	2,168	2,127	2,037	1,647	1,604	2,092
Total Assets	16,436	17,604	21,062	21,702	6,038	6,278	6,153	5,896	5,825	6,407
Current Liabilities	4,167	4,472	4,607	4,705	1,507	1,632	1,872	1,525	1,701	2,341
Long Term Debt	7,022	7,968	8,502	9,192	1,406	1,579	1,634	2,020	1,875	2,008
Common Equity	2,887	2,581	5,953	5,306	2,619	2,511	2,210	2,009	1,918	1,793
Total Capital	10,522	10,549	14,455	15,006	4,079	4,240	3,986	4,146	3,873	3,831
Capital Expenditures	681	1,186	1,191	837	308	233	328	383	293	398
Cash Flow	1,350	-1,778	1,623	1,331	517	689	582	554	547	426
Current Ratio	0.9	0.9	0.9	0.9	1.4	1.3	1.1	1.1	0.9	0.9
% Long Term Debt of Capitalization	66.7	75.5	58.8	61.3	34.5	37.2	41.0	48.7	48.4	52.4
% Net Income of Revenue	1.0	NM	1.4	1.2	1.0	2.0	1.4	1.3	1.0	0.4
% Return on Assets	2.3	NM	2.8	3.2	3.3	6.2	4.6	4.4	3.4	1.3
% Return on Equity	14.4	NM	10.5	11.4	8.0	16.3	13.3	13.2	11.1	4.5

Data as orig reptd.; bef. results of disc opers/spec. items. Per share data adj. for stk. divs.; EPS diluted. E-Estimated. NA-Not Available. NM-Not Meaningful. NR-Not Ranked. UR-Under Review.

Office: 11840 Valley View Road, Eden Prairie, MN 55344.
Telephone: 952-828-4000.
Website: http://www.supervalu.com
Pres & CEO: C. Herkert

EVP & CIO: W. Shurts
SVP, CFO & Chief Acctg Officer: S.M. Smith
Treas: J. Stoffel
Secy & General Counsel: T.N. Sheldon

Investor Contact: K. Levy (952-828-4540)
Board Members: D. R. Chappel, I. Cohen, R. E. Daly, S. E. Engel, P. Francis, E. C. Gage, C. Herkert, C. M. Lillis, S. S. Rogers, M. E. Rubel, W. C. Sales, K. P. Seifert

Founded: 1871
Domicile: Delaware
Employees: 160,000

Symantec Corp

STANDARD
&POOR'S

S&P Recommendation	HOLD ★★★☆☆	Price $15.70 (as of Oct 22, 2010)	12-Mo. Target Price $14.00	Investment Style Large-Cap Blend

GICS Sector Information Technology
Sub-Industry Systems Software

Summary This company provides software solutions that enable customers to protect their network infrastructure from potential threats and to store their data.

Key Stock Statistics (Source S&P, Vickers, company reports)

52-Wk Range	$19.16–12.04	S&P Oper. EPS 2011E	0.73	Market Capitalization(B)	$12.393	Beta	0.80
Trailing 12-Month EPS	$0.99	S&P Oper. EPS 2012E	0.77	Yield (%)	Nil	S&P 3-Yr. Proj. EPS CAGR(%)	9
Trailing 12-Month P/E	15.9	P/E on S&P Oper. EPS 2011E	21.5	Dividend Rate/Share	Nil	S&P Credit Rating	BBB
$10K Invested 5 Yrs Ago	$6,947	Common Shares Outstg. (M)	789.3	Institutional Ownership (%)	91		

Price Performance

30-Week Mov. Avg. · · · 10-Week Mov. Avg. - - **GAAP Earnings vs. Previous Year** Volume Above Avg. STARS
12-Mo. Target Price — Relative Strength — ▲ Up ▼ Down ▶ No Change Below Avg. ★

Options: ASE, CBOE, P, Ph

Analysis prepared by **Jim Yin, CFA** on August 03, 2010, when the stock traded at **$ 12.96**.

Highlights

▶ We project flat revenues in FY 11 (Mar.), compared to a 2.7% decline in FY 10. Although we forecast 5% growth in overall IT spending in 2010, we think SYMC will grow slower than the industry average because we see most of the growth in hardware, not in software. We believe SYMC's sales cycles on large contracts will remain elongated, as customers negotiate for more favorable terms. We also think the company is losing market share in the business segment. We see these adverse factors being partially offset by stronger growth in endpoint management, however. We think SYMC will benefit from vendor consolidation, as customers prefer better-capitalized vendors during economic uncertainty.

▶ We project gross margins in FY 11 of 82%, the same as in FY 10. We look for operating expenses at 66% of revenues in FY 11, up from 64% in FY 10 due to added employees from acquired companies. We forecast FY 11 operating margins of 15%, down from about 16% in FY 10.

▶ Our FY 11 EPS estimate is $0.73, compared to $0.87 in FY 10. The decrease reflects our projections for flat revenues and lower operating margins amid a challenging sales environment.

Investment Rationale/Risk

▶ Our Hold recommendation reflects our concern about SYMC's sluggish revenue growth. We think SYMC will grow slower than the industry's average due to loss in market share and its reliance on large contracts, which we think will remain difficult to close. However, we are positive on the company's cost-savings efforts, which we think will partially offset the weakness in revenue growth. We also think the security software sector will be less affected than other IT sectors if the economy falters, because of security software's mission-critical nature.

▶ Risks to our recommendation and target price include a weaker-than-expected recovery in the global economy, lower enterprise IT spending, and integration problems associated with recent acquisitions.

▶ Our 12-month target price of $14 is based on a weighted blend of our discounted cash flow (DCF) and P/E analyses. Our DCF model assumes a 12% WACC and 3% terminal growth, yielding an intrinsic value of $16. From our P/E analysis, we derive a value of $12 based on an industry P/E-to-growth ratio of 1.8X, or 16X our FY 11 EPS estimate of $0.73.

Qualitative Risk Assessment

LOW	MEDIUM	HIGH

Our risk assessment for Symantec reflects the highly competitive market in which the company operates and integration risks from recent acquisitions.

Quantitative Evaluations

S&P Quality Ranking   B

D	C	B-	B	B+	A-	A	A+

Relative Strength Rank   MODERATE

66

LOWEST = 1   HIGHEST = 99

Revenue/Earnings Data

Revenue (Million $)

	1Q	2Q	3Q	4Q	Year
2011	1,433	--	--	--	--
2010	1,432	1,474	1,548	1,531	5,985
2009	1,650	1,518	1,514	1,468	6,150
2008	1,400	1,419	1,515	1,540	5,874
2007	1,259	1,262	1,313	1,357	5,199
2006	699.9	1,056	1,149	1,239	4,143

Earnings Per Share ($)

	1Q	2Q	3Q	4Q	Year
2011	0.20	E0.14	E0.20	E0.20	E0.73
2010	0.09	0.19	0.37	0.19	0.87
2009	0.22	0.16	-8.23	-0.30	-8.10
2008	0.10	0.06	0.15	0.22	0.52
2007	0.09	0.12	0.12	0.07	0.41
2006	0.27	-0.21	0.08	0.11	0.15

Fiscal year ended Mar. 31. Next earnings report expected: Late October. EPS Estimates based on S&P Operating Earnings; historical GAAP earnings are as reported.

Dividend Data

No cash dividends have been paid.

Please read the Required Disclosures and Analyst Certification on the last page of this report.

The McGraw-Hill Companies

Symantec Corp

Business Summary August 03, 2010

CORPORATE OVERVIEW. Symantec Corp. (SYMC) is a provider of security, storage and systems management solutions that enable enterprises and consumers to protect their network infrastructure from potential threats and to archive and recover their data. Its products include virus protection, firewall, virtual private network, data protection, compliance, vulnerability management, intrusion detection, remote management technologies, and security services.

The company is organized into five operating segments:

Consumer Products -- focuses on Internet security. Key products include Norton 360 and Norton Internet Security, which protect against viruses, worms and other security risks; Norton AntiVirus, which removes viruses, Trojan horses and worms; and Norton SystemWorks, which enables users to maintain and optimize their computers. The Consumer Products segment accounted for 29% and 31% of total revenue in FY 09 (Mar.) and FY 10, respectively.

Security and Compliance -- provides security throughout the network, including behind the gateway and at the client level including servers, desktop PCs, laptops and other mobile devices. Its Information Risk Management solutions enforce data security policies on email, storage systems, and archiving. The

company's enterprise security solutions address the following areas: Antivirus, Antispam, Compliance, and Managed Security Services. The Security and Compliance segment accounted for 24% and 24% of total revenue in FY 09 and FY 10, respectively.

Storage and Server Management -- provides software solutions designed to protect, back up, archive and restore data across the enterprise. It also helps customers manage heterogeneous storage and server environments. This segment accounted for 40% and 38% of total revenue in FY 09 and FY 10, respectively.

Services -- assists SYMC's customers in implementing, supporting and maintaining their security, storage and infrastructure software solutions. Services accounted for 7% and 7% of total revenues in FY 09 and FY 10, respectively.

The Other segment is comprised of products nearing the end of their life cycle. Revenues were insignificant during FY 09 and FY 10.

Company Financials Fiscal Year Ended Mar. 31

Per Share Data ($)	2010	2009	2008	2007	2006	2005	2004	2003	2002	2001
Tangible Book Value	NM	NM	NM	NM	0.63	3.07	1.97	2.89	1.26	0.97
Cash Flow	1.77	-7.09	1.46	1.24	0.48	0.86	0.62	0.45	0.37	0.18
Earnings	0.87	-8.10	0.52	0.41	0.15	0.74	0.54	0.38	-0.05	0.12
S&P Core Earnings	0.83	NA	0.55	0.40	-0.06	0.59	0.43	0.26	-0.19	0.03
Dividends	Nil	Nil	Nil	Nil	Nil	Nil	Nil	Nil	Nil	Nil
Payout Ratio	Nil	Nil	Nil	Nil	Nil	Nil	Nil	Nil	Nil	Nil
Calendar Year	2009	2008	2007	2006	2005	2004	2003	2002	2001	2000
Prices:High	18.28	22.80	21.86	22.19	26.60	34.05	17.50	11.55	9.19	10.20
Prices:Low	12.54	10.05	15.97	14.78	16.32	17.27	9.09	6.80	3.90	3.42
P/E Ratio:High	21	NM	42	54	NM	46	33	30	78	NM
P/E Ratio:Low	14	NM	31	36	NM	23	17	18	33	NM

Income Statement Analysis (Million $)										
Revenue	5,985	6,150	5,874	5,199	4,143	2,583	1,870	1,407	1,071	854
Operating Income	1,790	1,918	1,597	1,402	942	926	611	417	269	240
Depreciation	733	837	824	811	340	96.3	78.8	59.6	238	105
Interest Expense	129	29.7	29.5	27.2	18.0	12.3	21.2	21.2	9.17	Nil
Pretax Income	826	-6,507	713	632	363	858	542	364	45.5	141
Effective Tax Rate	13.6%	NM	34.9%	36.0%	56.8%	37.5%	31.6%	31.7%	NM	54.6%
Net Income	714	-6,729	464	404	157	536	371	248	-28.2	63.9
S&P Core Earnings	683	NA	488	393	-51.0	423	284	157	-106	14.8

Balance Sheet & Other Financial Data (Million $)										
Cash	3,044	1,991	2,427	2,559	2,316	1,091	2,410	1,706	1,375	557
Current Assets	4,351	3,300	3,730	4,071	3,908	3,688	2,842	1,988	1,563	782
Total Assets	11,232	10,645	18,092	17,751	17,913	5,614	4,456	3,266	2,503	1,792
Current Liabilities	3,771	3,514	3,800	3,318	3,478	1,701	1,287	895	579	413
Long Term Debt	1,871	2,100	2,100	2,100	24.9	4.41	606	607	604	2.36
Common Equity	4,548	3,948	10,973	11,602	13,668	3,705	2,426	1,764	1,320	1,377
Total Capital	6,419	6,100	13,293	14,045	14,187	3,798	3,077	2,371	1,924	1,379
Capital Expenditures	248	272	274	420	267	91.5	111	192	141	61.2
Cash Flow	1,447	-5,892	1,288	1,216	497	633	453	308	210	95.9
Current Ratio	1.2	0.9	1.0	1.2	1.1	2.2	2.2	2.2	31.3	1.9
% Long Term Debt of Capitalization	29.2	34.4	15.8	15.0	0.2	0.1	19.7	25.6	0.3	0.2
% Net Income of Revenue	11.9	NM	7.9	7.8	3.8	20.8	19.8	17.7	NM	7.5
% Return on Assets	6.5	NM	2.6	2.3	1.3	10.6	9.6	8.6	NM	4.8
% Return on Equity	16.8	NM	4.1	3.2	1.8	17.5	17.7	16.1	NM	6.4

Data as orig reptd.; bef. results of disc opers/spec. items. Per share data adj. for stk. divs.; EPS diluted. E-Estimated. NA-Not Available. NM-Not Meaningful. NR-Not Ranked. UR-Under Review.

Office: 350 Ellis Street, Mountain View, CA 94043.
Telephone: 650-527-8000.
Email: investor-relations@symantec.com
Website: http://www.symantec.com

Chrmn: J. Thompson
Pres & CEO: E.T. Salem
EVP & CFO: J. Beer
EVP & CTO: M.F. Bregman

EVP, Secy & General Counsel: S.C. Taylor
Investor Contact: H. Corcos (408-517-8324)
Board Members: S. M. Bennett, M. A. Brown, W. T. Coleman, III, F. E. Dangeard, G. B. Laybourne, D. L. Mahoney, R. S. Miller, Jr., E. T. Salem, D. H. Schulman, J. Thompson, V. P. Unruh

Founded: 1983
Domicile: Delaware
Employees: 17,400

The McGraw·Hill Companies

Sysco Corp

STANDARD
&POOR'S

S&P Recommendation HOLD ★★★☆☆	**Price** $29.56 (as of Oct 22, 2010)	**12-Mo. Target Price** $31.00	**Investment Style** Large-Cap Blend

GICS Sector Consumer Staples
Sub-Industry Food Distributors

Summary This company is the largest U.S. marketer and distributor of foodservice products.

Key Stock Statistics (Source S&P, Vickers, company reports)

52-Wk Range	$31.99– 25.93	S&P Oper. EPS 2011E	1.95	Market Capitalization(B)	$17.393	Beta	0.74
Trailing 12-Month EPS	$1.99	S&P Oper. EPS 2012E	NA	Yield (%)	3.38	S&P 3-Yr. Proj. EPS CAGR(%)	4
Trailing 12-Month P/E	14.9	P/E on S&P Oper. EPS 2011E	15.2	Dividend Rate/Share	$1.00	S&P Credit Rating	AA-
$10K Invested 5 Yrs Ago	$10,668	Common Shares Outstg. (M)	588.4	Institutional Ownership (%)	74		

Price Performance

30-Week Mov. Avg. · · · ·   10-Week Mov. Avg. – – – **GAAP Earnings vs. Previous Year**   Volume Above Avg. ▮▮▮ STARS
12-Mo. Target Price —   Relative Strength — ▲ Up ▼ Down ▶ No Change   Below Avg. ▮▮▮ ★

[Price chart showing 2007, 2008, 2009, 2010 with volume bars]

Options: ASE, CBOE, P

Analysis prepared by **Tom Graves, CFA** on August 19, 2010, when the stock traded at **$ 28.90**.

Highlights

➤ In FY 11 (June), we look for SYY's revenue to increase about 3% from $37.2 billion reported for FY 10, which included 53 weeks. We have a generally cautious outlook regarding SYY's most important end market -- restaurants.

➤ We look for productivity gains to bolster profit margins, but expect that costs related to a Business Transformation Project, including adoption of an SAP platform, will have a negative impact on margins in FY 11. Over time, we look for SYY's profitability to benefit from more consolidated purchasing, the addition of regional distribution centers, improved management of freight costs, and better inventory management.

➤ Our FY 11 EPS estimate is $1.95, vs. 53-week FY 10's $1.99. We expect some difficult EPS comparisons in FY 11 as FY 10 included roughly a $0.13 contribution from corporate-owned life insurance, a tax benefit, and an extra week. Also, in FY 11, we look for pension expense to be about $0.06 higher than it was in FY 10, and we expect higher spending in FY 11 related to a software system project.

Investment Rationale/Risk

➤ For the long term, we expect SYY to experience internal growth and to make additional acquisitions. We think SYY will at least maintain market share during the current difficult period for restaurant sales, which we believe is caused by the weak consumer discretionary environment. Restaurants accounted for 62% of SYY's FY 09 sales.

➤ Risks to our recommendation and target price include a slowing of growth rates given SYY's significant size and reach, sharp increases in gasoline prices, and a potential prolonged slowdown in restaurant sales.

➤ Our 12-month target price of $31 is a blend of our historical and relative analyses. Our historical analysis applies a P/E multiple toward the low end of the 10-year forward P/E range, to our calendar 2010 EPS estimate of $1.95. Our target multiple reflects what we see as the decreased likelihood of SYY consistently achieving its former sales growth rates, given its size and S&P's negative outlook for the restaurant sub-industry. Our peer analysis applies a premium P/E to the average of a small group of other food distributor stocks, suggesting a value of $31.

Qualitative Risk Assessment

LOW	MEDIUM	HIGH

Our risk assessment reflects SYY's operations in a relatively stable industry, in which we believe it has the largest market share.

Quantitative Evaluations

S&P Quality Ranking   A+

D	C	B-	B	B+	A-	A	A+

Relative Strength Rank   MODERATE

42

LOWEST = 1   HIGHEST = 99

Revenue/Earnings Data

Revenue (Million $)

	1Q	2Q	3Q	4Q	Year
2010	9,081	8,869	8,945	10,348	37,244
2009	9,877	9,150	8,739	9,087	36,853
2008	9,406	9,240	9,147	9,730	37,522
2007	8,672	8,569	8,573	9,228	35,042
2006	8,010	7,971	8,138	8,509	32,628
2005	7,532	7,331	7,437	7,981	30,282

Earnings Per Share ($)

2010	0.55	0.41	0.42	0.57	1.99
2009	0.46	0.40	0.38	0.53	1.77
2008	0.43	0.43	0.40	0.55	1.81
2007	0.37	0.39	0.35	0.49	1.60
2006	0.31	0.33	0.30	0.41	1.35
2005	0.35	0.36	0.34	0.44	1.47

Fiscal year ended Jun. 30. Next earnings report expected: Early November. EPS Estimates based on S&P Operating Earnings; historical GAAP earnings are as reported.

Dividend Data (Dates: mm/dd Payment Date: mm/dd/yy)

Amount ($)	Date Decl.	Ex-Div. Date	Stk. of Record	Payment Date
0.250	11/17	12/29	12/31	01/22/10
0.250	02/19	03/30	04/01	04/23/10
0.250	05/21	06/30	07/02	07/23/10
0.250	08/27	09/29	10/01	10/22/10

Dividends have been paid since 1970. Source: Company reports.

Please read the Required Disclosures and Analyst Certification on the last page of this report.

The McGraw·Hill Companies

Sysco Corp

STANDARD &POOR'S

Business Summary August 19, 2010

CORPORATE OVERVIEW. Sysco is the largest distributor of foodservice products in the U.S. and Canada. As of June 2009, it operated 186 distribution facilities in the U.S., Canada and Ireland. The company provides products and services to approximately 400,000 customers, including restaurants (62% of FY 09 sales), hospitals and nursing homes (11%), schools and colleges (5%), hotels and motels (6%), and others (16%).

Sysco distributes food products, including frozen foods such as meats, fully prepared entrees, fruits, vegetables and desserts; canned and dry foods; fresh meats; imported specialties; and fresh produce. The company also distributes non-food products. These include paper products, tableware such as china and silverware, cookware, restaurant and kitchen equipment and supplies, and cleaning supplies. The company stresses prompt and accurate delivery of orders, and close contact with customers, and also provides customers with ancillary services, such as providing product usage reports, menu-planning advice, food safety training, and assistance in inventory control. No single customer accounted for 10% or more of sales in FY 09.

CORPORATE STRATEGY. SYY seeks to expand its business by garnering an increased share of products purchased by existing customers, the development of new customers, the use of foldouts (new facilities built in established markets), and an acquisition program. SYY distributes nationally branded merchandise, as well as products packaged under SYY private brands. We believe that Sysco-branded products typically carry wider profit margins than other branded products distributed by the company. From its inception through the end of FY 09, the company had acquired about 150 companies or divisions of companies. At July 3, 2010, SYY's balance sheet included $1.550 billion of goodwill.

Over time, we look for SYY's profitability to benefit from an increased amount of consolidated purchasing, the addition of regional distribution centers, improved management of freight costs, and better inventory management. Among SYY's supply chain initiatives are (1) the construction of regional distribution centers (RDCs); SYY expects to build five to seven of these centers, with two already operational; and (2) improving the capability to view and manage all of SYY's inbound freight, both to RDCs and the operating companies, as a network and not as individual locations. FY 08 was the first full year SYY operated under this initiative. During FY 09, SYY began the design of an enterprise-wide project to implement an integrated software system to support the majority of its business processes.

Company Financials Fiscal Year Ended Jun. 30

Per Share Data ($)	2010	2009	2008	2007	2006	2005	2004	2003	2002	2001
Tangible Book Value	3.69	3.08	3.17	2.99	2.67	2.35	2.11	1.68	1.85	2.07
Cash Flow	2.64	2.41	2.41	2.23	1.89	1.96	1.80	1.59	1.47	1.27
Earnings	1.99	1.77	1.81	1.60	1.35	1.47	1.37	1.18	1.01	0.88
S&P Core Earnings	2.06	1.65	1.68	1.59	1.38	1.39	1.31	1.08	0.92	0.82
Dividends	0.99	1.16	0.82	0.72	0.64	0.56	0.48	0.40	0.32	0.23
Payout Ratio	50%	66%	45%	45%	47%	38%	35%	34%	32%	26%
Prices:High	31.99	29.48	35.00	36.74	37.04	38.04	41.27	37.57	32.58	30.12
Prices:Low	26.99	19.39	20.74	29.90	26.50	29.98	29.48	22.90	21.25	21.75
P/E Ratio:High	16	17	19	23	27	26	30	32	32	34
P/E Ratio:Low	14	11	11	19	20	20	22	19	21	25

Income Statement Analysis (Million $)	2010	2009	2008	2007	2006	2005	2004	2003	2002	2001
Revenue	37,244	36,853	37,522	35,042	32,628	30,282	29,335	26,140	23,351	21,784
Operating Income	2,366	2,255	2,246	2,071	1,840	1,906	1,816	1,597	1,439	1,286
Depreciation	390	382	366	363	345	317	284	273	278	248
Interest Expense	125	116	118	105	109	75.0	69.9	72.2	62.9	71.0
Pretax Income	1,850	1,771	1,791	1,621	1,395	1,525	1,475	1,260	1,101	967
Effective Tax Rate	NA	40.4%	38.3%	38.3%	39.3%	37.0%	38.5%	38.3%	38.3%	38.3%
Net Income	1,180	1,056	1,106	1,001	846	961	907	778	680	597
S&P Core Earnings	1,219	987	1,022	995	866	890	868	710	618	559

Balance Sheet & Other Financial Data (Million $)	2010	2009	2008	2007	2006	2005	2004	2003	2002	2001
Cash	609	1,087	552	208	202	192	200	421	230	136
Current Assets	5,076	5,271	5,175	4,676	4,400	4,002	3,851	3,630	3,185	2,985
Total Assets	10,314	10,322	10,082	9,519	8,992	8,268	7,848	6,937	5,990	5,469
Current Liabilities	3,009	3,150	3,499	3,415	3,226	3,458	3,127	2,701	2,239	2,090
Long Term Debt	2,473	2,467	1,975	1,758	1,627	956	1,231	1,249	1,176	961
Common Equity	3,828	3,450	3,409	3,278	3,052	2,759	2,565	2,198	2,133	2,148
Total Capital	6,308	6,444	5,925	5,037	5,403	4,440	4,483	3,945	3,750	3,379
Capital Expenditures	595	465	516	603	515	390	530	436	416	341
Cash Flow	1,570	1,438	1,473	1,364	1,191	1,278	1,191	1,051	958	845
Current Ratio	1.7	1.7	1.5	1.4	1.4	1.2	1.2	1.3	1.4	1.4
% Long Term Debt of Capitalization	39.2	38.3	33.3	34.9	30.1	21.5	27.4	31.7	31.4	28.4
% Net Income of Revenue	3.2	2.9	3.0	2.9	2.6	3.2	3.1	3.0	2.9	2.7
% Return on Assets	11.5	10.4	11.3	10.8	9.8	11.9	12.3	12.0	12.0	11.6
% Return on Equity	32.4	30.8	33.1	31.6	29.1	36.1	38.1	35.9	32.1	30.5

Data as orig reptd.; bef. results of disc opers/spec. items. Per share data adj. for stk. divs.; EPS diluted. E-Estimated. NA-Not Available. NM-Not Meaningful. NR-Not Ranked. UR-Under Review.

Office: 1390 Enclave Parkway, Houston, TX, USA 77077-2099.
Telephone: 281-584-1390.
Website: http://www.sysco.com
Chrmn: M.A. Fernandez

Pres & CEO: W.J. DeLaney, III
EVP & CFO: R.C. Kreidler
SVP, Chief Acctg Officer & Cntlr: G.M. Elmer
SVP & Treas: K.G. Drummond

Board Members: J. M. Cassaday, J. L. Craven, W. J. DeLaney, III, M. A. Fernandez, L. C. Glasscock, J. Golden, J. A. Hafner, Jr., H. Koerber, N. S. Newcomb, P. S. Sewell, R. G. Tilghman, J. M. Ward

Founded: 1969
Domicile: Delaware
Employees: 46,000

The McGraw-Hill Companies

Target Corp

S&P Recommendation	BUY ★★★★☆	Price $53.87 (as of Oct 22, 2010)	12-Mo. Target Price $60.00	Investment Style Large-Cap Growth

GICS Sector Consumer Discretionary
Sub-Industry General Merchandise Stores

Summary This company operates about 1,490 Target and 250 SuperTarget general merchandise stores across the U.S.

Key Stock Statistics (Source S&P, Vickers, company reports)

52-Wk Range	$58.52– 45.11	S&P Oper. EPS 2011**E**	3.90	Market Capitalization(B)	$38.864	Beta	1.00
Trailing 12-Month EPS	$3.64	S&P Oper. EPS 2012**E**	4.40	Yield (%)	1.86	S&P 3-Yr. Proj. EPS CAGR(%)	20
Trailing 12-Month P/E	14.8	P/E on S&P Oper. EPS 2011**E**	13.8	Dividend Rate/Share	$1.00	S&P Credit Rating	A+
$10K Invested 5 Yrs Ago	$10,476	Common Shares Outstg. (M)	721.4	Institutional Ownership (%)	87		

Price Performance

- 30-Week Mov. Avg. ···
- 10-Week Mov. Avg. --
- **GAAP Earnings vs. Previous Year**
- Volume Above Avg. ▮▮▮ STARS
- 12-Mo. Target Price —
- Relative Strength
- ▲ Up ▼ Down ► No Change
- Below Avg. ▮▮▮ ☆

Options: ASE, CBOE, Ph

Analysis prepared by **Jason N. Asaeda** on August 19, 2010, when the stock traded at **$ 51.97**.

Highlights

▶ We look for a low-single digit same-store sales increase in FY 11 (Jan.), supported by an accelerated remodel program that will add fresh food to 340 Target stores; a growing assortment of value-priced consumables, including new value-priced "up & up" private label merchandise (encompassing about 800 items across 40 categories); what we see as TGT's success in better marketing its value proposition to consumers; and steps the company is taking to better align store assortments with customer preferences and in matching competitor's pricing. Also factoring in our expectations of 10 net new store openings and lower credit revenues, we see revenues reaching $67.5 billion in FY 11.

▶ We look for faster sales growth in lower-margin consumables to be offset by higher merchandise markups, supported by direct imports and disciplined inventory management, a recovery in sales of discretionary categories, and well-controlled dollar expense growth. We also anticipate a reduction in bad debt expense.

▶ Assuming moderate share repurchase activity, we forecast EPS of $3.90 in FY 11.

Investment Rationale/Risk

▶ Our buy recommendation is based on valuation. While we anticipate a slow and uneven economic recovery, we look for TGT to accelerate same-store sales growth over the balance of FY 11 and into FY 12, supported by higher traffic and cross-shopping of categories the company is seeing in PFresh format stores; our view of improving apparel and home assortments; and incremental sales we expect from a new 5% discount REDcard (Target Credit Card, Target Visa Credit Card, or Target Check Card) holders will receive on all purchases beginning in mid-October. We also think TGT is doing a good job of managing its flow of goods, which is limiting markdown risk, and look for continued strengthening of credit card segment metrics.

▶ Risks to our recommendation and target price include a loss of business due to changes in consumer confidence, spending habits, and buying preferences, as well as increased promotional activity by competitors.

▶ Our 12-month target price of $60 is based on a peer-average forward P/E multiple of 15.3X applied to our FY 11 EPS estimate.

Qualitative Risk Assessment

LOW	MEDIUM	HIGH

Our risk assessment reflects our view of TGT's fairly consistent earnings track record, and its healthy balance sheet and cash flow, offset by our concerns over potential loss of market share as a result of lackluster merchandising and aggressive pricing by competitors.

Quantitative Evaluations

S&P Quality Ranking — A+

D	C	B-	B	B+	A-	A	A+

Relative Strength Rank — MODERATE

40

LOWEST = 1 HIGHEST = 99

Revenue/Earnings Data

Revenue (Million $)

	1Q	2Q	3Q	4Q	Year
2011	15,593	15,532	--	--	--
2010	14,833	15,067	15,276	20,181	65,357
2009	14,302	15,472	15,114	19,560	64,948
2008	14,041	14,620	14,835	19,872	63,367
2007	12,863	13,347	13,570	19,710	59,490
2006	11,477	11,990	12,206	16,947	52,620

Earnings Per Share ($)

2011	0.90	0.92	E0.69	E1.39	E3.90
2010	0.69	0.79	0.58	1.24	3.30
2009	0.74	0.82	0.49	0.81	2.86
2008	0.75	0.82	0.56	1.23	3.33
2007	0.63	0.70	0.59	1.29	3.21
2006	0.55	0.61	0.49	1.06	2.71

Fiscal year ended Jan. 31. Next earnings report expected: Mid November. EPS Estimates based on S&P Operating Earnings; historical GAAP earnings are as reported.

Dividend Data (Dates: mm/dd Payment Date: mm/dd/yy)

Amount ($)	Date Decl.	Ex-Div. Date	Stk. of Record	Payment Date
0.170	03/11	05/18	05/20	06/10/10
0.250	06/09	08/18	08/20	09/10/10
0.250	06/09	08/18	08/20	09/10/10
0.250	09/09	11/17	11/20	12/10/10

Dividends have been paid since 1965. Source: Company reports.

Please read the Required Disclosures and Analyst Certification on the last page of this report.

The McGraw-Hill Companies

Target Corp

Business Summary August 19, 2010

CORPORATE PROFILE. In FY 05 (Jan.), Target Corp. (TGT) shed its non-core legacy department store operations, retaining only its eponymous chain of upscale general merchandise stores that cater to middle- and upper-income consumers. As of July 31, 2010, the company operated 1,492 Target locations, and 251 SuperTarget stores. SuperTarget stores combine a full line of groceries with fashion apparel, electronics, home furnishings and other general merchandise found in Target stores. TGT's Web site serves as both a sales driver and a marketing vehicle. Target.com offers a more extensive selection of merchandise than the company's physical stores, including exclusive online products. To support sales and earnings growth, TGT offers credit to qualified customers. In FY 10, its credit card operations contributed $1.9 billion of revenues.

PRIMARY BUSINESS DYNAMICS. TGT's primary growth drivers are new store openings and same-store sales (sales results for stores open for over one year). From FY 05 through FY 10, the company increased its retail square footage at a compound annual growth rate (CAGR) of 5.9%, as its store count rose from 1,308 to 1,740. Having added a net of 46 Target and 12 SuperTarget locations to its store base in FY 10, TGT plans to add approximately 10 net new stores and to remodel 340 stores in FY 11.

Company Financials Fiscal Year Ended Jan. 31

Per Share Data ($)	2010	2009	2008	2007	2006	2005	2004	2003	2002	2001
Tangible Book Value	20.47	18.10	18.44	18.17	16.25	14.63	12.14	10.38	8.68	7.27
Cash Flow	5.98	5.22	5.30	4.93	4.29	3.45	3.45	3.14	2.70	2.41
Earnings	3.30	2.86	3.33	3.21	2.71	2.07	2.01	1.81	1.51	1.38
S&P Core Earnings	3.27	2.73	3.32	3.21	2.68	2.06	1.95	1.70	1.42	1.37
Dividends	0.66	0.60	0.44	0.36	0.30	0.26	0.26	0.24	0.21	0.20
Payout Ratio	20%	21%	13%	11%	11%	13%	13%	13%	14%	14%
Calendar Year	2009	2008	2007	2006	2005	2004	2003	2002	2001	2000
Prices:High	51.77	59.55	70.75	60.34	60.00	54.14	41.80	46.15	41.74	39.19
Prices:Low	25.00	25.60	48.85	44.70	45.55	36.63	25.60	24.90	26.00	21.63
P/E Ratio:High	16	21	21	19	22	26	21	25	28	28
P/E Ratio:Low	8	9	15	14	17	18	13	14	17	16

Income Statement Analysis (Million $)

	2010	2009	2008	2007	2006	2005	2004	2003	2002	2001
Revenue	65,357	64,948	63,367	59,490	52,620	46,839	48,163	43,917	39,888	36,903
Operating Income	6,696	6,228	6,931	6,565	5,732	4,860	4,839	4,476	3,759	3,418
Depreciation	2,023	1,826	1,659	1,496	1,409	1,259	1,320	1,212	1,079	940
Interest Expense	804	894	747	597	532	674	559	588	464	425
Pretax Income	3,872	3,536	4,625	4,497	3,860	3,031	2,960	2,676	2,216	2,053
Effective Tax Rate	35.7%	37.4%	38.4%	38.0%	37.6%	37.8%	37.8%	38.2%	38.0%	38.4%
Net Income	2,488	2,214	2,849	2,787	2,408	1,885	1,841	1,654	1,374	1,264
S&P Core Earnings	2,469	2,117	2,841	2,784	2,383	1,876	1,791	1,553	1,289	1,247

Balance Sheet & Other Financial Data (Million $)

	2010	2009	2008	2007	2006	2005	2004	2003	2002	2001
Cash	2,200	864	2,450	813	1,648	2,245	716	758	499	356
Current Assets	18,424	17,488	18,906	14,706	14,405	13,922	12,928	11,935	9,648	7,304
Total Assets	44,533	44,106	44,560	37,349	34,995	32,293	31,392	28,603	24,154	19,490
Current Liabilities	11,327	10,512	11,782	11,117	9,588	8,220	8,314	7,523	7,054	6,301
Long Term Debt	15,118	17,371	15,126	8,675	9,119	9,034	10,217	10,186	8,088	5,634
Common Equity	15,347	13,712	15,307	15,633	14,205	13,029	11,065	9,443	7,860	6,519
Total Capital	32,161	31,538	30,903	24,885	24,175	23,036	21,282	21,080	15,948	12,153
Capital Expenditures	1,729	3,547	4,369	3,928	3,388	3,068	3,004	3,221	3,163	2,528
Cash Flow	4,511	4,040	4,508	4,283	3,817	3,144	3,161	2,866	2,453	2,204
Current Ratio	1.6	1.7	1.6	1.3	1.5	1.7	1.6	1.6	1.4	1.2
% Long Term Debt of Capitalization	47.0	55.1	49.0	34.9	37.7	39.2	48.0	48.3	50.7	46.4
% Net Income of Revenue	3.8	3.4	4.5	4.7	4.5	4.0	3.8	3.8	3.4	3.4
% Return on Assets	5.6	5.0	7.0	7.7	7.1	5.9	6.1	6.3	6.3	6.9
% Return on Equity	17.1	15.3	18.4	18.7	17.6	15.6	18.0	19.1	19.1	20.4

Data as orig reptd.; bef. results of disc opers/spec. items. Per share data adj. for stk. divs.; EPS diluted. E-Estimated. NA-Not Available. NM-Not Meaningful. NR-Not Ranked. UR-Under Review.

Office: 1000 Nicollet Mall, Minneapolis, MN 55403-2467.
Telephone: 612-304-6073.
Website: http://www.target.com
Chrmn, Pres & CEO: G.W. Steinhafel

Investor Contact: D.A. Scovanner
EVP, CFO & Chief Acctg Officer: D.A. Scovanner
EVP, Secy & General Counsel: T.R. Baer
CTO & CIO: B.M. Jacob

Board Members: R. S. Austin, C. Darden, M. N. Dillon, J. A. Johnson, R. M. Kovacevich, M. E. Minnick, A. M. Mulcahy, D. W. Rice, S. W. Sanger, G. W. Steinhafel, J. G. Stumpf, S. Trujillo
Founded: 1902
Domicile: Minnesota
Employees: 351,000

TECO Energy Inc.

STANDARD &POOR'S

S&P Recommendation 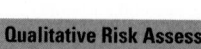 BUY ★★★★☆

Price	12-Mo. Target Price	Investment Style
$17.75 (as of Oct 22, 2010)	$18.00	Large-Cap Value

GICS Sector Utilities
Sub-Industry Multi-Utilities

Summary This company owns Tampa Electric Co., which serves the Tampa Bay region in west central Florida and has significant diversified operations related to its core business.

Key Stock Statistics (Source S&P, Vickers, company reports)

52-Wk Range	$18.11–13.71	S&P Oper. EPS 2010E	1.36	Market Capitalization(B)	$3.809	Beta	0.88
Trailing 12-Month EPS	$1.16	S&P Oper. EPS 2011E	1.42	Yield (%)	4.62	S&P 3-Yr. Proj. EPS CAGR(%)	9
Trailing 12-Month P/E	15.3	P/E on S&P Oper. EPS 2010E	13.1	Dividend Rate/Share	$0.82	S&P Credit Rating	BBB
$10K Invested 5 Yrs Ago	$14,044	Common Shares Outstg. (M)	214.6	Institutional Ownership (%)	55		

Price Performance

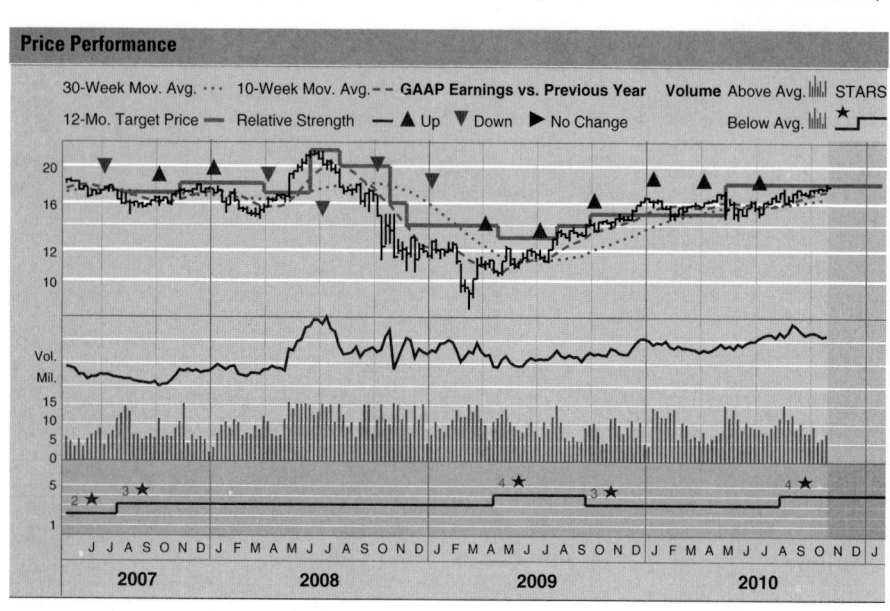

30-Week Mov. Avg. · · · 10-Week Mov. Avg. - - GAAP Earnings vs. Previous Year   Volume Above Avg. ▥ STARS
12-Mo. Target Price — Relative Strength   — ▲ Up ▼ Down ▶ No Change   Below Avg. ▥   ★

Options: Ph

Analysis prepared by **Justin McCann** on August 16, 2010, when the stock traded at **$ 16.33**.

Highlights

➤ Excluding one-time charges of $0.10, we expect operating EPS in 2010 to grow more than 25% from 2009's $1.08. In addition to the exceptionally cold weather in the first quarter and the unusually warm weather in the second, operating EPS in the first half of 2010 was aided by higher prices and demand for products at TECO Coal, largely driven by the recovery in the steel markets. Earnings at TE's Guatemala subsidiary remained essentially flat.

➤ For full-year 2010, we expect operating EPS to benefit from rate increases (partially offset by an expected $0.07 refund to customers), the very favorable weather, and the strength at the coal operations. While we remain cautious about the extent of the recovery, we are encouraged by signs of improvement in the local housing market. For 2011, we expect earnings to reflect a rate increase, a modest recovery in the economy, and a still strong coal market.

➤ Given the current strength of certain coal markets, we expect the TECO Coal subsidiary to have sales of approximately 9 million tons in 2010, at an average selling price of almost $77 a ton. The cost of production is expected to be $65 to $69 per ton.

Investment Rationale/Risk

➤ We recently raised our recommendation on the shares to buy, from hold. Given the attractive yield from the dividend (recently at 5.0%), we believe the stock has become attractive for above-average total return. The performance of the shares has been relatively flat year to date. This follows a gain of more than 30% in 2009 that reflected, in our view, the rate increases implemented in May 2009, the anticipation of the one implemented in January 2010, and a well-above-peers yield from the dividend. Earlier, we believe the stock was hurt by the weak economy and housing market, as well as by the rise in the coal operation's production costs and the slowing of international demand.

➤ Risks to our recommendation and target price include prolonged weakness in the housing market, a sharp decrease in the average P/E of the electric utility group as a whole, and much lower than anticipated earnings from the non-regulated coal operations.

➤ While TE's dividend represented 76% of its operating EPS in 2009, it is expected to represent only 60% of our EPS estimate for 2010. Our 12-month target price is $18, an approximate peer P/E of 12.7X our 2011 forecast.

Qualitative Risk Assessment

LOW	MEDIUM	HIGH

Our risk assessment reflects the steady cash flow we expect from the regulated electric and gas utilities, which operate within a generally supportive regulatory environment, offset by our view of the much less predictable earnings and cash flow from the unregulated coal and transport operations, particularly given uncertainties concerning tax credits related to the synthetic fuel operations.

Quantitative Evaluations

S&P Quality Ranking   B

D	C	B-	B	B+	A-	A	A+

Relative Strength Rank   MODERATE

56

LOWEST = 1   HIGHEST = 99

Revenue/Earnings Data

Revenue (Million $)

	1Q	2Q	3Q	4Q	Year
2010	912.3	898.8	--	--	--
2009	824.0	825.2	896.3	765.0	3,311
2008	791.7	887.2	926.1	770.3	3,375
2007	821.3	866.5	990.0	858.3	3,536
2006	836.4	862.6	922.9	826.2	3,448
2005	684.7	719.0	836.4	770.0	3,010

Earnings Per Share ($)

	1Q	2Q	3Q	4Q	Year
2010	0.26	0.35	E0.42	E0.25	E1.36
2009	0.16	0.29	0.30	0.25	1.00
2008	0.15	0.24	0.27	0.10	0.77
2007	0.35	0.28	0.44	0.83	1.90
2006	0.26	0.29	0.38	0.23	1.17
2005	0.25	0.04	0.45	0.24	1.00

Fiscal year ended Dec. 31. Next earnings report expected: Early November. EPS Estimates based on S&P Operating Earnings; historical GAAP earnings are as reported.

Dividend Data (Dates: mm/dd Payment Date: mm/dd/yy)

Amount ($)	Date Decl.	Ex-Div. Date	Stk. of Record	Payment Date
0.200	10/29	11/12	11/16	11/27/09
0.200	02/03	02/10	02/12	02/26/10
0.205	05/05	05/12	05/14	05/28/10
0.205	08/04	08/12	08/16	08/27/10

Dividends have been paid since 1900. Source: Company reports.

Please read the Required Disclosures and Analyst Certification on the last page of this report.

The McGraw·Hill Companies

TECO Energy Inc.

STANDARD &POOR'S

Business Summary August 16, 2010

CORPORATE OVERVIEW. TECO Energy (TE) is a holding company for a diverse set of energy companies including the regulated utility subsidiary Tampa Electric Company, which provides retail electric service in west central Florida. TE's other regulated utility is Peoples Gas System, which distributes natural gas in Florida's metropolitan areas. TE's unregulated businesses include TECO Coal, which has coal-mining operations, and TECO Guatemala, which participates in independent power projects and electric distribution in Guatemala. In December 2007, TE completed the sale of TECO Transport, which provided shipping and storage services for coal and other dry-bulk commodities. In 2009, Tampa Electric accounted for 66.0% of TE's consolidated revenues; TECO Coal 19.6%; Peoples Gas System 14.2%; and TECO Guatemala 0.2%.

CORPORATE STRATEGY. Despite the challenges and uncertainties related to the current state of the economy and housing market in Florida, TECO Energy plans to continue its strategy of investment in Tampa Electric. The company intends to remain focused on the reduction of its debt and to improve its already investment-grade status so as to ensure access to the credit markets and to meet its growing level of necessary capital investment. TE expects to continue its investment in the Peoples Gas infrastructure to serve more customers and to maintain its compliance with federal pipeline standards. The company believes the most significant factors affecting the results of TECO Coal in 2010 will be the cost of its coal production and the ability of its customers to accept their full contracted volumes.

Company Financials Fiscal Year Ended Dec. 31

Per Share Data ($)	2009	2008	2007	2006	2005	2004	2003	2002	2001	2000
Tangible Book Value	9.47	9.15	9.28	7.97	7.36	6.13	8.55	13.75	12.94	11.93
Earnings	1.00	0.77	1.90	1.17	1.00	-2.10	-0.08	1.95	2.24	1.97
S&P Core Earnings	0.98	0.67	1.25	1.19	1.00	-1.58	0.24	1.75	2.04	NA
Dividends	0.80	0.80	0.78	0.76	0.76	0.76	0.93	1.41	1.37	1.33
Payout Ratio	80%	103%	41%	65%	76%	NM	NM	72%	61%	68%
Prices:High	16.71	21.99	18.58	17.73	19.30	15.49	17.00	29.05	32.97	33.19
Prices:Low	8.41	10.50	14.84	14.40	14.87	11.30	9.47	10.02	24.75	17.25
P/E Ratio:High	17	29	10	15	19	NM	NM	15	15	17
P/E Ratio:Low	8	14	8	12	15	NM	NM	5	11	9

Income Statement Analysis (Million $)										
Revenue	3,311	3,375	3,536	3,448	3,010	2,669	2,740	2,676	2,649	2,295
Depreciation	288	266	264	282	282	282	326	303	298	268
Maintenance	188	174	184	183	168	141	152	162	151	140
Fixed Charges Coverage	2.28	1.80	2.06	1.42	1.25	1.26	2.30	2.43	2.51	2.59
Construction Credits	13.8	8.70	6.20	3.80	Nil	1.00	27.4	9.60	2.60	0.70
Effective Tax Rate	31.6%	36.8%	40.4%	40.2%	45.1%	NM	NM	NM	NM	6.87%
Net Income	214	162	399	246	211	-404	-14.7	298	304	251
S&P Core Earnings	210	143	260	248	212	-306	44.4	267	277	NA

Balance Sheet & Other Financial Data (Million $)										
Gross Property	7,778	7,311	6,894	7,084	6,755	6,723	8,040	8,215	7,544	6,560
Capital Expenditures	630	583	494	456	295	273	591	1,065	966	688
Net Property	5,544	5,221	4,888	4,767	4,567	4,658	5,679	5,464	4,838	3,970
Capitalization:Long Term Debt	3,202	3,207	3,158	3,213	3,709	3,880	4,393	3,973	2,043	1,575
Capitalization:% Long Term Debt	60.6	61.5	61.0	65.0	70.0	75.1	73.0	43.2	50.9	51.1
Capitalization:Preferred	Nil	Nil	Nil	Nil	Nil	Nil	Nil	Nil	Nil	Nil
Capitalization:% Preferred	Nil	Nil	Nil	Nil	Nil	Nil	Nil	Nil	Nil	Nil
Capitalization:Common	2,085	2,008	2,017	1,729	1,592	1,284	1,622	5,223	1,972	1,507
Capitalization:% Common	39.4	38.5	39.0	35.0	30.0	24.9	27.0	56.8	49.1	48.9
Total Capital	5,395	5,226	5,188	4,957	5,318	5,691	6,537	9,719	4,545	3,564
% Operating Ratio	89.9	91.4	94.3	91.9	91.4	80.2	83.7	84.0	83.7	82.8
% Earned on Net Property	9.0	7.6	8.6	9.0	7.7	NA	0.3	7.6	9.6	10.9
% Return on Revenue	6.5	4.8	11.3	7.1	7.0	NM	NM	11.1	11.5	10.9
% Return on Invested Capital	7.9	6.1	6.3	8.5	9.3	14.2	9.6	6.4	11.9	12.4
% Return on Common Equity	10.5	8.1	21.3	14.8	14.7	NM	NM	6.5	17.5	17.2

Data as orig reptd.; bef. results of disc opers/spec. items. Per share data adj. for stk. divs.; EPS diluted. E-Estimated. NA-Not Available. NM-Not Meaningful. NR-Not Ranked. UR-Under Review.

Office: Teco Plaza, 702 North Franklin Street, Tampa, FL 33602.
Telephone: 813-228-1111.
Website: http://www.tecoenergy.com
Chrmn: S.W. Hudson

Pres & CEO: J.B. Ramil
SVP & General Counsel: C. Attal, III
CFO & Chief Acctg Officer: S.W. Callahan
Treas: K.M. Caruso

Investor Contact: M.M. Kane (813-228-1772)
Board Members: D. Ausley, J. L. Ferman, Jr., S. W. Hudson, J. P. Lacher, L. A. Penn, J. B. Ramil, T. L. Rankin, W. Rockford, P. L. Whiting

Founded: 1899
Domicile: Florida
Employees: 4,073

The McGraw-Hill Companies

Tellabs Inc

STANDARD
&POOR'S

S&P Recommendation HOLD ★★★☆☆

Price	12-Mo. Target Price
$7.84 (as of Oct 22, 2010)	**$10.00**

GICS Sector Information Technology
Sub-Industry Communications Equipment

Summary This company manufactures voice and data equipment used in public and private communications networks worldwide.

Key Stock Statistics (Source S&P, Vickers, company reports)

52-Wk Range	$9.45–5.36	S&P Oper. EPS 2010**E**	0.50	Market Capitalization(B)	$2.990	Beta	0.82
Trailing 12-Month EPS	$0.52	S&P Oper. EPS 2011**E**	0.60	Yield (%)	1.02	S&P 3-Yr. Proj. EPS CAGR(%)	10
Trailing 12-Month P/E	15.1	P/E on S&P Oper. EPS 2010**E**	15.7	Dividend Rate/Share	$0.08	S&P Credit Rating	NA
$10K Invested 5 Yrs Ago	$7,833	Common Shares Outstg. (M)	381.4	Institutional Ownership (%)	79		

Price Performance

- 30-Week Mov. Avg. · · · · 10-Week Mov. Avg. - - **GAAP Earnings vs. Previous Year** Volume Above Avg. STARS
- 12-Mo. Target Price — Relative Strength — ▲ Up ▼ Down ▶ No Change Below Avg.

Options: ASE, CBOE, P, Ph

Analysis prepared by **Ari Bensinger** on July 28, 2010, when the stock traded at **$ 7.48**.

Highlights

➤ Following a 12% decline in 2009, we see sales advancing 9% in 2010, as improving customer demand for new products, such as the 7100 optical transport, 8600 managed edge, and 8800 multiservice router systems offset a continued decline in demand for legacy products, particularly the mature core 5500 cross connect solution. We see the broadband stimulus package boosting sales in the second half of 2010.

➤ We see 2010 gross margins widening nearly 800 basis points from 2009, to 52%, aided by a favorable product mix shift toward higher margin data products and the beneficial effects of cost reduction on new products. Despite restructuring initiatives, we expect 2010 operating expenses on an absolute basis to increase modestly from the prior year, primarily on the Wi-Chorus acquisition.

➤ We forecast 2010 operating margins of 18.5%, up from 10% in 2009. After a 32% tax rate and factoring in our projection for continued share repurchases, we look for 2010 EPS of $0.50, versus the $0.29 posted for 2009. Our 2010 estimate includes projected stock option expense of $0.08.

Investment Rationale/Risk

➤ While TLAB's large legacy product base (roughly 45% of total sales) continues to shrink, we are encouraged by the improving demand for the company's new growth products. We view a continuing rapid rise in mobile data traffic, which is fueling wireless backhaul product demand, as a strong underlying growth driver for the company. Still, we are wary of increasing competition, particularly for business at large customer AT&T.

➤ Risks to our recommendation and target price include the loss of a major customer, slowing market penetration for the company's new broadband products, and a sharp dropoff in its core transport products.

➤ Our 12-month target price of $10 equates to 1.8X book value and 2X our 2010 sales per share forecast, valuation multiples that are slightly below the peer means, reflecting our view of the company's below industry average sales growth profile. Our target price also represents a multiple of 20X our 2010 EPS estimate of $0.50, in line with the industry mean. Cash and investments per share amount to roughly $3.00.

Qualitative Risk Assessment

LOW	MEDIUM	HIGH

Our risk assessment reflects the competitive pressure the company faces, and its dependence on a consolidating telecom industry.

Quantitative Evaluations

S&P Quality Ranking B

D	C	B-	**B**	B+	A-	A	A+

Relative Strength Rank **MODERATE**

64

LOWEST = 1 HIGHEST = 99

Revenue/Earnings Data

Revenue (Million $)

	1Q	2Q	3Q	4Q	Year
2010	379.7	422.7	--	--	--
2009	361.7	385.4	389.3	389.3	1,526
2008	464.1	432.5	424.1	408.3	1,729
2007	451.9	534.5	457.9	469.1	1,913
2006	514.7	549.3	522.5	454.7	2,041
2005	435.6	462.5	463.9	521.4	1,883

Earnings Per Share ($)

2010	0.12	0.16	E0.12	E0.12	E0.50
2009	0.02	0.04	0.07	0.16	0.29
2008	0.04	-0.10	-2.51	0.03	-2.32
2007	0.06	0.07	0.01	0.02	0.15
2006	0.11	0.12	0.13	0.07	0.43
2005	Nil	0.09	0.09	0.20	0.39

Fiscal year ended Dec. 31. Next earnings report expected: Late October. EPS Estimates based on S&P Operating Earnings; historical GAAP earnings are as reported.

Dividend Data (Dates: mm/dd Payment Date: mm/dd/yy)

Amount ($)	Date Decl.	Ex-Div. Date	Stk. of Record	Payment Date
0.020	01/26	02/10	02/12	02/26/10
0.020	04/29	05/12	05/14	05/28/10
0.020	07/28	08/11	08/13	08/27/10

Dividends have been paid since 2010. Source: Company reports.

Please read the Required Disclosures and Analyst Certification on the last page of this report.

The **McGraw·Hill** Companies

Tellabs Inc

STANDARD
&POOR'S

Business Summary July 28, 2010

CORPORATE OVERVIEW. Tellabs designs, manufactures, markets and services optical networking, next-generation switching and broadband access solutions. The company's products enable the delivery of wireline and wireless voice, data and video services. Solutions are primarily focused on the last mile of the communications network, the part of the network that is closest to homes and businesses. International sales represented 34% of total sales in 2009, up from 32% in 2008. Results are reported in three business segments: broadband, transport and services.

The broadband segment, which accounts for 50% of total sales, enables service providers to deliver bundled voice, video and high-speed Internet data services over copper or fiber networks. Broadband access products include digital loop carriers, digital subscriber line access multiplexers, fiber-to-the-premise (FTTP) optical line terminals for broadband passive optical networks, and voice gateways for voice over Internet protocol (VoIP). Managed access products include aggregation and transport products that deliver wireless and business services outside of the United States. Data products include next-generation packet-switched products that enable wireline and wireless carriers to deliver business services and next-generation wireless services to their customers.

The transport segment, which represents one-third of total sales, enables service providers to transport services and manage bandwidth by adding capacity when and where it is needed. Wireline and wireless providers use these to support wireless services, business services for enterprises, and triple-play voice, video and data services for consumers. Products include the company's core digital cross-connect systems, voice-quality enhancement products, and optical transport systems.

The services segment (15%) delivers deployment, training, support services and professional consulting to customers. Services in the planning phase include network architecture and design, network and applications planning, network management design, migration planning and others. Building services include applications integration, program and project management, installation, testing, network integration, third-party systems integration and others.

Company Financials Fiscal Year Ended Dec. 31

Per Share Data ($)	2009	2008	2007	2006	2005	2004	2003	2002	2001	2000
Tangible Book Value	4.18	4.25	4.14	3.97	3.53	3.34	3.76	4.45	5.55	6.26
Cash Flow	0.48	-2.11	0.35	0.66	0.66	0.12	-0.32	-0.41	-0.06	2.09
Earnings	0.29	-2.32	0.15	0.43	0.39	-0.07	-0.58	-0.76	-0.44	1.82
S&P Core Earnings	0.28	-0.69	0.16	0.44	0.38	-0.14	-0.71	-1.03	-0.68	NA
Dividends	Nil	Nil	Nil	Nil	Nil	Nil	Nil	Nil	Nil	Nil
Payout Ratio	Nil	Nil	Nil	Nil	Nil	Nil	Nil	Nil	Nil	Nil
Prices:High	7.70	7.21	13.67	17.28	11.49	11.37	9.73	17.47	67.13	76.94
Prices:Low	3.52	3.10	6.52	8.84	6.56	7.40	5.07	4.00	8.98	37.63
P/E Ratio:High	27	NM	91	40	29	NM	NM	NM	NM	42
P/E Ratio:Low	12	NM	43	21	17	NM	NM	NM	NM	21

Income Statement Analysis (Million $)	2009	2008	2007	2006	2005	2004	2003	2002	2001	2000
Revenue	1,526	1,729	1,913	2,041	1,883	1,232	980	1,317	2,200	3,387
Operating Income	202	147	124	358	330	152	-77.1	-12.7	70.9	1,117
Depreciation	75.3	87.4	90.7	104	126	82.3	110	143	158	116
Interest Expense	NA	Nil	Nil	Nil	Nil	Nil	0.70	0.90	0.51	0.63
Pretax Income	113	-952	70.2	285	213	-10.2	-245	-328	-245	1,109
Effective Tax Rate	NM	NM	7.41%	31.8%	17.5%	NM	NM	NM	NM	31.5%
Net Income	114	-930	65.0	194	176	-29.8	-242	-313	-182	760
S&P Core Earnings	110	-279	68.7	198	171	-58.9	-295	-427	-277	NA

Balance Sheet & Other Financial Data (Million $)	2009	2008	2007	2006	2005	2004	2003	2002	2001	2000
Cash	1,358	1,331	1,510	154	1,371	293	246	1,019	1,102	1,022
Current Assets	1,898	1,936	2,112	2,233	1,873	1,819	1,499	1,534	1,945	2,322
Total Assets	2,623	2,508	3,747	3,922	3,515	3,523	2,608	2,623	2,866	3,073
Current Liabilities	609	541	673	762	525	524	208	257	320	412
Long Term Debt	NA	Nil	Nil	Nil	Nil	Nil	Nil	Nil	3.39	2.85
Common Equity	1,915	1,847	2,913	2,938	2,815	2,797	2,219	2,290	2,466	2,628
Total Capital	1,915	1,847	2,992	2,938	2,815	2,797	2,319	2,290	2,490	2,637
Capital Expenditures	45.9	50.1	57.7	67.2	61.8	41.4	9.50	34.1	208	208
Cash Flow	189	-843	156	298	302	52.5	-131	-171	-24.5	876
Current Ratio	3.1	3.6	3.1	2.9	3.6	3.5	7.2	6.0	6.1	5.6
% Long Term Debt of Capitalization	Nil	Nil	Nil	Nil	Nil	Nil	Nil	Nil	0.1	0.1
% Net Income of Revenue	7.5	NM	3.4	9.5	9.3	NM	NM	NM	NM	22.4
% Return on Assets	4.4	NM	1.7	5.2	5.0	NM	NM	NM	NM	28.0
% Return on Equity	6.0	NM	2.2	6.7	6.3	NM	NM	NM	NM	32.5

Data as orig reptd.; bef. results of disc opers/spec. items. Per share data adj. for stk. divs.; EPS diluted. E-Estimated. NA-Not Available. NM-Not Meaningful. NR-Not Ranked. UR-Under Review.

Office: 1415 W Diehl Rd, Naperville, IL 60563-2349.
Telephone: 630-798-8800.
Website: http://www.tellabs.com
Chrmn: M.J. Birck

Pres & CEO: R.W. Pullen
COO: J.M. Brots
EVP & CFO: T.J. Wiggins
EVP, Chief Admin Officer, Secy & General Counsel: J.M. Sheehan

Investor Contact: T. Scottino (630-798-3602)
Board Members: M. J. Birck, B. C. Hedfors, F. Ianna, L. W. Kahangi, M. E. Lavin, S. P. Marshall, R. W. Pullen, W. F. Souders, J. H. Suwinski, V. H. Tobkin

Founded: 1974
Domicile: Delaware
Employees: 3,295

Tenet Healthcare Corp

STANDARD &POOR'S

S&P Recommendation **HOLD** ★★★☆☆	Price	12-Mo. Target Price	Investment Style
	$4.33 (as of Oct 22, 2010)	$6.00	Large-Cap Value

GICS Sector Health Care
Sub-Industry Health Care Facilities

Summary This company is the second largest U.S. for-profit hospital manager.

Key Stock Statistics (Source S&P, Vickers, company reports)

52-Wk Range	$6.46– 3.92	S&P Oper. EPS 2010E	0.28	Market Capitalization(B)	$2.101	Beta		2.12
Trailing 12-Month EPS	$0.27	S&P Oper. EPS 2011E	0.31	Yield (%)	Nil	S&P 3-Yr. Proj. EPS CAGR(%)		5
Trailing 12-Month P/E	16.0	P/E on S&P Oper. EPS 2010E	15.5	Dividend Rate/Share	Nil	S&P Credit Rating		B
$10K Invested 5 Yrs Ago	$4,748	Common Shares Outstg. (M)	485.2	Institutional Ownership (%)	84			

Price Performance

30-Week Mov. Avg. · · · 10-Week Mov. Avg. – – GAAP Earnings vs. Previous Year   Volume Above Avg. STARS
12-Mo. Target Price — Relative Strength   — ▲ Up ▼ Down ▶ No Change   Below Avg.

Options: ASE, CBOE, P

Analysis prepared by **Steven Silver** on August 11, 2010, when the stock traded at **$ 4.41**.

Highlights

➤ We see revenues rising about 4% in both 2010 and 2011. We continue to view THC as operating in a difficult market environment and amid weak employment in key markets. As such, we see THC struggling with commercial managed care admissions, which we view as key to revenue growth prospects. We expect the passage of health care reform to be a positive for hospitals post-2014, but until then, we see margin pressure as rate cuts and givebacks are implemented before the uninsured obtain coverage.

➤ We see EBITDA margins widening modestly in 2010 to slightly above 11%, as THC aligns its cost structure with moderating revenue growth. We look for EBITDA margins to remain essentially flat with this level in 2011. We are encouraged by the firming of bad debt trends over the first half of 2010, and we forecast such charges of around 8% of revenues in 2010 and 2011, up modestly from 7.7% of 2009.

➤ We see adjusted EPS of $0.28 in 2010 and $0.31 in 2011, excluding one-time items. We assume about 559 million shares for 2010 and 561 million for 2011.

Investment Rationale/Risk

➤ We view 2010 as a transition year for THC as it deals with extended weak volume growth, particularly in commercial admits. While we see early signs of positive impacts from steps to improve service quality and physician and managed care payor relationships, we are looking for more consistency in quarterly results. We view favorably cost controls that have contributed to rising EBITDA margins, though we note that these levels remain below those of its peers. We are also wary of its strategic focus, after its planed acquisition of Australian hospital operator Healthscope was scrapped in June 2010 given investor scrutiny of the deal's potential value.

➤ Risks to our recommendation and target price include a less favorable government or third-party reimbursement environment and slower physician recruitment than expected. In addition, higher self-pay volumes could negatively affect bad debt expense more than we expect.

➤ Our 12-month target price of $6.00 assumes an EV/EBITDA multiple of about 6.0X our 2010 EBITDA estimate, a discount to historical levels given our view of a challenging admissions environment.

Qualitative Risk Assessment

LOW	MEDIUM	**HIGH**

Our risk assessment for THC reflects our view of its high level of debt and ongoing negative operating cash flow position. In addition, we are concerned by the company's strong dependence on third-party reimbursements, including Medicare and Medicaid, which can be unpredictable.

Quantitative Evaluations

S&P Quality Ranking   B-

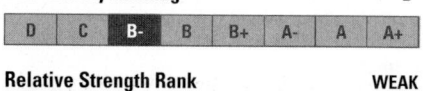

D	C	**B-**	B	B+	A-	A	A+

Relative Strength Rank   **WEAK**

22

LOWEST = 1   HIGHEST = 99

Revenue/Earnings Data

Revenue (Million $)

	1Q	2Q	3Q	4Q	Year
2010	2,339	2,303	--	--	--
2009	2,262	2,229	2,262	2,261	9,014
2008	2,178	2,132	2,158	2,195	8,663
2007	2,218	2,171	2,212	2,251	8,852
2006	2,414	2,195	2,117	2,179	8,701
2005	2,501	2,420	2,394	2,299	9,614

Earnings Per Share ($)

2010	0.16	0.07	E0.05	E0.06	E0.28
2009	0.39	Nil	Nil	0.04	0.43
2008	-0.02	-0.04	-0.24	-0.07	-0.13
2007	0.20	-0.06	-0.07	-0.18	-0.10
2006	-0.03	-0.95	-0.06	-0.83	-1.85
2005	0.04	Nil	-0.82	-0.54	-1.32

Fiscal year ended Dec. 31. Next earnings report expected: Early November. EPS Estimates based on S&P Operating Earnings; historical GAAP earnings are as reported.

Dividend Data

Dividends, initiated in 1973, were omitted beginning in 1993. A special dividend of $0.01 a share was paid in March 2000.

Please read the Required Disclosures and Analyst Certification on the last page of this report.

The McGraw-Hill Companies

STANDARD &POOR'S

Tenet Healthcare Corp

Business Summary August 11, 2010

CORPORATE OVERVIEW. Tenet Healthcare ranks as the second largest U.S. for-profit hospital manager. At December 31, 2009, it owned or operated 50 hospitals (including one hospital not yet divested but classified as discontinued operations), with 13,601 licensed beds. The largest concentrations of hospital beds were in California, Florida and Texas. THC also owns and operates a small number of rehabilitation hospitals, a specialty hospital, skilled nursing facilities, and medical office buildings located on or near the general hospital properties.

In January 2003, THC was sued by the U.S. Justice Department for allegedly submitting false claims to Medicare. In October 2003, the Justice Department served THC with a subpoena related to its investigation of Medicare outlier payments. In September 2003, the U.S. Senate launched an investigation into the company's corporate governance practices with respect to federal health care programs. In October 2004, additional investigations were announced into THC's medical directorship arrangements and physician relocation agreements.

In January 2006, THC reached an agreement to settle federal securities class

action lawsuits as well as shareholder derivative litigation for $215 million in cash; insurance proceeds covered $75 million of the this amount. The lawsuits were filed against the company beginning in 2002 and were consolidated in January 2003. In June 2006, THC and the U.S. Department of Justice reached an agreement to settle the ongoing investigation into Medicare outlier billing. The company agreed to pay $725 million over a period of four years, plus interest, and to waive its right to collect $175 million in Medicare payments for past services. In order to fund the settlement, at that time THC announced it would sell 11 hospitals. The settlement does not involve the Securities and Exchange Commission, which is investigating THC's financial disclosures surrounding the Medicare outlier payments. In our view, the Justice Department settlement removes some risk from the stock, but we expect its valuation to continue to be driven by the company's underlying operating fundamentals.

Company Financials Fiscal Year Ended Dec. 31

Per Share Data ($)	2009	2008	2007	2006	2005	2004	2003	2002	2001	2000
Tangible Book Value	NM	NM	NM	NM	NM	1.63	4.85	4.40	4.40	3.45
Cash Flow	0.01	0.83	0.59	-1.12	-0.51	-3.02	-2.00	1.54	3.24	2.51
Earnings	0.43	-0.13	-0.10	-1.85	-1.32	-3.85	-3.01	0.93	2.04	1.39
S&P Core Earnings	0.46	NA	-0.11	-0.34	-1.14	-2.28	0.27	1.54	1.24	NA
Dividends	Nil	Nil	Nil	Nil	Nil	Nil	Nil	Nil	Nil	Nil
Payout Ratio	Nil	Nil	Nil	Nil	Nil	Nil	Nil	Nil	Nil	Nil
Prices:High	6.39	6.88	7.80	9.27	13.06	18.73	19.25	52.50	41.85	30.50
Prices:Low	0.78	0.99	3.06	5.77	7.27	9.15	11.32	13.70	24.67	11.29
P/E Ratio:High	15	NM	NM	NM	NM	NM	NM	56	21	22
P/E Ratio:Low	2	NM	NM	NM	NM	NM	NM	15	12	8

Income Statement Analysis (Million $)	2009	2008	2007	2006	2005	2004	2003	2002	2001	2000
Revenue	9,014	8,663	8,852	8,701	9,614	9,919	13,212	8,743	13,913	12,053
Operating Income	982	694	669	687	571	434	1,072	1,676	2,797	2,244
Depreciation	386	335	330	342	382	388	471	302	604	554
Interest Expense	445	428	430	409	405	333	296	147	327	456
Pretax Income	205	43.0	-103	-1,129	-701	-1,616	-1,829	777	1,799	1,156
Effective Tax Rate	NM	NM	56.3%	NM	NM	NM	NM	38.5%	40.9%	40.1%
Net Income	218	62.0	-49.0	-871	-621	-1,797	-1,404	459	1,025	678
S&P Core Earnings	228	-1.05	-52.3	-159	-561	-1,061	123	760	607	NA

Balance Sheet & Other Financial Data (Million $)	2009	2008	2007	2006	2005	2004	2003	2002	2001	2000
Cash	703	523	592	784	1,373	654	619	210	38.0	62.0
Current Assets	2,472	2,709	2,560	3,025	3,508	3,992	4,248	3,792	3,394	3,226
Total Assets	7,953	8,174	8,393	8,539	9,812	10,078	12,298	13,780	13,814	12,995
Current Liabilities	1,783	1,949	2,048	1,925	2,292	2,130	2,394	2,381	2,584	2,166
Long Term Debt	4,272	4,778	4,771	4,760	4,784	4,395	4,039	3,872	3,919	4,202
Common Equity	312	103	54.0	995	1,760	2,460	4,361	5,723	5,619	5,079
Total Capital	4,971	4,982	4,944	5,862	6,756	7,166	8,404	10,121	10,227	9,835
Capital Expenditures	455	527	729	631	568	454	753	490	889	601
Cash Flow	598	397	281	-529	-239	-1,409	-933	761	1,629	1,232
Current Ratio	1.4	1.4	1.3	1.6	1.5	1.9	1.8	1.6	1.3	1.5
% Long Term Debt of Capitalization	85.9	95.9	96.5	81.2	70.8	61.3	48.1	38.3	38.3	42.7
% Net Income of Revenue	2.4	0.7	NM	NM	NM	NM	NM	5.2	7.4	5.6
% Return on Assets	2.7	0.8	NM	NM	NM	NM	NM	NM	7.6	5.2
% Return on Equity	105.1	79.0	NM	NM	NM	NM	NM	NM	19.2	14.8

Data as orig reptd.; bef. results of disc opers/spec. items. Per share data adj. for stk. divs.; EPS diluted. E-Estimated. NA-Not Available. NM-Not Meaningful. NR-Not Ranked. UR-Under Review.

Office: 1445 Ross Ave, Ste 1400, Dallas, TX 75202.
Telephone: 469-893-2200.
Email: feedback@tenethealth.com
Website: http://www.tenethealth.com

Chrmn: E.A. Kangas
Pres & CEO: T. Fetter
COO: S.L. Newman
EVP & CIO: S.F. Brown

SVP, Secy & General Counsel: G. Ruff
Investor Contact: T. Rice (469-893-2522)
Board Members: J. E. Bush, T. Fetter, B. J. Gaines, K. M. Garrison, E. A. Kangas, J. R. Kerrey, F. D. Loop, R. R. Pettingill, R. A. Rittenmeyer, J. A. Unruh

Founded: 1967
Domicile: Nevada
Employees: 57,613

The McGraw-Hill Companies

Teradata Corp

STANDARD &POOR'S

S&P Recommendation **HOLD** ★★★☆☆	Price	12-Mo. Target Price	Investment Style
	$38.35 (as of Oct 22, 2010)	$37.00	Large-Cap Blend

GICS Sector Information Technology
Sub-Industry IT Consulting & Other Services

Summary This Ohio-based company has global operations focused on data warehousing and enterprise analytics. Teradata was spun off from NCR Corporation in 2007.

Key Stock Statistics (Source S&P, Vickers, company reports)

52-Wk Range	$39.93–26.80	S&P Oper. EPS 2010**E**	1.70	Market Capitalization(B)	$6.416	Beta	0.91
Trailing 12-Month EPS	$1.68	S&P Oper. EPS 2011**E**	1.93	Yield (%)	Nil	S&P 3-Yr. Proj. EPS CAGR(%)	14
Trailing 12-Month P/E	22.8	P/E on S&P Oper. EPS 2010**E**	22.6	Dividend Rate/Share	Nil	S&P Credit Rating	NA
$10K Invested 5 Yrs Ago	NA	Common Shares Outstg. (M)	167.3	Institutional Ownership (%)	79		

Price Performance

30-Week Mov. Avg. · · ·   10-Week Mov. Avg. – –   GAAP Earnings vs. Previous Year   Volume Above Avg. ▮▮▮ STARS
12-Mo. Target Price —   Relative Strength —   ▲ Up ▼ Down ▶ No Change   Below Avg. ▮▮▮ ★

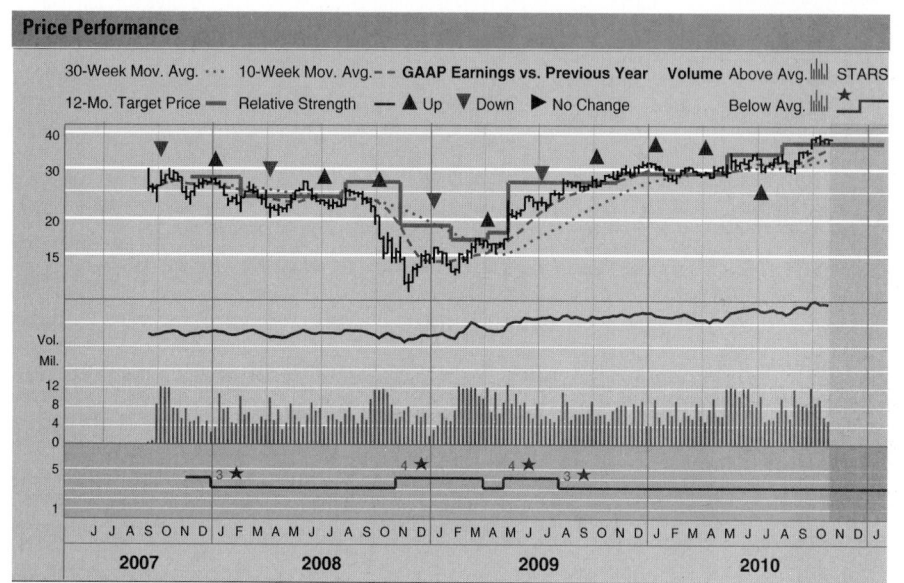

Options: CBOE, Ph

Analysis prepared by **Zaineb Bokhari** on August 12, 2010, when the stock traded at **$ 29.98**.

Highlights

➤ We expect revenues to rise 10% in 2010 to $1.88 billion, aided by easier year-to-year comparisons after a 3% decline in 2009, and some benefit seen from pent-up demand as the economic environment stabilizes. We think a more restrictive regulatory environment and the continuing demand for business intelligence solutions will also drive sales for TDC's solutions. We expect the pace of sales growth to slow in the 2010 second half, owing to tougher year-to-year comparisons. We see sales rising 6.6% in 2011.

➤ Despite the projected higher revenues, we expect 2010 gross margins to widen modestly as TDC gradually adds to professional services headcount. We see product gross margins impacted by the amortization of software development costs. We think operating margins will widen to 21% in 2010 from 20% in 2009, due to investment in R&D and sales. We anticipate modestly wider operating margins in 2011. A lack of long-term debt and the establishment of a $300 million credit facility indicates to us that currently negligible interest expense could rise.

➤ We estimate EPS of $1.70 for 2010 and $1.93 for 2011. We expect share repurchases to aid per-share results.

Investment Rationale/Risk

➤ We view Teradata as operating in a large niche of the information technology sector. A primary sales driver is rising interest among enterprises in using their transaction data to study and improve patterns of operation. The company aims to expand by entering new sales territories, and we believe it has the potential to do well based on its one-stop shopping approach to offering business intelligence hardware, software, and consulting. Despite this, we think competition remains intense, and will contribute to unpredictable and lengthy sales cycles. Based on our forward P/E analysis, we view TDC's valuation as reasonable relative to peers.

➤ Risks to our recommendation and target price include slowdowns in the general pace of spending on information technology for businesses, any failure to keep pace with rapidly evolving computer and analytical technology, and competition on price and quality of products and services.

➤ Our 12-month target price of $37 is derived from our discounted cash flow analysis. We incorporate assumptions for a 9% weighted average cost of capital and 3% terminal growth.

Qualitative Risk Assessment

LOW	MEDIUM	HIGH

Teradata participates in a large and growing global market we see for storing, retrieving, and analyzing data produced by businesses. While competition is high for technology and pricing, we believe a stream of revenue from services, and a lack of debt, lends some stability.

Quantitative Evaluations

S&P Quality Ranking NR

D	C	B-	B	B+	A-	A	A+

Relative Strength Rank STRONG

76

LOWEST = 1   HIGHEST = 99

Revenue/Earnings Data

Revenue (Million $)

	1Q	2Q	3Q	4Q	Year
2010	429.0	470.0	--	--	--
2009	367.0	421.0	425.0	496.0	1,709
2008	375.0	455.0	439.0	493.0	1,762
2007	367.0	430.0	439.0	466.0	1,702
2006	323.0	396.0	375.0	466.0	1,560
2005	347.0	357.0	358.0	405.0	1,467

Earnings Per Share ($)

2010	0.39	0.44	E0.41	E0.47	E1.70
2009	0.26	0.36	0.36	0.49	1.46
2008	0.23	0.38	0.33	0.45	1.39
2007	0.24	0.27	0.16	0.46	1.10
2006	0.20	0.28	0.31	0.31	1.09
2005	--	--	--	--	1.14

Fiscal year ended Dec. 31. Next earnings report expected: NA. EPS Estimates based on S&P Operating Earnings; historical GAAP earnings are as reported.

Dividend Data

No cash dividends have been paid.

The **McGraw·Hill** Companies

Teradata Corp

Business Summary August 12, 2010

CORPORATE OVERVIEW. Teradata Corporation aims to help its enterprise customers make smarter and faster use of their stored data to improve decision-making. It views itself as a global leader in data warehousing and enterprise analytic technologies. The company offers hardware and software, as well as services including consulting, customer support and training. In 2009, 45% of revenues were derived from products (48% for 2008), and 55% (52%) came from services.

Headquartered in Dayton, Ohio, the company has offices throughout the Americas and operates in 60 countries worldwide. It earned 49% of its revenues outside the U.S. in 2009 and 2008. Teradata has a broad customer base, in our view, with the top 10 customers in 2009 representing only about 16% of sales, down from 20% in 2008. In 2009, revenue came 57% from the Americas, 25% from EMEA (Europe, Middle East, Africa), and 18% from APJ (Asia Pacific/Japan), similar to the 2008 breakout. Gross margins have typically been widest for the Americas region, near 58% compared to a company average of 55% in 2008.

Data warehousing is the process of capturing, storing and analyzing data to

gain insight, according to the company. This activity can be a significant source of intelligence for the enterprise and become a competitive advantage. Beyond mere storage of data, modern solutions allow for near real-time information access and analysis. Predictive analytics on customer or business activity may be run. Both long-term strategic and short-term tactical inquiries may be pursued.

In one example of active data warehousing, a business's call center could produce raw data on call attributes (e.g., number of calls, duration, agent, customer, dropped calls, results), which could be a starting point for mapping and analyzing overall interactions with customers, including Internet communications, which could then become the basis for a plan to improve customer satisfaction. The company serves many large clients in the communications industry, as well as in media and entertainment, financial services, government, health care, manufacturing, retail, and transportation.

Company Financials Fiscal Year Ended Dec. 31

Per Share Data ($)	2009	2008	2007	2006	2005	2004	2003	2002	2001	2000
Tangible Book Value	4.14	3.30	2.91	2.15	NA	NA	NA	NA	NA	NA
Cash Flow	1.61	1.72	1.48	1.40	1.44	1.03	NA	NA	NA	NA
Earnings	1.46	1.39	1.10	1.09	1.14	0.76	NA	NA	NA	NA
S&P Core Earnings	1.48	1.40	1.18	1.09	1.10	NA	NA	NA	NA	NA
Dividends	Nil	Nil	Nil	NA	NA	NA	NA	NA	NA	NA
Payout Ratio	Nil	Nil	Nil	NA	NA	NA	NA	NA	NA	NA
Prices:High	32.24	27.90	30.08	NA	NA	NA	NA	NA	NA	NA
Prices:Low	12.75	11.11	22.35	NA	NA	NA	NA	NA	NA	NA
P/E Ratio:High	22	20	27	NA	NA	NA	NA	NA	NA	NA
P/E Ratio:Low	9	8	20	NA	NA	NA	NA	NA	NA	NA

Income Statement Analysis (Million $)	2009	2008	2007	2006	2005	2004	2003	2002	2001	2000
Revenue	1,709	1,762	1,702	1,560	1,467	1,349	NA	NA	NA	NA
Operating Income	364	393	405	367	339	247	NA	NA	NA	NA
Depreciation	63.0	60.0	68.0	55.0	55.0	48.0	NA	NA	NA	NA
Interest Expense	NA	Nil	Nil	Nil	Nil	Nil	NA	NA	NA	NA
Pretax Income	334	338	322	312	284	199	NA	NA	NA	NA
Effective Tax Rate	24.0%	26.0%	37.9%	36.5%	27.5%	30.7%	NA	NA	NA	NA
Net Income	254	250	200	198	206	138	NA	NA	NA	NA
S&P Core Earnings	256	252	213	198	200	NA	NA	NA	NA	NA

Balance Sheet & Other Financial Data (Million $)	2009	2008	2007	2006	2005	2004	2003	2002	2001	2000
Cash	661	442	270	200	NA	NA	NA	NA	NA	NA
Current Assets	1,152	1,015	873	645	444	NA	NA	NA	NA	NA
Total Assets	1,569	1,445	1,295	983	911	NA	NA	NA	NA	NA
Current Liabilities	543	540	572	428	370	NA	NA	NA	NA	NA
Long Term Debt	NA	Nil	Nil	Nil	NA	NA	NA	NA	NA	NA
Common Equity	910	782	631	477	517	NA	NA	NA	NA	NA
Total Capital	910	777	631	477	517	NA	NA	NA	NA	NA
Capital Expenditures	29.0	19.0	50.0	20.0	18.0	14.0	NA	NA	NA	NA
Cash Flow	280	310	268	253	261	186	NA	NA	NA	NA
Current Ratio	2.1	1.9	1.5	1.5	1.2	NA	NA	NA	NA	NA
% Long Term Debt of Capitalization	Nil	Nil	Nil	Nil	Nil	10.2	NA	NA	NA	NA
% Net Income of Revenue	14.9	14.2	11.8	12.7	14.0	10.2	NA	NA	NA	NA
% Return on Assets	16.9	18.3	17.4	NM	NM	10.2	NA	NA	NA	NA
% Return on Equity	30.1	35.4	32.6	NM	NM	NA	NA	NA	NA	NA

Data as orig reptd.; bef. results of disc opers/spec. items. Per share data adj. for stk. divs.; EPS diluted. E-Estimated. NA-Not Available. NM-Not Meaningful. NR-Not Ranked. UR-Under Review.

Office: 2835 Miami Village Drive, Dayton, OH 45342.
Telephone: 866-548-8348.
Website: http://www.teradata.com
Chrmn: J.M. Ringler

Pres & CEO: M.F. Koehler
COO: B.A. Langos
EVP, CFO & Chief Acctg Officer: S.M. Scheppmann
CTO: S.A. Brobst

Investor Contact: G. Swearingen (937-242-4600)
Board Members: E. P. Boykin, N. Cooper, C. T. Fu, D. E. Kepler, II, M. F. Koehler, V. L. Lund, J. M. Ringler, J. G. Schwarz, W. S. Stavropoulos

Founded: 1979
Domicile: Delaware

Teradyne Inc.

STANDARD &POOR'S

S&P Recommendation SELL ★★☆☆☆	Price $11.45 (as of Oct 22, 2010)	12-Mo. Target Price $9.50	Investment Style Large-Cap Blend

GICS Sector Information Technology
Sub-Industry Semiconductor Equipment

Summary This company makes automatic test equipment used primarily by the semiconductor and telecommunications industries.

Key Stock Statistics (Source S&P, Vickers, company reports)

52-Wk Range	$13.37– 8.09	S&P Oper. EPS 2010**E**	2.34	Market Capitalization(B)	$2.076	Beta	1.73
Trailing 12-Month EPS	$1.01	S&P Oper. EPS 2011**E**	1.89	Yield (%)	Nil	S&P 3-Yr. Proj. EPS CAGR(%)	NM
Trailing 12-Month P/E	11.3	P/E on S&P Oper. EPS 2010**E**	4.9	Dividend Rate/Share	Nil	S&P Credit Rating	NR
$10K Invested 5 Yrs Ago	$8,144	Common Shares Outstg. (M)	181.3	Institutional Ownership (%)	NM		

Price Performance

30-Week Mov. Avg. · · · · 10-Week Mov. Avg. - - **GAAP Earnings vs. Previous Year** Volume Above Avg. STARS
12-Mo. Target Price — Relative Strength — ▲ Up ▼ Down ► No Change Below Avg. ★

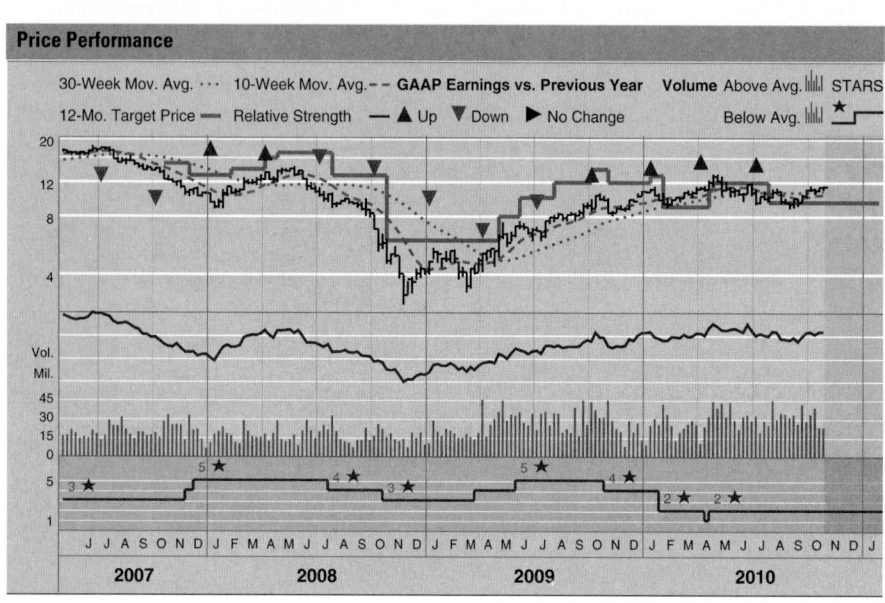

Options: ASE, CBOE, P, Ph

Analysis prepared by **Angelo Zino** on August 02, 2010, when the stock traded at **$ 11.10**.

Highlights

▶ We project revenues will decline 7% in 2011 following our forecast for an increase of 114% in 2010, which is being driven by a significant rebound in the system-on-chip (SOC) test equipment market. We think SOC bookings are nearing a peak and expect tester spending by wireless and power management manufacturers to begin to slow. In addition, we believe outsourced assembly and packaging customers will remain cautious with future capital spending plans. However, we expect memory test sales to increase from current levels.

▶ We expect gross margins to narrow to 51% in 2011, versus our projection of 54% margins in 2010. While we think TER has a much improved business model, our lower margin outlook for 2011 reflects our belief that volume will decline. We see research and development expenses absorbing 11% of sales in 2010 and 2011. We think prior cost cuts will provide considerable earnings leverage for TER in the future.

▶ We estimate operating EPS of $2.34 in 2010, excluding $0.22 of non-recurring charges, and $1.89 in 2011. We model an effective tax rate of 8% for the foreseeable future.

Investment Rationale/Risk

▶ Our sell recommendation primarily reflects our intermediate-term sales outlook for TER. While we believe revenues will remain strong in the near term, driven by its system-on-chip business, we think current demand is likely to be unsustainable. We see benefits from a rise in memory spending and note that TER's overall book-to-bill ratio remains above 1.0. We view favorably TER's commanding market share position in the test equipment SOC market. TER's leadership position in the business and what we view as its strong cash position, offset in part by the competitive and low-growth environment for testers, are incorporated into our opinion. We see multiples compressing near peak orders.

▶ Risks to our recommendation and target price include wider-than-anticipated margins, higher-than-projected customer capital spending plans, a strengthening global economy, and less competitive pressure.

▶ We derive our 12-month target price of $9.50 by applying a price-to-sales (P/S) multiple of 1.13X to our 2011 sales per share forecast of $8.40, near peers. The ratio is below TER's historical three- and five-year averages of 1.6X and 2.1X.

Qualitative Risk Assessment

LOW	MEDIUM	HIGH

Our risk assessment reflects the historical cyclicality of the semiconductor equipment industry, the lack of visibility in the medium term, and intense competition, which we think are only partially offset by Teradyne's market position and financial strength.

Quantitative Evaluations

S&P Quality Ranking C

D	C	B-	B	B+	A-	A	A+

Relative Strength Rank STRONG
74
LOWEST = 1   HIGHEST = 99

Revenue/Earnings Data

Revenue (Million $)

	1Q	2Q	3Q	4Q	Year
2010	329.6	454.8	--	--	--
2009	120.6	169.6	262.2	267.1	819.4
2008	297.3	317.7	297.3	194.8	1,107
2007	258.1	288.7	299.5	260.4	1,102
2006	362.9	391.6	359.1	263.2	1,377
2005	210.4	226.2	293.6	345.2	1,075

Earnings Per Share ($)

2010	0.24	0.55	E0.79	E0.54	E2.34
2009	-0.53	-0.39	0.04	0.09	-0.77
2008	0.01	0.06	-0.14	-0.33	-0.38
2007	-0.04	0.14	0.19	0.10	0.39
2006	0.23	0.40	0.33	0.06	1.03
2005	-0.28	-0.26	-0.22	0.44	-0.31

Fiscal year ended Dec. 31. Next earnings report expected: Late October. EPS Estimates based on S&P Operating Earnings; historical GAAP earnings are as reported.

Dividend Data

No cash dividends have been paid.

Teradyne Inc.

STANDARD
&POOR'S

Business Summary August 02, 2010

CORPORATE OVERVIEW. Founded in 1960, Teradyne is a leading global supplier of automatic test equipment (ATE) for the electronics industry. As electronic systems have become more complex, the need for products to test the systems has grown dramatically. TER's product segments include Semiconductor Test (67% of 2009 revenue, 81% in 2008) and Systems Test Group (33%, 19%).

Semiconductor Test products test system on a chip (SOC) semiconductor devices during the manufacturing process. These systems are used for wafer level and device packaging testing and span a broad range of end users and functionality. TER's systems help customers improve and control quality, reduce time to market, increase production yields, and improve product performance. TER's FLEX Test platform is designed for scalability and allows for simultaneous parallel testing, reducing costs. The J750 platform is designed to address the highest volume semiconductor devices such as microcontrollers, with a single circuit board providing up to 64 digital input/output channels. The J750 platform technology has been extended to create the IP 750 Image Sensor test system, which focuses on testing image sensor devices used in digital cameras and other imaging products. The J750 platform has been expanded to include critical new devices that include high-end microcontroller, LCD drivers, and the latest generation of cameras.

TER's acquisition of Nextest expanded its product base to include the Magnum test platform. The Magnum platform offers memory test products for the flash memory and dynamic random access memory (DRAM) markets. TER's Eagle Test acquisition expanded its product offerings to include the ETS platform. The ETS platform is used by chipmaker's and assembly and test subcontractors, primarily in the low pin count analog/mixed signal discrete markets that cover more cost sensitive applications. Its SmartPin technology enables multiple semiconductor devices to be tested simultaneously, or in parallel, on an individual test system, permitting greater test throughput.

Company Financials Fiscal Year Ended Dec. 31

Per Share Data ($)	2009	2008	2007	2006	2005	2004	2003	2002	2001	2000
Tangible Book Value	2.93	3.16	6.70	6.84	5.75	5.00	4.33	4.97	8.69	9.89
Cash Flow	-0.16	-1.92	0.71	1.35	0.16	1.47	-0.22	-3.06	-0.36	3.42
Earnings	-0.77	-0.38	0.39	1.03	-0.31	0.84	-1.03	-3.93	-1.15	2.86
S&P Core Earnings	-0.76	-1.21	0.37	0.92	-0.80	0.37	-1.44	-4.25	-1.65	NA
Dividends	Nil	Nil	Nil	Nil	Nil	Nil	Nil	Nil	Nil	Nil
Payout Ratio	Nil	Nil	Nil	Nil	Nil	Nil	Nil	Nil	Nil	Nil
Prices:High	10.96	14.50	18.53	18.08	17.33	30.70	26.31	40.20	47.21	115.44
Prices:Low	3.24	2.80	10.02	11.50	10.80	12.53	8.75	7.10	18.43	23.00
P/E Ratio:High	NM	NM	48	18	NM	37	NM	NM	NM	40
P/E Ratio:Low	NM	NM	26	11	NM	15	NM	NM	NM	8

Income Statement Analysis (Million $)	2009	2008	2007	2006	2005	2004	2003	2002	2001	2000
Revenue	819	1,107	1,102	1,377	1,075	1,792	1,353	1,222	1,441	3,044
Operating Income	35.7	89.6	117	236	27.1	318	47.3	-192	-1.54	813
Depreciation	106	71.3	59.4	73.5	91.2	124	152	160	139	102
Interest Expense	16.4	NA	0.69	11.1	16.2	18.8	20.9	21.8	4.09	1.84
Pretax Income	-143	-52.7	79.2	230	-80.1	188	-186	-561	-326	740
Effective Tax Rate	6.17%	NM	9.29%	12.0%	NM	12.1%	NM	NM	NM	30.0%
Net Income	-134	-65.3	71.9	203	-60.5	165	-194	-718	-202	518
S&P Core Earnings	-132	-206	68.3	179	-161	73.3	-270	-777	-290	NA

Balance Sheet & Other Financial Data (Million $)	2009	2008	2007	2006	2005	2004	2003	2002	2001	2000
Cash	464	323	638	945	695	285	586	541	586	464
Current Assets	762	679	945	889	1,095	806	769	809	1,207	1,378
Total Assets	1,235	1,560	1,555	1,721	1,860	1,923	1,785	1,895	2,542	2,356
Current Liabilities	283	367	223	260	515	277	281	279	296	619
Long Term Debt	141	Nil	Nil	Nil	1.82	399	408	451	452	8.35
Common Equity	665	1,039	1,229	1,361	1,243	1,134	950	1,028	1,764	1,707
Total Capital	808	706	1,229	1,361	1,244	1,532	1,357	1,479	2,216	1,737
Capital Expenditures	41.9	87.2	86.1	110	113	165	30.8	46.4	198	235
Cash Flow	-27.8	-327	131	276	30.7	290	-41.5	-559	-63.5	620
Current Ratio	2.7	1.9	4.2	3.4	2.1	2.9	2.7	2.9	4.1	2.2
% Long Term Debt of Capitalization	17.5	Nil	Nil	Nil	0.1	26.0	30.0	30.5	20.4	0.5
% Net Income of Revenue	NM	NM	6.5	14.7	NM	9.2	NM	NM	NM	17.0
% Return on Assets	NM	NM	4.4	11.3	NM	8.9	NM	NM	NM	26.4
% Return on Equity	NM	NM	5.6	15.6	NM	15.9	NM	NM	NM	36.2

Data as orig reptd.; bef. results of disc opers/spec. items. Per share data adj. for stk. divs.; EPS diluted. E-Estimated. NA-Not Available. NM-Not Meaningful. NR-Not Ranked. UR-Under Review.

Office: 600 Riverpark Dr, North Reading, MA 01864-2634.
Telephone: 978-370-2700.
Email: investorrelations@teradyne.com
Website: http://www.teradyne.com

Chrmn: A. Carnesale
Pres & CEO: M.A. Bradley
CFO, Chief Acctg Officer & Treas: G.R. Beecher
Secy & General Counsel: C.J. Gray

Investor Contact: A. Blanchard (978-370-2425)
Board Members: J. W. Bageley, M. A. Bradley, A. Carnesale, D. W. Christman, E. Gillis, P. Tufano, R. A. Vallee

Founded: 1960
Domicile: Massachusetts
Employees: 2,900

Tesoro Corp

S&P Recommendation	HOLD ★★★☆☆	Price $13.20 (as of Oct 22, 2010)	12-Mo. Target Price $14.00	Investment Style Large-Cap Blend

GICS Sector Energy
Sub-Industry Oil & Gas Refining & Marketing

Summary Tesoro is one of the largest independent refiners and marketers of petroleum products in the U.S., with operations focused on the West Coast.

Key Stock Statistics (Source S&P, Vickers, company reports)

52-Wk Range	$16.80– 10.40	S&P Oper. EPS 2010E	-0.44	Market Capitalization(B)	$1.884	Beta	1.28
Trailing 12-Month EPS	$-1.68	S&P Oper. EPS 2011E	1.30	Yield (%)	Nil	S&P 3-Yr. Proj. EPS CAGR(%)	NM
Trailing 12-Month P/E	NM	P/E on S&P Oper. EPS 2010E	NM	Dividend Rate/Share	Nil	S&P Credit Rating	BB+
$10K Invested 5 Yrs Ago	$5,080	Common Shares Outstg. (M)	142.7	Institutional Ownership (%)	90		

Price Performance

30-Week Mov. Avg. · · · ·   10-Week Mov. Avg. – –   **GAAP Earnings vs. Previous Year**   Volume Above Avg. STARS
12-Mo. Target Price —   Relative Strength —   ▲ Up   ▼ Down   ► No Change   Below Avg.

Options: ASE, CBOE, Ph

Analysis prepared by **Tina J. Vital** on August 09, 2010, when the stock traded at **$ 13.11**.

Highlights

➤ Second quarter refining throughputs fell 16%, to 474,000 b/d, but we look for an increase of about 10% from the second to the third quarter. The company's Anacortes refinery, shut down following a fatal fire on April 2, is scheduled for a restart in September. Results from a U.S. Chemical Safety and Hazard Investigation Board regarding this fire are expected in late August.

➤ Manufacturing costs (before depreciation and amortization) rose 24% in the second quarter, to $5.74 per throughput barrel, but we project second half costs will ease as throughput volumes rise. With signs of improved fuel demand as of July 2010, we projected U.S. Gulf Coast 3-2-1 crack spreads would widen by 9% in 2010 and another 3% in 2011.

➤ We expect an after-tax operating loss in 2010 on poor first quarter results reflecting high West Coast product inventory and high crude costs, but earnings reached positive ground in the second quarter. We expect this trend to continue into 2011 and 2012 on improved demand and cost initiatives.

Investment Rationale/Risk

➤ As a small independent refiner, TSO is vulnerable to challenging industry conditions. In July 2010, TSO said it was a conducting a strategic review of its assets; details are to be provided in the fall. And with about 58% of TSO's refining capacity concentrated in three refineries (Martinez and Los Angeles, CA, and Anacortes, WA), the company is exposed to increased operational risk as well. While a significant portion of TSO's refining capacity is of lower complexity, we believe its facilities are strategically sited to benefit from local markets, particularly in above-average margined California, and we expect TSO to achieve enhanced operational efficiencies from recent refining upgrades.

➤ Risks to our recommendation and target price include worse than expected economic, industry, and operating conditions that lead to narrower refining margins or decreased sales.

➤ A blend of our discounted cash flow ($15 per share, assuming a WACC of 9.8% and terminal growth of 3%) and relative market valuations leads to our 12-month target price of $14. This represents an expected enterprise value of about 4.0X our 2011 EBITDA estimate, a discount to U.S. refining peers.

Qualitative Risk Assessment

LOW	MEDIUM	HIGH

Our risk assessment reflects our view of TSO's satisfactory business profile in a competitive and volatile refining industry. While we believe the company has good asset quality, we believe it has moved into a cash conservation mode given difficult refining conditions.

Quantitative Evaluations

S&P Quality Ranking   B

D	C	B-	B	B+	A-	A	A+

Relative Strength Rank   MODERATE

49

LOWEST = 1   HIGHEST = 99

Revenue/Earnings Data

Revenue (Million $)

	1Q	2Q	3Q	4Q	Year
2010	4,607	5,072	--	--	--
2009	3,280	4,181	4,742	4,669	16,872
2008	6,531	8,754	8,698	4,326	28,309
2007	3,876	5,604	5,902	6,533	21,915
2006	3,877	4,929	5,278	4,020	18,104
2005	3,171	4,033	5,017	4,360	16,581

Earnings Per Share ($)

2010	-1.11	0.47	E0.21	E0.02	E-0.44
2009	0.37	-0.33	-0.24	-1.30	-1.01
2008	-0.60	-0.03	1.86	0.70	2.00
2007	0.84	3.17	0.34	-0.29	4.06
2006	0.31	2.33	1.96	1.14	5.73
2005	0.20	1.31	1.60	0.49	3.60

Fiscal year ended Dec. 31. Next earnings report expected: Early November. EPS Estimates based on S&P Operating Earnings; historical GAAP earnings are as reported.

Dividend Data (Dates: mm/dd Payment Date: mm/dd/yy)

Amount ($)	Date Decl.	Ex-Div. Date	Stk. of Record	Payment Date
0.050	11/09	11/27	12/01	12/15/09

Dividends have been paid since 2005. Source: Company reports.

Please read the Required Disclosures and Analyst Certification on the last page of this report.

The McGraw-Hill Companies

Tesoro Corp

STANDARD &POOR'S

Business Summary August 09, 2010

CORPORATE OVERVIEW. Tesoro Corp. (TSO; formerly Tesoro Petroleum Corp.) is one of the largest independent refiners and marketers of petroleum products in the U.S. The company operates in two business segments: Refining (83% of 2009 revenues; 40% of operating income) and Retail (17%; 60%).

The Refining segment refines crude oil and other feedstocks at its seven refineries (total refining capacity 664,500 b/d, as of December 31, 2009) in the U.S. West and Mid-Continent: California ("Wilmington" in Los Angeles, CA, 97,000 b/d; "Golden Eagle" in Martinez, CA, 166,000 b/d), the Pacific Northwest (Anacortes, WA, 120,000 b/d; and Kenai, AK, 72,000 b/d), the Mid-Pacific (Kapolei, HI, 93,500 b/d) and the Mid-Continent (Mandan, ND, 58,000 b/d; and Salt Lake City, UT, 58,000 b/d). As a result of falling demand and excess refining capacity, refining yields declined 7.4% to 579,000 b/d in 2009, and included gasoline 46%, jet fuel 12%, diesel fuel 20%, and heavy oils, residual products and other 22%.

The company purchases its crude oil and other feedstocks for its refineries from various domestic (about 62% of its 2009 crude oil, with a significant amount from Alaska's North Slope) and foreign (around 38%, with a significant amount from Canada) sources through term agreements (30%), which are mainly short term, and in the spot market. TSO charters tankers to ship crude oil from foreign and domestic sources to its California, Mid-Pacific and Pacific Northwest refineries. About 32% of its total refining throughput was heavy oil (API specific gravity of 24 or less) in 2009, steady with levels in 2008.

TSO's crude pipeline system in North Dakota and in Alaska are common carriers subject to regulation by various federal, state and local agencies, including the FERC under the Interstate Commerce Act.

MARKET PROFILE. TSO is one of the largest independent refiners in the U.S. The company operates the largest refineries in Hawaii and Utah, and the second largest in northern California and Alaska. Through its network of retail stations, TSO sells gasoline and diesel fuel in the western and mid-continental U.S. As of December 31, 2009, TSO's retail segment included 886 branded retail stations (under the Tesoro, Mirastar, Shell and USA Gasoline brands), comprising 387 company-operated retail gasoline stations and 499 jobber/dealer stations. Reflecting market conditions, retail fuel sales declined 1.8%, to 1.33 billion gallons, in 2009.

Company Financials Fiscal Year Ended Dec. 31

Per Share Data ($)	2009	2008	2007	2006	2005	2004	2003	2002	2001	2000
Tangible Book Value	19.84	20.78	19.48	17.09	12.12	8.31	5.70	5.00	6.75	7.17
Cash Flow	1.14	3.97	5.82	7.50	4.92	3.50	1.72	0.11	2.07	1.28
Earnings	-1.01	2.00	4.06	5.73	3.60	2.38	0.58	-0.97	1.05	0.88
S&P Core Earnings	-0.57	1.73	4.12	5.73	3.65	2.42	0.78	-0.97	1.00	NA
Dividends	0.35	0.40	0.35	0.20	0.10	Nil	Nil	Nil	Nil	Nil
Payout Ratio	NM	20%	9%	3%	3%	Nil	Nil	Nil	Nil	Nil
Prices:High	19.16	48.35	65.98	38.40	35.91	17.33	7.56	7.65	8.25	6.50
Prices:Low	10.62	6.71	31.47	26.48	14.13	7.00	1.69	0.62	4.85	4.47
P/E Ratio:High	NM	24	16	7	10	7	13	NM	8	7
P/E Ratio:Low	NM	3	8	5	4	3	3	NM	5	5

Income Statement Analysis (Million $)	2009	2008	2007	2006	2005	2004	2003	2002	2001	2000
Revenue	16,872	28,309	21,915	18,104	16,581	12,262	8,846	7,119	5,218	5,104
Operating Income	NA	787	1,473	1,614	1,232	881	638	120	290	205
Depreciation, Depletion and Amortization	297	274	246	247	186	154	148	131	91.2	45.5
Interest Expense	130	111	125	77.0	211	167	212	166	52.8	32.7
Pretax Income	-188	429	905	1,286	831	547	123	-181	147	124
Effective Tax Rate	25.5%	35.2%	37.5%	37.7%	39.0%	40.0%	38.2%	NM	40.1%	40.6%
Net Income	-140	278	566	801	507	328	76.1	-117	88.0	73.3
S&P Core Earnings	-79.6	241	574	800	514	333	101	-117	77.2	NA

Balance Sheet & Other Financial Data (Million $)	2009	2008	2007	2006	2005	2004	2003	2002	2001	2000
Cash	413	20.0	23.0	986	440	185	77.2	110	51.9	14.1
Current Assets	2,223	1,646	2,600	2,811	2,215	1,393	1,024	1,054	878	630
Total Assets	8,070	7,433	8,128	5,904	5,097	4,075	3,661	3,759	2,662	1,544
Current Liabilities	1,889	1,441	2,494	1,672	1,502	993	687	608	538	382
Long Term Debt	1,810	1,609	1,657	1,029	1,044	1,215	1,605	1,907	1,113	307
Common Equity	3,087	3,218	3,052	2,502	1,887	1,327	965	888	757	505
Total Capital	4,906	5,243	5,097	3,908	3,320	2,835	2,750	2,923	2,006	1,084
Capital Expenditures	437	650	747	436	258	179	101	204	210	94.0
Cash Flow	157	552	812	1,048	693	482	224	13.7	173	107
Current Ratio	1.2	1.1	1.0	1.7	1.5	1.4	1.5	1.7	1.6	1.6
% Long Term Debt of Capitalization	Nil	30.7	32.5	26.3	31.4	42.9	58.4	65.2	55.4	28.3
% Return on Assets	NM	3.6	8.1	14.6	11.1	8.5	2.1	NM	4.2	4.8
% Return on Equity	NA	16.5	20.4	36.5	31.5	28.6	8.2	NM	13.0	12.7

Data as orig reptd.; bef. results of disc opers/spec. items. Per share data adj. for stk. divs.; EPS diluted. E-Estimated. NA-Not Available. NM-Not Meaningful. NR-Not Ranked. UR-Under Review.

Office: 19100 Ridgewood Parkway, San Antonio, TX 78259-1828.
Telephone: 210-626-6000.
Email: investor_relations@tesoropetroleum.com
Website: http://www.tsocorp.com

Chrmn: S.H. Grapstein
Pres & CEO: G.J. Goff
COO & EVP: E.D. Lewis
EVP, Secy & General Counsel: C.S. Parrish

SVP, CFO & Treas: G.S. Spendlove
Investor Contact: S. Phipps (210-283-2882)
Board Members: R. F. Chase, G. J. Goff, R. W. Goldman, S. H. Grapstein, W. J. Johnson, J. W. Nokes, D. H. Schmude, M. E. Wiley

Founded: 1939
Domicile: Delaware
Employees: 5,500

The McGraw-Hill Companies

Texas Instruments Inc

STANDARD &POOR'S

S&P Recommendation HOLD ★★★★★	**Price** $28.66 (as of Oct 22, 2010)	**12-Mo. Target Price** $30.00	**Investment Style** Large-Cap Growth

GICS Sector Information Technology
Sub-Industry Semiconductors

Summary One of the world's largest manufacturers of semiconductors, this company also produces handheld graphing and scientific calculator products.

Key Stock Statistics (Source S&P, Vickers, company reports)

52-Wk Range	$28.98–22.28	S&P Oper. EPS 2010**E**	2.41	Market Capitalization(B)	$34.254	Beta	1.06
Trailing 12-Month EPS	$2.07	S&P Oper. EPS 2011**E**	2.46	Yield (%)	1.81	S&P 3-Yr. Proj. EPS CAGR(%)	21
Trailing 12-Month P/E	13.9	P/E on S&P Oper. EPS 2010**E**	11.9	Dividend Rate/Share	$0.52	S&P Credit Rating	A+
$10K Invested 5 Yrs Ago	$10,058	Common Shares Outstg. (M)	1,195.2	Institutional Ownership (%)	78		

Price Performance

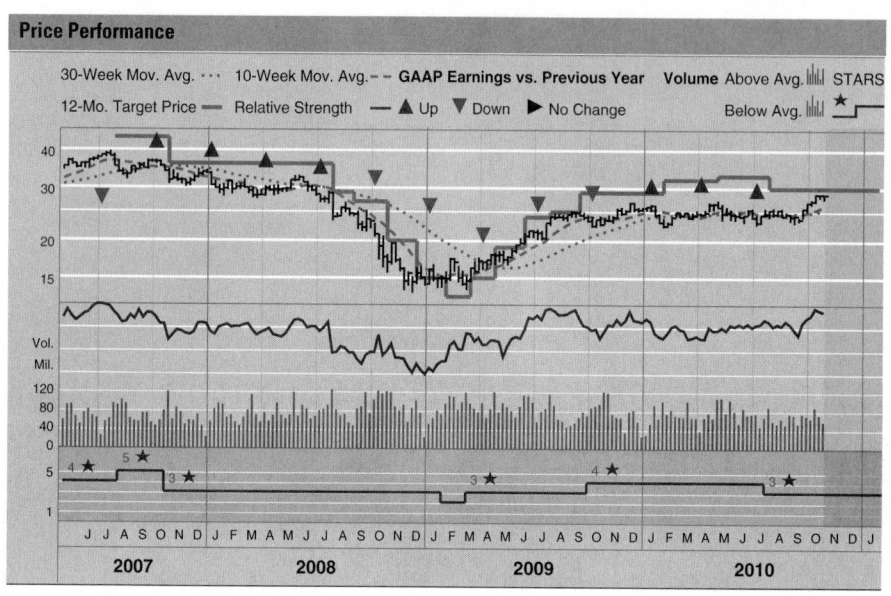

30-Week Mov. Avg. · · · · 10-Week Mov. Avg. — — **GAAP Earnings vs. Previous Year** Volume Above Avg. ▮▮▮ STARS
12-Mo. Target Price — Relative Strength — ▲ Up ▼ Down ▶ No Change Below Avg. ▮▮▮ ★

Options: ASE, CBOE, P, Ph

Analysis prepared by **Clyde Montevirgen** on September 10, 2010, when the stock traded at **$ 23.39**.

Highlights

► We forecast that sales will increase 2% in 2011, after a projected 33% rise in 2010. We look for sales to be aided by healthy demand from industrial markets, the telecom build-out in China, robust computer orders, and the general proliferation of semiconductors in consumer products. Furthermore, we believe that share gains for TXN's higher-margin analog and embedded businesses will help top-line results. However, we see sales growth limited by decreasing baseband revenues as the company winds down this business.

► We expect gross margins to remain around 54% for 2011, similar to what we see for 2010. We believe that a greater mix of analog and embedded chips and lower unit costs from 300 millimeter production will balance higher depreciation and other costs related to capacity expansion. With expenses rising to support TXN's goal of faster top-line growth, we believe operating margins will be around 31% for 2011.

► Our 2011 EPS estimate assumes an effective tax rate of 31% and a modest decline in the diluted share count.

Investment Rationale/Risk

► Our hold opinion reflects our view of fair valuations given anticipated below-industry growth. We believe that TXN's dedication to the analog and embedded markets will provide long-term growth through market share gains and wider margins. We also think TXN's return metrics compare favorably to the industry's. However, deteriorating baseband sales and higher costs related to ramping capacity, as well as anticipated higher expenses to support sales, could lead to sub-par earnings growth over the next several quarters, in our opinion. Also, considering risks due to contracting leadtimes and inventory concerns, we believe that multiples should be near the industry average.

► Risks to our recommendation and target price include a slower-than-peers growth in the analog market, faster-than-anticipated declines in its baseband business, and higher-than-expected costs and expenses related to capacity additions.

► Our 12-month target price of $30 is based on our price-to-earnings (P/E) analysis. We apply a P/E multiple of approximately 12X, near the industry average, to our 2011 EPS estimate.

Qualitative Risk Assessment

LOW	MEDIUM	HIGH

Our risk assessment reflects the cyclicality of the industry in which TXN operates, offset by the large number of company operations, TXN's diverse line of semiconductor products with exposure to many end markets and customers, our view of its low debt levels, and its long corporate history.

Quantitative Evaluations

S&P Quality Ranking B

D	C	B-	B	B+	A-	A	A+

Relative Strength Rank STRONG

79

LOWEST = 1   HIGHEST = 99

Revenue/Earnings Data

Revenue (Million $)

	1Q	2Q	3Q	4Q	Year
2010	3,205	3,496	--	--	--
2009	2,086	2,457	2,880	3,005	10,427
2008	3,272	3,351	3,387	2,491	12,501
2007	3,191	3,424	3,663	3,556	13,835
2006	3,334	3,697	3,761	3,463	14,255
2005	2,972	3,239	3,590	3,591	13,392

Earnings Per Share ($)

2010	0.52	0.63	E0.66	E0.60	E2.41
2009	0.01	0.20	0.42	0.52	1.15
2008	0.49	0.44	0.43	0.08	1.45
2007	0.35	0.42	0.52	0.54	1.83
2006	0.33	0.47	0.45	0.45	1.69
2005	0.24	0.38	0.38	0.40	1.39

Fiscal year ended Dec. 31. Next earnings report expected: NA. EPS Estimates based on S&P Operating Earnings; historical GAAP earnings are as reported.

Dividend Data (Dates: mm/dd Payment Date: mm/dd/yy)

Amount ($)	Date Decl.	Ex-Div. Date	Stk. of Record	Payment Date
0.120	01/21	01/28	02/01	02/22/10
0.120	04/14	04/28	04/30	05/17/10
0.120	07/15	07/28	07/30	08/16/10
0.130	09/16	10/28	11/01	11/22/10

Dividends have been paid since 1962. Source: Company reports.

Please read the Required Disclosures and Analyst Certification on the last page of this report.

The McGraw·Hill Companies

Texas Instruments Inc

Business Summary September 10, 2010

CORPORATE OVERVIEW. Texas Instruments is the world's fourth largest semi-conductor company, based on 2008 revenues. The company's semiconductors are used for various functions including: converting and amplifying signals, interfacing with other devices, managing and distributing power, processing data, canceling noise and improving signal resolution. TXN's product portfolio includes the types of products that are integral to almost all electronic equipment. It offers either custom or standard products. A custom product is designed for a specific customer for a specific application, is sold only to that customer, and is typically sold directly to the customer. A standard product is designed for use by many customers and/or many applications and is generally sold through both distribution and direct channels. Standard products include both proprietary and commodity products. TXN's product segments are analog (40% of sales in 2009), embedded processing (15%), wireless (25%), and other (20%).

Analog semiconductors change real-world signals - such as sound, temperature, pressure or images - by conditioning them, amplifying them, and often converting them to a stream of digital data so the signals can be processed by other semiconductors. Analog products can be further divided by high performance and high volume. High-performance analog products include standard

analog semiconductors, such as amplifiers, data converters, low-power radio frequency devices, and interface and power management semiconductors. High-performance analog products generally have long life cycles, often 10 to 20 years. The high-volume products include two product types. The first, high-volume analog, includes products for specific applications, including custom products for specific customers. The life cycles of TXN's high-volume analog products are generally shorter than those of its high-performance analog products. The second product type, standard linear and logic, includes commodity products marketed to many different customers for many different applications.

Embedded processing include digital signal processors (DSPs) and microcontrollers. DSPs perform mathematical computations almost instantaneously to process and improve digital data. Microcontrollers are microprocessors that are designed to control a set of specific tasks for electronic equipment.

Company Financials Fiscal Year Ended Dec. 31

Per Share Data ($)	2009	2008	2007	2006	2005	2004	2003	2002	2001	2000
Tangible Book Value	6.90	6.43	6.72	7.08	6.99	7.13	6.35	5.73	6.42	6.71
Cash Flow	1.89	2.25	2.57	2.37	2.32	1.93	1.54	0.78	0.94	2.49
Earnings	1.15	1.45	1.83	1.69	1.39	1.05	0.68	-0.20	-0.12	1.73
S&P Core Earnings	1.19	1.40	1.81	1.68	1.26	0.86	0.40	-0.16	-0.34	NA
Dividends	0.45	0.41	0.30	0.13	0.11	0.09	0.09	0.09	0.09	0.09
Payout Ratio	39%	28%	16%	8%	8%	9%	13%	NM	NM	5%
Prices:High	27.00	33.24	39.63	36.40	34.68	33.98	31.67	35.94	54.69	99.78
Prices:Low	13.70	13.38	28.24	26.77	20.70	18.06	13.90	13.10	20.10	35.00
P/E Ratio:High	23	23	22	22	25	32	47	NM	NM	58
P/E Ratio:Low	12	9	15	16	15	17	20	NM	NM	20

Income Statement Analysis (Million $)	2009	2008	2007	2006	2005	2004	2003	2002	2001	2000
Revenue	10,427	12,501	13,835	14,255	13,392	12,580	9,834	8,383	8,201	11,875
Operating Income	3,128	3,794	4,580	4,419	4,222	3,756	2,493	1,977	1,246	3,715
Depreciation	925	1,059	1,070	1,052	1,431	1,549	1,528	1,689	1,828	1,376
Interest Expense	NA	Nil	1.00	7.00	9.00	21.0	39.0	57.0	61.0	75.0
Pretax Income	2,017	2,481	3,692	3,625	2,988	2,421	1,250	-346	-426	4,578
Effective Tax Rate	27.1%	22.6%	28.5%	27.2%	22.2%	23.1%	4.16%	NM	NM	32.6%
Net Income	1,470	1,920	2,641	2,638	2,324	1,861	1,198	-344	-201	3,087
S&P Core Earnings	1,507	1,855	2,609	2,614	2,110	1,516	701	-275	-587	NA

Balance Sheet & Other Financial Data (Million $)	2009	2008	2007	2006	2005	2004	2003	2002	2001	2000
Cash	2,925	2,540	2,924	1,183	1,219	2,668	1,818	949	431	745
Current Assets	6,114	5,790	6,918	7,854	9,185	10,190	7,709	6,126	5,775	8,115
Total Assets	12,119	11,923	12,667	13,930	15,063	16,299	15,510	14,679	15,779	17,720
Current Liabilities	1,587	1,532	2,025	2,078	2,346	1,925	2,200	1,934	1,580	2,813
Long Term Debt	NA	Nil	Nil	Nil	360	368	395	833	1,211	1,216
Common Equity	9,722	9,326	9,975	11,711	11,937	13,063	11,864	10,734	11,879	12,588
Total Capital	9,722	9,385	10,024	11,734	12,320	13,471	12,318	11,696	13,421	14,273
Capital Expenditures	753	763	686	1,272	1,330	1,298	800	802	1,790	2,762
Cash Flow	2,395	2,979	3,711	3,690	3,882	3,410	2,726	1,345	1,627	4,463
Current Ratio	3.9	3.8	3.4	3.8	3.9	5.3	3.5	3.2	3.7	2.9
% Long Term Debt of Capitalization	Nil	Nil	Nil	Nil	2.9	2.7	3.2	7.1	9.0	8.5
% Net Income of Revenue	14.1	15.4	19.1	18.5	17.4	14.8	12.2	NM	NM	26.0
% Return on Assets	12.2	15.6	19.9	18.2	14.8	11.7	7.9	NM	NM	18.6
% Return on Equity	15.4	19.9	24.8	22.2	18.6	14.9	10.6	NM	NM	27.9

Data as orig reptd.; bef. results of disc opers/spec. items. Per share data adj. for stk. divs.; EPS diluted. E-Estimated. NA-Not Available. NM-Not Meaningful. NR-Not Ranked. UR-Under Review.

Office: PO Box 660199, Dallas, TX 75266-0199.
Telephone: 972-995-3773.
Website: http://www.ti.com
Chrmn, Pres & CEO: R.K. Templeton

SVP, CFO & Chief Acctg Officer: K.P. March
SVP, Secy & General Counsel: J.F. Hubach
Treas: B. Bull
Investor Contact: R. Slaymaker (972-995-3773)

Board Members: J. R. Adams, R. W. Babb, Jr., D. L. Boren, D. A. Carp, C. S. Cox, D. Goode, S. P. MacMillan, P. H. Patsley, W. R. Sanders, R. J. Simmons, R. K. Templeton, C. T. Whitman

Founded: 1930
Domicile: Delaware
Employees: 26,584

Textron Inc.

STANDARD
&POOR'S

S&P Recommendation HOLD ★ ★ ★ ★ ★

Price $20.95 (as of Oct 22, 2010)	**12-Mo. Target Price** $24.00	**Investment Style** Large-Cap Value

GICS Sector Industrials
Sub-Industry Industrial Conglomerates

Summary This aerospace and industrial conglomerate makes Cessna business jets, Bell helicopters, and industrial equipment and components. It also operates a diversified commercial finance company.

Key Stock Statistics (Source S&P, Vickers, company reports)

52-Wk Range	$25.30– 15.88	S&P Oper. EPS 2010**E**	0.33	Market Capitalization(B)	$5.745	Beta	2.82
Trailing 12-Month EPS	$0.05	S&P Oper. EPS 2011**E**	1.20	Yield (%)	0.38	S&P 3-Yr. Proj. EPS CAGR(%)	NM
Trailing 12-Month P/E	NM	P/E on S&P Oper. EPS 2010**E**	63.5	Dividend Rate/Share	$0.08	S&P Credit Rating	BBB-
$10K Invested 5 Yrs Ago	$6,262	Common Shares Outstg. (M)	274.2	Institutional Ownership (%)	85		

Price Performance

30-Week Mov. Avg. · · ·   10-Week Mov. Avg. - - **GAAP Earnings vs. Previous Year**   Volume Above Avg. ⅡⅢ STARS
12-Mo. Target Price —   Relative Strength —   ▲ Up ▼ Down ▶ No Change   Below Avg. ⅡⅢ ★

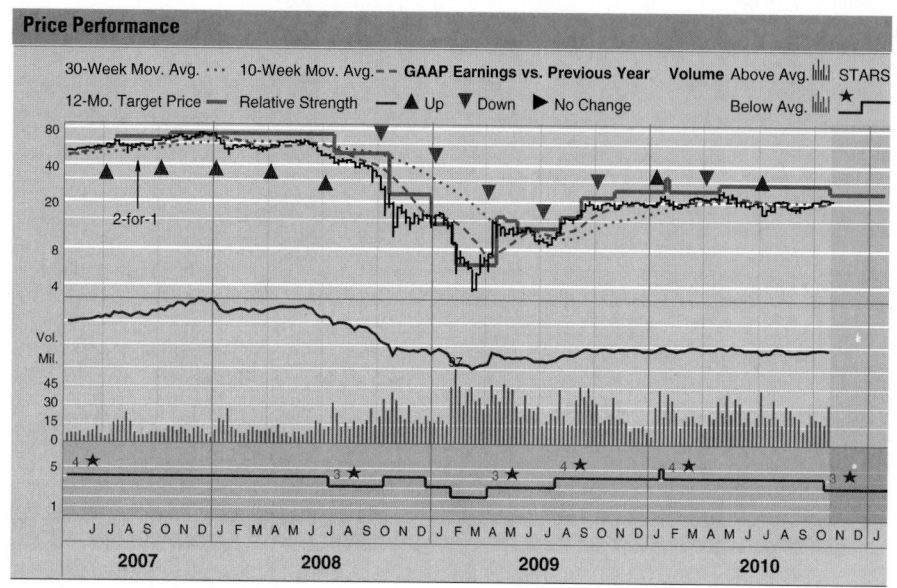

Options: ASE, CBOE, P, Ph

Highlights

> ► The STARS recommendation for TXT has recently been changed to 3 (hold) from 4 (buy) and the 12-month target price has recently been changed to $24.00 from $28.00. The Highlights section of this Stock Report will be updated accordingly.

Investment Rationale/Risk

> ► The Investment Rationale/Risk section of this Stock Report will be updated shortly. For the latest News story on TXT from MarketScope, see below.

> ► 10/21/10 10:47 am ET ... S&P ADDS SHARES OF DOMINO'S PIZZA TO TOP TEN PORTFOLIO (DPZ 15.23*****): We foresee strong customer traffic trends for DPZ as it promotes new pizza items with an extensive advertising campaign. Results for Q3 released Oct. 19 showed an impressive gain in same-store sales of almost 12%. We see opportunities for international growth. Cost controls across the organization should aid margins. We estimate EPS of $1.25 for 2010, with improvement to $1.55 for 2011. Our DCF-based 12-month target price is $22. The shares replace those of aerospace and industrial conglomerate Textron (TXT 21***) which was downgraded to Hold from Buy on Oct. 20. /T.Smith-CFA

Qualitative Risk Assessment

LOW	MEDIUM	**HIGH**

Our risk assessment reflects our view of TXT's history of cyclical earnings, as well as its significant debt burden and exposure to bad loans.

Quantitative Evaluations

S&P Quality Ranking   B

D	C	B-	**B**	B+	A-	A	A+

Relative Strength Rank   MODERATE

58

LOWEST = 1   HIGHEST = 99

Revenue/Earnings Data

Revenue (Million $)

	1Q	2Q	3Q	4Q	Year
2010	2,210	2,709	--	--	--
2009	2,526	2,612	2,549	2,813	10,500
2008	3,518	3,919	3,533	3,606	14,246
2007	2,964	3,235	3,263	3,763	13,225
2006	2,632	2,820	2,837	3,201	11,490
2005	2,791	3,188	2,862	2,701	10,043

Earnings Per Share ($)

2010	-0.01	0.27	E-0.17	E0.22	E0.33
2009	0.18	-0.23	0.02	-0.22	-0.28
2008	0.93	1.03	0.85	-1.44	1.38
2007	0.78	0.85	0.95	1.02	3.59
2006	0.60	0.67	0.68	0.77	2.72
2005	0.29	0.47	-0.63	0.63	1.89

Fiscal year ended Dec. 31. Next earnings report expected: Late October. EPS Estimates based on S&P Operating Earnings; historical GAAP earnings are as reported.

Dividend Data (Dates: mm/dd Payment Date: mm/dd/yy)

Amount ($)	Date Decl.	Ex-Div. Date	Stk. of Record	Payment Date
0.020	10/21	12/09	12/11	01/01/10
0.020	02/24	03/10	03/12	04/01/10
0.020	04/28	06/09	06/11	07/01/10
0.020	07/29	09/08	09/10	10/01/10

Dividends have been paid since 1942. Source: Company reports.

Textron Inc.

Business Summary August 04, 2010

CORPORATE OVERVIEW. Textron, an $11 billion in estimated 2010 revenue aerospace and industrial conglomerate, conducts business through five operating segments.

The Cessna segment (32% of sales and 42% of operating profits in 2009) primarily makes the Cessna brand aircraft. Business lines include Citation business jets, Caravan single-engine turboprops, Cessna single-engine piston aircraft, and aftermarket services. Based on revenues, Cessna is the world's third largest corporate jet maker, behind Canada's Bombardier and General Dynamics' Gulfstream division; however, it is the world's largest business jet maker in unit volume. The family of business jets currently produced by Cessna includes the Mustang, the Citation CJ1+, CJ2+, CJ3, and CJ4, the Citation Encore+, the Citation XLS+, the Citation Sovereign, and Citation X. The Citation X is the world's fastest business jet, with a maximum speed of Mach 0.92. First customer deliveries of the Citation CJ4 are scheduled to begin in 2010. The Cessna Caravan (four models) is the world's best-selling utility turboprop. Cessna also offers nine models in its single-engine piston product line.

Bell Helicopter (27%; 64%) is the world's third largest rotary-wing aircraft maker, behind United Technologies' Sikorsky Unit and EADS's Eurocopter unit. Bell makes helicopters and tiltrotor aircraft (the V-22 Osprey) for both military and commercial applications, and provides spare parts and service. Bell supplies advanced military helicopters and support (including spare parts, support equipment, technical data, trainers, etc.) to the U.S. government and to military customers outside the U.S. Bell is also a leading supplier of commercially certified helicopters to corporate, offshore petroleum exploration and development, utility, charter, police, fire, rescue and emergency medical helicopter operators. The V-22 Osprey is a military tiltrotor aircraft built in conjunction with Boeing, with contracts for 285 units (116 of which had been delivered as of year-end 2009). Bell also makes the Marine Corps. H-1 helicopter (AH-1Z and UH-1Z), with a program of record that calls for 349 production units. Bell's commercial offerings include the 206, 407, 412, and 429.

Company Financials Fiscal Year Ended Dec. 31

Per Share Data ($)	2009	2008	2007	2006	2005	2004	2003	2002	2001	2000
Tangible Book Value	4.42	2.06	2.77	4.86	8.02	7.35	8.09	6.46	6.20	5.80
Cash Flow	1.28	2.81	4.91	3.95	3.15	2.69	2.32	2.61	2.38	2.64
Earnings	-0.28	1.38	3.59	2.72	1.89	1.33	1.03	1.30	0.58	0.95
S&P Core Earnings	-0.23	1.11	3.51	2.66	2.06	1.01	0.59	0.14	-0.70	NA
Dividends	0.08	0.92	0.85	0.78	0.70	0.66	0.65	0.65	0.65	0.65
Payout Ratio	NM	67%	24%	29%	37%	50%	63%	50%	NM	68%
Prices:High	21.00	70.14	74.40	49.48	40.36	37.46	29.00	26.80	30.24	38.75
Prices:Low	3.57	10.09	43.60	37.76	32.60	25.30	13.00	16.10	15.65	20.34
P/E Ratio:High	NM	51	21	18	21	28	28	21	52	41
P/E Ratio:Low	NM	7	12	14	17	19	13	12	27	21

Income Statement Analysis (Million $)										
Revenue	10,500	14,246	13,225	11,490	10,043	10,242	9,859	10,658	12,321	13,090
Operating Income	830	1,974	2,120	1,703	1,450	1,260	1,171	1,285	1,461	2,074
Depreciation	409	358	336	290	303	353	356	368	514	494
Interest Expense	309	432	484	438	290	248	283	330	459	492
Pretax Income	-149	658	1,300	437	739	528	388	464	393	585
Effective Tax Rate	51.0%	47.7%	29.6%	NM	30.2%	29.4%	27.6%	21.6%	57.8%	52.6%
Net Income	-73.0	344	915	706	516	373	281	364	166	277
S&P Core Earnings	-63.9	272	895	690	565	282	161	38.6	-202	NA

Balance Sheet & Other Financial Data (Million $)										
Cash	1,748	531	531	780	796	732	843	307	260	289
Current Assets	12,761	4,766	4,846	4,287	4,975	4,168	3,592	3,887	4,017	3,914
Total Assets	18,940	20,020	19,956	17,550	16,499	15,875	15,090	15,505	16,052	16,370
Current Liabilities	4,905	7,406	7,248	2,994	3,147	2,975	2,256	2,239	3,075	3,263
Long Term Debt	3,450	6,779	6,384	6,150	7,079	6,141	6,144	7,038	5,962	6,648
Common Equity	2,826	2,366	3,505	2,639	3,266	3,642	3,680	3,395	3,923	3,982
Total Capital	6,410	3,924	10,363	8,799	10,816	10,246	10,224	10,842	10,253	10,957
Capital Expenditures	238	550	401	431	365	302	301	296	532	527
Cash Flow	336	702	1,251	996	819	726	637	732	680	771
Current Ratio	2.1	1.8	1.2	1.4	1.6	1.4	1.6	1.7	1.3	1.2
% Long Term Debt of Capitalization	53.8	172.7	61.6	69.9	65.4	59.9	60.1	64.9	58.1	60.7
% Net Income of Revenue	NM	2.4	6.9	6.1	5.1	3.6	2.9	3.4	1.3	2.1
% Return on Assets	NM	1.7	4.9	4.1	3.2	2.4	1.8	2.3	1.0	1.7
% Return on Equity	NM	11.7	29.8	23.9	14.9	10.2	7.9	9.9	4.2	6.6

Data as orig reptd.; bef. results of disc opers/spec. items. Per share data adj. for stk. divs.; EPS diluted. E-Estimated. NA-Not Available. NM-Not Meaningful. NR-Not Ranked. UR-Under Review.

Office: 40 Westminster Street, Providence, RI 02903-2525.
Telephone: 401-421-2800.
Website: http://www.textron.com
Chrmn, Pres & CEO: S. Donnelly

EVP & CFO: F.T. Connor
EVP, Secy & General Counsel: T. O'Donnell
SVP, Chief Acctg Officer & Cntlr: D. Yates
Chief Admin Officer: J.D. Butler

Investor Contact: D.R. Wilburne (401-457-2353)
Board Members: K. M. Bader, R. K. Clark, S. Donnelly, I. J. Evans, L. Fish, J. T. Ford, P. Gagne, D. M. Hancock, C. D. Powell, L. G. Trotter, T. B. Wheeler, J. Ziemer
Founded: 1928
Domicile: Delaware
Employees: 32,000

Thermo Fisher Scientific Inc

STANDARD &POOR'S

S&P Recommendation	**STRONG BUY** ★★★★	Price $49.66 (as of Oct 22, 2010)	12-Mo. Target Price $68.00	Investment Style Large-Cap Growth

GICS Sector Health Care
Sub-Industry Life Sciences Tools & Services

Summary Formed through the November 2006 merger of Thermo Electron and Fisher Scientific, TMO is a leading manufacturer and developer of analytical and laboratory instruments and supplies for life science, drug discovery, and industrial applications.

Key Stock Statistics (Source S&P, Vickers, company reports)

52-Wk Range	$57.40– 41.74	S&P Oper. EPS 2010**E**	3.49	Market Capitalization(B)	$20.233	Beta		0.80
Trailing 12-Month EPS	$2.30	S&P Oper. EPS 2011**E**	3.92	Yield (%)	Nil	S&P 3-Yr. Proj. EPS CAGR(%)		13
Trailing 12-Month P/E	21.6	P/E on S&P Oper. EPS 2010**E**	14.2	Dividend Rate/Share	Nil	S&P Credit Rating		A-
$10K Invested 5 Yrs Ago	$16,438	Common Shares Outstg. (M)	407.4	Institutional Ownership (%)	91			

Price Performance

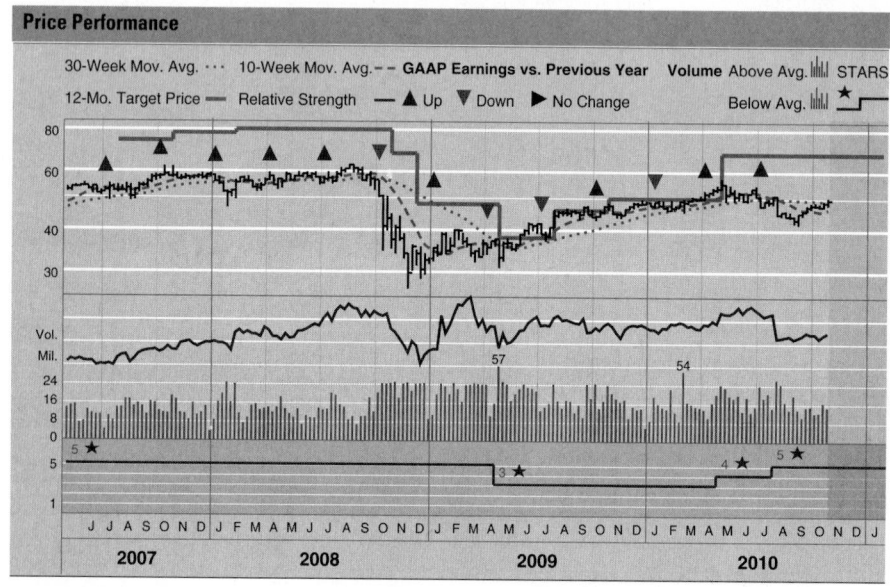

30-Week Mov. Avg. · · · 10-Week Mov. Avg. - - GAAP Earnings vs. Previous Year   Volume Above Avg. STARS
12-Mo. Target Price — Relative Strength — ▲ Up ▼ Down ► No Change   Below Avg. ★

Options: ASE, CBOE, Ph

Analysis prepared by **Jeffrey Loo, CFA** on August 20, 2010, when the stock traded at **$ 44.09.**

Highlights

➤ We expect 2010 and 2011 sales, with a neutral foreign exchange impact, to increase 6% each year to $10.7 billion and $11.35 billion, rebounding from a 4% decline in 2009. We look for 2010 sales within the laboratory products unit to rise 6% and analytical technologies to advance 8%. We expect better instrument sales as we see improvement in industrial end-markets, but we forecast only a flat or modest advance in the pharmaceutical sector as R&D spending remains modest amid a cautious environment. We believe pharmaceutical spending will improve in 2011.

➤ TMO has also made significant inroads in China, and we believe that country will become a key growth driver over the next several years. We see 2010 gross margins widening 80 basis points, mainly on improved efficiency and facility closures, and operating margins improving 100 basis points, after the 90 basis point decline in 2009, on leverage and improvement from global sourcing.

➤ We estimate EPS of $3.49 and $3.92 in 2010 and 2011, before amortization of intangible assets.

Investment Rationale/Risk

➤ We recently raised our opinion on the shares to strong buy from buy. At 12.7X and 11.3X our 2010 and 2011 EPS estimates, respectively, below peers and well below historical levels, TMO is undervalued, in our view. Although the economic environment remains challenging, we believe TMO, with its comprehensive product offering and broad geographic coverage, will be able to capture market share and grow faster than the market. We believe several of TMO's end-markets are beginning to stabilize, and we think its industrial end-markets are recovering faster than we had anticipated. We think clients continue to seek efficiency and consolidate suppliers, and we believe TMO will be a main beneficiary as the challenging environment has adversely affected TMO's smaller peers to a greater extent.

➤ Risks to our opinion and target price include a slower than expected recovery in TMO's end-markets and loss of market share.

➤ Our 12-month target price of $68 assumes a PEG ratio of 1.5X, in line with peers, based on our 2010 EPS estimate of $3.49 and a projected three-year EPS growth rate of 13%.

Qualitative Risk Assessment

LOW	**MEDIUM**	HIGH

Our risk assessment reflects TMO's broad product lines and geographic coverage, spread across the life sciences, health care, and industrial markets, which we believe reduces risk. However, TMO has a proactive acquisition strategy that we believe raises its risk profile.

Quantitative Evaluations

S&P Quality Ranking   **B-**

D	C	**B-**	B	B+	A-	A	A+

Relative Strength Rank   **MODERATE**

	59	
LOWEST = 1		HIGHEST = 99

Revenue/Earnings Data

Revenue (Million $)

	1Q	2Q	3Q	4Q	Year
2010	2,675	2,649	--	--	--
2009	2,255	2,484	2,531	2,839	10,110
2008	2,554	2,710	2,588	2,646	10,498
2007	2,338	2,386	2,401	2,621	9,746
2006	684.3	713.5	725.0	1,669	3,792
2005	559.2	653.6	679.4	740.8	2,633

Earnings Per Share ($)

2010	0.55	0.57	E0.84	E0.97	E3.49
2009	0.35	0.49	0.53	0.65	2.01
2008	0.54	0.56	0.50	0.68	2.27
2007	0.31	0.42	0.51	0.53	1.76
2006	0.26	0.30	0.30	0.08	0.82
2005	0.28	0.35	0.25	0.34	1.21

Fiscal year ended Dec. 31. Next earnings report expected: Late October. EPS Estimates based on S&P Operating Earnings; historical GAAP earnings are as reported.

Dividend Data

No cash dividends have been paid.

Please read the Required Disclosures and Analyst Certification on the last page of this report.

The McGraw·Hill Companies

Thermo Fisher Scientific Inc

STANDARD
&POOR'S

Business Summary August 20, 2010

CORPORATE OVERVIEW. In November 2006, Thermo Electron Corp. and Fisher Scientific completed a stock-for-stock merger. The combined company was renamed Thermo Fisher Scientific (TMO) and is a leading provider of life science and laboratory analytical instruments, equipment, reagents and consumables, software and services for research, analysis, discovery and diagnosis. Following the merger the company had annual revenues in excess of $9 billion, with over 30,000 employees in 38 countries providing services and sales in over 150 countries. Major end-markets served include drug discovery, proteomics research, biopharma services, molecular diagnostics, immunohistochemistry, cell screening, environmental regulatory compliance, and food safety. TMO believes these markets represent a combined $70 billion to $80 billion annual marketplace. We believe TMO is the largest company within its marketplace, with the broadest product offering and geographic coverage.

The legacy Thermo Electron business focuses primarily on the development and manufacture of analytical systems, instruments and components and provides solutions to monitor, collect and analyze data. These instruments are used primarily in life science, drug discovery, clinical, environmental and industrial laboratory applications. The legacy Fisher Scientific business focuses

on providing a broad range of over 600,000 scientific research, health care and safety-related products and services. Customers included pharmaceutical and biotechnology companies, colleges and universities, medical research institutions, hospitals and reference labs, and research and development labs.

The company now reports through two business segments: Analytical Technologies and Laboratory Products and Services. Analytical Technologies should account for about 40% of sales and focuses on scientific instruments, bioscience reagents, lab informatics and automation, diagnostics, environmental monitoring instruments and industrial process instruments. Analytical Technologies is comprised primarily of the legacy Thermo Electron business. Laboratory Products and Services, comprised primarily of legacy Fisher Scientific business should account for about 60% of sales and focuses on lab equipment and consumables and biopharma outsourcing services.

Company Financials Fiscal Year Ended Dec. 31

Per Share Data ($)	2009	2008	2007	2006	2005	2004	2003	2002	2001	2000
Tangible Book Value	0.27	NM	NM	NM	2.32	6.19	5.00	3.79	1.33	6.34
Cash Flow	3.88	4.10	3.46	2.00	1.95	1.70	1.35	1.35	0.81	0.94
Earnings	2.01	2.27	1.76	0.82	1.21	1.31	1.04	1.12	0.27	0.36
S&P Core Earnings	1.99	2.16	1.78	0.83	1.01	1.18	0.79	0.50	0.02	NA
Dividends	Nil	Nil	Nil	Nil	Nil	Nil	Nil	Nil	Nil	Nil
Payout Ratio	Nil	Nil	Nil	Nil	Nil	Nil	Nil	Nil	Nil	Nil
Prices:High	49.70	62.77	62.02	46.34	31.87	31.40	25.40	24.60	30.62	31.24
Prices:Low	30.83	26.65	43.60	29.95	23.94	24.00	16.89	14.33	16.55	14.00
P/E Ratio:High	25	28	35	57	26	24	24	22	NM	87
P/E Ratio:Low	15	12	25	37	20	18	16	13	NM	39

Income Statement Analysis (Million $)										
Revenue	10,110	10,498	9,746	3,792	2,633	2,206	2,097	2,086	2,188	2,281
Operating Income	1,905	2,059	1,823	528	404	319	292	264	265	296
Depreciation	787	793	757	241	123	66.1	58.5	56.4	98.5	97.5
Interest Expense	118	130	140	51.9	26.7	11.0	18.7	Nil	71.8	Nil
Pretax Income	927	1,150	881	209	286	259	219	288	70.7	185
Effective Tax Rate	8.18%	14.0%	11.5%	20.6%	30.6%	15.8%	21.0%	32.3%	38.1%	60.7%
Net Income	851	989	780	166	198	218	173	195	49.6	62.0
S&P Core Earnings	847	941	785	169	164	196	131	79.3	5.63	NA

Balance Sheet & Other Financial Data (Million $)										
Cash	1,571	1,288	639	667	214	327	304	339	298	506
Current Assets	4,531	4,346	3,665	3,660	1,354	1,470	1,395	1,772	1,965	2,466
Total Assets	21,601	21,090	21,207	21,262	4,252	3,577	3,389	3,647	3,825	4,863
Current Liabilities	1,639	1,540	1,902	2,152	792	579	685	1,104	1,142	729
Long Term Debt	2,066	2,044	2,046	2,181	469	226	230	451	728	1,528
Common Equity	15,431	14,927	14,488	13,912	2,793	2,666	2,383	2,033	1,908	2,534
Total Capital	17,497	16,979	18,814	18,650	3,327	2,907	2,624	2,495	2,650	4,098
Capital Expenditures	208	264	176	76.8	43.5	50.0	46.1	51.2	84.8	74.0
Cash Flow	1,639	1,781	1,536	407	322	285	231	252	148	160
Current Ratio	2.8	2.8	1.9	1.7	1.7	2.5	2.0	1.6	1.7	3.4
% Long Term Debt of Capitalization	11.8	12.0	10.9	11.7	14.1	7.8	8.7	18.1	27.4	37.3
% Net Income of Revenue	8.4	9.4	8.0	4.4	7.5	9.9	8.2	9.4	2.3	2.7
% Return on Assets	4.0	4.7	3.7	1.3	5.1	6.3	4.9	5.2	1.1	1.2
% Return on Equity	5.6	6.7	5.5	2.0	7.3	8.7	7.8	9.9	2.2	2.7

Data as orig reptd.; bef. results of disc opers/spec. items. Per share data adj. for stk. divs.; EPS diluted. E-Estimated. NA-Not Available. NM-Not Meaningful. NR-Not Ranked. UR-Under Review.

Office: 81 Wyman St PO Box 9046, Waltham, MA 02254-9046.
Telephone: 781-622-1000.
Website: http://www.fishersci.com
Chrmn: J.P. Manzi

Pres & CEO: M.N. Casper
SVP & CFO: P.M. Wilver
SVP, Secy & General Counsel: S.H. Hoogasian
Chief Acctg Officer: P.E. Hornstra

Investor Contact: K.J. Apicerno (781-622-1111)
Board Members: M. N. Casper, T. Jacks, J. C. Lewent, T. Lynch, P. J. Manning, J. P. Manzi, W. G. Parrett, M. E. Porter, S. M. Sperling, E. S. Ullian

Founded: 1956
Domicile: Delaware
Employees: 35,400

3M Co

STANDARD &POOR'S

S&P Recommendation	BUY ★★★★☆	Price $90.44 (as of Oct 22, 2010)	12-Mo. Target Price $101.00	Investment Style Large-Cap Growth

GICS Sector Industrials
Sub-Industry Industrial Conglomerates

Summary This diversified global company provides enhanced product functionality in electronics, healthcare, industrial, consumer, office, telecommunications, safety & security and other markets via coatings, sealants, adhesives, and other chemical properties.

Key Stock Statistics (Source S&P, Vickers, company reports)

52-Wk Range	$90.90– 67.98	S&P Oper. EPS 2010E	5.79	Market Capitalization(B)	$64.496	Beta	0.82
Trailing 12-Month EPS	$5.48	S&P Oper. EPS 2011E	6.16	Yield (%)	2.32	S&P 3-Yr. Proj. EPS CAGR(%)	10
Trailing 12-Month P/E	16.5	P/E on S&P Oper. EPS 2010E	15.6	Dividend Rate/Share	$2.10	S&P Credit Rating	AA-
$10K Invested 5 Yrs Ago	$13,793	Common Shares Outstg. (M)	713.1	Institutional Ownership (%)	69		

Price Performance

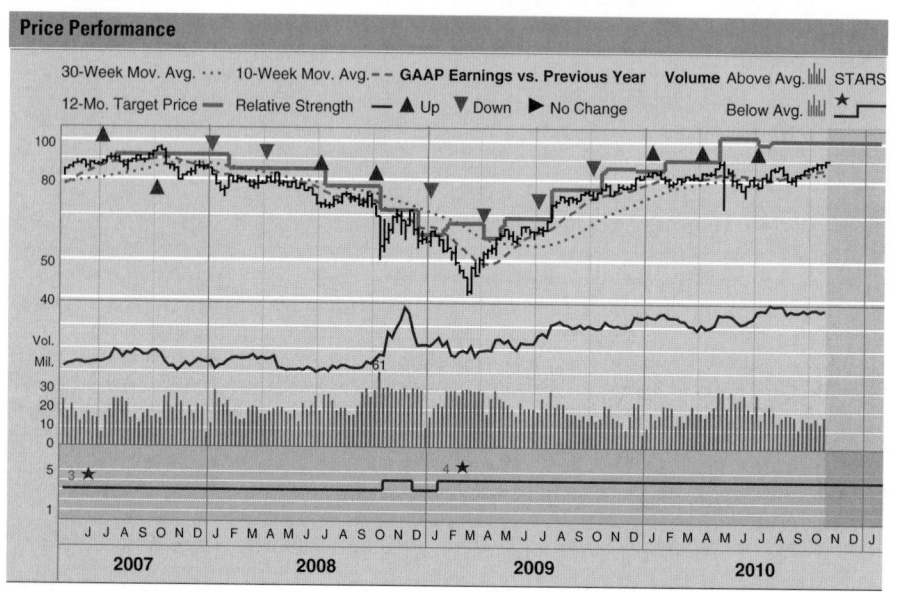

30-Week Mov. Avg. · · · · 10-Week Mov. Avg. – – GAAP Earnings vs. Previous Year Volume Above Avg. STARS
12-Mo. Target Price — Relative Strength — ▲ Up ▼ Down ▶ No Change Below Avg.

Options: ASE, CBOE, P, Ph

Analysis prepared by **Mathew Christy, CFA** on September 15, 2010, when the stock traded at **$ 84.29**.

Qualitative Risk Assessment

LOW	MEDIUM	HIGH

Our risk assessment reflects our view of the company's strong historical earnings and dividend growth, its leading position in many of the markets it serves, its strong balance sheet with a relatively low amount of debt, and free cash flow that has averaged more than net income over the past 10 years.

Quantitative Evaluations

S&P Quality Ranking A+

D	C	B-	B	B+	A-	A	A+

Relative Strength Rank MODERATE

64

LOWEST = 1 HIGHEST = 99

Revenue/Earnings Data

Revenue (Million $)

	1Q	2Q	3Q	4Q	Year
2010	6,348	6,731	--	--	--
2009	5,089	5,719	6,193	6,122	23,123
2008	6,463	6,739	6,558	5,509	25,269
2007	5,937	6,142	6,177	6,206	24,462
2006	5,595	5,688	5,858	5,782	22,923
2005	5,166	5,294	5,382	5,325	21,167

Earnings Per Share ($)

	1Q	2Q	3Q	4Q	Year
2010	1.29	1.55	E1.50	E1.46	E5.79
2009	0.74	1.12	1.35	1.30	4.52
2008	1.38	1.33	1.41	0.77	4.89
2007	1.85	1.25	1.32	1.17	5.60
2006	1.17	1.15	1.18	1.57	5.06
2005	1.03	1.00	1.10	1.04	4.16

Fiscal year ended Dec. 31. Next earnings report expected: NA. EPS Estimates based on S&P Operating Earnings; historical GAAP earnings are as reported.

Highlights

▶ Following an 8.5% decline in 2009 revenues due to the weak global economy, we project that revenues will increase more than 14% this year as a result of greater volumes, pricing, and the positive effects of currency translation. In addition, our forecast is based on projected strength across all of 3M's business units -- especially higher results at the industrial, electronics, display & graphics and consumer & office units -- as the economy continues to recover. In 2011, we forecast that revenue will rise more than 5%, and we expect modest gains across the business platform.

▶ We think 3M's strong product portfolio, innovation-based culture and continual investment in research and development provide operating margin resilience, which we believe was seen in 2009's operating margin performance, down only 80 basis points. We expect that 3M will continue to pursue innovation, and see this leading to higher pricing and margins in 2010 and 2011.

▶ Assuming an effective tax rate of about 28% this year and next year, we estimate EPS of $5.79 rising to $6.16 in the respective years.

Investment Rationale/Risk

▶ We view positively 3M's ability to generate strong returns on capital and free cash flows. In addition, we like the company's early cycle, innovative, consumable-product business mix, and believe the company's strategy of marketing new and innovative products to capture market share and increase operating margins will continue to benefit results. We view the shares, recently trading at about 15X our 2010 EPS estimate, below the peer average but at a historical premium, as attractively valued.

▶ Risks to our recommendation and target price include slower global economic growth, execution risk associated with acquisitions, failure to market new and innovative products, and inability to promote growth in developing markets.

▶ Our 12-month target price of $101 is based on a blend of valuations. Our DCF model, which assumes 3% growth in perpetuity and a 9.1% discount rate, indicates intrinsic value of $95. In terms of relative valuation, we apply a multiple of about 18.5X, ahead of peers, to our 2010 EPS estimate, suggesting a value of $107.

Dividend Data (Dates: mm/dd Payment Date: mm/dd/yy)

Amount ($)	Date Decl.	Ex-Div. Date	Stk. of Record	Payment Date
0.510	11/10	11/18	11/20	12/12/09
0.525	02/09	02/17	02/19	03/12/10
0.525	05/11	05/19	05/21	06/12/10
0.525	08/09	08/18	08/20	09/12/10

Dividends have been paid since 1916. Source: Company reports.

Please read the Required Disclosures and Analyst Certification on the last page of this report.

The **McGraw·Hill** Companies

3M Co

Business Summary September 15, 2010

CORPORATE OVERVIEW. 3M Co. is a global manufacturer operating a broadly diversified business. The company classifies its business into six reportable segments -- Industrial & Transportation, Health Care, Display & Graphics, Consumer & Office, Electro & Communications, and Safety, Security and Protection. Most 3M products involve expertise in product development, manufacturing and marketing with many of the company's products involving some form of coating, sealant, adhesive, film, or chemical additive that increases the products overall functionality. As of the end of 2009, the company employed nearly 75,000 people.

The Industrial & Transportation segment (30% of 2009 revenues, with an 18.6% operating margin) serves a broad range of markets, from appliances and electronics to paper and packaging, food and beverages, automotive, automotive aftermarket, aerospace and marine, and other transportation-related industries. Products include pressure-sensitive tapes, abrasives, adhesives, specialty materials, supply chain management software and solutions, insulation components, films, masking tapes, fasteners and adhesives, to name a few.

The Health Care segment (18% and 31.9%) serves markets worldwide, including medical and surgical, pharmaceutical, dental, health information systems and personal care, with a variety of medical and surgical, infection prevention, pharmaceutical, drug delivery, dental, personal care and other products and systems.

The Display & Graphics segment (13% and 19.5%) serves markets that include electronic display, touch screen, commercial graphics and traffic control materials. Optical products include Vikkuiti display enhancement films for electronic displays, lens systems for projection televisions, and 3M MicroTouch touch screens and touch monitors.

Company Financials Fiscal Year Ended Dec. 31

Per Share Data ($)	2009	2008	2007	2006	2005	2004	2003	2002	2001	2000
Tangible Book Value	7.87	3.93	13.40	7.04	8.13	9.62	6.62	4.91	6.23	7.17
Cash Flow	6.16	6.52	7.06	6.48	5.43	5.01	4.23	3.70	3.15	3.60
Earnings	4.52	4.89	5.60	5.06	4.16	3.75	3.02	2.49	1.79	2.32
S&P Core Earnings	4.40	3.77	4.68	4.26	4.13	3.66	2.91	1.71	0.94	NA
Dividends	2.04	2.00	1.92	1.84	1.68	1.44	1.32	1.24	1.20	1.16
Payout Ratio	45%	41%	34%	36%	40%	38%	44%	50%	67%	50%
Prices:High	84.32	84.76	97.00	88.35	87.45	90.29	85.40	65.78	63.50	61.47
Prices:Low	40.87	50.10	72.90	67.05	69.71	73.31	59.73	50.00	42.93	39.09
P/E Ratio:High	19	17	17	17	21	24	28	26	35	26
P/E Ratio:Low	9	10	13	13	17	20	20	20	24	17

Income Statement Analysis (Million $)	2009	2008	2007	2006	2005	2004	2003	2002	2001	2000
Revenue	23,123	25,269	24,462	22,923	21,167	20,011	18,232	16,332	16,079	16,724
Operating Income	6,180	6,640	6,584	6,252	5,995	5,577	4,677	4,000	3,274	3,898
Depreciation	1,157	1,153	1,072	1,079	986	999	964	954	1,089	1,025
Interest Expense	219	215	210	122	82.0	69.0	84.0	80.0	124	111
Pretax Income	4,632	5,108	6,115	5,625	4,983	4,555	3,657	3,005	2,186	2,974
Effective Tax Rate	30.0%	31.1%	32.1%	30.6%	34.0%	33.0%	32.9%	32.1%	32.1%	34.5%
Net Income	3,193	3,460	4,096	3,851	3,234	2,990	2,403	1,974	1,430	1,857
S&P Core Earnings	3,110	2,672	3,418	3,242	3,227	2,918	2,319	1,356	750	NA

Balance Sheet & Other Financial Data (Million $)	2009	2008	2007	2006	2005	2004	2003	2002	2001	2000
Cash	3,784	2,222	2,475	1,918	1,072	2,757	1,836	618	616	302
Current Assets	10,795	9,598	9,838	8,946	7,115	8,720	7,720	6,059	6,296	6,379
Total Assets	27,250	25,646	24,694	21,294	20,513	20,708	17,600	15,329	14,606	14,522
Current Liabilities	4,897	5,839	5,362	7,323	5,238	6,071	5,082	4,457	4,509	4,754
Long Term Debt	5,097	5,224	4,088	1,047	1,309	727	1,735	2,140	1,520	971
Common Equity	13,302	9,879	11,747	10,097	10,100	10,378	7,885	5,993	6,086	6,531
Total Capital	18,399	15,548	16,515	11,433	11,409	11,105	9,620	8,133	7,606	7,502
Capital Expenditures	903	1,471	1,422	1,168	943	937	677	763	980	1,115
Cash Flow	4,350	4,613	5,168	4,930	4,220	3,989	3,367	2,928	2,519	2,882
Current Ratio	2.2	1.6	1.8	1.2	1.4	1.4	1.5	1.4	1.4	1.3
% Long Term Debt of Capitalization	27.7	33.6	24.8	9.4	11.5	6.5	18.0	26.3	20.0	12.9
% Net Income of Revenue	13.8	13.7	16.7	16.8	15.3	14.9	13.2	12.1	8.9	11.1
% Return on Assets	12.1	13.8	17.8	18.4	15.7	15.6	14.6	13.2	9.8	13.1
% Return on Equity	27.6	32.0	37.7	37.3	31.6	32.7	34.6	32.7	22.7	29.0

Data as orig reptd.; bef. results of disc opers/spec. items. Per share data adj. for stk. divs.; EPS diluted. E-Estimated. NA-Not Available. NM-Not Meaningful. NR-Not Ranked. UR-Under Review.

Office: 3M Center, St. Paul, MN 55144-1000.
Telephone: 651-733-1110.
Email: innovation@mmm.com
Website: http://www.3m.com

Chrmn, Pres & CEO: G.W. Buckley
COO: I.G. Thulin
EVP & CTO: F.J. Palensky
SVP & CFO: P.D. Campbell

SVP & General Counsel: M.I. Smith
Investor Contact: M. Colin (651-733-8206)
Board Members: L. G. Alvarado, G. W. Buckley, V. D. Coffman, M. L. Eskew, W. J. Farrell, H. L. Henkel, E. M. Liddy, R. S. Morrison, A. L. Peters, R. J. Ulrich

Founded: 1902
Domicile: Delaware
Employees: 74,835

Tiffany & Co.

STANDARD &POOR'S

S&P Recommendation **BUY** ★★★★☆	Price $50.48 (as of Oct 22, 2010)	12-Mo. Target Price $55.00	Investment Style Large-Cap Growth

GICS Sector Consumer Discretionary
Sub-Industry Specialty Stores

Summary Tiffany is a leading international retailer, designer, manufacturer and distributor of fine jewelry and gift items.

Key Stock Statistics (Source S&P, Vickers, company reports)

52-Wk Range	$52.19–35.81	S&P Oper. EPS 2011E	2.61	Market Capitalization(B)	$6.374	Beta	1.76
Trailing 12-Month EPS	$2.48	S&P Oper. EPS 2012E	3.02	Yield (%)	1.98	S&P 3-Yr. Proj. EPS CAGR(%)	10
Trailing 12-Month P/E	20.4	P/E on S&P Oper. EPS 2011E	19.3	Dividend Rate/Share	$1.00	S&P Credit Rating	NR
$10K Invested 5 Yrs Ago	$14,405	Common Shares Outstg. (M)	126.3	Institutional Ownership (%)	95		

Price Performance

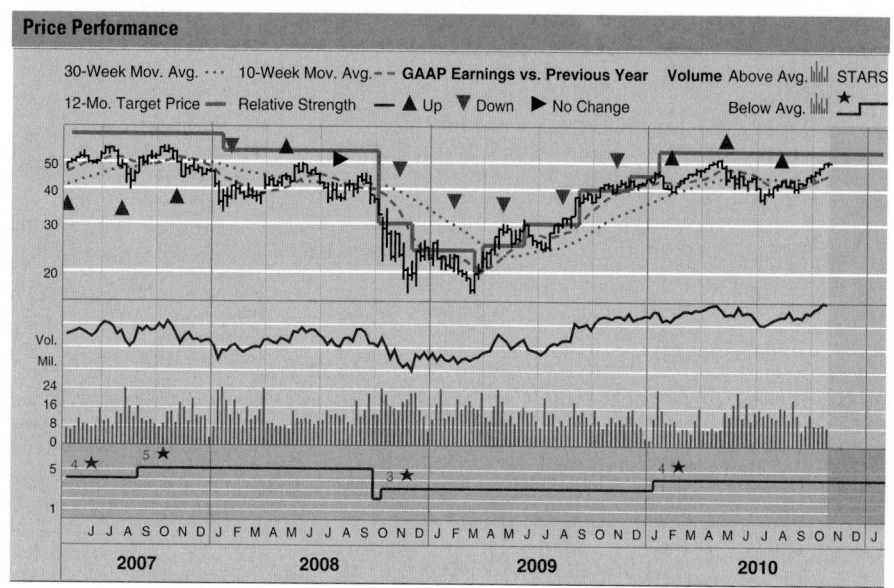

30-Week Mov. Avg. · · · 10-Week Mov. Avg. – – **GAAP Earnings vs. Previous Year** Volume Above Avg. STARS
12-Mo. Target Price — Relative Strength — ▲ Up ▼ Down ▶ No Change Below Avg. ★

Options: CBOE, P, Ph

Analysis prepared by **Marie Driscoll, CFA** on September 02, 2010, when the stock traded at **$ 41.13**.

Highlights

➤ We see global expansion along with innovative new collections and categories supporting sales and profit gains in FY 11 (Jan.) and beyond. First half consolidated same store sales rose 7%, led by an 18% gain in Europe and 14% in Asia-Pacific. A modest slowdown in merchandise sales under $500 suggests the entry level/aspirational shopper is splurging less on silver trinkets and is focused on paying down debt. Despite this, we see double digit growth with continued European and Asian expansion.

➤ We see an 11% sales advance in FY 11 and FY 12, led by double-digit gains in Asia/Pacific, Europe and the Americas as TIF opens 14 stores in FY 11 and same-store sales increase an estimated 7%. Japan remains a weak link, and we see sales declining about 10% in constant currency. We look for about a 210 basis point EBIT margin improvement to 18.4% reflecting gross margin expansion in FY 11 and see another 100 basis point EBIT margin expansion in FY 12.

➤ We estimate FY 11 EPS of $2.61 after net interest expense of $49 million and a 34% effective tax rate (32% in FY 10) and estimate $3.02 for FY 12 with a 35% effective tax rate.

Investment Rationale/Risk

➤ Despite weak economic fundamentals that we see limiting a strong recovery in discretionary spending this year, we expect TIF to gain domestic market share as the retail jewelry industry contracts and benefits from the return of the luxury shopper. Globally, we believe TIF's strong brand is under-penetrated, with lucrative expansion opportunities in Asia, Europe and Eastern Europe. We believe these trends support our buy recommendation.

➤ Risks to our recommendation and target price include lower-than-expected sales; a double-dip recession; weaker-than-expected global consumer demand for luxury goods; and increased competition from European luxury brands and independent high-end jewelers.

➤ We employ DCF methodology to derive our 12-month target price of $55, incorporating our assumptions of a 2% terminal growth rate and an 8% weighted average cost of capital. This is supported by our P/E valuation in which we apply TIF's historical 3-year forward peer forward multiple of 18X to our FY 12 EPS estimate, in line with global luxury peers. This leads to a $54 valuation.

Qualitative Risk Assessment

LOW	MEDIUM	HIGH

Our risk assessment reflects our view of TIF's favorable market position as a premier global luxury brand, offset by a weak outlook for U.S. consumer discretionary spending.

Quantitative Evaluations

S&P Quality Ranking A-

D	C	B-	B	B+	A-	A	A+

Relative Strength Rank STRONG
83
LOWEST = 1 HIGHEST = 99

Revenue/Earnings Data

Revenue (Million $)

	1Q	2Q	3Q	4Q	Year
2011	633.6	668.8	--	--	--
2010	517.6	612.5	598.2	981.4	2,710
2009	668.2	732.4	618.2	841.2	2,860
2008	595.7	662.6	627.3	1,053	2,939
2007	539.2	574.9	547.8	986.4	2,648
2006	509.9	526.7	500.1	858.5	2,395

Earnings Per Share ($)

	1Q	2Q	3Q	4Q	Year
2011	0.50	0.53	E0.37	E1.21	E2.61
2010	0.22	0.46	0.34	1.09	2.12
2009	0.50	0.63	0.35	0.25	1.74
2008	0.36	0.63	0.73	0.89	2.40
2007	0.30	0.29	0.21	1.02	1.80
2006	0.27	0.35	0.16	0.97	1.75

Fiscal year ended Jan. 31. Next earnings report expected: Late November. EPS Estimates based on S&P Operating Earnings; historical GAAP earnings are as reported.

Dividend Data (Dates: mm/dd Payment Date: mm/dd/yy)

Amount ($)	Date Decl.	Ex-Div. Date	Stk. of Record	Payment Date
0.170	11/19	12/17	12/21	01/11/10
0.200	02/18	03/18	03/22	04/12/10
0.250	05/20	06/17	06/21	07/12/10
0.250	08/19	09/16	09/20	10/11/10

Dividends have been paid since 1988. Source: Company reports.

Please read the Required Disclosures and Analyst Certification on the last page of this report.

The **McGraw·Hill** Companies

Tiffany & Co.

STANDARD &POOR'S

Business Summary September 02, 2010

CORPORATE OVERVIEW. Charles Lewis Tiffany founded Tiffany & Co. in 1837. Jewelry is the company's primary sales driver, accounting for 90% of FY 10 (Jan.) net sales. The Tiffany & Co. brand also encompasses timepieces, sterling silver merchandise, china, crystal, stationery, fragrances and personal accessories. Additionally, TIF sells other brands of timepieces and tableware in its U.S. stores.

TIF divides its worldwide business into four reportable segments: Americas (52% of FY 10 net sales), comprised of 91 company-owned stores, catalog and Internet, business-to-business and wholesale distribution; Asia-Pacific (35%), including 102 retail locations, Internet, business-to-business and wholesale distribution, with its wholly owned subsidiary, Tiffany & Co. Japan , Inc. accounting for 19% of FY 10 net sales; Europe (12%), with 27 retail locations and a limited amount of business-to-business and Internet and wholesale sales; and other (1%), consisting primarily of wholesale sales of diamonds and earnings and fees received from a licensing agreement with Luxottica and The Swatch Group, respectively, for sales transacted under Tiffany & Co. trademarks.

CORPORATE STRATEGY. Diamonds are at the heart of TIF's merchandise offering, which also includes colored gemstones and silver and gold fashion jewelry. In FY 10, TIF produced approximately 60% of Tiffany merchandise

sold, and purchased the remaining and almost all non-jewelry merchandise from third-party vendors. Products containing one or more diamonds accounted for 48% of FY 10 sales. In FY 10 TIF increased the proportion of polished diamonds it produced from rough diamonds to 70% from 40%, significantly reducing those purchased from third parties. To drive sales, TIF introduces new products annually; however, we believe outside designers, whose jewelry is licensed and sold exclusively under the Tiffany & Co. brand such as Jean Schlumberger, Elsa Peretti and Paloma Picasso, are important differentiators for TIF.

TIF believes that its multi-channel distribution represents a competitive advantage in a large and fragmented industry. In recent years, TIF has expanded its direct marketing business, with a focus on e-commerce. In FY 09, TIF reduced U.S. catalog distribution 7%, to 18.2 million, and in FY 10, another 35% or about 6 million catalogs, to 12 million catalogs distributed. Its U.S. consumer website, www.tiffany.com, was launched in FY 00, and e-commerce purchase capabilities were extended to the U.K. in FY 02 and to Japan and Canada in FY 06. An informational website for China was launched in FY 07.

Company Financials Fiscal Year Ended Jan. 31

Per Share Data ($)	2010	2009	2008	2007	2006	2005	2004	2003	2002	2001
Tangible Book Value	14.79	12.70	12.92	13.28	12.85	11.77	10.01	8.34	7.15	6.34
Cash Flow	3.23	2.83	3.28	2.64	2.50	2.79	2.06	1.80	1.58	1.56
Earnings	2.12	1.74	2.40	1.80	1.75	2.05	1.45	1.28	1.15	1.26
S&P Core Earnings	2.17	1.99	1.95	1.84	1.80	1.22	1.37	1.16	1.09	1.20
Dividends	NA	0.66	0.38	0.38	0.30	0.23	0.19	0.16	0.16	0.15
Payout Ratio	NA	31%	16%	16%	17%	11%	13%	13%	14%	12%
Calendar Year	2009	2008	2007	2006	2005	2004	2003	2002	2001	2000
Prices:High	44.49	49.98	57.34	41.29	43.80	45.22	49.45	41.00	38.25	45.38
Prices:Low	16.70	16.75	38.17	29.63	28.60	27.00	21.60	19.40	19.90	27.09
P/E Ratio:High	21	29	24	23	25	22	34	32	33	36
P/E Ratio:Low	8	10	16	16	16	13	15	15	17	22

Income Statement Analysis (Million $)	2010	2009	2008	2007	2006	2005	2004	2003	2002	2001
Revenue	2,710	2,860	2,939	2,648	2,395	2,205	2,000	1,707	1,607	1,668
Operating Income	579	633	640	533	492	403	446	397	375	374
Depreciation	139	138	122	118	109	108	90.4	78.0	64.6	46.7
Interest Expense	50.5	29.0	16.2	26.1	23.1	22.0	14.9	15.1	19.8	16.2
Pretax Income	390	346	522	404	368	472	343	300	289	318
Effective Tax Rate	31.9%	36.4%	36.6%	37.2%	30.8%	35.6%	37.1%	36.6%	40.0%	40.0%
Net Income	266	220	331	254	255	304	216	190	174	191
S&P Core Earnings	271	252	269	260	261	181	204	173	164	181

Balance Sheet & Other Financial Data (Million $)	2010	2009	2008	2007	2006	2005	2004	2003	2002	2001
Cash	786	160	247	177	394	188	276	156	174	196
Current Assets	2,446	2,049	1,844	1,707	1,699	1,608	1,348	1,070	954	1,005
Total Assets	3,488	3,102	2,922	2,846	2,777	2,666	2,391	1,924	1,630	1,568
Current Liabilities	600	602	585	453	365	400	395	300	341	337
Long Term Debt	520	425	343	406	427	398	393	297	179	242
Common Equity	1,883	1,588	1,637	1,805	1,831	1,701	1,468	1,208	1,037	925
Total Capital	2,610	2,014	2,046	2,211	2,257	2,132	1,884	1,505	1,216	1,168
Capital Expenditures	75.4	154	186	182	157	142	273	220	171	108
Cash Flow	405	358	453	372	364	412	306	268	238	237
Current Ratio	4.1	3.4	3.2	3.8	4.7	4.0	3.4	3.6	2.8	3.0
% Long Term Debt of Capitalization	19.9	21.1	16.8	18.4	18.9	18.7	20.9	19.7	14.7	20.7
% Net Income of Revenue	9.8	7.7	11.3	9.6	10.6	13.8	10.8	11.1	10.8	11.4
% Return on Assets	8.1	7.3	11.5	9.0	9.4	12.0	10.0	10.7	10.9	13.1
% Return on Equity	15.3	13.6	19.3	14.0	14.4	19.2	16.1	16.9	17.7	22.7

Data as orig reptd.; bef. results of disc opers/spec. items. Per share data adj. for stk. divs.; EPS diluted. E-Estimated. NA-Not Available. NM-Not Meaningful. NR-Not Ranked. UR-Under Review.

Office: 727 Fifth Avenue, New York, NY 10022.
Telephone: 212-755-8000.
Website: http://www.tiffany.com
Chrmn & CEO: M.J. Kowalski

Pres: J.E. Quinn
EVP & CFO: J.N. Fernandez
SVP, Secy & General Counsel: P.B. Dorsey
Chief Acctg Officer & Cntlr: H. Iglesias

Investor Contact: M.L. Aaron (212-230-5301)
Board Members: R. M. Bravo, G. E. Costley, L. Fish, A. F. Kohnstamm, M. J. Kowalski, C. K. Marquis, P. W. May, J. T. Presby, W. A. Shutzer

Founded: 1837
Domicile: Delaware
Employees: 8,400

The McGraw-Hill Companies

Time Warner Cable Inc

STANDARD &POOR'S

S&P Recommendation HOLD ★★★☆☆	**Price** $57.39 (as of Oct 22, 2010)
	12-Mo. Target Price $60.00
	Investment Style Large-Cap Growth

GICS Sector Consumer Discretionary
Sub-Industry Cable & Satellite

Summary This company is the largest pure-play U.S. cable multiple system operator (MSO), recently counting more than 12.8 million customers, mostly located in New York, the Carolinas, Ohio, Southern California and Texas.

Key Stock Statistics (Source S&P, Vickers, company reports)

52-Wk Range	$59.47– 38.24	S&P Oper. EPS 2010**E**	3.62	Market Capitalization(B)	$20.397	Beta	0.65
Trailing 12-Month EPS	$3.20	S&P Oper. EPS 2011**E**	4.15	Yield (%)	2.79	S&P 3-Yr. Proj. EPS CAGR(%)	12
Trailing 12-Month P/E	17.9	P/E on S&P Oper. EPS 2010**E**	15.9	Dividend Rate/Share	$1.60	S&P Credit Rating	BBB
$10K Invested 5 Yrs Ago	NA	Common Shares Outstg. (M)	355.4	Institutional Ownership (%)	87		

Price Performance

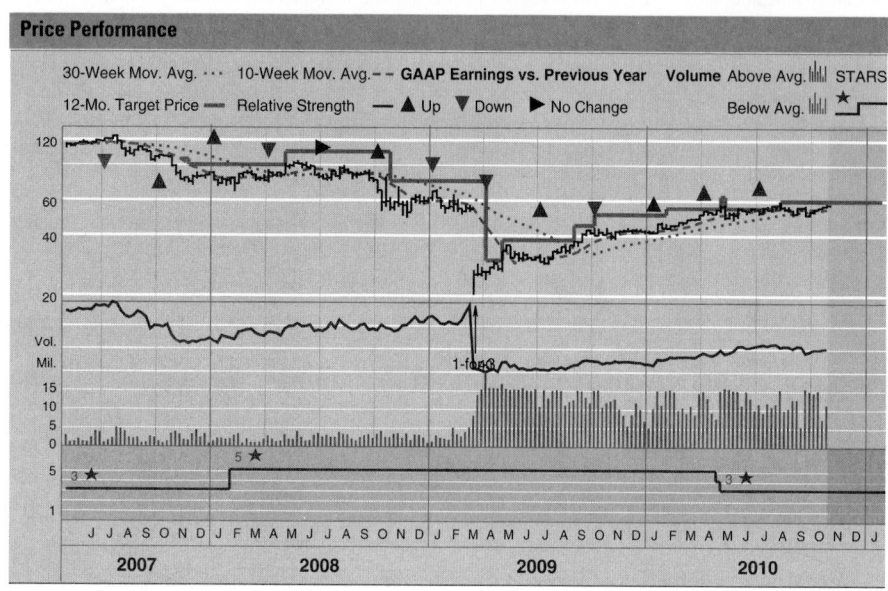

30-Week Mov. Avg. · · · 10-Week Mov. Avg. – – **GAAP Earnings vs. Previous Year** Volume Above Avg. STARS
12-Mo. Target Price — Relative Strength — ▲ Up ▼ Down ► No Change Below Avg. ★

Analysis prepared by **Tuna N. Amobi, CFA, CPA** on August 25, 2010, when the stock traded at **$ 50.67**.

Highlights

► We expect consolidated revenues to advance 6.0% in 2010, to more than $18.9 billion, and 4.5% in 2011, to almost $19.8 billion, mainly on further penetration of bundled residential (and increasingly commercial) high-speed data and digital phone products. We project relatively modest gains in video revenues, with the potential benefits of annual rate hikes and higher average pricing on advanced video offerings (HD and DVR), while assuming relatively moderate levels of basic subscriber losses. We also expect a strong rebound in advertising revenues (local and national) over the next two years.

► We see margins being slightly pressured by programming and marketing expenses, versus some cost savings (lower head count, call center consolidation and efficiency gains) and higher-margin ad revenues. We project 2010 and 2011 adjusted EBITDA up 6.2% and 4.7%, to about $6.9 billion and $7.2 billion, respectively.

► After higher D&A and interest expense (with $21 billion of long-term debt), and taxes at an effective rate of 37%-38%, we forecast 2010 and 2011 operating EPS of $3.62 and $4.15, respectively.

Investment Rationale/Risk

► Despite somewhat softer-than-expected unit growth in a seasonally slow second quarter, we think TWC's encouraging results for the 2010 first half showed continued traction from the nascent commercial market, as the company also pursues digital video and wireless broadband initiatives. With TWC's declining capital intensity and a strong management team, we see potentially sustainable double-digit free cash flow growth in the next few years. Having recently achieved its target leverage ratio -- following its 2009 spin-off that we think also enhanced its corporate governance -- TWC appears to have regained ample financial flexibility for sustainable dividends.

► Risks to our recommendation and target price include heightened regulatory overhang on a potential reclassification of broadband (Title II); a slower-than-expected economic (and housing) recovery; increased competition from satellite TV/telcos; and dilutive acquisitions.

► Our 12-month target price of $60 reflects 6.1X 2010E EV/EBITDA, or $3,200 per subscriber, which we view as adequate relative to peers -- noting the stock's ample dividend yield of 3.0%.

Qualitative Risk Assessment

LOW	MEDIUM	HIGH

Our risk assessment reflects what we view as the company's strong leadership position in a highly consolidated pay TV industry and a relatively strong balance sheet, combined with increased flexibility after a separation from its parent company, offset by increased competition and regulatory risk factors.

Quantitative Evaluations

S&P Quality Ranking NR

D	C	B-	B	B+	A-	A	A+

Relative Strength Rank MODERATE

60

LOWEST = 1 HIGHEST = 99

Revenue/Earnings Data

Revenue (Million $)

	1Q	2Q	3Q	4Q	Year
2010	4,599	4,734	--	--	--
2009	4,364	4,474	4,498	4,532	17,868
2008	4,160	4,298	4,340	4,402	17,200
2007	3,851	4,014	4,001	4,089	15,955
2006	2,385	2,721	3,209	3,651	11,767
2005	2,302	2,357	2,227	2,315	9,498

Earnings Per Share ($)

2010	0.60	0.94	E0.86	E0.97	E3.62
2009	0.48	0.89	0.76	0.91	3.05
2008	0.75	0.84	0.93	-25.08	-22.56
2007	0.84	0.84	0.75	0.99	3.45
2006	0.60	0.87	0.69	0.75	2.85
2005	0.90	1.29	0.60	1.20	3.75

Fiscal year ended Dec. 31. Next earnings report expected: Early November. EPS Estimates based on S&P Operating Earnings; historical GAAP earnings are as reported.

Dividend Data (Dates: mm/dd Payment Date: mm/dd/yy)

Amount ($)	Date Decl.	Ex-Div. Date	Stk. of Record	Payment Date
0.400	01/28	01/24	02/26	03/15/10
0.400	04/26	05/26	05/28	06/15/10
0.400	07/30	08/27	08/31	09/15/10

Dividends have been paid since 2010. Source: Company reports.

Please read the Required Disclosures and Analyst Certification on the last page of this report.

The McGraw·Hill Companies

Time Warner Cable Inc

STANDARD &POOR'S

Business Summary August 25, 2010

CORPORATE OVERVIEW. Time Warner Cable Inc. (TWC) is the second largest cable operator in the U.S., with more than 12.8 million video subscribers as of June 30, 2010. After its July 2006 acquisition of Adelphia Communications (for about $8.9 billion in cash plus 16% of its common stock) -- which added a net 3.2 million subscribers -- TWC became a public company on February 13, 2007 (effective date of Adelphia's reorganization plan), and its Class A shares began trading as of March 1, 2007 (the non-trading Class B shares are held by its parent). In March 2009, TWC was spun off from its former 84% equity owner Time Warner (TWX 34, Buy).

As of June 30, 2010, TWC's cable systems passed over 27 million U.S. homes (including the distribution on January 1, 2007, of the Texas/Kansas City JV), nearly 85% of which were located in New York, the Carolinas, Ohio, Southern California and Texas. Nearly 9.3 million (34.2% penetration) of TWC's homes passed subscribed to a residential high-speed data service such as Road Runner, and over 4.3 million (or 15.8%) to residential digital phone service. Also, there were 405,000 commercial customers (315,000 for data and 90,000 for digital phone). Nearly all of the homes passed in its legacy systems and more than 94% in the acquired systems were served by a system with at least 750 MHz of capacity.

CORPORATE STRATEGY. After its 2004 initial launch of digital phone service, TWC now offers the triple-play bundle substantially across its footprint, while it is in the relatively early stages of launching data and digital phone services to small to medium-sized businesses -- a potential opportunity that the company recently quantified at about $10 billion). In May 2008, TWC invested $550 million in a JV to build a nationwide WiMAX network with Sprint, Clearwire and others. In 2006, a cable consortium including TWC won 137 Advanced Wireless Spectrum (AWS) licenses in an FCC auction. An industry leader in advanced digital services (so-called Enhanced TV offerings), TWC is also pursuing a number of network-bandwidth reclamation initiatives (e.g., all-digital, switched digital video etc.), while adding a growing number of HD channels (now up to 100 in some of its systems). In August 2009, TWX unveiled pilot testing of its Web TV authentication technology with about a dozen TV programmers under the TV Everywhere initiative.

Company Financials Fiscal Year Ended Dec. 31

Per Share Data ($)	2009	2008	2007	2006	2005	2004	2003	2002	2001	2000
Tangible Book Value	NM	NM	NM	NM	NA	NA	NA	NA	NA	NA
Cash Flow	11.84	-2.32	12.60	9.05	8.75	6.72	6.29	NA	NA	NA
Earnings	3.05	-22.56	3.45	2.85	3.75	2.19	1.71	NA	NA	NA
S&P Core Earnings	3.14	7.68	3.12	2.88	NA	NA	NA	NA	NA	NA
Dividends	Nil	Nil	Nil	NA	NA	NA	NA	NA	NA	NA
Payout Ratio	Nil	Nil	Nil	NA	NA	NA	NA	NA	NA	NA
Prices:High	68.23	94.68	126.34	NA	NA	NA	NA	NA	NA	NA
Prices:Low	20.19	48.90	70.81	NA	NA	NA	NA	NA	NA	NA
P/E Ratio:High	22	NM	37	NA	NA	NA	NA	NA	NA	NA
P/E Ratio:Low	7	NM	21	NA	NA	NA	NA	NA	NA	NA

Income Statement Analysis (Million $)										
Revenue	17,868	17,200	15,955	11,767	9,498	8,484	7,699	NA	NA	NA
Operating Income	NA	76.0	5,765	4,285	NA	NA	NA	NA	NA	NA
Depreciation	NA	33.5	2,976	2,050	1,664	1,514	1,461	NA	NA	NA
Interest Expense	1,324	25.8	907	646	501	491	514	NA	NA	NA
Pretax Income	1,912	-13,072	2,028	1,664	1,535	1,305	987	NA	NA	NA
Effective Tax Rate	42.9%	NM	36.5%	37.3%	13.8%	39.6%	38.9%	NA	NA	NA
Net Income	1,070	-7,344	1,123	936	1,253	726	541	NA	NA	NA
S&P Core Earnings	1,104	2,511	1,019	945	NA	NA	NA	NA	NA	NA

Balance Sheet & Other Financial Data (Million $)										
Cash	1,048	5,552	232	51.0	12.0	102	NA	NA	NA	NA
Current Assets	NA	57.1	1,163	910	NA	NA	NA	NA	NA	NA
Total Assets	43,694	47,889	56,600	55,743	43,677	43,138	NA	NA	NA	NA
Current Liabilities	NA	387	2,536	2,490	NA	NA	NA	NA	NA	NA
Long Term Debt	22,631	17,727	13,877	300	4,455	4,898	NA	NA	NA	NA
Common Equity	8,685	17,164	24,706	23,564	21,331	20,039	NA	NA	NA	NA
Total Capital	NA	36,301	53,598	38,390	29,193	28,304	NA	NA	NA	NA
Capital Expenditures	NA	3,522	3,433	2,718	1,975	1,712	1,637	NA	NA	NA
Cash Flow	4,155	-59.1	4,099	2,986	2,917	2,240	2,002	NA	NA	NA
Current Ratio	0.7	2.3	0.5	0.4	0.3	0.3	NA	NA	NA	NA
% Long Term Debt of Capitalization	72.3	48.8	25.9	0.8	17.3	19.6	Nil	NA	NA	NA
% Net Income of Revenue	6.0	NM	7.0	8.0	13.2	8.6	7.0	NA	NA	NA
% Return on Assets	2.3	NM	2.0	1.9	2.9	NA	NA	NA	NA	NA
% Return on Equity	8.3	NM	4.7	4.2	6.1	NA	NA	NA	NA	NA

Data as orig reptd.; bef. results of disc opers/spec. items. Per share data adj. for stk. divs.; EPS diluted. E-Estimated. NA-Not Available. NM-Not Meaningful. NR-Not Ranked. UR-Under Review.

Office: 60 Columbus Cir, New York, NY 10023-5802.
Telephone: 212-364-8200.
Website: http://www.timewarnercable.com
Chrmn, Pres & CEO: G.A. Britt

COO: L.C. Hobbs
EVP & CFO: R.D. Marcus
EVP & CTO: M. LaJoie
EVP, Secy & General Counsel: M. Lawrence-Apfelbaum

Investor Contact: W. Osbourn, Jr. (203-351-2015)
Board Members: C. Black, G. A. Britt, T. H. Castro, D. C. Chang, J. E. Copeland, Jr., P. R. Haje, D. A. James, D. Logan, N. J. Nicholas, Jr., W. H. Pace, E. D. Shirley, J. E. Sununu

Founded: 2003
Domicile: Delaware
Employees: 47,000

The McGraw-Hill Companies

Time Warner Inc.

S&P Recommendation	BUY ★★★★☆	Price $31.52 (as of Oct 22, 2010)	12-Mo. Target Price $38.00	Investment Style Large-Cap Blend

GICS Sector Consumer Discretionary
Sub-Industry Movies & Entertainment

Summary This company owns some of the world's leading media and entertainment brands, including Warner Bros. (film/TV studio), Turner cable networks (TNT, TBS, CNN), HBO/Cinemax premium channels, as well as several newspaper and magazine brands through its Time Inc. publishing businesses.

Key Stock Statistics (Source S&P, Vickers, company reports)

52-Wk Range	$34.07–26.43	S&P Oper. EPS 2010E	2.30	Market Capitalization(B)	$35.435	Beta	1.09
Trailing 12-Month EPS	$2.18	S&P Oper. EPS 2011E	2.58	Yield (%)	2.70	S&P 3-Yr. Proj. EPS CAGR(%)	12
Trailing 12-Month P/E	14.5	P/E on S&P Oper. EPS 2010E	13.7	Dividend Rate/Share	$0.85	S&P Credit Rating	BBB
$10K Invested 5 Yrs Ago	NA	Common Shares Outstg. (M)	1,124.2	Institutional Ownership (%)	82		

Price Performance

30-Week Mov. Avg. · · · 10-Week Mov. Avg. - - **GAAP Earnings vs. Previous Year** Volume Above Avg. STARS
12-Mo. Target Price — Relative Strength — ▲ Up ▼ Down ▶ No Change Below Avg. ★

Options: ASE, CBOE, P, Ph

Analysis prepared by **Tuna N. Amobi, CFA, CPA** on August 05, 2010, when the stock traded at **$ 32.87.**

Highlights

▶ We see consolidated revenues rising about 7% in 2010, to $27.1 billion, and 5% in 2011, to more than $28.4 billion, mainly on affiliate revenues and improved ad sales at the Turner networks (TNT, TBS, CNN), HBO subscriptions, and healthy film/TV studio contributions (theatrical/home video releases and growing video games revenues). Also, the publishing division should see a gradual recovery in print ads, as well as growing online revenues, versus stagnant circulation.

▶ We expect recent restructuring actions to significantly enhance TWX's operating leverage over the next two years, resulting in sizable margin expansion. Results should also reflect increased contributions from higher-margin digital revenues, as well as merchandise licensing and other ancillary businesses.

▶ After D&A and lower net interest expense (on debt paydown and ample cash), we estimate 2010 operating EPS of $2.30 (consistent with TWX's guidance of at least 20% growth). With further share buybacks under a current $3 billion plan, we see 2011 EPS of $2.58.

Investment Rationale/Risk

▶ We think TWX's stronger-than-expected results for the 2010 second quarter showed continued overall improvement in underlying business trends across its core content-oriented businesses. Other potential catalysts we see include Turner networks' strong upfront sales, gains from international expansion, a film slate featuring the final two installments of Harry Potter (among other 3D releases), and growing contributions from video games, e-readers and other digital initiatives. We see ample financial capacity for dividends and share buybacks.

▶ Risks to our recommendation and target price include a slower-than-expected economic and ad rebound; potential ratings issues for the Turner networks; a sharp slowdown in the home video market; dilutive acquisitions; and continued secular challenges for publishing.

▶ Our 12-month target price of $38 is a blend of what we view as an ample EV/EBITDA of 10.2X our 2010 estimate and our sum-of-the-parts valuation. The dividend recently yielded 2.6%. We expect TWX to generate over $5 million in aggregate free cash flow in 2010 and 2011.

Qualitative Risk Assessment

LOW	MEDIUM	HIGH

Our risk assessment reflects our view of the company's leading content-oriented businesses, ample financial flexibility, and what we view as an adequate governance framework, offset by cyclical and secular pressures and a relatively volatile earnings stream.

Quantitative Evaluations

S&P Quality Ranking B-

D	C	B-	B	B+	A-	A	A+

Relative Strength Rank MODERATE

41

LOWEST = 1   HIGHEST = 99

Revenue/Earnings Data

Revenue (Million $)

	1Q	2Q	3Q	4Q	Year
2010	6,322	6,377	--	--	--
2009	6,086	6,013	6,366	7,320	25,785
2008	11,417	11,555	11,706	12,306	46,984
2007	11,184	10,980	11,676	12,642	46,482
2006	10,327	10,519	10,912	12,466	44,224
2005	10,483	10,744	10,538	11,887	43,652

Earnings Per Share ($)

2010	0.62	0.48	E0.62	E0.57	E2.30
2009	0.39	0.35	0.49	0.51	1.74
2008	0.63	0.66	0.90	-13.41	-11.22
2007	0.90	0.75	0.72	0.84	3.24
2006	0.78	0.60	0.99	1.29	3.63
2005	0.60	-0.21	0.57	0.87	1.86

Fiscal year ended Dec. 31. Next earnings report expected: Early November. EPS Estimates based on S&P Operating Earnings; historical GAAP earnings are as reported.

Dividend Data (Dates: mm/dd Payment Date: mm/dd/yy)

Amount ($)	Date Decl.	Ex-Div. Date	Stk. of Record	Payment Date
0.188	04/22	11/24	11/27	12/09/09
Stk.	11/16	08/27	08/31	09/15/10

Dividends have been paid since 2005. Source: Company reports.

Please read the Required Disclosures and Analyst Certification on the last page of this report.

The McGraw-Hill Companies

Time Warner Inc.

Business Summary August 05, 2010

CORPORATE OVERVIEW. Time Warner is one of the major media conglomerates -- creating and providing entertainment and information content across its key film, television and publishing divisions. The company's revenues are derived from three primary sources: content (43% of 2009 revenues), subscriptions (34%), advertising (20%), and other (3%).

In March 2009, the company completed a full spin-off of its cable systems businesses owned by Time Warner Cable (TWC 59, Hold). In December 2009, the company also spun off its online subscription and advertising businesses owned by AOL (AOL 23, NR).

For the company as presently constituted, the Filmed Entertainment segment (42% of 2009 revenues) includes the Warner Bros. and New Line Cinema studios, and home entertainment businesses, with key franchises such as Harry Potter, Lord of the Rings and Batman. In 2008, the company closed its two specialty film labels -- Warner Independent Films, and Picturehouse.

The Networks segment (44%) includes cable networks CNN, HBO/Cinemax and Turner (TNT, TBS). In September 2006, TWX's WB broadcast network merged with CBS's UPN to create the CW network. The Publishing segment

(14%) includes Time Inc., with 112 magazine titles worldwide (20 in the U.S., 90 outside the U.S.) -- including Time, People, Sports Illustrated, and Fortune.

CORPORATE STRATEGY. CEO Jeffrey Bewkes recently articulated several key priorities, including continued delivery of quality content, improved operating efficiency, international expansion, and exploiting advances in digital technology. Over the next few years, TWX plans up to 20 3-D films in the Imax format. The company provides its titles to Netflix and Redbox after a 28-day DVD window. In so doing, TWX aims balance the dynamics of its content distribution strategy -- optimizing incremental payoff from emerging VOD platforms, electronic sell-through outlets like Apple's iTunes, Amazon.com and Wal-Mart's Vudu (as well as Netflix and Redbox) -- with minimal jeopardy to the traditional DVD window.

Separately, in May 2009, TWX invested $241.5 million in Central European Media Enterprises for about a 31% equity stake in the European broadcaster.

Company Financials Fiscal Year Ended Dec. 31

Per Share Data ($)	2009	2008	2007	2006	2005	2004	2003	2002	2001	2000
Tangible Book Value	NM	NM	NM	NM	NM	NM	NM	NM	NM	7.53
Cash Flow	2.54	-2.46	11.58	8.57	6.18	6.39	6.00	-27.96	2.90	1.85
Earnings	1.74	-11.22	3.24	3.63	1.86	2.07	2.04	-28.29	-3.60	1.35
S&P Core Earnings	1.86	-6.72	2.85	3.21	2.49	1.86	1.26	-10.32	-3.24	NA
Dividends	0.75	0.75	0.71	0.63	0.30	Nil	Nil	Nil	Nil	Nil
Payout Ratio	43%	NM	22%	17%	16%	Nil	Nil	Nil	Nil	Nil
Prices:High	33.45	50.70	69.46	66.76	58.93	59.71	54.97	98.77	175.55	250.15
Prices:Low	17.81	21.00	48.51	47.10	48.30	46.23	29.70	26.10	82.21	98.26
P/E Ratio:High	19	NM	21	18	32	29	27	NM	NM	NM
P/E Ratio:Low	10	NM	15	13	26	22	15	NM	NM	NM

Income Statement Analysis (Million $)

	2009	2008	2007	2006	2005	2004	2003	2002	2001	2000
Revenue	25,785	46,984	46,482	44,224	43,652	42,081	39,496	36,955	33,765	7,703
Operating Income	6,092	19,229	19,217	14,837	14,312	13,535	11,839	NA	NA	2,271
Depreciation	998	10,481	10,488	6,953	6,781	6,743	6,086	NA	NA	444
Interest Expense	1,293	2,275	2,509	1,971	1,622	1,754	1,926	1,900	1,576	55.0
Pretax Income	3,283	-18,623	6,795	6,826	4,007	5,206	4,763	-44,156	-4,465	1,884
Effective Tax Rate	36.4%	NM	34.4%	19.6%	27.2%	33.0%	29.0%	NM	NM	38.9%
Net Income	2,040	-13,402	4,051	5,114	2,921	3,239	3,164	-42,003	-5,313	1,152
S&P Core Earnings	2,212	-7,981	3,579	4,551	3,929	2,938	1,999	-15,240	-4,771	NA

Balance Sheet & Other Financial Data (Million $)

	2009	2008	2007	2006	2005	2004	2003	2002	2001	2000
Cash	4,800	6,682	1,516	1,549	4,220	6,139	3,040	1,730	771	2,610
Current Assets	13,007	16,602	12,451	10,851	13,463	14,639	12,268	11,155	10,274	4,671
Total Assets	65,730	113,896	133,830	131,669	122,745	123,149	121,748	115,508	209,429	10,827
Current Liabilities	8,765	13,976	12,193	12,780	12,608	14,673	15,518	13,395	12,972	2,328
Long Term Debt	15,357	37,916	37,304	35,233	20,238	20,703	23,458	27,354	22,792	1,411
Common Equity	33,383	42,288	58,536	60,389	62,679	60,719	56,131	52,891	150,667	6,778
Total Capital	49,142	92,379	113,898	112,857	103,760	103,285	NA	NA	NA	8,189
Capital Expenditures	561	4,377	4,430	4,085	3,246	3,024	2,761	3,023	3,634	485
Cash Flow	3,038	-2,921	14,539	12,067	9,702	9,982	9,250	-41,515	4,282	1,596
Current Ratio	1.5	1.2	1.0	0.8	1.1	1.0	0.8	0.8	0.8	2.0
% Long Term Debt of Capitalization	31.3	41.0	32.8	31.2	19.5	20.0	NA	NA	NA	17.2
% Net Income of Revenue	7.9	NM	8.7	11.6	6.7	7.7	8.0	NM	NM	15.0
% Return on Assets	2.3	NM	3.1	4.0	2.4	2.6	2.7	NM	NM	10.9
% Return on Equity	5.4	NM	6.8	8.2	4.7	5.5	5.8	NM	NM	17.6

Data as orig reptd.; bef. results of disc opers/spec. items. Per share data adj. for stk. divs.; EPS diluted. E-Estimated. NA-Not Available. NM-Not Meaningful. NR-Not Ranked. UR-Under Review.

Office: 1 Time Warner Ctr, New York, NY 10019-6038.
Telephone: 212-484-8000.
Email: aoltwir@aoltw.com
Website: http://www.timewarner.com

Chrmn & CEO: J.L. Bewkes
Pres: R.E. Grant
EVP & CFO: J.K. Martin, Jr.
EVP & General Counsel: P.T. Cappuccio

SVP, Chief Acctg Officer & Cntlr: P. Desroches
Investor Contact: J.E. Burtson
Board Members: J. L. Barksdale, W. P. Barr, J. L. Bewkes, S. F. Bollenbach, F. J. Caufield, R. C. Clark, M. Dopfner, J. P. Einhorn, F. Hassan, M. A. Miles, K. J. Novack, D. C. Wright

Founded: 1985
Domicile: Delaware
Employees: 31,000

The McGraw·Hill Companies

Titanium Metals Corp

STANDARD &POOR'S

S&P Recommendation **SELL** ★★★★★	Price $18.84 (as of Oct 22, 2010)	12-Mo. Target Price $15.00	Investment Style Large-Cap Blend

GICS Sector Materials
Sub-Industry Diversified Metals & Mining

Summary This company is a worldwide integrated producer of titanium metal products.

Key Stock Statistics (Source S&P, Vickers, company reports)

52-Wk Range	$22.93– 8.39	S&P Oper. EPS 2010**E**	0.46	Market Capitalization(B)	$3.394	Beta	1.76
Trailing 12-Month EPS	$0.23	S&P Oper. EPS 2011**E**	0.78	Yield (%)	Nil	S&P 3-Yr. Proj. EPS CAGR(%)	69
Trailing 12-Month P/E	81.9	P/E on S&P Oper. EPS 2010**E**	41.0	Dividend Rate/Share	Nil	S&P Credit Rating	NR
$10K Invested 5 Yrs Ago	$18,184	Common Shares Outstg. (M)	180.2	Institutional Ownership (%)	32		

Price Performance

30-Week Mov. Avg. · · · 10-Week Mov. Avg. - - GAAP Earnings vs. Previous Year   Volume Above Avg. ▐▍▍ STARS
12-Mo. Target Price — Relative Strength — ▲ Up ▼ Down ► No Change   Below Avg. ▐▍▍ ★

Options: ASE, CBOE, Ph

Analysis prepared by **Leo J. Larkin** on August 19, 2010, when the stock traded at **$ 19.75.**

Highlights

► Following a sales decline of 33% in 2009, we look for a rise of 18% in 2010, with a forecasted increase in the volume of shipments for both segments offsetting an anticipated drop in average realized selling prices for both melted and mill products. Our sales outlook assumes GDP growth of 2.8% in 2010, versus a decline of 2.6% in 2009, which we see boosting demand for durable goods. Also, we expect demand to be aided by the rebuilding of inventories in the aerospace supply chain following large destocking through nearly all of 2009.

► We look for margin expansion and a sizable gain in operating profit in 2010, as an increased volume of shipments offsets a decline in selling prices. After minimal interest expense and taxes, we project operating EPS of $0.46 in 2010, versus EPS of $0.19 in 2009.

► Longer term, we forecast higher earnings on an eventual rebound in the commercial aerospace industry, growing use of titanium in other industrial applications, and a secular rise in titanium consumption in Asia.

Investment Rationale/Risk

► We believe TIE shares are overvalued, recently trading at close to 26X our 2011 EPS estimate. In our view, the P/E is excessive and the stock is vulnerable to a decline on that basis. Longer term, we have a favorable view of TIE as a beneficiary of a recovery in commercial aerospace, growing acceptance of titanium in other industrial markets, and a secular rise in Asian demand for titanium. While its EPS substantially declined in 2009, TIE remained free cash flow positive, reflecting lower capital spending and reduced working capital. We believe this, combined with its low debt levels, should enable TIE to capitalize on a cyclical upturn in titanium demand.

► Risks to our recommendation and target price include increases in volume and pricing for both segments in 2011 in excess of what we project.

► Our 12-month target price of $15 is 19.2X our 2011 EPS estimate, which is the mid-point of the company's 10-year historical range. Based on our target multiple, TIE would trade about in line with the P/E we apply to its specialty metals peers.

Qualitative Risk Assessment

LOW	MEDIUM	HIGH

Our risk assessment reflects the company's low debt levels and its large share of the markets it serves. Partly offsetting this is its heavy reliance on aerospace industry demand and the volatility of raw material costs.

Quantitative Evaluations

S&P Quality Ranking   B-

D	C	B-	B	B+	A-	A	A+

Relative Strength Rank   WEAK

21

LOWEST = 1   HIGHEST = 99

Revenue/Earnings Data

Revenue (Million $)

	1Q	2Q	3Q	4Q	Year
2010	217.5	212.0	--	--	--
2009	203.4	205.7	181.4	183.5	774.0
2008	293.7	297.3	295.4	265.2	1,152
2007	341.7	341.2	297.3	298.6	1,279
2006	286.9	300.9	271.8	323.5	1,183
2005	155.2	183.8	190.0	220.8	749.8

Earnings Per Share ($)

2010	0.09	0.11	E0.13	E0.14	E0.46
2009	0.11	0.05	0.01	0.03	0.19
2008	0.22	0.26	0.22	0.19	0.89
2007	0.41	0.42	0.29	0.61	1.46
2006	0.32	0.31	0.29	0.61	1.53
2005	0.23	0.21	0.20	0.23	0.86

Fiscal year ended Dec. 31. Next earnings report expected: Early November. EPS Estimates based on S&P Operating Earnings; historical GAAP earnings are as reported.

Dividend Data

No cash dividends have been paid since 2008.

Please read the Required Disclosures and Analyst Certification on the last page of this report.

The McGraw·Hill Companies

Titanium Metals Corp

Business Summary August 19, 2010

CORPORATE OVERVIEW. Titanium Metals Corp. is the one of the world's largest producers of titanium melted and mill products and the largest U.S. producer of titanium sponge (the raw material for titanium). TIE estimates that it accounted for some 18% of global industry shipments of titanium mill products in 2009 and 6% of worldwide sponge production. Melted and mill products and sponge are sold principally to the commercial aerospace industry. Other sources of product demand include the military, industrial and emerging markets. As of December 31, 2009, 27.5% of TIE's common shares were held by Contran Corporation and its subsidiaries, and an additional 8.6% were held by a trust sponsored by Contran.

Products include titanium sponge; melted products (ingot, electrodes and slab); mill products, including billet and bar, plate, strip and pipe; and fabricated products such as spools, pipe fittings, manifolds and vessels. In 2009, mill products accounted for 82% of sales, melted products 9%, and other products

(titanium fabrications, titanium scrap and titanium tetrachloride), 9%.

Sales by market sector in 2009 were: aerospace, 60%; military, 20%; industrial and emerging markets, 11%; and other, 9%.

In 2009, North America accounted for 65% of sales, Europe for 27% and other regions for 8%.

CORPORATE STRATEGY. The company's long-term strategy is to maximize the value of its core aerospace business while expanding its presence in non-aerospace markets. Additionally, the company seeks to develop new applications for its products.

Company Financials Fiscal Year Ended Dec. 31

Per Share Data ($)	2009	2008	2007	2006	2005	2004	2003	2002	2001	2000
Tangible Book Value	6.15	5.94	6.16	4.92	2.91	1.41	1.20	1.18	1.92	2.32
Cash Flow	0.47	1.15	1.65	1.68	0.96	0.47	0.19	-0.24	-0.01	0.03
Earnings	0.19	0.89	1.46	1.53	0.86	0.28	-0.11	-0.53	-0.33	-0.30
S&P Core Earnings	0.23	0.80	1.35	1.29	0.82	0.29	-0.08	-0.37	-0.41	NA
Dividends	Nil	0.30	0.08	Nil	Nil	Nil	Nil	Nil	Nil	Nil
Payout Ratio	Nil	34%	5%	Nil	Nil	Nil	Nil	Nil	Nil	Nil
Prices:High	13.18	26.79	39.80	47.63	19.86	3.33	1.51	1.35	3.60	2.23
Prices:Low	4.04	5.31	25.26	15.96	2.91	1.06	0.39	0.23	0.59	0.78
P/E Ratio:High	69	30	27	31	23	12	NM	NM	NM	NM
P/E Ratio:Low	21	6	17	10	3	4	NM	NM	NM	NM

Income Statement Analysis (Million $)										
Revenue	774	1,152	1,279	1,183	750	502	385	367	487	427
Operating Income	106	269	420	403	177	43.8	17.2	-9.02	28.2	1.81
Depreciation	51.5	47.7	41.1	34.1	31.5	32.8	36.6	37.1	40.1	41.9
Interest Expense	0.80	1.80	2.60	3.43	3.96	12.5	16.4	3.38	4.06	7.70
Pretax Income	56.5	237	394	418	185	39.0	-11.3	-54.5	4.47	-43.1
Effective Tax Rate	36.6%	29.1%	29.7%	30.7%	13.2%	NM	NM	NM	NM	NM
Net Income	34.5	163	268	281	156	39.9	-12.9	-67.2	-41.8	-38.0
S&P Core Earnings	42.5	145	243	230	136	37.9	-9.92	-46.4	-51.7	NA

Balance Sheet & Other Financial Data (Million $)										
Cash	169	45.0	90.0	86.2	17.6	54.4	35.0	6.21	24.5	9.80
Current Assets	807	789	898	758	550	344	276	263	309	248
Total Assets	1,379	1,368	1,420	1,217	907	666	567	564	699	759
Current Liabilities	105	152	178	211	167	162	78.5	92.6	122	116
Long Term Debt	NA	0.20	0.50	Nil	57.2	12.2	9.77	217	221	229
Common Equity	1,104	1,076	1,129	804	430	206	159	159	298	357
Total Capital	1,124	1,101	1,168	918	660	404	180	388	533	604
Capital Expenditures	33.0	121	101	101	61.1	23.6	12.5	7.77	16.1	11.2
Cash Flow	85.8	210	304	309	175	68.4	23.7	-30.1	-1.63	3.91
Current Ratio	7.7	5.2	5.1	3.6	3.3	2.1	3.5	2.8	2.5	2.1
% Long Term Debt of Capitalization	Nil	Nil	Nil	Nil	8.7	3.0	5.4	56.0	41.4	37.9
% Net Income of Revenue	4.5	14.1	21.0	23.8	20.8	8.0	NM	NM	NM	NM
% Return on Assets	NA	11.7	20.3	26.5	19.4	6.5	NM	NM	NM	NM
% Return on Equity	NA	14.7	27.2	44.5	43.4	19.5	NM	NM	NM	NM

Data as orig reptd.; bef. results of disc opers/spec. items. Per share data adj. for stk. divs.; EPS diluted. E-Estimated. NA-Not Available. NM-Not Meaningful. NR-Not Ranked. UR-Under Review.

Office: 5430 LBJ Freeway, Suite 1700, Dallas, TX 75240-2697.
Telephone: 972-233-1700.
Website: http://www.timet.com
Chrmn: H.C. Simmons

Pres & CEO: B.D. O'Brien
Vice Chrmn: S.L. Watson
CFO: J.W. Brown
CTO: M.W. Kearns

Board Members: K. R. Coogan, G. R. Simmons, H. C. Simmons, T. P. Stafford, S. L. Watson, T. N. Worrell, P. J. Zucconi

Founded: 1950
Domicile: Delaware
Employees: 2,205

TJX Companies Inc (The)

STANDARD &POOR'S

S&P Recommendation **BUY** ★★★★☆	Price $44.86 (as of Oct 22, 2010)	12-Mo. Target Price $48.00	Investment Style Large-Cap Growth

GICS Sector Consumer Discretionary
Sub-Industry Apparel Retail

Summary TJX operates eight chains of off-price apparel and home fashion specialty stores in the U.S., Canada, Germany, Ireland and the U.K.

Key Stock Statistics (Source S&P, Vickers, company reports)

52-Wk Range	$48.50–35.75	S&P Oper. EPS 2011**E**	3.35	Market Capitalization(B)	$17.974	Beta	0.60
Trailing 12-Month EPS	$3.30	S&P Oper. EPS 2012**E**	3.70	Yield (%)	1.34	S&P 3-Yr. Proj. EPS CAGR(%)	14
Trailing 12-Month P/E	13.6	P/E on S&P Oper. EPS 2011**E**	13.4	Dividend Rate/Share	$0.60	S&P Credit Rating	A
$10K Invested 5 Yrs Ago	$23,115	Common Shares Outstg. (M)	400.7	Institutional Ownership (%)	93		

Price Performance

- 30-Week Mov. Avg. · · ·
- 10-Week Mov. Avg. - -
- **GAAP Earnings vs. Previous Year**
- Volume Above Avg. STARS
- 12-Mo. Target Price —
- Relative Strength —
- ▲ Up ▼ Down ▶ No Change
- Below Avg. ★

Options: ASE, CBOE

Analysis prepared by **Jason N. Asaeda** on August 18, 2010, when the stock traded at **$ 42.14**.

Highlights

▶ Following a 6% increase in FY 10 (Jan.), we look for consolidated same-store sales on a constant currency basis to rise 3% in FY 11. We think TJX's strong value proposition across brands, focus on off-price buys (purchases made opportunistically and closer to need during a season), and ability to quickly respond to changes in customer buying preferences position the company solidly for continued growth. Coupled with planned global addition of 130 net new stores, we expect net sales to reach $21.5 billion in FY 11.

▶ We forecast gross margin expansion, supported by an increase in off-price buys, which carry higher mark-ups than upfront buys (purchases made before or early in a season), and lower markdowns as a result of improved inventory management. We also look for TJX to partially offset new store expenses and higher marketing spend with cost controls.

▶ FY 11 second quarter results included a $0.01 benefit from a reduction in the company's provision for computer intrusion related costs. Excluding this non-operating items but factoring in planned share repurchase activity, we project 18% EPS growth in FY 11, to $3.35.

Investment Rationale/Risk

▶ Our buy recommendation is based on valuation. We think TJX, with what we view as its compelling values on brand-name merchandise, is gaining marketshare at a time when consumers are growing increasingly cost-conscious. We see the company's core Marmaxx division generating ample operating cash flow to fund various growth initiatives such as expansion of T.K. Maxx and HomeSense in Europe; further testing of the Marshalls Shoe Mega Shop (U.S.) and StyleSense (Canada) family footwear and accessories retail concepts; investments in infrastructure; and $900 million to $1 billion in additional share buybacks in FY 11.

▶ Risks to our recommendation and target price include sales shortfalls due to changes in consumer spending habits and buying preferences; merchandise availability; increased promotional activity by competitors, particularly bankruptcy-related clearance sales in the U.S.; and difficult same-store sales comparisons in FY 11.

▶ Our 12-month target price of $48 applies a forward P/E multiple of 14.4X, near TJX's 10-year historical median, to our FY 11 EPS estimate.

Qualitative Risk Assessment

LOW	MEDIUM	HIGH

Our risk assessment reflects our view of TJX's leadership position in off-price retail and promising new merchandising and productivity initiatives that could boost sales and profit margins. This is offset by what we see as an inconsistent earnings track record and an uncertain outlook for consumer discretionary spending.

Quantitative Evaluations

S&P Quality Ranking A+

D	C	B-	B	B+	A-	A	A+

Relative Strength Rank MODERATE

52

LOWEST = 1   HIGHEST = 99

Revenue/Earnings Data

Revenue (Million $)

	1Q	2Q	3Q	4Q	Year
2011	5,017	5,068	--	--	--
2010	4,354	4,748	5,245	5,942	20,288
2009	4,364	4,621	4,762	5,380	19,000
2008	4,108	4,313	4,737	5,488	18,647
2007	3,871	3,964	4,473	5,097	17,405
2006	3,652	3,648	4,042	4,716	16,058

Earnings Per Share ($)

2011	0.80	0.74	E0.89	E0.93	E3.35
2010	0.49	0.61	0.81	0.94	2.84
2009	0.43	0.45	0.58	0.58	2.07
2008	0.34	0.45	0.54	0.66	1.66
2007	0.34	0.29	0.48	0.51	1.63
2006	0.28	0.23	0.32	0.60	1.41

Fiscal year ended Jan. 31. Next earnings report expected: Mid November. EPS Estimates based on S&P Operating Earnings; historical GAAP earnings are as reported.

Dividend Data (Dates: mm/dd Payment Date: mm/dd/yy)

Amount ($)	Date Decl.	Ex-Div. Date	Stk. of Record	Payment Date
0.120	12/01	02/09	02/11	03/04/10
0.150	04/06	05/11	05/13	06/03/10
0.150	06/02	08/10	08/12	09/02/10
0.150	09/09	11/08	11/11	12/02/10

Dividends have been paid since 1980. Source: Company reports.

Please read the Required Disclosures and Analyst Certification on the last page of this report.

TJX Companies Inc (The)

Business Summary August 18, 2010

COMPANY PROFILE. With over $20 billion in annual revenues, TJX Companies is the largest U.S. off-price family apparel and home fashion retailer via its eight retail concepts. As of August 17, 2010, the company's core Marmaxx Group division operated 903 T.J. Maxx and 820 Marshalls stores. TJX also operated 154 A.J. Wright units and 328 HomeGoods stores in the U.S.; 21 HomeSense and 283 T.K. Maxx stores in Europe; and 79 HomeSense, 208 Winners and three StyleSense (a new family footwear and accessories test concept) stores in Canada. The company sold its 34-store Bob's Store chain to private equity firms Versa Capital Management and Crystal Capital in August 2008.

TJX believes it derives a competitive advantage by offering rapidly changing assortments of quality brand name and designer merchandise at prices usually 20% to 60% below department and specialty store regular prices. With over 2,700 stores, the company has substantial buying power with more than 12,000 vendors worldwide. TJX purchases later in the buying cycle than department and specialty stores. Generally, purchases are for current selling seasons, with a limited quantity of packaway inventory intended for a future selling season. A combination of opportunistic buying, an expansive distribution in-frastructure, and a low expense structure enable the company to offer every-day savings to its customers.

PRIMARY BUSINESS DYNAMICS. TJX's primary growth drivers are new store openings and same-store sales (sales results for stores open for all or a portion of two consecutive fiscal years). From FY 06 through FY 09, the company increased its retail selling square footage at a compound annual growth rate (CAGR) of 5%, as its total store count rose from 2,192 to 2,652. In FY 10, TJX saw opportunities to negotiate more favorable leases and to relocate stores to better locations. As a result, the company committed to fewer new store openings and retail square footage grew by only an estimated 3.5%. TJX ended FY 10 with 2,743 stores. The company is targeting 5% to 6% annual retail square footage growth from FY 11 through FY 13.

Company Financials Fiscal Year Ended Jan. 31

Per Share Data ($)	2010	2009	2008	2007	2006	2005	2004	2003	2002	2001
Tangible Book Value	6.62	4.74	4.55	4.65	3.71	3.06	2.74	2.36	2.14	1.85
Cash Flow	3.86	2.97	2.43	2.35	2.23	1.86	1.75	1.46	1.34	1.23
Earnings	2.84	2.07	1.66	1.63	1.41	1.30	1.28	1.08	0.97	0.93
S&P Core Earnings	2.88	2.03	1.63	1.64	1.40	1.22	1.21	1.01	0.91	0.90
Dividends	0.47	0.42	0.27	0.23	0.17	0.14	0.13	0.12	0.11	0.07
Payout Ratio	17%	15%	16%	14%	12%	10%	10%	11%	11%	7%
Calendar Year	2009	2008	2007	2006	2005	2004	2003	2002	2001	2000
Prices:High	40.64	37.52	32.46	29.84	25.96	26.82	23.70	22.45	20.30	15.75
Prices:Low	19.16	17.80	25.74	22.16	19.95	20.64	15.54	15.30	13.56	6.97
P/E Ratio:High	14	18	20	18	18	21	19	21	21	17
P/E Ratio:Low	7	9	16	14	14	16	12	14	14	7

Income Statement Analysis (Million $)

	2010	2009	2008	2007	2006	2005	2004	2003	2002	2001
Revenue	20,288	19,000	18,647	17,405	16,058	14,913	13,328	11,981	10,709	9,579
Operating Income	2,426	1,833	1,811	1,616	1,444	1,394	1,334	1,171	1,104	1,064
Depreciation	435	398	365	353	405	288	238	208	204	176
Interest Expense	39.5	38.1	39.9	39.2	39.0	33.5	27.3	25.4	25.6	34.7
Pretax Income	1,952	1,451	1,243	1,247	1,009	1,080	1,068	938	874	865
Effective Tax Rate	37.8%	37.0%	37.9%	37.7%	31.6%	38.5%	38.4%	38.3%	38.2%	37.8%
Net Income	1,214	915	772	777	690	664	658	578	540	538
S&P Core Earnings	1,229	893	756	778	687	615	619	546	506	519

Balance Sheet & Other Financial Data (Million $)

	2010	2009	2008	2007	2006	2005	2004	2003	2002	2001
Cash	1,745	454	733	857	466	307	246	492	493	133
Current Assets	4,804	3,626	3,992	3,749	3,140	2,905	2,452	2,241	2,116	1,722
Total Assets	7,464	6,178	6,600	6,086	5,496	5,075	4,397	3,940	3,596	2,932
Current Liabilities	2,895	2,768	2,761	2,383	2,252	2,204	1,691	1,566	1,315	1,229
Long Term Debt	774	384	853	808	807	599	692	694	702	319
Common Equity	2,889	2,135	2,131	2,290	1,893	1,653	1,552	1,409	1,341	1,219
Total Capital	3,664	2,646	3,028	3,120	2,700	2,405	2,369	2,145	2,043	1,538
Capital Expenditures	429	583	527	378	496	429	409	397	449	257
Cash Flow	1,649	1,313	1,137	1,130	1,096	953	897	786	744	714
Current Ratio	1.7	1.3	1.5	1.6	1.4	1.3	1.5	1.4	1.6	1.4
% Long Term Debt of Capitalization	21.1	14.5	28.2	25.9	29.9	24.9	29.2	32.3	34.4	20.8
% Net Income of Revenue	6.0	4.8	4.1	4.5	4.3	4.5	4.9	4.8	5.0	5.6
% Return on Assets	17.8	14.3	12.2	13.4	13.1	14.0	15.8	15.3	16.6	18.8
% Return on Equity	48.3	42.9	34.9	37.1	37.9	41.4	44.5	42.1	42.2	46.0

Data as orig reptd.; bef. results of disc opers/spec. items. Per share data adj. for stk. divs.; EPS diluted. E-Estimated. NA-Not Available. NM-Not Meaningful. NR-Not Ranked. UR-Under Review.

Office: 770 Cochituate Road, Framingham, MA 01701-4666.
Telephone: 508-390-1000.
Website: http://www.tjx.com
Chrmn: B. Cammarata

Pres & CEO: C.M. Meyrowitz
EVP, CFO, Chief Admin Officer & Chief Acctg Officer: J.G. Naylor
EVP, Secy & General Counsel: A. McCauley
Investor Contact: S. Lang (508-390-2323)

Board Members: J. B. Alvarez, A. Bennett, D. A. Brandon, B. Cammarata, D. T. Ching, M. Hines, A. B. Lane, C. M. Meyrowitz, J. F. O'Brien, W. B. Shire, F. H. Wiley

Founded: 1956
Domicile: Delaware
Employees: 154,000

Torchmark Corp

STANDARD & POOR'S

S&P Recommendation SELL ★★☆☆☆	**Price** $55.37 (as of Oct 22, 2010)	**12-Mo. Target Price** $47.00	**Investment Style** Large-Cap Blend

GICS Sector Financials
Sub-Industry Life & Health Insurance

Summary This financial services company derives most of its earnings from its life and health insurance operations.

Key Stock Statistics (Source S&P, Vickers, company reports)

52-Wk Range	$56.54–39.61	S&P Oper. EPS 2010**E**	6.30	Market Capitalization(B)	$4.475	Beta	1.66
Trailing 12-Month EPS	$5.57	S&P Oper. EPS 2011**E**	6.75	Yield (%)	1.16	S&P 3-Yr. Proj. EPS CAGR(%)	4
Trailing 12-Month P/E	9.9	P/E on S&P Oper. EPS 2010**E**	8.8	Dividend Rate/Share	$0.64	S&P Credit Rating	A
$10K Invested 5 Yrs Ago	$11,270	Common Shares Outstg. (M)	80.8	Institutional Ownership (%)	77		

Price Performance

30-Week Mov. Avg. ··· 10-Week Mov. Avg.-- **GAAP Earnings vs. Previous Year** Volume Above Avg. STARS
12-Mo. Target Price — Relative Strength — ▲ Up ▼ Down ▶ No Change Below Avg. ★

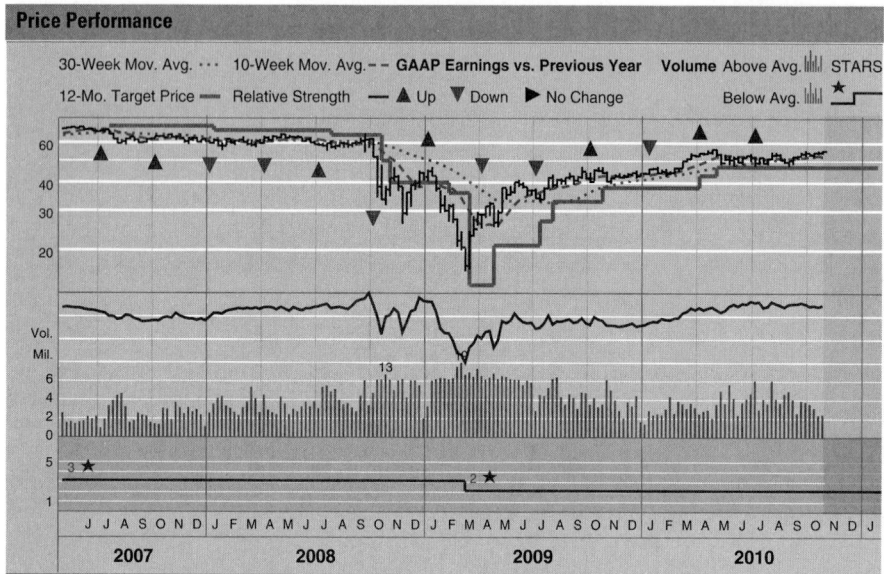

2007 2008 2009 2010

Options: ASE

Analysis prepared by **Bret Howlett** on August 02, 2010, when the stock traded at **$ 54.38**.

Qualitative Risk Assessment

LOW	**MEDIUM**	HIGH

Our risk assessment reflects our view of the company's below peer average capital cushion and potential for further investment losses and adverse credit migration in its fixed income portfolio. This is offset by TMK's varied product lineup and limited exposure to structured investments. Also, we think TMK generates strong cash flow and statutory earnings and uses excess cash flow to pay its dividend and repurchase shares.

Quantitative Evaluations

S&P Quality Ranking A

D	C	B-	B	B+	A-	**A**	A+

Relative Strength Rank MODERATE

58

LOWEST = 1 HIGHEST = 99

Highlights

> We forecast that total life sales will increase 8%-9% in 2010, on higher producing agent counts and strong results from the American Income Agency channel, tempered by poor consumer confidence and a decline in LNL Agency sales. We expect sales at American Income to increase 15%-20%, although we are concerned about agent retention. We expect life underwriting margins to increase 9%-10% in 2010 on solid premium growth, favorable mortality, lower commission expense and improved persistency. We see sluggish sales growth in direct response, although that segment should benefit from improved claims costs.

> We expect health segment sales to continue to decline in 2010 as TMK de-emphasizes that business. However, we forecast strong sales of medical supplemental products. We believe new health business written will improve margins, but we do not anticipate underwriting margin expansion until early next year. We think administrative expenses will likely grow 2%-3%.

> We forecast EPS of $6.30 for 2010 and $6.75 for 2011. Our estimates exclude realized investment gains or losses.

Investment Rationale/Risk

> Although TMK generates solid cash flow, produces consistent earnings, and is repurchasing its shares, we believe the company's growth prospects are relatively weak versus the group. We view positively TMK's reducing its below investment grade bonds to 8% of total fixed maturities, from 15% at the end of the second quarter of 2009, although we expect elevated investment losses, and capital charges stemming from adverse credit migration, to weigh on TMK's stock. In addition, we believe fundamentals in the health business are poor and expect lower health income to remain a drag on earnings. At current levels, we believe the shares are overvalued, as they trade at a sizable premium to the group on a price-to-book value basis.

> Risks to our recommendation and target price include lower than expected investment losses, less competition for some products, lower loss ratios for TMK's Medicare Part D business, and favorable mortality experience.

> Our 12-month target price of $47 is based on 1.0X our 2010 book value estimate, in line with the peer group average, but below historical levels.

Revenue/Earnings Data

Revenue (Million $)

	1Q	2Q	3Q	4Q	Year
2010	874.8	865.0	--	--	--
2009	809.6	819.7	784.9	808.2	2,687
2008	872.4	860.5	753.4	840.6	2,758
2007	906.0	876.6	863.6	840.5	3,487
2006	857.0	869.1	837.9	857.1	3,421
2005	783.0	804.8	769.0	769.1	3,126

Earnings Per Share ($)

	1Q	2Q	3Q	4Q	Year
2010	1.46	1.53	E1.61	E1.58	E6.30
2009	0.91	1.38	1.22	1.36	4.88
2008	1.29	1.47	0.72	1.61	5.11
2007	1.37	1.32	1.41	1.41	5.50
2006	1.16	1.26	1.28	1.43	5.13
2005	1.09	1.25	1.14	1.21	4.68

Fiscal year ended Dec. 31. Next earnings report expected: Late October. EPS Estimates based on S&P Operating Earnings; historical GAAP earnings are as reported.

Dividend Data (Dates: mm/dd Payment Date: mm/dd/yy)

Amount ($)	Date Decl.	Ex-Div. Date	Stk. of Record	Payment Date
0.150	10/23	01/04	01/06	02/01/10
0.150	03/01	03/30	04/02	04/30/10
0.150	06/24	06/30	07/02	07/30/10
0.160	08/12	09/29	10/02	11/01/10

Dividends have been paid since 1933. Source: Company reports.

Please read the Required Disclosures and Analyst Certification on the last page of this report.

The **McGraw-Hill** Companies

Torchmark Corp

Business Summary August 02, 2010

CORPORATE OVERVIEW. TMK's subsidiaries offer a full line of nonparticipating ordinary individual life products and health insurance, as well as fixed and variable annuities (VAs), although its VA offering is small. Traditional whole life insurance constituted 61% of life insurance in force at the end of 2009 as measured by annualized premiums, interest-sensitive whole life 5.9%, term life 30%, and other life products 3.5%. Medicare supplemental insurance accounted for 46% of supplemental health insurance in force at the end of 2009, as measured by annualized premiums, limited-benefit plans 35%, and Medicare Part D 19%. The number of individual health policies in force (excluding Medicare Part D) was 1.66 million at December 31, 2009, versus 1.54 million at prior year-end. Medicare Part D enrollees to begin the 2010 plan year were 158,000 at December 31, 2009, and the company believes enrollees are not expected to increase for the 2010 plan. Annuity separate account assets totaled $793.0 million at December 31, 2009, up nearly 4.6% from the year-earlier level.

Life segment premium revenue accounted for 62% of total premium revenue in 2009 (59% in 2008), the health segment 38% (41%), and the annuity segment 0.4% (0.5%).

CORPORATE STRATEGY. A key corporate strategy for TMK is to improve its

distribution system. Distribution is through direct solicitation, independent agents, and exclusive agents. The Liberty National exclusive agency markets products to middle-income families in the Southeastern U.S. through full-time sales representatives. In 2009, TMK combined its United American Agency Branch with its Liberty National Exclusive Agency and focused the combined sales force on writing life and supplemental health products in middle income markets. The United American branch office agency focused on health insurance to over-age-50 individuals through exclusive producing agents. The American Income exclusive agency focuses on members of labor unions, credit unions, and other associations in the U.S., Canada and New Zealand. The United Investors agency markets to middle-income Americans through independent agents. The military agency consists of a nationwide independent agency comprised of former commissioned and noncommissioned military officers who sell exclusively to military officers and their families. The United American independent agency focuses primarily on health insurance in the U.S. and Canada to individuals over the age of 50.

Company Financials Fiscal Year Ended Dec. 31

Per Share Data ($)	2009	2008	2007	2006	2005	2004	2003	2002	2001	2000
Tangible Book Value	77.55	19.52	31.74	31.39	29.49	28.16	25.39	20.91	17.24	14.34
Operating Earnings	NA	NA	NA	NA	NA	NA	3.87	3.51	3.12	2.85
Earnings	4.88	5.11	5.50	5.13	4.68	4.25	3.73	3.18	3.11	2.82
S&P Core Earnings	6.08	5.81	5.35	5.07	4.29	4.03	3.68	3.39	2.73	NA
Dividends	0.42	0.69	0.52	0.48	0.44	0.44	0.38	0.36	0.36	0.36
Payout Ratio	9%	14%	9%	9%	9%	10%	10%	11%	12%	13%
Prices:High	47.25	66.00	70.54	64.59	57.50	57.57	45.75	42.17	43.25	41.19
Prices:Low	16.16	26.27	58.50	53.91	50.05	44.61	33.00	30.02	32.56	18.75
P/E Ratio:High	10	13	13	13	12	14	12	13	14	15
P/E Ratio:Low	3	5	11	11	11	10	9	9	10	7

Income Statement Analysis (Million $)

	2009	2008	2007	2006	2005	2004	2003	2002	2001	2000
Life Insurance in Force	152,525	147,780	145,349	141,134	139,233	134,640	126,737	118,660	113,055	108,319
Premium Income:Life	1,660	1,617	1,570	1,524	1,468	1,396	1,246	1,221	1,144	1,082
Premium Income:A & H	1,018	1,127	1,237	1,238	1,015	1,049	1,034	1,019	1,011	911
Net Investment Income	675	671	649	629	603	577	557	519	492	472
Total Revenue	3,222	3,327	3,487	3,421	3,126	3,072	2,931	2,738	2,707	2,516
Pretax Income	660	715	797	774	732	721	655	580	597	553
Net Operating Income	NA	NA	NA	NA	NA	NA	446	424	393	365
Net Income	405	452	528	519	495	476	430	383	391	362
S&P Core Earnings	505	514	514	512	455	452	424	408	343	NA

Balance Sheet & Other Financial Data (Million $)

	2009	2008	2007	2006	2005	2004	2003	2002	2001	2000
Cash & Equivalent	411	223	193	185	178	164	155	140	129	154
Premiums Due	197	152	96.8	78.8	67.3	73.4	80.7	70.4	67.5	75.0
Investment Assets:Bonds	9,696	7,817	9,226	9,127	8,837	8,715	8,103	7,194	6,526	5,950
Investment Assets:Stocks	16.7	16.3	21.3	41.2	48.0	36.9	57.4	24.5	0.57	0.54
Investment Assets:Loans	384	360	344	329	317	338	704	401	393	374
Investment Assets:Total	10,507	8,489	9,772	9,703	9,649	9,405	8,795	7,784	7,154	6,471
Deferred Policy Costs	3,457	3,395	3,159	2,956	2,768	2,506	2,330	2,184	2,066	1,942
Total Assets	16,024	13,529	15,241	14,980	14,769	14,252	13,461	12,361	12,428	12,963
Debt	796	499	598	598	353	540	693	552	681	366
Common Equity	3,399	2,223	3,325	3,459	3,433	6,840	3,240	2,851	2,497	2,202
% Return on Revenue	12.6	13.6	15.1	15.2	15.8	15.5	14.7	14.0	14.4	14.4
% Return on Assets	2.7	3.1	3.5	3.5	3.4	3.4	3.3	3.1	3.1	2.9
% Return on Equity	14.4	16.2	15.6	15.1	14.5	7.1	14.1	14.3	16.6	17.2
% Investment Yield	7.1	7.3	6.7	6.5	6.3	6.4	6.7	7.0	7.2	7.5

Data as orig reptd.; bef. results of disc opers/spec. items. Per share data adj. for stk. divs.; EPS diluted. E-Estimated. NA-Not Available. NM-Not Meaningful. NR-Not Ranked. UR-Under Review.

Office: 3700 S Stonebridge Dr, McKinney, TX 75070-5934.
Telephone: 972-569-4000.
Website: http://www.torchmarkcorp.com
Chrmn & CEO: M.S. McAndrew

EVP & CFO: G.L. Coleman
EVP & Chief Admin Officer: V.D. Herbel
EVP & General Counsel: L.M. Hutchison
Chief Acctg Officer: D.H. Almond

Investor Contact: J.L. Lane (972-569-3627)
Board Members: C. E. Adair, D. L. Boren, J. M. Buchan, R. W. Ingram, M. S. McAndrew, L. W. Newton, S. R. Perry, D. M. Rebelez, L. Smith, P. J. Zucconi

Founded: 1900
Domicile: Delaware
Employees: 3,505

Total System Services Inc.

STANDARD &POOR'S

S&P Recommendation HOLD ★★★☆☆

Price	12-Mo. Target Price	Investment Style
$15.98 (as of Oct 22, 2010)	$17.00	Large-Cap Growth

GICS Sector Information Technology
Sub-Industry Data Processing & Outsourced Services

Summary This company processes data, transactions, and payments for domestic and international issuers of credit, debit, commercial, and private-label cards.

Key Stock Statistics (Source S&P, Vickers, company reports)

52-Wk Range	$17.75–13.41	S&P Oper. EPS 2010E	0.98	Market Capitalization(B)	$3.155	Beta		0.99
Trailing 12-Month EPS	$1.10	S&P Oper. EPS 2011E	1.05	Yield (%)	1.75	S&P 3-Yr. Proj. EPS CAGR(%)		8
Trailing 12-Month P/E	14.5	P/E on S&P Oper. EPS 2010E	16.3	Dividend Rate/Share	$0.28	S&P Credit Rating		NA
$10K Invested 5 Yrs Ago	$9,278	Common Shares Outstg. (M)	197.4	Institutional Ownership (%)	66			

Price Performance

- 30-Week Mov. Avg. · · · ·
- 10-Week Mov. Avg. – –
- 12-Mo. Target Price —
- Relative Strength —
- GAAP Earnings vs. Previous Year
- ▲ Up ▼ Down ► No Change
- Volume Above Avg. ▊▊▏ STARS
- Below Avg. ▏▊▏ ★

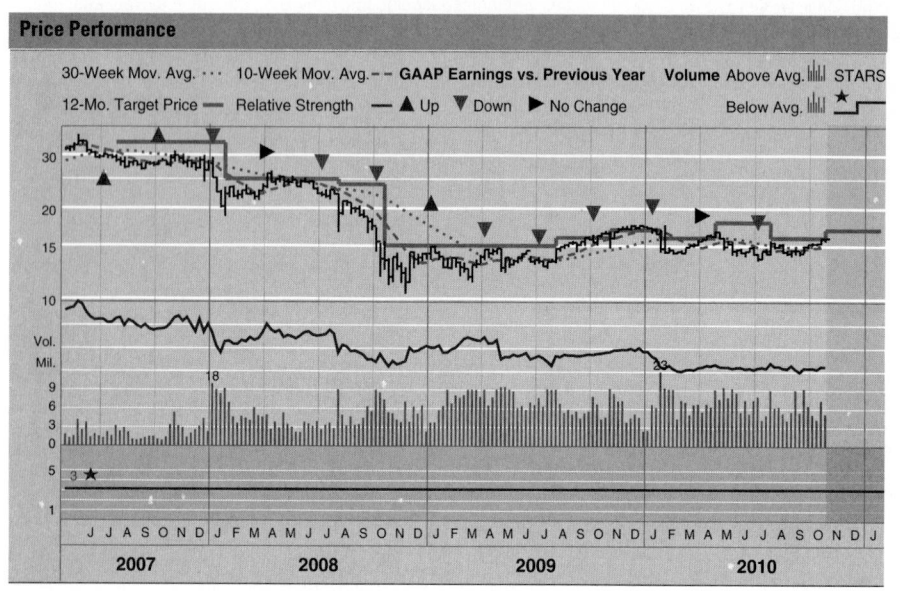

Options: CBOE, Ph

Analysis prepared by **Zaineb Bokhari** on October 22, 2010, when the stock traded at **$ 15.77**.

Highlights

► We forecast operating revenues (before reimbursable items) of $1.4 billion in 2010, about 2% greater than 2009, aided by contributions from a recent joint venture with First National Bank of Omaha. We think TSS sees growth opportunities in international markets, but we look for this to be offset by year-over-year declines in domestic operations, attributable to slowing internal growth, customer loss, price erosion, and the domestic economy. We forecast growth of about 5% for operating revenues in 2011. We see total revenue rising 2% and 4% in 2010 and 2011, respectively.

► We look for operating margins to narrow to approximately 18.5% in 2010, from 20.3% in 2009 (on a restated basis), reflecting our outlook for lower North American Services revenues and anticipated shifts in TSS's customer base, which the company is responding to with planned headcount and expense reductions. We expect ongoing investment in international operations to limit benefits from anticipated expense reductions. We see modestly wider operating margins in 2011 reflecting our revenue growth outlook.

► We see EPS of $0.98 in 2010 and $1.05 in 2011.

Investment Rationale/Risk

► TSS continues to navigate through a difficult period for its financial institution customers, some of whom experienced considerable financial losses in the recent recession. In this environment and after the recent credit card regulation, card issuance has declined and issuers have purged inactive consumer card accounts. Business has also been lost due to client consolidation. TSS continues to add new customers, but we think the revenue hole created by recent business losses will be replaced slowly. We see TSS continuing to manage costs until the economic recovery becomes firmer, but as it expands overseas, we expect investment.

► Risks to our recommendation and target price include greater competition from other payment processors, and an increased potential for business disruptions or loss due to ongoing industry consolidation. We expect the pace of economic recovery and the prevailing regulatory environment to impact card growth.

► We derive our 12-month target price of $17 by applying a 16.4 P/E to our 2011 estimate, consistent with the recent average for data processing and outsourced services peers.

Qualitative Risk Assessment

LOW	MEDIUM	HIGH

Our risk assessment reflects our view that the company is navigating past a difficult period with sizable customer losses. We continue to view TSS as a leading provider of card processing services, but we expect the environment to improve gradually as organic growth remains modest.

Quantitative Evaluations

S&P Quality Ranking A-

D	C	B-	B	B+	A-	A	A+

Relative Strength Rank MODERATE

68

LOWEST = 1   HIGHEST = 99

Revenue/Earnings Data

Revenue (Million $)

	1Q	2Q	3Q	4Q	Year
2010	415.4	433.8	--	--	--
2009	408.9	412.0	432.3	434.8	1,688
2008	461.7	483.1	500.4	493.4	1,939
2007	429.6	460.2	457.6	458.5	1,806
2006	412.3	429.2	441.8	503.9	1,787
2005	350.0	410.2	422.0	420.7	1,603

Earnings Per Share ($)

	1Q	2Q	3Q	4Q	Year
2010	0.26	0.25	E0.24	E0.24	E0.98
2009	0.26	0.27	0.29	0.31	1.12
2008	0.29	0.32	0.33	0.34	1.27
2007	0.29	0.33	0.35	0.23	1.20
2006	0.26	0.29	0.28	0.44	1.26
2005	0.23	0.26	0.24	0.25	0.99

Fiscal year ended Dec. 31. Next earnings report expected: Late October. EPS Estimates based on S&P Operating Earnings; historical GAAP earnings are as reported.

Dividend Data (Dates: mm/dd Payment Date: mm/dd/yy)

Amount ($)	Date Decl.	Ex-Div. Date	Stk. of Record	Payment Date
0.070	12/08	12/21	12/23	01/04/10
0.070	02/25	03/16	03/18	04/01/10
0.070	06/01	06/15	06/17	07/01/10
0.070	08/26	09/14	09/16	10/01/10

Dividends have been paid since 1990. Source: Company reports.

Please read the Required Disclosures and Analyst Certification on the last page of this report.

The McGraw-Hill Companies

Total System Services Inc.

STANDARD &POOR'S

Business Summary October 22, 2010

CORPORATE PROFILE. Total System Services provides electronic payment processing, merchant processing and associated services to financial and non-financial institutions in the U.S., Canada, Mexico, Europe, and the Caribbean. Electronic payment processing services are generated primarily from charges based on the number of accounts on file, transactions and authorizations processed, statements mailed, and other processing services for cardholder accounts on file. These services are provided to issuers of consumer credit, debit, retail, stored value cards as well as government services and commercial card accounts. As of December 2009, TSS had 344.8 million accounts on file, down from 352.5 million in 2008 and 375.5 million in 2007. The company divides its services into three operating segments: North America Services (60% of 2009 revenues), Global (or International) Services (20%), and Merchant Services (20%).

PRIMARY BUSINESS DYNAMICS. TSS serves large financial institutions under long-term contracts. This results in revenue concentration that we view as a risk, since these large customers can be acquired, move to a competitor, or in some case, move processing of transactions in-house. In 2008, 2007 and 2006, the company's three largest customers contributed 32.4%, 32.4% and 39.2%, respectively, of total revenues. In 2006, Bank of America moved

processing on its consumer card portfolio of about 46 million accounts in-house. In 2007, customer JPMorgan Chase ended its outsourcing agreement with TSS and moved its processing in-house, using a system licensed from TSS. Recent consolidation among financial institutions involving TSS clients include JPMorgan's acquisition of Washington Mutual Bank and Wells Fargo's acquisition of TSS client Wachovia. In 2009, Bank of America accounted for 12.9% of TSS's total revenues.

MARKET PROFILE. The domestic market for third-party card processing is fairly concentrated, with three vendors serving most of the national market. In 2008, TSS believed that 42% of the domestic credit card processing was done using its systems. The company includes cards that are processed in-house, but using software licensed from TSS in this assessment of market share. In 2009, the comparable market share number was 19%, reflecting business losses. TSS's market share was 42% in 2007, 39% in 2006 and 2005 and 21% in 2004.

Company Financials Fiscal Year Ended Dec. 31

Per Share Data ($)	2009	2008	2007	2006	2005	2004	2003	2002	2001	2000
Tangible Book Value	4.04	3.07	3.51	5.40	4.49	4.01	3.57	3.06	2.57	2.10
Cash Flow	1.83	1.53	1.44	2.20	1.75	1.31	1.21	1.01	0.82	0.70
Earnings	1.12	1.27	1.20	1.26	0.99	0.76	0.71	0.64	0.53	0.44
S&P Core Earnings	1.12	1.27	1.20	1.26	0.95	0.74	0.69	0.60	0.51	NA
Dividends	0.28	0.28	3.31	0.27	0.22	0.14	0.08	0.07	0.06	0.05
Payout Ratio	25%	22%	NM	21%	22%	18%	11%	11%	11%	11%
Prices:High	17.71	28.19	35.05	26.61	25.88	31.27	31.50	29.44	35.84	22.75
Prices:Low	11.33	10.36	24.35	17.87	17.76	19.47	13.25	11.01	18.91	14.88
P/E Ratio:High	16	22	29	21	26	41	44	46	68	52
P/E Ratio:Low	10	8	20	14	18	26	19	17	36	34

Income Statement Analysis (Million $)										
Revenue	1,688	1,939	1,806	1,787	1,603	1,187	1,053	955	650	601
Operating Income	481	433	415	542	438	311	289	232	193	164
Depreciation	156	50.5	47.1	185	151	109	98.4	74.5	57.4	51.6
Interest Expense	4.10	11.3	3.13	0.57	0.37	0.94	Nil	1.10	Nil	Nil
Pretax Income	346	383	383	376	298	228	212	184	156	132
Effective Tax Rate	35.1%	34.4%	37.5%	33.6%	34.7%	33.9%	33.4%	31.5%	33.9%	35.0%
Net Income	220	250	237	249	195	151	141	126	103	85.6
S&P Core Earnings	219	250	237	249	188	145	136	119	99.5	NA

Balance Sheet & Other Financial Data (Million $)										
Cash	450	220	240	389	238	232	123	113	56.0	80.1
Current Assets	811	625	587	745	512	448	274	266	206	211
Total Assets	1,711	1,539	1,479	1,634	1,411	1,282	1,001	783	652	604
Current Liabilities	221	249	274	296	277	278	147	114	103	147
Long Term Debt	192	210	257	3.63	3.56	4.51	29.7	0.07	Nil	Nil
Common Equity	1,176	989	844	1,217	1,013	865	733	602	501	409
Total Capital	1,389	1,260	1,177	1,296	1,106	1,004	854	668	550	446
Capital Expenditures	34.0	48.0	55.3	26.5	40.9	53.9	125	14.8	30.8	31.8
Cash Flow	359	301	285	434	346	259	239	200	160	137
Current Ratio	3.7	2.5	2.1	2.5	1.8	1.6	1.9	2.3	2.0	1.4
% Long Term Debt of Capitalization	13.9	16.7	21.8	0.3	0.3	0.4	3.5	0.0	Nil	Nil
% Net Income of Revenue	13.1	12.9	13.2	13.9	12.1	12.7	13.4	13.2	15.8	14.2
% Return on Assets	13.5	16.6	15.3	16.4	14.4	13.2	15.8	17.5	16.4	16.0
% Return on Equity	20.3	27.3	23.0	22.3	20.7	18.9	21.1	22.7	22.6	23.0

Data as orig reptd.; bef. results of disc opers/spec. items. Per share data adj. for stk. divs.; EPS diluted. E-Estimated. NA-Not Available. NM-Not Meaningful. NR-Not Ranked. UR-Under Review.

Office: One TSYS Wy, Columbus, GA 31902.
Telephone: 706-649-2267.
Email: ir@tsys.com
Website: http://www.tsys.com

Chrmn & CEO: P.W. Tomlinson
Pres & COO: M.T. Woods
EVP & CFO: J.B. Lipham
EVP & CTO: S.W. Humber

EVP, Chief Acctg Officer & Cntlr: D.K. Weaver
Investor Contact: S. Roberts (706-644-6081)
Board Members: R. E. Anthony, J. H. Blanchard, R. Y. Bradley, K. Cloninger, III, W. W. Driver, Jr., G. W. Garrard, Jr., S. E. Harris, M. H. Lampton, W. W. Miller, Jr., H. L. Page, P. W. Tomlinson, J. T. Turner, R. W. Ussery, M. T. Woods, J. D. Yancey, R. K. Yarbrough

Founded: 1982
Domicile: Georgia
Employees: 7,620

Travelers Companies Inc (The)

STANDARD &POOR'S

S&P Recommendation STRONG BUY ★★★★★

Price	12-Mo. Target Price	Investment Style
$55.10 (as of Oct 22, 2010)	$65.00	Large-Cap Value

GICS Sector Financials
Sub-Industry Property & Casualty Insurance

Summary Formed via the 2004 merger of Travelers Property Casualty Corp. and Saint Paul Cos., TRV is a leading provider of commercial property-liability and homeowners and auto insurance.

Key Stock Statistics (Source S&P, Vickers, company reports)

52-Wk Range	$55.70– 47.35	S&P Oper. EPS 2010E	5.85	Market Capitalization(B)	$25.896	Beta	0.58
Trailing 12-Month EPS	$6.66	S&P Oper. EPS 2011E	6.25	Yield (%)	2.61	S&P 3-Yr. Proj. EPS CAGR(%)	3
Trailing 12-Month P/E	8.3	P/E on S&P Oper. EPS 2010E	9.4	Dividend Rate/Share	$1.44	S&P Credit Rating	A-
$10K Invested 5 Yrs Ago	$14,269	Common Shares Outstg. (M)	470.0	Institutional Ownership (%)	84		

Price Performance

30-Week Mov. Avg. · · · · 10-Week Mov. Avg. – – **GAAP Earnings vs. Previous Year** Volume Above Avg. STARS
12-Mo. Target Price — Relative Strength — ▲ Up ▼ Down ► No Change Below Avg.

Options: ASE, CBOE, Ph

Analysis prepared by **Cathy A. Seifert** on October 21, 2010, when the stock traded at **$ 54.78**.

Highlights

➤ We expect earned premium growth of 1% to 3% in 2010 and in 2011, versus a fractional decline in 2009. This reflects our view of ongoing price competition in many core lines and the impact of a weak economic climate in 2009. Our forecast of modestly higher premiums in coming periods is predicated on a modest economic recovery, coupled with TRV's ability to retain its existing client base and leverage new business opportunities.

➤ We believe net investment income trends will be mixed in 2010, as a recovery in the non fixed-income portfolio is offset by pressure in the fixed income portfolio due to lower reinvestment rates.

➤ We estimate operating EPS of $5.85 in 2010 and $6.25 in 2011, versus $6.29 in 2009. Our 2010 estimate assumes that underwriting results will remain under pressure (but remain profitable) due to competitive pricing pressures and a resumption of "normal" catastrophe loss trends. We also assume per-share results will continue to be aided by share buybacks, which totaled 69.4 million during 2009 and 66.8 million in the first nine months of 2010.

Investment Rationale/Risk

➤ Although our outlook remains tempered by concerns we have that both the underwriting and investment environments will remain challenging through 2010 and possibly into 2011, we believe TRV's shares do not adequately reflect the actions the company has taken in recent years to improve its underwriting results and to better capitalize on what we see as a flight to quality within the property-casualty insurance market. We also view TRV as a prudent underwriter with an above-average quality balance sheet.

➤ Risks to our recommendation and target price include deterioration in asbestos and environmental claims and reserve development, erosion in underwriting trends, a surge in catastrophe losses, and erosion in the credit quality of TRV's investment portfolio.

➤ Our 12-month target price of $65 assumes a multiple of 10.4X our 2011 operating EPS estimate. Our target multiple reflects our assumption that TRV shares will trade at the midpoint of their historical valuation range, but at a premium to some peers.

Qualitative Risk Assessment

LOW	MEDIUM	HIGH

Our risk assessment reflects our view of TRV as a leading property-casualty underwriter with a diversified mix of business and sound capital management practices. Offsetting this is our view that TRV may have to add to loss reserves for certain "long tail" liability lines of coverage, and could see impairments to its fixed income investment portfolio.

Quantitative Evaluations

S&P Quality Ranking   NR

D	C	B-	B	B+	A-	A	A+

Relative Strength Rank   MODERATE

68

LOWEST = 1   HIGHEST = 99

Revenue/Earnings Data

Revenue (Million $)

	1Q	2Q	3Q	4Q	Year
2010	6,119	6,179	--	--	--
2009	5,735	6,162	6,327	6,456	24,680
2008	6,232	6,295	6,145	5,805	24,477
2007	6,427	6,612	6,526	6,491	26,017
2006	6,050	6,255	6,316	6,469	25,090
2005	6,105	6,037	6,042	6,181	24,365

Earnings Per Share ($)

2010	1.25	1.35	E1.81	E1.43	E5.85
2009	1.11	1.27	1.65	2.36	6.33
2008	1.54	1.54	0.36	1.35	4.82
2007	1.56	1.86	1.81	1.64	6.86
2006	1.41	1.36	1.47	1.68	5.91
2005	1.25	1.33	0.11	0.26	2.95

Fiscal year ended Dec. 31. Next earnings report expected: Late October. EPS Estimates based on S&P Operating Earnings; historical GAAP earnings are as reported.

Dividend Data (Dates: mm/dd Payment Date: mm/dd/yy)

Amount ($)	Date Decl.	Ex-Div. Date	Stk. of Record	Payment Date
0.330	10/22	12/08	12/10	12/31/09
0.330	02/03	03/08	03/10	03/31/10
0.360	04/23	06/08	06/10	06/30/10
0.360	08/04	09/08	09/10	09/30/10

Dividends have been paid since 2003. Source: Company reports.

Please read the Required Disclosures and Analyst Certification on the last page of this report.

The **McGraw·Hill** Companies

Travelers Companies Inc (The)

Business Summary October 21, 2010

CORPORATE OVERVIEW. The Travelers Companies (TRV) is a leading property-casualty underwriter. Net written premiums of $21.3 billion in 2009 (versus $21.7 billion in 2008) were divided as follows: business insurance 51%; personal lines 34%; and financial, professional and international lines 15% (all of which were not significantly different from the business mix in 2008).

The business insurance lines segment offers a broad array of coverages distributed through about 6,300 independent brokers and agencies in the U.S. Business insurance net written premiums of $10.9 billion in 2009 were divided as follows: commercial multi-peril 27%, workers' compensation 23%, commercial automobile 18%, commercial property 16%, and general liability and other 16%. This segment's underwriting results in 2009 improved largely due to a decline in catastrophe losses. The combined loss and expense ratio declined to 86.1% in 2009 (consisting of a loss ratio of 53.9% and an expense ratio of 32.2%), from 90.2% in 2008 (consisting of a loss ratio of 57.7% and an expense ratio of 32.5%).

The financial, professional and international lines segment underwrites a number of specialized lines of business, including lines of coverage related to the surety bond business, the construction industry, and certain types of professional and managerial liability. This unit operates throughout the U.S. and

in the U.K., Canada and Ireland. Net written premiums of $3.3 billion in 2009 (versus $3.5 billion in 2008) were divided as follows: general liability 28%, fidelity and surety 30%, international 38%, and other 4%. Underwriting results in this segment deteriorated slightly in 2009. As a result, the combined (loss and expense) ratio equaled 88.1% in 2009, versus 87.2% in 2008.

The personal lines segment underwrites an array of coverage for personal risks (primarily personal automobile and homeowners' coverage) via a network of independent agencies. Net premiums written of $7.1 billion in 2009 were divided as follows: personal auto 51%, and homeowners' and other 49%. At year-end 2009, the personal lines segment had approximately 7.5 million policies in force (consisting primarily of personal auto and homeowners' insurance policies). Underwriting results in 2009 improved, largely due to a decline in the level of catastrophe losses, partly offset by a rise in non-catastrophe loss costs. Consequently, the combined ratio in 2009 was 94.6%, versus 97.0% in 2008.

Company Financials Fiscal Year Ended Dec. 31

Per Share Data ($)	2009	2008	2007	2006	2005	2004	2003	2002	2001	2000
Tangible Book Value	48.03	36.08	35.56	31.85	25.66	20.93	9.52	10.29	6.66	NA
Operating Earnings	NA	NA	NA	NA	NA	NA	NA	NA	NA	NA
Earnings	6.33	4.82	6.86	5.91	2.95	1.53	1.68	0.23	1.06	1.71
S&P Core Earnings	6.25	5.10	6.67	5.87	2.87	1.50	3.71	0.14	2.42	NA
Dividends	1.23	1.19	1.13	1.01	0.91	0.74	0.28	Nil	NA	NA
Payout Ratio	19%	25%	16%	17%	31%	48%	17%	Nil	NA	NA
Prices:High	54.47	58.57	56.99	55.00	46.97	43.31	17.42	19.50	NA	NA
Prices:Low	33.07	28.91	47.26	40.23	33.70	16.55	12.98	12.09	NA	NA
P/E Ratio:High	9	12	8	9	16	28	10	85	NA	NA
P/E Ratio:Low	5	6	7	7	11	11	8	53	NA	NA

Income Statement Analysis (Million $)										
Premium Income	21,418	21,579	21,470	20,760	20,341	19,038	12,545	11,155	9,411	NA
Net Investment Income	2,776	2,792	3,761	3,517	3,165	2,663	1,869	1,881	2,034	NA
Other Revenue	486	106	825	813	859	20,271	725	1,234	786	NA
Total Revenue	24,680	24,477	26,017	25,090	24,365	22,934	15,139	14,270	12,231	11,071
Pretax Income	4,711	3,716	6,216	5,725	2,671	1,128	2,229	-260	1,389	1,864
Net Operating Income	NA	NA	NA	NA	NA	NA	NA	NA	NA	NA
Net Income	3,622	2,924	4,601	4,208	2,061	955	1,696	216	1,062	1,312
S&P Core Earnings	3,548	3,087	4,464	4,171	2,001	937	1,615	41.1	803	NA

Balance Sheet & Other Financial Data (Million $)										
Cash & Equivalent	1,080	1,173	1,132	1,286	1,098	933	714	432	865	196
Premiums Due	5,471	5,954	6,142	6,181	6,124	6,201	4,090	3,861	NA	NA
Investment Assets:Bonds	65,847	61,275	64,920	62,666	58,983	54,256	33,046	30,003	NA	NA
Investment Assets:Stocks	451	379	488	476	579	791	733	852	NA	NA
Investment Assets:Loans	Nil	Nil	Nil	Nil	145	191	211	258	32,843	NA
Investment Assets:Total	74,403	70,199	74,818	72,268	68,287	64,710	38,652	38,425	32,619	30,754
Deferred Policy Costs	1,758	1,774	1,809	1,615	1,527	1,559	925	873	NA	NA
Total Assets	109,824	109,751	115,224	113,761	113,187	111,815	64,872	64,138	57,599	53,850
Debt	6,527	6,181	6,242	4,588	5,850	5,709	2,675	2,744	3,755	NA
Common Equity	27,336	25,230	26,504	25,006	33,077	32,323	11,987	10,137	9,729	9,214
Property & Casualty:Loss Ratio	57.3	59.4	56.6	57.5	71.9	NA	NA	NA	80.7	NA
Property & Casualty:Expense Ratio	31.9	32.5	30.8	30.6	29.4	NA	NA	NA	27.3	NA
Property & Casualty Combined Ratio	89.2	91.9	87.4	88.1	101.3	107.7	96.9	117.4	108.0	100.2
% Return on Revenue	14.7	12.0	17.8	20.3	8.5	4.2	11.2	1.6	8.7	11.9
% Return on Equity	13.8	11.3	17.9	17.8	6.3	3.7	15.3	NA	10.7	NA

Data as orig reptd.; bef. results of disc opers/spec. items. Per share data adj. for stk. divs.; EPS diluted. E-Estimated. NA-Not Available. NM-Not Meaningful. NR-Not Ranked. UR-Under Review.

Office: 385 Washington Street, Saint Paul, MN 55102.
Telephone: 651-310-7911.
Website: http://www.stpaultravelers.com
Chrmn & CEO: J.S. Fishman

Pres & COO: B.W. MacLean
EVP & Chief Admin Officer: A. Bessette
EVP & Treas: M. Olivo
EVP & General Counsel: A.D. Schnitzer

Investor Contact: M. Parr (860-277-0779)
Board Members: A. L. Beller, J. H. Dasburg, J. M. Dolan, K. M. Duberstein, J. S. Fishman, L. G. Graev, P. L. Higgins, T. R. Hodgson, C. L. Killingsworth, Jr., B. J. McGarvie, D. J. Shepard, L. J. Thomsen

Auditor: KPMG LLP
Founded: 1853
Domicile: Minnesota
Employees: 32,000

T. Rowe Price Group Inc

STANDARD
&POOR'S

S&P Recommendation HOLD ★★★☆☆ | **Price** $54.69 (as of Oct 25, 2010) | **12-Mo. Target Price** $55.00 | **Investment Style** Large-Cap Growth

GICS Sector Financials
Sub-Industry Asset Management & Custody Banks

Summary This company (formerly T. Rowe Price Associates) operates one of the largest no-load mutual fund complexes in the United States.

Key Stock Statistics (Source S&P, Vickers, company reports)

52-Wk Range	$59.44– 42.81	S&P Oper. EPS 2010E	2.48	Market Capitalization(B)	$1.447	Beta	1.71
Trailing 12-Month EPS	$2.39	S&P Oper. EPS 2011E	2.72	Yield (%)	1.97	S&P 3-Yr. Proj. EPS CAGR(%)	26
Trailing 12-Month P/E	22.9	P/E on S&P Oper. EPS 2010E	22.1	Dividend Rate/Share	$1.08	S&P Credit Rating	NA
$10K Invested 5 Yrs Ago	$19,057	Common Shares Outstg. (M)	26.5	Institutional Ownership (%)	69		

Price Performance

30-Week Mov. Avg. · · · · 10-Week Mov. Avg. - - - GAAP Earnings vs. Previous Year Volume Above Avg. ▮▮▮ STARS
12-Mo. Target Price — Relative Strength — ▲ Up ▼ Down ▶ No Change Below Avg. ▮▮▮ ★

Options: ASE, CBOE, P, Ph

Analysis prepared by **Christopher Maimone** on October 25, 2010, when the stock traded at **$ 54.96**.

Highlights

➤ Recent stock market appreciation and increased advisory fees drove strong third quarter revenues as assets under management grew at a faster pace than peers. We look for continued robust flows into TROW's target-date retirement and fixed income funds as baby boomers approach retirement and retail investors remain concerned about economic growth. We see TROW's robust net sales continuing as strong marketing and a growing international presence attract more inflows.

➤ We think the pretax margin will rise modestly in 2011, even as TROW boosts advertising and promotion spending by 40%. We think TROW's investment to strengthen its already strong brand will bolster mutual fund inflows. Assuming economic conditions improve, we see operating margins widening in 2011 to roughly 46.9%, from our 2010 estimate of 44.9%. We see future compensation expense and advertising expense ratios below historical norms as advisory fee and net inflow revenue growth converge to offset growth in expenses.

➤ We project EPS of $2.48 in 2010 and $2.72 in 2011.

Investment Rationale/Risk

➤ We believe TROW's relative investment performance is strong, with 89%, 86% and 71% of funds outperforming their comparable Lipper averages on a one-, three- and five-year performance basis. We think this will help attract client assets into its mutual funds and separately managed accounts as market conditions improve. We also view favorably its low debt levels, consistent dividend payout and continued share repurchases. We view TROW's stock option grants as generous, especially given reductions at competitors, and we would like to see more independent directors on the board.

➤ Risks to our recommendation and target price include stock and bond market depreciation, heightened regulatory scrutiny, and increased competition.

➤ Our 12-month target price of $55 assumes a multiple of 20.2X our 2011 EPS estimate of $2.72. We value TROW at a premium to its peer multiple of 14X to reflect our view of TROW's low debt levels, strong relative fund performance, and an asset mix that favors equities in an improving market environment.

Qualitative Risk Assessment

LOW	MEDIUM	HIGH

Our risk assessment reflects the company's strong market share and our view of its consistent net client inflows and impressive relative investment performance, offset by industry cyclicality.

Quantitative Evaluations

S&P Quality Ranking A-

D	C	B-	B	B+	A-	A	A+

Relative Strength Rank STRONG

79

LOWEST = 1   HIGHEST = 99

Revenue/Earnings Data

Revenue (Million $)

	1Q	2Q	3Q	4Q	Year
2010	556.2	577.4	586.1	--	--
2009	384.5	442.2	498.1	542.6	1,872
2008	560.4	587.7	555.9	417.3	2,121
2007	508.4	551.1	571.0	597.8	2,233
2006	429.3	446.0	450.6	489.1	1,819
2005	358.0	364.5	389.6	403.8	1,516

Earnings Per Share ($)

	1Q	2Q	3Q	4Q	Year
2010	0.57	0.59	0.64	E0.68	E2.48
2009	0.19	0.38	0.50	0.57	1.65
2008	0.55	0.60	0.56	0.09	1.82
2007	0.51	0.58	0.63	0.68	2.40
2006	0.42	0.49	0.46	0.53	1.90
2005	0.35	0.38	0.43	0.43	1.58

Fiscal year ended Dec. 31. Next earnings report expected: Late January. EPS Estimates based on S&P Operating Earnings; historical GAAP earnings are as reported.

Dividend Data (Dates: mm/dd Payment Date: mm/dd/yy)

Amount ($)	Date Decl.	Ex-Div. Date	Stk. of Record	Payment Date
0.270	02/18	03/12	03/16	03/29/10
0.270	06/03	06/10	06/14	06/28/10
0.270	09/03	09/10	09/14	09/28/10
0.270	10/18	12/10	12/14	12/28/10

Dividends have been paid since 1986. Source: Company reports.

Please read the Required Disclosures and Analyst Certification on the last page of this report.

The McGraw-Hill Companies

T. Rowe Price Group Inc

STANDARD &POOR'S

Business Summary October 25, 2010

CORPORATE OVERVIEW. T. Rowe Price Group (TROW) is the successor to an investment counseling business formed by the late Thomas Rowe Price, Jr. in 1937. It is now the investment adviser to the T. Rowe Price family of no-load mutual funds, and is one of the largest publicly held U.S. mutual fund complexes. At the end of 2009, TROW had about $391 billion in assets under management, up from $276 billion at the end of 2008, but still below the $400 billion under management at the end of 2007. As of year-end 2009, 74% of assets under management were invested in stock and blended asset portfolios, and 26% were invested in bond and money market portfolios.

T. Rowe Price offers mutual funds and separate accounts that employ a broad range of investment styles, including growth, value, sector-focused, tax-efficient, and quantitative index-oriented approaches. The company's investment approach is based upon a strong commitment to proprietary research, sophisticated risk-management processes, and a strict adherence to stated investment objectives. The company employs both fundamental and quantitative methods in performing security analyses, using internal equity and fixed income investment research capabilities. We believe T. Rowe Price's broad

line of no-load mutual funds makes it easy for investors to reallocate assets among funds (which is not the case at some smaller fund companies), contributing to increased client retention.

All of the company's Investor class funds are sold without a sales commission, known as no-load funds. Its Advisors and R class funds, distributed through third-party financial intermediaries, carry 12b-1 fees to cover distribution costs. TROW also manages private accounts for individuals and institutions. Revenues primarily come from investment advisory fees for managing portfolios, which depend largely on the total value and composition of assets under management. At December 31, 2009, the six largest Price funds -- Growth Stock, Equity Income, Mid-Cap Growth, Blue Chip Growth, Value, and Capital Appreciation -- accounted for 26% of investment advisory revenues in 2009 and 21% of assets under management.

Company Financials Fiscal Year Ended Dec. 31

Per Share Data ($)	2009	2008	2007	2006	2005	2004	2003	2002	2001	2000
Tangible Book Value	8.57	7.09	7.97	6.63	5.21	3.98	2.66	1.91	1.68	1.21
Cash Flow	1.90	2.05	2.60	2.07	1.80	1.48	1.11	0.96	20.71	1.33
Earnings	1.65	1.82	2.40	1.90	1.58	1.26	0.89	0.76	0.76	1.04
S&P Core Earnings	1.72	2.03	2.40	1.90	1.43	1.16	0.78	0.67	0.65	NA
Dividends	1.00	0.96	0.75	0.59	0.49	0.40	0.35	0.33	0.31	0.27
Payout Ratio	61%	53%	31%	31%	31%	32%	40%	43%	40%	26%
Prices:High	55.48	70.20	65.46	48.50	37.70	31.70	23.80	21.35	21.97	24.97
Prices:Low	20.09	24.26	44.59	34.87	27.10	21.92	19.19	10.63	11.72	15.03
P/E Ratio:High	34	39	27	26	24	25	27	28	29	24
P/E Ratio:Low	12	13	19	18	17	17	22	14	15	14

Income Statement Analysis (Million $)	2009	2008	2007	2006	2005	2004	2003	2002	2001	2000
Income Interest	7.00	6.40	5.90	5.40	4.28	3.78	3.91	3.06	32.8	59.1
Income Other	1,865	2,115	2,227	1,814	1,512	1,277	995	923	995	1,153
Total Income	1,872	2,121	2,233	1,819	1,516	1,280	999	926	1,028	1,212
General Expenses	1,101	1,206	1,179	982	814	638	585	552	603	690
Interest Expense	4.50	5.00	4.80	4.30	4.03	3.30	3.29	4.96	12.7	9.72
Depreciation	65.2	61.7	54.0	47.0	42.0	40.0	45.3	50.6	80.5	53.7
Net Income	434	491	671	530	431	337	227	194	196	269
S&P Core Earnings	451	548	671	530	391	309	198	169	167	NA

Balance Sheet & Other Financial Data (Million $)	2009	2008	2007	2006	2005	2004	2003	2002	2001	2000
Cash	743	619	785	773	804	500	237	111	79.7	80.5
Receivables	246	177	265	224	175	158	121	96.8	104	131
Cost of Investments	906	721	1,002	762	378	329	273	216	154	250
Total Assets	3,210	2,819	3,177	2,765	2,311	1,929	1,547	1,370	1,313	1,469
Loss Reserve	Nil	Nil	Nil	Nil	Nil	Nil	Nil	Nil	Nil	Nil
Short Term Debt	Nil	Nil	Nil	Nil	Nil	Nil	Nil	Nil	Nil	Nil
Capitalization:Debt	Nil	Nil	Nil	Nil	Nil	Nil	Nil	Nil	104	312
Capitalization:Equity	2,882	2,489	2,777	2,427	2,036	1,697	1,329	1,189	1,078	991
Capitalization:Total	2,882	2,489	2,777	2,427	2,036	1,697	1,329	1,189	1,181	1,304
Price Times Book Value:High	6.5	9.0	8.2	7.3	7.2	7.9	9.0	11.2	13.1	20.6
Price Times Book Value:Low	2.3	3.4	5.6	5.3	5.2	5.5	7.2	5.6	7.0	12.4
Cash Flow	499	553	725	577	473	377	273	245	276	323
% Expense/Operating Revenue	62.5	56.8	55.4	52.3	56.7	63.8	65.8	65.7	67.8	62.2
% Earnings & Depreciation/Assets	16.5	18.4	24.4	22.7	22.3	21.7	18.7	18.3	19.9	26.2

Data as orig reptd.; bef. results of disc opers/spec. items. Per share data adj. for stk. divs.; EPS diluted. E-Estimated. NA-Not Available. NM-Not Meaningful. NR-Not Ranked. UR-Under Review.

Office: 100 East Pratt Street, Baltimore, MD 21202.
Telephone: 410-345-2000.
Email: info@troweprice.com
Website: http://www.troweprice.com

Chrmn: B.C. Rogers
Pres & CEO: J.A. Kennedy
Vice Chrmn: E.C. Bernard
CFO: K.V. Moreland

Chief Acctg Officer & Treas: J.M. Hiebler
Board Members: E. C. Bernard, J. T. Brady, J. A. Broaddus, Jr., D. B. Hebb, Jr., J. A. Kennedy, R. F. MacLellan, B. C. Rogers, A. Sommer, D. S. Taylor, A. M. Whittemore

Founded: 1937
Domicile: Maryland
Employees: 4,802

STANDARD &POOR'S

Tyco International Ltd

S&P Recommendation HOLD ★★★★★	Price $38.54 (as of Oct 22, 2010)	12-Mo. Target Price $40.00	Investment Style Large-Cap Blend

GICS Sector Industrials
Sub-Industry Industrial Conglomerates

Summary Tyco split into three separate publicly traded companies in June 2007, with the company maintaining its former Fire & Security and Engineered Products divisions.

Key Stock Statistics (Source S&P, Vickers, company reports)

52-Wk Range	$40.61– 32.94	S&P Oper. EPS 2010E	2.60	Market Capitalization(B)	$19.181	Beta	1.30
Trailing 12-Month EPS	$2.23	S&P Oper. EPS 2011E	3.00	Yield (%)	2.18	S&P 3-Yr. Proj. EPS CAGR(%)	13
Trailing 12-Month P/E	17.3	P/E on S&P Oper. EPS 2010E	14.8	Dividend Rate/Share	$0.84	S&P Credit Rating	BBB
$10K Invested 5 Yrs Ago	NA	Common Shares Outstg. (M)	497.7	Institutional Ownership (%)	88		

Price Performance

30-Week Mov. Avg. · · · 10-Week Mov. Avg. – – GAAP Earnings vs. Previous Year Volume Above Avg. STARS
12-Mo. Target Price — Relative Strength — ▲ Up ▼ Down ► No Change Below Avg.

Options: ASE, CBOE, P, Ph

Analysis prepared by **Michael W. Jaffe** on August 13, 2010, when the stock traded at **$ 36.57**.

Highlights

➤ In April 2010, TYC announced plans to spin off its Electrical & Metal Products businesses. We will include the segment in our forecast until the transaction takes place, which is expected in the first half of FY 11 (Sep.). We see an 8% increase in revenues in FY 11, largely reflecting benefits that we see from the apparent start of a recovery in the global economy, and expected stabilization of U.S. housing markets. We also expect revenues to be aided by the full-year inclusion of Broadview Security (formerly Brink's Home Security), which was acquired in May 2010.

➤ We forecast improved margins in FY 11, aided largely by the expected start of a revival in demand for TYC's products and services. We also see profitability being aided by cost controls, and further incremental savings related to TYC's restructuring actions.

➤ Our FY 11 forecast compares with an FY 10 estimate that excludes total charges of $0.18 a share in the first nine months, mostly from restructuring activities and a loss on the extinguishment of debt. Operating EPS was $2.36 in FY 09.

Investment Rationale/Risk

➤ We think TYC's results will soon start to benefit from the likely ongoing recovery of the global economy. We also think Tyco's executive team is making solid decisions, including its May 2010 expansion of its electronic security business through the purchase of Brink's Home Security, and its plan to spin off its very volatile Electrical and Metal Products division. Yet, despite these mostly positive views, our valuation model finds the shares fairly valued.

➤ Risks to our opinion and target price include a resumption of the downturn in global economies, and a lack of success with TYC's current business initiatives.

➤ The stock recently traded at 12X our calendar 2011 EPS forecast of $3.09, in line with the S&P 500. We think this is near an appropriate level. We have positive views of TYC's actions over the past few years, and think major concerns were resolved by its class action settlement in June 2007. At the same time, we think mixed conditions in Tyco's various businesses will limit the level of its expected business rebound in the coming year. Based on these factors, our 12-month target price is $40, or about 13X our calendar 2011 forecast.

Qualitative Risk Assessment

LOW	MEDIUM	HIGH

Our risk assessment reflects what we see as strong cash flow characteristics and high levels of recurring revenues in a number of Tyco's businesses. However, at the same time, we believe that many of Tyco's business segments are highly cyclical in nature.

Quantitative Evaluations

S&P Quality Ranking NR

D	C	B-	B	B+	A-	A	A+

Relative Strength Rank MODERATE

44

LOWEST = 1   HIGHEST = 99

Revenue/Earnings Data

Revenue (Million $)

	1Q	2Q	3Q	4Q	Year
2010	4,246	4,169	4,274	--	--
2009	4,426	4,150	4,240	4,421	17,237
2008	4,870	4,866	5,215	5,284	20,199
2007	10,329	10,838	5,085	5,028	18,781
2006	9,603	10,093	10,504	10,760	40,960
2005	10,065	10,456	10,562	10,030	39,727

Earnings Per Share ($)

2010	0.63	0.65	0.50	E0.66	E2.60
2009	0.57	-5.40	0.51	0.44	-3.87
2008	0.74	0.56	0.41	0.55	2.25
2007	1.48	1.68	-6.13	0.42	-5.09
2006	1.56	2.08	1.72	2.52	7.88
2005	1.40	0.44	2.24	1.68	6.04

Fiscal year ended Sep. 30. Next earnings report expected: Mid November. EPS Estimates based on S&P Operating Earnings; historical GAAP earnings are as reported.

Dividend Data (Dates: mm/dd Payment Date: mm/dd/yy)

Amount ($)	Date Decl.	Ex-Div. Date	Stk. of Record	Payment Date
0.226	--	10/28	10/30	11/24/09
0.224	12/10	01/27	01/29	02/24/10
0.211	07/08	07/28	07/30	08/25/10
0.211	09/09	10/27	10/29	11/23/10

Dividends have been paid since 1975. Source: Company reports.

Please read the Required Disclosures and Analyst Certification on the last page of this report.

The McGraw-Hill Companies

Tyco International Ltd

STANDARD &POOR'S

Business Summary August 13, 2010

CORPORATE OVERVIEW. At the close of trading on June 29, 2007, Tyco International divided its portfolio of businesses into three separate publicly traded companies. TYC maintained the units that had been part of its Fire & Security and Engineered Products & Services divisions, and spun off its Healthcare (now Covidien; COV) and Electronics (trading as Tyco Electronics; TEL) units. Tyco now divides its businesses into five separate segments, ADT Worldwide; Fire Protection Services; Flow Control; Safety Products; and Electrical and Metal Products. In April 2010, Tyco announced plans to spin-off its Electrical and Metals Products businesses; it expected to complete that transaction in the first half of FY 11 (Sep.). The company derived 52% of its revenues outside the U.S. in FY 09, with more than half of that total in the Europe, Middle East and Africa region.

ADT Worldwide (41% of TYC's revenues in FY 09) sells, installs, services and monitors electronic security systems. The Fire Protection Services segment (20%) provides and services fire detection and fire suppression systems. Both ADT and Fire Protection serve commercial, industrial and governmental customers, while ADT also serves residential clients. Safety Products (9%) makes

fire protection, security and life safety products, including fire suppression products, breathing apparatus, intrusion security, access control and video management systems. Tyco expanded its ADT business through the May 2010 acquisition of Brink's Home Security Holdings (now operating as Broadview Security), a monitored North American security company (about $565 million of annual revenues), for a total of about $2.0 billion in cash and stock.

The company's Flow Control division (22% of FY 09 revenues) manufactures and services valves, pipe fittings, valve automation and heat tracing products for the water and wastewater, oil, gas and other energy, and general process industries. The Electrical and Metal Products division (8%) makes steel tubing, armored wire and cable and other cable products, used primarily by trade contractors in the construction and modernization of non-residential structures.

Company Financials Fiscal Year Ended Sep. 30

Per Share Data ($)	2009	2008	2007	2006	2005	2004	2003	2002	2001	2000
Tangible Book Value	3.17	2.84	2.49	10.92	5.56	NM	NM	NM	NM	1.68
Cash Flow	-1.48	4.61	-2.76	11.79	9.78	9.35	5.01	-2.09	14.88	14.39
Earnings	-3.87	2.25	-5.09	7.88	6.04	5.64	2.08	-6.16	10.20	10.56
Dividends	0.61	0.35	1.90	1.20	1.60	0.20	0.20	0.20	0.20	0.20
Payout Ratio	NM	16%	NM	15%	26%	4%	10%	NM	2%	2%
Prices:High	37.33	47.95	137.92	127.44	146.32	145.68	108.72	235.24	252.84	236.75
Prices:Low	17.25	15.17	37.46	98.60	102.64	104.04	44.80	27.92	156.96	128.00
P/E Ratio:High	NM	21	NM	16	24	26	52	NM	25	22
P/E Ratio:Low	NM	7	NM	13	17	18	22	NM	15	12

Income Statement Analysis (Million $)	2009	2008	2007	2006	2005	2004	2003	2002	2001	2000
Revenue	17,237	20,199	18,781	40,960	39,727	40,153	36,801	35,644	34,037	28,932
Operating Income	2,570	3,324	1,720	7,754	7,637	7,957	5,568	6,509	8,865	7,393
Depreciation	1,133	1,154	1,151	2,065	2,100	2,176	1,472	2,033	2,141	1,644
Interest Expense	301	396	313	713	815	963	1,148	1,077	776	845
Pretax Income	-1,751	1,431	-2,181	4,884	4,192	4,159	1,803	-2,811	6,004	6,465
Effective Tax Rate	NM	23.4%	NM	16.4%	23.5%	27.4%	42.4%	NM	21.4%	29.8%
Net Income	-1,833	1,095	-2,519	4,075	3,199	3,005	1,035	-3,070	4,671	4,520

Balance Sheet & Other Financial Data (Million $)	2009	2008	2007	2006	2005	2004	2003	2002	2001	2000
Cash	2,354	1,519	1,894	2,926	3,196	4,467	4,329	6,383	2,587	1,265
Current Assets	7,967	8,541	12,345	18,785	18,537	18,545	17,240	19,765	NA	12,816
Total Assets	25,553	28,804	32,815	63,722	62,621	63,667	63,545	66,414	111,287	40,404
Current Liabilities	4,716	5,657	9,101	11,066	11,835	11,152	10,572	19,632	NA	11,679
Long Term Debt	4,029	3,709	4,076	9,365	10,600	14,617	18,251	16,487	38,503	9,462
Common Equity	12,941	15,494	15,624	35,419	32,450	30,292	26,369	24,791	31,737	17,033
Total Capital	16,983	19,217	19,767	44,838	43,111	44,977	44,733	41,320	70,542	27,630
Capital Expenditures	709	734	669	1,569	1,272	1,015	1,170	1,709	1,798	1,704
Cash Flow	-700	2,249	-1,368	6,140	5,299	5,181	2,507	-1,037	6,812	6,165
Current Ratio	1.7	1.5	1.4	1.7	1.6	1.7	1.6	1.0	1.3	1.1
% Long Term Debt of Capitalization	23.7	19.3	20.6	20.9	24.6	32.5	40.8	39.9	54.6	34.2
% Net Income of Revenue	NM	5.4	NM	9.9	8.1	7.5	2.8	NM	13.7	15.6
% Return on Assets	NM	3.6	NM	6.4	5.1	4.7	1.6	NM	6.2	12.4
% Return on Equity	NM	7.0	NM	12.0	10.2	10.6	4.1	NM	19.2	30.7

Data as orig reptd.; bef. results of disc opers/spec. items. Per share data adj. for stk. divs.; EPS diluted. E-Estimated. NA-Not Available. NM-Not Meaningful. NR-Not Ranked. UR-Under Review.

Office: Freier Platz 10, Schaffhausen, Switzerland 8200.
Telephone: 41 52 633 02 44.
Email: info@tyco.com
Website: www.tyco.com

Chrmn & CEO: E.D. Breen
EVP & CFO: C.J. Coughlin
EVP & General Counsel: J.A. Reinsdorf
SVP, Chief Acctg Officer & Cntlr: C.A. Davidson

SVP & Treas: A. Nayar
Investor Contact: E.C. Arditte (609-720-4621)
Board Members: E. D. Breen, M. E. Daniels, T. M. Donahue, B. Duperreault, B. S. Gordon, R. L. Gupta, J. Krol, B. R. O'Neill, W. S. Stavropoulos, S. S. Wijnberg, R. D. Yost

Founded: 1960
Domicile: Bermuda
Employees: 106,000

Tyson Foods Inc.

STANDARD
&POOR'S

| S&P Recommendation | **STRONG BUY** ★★★★★ | Price $15.63 (as of Oct 22, 2010) | 12-Mo. Target Price $21.00 | Investment Style Large-Cap Blend |

GICS Sector Consumer Staples
Sub-Industry Packaged Foods & Meats

Summary Tyson is one of the world's largest suppliers of beef, chicken and pork products.

Key Stock Statistics (Source S&P, Vickers, company reports)

52-Wk Range	$20.57–11.94	S&P Oper. EPS 2010E	2.06	Market Capitalization(B)	$4.805	Beta	1.17
Trailing 12-Month EPS	$0.32	S&P Oper. EPS 2011E	2.00	Yield (%)	1.02	S&P 3-Yr. Proj. EPS CAGR(%)	UR
Trailing 12-Month P/E	48.8	P/E on S&P Oper. EPS 2010E	7.6	Dividend Rate/Share	$0.16	S&P Credit Rating	BB+
$10K Invested 5 Yrs Ago	$9,332	Common Shares Outstg. (M)	377.5	Institutional Ownership (%)	87		

Price Performance

30-Week Mov. Avg. · · · · 10-Week Mov. Avg. – – GAAP Earnings vs. Previous Year   Volume Above Avg. STARS
12-Mo. Target Price — Relative Strength   ▲ Up ▼ Down ► No Change   Below Avg.   ★

Options: ASE, CBOE, P

Analysis prepared by **Tom Graves, CFA** on August 30, 2010, when the stock traded at **$ 16.53**.

Highlights

► We look for sales of $29.3 billion in FY 11 (Sep.), up about 4% from the $28.4 billion that we project for FY 10, reflecting prospects for a more stable global economic environment and some improved pricing power. In FY 09, TSN's fiscal year had a 53rd week.

► In FY 11, with the prospect of higher grain feed costs and a possible rise in chicken industry production, we look for operating profit to decline about 5%, but for this to be partly offset by lower interest expense (excluding losses on FY 10 note repurchases). In FY 10, we expect the chicken segment profit margin to improve significantly from what it was in FY 09, at least partly due to the expiration of adverse commodity hedging contracts in mid-FY 09. Also, in FY 10, in both the beef and the pork segments, we look for wider margins and sizable profit improvement.

► We estimate FY 11 EPS of $2.00, down from the $2.06 that we project for FY 10, which excludes a net adverse impact of about $0.06 a share from special items in the first nine months of FY 10.

Investment Rationale/Risk

► Over time, we think TSN, as a major diversified protein supplier, is positioned to benefit from improving economic conditions, including rising incomes and changing diets in developing international markets. We also expect TSN's strategy to include a focus on expansion in value-added food products. We have some concern about the prospect of restrictions or tariffs on sales to Russia and China, but we look for TSN to benefit over time from changing diets in developing markets.

► Risks to our recommendation and target price include weaker-than-expected demand and prices, industry production that is higher than anticipated, and an adverse impact from currency exchange rate fluctuations.

► Our 12-month target price of $21 is based on our view that an outlook for improving economic environments, and expected rising demand for protein-related products, should help the stock to trade at a P/E of 10.4X our four-quarter forward EPS estimate of $2.01, which is a discount to the median such P/E in recent years.

Qualitative Risk Assessment

| LOW | MEDIUM | **HIGH** |

Our risk assessment reflects the company's cyclical operations, which can be significantly affected by exposure to commodity crop and meat markets, and regulations related to international trade.

Quantitative Evaluations

S&P Quality Ranking   B-

| D | C | **B-** | B | B+ | A- | A | A+ |

Relative Strength Rank   WEAK

| 20 |
LOWEST = 1   HIGHEST = 99

Revenue/Earnings Data

Revenue (Million $)

	1Q	2Q	3Q	4Q	Year
2010	6,635	6,916	7,438	--	--
2009	6,521	6,307	66,620	7,214	26,704
2008	6,766	6,612	6,849	7,201	26,862
2007	6,558	6,501	6,958	6,883	26,900
2006	6,454	6,251	6,383	6,471	25,559
2005	6,452	6,359	6,708	6,495	26,014

Earnings Per Share ($)

2010	0.44	0.42	0.68	E0.50	E2.06
2009	-0.30	-0.24	0.37	-1.22	-1.47
2008	0.10	-0.01	-0.01	0.13	0.24
2007	0.16	0.20	0.31	0.09	0.75
2006	0.11	-0.37	-0.15	-0.15	-0.56
2005	0.14	0.21	0.36	0.28	0.99

Fiscal year ended Sep. 30. Next earnings report expected: Late November. EPS Estimates based on S&P Operating Earnings; historical GAAP earnings are as reported.

Dividend Data (Dates: mm/dd Payment Date: mm/dd/yy)

Amount ($)	Date Decl.	Ex-Div. Date	Stk. of Record	Payment Date
0.040	11/23	02/25	03/01	03/15/10
0.040	02/04	05/27	06/01	06/15/10
0.040	05/06	08/30	09/01	09/15/10
0.040	08/04	11/29	12/01	12/15/10

Dividends have been paid since 1976. Source: Company reports.

Please read the Required Disclosures and Analyst Certification on the last page of this report.

The **McGraw·Hill** Companies

Tyson Foods Inc.

STANDARD &POOR'S

Business Summary August 30, 2010

CORPORATE OVERVIEW. Tyson Foods is one of the world's largest suppliers of beef, chicken and pork products. It produces a wide variety of brand name protein-based and prepared food products, marketed in the U.S. and about 90 countries around the world.

Most of TSN's operations are in the U.S., and about 97% of FY 09 (Sep.) sales to external customers were sourced from the U.S. TSN's export sales totaled $2.7 billion in FY 09, down from $3.2 billion in FY 08. Major export markets include Canada, Central America, China, the European Union, Japan, Mexico, the Middle East, Russia, South Korea, Taiwan and Vietnam. In FY 09, TSN's largest customer, Wal-Mart Stores, Inc., accounted for 13.8% of FY 09's consolidated sales

CORPORATE STRATEGY. TSN's seeks to identify target markets for value-added products; concentrate production, sales and marketing efforts to enhance product demand; and utilize national distribution systems and customer support services. We think the company's scale and diversified product mix is a competitive advantage.

The beef segment (40% of FY 09 revenues) includes the slaughter of live cattle and fabrication into primal and sub-primal meat cuts and case-ready prod-

ucts. Operations include sales from allied products such as hides and variety meats. The company's products are marketed to various channels, including food retailers, foodservice distributors, restaurant operators and others. The company does not have facilities of its own to raise cattle, but has cattle buyers located in cattle producing areas who visit independent feed yards and buy live cattle on the open spot market.

The chicken segment (36%) includes fresh, frozen and value-added chicken products sold domestically through various channels, including retailers, foodservice distributors, restaurant operators and foodservice establishments such as schools, hotel chains, health care facilities and the military; and also to international markets. Included in this segment are sales from allied products and TSN's chicken breeding stock subsidiary. The segment's raw material includes live chickens that are raised primarily by independent contractors. Also, corn and soybean meal are major production costs, and in FY 09 represented roughly 45% of TSN's cost of growing a live chicken.

Company Financials Fiscal Year Ended Sep. 30

Per Share Data ($)	2009	2008	2007	2006	2005	2004	2003	2002	2001	2000
Tangible Book Value	5.98	6.30	5.96	5.05	5.66	4.49	3.17	2.92	1.71	NM
Cash Flow	-0.22	1.57	2.20	1.31	2.39	2.50	2.26	2.39	1.91	-1.97
Earnings	-1.47	0.24	0.75	-0.56	0.99	1.13	0.96	1.08	0.40	0.68
S&P Core Earnings	0.05	0.20	0.64	-0.56	1.06	1.10	0.64	1.02	0.39	NA
Dividends	0.16	0.16	0.16	0.16	0.16	0.16	0.16	0.16	0.16	0.16
Payout Ratio	NM	67%	21%	NM	16%	14%	17%	15%	40%	24%
Prices:High	14.25	67.00	24.32	17.33	19.91	21.28	15.10	15.71	14.20	17.38
Prices:Low	7.51	4.40	13.50	12.57	12.50	12.97	7.25	9.27	8.10	8.50
P/E Ratio:High	NM	81	32	NM	20	19	16	15	35	26
P/E Ratio:Low	NM	18	18	NM	13	11	8	9	20	13

Income Statement Analysis (Million $)										
Revenue	26,704	26,862	26,900	25,559	26,014	26,441	24,549	23,367	10,751	7,268
Operating Income	817	878	1,130	510	1,266	1,415	837	1,407	650	643
Depreciation	455	471	514	517	501	490	458	467	335	294
Interest Expense	313	218	232	268	227	275	592	305	144	116
Pretax Income	-526	154	410	-293	528	635	523	593	165	234
Effective Tax Rate	NM	44.2%	34.6%	NM	33.1%	36.5%	35.6%	35.4%	35.2%	35.5%
Net Income	-536	86.0	268	-191	353	403	337	383	88.0	151
S&P Core Earnings	21.4	71.1	228	-190	379	392	224	365	87.5	NA

Balance Sheet & Other Financial Data (Million $)										
Cash	1,004	250	42.0	28.0	40.0	33.0	25.0	51.0	70.0	43.0
Current Assets	4,375	4,361	3,596	4,187	3,485	3,532	3,371	3,144	3,290	1,576
Total Assets	10,595	10,850	10,227	11,121	10,504	10,464	10,486	10,372	10,632	4,854
Current Liabilities	1,993	2,103	2,115	2,846	2,157	2,293	2,475	2,093	2,416	886
Long Term Debt	3,333	2,888	2,642	2,987	2,869	3,024	3,114	3,733	4,016	1,357
Common Equity	4,352	5,014	4,731	4,900	4,615	4,912	3,954	3,662	3,354	2,175
Total Capital	8,002	8,193	7,740	8,382	8,141	8,631	7,790	8,038	7,979	3,917
Capital Expenditures	368	425	285	531	571	486	402	433	261	196
Cash Flow	-81.0	557	782	326	854	893	795	850	423	445
Current Ratio	2.2	2.1	1.7	1.5	1.6	1.5	1.4	1.5	1.4	1.8
% Long Term Debt of Capitalization	41.7	35.3	34.1	35.6	35.2	35.0	40.0	46.4	50.3	34.6
% Net Income of Revenue	NM	0.3	1.0	NM	1.4	1.5	1.4	1.6	0.8	2.1
% Return on Assets	NM	0.8	2.5	NM	3.4	3.8	3.2	3.6	1.1	3.0
% Return on Equity	NM	1.8	5.6	NM	7.9	8.5	8.8	10.9	3.2	7.0

Data as orig reptd.; bef. results of disc opers/spec. items. Per share data adj. for stk. divs.; EPS diluted. E-Estimated. NA-Not Available. NM-Not Meaningful. NR-Not Ranked. UR-Under Review.

Office: 2200 Don Tyson Pkwy, Springdale, AR 72762-6999.
Telephone: 479-290-4000.
Email: tysonir@tyson.com
Website: http://www.tyson.com

Chrmn: J.H. Tyson
Pres & CEO: D. Smith
COO: J.V. Lochner
EVP & CFO: D. Leatherby

EVP & General Counsel: D.L. Van Bebber
Investor Contact: R. Wisener
Board Members: L. V. Hackley, J. D. Kever, K. M. McNamara, B. T. Sauer, R. C. Thurber, B. A. Tyson, D. Tyson, J. H. Tyson, A. C. Zapanta

Founded: 1935
Domicile: Delaware
Employees: 117,000

The McGraw·Hill Companies

Union Pacific Corp

STANDARD &POOR'S

S&P Recommendation `HOLD` ★★★☆☆

Price $86.31 (as of Oct 22, 2010)	**12-Mo. Target Price** $86.00	**Investment Style** Large-Cap Blend

GICS Sector Industrials
Sub-Industry Railroads

Summary Union Pacific operates the largest U.S. railroad, with over 32,000 miles of rail serving the western two-thirds of the country.

Key Stock Statistics (Source S&P, Vickers, company reports)

52-Wk Range	$87.32– 54.20	S&P Oper. EPS 2010**E**	5.37	Market Capitalization(B)	$42.945	Beta	1.18
Trailing 12-Month EPS	$4.53	S&P Oper. EPS 2011**E**	5.78	Yield (%)	1.53	S&P 3-Yr. Proj. EPS CAGR(%)	16
Trailing 12-Month P/E	19.1	P/E on S&P Oper. EPS 2010**E**	16.1	Dividend Rate/Share	$1.32	S&P Credit Rating	BBB
$10K Invested 5 Yrs Ago	$27,881	Common Shares Outstg. (M)	497.6	Institutional Ownership (%)	84		

Price Performance

30-Week Mov. Avg. · · · · 10-Week Mov. Avg. – – **GAAP Earnings vs. Previous Year** Volume Above Avg. STARS
12-Mo. Target Price — Relative Strength — ▲ Up ▼ Down ▶ No Change Below Avg. ★

Options: CBOE, Ph

Analysis prepared by **Kevin Kirkeby** on October 07, 2010, when the stock traded at **$ 83.63**.

Highlights

➤ We look for revenues to rise nearly 19% in 2010, incorporating a 13% increase in volume, with intermodal and automotive-related shipments being the primary contributors. For 2011, we expect revenues to rise another 6%, reflecting a 4% volume increase and a modest improvement in core pricing and fuel surcharges. The impact of customer wins and contract renewals achieved in 2010 will carry over into 2011, in our view. However, we expect volumes to become more balanced as both coal and grain are forecast to rise.

➤ We expect operating expenses to rise as volumes recover into 2011, due to higher wages and incentive compensation. However, we still anticipate a widening of margins due to improved pricing and greater asset utilization, like increases in both cars per train and ton-miles per employee. We also look for UNP's focus on fuel efficiency and distributed power to reduce overall fuel consumption.

➤ Our EPS estimate for 2010 of $5.22 incorporates an effective tax rate of 38%, as well as the buyback of about 10 million shares made during the April through July period.

Investment Rationale/Risk

➤ Recent data suggests the economy is recovering, and is contributing to growth in nearly all of UNP's freight categories. At this point, we think a valuation above the midpoint of the historical range is warranted, as we balance near-term volume gains and our expectation that operating costs will start to rise as certain volume thresholds are reached with what we see as UNP's above peer average investment requirements.

➤ Risks to our recommendation and target price include a slower-than-expected recovery in the economy, reduced coal consumption by utilities as a result of government efforts to control carbon dioxide emissions, and more regulatory oversight of railroad pricing.

➤ Our relative valuation model suggests an enterprise value-to-EBITDA multiple, using our four-quarter forward estimate, of about 8.3X, which is above the 10-year average, and produces a value of $91. Our discounted cash flow model, which assumes a 10.5% cost of equity, annual free cash flow growth of 5% for five years, and a 3.5% terminal growth rate, estimates an intrinsic value of $81. Blending, we arrive at our 12-month target price of $86.

Qualitative Risk Assessment

LOW	MEDIUM	HIGH

Our risk assessment reflects UNP's exposure to economic cycles, regulations, and labor and fuel costs, coupled with significant capital expenditure requirements, offset by our view of the company's historically positive cash flow generation and moderate financial leverage.

Quantitative Evaluations

S&P Quality Ranking A

D	C	B-	B	B+	A-	A	A+

Relative Strength Rank STRONG

77

LOWEST = 1   HIGHEST = 99

Revenue/Earnings Data

Revenue (Million $)

	1Q	2Q	3Q	4Q	Year
2010	3,965	4,182	--	--	--
2009	3,415	3,303	3,671	3,754	14,143
2008	4,270	4,568	4,846	4,286	17,970
2007	3,849	4,046	4,191	4,197	16,283
2006	3,710	3,923	3,983	3,962	15,578
2005	3,152	3,344	3,461	3,621	13,578

Earnings Per Share ($)

2010	1.01	1.40	E1.56	E1.33	E5.37
2009	0.72	0.92	1.02	1.08	3.75
2008	0.85	1.02	1.38	1.31	4.54
2007	0.71	0.83	1.00	0.93	3.46
2006	0.58	0.72	0.77	0.89	2.96
2005	0.24	0.44	0.69	0.55	1.93

Fiscal year ended Dec. 31. Next earnings report expected: Late October. EPS Estimates based on S&P Operating Earnings; historical GAAP earnings are as reported.

Dividend Data (Dates: mm/dd Payment Date: mm/dd/yy)

Amount ($)	Date Decl.	Ex-Div. Date	Stk. of Record	Payment Date
0.270	11/19	11/25	11/30	01/04/10
0.270	02/04	02/24	02/26	04/01/10
0.330	05/06	05/26	05/28	07/01/10
0.330	07/29	08/27	08/31	10/01/10

Dividends have been paid since 1900. Source: Company reports.

Please read the Required Disclosures and Analyst Certification on the last page of this report.

The McGraw-Hill Companies

Union Pacific Corp

Business Summary October 07, 2010

CORPORATE OVERVIEW. Union Pacific operates the largest U.S. railroad, with a network that spans about 32,200 miles, linking Pacific Coast and Gulf Coast ports to midwestern and eastern gateways. The rail lines touch 23 states, as well as the Mexican and Canadian borders. Energy accounted for 23% of freight revenues and 26% of carloadings in 2009. UNP is a major transporter of low-sulfur coal, with about 67% of its energy traffic consisting of coal originating in the Powder River Basin of Wyoming and Montana, primarily delivered to power utilities. In 2009, UNP's intermodal business represented 19% of freight revenue, and accounted for a much larger 36% of total carloads. The industrial products category represented another 16% of freight revenues, while chemicals, agricultural products and automotive contributed 16%, 20% and 6%, respectively, of 2009 freight revenues.

COMPETITIVE LANDSCAPE. The U.S. rail industry has an oligopoly-like structure, with over 80% of revenues generated by the four largest railroads: UNP and Burlington Northern Santa Fe Corp. operating on the West Coast, and CSX Corp. and Norfolk Southern Corp. operating on the East Coast. Railroads simultaneously compete for customers while cooperating by sharing assets, interfacing systems, and completing customer movements. Railroads also compete with trucking, shipping, and pipeline transportation. Rail rates are generally lower than trucking rates, as service is slower and less flexible, in our view, than trucking, which provides most U.S. transportation. We believe the rising price of fuel increases the cost attractiveness of railroads over less fuel-efficient trucking, which should help support industry volumes over the next five years. While large freight integrators, coal and utility companies may exert more pricing power than smaller customers, there has been an increase in shippers across the rail industry filing complaints with the Surface Transportation Board (STB) alleging excessive pricing. In a July 2009 ruling, the STB determined that UNP was seeking rate increases from Oklahoma Gas & Electric that exceeded permissible levels. The STB ordered UNP to reimburse the shipper for amounts already collected, and effectively capped the rate on those particular moves through 2018. We note that 67% of UNP's contracts that have not been repriced since 2004 are in the energy (coal) category.

Company Financials Fiscal Year Ended Dec. 31

Per Share Data ($)	2009	2008	2007	2006	2005	2004	2003	2002	2001	2000
Tangible Book Value	33.00	30.70	31.73	28.34	25.58	24.25	23.93	21.00	19.15	17.54
Cash Flow	6.61	7.23	5.92	5.23	4.13	3.27	3.96	4.60	3.93	3.67
Earnings	3.75	4.54	3.46	2.96	1.93	1.15	2.04	2.53	1.89	1.67
S&P Core Earnings	3.52	4.29	3.37	2.86	1.66	1.05	1.88	1.92	1.41	NA
Dividends	1.08	0.98	0.75	0.60	0.60	0.60	0.50	0.42	0.40	0.40
Payout Ratio	29%	22%	22%	20%	31%	52%	24%	16%	21%	24%
Prices:High	66.73	85.80	68.78	48.75	40.63	34.78	34.75	32.58	30.35	26.41
Prices:Low	33.28	41.84	44.79	38.81	29.09	27.40	25.45	26.50	21.88	17.13
P/E Ratio:High	18	19	20	16	21	30	17	13	16	16
P/E Ratio:Low	9	9	13	13	15	24	13	10	12	10

Income Statement Analysis (Million $)	2009	2008	2007	2006	2005	2004	2003	2002	2001	2000
Revenue	14,143	17,970	16,283	15,578	13,578	12,215	11,551	12,491	11,973	11,878
Operating Income	4,836	5,462	4,696	4,121	2,970	2,406	3,200	3,530	2,072	2,043
Depreciation	1,444	1,387	1,321	1,237	1,175	1,111	1,067	1,206	1,174	1,140
Interest Expense	600	511	482	477	504	527	574	633	701	723
Pretax Income	2,987	3,656	3,009	2,525	1,436	856	1,637	2,016	1,533	1,310
Effective Tax Rate	36.5%	36.1%	38.4%	36.4%	28.6%	29.4%	35.5%	33.5%	37.0%	35.7%
Net Income	1,898	2,338	1,855	1,606	1,026	604	1,056	1,341	966	842
S&P Core Earnings	1,782	2,209	1,808	1,553	886	551	972	1,003	708	NA

Balance Sheet & Other Financial Data (Million $)	2009	2008	2007	2006	2005	2004	2003	2002	2001	2000
Cash	1,850	1,249	878	827	773	977	527	369	113	105
Current Assets	3,680	2,813	2,594	2,411	2,325	2,290	2,089	2,152	1,542	1,285
Total Assets	42,410	39,722	38,033	36,515	35,620	34,589	33,460	32,764	31,551	30,499
Current Liabilities	2,682	2,880	3,041	3,539	3,384	2,516	2,456	2,701	2,692	2,962
Long Term Debt	9,636	8,607	7,543	6,000	6,760	7,981	7,822	8,928	9,386	9,644
Common Equity	16,941	15,447	15,585	15,312	13,707	12,655	12,354	10,651	9,575	8,662
Total Capital	26,789	34,336	33,178	31,008	29,949	29,816	29,345	28,057	26,843	25,449
Capital Expenditures	2,384	2,780	2,496	2,242	2,169	1,876	1,752	1,887	1,736	1,783
Cash Flow	3,342	3,725	3,176	2,843	2,201	1,715	2,123	2,547	2,140	1,982
Current Ratio	1.4	1.0	0.9	0.7	0.7	0.9	0.9	0.8	0.6	0.4
% Long Term Debt of Capitalization	36.0	25.1	22.7	19.3	22.6	26.8	26.7	31.8	35.0	37.9
% Net Income of Revenue	13.4	13.0	11.4	10.3	7.6	4.9	9.1	10.7	8.1	7.1
% Return on Assets	4.6	6.0	5.0	4.5	2.9	1.8	3.2	4.2	3.1	2.8
% Return on Equity	11.7	15.1	12.0	11.1	7.8	4.8	9.2	13.3	10.6	10.1

Data as orig reptd.; bef. results of disc opers/spec. items. Per share data adj. for stk. divs.; EPS diluted. E-Estimated. NA-Not Available. NM-Not Meaningful. NR-Not Ranked. UR-Under Review.

Office: 1400 Douglas Street, Omaha, NE 68179.
Telephone: 402-544-5000.
Website: http://www.up.com
Chrmn, Pres, CEO & COO: J.R. Young

EVP & CFO: R.M. Knight, Jr.
SVP & Chief Admin Officer: C.R. Eisele
SVP & Secy: B.W. Schaefer
SVP & General Counsel: J.M. Hemmer

Investor Contact: J. Hamann (402-544-4227)
Board Members: A. H. Card, Jr., E. B. Davis, Jr., T. J. Donohue, Jr., A. W. Dunham, J. R. Hope, C. C. Krulak, M. R. McCarthy, M. W. McConnell, T. F. McLarty, III, S. Rogel, J. H. Villarreal, J. R. Young

Founded: 1862
Domicile: Utah
Employees: 43,531

UnitedHealth Group Inc

STANDARD &POOR'S

S&P Recommendation	**BUY** ★★★★☆	Price $37.26 (as of Oct 22, 2010)	12-Mo. Target Price $40.00	Investment Style Large-Cap Growth

GICS Sector Health Care
Sub-Industry Managed Health Care

Summary This leading health care services company was providing health benefit services to over 32 million individuals across the U.S. as of March 31, 2010.

Key Stock Statistics (Source S&P, Vickers, company reports)

52-Wk Range	**$37.26– 25.19**	S&P Oper. EPS 2010**E**	**3.95**	Market Capitalization(B)	**$41.890**	Beta	**0.93**
Trailing 12-Month EPS	**$3.72**	S&P Oper. EPS 2011**E**	**3.45**	Yield (%)	**1.34**	S&P 3-Yr. Proj. EPS CAGR(%)	**4**
Trailing 12-Month P/E	**10.0**	P/E on S&P Oper. EPS 2010**E**	**9.4**	Dividend Rate/Share	**$0.50**	S&P Credit Rating	**A-**
$10K Invested 5 Yrs Ago	**$6,600**	Common Shares Outstg. (M)	**1,124.3**	Institutional Ownership (%)	**84**		

Price Performance

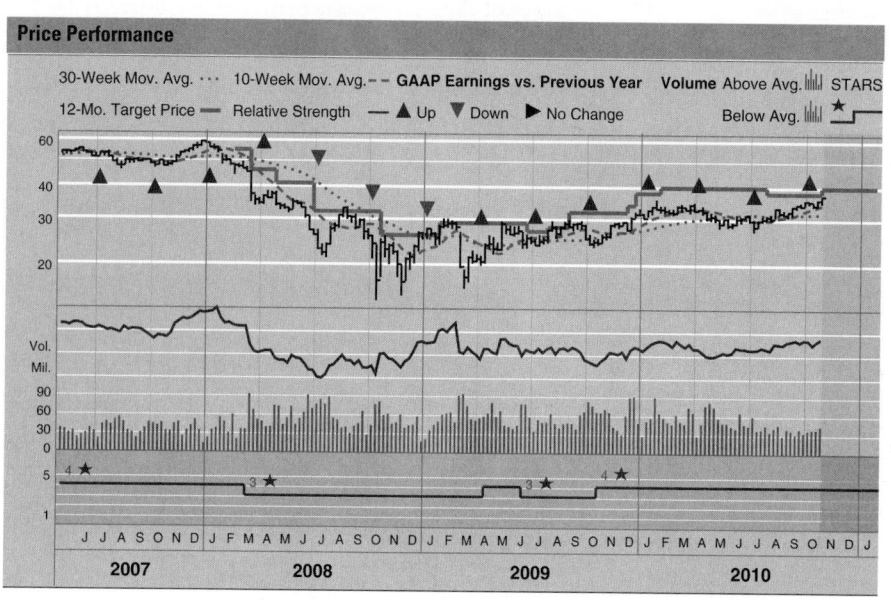

30-Week Mov. Avg. ··· 10-Week Mov. Avg.-- **GAAP Earnings vs. Previous Year** Volume Above Avg. ▏▍▊ STARS
12-Mo. Target Price— Relative Strength— ▲ Up ▼ Down ▶ No Change   Below Avg. ▏▍▊ ★

Options: ASE, CBOE, P

Analysis prepared by **Phillip M. Seligman** on October 21, 2010, when the stock traded at **$ 36.41**.

Highlights

➤ We look for operating revenues to rise 5.0% in 2011, to $98.4 billion, following an 8.2% rise we see in 2010, to $93.6 billion. Contributors we see include premium rate hikes, a modest rise in commercial membership, assuming a gradual decline in the unemployment rate, and continued increases in Medicare Advantage (MA; Medicare managed care), Medicaid and Medicare Part D (drug plan) enrollment.

➤ We expect medical costs to rise as a percentage of premium revenues (medical loss ratio, or MLR) by 240 basis points (bps) in 2011. The health care reform law requires health insurers to spend a minimum portion of the premium proceeds to cover medical costs (80% for individuals/small groups, 85% for large groups) for commercial members starting that year. In addition, we believe medical cost trends will pick up after moderating in 2010, and we see a further decrease in MA rates, albeit slower than the drop in 2010. On a positive note, we believe the SG&A cost ratio will decline slightly, as revenue leverage outweighs IT upgrade spending.

➤ We look for EPS of $3.45 in 2011, versus our operating EPS estimate of $3.95 in 2010. Operating EPS in 2009 was $3.24.

Investment Rationale/Risk

➤ In our view, UNH has been executing well in a weak economic environment, and we expect it to continue to do so. We think its scale, cash flow and diversification should temper the margin pressure and enable it to manage better than most peers amid health care reform. In this regard, we believe UNH will be a consolidator should reform lead to a shake-out in the health insurance industry. We also believe UNH's ability so far to realize MLRs below the required floors provides it with the opportunity to add benefits, thereby increasing its competitive strength and reducing the rebate it may have to return to policyholders. Headwinds we see in 2011 include a still-high unemployment rate, state budget pressures clouding the Medicaid reimbursement environment, and a shortened Medicare selling season. Our 2011 EPS outlook is clouded by the final MLR regulations not yet having been released by the U.S. Dept. of Health & Human Services.

➤ Risks to our recommendation and target price include a sharp rise in medical costs and intensified competition.

➤ Our 12-month target price of $40 assumes an above-peer P/E of 11.5X our 2011 EPS estimate.

Qualitative Risk Assessment

LOW	**MEDIUM**	HIGH

Our risk assessment reflects UNH's leadership in the highly fragmented managed care market and its wide geographic, market and product diversity, which we believe permits stable operational performance even during periods of economic downturn. However, we see commercial enrollment growth slowing from an expanding base and from intensifying competition.

Quantitative Evaluations

S&P Quality Ranking A+

D	C	B-	B	B+	A-	A	**A+**

Relative Strength Rank **STRONG**

81

LOWEST = 1   HIGHEST = 99

Revenue/Earnings Data

Revenue (Million $)

	1Q	2Q	3Q	4Q	Year
2010	23,193	23,264	23,668	--	--
2009	22,004	21,655	21,695	21,784	87,138
2008	20,304	20,272	20,156	20,454	81,186
2007	19,047	18,926	18,679	18,705	75,431
2006	17,581	17,863	17,970	18,128	71,542
2005	10,887	11,111	11,322	12,045	45,365

Earnings Per Share ($)

	1Q	2Q	3Q	4Q	Year
2010	1.03	0.99	1.14	E0.79	E3.95
2009	0.81	0.73	0.89	0.81	3.24
2008	0.78	0.27	0.75	0.60	2.40
2007	0.66	0.87	0.95	0.92	3.42
2006	0.63	0.70	0.80	0.84	2.97
2005	0.58	0.61	0.64	0.65	2.48

Fiscal year ended Dec. 31. Next earnings report expected: Late January. EPS Estimates based on S&P Operating Earnings; historical GAAP earnings are as reported.

Dividend Data (Dates: mm/dd Payment Date: mm/dd/yy)

Amount ($)	Date Decl.	Ex-Div. Date	Stk. of Record	Payment Date
0.030	02/10	04/01	04/06	04/20/10
0.125	05/26	06/03	06/07	06/21/10
0.125	08/04	09/10	09/14	09/28/10

Dividends have been paid since 1990. Source: Company reports.

Please read the Required Disclosures and Analyst Certification on the last page of this report.

The McGraw-Hill Companies

UnitedHealth Group Inc

STANDARD &POOR'S

Business Summary October 21, 2010

CORPORATE OVERVIEW. UnitedHealth Group, a U.S. leader in health care management, provides a broad range of health care products and services, including health maintenance organizations (HMOs), point of service (POS) plans, preferred provider organizations (PPOs), and managed fee for service programs.

The company reports results in four business segments, organized by product basis:

The Health Benefits Services segment (79% of 2009 revenues and 73% of operating earnings before eliminations) consists of the following business units: UnitedHealthcare coordinates network-based health and well-being services on behalf of multistate mid-sized and local employers and for individuals. Uniprise provides these services to large, self-insured accounts in return for administrative fees; it generally assumes no responsibility for health care costs. AmeriChoice facilitates and manages health care services for state Medicaid programs and their beneficiaries. Ovations delivers health and well-being services to Americans over the age of 50. At September 30, 2010, risk and fee-based Health Care Services enrollment totaled 32,745,000, versus 31,995,000 at December 31, 2009, including commercial risk-based (9,330,000 versus 9,415,000), commercial fee-based (15,370,000 versus 15,210,000), Medicare Advantage (2,060,000 versus 1,790,000), Medicaid (3,235,000 versus

2,900,000), and Standardized Medicare Supplement (2,750,000 versus 2,680,000). In addition, there are 6,480,000 Medicare Part D Prescription Drug Plan members, versus 5,935,000.

OptumHealth (5% and 10%) provides specialized benefits such as behavioral, dental and vision offerings, and financial services.

Ingenix (2% and 5%) is a leader in the field of health care data, analysis and application, serving pharmaceutical companies, health insurers and other payers, physicians and other health care providers, large employers and governments. We view Ingenix as key to the other segments' competitive strengths.

Prescription Solutions (14% and 12%) offers pharmacy benefit management and specialty pharmacy management services to employer groups, union trusts, seniors -- through Medicare prescription drug plans, and commercial health plans.

Company Financials Fiscal Year Ended Dec. 31

Per Share Data ($)	2009	2008	2007	2006	2005	2004	2003	2002	2001	2000
Tangible Book Value	NM	NM	1.18	1.55	NM	0.04	1.24	0.79	0.88	0.61
Cash Flow	NA	3.19	4.00	3.44	2.82	2.26	1.72	1.26	0.90	0.73
Earnings	3.24	2.40	3.42	2.97	2.48	1.97	1.48	1.07	0.70	0.55
S&P Core Earnings	3.23	2.95	3.40	2.94	2.36	1.86	1.37	0.99	0.62	NA
Dividends	0.03	0.03	0.03	0.03	0.02	0.02	0.01	0.01	0.01	0.00
Payout Ratio	1%	1%	1%	1%	1%	1%	1%	1%	1%	1%
Prices:High	33.25	57.86	59.46	62.93	64.61	44.38	29.34	25.25	18.20	15.86
Prices:Low	16.18	14.51	45.82	41.44	42.63	27.73	19.60	16.96	12.63	5.80
P/E Ratio:High	10	24	17	21	26	23	20	24	26	29
P/E Ratio:Low	5	6	13	14	17	14	13	16	18	11

Income Statement Analysis (Million $)	2009	2008	2007	2006	2005	2004	2003	2002	2001	2000
Revenue	87,138	81,186	75,431	71,542	45,365	37,218	28,823	25,020	23,454	21,122
Operating Income	NA	7,281	8,821	6,783	5,826	4,475	3,234	2,441	1,831	1,215
Depreciation	NA	981	796	670	453	374	299	255	265	247
Interest Expense	551	639	544	456	241	128	95.0	90.0	94.0	72.0
Pretax Income	5,808	4,624	7,305	6,528	5,132	3,973	2,840	2,096	1,472	1,155
Effective Tax Rate	34.2%	35.6%	36.3%	36.3%	35.7%	34.9%	35.7%	35.5%	38.0%	36.3%
Net Income	3,822	2,977	4,654	4,159	3,300	2,587	1,825	1,352	913	736
S&P Core Earnings	3,815	3,655	4,629	4,108	3,137	2,443	1,689	1,260	812	NA

Balance Sheet & Other Financial Data (Million $)	2009	2008	2007	2006	2005	2004	2003	2002	2001	2000
Cash	9,800	7,426	9,619	10,940	5,421	3,991	2,262	1,130	1,540	1,419
Current Assets	NA	14,990	15,544	16,044	10,640	8,241	6,120	5,174	4,946	4,405
Total Assets	59,045	55,815	50,899	48,320	41,374	27,879	17,634	14,164	12,486	11,053
Current Liabilities	NA	19,761	18,492	18,497	16,644	11,329	8,768	8,379	7,491	6,570
Long Term Debt	9,858	11,338	9,063	5,973	3,850	3,350	1,750	950	900	650
Common Equity	23,606	20,780	20,063	20,810	17,733	10,717	5,128	4,428	3,891	3,688
Total Capital	NA	33,473	29,126	26,783	21,583	14,067	6,878	5,378	4,791	4,338
Capital Expenditures	NA	791	871	728	5,876	350	352	419	425	245
Cash Flow	NA	3,958	5,450	4,829	3,753	2,961	2,124	1,607	1,178	983
Current Ratio	0.9	0.8	0.8	0.9	0.6	0.7	0.7	0.6	0.7	0.7
% Long Term Debt of Capitalization	29.5	33.9	31.1	22.3	17.8	23.8	25.4	17.7	18.8	15.0
% Net Income of Revenue	4.4	3.7	6.2	5.9	7.3	7.0	6.3	5.4	3.9	3.5
% Return on Assets	6.7	5.6	9.4	9.3	9.5	11.4	11.5	10.1	7.8	6.9
% Return on Equity	17.2	14.6	22.8	21.5	23.2	32.7	38.2	32.5	24.1	19.5

Data as orig reptd.; bef. results of disc opers/spec. items. Per share data adj. for stk. divs.; EPS diluted. E-Estimated. NA-Not Available. NM-Not Meaningful. NR-Not Ranked. UR-Under Review.

Office: 9900 Bren Rd E, Minnetonka, MN 55343.
Telephone: 952-936-1300.
Website: http://www.unitedhealthgroup.com
Chrmn: R.T. Burke

Pres & CEO: S.J. Hemsley
COO & EVP: D.S. Wichmann
EVP & CFO: G.L. Mikan, III
SVP & Chief Acctg Officer: E. Rangen

Board Members: W. C. Ballard, Jr., R. T. Burke, R. J. Darretta, S. J. Hemsley, M. J. Hooper, D. W. Leatherdale, G. M. Renwick, K. I. Shine, G. Wilensky

Founded: 1974
Domicile: Minnesota
Employees: 80,000

The McGraw-Hill Companies

United Parcel Service Inc

STANDARD &POOR'S

S&P Recommendation BUY ★★★★☆

Price	12-Mo. Target Price	Investment Style
$69.83 (as of Oct 22, 2010)	$84.00	Large-Cap Growth

GICS Sector Industrials
Sub-Industry Air Freight & Logistics

Summary UPS is the world's largest express delivery company, and has established itself as a facilitator of e-commerce.

Key Stock Statistics (Source S&P, Vickers, company reports)

52-Wk Range	$70.89–53.17	S&P Oper. EPS 2010E	3.54	Market Capitalization(B)	$50.628
Trailing 12-Month EPS	$2.67	S&P Oper. EPS 2011E	4.00	Yield (%)	2.69
Trailing 12-Month P/E	26.2	P/E on S&P Oper. EPS 2010E	19.7	Dividend Rate/Share	$1.88
$10K Invested 5 Yrs Ago	$11,123	Common Shares Outstg. (M)	990.7	Institutional Ownership (%)	68

Beta	0.85
S&P 3-Yr. Proj. EPS CAGR(%)	14
S&P Credit Rating	AA-

Price Performance

30-Week Mov. Avg. · · · 10-Week Mov. Avg. - - GAAP Earnings vs. Previous Year Volume Above Avg. ▮▮▮ STARS
12-Mo. Target Price — Relative Strength — ▲ Up ▼ Down ► No Change Below Avg. ▮▮▮ ★

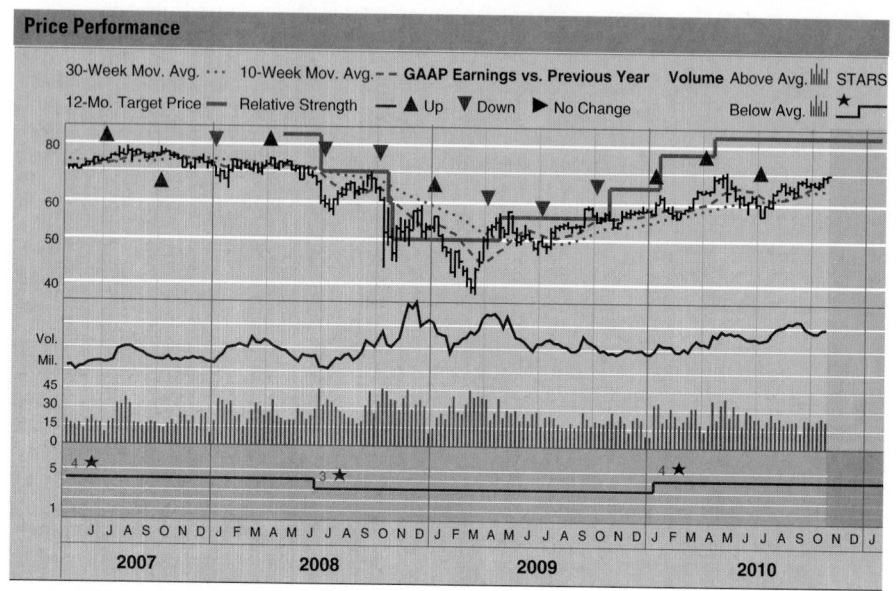

Options: ASE, CBOE, P, Ph

Analysis prepared by **Jim Corridore** on July 28, 2010, when the stock traded at **$ 64.66**.

Qualitative Risk Assessment

LOW	MEDIUM	HIGH

Our risk assessment reflects what we see as UPS's geographically diversified and increasing revenue base, a strong balance sheet with ample cash and low debt relative to total capitalization, and a track record of earnings and cash flow growth.

Quantitative Evaluations

S&P Quality Ranking B

D	C	B-	B	B+	A-	A	A+

Relative Strength Rank MODERATE

62

LOWEST = 1   HIGHEST = 99

Revenue/Earnings Data

Revenue (Million $)

	1Q	2Q	3Q	4Q	Year
2010	11,728	12,204	--	--	--
2009	10,938	10,829	11,153	12,377	45,297
2008	12,675	13,001	13,113	12,697	51,486
2007	11,906	12,189	12,205	12,697	49,692
2006	11,521	11,736	11,662	12,628	47,547
2005	9,886	10,191	10,550	11,954	42,581

Earnings Per Share ($)

2010	0.53	0.84	E0.93	E1.06	E3.54
2009	0.40	0.44	0.55	0.75	2.14
2008	0.87	0.85	0.96	0.25	2.94
2007	0.78	1.04	1.02	-2.52	0.36
2006	0.89	0.97	0.96	1.04	3.86
2005	0.78	0.88	0.86	0.95	3.47

Fiscal year ended Dec. 31. Next earnings report expected: Late October. EPS Estimates based on S&P Operating Earnings; historical GAAP earnings are as reported.

Highlights

➤ We expect 2010 revenues to rise 11%, following a 12% decline in 2009. We see gains in U.S. domestic as well as international shipping, driven by strengthening in the U.S. and global economies. We see a 14% rise in supply chain and freight revenues after a 14% drop in 2009. Fuel surcharges are likely to be a drag on revenues, since fuel prices have come down sharply. Should oil prices start to move back up, revenue growth would pick up on increased fuel surcharges.

➤ We see operating margins improving in 2010, mainly from fixed cost leverage on a higher number of package deliveries. UPS should also benefit from an improved package mix, as we think consumers are likely to shift toward faster delivery methods as the economy strengthens. We also see productivity gains from new technology and reduced costs from restructuring actions. The company froze management salaries in 2009 and suspended its 401k matching program, which is likely to be restored in 2010, leading to a rise in compensation costs.

➤ We estimate 2010 EPS of $3.45, up 49% from 2009 operating EPS of $2.31. For 2011, we see EPS of $4.00.

Investment Rationale/Risk

➤ We think UPS will likely see increased international and domestic volumes and higher pricing once the economy starts to show improvement, leading to our forecast of material EPS improvement in 2010. We think the company is a strong generator of cash, and we favor its historical use of its funds to pay dividends and repurchase stock. These positives support our buy opinion on the stock, despite a valuation being toward the high end of its historical P/E range. UPS has temporarily slowed its share repurchase program, but we expect it to eventually resume buybacks, which should provide support for the stock.

➤ Risks to our recommendation and target price include a much slower economic recovery than we expect, and a possible price war with competitors. Regarding corporate governance, we are concerned that Class A shareholders have 10 votes per share on many matters.

➤ Our 12-month target price of $84 values the stock at 21X our 2011 EPS estimate, in the middle of UPS's five-year historical P/E range. We view positively return on assets and cash flow from operations.

Dividend Data (Dates: mm/dd Payment Date: mm/dd/yy)

Amount ($)	Date Decl.	Ex-Div. Date	Stk. of Record	Payment Date
0.450	11/05	11/12	11/16	12/03/09
0.470	02/04	02/11	02/16	03/03/10
0.470	05/06	05/13	05/17	06/02/10
0.470	08/05	08/12	08/16	09/01/10

Dividends have been paid since 2000. Source: Company reports.

Please read the Required Disclosures and Analyst Certification on the last page of this report.

The McGraw-Hill Companies

United Parcel Service Inc

Business Summary July 28, 2010

CORPORATE OVERVIEW. United Parcel Service is the world's largest express and package delivery company. It is also a leading commerce facilitator, offering various logistics and financial services. The company, which was privately held since its founding in 1907, had its IPO of Class B stock in November 1999.

CORPORATE STRATEGY. The company seeks to position itself as the primary coordinator of the flow of goods, information and funds throughout the entire supply chain (the movement from the raw materials and parts stage through final consumption of the finished product).

Domestic package delivery services accounted for 62% of revenues in 2009, up from 61% in 2008. About 83% of the 13.1 million daily domestic shipments handled by the company in 2009 were moved by its ground delivery service, which is available to every address in the 48 contiguous states in the U.S. Domestic air delivery is provided throughout the U.S., including next-day air, which is guaranteed by 10:30 a.m. to more than 75% of the U.S. population, and by noon to an additional 15% of the population.

UPS entered the international arena in 1975. In 2009, it handled 2.0 million international shipments per day. S&P believes the international package delivery service (21% of total revenues in 2009) is likely to grow faster than its domestic business over the next several years, though it declined 14% in 2009. UPS delivers international shipments to more than 200 countries and territories worldwide and provides delivery within one to two business days to the world's major business centers. Services include export (packages that cross national borders) and domestic (packages that stay within a single country's boundaries). UPS has a portfolio of domestic services in 20 major countries. Transborder services within the European Union are expected to continue to be a growth engine for the company. Asia continues to be an area in which UPS is investing in infrastructure and technology.

Company Financials Fiscal Year Ended Dec. 31

Per Share Data ($)	2009	2008	2007	2006	2005	2004	2003	2002	2001	2000
Tangible Book Value	4.96	4.29	9.04	11.46	12.44	12.84	12.03	11.09	9.14	8.58
Cash Flow	3.88	4.71	2.00	5.46	4.94	4.33	3.91	4.20	3.41	3.50
Earnings	2.14	2.94	0.36	3.86	3.47	2.93	2.55	2.87	2.12	2.50
S&P Core Earnings	2.09	2.61	0.20	3.78	3.40	2.87	2.46	2.48	1.70	NA
Dividends	1.80	1.80	1.68	1.52	1.32	1.12	0.92	0.76	0.76	0.81
Payout Ratio	84%	61%	NM	39%	38%	38%	36%	26%	36%	32%
Prices:High	59.75	75.08	78.99	83.99	85.84	89.11	74.87	67.10	62.50	69.75
Prices:Low	37.99	43.32	68.66	65.50	66.10	67.51	53.00	54.25	46.15	49.50
P/E Ratio:High	28	26	NM	22	25	30	29	23	29	28
P/E Ratio:Low	18	15	NM	17	19	23	21	19	22	20

Income Statement Analysis (Million $)										
Revenue	45,297	51,486	49,692	47,547	42,581	36,582	33,485	31,272	30,646	29,771
Operating Income	5,789	7,771	8,758	8,383	7,787	6,532	5,994	5,560	5,358	5,685
Depreciation	1,747	1,814	1,745	1,748	1,644	1,543	1,549	1,464	1,396	1,173
Interest Expense	445	490	313	211	172	149	121	173	184	205
Pretax Income	3,366	5,015	431	6,510	6,075	4,922	4,370	5,009	3,937	4,834
Effective Tax Rate	36.1%	40.1%	11.4%	35.5%	36.3%	32.3%	33.7%	35.0%	38.4%	39.3%
Net Income	2,152	3,003	382	4,202	3,870	3,333	2,898	3,254	2,425	2,934
S&P Core Earnings	2,107	2,664	212	4,109	3,784	3,261	2,790	2,820	1,948	NA

Balance Sheet & Other Financial Data (Million $)										
Cash	2,100	1,049	2,604	794	1,369	5,197	2,951	2,211	1,616	1,952
Current Assets	9,275	8,845	11,760	9,377	11,003	12,605	9,853	8,738	7,597	7,124
Total Assets	31,883	31,879	39,042	33,210	35,222	33,026	28,909	26,357	24,636	21,662
Current Liabilities	6,239	7,817	9,840	6,719	6,793	6,483	5,518	5,555	4,629	4,501
Long Term Debt	8,420	7,797	7,506	3,133	3,159	3,261	3,149	3,495	4,648	2,981
Common Equity	7,630	6,780	12,183	15,482	16,884	16,384	14,852	12,455	10,248	9,735
Total Capital	16,863	16,231	22,309	21,144	20,043	25,027	18,001	15,950	14,896	12,716
Capital Expenditures	1,602	2,636	2,820	3,085	2,187	2,127	1,947	1,658	2,372	2,147
Cash Flow	3,899	4,817	2,127	5,950	5,514	4,876	4,447	4,718	3,821	4,107
Current Ratio	1.5	1.1	1.2	1.4	1.6	1.9	1.8	1.6	1.6	1.6
% Long Term Debt of Capitalization	Nil	48.0	33.7	14.8	15.8	13.0	17.5	21.9	31.2	23.4
% Net Income of Revenue	4.8	5.8	0.8	8.8	9.1	9.1	8.7	10.4	7.9	9.9
% Return on Assets	NA	8.5	1.1	12.3	11.3	10.6	10.5	12.8	10.5	13.1
% Return on Equity	NA	31.7	2.8	26.0	23.3	21.3	21.2	28.7	24.3	26.4

Data as orig reptd.; bef. results of disc opers/spec. items. Per share data adj. for stk. divs.; EPS diluted. E-Estimated. NA-Not Available. NM-Not Meaningful. NR-Not Ranked. UR-Under Review.

Office: 55 Glenlake Parkway NE, Atlanta, GA 30328.
Telephone: 404-828-6000.
Website: http://www.ups.com
Chrmn & CEO: D.S. Davis

COO & SVP: D.P. Abney
SVP, CFO, Chief Acctg Officer & Treas: K. Kuehn
SVP, Secy & General Counsel: T.P. McClure
SVP & CIO: D. Barnes

Investor Contact: M. Vale (404-828-6703)
Board Members: F. D. Ackerman, M. J. Burns, D. S. Davis, S. E. Eizenstat, M. L. Eskew, W. R. Johnson, A. M. Livermore, R. Markham, C. T. Randt, Jr., J. Thompson, C. B. Tome

Founded: 1907
Domicile: Delaware
Employees: 408,000

U.S. Bancorp

STANDARD &POOR'S

S&P Recommendation BUY ★★★★☆

Price $23.59 (as of Oct 22, 2010)	**12-Mo. Target Price** $26.00	**Investment Style** Large-Cap Blend

GICS Sector Financials
Sub-Industry Diversified Banks

Summary This bank holding company was formed through the February 2001 merger of Minneapolis-based U.S. Bancorp and Milwaukee-based Firstar Corp.

Key Stock Statistics (Source S&P, Vickers, company reports)

52-Wk Range	$28.43– 20.44	S&P Oper. EPS 2010**E**	1.69	Market Capitalization(B)	$45.226	Beta	0.98
Trailing 12-Month EPS	$1.39	S&P Oper. EPS 2011**E**	1.98	Yield (%)	0.85	S&P 3-Yr. Proj. EPS CAGR(%)	35
Trailing 12-Month P/E	17.0	P/E on S&P Oper. EPS 2010**E**	14.0	Dividend Rate/Share	$0.20	S&P Credit Rating	A+
$10K Invested 5 Yrs Ago	$9,721	Common Shares Outstg. (M)	1,917.2	Institutional Ownership (%)	66		

Price Performance

30-Week Mov. Avg. ··· 10-Week Mov. Avg. – – GAAP Earnings vs. Previous Year   Volume Above Avg. STARS
12-Mo. Target Price — Relative Strength   ▲ Up ▼ Down ► No Change   Below Avg. ★

Options: ASE, CBOE, Ph

Qualitative Risk Assessment

LOW	MEDIUM	HIGH

Our risk assessment for U.S. Bancorp reflects our view of the company's solid fundamentals and prudent underwriting practices, along with good geographic and product diversification.

Quantitative Evaluations

S&P Quality Ranking   **B+**

D	C	B-	B	B+	A-	A	A+

Relative Strength Rank   **MODERATE**

57

LOWEST = 1   HIGHEST = 99

Revenue/Earnings Data

Revenue (Million $)

	1Q	2Q	3Q	4Q	Year
2010	4,911	5,105	--	--	--
2009	4,655	4,895	4,950	4,990	19,490
2008	5,249	4,907	4,469	4,604	19,229
2007	4,883	5,091	5,178	5,156	20,308
2006	4,505	4,773	4,897	4,934	19,109
2005	3,817	4,106	4,294	4,379	16,596

Earnings Per Share ($)

	1Q	2Q	3Q	4Q	Year
2010	0.34	0.45	E0.45	E0.45	E1.69
2009	0.24	0.12	0.30	0.30	0.97
2008	0.62	0.53	0.32	0.15	1.61
2007	0.63	0.65	0.62	0.53	2.43
2006	0.63	0.66	0.66	0.66	2.61
2005	0.57	0.60	0.62	0.62	2.42

Fiscal year ended Dec. 31. Next earnings report expected: NA. EPS Estimates based on S&P Operating Earnings; historical GAAP earnings are as reported.

Highlights

► The STARS recommendation for USB has recently been changed to 4 (buy) from 3 (hold). The Highlights section of this Stock Report will be updated accordingly.

Investment Rationale/Risk

► The Investment Rationale/Risk section of this Stock Report will be updated shortly. For the latest News story on USB from MarketScope, see below.

► 10/20/10 09:23 am ET ... S&P RAISES OPINION ON SHARES OF U.S. BANCORP TO BUY FROM HOLD (USB 22.81****): Q3 EPS of $0.45, vs. $0.30, beats our $0.44 EPS estimate on better than expected net interest income driven by increased lending activity, which was better than at peers who have already reported Q3 results. On Q3 results, we are raising our '10 EPS estimate to $1.69 from $1.68. We have a positive view of USB's ability to grow net interest income faster than peers while maintaining credit quality. We keep our target price of $26, which is based on a slight premium to peers 13.1X multiple on our unchanged '11 EPS estimate of $1.98. /E. Oja

Dividend Data (Dates: mm/dd Payment Date: mm/dd/yy)

Amount ($)	Date Decl.	Ex-Div. Date	Stk. of Record	Payment Date
0.050	12/08	12/29	12/31	01/15/10
0.050	03/16	03/29	03/31	04/15/10
0.050	06/15	06/28	06/30	07/15/10
0.050	09/21	09/28	09/30	10/15/10

Dividends have been paid since 1863. Source: Company reports.

Please read the Required Disclosures and Analyst Certification on the last page of this report.

The McGraw-Hill Companies

U.S. Bancorp

Business Summary July 22, 2010

CORPORATE OVERVIEW. U.S. Bancorp (USB) consists of several major lines of business, which include wholesale banking, consumer banking, wealth management & securities services, payment services, and treasury and corporate support. Wholesale banking offers lending, equipment finance and small ticket leasing, depository, treasury management, capital markets, foreign exchange, international trade services and other financial services to middle-market, large corporate and public sector clients. Consumer banking delivers products and services through banking offices, telephone servicing and sales, online services, direct mail and ATMs. It encompasses community banking, metropolitan banking, in-store banking, small business banking, including lending guaranteed by the Small Business Administration, consumer lending, mortgage banking, consumer finance, workplace banking, student banking, and 24-hour banking.

Wealth management & securities services provides trust, custody, private banking, financial advisory, investment management, retail brokerage services, insurance, custody and mutual fund servicing through five businesses:

wealth management, corporate trust, FAF Advisors, institutional trust and custody, and fund services. Payment services includes consumer and business credit cards, stored-value cards, debit cards, corporate and purchasing card services, consumer lines of credit, and merchant processing.

CORPORATE STRATEGY. USB has several goals in order to achieve long-term success, including: 10%-plus EPS growth, a 20%-plus ROE, reducing credit and earnings volatility, providing high-quality customer service, investing in future growth, and targeting an 80% return on earnings to shareholders. In banking, USB is maintaining what we view as its low-cost, highly efficient model and plans to grow organically and through smaller, fill-in acquisitions in higher-growth markets.

Company Financials Fiscal Year Ended Dec. 31

Per Share Data ($)	2009	2008	2007	2006	2005	2004	2003	2002	2001	2000
Tangible Book Value	7.21	3.97	6.31	5.34	5.62	5.87	5.77	4.93	4.64	7.11
Earnings	0.97	1.61	2.43	2.61	2.42	2.18	1.92	1.73	0.88	1.32
S&P Core Earnings	0.96	1.49	2.54	2.59	2.41	2.16	1.89	1.59	0.66	NA
Dividends	0.20	1.70	1.63	1.39	1.23	1.02	0.86	0.78	0.75	0.65
Payout Ratio	21%	106%	67%	53%	51%	47%	45%	45%	85%	49%
Prices:High	25.59	42.23	36.84	36.85	31.36	31.65	30.00	24.50	26.06	28.00
Prices:Low	8.06	20.22	29.09	28.99	26.80	24.89	18.56	16.05	16.50	15.38
P/E Ratio:High	26	26	15	14	13	15	16	14	30	21
P/E Ratio:Low	8	13	12	11	11	11	10	9	19	12

Income Statement Analysis (Million $)										
Net Interest Income	8,518	7,732	6,689	6,741	7,055	7,111	7,189	6,840	6,409	2,699
Tax Equivalent Adjustment	198	134	75.0	49.0	33.0	28.6	28.2	36.6	55.9	45.1
Non Interest Income	7,952	6,811	7,157	6,832	6,151	5,624	5,068	5,569	5,030	1,505
Loan Loss Provision	5,557	3,096	792	544	666	670	1,254	1,349	2,529	222
% Expense/Operating Revenue	50.3%	47.4%	49.6%	45.4%	44.3%	45.3%	45.7%	83.7%	57.5%	55.0%
Pretax Income	2,632	4,033	6,207	6,863	6,571	6,176	5,651	5,103	2,634	1,927
Effective Tax Rate	15.0%	27.0%	30.3%	30.8%	31.7%	32.5%	34.4%	34.8%	35.2%	31.4%
Net Income	2,205	2,946	4,324	4,751	4,489	4,167	3,710	3,326	1,707	1,284
% Net Interest Margin	3.67	3.66	3.47	3.65	3.97	4.25	4.49	4.61	4.45	4.73
S&P Core Earnings	1,783	2,606	4,470	4,674	4,470	4,135	3,655	3,062	1,280	NA

Balance Sheet & Other Financial Data (Million $)										
Money Market Assets	Nil	Nil	Nil	Nil	Nil	Nil	Nil	1,332	1,607	200
Investment Securities	44,768	39,521	43,116	40,117	39,768	41,481	43,334	28,488	26,608	13,866
Commercial Loans	82,885	89,831	80,281	74,835	71,405	67,758	65,768	68,811	71,703	28,498
Other Loans	112,523	95,398	73,546	68,762	66,401	58,557	52,467	47,440	42,702	25,208
Total Assets	281,176	265,912	237,615	219,232	209,465	195,104	189,286	180,027	171,390	77,585
Demand Deposits	38,186	37,494	33,334	32,128	32,214	30,756	32,470	35,106	31,212	10,980
Time Deposits	145,056	121,856	98,111	92,754	92,495	89,985	86,582	80,428	74,007	45,298
Long Term Debt	32,580	38,359	43,440	37,602	37,069	22,807	33,816	31,582	28,542	3,877
Common Equity	24,463	18,369	20,046	20,197	20,086	19,539	19,242	18,101	16,461	6,528
% Return on Assets	0.8	1.2	1.9	2.2	2.2	2.2	2.0	1.9	1.0	1.7
% Return on Equity	10.3	15.3	21.2	23.6	22.7	21.5	19.7	19.2	10.8	20.0
% Loan Loss Reserve	2.6	1.9	1.3	1.4	1.5	1.6	2.0	2.0	2.1	1.3
% Loans/Deposits	106.6	116.2	118.1	117.6	111.9	105.8	100.5	100.6	111.4	95.4
% Equity to Assets	7.8	7.6	8.8	9.4	9.8	10.1	10.2	9.8	9.4	8.5

Data as orig reptd.; bef. results of disc opers/spec. items. Per share data adj. for stk. divs.; EPS diluted. E-Estimated. NA-Not Available. NM-Not Meaningful. NR-Not Ranked. UR-Under Review.

Office: US Bancorp Center, 800 Nicollet Mall, Minneapolis, MN 55402.
Telephone: 651-466-3000.
Website: http://www.usbank.com
Chrmn, Pres & CEO: R.K. Davis

COO & CTO: J. von Gillern
EVP & Treas: K.D. Nelson
EVP, Secy & General Counsel: L.R. Mitau
SVP & Chief Acctg Officer: C.E. Gifford

Investor Contact: J.T. Murphy (612-303-0783)
Board Members: D. M. Baker, Jr., Y. M. Belton, A. D. Collins, Jr., R. K. Davis, V. B. Gluckman, J. W. Johnson, O. F. Kirtley, J. W. Levin, D. B. O'Maley, O. M. Owens, R. G. Reiten, C. D. Schnuck, P. T. Stokes

Founded: 1929
Domicile: Delaware
Employees: 58,229

United States Steel Corp

STANDARD &POOR'S

S&P Recommendation BUY ★★★★☆	**Price** $42.28 (as of Oct 22, 2010)	**12-Mo. Target Price** $57.00	**Investment Style** Large-Cap Value

GICS Sector Materials
Sub-Industry Steel

Summary This company manufactures and sells a wide variety of steel sheet, plate, tubular and tin products, coke, and taconite pellets.

Key Stock Statistics (Source S&P, Vickers, company reports)

52-Wk Range	$70.95– 33.25	S&P Oper. EPS 2010**E**	-1.33	Market Capitalization(B)	$6.070	Beta	2.70
Trailing 12-Month EPS	$-5.24	S&P Oper. EPS 2011**E**	5.52	Yield (%)	0.47	S&P 3-Yr. Proj. EPS CAGR(%)	NM
Trailing 12-Month P/E	NM	P/E on S&P Oper. EPS 2010**E**	NM	Dividend Rate/Share	$0.20	S&P Credit Rating	BB
$10K Invested 5 Yrs Ago	$12,790	Common Shares Outstg. (M)	143.6	Institutional Ownership (%)	81		

Price Performance

- 30-Week Mov. Avg. · · ·
- 10-Week Mov. Avg. - -
- **GAAP Earnings vs. Previous Year**
- Volume Above Avg. ▦ STARS
- 12-Mo. Target Price —
- Relative Strength —
- ▲ Up ▼ Down ▶ No Change
- Below Avg. ▦ ★

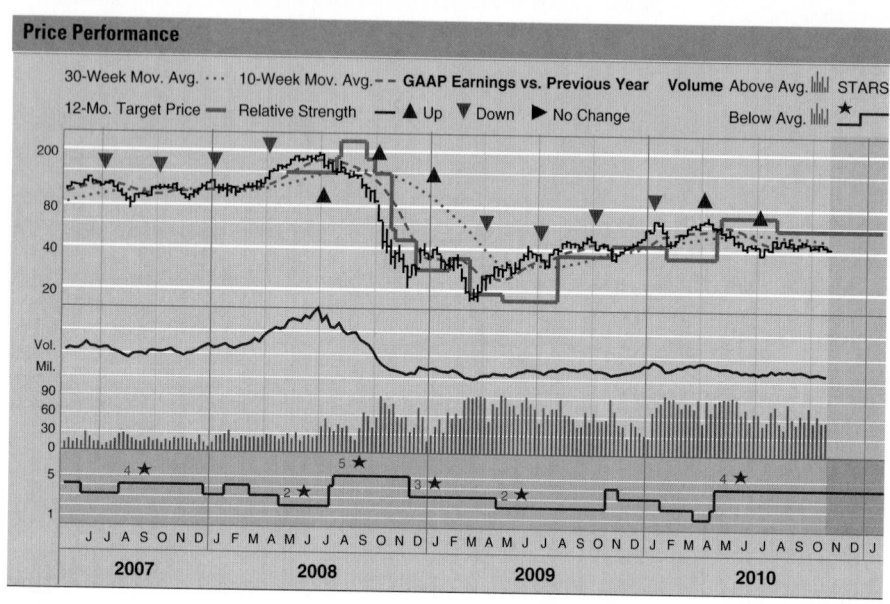

Analysis prepared by **Leo J. Larkin** on July 30, 2010, when the stock traded at **$ 43.77**.

Options: ASE, CBOE

Highlights

▶ Following a sales decrease of 53% in 2009, we look for a 55% rise in 2010, on an anticipated rebound in tons shipped and steel prices. Our forecast rests on several assumptions. First, S&P forecasts GDP growth of 3.1% in 2010, versus a 2.6% decrease in GDP in 2009. We see a resumption of GDP growth leading to rising demand for durable goods. Second, we think demand for oil country tubular goods will rise from 2009's depressed levels as drilling activity picks up. Third, we see distributors adding to inventory in 2010 after destocking through most of 2009. Fourth, we expect that demand for durable goods in Europe will recover from 2009's depressed levels.

▶ We look for a return to operating profit in 2010 on higher volume and increased revenue per ton. But, after interest expense, taxes and more shares outstanding, we estimate a loss per share of $1.33, versus a per-share loss of $10.48 in 2009, which excludes special gains of $0.06.

▶ We think earnings over the long term will increase on industry consolidation, rising demand for oil country tubular goods, and a gradual decline in costs for employee pensions and health care.

Investment Rationale/Risk

▶ We look for a solid recovery in sales and a much smaller loss in 2010, and EPS in 2011. Beyond 2011, we see X's earnings generally rising on a gradual decline in pension and health care costs, well controlled raw material costs in domestic operations, consolidation of the global steel industry, and a secular increase in demand for oil country tubular goods used for oil and gas exploration. In particular, we believe that the concentration of steel output in the hands of fewer companies should result in greater pricing and production discipline. In turn, we think this will lead to less volatile swings in pricing and profits over the course of the business cycle and result in generally higher valuations for steel companies.

▶ Risks to our recommendation and target price include a decline in steel prices and steel shipments in 2011 instead of the gains we project.

▶ Our 12-month target price of $57 is based on our view that the shares should trade at a multiple of 10.3X our 2011 EPS estimate. On this projected multiple, X's valuation would be just above the mid-point of its historical range of the past 10 years and would be at a discount to the P/E we apply to its peers.

Qualitative Risk Assessment

LOW	MEDIUM	HIGH

Our risk assessment reflects the company's exposure to highly cyclical industries such as autos and construction along with what we view as its high ratio of liabilities to assets and its unfunded pension and health care liabilities of $4.6 billion at the end of 2009.

Quantitative Evaluations

S&P Quality Ranking   B

D	C	B-	**B**	B+	A-	A	A+

Relative Strength Rank   **WEAK**

16

LOWEST = 1   HIGHEST = 99

Revenue/Earnings Data

Revenue (Million $)

	1Q	2Q	3Q	4Q	Year
2010	3,896	4,681	--	--	--
2009	2,750	2,127	2,817	3,354	11,048
2008	5,196	6,744	7,312	4,502	23,754
2007	3,756	4,228	4,354	4,535	16,873
2006	3,728	4,107	4,106	3,774	15,715
2005	3,787	3,582	3,200	3,470	14,039

Earnings Per Share ($)

	1Q	2Q	3Q	4Q	Year
2010	-1.10	-0.17	E-0.20	E0.15	E-1.33
2009	-3.78	-2.92	-2.11	-1.86	-10.42
2008	1.98	5.65	7.79	2.50	17.96
2007	2.30	2.54	2.27	0.30	7.40
2006	2.04	3.22	3.42	2.50	11.18
2005	3.51	1.91	0.71	0.85	7.00

Fiscal year ended Dec. 31. Next earnings report expected: Late October. EPS Estimates based on S&P Operating Earnings; historical GAAP earnings are as reported.

Dividend Data (Dates: mm/dd Payment Date: mm/dd/yy)

Amount ($)	Date Decl.	Ex-Div. Date	Stk. of Record	Payment Date
0.050	10/27	11/06	11/11	12/10/09
0.050	01/26	02/08	02/10	03/10/10
0.050	04/27	05/10	05/12	06/10/10
0.050	07/27	08/09	08/11	09/10/10

Dividends have been paid since 1991. Source: Company reports.

Please read the Required Disclosures and Analyst Certification on the last page of this report.

The McGraw-Hill Companies

STANDARD & POOR'S

United States Steel Corp

Business Summary July 30, 2010

CORPORATE OVERVIEW. Following its acquisition of Stelco Inc. and Lone Star Technologies in 2007, U.S. Steel is the fifth largest steel producer in the world, the largest integrated steel producer headquartered in North America, and one of the largest integrated flat-rolled producers in Central Europe. In 2009, X produced 11.7 million tons of steel in North America and 5.1 million tons of steel in Europe. By way of comparison, X produced 19.2 million tons of steel in North America and 6.4 million tons in Europe in 2008.

The company's other business activities include the production of coke in North America and Central Europe; and the production of iron ore pellets from taconite, transportation services (railroad and barge operations), real estate operations, and engineering and consulting services in North America.

CORPORATE STRATEGY. The company seeks to boost its revenues and earnings by expanding its value-added product mix, becoming a prime supplier of steel to growing European markets, strengthening its balance sheet, and becoming more cost competitive.

MARKET PROFILE. The primary factor affecting demand for steel products is economic growth in general, and growth in demand for durable goods in par-

ticular. The two largest end markets for steel products in the U.S. are autos and construction, which together accounted for 28.3% of shipments in 2009. Other end markets include appliances, containers, machinery, and oil and gas. Distributors, also known as service centers, accounted for 20.6% of industry shipments in the U.S. in 2009. Distributors are the largest single market for the steel industry in the U.S. Because distributors sell to a wide variety of OEMs, it is impossible to trace the final destination of much of the industry's shipments. Consequently, consumption of steel by the auto, construction and other industries may be higher than the shipment data would suggest. U.S. production was 64.2 million tons in 2009. X's largest end markets in 2009 were distributors (19.2% of tons shipped), appliances (6.7%), converters (26.4%), construction (15.3%), automotive (11.0%), containers (12.1%), oil and gas (4.3%), and other (5.0%). U.S. consumption decreased at a compound annual rate (CAGR) of 7.9% from 2000 through 2009. Global steel production totaled 1.22 billion metric tons in 2009, versus 1.33 billion metric tons in 2008.

Company Financials Fiscal Year Ended Dec. 31

Per Share Data ($)	2009	2008	2007	2006	2005	2004	2003	2002	2001	2000
Tangible Book Value	18.62	25.85	28.81	36.82	25.63	32.30	7.98	15.81	28.16	21.54
Cash Flow	-5.50	23.26	11.66	14.69	11.54	11.17	-0.57	4.24	1.42	3.72
Earnings	-10.42	17.96	7.40	11.18	7.00	8.37	-4.09	0.62	-2.45	-0.33
S&P Core Earnings	-9.64	14.34	7.42	11.76	6.64	8.74	-1.06	-4.10	-8.47	NA
Dividends	0.45	1.10	0.60	0.25	0.28	0.20	0.20	0.20	0.55	1.00
Payout Ratio	NM	6%	8%	2%	4%	2%	NM	32%	NM	NM
Prices:High	58.19	196.00	127.26	79.01	63.90	54.06	37.05	22.00	22.00	32.94
Prices:Low	16.66	20.71	68.83	48.05	33.59	25.22	9.61	10.66	13.00	12.69
P/E Ratio:High	NM	11	17	7	9	6	NM	35	NM	NM
P/E Ratio:Low	NM	1	9	4	5	3	NM	17	NM	NM

Income Statement Analysis (Million $)										
Revenue	11,048	23,754	16,873	15,715	14,039	14,108	9,458	7,054	6,375	6,090
Operating Income	-1,056	3,406	1,804	2,143	1,740	1,964	316	478	-61.0	422
Depreciation	661	605	506	441	366	382	363	350	344	360
Interest Expense	159	176	163	117	107	138	148	136	153	115
Pretax Income	-1,845	3,007	1,108	1,723	1,312	1,461	-860	13.0	-546	-1.00
Effective Tax Rate	23.8%	28.4%	19.7%	18.8%	27.8%	24.0%	NM	NM	NM	NM
Net Income	-1,401	2,112	879	1,374	910	1,077	-406	61.0	-218	-21.0
S&P Core Earnings	-1,296	1,686	882	1,438	847	1,104	-109	-398	-755	NA

Balance Sheet & Other Financial Data (Million $)										
Cash	1,218	724	401	1,422	1,479	1,037	316	243	147	219
Current Assets	5,015	5,732	4,959	5,196	4,831	4,243	3,107	2,440	2,073	2,717
Total Assets	15,422	16,087	15,632	10,586	9,822	10,956	7,838	7,977	8,337	8,711
Current Liabilities	2,474	2,778	3,003	2,702	2,749	2,531	2,130	1,372	1,259	1,391
Long Term Debt	3,345	3,064	3,147	943	1,363	1,363	1,890	1,408	1,434	2,485
Common Equity	4,676	4,895	5,531	4,365	3,108	3,754	867	2,027	2,506	1,917
Total Capital	8,343	8,132	8,736	5,346	4,719	5,959	2,989	3,658	4,672	5,070
Capital Expenditures	619	896	692	612	741	579	316	258	287	244
Cash Flow	-740	2,735	1,385	1,807	1,258	1,441	-59.0	411	126	331
Current Ratio	2.1	2.1	1.7	1.9	1.8	1.7	1.5	1.8	1.6	2.0
% Long Term Debt of Capitalization	40.1	37.7	36.0	17.6	28.9	22.9	63.2	38.5	30.7	49.0
% Net Income of Revenue	NM	8.9	5.2	8.7	6.5	7.8	NM	0.9	NM	NM
% Return on Assets	NM	13.3	6.7	13.5	8.7	11.5	NM	0.7	NM	NM
% Return on Equity	NM	40.5	17.8	36.6	25.6	45.8	NM	2.7	NM	NM

Data as orig reptd.; bef. results of disc opers/spec. items. Per share data adj. for stk. divs.; EPS diluted. E-Estimated. NA-Not Available. NM-Not Meaningful. NR-Not Ranked. UR-Under Review.

Office: 600 Grant Street, Pittsburgh, PA 15219-2702.
Telephone: 412-433-1121.
Email: shareholderservices@uss.com
Website: http://www.ussteel.com

Chrmn & CEO: J.P. Surma, Jr.
COO & EVP: J.H. Goodish
EVP & CFO: G.R. Haggerty
SVP & General Counsel: J.D. Garraux

Chief Admin Officer: D.H. Lohr
Investor Contact: N. Harper (412-433-1184)
Board Members: D. O. Dinges, J. G. Drosdick, R. A. Gephardt, C. R. Lee, J. M. Lipton, F. J. Lucchino, G. G. McNeal, S. E. Schofield, G. Spanier, J. P. Surma, Jr., D. S. Sutherland, P. A. Tracey

Founded: 2001
Domicile: Delaware
Employees: 43,000

The McGraw-Hill Companies

United Technologies Corp

STANDARD &POOR'S

S&P Recommendation BUY ★★★★☆

Price	12-Mo. Target Price	Investment Style
$74.94 (as of Oct 22, 2010)	$85.00	Large-Cap Growth

GICS Sector Industrials
Sub-Industry Aerospace & Defense

Summary This aerospace-industrial conglomerate's portfolio includes Pratt & Whitney jet engines, Sikorsky helicopters, Otis elevators and Carrier air conditioners, among other products.

Key Stock Statistics (Source S&P, Vickers, company reports)

52-Wk Range	$77.09– 61.42	S&P Oper. EPS 2010**E**	4.72	Market Capitalization(B)	$69.625	Beta		1.03
Trailing 12-Month EPS	$4.42	S&P Oper. EPS 2011**E**	5.25	Yield (%)	2.27	S&P 3-Yr. Proj. EPS CAGR(%)		10
Trailing 12-Month P/E	17.0	P/E on S&P Oper. EPS 2010**E**	15.9	Dividend Rate/Share	$1.70	S&P Credit Rating		A
$10K Invested 5 Yrs Ago	$16,345	Common Shares Outstg. (M)	929.1	Institutional Ownership (%)	82			

Price Performance

30-Week Mov. Avg. · · · 10-Week Mov. Avg. - - **GAAP Earnings vs. Previous Year** Volume Above Avg. STARS
12-Mo. Target Price — Relative Strength — ▲ Up ▼ Down ► No Change Below Avg.

Options: ASE, CBOE, P, Ph

Analysis prepared by **Richard Tortoriello** on October 21, 2010, when the stock traded at **$ 74.99**.

Highlights

▶ We estimate a 3% sales increase in 2010, following a 10% decline in 2009. For 2011, we project a 6% increase, with 7% growth at Carrier on a moderate recovery in U.S. residential housing as well as demand for repair and replacement, 5% growth at Otis, and 7% growth at Fire & Security, aided by the GE Security acquisition (which closed in March 2010). On the aerospace side, we project 6% growth at Hamilton Sundstrand and 5% at Pratt & Whitney, driven by increases in both OEM and aftermarket demand as commercial aerospace continues to recover, and 4% growth at Sikorsky, driven by military helicopter demand.

▶ We estimate operating margins of 13.6% in 2010, up from 12.2% in 2009, and a further increase to 14.4% in 2011, on much lower restructuring spending, significantly improved operating leverage as a result of prior restructuring activities, and volume increases.

▶ We estimate EPS of $4.72 in 2010, rising to $5.25 in 2011. Our outlook for 2011 includes projected significant increases in both income tax rates and pension expense.

Investment Rationale/Risk

▶ We see the following trends positively affecting UTX's business: large backlogs of commercial aircraft at both Airbus and Boeing, which we view as providing good production levels through at least 2011; the expected service entry of the 787 in early 2011; an expected large rise in commercial aerospace aftermarket spending; continued strong growth in emerging economies; and improvement in the U.S. residential housing market. We expect headwinds of commodity price inflation and increased pension and tax expense to be offset by our view of UTX's strong operating leverage.

▶ Risks to our opinion and target price include the possibility that the U.S. economy re-enters recession, operational issues in UTX's business segments, and a sustained rise in the dollar.

▶ Our 12-month target price of $85 is based on an enterprise value-to-estimated 2011 EBITDA multiple of about 9X, above the 20-year historical average multiple of 8X, reflecting our view that UTX's strong operating leverage and anticipated 2011 record EPS merit an above-average valuation.

Qualitative Risk Assessment

LOW	MEDIUM	HIGH

Our risk assessment is based on our view of UTX's history of steady growth in both earnings and dividends over the past 10 years, as reflected in its S&P Quality Ranking of A+. We also consider UTX's balance sheet to be strong, with long-term debt at 31% of total capital and cash at 9% of assets as of September 2010.

Quantitative Evaluations

S&P Quality Ranking A+

D	C	B-	B	B+	A-	A	A+

Relative Strength Rank MODERATE

66

LOWEST = 1 HIGHEST = 99

Revenue/Earnings Data

Revenue (Million $)

	1Q	2Q	3Q	4Q	Year
2010	12,091	13,890	--	--	--
2009	12,199	13,060	13,187	13,979	52,920
2008	13,577	15,535	14,702	14,299	58,681
2007	12,278	13,904	13,863	14,714	54,759
2006	10,446	12,046	11,972	12,654	47,829
2005	9,309	10,974	10,832	11,172	42,725

Earnings Per Share ($)

	1Q	2Q	3Q	4Q	Year
2010	0.93	1.20	E1.30	E1.29	E4.72
2009	0.78	1.05	1.14	1.15	4.12
2008	1.03	1.32	1.33	1.23	4.90
2007	0.82	1.16	1.21	1.08	4.27
2006	0.76	1.09	0.99	0.87	3.71
2005	0.64	0.95	0.81	0.71	3.12

Fiscal year ended Dec. 31. Next earnings report expected: NA. EPS Estimates based on S&P Operating Earnings; historical GAAP earnings are as reported.

Dividend Data (Dates: mm/dd Payment Date: mm/dd/yy)

Amount ($)	Date Decl.	Ex-Div. Date	Stk. of Record	Payment Date
0.425	02/08	02/17	02/19	03/10/10
0.425	04/14	05/12	05/14	06/10/10
0.425	06/09	08/18	08/20	09/10/10
0.425	10/13	11/17	11/19	12/10/10

Dividends have been paid since 1936. Source: Company reports.

Please read the Required Disclosures and Analyst Certification on the last page of this report.

The McGraw·Hill Companies

United Technologies Corp

Business Summary October 21, 2010

CORPORATE OVERVIEW. United Technologies is a multi-industry holding company that conducts business through six business segments: Carrier, Otis, Pratt & Whitney, UTC Fire & Security, Hamilton Sundstrand, and Sikorsky.

Carrier (21% of sales and 11% of operating profits in 2009) is the world's largest maker of heating, ventilating and air-conditioning (HVAC) and refrigeration systems. It offers HVAC, refrigeration systems and food service equipment, and refrigeration-related controls for residential, commercial, industrial and transportation applications. In addition, Carrier provides installation, retrofit, and parts and services for its products, as well as those of other HVAC and refrigeration makers. International sales, including U.S. export sales, accounted for 55% of segment sales in 2009.

Otis (22% of sales and 35% of operating profits) is the world's largest maker of elevators and escalators. Otis designs, manufactures, sells, installs, maintains and modernizes a wide range of passenger and freight elevators for low-, medium- and high-speed applications, as well as a broad line of escalators and moving walkways. International revenues were 80% of total segment revenues in 2009.

Pratt & Whitney (24% and 26%) is a major supplier of jet engines for commer-

cial, business & general aviation, and military aircraft. P&W also sells industrial gas turbines (for industrial power generation) and space propulsion systems. P&W's Global Services provides maintenance, repair and overhaul services, and fleet management services for large commercial engines. Airbus accounted for 11% of segment sales in 2009, and the U.S. government accounted for 31%. International revenues were 51% of total segment revenues in 2009.

UTC Fire & Security (10% and 7%) is a global provider of security and fire safety products and services, including intruder alarms, access control systems and video surveillance systems, specialty hazard detection and fixed suppression products, portable fire extinguishers, and other firefighting equipment. In March 2010, UTX purchased GE Security, from General Electric, for $1.8 billion. International sales accounted for 82% of total segment sales in 2009.

Company Financials Fiscal Year Ended Dec. 31

Per Share Data ($)	2009	2008	2007	2006	2005	2004	2003	2002	2001	2000
Tangible Book Value	0.25	NM	2.45	NM	0.91	1.84	2.32	1.46	1.66	0.95
Cash Flow	5.48	6.19	5.38	4.74	4.09	3.73	3.14	2.93	2.81	2.63
Earnings	4.12	4.90	4.27	3.71	3.12	2.76	2.35	2.21	1.92	1.78
S&P Core Earnings	4.05	3.81	4.17	3.64	3.05	2.59	2.16	1.32	1.14	NA
Dividends	1.54	1.35	1.17	1.02	0.88	0.70	0.57	0.49	0.45	0.41
Payout Ratio	37%	27%	27%	27%	28%	25%	24%	22%	23%	23%
Prices:High	70.89	77.14	82.50	67.47	58.89	53.14	48.38	38.88	43.75	39.88
Prices:Low	37.40	41.76	61.85	54.20	48.43	40.34	26.76	24.42	20.05	23.25
P/E Ratio:High	17	16	19	18	19	19	21	18	23	22
P/E Ratio:Low	9	9	14	15	16	15	11	11	10	13

Income Statement Analysis (Million $)										
Revenue	52,920	58,681	54,759	47,829	42,725	37,445	31,034	28,212	27,897	26,583
Operating Income	8,488	9,031	8,223	7,131	6,166	5,448	4,644	4,384	4,138	3,999
Depreciation	1,258	1,228	1,173	1,033	984	978	799	727	905	859
Interest Expense	705	689	666	606	498	363	375	381	426	382
Pretax Income	5,760	6,936	6,384	5,492	4,684	4,107	3,470	3,276	2,807	2,758
Effective Tax Rate	27.5%	27.2%	28.8%	27.2%	26.8%	26.4%	27.1%	27.1%	26.9%	30.9%
Net Income	3,829	4,689	4,224	3,732	3,164	2,788	2,361	2,236	1,938	1,808
S&P Core Earnings	3,756	3,648	4,125	3,653	3,089	2,619	2,147	1,298	1,113	NA

Balance Sheet & Other Financial Data (Million $)										
Cash	4,449	4,327	2,904	2,546	2,247	2,265	1,623	2,080	1,558	748
Current Assets	23,194	24,099	22,071	18,844	17,206	15,522	12,364	11,751	11,263	10,662
Total Assets	55,762	56,469	54,575	47,141	45,925	40,035	34,648	29,090	26,969	25,364
Current Liabilities	17,913	19,434	17,469	15,208	15,345	12,947	10,295	7,903	8,371	9,344
Long Term Debt	8,257	9,337	8,015	7,037	5,935	4,231	4,257	4,632	4,237	3,476
Common Equity	20,066	15,917	21,355	17,297	16,991	14,008	11,707	10,506	8,369	7,662
Total Capital	29,645	27,379	30,282	25,170	23,704	19,149	16,673	16,445	13,899	12,514
Capital Expenditures	826	1,216	1,153	954	929	795	530	586	793	937
Cash Flow	5,087	5,917	5,319	4,765	4,148	3,766	3,160	2,963	2,843	2,667
Current Ratio	1.3	1.2	1.3	1.2	1.1	1.2	1.2	1.5	1.3	1.1
% Long Term Debt of Capitalization	27.9	35.6	26.5	28.0	25.0	22.1	25.5	28.2	30.5	27.8
% Net Income of Revenue	7.2	8.0	7.7	7.8	7.4	7.4	7.6	7.9	6.9	6.8
% Return on Assets	6.8	8.5	8.3	8.0	7.3	7.4	7.4	8.0	7.4	7.3
% Return on Equity	21.3	25.2	21.9	21.8	20.2	21.7	23.9	23.0	24.2	24.5

Data as orig reptd.; bef. results of disc opers/spec. items. Per share data adj. for stk. divs.; EPS diluted. E-Estimated. NA-Not Available. NM-Not Meaningful. NR-Not Ranked. UR-Under Review.

Office: 1 Financial Plz, Hartford, CT 06103.
Telephone: 860-728-7000.
Email: invrelations@corphq.utc.com
Website: http://www.utc.com

Chrmn, Pres & CEO: L.R. Chenevert
SVP & CFO: G.J. Hayes
SVP & General Counsel: C.D. Gill, Jr.
CTO: J.M. McQuade

Treas: T.I. Rogan
Investor Contact: J. Moran (860-728-7062)
Board Members: L. R. Chenevert, J. V. Faraci, J. P. Garnier, J. S. Gorelick, C. M. Gutierrez, E. A. Kangas, C. R. Lee, R. D. McCormick, H. McGraw, III, R. B. Myers, H. P. Swygert, A. Villeneuve, C. T. Whitman

Founded: 1934
Domicile: Delaware
Employees: 206,700

Unum Group

S&P Recommendation HOLD ★★★☆☆

Price	**12-Mo. Target Price**	**Investment Style**
$22.42 (as of Oct 22, 2010)	$24.00	Large-Cap Value

GICS Sector Financials
Sub-Industry Life & Health Insurance

Summary The largest provider of individual and group disability insurance products in the U.S. and the U.K., Unum provides other products and services as well.

Key Stock Statistics (Source S&P, Vickers, company reports)

52-Wk Range	$26.42– 18.48	S&P Oper. EPS 2010**E**	2.79	Market Capitalization(B)	$7.326	Beta	1.72
Trailing 12-Month EPS	$2.58	S&P Oper. EPS 2011**E**	3.10	Yield (%)	1.65	S&P 3-Yr. Proj. EPS CAGR(%)	5
Trailing 12-Month P/E	8.7	P/E on S&P Oper. EPS 2010**E**	8.0	Dividend Rate/Share	$0.37	S&P Credit Rating	BBB-
$10K Invested 5 Yrs Ago	$12,257	Common Shares Outstg. (M)	326.8	Institutional Ownership (%)	93		

Price Performance

30-Week Mov. Avg. · · · 10-Week Mov. Avg. – – GAAP Earnings vs. Previous Year   Volume Above Avg. STARS
12-Mo. Target Price — Relative Strength ▲ Up ▼ Down ► No Change   Below Avg. ★

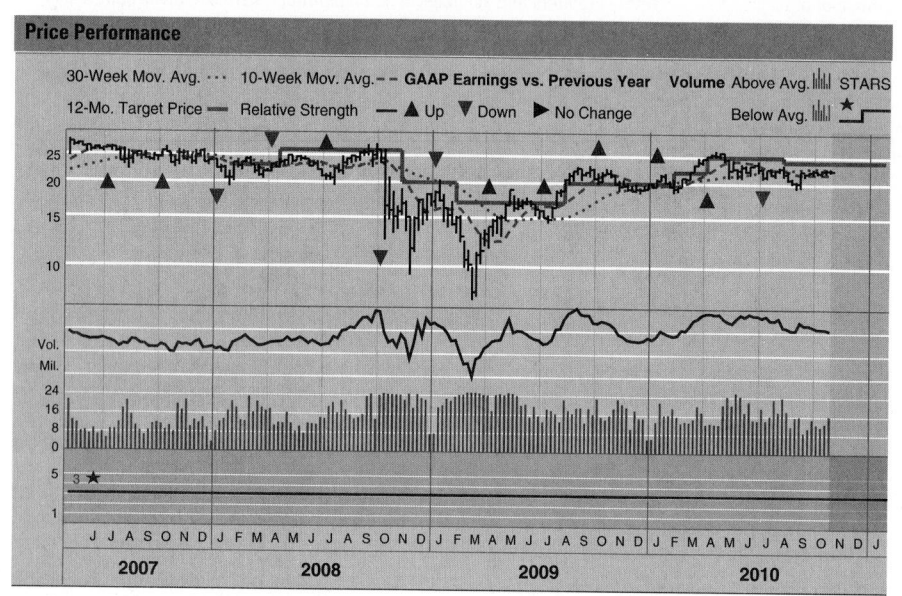

Options: ASE, CBOE, P

Analysis prepared by **Bret Howlett** on August 17, 2010, when the stock traded at **$ 21.03**.

Highlights

➤ We project earnings for Unum US to increase 5% to 7% on a lower expense ratio and higher investment income, although premium growth should be tempered by the weak economy and mixed sales results. While we expect persistency to hold steady, we see the benefit ratio rising due to high unemployment. In 2009, Unum US benefited from reduced claim activity, which we do not believe is sustainable. We expect sales to be challenged in the core market due to the weak labor market and the reluctance of employers to add new benefits to existing accounts. We expect earnings to decline in the mid-single digits in supplemental and voluntary lines, as we believe these products are more economically sensitive.

➤ We look for earnings to rise modestly at Colonial, as favorable agent recruitment trends and lower expenses should more than offset pricing pressure and an increase in the benefit ratio. We expect earnings at Unum UK to decline modestly on higher claims and unfavorable foreign currency shifts.

➤ We project operating EPS of $2.79 in 2010 and $3.10 in 2011. Our estimates exclude realized investment gains or losses.

Investment Rationale/Risk

➤ While we are encouraged by UNM's recent solid underwriting results, we believe that the challenging macro environment will temper sales growth, increase claims, and restrict disability margins and enrollment levels. We believe UNM will continue to experience a decline in sales and poor risk results in the large case market. However, UNM maintains a conservative investment portfolio, and we think its strong capital position will be a competitive advantage that should enable the company to gain market share in some businesses. We expect UNM to use its excess capital and liquidity to repurchase its shares in 2010. We view favorably UNM's lack of exposure to the equity markets in this environment.

➤ Risks to our recommendation and target price include worse-than-expected client retention and sales following income protection product price increases; unfavorable claims handling in the group income protection area; higher-than-forecast costs for reassessed claims; and investment losses.

➤ Our 12-month target price of $24 is 0.9X our 2010 book value per share (ex-FAS 115) estimate, below UNM's historical multiple.

Qualitative Risk Assessment

LOW	MEDIUM	HIGH

Our risk assessment reflects regulatory scrutiny surrounding certain claims practices. Although the largest lawsuits have been settled, UNM faces the possibility of additional suits and increased reserving for benefit costs in its claims reassessment. Our risk assessment also reflects the poor macro environment and the possibility of lower sales going forward. However, we believe UNM maintains a strong financial position relative to peers, and we believe its investment losses will be lower than the group's.

Quantitative Evaluations

S&P Quality Ranking   B

D	C	B-	**B**	B+	A-	A	A+

Relative Strength Rank   MODERATE

43

LOWEST = 1   HIGHEST = 99

Revenue/Earnings Data

Revenue (Million $)

	1Q	2Q	3Q	4Q	Year
2010	2,562	2,511	--	--	--
2009	2,449	2,628	2,518	2,497	10,091
2008	2,541	2,675	2,443	2,324	9,982
2007	2,601	2,666	2,610	2,644	10,520
2006	2,600	2,622	2,617	2,696	10,535
2005	2,572	2,657	2,544	2,665	10,437

Earnings Per Share ($)

2010	0.69	0.63	E0.66	E0.76	E2.79
2009	0.50	0.80	0.67	0.60	2.57
2008	0.46	0.69	0.32	0.13	1.62
2007	0.49	0.43	0.52	0.45	1.89
2006	0.23	0.37	-0.19	0.79	1.21
2005	0.49	0.55	0.17	0.43	1.64

Fiscal year ended Dec. 31. Next earnings report expected: Early November. EPS Estimates based on S&P Operating Earnings; historical GAAP earnings are as reported.

Dividend Data (Dates: mm/dd Payment Date: mm/dd/yy)

Amount ($)	Date Decl.	Ex-Div. Date	Stk. of Record	Payment Date
0.083	01/11	01/21	01/25	02/19/10
0.083	04/12	04/22	04/26	05/21/10
0.093	07/16	07/28	07/30	08/20/10
0.093	10/07	10/21	10/25	11/19/10

Dividends have been paid since 1925. Source: Company reports.

Please read the Required Disclosures and Analyst Certification on the last page of this report.

Unum Group

Business Summary August 17, 2010

CORPORATE OVERVIEW. UNM is the largest provider of disability insurance products in the United States and the U.K. through its subsidiaries. The company offers other products, including long-term care insurance, life insurance, group benefits, and related services.

The company has five operating segments: Unum US, Unum UK, Colonial, Individual Disability - Closed Block, and Corporate and Other. Unum US accounted for 61% of operating revenue in 2009, Unum UK 8.8%, Colonial 11%, Individual Disability - Closed Block 17%, and Corporate and Other 2.0%. In 2009, premium income for Unum US declined 3.1%, Unum UK premium income declined roughly 1.3%, and Colonial premium income increased 3.3%.

The Unum US segment includes group income protection insurance, group life and accidental death and dismemberment products, and supplemental and voluntary lines of business. The Unum UK segment includes group long-term income protection insurance, group life products, and individual income protection products issued by Unum Limited and sold primarily in the U.K. through field sales personnel and independent brokers and consultants. The Colonial segment includes a broad line of products sold mainly to employees at their workplaces, including income protection, life, and cancer and critical illness products. The Corporate and Other segment includes investment income on unallocated corporate assets, interest expense, and certain unallocated corporate income and expense items. In addition, the segment includes products that are no longer actively marketed, with the exception of the closed block business, including individual life and corporate-owned life insurance, reinsurance pools and management operations, group pension, health insurance, and individual annuities.

The Individual Disability Closed Block segment mainly includes individual income protection insurance written on a noncancelable basis with a fixed annual premium. Generally, the policies are individual disability insurance policies designed to be distributed to individuals in a non-workplace setting and written prior to UNM's restructuring of its individual disability business, where the focus was changed to workplace distribution.

Company Financials Fiscal Year Ended Dec. 31

Per Share Data ($)	2009	2008	2007	2006	2005	2004	2003	2002	2001	2000
Tangible Book Value	32.48	18.34	21.72	21.93	23.76	23.45	22.94	25.58	21.74	20.29
Operating Earnings	NA	NA	NA	NA	NA	NA	NA	2.52	2.44	2.37
Earnings	2.57	1.62	1.89	1.21	1.64	-0.65	-0.96	1.68	2.39	2.33
S&P Core Earnings	2.64	2.43	2.10	1.29	1.81	-0.26	-0.54	2.35	2.30	NA
Dividends	0.31	0.30	0.30	0.30	0.30	0.30	0.37	0.59	0.59	0.59
Payout Ratio	12%	19%	16%	25%	18%	NM	NM	35%	25%	25%
Prices:High	23.25	27.50	28.20	24.44	22.90	18.25	19.54	29.70	33.75	31.94
Prices:Low	7.61	9.33	19.79	16.15	15.50	11.41	5.91	16.30	22.25	11.94
P/E Ratio:High	9	17	15	20	14	NM	NM	18	14	14
P/E Ratio:Low	3	6	10	13	9	NM	NM	10	9	5

Income Statement Analysis (Million $)	2009	2008	2007	2006	2005	2004	2003	2002	2001	2000
Life Insurance in Force	677,278	629,069	692,012	773,070	833,363	908,034	787,199	712,826	642,988	583,848
Premium Income:Life	1,603	1,620	1,641	1,761	7,816	5,985	1,800	1,683	1,554	1,448
Premium Income:A & H	5,873	6,163	6,261	6,187	1,787	1,855	5,816	5,770	5,524	5,608
Net Investment Income	2,347	2,389	2,410	2,321	2,188	2,159	2,158	2,086	2,003	2,060
Total Revenue	10,091	9,982	10,520	10,535	10,437	10,465	9,992	9,613	9,395	9,432
Pretax Income	1,292	824	997	465	710	-260	-435	1,019	825	866
Net Operating Income	NA	NA	NA	NA	NA	NA	NA	614	593	NA
Net Income	853	553	672	404	514	-192	-265	817	582	564
S&P Core Earnings	878	824	748	428	570	-77.1	-150	568	564	NA

Balance Sheet & Other Financial Data (Million $)	2009	2008	2007	2006	2005	2004	2003	2002	2001	2000
Cash & Equivalent	714	656	791	768	688	719	663	734	2,515	NA
Premiums Due	1,732	1,785	1,915	2,057	NA	NA	NA	NA	NA	NA
Investment Assets:Bonds	37,914	31,926	35,655	35,002	34,857	32,488	31,187	27,486	24,393	22,589
Investment Assets:Stocks	Nil	208	Nil	Nil	13.6	12.9	39.1	27.9	10.9	24.5
Investment Assets:Loans	4,282	4,029	3,705	944	3,941	3,572	3,353	3,344	3,510	3,679
Investment Assets:Total	43,295	37,866	40,951	40,163	39,357	36,588	35,028	31,152	28,324	26,604
Deferred Policy Costs	2,483	2,472	2,381	2,983	2,913	2,883	3,052	2,982	2,675	2,424
Total Assets	54,506	49,417	52,433	52,823	51,867	50,832	49,718	45,260	42,443	40,364
Debt	2,550	2,259	2,515	2,660	3,262	2,862	2,789	1,914	2,304	1,915
Common Equity	8,500	6,398	8,040	7,719	7,364	7,224	7,271	9,398	5,940	5,576
% Return on Revenue	8.5	5.5	6.4	3.9	4.9	NM	NM	8.5	6.2	6.0
% Return on Assets	1.6	1.1	1.3	0.8	1.0	NM	NM	1.9	1.4	1.4
% Return on Equity	11.5	7.7	8.5	5.4	7.0	NM	NM	9.1	10.1	10.7
% Investment Yield	5.8	6.1	5.9	5.8	5.8	6.0	6.5	7.0	7.3	7.8

Data as orig reptd.; bef. results of disc opers/spec. items. Per share data adj. for stk. divs.; EPS diluted. E-Estimated. NA-Not Available. NM-Not Meaningful. NR-Not Ranked. UR-Under Review.

Office: 1 Fountain Square, Chattanooga, TN 37402-1307.
Telephone: 423-294-1011.
Website: http://www.unum.com
Chrmn: J.S. Fossel

Pres & CEO: T.R. Watjen
Pres, CEO & EVP: J.F. McGarry
EVP, CFO & Chief Acctg Officer: R.P. McKenney
EVP & General Counsel: E.L. Bishop, III

Investor Contact: T.A. White (423-294-8996)
Board Members: E. M. Caulfield, J. S. Fossel, P. H. Godwin, R. E. Goldsberry, K. T. Kabat, T. A. Kinser, G. C. Larson, A. MacMillan, Jr., E. J. Muhl, M. J. Passarella, W. J. Ryan, T. R. Watjen

Founded: 1887
Domicile: Delaware
Employees: 9,700

Urban Outfitters Inc

STANDARD &POOR'S

S&P Recommendation	BUY ★★★★★	Price $30.28 (as of Oct 22, 2010)	12-Mo. Target Price $44.00	Investment Style Large-Cap Growth

GICS Sector Consumer Discretionary
Sub-Industry Apparel Retail

Summary This company primarily operates three specialty retail brands -- Urban Outfitters, Anthropologie, and Free People -- in multi-channel settings.

Key Stock Statistics (Source S&P, Vickers, company reports)

52-Wk Range	$40.84– 29.03	S&P Oper. EPS 2011**E**	1.69	Market Capitalization(B)	$4.999	Beta	1.05
Trailing 12-Month EPS	$1.54	S&P Oper. EPS 2012**E**	1.95	Yield (%)	Nil	S&P 3-Yr. Proj. EPS CAGR(%)	15
Trailing 12-Month P/E	19.7	P/E on S&P Oper. EPS 2011**E**	17.9	Dividend Rate/Share	Nil	S&P Credit Rating	NA
$10K Invested 5 Yrs Ago	$9,631	Common Shares Outstg. (M)	165.1	Institutional Ownership (%)	86		

Price Performance

30-Week Mov. Avg. ··· 10-Week Mov. Avg. --- **GAAP Earnings vs. Previous Year** Volume Above Avg. |||||| STARS
12-Mo. Target Price — Relative Strength — ▲ Up ▼ Down ► No Change Below Avg. |||||| ★

Options: ASE, CBOE, P, Ph

Analysis prepared by **Marie Driscoll, CFA** on August 20, 2010, when the stock traded at **$ 32.95**.

Highlights

► URBN's broad and shallow merchandise strategy with frequent inventory flows delivers newness to the stores, while perpetuating exclusivity and driving full-price sales. That's a strategy we like. Moreover, we are impressed with caliber of the URBN management team, and its approach to brand development. URBN has numerous concepts in various stages including a wedding lifestyle concept planned for 2011. We see URBN doubling its retail brand portfolio over the next five years.

► We look for 18% sales growth in FY 11 (Jan.), assuming a high single digit comp, about 45 new stores, and 20% growth in the DTC channel. For FY 12, we project 15% sales growth.

► We see 190 basis points (bps) of EBIT margin improvement in FY 11, to 19.4% (on top of 140 bps of expansion in FY 10) on improved initial markups (IMUs) and continued gains in inventory management, resulting in reduced markdowns. We see another 10 bps in FY 12. Longer term, URBN's increasing scale and improved sourcing should support further IMU expansion and drive a 20% operating margin. New concept development is expected to reduce FY 11 EPS by about $0.03.

Investment Rationale/Risk

► We regard URBN's retail concepts and growth opportunities as superior, given its strong management and merchant and design teams, and under-penetrated niche brands that we see providing above-average long-term sales and earnings growth. We see URBN benefiting from a growing demand for authenticity and value, and its relatively small base of 341 stores across its three main retail brands provide ample opportunity for store expansion globally. URBN has communicated a 1,000-store goal, which we regard as appropriate and conservative.

► Risks to our recommendation and target price include the possibility that URBN will fail to continue to source brand-appropriate merchandise while executing an aggressive growth strategy. A slowdown in store level productivity would likely adversely affect sales and profits.

► Our 12-month target price of $44 is based on a 26X multiple of our FY 11 EPS estimate, which is about a 35% premium to peers and compares with URBN's average forward multiple over the past 60 months of 27X (in a range of 10X to 41X).

Qualitative Risk Assessment

LOW	MEDIUM	HIGH

Our risk assessment reflects what we view as URBN's strong balance sheet and rising cash flow, offset by fashion risk.

Quantitative Evaluations

S&P Quality Ranking B+

D	C	B-	B	B+	A-	A	A+

Relative Strength Rank WEAK

14

LOWEST = 1   HIGHEST = 99

Revenue/Earnings Data

Revenue (Million $)

	1Q	2Q	3Q	4Q	Year
2011	480.0	552.2	--	--	--
2010	384.8	458.6	505.9	588.5	1,938
2009	394.3	454.3	478.0	508.1	1,835
2008	314.5	348.5	379.3	465.4	1,508
2007	270.0	285.6	308.4	360.8	1,225
2006	231.3	253.4	288.8	318.6	1,092

Earnings Per Share ($)

2011	0.31	0.42	E0.44	E0.53	E1.69
2010	0.18	0.29	0.36	0.45	1.28
2009	0.25	0.33	0.35	0.24	1.17
2008	0.17	0.33	0.27	0.32	0.95
2007	0.12	0.15	0.21	0.21	0.69
2006	0.16	0.18	0.22	0.21	0.77

Fiscal year ended Jan. 31. Next earnings report expected: NA. EPS Estimates based on S&P Operating Earnings; historical GAAP earnings are as reported.

Dividend Data

No cash dividends have been paid.

Please read the Required Disclosures and Analyst Certification on the last page of this report.

The McGraw·Hill Companies

Urban Outfitters Inc

STANDARD &POOR'S

Business Summary August 20, 2010

CORPORATE OVERVIEW. Urban Outfitters operates specialty retail stores under the Urban Outfitters, Anthropologie and Free People brands, as well as a wholesale division. The company opened its first store in Philadelphia in 1970, near the University of Pennsylvania. URBN's strategy is to provide unified store environments that establish emotional bonds with the customer. The company also offers products directly to the consumer through its e-commerce websites (www.urbn.com, www.anthropologie.com and www.freepeople.com) and the Urban Outfitters, Anthropologie and Free People catalogs.

MARKET PROFILE. The U.S. apparel market generated $188.5 billion in sales at retail in 2009, down 4%, according to NPD Fashionworld consumer estimated data. Sales of women's apparel represented 55%, men's 27%, and kids' the remaining 18%. While the U.S. apparel market is mature, it is fragmented, with national brands marketed by 20 companies accounting for about 30% of total apparel sales. Private label (or store) brands account for an estimated 40% of apparel sales. With 17 Urban Outfitters stores in Europe and its direct-to-consumer catalogs and websites, URBN's breadth is international. In addition to URBN's apparel and accessories product offerings, its merchandise mix includes furniture and home ware and apartment ware, a more fragmented, faster-growing market that S&P estimates at $120 billion at retail.

COMPETITIVE LANDSCAPE. The retail landscape is consolidating, with share accruing to mass merchants and specialty chains as traditional department stores lose ground. Specialty chains, we believe, compete on customer knowledge garnered in daily interactions, focus groups and market intelligence, with this knowledge combined with high customer service levels resulting in an attractive price/value equation for consumers, in our view. By channel, specialty stores account for the largest share of apparel sales, at about 31% of 2009 apparel sales. This penetration varies by age for a high of 42% for teenagers (13-19 year olds), to less than 20% for those 45 years and older. Upheaval in the department store and specialty retail channels creates a window of opportunity over the coming 18-24 months for adept retailers and apparel brands to capture increased share. In the past few years, a number of new concepts targeting the 25+ age group launched to questionable success. We believe URBN's distinct market positioning is an ample barrier to new competition, and its design and merchandising competency is not easily replicated.

Company Financials Fiscal Year Ended Jan. 31

Per Share Data ($)	2010	2009	2008	2007	2006	2005	2004	2003	2002	2001
Tangible Book Value	7.69	6.28	5.14	4.09	3.40	2.47	1.82	1.45	1.05	0.94
Cash Flow	1.79	1.63	1.35	1.02	1.00	0.73	0.44	0.29	0.22	0.16
Earnings	1.28	1.17	0.95	0.94	0.77	0.54	0.30	0.18	0.11	0.08
S&P Core Earnings	1.28	1.19	0.94	0.69	0.42	0.40	0.27	0.17	0.10	0.06
Dividends	NA	Nil	Nil	Nil	Nil	Nil	Nil	Nil	Nil	Nil
Payout Ratio	Nil	Nil	Nil	Nil	Nil	Nil	Nil	Nil	Nil	Nil
Calendar Year	2009	2008	2007	2006	2005	2004	2003	2002	2001	2000
Prices:High	35.84	38.40	29.40	29.89	33.77	24.24	10.32	4.65	3.11	3.68
Prices:Low	13.63	12.33	19.20	13.65	18.93	9.17	2.09	2.21	0.95	0.80
P/E Ratio:High	28	33	31	43	44	43	34	13	29	48
P/E Ratio:Low	11	11	20	20	25	16	7	NA	9	11

Income Statement Analysis (Million $)										
Revenue	1,938	1,835	1,508	1,225	1,092	828	548	423	349	295
Operating Income	425	379	294	220	247	180	103	63.6	41.0	29.9
Depreciation	86.2	79.5	68.7	55.7	39.3	31.9	22.4	18.2	15.5	12.0
Interest Expense	NA	Nil	Nil	Nil	Nil	Nil	Nil	Nil	Nil	Nil
Pretax Income	344	309	234	170	212	150	81.3	46.1	25.2	17.8
Effective Tax Rate	36.2%	35.6%	31.6%	31.7%	38.4%	39.8%	40.5%	40.5%	40.5%	41.0%
Net Income	220	199	160	116	131	90.5	48.4	27.4	15.0	10.5
S&P Core Earnings	219	203	160	116	71.0	65.9	43.7	25.8	13.6	8.81

Balance Sheet & Other Financial Data (Million $)										
Cash	502	366	185	222	257	219	139	95.1	28.3	16.6
Current Assets	806	624	434	366	385	288	176	145	82.1	65.0
Total Assets	1,636	1,323	1,143	899	769	557	360	278	195	169
Current Liabilities	189	141	167	135	134	98.3	57.8	43.1	40.8	33.3
Long Term Debt	NA	Nil	Nil	Nil	Nil	Nil	Nil	Nil	Nil	Nil
Common Equity	1,297	1,054	853	675	561	402	290	224	146	130
Total Capital	1,297	1,054	853	675	561	402	290	224	146	130
Capital Expenditures	109	113	115	212	128	75.1	33.1	22.2	22.3	36.9
Cash Flow	306	279	229	172	170	122	70.8	45.6	30.5	22.5
Current Ratio	4.3	4.4	2.6	2.7	2.9	2.9	3.0	3.4	2.0	2.0
% Long Term Debt of Capitalization	Nil	Nil	Nil	Nil	Nil	Nil	Nil	Nil	Nil	Nil
% Net Income of Revenue	11.4	10.9	10.6	9.5	12.0	10.9	8.8	6.5	4.3	3.6
% Return on Assets	14.8	16.2	15.7	13.9	19.7	19.2	15.1	11.6	8.2	6.5
% Return on Equity	18.7	20.9	21.0	18.8	27.2	26.1	18.8	14.8	10.9	8.4

Data as orig reptd.; bef. results of disc opers/spec. items. Per share data adj. for stk. divs.; EPS diluted. E-Estimated. NA-Not Available. NM-Not Meaningful. NR-Not Ranked. UR-Under Review.

Office: 5000 S Broad St, Philadelphia, PA 19112-1495.
Telephone: 215-454-5500.
Website: http://www.urbanoutfitters.com
Chrmn & Pres: R.A. Hayne

CEO: G.T. Senk
CFO: E. Artz
Chief Admin Officer: F. Zausner
Chief Acctg Officer & Cntlr: F.J. Conforti

Investor Contact: J.E. Kyees
Board Members: S. A. Belair, H. S. Cherken, Jr., R. A. Hayne, J. S. Lawson, III, G. T. Senk, R. H. Strouse

Founded: 1976
Domicile: Pennsylvania
Employees: 14,000

The McGraw-Hill Companies

Valero Energy Corp

S&P Recommendation HOLD ★★★☆☆ | **Price** $17.65 (as of Oct 22, 2010) | **12-Mo. Target Price** $19.00 | **Investment Style** Large-Cap Blend

GICS Sector Energy
Sub-Industry Oil & Gas Refining & Marketing

Summary This company is North America's largest oil refiner, one of the largest independent U.S. refined petroleum products retailers, and operates refineries that can process sour and acidic crudes.

Key Stock Statistics (Source S&P, Vickers, company reports)

52-Wk Range	$21.49–15.49	S&P Oper. EPS 2010E	1.51	Market Capitalization(B)	$9.994	Beta	1.09
Trailing 12-Month EPS	$-2.79	S&P Oper. EPS 2011E	2.68	Yield (%)	1.13	S&P 3-Yr. Proj. EPS CAGR(%)	NM
Trailing 12-Month P/E	NM	P/E on S&P Oper. EPS 2010E	11.7	Dividend Rate/Share	$0.20	S&P Credit Rating	BBB
$10K Invested 5 Yrs Ago	$3,999	Common Shares Outstg. (M)	566.3	Institutional Ownership (%)	74		

Price Performance

30-Week Mov. Avg. · · · · 10-Week Mov. Avg. – – **GAAP Earnings vs. Previous Year** Volume Above Avg. STARS
12-Mo. Target Price — Relative Strength — ▲ Up ▼ Down ► No Change Below Avg. ★

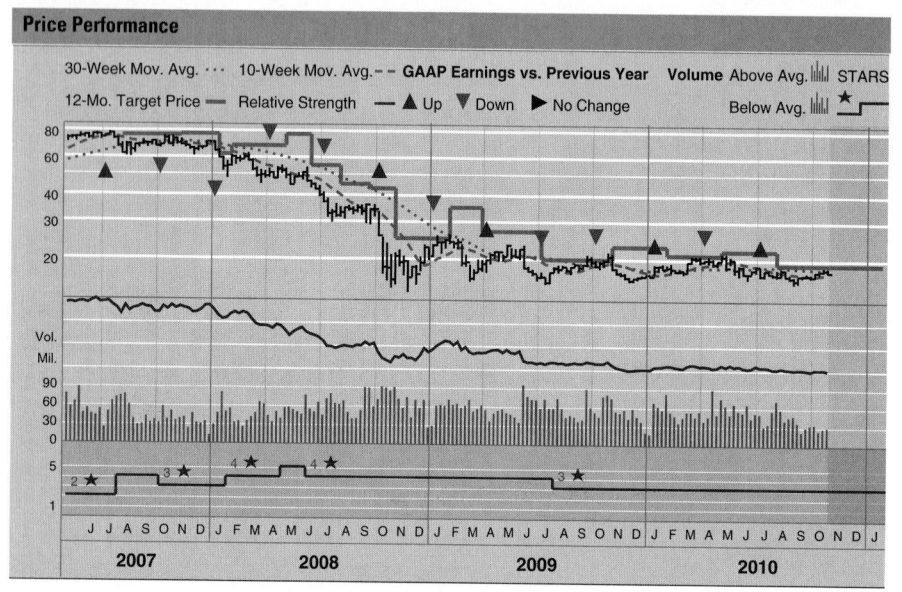

Options: ASE, CBOE, P, Ph

Analysis prepared by **Tina J. Vital** on September 29, 2010, when the stock traded at **$ 17.43**.

Highlights

► Light-heavy crude differentials widened in the first half of 2010, and diesel and secondary product margins widened sequentially in the second quarter on improved demand. We expect third-quarter throughput rates to rise 4% from the second quarter. Overall, we project that U.S. Gulf Coast 3-2-1 crack spreads will narrow 5% in 2010, but widen 16% in 2011.

► In June 2010, VLO sold its discontinued operations at Delaware City to PBF Energy Partners for $220 million (or $1,048 per barrel of crude production capacity), and in September 2010, agreed to sell its Paulsboro refinery to PBR Energy Partners for $360 million (or $1,946 per barrel); we view both deal values as fair considering difficult market conditions. VLO is exploring options for its Aruba refinery. In June, maintenance began at the refinery (shut down in July 2009) with the potential to restart in 2010.

► VLO posted an after-tax operating loss in the first quarter on narrowed margins, but profitability was restored in the second quarter. We expect continued improvement through 2012 on a better economic outlook and strategic actions.

Investment Rationale/Risk

► VLO is focused on the refining of heavy and sour crudes. While we look for refining margins to remain pressured through 2016 on surplus global refining capacity, we expect the discounts on heavy sour crude to improve as oil prices rise. With fuel demand strengthening, we expect refining throughputs to rise (which should permit lower operating expenses per barrel), and retail marketing and ethanol to contribute to solid earnings in 2010. Over the long term, we believe VLO's size and ability to refine lower cost and quality crude oils offer strategic advantages.

► Risks to our recommendation and target price include weaker economic conditions, excess industry refining capacity, and changes in operating conditions that lead to a narrowing of margins or reduced throughput rates.

► A blend of our discounted cash flow ($19 per share, assuming a WACC of 7.4% and terminal growth of 3%) and relative market valuations leads to our 12-month target price of $19. This represents an expected enterprise value of about 3.9X our 2011 EBITDA estimate, a discount to the peer average.

Qualitative Risk Assessment

LOW	MEDIUM	HIGH

Our risk assessment reflects our view of VLO's strong business profile in the volatile and competitive oil refining industry. The company possesses above-average refining complexity, which allows it to process a large amount of lower-cost heavy and sour crudes.

Quantitative Evaluations

S&P Quality Ranking B

D	C	B-	B	B+	A-	A	A+

Relative Strength Rank MODERATE

39

LOWEST = 1   HIGHEST = 99

Revenue/Earnings Data

Revenue (Million $)

	1Q	2Q	3Q	4Q	Year
2010	19,435	21,550	--	--	--
2009	13,329	17,375	18,523	18,867	68,144
2008	27,945	36,436	35,753	18,358	118,298
2007	18,755	24,202	23,699	28,671	95,327
2006	20,941	26,781	24,319	19,792	91,833
2005	14,943	18,032	23,283	25,894	82,162

Earnings Per Share ($)

	1Q	2Q	3Q	4Q	Year
2010	-0.18	0.94	E0.51	E0.24	E1.51
2009	0.59	-0.48	-1.12	-0.32	-0.65
2008	0.48	1.38	2.18	-6.36	-2.16
2007	1.86	3.57	1.34	1.02	7.72
2006	1.32	2.98	2.55	1.80	8.64
2005	0.96	1.53	1.47	2.06	6.10

Fiscal year ended Dec. 31. Next earnings report expected: Late October. EPS Estimates based on S&P Operating Earnings; historical GAAP earnings are as reported.

Dividend Data (Dates: mm/dd Payment Date: mm/dd/yy)

Amount ($)	Date Decl.	Ex-Div. Date	Stk. of Record	Payment Date
0.150	10/15	11/06	11/11	12/09/09
0.050	01/27	02/12	02/17	03/17/10
0.050	04/29	05/17	05/19	06/16/10
0.050	07/29	08/16	08/18	09/15/10

Dividends have been paid since 1997. Source: Company reports.

Please read the Required Disclosures and Analyst Certification on the last page of this report.

Valero Energy Corp

Business Summary September 29, 2010

CORPORATE OVERVIEW. Incorporated in 1981 under the name Valero Refining and Marketing Co., the company changed its name to Valero Energy Co. (VLO) in 1997. In 2001, VLO merged with Ultramar Diamond Shamrock, and in 2005 with Premcor Inc., creating the largest refiner in North America, based on atmospheric distillation capacity.

The company operates in three business segments: Refining (87% of 2009 operating revenues, 19% of 2009 operating income), Ethanol (11%; 52%), and Retail (2%, 29%). VLO serves customers in the U.S. (86% of 2009 revenues), Canada (9%), and other countries (5%); no single customer accounted for over 10% of consolidated operating revenues.

The Refining segment includes refining operations, wholesale marketing, product supply and distribution, and transportation operations. As of year-end 2009, the company owned and operated 15 refineries in the U.S., Canada and Aruba, with a combined throughput capacity of 2.78 million barrels per day (b/d). These capacities by region include: Gulf Coast (eight refineries, 58% of 2009 throughput capacity), the Mid-Continent (three, 16%), the West Coast (two, 11%), and the Northeast (two, 15%).

During 2009, sour crude oils, acidic sweet crude oils and residuals represent-

ed 53% of VLO's throughput volumes; sweet crude oil 28%; and blendstocks and other feedstocks 19%. About 55% of VLO's current crude oil feedstock requirements were purchased through term contracts, with the remainder generally purchased on the spot market. About 75% of 2009 crude oil feedstocks were imported from foreign sources.

The Ethanol segment includes sales of internally produced ethanol and distillers grains. As of April 2010, VLO owned 10 ethanol plants with production capacity of about 1.11 billion gallons per year; three of these facilities were acquired in the 2010 first quarter. Operations are located in the central plains region of the U.S.

VLO is one of the largest independent retailers of refined products in the central and southwest U.S. and eastern Canada. Its retail operations are segregated geographically into two groups: Retail-U.S. System (991 company-operated sites - 79% owned, 21% leased - in 2009) and Retail-Canada (479 retail stores or cardlocks, owned or leased).

Company Financials Fiscal Year Ended Dec. 31

Per Share Data ($)	2009	2008	2007	2006	2005	2004	2003	2002	2001	2000
Tangible Book Value	25.67	29.82	31.75	23.33	15.82	9.55	5.86	3.24	3.90	6.28
Cash Flow	2.17	0.18	9.55	10.47	7.57	3.24	2.31	1.23	2.75	1.86
Earnings	-0.65	-2.16	7.72	8.64	6.10	3.27	1.27	0.21	2.21	1.40
S&P Core Earnings	-0.67	2.32	7.73	8.32	6.02	3.25	1.25	0.14	2.14	NA
Dividends	0.60	0.57	0.48	0.30	0.19	0.15	0.15	0.10	0.09	0.08
Payout Ratio	NM	NM	6%	3%	3%	4%	11%	48%	4%	6%
Prices:High	26.20	71.12	78.68	70.75	58.63	23.91	11.77	12.49	13.15	9.66
Prices:Low	15.29	13.94	47.66	46.84	21.01	11.43	8.05	5.79	7.88	4.63
P/E Ratio:High	NM	NM	10	8	10	7	9	60	6	7
P/E Ratio:Low	NM	NM	6	5	3	3	6	28	4	3

Income Statement Analysis (Million $)										
Revenue	67,271	118,298	95,327	91,833	82,162	54,619	37,969	26,976	14,988	14,671
Operating Income	NA	20.4	8,278	9,165	6,334	2,979	1,733	920	1,139	723
Depreciation, Depletion and Amortization	1,527	1,038	1,360	1,155	875	618	511	449	138	112
Interest Expense	408	340	466	210	266	260	278	256	102	83.0
Pretax Income	-449	336	6,726	8,196	5,287	2,710	989	164	895	528
Effective Tax Rate	21.6%	NM	32.1%	33.3%	32.1%	33.4%	36.9%	35.5%	37.0%	35.8%
Net Income	-352	-1,131	4,565	5,463	3,590	1,804	622	91.5	564	339
S&P Core Earnings	-366	1,212	4,572	5,258	3,534	1,785	604	60.0	547	NA

Balance Sheet & Other Financial Data (Million $)										
Cash	825	940	2,495	1,590	436	864	369	409	346	14.6
Current Assets	10,923	9,450	14,792	10,760	8,276	5,264	3,817	3,536	4,113	1,285
Total Assets	35,629	34,417	42,722	37,753	32,728	19,392	15,664	14,465	14,337	4,308
Current Liabilities	7,798	6,209	11,914	8,822	7,305	4,534	3,064	3,007	4,730	1,039
Long Term Debt	7,163	6,264	6,470	4,657	5,156	3,901	4,245	4,867	2,805	1,042
Common Equity	14,725	15,620	18,507	18,605	14,982	7,590	5,535	4,308	4,203	1,527
Total Capital	22,125	26,047	28,998	27,309	20,206	13,710	11,585	10,592	8,884	3,149
Capital Expenditures	2,327	2,790	2,260	3,187	2,133	1,292	976	628	394	195
Cash Flow	1,175	93.0	5,529	6,616	4,452	1,791	1,128	541	701	451
Current Ratio	1.4	1.5	1.2	1.2	1.1	1.2	1.2	1.2	0.9	1.2
% Long Term Debt of Capitalization	Nil	24.0	22.3	17.1	25.5	28.5	36.6	45.9	31.6	33.0
% Return on Assets	NM	NM	11.4	15.5	13.8	10.3	4.1	0.6	6.0	9.3
% Return on Equity	NA	NM	24.6	32.5	31.7	27.3	12.5	2.2	19.7	26.0

Data as orig reptd.; bef. results of disc opers/spec. items. Per share data adj. for stk. divs.; EPS diluted. E-Estimated. NA-Not Available. NM-Not Meaningful. NR-Not Ranked. UR-Under Review.

Office: 1 Valero Way, San Antonio, TX 78249-1616.
Telephone: 210-345-2000.
Email: investorrelations@valero.com
Website: http://www.valero.com

Chrmn, Pres & CEO: W.R. Klesse
COO & EVP: R.J. Marcogliese
Investor Contact: M.S. Ciskowski (210-345-2000)
EVP, CFO & Chief Acctg Officer: M.S. Ciskowski

EVP & General Counsel: K.S. Bowers
Board Members: R. K. Calgaard, J. D. Choate, I. F. Engelhardt, R. M. Escobedo, W. R. Klesse, B. Marbut, D. L. Nickles, R. Profusek, S. K. Purcell, S. M. Waters

Founded: 1955
Domicile: Delaware
Employees: 20,920

Varian Medical Systems Inc

S&P Recommendation HOLD ★★★★★

Price	12-Mo. Target Price	Investment Style
$61.03 (as of Oct 22, 2010)	$61.00	Large-Cap Growth

GICS Sector Health Care
Sub-Industry Health Care Equipment

Summary This leading maker of radiotherapy cancer systems also supplies X-ray tubes and flat-panel digital subsystems for imaging in medical, scientific and industrial applications.

Key Stock Statistics (Source S&P, Vickers, company reports)

52-Wk Range	$62.60– 35.50	S&P Oper. EPS 2010E	2.93	Market Capitalization(B)	$7.423	Beta	0.76
Trailing 12-Month EPS	$2.82	S&P Oper. EPS 2011E	3.20	Yield (%)	Nil	S&P 3-Yr. Proj. EPS CAGR(%)	9
Trailing 12-Month P/E	21.6	P/E on S&P Oper. EPS 2010E	20.8	Dividend Rate/Share	Nil	S&P Credit Rating	NA
$10K Invested 5 Yrs Ago	$13,687	Common Shares Outstg. (M)	121.6	Institutional Ownership (%)	92		

Price Performance

30-Week Mov. Avg. · · · · 10-Week Mov. Avg. – – **GAAP Earnings vs. Previous Year** Volume Above Avg. STARS
12-Mo. Target Price — Relative Strength — ▲ Up ▼ Down ► No Change Below Avg. ★

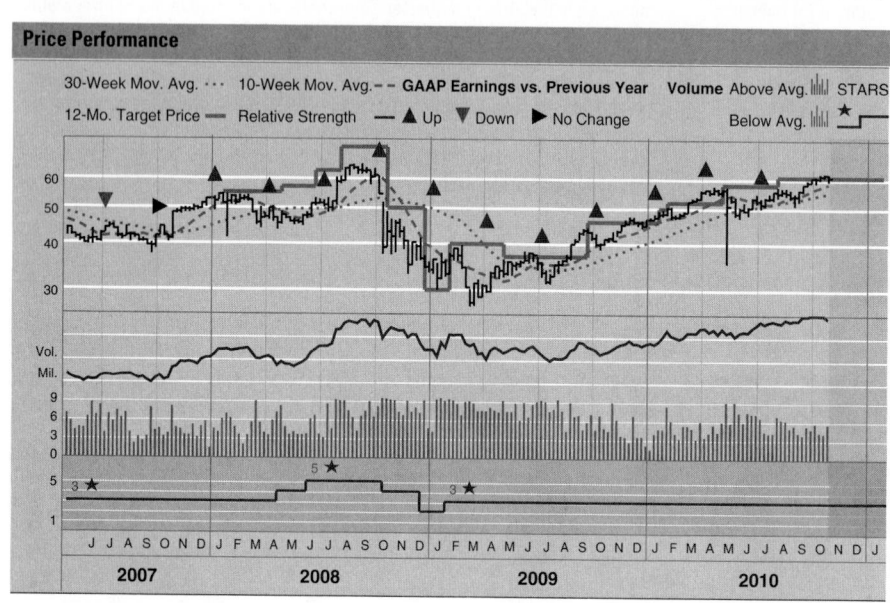

Options: ASE

Analysis prepared by **Phillip M. Seligman** on August 06, 2010, when the stock traded at **$ 55.47**.

Highlights

➤ We look for total sales in FY 11 (Sep.) to rise about 6%, following a 7% increase we see in FY 10. We see a modest pickup in demand for RapidArc, partly on demand for the new TrueBeam platform in the U.S., and continued strength in lower-end radiation oncology systems, particularly outside the U.S. We expect strong demand for VAR's X-ray products to continue, assuming the diagnostic imaging market recovery is sustainable, but think sales comparisons become tougher in FY 11. We assume currency exchange will remain unfavorable to FY 10 growth through year end, but will be neutral in FY 11.

➤ We see gross margins continuing to widen through FY 11, mainly as the benefits of product mix shifts and cost-control initiatives outweigh pricing pressures. We also expect the SG&A cost ratio to be stable in FY 11, after declining in FY 10 on cost control, but we see the R&D cost ratio gradually rising, reflecting VAR's intention to boost R&D spending.

➤ Our FY 10 EPS estimate for continuing operations is $2.93, versus $2.65 earned FY 09, and we look for $3.20 in FY 11.

Investment Rationale/Risk

➤ VAR's radiation oncology systems are big-ticket items and their order rates have been hurt in the U.S., where hospitals face tightened capital budgets. We see U.S. hospitals prioritizing radiation oncology modernization assuming their budgets expand meaningfully, which we do not see in the near term. Oncology orders grew in the U.S. in the second quarter after a year of declines, reflecting interest in VAR's new TrueBeam linear accelerator. Still, a significant number of the TrueBeam orders were backlog upgrades. Although more than half were new orders, we are cautious regarding the sustainability of growth of new systems following purchases by early adopters. However, VAR is seeing healthy orders from overseas markets where healthcare is government-run.

➤ Risks to our recommendation and target price include unfavorable changes in Medicare reimbursements, competitive pricing, and further deterioration in the outlook for hospital spending plans in 2010.

➤ Our 12-month target price of $61 is 20.5X our calendar 2010 EPS estimate of $2.97, a valuation discount to VAR's historical averages.

Qualitative Risk Assessment

LOW	MEDIUM	HIGH

Our risk assessment reflects that while Varian offers some of the more technologically advanced products in the oncology equipment industry, it operates in a competitive industry characterized by technological innovation and new product entrants. In addition, although we believe radiation therapy will continue to be an integral component of global cancer treatment protocols, the continued development of drug-based oncology treatments represents a substantial threat to the company's radiation therapy equipment business. In our view, tight credit market conditions globally could also negatively affect capital expenditure decisions by Varian's customers.

Quantitative Evaluations

S&P Quality Ranking B+

D	C	B-	B	B+	A-	A	A+

Relative Strength Rank MODERATE

59

LOWEST = 1   HIGHEST = 99

Revenue/Earnings Data

Revenue (Million $)

	1Q	2Q	3Q	4Q	Year
2010	540.9	585.6	578.0	--	--
2009	508.7	553.6	509.8	642.0	2,214
2008	451.2	518.4	507.4	592.7	2,070
2007	387.9	442.6	423.7	522.4	1,777
2006	334.2	413.9	395.7	454.0	1,598
2005	299.0	350.8	346.5	386.2	1,383

Earnings Per Share ($)

2010	0.63	0.73	0.74	E0.83	E2.93
2009	0.56	0.64	0.68	0.78	2.65
2008	0.46	0.57	0.61	0.68	2.31
2007	0.37	0.46	0.39	0.61	1.83
2006	0.30	0.41	0.49	0.61	1.80
2005	0.29	0.39	0.37	0.45	1.50

Fiscal year ended Sep. 30. Next earnings report expected: Late October. EPS Estimates based on S&P Operating Earnings; historical GAAP earnings are as reported.

Dividend Data

Cash dividends were last paid in 1999.

Varian Medical Systems Inc

STANDARD &POOR'S

Business Summary August 06, 2010

CORPORATE OVERVIEW. Varian is one of the largest manufacturers of oncology diagnostic products, X-ray tubes, and imaging subsystems. The company is focused primarily on capturing share in the global oncology radiation therapy markets. Cancer rates are expected to increase 50% by 2020.

MARKET PROFILE. Driven by an aging global population and improved diagnostic methods, the number of newly diagnosed cancer cases continues to increase. According to estimates published in February 2005 by the Annals of Oncology, nearly 2.9 million new cancer cases were diagnosed during 2004, and the U.S. National Cancer Institute estimates that cancer diagnoses will rise 1.6 million per year by 2010, a 23% increase from the 1.3 million cancers per year seen in 2000. Radiation therapy is commonly used in the treatment of cancer, alone or in combination with surgery or chemotherapy. The most common type of radiotherapy uses X-rays delivered by external beams, and is administered using linear accelerators. In addition to external radiation, radioactive seeds, wires or ribbons are sometimes inserted into a tumor or into a body cavity (brachytherapy), a modality that does not require radiation to pass through healthy tissues.

Varian's oncology systems group (81% of FY 09 (Sep.) revenues) designs, mar-

kets and services hardware and software products for cancer radiation treatment, including linear accelerators, treatment simulators and verification products, and software systems for planning cancer treatment and managing information and images for radiation oncology. Products focus on enabling a new therapy that delivers high doses of radiation to tumors while reducing risk to surrounding tissues. This three-dimensional conformal radiation therapy, called Intensity Modulation Radiation Therapy (IMRT), links treatment planning, information management and driver software to the treatment delivery device, the linear accelerator. This is designed to allow clinicians to determine and deliver a clinically optimized plan of radiation for each patient. IMRT is used to treat head and neck, breast, prostate, pancreatic, lung, liver, gynecological and central nervous system cancers. VAR has also developed image-guided radiation therapy (IGRT), which improves radiation therapy precision by using technologies that compensate for tumor changes and movements during and between treatments.

Company Financials Fiscal Year Ended Sep. 30

Per Share Data ($)	2009	2008	2007	2006	2005	2004	2003	2002	2001	2000
Tangible Book Value	8.72	6.43	4.92	5.21	4.11	3.74	3.71	3.05	2.93	2.13
Cash Flow	3.01	2.60	2.08	2.02	1.70	1.32	1.06	0.81	0.64	0.55
Earnings	2.65	2.31	1.83	1.80	1.50	1.18	0.92	0.66	0.50	0.41
S&P Core Earnings	2.63	2.28	1.83	1.80	1.34	1.04	0.78	0.54	0.40	NA
Dividends	Nil	Nil	Nil	Nil	Nil	Nil	Nil	Nil	Nil	Nil
Payout Ratio	Nil	Nil	Nil	Nil	Nil	Nil	Nil	Nil	Nil	Nil
Prices:High	47.78	65.84	53.22	61.70	52.92	46.49	35.65	25.66	19.31	17.75
Prices:Low	27.10	33.12	37.30	41.10	31.65	29.63	23.70	15.80	13.50	6.88
P/E Ratio:High	18	29	29	34	35	39	39	39	39	43
P/E Ratio:Low	10	14	20	23	21	25	26	24	27	17

Income Statement Analysis (Million $)

	2009	2008	2007	2006	2005	2004	2003	2002	2001	2000
Revenue	2,214	2,070	1,777	1,598	1,383	1,236	1,042	873	774	690
Operating Income	519	456	367	339	332	277	219	165	129	108
Depreciation	44.6	36.7	32.2	29.6	27.1	20.8	20.3	20.4	19.3	17.8
Interest Expense	4.10	4.88	4.79	4.65	4.70	4.67	4.38	4.49	4.13	5.16
Pretax Income	475	426	343	319	308	257	201	146	107	84.9
Effective Tax Rate	30.2%	30.7%	30.1%	23.6%	33.0%	35.0%	35.0%	36.0%	36.5%	37.5%
Net Income	332	295	239	244	207	167	131	93.6	68.0	53.0
S&P Core Earnings	329	292	240	245	184	148	111	75.9	54.2	NA

Balance Sheet & Other Financial Data (Million $)

	2009	2008	2007	2006	2005	2004	2003	2002	2001	2000
Cash	554	397	263	366	378	352	323	299	219	83.3
Current Assets	1,672	1,394	1,160	1,156	1,017	885	806	651	620	451
Total Assets	2,308	1,976	1,684	1,512	1,317	1,170	1,053	910	759	603
Current Liabilities	842	782	782	644	544	461	409	358	285	250
Long Term Debt	23.4	32.4	40.4	49.4	57.3	53.3	58.5	58.5	58.5	58.5
Common Equity	1,312	1,027	821	797	659	614	564	504	418	270
Total Capital	1,344	1,060	862	847	716	667	622	562	477	329
Capital Expenditures	62.6	81.4	64.1	41.4	43.9	24.2	18.9	25.9	16.5	19.2
Cash Flow	376	332	272	273	234	188	151	114	87.3	70.8
Current Ratio	2.0	1.8	1.5	1.8	1.9	1.9	2.0	1.8	2.2	1.8
% Long Term Debt of Capitalization	1.7	3.1	4.7	5.8	8.0	8.0	9.4	10.4	12.3	17.8
% Net Income of Revenue	15.0	14.3	13.5	15.2	14.9	13.5	12.6	10.7	8.8	7.7
% Return on Assets	15.5	16.1	15.0	17.2	16.5	15.0	13.3	11.2	10.0	9.3
% Return on Equity	28.4	32.0	29.6	33.4	32.2	28.4	25.3	20.3	19.2	23.3

Data as orig reptd.; bef. results of disc opers/spec. items. Per share data adj. for stk. divs.; EPS diluted. E-Estimated. NA-Not Available. NM-Not Meaningful. NR-Not Ranked. UR-Under Review.

Office: 3100 Hansen Way, Palo Alto, CA 94304-1030.
Telephone: 650-493-4000.
Website: http://www.varian.com
Chrmn: R.M. Levy

Pres & CEO: T.E. Guertin
SVP & CFO: E.W. Finney
CTO: G.A. Zdasiuk
Chief Acctg Officer & Cntlr: T. Chen

Investor Contact: S. Sias (650-424-5782)
Board Members: S. L. Bostrom, J. S. Brown, R. Eckert, T. E. Guertin, M. Laret, R. M. Levy, D. W. Martin, Jr., R. Naumann-Etienne, V. Thyagarajan

Founded: 1976
Domicile: Delaware
Employees: 5,100

Ventas Inc.

**STANDARD
&POOR'S**

| S&P Recommendation | HOLD ★★★☆☆ | Price $52.35 (as of Oct 22, 2010) | 12-Mo. Target Price $54.00 | Investment Style Large-Cap Blend |

GICS Sector Financials
Sub-Industry Specialized REITS

Summary This real estate investment trust invests in health care facilities, including seniors housing, specialty care facilities, hospitals, and medical office buildings.

Key Stock Statistics (Source S&P, Vickers, company reports)

52-Wk Range	$55.38–38.87	S&P FFO/Sh. 2010E	2.78	Market Capitalization(B)	$8.223	Beta	1.43
Trailing 12-Month FFO/Share	NA	S&P FFO/Sh. 2011E	3.07	Yield (%)	4.09	S&P 3-Yr. FFO/Sh. Proj. CAGR(%)	3
Trailing 12-Month P/FFO	NA	P/FFO on S&P FFO/Sh. 2010E	18.8	Dividend Rate/Share	$2.14	S&P Credit Rating	BBB-
$10K Invested 5 Yrs Ago	$22,137	Common Shares Outstg. (M)	157.1	Institutional Ownership (%)	NM		

Price Performance

30-Week Mov. Avg. ··· 10-Week Mov. Avg. --- GAAP Earnings vs. Previous Year   Volume Above Avg. STARS
12-Mo. Target Price — Relative Strength   ▲ Up ▼ Down ► No Change   Below Avg.

Analysis prepared by **Robert McMillan** on July 30, 2010, when the stock traded at **$ 50.91**.

Highlights

▶ We believe VTR has assembled a portfolio of health care properties that is well diversified in terms of asset type, geography, and tenant base. With its core focus on senior housing, we think VTR will benefit from increased demand driven by the aging baby boomer population. After revenue increases of 23% in 2008, on acquisitions, and 1.7% in 2009, we see 2010 revenue growth in VTR's need-based businesses of 7.3%, helped by acquisitions.

▶ Net operating income, occupancy levels and coverage levels improved for VTR's overall portfolio during the second quarter of 2010 versus the 2009 quarter. In VTR's Sunrise senior housing portfolio, average occupancy rose to 88.4% from 87.2%, while the average daily rate (ADR) rose 3.5%. In the medical office portfolio, same-space occupancy remained flat at 93.5%, while net operating income rose 2.2%. We are optimistic that VTR's recent acquisition of a large portfolio of medical office buildings will position it to benefit from an aging population and increased demand for medical services due to health care reform.

▶ We forecast per-share funds from operations (FFO) of $2.78 in 2010 and $3.07 in 2011.

Investment Rationale/Risk

▶ We like the predictable nature of VTR's long-term triple net lease revenue stream, and believe the stock correlates less with macroeconomic trends than most other REITs. Amid an anemic economy, we favor what we see as VTR's stable revenue stream with minimal short-term lease expirations, its solid balance sheet, and its relatively secure dividend payout.

▶ Risks to our recommendation and target price include a faster-than-expected decline in seniors housing occupancy, and a decrease in government reimbursement rates.

▶ The stock recently traded at about 18.9X trailing 12-month FFO per share. Our 12-month target price of $54 is about 18.3X our forward four-quarter FFO per share estimate of $2.94, a moderately high multiple by historical standards, but reasonable, we believe, given VTR's portfolio and operating performance as well as its strong balance sheet and liquidity position. We see the valuation multiple narrowing to a more modest level over time, although we still see continued improvements in operating results, which should benefit from an aging population and a greater need for space in health care facilities.

Qualitative Risk Assessment

| LOW | MEDIUM | HIGH |

Our risk assessment reflects VTR's position as the owner of a large and diversified portfolio of health care-related properties that provide what we see as a steady and predictable stream of income.

Quantitative Evaluations

S&P Quality Ranking B+

| D | C | B- | B | B+ | A- | A | A+ |

Relative Strength Rank MODERATE

37

LOWEST = 1   HIGHEST = 99

Revenue/FFO Data

Revenue (Million $)

	1Q	2Q	3Q	4Q	Year
2010	241.6	244.0	--	--	--
2009	229.4	231.9	235.8	239.0	936.1
2008	231.8	233.5	238.6	234.0	929.8
2007	119.2	193.8	226.3	232.6	771.8
2006	97.81	100.3	109.7	120.6	428.4
2005	63.80	74.95	95.93	98.30	333.0

FFO Per Share ($)

2010	0.66	0.64	E0.68	E0.73	E2.78
2009	0.66	0.68	0.66	0.66	2.58
2008	0.75	0.73	0.81	0.69	2.74
2007	0.68	0.70	0.66	0.66	2.69
2006	0.55	0.57	0.64	0.69	2.44
2005	0.48	0.51	0.54	0.55	2.09

Fiscal year ended Dec. 31. Next earnings report expected: Late October. FFO Estimates based on S&P Funds From Operations Est..

Dividend Data (Dates: mm/dd Payment Date: mm/dd/yy)

Amount ($)	Date Decl.	Ex-Div. Date	Stk. of Record	Payment Date
0.513	12/04	12/14	12/16	12/30/09
0.535	02/17	03/10	03/12	03/31/10
0.535	05/03	06/09	06/11	06/30/10
0.535	09/02	09/15	09/17	09/30/10

Dividends have been paid since 1999. Source: Company reports.

Please read the Required Disclosures and Analyst Certification on the last page of this report.

The **McGraw·Hill** Companies

Ventas Inc.

Business Summary July 30, 2010

CORPORATE OVERVIEW. Ventas Inc. is a health care REIT (real estate investment trust) that specializes in acquiring, financing and owning seniors housing and health care properties and leasing those properties to third parties or operating them through independent third party managers. At the end of 2009, its portfolio consisted of interests in 505 properties in the United States and Canada, including 244 seniors housing communities, 187 skilled nursing facilities, 40 hospitals and 34 medical office buildings (MOBs) and other properties in 43 states and two Canadian provinces. With the exception of its seniors housing communities, which are managed by Sunrise Medical Systems pursuant to long-term management agreements, and the majority of its MOBs, VTR leases its properties to health care operating companies under triple-net or absolute-net leases, which require the tenants to pay all property-related expenses. The trust also had real estate loan investments relating to senior housing and health care companies or properties at the end of 2009.

VTR's seniors housing communities (65.8% of 2009 total revenues) include independent and assisted living communities, and communities providing care for individuals with Alzheimer's disease and other forms of dementia or memory loss. These communities offer residential units on a month-to-month basis primarily to elderly individuals requiring various levels of assistance. Basic services for residents of these communities include housekeeping, meals in a central dining area and group activities organized by the staff with input from the residents. More extensive care and personal supervision, at additional fees, are also available for such needs as eating, bathing, grooming, transportation, limited therapeutic programs and medication administration, all of which encourage the residents to live as independently as possible according to their abilities. These needs are often met by home health providers in close coordination with the resident's physician and skilled nursing facilities. The skilled nursing facilities (18.8%) typically provide nursing care services to the elderly and rehabilitation and restoration services, including physical, occupational and speech therapies, and other medical treatment for patients and residents who do not require the high technology, care-intensive setting of an acute care or rehabilitation hospital.

Company Financials Fiscal Year Ended Dec. 31

Per Share Data ($)	2009	2008	2007	2006	2005	2004	2003	2002	2001	2000
Tangible Book Value	15.74	14.99	13.65	6.51	6.28	1.73	0.53	NM	NM	NM
Earnings	1.27	1.30	1.15	1.25	1.31	1.19	1.21	0.75	0.75	-0.90
S&P Core Earnings	1.27	1.30	1.15	1.25	1.14	1.18	1.08	0.70	0.56	NA
Dividends	2.05	2.05	2.05	1.58	1.44	1.30	1.07	0.95	0.92	0.62
Payout Ratio	161%	158%	105%	126%	110%	109%	88%	127%	123%	NM
Prices:High	44.91	52.00	47.97	42.40	32.71	29.48	22.98	13.76	12.85	5.81
Prices:Low	19.13	17.31	23.98	29.54	24.43	20.56	11.08	10.06	5.56	2.68
P/E Ratio:High	35	40	42	34	25	25	19	18	17	NM
P/E Ratio:Low	15	13	21	24	19	17	9	13	7	NM

Income Statement Analysis (Million $)										
Rental Income	501	487	484	418	NA	NA	191	190	185	233
Mortgage Income	Nil	Nil	Nil	Nil	NA	NA	Nil	Nil	Nil	Nil
Total Income	936	930	772	428	333	237	205	197	205	242
General Expenses	342	348	234	36.7	115	18.3	15.2	54.9	16.6	20.5
Interest Expense	179	203	204	141	106	66.8	66.7	82.0	91.6	95.3
Provision for Losses	Nil	Nil	Nil	Nil	NA	NA	Nil	Nil	Nil	Nil
Depreciation	201	232	234	120	91.9	49.0	81.7	42.1	42.0	43.5
Net Income	195	182	147	131	125	100	96.7	53.0	51.9	-61.2
S&P Core Earnings	195	182	141	131	108	99.3	87.4	49.1	38.6	NA

Balance Sheet & Other Financial Data (Million $)										
Cash	107	177	82.4	1.25	2,528	3.37	82.1	39.1	880	114
Total Assets	5,616	5,770	5,717	3,254	2,639	1,127	813	896	942	981
Real Estate Investment	6,293	NA	6,290	6,161	NA	NA	1,090	1,221	1,231	1,176
Loss Reserve	Nil	Nil	Nil	Nil	NA	NA	Nil	Nil	Nil	Nil
Net Investment	5,115	5,173	5,494	3,084	2,526	1,058	681	829	861	849
Short Term Debt	203	118	Nil	Nil	NA	NA	Nil	Nil	Nil	Nil
Capitalization:Debt	2,467	3,030	3,360	2,199	1,803	843	641	708	848	886
Capitalization:Equity	2,466	2,148	1,824	710	667	160	56.3	78.3	-91.1	-118
Capitalization:Total	4,951	5,456	5,320	2,939	2,470	1,034	56.3	816	788	799
% Earnings & Depreciation/Assets	6.9	7.2	8.4	8.5	NA	NA	20.9	10.4	9.8	NM
Price Times Book Value:High	2.9	3.5	3.5	6.5	NA	NA	43.3	NM	NM	NM
Price Times Book Value:Low	1.2	1.2	1.8	4.5	NA	NA	20.9	NM	NM	NM

Data as orig reptd.; bef. results of disc opers/spec. items. Per share data adj. for stk. divs.; EPS diluted. E-Estimated. NA-Not Available. NM-Not Meaningful. NR-Not Ranked. UR-Under Review.

Office: 111 South Wacker Drive, Suite 4800, Chicago, IL 60606.
Telephone: 877-483-6827.
Email: info@ventasreit.com
Website: http://www.ventasreit.com

Chrmn, Pres & CEO: D.A. Cafaro
EVP & CFO: R.A. Schweinhart
EVP, Chief Admin Officer, Secy & General Counsel: T.R. Riney
Chief Acctg Officer & Cntlr: R.J. Brehl

Investor Contact: L. Weiner (312-765-0390)
Board Members: D. A. Cafaro, D. Crocker, II, R. G. Geary, J. M. Gellert, R. D. Reed, S. Z. Rosenberg, G. J. Rufrano, J. D. Shelton, T. C. Theobald

Founded: 1983
Domicile: Delaware
Employees: 61

VeriSign Inc

STANDARD &POOR'S

S&P Recommendation	Price	12-Mo. Target Price	Investment Style
STRONG SELL ★ ☆ ☆ ☆ ☆	$32.86 (as of Oct 22, 2010)	$26.00	Large-Cap Blend

GICS Sector Information Technology
Sub-Industry Internet Software & Services

Summary This leading provider of infrastructure services that enable secure digital communications and commerce has recently sold many of its businesses to focus on core operations.

Key Stock Statistics (Source S&P, Vickers, company reports)

52-Wk Range	$32.93–21.21	S&P Oper. EPS 2010E	0.69	Market Capitalization(B)	$5.722	Beta	0.74
Trailing 12-Month EPS	$1.24	S&P Oper. EPS 2011E	1.00	Yield (%)	Nil	S&P 3-Yr. Proj. EPS CAGR(%)	20
Trailing 12-Month P/E	26.5	P/E on S&P Oper. EPS 2010E	47.6	Dividend Rate/Share	Nil	S&P Credit Rating	NA
$10K Invested 5 Yrs Ago	$14,617	Common Shares Outstg. (M)	174.1	Institutional Ownership (%)	NM		

Price Performance

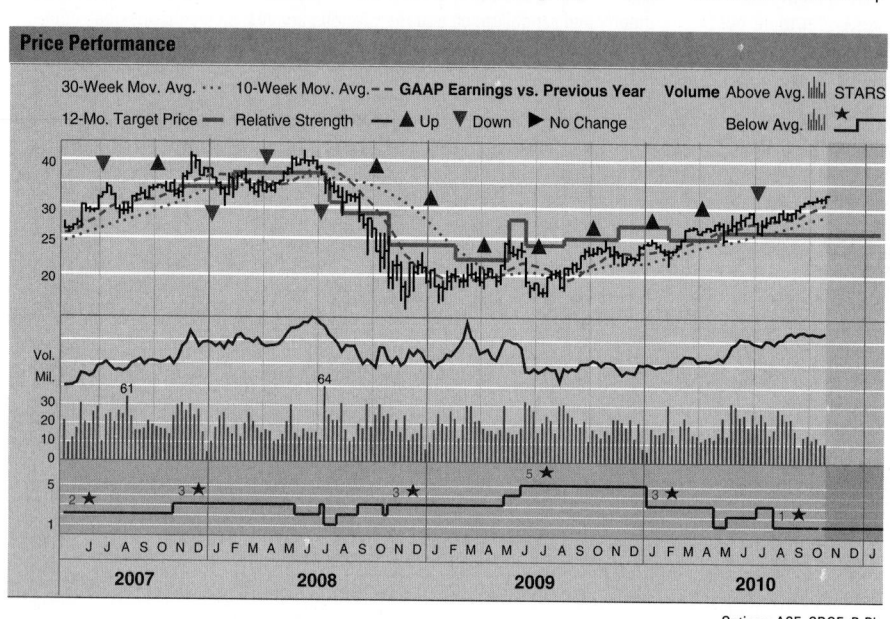

30-Week Mov. Avg. · · · · 10-Week Mov. Avg. – – GAAP Earnings vs. Previous Year Volume Above Avg. STARS
12-Mo. Target Price — Relative Strength — ▲ Up ▼ Down ▶ No Change Below Avg. ★

Options: ASE, CBOE, P, Ph

Analysis prepared by **Scott H. Kessler** on August 05, 2010, when the stock traded at **$29.55.**

Highlights

➤ Revenues from continuing operations rose 6% from 2009, despite the adverse effects of the global recession, including some pricing pressures. We project growth of around 10% for 2010 and 8% for 2011.

➤ We believe annual margins bottomed in 2009, reflecting a challenging economic backdrop and expenses related to notable divestiture activity. We think a more focused VRSN will be able to more effectively pursue sales opportunities and efficiencies, and we project higher margins in 2010 and 2011.

➤ VRSN continues to focus on significant stock-buyback activity, with an additional authorization of $1.1 billion in July 2010 (bringing the amount authorized and available to $1.5 billion). VRSN has pursued notable divestitures in recent years, including the late 2008 sale of a joint venture stake for some $200 million and the May 2009 sale of its communications unit for about $230 million. In May 2010, VRSN announced a proposed agreement to sell its authentication security business for $1.3 billion.

Investment Rationale/Risk

➤ Four high level executives left in 2008, including former CEO Bill Roper. Former VRSN executive Mark McLaughlin re-joined VRSN as president and COO in early 2009 and was named CEO in August 2009. We see VRSN as a more focused and profitable market leader. However, we believe the stock already reflects benefits related to divestiture and buyback activity, and we see it as notably overvalued in light of a largely mature business and substantial P/E and P/E-to-growth multiples.

➤ Risks to our opinion and target price include sustained strength in its core business, and more successful actions intended to generate shareholder value than we foresee.

➤ Applying a 37% premium to the P/E-to-growth multiple of the S&P 500 Internet Software & Services sub-industry results leads to our 12-month target price of $26. We believe VRSN should trade at a premium to peers given the barriers to entry in, and considerable profitability of its operations. However, we see the recent premium of more than 50% as excessive, especially given so much recent change at the company and a notable pending lawsuit.

Qualitative Risk Assessment

LOW	MEDIUM	**HIGH**

Our risk assessment reflects what we consider the emerging nature of, and notable competition in, many of the company's businesses, substantial corporate transactional activity since 2004, and numerous one-time items appearing in the company's recent financials.

Quantitative Evaluations

S&P Quality Ranking   **B-**

D	C	**B-**	B	B+	A-	A	A+

Relative Strength Rank   **STRONG**

72

LOWEST = 1   HIGHEST = 99

Revenue/Earnings Data

Revenue (Million $)

	1Q	2Q	3Q	4Q	Year
2010	264.4	168.7	--	--	--
2009	255.0	256.6	258.0	262.7	1,031
2008	232.5	239.2	243.0	247.0	961.7
2007	373.1	363.2	373.6	386.4	1,496
2006	372.8	390.7	399.5	412.2	1,575
2005	401.0	444.8	414.8	392.1	1,609

Earnings Per Share ($)

	1Q	2Q	3Q	4Q	Year
2010	0.29	0.14	E0.17	E0.21	E0.69
2009	0.24	0.22	0.25	0.33	1.03
2008	0.08	-0.07	0.21	0.24	0.46
2007	0.24	-0.02	0.07	-0.88	-0.61
2006	0.06	1.52	0.06	-0.12	1.53
2005	0.17	0.14	0.17	0.07	0.53

Fiscal year ended Dec. 31. Next earnings report expected: Early November. EPS Estimates based on S&P Operating Earnings; historical GAAP earnings are as reported.

Dividend Data

No cash dividends have been paid.

VeriSign Inc

Business Summary August 05, 2010

CORPORATE OVERVIEW. VeriSign, Inc. provides Internet infrastructure services for the networked world, offering products and services that help organizations communicate and conduct commerce. After notable divestiture activity, as of December 2008, VRSN's had two operating segments: Internet Infrastructure and Identity Services (3IS) and Other Services.

3IS consists of Naming Services, SSL Certificate Services, Identity and Authentication Services (IAS) and VeriSign Japan. Other Services includes continuing operations of non-core businesses and legacy products and services from divested businesses.

In May 2010, VRSN announced the proposed sale of its authentication security businesses, including the SSL and IAS units and VeriSign Japan, for some $1.3 billion. We expect this transaction to close in August 2010.

Naming Services is the directory provider for all .com, .net, .cc., .tv, .name and .jobs domain names. SSL Certificate Services enables enterprises and online merchants to implement and operate secure networks and websites, allowing customers to authenticate themselves and encrypt communications. IAS includes identity protection services, fraud detection services, managed public key infrastructure (PKI) services, and unified authentication services, all of

which are intended to help enterprises secure intranets, extranets and other applications and devices, and provide for authentication. VeriSign Japan is a majority-owned subsidiary with offerings similar to SSL Certificate Services and IAS.

In June 2009, an antitrust suit filed against the company in 2005 was essentially reinstated, in our view. It challenges VRSN's .com contract, and we think that even though the company will retain this key business, this development could result in restrained price increases or even reductions. We also see significant associated legal expenses. In June 2010, a federal appeals court allowed the case to proceed.

Nonetheless, in December 2009, VRSN announced registry increases, effective July 1, 2010, for the fees for .com to $7.34 from $6.86, and .net to $4.65 from $4.23, consistent with the company's agreements with ICANN (Internet Corporation for Assigned Names and Numbers), the related oversight authority.

Company Financials Fiscal Year Ended Dec. 31

Per Share Data ($)	2009	2008	2007	2006	2005	2004	2003	2002	2001	2000
Tangible Book Value	1.29	NM	2.17	2.44	2.98	2.92	3.16	1.89	3.50	4.15
Cash Flow	1.47	1.10	0.36	2.47	1.25	1.05	-0.61	0.16	1.63	0.64
Earnings	1.03	0.46	-0.61	1.53	0.53	0.72	-1.08	-20.97	-65.64	-19.57
S&P Core Earnings	1.02	0.73	-0.30	1.45	NA	0.01	-1.75	-8.79	-35.05	NA
Dividends	Nil	Nil	Nil	Nil	Nil	Nil	Nil	Nil	Nil	Nil
Payout Ratio	Nil	Nil	Nil	Nil	Nil	Nil	Nil	Nil	Nil	Nil
Prices:High	24.99	42.50	41.96	26.77	33.67	36.09	17.55	39.23	97.75	258.50
Prices:Low	16.89	16.23	22.92	15.95	19.01	14.94	6.55	3.92	26.25	65.38
P/E Ratio:High	24	92	NM	17	64	50	NM	NM	NM	NM
P/E Ratio:Low	16	35	NM	10	36	21	NM	NM	NM	NM

Income Statement Analysis (Million $)										
Revenue	1,031	962	1,496	1,575	1,609	1,166	1,055	1,222	984	475
Operating Income	416	387	309	340	416	242	304	287	277	70.0
Depreciation	86.3	128	231	232	191	85.6	114	5,000	13,687	3,217
Interest Expense	47.4	41.1	18.3	Nil	Nil	Nil	Nil	149	20.7	Nil
Pretax Income	281	119	-130	140	248	214	-237	-4,951	-13,433	-3,114
Effective Tax Rate	28.5%	39.5%	NM	NM	42.2%	12.9%	NM	NM	NM	NM
Net Income	198	88.3	-145	378	139	186	-260	-4,961	-13,356	-3,115
S&P Core Earnings	195	146	-72.0	359	-1.39	2.76	-421	-2,080	-7,134	NA

Balance Sheet & Other Financial Data (Million $)										
Cash	1,477	789	1,378	501	477	331	394	282	306	460
Current Assets	1,709	1,625	1,750	1,332	1,228	1,006	880	604	1,091	1,186
Total Assets	2,470	2,726	4,023	3,974	3,173	2,593	2,100	2,391	7,538	19,195
Current Liabilities	886	977	946	1,359	938	700	555	665	834	665
Long Term Debt	574	1,262	1,265	Nil	Nil	Nil	Nil	Nil	Nil	Nil
Common Equity	550	169	1,528	2,377	2,032	1,692	1,414	1,579	6,506	18,471
Total Capital	1,173	1,362	2,851	2,449	2,092	1,728	1,443	1,579	6,533	18,471
Capital Expenditures	117	104	152	182	140	92.5	108	176	380	58.8
Cash Flow	284	221	85.9	609	330	272	-145	38.9	331	101
Current Ratio	1.9	1.7	1.9	1.0	1.3	1.4	1.6	0.9	1.3	1.8
% Long Term Debt of Capitalization	49.0	92.6	44.4	Nil	Nil	Nil	Nil	Nil	Nil	Nil
% Net Income of Revenue	19.2	9.2	NM	24.0	8.6	16.0	NM	NM	NM	NM
% Return on Assets	7.8	2.6	NM	10.6	4.8	7.9	NM	NM	NM	NM
% Return on Equity	65.8	10.4	NM	17.1	7.4	12.1	NM	NM	NM	NM

Data as orig reptd.; bef. results of disc opers/spec. items. Per share data adj. for stk. divs.; EPS diluted. E-Estimated. NA-Not Available. NM-Not Meaningful. NR-Not Ranked. UR-Under Review.

Office: 487 East Middlefield Road, Mountain View, CA 94043.
Telephone: 650-961-7500.
Website: http://www.verisign.com
Chrmn: D.J. Bidzos

Pres & CEO: M.D. McLaughlin
EVP, CFO & Chief Acctg Officer: B.G. Robins
SVP & CTO: K.J. Silva
SVP, Secy & General Counsel: R.H. Goshorn

Investor Contact: K. Bond (650-426-3744)
Board Members: D. J. Bidzos, W. Chenevich, K. A. Cote, M. D. McLaughlin, R. H. Moore, J. D. Roach, L. A. Simpson, T. Tomlinson

Founded: 1995
Domicile: Delaware
Employees: 2,328

Verizon Communications Inc

STANDARD &POOR'S

S&P Recommendation HOLD ★★★☆☆	**Price** $32.35 (as of Oct 25, 2010)	**12-Mo. Target Price** $32.00	**Investment Style** Large-Cap Value

GICS Sector Telecommunication Services
Sub-Industry Integrated Telecommunication Services

Summary VZ offers wireline, wireless and broadband services primarily in the northeastern United States. It acquired MCI Inc in 2006 and has since sold or spun off non-core assets. Alltel was acquired in early 2009.

Key Stock Statistics (Source S&P, Vickers, company reports)

52-Wk Range	$34.13– 25.99	S&P Oper. EPS 2010E	2.28	Market Capitalization(B)	$91.445	Beta	0.63
Trailing 12-Month EPS	$0.26	S&P Oper. EPS 2011E	2.42	Yield (%)	6.03	S&P 3-Yr. Proj. EPS CAGR(%)	6
Trailing 12-Month P/E	NM	P/E on S&P Oper. EPS 2010E	14.2	Dividend Rate/Share	$1.95	S&P Credit Rating	A
$10K Invested 5 Yrs Ago	NA	Common Shares Outstg. (M)	2,826.7	Institutional Ownership (%)	52		

Price Performance

- 30-Week Mov. Avg. ···
- 10-Week Mov. Avg. - - -
- GAAP Earnings vs. Previous Year
- Volume Above Avg. ▐▐▐ STARS
- 12-Mo. Target Price —
- Relative Strength —
- ▲ Up ▼ Down ▶ No Change
- Below Avg. ▐▐▐ ★

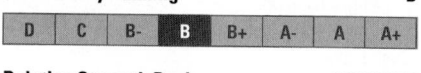

Options: ASE, CBOE, P, Ph

Analysis prepared by **Todd Rosenbluth** on October 25, 2010, when the stock traded at **$ 32.43**.

Highlights

▶ We forecast revenues of $107 billion in 2010 and $108 billion in 2011, driven by increases in wireless and data services. On the wireline side, we think the penetration of FiOS services will offset pressure in the mass markets consumer group, but overall segment revenues will be hurt by weakness in wholesale. Meanwhile, we expect the enterprise segment to be stable, even as unemployment remains high.

▶ We estimate that the EBITDA margin will average 33% in 2011, down slightly from the 34% we project for the 2010 fourth quarter. We expect higher pension expenses, due to weakness in VZ's investments in prior years and increased handset subsidies. However, we believe cost synergies in wireless and work force reduction benefits will provide an offset.

▶ We forecast operating EPS of $2.28 for 2010 and see growth to $2.42 in 2011, excluding the impact of one-time items related to taxes and work force reductions. During the first half of 2010, VZ generated $0.12 of EPS from assets that have since been spun off or sold.

Investment Rationale/Risk

▶ We believe VZ's wireless business remains in strong shape despite competitive and economic pressures. The global enterprise segment is facing some macroeconomic headwinds including high unemployment and should lag a broader market recovery. However, we are encouraged by the relative stability in VZ's wireline segment in the first nine months of 2010, helped by FiOS gains. In our view, VZ's dividend is secure and well supported by its free cash flow. We view the shares as fairly valued.

▶ Risks to our recommendation and target price include a greater impact from a depressed economy, pricing pressures, a weaker balance sheet, and the cost and level of success of fiber-based services.

▶ Our blended 12-month target price of $32 is based on a forward P/E multiple of 13X, a slight premium to the broader market to reflect VZ's relatively stronger balance sheet and the stability of its dividend payments. VZ has a 6% dividend yield, which we think offers support to the shares, given low Treasury bond yields.

Qualitative Risk Assessment

LOW	MEDIUM	HIGH

Our risk assessment reflects our view of VZ's strong cash flow generation and the pricing power it has over its suppliers, offset by the competitive conditions it faces offering telecom services.

Quantitative Evaluations

S&P Quality Ranking B

D	C	B-	B	B+	A-	A	A+

Relative Strength Rank MODERATE

53

LOWEST = 1   HIGHEST = 99

Revenue/Earnings Data

Revenue (Million $)

	1Q	2Q	3Q	4Q	Year
2010	26,913	26,773	--	--	--
2009	26,591	26,861	27,265	27,091	107,808
2008	23,833	24,124	24,752	24,645	97,354
2007	22,584	23,273	23,772	23,840	93,469
2006	21,221	21,876	22,449	22,598	88,144
2005	18,179	18,569	19,038	19,326	75,112

Earnings Per Share ($)

	1Q	2Q	3Q	4Q	Year
2010	0.14	-0.07	E0.53	E0.58	E2.28
2009	0.58	0.52	0.41	-0.23	1.29
2008	0.57	0.65	0.59	0.43	2.26
2007	0.51	0.58	0.44	0.37	1.90
2006	0.57	0.43	0.53	0.48	1.87
2005	0.63	0.75	0.67	0.59	2.65

Fiscal year ended Dec. 31. Next earnings report expected: Late October. EPS Estimates based on S&P Operating Earnings; historical GAAP earnings are as reported.

Dividend Data (Dates: mm/dd Payment Date: mm/dd/yy)

Amount ($)	Date Decl.	Ex-Div. Date	Stk. of Record	Payment Date
0.475	03/05	04/07	04/09	05/03/10
Stk.	06/01	07/02	06/07	07/01/10
0.475	06/03	07/07	07/09	08/02/10
0.488	09/02	10/06	10/08	11/01/10

Dividends have been paid since 1984. Source: Company reports.

Please read the Required Disclosures and Analyst Certification on the last page of this report.

The McGraw-Hill Companies

Verizon Communications Inc

STANDARD &POOR'S

Business Summary October 25, 2010

CORPORATE OVERVIEW. As of September 2010, Verizon Communications (VZ) provided wireline service to 26.5 million access lines (down 8.5% from a year earlier excluding those sold), and, through its joint venture with Vodafone Group, had 93 million wireless customers plus approximately 8 million additional other connected devices on its network. We think the relationship with Vodafone remains strong and is unlikely to change.

MARKET PROFILE. Verizon Wireless added 1 million net subscribers in the third quarter of 2010 (584,000 retail post-paid customers), and, together with peer AT&T, we think it continued to capture market share as it did in 2009. Strong wireless rivalry has raised the level of competition, in our view, with new unlimited service plans and data-equipped devices gaining significant appeal in a highly penetrated market. As of September 2010, Verizon Wireless had a 1.4% monthly total churn rate, and its retail post-paid monthly service revenue per user was $52, up 2% from a year earlier. Wireless data average revenue per user rose 19% in the third quarter of 2010 and comprised 36% of service revenues. The segment's EBITDA service margin of 47% was the best in the industry. As of September 2010, 23% of Verizon Wireless's retail post-paid customers had a smartphone, and as this percentage grows, particularly helped by Android devices, we expect data revenues to increase.

Verizon also serves the Internet market through its wireline broadband offerings (8.3 million connections) and has increased the speed of its connectivity in what we view as an effort to upgrade DSL subscribers. However, the traditional DSL customer base began to decline in early 2009, slowed by the effects of the economy and new, faster fiber offerings gaining traction; this has continued in 2010.

In the first nine months of 2010, revenues at VZ's global enterprise segment declined only 0.4%, year to year, versus the 4.5% decrease in the fourth quarter of 2009. In April 2010, VZ said it experienced improving long distance volume trends during the first quarter, but we still believe the segment will lag an economic recovery.

COMPETITIVE LANDSCAPE. VZ's wireline segment competes for broadband and now telephony customers against cable companies Cablevision and Comcast. At the end of September 2010, nearly 13 million homes and businesses were able to buy VZ's advanced fiber-based broadband services (FiOS), many of which also had access to FiOS video.

Company Financials Fiscal Year Ended Dec. 31

Per Share Data ($)	2009	2008	2007	2006	2005	2004	2003	2002	2001	2000
Tangible Book Value	NM	NM	NM	NM	NM	NM	NM	NM	NM	12.79
Cash Flow	7.10	7.37	6.85	1.87	7.61	7.67	6.14	6.56	5.22	8.43
Earnings	1.29	2.26	1.90	1.87	2.65	2.59	1.27	1.67	0.22	3.95
S&P Core Earnings	2.03	1.72	1.85	1.87	2.42	2.76	1.76	1.91	0.58	NA
Dividends	1.85	1.75	1.65	1.62	1.60	1.54	1.54	1.54	1.54	1.54
Payout Ratio	144%	77%	88%	86%	60%	60%	121%	92%	NM	39%
Prices:High	34.76	44.32	46.24	38.95	41.06	42.27	44.31	51.09	57.40	66.00
Prices:Low	26.10	23.07	35.60	30.04	29.13	34.13	31.10	26.01	43.80	39.06
P/E Ratio:High	27	20	25	21	15	16	35	31	NM	17
P/E Ratio:Low	20	10	19	16	11	13	24	16	NM	10

Income Statement Analysis (Million $)	2009	2008	2007	2006	2005	2004	2003	2002	2001	2000
Revenue	107,808	97,354	93,469	88,144	75,112	71,283	67,752	67,625	67,190	64,707
Depreciation	16,532	14,565	14,377	14,545	14,047	13,910	13,617	13,423	13,657	12,261
Maintenance	NA	NA	NA	NA	NA	NA	NA	NA	NA	NA
Construction Credits	NA	NA	NA	NA	NA	NA	NA	NA	NA	NA
Effective Tax Rate	10.5%	20.9%	27.4%	21.9%	23.5%	22.8%	19.7%	21.7%	64.2%	38.9%
Net Income	3,651	6,428	5,510	5,480	7,397	7,261	3,509	4,584	590	10,810
S&P Core Earnings	5,778	4,893	5,370	5,467	6,774	7,724	4,859	5,250	1,557	NA

Balance Sheet & Other Financial Data (Million $)	2009	2008	2007	2006	2005	2004	2003	2002	2001	2000
Gross Property	228,518	215,605	213,994	204,109	193,610	185,522	180,975	178,028	169,586	158,957
Net Property	91,466	86,546	85,294	82,356	75,305	74,124	75,316	74,496	74,419	69,504
Capital Expenditures	17,047	17,238	17,538	17,101	15,324	13,259	11,884	11,984	17,371	17,633
Total Capital	145,523	137,633	125,856	121,788	120,714	120,819	118,935	122,120	116,888	115,923
Fixed Charges Coverage	4.6	9.4	8.6	5.9	6.7	5.1	2.5	5.5	3.6	3.7
Capitalization:Long Term Debt	55,051	46,959	28,203	28,646	31,869	35,674	39,413	44,791	45,657	42,491
Capitalization:Preferred	Nil	Nil	Nil	Nil	Nil	Nil	Nil	Nil	Nil	Nil
Capitalization:Common	41,606	41,706	50,581	48,535	39,680	37,560	33,466	33,720	32,539	36,342
% Return on Revenue	3.4	6.6	5.9	6.2	9.8	10.2	5.2	6.8	0.9	16.7
% Return on Invested Capital	9.4	10.5	9.5	9.8	10.5	8.6	5.1	7.6	4.0	15.4
% Return on Common Equity	8.8	13.9	11.1	12.4	19.2	20.4	10.6	13.5	1.8	33.5
% Earned on Net Property	15.8	19.7	18.6	17.2	37.9	36.2	28.1	34.5	50.5	38.3
% Long Term Debt of Capitalization	57.0	53.0	35.8	37.1	44.5	48.7	54.1	36.6	58.4	53.9
Capital % Preferred	Nil	Nil	Nil	Nil	Nil	Nil	Nil	Nil	Nil	Nil
Capitalization:% Common	43.0	47.0	64.2	62.9	55.5	51.3	45.9	42.9	41.6	46.1

Data as orig reptd.; bef. results of disc opers/spec. items. Per share data adj. for stk. divs.; EPS diluted. E-Estimated. NA-Not Available. NM-Not Meaningful. NR-Not Ranked. UR-Under Review.

Office: 1095 Avenue of the Americas, New York, NY 10036.
Telephone: 212-395-2121.
Website: http://www.verizon.com
Chrmn & CEO: I.G. Seidenberg

Pres & COO: L.C. McAdam
EVP & CFO: J.F. Killian
EVP & CTO: R.J. Lynch
EVP & General Counsel: R.S. Milch

Investor Contact: C. Webster (212-395-1000)
Board Members: R. L. Carrion, M. F. Keeth, R. W. Lane, S. O. Moose, J. Neubauer, D. T. Nicolaisen, T. H. O'Brien, Jr., C. Otis, Jr., H. B. Price, I. G. Seidenberg, R. E. Slater, J. W. Snow, J. R. Stafford

Founded: 1983
Domicile: Delaware
Employees: 222,927

The McGraw-Hill Companies

V.F. Corp

STANDARD &POOR'S

S&P Recommendation STRONG BUY ★★★★★

Price	12-Mo. Target Price	Investment Style
$86.00 (as of Oct 22, 2010)	$106.00	Large-Cap Blend

GICS Sector Consumer Discretionary
Sub-Industry Apparel, Accessories & Luxury Goods

Summary This global apparel company, with leading shares in denim and daypacks, is transforming itself into a designer and marketer of lifestyle apparel brands.

Key Stock Statistics (Source S&P, Vickers, company reports)

52-Wk Range	$89.30– 69.24	S&P Oper. EPS 2010E	6.32	Market Capitalization(B)	$9.289	Beta	0.98
Trailing 12-Month EPS	$5.01	S&P Oper. EPS 2011E	6.75	Yield (%)	2.93	S&P 3-Yr. Proj. EPS CAGR(%)	8
Trailing 12-Month P/E	17.2	P/E on S&P Oper. EPS 2010E	13.6	Dividend Rate/Share	$2.52	S&P Credit Rating	A-
$10K Invested 5 Yrs Ago	$18,760	Common Shares Outstg. (M)	108.0	Institutional Ownership (%)	88		

Price Performance

30-Week Mov. Avg. ··· 10-Week Mov. Avg. - - GAAP Earnings vs. Previous Year Volume Above Avg. STARS
12-Mo. Target Price — Relative Strength — ▲ Up ▼ Down ▶ No Change Below Avg. ★

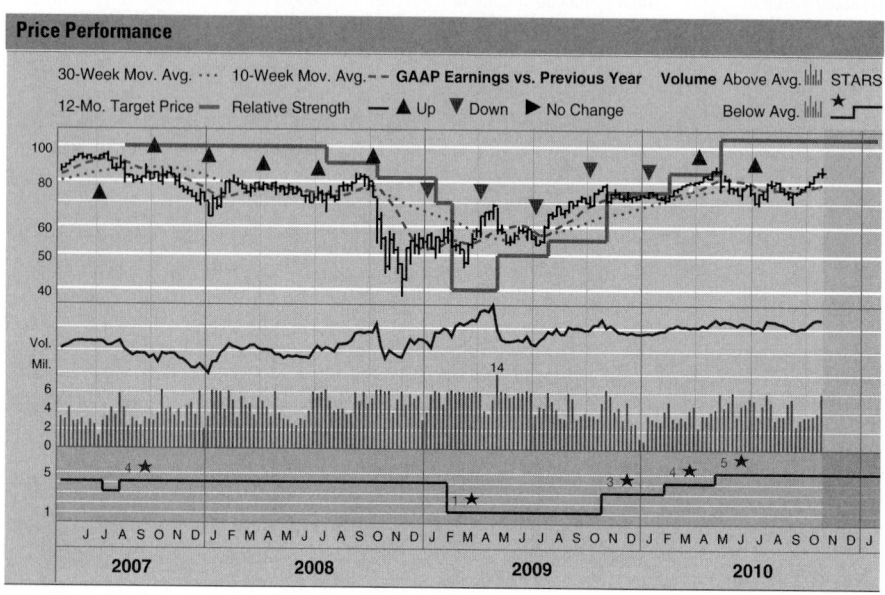

Options: CBOE

Analysis prepared by **Marie Driscoll, CFA** on October 22, 2010, when the stock traded at **$ 85.50**.

Highlights

► With improving trends across its brand portfolio, we see VFC taking the offensive to expand and support its multiple growth opportunities, specifically in the areas of outdoors and action sports and contemporary brands. We view Asia, new store growth, and VFC's power brands, Vans and The North Face, as 2010 and 2011 growth drivers.

► We see 2010 sales up 5%, to $7.6 billion, with outdoors and action sports up 13%, jeanswear flat, imagewear up 5%, and contemporary and sportswear down 1% and 2%, respectively. We estimate 150 bps of EBIT margin expansion in 2010, to 13.4%, following the 140 bps contraction of the past two years. We see 250 bps of gross margin expansion somewhat being offset by a 100 bps increase in the SG&A expense ratio, as VFC boosts marketing spending by $95 million to support its growth brands and growing regions. We see 6% sales growth in 2011 and 90 bps of gross margin contraction on higher input costs.

► After lower pension expense, which is expected to benefit EPS by $0.20, and a 25% effective tax rate, we estimate EPS of $6.32 for 2010 and $6.75 for 2011.

Investment Rationale/Risk

► While we assume weak global employment will affect consumer spending trends, we think a number of VFC's brands will continue to enjoy strong momentum going forward. We believe VFC's recent lifestyle brand acquisitions have superior long-term growth potential. In addition to outdoors and action sports and contemporary brands, 2010 growth priorities include China, social media, retail expansion, and e-commerce. EPS advanced 32% in the first nine months of 2010, on a 5% sales increase. With clean inventories entering the final quarter, we see continued opportunity for gross margin expansion.

► Risks to our recommendation and target price include worse than expected and/or slower economic and consumer rebounds.

► Our 12-month target price of $106 is derived by blending historical, peer and DCF valuation methodologies. Applying a peer forward P/E multiple of 19X to our 2011 EPS estimate of $6.75 generates a $128 value; VFC's five-year average forward multiple of 13.3X (in a range of 7X to 18X) produces a $90 value; and our DCF model generates a present value of $102, assuming a 10.7% WACC and a 3% terminal growth rate.

Qualitative Risk Assessment

LOW	MEDIUM	HIGH

Our risk assessment reflects our view of VFC's strong cash flow, offset by integration risk as VFC pursues growth via acquisitions.

Quantitative Evaluations

S&P Quality Ranking A

D	C	B-	B	B+	A-	A	A+

Relative Strength Rank STRONG

73

LOWEST = 1   HIGHEST = 99

Revenue/Earnings Data

Revenue (Million $)

	1Q	2Q	3Q	4Q	Year
2010	1,750	1,594	--	--	--
2009	1,725	1,486	2,094	1,915	7,220
2008	1,846	1,677	2,207	1,912	7,643
2007	1,674	1,517	2,073	1,955	7,219
2006	1,456	1,351	1,810	1,599	6,216
2005	1,582	1,452	1,822	1,646	6,502

Earnings Per Share ($)

2010	1.47	1.00	E2.07	E1.61	E6.32
2009	0.91	0.68	1.94	0.60	4.13
2008	1.33	0.94	2.10	1.05	5.42
2007	1.17	0.93	1.86	1.46	5.41
2006	1.05	0.80	1.64	1.24	4.73
2005	1.00	0.85	1.57	1.13	4.54

Fiscal year ended Dec. 31. Next earnings report expected: Late October. EPS Estimates based on S&P Operating Earnings; historical GAAP earnings are as reported.

Dividend Data (Dates: mm/dd Payment Date: mm/dd/yy)

Amount ($)	Date Decl.	Ex-Div. Date	Stk. of Record	Payment Date
0.600	02/11	03/05	03/09	03/19/10
0.600	04/30	06/04	06/08	06/18/10
0.600	07/22	09/08	09/10	09/20/10
0.630	10/21	12/08	12/10	12/20/10

Dividends have been paid since 1941. Source: Company reports.

Please read the Required Disclosures and Analyst Certification on the last page of this report.

The **McGraw·Hill** Companies

V.F. Corp

Business Summary October 22, 2010

CORPORATE OVERVIEW. VF Corp. is the world's largest apparel manufacturer, and holds the leading position in several market categories, including jean-swear, workwear and daypacks. In early 2004, VFC developed a growth plan to support its long-term sales growth target of 8%-10% annually, its 15% operating margin goal, and a 17% return on invested capital goal. The growth strategy consists of six drivers: building new, growing lifestyle brands; expanding share with successful retailers; growing internationally; leveraging supply chain and information technology; identifying, developing and recruiting qualified leaders; and expanding its direct to consumer business.

MARKET PROFILE. VFC participates in the broad apparel market, spanning product categories from women's activewear to denim, as well as the outdoor market for apparel and accessories via its lifestyle brands. Apparel is a mature market, with demand mirroring population growth and a modicum related to fashion; it is fragmented, with national brands marketed by 20 companies accounting for about 30% of total apparel sales and the remaining 70% comprised of smaller and/or private label "store" brands. Deflationary pricing pressure is, we think, a function of channel competition and production steadily moving offshore to low-cost producers in Asia, especially India and China.

S&P forecast a 2% increase in 2010 apparel sales, following the 5% decrease of 2009, a 4% decline in 2008 and 4% gains in 2007 and 2006.

According to the SGMA (Sporting Goods Manufacturers Association), wholesale sales of sporting goods and fitness equipment (excluding recreational transport such as bikes, boats and snowmobiles), sports apparel, athletic footwear and licensed merchandise in the U.S. declined 4%, to $71.8 billion in 2009. Apparel represents about 39% of the mix, footwear 18%, equipment 33%, and licensed merchandise 10%. Sports apparel and footwear brands more frequently serve a fashion market than a true athletic or active sports market; generally only a third of sports apparel and footwear is purchased with the intent that it will be used in an active sport, according to the NPD Group. For 2010, SGMA projects a 2% gain in branded sports apparel at wholesale and 3% for athletic footwear.

Company Financials Fiscal Year Ended Dec. 31

Per Share Data ($)	2009	2008	2007	2006	2005	2004	2003	2002	2001	2000
Tangible Book Value	7.90	7.54	7.86	13.18	8.78	7.56	8.61	10.91	9.97	9.71
Cash Flow	5.66	6.72	6.48	5.74	5.56	5.53	4.64	4.35	0.00	3.73
Earnings	4.13	5.42	5.41	4.73	4.54	4.21	3.61	3.24	1.19	2.27
S&P Core Earnings	5.20	4.98	5.31	4.82	4.67	4.36	3.70	2.75	0.77	NA
Dividends	2.37	2.33	2.23	1.94	1.10	1.05	1.01	0.97	0.93	0.89
Payout Ratio	57%	43%	41%	41%	24%	25%	28%	30%	78%	39%
Prices:High	79.79	84.60	96.20	83.10	61.61	55.61	44.08	45.64	42.70	36.90
Prices:Low	46.06	38.22	68.15	53.25	50.44	42.06	32.62	31.50	28.15	20.94
P/E Ratio:High	19	16	18	18	14	13	12	14	36	16
P/E Ratio:Low	11	7	13	11	11	10	9	10	24	9

Income Statement Analysis (Million $)	2009	2008	2007	2006	2005	2004	2003	2002	2001	2000
Revenue	7,220	7,643	7,219	6,216	6,502	6,055	5,207	5,084	5,519	5,748
Operating Income	1,029	1,124	1,081	935	944	874	718	729	516	683
Depreciation	170	144	122	108	116	141	104	107	169	173
Interest Expense	85.9	94.1	72.1	57.3	70.6	76.1	61.4	71.3	93.4	88.7
Pretax Income	655	848	906	777	771	712	599	562	263	432
Effective Tax Rate	30.0%	28.9%	32.3%	31.2%	32.7%	33.3%	33.5%	35.1%	47.6%	38.1%
Net Income	461	603	613	535	519	475	398	364	138	267
S&P Core Earnings	581	554	602	544	532	490	406	303	84.6	NA

Balance Sheet & Other Financial Data (Million $)	2009	2008	2007	2006	2005	2004	2003	2002	2001	2000
Cash	732	382	322	343	297	486	515	496	332	119
Current Assets	2,629	2,653	2,645	2,578	2,365	2,379	2,209	2,075	2,031	2,110
Total Assets	6,488	6,434	6,447	5,466	5,171	5,004	4,246	3,503	4,103	4,358
Current Liabilities	1,093	1,012	1,134	1,015	1,152	1,372	872	875	814	1,006
Long Term Debt	938	1,104	1,145	635	648	557	956	602	904	905
Common Equity	3,832	3,556	3,577	3,265	2,808	2,513	1,951	1,658	2,113	2,192
Total Capital	4,971	4,662	4,722	3,901	3,479	3,096	2,938	2,297	3,062	3,145
Capital Expenditures	85.9	124	114	127	110	81.4	86.6	64.5	81.6	125
Cash Flow	632	747	735	643	635	615	502	472	304	437
Current Ratio	2.4	2.6	2.3	2.5	2.1	1.7	2.5	2.4	2.5	2.1
% Long Term Debt of Capitalization	18.9	24.3	24.2	16.3	18.6	18.0	32.6	26.2	29.5	28.8
% Net Income of Revenue	6.4	7.9	8.5	8.6	7.9	7.8	7.6	7.2	2.5	4.6
% Return on Assets	7.1	9.4	10.3	10.1	10.2	10.3	10.3	9.6	3.3	6.4
% Return on Equity	12.5	16.9	17.9	17.6	19.5	21.3	22.1	19.3	6.3	12.1

Data as orig reptd.; bef. results of disc opers/spec. items. Per share data adj. for stk. divs.; EPS diluted. E-Estimated. NA-Not Available. NM-Not Meaningful. NR-Not Ranked. UR-Under Review.

Office: 105 Corporate Center Boulevard, Greensboro, NC 27408.
Telephone: 336-424-6000.
Email: irrequest@vfc.com
Website: http://www.vfc.com

Chrmn, Pres & CEO: E.C. Wiseman
SVP & CFO: R.K. Shearer
Chief Admin Officer, Secy & General Counsel: C.S. Cummings
Chief Acctg Officer & Cntlr: B.W. Batten

Treas: F.C. Pickard, III
Investor Contact: C. Knoebel (336-424-6189)
Board Members: C. V. Bergh, R. T. Carucci, J. L. Chugg, J. E. De Bedout, U. O. Fairbairn, G. Fellows, R. J. Hurst, W. A. McCollough, C. Otis, Jr., M. R. Sharp, R. Viault, E. C. Wiseman

Founded: 1899
Domicile: Pennsylvania
Employees: 45,700

Viacom Inc

STANDARD &POOR'S

S&P Recommendation HOLD ★★★☆☆	**Price** $37.18 (as of Oct 22, 2010)	**12-Mo. Target Price** $38.00	**Investment Style** Large-Cap Blend

GICS Sector Consumer Discretionary
Sub-Industry Movies & Entertainment

Summary Among the well-known assets of this pure-play global provider of branded entertainment content are the MTV (domestic and international) and BET networks, Paramount Pictures (film studio), and Rock Band (casual online gaming).

Key Stock Statistics (Source S&P, Vickers, company reports)

52-Wk Range	$38.00–27.35	S&P Oper. EPS 2010E	2.98	Market Capitalization(B)	$20.679	Beta	1.26
Trailing 12-Month EPS	$2.99	S&P Oper. EPS 2011E	3.57	Yield (%)	1.61	S&P 3-Yr. Proj. EPS CAGR(%)	9
Trailing 12-Month P/E	12.4	P/E on S&P Oper. EPS 2010E	12.5	Dividend Rate/Share	$0.60	S&P Credit Rating	BBB+
$10K Invested 5 Yrs Ago	NA	Common Shares Outstg. (M)	608.2	Institutional Ownership (%)	90		

Price Performance

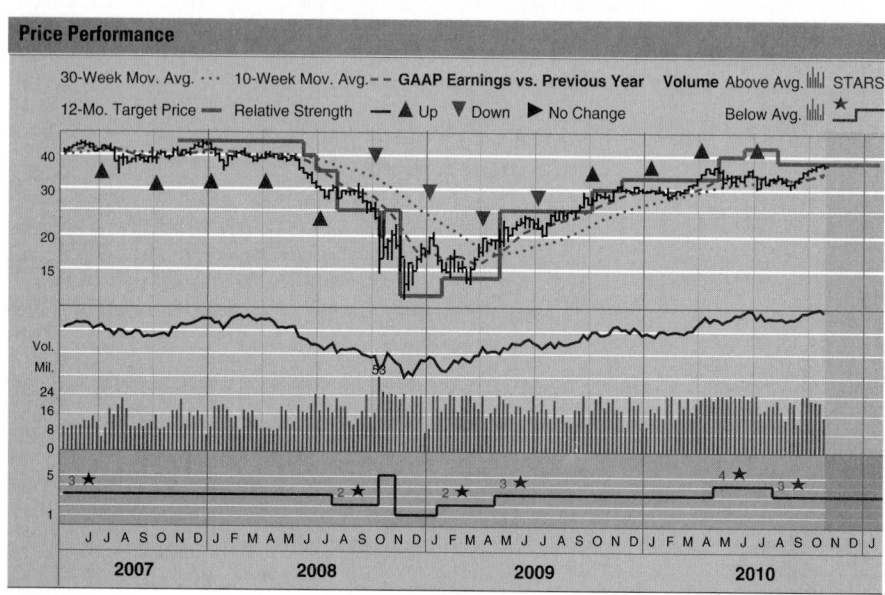

30-Week Mov. Avg. · · · 10-Week Mov. Avg. – – GAAP Earnings vs. Previous Year Volume Above Avg. STARS
12-Mo. Target Price — Relative Strength — ▲ Up ▼ Down ► No Change Below Avg. ★

2007 2008 2009 2010

Options: ASE, CBOE, P, Ph

Analysis prepared by **Tuna N. Amobi, CFA, CPA** on August 20, 2010, when the stock traded at **$ 31.68**.

Highlights

➤ Reflecting a pending transition to a new fiscal year end, we see FY 10 (Sep.) consolidated revenues down 1.7%, to $13.5 billion, then advancing 4.5% in FY 11, to almost $14.1 billion. Our overall outlook factors in a rebounding advertising environment, continued solid growth in worldwide affiliate fees, and relatively healthy contributions from worldwide TV licensing and ancillary revenues (assuming improved sales of Rock Band video games) -- versus difficult FY 10 film comparisons that should ease in FY 11.

➤ Still, improved overall results should benefit from enhanced operating leverage, reflecting recent restructuring measures. However, overall margins could be further adversely affected by continued losses on the Rock Band franchise, partly offset by higher-margin ads and growing digital revenues.

➤ We see total adjusted EBIT of about $3.6 billion and $3.7 billion in FY 10 and FY 11, respectively, and after interest and taxes, FY 10 and FY 11 operating EPS of $2.96 and $3.39 ($2.98 and $3.57 calendarized EPS for 2010 and 2011). In June, VIA.B reinstituted a $4 billion share buyback plan that was suspended in early 2009.

Investment Rationale/Risk

➤ While VIA.B's mixed results in the 2010 first half showed a relatively slow pace of domestic ads recovery, we expect the MTV and BET networks to further capitalize on gains from the recent upfront sales and a continued strong scatter market. While the upcoming film slate seems somewhat weak, we see further upside on key summer titles (Iron Man 2, The Last Airbender, Shrek 4) across the DVD and ancillary windows, while encouraged by the EPIX channel's new multi-year online streaming deal with Netflix. We see ample financial flexibility for modest dividend payouts and share buybacks.

➤ Risks to our recommendation and target price include a severe macroeconomic slowdown (for ads and DVD sales); a sharp ratings decline for the domestic networks; lingering strategic challenges for Rock Band; potential loss of film distribution deals with Dreamworks Animation and/or Marvel; and currency exposure.

➤ Our 12-month target price is $38, blending sum-of-the-parts analysis, 9X 2010E EV/EBITDA, and 1.4X P/E-to-growth, in line with less niche-focused entertainment peers -- also noting a recent 1.9% dividend yield on the shares.

Qualitative Risk Assessment

LOW	MEDIUM	HIGH

Our risk assessment reflects the company's leading demographically targeted brands, as well as our view of relatively encouraging but recently decelerating growth prospects and ample financial flexibility, offset by exposure to cyclical advertising and a volatile, hit-driven filmed entertainment business.

Quantitative Evaluations

S&P Quality Ranking   NR

D	C	B-	B	B+	A-	A	A+

Relative Strength Rank   **MODERATE**

68

LOWEST = 1   HIGHEST = 99

Revenue/Earnings Data

Revenue (Million $)

	1Q	2Q	3Q	4Q	Year
2010	2,786	3,301	--	--	--
2009	2,905	3,299	3,317	4,098	13,619
2008	3,117	3,857	3,408	4,243	14,625
2007	2,746	3,186	3,271	4,248	13,423
2006	2,368	2,847	2,660	3,593	11,467
2005	2,107	2,302	2,478	2,724	9,610

Earnings Per Share ($)

2010	0.40	0.68	E0.79	E1.11	E2.98
2009	0.29	0.46	0.73	1.14	2.62
2008	0.42	0.64	0.62	0.28	1.97
2007	0.29	0.63	0.67	0.84	2.41
2006	0.43	0.58	0.50	0.69	2.19
2005	0.48	0.48	--	0.29	1.73

Fiscal year ended Dec. 31. Next earnings report expected: Early November. EPS Estimates based on S&P Operating Earnings; historical GAAP earnings are as reported.

Dividend Data (Dates: mm/dd Payment Date: mm/dd/yy)

Amount ($)	Date Decl.	Ex-Div. Date	Stk. of Record	Payment Date
0.150	06/09	06/17	06/21	07/01/10
0.150	07/27	08/27	08/31	10/01/10

Dividends have been paid since 2010. Source: Company reports.

Please read the Required Disclosures and Analyst Certification on the last page of this report.

The McGraw·Hill Companies

Viacom Inc

Business Summary August 20, 2010

CORPORATE OVERVIEW. Viacom is one of the two public companies created after the January 2006 separation of the "old" Viacom into two independent public entities (the "old" Viacom was renamed CBS Corp.). Each Class A and B shareholder of the "old" Viacom received 0.5 of a share of the corresponding A or B stock of each of the new entities. We believe that the company is the faster growing of the two companies resulting from the separation, and is specifically targeted to growth-oriented investors.

The company's media networks segment (58% of 2009 revenues) is mainly comprised of MTV Networks (including MTV, Nickelodeon, VH1, Comedy Central, Country Music Television, Spike TV, TV Land, Logo, Neopets, Xfire and VIVA) and BET Networks. In November 2007, Viacom launched its Rock Band music video games franchise (which had passed $1 billion in sales as of March 2009). The entertainment segment (42%) mainly comprises Paramount Pictures film studio (and home entertainment). About 34% of 2009 revenues were derived from ad sales, 29% from feature films (theatrical and home video), 22% from affiliate fees, 11% from TV licensing, and 4% from other ancillary sources (including merchandise licensing).

CORPORATE STRATEGY. We see various digital initiatives, aided by partnerships with Internet and technology companies, such as pacts with Microsoft, Yahoo, Comcast/Fancast, AOL, Bebo, Dailymotion, Veoh, GoFish, and MeeVee. The company recently operated over 500 web sites, and has made several selective digital acquisitions since 2006 (mostly in online gaming and films) -- including Xfire, Y2M, Atom Entertainment, Harmonic Music, Quizilla, Teenage Mutant Ninja Turtles and Social Express. The company's global footprint traverses Europe and emerging markets (India and China) -- with over 166 MTVN channels across 161 countries in 28 languages, reaching nearly 450 million homes. The company recently made some strategic changes aimed to stem further downside risk on its Rock Band franchise, while making a broader strategic push into the casual gaming arena through some "tuck-in" acquisitions.

Company Financials Fiscal Year Ended Dec. 31

Per Share Data ($)	2009	2008	2007	2006	2005	2004	2003	2002	2001	2000
Tangible Book Value	NM	NM	NM	NM	NM	NM	NA	NA	NA	NA
Cash Flow	3.16	2.55	2.99	2.70	2.08	1.78	NA	NA	NA	NA
Earnings	2.62	1.97	2.41	2.19	1.73	1.48	NA	NA	NA	NA
S&P Core Earnings	2.65	2.01	2.34	2.22	1.46	1.47	NA	NA	NA	NA
Dividends	Nil	Nil	Nil	Nil	Nil	NA	NA	NA	NA	NA
Payout Ratio	Nil	Nil	Nil	Nil	Nil	NA	NA	NA	NA	NA
Prices:High	31.56	44.19	45.40	43.90	44.95	NA	NA	NA	NA	NA
Prices:Low	13.25	11.60	33.74	32.42	39.78	NA	NA	NA	NA	NA
P/E Ratio:High	12	22	19	20	26	NA	NA	NA	NA	NA
P/E Ratio:Low	5	6	14	15	23	NA	NA	NA	NA	NA

Income Statement Analysis (Million $)

	2009	2008	2007	2006	2005	2004	2003	2002	2001	2000
Revenue	13,619	14,625	13,423	11,467	9,610	8,132	7,304	6,051	NA	NA
Operating Income	3,295	3,341	3,404	3,137	2,625	2,534	2,218	1,932	NA	NA
Depreciation	331	364	393	366	259	2,522	198	195	NA	NA
Interest Expense	440	514	487	472	23.0	20.0	23.2	40.9	NA	NA
Pretax Income	2,276	1,855	2,579	2,322	2,328	2,017	1,938	1,641	NA	NA
Effective Tax Rate	31.1%	32.6%	36.0%	31.8%	43.8%	36.4%	40.6%	39.3%	NA	NA
Net Income	1,591	1,233	1,630	1,570	1,304	1,281	1,147	994	NA	NA
S&P Core Earnings	1,607	1,257	1,588	1,592	1,165	1,282	NA	NA	NA	NA

Balance Sheet & Other Financial Data (Million $)

	2009	2008	2007	2006	2005	2004	2003	2002	2001	2000
Cash	298	792	920	706	361	99.2	58.3	NA	NA	NA
Current Assets	4,430	4,502	4,833	4,211	3,513	2,384	3,213	NA	NA	NA
Total Assets	21,900	22,487	22,904	21,797	19,116	18,400	22,304	NA	NA	NA
Current Liabilities	3,751	4,842	5,273	4,617	3,269	2,617	3,766	NA	NA	NA
Long Term Debt	6,650	7,897	8,060	7,584	5,702	3,718	NA	NA	NA	NA
Common Equity	8,704	7,033	7,111	7,166	7,788	9,905	15,816	NA	NA	NA
Total Capital	15,450	14,980	15,312	14,932	13,534	13,623	16,441	NA	NA	NA
Capital Expenditures	141	288	237	210	193	NA	114	122	NA	NA
Cash Flow	1,922	1,597	2,023	1,936	1,563	1,533	1,345	1,189	NA	NA
Current Ratio	1.2	0.9	0.9	0.9	1.1	0.9	0.9	NA	NA	NA
% Long Term Debt of Capitalization	43.0	52.7	52.6	50.8	42.1	27.3	Nil	Nil	NA	NA
% Net Income of Revenue	11.7	8.4	12.2	13.7	13.6	15.8	15.7	16.4	NA	NA
% Return on Assets	7.2	5.4	7.3	7.7	6.9	NA	NA	NA	NA	NA
% Return on Equity	20.2	17.4	22.8	21.0	12.3	NA	NA	NA	NA	NA

Data as orig reptd.; bef. results of disc opers/spec. items. Per share data adj. for stk. divs.; EPS diluted. E-Estimated. NA-Not Available. NM-Not Meaningful. NR-Not Ranked. UR-Under Review.

Office: 1515 Broadway, New York, NY 10036.
Telephone: 212-258-6000.
Website: http://www.viacom.com
Chrmn: S.M. Redstone

Pres & CEO: P.P. Dauman
Vice Chrmn: S.E. Redstone
COO: T.E. Dooley
EVP, CFO & Chief Acctg Officer: J.W. Barge

Investor Contact: J. Bombassei (212-258-6700)
Board Members: G. S. Abrams, P. P. Dauman, T. E. Dooley, A. C. Greenberg, R. K. Kraft, B. J. McGarvie, C. E. Phillips, Jr., S. E. Redstone, S. M. Redstone, F. V. Salerno, W. Schwartz

Founded: 2005
Domicile: Delaware
Employees: 11,200

Visa Inc

STANDARD &POOR'S

S&P Recommendation	STRONG BUY ★★★★★	Price $79.29 (as of Oct 22, 2010)	12-Mo. Target Price $91.00	Investment Style Large-Cap Growth

GICS Sector Information Technology
Sub-Industry Data Processing & Outsourced Services

Summary Visa is the world's largest electronics payment network and leading payments brand, and provides services to consumers, businesses, and governments in more than 200 countries.

Key Stock Statistics (Source S&P, Vickers, company reports)

52-Wk Range	$97.19– 64.90	S&P Oper. EPS 2010**E**	3.86	Market Capitalization(B)	$39.381	Beta	0.86
Trailing 12-Month EPS	$3.71	S&P Oper. EPS 2011**E**	4.65	Yield (%)	0.76	S&P 3-Yr. Proj. EPS CAGR(%)	20
Trailing 12-Month P/E	21.4	P/E on S&P Oper. EPS 2010**E**	20.5	Dividend Rate/Share	$0.60	S&P Credit Rating	NA
$10K Invested 5 Yrs Ago	NA	Common Shares Outstg. (M)	840.1	Institutional Ownership (%)	84		

Price Performance

30-Week Mov. Avg. ··· 10-Week Mov. Avg. -- **GAAP Earnings vs. Previous Year** Volume Above Avg. STARS
12-Mo. Target Price — Relative Strength — ▲ Up ▼ Down ▶ No Change Below Avg. ★

Options: ASE, CBOE, Ph

Analysis prepared by **Zaineb Bokhari** on August 12, 2010, when the stock traded at **$ 73.54**.

Highlights

► We expect operating revenues to rise 15% in FY 10 (Sep.), to $7.95 billion. Domestically, we think solid growth in debit payment volumes and incremental improvements in credit volumes will drive service fees. We look for rising cross border payment volumes to drive international transaction fees. We are encouraged by the increasing volumes of transactions processed on Visa's platform, but note potential for some headwind arising from U.S. debit interchange regulation. In FY 11, we see operating revenues rising 13%.

► We see rebates and incentives rising to 17% of gross operating revenue in FY 10 and staying near this level in FY 11. Factors driving this outlook include the impact of bank consolidations on the size of card portfolios at V's largest clients, rising card usage, the greater proportion of multi-year contracts, and pricing. Given V's operating leverage and scale, we look for operating margins to widen to roughly 58% in FY 10, from 51% in FY 09. We expect operating margins to widen more modestly in FY 11.

► We estimate EPS of $3.86 in FY 10, and an increase to $4.65 in FY 11.

Investment Rationale/Risk

► We see a pickup in payment volumes in FY 10 and FY 11, aided by the secular trend toward non-cash payments and strong growth prospects for cards in emerging markets, which we think will help as the global economy continues to recover. V's preponderance of debit cards, which replace cash currency and are used for everyday purchases, is a positive, in our view, although we note the uncertainty created by domestic regulation aimed at regulating interchange on debit cards. V's ability to curtail expense growth will also help boost earnings. We are optimistic about growth initiatives that include expansion in prepaid cards and newer initiatives, such as mobile payments, money transfer, and e-commerce capabilities.

► Risks to our opinion and target price include regulations limiting interchange fees, negative outcomes to pending litigation, customer loss, and a sharp slowdown in consumer spending.

► Our 12-month target price of $91 is 19.5X our FY 11 EPS estimate, above the recent mean for Data Processing and Outsourced Services peers, warranted, we think, by V's market position and EPS growth.

Qualitative Risk Assessment

LOW	MEDIUM	HIGH

Our risk assessment reflects what we view as a dynamic market environment, tempered somewhat by pending litigation risks, an evolving competitive and regulatory environment, and prospect of sluggish domestic consumer spending.

Quantitative Evaluations

S&P Quality Ranking NR

D	C	B-	B	B+	A-	A	A+

Relative Strength Rank STRONG

73

LOWEST = 1   HIGHEST = 99

Revenue/Earnings Data

Revenue (Million $)

	1Q	2Q	3Q	4Q	Year
2010	1,960	1,959	2,029	--	--
2009	1,739	1,647	1,646	1,879	6,911
2008	1,488	1,453	1,613	1,709	6,263
2007	845.0	813.0	1,363	1,466	5,193
2006	--	--	--	--	3,899
2005	--	--	--	--	--

Earnings Per Share ($)

	1Q	2Q	3Q	4Q	Year
2010	1.02	0.96	0.97	E0.90	E3.86
2009	0.74	0.71	0.97	0.69	3.10
2008	0.55	0.39	0.51	-0.45	0.96
2007	--	0.23	0.42	-2.25	-1.15
2006	--	--	--	--	0.60
2005	--	--	--	--	--

Fiscal year ended Sep. 30. Next earnings report expected: Late October. EPS Estimates based on S&P Operating Earnings; historical GAAP earnings are as reported.

Dividend Data (Dates: mm/dd Payment Date: mm/dd/yy)

Amount ($)	Date Decl.	Ex-Div. Date	Stk. of Record	Payment Date
0.125	01/21	02/10	02/12	03/02/10
0.125	04/20	05/12	05/14	06/02/10
0.125	07/22	08/11	08/13	09/01/10
0.150	10/20	11/17	11/19	12/07/10

Dividends have been paid since 2008. Source: Company reports.

The McGraw·Hill Companies

Business Summary August 12, 2010

CORPORATE OVERVIEW. Visa Inc. (V) operates the world's largest retail electronic payments network, providing financial institutions with a broad range of platforms for consumer credit, debit, prepaid and commercial payments. In October 2007, V completed a reorganization via which Visa U.S.A., Visa International, Visa Canada and Inovant, which operated the VisaNet transaction processing system and other related processing systems, became subsidiaries of V.

V derives revenues primarily from card service fees, data processing fees, and international transaction fees. Service fees (39% of FY 09 (Sep.) gross operating revenue) reflect payments by customers for their participation in card programs carrying Visa brands. They also include acceptance fees, which are used to support merchant acceptance and ongoing volume growth initiatives. Data processing fees (30%) consist of fees charged to customers for providing transaction processing and other payment services, including processing services provided under V's bilateral services agreement with Visa Europe. International transaction fees (23%) are charged to customers on transactions where the issuer and the merchant are located in different countries. Its other revenues (8%) consist primarily of optional service or product enhancements, such as extended cardholder protection and concierge services, cardholder services and fees for licensing and certification, as well as licensing and other service-related fees from Visa Europe.

Payments volume, the basis for card service fee revenue, and transactions, which drive data processing revenue, are key drivers of V's business. Payments volume increased 1% to $2.67 trillion in FY 09, driven by 8% growth in transactions processed to $40.0 billion. V's operating revenues from its five largest customers represented approximately 32% (26% in FY 08) of its total operating revenues in FY 09. In addition, its operating revenues from its largest customer, JPMorgan Chase, accounted for 10% (8%) in FY 09.

CORPORATE STRATEGY. V seeks to grow by expanding its core payments business in new and established geographies and market segments, as well as by broadening its processing capabilities and value-added service offerings for payments and related opportunities. The company intends to continue to expand the size of its payments network to drive the issuance, acceptance and usage of its products globally. V believes that there is a significant opportunity for expanding the usage of its products and services in high-growth geographies in which it currently operates.

Company Financials Fiscal Year Ended Sep. 30

Per Share Data ($)	2009	2008	2007	2006	2005	2004	2003	2002	2001	2000
Tangible Book Value	2.48	NM	NM	NA	NA	NA	NA	NA	NA	NA
Cash Flow	3.40	0.95	NA	NA	NA	NA	NA	NA	NA	NA
Earnings	3.10	0.96	-1.15	0.60	NA	NA	NA	NA	NA	NA
S&P Core Earnings	1.91	1.63	1.87	0.57	NA	NA	NA	NA	NA	NA
Dividends	0.42	0.11	NA	NA	NA	NA	NA	NA	NA	NA
Payout Ratio	14%	11%	NA	NA	NA	NA	NA	NA	NA	NA
Prices:High	89.69	89.84	NA	NA	NA	NA	NA	NA	NA	NA
Prices:Low	41.78	43.54	NA	NA	NA	NA	NA	NA	NA	NA
P/E Ratio:High	29	94	NA	NA	NA	NA	NA	NA	NA	NA
P/E Ratio:Low	13	45	NA	NA	NA	NA	NA	NA	NA	NA

Income Statement Analysis (Million $)	2009	2008	2007	2006	2005	2004	2003	2002	2001	2000
Revenue	6,911	6,263	5,193	3,899	NA	NA	NA	NA	NA	NA
Operating Income	3,766	3,106	NA	NA	NA	NA	NA	NA	NA	NA
Depreciation	226	237	NA	NA	NA	NA	NA	NA	NA	NA
Interest Expense	115	143	NA	104	NA	NA	NA	NA	NA	NA
Pretax Income	4,000	1,336	-1,007	738	NA	NA	NA	NA	NA	NA
Effective Tax Rate	41.2%	39.8%	NM	37.0%	NA	NA	NA	NA	NA	NA
Net Income	2,353	804	-892	465	NA	NA	NA	NA	NA	NA
S&P Core Earnings	2,033	1,787	1,574	476	NA	NA	NA	NA	NA	NA

Balance Sheet & Other Financial Data (Million $)	2009	2008	2007	2006	2005	2004	2003	2002	2001	2000
Cash	4,732	6,287	7,935	NA	NA	NA	NA	NA	NA	NA
Current Assets	9,241	11,174	11,321	NA	NA	NA	NA	NA	NA	NA
Total Assets	32,281	34,981	33,250	NA	NA	NA	NA	NA	NA	NA
Current Liabilities	4,442	7,165	6,541	NA	NA	NA	NA	NA	NA	NA
Long Term Debt	44.0	55.0	40.0	NA	NA	NA	NA	NA	NA	NA
Common Equity	23,189	21,141	19,747	NA	NA	NA	NA	NA	NA	NA
Total Capital	23,249	26,143	24,560	NA	NA	NA	NA	NA	NA	NA
Capital Expenditures	306	415	NA	NA	NA	NA	NA	NA	NA	NA
Cash Flow	2,579	1,041	NA	NA	NA	NA	NA	NA	NA	NA
Current Ratio	2.1	1.6	1.7	NA	NA	NA	NA	NA	NA	NA
% Long Term Debt of Capitalization	0.2	0.2	0.2	Nil	NA	NA	NA	NA	NA	NA
% Net Income of Revenue	34.1	12.8	NM	11.9	NA	NA	NA	NA	NA	NA
% Return on Assets	7.0	2.4	NA	NA	NA	NA	NA	NA	NA	NA
% Return on Equity	10.6	3.9	NA	NA	NA	NA	NA	NA	NA	NA

Data as orig reptd.; bef. results of disc opers/spec. items. Per share data adj. for stk. divs.; EPS diluted. 2007 pro forma bal. sheet (as of Dec. 31, 2007) and income statement; per share data based on Class A and Class C common stock. E-Estimated. NA-Not Available. NM-Not Meaningful. NR-Not Ranked. UR-Under Review.

Office: P.O. Box 8999, San Francisco, CA 94128-8999.
Telephone: 415-932-2100.
Website: http://www.visa.com
Chrmn & CEO: J.W. Saunders

Pres: J. Partridge
CFO & Chief Acctg Officer: B.H. Pollitt, Jr.
Secy & General Counsel: J. Floum
Investor Contact: B.H. Pollitt (415-932-2213)

Board Members: H. Al-Qadi, G. P. Coughlan, M. B. Cranston, C. T. Doyle, J. F. Fernandez-Carbajal, P. Hawkins, S. N. Johnson, R. W. Matschullat, D. I. McKay, C. Minehan, D. J. Pang, J. W. Saunders, C. W. Scharf, S. Schulin-Zeuthen, W. S. Shanahan, J. A.

Founded: 2007
Domicile: Delaware
Employees: 5,700

The McGraw·Hill Companies

Vornado Realty Trust

S&P Recommendation HOLD ★★★☆☆

Price	12-Mo. Target Price	Investment Style
$91.06 (as of Oct 22, 2010)	$86.00	Large-Cap Blend

GICS Sector Financials
Sub-Industry Diversified REITS

Summary This real estate investment trust owns a diverse group of properties, including Northeast retail properties, New York City office buildings, and other interests.

Key Stock Statistics (Source S&P, Vickers, company reports)

52-Wk Range	$91.25– 56.54	S&P FFO/Sh. 2010E	5.25	Market Capitalization(B)	$16.599	Beta	1.78
Trailing 12-Month FFO/Share	NA	S&P FFO/Sh. 2011E	5.35	Yield (%)	1.67	S&P 3-Yr. FFO/Sh. Proj. CAGR(%)	3
Trailing 12-Month P/FFO	NA	P/FFO on S&P FFO/Sh. 2010E	17.3	Dividend Rate/Share	$1.52	S&P Credit Rating	BBB+
$10K Invested 5 Yrs Ago	$14,203	Common Shares Outstg. (M)	182.3	Institutional Ownership (%)	87		

Price Performance

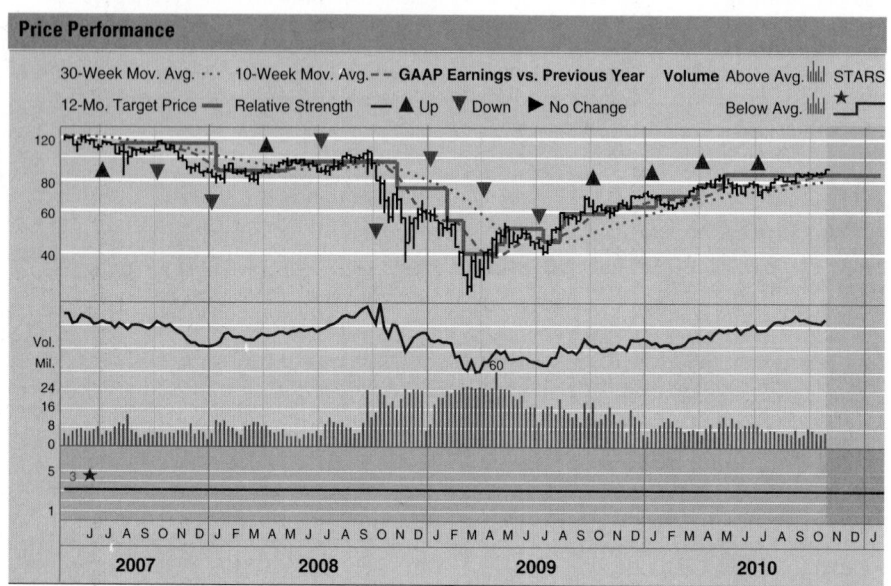

30-Week Mov. Avg. · · · 10-Week Mov. Avg. - - **GAAP Earnings vs. Previous Year** **Volume** Above Avg. STARS
12-Mo. Target Price — Relative Strength — ▲ Up ▼ Down ▶ No Change Below Avg.

Analysis prepared by **Royal F. Shepard, CFA** on August 10, 2010, when the stock traded at **$ 83.86**.

Highlights

➤ We expect a challenging economic environment to limit the opportunity to sign new office tenants through 2010. However, we think leasing activity is stabilizing in the trust's core New York City and Washington, DC markets and should keep 2010 occupancy levels close to 95%. VNO's retail portfolio is also performing well in view of competition from space vacated by bankrupt retailers. We think its strength in street-level retail in urban markets will help keep occupancy close to 92% in 2010.

➤ In the second half of 2010, we expect VNO to become more aggressive in pursuing new acquisitions. In July, the trust raised $550 million for a new real estate investment fund in which its owns a 36% interest. In addition, VNO invested $116 million in LNR Property Corp., a leader servicer of commercial mortgage loans. We think the trust may use its LNR investment to help identify distressed mortgage investment opportunities.

➤ VNO has restored an all cash quarterly dividend of $0.65 in 2010, after paying a portion of its 2009 payout in common stock. With our view of its strong balance sheet, we think VNO will maintain the cash payout over the next 12 months.

Investment Rationale/Risk

➤ We think VNO has the financial resources to expand a strong portfolio of office and retail assets in supply-limited markets. The trust has begun to put excess cash balances to work in buying select assets, including properties from distressed sellers. In our view, new development opportunities will remain on hold until the economy recovery gains steam. In the near term, we think a well-diversified operating platform will produce a steady stream of cash flow. With the shares recently trading at a premium to diversified peers based on price to estimated 2010 FFO, we think they appropriately reflect VNO's long-term growth prospects.

➤ Risks to our opinion and target price include rising interest rates, and economic declines in New York and/or Washington, DC. We also have corporate governance concerns related to anti-takeover defenses, including a classified board and blank check preferred stock.

➤ Our 12-month target price of $86 represents a multiple of 16.4X our 2010 FFO per share forecast, a moderate premium to peers. We consider the premium justified by VNO's portfolio of high-quality assets earning relatively consistent investment returns.

Qualitative Risk Assessment

LOW	MEDIUM	HIGH

Our risk assessment reflects VNO's large market capitalization, and what we see as its financial strength, diversified asset portfolio, and low share price volatility.

Quantitative Evaluations

S&P Quality Ranking B

D	C	B-	B	B+	A-	A	A+

Relative Strength Rank STRONG

73

LOWEST = 1   HIGHEST = 99

Revenue/FFO Data

Revenue (Million $)

	1Q	2Q	3Q	4Q	Year
2010	827.1	696.1	--	--	--
2009	678.6	673.8	671.2	719.0	2,743
2008	649.3	674.4	677.2	696.3	2,697
2007	736.3	792.8	853.0	888.5	3,271
2006	647.3	663.0	678.5	723.3	2,712
2005	598.7	594.8	657.0	697.2	2,548

FFO Per Share ($)

	1Q	2Q	3Q	4Q	Year
2010	1.89	1.11	E1.26	E0.95	E5.25
2009	1.63	0.54	1.25	E1.04	3.36
2008	3.27	1.27	1.06	-0.50	5.16
2007	1.65	1.72	1.35	1.18	5.89
2006	1.37	1.49	1.31	1.34	5.51
2005	1.84	1.51	0.65	1.26	5.21

Fiscal year ended Dec. 31. Next earnings report expected: Early November. FFO Estimates based on S&P Funds From Operations Est..

Dividend Data (Dates: mm/dd Payment Date: mm/dd/yy)

Amount ($)	Date Decl.	Ex-Div. Date	Stk. of Record	Payment Date
0.650	10/29	11/06	11/10	12/14/09
0.650	01/13	01/26	01/28	02/22/10
0.650	04/29	05/06	05/10	05/24/10
0.650	07/29	08/09	08/11	08/23/10

Dividends have been paid since 1990. Source: Company reports.

Please read the Required Disclosures and Analyst Certification on the last page of this report.

Vornado Realty Trust

Business Summary August 10, 2010

CORPORATE OVERVIEW. Vornado Realty Trust is a diversified REIT that has interests in a wide range of properties, including office buildings, retail properties, refrigerated warehouses, a hotel, and dry warehouses, among others, primarily in the Northeast. The company conducts its business through, was the sole general partner of, and, as of December 31, 2009, owned 92.5% of the limited partnership interests in, Vornado Realty L.P.

MARKET PROFILE. During 2009, VNO derived 63% of operating segment EBITDA from office properties. The market for office leases is inherently cyclical. The U.S. office market tends to track the overall economy on a lagged basis. At year-end 2009, we believe the national vacancy rate was about 17.0%, reflecting deterioration since its cyclical low of about 12.5% at the end of 2007.

Local economic conditions, particularly the employment level, play an important role in determining competitive dynamics. In our opinion, VNO's principal target markets, the New York City metropolitan area and Washington DC, have vacancy rates below the average nationwide. In addition, unlike many markets, rates on new or renewed leases in Washington are often at higher rates than those previously in place. At December 31, 2009, VNO owned or had an interest in 113 office properties totaling 36.6 million sq. ft. The New

York portfolio was 95.5% occupied at December 31, 2009; the Washington, DC, portfolio was 94.9% occupied.

In 2009, VNO derived about 19% of EBITDA from its retail segment. As of December 31, 2009, the retail portfolio included about 22.6 million sq. ft. in northeast U.S. states, Washington DC, and Puerto Rico. For VNO, as well as other retail oriented REITs, location and the financial health and growth of its retail tenants are among the most important factors affecting the success of its portfolio. Further, the companies in this industry enjoy relatively high barriers to entry, since developing new shopping centers requires large amounts of capital as well as time-consuming regulatory approvals which have been difficult to obtain in the recent past amid concerns about traffic and pollution. We expect VNO to focus on the re-development of acquired properties, including the Manhattan Mall, in New York City, and shopping centers acquired in Northern New Jersey and Long Island, New York.

Company Financials Fiscal Year Ended Dec. 31

Per Share Data ($)	2009	2008	2007	2006	2005	2004	2003	2002	2001	2000
Tangible Book Value	27.46	27.79	34.57	35.22	31.38	26.86	24.15	21.68	21.15	18.31
Earnings	Nil	1.16	2.86	3.13	3.27	3.75	2.29	2.18	2.50	2.21
S&P Core Earnings	-0.01	1.13	2.69	2.62	3.09	3.62	3.63	2.15	2.58	NA
Dividends	3.20	3.65	3.45	3.25	3.85	2.89	2.91	2.97	2.31	1.97
Payout Ratio	NM	NM	107%	104%	118%	77%	127%	136%	92%	89%
Prices:High	73.96	108.15	136.55	131.35	89.70	76.99	55.84	47.20	42.03	40.75
Prices:Low	27.01	36.66	82.82	83.28	68.25	47.00	33.25	33.20	34.47	29.87
P/E Ratio:High	NM	93	42	42	27	21	24	22	17	18
P/E Ratio:Low	NM	32	26	27	21	13	15	15	14	14

Income Statement Analysis (Million $)										
Rental Income	2,222	2,211	1,989	1,568	1,397	1,345	1,261	1,249	842	695
Mortgage Income	Nil	Nil	Nil	Nil	Nil	Nil	Nil	Nil	Nil	Nil
Total Income	2,743	2,697	3,271	2,712	2,548	1,707	1,503	1,435	986	827
General Expenses	1,320	1,264	2,935	1,588	1,488	825	706	668	472	366
Interest Expense	634	608	635	478	341	242	230	240	173	170
Provision for Losses	Nil	Nil	Nil	Nil	Nil	Nil	Nil	Nil	Nil	Nil
Depreciation	540	537	530	397	335	243	215	206	124	99.8
Net Income	54.3	241	510	607	507	514	285	263	267	235
S&P Core Earnings	-1.06	178	426	393	435	476	421	236	238	NA

Balance Sheet & Other Financial Data (Million $)										
Cash	535	1,527	1,858	2,690	763	NA	NA	NA	NA	NA
Total Assets	20,185	21,418	22,479	17,954	13,637	11,581	9,519	9,018	6,777	6,370
Real Estate Investment	17,950	17,870	18,972	13,553	11,449	9,757	7,748	7,560	4,690	4,295
Loss Reserve	Nil	Nil	Nil	Nil	Nil	Nil	Nil	Nil	Nil	Nil
Net Investment	15,455	15,709	16,565	11,585	9,776	8,349	6,879	6,822	4,184	3,901
Short Term Debt	852	357	527	778	398	Nil	Nil	Nil	Nil	425
Capitalization:Debt	10,088	12,292	12,426	9,056	5,857	4,937	3,768	3,622	1,643	2,232
Capitalization:Equity	5,419	4,841	5,293	5,322	4,260	3,301	2,827	2,362	2,101	1,597
Capitalization:Total	17,989	19,567	20,038	16,335	12,208	8,238	8,767	8,287	5,693	5,767
% Earnings & Depreciation/Assets	2.9	3.5	5.1	6.3	6.6	7.1	5.4	5.9	5.9	5.6
Price Times Book Value:High	2.7	3.9	3.9	3.7	2.9	2.9	2.3	2.2	2.0	2.2
Price Times Book Value:Low	1.0	1.3	2.4	2.4	2.2	1.7	1.4	1.5	1.6	1.6

Data as orig reptd.; bef. results of disc opers/spec. items. Per share data adj. for stk. divs.; EPS diluted. E-Estimated. NA-Not Available. NM-Not Meaningful. NR-Not Ranked. UR-Under Review.

Vulcan Materials Co

STANDARD & POOR'S

S&P Recommendation HOLD ★★★☆☆

Price	**12-Mo. Target Price**	**Investment Style**
$36.70 (as of Oct 22, 2010)	$48.00	Large-Cap Growth

GICS Sector Materials
Sub-Industry Construction Materials

Summary This company is the nation's largest producer of aggregates in the United States, and is also a major supplier of asphalt and concrete used in road construction and the building of commercial, residential and public buildings and infrastructure.

Key Stock Statistics (Source S&P, Vickers, company reports)

52-Wk Range	$59.90– 35.40	S&P Oper. EPS 2010**E**	0.30	Market Capitalization(B)	$4.708	Beta	1.37
Trailing 12-Month EPS	$-0.17	S&P Oper. EPS 2011**E**	1.25	Yield (%)	2.72	S&P 3-Yr. Proj. EPS CAGR(%)	NM
Trailing 12-Month P/E	NM	P/E on S&P Oper. EPS 2010**E**	NM	Dividend Rate/Share	$1.00	S&P Credit Rating	BBB-
$10K Invested 5 Yrs Ago	$6,162	Common Shares Outstg. (M)	128.3	Institutional Ownership (%)	81		

Price Performance

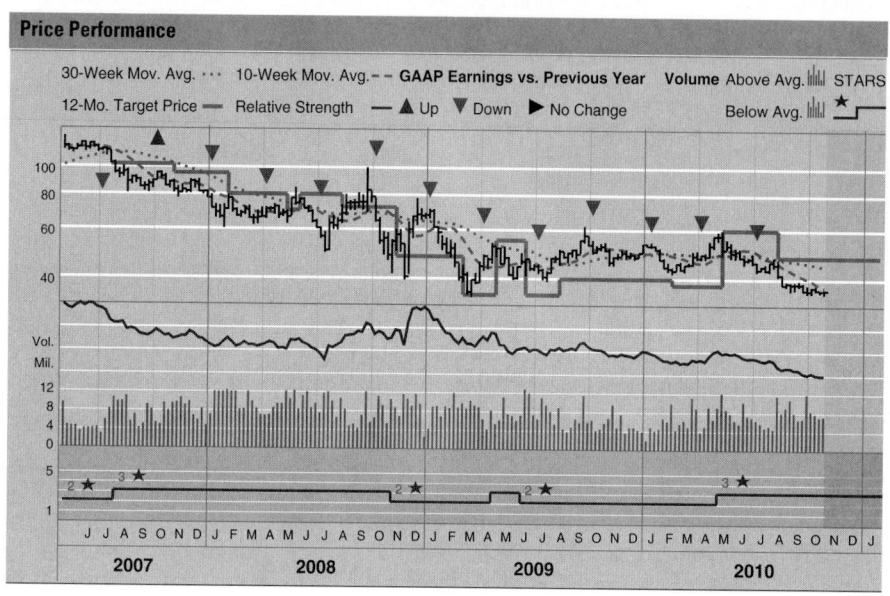

30-Week Mov. Avg. · · · 10-Week Mov. Avg. – – GAAP Earnings vs. Previous Year Volume Above Avg. STARS
12-Mo. Target Price — Relative Strength — ▲ Up ▼ Down ► No Change Below Avg. ★

Options: P

Analysis prepared by **Stuart J. Benway, CFA** on August 10, 2010, when the stock traded at **$ 40.72**.

Qualitative Risk Assessment

LOW	MEDIUM	HIGH

Our risk assessment reflects that while VMC's earnings are exposed to the construction industry, about half of the aggregates volume comes from public construction, which is more stable than commercial construction. In addition, we view VMC's free cash flow generation as strong.

Quantitative Evaluations

S&P Quality Ranking B+

D	C	B-	B	B+	A-	A	A+

Relative Strength Rank WEAK

16

LOWEST = 1   HIGHEST = 99

Revenue/Earnings Data

Revenue (Million $)

	1Q	2Q	3Q	4Q	Year
2010	493.3	736.2	--	--	--
2009	600.3	721.9	778.2	590.1	2,690
2008	817.3	1,022	1,013	799.2	3,651
2007	687.2	878.8	904.9	856.9	3,328
2006	708.7	888.2	929.3	816.3	3,342
2005	528.6	782.1	830.0	754.6	2,895

Earnings Per Share ($)

2010	-0.35	-0.18	E0.40	E0.15	E0.30
2009	-0.29	0.14	0.38	-0.10	0.16
2008	0.13	1.27	0.54	0.14	2.08
2007	0.91	1.46	1.47	0.83	4.66
2006	0.70	1.47	1.45	1.19	4.79
2005	0.21	0.98	1.23	0.89	3.30

Fiscal year ended Dec. 31. Next earnings report expected: Early November. EPS Estimates based on S&P Operating Earnings; historical GAAP earnings are as reported.

Dividend Data (Dates: mm/dd Payment Date: mm/dd/yy)

Amount ($)	Date Decl.	Ex-Div. Date	Stk. of Record	Payment Date
0.250	02/12	02/24	02/26	03/10/10
0.250	05/14	05/26	05/28	06/10/10
0.250	07/09	08/24	08/26	09/10/10
0.250	10/08	11/02	11/04	12/10/10

Dividends have been paid since 1934. Source: Company reports.

Highlights

► After a 26% revenue decline in 2009, we look for little change in 2010 levels. Demand for construction aggregates is likely to rise slightly from low levels in 2009, as we forecast that housing starts will increase 15%. However, commercial construction is likely to remain very weak. We expect spending on highways and other public infrastructure to rise due to increased federal spending, but prices for aggregates could decrease by about 2%.

► Operating margins fell 640 basis points in 2009, to 5.7%. Despite progress on reducing administrative costs and a relatively flexible cost structure, margins at VMC have suffered from significantly underutilized capacity. The modest recovery that we expect in 2010, coupled with the lower cost base, should lead to about a 150 basis point increase in operating margins.

► We project EPS of $0.30 in 2010, up from a very weak level of $0.16 in 2009. The solid growth trends that Vulcan has historically exhibited have been disrupted over the past two years, although we think the worst may be over. Our EPS estimate for 2011 is $1.25.

Investment Rationale/Risk

► We expect conditions in most of Vulcan's markets to remain weak in 2010. Our forecast is for improvement in home starts, although activity is likely to remain well below historical levels. We project that commercial construction will decline again in 2010. Industrial markets should provide some stability as they are more long term in nature. We look for an increase in government infrastructure spending to moderately boost demand for construction aggregates. The shares are trading well above their average forward P/E ratio of about 20X.

► Risks to our recommendation and target price include demand being weaker than we project due to a lack of recovery in residential construction activity, and public infrastructure spending being boosted less than expected by a government-sponsored stimulus plan.

► Our discounted cash flow model, which assumes a 10.0% weighted average cost of capital, lower capital spending again in 2010, lower cash flow generation in 2010, and 3% cash flow growth in perpetuity, indicates intrinsic value of $48, which is our 12-month target price.

Please read the Required Disclosures and Analyst Certification on the last page of this report.

The **McGraw·Hill** Companies

Vulcan Materials Co

Business Summary August 10, 2010

CORPORATE OVERVIEW. Vulcan Materials is the largest U.S. producer of construction aggregates, primarily crushed stone, sand, and gravel. It is also a major producer of asphalt and ready-mix concrete and a leading producer of cement in Florida. Proven and probable reserves of aggregates were estimated at 14.2 billion tons at the end of 2009. Vulcan shipped 151 million tons of aggregates in 2009 to 23 states, the District of Columbia, Mexico, the Bahamas, Canada, the Cayman Islands and Chile from 331 production facilities and distribution points. Construction aggregates were 66% of sales in 2009, asphalt mix and concrete 33%, and cement was 1%. VMC estimates that 50% of its aggregates shipments in 2009 went to publicly funded construction projects and 50% was used for privately funded residential and nonresidential construction.

PRIMARY BUSINESS DYNAMICS. Public sector construction spending is generally more stable than in the private sector, in part because public sector spending is less sensitive to interest rates and is often supported by multi-year legislation and programs. Public construction is typically funded through a combination of federal state and local sources. The federal transportation bill is the principal source of federal funding for public infrastructure and transportation projects. For over two decades, the federal funding component

of these projects has been provided through a series of six-year bills. The multi-year aspect of these bills is critically important because it provides state departments of transportation with the ability to plan and execute long-term and complex highway projects. Federal highway spending is primarily determined by this six-year authorization bill and annual budget appropriations using funds largely taken from the Federal Highway Trust Fund, which receives taxes on gasoline and other levies. State highway and bridge projects supplement federal funding with state fuel taxes and vehicle registration fees. Private nonresidential construction includes a wide array of project types and generally is more aggregates intensive than residential construction but less so than public construction. Demand in private nonresidential construction is driven by job growth, vacancy rates, private infrastructure needs, and demographic trends. The majority of residential construction activity is for single-family houses with the remainder consisting of multi-family construction. Household formation is a primary driver of housing demand along with mortgage rates.

Company Financials Fiscal Year Ended Dec. 31

Per Share Data ($)	2009	2008	2007	2006	2005	2004	2003	2002	2001	2000
Tangible Book Value	2.19	NM	NM	14.60	15.05	13.77	12.01	11.04	10.02	9.00
Cash Flow	3.46	3.53	7.33	7.04	5.43	4.88	4.87	4.47	4.89	4.43
Earnings	0.16	2.08	4.66	4.79	3.30	2.52	2.18	1.86	2.17	2.29
S&P Core Earnings	NA	1.20	4.22	4.53	3.17	2.29	1.89	1.51	1.81	NA
Dividends	1.48	1.96	1.84	1.48	1.16	1.04	0.97	0.94	0.90	0.84
Payout Ratio	NM	94%	39%	31%	35%	41%	44%	51%	41%	37%
Prices:High	71.26	100.25	128.62	93.85	76.31	55.53	48.60	49.95	55.30	48.88
Prices:Low	34.30	39.52	77.04	65.85	52.36	41.94	28.75	32.35	37.50	36.50
P/E Ratio:High	NM	48	28	20	23	22	22	27	25	21
P/E Ratio:Low	NM	19	17	14	16	17	13	17	17	16

Income Statement Analysis (Million $)										
Revenue	2,690	3,651	3,328	3,342	2,895	2,454	2,892	2,797	3,020	2,492
Operating Income	516	814	954	914	690	623	618	560	649	573
Depreciation	395	389	266	225	221	245	277	268	278	232
Interest Expense	175	187	53.4	26.3	37.1	40.3	54.1	55.0	61.3	48.1
Pretax Income	-19.2	327	668	703	480	376	311	260	324	312
Effective Tax Rate	197.0%	29.5%	30.6%	32.1%	28.4%	30.4%	28.3%	25.8%	31.3%	29.6%
Net Income	18.7	231	463	477	344	261	223	190	223	220
S&P Core Earnings	-0.71	132	419	452	328	236	194	155	186	NA

Balance Sheet & Other Financial Data (Million $)										
Cash	26.4	46.9	34.9	55.2	275	271	417	171	101	55.3
Current Assets	743	894	1,157	731	1,165	1,418	1,050	790	730	695
Total Assets	8,534	9,176	8,936	3,424	3,589	3,665	3,637	3,448	3,398	3,229
Current Liabilities	857	1,663	2,528	494	579	427	543	298	344	572
Long Term Debt	2,116	2,154	1,530	322	323	605	339	858	906	685
Common Equity	4,052	3,784	3,760	2,001	2,127	2,014	1,803	1,697	1,604	1,471
Total Capital	6,554	6,626	5,961	2,611	2,725	2,967	2,573	2,993	2,829	2,426
Capital Expenditures	110	401	483	435	216	204	194	249	287	340
Cash Flow	413	387	729	702	565	506	501	458	501	452
Current Ratio	0.9	0.5	0.5	1.5	2.0	3.3	1.9	2.7	2.1	1.2
% Long Term Debt of Capitalization	32.3	32.5	25.7	12.3	11.9	20.4	13.2	28.7	32.0	28.3
% Net Income of Revenue	0.7	6.3	13.9	14.3	11.9	10.6	7.7	6.8	7.4	8.8
% Return on Assets	0.2	2.6	7.5	13.6	9.5	7.2	6.3	5.6	6.7	7.2
% Return on Equity	0.5	6.1	16.1	23.1	16.6	13.7	12.8	11.5	14.5	15.7

Data as orig reptd.; bef. results of disc opers/spec. items. Per share data adj. for stk. divs.; EPS diluted. E-Estimated. NA-Not Available. NM-Not Meaningful. NR-Not Ranked. UR-Under Review.

Office: 1200 Urban Center Drive, Birmingham, AL 35242.
Telephone: 205-298-3000.
Email: ir@vmcmail.com
Website: http://www.vulcanmaterials.com

Chrmn & CEO: D.M. James
SVP & CFO: D. Sansone
SVP & General Counsel: R.A. Wason, IV
Chief Acctg Officer, Cntlr & CIO: E.A. Khan

Treas: J.P. Alford
Investor Contact: M. Warren (205-298-3220)
Board Members: P. W. Farmer, H. A. Franklin, D. M. James, A. M. Korologos, D. J. McGregor, J. V. Napier, R. O'Brien, J. T. Prokopanko, D. B. Rice, V. J. Trosino, K. Wilson-Thompson

Founded: 1910
Domicile: New Jersey
Employees: 8,479

Walgreen Co

STANDARD
&POOR'S

S&P Recommendation **BUY** ★★★★☆	Price $34.07 (as of Oct 22, 2010)	12-Mo. Target Price $38.00	Investment Style Large-Cap Growth

GICS Sector Consumer Staples
Sub-Industry Drug Retail

Summary The largest U.S. retail drug chain in terms of revenues, this company operates more than 8,000 drug stores throughout the U.S. and Puerto Rico.

Key Stock Statistics (Source S&P, Vickers, company reports)

52-Wk Range	$40.26– 26.26	S&P Oper. EPS 2011**E**	2.50	Market Capitalization(B)	$33.156	Beta	0.83
Trailing 12-Month EPS	$2.12	S&P Oper. EPS 2012**E**	2.79	Yield (%)	2.05	S&P 3-Yr. Proj. EPS CAGR(%)	15
Trailing 12-Month P/E	16.1	P/E on S&P Oper. EPS 2011**E**	13.6	Dividend Rate/Share	$0.70	S&P Credit Rating	A
$10K Invested 5 Yrs Ago	$8,026	Common Shares Outstg. (M)	973.2	Institutional Ownership (%)	67		

Price Performance

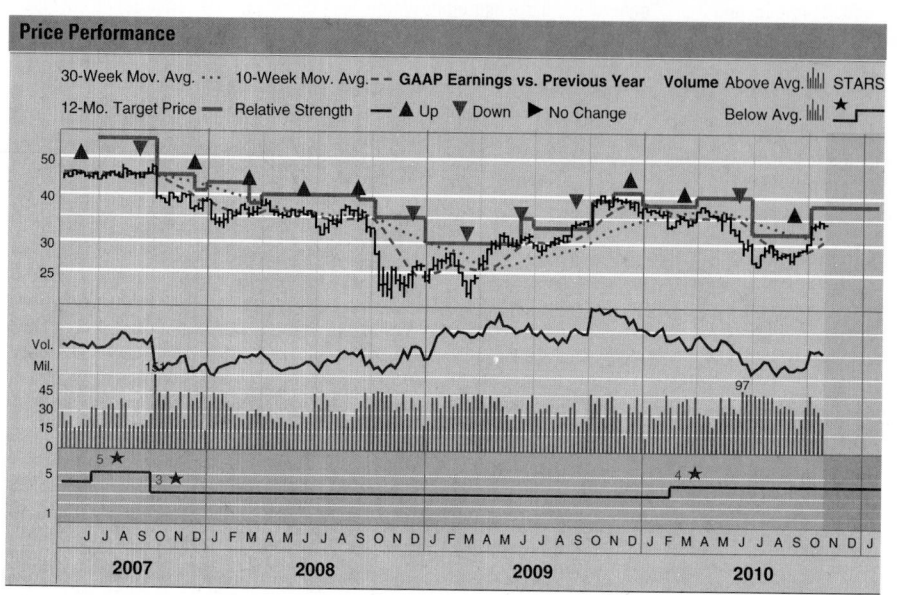

30-Week Mov. Avg. · · · 10-Week Mov. Avg. - - GAAP Earnings vs. Previous Year Volume Above Avg. ▮▮▮ STARS
12-Mo. Target Price — Relative Strength — ▲ Up ▼ Down ▶ No Change Below Avg. ▮▮▮ ★

Options: ASE, CBOE, P

Analysis prepared by **Joseph Agnese** on September 28, 2010, when the stock traded at **$ 33.75**.

Highlights

➤ We see sales advancing 7.1% in FY 11 (Aug.), to roughly $72.2 billion, from $67.4 billion in FY 10, fueled by about 250 net new store openings (approximately 3.0% square footage growth), acquisitions, a pharmacy same-store sales gain of about 3%, and front-end same-store sales growth of about 2%. We see front-end growth benefiting from the rollout of store remodelings across a majority of stores, including new merchandising initiatives that we expect to significantly boost non-pharmacy sales.

➤ We expect margins to expand on an improved product mix, lower labor costs, reduced inventory markdowns and increased sales of wider-margin generic drugs, partially offset by increased drug reimbursement pressures. We think the company's investment in health clinics will be accretive to earnings in FY 11, versus a dilutive impact in FY 10. We expect interest expense to decline slightly, reflecting lower interest rates.

➤ We look for EPS to increase 17% in FY 11, to $2.50, from $2.13 (including $0.03 in restructuring and related costs associated with the rewiring for growth initiative) in FY 10.

Investment Rationale/Risk

➤ The company acquired drug store chain Duane Reade in April 2010 for a total enterprise value of $1.1 billion in cash. The acquisition gives the company a leading market share position in New York City, the largest drug store market in the U.S. We see benefits from the sharing of best practices, with Duane Reade's strengths in non-pharmacy merchandising and Walgreen's strengths in pharmacy, in addition to purchasing benefits and overhead cost reductions.

➤ Risks to our recommendation and target price include a weaker-than-expected economy, increased competition from peers and other retail formats, and legislative changes that may affect drug reimbursements.

➤ We believe the shares should trade in line with their historical premium to the S&P 500 as the company makes progress on initiatives to improve merchandising and remodel existing stores, leading to an acceleration of earnings growth. Applying a multiple of 15.1X to our FY 11 EPS estimate of $2.50, in line with its historical 3% premium to the P/E multiple on the S&P 500, results in a value of $38, which is our 12-month target price.

Qualitative Risk Assessment

LOW	MEDIUM	HIGH

Our risk assessment reflects the company's strong market share positions in the relatively stable U.S. retail drug industry, offset by growth of non-traditional competitors and potential adverse legislation.

Quantitative Evaluations

S&P Quality Ranking A+

D	C	B-	B	B+	A-	A	A+

Relative Strength Rank STRONG

78

LOWEST = 1   HIGHEST = 99

Revenue/Earnings Data

Revenue (Million $)

	1Q	2Q	3Q	4Q	Year
2010	16,364	16,987	17,199	16,870	67,420
2009	14,947	16,475	16,210	15,703	63,335
2008	14,028	15,394	15,016	14,597	59,034
2007	12,709	13,934	13,698	13,422	53,762
2006	10,900	12,163	12,175	12,170	47,409
2005	9,889	10,987	10,831	10,495	42,202

Earnings Per Share ($)

2010	0.49	0.68	0.47	0.49	2.12
2009	0.41	0.65	0.53	0.44	2.02
2008	0.46	0.69	0.58	0.45	2.17
2007	0.43	0.65	0.56	0.40	2.03
2006	0.34	0.51	0.46	0.41	1.72
2005	0.32	0.48	0.40	0.32	1.52

Fiscal year ended Aug. 31. Next earnings report expected: Late December. EPS Estimates based on S&P Operating Earnings; historical GAAP earnings are as reported.

Dividend Data (Dates: mm/dd Payment Date: mm/dd/yy)

Amount ($)	Date Decl.	Ex-Div. Date	Stk. of Record	Payment Date
0.138	01/15	02/16	02/18	03/12/10
0.138	04/12	05/18	05/20	06/12/10
0.175	07/14	08/17	08/19	09/11/10
0.175	10/13	11/10	11/15	12/11/10

Dividends have been paid since 1933. Source: Company reports.

Please read the Required Disclosures and Analyst Certification on the last page of this report.

The McGraw-Hill Companies

Walgreen Co

STANDARD
&POOR'S

Business Summary September 28, 2010

CORPORATE OVERVIEW. Walgreen Co. is one of the largest drug store chains in the U.S., based on sales and store count. In 1909, the company's founder, Charles Rudolph Walgreen Sr., purchased one of the busiest drug stores on Chicago's South Side, and transformed it by constructing an ice cream fountain that featured his own brand of ice cream. The ice cream fountain was the forerunner of the famous Walgreen's soda fountain, which became the main attraction for customers from the 1920s through the 1950s. People lined up to buy a product that WAG invented in the early 1920s: the milkshake. The company continued to be innovative by pioneering computerized pharmacies connected by satellite in 1981, completing chain wide point-of-sale scanning in 1991, and introducing freestanding stores with drive-thru pharmacies in 1992.

MARKET PROFILE. Walgreen operates one of the largest U.S. drug store chain based on sales, generating $63.3 billion in sales in FY 09 (Aug.). According to

our analysis, the company filled about 650 million prescriptions in FY 09, accounting for about 18% of the U.S. retail market. The company experienced a 6.9% growth rate in prescription volume in FY 09, outpacing our estimate of a low single digit growth rate for the industry. WAG pharmacy sales rose 7.8% in FY 09, to about $42 billion, versus our estimate of a low single digit growth rate for the total industry, on comparable prescription sales growth of 3.5%. Sales of non-pharmacy items outperformed competitors, with the company increasing market share in most of its core categories versus drug store, grocery and mass merchant competition.

Company Financials Fiscal Year Ended Aug. 31

Per Share Data ($)	2010	2009	2008	2007	2006	2005	2004	2003	2002	2001
Tangible Book Value	NA	13.06	11.56	10.13	9.61	8.69	8.04	7.02	6.08	5.11
Cash Flow	3.16	3.01	3.01	2.70	2.28	1.99	1.71	1.47	1.29	1.12
Earnings	2.12	2.02	2.17	2.03	1.72	1.52	1.32	1.14	0.99	0.86
S&P Core Earnings	NA	2.01	2.17	2.03	1.71	1.44	1.27	1.07	0.93	0.80
Dividends	0.59	0.48	0.40	0.33	0.27	0.22	0.18	0.16	0.15	0.14
Payout Ratio	28%	24%	18%	16%	16%	15%	14%	14%	15%	16%
Prices:High	37.95	40.69	39.00	49.10	51.60	49.01	39.51	37.42	40.70	45.29
Prices:Low	26.26	21.39	21.28	35.80	39.55	39.66	32.00	26.90	27.70	28.70
P/E Ratio:High	18	20	18	24	30	32	30	33	41	53
P/E Ratio:Low	12	11	10	18	23	26	24	24	28	33

Income Statement Analysis (Million $)	2010	2009	2008	2007	2006	2005	2004	2003	2002	2001
Revenue	67,420	63,335	59,034	53,762	47,409	42,202	37,508	32,505	28,681	24,623
Operating Income	4,488	4,442	4,202	3,827	3,274	2,906	2,546	2,194	1,932	1,668
Depreciation	1,030	975	840	676	572	482	403	346	307	269
Interest Expense	85.0	99.0	30.0	Nil	Nil	Nil	Nil	Nil	Nil	3.10
Pretax Income	3,373	3,164	3,430	3,189	2,754	2,456	2,176	1,889	1,637	1,423
Effective Tax Rate	NA	36.6%	37.1%	36.0%	36.4%	36.5%	37.5%	37.8%	37.8%	37.8%
Net Income	2,091	2,006	2,157	2,041	1,751	1,560	1,360	1,176	1,019	886
S&P Core Earnings	NA	1,997	2,158	2,042	1,754	1,478	1,302	1,104	955	820

Balance Sheet & Other Financial Data (Million $)	2010	2009	2008	2007	2006	2005	2004	2003	2002	2001
Cash	1,880	2,587	443	255	920	577	1,696	1,017	450	16.9
Current Assets	11,922	12,049	10,433	9,511	9,705	8,317	7,764	6,358	5,167	4,394
Total Assets	26,275	25,142	22,410	19,314	17,131	14,609	13,342	11,406	9,879	8,834
Current Liabilities	7,433	6,769	6,644	6,744	5,755	4,481	4,078	3,421	2,955	3,012
Long Term Debt	2,389	2,336	1,377	Nil	Nil	Nil	Nil	Nil	Nil	Nil
Common Equity	14,400	14,376	12,869	11,104	10,116	8,890	8,228	7,196	6,230	5,207
Total Capital	16,789	16,712	14,396	11,263	10,257	9,130	8,556	7,424	6,407	5,344
Capital Expenditures	1,014	1,927	2,225	1,785	1,338	1,238	940	795	934	1,237
Cash Flow	3,121	2,981	2,997	2,717	2,323	2,042	1,763	1,522	1,327	1,155
Current Ratio	1.6	1.8	1.6	1.4	1.7	1.9	1.9	1.9	1.7	1.5
% Long Term Debt of Capitalization	14.2	14.0	9.6	Nil	Nil	Nil	Nil	Nil	Nil	Nil
% Net Income of Revenue	3.1	3.2	3.7	3.8	3.7	3.7	3.6	3.6	3.6	3.6
% Return on Assets	8.1	8.4	10.3	11.2	11.0	11.2	10.9	11.0	10.9	11.1
% Return on Equity	14.5	14.7	18.0	19.2	18.4	18.3	17.6	17.5	17.8	18.8

Data as orig reptd.; bef. results of disc opers/spec. items. Per share data adj. for stk. divs.; EPS diluted. E-Estimated. NA-Not Available. NM-Not Meaningful. NR-Not Ranked. UR-Under Review.

Office: 200 Wilmot Road, Deerfield, IL 60015.
Telephone: 847-940-2500.
Email: investor.relations@walgreens.com
Website: http://www.walgreens.com

Chrmn: A.G. McNally
Pres, CEO & COO: G.D. Wasson
EVP & CFO: W.D. Miquelon
EVP, Secy & General Counsel: D.I. Green

SVP & CIO: T.J. Theriault
Investor Contact: R.J. Hans (847-940-2500)
Board Members: D. J. Brailer, S. A. Davis, W. C. Foote, M. P. Frissora, G. L. Graham, A. G. McNally, N. M. Schlichting, D. Y. Schwartz, A. Silva, J. Skinner, G. D. Wasson

Founded: 1901
Domicile: Illinois
Employees: 238,000

Wal-Mart Stores Inc

STANDARD &POOR'S

S&P Recommendation **STRONG BUY** ★★★★★	Price $54.06 (as of Oct 22, 2010)	12-Mo. Target Price $63.00	Investment Style Large-Cap Blend

GICS Sector Consumer Staples
Sub-Industry Hypermarkets & Super Centers

Summary The largest retailer in North America, WMT operates a chain of discount department stores, wholesale clubs, and combination discount stores and supermarkets.

Key Stock Statistics (Source S&P, Vickers, company reports)

52-Wk Range	$56.27– 47.77	S&P Oper. EPS 2011E	4.03	Market Capitalization(B)	$196.592	Beta	0.28
Trailing 12-Month EPS	$3.89	S&P Oper. EPS 2012E	4.40	Yield (%)	2.24	S&P 3-Yr. Proj. EPS CAGR(%)	9
Trailing 12-Month P/E	13.9	P/E on S&P Oper. EPS 2011E	13.4	Dividend Rate/Share	$1.21	S&P Credit Rating	AA
$10K Invested 5 Yrs Ago	$12,975	Common Shares Outstg. (M)	3,636.5	Institutional Ownership (%)	34		

Price Performance

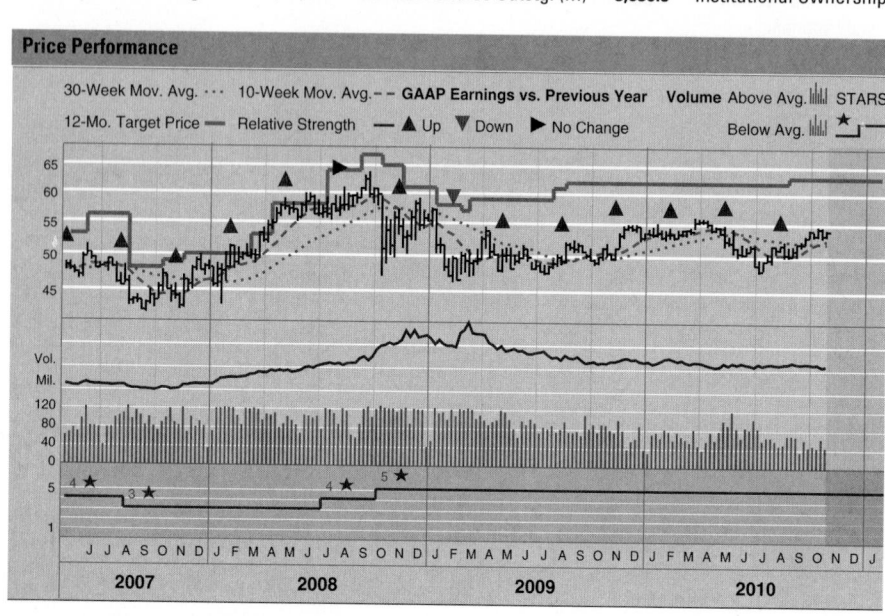

30-Week Mov. Avg. ···· 10-Week Mov. Avg. - - GAAP Earnings vs. Previous Year Volume Above Avg. STARS
12-Mo. Target Price — Relative Strength ▲ Up ▼ Down ▶ No Change Below Avg. ★

Options: ASE, CBOE, P, Ph

Analysis prepared by **Joseph Agnese** on October 14, 2010, when the stock traded at **$ 53.40.**

Highlights

▶ We expect net revenues to increase 4.3% in FY 11 (Jan.), driven by 10% growth in international sales and the addition of about 4% in new retail square footage, with square footage growth (excluding acquisitions) shifting toward international markets (25 million square feet) from domestic expansion (12 million square feet), partially offset by store closures. We expect U.S. same store sales to decline 1% reflecting more aggressive price rollbacks and weak consumer demand. We do not expect food inflation to return in FY 11.

▶ We estimate that EBIT margins will widen slightly, reflecting higher sales of wider margin private label merchandise, increased sales leverage and well controlled inventory levels, partially offset by a shift in the product mix due to higher sales of food and pharmacy products and sluggish sales growth in discretionary categories such as apparel and home departments. Additionally, we see continued benefits from improved labor productivity due to the rollout of scheduling software.

▶ We project EPS of $4.03 for FY 11, up 10% from operating EPS of $3.66 in FY 10, excluding one-time tax benefits and restructuring costs.

Investment Rationale/Risk

▶ We believe the company is well positioned to grow market share despite a more stable economic environment in FY 11, as we think consumers will continue to seek good values and take advantage of its one-stop shopping convenience. We believe WMT's significant staples product offerings and basics discretionary offerings position it well despite weak consumer spending.

▶ Risks to our recommendation and target price include economic pressures such as rising unemployment or lower consumer confidence, which we think would negatively affect WMT's core customers and the company's results, and unfavorable foreign currency exchange rates.

▶ Our 12-month target price of $63 reflects our analysis of relative P/E ratios. Based on our expectation for the company to grow market share in a stable economic environment, we believe the stock should trade in line with its historical median forward P/E. Applying a multiple of 15.3X, in line with its five-year median P/E but at a 7% premium to the forward 12-month P/E for the S&P 500, to our forward 12-month EPS estimate of $4.11 implies a value of $63.

Qualitative Risk Assessment

LOW	MEDIUM	HIGH

Our risk assessment of Wal-Mart Stores, Inc. reflects our view of the company's high-quality earnings, as reflected in its S&P Quality Ranking of A+, its dominant market share positions, continued price leadership and strong cash flow generation.

Quantitative Evaluations

S&P Quality Ranking A+

D	C	B-	B	B+	A-	A	A+

Relative Strength Rank MODERATE

49

LOWEST = 1 HIGHEST = 99

Revenue/Earnings Data

Revenue (Million $)

	1Q	2Q	3Q	4Q	Year
2011	99,848	103,726	--	--	--
2010	94,242	100,910	99,411	113,651	408,214
2009	94,070	101,544	97,634	107,996	405,607
2008	85,387	91,990	90,880	106,269	378,799
2007	79,613	85,430	84,467	99,078	348,650
2006	71,680	76,811	75,436	89,273	312,427

Earnings Per Share ($)

2011	0.88	0.97	E0.91	E1.27	E4.03
2010	0.77	0.88	0.84	1.23	3.72
2009	0.76	0.86	0.77	0.96	3.35
2008	0.68	0.86	0.70	1.03	3.16
2007	0.64	0.72	0.62	0.95	2.92
2006	0.58	0.67	0.57	0.86	2.68

Fiscal year ended Jan. 31. Next earnings report expected: Mid November. EPS Estimates based on S&P Operating Earnings; historical GAAP earnings are as reported.

Dividend Data (Dates: mm/dd Payment Date: mm/dd/yy)

Amount ($)	Date Decl.	Ex-Div. Date	Stk. of Record	Payment Date
0.303	03/04	03/10	03/12	04/05/10
0.303	03/04	05/12	05/14	06/01/10
0.303	03/04	08/11	08/13	09/07/10
0.303	03/04	12/08	12/10	01/03/11

Dividends have been paid since 1973. Source: Company reports.

Please read the Required Disclosures and Analyst Certification on the last page of this report.

The McGraw-Hill Companies

Wal-Mart Stores Inc

STANDARD &POOR'S

Business Summary October 14, 2010

CORPORATE OVERVIEW. Walmart, the largest retailer in North America, has set its sights on other parts of the world. The company's operations are divided into three divisions: Walmart U.S. (FY 10 (Jan.) sales $258.2 billion), Sam's Club ($46.7 billion), and Walmart International ($100.1 billion). Internationally, WMT recently operated 44 units in Argentina, 436 in Brazil, 317 in Canada, 519 in Central America, 254 in Chile, 283 in China (through joint ventures), 371 in Japan, 1,472 in Mexico, and 371 in the U.K.

MARKET PROFILE. With over 100 million people walking into Walmart stores every week, the company is a dominant player in many of the markets in which it competes. With FY 10 sales of about $155 billion within supermarket-related categories (grocery, health & wellness), the Walmart U.S. division is the largest supermarket operator in the U.S., commanding over 25% market share of the $500+ billion supermarket industry. Other major product categories within the Walmart division include entertainment ($34 billion in estimated sales in FY 10), hardlines ($28 billion), apparel ($26 billion), and home ($13 billion). Sam's Club is the second largest warehouse club in the U.S., with sales of $46.7 billion in FY 10. About 58% of Sam's Club sales were generated from food, beverage health and wellness categories.

Company Financials Fiscal Year Ended Jan. 31

Per Share Data ($)	2010	2009	2008	2007	2006	2005	2004	2003	2002	2001
Tangible Book Value	14.43	12.75	12.22	11.57	9.84	9.12	7.83	6.78	5.95	4.99
Cash Flow	5.56	5.06	4.72	4.23	3.81	3.44	2.91	2.58	2.22	2.04
Earnings	3.72	3.35	3.16	2.92	2.68	2.41	2.03	1.81	1.50	1.40
S&P Core Earnings	3.72	3.42	3.16	2.92	2.66	2.41	2.03	1.79	1.47	1.39
Dividends	1.09	0.95	0.67	0.67	0.60	0.52	0.36	0.30	0.28	0.24
Payout Ratio	29%	28%	21%	23%	22%	22%	18%	17%	19%	17%
Calendar Year	2009	2008	2007	2006	2005	2004	2003	2002	2001	2000
Prices:High	57.51	63.85	51.44	52.15	54.60	61.31	60.20	63.94	58.75	69.00
Prices:Low	46.25	43.11	42.09	42.31	42.31	51.08	46.25	43.72	42.00	41.44
P/E Ratio:High	15	19	16	18	20	25	30	35	39	49
P/E Ratio:Low	12	13	13	14	16	21	23	24	28	30

Income Statement Analysis (Million $)										
Revenue	408,214	405,607	378,799	348,650	312,427	285,222	256,329	244,524	217,799	191,329
Operating Income	31,663	26,580	24,784	22,298	23,247	18,729	16,525	15,075	15,367	12,392
Depreciation	7,157	6,739	6,317	5,459	4,717	4,405	3,852	3,432	3,290	2,868
Interest Expense	2,065	2,272	1,467	1,809	1,420	1,187	996	1,063	1,326	1,374
Pretax Income	22,066	20,898	20,198	18,968	17,358	16,105	14,193	12,719	10,751	10,116
Effective Tax Rate	32.4%	34.2%	34.2%	33.6%	33.4%	34.7%	36.1%	35.3%	36.2%	36.5%
Net Income	14,414	13,254	12,884	12,178	11,231	10,267	8,861	8,039	6,671	6,295
S&P Core Earnings	14,414	13,505	12,880	12,178	11,134	10,267	8,861	7,955	6,592	6,235

Balance Sheet & Other Financial Data (Million $)										
Cash	7,907	7,275	5,569	7,373	6,414	5,488	5,199	2,758	2,161	2,054
Current Assets	48,331	48,949	47,585	46,588	43,824	38,491	34,421	30,483	28,246	26,555
Total Assets	170,706	163,429	163,514	151,193	138,187	120,223	104,912	94,685	83,451	78,130
Current Liabilities	55,561	55,390	58,454	51,754	48,826	42,888	37,418	32,617	27,282	28,949
Long Term Debt	33,231	31,349	29,799	30,735	30,171	23,669	20,099	19,608	18,732	15,655
Common Equity	70,749	65,285	64,608	61,573	53,171	49,396	43,623	39,337	35,102	31,343
Total Capital	110,517	104,673	102,259	94,468	84,809	74,388	65,206	60,307	55,041	48,138
Capital Expenditures	12,184	11,499	14,937	15,666	14,563	12,893	10,308	9,355	8,383	8,042
Cash Flow	21,571	19,993	19,201	17,637	15,948	14,672	12,713	11,471	9,961	9,163
Current Ratio	0.9	0.9	0.8	0.9	0.9	0.9	0.9	0.9	1.0	0.9
% Long Term Debt of Capitalization	30.1	30.0	29.1	32.5	35.6	31.8	30.8	32.5	34.0	32.5
% Net Income of Revenue	3.5	3.3	3.4	3.5	3.5	3.6	3.5	3.3	3.1	3.3
% Return on Assets	8.6	8.1	8.2	8.4	8.7	9.1	8.9	9.0	8.3	8.5
% Return on Equity	21.2	20.4	20.4	21.2	21.9	22.1	21.3	21.6	20.1	22.0

Data as orig reptd.; bef. results of disc opers/spec. items. Per share data adj. for stk. divs.; EPS diluted. E-Estimated. NA-Not Available. NM-Not Meaningful. NR-Not Ranked. UR-Under Review.

Office: 702 S.W. 8th Street, Bentonville, AR 72716.
Telephone: 479-273-4000.
Website: http://www.walmartstores.com
Chrmn: S.R. Walton

Pres & CEO: M. Duke
EVP & CFO: T.M. Schoewe
EVP & Chief Admin Officer: T.A. Mars
EVP & Treas: C.M. Holley, Jr.

Investor Contact: M. Beckstead (479-277-9558)
Board Members: A. M. Alvarez, J. W. Breyer, M. M. Burns, J. I. Cash, Jr., R. C. Corbett, D. N. Daft, M. Duke, G. B. Penner, H. L. Scott, Jr., A. M. Sorenson, J. Walton, S. R. Walton, C. J. Williams, L. S. Wolf

Founded: 1945
Domicile: Delaware
Employees: 2,100,000

The McGraw-Hill Companies

Washington Post Co (The)

STANDARD &POOR'S

S&P Recommendation	HOLD ★★★☆☆	Price $372.63 (as of Oct 22, 2010)	12-Mo. Target Price $411.00	Investment Style Large-Cap Growth

GICS Sector Consumer Discretionary
Sub-Industry Publishing

Summary WPO publishes The Washington Post newspaper, operates TV stations and cable systems, and provides education and database services.

Key Stock Statistics (Source S&P, Vickers, company reports)

52-Wk Range	$547.58– 295.56	S&P Oper. EPS 2010**E**	33.55	Market Capitalization(B)	$2.935	Beta	0.90
Trailing 12-Month EPS	$25.42	S&P Oper. EPS 2011**E**	36.25	Yield (%)	2.42	S&P 3-Yr. Proj. EPS CAGR(%)	8
Trailing 12-Month P/E	14.7	P/E on S&P Oper. EPS 2010**E**	11.1	Dividend Rate/Share	$9.00	S&P Credit Rating	A
$10K Invested 5 Yrs Ago	$5,297	Common Shares Outstg. (M)	9.2	Institutional Ownership (%)	89		

Price Performance

30-Week Mov. Avg. · · · 10-Week Mov. Avg. - - GAAP Earnings vs. Previous Year Volume Above Avg. |ılıl| STARS
12-Mo. Target Price — Relative Strength — ▲ Up ▼ Down ► No Change Below Avg. |ılıl| ★

Analysis prepared by **Joseph Agnese** on September 17, 2010, when the stock traded at **$ 357.16**.

Highlights

➤ We look for revenues to rise about 6.2% in 2010. We project growth in education segment revenues to be driven by a mix of organic gains and acquisitions. We forecast an increase in cable segment revenues from the addition of new cable modem, telephone and digital video subscribers. We expect television segment revenues to improve this year on easier comparisons, increased political advertising and more stable advertising demand. Although we see declines in the newspaper segment amid persisting secular challenges, we look for cyclical challenges to ease as the year progresses.

➤ We expect operating margins to widen in 2010. We see margin improvements in the cable division, coupled with less severe losses in the company's publishing businesses, offsetting a shift in mix toward the lower-margin education business. We believe publishing margins will be supported by more stable advertising demand and benefits from cost-cutting efforts.

➤ After a moderate reduction in share count due to an active share repurchase program, we see EPS of $33.55 in 2010, up from operating EPS of $22.40 in 2009, excluding restructuring and early retirement charges of $10.60.

Investment Rationale/Risk

➤ In August 2010, the company agreed to sell Newsweek magazine to Harman Media. Nevertheless, we believe diverse media and educational service operations position WPO better than many peers despite significant cyclical and secular pressures. The company's newspaper operations continue to be negatively impacted by a long-term shift of advertising revenues to digital media. However, we think an improved economic environment is helping ease cyclical pressures on ad spending.

➤ Risks to our recommendation and target price include the potential for federal rule changes to result in a significant reduction in Title IV funding for Kaplan schools. Regarding corporate governance, 28 holders of non-publicly traded Class A shares (as of January 31, 2010) have the right to elect a majority of the directors, which we believe may not be in the best interests of common (Class B) stockholders.

➤ We think WPO should trade at a discount to its peers' median EV/EBITDA multiple due to what we see as its higher risk profile. Applying a 17% peer discounted EV/EBITDA multiple of 4.0X to our 2010 EBITDA estimate of $818 million, results in our 12-month target price of $411.

Qualitative Risk Assessment

LOW	MEDIUM	HIGH

Our risk assessment incorporates our view of a highly competitive environment for advertising among publishers and other media, and a significant negative trend in print advertising and circulation, partially offset by the recurring nature of a significant portion of company revenues.

Quantitative Evaluations

S&P Quality Ranking   B+

D	C	B-	B	B+	A-	A	A+

Relative Strength Rank   WEAK

    17

LOWEST = 1   HIGHEST = 99

Revenue/Earnings Data

Revenue (Million $)

	1Q	2Q	3Q	4Q	Year
2010	1,171	1,202	--	--	--
2009	1,054	1,128	1,149	1,238	4,570
2008	1,063	1,106	1,129	1,164	4,462
2007	985.6	1,047	1,023	1,126	4,180
2006	948.3	969.0	946.9	1,041	3,905
2005	833.9	897.6	873.7	948.7	3,554

Earnings Per Share ($)

	1Q	2Q	3Q	4Q	Year
2010	4.91	10.25	E8.79	E9.62	E33.55
2009	-2.04	1.30	1.81	8.71	9.78
2008	4.08	-0.31	1.08	2.01	6.87
2007	6.70	7.19	7.60	8.72	30.19
2006	8.48	8.17	7.60	9.97	34.21
2005	6.87	8.16	6.89	10.65	32.59

Fiscal year ended Dec. 31. Next earnings report expected: Early November. EPS Estimates based on S&P Operating Earnings; historical GAAP earnings are as reported.

Dividend Data (Dates: mm/dd Payment Date: mm/dd/yy)

Amount ($)	Date Decl.	Ex-Div. Date	Stk. of Record	Payment Date
2.250	01/21	01/25	01/27	02/05/10
2.250	02/23	04/22	04/26	05/07/10
2.250	06/10	07/22	07/26	08/06/10
2.250	09/23	10/21	10/25	11/05/10

Dividends have been paid since 1956. Source: Company reports.

Please read the Required Disclosures and Analyst Certification on the last page of this report.

The McGraw·Hill Companies

Washington Post Co (The)

Business Summary September 17, 2010

CORPORATE OVERVIEW. The Washington Post operates principally in four areas of the media business: newspaper publishing, television broadcasting, magazine publishing, and cable television. Through its subsidiary Kaplan, Inc., the company also provides educational services for individuals, schools and businesses.

The company divides Kaplan's various educational businesses (58% of 2009 revenues) into four categories: higher education (58% of segment revenues), test preparation (17%), international (20%),and Kaplan ventures (4.7%). Higher education includes Kaplan's domestic post-secondary education businesses, including fixed facility colleges and online post-secondary and career programs. We note that approximately 71% of Kaplan's higher education revenues came from Title IV (federal financial aid) programs in 2009, and thus we believe the segment is vulnerable to budget cuts for education spending. Test preparation includes standardized test prep for college, graduate school and professional licensing and advanced designation exams and includes live tutoring services. International includes U.K., Ireland, Singapore, Australia, Hong Kong and China businesses. Kaplan ventures division manages and de-

velops business lines in markets adjacent to Kaplan's core educational businesses such as compliance training in the pharmaceutical and medical technology industries and assistance in licensure and registration filings for insurance carriers, agencies and brokers/dealers. Part of the company's strategy in the education business is to grow through acquisition; along those lines, Kaplan made two acquisitions in 2009, following nine in both 2008 and 2007.

The Newspaper division (15%) includes The Washington Post, Express (a free weekly tabloid), Post-Newsweek Media, the Slate group, and other publications. WPNI holds an interest in Classified Ventures, a company that provides online classified advertising databases for cars, apartment rentals and residential real estate. Advertising represented 68% of The Washington Post's revenue, with subscription fees contributing 29%.

Company Financials Fiscal Year Ended Dec. 31

Per Share Data ($)	2009	2008	2007	2006	2005	2004	2003	2002	2001	2000
Tangible Book Value	97.63	89.89	NM	143.64	103.66	92.76	64.70	59.82	50.31	50.03
Cash Flow	44.12	37.42	55.26	57.76	53.26	54.04	43.38	40.93	38.62	26.79
Earnings	9.78	6.87	30.19	34.21	32.59	34.59	25.12	22.61	24.06	14.32
S&P Core Earnings	13.26	15.82	25.02	30.53	26.50	29.88	15.68	12.98	-1.24	NA
Dividends	8.60	8.60	8.20	7.80	7.40	7.00	5.80	5.60	5.60	5.40
Payout Ratio	88%	125%	27%	23%	23%	20%	23%	25%	23%	38%
Prices:High	495.60	823.25	885.23	815.00	982.03	999.50	819.50	743.00	651.50	628.75
Prices:Low	300.16	320.00	726.93	690.00	716.00	790.21	650.03	516.00	470.00	467.25
P/E Ratio:High	51	NM	29	24	30	29	33	33	27	44
P/E Ratio:Low	31	NM	24	20	22	23	26	23	20	33

Income Statement Analysis (Million $)										
Revenue	4,570	4,462	4,180	3,905	3,554	3,300	2,839	2,584	2,417	2,412
Operating Income	542	598	716	682	713	748	497	549	358	458
Depreciation	323	288	239	222	198	185	174	172	138	118
Interest Expense	31.6	24.7	24.1	25.3	26.8	28.0	27.8	33.8	49.6	54.7
Pretax Income	149	145	481	519	500	542	383	354	388	230
Effective Tax Rate	38.7%	54.7%	40.0%	36.5%	37.1%	38.7%	37.0%	38.8%	40.7%	40.6%
Net Income	92.8	65.7	289	330	314	333	241	216	230	136
S&P Core Earnings	124	148	238	293	255	287	150	124	-13.4	NA

Balance Sheet & Other Financial Data (Million $)										
Cash	863	748	373	348	216	119	87.4	28.8	31.5	20.3
Current Assets	1,388	1,352	995	935	818	754	496	383	397	405
Total Assets	5,186	5,158	6,005	5,381	4,585	4,317	3,902	3,584	3,559	3,201
Current Liabilities	990	1,094	1,013	803	695	688	712	736	434	409
Long Term Debt	396	400	401	402	404	426	422	406	1,862	873
Common Equity	2,940	2,858	3,461	3,160	2,638	2,412	2,075	1,837	1,683	1,481
Total Capital	3,358	3,630	4,583	4,173	3,477	3,254	2,814	2,517	3,781	2,485
Capital Expenditures	258	289	290	284	238	205	126	153	224	130
Cash Flow	414	353	526	551	511	518	414	387	367	253
Current Ratio	1.4	1.2	1.0	1.2	1.2	1.1	0.7	0.5	0.9	1.0
% Long Term Debt of Capitalization	Nil	11.0	8.7	9.6	11.6	13.1	15.0	16.1	49.3	35.1
% Net Income of Revenue	2.0	1.5	6.9	8.4	8.8	10.1	8.5	8.4	9.5	5.7
% Return on Assets	NA	1.2	5.1	6.6	7.1	8.0	6.4	6.1	6.8	4.4
% Return on Equity	NA	2.1	8.7	11.3	12.4	14.9	12.3	12.2	14.4	9.5

Data as orig reptd.; bef. results of disc opers/spec. items. Per share data adj. for stk. divs.; EPS diluted. E-Estimated. NA-Not Available. NM-Not Meaningful. NR-Not Ranked. UR-Under Review.

Office: 1150 15th Street NW, Washington, DC 20071.
Telephone: 202-334-6000.
Website: http://www.washpostco.com
Chrmn & CEO: D. Graham

Vice Chrmn: B. Jones, Jr.
SVP & CFO: H. Jones
SVP, Secy & General Counsel: V. Dillon
CTO: Y. Kochar

Investor Contact: J.B. Morse, Jr. (202-334-6662)
Board Members: L. C. Bollinger, W. E. Buffett, C. C. Davis, B. Diller, J. L. Dotson, Jr., M. F. Gates, T. S. Gayner, D. Graham, B. Jones, Jr., A. M. Mulcahy, R. L. Olson, G. R. Wagoner, Jr., K. Weymouth

Founded: 1947
Domicile: Delaware
Employees: 21,500

Waste Management Inc.

STANDARD &POOR'S

S&P Recommendation BUY ★★★★☆	**Price** $36.79 (as of Oct 22, 2010)	**12-Mo. Target Price** $40.00	**Investment Style** Large-Cap Blend

GICS Sector Industrials
Sub-Industry Environmental & Facilities Services

Summary This Houston-based company is the largest U.S. trash hauling/disposal concern.

Key Stock Statistics (Source S&P, Vickers, company reports)

52-Wk Range	$37.25– 29.75	S&P Oper. EPS 2010**E**	2.15	Market Capitalization(B)	$17.565	Beta		0.60
Trailing 12-Month EPS	$2.09	S&P Oper. EPS 2011**E**	2.45	Yield (%)	3.42	S&P 3-Yr. Proj. EPS CAGR(%)		11
Trailing 12-Month P/E	17.6	P/E on S&P Oper. EPS 2010**E**	17.1	Dividend Rate/Share	$1.26	S&P Credit Rating		BBB
$10K Invested 5 Yrs Ago	$15,732	Common Shares Outstg. (M)	477.4	Institutional Ownership (%)	80			

Price Performance

30-Week Mov. Avg. · · · 10-Week Mov. Avg. — — **GAAP Earnings vs. Previous Year** **Volume** Above Avg. ▦ STARS
12-Mo. Target Price — Relative Strength — ▲ Up ▼ Down ▶ No Change Below Avg. ▦ ★

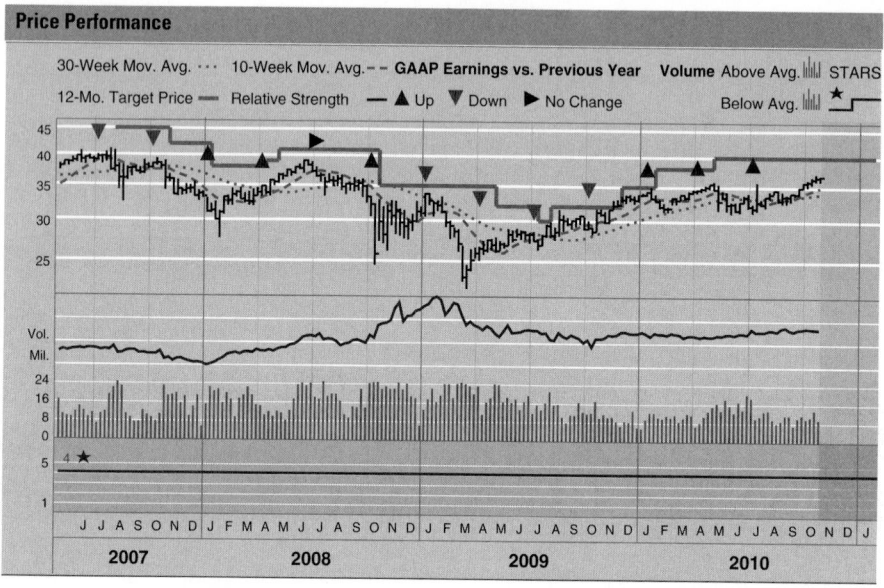

Options: ASE, CBOE, P, Ph

Analysis prepared by **Stewart Scharf** on August 05, 2010, when the stock traded at **$ 34.29**.

Highlights

➤ We expect organic revenues to rise modestly in 2010, as at least 2% higher core prices, and rising commodity recycling prices should outweigh lower volume. We think volume will turn positive in the second half of 2010, driven by growth in special waste in landfill, and improving commercial and residential collection. Industrial and C&D waste (construction & demolition) should also slowly recover. We see revenue growth returning in 2011.

➤ In our view, gross margins (before D&A) will widen further in 2010, from 38.6% in 2009, based on price hikes, cost savings from routing initiatives and an improving landfill mix. We see the EBITDA margin expanding from 27% in 2009, as restructuring efforts, improved productivity, and lower maintenance and safety costs outweigh higher salary and information technology expenses. We also expect interest expense to rise, primarily due to interest on senior notes.

➤ We project a lower effective tax rate of below 37% for 2010, with operating EPS of $2.15 (before at least $0.07 of charges), and then an advance of 14% to $2.45 for 2011.

Investment Rationale/Risk

➤ Our Buy recommendation is based on our valuation metrics, the company's pricing and expansion strategy, and more favorable economic trends. We expect strong cash generation to be used for niche acquisitions, alternative energy projects, share buybacks, and dividends.

➤ Risks to our opinion and target price include a significant rise in fuel costs, a prolonged downturn in the U.S. economy, a sharp drop in recycling prices and demand, a lower customer retention rate, and an inability to raise prices enough to meet return on invested capital (ROIC) goals.

➤ We view the stock's recent dividend yield of 3.7%, above the 2.1% yield of the S&P 500, as attractive. Correlating various relative metrics, including its historical five-year average P/E multiple, we believe the shares should trade at an above-peer average P/E of near 19X our EPS estimate for 2010, valuing the stock at $41. Based on our discounted cash flow model, assuming a 7.5% weighted average cost of capital and 3% terminal growth rate, our intrinsic value estimate is $39. Blending these metrics, we derive our 12-month target price of $40.

Qualitative Risk Assessment

LOW	**MEDIUM**	HIGH

Our risk assessment reflects soft volume due to weak economic conditions, offset by our view of a solid balance sheet, with strong cash generation for dividends, share buybacks, debt paydowns, and niche acquisitions. In addition, we view corporate governance practices as sound.

Quantitative Evaluations

S&P Quality Ranking B+

D	C	B-	B	**B+**	A-	A	A+

Relative Strength Rank MODERATE

62

LOWEST = 1   HIGHEST = 99

Revenue/Earnings Data

Revenue (Million $)

	1Q	2Q	3Q	4Q	Year
2010	2,935	3,158	--	--	--
2009	2,810	2,952	3,023	3,006	11,791
2008	3,266	3,489	3,525	3,108	13,388
2007	3,188	3,358	3,403	3,361	13,310
2006	3,229	3,410	3,441	3,283	13,363
2005	3,038	3,289	3,375	3,372	13,074

Earnings Per Share ($)

	1Q	2Q	3Q	4Q	Year
2010	0.37	0.51	E0.65	E0.55	E2.15
2009	0.31	0.50	0.56	0.64	2.01
2008	0.48	0.64	0.63	0.44	2.19
2007	0.42	0.64	0.54	0.61	2.23
2006	0.34	0.76	0.55	0.46	2.10
2005	0.26	0.92	0.38	0.52	2.09

Fiscal year ended Dec. 31. Next earnings report expected: Late October. EPS Estimates based on S&P Operating Earnings; historical GAAP earnings are as reported.

Dividend Data (Dates: mm/dd Payment Date: mm/dd/yy)

Amount ($)	Date Decl.	Ex-Div. Date	Stk. of Record	Payment Date
0.290	11/10	11/30	12/02	12/18/09
0.315	02/26	03/01	03/03	03/19/10
0.315	05/11	05/27	06/01	06/18/10
0.315	08/20	09/02	09/07	09/24/10

Dividends have been paid since 1998. Source: Company reports.

Please read the Required Disclosures and Analyst Certification on the last page of this report.

The McGraw-Hill Companies

Waste Management Inc.

STANDARD &POOR'S

Business Summary August 05, 2010

CORPORATE OVERVIEW. Waste Management, the largest waste disposal company in North America, provides collection, transfer, recycling and re-source recovery, as well as disposal services. It also owns U.S. waste-to-energy facilities. As of December 31, 2009, it served nearly 20 million cus-tomers through 345 transfer stations and 273 owned or operated landfills (five hazardous waste landfills), 16 waste-to-energy plants, 98 recycling plants, five independent power production plants and 108 beneficial-use landfill gas projects. In 2009, revenues from the North American solid waste (NASW) business were: 58% collection; 19% landfill; 6.1% waste-to-energy (Wheelabrator Technologies unit); 10% transfer; 5.4% recycling; and 1.8% oth-er. WM's average remaining landfill life at December 31, 2009, was 35 years, and 41 years when considering remaining permitted capacity and projected annual disposal volume. WM's internalization rate at June 30, 2010 was 68.4%, down slightly from 68.7% at 2009 year end. WM believes that for every 1% re-duction in its "churn" ratio (customer turnover; 11% at June 30, 2010, up from 9% three months earlier), it adds $25 million to EBIT (earnings before interest and taxes).

We project free cash flow near $1.3 billion for 2010, up from $1.21 billion in 2009, with WM targeting about $685 million for share buybacks and $615 mil-lion for dividends. WM resumed its stock repurchase program in the third quarter of 2009, buying back about 4.6 million shares for $226 million. It spent $286 million on buybacks in the first half of 2010. The company sees a strong

acquisition pipeline and more attractive valuations over the next 9 to 15 months, targeting $250 million to $350 million for mostly solid waste "tuck-in" deals, while also considering some medical waste operations. In 2009, WM spent $281 million ($200 million annualized revenues) on acquisitions. We be-lieve capital spending for 2010 will be close to $1.2 billion, versus $1.18 billion in 2009. While the company can lose 3% to 5% of volume for every 1% price increase, it believes this method still boosts profit.

CORPORATE STRATEGY. In our view, WM will use its strong cash generation primarily for acquisitions, dividends and share buybacks, with more favorable acquisition multiples leading to a rise in acquired revenues. In October 2007, the company announced an environmental initiative under which it plans to invest in waste-based energy production, recycling and new waste technolo-gies, including up to $500 million a year for 10 years to increase the fuel effi-ciency of its fleet. We view this as a positive long-term environmental strategy as more methane in landfills is converted into energy. In March 2010, WM ac-quired a 40% interest in Shanghai Environment Group (SEG), a leading waste-to-energy company in China, for $142 million. In April 2010, it bought a waste-to-energy plant in Virginia for $150 million.

Company Financials Fiscal Year Ended Dec. 31

Per Share Data ($)	2009	2008	2007	2006	2005	2004	2003	2002	2001	2000
Tangible Book Value	0.85	0.57	0.52	1.52	1.10	0.91	0.24	0.21	0.43	NM
Cash Flow	4.38	4.87	4.64	4.66	4.50	3.90	3.44	5.29	2.97	2.14
Earnings	2.01	2.19	2.23	2.10	2.09	1.60	1.21	1.33	0.80	-0.16
S&P Core Earnings	2.01	2.15	2.18	2.08	1.90	1.48	1.09	1.17	1.04	NA
Dividends	1.16	1.08	0.96	0.88	0.80	0.75	0.01	0.01	0.01	0.01
Payout Ratio	58%	49%	43%	42%	38%	47%	1%	1%	1%	NM
Prices:High	34.18	39.25	41.19	38.64	31.03	31.42	29.72	31.25	32.50	28.31
Prices:Low	22.10	24.51	32.40	30.08	26.80	25.67	19.39	20.20	22.51	13.00
P/E Ratio:High	17	18	18	18	15	20	25	23	41	NM
P/E Ratio:Low	11	11	15	14	13	16	16	15	28	NM

Income Statement Analysis (Million $)	2009	2008	2007	2006	2005	2004	2003	2002	2001	2000
Revenue	11,791	13,388	13,310	13,363	13,074	12,516	11,574	11,142	11,322	12,492
Operating Income	3,186	3,577	3,746	3,388	3,167	3,021	2,841	2,870	3,034	3,216
Depreciation	1,166	1,323	1,259	1,334	1,361	1,336	1,265	2,444	1,371	1,429
Interest Expense	426	472	521	545	496	455	439	462	541	748
Pretax Income	1,473	1,797	1,784	1,518	1,140	1,214	1,129	1,240	792	344
Effective Tax Rate	28.0%	37.2%	30.2%	21.4%	NM	20.3%	35.8%	34.2%	35.9%	NM
Net Income	994	1,087	1,163	1,149	1,182	931	719	823	503	-97.0
S&P Core Earnings	994	1,066	1,133	1,139	1,072	864	643	725	653	NA

Balance Sheet & Other Financial Data (Million $)	2009	2008	2007	2006	2005	2004	2003	2002	2001	2000
Cash	1,153	480	348	614	666	443	135	264	730	94.0
Current Assets	3,010	2,335	2,480	3,182	3,451	2,819	2,588	2,700	3,124	2,457
Total Assets	21,154	20,227	20,175	20,600	21,135	20,905	20,656	19,631	19,490	18,565
Current Liabilities	2,901	3,036	2,598	3,268	3,257	3,205	3,332	3,173	3,721	2,937
Long Term Debt	8,124	7,491	8,008	7,495	8,165	8,182	7,997	8,062	7,709	8,372
Common Equity	6,285	5,902	5,792	6,222	6,121	5,971	5,563	5,308	5,392	4,801
Total Capital	15,464	15,160	15,521	15,357	15,931	14,435	15,473	13,389	14,241	14,067
Capital Expenditures	1,179	1,221	1,211	1,329	1,180	1,258	1,200	1,287	1,328	1,313
Cash Flow	2,160	2,410	2,422	2,483	2,543	2,267	1,984	3,267	1,874	1,332
Current Ratio	1.0	0.8	1.0	1.0	1.1	0.9	0.8	0.9	0.8	0.8
% Long Term Debt of Capitalization	52.5	49.4	51.5	48.8	51.3	56.7	51.7	60.2	54.1	59.5
% Net Income of Revenue	8.4	8.1	8.7	8.6	9.0	7.4	6.2	7.4	4.4	NM
% Return on Assets	4.8	5.4	5.7	5.5	5.6	4.5	3.5	4.2	2.6	NM
% Return on Equity	16.3	18.6	19.3	18.6	19.6	16.1	13.2	15.4	9.9	NM

Data as orig reptd.; bef. results of disc opers/spec. items. Per share data adj. for stk. divs.; EPS diluted. E-Estimated. NA-Not Available. NM-Not Meaningful. NR-Not Ranked. UR-Under Review.

Office: 1001 Fannin, Suite 4000, Houston, TX 77002.
Telephone: 713-512-6200.
Website: http://www.wm.com
Chrmn: J.C. Pope

Pres & CEO: D.P. Steiner
SVP & CFO: R. Simpson
SVP & General Counsel: R.L. Wittenbraker
SVP & CIO: P. Bhasin

Investor Contact: J. Alderson (713-394-2281)
Board Members: P. S. Cafferty, F. M. Clark, Jr., P. W. Gross, J. C. Pope, W. R. Reum, S. G. Rothmeier, D. P. Steiner, T. H. Weidemeyer

Founded: 1894
Domicile: Delaware
Employees: 43,400

The **McGraw-Hill** Companies

Waters Corp

STANDARD &POOR'S

S&P Recommendation HOLD ★★★☆☆

Price	12-Mo. Target Price	Investment Style
$72.53 (as of Oct 22, 2010)	$74.00	Large-Cap Growth

GICS Sector Health Care
Sub-Industry Life Sciences Tools & Services

Summary This company manufactures scientific and industrial analytical equipment such as liquid chromatography, thermal analysis and mass spectrometry products.

Key Stock Statistics (Source S&P, Vickers, company reports)

52-Wk Range	$73.78– 55.94	S&P Oper. EPS 2010**E**	3.96	Market Capitalization(B)	$6.676	Beta		1.07
Trailing 12-Month EPS	$3.56	S&P Oper. EPS 2011**E**	4.40	Yield (%)	Nil	S&P 3-Yr. Proj. EPS CAGR(%)		13
Trailing 12-Month P/E	20.4	P/E on S&P Oper. EPS 2010**E**	18.3	Dividend Rate/Share	Nil	S&P Credit Rating		NA
$10K Invested 5 Yrs Ago	$20,036	Common Shares Outstg. (M)	92.0	Institutional Ownership (%)	90			

Price Performance

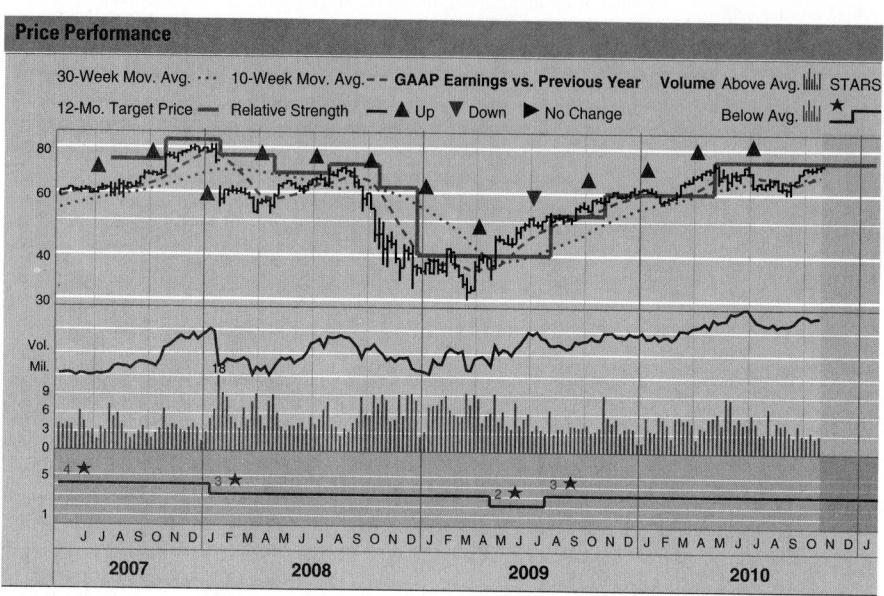

- 30-Week Mov. Avg. · · · · 10-Week Mov. Avg. - - - **GAAP Earnings vs. Previous Year** Volume Above Avg. ▮▮▮ STARS
- 12-Mo. Target Price —— Relative Strength — ▲ Up ▼ Down ► No Change Below Avg. ▮▮▮ ★

Options: ASE, CBOE, Ph

Analysis prepared by **Jeffrey Loo, CFA** on August 09, 2010, when the stock traded at **$ 66.58**.

Highlights

▶ We see sales growing 7% in both 2010 and 2011, to $1.6 billion and $1.72 billion, respectively, rebounding from the 5% decline of 2009. We believe WAT's end-markets are improving, albeit slowly, and we expect modest improvement throughout the year. Instrument sales to the pharmaceutical and life sciences end-markets should grow modestly as strong sales to generic pharmaceutical and specialty biopharmaceutical firms are partially offset by continued slow sales to large pharmaceutical firms due to capital constraints. Sales to government and academic customers are slower than we had initially anticipated as NIH funding from the economic stimulus package has been rolling out slowly. But we expect WAT to benefit from stimulus packages in other countries. WAT's industrial end-markets, particularly the chemical sector, should recover nicely following the double digit decline in 2009.

▶ We expect gross margins to improve 60 basis points (bps) on manufacturing cost reductions in both 2010 and 2011, while we see operating margins improving 200 bps and 140 bps on leverage and a lower cost structure.

▶ We see 2010 EPS of $3.96, and 2011 at $4.40.

Investment Rationale/Risk

▶ We believe the shares, recently trading at 16.8X our 2010 EPS estimate and at a 1.3X P/E-to-growth ratio, both in line with peers, are fairly valued. We see a recover within WAT's industrial end-markets, but see only modest growth within the life sciences and pharmaceutical markets. We look for continued solid growth in consumables and services sales. However, we are encouraged by WAT's introduction of new products including the mid-range Acquity UPLC H-Class, which we believe will appeal more to the mainstream laboratories. Early indications show robust interest in this instrument. Toward the end of the second quarter 2010, WAT began shipping two of its latest high performance systems, the Xevo G2 QT and Xevo TQ-S.

▶ Risks to our recommendation and target price include weaker-than-expected equipment sales to the life sciences and pharmaceutical end-markets and slower-than-expected recovery in the industrial end-markets.

▶ Based on our P/E-to-growth (PEG) analysis, using our 2010 EPS forecast, a PEG ratio of 1.4X, in line with peers, and a 13% projected three-year growth rate, our 12-month target price is $74.

Qualitative Risk Assessment

LOW	MEDIUM	HIGH

Our risk assessment reflects WAT's strong market share in the liquid chromatography and mass spectrometry markets, offset by a highly competitive marketplace and a reliance on customer demand for expensive instruments.

Quantitative Evaluations

S&P Quality Ranking B+

D	C	B-	B	B+	A-	A	A+

Relative Strength Rank MODERATE

67

LOWEST = 1   HIGHEST = 99

Revenue/Earnings Data

Revenue (Million $)

	1Q	2Q	3Q	4Q	Year
2010	367.7	391.1	--	--	--
2009	333.1	362.8	374.0	428.9	1,499
2008	371.7	398.8	386.3	418.3	1,575
2007	330.8	352.6	352.6	437.0	1,473
2006	290.2	301.9	301.2	386.9	1,280
2005	268.3	284.6	273.0	332.3	1,158

Earnings Per Share ($)

	1Q	2Q	3Q	4Q	Year
2010	0.79	0.90	E0.94	E1.30	E3.96
2009	0.75	0.72	0.79	1.08	3.34
2008	0.67	0.82	0.71	1.01	3.21
2007	0.54	0.59	0.52	0.96	2.62
2006	0.42	0.46	0.49	0.78	2.13
2005	0.38	0.46	0.22	0.71	1.74

Fiscal year ended Dec. 31. Next earnings report expected: Late October. EPS Estimates based on S&P Operating Earnings; historical GAAP earnings are as reported.

Dividend Data

No cash dividends have been paid.

Please read the Required Disclosures and Analyst Certification on the last page of this report.

The **McGraw-Hill** Companies

Waters Corp

Business Summary August 09, 2010

CORPORATE OVERVIEW. Waters manufactures, distributes, and services analytical instruments to the pharmaceutical, life sciences, biochemical, industrial, academic, and government end-markets. Analytical instruments and components manufactured include high-performance liquid chromatography (HPLC) instruments, columns and other consumables, mass spectrometry (MS) instruments that can be integrated with other analytical instruments, and thermal analysis (TA) and rheology instruments. HPLC is the standard technique to identify and analyze constituent components of various chemicals and materials. Its unique performance capabilities let it separate and identify 80% of known chemicals and materials. HPLC is used to analyze substances in a variety of industries for R&D, quality control, and process engineering applications. Pharmaceutical and life science industries use HPLC primarily to identify new drugs.

In March 2004, WAT introduced a novel technology that it describes as Ultra Performance Chromatography, the Acquity UPLC. WAT believes the Acquity UPLC provides more comprehensive chemical separation and faster analysis times compared to the HPLC. MS is an analytical technique used to identify unknown compounds, quantify known materials, and elucidate the structural and chemical properties of molecules by measuring the masses of individual molecules that have been converted into ions. These products serve diverse markets, including pharmaceutical and environmental industries. The TA In-

struments division makes and services thermal analysis and rheology instruments used for the physical characterization of polymers and related materials. Thermal analysis measures physical characteristics of materials as a function of temperature. Changes in temperature affect several characteristics of materials, such as their physical state, weight, dimension and mechanical and electrical properties, which may be measured using thermal analysis techniques. As a result, thermal analysis is widely used to develop, produce and characterize materials in industries such as plastics, chemicals and pharmaceuticals.

WAT has supplemented its internal growth with various strategic acquisitions. In March 2004, it acquired NuGenesis Technologies Corp. for about $43 million. NuGenesis and Creon Lab formed the company's new Lab Informatics market segment. In March 2006, WAT acquired VICAM, a provider of bioseparation and rapid detection instruments for food safety. In August 2006, WAT acquired Thermometric AB, and in November 2006, it acquired Environmental Resource Associates, a provider of environmental testing and services. In 2007 WAT acquired Calorimetry Sciences Corporation.

Company Financials Fiscal Year Ended Dec. 31

Per Share Data ($)	2009	2008	2007	2006	2005	2004	2003	2002	2001	2000
Tangible Book Value	3.97	2.48	5.71	NM	NM	3.05	2.67	NM	3.19	2.21
Cash Flow	3.93	3.50	2.88	2.57	2.12	2.16	1.60	1.40	1.08	1.36
Earnings	3.34	3.21	2.62	2.13	1.74	1.82	1.34	1.12	0.84	1.14
S&P Core Earnings	3.34	3.21	2.62	2.18	1.57	1.45	1.18	0.99	1.07	NA
Dividends	Nil	Nil	Nil	Nil	Nil	Nil	Nil	Nil	Nil	Nil
Payout Ratio	Nil	Nil	Nil	Nil	Nil	Nil	Nil	Nil	Nil	Nil
Prices:High	63.09	81.84	81.53	51.64	51.57	49.80	33.42	39.25	85.38	90.94
Prices:Low	30.00	32.21	48.55	37.06	33.99	33.10	19.79	17.86	22.33	21.97
P/E Ratio:High	19	25	31	24	30	27	25	35	NM	80
P/E Ratio:Low	9	10	19	17	20	18	15	16	NM	19

Income Statement Analysis (Million $)	2009	2008	2007	2006	2005	2004	2003	2002	2001	2000
Revenue	1,499	1,575	1,473	1,280	1,158	1,105	958	890	859	795
Operating Income	452	436	389	355	330	321	271	251	258	240
Depreciation	57.3	29.1	27.5	46.2	43.7	41.9	33.8	37.2	34.0	29.4
Interest Expense	11.0	38.5	56.5	51.7	24.7	10.1	2.37	2.48	1.26	Nil
Pretax Income	387	372	323	263	275	286	224	195	147	211
Effective Tax Rate	16.4%	13.4%	17.1%	15.5%	26.4%	21.6%	23.6%	22.1%	22.3%	26.0%
Net Income	323	322	268	222	202	224	171	152	115	156
S&P Core Earnings	324	322	268	227	183	179	150	134	147	NA

Balance Sheet & Other Financial Data (Million $)	2009	2008	2007	2006	2005	2004	2003	2002	2001	2000
Cash	630	429	693	514	494	539	357	313	227	75.5
Current Assets	1,172	956	1,237	1,000	913	974	715	636	523	344
Total Assets	1,916	1,623	1,881	1,617	1,429	1,460	1,131	1,011	887	692
Current Liabilities	395	290	658	686	604	493	379	320	281	221
Long Term Debt	500	500	500	500	500	250	125	Nil	Nil	Nil
Common Equity	848	661	586	362	284	679	590	665	582	452
Total Capital	1,348	1,161	1,086	862	784	929	715	665	582	452
Capital Expenditures	93.8	69.1	60.3	51.4	51.0	66.2	34.6	37.9	42.4	35.4
Cash Flow	381	352	296	268	246	266	205	189	148	186
Current Ratio	2.9	3.3	1.9	1.5	1.5	2.0	1.9	2.0	1.9	1.6
% Long Term Debt of Capitalization	37.1	43.1	46.0	58.0	63.8	26.9	17.5	Nil	Nil	Nil
% Net Income of Revenue	21.6	20.5	18.2	17.4	17.4	20.3	17.8	17.1	13.3	19.6
% Return on Assets	18.3	18.4	15.3	14.6	14.0	17.3	15.9	16.0	14.5	24.4
% Return on Equity	42.9	51.7	56.5	68.8	42.0	35.3	27.2	24.3	22.2	42.0

Data as orig reptd.; bef. results of disc opers/spec. items. Per share data adj. for stk. divs.; EPS diluted. E-Estimated. NA-Not Available. NM-Not Meaningful. NR-Not Ranked. UR-Under Review.

Office: 34 Maple Street, Milford, MA 01757-3696.
Telephone: 508-478-2000.
Email: info@waters.com
Website: http://www.waters.com

Chrmn, Pres & CEO: D.A. Berthiaume
CFO, Chief Admin Officer & Chief Acctg Officer: J.A. Ornell
Secy & General Counsel: M.T. Beaudouin
Cntlr: W. Curry

Board Members: J. Bekenstein, M. Berendt, D. A. Berthiaume, E. W. Conard, L. H. Glimcher, C. A. Kuebler, W. J. Miller, J. A. Reed, T. P. Salice

Founded: 1991
Domicile: Delaware
Employees: 5,216

Watson Pharmaceuticals Inc.

STANDARD &POOR'S

S&P Recommendation BUY ★★★★☆

Price	**12-Mo. Target Price**	**Investment Style**
$46.76 (as of Oct 22, 2010)	$50.00	Large-Cap Blend

GICS Sector Health Care
Sub-Industry Pharmaceuticals

Summary This company produces generic and branded drugs. In December 2009, Watson acquired international generic drugmaker Arrow Group for about $1.8 billion in cash and stock.

Key Stock Statistics (Source S&P, Vickers, company reports)

52-Wk Range	$47.53–33.88	S&P Oper. EPS 2010**E**	3.40	Market Capitalization(B)	$5.839	Beta		0.48
Trailing 12-Month EPS	$2.20	S&P Oper. EPS 2011**E**	3.80	Yield (%)	Nil	S&P 3-Yr. Proj. EPS CAGR(%)		13
Trailing 12-Month P/E	21.3	P/E on S&P Oper. EPS 2010**E**	13.8	Dividend Rate/Share	Nil	S&P Credit Rating		BBB
$10K Invested 5 Yrs Ago	$13,243	Common Shares Outstg. (M)	124.9	Institutional Ownership (%)	78			

Price Performance

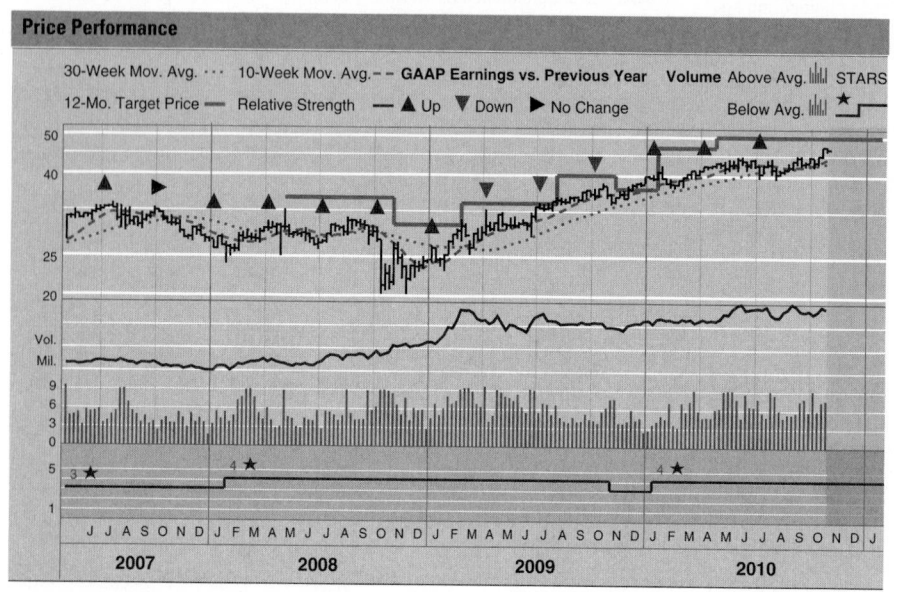

Options: ASE, CBOE, Ph

Analysis prepared by **Herman B. Saftlas** on September 03, 2010, when the stock traded at **$ 44.39**.

Highlights

➤ We project revenues of about $3.5 billion in 2010, up from 2009's $2.8 billion, largely reflecting the December 2009 acquisition of Arrow Group. The latter markets some 50 generic drugs in over 20 countries. Generic volume should also reflect greater contributions from new products, with 36 ANDAs filed in 2009. Key new products, in our opinion, include generic versions of Toprol XL, Cardizem LA, Concerta, Lovenox and Lotrel. Distribution revenues are likely to increase, but branded sales are expected to decline sharply, reflecting the absence of Ferrlecit.

➤ We expect 2010 gross margins to hold up relatively well, benefiting from manufacturing efficiencies and other supply chain improvements. We also see SG&A and R&D spending declining as a percentage of sales. Interest expense, however, will likely be sharply higher.

➤ After an estimated tax rate of about 36%, versus 2009's 37%, we project adjusted cash EPS (before amortization) of $3.40 for 2010, up from $3.04 in 2009. GAAP EPS in 2009 were $1.96. Boosted by new products, we forecast cash EPS of $3.80 in 2011.

Investment Rationale/Risk

➤ We believe that WPI's diversified business platform, which comprises growing positions in generics, branded drugs and drug distribution, coupled with ongoing cost-streamlining measures, will provide the underpinnings for EPS growth over the coming years. We view the December 2009 acquisition of Arrow Group as a key strategic move, expanding Watson's generic lines and geographic base, and providing important cost synergies. Despite the recent loss of Ferrlecit, we continue to see long-term opportunities for the branded business, especially in the areas of urology and women's health.

➤ Risks to our recommendation and target price include greater-than-expected competitive pressures in principal generic and branded product lines, as well as possible R&D pipeline disappointments.

➤ Our 12-month target price of $50 applies a near-peers P/E of 13.2X to our 2011 cash EPS estimate. This is supported by our DCF model, which assumes decelerating cash flow growth over the next 10 years, a WACC of 7.0%, and perpetuity growth of 2%, indicating intrinsic value of $50.

Qualitative Risk Assessment

LOW	MEDIUM	HIGH

Our risk assessment reflects risks common to the generic pharmaceutical business, which include the need to successfully develop generic products, obtain regulatory approvals and legally challenge branded patents. However, we believe these risks are offset by the company's wide and diverse generic portfolio and the balance afforded by WPI's branded drug business.

Quantitative Evaluations

S&P Quality Ranking   B-

D	C	B-	B	B+	A-	A	A+

Relative Strength Rank   MODERATE

68

LOWEST = 1   HIGHEST = 99

Revenue/Earnings Data

Revenue (Million $)

	1Q	2Q	3Q	4Q	Year
2010	856.5	875.3	--	--	--
2009	667.4	677.8	662.1	785.7	2,793
2008	627.0	622.6	640.7	645.2	2,536
2007	671.6	603.0	594.7	627.3	2,497
2006	407.2	510.4	440.5	621.2	1,979
2005	400.8	416.3	410.3	418.8	1,646

Earnings Per Share ($)

2010	0.57	0.57	E0.86	E0.90	E3.40
2009	0.43	0.46	0.55	0.51	1.96
2008	0.45	0.53	0.62	0.50	2.09
2007	0.29	0.33	0.31	0.34	1.27
2006	0.23	-0.15	0.31	-4.80	-4.37
2005	0.32	0.35	0.35	0.19	1.21

Fiscal year ended Dec. 31. Next earnings report expected: Early November. EPS Estimates based on S&P Operating Earnings; historical GAAP earnings are as reported.

Dividend Data

No cash dividends have been paid.

Watson Pharmaceuticals Inc.

STANDARD
&POOR'S

Business Summary September 03, 2010

CORPORATE PROFILE. Watson Pharmaceuticals is a leading maker of generic pharmaceuticals that targets difficult to produce niche off-patent drugs. WPI significantly expanded its U.S. generic business with the acquisitions of Andrx Corp. in 2006, and U.K.-based Arrow Group in late 2009. WPI also offers a line of specialty branded pharmaceuticals, largely in the areas of urology, cancer and women's health.

Many WPI pharmaceuticals incorporate the company's novel proprietary drug delivery systems, such as transmucosal, vaginal and transdermal systems that allow for defined rates of drug release. Generic drugs accounted for about 60% of revenues and 72% of operating income in 2009, branded drugs for 16% and 23%, and distribution operations for 24% and 5%. Third-party manufactured products accounted for about 55% of Watson's net revenues in 2009.

WPI markets some 170 generic drug products in the U.S. and 49 in Canada, comprising a broad cross section of therapeutic categories. Key segments include oral contraceptives, analgesics, antihypertensives, diuretics, antiulcers, antipsychotics, anti-inflammatories, analgesics, hormone replacements, antispasmodics and antidiarrheals. Arrow Group markets some 50 generic products in Europe, Asia, South Africa and Australia.

During 2009, WPI launched eight new generic products in the U.S. and filed 36 Abbreviated New Drug Applications (ANDAs) with the FDA. In total, Watson has about 110 ANDAs pending at the FDA, and over 900 applications pending outside of the U.S.

Branded pharmaceuticals comprise treatments for incontinence, cancer, pain management and other conditions. Key products include Trelstar, a treatment for prostate cancer; Oxytrol oxybutynin transdermal patch and Gelnique oxytrol gel to treat urinary incontinence; Androderm, a testosterone transdermal patch; and Rapaflo, a treatment for enlarged prostates. WPI's branded rights to Ferrlecit, a nephrology product used to treat iron deficiency anemia, ended at the end of 2009.

The company sells its products primarily through distributors and chain drug stores, such as McKesson Corp. (11% of net revenues in 2009) and Walgreen (13%).

Company Financials Fiscal Year Ended Dec. 31

Per Share Data ($)	2009	2008	2007	2006	2005	2004	2003	2002	2001	2000
Tangible Book Value	3.06	6.51	3.56	0.09	8.81	7.97	5.54	4.33	3.79	0.98
Cash Flow	3.53	3.48	3.37	-2.23	2.87	2.07	2.78	2.45	2.01	2.34
Earnings	1.96	2.09	1.27	-4.37	1.21	1.27	1.86	1.64	1.07	1.65
S&P Core Earnings	2.12	1.96	1.24	-4.32	1.09	1.16	1.64	1.36	0.52	NA
Dividends	Nil	Nil	Nil	Nil	Nil	Nil	Nil	Nil	Nil	Nil
Payout Ratio	Nil	Nil	Nil	Nil	Nil	Nil	Nil	Nil	Nil	Nil
Prices:High	40.25	32.70	33.91	35.27	36.93	49.19	50.12	33.25	66.39	71.50
Prices:Low	23.05	20.17	25.02	21.35	27.99	24.50	26.90	17.95	26.50	33.69
P/E Ratio:High	21	16	27	NM	31	39	27	20	62	43
P/E Ratio:Low	12	10	20	NM	23	19	14	11	25	20

Income Statement Analysis (Million $)	2009	2008	2007	2006	2005	2004	2003	2002	2001	2000
Revenue	2,793	2,536	2,497	1,979	1,646	1,641	1,458	1,223	1,161	812
Operating Income	638	539	515	364	450	419	439	386	404	227
Depreciation	189	171	254	218	207	107	100	86.6	101	71.4
Interest Expense	34.2	28.2	44.5	22.1	14.5	13.3	25.8	22.1	27.8	24.3
Pretax Income	363	358	224	-411	219	237	318	279	199	355
Effective Tax Rate	38.8%	33.5%	37.1%	NM	37.0%	36.1%	36.2%	37.0%	41.5%	52.0%
Net Income	222	238	141	-445	138	151	203	176	116	171
S&P Core Earnings	240	222	138	-441	123	137	178	146	56.3	NA

Balance Sheet & Other Financial Data (Million $)	2009	2008	2007	2006	2005	2004	2003	2002	2001	2000
Cash	215	521	216	161	630	680	574	273	329	238
Current Assets	1,771	1,458	1,174	1,262	1,360	1,370	1,323	921	890	831
Total Assets	5,992	3,678	3,472	3,761	3,080	3,244	3,283	2,663	2,528	2,580
Current Liabilities	1,052	482	445	690	246	256	339	375	245	280
Long Term Debt	1,150	825	899	1,124	588	588	723	332	416	438
Common Equity	3,023	2,109	1,849	1,680	2,104	2,243	2,057	1,798	1,672	1,548
Total Capital	4,481	3,108	2,928	3,008	2,692	2,831	2,924	2,282	2,274	2,242
Capital Expenditures	71.9	100	75.1	44.4	78.8	69.2	151	87.5	62.0	34.3
Cash Flow	411	409	395	-227	345	258	303	262	218	242
Current Ratio	1.7	3.0	2.6	1.8	5.5	5.4	3.9	2.5	3.6	3.0
% Long Term Debt of Capitalization	25.7	26.5	30.7	37.4	21.8	20.8	24.7	14.5	18.3	19.6
% Net Income of Revenue	8.0	9.4	5.7	NM	8.4	9.2	13.9	14.4	10.0	21.0
% Return on Assets	4.6	6.7	3.9	NM	4.4	4.6	6.8	6.8	4.6	8.4
% Return on Equity	8.7	12.1	8.0	NM	6.4	7.0	10.5	10.1	7.2	13.1

Data as orig reptd.; bef. results of disc opers/spec. items. Per share data adj. for stk. divs.; EPS diluted. E-Estimated. NA-Not Available. NM-Not Meaningful. NR-Not Ranked. UR-Under Review.

Office: 311 Bonnie Circle, Corona, CA 92880-2882.
Telephone: 951-493-5300.
Website: http://www.watson.com
Chrmn: A.L. Turner

Pres & CEO: P.M. Bisaro
COO: R.A. Stewart
SVP, CFO, Chief Acctg Officer & Treas: R.T. Joyce
SVP, Secy & General Counsel: D.A. Buchen

Investor Contact: P. Eisenhaur (973-355-8310)
Board Members: P. M. Bisaro, C. W. Bodine, M. Fedida, M. J. Feldman, A. F. Hummel, C. M. Klema, J. Michelson, A. S. Tabatznik, R. R. Taylor, A. L. Turner, F. G. Weiss

Founded: 1983
Domicile: Nevada
Employees: 5,830

WellPoint Inc

STANDARD &POOR'S

S&P Recommendation **BUY** ★★★★☆	Price $57.54 (as of Oct 22, 2010)	12-Mo. Target Price $63.00	Investment Style Large-Cap Growth

GICS Sector Health Care
Sub-Industry Managed Health Care

Summary This managed health organization is the largest in the U.S., serving 33.5 million members mainly under the Blue Cross and/or Blue Shield license in 14 states.

Key Stock Statistics (Source S&P, Vickers, company reports)

52-Wk Range	$70.00– 44.58	S&P Oper. EPS 2010E	6.25	Market Capitalization(B)	$23.001	Beta	0.97
Trailing 12-Month EPS	$11.23	S&P Oper. EPS 2011E	6.65	Yield (%)	Nil	S&P 3-Yr. Proj. EPS CAGR(%)	6
Trailing 12-Month P/E	5.1	P/E on S&P Oper. EPS 2010E	9.2	Dividend Rate/Share	Nil	S&P Credit Rating	A-
$10K Invested 5 Yrs Ago	$7,377	Common Shares Outstg. (M)	399.7	Institutional Ownership (%)	86		

Price Performance

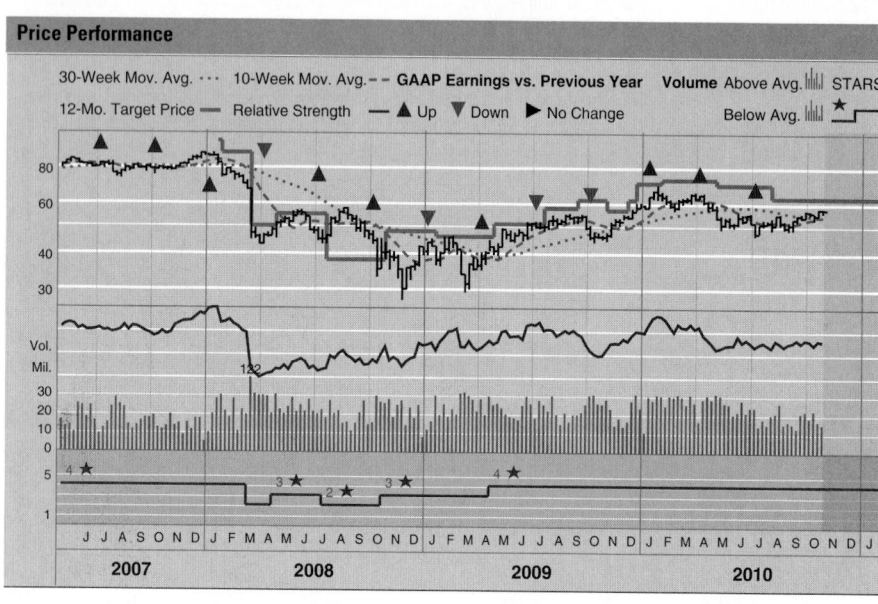

30-Week Mov. Avg. · · · · 10-Week Mov. Avg. - - **GAAP Earnings vs. Previous Year** Volume Above Avg. STARS
12-Mo. Target Price — Relative Strength — ▲ Up ▼ Down ▶ No Change Below Avg. ★

2007 2008 2009 2010

Options: ASE, CBOE, Ph

Analysis prepared by **Phillip M. Seligman** on August 06, 2010, when the stock traded at **$ 54.51**.

Highlights

▶ We see 2010's operating revenues declining 5.5%, to $57.5 billion, mainly on the sale of the pharmacy benefit management (PBM) unit, the divestiture of non-Blues health plans in two states, the transition of a large, fully insured account to self-funded status, and membership attrition amid the still-soft economy. We see these partly offset by 300,000 net new National Accounts members by year end and slightly higher Medicare Advantage (MA) and Medicaid membership.

▶ We expect benefit expenses as a percentage of premiums (medical loss ratio, or MLR) to rise 80 basis points (bps), mainly on the change in enrollment mix, the California rate delay, and health care reform implementation, partly offset by favorable claims reserve development. We expect the SG&A expense ratio to decline 30 bps, partly on cost control.

▶ All told, we expect net income to decline in 2010, but we look for EPS of $6.25, versus non-GAAP 2009 EPS of $6.09 (before $3.79 of net one-time gains, mainly on the PBM sale), on share buybacks. We see $6.65 in 2011, assuming a higher MLR is outweighed by additional buybacks.

Investment Rationale/Risk

▶ We think WLP has been executing well in a soft economy. It has exited underperforming markets, and eliminated 1,500 positions. We also believe it has been applying pricing discipline, although its California individual account premium rate hikes remain delayed, yielding losses in that market. In addition, we are encouraged by its growth in national accounts, and we believe it has the scale, diversity and strong cash flow to manage better than most insurers amid health care reform. Meanwhile, we expect the stock to be volatile, while WLP waits for the rules on what constitutes medical costs starting 2011, given health care reform's required MLR floors. WLP is heavily exposed to individual and small group markets, many with MLRs well below the floors. The benefit mandates will raise the MLRs, but we think WLP may also have room to add competitive benefits.

▶ Risks to our recommendation and target price include enrollment losses above our expectations, higher medical cost trends, and unfavorable regulatory changes.

▶ Our 12-month target price of $63 reflects a slightly above-peer multiple of 10X our 2010 EPS estimate.

Qualitative Risk Assessment

LOW	**MEDIUM**	HIGH

Our risk assessment reflects WLP's leadership in the highly fragmented managed care market. We believe that its geographic, market and product diversity and Blue Cross/Blue Shield tie are competitive strengths. However, we think enrollment growth going forward will be limited by heightened competition that we expect following consolidation in the managed care industry and from the difficult economic environment.

Quantitative Evaluations

S&P Quality Ranking B+

D	C	B-	B	**B+**	A-	A	A+

Relative Strength Rank MODERATE

64

LOWEST = 1 HIGHEST = 99

Revenue/Earnings Data

Revenue (Million $)

	1Q	2Q	3Q	4Q	Year
2010	15,099	14,457	--	--	--
2009	15,143	15,413	15,425	19,047	65,028
2008	15,554	15,667	14,961	15,070	61,251
2007	15,079	15,260	15,234	15,561	61,134
2006	13,820	14,152	14,426	14,556	56,953
2005	11,100	11,299	11,305	11,432	45,136

Earnings Per Share ($)

2010	1.96	1.71	E1.58	E1.01	E6.25
2009	1.16	1.43	1.53	5.95	9.88
2008	1.07	1.44	1.60	0.65	4.76
2007	1.26	1.35	1.45	1.51	5.56
2006	1.09	1.17	1.29	1.28	4.82
2005	0.98	0.90	1.02	1.04	3.94

Fiscal year ended Dec. 31. Next earnings report expected: Late October. EPS Estimates based on S&P Operating Earnings; historical GAAP earnings are as reported.

Dividend Data

No cash dividends have been paid.

Please read the Required Disclosures and Analyst Certification on the last page of this report.

The **McGraw·Hill** Companies

WellPoint Inc

Business Summary August 06, 2010

CORPORATE OVERVIEW. WellPoint, Inc. was formed by the merger consummated on November 30, 2004, between publicly traded managed care giants Anthem, Inc. and WellPoint Health Networks Inc. (WHN). All prior historical data in this report are for Anthem. WLP is the largest publicly traded commercial health benefits company in the U.S., serving 33.5 million members as of June 30, 2010 (versus 33.7 million at December 31, 2009), and an independent licensee of the Blue Cross and Blue Shield Association. It serves members as the Blue Cross licensee for California and the Blue Cross or Blue Cross and Blue Shield (BCBS) licensee in all or parts of 13 other states. WLP also serves members in various parts of the U.S. as UniCare and conducts insurance operations in all 50 states and Puerto Rico through an affiliate.

WLP's network-based managed care plans include preferred provider organizations (PPOs), health maintenance organizations (HMOs), point-of-service plans (POS), traditional indemnity plans and other hybrid plans, including consumer-driven health plans (CDHPs), hospital only, and limited benefit products. It also provides managed care services to self-funded customers. In addition, WLP provides specialty and other products and services, including

pharmacy benefit management, group life and disability insurance, dental, vision, behavioral health, workers compensation and long-term care insurance. Approximately 93% of 2009 operating revenue was derived from premium income and 6% from administrative services and other revenues.

The customer base includes local groups (15,198,000 members as of June 30, 2010, versus 15,643,000 as of December 31, 2009); individuals under age 65 (1,953,000 versus 2,131,000); National Accounts (multi-state employers primarily headquartered in WLP's service area with 1,000 or more eligible employees, with 5% or more located outside headquarters state -- 7,108,000 versus 6,813,000); BlueCard (enrollees of non-owned BCBS plans who receive benefits in WLP's BCBS markets -- 4,782,000 versus 4,744,000); Seniors (1,252,000 versus 1,215,000); State Sponsored (1,750,000 versus 1,733,000); and Federal Employee Program (1,449,000 versus 1,391,000).

Company Financials Fiscal Year Ended Dec. 31

Per Share Data ($)	2009	2008	2007	2006	2005	2004	2003	2002	2001	2000
Tangible Book Value	7.42	NM	0.60	2.92	2.78	2.03	8.44	5.76	7.71	7.66
Cash Flow	NA	5.84	6.24	4.82	3.94	2.05	3.59	2.90	2.23	1.55
Earnings	9.88	4.76	5.56	4.82	3.94	3.05	2.73	2.26	1.65	1.05
S&P Core Earnings	5.82	6.00	5.50	4.79	3.82	2.69	2.49	1.93	1.16	NA
Dividends	Nil	Nil	Nil	Nil	Nil	Nil	Nil	Nil	Nil	NA
Payout Ratio	Nil	Nil	Nil	Nil	Nil	Nil	Nil	Nil	Nil	NA
Prices:High	60.89	90.00	89.95	80.37	80.40	58.88	41.45	37.75	25.95	NA
Prices:Low	29.32	27.50	72.90	65.50	54.58	36.10	26.50	23.20	18.00	NA
P/E Ratio:High	6	19	16	17	20	19	15	17	16	NA
P/E Ratio:Low	3	6	13	14	14	12	10	10	11	NA

Income Statement Analysis (Million $)	2009	2008	2007	2006	2005	2004	2003	2002	2001	2000
Revenue	65,028	61,251	61,134	56,953	45,136	20,815	16,771	13,282	10,445	8,771
Operating Income	NA	4,297	6,117	5,748	4,750	2,072	1,595	1,093	733	487
Depreciation	NA	564	411	430	634	279	245	157	121	102
Interest Expense	447	470	448	404	226	142	131	98.5	60.2	69.6
Pretax Income	7,403	3,122	5,258	4,914	3,890	1,443	1,219	808	525	315
Effective Tax Rate	35.9%	20.2%	36.4%	37.0%	36.7%	33.5%	36.1%	31.6%	35.0%	30.8%
Net Income	4,746	2,491	3,345	3,095	2,464	960	774	549	342	216
S&P Core Earnings	2,797	3,143	3,308	3,077	2,402	842	708	467	240	NA

Balance Sheet & Other Financial Data (Million $)	2009	2008	2007	2006	2005	2004	2003	2002	2001	2000
Cash	4,816	2,208	6,535	2,602	2,897	1,457	523	744	406	421
Current Assets	NA	12,130	13,032	11,807	25,945	19,358	8,865	7,877	5,300	5,025
Total Assets	52,125	48,403	52,060	51,760	51,405	39,738	13,439	12,293	6,277	6,021
Current Liabilities	NA	15,020	14,388	15,323	14,857	11,571	4,772	4,449	2,963	2,784
Long Term Debt	8,338	7,834	9,024	6,493	6,325	4,277	1,663	1,659	818	789
Common Equity	24,863	21,432	22,990	25,299	25,755	20,331	6,000	5,362	2,060	2,055
Total Capital	NA	31,365	35,018	35,142	35,386	27,204	8,188	7,412	2,878	2,844
Capital Expenditures	NA	346	322	194	162	137	111	123	70.4	73.3
Cash Flow	NA	3,054	3,756	3,095	2,464	1,239	1,019	706	463	318
Current Ratio	1.9	0.8	0.9	0.8	1.7	1.7	1.9	1.8	1.8	1.8
% Long Term Debt of Capitalization	25.1	25.0	25.8	18.5	17.9	15.7	20.3	22.4	28.4	27.7
% Net Income of Revenue	7.3	4.1	5.5	62.1	5.5	4.7	4.6	50.8	35.6	2.5
% Return on Assets	9.4	5.0	6.5	6.0	5.4	3.6	6.0	5.9	5.7	4.3
% Return on Equity	20.5	11.2	14.1	12.1	10.7	7.2	13.6	14.8	17.2	12.6

Data as orig reptd.; bef. results of disc opers/spec. items. Per share data adj. for stk. divs.; EPS diluted. E-Estimated. NA-Not Available. NM-Not Meaningful. NR-Not Ranked. UR-Under Review.

Office: 120 Monument Circle, Indianapolis, IN 46204-4903.
Telephone: 317-488-6000.
Email: anthem.corporate.communications@anthem.com
Website: http://www.wellpoint.com

Chrmn, Pres & CEO: A.F. Braly
Investor Contact: W.S. Deveydt (317-488-6390)
EVP & CFO: W.S. Deveydt
EVP, Secy & General Counsel: J. Cannon, III

SVP, Chief Acctg Officer & Cntlr: M.L. Miller
Board Members: L. D. Baker, Jr., S. B. Bayh, A. F. Braly, S. P. Burke, W. H. Bush, J. A. Hill, W. Y. Jobe, W. G. Mays, R. G. Peru, J. G. Pisano, D. W. Riegle, Jr., W. J. Ryan, G. A. Schaefer, Jr., J. M. Ward

Founded: 1944
Domicile: Indiana
Employees: 40,500

Wells Fargo & Co

STANDARD &POOR'S

S&P Recommendation **BUY** ★★★★☆	Price $26.11 (as of Oct 22, 2010)	12-Mo. Target Price $30.00	Investment Style Large-Cap Blend

GICS Sector Financials
Sub-Industry Diversified Banks

Summary This bank holding company provides banking, insurance, investment, mortgage and consumer finance services throughout North America.

Key Stock Statistics (Source S&P, Vickers, company reports)

52-Wk Range	$34.25– 23.02	S&P Oper. EPS 2010E	2.20	Market Capitalization(B)	$136.645
Trailing 12-Month EPS	$1.66	S&P Oper. EPS 2011E	2.48	Yield (%)	0.77
Trailing 12-Month P/E	15.7	P/E on S&P Oper. EPS 2010E	11.9	Dividend Rate/Share	$0.20
$10K Invested 5 Yrs Ago	$10,224	Common Shares Outstg. (M)	5,233.4	Institutional Ownership (%)	75

Beta	1.39
S&P 3-Yr. Proj. EPS CAGR(%)	21
S&P Credit Rating	AA-

Price Performance

30-Week Mov. Avg. · · · · 10-Week Mov. Avg. - - **GAAP Earnings vs. Previous Year** Volume Above Avg. STARS
12-Mo. Target Price — Relative Strength — ▲ Up ▼ Down ▶ No Change Below Avg.

Options: ASE, CBOE, P, Ph

Qualitative Risk Assessment

LOW	MEDIUM	HIGH

Our risk assessment reflects what we see as solid business fundamentals and a strong customer base, offset by increased risk stemming from the Wachovia acquisition combined with declining tangible capital levels.

Quantitative Evaluations

S&P Quality Ranking A-

D	C	B-	B	B+	A-	A	A+

Relative Strength Rank MODERATE

38

LOWEST = 1   HIGHEST = 99

Highlights

► The 12-month target price for WFC has recently been changed to $30.00 from $34.00. The Highlights section of this Stock Report will be updated accordingly.

Investment Rationale/Risk

► The Investment Rationale/Risk section of this Stock Report will be updated shortly. For the latest News story on WFC from MarketScope, see below.

► 10/20/10 09:00 am ET ... S&P MAINTAINS BUY RECOMMENDATION ON SHARES OF WELLS FARGO (WFC 24.55****): Q3 EPS of $0.60, vs. $0.56, beats our $0.45 estimate on higher than expected noninterest income and a lower than expected loan loss provision, which offset lower than expected net interest income. On the results, are raising our '10 EPS estimate to $2.20 from $1.99. We see credit quality improving, and think that the national foreclosure issue is manageable for WFC. We reiterate our $30 target price, which is based on slight premium to peers multiples of 1.7X our year-end tangible book value per share estimate, and 12.1X our unchanged '11 EPS estimate of $2.48. /E. Oja

Revenue/Earnings Data

Revenue (Million $)

	1Q	2Q	3Q	4Q	Year
2010	23,526	23,417	--	--	--
2009	23,954	25,044	24,750	24,888	98,636
2008	13,652	13,728	12,772	11,828	51,980
2007	12,570	13,268	13,796	13,959	53,596
2006	11,217	11,882	12,286	12,594	47,979
2005	9,509	9,529	10,427	10,897	40,407

Earnings Per Share ($)

2010	0.45	0.55	E0.60	E0.60	E2.20
2009	0.56	0.57	0.56	0.08	1.75
2008	0.60	0.53	0.49	-0.79	0.75
2007	0.66	0.67	0.68	0.37	2.38
2006	0.60	0.61	0.64	0.64	2.49
2005	0.54	0.56	0.58	0.57	2.25

Fiscal year ended Dec. 31. Next earnings report expected: NA. EPS Estimates based on S&P Operating Earnings; historical GAAP earnings are as reported.

Dividend Data (Dates: mm/dd Payment Date: mm/dd/yy)

Amount ($)	Date Decl.	Ex-Div. Date	Stk. of Record	Payment Date
0.050	10/27	11/04	11/06	12/01/09
0.050	01/26	02/03	02/05	03/01/10
0.050	04/27	05/05	05/07	06/01/10
0.050	07/27	08/04	08/06	09/01/10

Dividends have been paid since 1939. Source: Company reports.

Wells Fargo & Co

Business Summary July 22, 2010

CORPORATE OVERVIEW. Wells Fargo & Co. (WFC) has three lines of business for management reporting: community banking, wholesale banking, and Wells Fargo Financial. The community banking group offers a complete line of banking and diversified financial products and services to consumers and small businesses with annual sales generally up to $20 million, in which the owner generally is the financial decision maker. Community banking also offers investment management and other services to retail customers and high-net-worth individuals, insurance, securities brokerage through affiliates, and venture capital financing.

Community banking serves customers through a wide range of channels, including traditional banking stores, in-store banking centers, business centers and ATMs. In addition, Phone Bank centers and the National Business Banking Center provide 24-hour telephone service.

The wholesale banking group serves businesses across the U.S. with annual sales generally in excess of $10 million. Wholesale banking provides a complete line of commercial, corporate and real estate banking products and ser-

vices. These include traditional commercial loans and lines of credit; letters of credit; asset-based lending; equipment leasing; mezzanine financing; high-yield debt; international trade facilities; foreign exchange services; treasury management; investment management; institutional fixed income and equity sales; interest rate, commodity and equity risk management; online/electronic products; insurance, corporate trust fiduciary and agency services and investment banking services.

Wholesale banking manages and administers institutional investments, employee benefit trusts and mutual funds, including the Wells Fargo Advantage Funds. Wholesale banking includes the majority ownership interest in the Wells Fargo SC Trade Bank, which provides trade financing, letters of credit, and collection services, and is sometimes supported by the Export-Import Bank of the United States.

Company Financials Fiscal Year Ended Dec. 31

Per Share Data ($)	2009	2008	2007	2006	2005	2004	2003	2002	2001	2000
Tangible Book Value	12.74	3.31	5.55	10.13	8.76	7.95	7.04	6.11	4.90	4.59
Earnings	1.75	0.75	2.38	2.49	2.25	2.05	1.83	1.66	0.99	1.17
S&P Core Earnings	1.77	0.57	2.39	2.47	2.18	1.96	1.78	1.57	0.84	NA
Dividends	0.49	1.30	1.18	1.08	1.00	0.93	0.75	0.55	0.50	0.45
Payout Ratio	28%	173%	50%	43%	44%	45%	41%	33%	51%	39%
Prices:High	31.53	44.69	37.99	36.99	32.35	32.02	29.59	26.72	27.41	28.19
Prices:Low	7.80	19.89	29.29	30.31	28.81	27.16	21.64	21.65	19.13	15.69
P/E Ratio:High	18	63	16	15	14	16	16	16	28	24
P/E Ratio:Low	4	27	12	12	13	13	12	13	19	13

Income Statement Analysis (Million $)	2009	2008	2007	2006	2005	2004	2003	2002	2001	2000
Net Interest Income	46,324	25,143	20,974	19,951	18,504	17,150	16,007	14,855	12,460	10,865
Tax Equivalent Adjustment	706	321	146	116	110	104	NA	NA	NA	65.0
Non Interest Income	42,362	16,776	17,473	15,021	14,054	12,530	12,323	9,348	7,227	9,565
Loan Loss Provision	21,668	15,979	4,939	2,204	2,383	1,717	1,722	1,733	1,780	1,329
% Expense/Operating Revenue	55.3%	54.1%	59.4%	59.3%	58.2%	64.8%	60.7%	52.2%	65.5%	57.7%
Pretax Income	17,998	3,585	11,627	12,745	11,548	10,769	9,477	8,854	5,479	6,549
Effective Tax Rate	29.6%	20.7%	30.7%	33.4%	33.6%	34.9%	34.6%	35.5%	37.5%	38.5%
Net Income	12,275	2,842	8,057	8,482	7,671	7,014	6,202	5,710	3,423	4,026
% Net Interest Margin	4.28	4.83	4.74	4.83	4.86	4.89	5.08	5.57	5.36	5.35
S&P Core Earnings	8,084	1,937	8,099	8,401	7,423	6,722	6,055	5,374	2,894	NA

Balance Sheet & Other Financial Data (Million $)	2009	2008	2007	2006	2005	2004	2003	2002	2001	2000
Money Market Assets	83,924	104,317	10,481	11,685	16,211	14,020	2,745	3,174	2,530	1,598
Investment Securities	172,710	151,569	72,951	42,629	41,834	33,717	32,953	27,947	40,308	38,655
Commercial Loans	172,562	218,298	152,841	122,065	108,903	98,515	48,729	47,292	47,547	60,541
Other Loans	610,208	625,519	229,354	273,069	201,934	189,071	204,344	149,342	124,952	10,583
Total Assets	1,243,646	1,309,639	575,442	481,996	481,741	427,849	387,798	349,259	307,569	272,426
Demand Deposits	181,356	150,837	84,348	89,119	87,712	81,082	74,387	74,094	65,362	55,096
Time Deposits	642,662	630,565	260,112	221,124	226,738	193,776	173,140	142,822	121,904	114,463
Long Term Debt	203,861	267,158	99,393	72,404	79,668	73,580	63,642	50,205	38,530	32,981
Common Equity	103,743	68,307	47,660	45,492	40,335	37,596	34,255	30,107	26,996	26,103
% Return on Assets	1.0	0.3	1.5	1.8	1.7	1.7	1.7	1.7	1.2	1.6
% Return on Equity	14.3	4.9	17.2	19.8	19.7	19.5	19.3	20.0	12.8	16.2
% Loan Loss Reserve	3.1	2.4	1.4	1.1	1.1	1.2	1.3	1.5	1.8	2.1
% Loans/Deposits	95.0	110.7	107.1	113.8	111.9	118.6	117.0	117.3	110.9	104.7
% Equity to Assets	6.7	6.2	8.9	8.9	8.6	8.8	8.7	8.7	9.2	9.7

Data as orig reptd.; bef. results of disc opers/spec. items. Per share data adj. for stk. divs.; EPS diluted. E-Estimated. NA-Not Available. NM-Not Meaningful. NR-Not Ranked. UR-Under Review.

Office: 420 Montgomery Street, San Francisco, CA 94104-1207.
Telephone: 800-411-4932.
Website: http://www.wellsfargo.com
Chrmn, Pres & CEO: J.G. Stumpf

EVP & CFO: H.I. Atkins
EVP, Chief Acctg Officer & Cntlr: R.D. Levy
EVP & Treas: P.R. Ackerman
EVP & Secy: L.A. Holschuh

Board Members: J. D. Baker, II, J. S. Chen, L. H. Dean, S. E. Engel, E. Hernandez, Jr., D. M. James, R. D. McCormick, M. J. Mcdonald, C. H. Milligan, N. G. Moore, P. J. Quigley, J. M. Runstad, S. W. Sanger, J. G. Stumpf, S. G. Swenson

Founded: 1929
Domicile: Delaware
Employees: 267,300

Western Digital Corp

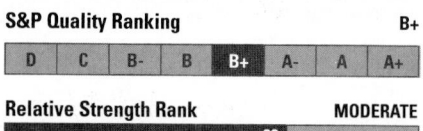

STANDARD &POOR'S

S&P Recommendation **SELL** ★★☆☆☆	Price $30.43 (as of Oct 22, 2010)	12-Mo. Target Price $28.00	Investment Style Large-Cap Blend

GICS Sector Information Technology
Sub-Industry Computer Storage & Peripherals

Summary This company designs and manufactures hard disk drives for personal computing.

Key Stock Statistics (Source S&P, Vickers, company reports)

52-Wk Range	$47.44–23.06	S&P Oper. EPS 2011**E**	2.30	Market Capitalization(B)	$6.978	Beta	1.41
Trailing 12-Month EPS	$5.52	S&P Oper. EPS 2012**E**	3.33	Yield (%)	Nil	S&P 3-Yr. Proj. EPS CAGR(%)	6
Trailing 12-Month P/E	5.5	P/E on S&P Oper. EPS 2011**E**	13.2	Dividend Rate/Share	Nil	S&P Credit Rating	NA
$10K Invested 5 Yrs Ago	$26,811	Common Shares Outstg. (M)	229.3	Institutional Ownership (%)	90		

Price Performance

30-Week Mov. Avg. · · · 10-Week Mov. Avg. - - **GAAP Earnings vs. Previous Year** Volume Above Avg. STARS
12-Mo. Target Price — Relative Strength — ▲ Up ▼ Down ▶ No Change Below Avg. ★

Options: ASE, CBOE, P

Highlights

▶ The STARS recommendation for WDC has recently been changed to 2 (sell) from 3 (hold) and the 12-month target price has recently been changed to $28.00 from $36.00. The Highlights section of this Stock Report will be updated accordingly.

Investment Rationale/Risk

▶ The Investment Rationale/Risk section of this Stock Report will be updated shortly. For the latest News story on WDC from MarketScope, see below.

▶ 10/20/10 09:21 am ET ... S&P LOWERS RECOMMENDATION ON SHARES OF WESTERN DIGITAL TO SELL FROM HOLD (WDC 30.2**): Sep-Q EPS of $0.84, vs. $1.25, misses our EPS estimate of $0.90. Revenues rose 8.5% to $2.4B, $33M above our forecast. Gross margins fell to 18.2% from 22.5% in Jun-Q due to pricing pressures of excess industry production capacity. We believe the excess capacity issue will persist, reflecting our view of slower PC unit growth. We are also concerned about the growth of tablet computers and increased usage of flash memory. We project lower gross margins for the next few quarters and cut our FY 11 (Jun.) EPS estimate by $1.67 to $2.30. We reduce our target price by $8 to $28. /J.Yin-CFA

Qualitative Risk Assessment

LOW	MEDIUM	**HIGH**

Our risk assessment reflects the volatility of the disk drive industry, including significant exposure to the PC sector and ongoing erosion of average selling prices.

Quantitative Evaluations

S&P Quality Ranking B+

D	C	B-	B	**B+**	A-	A	A+

Relative Strength Rank MODERATE

68

LOWEST = 1 HIGHEST = 99

Revenue/Earnings Data

Revenue (Million $)

	1Q	2Q	3Q	4Q	Year
2011	2,396	--	--	--	--
2010	2,208	2,619	2,641	2,382	9,850
2009	2,109	1,823	1,592	1,928	7,453
2008	1,766	2,204	2,111	1,993	8,074
2007	1,264	1,428	1,410	1,367	5,468
2006	1,010	1,117	1,129	1,086	4,341

Earnings Per Share ($)

2011	0.84	E0.60	E0.43	E0.43	E2.30
2010	1.25	1.85	1.71	1.13	5.93
2009	0.93	0.06	0.22	0.86	2.08
2008	0.31	1.39	1.23	0.94	3.84
2007	0.46	0.57	0.53	0.94	2.50
2006	0.31	0.47	0.45	0.53	1.76

Fiscal year ended Jun. 30. Next earnings report expected: Late January. EPS Estimates based on S&P Operating Earnings; historical GAAP earnings are as reported.

Dividend Data

No cash dividends have been paid.

Western Digital Corp

STANDARD &POOR'S

Business Summary August 04, 2010

CORPORATE OVERVIEW. Western Digital designs, develops, manufactures and markets hard disk drives. The company's hard drives are used in desktop PC, notebook computers, enterprise servers, network attached storage devices, and consumer electronics products such as personal/digital video recorders, and satellite and cable set-top boxes. WDC's hard drive products include 3.5- and 2.5-inch form factor drives with capacities ranging from 40 gigabytes to 2 terabyte and rotation speeds up to 10,000 revolutions per minute. The company believes that these form factors represent its major growth areas, with 3.5-inch form factor hard drives used in the desktop, enterprise, consumer electronic and external storage markets, and 2.5-inch form factor hard drives serving the mobile PC/laptop, consumer electronic and external storage markets.

WDC entered the solid-state drive market by acquiring SiliconSystems in the first quarter of 2009. A solid-state drive is a storage device that uses semiconductor rather than magnetic disks and heads to store data and is more commonly used in notebooks because of its lighter weight and higher durability. We expect the solid-state drive market segment to grow faster than the rest of the industry given the rapid growth of netbooks. However, we think solid-

state drives represented less than 3% of WDC's FY 10 (Jun.) total sales.

Drives are sold globally to OEMs, distributors and retailers. Sales to OEMs accounted for 54% of revenues in FY 09, up from 51% in FY 08. Distributors made up 26% (31%) and retailers 20% (18%).

Historically, WDC believes that sales of PCs and hard disk drives were similar in volume. However, over the past five years, the company's research indicates that growth in hard drives has outpaced the PC market. This shifting dynamic is based on a number of factors, including the growth of alternative products such as consumer electronics devices, the expansion of the external hard drive market, which allows for a more convenient way to store music and photos, and the increased use of multiple hard drives to deal with capacity constraints and safety issues.

Company Financials Fiscal Year Ended Jun. 30

Per Share Data ($)	2010	2009	2008	2007	2006	2005	2004	2003	2002	2001
Tangible Book Value	19.37	13.17	11.16	7.73	5.24	3.29	2.36	1.61	0.54	0.04
Cash Flow	8.12	4.20	5.66	3.42	2.48	1.54	1.17	1.13	0.51	-0.21
Earnings	5.93	2.08	3.84	2.50	1.76	0.91	0.70	0.88	0.28	-0.71
S&P Core Earnings	6.01	2.01	3.88	2.50	1.82	0.87	0.58	0.81	0.14	-0.69
Dividends	NA	Nil	Nil	Nil	Nil	Nil	Nil	Nil	Nil	Nil
Payout Ratio	Nil	Nil	Nil	Nil	Nil	Nil	Nil	Nil	Nil	Nil
Prices:High	47.44	44.96	40.00	31.70	24.70	19.15	13.55	14.95	8.96	6.79
Prices:Low	23.06	11.49	9.48	16.21	15.90	9.84	6.39	6.44	2.98	1.95
P/E Ratio:High	8	22	10	13	14	21	19	17	32	NM
P/E Ratio:Low	4	6	2	6	9	11	9	7	11	NM

Income Statement Analysis (Million $)										
Revenue	9,850	7,453	8,074	5,468	4,341	3,639	3,047	2,719	2,151	1,953
Operating Income	2,035	1,106	1,468	625	526	332	257	237	96.5	18.0
Depreciation	510	479	413	210	160	135	102	50.4	45.8	51.9
Interest Expense	5.00	17.0	52.0	4.00	3.70	Nil	Nil	Nil	8.13	8.94
Pretax Income	1,520	501	981	443	382	202	155	188	52.1	-88.3
Effective Tax Rate	NA	6.19%	11.6%	NM	NM	1.93%	2.51%	4.03%	NM	NM
Net Income	1,382	470	867	564	395	198	151	181	53.2	-87.1
S&P Core Earnings	1,400	454	875	564	407	186	125	166	27.0	-117

Balance Sheet & Other Financial Data (Million $)										
Cash	2,734	1,794	1,107	700	551	485	378	393	224	168
Current Assets	4,720	3,230	2,731	2,029	1,492	1,181	857	744	528	386
Total Assets	7,328	5,291	4,871	2,901	2,073	1,589	1,159	866	637	508
Current Liabilities	2,023	1,525	1,564	1,130	859	818	587	506	493	340
Long Term Debt	294	400	482	10.0	19.4	32.6	52.7	Nil	Nil	112
Common Equity	4,709	3,192	2,696	1,716	1,157	702	488	327	103	6.80
Total Capital	5,109	3,592	3,205	1,726	1,177	735	540	327	103	129
Capital Expenditures	737	519	615	324	302	233	132	61.9	47.7	50.7
Cash Flow	1,892	949	1,280	774	554	333	253	231	99.0	-35.2
Current Ratio	2.3	2.1	1.8	1.8	1.7	1.4	1.5	1.5	1.1	1.1
% Long Term Debt of Capitalization	5.8	11.1	15.0	0.6	1.6	4.4	9.8	Nil	Nil	87.4
% Net Income of Revenue	14.0	6.3	10.7	10.3	9.1	5.5	5.0	6.7	2.5	NM
% Return on Assets	21.9	9.3	22.3	22.6	21.6	14.4	14.9	24.1	9.3	NM
% Return on Equity	35.0	16.0	39.3	39.3	42.5	33.4	37.1	84.0	97.1	NM

Data as orig reptd.; bef. results of disc opers/spec. items. Per share data adj. for stk. divs.; EPS diluted. E-Estimated. NA-Not Available. NM-Not Meaningful. NR-Not Ranked. UR-Under Review.

Office: 20511 Lake Forest Drive, Lake Forest, CA 92630-7741.
Telephone: 949-672-7000.
Website: http://www.westerndigital.com
Chrmn: T.E. Pardun

Pres & CEO: J.F. Coyne
COO: T.M. Leyden
SVP & CFO: W. Nickl
Chief Acctg Officer & Cntlr: J.R. Carrillo

Investor Contact: R. Blair
Board Members: P. D. Behrendt, K. A. Cote, J. F. Coyne, H. T. DeNero, W. L. Kimsey, M. D. Lambert, L. J. Lauer, M. E. Massengill, R. H. Moore, T. E. Pardun, A. Shakeel

Founded: 1970
Domicile: Delaware
Employees: 62,500

The McGraw·Hill Companies

Western Union Co

STANDARD &POOR'S

S&P Recommendation	BUY ★★★★☆	Price	12-Mo. Target Price	Investment Style
		$17.90 (as of Oct 22, 2010)	$20.00	Large-Cap Blend

GICS Sector Information Technology
Sub-Industry Data Processing & Outsourced Services

Summary Spun off from First Data Corp. in September 2006, Western Union is a leading independent provider of consumer money transfer services.

Key Stock Statistics (Source S&P, Vickers, company reports)

52-Wk Range	$20.26– 14.65	S&P Oper. EPS 2010**E**	1.36	Market Capitalization(B)	$11.816	Beta	1.46
Trailing 12-Month EPS	$1.21	S&P Oper. EPS 2011**E**	1.48	Yield (%)	1.34	S&P 3-Yr. Proj. EPS CAGR(%)	10
Trailing 12-Month P/E	14.8	P/E on S&P Oper. EPS 2010**E**	13.2	Dividend Rate/Share	$0.24	S&P Credit Rating	A-
$10K Invested 5 Yrs Ago	NA	Common Shares Outstg. (M)	660.1	Institutional Ownership (%)	91		

Price Performance

30-Week Mov. Avg. · · · 10-Week Mov. Avg. – – GAAP Earnings vs. Previous Year   Volume Above Avg. STARS
12-Mo. Target Price — Relative Strength — ▲ Up ▼ Down ▶ No Change   Below Avg. ★

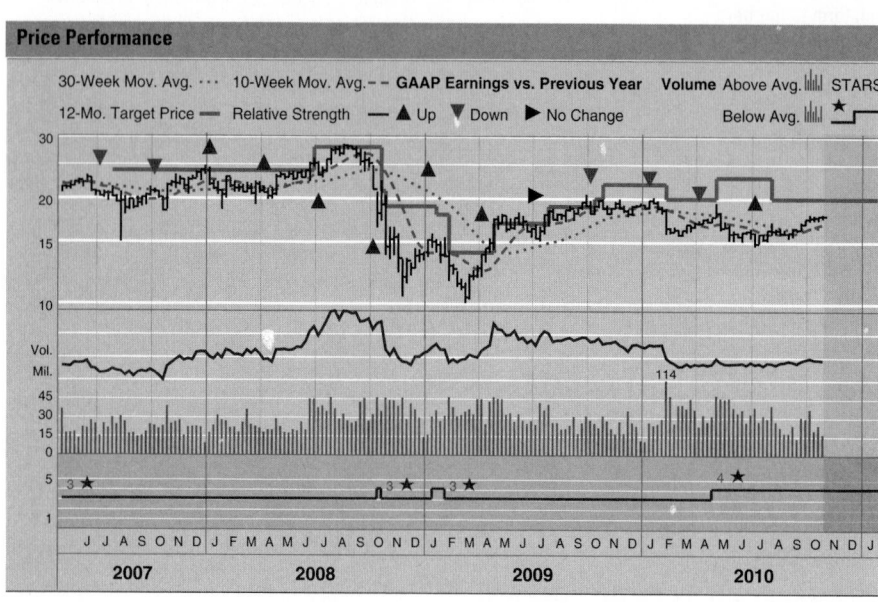

Options: ASE, CBOE, P, Ph

Analysis prepared by **Zaineb Bokhari** on July 30, 2010, when the stock traded at **$ 16.25.**

Highlights

➤ We expect revenue to rise 1% in 2010, to $5.1 billion, versus the 4% decline in 2009. We think some of the global remittance markets that WU serves have begun to stabilize as macroeconomic conditions gradually improve. We see slower growth in geographies such as the Persian Gulf states, but we expect regions such as Asia to show greater resilience and growth. In addition, we look for WU to invest up to 4% of sales (vs. 2 to 3% historically) in pricing and promotional initiatives as it repositions its domestic money transfer business. Finally, we see growth held back by lower volumes of U.S. consumer bill payments tied to consumer credit, including mortgages, auto loans and credit cards. We project 4% revenue growth for 2011, to $5.35 billion.

➤ We project gross and operating margins to remain flat in 2010, reflecting our outlook for investments in technology, marketing and distribution, the acquisition of Custom House, and the impact of the company's assumption of the retail money order portfolio from First Data (October 2009). We see margins benefiting in 2011 from a restructuring in 2010.

➤ We estimate EPS of $1.36 in 2010.

Investment Rationale/Risk

➤ We expect transaction volumes to recover in many of the regions WU serves in keeping with a gradual improvement in the global economy. We see WU benefiting from a recent restructuring but expect the company to invest in technology, marketing and pricing initiatives as it invests ahead of a recovery in demand. We view favorably agreements through which WU provides consumer money transfer services through banks, thus expanding the distribution of its services. We think WU, with more than $800 million in cash from operations estimated for 2010, has adequate near-term liquidity, and we view the shares as attractive.

➤ Risks to our recommendation and target price include worsening global economic trends, accelerating consumer adoption of digital alternatives to WU's money transfer offerings, and competition from traditional financial institutions and money transfer peers.

➤ We derive our 12-month target price of $20 by applying a 13.5X P/E multiple to our 2011 EPS estimate, within the historical average range for the shares of 9.4X-17.5X, but below the 15.7X mean for peers, reflecting our view of modest near-term revenue growth.

Qualitative Risk Assessment

LOW	MEDIUM	HIGH

Our risk assessment reflects the sluggish global macroeconomy, which we expect will impact transaction volumes, offset by what we see as relatively high barriers to entry in WU's businesses and potential for operating margin expansion.

Quantitative Evaluations

S&P Quality Ranking   NR

D	C	B-	B	B+	A-	A	A+

Relative Strength Rank   MODERATE

63

LOWEST = 1   HIGHEST = 99

Revenue/Earnings Data

Revenue (Million $)

	1Q	2Q	3Q	4Q	Year
2010	1,233	1,273	--	--	--
2009	1,201	1,254	1,314	1,314	5,084
2008	1,266	1,347	1,377	1,292	5,282
2007	1,131	1,203	1,257	1,309	4,900
2006	1,043	1,114	1,140	1,173	4,470
2005	919.6	980.8	1,019	1,068	3,988

Earnings Per Share ($)

	1Q	2Q	3Q	4Q	Year
2010	0.30	0.33	E0.34	E0.35	E1.36
2009	0.32	0.31	0.26	0.32	1.21
2008	0.27	0.31	0.33	0.34	1.24
2007	0.25	0.26	0.28	0.32	1.11
2006	0.29	0.29	0.34	0.28	1.19
2005	--	--	0.32	0.31	0.96

Fiscal year ended Dec. 31. Next earnings report expected: NA. EPS Estimates based on S&P Operating Earnings; historical GAAP earnings are as reported.

Dividend Data (Dates: mm/dd Payment Date: mm/dd/yy)

Amount ($)	Date Decl.	Ex-Div. Date	Stk. of Record	Payment Date
0.060	12/09	12/17	12/21	12/30/09
0.060	02/25	03/17	03/19	03/31/10
0.060	05/14	06/16	06/18	06/30/10
0.060	09/22	09/30	10/04	10/14/10

Dividends have been paid since 2006. Source: Company reports.

Please read the Required Disclosures and Analyst Certification on the last page of this report.

The **McGraw·Hill** Companies

Western Union Co

STANDARD &POOR'S

Business Summary July 30, 2010

CORPORATE OVERVIEW. Western Union is a leading independent provider of consumer money transfer services. WU offers its services through a network of about 410,000 agent locations (at December 31, 2009) spanning more than 200 countries and territories. The company provides its services globally, mainly under the Western Union brand name and also under the Orlandi Valuta and Vigo brands. WU derives the majority of revenues from fees that consumers pay when they send money. The company's main segments include consumer-to-consumer (C2C; 85% of 2009 revenues) and Global Business Payments (formerly consumer-to-business or C2B; 14%).

WU's core C2C services allow customers to transfer money to other individuals. The majority of these transfers are originated in cash at Western Union agent locations, although consumers can also send money via the Internet, telephone, credit or debit card and, in some cases, through bank debits. In 2009, C2C transactions increased 4%, to 196 million, while C2C transaction fees fell about 5%.

Through its Global Business Payments segment, consumers or businesses can make payments to businesses electronically, over the telephone, via the Internet, or at one of WU's agent locations. The company has long-standing relationships with billers such as utilities, auto finance companies, mortgage servicers, financial service providers and government agencies who accept such payments. In 2009, WU's Global Business Payment transactions increased less than 1%, to 415 million, while transaction fees fell 7%.

CORPORATE STRATEGY. The pursuit of growth through international expansion is a key tenet of Western Union's growth strategy. The company believes that a majority of its C2C transactions involve at least one non-U.S. location. Outside the United states, WU's revenue base is well-diversified geographically. Building on and maintaining its well-recognized consumer brand is another key element to the company's strategy. WU spent between 5%-6% of revenues on marketing, advertising and developing customer loyalty programs in 2007, 2008 and 2009. The company also invested about 3% of annual revenues in selective price reductions on its C2C services in individual markets depending on the dynamics within those markets in 2006 and 2007; in 2008, such reductions accounted for 1% of revenues and 2% in 2009. We think the difference in growth between transaction fees and transaction volumes is evidence of this strategy.

Company Financials Fiscal Year Ended Dec. 31

Per Share Data ($)	2009	2008	2007	2006	2005	2004	2003	2002	2001	2000
Tangible Book Value	NM	NM	NM	NM	NM	NA	NA	NA	NA	NA
Cash Flow	1.43	1.33	1.17	1.32	NA	NA	NA	NA	NA	NA
Earnings	1.21	1.24	1.11	1.19	0.96	NA	NA	NA	NA	NA
S&P Core Earnings	1.29	1.22	1.11	1.18	1.10	0.95	NA	NA	NA	NA
Dividends	0.06	0.04	0.04	0.01	NA	NA	NA	NA	NA	NA
Payout Ratio	5%	3%	4%	1%	NA	NA	NA	NA	NA	NA
Prices:High	20.64	28.62	24.83	24.14	NA	NA	NA	NA	NA	NA
Prices:Low	10.05	10.48	15.00	16.85	NA	NA	NA	NA	NA	NA
P/E Ratio:High	17	23	22	20	NA	NA	NA	NA	NA	NA
P/E Ratio:Low	8	8	14	14	NA	NA	NA	NA	NA	NA
Income Statement Analysis (Million $)										
Revenue	5,084	5,282	4,900	4,470	3,988	3,524	3,121	NA	NA	NA
Operating Income	1,437	1,500	1,393	1,415	NA	1,168	1,051	NA	NA	NA
Depreciation	154	61.7	49.1	104	NA	79.2	78.4	NA	NA	NA
Interest Expense	158	171	189	53.0	202	6.40	NA	NA	NA	NA
Pretax Income	1,132	1,239	1,222	1,335	1,063	1,098	970	NA	NA	NA
Effective Tax Rate	25.0%	25.8%	29.9%	31.5%	29.5%	31.5%	34.1%	NA	NA	NA
Net Income	849	919	857	914	749	752	639	NA	NA	NA
S&P Core Earnings	904	908	857	913	859	734	NA	NA	NA	NA
Balance Sheet & Other Financial Data (Million $)										
Cash	1,685	1,296	2,030	1,422	1,186	470	NA	NA	NA	NA
Current Assets	1,985	1,850	1,959	1,631	NA	1,520	NA	NA	NA	NA
Total Assets	7,353	5,578	5,784	5,321	4,659	3,307	NA	NA	NA	NA
Current Liabilities	1,020	1,350	1,468	882	NA	218	NA	NA	NA	NA
Long Term Debt	3,049	2,561	2,500	2,996	3,500	9.90	NA	NA	NA	NA
Common Equity	354	-8.10	50.7	-315	-687	1,909	NA	NA	NA	NA
Total Capital	3,402	2,823	2,814	2,681	2,183	1,919	NA	NA	NA	NA
Capital Expenditures	59.7	53.9	83.5	64.0	NA	26.5	23.6	NA	NA	NA
Cash Flow	1,003	981	906	1,018	NA	831	717	NA	NA	NA
Current Ratio	1.7	2.1	1.3	1.9	NA	7.0	NA	NA	NA	NA
% Long Term Debt of Capitalization	89.6	90.7	88.8	112.0	160.3	0.5	Nil	NA	NA	NA
% Net Income of Revenue	16.7	17.4	17.5	20.4	18.8	21.3	20.5	NA	NA	NA
% Return on Assets	13.1	16.2	15.4	18.3	NA	NA	NA	NA	NA	NA
% Return on Equity	NM	NM	NM	NM	NA	NA	NA	NA	NA	NA

Data as orig reptd.; bef. results of disc opers/spec. items. Per share data adj. for stk. divs.; EPS diluted. Pro forma data in 2005; balance sheet and book value as of Jun. 30, 2006. E-Estimated. NA-Not Available. NM-Not Meaningful. NR-Not Ranked. UR-Under Review.

Office: 12500 East Belford Avenue, Englewood, CO 80112.
Telephone: 866-405-5012.
Website: http://www.westernunion.com
Chrmn: J.M. Greenberg

Pres & CEO: H. Ersek
EVP & CFO: S.T. Scheirman
EVP, Secy & General Counsel: M.J. Wong
SVP, Chief Acctg Officer & Cntlr: A.T. Schenkel

Investor Contact: G. Kohn (720-332-8276)
Board Members: D. S. Devitre, H. Ersek, J. M. Greenberg, B. D. Holden, A. J. Lacy, R. Mendoza, M. Miles, Jr., D. Stevenson, L. F. levinson, W. von Schimmelmann

Founded: 1851
Domicile: Delaware
Employees: 6,800

The McGraw-Hill Companies

Weyerhaeuser Co

STANDARD &POOR'S

S&P Recommendation HOLD ★★★★★

Price	$15.72 (as of Oct 22, 2010)
12-Mo. Target Price	$17.00
Investment Style	Large-Cap Blend

GICS Sector Financials
Sub-Industry Specialized REITS

Summary One of the world's largest integrated forest products companies, WY grows timber; makes and sells forest products and pulp; and engages in real estate construction and development.

Key Stock Statistics (Source S&P, Vickers, company reports)

52-Wk Range	$53.69– 15.06	S&P Oper. EPS 2010E	0.30	Market Capitalization(B)	$3.327	Beta	1.16
Trailing 12-Month EPS	$-0.86	S&P Oper. EPS 2011E	0.80	Yield (%)	1.27	S&P 3-Yr. Proj. EPS CAGR(%)	NM
Trailing 12-Month P/E	NM	P/E on S&P Oper. EPS 2010E	52.4	Dividend Rate/Share	$0.20	S&P Credit Rating	BBB-
$10K Invested 5 Yrs Ago	$7,990	Common Shares Outstg. (M)	211.6	Institutional Ownership (%)	82		

Price Performance

- 30-Week Mov. Avg. · · ·
- 10-Week Mov. Avg. - -
- **GAAP Earnings vs. Previous Year**
- Volume Above Avg. STARS
- 12-Mo. Target Price —
- Relative Strength —
- ▲ Up ▼ Down ▶ No Change
- Below Avg.

Options: CBOE, P

Analysis prepared by **Stuart J. Benway, CFA** on August 03, 2010, when the stock traded at **$ 16.91**.

Highlights

➤ We see sales rising 15%-20% in 2010 following the 41% decline in 2009 from continuing operations. Divestitures have helped reduce WY's revenue base by a third over the past two years. S&P expects the residential housing market to begin to recover this year, with housing starts seen increasing by 15%. This should lead to higher prices for lumber and panels and to higher closings in homebuilding. Pulp prices are also expected to be much higher in 2010.

➤ We look for conditions to improve somewhat in 2010. Timberland margins are likely to remain below normal due to deferred harvests. However, margins in wood products should improve, reflecting steep cost reductions and higher prices. We also look for higher volume and land sales in the real estate sector to aid profits. Our estimate is for positive operating margins in 2010 after two years of negative margins.

➤ For 2010, we see an operating profit of $0.30 per share, excluding unusual items but including land sales gains, compared to the operating loss of $2.12 in 2009. In 2011, we project a further earnings recovery to $0.80 per share.

Investment Rationale/Risk

➤ WY has divested assets to focus on its timber, wood products, real estate and fiber businesses. Although these sales generated significant proceeds, its lumber and homebuilding businesses have been hurt badly by the downturn in residential real estate. WY has reduced its annual dividend by over 90%. However, it is in the process of adopting the REIT form of corporate structure, which will likely result in higher cash flows over time due to a lower tax rate.

➤ Risks to our recommendation and target price include the lack of a housing recovery, a significant decline in wood product and pulp prices, and decreased values for timberland.

➤ Given the company's recent and potential corporate repositioning moves, we believe it is appropriate to value WY shares on a sum-of-the-parts basis. Our model recognizes the cyclical characteristics of the wood products and real estate businesses, the relative stability of the fibers unit, and what we view as the significant value of the timberlands. Considering these factors, we derive a value of $17, which is our 12-month target price.

Qualitative Risk Assessment

LOW	MEDIUM	HIGH

Our risk assessment reflects that Weyerhaeuser operates in a cyclical industry, with large capital requirements and significant variability in both costs and prices. However, the company is one of the largest in the industry, and we believe it has a major base of assets and modest debt levels.

Quantitative Evaluations

S&P Quality Ranking B-

D	C	B-	B	B+	A-	A	A+

Relative Strength Rank WEAK

7

LOWEST = 1   HIGHEST = 99

Revenue/Earnings Data

Revenue (Million $)

	1Q	2Q	3Q	4Q	Year
2010	1,419	1,805	--	--	--
2009	1,275	1,391	1,407	1,455	5,528
2008	2,096	2,174	2,107	1,760	8,018
2007	3,891	4,334	4,146	3,937	16,308
2006	5,256	5,657	5,328	5,655	21,896
2005	5,404	5,838	5,604	5,868	22,629

Earnings Per Share ($)

	1Q	2Q	3Q	4Q	Year
2010	-0.09	0.07	E0.13	E0.04	E0.30
2009	-1.25	-0.50	Nil	-0.83	-2.58
2008	-1.08	-0.98	-0.95	-5.67	-8.61
2007	-0.07	0.17	0.34	-0.21	0.23
2006	-2.36	1.20	0.75	1.67	1.44
2005	0.98	1.22	1.16	-1.00	2.36

Fiscal year ended Dec. 31. Next earnings report expected: Early November. EPS Estimates based on S&P Operating Earnings; historical GAAP earnings are as reported.

Dividend Data (Dates: mm/dd Payment Date: mm/dd/yy)

Amount ($)	Date Decl.	Ex-Div. Date	Stk. of Record	Payment Date
0.050	01/04	01/27	01/29	03/01/10
0.050	04/15	04/28	04/30	06/01/10
26.420	07/12	07/20	07/22	09/01/10
0.050	10/15	11/03	11/05	12/01/10

Dividends have been paid since 1933. Source: Company reports.

Please read the Required Disclosures and Analyst Certification on the last page of this report.

The McGraw·Hill Companies

Weyerhaeuser Co

STANDARD &POOR'S

Business Summary August 03, 2010

CORPORATE OVERVIEW. Weyerhaeuser, one of the world's largest integrated forest products companies, is primarily engaged in growing and harvesting timber; the production, distribution and sale of wood and paper products; and real estate development. Through its timberlands segment (13% of 2009 sales), WY manages 22 million acres of forestland through company-owned or leased property in eight states and Canada. The wood products businesses (42%) produce and sell softwood and hardwood lumber, plywood and veneer, composite panels, oriented strand board, and engineered lumber. Products made by the pulp and paper unit (28%) include paper grade, absorbent, dissolving and specialty pulp grades. Paper products include liquid packaging board used for milk, juice, and tea. Through Weyerhaeuser Real Estate Company (17%), the company is involved in the development of single-family housing and residential lots, including the development of master-planned communities.

MARKET PROFILE. Weyerhaeuser operates in a highly cyclical and capital-intensive industry. Demand for the company's products is dependent on a number of factors including consumer spending, white collar employment levels, domestic and Japanese new home construction and repair and remodeling activity, and movements in currency exchange rates. Historical prices for pulp and wood products have been volatile, and, despite its size, Weyerhaeuser has had only a limited direct influence over the timing and extent of price changes for its products. Pricing is significantly affected by the relationship between supply and demand, and supply is influenced primarily by fluctuations in available manufacturing capacity.

Company Financials Fiscal Year Ended Dec. 31

Per Share Data ($)	2009	2008	2007	2006	2005	2004	2003	2002	2001	2000
Tangible Book Value	19.00	22.58	27.35	28.92	27.81	24.84	17.44	15.80	25.45	25.95
Cash Flow	-0.18	-5.80	4.43	6.88	7.80	10.76	7.23	6.63	5.94	7.52
Earnings	-2.58	-8.61	0.23	1.44	2.36	5.43	1.30	1.09	1.61	3.72
S&P Core Earnings	-3.55	-7.30	-0.25	2.97	1.79	4.37	0.70	-0.75	NA	NA
Dividends	0.60	2.40	2.40	2.20	1.90	1.60	1.60	1.60	1.60	1.60
Payout Ratio	NM	NM	NM	182%	81%	29%	123%	147%	99%	43%
Prices:High	46.80	73.75	87.09	75.50	71.85	68.59	64.70	68.09	63.50	74.50
Prices:Low	18.67	28.68	59.67	54.25	60.62	55.06	45.40	37.35	42.77	36.06
P/E Ratio:High	NM	NM	NM	62	30	13	50	62	39	20
P/E Ratio:Low	NM	NM	NM	45	26	10	35	34	27	10

Income Statement Analysis (Million $)										
Revenue	5,528	8,018	16,308	21,896	22,629	22,665	19,873	18,521	14,545	15,980
Operating Income	158	38.0	1,628	2,914	3,443	4,028	2,716	2,455	1,689	2,536
Depreciation	508	593	925	1,283	1,337	1,322	1,318	1,225	876	859
Interest Expense	434	550	586	531	730	829	796	771	344	351
Pretax Income	-842	-2,707	59.0	826	906	1,945	436	371	516	1,323
Effective Tax Rate	32.5%	NM	13.6%	57.0%	35.8%	34.0%	33.9%	35.0%	31.4%	36.5%
Net Income	-545	-1,819	51.0	355	582	1,283	288	241	354	840
S&P Core Earnings	-762	-1,542	-53.0	728	444	1,029	156	-168	2.35	NA

Balance Sheet & Other Financial Data (Million $)										
Cash	1,918	2,432	114	243	1,104	1,197	202	122	204	123
Current Assets	5,221	6,085	5,990	4,121	4,876	5,293	4,021	3,888	3,061	3,288
Total Assets	15,250	16,735	23,806	26,862	28,229	29,954	28,109	28,219	18,293	18,195
Current Liabilities	995	1,864	2,921	3,129	3,255	3,149	2,525	2,994	1,863	2,704
Long Term Debt	5,683	5,557	6,522	7,675	8,262	10,144	12,397	12,721	5,715	5,114
Common Equity	4,044	4,814	7,981	9,095	9,800	9,255	7,109	6,623	6,695	6,832
Total Capital	9,740	12,228	17,830	20,461	22,097	23,932	23,800	23,400	14,787	14,323
Capital Expenditures	239	608	880	837	861	492	608	930	660	848
Cash Flow	-37.0	-1,226	976	1,638	1,919	2,605	1,606	1,466	1,230	1,699
Current Ratio	5.5	3.4	2.1	1.3	1.5	1.7	1.6	1.3	1.6	1.2
% Long Term Debt of Capitalization	58.4	45.4	36.6	37.5	37.4	42.4	52.1	54.4	38.6	35.7
% Net Income of Revenue	NM	NM	0.3	1.6	2.6	5.7	1.4	1.3	2.4	5.3
% Return on Assets	NM	NM	0.2	1.3	2.0	4.4	1.0	1.0	1.9	4.6
% Return on Equity	NM	NM	0.6	3.8	6.1	15.7	4.2	3.6	5.2	12.0

Data as orig reptd.; bef. results of disc opers/spec. items. Per share data adj. for stk. divs.; EPS diluted. E-Estimated. NA-Not Available. NM-Not Meaningful. NR-Not Ranked. UR-Under Review.

Office: 33663 Weyerhaeuser Way South, Federal Way, WA 98063-9777.
Telephone: 253-924-2345.
Email: invrelations@weyerhaeuser.com
Website: http://www.weyerhaeuser.com

Chrmn: C.R. Williamson
Pres & CEO: D.S. Fulton
COO: J.M. Hillman
EVP & CFO: P. Bedient

SVP & CTO: M.P. Drake
Investor Contact: K.F. McAuley (253-924-2058)
Board Members: D. A. Cafaro, M. A. Emmert, D. S. Fulton, J. I. Kieckhefer, A. G. Langbo, W. Murdy, N. Piasecki, R. H. Sinkfield, D. M. Steuert, K. Williams, C. R. Williamson

Founded: 1900
Domicile: Washington
Employees: 14,888

The McGraw-Hill Companies

Whirlpool Corp

STANDARD &POOR'S

S&P Recommendation	BUY ★★★★☆	Price $85.56 (as of Oct 22, 2010)	12-Mo. Target Price $108.00	Investment Style Large-Cap Blend

GICS Sector Consumer Discretionary
Sub-Industry Household Appliances

Summary Whirlpool, which acquired Maytag in 2006, is the world's largest manufacturer of home appliances. Sears, Roebuck is its biggest customer.

Key Stock Statistics (Source S&P, Vickers, company reports)

52-Wk Range	$118.44– 68.90	S&P Oper. EPS 2010**E**	9.44	Market Capitalization(B)	$6.503	Beta	1.99
Trailing 12-Month EPS	$7.17	S&P Oper. EPS 2011**E**	9.40	Yield (%)	2.01	S&P 3-Yr. Proj. EPS CAGR(%)	18
Trailing 12-Month P/E	11.9	P/E on S&P Oper. EPS 2010**E**	9.1	Dividend Rate/Share	$1.72	S&P Credit Rating	BBB-
$10K Invested 5 Yrs Ago	$13,008	Common Shares Outstg. (M)	76.0	Institutional Ownership (%)	100		

Price Performance

30-Week Mov. Avg. · · · 10-Week Mov. Avg. - - GAAP Earnings vs. Previous Year   Volume Above Avg. STARS
12-Mo. Target Price — Relative Strength   ▲ Up ▼ Down ► No Change   Below Avg.

Options: CBOE, P

Analysis prepared by **Erik Kolb** on October 19, 2010, when the stock traded at **$ 85.16**.

Highlights

➤ Following a sales decline of 10% in 2009, we forecast increases of 6.2% for 2010 and 4.6% for 2011, as the general economy rebounds. For 2010, the company estimates industry unit shipments will rise 10% in Brazil, compared to a 5% rise in the U.S. market, and no growth forecasted for Europe. We believe customer demand for large kitchen and laundry appliances is beginning to pick up for upgrades and replacements.

➤ We think WHR's addressable markets for appliances will also benefit from demand for energy savings performance spurred by federal tax credits. With improved cost controls, WHR's gross margins widened to 14% in 2009 from 13.3% in 2008, and we estimate gross margins will improve to about 15.7% in both 2010 and 2011.

➤ Following operating margins of 4.8% in 2009, we expect operating margins to rise to 6.9% in 2010. For the long term, we believe WHR will benefit from its larger scale and purchasing power. With material federal energy tax credits, we see operating EPS of $9.44 for 2010 and $9.40 for 2011.

Investment Rationale/Risk

➤ We believe the industry association for U.S. appliances will report positive monthly shipments of major appliances in 2010. We also see sustainable strong demand for appliances in non-U.S. markets, especially in Asia and Latin America. In our opinion, WHR can gain market share with its scale advantages and price competitively without hurting margins.

➤ Risks to our opinion and target price include another economic recession that further weakens business conditions or growth prospects in WHR's major markets, particularly in the Americas and Europe; more competition and/or market share losses; and, narrower margins resulting from higher raw material costs.

➤ Our 12-month target price of $108 is based on a target P/E of 11.5X, slightly below the midpoint of the historical range for WHR and peers, applied to our 2011 EPS projection, which excludes non-recurring items. Given our view of an improving sales outlook, we think the Maytag merger is paying dividends through better economies of scale.

Qualitative Risk Assessment

LOW	MEDIUM	HIGH

Our risk assessment reflects WHR's leading market share across many brands, offset by intense industry rivalry and heightened competition from foreign companies. We view home appliances to be cyclical, but less so than other large-ticket items, like home furnishings or automobiles.

Quantitative Evaluations

S&P Quality Ranking B+

D	C	B-	B	B+	A-	A	A+

Relative Strength Rank MODERATE

57

LOWEST = 1   HIGHEST = 99

Revenue/Earnings Data

Revenue (Million $)

	1Q	2Q	3Q	4Q	Year
2010	4,272	4,534	--	--	--
2009	3,569	4,169	4,497	4,864	17,099
2008	4,614	5,076	4,902	4,315	18,907
2007	4,389	4,854	4,840	5,325	19,408
2006	3,536	4,747	4,843	4,954	18,080
2005	3,208	3,556	3,599	3,954	14,317

Earnings Per Share ($)

2010	2.13	2.64	E2.25	E2.41	E9.44
2009	-0.91	1.04	1.15	1.24	4.34
2008	1.22	1.53	2.15	0.60	5.50
2007	1.55	2.00	2.20	2.39	8.10
2006	1.70	1.26	1.68	1.67	6.35
2005	1.26	1.42	1.66	1.83	6.19

Fiscal year ended Dec. 31. Next earnings report expected: Late October. EPS Estimates based on S&P Operating Earnings; historical GAAP earnings are as reported.

Dividend Data (Dates: mm/dd Payment Date: mm/dd/yy)

Amount ($)	Date Decl.	Ex-Div. Date	Stk. of Record	Payment Date
0.430	02/16	02/24	02/26	03/15/10
0.430	04/20	05/19	05/21	06/15/10
0.430	08/17	08/25	08/27	09/15/10
0.430	10/19	11/17	11/19	12/15/10

Dividends have been paid since 1929. Source: Company reports.

Whirlpool Corp

Business Summary October 19, 2010

CORPORATE OVERVIEW. Whirlpool Corp. (WHR) manufactures and markets a full line of major appliances and related products, primarily for home use. Products are manufactured in 12 countries and marketed worldwide under 13 main brand names. The company's growth strategy over the past several years has been to introduce innovative new products, strengthen customer loyalty, expand its global footprint, enhance distribution channels, and make strategic acquisitions where appropriate.

MARKET PROFILE. Of WHR's total sales in 2009, 56% were from North America. As the market leader, WHR's major product brands in the U.S. include Whirlpool, Maytag, KitchenAid, Jenn-Air, Roper, Estate, Admiral, Magic Chef, Amana, and Inglis. In Europe, which generated 19% of sales, products are marketed under the Whirlpool, Maytag, Amana, Bauknecht, Ignis, Laden, Polar and KitchenAid brand names. Markets also include Latin America and Asia.

About 22% of total sales in 2009 were from Latin America which is its fastest-growing market. In this region, WHR markets and distributes its major home appliances under the Whirlpool, Maytag, KitchenAid, Brastemp, Consul, and

Eslabon de Lujo brand names. It manages appliance sales and distribution in Brazil, Argentina, Chile, and Peru through a Brazilian subsidiary, and in Bolivia, Paraguay, and Uruguay through outside distributors. Also, WHR manages appliance sales and distribution in Central American countries, the Caribbean, Venezuela, Colombia, Guatemala, and Ecuador through its Brazilian subsidiary and through distributors. In Latin America, Whirlpool has manufacturing facilities only in Brazil.

COMPETITIVE LANDSCAPE. The company has been able to retain a number one position in brand and market share in most global regions. Combined with high reliability, WHR has developed strong customer loyalty. Competitors in the appliance industry include long-time incumbents Electrolux and General Electric, as well as expanding foreign operations such as LG Electronics, Bosch Siemens, Samsung, Fisher & Paykel, and Haier from China.

Company Financials Fiscal Year Ended Dec. 31

Per Share Data ($)	2009	2008	2007	2006	2005	2004	2003	2002	2001	2000
Tangible Book Value	1.86	NM	6.06	NM	21.49	19.85	15.23	5.82	11.10	13.97
Cash Flow	11.28	13.36	15.52	13.54	12.65	12.35	12.00	9.62	6.32	10.39
Earnings	4.34	5.50	8.10	6.35	6.19	5.90	5.91	3.78	0.50	5.20
S&P Core Earnings	4.34	3.17	7.33	6.33	5.99	5.58	5.71	2.12	-1.91	NA
Dividends	1.72	1.72	1.72	2.15	1.72	1.72	1.36	1.36	1.02	1.36
Payout Ratio	40%	31%	21%	34%	28%	29%	23%	36%	NM	26%
Prices:High	85.01	98.00	118.00	96.00	86.52	80.00	73.35	79.80	74.20	68.31
Prices:Low	19.19	30.19	72.10	74.07	60.78	54.53	42.80	39.23	45.88	31.50
P/E Ratio:High	20	18	15	15	14	14	12	21	NM	13
P/E Ratio:Low	4	5	9	12	10	9	7	10	NM	6

Income Statement Analysis (Million $)	2009	2008	2007	2006	2005	2004	2003	2002	2001	2000
Revenue	17,099	18,907	19,408	18,080	14,317	13,220	12,176	11,016	10,343	10,325
Operating Income	1,257	1,347	1,717	1,428	1,291	1,218	1,219	1,207	1,147	1,178
Depreciation	525	597	593	550	442	445	427	405	396	371
Interest Expense	219	203	203	202	130	128	137	143	162	180
Pretax Income	293	246	786	620	598	615	652	468	89.0	580
Effective Tax Rate	NM	NM	14.9%	20.3%	28.6%	34.0%	35.0%	41.2%	48.3%	34.5%
Net Income	328	418	647	486	422	406	414	262	34.0	367
S&P Core Earnings	327	241	587	484	408	384	401	147	-130	NA

Balance Sheet & Other Financial Data (Million $)	2009	2008	2007	2006	2005	2004	2003	2002	2001	2000
Cash	1,380	146	201	262	524	243	249	192	316	114
Current Assets	7,025	6,044	6,555	6,476	4,710	4,514	3,865	3,327	3,311	3,237
Total Assets	15,094	13,532	14,009	13,878	8,248	8,181	7,361	6,631	6,967	6,902
Current Liabilities	5,941	5,563	5,893	6,002	4,301	3,985	3,589	3,505	3,082	3,303
Long Term Debt	2,502	2,002	1,668	1,798	745	1,160	1,134	1,092	1,295	795
Common Equity	3,664	3,006	3,911	3,283	1,745	1,606	1,301	796	2,126	1,684
Total Capital	6,640	5,277	5,648	5,481	2,749	3,074	2,734	2,083	3,725	2,801
Capital Expenditures	541	547	536	576	484	511	423	430	378	375
Cash Flow	853	1,015	1,240	1,036	864	851	841	667	430	738
Current Ratio	1.2	1.1	1.1	1.1	1.1	1.1	1.1	0.9	1.1	1.0
% Long Term Debt of Capitalization	37.7	37.9	29.5	32.8	27.1	37.8	41.5	52.4	34.8	28.4
% Net Income of Revenue	1.9	2.2	3.3	2.7	2.9	3.1	3.4	2.4	0.3	3.6
% Return on Assets	2.3	3.0	4.6	4.4	5.1	5.2	5.9	3.9	0.5	5.3
% Return on Equity	9.8	12.1	18.0	19.3	25.2	27.9	40.6	22.8	1.5	20.7

Data as orig reptd.; bef. results of disc opers/spec. items. Per share data adj. for stk. divs.; EPS diluted. E-Estimated. NA-Not Available. NM-Not Meaningful. NR-Not Ranked. UR-Under Review.

Office: 2000 N M 63, Benton Harbor, MI 49022-2692.
Telephone: 269-923-5000.
Email: info@whirlpool.com
Website: http://www.whirlpool.com

Chrmn & CEO: J.M. Fettig
EVP & CFO: R. Templin
SVP, Chief Acctg Officer & Cntlr: L.M. Venturelli
CTO: S. Sarraf

Secy & General Counsel: R.J. LaForest
Investor Contact: G. Fritz (269-923-2641)
Board Members: S. R. Allen, H. Cain, G. T. DiCamillo, J. M. Fettig, K. J. Hempel, M. F. Johnston, W. T. Kerr, J. D. Liu, M. L. Marsh, W. D. Perez, P. G. Stern, J. D. Stoney, M. A. Todman, M. D. White

Founded: 1906
Domicile: Delaware
Employees: 66,884

Whole Foods Market Inc

STANDARD &POOR'S

S&P Recommendation **BUY** ★★★★☆	Price $39.89 (as of Oct 22, 2010)	12-Mo. Target Price $44.00	Investment Style Large-Cap Blend

GICS Sector Consumer Staples
Sub-Industry Food Retail

Summary This company owns and operates the largest U.S. chain of natural and organic foods supermarkets.

Key Stock Statistics (Source S&P, Vickers, company reports)

52-Wk Range	$43.18–24.94	S&P Oper. EPS 2010**E**	1.39	Market Capitalization(B)	$6.857	Beta	1.07
Trailing 12-Month EPS	$1.31	S&P Oper. EPS 2011**E**	1.63	Yield (%)	Nil	S&P 3-Yr. Proj. EPS CAGR(%)	15
Trailing 12-Month P/E	30.5	P/E on S&P Oper. EPS 2010**E**	28.7	Dividend Rate/Share	Nil	S&P Credit Rating	BB
$10K Invested 5 Yrs Ago	$6,336	Common Shares Outstg. (M)	171.9	Institutional Ownership (%)	92		

Price Performance

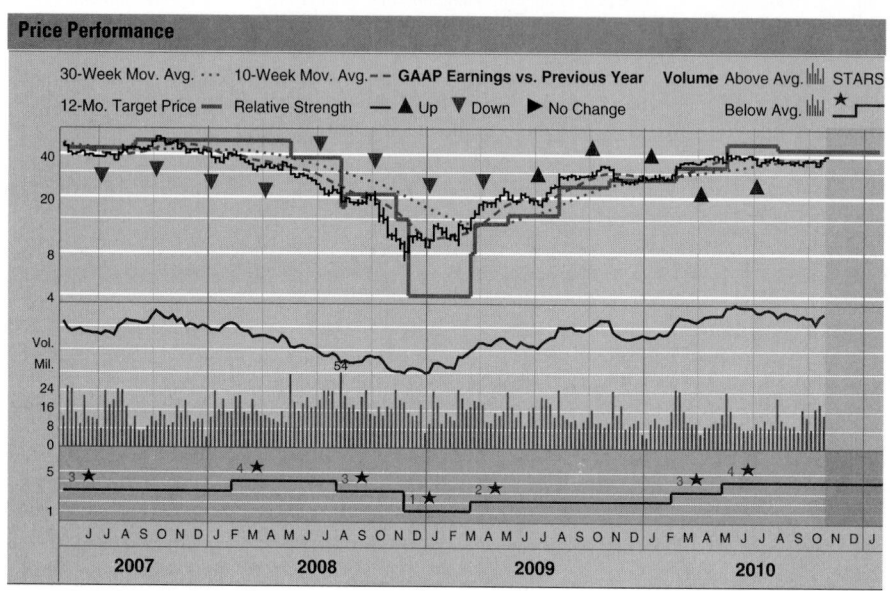

30-Week Mov. Avg. · · · 10-Week Mov. Avg. – – GAAP Earnings vs. Previous Year   Volume Above Avg. STARS
12-Mo. Target Price — Relative Strength — ▲ Up ▼ Down ► No Change   Below Avg.

Options: ASE

Analysis prepared by **Joseph Agnese** on August 05, 2010, when the stock traded at **$ 36.16**.

Highlights

➤ We expect FY 11 (Sep.) sales to increase 11.5% to $10.0 billion, from our estimate of $9.0 billion in FY 10, reflecting square footage growth of 5.0% from the opening of 11 net new stores, and as easier comparisons, an increased selection of low-priced products, and food inflation result in a comparable-store sales increase of about 6.0%.

➤ We believe margins will expand in both FY 10 and FY 11, reflecting increased operating leverage and our projection for lower new store opening costs in FY 10, as the company opens smaller and a fewer number of stores, and a 10% rise in FY 11 due to an acceleration in new store openings. We see improved inventory management leading to lower shrink expense and contributing to increased labor productivity. We expect net interest expense to decline significantly in FY 11 due to lower debt levels and the expiration of an interest rate swap agreement in October 2010.

➤ We project that FY 11 EPS will increase 17%, to $1.63, up from our estimate of $1.39 in FY 10.

Investment Rationale/Risk

➤ We believe the adoption of a new pricing strategy, a focus on lower-priced (value) products, and a significant slowdown in square footage expansion will lead to a strengthening of the company's balance sheet and above-average industry sales growth levels in FY 10. Longer term, we expect plans to reaccelerate square footage growth while utilizing free cash flow to pay down debt will lead to both an acceleration in EPS growth and a reduction in risks.

➤ Risks to our recommendation and target price include lower-than-expected comparable-store sales growth on weaker-than-expected consumer demand.

➤ Due to a stronger-than-expected rebound in comparable-store sales results in the first three quarters of 2010 and our expectation for sales strength to continue, we believe the stock should trade in line with its 10-year historical average premium of 1.9X compared to the S&P 500, but below its long-term P/E average of 35X as our projected EPS growth estimates are still below historical levels. We apply a P/E multiple of 27X to our FY 11 EPS estimate of $1.63, to reach our 12-month target price of $44.

Qualitative Risk Assessment

LOW	**MEDIUM**	HIGH

Our risk assessment reflects the intensely competitive environment in the retail food industry, partly offset by our view of WFMI's strong balance sheet and growing natural and organic food industry sales momentum.

Quantitative Evaluations

S&P Quality Ranking   B

D	C	B-	**B**	B+	A-	A	A+

Relative Strength Rank   STRONG

77

LOWEST = 1   HIGHEST = 99

Revenue/Earnings Data

Revenue (Million $)

	1Q	2Q	3Q	4Q	Year
2010	2,639	2,106	2,163	--	--
2009	2,467	1,858	1,878	1,829	8,032
2008	2,457	1,866	1,841	1,789	7,954
2007	1,871	1,463	1,514	1,743	6,592
2006	1,667	1,312	1,338	1,291	5,607
2005	1,368	1,085	1,133	1,115	4,701

Earnings Per Share ($)

2010	0.32	0.39	0.38	E0.30	E1.39
2009	0.20	0.19	0.25	0.20	0.85
2008	0.28	0.29	0.24	0.01	0.82
2007	0.38	0.32	0.35	0.24	1.29
2006	0.40	0.36	0.37	0.28	1.41
2005	0.35	0.29	0.29	0.07	0.99

Fiscal year ended Sep. 30. Next earnings report expected: Early November. EPS Estimates based on S&P Operating Earnings; historical GAAP earnings are as reported.

Dividend Data

No cash dividends have been paid since 2008.

Whole Foods Market Inc

STANDARD &POOR'S

Business Summary August 05, 2010

CORPORATE OVERVIEW. Whole Foods Market, established in 1980, has grown into the largest U.S. retailer of natural and organic foods, with $8.0 billion in sales in FY 09 (Sep.). Reflecting a series of store openings and acquisitions, the company has expanded from a single Austin, TX, store in 1980 to a chain of more than 280 stores in 37 states plus Washington, DC; six stores in Canada; and five stores in the United Kingdom. The company strives to differentiate its stores from those of its competitors by tailoring its product mix, customer service attitude and store environment to appeal to health conscious and gourmet customers.

CORPORATE STRATEGY. The company opens or acquires stores in existing regions, and in metropolitan areas in which it believes it can become the leading natural foods supermarket retailer. In developing new stores, WFMI seeks to open large format units of 35,000 sq. ft. to 50,000 sq. ft., located on premium sites, often in urban, highly populated areas. Although approximately 30% of its store base consists of acquired stores, the company expects more of its future growth to come from developing new stores. As of June 2010, WFMI had signed leases for 48 stores averaging approximately 41,600 square feet in size,

which is about 11% larger than its existing store base average. It operated about 11.2 million square feet of retail space, and had about 2.0 million square feet (18% of existing sq. ft.) of retail space under development at June 2010

Stores average about 37,500 sq. ft., and offer a selection of some 30,000 food and non-food products. Each store contributes an average of almost $30 million in annual sales and averages about 7.6 years old. Products sold include natural and organic foods and beverages; dietary supplements; natural personal care products; natural household goods; and educational products. Natural foods can be defined as foods that are minimally processed, largely or completely free of artificial ingredients, preservatives and other non-naturally occurring chemicals, and as near as possible to their whole, natural state. Organic foods are based on the minimal use of off-farm inputs and on management practices that restore, maintain and enhance the ecology.

Company Financials Fiscal Year Ended Sep. 30

Per Share Data ($)	2009	2008	2007	2006	2005	2004	2003	2002	2001	2000
Tangible Book Value	6.38	5.47	4.97	9.00	9.06	6.82	5.57	4.21	2.98	2.11
Cash Flow	2.66	2.49	2.60	2.48	1.93	1.84	1.54	1.34	1.16	0.85
Earnings	0.85	0.82	1.29	1.41	0.99	1.05	0.83	0.70	0.61	0.26
S&P Core Earnings	0.92	0.82	1.29	1.40	-0.21	0.85	0.70	0.58	0.38	NA
Dividends	Nil	0.78	0.69	0.88	0.42	0.23	Nil	Nil	Nil	Nil
Payout Ratio	Nil	95%	53%	62%	42%	22%	Nil	Nil	Nil	Nil
Prices:High	34.40	42.48	53.65	78.27	79.90	48.74	33.81	27.30	23.25	15.94
Prices:Low	9.06	7.04	36.00	45.56	44.14	32.96	22.39	17.74	9.73	8.59
P/E Ratio:High	40	52	42	56	81	47	41	39	38	60
P/E Ratio:Low	11	9	28	32	45	32	27	25	16	32

Income Statement Analysis (Million $)	2009	2008	2007	2006	2005	2004	2003	2002	2001	2000
Revenue	8,032	7,954	6,592	5,607	4,701	3,865	3,149	2,690	2,272	1,839
Operating Income	559	470	484	475	363	341	285	248	209	181
Depreciation	255	234	186	156	134	112	98.0	85.9	78.8	63.9
Interest Expense	42.1	42.4	4.21	0.03	2.22	7.25	8.11	10.4	17.9	15.1
Pretax Income	251	207	305	340	237	229	173	141	89.8	63.5
Effective Tax Rate	41.5%	44.6%	40.0%	40.0%	42.5%	40.0%	40.0%	40.0%	42.5%	54.5%
Net Income	147	115	183	204	136	137	104	84.5	51.6	28.9
S&P Core Earnings	128	115	183	202	-28.0	109	85.0	70.4	43.0	NA

Balance Sheet & Other Financial Data (Million $)	2009	2008	2007	2006	2005	2004	2003	2002	2001	2000
Cash	430	30.5	Nil	2.25	309	198	166	12.6	1.84	0.40
Current Assets	1,055	623	668	624	673	485	364	172	145	152
Total Assets	3,783	3,381	3,213	2,043	1,889	1,520	1,197	943	829	760
Current Liabilities	684	666	785	510	418	331	240	176	156	143
Long Term Debt	739	929	736	8.61	12.9	165	163	162	251	298
Common Equity	1,628	1,506	1,459	1,404	1,366	988	776	589	409	307
Total Capital	2,780	2,435	2,195	1,413	1,379	1,173	942	751	660	605
Capital Expenditures	315	522	140	132	116	110	84.1	61.4	49.0	111
Cash Flow	374	348	369	360	270	249	202	170	130	92.8
Current Ratio	1.5	0.9	0.9	1.2	1.6	1.5	1.5	1.0	0.9	1.1
% Long Term Debt of Capitalization	26.6	38.2	33.5	0.6	0.9	14.0	17.3	21.6	38.0	49.2
% Net Income of Revenue	1.8	1.4	2.8	3.6	2.9	3.5	3.3	3.1	2.3	1.6
% Return on Assets	4.1	3.5	7.0	10.4	8.0	10.1	9.7	9.5	6.5	4.1
% Return on Equity	9.4	7.7	12.8	14.7	11.8	15.5	15.2	16.9	14.4	9.4

Data as orig reptd.; bef. results of disc opers/spec. items. Per share data adj. for stk. divs.; EPS diluted. E-Estimated. NA-Not Available. NM-Not Meaningful. NR-Not Ranked. UR-Under Review.

Office: 550 Bowie St, Austin, TX 78703-4644.
Telephone: 512-477-4455.
Website: http://www.wholefoods.com
Chrmn: J.B. Elstrott

Pres & COO: A.C. Gallo
Co-CEO: J.P. Mackey
Co-CEO: W. Robb
EVP, CFO, Chief Acctg Officer & Secy: G.J. Chamberlain

Investor Contact: C. McCann (512-477-4455)
Board Members: J. B. Elstrott, G. E. Greene, S. M. Hassan, S. Kugelman, J. P. Mackey, W. Robb, J. A. Seiffer, M. Siegel, J. D. Sokoloff, R. Sorenson, W. A. Tindell, III

Founded: 1978
Domicile: Texas
Employees: 52,500

The McGraw-Hill Companies

Williams Cos Inc. (The)

STANDARD & POOR'S

S&P Recommendation BUY ★★★★☆	**Price** $20.99 (as of Oct 22, 2010)	**12-Mo. Target Price** $23.00	**Investment Style** Large-Cap Blend

GICS Sector Energy
Sub-Industry Oil & Gas Storage & Transportation

Summary As an integrated natural gas company, Williams produces, gathers, processes and transports natural gas across the country.

Key Stock Statistics (Source S&P, Vickers, company reports)

52-Wk Range	$24.66– 17.53	S&P Oper. EPS 2010E	1.17	Market Capitalization(B)	$12.272	Beta	1.19
Trailing 12-Month EPS	$0.53	S&P Oper. EPS 2011E	1.35	Yield (%)	2.38	S&P 3-Yr. Proj. EPS CAGR(%)	-14
Trailing 12-Month P/E	39.6	P/E on S&P Oper. EPS 2010E	17.9	Dividend Rate/Share	$0.50	S&P Credit Rating	BBB-
$10K Invested 5 Yrs Ago	$10,695	Common Shares Outstg. (M)	584.7	Institutional Ownership (%)	99		

Price Performance

30-Week Mov. Avg. · · · 10-Week Mov. Avg. – – GAAP Earnings vs. Previous Year   Volume Above Avg. STARS
12-Mo. Target Price — Relative Strength — ▲ Up ▼ Down ► No Change   Below Avg.

Options: ASE, CBOE, P

Analysis prepared by **Michael Kay** on August 10, 2010, when the stock traded at **$ 20.35.**

Qualitative Risk Assessment

LOW	MEDIUM	HIGH

Our risk assessment reflects our view of the volatility of WMB's E&P segment, offset by a business portfolio focused on regulated industries with largely fixed returns.

Quantitative Evaluations

S&P Quality Ranking   B

D	C	B-	B	B+	A-	A	A+

Relative Strength Rank   MODERATE

70

LOWEST = 1   HIGHEST = 99

Revenue/Earnings Data

Revenue (Million $)

	1Q	2Q	3Q	4Q	Year
2010	2,596	2,292	--	--	--
2009	1,922	1,909	2,098	2,326	8,255
2008	3,204	3,701	3,245	2,202	12,352
2007	2,368	2,824	2,860	2,506	10,558
2006	3,028	2,715	3,300	2,770	11,813
2005	2,954	2,871	3,082	3,676	12,584

Earnings Per Share ($)

	1Q	2Q	3Q	4Q	Year
2010	-0.33	0.32	E0.26	E0.28	E1.17
2009	-0.29	0.21	0.24	0.29	0.75
2008	0.70	0.70	0.62	0.23	2.26
2007	0.28	0.40	0.38	0.34	1.39
2006	0.22	-0.11	0.19	0.25	0.55
2005	0.34	0.07	0.01	0.12	0.53

Fiscal year ended Dec. 31. Next earnings report expected: Late October. EPS Estimates based on S&P Operating Earnings; historical GAAP earnings are as reported.

Highlights

► Despite a pullback in activity throughout 2009, as lower prices warranted reduced drilling plans, WMB saw an 8% boost in production. On improved Piceance Basin economics and bolt-on acquisitions made in 2009, we expect WMB to accelerate production growth in 2010. After making its initial investment in the Marcellus Shale in 2009, WMB plans to expand midstream capabilities in the play through Williams Partners (WPZ 45, NR). Longer term, we look for E&P to benefit from the development of drilling prospects, especially in the Piceance Basin, the Powder River Basin and the Marcellus Shale, where WMB is acquiring acreage.

► WMB spent $2.4 billion on expansion in 2009, with 60% for E&P, 20% for midstream, and 19% for pipelines. Capex is budgeted at $3.475 billion-$3.975 billion in 2010 and $2.4 billion-$3.7 billion in 2011. EPS guidance is $1.00-$1.45 for 2010 and $1.15-$2.50 for 2011. WMB is allocating about 50%-55% of future capex to E&P and 32%-35% to WPZ.

► Operating EPS of $0.94 in 2009 fell 56%, mainly on lower gas prices. We see 2010 and 2011 EPS of $1.25 and $1.52, respectively, on improved pricing and lower operating costs.

Investment Rationale/Risk

► In February, WMB completed a $12 billion restructuring, contributing gas pipeline and U.S. midstream assets and L.P. and G.P. interests in Williams Pipeline Partners (WMZ 33, NR) to WPZ. WMB now owns 84% of the new WPZ, versus 24% of WMZ previously. We see a growing midstream business, 3 major pipelines and solid E&P prospects driving future growth. WMB sees lower NGL prices and delays at the deepwater Gulf of Mexico Perdido Norte project, but higher capex on Marcellus acquisitions, increased interest in Overland Pass and a new Parachute facility in the Piceance Basin.

► Risks to our recommendation and target price include sharply higher interest rates, slower-than-projected economic growth, a sustained decline in natural gas prices, and lower rates for FERC regulated pipelines.

► We see improving fundamentals in all business segments in 2010. Our 12-month target price of $23 reflects a blend of peer-average relative metrics, given our view of high-quality pipelines and a strong asset base in E&P, including an enterprise value to projected 2011 EBITDA multiple of 6X, a target P/E of 15X our 2011 EPS forecast, and our proved reserve NAV of $23.

Dividend Data (Dates: mm/dd Payment Date: mm/dd/yy)

Amount ($)	Date Decl.	Ex-Div. Date	Stk. of Record	Payment Date
0.110	11/19	12/09	12/11	12/28/09
0.110	01/21	03/10	03/12	03/29/10
0.125	04/27	06/09	06/11	06/28/10
0.125	07/14	08/25	08/27	09/13/10

Dividends have been paid since 1974. Source: Company reports.

Please read the Required Disclosures and Analyst Certification on the last page of this report.

The McGraw-Hill Companies

Williams Cos Inc. (The)

STANDARD & POOR'S

Business Summary August 10, 2010

CORPORATE OVERVIEW. The Williams Companies (WMB) primarily finds, produces, gathers, processes and transports natural gas. Operations are concentrated in the Pacific Northwest, Rocky Mountains, Gulf Coast, Southern California and Eastern Seaboard.

In February 2009, WMB announced a business strategy focused on migrating to an integrated natural gas business comprised of a smaller portfolio of natural gas businesses, reducing debt and increasing liquidity via asset sales, strategic levels of financing, and reductions in operating costs. Beginning with the first quarter of 2010, WMB's business segments will be Exploration & Production, Williams Partners and Other.

CORPORATE STRATEGY. WMB has transitioned toward aggressively focusing on the market in which it perceives a sustainable competitive advantage, primarily its E&P segment and its midstream segment. WMB has about 4.5 Tcfe of proved reserves (97% natural gas, 57% proved developed), with natural gas produced from tight sands formations and coal bed methane. Proved reserves were flat with 2008.

E&P profit fell about 67% in 2009 on a drop in natural gas prices. In 2010, WMB plans to accelerate drilling activity and sees production growth of about 12%, but believes it can return to over 20% growth should prices spike. WMB grew natural gas production by 8% in 2009, despite a pull-back in drilling activity reflecting a weak economy and plummeting natural gas prices. In the Piceance Basin, which represents about 56% of total WMB volumes, production grew 7%. Piceance production is expected to grow 12% in 2010, to about 781 MMcfe/day, as WMB accelerates its drilling program in the play. In the Powder River Basin, WMB is producing about 244 MMcfe/day, up 7% in 2009. WMB made its initial investment at Marcellus Shale in 2010, in a joint venture with Rex Energy Corp. (REXX 10, NR), with 44,000 net acres for $33 million. WMB expects $1.9 billion-$2.1 billion of E&P capex in 2010.

Company Financials Fiscal Year Ended Dec. 31

Per Share Data ($)	2009	2008	2007	2006	2005	2004	2003	2002	2001	2000
Tangible Book Value	12.75	12.85	9.51	8.48	7.70	7.06	5.96	7.15	9.43	13.26
Cash Flow	3.35	4.46	3.16	1.97	1.75	1.37	1.27	0.53	3.17	3.80
Earnings	0.75	2.26	1.39	0.55	0.53	0.18	-0.03	-1.14	1.67	1.95
S&P Core Earnings	0.80	2.14	1.41	0.78	0.64	0.05	-0.26	-1.34	1.40	NA
Dividends	0.44	0.43	0.39	0.35	0.25	0.08	0.04	0.42	0.68	0.60
Payout Ratio	59%	19%	28%	63%	47%	44%	NM	NM	41%	31%
Prices:High	21.54	40.75	37.74	28.32	25.72	17.18	10.73	26.35	46.44	49.75
Prices:Low	9.52	11.69	25.17	19.35	15.18	8.49	2.51	0.78	20.80	29.50
P/E Ratio:High	29	18	27	51	49	95	NM	NM	28	26
P/E Ratio:Low	13	5	18	35	29	47	NM	NM	12	15

Income Statement Analysis (Million $)										
Revenue	8,255	12,352	10,558	11,813	12,584	12,461	16,834	5,608	11,035	10,398
Operating Income	NA	3,853	2,938	2,124	1,972	1,903	1,849	1,566	3,389	2,602
Depreciation	1,469	1,310	1,082	866	740	668	671	775	798	832
Interest Expense	585	594	685	659	664	833	1,241	1,325	747	1,010
Pretax Income	943	2,221	1,461	579	557	246	71.0	-617	1,533	1,415
Effective Tax Rate	38.1%	32.1%	35.9%	35.6%	38.4%	53.4%	51.3%	NM	41.1%	39.1%
Net Income	508	1,334	847	333	317	93.2	15.2	-502	835	873
S&P Core Earnings	471	1,266	852	480	388	27.3	-144	-699	703	NA

Balance Sheet & Other Financial Data (Million $)										
Cash	1,188	800	1,699	2,269	1,597	930	2,316	2,019	1,301	1,211
Current Assets	3,793	4,411	5,538	6,322	9,697	6,044	8,795	12,886	12,938	15,477
Total Assets	25,280	26,006	25,061	25,402	29,443	23,993	27,022	34,989	38,906	40,197
Current Liabilities	2,477	3,519	4,431	4,694	8,450	5,146	6,270	11,309	13,495	16,804
Long Term Debt	8,258	7,683	7,757	7,622	7,591	7,712	11,040	11,896	10,621	10,532
Common Equity	8,447	8,440	6,375	6,073	5,428	4,956	4,102	4,778	6,044	5,892
Total Capital	17,292	20,127	18,558	17,656	15,741	15,238	17,595	20,723	21,532	20,693
Capital Expenditures	2,314	3,475	2,816	-2,509	1,299	787	957	1,824	1,922	4,904
Cash Flow	1,977	2,644	1,929	1,198	1,057	762	657	274	1,633	1,705
Current Ratio	1.5	1.3	1.3	1.3	1.1	1.2	1.4	1.1	1.0	0.9
% Long Term Debt of Capitalization	Nil	38.2	41.8	43.2	48.2	50.6	62.7	57.4	49.3	50.9
% Net Income of Revenue	6.2	10.8	8.0	2.8	2.5	0.7	0.1	NM	7.6	8.4
% Return on Assets	2.0	5.2	3.4	1.2	1.2	0.4	0.0	NM	2.3	2.7
% Return on Equity	NA	18.0	13.6	5.8	6.1	2.1	0.0	NM	14.0	15.2

Data as orig reptd.; bef. results of disc opers/spec. items. Per share data adj. for stk. divs.; EPS diluted. E-Estimated. NA-Not Available. NM-Not Meaningful. NR-Not Ranked. UR-Under Review.

Office: 1 Williams Ctr, Tulsa, OK 74172-0140.
Telephone: 918-573-2000.
Website: http://www.williams.com
Chrmn, Pres & CEO: S.J. Malcolm

Pres: J.C. Bumgarner, Jr.
SVP & CFO: D.R. Chappel
SVP & Chief Admin Officer: R.L. Ewing
SVP & General Counsel: J.J. Bender

Investor Contact: T.N. Campbell (918-573-2944)
Board Members: J. R. Cleveland, K. B. Cooper, I. F. Engelhardt, W. R. Granberry, W. E. Green, J. H. Hinshaw, W. R. Howell, G. A. Lorch, W. G. Lowrie, F. T. MacInnis, S. J. Malcolm, J. D. Stoney

Founded: 1908
Domicile: Delaware
Employees: 4,801

Windstream Corp

STANDARD &POOR'S

S&P Recommendation **STRONG BUY** ★★★★★	Price $12.45 (as of Oct 22, 2010)	12-Mo. Target Price $13.00	Investment Style Large-Cap Value

GICS Sector Telecommunication Services
Sub-Industry Integrated Telecommunication Services

Summary This company was formed through the July 2006 combination of former Alltel wireline assets and Valor Communications and continues to grow via acquisitions. It provides telephone service to 3 million lines in rural markets.

Key Stock Statistics (Source S&P, Vickers, company reports)

52-Wk Range	$13.05– 6.02	S&P Oper. EPS 2010E	0.87	Market Capitalization(B)	$6.015	Beta	0.92
Trailing 12-Month EPS	$0.69	S&P Oper. EPS 2011E	0.91	Yield (%)	8.03	S&P 3-Yr. Proj. EPS CAGR(%)	5
Trailing 12-Month P/E	18.0	P/E on S&P Oper. EPS 2010E	14.3	Dividend Rate/Share	$1.00	S&P Credit Rating	BB-
$10K Invested 5 Yrs Ago	NA	Common Shares Outstg. (M)	483.2	Institutional Ownership (%)	53		

Price Performance

30-Week Mov. Avg. · · · · 10-Week Mov. Avg. - - - **GAAP Earnings vs. Previous Year** Volume Above Avg. STARS
12-Mo. Target Price — Relative Strength — ▲ Up ▼ Down ▶ No Change Below Avg. ★

Options: CBOE, Ph

Analysis prepared by **Todd Rosenbluth** on August 19, 2010, when the stock traded at **$ 11.18**.

Highlights

▸ We project revenues of $3.7 billion in 2010 and $3.8 billion in 2011, including contributions from recently closed acquisitions. On an organic basis, we see broadband customer additions nearly offsetting the impact of increasing access line losses, but growth will likely slow given an above-average penetration rate. We expect lower universal service funding, from the loss of access lines, and we see this pressuring revenues.

▸ We expect WIN to generate EBITDA of $1.83 billion in 2010 and $1.91 billion in 2011, similarly helped by acquisitions, as well as cost synergies from consolidated billing systems. We forecast that EBITDA margins will stay near 50%, despite synergies due in part to the loss of higher-margin voice revenues and addition of lower-margin NuVox operations.

▸ We look for interest expense to be higher in 2010, as new debt was taken on to complete the acquisitions. We forecast operating EPS of $0.87 in 2010 and $0.91 in 2011, with modest share repurchases in late 2009 offset by stock issued in mergers.

Investment Rationale/Risk

▸ With approximately 65% of WIN's expected free cash flow in 2010 being used to support its dividend, we see the dividend as secure. In our view, due to its rural operations and high broadband penetration, WIN's access line base has been much more stable than that of peers, and we expect improved demand from business customers when the economy becomes stronger. We believe recent acquisitions are being integrated smoothly. Despite our view of risks from the company's acquisition strategy and potential new regulations for rural telecom companies, we see the stock as attractive.

▸ Risks to our recommendation and target price include increased cable telephony competition, federal or state regulatory changes that pressure cash flow, and inability to support the dividend.

▸ Using a projected enterprise value/EBITDA multiple of 6.4X, in line with rural telecom peers with similar operating structures, we have a 12-month target price of $13. At our target price, WIN's dividend yield would still be an above-average 7.7% and its P/E multiple a slightly higher than peers 14X.

Qualitative Risk Assessment

LOW	MEDIUM	HIGH

Our risk assessment reflects the stable rural markets that WIN serves and our view of its lower-than-peer debt leverage, offset by potential risks in integrating acquisitions.

Quantitative Evaluations

S&P Quality Ranking NR

D	C	B-	B	B+	A-	A	A+

Relative Strength Rank MODERATE

54

LOWEST = 1   HIGHEST = 99

Revenue/Earnings Data

Revenue (Million $)

	1Q	2Q	3Q	4Q	Year
2010	847.9	917.3	--	--	--
2009	755.0	752.9	734.3	754.4	2,997
2008	811.7	799.9	794.1	777.5	3,172
2007	783.7	826.7	822.6	827.8	3,261
2006	703.0	125.5	771.4	827.6	3,033
2005	712.6	736.5	728.9	745.5	3,414

Earnings Per Share ($)

	1Q	2Q	3Q	4Q	Year
2010	0.17	0.17	E0.23	E0.25	E0.87
2009	0.20	0.21	0.18	0.18	0.77
2008	0.28	0.27	0.24	0.21	0.98
2007	0.21	0.24	0.25	1.25	1.94
2006	--	0.22	0.21	0.25	1.02
2005	--	--	0.27	0.23	0.83

Fiscal year ended Dec. 31. Next earnings report expected: Early November. EPS Estimates based on S&P Operating Earnings; historical GAAP earnings are as reported.

Dividend Data (Dates: mm/dd Payment Date: mm/dd/yy)

Amount ($)	Date Decl.	Ex-Div. Date	Stk. of Record	Payment Date
0.250	11/04	12/29	12/31	01/15/10
0.250	02/18	03/29	03/31	04/15/10
0.250	05/05	06/28	06/30	07/15/10
0.250	08/04	09/28	09/30	10/15/10

Dividends have been paid since 2006. Source: Company reports.

Please read the Required Disclosures and Analyst Certification on the last page of this report.

The **McGraw·Hill** Companies

STANDARD &POOR'S

Windstream Corp

Business Summary August 19, 2010

CORPORATE OVERVIEW. In July 2006, Alltel Corp. spun off its wireline opera-tions into a separate entity. Immediately after the consummation of the tax free spin-off, the entity merged with Valor Communications, and the resulting company was renamed Windstream Corporation. As of June 2010, WIN had 3.1 million access lines. The company also had just under 2 million long dis-tance customers and 1.3 million broadband customers (41% of total access lines), up 9% on a pro forma basis from a year earlier. WIN operates primarily in rural markets in the southern U.S., such as Lexington, KY, and Lincoln, NE, with an average of about 20 access lines per square mile.

CORPORATE STRATEGY. Since becoming a public company, WIN has looked to make small acquisitions and benefit from expense savings (consolidating call centers and IT systems) and expanding service bundles via broadband and digital TV. WIN completed its acquisition of D&E Communications (114,000 incumbent access lines), a deal worth $170 million, in November 2009. In the fourth quarter of 2009, WIN acquired Lexcom Inc. (23,000 lines) for $141 mil-lion, and in February 2010, it acquired, for $460 million, NuVox, which offers phone services to business customers. In June 2010, WIN acquired Iowa Telecom Services (240,000 lines) in a larger $1.1 billion deal. Combined, the four recent deals should provide $55 million in synergies, according to the company.

WIN provides a wholesale satellite TV product from Echostar with 382,000 customers (up 21% from a year earlier), to retain its wireline customers and improve revenue per customer. During 2009, WIN also had success in upgrad-ing existing DSL customers with higher-speed offerings and was offering 12 Mbps of broadband service, 10 times the speed of traditional DSL service, in certain markets. WIN has also targeted its broadband product to customers without a wireline phone.

COMPETITIVE LANDSCAPE. We believe that WIN's access line count, which fell 4% in the 12 months ended June 2010, has been hurt by increased compe-tition. Wireless coverage in rural markets has improved in recent years, and we think that many customers have dropped their landlines. However, the line loss percentage has improved from 5% in mid-2009 and is less severe than at peers.

Company Financials Fiscal Year Ended Dec. 31

Per Share Data ($)	2009	2008	2007	2006	2005	2004	2003	2002	2001	2000
Tangible Book Value	NM	NM	NM	NM	NM	NA	NA	NA	NA	NA
Cash Flow	2.02	2.10	3.08	1.88	2.08	2.22	NA	NA	NA	NA
Earnings	0.77	0.98	1.94	1.02	0.83	0.96	NA	NA	NA	NA
S&P Core Earnings	0.88	0.87	0.98	0.95	0.80	0.80	NA	NA	NA	NA
Dividends	1.00	1.00	1.00	0.38	NA	NA	NA	NA	NA	NA
Payout Ratio	130%	102%	52%	37%	NA	NA	NA	NA	NA	NA
Prices:High	11.65	14.05	15.63	14.43	NA	NA	NA	NA	NA	NA
Prices:Low	6.28	6.37	12.38	11.13	NA	NA	NA	NA	NA	NA
P/E Ratio:High	15	14	8	14	NA	NA	NA	NA	NA	NA
P/E Ratio:Low	8	7	6	11	NA	NA	NA	NA	NA	NA

Income Statement Analysis (Million $)										
Revenue	2,997	3,172	3,261	3,033	3,414	2,934	NA	NA	NA	NA
Operating Income	NA	1,646	1,705	1,398	1,617	NA	NA	NA	NA	NA
Depreciation	538	493	540	450	593	509	NA	NA	NA	NA
Interest Expense	410	416	443	210	391	35.6	NA	NA	NA	NA
Pretax Income	546	718	1,169	722	662	646	NA	NA	NA	NA
Effective Tax Rate	38.7%	39.4%	21.6%	38.3%	40.5%	40.2%	NA	NA	NA	NA
Net Income	335	435	917	446	394	386	NA	NA	NA	NA
S&P Core Earnings	379	385	462	451	382	382	NA	NA	NA	NA

Balance Sheet & Other Financial Data (Million $)										
Cash	1,063	297	72.0	387	119	NA	NA	NA	NA	NA
Current Assets	1,456	709	498	877	533	NA	NA	NA	NA	NA
Total Assets	9,145	8,009	8,211	8,031	7,751	NA	NA	NA	NA	NA
Current Liabilities	709	665	641	685	459	NA	NA	NA	NA	NA
Long Term Debt	6,271	5,358	5,331	5,456	5,525	NA	NA	NA	NA	NA
Common Equity	261	252	700	470	533	NA	NA	NA	NA	NA
Total Capital	6,556	6,681	7,137	6,917	7,064	NA	NA	NA	NA	NA
Capital Expenditures	298	318	366	374	NA	338	NA	NA	NA	NA
Cash Flow	872	928	1,457	895	987	895	NA	NA	NA	NA
Current Ratio	2.1	1.1	0.8	1.3	1.2	NA	NA	NA	NA	NA
% Long Term Debt of Capitalization	95.7	80.2	74.7	78.9	78.2	Nil	NA	NA	NA	NA
% Net Income of Revenue	11.2	13.7	28.1	14.7	11.5	13.2	NA	NA	NA	NA
% Return on Assets	3.9	5.4	11.3	6.9	NA	NA	NA	NA	NA	NA
% Return on Equity	130.4	91.4	156.8	22.5	NA	NA	NA	NA	NA	NA

Data as orig reptd.; bef. results of disc opers/spec. items. Per share data adj. for stk. divs.; EPS diluted. E-Estimated. NA-Not Available. NM-Not Meaningful. NR-Not Ranked. UR-Under Review.

Office: 4001 N Rodney Parham Rd, Little Rock, AR 72212-2442.
Telephone: 501-748-7000.
Website: http://www.windstream.com
Chrmn: D.E. Foster

Pres & CEO: J. Gardner
COO: B.K. Whittington
EVP, Secy & General Counsel: J.P. Fletcher
CFO: A.W. Thomas

Investor Contact: M. Michaels (501-748-7578)
Board Members: C. Armitage, S. E. Beall, III, D. E. Foster, F. X. Frantz, J. Gardner, J. T. Hinson, J. K. Jones, W. A. Montgomery, A. L. Wells

Founded: 2000
Domicile: Delaware
Employees: 7,385

The McGraw-Hill Companies

Wisconsin Energy Corp

STANDARD
&POOR'S

S&P Recommendation HOLD ★★★★★	Price $59.49 (as of Oct 22, 2010)	12-Mo. Target Price $56.00	Investment Style Large-Cap Blend

GICS Sector Utilities
Sub-Industry Multi-Utilities

Summary WEC serves more than 1.1 million electric customers in Wisconsin and Michigan's Upper Peninsula, and more than 1 million natural gas customers in Wisconsin.

Key Stock Statistics (Source S&P, Vickers, company reports)

52-Wk Range	$60.00– 42.89	S&P Oper. EPS 2010**E**	3.78	Market Capitalization(B)	$6.954	Beta	0.40
Trailing 12-Month EPS	$3.35	S&P Oper. EPS 2011**E**	4.16	Yield (%)	2.69	S&P 3-Yr. Proj. EPS CAGR(%)	11
Trailing 12-Month P/E	17.8	P/E on S&P Oper. EPS 2010**E**	15.7	Dividend Rate/Share	$1.60	S&P Credit Rating	BBB+
$10K Invested 5 Yrs Ago	$17,957	Common Shares Outstg. (M)	116.9	Institutional Ownership (%)	70		

Price Performance

- 30-Week Mov. Avg. · · ·
- 10-Week Mov. Avg. – –
- **GAAP Earnings vs. Previous Year**
- Volume Above Avg. STARS
- 12-Mo. Target Price —
- Relative Strength
- ▲ Up ▼ Down ▶ No Change
- Below Avg.

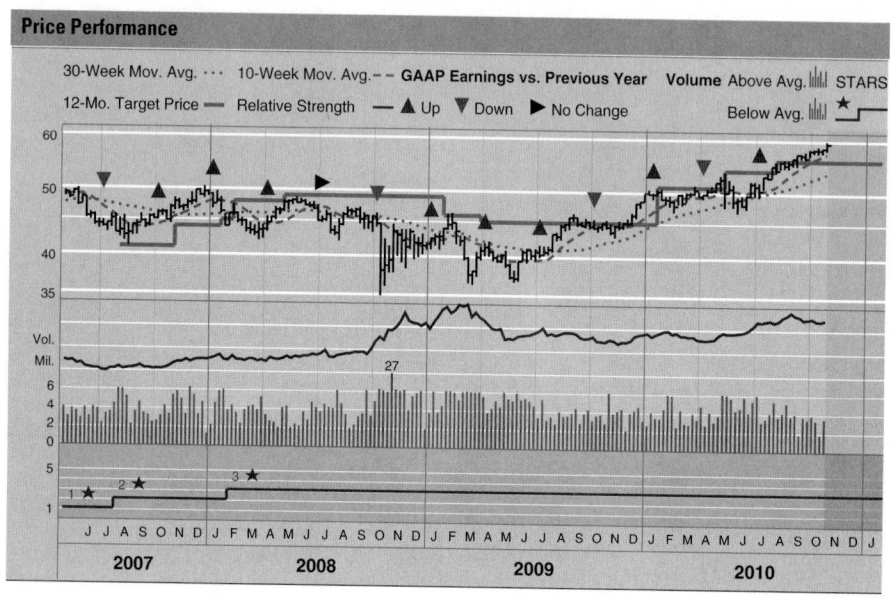

Qualitative Risk Assessment

LOW	MEDIUM	HIGH

Our risk assessment reflects our view of the company's strong and steady cash flow from the regulated utility operations, and a regulatory environment that has historically been supportive. We believe this is only partially offset by the higher risk profile of the company's non-regulated power generating subsidiary, as well as by the high level of capital expenditures the company expects to incur over the next five years.

Quantitative Evaluations

S&P Quality Ranking A-

D	C	B-	B	B+	A-	A	A+

Relative Strength Rank MODERATE

61

LOWEST = 1   HIGHEST = 99

Analysis prepared by **Justin McCann** on August 04, 2010, when the stock traded at **$ 54.83**.

Highlights

- Excluding a one-time gain of $0.02, we expect operating EPS in 2010 to rise about 18% from 2009's $3.20, which grew more than 5% from 2008's $3.03. In addition to increases in electric and gas rates, a sharp decline in natural gas costs and the more favorable weather in the second quarter, results in the first half of 2010 were aided by the new Oak Creek Unit 1 power plant, which commenced operations in February 2010. We do not expect WEC to issue any new common shares in 2010.

- For full-year 2010, operating EPS is expected to benefit from the rate increases implemented in the first half and a gradual recovery in the local economy. For 2011, we expect earnings to benefit from higher returns from the utilities, increased earnings from WEC's investment in a transmission company, and from a full year of the Oak Creek Unit 2 power plant that is scheduled to become operational in November 2010.

- Under the company's current dividend policy, WEC has targeted a dividend payout ratio of between 40% and 45% of earnings for the years 2010 and 2011. Starting in 2012, the company plans to target a payout ratio of 45% to 50%.

Investment Rationale/Risk

- The stock is up about 9% year to date, outperforming WEC's electric as well as gas utility peers. This follows a nearly 20% gain in 2009, which substantially outperformed WEC's electric utility peers, and only slightly underperformed its gas utility peers. The yield from WEC's dividend (2.9%) and its dividend payout ratio (50% of its 2009 operating EPS) are still well below those of peers (4.8% and 64%, respectively), but we believe that WEC's current dividend policy will result in additional increases over the next couple of years. We look for the shares to realize a modest total return.

- Risks to our investment recommendation and target price include unfavorable regulatory rulings, as well as further delays in bringing the second Oak Creek power plant into operation, which could result in sharply higher costs.

- The company increased its dividend more than 18% with the March 2010 payment and, under its current policy, plans to raise the annual dividend at a rate of about half that of its EPS growth. Our 12-month target price is $56, reflecting a premium-to-peers P/E of 13.5X our operating EPS estimate for 2011.

Revenue/Earnings Data

Revenue (Million $)

	1Q	2Q	3Q	4Q	Year
2010	1,256	890.9	--	--	--
2009	1,396	842.5	821.9	1,067	4,128
2008	1,432	946.1	852.5	1,201	4,431
2007	1,301	906.5	881.5	1,149	4,238
2006	1,247	814.4	839.8	1,095	3,996
2005	1,095	788.5	797.3	1,135	3,816

Earnings Per Share ($)

2010	1.10	0.74	E0.85	E1.09	E3.78
2009	1.20	0.54	0.50	0.96	3.20
2008	1.04	0.49	0.65	0.85	3.03
2007	0.85	0.49	0.70	0.80	2.84
2006	0.88	0.50	0.60	0.65	2.64
2005	0.76	0.48	0.56	0.77	2.56

Fiscal year ended Dec. 31. Next earnings report expected: Late October. EPS Estimates based on S&P Operating Earnings; historical GAAP earnings are as reported.

Dividend Data (Dates: mm/dd Payment Date: mm/dd/yy)

Amount ($)	Date Decl.	Ex-Div. Date	Stk. of Record	Payment Date
0.400	01/21	02/10	02/12	03/01/10
0.400	04/22	05/12	05/14	06/01/10
0.400	07/22	08/11	08/13	09/01/10
0.400	10/14	11/09	11/12	12/01/10

Dividends have been paid since 1939. Source: Company reports.

Wisconsin Energy Corp

STANDARD &POOR'S

Business Summary August 04, 2010

CORPORATE OVERVIEW. Wisconsin Energy Corporation (WEC) is a holding company that primarily operates in two segments: utility energy and non-utility energy. The principal utilities (under the trade name We Energies) are Wisconsin Electric Power Company and Wisconsin Gas LLC). On October 29, 2009, WEC announced that it had reached a definitive agreement to sell the Edison Sault Electric Company for $61.5 million. In April 2009, WEC sold its water utility for $14.5 million. WEC's non-regulated segment consists primarily of We Power, which was formed to design, construct, own and lease to Wisconsin Electric the new generating capacity included in the company's "Power the Future" strategy. In 2009, utility operations contributed 99.8% of total operating revenues.

CORPORATE STRATEGY. WEC's goal is to strengthen its utility business through the development of a reliable power supply and the upgrade of its infrastructure, and to continue the divestiture of its non-energy and real estate operations. The company has initiated its "Power the Future" strategy, which is expected to significantly improve the supply and reliability of power. The company has invested in four new electric generation facilities (three of which have been completed) and is also upgrading the existing ones. The strategy also includes an upgrade of existing distribution facilities. WEC is working to achieve operational synergies by integrating the businesses of

Wisconsin Electric and Wisconsin Gas, which it believes will result in improved customer satisfaction.

MARKET PROFILE. In 2008, We Energies served nearly 1.12 million electric customers in Wisconsin and (through its Edison Sault unit) the Upper Peninsula of Michigan, nearly 1.06 million gas customers in Wisconsin, and about 465 steam customers in Milwaukee. Over the next five years, WEC estimates that the utility energy segment in the service territories will grow at an annual rate of 0.5% to 1.0%; annual peak electric demand is projected to grow at a rate of 1.0% to 1.5%. In 2009, residential customers accounted for 36.6% of electric utility revenues; small commercial/industrial customers 32.5%; large commercial and industrial users 22.6%; other retail 0.8%; other wholesale 3.6%; resale-utilities 1.8%; and other 2.1%. Residential customers accounted for 62.6% of gas utility revenues in 2009; commercial/industrial customers, 32.4%; transported gas, 3.2%; and other, 1.8%. In 2009, coal accounted for 52.3% of the company's total fuel sources; purchased power 37.6%; natural gas 7.7%; hydroelectric 1.3%; and wind 1.1%.

Company Financials Fiscal Year Ended Dec. 31

Per Share Data ($)	2009	2008	2007	2006	2005	2004	2003	2002	2001	2000
Tangible Book Value	26.73	24.76	22.72	20.92	0.71	17.53	12.86	11.26	10.61	10.03
Earnings	3.20	3.03	2.84	2.64	2.56	1.03	2.06	1.44	1.77	1.27
S&P Core Earnings	1.93	-0.16	2.70	2.70	2.55	0.84	1.97	0.93	1.19	NA
Dividends	1.35	1.08	1.00	0.92	0.88	0.83	0.80	0.80	0.80	1.37
Payout Ratio	42%	36%	35%	35%	34%	81%	39%	56%	45%	108%
Prices:High	50.62	49.61	50.48	48.70	40.83	34.60	33.68	26.48	24.62	23.56
Prices:Low	36.31	34.89	41.06	38.16	33.35	29.50	22.56	20.17	19.13	16.81
P/E Ratio:High	16	16	18	18	16	34	16	18	14	19
P/E Ratio:Low	11	12	14	14	13	29	11	14	11	13

Income Statement Analysis (Million $)										
Revenue	4,128	4,431	4,238	3,996	3,816	3,431	4,054	3,736	3,929	3,355
Depreciation	349	332	328	326	332	327	332	321	342	336
Maintenance	NA	NA	NA	NA	NA	NA	NA	NA	NA	NA
Fixed Charges Coverage	4.42	4.41	4.00	3.60	3.61	2.64	2.68	2.03	2.17	1.64
Construction Credits	NA	NA	NA	NA	NA	2.80	18.6	11.2	15.2	16.2
Effective Tax Rate	36.6%	37.7%	39.1%	35.9%	33.0%	39.7%	35.6%	38.8%	41.9%	44.9%
Net Income	377	359	337	313	304	122	244	167	209	154
S&P Core Earnings	227	-18.7	320	319	302	98.5	233	108	142	NA

Balance Sheet & Other Financial Data (Million $)										
Gross Property	12,543	11,832	10,805	10,476	9,651	9,025	9,017	8,406	8,014	8,065
Capital Expenditures	818	1,137	1,212	929	745	637	659	557	672	611
Net Property	9,071	8,517	7,681	7,053	6,363	5,903	5,926	4,399	4,188	4,152
Capitalization:Long Term Debt	3,906	4,105	3,203	3,104	3,061	3,270	3,605	3,261	3,468	2,933
Capitalization:% Long Term Debt	52.3	55.2	50.8	51.8	50.9	55.3	60.1	60.4	62.8	59.3
Capitalization:Preferred	Nil	Nil	Nil	Nil	Nil	Nil	Nil	Nil	Nil	Nil
Capitalization:% Preferred	Nil	Nil	Nil	Nil	Nil	Nil	Nil	Nil	Nil	Nil
Capitalization:Common	3,567	3,337	3,099	2,889	2,955	2,645	2,393	2,139	2,056	2,017
Capitalization:% Common	47.7	44.8	49.2	48.2	49.1	44.7	39.9	39.6	37.2	40.7
Total Capital	7,769	8,298	6,902	6,618	6,666	6,507	6,712	6,039	6,147	5,617
% Operating Ratio	89.2	90.0	90.4	90.2	89.2	86.9	88.6	86.8	88.4	90.5
% Earned on Net Property	7.6	8.2	8.4	8.5	9.2	6.5	9.6	10.7	14.5	11.1
% Return on Revenue	9.1	8.1	7.9	7.8	8.0	3.6	6.0	4.5	5.3	4.6
% Return on Invested Capital	6.2	6.1	6.8	7.5	7.2	7.1	8.1	13.6	8.0	7.9
% Return on Common Equity	10.9	11.1	11.2	11.2	10.8	4.9	10.5	8.0	10.2	7.7

Data as orig reptd.; bef. results of disc opers/spec. items. Per share data adj. for stk. divs.; EPS diluted. E-Estimated. NA-Not Available. NM-Not Meaningful. NR-Not Ranked. UR-Under Review.

Office: 231 West Michigan Street, Milwaukee, WI 53201.
Telephone: 414-221-2345.
Website: http://www.wisconsinenergy.com
Chrmn, Pres & CEO: G.E. Klappa

EVP & CFO: A.L. Leverett
EVP & General Counsel: J.C. Fleming
SVP & Chief Admin Officer: K.A. Rappe
Chief Acctg Officer & Cntlr: S.P. Dickson

Investor Contact: C.F. Henderson (414-221-2592)
Board Members: J. F. Bergstrom, B. L. Bowles, P. W. Chadwick, R. A. Cornog, C. S. Culver, T. Fischer, G. E. Klappa, U. Payne, Jr., C. P. Stratton, Jr.

Founded: 1981
Domicile: Wisconsin
Employees: 4,692

The McGraw-Hill Companies

Wyndham Worldwide Corp

STANDARD &POOR'S

S&P Recommendation SELL ★★★★★

Price $29.49 (as of Oct 22, 2010)	**12-Mo. Target Price** $21.00	**Investment Style** Large-Cap Blend

GICS Sector Consumer Discretionary
Sub-Industry Hotels, Resorts & Cruise Lines

Summary This company sells interests in vacation ownership resorts, facilitates the exchange and rental of access to vacation properties, and franchises hotels.

Key Stock Statistics (Source S&P, Vickers, company reports)

52-Wk Range	$29.77– 16.39	S&P Oper. EPS 2010**E**	1.80	Market Capitalization(B)	$5.268	Beta		3.33
Trailing 12-Month EPS	$1.74	S&P Oper. EPS 2011**E**	2.00	Yield (%)	1.63	S&P 3-Yr. Proj. EPS CAGR(%)		5
Trailing 12-Month P/E	17.0	P/E on S&P Oper. EPS 2010**E**	16.4	Dividend Rate/Share	$0.48	S&P Credit Rating		BBB-
$10K Invested 5 Yrs Ago	NA	Common Shares Outstg. (M)	178.6	Institutional Ownership (%)	NM			

Price Performance

30-Week Mov. Avg. · · · · 10-Week Mov. Avg. – – GAAP Earnings vs. Previous Year   Volume Above Avg. STARS
12-Mo. Target Price — Relative Strength   ▲ Up ▼ Down ▶ No Change   Below Avg. ★

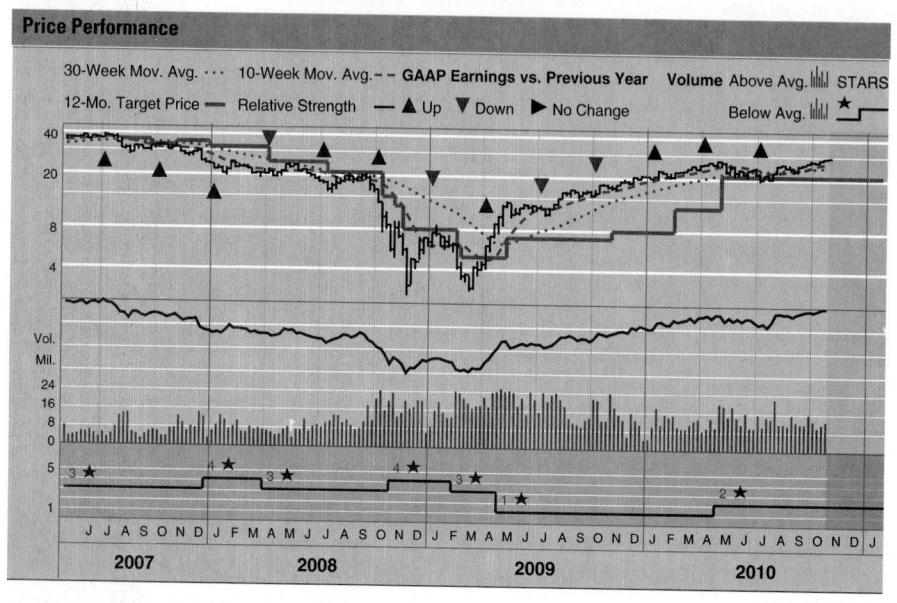

Options: CBOE, Ph

Analysis prepared by **Mark S. Basham** on August 04, 2010, when the stock traded at **$ 25.85**.

Highlights

► For 2010, we forecast WYN revenues will increase about 3.0%-3.5%, with growth held down by no deferred timeshare sales being recognized in 2010, versus $190 million of deferred revenues in 2009. This should be partly offset by a lower provision for losses on timeshare finance contracts. We expect vacation exchange and rental revenues to increase by a high single digit percentage, and project lodging revenues will rise about 2%.

► Expenses are likely to be slightly higher in 2010 compared to 2009, primarily reflecting the effects of cost cuts enacted in 2009 being somewhat outweighed by modest cost inflation. Interest expense is likely to rise by nearly 50%, due to higher rates under WYN's renegotiated credit facilities. On a tax rate projected to be 365 basis points lower than in 2009, we expect EPS to advance to $1.80, from $1.61 in 2009.

► We estimate unadjusted EBITDA in 2010 will approximate $825 million to $850 million. We note that this is not comparable to "adjusted EBITDA" as presented by WYN. In 2011, we expect revenues in all three operating segments to increase in the low single digits, with EPS of $2.00 and EBITDA of $900 million.

Investment Rationale/Risk

► Our Sell opinion reflects our view that the stock is overvalued after the sharp rise in share price since the S&P 500 bottomed in early March 2009. We believe that lodging industry fundamentals will likely improve modestly in 2010, with a full recovery not until 2012 at the earliest. Although the cost reductions WYN has achieved may serve it well through the downturn, we think substantial operating and financial risks remain.

► Risks to our recommendation and target price include a quick positive turnaround in consumer confidence and a related boost to travel spending. Also, future travel activity could be aided by additional stimulus measures.

► We believe the stock should have a slightly lower P/E and enterprise value-to-EBITDA multiple than some lodging industry peers in our coverage universe given the company's higher revenue mix of vacation exchange, ownership sales and financing, as well as legacy tax liabilities. Our 12-month target price of $21 reflects an enterprise value/EBITDA multiple of 8.0X applied to our 2011 EBITDA estimate.

Qualitative Risk Assessment

LOW	MEDIUM	**HIGH**

Our risk assessment reflects our view that the company's business is sensitive to changes in consumer confidence and hotel room demand, as well as the receptivity of credit markets to its securitized vacation ownership receivables.

Quantitative Evaluations

S&P Quality Ranking   NR

D	C	B-	B	B+	A-	A	A+

Relative Strength Rank   STRONG

83

LOWEST = 1   HIGHEST = 99

Revenue/Earnings Data

Revenue (Million $)

	1Q	2Q	3Q	4Q	Year
2010	886.0	963.0	--	--	--
2009	901.0	920.0	1,016	913.0	3,750
2008	1,012	1,132	1,226	911.0	4,281
2007	1,012	1,100	1,216	1,032	4,360
2006	870.0	955.0	1,047	970.0	3,842
2005	795.0	867.0	948.0	861.0	3,471

Earnings Per Share ($)

	1Q	2Q	3Q	4Q	Year
2010	0.27	0.51	E0.61	E0.41	E1.80
2009	0.25	0.39	0.57	0.40	1.61
2008	0.24	0.55	0.80	-7.62	-6.03
2007	0.45	0.52	0.65	0.59	2.20
2006	0.46	0.37	0.45	0.48	1.77
2005	--	0.44	0.61	0.46	1.73

Fiscal year ended Dec. 31. Next earnings report expected: Late October. EPS Estimates based on S&P Operating Earnings; historical GAAP earnings are as reported.

Dividend Data (Dates: mm/dd Payment Date: mm/dd/yy)

Amount ($)	Date Decl.	Ex-Div. Date	Stk. of Record	Payment Date
0.120	02/24	03/04	03/08	03/15/10
0.120	05/13	05/25	05/27	06/11/10
0.120	07/22	08/24	08/26	09/10/10
0.120	10/21	11/22	11/24	12/10/10

Dividends have been paid since 2007. Source: Company reports.

Please read the Required Disclosures and Analyst Certification on the last page of this report.

The McGraw-Hill Companies

Wyndham Worldwide Corp

Business Summary August 04, 2010

CORPORATE OVERVIEW. Wyndham Worldwide (WYN) operates lodging, vacation exchange and rental and vacation ownership businesses.

The Wyndham Hotel Group franchises hotels in various segments of the lodging industry under brands such as Super 8, Days Inn, Ramada, Travelodge, and Wyndham Hotels. As of December 31, 2009, WYN's lodging business had 7,114 franchised hotels with 597,674 rooms in operation. As of December 31, 2009, there were also about 950 hotels with about 108,100 rooms in the development pipeline, of which 51% represented new construction and 43% were in international markets.

On July 21, 2008, WYN acquired U.S. Franchise Systems, Inc. for $131 million. Previously part of the Hyatt hotel business, U.S. Franchise Systems includes the Microtel Inns & Suites and Hawthorn Suites brands. At the time of purchase, the Microtel system included 298 all new construction economy hotels with 35 more under construction, and the Hawthorn chain was comprised of 91 all-suites, extended-stay hotels.

Wyndham Exchange and Rentals (previously Group RCI) provides vacation exchange products and services to developers, managers and owners of intervals of vacation ownership interests, and markets vacation rental properties.

WYN's vacation exchange and rental business has access for specified periods, often on an exclusive basis, to about 65,000 vacation properties located in approximately 100 countries. Membership as of December 31, 2009, was 3.8 million.

Wyndham Vacation Ownership markets and sells vacation ownership interests, provides consumer financing in connection with the purchase by individuals of vacation ownership interests, manages properties for property owners' associations, and develops and acquires vacation ownership resorts. It operates principally under its two primary brands, Wyndham Vacation Resorts and WorldMark by Wyndham. WYN has developed or acquired over 155 vacation ownership resorts in North America, the Caribbean and the South Pacific that serve over 820,000 owners of vacation ownership and other real estate interests. WYN's gross sales of vacation ownership interests totaled $1.3 billion in 2009, down from $2.0 billion in 2008. Inventory of unsold interests was approximately $1.3 billion as of December 31, 2009.

Company Financials Fiscal Year Ended Dec. 31

Per Share Data ($)	2009	2008	2007	2006	2005	2004	2003	2002	2001	2000
Tangible Book Value	1.41	NM	NM	NM	NM	NA	NA	NA	NA	NA
Cash Flow	2.59	-5.00	2.96	2.63	2.37	NA	NA	NA	NA	NA
Earnings	1.61	-6.03	2.20	1.77	1.73	NA	NA	NA	NA	NA
S&P Core Earnings	1.61	1.47	2.20	1.75	1.97	NA	NA	NA	NA	NA
Dividends	0.16	0.16	0.08	Nil	Nil	NA	NA	NA	NA	NA
Payout Ratio	10%	NM	4%	Nil	Nil	NA	NA	NA	NA	NA
Prices:High	21.45	25.00	39.40	34.87	NA	NA	NA	NA	NA	NA
Prices:Low	2.77	2.55	23.28	25.48	NA	NA	NA	NA	NA	NA
P/E Ratio:High	13	NM	18	20	NA	NA	NA	NA	NA	NA
P/E Ratio:Low	2	NM	11	14	NA	NA	NA	NA	NA	NA

Income Statement Analysis (Million $)										
Revenue	3,750	4,281	4,360	3,842	3,471	3,014	2,652	NA	NA	NA
Operating Income	834	865	821	824	699	719	602	NA	NA	NA
Depreciation	178	184	139	148	135	119	107	NA	NA	NA
Interest Expense	114	99.0	96.0	67.0	41.0	34.0	6.00	NA	NA	NA
Pretax Income	493	-887	655	542	523	587	500	NA	NA	NA
Effective Tax Rate	40.6%	NM	38.5%	35.1%	29.8%	39.9%	37.2%	NA	NA	NA
Net Income	293	-1,074	403	352	367	349	299	NA	NA	NA
S&P Core Earnings	293	261	404	352	419	NA	NA	NA	NA	NA

Balance Sheet & Other Financial Data (Million $)										
Cash	155	136	276	269	106	94.0	NA	NA	NA	NA
Current Assets	1,740	1,914	2,056	2,052	1,874	2,075	NA	NA	NA	NA
Total Assets	9,352	9,573	10,459	9,520	8,590	8,343	NA	NA	NA	NA
Current Liabilities	1,885	2,169	2,180	1,977	2,212	1,179	NA	NA	NA	NA
Long Term Debt	3,183	3,331	3,195	1,322	1,733	1,478	NA	NA	NA	NA
Common Equity	2,688	2,342	3,516	3,559	3,464	4,679	NA	NA	NA	NA
Total Capital	6,255	6,136	7,638	5,663	5,987	6,447	NA	NA	NA	NA
Capital Expenditures	135	187	194	191	134	116	102	NA	NA	NA
Cash Flow	471	-890	542	500	502	468	406	NA	NA	NA
Current Ratio	0.9	0.9	0.9	1.0	0.9	1.8	NA	NA	NA	NA
% Long Term Debt of Capitalization	Nil	54.3	41.8	23.3	28.9	22.9	Nil	NA	NA	NA
% Net Income of Revenue	7.8	NM	9.2	9.2	10.5	11.6	11.3	NA	NA	NA
% Return on Assets	NA	NM	4.0	3.8	NA	NA	NA	NA	NA	NA
% Return on Equity	NA	NM	11.4	8.2	NA	NA	NA	NA	NA	NA

Data as orig reptd.; bef. results of disc opers/spec. items. Per share data adj. for stk. divs.; EPS diluted. E-Estimated. NA-Not Available. NM-Not Meaningful. NR-Not Ranked. UR-Under Review.

Office: 22 Sylvan Wy, Parsippany, NJ 07054.
Telephone: 973-753-6000.
Website: http://www.wyndhamworldwide.com
Chrmn & CEO: S.P. Holmes

EVP & CFO: T.G. Conforti
EVP, Secy & General Counsel: S.G. McLester
SVP & Chief Acctg Officer: N. Rossi
SVP & CIO: D. Kornick

Investor Contact: M. Happer (973-753-5500)
Board Members: M. J. Biblowit, J. E. Buckman, G. Herrera, S. P. Holmes, B. R. Mulroney, P. Richards, M. H. Wargotz

Founded: 2003
Domicile: Delaware
Employees: 24,600

Wynn Resorts Ltd

STANDARD &POOR'S

S&P Recommendation BUY ★★★★☆

Price	12-Mo. Target Price	Investment Style
$104.42 (as of Oct 22, 2010)	$115.00	Large-Cap Growth

GICS Sector Consumer Discretionary
Sub-Industry Casinos & Gaming

Summary This company is involved in the design, development, financing and construction of gaming projects in Las Vegas and Macau.

Key Stock Statistics (Source S&P, Vickers, company reports)

52-Wk Range	$107.36– 51.73	S&P Oper. EPS 2010**E**	1.70	Market Capitalization(B)	$12.897	Beta	2.70
Trailing 12-Month EPS	$0.88	S&P Oper. EPS 2011**E**	2.00	Yield (%)	0.96	S&P 3-Yr. Proj. EPS CAGR(%)	NM
Trailing 12-Month P/E	NM	P/E on S&P Oper. EPS 2010**E**	61.4	Dividend Rate/Share	$1.00	S&P Credit Rating	BB
$10K Invested 5 Yrs Ago	$26,142	Common Shares Outstg. (M)	123.5	Institutional Ownership (%)	48		

Price Performance

30-Week Mov. Avg. · · · · 10-Week Mov. Avg. – – GAAP Earnings vs. Previous Year Volume Above Avg. ▮▮▮ STARS
12-Mo. Target Price — Relative Strength — ▲ Up ▼ Down ▶ No Change Below Avg. ▮▮▮ ★

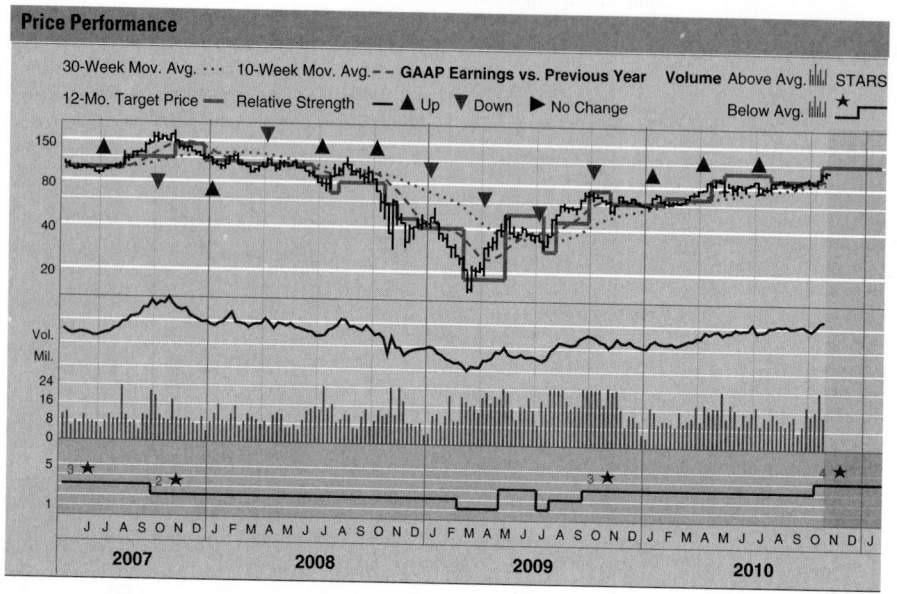

Options: ASE, CBOE, P, Ph

Analysis prepared by **Esther Y. Kwon, CFA** on October 11, 2010, when the stock traded at **$ 102.33**.

Highlights

➤ We estimate that net revenue in 2010 will rise approximately 33% from the $3.0 billion reported for 2009, bolstered by the April 2010 opening of Encore at Wynn Macau, which includes approximately 410 luxury suites and four villas in addition to restaurants and retail and gaming space. In the U.S., we believe revenue will be pressured by increased price competition on an excess supply of hotel rooms and lower spending per visit, despite improvement in the second half. In Macau, we forecast revenue rising over 50%, while we see Las Vegas increasing at a low to mid-single digit pace.

➤ For 2010, we estimate higher EBITDA, driven by the opening of the Encore in Macau, and wider property margins, with general strength in the Macau market more than offsetting operating inefficiencies at Encore. With Las Vegas revenues likely to struggle until the second half, we look for expense deleveraging in the first half but steady improvement in the third and fourth quarters and into 2011.

➤ With our projection for more shares outstanding, we see EPS of $1.70 in 2010, up significantly from 2009's operating EPS of $0.26. For 2011, we forecast EPS of $2.00.

Investment Rationale/Risk

➤ We see WYNN's results benefiting from strength in its Macau operations, which we estimate will account for over 75% of 2010 total property EBITDA. We also forecast improving Las Vegas Strip fundamentals in the second half of 2010 and 2011 as higher margin convention visitation accelerates and the hotel room supply outlook becomes more benign in 2011 and 2012, after large increases in 2008 and 2009.

➤ Risks to our opinion and target price include the possibility that profit contributions from Macau will be lower than we anticipate, or that Las Vegas properties will experience an accelerated decline in room revenue or gaming handle.

➤ Our 12-month target price of $115 is based on an EV/EBITDA multiple of approximately 15X our 2011 EBITDA estimate, a premium to gaming peers but below the historical average. We believe a higher-than-peers multiple is warranted based on WYNN's exposure to the Macau market, which we see as having better prospects over the long term, and what we view as its solid balance sheet compared to peers.

Qualitative Risk Assessment

LOW	MEDIUM	HIGH

In our view, there is likely to be an opportunity for additional expansion by WYNN in Macau. However, we see uncertainty surrounding the regulatory environment there and the extent to which demand in that market will develop, adding to risk.

Quantitative Evaluations

S&P Quality Ranking NR

D	C	B-	B	B+	A-	A	A+

Relative Strength Rank STRONG

90

LOWEST = 1   HIGHEST = 99

Revenue/Earnings Data

Revenue (Million $)

	1Q	2Q	3Q	4Q	Year
2010	908.9	1,033	--	--	--
2009	740.0	723.3	773.1	809.3	3,046
2008	778.7	825.2	769.2	614.3	2,987
2007	635.3	687.5	653.4	711.3	2,688
2006	277.2	273.4	318.1	563.6	1,432
2005	Nil	201.1	251.4	269.4	722.0

Earnings Per Share ($)

	1Q	2Q	3Q	4Q	Year
2010	0.22	0.42	E0.43	E0.48	E1.70
2009	-0.30	0.21	0.28	-0.04	0.17
2008	0.41	2.42	0.49	-1.49	1.92
2007	0.54	0.82	0.41	0.57	2.34
2006	-0.12	-0.20	6.43	-0.51	6.24
2005	-0.30	-0.43	-0.09	-0.10	-0.92

Fiscal year ended Dec. 31. Next earnings report expected: Late October. EPS Estimates based on S&P Operating Earnings; historical GAAP earnings are as reported.

Dividend Data (Dates: mm/dd Payment Date: mm/dd/yy)

Amount ($)	Date Decl.	Ex-Div. Date	Stk. of Record	Payment Date
4.0 Spl.	11/09	11/17	11/19	12/08/09
0.250	04/29	05/10	05/12	05/26/10
0.250	07/29	08/10	08/12	08/26/10

Dividends have been paid since 2006. Source: Company reports.

Please read the Required Disclosures and Analyst Certification on the last page of this report.

The **McGraw·Hill** Companies

STANDARD &POOR'S

Wynn Resorts Ltd

Business Summary October 11, 2010

CORPORATE OVERVIEW. Wynn Resorts is involved in the design, development, financing and construction of gaming projects in Las Vegas and Macau. The company's first such project, Wynn Las Vegas, opened in April 2005. We believe that the cost of this project was about $2.7 billion.

Wynn Las Vegas, which occupies about 215 acres of land, includes 2,716 guest rooms and suites, an approximate 110,000 sq. ft. casino with 1,920 slot machines, 22 food and beverage outlets, an 18-hole golf course, about 223,000 sq. ft. of meeting space, a Ferrari and Maserati dealership, and about 74,000 sq. ft. of retail space.

The company also operates the Encore at Wynn Las Vegas, which includes about 2,034 guest suites, plus an approximately 76,000 square foot casino with 790 slot machines, entertainment and other facilities. This facility opened in December 2008.

In China, the company is operating Wynn Macau under a 20-year concession agreement with the government of Macau. The initial stage of Wynn Macau opened in September 2006, and included about 600 hotel rooms or suites, about 100,000 sq. ft. of gaming space, seven restaurants, and additional facilities. A second phase included additional casino space and other facilities. We believe that Wynn Macau, including the second phase, had a project budget of about $1.2 billion.

The Encore at Wynn Macau, which opened in April 2010, includes approximately 410 luxury suites and villas in addition to restaurants, retail and gaming space.

Also, the company has submitted an application for a land concession on 52 acres in Macau's Cotai Strip area, where we expect additional WYNN-related development could occur. There are a limited number of companies with casino operating rights in Macau.

Company Financials Fiscal Year Ended Dec. 31

Per Share Data ($)	2009	2008	2007	2006	2005	2004	2003	2002	2001	2000
Tangible Book Value	24.39	13.75	16.79	14.75	14.16	15.64	11.38	11.70	12.92	NA
Cash Flow	3.59	4.32	4.24	7.20	0.13	-2.29	-0.54	-0.49	-0.25	-49.28
Earnings	0.17	1.92	2.34	6.24	-0.92	-2.37	-0.62	-0.68	-0.45	-79.62
S&P Core Earnings	0.17	1.92	2.29	1.00	-1.00	-2.41	-0.64	-0.69	NA	NA
Dividends	4.00	Nil	6.00	6.00	Nil	Nil	Nil	Nil	NA	NA
Payout Ratio	NM	Nil	256%	96%	Nil	Nil	Nil	Nil	NA	NA
Prices:High	74.90	124.77	176.14	98.45	76.45	72.99	28.61	14.39	NA	NA
Prices:Low	14.50	28.06	85.53	52.44	42.06	27.50	12.76	10.76	NA	NA
P/E Ratio:High	NM	65	75	16	NM	NM	NM	NM	NA	NA
P/E Ratio:Low	NM	15	37	8	NM	NM	NM	NM	NA	NA

Income Statement Analysis (Million $)										
Revenue	3,046	2,987	2,688	1,432	722	0.20	1.02	1.16	1.16	0.13
Operating Income	674	608	708	249	77.5	-81.5	-46.9	-24.8	0.73	-10.2
Depreciation	411	263	220	175	103	6.98	5.74	8.93	8.16	6.07
Interest Expense	211	260	188	206	103	2.69	9.03	1.90	NA	0.03
Pretax Income	42.1	149	327	799	-90.8	-207	-45.8	-30.8	-17.7	-15.9
Effective Tax Rate	7.12%	NM	21.1%	21.3%	NM	NM	NM	NM	NM	NA
Net Income	20.7	210	258	629	-90.8	-206	-48.9	-31.7	-17.7	-15.9
S&P Core Earnings	20.7	210	252	44.1	-98.6	-210	-50.9	-32.0	-17.3	NA

Balance Sheet & Other Financial Data (Million $)										
Cash	1,992	1,134	1,275	789	434	330	342	110	39.3	54.4
Current Assets	2,283	1,411	1,582	1,096	685	451	402	112	41.6	56.6
Total Assets	7,582	6,743	6,299	4,660	3,945	3,464	1,733	1,399	389	387
Current Liabilities	726	724	585	511	270	170	71.2	20.7	4.02	4.80
Long Term Debt	3,587	4,290	3,539	2,381	2,091	1,628	730	382	1,501	0.33
Common Equity	3,034	1,593	1,948	1,646	1,563	1,644	1,002	992	972	382
Total Capital	6,750	5,886	5,640	4,123	3,654	3,272	1,733	1,378	2,473	382
Capital Expenditures	541	1,333	1,007	643	877	1,008	415	66.3	29.1	85.7
Cash Flow	431	473	478	804	12.5	-199	-43.1	-22.8	-9.56	-9.86
Current Ratio	3.2	2.0	2.7	2.1	2.5	2.7	5.7	5.4	10.4	11.8
% Long Term Debt of Capitalization	Nil	72.9	62.8	57.7	57.2	49.8	42.1	27.7	0.1	0.1
% Net Income of Revenue	0.7	7.0	9.6	43.9	NM	NM	NM	NM	NM	NM
% Return on Assets	NA	3.2	4.7	14.6	NM	NM	NM	NM	NM	NA
% Return on Equity	NA	11.9	14.4	39.2	NM	NM	NM	NM	NM	NA

Data as orig reptd.; bef. results of disc opers/spec. items. Per share data adj. for stk. divs.; EPS diluted. E-Estimated. NA-Not Available. NM-Not Meaningful. NR-Not Ranked. UR-Under Review.

Office: 3131 Las Vegas Blvd S, Las Vegas, NV 89109.
Telephone: 702-733-4444.
Email: investorrelations@wynnresorts.com
Website: http://www.wynnresorts.com

Chrmn & CEO: S.A. Wynn
Vice Chrmn: K. Okada
COO: M.D. Schorr
Investor Contact: J. Strzemp (702-770-7555)

EVP & Chief Admin Officer: J. Strzemp
Board Members: L. Chen, R. Goldsmith, R. R. Irani, R. J. Miller, J. A. Moran, K. Okada, M. D. Schorr, A. V. Shoemaker, D. B. Wayson, E. P. Wynn, S. A. Wynn, A. Zeman

Founded: 2002
Domicile: Nevada
Employees: 18,900

The McGraw-Hill Companies

Xcel Energy Inc.

STANDARD &POOR'S

S&P Recommendation HOLD ★★★☆☆

Price	12-Mo. Target Price	Investment Style
$23.89 (as of Oct 22, 2010)	$23.00	Large-Cap Value

GICS Sector Utilities
Sub-Industry Multi-Utilities

Summary This company offers energy-related products and services to 3.4 million electricity customers and 1.9 million natural gas customers in eight western and midwestern states.

Key Stock Statistics (Source S&P, Vickers, company reports)

52-Wk Range	$24.00– 18.53	S&P Oper. EPS 2010E	1.65	Market Capitalization(B)	$10.981	Beta	0.45
Trailing 12-Month EPS	$1.51	S&P Oper. EPS 2011E	1.71	Yield (%)	4.23	S&P 3-Yr. Proj. EPS CAGR(%)	6
Trailing 12-Month P/E	15.8	P/E on S&P Oper. EPS 2010E	14.5	Dividend Rate/Share	$1.01	S&P Credit Rating	A-
$10K Invested 5 Yrs Ago	$16,386	Common Shares Outstg. (M)	459.6	Institutional Ownership (%)	59		

Price Performance

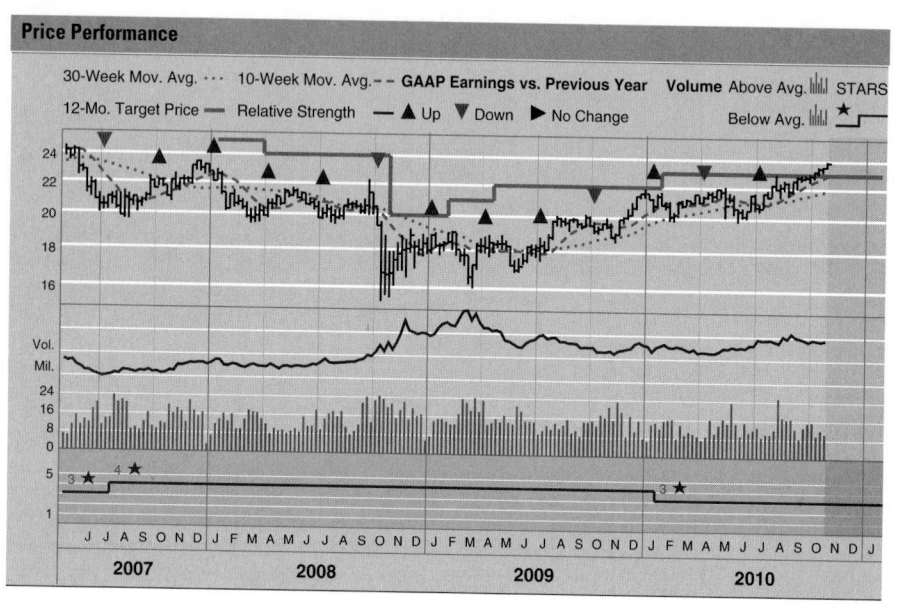

30-Week Mov. Avg. · · · · 10-Week Mov. Avg. – – **GAAP Earnings vs. Previous Year** Volume Above Avg. STARS
12-Mo. Target Price — Relative Strength — ▲ Up ▼ Down ► No Change Below Avg. ★

Options: ASE, CBOE

Analysis prepared by **Justin McCann** on October 11, 2010, when the stock traded at **$ 23.47**.

Highlights

▶ Excluding $0.05 of net one-time charges, we expect 2010 EPS from continuing operations to grow about 10% from 2009's $1.50, which excluded $0.02 of one-time charges. In the first half of 2010, operating EPS was aided by electric rate increases in Colorado and South Dakota and more favorable weather in the second quarter. This was partially offset by higher operating and maintenance expenses.

▶ For the second half of 2010, we believe that in addition to the rate hikes in Colorado and South Dakota, EPS will benefit from the increased demand due to the above normal summer temperatures. For 2011, we expect growth to be driven by a gas rate increase in Minnesota, and electric rate increases in Texas and Wisconsin.

▶ On January 5, 2010, XEL was authorized an $8 million increase in its South Dakota electric rates (effective January 18). Earlier, on December 4, 2009, its Public Service of Colorado utility was authorized a $128.3 million increase. However, due to the delay in placing a power plant into service, only $67 million was implemented on January 1, 2010; $121 million would be implemented upon the plant being placed in service, and the full $128.3 million on January 1, 2011.

Investment Rationale/Risk

▶ The stock is up more than 10% year to date. In addition to the strong recovery in the utility sector, we believe the 2009 and 2010 rebound in the stock price has reflected the expectation of a gradual recovery in the economy. As of July April 26, 2010, XEL had available credit lines of $1.97 billion and cash of $18.4 million. We believe this $1.98 billion of total liquidity is more than adequate for XEL's near-term requirements. We believe the stock is fairly valued at its current level.

▶ Risks to our recommendation and target price include the possibility of a severe economic downturn in the company's service territory, unfavorable legislative or regulatory decisions, and/or a sharp decline in the average P/E of XEL's electric and gas utility peers.

▶ We expect the shares to be partially supported by the yield from the dividend (recently 4.3%), which is just slightly below the recent electric and gas utility peer average (4.6%). We expect the company to increase its dividend at a rate of 2% to 4% a year. Our 12-month target price of $23 reflects a premium-to-peers P/E of 13.5X our operating EPS estimate for 2011.

Qualitative Risk Assessment

LOW	MEDIUM	HIGH

Our risk assessment reflects the steady cash flow that we expect from the regulated electric and gas utility operations, which have a relatively low-cost power supply, our view of a relatively healthy economy in most of the company's service territory, and a generally supportive regulatory environment.

Quantitative Evaluations

S&P Quality Ranking B

D	C	B-	B	B+	A-	A	A+

Relative Strength Rank MODERATE

61

LOWEST = 1   HIGHEST = 99

Revenue/Earnings Data

Revenue (Million $)

	1Q	2Q	3Q	4Q	Year
2010	2,807	2,308	--	--	--
2009	2,696	2,016	2,315	2,618	9,644
2008	3,028	2,616	2,852	2,708	11,203
2007	2,764	2,267	2,400	2,603	10,034
2006	2,888	2,074	2,412	2,467	9,840
2005	2,381	2,074	2,289	2,882	9,625

Earnings Per Share ($)

	1Q	2Q	3Q	4Q	Year
2010	0.36	0.29	E0.55	E0.39	E1.65
2009	0.38	0.25	0.48	0.37	1.49
2008	0.35	0.24	0.51	0.36	1.46
2007	0.28	0.16	0.59	0.31	1.34
2006	0.36	0.24	0.53	0.23	1.35
2005	0.31	0.18	0.47	0.24	1.20

Fiscal year ended Dec. 31. Next earnings report expected: Late October. EPS Estimates based on S&P Operating Earnings; historical GAAP earnings are as reported.

Dividend Data (Dates: mm/dd Payment Date: mm/dd/yy)

Amount ($)	Date Decl.	Ex-Div. Date	Stk. of Record	Payment Date
0.245	12/16	12/22	12/24	01/20/10
0.245	02/17	03/23	03/25	04/20/10
0.253	05/19	06/22	06/24	07/20/10
0.253	08/25	09/21	09/23	10/20/10

Dividends have been paid since 1910. Source: Company reports.

Please read the Required Disclosures and Analyst Certification on the last page of this report.

The McGraw-Hill Companies

Xcel Energy Inc.

STANDARD &POOR'S

Business Summary October 11, 2010

CORPORATE OVERVIEW. Xcel Energy Inc. (XEL) is a holding company with a diverse portfolio of regulated and nonregulated subsidiaries. The company's utility subsidiaries are Northern States Power Company of Minnesota and Wisconsin (NSPM and NSPW, respectively), Public Service Company of Colorado (PSCo), and Southwestern Public Service Co. (SPS), which provide electric and gas services in eight western and midwestern states, and West-Gas Interstate Inc. (WGI), an interstate natural gas pipeline. XEL's nonregulated subsidiaries include Eloigne Co., which operates rental housing projects. The electric utility operations accounted for 79.9% of operating revenues in 2009; the natural gas utility operations for 19.3%; and non-regulated and other for 0.8%.

CORPORATE STRATEGY. XEL plans to continue investing in the core utility business and to earn the authorized returns. The company has a strong focus on system reliability and continues to invest in transmission and distribution systems. To recover the cost without the delay caused by the filing of rate cases, XEL gets regulatory approval for rate riders. This ensures fair returns on the company's investment. The company is also working to apply intelligence technology to its electric grid, creating a "smart grid" that will provide customers with more reliability, choice and control over their energy use. Given the current economic environment, XEL remains committed to maintaining a strong balance sheet to provide it with the financial flexibility to respond appropriately to the challenges and opportunities it will face.

Company Financials Fiscal Year Ended Dec. 31

Per Share Data ($)	2009	2008	2007	2006	2005	2004	2003	2002	2001	2000
Tangible Book Value	15.92	15.35	14.70	14.28	13.11	12.99	12.95	11.44	17.91	15.79
Earnings	1.49	1.46	1.34	1.35	1.20	1.27	1.23	-4.36	2.27	1.54
S&P Core Earnings	1.51	1.11	1.31	1.35	1.15	1.21	1.03	-4.57	1.68	NA
Dividends	0.97	0.94	0.91	0.88	0.85	0.81	0.75	1.13	1.50	1.47
Payout Ratio	65%	65%	68%	65%	71%	64%	61%	NM	66%	96%
Prices:High	21.94	22.90	25.03	23.63	20.19	18.78	17.40	28.49	31.85	30.00
Prices:Low	16.01	15.32	19.59	17.80	16.50	15.48	10.40	5.12	24.19	16.13
P/E Ratio:High	15	16	19	18	17	15	14	NM	14	19
P/E Ratio:Low	11	10	15	13	14	12	8	NM	11	10

Income Statement Analysis (Million $)	2009	2008	2007	2006	2005	2004	2003	2002	2001	2000
Revenue	9,644	11,203	10,034	9,840	9,625	8,345	7,938	9,524	15,028	11,592
Depreciation	916	948	827	822	782	708	756	1,037	949	792
Maintenance	NA	NA	NA	NA	NA	NA	NA	NA	NA	NA
Fixed Charges Coverage	2.98	2.92	2.62	2.43	2.43	2.36	2.50	1.54	2.37	2.54
Construction Credits	116	103	71.8	56.0	0.88	33.6	NA	NA	NA	NA
Effective Tax Rate	35.1%	34.4%	33.8%	24.2%	25.8%	23.2%	23.7%	NM	28.2%	34.2%
Net Income	686	646	576	569	499	527	510	-1,661	785	546
S&P Core Earnings	688	487	554	566	472	498	417	-1,745	579	NA

Balance Sheet & Other Financial Data (Million $)	2009	2008	2007	2006	2005	2004	2003	2002	2001	2000
Gross Property	30,858	29,546	26,726	25,219	24,054	23,160	22,371	29,119	31,770	25,000
Capital Expenditures	1,711	2,050	2,096	1,626	1,304	1,274	951	1,503	5,366	2,196
Net Property	18,508	17,689	16,676	15,549	14,696	14,096	13,667	18,816	21,165	15,273
Capitalization:Long Term Debt	7,889	7,732	6,342	6,450	5,898	6,493	6,519	7,044	12,612	8,060
Capitalization:% Long Term Debt	51.6	52.2	49.8	52.1	51.3	55.0	55.0	59.6	66.7	58.7
Capitalization:Preferred	105	105	105	105	105	105	105	105	105	105
Capitalization:% Preferred	0.70	0.70	0.80	0.85	0.91	0.89	0.89	0.89	0.56	0.76
Capitalization:Common	7,283	6,964	6,301	5,817	5,484	5,203	5,222	4,665	6,194	5,562
Capitalization:% Common	47.7	47.1	49.4	47.0	47.7	44.1	44.1	39.5	32.8	40.5
Total Capital	15,821	17,699	15,415	14,751	13,813	14,019	14,017	13,303	22,040	15,996
% Operating Ratio	88.6	90.6	89.5	89.9	98.6	88.8	88.1	78.0	87.1	87.0
% Earned on Net Property	8.1	8.1	8.4	7.8	13.0	7.8	8.0	13.0	10.7	11.2
% Return on Revenue	7.1	5.8	5.7	5.8	5.2	6.3	6.4	NM	5.2	4.7
% Return on Invested Capital	7.6	7.0	7.4	7.4	6.9	7.0	7.3	12.4	10.9	10.3
% Return on Common Equity	9.6	9.7	9.4	10.1	9.2	10.1	10.1	NM	13.5	10.0

Data as orig reptd.; bef. results of disc opers/spec. items. Per share data adj. for stk. divs.; EPS diluted. E-Estimated. NA-Not Available. NM-Not Meaningful. NR-Not Ranked. UR-Under Review.

Office: 414 Nicollet Mall, Minneapolis, MN 55401-1993.
Telephone: 612-330-5500.
Website: http://www.xcelenergy.com
Chrmn & CEO: R.C. Kelly

Pres & COO: B.G. Fowke, III
CFO: D.M. Sparby
Chief Admin Officer: M. McDaniel
Treas: G.E. Tyson, II

Investor Contact: P. Johnson (612-215-4535)
Board Members: F. W. Corrigan, R. K. Davis, B. G. Fowke, III, R. C. Kelly, A. F. Moreno, C. J. Policinski, A. P. Sampson, D. A. Westerlund, K. Williams, T. V. Wolf

Founded: 1909
Domicile: Minnesota
Employees: 11,351

The McGraw-Hill Companies

Xerox Corp

STANDARD &POOR'S

S&P Recommendation	**STRONG BUY** ★★★★★	Price $11.42 (as of Oct 22, 2010)	12-Mo. Target Price $14.00	Investment Style Large-Cap Blend

GICS Sector Information Technology
Sub-Industry Office Electronics

Summary This company serves the worldwide document processing market, offering a complete line of copiers, printers and other office equipment, as well as business process outsourcing services.

Key Stock Statistics (Source S&P, Vickers, company reports)

52-Wk Range	$11.72– 7.32	S&P Oper. EPS 2010**E**	0.92	Market Capitalization(B)	$15.794
Trailing 12-Month EPS	$0.44	S&P Oper. EPS 2011**E**	1.10	Yield (%)	1.49
Trailing 12-Month P/E	26.0	P/E on S&P Oper. EPS 2010**E**	12.4	Dividend Rate/Share	$0.17
$10K Invested 5 Yrs Ago	$8,982	Common Shares Outstg. (M)	1,383.0	Institutional Ownership (%)	85

Beta	1.57
S&P 3-Yr. Proj. EPS CAGR(%)	29
S&P Credit Rating	BBB-

Price Performance

30-Week Mov. Avg. · · · · 10-Week Mov. Avg. - - GAAP Earnings vs. Previous Year   Volume Above Avg. STARS
12-Mo. Target Price — Relative Strength — ▲ Up ▼ Down ▶ No Change   Below Avg.

Options: ASE, CBOE, P, Ph

Analysis prepared by **Thomas W. Smith, CFA** on October 21, 2010, when the stock traded at **$ 11.21.**

Highlights

► We expect revenues to rise 43% in 2010, reflecting our forecast of a printer industry rebound and the acquisition of information services provider Affiliated Computer Services (ACS) in February 2010 in a stock and cash deal valued at approximately $6.4 billion plus $2 billion in assumed debt. We believe the combination is broadening geographic sales territories for ACS services via XRX's global sales network, and helping to smooth revenue flows for XRX. For 2011, we project a revenue increase of 7%, based on a further printer industry recovery and growth in ACS's traditional markets in business process outsourcing services.

► Following a deep downturn for the printer industry in 2009, we expect net margins, excluding acquisition and restructuring-related charges, to widen in 2010 and 2011, as unit volumes rise, cost control initiatives continue, and higher-margin operations acquired from ACS are brought into the mix.

► We estimate operating EPS of $0.92 in 2010 and $1.10 in 2011, excluding acquisition and restructuring charges.

Investment Rationale/Risk

► We believe XRX is recovering from cyclically low demand for printers seen in 2009, and is benefiting from having more service offerings, a result of the ACS acquisition. We foresee more stability in overall results, as well as opportunities for new sales on an expanded customer list. We think XRX is realizing some of the potential savings from several rounds of restructuring and from sales of new color printing products.

► Risks to our recommendation and target price include integration risks arising from the ACS acquisition, an aggressive pricing environment, and challenges in deploying new products and services effectively. The company's cost efficiency efforts could prove less effective than we project.

► We apply a target P/E multiple of 13X, a discount to the level for Information Technology sector peers in the S&P 500 Index, to our 2011 operating EPS estimate of $1.10 to obtain a value of $14.30, and round down to $14 for our 12-month target price. We see a compelling valuation based on our view of rising earnings amid steadier revenue patterns.

Qualitative Risk Assessment

LOW	MEDIUM	HIGH

Xerox operates in a cyclical industry marked by lively price and marketing competition for often commoditized printer and copier products. We observe a trend toward lackluster organic revenue growth, although we note XRX's efforts to improve profitability through acquisitions and cost control.

Quantitative Evaluations

S&P Quality Ranking   **B**

D	C	B-	**B**	B+	A-	A	A+

Relative Strength Rank   **STRONG**

88

LOWEST = 1   HIGHEST = 99

Revenue/Earnings Data

Revenue (Million $)

	1Q	2Q	3Q	4Q	Year
2010	4,721	5,508	--	--	--
2009	3,554	3,731	3,675	4,219	15,179
2008	4,335	4,533	4,370	4,370	17,608
2007	3,836	4,208	4,302	4,882	17,228
2006	3,695	3,977	3,844	4,379	15,895
2005	3,771	3,921	3,759	4,250	15,701

Earnings Per Share ($)

	1Q	2Q	3Q	4Q	Year
2010	-0.04	0.16	E0.22	E0.28	E0.92
2009	0.05	0.16	0.14	0.20	0.55
2008	-0.27	0.24	0.29	Nil	0.26
2007	0.24	0.28	0.27	0.41	1.19
2006	0.20	0.26	0.54	0.22	1.22
2005	0.20	0.35	0.06	0.27	0.90

Fiscal year ended Dec. 31. Next earnings report expected: Late October. EPS Estimates based on S&P Operating Earnings; historical GAAP earnings are as reported.

Dividend Data (Dates: mm/dd Payment Date: mm/dd/yy)

Amount ($)	Date Decl.	Ex-Div. Date	Stk. of Record	Payment Date
0.043	02/25	03/29	03/31	04/30/10
0.043	05/20	06/28	06/30	07/30/10
0.043	07/15	09/28	09/30	10/29/10
0.043	10/14	12/29	12/31	01/28/11

Dividends have been paid since 2008. Source: Company reports.

STANDARD &POOR'S

Xerox Corp

Business Summary October 21, 2010

CORPORATE OVERVIEW. Xerox is a large operator in the global document markets, providing document equipment such as printing and publishing systems; digital copiers; laser and solid ink printers; fax machines; and digital multifunctional devices, which can print, copy, scan and fax. Increasingly, the company has also aimed at related service markets, including traditional supplies and printer support, and newer areas such as document management and business processes. The latter range from claims reimbursement and electronic toll transactions to customer call centers and HR benefits management. By improving clients' document systems, the company claims it can save an enterprise up to 30% on its printing costs.

In 2009, equipment sales represented 23% (27% of sales in 2008) of total revenue, with the remaining 77% (73%) coming from post-sale operations including maintenance, services, supplies and financing.

The company reported in three operating segments in 2009, according to the type of customer served. Production represented 30% of 2009 revenues (30% in 2008), Office 56% (56%), and Other 14% (14%). Production provides large enterprises and companies in the graphic communications industry with high-end devices that enable digital on-demand printing, digital full-color printing, digital monochrome printing, and enterprise printing. Office serves global, national and small to medium-size commercial customers with a lineup of digital printers, and copiers. The Other segment includes revenue from paper sales, value-added services, wide-format systems and global imaging system network integration solutions and electronic presentations systems.

The company operates in over 160 countries and derived 54% of revenues in 2009 (52% in 2008) from the U.S., 33% (34%) from Europe, and 13% (14%) from other areas. The company has manufacturing plants in the U.S. and Europe, and also outsources manufacturing via a multi-year master supply agreement with Flextronics, which accounts for about 20% of XRX's worldwide production.

Company Financials Fiscal Year Ended Dec. 31

Per Share Data ($)	2009	2008	2007	2006	2005	2004	2003	2002	2001	2000
Tangible Book Value	3.08	2.50	4.93	5.04	4.68	4.29	1.57	NM	0.52	2.86
Cash Flow	0.91	0.94	1.88	1.95	1.62	1.45	1.25	1.38	1.72	0.96
Earnings	0.55	0.26	1.19	1.22	0.90	0.78	0.36	0.10	-0.17	-0.44
S&P Core Earnings	0.52	0.73	1.16	1.27	0.88	0.75	0.53	-0.17	-1.33	NA
Dividends	0.17	0.17	0.04	Nil	Nil	Nil	Nil	Nil	0.05	0.65
Payout Ratio	31%	65%	3%	Nil	Nil	Nil	Nil	Nil	NM	NM
Prices:High	9.75	16.43	20.18	17.31	17.02	17.24	13.89	11.45	11.35	29.31
Prices:Low	4.12	4.83	15.26	13.16	12.40	12.55	7.90	4.20	4.69	3.75
P/E Ratio:High	18	63	17	14	19	22	39	NM	NM	NM
P/E Ratio:Low	7	19	13	11	14	16	22	NM	NM	NM

Income Statement Analysis (Million $)	2009	2008	2007	2006	2005	2004	2003	2002	2001	2000
Revenue	15,179	17,608	17,228	15,895	15,701	15,722	15,701	15,849	17,008	18,701
Operating Income	1,347	2,340	2,699	2,165	2,159	2,451	2,585	2,803	3,011	1,946
Depreciation	698	613	656	636	637	686	748	1,035	1,332	948
Interest Expense	256	567	316	305	231	708	362	401	457	605
Pretax Income	668	-1.00	1,535	922	928	1,116	494	306	418	-323
Effective Tax Rate	22.8%	NM	26.0%	NM	NM	30.5%	27.1%	19.6%	NM	NM
Net Income	485	230	1,135	1,210	933	776	360	154	-109	-257
S&P Core Earnings	457	670	1,101	1,235	862	666	434	-128	-931	NA

Balance Sheet & Other Financial Data (Million $)	2009	2008	2007	2006	2005	2004	2003	2002	2001	2000
Cash	3,799	1,229	1,099	1,399	1,322	3,218	2,477	2,887	3,990	1,741
Current Assets	9,731	8,150	8,540	8,754	8,736	10,928	10,335	11,019	12,600	13,022
Total Assets	24,032	22,447	23,543	21,709	21,953	24,884	24,591	25,458	27,689	29,475
Current Liabilities	4,461	5,450	4,077	4,698	4,346	6,300	7,569	7,787	10,260	6,268
Long Term Debt	8,925	7,422	7,571	6,284	6,765	7,767	8,739	11,485	11,815	16,042
Common Equity	7,050	6,238	8,588	7,080	6,319	6,244	3,291	1,893	1,820	3,493
Total Capital	17,104	15,329	16,159	13,364	13,973	14,900	13,418	14,001	14,313	20,323
Capital Expenditures	95.0	206	236	215	181	204	197	146	219	452
Cash Flow	796	843	1,791	1,846	1,512	1,389	1,037	1,116	1,209	638
Current Ratio	2.2	1.5	2.1	1.9	2.0	1.7	1.4	1.4	1.2	2.1
% Long Term Debt of Capitalization	52.2	48.4	46.8	47.0	48.4	52.1	65.1	82.0	82.5	78.9
% Net Income of Revenue	3.2	1.3	6.5	7.6	5.9	4.9	2.3	1.0	NM	NM
% Return on Assets	2.1	1.0	5.0	5.5	4.0	3.1	1.4	0.6	NM	NM
% Return on Equity	7.3	3.1	14.4	18.1	13.9	14.7	11.1	4.4	NM	NM

Data as orig reptd.; bef. results of disc opers/spec. items. Per share data adj. for stk. divs.; EPS diluted. E-Estimated. NA-Not Available. NM-Not Meaningful. NR-Not Ranked. UR-Under Review.

Office: 45 Glover Ave, Norwalk, CT 06856-4505.
Telephone: 203-968-3000.
Website: http://www.xerox.com
Chrmn & CEO: U.M. Burns

COO & EVP: J.A. Firestone
SVP, Secy & General Counsel: D.H. Liu
CFO: L. Zimmerman
CTO: S.V. Vandebroek

Investor Contact: J.H. Lesko (800-828-6396)
Board Members: G. A. Britt, U. M. Burns, R. J. Harrington, W. C. Hunter, R. A. McDonald, N. J. Nicholas, Jr., C. Prince, III, A. N. Reese, M. A. Wilderotter

Founded: 1906
Domicile: New York
Employees: 53,600

The McGraw·Hill Companies

Xilinx Inc

STANDARD &POOR'S

S&P Recommendation	HOLD ★★★☆☆	Price	12-Mo. Target Price	Investment Style
		$25.20 (as of Oct 22, 2010)	$28.00	Large-Cap Growth

GICS Sector Information Technology
Sub-Industry Semiconductors

Summary This company is the world's largest supplier of programmable logic chips and related development system software.

Key Stock Statistics (Source S&P, Vickers, company reports)

52-Wk Range	$29.40– 21.01	S&P Oper. EPS 2011E	2.41	Market Capitalization(B)	$6.523	Beta	0.96
Trailing 12-Month EPS	$1.73	S&P Oper. EPS 2012E	2.36	Yield (%)	2.54	S&P 3-Yr. Proj. EPS CAGR(%)	29
Trailing 12-Month P/E	14.6	P/E on S&P Oper. EPS 2011E	10.5	Dividend Rate/Share	$0.64	S&P Credit Rating	BBB-
$10K Invested 5 Yrs Ago	$11,844	Common Shares Outstg. (M)	258.8	Institutional Ownership (%)	99		

Price Performance

30-Week Mov. Avg. · · · 10-Week Mov. Avg. - - **GAAP Earnings vs. Previous Year** Volume Above Avg. STARS
12-Mo. Target Price — Relative Strength — ▲ Up ▼ Down ► No Change Below Avg.

Options: ASE, CBOE, P

Analysis prepared by **Clyde Montevirgen** on October 22, 2010, when the stock traded at **$ 25.12**.

Highlights

► We project that revenues will rise 33% in FY 11 (Mar.), compared to essentially flat sales in FY 10. Although we are concerned about rising inventory throughout the supply chain slowing orders over the near-term, we believe longer-term growth will be supported by improving global economic conditions and as FPGAs replace ASICs. We are positive about XLNX's proprietary nature of its products, long product cycles, and 40 and 45 nanometer (nm) products, which should provide a reliable sales base.

► We think XLNX will be able to maintain fairly steady gross margins in the mid-60% area due to what we view as its cost-effective manufacturing partnerships with chip foundries and its product portfolio of higher-margin programmable devices. However, we see minor fluctuations based on varying customer and product mixes and yields. Although we expect rising expenses to support new products and related sales, we look for operating margins to widen to 35% in FY 11, from 24% in FY 10.

► Our EPS projections assume an effective tax rate of 23% and a decrease in the diluted share count of around 4%.

Investment Rationale/Risk

► Our hold recommendation reflects our view of healthy fundamentals and fair valuations. XLNX has enough business with products using older geometries to support growth, in our opinion. Having improved its cost structure, it boasts above industry profitability and returns, and also has what we see as a strong balance sheet and cash flows. However, we are concerned about new offerings from its main rival Altera (ALTR 29, Hold) leading to market share loss and below-industry growth over the next few quarters as inventory builds throughout the supply-chain. Overall, we think valuations should be similar to the industry's.

► Risks to our recommendation and target price include weaker-than-expected economic conditions, dependence on chip foundry partners, and fluctuations in chip inventories.

► Our 12-month target price of $28 is based on a price-to-earnings multiple of approximately 12X, near the industry average to account for our view of relative growth, return on equity, and risk, applied to our calendar 2011 EPS estimate.

Qualitative Risk Assessment

LOW	MEDIUM	HIGH

Our risk assessment reflects the cyclicality of the semiconductor industry, offset by the company's position as the largest competitor in a fast-growing niche, its diverse end markets, and its sharing of factory operations risk with chip foundry partners.

Quantitative Evaluations

S&P Quality Ranking B

D	C	B-	B	B+	A-	A	A+

Relative Strength Rank WEAK

20

LOWEST = 1   HIGHEST = 99

Revenue/Earnings Data

Revenue (Million $)

	1Q	2Q	3Q	4Q	Year
2011	594.7	--	--	--	--
2010	376.2	415.0	513.4	529.0	1,834
2009	488.3	483.5	458.4	395.0	1,825
2008	445.9	444.9	474.8	475.8	1,841
2007	481.4	467.2	450.7	443.5	1,843
2006	405.4	398.9	449.6	472.3	1,726

Earnings Per Share ($)

	1Q	2Q	3Q	4Q	Year
2011	0.58	E0.65	E0.60	E0.58	E2.41
2010	0.14	0.23	0.38	0.54	1.29
2009	0.30	0.29	0.51	0.26	1.36
2008	0.28	0.30	0.35	0.34	1.25
2007	0.24	0.27	0.26	0.27	1.02
2006	0.21	0.24	0.23	0.32	1.00

Fiscal year ended Mar. 31. Next earnings report expected: NA. EPS Estimates based on S&P Operating Earnings; historical GAAP earnings are as reported.

Dividend Data (Dates: mm/dd Payment Date: mm/dd/yy)

Amount ($)	Date Decl.	Ex-Div. Date	Stk. of Record	Payment Date
0.160	01/20	02/08	02/10	03/03/10
0.160	04/28	05/17	05/19	06/09/10
0.160	07/21	08/09	08/11	09/01/10
0.160	10/20	11/08	11/10	12/01/10

Dividends have been paid since 2004. Source: Company reports.

Please read the Required Disclosures and Analyst Certification on the last page of this report.

The **McGraw-Hill** Companies

Xilinx Inc

Business Summary October 22, 2010

CORPORATE OVERVIEW. Founded in 1984, Xilinx is the world's leading supplier of programmable logic devices (PLDs) based on market share. These devices include field programmable gate arrays (FPGAs) and complex programmable logic devices (CPLDs). They are standard integrated circuits (ICs) that are programmed by customers to perform desired logic operations. The company believes it provides high levels of integration and creates significant time and cost savings for electronic equipment manufacturers in the telecommunications, networking, computing and industrial markets.

Xilinx's FPGAs are proprietary ICs designed by the company; they provide a combination of the high logic density usually associated with custom gate arrays, the time-to-market advantages of programmable logic, and the availability of a standard product. Like other chipmakers, Xilinx utilizes manufacturing process technologies that enable the PLD to increase functionality. Generally, the smaller the process technology, the higher the chip's performance and density and the lower the power consumption. XLNX has several product families, including the Virtex, Spartan and CoolRunner lines. The Virtex-6 is the latest generation FPGA produced on 40 nanometer (nm) process technology.

Older generations include the Virtex-5 (65nm) and Virtex 4 (90nm).

Products are classified as new, mainstream, base and support. New products accounted for 47% of FY 09 (Mar.) sales (33% in FY 08), mainstream products 37% (46%), base products 11% (15%), and support products 5% (6%). Revenue by end market in FY 09 broke down as follows: 44% (43% in FY 08) communications, 32% (32%) industrial and other, 16% (17%) consumer and automotive, and 8% (8%) data processing.

Xilinx sells its products globally to OEMs and to electronic components distributors that resell them. Avnet distributes the majority of the company's products worldwide and accounted for 81% of XLNX's accounts receivable in FY 09. However, no single end customer accounted for more than 10% of Xilinx's revenues.

Company Financials Fiscal Year Ended Mar. 31

Per Share Data ($)	2010	2009	2008	2007	2006	2005	2004	2003	2002	2001
Tangible Book Value	7.26	5.74	5.45	5.54	7.53	7.24	6.79	5.44	5.26	5.82
Cash Flow	1.53	1.58	1.46	1.24	1.19	1.05	1.05	0.57	-0.02	0.36
Earnings	1.29	1.36	1.25	1.02	1.00	0.87	0.85	0.36	-0.34	0.10
S&P Core Earnings	1.30	1.48	1.28	1.01	0.78	0.58	0.57	0.05	-0.31	0.35
Dividends	0.60	0.56	0.36	0.36	0.28	0.20	Nil	Nil	Nil	Nil
Payout Ratio	47%	41%	29%	35%	28%	23%	Nil	Nil	Nil	Nil
Calendar Year	2009	2008	2007	2006	2005	2004	2003	2002	2001	2000
Prices:High	25.45	28.21	30.50	29.98	32.30	45.40	39.20	47.15	59.25	98.31
Prices:Low	15.00	14.28	21.14	18.35	21.25	25.21	18.50	13.50	19.52	35.25
P/E Ratio:High	20	21	24	29	32	47	46	NM	NM	NM
P/E Ratio:Low	12	10	17	18	21	26	22	NM	NM	NM

Income Statement Analysis (Million $)										
Revenue	1,834	1,825	1,841	1,843	1,726	1,573	1,398	1,156	1,016	1,659
Operating Income	527	513	485	424	489	442	412	283	87.3	568
Depreciation	65.2	61.0	61.0	73.9	69.5	63.1	67.9	72.5	106	93.5
Interest Expense	6.58	29.0	0.17	Nil	Nil	Nil	Nil	Nil	0.06	0.17
Pretax Income	422	498	474	431	457	401	351	170	-193	61.1
Effective Tax Rate	15.2%	24.6%	21.1%	18.7%	22.4%	21.9%	13.6%	26.0%	NM	42.3%
Net Income	357	376	374	351	354	313	303	126	-114	35.3
S&P Core Earnings	360	409	382	348	277	205	204	18.1	-103	132

Balance Sheet & Other Financial Data (Million $)										
Cash	1,387	1,325	1,296	636	783	449	337	214	230	209
Current Assets	1,907	1,752	1,820	1,700	1,648	1,466	1,302	1,175	999	1,102
Total Assets	3,184	2,826	3,137	3,179	3,174	3,039	2,937	2,422	2,335	2,502
Current Liabilities	357	233	341	303	345	298	381	314	196	350
Long Term Debt	355	690	1,000	1,000	Nil	Nil	Nil	Nil	Nil	Nil
Common Equity	2,120	1,738	1,672	1,773	2,729	2,674	2,483	1,951	1,904	1,918
Total Capital	2,475	2,511	2,756	2,875	2,821	2,741	2,556	2,108	2,140	2,152
Capital Expenditures	28.2	39.1	45.6	111	67.0	61.4	41.0	46.0	94.9	223
Cash Flow	423	437	435	425	424	376	371	198	-7.51	129
Current Ratio	5.3	7.5	5.3	5.6	4.8	4.9	3.4	3.7	5.1	3.1
% Long Term Debt of Capitalization	14.3	27.5	36.3	34.8	Nil	Nil	Nil	Nil	Nil	Nil
% Net Income of Revenue	19.5	20.6	20.3	19.0	20.5	19.8	21.7	10.9	NM	2.1
% Return on Assets	11.9	12.6	11.8	11.0	11.4	10.5	11.3	5.3	NM	1.5
% Return on Equity	18.5	22.0	21.7	15.6	13.1	12.1	13.7	6.5	NM	1.9

Data as orig reptd.; bef. results of disc opers/spec. items. Per share data adj. for stk. divs.; EPS diluted. E-Estimated. NA-Not Available. NM-Not Meaningful. NR-Not Ranked. UR-Under Review.

Office: 2100 Logic Drive, San Jose, CA, USA 95124-3400.
Telephone: 408-559-7778.
Email: ir@xilinx.com
Website: http://www.xilinx.com

Chrmn: P.T. Gianos
Pres & CEO: M.N. Gavrielov
COO: R.G. Petrakian
Investor Contact: J.A. Olson (408-559-7778)

SVP, CFO & Chief Acctg Officer: J.A. Olson
Board Members: J. L. Doyle, J. G. Fishman, M. N. Gavrielov, P. T. Gianos, W. G. Howard, Jr., J. M. Patterson, A. A. Pimentel, M. Turner, Jr., E. W. Vanderslice

Founded: 1984
Domicile: Delaware
Employees: 2,948

XL Group Plc

STANDARD
&POOR'S

S&P Recommendation	BUY ★★★★☆	Price $21.98 (as of Oct 22, 2010)	12-Mo. Target Price $21.00	Investment Style Large-Cap Blend

GICS Sector Financials
Sub-Industry Property & Casualty Insurance

Summary Bermuda-based XL, which originally provided excess liability coverage, has expanded into providing a broad array of commercial lines insurance, reinsurance, and other risk management services.

Key Stock Statistics (Source S&P, Vickers, company reports)

52-Wk Range	$22.52– 15.59	S&P Oper. EPS 2010**E**	2.30	Market Capitalization(B)	$7.519	Beta	2.68
Trailing 12-Month EPS	$0.46	S&P Oper. EPS 2011**E**	2.55	Yield (%)	1.82	S&P 3-Yr. Proj. EPS CAGR(%)	NA
Trailing 12-Month P/E	47.8	P/E on S&P Oper. EPS 2010**E**	9.6	Dividend Rate/Share	$0.40	S&P Credit Rating	NA
$10K Invested 5 Yrs Ago	$3,932	Common Shares Outstg. (M)	342.1	Institutional Ownership (%)	88		

Price Performance

30-Week Mov. Avg. · · · 10-Week Mov. Avg. – – GAAP Earnings vs. Previous Year   Volume Above Avg. STARS
12-Mo. Target Price — Relative Strength   ▲ Up ▼ Down ▶ No Change   Below Avg. ★

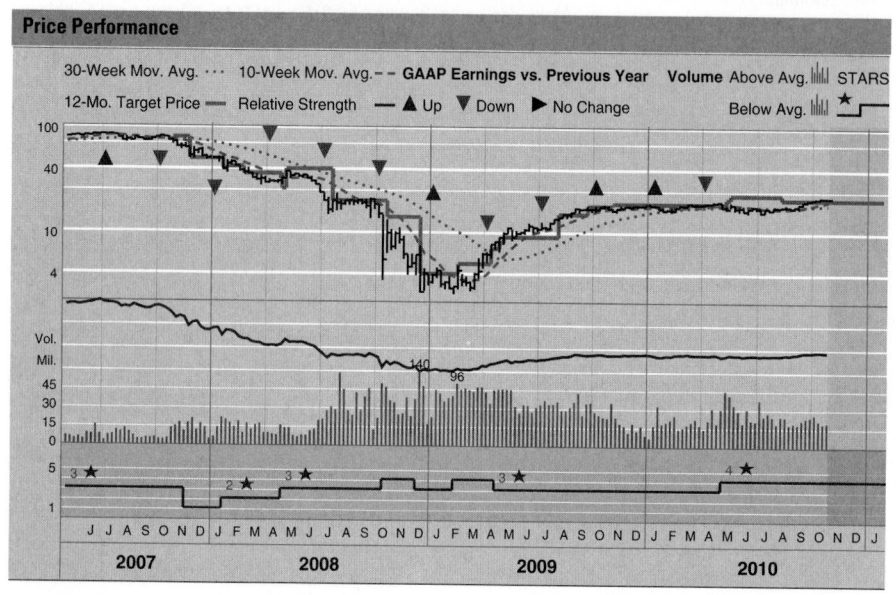

Options: CBOE, P, Ph

Analysis prepared by **Cathy A. Seifert** on August 06, 2010, when the stock traded at **$ 17.99**.

Highlights

➤ We expect earned premiums to decline by 2% to 5% in 2010, and to be fractionally lower in 2011, following declines of 14% in 2009 and 7.8% in 2008. Our forecast reflects our view of improved stability of the XL franchise, offset by the impact of competitive pricing in the core property casualty line, coupled with reduced writings in the life insurance and financial guarantee lines. Net written premiums declined 17% in 2009.

➤ We expect net investment income to be flat to modestly lower in 2010, following a decline of 21% in 2009. The decline experienced in 2009 reflected a challenging investment environment and steps XL took to lower the risk profile of its investment portfolio.

➤ We estimate operating EPS of $2.30 for 2010 and $2.55 for 2011, versus $2.69 of operating EPS reported for 2009 and $3.49 of operating EPS in 2008. Our estimates exclude realized investment gains/losses. XL reported a 2008 net loss of $11.02 a share, due mainly to a $1.4 billion charge taken to (among other things) terminate a reinsurance agreement with Syncora Holdings (formerly Security Capital Assurance).

Investment Rationale/Risk

➤ Our Buy recommendation reflects our view that the shares are undervalued versus peers, particularly in light of what we see as progress XL is making in rebuilding its franchise and de-risking its balance sheet. At current levels, the shares are trading at about 0.8X June 30, 2010, tangible common equity, versus 1.3X to 1.5X for most of XL's peers.

➤ Risks to our recommendation and target price include a greater-than-anticipated decline in premium rates and underwriting margins; a more significant deterioration in the credit quality of XL's investment portfolio; and not fully executing on its balance sheet restructuring.

➤ Our 12-month target price of $21 assumes that the shares will trade at approximately 8.2X our operating earnings per share estimate for 2011. This represents a discount (albeit less of one than before) to most of XL's peers.

Qualitative Risk Assessment

LOW	MEDIUM	HIGH

Our risk assessment reflects our concerns about XL's exposure to catastrophe losses and the adequacy of its loss reserves in certain liability lines of business, and our view that XL could face writedowns of its fixed income investment portfolio and certain other investments.

Quantitative Evaluations

S&P Quality Ranking   NR

D	C	B-	B	B+	A-	A	A+

Relative Strength Rank   STRONG

LOWEST = 1   78   HIGHEST = 99

Revenue/Earnings Data

Revenue (Million $)

	1Q	2Q	3Q	4Q	Year
2010	1,637	--	--	--	--
2009	1,555	1,725	1,486	1,448	6,194
2008	2,174	2,125	1,744	1,106	7,148
2007	2,483	2,597	2,153	1,902	9,136
2006	2,473	2,499	2,364	2,496	9,833
2005	2,401	4,108	2,296	2,479	11,285

Earnings Per Share ($)

	1Q	2Q	3Q	4Q	Year
2010	0.37	E0.64	E0.53	E0.69	E2.30
2009	0.53	0.23	-0.03	-0.12	0.61
2008	1.20	1.34	-6.09	-4.36	-11.02
2007	3.06	3.00	1.82	-6.88	1.15
2006	2.56	2.10	2.32	2.62	9.60
2005	3.18	0.97	-7.53	-5.51	-9.14

Fiscal year ended Dec. 31. Next earnings report expected: NA. EPS Estimates based on S&P Operating Earnings; historical GAAP earnings are as reported.

Dividend Data (Dates: mm/dd Payment Date: mm/dd/yy)

Amount ($)	Date Decl.	Ex-Div. Date	Stk. of Record	Payment Date
0.100	10/23	12/11	12/15	12/31/09
0.100	02/26	03/11	03/15	03/31/10
0.100	04/30	06/11	06/15	06/30/10
0.100	07/26	09/13	09/15	09/30/10

Dividends have been paid since 1992. Source: Company reports.

Please read the Required Disclosures and Analyst Certification on the last page of this report.

The McGraw-Hill Companies

XL Group Plc

Business Summary August 06, 2010

CORPORATE OVERVIEW. Bermuda-based XL Capital was formed in 1986 by a consortium of Fortune 500 companies to provide excess liability coverage. Since then, XL has expanded (mostly via acquisitions) to include insurance, reinsurance, and other financial services. In January 2010, XL announced plans to redomesticate its holding company to Ireland from the Cayman Islands. Gross written premiums of nearly $6.7 billion in 2009 (down 19% from $8.3 billion in 2008) were divided: insurance 63%, reinsurance 28%, and life operations 9%.

Insurance business written includes general liability, as well as other specialized types of liability coverage, such as directors' and officers' liability and professional and employment practices liability coverage. An array of property coverage, as well as marine and aviation coverage, is also offered. Insurance net written premiums of $3.27 billion in 2009 were divided: professional liability 41%, casualty 17%, property 11%, marine/energy/aviation/satellite 16%, and other specialty lines 15%.

Reinsurance business written includes treaty and facultative reinsurance to primary insurers of casualty risk. Reinsurance net written premiums totaled $1.47 billion in 2009 and were divided: property 38%, casualty 15%, property catastrophe 21%, professional lines 11%, marine, energy aviation and satellite 6%, and other lines (including political risk, surety and structured indemnity) 9%.

Life operations include reinsurance written from other life insurers, principally to help in managing mortality, morbidity, survivorship, investment and lapse risks. Net written premiums totaled $532.9 million in 2009 and were divided: annuity risks 25%, life insurance 75%. In December 2008, XL completed a strategic review of its life reinsurance business, which is now in runoff mode.

In July 2001, the company acquired Winterthur International, for about $330.2 million in cash (as adjusted). As part of the transaction, XL received certain post-closing arrangements protecting it against (among other things) certain types of adverse loss development. XL valued the post-closing payment at $1.45 billion, and Winterthur Swiss Insurance Co. (the seller) believed the post-closing payment was $541 million. In December 2005, an independent actuarial review concluded that Winterthur's estimate was closer than the estimate submitted by XL. As a result of this difference, XL recorded a fourth-quarter 2005 after-tax charge of $834.2 million.

Company Financials Fiscal Year Ended Dec. 31

Per Share Data ($)	2009	2008	2007	2006	2005	2004	2003	2002	2001	2000
Tangible Book Value	25.09	16.74	41.31	45.93	37.08	42.55	37.07	36.13	28.35	31.86
Operating Earnings	NA	NA	NA	NA	NA	NA	NA	5.10	-3.67	4.52
Earnings	0.61	-11.02	1.15	9.60	-9.14	8.13	2.69	2.88	-4.55	4.03
Dividends	0.40	1.14	1.52	1.52	2.00	1.96	1.92	1.88	1.84	1.80
Payout Ratio	66%	NM	76%	16%	NM	24%	71%	65%	NM	45%
Prices:High	19.03	52.26	85.67	72.90	79.80	82.00	88.87	98.48	96.50	89.25
Prices:Low	2.56	2.65	48.16	59.82	60.03	66.70	63.49	58.45	61.50	39.00
P/E Ratio:High	31	NM	43	8	NM	10	33	34	NM	22
P/E Ratio:Low	4	NM	24	6	NM	8	24	20	NM	10

Income Statement Analysis (Million $)	2009	2008	2007	2006	2005	2004	2003	2002	2001	2000
Premium Income	5,707	6,640	7,205	7,570	2,238	1,406	6,969	5,990	3,476	2,035
Net Investment Income	1,320	1,769	2,249	1,978	1,475	995	780	735	563	542
Other Revenue	-833	-1,261	-318	8,904	8,864	7,426	268	-147	18.0	140
Total Revenue	6,194	7,148	9,136	9,833	11,285	10,028	8,017	6,578	4,057	2,717
Pretax Income	195	-2,331	534	2,007	-1,194	1,260	451	442	-764	451
Net Operating Income	NA	NA	NA	NA	NA	NA	NA	701	-465	NA
Net Income	75.0	-2,554	276	1,763	-1,252	1,167	412	406	-576	506

Balance Sheet & Other Financial Data (Million $)	2009	2008	2007	2006	2005	2004	2003	2002	2001	2000
Cash & Equivalent	3,994	4,717	4,328	2,656	4,085	2,631	2,698	3,785	2,044	1,074
Premiums Due	2,598	4,273	4,610	4,698	4,842	4,934	4,847	4,833	2,182	1,120
Investment Assets:Bonds	28,058	25,636	33,608	36,121	32,310	25,100	19,494	14,483	10,832	8,605
Investment Assets:Stocks	17.8	361	855	891	869	963	583	575	548	557
Investment Assets:Loans	Nil	Nil	Nil	Nil	Nil	Nil	Nil	Nil	Nil	Nil
Investment Assets:Total	31,822	29,477	39,585	42,137	38,171	30,066	22,821	17,956	13,741	10,472
Deferred Policy Costs	654	714	755	870	866	845	778	688	394	309
Total Assets	45,580	45,682	57,762	59,309	58,455	49,015	40,764	35,647	27,963	16,942
Debt	2,451	3,190	2,869	3,368	3,413	2,721	1,905	1,878	1,605	450
Common Equity	9,432	6,615	9,948	16,422	14,078	12,286	10,171	6,569	5,437	5,574
Property & Casualty:Loss Ratio	61.5	66.1	59.8	60.7	107.1	68.6	75.3	68.0	105.0	70.4
Property & Casualty:Expense Ratio	32.1	29.6	29.0	27.8	25.8	27.4	27.3	29.0	34.9	36.4
Property & Casualty Combined Ratio	93.6	95.7	88.8	88.5	132.9	96.0	102.6	97.0	139.9	106.8
% Return on Revenue	1.2	NM	3.0	18.6	NM	11.9	5.2	6.0	NM	18.6
% Return on Equity	1.0	NM	2.1	11.3	NM	10.0	3.9	6.6	NM	9.1

Data as orig reptd.; bef. results of disc opers/spec. items. Per share data adj. for stk. divs.; EPS diluted. E-Estimated. NA-Not Available. NM-Not Meaningful. NR-Not Ranked. UR-Under Review.

Office: 1 Hatch Street Upper, Dublin, Ireland 2.
Telephone: 441-292-8515.
Website: http://www.xlgroup.com
Chrmn: R.R. Glauber

Pres: P. Rochaix
CEO: M.S. McGavick
EVP & CFO: I.M. Esteves
EVP, Secy & General Counsel: K.R. Gould

Investor Contact: D.R. Radulski (441-294-7460)
Board Members: D. R. Comey, R. R. Glauber, H. N. Haag, J. Mauriello, M. S. McGavick, E. M. McQuade, C. S. Rose, E. E. Thrower, J. Vereker

Founded: 1986
Domicile: Cayman Islands
Employees: 3,565

Yahoo! Inc

STANDARD &POOR'S

S&P Recommendation	**STRONG BUY** ★★★★★	Price $16.31 (as of Oct 22, 2010)	12-Mo. Target Price $19.00	Investment Style Large-Cap Growth

GICS Sector Information Technology
Sub-Industry Internet Software & Services

Summary This company is one of the world's largest providers of online content and services.

Key Stock Statistics (Source S&P, Vickers, company reports)

52-Wk Range	$19.12– 12.94	S&P Oper. EPS 2010**E**	0.71	Market Capitalization(B)	$21.984	Beta	0.81
Trailing 12-Month EPS	$0.77	S&P Oper. EPS 2011**E**	0.87	Yield (%)	Nil	S&P 3-Yr. Proj. EPS CAGR(%)	43
Trailing 12-Month P/E	21.2	P/E on S&P Oper. EPS 2010**E**	23.0	Dividend Rate/Share	Nil	S&P Credit Rating	NR
$10K Invested 5 Yrs Ago	$4,620	Common Shares Outstg. (M)	1,348.3	Institutional Ownership (%)	72		

Price Performance

30-Week Mov. Avg. · · · 10-Week Mov. Avg. - - **GAAP Earnings vs. Previous Year** Volume Above Avg. STARS
12-Mo. Target Price — Relative Strength — ▲ Up ▼ Down ▶ No Change Below Avg. ★

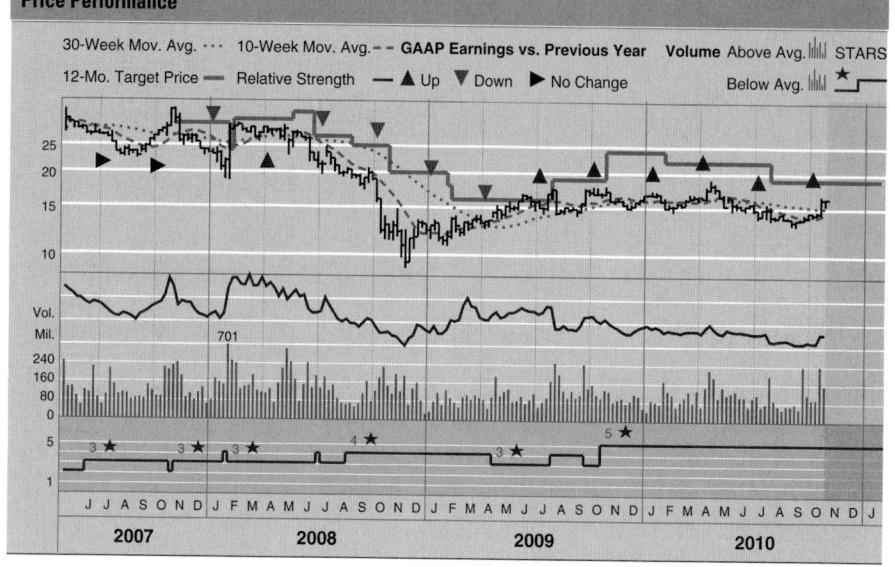

Options: ASE, CBOE, P, Ph

Analysis prepared by **Scott H. Kessler** on October 21, 2010, when the stock traded at **$ 15.80**.

Highlights

➤ We project that revenues will increase 2% to 5% annually through 2012, reflecting a healthier global economy, greater demand for display advertising, benefits of a search advertising deal with Microsoft (MSFT 25, Hold), and challenges in terms of usage and in the fees area.

➤ We believe revenues will continue to benefit from secular growth in online advertising. We think annual operating margins bottomed in 2008, due to changed broadband alliances and aggressive investments in new initiatives, and we see improvements through 2012. EPS should benefit from a $3 billion share repurchase program announced in June 2010.

➤ YHOO announced a search technology and advertising agreement with MSFT in July 2009. MSFT powers YHOO's search results and non-premium related advertising, and YHOO sells the companies' premium search inventory. Although the deal was initially perceived by some as disappointing for YHOO, we think it will enable YHOO to better focus and invest in its core media operations, and we see notable financial benefits.

Investment Rationale/Risk

➤ We think an increasing percentage of advertising budgets are being spent online. We also see multiple potential positive catalysts for YHOO, including possible monetization efforts around its major investments in Asia-based businesses, continuing benefits from the MSFT deal, and improvements associated with new content and social media-related efforts.

➤ Risks to our opinion and target price include the potential for continuing user activity declines, issues related to the search partnership with MSFT, and global economic weakness.

➤ After excluding the value of YHOO's Asia-based equity investments, our relative P/E and P/E-to-growth analyses (including a discount given recent company changes and challenges) yields a value of $13. Our DCF analysis, with assumptions including a WACC of 12.7%, projected annual FCF growth of 9% from 2010 to 2014, and a perpetuity growth rate of 3%, results in an intrinsic value of $7. Weighing these assessments, and adding the value of YHOO's investments in Asia-based companies that we estimate at about $9 per share, results in our 12-month target price of $19.

Qualitative Risk Assessment

LOW	MEDIUM	**HIGH**

The company is a large and well-capitalized leader in a number of areas related to Internet content and services. However, in our view, the markets in which it participates change rapidly and have relatively low barriers to entry, which has contributed to the notable competition and inconsistent financial execution that we have observed.

Quantitative Evaluations

S&P Quality Ranking B

D	C	B-	**B**	B+	A-	A	A+

Relative Strength Rank **STRONG**

86

LOWEST = 1 HIGHEST = 99

Revenue/Earnings Data

Revenue (Million $)

	1Q	2Q	3Q	4Q	Year
2010	1,597	1,601	1,601	--	--
2009	1,580	1,573	1,575	1,732	6,460
2008	1,818	1,798	1,786	1,806	7,209
2007	1,672	1,698	1,768	1,832	6,969
2006	1,567	1,576	1,580	1,702	6,426
2005	1,174	1,253	1,330	1,501	5,258

Earnings Per Share ($)

	1Q	2Q	3Q	4Q	Year
2010	0.22	0.15	0.30	E0.24	E0.71
2009	0.08	0.10	0.13	0.11	0.42
2008	0.37	0.09	0.04	-0.22	0.29
2007	0.10	0.11	0.11	0.15	0.47
2006	0.11	0.11	0.11	0.19	0.52
2005	0.14	0.51	0.17	0.46	1.28

Fiscal year ended Dec. 31. Next earnings report expected: Late January. EPS Estimates based on S&P Operating Earnings; historical GAAP earnings are as reported.

Dividend Data

No cash dividends have been paid.

Please read the Required Disclosures and Analyst Certification on the last page of this report.

The **McGraw·Hill** Companies

Yahoo! Inc

STANDARD &POOR'S

Business Summary October 21, 2010

CORPORATE OVERVIEW. Yahoo! is one of the world's largest Internet companies. It classifies properties in six categories: Front Doors (including the Yahoo front page, My Yahoo, and the Yahoo Toolbar), Communities (including Yahoo Groups and Flickr), Search, Communications (including mail and messaging offerings), Audience (consisting of offerings in areas such as information/entertainment offerings related to news, finance, sports, music, movies, television, games, autos, real estate, food, consumer technology, kids and health), and Connected Life (including Yahoo Mobile and Yahoo Digital Home).

Hundreds of millions of users every month visit the online properties of YHOO and its unconsolidated subsidiaries (excluding the 35% stake in Yahoo Japan and 43% interest in privately held Chinese Internet conglomerate Alibaba Group), making it one of the world's most popular Internet destinations.

Blake Jorgensen became CFO in June 2007. Soon thereafter, co-founder Jerry Yang replaced Terry Semel as CEO, and long-time CFO Sue Decker became President and COO. Many other important executives have also left YHOO since early 2007, and the pace and magnitude of these departures increased around mid-2008, in our view. Carol Bartz replaced Jerry Yang as CEO and Sue Decker left in January 2009, and Tim Morse replaced Jorgensen as CFO in July 2009.

Company Financials Fiscal Year Ended Dec. 31

Per Share Data ($)	2009	2008	2007	2006	2005	2004	2003	2002	2001	2000
Tangible Book Value	6.18	5.26	3.70	4.25	3.59	2.94	1.64	1.47	1.52	1.69
Cash Flow	0.94	0.87	0.94	0.89	1.54	0.79	0.31	0.18	0.03	0.11
Earnings	0.42	0.29	0.47	0.52	1.28	0.58	0.19	0.09	-0.08	0.06
S&P Core Earnings	0.33	0.33	0.46	0.51	0.56	0.24	0.03	-0.32	-0.85	NA
Dividends	Nil	Nil	Nil	Nil	Nil	Nil	Nil	Nil	Nil	Nil
Payout Ratio	Nil	Nil	Nil	Nil	Nil	Nil	Nil	Nil	Nil	Nil
Prices:High	18.02	30.25	34.08	43.66	43.45	39.79	22.74	10.68	21.69	125.03
Prices:Low	10.81	8.94	22.27	22.65	30.30	20.57	8.25	4.47	4.01	12.53
P/E Ratio:High	43	NM	73	84	34	69	NM	NM	NM	NM
P/E Ratio:Low	26	NM	47	44	24	35	NM	NM	NM	NM

Income Statement Analysis (Million $)										
Revenue	6,460	7,209	6,969	6,426	5,258	3,575	1,625	953	717	1,110
Operating Income	1,252	1,477	1,355	1,481	1,505	1,000	455	198	34.5	390
Depreciation	739	790	659	540	397	311	160	109	131	69.1
Interest Expense	NA	NA	Nil	Nil	Nil	Nil	Nil	Nil	Nil	Nil
Pretax Income	825	693	1,000	293	2,672	1,280	391	180	-81.1	264
Effective Tax Rate	26.6%	37.9%	33.7%	NM	28.7%	34.2%	37.6%	39.7%	NM	71.2%
Net Income	598	424	660	751	1,896	840	238	107	-92.8	70.8
S&P Core Earnings	470	464	651	744	840	353	35.5	-377	-966	NA

Balance Sheet & Other Financial Data (Million $)										
Cash	3,291	3,452	2,001	2,601	2,561	3,512	1,310	774	926	1,120
Current Assets	4,595	4,746	3,238	3,750	3,450	4,090	1,722	970	1,052	1,291
Total Assets	14,936	13,690	12,230	11,514	10,832	9,178	5,932	2,790	2,379	2,270
Current Liabilities	1,718	1,705	2,300	1,474	1,204	1,181	708	412	359	311
Long Term Debt	NA	43.0	Nil	750	750	750	750	Nil	Nil	Nil
Common Equity	12,493	11,242	9,533	9,161	8,566	7,101	4,363	2,262	1,967	1,897
Total Capital	12,519	11,269	9,545	9,919	9,316	7,896	5,151	2,294	1,997	1,926
Capital Expenditures	434	675	602	689	409	246	117	51.6	86.2	94.4
Cash Flow	1,337	1,214	1,319	1,291	2,293	1,151	398	216	37.8	140
Current Ratio	2.7	2.8	1.4	2.5	2.9	3.5	2.4	2.4	2.9	4.1
% Long Term Debt of Capitalization	Nil	0.4	Nil	7.6	8.0	9.5	14.6	Nil	Nil	Nil
% Net Income of Revenue	9.3	5.9	9.5	11.7	36.0	23.5	14.6	11.2	NM	6.4
% Return on Assets	4.2	3.3	5.6	6.7	18.9	11.1	5.5	4.1	NM	3.7
% Return on Equity	5.0	4.1	7.1	8.5	24.2	14.6	7.2	5.1	NM	4.5

Data as orig reptd.; bef. results of disc opers/spec. items. Per share data adj. for stk. divs.; EPS diluted. E-Estimated. NA-Not Available. NM-Not Meaningful. NR-Not Ranked. UR-Under Review.

Office: 701 First Avenue, Sunnyvale, CA 94089.
Telephone: 408-349-3300.
Email: investor_relations@yahoo-inc.com
Website: http://www.yahoo.com

Chrmn: R.J. Bostock
Pres & CEO: C.A. Bartz
COO: J. Marcom, Jr.
EVP & CFO: T.R. Morse

EVP, Secy & General Counsel: M.J. Callahan
Board Members: C. A. Bartz, R. J. Bostock, P. S. Hart, E. C. Hippeau, S. M. James, V. I. Joshi, A. Kern, B. D. Smith, G. L. Wilson, J. Yang

Founded: 1995
Domicile: Delaware
Employees: 13,900

YUM! Brands Inc.

STANDARD &POOR'S

S&P Recommendation	HOLD ★★★☆☆	Price $49.57 (as of Oct 22, 2010)	12-Mo. Target Price $50.00	Investment Style Large-Cap Growth

GICS Sector Consumer Discretionary
Sub-Industry Restaurants

Summary This company operates, franchises, has interests in or licenses the largest number of fast food restaurants in the world, with more than 37,000 units in over 110 countries, including the KFC, Pizza Hut and Taco Bell chains.

Key Stock Statistics (Source S&P, Vickers, company reports)

52-Wk Range	$49.63– 32.49	S&P Oper. EPS 2010E	2.49	Market Capitalization(B)	$23.228	Beta	1.02
Trailing 12-Month EPS	$2.27	S&P Oper. EPS 2011E	2.67	Yield (%)	2.02	S&P 3-Yr. Proj. EPS CAGR(%)	7
Trailing 12-Month P/E	21.8	P/E on S&P Oper. EPS 2010E	19.9	Dividend Rate/Share	$1.00	S&P Credit Rating	BBB-
$10K Invested 5 Yrs Ago	$21,247	Common Shares Outstg. (M)	468.6	Institutional Ownership (%)	76		

Price Performance

30-Week Mov. Avg. · · · ·   10-Week Mov. Avg. - -   **GAAP Earnings vs. Previous Year**   **Volume** Above Avg.|||| STARS
12-Mo. Target Price —   Relative Strength —   ▲ Up ▼ Down ▶ No Change   Below Avg.|||| ★

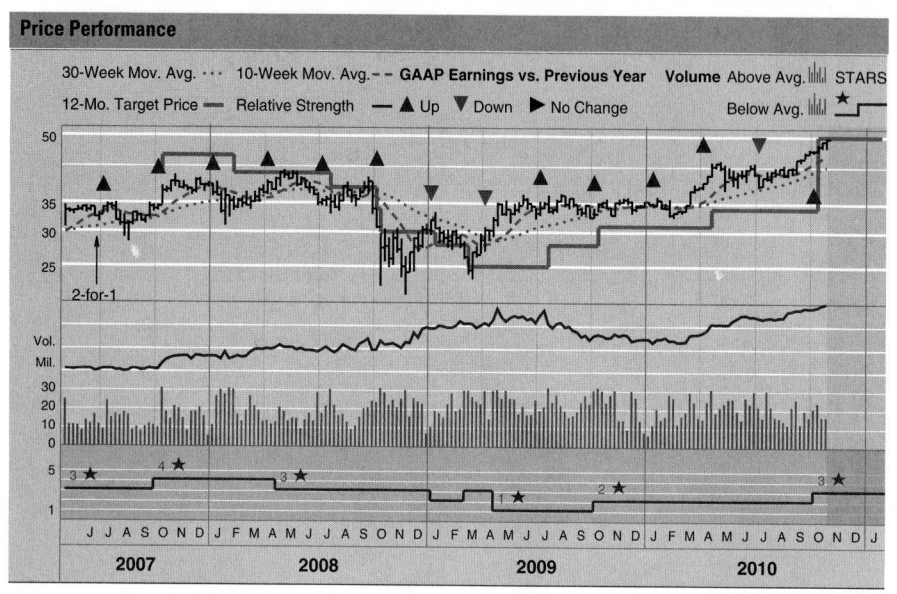

Options: ASE, CBOE, Ph

Analysis prepared by **Erik Kolb** on October 08, 2010, when the stock traded at **$ 47.24**.

Qualitative Risk Assessment

LOW	**MEDIUM**	HIGH

YUM competes primarily in the fast food industry, in which its concepts possess a very strong brand name presence domestically and in certain foreign markets. However, operating margins can vary widely due to fluctuations in food costs. Furthermore, YUM's profits can be affected by changing currency exchange rates given its large and fast-growing international business.

Quantitative Evaluations

S&P Quality Ranking **A**

D	C	B-	B	B+	A-	**A**	A+

Relative Strength Rank **STRONG**

81

LOWEST = 1 HIGHEST = 99

Revenue/Earnings Data

Revenue (Million $)

	1Q	2Q	3Q	4Q	Year
2010	2,345	2,574	2,862	--	--
2009	2,217	2,476	2,778	3,365	10,836
2008	2,408	2,653	2,835	3,383	11,279
2007	2,223	2,367	2,564	3,262	10,416
2006	2,085	2,182	2,278	3,016	9,561
2005	2,054	2,153	2,243	2,899	9,349

Earnings Per Share ($)

2010	0.50	0.59	0.74	E0.57	E2.49
2009	0.46	0.63	0.69	0.45	2.22
2008	0.50	0.45	0.58	0.43	1.96
2007	0.35	0.39	0.50	0.44	1.68
2006	0.29	0.34	0.42	0.42	1.46
2005	0.25	0.29	0.35	0.39	1.28

Fiscal year ended Dec. 31. Next earnings report expected: Early February. EPS Estimates based on S&P Operating Earnings; historical GAAP earnings are as reported.

Dividend Data (Dates: mm/dd Payment Date: mm/dd/yy)

Amount ($)	Date Decl.	Ex-Div. Date	Stk. of Record	Payment Date
0.210	11/20	01/13	01/15	02/05/10
0.210	03/12	04/14	04/16	05/07/10
0.210	05/20	07/14	07/16	08/06/10
0.250	09/14	10/13	10/15	11/05/10

Dividends have been paid since 2004. Source: Company reports.

Highlights

➤ YUM's growth strategy is focused primarily on developing markets. YUM's most recent 2010 new restaurant guidance for each division is for about 475 new units in its China division and about 900 in the Yum Restaurants International division (YRI). In the U.S., YUM expects about 200 openings, offset by a similar number of closings.

➤ Year-to-date 2010 results through September benefited from continued aggressive expansion in China, positive foreign currency translation at YRI, and food and other commodity cost deflation. This was particularly so in China, where food and paper margins improved by 220 basis points (bps). Same-store sales grew 5% in China. In the U.S., same-store results were flat, as strength at Pizza Hut offset weakness at KFC.

➤ We expect costs, as well as forex, to become less favorable in the fourth quarter of 2010 and into 2011. However, we think continued international expansion will more than offset domestic weakness, and project that 2010 EPS of $2.49, compared to $2.22 in 2009. For 2011, we see an increase in EPS to $2.67.

Investment Rationale/Risk

➤ We think YUM is making steady progress expanding internationally, especially in China, but also in other areas. We think areas with low stores per capita, but rising incomes, such as in certain sections of Africa, represent further growth opportunities. But we believe additional efforts are needed to reinvigorate results at U.S. KFC restaurants, which have lagged of late. While food costs have been relatively low to date in 2010, we expect less favorable conditions in 2011 as the worldwide economic recovery likely continues.

➤ Risks to our recommendation and target price include less favorable energy, food and labor costs, a material strengthening of the dollar (making foreign profits worth less in dollars), and slower growth in international markets.

➤ Our 12-month target price of $50 is based on our relative P/E analysis. We apply an 18.7X multiple to our $2.67 2011 EPS estimate to derive a $50 value. Although this multiple is slightly above peers, we think this is warranted given our view of YUM's attractive international growth prospects.

YUM! Brands Inc.

STANDARD &POOR'S

Business Summary October 08, 2010

CORPORATE PROFILE. Yum! Brands has the world's largest quick service restaurant (QSR) system, with over 37,000 restaurants, including licensee units, in more than 110 countries and territories. The company operates and franchises restaurants under the KFC, Pizza Hut, Taco Bell, Long John Silver's and A&W All American Food concepts. In 2009, the company's brands generated close to $36 billion in systemwide sales (up 1% in constant currencies) and $10.8 billion in worldwide revenues, down 4.1% from 2008.

KFC (originally Kentucky Fried Chicken) is the leader in the U.S. chicken QSR segment, with about a 42% market share at year-end 2009 (44% in 2008), according to NPD Group CREST. At the end of 2009, there were 5,162 units in the U.S. and 11,102 units internationally, of which 17% in the U.S. and 31% internationally were operated by the company.

Pizza Hut is the world's largest restaurant chain specializing in ready-to-eat pizza products. At December 31, 2009, it led the U.S. pizza QSR segment with about a 14% market share (15%). As of December 2009, there were 7,566 units

in the U.S. and 5,715 units internationally, of which 8% in the U.S. and 25% of the non-U.S. units were operated by the company.

Taco Bell is the leader in the U.S. Mexican food QSR segment, with about a 52% market share (54%). At the end of 2009, it had 5,604 units in the U.S. and 251 units internationally. About 23% of U.S. and 1% of international locations were operated by YUM.

Long John Silver's operates mostly in the U.S., with 1,134 franchised-operated restaurants in total, including 110 multi-brand locations that include LJS. LJS had a 36% market share of the U.S. QSR seafood segment in 2009. A&W operates 344 units in the U.S. and 293 outside the U.S.

Company Financials Fiscal Year Ended Dec. 31

Per Share Data ($)	2009	2008	2007	2006	2005	2004	2003	2002	2001	2000
Tangible Book Value	NM	NM	0.27	0.81	1.04	1.20	0.42	NM	NM	NM
Cash Flow	3.42	3.10	2.67	2.46	2.07	1.95	1.67	1.54	1.39	1.29
Earnings	2.22	1.96	1.68	1.46	1.28	1.21	1.01	0.94	0.81	0.69
S&P Core Earnings	2.16	1.76	1.69	1.51	1.26	1.15	1.04	0.80	0.68	NA
Dividends	0.78	0.68	0.52	0.26	0.22	0.10	Nil	Nil	Nil	Nil
Payout Ratio	35%	35%	31%	18%	17%	8%	Nil	Nil	Nil	Nil
Prices:High	36.96	41.73	40.60	31.84	26.90	23.74	17.71	16.58	13.33	9.64
Prices:Low	23.37	21.50	27.51	22.11	22.37	16.07	10.77	10.18	7.89	5.89
P/E Ratio:High	17	21	24	22	21	20	18	18	16	14
P/E Ratio:Low	11	11	16	15	18	13	11	11	10	9

Income Statement Analysis (Million $)	2009	2008	2007	2006	2005	2004	2003	2002	2001	2000
Revenue	10,836	11,279	10,416	9,561	9,349	9,011	8,380	7,757	6,953	7,093
Operating Income	2,185	1,971	1,808	1,724	1,538	1,518	1,471	1,375	1,220	1,217
Depreciation	580	560	533	479	469	448	401	370	354	354
Interest Expense	212	253	199	154	127	129	173	172	158	176
Pretax Income	1,396	1,280	1,191	1,108	1,026	1,026	886	858	733	684
Effective Tax Rate	22.4%	24.7%	23.7%	25.6%	25.7%	27.9%	30.2%	32.1%	32.9%	39.6%
Net Income	1,071	964	909	824	762	740	618	583	492	413
S&P Core Earnings	1,041	863	913	849	754	704	635	494	416	NA

Balance Sheet & Other Financial Data (Million $)	2009	2008	2007	2006	2005	2004	2003	2002	2001	2000
Cash	353	164	789	319	158	62.0	192	130	110	133
Current Assets	1,208	951	1,481	901	837	747	806	730	547	688
Total Assets	7,148	6,506	7,242	6,353	5,698	5,696	5,620	5,400	4,388	4,149
Current Liabilities	1,653	1,722	2,062	1,724	1,605	1,376	1,461	1,520	1,805	1,216
Long Term Debt	3,207	3,564	2,924	2,045	1,649	1,731	2,056	2,299	1,552	2,397
Common Equity	1,025	-112	1,139	1,437	1,449	1,595	1,120	594	104	-322
Total Capital	4,321	3,509	4,063	3,482	3,098	3,326	3,176	2,893	1,656	2,085
Capital Expenditures	797	935	742	614	609	645	663	760	636	572
Cash Flow	1,651	1,524	1,442	1,303	1,231	1,188	1,019	953	846	767
Current Ratio	0.7	0.6	0.7	0.5	0.5	0.5	0.6	0.5	0.3	0.6
% Long Term Debt of Capitalization	74.2	101.6	71.9	58.7	53.2	52.0	64.7	79.5	93.7	115.0
% Net Income of Revenue	9.9	8.6	8.7	8.6	8.2	8.2	7.4	7.5	7.1	5.8
% Return on Assets	15.7	14.0	14.0	13.4	13.6	13.4	13.1	11.2	11.5	10.2
% Return on Equity	NM	NM	70.6	57.1	50.1	54.5	72.1	167.0	NM	NM

Data as orig reptd.; bef. results of disc opers/spec. items. Per share data adj. for stk. divs.; EPS diluted. E-Estimated. NA-Not Available. NM-Not Meaningful. NR-Not Ranked. UR-Under Review.

Office: 1441 Gardiner Lane, Louisville, KY 40213.
Telephone: 502-874-8300.
Email: yum.investors@yum.com
Website: http://www.yum.com

Chrmn, Pres & CEO: D.C. Novak
Vice Chrmn: J.S. Su
COO: E.J. Brolick
SVP, Chief Acctg Officer & Cntlr: T.F. Knopf

SVP, Secy & General Counsel: C.L. Campbell
Investor Contact: B. Bishop (502-874-8905)
Board Members: D. W. Dorman, M. Ferragamo, J. D. Grissom, B. G. Hill, R. Holland, Jr., K. G. Langone, J. S. Linen, T. C. Nelson, D. C. Novak, T. M. Ryan, J. S. Su, R. D. Walter

Founded: 1997
Domicile: North Carolina
Employees: 350,000

The **McGraw·Hill** Companies

Zimmer Holdings Inc.

STANDARD &POOR'S

S&P Recommendation	**BUY** ★★★★☆	Price $51.29 (as of Oct 22, 2010)	12-Mo. Target Price $62.00	Investment Style Large-Cap Growth

GICS Sector Health Care
Sub-Industry Health Care Equipment

Summary This company, spun off by Bristol-Myers Squibb in August 2001, manufactures orthopedic reconstructive implants, fracture management products, and dental implants.

Key Stock Statistics (Source S&P, Vickers, company reports)

52-Wk Range	$64.77– 46.27	S&P Oper. EPS 2010**E**	4.32	Market Capitalization(B)	$10.307	Beta	1.05
Trailing 12-Month EPS	$3.25	S&P Oper. EPS 2011**E**	4.75	Yield (%)	Nil	S&P 3-Yr. Proj. EPS CAGR(%)	10
Trailing 12-Month P/E	15.8	P/E on S&P Oper. EPS 2010**E**	11.9	Dividend Rate/Share	Nil	S&P Credit Rating	A-
$10K Invested 5 Yrs Ago	$8,255	Common Shares Outstg. (M)	201.0	Institutional Ownership (%)	79		

Price Performance

30-Week Mov. Avg. · · · 10-Week Mov. Avg. – – GAAP Earnings vs. Previous Year   Volume Above Avg. ▮▮▮ STARS
12-Mo. Target Price — Relative Strength — ▲ Up ▼ Down ▶ No Change   Below Avg. ▮▮▮ ★

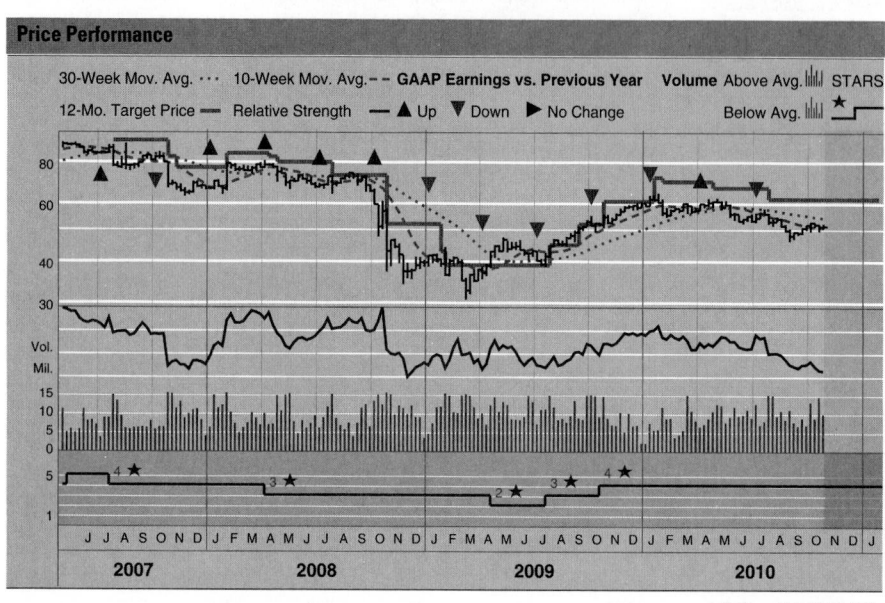

Options: ASE, CBOE, P, Ph

Analysis prepared by **Phillip M. Seligman** on July 28, 2010, when the stock traded at **$ 53.46**.

Highlights

➤ We estimate revenues will climb 3.6% in 2010 to over $4.2 billion, with knee implant sales of more than $1.8 billion, hip implant sales of almost $1.3 billion, other reconstructive sales of $363 million, spinal sales of $253 million, trauma (fracture management) sales of $243 million, and other surgical product sales of $306 million. We assume unfavorable foreign exchange will subtract 50 basis points (bps) from the top line, but that revenue growth, in constant currency, accelerates through the year, mainly on new hip and knee products.

➤ We believe gross margins will widen by 30 bps in 2010, on improved manufacturing efficiency, new products, and currency hedge gains. We expect the R&D cost ratio to rise by 10 bps reflecting ZMH's need to fill in product-line gaps, while the SG&A cost ratio declines by 30 bps on cost controls. Interest expense should be above 2009 levels, due to the $1 billion note offering ZMH completed in 2009's fourth quarter.

➤ We forecast EPS of $4.32 (before $0.28 in net one-time costs) in 2010, versus $3.94 in 2009 (before $0.62 in net one-time costs). We look for $4.75 in 2011.

Investment Rationale/Risk

➤ We think the long-term global demand drivers for ZMH's orthopedic implants remain intact, given aging populations and the rise of obesity levels. In addition, we think eventual insurance coverage for up to 32 million additional Americans via health care reform may expand ZMH's potential market down the road. We also think ZMH's share losses in the global hip and knee markets have slowed, and we expect the company to shortly return to market growth rates in both arenas on new products. In the interim, orthopedic procedure volume growth has slowed in the U.S. and Europe amid challenging economic conditions, but we see a seasonal pickup in 2010's fourth quarter. They remain strong in Asia Pacific, where we are positive on ZMH's planned acquisition of a Chinese firm, pending approvals.

➤ Risks to our recommendation and target price include lower Medicare reimbursement and significant device reimbursement cuts in key overseas markets.

➤ Our 12-month target price is $62, or 14.4X our 2010 EPS estimate. This multiple represents a discount to the stock's historical levels to reflect our view of recent market share losses.

Qualitative Risk Assessment

LOW	**MEDIUM**	HIGH

Our risk assessment reflects Zimmer's operations in a highly competitive industry characterized by relatively short product life cycles, requiring a significant number of new product introductions to maintain market share and gross profit margins. Many of the company's customers are reimbursed by the federal government through Medicare, and a more restrictive budgetary environment could result in lower prices paid to medical device suppliers such as Zimmer. However, this is offset by the company's position as one of the dominant manufacturers in the orthopedic device industry, with substantial global sales force capabilities and an expansive product line.

Quantitative Evaluations

S&P Quality Ranking B+

D	C	B-	B	**B+**	A-	A	A+

Relative Strength Rank WEAK

29

LOWEST = 1   HIGHEST = 99

Revenue/Earnings Data

Revenue (Million $)

	1Q	2Q	3Q	4Q	Year
2010	1,063	1,058	--	--	--
2009	992.6	1,020	975.6	1,107	4,095
2008	1,059	1,080	952.2	1,030	4,121
2007	950.2	970.6	903.2	1,074	3,898
2006	860.4	881.6	819.8	933.6	3,495
2005	828.5	846.8	762.5	848.3	3,286

Earnings Per Share ($)

2010	1.01	0.82	E0.97	E1.24	E4.32
2009	0.91	0.98	0.70	0.74	3.32
2008	1.02	0.99	0.95	0.75	3.72
2007	0.98	0.97	0.19	1.12	3.26
2006	0.82	0.81	0.76	1.02	3.40
2005	0.70	0.76	0.67	0.80	2.93

Fiscal year ended Dec. 31. Next earnings report expected: Late October. EPS Estimates based on S&P Operating Earnings; historical GAAP earnings are as reported.

Dividend Data

No cash dividends have been paid.

Zimmer Holdings Inc.

STANDARD
&POOR'S

Business Summary July 28, 2010

CORPORATE OVERVIEW. Zimmer Holdings primarily designs, develops, manufactures and markets orthopedic reconstructive implants and fracture management products. The former division of Bristol-Myers Squibb was spun off to BMY shareholders in August 2001.

Zimmer's reconstructive implants (81% of 2009 sales) are used to restore function lost due to disease or trauma in joints such as knees, hips, shoulders and elbows. The company offers a wide range of products for specialized knee procedures, including The NexGen Complete Knee Solution, NexGen Legacy, NexGen Revision Knee, Innex Total Knee System, M/G Unicompartmental Knee System, and Prolong Highly Crosslinked Polyethylene Articular Surface material. Hip replacement products include the VerSys Hip System, the ZMR Hip System, the Trilogy Acetabular System and a line of specialty hip products. The company also continues to develop a portfolio of minimally invasive hip replacement procedures. ZMH sells the Coonrad/Morrey product line of elbow replacement implant products, along with a line of restorative dental products.

In the spine/trauma area (12%), the company sells devices used to reattach or

stabilize damaged bone and tissue to support the body's natural healing process. The most common stabilization of bone fractures concerns the internal fixation of bone fragments, which can involve the use of an assortment of plates, screws, rods, wires and pins. ZMH offers a line of products designed for use in fracture fixation. In October 2008, the company acquired the spinal business of Abbott Labs for $360 million in cash.

ZMH makes and markets other orthopedic surgical products (7%) used by surgeons for orthopedic as well as non-orthopedic procedures. Products include tourniquets, blood management systems, wound debridgement products, powered surgical instruments, pain management devices, and orthopedic soft goods that provide support and/or heat retention and compression for trauma of the knee, ankle, back and upper extremities, including the shoulder, elbow, neck and wrist.

Company Financials Fiscal Year Ended Dec. 31

Per Share Data ($)	2009	2008	2007	2006	2005	2004	2003	2002	2001	2000
Tangible Book Value	9.78	8.96	9.76	7.15	7.94	2.52	0.38	1.88	0.41	NM
Cash Flow	4.89	4.92	4.22	4.21	3.68	2.92	1.87	1.43	0.89	0.92
Earnings	3.32	3.72	3.26	3.40	2.93	2.19	1.38	1.31	0.77	0.81
S&P Core Earnings	3.67	3.56	3.94	3.36	2.73	2.08	1.31	1.24	0.70	NA
Dividends	Nil	Nil	Nil	Nil	Nil	Nil	Nil	Nil	Nil	NA
Payout Ratio	Nil	Nil	Nil	Nil	Nil	Nil	Nil	Nil	Nil	NA
Prices:High	60.64	80.92	94.38	79.11	89.10	89.44	71.85	43.00	33.30	NA
Prices:Low	30.67	34.10	63.00	52.20	60.19	64.40	38.02	28.00	24.70	NA
P/E Ratio:High	18	22	29	23	30	41	52	33	43	NA
P/E Ratio:Low	9	9	19	15	21	29	28	21	32	NA

Income Statement Analysis (Million $)	2009	2008	2007	2006	2005	2004	2003	2002	2001	2000
Revenue	4,095	4,121	3,898	3,495	3,286	2,981	1,901	1,372	1,179	1,041
Operating Income	1,480	1,510	1,553	1,369	1,297	1,026	633	426	272	291
Depreciation	337	275	230	197	186	181	103	25.0	23.4	23.0
Interest Expense	20.6	7.00	NA	4.00	14.0	32.0	13.0	12.0	7.40	29.0
Pretax Income	998	1,122	1,132	1,169	1,040	732	438	389	241	239
Effective Tax Rate	28.1%	24.3%	31.6%	28.5%	29.5%	25.9%	33.6%	33.7%	37.8%	34.3%
Net Income	717	849	773	835	733	542	291	258	150	157
S&P Core Earnings	789	812	936	823	682	515	277	244	137	NA

Balance Sheet & Other Financial Data (Million $)	2009	2008	2007	2006	2005	2004	2003	2002	2001	2000
Cash	758	213	466	266	233	155	78.0	16.0	18.4	50.0
Current Assets	2,738	2,179	2,083	1,746	1,576	1,561	1,339	612	509	487
Total Assets	7,786	7,239	6,634	5,974	5,722	5,696	5,156	859	745	669
Current Liabilities	691	771	749	628	607	701	645	401	373	217
Long Term Debt	1,128	460	104	100	82.0	624	1,008	Nil	214	500
Common Equity	5,639	5,650	5,450	4,921	4,683	3,943	3,143	366	78.7	-48.0
Total Capital	6,766	6,114	5,554	5,024	4,767	4,574	4,158	366	293	452
Capital Expenditures	229	488	331	142	105	101	45.0	34.0	54.7	NA
Cash Flow	1,055	1,124	1,003	1,032	919	723	394	283	173	180
Current Ratio	4.0	2.8	2.8	2.8	2.6	2.2	2.1	1.5	1.4	2.2
% Long Term Debt of Capitalization	16.7	7.5	1.8	1.9	1.7	13.6	24.2	Nil	73.0	110.6
% Net Income of Revenue	17.5	20.6	19.8	23.8	22.3	18.1	15.3	18.9	12.7	15.1
% Return on Assets	9.6	12.2	12.3	14.2	12.8	9.9	9.7	32.1	22.4	NA
% Return on Equity	12.7	15.3	14.9	17.3	16.9	15.2	10.6	115.0	NM	NA

Data as orig reptd.; bef. results of disc opers/spec. items. Per share data adj. for stk. divs.; EPS diluted. E-Estimated. NA-Not Available. NM-Not Meaningful. NR-Not Ranked. UR-Under Review.

Office: 345 East Main Street, Warsaw, IN 46580.
Telephone: 574-267-6131.
Email: zimmer.infoperson@zimmer.com
Website: http://www.zimmer.com

Chrmn: J.L. McGoldrick
Pres & CEO: D. Dvorak
COO: R.C. Stair
EVP & CFO: J.T. Crines

SVP & CSO: C.R. Blanchard
Investor Contact: P. Blair (574-371-8042)
Board Members: B. J. Bernard, M. N. Casper, D. Dvorak, L. C. Glasscock, R. A. Hagemann, A. J. Higgins, J. L. McGoldrick, C. B. Pickett

Founded: 1927
Domicile: Delaware
Employees: 8,200

Zions BanCorp

STANDARD &POOR'S

S&P Recommendation **HOLD** ★★★☆☆	Price	12-Mo. Target Price	Investment Style
	$21.69 (as of Oct 22, 2010)	$26.00	Large-Cap Blend

GICS Sector Financials
Sub-Industry Regional Banks

Summary ZION has more than 500 full-service banking offices in Utah, California, Texas, Nevada, Arizona, and five other western states. At mid 2010, it had assets of $52.1 billion and deposits of $42.0 billion.

Key Stock Statistics (Source S&P, Vickers, company reports)

52-Wk Range	$30.29– 12.50	S&P Oper. EPS 2010**E**	-2.14	Market Capitalization(B)	$3.760	Beta	1.00
Trailing 12-Month EPS	$-4.00	S&P Oper. EPS 2011**E**	0.56	Yield (%)	0.18	S&P 3-Yr. Proj. EPS CAGR(%)	NA
Trailing 12-Month P/E	NM	P/E on S&P Oper. EPS 2010**E**	NM	Dividend Rate/Share	$0.04	S&P Credit Rating	BBB-
$10K Invested 5 Yrs Ago	$3,371	Common Shares Outstg. (M)	173.3	Institutional Ownership (%)	86		

Price Performance

30-Week Mov. Avg. ···   10-Week Mov. Avg.   **GAAP Earnings vs. Previous Year**   Volume Above Avg. STARS
12-Mo. Target Price   Relative Strength   ▲ Up ▼ Down ▶ No Change   Below Avg.

Options: CBOE, Ph

Analysis prepared by **Erik Oja** on July 22, 2010, when the stock traded at **$ 20.04**.

Highlights

➤ We expect the reported net interest margin to rebound to nearly 4.0%, after a second quarter dip to 3.58%, caused by expenses related to debt, and we forecast 2010 net interest income of $1.80 billion, down 5.4% from 2009, caused by loan shrinkage. We expect core non-interest income to increase 3.5% in 2010.

➤ Second quarter net chargeoffs rose from first quarter levels, breaking a string of quarterly improvements, and we think casting doubt on how rapidly ZION's credit quality will return to normalized levels of health. However, provisions fell for the fourth consecutive quarter, and provisions to net chargeoffs were only 0.93, indicating ZION has begun releasing reserves for the first time in several years, a positive. However, continuance of reserve releases will require meaningful future declines in chargeoffs, which we think will happen, barring a major economic downturn. We forecast 2010 net chargeoffs of $915 million, down from $1.175 billion in 2009. Our 2010 provisioning forecast is $830 million, down from $2.02 billion in 2009.

➤ We project a loss per share of $1.93 in 2010, EPS of $0.56 in 2011, and EPS of $1.17 in 2012.

Investment Rationale/Risk

➤ ZION's second quarter results missed expectation, as net chargeoffs increased from first quarter levels, thus limiting how quickly loan loss provisions could decline. Management also delayed, to late 2010, from mid-2010, its expectation of when the company would be able to return to profitability, citing provisions, net interest margins, and loan growth. However, we point to positive trends such as a lower formation of new nonperforming loans, and lower securities writeoffs, as indicators that ZION's recovery is still on track. The U.S. economic recovery is likely dependent on numerous government support programs. It is very uncertain how the U.S. economy and ZION's credit quality will improve as these programs are withdrawn.

➤ Risks to our recommendation and target price include worsening employment trends and declining housing industry indicators.

➤ Our 12-month target price of $26 equals a below-peers multiple of 1.4X our year-end estimate of tangible book value per share of $18.60. This equals an above-peers 46.4X our 2011 EPS estimate, and a premium 22.2X our 2012 estimate, a reflection of recovering earnings.

Qualitative Risk Assessment

LOW	**MEDIUM**	HIGH

Our risk assessment reflects the company's credit exposure to housing and commercial real estate in California, Arizona, and Nevada, offset by its sizeable capital levels and recent progress towards resolution of much of the nonperforming assets.

Quantitative Evaluations

S&P Quality Ranking B+

D	C	B-	B	**B+**	A-	A	A+

Relative Strength Rank MODERATE

47

LOWEST = 1   HIGHEST = 99

Revenue/Earnings Data

Revenue (Million $)

	1Q	2Q	3Q	4Q	Year
2010	673.3	693.2	--	--	--
2009	494.4	1,250	902.5	672.0	3,319
2008	901.1	795.3	825.3	642.9	3,165
2007	915.9	931.0	963.6	807.3	3,776
2006	767.1	824.1	876.9	901.2	3,369
2005	525.8	562.3	594.5	666.5	2,349

Earnings Per Share ($)

	1Q	2Q	3Q	4Q	Year
2010	-0.57	-0.84	E-0.47	E-0.26	E-2.14
2009	-7.47	-0.21	-1.43	-1.26	-9.92
2008	0.98	0.65	0.31	-4.37	-2.66
2007	1.36	1.43	1.22	0.40	4.42
2006	1.28	1.35	1.42	1.32	5.36
2005	1.20	1.30	1.34	1.32	5.16

Fiscal year ended Dec. 31. Next earnings report expected: NA. EPS Estimates based on S&P Operating Earnings; historical GAAP earnings are as reported.

Dividend Data (Dates: mm/dd Payment Date: mm/dd/yy)

Amount ($)	Date Decl.	Ex-Div. Date	Stk. of Record	Payment Date
0.010	10/30	11/09	11/12	11/20/09
0.010	01/29	02/08	02/10	02/24/10
0.010	04/23	05/06	05/10	05/26/10
0.010	07/23	08/06	08/10	08/25/10

Dividends have been paid since 1966. Source: Company reports.

Zions BanCorp

STANDARD
&POOR'S

Business Summary July 22, 2010

CORPORATE OVERVIEW. ZION provides a full range of banking and related services through banking subsidiaries in ten Western and Southwestern states as follows: Zions First National Bank in Utah and Idaho; California Bank & Trust, Amegy Corporation and its subsidiary, Amegy Bank, in Texas, National Bank of Arizona, Nevada State Bank, Vectra Bank Colorado, in Colorado and New Mexico, The Commerce Bank of Washington, and The Commerce Bank of Oregon. ZION's parent company also owns and operates certain non-bank subsidiaries that engage in the development and sale of financial technologies and related services, and in wealth management services.

MARKET PROFILE. As of June 30, 2009 (latest available FDIC branch-level data), ZION had 506 branches, and about $42.3 billion in deposits. About 53.6% of deposits were concentrated in Utah and California. In Utah, ZION had 111 branches, $12.7 billion in deposits, up from $9.7 billion a year earlier, and a de-

posit market share of about 4.6%, up from 4.0% a year earlier, ranking sixth. In California, ZION had 110 branches, $10.0 billion in deposits, up from $8.2 billion a year earlier, and a deposit market share of about 1.2%, ranking 12th. In Texas, ZION had 84 branches, $8.3 billion in deposits, up from $6.8 billion a year earlier, and a market share of 1.8%, ranking seventh. In Arizona, ZION had 76 branches, almost $4.0 billion of deposits, and a deposit market share of about 4.8%, ranking fourth. In addition, ZION had a total of 64 branches and $3.6 billion in deposits in Colorado, Idaho, Washington State, New Mexico and Oregon.

Company Financials Fiscal Year Ended Dec. 31

Per Share Data ($)	2009	2008	2007	2006	2005	2004	2003	2002	2001	2000
Tangible Book Value	20.35	27.24	27.02	25.15	20.45	23.29	20.96	17.21	15.19	13.06
Earnings	-9.92	-2.67	4.42	5.36	5.16	4.47	3.74	3.44	3.15	1.86
S&P Core Earnings	-5.65	-0.67	4.46	5.36	5.04	4.33	4.42	3.17	2.42	NA
Dividends	0.10	1.61	1.68	1.47	1.44	1.26	1.02	0.80	0.80	0.89
Payout Ratio	NM	NM	38%	27%	28%	28%	27%	23%	25%	48%
Prices:High	25.52	57.05	88.56	85.25	77.67	69.29	63.86	59.65	64.00	62.88
Prices:Low	5.90	21.07	45.70	75.13	63.33	54.08	39.31	34.14	42.30	32.00
P/E Ratio:High	NM	NM	20	16	15	16	17	17	20	34
P/E Ratio:Low	NM	NM	10	14	12	12	11	10	13	17

Income Statement Analysis (Million $)										
Net Interest Income	1,898	1,972	1,882	1,765	1,361	1,174	1,095	1,035	950	803
Tax Equivalent Adjustment	22.8	23.7	26.1	24.3	21.1	NA	NA	NA	NA	NA
Non Interest Income	126	191	395	527	439	425	426	402	388	274
Loan Loss Provision	2,017	650	152	72.6	43.0	44.1	69.9	71.9	73.2	31.8
% Expense/Operating Revenue	NA	58.9%	61.7%	57.4%	56.4%	57.8%	63.7%	59.8%	63.9%	75.9%
Pretax Income	-1,623	-315	738	913	742	624	546	481	440	243
Effective Tax Rate	NM	NM	32.0%	34.8%	35.5%	35.3%	39.1%	34.9%	35.8%	32.8%
Net Income	-1,216	-266	494	583	480	406	340	317	290	162
% Net Interest Margin	3.94	4.18	4.43	4.63	4.58	4.32	4.45	4.56	4.64	4.27
S&P Core Earnings	-703	-73.1	483	579	469	394	402	292	223	NA

Balance Sheet & Other Financial Data (Million $)										
Money Market Assets	732	2,703	1,500	369	667	593	569	543	280	528
Investment Securities	4,548	4,509	6,895	6,790	6,996	5,786	5,402	4,238	3,463	4,188
Commercial Loans	19,139	34,333	31,508	27,559	23,122	16,337	10,404	13,648	4,110	3,615
Other Loans	NA	7,659	7,744	7,260	7,131	6,395	9,613	5,195	13,304	10,843
Total Assets	51,123	55,093	52,947	46,970	42,780	31,470	28,558	26,566	24,304	21,939
Demand Deposits	12,324	9,683	9,618	25,869	9,954	6,822	5,883	5,117	4,481	3,586
Time Deposits	29,517	31,633	27,305	9,113	22,689	16,471	15,014	15,015	13,361	11,484
Long Term Debt	2,033	2,657	2,815	2,495	2,746	1,919	1,843	1,310	781	420
Common Equity	4,190	4,920	5,053	4,747	4,237	2,790	2,540	2,374	2,281	1,779
% Return on Assets	NM	NM	1.0	1.3	1.3	2.0	1.2	1.2	1.3	0.8
% Return on Equity	NM	NM	9.8	12.9	13.7	15.2	13.8	13.6	14.3	9.4
% Loan Loss Reserve	3.8	1.6	1.2	1.1	1.1	1.2	0.9	1.4	1.5	1.3
% Loans/Deposits	96.4	101.2	103.1	99.1	92.3	97.1	142.6	96.0	97.0	96.6
% Equity to Assets	8.6	9.2	9.8	10.0	9.5	13.3	8.9	9.2	8.8	8.1

Data as orig reptd.; bef. results of disc opers/spec. items. Per share data adj. for stk. divs.; EPS diluted. E-Estimated. NA-Not Available. NM-Not Meaningful. NR-Not Ranked. UR-Under Review.

Office: 1 S Main St 15th Fl, Salt Lake City, UT, USA 84133.
Telephone: 801-524-4787.
Website: http://www.zionsbancorporation.com
Chrmn, Pres & CEO: H.H. Simmons

Vice Chrmn, EVP & CFO: D.L. Arnold
EVP, Secy & General Counsel: T.E. Laursen
EVP & CIO: J.T. Itokazu
SVP & Cntlr: A.J. Hume

Investor Contact: C.B. Hinckley (801-524-4787)
Board Members: D. L. Arnold, J. C. Atkin, R. D. Cash, P. Frobes, J. D. Heaney, R. B. Porter, S. D. Quinn, H. H. Simmons, L. E. Simmons, S. Wheelwright, S. T. Williams

Founded: 1961
Domicile: Utah
Employees: 10,529